# Freedom of Information Act Guide

## *March 2007 Edition*

Office of Information and Privacy
U.S. Department of Justice
Washington, D.C. 20530

**Director**
Melanie Ann Pustay

**Chief of Staff**
Carmen L. Mallon

**Associate Director**
Janice Galli McLeod

**Senior Counsel**
Brentin V. Evitt

For sale by the Superintendent of Documents, U.S. Government Printing Office
Internet: bookstore.gpo.gov  Phone: toll free (866) 512-1800;  DC area (202) 512-1800
Fax: (202) 512-2104 Mail: Stop IDCC, Washington, DC 20402-0001

ISBN 978-0-16-077206-1

# FREEDOM OF INFORMATION ACT GUIDE

## MARCH 2007 EDITION

## ACKNOWLEDGMENT

This newly updated edition of the *Freedom of Information Act Guide* was made possible by the dedication and commitment of the staff of the Office of Information and Privacy. The authors and editors of the March 2007 edition are -- Jennifer H. Ashworth, Allan L. Blutstein, Nicholas D. Delaney, Brentin V. Evitt, Ramona M. Fine, Kenneth A. Hendricks, Thomas E. Hitter, Dione C. Jackson Stearns, Catherine Lev, Janice G. McLeod, Kathleen McNabb, Kathleene A. Molen, Sean R. O'Neill, Joshua T. Raines, Michael J. Sherman, Caroline A. Smith, Sean J. Vanek, Jonathan P. Wentz, and Anne Davis Work. Together with publications editor Bertina Adams Cleveland, they have made this extraordinary publication possible.

*Melanie Ann Pustay*
Melanie Ann Pustay
Acting Director
Office of Information and Privacy

## JUSTICE DEPARTMENT GUIDE TO THE FREEDOM OF INFORMATION ACT

The Freedom of Information Act Guide is an overview discussion of the FOIA's exemptions, its law enforcement record exclusions, and its most important procedural aspects. Prepared by the staff of the Office of Information and Privacy, it is updated and revised biennially. Any inquiry about the points addressed below, or regarding matters of FOIA administration or interpretation, should be made to the Office of Information and Privacy through its FOIA Counselor service, at (202) 514-3642 (514-FOIA), ordinarily after initial consultation with an agency FOIA officer. A word-searchable version of this Guide is available on the Department of Justice's FOIA Web site at http://www.usdoj.gov/ 04foia/04_7.html.

## TABLE OF CONTENTS

INTRODUCTION . . . . . . . . . . . . . . . . . . . . . . . . . . . . . . . . . . . . . . . . . . . . . .   5

FOIA READING ROOMS AND WEB SITES . . . . . . . . . . . . . . . . . . . . . . .  22
    FOIA Reading Rooms . . . . . . . . . . . . . . . . . . . . . . . . . . . . . . . . . . . . . . .  23
    FOIA Web Sites . . . . . . . . . . . . . . . . . . . . . . . . . . . . . . . . . . . . . . . . . . . .  33

PROCEDURAL REQUIREMENTS . . . . . . . . . . . . . . . . . . . . . . . . . . . . . . .  38
    Executive Order 13,392 . . . . . . . . . . . . . . . . . . . . . . . . . . . . . . . . . . . . . . .  39
    Entities Subject to the FOIA . . . . . . . . . . . . . . . . . . . . . . . . . . . . . . . . . .  46
    "Agency Records" . . . . . . . . . . . . . . . . . . . . . . . . . . . . . . . . . . . . . . . . . . .  53
    FOIA Requesters . . . . . . . . . . . . . . . . . . . . . . . . . . . . . . . . . . . . . . . . . . . .  62
    Proper FOIA Requests . . . . . . . . . . . . . . . . . . . . . . . . . . . . . . . . . . . . . . .  69
    Time Limits . . . . . . . . . . . . . . . . . . . . . . . . . . . . . . . . . . . . . . . . . . . . . . . .  91
    Expedited Processing . . . . . . . . . . . . . . . . . . . . . . . . . . . . . . . . . . . . . . . .  98
    Searching for Responsive Records . . . . . . . . . . . . . . . . . . . . . . . . . . . . 103
    "Reasonably Segregable" Obligation . . . . . . . . . . . . . . . . . . . . . . . . . . . 113
    Referrals and Consultations . . . . . . . . . . . . . . . . . . . . . . . . . . . . . . . . . . 119
    Responding to FOIA Requests . . . . . . . . . . . . . . . . . . . . . . . . . . . . . . . . 123

FEES AND FEE WAIVERS . . . . . . . . . . . . . . . . . . . . . . . . . . . . . . . . . . . . 130
    Fees . . . . . . . . . . . . . . . . . . . . . . . . . . . . . . . . . . . . . . . . . . . . . . . . . . . . . . 133
    Fee Waivers . . . . . . . . . . . . . . . . . . . . . . . . . . . . . . . . . . . . . . . . . . . . . . . 162

EXEMPTION 1 . . . . . . . . . . . . . . . . . . . . . . . . . . . . . . . . . . . . . . . . . . . . . . 195
    Standard of Review . . . . . . . . . . . . . . . . . . . . . . . . . . . . . . . . . . . . . . . . . 199
    Deference to Agency Expertise . . . . . . . . . . . . . . . . . . . . . . . . . . . . . . . . 205
    In Camera Submissions and Adequate Public Record . . . . . . . . . . . . . 213
    Waiver of Exemption Protection . . . . . . . . . . . . . . . . . . . . . . . . . . . . . . . 218
    Executive Order 12,958, as Amended . . . . . . . . . . . . . . . . . . . . . . . . . . . 227
    Duration of Classification and Declassification . . . . . . . . . . . . . . . . . . 240
    Additional Considerations . . . . . . . . . . . . . . . . . . . . . . . . . . . . . . . . . . . . 246

    "Operational Files" Statutes .................................... 250
    Homeland Security-Related Information ........................ 253

EXEMPTION 2 ............................................... 257
    Initial Considerations ........................................ 259
    "Low 2": Trivial Matters ...................................... 262
    "High 2": Risk of Circumvention ............................. 273
    Homeland Security-Related Information ........................ 299

EXEMPTION 3 ............................................... 305
    Initial Considerations ........................................ 306
    Exemption 3 Statutes ........................................ 312
    FOIA-Specific Nondisclosure Statutes ........................ 344
    Nondisclosure Results Under Appropriations Acts ............... 346
    "Operational Files" Provisions ................................ 348
    Additional Consideration ̄ .................................... 349

EXEMPTION 4 ............................................... 355
    Trade Secrets ............................................... 355
    Commercial or Financial Information ......................... 358
    Obtained from a "Person" .................................... 364
    "Confidential" Information ................................... 367
    The Critical Mass Decision ................................... 369
    Applying Critical Mass ...................................... 372
    Impairment Prong of National Parks ......................... 396
    Competitive Harm Prong of National Parks .................... 406
    Third Prong of National Parks ............................... 455
    Privileged Information ...................................... 460
    Interrelation with the Trade Secrets Act ..................... 463

EXEMPTION 5 ............................................... 465
    "Inter-Agency or Intra-Agency" Threshold Requirement .......... 468
    Deliberative Process Privilege ............................... 478
    Attorney Work-Product Privilege ............................. 510
    Attorney-Client Privilege .................................... 525
    Other Privileges ............................................ 529

EXEMPTION 6 ............................................... 540
    Initial Considerations ........................................ 541
    The Reporters Committee Decision ........................... 545
    Privacy Considerations ...................................... 548
    Factoring in the Public Interest .............................. 578
    The Balancing Process ...................................... 605

EXEMPTION 7 ............................................... 636

EXEMPTION 7(A) ............................................ 677

EXEMPTION 7(B) ............................................ 721

EXEMPTION 7(C) ............................................ 722

EXEMPTION 7(D) ................................................ 771

EXEMPTION 7(E) ............................................... 813

EXEMPTION 7(F) ............................................... 831

EXEMPTION 8 ................................................. 840

EXEMPTION 9 ................................................. 848

EXCLUSIONS ................................................. 851
   The (c)(1) Exclusion ......................................... 852
   The (c)(2) Exclusion ......................................... 856
   The (c)(3) Exclusion ......................................... 859
   Procedural Considerations ................................... 861

DISCRETIONARY DISCLOSURE AND WAIVER .................. 864
   Discretionary Disclosure ..................................... 866
   Waiver ...................................................... 875

LITIGATION CONSIDERATIONS ............................... 898
   Jurisdiction, Venue, and Other Preliminary Matters .............. 899
   Pleadings .................................................... 920
   Exhaustion of Administrative Remedies ...................... 927
   "Open America" Stays of Proceedings ........................ 944
   Adequacy of Search ......................................... 954
   Mootness and Other Grounds for Dismissal .................... 976
   "Vaughn Index" .............................................. 986
   "Reasonably Segregable" Requirements ....................... 1005
   In Camera Inspection ........................................ 1010
   Summary Judgment .......................................... 1020
   Discovery .................................................... 1029
   Waiver of Exemptions in Litigation ........................... 1037
   Sanctions .................................................... 1045
   Considerations on Appeal .................................... 1052

ATTORNEY FEES ............................................. 1064
   Attorney Fees and Litigation Costs: Eligibility Generally ........ 1064
   Attorney Fees and Litigation Costs: The Buckhannon Standard ... 1070
   Attorney Fees and Litigation Costs: Entitlement ............... 1075
   Attorney Fees and Litigation Costs: Calculations .............. 1086

"REVERSE" FOIA ............................................. 1091
   Standard of Review .......................................... 1100
   Executive Order 12,600 ...................................... 1108

BASIC FOIA REFERENCES .................................... 1113
   Congressional References .................................... 1114
   Executive Branch Materials .................................. 1117
   Nongovernment Publications ................................. 1120

TEXT OF THE FREEDOM OF INFORMATION ACT ............... 1123

-3-

# INTRODUCTION

The Freedom of Information Act[1] generally provides that any person has a right, enforceable in court, to obtain access to federal agency records, except to the extent that such records (or portions of them) are protected from public disclosure by one of nine exemptions or by one of three special law enforcement record exclusions.

Enacted in 1966, and taking effect on July 5, 1967, the FOIA firmly established an effective statutory right of public access to executive branch information in the federal government.[2] The principles of government openness and accountability underlying the FOIA, however, are inherent in the democratic ideal: "The basic purpose of [the] FOIA is to ensure an informed citizenry, vital to the functioning of a democratic society, needed to check against corruption and to hold the governors accountable to the governed."[3] The United States Supreme Court has emphasized that only "[o]fficial information that sheds light on an agency's performance of its statutory duties falls squarely within that statutory purpose."[4]

To be sure, achieving an informed citizenry is a goal often counterpoised against other vital societal aims. Society's strong interest in an open government can conflict with other fundamental societal values, "[a]mong [which] are safeguarding our national security, enhancing the effectiveness of our law enforcement agencies, protecting sensitive business information and, not least, preserving personal privacy."[5] Though tensions among these competing interests are characteristic of a democratic society, their resolution lies in providing a workable scheme that encompasses, balances, and appropriately protects all interests -- while placing primary

---

[1] 5 U.S.C. § 552 (2000 & Supp. IV 2004).

[2] See _FOIA Post_, "World Now Celebrates 'International Right-to-Know Day'" (posted 9/28/04) (observing that "when the Freedom of Information Act was enacted, the United States stood nearly alone in the world in providing an enforceable legal mechanism for public access to the official records of a national government").

[3] NLRB v. Robbins Tire & Rubber Co., 437 U.S. 214, 242 (1978); see also NARA v. Favish, 541 U.S. 157, 171-72 (emphasizing that the FOIA's underlying purpose of allowing "citizens to know 'what their government is up to'" is "a structural necessity in a real democracy" (quoting U.S. Dep't of Justice v. Reporters Comm. for Freedom of the Press, 489 U.S. 749, 773 (1989))), reh'g denied, 541 U.S. 1057 (2004).

[4] Reporters Comm., 489 U.S. at 773.

[5] See Attorney General's Memorandum for Heads of All Federal Departments and Agencies Regarding the Freedom of Information Act (Oct. 12, 2001) [hereinafter Attorney General Ashcroft's FOIA Memorandum], reprinted in _FOIA Post_ (posted 10/15/01).

emphasis on the most responsible disclosure possible.[6] It is this accommodation of strongly countervailing public concerns, with disclosure as the animating objective, that the FOIA seeks to achieve.

The FOIA evolved after a decade of debate among agency officials, legislators, and public interest group representatives.[7] It revised the public disclosure section of the Administrative Procedure Act,[8] which generally had been recognized as "falling far short" of its disclosure goals[9] and had come to be looked upon as more a withholding statute than a disclosure statute.[10]

By contrast, under the thrust and structure of the FOIA, virtually every record of a federal executive branch agency must be made available to the public in one form or another, unless it is specifically exempted from disclosure or specially excluded from the Act's coverage in the first place.[11] The nine exemptions of the FOIA ordinarily provide the only bases for nondisclosure,[12] and generally they are discretionary, not mandatory, in nature.[13] (For a discussion of the discretionary nature of FOIA exemptions, see Discretionary Disclosure and Waiver, below.) Dissatisfied record re-

---

[6] See S. Rep. No. 89-813, at 3 (1965) (stating the FOIA's statutory objective as that of achieving "the fullest responsible disclosure"); see also Attorney General's Memorandum on the 1986 Amendments to the Freedom of Information Act 30 (Dec. 1987) [hereinafter Attorney General's 1986 Amendments Memorandum] (same) (quoting Chrysler Corp. v. Brown, 441 U.S. 281, 292 (1979)); cf. 5 U.S.C. § 552b note (2000 & Supp. III 2003) (policy statement enacted as part of the Government in the Sunshine Act specifying that it is "the policy of the United States that the public is entitled to the fullest practicable information regarding the decisionmaking processes of the Federal Government").

[7] See 112 Cong. Rec. H13641 (daily ed. June 20, 1966) (statement of Rep. John Moss describing protracted legislative efforts, including decade of media-driven hearings, required to develop and achieve enactment of FOIA).

[8] 5 U.S.C. § 1002 (1964) (enacted in 1946, amended in 1966, and now codified at 5 U.S.C. § 552).

[9] EPA v. Mink, 410 U.S. 73, 79 (1973).

[10] See S. Rep. No. 89-813, at 5 (1965).

[11] See NLRB v. Sears, Roebuck & Co., 421 U.S. 132, 136 (1975).

[12] See 5 U.S.C. § 552(d); see also FOIA Update, Vol. V, No. 4, at 1-2 (describing first of several "operational files" provisions enacted by Congress to remove, as a threshold matter, such national security-classified files at certain intelligence agencies from FOIA's reach).

[13] See Chrysler Corp., 441 U.S. at 293.

questers are given a relatively speedy remedy in the United States district courts, where judges determine the propriety of agency withholdings de novo and agencies bear the burden of proof in defending their nondisclosure actions.[14]

The FOIA contains seven subsections, the first two of which establish certain categories of information that must "automatically" be disclosed by federal agencies.[15] Subsection (a)(1) of the FOIA[16] requires disclosure (through publication in the Federal Register) of information such as descriptions of agency organizations, functions, and procedures; substantive agency rules; and statements of general agency policy.[17] This requirement provides the public with automatic access to very basic information regarding the transaction of agency business.[18]

Subsection (a)(2) of the FOIA[19] requires that certain types of records -- final agency opinions and orders rendered in the adjudication of cases, specific policy statements, certain administrative staff manuals, and some records previously processed for disclosure under the Act[20] -- be routinely

---

[14] See 5 U.S.C. § 552(a)(4)(B)-(C).

[15] See FOIA Update, Vol. XIII, No. 3, at 3-4 ("OIP Guidance: The 'Automatic' Disclosure Provisions of FOIA: Subsections (a)(1) & (a)(2)").

[16] 5 U.S.C. § 552(a)(1).

[17] See, e.g., Splane v. West, 216 F.3d 1058, 1065 (Fed. Cir. 2000); Aulenback, Inc. v. Fed. Highway Admin., 103 F.3d 156, 168 (D.C. Cir. 1997); Hughes v. U.S., 953 F.2d 531, 539 (9th Cir. 1992); NI Indus., Inc. v. United States, 841 F.2d 1104, 1107 (Fed. Cir. 1988); Bright v. INS, 837 F.2d 1330, 1331 (5th Cir. 1988); see also DiCarlo v. Comm'r, T.C. Memo 1992-280, slip op. at 9-10 (May 14, 1992) (holding that publication in United States Government Manual, special edition of Federal Register, satisfies publication requirement of subsection (a)(1)(A) (citing 1 C.F.R. § 9 (1991))); cf. Nat'l Leased Housing Ass'n v. United States, 105 F.3d 1423, 1433 & n.13 (Fed. Cir. 1997) (noting difficulty in determining which government documents fall within FOIA's publication requirements as opposed to APA's notice-and-comment requirements, and describing distinction as "'fuzzy,'" "'blurred,'" "'enshrouded by smog,'" and "'baffling'" (quoting Cmty. Nutrition Inst. v. Young, 818 F.2d 943, 946 (D.C. Cir. 1987))).

[18] See FOIA Update, Vol. XIII, No. 3, at 3-4 (advising agencies to meet their subsection (a)(1) responsibilities on no less than quarterly basis).

[19] 5 U.S.C. § 552(a)(2).

[20] See id. § 552(a)(2)(A)-(D); see also FOIA Post, "FOIA Counselor Q&A: 'Frequently Requested' Records" (posted 7/25/03).

made "available for public inspection and copying."[21] This is commonly referred to as the "reading room" provision of the FOIA,[22] and it requires that some such records be made available by agencies in "electronic reading rooms" as well.[23] (For a discussion of the operation of this FOIA subsection, see FOIA Reading Rooms and Web Sites, below.)

The courts have held that providing official notice and guidance to the general public is the fundamental purpose of the publication requirement of subsection (a)(1) and the "reading room" availability requirement of subsection (a)(2).[24] Failure to comply with the requirements of either subsection can result in invalidation of related agency action,[25] unless the

---

[21] 5 U.S.C. § 552(a)(2); see Fed. Open Market Comm. v. Merrill, 443 U.S. 340, 360 n.23 (1979) (acknowledging that portions of subsection (a)(2) records may nevertheless be protected by FOIA exemptions).

[22] See FOIA Update, Vol. XIII, No. 3, at 4; see also FOIA Update, Vol. XIX, No. 1, at 3-4; FOIA Update, Vol. XVIII, No. 1, at 3-5.

[23] See FOIA Update, Vol. XVII, No. 4, at 1-2 (discussing provisions of Electronic Freedom of Information Act Amendments of 1996, Pub. L. No. 104-231, 110 Stat. 3048); see also FOIA Update, Vol. XIX, No. 3, at 3-4 ("OIP Guidance: Recommendations for FOIA Web Sites"); FOIA Update, Vol. XVIII, No. 3, at 1-2 (describing early agency development of World Wide Web sites for "electronic reading room" purposes). See generally FOIA Post, "Follow-Up Report on E-FOIA Implementation Issued" (posted 9/27/02) (discussing need for agencies to devote further attention to compliance with FOIA's electronic availability obligations); FOIA Post, "GAO E-FOIA Implementation Report Issued" (posted 3/23/01) (reminding agencies to take all steps necessary to both attain and maintain full compliance with their electronic availability obligations through their FOIA Web sites).

[24] See, e.g., Welch v. United States, 750 F.2d 1101, 1111 (1st Cir. 1985).

[25] See, e.g., Kennecott Utah Copper Corp. v. U.S. Dep't of the Interior, 88 F.3d 1191, 1203 (D.C. Cir. 1996) ("Congress has provided [a] means for encouraging agencies to fulfill their obligation to publish materials in the Federal Register" by "protect[ing] a person from being adversely affected" by an unpublished regulation.); Checkosky v. SEC, 23 F.3d 452, 459, 482 (D.C. Cir. 1994) (per curiam) (finding that SEC cannot rely on unpublished opinion as precedent) (Silberman & Randolph, JJ., filing separate opinions); NI Indus., 841 F.2d at 1108 (holding that agency could not rely on unpublished policy pertaining to its "value engineering change program" to deny contractor its share of savings from that program); D&W Food Ctrs. v. Block, 786 F.2d 751, 757-58 (6th Cir. 1986) (ruling that agency's interpretation of statute requiring certain businesses to be continuously inspected could not be enforced against noncomplying parties because it was not published); Anderson v. Butz, 550 F.2d 459, 462-63 (9th Cir. 1977) (holding HUD instruction describing what must be treated as income for food stamp
(continued...)

complaining party had actual and timely notice of the unpublished agency policy,[26] unless he is unable to show that he was adversely affected by the lack of publication,[27] or unless he fails to show that he would have been able to pursue "an alternative course of conduct" had the information been published.[28] However, unpublished interpretive guidelines that were available for copying and inspection in an agency program manual have been held not to violate subsection (a)(1),[29] and it also has been held that regula-

---

[25](...continued)
purposes void for failure to publish in Federal Register); Lewis v. Weinberger, 415 F. Supp. 652, 661 (D.N.M. 1976) (finding that an agency's policy regarding eligibility for an Indian Health Service program "has no effect for lack of publication in the Federal Register"); see also Tex. Health Care Ass'n v. Bowen, 710 F. Supp. 1109, 1113-14, 1116 (W.D. Tex. 1989) (enjoining agency from enforcing criteria established to implement Medicaid law, because criteria were not published and offered for comment).

[26] See, e.g., Splane, 216 F.3d at 1065 (finding it unnecessary to decide whether publishing only summary of agency opinion violated subsection (a)(1), because plaintiff had actual notice of entire opinion); United States v. F/V Alice Amanda, 987 F.2d 1078, 1084-85 (4th Cir. 1993) (denying statutory defense of subsection (a)(1) when defendant had copy of unpublished regulations); United States v. Bowers, 920 F.2d 220, 222 (4th Cir. 1990) (finding that the IRS's failure to publish tax forms did not preclude the defendants' convictions for income tax evasion, as the defendants had notice of their duty to pay those taxes, that duty was "manifest on the face" of the statutes, a listing of places where forms can be obtained is published in Code of Federal Regulations, and those defendants had filed tax returns before); Lonsdale v. United States, 919 F.2d 1440, 1447 (10th Cir. 1990); Tearney v. NTSB, 868 F.2d 1451, 1454 (5th Cir. 1989); Bright, 837 F.2d at 1331; Mada-Luna v. Fitzpatrick, 813 F.2d 1006, 1018 (9th Cir. 1987); Sierra Club N. Star Chapter v. Peña, 1 F. Supp. 2d 971, 980 (D. Minn. 1998) (holding organization subject to unpublished agency interpretation when it was "repeatedly informed" of agency's position); see also United States v. $200,000 in U.S. Currency, 590 F. Supp. 866, 874-75 (S.D. Fla. 1984) (alternative holding) (determining that published regulations adequately apprised individuals of obligation to use unpublished reporting form).

[27] See, e.g., Splane, 216 F.3d at 1065; Lake Mohave Boat Owners Ass'n v. Nat'l Park Serv., 78 F.3d 1360, 1368 (9th Cir. 1996); Alliance for Cannabis Therapeutics v. DEA, 15 F.3d 1131, 1136 (D.C. Cir. 1994); Bowers, 920 F.2d at 222; Sheppard v. Sullivan, 906 F.2d 756, 762 (D.C. Cir. 1990); Nguyen v. United States, 824 F.2d 697, 702 (9th Cir. 1987); Coos-Curry Elec. Coop., Inc. v. Jura, 821 F.2d 1341, 1347 (9th Cir. 1987).

[28] Alliance for Cannabis Therapeutics, 15 F.3d at 1136 (citing Zaharakis v. Heckler, 744 F.2d 711, 714 (9th Cir. 1984)).

[29]See McKenzie v. Bowen, 787 F.2d 1216, 1222-23 (8th Cir. 1986); see
(continued...)

tions pertaining solely to internal personnel matters that do not affect members of the public need not be published.[30] Of course, an agency is not required to publish substantive rules and policy statements of general applicability that it has not adopted.[31]

---

[29](...continued)
also Cathedral Candle Co. v. U.S. Int'l Trade Comm'n, 400 F.3d 1352, 1372 (Fed. Cir. 2005) (finding that agency was not required to publish interpretive letter once it published Federal Register notice directing affected parties to agency Web site where letter was located); Lake Mohave Boat Owners, 78 F.3d at 1368 (finding rate-setting guidelines to be "an agency staff manual governed by § 552(a)(2)," requiring only public availability, not Federal Register publication under subsection (a)(1)); Capuano v. NTSB, 843 F.2d 56, 57-58 (1st Cir. 1988); Pagan-Astacio v. Dep't of Educ., No. 93-2173, slip op. at 9 (D.P.R. June 1, 1995) (determining that agency need not publish directory explaining existing regulation when it publishes Federal Register notice explaining where directory is available), aff'd, 81 F.3d 147 (1st Cir. 1996) (unpublished table decision); Medics, Inc. v. Sullivan, 766 F. Supp. 47, 52-53 (D.P.R. 1991); Sturm v. James, 684 F. Supp. 1218, 1223 n.6 (S.D.N.Y. 1988).

[30] See Hamlet v. United States, 63 F.3d 1097, 1103 (Fed. Cir. 1995) (holding that publication is not required for personnel manuals "related solely to the [agency's] internal personnel rules and practices"); Pruner v. Dep't of the Army, 755 F. Supp. 362, 365 (D. Kan. 1991) (holding that Army regulation governing procedures for applications for conscientious objector status concerned internal personnel matters and were not required to be published); see also Dilley v. NTSB, 49 F.3d 667, 669-70 (10th Cir. 1995) (holding that publication of policy regarding FAA's authority to suspend pilot certificates is not required when statute clearly grants agency broad disciplinary powers); Lonsdale, 919 F.2d at 1446-47 (holding that FOIA does not require publication of Treasury Department orders that internally delegate authority to enforce internal agency revenue laws); cf. Smith v. NTSB, 981 F.2d 1326, 1328-29 (D.C. Cir. 1993) (holding that unpublished policy bulletin regarding sanctions was not valid basis for suspension of license because sanctions policy affects public by altering public's behavior).

[31] See 5 U.S.C. § 552(a)(1); see, e.g., Xin-Chang Zhang v. Slattery, 55 F.3d 732, 749 (2d Cir. 1995) (reversing a district court's order that had required the agency to give effect to an unpublished rule based upon the lower court's finding that the plaintiff had been adversely affected by lack of publication, because the rule actually was to be effective only on the date of its publication and "[b]y its own terms, the [r]ule never became effective"); Clarry v. United States, 891 F. Supp. 105, 110-11 (E.D.N.Y. 1995) (stating that failure to publish notice of ban for reemployment of strikers did not violate FOIA's notice requirement when rule was not "formulated and adopted" by agency but was authorized by presidential directive and by statute); Peng-Fei Si v. Slattery, 864 F. Supp. 397, 405 (S.D.N.Y. 1994) ("The FOIA cannot be used to force an agency to adopt a new regulation that it with-

(continued...)

Under subsection (a)(3) of the FOIA -- by far the most commonly utilized part of the Act -- all records not made available to the public under subsections (a)(1) or (a)(2), or exempted from mandatory disclosure under subsection (b), or excluded under subsection (c), are subject to disclosure upon an agency's receipt of a proper FOIA request from any person.[32] (See the discussions of the procedural aspects of subsection (a)(3) (including fees and fee waivers), the exemptions of subsection (b), and the exclusions of subsection (c), below.)

Subsection (c) of the FOIA,[33] which was added as part of the Freedom of Information Reform Act of 1986,[34] establishes three special categories of law enforcement-related records that are entirely excluded from the coverage of the FOIA in order to safeguard against unique types of harm.[35] The extraordinary protection embodied in subsection (c) permits an agency to respond to a request for such records as if the records in fact did not ex-

---

[31](...continued) drew from publication for the specific purpose of determining whether or not it should be adopted."); Xiu Qin Chen v. Slattery, 862 F. Supp. 814, 822 (E.D.N.Y. 1994) ("[A]n agency cannot be bound by [an un]published rule in a situation in which the agency never actually adopted the rule."); cf. Kennecott, 88 F.3d at 1202-03 (finding that FOIA does not authorize district court to order publication of regulation that was withdrawn by new Administration before it could be published).

[32] See 5 U.S.C. § 552(a)(3)(A) (stating that FOIA requests under subsection (a)(3) cannot be made for any records "made available" under subsections (a)(1) or (a)(2)); see also FOIA Update, Vol. XVI, No. 1, at 2; FOIA Update, Vol. XIII, No. 3, at 4; FOIA Update, Vol. XII, No. 2, at 5. But see FOIA Update, Vol. XVIII, No. 1, at 3 (advising that while ordinary rule is that records placed in reading room under subsection (a)(2) cannot be subject of regular FOIA request, Congress made clear that this rule does not apply to subsection (a)(2)(D) category of FOIA-processed records (citing H.R. Rep. No. 104-795, at 21 (1996))); see also FOIA Post, "FOIA Amended by Intelligence Authorization Act" (posted 12/23/02) (describing second exception, applicable to certain intelligence agencies only); cf. FOIA Post, "NTIS: An Available Means of Record Disclosure" (posted 8/30/02; supplemented 9/23/02) (describing how the National Technical Information Service "occupies a special status" with respect to making records available to the public, pursuant to a provision of the 1986 FOIA amendments, 5 U.S.C. § 552(a)(4)(A)(vi)).

[33] 5 U.S.C. § 552(c).

[34] Pub. L. No. 99-570, §§ 1801-1804, 100 Stat. 3207, 3207-48.

[35] See generally Attorney General's 1986 Amendments Memorandum 18-30; see also Favish, 541 U.S. at 169 (evincing the Supreme Court's reliance on "the Attorney General's consistent interpretation of" the FOIA in successive such Attorney General memoranda).

ist.[36] (See the discussion of the operation of these special provisions under Exclusions, below.)

Subsection (d) of the FOIA[37] makes clear that the Act was not intended to authorize any new withholding of information, including from Congress. While individual Members of Congress possess merely the same rights of access as those guaranteed to "any person" under subsection (a)(3), Congress as a body (or through its committees and subcommittees) cannot be denied access to information on the grounds of FOIA exemptions.[38]

Subsection (e) of the FOIA,[39] which was modified as part of the Electronic Freedom of Information Act Amendments of 1996,[40] requires an annual report from each federal agency regarding its FOIA operations and an annual report from the Department of Justice to Congress regarding both FOIA litigation and the Department of Justice's efforts (primarily through the Office of Information and Privacy) to encourage agency compliance with the FOIA.[41] Agencies now prepare annual reports of their FOIA sta-

---

[36] See Attorney General's 1986 Amendments Memorandum 18, 27.

[37] 5 U.S.C. § 552(d).

[38] See FOIA Update, Vol. V, No. 1, at 3-4 ("OIP Guidance: Congressional Access Under FOIA" (citing, e.g., H.R. Rep. No. 89-1497, at 11-12 (1966) and 5 U.S.C. § 552a(b)(9) (2000 & Supp. IV 2004) (counterpart provision of Privacy Act of 1974) to advise that "[e]ven where a FOIA request is made by a Member clearly acting in a completely official capacity, such a request does not properly trigger the special access rule of subsection ([d]) unless it is made by a committee or subcommittee chairman, or otherwise under the authority of a committee or subcommittee")); Application of Privacy Act Congressional-Disclosure Exception to Disclosures to Ranking Minority Members, Op. Off. Legal Counsel (Dec. 5, 2001), available at http://www. usdoj.gov/olc/2001/privacy_act_opinion.pdf (discussing congressional access under the Privacy Act); see also Leach v. RTC, 860 F. Supp. 868, 878-79 & n.13 (D.D.C. 1994) (treating contrary statements in Murphy v. Dep't of the Army, 613 F.2d 1151, 1155-59 (D.C. Cir. 1979), as no better than "mere dicta"), appeal dismissed per stipulation, No. 94-5279 (D.C. Cir. Dec. 22, 1994).

[39] 5 U.S.C. § 552(e).

[40] Pub. L. No. 104-231, 110 Stat. 3048.

[41] See 5 U.S.C. § 552(e)(5); see, e.g., FOIA Update, Vol. XIX, No. 3, at 6 (describing range of OIP policy activities in connection with government-wide implementation of Electronic FOIA amendments); FOIA Update, Vol. XIV, No. 3, at 8-9 (describing range of OIP policy activities, including its "ombudsman" function); see also FOIA Update, Vol. VIII, No. 3, at 2 (further description of same); FOIA Post, "FOIA Conferences Held by Growing

(continued...)

tistics for submission to the Department of Justice,[42] which reviews them for completeness[43] and then makes them available to the public, in a consolidated compilation, at a single World Wide Web site.[44] Each agency also must make its annual FOIA report readily available on its own FOIA Web site,[45] and it should do so promptly in order to facilitate the Department of Justice's preparation of summary compilations of all agencies' aggregate annual report data.[46] Significantly, as is further described below, as a result of the President's issuance of Executive Order 13,392, agency

---

[41](...continued)
Numbers of Agencies" (posted 2/22/05) (describing OIP's efforts to strongly encourage and support agencywide FOIA conferences throughout executive branch); cf. *FOIA Post*, "World Now Celebrates 'International Right to Know Day'" (posted 9/28/04) (describing OIP's extensive "implementation and training assistance" to several other nations with new FOIA-like regimes).

[42] See 5 U.S.C. § 552(e)(1); FOIA Update, Vol. XVIII, No. 3, at 3-7 ("OIP Guidance: Guidelines for Agency Preparation and Submission of Annual FOIA Reports"); *FOIA Post*, "Executive Order 13,392 Implementation Guidance" (posted 4/27/06) (detailing requirements for new Section XII in annual FOIA reports describing agency progress in implementing its FOIA Improvement Plan pursuant to Executive Order 13,392); see also *FOIA Post*, "FOIA Counselor Q&A: Annual FOIA Reports" (posted 12/19/03); *FOIA Post*, "Annual Report Guidance for DHS-Related Agencies" (posted 8/8/03); *FOIA Post*, "Supplemental Guidance on Annual FOIA Reports" (posted 8/13/01); FOIA Update, Vol. XIX, No. 3, at 2 (advising agencies on additional aspect of annual FOIA reports).

[43] See *FOIA Post*, "GAO E-FOIA Implementation Report Issued" (posted 3/23/01) (describing Office of Information and Privacy's process of reviewing all annual FOIA reports and contacting individual agencies to resolve any discrepancies found); see also *FOIA Post*, "Follow-Up Report on E-FOIA Implementation Issued" (posted 9/27/02) (describing progress made by agencies in improving quality of their annual FOIA reports).

[44] See FOIA Update, Vol. XIX, No. 3, at 2 (advising agencies on proper FOIA Web site treatment of their annual FOIA reports in compliance with electronic availability requirements of 5 U.S.C. § 552(e)(2)-(3), including through agency identification of URL (Uniform Resource Locator) for each report, and also referencing Department of Justice's FOIA Web site at http://www.usdoj.gov/04foia).

[45] See 5 U.S.C. § 552(e)(2); see also *FOIA Post*, "FOIA Counselor Q&A: Annual FOIA Reports" (advising agencies to correct any annual report error on Web site as well as in paper form); FOIA Update, Vol. XIX, No. 3, at 4 (advising agencies to "clearly indicate the year of each of [their annual FOIA] reports" on their FOIA Web sites).

[46] See, e.g., *FOIA Post*, "Summary of Annual FOIA Reports for Fiscal Year 2003" (posted 7/29/04).

annual FOIA reports now include a narrative description of the agency's progress in implementing the milestones and goals of its FOIA Improvement Plan, including highlights of agency achievements, a description of any deficiencies in meeting plan milestones, as well as the time range of pending requests and consultations.[47]

Subsection (f) of the FOIA[48] defines the term "agency" so as to subject the records of nearly all executive branch entities to the Act and defines the term "record" to include information maintained in an electronic format. (See the discussions of these terms under Procedural Requirements, Entities Subject to the FOIA, below, and Procedural Requirements, "Agency Records," below.) Lastly, subsection (g) of the FOIA[49] requires agencies to prepare FOIA reference guides describing their information systems and their processes of FOIA administration, as an aid to potential FOIA requesters.[50]

As originally enacted in 1966, the FOIA contained, in the views of many, several weaknesses that detracted from its ideal operation. In response, the courts fashioned certain procedural devices, such as the requirement of a "Vaughn Index" -- a detailed index of withheld documents and the justification for their exemption, established in Vaughn v. Rosen[51] -- and the requirement that agencies release reasonably segregable, non-exempt portions of a partially exempt record, which was first articulated in EPA v. Mink.[52]

---

[47] See 70 Fed. Reg. 75,373 (Dec. 14, 2005).

[48] 5 U.S.C. § 552(f)(1)-(2).

[49] Id. § 552(g).

[50] See Exec. Order No. 13,392, Sec. 2(b)(v) (referencing requirement to prepare handbook and linking that to facilitation of public understanding of FOIA operations); FOIA Update, Vol. XIX, No. 3, at 3 (referencing revised Office of Management and Budget guidance to agencies on contents of FOIA reference guides); FOIA Update, Vol. XVIII, No. 2, at 1 (discussing electronic availability of Justice Department's FOIA Reference Guide); see also Mount of Olives' Paralegals v. Bush, No. 04-CV-0044, 2004 U.S. Dist. LEXIS 8504, at 6 (S.D. Ill. Jan. 23, 2004) (suggesting to plaintiff that it consult Justice Department's FOIA Reference Guide in future); Pub. Citizen v. Lew, 127 F. Supp. 2d 1, 21 (D.D.C. 2000) (finding that several agencies initially misapplied OMB guidance on what constitutes "major information system").

[51] 484 F.2d 820, 827 (D.C. Cir. 1973).

[52] 410 U.S. at 91; see 5 U.S.C. § 552(b) (sentence immediately following exemptions) (requiring disclosure of any "reasonably segregable" nonexempt information); see also FOIA Update, Vol. XIV, No. 3, at 11-12 ("OIP Guidance: The 'Reasonable Segregation' Obligation"); cf. FOIA Update, Vol.
(continued...)

In an effort to further extend the FOIA's disclosure requirements, and also as a reaction to the abuses of the "Watergate era,"[53] the FOIA was substantially amended in 1974.[54] The 1974 FOIA amendments considerably narrowed the overall scope of the Act's law enforcement and national security exemptions, and also broadened many of its procedural provisions -- such as those relating to fees, time limits, segregability, and in camera inspection by the courts.[55] At the same time, Congress enacted the Privacy Act of 1974,[56] which supplements the FOIA when requests are made by individuals for access to records about themselves[57] and also contains a variety of separate privacy protections.[58] (For an extensive discussion of the Privacy Act's provisions, see the Department of Justice's "Overview of the Privacy Act of 1974," the most recent edition of which is contained in the Freedom of Information Act Guide & Privacy Act Overview (May 2004 ed.).)

In 1976, Congress again limited what could be withheld as exempt from disclosure under the FOIA, this time by narrowing the Act's incorpo-

---

[52](...continued)
XVII, No. 1, at 1-2 (describing agency use of document imaging in automated FOIA processing).

[53] See, e.g., Fund for Constitutional Gov't v. Nat'l Archives & Records Serv., 656 F.2d 856, 860 (D.C. Cir. 1981) (dealing with records of Watergate Special Prosecution Force); Congressional News Syndicate v. U.S. Dep't of Justice, 438 F. Supp. 538, 544 (D.D.C. 1977) (speaking of "aura of Watergate" in applying provisions of 1974 FOIA amendments).

[54] See Pub. L. No. 93-502, 88 Stat. 1561.

[55] See Attorney General's Memorandum on the 1974 Amendments to the Freedom of Information Act 1-26 (Feb. 1975) (addressing provisions of 1974 FOIA amendments); see also James T. O'Reilly, Federal Information Disclosure § 3.8 (3d ed. 2000) (summarizing 1974 FOIA amendments' provisions).

[56] 5 U.S.C. § 552a (2000 & Supp. IV 2004).

[57] See id. § 552a(d); see, e.g., Martin v. Office of Special Counsel, 819 F.2d 1181, 1184 (D.C. Cir. 1987) (discussing relation between two acts); see also 5 U.S.C. § 552a(t) (addressing interrelationship of exemptions in two acts); FOIA Update, Vol. VII, No. 1, at 6 (advising agencies to treat all first-party access requests as FOIA requests as well as Privacy Act requests).

[58] See 5 U.S.C. § 552a; see also Memorandum on Privacy and Personal Information in Federal Records, 34 Weekly Comp. Pres. Doc. 870 (May 14, 1998), available in Westlaw, 1998 WL 241263 (May 14, 1998) (executive memorandum to heads of all federal departments and agencies on Privacy Act-related matters); FOIA Update, Vol. XIX, No. 2, at 1 (describing executive memorandum).

# INTRODUCTION

ration of the nondisclosure provisions of other statutes.[59] (See the discussion of Exemption 3, below.) A technical change was made in 1978 to update the FOIA's provision for administrative disciplinary proceedings,[60] and in 1984 Congress repealed the expedited judicial review provision previously contained in former subsection (a)(4)(D) of the Act, replacing it with a more general statutory provision that allows courts to expedite a FOIA lawsuit only if "good cause therefor is shown."[61]

In 1986, after many years of administrative experience with the FOIA demonstrated that the Act was in need of both substantive and procedural reform,[62] Congress enacted the Freedom of Information Reform Act of 1986,[63] which amended the FOIA to provide broader exemption protection for law enforcement information, plus special law enforcement record exclusions, and also created a new fee and fee waiver structure.[64] The Department of Justice and other federal agencies took several steps to implement the provisions of the 1986 FOIA amendments.[65]

In 1996, after several years of legislative consideration of "electronic

---

[59] See Pub. L. No. 94-409, 90 Stat. 1241, 1247 (1976) (single FOIA amendment enacted together with the Government in the Sunshine Act in 1976, 5 U.S.C. § 552b (2000 & Supp. III 2003)). See generally FOIA Post, "Agencies Rely on Wide Range of Exemption 3 Statutes" (posted 12/16/03).

[60] See 5 U.S.C. § 552(a)(4)(F).

[61] See Federal Courts Improvement Act of 1984, Pub. L. No. 98-620, § 402, 98 Stat. 3335, 3357 (codified at 28 U.S.C. § 1657 (2000)) (repealing provision formerly codified at 5 U.S.C. § 552(a)(4)(D) (1982)); see also FOIA Update, Vol. VI, No. 2, at 6.

[62] See generally Freedom of Information Act: Hearings on S. 587, S. 1235, S. 1247, S. 1730, and S. 1751 Before the Subcomm. on the Constitution of the Senate Comm. on the Judiciary, 97th Cong., 1st Sess. (1981) (two volumes); see also FOIA Update, Vol. VII, No. 2, at 1; FOIA Update, Vol. V, No. 4, at 1; FOIA Update, Vol. V, No. 3, at 1, 4; FOIA Update, Vol. V, No. 1, at 1, 6; FOIA Update, Vol. IV, No. 3, at 1-2; FOIA Update, Vol. IV, No. 2, at 1; FOIA Update, Vol. III, No. 3, at 1-2; FOIA Update, Vol. III, No. 2, at 1-2; FOIA Update, Vol. III, No. 1, at 1-2, 3-8; FOIA Update, Vol. II, No. 4, at 1-2; FOIA Update, Vol. II, No. 3, at 1-2.

[63] Pub. L. No. 99-570, 100 Stat. 3207.

[64] See FOIA Update, Vol. VII, No. 4, at 1-2; see also id. at 3-6 (setting out statute in its amended form, interlineated to show exact changes made).

[65] See FOIA Update, Vol. VIII, No. 1, at 1-2; FOIA Update, Vol. IX, No. 3, at 1-14; FOIA Update, Vol. IX, No. 1, at 2; see also Attorney General's 1986 Amendments Memorandum 1-30.

record" issues,[66] Congress enacted the Electronic Freedom of Information Act Amendments of 1996,[67] which addressed the subject of electronic records, as well as the subject areas of FOIA reading rooms and agency backlogs of FOIA requests, among other procedural provisions.[68] (See the discussions of the various provisions of the Electronic FOIA amendments under FOIA Reading Rooms and Web Sites, Procedural Requirements, Fees and Fee Waivers, and Litigation Considerations, below.) The Department of Justice and other federal agencies took a number of steps to implement the provisions of the Electronic FOIA amendments.[69]

---

[66] See, e.g., FOIA Update, Vol. XIII, No. 2, at 1, 3-10 (congressional testimony discussing need to modify FOIA to accommodate "electronic record" environment); see FOIA Update, Vol. XVII, No. 3, at 1-2 (describing electronic record legislative proposal); FOIA Update, Vol. XVII, No. 2, at 1 (same); see also FOIA Update, Vol. XV, No. 4, at 1-6; FOIA Update, Vol. XV, No. 3, at 1-2; FOIA Update, Vol. XV, No. 1, at 1; FOIA Update, Vol. XII, No. 4, at 1-2.

[67] Pub. L. No. 104-231, 110 Stat. 3048.

[68] See FOIA Update, Vol. XVII, No. 4, at 1-2, 10-11 (discussing statutory changes); see also id. at 3-9 (setting out statute in its amended form, interlineated to show exact changes made); President's Statement on Signing the Electronic Freedom of Information Act Amendments of 1996, 32 Weekly Comp. Pres. Doc. 1949 (Oct. 7, 1996), reprinted in FOIA Update, Vol. XVII, No. 4, at 9.

[69] See FOIA Post, "Electronic Compilation of E-FOIA Implementation Guidance" (posted 2/28/03); FOIA Post, "FOIA Officers Conference Scheduled" (posted 9/17/02); FOIA Post, "GAO to Update Its E-FOIA Implementation Study" (posted 3/8/02); FOIA Post, "GAO E-FOIA Implementation Report Issued" (posted 3/23/01) (discussing governmentwide Electronic FOIA amendment implementation activities); FOIA Update, Vol. XIX, No. 3, at 5-6 (Department of Justice congressional testimony describing agency's amendment-implementation activities); id. at 3-4 ("OIP Guidance: Recommendations for FOIA Web Sites"); FOIA Update, Vol. XIX, No. 1, at 3-5 ("OIP Guidance: Electronic FOIA Amendments Implementation Guidance Outline"); FOIA Update, Vol. XVIII, No. 3, at 1-2 (describing agency amendment-implementation activities involving development of World Wide Web sites); id. at 3-7 (Department of Justice guidelines on implementation of new annual reporting requirements); FOIA Update, Vol. XVIII, No. 2, at 1 (describing Justice Department's amendment-implementation activities, including development of FOIA Reference Guide); FOIA Update, Vol. XVIII, No. 1, at 3-7 (addressing amendment-implementation questions); FOIA Update, Vol. XVII, No. 4, at 1-11 (describing amendments); see also FOIA Post, "FOIA Counselor Q&A: Annual FOIA Reports" (posted 12/19/03); FOIA Post, "Annual Report Guidance for DHS-Related Agencies" (posted 8/8/03); FOIA Post, "Supplemental Guidance on Annual FOIA Reports" (posted 8/13/01); FOIA Post, "Agencies Continue E-FOIA Implementation"

(continued...)

# INTRODUCTION

A more recent significant Freedom of Information Act development was the issuance in October 2001 of a statement of FOIA policy by Attorney General John Ashcroft.[70] The Ashcroft FOIA Memorandum emphasizes the Bush Administration's commitment to full compliance with the FOIA as an important means of maintaining an open and accountable system of government.[71] At the same time, it recognizes the importance of protecting the sensitive institutional, commercial, and personal interests that can be implicated in government records -- such as the need to safeguard national security, to enhance law enforcement effectiveness, to respect business confidentiality, to protect internal agency deliberations, and to preserve personal privacy.[72]

The Ashcroft FOIA Memorandum establishes a "sound legal basis" standard governing the Department of Justice's decisions on whether to defend agency actions under the FOIA when they are challenged in court.[73] Under this newer standard, agencies should reach the judgment that their

---

[69](...continued)
(posted 3/14/01); FOIA Update, Vol. XIX, No. 4, at 4-5 (emphasizing importance of "new partnership" between agency FOIA officers and agency Information Technology (IT) personnel in Electronic FOIA amendment implementation); FOIA Update, Vol. XIX, No. 3, at 2 (addressing additional amendment-implementation questions); FOIA Update, Vol. XIX, No. 2, at 2 ("Web Site Watch" discussion of agency FOIA Web sites); FOIA Update, Vol. XIX, No. 1, at 2 (same); FOIA Update, Vol. XIX, No. 1, at 6 (addressing additional amendment-implementation questions); FOIA Update, Vol. XVIII, No. 2, at 2 (same); cf. FOIA Post, "Summary of Annual FOIA Reports for Fiscal Year 2003" (posted 7/29/04). See generally Department of Justice FOIA Regulations, 28 C.F.R. pt. 16 (2006); FOIA Post, "Follow-Up Report on E-FOIA Implementation Issued" (posted 9/27/02) (describing GAO supplemental review of agency amendment-implementation activities); FOIA Update, Vol. XIX, No. 3, at 1 (describing 1998 congressional hearing on agency amendment-implementation activities).

[70] Attorney General Ashcroft's FOIA Memorandum, reprinted in *FOIA Post* (posted 10/15/01) (superseding predecessor Attorney General FOIA policy memorandum that had been in effect since 1993).

[71] See *FOIA Post*, "New Attorney General FOIA Memorandum Issued" (posted 10/15/01) (describing Attorney General Ashcroft's FOIA Memorandum); see also Presidential Memorandum for Heads of Departments and Agencies Regarding the Freedom of Information Act, 29 Weekly Comp. Pres. Doc. 1999 (Oct. 4, 1993), reprinted in FOIA Update, Vol. XIV, No. 3, at 3 (emphasizing importance of FOIA).

[72] See Attorney General Ashcroft's FOIA Memorandum, reprinted in *FOIA Post* (posted 10/15/01) (recognizing protection of such interests as among "fundamental values that are held by our society").

[73] Id.

use of a FOIA exemption is on sound footing, both factually and legally, whenever they withhold requested information.[74] Significantly, the Ashcroft FOIA Memorandum also recognizes the continued agency practice of considering whether to make "discretionary disclosures" of information that is exempt under the Act, upon "full and deliberate consideration" of all interests involved.[75] The Ashcroft FOIA Memorandum describes the "institutional, commercial, and personal privacy" interests that are protected by the Act's exemptions,[76] and reminds agencies "to carefully consider the protection of all such values and interests when making disclosure determinations under the FOIA."[77]

Most significantly, during this past year the FOIA landscape saw an unprecedented development in the issuance of Executive Order 13,392, which is entitled "Improving Agency Disclosure of Information."[78] This first-of-its-kind FOIA executive order establishes a "citizen-centered" and "results-oriented" policy for improving the Act's administration throughout the executive branch and it draws new attention to the challenges presented by agency backlogs of pending FOIA requests.[79] Fundamentally, Executive Order 13,392 emphasizes the FOIA's importance to "[t]he effective

---

[74] See *FOIA Post*, "New Attorney General FOIA Memorandum Issued" (posted 10/15/01) (discussing new FOIA policy).

[75] Attorney General Ashcroft's FOIA Memorandum, reprinted in *FOIA Post* (posted 10/15/01); see also *FOIA Post*, "New Attorney General FOIA Memorandum Issued" (posted 10/15/01) (reminding agencies that much FOIA-exempt information is subject to statutory disclosure prohibitions as well as standard prudential considerations).

[76] See Attorney General Ashcroft's FOIA Memorandum, reprinted in *FOIA Post* (posted 10/15/01); see also *FOIA Post*, "New Attorney General FOIA Memorandum Issued" (posted 10/15/01).

[77] Attorney General Ashcroft's FOIA Memorandum, reprinted in *FOIA Post* (posted 10/15/01); see White House Memorandum for Heads of Executive Departments and Agencies Concerning Safeguarding Information Related to Homeland Security (Mar. 19, 2002), reprinted in *FOIA Post* (posted 3/21/02) (focusing on need to protect sensitive homeland security-related information); *FOIA Post*, "New Attorney General FOIA Memorandum Issued" (posted 10/15/01) (highlighting government's "need to protect critical systems, facilities, stockpiles, and other assets from security breaches and harm -- and in some instances from their potential use as weapons of mass destruction in and of themselves"); see also *FOIA Post*, "FOIA Officers Conference Held on Homeland Security" (posted 7/3/03) (discussing the Ashcroft FOIA Memorandum in the context of homeland security-related considerations and the protection of "information viewed as sensitive through a post-9/11 lens").

[78] 70 Fed. Reg. 75,373.

[79] Exec. Order No. 13,392, Sec. 1(b), (c).

functioning of our constitutional democracy," and it pointedly reminds all federal agencies that "FOIA requesters are seeking a service from the federal government and should be treated as such."[80]

Accordingly, the Executive Order states an overall policy of responding to FOIA requests "courteously and appropriately" and in ways that permit FOIA requesters to "learn about the FOIA process," most particularly "about the status of a person's FOIA request."[81] It calls upon all federal agencies to discharge their FOIA responsibilities in an efficient and "results-oriented" manner and to "achieve tangible, measurable improvements in FOIA processing."[82] Its stated goal is to "improve service and performance" and "increase efficiency" in agency FOIA operations, "thereby strengthening compliance with the FOIA" and minimizing both "disputes and related litigation" arising under it.[83] It takes great strides toward that goal through the establishment of such creative new mechanisms as Chief FOIA Officers, FOIA Requester Service Centers, FOIA Public Liaisons, and FOIA Improvement Plans at all federal agencies.[84]

Under Executive Order 13,392, each of the ninety-two federal agencies subject to the Act now has a Chief FOIA Officer, all of whom are listed on the Department of Justice's FOIA site on the World Wide Web.[85] In accordance with the Executive Order's requirements, during the first half of 2006 these newly designated high-level agency officials undertook wide-ranging reviews of their agencies' FOIA operations, in order to develop detailed FOIA Improvement Plans.[86] These plans were developed in close coordination with the Department of Justice, which issued extensive written guidance and conducted several governmentwide meetings in order to fa-

---

[80] Id. at Sec. 1(a), (b).

[81] Id. at Sec. 1(b).

[82] Id. at Sec. 1(c).

[83] Id. at Sec. 1(c), (d).

[84] See id. at Sec. 2(a), (c); id. at Sec. 3(b).

[85] See http://www.usdoj.gov/04foia/chieffoiaofficers.html.

[86] See Exec. Order No. 13,392, Sec. 3(a)-(b); see also Attorney General's Report to the President Pursuant to Executive Order 13,392, Entitled "Improving Agency Disclosure of Information," 4 (Oct. 16, 2006), available at http://www.usdoj.gov/oip/ag_report_to_president_13392.pdf (noting that "OIP has compiled these plans and makes them available for convenient public access at a single location on its FOIA Web site" and that "any interested person can examine all agency FOIA improvement plans under Executive Order 13,392, side by side, through a standard format recommended for ease of reference, just as they are able to do with the annual FOIA reports that agencies file").

cilitate full and proper Executive Order 13,392 implementation.[87] Agencies then reported on their progress under their FOIA Improvement Plans in their annual FOIA reports for fiscal year 2006, which are made available on the Department of Justice's FOIA Web site.[88] (For further discussions of Executive Order 13,392, see FOIA Reading Rooms and Web Sites, below, Procedural Requirements, Executive Order 13,392, below, and Fees and Fee Waivers, below.)

Lastly, it should be noted that the FOIA was amended by the Intelligence Authorization Act of 2003, effective as of November 27, 2002.[89] The FOIA now contains language that precludes agencies of the "intelligence community"[90] from disclosing records in response to any FOIA request that

---

[87] See *FOIA Post*, "Executive Order 13,392 Implementation Guidance" (posted 4/27/06) (providing more than two dozen potential improvement areas for possible inclusion in agency plans); accord Exec. Order No. 13,392, Sec. 4(b) (directing Department of Justice to "issue such instructions and guidance . . . as may be appropriate" to implement certain provisions of Executive Order).

[88] See Annual FOIA Reports, available at http://www.usdoj.gov/oip /fy06.html; see also *FOIA Post*, "Executive Order 13,392 Implementation Guidance" (posted 4/27/06) (establishing uniform template for reporting Executive Order 13,392 results as part of annual FOIA reports); Attorney General's Report to the President Pursuant to Executive Order 13,392, Entitled "Improving Agency Disclosure of Information," 15 (Oct. 16, 2006), available at http://www.usdoj.gov/oip/ag_report_to_president_13392.pdf (recommending special conference of agency Chief FOIA Officers, subsequently conducted by Department of Justice on Nov. 9, 2006, for purpose of placing pointed emphasis on importance of meeting then-upcoming executive order deadlines); Implementing FOIA [Freedom of Information Act] - Assessing Agency Efforts to meet FOIA Requirements: Hearing Before the Subcomm. on Information Policy, Census, and National Archives of the Comm. on Oversight and Government Reform, 110th Cong. (2007) (statement of Melanie Ann Pustay, Acting Director, Office of Information and Privacy), available at http://www.usdoj.gov/oip /foia30.pdf (describing OIP's extensive executive order implementation efforts, including its "public outreach activities"); Implementing FOIA [Freedom of Information Act] - Does the Bush Administration Executive Order Improve Processing?: Hearing Before the Subcomm. on Government Management, Finance and Accountability of the Comm. on Government Reform, 109th Cong. (2006), available at http://www.usdoj.gov/oip/ metcalfe_foia_ testimony07252006.pdf (same).

[89] Pub. L. No. 107-306, 116 Stat. 2383 (2002).

[90] See 50 U.S.C.A. § 401a(4) (2003 & West Supp. 2006) (provision of the National Security Act of 1947, as amended, that specifies the federal agencies and agency subparts that are deemed "elements of the intelligence (continued...)

is made by any foreign government or international governmental organization, either directly or through a representative.[91] Significantly, this is the first time that Congress has departed from the general rule that "any person" may submit a FOIA request.[92]

In sum, the FOIA is a vital and continuously developing government disclosure mechanism which, with refinements over time to accommodate both technological advancements and society's maturing interests in an open and fully responsible government, truly enhances our democratic way of life.[93]

## FOIA READING ROOMS AND WEB SITES

Subsection (a)(2) of the FOIA,[1] which provides for what is commonly referred to as "reading room" access to certain agency records,[2] serves an increasingly vital role in achieving the "informed citizenry" that is the cen-

---

[90](...continued)
community").

[91] Pub. L. No. 107-306, 116 Stat. 2383, § 312 (codified at 5 U.S.C. § 552(a)(3)(A), (E) (2000 & Supp. IV 2004)); see also FOIA Post, "FOIA Amended by Intelligence Authorization Act" (posted 12/23/02) (advising that "for any FOIA request that by its nature appears as if it might have been made by or on behalf of a non-U.S. governmental entity, a covered agency may inquire into the particular circumstances of the requester in order to properly implement this new FOIA provision").

[92] 5 U.S.C. § 552(a)(3)(A); see Favish, 541 U.S. at 170 (observing that the FOIA has "a general rule" that "the identity of the requester" is not taken into consideration) (emphasis added).

[93] See FOIA Post, "FOIA Post Interview: Chairman Stephen Horn" (posted 12/23/03) (publicizing observations by the outgoing chairman of the FOIA subcommittee of the House of Representatives regarding, inter alia, "the critical role that public access to Government information plays in our democracy"); see also Attorney General's Report to the President Pursuant to Executive Order 13,392, Entitled "Improving Agency Disclosure of Information," 1 (Oct. 16, 2006), available at http://www.usdoj.gov/oip/ag_report_to_president_13392.pdf (describing the FOIA as "a fundamental cornerstone of our modern democratic system of government"); Favish, 541 U.S. at 172 (emphasizing that the FOIA is vital to "a real democracy"); FOIA Post, "OIP Gives Implementation Advice to Other Nations" (posted 12/12/02) (describing progress in establishing "transparency in government" worldwide).

[1] 5 U.S.C. § 552(a)(2) (2000 & Supp. IV 2004).

[2] See FOIA Update, Vol. XIII, No. 3, at 3-4 ("OIP Guidance: The 'Automatic' Disclosure Provisions of FOIA: Subsections (a)(1) & (a)(2)").

tral purpose of the FOIA.[3] While the usefulness of this provision historically has depended on the public's ability to visit an agency's reading room in person, agencies now are required to maintain these records on the World Wide Web in "electronic reading rooms"[4] and now use FOIA Web sites as a major part of their processes of FOIA administration -- which has brought ever-increasing attention to this FOIA provision in particular and to agency FOIA Web sites overall.[5]

## FOIA Reading Rooms

Subsection (a)(2) of the FOIA applies to certain basic agency records that, while not automatically published under subsection (a)(1) of the Act,[6] must routinely be made "available for public inspection and copying" in agency reading rooms.[7] This public inspection obligation applies to all federal agencies, it governs all records covered by subsection (a)(2) except those "offered for sale,"[8] and it extends to the maintenance of "electronic reading rooms" as well.[9] By the same token, records required to be made publicly available pursuant to subsection (a)(2) ordinarily cannot be the

---

[3] NLRB v. Robbins Tire & Rubber Co., 437 U.S. 214, 242 (1978); see also *FOIA Post*, "Executive Order 13,392 Implementation Guidance" (posted 4/27/06) (emphasizing importance of "reading room" access under first-of-its-kind FOIA executive order, Exec. Order No. 13,392, 70 Fed. Reg. 75,373 (Dec. 14, 2005)).

[4] 5 U.S.C. § 552(a)(2).

[5] See, e.g., *FOIA Post*, "GAO E-FOIA Implementation Report Issued" (posted 3/23/01) (describing GAO report's emphasis on agency compliance with "electronic reading room" obligations); *FOIA Post*, "Agencies Continue E-FOIA Implementation" (posted 3/14/01) (advising of growing attention being paid to agencies' "electronic reading rooms"); see also Exec. Order No. 13,392 (requiring agencies to review practices relating to making information available on agency Web sites).

[6] 5 U.S.C. § 552(a)(1) (2000 & Supp. IV 2004) (providing for Federal Register publication of very basic agency information, as discussed under Introduction, above).

[7] Id. § 552(a)(2); see Jordan v. U.S. Dep't of Justice, 591 F.2d 753, 756 (D.C. Cir. 1978) (en banc) (observing that subsection (a)(2) records must be made "automatically available for public inspection; no demand is necessary"); see also FOIA Update, Vol. XVIII, No. 1, at 4 (advising that large agencies with decentralized FOIA operations may maintain separate reading rooms for agency components).

[8] 5 U.S.C. § 552(a)(2).

[9] See FOIA Update, Vol. XVII, No. 4, at 1-2 (describing "electronic reading room" requirements under Electronic Freedom of Information Act Amendments of 1996, Pub. L. No. 104-231, 110 Stat. 3048).

FOIA READING ROOMS AND WEB SITES

subject of regular "FOIA requests."[10]

For the first thirty years of the FOIA's operation, three categories of records -- "final opinions [and] . . . orders" rendered in the adjudication of administrative cases,[11] specific agency policy statements,[12] and certain ad-

---

[10] See 5 U.S.C. § 552(a)(3)(A) (stating general rule that "FOIA request" under subsection (a)(3) cannot be made for any record that is "made available" under subsections (a)(1) or (a)(2)); see also U.S. Dep't of Justice v. Tax Analysts, 492 U.S. 136, 152 (1989) ("Under subsection (a)(3) . . . an agency need not make available those materials that have already been disclosed under subsections (a)(1) and (a)(2)."); Schwarz v. U.S. Patent & Trademark Office, No. 95-5349, 1996 U.S. App. LEXIS 4609, at *1 (D.C. Cir. Feb. 22, 1996) (finding that agency was not required to disclose records from patent files in response to a subsection (a)(3) request because patent files are available for public inspection and copying under subsection (a)(2)); Crews v. Internal Revenue, No. 99-8388, 2000 U.S. Dist. LEXIS 21077, at *16 (C.D. Cal. Apr. 26, 2000) (declaring that policy statements and administrative staff manuals made available under subsection (a)(2) are not required to be made available in response to subsection (a)(3) requests); Reeves v. United States, No. 94-1291, 1994 WL 782235, at *1-2 (E.D. Cal. Nov. 16, 1994) (dismissing lawsuit because FOIA requests sought publicly available agency regulations). But see FOIA Update, Vol. XVIII, No. 1, at 3 (advising of major exception to general rule for records falling within subsection (a)(2)(D)).

[11] 5 U.S.C. § 552(a)(2)(A); see, e.g., NLRB v. Sears, Roebuck & Co., 421 U.S. 132, 155-59 (1975) (holding that NLRB "advice and appeals" memorandum deciding not to file unfair labor complaint was "final opinion" when decision not to file effectively put an end to formal complaint procedure); Rockwell Int'l Corp. v. U.S. Dep't of Justice, 235 F.3d 598, 603 (D.C. Cir. 2001) (finding that agency report of voluntarily conducted internal investigation into propriety of Rocky Flats prosecution was not "final opinion" because determination of propriety of prosecution was neither "case" nor "adjudication"); Nat'l Prison Project v. Sigler, 390 F. Supp. 789, 792-93 (D.D.C. 1975) (determining that parole board decisions denying inmate applications for parole were "reading room" records).

[12] 5 U.S.C. § 552(a)(2)(B); see, e.g., Bailey v. Sullivan, 885 F.2d 52, 62 (3d Cir. 1977) (stating that Social Security Ruling providing examples of medical conditions to be treated as "per se nonsevere" fell under subsection (a)(2)(B)); Pa. Dep't of Pub. Welfare v. United States, No. 99-175, 2001 U.S. Dist. LEXIS 3492, at *90 (W.D. Pa. Feb. 7, 2001) (holding that HHS documents that advised regional offices of agency's view on policy matters pertaining to certain welfare programs were "interpretations adopted by the agency"); Tax Analysts v. IRS, No. 94-923, 1996 U.S. Dist. LEXIS 3259, at *9 (D.D.C. Mar. 15, 1996) (holding that IRS Field Service Advice Memoranda, even though not binding on IRS personnel, were "statements of policy"), aff'd on other grounds, 117 F.3d 607 (D.C. Cir. 1997); Pub. Citizen v. Office of U.S. Trade Representative, 804 F. Supp. 385, 387 (D.D.C. 1992) (conclud-
(continued...)

ministrative staff manuals "that affect a member of the public"[13] -- have
been made available routinely in agency reading rooms.[14] Such records
must be indexed by agencies in order to facilitate the public's convenient
access to them.[15]

---

[12](...continued)
ing that agency submissions to a trade panel containing an agency's interpretation of U.S.'s international legal obligations were "statements of policy
and interpretations adopted by the [agency]"); see also Vietnam Veterans
of Am. v. Dep't of the Navy, 876 F.2d 164, 165 (D.C. Cir. 1989) (finding that
opinions in which Judge Advocates General of Army and Navy have authority only to dispense legal advice -- rendered in subject areas for which
those officials do not have authority to act on behalf of agency -- were not
"statements of policy or interpretations adopted by" those agencies and
were not required to be published or made available for public inspection).

[13] 5 U.S.C. § 552(a)(2)(C); see, e.g., Sladek v. Bensinger, 605 F.2d 899, 901
(5th Cir. 1979) (finding DEA agents' manual concerning treatment of confidential informants and search warrant procedures to be subsection
(a)(2)(C) record); Stokes v. Brennan, 476 F.2d 699, 701 (5th Cir. 1973) (determining that "Training Course for Compliance Safety and Health Officers,"
including all instructor and student manuals, training slides, films, and vis-
ual aids, must be made available for public inspection and copying); Fire-
stone Tire & Rubber Co. v. Coleman, 432 F. Supp. 1359, 1364-65 (N.D. Ohio
1976) (ruling that memoranda approved by Office of Standards Enforcement, which set forth agency's policy regarding sampling plans that office
must follow when tire fails lab test under Federal Motor Vehicle Safety
Standards, were "reading room" records); see also Stanley v. DOD, No. 98-
CV-4116, slip op. at 9-10 (S.D. Ill. June 22, 1999) (finding that administrative staff manuals pertaining to military hospital procedures did not "affect
the public" and were not required to be given "reading room" treatment).

[14] See FOIA Update, Vol. XIII, No. 3, at 4 (describing categories of records required to be placed in agency reading rooms).

[15] See 5 U.S.C. § 552(a)(2); see, e.g., Irons & Sears v. Dann, 606 F.2d 1215,
1223 (D.C. Cir. 1979) (requiring agency to provide "reasonable index" of requested decisions); Taxation With Representation Fund v. IRS, 2 Gov't Disclosure Serv. (P-H) ¶ 81,028, at 81,080 (D.D.C. Apr. 22, 1980) (recognizing
agency's "continuing duty" to make subsection (a)(2) records and indices
available); see also Pa. Dep't of Pub. Welfare, 2001 U.S. Dist. LEXIS 3492, at
*82 (finding agency in violation of indexing requirement because index
was incomplete and it was "nearly impossible" to distinguish precedential
material from obsolete material). See generally FOIA Update, Vol. XVII,
No. 4, at 2 (discussing statutory indexing requirements under Electronic
FOIA amendments). But cf. Tax Analysts v. IRS, No. 94-923, 1998 WL
419755, at *5 (D.D.C. May 1, 1998) (concluding that court has "no statutory
authority for actually ordering . . . a remedy" regarding indexing requirement), appeal dismissed voluntarily, No. 94-5252 (D.C. Cir. Aug. 11, 1998).

Routine public access to such records serves to guard against the development of agency "secret law" known to agency personnel but not to members of the public who deal with agencies, so records that have no precedential value and do not constitute the working law of the agency are not required to be made available under this part of the Act.[16] In addition, agencies may "withhold" (i.e., not make available) a subsection (a)(2) record (or portion of such a record) if it falls within a FOIA exemption, just as

---

[16] See Sears, 421 U.S. at 153-54 (observing that the reading room provision "represents a strong congressional aversion to 'secret [agency] law,' . . . and represents an affirmative congressional purpose to require disclosure of documents which have 'the force and effect of law'" (quoting H.R. Rep. No. 89-1497, at 7 (1966))); Skelton v. USPS, 678 F.2d 35, 41 (5th Cir. 1982) ("That requirement was designed to help the citizen find agency statements 'having precedential significance' when he becomes involved in 'a controversy with an agency.'" (quoting H.R. Rep. No. 89-1497, at 8)); Attorney General's Memorandum on the 1974 Amendments to the Freedom of Information Act 19 (Feb. 1975) (explaining that the "primary purpose of subsection (a)(2) was to compel disclosure of what has been called 'secret law,' or as the 1966 House Report put it, agency materials which have 'the force and effect of law in most cases'" (quoting H.R. Rep. No. 89-1497, at 7)); Attorney General's Memorandum on the Public Information Section of the Administrative Procedure Act 15 (June 1967) [hereinafter Attorney General's 1967 FOIA Memorandum] (advising that keeping "orders available in reading rooms . . . [that] have no precedential value, often would be impracticable and would serve no useful purpose"); see also Smith v. NTSB, 981 F.2d 1326, 1328 (D.C. Cir. 1993) (stating that the purpose of this "requirement is obviously to give the public notice of what the law is so that each individual can act accordingly"); Vietnam Veterans of Am., 876 F.2d at 165 (rejecting argument that legal opinions issued by Judge Advocates General of Army and Navy must be placed in agency reading room, because those opinions are not statements of policy that "operate as law"); Doe v. U.S. Dep't of Labor, No. 05-2449, 2006 WL 2615101, at *13 (D.D.C. Sept. 6, 2006) (finding that Employee Compensation Appeals Board decisions "form an essential corpus of administrative precedent" and are properly placed in an agency's reading room); Pa. Dep't of Pub. Welfare, 2001 U.S. Dist. LEXIS 3492, at *78 (holding that a FOIA reading room index "must include those matters that the agency considers to be of precedential value"); Stanley, No. 98-CV-4116, slip op. at 9-10 (S.D. Ill. June 22, 1999) (holding that administrative staff manuals that do not have any "precedential significance" and would not assist members of the public in "tailor[ing] their behavior to the law" are not required to be made publicly available in an agency reading room). But see Nat'l Prison Project, 390 F. Supp. at 793 (ruling otherwise prior to Supreme Court's instructive emphasis on legislative history of subsection (a)(2) in Sears); Tax Analysts & Advocates v. IRS, 362 F. Supp. 1298, 1303 (D.D.C. 1973) (same), modified & remanded on other grounds, 505 F.2d 350 (D.C. Cir. 1974).

they can do in response to FOIA requests.[17] Likewise, records that are published and offered for sale by an agency, either directly or indirectly,[18] are not required to be placed in an agency's reading room.[19]

---

[17] See, e.g., Fed. Open Market Comm. v. Merrill, 443 U.S. 340, 360 n.23 (1979) (applying commercial privilege to subsection (a)(1) record and recognizing that subsection (a)(2) records likewise may be protected by FOIA exemptions); Renegotiation Bd. v. Grumman Aircraft Eng'g Corp., 421 U.S. 168, 184 n.21 (1975) (acknowledging that subsection (a)(2) records may be protected by FOIA exemptions); Sears, 421 U.S. at 160 (finding it unnecessary to decide whether documents were subsection (a)(2) records, because attorney work-product privilege protected them in any event); Sladek, 605 F.2d at 901 (applying Exemption 2 to portions of subsection (a)(2)(C) record); Doe, 2006 WL 2615101, at *13 (finding that agency's placement of subsection (a)(2)(A) decisions in reading room without redacting claimants' names violated Privacy Act of 1974, 5 U.S.C. § 552a (2000 & Supp. IV 2004)); Peter S. Herrick's Customs & Int'l Trade Newsletter v. U.S. Customs & Border Prot., No. 04-3777, 2006 WL 1826185, at *3 n.2 (D.D.C. June 30, 2006) (recognizing that contents of subsection (a)(2)(C) documents can be withheld pursuant to FOIA exemptions) (appeal pending); Tax Analysts, 1996 U.S. Dist. LEXIS 3259, at *9-10 (applying attorney work-product privilege to subsection (a)(2)(B) records); see also FOIA Update, Vol. XIII, No. 3, at 4 (advising that "an agency may withhold any record or record portion falling within subsection (a)(2) . . . if it is of such sensitivity as to fall within a FOIA exemption").

[18] See, e.g., FOIA Post, "NTIS: An Available Means of Record Disclosure" (posted 8/30/02) (describing operation of National Technical Information Service (commonly known as "NTIS") in governmentwide process of record dissemination); Uniform Freedom of Information Act Fee Schedule and Guidelines, 52 Fed. Reg. 10,018 (1987) (recognizing NTIS as "statutor[il]y-based" government record distribution program); cf. White House Memorandum for Heads of Executive Departments and Agencies Concerning Safeguarding Information Regarding Weapons of Mass Destruction and Other Sensitive Documents Related to Homeland Security (Mar. 19, 2002) [hereinafter White House Homeland Security Memorandum], reprinted in FOIA Post (posted 3/21/02) (requiring agencies to exercise special care in distributing information through Defense Technical Information Center (commonly known as "DTIC"), particularly regarding information relating to development of weapons of mass destruction, in light of heightened homeland security concerns).

[19] See, e.g., Gaunce v. Burnett, 849 F.2d 1475, 1475 (9th Cir. 1988) (unpublished table decision) (finding assessment of $13.25 for copy of FAA order proper, notwithstanding its subsection (a)(2) character, because "FOIA allows copies of orders to be 'offered for sale'"); Jackson v. Heckler, 580 F. Supp. 1077, 1081 (E.D. Pa. 1984) (holding that Social Security Ruling relied on by administrative law judge need not be made "available for inspection and copying" pursuant to subsection (a)(2)(B) because it was

(continued...)

Agencies have made good use of their FOIA reading rooms in achieving efficient "affirmative" disclosure of records that otherwise might be sought through less efficient FOIA requests.[20] In so doing, though, they must be mindful of the distinction between subsection (a)(2) records (i.e., "reading room" records) and subsection (a)(3) records (i.e., records subject to standard "FOIA requests") under the Act.[21]

The Electronic Freedom of Information Act Amendments of 1996[22] heavily modified the requirements of subsection (a)(2) by creating a fourth category of "reading room" records,[23] and by establishing a requirement for the electronic availability of "reading room" records in what are referred to

---

[19](...continued)
"published for sale"); see also FOIA Update, Vol. XVII, No. 4, at 1 (noting that "reading room" obligation does not apply to any records that "are promptly published and [are] offered for sale" (quoting 5 U.S.C. § 552(a)(2))); Attorney General's 1967 FOIA Memorandum 15 (noting that "[t]his is to afford the agency 'an alternative means of making these materials available through publication'" (quoting S. Rep. No. 89-813, at 7 (1966))); cf. NARA v. Favish, 541 U.S. 157, 169 (evincing the Supreme Court's reliance on "the Attorney General's consistent interpretation of" the FOIA in successive such Attorney General memoranda), reh'g denied, 541 U.S. 1057 (2004).

[20] See, e.g., FOIA Update, Vol. XVI, No. 1, at 1-2 (promoting "affirmative" agency disclosure practices through "reading room" access, among other means); FOIA Update, Vol. XIX, No. 1, at 1 (discussing Department of the Air Force affirmative electronic information disclosure program); see also Exec. Order No. 13,392, Sec. 3(b)(ii) (requiring agencies' FOIA Implementation Plans to include increased reliance on affirmative availability of records); FOIA Post, "Executive Order 13,392 Implementation Guidance" (posted 4/27/06) (discussing importance of continuing obligation to make subsection (a)(2) records affirmatively available); FOIA Post, "FOIA Counselor Q&A: 'Frequently Requested' Records" (posted 7/25/03) (emphasizing that bringing any "pre-existing reading room availability" to "FOIA requesters' attention . . . could be a basis for resolving their requests most efficiently").

[21] See, e.g., FOIA Update, Vol. XVI, No. 1, at 2 (reminding that "an agency cannot convert a subsection (a)(3) record into a subsection (a)(2) record (which cannot be the subject of a FOIA request under subsection (a)(3)) just by voluntarily placing it into its reading room"); FOIA Update, Vol. XII, No. 2, at 5 (advising that FOIA requesters may not be deprived of subsection (a)(3) access rights through voluntary "reading room" availability). But cf. Tax Analysts, 1998 WL 419755, at *4 (failing to distinguish between records subject to subsection (a)(2) and those subject to subsection (a)(3)).

[22] Pub. L. No. 104-231, 110 Stat. 3048.

[23] See 5 U.S.C. § 552(a)(2)(D).

as "electronic reading rooms."[24] The Electronic FOIA amendments greatly elevated the role of agency reading rooms -- and, in turn, agency sites on the World Wide Web -- in the processes of FOIA administration.[25]

First, in addition to the traditional three categories of "reading room" records discussed above, agencies must also include any records processed and disclosed in response to a FOIA request that "the agency determines have become or are likely to become the subject of subsequent requests for substantially the same records."[26] Under this provision, when records are disclosed in response to a FOIA request, an agency is required to determine whether they have been the subject of multiple FOIA requests (i.e., two or more additional ones) or, in the agency's best judgment based upon the nature of the records and the types of requests regularly received, are likely to be the subject of multiple requests in the future.[27]

Inasmuch as this requirement by definition begins with the processing of records disclosed in response to a FOIA request, and then is met by multiple other such "requests,"[28] it is either the receipt or the anticipation of the third such request that triggers it.[29] If either is the case,[30] then those

---

[24] See id. § 552(a)(2); see also FOIA Update, Vol. XIX, No. 4, at 4-5 (emphasizing importance of "electronic reading rooms" in satisfying FOIA obligations); FOIA Update, Vol. XVII, No. 4, at 1-2 (discussing statutory changes).

[25] See FOIA Post, "Agencies Continue E-FOIA Implementation" (posted 3/14/01) (advising of growing attention being paid to agencies' "electronic reading rooms"); see also FOIA Post, "Follow-Up Report on E-FOIA Implementation Issued" (posted 9/27/02) (describing results of GAO's updated review of agency compliance with "electronic reading room" requirements); FOIA Post, "GAO E-FOIA Implementation Report Issued" (posted 3/23/01) (describing GAO report's emphasis on agency compliance with "electronic reading room" obligations); FOIA Update, Vol. XIX, No. 3, at 1 (describing 1998 congressional hearing on agency amendment-implementation activities).

[26] 5 U.S.C. § 552(a)(2)(D).

[27] See FOIA Update, Vol. XVIII, No. 1, at 3-4 (advising on processes for exercise of agency judgment under fourth "reading room" category).

[28] 5 U.S.C. § 552(a)(2)(D) (speaking of "requests" in plural form, above and beyond FOIA request already received).

[29] See FOIA Post, "FOIA Counselor Q&A: 'Frequently Requested' Records" (posted 7/25/03) (explaining the "rule of three" that is employed to determine the applicability of subsection (a)(2)(D)); see also FOIA Update, Vol. XVII, No. 4, at 1 (describing subsection (a)(2)(D) obligations); FOIA Update, Vol. XVIII, No. 1, at 3-4 (same). But see FOIA Update, Vol. XVIII, No. 2, at 2 (advising that agencies need not include records processed for "flur-
(continued...)

records in their FOIA-processed form become "reading room" records,[31] which must automatically be made available to potential FOIA request-ers.[32] Ideally, this availability will satisfy much of the future public de-mand for those processed records in a more efficient fashion.[33] Neverthe-less, any subsequent FOIA request received for such records has to be re-sponded to in the regular way as well, if the requester so chooses.[34]

---

[29](...continued)
ry" of contemporaneous multiple requests when they are not likely to be re-quested again -- e.g., requests for certain types of routine government con-tract submissions); see also FOIA Post, "FOIA Counselor Q&A: 'Frequently Requested' Records" (posted 7/25/03) (addressing the "comparable circum-stances" in which agencies may determine likewise over time).

[30] See FOIA Post, "FOIA Counselor Q&A: 'Frequently Requested' Rec-ords" (posted 7/25/03) (discussing placement of records in a reading room based upon the subsection's "likely to become the subject of subsequent requests" standard).

[31] See id. (reminding that "an agency's (a)(2)(D) obligation arises only with respect to any FOIA-processed record that is disclosed at least in some part," and at the same time advising that with slightly different mul-tiple requests only "'overlap' records" are included within the obligation).

[32] See FOIA Update, Vol. XVII, No. 4, at 1-2 (discussing operation of subsection (a)(2)); see also FOIA Update, Vol. XIX, No. 1, at 3-4 (compila-tion of OIP policy guidance regarding "reading room" matters); cf. Tax Ana-lysts, 1998 WL 419755, at *4, 6 (requiring agency to place exceptionally large volume of FOIA-processed records in reading room on weekly basis, as they are processed, rather than all at once at conclusion of lengthy proc-essing period). But see FOIA Update, Vol. XVIII, No. 1, at 3 (cautioning that any information about any first-party requester that would not be disclosed to any other FOIA requester, such as information protected by Privacy Act of 1974 or Trade Secrets Act, 18 U.S.C. § 1905 (2000 & Supp. IV 2004), would not be appropriate for automatic public disclosure under fourth "reading room" category).

[33] See FOIA Update, Vol. XVIII, No. 2, at 2 (citing H.R. Rep. No. 104-795, at 21 (1996)); see also FOIA Post, "FOIA Counselor Q&A: 'Frequently Re-quested' Records" (posted 7/25/03) (discussing underlying purpose of fourth "reading room" category); FOIA Update, Vol. XVII, No. 4, at 1 (em-phasizing connection between fourth "reading room" category and "elec-tronic reading room" mechanism in meeting public access demands); cf. President's Statement on Signing the Electronic Freedom of Information Act Amendments of 1996, 32 Weekly Comp. Pres. Doc. 1949 (Oct. 7, 1996), reprinted in FOIA Update, Vol. XVII, No. 4, at 9 (expressing "hope that there will be less need to use FOIA to obtain government information").

[34] See FOIA Update, Vol. XVIII, No. 1, at 3 (advising that while ordinary rule is that records placed in reading room under subsection (a)(2) cannot
(continued...)

Second, the Electronic FOIA amendments require agencies to use electronic information technology to enhance the availability of their "reading room" records: Agencies must make the records created by them on or after November 1, 1996[35] in all four "reading room" categories available to the public by "electronic means."[36] The Electronic FOIA amendments embodied a strong statutory preference that electronic availability be provided by agencies in the form of online, World Wide Web access -- which is most efficient for both agencies and the public alike[37] -- and this expectation has been met by the development of agency FOIA sites on the World Wide Web.[38]

Agencies therefore must maintain in their conventional "paper" reading rooms copies of any FOIA-processed records determined to fall within

---

[34](...continued)
be subject of regular FOIA request, Congress made clear that such rule does not apply to fourth "reading room" category of FOIA-processed records (citing H.R. Rep. No. 104-795, at 21 (1996))); see also *FOIA Post*, "FOIA Counselor Q&A: 'Frequently Requested' Records" (posted 7/25/03) (advising that "the pre-existing reading room availability of records responsive to those subsequent requests in an electronic reading room on an agency's FOIA Web site, once brought to those FOIA requesters' attention, could be a basis for resolving those requests most efficiently").

[35] See 5 U.S.C. § 552(a)(2); see also *FOIA Post*, "Electronic Compilation of E-FOIA Implementation Guidance" (posted 2/28/03); FOIA Update, Vol. XVIII, No. 1, at 4-5.

[36] 5 U.S.C. § 552(a)(2); see also FOIA Update, Vol. XVIII, No. 1, at 3 (advising that records made available in "electronic reading rooms" must nevertheless be made available in conventional "paper" reading rooms as well (citing H.R. Rep. No. 104-795, at 21 (1996))).

[37] See 5 U.S.C. § 552(a)(2) (stressing use of "computer telecommunications," and establishing absolute requirement of World Wide Web use by all agencies); see also FOIA Update, Vol. XIX, No. 4, at 4-5 (emphasizing importance of "new partnership" between agency FOIA officers and agency Information Technology (IT) personnel to achieve efficient disclosure through electronic means); FOIA Update, Vol. XVIII, No. 3, at 1-2 (describing efficiency of online public access).

[38] See *FOIA Post*, "Follow-Up Report on E-FOIA Implementation Issued" (posted 9/27/02) (discussing GAO conclusion that agencies are not devoting sufficient attention to on-line electronic availability requirements); *FOIA Post*, "GAO E-FOIA Implementation Report Issued" (posted 3/23/01) (recognizing universal development of agency FOIA Web sites, but nonetheless urging "careful vigilance in both the establishment and the augmentation of agency FOIA Web sites with the passage of time").

the fourth subsection (a)(2) category,[39] and must identify such records that were created by them on or after the November 1, 1996 "cut-off" date in order to make them available through their "electronic reading rooms" as well.[40] In doing so, they should be mindful that some of the records falling under this fourth category might not have been created by the agency and instead might have been generated elsewhere; while such records may be determined by the agency to fall within subsection (a)(2)(D), they are not "created" by the agency and should not be regarded as subject to the electronic availability requirement.[41] However, an agency may as a matter of administrative discretion choose to make such records available electronically even though they were not generated by the agency, or not created after November 1, 1996, when to do so would be most cost-effective in serving public access needs under subsection (a)(2)(D).[42]

Furthermore, agencies should make clear to the users of their "electronic reading rooms" that while all of their subsection (a)(2) records are

---

[39] See FOIA Update, Vol. XIX, No. 1, at 3 (advising that agencies "should use their judgment as to the length of time that records determined to fall within the new reading room category should continue to be maintained in a reading room"); FOIA Update, Vol. XVIII, No. 1, at 4 (advising that agencies may determine that records no longer fall within fourth "reading room" category after passage of time); see also FOIA Post, "FOIA Counselor Q&A: 'Frequently Requested' Records" (posted 7/25/03) (advising that agencies "certainly can consider the absence of predicted FOIA requests as a factor in determining whether the continued maintenance of a record as a 'frequently requested' record is warranted").

[40] See FOIA Update, Vol. XVIII, No. 1, at 5 (advising that redaction of record during FOIA processing does not amount to record "creation" for purposes of determining applicability of electronic availability requirement); see also FOIA Update, Vol. XVII, No. 4, at 2 (observing that in case of FOIA-processed records, very large proportion of those records would have been created prior to Nov. 1, 1996 "cut-off" date, until long after Electronic FOIA amendments' initial implementation, and therefore would not have been subject to electronic availability requirement); cf. FOIA Post, "Use of 'Cut-Off' Dates in FOIA Searches" (posted 5/6/04) (advising in comparable FOIA-request context that "scope" of agency's search obligation "has both substantive and temporal aspects").

[41] See FOIA Update, Vol. XVIII, No. 1, at 4-5 (citing U.S. Dep't of Justice v. Tax Analysts, 492 U.S. 136, 144 (1989)); see also 63 Fed. Reg. 29,591, 29,592 (June 1, 1998) (discussing Department of Justice regulation on point, currently at 28 C.F.R. § 16.2(c) (2006)).

[42] See FOIA Update, Vol. XIX, No. 1, at 4; see, e.g., FOIA Update, Vol. XIX, No. 3, at 5; accord Exec. Order No. 13,392, Sec. 3(a)(iv). But see FOIA Update, Vol. XVIII, No. 1, at 5 (cautioning agencies to guard against possibility that "electronic reading room" treatment of record generated by outside party might be regarded as copyright infringement by that party).

available in their conventional reading rooms,[43] generally only those records created on or after November 1, 1996 are available in their electronic ones.[44] In addition, they should utilize indices to facilitate use of both types of reading rooms;[45] indeed, they are required by the Electronic FOIA amendments to maintain indexes of the FOIA-processed records in the fourth "reading room" category and to make them available on their FOIA Web sites.[46]

### FOIA Web Sites

Under the Electronic FOIA amendments, all federal agencies have FOIA sites on the World Wide Web to serve the "electronic reading room" function,[47] as well as for other FOIA-related purposes.[48] Especially now

---

[43] See FOIA Update, Vol. XVIII, No. 1, at 3 (advising agencies of utility of using computer terminals to meet statutory obligation, thus beginning trend that is becoming universal among agencies).

[44] See FOIA Update, Vol. XIX, No. 3, at 4; FOIA Update, Vol. XVII, No. 4, at 2; see also FOIA Update, Vol. XVIII, No. 2, at 2 (advising agencies on practical treatment of written signatures on adjudicatory orders for "electronic reading room" purposes).

[45] See FOIA Update, Vol. XIX, No. 3, at 4 (recommending use of "visible links" for electronic indexing purposes); cf. FOIA Update, Vol. XVIII, No. 3, at 1-2 (describing early agency use of home pages and electronic links for FOIA-related purposes on agency World Wide Web sites).

[46] 5 U.S.C. § 552(a)(2)(E); cf. FOIA Post, "Executive Order 13,392 Implementation Guidance" (posted 4/27/06) (setting forth guidelines for new section in annual FOIA reports describing agency's progress under its FOIA Improvement Plan, in accordance with Executive Order 13,392); FOIA Update, Vol. XVIII, No. 3, at 3-7 (setting forth Justice Department guidelines for agency preparation and submission of revised form of annual FOIA reports, as required to be prepared by all agencies electronically and made available on FOIA Web sites); FOIA Update, Vol. XIX, No. 3, at 2 (advising agencies on proper FOIA Web site treatment of annual FOIA reports, in compliance with electronic availability requirements of 5 U.S.C. § 552(e)(2)-(3), including through agency identification of URL (Uniform Resource Locator) for each report); see also FOIA Post, "FOIA Counselor Q&A: Annual FOIA Reports" (posted 12/19/03) (providing additional guidance regarding posting of annual FOIA reports).

[47] 5 U.S.C. § 552(a)(2) (2000 & Supp. IV 2004); see FOIA Post, "Supplemental Guidance on Annual FOIA Reports" (posted 8/13/01) (recognizing that all federal agencies now have established Web sites for FOIA purposes); FOIA Update, Vol. XIX, No. 3, at 3-4 ("OIP Guidance: Recommendations for FOIA Web Sites"); FOIA Update, Vol. XIX, No. 2, at 2 ("Web Site Watch" discussion of agency FOIA Web sites); FOIA Update, Vol. XIX, No.

(continued...)

under Executive Order 13,392,[49] special attention should be paid to FOIA Web sites by all agencies because they are a matter of great and growing importance to the processes of FOIA administration.[50]

There are two distinct elements of a well-designed FOIA page of which agencies should be mindful.[51] First and foremost is the ease of locating and accessing agency FOIA information.[52] In order for Web users to be able to access an agency's FOIA home page quickly and simply, every agency's main home page should have a clear, unmistakable link to its main FOIA page.[53] Furthermore, agencies' "electronic reading rooms"

---

[47](...continued)
1, at 2 (same); FOIA Update, Vol. XVIII, No. 3, at 1-2 (describing early agency development of World Wide Web sites for FOIA-related purposes, including "electronic reading rooms").

[48] See, e.g., 5 U.S.C. § 552(e)(2) (setting forth requirement that each agency make its annual FOIA report available to public electronically); see also FOIA Update, Vol. XIX, No. 3, at 3-4 (recommending that FOIA Web sites include links to agency's FOIA Reference Guide and its FOIA/Privacy Act regulations); cf. FOIA Update, Vol. XIX, No. 1, at 6 (encouraging agencies to consider as matter of administrative discretion establishing capability to receive FOIA requests via World Wide Web).

[49] 70 Fed. Reg. 75,373 (Dec. 14, 2005) (requiring agencies to review practices relating to making information available on agency Web sites); see also FOIA Post, "Executive Order 13,392 Implementation Guidance" (posted 4/27/06) (emphasizing importance of agency FOIA Web sites to processes of FOIA administration).

[50] See Attorney General's Report to the President Pursuant to Executive Order 13,392, Entitled "Improving Agency Disclosure of Information," 8 (Oct. 16, 2006), available at http://www.usdoj.gov/oip/ag_report_to_president_13392.pdf (recognizing significance of agency Web sites to "modern agency administration" of FOIA); FOIA Update, Vol. XIX, No. 4, at 5 (observing that "an agency's FOIA Web site has become an essential means by which its FOIA obligations are satisfied," so FOIA Web site support "should be a primary mission of each agency's IT staff"); FOIA Update, Vol. XIX, No. 3, at 1 (describing congressional interest in agency Web site development for purposes of FOIA administration); id. at 1, 3 (describing governmentwide attention to same). See generally FOIA Post, "GAO to Update Its E-FOIA Implementation Study" (posted 3/8/02).

[51] See FOIA Update, Vol. XIX, No. 3, at 3-4 (recommending basic elements and features of agency FOIA Web sites).

[52] See FOIA Update, Vol. XIX, No. 3, at 3 (advising that "[c]larity to the [W]eb site user is essential to the effectiveness of the site").

[53] See FOIA Update, Vol. XIX, No. 3, at 3-4 (emphasizing vital impor-
(continued...)

should be clearly designated as such and should contain index listings of agency reading room contents with direct links to those records that are available electronically.[54] Agencies of such size that they contain sub-agencies or major agency components that administer the FOIA on a de-centralized basis and have their own Web sites may maintain multiple "electronic reading rooms," so long as they are linked together clearly and efficiently for Web site users.[55]

Second, agencies should pay very close attention to both the accura-cy and the timeliness of the information that they maintain on their FOIA Web site pages.[56] The very nature of this FOIA obligation is such that without continuous diligent attention to it an agency can quickly fall out of compliance with the passage of time.[57] This can best be achieved by thor-oughly reviewing each aspect of agency FOIA pages on no less than a quarterly basis, if not more frequently.[58]

The need to consistently review and update agency Web sites has become even more important after the issuance of Executive Order 13,392, which specifically addressed the use of agency Web sites in making more

---

[53](...continued)
tance of ability to access agency's FOIA Web site directly from agency's main home page); see also Office of Management and Budget Memoran-dum for Heads of Executive Departments and Agencies Concerning Poli-cies for Federal Agency Public Websites (Dec. 17, 2004) (requiring agen-cies to link to certain basic information from main agency home page, in-cluding FOIA information).

[54] See FOIA Update, Vol. XIX, No. 3, at 4 (recommending that part of FOIA Web site be specifically designated as agency "reading room" and that reading room records be grouped according to category).

[55] See FOIA Update, Vol. XIX, No. 1, at 6 (advising on use of FOIA Web sites by all agency components "once an agency has established its World Wide Web capability"); FOIA Update, Vol. XVIII, No. 1, at 4 (advising that agencies with separate "electronic reading rooms" for separate components "should ensure that [they] are linked together electronically so as to facili-tate efficient user access").

[56] See FOIA Update, Vol. XIX, No. 2, at 2 (emphasizing importance of keeping Web sites accurate and up-to-date).

[57] See FOIA Post, "GAO E-FOIA Implementation Report Issued" (posted 3/23/01) (emphasizing that, with passage of time, "careful vigilance" is needed in maintaining FOIA Web sites).

[58] See FOIA Update, Vol. XIX, No. 3, at 4 (recommending that agencies check both accuracy and viability of their FOIA Web site links and text content of their FOIA Web site home pages on regular basis).

information available to the public.[59]

All agencies were required by Executive Order 13,392 to review their FOIA operations with both efficiency and customer service in mind, and to develop plans to improve their administration of the FOIA.[60] Agencies were specifically called upon to review the use of their World Wide Web sites in making subsection (a)(2) records available, as well as in making proactive disclosures of other information.[61] They also were required to include in their FOIA Improvement Plans specific information regarding the dissemination of information through the agency's Web site.[62]

Significantly, Executive Order 13,392 addressed both the spontaneous disclosure of records to the public pursuant to subsection (a)(2) of the FOIA and the public disclosure of information on a voluntary basis.[63] In

---

[59] See Executive Order 13,392, Sec. 1(b).

[60] See id. at Sec. 1(b), (c); see also FOIA Post, "Executive Order 13,392 Implementation Guidance" (posted 4/27/06) (containing more than two dozen potential improvement areas for possible inclusion in agency FOIA Improvement Plans).

[61] See Exec. Order No. 13,392, Sec. 3(a)(iv) (requiring agencies to "review the agency's policies and practices relating to the availability of public information through websites and other means, including the use of websites to make available the records described in section 552(a)(2)"); see also FOIA Post, "Executive Order 13,392 Implementation Guidance" (posted 4/27/06) (urging agencies to consider related areas of affirmative disclosure and proactive disclosure, as well as overall FOIA Web site improvement, in developing their FOIA Improvement Plans).

[62] See Exec. Order No. 13,392, Sec. 3(b)(ii) ("The plan shall include specific activities that the agency will implement to eliminate or reduce the agency's FOIA backlog, including . . . increased reliance on the dissemination of records that can be made available to the public through a website or other means that do not require the public to make a request for the records under the FOIA."); cf. Department of Justice FOIA Improvement Plan at 10-11, 21, 117-18 (describing goals to use component FOIA Web sites for both affirmative and proactive disclosures); Federal Deposit Insurance Corporation FOIA Improvement Plan at 7-10 (describing significant efforts in improving affirmative disclosure of subsection (a)(2) information as well as proactive disclosure of other information of interest to public).

[63] See Exec. Order 13,392, Sec. 3(a)(iv), (b)(ii); see also Attorney General's Report to the President Pursuant to Executive Order 13,392, Entitled "Improving Agency Disclosure of Information," 8 (Oct. 16, 2006), available at http://www.usdoj.gov/oip/ag_report_to_president_13392.pdf (explaining that affirmative disclosure "involves the spontaneous disclosure of information to the public pursuant to subsection (a)(2)," while proactive disclosure
(continued...)

both cases, the agency's disclosure efforts can meet the public demand for information and thereby greatly reduce the need for the public to make FOIA requests.[64] (For a further detailed discussion of Executive Order 13,392 see Procedural Requirements, Executive Order 13,392, below.)

In accordance with Executive Order 13,392, agencies are encouraged to make a wide range of records available through their World Wide Web sites as a matter of administrative discretion.[65] But in so doing, of course, they should make sure that all possible security concerns regarding these records have been carefully considered.[66]

In sum, all agencies should continue to be vigilant in maintaining and augmenting their FOIA Web sites in order to ensure consistent compliance with both the Electronic FOIA amendments' and Executive Order 13,392's important electronic availability requirements.[67]

------

[63](...continued)
"refers to the public disclosure of records or information on a voluntary (i.e., not FOIA-compelled) basis"); *FOIA Post*, "Executive Order 13,392 Implementation Guidance" (posted 4/27/06) (encouraging proactive disclosure "when an agency has public information that does not fall into any subsection (a)(2) category but nevertheless could be made readily available to the public").

[64] See *FOIA Post*, "Executive Order 13,392 Implementation Guidance" (posted 4/27/06) (emphasizing that proactive disclosure of information can reduce need for FOIA requests).

[65] See Information Policy in the 21st Century: A Review of the Freedom of Information Act: Hearing Before the Subcommittee on Government Management, Finance, and Accountability, Committee on Government Reform, House of Representatives, 109th Cong. 72 (2005) (statement of Department of Justice describing difference between removal from agency Web site of information not required to be there in first place -- which is not FOIA issue -- and removal of information required by FOIA to be made available in electronic reading room).

[66] See, e.g., White House Homeland Security Memorandum, reprinted in *FOIA Post* (posted 3/21/02) (requiring agencies to ensure appropriate protection of information relating to weapons of mass destruction and of other sensitive homeland security-related information); accord Attorney General's Memorandum for Heads of All Federal Departments and Agencies Regarding the Freedom of Information Act (Oct. 12, 2001), reprinted in *FOIA Post* (posted 10/15/01) (urging agencies to "carefully consider" the protection of fundamental societal values, including "safeguarding our national security").

[67] See Exec. Order No. 13,392, Sec. 3(a)(iv), (b)(ii); see also Attorney General's Report to the President Pursuant to Executive Order 13,392, Entitled
(continued...)

## PROCEDURAL REQUIREMENTS

The Freedom of Information Act requires federal agencies to make their records promptly available to any person who makes a proper request for them.[1] To provide a general overview of the Act's procedural requirements, this section first will discuss the new executive order on the FOIA, Executive Order 13,392,[2] followed by a roughly chronological discussion of how a typical FOIA request is processed -- from the point of determining whether an entity in receipt of a request is subject to the FOIA in the first place to the review of an agency's initial decision regarding a FOIA request on administrative appeal. (The subject of fees under the Act is discussed more fully and separately under Fees and Fee Waivers, below.) In administering the Act's procedural requirements, agencies should remember Executive Order 13,392's reminder that "FOIA requesters are seeking a

---

[67](...continued)
"Improving Agency Disclosure of Information," 8, 12 (Oct. 16, 2006), available at http://www.usdoj.gov/oip/ag_report_to_president_13392.pdf (emphasizing "particular[] importan[ce]" of FOIA Web sites and also agency use of "FOIA Intranet site[s]" for more efficient FOIA administration); *FOIA Post*, "Executive Order 13,392 Implementation Guidance" (posted 4/27/06) (advising that overall FOIA Web site improvement is "particularly worthwhile area for agency attention"); *FOIA Post*, "Electronic Compilation of E-FOIA Implementation Guidance" (posted 2/28/03) (urging agencies to "redouble their efforts to ensure complete E-FOIA compliance"); *FOIA Post*, "Follow-Up Report on E-FOIA Implementation Issued" (posted 9/27/02) (discussing continued congressional focus on governmentwide implementation of FOIA's electronic availability requirements); *FOIA Post*, "FOIA Officers Conference Scheduled" (posted 9/17/02) (scheduling governmentwide FOIA officers conference to focus on 2002 GAO Report as "basis for all agencies to review and improve wherever necessary their compliance with E-FOIA's requirements"); *FOIA Post*, "GAO E-FOIA Implementation Report Issued" (posted 3/23/01) (advising that agencies must take all steps necessary to "both attain[] and maintain[] proper compliance with all of [the FOIA's] electronic availability requirements"); *FOIA Post*, "Agencies Continue E-FOIA Implementation" (posted 3/14/01) (identifying prospective GAO report as "excellent basis upon which all agencies can review their E-FOIA implementation compliance").

[1] 5 U.S.C. § 552(a)(3)(A) (2000 & Supp. IV 2004) (providing that "each agency, upon any request for records which (i) reasonably describes such records and (ii) is made in accordance with published rules stating the time, place, fees (if any), and procedures to be followed, shall make the records promptly available to any person"). But see id. at § 552(a)(3)(E) (prohibiting, as of 2002, certain agency FOIA disclosures to foreign governments or representatives of such governments); see also *FOIA Post*, "FOIA Amended by Intelligence Authorization Act" (posted 12/23/02) (advising on 2002 FOIA amendments' implementation).

[2] Exec. Order No. 13,392, 70 Fed. Reg. 75,373 (Dec. 14, 2005).

service from the Federal Government and should be treated as such."[3] Accordingly, agencies should strive to "carefully consider [all] FOIA requests"[4] and handle them "courteously and appropriately."[5]

### Executive Order 13,392

On December 14, 2005, the President issued Executive Order 13,392, entitled "Improving Agency Disclosure of Information," which contains several statements of governmentwide FOIA policy as well as many specific requirements in the areas of customer service, planning, and reporting that affect all federal agencies in their administration of the Act.[6] This first-of-its-kind FOIA executive order established a "citizen-centered"[7] and "results-oriented"[8] policy for improving the Act's administration throughout the executive branch; it draws new attention to the difficulties presented by agency backlogs of pending FOIA requests;[9] and it places new obligations

---

[3] Id. at Sec. 1(b).

[4] Attorney General's Memorandum for Heads of All Federal Departments and Agencies Regarding the Freedom of Information Act (Oct. 12, 2001), reprinted in *FOIA Post* (posted 10/15/01) (Attorney General FOIA policy memorandum encouraging all federal agencies to make "careful[] . . . disclosure determinations under the FOIA" and also to "consult with the Department of Justice's Office of Information and Privacy when significant FOIA issues arise").

[5] Exec. Order No. 13,392, Sec. 1(b); see also id. at Sec. 2(c) (establishing FOIA Requester Service Centers and FOIA Public Liaisons in order to "ensure appropriate communication with FOIA requesters"); id. at Sec. 2(c)(ii) (directing that FOIA Public Liaisons must seek to ensure service-oriented responses to FOIA requests and FOIA-related inquiries); *FOIA Post*, "Executive Order 13,392 Implementation Guidance" (posted 4/27/06) (Part I.13.) (advising that politeness and courtesy are "integral to the overall 'customer-service' policy of the executive order"); id. at (Part IV.8.) (encouraging agencies to include in their improvement plans even "seemingly small or slight improvements" in areas such as politeness and courtesy); Presidential Memorandum for Heads of Departments and Agencies Regarding the Freedom of Information Act, 29 Weekly Comp. Pres. Doc. 1999 (Oct. 4, 1993), reprinted in FOIA Update, Vol. XIV, No. 3, at 3.

[6] Exec. Order No. 13,392, 70 Fed. Reg. 75,373 (Dec. 14, 2005).

[7] Id. at Sec. 1(b), (d).

[8] Id. at Sec. 1(c), (d).

[9] See id. at Sec. 3(a)(i) (instructing the newly appointed Chief FOIA Officer of each agency to conduct a review of FOIA operations in order to evaluate "the extent to which . . . requests for records have not been responded to within the statutory time limit"); id. at Sec. 3(a)(v) (instructing
(continued...)

on all agencies to be met by specified deadlines.[10]

Most fundamentally, Executive Order 13,392 emphasizes the importance of the Freedom of Information Act to "[t]he effective functioning of our constitutional democracy"[11] and reminds all agencies that "FOIA requesters are seeking a service from the Federal Government and should be treated as such."[12] Accordingly, it states an overall policy of responding to FOIA requests "courteously and appropriately" and in ways that permit FOIA requesters to "learn about the FOIA process" -- most particularly, "about the status of a person's FOIA request."[13] It calls upon all federal agencies to discharge their FOIA responsibilities in an efficient as well as "results-oriented" manner and to "achieve tangible, measurable improvements in FOIA processing."[14] Its goal is to "improve service and performance" and "increase efficiency" in agency FOIA operations, "thereby strengthening compliance with the FOIA" and minimizing both "disputes and related litigation" arising under it.[15]

Toward that end, Executive Order 13,392 directed all federal agencies subject to the FOIA to, among other things, take the following basic steps:

(1) Designate within thirty days a senior official of each agency (at the Assistant Secretary or equivalent level), to serve as the Chief FOIA

---

[9](...continued)
each Chief FOIA Officer to "identify ways to eliminate or reduce [agency's] backlog"); id. at Sec. 3(b)(ii) (requiring that Chief FOIA Officer's improvement plan include "specific activities that the agency will implement to eliminate or reduce" its backlog); see also FOIA Post, "Executive Order 13,392 Implementation Guidance" (posted 4/27/06) (Part I.12.) (stating that backlog reduction/elimination "should be a major underpinning of the implementation plans" of all agencies with backlogs).

[10] See, e.g., Exec. Order No. 13,392, Sec. 2(a) (requiring designation of Chief FOIA Officer in each agency); id. at Sec. 3(c)(i) (requiring development of individual agency FOIA Improvement Plans); id. at Sec. 4(a) (requiring Attorney General report to President on agency FOIA implementation).

[11] Id. at Sec. 1(a).

[12] Id. at Sec. 1(b).

[13] Id.; see also FOIA Post, "Executive Order 13,392 Implementation Guidance" (posted 4/27/06) (Part I.4.) (stating that agencies should ensure that FOIA Reference Guides "remain comprehensive and up to date" in light of effectiveness of guides in increasing public awareness of FOIA).

[14] Exec. Order No. 13,392, Sec. 1(c).

[15] Id. at Sec. 1(c), (d).

Officer of that agency.[16]

(2) Establish one or more FOIA Requester Service Centers (Center), as appropriate, to serve as the first place that FOIA requesters can contact in order to seek information concerning the status of their FOIA requests and appropriate information about the agency's FOIA responses. The Center must include appropriate staff to receive and respond to inquiries from FOIA requesters.[17]

(3) Designate one or more agency officials, as appropriate, as FOIA Public Liaisons, who may serve in the Center or who may serve in a separate office. FOIA Public Liaisons serve as supervisory officials to whom a FOIA requester can raise concerns about the service the FOIA requester received from the Center, following an initial response from the Center staff.[18]

(4) Conduct a review of the agency's FOIA operations in order to determine whether agency practices are consistent with the policies set forth in the Executive Order.[19]

(5) Develop, in consultation as appropriate with the staff of the agency (including the FOIA Public Liaisons), the Attorney General, and the OMB Director, an agency-specific plan to ensure that the agency's administration of the FOIA is in accordance with applicable law and the policies set forth in the Executive Order.[20]

(6) Submit a report to the Attorney General and the OMB Director that summarizes the results of the agency's review and encloses a copy of the agency's FOIA Improvement Plan under the Executive Order.[21]

(7) Include in the agency's annual FOIA reports for fiscal years 2006 and 2007 a report on the agency's development and implementation of its FOIA Improvement Plan and on the agency's performance in meeting the milestones set forth in that plan, consistent with Department of Justice guidance.[22]

To facilitate the reviews, the development of FOIA Improvement

---

[16] Id. at 2(a).

[17] Id. at 2(c)(i).

[18] Id. at 2(c)(ii).

[19] See id. at 3(a).

[20] See id. at 3(b)(i).

[21] See id. at 3(c)(i).

[22] See id. at 3(c)(ii).

## PROCEDURAL REQUIREMENTS

Plans, and other implementation efforts required under Executive Order 13,392, the Department of Justice conducted several governmentwide conferences for Chief FOIA Officers and key FOIA personnel.[23] The Department of Justice also provided extensive written guidance to all agencies on their implementation of Executive Order 13,392, in the further exercise of the Attorney General's guidance authority under it.[24] This formal guidance, which was issued on April 26, 2006, was distributed to all agencies at one of the earliest guidance conferences and also is widely available on the Justice Department's FOIA Web site.[25] It contained discussions of more than two dozen potential improvement areas for possible inclusion in agency plans, set forth a standard template for the uniform development and presentation of all plans, included supplemental guidelines on the use of agency annual FOIA reports for reporting the results of Executive Order 13,392's implementation, and also addressed a breadth of questions and guidance points in further aid of the executive order's implementation.[26]

Under Executive Order 13,392, an agency's Chief FOIA Officer holds "agency-wide responsibility for efficient and appropriate compliance with the FOIA."[27] The Department of Justice maintains a comprehensive list of all Chief FOIA Officers on its FOIA Web site.[28] Each agency also must have established one or more operating groups or units (depending upon agency size and degree of decentralization), called "FOIA Requester Service Centers," for the purpose of facilitating better agency communications with

---

[23] See Implementing FOIA [Freedom of Information Act] - Assessing Agency Efforts to meet FOIA Requirements: Hearing Before the Subcomm. on Information Policy, Census, and National Archives of the Comm. on Oversight and Government Reform, 110th Cong. (2007) (statement of Melanie Ann Pustay, Acting Director, Office of Information and Privacy), available at http://www.usdoj.gov/oip /foia30.pdf (discussing extensive Department of Justice executive order coordination efforts); Implementing FOIA [Freedom of Information Act] - Does the Bush Administration Executive Order Improve Processing?: Hearing Before the Subcomm. on Government Management, Finance and Accountability of the Comm. on Government Reform, 109th Cong. (2006), available at http://www.usdoj.gov/oip/ metcalfe_foia_ testimony07252006.pdf (same)

[24] See id. at Sec. 4(b); see also id. at Sec. 3(b)(i).

[25] See FOIA Post, "Executive Order 13,392 Implementation Guidance" (posted 4/27/06) (containing potential improvement areas for possible inclusion in FOIA Improvement Plans).

[26] See id.

[27] Exec. Order No. 13,392, Sec. 2(b)(i).

[28] See http://www.usdoj.gov/04foia/chieffoiaofficers.html.

FOIA requesters.[29] Under Executive Order 13,392, each such Center "shall serve as the first place that a FOIA requester can contact to seek information concerning the status of the person's FOIA request."[30] Executive Order 13,392 emphasizes that all such FOIA Centers must have "appropriate staff to receive and respond to inquiries from FOIA requesters."[31]

In addition to the basic staff to be made available to respond to FOIA requesters' inquiries about their requests in these new FOIA Requester Service Centers, each agency also must designate one or more supervisory-level employees to serve as "FOIA Public Liaisons" either inside or outside of its FOIA Requester Service Center.[32] Executive Order 13,392 states that in establishing and maintaining these FOIA positions, agencies "shall use, as appropriate, existing agency staff and resources."[33] As further specified by Executive Order 13,392, FOIA Public Liaisons must among other things serve as "supervisory officials to whom a FOIA requester can raise concerns about the service the FOIA requester has received from the FOIA Requester Service Center, following an initial response from the FOIA Requester Service Center staff."[34] Furthermore, the Department of Justice has called upon all FOIA Public Liaisons to take responsibility for ensuring that absolutely all personnel at their agencies who work with the FOIA (i.e., even "program personnel" whose primary job responsibilities are not FOIA-related) have been fully educated about Executive Order 13,392's policies and customer-service principles.[35] Both agencies and requesters should

---

[29] See Exec. Order No. 13,392, Sec. 2(c)(i); see also FOIA Post, "Executive Order 13,392 Implementation Guidance" (posted 4/27/06) (observing that FOIA Requester Service Center will perform "customer feedback" function).

[30] Exec. Order No. 13,392, Sec. 2(c)(i); see also FOIA Post, "Executive Order 13,392 Implementation Guidance" (posted 4/27/06) (recognizing that a FOIA Requester Service Center may answer questions other than those relating to the status of a FOIA request "where appropriate as a matter of discretion").

[31] Exec. Order No. 13,392, Sec. 2(c)(i); see also id. at Sec. 2(c)(iv) (placing emphasis on staffing requirement).

[32] See id. at Sec. 2(c)(ii) (noting that FOIA Public Liaisons "may serve in a separate office").

[33] Id. at Sec. 2(c)(iv).

[34] Id. at Sec. 2(c)(ii).

[35] See FOIA Post, "Executive Order 13,392 Implementation Guidance" (posted 4/27/06) (stressing that the Office of Information and Privacy would be "urging any agency that has not already done so to conduct an in-house training session on the policies of Executive Order 13,392 for all of its FOIA personnel"); Implementing FOIA [Freedom of Information Act] - Assessing Agency Efforts to meet FOIA Requirements: Hearing Before the Subcomm.
(continued...)

bear in mind that neither the FOIA Requester Service Centers nor the FOIA Public Liaisons are avenues of administrative appeal.[36]

Most significantly, Executive Order 13,392 required each Chief FOIA Officer to "conduct a review of the agency's FOIA operations to determine whether agency practices are consistent with the policies" that it set forth.[37] Each Chief FOIA Officer was required to examine and evaluate a range of the agency's FOIA-related activities, including "ways to eliminate or reduce its FOIA backlog" where applicable.[38]

Executive Order 13,392 next required all agencies, based upon the reviews conducted by their new Chief FOIA Officers, to prepare "agency-specific plan[s]" for improvement of their administration of the Act.[39] Each agency's plan was required to be sent to both the Justice Department and OMB, together with a report that "summarizes the results of" the agency's FOIA review, by June 14, 2006.[40] The Department of Justice has received those reports and has made them available at a single location on its FOIA Web site for convenient reference as well.[41]

---

[35](...continued)
on Information Policy, Census, and National Archives of the Comm. on Oversight and Government Reform, 110th Cong. (2007) (statement of Melanie Ann Pustay, Acting Director, Office of Information and Privacy), available at http://www.usdoj.gov/oip /foia30.pdf (describing special training conference conducted by OIP for FOIA Public Liaisons at all federal agencies).

[36] See Exec. Order No. 13,392, Sec. 7(b)(iii) (emphasizing that Executive Order 13,392 "is not intended to, and does not, create any right or benefit, substantive or procedural, enforceable at law or in equity").

[37] Id. at Sec. 3(a).

[38] Id. at Sec. 3(a)(v); see also id. at Sec. 3(a)(i)-(v) (specifying range of matters to be reviewed).

[39] Id. at Sec. 3(b)(i); see also FOIA Post, "Executive Order 13,392 Implementation Guidance" (posted 4/27/06) (listing twenty-seven possible areas of improvement).

[40] Exec. Order No. 13,392, Sec. 3(c)(i) (requiring head of each agency to submit FOIA Improvement Plans "no later than 6 months from the date of this order [December 14, 2005]"); see also FOIA Post, "Executive Order 13,392 Implementation Guidance" (posted 4/27/06) (urging all agencies to submit improvement plans by "no later than" June 14).

[41] See U.S. Department of Justice, "Agency FOIA Improvement Plans Under E.O. 13,392," available at http://www.usdoj.gov/04foia/agency_ improvement.html; see also Attorney General's Report to the President Pursuant to Executive Order 13,392, Entitled "Improving Agency Disclosure
(continued...)

Under Executive Order 13,392, each agency then was required to report on the results it had achieved under its plan in a new section of its regular annual FOIA report.[42] The new Section XII for Fiscal Year 2006 contained a narrative description of each agency's progress in meeting its milestones and goals under its FOIA Improvement Plan, as well as a description of any failure to meet a milestone or goal.[43] These annual reports have been posted on the Department of Justice's Web site.[44]

Notably, Executive Order 13,392 provides for specific consequences and corrective actions in the event that a milestone in an agency's plan is not met.[45] For any agency that does not meet a milestone set forth in its FOIA Improvement Plan, "the head of the agency shall: (A) identify this deficiency in the annual FOIA report to the Attorney General; (B) explain in the annual report the reasons for the agency's failure to meet the milestone; (C) outline in the annual report the steps that the agency has already taken, and will be taking, to address the deficiency; and (D) report this deficiency to the President's Management Council."[46]

Lastly, Executive Order 13,392 authorized the Attorney General to review these agency FOIA Improvement Plans in order to provide to the President "appropriate recommendations on administrative or other agency actions" for purposes of future governmentwide FOIA administration.[47] Under the Executive Order, the Attorney General timely submitted his first such report and recommendations to the President on October 16, 2006.[48]

---

[41](...continued)
of Information," 6 & n.14 (Oct. 16, 2006), available at http://www.usdoj.gov/ oip/ag_report_ to_president_13392.pdf (describing "ease of reference" afforded).

[42] Exec. Order No. 13,392, Sec. 3(c)(ii); see also 5 U.S.C. § 552(e)(1) (2000 & Supp. IV 2004) (establishing February 1 of each year as deadline for filing annual FOIA reports).

[43] See Annual FOIA Reports, available at http://www.usdoj.gov/oip /fy06.html.

[44] Id.

[45] See Exec. Order No. 13,392, Sec. 3(c)(iii)(A)-(D).

[46] Id.; see also FOIA Post, "Executive Order 13,392 Implementation Guidance" (posted 4/27/06) (emphasizing that notwithstanding consequences contemplated in order for any deficiency, agencies should strive to set "reasonably aggressive goals").

[47] Id. at Sec. 4(a).

[48] See Attorney General's Report to the President Pursuant to Executive Order 13,392, Entitled "Improving Agency Disclosure of Information," 15-16
(continued...)

## PROCEDURAL REQUIREMENTS

Executive Order 13,392 provides for two further such Attorney General reports to the President, first on June 1, 2007 and again on June 1, 2008.[49] These reports will be based on a comprehensive review of each agency's implementation activities as reflected in the new Section XII of their annual FOIA reports.[50]

### Entities Subject to the FOIA

Agencies within the executive branch of the federal government, including the Executive Office of the President and independent regulatory agencies, are subject to the provisions of the FOIA.[51] However, the FOIA does not apply to entities that "are neither chartered by the federal government [n]or controlled by it."[52] Thus, it is settled that state, local, and for-

---

[48](...continued)
(Oct. 16, 2006), available at http://www.usdoj.gov/oip/ag_report_to_president_13392.pdf (recommending governmentwide general FOIA administration improvements in areas of acknowledgment letters, FOIA form reviews, and technology initiatives).

[49] See Exec. Order No. 13,392, Sec. 4(a).

[50] Id.

[51] 5 U.S.C. § 552(f)(1) (2000 & Supp. IV 2004).

[52] H.R. Rep. No. 93-1380, at 14 (1974), reprinted in House Comm. on Gov't Operations and Senate Comm. on the Judiciary, 94th Cong., 1st Sess., Freedom of Information Act and Amendments of 1974 (P.L. 93-502) Source Book: Legislative History, Texts, and Other Documents at 231-32 (1975); see Forsham v. Harris, 445 U.S. 169, 179-80 (1980) (holding that private grantee of federal agency is not itself subject to FOIA); Missouri v. U.S. Dep't of Interior, 297 F.3d 745, 750 (8th Cir. 2002) ("The provision of federal resources, such as federal funding, is insufficient to transform a private organization into a federal agency."); Pub. Citizen Health Research Group v. HEW, 668 F.2d 537, 543-44 (D.C. Cir. 1981) (stating that medical peer review committees are not agencies under FOIA); Irwin Mem'l Blood Bank v. Am. Nat'l Red Cross, 640 F.2d 1051, 1057 (9th Cir. 1981) (determining that American National Red Cross is not an agency under FOIA); Holland v. FBI, No. 04-2593, slip op. at 8 (N.D. Ala. June 30, 2005) (concluding that American National Red Cross is not federal agency under FOIA (citing Irwin Mem'l Blood Bank, 640 F. Supp. 2d 1051)); Gilmore v. U.S. Dep't of Energy, 4 F. Supp. 2d 912, 919-20 (N.D. Cal. 1998) (finding that privately owned laboratory that developed electronic conferencing software, for which government owned nonexclusive license regarding its use, is not "a government-controlled corporation" as it is not subject to day-to-day supervision by federal government, nor are its employees or management considered government employees); Leytman v. N.Y. Stock Exch., No. 95 CV 902, 1995 WL 761843, at *2 (E.D.N.Y. Dec. 6, 1995) (relying on Indep. Investor Protective
(continued...)

-46-

eign governments,[53] municipal corporations,[54] the courts,[55] Congress,[56]

---

[52](...continued)
League v. N.Y. Stock Exch., 367 F. Supp. 1376, 1377 (S.D.N.Y. 1973), to find that although "[t]he Exchange is subject to significant federal regulation . . . it is not an agency of the federal government"); Rogers v. U.S. Nat'l Reconnaissance Office, No. 94-B-2934, slip op. at 7 (N.D. Ala. Sept. 13, 1995) (observing that "[t]he degree of government involvement and control over [private organizations which contracted with government to construct office facility is] insufficient to establish companies as federal agencies for purposes of the FOIA"); see also FOIA Update, Vol. XIX, No. 4, at 2 (noting the FOIA's applicability to certain research data generated by private grantees of federal agencies, pursuant to the Omnibus Consolidated and Emergency Supplemental Appropriations Act for Fiscal Year 1999, Pub. L. No. 105-277, 112 Stat. 2681 (1998), as implemented by OMB Circular A-110, "Uniform Administrative Requirements for Grants and Agreements with Institutions of Higher Education, Hospitals, and Other Non-Profit Organizations," 64 Fed. Reg. 54,926 (Oct. 8, 1999)). But see Moye, O'Brien, O'Rourke, Hogan & Pickert v. Nat'l R.R. Passenger Corp., 376 F.3d 1270, 1277 n.5 (11th Cir. 2004) (Although [defendant] Amtrak is not a federal agency, it must comply with FOIA" (citing 49 U.S.C. § 24301(e) (2000))); Cotton v. Adams, 798 F. Supp. 22, 24 (D.D.C. 1992) (holding that the Smithsonian Institution is an agency under the FOIA on basis that it "performs governmental functions as a center of scholarship and national museum responsible for the safe-keeping and maintenance of national treasures"), holding questioned on appeal of award of attorney fees sub nom. Cotton v. Heyman, 63 F.3d 1115, 1123 (D.C. Cir. 1995) (noting that the Smithsonian Institution could "reasonably interpret our precedent to support its position that it is not an agency under FOIA"); Ass'n of Cmty. Orgs. for Reform Now v. Barclay, No. 3-89-409T, slip op. at 8 (N.D. Tex. June 9, 1989) (holding that federal home loan banks are agencies under FOIA); cf. Dong v. Smithsonian Inst., 125 F.3d 877, 879 (D.C. Cir. 1997) (holding that the Smithsonian Institution is not an agency for purposes of the Privacy Act of 1974 (5 U.S.C. § 552a (2000 & Supp. IV 2004)), as it is neither an "establishment of the executive branch" nor a "government-controlled corporation").

[53] See, e.g., Blankenship v. Claus, 149 F. App'x 897, 898 (11th Cir. Sept. 7, 2005); Wright v. Curry, 122 F. App'x 724, 725 (5th Cir. 2004) (explaining that state agencies are "expressly exclude[d]" from scope of FOIA); Moore v. United Kingdom, 384 F.3d 1079, 1089-90 (9th Cir. 2004) (finding that "[n]o cause of action lies under FOIA against a foreign government"); Lau v. Sullivan County Dist. Att'y, No. 99-7341, 1999 WL 1069966, at *2 (2d Cir. Nov. 12, 1999); Martinson v. DEA, No. 96-5262, 1997 WL 634559, at *1 (D.C. Cir. July 3, 1997); Ortez v. Wash. County, 88 F.3d 804, 811 (9th Cir. 1996); Davidson v. Georgia, 622 F.2d 895, 897 (5th Cir. 1980); see also Foley v. Village of Weston, No. 06-350, 2006 WL 3449414, at *5 (W.D. Wis. Nov. 28, 2006) (holding that local county government, sheriff's department, and sheriff are not agencies under FOIA); Moreno v. Curry, No. 06-238, 2006 U.S. Dist. LEXIS 81416, at *6 (N.D. Tex. Nov. 7, 2006) (stating that FOIA
(continued...)

[53](...continued)
does not apply to state or municipal agencies); Conlin v. Davis, No. 06-3305, 2006 U.S. Dist. LEXIS 76975, at *4 (S.D. Tex. Oct. 23, 2006) (FOIA claim against state officials is "patently frivolous" because only federal agencies are subject to FOIA); Brown v. City of Detroit, No. 05-60162, 2006 WL 3196297, at *1 (E.D. Mich. Sept. 11, 2006) (magistrate's recommendation) (stating that FOIA "does not apply to state or local governments or agencies"), adopted 2006 WL 3086909 (E.D. Mich. Oct. 30, 2006); Gabbard v. Hall County, Ga., No. 06-37, 2006 U.S. Dist. LEXIS 56662, at *4 (M.D. Ga. Aug. 14, 2006) (FOIA does not apply to state or local agencies); Nnabuihe v. Dallas County Criminal Courts, No. 05-2115, slip op. at 2 (N.D. Tex. Jan. 25, 2006) (magistrate's recommendation) (finding no jurisdiction as FOIA does not apply to request for state records), adopted, 2006 U.S. Dist. LEXIS 2716, at *1 (N.D. Tex. Jan. 25, 2006) (dismissing case "for want of jurisdiction"); Davis v. Johnson, No. 05-2060, 2005 U.S. Dist. LEXIS 12475, at *1 (N.D. Cal. June 20, 2005) (stating that a requester seeking state public defender records cannot use the FOIA because the Act "does not apply to the records of an individual attorney, or of a state or county agency"); Dipietro v. Executive Office for U.S. Attorneys, 357 F. Supp. 2d 177, 182 (D.D.C. 2004) (finding that county sheriff's department is not agency subject to FOIA (citing Beard v. Dep't of Justice, 917 F. Supp. 61, 63 (D.D.C. 1996))); Mount of Olives Paralegals v. Bush, No. 04-C-620, 2004 U.S. Dist. LEXIS 8085, at *6 (N.D. Ill. May 6, 2004) ("[T]he federal FOIA statute may not be used against state agencies."); Rodgers v. Texas, No. 03-2015, 2004 WL 764946, at *2 n.1 (N.D. Tex. Apr. 7, 2004) ("FOIA does not apply to state agencies.") (non-FOIA case); Daniel v. Safir, 175 F. Supp. 2d 474, 481 (E.D.N.Y. 2001) ("[T]here is no right of action under FOIA against state actors or officials."), aff'd, 42 F. App'x 528 (2d Cir. 2002); Ali v. Przbyl, No. 04-03459E, 2004 WL 1682774, at *2 (W.D.N.Y. July 26, 2004) ("FOIA does not apply to state or local agencies or state or local individuals."); McClain v. U.S. Dep't of Justice, No. 97-C-0385, 1999 WL 759505, at *2 (N.D. Ill. Sept. 1, 1999) (dismissing FOIA claims against state attorney general because "[p]laintiff may assert Privacy Act and Freedom of Information Act claims against . . . federal defendants only"), aff'd, 17 F. App'x 471 (7th Cir. 2001); Beard, 917 F. Supp. at 63 (holding District of Columbia Police Department to be "local" law enforcement agency not subject to FOIA); Gillard v. U.S. Marshals Serv., No. 87-0689, 1987 WL 11218, at *1 (D.D.C. May 11, 1987) (holding that District of Columbia Government records are not covered by FOIA).

[54] See Lau, 1999 WL 1069966, at *2 (affirming dismissal of FOIA claims against county officials); Cruz v. Superior Court Judges, No. 04-1103, 2006 WL 547930, at *1 (D. Conn. Mar. 1, 2006) (noting that "[a] municipal police department is not a federal agency"); Jones v. City of Indianapolis, 216 F.R.D. 440, 443 (S.D. Ind. 2003) ("The term 'agency' in the FOIA does not apply to municipal agencies."); Essily v. Giuliani, No. 00-5271, 2000 WL 1154313, at *1 (S.D.N.Y. Aug. 14, 2000) ("FOIA does not apply to city agencies."), aff'd, 22 F. App'x 77 (2d Cir. 2001); McClain, 1999 WL 759505, at *2
(continued...)

[54](...continued)
(dismissing plaintiff's FOIA claims against county attorney).

[55] See, e.g., Megibow v. Clerk of the U.S. Tax Court, 432 F.3d 387, 388 (2d Cir. 2005) (per curiam) (affirming district court's conclusion that United States Tax Court is not subject to FOIA); United States v. Casas, 376 F.3d 20, 22 (1st Cir. 2004) (stating that "[t]he judicial branch is exempt from the Freedom of Information Act"); United States v. Choate, 102 F. App'x 634, 635 (10th Cir. 2004) (affirming district court holding that FOIA does not apply to federal courts); United States v. Mitchell, No. 03-6938, 2003 WL 22999456, at *1 (4th Cir. Dec. 23, 2003) ("[F]ederal courts do not fall within the definition of 'agency' under FOIA.") (non-FOIA case); United States v. Alcorn, 6 F. App'x 315, 317 (6th Cir. 2001) (holding that "the federal courts are specifically excluded from FOIA's definition of 'agency'") (non-FOIA case); Gaydos v. Mansmann, No. 98-5002, 1998 WL 389104, at *1 (D.C. Cir. June 24, 1998) (per curiam); Warth v. Dep't of Justice, 595 F.2d 521, 523 (9th Cir. 1979); United States v. Neal, No. 90-0003, 2007 U.S. Dist. LEXIS 10176, at *2 (D. Ariz. Feb. 13, 2007) (federal district courts are not agencies under FOIA); Scott v. United States, No. 98-CR-00079, 2006 WL 4031428, at *1 (E.D.N.C. May 9, 2006) (federal courts are not agencies under FOIA), aff'd, No. 06-7197, 2006 WL 2852999 (4th Cir. Oct. 3, 2006); Benjamin v. U.S. Dist. Court, No. 05-941, 2005 WL 1136864, at *1 (M.D. Pa. May 13, 2005) (explaining that United States courts are not "agencies" under FOIA); see also Andrade v. U.S. Sentencing Comm'n, 989 F.2d 308, 309-10 (9th Cir. 1993) (Sentencing Commission, as independent body within judicial branch, is not subject to FOIA); United States v. Richardson, No. 2001-10, 2007 U.S. Dist. LEXIS 77, at *3 (W.D. Pa. Jan. 3, 2007) (federal grand jury is not agency under FOIA); Carter v. U.S. 6th Circuit of Appeal, No. 05-134, 2005 WL 1138828, at *1 (E.D. Tenn. May 12, 2005); Woodruff v. Office of the Pub. Defender, No. 03-791, slip op. at 3 (N.D. Cal. June 3, 2004) (Federal Public Defender's Office, which is controlled by courts, is not agency under FOIA); Wayne Seminoff Co. v. Mecham, No. 02-2445, 2003 U.S. Dist. LEXIS 5829, at *20 (E.D.N.Y. Apr. 10, 2003) ("[T]he Administrative Office of the United States Courts is not an agency for purposes of FOIA."), aff'd, 82 F. App'x 740 (2d Cir. 2003); Maydak v. U.S. Dep't of Justice, 254 F. Supp. 2d 23, 40 (D.D.C. 2003) ("[A] United States probation office is not subject to the FOIA's disclosure requirements because it is an arm of the federal courts."); United States v. Ford, No. 96-00271-01, 1998 U.S. Dist. LEXIS 16438, at *1 (E.D. Pa. Oct. 21, 1998) ("The Clerk of Court, as part of the judicial branch, is not an agency as defined by FOIA."); cf. Callwood v. Dep't of Prob., 982 F. Supp. 341, 342 (D.V.I. 1997) ("[T]he Office of Probation is an administrative unit of [the] Court . . . [and] is not subject to the terms of the Privacy Act.").

[56] See, e.g., United We Stand Am. v. IRS, 359 F.3d 595, 597 (D.C. Cir. 2004) ("The Freedom of Information Act does not cover congressional documents."); Dow Jones & Co. v. Dep't of Justice, 917 F.2d 571, 574 (D.C. Cir. 1990) (holding that Congress is not an agency for any purpose under FOIA); Dunnington v. DOD, No. 06-0925, 2007 U.S. Dist. LEXIS 715, at *3
(continued...)

and private citizens[57] are not subject to the FOIA.  Nor does the FOIA apply to a presidential transition team.[58]

---

[56](...continued)
(D.D.C. Jan. 8, 2007) (ruling that United States Senate and House of Representatives are not agencies under FOIA); see also Mayo v. U.S. Gov't Printing Office, 9 F.3d 1450, 1451 (9th Cir. 1994) (deciding that Government Printing Office is part of congressional branch and therefore is not subject to FOIA); Owens v. Warner, No. 93-2195, slip op. at 1 (D.D.C. Nov. 24, 1993) (ruling that office of Senator John Warner is not subject to FOIA), summary affirmance granted, No. 93-5415, 1994 WL 541335 (D.C. Cir. May 25, 1994).

[57] See, e.g., Henderson v. Office & Prof'l Employees Int'l Union, 143 F. App'x 741, 744 (9th Cir. 2005) (finding that the "district court properly dismissed [the FOIA claim] because the defendants are not 'agencies' and therefore cannot be held liable under the FOIA"); Henderson v. Sony Pictures Entm't, Inc., 135 F. App'x 934, 935 (9th Cir. 2005) (finding that the "district court properly dismissed [a FOIA claim] because the defendants are not 'agencies' and therefore cannot be held liable under the FOIA"); Mitchell, 2003 WL 22999456, at *1 ("[P]rivate counsel and law firms are not subject to FOIA."); In re Olsen, No. UT-98-088, 1999 Bankr. LEXIS 791, at *11 (B.A.P. 10th Cir. June 24, 1999) (holding that chapter seven bankruptcy trustee is not an agency under FOIA); Buemi v. Lewis, No. 94-4156, 1995 WL 149107, at *2 (6th Cir. Apr. 4, 1995) (concluding that the FOIA applies only to federal agencies and not to private individuals); Furlong v. Cochran, No. 06-05443, 2006 WL 3254505, at *1 (W.D. Wash. Nov. 9, 2006) (ruling that lawyer and law firm are not agencies under FOIA); Torres v. Howell, No. 03-2227, 2004 U.S. Dist. LEXIS, at *8 (D. Conn. Dec. 6, 2004) (concluding that plaintiff cannot state FOIA claim against private business and nonfederal attorney); BDX Inc. v. U.S. Dep't of Justice, No. 02-0826, slip op. at 17-18 (N.D. Ind. June 2, 2004) (concluding that because a private trustee was "neither a Department employee nor its agent" his records were not agency records); Allnutt v. U.S. Dep't of Justice, 99 F. Supp. 2d 673, 678 (D. Md. 2000) (holding that records possessed by private trustee acting as agent of United States Trustee are not "agency records" subject to FOIA), aff'd sub nom. Allnut v. Handler, 8 F. App'x 225 (4th Cir. 2001); Simon v. Miami County Incarceration Facility, No. 05-191, 2006 WL 1663689, at *1 (S.D. Ohio May 5, 2006) (stating that a communications company "is not subject to the FOIA") (appeal pending); Germosen v. Cox, No. 98 Civ. 1294, 1999 WL 1021559, at *20 (S.D.N.Y. Nov. 9, 1999) (noting that "there is no authority in the FOIA or Privacy Act obligating . . . private individuals to maintain or make available documents to the public"); Allnutt v. U.S. Trustee, Region Four, No. 97-02414, slip op. at 6 (D.D.C. July 31, 1999) (holding private trustee of bankruptcy estates is not subject to FOIA even though trustee "cooperates [with] and submits regular reports to the United States Trustee," who is subject to FOIA), appeal dismissed for lack of juris., No. 99-5410 (D.C. Cir. Feb. 2, 2000).

[58] See Ill. Inst. for Continuing Legal Educ. v. U.S. Dep't of Labor, 545 F.
(continued...)

Offices within the Executive Office of the President whose functions are limited to advising and assisting the President also do not fall within the definition of "agency";[59] such offices include the Offices of the President and of the Vice President, as well as their respective staffs.[60] The Court of Appeals for the District of Columbia Circuit illustrated this functional definition of "agency" when it held that the former Presidential Task Force on Regulatory Relief -- chaired by the Vice President and composed of several cabinet members -- was not an agency subject to the FOIA because the

---

[58](...continued)
Supp. 1229, 1231-33 (N.D. Ill. 1982); see also FOIA Update, Vol. IX, No. 4, at 3-4 ("FOIA Counselor: Transition Team FOIA Issues"); cf. Wolfe v. HHS, 711 F.2d 1077, 1079 (D.C. Cir. 1983) (treating presidential transition team as not agency subject to FOIA and citing with approval Ill. Inst., 545 F. Supp. at 1231-33) (dicta).

[59] S. Conf. Rep. No. 93-1200, at 14 (1974), reprinted in 1974 U.S.C.C.A.N. 6285, 6293; see, e.g., Judicial Watch, Inc. v. Dep't of Energy, 412 F.3d 125, 127 (D.C. Cir. 2005) (concluding that the National Energy Policy Development Group was not an agency subject to the FOIA, because "its sole function [was] to advise and assist the President" (citing Meyer v. Bush, 981 F.2d 1288, 1292 (D.C. Cir. 1993))); Rushforth v. Council of Econ. Advisers, 762 F.2d 1038, 1042-43 (D.C. Cir. 1985) (ruling that Council of Economic Advisers is not an agency under FOIA); Nation Co. v. Archivist of the United States, No. 88-1939, slip op. at 5-6 (D.D.C. July 24, 1990) (finding that Tower Commission is not an agency under FOIA); Nat'l Sec. Archive v. Executive Office of the President, 688 F. Supp. 29, 31 (D.D.C. 1988) (concluding that Office of Counsel to President is not an agency under FOIA), aff'd sub nom. Nat'l Sec. Archive v. Archivist of the United States, 909 F.2d 541 (D.C. Cir. 1990); see also FOIA Update, Vol. XIV, No. 3, at 6-8 (Department of Justice memorandum specifying consultation process for agencies possessing White House-originated records or White House-originated information located in response to FOIA requests).

[60] See Nat'l Sec. Archive v. Archivist of the United States, 909 F.2d 541, 544 (D.C. Cir. 1990) ("The Supreme Court has made clear that the Office of the President is not an 'agency' for purposes of the FOIA." (citing Kissinger v. Reporters Comm. for Freedom of the Press, 445 U.S. 136, 156 (1980))); Judicial Watch, Inc. v. Nat'l Energy Policy Dev. Group, 219 F. Supp. 2d 20, 55 (D.D.C. 2002) ("[T]he Vice President and his staff are not 'agencies' for purposes of the FOIA.") (non-FOIA case); McDonnell v. Clinton, No. 97-1535, 1997 WL 33321085, at *1 (D.D.C. July 3, 1997) (holding that "Office of the President, including its personal staff . . . whose sole function is to advise and assist the President, does not fall within the definition of agency" (citing Kissinger v. Reporters Comm. for Freedom of the Press, 445 U.S. 136, 150-55 (1980))), aff'd, 132 F.3d 1481 (D.C. Cir. 1997) (unpublished table decision); cf. Sweetland v. Walters, 60 F.3d 852, 855-56 (D.C. Cir. 1995) (finding that the Executive Residence staff, which is "exclusively dedicated to assisting the President in maintaining his home and carrying out his various ceremonial duties," is not an agency under the FOIA).

cabinet members acted not as heads of their departments "but rather as the functional equivalents of assistants to the President."[61]

Under this functional definition of "agency," however, executive branch entities whose responsibilities exceed merely advising and assisting the President generally are considered "agencies" under the FOIA.[62] For example, the D.C. Circuit concluded that the Council on Environmental Quality (a unit within the Executive Office of the President) was an agency subject to the FOIA because its investigatory, evaluative, and recommendatory functions exceeded merely advising the President.[63] On the other hand, when the D.C. Circuit evaluated the structure of the NSC, its proximity to the President, and the nature of the authority delegated to it, the D.C. Circuit determined that the NSC is not an agency subject to the FOIA.[64]

Finally, it should be noted that Congress has removed from the scope of the FOIA certain parts of the operations of some intelligence agencies. Most recently, through the National Defense Authorization Act for Fiscal Year 2006,[65] Congress placed the "operational files" of the Defense Intelligence Agency beyond the scope of the FOIA.[66] Section 933(a) of that Act adds a new section to the National Security Act of 1947 that provides that "[t]he Director of the Defense Intelligence Agency, in coordination with the Director of National Intelligence, may exempt operational files of the De-

---

[61] Meyer v. Bush, 981 F.2d 1288, 1294 (D.C. Cir. 1993); cf. Judicial Watch, Inc. v. Clinton, 76 F.3d 1232, 1234 (D.C. Cir. 1996) (holding that trust established to assist President Clinton with personal legal expenses is not subject to Federal Advisory Committee Act, 5 U.S.C. app. 2 (2000), because "[a]dvice on the legal or ethical implications of presidential fund-raising for personal purposes . . . does not involve 'policy'"); Ass'n of Am. Physicians & Surgeons v. Clinton, 997 F.2d 898, 911 (D.C. Cir. 1993) (declaring that President's Task Force on National Health Care Reform, composed of cabinet officials and chaired by First Lady, was not subject to Federal Advisory Committee Act).

[62] See Soucie v. David, 448 F.2d 1067, 1075 (D.C. Cir. 1971); see also Ryan v. Dep't of Justice, 617 F.2d 781, 784-89 (D.C. Cir. 1980).

[63] Pac. Legal Found. v. Council on Envtl. Quality, 636 F.2d 1259, 1263 (D.C. Cir. 1980) (holding that Council on Environmental Quality is an agency under FOIA); cf. Energy Research Found. v. Def. Nuclear Facilities Safety Bd., 917 F.2d 581, 584-85 (D.C. Cir. 1990) (determining that Defense Nuclear Facilities Safety Board is an agency because of its multiple functions).

[64] Armstrong v. Executive Office of the President, 90 F.3d 553, 559-65 (D.C. Cir. 1996).

[65] Pub. L. No. 109-163, § 933(a), 119 Stat. 34 (2006) (codified at 50 U.S.C.A. § 432c (West Supp. 2006).

[66] Id.; see also 50 U.S.C.A. § 432b (West Supp. 2006) (providing same protective treatment to "operational files" of NSA).

fense Intelligence Agency from the provisions of [the FOIA], which require publication, disclosure, search, or review in connection therewith."[67]

This special statutory protection is quite similar to counterpart Exemption 3 provisions that have been relied on by such other intelligence agencies as the CIA, the NSA, the National Reconnaissance Office, and the National Geospatial-Intelligence Agency (formerly the National Imaging and Mapping Agency and before that the Defense Mapping Agency).[68] In fact, it was more than two decades ago that the CIA became the first entity to obtain such special FOIA treatment for its "operational files" through the Central Intelligence Agency Information Act of 1984.[69] Under these unique "operational file" protective aspects of FOIA administration, these specific intelligence agencies, once any regulatory implementation is conducted, are not subject to the FOIA for these areas of their operations. (For further discussions of this subject, see Exemption 1, "Operational Files" Statutes, below, and Exemption 3, "Operational Files" Provisions, below.)

### "Agency Records"

The Supreme Court has articulated a basic, two-part test for determining what constitutes "agency records" under the FOIA: "Agency records" are records that are (1) either created or obtained by an agency, and (2) under agency control at the time of the FOIA request.[70] Inasmuch as the "agency record" analysis usually hinges upon whether an agency has sufficient "control" over a record,[71] courts have identified four relevant fac-

---

[67] 50 U.S.C.A. § 432c (West Supp. 2006).

[68] See 50 U.S.C.A. §§ 403-5b, 403-5d (2000 & Supp. III 2003); see also FOIA Post, "Agencies Rely on Wide-Range of Exemption 3 Statutes" (posted 12/16/03) (observing that 2003 enactment regarding NSA parallels other Exemption 3 statutes that intelligence agencies such as CIA, National Reconnaissance Office, and National Geospatial-Intelligence Agency have relied on for number of years).

[69] 50 U.S.C.A. § 431 (2003 & West Supp. 2006); see also FOIA Update, Vol. V, No. 4, at 1-2 (discussing statutory removal of CIA "operational files" from scope of FOIA as threshold matter).

[70] U.S. Dep't of Justice v. Tax Analysts, 492 U.S. 136, 144-45 (1989) (holding that court opinions in agency files are agency records); Judicial Watch, Inc. v. U.S. Dep't of Energy, 412 F.3d 125, 132 (D.C. Cir. 2005) (holding that records of agency employees detailed to the National Energy Policy Development Group (NEPDG), chaired by the Vice President, were not agency records when "as a practical matter," the detailees were employees of the NEPDG, not of the agency).

[71] See, e.g., Int'l Bhd. of Teamsters v. Nat'l Mediation Bd., 712 F.2d 1495, 1496 (D.C. Cir. 1983) (determining that submission of gummed-label mail-
(continued...)

tors for an agency to consider when making such a determination:

(1) the intent of the record's creator to retain or relinquish control over the record;[72]

(2) the ability of the agency to use and dispose of the record as it sees fit;[73]

(3) the extent to which agency personnel have read or relied upon the record;[74] and

(4) the degree to which the record was integrated into the agency's

---

[71](...continued)
ing list as required by court were not sufficient to give "control" over record to agency); McErlean v. U.S. Dep't of Justice, No. 97-7831, 1999 WL 791680, at *11 (S.D.N.Y. Sept. 30, 1999) (finding that agency had no "control" over requested records because it assented to restrictions on their dissemination and use that were requested by confidential source who provided them); KDKA v. Thornburgh, No. 90-1536, 1992 U.S. Dist. LEXIS 22438, at *16-17 (D.D.C. Sept. 30, 1992) (concluding that Canadian Safety Board report of aircrash, although possessed by NTSB, is not under agency "control," because of restrictions on its dissemination imposed by Convention on International Civil Aviation); Teich v. FDA, 751 F. Supp. 243, 248-49 (D.D.C. 1990) (holding that documents submitted to FDA in "'legitimate conduct of its official duties'" are agency records notwithstanding FDA's presubmission review regulation allowing submitters to withdraw their documents from agency's files (quoting Tax Analysts, 492 U.S. at 145)); Rush v. Dep't of State, 716 F. Supp. 598, 600 (S.D. Fla. 1989) (finding that correspondence between former ambassador and Henry Kissinger (then Assistant to the President) were agency records of Department of State as it exercised control over them); McCullough v. FDIC, No. 79-1132, 1980 U.S. Dist. LEXIS 17685, at *6 (D.D.C. July 28, 1980) (concluding that state report transmitted to FDIC remains under control of state and is not agency record under FOIA in light of state confidentiality statute, but that other reports transmitted to agency by state regulatory authorities might be agency records because "it is questionable whether [state authorities] retained control" over them); see also FOIA Update, Vol. XIII, No. 3, at 5 (advising that records subject to "protective order" issued by administrative law judge remain within agency control and are subject to FOIA).

[72] Burka v. HHS, 87 F.3d 508, 515 (D.C. Cir. 1996) (quoting Tax Analysts v. U.S. Dep't of Justice, 845 F.2d 1060, 1069 (D.C. Cir. 1988)).

[73] Id.

[74] Id.

record systems or files.[75]

Agency "control" is also the predominant consideration in determining the "agency record" status of records that are either generated[76] or main-

---

[75] Id.; see also Consumer Fed'n of Am. v. USDA, 455 F.3d 283, 288 n.7 (D.C. Cir. 2006) (noting four relevant factors discussed in Burka, 87 F.3d at 515); Judicial Watch, Inc. v. Dep't of Energy, 412 F.3d 125, 127 (D.C. Cir. 2005) (holding that "records created or obtained by employees detailed from an agency to the NEPDG [an advisory group within the Office of the Vice President] are not 'agency records' subject to disclosure under the FOIA"); Missouri v. U.S. Dep't of Interior, 297 F.3d 745, 750-51 (8th Cir. 2002) (holding that records maintained in an agency office by an agency employee who was acting as the full-time coordinator of a nonprofit organization that had a "cooperative" relationship with the agency were not "agency records," because they were not integrated into agency files and were not used by the agency in the performance of its official functions); Katz v. NARA, 68 F.3d 1438, 1442 (D.C. Cir. 1995) (holding that autopsy x-rays and photographs of President Kennedy, created and handled as personal property of Kennedy estate, are presidential papers, not records of any agency); Gen. Elec. Co. v. NRC, 750 F.2d 1394, 1400-01 (7th Cir. 1984) (determining that agency "use" of internal report submitted in connection with licensing proceedings renders report an agency record); Wolfe v. HHS, 711 F.2d 1077, 1079-82 (D.C. Cir. 1983) (holding that transition team records, although physically maintained within "four walls" of agency, were not agency records under FOIA); Judicial Watch, Inc. v. Clinton, 880 F. Supp. 1, 11-12 (D.D.C. 1995) (following Wash. Post v. DOD, 766 F. Supp. 1, 17 (D.D.C. 1991), to find that transcript of congressional testimony provided "solely for editing purposes," with cover sheet restricting dissemination, is not an agency record), aff'd on other grounds, 76 F.3d 1232 (D.C. Cir. 1996); Marzen v. HHS, 632 F. Supp. 785, 801 (N.D. Ill. 1985) (declaring that records created outside federal government which "agency in question obtained without legal authority" are not agency records), aff'd on other grounds, 825 F.2d 1148 (7th Cir. 1987); Ctr. for Nat'l Sec. Studies v. CIA, 577 F. Supp. 584, 586-90 (D.D.C. 1983) (holding that agency report, prepared "at the direct request of Congress" with intent that it remain secret and transferred to agency with congressionally imposed "conditions" of secrecy, is not an agency record); cf. SDC Dev. Corp. v. Mathews, 542 F.2d 1116, 1120 (9th Cir. 1976) (reaching "displacement-type" result for records governed by National Library of Medicine Act (last codified at 42 U.S.C. §§ 275-280a-1 (1982)); Baizer v. U.S. Dep't of the Air Force, 887 F. Supp. 225, 228-29 (N.D. Cal. 1995) (holding that database of Supreme Court decisions, used for reference purposes or as research tool, is not an agency record); Waters v. Pan. Canal Comm'n, No. 85-2029, slip op. at 5-6 (D.D.C. Nov. 26, 1985) (finding that Internal Revenue Code is not an agency record); FOIA Update, Vol. XI, No. 3, at 7-8 n.32 (discussing "'displacement-type'" decision in SDC Dev. Corp. v. Mathews, 542 F.2d 1116, 1120 (9th Cir. 1976)).

[76] See Hercules, Inc. v. Marsh, 839 F.2d 1027, 1029 (4th Cir. 1988) (hold-

(continued...)

tained[77] by a government contractor.

Another important consideration in the "agency record" analysis sometimes is whether Congress, whose records are not subject to the FOIA,[78] has manifested an intent to exert control over certain records in an

---

[76](...continued)
ing that an army ammunition plant telephone directory prepared by a contractor at government expense, bearing a "property of the U.S." legend, is an agency record); Gilmore v. U.S. Dep't of Energy, 4 F. Supp. 2d 912, 922 (N.D. Cal. 1998) (finding that video conferencing software created by privately owned laboratory is not an agency record); Tax Analysts v. U.S. Dep't of Justice, 913 F. Supp. 599, 607 (D.D.C. 1996) (finding that electronic legal research database contracted by agency is not an agency record because licensing provisions specifically precluded agency control), aff'd, 107 F.3d 923 (D.C. Cir. 1997) (unpublished table decision); Lewisburg Prison Project, Inc. v. Fed. Bureau of Prisons, No. 86-1339, slip op. at 4-5 (M.D. Pa. Dec. 16, 1986) (holding that training videotape provided by contractor is not an agency record).

[77] See, e.g., Burka, 87 F.3d at 515 (finding data tapes created and possessed by contractor to be agency records because of extensive supervision exercised by agency, which evidenced "constructive control"); Los Alamos Study Group v. Dep't of Energy, No. 97-1412, slip op. at 4 (D.N.M. July 22, 1998) (determining that records created by contractor are agency records within meaning of FOIA because government contract "establishes [agency] intent to retain control over the records and to use or dispose of them as they see fit" and agency regulation "reinforces the conclusion that [the agency] intends to exercise control over the material"); Chi. Tribune Co. v. HHS, No. 95-C-3917, 1997 U.S. Dist. LEXIS 2308, at *33 (N.D. Ill. Feb. 26, 1997) (magistrate's recommendation) (finding that notes and audit analysis file created by independent contractor are agency records because they were created on behalf of (and at request of) agency and agency maintained "effective control" over them), adopted (N.D. Ill. Mar. 28, 1997); Rush Franklin Publ'g, Inc. v. NASA, No. 90-CV-2855, slip op. at 10 (E.D.N.Y. Apr. 13, 1993) (finding that computer tape maintained by contractor is not an agency record in absence of agency control); see also Sangre de Cristo Animal Prot., Inc. v. U.S. Dep't of Energy, No. 96-1059, slip op. at 3-6 (D.N.M. Mar. 10, 1998) (holding that records that agency neither possessed nor controlled and that were created by entity under contract with agency, although not agency records, were accessible under agency regulation, 10 C.F.R. § 1004.3 (currently 2006), that specifically provided for public availability of contractor records).

[78] See, e.g., United We Stand Am. v. IRS, 359 F.3d 595, 597 (D.C. Cir. 2004) (observing that "[t]he Freedom of Information Act does not cover congressional documents").

agency's possession.[79] "Congressional records" may include records received by an agency from Congress,[80] or records generated by an agency in response to a confidential congressional inquiry,[81] and their status will depend on the particular contours of the congressional reservation of control over those records.[82] In all such cases, Congress's manifestation of its intent to control such records cannot be accomplished on a "post hoc" basis "long after the original creation [or] transfer of the requested documents."[83] Instead, Congress's intent to exert control over the records must be evident from the circumstances surrounding their creation or transmittal.[84] Other-

---

[79] See, e.g., Paisley v. CIA, 712 F.2d 686, 693 (D.C. Cir. 1983), vacated in part on other grounds, 724 F.2d 201 (D.C. Cir. 1984) (per curiam) (noting that if "Congress has manifested its own intent to retain control [of records in the agency's possession], then the agency -- by definition -- cannot lawfully 'control' the documents . . . and hence they are not 'agency records'").

[80] See, e.g., Goland v. CIA, 607 F.2d 339, 347 (D.C. Cir. 1978) (holding that the agency was acting merely "as a 'trustee' for Congress" in retaining a copy of a hearing transcript over which Congress "plainly" manifested an intent to control by denominating it as "'secret'"); Hall v. CIA, No. 98-1319, slip op. at 15 (D.D.C. Aug. 10, 2000) (finding that Senate committee "unequivocally" stated its intent in writing to retain control over committee documents that it entrusted to National Archives).

[81] See Holy Spirit Ass'n v. CIA, 636 F.2d 838, 842-43 (D.C. Cir. 1980) (recognizing that agency-created records can become "congressional records"), vacated in part on other grounds, 455 U.S. 997 (1982); Judicial Watch, Inc. v. Clinton, 880 F. Supp. 1, 12 (D.D.C. 1995) ("Even documents created by the agencies themselves may elude FOIA's reach if prepared on request of Congress with confidentiality restrictions."), aff'd, 76 F.3d 1232 (D.C. Cir. 1996).

[82] See United We Stand Am., 359 F.3d at 604 (concluding that only certain portions of an agency-created response to a confidential congressional inquiry were "congressional records" not subject to the FOIA, "because Congress manifested its intent [to exert control] with respect to at most only a part" of those records).

[83] United We Stand Am., 359 F.3d at 602; see Holy Spirit Ass'n, 636 F.2d at 843 (concluding that Congress's "post hoc" assertion of control, which came about "as a result of . . . the FOIA request and this litigation long after the actual transfer" of the requested records, was "insufficient evidence of Congress'[s] intent to retain control over th[o]se records").

[84] See United We Stand Am., 359 F.3d at 600 (holding that "under all of the circumstances surrounding the [agency's] creation and possession of the documents," there were "sufficient indicia of congressional intent to control" certain portions of those documents); see also Paisley, 712 F.2d at 694 ("[W]e find that neither the circumstances surrounding the creation of the documents nor the conditions under which they were transferred to the

(continued...)

wise, the records may not be considered to be "congressional records" beyond the reach of the FOIA.[85]

In a similar vein, agencies should take care to distinguish "agency records" from "personal records," which are maintained by agency employees but are not subject to the FOIA.[86] In determining the "personal record" status of a record, an agency should examine "the totality of the circumstances surrounding the creation, maintenance, and use" of the record.[87] Factors relevant to this inquiry include the purpose for which the document was created, the degree of integration of the record into the agency's filing system, and the extent to which the record's author or other employ-

---

[84](...continued)
agencies manifests a clear congressional intent to maintain control."); Holy Spirit Ass'n, 636 F.2d at 842 ("Nothing here either in the circumstances of the documents' creation or in the conditions under which they were sent to the [agency] indicates Congress'[s] intent to retain control over the records."); Goland, 607 F.2d at 348 (holding that a congressional hearing transcript maintained by an agency was "not an 'agency record' but a Congressional document to which FOIA does not apply . . . because we believe that on all the facts of the case Congress'[s] intent to retain control of the document is clear").

[85] See, e.g., Paisley, 712 F.2d at 692-93 ("In the absence of any manifest indications that Congress intended to exert control over documents in an agency's possession, the court will conclude that such documents are not congressional records.").

[86] See, e.g., Consumer Fed'n of Am., 455 F.3d at 288-93 (holding that calendars of five officials were agency records where calendars were distributed to other staff for business use, but that calendar of sixth official was personal record created and used for sixth official's convenience where it was distributed only to his secretarial staff); Bureau of Nat'l Affairs, Inc. v. U.S. Dep't of Justice, 742 F.2d 1484, 1488-96 (D.C. Cir. 1984) (holding that uncirculated appointment calendars and telephone message slips of agency official were not agency records); Spannaus v. U.S. Dep't of Justice, 942 F. Supp. 656, 658 (D.D.C. 1996) (finding that "'personal' files" of attorney no longer employed with agency were "beyond the reach of FOIA" if they were not turned over to agency at end of employment); Forman v. Chapotan, No. 88-1151, slip op. at 14 (W.D. Okla. Dec. 12, 1988) (rejecting contention that materials distributed to agency officials at privately sponsored seminar are agency records), aff'd, No. 89-6035 (10th Cir. Oct. 31, 1989); see also FOIA Update, Vol. IX, No. 4, at 3-4 (discussing circumstances under which presidential transition team documents can be regarded as "personal records" when brought into federal agency); FOIA Update, Vol. V, No. 4, at 3-4 ("OIP Guidance: 'Agency Records' vs. 'Personal Records'").

[87] Bureau of Nat'l Affairs, 742 F.2d at 1492; see also Consumer Fed'n of Am., 455 F.3d at 287-88 (deciding case by using "totality" test articulated in, and "template" provided by, Bureau of Nat'l Affairs, 742 F.2d at 1488-96).

ees used the record to conduct agency business.[88]

---

[88] Consumer Fed'n of Am., 455 F.3d at 287 (citing Bureau of Nat'l Affairs, 742 F.2d at 1490)); Bureau of Nat'l Affairs, 742 F.2d at 1492-93; FOIA Update, Vol. V, No. 4, at 3-4; see, e.g., Gallant v. NLRB, 26 F.3d 168, 171-72 (D.C. Cir. 1994) (ruling that letters written on agency time on agency equipment by board member seeking renomination, which had been reviewed by other agency employees but not integrated into agency record system and over which author had not relinquished control, are not agency records); Fortson v. Harvey, 407 F. Supp. 2d 13, 16 (D.D.C. 2005) (finding that Army officer's notes of investigation were personal records because notes were used only to refresh officer's memory and were neither integrated into agency files nor relied on by other agency employees), appeal dismissed, No. 05-5193, 2005 WL 3789054, at *1 (D.C. Cir. Oct. 31, 2005); Bloomberg, L.P. v. SEC, 357 F. Supp. 2d 156, 163-67 (D.D.C. 2004) (concluding that computer calendar, telephone logs, and message slips of SEC Chairman, and meeting notes of Chairman's chief of staff, were personal records where they were created for personal use of Chairman or chief of staff, were not incorporated into SEC files, and were not under SEC control, even though some records were maintained by SEC personnel and were automatically "backed-up" onto SEC computer server at regular intervals); Inner City Press/Cmty. on the Move v. Bd. of Governors of the Fed. Reserve Sys., No. 98-4608, 1998 U.S. Dist. LEXIS 15333, at *17 (S.D.N.Y. Sept. 30, 1998) (ruling that handwritten notes neither shared with other agency employees nor placed in agency files were not "agency records" even though they may have furthered their author's performance of his agency duties), aff'd, 182 F.3d 900 (2d Cir. 1999) (unpublished table decision); Clarkson v. Greenspan, No. 97-2035, slip op. at 14 (D.D.C. June 30, 1998) (holding that notes taken by Federal Reserve Banks' employees are "personal" because they were maintained by authors for their own use, were not intended to be shared with other employees, and were not made part of Banks' filing systems), summary affirmance granted, No. 98-5349, 1999 WL 229017 (D.C. Cir. Mar. 2, 1999); Judicial Watch, 880 F. Supp. at 11 (concluding that "telephone logs, calendar markings, [and] personal staff notes" not incorporated into agency recordkeeping system are not agency records); Dow Jones & Co. v. GSA, 714 F. Supp. 35, 39 (D.D.C. 1989) (determining that agency head's recusal list, shared only with personal secretary and chief of staff, is not an agency record); AFGE v. U.S. Dep't of Commerce, 632 F. Supp. 1272, 1277 (D.D.C. 1986) (finding that employee logs created voluntarily to facilitate work are not agency records even though they contained substantive information), aff'd, 907 F.2d 203 (D.C. Cir. 1990). But cf. Grand Cent. P'ship, Inc. v. Cuomo, 166 F.3d 473, 481 (2d Cir. 1999) (rejecting agency affidavit concerning "personal" records as insufficient and remanding case for further development through affidavits by records' authors explaining their intended use of records in question); Ethyl Corp. v. EPA, 25 F.3d 1241, 1247-48 (4th Cir. 1994) (finding record search inadequate because employees were "not properly instructed on how to distinguish personal records from agency records").

## PROCEDURAL REQUIREMENTS

While courts continue to apply longstanding precedent regarding the kinds of records considered to be "personal records" in nature,[89] recent case law in this area indicates that some courts are holding agencies to closer scrutiny regarding "personal record" determinations.[90] Any agency engaging in an analysis to distinguish "agency records" from "personal records" should therefore carefully consider all criteria appropriate to reaching a conclusion[91] and should memorialize the careful consideration given to such issues by agency personnel with knowledge of the requisite considerations involved in such determinations.[92]

Agencies also should be mindful of the "agency record" status of research data generated through federal grants. The Omnibus Consolidated and Emergency Supplemental Appropriations Act for Fiscal Year 1999,[93] which partly overruled the longstanding Supreme Court precedent of For-sham v. Harris,[94] made certain research data generated through federal grants subject to the FOIA.[95] In Forsham, the Supreme Court held that data generated and maintained by private research institutions receiving federal grants are not "agency records" subject to the FOIA, and that a grantor agency is not obligated to demand such data in order to respond to any

---

[89] See, e.g., Consumer Fed'n of Am., 455 F.3d at 287-88 (relying on Bureau of Nat'l Affairs, 742 F.2d 1484).

[90] See Ethyl Corp., 25 F.3d at 1247 (stating that agency "employees were not properly instructed on how to distinguish personal records from agency records" because agency provided guidance to employees on only some considerations necessary for such analysis); Kempker-Cloyd v. U.S. Dep't of Justice, No. 5:97-253, 1999 U.S. Dist. LEXIS 4813, at *12, *24 (W.D. Mich. Mar. 12, 1999) (finding that agency's "initial search efforts . . . were incomplete and untimely," in part, because FOIA office did not actually review documents that field employee asserted were personal records in order to determine whether assertion was correct).

[91] See Ethyl Corp., 25 F.3d at 1247-48 (finding that agency did not demonstrate adequate search when, inter alia, "employees were not properly instructed on how to distinguish personal records from agency records" when agency provided guidance to employees on only some considerations necessary for such analysis); see also FOIA Update, Vol. V, No. 4, at 1-4 ("OIP Guidance: 'Agency Records' vs. 'Personal Records'") (advising of ten criteria "that should be evaluated by agencies in making all 'agency record/personal record' determinations").

[92] See, e.g., Ethyl Corp., 25 F.3d at 1247-48 (questioning agency's methodology where agency provided instructions to employees on only four out of ten criteria appropriate to "agency record/personal record" analysis).

[93] Pub. L. No. 105-277, 112 Stat. 2681 (1998).

[94] 445 U.S. 169 (1980).

[95] See FOIA Update, Vol. XIX, No. 4, at 2 (describing legislative change).

FOIA request for them.[96] This statutory provision, however, required OMB to revise its Circular A-110 (the regulatory publication by which OMB sets the rules governing grants from all federal agencies to institutions of higher education, hospitals, and nonprofit institutions) so that "all data produced under an award will be made available to the public through the procedures established under the Freedom of Information Act."[97] The final revised version of Circular A-110 requires agencies to respond to FOIA requests for certain grantee research findings by obtaining the requested data from the grantee and processing it for release to the requester.[98] (In accordance with OMB's statutory authority over such matters, questions concerning the processing of FOIA requests for grantee research data should be directed to OMB's Office of Information and Regulatory Affairs, Information Policy and Technology Branch, at (202) 395-3052.)

At a more fundamental level, the FOIA applies only to "records," not to tangible, evidentiary objects.[99] The courts initially defined "record" by relying on the traditional dictionary meaning of the term.[100] However, the Supreme Court subsequently broadened the meaning of "record" by incorporating the more modern record media referenced in the Records Disposal

---

[96] 445 U.S. at 178-81.

[97] Omnibus Consolidated and Emergency Supplemental Appropriations Act for Fiscal Year 1999, Pub. L. No. 105-277, 112 Stat. 2681 (1998).

[98] See OMB Circular A-110, "Uniform Administrative Requirements for Grants and Agreements with Institutions of Higher Education, Hospitals, and Other Non-Profit Organizations," 64 Fed. Reg. 54,926 (Oct. 8, 1999); see also FOIA Update, Vol. XIX, No. 4, at 2 (discussing grantee records subject to FOIA under Circular A-110's definition of "research data").

[99] See Matthews v. U.S. Postal Serv., No. 92-1208, slip op. at 4 n.3 (W.D. Mo. Apr. 14, 1994) (holding that computer hardware is not "record"); Nichols v. United States, 325 F. Supp. 130, 135-36 (D. Kan. 1971) (holding that archival exhibits consisting of guns, bullets, and clothing pertaining to assassination of President Kennedy are not "records"), aff'd on other grounds, 460 F.2d 671 (10th Cir. 1972); see also FOIA Update, Vol. XIV, No. 1, at 1 (discussing implementation of President John F. Kennedy Assassination Records Collection Act of 1992, 44 U.S.C. § 2107 note (2000)); cf. FOIA Update, Vol. XIX, No. 4, at 2 (discussing provisions of "somewhat akin" FOIA-related statute, Nazi War Crimes Disclosure Act, 5 U.S.C. § 552 note (2000 & Supp. IV 2004).

[100] See DiViaio v. Kelley, 571 F.2d 538, 542 (10th Cir. 1978) ("[R]eliance may be placed on the dictionary meaning . . . as that which is written or transcribed to perpetuate knowledge."); Nichols, 325 F. Supp. at 135 (stating that reliance "placed on a dictionary of respected ancestry [(i.e., Webster's)]").

Act[101] into its definition of the term.[102] As information technology evolved, computer software increasingly could be considered as generally within the definition of "record."[103] With the passage of the Electronic Freedom of Information Act Amendments of 1996,[104] the FOIA now defines the term "record" as simply "includ[ing] any information that would be an agency record . . . when maintained by an agency in any format, including an electronic format."[105]

## FOIA Requesters

A FOIA request can be made by "any person," a broad term that encompasses individuals (including foreign citizens), partnerships, corporations, associations, and foreign or domestic governments.[106] Requests may

---

[101] 44 U.S.C. § 3301 (2000).

[102] See Forsham, 445 U.S. at 183 (treating "record" as including "'machine readable materials . . . regardless of physical form or characteristics'" (quoting Records Disposal Act, 44 U.S.C. § 3301 (1980)); see also N.Y. Times Co. v. NASA, 920 F.2d 1002, 1005 (D.C. Cir. 1990) (holding that audiotape of Space Shuttle Challenger astronauts is "record," as "FOIA makes no distinction between information in lexical and . . . non-lexical form"); Save the Dolphins v. U.S. Dep't of Commerce, 404 F. Supp. 407, 410-11 (N.D. Cal. 1975) (finding that motion picture film is "record" for purposes of FOIA).

[103] Cleary, Gottlieb, Steen & Hamilton v. HHS, 844 F. Supp. 770, 782 (D.D.C. 1993) ("These [computer] programs preserve information and 'perpetuate knowledge.'" (quoting DiViaio, 571 F.2d at 542)); see also FOIA Update, Vol. XV, No. 4, at 4-5 (proposed electronic record FOIA principles); Department of Justice "Electronic Record" Report, reprinted in abridged form in FOIA Update, Vol. XI, No. 3, at 6-12 (discussing issue of "record" status of computer software). But see Gilmore, 4 F. Supp. 2d at 919-20 (holding alternatively that video conferencing software developed by privately owned laboratory may not be regarded as "record" on basis that such software "does not illuminate the structure, operation, or decisionmaking structure" of agency); Essential Info., Inc. v. USIA, 134 F.3d 1165, 1166 n.3 (D.C. Cir. 1998) (dictum) (suggesting, without authority, that Internet addresses "seem to be" not records, but "simply 'a means to access' records").

[104] Pub. L. No. 104-231, § 3, 110 Stat. 3048, 3049 (codified as amended at 5 U.S.C. § 552(f)(2) (2000 & Supp. IV 2004)).

[105] 5 U.S.C. § 552(f)(2); see FOIA Update, Vol. XVII, No. 4, at 2 (discussing statutory amendment); see also FOIA Post, "FOIA Counselor Q&A" (posted 1/24/06) (advising that "electronic databases to which an agency has no more than 'read only' access" -- e.g., "LexisNexis, Westlaw, and other such data services" -- are not "'agency records'" under the FOIA).

[106] 5 U.S.C. § 551(2) (2000); cf. Judicial Watch v. U.S. Dep't of Justice, 102

(continued...)

also be made through an attorney or other representative on behalf of "any person."[107] Individual members of Congress possess the same rights of access as those guaranteed to "any person."[108] Although the statute

---

[106](...continued)
F. Supp. 2d 6, 10 (D.D.C. 2000) (holding that because two related organizations "are separate corporations, . . . each is entitled to request documents under FOIA in its own right").

[107] See, e.g., Constangy, Brooks & Smith v. NLRB, 851 F.2d 839, 840 n.2 (6th Cir. 1988) (recognizing standing of attorney to request documents on behalf of client); see also Doherty v. U.S. Dep't of Justice, 596 F. Supp. 423, 427 n.4 (S.D.N.Y. 1984) (reviewing legislative history), aff'd on other grounds, 775 F.2d 49 (2d Cir. 1985). See generally Burka v. HHS, 142 F.3d 1286, 1290 (D.C. Cir. 1998) (holding that when an attorney makes a request in his own name without disclosing that he is acting on behalf of a client, he may not later seek attorney fees for his legal work); McDonnell v. United States, 4 F.3d 1227, 1237-38 (3d Cir. 1993) (holding that person whose name does not appear on request does not have standing); Brown v. EPA, 384 F. Supp. 2d 271, 276-78 (D.D.C. 2005) (finding that plaintiff has standing where request stated that attorney was making request on behalf of client, and where "other correspondence . . . confirm[ed]" that all parties understood attorney to be acting on behalf of client); Mahtesian v. OPM, 388 F. Supp. 2d 1047, 1050 (N.D. Cal. 2005) (finding that a lawyer's "reference to an anonymous client in a FOIA request, can not [sic], alone, confer standing on that client"); Hall v. CIA, No. 04-00814, 2005 WL 850379, at *4 (D.D.C. Apr. 13, 2005) (finding that requester organization was party to request where request letter stated that organization was "joining" request, even though organization's attorney did not sign letter); Three Forks Ranch Corp. v. Bureau of Land Mgmt., 358 F. Supp. 2d 1, 3 (D.D.C. 2005) (finding that corporation lacked standing to pursue FOIA action where its attorney did not indicate specifically that he was making FOIA request "on behalf of" corporation); Scaife v. IRS, No. 02-1805, 2003 U.S. Dist. LEXIS 22661, at *5 (D.D.C. Nov. 20, 2003) (finding that powers-of-attorney submitted with FOIA request were insufficient to vest requester with right to receive requested records); Archibald v. Roche, No. 01-1492, slip op. at 1-2 (D.D.C. Mar. 29, 2002) (concluding that the request "appears to [have been] filed on behalf of the attorney" who signed the request, rather than on behalf of the client, because "nowhere in [the request] does [the attorney] ever state that he [was] filing this request on behalf of" the client); Dale v. IRS, 238 F. Supp. 2d 99, 107 (D.D.C. 2002) ("A party's counsel is not the 'requester' for purposes of a fee waiver."); MAXXAM, Inc. v. FDIC, 1999 WL 33912624, at *2 (D.D.C. Jan. 29, 1999) (finding that a corporate plaintiff whose name did not appear on a FOIA request made by its attorney "'has not administratively asserted a right to receive [the requested records] in the first place'" (quoting McDonnell, 4 F.3d at 1237)).

[108] See FOIA Update, Vol. V, No. 1, at 3-4 (distinguishing between individual Members of Congress and Congress as an institutional entity, which
(continued...)

specifically excludes federal agencies from the definition of a "person,"[109] states and state agencies can make FOIA requests.[110]

There are two narrow, noteworthy exceptions to this broad "any person" standard, however. First, courts have denied relief under the FOIA to fugitives from justice if the requested records relate to the requester's fugitive status.[111] This holds true also when the FOIA plaintiff is an agent act-

---

[108](...continued)
exercises its authority through its committee chairs); see also Congressional Oversight Manual, T.J. Halstead, Frederick M. Kaiser, Walter J. Oleszek, Morton Rosenberg, Todd B. Tatelman, Congressional Research Service, Report RL30240, Sec. III.G., at CRS-56 ("Role of Minority-Party Members in the Investigative Process") (Jan. 3, 2007) (discussing, inter alia, minority-party avenues of information access); Application of Privacy Act Congressional-Disclosure Exception to Disclosures to Ranking Minority Members, Op. Off. Legal Counsel (Dec. 5, 2001), available at http://www.usdoj.gov/olc/2001/privacy_act_opinion.pdf (discussing congressional access under the Privacy Act).

[109] 5 U.S.C. § 551(2); see also FOIA Update, Vol. VI, No. 1, at 6 (advising that information requests from agencies within executive branch of federal government cannot be considered FOIA requests).

[110] See, e.g., Texas v. ICC, 935 F.2d 728, 728 (5th Cir. 1991); Massachusetts v. HHS, 727 F. Supp. 35, 35 (D. Mass. 1989).

[111] See Maydak v. U.S. Dep't of Educ., 150 F. App'x 136, 138 (3d Cir. 2005) (affirming the district court's dismissal with prejudice as "there was enough of a connection between Maydak's fugitive status and his FOIA case"); Maydak v. United States, No. 02-5168, slip op. at 1 (D.C. Cir. Dec. 11, 2003) (refusing to dismiss the case because "[t]here is no substantial connection between [the requester's] alleged fugitive status and his current [FOIA] action," which was filed four years before the requester became a fugitive) (citing Daccarett-Ghia v. IRS, 70 F.3d 621, 626 (D.C. Cir. 1995)); Doyle v. U.S. Dep't of Justice, 668 F.2d 1365, 1365-66 (D.C. Cir. 1981) (holding that fugitive is not entitled to enforcement of FOIA's access provisions because he cannot expect judicial aid in obtaining government records related to sentence that he was evading); Meddah v. Reno, No. 98-1444, slip op. at 2 (E.D. Pa. Dec. 3, 1998) (dismissing escapee's FOIA claim because escapee "request[ed] documents which were used to determine that he should be detained"); see also Daccarett-Ghia, 70 F.3d at 626 n.4 (limiting the applicability of the "fugitive disentitlement doctrine" generally, but explaining that the "holding in this case does not disturb that aspect of Doyle" in which the court "recognize[d] one universally applied constraint on the fugitive disentitlement doctrine" -- namely, that "[d]ismissal was appropriate in part because the fugitive's [FOIA] suit sought records that were 'not devoid of a relationship' to the criminal charges pending against him") (non-FOIA case). But cf. O'Rourke v. U.S. Dep't of Justice, 684 F.

(continued...)

ing on behalf of a fugitive.[112]

Second, the Intelligence Authorization Act of 2003[113] amended the FOIA to now preclude agencies of the intelligence community[114] from disclosing records in response to any FOIA request that is made by any foreign government or international governmental organization, either directly or through a representative.[115] This means that agencies such as the CIA, the NSA, and even some parts of the FBI and the DHS may refuse to process such requests.[116]

Inasmuch as FOIA requests can be made for any reason whatsoever, FOIA requesters generally do not have to justify or explain their reasons for making requests.[117] Consistent with this, the Supreme Court has stated that a FOIA requester's basic access rights are neither increased nor decreased because the requester claims to have a particular interest in the records sought.[118] Yet despite repeated Supreme Court admonitions for re-

---

[111](...continued)
Supp. 716, 718 (D.D.C. 1988) (holding that convicted criminal, fugitive from his home country and undergoing U.S. deportation proceedings, qualified as "any person" for purpose of making FOIA request); Doherty, 596 F. Supp. at 424-29 (same).

[112] See Javelin Int'l, Ltd. v. U.S. Dep't of Justice, 2 Gov't Disclosure Serv. (P-H) ¶ 82,141, at 82,479 (D.D.C. Dec. 9, 1981).

[113] Pub. L. No. 107-306, 116 Stat. 2383 (2002).

[114] See 50 U.S.C.A. § 401a(4) (2003 & West Supp. 2006) (provision of the National Security Act of 1947, as amended, that specifies the federal agencies and agency subparts that are deemed "elements of the intelligence community").

[115] Pub. L. No. 107-306, 116 Stat. 2383, § 312 (codified at 5 U.S.C. § 552(a)(3)(A), (E) (2000 & Supp. IV 2004)).

[116] See FOIA Post, "FOIA Amended by Intelligence Authorization Act" (posted 12/23/02) (advising that "for any FOIA request that by its nature appears as if it might have been made by or on behalf of a non-U.S. governmental entity, a covered agency may inquire into the particular circumstances of the requester in order to properly implement this new FOIA provision").

[117] See, e.g., NARA v. Favish, 541 U.S. 157, 172 ("[A]s a general rule, when documents are within FOIA's disclosure provisions, citizens should not be required to explain why they seek the information."), reh'g denied, 541 U.S. 1057 (2004).

[118] See NLRB v. Sears, Roebuck & Co., 421 U.S. 132, 143 n.10 (1975) (recognizing that a requester's "rights under the Act are neither increased nor

(continued...)

straint,[119] requesters have invoked the FOIA successfully as a substitute for, or a supplement to, document discovery in the contexts of both civil[120]

---

[118](...continued)
decreased by reason of the fact that [he or she] claims an interest in the [requested records] greater than that shared by the average member of the public"); see also U.S. Dep't of Justice v. Reporters Comm. for Freedom of the Press, 489 U.S. 749, 771 (1989) ("As we have repeatedly stated, Congress 'clearly intended' the FOIA 'to give any member of the public as much right to disclosure as one with a special interest [in a particular document].'" (quoting Sears, 421 U.S. at 149)); EPA v. Mink, 410 U.S. 73, 86 (1973) (declaring that the FOIA "is largely indifferent to the intensity of a particular requester's need"); cf. Parsons v. Freedom of Info. Act Officer, No. 96-4128, 1997 WL 461320, at *1 (6th Cir. Aug. 12, 1997) (rejecting plaintiff's argument that his "legitimate need for the documents superior to that of the general public or the press" warranted disclosure of exempt information); North v. Walsh, 881 F.2d 1088, 1096 (D.C. Cir. 1989) ("In sum, [the FOIA requester's] need or intended use for the documents is irrelevant."); Ctr. for Individual Rights v. U.S. Dep't of Justice, No. 03-1706, slip op. at 5-6 (D.D.C. June 29, 2004) (stating that requester's rights under FOIA are not affected by his involvement in other cases in litigation, even where discovery process would not provide access to requested documents).

[119] See United States v. Weber Aircraft Corp., 465 U.S. 792, 801-02 (1984); Baldrige v. Shapiro, 455 U.S. 345, 360 n.14 (1982); NLRB v. Robbins Tire & Rubber Co., 437 U.S. 214, 242 (1978); Sears, 421 U.S. at 143 n.10; Renegotiation Bd. v. Bannercraft Clothing Co., 415 U.S. 1, 24 (1974).

[120] See, e.g., Jackson v. First Fed. Sav., 709 F. Supp. 887, 889 (E.D. Ark. 1989); see also In re F&H Barge Corp., 46 F. Supp. 2d 453, 454-55 (E.D. Va. 1998) (noting that "courts have allowed private litigants to obtain documents in discovery via the FOIA"); FOIA Update, Vol. III, No. 1, at 10 (acknowledging that "[u]nder present law there is no statutory prohibition to the use of FOIA as a discovery tool"). But see also Martinez v. EEOC, No. 04-0391, 2004 WL 2359895, at *6 (W.D. Tex. Oct. 19, 2004) (concluding that a requester "may not use the FOIA to circumvent the discovery process and thereby frustrate the investigative procedures of the EEOC"); Cantres v. FBI, No. 01-1115, slip op. at 5 (D. Minn. June 21, 2002) (magistrate's recommendation) (avouching that "[a] FOIA request is not a substitute for discovery in a habeas case," nor was the FOIA "designed to supplement the rules of civil discovery"), adopted (D. Minn. July 16, 2002); Comer v. IRS, No. 97-76329, 2000 WL 1566279, at *2 (E.D. Mich. Aug. 17, 2000) (opining that "while documents obtained through FOIA requests may ultimately prove helpful in litigation by permitting a citizen to more precisely target his discovery requests, FOIA is not intended to be a substitute for discovery"); Envtl. Crimes Project v. EPA, 928 F. Supp. 1, 2 (D.D.C. 1995) (ordering a stay of a FOIA case "pending the resolution of the discovery disputes" in the parties' related lawsuit in order to foreclose the requester's attempt to "end run" or interfere with discovery); cf. Injex Indus. v. NLRB, 699 F. Supp.

(continued...)

and criminal[121] litigation.

Nevertheless, there are two types of circumstances in which a requester's reason for making a FOIA request can properly affect the manner in which it is processed, either procedurally or substantively. First, the resolution of certain procedural issues -- i.e., expedited access, the assessment or waiver of fees, and the award of attorney fees and costs to a successful FOIA plaintiff -- can depend upon the reason for which the request was made.[122] Second, a requester's reason for making a FOIA request -- as it is reflected in an evidentiary showing of "public interest" -- can substantively affect the agency's decision to disclose or withhold information that is potentially subject to the FOIA's privacy exemptions.[123] (For discussions

---

[120](...continued)
1417, 1419 (N.D. Cal. 1986) (holding that FOIA cannot be used to circumvent nonreviewable decision to impound requested documents); Morrison-Knudsen Co. v. Dep't of the Army of the United States, 595 F. Supp. 352, 356 (D.D.C. 1984) ("[T]he use of FOIA to unsettle well established procedures governed by a comprehensive regulatory scheme must be . . . viewed not only 'with caution' but with concern."), aff'd, 762 F.2d 138 (D.C. Cir. 1985) (unpublished table decision).

[121] See, e.g., North, 881 F.2d at 1096; Bright v. Attorney Gen. John Ashcroft, 259 F. Supp. 2d 502, 503 & n.1 (E.D. La. 2003) (concluding erroneously that Brady v. Maryland "demands" that information withheld under Exemption 7(D) of FOIA be released to plaintiff). But see United States v. U.S. Dist. Court, Cent. Dist. of Cal., 717 F.2d 478, 480 (9th Cir. 1983) (holding that FOIA does not expand scope of criminal discovery permitted under Rule 16 of Federal Rules of Criminal Procedure); United States v. Agunbiade, No. 90-CR-610, 1995 WL 351058, at *7 (E.D.N.Y. May 10, 1995) (stating that a FOIA requester "cannot employ the statute as a means to enlarge his right to discovery" in his criminal case); Johnson v. U.S. Dep't of Justice, 758 F. Supp. 2, 5 (D.D.C. 1991) ("Resort to Brady v. Maryland as grounds for waiving confidentiality is . . . outside the proper role of FOIA."); Stimac v. U.S. Dep't of Justice, 620 F. Supp. 212, 213 (D.D.C. 1985) ("Brady v. Maryland . . . provides no authority for releasing material under FOIA."); cf. Jones v. FBI, 41 F.3d 238, 250 (6th Cir. 1994) ("FOIA's scheme of exemptions does not curtail a plaintiff's right to discovery in related non-FOIA litigation; but neither does that right entitle a FOIA plaintiff to circumvent the rules limiting release of documents under FOIA.").

[122] Cf. Forsham v. Califano, 587 F.2d 1128, 1134 (D.C. Cir. 1978) (recognizing that "considerations such as need, interest, or public interest may bear on the agency's determination" to process pending FOIA requests in a certain order), aff'd on other grounds sub nom. Forsham v. Harris, 445 U.S. 169 (1980).

[123] See Favish, 541 U.S. at 172 (declaring that "[w]here the privacy concerns addressed by Exemption 7(C) are present, the exemption requires
(continued...)

of the proper application of those exemptions, see Exemption 6, below, and Exemption 7(C), below.)

On a related note, the Supreme Court has observed that a FOIA requester's identity generally "has no bearing on the merits of his or her FOIA request."[124] However, the Court has recognized an exception to this general rule by noting that the requester's identity can be significant in one substantive respect: "The fact that no one need show a particular need for information in order to qualify for disclosure under the FOIA does not mean

---

[123](...continued)
the person requesting the information to establish a sufficient reason for the disclosure" by showing that "the public interest sought to be advanced [by the requested disclosure] is a significant one" and that disclosure of "the information is likely to advance that interest"); see also FOIA Post, "Supreme Court Rules for 'Survivor Privacy' in Favish" (posted 4/9/04) ("Favish thus stands as a reminder to all agencies that their consideration of potential privacy invasions must include . . . what the requester might do with the information at hand.").

[124] Reporters Comm., 489 U.S. at 771; see Favish, 541 U.S. at 170 ("As a general rule, withholding information under FOIA cannot be predicated on the identity of the requester."); see also Lynch v. Dep't of the Treasury, No. 98-56368, 2000 WL 123236, at *4 (9th Cir. Jan. 28, 2000) (upholding district court's decision to not consider identity of requester in determining whether records were properly withheld under Exemption 7(A)); Parsons, 1997 WL 461320, at *1 ("[T]he identity of the requestor is irrelevant to the determination of whether an exemption applies."); United Techs. v. FAA, 102 F.3d 688, 692 (2d Cir. 1996) (rejecting plaintiff's argument that Exemption 4 should be applied "on a requester-specific basis," because "[u]nder that rule, the Government would be required in every FOIA case to conduct an inquiry regarding the identity of the requester and the circumstances surrounding its request," and "[t]he FOIA was not intended to be applied on such an individualized basis"); Swan v. SEC, 96 F.3d 498, 499 (D.C. Cir. 1996) ("Whether [a particular exemption] protects against disclosure to 'any person' is a judgment to be made without regard to the particular requester's identity."); Durns v. Bureau of Prisons, 804 F.2d 701, 706 (D.C. Cir. 1986) ("Congress granted the scholar and the scoundrel equal rights of access to agency records."), cert. granted, judgment vacated on other grounds & remanded, 486 U.S. 1029 (1988); FOIA Update, Vol. VI, No. 3, at 5 ("It is also well established that a FOIA requester cannot rely upon his status as a private party litigant -- in either civil or criminal litigation -- to claim an entitlement to greater FOIA access than would be available to the average requester."); cf. Calder v. IRS, 890 F.2d 781, 783 (5th Cir. 1989) (holding that historian denied access under FOIA also has no "constitutional right of access" to Al Capone's tax records); Leach v. RTC, 860 F. Supp. 868, 871, 878-79 & n.13 (D.D.C. 1994) (recognizing, in dicta, that individual Members of Congress are granted no greater access to agency records by virtue of their position than are other FOIA requesters), appeal dismissed per stipulation, No. 94-5279 (D.C. Cir. Dec. 22, 1994).

that in no situation whatever will there be valid reasons for treating [an exemption] differently as to one class of those who make requests than as to another class."[125] In short, this means that an agency should not invoke a FOIA exemption to protect a requester from himself.[126]

Finally, the Court of Appeals for the District of Columbia Circuit has held that under some circumstances a FOIA claim in litigation may survive even if the FOIA requester dies before the case is put to rest.[127]

## Proper FOIA Requests

The FOIA specifies only two requirements for an access request: It must "reasonably describe" the records sought[128] and it must be made in accordance with the agency's published FOIA regulations.[129] Because "a

---

[125] U.S. Dep't of Justice v. Julian, 486 U.S. 1, 14 (1988); accord Reporters Comm., 489 U.S. at 771 (recognizing single exception to general FOIA-disclosure rule in case of "first-party" requester).

[126] See FOIA Update, Vol. X, No. 2, at 5 (advising agencies to treat first-party FOIA requesters in accordance with protectible interests that requesters can have in their own information, such as personal privacy information, and to treat third-party FOIA requesters differently).

[127] See Sinito v. U.S. Dep't of Justice, 176 F.3d 512, 513 (D.C. Cir. 1999) (holding that FOIA claim can survive death of original requester and remanding case for determination regarding who could properly be substituted for decedent); see also D'Aleo v. Dep't of the Navy, No. 89-2347, 1991 U.S. Dist. LEXIS 3884, at *4 (D.D.C. Mar. 21, 1991) (allowing decedent's executrix to be substituted as plaintiff). But see Hayles v. U.S. Dep't of Justice, No. H-79-1599, slip op. at 3 (S.D. Tex. Nov. 2, 1982) (dismissing case upon death of plaintiff because no timely motion for substitution was filed).

[128] 5 U.S.C. § 552(a)(3)(A) (2000 & Supp. IV 2004).

[129] Id. § 552(a)(3)(A)(ii); see, e.g., Maxwell v. Snow, 409 F.3d 354, 358-59 (D.C. Cir. 2005) (affirming district court's holding that "FOIA procedures should apply to requests for [tax] return information under 26 U.S.C. § 6103"); Borden v. FBI, No. 94-1029, slip op. at 2 (1st Cir. June 28, 1994) (per curiam) (affirming dismissal of case because requester failed to comply with agency's published regulations); McDonnell v. United States, 4 F.3d 1227, 1236-37 (3d Cir. 1993) ("[A] person whose name does not appear on [FOIA] request [as required by agency regulations] . . . has not made a formal request for documents within the meaning of the statute [and therefore] has no right to [the documents or to] sue in district court when the agency refuses to release requested documents."); Church of Scientology v. IRS, 792 F.2d 146, 150 (D.C. Cir. 1986) (stating that requesters must follow "the statutory command that requests be made in accordance with published rules"); Harris v. Freedom of Info. Unit, DEA, No. 06-00176, slip op. at

(continued...)

person need not title a request for government records a 'FOIA request,'"[130] agencies should use sound administrative discretion when determining the nature of an access request.[131] For example, a first-party access request that cites only the Privacy Act of 1974[132] should be processed under both that statute and the FOIA.[133]

The legislative history of the 1974 FOIA amendments indicates that a description of a requested record that enables a professional agency em-

---

[129](...continued)
10 (N.D. Tex. Oct. 3, 2006) (magistrate's recommendation) (finding that plaintiff failed to exhaust administrative remedies where request did not comply with agency's regulations), adopted, 2006 WL 3342598 (N.D. Tex. Nov. 17, 2006) (appeal pending); Smith v. FBI, No. 06-1026, slip op. at 7 n.5 (D.D.C. Sept. 19, 2006) (recognizing that the FBI's Headquarters "lacks the regulatory authority to search field office records" in light of 28 C.F.R. § 16.3(a) (2006), which requires requesters to submit field office requests directly to field offices); Antonelli v. ATF, No. 04-1180, 2006 WL 141732, at *2 (D.D.C. Mar. 17, 2006) (granting agency's motion for summary judgment, because requester failed to exhaust administrative remedies when he refused to identify which of more than 100 systems of records his request concerned); Duggan v. U.S. Dep't of Justice, No. 03-10260, slip op. at 2 (D. Mass. Jan. 28, 2004) (stating that "FOIA does not entitle the plaintiff to direct the Criminal Division to search the records of other agencies and agency components; and [that] the plaintiff must exhaust his administrative remedies by directing his requests to the agencies that possess the records he seeks"), aff'd per curiam, No. 04-1455, slip op. at 2 (1st Cir. Sept. 29, 2004). But see Summers v. U.S. Dep't of Justice, 999 F.2d 570, 572-73 (D.C. Cir. 1993) (holding that 28 U.S.C. § 1746 (2000) -- which requires that unsworn declarations be treated with "like force and effect" as sworn declarations -- can be used in place of notarized-signature requirement of agency regulation for verification of FOIA privacy waivers); Kennedy v. U.S. Dep't of Justice, No. 03-CV-6077, 2004 WL 2284691, at *4 (W.D.N.Y. Oct. 8, 2004) (ruling that search was inadequate when it did not include field office, even though request was not sent to field office).

[130] Newman v. Legal Servs. Corp., 628 F. Supp. 535, 543 (D.D.C. 1986). But see Blackwell v. EEOC, No. 2:98-38, 1999 U.S. Dist. LEXIS 3708, at *5 (E.D.N.C. Feb. 12, 1999) (finding that request was not properly made because plaintiff failed to follow agency regulation requiring that request be denominated explicitly as request for information under FOIA).

[131] See FOIA Update, Vol. VII, No. 1, at 6 (advising that "agencies are expected to honor a requester's obvious intent").

[132] 5 U.S.C. § 552a (2000 & Supp. IV 2004).

[133] See FOIA Update, Vol. VII, No. 1, at 6 (advising that it is "good policy for agencies to treat all first-party access requests as FOIA requests" regardless of whether FOIA is cited by requester).

ployee familiar with the subject area to locate the record with a "reasonable amount of effort" is sufficient.[134] Courts have explained that "[t]he rationale for this rule is that FOIA was not intended to reduce government agencies to full-time investigators on behalf of requesters,"[135] or to allow requesters to conduct "fishing expeditions" through agency files.[136] Accord-

---

[134] H.R. Rep. No. 93-876, at 6 (1974), reprinted in 1974 U.S.C.C.A.N. 6267, 6271; see, e.g., Truitt v. Dep't of State, 897 F.2d 540, 544-45 (D.C. Cir. 1990) (discussing legislative history of 1974 FOIA amendments as related to requirements for describing requested records); Gaunce v. Burnette, 849 F.2d 1475, 1475 (9th Cir. 1988) (affirming the lower court's grant of summary judgment, and stating that the request did not reasonably describe the records sought, where the request sought "'every scrap of paper wherever located within the agency'" related to the requester's aviation activities (citing Marks v. U.S. Dep't of Justice, 578 F.2d 261, 263 (9th Cir. 1978))); Goland v. CIA, 607 F.2d 339, 353 (D.C. Cir. 1978); Marks v. U.S. Dep't of Justice, 578 F.2d 261, 263 (9th Cir. 1978); Mason v. Callaway, 554 F.2d 129, 131 (4th Cir. 1977) (affirming lower court finding that request did not reasonably describe records sought); Stuler v. IRS, No. 06-2251, 2007 WL 485230, at *2 (3d Cir. Feb. 15, 2007) (per curiam) (affirming district court's grant of summary judgment, where requester failed to comply with agency regulations requiring "reasonably described" requests); Ferri v. U.S. Dep't of Justice, 573 F. Supp. 852, 859 (W.D. Pa. 1983) (granting summary judgment where the plaintiff failed to provide sufficient information to allow the agency to retrieve the requested information "with a reasonable amount of effort" (citing Marks, 578 F.2d at 263)).

[135] Assassination Archives & Research Ctr. v. CIA, 720 F. Supp. 217, 219 (D.D.C. 1989), aff'd in pertinent part, No. 89-5414 (D.C. Cir. Aug. 13, 1990); Nurse v. Sec'y of the Air Force, 231 F. Supp 2d 323, 329 (D.D.C. 2002) (quoting Assassination Archives & Research Ctr., 720 F. Supp. at 219); see Frank v. U.S. Dep't of Justice, 941 F. Supp. 4, 5 (D.D.C. 1996) (stating that an agency is not required to "dig out all the information that might exist, in whatever form or place it might be found, and to create a document that answers plaintiff's questions"); Blakey v. Dep't of Justice, 549 F. Supp. 362, 366-67 (D.D.C. 1982) ("The FOIA was not intended to compel agencies to become ad hoc investigators for requesters whose requests are not compatible with their own information retrieval systems."), aff'd, 720 F.2d 215 (D.C. Cir. 1983) (unpublished table decision); see also Trenerry v. Dep't of the Treasury, No. 92-5053, 1993 WL 26813, at *3 (10th Cir. Feb. 5, 1993) (holding that agency not required to provide personal services such as legal research); Satterlee v. IRS, No. 05-3181, 2006 U.S. Dist. LEXIS 78775, at *9 (W.D. Mo. Oct. 30, 2006) (finding that request was improper where it would require agency to "conduct legal research" and answer questions "disguised as . . . FOIA request"); Lamb v. IRS, 871 F. Supp. 301, 304 (E.D. Mich. 1994) (finding requests outside scope of FOIA when they require legal research, are unspecific, or seek answers to interrogatories).

[136] Immanuel v. Sec'y of the Treasury, No. 94-884, 1995 WL 464141, at *1
(continued...)

ingly, one FOIA request was held invalid because it required an agency's FOIA staff either to have "clairvoyant capabilities" to discern the requester's needs or to spend "countless numbers of personnel hours seeking needles in bureaucratic haystacks."[137]

---

[136](...continued)
(D. Md. Apr. 4, 1995), aff'd, 81 F.3d 150 (4th Cir. 1996) (unpublished table decision); see also Dale v. IRS, 238 F. Supp. 2d 99, 104-05 (D.D.C. 2002) (concluding that a request that sought "'any and all documents . . . that refer or relate in any way'" to the requester failed to reasonably describe the records sought and "amounted to an all-encompassing fishing expedition of files at [the agency's] offices across the country, at taxpayer expense"); Freeman v. U.S. Dep't of Justice, No. 90-2754, slip op. at 3 (D.D.C. Oct. 16, 1991) ("The FOIA does not require that the government go fishing in the ocean for fresh water fish.").

[137] Devine v. Marsh, 2 Gov't Disclosure Serv. (P-H) ¶ 82,022, at 82,186 (E.D. Va. Aug. 27, 1981); see also Goldgar v. Office of Admin., 26 F.3d 32, 35 (5th Cir. 1994) (holding that the agency was not required to produce information sought by the requester -- "the identity of the government agency that is reading his mind" -- that does not exist in record form); Satterlee, 2006 U.S. Dist. LEXIS 78775, at *9 (finding that requester did not reasonably describe records sought where his request asked IRS to "prove that it has jurisdiction over him"); Segal v. Whitmyre, No. 04-809795, 2005 WL 1406171, at *2 (S.D. Fla. Apr. 6, 2005) (finding that court lacks jurisdiction under FOIA because request "failed to assert exactly what records/documents" requester sought, but instead asked for "proof/documentation" that requester was not entitled to IRS tax hearing), aff'd on other grounds sub nom. Segal v. Comm'r, No. 05-13278 (11th Cir. Apr. 13, 2006); Benneville v. U.S. Dep't of Justice, No. 98-6137, slip op. at 10 (D. Or. June 11, 2003) (rejecting plaintiff's contention that the agency should have provided him with information on all environmental groups, rather than just the single group specifically named in his request letter, because "the government should not be expected to determine [the unnamed groups'] identit[ies] and determine if they should be involved in the search"); Malak v. Tenet, No. 01-3996, 2001 WL 664451, at *1 (N.D. Ill. June 12, 2001) (concluding that request's "discursive narrative doesn't even begin to approach the necessary job to permit performance of [agency's] FOIA responsibilities"); Judicial Watch v. Exp.-Imp. Bank, 108 F. Supp. 2d 19, 27-28 (D.D.C. 2000) (ruling that a request did not reasonably describe the records sought because the plaintiff "fail[ed] to state its request with sufficient particularity, [and] it also declined [the agency's] repeated attempts to clarify the request"); Keenan v. U.S. Dep't of Justice, No. 94-1909, slip op. at 1 (D.D.C. Nov. 12, 1996) ("Plaintiff can not [sic] place a request for one search and then, when nothing is found, convert that request into a different search."); Graphics of Key W. v. United States, 1996 WL 167861, at *7 (D. Nev. 1996) (finding plaintiff's request letters to be "more arguments than clear requests for information"); Kubany v. Bd. of Governors of the Fed. Reserve Sys., No. 93-1428, slip op. at 6-8 (D.D.C. July 19, 1994) (holding that request relying on exhibits contain-
(continued...)

Depending upon the particular type of FOIA activity that is involved, an agency might be required to make translations of requests or records that are written in a language other than English.[138] When reading a request not written in English, an agency may attempt to translate the request; but an agency unable to make such a translation should, at a minimum, attempt to contact the requester in order to "clarify" the request -- i.e., to obtain from the requester a translation of the request.[139] Further, in processing non-English records in response to a FOIA request, an agency should make all "scoping" and disclosure determinations with great care so that it is able to fulfill its obligations under the Act.[140] When processing non-English responsive records, agencies should not run the risk of disclosing sensitive information that should be withheld.[141] Rather, an agency in such a situation should bear the burden of translation so that it can properly determine exemption applicability, and so that it can fairly defend such determinations should litigation arise.[142] Finally, while agencies might

---

[137](...continued)
ing "multiple, unexplained references to hundreds of accounts, and various flowcharts, and schematics" is "entirely unreasonable"). But cf. Doolittle v. U.S. Dep't of Justice, 142 F. Supp. 2d 281, 285 (N.D.N.Y. 2001) (concluding that so long as description of records sought is otherwise reasonable, agency cannot refuse to search for records simply because requester did not also identify them by the date on which they were created).

[138] See FOIA Post, "The Limits of Agency Translation Obligations Under the FOIA" (posted 12/1/04) (discussing agency translation obligations in determining responsiveness of records, determining applicability of exemptions, and providing records in response to FOIA requests).

[139] Cf. Ruotolo v. Dep't of Justice, 53 F.3d 4, 10 (2d Cir. 1995) (concluding that agency failed to perform its "duty" to assist requester in reformulating request); Exec. Order No. 13,392, Sec. 1(b), 70 Fed. Reg. 75,373 (Dec. 14, 2005) (directing that agencies respond to FOIA requesters "courteously and appropriately"); id. at Sec. 2(c) (establishing FOIA Requester Service Center and FOIA Public Liaison in order to "ensure appropriate communication with FOIA requesters"); id. at Sec. 2(c)(ii) (directing that FOIA Public Liaisons must seek to ensure service-oriented response to FOIA requests and FOIA-related inquiries).

[140] See FOIA Post, "The Limits of Agency Translation Obligations Under the FOIA" (posted 12/1/04) (discussing the importance of understanding the contents of records believed to be responsive, and advising agencies to obtain translations of responsive records rather than making disclosure determinations "in the dark").

[141] See id.

[142] See id. (stating that "if a FOIA request were to proceed to litigation in a case in which records were withheld without the agency's knowledge of their contents, then that case could not properly be defended" (citing Lion
(continued...)

translate releasable records when making a response as a matter of administrative discretion, nothing in the FOIA requires such action.[143]

The fact that a FOIA request is very broad or "burdensome" in its magnitude does not, in and of itself, entitle an agency to deny that request on the basis that it does not "reasonably describe" the records sought.[144] The key factor is the ability of an agency's staff to reasonably ascertain exactly which records are being requested and then locate them.[145] The

---

[142](...continued)
Raisins Inc. v. USDA, 354 F.3d 1072, 1082 n.10 (9th Cir. 2004) (finding it "perplexing that the government would choose to assign counsel to defend its position on appeal . . . who is totally unfamiliar with (and, presumably, denied access to) the facts upon which the government bases its claim" to exemption))).

[143] See FOIA Post, "The Limits of Agency Translation Obligations Under the FOIA" (posted 12/1/04) (advising that agencies have no obligation to "provide a requester with more than what the requested record contains on its face").

[144] See 53 F.3d at 10 (finding that request that required 803 files to be searched was not "unreasonably burdensome"); see also FOIA Update, Vol. IV, No. 3, at 5 ("The sheer size or burdensomeness of a FOIA request, in and of itself, does not entitle an agency to deny that request on the ground that it does not 'reasonably describe' records within the meaning of 5 U.S.C. § 552(a)(3)(A)."). But see Domingues v. FBI, No. 98-74612, slip op. at 11 (E.D. Mich. July 24, 1999) (magistrate's recommendation) (determining that "a request directed to an agency's headquarters which does not request a search of its field offices, or which requests a blanket search of all field offices without specifying which offices should be searched, does not 'reasonably describe' any records which may be in those field offices, and an agency's search of just the headquarters records complies with the FOIA"), adopted (E.D. Mich. July 29, 1999), aff'd, 229 F.3d 1151 (6th Cir. 2000) (unpublished table decision); Massachusetts v. HHS, 727 F. Supp. 35, 36 n.2 (D. Mass. 1989) (holding that a request for all records "relating to" a particular subject is overbroad, "thus unfairly plac[ing] the onus of non-production on the recipient of the request and not where it belongs -- upon the person who drafted such a sloppy request").

[145] See Yeager v. DEA, 678 F.2d 315, 322, 326 (D.C. Cir. 1982) (holding request encompassing over 1,000,000 computerized records to be valid because "[t]he linchpin inquiry is whether the agency is able to determine 'precisely what records [are] being requested'" (quoting legislative history)); Weewee v. IRS, No. 99-475, 2001 WL 283801, at *12 (D. Ariz. Feb. 13, 2001) (finding that request for records related to each occurrence of specific actions related to requester's tax return "does not appear to be too broad" given that agency already had processed request that was "identically worded"). But see AFGE v. U.S. Dep't of Commerce, 907 F.2d 203, 209
(continued...)

courts have held only that agencies are not required to conduct wide-ranging, "unreasonably burdensome" <u>searches</u> for records.[146] An agency in re-

---

[145](...continued)
(D.C. Cir. 1990) (holding that "while [plaintiff's requests] might identify the documents requested with sufficient precision to enable the agency to identify them . . . it is clear that these requests are so broad as to impose an unreasonable burden upon the agency," because the agency would have "to locate, review, redact, and arrange for inspection a vast quantity of material").

[146] <u>See</u> <u>Solar Sources, Inc. v. United States</u>, 142 F.3d 1033, 1039 (7th Cir. 1998) (refusing to order agency to identify and segregate nonexempt documents from millions of pages of files in light of government's estimate that doing so would take eight work-years); <u>Nation Magazine v. U.S. Customs Serv.</u>, 71 F.3d 885, 892 (D.C. Cir. 1995) (agreeing that search which would require review of twenty-three years of unindexed files would be unreasonably burdensome, but disagreeing that search through chronologically indexed agency files for dated memorandum would be burdensome); <u>Van Strum v. EPA</u>, No. 91-35404, 1992 WL 197660, at *1 (9th Cir. Aug. 17, 1992) (accepting agency justification in denying or seeking clarification of overly broad requests which would place inordinate search burden on agency resources); <u>Marks</u>, 578 F.2d at 263 (ruling that FBI is not required to search every one of its field offices); <u>Ray v. FBI</u>, 441 F. Supp. 2d 27, 32 (D.D.C. 2006) (stating that the "FBI is not obligated to undertake a search of its field offices' records when a requester submits his request only to its headquarters" (citing <u>Oglesby</u>, 920 F.2d at 68)); <u>Schrecker v. U.S. Dep't of Justice</u>, 217 F. Supp. 2d 29, 35 (D.D.C. 2002) (finding "that to require an agency to hand search through millions of documents is not reasonable and therefore not necessary," as the agency already had searched "the most likely place responsive documents would be located"), <u>aff'd</u>, 349 F.3d 657 (D.C. Cir. 2003); <u>Burns v. U.S. Dep't of Justice</u>, No. 99-3173, slip op. at 2 (D.D.C. Feb. 5, 2001) (concluding that "given the capacity of the reels and the absence of any index," a request for specific telephone conversations recorded on reel-to-reel tapes was "unreasonably burdensome" because "it would take an inordinate [amount of] time to listen to the reels in order to locate any requested conversations that might exist"); <u>Blackman v. U.S. Dep't of Justice</u>, No. 00-3004, slip op. at 5 (D.D.C. July 5, 2001) (declaring request that would require a manual search through 37 million pages to be "unreasonable in light of the resources needed" to process it), <u>appeal dismissed for lack of prosecution</u>, No. 01-5431 (D.C. Cir. Jan. 2, 2003); <u>Peyton v. Reno</u>, No. 98-1457, 1999 U.S. Dist. LEXIS 12125, at *4-5 (D.D.C. July 19, 1999) (finding that request for all records indexed under subject's name reasonably described records sought because agency failed to demonstrate that name search would be unduly burdensome); <u>O'Harvey v. Office of Workers' Comp. Programs</u>, No. 95-0187, slip op. at 3 (E.D. Wash. Dec. 29, 1997) (finding a request to be unreasonably burdensome because a search would require the agency "to review all of the case files maintained by the agency" and "would entail review of millions of pages of hard copies"), <u>aff'd sub</u>
(continued...)

ceipt of a request that it deems burdensome may contact the requester in an attempt to clarify or narrow the breadth of the request[147] -- and it should do so of course whenever such action is required by agency regulations.[148]

By the same token, an agency should "carefully consider" the nature of each FOIA request[149] and give reasonable import to its terms and full content overall, even if the request "is not a model of clarity."[150]  Likewise,

---

[146](...continued)
nom. O'Harvey v. Comp. Programs Workers, 183 F.3d 514 (9th Cir. 1999) (unpublished table decision); Spannaus v. U.S. Dep't of Justice, No. 92-372, slip op. at 6 (D.D.C. June 20, 1995) (finding that agency is not required to determine all persons having ties to associations targeted in bankruptcy proceedings "and then search any and all civil or criminal files relating to those persons"), summary affirmance granted in pertinent part, No. 95-5267 (D.C. Cir. Aug. 16, 1996).

[147] Accord Pub. L. No. 104-231, § 4, 110 Stat. 3048, 3050-51 (1996) (codified as amended at 5 U.S.C. § 552(a)(6)(B) (amending Act to provide for agency invocation of ten working-day extension to response time for "unusual circumstances" in tandem with agency providing requester with full opportunity to narrow request).

[148] See, e.g., Ruotolo, 53 F.3d at 10 (stating that agency failed to perform its "duty" to assist requester in reformulating request); Pub. Citizen Health Research Group v. FDA, No. 94-0018, slip op. at 2-3 (D.D.C. Feb. 9, 1996) (criticizing agency for failing to seek narrowing of request as required by agency regulations, and ordering parties to "seek to agree" on search breadth).

[149] Attorney General's Memorandum for Heads of All Federal Departments and Agencies Regarding the Freedom of Information Act (Oct. 12, 2001), reprinted in FOIA Post (posted 10/15/01); see also Presidential Memorandum for Heads of Departments and Agencies Regarding the Freedom of Information Act, 29 Weekly Comp. Pres. Doc. 1999 (Oct. 4, 1993), reprinted in FOIA Update, Vol. XIV, No. 3, at 3 (encouraging agencies to handle FOIA requests "in a customer-friendly manner").

[150] LaCedra v. Executive Office for U.S. Attorneys, 317 F.3d 345, 347-48 (D.C. Cir. 2003) (concluding that the agency failed to "liberally construe" a request for "all documents pertaining to [plaintiff's] case" when it limited that request's scope to only those records specifically and individually listed in the request letter, because "[t]he drafter of a FOIA request might reasonably seek all of a certain set of documents while nonetheless evincing a heightened interest in a specific subset thereof" (citing Nation Magazine, 71 F.3d at 890)); see Horsehead Indus. v. EPA, No. 94-1299, slip op. at 4 n.2 (D.D.C. Jan. 3, 1997) (ruling that "[b]y construing the FOIA request narrowly, [the agency] seeks to avoid disclosing information"); FOIA Update, Vol. XVI, No. 3, at 3 (advising agencies on interpretation of terms of FOIA re-
(continued...)

an agency "must be careful not to read [a] request so strictly that the requester is denied information the agency well knows exists in its files, albeit in a different form from that anticipated by the requester."[151] Specifically, agencies should be careful to undertake any "scoping" of documents found in response to a request only with full communication with the FOIA requester.[152]

Although the scope of a FOIA request is most commonly thought of

---

[150](...continued)
quests); see also Miller v. Casey, 730 F.2d 773, 777 (D.C. Cir. 1984) (emphasizing that an agency is required to read a FOIA request as drafted, "not as either [an] agency official or [the requester] might wish it was drafted"); Landes v. Yost, No. 89-6338, slip op. at 4-5 (E.D. Pa. Apr. 11, 1990) (finding that request was "reasonably descriptive" when it relied on agency's own outdated identification code), aff'd, 922 F.2d 832 (3d Cir. 1990) (unpublished table decision).

[151] Hemenway v. Hughes, 601 F. Supp. 1002, 1005 (D.D.C. 1985); see Allen v. Fed. Bureau of Prisons, No. 00-342, slip op. at 7-9 (D.D.C. Mar. 1, 2001) (concluding that the agency took "an extremely constricted view" of plaintiff's FOIA request for all "records or transcripts" of intercepted phone calls by failing to construe audiotape recordings of those calls as being within the request's scope), aff'd, 89 F. App'x 276 (D.C. Cir. 2004). But see also Judicial Watch, Inc. v. DOD, No. 05-00390, 2006 WL 1793297, at *3 (D.D.C. June 28, 2006) (concluding that agency need not construe request for names of corporations related to particular subject to be request for all records related to that subject); Nat'l Ass'n of Criminal Def. Lawyers v. U.S. Dep't of Justice, No. 04-0697, 2006 WL 666938, at *2 (D.D.C. Mar. 15, 2006) (concluding that agency "reasonably" read request as seeking "'any reports or studies'" and that requester's attempt to narrow request resulted in request that is "substantially different" from original request).

[152] See FOIA Update, Vol. XVI, No. 3, at 3-5 ("OIP Guidance: Determining the Scope of a FOIA Request") (advising of procedures and underlying considerations for document "scoping"), supplemented by FOIA Post, "FOIA Counselor Q&A" (posted 1/24/06) (addressing "scoping" in context of, e.g., "lengthy chains of 'electronic mail'" (citing St. Andrews Park, Inc. v. U.S. Dep't of the Army Corps of Eng'rs, 299 F. Supp. 2d 1264, 1271 (S.D. Fla. 2003))); see also Halpern v. FBI, 181 F.3d 279, 289 (2d Cir. 1999) (holding cross-referenced files to be beyond the scope of a request because once the agency "had requested clarification [about the requester's interest in receiving such records], it could then in good faith ignore the cross-referenced files until it received an affirmative response" from the requester); Hamilton Sec. Group v. HUD, 106 F. Supp. 2d 23, 27 (D.D.C. 2000) ("Given the exchange of correspondence between counsel and the agency relating to the scope of the request, there is no basis for plaintiff's claim that defendant should have understood that the request for a [single, specific record] was meant to include additional [records].")), aff'd per curiam, No. 00-5331, 2001 WL 238162 (D.C. Cir. Feb. 23, 2001).

as being defined by the subject matter of the records that it seeks, a request's scope also depends on the time frame in which the requested records were created.[153] The temporal scope of a FOIA request typically is defined through the agency's use of a "cut-off" date, meaning that records created after that date are treated as not responsive to the request.[154] Generally speaking, an agency should use as its "cut-off" date the date that the search for records begins (i.e., a "date-of-search cut-off")[155] -- which courts have favored because it "results in a much fuller search and disclosure" than the use of a less inclusive "cut-off," such as one based on the date of the request or of its receipt by the agency.[156] While an agency may choose not to use a "date-of-search cut-off" if "specific circumstances" warrant,[157] it

---

[153] See FOIA Post, "Use of 'Cut-Off' Dates for FOIA Searches" (posted 5/6/04) (explaining that "[t]he scope of a FOIA request has both substantive and temporal aspects"); see also Church of Scientology v. IRS, 816 F. Supp. 1138, 1148 (W.D. Tex. 1993) (observing that "there has to be a temporal deadline for documents that satisfy [a FOIA] request"), appeal dismissed by stipulation, No. 93-8431 (5th Cir. Oct. 21, 1993).

[154] See Defenders of Wildlife v. U.S. Dep't of the Interior, 314 F. Supp. 2d 1, 12, n.10 (D.D.C. 2004) (recognizing that records created after date-of-search "cut-off" date specifically established by agency regulation "are not covered by [plaintiff's] request"); FOIA Update, Vol. IV, No. 4, at 14 (advising that records that "post-date" an agency's "cut-off" date are not included within the temporal scope of a request).

[155] See FOIA Post, "Use of 'Cut-Off' Dates for FOIA Searches" (posted 5/6/04) (explaining practical reasons for using date that agency's search begins as"cut-off" date for request).

[156] McGehee v. CIA, 697 F.2d 1095, 1104 (D.C. Cir.), vacated on other grounds on panel reh'g & reh'g en banc denied, 711 F.2d 1076 (D.C. Cir. 1983); see Pub. Citizen v. Dep't of State, 276 F.3d 634, 644 (D.C. Cir. 2002) (favoring a "date-of-search cut-off" because its use "might . . . result[] in the retrieval of more [responsive] documents" than would a cut-off based on the date of the request); Van Strum v. EPA, No. 91-35404, 1992 WL 197660, at *2 (9th Cir. Aug. 17, 1992) (agreeing that a date-of-search "cut-off" date is "the most reasonable date for setting the temporal cut-off in this case"); Edmonds Inst. v. U.S. Dep't of the Interior, 383 F. Supp. 2d 105, 110-11 (D.D.C. 2005) (rejecting requester's call for use of date-of-release "cut-off" date in favor of date-of-search "cut-off" date, in accordance with agency's regulations).

[157] Pub. Citizen, 276 F.3d at 643; see FOIA Post, "Use of 'Cut-Off' Dates for FOIA Searches" (posted 5/6/04) (describing circumstances under which use of different "cut-off" dates may be reasonable); see also, e.g., Blazy v. Tenet, 979 F. Supp. 10, 17 (D.D.C. 1997) (concluding that it was "reasonable under the circumstances" for the agency to apply a date-of-request "cut-off" to a request that sought records concerning events that already had oc-
(continued...)

may be required to articulate a "compelling justification" for doing so if challenged in court.[158]

No matter which type of "cut-off" date an agency adopts and ordinarily uses, it is obliged to inform FOIA requesters of that date.[159] The most efficient way in which an agency can give such notice is through "constructive notice" in its published FOIA regulations[160] and/or through its FOIA Reference Guide on its FOIA Web site.[161] Alternatively, an agency can give actual notice of its "cut-off" date policy in its correspondence with each FOIA requester individually.[162] An agency also can use such a letter whenever it departs from its ordinary practice for some reason, lest the request-

---

[157](...continued)
curred (and records that already had been created) by the time the request was made), summary affirmance granted, No. 97-5330, 1998 WL 315583 (D.C. Cir. May 12, 1998). But see Or. Natural Desert Ass'n v. Gutierrez, 419 F. Supp. 2d 1284, 1288 (D. Or. Mar. 2, 2006) (concluding that agency's date-of-request "cut-off" date regulation "is not reasonable on its face and violates FOIA").

[158] Pub. Citizen, 276 F.3d at 644; cf. McGehee, 647 F.2d at 1103-04 (rejecting agency's arguments that use of date-of-search cut-off would be "unduly burdensome, expensive, or productive of 'administrative chaos'" as lacking any "detailed substantiation").

[159] See, e.g., Judicial Watch, Inc. v. U.S. Dep't of Energy, No. 01-0981, 2004 WL 635180, at *21 (D.D.C. Mar. 31, 2004) ("Because the [agency] imposed the . . . cut-off date without informing [the requester] of its intention to do so, the court must conclude that [the agency's] search was inadequate."); see also FOIA Update, Vol. IV, No. 4, at 14 (advising more than two decades ago that "agencies should give requesters notice of the 'cut-off' dates they use"); cf. McGehee, 697 F.2d at 1105 (expressing doubt that the agency could establish that "it may 'reasonably' use any 'cut-off' date without so informing the requester").

[160] See, e.g., 28 C.F.R. § 16.4(a) (2006) (Department of Justice FOIA regulation notifying requesters of its "cut-off" date).

[161] See 5 U.S.C. § 552(g) (requiring each agency to prepare and make publicly available (including electronically) its own guide for ready use by FOIA requesters in making requests to it); see also FOIA Update, Vol. XIX, No. 3, at 4 (advising that "[a]n agency's FOIA Web site is an excellent means of affording widespread public availability to its FOIA and Privacy Act regulations").

[162] See, e.g., Pub. Citizen, 276 F.3d at 634 (noting that State Department provided notice of its "cut-off" date policy in letters sent to all requesters acknowledging receipt of their requests); cf. McGehee, 697 F.2d at 1105 (suggesting that actual notice of an agency's "cut-off" policy might be given where such notice "would involve an insignificant expenditure of time and effort on the part of the agency").

er mistakenly be on "constructive notice" to the contrary.[163] Simply put, a FOIA requester should know what "cut-off" date is being applied to his request, if for no other reason than to minimize the chance of any inefficient misunderstanding about its scope.[164] (For further discussions of search requirements, see Procedural Requirements, Searching for Responsive Records, below, and Litigation Considerations, Adequacy of Search, below.)

When determining the scope of a FOIA request, however, agencies should remember that they are not required to answer questions posed as FOIA requests.[165] Nor does the FOIA require agencies to respond to re-

---

[163] See, e.g., 28 C.F.R. § 16.4(a) (providing notice of the "cut-off" date that the Justice Department "ordinarily" uses, and specifying that "if any other date is used, the [Department] shall inform the requester of that date").

[164] See FOIA Update, Vol. XVI, No. 3, at 3 (reminding agencies of importance of FOIA requesters "being fully informed of all such scope matters").

[165] See, e.g., Zemansky v. EPA, 767 F.2d 569, 574 (9th Cir. 1985); DiViaio v. Kelley, 571 F.2d 538, 542-43 (10th Cir. 1978); Ivey v. U.S. Office of Special Counsel, No. 05-0176, 2005 U.S. Dist. LEXIS 18874, at *8 (D.D.C. Aug. 31, 2005) (finding that agency is not required to answer questions in response to request seeking reasons for closure of agency investigation); Stuler v. U.S. Dep't of Justice, No. 03-1525, 2004 WL 1304040, at *3 (W.D. Pa. June 30, 2004) (concluding that FOIA does not give requester "opportunity to relitigate his criminal case," and that agency was not obligated to answer requester's questions), aff'd, No. 06-2251, 2007 WL 485230, at *2 (3d Cir. Feb. 15, 2007) (per curiam); Barber v. Office of Info. & Privacy, No. 02-1748, slip op. at 4 (D.D.C. Sept. 4, 2003) (holding that the agency "had no duty to conduct research or to answer questions" that addressed the "'authentic[ity]' of federal jurisdiction over the location of his criminal prosecution"), aff'd per curiam, No. 03-5266 (D.C. Cir. Feb. 20, 2004); Gillin v. Dep't of the Army, No. 92-325, slip op. at 10 (D.N.H. May 28, 1993) ("FOIA creates only a right of access to records, not a right to require an agency to disclose its collective reasoning behind agency actions, nor does FOIA provide a mechanism to challenge the wisdom of substantive agency decisions."), aff'd, 21 F.3d 419 (1st Cir. 1994) (unpublished table decision); Patton v. U.S. R.R. Ret. Bd., No. ST-C-91-04, slip op. at 3 (W.D.N.C. Apr. 26, 1991) (stating that the FOIA "provides a means for access to existing documents and is not a way to interrogate an agency"), aff'd, 940 F.2d 652 (4th Cir. 1991) (unpublished table decision); Hudgins, 620 F. Supp. at 21 ("[The] FOIA creates only a right of access to records, not a right to personal services."); cf. Flowers v. IRS, 307 F. Supp. 2d 60, 71 (D.D.C. 2004) (declaring that the plaintiff "cannot use FOIA discovery to conduct an investigation into the [agency's] rationale" for auditing her). But see also Ferri v. Bell, 645 F.2d 1213, 1220 (3d Cir. 1981) (declaring that a request "inartfully presented in the form of questions" could not be dismissed, partly because the agency conceded that it could provide the requester with records containing the information he sought); FOIA Update, Vol. V, No. 1, at 5 (advising that "while agencies do
(continued...)

quests by creating records,[166] such as by modifying exempt information in order to make it disclosable.[167] Likewise, agencies need not add explana-

---

[165](...continued)
not have to create or compile new records in response to FOIA requests (whether formulated in question form or not), they should make good faith efforts to assist requesters in honing any requests for readily accessible records which are 'inartfully presented in the form of questions.'" (quoting Ferri, 645 F.2d at 1220)).

[166] See, e.g., Poll v. U.S. Office of Special Counsel, No. 99-4021, 2000 WL 14422, at *5 n.2 (10th Cir. Jan. 10, 2000) (recognizing that the FOIA does not require an agency "'to create documents or opinions in response to an individual's request for information'" (quoting Hudgins v. IRS, 620 F. Supp. 19, 21 (D.D.C. 1985))); Sorrells v. United States, No. 97-5586, 1998 WL 58080, at *1 (6th Cir. Feb. 6, 1998) (advising that agency is not required to compile document that "contain[s] a full, legible signature"); Krohn v. Dep't of Justice, 628 F.2d 195, 197-98 (D.C. Cir. 1980) (finding that agency "cannot be compelled to create the [intermediary records] necessary to produce" the information sought); Stuler v. IRS, No. 05-1717, 2006 WL 891073, at *3 (W.D. Pa. Mar. 31, 2006) (stating that agency "is not required to create documents that don't exist"); Sakamoto v. EPA, 443 F. Supp. 2d 1182, 1189 (N.D. Cal. 2006) (granting summary judgment because, inter alia, the "FOIA does not require an agency to create records in response to a request"); Jones v. Runyon, 32 F. Supp. 2d 873, 876 (N.D. W. Va. 1998) (concluding that "because the FOIA does not obligate the [agency] to create records," it "acted properly by providing access to those documents already created"), aff'd, 173 F.3d 850 (4th Cir. 1999) (unpublished table decision); Bartlett v. U.S. Dep't of Justice, 867 F. Supp. 314, 316 (E.D. Pa. 1994) (ruling that agency is not required to create handwriting analysis); see also FOIA Update, Vol. V, No. 1, at 5; cf. De Luca v. INS, No. 95-6240, 1996 U.S. Dist. LEXIS 2696, at *2 (E.D. Pa. Mar. 7, 1996) (noting that agency offered -- purely as matter of administrative discretion -- to create certification that it had no record that requester was naturalized citizen). But cf. Schladetsch v. HUD, No. 99-0175, 2000 WL 33372125, at *3 (D.D.C. Apr. 4, 2000) ("Because [the agency] has conceded that it possesses in its databases the discrete pieces of information which [plaintiff] seeks, extracting and compiling that data does not amount to the creation of a new record."), appeal dismissed voluntarily, No. 00-5220 (D.C. Cir. Oct. 12, 2000); Int'l Diatomite Producers, 1993 WL 137286, at *5 (N.D. Cal. Apr. 28, 1993) (giving agency choice of compiling responsive list or redacting existing lists containing responsive information); FOIA Update, Vol. XVIII, No. 1, at 5-6 (advising of particular statutory obligations regarding electronic record searches and format of disclosure).

[167] See FlightSafety Servs. Corp. v. Dep't of Labor, 326 F.3d 607, 613 (5th Cir. 2003) (per curiam) (recognizing that plaintiff's demand that the agency "simply insert new information in the place of the redacted information requires the creation of new agency records, a task that the FOIA does not
(continued...)

tory materials to any records disclosed in response to a FOIA request.[168] Agencies also cannot be required by FOIA requesters to seek the return of records over which they retain no "control"[169] (even records that were wrongfully removed from their possession);[170] to re-create records properly disposed of;[171] or to seek the delivery of records held by private entities.[172]

---

[167](...continued) require the government to perform"); Students Against Genocide v. Dep't of State, 257 F.3d 828, 837 (D.C. Cir. 2001) (rejecting plaintiff's argument that "even if the agencies do not want to disclose the photographs in their present state, they should produce new photographs at a different resolution in order to mask the [classified] capabilities of the reconnaissance systems that took them"). But see Jones v. OSHA, No. 94-3225, 1995 WL 435320, at *4 (W.D. Mo. June 6, 1995) (stating that agency must "retype," not withhold in full, documents required to be released by its own regulation, in order to delete FOIA-exempt information).

[168] See NLRB v. Sears, Roebuck & Co., 421 U.S. 132, 162 (1975) (holding that agency is not required to create explanatory materials); Jackman v. Dep't of Justice, No. 05-1889, 2006 WL 2598054, at *2 (D.D.C. Sept. 11, 2006) (stating that "questions about the authenticity and correctness of the released records are beyond the scope of the court's FOIA jurisdiction"); Citizens Progressive Alliance v. U.S. Bureau of Indian Affairs, 241 F. Supp. 2d 1342, 1365 (D.N.M. 2002) ("Defendants may be required to disclose material pursuant to FOIA, but Defendants are not required to . . . explain any records produced."); Tax Analysts v. IRS, No. 94-923, 1998 WL 419755, at *2 (D.D.C. May 1, 1998) (declaring that "an agency need not add explanatory material to a document to make it more understandable in light of the redactions"); Gabel v. Comm'r, 879 F. Supp. 1037, 1039 (N.D. Cal. 1994) (noting that FOIA does not require agency "to revamp documents or generate exegeses so as to make them comprehensible to a particular requestor"); cf. Essential Info., Inc. v. USIA, 134 F.3d 1165, 1172 (D.C. Cir. 1998) (Tatel, J., dissenting) (observing that "FOIA contains no . . . translation requirement"). But cf. McDonnell, 4 F.3d at 1261 n.21 (suggesting, in dictum, that agency might be compelled to create translation of any disclosable encoded information).

[169] See Steinberg v. U.S. Dep't of Justice, 801 F. Supp. 800, 802 (D.D.C. 1992) (holding that agency is not obligated to retrieve law enforcement records transferred for use in criminal prosecutions to Commonwealth of Virginia).

[170] See Kissinger v. Reporters Comm. for Freedom of the Press, 445 U.S. 136, 150-55 (1980); cf. Spannaus v. U.S. Dep't of Justice, 942 F. Supp. 656, 658 (D.D.C. 1996) (finding that "personal files" of attorney no longer employed with agency were "beyond the reach of FOIA" if they were not turned over to agency at end of employment).

[171] See, e.g., Jones v. FBI, 41 F.3d 238, 249 (6th Cir. 1994); see also Robert
(continued...)

[171](...continued)

v. HHS, 78 F. App'x 146, 147 (2d Cir. 2003) (finding no improper withholding of records that were destroyed in accordance with agency's record-retention schedule prior to agency's receipt of FOIA request); Flowers, 307 F. Supp. 2d at 71 (excusing agency's failure to locate file destroyed in accordance with published record- retention schedules); Laughlin v. Comm'r, 103 F. Supp. 2d 1219, 1224-25 (S.D. Cal. 1999) (refusing to order agency to re-create properly discarded document); Jones, 32 F. Supp. 2d at 875-76 (finding that agency did not improperly withhold requested report that was discarded in accordance with agency policies and practices); Rothschild v. Dep't of Energy, 6 F. Supp. 2d 38, 40 (D.D.C. 1998) (agreeing that because agency "is under no duty to disclose documents not in its possession," agency did not violate the FOIA by failing to provide discarded drafts of responsive documents); Green v. NARA, 992 F. Supp. 811, 817 (E.D. Va. 1998) (finding that agency met its FOIA obligation when it provided reasonable access to records sought by plaintiff prior to disposal of records under Records Disposal Act, 44 U.S.C. § 3301 (2000), and noting that "FOIA . . . does not obligate agencies to retain all records [in its possession], nor does it establish specified procedures designed to guide disposal determinations"); cf. Folstad v. Bd. of Governors of the Fed. Reserve Sys., No. 1:99-124, 1999 U.S. Dist. LEXIS 17852, at *5 (W.D. Mich. Nov. 16, 1999) (recognizing that "[e]ven if the agency failed to keep documents that it should have kept, that failure would create neither responsibility under the FOIA to reconstruct those documents nor liability for the lapse"), aff'd, 234 F.3d 1268 (6th Cir. 2000) (unpublished table decision); FOIA Update, Vol. XVIII, No. 1, at 5-6 (advising that FOIA does not govern agency records disposition practices). But cf. Schrecker v. U.S. Dep't of Justice, 254 F.3d 162, 165 (D.C. Cir. 2001) (holding that absent proof that requested records were destroyed, agency cannot refuse to search for such records simply because they were type of records not required to be retained); Valencia-Lucena v. U.S. Coast Guard, 180 F.3d 321, 328 (D.C. Cir. 1999) (rejecting agency's claim that it failed to locate requested records because they were type routinely destroyed, and declaring that "generalized claims of destruction or non-preservation cannot sustain summary judgment").

[172] See Folstad, 1999 U.S. Dist. LEXIS 17852, at *8 (finding that if agency "is no longer in possession of the documents, nothing in the FOIA requires the agency to obtain those documents from the private [banking] institution"); Rush Franklin Publ'g, Inc. v. NASA, No. 90-CV-2855, slip op. at 9-10 (E.D.N.Y. Apr. 13, 1993) (mailing list generated and held by federal contractor); Conservation Law Found. v. Dep't of the Air Force, No. 85-4377, 1986 U.S. Dist. LEXIS 24515, at *10 (D. Mass. June 6, 1986) (computer program generated and held by federal contractor); cf. U.S. v. Napper, 887 F.2d 1528, 1530 (11th Cir. 1989) (concluding that FBI was entitled to return of documents loaned to city law enforcement officials, notwithstanding fact that copies of some documents had been disclosed) (non-FOIA case). But see Chi. Tribune Co. v. HHS, No. 95 C 3917, 1999 WL 299875, at *3 (N.D. Ill. May 4, 1999) (ordering nonparty government contractor to disclose audit

(continued...)

Requesters also cannot use the FOIA as an "enforcement mechanism" to compel agencies to perform their missions.[173] Neither may requesters compel agencies to make automatic releases of records as they are created,[174] which means that requests cannot properly be made for "future"

---

[172](...continued) data because "the government whole-handedly controls and blatantly influences [the contractor's] action with respect to disclosure of the documents"), emergency stay denied, No. 99-2162 (7th Cir. June 9, 1999); Cal-Almond, Inc. v. USDA, No. 89-574, slip op. at 3-4 (E.D. Cal. Mar. 17, 1993) (ordering agency to reacquire records that mistakenly were returned to submitter upon closing of administrative appeal), appeal dismissed per stipulation, No. 93-16727 (9th Cir. Oct. 26, 1994); see also FOIA Update, Vol. XIX, No. 4, at 2 (discussing private grantee records that are uniquely made subject to FOIA under OMB Circular A-110, "Uniform Administrative Requirements for Grants and Agreements with Institutions of Higher Education, Hospitals, and Other Non-Profit Organizations," 64 Fed. Reg. 54,926 (1999)); cf. Nw. Coal. for Alternatives to Pesticides v. EPA, 254 F. Supp. 2d 125, 131 (D.D.C. 2003) (noting that a private entity's "voluntary provision" of a requested record to plaintiff "does not relieve the [agency] of [its] obligation to respond to plaintiff's [FOIA] request" for an identical record maintained in the agency's files).

[173] See, e.g., Niagara Mohawk Power Corp. v. U.S. Dep't of Energy, No. 95-0952, transcript at 10 (D.D.C. Feb. 23, 1996) (bench order) (admonishing that FOIA is not to be used to force agency to obtain information from another agency), vacated & remanded on other grounds, 169 F.3d 16 (D.C. Cir. 1999); Gillin, No. 92-325, slip op. at 5 (D.N.H. May 28, 1993) (The "[r]equest focused primarily upon the decisions made by the [agency] in granting [the administrative permit], rather than the documentation upon which the [agency] relied."). But cf. Nat'l Ass'n of Criminal Def. Lawyers v. U.S. Dep't of Justice, No. 97-372, slip op. at 8-10 (D.D.C. June 26, 1998) (concluding that plaintiff's FOIA suit caused agency to issue revised criminal prosecution policy and awarding interim attorney fees partly on such basis), interlocutory appeal dismissed for lack of juris., 182 F.3d 981 (D.C. Cir. 1999).

[174] See Tuchinsky v. Selective Serv. Sys., 418 F.2d 155, 158 (7th Cir. 1969) (holding that no automatic release is required of material related to occupational deferments until a request is in hand; "otherwise, [the agency] would be required to 'run [a] loose-leaf service' for every draft counselor in the country"); Mandel Grunfeld & Herrick v. U.S. Customs Serv., 709 F.2d 41, 43 (11th Cir. 1983) (determining that plaintiff not entitled to automatic mailing of materials as they are updated); Howard v. Sec'y of the Air Force, No. SA-89-CA-1008, slip op. at 6 (W.D. Tex. Oct. 2, 1991) (concluding that plaintiff's request for records on continuing basis would "create an enormous burden, both in time and taxpayers' money"); Lybarger v. Cardwell, 438 F. Supp. 1075, 1077 (D. Mass. 1977) (holding that "open-ended procedure" advanced by requester whereby records automatically disclosed not required by FOIA and "will not be forced" upon agency); see also FOIA

(continued...)

records not yet created.[175]

Likewise, both agencies and requesters alike should remember to distinguish between records that may be sought through FOIA requests[176] and records that are required to be made available in agency reading rooms (both conventional and "electronic") under subsection (a)(2) of the Act.[177] Agencies are not required to provide FOIA requesters with records that fall within subsection (a)(2) and are already available for "reading room" inspection and copying.[178] (For a discussion of "reading room" rec-

---

[174](...continued)
Update, Vol. VI, No. 2, at 6 ("[I]n the few cases to have raised the issue of 'prospective' FOIA requests the courts have uniformly held that such requests are not proper.").

[175] See, e.g., Tax Analysts v. IRS, No. 94-923, 1998 WL 419755, at *4 (D.D.C. May 1, 1998) (recognizing that court could not order relief concerning documents not yet created and "for which a request for release has not even been made and for which administrative remedies have not been exhausted"); cf. FOIA Update, Vol. XVI, No. 1, at 1 (citing OMB Circular A-130, "Management of Federal Information Resources," 59 Fed. Reg. 37,905 (1994) (prescribing policies to encourage agencies to affirmatively disseminate government information independent of FOIA context)). But cf. Nat'l Ass'n of Criminal Def. Lawyers, No. 97-372, slip op. at 17 (D.D.C. June 26, 1998) (granting interim attorney fees based in part upon novel finding that plaintiff prevailed when, during litigation, agency released report which was not yet in existence at time of plaintiff's request).

[176] See 5 U.S.C. § 552(a)(3) (generally excluding "reading room" records from Act's basic "FOIA request" provisions).

[177] Id. § 552(a)(2); see also FOIA Post, "GAO E-FOIA Implementation Report Issued" (posted 3/23/01) (outlining categories of records required to be affirmatively disclosed in "electronic" reading rooms); FOIA Update, Vol. XVII, No. 3, at 1-2 (discussing maintenance of both conventional and "electronic" reading rooms under Electronic FOIA amendments).

[178] See Schwarz v. U.S. Patent & Trademark Office, No. 95-5349, 1996 U.S. App. LEXIS 4609, at *2-3 (D.C. Cir. Feb. 22, 1996) (per curiam); Crews v. Internal Revenue, No. 99-8388, 2000 WL 900800, at *6 (C.D. Cal. Apr. 26, 2000) (holding that "documents that are publicly available either in the [agency's FOIA] reading room or on the [I]nternet" are "not subject to production via FOIA requests"); cf. Perales v. DEA, 21 F. App'x 473, 474-75 (7th Cir. 2001) (recognizing that under subsection (a)(3), agencies are not required to disclose in response to FOIA requests records already made available under subsection (a)(1) through publication in the Federal Register). But see also FOIA Update, Vol. XVIII, No. 1, at 3 (advising that Congress made clear that newly established "reading room" category of FOIA-processed records would stand as exception to general rule and be subject
(continued...)

PROCEDURAL REQUIREMENTS

ords, see FOIA Reading Rooms and Web Sites, FOIA Reading Rooms, above.)

   In addition to reasonably describing the records sought, a FOIA requester must follow an agency's regulations in making a request.[179] Each federal agency must publish in the Federal Register its procedural regulations governing access to its records under the FOIA.[180] These regulations must inform the public of where and how to address requests; its schedule of fees for search, review, and duplication; its fee waiver criteria; and its administrative appeal procedures.[181] The Electronic Freedom of Information Act Amendments of 1996[182] affected several procedural aspects of FOIA administration[183] (including matters concerning the timing of processing FOIA requests, which are discussed below).[184] Each federal agency is required to have implementing regulations published in the Federal

---

   [178](...continued)
to regular FOIA requests as well); FOIA Update, Vol. XVI, No. 1, at 2 (reminding that "an agency cannot convert a subsection (a)(3) record into a subsection (a)(2) record . . . just by voluntarily placing it into its reading room").

   [179] 5 U.S.C. § 552(a)(3)(A); see, e.g., Ivey v. Snow, No. 05-1095, 2006 WL 2051339, at *4 (D.D.C. 2006) (granting summary judgment to agency because plaintiff failed to exhaust administrative remedies when requests failed to comply with agency regulations); Wicks v. Coffrey, No. 01-3664, 2002 WL 1000975, at *2 (E.D. La. May 14, 2002) ("The first step in exhausting administrative remedies under the FOIA is filing a proper FOIA request."); Blackwell v. EEOC, No. 2:98-38, 1999 U.S. Dist. LEXIS 3708, at *5 (E.D.N.C. Feb. 12, 1999) (finding that request was not properly made because plaintiff failed to follow specific agency regulation requiring that request be denominated explicitly as request for information under FOIA).

   [180] See 5 U.S.C. § 552(a)(4)(A), (a)(6)(A), (a)(6)(D), (a)(6)(E); see also id. § 552(g) (requiring agencies to make available "reference material or a guide for requesting records or information from the agency"); FOIA Update, Vol. XIX, No. 3, at 3 (discussing availability of agency FOIA reference guides through agency FOIA sites on World Wide Web); FOIA Update, Vol. XVIII, No. 2, at 1 (discussing electronic availability of Justice Department's FOIA Reference Guide).

   [181] See, e.g., Department of Justice FOIA Regulations, 28 C.F.R. pt. 16 (2006).

   [182] Pub. L. No. 104-231, 110 Stat. 3048 (codified as amended at 5 U.S.C. § 552).

   [183] See FOIA Update, Vol. XIX, No. 1, at 3-5 ("OIP Guidance: Electronic FOIA Amendments Implementation Guidance Outline").

   [184] See FOIA Update, Vol. XVII, No. 4, at 1-2, 10-11 (discussing statutory changes).

Register that address these matters as well.[185]

Although an agency occasionally may waive some of its published procedures for reasons of public interest, speed, or simplicity, all agencies should remember that any "unnecessary bureaucratic hurdle has no place in [the Act's] implementation."[186] Accordingly, an agency may not impose any additional requirements on a requester beyond those prescribed in its regulations.[187] Of course, agencies should adhere strictly to their own regulations, especially when doing so would benefit the FOIA requester.[188]

Conversely, a requester's failure to comply with an agency's procedural regulations governing access to records -- such as those concerning

---

[185] 5 U.S.C. § 552(a)(6)(D), (a)(6)(E); see, e.g., 28 C.F.R. pt. 16; see also FOIA Post, "GAO E-FOIA Implementation Report Issued" (posted 3/23/01) (reminding agencies of their electronic access obligations for regulations); FOIA Update, Vol. XIX, No. 3, at 4 (discussing availability of agency regulations, including proposed regulations, through agency FOIA Web sites).

[186] Presidential FOIA Memorandum, reprinted in FOIA Update, Vol. XIV, No. 3, at 3; see, e.g., FOIA Update, Vol. XV, No. 3, at 6 (cautioning against practices that would cause unwarranted disadvantages to requesters in record-referral processes).

[187] See Zemansky, 767 F.2d at 574; see also FOIA Update, Vol. X, No. 3, at 5 (addressing submission of FOIA requests by "fax" in relation to agency regulation); cf. FOIA Post, "Anthrax Mail Emergency Delays FOIA Correspondence" (posted 11/30/01) (noting that agencies can mitigate the effects of anthrax-related mail disruption by "allow[ing] FOIA requesters to submit new requests by fax, or even electronically if they have established that capability"); FOIA Update, Vol. XIX, No. 1, at 6 (encouraging agencies to consider as matter of administrative discretion establishing capability to receive FOIA requests via World Wide Web).

[188] See, e.g., Ruotolo, 53 F.3d at 10 (charging that agency failed to comply with its own regulation requiring it to assist requesters in reformulating requests determined not to reasonably describe records sought); Pub. Citizen v. FDA, No. 94-0018, slip op. at 2 (D.D.C. Feb. 9, 1996) (criticizing agency for asserting that request did not reasonably describe "records which could be located in the FDA's record keeping system without an unduly burdensome search," and ignoring plaintiff's concession to limit scope of request, concluding that agency violated its own regulatory requirement to seek more specific information and to narrow scope of request); see also FOIA Post, "FOIA Counselor Q&A" (posted 1/24/06) (advising that agency FOIA regulations "creat[e] an expectation on the FOIA requester's part"); cf. FOIA Update, Vol. XIX, No. 1, at 5 (advising agencies to implement statutory provisions of Electronic FOIA amendments "without any disadvantage to FOIA requesters," regardless of status of implementing regulations).

properly addressed requests,[189] fees and fee waivers,[190] proof of identity,[191]

---

[189] See Thomas v. FAA, No. 05-2391, 2007 U.S. Dist. LEXIS 5260, at *12-14 (D.D.C. Jan. 25, 2007) (ruling that plaintiff has not exhausted administrative remedies where agency has not received FOIA request); West v. Jackson, No. 05-1441, 2006 WL 2660610, at *3-4 (D.D.C. Sept. 15, 2006) (finding that requester failed to exhaust administrative remedies where he could not show that agency received request letter and where purported request letter was addressed to incorrect address); Thorn v. Soc. Sec. Admin., No. 04-1282, 2005 WL 1398605, at *3 (D.D.C. June 11, 2005) (finding failure to exhaust where requester did not submit his requests to proper address); Thomas v. IRS, No. 03-2080, 2004 WL 3185316, at *2 (M.D. Pa. Nov. 2, 2004) (finding failure to exhaust where requester did not file proper request when he addressed his purported request to non-FOIA officer employee in incorrect state), aff'd, 153 F. App'x 89 (3d Cir. 2005); Maydak v. U.S. Dep't of Justice, 254 F. Supp. 2d 23, 40 (D.D.C. 2003) (ruling that because the agency's "regulations require FOIA requesters seeking records from field offices to write directly to the respective field office," the agency "had no statutory obligation to proceed with a search of all of its field offices"); Stanley v. DOD, No. 93-4247, slip op. at 10 (S.D. Ill. July 28, 1998) (holding that a request was not properly received when the agency returned -- unopened -- an improperly addressed request); Smith, 1996 U.S. Dist. LEXIS 5594, at *9 (N.D. Cal. Apr. 23, 1996) (stating that "National Records Administration is not a HUD information center," and holding that by directing FOIA request to wrong agency plaintiff failed to exhaust administrative remedies); Sands v. United States, No. 94-0537, 1995 U.S. Dist. LEXIS 9252, at *10-12 (S.D. Fla. June 16, 1995) (noting, in light of agency's clear rules and reasonable treatment of misdirected request, that plaintiff failed to exhaust administrative remedies by not directing request to appropriate office); United States v. Agunbiade, No. 90-CR-610, 1995 WL 351058, at *6 (E.D.N.Y. May 10, 1995) (ruling that plaintiff who did not direct request to "appropriate parties and agencies" in accordance with agency-specific rules failed to exhaust administrative remedies), aff'd sub nom. United States v. Osinowo, 100 F.3d 942 (2d Cir. 1996) (unpublished table decision). But see Coolman v. IRS, No. 98-6149, 1999 WL 675319, at *4 (W.D. Mo. July 12, 1999) (finding administrative remedies exhausted because "it cannot be said . . . that plaintiff's failure to use the address provided in [agency's] regulations prevented his request from arriving at the correct destination"), summary affirmance granted, No. 99-3963, 1999 WL 1419039 (8th Cir. Dec. 6, 1999); Raulerson v. Reno, No. 96-120, slip op. at 5 (D.D.C. Feb. 26, 1999) (finding search inadequate -- notwithstanding agency regulations requiring that requests be addressed to individual offices maintaining records sought -- because not all offices likely to contain responsive records were searched), summary affirmance granted, No. 99-5257, 1999 WL 1215968 (D.C. Cir. Nov. 23, 1999).

[190] See Pietrangelo v. Dep't of the Army, 155 F. App'x 526, 526 (2d Cir. 2005) (affirming district court decision which found that requester could not seek judicial review when he failed to meet fee-related exhaustion re-

(continued...)

[190](...continued)
quirements); Pollack v. Dep't of Justice, 49 F.3d 115, 119 (4th Cir. 1995) (concluding that plaintiff's refusal to pay anticipated fees constitutes failure to exhaust administrative remedies); Kumar v. U.S. Dep't of Justice, No. 06-714, 2007 U.S. Dist. LEXIS 11144, at *11-12 (D.D.C. Feb. 16, 2007) (holding that failure to pay fees under FOIA constitutes failure to exhaust administrative remedies); Kemmerly v. U.S. Dep't of Interior, No. 06-2386, 2006 WL 2990122, at *2 (E.D. La. Oct. 17, 2006) (stating that "administrative exhaustion does not occur until the required fees are paid or an appeal is taken from the refusal to waive fees" (citing Oglesby v. U.S. Dep't of the Army, 920 F.2d 57, 66 (D.C. Cir. 1990))); Judicial Watch v. FBI, 190 F. Supp. 2d 29, 33 (D.D.C. 2002) ("The D.C. Circuit has held that failure to pay FOIA fees constitutes a failure to exhaust administrative remedies"); Thorn v. United States, No. 04-1185, 2005 WL 3276285, at *3 (D.D.C. Aug. 11, 2005) (finding failure to exhaust when requester did not pay fees); Schwarz v. U.S. Dep't of Treasury, 131 F. Supp. 2d 142, 148 (D.D.C. 2000) ("Exhaustion of administrative remedies . . . includes payment of required fees or an appeal within the agency from a decision refusing to waive fees."); Grecco v. Dep't of Justice, No. 97-0419, slip op. at 5 (D.D.C. Apr. 1, 1999) (recognizing that requester's failure to pay fees or ask for fee waiver constitutes failure to exhaust administrative remedies); Smith v. IRS, No. 2:94-989, 1999 WL 357935, at *1 (D. Utah Mar. 24, 1999) (finding that plaintiff "failed to exhaust his administrative remedies in that he failed to pay the fees and costs in order to process his claims"); Stanley, No. 93-4247, slip op. at 9 (S.D. Ill. July 28, 1998) (finding request not properly received also because requester failed to follow agency regulations requiring agreement to pay fees); cf. Pub. Citizen, Inc. v. Dep't of Educ., 292 F. Supp. 2d 1, 4-5 & n.4 (D.D.C. 2003) (concluding that because the agency "failed to [respond] to plaintiff's fee waiver request when it was required by statute to do so," and then "proceed[ed] with a search without notifying plaintiff of the cost of that search," the agency could not subsequently in litigation demand payment of fees from plaintiff, which "had no reason to assume it would be required to pay fees . . . in view of [the agency's] silence in the face of plaintiff's specific fee waiver request").

[191] See Schwarz v. FBI, 31 F. Supp. 2d 540, 542 (N.D. W. Va. 1998) (recognizing that first-party requester's failure to follow agency regulations requiring her to submit fingerprints for positive identification constituted failure to exhaust administrative remedies), aff'd, 166 F.3d 334 (4th Cir. 1998) (unpublished table decision); cf. Martin v. U.S. Dep't of Justice, No. 96-2866, slip op. at 7-8 (D.D.C. Dec. 16, 1999) (ruling that requester who seeks law enforcement information about living third party and fails to provide subject's written authorization permitting disclosure of records has not failed to exhaust administrative remedies because agency regulations stated only that such authorization "will help the processing of [the] request"), rev'd & remanded in part on other grounds, No. 00-5389 (D.C. Cir. Apr. 23, 2002). But cf. Pusa v. FBI, No. 99-04603, slip op. at 5 (C.D. Cal. Aug. 3, 1999) (holding that plaintiff who failed to submit third party's privacy waiver "has

(continued...)

## PROCEDURAL REQUIREMENTS

and administrative appeals[192] -- may be held to constitute a failure to prop-

---

[191](...continued)
failed to exhaust administrative remedies under the FOIA by failing to comply with the agency's published procedures for obtaining third-party information").

[192] See, e.g., Lumarse v. HHS, No. 98-55880, 1999 WL 644355, at *5 (9th Cir. Aug. 24, 1999) (affirming dismissal of plaintiff's FOIA claim for failure to exhaust administrative remedies because plaintiff "does not allege that it [administratively] appealed the denials of its FOIA requests"); Teplitsky v. Dep't of Justice, No. 96-36208, 1997 WL 665705, at *1 (9th Cir. Oct. 24, 1997) (holding plaintiff had not exhausted administrative remedies when he did not administratively appeal denial of FOIA request even though agency notified him of procedure); RNR Enters. v. SEC, 122 F.3d 93, 98 (2d Cir. 1997) (ruling plaintiff had not exhausted his administrative remedies when he failed to appeal agency denial even though he was advised of his right to appeal and denial was issued during requisite time period); Dunnington v. DOD, No. 06-0925, 2007 U.S. Dist. LEXIS 715, at *4-5 (D.D.C. Jan. 8, 2007) (holding that requester failed to exhaust administrative remedies where he failed to perfect request or file administrative appeal); Ctr. for Biological Diversity v. Gutierrez, No. 05-1045, 2006 WL 2329330, at *6-8 (D.D.C. Aug. 10, 2006) (concluding that requester failed to exhaust administrative remedies when electronically submitted appeal was received twelve minutes after expiration of agency's regulatory appeal deadline); Fulton v. Executive Office for U.S. Attorneys, No. 05-1530, 2006 WL 1663526, at *3 (D.D.C. June 15, 2006) (concluding that requester failed to exhaust administrative remedies because he did not administratively appeal denial of fee waiver request); Schoenman v. FBI, No. 04-2202, 2006 WL 1582253, at *12 (D.D.C. Mar. 31, 2006) (stating that the requester "cannot establish an essential element of the statutory requirement under FOIA requiring an agency's actual receipt of the appeal as a precursor to exhausting all administrative remedies"); Bernard v. DOD, 362 F. Supp. 2d 272, 281-82 (D.D.C. 2005) (dismissing FOIA claims where requester did not exhaust Army Privacy Program's administrative appeal remedies); Thorn, 2005 WL 3276285, at *2-3 (finding failure to exhaust because requester's letter to Attorney General is not proper administrative appeal under agency regulations); Thomas, 2004 WL 3185316, at *3 (finding that the plaintiff's letters were not appeals where "neither document contains the word appeal, or any reference to a prior request or proceeding," meaning that the plaintiff failed to exhaust administrative remedies), reconsideration denied, 95 A.F.T.R. 2d 2005-559 (M.D. Pa. Nov. 16, 2004), motion to vacate denied, 95 A.F.T.R. 2d 2005-562 (M.D. Pa. Dec. 16, 2004), aff'd, 153 F. App'x 89 (3d Cir. 2005); N.Y. Times Co. v. U.S. Dep't of Labor, 340 F. Supp. 2d 394, 399 (S.D.N.Y. 2004) (finding that exhaustion was achieved where on appeal agency did not give "explicit denial" but gave "practical" denial by offering no alternative for burdensome request); Coleman v. U.S. Dep't of Justice, No. 02-79, slip op. at 5 (E.D. Va. Oct. 7, 2002) (holding that plaintiff "has not exhausted his administrative remedies with regard to the particular issue
(continued...)

erly exhaust administrative remedies. (For a further discussion of exhaustion of administrative remedies, see Litigation Considerations, Exhaustion of Administrative Remedies, below.)

## Time Limits

Until an agency (or the proper component of that agency) receives a FOIA request, it is not obligated to search for responsive records, meet time deadlines, or release any records.[193] Requests not filed in accordance

---

[192](...continued)
of whether the [agency's] search was adequate," because plaintiff failed to raise that issue on administrative appeal); Coates v. Dep't of Labor, 138 F. Supp. 2d 663, 668 (E.D. Pa. 2001) (deeming administrative remedies not exhausted due to plaintiff's failure to "engage in [administrative appeal] process, regardless of how frivolous he may have believed [that process] to be"); Hamilton Sec. Group v. HUD, 106 F. Supp. 2d 23, 29 (D.D.C. 2000) (holding that plaintiff failed to exhaust administrative remedies because it filed its administrative appeal one day after regulatory deadline for filing such appeals had passed), aff'd per curiam, No. 00-5331, 2001 WL 238162 (D.C. Cir. Feb. 23, 2001); Comer v. IRS, No. 97-76329, 1999 U.S. Dist. LEXIS 16268, at *11 (E.D. Mich. Sept. 30, 1999) (finding that although plaintiff previously appealed agency's failure to promptly respond to his request, "[u]pon receiving the documents and the bill, and prior to filing suit, plaintiff was [again] obliged to administratively appeal whatever dissatisfactions he may have had with that result"); Patterson, No. 96-0095, slip op. at 1 (D.D.C. Mar. 23, 1999) (dismissing case because plaintiff failed to exhaust administrative remedies by not administratively appealing denial of fee waiver request); Thomas v. Office of U.S. Attorney, 171 F.R.D. 53, 54 (E.D.N.Y. 1997) (ruling that administrative remedies were not exhausted when plaintiff made further request for documents in appeal of agency's denial of plaintiff's initial request). But cf. Wilbur v. CIA, 355 F.3d 675, 677 (D.C. Cir. 2004) (noting that "the policies underlying the exhaustion requirement have been served" when the agency "accepted" and then adjudicated an administrative appeal received four years after the regulatory deadline for its submission had passed); Jennings v. FBI, No. 03-1651, slip op. at 10-11 (D.D.C. May 6, 2004) (rejecting agency's failure-to-exhaust argument where, inter alia, requester produced appeal letter, even though agency attested that it did not receive that letter).

[193] See Brumley v. U.S. Dep't of Labor, 767 F.2d 444, 445 (8th Cir. 1985) (determining that agency complied with "FOIA's response time provisions" after advising plaintiff that routing of his request to appropriate office within agency would result in short delay "before the ten working day response period would begin running"); Blackwell v. EEOC, No. 2:98-38, 1999 U.S. Dist. LEXIS 3708, at *6 (E.D.N.C. Feb. 12, 1999) ("The time period for responding to a FOIA request . . . does not begin to run until the request is received by the appropriate office and officer in the agency, as set forth in the agency's published regulations."); see also Judicial Watch, Inc. v. U.S.
(continued...)

with published regulations are not deemed to have been received until they are identified as proper FOIA requests by agency personnel.[194] For example, under Department of Justice regulations,[195] a request is not considered received until the requester has promised to pay fees (above a minimum amount) or the receiving component has decided to waive all fees.[196] Moreover, if a requester agrees to pay properly assessed search, review, and/or duplication fees but later fails to pay those fees, an agency may refuse to process that requester's subsequent requests until the amount owed is paid.[197] (For a discussion of the assessment of fees, see Fees and Fee Waivers, below.)

Once an agency properly receives a FOIA request,[198] it has twenty

---

[193](...continued)
Dep't of Justice, No. 97-2089, slip op. at 10-11 (D.D.C. July 14, 1998) (finding that the court was without jurisdiction when plaintiff filed Complaint prior to lapse of statutory time limit); cf. Soghomonian v. United States, 82 F. Supp. 2d 1134, 1138 (E.D. Cal. 1999) (holding that twenty-day time period for responding to administrative appeal begins when agency receives appeal, not when requester mails it).

[194] See, e.g., Lykins v. U.S. Dep't of Justice, 3 Gov't Disclosure Serv. (P-H) ¶ 83,092, at 83,637 (D.D.C. Feb. 28, 1983).

[195] 28 C.F.R. § 16.11(e) (2006).

[196] See Irons v. FBI, 571 F. Supp. 1241, 1243 (D. Mass. 1983), rev'd on other grounds, 811 F.2d 681 (1987); see also Pollack v. Dep't of Justice, 49 F.3d 115, 120 (4th Cir. 1995); cf. Oglesby v. U.S. Dep't of the Army, 920 F.2d 57, 66 (D.C. Cir. 1990); Loomis v. Dep't of Energy, No. 96-149, 1999 WL 33541935, at *3-4 (N.D.N.Y. Mar. 9, 1999) (finding that plaintiff's request was properly received when he agreed to pay estimated fee that agency later revised upward), aff'd, 21 F. App'x 80 (2d Cir. 2001).

[197] See Trenerry v. IRS, No. 95-5150, 1996 WL 88459, at *2 (10th Cir. Mar. 1, 1996); Atkin v. EEOC, No. 92-3275, slip op. at 5 (D.N.J. June 24, 1993); Crooker v. U.S. Secret Serv., 577 F. Supp. 1218, 1219-20 (D.D.C. 1983); FOIA Update, Vol. VII, No. 2, at 2; see also 5 U.S.C. § 552(a)(4)(A)(v).

[198] See Dunnington v. DOD, No. 06-0925, 2007 U.S. Dist. LEXIS 715, at *5 (D.D.C. Jan. 8, 2007) (finding failure to state claim where plaintiff presented no evidence he submitted FOIA request to agency); Schoenman v. FBI, No. 04-2202, 2006 WL 1126813, at *13 (D.D.C. Mar. 31, 2006) (stating that an agency's FOIA obligations do not commence with the "averred mailing of a FOIA request," and dismissing counts where the plaintiff did not establish that the agency received the request); Carbe v. ATF, No. 03-1658, 2004 WL 2051359, at *8 (D.D.C. Aug. 12, 2004) (stating that agency "has no reason to search or produce records . . . and . . . has no basis to respond" if it does not receive FOIA request, even where requester claims to have submitted one); see also FOIA Post, "Anthrax Mail Emergency Delays FOIA Corres-

(continued...)

working days in which to make a determination on the request.[199] Previously, once an agency was in receipt of a proper FOIA request, it was required to inform the requester of its decision to grant or deny access to the requested records within ten working days, but the Electronic Freedom of Information Act Amendments of 1996 increased the Act's basic time limit for agency responses, lengthening it from ten to twenty working days.[200] Agencies are not necessarily required to release the records within the statutory time limit, but access to releasable records should, at a minimum, be granted promptly thereafter.[201]

In "unusual circumstances," an agency can extend the twenty-day time limit for processing a FOIA request if it tells the requester in writing why it needs the extension and when it will make a determination on the request.[202] The FOIA defines "unusual circumstances" as: (1) the need to search for and collect records from separate offices; (2) the need to examine a voluminous amount of records required by the request; and (3) the

---

[198](...continued)
pondence" (posted 11/30/01) (noting that "[t]he processing of a FOIA request, with all applicable statutory deadlines, is triggered by an agency's 'receipt of . . . such request'" (quoting 5 U.S.C. § 552(a)(6)(A)(i))).

[199] 5 U.S.C. § 552(a)(6)(A)(i) (2000 & Supp. IV 2004); see FOIA Update, Vol. XVII, No. 4, at 2, 10 (discussing Electronic FOIA amendments' modifications to FOIA's time-limit provisions); FOIA Update, Vol. XIII, No. 3, at 5 (advising that merely acknowledging request within statutory time period is simply insufficient); cf. Judicial Watch, 880 F. Supp. at 10 (rejecting requester's preposterous claim that response in less than ten working days is evidence of "bad faith").

[200] Pub. L. No. 104-231, § 8(b), 110 Stat. 3048, 3052 (codified as amended at 5 U.S.C. § 552(a)(6)(A)(i)).

[201] See 5 U.S.C. § 552(a)(6)(C)(i) (requiring that records be made available "promptly"); see also Larson v. IRS, No. 85-3076, slip op. at 2-3 (D.D.C. Dec. 11, 1985) (finding that the FOIA "does not require that the person requesting records be informed of the agency's decision within ten days, it only demands that the government make [and mail] its decision within that time"). But see Manos v. U.S. Dep't of the Air Force, No. C-92-3986, 1993 U.S. Dist. LEXIS 1501, at *14-15 (N.D. Cal. Feb. 10, 1993) (ruling that even mailing response within ten-day period was not sufficient and that requester must actually receive response within ten-day period).

[202] 5 U.S.C. § 552(a)(6)(B)(i); see Pub. Citizen, Inc. v. Dep't of Educ., No. 01-2351, slip op. at 17-23 (D.D.C. June 17, 2002) (ruling that because provisions of subsection (a)(6)(B)(i) are permissive rather than mandatory, agency is not obliged to send such notice, although such nonaction certainly will not extend time for making determination on request).

need to consult with another agency or agency component.[203] If the required extension exceeds ten days, the agency must allow the requester an opportunity to modify his or her request, or to arrange for an alternative time frame for completion of the agency's processing.[204]

In many instances, though, agencies cannot meet these time limits due to limitations on their resources,[205] or for other reasons.[206] Agencies therefore have adopted the court-sanctioned practice of generally handling backlogged FOIA requests on a "first-in, first-out" basis.[207] The Electronic

---

[203] 5 U.S.C. § 552(a)(6)(B)(iii); see also Al-Fayed v. CIA, No. 00-2092, slip op. at 5 (D.D.C. Jan. 16, 2001) (recognizing that circumstances "such as an agency's effort to reduce the number of pending requests, the amount of classified material, the size and complexity of other requests processed by the agency, the resources being devoted to the declassification of classified material of public interest, and the number of requests for records by courts or administrative tribunals are relevant to the Courts' determination as to whether [unusual] circumstances exist"), aff'd, 254 F.3d 300 (D.C. Cir. 2001); Sierra Club v. U.S. Dep't of Interior, 384 F. Supp. 2d 1, 31 (D.D.C. 2004) (finding that the "onerous request" and the requester's "refusal to reasonably modify it or to arrange an alternative timeframe for release of documents certainly constituted 'unusual circumstances' that relieved the [agency] of the normal timeliness for release of documents under FOIA").

[204] 5 U.S.C. § 552(a)(6)(B)(ii); see, e.g., 28 C.F.R. § 16.5(c) (Department of Justice FOIA regulation); cf. Al-Fayed, No. 00-2092, slip op. at 6 (D.D.C. Jan. 16, 2001) (observing that the Act "places the onus of modification [of a request's scope] squarely upon the requester, and does not indicate that an equal burden rests with the agency to 'negotiate' an agreeable 'deadline'").

[205] See, e.g., Zuckerman v. FBI, No. 94-6315, slip op. at 8 (D.N.J. Dec. 6, 1995) (noting effects of resource limitations on complying with statutory time limits); see also FOIA Update, Vol. XV, No. 2, at 2; FOIA Update, Vol. XIV, No. 3, at 5, 8-9; FOIA Update, Vol. XIII, No. 2, at 8-10; FOIA Update, Vol. XI, No. 1, at 1-2; cf. FOIA Update, Vol. XVI, No. 1, at 1-2 (promoting practice of making agency records "affirmatively" available to public, rather than providing them only in response to particular FOIA requests, in order to benefit overall process of FOIA administration).

[206] See, e.g., Tri-Valley Cares v. U.S. Dep't of Energy, No. 03-3926, 2004 WL 2043034, at *20 (N.D. Cal. Sept. 10, 2004) (recognizing that because requested FOIA response required "review from [Department of] Homeland Security," delay was not indication of bad faith), aff'd in pertinent part & rev'd on other grounds, No. 04-17232, 2006 WL 2971651, at *2-3 (9th Cir. Oct. 16, 2006).

[207] See Open Am. v. Watergate Special Prosecution Force, 547 F.2d 605, 614-16 (D.C. Cir. 1976) (citing 5 U.S.C. § 552(a)(6)(C)). But cf. Al-Fayed, No. 00-2092, slip op. at 9 n.5 (D.D.C. Jan. 16, 2001) (noting that "even if the

(continued...)

FOIA amendments expressly authorized agencies to promulgate regulations providing for "multitrack processing" of their FOIA requests -- which allows agencies to process requests on a first-in, first-out basis within each track, but also permits them to respond to relatively simple requests more quickly than requests involving complex and/or voluminous records.[208] (For a further discussion of these points, see Litigation Considerations, "Open America" Stays of Proceedings, below.)

An agency's failure to comply with the time limits for either an initial request or an administrative appeal may be treated as a "constructive exhaustion" of administrative remedies.[209] A requester may immediately thereafter seek judicial review if he or she wishes to do so.[210] However, the

---

[207](...continued)
[agency] did not adhere strictly to first-in, first-out processing, there is little support that Open America requires such a system" so long as the agency's processing system is fair overall); Summers v. CIA, No. 98-1682, slip op. at 4 (D.D.C. July 26, 1999) (recognizing that agency need not adhere strictly to "first-in, first-out process[ing]" so long as "it is proceeding in a manner designed to be fair and expeditious").

[208] Pub. L. No. 104-231, § 7(a), 110 Stat. 3048, 3050 (codified as amended at 5 U.S.C. § 552(a)(6)(D)); see, e.g., 28 C.F.R. § 16.5(b) (Department of Justice implementing regulation); see also FOIA Update, Vol. XVIII, No. 1, at 6 (discussing multitrack processing for agencies with decentralized FOIA operations); FOIA Update, Vol. XVII, No. 4, at 10 (discussing implementing regulations); cf. FOIA Post, "Supplemental Guidance on Annual FOIA Reports" (posted 8/13/01) (noting that agencies' annual FOIA reports must include "the number of requests that were accorded expedited processing . . . [and] should to the extent practicable also report the number of requests for expedited processing that are received each year"); FOIA Update, Vol. XVIII, No. 3, at 3-7 (advising agencies regarding reporting of multitrack-processing information in annual FOIA reports).

[209] See 5 U.S.C. § 552(a)(6)(C); Thomas v. FAA, No. 05-2391, 2007 U.S. Dist. LEXIS 5260, at *12 (D.D.C. Jan. 25, 2007) (stating that agency's failure to respond to FOIA request within twenty days constitutes constructive exhaustion of administrative remedies). But cf. Judicial Watch v. U.S. Naval Observatory, 160 F. Supp. 2d 111, 113 (D.D.C. 2001) (concluding that agency's "failure to timely respond to [a] request for expedited processing is not equivalent to constructive exhaustion of administrative remedies as to the request for documents").

[210] See, e.g., Spannaus v. U.S. Dep't of Justice, 824 F.2d 52, 58 (D.C. Cir. 1987); Perdue Farms v. NLRB, 927 F. Supp. 897, 904 (E.D.N.C. 1996), vacated on other grounds, 108 F.3d 519 (4th Cir. 1997); see also Walsh v. VA, No. 03-C-0225, slip op. at 3-4 (E.D. Wis. Feb. 10, 2004) ("The failure of an agency to comply with the [FOIA's] statutory time limits . . . constitutes constructive exhaustion of administrative remedies, thereby permitting the
(continued...)

## PROCEDURAL REQUIREMENTS

D.C. Circuit has interpreted this rule of constructive exhaustion by requiring that once the agency responds to the FOIA request -- after the statutory time limit but before the requester has filed suit -- the requester must administratively appeal the denial before proceeding to court.[211] (For a

---

[210](...continued)
requestor to seek relief in court."); McCall v. U.S. Marshals Serv., 36 F. Supp. 2d 3, 5 (D.D.C. 1999) (finding that plaintiff constructively exhausted his administrative remedies when court "provisionally filed" his FOIA complaint and application to proceed in forma pauperis before agency responded to his request, even though agency responded before court granted plaintiff's motion to proceed in forma pauperis); FOIA Update, Vol. IV, No. 1, at 6 (superseded in part). But cf. Pollack, 49 F.3d at 119 (holding that constructive exhaustion provision does not relieve requester of statutory obligation to pay fees that agency is authorized to collect).

[211] See Oglesby, 920 F.2d at 61-65; accord Hidalgo v. FBI, 344 F.3d 1256, 1259-60 (D.C. Cir. 2003) (ruling that plaintiff failed to exhaust his administrative remedies because his prematurely filed administrative appeal of the agency's failure to comply with the FOIA's time limits "did not promote the purposes of the exhaustion doctrine" with respect to the "substance" of the agency's ultimately timely response to his request); Teplitsky v. Dep't of Justice, No. 96-36208, 1997 WL 665705, at *1 (9th Cir. Oct. 24, 1997) (holding that plaintiff had not exhausted administrative remedies when he did not appeal denial of FOIA request even though agency notified him of procedure); RNR Enters. v. SEC, 122 F.3d 93, 98 (2d Cir. 1997) (ruling that plaintiff had not exhausted his administrative remedies when he failed to appeal agency denial even though he was advised of his right to appeal and denial was issued during requisite time period); Ruotolo v. Dep't of Justice, 53 F.3d 4, 9 (2d Cir. 1995) (finding administrative remedies exhausted when agency did not include notification of right to appeal its determination that request not reasonably described); Taylor v. Appleton, 30 F.3d 1365, 1370 (11th Cir. 1994) (stating that once party has waited for response from agency, actual exhaustion must occur before court has jurisdiction to review challenges); McDonnell v. United States, 4 F.3d 1227, 1240 (3d Cir. 1993) (upholding dismissal of claim as proper when plaintiff filed suit before filing appeal of denial received after exhaustion of statutory response period); see also Amaya-Flores v. DHS, No. 06-225, 2006 U.S. Dist. LEXIS 78735, at *7-8 (W.D. Tex. Oct. 30, 2006) (magistrate's recommendation) (recommending dismissal of FOIA claim as moot in light of agency's disclosure of documents); Lowry v. Soc. Sec. Admin., No. 00-1616, slip op. at 9-10 (D. Or. Aug. 29, 2001) (holding that requester had not constructively exhausted administrative remedies when he filed suit on day after agency mailed its denial letter, despite fact that he did not receive letter until several days thereafter); Bryce v. Overseas Private Inv. Corp., No. A-96-595, slip op. at 12 (W.D. Tex. Sept. 28, 1998) (recognizing that although agency's failure to respond within statutory time limit constitutes constructive exhaustion, "if the agency responds with a determination prior to the requester filing suit, then the requirement to exhaust administrative

(continued...)

discussion of this aspect of FOIA litigation, see Litigation Considerations, Exhaustion of Administrative Remedies, below.)

Under the law existing prior to the enactment of the Electronic FOIA amendments, an agency sued for not responding to a FOIA request could receive additional time to process that request if it could show that its failure to meet the statutory time limits resulted from "exceptional circumstances" and that it was applying "due diligence" in processing the request.[212] Previously, the need to process an extremely large volume of requests constituted "exceptional circumstances," and the commitment of large amounts of resources to process requests on a first-come, first-served basis was considered "due diligence."[213] The Electronic FOIA amendments, however, explicitly excluded "a predictable agency workload" of FOIA requests

---

[211](...continued)
review is revived"), appeal dismissed voluntarily, No. 99-50893 (5th Cir. Oct. 11, 1999); FOIA Update, Vol. XII, No. 2, at 3-4 ("OIP Guidance: Procedural Rules Under the D.C. Circuit's Oglesby Decision"). But see Mieras v. U.S. Forest Serv., No. 93-CV-74552, slip op. at 3 (E.D. Mich. Feb. 14, 1995) (misapplying D.C. Circuit rules on constructive exhaustion in declaring that plaintiff had not exhausted administrative remedies as he failed to file administrative appeal after agency response, even though he initiated lawsuit before agency response was made).

[212] See 5 U.S.C. § 552(a)(6)(C); see also FOIA Update, Vol. IX, No. 4, at 5.

[213] See Open Am. v. Watergate Special Prosecution Force, 547 F.2d 605, 615-16 (D.C. Cir. 1976); see also Gilmore v. NSA, No. 94-16165, 1995 WL 792079, at *1 (9th Cir. Dec. 11, 1995) (noting that even after agency's internal review of its FOIA operations to identify and correct deficiencies resulted in staff increase and implementation of "first-in/first-out" procedure, court determined it "unlikely that [agency] could process requests more quickly given that it must undertake a painstaking review of voluminous sensitive documents before disclosing requested information"); Jimenez v. FBI, 938 F. Supp. 21, 31 (D.D.C. 1996) ("In view of [the agency's] two-track system and the large volume of documents expected to be responsive to plaintiff's request, the Court finds that [the agency] has met the due diligence requirements for a stay."); Gilmore v. U.S. Dep't of State, No. 95-1098, slip op. at 27 (N.D. Cal. Feb. 9, 1996) (finding that in addition to other factors, "the recent and prolonged government shutdown provides a sufficient showing of exceptional circumstances"). But see Matlack, Inc. v. EPA, 868 F. Supp. 627, 633 (D. Del. 1994) (deciding that agency's response that it has a "'large docket of Freedom of Information Act appeals and [is] working as quickly as possible to resolve them,' without more, is simply insufficient to demonstrate 'exceptional circumstances'"). See generally FOIA Update, Vol. XIV, No. 3, at 8-9 (discussing possible solutions to backlog problem); FOIA Update, Vol. XII, No. 2, at 8-10 (discussing agency difficulties with FOIA time limits and administrative backlogs); FOIA Update, Vol. XI, No. 1, at 1-2 (discussing effects of budgetary constraints upon agency FOIA operations).

as "exceptional circumstances . . . unless the agency demonstrates reasonable progress in reducing its backlog of pending requests."[214] Nevertheless, a FOIA requester's refusal "to reasonably modify the scope of a request or arrange for an alternative time frame for processing the request," may be used as evidence of "exceptional circumstances."[215] (For a discussion of the litigation aspects of the FOIA's "exceptional circumstances" provision, see Litigation Considerations, "Open America" Stays of Proceedings, below.)

## Expedited Processing

Prior to the enactment of the Electronic Freedom of Information Act Amendments of 1996,[216] a FOIA request could have received "expedited"

---

[214] Pub. L. No. 104-231, § 7(c), 110 Stat. 3048, 3051 (codified as amended at 5 U.S.C. § 552(a)(6)(C)(ii)); see, e.g., Fiduccia, 185 F.3d at 1042 (finding no exceptional circumstances when only "a slight upward creep in the caseload" caused a backlog that the agency claimed resulted from employee cutbacks and rejection of its budget requests); Peltier v. FBI, No. 02-4328, slip op. at 8-10 (D. Minn. Aug. 15, 2003) (finding that agency made "reasonable progress in reducing its backlog" through additional staffing and technological enhancements to searching and processing functions); Appleton v. FDA, 254 F. Supp. 2d 6, 9-10 & n.4 (D.D.C. 2003) (declaring, despite the fact that the agency's "annual backlog reductions [were not] uniform," that the agency had demonstrated "reasonable progress in reducing its backlog" by committing additional resources and personnel and by implementing new electronic filing and redaction systems); Emerson v. CIA, No. 99-0274, 1999 U.S. Dist. LEXIS 19511, at *3 (D.D.C. Dec. 16, 1999) (finding that agency was exercising due diligence in reducing backlog through use of new FOIA task force, new databases, and new document-scanning mechanisms); Judicial Watch of Fla., Inc. v. U.S. Dep't of Justice, No. 97-cv-2869, slip op. at 6 (D.D.C. Aug. 25, 1998) (granting three-year stay of proceedings in light of agency's processing of FOIA requests on a "first-in/first out" basis, hiring of additional employees to handle requests, and reduction of backlog by twenty-five percent); Narducci v. FBI, No. 98-0130, slip op. at 1 (D.D.C. July 17, 1998) (observing that agency is "deluged with a volume of requests for information vastly in excess of that anticipated by Congress," and noting agency's "reasonable progress in reducing its backlog" of pending requests; granting agency request to stay proceedings for thirty-four months); see also FOIA Update, Vol. XVIII, No. 3, at 3-7 (advising agencies regarding reporting of backlog-related information in annual FOIA reports, beginning with annual report for Fiscal Year 1998).

[215] 5 U.S.C. § 552(a)(6)(C)(iii); see also H.R. Rep. No. 104-795, at 24-25 (1996) (elaborating on circumstances); see, e.g., Peltier, No. 02-4328, slip op. at 8-10 (D. Minn. Aug. 15, 2003) (finding exceptional circumstances due in large part to requester's "45,000 page large queue request").

[216] Pub. L. No. 104-231, 110 Stat. 3048 (codified as amended at 5 U.S.C.

(continued...)

treatment and be processed out of sequence if the requester could show an "exceptional need or urgency."[217] Courts granted expedited access when requests involved exceptional factors, such as jeopardy to life or personal safety,[218] or a threatened loss of substantial due process rights,[219] and

---

[216](...continued)
§ 552 (2000 & Supp. IV 2004)).

[217] Open Am., 547 F.2d at 616 (D.C. Cir. 1976) (citing 5 U.S.C. § 552(a)(6)(C) (1976)); see also Whitehurst v. FBI, No. 96-572, slip op. at 5 (D.D.C. Feb. 5, 1997) (finding that expedited processing is warranted where plaintiff's allegations regarding FBI crime laboratory potentially impact upon other criminal matters, where more than three years have elapsed, and where the agency has failed to release numerous documents it has already received and cleared for release to others); Schweihs v. FBI, 933 F. Supp. 719, 723 (N.D. Ill. 1996) (finding "no legal precedent or statutory or regulatory authority for prioritizing FOIA applicants by age or health status"); Gilmore v. FBI, No. 93-2117, slip op. at 3 (N.D. Cal. July 27, 1994) (ordering that request for information concerning government's key encryption and digital telephony initiative be expedited because material sought will "become less valuable if the FBI processes . . . on a first in-first out basis"); FOIA Update, Vol. IV, No. 3, at 3 ("OIP Guidance: When to Expedite FOIA Requests"); see also FOIA Update, Vol. XII, No. 3, at 5 (emphasizing need to promptly determine whether to expedite processing of request); cf. Fox v. U.S. Dep't of Justice, No. 94-4622, 1994 WL 923072, at *3 (C.D. Cal. Dec. 16, 1994) (ruling that agency is not required to disrupt its administrative routine unless requester has shown strong justification for obtaining documents in expedited manner), appeal dismissed, No. 94-56788 (9th Cir. Feb. 21, 1995).

[218] See, e.g., Exner v. FBI, 443 F. Supp. 1349, 1353 (S.D. Cal. 1978) (holding that plaintiff was entitled to expedited access after leak of information exposed her to harm from organized crime figures), aff'd, 612 F.2d 1202 (9th Cir. 1980); Cleaver v. Kelley, 427 F. Supp. 80, 81 (D.D.C. 1976) (determining that exceptional circumstances existed when plaintiff faced multiple criminal charges carrying possible death penalty in state court).

[219] See, e.g., Neely v. FBI, No. 7:97-0786, slip op. at 9 (W.D. Va. July 27, 1998) (granting expedited processing of FOIA request for plaintiff who had motion for new criminal trial pending and had made specific allegations related to agency documents); Ferguson v. FBI, 722 F. Supp. 1137, 1141-43 (S.D.N.Y. 1989) (noting that "due process interest must be substantial," and holding that plaintiff's request for information regarding his particular post-conviction proceeding required expedition); see also, e.g., NLRB v. Robbins Tire & Rubber Co., 437 U.S. 214, 242 & n.23 (1978) (making clear that FOIA is not intended to function as discovery tool); cf. Fiduccia v. U.S. Dep't of Justice, 185 F.3d 1035, 1041 (9th Cir. 1999) (rejecting argument that "requesters who sue agencies under the FOIA should have their requests handled before requesters who do not file lawsuits"); Ruiz v. U.S. Dep't of
(continued...)

PROCEDURAL REQUIREMENTS

thereby warranted such treatment.

Now the FOIA requires agencies to promulgate regulations providing for the expedited processing of requests if the requester demonstrates a "compelling need" (as defined by the amended statute), or in any other case the agency deems appropriate under its regulations.[220] Under the amended statute, a requester can show "compelling need" in one of two ways:  by establishing that his or her failure to obtain the records quickly "could reasonably be expected to pose an imminent threat to the life or physical safety of an individual"; or, if the requester is a "person primarily engaged in disseminating information,"[221] by demonstrating that an "urgency to inform the public concerning actual or alleged Federal Government activity" exists.[222] At their discretion, agencies may grant expedited treat-

---

[219](...continued)
Justice, No. 00-0105, slip op. at 3 (D.D.C. Sept. 27, 2001) ("To the extent that [the requested] records are intended for use in an attack on plaintiff's criminal conviction, this situation does not constitute an exceptional need."); Raulerson v. Reno, 95-cv-2053, slip op. at 4-6 (D.D.C. Mar. 30, 1998) (denying FBI's motion to stay proceedings for nearly three years when plaintiff had asserted he had only two years to appeal criminal conviction and requested documents may aid in preparation of appeal), plaintiff's appeal dismissed, No. 98-5112 (D.C. Cir. May 5, 1998); Edmond v. U.S. Attorney, 959 F. Supp. 1, 6 (D.D.C. 1997) ("In the absence of some other urgency, Plaintiff cannot meet his burden by merely making a naked assertion that the Government is withholding Brady material in order to accelerate his FOIA processing.").

[220] Pub. L. No. 104-231, § 8(a), 110 Stat. 3048, 3051-52 (codified as amended at 5 U.S.C. § 552(a)(6)(E)); see Judicial Watch, Inc. v. Rossotti, No. 01-2672, 2002 WL 31962775, at *2 n.8 (D. Md. Dec. 16, 2002) (denying plaintiff's request for expedited processing because its allegations "that it was the victim of ongoing criminal activity" and that "it would be unable to vindicate its rights without the requested documents . . . . do[] not meet the statutory definition of 'compelling need'"), aff'd sub nom. Judicial Watch, Inc. v. United States, 84 F. App'x 335 (4th Cir. 2004); see also FOIA Update, Vol. XIX, No. 1, at 5 (discussing significance of implementing regulations); FOIA Update, Vol. XVII, No. 4, at 10 (discussing statutory provision).

[221] See, e.g., Leadership Conference on Civil Rights v. Gonzales, 404 F. Supp. 2d 246, 260 (D.D.C. 2005) (concluding that "plaintiff is primarily engaged in disseminating information . . . regarding civil rights"), appeal dismissed, No. 06-5055 (D.C. Cir. Apr. 28, 2006); Tripp v. DOD, 193 F. Supp. 2d 229, 241 (D.D.C. 2002) ("To be sure, plaintiff has been the object of media attention and has at times provided information to the media, but there is no evidence . . . that she is 'primarily' engaged in such efforts.").

[222] 5 U.S.C. § 552(a)(6)(E)(v); see, e.g., 28 C.F.R. § 16.5(d)(ii) (2006) (Justice Department implementing regulation); see also Al-Fayed v. CIA, 254
(continued...)

ment under additional circumstances as well.[223]

In this regard, agencies should keep in mind the logical distinction between the public interest that can exist in the overall subject matter of a FOIA request (e.g., some matter of significant, perhaps even controversial, agency activity) and the public interest that might or might not be served by disclosure of the actual records that are at hand in that particular FOIA request.[224] For example, the District Court for the District of Columbia, in

---

[222](...continued)
F.3d at 310 (holding that to determine if an "urgency to inform" exists, a court must consider whether the request concerns a "matter of current exigency to the American public," whether the consequences of delaying the response would "compromise a significant recognized interest," whether the request concerns "federal government activity," and "credibility of [the] requester"); Long v. DHS, 436 F. Supp. 2d 38, 43 (D.D.C. 2006) (finding that requester failed to link need for records to "imminent action" that would affect usefulness of records); ACLU v. DOD, No. 06-1698, 2006 WL 1469418, at *7-8 (N.D. Cal. May 25, 2006) (finding that the requesters established a "public's need to know" as well as "urgency of the news" related to a Pentagon intelligence program, and stating that "extensive media interest usually is a fact supporting not negating urgency"); IEEE Spectrum v. Dep't of Justice, No. 05-0865, slip op. at 2 (D.D.C. Feb. 16, 2006) (finding that the requester failed to establish a "'current exigency'" when it merely demonstrated its own desire to publish the requested information, "a self-serving assertion that carries very little weight"); Leadership Conference on Civil Rights, 404 F. Supp. 2d at 260 (finding that "[p]laintiff's FOIA requests could have a vital impact on development of the substantive record" related to the issue of re-authorization of provisions of the Voting Rights Act); Elec. Privacy Info. Ctr. v. DOD, 355 F. Supp. 2d 98, 101 (D.D.C. 2004) (finding that, by demonstrating public interest in only general topic rather than specific subject of its requests, requester failed to demonstrate "urgency to inform"); Tripp, 193 F. Supp. 2d at 241 (holding that plaintiff's "job application to the Marshall Center and the resulting alleged Privacy Act violations by DOD are not the subject of any breaking news story"); FOIA Update, Vol. XIX, No. 4, at 2 (discussing Nazi War Crimes Disclosure Act, 5 U.S.C. § 552 note (2000 & Supp. IV 2004), which does not directly amend the FOIA, but which does "impact[] directly on the FOIA [in that it provides] that any person who was persecuted by the Nazi government of Germany or its allies 'shall be deemed to have a compelling need' under 'section 552(a)(6)(E) of title 5, United States Code'" in making requests for access to classified Nazi war-criminal records (quoting 5 U.S.C. § 552 note, § 4)).

[223] See, e.g., 22 C.F.R. § 171.12(b)(1) (2006) (Department of State regulation under which expedited processing may be granted if "[f]ailure to obtain requested information on an expedited basis could reasonably be expected to . . . harm substantial humanitarian interests").

[224] See FOIA Post, "FOIA Counselor Q&A" (posted 1/24/06).

PROCEDURAL REQUIREMENTS

Electronic Privacy Information Center v. Department of Defense,[225] recently employed such an analysis when deciding whether a public interest organization was entitled to expedited processing, on a "media urgency" basis, of its FOIA request for records relating to the general subject of "data mining."[226] Ruling against the FOIA requester, the court found that the requester had "failed to present the agency with evidence that there is a 'substantial interest' in the 'particular aspect' of [its] FOIA request."[227] In other words, the court said, "[t]he fact that [the requester] has provided evidence that there is some media interest in data mining as an umbrella issue does not satisfy the requirement that [it] demonstrate interest in the specific subject of [its] FOIA request."[228]

Agencies must determine whether to grant a request for expedited access within ten calendar days of its receipt by the proper FOIA office.[229] This is an important obligation that agencies must be sure to bear in mind.[230] Of course, agencies also should make their administrative appeal mechanism available to requesters whenever requests for expedited processing are denied and then act on those administrative appeals in a timely fashion commensurate with the nature of such matters.[231] (For a further

---

[225] 355 F. Supp. 2d 98 (D.D.C. 2004).

[226] Id. at 102.

[227] Id.; see also ACLU of N. Cal. v. Dep't of Justice, No. 04-4447, 2005 WL 588354, at *13 (N.D. Cal. Mar. 11, 2005) (likewise ruling in an "expedited processing" context that "it was not sufficient for the plaintiffs to show [public] interest in only the general subject area of the request").

[228] 355 F. Supp. 2d at 102 (emphasis added); see also FOIA Post, "FOIA Counselor Q&A" (posted 1/24/06) (advising on "the meaning of an 'umbrella issue' under the FOIA," and noting that "[t]he term 'umbrella issue' is a relatively new one that has been used by agencies and courts alike to make important distinctions when considering public interest issues" in FOIA decisionmaking).

[229] 5 U.S.C. § 552(a)(6)(C)(i); see, e.g., 28 C.F.R. § 16.5(d)(ii)(4) (Department of Justice implementing regulation).

[230] FOIA Post, "Executive Order 13,392 Implementation Guidance" (posted 4/27/06) (Part I.11.) (advising that agencies should review their expedited processing practices in order "to ensure that they are fully in compliance with the law and sound policy in this area").

[231] See 28 C.F.R. § 16.6(c) (Department of Justice regulation listing the types of "adverse determinations," including "a denial of a request for expedited treatment," for which the Department's appeal mechanism is made available). But cf. ACLU v. U.S. Dep't of Justice, 321 F. Supp. 2d 24, 29 (D.D.C. 2004) (stating that the requester's failure to appeal an agency's decision denying expedited processing "does not preclude judicial review

(continued...)

discussion of expedited access, see Litigation Considerations, "Open America" Stays of Proceedings, below.)

## Searching for Responsive Records

The adequacy of an agency's search under the FOIA is determined by a test of "reasonableness," which may vary from case to case.[232] As a general rule, an agency must undertake a search that is "reasonably calculated to uncover all relevant documents."[233] The reasonableness of an agency's

---

[231](...continued) of the decision").

[232] See Zemansky v. EPA, 767 F.2d 569, 571-73 (9th Cir. 1985) (observing that reasonableness of agency search depends upon facts of each case (citing Weisberg v. U.S. Dep't of Justice, 705 F.2d 1344, 1351 (D.C. Cir. 1983))).

[233] Weisberg, 705 F.2d at 1351; see, e.g., Williams v. U.S. Dep't of Justice, 177 F. App'x 231, 233 (3d Cir. 2006) (recognizing that an agency "has a duty to conduct a reasonable search for responsive records" (citing Oglesby v. U.S. Dep't of the Army, 920 F.2d 57, 68 (D.C. Cir. 1990))); Johnston v. U.S. Dep't of Justice, No. 97-2173, 1998 WL 518529, at *1 (8th Cir. Aug. 10, 1998) (concluding that agency demonstrated that it conducted search reasonably calculated to uncover all responsive documents); Campbell v. U.S. Dep't of Justice, 164 F.3d 20, 27 (D.C. Cir. 1998) (noting that an agency must search "'using methods which can be reasonably expected to produce the information requested'" (quoting Oglesby v. U.S. Dep't of the Army, 920 F.2d 57, 68 (D.C. Cir. 1990))); Miller v. U.S. Dep't of State, 779 F.2d 1378, 1383 (8th Cir. 1985) (recognizing that search must be "'reasonably calculated to uncover all relevant documents'" (quoting Weisberg, 705 F.2d at 1351)); Corbeil v. U.S. Dep't of Justice, No. 04-2265, 2005 WL 3275910, at *3 (D.D.C. Sept. 26, 2005) (declaring that "an agency's prompt report of the discovery of additional responsive materials may be viewed as evidence of its good faith efforts to comply with its obligations under the FOIA"); Friends of Blackwater v. U.S. Dep't of the Interior, 391 F. Supp. 2d 115, 121 (D.D.C. 2005) (finding that agency's search was inadequate where its declaration did not describe specific search terms used, where agency had evidence that documents existed that originated in leadership office, and where agency did not forward request to leadership office in accordance with agency's regulations requiring such forwarding); Nat'l Inst. of Military Justice v. DOD, 404 F. Supp. 2d 325, 333-34 (D.D.C. 2005) (stating that, standing alone, agency's initial lack of diligence does not rise to level of bad faith, especially given that agency engaged in subsequent search efforts); Van Mechelen v. U.S. Dep't of the Interior, No. 05-5393, 2005 WL 3007121, at *2 (W.D. Wash. Nov. 9, 2005) (recognizing that an "agency must show . . . that it has conducted a search reasonably calculated to uncover all relevant documents" (citing Weisberg, 705 F.2d at 1351)); Jackson v. U.S. Attorney's Office, Dist. of N.J., 362 F. Supp. 2d 39, 42 (D.D.C. 2005) (concluding that agency's search was inadequate where, inter alia, it sought records per-
(continued...)

search depends, in part, on how the agency conducted its search in light of the scope of the request[234] and the requester's description of the records

---

[233](...continued)
taining to requester instead of records pertaining to investigation that requester wanted initiated); Allen v. U.S. Secret Serv., 335 F. Supp. 2d 95, 99 (D.D.C. 2004) (concluding that the agency's search of its "comprehensive [Master Central Index] system is a search method that could be 'reasonably expected to produce the information requested'" (citing Ogelsby, 920 F.2d at 68)); Defenders of Wildlife v. USDA, 311 F. Supp. 2d 44, 55 (D.D.C. 2004) (stating that an agency's "bare assertion that the Deputy Under Secretary saw the FOIA request and that he stated that he had no responsive documents is inadequate because it does not indicate that he performed any search at all"); cf. Comer v. IRS, No. 97-76329, 2000 WL 1566279, at *2 (E.D. Mich. Aug. 17, 2000) ("[T]he government is not required to expend the same efforts under FOIA that it would in response to a litigation-specific document request."). But see Al Najjar v. Ashcroft, No. 00-1472, slip op. at 4-5 (D.D.C. July 22, 2003) (acknowledging that the agency's "affidavit on its face tends to establish the adequacy of the search," yet nonetheless requiring the agency to conduct a further search "in the interest of ensuring a complete resolution of this matter" and in light of the "limited burden" that the further search ostensibly would impose), motion to dismiss or for summary judgment granted as to some agencies (D.D.C. June 28, 2004), case dismissed with prejudice by stipulation (D.D.C. Mar. 31, 2005).

[234] See, e.g., Negley v. FBI, 169 F. App'x 591, 595 (D.C. Cir. 2006) (reversing and remanding because agency did not "clarify whether . . . [pertinent] file references are synonymous, and more important, whether it actually searched" particular file requested); Hayden v. Dep't of Justice, No. 03-5078, 2003 WL 22305071, at *1 (D.C. Cir. Oct. 6, 2003) (per curiam) (rejecting plaintiff's argument that the agency should have searched for records about him in the case file of another individual who was mentioned during his criminal trial, because "[b]ased on [plaintiff's] FOIA requests, the [agency] reasonably limited the scope of its search to [his own] criminal case file"); Coal. on Political Assassinations v. DOD, 12 F. App'x 13, 14 (D.C. Cir. 2001) (recognizing that search conducted using terms derived from "appellant's limited request" obviously would not have produced records that lacked any "apparent connection" to such a narrowly defined request); Voinche v. FBI, No. 96-5304, 1997 U.S. App. LEXIS 19089, at *3 (D.C. Cir. June 19, 1997) (ruling that agency was not obliged to "search for records beyond the scope of the request"); Maynard v. CIA, 986 F.2d 547, 560 (1st Cir. 1993) (finding that agency's search was properly limited to scope of FOIA request, with no requirement that secondary references or variant spellings be checked); Meeropol v. Meese, 790 F.2d 942, 956 (D.C. Cir. 1986) ("[A] search need not be perfect, only adequate, and adequacy is measured by the reasonableness of the effort in light of the specific request."); Knight v. NASA, No. 04-2054, 2006 WL 3780901, at *5 (E.D. Cal. Dec. 21, 2006) (stating that "there is no requirement that an agency search all possible sources in response to a FOIA request when it believes all re-
(continued...)

sought[235] -- particularly if the description includes specific details about the

---

[234](...continued)
sponsive documents are likely to be located in one place"); Askew v. United States, No. 05-00200, 2006 WL 3307469, at *10 (E.D. Ky. Nov. 13, 2006) (rejecting plaintiff's contention that FOIA requires an agency to search another agency's files); Gilchrest v. Dep't of Justice, No. 05-1540, 2006 U.S. Dist. LEXIS 78706, at *10 (D.D.C. Oct. 30, 2006) (stating that it is "not unreasonable" for agency to limit search to record specifically requested where requester sought only one record); Trentadue v. FBI, No. 04-772, slip op. at 20 (D. Utah Mar. 29, 2006) (ordering additional "limited searches" because, in part, agency failed to conduct search using particular acronym "often used" for subject organization); Reyes v. U.S. Customs Serv., No. 05-173, 2006 WL 123928, at *3 (D.D.C. Jan. 17, 2006) (finding that search was adequate where agency searched two systems likely to have responsive records); Wilderness Soc'y v. U.S. Dep't of the Interior, 344 F. Supp. 2d 1, 21 (D.D.C. 2004) (concluding that agency's search was inadequate when agency failed to search Office of Solicitor in response to request for lawsuit and settlement records); Wilderness Soc'y v. U.S. Bureau of Land Mgmt., No. 01-2210, 2003 WL 255971, at *5 (D.D.C. Jan. 15, 2003) (concluding that the agency's search was inadequate because "responsive documents [possibly maintained] in the locations searched may not have been produced as a result of the [agency's] narrow interpretation of plaintiffs' request"); Adams v. FBI, No. 97-2861, slip op. at 7 (D.D.C. Mar. 3, 1999) (finding that requester cannot object to agency's failure to search under aliases not mentioned in request); Rothschild v. Dep't of Energy, 6 F. Supp. 2d 38, 39 (D.D.C. 1998) (declaring that agency is not required to search for records that "do not mention or specifically discuss" subject of request); cf. Russell v. Barr, No. 92-2546, slip op. at 4 (D.D.C. Aug. 28, 1998) (determining that agency searched "all reasonable terms" and "exceeded the call of duty" when "out of an abundance of caution" it searched using subject's maiden name, which was not provided in request).  But see Jefferson v. Bureau of Prisons, No. 05-00848, 2006 WL 3208666, at *6 (D.D.C. Nov. 7, 2006) (finding search not reasonable when agency searched only its Central Records System database, but breadth of request warranted search of "I" drive database); Summers v. U.S. Dep't of Justice, 934 F. Supp. 458, 461 (D.D.C. 1996) (notwithstanding fact that plaintiff's request specifically sought access to former FBI Director J. Edgar Hoover's "commitment calendars," finding agency's search inadequate, as agency did not use additional search terms such as "appointment" or "diary" to locate responsive records); Canning v. U.S. Dep't of Justice, 919 F. Supp. 451, 460-61 (D.D.C. 1994) (indicating that when agency was aware that subject of request used two names, it should have conducted search under both names).

[235] See 5 U.S.C. § 552(a)(3)(A) (2000 & Supp. IV 2004) (statutory provision requiring that a FOIA request "reasonably describe[]" the records sought); see also, e.g., Ledesma v. U.S. Marshals Serv., No. 05-5150, 2006 U.S. App. LEXIS 11218, at *2 (D.C. Cir. Apr. 19, 2006) (finding that search was adequate where requester did not "specifically mention" cellblock video and
(continued...)

circumstances surrounding the agency's creation or maintenance of the records.[236] The reasonableness of an agency's search also can depend on

---

[235](...continued)
agency did not conduct search for video); Domingues v. FBI, No. 98-74612, slip op. at 11 (E.D. Mich. July 24, 1999) (magistrate's recommendation) (determining that "a request directed to an agency's headquarters which does not request a search of its field offices, or which requests a blanket search of all field offices without specifying which offices should be searched, does not 'reasonably describe' any records which may be in those field offices, and an agency's search of just the headquarters records complies with the FOIA"), adopted (E.D. Mich. July 29, 1999), aff'd, 229 F.3d 1151 (6th Cir. 2000) (unpublished table decision); Murphy v. IRS, 79 F. Supp. 2d 1180, 1185-86 (D. Haw. 1999) (holding that the agency "conducted a reasonable search in light of the fact that Plaintiff gave no indication as to what types of files could possibly contain documents responsive to this request or where they might be located"); Bricker v. FBI, No. 97-2742, slip op. at 7 (D.D.C. Mar. 26, 1999) (approving agency search of "files where responsive information would likely be located," given limited information that requester provided about subject of request); Greenberg v. Dep't of Treasury, 10 F. Supp. 2d 3, 13 (D.D.C. 1998) (excusing agency's inability to locate materials "as written" in request because agency records systems "are not indexed in a manner such that responsive records could have been located"); see also Citizens Against UFO Secrecy v. DOD, 21 F. App'x 774, 776 (9th Cir. 2001) (rejecting plaintiff's contention that search using additional terms not found within request was inadequate because agency's use of "extra terms [made] it more likely that responsive documents [would] be located"); cf. Truitt v. Dep't of State, 897 F.2d 540, 544-46 (D.C. Cir. 1990) (stating that when request was "reasonably clear as to the materials desired," agency failed to conduct adequate search as it did not include file likely to contain responsive records); Davidson v. EPA, 121 F. Supp. 2d 38, 39 (D.D.C. 2000) ("Because plaintiff is searching for a specific [record], defendant must, at minimum, explain its procedure for issuing and retaining [such records] and by what reasonable methods it used to locate the one requested by plaintiff."); cf. Kowalczyk v. Dep't of Justice, 73 F.3d 386, 389 (D.C. Cir. 1996) (finding search limited to agency headquarters files reasonable because plaintiff directed his request there).

[236] Valencia-Lucena v. U.S. Coast Guard, 180 F.3d 321, 328 (D.C. Cir. 1999) (finding that because requester provided agency with name of agency employee who possessed requested records during requester's criminal trial, "[w]hen all other sources fail to provide leads to the missing records, agency personnel should be contacted if there is a close nexus, as here, between the person and the particular record"); Afshari v. HHS, No. 05-0826, slip op. at 3 (D.D.C. May 2, 2006) (finding that agency affidavits failed to demonstrate adequate search where they contained no indication of contacting appropriate agency personnel in effort to find missing records); Hardy v. DOD, No. 99-523, 2001 WL 34354945, at *5 (D. Ariz. Aug. 27, 2001) (requiring the agency "to locate the presumably few witnesses who were

(continued...)

the standards that the agency applied in determining where responsive records were likely to be found,[237] especially if the agency fails to locate

---

[236](...continued)
responsible for operating the closed circuit television system, the robots, and any other video sources" that might have created the requested tapes); Comer v. IRS, No. 97-76329, 1999 U.S. Dist. LEXIS 16268, at *3 (E.D. Mich. Sept. 30, 1999) (rejecting agency's assertion that it conducted a reasonable search when plaintiff "listed a small number of specific persons who might have knowledge of [the requested documents] and specific places where they might be found" and the agency did not indicate that it searched there); see also Gilliland v. Bureau of Prisons, No. 03-5251, 2004 WL 885222, at *1 (D.C. Cir. Apr. 23, 2004) (rejecting the requester's claim that the agency "should have contacted the federal officials connected with [the] allegedly missing documents," because his FOIA requests "did not specify these officials or otherwise indicate that they might have responsive records"); Rugerio v. U.S. Dep't of Justice, 257 F.3d 534, 547-48 (6th Cir. 2001) (rejecting plaintiff's contention that the "agent [who] testified against him at trial" must have records about him because agency established that employee who testified had no such records), cert. denied, 534 U.S. 1134 (2002); Vigneau v. O'Brien, No. 99-37ML, slip op. at 5 (D.R.I. Aug. 3, 1999) (magistrate's recommendation) (finding search adequate when agency employee who plaintiff alleged wrote requested records provided affidavit stating that no such records ever existed), adopted (D.R.I. Sept. 9, 1999); cf. Doolittle v. U.S. Dep't of Justice, 142 F. Supp. 2d 281, 285 (N.D.N.Y. 2001) (concluding that so long as description of records sought is otherwise reasonable, agency cannot refuse to search for records simply because requester did not also identify them by the date on which they were created). But see Blanton v. U.S. Dep't of Justice, 182 F. Supp. 2d 81, 85 (D.D.C. 2002) ("[T]he FOIA does not impose an obligation on defendant to contact former employees to determine whether they know of the whereabouts of records that might be responsive to a FOIA request."), aff'd on other grounds, No. 02-5115, 2003 U.S. App. LEXIS 8429 (D.C. Cir. May 1, 2003); cf. Chilingirian v. U.S. Attorney Executive Office, 71 F. App'x 571, 572 (6th Cir. 2003) ("The record shows that defendants went beyond the requirements of a reasonable search by contacting the attorneys who might know of the existence of the [requested] records, even though they were no longer employed by defendants."); Atkin v. IRS, No. 04-0080, 2005 WL 1155127, at *3 (N.D. Ohio Mar. 30, 2005) (stating that "additional efforts to contact a former employee are irrelevant under the appropriate standard of reasonable effort" (citing Chilingirian, 71 F. App'x at 571, 572)).

[237] See Jones-Edwards v. NSA, No. 05-0962, 2006 WL 2620313, at *2 (2d Cir. Sept. 12, 2006) (stating that an "agency is not obliged to conduct a search of records outside its possession or control"); Lechliter v. Rumsfeld, 182 F. App'x 113, 115 (3d Cir. 2006) (stating that an agency "has a duty to conduct a reasonable search for responsive records," and concluding that the agency fulfilled that duty when it searched the two offices that it "determined to be the only ones likely to possess responsive documents" (cit-
(continued...)

records that it has reason to know might well exist,[238] or if the search re-

---

[237](...continued)
ing Oglesby, 920 F.2d at 68)); Jefferson v. Dep't of Justice, 168 F. App'x 448, 450 (D.C. Cir. 2005) (reversing district court's finding of reasonable search when agency "offered no plausible justification" for searching only its investigative database and agency "essentially acknowledged" that responsive files might exist in separate database); Juda v. U.S. Customs Serv., No. 00-5399, 2000 U.S. App. LEXIS 17985, at *2-3 (D.C. Cir. June 19, 2000) (concluding that the agency improperly limited its search to a single database when "the agency itself has identified at least one other record system . . . that is likely to produce the information [plaintiff] requests"); Oglesby, 920 F.2d at 68 (holding that agency may not limit search to one record system if others are likely to contain responsive records); Pac. Fisheries, Inc. v. IRS, No. 04-2436, 2006 WL 1635706, at *2-3 (W.D. Wash. June 1, 2006) (finding that agency's search was adequate when agency sent search queries to people "likely to have responsive documents," but did not ask people if they knew of others who might have responsive documents); Williams v. U.S. Attorney's Office, No. 03-674, 2006 WL 717474, at *5 (N.D. Okla. Mar. 16, 2006) (stating that search obligations under FOIA require agency to search "its own records," not "records of third parties"); Sakamoto v. EPA, 443 F. Supp. 2d 1182, 1198 (N.D. Cal. 2006) (finding agency's search within one region to be adequate when agency "reasonably concluded" that responsive documents would "most likely" be there); Antonelli v. ATF, No. 04-1180, 2006 WL 367893, at *7 (D.D.C. Feb. 16, 2006) (concluding that FBI's search of Central Records System was reasonable and that FBI was not obliged under FOIA to search its computer hard drives for preliminary work product when requester did not specifically request search of FBI's "I" drives); Blanton v. U.S. Dep't of Justice, 63 F. Supp. 2d 35, 41 (D.D.C. 1999) (noting that even though agency did not search individual informant files for references to requester, any responsive information in such files would have been identified by agency's "cross-reference" search using requester's name); Hall v. U.S. Dep't of Justice, 63 F. Supp. 2d 14, 17-18 (D.D.C. 1999) (finding that agency need not search for records concerning subject's husband even though such records may have also included references to subject); Iacoe v. IRS, No. 98-C-0466, 1999 U.S. Dist. LEXIS 12809, at *11 (E.D. Wis. July 23, 1999) (recognizing that the agency "diligently searched for the records requested in those places where [the agency] expected they could be located"); Nation Magazine v. U.S. Customs Serv., No. 94-00808, slip op. at 8, 13-14 (D.D.C. Feb. 14, 1997) (stating that reasonable search did not require agency to search individual's personnel file in effort to locate substantive document drafted by him); cf. Bennett v. DEA, 55 F. Supp. 2d 36, 39-40 (D.D.C. 1999) (holding search inadequate when agency failed to search investigatory files for cases in which subject of request acted as informant, even though agency did not track informant activity by case name, number, or judicial district), appeal dismissed voluntarily, No. 99-5300 (D.C. Cir. Dec. 23, 1999).

[238] Campbell, 164 F.3d at 27 (concluding that a search limited to the
(continued...)

quires the agency's FOIA personnel to distinguish any "personal" records from "agency" records.[239] Nevertheless, an agency's inability to locate every

---

[238](...continued)
agency's central records system was unreasonable because during the search the agency "discovered information suggesting the existence of documents that it could not locate without expanding the scope of its search"); NYC Apparel FZE v. U.S. Customs & Border Prot., No. 02-5130, 2006 WL 167833, at *7 (D.D.C. Jan. 23, 2006) (concluding that the agency must conduct a new search or "submit a supplemental declaration describing in substantially greater detail the procedure by which the FOIA processor" responded to the request); Natural Res. Def. Council, Inc. v. DOD, 388 F. Supp. 2d 1086, 1100-03 (C.D. Cal. 2005) (ordering new search where agency searched only one office and did not forward request to another office that agency knew to be lead office in subject area); Trentadue v. FBI, No. 04-772, slip op. at 5-6 (D. Utah May 5, 2005) (ordering additional search because, in part, agency conducted computer search only, even though agency previously limited ability of field offices to upload documents into computer database); Wolf v. CIA, 357 F. Supp. 2d 112, 119 (D.D.C. 2004) (ordering agency to conduct additional search of broader scope because agency failed to do that even though first search yielded indications that responsive records could be in another file) (appeal pending); Ctr. for Nat'l Security Studies v. U.S. Dep't of Justice, 215 F. Supp. 2d 94, 110 (D.D.C. 2002) (holding that the discovery of a document that "clearly indicates the existence of [other] relevant documents" creates an "obligation" on the agency to conduct a further search for those additional documents), aff'd in part, rev'd in part & remanded on other grounds, 331 F.3d 918 (D.C. Cir. 2003); Tarullo v. DOD, 170 F. Supp. 2d 271, 275 (D. Conn. 2001) (declaring the agency's search inadequate because "[w]hile hypothetical assertions as to the existence of unproduced responsive documents are insufficient to create a dispute of material fact as to the reasonableness of the search, plaintiff here has [himself provided a copy of an agency record] which appears to be responsive to the request"); Loomis v. Dep't of Energy, No. 96-149, 1999 WL 33541935, at *5 (N.D.N.Y. Mar. 9, 1999) (determining search inadequate in light of agency's admission that additional responsive records may exist in location not searched), aff'd, 199 F.3d 1322 (2d Cir. 1999) (unpublished table decision); Kronberg v. U.S. Dep't of Justice, 875 F. Supp. 861, 870-71 (D.D.C. 1995) (holding that search was inadequate when agency did not find records required to be maintained and plaintiff produced documents obtained by other FOIA requesters demonstrating that agency possessed files which may contain records sought); cf. Grace v. Dep't of the Navy, No. 99-4306, 2001 WL 940908, at *5 (N.D. Cal. Aug. 13, 2001) (concluding that although the agency apparently had misplaced the records requested under FOIA, "[d]efendants have discharged their burden [by] making a good faith attempt to locate the missing files"), aff'd, 43 F. App'x 76 (9th Cir. 2002).

[239] See Ethyl Corp. v. EPA, 25 F.3d 1241, 1247-48 (4th Cir. 1994) (citing agency's failure to follow Department of Justice guidance concerning "per-
(continued...)

single responsive record does not undermine an otherwise reasonable search.[240]

---

[239](...continued)
sonal record" considerations in FOIA Update, Vol. V, No. 4, at 3-4); see also Kempker-Cloyd v. U.S. Dep't of Justice, No. 5:97-253, 1999 U.S. Dist. LEXIS 4813, at *12-13 (W.D. Mich. Mar. 12, 1999) (determining that agency acted in bad faith because it failed to review responsive records that agency official asserted were "personal"); cf. Grand Cent. P'ship, Inc. v. Cuomo, 166 F.3d 473, 481 (2d Cir. 1999) (rejecting agency affidavit concerning "personal" records as insufficient, and remanding case for further development through affidavits by records' authors explaining their intended use of records in question).

[240] See Duenas Iturralde v. Comptroller of the Currency, 315 F.3d 311, 315 (D.C. Cir. 2003) ("[I]t is long settled that the failure of an agency to turn up one specific document in its search does not alone render a search inadequate . . . . After all, particular documents may have been accidentally lost or destroyed, or a reasonable and thorough search may have missed them."); Grand Cent. P'ship, 166 F.3d at 489 (declaring that the fact that "some documents were not discovered until a second, more exhaustive, search was conducted does not warrant overturning the district court's ruling" that the agency conducted a reasonable search); Schwarz v. FBI, No. 98-4036, 1998 WL 667643, at *2 (10th Cir. Nov. 5, 1998) (concluding that "the fact that the [agency's] search failed to turn up three documents is not sufficient to contradict the reasonableness of the FBI's search without evidence of bad faith"); Campbell, 164 F.3d at 28 n.6 (holding that "the inadvertent omission of three documents does not render a search inadequate when the search produced hundreds of pages that had been buried in archives for decades"); Citizens Comm'n on Human Rights v. FDA, 45 F.3d 1325, 1328 (9th Cir. 1995) (determining that search was adequate when agency spent 140 hours reviewing relevant files, notwithstanding fact that agency was unable to locate 137 of 1000 volumes of records); Manchester v. FBI, No. 96-0137, 2005 WL 3275802, at *3 (D.D.C. Aug. 9, 2005) (concluding that a "speculative allegation as to the existence of [a record] does not cast doubt on the adequacy of" the search); Campaign for Responsible Transplantation v. FDA, 219 F. Supp. 2d 106, 111 (D.D.C. 2002) (upholding the adequacy of the agency's search by declaring that the agency's belated production of fifty-five additional documents that it located using information contained in plaintiff's summary judgment motion "is a proverbial 'drop in the bucket'" relative to the 27,000 documents that the agency already had provided to plaintiff); cf. W. Ctr. for Journalism v. IRS, 116 F. Supp. 2d 1, 10 (D.D.C. 2000) (concluding that agency conducted reasonable search and acted in good faith by locating and releasing additional responsive records mistakenly omitted from its initial response, because "it is unreasonable to expect even the most exhaustive search to uncover every responsive file; what is expected of a law-abiding agency is that the agency admit and correct error when error is revealed"), aff'd, 22 F. App'x 14 (D.C. Cir. 2001). But see Oglesby v. U.S. Dep't of the Army, 79 F.3d 1172, 1185

(continued...)

Prior to the enactment of the Electronic FOIA amendments, several courts held that agencies do not have to organize or reorganize file systems in order to respond to particular FOIA requests,[241] to write new computer programs to search for "electronic" data not already compiled for agency purposes,[242] or to aggregate computerized data files so as to effectively create new, releasable records.[243] More than one court ruled, though, that agencies may be required to perform relatively simple computer searches to locate requested records, or to demonstrate why such searches are unreasonable in a given case.[244]

---

[240](...continued) (D.C. Cir. 1996) (acknowledging plaintiff's assertion that search was inadequate because of previous FOIA requester's claim that agency provided her with "well over a thousand documents," and holding that claim raises enough doubt to preclude summary judgment in absence of agency affidavit further describing its search); Accuracy in Media v. FBI, No. 97-2107, slip op. at 12 (D.D.C. Mar. 31, 1999) (directing agency to conduct further search for two unaccounted-for documents referenced in documents located by agency's otherwise reasonable search).

[241] See, e.g., Church of Scientology v. IRS, 792 F.2d 146, 150-51 (D.C. Cir. 1986); Miller v. U.S. Dep't of State, 779 F.2d 1378, 1385 (8th Cir. 1986).

[242] See Burlington N. R.R. v. EPA, No. 91-1636, slip op. at 4 (D.D.C. June 15, 1992); Clarke v. U.S. Dep't of the Treasury, No. 84-1873, 1986 WL 1234, at *1 (E.D. Pa. Jan. 24, 1986); see also FOIA Update, Vol. XIII, No. 2, at 3-7 (congressional testimony discussing "electronic record" FOIA issues).

[243] See Yeager v. DEA, 678 F.2d 315, 324 (D.C. Cir. 1982); see also "Department of Justice Report on 'Electronic Record' FOIA Issues" [hereinafter Department of Justice "Electronic Record" Report], reprinted in abridged form in FOIA Update, Vol. XI, No. 2, at 8-21 (discussing use of "computer programming" for FOIA search and processing purposes). But cf. Int'l Diatomite Producers Ass'n v. U.S. Soc. Sec. Admin., No. 92-1634, 1993 WL 137286, at *5 (N.D. Cal. Apr. 28, 1993) (ordering agency to respond to request for specific information, portions of which were maintained in four separate computerized listings, by either compiling new list or redacting existing lists), appeal dismissed, No. 93-16723 (9th Cir. Nov. 1, 1993).

[244] See Thompson Publ'g Group, Inc. v. Health Care Fin. Admin., No. 92-2431, 1994 WL 116141, at *1 (D.D.C. Mar. 15, 1994) (finding that relatively simple computer searches and computer queries are reasonable for data that do not exist "in a single computer 'document' or 'file'"); Belvy v. U.S. Dep't of Justice, No. 94-923, slip op. at 7-9 (S.D. Fla. Dec. 15, 1994) (magistrate's recommendation) (rejecting agency's claim that it did not have to undertake computer search because it failed "to establish that the creation of such a [computer] program would be unreasonable"), adopted (S.D. Fla. Jan. 27, 1995); see also Department of Justice "Electronic Record" Report, reprinted in abridged form in FOIA Update, Vol. XI, No. 2, at 8-17 (discuss-

(continued...)

## PROCEDURAL REQUIREMENTS

Consistent with these latter cases, and to promote electronic database searches, the Electronic FOIA amendments now require agencies to make "reasonable efforts" to search for requested records in electronic form or format "except when such efforts would significantly interfere with the operation of the agency's automated information system."[245] The Electronic

---

[244](...continued)
ing issue of computer programming for search purposes).

[245] Pub. L. No. 104-231, § 5, 110 Stat. 3048, 3050 (codified as amended at 5 U.S.C. § 552(a)(3)(c)); Sun-Sentinel Co. v. DHS, 431 F. Supp. 2d 1258, 1276 (S.D. Fla. 2006) (stating that subsection (a)(3)(C) "addresses problems with searching for records as opposed to producing records," and deciding that evidentiary hearing is needed to determine whether agency's claim of significant interference relates to agency's "inability . . . to search for these records or to produce these records"); see Baker & Hostetler LLP v. U.S. Dep't of Commerce, No. 02-2522, slip op. at 10-11 (D.D.C. Mar. 31, 2004) (finding database restoration would "significantly interfere with the operation of the agency's automated information system" where it would render servers unusable for other functions, and where database restoration attempts could fail due to absence of certain backup tapes), aff'd in pertinent part, No. 05-5185, 2006 WL 3751451 (D.C. Cir. Dec. 22, 2006); Albino v. USPS, No. 01-C-563-C, 2002 WL 32345674, at *7 (W.D. Wis. May 20, 2002) (declaring a search for responsive e-mail messages spanning five years to be inadequate because the agency "did not enlist the help of information technology personnel . . . [who] . . . would have access to e-mail message archives" possibly containing requested records"); Schladetsch v. HUD, No. 99-0175, 2000 WL 33372125, at *5 (D.D.C. Apr. 4, 2000) (rejecting as insufficient agency affidavit that failed to show how creation and use of computer program to perform electronic database search for responsive information would require "unreasonable efforts" or would "substantially interfere" with agency's computer system), appeal dismissed voluntarily, No. 00-5220 (D.C. Cir. Oct. 12, 2000); see also FOIA Update, Vol. XVII, No. 4, at 2 (discussing current electronic search requirements); cf. Hoffman v. U.S. Dep't of Justice, No. 98-1733-A, slip op. at 10-11 (W.D. Okla. Dec. 15, 1999) (finding that an agency is not required to conduct a physical search of records "if other computer-assisted search procedures available to [the] agency are more efficient and serve the same practical purpose of reviewing hard copies of documents"). But see Pub. Citizen, Inc. v. Dep't of Educ., 292 F. Supp. 2d 1, 8 (D.D.C. 2003) ("While a computerized search may well be far more efficient and less costly than a manual search . . . it is apparent [under the facts of this particular case] that only the more cumbersome procedure is likely to turn up the requested information."); cf. Davis v. Dep't of Justice, 460 F.3d 92, 105 (D.C. Cir. 2006) (remanding case "to provide the agency an opportunity to evaluate [search] alternatives" including non-agency Internet search tools); People for the Am. Way Found. v. U.S. Dep't of Justice, No. 04-1421, 2006 WL 2035656, at *8 (D.D.C. July 18, 2006) (ordering an agency to search a nonagency database because that database is "simply a tool to aid in identifying responsive records from [the agency's]
(continued...)

FOIA amendments expressly define the term "search" as meaning "to review, manually or by automated means, agency records for the purpose of locating those records which are responsive to a request."[246] (For a discussion of the litigation aspects of adequacy of search, see Litigation Considerations, Adequacy of Search, below.)

## "Reasonably Segregable" Obligation

The FOIA requires that "any reasonably segregable portion of a record" must be released after appropriate application of the Act's nine exemptions.[247] Agencies should pay particularly close attention to this "reasonably segregable" requirement because courts may closely examine the

---

[245](...continued)
database of case files"); Peltier v. FBI, No. 02-4328, 2005 WL 1009595, at *2 (D. Minn. Apr. 26, 2005) (finding it "inexcusable" that an agency withheld trial transcripts without first placing "a quick phone call to the Clerk's office" to determine whether the documents were publicly available).

[246] Pub. L. No. 104-231, § 5, 110 Stat. 3048, 3050 (codified as amended at 5 U.S.C. § 552(a)(3)(D)); see Dayton Newspapers, Inc. v. Dep't of the Air Force, 35 F. Supp. 2d 1033, 1035 (S.D. Ohio 1998) (preliminary ruling without entry of judgment) (concluding that an estimated fifty-one hours required to "assemble" requested information from an agency database "is a small price to pay" in light of the FOIA's presumption favoring disclosure); see also Schladetsch, No. 99-0175, 2000 WL 33372125, at *5 (D.D.C. Apr. 4, 2000) ("The programming necessary to conduct the [electronic database] search is a search tool and not the creation of a new record."); FOIA Update, Vol. XVIII, No. 1, at 6 (advising that search provisions of Electronic FOIA amendments do not involve record "creation" in Congress's eyes); cf. FOIA Post, "FOIA Counselor Q&A" (posted 1/24/06) (advising that agencies have no obligation to search through "electronic databases [i.e., 'distributed data'] to which [they] have no more than 'read only'" access). But cf. Jennings v. FBI, No. 03-1651, slip op. at 8-9 (D.D.C. May 6, 2004) (finding that agency's search was adequate even when "faulty computer mechanism" rendered identifiable tape recordings of telephone conversations irretrievable); Burns v. U.S. Dep't of Justice, No. 99-3173, slip op. at 2 (D.D.C. Feb. 5, 2001) (concluding that an agency need not search through reel-to-reel audiotapes containing requested recorded conversations, because "the equipment on which these reels could be played has broken and [has been] replaced with other, incompatible equipment," and the agency is "not required to obtain new equipment to process [p]laintiff's FOIA request"); Lepelletier v. FDIC, No. 96-1363, transcript at 8 (D.D.C. Mar. 3, 2000) (refusing to require agency to undertake "an enormous effort that may not even work to try to convert [obsolete] computer files that nobody knows how to read now to provide information that [plaintiff] would like to have"), appeal dismissed as moot, 23 F. App'x 4 (D.C. Cir. 2001).

[247] 5 U.S.C. § 552(b) (2000 & Supp. IV 2004) (sentence immediately following exemptions).

propriety of agency segregability determinations,[248] even if the requester does not raise the issue of segregability at the administrative level or before the court.[249] Accordingly, an agency must adequately demonstrate to

---

[248] See, e.g., Patterson v. IRS, 56 F.3d 832, 840 (7th Cir. 1995) (finding that an agency is certainly not entitled to withhold an entire document if only "portions" contain exempt information); Wightman v. ATF, 755 F.2d 979, 983 (1st Cir. 1985) (holding that detailed "process of segregation" is not unreasonable for request involving thirty-six document pages); Bristol-Myers Co. v. FTC, 424 F.2d 935, 938 (D.C. Cir. 1970) (stating that the "statutory scheme does not permit a bare claim of confidentiality to immunize agency [records] from scrutiny" in their entireties); ACLU v. FBI, 429 F. Supp. 2d 179, 193 (D.D.C. 2006) (finding that agency did not establish that factual portions of e-mail messages were inextricably intertwined with material exempt as deliberative); Dean v. FDIC, 389 F. Supp. 2d 780, 793 (E.D. Ky. 2005) (finding that agency failed to meet segregability burden when it withheld documents in entirety and it then declared that documents would be "unintelligible" if disclosed after redaction); Perry-Torres v. U.S. Dep't of State, 404 F. Supp. 2d 140, 144-45 (D.D.C. 2005) (ordering the agency to submit a renewed motion for summary judgment and an affidavit that includes a segregability explanation that "[a]t a minimum . . . should state that a line-by-line analysis of [the documents' ten pages] was conducted and that no information can reasonably be segregated"); Dorsett v. U.S. Dep't of the Treasury, No. 00-1730, slip op. at 25-26 (D.D.C. Mar. 10, 2004) (finding that agency's segregability demonstration was "wholly insufficient" as it failed to include descriptions of line-by-line or even page-by-page segregability reviews); see also FOIA Update, Vol. XIV, No. 3, at 11-12 ("OIP Guidance: The 'Reasonable Segregation' Obligation" (citing, e.g., Schiller v. NLRB, 964 F.2d 1205 (D.C. Cir 1992))).

[249] See, e.g., Trans-Pac. Policing Agreement v. U.S. Customs Serv., 177 F.3d 1022, 1028 (D.C. Cir. 1999) (indicating that district court had affirmative duty to consider reasonable segregability even though requester never sought segregability finding administratively or before district court); Isley v. Executive Office for U.S. Attorneys, No. 98-5098, 1999 WL 1021934, at *7 (D.C. Cir. Oct. 21, 1999) (remanding case to district court for segregability finding even though neither party raised segregability issue in district court); see also Kimberlin v. Dep't of Justice, 139 F.3d 944, 951 (D.C. Cir. 1998) (affirming application of exemption but nevertheless remanding case to district court for finding on segregability); Krikorian v. Dep't of State, 984 F.2d 461, 467 (D.C. Cir. 1993) (affirming general application of exemption but nevertheless remanding to district court for finding as to segregability); Schreibman v. U.S. Dep't of Commerce, 785 F. Supp. 164, 166 (D.D.C. 1991) (holding that segregation required for computer vulnerability assessment withheld under Exemption 2). But see Nicolaus v. FBI, 24 F. App'x 807, 808 (9th Cir. 2001) (concluding that plaintiff's "argument that the district court failed to make adequate factual findings concerning the segregability of documents is waived for failure to present it in his opening brief"); cf. Becker v. IRS, 34 F.3d 398, 406 (7th Cir. 1994) (noting that the district court's

(continued...)

the court that all reasonably segregable, nonexempt information -- perhaps even including individual numbers contained within multiple-digit codes[250] -- was disclosed.[251] If, however, an agency determines that nonexempt ma-

---

[249](...continued)
failure to make a segregability determination did not necessitate remand because it "did not simply rely on [agency] affidavits describing the documents, but conducted an in camera review").

[250] See Trans-Pac., 177 F.3d at 1027-28 (going so far as to remand case to district court for determination of releasability of "four or six digits" of ten-digit numbers withheld in full). But see Aftergood v. CIA, No. 02-1146, slip op. at 4 n.1 (D.D.C. Feb. 6, 2004) ("Because the plaintiff seeks the disclosure of a single [budget] number, the court concludes that it would be impossible to segregate information from this request."), motion to alter or amend judgment denied, 2004 U.S. Dist. LEXIS 27035, at *8 (D.D.C. Sept. 29, 2004); cf. Students Against Genocide v. Dep't of State, 257 F.3d 828, 837 (D.C. Cir. 2001) (declaring that an agency is not obligated to segregate and release images from classified photographs by "produc[ing] new photographs at a different resolution in order to mask the [classified] capabilities of the reconnaissance systems that took them"); Ho v. Dir., Executive Office for U.S. Attorneys, No. 00-1759, slip op. at 2 (D.D.C. Sept. 17, 2001) (concluding that it was not reasonable to segregate and release to first-party requester any portion of privacy-protected records that did not mention him); Emerson v. CIA, No. 99-0274, slip op. at 13-14 (D.D.C. May 8, 2000) ("Plaintiff's request [for records about three individuals] is not one for which redacted responses would adequately protect th[ose] individuals' privacy."); Schrecker v. U.S. Dep't of Justice, 74 F. Supp. 2d 26, 32 (D.D.C. 1999) (finding that confidential informant "source codes and symbols are assigned in such a specific manner that no portion of the code is reasonably segregable"), rev'd & remanded in part on other grounds, 254 F.3d 162 (D.C. Cir. 2001); Rockwell Int'l Corp. v. U.S. Dep't of Justice, No. 98-761, slip op. at 15-16 (D.D.C. Mar. 24, 1999) (rejecting plaintiff's unsupported assertion that documents withheld by defendant agency in full "must" contain segregable information, because "the documents at issue here are not of the type that are likely to contain" such information), aff'd, 235 F.3d 598 (D.C. Cir. 2001).

[251] See Judicial Watch, Inc. v. Dep't of Justice, 432 F.3d 366, 371-72 (D.C. Cir. 2005) (holding that Exemption 5 protects from disclosure attorney work-product documents in full, including factual portions, and that factual portions are not subject to segregability); Davin v. U.S. Dep't of Justice, 60 F.3d 1043, 1052 (3d Cir. 1995) ("The statements regarding segregability are wholly conclusory, providing no information that would enable [plaintiff] to evaluate the FBI's decisions to withhold."); Schiller v. NLRB, 964 F.2d 1205, 1209-10 (D.C. Cir. 1992) (noting that agency's affidavit referred to withholding of "documents, not information," and remanding for specific finding as to segregability); Geronimo v. Executive Office for U.S. Attorneys, No. 05-1057, 2006 WL 1992625, at *7 (D.D.C. July 14, 2006) (concluding that "categorical treatment" of document withheld in full under Exemption 7(C)

(continued...)

**PROCEDURAL REQUIREMENTS**

terial is so "inextricably intertwined" that disclosure of it would "leave only essentially meaningless words and phrases," then the entire record may be withheld.[252]

---

[251](...continued)
"raises doubt as to whether . . . document was properly reviewed for segregability"); Nat'l Sec. Archive Fund, Inc. v. CIA, 402 F. Supp. 2d 211, 221-22 (D.D.C. 2005) (concluding that agency's declaration "[t]aken in its entirety" shows that 2004 National Intelligence Estimate (NIE) on Iraq is summarization of classified material, and that the NIE contains no "segregable portions that might sensibly be released"); Manchester, 2005 WL 3275802, at *4 (finding that agency's declarations describing "extensive efforts" and its declarations' coded attachments show that agency met segregability obligations); Mokhiber v. U.S. Dep't of the Treasury, 335 F. Supp. 2d 65, 70 (D.D.C. 2004) (granting plaintiff's motion for summary judgment when agency declarations failed to show that agency "even attempted" to meet segregability obligations); Shacket v. United States, 339 F. Supp. 2d 1092, 1095-96 (S.D. Cal. 2004) (concluding that agency need not segregate factual material from records of nonattorney investigator that are exempt from disclosure under attorney work-product privilege); Neely v. FBI, No. 7:97-0786, Order at 1 (W.D. Va. Jan. 25, 1999) (finding that agency applied exemptions "in a wholesale fashion" and without adequate explanation), vacated & remanded on other grounds, 208 F.3d 461 (4th Cir. 2000); Carlton v. Dep't of the Interior, No. 97-2105, slip op. at 12 (D.D.C. Sept. 3, 1998) (requiring defendant agencies to provide further explanation of exemptions applied because agencies made "only a general statement that the withheld documents do not contain segregable portions"), appeal dismissed voluntarily, No. 98-5518 (D.C. Cir. Nov. 18, 1998); Church of Scientology v. IRS, 816 F. Supp. 1138, 1162 (W.D. Tex. 1993) ("The burden is on the agency to prove the document cannot be segregated for partial release."); cf. Anderson v. CIA, 63 F. Supp. 2d 28, 30 (D.D.C. 1999) (declining, "especially in the highly classified context of this case," to "infer from the absence of the word 'segregable' [in the agency's affidavit] that segregability was possible").

[252] Neufeld v. IRS, 646 F.2d 661, 663 (D.C. Cir. 1981); see, e.g., Local 3, Int'l Bhd. of Elec. Workers v. NLRB, 845 F.2d 1177, 1179 (2d Cir. 1988); Mead Data Cent., Inc. v. U.S. Dep't of the Air Force, 566 F.2d 242, 261 (D.C. Cir. 1977); see also Yeager v. DEA, 678 F.2d 315, 322 n.16 (D.C. Cir. 1982) (concluding that it was appropriate to consider "intelligibility" of document and burden imposed by editing and segregation of nonexempt matters); Swope v. U.S. Dep't of Justice, 439 F. Supp. 2d 1, 7 (D.D.C. 2006) (concluding that the requester's portion of recorded telephone calls "could not be reasonably segregated" where the agency "lacks the technical capability" to segregate information that is digitally recorded); Berman v. CIA, 378 F. Supp. 2d 1209, 1222 (E.D. Cal. 2005) (finding that Presidential Daily Briefs (PDBs) do not contain reasonably segregable information, as "the PDB is itself an intelligence method" because intelligible but unclassified information in the PDB "is part of a mosaic of PDB information that could provide

(continued...)

It is important to remember that while the FOIA's segregability requirement applies to all FOIA exemptions generally, it certainly does not apply to the factual portions of records that are wholly exempt under the attorney work-product privilege of Exemption 5.[253] The Court of Appeals for the D.C. Circuit recently reiterated "clear" and longstanding case law in stating that "factual material is itself privileged when it appears within documents that are attorney work product."[254] The D.C. Circuit's opinion reversed a district court order that had directed the Department of Justice to conduct a segregability analysis of documents that the district court it-

---

[252](...continued)
damaging insight" into intelligence practices and "the presidential communications privilege applies to documents in their entireties"); Jones v. DEA, No. 04-1690, 2005 WL 1902880, at *4 (D.D.C. July 13, 2005) (concluding that court could not make finding regarding segregability where record was not clear as to what exemptions agency was invoking); Pendergrass v. U.S. Dep't of Justice, No. 04-112, 2005 WL 1378724, at *6 (D.D.C. June 7, 2005) (finding that requester's portion of recorded telephone conversation with attorney is inextricably intertwined with attorney's portion of conversation, which is exempt from disclosure); W & T Offshore, Inc. v. U.S. Dep't of Commerce, No. 03-2285, 2004 WL 2115418, at *3 (E.D. La. Sept. 21, 2004) (recognizing that "some factual materials will fall within the deliberative process exemption if the manner in which the facts were selected would reveal the deliberative process or if the facts are inextricably intertwined with the policy-making process"); Warren v. Soc. Sec. Admin., No. 98-0116, 2000 WL 1209383, at *5 (W.D.N.Y. Aug. 22, 2000) (refusing to order segregation of standard forms containing personal information because "if the [agency] were to redact the requested documents in a manner that would remove all exempted . . . information, the resulting materials would be little more than templates"), aff'd in pertinent part, 10 F. App'x 20 (2d Cir. 2001); Eagle Horse v. FBI, No. 92-2357, slip op. at 5-6 (D.D.C. July 28, 1995) (finding disclosure of polygraph examination -- after protecting sensitive structure, pattern, and sequence of questions -- was not feasible without reducing product to "unintelligible gibberish").

[253] Judicial Watch, Inc. v. Dep't of Justice, 432 F.3d 366, 371-72 (D.C. Cir. 2005) (holding that Exemption 5 protects from disclosure attorney work-product documents in full, including factual portions, and that such portions are not subject to segregability); Shacket, 339 F. Supp. 2d at 1095-96 (concluding that agency need not segregate factual material from records of nonattorney investigator that are exempt from disclosure under attorney work-product privilege); see also FOIA Update, Vol. V, No. 4 ("FOIA Counselor: The Breadth of Work-Product Protection"). But cf. Mone v. Dep't of the Navy, 353 F. Supp. 2d 193, 196 (D. Mass. 2005) (ordering in camera review of work-product document, mistakenly, to determine if it contained segregable material).

[254] Judicial Watch, Inc., 432 F.3d at 371 (distilling quotations from Tax Analysts v. IRS, 117 F.3d 607, 620 (D.C. Cir. 1997), and Martin v. Office of Special Counsel, 819 F.2d 1181, 1187 (D.C. Cir. 1987)).

self found were properly exempt under Exemption 5 through the attorney work-product privilege.[255] In reversing this case, the D.C. Circuit stated that "the District Court's principal error was in conflating the deliberative process privilege and the attorney work-product doctrine."[256] This D.C. Circuit ruling makes it clear that an agency need not segregate factual portions from documents that are entirely exempt from disclosure under the attorney work-product privilege.[257] (For a further discussion of the applicability of protections under the attorney work-product privilege, see Exemption 5, Attorney Work-Product Privilege, below.)

In cases involving a large amount of records or an unreasonably high-cost, "line-by-line" review, agencies may withhold small segments of nonexempt data "if the proportion of nonexempt factual material is relatively small and is so interspersed with exempt material that separation by the agency and policing by the courts would impose an inordinate burden."[258]

---

[255] See Judicial Watch, Inc., 432 F.3d at 372.

[256] Id. at 371-72.

[257] See id.

[258] Lead Indus. Ass'n v. OSHA, 610 F.2d 70, 86 (2d Cir. 1979); see, e.g., FlightSafety Servs. Corp. v. Dep't of Labor, 326 F.3d 607, 613 (5th Cir. 2003) (per curiam) (reasoning that further segregation was not reasonable because "any disclosable information is so inextricably intertwined with the exempt, confidential information that producing it would require substantial agency resources and produce a document of little informational value"); Solar Sources, Inc. v. United States, 142 F.3d 1033, 1039 (7th Cir. 1998) (finding that because agency would require eight work-years to identify all nonexempt documents in millions of pages of files, the very small percentage of documents that could be released were not "reasonably segregable"); Doherty v. U.S. Dep't of Justice, 775 F.2d 49, 53 (2d Cir. 1985) ("The fact that there may be some nonexempt matter in documents which are predominantly exempt does not require the district court to undertake the burdensome task of analyzing approximately 300 pages of documents, line-by-line."); Neufeld, 646 F.2d at 666 (holding that segregation is not required when it "would impose significant costs on the agency and produce an edited document of little informational value"); Wilson v. DEA, 414 F. Supp. 2d 5, 15 (D.D.C. 2006) (finding without explanation that the agency "fulfilled its segregability obligation" even when it withheld in full one document rather than "undergo the time and expense of redacting all the information on that page except the [requester's] name"); Assassination Archives & Research Ctr. v. CIA, 177 F. Supp. 2d 1, 9 (D.D.C. Oct. 24, 2001) (declining to order the agency to segregate nonexempt information from documents withheld in full, because "[t]he necessary redaction would require the agency to commit significant time and resources to a task that would yield a product with little, if any, informational value"), aff'd, 334 F.3d 55 (D.C. Cir. 2003); Journal of Commerce v. U.S. Dep't of the Treasury, No. 86-1075, 1988 U.S.

(continued...)

Agencies nonetheless may make discretionary disclosures of exempt information, but should do so only upon "full and deliberate consideration of the . . . interests that could be implicated by disclosure of the information.[259] (For a discussion of discretionary disclosure, see Discretionary Disclosure and Waiver, below; for a further discussion of segregability, see Litigation Considerations, "Reasonably Segregable" Requirements, below.)

## Referrals and Consultations

When an agency locates records responsive to a FOIA request, it should determine whether any of those records, or information contained in those records, originated with another agency or agency component.[260] As a matter of sound administrative practice, an agency should consult with any other agency or other agency component whose information appears in the responsive records, especially if that other agency or component is better able to determine whether the information is exempt from disclosure.[261] An agency may also consult with any other agency that holds an equity in, or special expertise or knowledge concerning, a particular type of information.[262] If the response to the consultation is delayed, the agency or compo

---

[258](...continued)
Dist. LEXIS 17610, at *21 (D.D.C. Mar. 30, 1988) (finding that segregation was "neither useful, feasible nor desirable" when it would compel the agency "to pour through [literally millions of pages of documents] to segregate nonexempt material [and] would impose an immense administrative burden . . . that would in the end produce little in the way of useful nonexempt material"). But see Rugerio v. U.S. Dep't of Justice, 234 F. Supp. 2d 697, 707-09 (E.D. Mich. 2002) (concluding that "[i]n this case, the burden of segregation does not outweigh the significant value of the information to Plaintiff because it does not appear that the Government would have to expend a large amount of additional time and resources to provide Plaintiff with the segregable information" from 364 pages).

[259] Attorney General's Memorandum for Heads of All Departments and Agencies Regarding the Freedom of Information Act (Oct. 12, 2001), reprinted in FOIA Post (posted 10/15/01).

[260] Accord 5 U.S.C. § 552(a)(6)(B)(iii) (2000 & Supp. IV 2004).

[261] See, e.g., 28 C.F.R. § 16.4(c)(1) (2006) (Department of Justice regulation concerning consultations).

[262] See, e.g., White House Memorandum for Heads of Executive Departments and Agencies Concerning Safeguarding Information Related to Homeland Security (Mar. 19, 2002), reprinted in FOIA Post (posted 3/21/02) (directing all federal departments and agencies, in accordance with accompanying memorandum from the Information Security Oversight Office and the Office of Information and Privacy, to "consult with . . . the Department of Energy's Office of Security if the [requested] information concerns
(continued...)

PROCEDURAL REQUIREMENTS

nent in receipt of the FOIA request should notify the requester that a supplemental response will follow when the consultation is completed.[263]

If an agency or component locates entire records originating with another agency or component, it should refer those records to their originator for its direct response to the requester.[264] The referring agency or component ordinarily should advise the requester of the referral and of the name of the agency FOIA office to which it was made.[265] Some agencies have streamlined their practices of continually referring certain routine records or classes of records to other agencies or components by establishing standard processing protocols and agreements between them.[266]

---

[262](...continued)
nuclear or radiological weapons").

[263] See FOIA Update, Vol. XII, No. 3, at 3-4 ("OIP Guidance: Referral and Consultation Procedures"); see also FOIA Update, Vol. XIV, No. 3, at 6-8 (Department of Justice memorandum setting forth White House consultation process in which agency retains responsibility for responding to requester regarding any White House-originated records or White House-originated information located within scope of FOIA request that agency has received).

[264] See FOIA Update, Vol. XII, No. 3, at 3-4; FOIA Update, Vol. IV, No. 3, at 5; see also, e.g., Rzeslawski v. U.S. Dep't of Justice, No. 97-1156, slip op. at 6 (D.D.C. July 23, 1998) (observing that an agency's "referral procedure is generally faster than attempting to make an independent determination regarding disclosure" and that "by placing the request in the hands of the originating agency, discretionary disclosure is more likely"), aff'd, No. 00-5029, 2000 WL 621299 (D.C. Cir. Apr. 4, 2000); Stone v. Def. Investigative Serv., No. 91-2013, 1992 WL 52560, at *1 (D.D.C. Feb. 24, 1992) (recognizing that agencies may refer responsive records to originating agencies in responding to FOIA requests), aff'd, 978 F.2d 744 (D.C. Cir. 1992) (unpublished table decision); 28 C.F.R. § 16.4(c)(2) (Department of Justice regulation containing referral and consultation procedures). But cf. Maydak v. U.S. Dep't of Justice, 254 F. Supp. 2d 23, 40 (D.D.C. 2003) (noting that the agency's referral of records requested under the FOIA to an entity that is not subject to the FOIA -- a United States Probation Office -- "raises a genuine legal issue about the propriety" of the agency's action).

[265] See FOIA Update, Vol. XII, No. 2, at 6. But see id. (warning agencies not to notify requesters of identities of other agencies to which record referrals are made, in any exceptional case in which so doing would reveal sensitive abstract fact about record's existence).

[266] See, e.g., 28 C.F.R. § 16.4(h) (Department of Justice regulation authorizing its components to make agreements with other components or agencies to eliminate need for consultations or referrals for particular types of records).

All agencies should remember, however, that even after they make such record referrals in response to FOIA requests, they retain the responsibility of defending any agency action taken on those records if the matter proceeds to litigation.[267] Additionally, agencies receiving referrals should handle them on a "first-in, first-out" basis among their other FOIA requests -- but they should be sure to do so according to the date of the request's initial receipt at the referring agency, lest FOIA requesters be placed at an unfair timing disadvantage through agency referral practices.[268]

---

[267] See, e.g., Peralta v. U.S. Attorney's Office, 136 F.3d 169, 175 (D.C. Cir. 1998) (remanding case for further consideration of whether referral of FBI documents to FBI resulted in "improper withholding" of documents), on remand, 69 F. Supp. 2d 21, 29 (D.D.C. 1999) (holding that Executive Office for United States Attorneys' referral of documents to FBI was not improper); Williams v. FBI, No. 92-5176, 1993 WL 157679, at *1 (D.C. Cir. May 7, 1993) (illustrating that in litigation referring agency is nevertheless required to justify withholding of record that was referred to another agency); Hronek v. DEA, 16 F. Supp. 2d 1260, 1272 (D. Or. 1998) (noting that with respect to records referred to nonparty agencies "the ultimate responsibility for a full response lies with the [referring] agencies"), aff'd, 7 F. App'x 591 (9th Cir. 2001); see also FOIA Update, Vol. XV, No. 3, at 6 (advising on proper litigation practice for defending referrals of records to other agencies); cf. Goldstein v. Office of Indep. Counsel, No. 87-2028, 1999 WL 570862, at *14 (D.D.C. July 29, 1999) (magistrate's recommendation) (requiring referring agency to ask agency receiving referral to provide court with its position concerning releasability of records referred); Grove v. Dep't of Justice, 802 F. Supp. 506, 518 (D.D.C. 1992) (declaring that agency may not use "'consultation' as its reason for a deletion, without asserting a valid exemption").

[268] See FOIA Update, Vol. XV, No. 3, at 6 (observing that a requester should "receive her rightful place in line as of the date upon which her request was received," and advising likewise regarding "consultation" practices (citing Freeman v. Dep't of Justice, 822 F. Supp. 1064, 1067 (S.D.N.Y. 1993))); cf. Or. Natural Desert Ass'n v. Gutierrez, 409 F. Supp. 2d 1237, 1250 (D. Or. 2006) (concluding that the agency's referral regulation "does not significantly impair the ability to get records" and that that regulation is "reasonable"); Snyder v. CIA, 230 F. Supp. 2d 17, 26 (D.D.C. 2002) (concluding that the delayed response to plaintiff's request, which was caused by the agency's referral of records to another agency, did not constitute an improper withholding of the referred records); Boyd v. U.S. Marshals Serv., No. 99-2712, slip op. at 5-6 (D.D.C. Mar. 30, 2001) (approving agency's referral of records to originating agencies, because that referral "was done in accordance with agency regulation . . . and does not appear to have impaired plaintiff's ability to gain access to these records"), appeal dismissed for lack of juris., No. 01-5306, 2001 WL 1488181 (D.C. Cir. Oct. 10, 2001); Williams v. United States, 932 F. Supp. 354, 357 & n.7 (D.D.C. 1996) (urging the agency to set up an "express lane" for referred records so as to not "tie up other agencies by taking an inordinate period of time to review referred records [and] unnecessarily inhibit the smooth functioning of the [other]

(continued...)

**PROCEDURAL REQUIREMENTS**

It should be noted that if an agency or component determines that it does not maintain any record responsive to a particular FOIA request, that agency generally is under no obligation to "forward" that request to any other agency or component where such records might be located.[269] An agency must, however, undertake such a step of request "forwarding" (which is distinct from record "referral") if it has obligated itself to do so by creating such a required practice through its own FOIA regulations.[270] As a matter of administrative discretion, though, the agency may advise the requester of the name and address of such other agency.[271] Finally, as a matter of sound administrative practice, agencies should ensure that their referral and consultation procedures and practices are in keeping with Executive Order 13,392's mandate that agencies administer the FOIA with a "citizen-centered and results-oriented approach."[272]

---

[268](...continued) agencies' well oiled FOIA processing systems").

[269] See Hardy v. DOD, No. 99-523, 2001 WL 34354945, at *10 (D. Ariz. Aug. 27, 2001) (holding that an agency was not obligated to forward to OPM a FOIA request for personnel records that the agency did not maintain itself).

[270] See Friends of Blackwater v. U.S. Dep't of the Interior, 391 F. Supp. 2d 115, 122 (D.D.C. 2005); see also FOIA Post, "FOIA Counselor Q&A" (posted 1/24/06) (discussing referral obligations in light of Friends of Blackwater, and also emphasizing explicitly that "[t]he 'forwarding' of a FOIA request . . . involves nothing more than the discretionary transmittal of the request . . . [whereas a] 'referral' under the FOIA . . . involves the transfer of responsibility for processing certain requested records to an agency that originated those particular records, which usually involves only part of the responsibility for an entire FOIA request").

[271] Accord Presidential Memorandum for Heads of Departments and Agencies Regarding the Freedom of Information Act, 29 Weekly Comp. Pres. Doc. 1999 (Oct. 4, 1993) [hereinafter Presidential FOIA Memorandum], reprinted in FOIA Update, Vol. XIV, No. 3, at 3 ("[A]gencies should handle requests for information in a customer-friendly manner."); cf. Conteh v. FBI, No. 01-1330, slip op. at 4-5 (D.D.C. Apr. 1, 2002) (concluding that the response of an agency whose regulations require a requester to send separate requests to each individual field office that is believed to maintain responsive records was inadequate because the agency could have informed the requester of the existence and location of records maintained by two of its field offices "so that [the] plaintiff could direct his request to [those] offices pursuant to the [agency's] regulations"). But see also FOIA Update, Vol. XII, No. 2, at 6 (advising that in undertaking such requester communications agencies must take care not to compromise special secrecy interests and concerns held by law enforcement and intelligence agencies).

[272] Exec. Order No. 13,392, Sec. 1(d), 70 Fed. Reg. 75,373 (Dec. 14, 2005) (continued...)

## Responding to FOIA Requests

The FOIA provides that each agency "shall make [its disclosable] records promptly available" upon request.[273] Although the D.C. Circuit has suggested that an agency is not required to make requested records available by mailing copies of them to a FOIA requester if the agency prefers to make the "responsive records available in one central location for [the requester's] perusal," such as in a "reading room,"[274] the Department of Justice strongly advises agencies to decline to follow such a practice unless the requester prefers it as well.[275] However, agencies certainly may require

---

[272](...continued)
(stating that "[a] citizen-centered and results-oriented approach will improve service and performance, thereby strengthening compliance with the FOIA, and will help avoid disputes and related litigation"); see also FOIA Post, "Executive Order 13,392 Implementation Guidance" (posted 4/27/06) (Part I.16.) (stating that record-referral area of FOIA administration "warrants careful consideration" by agencies); id. (Part I.17.) (stating that administrative FOIA practice of consulting with other agencies is "deserving of considerable remedial attention" as "consultations have been known to consume large amounts of time and to contribute to agency backlogs of pending requests").

[273] 5 U.S.C. § 552(a)(3)(A) (2000 & Supp. IV 2004).

[274] Oglesby v. U.S. Dep't of the Army, 920 F.2d 57, 70 (D.C. Cir. 1990); cf. Chamberlain v. U.S. Dep't of Justice, 957 F. Supp. 292, 296 (D.D.C.) (holding that FBI's offer to make "visicorder charts" available to requester for review at FBI Headquarters met FOIA requirements due to exceptional fact that charts could be damaged if photocopied), summary affirmance granted, 124 F.3d 1309 (D.C. Cir. 1997) (unpublished table decision); Antonelli v. ATF, No. 04-1180, 2006 WL 3147675, at *2 (D.D.C. Nov. 1, 2006) (finding that agency satisfied FOIA's requirements by making available for viewing inmate requester's presentence report).

[275] See FOIA Update, Vol. XII, No. 2, at 5 ("OIP Guidance: Procedural Rules Under the D.C. Circuit's Oglesby Decision") (recognizing that "the effective administration of the FOIA relies quite heavily upon agency transmittal of disclosable record copies to FOIA requesters by mail"); see also Comer v. IRS, No. 97-76329, 1999 U.S. Dist. LEXIS 16268, at *3 (E.D. Mich. Sept. 30, 1999) (observing that although "FOIA does not require agencies to provide members of the public with information they can access themselves . . . [t]he Court is perplexed . . . why [defendant] refuses to simply copy this information and send it to plaintiff so long as he is willing to pay for the copies"); accord Presidential FOIA Memorandum, reprinted in FOIA Update, Vol. XIV, No. 3, at 3 ("[A]gencies should handle requests for information . . . [with no] unnecessary bureaucratic hurdles."); cf. Defenders of Wildlife v. U.S. Dep't of the Interior, 314 F. Supp. 2d 1, 10 (D.D.C. 2004) (opining that if an agency maintains duplicate copies of a document re-
(continued...)

requesters to pay any fees owed before releasing the processed records; otherwise, agencies "would effectively be bankrolling search and review, and duplicating expenses because there would never be any assurance whatsoever that payment would ever be made once the requesters had the documents in their hands."[276]

The FOIA does not provide for limited disclosure; rather, it "speaks in terms of disclosure and nondisclosure [and] ordinarily does not recognize degrees of disclosure, such as permitting viewing, but not copying, of documents."[277] Moreover, "[t]here is no mechanism under FOIA for a protective order allowing only the requester to see [the requested information] or for proscribing its general dissemination."[278] In short, "once there is disclosure,

---

[275](...continued) quested under the FOIA, then the agency need only provide one such copy in its response to the request, because "it would be illogical and wasteful to require an agency to produce multiple copies of the exact same document").

[276] Strout v. U.S. Parole Comm'n, 842 F. Supp. 948, 951 (E.D. Mich.), aff'd, 40 F.3d 136 (6th Cir. 1994); see also Taylor v. U.S. Dep't of the Treasury, No. A-96-CA-933, 1996 U.S. Dist. LEXIS 19909, at *5 (W.D. Tex. Dec. 17, 1996); Trueblood v. U.S. Dep't of the Treasury, 943 F. Supp. 64, 68 (D.D.C. 1996) (recognizing that agency may require payment before sending processed records); Putnam v. U.S. Dep't of Justice, 880 F. Supp. 40, 42 (D.D.C. 1995) (allowing agency to require payment of current and outstanding fees before releasing records); Crooker v. ATF, 882 F. Supp. 1158, 1162 (D. Mass. 1995) (finding no obligation to provide records until current and past-due fees are paid); cf. FOIA Post, "NTIS: An Available Means of Record Disclosure" (posted 8/30/02; supplemented 9/23/02) (advising that records that an agency chooses to distribute through the National Technical Information Service will be subject to that entity's statutorily based fee schedule, which "supersedes" the FOIA's fee provisions pursuant to 5 U.S.C. § 552(a)(4)(A)(vi)).

[277] Julian v. U.S. Dep't of Justice, 806 F.2d 1411, 1419 n.7 (9th Cir. 1986), aff'd, 486 U.S. 1 (1988); see NARA v. Favish, 541 U.S. 157, 172 (recognizing that information disclosed under FOIA "belongs to citizens to do with as they choose"), reh'g denied, 541 U.S. 1057 (2004); Berry v. Dep't of Justice, 733 F.2d 1343, 1355 n.19 (9th Cir. 1984); see also Seawell, Dalton, Hughes & Timms v. Exp.-Imp. Bank, No. 84-241-N, slip op. at 2 (E.D. Va. July 27, 1984) (stating that there is no "middle ground between disclosure and nondisclosure"); cf. FOIA Post, "Critical Infrastructure Information Regulations Issued by DHS" (posted 2/27/04) (emphasizing the critical distinction between "protecting information from public disclosure" and "the safeguarding of federal information").

[278] Favish, 541 U.S. at 174; see Maricopa Audobon Soc'y v. U.S. Forest Serv., 108 F.3d 1082, 1088-89 (9th Cir. 1997) (rejecting the plaintiff's offer to

(continued...)

the information belongs to the general public."[279]

An agency must "provide the [requested] record in any form or format requested by the person if the record is readily reproducible by the agency in that form or format" and "make reasonable efforts to maintain its records in forms or formats that are reproducible" for such purposes.[280] Together, these two provisions require agencies to honor a requester's specific choice among existing forms of a requested record (assuming no exceptional difficulty in reproducing an existing record form)[281] and to make "rea-

---

[278](...continued)
receive the requested documents under a confidentiality agreement because of the rule that "FOIA does not permit selective disclosure of information to only certain parties, and that once the information is disclosed to [the plaintiff], it must be made available to all members of the public who request it"); Swan v. SEC, 96 F.3d 498, 500 (D.C. Cir. 1996) ("Once records are released, nothing in the FOIA prevents the requester from disclosing the information to anyone else. The statute contains no provisions requiring confidentiality agreements or similar conditions."); Schiffer v. FBI, 78 F.3d 1405, 1410 (9th Cir. 1996) (reversing district court's conditional disclosure order, which is "not authorized by FOIA"); cf. Arieff v. U.S. Dep't of the Navy, 712 F.2d 1462, 1469 (D.C. Cir. 1983) (refusing to grant protective order that would allow plaintiff's counsel and medical expert to review exempt information, lest anyone think that "even in the process of sustaining an exemption the secrets to which it pertains will be compromised").

[279] Favish, 541 U.S. at 174; see also FOIA Post, "Supreme Court Rules for 'Survivor Privacy' in Favish" (posted 4/9/04) ("The well-known maxim under the FOIA that 'release to one is release to all' was firmly reinforced in the Favish decision.").

[280] 5 U.S.C. § 552(a)(3)(B); see also FOIA Update, Vol. XVII, No. 4, at 2 (discussing statutory provisions); cf. Department of Justice "Electronic Record" Report, reprinted in abridged form in FOIA Update, Vol. XI, No. 3, at 3-6 (discussing "choice of format" issues regarding "electronic records"). But see also Landmark Legal Found. v. EPA, 272 F. Supp. 2d 59, 63 (D.D.C. 2003) (concluding that the agency had not violated the FOIA's "readily reproducible" provision by failing to retain electronic copies of e-mails that were retained in paper form only, because "the agency may keep its files in a manner that best suits its needs"); cf. Martin & Merrell, Inc. v. U.S. Customs Serv., 657 F. Supp. 733, 734 (S.D. Fla. 1986) ("The [FOIA] in no way contemplates that agencies, in providing information to the public, should invest in the most sophisticated and expensive form of technology.") (pre-1996 FOIA amendment case).

[281] See, e.g., Lepelletier v. FDIC, No. 96-1363, transcript at 9 (D.D.C. Mar. 3, 2000) (refusing, with regard to information "maintained on an [agency] database incapable of being printed," to order agency "to render or attempt to render that database operational"), appeal dismissed as moot, 23 F.
(continued...)

sonable efforts" to disclose a record in a different form or format when that is requested, if the record is "readily reproducible" in that new form or format.[282]

Given "that computer-stored records, whether stored in the central processing unit, on magnetic tape, or in some other form, are records for the purposes of the FOIA,"[283] agencies should endeavor to use advanced technology to satisfy existing or potential FOIA demands most efficiently -- including through "affirmative" electronic disclosures.[284] To do so, and

---

[281](...continued)
App'x 4 (D.C. Cir. 2001); Chamberlain, 957 F. Supp. at 296 ("The substantial expense of reproducing the visicorder charts, as well as the possibility that the visicorder charts might be damaged if photocopied, make the Government's proposed form of disclosure [i.e., inspection] even more compelling.").

[282] See TPS, Inc. v. DOD, 330 F.3d 1191, 1195 (9th Cir. 2003) (stating, in light of a particular agency regulation, that the FOIA "requires that the agency satisfy a FOIA request [for the production of records in a certain format] when it has the capability to readily reproduce documents in the requested format"); see also Sample v. Bureau of Prisons, No. 05-5038, 2006 WL 3103009, at *1, *3 (D.C. Cir. Nov. 3, 2006) (finding that the statutory language "unambiguously requires" the agency to disclose records in the requested electronic format even though the agency's regulations prohibit an inmate from possessing such electronically formatted material, without making any finding with respect to inmate "access or possession" of such records, as those questions were "not before the court"); FOIA Update, Vol. XVIII, No. 1, at 5 (discussing agency obligations to produce records in requested forms or formats (citing H.R. Rep. No. 104-795, at 18, 21 (1996) (noting that amendments overrule Dismukes v. Dep't of the Interior, 603 F. Supp. 760, 761-63 (D.D.C. 1984), which previously allowed agency to chose format of disclosure if it chose "reasonably"))); see also FOIA Update, Vol. XIX, No. 1, at 6 (encouraging agencies to consider providing records in multiple forms as matter of administrative discretion if requested to do so).

[283] Yeager v. DEA, 678 F.2d 315, 321 (D.C. Cir. 1982); see Long v. IRS, 596 F.2d 362, 364-65 (9th Cir. 1979); see also FOIA Update, Vol. XVII, No. 4, at 2 (citing 5 U.S.C. § 552(f), as amended); FOIA Update, Vol. XI, No. 2, at 4 n.1.

[284] See FOIA Update, Vol. XIX, No. 3, at 1 (stressing congressional interest in "affirmative disclosures" of government information); id. at 5-6 (Department of Justice congressional testimony emphasizing same); FOIA Update, Vol. XIX, No. 1, at 1 (discussing Department of the Air Force affirmative electronic information disclosure program); FOIA Update, Vol. XVIII, No. 1, at 3 (advising that agencies may choose to meet their "paper" reading room responsibilities through placement of computer terminals in their "conventional" reading rooms); FOIA Update, Vol. XVI, No. 1, at 1-2 (promoting efficient agency disclosure through early Internet activity and other
(continued...)

also to meet their "electronic reading room" obligations under the Electronic FOIA amendments as well,[285] all federal agencies must pay increasing attention to the design and development of their sites on the World Wide Web for purposes of FOIA administration.[286] (For a discussion of "electronic reading rooms," see FOIA Reading Rooms and Web Sites, FOIA Reading Rooms, above.)

When an agency denies an initial request in full or in part, it must provide the requester with certain specific administrative information about the action taken on the request.[287] Pursuant to the requirements of the Electronic FOIA amendments, such information should include an estimate of the amount of denied information, unless doing so would undermine the protection provided by an exemption.[288] The Electronic FOIA

---

[284](...continued)
electronic means); FOIA Update, Vol. XV, No. 4, at 3 (proposed electronic record FOIA principles); see also FOIA Update, Vol. XVII, No. 1, at 1-2 (describing use of document imaging in automated FOIA processing).

[285] Pub. L. No. 104-231, § 4, 110 Stat. 3048, 3049 (codified as amended at 5 U.S.C. § 552(a)(2), (e)(2)); see also FOIA Update, Vol. XIX, No. 1, at 3-5 ("OIP Guidance: Electronic FOIA Amendments Implementation Guidance Outline").

[286] See Presidential FOIA Memorandum, reprinted in FOIA Update, Vol. XIV, No. 3, at 3 (noting that agencies have the responsibility "to enhance public access [to information] through the use of electronic information systems"); FOIA Update, Vol. XIX, No. 3, at 3-4 ("OIP Guidance: Recommendations for FOIA Web Sites"); FOIA Update, Vol. XIX, No. 2, at 2 ("Web Site Watch" discussion of agency FOIA Web sites); FOIA Update, Vol. XIX, No. 1, at 2 (same); FOIA Update, Vol. XVIII, No. 3, at 1-2 (describing early agency development of World Wide Web sites for FOIA purposes); see also FOIA Post, "GAO E-FOIA Implementation Report Issued" (posted 3/23/01) ("This [GAO] report provides an excellent basis for all agencies -- whether they were among the agencies examined by GAO as part of its study or not -- to review their current state of compliance with E-FOIA's requirements and to make any and all improvements that are needed."); FOIA Update, Vol. XIX, No. 3, at 2 (advising agencies on proper FOIA Web site treatment for annual FOIA reports, in compliance with newly enacted electronic availability requirements of 5 U.S.C. § 552(e)(2)-(3), including through agency identification of URL (Uniform Resource Locator) for each report).

[287] See 5 U.S.C. § 552(a)(6)(A)(i) (requiring agencies to notify requesters of disclosure determinations, of reasons for such determinations, and of administrative appeal rights); id. § 552(a)(6)(C)(i) (requiring agencies to notify requesters of name and title of person making determination regarding denials of requests for records).

[288] See 5 U.S.C. § 552(a)(6)(F); see, e.g., 28 C.F.R. § 16.6(c)(3) (2006); see
(continued...)

## PROCEDURAL REQUIREMENTS

amendments require agencies to also indicate the deletion of information at the point in the record where the deletion was made, wherever it is "technically feasible" to do so.[289]

While "[t]here is no requirement that administrative responses to FOIA requests contain the same documentation necessary in litigation,"[290] a decision to deny an initial request must inform the requester of the reasons for denial; of the right to appeal; and of the name and title of each person responsible for the denial.[291] Agencies also must include administra-

---

[288](...continued)
also FOIA Update, Vol. XVIII, No. 2, at 2 (discussing alternative methods of satisfying obligation to estimate volume of deleted or withheld information, including "forms of measurement" to be used); FOIA Update, Vol. XVII, No. 4, at 10-11 (discussing requirements of Electronic FOIA amendments).

[289] Pub. L. No. 104-231, § 4, 110 Stat. 3048, 3049 (codified as amended at 5 U.S.C. § 552(b) (2000 & Supp. IV 2004) (concluding sentences)); see, e.g., 28 C.F.R. § 16.6(c)(3); see also FOIA Update, Vol. XVIII, No. 1, at 6 (discussing use of "electronic markings to show the locations of electronic record deletions"); FOIA Update, Vol. XVII, No. 4, at 10 (advising that the statutory obligation "also codifies the sound administrative practice of marking records to show all deletions when records are disclosed in conventional paper form"); cf. Tax Analysts v. IRS, No. 94-923, 1998 WL 419755, at *2 (D.D.C. May 1, 1998) (declaring that "an agency need not add explanatory material to a document to make it more understandable in light of the redactions").

[290] Crooker v. CIA, No. 83-1426, 1984 U.S. Dist. LEXIS 23177, at *3-4 (D.D.C. Sept. 28, 1984); see Sakamoto v. EPA, 443 F. Supp. 2d 1182, 1189 (N.D. Cal. 2006) (granting summary judgment because, inter alia, "[i]nitial agency responses to FOIA requests are not required to contain a Vaughn index"); Judicial Watch, Inc. v. Clinton, 880 F. Supp. 1, 11-12 (D.D.C. 1995) (finding that agencies need not provide Vaughn Index until ordered by court after plaintiff has exhausted administrative process); Schaake v. IRS, No. 91-958, 1991 U.S. Dist. LEXIS 9418, at *9-10 (S.D. Ill. June 3, 1991) (ruling that court "lacks jurisdiction" to require agency to provide Vaughn Index at either initial request or administrative appeal stages); SafeCard Servs. v. SEC, No. 84-3073, 1986 U.S. Dist. LEXIS 26467, at *5 (D.D.C. Apr. 21, 1986) (noting that requester has no right to Vaughn Index during administrative process), aff'd on other grounds, 926 F.2d 1197 (D.C. Cir. 1991); see also FOIA Update, Vol. VII, No. 3, at 6.

[291] 5 U.S.C. § 552(a)(6)(A)(i), (a)(6)(C)(i); see Stanley v. DOD, No. 93-4247, slip op. at 14-15 (S.D. Ill. July 28, 1998) (finding constructive exhaustion when agency failed to provide requester with notice of administrative appeal rights regarding disputed fee estimate); Mayock v. INS, 714 F. Supp. 1558, 1567 (N.D. Cal. 1989) (denying plaintiff's request for Vaughn Index at administrative level, but suggesting that agency regulations then in effect

(continued...)

tive appeal notifications in all of their "no record" responses to FOIA requesters.[292]

Notifications to requesters should also contain other pertinent information: when and where records will be made available; what fees, if any, must be paid prior to the granting of access; what records are or are not responsive to the request; the date of receipt of the request or appeal; and the nature of the request or appeal and, when appropriate, the agency's interpretation of it.[293] Furthermore, because an agency is obligated to pro-

---

[291](...continued)
required "more information than just the number of pages withheld and an unexplained citation to the exemptions"), rev'd & remanded on other grounds sub nom. Mayock v. Nelson, 938 F.2d 1006 (9th Cir. 1991); Hudgins v. IRS, 620 F. Supp. 19, 20-21 (D.D.C. 1985) (suggesting that statement of appellate rights should be provided even when request was interpreted by agency as not reasonably describing records), aff'd, 808 F.2d 137 (D.C. Cir. 1987); see also FOIA Update, Vol. VI, No. 4, at 6 (discussing significance of apprising requesters of their rights to file administrative appeals of adverse FOIA determinations); cf. Kay v. FCC, 884 F. Supp. 1, 2-3 (D.D.C. 1995) (upholding notification that appeals were to be filed with general counsel even though Commission took final action on them).

[292] See Oglesby v. U.S. Dep't of the Army, 920 F.2d 57, 67 (D.C. Cir. 1990) (holding that an agency's "no record" response constitutes an "adverse determination" and therefore requires notification of appeal rights under 5 U.S.C. § 552(a)(6)(A)(i)); Dinsio v. FBI, 445 F. Supp. 2d 305, 311 (W.D.N.Y. 2006) (finding constructive exhaustion when agency response did not include notice of administrative appeal rights) (appeal pending); see also FOIA Update, Vol. XII, No. 2, at 5 ("OIP Guidance: Procedural Rules Under the D.C. Circuit's Oglesby Decision") (superseding FOIA Update, Vol. V, No. 3, at 2). But see Dorn v. IRS, No. 03-539, 2005 WL 1126653, at *3 (M.D. Fla. May 12, 2005) (stating erroneously that agency's response was not "adverse," even though response stated that requested records "did not exist, must be requested from another office, or could not be created").

[293] See FOIA Update, Vol. XVI, No. 3, at 3-5 ("OIP Guidance: Determining the Scope of a FOIA Request") (emphasizing importance of communication with requester); see, e.g., Astley v. Lawson, No. 89-2806, 1991 WL 7162, at *2 (D.D.C. Jan. 11, 1991) (suggesting that the agency "might have been more helpful" to requester by "explaining why the information he sought would not be provided"); see also FOIA Post, "Anthrax Mail Emergency Delays FOIA Correspondence" (posted 11/30/01) (suggesting that agencies inform requesters of the delayed receipt of their FOIA requests due to anthrax-related mail disruptions "by sending acknowledgment letters in response to all delayed FOIA correspondence as promptly as possible upon ultimate receipt, taking pains to specify the length of the delay that was incurred in each case"); FOIA Update, Vol. XV, No. 2, at 1 (describing Department of Justice "FOIA Form Review" as example for other agencies to fol-

vide a FOIA requester with the "best copy available" of a record,[294] an agency should address in its correspondence any problem with the quality of its photocopy of a disclosed record.[295]

Finally, a requester has the right to administratively appeal any adverse determination an agency makes on his or her FOIA request.[296] Under Department of Justice regulations, for example, adverse determinations include: denials of records in full or in part; "no records" responses; denials of requests for fee waivers; and denials of requests for expedited treatment.[297] An agency must make a determination on an administrative appeal within twenty working days after its receipt.[298] An administrative appeal decision upholding an adverse determination must also inform the requester of the provisions for judicial review of that determination in the federal courts.[299] (For discussions of the various aspects of judicial review of agency action under the FOIA, see Litigation Considerations, below.)

## FEES AND FEE WAIVERS

More than two decades ago, the Freedom of Information Reform Act of 1986[1] brought significant changes to the way in which fees are now assessed under the FOIA. A new fee structure was established, including a

---

[293](...continued)
low).

[294] See McDonnell v. United States, 4 F.3d 1227, 1262 n.21 (3d Cir. 1993) ("Of course, we anticipate that [plaintiff] will receive the best possible reproduction of the documents to which he is entitled."); Giles v. U.S. Dep't of Justice, No. 00-1497, slip op. at 5 (D.D.C. June 4, 2001) (accepting that agency provided plaintiff with "best copies available" even though plaintiff asserted that they were "unreadable"); see also FOIA Update, Vol. XVI, No. 3, at 5 (advising agencies that "before providing a FOIA requester with a photocopy of a record that is a poor copy or is not entirely legible," they should "make reasonable efforts to check for any better copy of a record that could be used to make a better photocopy for the requester").

[295] See FOIA Update, Vol. XVI, No. 3, at 5 (advising of procedures to be used in cases involving poor photocopies of records); cf. FOIA Post, "The Limits of Agency Translation Obligations Under the FOIA" (posted 12/1/04) (distinguishing "legibility" from "translatability" of disclosed records).

[296] 5 U.S.C. § 552(a)(6)(A); see Oglesby, 920 F.2d at 63-71.

[297] 28 C.F.R. § 16.6(c).

[298] 5 U.S.C. § 552(a)(6)(A)(ii).

[299] Id. § 552(a)(6)(A)(ii).

[1] Pub. L. No. 99-570, §§ 1801-04, 100 Stat. 3207.

new provision authorizing agencies to assess "review" charges when processing records in response to a commercial-use request.[2] Specific fee limitations and restrictions were placed on the assessment of certain fees both in general as well as for certain categories of requesters.[3] Additionally, the 1986 FOIA amendments replaced the statutory fee waiver provision with a revised standard.[4] These revised fee and fee waiver provisions were made effective as of mid-1987, but required implementing agency regulations to become fully effective.[5]

Under the FOIA Reform Act, the Office of Management and Budget was charged with the responsibility of promulgating, pursuant to notice and receipt of public comment, a "uniform schedule of fees"[6] for individual agencies to follow when promulgating their FOIA fee regulations.[7] In March 1987, OMB issued its Uniform Freedom of Information Act Fee Schedule and Guidelines [hereinafter OMB Fee Guidelines].[8] As mandated by the 1986 FOIA amendments, agencies are obligated to conform their fee schedules to these guidelines.[9]

The FOIA Reform Act also required agencies to promulgate specific "procedures and guidelines for determining when such fees should be

---

[2] § 1803, 100 Stat. at 3207-49.

[3] See id. at 3207-50.

[4] Id.

[5] Id. § 1804(b), 100 Stat. at 3207-50; see also FOIA Update, Vol. VIII, No. 1, at 2 (advising agencies that until implementing regulations were in place, they "should give FOIA requesters the full benefits of both . . . old and new" statutory provisions).

[6] 5 U.S.C. § 552(a)(4)(A)(i) (2000 & Supp. IV 2004); see Envtl. Prot. Info. Ctr. v. U.S. Forest Serv., 432 F.3d 945, 947 (9th Cir. 2005) ("FOIA calls for the Office of Management and Budget to promulgate [fee] guidelines for agencies to follow.") (citation omitted); cf. Media Access Project v. FCC, 883 F.2d 1063, 1069 (D.C. Cir. 1989) (rejecting plaintiff's claim that OMB's authority is limited to establishing "'price list'").

[7] § 1803, 100 Stat. at 3207-49 (codified as amended at 5 U.S.C. § 552(a)(4)(A)(i)); see Media Access Project, 883 F.2d at 1069 (finding that the FOIA expressly mandates that OMB establish a fee schedule and guidelines for statutory fee categories).

[8] 52 Fed. Reg. 10,012 (Mar. 27, 1987).

[9] 5 U.S.C. § 552(a)(4)(A)(i); see also 52 Fed. Reg. at 10,015 (explaining that issuance of governmentwide fee schedule is precluded by language of FOIA Reform Act requiring "each agency's fees to be based upon its direct reasonable operating costs of providing FOIA services").

waived or reduced."[10] The Department of Justice, in accordance with its statutory responsibility to encourage agency compliance with the FOIA,[11] developed new governmentwide policy guidance on the waiver of FOIA fees, to replace its previously issued guidance implementing the predecessor statutory fee waiver standard.[12] In April 1987, to assist federal agencies in addressing fee waivers in their revised FOIA fee regulations, the Department of Justice issued its New FOIA Fee Waiver Policy Guidance to the heads of all federal departments and agencies, which remains in effect.[13] While the Electronic Freedom of Information Act Amendments of 1996[14] made no direct changes to either the fee or fee waiver provisions of the FOIA,[15] several of those amendments can have an effect on fee matters.[16] In November 2002, the limited but significant amendment to the FOIA made by the Intelligence Authorization Act of 2003,[17] which was confined in scope to agencies within the intelligence community, had no direct effect on either the fee or fee waiver provisions.[18] (For discussions of this amendment, see Introduction, above, and Procedural Requirements, FOIA Requesters, above.)

More recently, Executive Order 13,392,[19] issued on December 14, 2005 and entitled "Improving Agency Disclosure of Information," places strong emphasis on the improvement of FOIA operations throughout the executive branch through greater efficiency of the FOIA administrative process and

---

[10] § 1803, 100 Stat. at 3207-49.

[11] See 5 U.S.C. § 552(e); see also FOIA Update, Vol. XIX, No. 3, at 6; FOIA Update, Vol. XIV, No. 3, at 8.

[12] See FOIA Update, Vol. VIII, No. 1, at 1-2; FOIA Update, Vol. VII, No. 3, at 3; FOIA Update, Vol. IV, No. 1, at 3-4.

[13] See FOIA Update, Vol. VIII, No. 1, at 3-10; Attorney General's Memorandum on the 1986 Amendments to the Freedom of Information Act 41-50 (Dec. 1987); see also, e.g., Department of Justice FOIA Regulations, 28 C.F.R. § 16.11 (2006) (example of fee regulation).

[14] Pub. L. No. 104-231, 110 Stat. 3048 (codified as amended at 5 U.S.C. § 552).

[15] 5 U.S.C. § 552(a)(4)(A).

[16] See, e.g., 5 U.S.C. § 552(a)(3)(B) (providing for information to be disclosed in requester's choice of form or format if "readily reproducible" by agency).

[17] Pub. L. No. 107-306, 116 Stat. 2383 (2002).

[18] See also FOIA Post, "FOIA Amended by Intelligence Authorization Act" (posted 12/23/02) (describing breadth and impact of 2002 FOIA amendment).

[19] Exec. Order No. 13,392, 70 Fed. Reg. 75,373 (Dec. 14, 2005).

better customer service within each federal agency.[20] These two policy goals may be accomplished in part through increased use of proactive disclosures and by improvements in the use of automated processing, and in time they can be expected to have an impact on the administration of both the FOIA's fee and fee waiver provisions.[21]

## Fees

As amended by the Freedom of Information Reform Act of 1986, the FOIA provides for three levels of fees that may be assessed in response to FOIA requests according to categories of FOIA requesters.[22] Within each fee level, the statute provides for limitations on the types of fees that an agency may assess.[23] An agency's determination of the appropriate fee level for an individual requester is dependent upon the identity of the re-

---

[20] Id. at Sec. 1(b), (c), (d).

[21] See FOIA Post, "Executive Order 13,392 Implementation Guidance" (posted 4/27/06) (Potential Improvement Areas #2 and #6); Attorney General's Report to the President Pursuant to Executive Order 13,392, Entitled "Improving Disclosure of Information," at 7-8, available at http://www. usdoj.gov/oip/ag_report_to_president_13392.pdf (observing that agencies "overwhelmingly recognized the value" of making proactive disclosures and embraced the use of automated processing either through "the establishment or the upgrading of automated systems" in their FOIA Improvement Plans).

[22] 5 U.S.C. § 552(a)(4)(A)(ii)(I)-(III) (2000 & Supp. IV 2004); see Long v. U.S. Dep't of Justice, 450 F. Supp. 2d 42, 82 (D.D.C.) (acknowledging that FOIA provides for three levels of fees), amended by 457 F. Supp. 2d 30 (D.D.C. 2006), amended further on reconsideration, Nos. 00-0211 & 02-2467, 2007 WL 293508 (D.D.C. Feb. 2, 2007), stay granted (D.D.C. Feb. 13, 2007); Hall v. CIA, No. 04-0814, 2005 WL 850379, at *6 (D.D.C. Apr. 13, 2005) (referencing three categories of fees that may be assessed under FOIA), subsequent opinion, No. 04-0814, 2006 WL 197462 (D.D.C. Jan. 25, 2006); McDade v. Executive Office for U.S. Attorneys, No. 03-1946, slip op. at 6 n.3 (D.D.C. Sept. 29, 2004) (recognizing that statute provides for three levels of fees), summary affirmance granted to agency, No. 04-5378, 2005 U.S. App. LEXIS 15259, at *1 (D.C. Cir. July 25, 2005), cert. denied, 126 S. Ct. 791 (2005).

[23] See 5 U.S.C. § 552(a)(4)(A)(ii)(I)-(III); Long, 450 F. Supp. 2d at 82 (recognizing limitations on fees imposed by statutory provisions); McDade, No. 03-1946, slip op. at 6 n.3 (D.D.C. Sept. 29, 2004) (noting statutory limitations on charging fees); see also Eagle v. U.S. Dep't of Commerce, No. C-01-20591, 2003 WL 21402534, at *4 (N.D. Cal. Apr. 28, 2003) (observing that the statutory limitations on the types of fees that may be charged do not per se disqualify a requester from obtaining a fee waiver under 5 U.S.C. § 552(a)(4)(A)(iii)).

quester and the intended use of the information sought.[24] The limitations placed on the types of fees that may be assessed are not the statutory equivalent of fee "waivers"[25] inasmuch as an agency cannot "waive" what it may not charge in the first place by statutory preclusion.[26] Rather, they are best characterized as statutory fee "limitations" in accordance with the structure of the statute.[27] (For a discussion of fee waivers under the FOIA, see Fee Waivers, below.)

The following discussion summarizes the FOIA's fee provisions. The Uniform Freedom of Information Act Fee Schedule and Guidelines [hereinafter OMB Fee Guidelines],[28] which provide general principles for how agencies should set fee schedules and make fee determinations, and include definitions of statutory fee terms, discuss these provisions in greater, authoritative detail. Anyone with a FOIA fee (as opposed to fee waiver) question should consult these guidelines in conjunction with the appropriate agency's FOIA regulations for the records at issue. Agency personnel should attempt to resolve such fee questions by consulting first with their FOIA officers. Whenever fee questions cannot be resolved in that way, agency FOIA officers should try to direct them to OMB's Office of Information and Regulatory Affairs, Information Policy and Technology Branch, at (202) 395-3785.

The first level of fees provided for by the FOIA encompasses charges for document search, review, and duplication, which are applicable "when records are requested for commercial use."[29] The OMB Fee Guidelines de-

---

[24] See 5 U.S.C. § 552(a)(4)(A)(ii); see also FOIA Update, Vol. VIII, No. 1, at 4.

[25] See 5 U.S.C. § 552(a)(4)(A)(iii).

[26] Id. § 552(a)(4)(A)(ii).

[27] See 5 U.S.C. § 552(a)(4)(A)(ii) (specifying in each fee level that "fees shall be limited to" search, review, and duplication (level one), duplication (level two), or search and duplication (level three)) (emphasis added); see also Judicial Watch v. U.S. Dep't of Energy, 310 F. Supp. 2d 271, 289 (D.D.C. 2004) (recognizing proper statutory distinction between "fee limitations" and "fee waivers"), aff'd in part, rev'd in part on other grounds & remanded, 412 F.3d 125 (D.C. Cir. 2005); Eagle, 2003 WL 21402534, at *2 (same).

[28] 52 Fed. Reg. 10,012 (Mar. 27, 1987).

[29] 5 U.S.C. § 552(a)(4)(A)(ii)(I); see Gavin v. SEC, No. 04-4522, 2006 U.S. Dist. LEXIS 75227, at *14 (D. Minn. Oct. 16, 2006) (reiterating that commercial-use requester pays for search, review, and duplication costs); see also Avondale Indus. v. NLRB, No. 96-1227, slip op. at 14 n.4 (E.D. La. Mar. 20, 1998) (noting that case law is "sparse" as to what constitutes "commercial use"). See generally L.A. Police Dep't v. United Reporting Publ'g Corp., 528 U.S. 32 (1999) (upholding state statute that denied commercial publishers

(continued...)

fine the term "commercial use" as "a use or purpose that furthers the commercial, trade, or profit interests of the requester or the person on whose behalf the request is being made,"[30] which can include furthering those interests through litigation.[31] Designation of a requester as a "commercial-use requester," therefore, will turn on the use to which the requested information would be put, rather than on the identity of the requester.[32] Agen-

---

[29](...continued)
access to arrest records but permitted journalists access to same records; tangentially raising questions as to how to define "commercial user" and "journalist" in electronic age) (non-FOIA case).

[30] OMB Fee Guidelines, 52 Fed. Reg. at 10,017-18; see Avondale, No. 96-1227, slip op. at 14 (E.D. La. Mar. 20, 1998) (embracing OMB's definition of "commercial use"); cf. OSHA Data/CIH, Inc. v. U.S. Dep't of Labor, 220 F.3d 153, 160 (3d Cir. 2000) (observing that under the 1986 FOIA amendments "commercial users shoulder more of the costs of FOIA requests"); Vote-Hemp, Inc. v. DEA, 237 F. Supp. 2d 59, 65 (D.D.C. 2002) (concluding that nonprofit organization, as advocate for free market in controlled substance, had commercial interest in requested records) (fee waiver context); Crain v. U.S. Customs Serv., No. 02-0341, slip op. at 7 (D.D.C. Mar. 25, 2003) (finding requester's status as commercial-use requester to be supported by administrative record before agency at time of its decision).

[31] See Rozet v. HUD, 59 F. Supp. 2d 55, 57 (D.D.C. 1999) (finding commercial interest where requester sought documents to defend his corporations in civil fraud action). But see McClellan Ecological Seepage Situation v. Carlucci, 835 F.2d 1282, 1285 (9th Cir. 1987) (finding no commercial interest in records sought in furtherance of requesters' tort claim); Muffoletto v. Sessions, 760 F. Supp. 268, 277-78 (E.D.N.Y. 1991) (finding no commercial interest when records were sought to defend against state court action to recover debts).

[32] See OMB Fee Guidelines, 52 Fed. Reg. at 10,018 (stating that "agencies must determine the use to which a requester will put the documents requested"); see also Comer v. IRS, No. 97-CV-76329, 1999 U.S. Dist. LEXIS 16268, at *12 (E.D. Mich. Sept. 30, 1999) (reiterating that requester's motives in seeking records relevant to "commercial user" determination); Hosp. & Physician Publ'g v. DOD, No. 98-CV-4117, 1999 WL 33582100, at *5 (S.D. Ill. June 22, 1999) (stating that requester's past commercial use of such records is not relevant to present case), remanded per joint stipulation, No. 99-3152 (7th Cir. Feb. 24, 2005) (remanding for purposes of adoption of parties' settlement agreement and dismissal of case); S.A. Ludsin & Co. v. SBA, No. 96 CV 5972, 1998 WL 355394, at *2 (E.D.N.Y. Apr. 2, 1998) (finding requester who sought documents to enhance prospect of securing government contract to be commercial requester); Avondale, No. 96-1227, slip op. at 14 (E.D. La. Mar. 20, 1998) (finding company's intent to use requested documents to contest union election results to be commercial use); cf. Rozet, 59 F. Supp. 2d at 57 (discounting plaintiff's assertion that infor-

(continued...)

cies are encouraged to seek additional information or clarification from the requester when the intended use is not clear from the request itself.[33]

Charges for document "search" include all the time spent looking for responsive material, including page-by-page or line-by-line identification of material within documents.[34] Additionally, agencies may charge for search time even if they fail to locate any records responsive to the request or even if the records located are subsequently determined to be exempt from disclosure.[35] Searches for responsive records should be done in the "most

---

[32](...continued)
mation was not of commercial interest where timing and content of requests in connection with other non-FOIA litigation conclusively demonstrated otherwise).

[33] See OMB Fee Guidelines, 52 Fed. Reg. at 10,018 (specifying that where the "use is not clear from the request . . . agencies should seek additional clarification before assigning the request to a specific category"); see also McClellan, 835 F.2d at 1287 ("Legislative history and agency regulations imply that an agency may seek additional information when establishing a requester's category for fee assessment."); cf. Long, 450 F. Supp. 2d at 85 (finding moot requester's challenge to agency's authority to request certain information in order to make fee category determination where no fee ultimately was assessed); Brown v. U.S. Patent & Trademark Office, 445 F. Supp. 2d 1347, 1354 (M.D. Fla. 2006) (observing in a fee waiver context that the requester provided no authority for the "proposition that an agency must conduct independent research" to make its determination), aff'd per curiam, No. 06-14716, 2007 WL 446601 (11th Cir. Feb. 13, 2007).

[34] See OMB Fee Guidelines, 52 Fed. Reg. at 10,017.

[35] See id. at 10,019; see also TPS, Inc. v. Dep't of the Air Force, No. C 01-4284, 2003 U.S. Dist. LEXIS 10925, at *8-9 (N.D. Cal. Mar. 28, 2003) ("'The fact that you did not receive any records from [the agency] . . . does not negate your responsibility to pay for programming services provided to you in good faith, at your request with your agreement to pay applicable fees.'" (quoting with approval exhibit to defendants' declaration)); Guzzino v. FBI, No. 95-1780, 1997 WL 22886, at *4 (D.D.C. Jan. 10, 1997) (upholding agency's assessment of search fees to conduct search for potentially responsive records within files of individuals "with names similar to" requester's when no files identifiable to requester were located), appeal dismissed for lack of prosecution, No. 97-5083 (D.C. Cir. Dec. 8, 1997); Linn v. U.S. Dep't of Justice, No. 92-1406, 1995 WL 417810, at *13 (D.D.C. June 6, 1995) (holding that there is no entitlement to refund of search fees when search unproductive); cf. Stabasefski v. United States, 919 F. Supp. 1570, 1573 (M.D. Ga. 1996) (holding that requester has no entitlement to reimbursement of copying fees when agency redacts portions of requested records).

efficient and least expensive manner."[36] As defined by the Electronic Freedom of Information Act Amendments of 1996,[37] the term "search" means locating records or information either "manually or by automated means"[38] and requires agencies to expend "reasonable efforts" in electronic searches, if requested to do so by requesters willing to pay for that search activity.[39]

The "review" costs which may be charged to commercial-use requesters consist of the "direct costs incurred during the initial examination of a document for the purposes of determining whether [it] must be disclosed [under the FOIA]."[40] Review time thus includes processing the documents

---

[36] OMB Fee Guidelines, 52 Fed. Reg. at 10,017; accord Exec. Order No. 13,392, Sec. 2(b)(i), 70 Fed. Reg. 75,373 (Dec. 14, 2005) (placing strong emphasis on FOIA efficiency); Presidential Memorandum for Heads of Departments and Agencies Regarding the Freedom of Information Act, 29 Weekly Comp. Pres. Doc. 1999 (Oct. 4, 1993), reprinted in FOIA Update, Vol. XIV, No. 3, at 3 ("Federal departments and agencies should handle requests for information in a customer-friendly manner."); see also FOIA Post, "Executive Order 13,392 Implementation Guidance" (posted 4/27/06) (explaining that "Executive Order 13,392 calls upon all federal agencies to improve their FOIA operations with both efficiency and customer service"); Attorney General's Memorandum for Heads of All Federal Departments and Agencies Regarding the Freedom of Information Act (Oct. 12, 2001) [hereinafter Attorney General Ashcroft's FOIA Memorandum], reprinted in FOIA Post (posted 10/15/01) (emphasizing that the citizenry has "a strong interest" in "efficient" government functioning).

[37] Pub. L. No. 104-231, 110 Stat. 3048 (codified as amended at 5 U.S.C. § 552).

[38] 5 U.S.C. § 552(a)(3)(D).

[39] Id. at § 552(a)(3)(C); see also FOIA Update, Vol. XVIII, No. 1, at 6 (analyzing 1996 FOIA amendment that requires agencies to "make reasonable efforts" to search for records electronically); Department of Justice FOIA Regulations, 28 C.F.R. § 16.11(b)(8) (2006) (stating that process of searching includes using "reasonable efforts to locate and retrieve information from records maintained in electronic form or format"); cf. OMB Fee Guidelines, 52 Fed. Reg. at 10,018, 10,019 (providing that agencies should charge "the actual direct cost of providing [computer searches]," but that for certain requester categories, the cost equivalent of two hours of manual search is provided without charge).

[40] 5 U.S.C. § 552(a)(4)(A)(iv); see also Carney v. U.S. Dep't of Justice, 19 F.3d 807, 814 n.2 (2d Cir. 1994) (noting that fee for document review is properly chargeable to commercial requesters); Gavin, 2006 U.S. Dist. LEXIS 75227, at *17-18 (finding that agency's court-ordered initial review of documents was chargeable to commercial-use requester); OMB Fee Guidelines, 52 Fed. Reg. at 10,018 (clarifying that records "withheld under an ex-

(continued...)

for disclosure, i.e., doing all that is necessary to prepare them for release,[41] but it does not include time spent resolving general legal or policy issues regarding the applicability of particular exemptions or reviewing on appeal exemptions that already are applied.[42] Records that have been withheld in full under a particular exemption that is later determined not to apply, however, may be "reviewed again to determine the application of other exemptions not previously considered."[43] Further, that subsequent review is properly chargeable to the requester as well.[44]

Under the 1986 FOIA amendments, "duplication" charges represent the reasonable "direct costs" of making copies of documents.[45] The OMB Fee Guidelines specifically require that agencies establish an "average agency-wide, per-page charge for paper copy reproduction."[46] Copies

---

[40](...continued)
emption which is subsequently determined not to apply may be reviewed again to determine the applicability of other exemptions not previously considered" and, further, that the "costs for such a subsequent review would be properly assessable"). But see AutoAlliance Int'l v. U.S. Customs Serv., No. 02-72369, slip op. at 7-8 (E.D. Mich. July 31, 2003) (finding, in fact-specific case, that where agency did not review all responsive documents during initial review -- and charged no fee -- it effectively waived agency's ability to charge commercial requester review fees for agency's "thorough review" conducted at administrative appeal level inasmuch as statute limits such fees to "initial examination" only).

[41] See OSHA Data, 220 F.3d at 168 (concluding in case of first impression that review fees include, in context of business-submitter information, costs of mandatory predisclosure notification to companies and evaluation of their responses by agency for purpose of determining applicability of exemption to companies' submitted business information); see also FOIA Post, "The Limits of Agency Translation Obligations Under the FOIA" (posted 12/1/04) (treating costs of translation of non-English records into English for purposes of applying FOIA exemptions as "part of agency's 'review' costs," which can be charged to commercial-use requester). But see Snyder v. DOD, No. C 03-4992, slip op. at 3 (N.D. Cal. Apr. 29, 2005) (reducing fee by $7.33, and finding that limited portion of activities described -- including updating workload-tracking database with request information -- did not encompass "review time" within meaning of FOIA).

[42] See OMB Fee Guidelines, 52 Fed. Reg. at 10,017, 10,018.

[43] Id. at 10,018.

[44] See id.

[45] 5 U.S.C. § 552(a)(4)(A)(iv); see OMB Fee Guidelines, 52 Fed. Reg. at 10,018.

[46] See OMB Fee Guidelines, 52 Fed. Reg. at 10,017, 10,018 (detailing ele-
(continued...)

can take various forms, including paper copies, microforms, or machine-readable documentation.[47] As further required by the Electronic FOIA amendments,[48] which were enacted a decade later, agencies must honor a requester's choice of form or format if the record is "readily reproducible" in that form or format with "reasonable efforts" by the agency.[49] For copies prepared by computer, such as printouts, disks, or other electronic media, agencies should charge the actual costs of production of that medium.[50] Agencies should consult with their technical support staff for assistance in determining their actual costs associated with producing copies of various types of media.[51] In this regard, it is standard practice that duplication charges are assessed only for those copies that are released, not for any responsive record withheld in its entirety.[52] (For further discussions of agency responsibilities when searching for or producing responsive records under the Electronic FOIA amendments, see Procedural Requirements, Searching for Records, above, and Procedural Requirements, Responding to FOIA Requests, above.)

The second level of fees limits charges to document duplication costs only, "when records are not sought for commercial use and the request is made by an educational or noncommercial scientific institution, whose purpose is scholarly or scientific research; or a representative of the news media."[53] FOIA requesters falling into one or more of these three subcategories of requesters under the 1986 FOIA amendments enjoy a complete

---

[46](...continued)
ments included in direct costs of duplication).

[47] See OMB Fee Guidelines, 52 Fed. Reg. at 10,017.

[48] Pub. L. No. 104-231, 110 Stat. 3048.

[49] 5 U.S.C. § 552(a)(3)(B); see FOIA Update, Vol. XVIII, No. 1, at 5-6 (advising agencies on new format disclosure obligations); FOIA Update, Vol. XVII, No. 4, at 2 (same); see also Exec. Order No. 13,392, Sec. 3(a)(iii)(A) (addressing use of "information technology" to respond to FOIA requests); FOIA Post, "Executive Order 13,392 Implementation Guidance" (posted 4/27/06) (Potential Improvement Area #7) (discussing potential use of World Wide Web to receive and respond to requests); FOIA Update, Vol. XIX, No. 1, at 6 (encouraging agencies to consider providing records in multiple forms as matter of administrative discretion if requested to do so).

[50] See OMB Fee Guidelines, 52 Fed. Reg. at 10,018; see also 28 C.F.R. § 16.11(c)(2); FOIA Update, Vol. XI, No. 3, at 4 & n.25.

[51] See OMB Fee Guidelines at 10,017-18 (advising agencies to "charge the actual cost, including computer operator time, of production of [a computer] tape or printout").

[52] See generally OMB Fee Guidelines, 52 Fed. Reg. at 10,017-19.

[53] 5 U.S.C. § 552(a)(4)(A)(ii)(II).

"exemption" from the assessment of search and review fees.[54] Their requests, like those made by any FOIA requester, still must "reasonably describe" the records sought in order to not impose upon an agency "'an unreasonably burdensome search.'"[55] (For a further discussion of this requirement, see Procedural Requirements, Proper FOIA Requests, above.)

The OMB Fee Guidelines define "educational institution" to include various categories of schools, as well as institutions of higher learning and vocational education.[56] This definition is limited, however, by the requirement that the educational institution be one "which operates a program or programs of scholarly research."[57] To qualify for inclusion in this fee category, the request must serve a scholarly research goal of the institution, not an individual goal.[58] The definition of a "noncommercial scientific institution" refers to a "noncommercial" institution that is "operated solely for the purpose of conducting scientific research the results of which are not intended to promote any particular product or industry."[59]

The definition of a "representative of the news media" refers to any person actively gathering information of current interest to the public for an organization that is organized and operated to publish or broadcast news to the general public.[60] Further, the OMB Guidelines specifically define "news" as "information that is about current events or that would be of current interest to the public."[61] The Court of Appeals for the District of Columbia Circuit has elaborated upon this by holding that "a representative of the news media is, in essence, a person or entity that gathers information of potential interest to a segment of the public, uses its editorial skills to turn the raw materials into a distinct work, and distributes that

---

[54] See 132 Cong. Rec. S14,298 (daily ed. Sept. 30, 1986) (statement of Sen. Leahy) (referring to requesters within the second level of fees as receiving the benefits of "the most favorable fee provision").

[55] AFGE v. U.S. Dep't of Commerce, 907 F.2d 203, 209 (D.C. Cir. 1990) (quoting Goland v. CIA, 607 F.2d 339, 353 (D.C. Cir. 1978)).

[56] See OMB Fee Guidelines, 52 Fed. Reg. at 10,018.

[57] Id.; see Nat'l Sec. Archive v. DOD, 880 F.2d 1381, 1383-85 (D.C. Cir. 1989) (approving implementation of this standard in DOD regulation).

[58] See OMB Fee Guidelines, 52 Fed. Reg. at 10,014 (distinguishing institutional from individual requests through use of examples).

[59] Id. at 10,018.

[60] Id.

[61] Id.

work to an audience."[62] In reaching its decision, the D.C. Circuit relied in large part on the legislative history of the 1986 FOIA amendments,[63] not finding the term "representative of the news media . . . self-evident [in] what [it] covers."[64] During the next decade, this category of FOIA requesters received scant additional attention by the courts.[65]

In more recent years, however, perhaps partly due to the passage of the Electronic FOIA amendments,[66] in conjunction with the ushering in of the "Information Age,"[67] there has been renewed interest in the question of what constitutes a "representative of the news media" both in the FOIA context[68] and with regard to non-FOIA matters as well.[69] Indeed, since

---

[62] Nat'l Sec. Archive, 880 F.2d at 1387; see also Elec. Privacy Info. Ctr. v. DOD, 241 F. Supp. 2d 5, 14 (D.D.C. 2003) (explaining that the fact that an entity distributes its publication "via Internet to subscribers' email addresses does not change the [news media] analysis"); cf. Hall, 2005 WL 850379, at *6 (finding that the organization's statement that "'news media status is pled,'" without mentioning the specific activities in which it is engaged, "misstates the burden that a party seeking a fee limitation . . . must carry . . . [o]therwise, every conceivable FOIA requester could simply declare itself a 'representative of the news media' to circumvent fees").

[63] See Nat'l Sec. Archive, 880 F.2d at 1385-87.

[64] See id. at 1385; see also 132 Cong. Rec. H9464 (daily ed. Oct. 8, 1986) (statement of Rep. English) (referring to "written explanatory materials that would have been included in a committee report" and that acknowledge that "no definition of 'news media' has been included in the [1986 FOIA amendments]").

[65] See Hosp. & Physician Publ'g, 1999 WL 33582100, at *4 (finding that the requester qualified under the test of National Security Archive as a "representative of the news media"); cf. Tax Analysts v. U.S. Dep't of Justice, 965 F.2d 1092, 1095 (D.C. Cir. 1992) (noting that, in the context of attorney fees, the plaintiff "is certainly a news organization").

[66] Pub. L. No. 104-231, 110 Stat. 3048.

[67] D.C. Technical Assistance Org. v. HUD, 85 F. Supp. 2d 46, 49 (D.D.C. 2000) (commenting on changes wrought by "Information Age"); see also Randall P. Bezanson, Taxes on Knowledge in America 2-3 (Univ. of Pa. Press 1994) (stating that "technology will force us to reexamine many of the most basic assumptions we hold about the role and, indeed, the meaning of the press").

[68] See, e.g., Brown, 445 F. Supp. 2d at 1356-57 (observing that at least two entities previously granted media status by courts had (unlike plaintiff) prior history of publication and had gathered information from several sources); Hall, 2005 WL 850379, at *6 (applying standard set forth in Nat'l Sec. Archive, 880 F.2d at 1387, as well as in agency regulation defining

(continued...)

2000, no fewer than eleven district court FOIA opinions have been issued (ten within the D.C. Circuit) on the "news media" question, and eight of those involved the same plaintiff organization. In the majority of these decisions, the court found that the organization before it was not such an entity.[70]

---

[68](...continued)
news media representative); Elec. Privacy Info. Ctr., 241 F. Supp. 2d at 14 n.7 (explaining that while the plaintiff qualified as a news media entity, "the Court is not convinced that a website is, by itself, sufficient to qualify a FOIA requester as a 'representative of the news media,'" and reasoning that virtually all organizations and many individuals in the metropolitan area have Web sites, "but certainly all are not entitled to news media status for fee determinations").

[69] Cf. In re Grand Jury Subpoenas, No. 01-20745, slip op. at 2, 5-6 (5th Cir. Aug. 17, 2001) (upholding contempt-of-court charge against "aspiring freelance writer" for failure to obey federal grand jury subpoenas, and finding that she was not in any event entitled to claim "journalist's privilege" in the case) (non-FOIA case); Tripp v. DOD, 284 F. Supp. 2d 50, 55-58 (D.D.C. 2003) (according newspaper status to military publication for purposes of First Amendment analysis, and finding that author of article was engaged in "newsgathering" activities entitling her to invoke "reporters privilege") (separate non-FOIA opinion in case brought under FOIA). See generally David A. Anderson, Freedom of the Press, 80 Tex. L. Rev. 429, 435-45 (2002) (discussing what constitutes "the press," and noting differences between information providers and providers of news).

[70] See Brown, 445 F. Supp. 2d at 1356-57 (holding that the plaintiff who provided no evidence of employment by a news organization or that he is a "freelance" journalist as defined by the agency's regulation, and has "not demonstrated a 'firm intention' of creating or publishing an editorialized work," does not qualify as a representative of the news media); Hall, 2005 WL 850379, at *6 (finding that the plaintiff's endeavors, including "'research contributions . . . email newsletters' . . . and a single magazine or newspaper article" were more akin to those of a middleman or information vendor; determining that second plaintiff offered only conclusory assertion that it was representative of news media and "mentioned no specific activities [that it] conducted"); Judicial Watch, Inc. v. Rossotti, No. 01-1612, 2002 WL 535803, at *5 (D.D.C. Mar. 18, 2002) (finding persuasive a prior district court decision on the same issue, adopting "the reasoning and conclusions set forth" therein, and holding that the plaintiff organization before it is not a representative of the news media), rev'd on other grounds, 326 F.3d 1309 (D.C. Cir. 2003); Judicial Watch, Inc. v. U.S. Dep't of Justice, 185 F. Supp. 2d 54, 59 (D.D.C. 2002) (concluding that the plaintiff organization did not qualify for media status as it was not organized to broadcast or publish news and was "at best a type of middleman or vendor of information that representatives of the news media can utilize when appropriate"); Judicial Watch, Inc. v. U.S. Dep't of Justice, No. 00-0745, slip op. at 15 (D.D.C. Feb. (continued...)

-142-

In addition to their reliance on the framework established by D.C. Circuit in National Security Archive, these numerous decisions also relied on the implementing regulations for the fee limitations/fee category portion of the statute.[71] Despite the direction taken (and given) by the District Court

---

[70](...continued)
12, 2001) (finding that the plaintiff organization is not "an entity organized to publish or broadcast news," and stating that the organization's "vague intention" to use the requested information is not specific enough "to establish the necessary firm intent to publish that is required [in order] to qualify as a representative of the news media"), partial summary judgment granted, slip op. at 22 (D.D.C. Apr. 20, 2001) (repeating that plaintiff's "vague intentions" to use requested information are insufficient to establish media status); Judicial Watch, Inc. v. U.S. Dep't of Justice, 122 F. Supp. 2d 13, 21 (D.D.C. 2000) (same); Judicial Watch, Inc. v. U.S. Dep't of Justice, 122 F. Supp. 2d 5, 12 (D.D.C. 2000) (commenting that by its own admission the requester is not "'an entity that is organized and operated to publish or broadcast news'" (quoting from definition found at 28 C.F.R. § 16.11(b)(6))); Judicial Watch, Inc. v. U.S. Dep't of Justice, No. 99-2315, 2000 WL 33724693, at *3-4 (D.D.C. Aug. 17, 2000) (stating that letting reporters view documents collected from government, faxing them to newspapers, and appearing on television or radio does not qualify the requester for news media status; concluding that if the requester's "vague intentions" to publish future reports "satisfied FOIA's requirements, any entity could transform itself into a 'representative of the news media' by including a single strategic sentence in its request"). But see Elec. Privacy Info. Ctr., 241 F. Supp. 2d at 9 (concluding that the publication activities of a public interest research center -- which included both print and other media -- satisfied the definition of "representative of the news media" under the agency's FOIA regulation); Judicial Watch, Inc. v. U.S. Dep't of Justice, 133 F. Supp. 2d 52, 53-54 (D.D.C. 2000) (finding that the requester qualified as a representative of the news media, but observing that the test for same that is set forth in National Security Archive did not "apparently anticipate[] the evolution of the Internet or the morphing of the 'news media' into its present indistinct form," thereby suggesting that under National Security Archive "arguably anyone with [a] website" could qualify for media status, and concluding that "if such a result is intolerable . . . the remedy lies with Congress"), appeal dismissed per curiam, No. 01-5019, 2001 WL 800022, at *1 (D.C. Cir. June 13, 2001) (ruling that the "district court's order holding that appellee is a representative of the news media for purposes of [the FOIA] is not final in the traditional sense and does not meet the requirements of the collateral order doctrine" for purposes of appeal).

[71] See 28 C.F.R. § 16.11; see also, e.g., Brown, 445 F. Supp. 2d at 1357 (relying heavily on agency's regulation defining representative of news media and "freelance" journalist); Hall, 2005 WL 850379, at *6 (applying standard set forth in Nat'l Sec. Archive, 880 F.2d at 1387, as well as in agency regulation defining news media representative); Judicial Watch, 185 F. Supp. 2d at 58-59 (noting that the agency, in accordance with congression-
(continued...)

for the District of Columbia on this issue though, it is likely to remain a somewhat unsettled area of law until it can be addressed by the D.C. Circuit, and other circuit courts as the issue develops, as well. Thus far, the only other circuit courts to have had before them the question of whether a FOIA requester was properly categorized as a representative of the news media are the Courts of Appeals for the Seventh and Eleventh Circuits.[72] In the Seventh Circuit, the Court did not reach the issue because the appeal was resolved through settlement, letting stand the district court's finding that the requester before it qualified for news media status.[73] In contrast, the Court of Appeals for the Eleventh Circuit recently concluded in a brief opinion, which affirmed the district court's more extensive findings, that the requester before it was not a representative of the news media.[74]

The D.C. Circuit did make clear at the time of its decision in National Security Archive, however, that the term "representative of the news media" excludes "'private librar[ies]' or 'private repositories'" of government records, or middlemen such as "'information vendors [or] data brokers,'" who request records for use by others.[75] This fee category, though, includes freelance journalists, when they can demonstrate a solid basis for expecting the information disclosed to be published by a news organiza-

---

[71](...continued) al directive, promulgated regulations that define "representative of the news media"); Judicial Watch, 122 F. Supp. 2d at 20 (considering the agency's regulatory definition of "representative of the news media" in its analysis, and finding to be "perhaps of utmost importance" the fact that the plaintiff organization "does not define itself as an 'entity that is organized and operated to publish or broadcast news'" (quoting from definition found at 28 C.F.R. § 16.11(b)(6))); Judicial Watch, 122 F. Supp. 2d at 12 (same); Judicial Watch, 2000 WL 33724693, at *3 (referring to and quoting from the agency's promulgated definition of "representative of the news media").

[72] Brown, 2007 WL 446601; Hosp. & Physician Publ'g, No. 99-3152 (7th Cir. Feb. 24, 2005) (remanding for purposes of adoption of parties' settlement agreement and dismissal of case).

[73] Hosp. & Physician Publ'g, 1999 WL 33582100, at *3 (ordering defendant to apply news media status to plaintiff even though it had not gathered news in past, nor did so at time of litigation, but had expressed its intention to "begin gathering news for dissemination . . . to news media via free news releases").

[74] Brown, 2007 WL 446601, at *2 (concluding that requester's "status as the publisher of a website does not make him a representative of the news media").

[75] Nat'l Sec. Archive, 880 F.2d at 1387; Hall, 2005 WL 850379, at *6 (finding plaintiff's activities to be more akin to those of middleman).

tion.[76]

It is well settled that a request from a representative of the news media that supports a news-dissemination function "shall not be considered to be a request that is for a commercial use."[77] A request from a representative of the news media that does not support its news-dissemination function, however, should not be accorded the favored fee treatment of this subcategory.[78]

Further, a request that is made to support an endeavor that merely makes the information received available to the public (or others) is not sufficient to qualify it for placement in this fee category.[79] Under the FOIA,

---

[76] See OMB Fee Guidelines, 52 Fed. Reg. at 10,018 (stating that for free-lancers, publication contract with news organization would be "clearest" proof for inclusion in news media category but that agencies may consider "past publication record" in this regard); Brown, 445 F. Supp. 2d at 1356-57 (finding that the plaintiff has not shown "that he is a freelance journalist with a 'solid basis for expecting publication'" (quoting agency regulation)). But see Hosp. & Physician Publ'g, 1999 WL 33582100, at *3, *5 (ordering, in a fact-specific case, the defendant to apply news media status to the plaintiff even though the plaintiff had not gathered news in the past but expressed intention to do so in the future; noting that the requester represented that the information received "will eventually be disseminated to the news media," that it will "not receive any income from its news gathering activities," and that "any windfall to the commercial aspect of its business will be negligible").

[77] OMB Fee Guidelines, 52 Fed. Reg. at 10,019; accord FOIA Update, Vol. VIII, No. 1, at 10; see also Nat'l Sec. Archive, 880 F.2d at 1387-88; 28 C.F.R. § 16.11(b)(6) (Department of Justice fee regulation defining "representative of the news media"); cf. Tax Analysts, 965 F.2d at 1096 (remarking that in the context of attorney fees, "[i]f newspapers and television news shows had to show the absence of commercial interests before they could win attorney[] fees in FOIA cases, very few, if any, would ever prevail").

[78] See Nat'l Sec. Archive, 880 F.2d at 1387 (stating that "there is no reason to treat an entity with news media activities in its portfolio . . . as a 'representative of the news media' when it requests documents . . . in aid of its nonjournalistic activities"); cf. Elec. Privacy Info. Ctr., 241 F. Supp. 2d at 14 n.6 (stating affirmatively that "not every organization with its own newsletter will necessarily qualify for news media status" and that, to qualify, a newsletter "must disseminate actual 'news' to the public, rather than solely self-promoting articles about that organization").

[79] See Nat'l Sec. Archive, 880 F.2d at 1386 (finding that "making information available to the public . . . is insufficient to establish an entitlement to preferred [fee] status"); see also Hall, 2005 WL 850379, at *6 (stating that plaintiff's endeavors "may establish" him as "vendor of information" but not
(continued...)

once a requester has gathered information of interest to the public it must, in some manner, "use its editorial skills to turn the raw materials into a distinct work" in order to qualify as a representative of the news media.[80] In the first case to construe this subcategory of requesters, the requester's status was not in dispute but rather where the news organization performed its media function. There the court held that even a foreign news service may qualify as a representative of the news media.[81]

The third level of fees, which applies to all requesters who do not fall within either of the preceding two fee levels, consists of reasonable charges for document search and duplication,[82] as was provided for in the statutory FOIA fee provision that was in place before the 1986 FOIA amendments.

When any FOIA request is submitted by someone on behalf of another person -- for example, by an attorney on behalf of a client -- it is nevertheless the underlying requester's identity and intended use that determines the level of fees.[83] When such information is not readily apparent from the request itself, agencies should seek clarification from the requester before assigning a requester to a specific requester category.[84]

An agency of course need not undertake a "fee category" analysis in any instance in which it has granted a full fee waiver.[85] Similarly, there is

---

[79](...continued)
as representative of news media).

[80] Id. at 1387; cf. Elec. Privacy Info. Ctr., 241 F. Supp. 2d at 12 ("Labels and titles alone . . . do not govern" the qualification for media status; rather, "the organization's substantive activities control.").

[81] Southam News v. INS, 674 F. Supp. 881, 892 (D.D.C. 1987).

[82] See 5 U.S.C. § 552(a)(4)(A)(ii)(III).

[83] See OMB Fee Guidelines, 52 Fed. Reg at 10,017-18; see also Dale v. IRS, 238 F. Supp. 2d 99, 107 (D.D.C. 2002) ("A party's counsel is not the 'requester' for purposes of a fee waiver request.").

[84] See id. at 10,013, 10,018 (explaining that under the FOIA Reform Act agencies will spend more time "determining what the requester intends to do with the records sought").

[85] See Carney, 19 F.3d at 814 n.3 (doubting requester's status as "news media" but stating that there was no need to resolve issue given his entitlement to fee waiver); Prison Legal News v. Lappin, 436 F. Supp. 2d 17, 27 (D.D.C. 2006) (finding "no need to analyze" entitlement to news media status where plaintiff was entitled to full fee waiver); Judicial Watch, Inc. v. U.S. Dep't of Transp., No. 02-566, 2005 WL 1606915, at *5 n.2 (D.D.C. July 5, 2005) (same); Judicial Watch, 310 F. Supp. at 293 n.3 (same); Long v. (continued...)

simply no need to determine a requester's fee category whenever the only assessable fee is a duplication fee, as that type of fee is properly chargeable to all three categories of requesters.[86] Nor is an agency required to establish at an earlier date a requester's proper fee category with regard to any future FOIA requests that it might make.[87] Agencies also should be alert to the fact that a requester's category can change over time.[88]

Additionally, the OMB Fee Guidelines authorize the recovery of the full costs of providing all categories of requesters with "special services" that are not required by the FOIA, such as when an agency complies with a request for certifying records as true copies or mailing records by express mail.[89] In this regard, agencies should strive to use the "most efficient and least costly" means of complying with a request.[90] This may include the

---

[85](...continued)
ATF, 964 F. Supp. 494, 498, 499 (D.D.C. 1997) (same); Project on Military Procurement v. Dep't of the Navy, 710 F. Supp 362, 368 (D.D.C. 1989) (same).

[86] See 5 U.S.C. § 552(a)(4)(A)(i)(I)-(III).

[87] See, e.g., Long, 450 F. Supp. 2d at 85 (concluding that "any declaration" by the court of a requester's fee status for future requests was not ripe, and that denial of "such a determination does not preclude a favorable outcome in the future, not least of all because an entity's status can change"); Long, 964 F. Supp. at 498, 499 (rejecting plaintiff's request for declaratory judgment as to requester category when no fee was at issue, and finding that question was not ripe as to future requests).

[88] See Nat'l Sec. Archive, 880 F.2d at 1388 (stating that court's determination of requester's news media status is "not chiselled in granite"); Long, 450 F. Supp. 2d at 85 (indicating that "an entity's status can change"); Long, 964 F. Supp. at 498 (same).

[89] OMB Fee Guidelines, 52 Fed. Reg. at 10,018; see, e.g., 28 C.F.R. § 16.11(f) (Department of Justice fee regulation); cf. OMB Fee Guidelines, 52 Fed Reg. at 10,016 (specifying that charges for ordinary packaging and mailing are to be borne by government); FOIA Update, Vol. XII, No. 2, at 4 ("[T]he effective administration of the FOIA relies quite heavily upon agency transmittal of disclosable record copies to FOIA requesters by mail.").

[90] See OMB Fee Guidelines, 52 Fed. Reg. at 10,018; see also Exec. Order No. 13,392, Sec. 3 (outlining several areas of FOIA administration to be considered by agencies in development of their FOIA Improvement Plans, including changes that will make processing of FOIA requests more streamlined and efficient); FOIA Post, "Executive Order 13,392 Implementation Guidance" (posted 4/27/06) (detailing the "potential improvement areas" of Executive Order 13,392, and emphasizing that "each agency should . . . consider its own individual circumstances in identifying particular areas in which it can improve its administration of the FOIA in accordance with Ex-
(continued...)

use of contractor services, as long as an agency does not relinquish responsibilities it alone must perform, such as making fee waiver determinations.[91] With regard to any contractor services that agencies may employ,
the OMB Fee Guidelines provide that agencies should ensure that the cost
to the requester "is no greater than it would be if the agency itself had performed the task."[92]

The fee structure also includes restrictions both on the assessment of
certain fees[93] and on the authority of agencies to ask for an advance payment of a fee.[94] No FOIA fee may be charged by an agency if the government's cost of collecting and processing the fee is likely to equal or exceed
the amount of the fee itself.[95] In addition, except with respect to commer-

---

[90](...continued)
ecutive Order 13,392"); FOIA Update, Vol. XVI, No. 1, at 1-2 (stressing importance of cost-efficiency to overall process of FOIA administration); Attorney General Ashcroft's FOIA Memorandum, reprinted in FOIA Post
(posted 10/15/01) (stressing importance of "efficien[cy]" in government);
Info. Handling Servs., Inc. v. Def. Automated Printing Servs., 338 F.3d 1024,
1027 (D.C. Cir. 2003) (referencing cost comparison required by 10 U.S.C.A.
§ 2462 (1998 & West Supp. 2006) to determine whether government could
produce documents at lower costs than private sector) (non-FOIA case).

[91] See OMB Fee Guidelines, 52 Fed. Reg. at 10,018; see also FOIA Update, Vol. IV, No. 1, at 2 (citing applicable Comptroller General decisions).

[92] OMB Fee Guidelines, 52 Fed. Reg. at 10,018; cf. FOIA Post, "The Use of
Contractors in FOIA Administration" (posted 9/30/04) (noting that encouraging agencies to extend "contracting out" beyond the duplication of records is in accordance with Comptroller General decisions, and observing
that "the trend clearly is in favor of allowing contractors to do any work
that does not require 'discretionary decision-making'"); FOIA Update, Vol.
IV, No. 1, at 2 (recounting early efforts by some agencies to use contractors
for duplication services under the FOIA, and encouraging agencies to extend "the concept of contracting out").

[93] Compare 132 Cong. Rec. H9464 (daily ed. Oct. 8, 1986) (statement of
Rep. English) (remarking that the restrictive statutory provisions were designed "to prevent agencies from using procedural ploys over fees to discourage requesters or delay the disclosure of information"), with Dep't of
Justice v. Tax Analysts, 492 U.S. 136, 146 (1989) (going so far, in the context of requested materials "that are readily available elsewhere," as to
pragmatically observe that "the fact that the FOIA allows agencies to
[properly] recoup the costs of processing requests from the requester may
discourage recourse to the FOIA," but nonetheless viewing that as a preferable result in such instances).

[94] See 5 U.S.C. § 552(a)(4)(A)(iv)-(v).

[95] Id. § 552(a)(4)(A)(iv)(I); see also OMB Fee Guidelines, 52 Fed. Reg. at
(continued...)

cial-use requesters, agencies must provide the first one hundred pages of duplication, as well as the first two hours of search time, without cost to the requester.[96] These two provisions work together so that, except with respect to commercial-use requesters, agencies should not begin to assess fees until after they provide this amount of free search and duplication; the assessable fee for any requester then must be greater than the agency's cost to collect and process it in order for the fee actually to be charged.[97]

Agencies also may not require a requester to make an advance payment, i.e., payment before work is begun or continued on a request, unless the agency first estimates that the assessable fee is likely to exceed $250, or unless the requester has previously failed to pay a properly assessed fee in a timely manner (i.e., within thirty days of the billing date).[98] Agencies

---

[95](...continued) 10,018.

[96] See 5 U.S.C. § 552(a)(4)(A)(iv)(II); see also OMB Fee Guidelines, 52 Fed. Reg. at 10,018-19; Carlson v. USPS, No. 02-05471, 2005 WL 756573, at *8 (N.D. Cal. Mar. 31, 2005) (upholding requester's statutory entitlement to two hours of search time and 100 pages of duplication without cost regardless of whether remainder of responsive records were to be processed); cf. Trupei v. DEA, No. 04-1481, 2005 WL 3276290, at *3 (D.D.C. Sept. 27, 2005) (upholding agency's refusal to expend additional search time without payment of fees where statutory allowance of two hours was already exceeded); Hicks v. Hardy, No. 04-0769, slip op. at 2 (D.D.C. Sept. 25, 2005) (observing that agency had apprised requester that "100-page limit on free releases" was reached and that commitment was needed to pay for remaining responsive records), renewed motion for summary judgment granted to agency, No. 04-0769, 2006 WL 949918 (D.D.C. Apr. 12, 2006); Pietrangelo v. U.S. Dep't of the Army, No. 2:04-CV-44, slip op. at 14 (D. Vt. Mar. 7, 2005) (quoting with implicit approval the agency's fee regulation requiring the requester to commit to pay fees in excess of the statutory allowances, and noting that if the requester fails to state a "'willingness to pay . . . then the request need not be processed'"), summary affirmance granted, 155 F. App'x 526 (2d Cir. 2005) (unpublished table decision).

[97] See 5 U.S.C. § 552(a)(4)(A)(iv)(I); see also OMB Fee Guidelines, 52 Fed. Reg. at 10,018; see, e.g., 28 C.F.R. § 16.11(d)(4) (Department of Justice fee regulation establishing fee threshold below which no fee will be charged).

[98] See 5 U.S.C. § 552(a)(4)(A)(v); see also OMB Fee Guidelines, 52 Fed. Reg. at 10,020; O'Meara v. IRS, No. 97-3383, 1998 WL 123984, at *1-2 (7th Cir. Mar. 17, 1998) (upholding agency's demand for advance payment when fees exceeded $800); Pietrangelo, No. 2:04-CV-44, slip op. at 14 (D. Vt. Mar. 7, 2005) ("Fees may be estimated by the agency and demanded in advance if the fee will exceed $250."); Idema v. U.S. Attorney, E. Dist. of N.C., No. 03-2493, slip op. at 2 (D.D.C. Feb. 25, 2005) (determining that there was no improper withholding where agency regulation required payment in advance
(continued...)

certainly may require requesters to make written agreements to pay the estimated or actual fees necessary to process a request as a condition precedent to a request being deemed received by the agency.[99] Estimated

---

[98](...continued)
of processing once total fee exceeded $250 but requester had not paid such fee); McDade, No. 03-1946, slip op. at 6 (D.D.C. Sept. 29, 2004) (citing with implicit approval agency regulation requiring requester to make advance payment before agency processes request once fees exceed $250); Jeanes v. U.S. Dep't of Justice, 357 F. Supp. 2d 119, 123 (D.D.C. 2004) (citing with implicit approval the agency's regulation requiring an advance fee payment, noting that "'the request shall not be considered received and further work will not be done on it until required payment is received'" (quoting 28 C.F.R. § 16.11(i)(4))); TPS, Inc., 2003 U.S. Dist. LEXIS 10925, at *8-9 (upholding agency's refusal to process further requests until all outstanding FOIA debts were paid) (appeal pending); Voinche v. FBI, No. 99-1931, slip op. at 6-7 (D.D.C. Nov. 17, 2000) (upholding agency's request for advance payment on basis of both statute and agency regulation where fees exceeded $250); Rothman v. Daschle, No. 96-5898, 1997 U.S. Dist. LEXIS 13009, at *2 (E.D. Pa. Aug. 20, 1997) (upholding agency's request for advance payment when fees exceeded $250); Mason v. Bell, No. 78-719-A, slip op. at 1 (E.D. Va. May 16, 1979) (finding dismissal of FOIA case proper when plaintiffs failed to pay fees to other federal agencies for prior requests). But cf. Ruotolo v. Dep't of Justice, 53 F.3d 4, 9-10 (2d Cir. 1995) (suggesting that agency should have processed request up to amount offered by requesters rather than state that estimated cost "would greatly exceed" $250 without providing an amount to be paid or offering assistance in reformulating request).

[99] See Kumar v. U.S. Dep't of Justice, No. 06-714, 2007 U.S. Dist. LEXIS 11144, at *6-7 (D.D.C. Feb. 16, 2007) (impliedly approving agency fee regulations with regard to notification to requester of fee estimate, requirement for commitment in writing by requester to pay anticipated fee, and agency's ability to require advance payment in certain circumstances); Hinojosa v. Dep't of Treasury, No. 06-0215, 2006 WL 2927095, at *4 (D.D.C. Oct. 11, 2006) (implicitly approving agency's requirement that requester make "firm promise" to pay fees); McDade, No. 03-1946, slip op. at 6 (D.D.C. Sept. 29, 2004) (citing with implicit approval agency's regulation requiring written agreement to pay fees before request is considered received); Dale, 238 F. Supp. 2d at 107 (dismissing case because plaintiff failed to make "firm commitment" to pay fees); cf. Kemmerly v. U.S. Dep't of Interior, No. 06-2386, 2006 WL 2990122, at *1 (E.D. La. Oct. 17, 2006) (finding requester's agreement to pay "reasonable fees" to be insufficient under FOIA and agency's implementing regulation); Hall, 2005 WL 850379, at *5 n.9 (noting that although plaintiff characterized agency's six-figure fee estimate as "ludicrous," he sought neither accounting nor relief from estimated fees from court). But see Hinojosa, 2006 WL 2927095, at *4-5 (finding that requesters' commitment to pay up to $50 per request "appears to satisfy" requirement of "firm promise" to pay); Baker & Hostetler LLP v. U.S. Dep't of Commerce,

(continued...)

fees, though, are not intended to be used to discourage requesters from exercising their access rights under the FOIA.[100] And an agency that fails to follow its own regulations which require furnishing requesters with notice of the estimated fees necessary to process a FOIA request and of their obligation to provide a written agreement to pay those fees may be precluded from collecting the full fee, if at all, from the requester.[101]

The statutory restriction prohibiting a demand for advance payments does not of course prevent agencies from requiring payment before records which have been processed are released.[102] Most notably in this regard,

---

[99](...continued)
No. 02-2522, slip op. at 30 (D.D.C. Mar. 31, 2004) (stating that where agency's fee determination found reasonable and law firm had expressed "willingness" to pay reasonable search and production fees, request for order directing plaintiff to pay remaining fees "presumably unnecessary").

[100] See Hall v. CIA, No. 04-0814, 2006 WL 197462, at *3 & n.4 (D.D.C. Jan. 25, 2006) (recognizing that it would be improper for agencies to inflate fees to discourage requests, but finding that propriety of fees assessed for records subject to prior court action cannot be put into question in current action); see also S. Rep. No. 93-864, at 11-12 (1974) (indicating that statutory fee waiver provision was amended to deter agencies from using fees to discourage requesters).

[101] See, e.g., 28 C.F.R. § 16.3(c); 28 C.F.R. § 16.11(e); cf. Sliney v. Fed. Bureau of Prisons, No. 04-1812, 2005 WL 839540, at *4 (D.D.C. Apr. 11, 2005) (characterizing agency's contention that requester failed to exhaust by paying fees as "disingenuous" where agency failed to notify requester of fee at administrative level as required by agency fee regulation), renewed motion for summary judgment granted, No. 04-1812, 2005 WL 3273567, at *4 (D.D.C. Sept. 28, 2005) (resolving that agency had corrected defect and that requester failed to exhaust administrative remedies with regard to processing fee); Cole-El v. U.S. Dep't of Justice, No. 03-1013, slip op. at 11-12 (D.D.C. Aug. 26, 2004) (finding search fee "unjustified" due to inadequacy of searches performed by agency), aff'd per curiam on other grounds sub nom. Cole v. U.S. Dep't of Justice, No. 04-5329, 2005 U.S. App. LEXIS 7358 (D.C. Cir. Apr. 27, 2005).

[102] See Strout v. U.S. Parole Comm'n, 40 F.3d 136, 139 (6th Cir. 1994) (finding that agency regulation requiring payment before release of processed records does not conflict with statutory prohibition against advance payment); Kong On Imp. & Exp. Co. v. U.S. Customs & Border Prot. Bureau, No. 04-2001, 2005 WL 1458279, at *1 (D.D.C. June 20, 2005) (citing with implicit approval agency's fee regulation that required payment before release of processed records); Farrugia v. Executive Office for U.S. Attorneys, 366 F. Supp. 2d 56, 57 (D.D.C. 2005) (explaining that where requested records are already processed, payment may be required by agency before sending them), subsequent opinion granting summary judgment to

(continued...)

when an agency reasonably believes that a requester is attempting to divide a request into a series of requests for the purpose of avoiding the assessment of fees, the agency may aggregate those requests and charge accordingly.[103] The OMB Fee Guidelines should be consulted for additional guidance on aggregating requests.[104]

The FOIA also provides that FOIA fees are superseded by "fees chargeable under a statute specifically providing for setting the level of fees for particular types of records."[105] Thus, when documents responsive

---

[102](...continued)
agency, No. 04-0294, 2006 WL 33577 (D.D.C. Feb. 14, 2006); Williams v. U.S. Dep't of Justice, No. 01-1009, slip op. at 3 (D.D.C. Jan. 22, 2003) (noting that agency may properly require payment before processed records are released); Voinche v. CIA, No. 98-1883, 2000 U.S. Dist. LEXIS 14291, at *13-14 (D.D.C. Sept. 27, 2000) (same); Taylor v. U.S. Dep't of the Treasury, No. A-96-CA-933, 1996 U.S. Dist. LEXIS 19909, at *5 (W.D. Tex. Dec. 17, 1996) (same); Crooker v. ATF, 882 F. Supp. 1158, 1162 (D. Mass. 1995) (finding no obligation to provide records until current and past due fees paid); see also, e.g., 28 C.F.R. § 16.11(i)(1) ("Payment owed for work already completed (i.e., a prepayment before copies are sent to the requester) is not an advance payment."); cf. Lee v. U.S. Dep't of Justice, 235 F.R.D. 274, 285 (W.D. Pa. 2006) (finding the agency's proposal to search a large number of district offices designated by the requester "three offices at a time" and, after the requester's payment was made for searching those three offices, "repeating the process until all districts had been searched," is permissible); Sliney, 2005 WL 3273567, at *4 (noting that no authority supported the plaintiff's proposal that his suggested "installment plan" for paying fees "constitutes an agreement to pay the total fee"); Hall, 2005 WL 850379, at *5 (finding that the requester's rationale for not paying fees -- i.e., that he did not "'wish to buy a pig in a poke'" -- did not "entitle him to resuscitate his previously filed, now-dismissed action"). But cf. Hemmings v. Freeh, No. 95-0738, 2005 WL 975626, at *3 (D.D.C. Apr. 25, 2005) (criticizing government's exhaustion argument as "form over substance" where none of its several requests for fee payment -- ultimately made by plaintiff after government filed motion to dismiss -- provided any "hard and fast deadline" for doing so).

[103] See OMB Fee Guidelines, 52 Fed. Reg. at 10,019; see also Atkin v. EEOC, No. 91-2508, slip op. at 20-21 (D.N.J. Dec. 4, 1992) (finding agency's decision to aggregate requests proper; reasonable for agency to believe that thirteen requests relating to same subject matter submitted within three-month period were made by requester to evade payment of fees), appeal dismissed for failure to timely prosecute sub nom. Atkin v. Kemp, No. 93-5548 (3d Cir. Dec. 6, 1993).

[104] OMB Fee Guidelines, 52 Fed. Reg. at 10,019-20.

[105] 5 U.S.C. § 552(a)(4)(A)(vi); see, e.g., Oglesby v. U.S. Dep't of the Army,
(continued...)

to a FOIA request are maintained for distribution by an agency according to a statutorily based fee schedule, requesters should obtain the documents from that source and pay the applicable fees in accordance with the fee schedule of that other statute.[106] This may at times result in the assessment of fees that are higher than those that would otherwise be chargeable under the FOIA,[107] but it ensures that such fees are properly borne by

---

[105](...continued)
79 F.3d 1172, 1177 (D.C. Cir. 1996) (stating that NARA's enabling statute, 44 U.S.C. § 2116 (2000), qualifies "as the genre of fee-setting provision not to be 'supersede[d]' under the FOIA's subsection (vi)" with regard to "the costs of making . . . reproductions of materials transferred to [requester's] custody"); see also FOIA Post, "NTIS: An Available Means of Record Disclosure" (posted 8/30/02; supplemented 9/23/02) (describing how the National Technical Information Service "occupies a special status" with respect to making records available to the public, pursuant to 1986 FOIA amendments, 5 U.S.C. § 552(a)(4)(A)(vi)); National Technical Information Act, 15 U.S.C. §§ 1151-57 (2000) (providing for dissemination of technological, scientific, and engineering information to business and industry); OMB Fee Guidelines, 52 Fed. Reg. at 10,017, 10,018; cf. Envtl. Prot. Info. Ctr., 432 F.3d at 947, 948 (finding the FOIA's superseding fee provision to be "ambiguous," relying instead on OMB's Guidelines that discuss that provision, and determining that the FOIA's reference to "a statute specifically providing for setting the level of fees" means "'any statute that specifically requires a government agency . . . to set the level of fees'" and not one that simply allows it to do so (quoting OMB Fee Guidelines) (emphasis added)).

[106] See OMB Fee Guidelines, 52 Fed. Reg. at 10,012-13, 10,017-18 (implementing 5 U.S.C. § 552(a)(4)(A)(vi), and advising agencies to "inform requesters of the steps necessary to obtain records from those sources"); id. at 10,017 (contemplating "statutor[il]y-based fee schedule programs . . . such as the NTIS [National Technical Information Service]"); Wade v. Dep't of Commerce, No. 96-0717, slip op. at 5-6 (D.D.C. Mar. 26, 1998) (concluding that fee was "properly charged by NTIS" under its fee schedule); cf. SDC Dev. Corp. v. Mathews, 542 F.2d 1116, 1120 (9th Cir. 1976) (in decision predating 1986 FOIA amendments and turning on issue of "agency records," holding that records for which charges were specifically authorized by another statute were not required to be made available under FOIA). But see Envtl. Prot. Info. Ctr., 432 F.3d at 948-49 (holding that a statute permitting the agency to sell maps and Geospatial Information System data "at not less than the estimated [reproduction] cost," or allowing the agency "to make other disposition of such . . . materials," was not a "superseding fee statute" given the discretionary nature of the agency's authority to charge fees, and recognizing that court's decision "may be at odds" with the D.C. Circuit's decision in Oglesby, 79 F.3d 1172).

[107] See, e.g., Wade, No. 96-0717, slip op. at 2, 6 (D.D.C. Mar. 26, 1998) (approving assessment of $1300 fee pursuant to National Technical Information Service's superseding fee statute and noting agency's return of re-
(continued...)

the requester and not by the general public.[108]

Given the increasing availability of low-cost and free government information through the Internet and other electronic sources,[109] it remains to be seen whether those agencies with such statutorily based fee schedules -- and which do not receive appropriated funds to support their record-distribution services, but are required by law to be self-sustaining -- will continue to be viable sources of government information.[110] The superseding of FOIA fees by the fee provisions of another statute raises a related question as to whether an agency with a statutorily based fee schedule for particular types of records is subject to the FOIA's fee waiver provision in those instances where it applies an alternate fee schedule.[111] Although this question has been raised, it has not yet been explicitly decided by an appellate court.[112]

---

[107](...continued) quester's $210 check for anticipated FOIA fees).

[108] See OMB Fee Guidelines, 52 Fed. Reg. at 10,017.

[109] See Exec. Order No. 13,392, Sec. 3 (providing that review of each agency's FOIA operations should include an examination of agency's use of information technology and review of policies and practices relating to availability of information through Web sites); see also FOIA Post, "Executive Order 13,392 Implementation Guidance" (posted 4/27/06) (potential improvement areas).

[110] See, e.g., id. at 10,018 (recognizing National Technical Information Service as "statutorily-based" government record distribution program). See generally White House Memorandum for Heads of Executive Departments and Agencies Concerning Safeguarding Information Related to Homeland Security (Mar. 19, 2002), reprinted in FOIA Post (posted 3/21/02) (recognizing sensitivity of records distributed through Defense Technical Information Center (commonly known as "DTIC"), Department of Defense counterpart to National Technical Information Service).

[111] See Envtl. Prot. Info. Ctr., 432 F.3d at 946, 948 (recognizing the FOIA's superseding fee provision as an "exception to the fee waiver provision of the FOIA," but stating that the statute in question did not qualify under the exception).

[112] Compare Oglesby, 79 F.3d at 1178 (refusing to rule on district court's finding that NARA's fee provision is exempt from FOIA's fee waiver requirement, because appellant failed to raise argument in timely manner), and Oglesby v. U.S. Dep't of the Army, 920 F.2d 57, 70 n.17 (D.C. Cir. 1990) (declining to reach fee waiver issue because plaintiff failed to exhaust administrative remedies), with Envtl. Prot. Info. Ctr., 432 F.3d at 946, 948 (recognizing the FOIA's superseding fee provision as an "exception to the fee waiver provision of the FOIA," and stating that "only statutes setting mandatory fees" meet that exception), and St. Hilaire v. Dep't of Justice, No. 91-
(continued...)

The FOIA requires that requesters follow the agency's published rules for making FOIA requests, including those pertaining to the payment of authorized fees.[113] Requesters have been found not to have exhausted their administrative remedies when fee requirements have not been met,[114]

---

[112](...continued) 0078, slip op. at 4-5 (D.D.C. Sept. 10, 1991) (avoiding fee waiver issue because requested records were made publicly available), summary judgment granted to agency (D.D.C. Mar. 18, 1992), aff'd per curiam, No. 92-5153 (D.C. Cir. Apr. 28, 1994).

[113] See 5 U.S.C. § 552(a)(3)(B); 28 C.F.R. § 16.11(e); Hinojosa, 2006 WL 2927095, at *4 (stating that a request must comply with the FOIA and with the agency's requirements, "including a firm promise to pay applicable processing fees"); Dinsio v. FBI, 445 F. Supp. 2d 305, 311 (W.D.N.Y. 2006) (reiterating that requester is required to follow agency rules "for requesting, reviewing and paying for documents"); see also Judicial Watch v. U.S. Dep't of Justice, No. 99-1883, slip op. at 16 (D.D.C. Sept. 11, 2003) (finding agency's closure of request proper where requester neither committed to pay processing fees nor made advance payment of fees as required by agency's fee regulations); Irons v. FBI, 571 F. Supp. 1241, 1243 (D. Mass. 1983); cf. Oglesby, 920 F.2d at 66; Lee, 235 F.R.D. at 285 (granting summary judgment on portion of defendant's motion that concerned requester's failure to comply with agency regulations governing where to send FOIA request) (non fee context); Casad v. HHS, No. 01-1911, 2003 U.S. Dist. LEXIS 13007, at *16-17 (D.D.C. June 20, 2003) (approving necessity of further response by requester in order to inform agency whether to proceed with request once agency advised requester of costs); DeCato v. Executive Office for U.S. Attorneys, No. 00-3053, slip op. at 4-5 & n.4 (D.D.C. Jan. 2, 2003) (emphasizing that the plaintiff's offer to pay fees under his "alternate payment plan "is not construed as his written agreement to pay the fees" as required by the agency's regulation), summary affirmance granted, No. 03-5044, 2003 WL 22433759, at *1 (D.C. Cir. Oct. 24, 2003); Dale, 238 F. Supp. 2d at 107 (dismissing case because plaintiff failed to make "firm commitment" to pay fees); O'Meara, 1998 WL 123984, at *1 ("Congress intended people making FOIA requests to bear the costs of processing such requests" unless they qualify for fee waiver). But cf. Keen v. FBI, No. 98-2658, slip op. at 4-5 (D.D.C. July 9, 2002) (magistrate's recommendation) (finding request "wrongfully terminated" where agency failed to advise requester that request would be closed if he did not respond to agency's letter that notified him of fees and suggested that he narrow scope of request), adopted (D.D.C. Aug. 26, 2002), renewed motion for summary judgment granted to agency, No. 98-2658, 2006 U.S. Dist. LEXIS 71860 (D.D.C. Sept. 29, 2006).

[114] See, e.g., Trenerry v. IRS, No. 95-5150, 1996 WL 88459, at *2 (10th Cir. Mar. 1, 1996) (explaining exhaustion includes payment of FOIA fees); Antonelli v. ATF, No. 04-1180, 2006 U.S. Dist. LEXIS 90923, at *6 (D.D.C. Dec. 18, 2006) (stating that fee exhaustion is jurisdictional prerequisite); Kemmerly, 2006 WL 2990122, at *1 (reiterating that requester's decision to

(continued...)

[114](...continued)
await agency's delayed response requires actual exhaustion of administration remedies before filing suit); Keen, 2006 U.S. Dist. LEXIS 71860, at *5 (concluding that where requester challenged portion of fee assessed by agency but did not dispute nor pay remainder, there was no exhaustion of administrative remedies as to unpaid portion; noting that requester provided no authority for proposition that until administrative appeal was adjudicated he had no legal obligation "to make [any] payment"); Dinsio, 445 F. Supp. 2d at 311 (determining that plaintiff was barred from seeking judicial review due to failure to agree to pay fees); Sells v. Executive Office for U.S. Attorneys, No. 06-0077, 2006 U.S. Dist. LEXIS 58446, at *4-5 (D.D.C. Aug. 21, 2006) (stating that exhaustion requirement was not met where plaintiff failed to pay or commit to pay fees); Ivey v. Snow, No. 05-1095, 2006 WL 2051339, at *4 (D.D.C. July 20, 2006) (finding that because plaintiff failed to pay fees or request waiver he had not exhausted administrative remedies); Green v. DEA, No. 03-2268, 2006 WL 826466, at *1 (D.D.C. Mar. 29, 2006) (reiterating that exhaustion of administrative remedies -- in this instance by paying assessed fees -- is "condition precedent" to filing FOIA suit); Antonelli v. ATF, No. 04-1108, 2006 WL 141732, at *3 (D.D.C. Jan. 18, 2006) (same), partial summary judgment granted, No. 04-1108, 2006 WL 695905, at *5 (D.D.C. Mar. 17, 2006) (same); Trani v. U.S. Dep't of Justice, No. 04-0399, 2005 WL3276178, at *1 (D.D.C. July 22, 2005) (stating that in absence of fee waiver request, failure to pay or to commit to pay is grounds for dismissal for failure to exhaust); Smith v. IRS, No. 2:94-CV-989, slip op. at 2 (D. Utah Mar. 24, 1999) (concluding that no exhaustion existed where requester failed to pay fees); see also Hicks, No. 04-0769, slip op. at 4 (D.D.C. Sept. 26, 2005) (finding that agency's failure to provide appeal rights -- in letter dated ten months after date of request and after litigation ensued -- defeated agency's exhaustion argument based on failure to pay fees); Loomis v. U.S. Dep't of Energy, No. 96-CV-149, slip op. at 9-10 (N.D.N.Y. Mar. 9, 1999) (stating that exhaustion occurred where plaintiff agreed to pay initial estimate for identified records which agency subsequently found covered only portion of fees), summary affirmance granted, 21 F. App'x 80 (2d Cir. 2000); Stanley v. DOD, No. 93-CV-4247 (S.D. Ill. July 28, 1998) (stating that agency's failure to inform plaintiff of right to administratively appeal its fee estimate amounted to constructive exhaustion where agency's regulations allowed appeal of such estimates); cf. OSHA Data, 220 F.3d at 168 (affirming district court's dismissal where requester was unable to pay $1.7 million estimated fee); Graves v. EEOC, No. 02-6842, slip op. at 23 (C.D. Cal. Apr. 1, 2004) (ruling that there is no improper withholding where requester did not pay required fee), aff'd, 144 F. App'x 626 (9th Cir. 2005); Judicial Watch v. FBI, 190 F. Supp. 2d 29, 33 n.7 (D.D.C. 2002) (declining to consider plaintiff's belated willingness to pay fees where court concluded that it lacked jurisdiction due to plaintiff's failure to exhaust). But see Wiggins v. Nat'l Credit Union Admin., No. 05-2332, 2007 U.S. LEXIS 6367, *12-13 (D.D.C. Jan. 30, 2007) (finding that, despite the requester's "apparent failure" to exhaust for nonpayment of processing fee, the Court may review merits of the

(continued...)

-156-

including taking an appeal of an adverse fee determination.[115] A requester's obligation to comply with the agency's fee requirements does not
cease after litigation has been initiated under the FOIA.[116] (For a further

---

[114](...continued)
FOIA claim where the responsive records already had been released as "no
purpose would be served by having this matter delayed until the [request-
er] pays the required fee"); cf. Hemmings, 2005 WL 975626, at *3 (denying
government's motion to dismiss where plaintiff tendered payment shortly
after government filed its motion; stating that case law "suggests that his
nonpayment of FOIA fees may be cured by payment" -- in particular,
where, as here, agency gave no deadline by which to do so); Sliney, 2005
WL 839540, at *4 (characterizing agency's contention that requester failed
to exhaust by paying fees as "disingenuous" where agency failed to notify
requester of fee at administrative level as required by agency fee regulation), subsequent opinion granting summary judgment to agency, 2005 WL
3273567, at *4 (resolving ultimately that agency had corrected defect and
that requester failed to exhaust with regard to processing fee).

[115] See, e.g., Oglesby, 920 F.2d at 66 & n.11, 71 ("Exhaustion does not occur until the required fees are paid or an appeal is taken from the refusal to
waive fees."); Gonzalez v. ATF, No. 04-2201, 2005 WL 3201009, at *6 (D.D.C.
Nov. 9, 2005) (finding that requester's inaction -- i.e., that he never paid assessed fee nor appealed agency's refusal of fee waiver denial -- precludes
judicial review of request); Sliney, 2005 WL 3273567, at *4 (reiterating that
where plaintiff neither agreed to pay processing fee nor appealed agency's
refusal of his "'installment' plan" offer, administrative exhaustion had not
occurred); Antonelli v. ATF, No. 04-1108, 2005 U.S. Dist. LEXIS 17089, at
*28 (D.D.C. Aug. 16, 2005) (finding requester's unsuccessful administrative
appeal challenging amount of fee to be insufficient to satisfy exhaustion requirement); Thorn v. United States, No. 04-1185, 2005 WL 3276285, at *3
(D.D.C. Aug. 11, 2005) (concluding that the plaintiff failed to exhaust because he "neither paid required fees . . . nor appealed the initial agency determinations"); Jeanes, 357 F. Supp. 2d at 122 (reiterating that exhaustion
does not occur until either fees are paid or appeal is taken from fee waiver
denial); Tinsley v. Comm'r, No. 3:96-1769-P, 1998 WL 59481, at *4 (N.D. Tex.
Feb. 9, 1998) (finding that because plaintiff failed to appeal fee waiver denial, exhaustion was not achieved). But cf. Payne v. Minihan, No. 97-0266,
slip op. at 34 n.17 (D.N.M. Apr. 30, 1998) (holding, in fact-specific case, that
plaintiff was not required to exhaust by appealing fee waiver denial when
requester's right to sue already was perfected on different issue), summary
judgment granted (D.N.M. Oct. 27, 1999), aff'd, 232 F.3d 902 (10th Cir. 2000)
(unpublished table decision).

[116] See Pollack v. Dep't of Justice, 49 F.3d 115, 119-20 (4th Cir. 1995) (providing that commencement of FOIA action does not relieve requester of obligation to pay for documents); Kemmerly, 2006 WL 2990122, at *2 (emphasizing that whether the request for payment is made by the agency pre- or
post-litigation, "'the plaintiff has an obligation to pay'" (quoting Trueblood
(continued...)

discussion of the exhaustion requirement, including exhaustion of "fee" issues, see Litigation Considerations, Exhaustion of Administrative Remedies, below.)

Further, the Act contains no provision for reimbursement of fees if the requester is dissatisfied with the agency's response.[117] Nor does the FOIA provide for penalties to be assessed against an agency or its administrators for delays in refunding a requester's overpayment.[118] In addition, ab-

---

[116](...continued)
v. U.S. Dep't of the Treasury, 943 F. Supp. 64, 68 (D.D.C. 1996))); Gavin, 2006 U.S. Dist. LEXIS 75227, at *16 (stating that FOIA fees may be assessed post-litigation); Hicks, 2006 WL 949918, at *2 (same); Pietrangelo, No. 2:04-CV-44, slip op. at 13 (D. Vt. Mar. 7, 2005) (explaining that constructive exhaustion based on agency's failure to respond "'did not relieve [requester] of statutory obligation to pay any and all fees'" (quoting Pollack, 49 F.3d at 119)); Jeanes, 357 F. Supp. 2d at 123 (observing that although plaintiff did not receive notice of fees until after litigation ensued, obligation to pay fees remained); Maydak v. U.S. Dep't of Justice, 254 F. Supp. 2d 23, 50 (D.D.C. 2003) (noting that plaintiff is still obligated to pay fee or seek waiver even if agency's fee assessment is made after plaintiff files suit); Goulding v. IRS, No. 97 C 5628, 1998 WL 325202, at *9 (N.D. Ill. June 8, 1998) (finding plaintiff's constructive exhaustion did not relieve his obligation to pay authorized fees), summary judgment granted, No. 97 C 5628 (N.D. Ill. July 30, 1998) (restating that plaintiff's failure to comply with fee requirements is fatal to claim against government); Trueblood v. U.S. Dep't of the Treasury, 943 F. Supp. 64, 68 (D.D.C. 1996) (stating even if request for payment not made until after litigation commences, that fact does not relieve requester of obligation to pay reasonably assessed fees); cf. Pub. Citizen, Inc. v. Dep't of Educ., 292 F. Supp. 2d 1, 5 (D.D.C. 2003) (disallowing assessment of fees after litigation ensued where agency failed to inform requester that fees were in excess of amount to which it agreed, failed to give notice that fees would exceed $250 as required by regulation, and failed to address request for fee waiver); Judicial Watch of Fla., Inc. v. U.S. Dep't of Justice, No. 01-0212, slip op. at 3 (D.D.C. Oct. 19, 2001) (finding that plaintiff, through its actions, including its ambiguous response to court's order to notify agency of its intent with regard to payment of fees, "constructively abandoned its FOIA request").

[117] See Stabasefski, 919 F. Supp. at 1573 (stating that FOIA does not provide for reimbursement of fees when agency redacts portions of records that are released). But see FOIA Update, Vol. IV, No. 1, at 2 (explaining to agencies and assuring requesters that if requester prevails on administrative appeal, "fees previously paid will be reimbursed").

[118] See Johnson v. Executive Office for U.S. Attorneys, No. 98-0729, 2000 U.S. Dist. LEXIS 6095, at *8 (D.D.C. May 2, 2000) (observing that despite delay in refunding overpayment, FOIA does not provide for award of damages to requester, nor does delay rise to level of constitutional violation by
(continued...)

sent specific statutory authority allowing an agency (or a subdivision of it) to do so,[119] all fees collected in the course of providing FOIA services are to be deposited into the Treasury of the United States.[120]

Because the FOIA Reform Act was silent with respect to the standard and scope of judicial review of FOIA fee issues, including a requester's fee category,[121] the standard and scope of review should remain the same as that under the predecessor statutory fee provision -- i.e., agency action should be upheld unless it is found to be "arbitrary or capricious," in accordance with the Administrative Procedure Act.[122] Perhaps due to this

---

[118](...continued) agency or its employees), aff'd, 310 F.3d 771 (D.C. Cir. 2002); cf. FOIA Update, Vol. IV, No. 1, at 4 (providing for reimbursement of fees previously paid where requester ultimately prevails on fee waiver or fee reduction issue).

[119] See Food and Drug Administration Revitalization Act, Pub. L. No. 101-635, § 201, 104 Stat. 4584 (1990) (codified as amended at 21 U.S.C. § 379(f) (2000)) (authorizing FDA to "retain all fees charged for [FOIA] requests"); see also FOIA Update, Vol. XIII, No. 2, at 1, 9 n.30 (recounting Justice Department testimony that explained to Senate multiple practical difficulties with such legislative proposals).

[120] See OMB Fee Guidelines, 52 Fed. Reg. at 10,012, 10,017 (reminding agencies that funds collected for providing FOIA services must be deposited into general revenues of United States and not into agency accounts).

[121] See 5 U.S.C. § 552(a)(4)(A)(vii) (establishing revised de novo/administrative record standard and scope of review for fee waiver issues); cf. Hall, 2005 WL 850379, at *6 n.10 (deciding sua sponte, inasmuch as there was no administrative action to review because agency made no decision with regard to fee limitation, that plaintiffs failed to show "eligibility for fee limitations based on news media status").

[122] 5 U.S.C. §§ 701-706 (2000); see Snyder, No. C 03-4992, slip op. at 13-14 (N.D. Cal. Feb. 2, 2005) (agreeing that the FOIA does not provide a cause of action for a fee issue but observing that the plaintiff "surely states a claim under the Administrative Procedure Act['s] . . . more deferential [i.e., to agency] arbitrary and capricious standard of review"), subsequent opinion (N.D. Cal. Apr. 29, 2005); Judicial Watch, 122 F. Supp. 2d at 20 (applying arbitrary and capricious standard of review "based on [court's] prior analysis" in Judicial Watch, 122 F. Supp. 2d at 11); Judicial Watch, 122 F. Supp. 2d at 11 (acknowledging that standard of review for fee issue is not "as well settled" as other areas of FOIA but that this issue is "not difficult" under well-established principle of statutory construction; reasoning that because the FOIA Reform Act "only changed the standard of review for fee-waiver decisions, this court presumes that Congress retained the arbitrary and capricious standard of review for fee-category decisions"); Trainer v. IRS, No. 90-
(continued...)

lack of statutory clarity, the appropriate standard of review has yet to be clearly established in the decisions that have considered this issue.[123] Despite statutory language that seems to specify to the contrary,[124] the majority of courts that have reviewed fee issues under the FOIA have applied a single review standard (i.e., de novo review) to both fee and fee waiver matters, and they have done so with little or no discussion.[125] As for the

---

[122](...continued)
C-444-B, 1993 WL 56534, at *6 (N.D. Okla. Oct. 28, 1993) (finding assessed fees reasonable, in accordance with agency regulations, and not arbitrary and capricious); see also Rozet, 59 F. Supp. 2d at 56 n.2 (D.D.C. 1999) (noting that before 1986, courts reviewed all FOIA fee issues under arbitrary and capricious standard); cf. Long, 964 F. Supp. at 497 (finding plaintiff's allegation that assessment of fees was arbitrary and capricious was mooted by subsequent grant of fee waiver). But see Judicial Watch, 133 F. Supp. 2d at 53 (stating that agency's argument that arbitrary and capricious standard applies to requester's fee category "is unsupported").

[123] Compare Hall, 2005 WL 850379, at *6 n.10 (acknowledging that there is "some dispute" as to review standard for fee limitation based on news media status (citing Judicial Watch, 122 F. Supp. 2d at 11-12 (applying arbitrary and capricious standard), and Judicial Watch, 133 F. Supp. 2d at 53 (applying de novo standard))), Crain, No. 02-0341, slip op. at 5 & n.5 (D.D.C. Mar. 25, 2003) (stating that there is uncertainty within D.C. Circuit as to standard of review regarding fee category status), Judicial Watch, 185 F. Supp. 2d at 59 (conceding that there is "some disagreement as to the correct standard" for review of the agency's denial of media status), Judicial Watch, 2002 WL 535803, at *5 & nn. 6-7 (same), and Rozet, 59 F. Supp. 2d at 56 (emphasizing that although denial of fee waiver requests are reviewed de novo, "the appropriate standard of review for an agency determination of fee status under FOIA . . . has not been decided in this Circuit"), with Brown, 445 F. Supp. 2d at 1356 (acknowledging some disagreement as to the appropriate standard of review for the media category but applying the de novo standard "because review under the de novo standard or under some more deferential standard leads to the same conclusion" in the instant case), Elec. Privacy Info. Ctr., 241 F. Supp. 2d at 9 (concluding that "the statutory language, judicial authority, and [FOIA Reform Act's] legislative history . . . support the view that determinations regarding preferred fee status are reviewed de novo" while acknowledging that at least one recent court has applied the "arbitrary and capricious" standard), and Hosp. & Physician Publ'g, 1999 WL 33582100, at *2 (stating in single sentence that court review of fee category is de novo, yet citing to statutory provision for de novo review of fee waivers).

[124] See 5 U.S.C. § 552(a)(4)(A)(vii) ("[I]n any action by a requester regarding the waiver of fees . . . the court shall determine the matter de novo.") (emphasis added).

[125] See, e.g., Judicial Watch, No. 00-0745, slip op. at 14-15 (D.D.C. Feb.
(continued...)

scope of the court's review, it should be limited to the administrative record before the agency at the time of its decision, not some new record made before the reviewing court.[126]

In 1989, in an important case brought in the D.C. Circuit,[127] the government argued that the defendant agency's interpretation of the 1986 fee amendments to the FOIA, reflected by the agency's implementing regulations, was owed great deference under the rule established by the Supreme Court in Chevron USA, Inc. v. Natural Resources Defense Council.[128] The D.C. Circuit avoided addressing the judicial review issue, however, by finding that with reference to the underlying fee issue, "the statute, read in

---

[125](...continued)
12, 2001) (applying de novo standard to both fee category and fee waiver issues) (same); Judicial Watch, 133 F. Supp. 2d at 53 (rejecting government's argument that arbitrary and capricious standard applied to matter of fee category; undertaking de novo review on both fee and fee waiver issues); Judicial Watch, 2000 WL 33724693, at *3-4 (applying de novo standard to fee category and fee waiver issues); cf. Hosp. & Physician Publ'g, 1999 WL 33582100, at *2 (using de novo standard for media issue, without discussion).

[126] See Crain, No. 02-0341, slip op. at 7 (D.D.C. Mar. 25, 2003) (saying that "this Court's review of fee categorization is limited to the record that was before the agency at the time it made its decision"); Judicial Watch, 122 F. Supp. 2d at 12 (stating that scope of court's review is limited to administrative record); Judicial Watch, 122 F. Supp. 2d at 20 (same); see also NTEU v. Griffin, 811 F.2d 644, 648 (D.C. Cir. 1987) (stating that the reasonableness of the agency's position "depends on the information before it at the time of its decision") (fee waiver case); cf. Camp v. Pitts, 411 U.S. 138, 142 (1973) ("In applying [the arbitrary and capricious] standard, the focal point for judicial review should be the administrative record already in existence, not some new record made initially in the reviewing court.") (non-FOIA case); IMS, P.C. v. Alvarez, 129 F.3d 618, 623 (D.C. Cir. 1997) ("It is a widely accepted principle of administrative law that the courts base their review of an agency's actions on the materials that were before the agency at the time its decision was made.") (non-FOIA case); Hall, 2005 WL 850379, at *6 n.10 (deciding issue of fee limitation sua sponte inasmuch as there was no administrative action to review because agency had made no decision).

[127] See Nat'l Sec. Archive, 880 F.2d at 1383.

[128] 467 U.S. 837, 844 (1984) (emphasizing that where the agency's statutory interpretation "fills a gap or defines a term in a way that is reasonable in light of the legislature's revealed design, [the court] give[s] that judgment 'controlling weight'") (non-FOIA case).

light of the legislative history . . . [was] clear."[129] Thus, some seventeen years later, the extent of judicial deference given to agency fee regulations that are based upon the OMB Fee Guidelines still remains unclear.[130]

## Fee Waivers

The Freedom of Information Reform Act of 1986[131] established the current fee waiver standard, which in contrast to its predecessor[132] more specifically defines the term "public interest" by providing that fees should be waived or reduced "if disclosure of the information is in the public interest because it is likely to contribute significantly to public understanding of the operations or activities of the government and is not primarily in the commercial interest of the requester."[133] In accordance with this provision, the Department of Justice issued revised fee waiver policy guidance on April 2, 1987 -- which superseded its previous 1983 substantive fee waiver guidance,[134] as well as that issued in 1986 (concerning institutions and rec-

---

[129] Nat'l Sec. Archive, 880 F.2d at 1383.

[130] Compare Media Access Project v. FCC, 883 F.2d 1063, 1071 (D.C. Cir. 1989) (stating that agency's interpretation of its own fee regulations "must be given at least some deference"), with Judicial Watch, Inc. v. Rossotti, 326 F.3d 1309, 1313 (D.C. Cir. 2003) (emphasizing that the court owes "no particular deference to the [agency's] interpretation of [the] FOIA") (fee waiver case), Edmonds Inst. v. U.S. Dep't of Interior, 460 F. Supp. 2d 63, 74 n.6 (D.D.C. 2006) (same), Inst. for Wildlife Prot. v. U.S. Fish & Wildlife Serv., 290 F. Supp. 2d 1226, 1230 (D. Or. 2003) (stating that court owes no particular deference to agency's interpretation of FOIA (citing Judicial Watch, 326 F.3d at 1313)), and Nat'l Sec. Archive, 880 F.2d at 1383 (failing to resolve question of deference owed to agency's fee regulations ).

[131] Pub. L. No. 99-570, § 1803, 100 Stat. 3207, 3207-50 (codified as amended at 5 U.S.C. § 552(a)(4)(A)(iii) (2000 & Supp. IV 2004)).

[132] Pub. L. No. 93-502, §§ 1-3, 88 Stat. 1561-64 (1974) (subsequently amended) (authorizing the waiver of fees when it was determined that such action was "in the public interest because furnishing the information can be considered as primarily benefitting the general public").

[133] § 1803, 100 Stat. at 3207-50; cf. Piper v. U.S. Dep't of Justice, 294 F. Supp. 2d 16, 24 (D.D.C. 2003) (explaining, in the context of Exemption 7(C), that disclosure "turn[s] on the nature of the requested document and its relationship to 'the basic purpose of [FOIA] to open agency action to the light of public scrutiny'" (quoting U.S. Dep't of Justice v. Reporters Comm. for Freedom of the Press, 489 U.S. 749, 772 (1989)), reconsideration denied, No. 98-1161, 2004 WL 764587 (D.D.C. Mar. 26, 2004).

[134] See FOIA Update, Vol. IV, No. 1, at 3-4 (establishing governmentwide fee waiver guidelines consisting of specific criteria developed in numerous court decisions for federal agencies to apply in determining whether public

(continued...)

ord repositories)[135] -- and it advised agencies of six analytical factors to be considered in applying this statutory fee waiver standard.[136] These six factors were applied and implicitly approved by the Court of Appeals for the Ninth Circuit in McClellan Ecological Seepage Situation v. Carlucci.[137]

The statutory fee waiver standard as amended in 1986 contains two basic requirements -- the public interest requirement and the requirement that the requester's commercial interest in the disclosure, if any, must be less than the public interest in it.[138] Both of these statutory requirements must be satisfied by the requester before properly assessable fees are waived or reduced under the statutory standard.[139] In this regard, of

---

[134](...continued)
interest warranted a statutory waiver or reduction of fees).

[135] See FOIA Update, Vol. VII, No. 3, at 4.

[136] See FOIA Update, Vol. VIII, No. 1, at 3-10; see also id. at 10 (specifying that previous "procedural" guidance on fee waiver issues remains in effect); FOIA Update, Vol. IV, No. 1, at 4. But cf. Cmty. Legal Servs., Inc. v. HUD, 405 F. Supp. 2d 553, 557-58 (E.D. Pa. 2005) (suggesting that statutory fee waiver provision does not contain "legal" test).

[137] 835 F.2d 1282, 1286 (9th Cir. 1987); see also, e.g., Judicial Watch, Inc. v. Rossotti, 326 F.3d 1309, 1313-15 (D.C. Cir. 2003); Brown v. U.S. Patent & Trademark Office, 445 F. Supp. 2d 1347, 1358 (M.D. Fla. 2006), aff'd per curiam, No. 06-14716, 2007 WL 446601 (11th Cir. Feb. 13, 2007); Judicial Watch, Inc. v. U.S. Dep't of Transp., No. 02-566, 2005 WL 1606915, at *4 (D.D.C. July 5, 2005); VoteHemp, Inc. v. DEA, 237 F. Supp. 2d 55, 59-66 (D.D.C. 2002); Judicial Watch, Inc. v. U.S. Dep't of Justice, 122 F. Supp. 2d 5, 16-17 (D.D.C. 2000); Pederson v. RTC, 847 F. Supp. 851, 855 (D. Colo. 1994); Sloman v. U.S. Dep't of Justice, 832 F. Supp. 63, 68 (S.D.N.Y. 1993); cf. Cmty. Legal Servs., 405 F. Supp. 2d at 557-58 (considering among other factors in fact-specific case requester's reputation in public and private sector).

[138] 5 U.S.C. § 552(a)(4)(A)(iii) (2000); see also Inst. for Wildlife Prot. v. U.S. Fish & Wildlife Serv., 290 F. Supp. 2d 1226, 1228 (D. Or. 2003) (recognizing that statute establishes two-part test for fee waiver); VoteHemp, 237 F. Supp. 2d at 58 (reiterating "two-prong analysis" required for fee waiver requests); Department of Justice FOIA Regulations, 28 C.F.R. § 16.11(k) (2006).

[139] See FOIA Update, Vol. VIII, No. 1, at 4; see also Kumar v. U.S. Dep't of Justice, No. 06-714, 2007 U.S. Dist. LEXIS 11144, at *9 (D.D.C. Feb. 16, 2007) (indicating that burden of "showing that disclosure . . . is likely to make a significant contribution to the public's understanding of identifiable operations or activities of the federal government" is on the requester); Brown, 445 F. Supp. 2d at 1354 (stating that the requester "bears the burden of providing information that supports his fee waiver request with the
(continued...)

FEES AND FEE WAIVERS

course, it is the requester, not the requester's representative or counsel, who must demonstrate his entitlement to a fee waiver.[140] Requests for a waiver or reduction of fees must be considered on a case-by-case basis[141]

---

[139](...continued)
initial FOIA request," and noting that the plaintiff provided no authority for the "proposition that an agency must conduct independent research in making a fee waiver determination"); S. Utah Wilderness Alliance v. U.S. Bureau of Land Mgmt., 402 F. Supp. 2d 82, 87 (D.D.C. 2005) (reiterating that requester bears burden of showing entitlement to fee waiver); Judicial Watch, 2005 WL 1606915, at *3 (same); McQueen v. United States, 264 F. Supp. 2d 502, 524 (S.D. Tex. 2003) (reiterating that burden is on requester to prove entitlement to fee waiver), aff'd per curiam in pertinent part, 100 F. App'x 964 (5th Cir. 2004); Citizens Progressive Alliance v. U.S. Bureau of Indian Affairs, 241 F. Supp. 2d 1342, 1366 (D.N.M. 2002) (same); Klamath Water Users Protective Ass'n v. U.S. Dep't of the Interior, No. 96-3077, slip op. at 47 (D. Or. June 19, 1997) (magistrate's recommendation) (observing that burden is on requester to show eligibility for fee waiver), adopted (D. Or. Oct. 16, 1997), rev'd on other grounds, 189 F.3d 1034 (9th Cir. 1999), aff'd on other grounds sub nom. Dep't of the Interior v. Klamath Water Users Protective Ass'n, 532 U.S. 1 (2001); S.A. Ludsin & Co. v. SBA, No. 96 Civ. 2146, 1997 U.S. Dist. LEXIS 8617, at *10-11 (S.D.N.Y. June 19, 1997) (noting that fee waiver provision contains two requirements and that requester carries burden of proof on both), summary affirmance granted, 162 F.3d 1148 (2d Cir. 1998) (unpublished table decision); Anderson v. DEA, No. 93-253, slip op. at 4 (W.D. Pa. May 11, 1995) (magistrate's recommendation) (stating that burden is on requester to establish fee waiver standard met), adopted (W.D. Pa. June 21, 1995); Sloman, 832 F. Supp. at 67 (acknowledging that two-pronged statutory test should be used to determine when fees should be waived); cf. Cole-El v. U.S. Dep't of Justice, No. 03-1013, slip op. at 11-12 (D.D.C. Aug. 26, 2004) (recognizing that plaintiff bears burden of establishing entitlement to fee waiver, and finding fee in this instance to be "unjustified" due to administrative processing irregularities), aff'd per curiam on other grounds sub nom. Cole v. U.S. Dep't of Justice, No. 04-5329, 2005 U.S. App. LEXIS 7358 (D.C. Cir. Apr. 27, 2005); Tripp v. DOD, 193 F. Supp. 2d 229, 242 (D.D.C. 2002) (remanding request to agency for further consideration as agency applied incorrect fee waiver standard).

[140] See Dale v. IRS, 238 F. Supp. 2d 99, 107 (D.D.C. 2002) ("A party's counsel is not the 'requester' for purposes of a fee waiver request."); cf. Trulock v. U.S. Dep't of Justice, 257 F. Supp. 2d 48, 52 (D.D.C. 2003) (finding that plaintiff has not exhausted administrative remedies where "blanket" fee waiver request was submitted to agency in plaintiff's counsel's name, not his own); OMB Fee Guidelines, 52 Fed. Reg. 10,012, 10,017-18 (Mar. 27, 1987) (addressing same matter in fee-category context).

[141] See FOIA Update, Vol. VIII, No. 1, at 6; Media Access Project v. FCC, 883 F.2d 1063, 1065 (D.C. Cir. 1989) (remarking that any requester may seek waiver of assessed fees on "case-by-case" basis); Nat'l Sec. Archive v. (continued...)

and should address both of the statutory requirements in sufficient detail for the agency to make an informed decision as to whether it can appropriately waive or reduce the fees in question.[142]

---

[141](...continued)
DOD, 880 F.2d 1381, 1383 (D.C. Cir. 1989) (dictum) (noting that fee waiver decisions are made on "case-by-case" basis); Edmonds Inst. v. U.S. Dep't of Interior, 460 F. Supp. 2d 63, 75 (D.D.C. 2006) (stating that "applications for fee waivers are considered on a case-by-case basis"); Nat'l Wildlife Fed'n v. Hamilton, No. 95-017-BU, slip op. at 2 (D. Mont. July 15, 1996) (same); see also Judicial Watch, Inc. v. GSA, No. 98-2223, slip op. at 14 (D.D.C. Sept. 25, 2000) (reiterating that prior judicial recognition of requester's "ability to disseminate FOIA-disclosed information is not binding in this case," but that agency should consider requester's "track record" and reputation for disseminating information); Judicial Watch, Inc. v. U.S. Dep't of Justice, No. 99-2315, 2000 WL 33724693, at *5 (D.D.C. Aug. 17, 2000) (noting that requester's "past record in uncovering information is simply irrelevant").

[142] See, e.g., Judicial Watch, 326 F.3d at 1312 (reiterating that requests for fee waivers "must be made with reasonable specificity . . . and based on more than conclusory allegations" (quotation marks and citations omitted)); Prison Legal News v. Lappin, 436 F. Supp. 2d 17, 25 (D.D.C. 2006) (reiterating that the requester bears the initial burden "of identifying, with reasonable specificity, the public interest to be served"); Judicial Watch v. U.S. Dep't of Energy, 310 F. Supp. 2d 271, 290-91 (D.D.C. 2004) (stating that fee waiver requests must be made with "'reasonable specificity'" and be based on more than "'conclusory allegations'" (quoting Judicial Watch, 326 F.3d at 1312)), aff'd in part, rev'd in part on other grounds & remanded, 412 F.3d 125 (D.C. Cir. 2005); McQueen, 264 F. Supp. at 525 (emphasizing that "[c]onclusory statements on their face are insufficient" to prove entitlement to fee waiver); Judicial Watch, Inc. v. U.S. Dep't of Justice, No. 00-0745, slip op. at 14-15 (D.D.C. Feb. 12, 2001) (finding that the plaintiff failed to provide any specific information in support of its general statement that its organization's purpose was to "expose government activities that are contrary to the law"), partial summary judgment granted (D.D.C. Apr. 20, 2001); see also McClellan, 835 F.2d at 1285 (stating that conclusory statements will not support fee waiver request); Judicial Watch, Inc. v. U.S. Dep't of Justice, 133 F. Supp. 2d 52, 54 (D.D.C. 2000) (finding a requester's statements in support of his fee waiver request to be "perfunctory assertions [that] were too 'ephemeral' to satisfy the 'reasonable specificity' standard"). But see Edmonds Inst., 460 F. Supp. 2d at 74 (finding that the plaintiff's failure to "state affirmatively" that it would use "the various means" described in its request in order to disseminate the requested information was not fatal to its fee waiver request); Prison Legal News, 436 F. Supp. 2d at 26 (finding that requester had provided reasonable specificity how requested records would benefit public); cf. Judicial Watch, 326 F.3d at 1314 (concluding that requiring requester to provide "specific plan" for dissemination in addition to its methods of publication would be "pointless specificity"); Judicial Watch, 2005 WL 1606915, at *5 (stating that where

(continued...)

Further, when a requester fails to provide sufficient information for the agency to make that decision, the agency may of course defer consideration of a fee waiver request in order to ask the requester for all necessary supplemental or clarifying information.[143] As an additional threshold matter, and just as with disclosures made under the FOIA,[144] agencies analyzing fee waiver requests are not strictly bound by previous administrative decisions.[145]

In order to determine whether the first fee waiver requirement has been met -- i.e., that disclosure of the requested information is in the public interest because it is likely to contribute significantly to public understanding of government operations or activities[146] -- agencies should consider

---

[142](...continued)
requester had detailed its ability to disseminate, its failure to provide specific dissemination plan was not fatal); Judicial Watch, 310 F. Supp. 2d at 291 (same).

[143] See McClellan, 835 F.2d at 1287 (noting that "[t]he fee waiver statute nowhere suggests that an agency may not ask for more information if the requester fails to provide enough"); Citizens, 241 F. Supp. 2d at 1366 (recognizing that the agency "is entitled to ask for more information with regards to a fee waiver request, where the information provided is not sufficient"); cf. Judicial Watch, 326 F.3d at 1315 (concluding that initial request demonstrated eligibility for fee waiver, thus effectively rejecting propriety of agency's request for additional information).

[144] See, e.g., Mobil Oil Corp. v. EPA, 879 F.2d 698, 700-01 (9th Cir. 1989) (discretionary release of document does not require similar release of similar documents).

[145] See, e.g., Judicial Watch, Inc. v. U.S. Dep't of Justice, No. 97-2089, slip op. at 14 (D.D.C. July 14, 1998) (finding, in case at hand, that it was "wholly irrelevant" that requester received fee waivers in other cases); Dollinger v. USPS, No. 95-CV-6174T, slip op. at 7-8 (W.D.N.Y. Aug. 24, 1995) (concluding that agency is not bound by previous decision on fee waiver for similar request from same requester).

[146] See, e.g., Judicial Watch, 326 F.3d at 1312 (stating that the case turns on whether the public interest requirement is met, and noting that the agency's implementing regulation included a "non-exclusive list of factors the agency 'shall consider'" (quoting agency's regulation)); S.A. Ludsin & Co. v. SBA, No. 97-7884, 1998 WL 642416, at *1 (2d Cir. Mar. 26, 1998) (reiterating that first requirement not met when requester "merely paraphrased" fee waiver provision); Oglesby v. U.S. Dep't of the Army, 920 F.2d 57, 66 n.11 (D.C. Cir. 1990) (conclusory statements insufficient to make public interest showing); Edmonds Inst., 460 F. Supp. 2d at 74 (noting that the requester's initial fee waiver request "represents the type of overly general, conclusory justification that does not support a fee waiver"); Judicial
(continued...)

the following four factors,[147] in sequence:

    1. First, the subject matter of the requested records, in the context of the request, must specifically concern identifiable "operations or activities

---

[146](...continued)
Watch, 310 F. Supp. 2d at 291 n.2 (applying public interest test, and noting that D.C. Circuit decision that applied this test "is binding precedent" (citing Judicial Watch, 326 F.3d at 1312)); Judicial Watch, 122 F. Supp. 2d at 9 (finding that nonprofit group's "general description of [its] organizational mission" failed to identify public interest to be served by release of specific information requested); S.A. Ludsin & Co. v. SBA, No. 96-5972, 1998 WL 355394, at *2 (E.D.N.Y. Apr. 2, 1998) (observing that mere recitation of statute does not satisfy requester's burden); Trueblood v. U.S. Dep't of the Treasury, 943 F. Supp. 64, 69 (D.D.C. 1996) (rejecting contention that public interest requirement met by identifying personal benefit to requester); Sloman, 832 F. Supp. at 68 (finding that public interest requirement is not met merely by quoting statutory standard); cf. S.A. Ludsin, 1998 WL 642416, at *1 (noting that requester's claim that disclosure to it would "create[] revenue for the federal government" does not demonstrate that disclosure "is in the public interest" for fee waiver purposes); Sierra Club Legal Def. Fund v. Bibles, No. 93-35383, slip op. at 3-4 (9th Cir. Aug. 29, 1994) (reasoning that disclosure to a group that is "in the public interest" is not the same as saying that disclosure without fees is likely to contribute to public understanding, and that the requester's status as a public interest law firm does not automatically entitle it to a fee waiver at taxpayer expense); NTEU v. Griffin, 811 F.2d 644, 647 (D.C. Cir. 1987) (observing under previous standard that requester seeking fee waiver bears burden of identifying "public interest" involved); Judicial Watch, Inc. v. U.S. Dep't of Justice, No. 01-0639, slip op. at 7 (D.D.C. Mar. 31, 2003) (admitting that given the evidence on the record at the time of the court's earlier decision -- including the plaintiff's failure to provide evidence "that further, free release of documents" was in the public interest -- "the Court's previous decision improperly shifted the burden of establishing eligibility for a FOIA fee waiver from Plaintiff to Defendant"). But cf. Judicial Watch of Fla., Inc. v. U.S. Dep't of Justice, No. 97-2869, slip op. at 4-5 (D.D.C. Aug. 25, 1998) (despite fact that disclosed information was "not necessarily all new," finding public interest served "by exposing government actions through litigation").

[147] See Judicial Watch, Inc. v. Dep't of Justice, No. 03-5093, 2004 WL 980826, at *18 (D.C. Cir. May 7, 2004) (invoking the agency's four-factor fee waiver test, and stating that "[the] four criteria must be satisfied" in order "for a request to be in the 'public interest'"); Judicial Watch, 326 F.3d at 1312 (applying agency's four-factor analysis of fee waivers, but referring to factors as "non-exclusive list"); Judicial Watch, 310 F. Supp. 2d at 291 n.2 (applying four-factor public interest test; observing that same test used in Judicial Watch, 326 F.3d at 1312, and stating that this decision then "is binding precedent"); Inst. for Wildlife Prot., 290 F. Supp. 2d at 1229 (recognizing that "agency is to consider [four fee waiver] factors in sequence"); VoteHemp, 237 F. Supp. 2d at 59 (same).

of the government."[148]  As the D.C. Circuit specifically indicated in applying the predecessor fee waiver standard, "the links between furnishing the requested information and benefitting the general public" should not be "tenuous."[149]  Although in most cases records possessed by a federal agency will meet this threshold, the records must be sought for their informative value with respect to specifically identified government operations or activities;[150] a request for access to records for their intrinsic informational

---

[148] 5 U.S.C. § 552(a)(4)(A)(iii); see Dollinger, No. 95-CV-6174T, slip op. at 4 (W.D.N.Y. Aug. 24, 1995) (concluding that "government" as used in fee waiver standard refers to federal government); see also Oglesby v. Dep't of Justice, No. 02-0603, slip op. at 4 (D.D.C. Sept. 3, 2002) (finding that a requester's statement that records pertaining to him would show "which [of his] activities were of interest to the Government and what actions it took with respect to them" was conclusory and did not identify "the link between identifiable government operations and the information requested").

[149] NTEU, 811 F.2d at 648; see also FOIA Post, "FOIA Counselor Q&A" (posted 1/24/06) (advising on "the meaning of an 'umbrella issue' under the FOIA," and noting that "the term 'umbrella issue' is a relatively new one that has been used by agencies and courts alike to make important distinctions" when considering public benefit in FOIA decisionmaking (citing NTEU)).  But see also Forest Guardians v. U.S. Dep't of the Interior, 416 F.3d 1173, 1178 (10th Cir. 2005) (accepting the requester's assertion that the requested records would indirectly pertain to agency policy by "shedding light on the potential influence private groups have over agency policy," and stating that requiring the requester "to provide more concrete factual support for its assertions would be setting the bar too high").

[150] See, e.g., Brown, 445 F. Supp. 2d 1358-59 (finding that allegations made in lawsuits brought against agency did not concern operations or activities of agency); DeCato v. Executive Office for U.S. Attorneys, No. 00-3053, slip op. at 7 (D.D.C. Jan. 2, 2003) (emphasizing that "important[ly], plaintiff does not explain the connection between the requested records about himself" and a governmental activity), summary affirmance granted, No. 03-5044, 2003 WL 22433759, at *1 (D.C. Cir. Oct. 24, 2003); Judicial Watch, Inc. v. Reno, No. 00-0723, 2001 WL 1902811, at *10 (D.D.C. Mar. 30, 2001) (upholding agency's assessment of fees, reasoning that while agency's response to citizen letters regarding Cuban emigré Elian Gonzales would likely contribute to understanding of agency actions, citizen letters to agency on that topic do not), summary judgment granted on other grounds (D.D.C. Sept. 25, 2001); Van Fripp v. Parks, No. 97-0159, slip op. at 10 (D.D.C. Mar. 16, 2000) (characterizing the request as a "fishing expedition that does not relate to defined operations or activities of the [agency]"); S.A. Ludsin, 1997 U.S. Dist. LEXIS 8617, at *14 (holding that disclosure of appraisals of government property do not "in any readily apparent way" contribute to public's understanding of operations or activities of government); Atkin v. EEOC, No. 91-2508, slip op. at 27-28 (D.N.J. Dec. 4, 1992) (finding requested list of agency attorneys and their bar affiliations "clearly

(continued...)

content alone would not satisfy this threshold consideration.[151]

2. Second, in order for the disclosure to be "likely to contribute" to an understanding of specific government operations or activities, the disclosable portions of the requested information must be meaningfully informative in relation to the subject matter of the request.[152] Requests for infor-

---

[150](...continued)
does not concern identifiable government activities or operations"), appeal dismissed for failure to timely prosecute sub nom. Atkin v. Kemp, No. 93-5548 (3d Cir. 1993); Nance v. USPS, No. 91-1183, 1992 WL 23655, at *2 (D.D.C. Jan. 24, 1992) (reiterating that disclosure of illegally cashed money orders will not contribute significantly to public understanding of operations of government); cf. Judicial Watch, 122 F. Supp. 2d at 9 (indicating that "a requester must do more to be eligible for a fee waiver than simply assert that its request somehow relates to government operations"). But see Forest Guardians, 416 F.3d at 1178 (finding that lienholder agreements that derived from private transactions have connection to activities of government where government maintains copies of those records and notifies submitters of agency actions that "might affect" their value); Inst. for Wildlife Prot., 290 F. Supp. 2d at 1231 (ordering fee waiver where requested documents consisted of petitions submitted to agency by outside parties seeking to list particular species as endangered and where requester "theorized" that such petitions were "likely to contain marginal notes" by agency employees whose "opinions are often ignored or overturned" by agency personnel of higher authority); Landmark Legal Found. v. IRS, No. 97-1474, slip op. at 8 (D.D.C. Sept. 22, 2000) (finding that "[although [the] disclosure . . . standing alone may reveal very little about the [agency], this information, coupled with information already in the public domain, may contribute to an understanding of the" agency's operations or activities), partial summary judgment granted on other grounds, 87 F. Supp. 2d 21 (D.D.C. 2000), aff'd, 267 F.3d 1132 (D.C. Cir. 2001).

[151] See FOIA Update, Vol. VIII, No. 1, at 6.

[152] See id.; Carney v. U.S. Dep't of Justice, 19 F.3d 807, 814 (2d Cir. 1994) (stating that it is relevant to consider subject matter of fee waiver request); Larson v. CIA, 843 F.2d 1481, 1483 (D.C. Cir. 1988) (noting that character of information is proper factor to consider); Klein v. Toupin, No. 05-647, 2006 U.S. Dist. LEXIS 32478, at *11-12 (D.D.C. May 24, 2006) (reiterating that conclusory and unsupported assertions of misconduct are not "meaningfully informative" of government operations); McDade v. Executive Office for U.S. Attorneys, No. 03-1946, slip op. at 8-9 (D.D.C. Sept. 29, 2004) (stating that the "informative value of the records to be disclosed" is considered by the agency under this factor, and concluding that the plaintiff had not shown how information that pertained only to himself would be "meaningfully informative about government operations" (citing agency's fee waiver regulation)), summary affirmance granted, No. 04-5378, 2005 U.S. App. LEXIS 15259, at *1 (D.C. Cir. July 25, 2005), cert. denied, 126 S. Ct. 791 (continued...)

mation that is already in the public domain, either in a duplicative or a substantially identical form, may not warrant a fee waiver because the disclosure would not be likely to contribute to an understanding of government operations or activities when nothing new would be added to the public's understanding.[153] Under existing case law, however, there is no clear con-

---

[152](...continued)
(2005); VoteHemp, 237 F. Supp. 2d at 61 (rejecting as "rank speculation" plaintiff's allegations that agency had "ulterior motive" when it published interpretive rule); Citizens, 241 F. Supp. 2d at 1366 (reiterating that when applying fee waiver standard, it is relevant to consider subject matter of request); Conklin v. United States, 654 F. Supp. 1104, 1106 (D. Colo. 1987) (finding that mere allegations of agency "oppression" did not justify fee waiver under predecessor fee waiver standard); AFGE v. U.S. Dep't of Commerce, 632 F. Supp. 1272, 1278 (D.D.C. 1986) (finding union's allegations of malfeasance to be too ephemeral to warrant waiver of search fees without further evidence that informative material will be found), aff'd on other grounds, 907 F.2d 203 (D.C. Cir. 1990); cf. NARA v. Favish, 541 U.S. 157, 174 (holding, in the context of Exemption 7(C)'s closely related public interest balancing test, that where the "public interest" asserted is to show negligent or improper performance of the agency officials' duties, "the requester must establish more than a bare suspicion in order to obtain disclosure"), reh'g denied, 541 U.S. 1057 (2004); Crawford-El v. Britton, 523 U.S. 574, 585 (1998) ("Allegations of government misconduct are 'easy to allege and hard to disprove.'" (quoting Crawford-El v. Britton, 93 F.3d 813, 816, 821 (D.C. Cir. 1996))) (non-FOIA case); Cole-El, No. 03-1013, slip op. at 10 (D.D.C. Aug. 26, 2004) (finding in context of Exemption 7(C) analysis that as primary beneficiary of records sought, plaintiff's interest in records did not overcome third-party's privacy interests); Judicial Watch v. Rossotti, No. 01-2672, 2002 WL 31962775, *6 (D. Md. Dec. 16, 2002) (finding, in the context of Exemption 7(C)'s balancing test, that the plaintiff's request for the names of persons who submitted concerns to the IRS about the plaintiff, made to further the plaintiff's investigation into the alleged "'connection between the volunteer tipsters and the retaliatory, political motivation for the unconstitutional audit and investigation,'" did not rise to a FOIA "public interest"), aff'd sub nom. Judicial Watch v. United States, 84 F. App'x 335 (4th Cir. 2004). But see Judicial Watch, 2005 WL 1606915, at *4 (noting that fee waiver request should have been evaluated on "potential contribution" of requested records and not on agency's determination that majority of information was exempt).

[153] See Judicial Watch, Inc., 2004 WL 980826, at *18 (emphasizing that the plaintiff received "thousands of pages of requested documents" but "has made no showing" to counter the government's representations that the requested information "was already in the public domain and thus not likely to contribute significantly to the public's understanding" of a governmental activity; further finding "no basis to conclude that [plaintiff] is entitled to a blanket fee waiver" where the plaintiff did not take issue with the reasonableness of the district court's finding of the public availability of the
(continued...)

[153](...continued)
documents already released; upholding government's refusal to process additional documents without payment of fees); Sierra Club Legal Def. Fund, No. 93-35383, slip op. at 4 (9th Cir. Aug. 29, 1994) (determining that plaintiff failed to explain "how its work would add anything to 'public understanding'" where requested material already widely disseminated and publicized); Carney, 19 F.3d at 815 (observing that "where records are readily available from other sources . . . further disclosure by the agency will not significantly contribute to public understanding"); McClellan, 835 F.2d at 1286 (recognizing new information has more potential to contribute to public understanding); Brown, 445 F. Supp. 2d at 1359-60 (holding that mere assertion that information will likely contribute to public understanding is insufficient under fee waiver factor two; citing with implicit approval an agency regulation specifying that the disclosure of information already in the public domain, such as that found "in open records and available to the public in court documents," is not likely to contribute to public understanding); Judicial Watch, No. 01-0639, slip op. at 7-8 (D.D.C. Mar. 31, 2003) (finding that the plaintiff failed to prove that disclosable documents were "likely to contribute significantly" to the public interest where "a vast majority of the responsive documents . . . were . . . publicly available"); VoteHemp, 237 F. Supp. 2d at 60 (concluding that plaintiff has not shown how requested documents would give public greater understanding of agency policy concerning controlled substance than was already available); Judicial Watch, 2001 WL 1902811, at *10 (sustaining the agency's assessment of fees for duplication of court documents, press clippings, and citizen letters where the material was "'easily accessible and available to everyone else for a fee'" (quoting Durham v. U.S. Dep't of Justice, 829 F. Supp. 428, 434-35 (D.D.C. 1993))); Durham, 829 F. Supp. at 434-35 (denying fee waiver for 2340 pages of public court records), appeal dismissed for failure to timely file, No. 93-5354 (D.C. Cir. Nov. 29, 1994); Sloman, 832 F. Supp. at 68 (stating that public's understanding would not be enhanced to a significant extent where material was previously released to other writers and "more important[ly]" was available in the agency's public reading room "where the public has access and has used the information extensively"); cf. Tax Analysts v. U.S. Dep't of Justice, 965 F.2d 1092, 1094-96 (D.C. Cir. 1992) (finding that news organization was not entitled to attorney fees because, inter alia, requested information was already in public domain). But see Campbell v. U.S. Dep't of Justice, 164 F.3d 20, 35 (D.C. Cir. 1998) ("declin[ing] to hold that the FBI cannot charge . . . any copying fees," but finding the agency's fee waiver analysis "flawed" with regard to summaries of public domain information, information that was repetitious but not asserted to be duplicative, and nonsubstantive administrative information); Prison Legal News, 436 F. Supp. 2d at 24 (concluding that publicly available court documents were "likely dispersed throughout the . . . federal courthouses in this country," thus compelling the conclusion that such records are not "readily available" to the public; further noting that electronic access to requested records on court electronic case filing system was not

(continued...)

sensus yet as to what "is and what is not" considered information in the public domain.[154]

Further, it should be noted that any denial of a fee waiver for records that are said to be already in the public domain is not a denial of access to them under the FOIA, despite what seemingly has been suggested by some courts;[155] rather, such records merely must be paid for by the requester. (For discussions of records considered to be in the "public domain," and the impact of the "public availability" on agency records in other FOIA contexts, see Exemption 1, "Public Domain" Information, below, Exemption 4, Competitive Harm Prong of National Parks, below, and Discretionary Disclosure and Waiver, below).[156]

---

[153](...continued)
yet fully implemented nationally).

[154] Schrecker v. Dep't of Justice, 970 F. Supp. 49, 50 (D.D.C. 1997). Compare Forest Guardians, 416 F.3d at 1181 (noting that public availability of information generally weighs against fee waiver), Conner v. CIA, No. 84-3625, slip op. at 2 (D.D.C. Jan. 31, 1986) (upholding denial of fee waiver for records available in agency's public reading room), appeal dismissed for lack of prosecution, No. 86-5221 (D.C. Cir. Jan. 23, 1987), and Blakey v. Dep't of Justice, 549 F. Supp. 362, 364-65 (D.D.C. 1982) (applying same principle under previous statutory fee waiver standard), aff'd, 720 F.2d 215 (D.C. Cir. 1983) (unpublished table decision), with Forest Guardians, 416 F.3d at 1181 (finding that information in courthouses, newspapers, and affidavits, while in the public domain, is "publicly accessible in only the grossest sense"), Friends of the Coast Fork v. U.S. Dep't of the Interior, 110 F.3d 53, 55 (9th Cir. 1997) (holding that availability in agency's public reading room alone does not justify denial of fee waiver), Carney, 19 F.3d at 815 (finding that mere fact records released to others does not mean same information is readily available to public), VoteHemp, 237 F. Supp. 2d at 61 (observing that fee waiver is not necessarily precluded solely on basis that information already is in public domain), Judicial Watch, No. 97-2869, slip op. at 4 (D.D.C. Aug 25, 1998) (same), and Fitzgibbon v. Agency for Int'l Dev., 724 F. Supp. 1048, 1051 & n.10 (D.D.C. 1989) (stating that agencies failed to demonstrate "public's understanding" of information publicly available in public reading rooms and reports to Congress).

[155] See, e.g., Prison Legal News, 436 F. Supp. 2d at 24 (concluding that publicly available court documents were "likely dispersed throughout the . . . federal courthouses in this country" compelling conclusion that such records not "readily available" to public); Forest Guardians, 416 F.3d at 1181 (stating that information found in courthouses, newspapers, and affidavits while in public domain is "publicly accessible in only the grossest sense").

[156] Compare OSHA Data/CIH, Inc. v. U.S. Dep't of Labor, 220 F.3d 153, 163 n.25 (3d Cir. 2000) (agreeing with the agency that "a limited disclosure
(continued...)

3. Third, the disclosure must contribute to the understanding of the public at large, as opposed to the individual understanding of the request-er or a narrow segment of interested persons.[157] In the past, courts have generally not defined the "public-at-large" to include the prison popula-tion.[158] More recently, courts have considered prisoners as the "public"

---

[156](...continued)
to a limited audience" at a private sector worksite "is surely insufficient" to render the data publicly available), and N.Y. Times v. U.S. Dep't of Labor, 340 F. Supp. 2d 394, 401-02 & n.9 (S.D.N.Y. 2004) (finding that required postings of government information by private employers at their work sites for limited periods of time does not make such postings "public") (in context of Exemption 4 analysis of confidential business information), with Cottone v. Reno, 193 F.3d 550, 554 (D.C. Cir. 1999) (identifying documents that have been "disclosed and preserved in a permanent public record" within the public domain doctrine) (waiver of exemption case).

[157] See Forest Guardian, 416 F.3d at 1179 (emphasizing that "FOIA fee waivers are limited to disclosures that will enlighten more than just the individual requester"); Carney, 19 F.3d at 814 (observing that the relevant inquiry is "whether requester will disseminate the disclosed records to a reasonably broad audience of persons interested in the subject"); Wagner v. U.S. Dep't of Justice, No. 86-5477, slip op. at 2 (D.C. Cir. Mar. 24, 1987) (reiterating that general public must benefit from release); Cmty. Legal Servs., 405 F. Supp. 2d at 557 (acknowledging that while the requester's limited dissemination methods are unlikely to reach a general audience "there is a segment of the public interested in requester's work"); Judicial Watch, Inc. v. U.S. Dep't of Justice, 185 F. Supp. 2d 54, 59 (D.D.C. 2002) (stating that requester must show that disclosure will contribute to under-standing of "reasonably broad audience of persons"); Judicial Watch, 122 F. Supp. 2d at 10 (same); Judicial Watch, 2000 WL 33724693, at *5 (same); Crooker v. Dep't of the Army, 577 F. Supp. 1220, 1223 (D.D.C. 1984) (reject-ing fee waiver under previous standard for information of interest to "a small segment of the scientific community," which would not "benefit the public at large"), appeal dismissed as frivolous, No. 84-5089 (D.C. Cir. June 22, 1984); see also NTEU, 811 F.2d at 648 (rejecting "union's suggestion that its size insures that any benefit to it amounts to a public benefit"); Citizens, 241 F. Supp. 2d at 1367 (holding that a requester's intent to re-lease the information obtained "to the media is not sufficient to demon-strate that disclosure would contribute significantly to public understand-ing"); Fazzini v. U.S. Dep't of Justice, No. 90-C-3303, 1991 WL 74649, at *5 (N.D. Ill. May 2, 1991) (finding that requester cannot establish public bene-fit merely by alleging he has "corresponded" with members of media and intends to share requested information with them), summary affirmance granted, No. 91-2219 (7th Cir. July 26, 1991).

[158] See, e.g., Wagner, No. 86-5477, slip op. at 2 (D.C. Cir. Mar. 24, 1987) (stating that general public must benefit from release); Cox v. O'Brien, No. 86-1639, slip op. at 2 (D.D.C. Dec. 16, 1986) (upholding denial of fee waiver
(continued...)

within the meaning of the FOIA,[159] though the issue has not yet been conclusively decided. Further, whether the "public-at-large" encompasses only the population of the United States has not been clearly resolved by the courts either. Only one case has directly raised this issue, one in which it was held that disclosure to a foreign news syndicate that publishes only in Canada satisfies the requirement that it contribute to "public understanding."[160]

As the proper focus must be on the benefit to be derived by the public, any personal benefit to be derived by the requester, or the requester's particular financial situation, are not factors entitling him or her to a fee waiver.[161] Indeed, it is well settled that indigence alone, without a show-

---

[158](...continued)
where prisoners, not general public, would be beneficiaries of release).

[159] See Ortloff v. U.S. Dep't of Justice, No. 98-2819, slip op. at 21 (D.D.C. Mar. 22, 2002) (stressing that to qualify him for a fee waiver, the requester's ability to disseminate information "to the general public, or even to a limited segment of the public such as prisoners" must be demonstrated); Van Fripp, No. 97-0159, slip op. at 8 (D.D.C. Mar. 16, 2000) (construing term "public" to include those who are incarcerated); Linn v. U.S. Dep't of Justice, No. 92-1406, 1995 WL 631847, at *14 (D.D.C. Aug. 22, 1995) (rejecting agency's position that dissemination to prison population is not to public at large; statute makes no distinction between incarcerated and nonincarcerated public).

[160] Southam News v. INS, 674 F. Supp. 881, 892-93 (D.D.C. 1987); cf. Edmonds Inst., 460 F. Supp. 2d at 74 n.7 (refraining from addressing the agency's claim that the meaning of "public" for fee waiver purposes "does not include members of the international community" given that there were a sufficient number of U.S.-based organizations involved in supporting the request before the agency). But cf. Reporters Comm., 489 U.S. at 773 (establishing that the core purpose of the FOIA is the people's right "to know what their government is up to") (emphasis added); NLRB v. Robbins Tire & Rubber Co., 437 U.S. 214, 242 (1978) (observing that the basic purpose of the FOIA is "to hold the governors accountable to the governed").

[161] See, e.g., McClain v. U.S. Dep't of Justice, 13 F.3d 220, 220-21 (7th Cir. 1993) (stating that a fee waiver was inappropriate when the requester sought to serve a private interest rather than "public understanding of operations or activities of the government"); Carney, 19 F.3d at 816 (finding fee waiver inappropriate for portion of responsive records that concerned processing of plaintiff's own FOIA requests); Kumar, 2007 U.S. Dist. LEXIS 1144, at *11 (private interests of requester not relevant to fee waiver consideration); Klein, 2006 U.S. Dist. LEXIS 32478, at *1, *12 (observing that plaintiff presented no evidence to show how records related to his suspension from practice before agency "would benefit anyone other than himself"); Hicks v. Hardy, No. 04-0769, 2006 WL 949918, at *2 (D.D.C. Apr. 12, (continued...)

ing of a public benefit, is insufficient to warrant a fee waiver.[162]

---

[161](...continued)
2006) (denying fee waiver partly because of requester's personal interest in records); McDade, No. 03-1946, slip op. at 9 (D.D.C. Sept. 29, 2004) (concluding that where intended audience is requester only, third fee waiver factor is not met); McQueen, 264 F. Supp. 2d at 525 (acknowledging that plaintiff asserted more than one basis in support of fee waiver, but concluding that his "primary purposes" served private interests and thus disqualified him on that basis alone); Mells v. IRS, No. 99-2030, 2002 U.S. Dist. LEXIS 24275, at *5-7 (D.D.C. Nov. 21, 2002) (noting that requester's reasons for fee waiver were "overwhelmingly personal in nature" where he claimed that disclosure "would yield exculpatory evidence pertaining to his criminal conviction"); Crooker, 577 F. Supp. at 1223-24 (finding that prison inmate's intent to write book about brother's connection with dangerous toxin was not proper benefit to public); see also Forest Guardians, 416 F.3d at 1179 (stating that records "that may show how, if at all" agency policy is influenced by special interest groups important to public's understanding of government operations); Judicial Watch, 326 F.3d at 1313-14 (emphasizing that contribution to public understanding of agency records related to possible conflict of interest by government official is not dependent on whether conflict actually exists); Ortloff, No. 98-2819, slip op. at 21 (D.D.C. Mar. 22, 2002) (stating questionably that cases are in conflict as to whether public interest is served where requester seeks records to challenge conviction); cf. Appleton v. FDA, 254 F. Supp. 2d 6, 10 n.5 (D.D.C. 2003) (explaining that FOIA does not provide for expedited processing on basis of age of requester). But see Johnson v. U.S. Dep't of Justice, No. 89-2842, slip op. at 3 (D.D.C. May 2, 1990) (stressing that death-row prisoner seeking previously unreleased and possibly exculpatory information was entitled to a partial fee waiver on the rationale that a potential "miscarriage of justice . . . is a matter of great public interest"), summary judgment granted, 758 F. Supp. 2, 5 (D.D.C. 1991) (holding that, ultimately, FBI is not required to review records or else forego FOIA exemption for possibly exculpatory information); see also Pederson, 847 F. Supp. at 856 (concluding that requester's personal interest in disclosure of requested information did not undercut fee waiver request when requester established existence of concurrent public interest); cf. Harper v. DOD, No. 93-35876, 1995 WL 392032, at *2 (9th Cir. July 3, 1995) (explaining that prisoner presented no evidence that requested technical reports might contain exculpatory material which would entitle him to consideration for fee waiver).

[162] See, e.g., DeCato v. Executive Office for the U.S. Attorneys, No. 03-5044, 2003 WL 22433759, at *1 (D.C. Cir. Oct. 24, 2003) (reiterating that "this court has held that indigence is not a justification for waiving fees" (citing Ely v. USPS, 753 F.2d 163, 165 (D.C. Cir. 1985))); Wagner, No. 86-5477, slip op. at 2 (D.C. Cir. Mar. 24, 1987) (observing that "indigency does not ipso facto require a fee waiver"); Ely, 753 F.2d at 165 ("Congress rejected a fee waiver provision for indigents."); Kumar, 2007 U.S. Dist. LEXIS 11144, at *10-11 (recognizing that indigence alone not sufficient to justify

(continued...)

Additionally, agencies should evaluate the identity and qualifications of the requester -- e.g., expertise in the subject area of the request and ability and intention to disseminate the information to the public -- in order to determine whether the public would benefit from disclosure to that requester.[163] Specialized knowledge may be required to extract, synthesize,

---

[162](...continued) fee waiver (citing Ely, 753 F.2d at 165); McDade, No. 03-1946, slip op. at 7 (D.D.C. Sept. 29, 2004) (same); Durham, 829 F. Supp. at 435 n.10 (finding indigence alone does not constitute adequate grounds for fee waiver); Rodriguez-Estrada v. United States, No. 92-2360, slip op. at 2 (D.D.C. Apr. 16, 1993) (explaining no entitlement to fee waiver on basis of in forma pauperis status under 28 U.S.C. § 1915 (2000); Crooker, 577 F. Supp. at 1224 (holding indigence alone does not automatically entitle requester to fee waiver); see also S. Conf. Rep. No. 93-1200, at 8 (1974), reprinted in 1974 U.S.C.C.A.N. 6285, 6287 (specific fee waiver provision for indigents eliminated; "such matters are properly the subject for individual agency determination in regulations"); cf. United States v. Tyree, No. 2:05-cr-0728, slip op. at 5-6 (E.D. Pa. Mar. 29, 2006) (pointing out that neither Federal Rules of Criminal Procedure nor Brady v. Maryland, 373 U.S. 83 (1963), imposes "affirmative duty" on government to provide free copies of records during discovery) (non-FOIA case).

[163] Compare Brown, 2007 WL 446601, at *2 (determining that the requester's stated purpose of his Web site, its traffic, and the attention it has received "do not establish that he . . . disseminates news to the public at large"), McClain, 13 F.3d at 221 (stating that fee waiver must be assessed in light of identity and objectives of requester), Larson, 843 F.2d at 1483 & n.5 (holding that inability to disseminate information alone is sufficient basis for denying fee waiver request; requester cannot rely on tenuous link to newspaper to establish dissemination where administrative record failed to identify the recipient news media outlet to which he intended to release information, his purpose for seeking requested material, or his . . . contacts with any major newspaper companies"), Brown, 445 F. Supp. 2d at 1360 ("Simply maintaining a website is not disseminating information to a broad audience of interested persons."), Hall v. CIA, No. 04-0814, 2005 WL 850379, at *7 (D.D.C. Apr. 13, 2005) (reiterating that the "'ability to convey information' to others [is] insufficient without some details of how the requester will actually do so" (citations omitted), and viewing the requester's statement that he "'makes pertinent information available to newspapers and magazines' . . . [as] exactly the kind of vague statement that will preclude a fee waiver"), subsequent opinion, No. 04-0814, 2006 WL 197462 (D.D.C. Jan. 25, 2006), Citizens, 241 F. Supp. 2d at 1366 (stating that when applying fee waiver standard, it is relevant to consider ability of requester to disseminate information), Ortloff, No. 98-2819, slip op. at 21 (D.D.C. Mar. 22, 2002) (reiterating that inability to disseminate is fatal to fee waiver request; expressing skepticism about viability of plaintiff's claim of maintaining future Web site on which requested documents could be posted), Anderson, No. 93-253, slip op. at 4 (W.D. Pa. May 11, 1995) (finding requester's (continued...)

and effectively convey the information to the public, and requesters certainly vary in their ability to do so.[164]

---

[163](...continued)
inability to disseminate fatal to fee waiver), and Larson v. CIA, 664 F. Supp. 15, 19 n.3 (D.D.C. 1987) (stating that "even if" it was appropriately before the court, the court would reject a letter from a newspaper to the requester indicating an interest in "anything you get" on the subject of the request "as evidence of [the requester's] ability to disseminate" because "such a rule would enable requesters to avoid fees simply by asserting an intention to give the released documents to a newspaper"), aff'd, 843 F.2d 1481 (D.C. Cir. 1988), with Forest Guardians, 416 F.3d at 1180 (finding requester's publication of online newsletter and its intent to create interactive Web site using requested records, "among other things," to be sufficient for dissemination purposes), Judicial Watch, 326 F.3d at 1314 (granting fee waiver where requester did not specifically state its intent to disseminate requested information but had presented multiple ways in which it could convey information to public), Carney, 19 F.3d at 814-15 (characterizing dissemination requirement as the ability to reach "a reasonably broad audience of persons interested in the subject" and not the need to "reach a broad cross-section of the public"), Prison Legal News, 436 F. Supp. 2d at 26-27 (viewing viability of requester's Web site as not relevant where estimated readership of requester's newsletter demonstrated ability to disseminate), Cmty. Legal Servs., 405 F. Supp. 2d at 557 n.3 (noting that agency's demand for "detailed numbers" with regard to requester's dissemination plan is not required by at least three other courts), Judicial Watch, 310 F. Supp. 2d at 292 (finding that requester's "litany of means by which it [could] publicize[] information" without any specific representation that it intended to do so in instant case satisfied dissemination requirement), W. Watersheds Project v. Brown, 318 F. Supp. 2d 1036, 1040-41 (D. Idaho 2004) (concluding that the requester had adequately demonstrated its intent and ability "to reach a large audience" through multiple means including its regular newsletter, radio and newspapers, Web site, presentations to diverse groups, and participation in conferences and nationwide public events; stating that the agency's position on dissemination "would set the bar for fee waivers impermissibly high"), Eagle v. U.S. Dep't of Commerce, No. C-01-20591, 2003 WL 21402534, at *3, *5 (N.D. Cal. Apr. 28, 2003) (finding that educator-requester made adequate showing of his ability to disseminate through his proposed distribution of newsletter to Congress, through publication in academic journals, and through publication on Web site), and VoteHemp, 237 F. Supp. 2d at 62 (finding requester's tri-part dissemination plan -- using its Web site, issuing press releases, and communicating with federal and state legislators -- sufficient to show that information would reach public).

[164] See McClellan, 835 F.2d at 1286 (observing that fee waiver request gave no indication of requesters' ability to understand and process information nor whether they intended to actually disseminate it); Cmty. Legal Servs., 405 F. Supp. 2d at 561 (finding with respect to requester's twenty-
(continued...)

Although established representatives of the news media, as defined in the Uniform Freedom of Information Act Fee Schedule and Guidelines [hereinafter OMB Fee Guidelines],[165] should be readily able to meet this aspect of the statutory requirement by showing their connection to a ready means of effective dissemination,[166] other requesters should be required to describe with greater substantiation their expertise in the subject area and their ability and intention to disseminate the information.[167]

---

[164](...continued)
four-point request that "comprehensiveness does not equal complexity"); S. Utah, 402 F. Supp. 2d at 87 (finding that requester's past publication history in area of cultural resources, its recent report on related issues, and its periodic comments to federal agencies on same were sufficient to establish for fee waiver purposes its expertise in "analyzing and disseminating records"); W. Watersheds, 318 F. Supp. 2d at 1038, 1040 (accepting the requester's statement that it could put the requested ecological information -- characterized by the requester as "tedious to read and difficult to understand" -- into a more user-friendly format given its past analysis of similar information, and noting there was no evidence in the record demonstrating that "the information requested was highly technical"); Eagle, 2003 WL 21402534, at *5 (granting a fee waiver and emphasizing that the agency ignored the educational institution requester's intent to review, evaluate, synthesize, and present "the otherwise raw information into a more usable form"); Klamath Water Users Protective Ass'n, No. 96-3077, slip op. at 47 (D. Or. June 19, 1997) (stating that requester provided insufficient information to establish its ability to understand, make use of, and disseminate requested information); S.A. Ludsin, 1997 U.S. Dist. LEXIS 8617, at *16 (finding requester's intention to make raw appraisal data available on computer network, without analysis, to be insufficient to meet public interest requirement); see also FOIA Update, Vol. VIII, No. 1, at 7.

[165] 52 Fed. Reg. at 10,018; cf. Nat'l Sec. Archive, 880 F.2d at 1387 (elaborating on OMB definition of news media representative to include requester organization).

[166] See FOIA Update, Vol. VIII, No. 1, at 8 & n.5; see also Oglesby, No. 02-0603, slip op. at 5 (D.D.C. Sept. 3, 2002) (reiterating that member of news media presumptively meets dissemination factor).

[167] See FOIA Update, Vol. VIII, No. 1, at 8 & n.5; see also, e.g., Oglesby, 920 F.2d at 66 n.11 (explaining that requester's assertion that he was writer and had disseminated in past, coupled with bare statement of public interest, was insufficient to meet statutory standard); McClellan, 835 F.2d at 1286-87 (stating agency may request additional information; finding twenty-three questions not burdensome); Burriss v. CIA, 524 F. Supp. 448, 449 (M.D. Tenn. 1981) (holding that denial of the plaintiff's fee waiver request "based upon mere representation that he is a researcher who plans to write a book" was not abuse of discretion); cf. Edmonds Inst., 460 F. Supp. 2d at 75 (finding that evidence of the requester's past use of FOIA
(continued...)

Some decisions under the former fee waiver standard suggested that journalists should presumptively be granted fee waivers.[168] The Department of Justice encourages agencies to give special weight to journalistic credentials under this factor,[169] though the statute provides no specific presumption that journalistic status alone is to be dispositive under the fee waiver standard overall and such a presumption would run counter to the 1986 amendments that set forth a special fee category for representatives of the news media.[170] (For a discussion of news media requesters in the context of attorney fee awards under the FOIA, see Tax Analysts v. United

---

[167](...continued) materials "can be relevant to a fee-waiver determination" but that there is no statutory or regulatory requirement that the requester provide it). But see Carney, 19 F.3d at 815 (noting that while the requester had only tentative book publication plans, "fact that he is working on a related dissertation is sufficient evidence . . . that his book will be completed"); S. Utah, 402 F. Supp. 2d at 87-88 (finding requester's specific examples of its involvement in area of cultural resources, including its submission of public comments about impact to such resources on federal land to federal agencies, publication of articles and reports, and use of archaeologists for its work, to be "sufficient evidence" of its expertise in field); W. Watersheds, 318 F. Supp. 2d at 1038, 1040 (stating that where no evidence was presented that the information sought was "highly technical," the requester's past experience analyzing agency records was sufficient to demonstrate its ability to "process the information" and to present it to the public in summarized form); cf. D.C. Technical Assistance Org. v. HUD, 85 F. Supp. 2d 46, 49 (D.D.C. 2000) (suggesting that in "this Information Age, technology has made it possible for almost anyone to fulfill [the fee waiver dissemination] requirement").

[168] See NTEU, 811 F.2d at 649; Goldberg v. U.S. Dep't of State, No. 85-1496, slip op. at 3-4 (D.D.C. Apr. 29, 1986), modified (D.D.C. July 25, 1986); Badhwar v. U.S. Dep't of the Air Force, 615 F. Supp. 698, 708 (D.D.C. 1985); Rosenfeld v. U.S. Dep't of Justice, No. C-85-2247, slip op. at 4-5 (N.D. Cal. Oct. 29, 1985), reconsideration denied (N.D. Cal. Mar. 25, 1986).

[169] See FOIA Update, Vol. VIII, No. 1, at 8; accord FOIA Update, Vol. IV, No. 4, at 14.

[170] 5 U.S.C. § 552(a)(4)(A)(ii)(II); OMB Fee Guidelines, 52 Fed. Reg. at 10,019; see also Hall, 2005 WL 850379, at *7 n.13 (noting that qualification as news media entity "would not automatically" entitle requester to public interest fee waiver); McClain, 13 F.3d at 221 (dictum) (concluding that status as newspaper or nonprofit institution does not lead to automatic waiver of fee); cf. Media Access Project, 883 F.2d at 1065 (remarking that any requester may seek waiver of assessed fees on "case-by-case" basis); Nat'l Sec. Archive, 880 F.2d at 1383 (dictum) (observing that fee waiver decisions are to be made on "case-by-case" basis).

States Department of Justice[171] as discussed in Attorney Fees and Other Sanctions, Attorney Fees and Litigation Costs: Entitlement, below.)

Additionally, in this regard, while nonprofit organizations and public interest groups often are capable of disseminating information, they do not by virtue of their status presumptively qualify for fee waivers; rather they must, like any requester, meet the statutory requirements for a full waiver of all fees.[172]

Further, the requirement that a requester demonstrate a contribution to the understanding of the public at large is not satisfied simply because a fee waiver request is made by a library or other record repository, or by a requester who intends merely to disseminate the information to such an institution.[173] Requests that make no showing of how the information would be disseminated, other than through passively making it available to anyone who might seek access to it, do not meet the burden of demonstrating with particularity that the information will be communicated to the public.[174] These requests, like those of other requesters, should be analyzed to

---

[171] 965 F.2d at 1095-96 (holding that litigant's status as news organization does not render award of attorney fees automatic).

[172] 5 U.S.C. § 552(a)(4)(A)(iii); see Forest Guardians, 416 F.3d at 1178 (reiterating that public interest groups "must still satisfy the statutory standard to obtain a fee waiver"); Sierra Club Legal Def. Fund, No. 93-35383, slip op. at 4 (9th Cir. Aug. 29, 1994) (explaining that status as public interest law firm does not entitle requester to fee waiver); McClain, 13 F.3d at 221 (stating that status as newspaper or nonprofit institution does not lead to "automatic" waiver of fee); McClellan, 835 F.2d at 1284 (stating that legislative history makes plain that "public interest" groups must satisfy statutory test); VoteHemp, 237 F. Supp. 2d at 59 (explaining that nonprofit status "does not relieve [the requester] of its obligation to satisfy the statutory requirements for a fee waiver"); Judicial Watch, No. 97-2089, slip op. at 13 (D.D.C. July 14, 1998) (emphasizing that requester's status as public interest group does not entitle it to fee waiver); Nat'l Wildlife Fed'n, No. 95-017-BU, slip op. at 3-4 (D. Mont. July 15, 1996) (finding that public interest groups must satisfy the statutory test and that a requester does not qualify for a fee waiver by "basically" relying on its status "as one of the nation's largest" conservation organizations).

[173] See FOIA Update, Vol. VIII, No. 1, at 8.

[174] See, e.g., Van Fripp, No. 97-0159, slip op. at 12 (D.D.C. Mar. 16, 2000) (emphasizing that placement in library amounts to, "at best, a passive method of distribution" that does not establish entitlement to fee waiver); Klamath Water Users Protective Ass'n, No. 96-3077, slip op. at 47 (D. Or. June 19, 1997) (finding placement in library insufficient in itself to establish entitlement to fee waiver); cf. S.A. Ludsin, 1997 U.S. Dist. LEXIS 8617, at *16 (indicating that requester, who intended merely to make raw appraisal
(continued...)

identify a particular person or persons who actually will use the requested information in scholarly or other analytic work and then disseminate it to the general public.[175]

4. Fourth, the disclosure must contribute "significantly" to public understanding of government operations or activities.[176] To warrant a waiver or reduction of fees, the public's understanding of the subject matter in question, as compared to the level of public understanding existing prior to the disclosure, must be likely to be enhanced by the disclosure to a significant extent.[177] Such a determination must be an objective one; agencies

---

[174](...continued) data available in electronic form, failed to explain how disclosure would provide explanation to public about government activities); see also FOIA Update, Vol. VIII, No. 1, at 8.

[175] See FOIA Update, Vol. VIII, No. 1, at 8.

[176] See 5 U.S.C. § 552(a)(4)(A)(iii); see also Cmty. Legal Servs., 405 F. Supp. 2d at 558 (noting that the statute provides no guidance "as to what constitutes a 'significant' contribution"); McDade, No. 03-1946, slip op. at 9 (D.D.C. Sept. 29, 2004) (paraphrasing with approval the agency's regulation that provides that the "public's understanding of the subject after disclosure must be enhanced significantly when compared to the level of public understanding prior to disclosure"); cf. Favish, 541 U.S. at 172 (emphasizing, in the Exemption 7(C) context, that the requester "must establish a sufficient reason for the disclosure" by showing "that the public interest sought to be advanced is a significant one" and that the information sought is "likely to advance that interest"); FOIA Post, "Supreme Court Rules for 'Survivor Privacy' in Favish" (posted 4/9/04) (advising further on nexus requirement); Tomscha v. GSA, No. 04-4804, 2005 WL 3406575, at *2 (2d Cir. Dec. 12, 2005) (determining, in an Exemption 6 context, that where the requester sought justifications for a federal employee's performance awards but provided no evidence of wrongdoing by the agency in granting such awards, disclosure would not "contribut[e] significantly to the public understanding of the operations or activities of the government") (citations omitted).

[177] See FOIA Update, Vol. VIII, No. 1, at 8; Brown v. U.S. Patent & Trademark Office, No. 06-14716, 2007 WL 446601, at *2 (11th Cir. Feb. 13, 2007) (holding that the requester failed to adequately explain how the requested records were "related to the activities or operations" of the agency or how they "would contribute to the public's understanding of that agency"); Sierra Club Legal Def. Fund, No. 93-35383, slip op. at 4 (9th Cir. Aug. 29, 1994) (concluding that requester failed to explain how disclosure to it "would add anything to 'public understanding' in light of vast amount of material already disseminated and publicized"); Carney, 19 F.3d at 815 (observing that when requested records are readily available from other sources, further disclosure will not significantly contribute to public

(continued...)

are not permitted to make separate value judgments as to whether any information that would in fact contribute significantly to public understanding of government operations or activities is "important" enough to be made

---

[177](...continued)
understanding); <u>Brown</u>, 445 F. Supp. 2d at 1361 (emphasizing that because plaintiff did not address how disclosure of allegations made against agency in litigation is likely to contribute "significantly" to public understanding of agency's operations, he failed factor four); <u>Klein</u>, 2006 U.S. Dist. LEXIS 32478, at *12 (finding that no showing was made of how disclosure "would contribute significantly to public understanding of government operations"); <u>Hall</u>, 2005 WL 850379, at *7 (finding that no showing was made that requested records would "meaningfully enhance" public understanding of subject of request); <u>Judicial Watch</u>, 185 F. Supp. 2d at 62 (finding that the plaintiff failed to describe with specificity how disclosure of "these particular documents will 'enhance' public understanding 'to a significant extent'"); <u>Judicial Watch</u>, 122 F. Supp. 2d at 10 (explaining that the plaintiff's failure to provide information relevant to other fee waiver factors "makes it impossible to determine that disclosing the requested information will significantly contribute to public understanding of that operation or activity"); <u>D.C. Technical Assistance Org.</u>, 85 F. Supp. 2d at 49 (noting that while plaintiff demonstrated ability to disseminate information, it failed to establish that disclosure would contribute significantly to public's understanding of government activities or operations); <u>Dollinger</u>, No. 95-CV-6174T, slip op. at 5-6 (W.D.N.Y. Aug. 24, 1995) (finding that routine, generic information "lacks substantial informative value" and would not significantly contribute to public understanding); <u>Sloman</u>, 832 F. Supp. at 68 (stating information previously released to other writers and "more important[ly]" available in agency's reading room will not contribute significantly to public understanding of operations of government); see also <u>Forest Guardians</u>, 416 F.3d at 1181-82 (acknowledging that the significance of the contribution to be made by the "release of the records" at issue "is concededly a close question," and finding that the requester "should get the benefit of the doubt" and therefore is entitled to a fee waiver); <u>Cmty. Legal Servs.</u>, 405 F. Supp. 2d at 559 (finding that extent to which requested information already is available, its newness, and whether request is pretext for discovery all were proper considerations in applying "significance factor" where agency's regulation did not address statutory provision). But see <u>W. Watersheds</u>, 318 F. Supp. 2d at 1039 n.2 (finding that significance factor was met where requester's statements that information sought either was not readily available or had never been provided to public were not contradicted in the administrative record by agency); <u>Landmark</u>, No. 97-1474, slip op. at 10 (D.D.C. Sept. 22, 1998) (finding "untenable" agency's position that possible prospective release" of same material by congressional committee diminishes significance of current release); <u>Pedersen</u>, 847 F. Supp. at 855 (finding that despite requesters' failure to specifically assert such significance, widespread media attention referenced in appeal letter sufficient to demonstrate information's significant contribution to public understanding).

public.[178]

Once an agency determines that the "public interest" requirement for a fee waiver has been met -- through its consideration of fee waiver factors one through four -- the statutory standard's second requirement calls for the agency to determine whether "disclosure of the information . . . is not primarily in the commercial interest of the requester."[179] In order to decide whether this requirement has been satisfied, agencies should consider the final two of the six fee waiver factors -- factors five and six -- in sequence:

5. Accordingly, to apply the fifth factor an agency must next determine as a threshold matter whether the request involves any commercial interest of the requester which would be furthered by the disclosure.[180] A "commercial interest" is one that furthers a commercial, trade, or profit interest as those terms are commonly understood.[181] Information sought in furtherance of a tort claim for compensation or retribution for the requester is not considered to involve a "commercial interest."[182] However, not only profit-making corporations but also individuals or other organizations may have a commercial interest to be furthered by the disclosure, depending

---

[178] Cf. 132 Cong. Rec. S14,298 (daily ed. Sept. 30, 1986) (statement of Sen. Leahy) (emphasizing that agencies should administer the fee waiver provision in "an objective manner and should not rely on their own, subjective view as to the value of the information"); Cmty. Legal Servs., 405 F. Supp. 2d at 560 (finding that the agency's inferences that the request was a pretext for discovery and the requester's use of "information in advising clients suggests a litigious motive" were speculative where there was no evidence of any pending lawsuits); see also Ettlinger v. FBI, 596 F. Supp. 867, 875 (D. Mass. 1984); FOIA Update, Vol. VIII, No. 1, at 8.

[179] 5 U.S.C. § 552(a)(4)(A)(iii).

[180] See FOIA Update, Vol. VIII, No. 1, at 9 (discussing analysis required to determine whether requester has commercial interest); see also Vote-Hemp, 237 F. Supp. 2d at 64 (citing to the agency's regulation and noting that "agencies are instructed to consider 'the existence and magnitude' of a commercial interest").

[181] See id.; OMB Fee Guidelines, 52 Fed. Reg. at 10,017-18; cf. Am. Airlines, Inc. v. Nat'l Mediation Bd., 588 F.2d 863, 870 (2d Cir. 1978) (defining term "commercial" in Exemption 4 as meaning anything "pertaining or relating to or dealing with commerce").

[182] See McClellan, 835 F.2d at 1285; cf. Detroit Free Press, Inc. v. Dep't of Justice, 73 F.3d 93, 98 (6th Cir. 1996) (stating, in context of attorney fees, that "'news interests should not be considered commercial interests'" when examining commercial benefit to requester (quoting Fenster v. Brown, 617 F.2d 740, 742 n.4 (D.C. Cir. 1979))).

upon the circumstances involved.[183] Agencies may properly consider the requester's identity and the circumstances surrounding the request and draw reasonable inferences regarding the existence of a commercial interest.[184]

When a commercial interest is found to exist and that interest would be furthered by the requested disclosure, an agency must assess the magnitude of such interest in order subsequently to compare it to the "public interest" in disclosure.[185] In assessing the magnitude of the commercial interest, the agency should reasonably consider the extent to which the FOIA disclosure will serve the requester's identified commercial interest.[186]

6. Lastly the agency must balance the requester's commercial interest against the identified public interest in disclosure and determine which interest is "primary." A fee waiver or reduction must be granted when the public interest in disclosure is greater in magnitude than the requester's commercial interest.[187] Or as one court phrased it when considering the balance to be struck under the predecessor fee waiver standard: "[I]n simple terms, the public should not foot the bill unless it will be the primary beneficiary of the [disclosure]."[188]

Although news gathering organizations ordinarily have a commercial interest in obtaining information, agencies may generally presume that when a news media requester has satisfied the "public interest" standard,

---

[183] See OMB Fee Guidelines, 52 Fed. Reg. at 10,013; FOIA Update, Vol. VIII, No. 1, at 9; see also VoteHemp, 237 F. Supp. 2d at 65 (concluding that nonprofit organization, as advocate for free market in controlled substance, had commercial interest in requested records); Judicial Watch, No. 97-2869, slip op. at 5 (D.D.C. Aug. 25, 1998) (stating that nonprofit status "does not determine the character of the information"); cf. Critical Mass Energy Project v. NRC, 830 F.2d 278, 281 (D.C. Cir. 1987) (recognizing that entity's "non-profit status is not determinative" of commercial status) (Exemption 4 case).

[184] See FOIA Update, Vol. VIII, No. 1, at 9; see also VoteHemp, 237 F. Supp. 2d at 65 ("A review of plaintiff's website pages demonstrates that indeed it has a commercial interest in the information it is seeking to obtain."); cf. Tax Analysts, 965 F.2d at 1096 (clarifying that in the context of attorney fees, the status of a requester as a news organization does not "render[] irrelevant the news organization's other interests in the information").

[185] See FOIA Update, Vol. VIII, No. 1, at 9.

[186] Id.

[187] Id.

[188] Burriss, 524 F. Supp. at 449.

that will be the primary interest served.[189] On the other hand, disclosure to private repositories of government records or data brokers may not be presumed to primarily serve the public interest; rather, requests on behalf of such entities can more readily be considered as primarily in their commercial interest, depending upon the nature of the records and their relation to the exact circumstances of the enterprise.[190]

When agencies analyze fee waiver requests by considering these six factors, they can rest assured that they have carried out their statutory obligation to determine whether a waiver is in the public interest.[191] When an agency has relied on factors unrelated to the public benefit standard to deny a fee waiver request, however, courts have found an abuse of discretion.[192] Additionally, when only some of the requested records satisfy the statutory test, a waiver should be granted for those records.[193]

---

[189] See FOIA Update, Vol. VIII, No. 1, at 10; see also Nat'l Sec. Archive, 880 F.2d at 1388 (requests from news media entities, in furtherance of their newsgathering function, are not for "commercial use").

[190] See FOIA Update, Vol. VIII, No. 1, at 10; see also Nat'l Sec. Archive, 880 F.2d at 1387-88.

[191] See FOIA Update, Vol. VIII, No. 1, at 10; cf. Friends of the Coast Fork, 110 F.3d at 55 (emphasizing that where agency's regulations provide for multifactor test, it is inappropriate to rely on single factor); Or. Natural Desert Ass'n v. U.S. Dep't of the Interior, 24 F. Supp. 2d 1088, 1095 (D. Or. 1998) (finding that fee waiver denial must fail when agency did not fully follow its multifactor regulation).

[192] See, e.g., Goldberg, No. 85-1496, slip op. at 3-5 (D.D.C. Apr. 29, 1986) (holding that an agency policy of granting a waiver of search fees but not of duplication fees is "both irrational and in violation of the statute"); Idaho Wildlife Fed'n v. U.S. Forest Serv., 3 Gov't Disclosure Serv. (P-H) ¶ 83,271, at 84,056 (D.D.C. July 21, 1983) (emphasizing that reliance on regulation that proscribes granting of fee waiver when records are sought for litigation is abuse of discretion because regulation is overbroad in that it ignores "public interest" in certain litigation); Diamond v. FBI, 548 F. Supp. 1158, 1160 (S.D.N.Y. 1982) (maintaining that agency may not decline to waive fees based merely upon perceived obligation to collect them); Eudey v. CIA, 478 F. Supp. 1175, 1177 (D.D.C. 1979) (stating that agency may not consider quantity of documents to be released).

[193] See 28 C.F.R. § 16.11(k)(4) ("Where only some of the records to be released satisfy the requirements for a waiver of fees, a waiver shall be granted for those records."); cf. Samuel Gruber Educ. Project v. U.S. Dep't of Justice, 24 F. Supp. 2d 1, 2 (D.D.C. 1998) (upholding, without discussion, seventy-percent fee waiver granted by agency). But see Schrecker, 970 F. Supp. at 50-51 (granting full fee waiver despite agency's determination that portion of requested information already was in public domain); cf. Camp-
(continued...)

## FEES AND FEE WAIVERS

An analysis of the foregoing factors routinely requires an agency to first assess the nature of the information likely to be released in response to an access request, because the statutory standard speaks to whether "disclosure" of the responsive information will significantly contribute to public understanding.[194] This assessment necessarily focuses on the information that would be disclosed,[195] which in turn logically requires an estimation of the applicability of any relevant FOIA exemption(s).

In an atypical decision, a question of whether an agency should be required to establish at the fee waiver determination stage the precise contours of its anticipated withholdings was raised during the late 1980s in Project on Military Procurement v. Department of the Navy.[196] There the district court seemed to suggest that an agency must defend an anticipated application of FOIA exemptions in the fee waiver context with an index pursuant to the requirements of Vaughn v. Rosen.[197] Such a requirement not only was unprecedented, it also is unworkable -- as it would compel an agency to actually process responsive records at the threshold fee waiver determination stage in order to compile the Vaughn Index; it would turn the normal, longstanding procedure for responding to FOIA/fee waiver requests on its head.[198] Until a fee waiver determination has been made and (if a full fee waiver is not granted) the requester has agreed to pay all the assessable fees, the request is not yet ripe for processing because there has been no compliance with the fee requirements of the FOIA.[199] The de-

---

[193](...continued)
bell, 164 F.3d at 35 (finding fault with analysis used by agency to award partial fee waiver; remanding case for reconsideration but declining to hold that agency may not charge any fee).

[194] 5 U.S.C. § 552(a)(4)(A)(iii); see also, e.g., 28 C.F.R. § 16.11(k)(2).

[195] See Hall, 2005 WL 850379, at *7 (reiterating that FOIA fee waiver provision is applicable to "properly disclosed documents"); Judicial Watch, 2000 WL 33724693, at *5 (explaining that "under the FOIA, the [fee waiver] analysis focuses on the subject and impact of the particular disclosure"); Van Fripp, No. 97-159, slip op. at 10 (D.D.C. Mar. 16, 2000) (stating that "reviewing agencies and courts should consider . . . whether the disclosable portions of requested information are meaningfully informative in relation to the subject matter requested" (citing agency's fee waiver regulation)).

[196] 710 F. Supp. 362, 366-68 (D.D.C. 1989).

[197] 484 F.2d 820, 826-28 (D.C. Cir. 1973).

[198] Cf. LaCedra v. Executive Office for U.S. Attorneys, No. 99-0273, slip op. at 1 (D.D.C. Nov. 5, 2003) ("Unless the agency waives fees, the payment of assessed fees or the administrative appeal from the denial of a fee waiver request is a jurisdictional prerequisite to maintaining a FOIA lawsuit.").

[199] See 5 U.S.C. § 552(a)(3); see also, e.g., Pollack v. Dep't of Justice, 49
(continued...)

cision on this issue in Project on Military Procurement would thus yield impracticable results.[200] Indeed, the court in Project on Military Procure-

---

[199](...continued)
F.3d 115, 120 (4th Cir. 1995) (finding when the requester refused to commit to pay fees, the agency "had the authority to cease processing [his] request"); Vennes v. IRS, No. 89-5136, slip op. at 2-3 (8th Cir. Oct. 13, 1989) (explaining agency under no obligation to produce material until either requester agrees to pay fee or fee waiver is approved); Casad, 2003 U.S. Dist. LEXIS 13007, at *18 (recognizing that where fee waiver is denied, no action by agency is required until requester agrees to pay fee associated with request); Woodfolk v. DEA, No. 97-0634, slip op. at 2 (D.D.C. Jan. 29, 2002) (finding that agency had no obligation to produce records where requester had neither paid fee nor applied for fee waiver); Daniel v. U.S. Dep't of Justice, No. 99-2423, slip op. at 2 (D.D.C. Mar. 30, 2001) (dismissing complaint for production of records where plaintiff had failed to pay fee after fee waiver was denied), summary affirmance granted, No. 01-5119, 2001 WL 1029156, at *1 (D.C. Cir. Aug 28, 2001); Irons v. FBI, 571 F. Supp. 1241, 1243 (D. Mass. 1983) (upholding regulation requiring payment of fees or waiver of fees before FOIA request is deemed to have been received); cf. Judicial Watch, No. 01-0639, slip op. at 7-8 (D.D.C. Mar. 31, 2003) (recognizing that court's prior opinion "essentially requiring [agency] to process Plaintiff's entire FOIA request for free without requiring Plaintiff to meet its burden of proof" of entitlement to fee waiver was improper); Johnston v. United States, No. 93-CV-5605, 1997 U.S. Dist. LEXIS 597, at *4 (E.D. Pa. Jan. 27, 1997) (upholding agency's decision to make availability of records contingent upon agreement to pay estimated fees); FOIA Update, Vol. XIX, No. 3, at 2 (advising agencies how to count requests closed for nonpayment of fees, for purposes of annual FOIA reports). But see S. Utah, 402 F. Supp. 2d at 88-91 (discounting defendant's claim that majority of information at issue was "patently exempt" under Exemption 3 and that remaining information would be of no public significance, where agency official had "substantial discretion" to disclose or withhold information based on assessment of benefits and risks of such disclosure); Judicial Watch, 310 F. Supp. 2d at 295 (ruling, where the agency granted a fee waiver for all documents other than those to be withheld, that it "'invert[s] the burden of proof'" to require the plaintiff to show that the agency's "contemplated withholdings" are not proper (quoting Project on Military Procurement, 710 F. Supp. at 367)); see also Carney, 19 F.3d at 815 (finding it not proper to deny fee waiver request on basis that records may have been exempt; fee waiver "should be evaluated on face of request"); Wilson v. CIA, No. 89-3356, slip op. at 3-4 (D.D.C. Mar. 25, 1991) (stating that agency may not deny fee waiver request based upon "likelihood" that information will be withheld); cf. Landmark, No. 97-1474, slip op. at 7 (D.D.C. Sept. 22, 1998) (finding it proper to deny fee waiver based on the agency's preliminary determination of exempt status of the records "'only if the request was for patently exempt documents'" (quoting Carney, 19 F.3d at 814)).

[200] See Judicial Watch, Inc., 2004 WL 980826, at *18 (implicitly rejecting
(continued...)

ment itself ultimately acknowledged that the government "may be correct" that a fee waiver determination depends in part on applicability of FOIA exemptions to the responsive records.[201]

With limited exceptions,[202] Project on Military Procurement was largely ignored during the next decade. In recent years, however, three district court opinions, all within the D.C. Circuit, have revisited this and have concluded that fee wavier requests should not be evaluated on the basis that the requested records may well ultimately be found to be exempt from disclosure.[203] Additionally, two of these three opinions appear to suggest that an agency should not consider what information will be disclosed to a requester in its analysis of its fee waiver request, but rather that a fee waiver request should be evaluated "based on the face of the request."[204] The language of the statute, however, authorizes agencies to waive or reduce fees only when "disclosure" of the information is likely to contribute significantly to the public's understanding of government op-

---

[200](...continued)
plaintiff's "catch-22" argument -- i.e., that it was being asked to identify documents qualifying for fee waiver before getting access to them -- and thus both exposing and logically undermining flawed rationale of Project on Military Procurement); cf., e.g., Favish, 541 U.S. at 172 (evincing Supreme Court's emphasis on "giv[ing] practical meaning" to FOIA provisions).

[201] 710 F. Supp. at 367 n.11.

[202] Carney, 19 F.3d at 815 (finding that the agency's denial of a fee waiver was not proper when made simply on the basis that the requested records "may [be] exempt from disclosure . . . , [because a] fee waiver should be evaluated based on the face of the request and the reasons given by the requester" (citing Project on Military Procurement)); Wilson v. CIA, No. 89-3356, slip op. at 3-4 (D.D.C. Mar. 25, 1991) (stating that agency may not deny fee waiver request based upon "likelihood" that information will be withheld).

[203] S. Utah, 402 F. Supp. 2d at 90 (opining that agency cannot base fee waiver decision on anticipated redactions to responsive records); Judicial Watch, 2005 WL 1606915, at *4 (saying that a fee waver decision should not be made on the basis of the agency's "determination that most of the information was exempt from disclosure"); Judicial Watch, 310 F. Supp. 2d at 295 (same).

[204] Judicial Watch, 2005 WL 1606915, at *4 ("A fee waiver request should be evaluated based on the face of the request and the reasons given by the requester in support of the waiver, 'not on the possibility that the records may ultimately be determined to be exempt from disclosure.'") (citations omitted); Judicial Watch, 310 F. Supp. 2d at 295 (same).

erations.[205] Further, in none of these recent opinions is any consideration given to the fees that would be owed for the processing of records properly withheld.[206]

The FOIA does not explicitly reference any time period within which an agency must resolve a fee waiver issue.[207] The extension of the statutory twenty-working day compliance requirement to include the resolution of fee waiver (and fee) issues, however, is a logical application of the statutory twenty-day provision; indeed, several courts, including the D.C. Circuit, have implicitly approved such application.[208] (For a discussion of when the need to resolve a procedural issue, including a fee-related matter, may extend the time period within which an agency must determine whether to comply with a request, see Procedural Requirements, Time Limits, above.)

---

[205] See 5 U.S.C. § 552(a)(4)(A)(iii).

[206] See, e.g., Judicial Watch, 2005 WL 1606915, at *3-11 (simultaneously granting plaintiff full fee waiver for "those records already released" -- approximately twenty percent of responsive records -- and upholding each of agency's claims of exemptions for remainder of processed records, with no consideration given to government's entitlement to reimbursement for processing fees government incurred for those records withheld); see also OMB Fee Guidelines, 52 Fed. Reg. at 10,019 (advising agencies that they may charge for search time even if they "fail to locate the records or if records located are determined to be exempt from disclosure").

[207] See 5 U.S.C. § 552(a)(4)(A).

[208] See Judicial Watch, 326 F.3d at 1311 ("A requester is considered to have constructively exhausted administrative remedies and may seek judicial review immediately if . . . the agency fails to answer the [fee waiver] request within twenty days.") (citations omitted); Judicial Watch, 310 F. Supp. 2d at 293 (commenting that where agency fails to respond to fee waiver request within twenty working days, requester has constructively exhausted administrative remedies and may seek judicial review); Pub. Citizen, Inc. v. Dep't of Educ., 292 F. Supp. 2d 1, 4 (D.D.C. 2003) (stating that "if the agency fails to respond to a waiver request within twenty days, the requester is deemed to have constructively exhausted" administrative remedies); cf. Long v. U.S. Dep't of Justice, 450 F. Supp. 2d 42 (D.D.C.) (finding the defendant's failure to render fee waiver determination within reasonable period of time to be mooted by the agency's ultimate release of records without charge; "'we cannot order the [agency] to do something [it] has already done'" (quoting Better Gov't Ass'n v. Dep't of State, 780 F.2d 86, 91 (D.C. Cir. 1986))), amended by 457 F. Supp. 2d 30 (D.D.C. 2006), amended further on reconsideration, Nos. 00-0211 & 02-2467, 2007 WL 293508 (D.D.C. Feb. 2, 2007), stay granted (D.D.C. Feb. 13, 2007); Citizens for Responsibility & Ethics in Wash. v. U.S. Dep't of Justice, No. 05-2078, 2006 WL 1518964, at *4 (D.D.C. June 1, 2006) (criticizing agency for time taken in adjudicating fee waiver appeal).

Nor does the FOIA explicitly provide for administrative appeals of denials of requests for fee waivers. Nevertheless, many agencies, either by regulation or by practice, have appropriately considered appeals of such actions.[209] The Courts of Appeals for the D.C. and Fifth Circuits have made it clear, moreover, that appellate administrative exhaustion is required for any adverse determination, including fee waiver denials.[210]

---

[209] See, e.g., 28 C.F.R. § 16.9(a) ("If you are dissatisfied with [the agency's] response to your request, you may appeal an adverse determination denying your request . . . ."); see also, e.g., id. at § 16.6(c) (including in its listing of adverse determinations "a denial of a request for a fee waiver").

[210] See Pruitt v. Executive Office for the U.S. Attorneys, No. 01-5453, 2002 WL 1364365, at *1 (D.C. Cir. Apr. 19, 2002) (reiterating that judicial review is not appropriate until requester either appeals fee waiver denial or pays assessed fee); Voinche v. U.S. Dep't of the Air Force, 983 F.2d 667, 669 (5th Cir. 1993) (emphasizing that requester seeking fee waiver under FOIA must exhaust administrative remedies before seeking judicial review); Oglesby, 920 F.2d at 66 & n.11, 71 ("Exhaustion does not occur until fees are paid or an appeal is taken from the refusal to waive fees."); Kumar, 2007 U.S. Dist. LEXIS 11144, at *11 (concluding that plaintiff's failure to make advance payment constituted failure to exhaust); Hall, 2005 WL 850379, at *2 (emphasizing that requester may seek judicial review "only after" exhaustion of administrative remedies through payment of fees or appeal taken from fee waiver denial); Boyd v. Criminal Div., U.S. Dep't of Justice, No. 04-1100, 2005 WL 555412, at *5 (D.D.C. Mar. 9, 2005) (noting that requester's failure to request fee waiver (or pay assessed fee) precluded judicial review); Pub. Citizen, 292 F. Supp. 2d at 4 ("A requester who disagrees with the denial of a waiver must pursue administrative remedies."); Judicial Watch, No. 99-1883, slip op. at 10-12 (D.D.C. Sept. 11, 2003) (concluding that although plaintiff "may have" exhausted its administrative remedies as to other issues, it had failed to administratively exhaust as to agency's denial of fee waiver, so its claims related to fee waiver were not properly before court; rejecting plaintiff's argument that its failure was irrelevant because of claimed entitlement to full waiver of fees); Trulock, 257 F. Supp. 2d at 52-53 (reiterating that where plaintiff has neither appealed fee waiver denial nor paid estimated fee, court cannot address entitlement to fee waiver until plaintiff exhausts administrative remedies with respect to fee issue); see also AFGE, 907 F.2d at 209 (declining consideration of fee waiver request when not pursued during agency administrative proceeding); Schoenman v. FBI, No. 04-2202, 2006 WL 1582253, at *16 (D.D.C. June 5, 2006) (finding agency's voluntary withdrawal of motion to dismiss appropriate where agency denied fee waiver and requester administratively appealed that decision); Kong On Imp. & Exp. Co. v. U.S. Customs & Border Prot. Bureau, No. 04-2001, 2005 WL 1458279, at *1 (D.D.C. June 20, 2005) (determining that because plaintiff failed to exhaust administrative remedies, court need not reach issue of whether requester's purported withdrawal of request was grounds for dismissal); Oguaju v. Executive Office for U.S. Attorneys, No. 00-1930, slip op. at 1 n.1 (D.D.C. Sept. 25, 2003)

(continued...)

Prior to the 1986 FOIA amendments, the discretionary nature of the FOIA's fee waiver provision led the majority of courts to conclude that the proper standard for judicial review of an agency denial of a fee waiver is whether that decision was arbitrary and capricious,[211] in accordance with the Administrative Procedure Act.[212] This meant that a court could not "replace its own judgment for that of [an agency] without first concluding that the [agency's] decision was completely unreasonable and unfair."[213]

This standard was changed, however, when a specific judicial review

---

[210](...continued) (denying motion for fee waiver by stating that "Court cannot compel agency to waive fees" but rather reviews agency's decision to deny fee waiver), summary affirmance granted, No. 04-5407, 2005 U.S. App. LEXIS 23891 (D.C. Cir. Nov. 3, 2005); Maydak v. U.S. Dep't of Justice, 254 F. Supp. 2d 23, 50 (D.D.C. 2003) (stating that payment or waiver of fees is jurisdictional prerequisite to filing suit); 28 C.F.R. § 16.9(c) (Department of Justice regulation providing for administrative appeal exhaustion before court review); cf. Campbell v. Unknown Power Superintendent of Flathead Irrigation & Power Project, No. 91-35104, slip op. at 3 (9th Cir. Apr. 22, 1992) (explaining exhaustion requirement not imposed when agency ignored fee waiver request). But see Judicial Watch, 2005 WL 1606915, at *3 (finding that constructive exhaustion occurred when agency failed to respond to fee waiver request within statutory time period); Hall, 2005 WL 850379, at *4 n.7 (noting that agency's request for fee deposit subsequent to litigation, and after requester had constructively exhausted administrative remedies, was not grounds for dismissal); Pub. Citizen, 292 F. Supp. 2d at 4 (finding that requester constructively exhausted administrative remedies where agency failed to respond to fee waiver request within twenty working days).

[211] See, e.g., NTEU, 811 F.2d at 647 (stating that agency's denial of fee waiver will be upheld unless finding is arbitrary or capricious); Burke v. U.S. Dep't of Justice, 559 F.2d 1182, 1182 (10th Cir. 1977) (same); Allen v. FBI, 551 F. Supp. 694, 696 (D.D.C. 1982) (same); Diamond, 548 F. Supp. at 1160 (same); Sellers v. Webster, 2 Gov't Disclosure Serv. (P-H) ¶ 81,243, at 81,699 (S.D. Ill. Feb. 6, 1981) (same); Eudey, 478 F. Supp. at 1176 (same); Fellner v. U.S. Dep't of Justice, No. 75-C-430, slip op. at 7 (W.D. Wisc. Apr. 28, 1976) (same); see also McClellan, 835 F.2d at 1248 (noting that for judicial review of fee waivers after the 1986 FOIA amendments "a court no longer applies the 'arbitrary and capricious' standard to an agency's action"); Ely, 753 F.2d at 165; Ettlinger, 596 F. Supp. at 871; cf. Walker v. IRS, No. 86-0073, 1986 WL 12049, at *2 (M.D. Pa. June 16, 1986) (noting that FOIA gives agency broad discretion to waive fees).

[212] 5 U.S.C. §§ 701-706 (2000).

[213] Crooker, 577 F. Supp. at 1224.

provision was included in the FOIA,[214] which provides for the review of agency fee waiver denials according to a de novo standard.[215] Yet this provision also explicitly provides that the scope of judicial review remains limited to the administrative record established before the agency,[216] and thus it is crucial that the agency's fee waiver denial letter create a comprehensive administrative record of all of the reasons for the denial.[217]

---

[214] 5 U.S.C. § 552(a)(4)(A)(vii).

[215] See Judicial Watch, 326 F.3d at 1311 (recognizing that review of agency's fee waiver denial is de novo); Campbell, 164 F.3d at 35 (stating that judicial review for action regarding wavier of fees is de novo); Kumar, 2007 U.S. Dist. LEXIS 11144, at *9 (same); Brown, 445 F. Supp. 2d at 1353 (same); Prison Legal News, 436 F. Supp. 2d at 22 (same); Cmty. Legal Servs., 405 F. Supp. 2d at 555 (same); S. Utah, 402 F. Supp. 2d at 87 (same); McDade, No. 03-1946, slip op. at 7 (D.D.C. Sept. 29, 2004) (same); Judicial Watch, 310 F. Supp. 2d at 290 (same); W. Watersheds, 318 F. Supp. 2d at 1039 (same); Inst. for Wildlife Prot., 290 F. Supp. 2d at 1228 (same); Eagle, 2003 WL 21402534, at *2 (same); McQueen, 264 F. Supp. 2d at 424 (same); Crain v. U.S. Customs Serv., No. 02-0341, slip op. at 5 n.5 (D.D.C. Mar. 25, 2003) (noting that "uncertainty present in review of fee status determinations is in contrast to review of denials of fee waiver requests, which must be done [de novo]").

[216] 5 U.S.C. § 552(a)(4)(A)(vii); see also, e.g., Judicial Watch, 326 F.3d at 1311 (stating that review is "limited to the record before the agency"); Campbell, 164 F.3d at 35 (same); Friends of the Coast Fork, 110 F.3d at 55 (stating that court's consideration of fee waiver must be limited to administrative record before agency); Carney, 19 F.3d at 814 (same); AFGE, 907 F.2d at 209 (same); Kumar, 2007 U.S. Dist. LEXIS 11144, at *9 (same); Brown, 445 F. Supp. 2d at 1353 (same); Prison Legal News, 436 F. Supp. 2d at 22, 26 n.4 (rejecting submissions not provided to agency administratively); Cmty. Legal Servs., 405 F. Supp. 2d at 555 (reiterating that review is limited to administrative record before agency); S. Utah, 402 F. Supp. 2d at 87 (same); McDade, No. 03-1946, slip op. at 7 (D.D.C. Sept. 29, 2004) (same); Judicial Watch, 310 F. Supp. 2d at 290 (same); W. Watersheds, 318 F. Supp. 2d at 1039 (same); Eagle, 2003 WL 21402534, at *4 (acknowledging that the agency ordinarily is not permitted "to rely on justifications for its decision that were not articulated during the administrative proceedings," but finding that here the agency was "simply clarifying and explaining" its earlier position); Judicial Watch, 133 F. Supp. 2d at 53 & n.1 (disallowing consideration of information not provided by plaintiff in administrative record).

[217] See, e.g., Friends of the Coast Fork, 110 F.3d at 55 (reiterating that the agency's letter "must be reasonably calculated to put the requester on notice" as to reasons for the fee waiver denial); Larson, 843 F.2d at 1483 (information not part of administrative record may not be considered by district court when reviewing agency fee waiver denial); NTEU, 811 F.2d at (continued...)

A requester wishing to challenge an agency's denial of a fee waiver may seek judicial review of the agency's decision.[218] In this regard, agencies should also be aware that a challenge to an agency's fee waiver policy is not automatically rendered moot when the agency reverses itself and grants the specific fee waiver request; courts may still entertain challenges when they concern the legality of the standards used.[219] An agency's belated grant of a fee waiver, however, can render moot a requester's challenge to its fee waiver denial when it is the agency's specific denial that is at issue,[220] not the underlying fee waiver policy used by the agency to

---

[217](...continued)
648 (holding that court can consider only information before agency at time of decision); Brown, 445 F. Supp. 2d at 1354 (observing that the "administrative record should consist of those documents which the [agency] used to determine whether Plaintiff's fees should be waived"); Pub. Citizen, 292 F. Supp. 2d at 5 (criticizing the agency for its failure to adjudicate fee waiver by emphasizing that "this Court has no record upon which to evaluate plaintiff's claims that it is entitled to a waiver"); S.A. Ludsin, 1997 U.S. Dist. LEXIS 8617, at *16 (stating that court cannot consider reasons not provided by agency); Fitzgibbon, 724 F. Supp. at 1051 n.10 (finding government's "post hoc rationales" offered in response to lawsuit untimely); see also FOIA Update, Vol. VIII, No. 1, at 10; FOIA Update, Vol. VI, No. 1, at 6.

[218] See 5 U.S.C. § 552(a)(4)(B); see also, e.g., 28 C.F.R. § 16.9(b) (requiring agency to inform requester of right to judicial review of agency's adverse determination); id. at § 16.6(c) (providing that adverse determinations include "a denial of a fee waiver request"); cf. Klein v. U.S. Patent & Trademark Office, No. 97-5285, 1998 U.S. App. LEXIS 4720, at *2 (D.C. Cir. Feb. 9, 1998) (holding that review of fee waiver denial may not be sought in appellate court in first instance); Kansi v. U.S. Dep't of Justice, 11 F. Supp. 2d 42, 43 (D.D.C. 1998) (refusing to consider fee waiver request when it was not raised in Complaint or adequately justified before agency).

[219] See Better Gov't Ass'n, 780 F.2d at 91-92 (concluding that arguments concerning facial validity of fee waiver guidelines not moot when agency intends to apply same standards to future requests); Pub. Citizen v. OSHA, No. 86-705, slip op. at 2-3 (D.D.C. Aug. 5, 1987) (same).

[220] See Hall v. CIA, 437 F.3d 94, 97-100 (D.C. Cir. 2006) (finding that in this "disconcertingly complex" case agency's decision to release documents without payment of fees moots requester's appeal of the fee waiver denial; vacating "each of the district court's decisions to the extent that they relate to the payment of fees"), reh'g denied, No. 04-5235, 2006 U.S. App. LEXIS 11103, at *1 (D.C. Cir. Apr. 19, 2006); Long, 450 F. Supp. 2d at 84 ("Once a fee waiver has been granted, neither the FOIA nor the agency's regulations create an independent right to an adjudication of [media] status."); Prison Legal News, 436 F. Supp. 2d at 27 n.5 (noting that because requester was entitled to blanket fee waiver there was no need to analyze its claimed entitlement to media status); Wilderness Soc'y v. U.S. Dep't of the Interior, No.

(continued...)

make that administrative determination.[221]

With regard to fee waiver matters, agencies should retain the general discretion, though, to consider the cost-effectiveness of their investment of administrative resources in their fee waiver determinations.[222] For additional guidance on any particular fee waiver issue, agency FOIA officers may contact OIP's FOIA Counselor service, at (202) 514-3642.

---

[220](...continued)
04-0650, 2005 U.S. Dist. LEXIS 20042, at *26-27 (D.D.C. Sept. 12, 2005) (ruling that agency's reversal of initial decision to deny fee waiver mooted that portion of lawsuit); Judicial Watch, 2005 WL 1606915, at *5 n.2 (finding that where requester was entitled to fee waiver "there was no need to address . . . news media" status); cf. Hall, 437 F.3d at 99 (refusing to consider requester's media status claim when it was rendered moot by agency's voluntary release of documents without requester's payment of fees); Tooley v. Bush, No. 06-306, 2006 WL 3783142, at *11 n.2 (D.D.C. Dec. 21, 2006) (stating that request for fee waiver moot where agencies charged no fees); Long, 450 F. Supp. 2d at 83-84 (resolving that where agency ultimately released records without imposing fee, requester's "arbitrary and capricious" claim with regard to agency's delay in processing fee waiver request was moot); Judicial Watch, 310 F. Supp. 2d at 293 n.3 (explaining that because requester was entitled to full fee waiver "it was unnecessary to determine" its fee category); Long v. ATF, 964 F. Supp. 494, 497-98 (D.D.C. 1997) (holding that there is no "independent right" to fee category determination once fee waiver is granted); Project on Military Procurement, 710 F. Supp. at 368 (finding no need to determine requester category where requester was going to receive full fee waiver).

[221] See Payne Enters. v. United States, 837 F.2d 486, 491-92 (D.C. Cir. 1988) (stating that when a party's lawsuit is a "challenge to the policy or practice" of the agency, such that the agency action reasonably would be expected to "recur" absent judicial review, and not to the specific action taken by the agency in a particular instance, it "cannot be mooted by the release of the specific documents that prompted the suit") (non-fee context).

[222] See Rodriguez v. USPS, No. 90-1886, slip op. at 3 n.1 (D.D.C. Oct. 2, 1991) (suggesting agency "consider" waiving de minimis fee despite requester's failure to comply with exhaustion requirement); see also OMB Fee Guidelines, 52 Fed. Reg. at 10,018 (encouraging agencies, with regard to fee matters, to use "most efficient and least costly methods" to comply with FOIA requests).

EXEMPTION 1

Beginning with President Harry S. Truman in 1951,[1] the uniform policy of the executive branch concerning the protection of national security information traditionally has been set by the President with the issuance of a new or revised national security classification executive order.[2] Exemption 1 of the FOIA integrates the national security protections provided by this executive order with the FOIA's disclosure mandate by protecting from disclosure all national security information concerning intelligence collection, the national defense, or foreign policy that has been properly classified in accordance with the substantive and procedural requirements of the current executive order.[3] As such, of course, Exemption 1 does not protect information that is merely "classifiable" -- that is, meets the substantive requirements of the current such order but has not been actually reviewed and classified under it.[4] The executive order currently in effect is Executive Order 12,958, as amended, which was signed by President George W. Bush on March 25, 2003.[5] This amended order replaced the original version of

---

[1] See Exec. Order No. 10,290, 16 Fed. Reg. 9795 (Sept. 24, 1951). But see also Exec. Order No. 8381, 5 Fed. Reg. 1147 (Mar. 22, 1940) (establishing initial classification structure within military to protect information related to "vital military installations and equipment").

[2] See, e.g., Exec. Order No. 10,501, 3 C.F.R. 398 (1949-1953) (Eisenhower Administration order); Exec. Order No. 10,985, 27 Fed. Reg. 439 (Jan. 2, 1962) (Kennedy Administration order); Exec. Order No. 11,652, 3 C.F.R. 678 (1971-1975) (Nixon Administration order); Exec. Order 11,862, 40 Fed. Reg. 25,197 (June 11, 1975) (Ford Administration amendment); Exec. Order No. 12,065, 3 C.F.R. 190 (1978) (Carter Administration order); Exec. Order No. 12,356, 3 C.F.R. 166 (1983) (Reagan Administration order), excerpted in FOIA Update, Vol. III, No. 3, at 6-7.

[3] 5 U.S.C. § 552(b)(1) (2000 & Supp. IV 2004).

[4] See, e.g., Assassination Archives & Research Ctr. v. CIA, 177 F. Supp. 2d 1, 8-9 (D.D.C. 2001) (explaining that agencies must follow procedural requirements of national security classification executive order to invoke Exemption 1), aff'd, 334 F.2d 55 (D.C. Cir. 2003); Lesar v. U.S. Dep't of Justice, 636 F.2d 474, 485 (D.D.C. 1980) (same). But see Goldberg v. U.S. Dep't of State, 818 F.2d 71, 77 (D.C. Cir. 1987) (finding that agency properly classified information under procedural requirements of existing executive order, subsequent to its receipt of FOIA request, despite its original marking of the information as "unclassified").

[5] See Exec. Order No. 13,292, 68 Fed. Reg. 15,315 (Mar. 28, 2003) [hereinafter Exec. Order No. 12,958, as amended], reprinted in 50 U.S.C. § 435 note (2000 & Supp. III 2003) and summarized in FOIA Post (posted 4/11/03); see also, e.g., ACLU v. FBI, 429 F. Supp. 2d 179, 188 (D.D.C. 2006) (applying Executive Order 12,958, as amended); Judicial Watch v. U.S.
(continued...)

# EXEMPTION 1

Executive Order 12,958, which was issued in 1995 by President William J. Clinton.[6] The provisions of this amended executive order are discussed below.

The issuance of each classification executive order, or the amendment of an existing executive order, raises the question of the applicability of successive executive orders to records that were in various stages of administrative or litigative handling as of the current executive order's effective date.[7] The appropriate executive order to apply, with its particular procedural and substantive standards, depends upon when the responsible agency official takes the final classification action on the record in question.[8]

---

[5](...continued)
Dep't of Justice, 306 F. Supp. 2d 58, 64-65 (D.D.C. 2004) (same).

[6] 3 C.F.R. 333 (1996), reprinted in 50 U.S.C. § 435 note and reprinted in abridged form in FOIA Update, Vol. XVI, No. 2, at 5-10.

[7] See FOIA Update, Vol. XVI, No. 2, at 3, 12 ("OIP Guidance: The Timing of New E.O. Applicability").

[8] See Halpern v. FBI, 181 F.3d 279, 289-90 (2d Cir. 1999); Campbell v. U.S. Dep't of Justice, 164 F.3d 20, 29 (D.C. Cir. 1998) ("[A]bsent a request by the agency to reevaluate an Exemption 1 determination based on a new executive order . . . the court must evaluate the agency's decision under the executive order in force at the time the classification was made."); Lesar, 636 F.2d at 480 (concluding that "a reviewing court should assess the agency's classification decision according to the guidelines established in the Executive Order in effect at the time classification took place"); see also Bonner v. U.S. Dep't of State, 928 F.2d 1148, 1152 (D.C. Cir. 1991) (rejecting plaintiff's suggestion that court assess propriety of agency's classification determination at time of court's review, because to do so would subject agencies and courts to "an endless cycle of judicially mandated reprocessing"); King v. Dep't of Justice, 830 F.2d 210, 217 (D.C. Cir. 1987) (finding that "[o]nly when a reviewing court contemplates remanding the case to the agency to correct a deficiency in its classification determination is it necessary to discriminate between the order governing for purposes of review and any that may have superseded it"); Assassination Archives, 177 F. Supp. 2d at 8-9 (finding that CIA properly classified subject records under Executive Order 10,501 because that order was in effect when agency made classification decision); Keenan v. Dep't of Justice, No. 94-1909, slip op. at 7-8 (D.D.C. Mar. 24, 1997) (rejecting argument that agency should apply Executive Order 12,958 because it did not produce supporting affidavit until after effective date of new order), renewed motion for summary judgment granted in part & denied in part on other grounds (D.D.C. Dec. 16, 1997); cf. Summers v. Dep't of Justice, 140 F.3d 1077, 1082 (D.C. Cir. 1998) (remanding to district court because district court failed to articulate whether it was applying Executive Order 12,356 or Executive Order 12,958

(continued...)

Under the precedents established by the Court of Appeals for the District of Columbia Circuit, the accepted rule is that a reviewing court will assess the propriety of Exemption 1 withholdings under the executive order in effect when "the agency's ultimate classification decision is actually made."[9] Only when "a reviewing court contemplates remanding the case to the agency to correct a deficiency in its classification determination is it necessary" to comply with a superseding executive order.[10] It also is important to note that agencies may, as a matter of discretion, reexamine their classification decisions under a newly issued or amended executive order in order to take into account "changed international and domestic circumstances."[11] This type of re-examination allows federal agencies to apply current executive branch national security policies in the protection of

---

[8](...continued)
to evaluate Exemption 1 withholdings, even though district court record made it clear), on remand, No. 87-3168, slip op. at 2 (D.D.C. Apr. 19, 2000) (applying Executive Order 12,958 to uphold Exemption 1 withholdings).

[9] King, 830 F.2d at 217.

[10] Id.; see also Campbell, 164 F.3d at 31 n.11 (recognizing that when court remands to agency for rereview of classification, such review is performed under superseding executive order); Kern v. FBI, No. 94-0208, slip op. at 5-6 & n.2 (C.D. Cal. Sept. 14, 1998) (remanding due to lack of specificity of Vaughn Index; classified information to be reviewed under current Executive Order 12,958); Greenberg v. U.S. Dep't of Treasury, 10 F. Supp. 2d 3, 12 (D.D.C. 1998) (applying Executive Order 12,356 to records at issue, but noting that Executive Order 12,958 would apply if court "[found] that the agencies improperly withheld information pursuant to Exemption 1"); cf. FOIA Update, Vol. XVI, No. 2, at 4, 12 (summarizing history of Exemption 1 disclosure orders and urging careful attention to classification determinations accordingly).

[11] Baez v. U.S. Dep't of Justice, 647 F.2d 1328, 1233 (D.C. Cir. 1980) (upholding agency's classification reevaluation under executive order issued during course of district court litigation); see, e.g., Miller v. U.S. Dep't of State, 779 F.2d 1378, 1388 (8th Cir. 1985) (agency chose to reevaluate under new Executive Order 12,356); Military Audit Project v. Casey, 656 F.2d 724, 737 & n.41 (D.C. Cir. 1981) (agency chose to reevaluate under new Executive Order 12,065); Nat'l Sec. Archive v. CIA, No. 99-1160, slip op. at 7 (D.D.C. July 31, 2000) ("[E]ven though the existence of [subject] documents was originally classified under Executive Order 12,356, the fact that they were reevaluated under Executive Order 12,958 means that Executive Order 12,958 controls."); Keenan, No. 94-1909, slip op. at 7 (D.D.C. Mar. 24, 1997) (finding that although agency could "voluntarily reassess" its classification decision under Executive Order 12,958, issued during pendency of lawsuit, agency not required to do so).

national security information.[12] For example, agencies may find it particularly beneficial to re-examine some classification decisions under amended Executive Order 12,958, as it provides additional protections for information related to weapons of mass destruction and the threat of transnational terrorism through provisions that did not exist in the original version of the order.[13]

Before examining the principles that courts apply in Exemption 1 cases, it is useful to review briefly the early decisions construing this exemption, as well as its legislative history. Doing so illustrates the difficult dilemma facing courts in reviewing the propriety of the government's withholding decisions regarding national security information. In an early case on this dilemma in 1973, the Supreme Court in EPA v. Mink[14] held that records classified under proper procedures were exempt from disclosure per se, without any further judicial review, thereby obviating the need for in camera review of information withheld under this exemption.[15] In Mink the Supreme Court recognized that a great amount of deference should be accorded to the agency's decision to protect national security information from disclosure.[16] Responding in large part to the thrust of that decision, Congress amended the FOIA in 1974 to provide expressly for de novo review by the courts and for in camera review of documents, including classified documents, where appropriate.[17] In so doing, Congress sought to ensure that agencies properly classify national security records and that reviewing courts remain cognizant of their authority to verify the correct-

---

[12] See Information Security Oversight Office Ann. Rep. 2 (2003) (comments of ISOO Director referring to "new priorities resulting from the events of September 11, 2001"). But see Wiener v. FBI, No. 83-1720, slip op. at 3 (C.D. Cal. Aug. 25, 2005) (denying FBI's request to reevaluate classified information under executive order as amended after court's earlier decision, and finding that FBI's decision not to conduct such review earlier suggests that such reconsideration "was not crucial to national security"), appeal dismissed per stipulation, No. 05-56652 (9th Cir. Jan. 3, 2007).

[13] Compare Exec. Order No. 12,958, as amended, §§ 1.1(a)(4), 1.4(e), (g), (h) (current version), with Exec. Order No. 12,958, §§ 1.2(a)(4), 1.5(e), (g) (original version); see also FOIA Post (posted 4/11/03). But cf. Primorac v. CIA, 277 F. Supp. 117, 120 (D.D.C. 2003) (recognizing that FOIA plaintiffs may not compel agencies to re-examine proper classification decisions under new executive order).

[14] 410 U.S. 73 (1973).

[15] Id. at 84.

[16] Id. at 84, 94.

[17] See 5 U.S.C. § 552(a)(4)(B).

ness of agency classification determinations.[18]

## Standard of Review

After Congress amended the FOIA in 1974, numerous litigants challenged the sufficiency of agency affidavits in Exemption 1 cases, requesting in camera review by the courts and hoping to obtain disclosure of challenged documents. Nevertheless, courts initially upheld agency classification decisions in reliance upon agency affidavits, as a matter of routine, in the absence of evidence of bad faith on the part of an agency.[19] In 1978, however, the Court of Appeals for the District of Columbia Circuit departed somewhat from such routine reliance on agency affidavits, prescribing in camera review to facilitate full de novo adjudication of Exemption 1 issues, even when there is no showing of bad faith on the part of the agency.[20] This decision nevertheless recognized that the courts should "first 'accord substantial weight to an agency's affidavit concerning the details of the classified status of the disputed record.'"[21]

The D.C. Circuit further refined the appropriate standard for judicial review of national security claims under Exemption 1 (or under Exemption 3, in conjunction with certain national security protection statutes), finding that summary judgment is entirely proper if an agency's affidavits are reasonably specific and there is no evidence of bad faith.[22] Rather than con-

---

[18] See H.R. Rep. No. 93-876, at 7-8 (1974), reprinted in 1974 U.S.C.C.A.N. 6267, 6272-73, and in House Comm. on Gov't Operations and Senate Comm. on the Judiciary, 94th Cong., 1st Sess., Freedom of Information Act and Amendments of 1974 (P.L. 93-502) Source Book: Legislative History, Texts, and Other Documents at 121, 127-28 (1975).

[19] See, e.g., Weissman v. CIA, 565 F.2d 692, 698 (D.C. Cir. 1977).

[20] Ray v. Turner, 587 F.2d 1187, 1194-95 (D.C. Cir. 1978).

[21] Id. at 1194 (quoting legislative history); see also Spirko v. USPS, 147 F.3d 992, 997 (D.C. Cir. 1998) (explaining that district court should first consider agency affidavits before resorting to in camera review); ACLU v. FBI, 429 F. Supp. 2d 179, 187 (D.D.C. 2006) (holding that "reviewing court must give 'substantial weight' to [agency] affidavits" (citing King v. Dep't of Justice, 830 F.2d 210, 217 (D.C. Cir. 1987))); Nat'l Sec. Archive Fund, Inc. v. CIA, 402 F. Supp. 2d 211, 216 (D.D.C. 2005) (same).

[22] See Halperin v. CIA, 629 F.2d 144, 148 (D.C. Cir. 1980); see, e.g., Pub. Citizen v. Dep't of State, 276 F.3d 634, 645 (D.C. Cir. 2002) (finding agency's affidavits sufficiently detailed to support Exemption 1 withholding and determining that subsequent release of some previously classified information was not evidence of bad faith); Students Against Genocide v. Dep't of State, 257 F.3d 828, 837 (D.C. Cir. 2001) (applying Halperin standard to waiver issue and finding that Department of State adequately explained
(continued...)

duct a detailed inquiry, the court deferred to the expert opinion of the

---

[22](...continued)
how national security concerns were not undermined -- and Exemption 1 was not waived -- by display of intelligence photographs to United Nations Security Council representatives from other countries); Wheeler v. CIA, 271 F. Supp. 2d 132, 139 (D.D.C. 2003) (denying plaintiff discovery to gather information on agency's classification decisionmaking process because plaintiff failed to demonstrate any agency bad faith); Ctr. for Int'l Envtl. Law v. Office of the U.S. Trade Representative, 237 F. Supp. 2d 17, 20 (D.D.C. 2002) (affirming agency's withholding when its affidavits sufficiently explained application of Exemption 1 and were not contradicted by any evidence of bad faith); Falwell v. Executive Office of the President, 158 F. Supp. 2d 734, 738 (W.D. Va. 2001) (finding Exemption 1 applicable based on affidavit that "fairly described the contents of the material withheld and adequately stated . . . reasons for nondisclosure"); Schrecker v. U.S. Dep't of Justice, 74 F. Supp. 2d 26, 30 (D.D.C. 1999) (granting summary judgment as agency "affidavits and indices pertaining to nondisclosure under Exemption 1 . . . [are] reasonably detailed and submitted in good faith"), aff'd in pertinent part, 254 F.3d 162 (D.C. Cir. 2001); Judicial Watch, Inc. v. Comm'n on U.S.-Pac. Trade & Inv. Policy, No. 97-0099, slip op. at 33 (D.D.C. Sept. 30, 1999) (finding that the agency's "entries explain with substantial specificity what material it has withheld, why it withheld it, and the risk to U.S. foreign policy should the information be revealed," and that therefore the court "need not attempt to second guess the department's decision"); Voinche v. FBI, 46 F. Supp. 2d 26, 29 (D.D.C. 1999) (declaring that agency properly invoked Exemption 1 when declaration "show[ed], with reasonable specificity, why the documents fall within the exemption" and when "there is no evidence of agency bad faith"); Billington v. Dep't of Justice, 11 F. Supp. 2d 45, 54, 58 (D.D.C. 1998) (finding that plaintiff's evidence "whittles down to a string of if-then statements and suggestions of government conspiracy," which provide "no basis upon which to . . . warrant a probe of bad faith"), summary judgment granted in pertinent part, 69 F. Supp. 2d 128, 135 (D.D.C. 1999), aff'd in part, vacated in part & remanded all on other grounds, 233 F.3d 581 (D.C. Cir. 2000) (Exemption 1 decision not challenged on appeal); cf. Pipko v. CIA, 312 F. Supp. 2d 669, 674 (D.N.J. 2004) (commenting that agency affidavits must provide more than "merely glib assertions" to support withholding); Coldiron v. Dep't of Justice, 310 F. Supp. 2d 44, 52 (D.D.C. 2004) (observing that courts do not expect "anything resembling poetry," but nonetheless expressing dissatisfaction with agency's "cut and paste" affidavits); Voinche v. FBI, 940 F. Supp. 323, 328 (D.D.C. 1996) (granting summary judgment despite "troubling" and "vague" affidavits in light of thoroughness of agency's other submissions and fact that Vaughn affidavits in Exemption 1 cases "inherently require a degree of generalization" to prevent compromise of national security interests), aff'd per curiam, No. 96-5304, 1997 WL 411685 (D.C. Cir. June 19, 1997); Ajluni v. FBI, 947 F. Supp. 599, 607 (N.D.N.Y. 1996) (rejecting plaintiff's request for discovery of procedure by which documents are classified, because Vaughn Index was "sufficient").

agency, noting that judges "lack the expertise necessary to second-guess such agency opinions in the typical national security FOIA case."[23] This review standard has been reaffirmed by the D.C. Circuit on several occasions,[24] and it has been adopted by other circuit courts as well.[25] Of

---

[23] Halperin, 629 F.2d at 148; see also Bowers v. U.S. Dep't of Justice, 930 F.2d 350, 357 (4th Cir. 1991) (stating that "a court should hesitate to substitute its judgment of the sensitivity of the information for that of the agency"); Military Audit Project v. Casey, 656 F.2d 724, 738 (D.C. Cir. 1981) (emphasizing that deference is due agency's classification judgment); Edmonds v. U.S. Dep't of Justice, 405 F. Supp. 2d 23, 27 (D.D.C. 2005) (same); Nat'l Sec. Archive, 402 F. Supp. 2d at 216 (same); ACLU v. DOD, 389 F. Supp. 2d 547, 565 (S.D.N.Y. 2005) (same); Snyder v. CIA, 230 F. Supp. 2d 17, 24 (D.D.C. 2002) (observing that agency is in best position to make "ultimate assessment of harm to intelligence sources and methods").

[24] See, e.g., Stillman v. CIA, 319 F.3d 546, 548 (D.C. Cir. 2003) (criticizing the district court because it failed "to evaluate the pleadings and affidavits to be submitted by the Government in defense of its classification decision," thereby erroneously withholding the deference that ordinarily is owed to national security officials) (non-FOIA case); King, 830 F.2d at 217 (concluding that "the court owes substantial weight to detailed agency explanations in the national security context"); Goldberg v. U.S. Dep't of State, 818 F.2d 71, 79-80 (D.C. Cir. 1987); see also Ctr. for Nat'l Sec. Studies v. U.S. Dep't of Justice, 331 F.3d 918, 928 (D.C. Cir. 2003) (accepting that "the judiciary is in an extremely poor position to second-guess the executive's judgment in this area") (Exemption 7(A)); Edmonds, 405 F. Supp. 2d at 33 (explaining that "this court must respect the experience of the agency and stay within the proper limits of the judicial role in FOIA review"); Wheeler, 271 F. Supp. 2d at 140 (declining to substitute judgment of plaintiff or court for that of agency classification authority simply on basis that classification action required exercise of some discretion); ACLU v. U.S. Dep't of Justice, 265 F. Supp. 2d 20, 27 (D.D.C. 2003) (reminding that although the agency's declarations "are entitled to substantial weight, they must nevertheless afford the requester an ample opportunity to contest, and the Court to review, the soundness of the withholding"); Linn v. U.S. Dep't of Justice, No. 92-1406, 1995 WL 631847, at *26 (D.D.C. Aug. 22, 1995) (indicating that role of courts in reviewing Exemption 1 claims "is to determine whether the agency has presented a logical connection between its use of the exemption and the legitimate national security concerns involved; the Court does not have to ascertain whether the underlying facts of each specific application merit the agency's national security concerns"); cf. Dep't of the Navy v. Egan, 484 U.S. 518, 529-30 (1988) (allowing deference to agency expertise in granting of security clearances) (non-FOIA case).

[25] See, e.g., Tavakoli-Nouri v. CIA, No. 00-3620, 2001 U.S. App. LEXIS 24676, at *9 (3d Cir. Oct. 18, 2001) (recognizing that courts give "substantial weight to agency's affidavit regarding details of classified status of a disputed document" (referencing McDonnell v. United States, 4 F.3d 1227,
(continued...)

course, where agency affidavits have been found to be insufficiently detailed, courts have withheld summary judgment in Exemption 1 cases on procedural grounds.[26]

---

[25](...continued)
1242 (3d Cir. 1993))); Maynard v. CIA, 986 F.2d 547, 555-56 & n.7 (1st Cir. 1993) (recognizing that courts must accord "substantial deference" to agency withholding determinations and "uphold the agency's decision" so long as withheld information logically falls into the exemption category cited and there exists no evidence of agency "bad faith"); Bowers, 930 F.2d at 357 (stating that "[w]hat fact or bit of information may compromise national security is best left to the intelligence experts"); cf. Hunt, 981 F.2d at 1119 (applying similar deference in Exemption 3 case involving national security). But see Minier v. CIA, 88 F.3d 796, 800 (9th Cir. 1996) (considering whether district court had "adequate factual basis upon which to base its decision" before undertaking de novo review (citing Painting Indus. of Haw. Mkt. Recovery Fund v. U.S. Dep't of the Air Force, 26 F.3d 1479, 1482 (9th Cir. 1994), and Schiffer v. FBI, 78 F.3d 1405, 1409 (9th Cir. 1996))) (Exemption 3).

[26] Halpern v. FBI, 181 F.3d 279, 293 (2d Cir. 1999) (declaring that agency's "explanations read more like a policy justification" for Executive Order 12,356, that the "affidavit gives no contextual description," and that it fails to "fulfill the functional purposes addressed in Vaughn"); Campbell v. U.S. Dep't of Justice, 164 F.3d 20, 31, 37 (D.C. Cir. 1998) (remanding to district court to allow the FBI to "further justify" its Exemption 1 claim because its declaration failed to "draw any connection between the documents at issue and the general standards that govern the national security exemption"), on remand, 193 F. Supp. 2d 29, 37 (D.D.C. 2001) (finding declaration insufficient where it merely concluded, without further elaboration, that "disclosure of [intelligence information] . . . could reasonably be expected to cause serious damage to the national security"); Oglesby v. U.S. Dep't of the Army, 79 F.3d 1172, 1179-84 (D.C. Cir. 1996) (rejecting as insufficient certain Vaughn Indexes because agencies must itemize each document and adequately explain reasons for nondisclosure); Rosenfeld v. U.S. Dep't of Justice, 57 F.3d 803, 807 (9th Cir. 1995) (affirming district court disclosure order based upon finding that government failed to show with "any particularity" why classified portions of several documents should be withheld); Wiener v. FBI, 943 F.2d 972, 978-79 (9th Cir. 1991) (rejecting as inadequate agency justifications contained in coded Vaughn affidavits, based upon view that they consist of "boilerplate" explanations not "tailored" to particular information being withheld pursuant to Exemption 1); Oglesby v. U.S. Dep't of the Army, 920 F.2d 57, 66 n.12 (D.C. Cir. 1990) (articulating degree of specificity required in public Vaughn affidavit in Exemption 1 case, especially with regard to agency's obligation to segregate and release nonexempt material); Greenberg v. U.S. Dep't of Treasury, 10 F. Supp. 2d 3, 15, 26-27 (D.D.C. 1998) (reserving judgment on Exemption 1 claims of CIA and FBI, and ordering new affidavits because agencies' Vaughn Indexes were found to be insufficient to permit court to engage in proper evaluation);

(continued...)

If an agency affidavit passes muster under this standard, in camera review may be inappropriate because substantial weight must be accorded that affidavit.[27] In a 1996 decision, the D.C. Circuit stated that in a na-

---

[26](...continued)
Keenan v. Dep't of Justice, No. 94-1909, slip op. at 8-11 (D.D.C. Mar. 24, 1997) (finding to be insufficient coded Vaughn Index that merely recited executive order's language without providing information about contents of withheld information), renewed motion for summary judgment denied in pertinent part (D.D.C. Dec. 16, 1997).

[27] See, e.g., Doherty v. U.S. Dep't of Justice, 775 F.2d 49, 53 (2d Cir. 1985) (adjudging that "the court should restrain its discretion to order in camera review"); Hayden v. NSA, 608 F.2d 1381, 1387 (D.C. Cir. 1979) (stating that "[w]hen the agency meets its burden by means of affidavits, in camera review is neither necessary nor appropriate"); Pub. Educ. Ctr., Inc. v. DOD, 905 F. Supp. 19, 22 (D.D.C. 1995) (declining in camera review of withheld videotapes after according substantial weight to agency's affidavit that public disclosure would harm national security); King v. U.S. Dep't of Justice, 586 F. Supp. 286, 290 (D.D.C. 1983) (characterizing in camera review as last resort), aff'd in part & rev'd in part on other grounds, 830 F.2d 210 (D.C. Cir. 1987); cf. Stillman, 319 F.3d at 548 (finding in general that in camera affidavits can effectively supplement public affidavits to explain agency classification decisions) (non-FOIA case); Young v. CIA, 972 F.2d 536, 538-39 (4th Cir. 1992) (holding that district court did not abuse its discretion by refusing to review documents in camera -- despite small number -- because agency's affidavits found sufficiently specific to meet required standards for proper withholding). But see, e.g., Patterson v. FBI, 893 F.2d 595, 599 (3d Cir. 1990) (finding in camera review of two documents appropriate when agency description of records was insufficient to permit meaningful review and to verify good faith of agency in conducting its investigation); Allen v. CIA, 636 F.2d 1287, 1291 (D.C. Cir. 1980) (holding that conclusory affidavit by agency requires remand to district court for in camera inspection of fifteen-page document); Trulock v. U.S. Dep't of Justice, 257 F. Supp. 2d 48, 51 (D.D.C. 2003) (observing that documents should be reviewed in camera when declarations are insufficient to demonstrate validity of withholdings); Armstrong v. Executive Office of the President, No. 89-142, slip op. at 4-8 (D.D.C. July 28, 1995) (ordering in camera review of four of seventeen documents at issue because government's explanation for withholdings was insufficient, but denying plaintiff's request that court review documents merely on basis that government subsequently released previously withheld material), aff'd on other grounds, 97 F.3d 575 (D.C. Cir. 1996); Moore v. FBI, No. 83-1541, 1984 U.S. Dist. LEXIS 18732, at *9 (D.D.C. Mar. 9, 1984) (finding in camera review particularly appropriate when only small volume of documents were involved and government made proffer), aff'd, 762 F.2d 138 (D.C. Cir. 1985) (unpublished table decision); cf. Jones v. FBI, 41 F.3d 238, 242-44 (6th Cir. 1994) (finding in camera inspection necessary, not because FBI acted in bad faith with regard to plaintiff's FOIA request, but due to evidence of illegality with regard to FBI's underlying investiga-

(continued...)

tional security case, a district court exercises "wise discretion" when it limits the number of documents it reviews in camera.[28] In upholding the district court's decision not to review certain documents in camera, the D.C. Circuit opined that limiting the number of documents examined by a court "makes it less likely that sensitive information will be disclosed" and, if there is an unauthorized disclosure of classified information, "makes it easier to pinpoint the source of the leak."[29]

In another case, the Court of Appeals for the Seventh Circuit analyzed the legislative history of the 1974 FOIA amendments and went so far as to conclude that "Congress did not intend that the courts would make a true de novo review of classified documents, that is, a fresh determination of the legitimacy of each classified document."[30] It also is noteworthy that the only Exemption 1 FOIA decision to find agency "bad faith,"[31] one in which an appellate court initially held that certain CIA procedural shortcomings amounted to "bad faith," was subsequently vacated on panel rehearing.[32]

Despite the courts' general reluctance to "second-guess" agency decisions on national security matters, agencies still have the responsibility to justify classification decisions in supporting affidavits.[33] In Exemption 1

---

[27](...continued) tion); Wiener, 943 F.2d at 979 & n.9 (holding that in camera review by district court cannot "replace" requirement for sufficient Vaughn Index and can only "supplement" agency's justifications contained in affidavits).

[28] Armstrong v. Executive Office of the President, 97 F.3d 575, 580 (D.C. Cir. 1996).

[29] Id.

[30] Stein v. Dep't of Justice, 662 F.2d 1245, 1253 (7th Cir. 1981).

[31] McGehee v. CIA, 697 F.2d 1095, 1113 (D.C. Cir. 1983).

[32] McGehee v. CIA, 711 F.2d 1076, 1077 (D.C. Cir. 1983); see also Wheeler, 271 F. Supp. 2d at 139 (finding that it was not at all proof of bad faith to show merely that agency handled two similar FOIA requests in different manner); Wash. Post Co. v. DOD, No. 84-2949, 1987 U.S. Dist. LEXIS 16108, at *12 (D.D.C. Feb. 25, 1987) (deciding that addition of second classification category at time of litigation "does not create an inference of 'bad faith' concerning the processing of plaintiff's request or otherwise implicating the affiant's credibility").

[33] See ACLU v. U.S. Dep't of Justice, 321 F. Supp. 2d 24, 35 (D.D.C. 2004) (declaring that "it is not a question of whether the Court agrees with the defendant's assessment of the danger, but rather, 'whether on the whole record the Agency's judgment objectively survives the test of reasonableness, good faith, specificity, and plausibility in this field of foreign intelligence in which the [agency] is expert and given by Congress a special

(continued...)

cases, courts are likely to require that the affidavit be provided by an agency official with direct knowledge of the classification decision.[34] When an affidavit contains sufficient explanation, however, it is generally accepted that "the court will not conduct a detailed inquiry to decide whether it agrees with the agency's opinions."[35]

## Deference to Agency Expertise

As indicated above, while the standard of judicial review often is expressed in different ways, courts generally have heavily deferred to agency expertise in national security cases.[36] Such deference is based upon the

---

[33](...continued)
role'" (quoting Gardels v. CIA, 689 F.2d 1100, 1105 (D.C. Cir. 1982))).

[34] See Hudson v. Dep't of Justice, No. C 04-4079, 2005 WL 1656909, at *3 (N.D. Cal. July 11, 2005) (accepting that affiant had requisite knowledge of classification decision despite fact that she did not possess original classification authority); Judicial Watch, Inc. v. U.S. Dep't of Transp., No. 02-566, 2005 WL 1606915, at *8 (D.D.C. July 7, 2005) (finding that affiant, while not original classification authority, had personal knowledge of matters set forth in his declaration). But see also Wickwire Gavin, P.C. v. Def. Intelligence Agency, 330 F. Supp. 2d 592, 600 (E.D. Va. 2004) (holding that "in order to sustain a claim of FOIA Exemption One under Exec. Order 12,958, courts require an affidavit from an individual with classifying authority").

[35] Edmonds, 405 F. Supp. 2d at 33; see also Larson v. Dep't of State, No. 02-1937, 2005 WL 3276303, at *11 (D.D.C. Aug. 10, 2005) (explaining that "[g]iven the weight of authority counseling deference . . in matters involving national security, this court must defer to the agency's judgment"); Fla. Immigrant Advocacy Ctr. v. NSA, 380 F. Supp. 2d 1332, 1334 (S.D. Fla. 2005) (declaring that Exemption 1, properly applied, serves as "absolute bar" to release of classified information); Judicial Watch, Inc. v. U.S. Dep't of Commerce, 337 F. Supp. 2d 146, 162 (D.D.C. 2004) (ruling that "a reviewing court is prohibited from conducting a detailed analysis of the agency's invocation of Exemption 1" (citing Halperin v. CIA, 629 F.2d 144, 148 (D.C. Cir. 1980))); Wolf v. CIA, 357 F. Supp. 2d 112, 116 (D.D.C. 2004) (commenting that "this Circuit has required little more than a showing that the agency's rationale is logical"), aff'd in pertinent part & remanded, 473 F.3d 370, 376 (D.C. Cir. 2007) (concluding that "[i]n light of the substantial weight accorded agency assertions of potential harm made in order to invoke the protection of FOIA Exemption 1, the [agency a]ffidavit both logically and plausibly suffices").

[36] See, e.g., Students Against Genocide v. Dep't of State, 257 F.3d 828, 837 (D.C. Cir. 2001) (holding that because courts lack expertise in national security matters, they must give "'substantial weight to agency statements'" (quoting Halperin v. CIA, 629 F.2d 144, 148 (D.C. Cir. 1980))); Bowers v. U.S. Dep't of Justice, 930 F.2d 350, 357 (4th Cir. 1991) (observing that
(continued...)

# EXEMPTION 1

"magnitude of the national security interests and potential risks at stake,"[37] and it is extended by courts because national security officials are uniquely positioned to view "the whole picture" and "weigh the variety of subtle and complex factors" in order to determine whether the disclosure of information would damage the national security.[38] Indeed, courts ordinarily are

---

[36](...continued)
"[w]hat fact . . . may compromise national security is best left to the intelligence experts"); Doherty v. U.S. Dep't of Justice, 775 F.2d 49, 52 (2d Cir. 1985) (according "substantial weight" to agency declaration); Taylor v. Dep't of the Army, 684 F.2d 99, 109 (D.C. Cir. 1982) (holding that classification affidavits are entitled to "the utmost deference") (reversing district court disclosure order); Edmonds v. FBI, 272 F. Supp. 2d 35, 46, 49 (D.D.C. 2003) (opining that courts should not challenge "the predictive judgments" of national security officials without cause to do so); ACLU v. U.S. Dep't of Justice, 429 F. Supp. 2d 179, 188 (D.D.C. 2006) (holding that "the court must recognize that the executive branch departments responsible for national security and national defense have unique insights and special expertise concerning the kind of disclosures that may be harmful" (citing Krikorian v. Dep't of State, 984 F.2d 461, 464 (D.C. Cir. 1993))); Assassination Archives & Research Ctr. v. CIA, 177 F. Supp. 2d 1, 7 (D.D.C. 2001) (recognizing that district courts must "defer to federal agencies in questions of national security and intelligence"), aff'd, 334 F.2d 55 (D.C. Cir. 2003); Canning v. U.S. Dep't of Justice, 848 F. Supp. 1037, 1042 (D.D.C. 1994) (describing how in according such deference, courts "credit agency expertise in evaluating matters of national security"); cf. Stillman v. CIA, 319 F.3d 546, 549 (D.C. Cir. 2003) (instructing that agency affidavits should be reviewed "with the appropriate degree of deference owed to the Executive Branch concerning classification decisions") (non-FOIA case); Wiener v. FBI, No. 83-1720, slip op. at 5 (C.D. Cal. Mar. 5, 2001) (rejecting the plaintiff's request to review redacted versions of the withheld documents in order to "independently verify" the government's characterization of their content, because to grant it would "remove all deference to the FBI's classification of its documents"), summary judgment for plaintiff granted (C.D. Cal. Sept. 27, 2004), reh'g denied (C.D. Cal. Aug. 25, 2005), appeal dismissed per stipulation, No. 05-56652 (9th Cir. Jan. 3, 2007). But see also FOIA Update, Vol. XVI, No. 2, at 4, 12 (summarizing history of Exemption 1 disclosure orders and urging careful attention to classification determinations accordingly).

[37] Ctr. for Nat'l Sec. Studies v. U.S. Dep't of Justice, 331 F.3d 918, 928 (D.C. Cir. 2003) (quoting CIA v. Sims, 471 U.S. 159, 179 (1985)) (Exemption 7(A)); see also L.A. Times Commc'ns, LLC v. Dep't of the Army, No. CV 05-8293, 2006 WL 2336457, at *14 (C.D. Cal. July 24, 2006) (deferring to judgment of senior Army officers regarding risks posed to soldiers and contractors by enemy forces in Iraq); ACLU v. DOD, 406 F. Supp. 2d 330, 333 (D.D.C. 2006) (acknowledging that "one may criticize the deference extended by the courts as excessive," but holding that such deference is the rule).

[38] Sims, 471 U.S. at 179-80; see also, e.g., Zadvydas v. Davis, 533 U.S.
(continued...)

very reluctant to substitute their judgment in place of the agency's "unique insights"[39] in the areas of national defense and foreign relations.[40] This is

---

[38](...continued)
678, 696 (2001) (commenting that "terrorism or other special circumstances" may warrant "heightened deference") (non-FOIA case); Dep't of the Navy v. Egan, 484 U.S. 518, 530 (1988) (explaining that "courts traditionally have been reluctant to intrude upon the authority of the executive in national security affairs") (non-FOIA case); Ctr. for Nat'l Sec. Studies, 331 F.3d at 918 (rejecting "artificial limits" on deference, and explaining that "deference depends on the substance of the danger posed by disclosure -- that is, harm to the national security -- not the FOIA exemption invoked").

[39] Miller v. U.S. Dep't of State, 779 F.2d 1378, 1387 (8th Cir. 1985).

[40] See, e.g., Maynard v. CIA, 986 F.2d 547, 556 n.9 (1st Cir. 1993) (stating that court "not in a position to 'second-guess'" agency's determination regarding need for continued classification of material); Krikorian, 984 F.2d at 464-65 (acknowledging agency's "unique insights" in areas of national defense and foreign relation and further explaining that because judges "'lack the expertise necessary to second-guess . . . agency opinions in the typical national security FOIA case,'" they must accord substantial deference to an agency's affidavit (quoting Halperin, 629 F.2d at 148)); ACLU v. FBI, 429 F. Supp. 2d 179, 188 (D.D.C. 2006) (reasoning that "while a court is ultimately to make its own decision, that decision must take seriously the government's predictions" of harm to national security); Nat'l Sec. Archive v. CIA, No. 99-1160, slip op. at 8 (D.D.C. July 31, 2000) ("Agencies have more experience in the national security arena than courts do, and therefore their judgment warrants deference as long as the agency can demonstrate a logical connection between a withheld document and an alleged harm to national security."); Aftergood v. CIA, No. 98-2107, 1999 U.S. Dist. LEXIS 18135, at *9-10 (D.D.C. Nov. 12, 1999) (declaring that courts must respect agency predictions concerning potential national security harm from disclosure, and recognizing that these predictions "must always be speculative to some extent"); Braslavsky v. FBI, No. 92 C 3027, 1994 WL 247078, at *2 (N.D. Ill. June 6, 1994) (commenting that "[a] court has neither the experience nor expertise to determine whether a classification [decision] is substantively correct"), aff'd, 57 F.3d 1073 (7th Cir. 1995) (unpublished table decision). But see King, 830 F.2d at 226 (holding that trial court erred in deferring to agency's judgment that information more than thirty-five years old remained classified when executive order presumed declassification of information over twenty years old and agency merely indicated procedural compliance with order); Coldiron v. Dep't of Justice, 310 F. Supp. 2d 44, 53 (D.D.C. 2004) (cautioning that court's deference should not be used as "wet blanket" to avoid proper justification of exemptions); Lawyers Comm. for Human Rights v. INS, 721 F. Supp. 552, 561 (S.D.N.Y. 1989) (reminding that such deference does not give agency "carte blanche" to withhold responsive documents without "valid and thorough affidavit"), subsequent decision, No. 87-Civ-1115, slip op. at 1-2 (S.D.N.Y. June 7, 1990) (up-
(continued...)

because courts have recognized that national security is a "uniquely executive purview"[41] and that "the judiciary is in an extremely poor position to
second-guess the executive's judgment" on national security issues.[42] The
tragic events of September 11, 2001, and their aftermath, have served to
make courts more aware of the need for deference when considering issues
related to national security, with one court observing that "America faces
an enemy just as real as its former Cold War foes, with capabilities beyond
the capacity of the judiciary to explore."[43]

Nevertheless, some FOIA plaintiffs have argued -- and in some cases
courts have agreed -- that the nature of judicial review should involve
questioning the underlying basis for the agency's classification decision.[44]
However, the majority of courts have firmly rejected the idea that judicial
review is to serve as a quality-control measure to reassure a doubtful re-

---

[40](...continued)
holding Exemption 1 excisions after in camera review of certain documents
and classified Vaughn affidavit).

[41] Ctr. for Nat'l Sec. Studies, 331 F.3d at 927; see also L.A. Times
Commc'ns, 2006 WL 2336457, at *15 (echoing the belief that national
security is "a uniquely executive purview" (citing Zadvydas, 533 U.S. at
696)).

[42] Ctr. for Nat'l Sec. Studies, 331 F.3d at 928. But see Larson v. Dep't of
State, No. 02-1937, 2005 WL 3276303, at *9 (D.D.C. Aug. 10, 2005) (observing that deference "does not mean acquiescence").

[43] Ctr. for Nat'l Sec. Studies, 331 F.3d at 928; see also Morley v. CIA, No.
03-2545, 2006 WL 2806561, at *3 (D.D.C. Sept. 29, 2006) (expressing deferential standard on national security issues); L.A. Times Commc'ns, LLC v.
Dep't of the Army, No. CV 05-8293, 2006 WL 2336457, at *14 (C.D. Cal. July
24, 2006) (explaining that "[t]he test is not whether the court personally
agrees in full with the [agency's] evaluation of the danger -- rather, the issue is whether on the whole record the Agency's judgment objectively survives the test of reasonableness, good faith, specificity, and plausibility in
this field of foreign intelligence in which the [agency] is expert and given
by Congress a special role"); Bassiouni v. CIA, No. 02-C-4049, 2004 WL
1125919, at *6 (N.D. Ill. Mar. 31, 2004) (deferring to the agency's determination of harm, and further noting that "[i]n the realm of intelligence, a lot can
occur in a short period of time"), aff'd, 392 F.3d 244 (7th Cir. 2004), cert. denied, 545 U.S. 1129 (2005).

[44] See ACLU, 429 F. Supp. 2d at 186 (concluding that "the importance of
the issues raised by this case" make in camera review necessary); Fla. Immigrant Advocacy Ctr. v. NSA, 380 F. Supp. 2d 1332, 1338 (S.D. Fla. 2005)
(granting in camera review "to satisfy an 'uneasiness' or 'doubt' that the exemption claim may be overbroad given the nature of Plaintiff's arguments").

quester.[45] Further, courts have overwhelmingly rejected the notion that additional judicial review should be triggered by a requester's unsupported allegations of wrongdoing against the government in a national security case.[46] By the same token, though, courts may not readily apply too much deference where an agency has merely raised a national security concern without providing an adequate explanation of it.[47]

Courts have demonstrated this deference to agency expertise also by according little or no weight to opinions of persons other than the agency classification authority when reviewing the propriety of agency classification determinations.[48] Persons whose opinions have been rejected by the

---

[45] See, e.g., Nat'l Sec. Archive Fund, Inc. v. CIA, 402 F. Supp. 2d 211, 221 (D.D.C. 2005) (declining to conduct in camera review merely "to verify the agency's descriptions and provide assurances, beyond a presumption of administrative good faith, to FOIA plaintiffs that the descriptions are accurate and as complete as possible"); Haddam v. FBI, No. 01-434, slip op. at 21 (D.D.C. Sept. 8, 2004) (observing that "[w]hile Plaintiff understandably would like to review the FBI's decisions for classifying the material, nothing in FOIA entitles Plaintiff to do so"); Wiener, No. 83-1720, slip op. at 5 (C.D. Cal. Mar. 5, 2001) (rejecting plaintiff's request that court "independently verify" government's characterization of records).

[46] See NARA v. Favish, 541 U.S. 157, 174 (reminding that "[a]llegations of government misconduct are 'easy to allege and hard to disprove'" (quoting Crawford-El v. Britton, 523 U.S. 574, 585 (1998))) (Exemption 7(C) case)), reh'g denied, 541 U.S. 1057 (2004); Bassiouni v. CIA, 392 F.3d 244, 247 (7th Cir. 2004) (commenting that "Exemption 1 would not mean much if all anyone had to do, to see the full list of the CIA's holdings, was allege that the agency had some documents showing how he 'exercises rights guaranteed by the First Amendment'"), cert. denied, 545 U.S. 1129 (2005); Nat'l Sec. Archive Fund, 402 F. Supp. 2d 211, 222 (D.D.C. 2005) (holding that a plaintiff had not proven its assertions of waiver, and explaining that "courts do not play a 'guessing game' with such sensitive and potentially dangerous information" (citing Assassination Archives at district and appellate court levels, 177 F. Supp. 2d at 10; 334 F.3d at 60-61 & n.6)); Peltier v. FBI, No. 03-CV-905, 2005 WL 735964, at *7 (W.D.N.Y. Mar. 31, 2005) (finding that plaintiff's bare claim that agency classified requested records solely in order to prevent embarrassment does not alone necessitate greater judicial scrutiny).

[47] See, e.g., ACLU v. DOD, 339 F. Supp. 2d 501, 504 (S.D.N.Y. 2004) (finding that "[m]erely raising national security concerns can not [sic] justify unlimited delay," and considering "the public's right to receive information on government activity in a timely manner").

[48] See, e.g., Van Atta v. Def. Intelligence Agency, No. 87-1508, 1988 WL 73856, at *1-2 (D.D.C. July 6, 1988) (rejecting opinion of requester about willingness of foreign diplomat to discuss issue); Wash. Post v. DOD, No. (continued...)

EXEMPTION 1

courts in this context include:

(1) a former ambassador who had personally prepared some of the records at issue;[49]

(2) a retired admiral;[50]

(3) a former CIA agent;[51]

(4) a retired CIA staff historian;[52]

(5) a retired member of the CIA's Historical Advisory Committee;[53] and

(6) a former Special Assistant to the President of the United States.[54]

---

[48](...continued) 84-2949, 1987 U.S. Dist. LEXIS 16108, at *19-20 (D.D.C. Feb. 25, 1987) (rejecting opinion of U.S. Senator who read document in official capacity as member of Committee on Foreign Relations); cf. Lawyers Alliance for Nuclear Arms Control v. Dep't of Energy, No. 88-CV-7635, 1991 WL 274860, at *1-2 (E.D. Pa. Dec. 18, 1991) (holding that requester provided no "admissible evidence" that officials of former Soviet Union consented to release of requested nuclear test results). But cf. Wash. Post v. DOD, 766 F. Supp. 1, 13-14 (D.D.C. 1991) (adjudging that "non-official releases" contained in books by participants involved in Iranian hostage rescue attempt -- including ground assault commander and former President Carter -- have "good deal of reliability" and require government to explain "how official disclosure" of code names "at this time would damage national security").

[49] See Rush v. Dep't of State, 748 F. Supp. 1548, 1554 (S.D. Fla. 1990) (finding that plaintiff, who retired from government service in 1977, failed to rebut opinion of current government officials on necessity of continued classification); cf. Goldberg v. U.S. Dep't of State, 818 F.2d 71, 79-80 (D.C. Cir. 1987) (accepting classification officer's national security determination even though more than 100 ambassadors did not initially classify information).

[50] See Hudson River Sloop Clearwater, Inc. v. Dep't of the Navy, 891 F.2d 414, 421-22 (2d Cir. 1989).

[51] See Gardels v. CIA, 689 F.2d 1100, 1106 n.5 (D.C. Cir. 1982).

[52] See Pfeiffer v. CIA, 721 F. Supp. 337, 340-41 (D.D.C. 1989).

[53] See Berman v. CIA, 378 F. Supp. 2d 1209, 1219 (E.D. Cal. 2005) (referring to declarations submitted by plaintiff in support of argument that information no longer warranted national security classification).

[54] See id.

And in a further example of deference to agency expertise, a court considering the sensitivity of CIA budget information not long ago concluded that it "must defer to . . . [the agency's] decision that release . . . amidst the information already publicly-available, provides too much trend information and too great a basis for comparison and analysis for our adversaries."[55]

Nevertheless, while judicial deference to agency expertise is the norm in Exemption 1 litigation, in some cases courts have rejected an agency's classification decision.[56] An example of this occurred in Weatherhead v. United States,[57] a case decided under the original version of Executive Order 12,958 in which a district court initially ordered the disclosure of a letter sent by the British Home Office to the Department of Justice, which was not classified until after receipt of the FOIA request.[58] On a motion for reconsideration, the district court rejected the government's arguments that the court had failed to give the agency's determination of harm sufficient deference.[59] The court "reluctantly" agreed to review the letter in camera because "of the danger that highly sensitive . . . material might be

---

[55] Aftergood, No. 98-2107, 1999 U.S. Dist. LEXIS 18135, at *11-12 (D.D.C. Jan. 12, 1999) (deferring to Director of Central Intelligence's determination that release of 1999 CIA budget data could reasonably be expected to harm intelligence activities, despite fact that the President had encouraged disclosure of previous budget data); see also Aftergood v. CIA, No. 02-1146, slip op. at 3 (D.D.C. Feb. 6, 2004) (finding CIA's aggregate intelligence budget data for 2002 to be exempt from disclosure, because it reveals the allocation, transfer, and funding of intelligence programs) (Exemption 3), reconsideration denied (D.D.C. Sept. 29, 2004).

[56] See FOIA Update, Vol. XVI, No. 2, at 4, 7 (compiling and discussing cases in which courts have rejected Exemption 1 claims and in some cases have ordered disclosure, but commenting that such disclosure orders nearly always were overturned on appeal); cf. AFL-CIO v. FEC, 333 F.3d 168, 179 (D.C. Cir. 2003) (concluding that the agency's disclosure policies in relation to the FOIA might be unconstitutional as applied, and requiring agency to "provide a separate First Amendment justification for publicly disclosing" information "relating to speech or political activity" that it compiled for law enforcement purposes) (Exemption 7(C)).

[57] Weatherhead v. United States, No. 95-519, slip op. at 5-6 (E.D. Wash. Mar. 29, 1996), reconsideration granted in pertinent part (E.D. Wash. Sept. 9, 1996) (upholding classification upon in camera inspection), rev'd, 157 F.3d 735 (9th Cir. 1998), appellate decision vacated & case remanded for dismissal, 528 U.S. 1042 (1999); see also Wiener v. FBI, No. 83-1720, slip op. at 9 (C.D. Cal. Sept. 27, 2004) (rejecting FBI's determination that national security harm would result from release), reh'g denied (C.D. Cal. Aug. 25, 2005).

[58] Id. at 2.

[59] Weatherhead, No. 95-519, slip op. at 3-4 (E.D. Wash. Sept. 9, 1996).

released only because [the agency was] unable to articulate a factual basis for their concerns without giving away the information itself."[60] When this proved to be the case upon the court's in camera review of the document, the court granted the motion for reconsideration and upheld the letter's classification.[61]

On appeal, however, the Court of Appeals for the Ninth Circuit, in a two-to-one decision, flatly refused to defer to the State Department's judgment of foreign relations harm and ordered the letter disclosed.[62] The Solicitor General then petitioned the Supreme Court to grant certiorari review of the Ninth Circuit's ruling, which it did, and the case was scheduled for Supreme Court argument.[63] During the briefing of the case, however, the requester suddenly revealed that he was in possession of a subsequent letter from a local British Consul that addressed the same subject.[64] In response to this revelation, the State Department brought this new information to the attention of the British Government, which then decided to no longer insist on confidentiality for the letter.[65] Accordingly, and on an expedited basis, the letter was declassified and disclosed to the requester.[66] The Solicitor General then successfully moved to have the Supreme Court nullify the Ninth Circuit's adverse precedent on the ground that it no longer could be appealed.[67]

---

[60] Id. at 7-8.

[61] Id. at 8. But see Keenan v. Dep't of Justice, No. 94-1909, slip op. at 8-9 (D.D.C. Dec. 16, 1997) (ordering upon in camera inspection the release of document segments that the agency withheld pursuant to Exemption 1, because the agency "failed to demonstrate" how disclosure of information ranging from thirty-two to forty-six years old could "continue to damage the national security"); Springmann v. U.S. Dep't of State, No. 93-1238, slip op. at 9-11 (D.D.C. Apr. 21, 1997) (ruling that disclosure of two paragraphs in embassy report about American employee engaging in religiously offensive behavior in Saudi Arabia would not harm national security), summary judgment granted to defendant upon reconsideration (D.D.C. Feb. 24, 2000) (ruling ultimately in agency's favor based upon in camera declaration).

[62] Weatherhead v. United States, 157 F.3d 735, 742 (9th Cir. 1998).

[63] See Weatherhead v. United States, 527 U.S. 1063 (1999).

[64] See FOIA Update, Vol. XX, No. 1, at 1.

[65] See id.

[66] See id.

[67] See United States v. Weatherhead, 528 U.S. 1042 (1999) (vacating Ninth Circuit decision).

## In Camera Submissions and Adequate Public Record

There are numerous instances in which courts have permitted agencies to submit explanatory in camera affidavits in order to protect certain national security information that could not be discussed in a public affidavit.[68] It is entirely clear, though, that agencies taking such a special step are under a duty to "create as complete a public record as is possible" before doing so.[69] This public record is intended to provide a meaningful and fair opportunity for a plaintiff to challenge, and an adequate evidentiary ba-

---

[68] See, e.g., Patterson v. FBI, 893 F.2d 595, 599-600 (3d Cir. 1990); Simmons v. U.S. Dep't of Justice, 796 F.2d 709, 711 (4th Cir. 1986); Ingle v. Dep't of Justice, 698 F.2d 259, 264 (6th Cir. 1983) (ruling that in camera review should be secondary to testimony or affidavits); Salisbury v. United States, 690 F.2d 966, 973 n.3 (D.C. Cir. 1982); Stein v. Dep't of Justice, 662 F.2d 1245, 1255-56 (7th Cir. 1981); cf. Stillman v. CIA, 319 F.3d 546, 548 (D.C. Cir. 2003) (holding that in camera affidavits are effective tools for justifying national security withholdings) (non-FOIA case); Armstrong v. Executive Office of the President, 97 F.3d 575, 580-81 (D.C. Cir. 1996) (finding that although district court may have erred by not explaining reasons for using in camera affidavit, any such error was "harmless" because agency adequately explained why it could not release withheld information).

[69] Phillippi v. CIA, 546 F.2d 1009, 1013 (D.C. Cir. 1976); see also Armstrong, 97 F.3d at 580 (holding that when district court uses an in camera affidavit, even in national security cases, "it must both make its reasons for doing so clear and make as much as possible of the in camera submission available to the opposing party" (citing Lykins v. U.S. Dep't of Justice, 725 F.2d 1455, 1465 (D.C. Cir. 1984))); Patterson, 893 F.2d at 600; Simmons, 796 F.2d at 710; Pub. Citizen v. Dep't of State, 100 F. Supp. 2d 10, 27-28 (D.D.C. 2000) (ordering submission of an in camera affidavit after first finding that agency's public affidavit was as complete as possible and that any further description "would reveal the [very] information the agency is trying to withhold"), aff'd on other grounds, 276 F.3d 674 (D.C. Cir. 2002); Scott v. CIA, 916 F. Supp. 42, 48-49 (D.D.C. 1996) (denying request for in camera review until agency "creates as full a public record as possible"); Pub. Educ. Ctr., Inc. v. DOD, 905 F. Supp. 19, 22 (D.D.C. 1995) (ordering in camera review only after the agency created "as full a public record as possible" (citing Hayden v. NSA, 608 F.2d 1381, 1384 (D.C. Cir. 1979))); Nat'l Sec. Archive v. Office of Indep. Counsel, No. 89-2308, 1992 WL 1352663, at *3-4 (D.D.C. Aug. 28, 1992) (applying Phillippi standards, and refusing to review in camera affidavits until agency "has stated publicly 'in as much detail as possible' . . . reasons for non-disclosure"); Moessmer v. CIA, No. 86-948, slip op. at 9-11 (E.D. Mo. Feb. 17, 1987) (finding in camera review appropriate when record contains contradictory evidence), aff'd, 871 F.2d 1092 (6th Cir. 1988) (unpublished table decision); cf. Lion Raisins Inc. v. USDA, 354 F.3d 1072, 1083 (9th Cir. 2004) (approving the "use of in camera affidavits in order to supplement prior public affidavits that were too general," but rejecting the district court's use of in camera affidavits as "the sole factual basis for a district court's decision").

sis for a court to rule on, an agency's invocation of Exemption 1.[70]

In this regard, it is reasonably well settled that counsel for plaintiffs are not entitled to participate in such in camera proceedings.[71] Several years ago, though, one court took the unprecedented step of appointing a special master to review and categorize a large volume of classified records.[72] In other instances involving voluminous records, courts have on occasion ordered agencies to submit samples of the documents at issue for in camera review.[73]

In a decision that highlights some of the difficulties of Exemption 1 litigation practice, the Court of Appeals for the Fourth Circuit issued a writ

---

[70] See Campbell v. U.S. Dep't of Justice, 164 F.3d 20, 30 (D.C. Cir. 1999) (requiring defendant to provide plaintiff with "'a meaningful opportunity to contest, and the district court [with] an adequate foundation to review, the soundness of the withholding'" (quoting King v. U.S. Dep't of Justice, 830 F.2d 210, 218 (D.C. Cir. 1987))); Coldiron v. Dep't of Justice, 310 F. Supp. 2d 44, 49 (D.D.C. 2004) (same); Campbell v. U.S. Dep't of Justice, 193 F. Supp. 2d 29, 37 (D.D.C. 2001) (same), partial reconsideration denied, 231 F. Supp. 2d 1 (D.D.C. 2002); see also ACLU v. U.S. Dep't of Justice, 265 F. Supp. 2d 20, 27 (D.D.C. 2003) (acknowledging that agency affidavits "are entitled to substantial weight," but finding that they "must nevertheless afford the requester an ample opportunity to contest" them).

[71] See Salisbury, 690 F.2d at 973 n.3; Weberman v. NSA, 668 F.2d 676, 678 (2d Cir. 1982); Hayden, 608 F.2d at 1385-86; see also Ellsberg v. Mitchell, 709 F.2d 51, 61 (D.C. Cir. 1983) (holding that plaintiff's counsel not permitted to participate in in camera review of documents arguably covered by state secrets privilege); Pollard v. FBI, 705 F.2d 1151, 1154 (9th Cir. 1983) (finding no reversible error where court not only reviewed affidavit and documents in camera, but also received authenticating testimony ex parte); cf. Arieff v. U.S. Dep't of the Navy, 712 F.2d 1462, 1470-71 & n.2 (D.C. Cir. 1983) (denying participation by plaintiff's counsel even when information withheld was personal privacy information). But cf. Lederle Lab. v. HHS, No. 88-249, 1988 WL 47649, at *1 (D.D.C. May 2, 1988) (granting restrictive protective order in Exemption 4 case permitting counsel for requester to review contested business information).

[72] See Wash. Post v. DOD, No. 84-3400, slip op. at 2 (D.D.C. Jan. 15, 1988), petition for mandamus denied sub nom. In re DOD, 848 F.2d 232 (D.C. Cir. 1988); cf. Bay Area Lawyers Alliance for Nuclear Arms Control v. Dep't of State, 818 F. Supp. 1291, 1301 (N.D. Cal. 1992) (holding that court "will not hesitate" to appoint special master to assist with in camera review of documents if agency fails to submit adequate Vaughn declaration).

[73] See, e.g., Wilson v. CIA, No. 89-3356, 1991 WL 226682, at *3 (D.D.C. Oct. 15, 1991) (ordering in camera submission of "sample" of fifty documents because it was "neither necessary nor practicable" for court to review all 1000 processed ones).

of mandamus that required court personnel who would have access to classified materials submitted in camera in an Exemption 1 case to obtain security clearances prior to the submission of any such materials to the court.[74] On remand, the district court judge reviewed the disputed documents entirely on his own.[75] Consistent with the special precautions taken by courts in Exemption 1 cases, the government also has been ordered to provide a court reporter with the requisite security clearances to transcribe in camera proceedings, in order "to establish a complete record for meaningful appellate review."[76]

In other cases, courts have compelled agencies to submit in camera affidavits when disclosure in a public affidavit would vitiate the very protection afforded by Exemption 1.[77] Affidavits -- whether public, in camera,

---

[74] In re U.S. Dep't of Justice, No. 87-1205, slip op. at 4-5 (4th Cir. Apr. 7, 1988).

[75] Bowers v. U.S. Dep't of Justice, No. C-C-86-336, 1990 WL 41893, at *1 (W.D.N.C. Mar. 9, 1990), rev'd on other grounds, 930 F.2d 350 (4th Cir. 1991).

[76] Willens v. NSC, 720 F. Supp. 15, 16 (D.D.C. 1989); cf. Physicians for Soc. Responsibility, Inc. v. U.S. Dep't of Justice, No. 85-169, slip op. at 3-4 (D.D.C. Aug. 25, 1985) (placing transcript of in camera proceedings -- from which plaintiff's counsel was excluded -- under seal). But cf. Pollard, 705 F.2d at 1154 (finding no reversible error when no transcript made of ex parte testimony of FBI Special Agent who merely "authenticated and described" documents at issue).

[77] See, e.g., Pub. Citizen, 100 F. Supp. 2d at 27-28 (ordering submission of an in camera affidavit because further description in a public affidavit "would reveal the [very] information the agency is trying to withhold"); Pub. Educ. Ctr., 905 F. Supp. at 22 (ordering in camera affidavit because "'extensive public justification would threaten to reveal the very information for which . . . [Exemption 1 was] claimed'" (quoting Lykins, 725 F.2d at 1463)); cf. Maynard v. CIA, 986 F.2d 547, 557 (1st Cir. 1993) (reasoning that "a more detailed affidavit could have revealed the very intelligence sources and methods the CIA wished to keep secret"); Gilmore v. NSA, No. C92-3646, 1993 U.S. Dist. LEXIS 7694, at *18-19 (N.D. Cal. May 3, 1993) (ruling that agency has provided as much information as possible in public affidavit without "thwarting" purpose of Exemption 1 (citing King, 830 F.2d at 224)); Krikorian v. Dep't of State, No. 88-3419, 1990 WL 236108, at *3 (D.D.C. Dec. 19, 1990) (declaring agency's public affidavits sufficient because requiring more detailed descriptions of information would give foreign governments and confidential intelligence sources "reason to pause" before offering advice or useful information to agency officials in future), aff'd in pertinent part, 984 F.2d 461, 464-65 (D.C. Cir. 1993); Green v. U.S. Dep't of State, No. 85-0504, slip op. at 17-18 (D.D.C. Apr. 17, 1990) (determining that a public Vaughn affidavit containing additional information could "well have the ef-
(continued...)

or a combination of the two -- have been employed when even the confirmation or denial of the existence of records at issue would pose a threat to
national security, which is the so-called "Glomar" situation.[78] Indeed,

_____

[77](...continued)
fect of prematurely letting the cat out of the bag").

[78] See Phillippi, 546 F.2d at 1013 (dealing with request for records regarding Glomar Explorer submarine-retrieval ship, so "neither confirm nor
deny" response is now known as a "Glomar" response or as "Glomarization"); see, e.g., Frugone v. CIA, 169 F.3d 772, 775 (D.C. Cir. 1999) (finding
that the CIA properly refused to confirm or deny whether plaintiff was ever
employed by the CIA, on the basis that disclosure could cause "diplomatic
tension between Chile and the United States" or could "lessen the burden
facing a foreign intelligence agency attempting to track the CIA's covert
activities abroad"); Miller v. Casey, 730 F.2d 773, 776 (D.C. Cir. 1984) (applying response to request for any record reflecting any attempt by Western countries to overthrow Albanian government); Gardels v. CIA, 689 F.2d
1100, 1105 (D.C. Cir. 1982) (applying response to request for any record revealing any covert CIA connection with University of California); Wheeler
v. CIA, 271 F. Supp. 2d 132, 140 (D.D.C. 2003) (allowing the agency to give
a "Glomar" response to a request for records concerning plaintiff's activities
as a journalist in Cuba during the 1960s); Hogan v. Huff, No. 00-6753, 2002
WL 1359722, at *7 (S.D.N.Y. June, 21, 2002) (ruling that the agency may use
a "Glomar" response to protect information "whenever the fact of [the information's] existence is itself classified") (decided under original version of
Executive Order 12,958); Rubin v. CIA, No. 01 CIV 2274, 2001 WL 1537706,
at *4 (S.D.N.Y. Dec. 3, 2001) (holding that CIA properly refused to confirm
or deny existence of records concerning two deceased British poets, because acknowledgment would negatively impact foreign relations and
compromise intelligence sources); Nat'l Sec. Archive v. CIA, No. 99-1160,
slip op. at 9 (D.D.C. July 31, 2000) (finding that a "Glomar" response would
have been appropriate for a request for CIA biographies on seven living
former East European leaders, because disclosing which leaders were the
subjects of biographic intelligence "would reveal how the CIA allocates its
resources" and thus help adversaries "subvert CIA efforts," but concluding
that the CIA waived its Glomar position through prior disclosure of the existence of records); Arabian Shield Dev. Co. v. CIA, No. 3-98-0624, 1999 WL
118796, at *9 (N.D. Tex. Feb. 26, 1999) (holding that agency properly refused to confirm or deny whether it "has collected intelligence regarding
specific individuals or corporations, or has an intelligence interest or a facility in a particular foreign location"), aff'd per curiam, 208 F.3d 1007 (5th
Cir. 2000) (unpublished table decision); Roman v. Dailey, No. 97-1164, 1998
U.S. Dist. LEXIS 6708, at *7-10 (D.D.C. May 11, 1998) (finding that agencies
properly refused to confirm or deny existence of records about alleged satellite capabilities) (Exemptions 1 and 3); Earth Pledge Found. v. CIA, 988 F.
Supp. 623, 627 (S.D.N.Y. 1996) (ruling that agency properly refused to confirm or deny existence of correspondence between CIA headquarters and
alleged CIA station in Dominican Republic, because fact of station's exis-
(continued...)

"Glomarization" has become a major part of the overall landscape for Exemption 1.[79] (For a further discussion of in camera review, see Litigation

---

[78](...continued)
tence itself was classified and disclosure would reveal agency's intelligence methods and could cause damage to U.S. foreign relations), aff'd per curiam, 128 F.3d 788 (2d Cir. 1997); Nayed v. INS, No. 91-805, 1993 WL 524541, at *2 (D.D.C. Nov. 29, 1993) (finding "Glomar" response appropriate for request for records on former Libyan national denied entry into United States because "confirmation that information exists would . . . be admission of identity of CIA intelligence interest . . . [while] denial . . . would allow interested parties to ascertain [such] interests based on their analysis of patterns of CIA answers in different FOIA cases"); D'Aleo v. Dep't of the Navy, No. 89-2347, 1991 U.S. Dist. LEXIS 3884, at *4-5 (D.D.C. Mar. 27, 1991) (holding that any confirmation or denial of existence of nondisclosure agreement allegedly signed by plaintiff would cause serious damage to national security); Marrera v. U.S. Dep't of Justice, 622 F. Supp. 51, 53-54 (D.D.C. 1985) (applying "Glomar" response to request for any record which would reveal whether requester was target of surveillance pursuant to Foreign Intelligence Surveillance Act); see also Exec. Order No. 12,958, as amended, § 3.6(a), 68 Fed. Reg. 15,315 (Mar. 28, 2003), reprinted in 50 U.S.C. § 435 note (2000 & Supp. III 2003) and summarized in FOIA Post (posted 4/11/03); cf. Minier v. CIA, 88 F.3d 796, 801-02 (9th Cir. 1996) (finding "neither confirm nor deny" response proper for request seeking records on individual's employment relationship with CIA because to reveal such information would "provide a window into the [agency's] 'sources and methods'") (Exemption 3); Hunt v. CIA, 981 F.2d 1116, 1120 (9th Cir. 1992) (holding "Glomar" response proper for request for records on murdered Iranian national) (Exemption 3); Bassiouni v. CIA, No. 02-C-4049, 2004 WL 1125919, at *7 (N.D. Ill. Mar. 31, 2004) (allowing agency to give "no number, no list" response -- i.e., admission that records existed, coupled with refusal to further describe them -- to protect classified national security information even though agency previously acknowledged existence of records), aff'd, 392 F.3d 244 (7th Cir. 2004), cert. denied, 545 U.S. 1129 (2005); Levy v. CIA, No. 95-1276, slip op. at 11-14 (D.D.C. Nov. 16, 1995) (finding a "Glomar" response appropriate regarding a request for CIA records on a foreign national because "[c]onsistent treatment of all requests relating to foreign nationals is a critical element to the CIA's protective strategy to safeguard its intelligence sources and methods") (Exemption 3), summary affirmance granted, No. 96-5004, 1997 WL 68328 (D.C. Cir. Jan. 15, 1997).

[79] See ACLU v. DOD, 406 F. Supp. 2d 330, 333 (D.D.C. 2006) (holding that limited disclosure in news reports did not waive agency's use of "Glomar" response); Wheeler v. CIA, 271 F. Supp. 2d 132, 140 (D.D.C. 2003) (allowing agency to give "Glomar" response to request for records concerning plaintiff's activities as journalist in Cuba during 1960s); Hogan v. Huff, No. 00-6753, 2002 WL 1359722, at *7 (S.D.N.Y. June, 21, 2002) (ruling that the agency may use a "Glomar" response to protect information "whenever the fact of [the information's] existence is itself classified") (decided under pre-
(continued...)

Considerations, In Camera Inspection, below.)

## Waiver of Exemption Protection

Several courts have had occasion to consider whether agencies have a duty to disclose classified information that purportedly has found its way into the public domain.[80] This issue most commonly arises when a plaintiff argues that an agency has waived its ability to invoke Exemption 1 as a result of prior disclosure of similar or related information.[81] In this regard, courts have held that, in making an argument of waiver through some prior public disclosure, a FOIA plaintiff bears "the initial burden of pointing to specific information in the public domain that appears to duplicate that be-

---

[79](...continued)
vious version of Executive Order 12,958); Rubin, 2001 WL 1537706, at *4 (holding that CIA properly refused to confirm or deny existence of records concerning two deceased British poets, because acknowledgment would negatively impact foreign relations and compromise intelligence sources); Nat'l Sec. Archive v. CIA, No. 99-1160, slip op. at 9 (D.D.C. July 31, 2000) (finding that a "Glomar" response would have been appropriate for a request for CIA biographies on seven living former East European leaders, because disclosing which leaders were the subjects of biographic intelligence "would reveal how the CIA allocates its resources" and thereby help adversaries "subvert CIA efforts," but concluding that the CIA waived its "Glomar" position through its prior disclosure of the existence of such records). But see ACLU v. DOD, 389 F. Supp. 2d 547, 561 (S.D.N.Y. 2005) (commenting that the "danger of Glomar responses is that they encourage an unfortunate tendency of government officials to over-classify information, frequently keeping secret that which the public already knows, or that which is more embarrassing that revelatory of intelligence sources or methods").

[80] See, e.g., Pub. Citizen v. Dep't of State, 276 F.3d 634, 645 (D.C. Cir. 2002) (reaffirming that burden is on requester to establish that specific record in public domain duplicates that being withheld (citing Afshar v. Dep't of State, 702 F.2d 1125, 1132 (D.C. Cir. 1983))); Frugone v. CIA, 169 F.3d 772, 774 (D.C. Cir. 1999) (finding that disclosure made by employee of agency other than agency from which information is sought is not official and thus does not constitute waiver).

[81] See, e.g., Assassination Archives & Research Ctr. v. CIA, 334 F.3d 55, 60 (D.C. Cir. 2003) (holding that FOIA plaintiff must show that previous disclosure duplicates specificity of withheld material to establish waiver of exemptions, and determining that CIA's prior disclosure of some intelligence methods employed in Cuba does not waive use of exemptions for all such methods); Wheeler v. CIA, 271 F. Supp. 2d 132, 140 (D.D.C. 2003) (rejecting plaintiff's contention that foreign nation's knowledge of past U.S. intelligence activities creates general waiver of all intelligence activities related to that nation).

ing withheld."[82] Accordingly, Exemption 1 claims should not be under-mined by generalized allegations that classified information has been leaked to the press or otherwise made available to members of the public.[83]

---

[82] Afshar, 702 F.2d at 1130; see James Madison Project v. NARA, No. 02-5089, 2002 WL 31296220, at *1 (D.C. Cir. Oct. 11, 2002) (affirming that the "party claiming that public disclosure prevents withholding the same infor-mation bears the burden of showing that the specific information at issue has been officially disclosed"); Pub. Citizen, 276 F.3d at 645 (rejecting plaintiff's waiver claim as "speculation" where plaintiff failed to demon-strate that specific information had been released into public domain, even though records were publicly accessible in NARA reading room upon re-quest); Ctr. for Int'l Envtl. Law v. Office of the U.S. Trade Representative, 237 F. Supp. 2d 17, 20 (D.D.C. 2002) (holding that plaintiff failed to show that information was in public domain when it merely pointed to other publicly available documents dealing with same general subject matter); Billington v. Dep't of Justice, 11 F. Supp. 2d 45, 54-56 (D.D.C. 1998) (reject-ing plaintiff's unsubstantiated allegations that agency had previously re-leased subject information, and concluding that because FBI "may have re-leased similar types of information in one case does not warrant disclosure" in this case), summary judgment granted in pertinent part, 69 F. Supp. 2d 128, 135 (D.D.C. 1999), aff'd in part, vacated in part & remanded all on other grounds, 233 F.3d 581 (D.C. Cir. 2000) (Exemption 1 decision not challeng-ed on appeal); Meeropol v. Reno, No. 75-1121, slip op. at 6-7 (D.D.C. Mar. 26, 1998) (ruling that plaintiffs failed to carry "burden of production" in as-serting that withheld information about atomic bomb spies Julius and Ethel Rosenberg was available in public domain) (Exemptions 1 and 7(D)); Scott v. CIA, 916 F. Supp. 42, 50 (D.D.C. 1996) (ordering plaintiff to compile list of information allegedly in public domain "with specific documentation demonstrating the legitimacy of such claims" and requiring release of that information if actually in public domain unless government demonstrates its release "threatens the national security"); Pfeiffer v. CIA, 721 F. Supp. 337, 342 (D.D.C. 1989) (holding that plaintiff must do more than simply identify "information that happens to find its way into a published account" to meet this burden); cf. Davis v. U.S. Dep't of Justice, 968 F.2d 1276, 1279 (D.C. Cir. 1992) (stating that a "party who asserts . . . material publicly available carries the burden of production on that issue . . . because the task of proving the negative -- that the information has not been revealed -- might require the government to undertake an exhaustive, potentially limit-less search") (Exemptions 3, 7(C), and 7(D)). But see Wash. Post v. DOD, 766 F. Supp. 1, 12-13 (D.D.C. 1991) (suggesting that agency has ultimate burden of proof when comparing publicly disclosed information with in-formation being withheld, determining whether information is identical and, if not, determining whether release of slightly different information would harm national security).

[83] See Exec. Order No. 12,958, as amended, § 1.1(b), 68 Fed. Reg. 15,315 (Mar. 28, 2003) (stating that "[c]lassified information shall not be declassi-fied automatically as a result of any unauthorized disclosure of identical or

(continued...)

EXEMPTION 1

Courts have carefully distinguished between a bona fide declassification action or official release on the one hand and unsubstantiated speculation lacking official confirmation on the other, refusing to consider classified information to be in the public domain unless it has been officially disclosed.[84] While this yields an especially narrow concept of "waiver" in the

---

[83](...continued)
similar information"), reprinted in 50 U.S.C. § 435 note (2000 & Supp. III 2003) and summarized in FOIA Post (posted 4/11/03); see also Pub. Citizen v. Dep't of State, 11 F.3d 198, 201 (D.C. Cir. 1993) (holding that "an agency official does not waive FOIA exemption 1 by publicly discussing the general subject matter of documents which are otherwise properly exempt from disclosure under that exemption") (decided under Executive Order 12,356); Nat'l Sec. Archive Fund, Inc. v. CIA, 402 F. Supp. 2d 211, 222 (D.D.C. 2005) (ruling that plaintiff's "bald assertions" of public disclosure do not satisfy waiver standard).

[84] See, e.g., Hoch v. CIA, No. 88-5422, 1990 WL 102740, at *1 (D.C. Cir. July 20, 1990) (concluding that without official confirmation, "clear precedent establishes that courts will not compel [an agency] to disclose information even though it has been the subject of media reports and speculation"); see also Frugone, 169 F.3d at 775 (holding that letter from OPM advising plaintiff that his employment records were in CIA custody is not "tantamount to an official statement of the CIA"); Hunt v. CIA, 981 F.2d 1116, 1120 (9th Cir. 1992) (finding that although some information about subject of request may have been made public by other governmental agencies, CIA's "Glomar" response in Exemption 3 context was not defeated); Simmons v. U.S. Dep't of Justice, 796 F.2d 709, 712 (4th Cir. 1986) (ruling that there had been no "widespread dissemination" of information in question); Abbotts v. NRC, 766 F.2d 604, 607-08 (D.C. Cir. 1985) (reasoning that even if the withheld data were the same as an estimate in the public domain, that is not the same as knowing the NRC's official policy as to the "proper level of threat a nuclear facility should guard against"); Afshar, 702 F.2d at 1130-31 (observing that a foreign government can ignore "[u]nofficial leaks and public surmise . . . but official acknowledgment may force a government to retaliate"); Philippi v. CIA, 665 F.2d 1325, 1332 (D.C. Cir. 1981) (concluding that a disclosure by a former Director of Central Intelligence did not result in waiver, and reasoning perceptively that "without the disclosure of the documents demanded by [plaintiff], foreign analysts remain in the dark as to the provenience of the information appearing in published reports"); Edmonds v. FBI, 272 F. Supp. 2d 35, 49 (D.D.C. 2003) (holding that anonymous leak of information concerning FBI counterterrorism activities did not prevent agency from invoking exemption, because disclosures in tandem would amount to official confirmation of authenticity); Rubin v. CIA, No. 01 CIV 2274, 2001 WL 1537706, at *5 (S.D.N.Y. Dec. 3, 2001) (finding that plaintiff's mere showing that some private publication alleged that CIA maintained files on subject was not evidence of official disclosure and, therefore, that agency's "Glomar" position was not defeated); Arabian Shield Dev. Co. v. CIA, No. 3-98-0624, 1999 WL 118796, at *3
(continued...)

national security context, courts have recognized the importance of protecting sensitive national security information through such an approach.[85] Indeed, this approach firmly comports with the amended Executive Order 12,958, which allows agencies to classify or reclassify information following an access request if it "has not previously been disclosed to the public under proper authority."[86] (For a discussion of the requirements for such belated classification, see Exemption 1, Executive Order 12,958, as Amended, below.)

---

[84](...continued)
n.5 (N.D. Tex. Feb. 26, 1999) (rejecting plaintiff's citation to "unspecified public news reports" identifying individuals as CIA agents and holding that "public speculation and disclosure . . . is quite different from official disclosure"), aff'd per curiam, 208 F.3d 1007 (5th Cir. 2000) (unpublished table decision); Steinberg v. U.S. Dep't of Justice, 801 F. Supp. 800, 802 (D.D.C. 1992) (recognizing that "[p]assage of time, media reports and informed or uninformed speculation based on statements by participants cannot be used . . . to undermine [government's] legitimate interest in protecting international security [information]"), aff'd in pertinent part, 23 F.3d 548, 553 (D.C. Cir. 1994); Van Atta v. Def. Intelligence Agency, No. 87-1508, 1988 WL 73856, at *2-3 (D.D.C. July 6, 1988) (holding that disclosure of information to foreign government during diplomatic negotiations was not "public disclosure"). But see Lawyers Comm. for Human Rights v. INS, 721 F. Supp. 552, 569 (S.D.N.Y. 1989) (ruling that Exemption 1 protection is not available when same documents were disclosed by foreign government or when same information was disclosed to media in "off-the-record exchanges").

[85] See Frugone v. CIA, 169 F.3d 772, 774 (D.C. Cir. 1999) (ruling that disclosure made by employee from agency other than one from which information was sought is not official and thus does not constitute waiver); Edmonds v. U.S. Dep't of Justice, 405 F. Supp. 2d 23, 29 (D.D.C. 2005) (finding that even agency's disclosure to plaintiff's counsel during meeting does not constitute declassification action that waives Exemption 1); Nat'l Sec. Archive v. CIA, No. 99-1160, slip op. at 12-13 (D.D.C. July 31, 2000) (ruling that Exemption 1 can be waived only through "the stamp of truth that accompanies official disclosure," even where requested information is otherwise "common knowledge in the public domain," and that "[d]isclosure by other agencies of CIA information does not preempt the CIA's ability to withhold that information"); see also Carson v. U.S. Dep't of Justice, 631 F.2d 1008, 1016 n.30 (D.C. Cir. 1980) (explaining that "the extent to which prior agency disclosure may constitute a waiver of the FOIA exemptions must depend both on the circumstances of prior disclosure and on the particular exemptions claimed").

[86] Exec. Order No. 12,958, as amended, § 1.7(d), see also White House Memorandum for Heads of Executive Departments and Agencies Concerning Safeguarding Information Regarding Weapons of Mass Destruction and Other Sensitive Documents Related to Homeland Security (Mar. 19, 2002), reprinted in FOIA Post (posted 3/21/02).

EXEMPTION 1

A recurring issue in the waiver arena is whether public statements by former government officials constitute such an "official disclosure," and thus prevent an agency from invoking Exemption 1 to withhold information that it determines still warrants national security protection. In this regard, the Court of Appeals for the Second Circuit has rejected the argument that a retired admiral's statements constituted an authoritative disclosure by the government.[87] It pointedly stated: "Officials no longer serving with an executive branch department cannot continue to disclose official agency policy, and certainly they cannot establish what is agency policy through speculation, no matter how reasonable it may appear to be."[88] Additionally, the Second Circuit affirmed the decision of the district court in holding that the congressional testimony of high-ranking Navy officials did not constitute official disclosure because it did not concern the specific information being sought.[89]

Similarly, courts have rejected the view that widespread reports in the media about the general subject matter involved are sufficient to overcome an agency's Exemption 1 claim for related records. Indeed, in one case, the court went so far as to hold that 180,000 pages of CIA records concerning Guatemala were properly classified despite the fact that the public domain contained significant information and speculation about CIA involvement in the 1954 coup in Guatemala: "CIA clearance of books and articles, books written by former CIA officials, and general discussions in [c]ongressional publications do not constitute official disclosures."[90] In a subsequent case, one court went even further, holding that documents were properly withheld under Exemption 1 even though they previously had been disclosed "involuntarily as a result of [a] tragic accident such as an aborted rescue mission [in Iran], or used in evidence to prosecute espionage."[91]

---

[87] See Hudson River Sloop Clearwater, Inc. v. Dep't of the Navy, 891 F.2d 414, 421-22 (2d Cir. 1989).

[88] Id. at 422.

[89] Id. at 421; see also Edmonds, 272 F. Supp. 2d at 49 (declaring that when an agency provides classified information to a congressional committee it "does not deprive [itself] of the right to classify the information under Exemption 1").

[90] Schlesinger v. CIA, 591 F. Supp. 60, 66 (D.D.C. 1984); see Pfeiffer v. CIA, 721 F. Supp. at 342; see also Wash. Post, 766 F. Supp. at 11-12 (finding no "presumption of reliability" for facts contained in books subject to prepublication review by government agency); cf. McGehee v. Casey, 718 F.2d 1137, 1141 & n.9 (D.C. Cir. 1983) (determining that CIA cannot reasonably bear burden of conducting exhaustive search to prove that particular items of classified information have never been published) (non-FOIA case).

[91] Wash. Post Co. v. DOD, No. 84-3400, slip op. at 3 (D.D.C. Sept. 22,

(continued...)

Another issue that has arisen in this regard has been the possible argument for waiver created when a government agency releases limited information on a subject while retaining additional information on the same subject as classified.[92] In a 1990 decision, the Court of Appeals for the District of Columbia Circuit held that for information to be "officially acknowledged" in the context of Exemption 1, it must: (1) be as "specific" as the information previously released; (2) "match" the information previously disclosed; and (3) have been made public through an "official and documented" disclosure.[93] Applying these criteria, the D.C. Circuit reversed the low-

---

[91](...continued)
1986) (refusing to find official disclosure through abandonment of documents in Iranian desert following aborted rescue mission or through government's introduction of them into evidence in espionage trial).

[92] See, e.g., Whalen v. U.S. Marine Corps, 407 F. Supp. 2d 54, 57 (D.D.C. 2005) (holding that the defendant agency's prior disclosures on a subject did not constitute a waiver of all information on that subject, and noting that "it seems equally as likely that the government's prior voluminous disclosures indicate diligent respect by the coordinate agencies to Executive Order 12,958 and bolster the defendant's position that it has withheld only that information which it must under the applicable exemptions").

[93] Fitzgibbon v. CIA, 911 F.2d 755, 765 (D.C. Cir. 1990); see also Wolf v. CIA, 473 F.3d 370, 378 (D.C. Cir. 2007) (reaffirming the rule in Fitzgibbon and the necessity of an "insistence on exactitude" when considering potential waiver of national security information and holding that in that case the "'specific information at issue,'" i.e. the existence of particular records, had been officially acknowledged by the agency during congressional testimony"); Assassination Archives & Research Ctr., 334 F.3d at 61 (determining that previous disclosure concerning Cuban operatives pursuant to John F. Kennedy Assassination Records Collection Act, 44 U.S.C. § 2107 note (2000), did not waive exemptions for specific CIA compendium of information); Students Against Genocide v. Dep't of State, 257 F.3d 828, 835 (D.C. Cir. 2001) (holding that a prior release of photographs similar to those withheld did not waive Exemption 1, because the fact that "some 'information resides in the public domain does not eliminate the possibility that further disclosures can cause harm to [national security]'" (quoting Fitzgibbon, 911 F.2d at 766)); Afshar, 702 F.2d at 1130, 1133-34 (determining that agency review of books written by former agency officials does not create official acknowledgment of information or waive applicability of FOIA exemptions); Kelly v. CIA, No. 00-2498, slip op. at 10, 12 (D.D.C. Aug. 8, 2002) (holding that official release of general agency memo concerning "agency-academic relations" did not waive Exemption 1 protection with regard to specific and detailed agency-academic information (citing Fitzgibbon, 911 F.2d at 765-66)), modified on other grounds, No. 00-2498, slip op. at 1 (D.D.C. Sept. 25, 2002), appeal on adequacy of search dismissed on procedural grounds, No. 02-5384, 2003 WL 21804101 (D.C. Cir. July 31, 2003). But see Nat'l Sec. Archive, No. 99-1160, slip op. at 15-16 (D.D.C. July 31,
(continued...)

er court's disclosure order and held that information published in a congressional report did not constitute "official acknowledgment" of the purported location of a CIA station, because the information sought related to an earlier time period than that discussed in the report.[94]

In so ruling, the D.C. Circuit did not address the broader question of whether congressional release of the identical information relating to intelligence sources and methods could ever constitute "official acknowledgment," thus requiring disclosure under the FOIA.[95] However, the D.C. Circuit had previously considered this broader question and had concluded that congressional publications do not constitute "official acknowledgment" for purposes of the FOIA.[96]

In 1993, the D.C. Circuit had another opportunity to consider the issue of whether an agency had "waived" its ability to properly withhold records pursuant to Exemption 1. The case involved the question of whether the public congressional testimony of the U.S. Ambassador to Iraq constituted such a "waiver" so as to prevent the agency from invoking the FOIA's national security exemption to withhold related records.[97] The district court had held -- after reviewing the seven documents at issue in camera -- that the public testimony had not "waived" Exemption 1 protection because the "context" of the information in the documents was sufficiently "different"

---

[93](...continued)
2000) (ordering CIA to disclose fact that it kept biographies on seven former East European heads of state because "Glomar" response was waived by CIA's 1994 admission that it kept biographies on all "heads of state" -- a "clear and narrowly defined term that is not subject to multiple interpretations," but noting that CIA's "Glomar" response otherwise would have been appropriate), reconsideration denied (D.D.C. Feb. 26, 2001); Krikorian v. Dep't of State, 984 F.2d 461, 467-68 (D.C. Cir. 1993) (remanding to district court to determine whether information excised in one document had been "officially acknowledged" by comparing publicly available record with record withheld; leaving to district court's discretion whether this could best be done by supplemental agency affidavit or by in camera inspection).

[94] Fitzgibbon, 911 F.2d at 765-66.

[95] Id.

[96] See, e.g., Salisbury v. United States, 690 F.2d 966, 971 (D.C. Cir. 1982) (holding that inclusion of information in Senate report "cannot be equated with disclosure by the agency itself"); Military Audit Project v. Casey, 656 F.2d 724, 744 (D.C. Cir. 1981) (finding that publication of Senate report does not constitute official release of agency information); see also Earth Pledge Found. v. CIA, 988 F. Supp. 623, 628 (S.D.N.Y. 1996) (same), aff'd per curiam, 128 F.3d 788 (2d Cir. 1997).

[97] Pub. Citizen v. Dep't of State, 11 F.3d 198, 199 (D.C. Cir. 1993).

so as to not "negate" their "confidentiality."[98] Terming this an "unusual FOIA case" because the requester did not challenge the district court's conclusion that the documents were properly exempt from disclosure under Exemption 1 and because the requester also conceded that it could not meet the strict test for "waiver," the D.C. Circuit firmly rejected the requester's argument that the facts of this case distinguished it from the court's prior decisions on this question.[99]

The requester contended first that the court's prior decisions concerned attempts by FOIA requesters to compel agencies to confirm or deny the truth of information that others had already publicly disclosed.[100] The plaintiff then argued that the Ambassador's public statements about her meeting with the Iraqi leader prior to the invasion of Kuwait were far more detailed than those that the D.C. Circuit had found did not constitute "waiver" in previous cases.[101] The D.C. Circuit repudiated both of the requester's points and, in affirming the district court's decision, grounded its own decision in the fact that the requester "conceded" it could not "meet [the] requirement that it show that [the Ambassador's] testimony was 'as specific as' the documents it [sought] in this case, or that her testimony 'matche[d]' the information contained in the documents."[102] Acknowledging that such a stringent standard is a "high hurdle for a FOIA plaintiff to clear," the D.C. Circuit concluded that the government's "vital interest in information relating to the national security and foreign affairs dictates that it must be."[103] To hold otherwise in a situation where the government had affirmatively disclosed some information about a classified matter would, in the court's view, give the agency "a strong disincentive ever to provide the citizenry with briefings of any kind on sensitive topics."[104] Indeed, in an opinion following this D.C. Circuit decision, the United States Court of Appeals for the Seventh Circuit reasoned that the public "is better off under a system that permits [the agency] to reveal some things without revealing everything; if even a smidgen of disclosure required [the agency] to open its files, there would be no smidgens."[105]

---

[98] Pub. Citizen v. Dep't of State, 787 F. Supp. 12, 13, 15 (D.D.C. 1992).

[99] Pub. Citizen, 11 F.3d at 201.

[100] Id. at 201-03.

[101] Id. at 203.

[102] Id.

[103] Id.

[104] Id.

[105] Bassiouni v. CIA, 392 F.3d 244, 247 (7th Cir. 2004), cert. denied, 545 U.S. 1129 (2005). But see Wolf, 473 F.3d at 379-80 (remanding for determination of whether CIA Director's 1948 testimony before Congress, which

(continued...)

**EXEMPTION 1**

In a case decided nearly a decade later, the D.C. Circuit once again visited the issue of claimed public disclosure of classified information. In Public Citizen v. Department of State,[106] it considered whether an Exemption 1 claim was defeated because the requested documents were, prior to their classification, publicly accessible upon request at the National Archives and Records Administration.[107] The district court earlier had rejected the plaintiff's waiver argument because the documents, while accessible, were not maintained in a public access area and were not likely to have been accessed by a researcher.[108] The district court had explained that such a "remote possibility of very limited disclosure" was not the type of "widespread" official dissemination capable of defeating an Exemption 1 claim.[109] Agreeing with this, the D.C. Circuit began its discussion of the issue by observing that, as an initial matter, the party claiming prior disclosure must point to "'specific information in the public domain that appears to duplicate that being withheld,'"[110] lest the defendant agency unrealistically bear "the task of proving the negative."[111] The D.C. Circuit concluded that the plaintiff had failed to meet this burden, and it dismissed the public disclosure claim as nothing more than "speculation."[112] (For a further discussion of this issue, see Discretionary Disclosure and Waiver, below.)

A final, seemingly obvious point -- but one nevertheless not accepted by all FOIA requesters -- is that classified information will not be released under the FOIA even to a requester of "unquestioned loyalty."[113] In a case

---

[105](...continued) was found to constitute "official acknowledgment" of "existence" of requested records, had also waived exemption protection for their "contents").

[106] 276 F.3d 634 (D.C. Cir. 2002).

[107] Id. at 644-45.

[108] Pub. Citizen v. Dep't of State, 100 F. Supp. 2d 10, 29 (D.D.C. 2000).

[109] Id. at 28-29.

[110] Pub. Citizen, 276 F.3d at 645 (quoting Afshar, 702 F.2d at 1129).

[111] Id. (quoting Davis v. Dep't of Justice, 968 F.2d 1276, 1279 (D.C. Cir. 1992). But see also NARA v. Favish, 541 U.S. 157, 167, 174 (accepting that unofficial leak and subsequent publication of photograph did not constitute waiver) (Exemption 7(C)), reh'g denied, 541 U.S. 1057 (2004); U.S. Dep't of Justice v. Reporters Comm. for Freedom of the Press, 489 U.S. 749, 762-63, 780 (1989) (introducing "practical obscurity" standard, and commenting that if such items of information actually "were 'freely available,' there would be no reason to invoke the FOIA to obtain access" to them).

[112] Id.

[113] Levine v. Dep't of Justice, No. 83-1685, slip op. at 6 (D.D.C. Mar. 30,
(continued...)

decided in 1990, a government employee with a current "Top Secret" security clearance was denied access to classified records concerning himself because Exemption 1 protects "information from disclosure based on the nature of the material, not on the nature of the individual requester."[114]

## Executive Order 12,958, as Amended

As is mentioned above, Executive Order 12,958, which was amended on March 25, 2003,[115] sets forth the standards governing national security classification and the mechanisms for declassification.[116] As with prior executive orders, the amended Executive Order 12,958 recognizes both the right of the public to be informed about activities of its government and the need to protect national security information from unauthorized or untimely disclosure.[117] Accordingly, information may not be classified unless "the unauthorized disclosure of the information reasonably could be expected to result in damage to the national security, which includes defense against transnational terrorism."[118] Courts grappling with the degree of certainty

---

[113](...continued)
1984) (concluding that regardless of a requester's loyalty, the release of documents to him could "open the door to secondary disclosure to others").

[114] Martens v. U.S. Dep't of Commerce, No. 88-3334, 1990 U.S. Dist. LEXIS 10351, at *10 (D.D.C. Aug. 6, 1990) (Privacy Act case); see also Miller v. Casey, 730 F.2d 773, 778 (D.C. Cir. 1984) (accepting that plaintiff's security clearance was not an issue in denying access to requested information); cf. U.S. Dep't of Justice v. Reporters Comm. for Freedom of the Press, 489 U.S. 749, 771 (1989) (stating that "the identity of the requester has no bearing on the merits of his or her FOIA request") (Exemption 7(C)); FOIA Update, Vol. X, No. 2, at 5 (advising that as general rule all FOIA requesters should be treated alike).

[115] See Exec. Order No. 12,958, as amended, 68 Fed. Reg. 15,315 (Mar. 28, 2003), reprinted in 50 U.S.C. § 435 note (2000 & Supp. III 2003) and summarized in FOIA Post (posted 4/11/03).

[116] See generally id.

[117] See Exec. Order No. 12,958, as amended (commenting in introductory statement that "our Nation's progress depends on the free flow of information"); see also Information Security Oversight Office Ann. Rep. 6 (2003) (explaining that "what is most notable about the new amendment is what did not change with respect to the fundamentals that make the security classification system work"); FOIA Post, "Executive Order on National Security Classification Amended" (posted 4/11/03) (discussing amendments to Executive Order 12,958).

[118] Exec. Order No. 12,958, as amended, § 1.1(a)(4); see also 32 C.F.R. § 2001.10(c) (2006) (ISOO directive explaining that ability of agency classifier to identify and describe damage to national security caused by un-
(continued...)

necessary to demonstrate the contemplated damage under this standard have recognized that an agency's articulation of the threatened harm must always be speculative to some extent and that to require a showing of actual harm would be judicial "overstepping."[119] In the area of intelligence sources and methods, for example, courts are strongly inclined to accept the agency's position that disclosure of this type of information will cause damage to national security interests because this is "necessarily a region for forecasts in which [the agency's] informed judgment as to potential future harm should be respected."[120]

This standard is elaborated upon in section 1.4 of the amended order, which specifies the types of information that may be considered for classification. The information categories identified as proper bases for classification in the amended Executive Order 12,958 consist of:

(1) foreign government information;[121]

---

[118](...continued)
authorized disclosure is critical aspect of classification system).

[119] Halperin v. CIA, 629 F.2d 144, 149 (D.C. Cir. 1980); see Aftergood v. CIA, No. 98-2107, 1999 U.S. Dist. LEXIS 18135, at *9 (D.D.C. Nov. 12, 1999) (declaring that "the law does not require certainty or a showing of harm" that has already occurred); cf. Snepp v. United States, 444 U.S. 507, 513 n.8 (1980) (articulating that "[t]he problem is to ensure, in advance, and by proper [CIA prepublication review] procedures, that information detrimental to the national interest is not published") (non-FOIA case); ACLU v. U.S. Dep't of Justice, 265 F. Supp. 2d 20, 30 (D.D.C. 2003) (reiterating that "'[t]he test is not whether the court personally agrees in full with the [agency's] evaluation of the danger -- rather, the issue is whether on the whole record the Agency's judgment objectively survives the test of reasonableness, good faith, specificity, and plausibility in this field of foreign intelligence in which the [agency] is expert'" (quoting Gardels v. CIA, 689 F.2d 1100, 1105 (D.C. Cir. 1982))).

[120] Gardels, 689 F.2d at 1106; see also Bassiouni v. CIA, 392 F.3d 244, 245 (7th Cir. 2004) (commenting that to protect sources, intelligence agencies must often protect "how" a document came to its records system, because "in the intelligence business, 'how' often means 'from whom'"), cert. denied, 545 U.S. 1129 (2005); Wash. Post v. DOD, 766 F. Supp. 1, 7 (D.D.C. 1991) (observing that disclosure of the working files of a failed Iranian hostage rescue attempt containing intelligence planning documents would "serve as a model of 'do's and don't's'" for future counterterrorist missions "with similar objectives and obstacles").

[121] See, e.g., Krikorian v. Dep't of State, 984 F.2d 461, 465 (D.C. Cir. 1993) (finding that telegram reporting discussion between agency official and high-ranking foreign diplomat regarding terrorism was properly withheld as foreign government information; release would "jeopardize 'reciprocal
(continued...)

(2) vulnerabilities or capabilities of systems, installations, projects, or plans relating to national security;[122]

(3) intelligence activities, sources, or methods;[123]

---

[121](...continued)
confidentiality'" between governments) (decided under Executive Order 12,356); Pinnavaia v. FBI, No. 03-112, slip op. at 8 (D.D.C. Feb. 25, 2004) (holding that it was reasonable to classify "sensitive information gathered by the United States either about or by a foreign country," because the disclosure "could have negative diplomatic consequences"); McErlean v. Dep't of Justice, No. 97-7831, 1999 WL 791680, at *5 (S.D.N.Y. Sept. 30, 1999) (protecting identities and information obtained from foreign governments) (decided under original version of Executive Order 12,958); Ajluni v. FBI, No. 94-325, 1996 WL 776996, at *4 (N.D.N.Y. July 13, 1996) (rejecting plaintiff's assertion that for withheld information to qualify as foreign government information the agency "should be forced to identify at least which government supplied the information," because to do so would cause such sources of information "to dry up") (decided under Executive Order 12,356); Badalementi v. Dep't of State, 899 F. Supp. 542, 546-47 (D. Kan. 1995) (categorizing record reflecting negotiations among United States, Spain, and Italy regarding extradition of alleged drug smuggler as foreign government information) (decided under Executive Order 12,356). But see Weiner v. FBI, No. 83-1720, slip op. at 9 (C.D. Cal. Sept. 27, 2004) (opining that foreign government's request for confidentiality alone is "not sufficient to justify non-disclosure of foreign government information"), appeal dismissed per stipulation, No. 05-56652 (9th Cir. Jan. 3, 2007).

[122] See, e.g., Judicial Watch, Inc. v. United States Dep't of Transp., No. 02-566, 2005 WL 1606915, at *8 (D.D.C. July 7, 2005) (holding that disclosure of testing data, minimum detection rates, and false alarm rates for explosive-detection systems would harm national security by exposing vulnerabilities in airport security); Pub. Educ. Ctr., Inc. v. DOD, 905 F. Supp. 19, 21 (D.D.C. 1995) (identifying videotapes made during raid by U.S. forces in Somalia as relating to vulnerabilities or capabilities of projects concerning national security) (decided under Executive Order 12,356); Gottesdiener v. Secret Serv., No. 86-576, slip op. at 5 (D.D.C. Feb. 21, 1989) (determining that agency had properly classified certain information related to government emergency-preparedness programs) (decided under Executive Order 12,356); cf. U.S. News & World Report v. Dep't of the Treasury, No. 84-2303, 1986 U.S. Dist. LEXIS 27634, at *3 (D.D.C. Mar. 26, 1986) (providing protection for information regarding armored limousines for the President) (Exemptions 1 and 7(E)) (decided under Executive Order 12,356).

[123] See, e.g., Schrecker v. U.S. Dep't of Justice, 254 F.3d 162, 166 (D.C. Cir. 2001) (protecting intelligence sources because release would harm national security by "dissuading current and future sources from cooperating"); Jones v. FBI, 41 F.3d 238, 244 (6th Cir. 1994) (protecting "numerical designators" assigned to national security sources) (decided under Execu-
(continued...)

EXEMPTION 1

(4) cryptology;[124]

(5) foreign relations or foreign activities, including confidential

---

[123](...continued)
tive Order 12,356); Patterson v. FBI, 893 F.2d 595, 597, 601 (3d Cir. 1990)
(protecting information concerning intelligence sources and methods FBI
used in investigation of student who corresponded with 169 foreign nations) (decided under Executive Order 12,356); Rubin v. CIA, No. 01-CIV-
2274, 2001 WL 1537706, at *3 (S.D.N.Y. Dec. 3, 2001) (holding that CIA
properly refused to confirm or deny existence of records concerning two
deceased British poets, because "intelligence collection may be compromised if sources are not confident that . . . their cooperation will remain for-
ever secret"); Falwell v. Executive Office of the President, 158 F. Supp. 2d
734, 738 (W.D. Va. 2001) (protecting information that could hamper efforts
to protect and recruit intelligence sources"); Halpern v. FBI, No. 94-CV-
365A, 2002 WL 31012157, at *8 (W.D.N.Y. Aug. 31, 2001) (magistrate's recommendation) (protecting information about covert CIA intelligence stations in foreign country because disclosure could harm national security
through "retaliation against American citizens or other American interests"), adopted (W.D.N.Y. Oct. 12, 2001); Cozier v. FBI, No. 99-0312, slip op.
at 10-11 (N.D. Ga. Sept. 25, 2000) (finding that internal code, numerical designators, and identifiers for intelligence gathering units "clearly fall within
category of intelligence activities, source[s], and methods"); Aranha v. CIA,
No. 99-8644, 2000 WL 1051908, at *1 (S.D.N.Y. July 31, 2000) (finding that
confirmation of any records concerning plaintiff's alleged employment as
CIA case agent would "provide information about CIA's intelligence sources and methods"); Emerson v. CIA, No. 99-00274, slip op. at 5 (D.D.C. May
8, 2000) (holding that the "CIA's covert intelligence interest in a specific individual represents an intelligence activity, source, and/or method"); Blazy
v. Tenet, 979 F. Supp. 10, 23 (D.D.C. 1997) (finding that former CIA employee's polygraphs constitute "intelligence method") (Exemptions 1 and 3) (decided under Executive Order 12,356), summary affirmance granted, No. 97-
5330, 1998 WL 315583 (D.C. Cir. May 12, 1998); cf. Schrecker v. U.S. Dep't of
Justice, 14 F. Supp. 2d 111, 117-18 (D.D.C. 1998) (observing that identities
of intelligence sources are protectible pursuant to Exemption 1 regardless
of whether individuals are alive or deceased), summary judgment granted,
74 F. Supp. 2d 26 (D.D.C. 1999), aff'd, 254 F.3d 162 (D.C. Cir. 2001).

[124] See McDonnell v. United States, 4 F.3d 1227, 1244 (3d Cir. 1993) (upholding classification of cryptographic information dating back to 1934
when release "could enable hostile entities to interpret other, more sensitive documents similarly encoded") (decided under Executive Order
12,356); Gilmore v. NSA, No. C92-3646, 1993 U.S. Dist. LEXIS 7694, at *18-
19, *22-23 (N.D. Cal. May 3, 1993) (finding mathematical principles and
techniques in agency treatise protectible under this executive order
category) (decided under Executive Order 12,356).

sources;[125]

    (6) military plans, weapons, or operations;[126]

---

[125] See, e.g., Bassiouni, 392 F.3d at 246 (observing that "[e]ven allies could be unpleasantly surprised" by disclosure of CIA espionage information involving one of its citizens); Wheeler v. U.S. Dep't of Justice, 403 F. Supp. 2d 1, 12 (D.D.C. 2005) (holding that "foreign relations between Cuba and the United States remain tenuous at best," and that it would follow that information about persons in Cuba who provided information to the United States could still be very dangerous and, if disclosed, result in "embarrassment or imprisonment, if not death"); ACLU v. DOD, 389 F. Supp. 2d 547, 561 (S.D.N.Y. 2005) (reasoning that "even if the only question was whether to recognize officially that which was informally or unofficially believed to exist, the niceties of international diplomacy sometimes make it important not to embarrass a foreign country or its leaders, and exemptions from FOIA protect that concern as well"); Wolf v. CIA, 357 F. Supp. 2d 112, 116 (D.D.C. 2004) (reasoning that the fact of the CIA's covert interest in a foreign citizen "could adversely affect relations with a foreign government because that government might believe that the CIA has collected intelligence information on or recruited one of its citizens or resident aliens"), aff'd in pertinent part & remanded on other grounds, 473 F.3d 370, 377-80 (D.C. Cir. 2007); Springmann v. U.S. Dep't of State, No. 93-1238, slip op. at 2-3 (D.D.C. Feb. 24, 2000) (accepting agency's judgment that disclosure of information about American employees' religiously offensive behavior in Saudi Arabia would adversely affect relations between United States and that country) (decided under original version of Executive Order 12,958); Linn v. U.S. Dep't of Justice, No. 92-1406, 1995 WL 631847, at *26 (D.D.C. Aug. 22, 1995) (finding Exemption 1 withholdings proper because the agency demonstrated that it has "a present understanding" with the foreign government that any shared information will not be disclosed) (decided under Executive Order 12,356); U.S. Comm. for Refugees v. Dep't of State, No. 91-3303, 1993 WL 364674, at *2 (D.D.C. Aug. 30, 1993) (holding that disclosure of withheld information could damage nation's foreign policy by jeopardizing success of negotiations with Haiti on refugee issues "[because] documents contain . . . frank assessments about the Haitian government") (decided under Executive Order 12,356); Van Atta v. Def. Intelligence Agency, No. 87-1508, 1988 WL 73856, at *2 (D.D.C. July 6, 1988) (protecting information compiled at request of foreign government for purpose of negotiations) (decided under Executive Order 12,356). But see Keenan v. Dep't of Justice, No. 94-1909, slip op. at 9-11 (D.D.C. Dec. 16, 1997) (ordering release of document segments withheld by the agency pursuant to Exemption 1, because the agency failed to show that the foreign governments named in documents more than thirty years old "still wish to maintain the secrecy of their cooperative efforts with" U.S.).

[126] See, e.g., Taylor v. Dep't of the Army, 684 F.2d 99, 109 (D.C. Cir. 1982) (protecting combat-ready troop assessments) (decided under Executive Order 12,065); Tawalbeh v. U.S. Dep't of the Air Force, No. 96-6241, slip op. at
(continued...)

EXEMPTION 1

(7) scientific, technological, or economic matters relating to national security;[127] and

(8) government programs for safeguarding nuclear materials and facilities.[128]

The amendment of Executive Order 12,958 also added a new classification category protecting information concerning "weapons of mass destruction,"[129] and it further expanded two previously existing categories to in-

---

[126](...continued)
10-11 (C.D. Cal. Aug. 8, 1997) (protecting information about military readiness and operational security related to operations Desert Shield and Desert Storm) (decided under original version of Executive Order 12,958); Pub. Educ. Ctr., 905 F. Supp. at 21 (protecting videotapes made during U.S. military action in Somalia) (decided under Executive Order 12,356); Wash. Post Co. v. DOD, No. 84-2403, slip op. at 3 (D.D.C. Apr. 15, 1988) (protecting foreign military information) (decided under Executive Order 12,356); Hudson River Sloop Clearwater, Inc. v. Dep't of the Navy, 891 F.2d 414, 417 (2d Cir. 1989) (concluding that refusal to confirm or deny presence of nuclear weapons aboard warships in homeports under the FOIA does not conflict with requirements of National Environmental Policy Act of 1969, 42 U.S.C. § 4321 (2000), that agencies consider environmental impact) (decided under Executive Order 12,356).

[127] See Exec. Order No. 12,958, as amended, § 1.4(e).

[128] See id. § 1.4(f); see, e.g., Weinberger v. Catholic Action of Haw., 454 U.S. 139, 144-45 (1981) (protecting "information relating to the storage of nuclear weapons"); Abbots v. NRC, 766 F.2d 604, 607 (D.C. Cir. 1985) (protecting "the NRC's determination as to the number of attackers a nuclear facility should be able to defend against successfully," because release of this information would allow potential attackers to "compute the size of the assault force needed for optimum results") (decided under Executive Order 12,356); Loomis v. U.S. Dep't of Energy, No. 96-149, 1999 WL 33541935, at *6 (N.D.N.Y. Mar. 9, 1999) (protecting nuclear containment layout plan and referenced document on propagation of radiological requirements and procedures) (decided under original version of Executive Order 12,958), summary affirmance granted, 21 F. App'x 80 (2d Cir. 2001).

[129] See Exec. Order No. 12,958, as amended, § 1.4(h); see also White House Memorandum for Heads of Executive Departments and Agencies Concerning Safeguarding Information Regarding Weapons of Mass Destruction and Other Sensitive Documents Related to Homeland Security [hereinafter White House Homeland Security Memorandum] (Mar. 19, 2002), reprinted in FOIA Post (posted 3/21/02) (emphasizing "obligation to safeguard" homeland security-related records).

clude information regarding "defense against transnational terrorism."[130]

Under the original version of Executive Order 12,958, there was no presumption that disclosure of information in any of the above categories could harm national security; hence, there was no presumption that such information is classified.[131] However, Executive Order 12,958, as amended, established a presumption of harm to national security from the release of information provided by or related to foreign governments.[132]

The addition of this presumption of harm might ultimately help to resolve a conflict between two decisions in the District Court for the District of Columbia, in which two judges took opposing views as to what agencies must demonstrate to protect national security-related information exchanged with foreign governments.[133] In the first case, in which the agency's Vaughn Index contained no indication of an explicit promise of confidentiality between the agency and the foreign government, the court ordered the FBI to "disclose the circumstances from which it deduces, and from which the court might as well, that the information was shared in confidence."[134] Using the relatively stringent standard for the protection of foreign government information that is applied to the protection of confidential informants in the law enforcement context,[135] the court required the government to fully explain the circumstances from which confidentiality is inferred.[136] It imposed this burden despite the fact that this case was decided under Executive Order 12,356, which, like the amended Executive

---

[130] See Exec. Order No. 12,958, as amended, § 1.4(e), (g); see also id. § 1.1(a)(4) (incorporating "defense against transnational terrorism" into classification standards).

[131] See Exec. Order No. 12,958, § 1.5, 3 C.F.R. 333 (1996), reprinted in 50 U.S.C. § 435 note and reprinted in abridged form in FOIA Update, Vol. XVI, No. 2, at 5-10.

[132] See Exec. Order No. 12,958, as amended, § 1.1(c).

[133] Compare Steinberg v. U.S. Dep't of Justice, 179 F.R.D. 357, 362-63 (D.D.C. 1998) (ordering FBI to submit further evidence to support confidentiality claim), with Billington v. Dep't of Justice, 11 F. Supp. 2d 45, 54-56 (D.D.C. 1998) (finding agency not required to demonstrate explicit confidentiality understanding), summary judgment granted in pertinent part, 69 F. Supp. 2d 128 (D.D.C. 1999), aff'd in part, vacated in part & remanded all on other grounds, 233 F.3d 581 (D.C. Cir. 2000) (Exemption 1 decision not challenged on appeal).

[134] Steinberg, 179 F.R.D. at 362-63.

[135] See U.S. Dep't of Justice v. Landano, 508 U.S. 165, 179 (1993) (requiring law enforcement agencies to demonstrate confidentiality basis for protecting law enforcement informants).

[136] Steinberg, 179 F.R.D. at 362.

Order 12,958, instructed agencies to presume harm to the national security in releasing foreign government information.[137] The court subsequently granted the FBI's motion for summary judgment based upon the agency's supplemental affidavit -- which demonstrated that the FBI's relationship with the foreign government was based on an express understanding of confidentiality.[138]

In the second case, the court specifically rejected the requester's argument that, in order to qualify for Exemption 1 protection, the agency's affidavit must demonstrate that there were explicit understandings of confidentiality between the agency and the foreign government regarding the information at issue.[139] In the court's view, "to compel the agency to supply more information would muddle the purpose of the exemption."[140] The court found no similarity between the protection of foreign government information for national security reasons and the protection of confidential informants in the law enforcement context.[141] It ruled that the government was not required to provide evidence of either an explicit or implicit confidentiality understanding with the foreign government, despite the fact that the information was classified under the original version of Executive Order 12,958, which did <u>not</u> permit agencies to presume harm to national security from the release of foreign government information.[142]

With the addition of a presumption of harm in the amended Executive Order 12,958, it now can be anticipated that future such decisions will adopt the latter court's view for the protection of foreign government information.[143] This latter view also corresponds more closely to the deferential approach that courts ordinarily take when reviewing cases involving Exemption 1. (For further discussions of the appropriate judicial standard in evaluating Exemption 1 claims, see Exemption 1, Standard of Review, above, and Exemption 1, Deference to Agency Expertise, above.)

As with prior orders, the amended Executive Order 12,958 contains a

---

[137] Exec. Order No. 12,356, § 1.3(c), 3 C.F.R. 166 (1983), excerpted in FOIA Update, Vol. III, No. 3, at 6.

[138] Steinberg, 179 F.R.D. at 368-69.

[139] See Billington, 11 F. Supp. 2d at 57-58.

[140] Id.

[141] Id. at 57.

[142] Id.

[143] But see Wiener v. FBI, No. 83-1720, slip op. at 9 (C.D. Cal. Sept. 27, 2004) (determining that "the FBI cannot merely rely on a foreign government request for confidentiality to justify non-disclosure"), reconsideration denied (C.D. Cal. Aug. 25, 2005).

number of distinct limitations on classification.[144] Specifically, information may not be classified in order to:

(1) conceal violations of law, inefficiency, or administrative error;[145]

(2) prevent embarrassment to a person, organization, or agency;[146]

(3) restrain competition;[147]

(4) prevent or delay the disclosure of information that does not require national security protection;[148] or

(5) protect basic scientific research not clearly related to the national

---

[144] Exec. Order No. 12,958, as amended, § 1.7.

[145] Id. § 1.7(a)(1); see also Billington, 11 F. Supp. 2d at 57-58 (dismissing plaintiff's "unsubstantiated accusations" that information should be disclosed because FBI engaged in illegal "dirty tricks" campaign); Computer Prof'ls for Soc. Responsibility v. Nat'l Inst. of Standards & Tech., No. 92-0972, slip op. at 1-2 (D.D.C. Apr. 11, 1994) (finding no basis to conclude that NSA improperly classified computer security guidelines in violation of law to "conceal its role" in developing such guidelines) (decided under Executive Order 12,356), summary affirmance granted, No. 94-5153, 1995 WL 66803, at *1 (D.C. Cir. Jan. 13, 1995); cf. NARA v. Favish, 541 U.S. 157, 174 (reminding that "[a]llegations of government misconduct are 'easy to allege and hard to disprove'" (quoting Crawford-El v. Britton, 523 U.S. 574, 585 (1998)) (Exemption 7(C) case)), reh'g denied, 541 U.S. 1057 (2004).

[146] Exec. Order No. 12,958, as amended, § 1.7(a)(2); see also Billington, 11 F. Supp. 2d at 58-59 (rejecting plaintiff's argument that information was classified by FBI to shield agency and foreign government from embarrassment); Canning v. U.S. Dep't of Justice, 848 F. Supp. 1037, 1047-48 (D.D.C. 1994) (finding no credible evidence that the FBI improperly withheld information to conceal the existence of "potentially inappropriate investigation" of a French citizen, and noting that "if anything, the agency released sufficient information to facilitate such speculation") (decided under Executive Order 12,356); Wilson v. Dep't of Justice, No. 87-2415, 1991 WL 111457, at *2 (D.D.C. June 13, 1991) (rejecting requester's unsupported claim that information at issue was classified in order to prevent embarrassment to foreign government official, and holding that "even if some . . . information . . . were embarrassing to Egyptian officials, it would nonetheless be covered by Exemption 1 if, independent of any desire to avoid embarrassment, the information withheld [was] properly classified") (decided under Executive Order 12,356).

[147] Exec. Order No. 12,958, as amended, § 1.7(a)(3).

[148] Id. § 1.7(a)(4).

EXEMPTION 1

security.[149]

Additionally, the amendment of Executive Order 12,958 removed the requirement in the original version of the order that agencies not classify information if there is "significant doubt" about the national security harm.[150]

Following the amendment of Executive Order 12,958, and subject to strict conditions, agencies may reclassify information after it has been declassified and released to the public.[151] The action must be taken under the "personal authority of the agency head or deputy agency head," who must determine in writing that the reclassification is necessary to protect national security.[152] Further, the information previously declassified and released must be "reasonably recovered" by the agency from all public holders, and it must be withdrawn from public access in archives and reading rooms.[153] Finally, the agency head or deputy agency head must report any agency reclassification action to the Director of the Information Security Oversight Office within thirty days, along with a description of the agency's recovery efforts, the number of public holders of the information, and the agency's efforts to brief any such public holders.[154] Similarly, the amended Executive Order 12,958 also authorizes the classification of a record after an agency has received a FOIA request for it, although such belated classification is permitted only through the "personal participation" of designated high-level officials and only on a "document-by-document ba-

---

[149] Id. § 1.7(b); see also White House Homeland Security Memorandum, reprinted in FOIA Post (posted 3/21/02) (directing agencies to review procedures for safeguarding information concerning "chemical, biological, radiological, and nuclear weapons, but at the same time emphasizing that "the need to protect such sensitive information from inappropriate disclosure should be carefully considered, on a case-by-case basis, together with the benefits that result from the open and efficient exchange of scientific, technical, and like information").

[150] Compare Exec. Order No. 12,958, as amended, § 1.1 (current version), with Exec. Order No. 12,958, § 1.2(b) (original version).

[151] See Exec. Order No. 12,958, as amended, § 1.7(c); see also Exec. Order No. 12,356, § 1.6(c).

[152] Exec. Order No. 12,958, as amended, § 1.7(c)(1); see also 32 C.F.R. § 2001.13(a) (2006) (directive issued by Information Security Oversight Office describing procedures for reclassifying information pursuant to section 1.7(c) of Executive Order 12,958, as amended).

[153] Exec. Order No. 12,958, as amended, § 1.7(c)(2); see also 32 C.F.R. § 2001.13(a)(1).

[154] Exec. Order No. 12,958, as amended, § 1.7(c)(3); see also 32 C.F.R. § 2001.13(b).

sis."[155] (For a further discussion of official disclosure, see Exemption 1, Waiver of Exemption Protection, above, and Discretionary Disclosure and Waiver, below.)

Executive Order 12,958, as amended, also contains a provision establishing a mechanism through which classification determinations can be challenged within the federal government.[156] Under this provision, "authorized holders of information" -- individuals who are authorized to have access to such information -- who, in good faith, believe that its classification is improper are "encouraged and expected" to challenge that classification.[157] Furthermore, agencies are required to set up internal procedures to implement this program, in order to ensure that holders are able to make such challenges without fear of retribution and that the information in question is reviewed by an impartial official or panel.[158] Additionally, an agency head or designee may authorize an "emergency" disclosure of information to individuals who are not eligible for access to classified infor-

---

[155] Exec. Order No. 12,958, as amended, § 1.7(d); see also 32 C.F.R. § 2001.13(a); see, e.g., Pub. Citizen v. Dep't of State, 100 F. Supp. 2d 10, 26 (D.D.C. 2000) (finding that agency official had "power to classify documents" following receipt of FOIA request) (decided under original version of Executive Order 12,958), aff'd on other grounds, 276 F.3d 674 (D.C. Cir. 2002); Council for a Livable World v. U.S. Dep't of State, No. 96-1807, slip op. at 8-9 (D.D.C. Nov. 23, 1998) (ordering disclosure of documents where agency official did not have special classification authority under section 1.8(d) of Executive Order 12,958 and did not take classification action under direction of official with such authority) (decided under original version of Executive Order 12,958), summary judgment granted (D.D.C. June 27, 2000), case dismissed (D.D.C. Aug. 22, 2000) (upholding Exemption 1 claim and dismissing case following classification of records by different agency official with proper authority and subsequent submission of further declaration); see also White House Homeland Security Memorandum, reprinted in FOIA Post (posted 3/21/02) (directing heads of federal departments and agencies to ensure appropriate protection of sensitive homeland security-related information; distributing implementing guidance, in attached memorandum from Information Security Oversight Office and Office of Information and Privacy, to effect that such information should be classified or reclassified pursuant to requirements of section 1.8(d) (now 1.7(d)) of Executive Order 12,958, as appropriate, if it has been subject of prior access request).

[156] Exec. Order No. 12,958, as amended, § 1.8.

[157] Id. § 1.8(a).

[158] See id. § 1.8(b); see also id. § 5.3(b) (authorizing Interagency Security Classification Appeals Panel to "decide on [sic] appeals by persons who have filed classification challenges"); 32 C.F.R. § 2001.14 (directive issued by Information Security Oversight Office describing procedures that agencies must establish in order to consider classification challenges).

EXEMPTION 1

mation, as may be necessary under exceptional circumstances "to respond to an imminent threat to life or in defense of the homeland."[159]

In addition to satisfying the substantive criteria outlined in the applicable executive order, information also must adhere to the order's procedural requirements to qualify for Exemption 1 protection.[160] In other words, the information has to be more than "classifiable" under the executive order -- it has to be actually classified under the order.[161] This requirement recognizes that proper classification is actually a review process to identify potential harm to national security.[162] Executive Order 12,958, as amended, prescribes the current procedural requirements that agencies must employ.[163] These requirements include such matters as the proper markings to be applied to classified documents,[164] as well as the manner in which

---

[159] See Exec. Order No. 12,958, as amended, § 4.2(b) (providing that an emergency disclosure does not constitute declassification); see also 32 C.F.R. § 2001.51 (describing transmission and reporting procedures for disclosure "in emergency situations, in which there is an imminent threat to life or in defense of the homeland").

[160] See, e.g., Assassination Archives & Research Ctr. v. CIA, 177 F. Supp. 2d 1, 8 (D.D.C. 2001) (finding that CIA properly classified subject records under procedures outlined in Executive Order 10,501, which was in force when classification decision was made), aff'd, 334 F.2d 55 (D.C. Cir. 2003); Tawalbeh, No. 96-6241, slip op. at 9 (C.D. Cal. Aug. 8, 1997) (ruling that classification procedures set forth in Executive Order 12,958 properly applied); Canning, 848 F. Supp. at 1048-49 (finding that agency adhered to appropriate classification procedures established by Executive Order 12,356).

[161] See, e.g., Exec. Order No. 12,958, as amended, §§ 1.1-.4, 1.6; see also 32 C.F.R. § 2001.10-.11, .20-.21, .23.

[162] See, e.g., Hayden v. NSA, 608 F.2d 1381, 1386-87 (D.C. Cir. 1979) (finding that information must have been classified according to procedures outlined in national security classification executive order); Peltier v. FBI, No. 02-4328, slip op. at 12, 15 (D. Minn. Oct. 24, 2006) (magistrate's recommendation) (same), adopted (D. Minn. Feb. 9, 2007); Riquelme v. CIA, No. 02-2382, 2006 U.S. Dist. LEXIS 70992, at *12 (D.D.C. Sept. 29, 2006) (same).

[163] See, e.g., Exec. Order No. 12,958, as amended, §§ 1.5, 1.6, 2.1; see also 32 C.F.R. § 2001.20-.24.

[164] See Exec. Order No. 12,958, as amended, § 1.6; see also Cohen v. FBI, No. 93-1701, slip op. at 5-6 (D.D.C. Oct. 11, 1994) (rejecting plaintiff's argument that subsequent marking of two documents during agency's second classification review rendered FBI's classification action ineffective; to require agencies "to perform every classification review perfectly on the first attempt" would be "a very strict and unforgiving standard") (decided under
(continued...)

agencies designate officials to classify information in the first instance.[165]

Regarding proper national security markings, Executive Order 12,958, as amended, requires that each classified document be marked with the appropriate classification level,[166] the identity of the original classification authority,[167] the identity of the agency and office classifying the document,[168] as well as with "a concise reason for classification" that cites the applicable classification category or categories.[169] It also requires that a date or event for declassification be specified on the document.[170] In addition, amended Executive Order 12,958 requires agencies to use portion markings to indicate levels of classification within documents,[171] and it advocates the use of classified addenda in cases in which classified informa-

---

[164](...continued)
Executive Order 12,356).

[165] See Exec. Order No. 12,958, as amended, § 1.3; see, e.g., Presidential Order of Sept. 17, 2003, 68 Fed. Reg. 55,257 (Sept. 17, 2003), reprinted in 50 U.S.C. § 435 note (granting classification authority to Director of Office of Science and Technology Policy); Exec. Order No. 13,284, § 20, 68 Fed. Reg. 4075 (Jan. 23, 2003) (granting classification authority to Secretary of Homeland Security); Presidential Order of Sept. 26, 2002, 67 Fed. Reg. 61,463 (Sept. 26, 2002), reprinted in 50 U.S.C. § 435 note (granting classification authority to Secretary of Agriculture); Presidential Order of May 6, 2002, 67 Fed. Reg. 31,109 (May 6, 2002), reprinted in 50 U.S.C. § 435 note (granting classification authority to Administrator of Environmental Protection Agency); Presidential Order of Dec. 10, 2001, 66 Fed. Reg. 64,347 (Dec. 10, 2001), reprinted in 50 U.S.C. § 435 note (granting classification authority to Secretary of Health and Human Services); Presidential Order of Oct. 13, 1995, 3 C.F.R. 513 (1996), reprinted in 50 U.S.C. § 435 note (designating those executive branch officials who are authorized to classify national security information under Executive Order 12,958 in first instance).

[166] See Exec. Order No. 12,958, as amended, § 1.6(a)(1); see also id. § 1.2 (directing that information may be classified at: (1) the "Top Secret" level, when disclosure could be expected to cause "exceptionally grave damage" to the national security; (2) the "Secret" level, when disclosure could be expected to cause "serious damage" to the national security; and (3) the "Confidential" level, when disclosure could be expected to cause "damage" to the national security).

[167] Id. § 1.6(a)(2).

[168] Id. § 1.6(a)(3).

[169] Id. § 1.6(a)(5).

[170] Id. § 1.6(a)(4).

[171] Id. § 1.6(c) (specifying that only Director of ISOO is authorized to grant portion-marking waivers).

tion comprises only "a small portion of an otherwise unclassified document."[172] The Information Security Oversight Office (ISOO) has issued governmentwide guidelines on these marking requirements.[173]

Executive Order 12,958 also establishes a government entity to provide oversight of agencies' classification determinations and their implementation of the order. The Interagency Security Classification Appeals Panel consists of senior-level representatives of the Secretaries of State and Defense, the Attorney General, the Director of Central Intelligence, the Archivist of the United States, and the Assistant to the President for National Security Affairs.[174] Among other things, this body adjudicates classification challenges filed by agency employees and decides appeals from persons who have filed requests under the mandatory declassification review provisions of the order.[175]

Agencies with questions about the proper implementation of the substantive or procedural requirements of Executive Order 12,958, as amended, may consult with the Information Security Oversight Office, located within the National Archives and Records Administration, at (202) 357-5259, which holds governmentwide oversight responsibility for classification matters under the executive order.[176]

### Duration of Classification and Declassification

Other important provisions of amended Executive Order 12,958 are those that establish (1) limitations on the length of time information may

---

[172] Id. § 1.6(g).

[173] See 32 C.F.R. § 2001.20-.24 (ISOO directive providing detailed guidance on identification and marking requirements of amended Executive Order 12,958).

[174] See Exec. Order No. 12,958, as amended, § 5.3(a)(1); see also 32 C.F.R. pt. 2001 app. A (bylaws of Interagency Security Classification Appeals Panel); see also FOIA Post, "FOIA Officers Conference Held on Homeland Security" (posted 7/3/03) (referring to Chairman of Interagency Security Classification Appeals Panel).

[175] See Exec. Order No. 12,958, as amended, § 5.3(b); see also id. § 3.5 (establishing mandatory declassification review program as non-FOIA mechanism for persons to seek access to classified information generated or maintained by agencies, including papers maintained by presidential libraries not yet accessible under FOIA).

[176] See id. § 5.2; see also FOIA Update, Vol. XVI, No. 2, at 15 (describing responsibilities of ISOO Director under original version of Executive Order 12,958); FOIA Update, Vol. VI, No. 1, at 1-2 (describing responsibilities of ISOO under Executive Order 12,356).

remain classified,[177] and (2) procedures for the declassification of older government information.[178] The order requires agencies to "attempt to establish a specific date or event for declassification based upon the duration of the national security sensitivity."[179] The order also limits the duration of classification to no longer than is necessary in order to protect national security.[180] If the agency is unable to determine a date or event that will trigger declassification, however, then amended Executive Order 12,958 instructs the original classification authority to set a ten-year limit on new classification actions.[181] The classification authority alternatively may determine that the sensitivity of the information justifies classification for a period of twenty-five years.[182]

The amendment of Executive Order 12,958 also continues the automatic declassification mechanism that was established by the original version of the order in 1995.[183] Upon implementation of the first provision of that automatic declassification mechanism on December 31, 2006,[184] Executive Order 12,958 required the automatic declassification of information that is more than twenty-five years old,[185] with exceptions limited to

---

[177] Exec. Order No. 12,958, as amended, § 1.5, 68 Fed. Reg. 15,315 (Mar. 28, 2003), reprinted in 50 U.S.C. § 435 note (2000 & Supp. III 2003) and summarized in FOIA Post (posted 4/11/03).

[178] See id. § 3.3.

[179] Id. § 1.5(a).

[180] See id.; see also 32 C.F.R. § 2001.12(a)(1) (2006) (establishing guidelines for the duration of the classification, and requiring that a "classification authority shall attempt to determine a date or event that is less than ten years from the date of the original classification and which coincides with the lapse of the information's national security sensitivity"); Information Security Oversight Office Ann. Rep. 6 (2003) (noting that "one of the principal procedures for maintaining the effectiveness of the classification system is to remove from the safeguarding system information that no longer requires protection").

[181] Exec. Order No. 12,958, as amended, § 1.5(b); see also 32 C.F.R. § 2001.12(a)(1).

[182] Exec. Order No. 12,958, as amended, § 1.5(b).

[183] Compare Exec. Order No. 12,958, as amended, § 3.3 (current version), with Exec. Order No. 12,958, § 3.4 (original version).

[184] See Exec. Order No. 12,958, as amended, § 3.3(a) (establishing December 31, 2006 as deadline for automatic declassification).

[185] Id. (applying twenty-five-year rule to classified information determined by Archivist of the United States to have "permanent historical value");

(continued...)

especially sensitive information designated as such by the heads of agencies.[186] These exceptions serve to narrow the categories of information that may be classified beyond twenty-five years.[187] As with an original classification decision, the application of these exceptions to automatic declassification requires a thorough review of the continued sensitivity of the information by an official with the expertise to make such determinations of national security harm.[188] This declassification mechanism did not exist under previous orders,[189] and its implementation certainly has taken longer than was originally anticipated.

Indeed, the original effective date for the automatic declassification mechanism under the original version of Executive Order 12,958 was October 17, 2001.[190] For certain identified records, however, the effective date for automatic declassification was extended to April 17, 2003 by Executive

---

[185](...continued)
see also 32 C.F.R. § 2001.30 (Information Security Oversight Office directive explaining requirements of automatic declassification program).

[186] Exec. Order No. 12,958, as amended, § 3.3(b) (specifying categories of sensitive information qualifying for exception to twenty-five-year rule); see also id. § 3.3(c), (d) (specifying manner in which agencies are to notify President of, and receive approval for, exceptions to automatic declassification for specific file series); White House Homeland Security Memorandum (directing heads of federal departments and agencies to ensure appropriate protection of sensitive homeland security-related information; distributing implementing guidance, in attached memorandum, to effect that such information should be exempted from automatic declassification).

[187] Compare Exec. Order No. 12,958, as amended, § 1.4(a)-(h), with Exec. Order No. 12,958, as amended, § 3.3(b)(1)-(9).

[188] Exec. Order No. 12,958, as amended, §§ 2.2(b), 3.3(b); see also 32 C.F.R. § 2001.21(e), 2001.32(a).

[189] Compare Exec. Order No. 12,958, § 3.4(a) (mandating automatic declassification for twenty-five-year-old information), with Exec. Order No. 12,356, § 3.1(a) (specifying that passage of time alone does not compel declassification); see also Exec. Order No. 12,936, 3 C.F.R. 949 (1994) (separate executive order issued by President Clinton automatically declassifying millions of pages of old records held by NARA). But see 50 U.S.C. § 435 note (requiring Secretary of Energy and Archivist of the United States to ensure that information concerning atomic weapons and special nuclear material is not inadvertently released during automatic declassification of voluminous records under original version of Executive Order 12,958).

[190] Exec. Order No. 13,142, § 1, 64 Fed. Reg. 66089 (Nov. 23, 1999) (extending automatic declassification deadline).

Order 13,142.[191] The amended Executive Order 12,958 further extended the deadline for automatic declassification to December 31, 2006, in order to allow government agencies additional time to properly review millions of pages of classified materials.[192] The amended Executive Order provided that on that date, all classified records containing the equities of a single agency only -- i.e., those not requiring referral to another agency for an equity review -- that are more than twenty-five years old, and have been determined to have permanent historical value, were automatically declassified even if those records have not yet been reviewed for declassification.[193] On the other hand, it specifically grants agencies an additional three years, until December 31, 2009, to review referrals sent from other agencies for declassification review.[194] And it further provides that "special media information" -- such as, microfilm, electronic records, and audiotape and videotape materials -- is to be processed for automatic declassification by December 31, 2011.[195] Notably, in addressing automatic declassification, courts have refused to order disclosure of information more than twenty-five years old until the applicable automatic disclosure provision takes effect.[196]

The automatic declassification mechanism applies to information currently classified under any predecessor executive order[197] and is intended to ultimately lead to the creation of a governmentwide declassification database within the National Archives and Records Administration.[198] For

---

[191] See id. § 2 (specifying that April 17, 2003, deadline pertains to "records otherwise subject to this paragraph for which a review or assessment conducted by the agency and confirmed by the Information Security Oversight Office has determined that they: (1) contain information that was created by or is under the control of more than one agency, or (2) are within file series containing information that almost invariably pertains to intelligence sources or methods").

[192] Exec. Order No. 12,958, as amended, § 3.3(a).

[193] Id.

[194] Id. at § 3.3(e)(3).

[195] Id. at § 3.3(e)(2).

[196] See Schrecker v. U.S. Dep't of Justice, 74 F. Supp. 2d 26, 30 (D.D.C. 1999), aff'd on other grounds, 254 F.3d 162 (D.C. Cir. 2001); Billington v. Dep't of Justice, 69 F. Supp. 2d 128, 134 (D.D.C. 1999), aff'd in part, vacated in part & remanded all on other grounds, 233 F.3d 581 (D.C. Cir. 2000) (Exemption 1 determination not challenged on appeal); Hall v. U.S. Dep't of Justice, 26 F. Supp. 2d 78, 80 (D.D.C. 1998).

[197] See Exec. Order No. 12,958, as amended, § 3.3(a).

[198] See id. § 3.7 (directing Archivist to establish database of information

(continued...)

records that fall within any exception to amended Executive Order 12,958's automatic declassification mechanism, agencies are required to establish "a program for systematic declassification review" that focuses on any need for continued classification of such records.[199] In his 2005 Report to the President, the Director of the Information Security Oversight Office suggested "key elements of a better way" to handle declassification and noted that "challenges for full implementation by December 31, 2009, remain."[200]

As did prior executive orders, amended Executive Order 12,958 provides for a "mandatory declassification review" program.[201] This mechanism allows any person -- entirely apart from the FOIA context -- to request that an agency review its national security records for declassification.[202] Traditionally, the mandatory declassification review program has been used by researchers interested in gaining access to papers maintained by presidential libraries, some of which are not accessible under the FOIA; under this provision, however, any person may submit a mandatory review request to an agency.[203] Unlike under the FOIA, though, such requesters do not have the right to judicial review of the agency's action.[204] Instead, amended Executive Order 12,958 authorizes persons to appeal an agency's final decision under this program to the Interagency Security Classification Appeals Panel.[205] To alleviate some of the burden of this program, Executive Order 12,958 contains a provision that allows an agency to deny a mandatory review request if it has already reviewed the information for declassification within the past two years.[206]

For declassification decisions, amended Executive Order 12,958 authorizes agencies to apply a balancing test -- i.e., to determine "whether

---

[198](...continued) that has been declassified by agencies, and instructing agency heads to cooperate in this governmentwide effort).

[199] Id. § 3.4(a).

[200] See Information Security Oversight Office Ann. Rep. 1, 3 (2005) (commenting generally on the executive branch's efforts to meet the automatic declassification deadline).

[201] Id. § 3.5.

[202] See id.

[203] See id.

[204] Id.; cf. Miller v. Casey, 730 F.2d 773, 778 (D.C. Cir. 1984) (refusing to review CIA decision to deny access to records under agency's discretionary "historical research program").

[205] See Exec. Order No. 12,958, as amended, § 3.5(b)(4), (d).

[206] Id. § 3.5(a)(3).

the public interest in disclosure outweighs the damage to national security that might reasonably be expected from disclosure."[207] Though Executive Order 12,958, as amended, specifies that this provision is implemented solely as a matter of administrative discretion and creates no new right of judicial review, it is significant that no such provision existed under prior orders.[208] Although a few courts have attempted to apply the balancing test to the review of classification decisions in litigation,[209] most have firmly held that national security officials are responsible for applying this balancing test at the time of the original classification decision, and that these officials logically are in the best position to weigh the public interest in disclosure against the threat to national security.[210]

It is worth noting in this regard that government policy on national security classification receives even greater attention and scrutiny during times of crisis -- often focused on the inherent tension between national security and open government.[211] In his 2005 Report to the President, the Director of the Information Security Oversight Office reiterated his belief that a "responsible security classification system and a committed declassification program are the cornerstones of an open and efficient government that serves to protect and inform its citizens" and require "diligence and integrity with regard to the American ideals of providing for our national security

---

[207] Id. § 3.1(b).

[208] See FOIA Update, Vol. XVI, No. 2, at 11 (chart comparing provisions of original version of Executive Order 12,958 with those of predecessor Executive Order 12,356).

[209] See, e.g., L.A. Times Commc'ns, LLC v. Dep't of the Army, No. CV 05-8293, 2006 WL 2336457, at *18 (C.D. Cal. July 24, 2006) (explaining that the court was attempting to achieve the "balance Congress sought to preserve between the public's right to know and the government's legitimate interest in keeping certain information confidential").

[210] See, e.g., ACLU v. U.S. Dep't of Justice, 265 F. Supp. 2d 20, 32 (D.D.C. 2003) (holding that even a "significant and entirely legitimate" public desire to view classified information "simply does not, in an Exemption 1 case, alter the analysis"); Kelly v. CIA, No. 00-2498, slip op. at 15 (D.D.C. Aug. 8, 2002) (observing that agency should factor in public interest at time that classification decision is made, and further noting that requester's asserted public interest in disclosure of requested information will not undermine proper classification because it certainly is in public interest to withhold information that would damage national security), modified in other respects, No. 00-2498, slip op. at 1 (D.D.C. Sept. 25, 2002), appeal on adequacy of search dismissed on procedural grounds, No. 02-5384, 2003 WL 21804101 (D.C. Cir. July 31, 2003).

[211] See, e.g., Information Security Oversight Office Ann. Rep. 2 (2003) (commenting on tension between informing and protecting American public and noting that classification system "is designed to promote" both).

**EXEMPTION 1**

within the context of a free and open society."[212]

### Additional Considerations

Two additional considerations addressed initially by the original version of Executive Order 12,958, and then continued in the amended version, have already been recognized by the courts. First, the "Glomar" response is explicitly incorporated into the order: "An agency may refuse to confirm or deny the existence or nonexistence of requested records whenever the very fact of their existence or nonexistence is itself classified under this order."[213] (For a further discussion of this point, see Exemption 1, In Camera Submissions, above.)

Second, the "mosaic" or "compilation" approach -- the concept that apparently harmless pieces of information, when assembled together, could reveal a damaging picture -- is recognized in amended Executive Order 12,958.[214] It is also a concept that has been widely recognized by courts in Exemption 1 cases.[215] Compilations of otherwise unclassified information

---

[212] See Information Security Oversight Office Ann. Rep. 1, 3 (2005).

[213] Exec. Order No. 12,958, as amended, § 3.6(a), 68 Fed. Reg. 15,315 (Mar. 28, 2003), reprinted in 50 U.S.C. § 435 note (2000 & Supp. III 2003) and summarized in FOIA Post (posted 4/11/03); see also Hogan v. Huff, No. 00-6753, 2002 WL 1359722, at *7 (S.D.N.Y. June, 21, 2002) (ruling that the executive order "authorizes agencies to refuse to confirm or deny the existence or non-existence of requested information whenever the fact of its existence is itself classified") (decided under original version of Executive Order 12,958).

[214] See Exec. Order No. 12,958, as amended, § 1.7(e).

[215] See Edmonds v. U.S. Dep't of Justice, 405 F. Supp. 2d 23, 33 (D.D.C. 2005) (upholding the agency's mosaic argument, and finding that it "comports with the legal framework"); Berman v. CIA, 378 F. Supp. 2d 1209, 1215-17 (E.D. Cal. 2005) (observing that "numerous courts have recognized the legitimacy of the mosaic theory in the context of the FOIA," and holding that CIA's Presidential Daily Briefs could fairly be viewed as "an especially large piece of the 'mosaic' because it is the only finished intelligence product that synthesizes all of the best available intelligence" for the President (citing CIA v. Sims, 471 U.S. 159, 178 (1985))); ACLU v. U.S. Dep't of Justice, 321 F. Supp. 2d 24, 37 (D.D.C. 2004) (affirming that "this Circuit has embraced the government's 'mosaic' argument in the context of FOIA requests that implicate national security concerns"); Edmonds v. FBI, 272 F. Supp. 2d 35, 47-48 (D.D.C. 2003) (accepting that "some information required classification because it was intertwined with the sensitive matters at the heart of the case" and "would tend to reveal matters of national security even though the sensitivity of the information may not be readily apparent in isolation") (decided under original version of Executive Order 12,958);

(continued...)

may be classified if the "compiled information reveals an additional association or relationship that: (1) meets the [order's classification] standards, and (2) is not otherwise revealed in the individual items of information."[216] This "mosaic" approach was presaged by a decision of the Court of Appeals for the District of Columbia Circuit in 1980,[217] and it has been endorsed by courts consistently on a case-by-case basis since that time.[218]  The D.C.

---

[215](...continued)
ACLU v. U.S. Dep't of Justice, 265 F. Supp. 2d 20, 29 (D.D.C. 2003) (allowing the agency to withhold statistical intelligence-collection data, commenting that "even aggregate data is revealing," and concluding that disclosure "could permit hostile governments to accurately evaluate the FBI's counterintelligence capabilities") (decided under original version of Executive Order 12,958); see also Bassiouni v. CIA, 392 F.3d 244, 246 (7th Cir. 2004) (recognizing properly that "[w]hen a pattern of responses itself reveals classified information, the only way to keep secrets is to maintain silence uniformly"), cert. denied, 545 U.S. 1129 (2005); cf. Ctr. for Nat'l Sec. Studies v. U.S. Dep't of Justice, 331 F.3d 918, 928 (D.C. Cir. 2003) (accepting government's mosaic argument in context of a criminal terrorism investigation) (Exemption 7(A)).

[216] See Exec. Order No. 12,958, as amended, § 1.7(e); see also Billington v. Dep't of Justice, 11 F. Supp. 2d 45, 55 (D.D.C. 1998) (applying cited provision of executive order to rule that "aggregate result" does not need to be "self-evident" to qualify for Exemption 1 protection), summary judgment granted in pertinent part, 69 F. Supp. 2d 128 (D.D.C. 1999), aff'd in part, vacated in part & remanded all on other grounds, 233 F.3d 581 (D.C. Cir. 2000).

[217] Halperin v. CIA, 629 F.2d 144, 150 (D.C. Cir. 1980) (observing that "[e]ach individual piece of intelligence information, much like a piece of a jigsaw puzzle, may aid in piecing together other bits of information even when the individual piece is not of obvious importance in itself").

[218] See Salisbury v. United States, 690 F.2d 966, 971 (D.C. Cir. 1982) (explicitly acknowledging "mosaic-like nature of intelligence gathering") (decided under Executive Order 12,065); Loomis v. U.S. Dep't of Energy, No. 96-149, 1999 WL 33541935, at *7 (N.D.N.Y. Mar. 9, 1999) (finding that safety measures regarding nuclear facilities set forth in manuals and lay-out plans contain highly technical information and that "such information in the aggregate could reveal sensitive aspects of operations") (decided under original version of Executive Order 12,958), summary affirmance granted, 21 F. App'x 80 (2d Cir. 2001); see also Am. Friends Serv. Comm. v. DOD, 831 F.2d 441, 444-45 (3d Cir. 1987) (recognizing validity of "compilation" theory, and ruling that certain "information harmless in itself might be harmful when disclosed in context") (decided under Executive Order 12,356); Taylor v. Dep't of the Army, 684 F.2d 99, 105 (D.C. Cir. 1982) (upholding classification of compilation of information on army combat units) (decided under Executive Order 12,065); Nat'l Sec. Archive v. FBI, 759 F. Supp. 872, 877
(continued...)

Circuit has also reaffirmed that even if there is other information that if released "would pose a greater threat to the national security," Exemption 1 "'bars the court from prying loose from the government even the smallest bit of information that is properly classified.'"[219]

In one recent case, the United States District Court for the District of Columbia commented that while the mosaic argument may be seen to "cast too wide a net," it is today accepted that "what may seem trivial to the uninformed, may appear of great moment to one who has a broad view of the scene."[220] The court held that situations may exist, in the national security context particularly, where even "'bits and pieces' of data 'may aid in piecing together bits of other information even when the individual piece is not of obvious importance itself.'"[221] As with other agency decisions regarding harm to national security, it is also reasonable for courts to grant an agency the appropriate degree of deference with regard to the practical applicability of their mosaic analysis.[222]

Another aspect of invoking Exemption 1 is the FOIA's general requirement that agencies segregate and release nonexempt information, unless the segregated information would have no meaning.[223] The duty to

---

[218](...continued)
(D.D.C. 1991) (adjudging that disclosure of code names and designator phrases could provide hostile intelligence analyst with "common denominator" permitting analyst to piece together seemingly unrelated data into snapshot of specific FBI counterintelligence activity) (decided under Executive Order 12,356); Jan-Xin Zang v. FBI, 756 F. Supp. 705, 709-10 (W.D.N.Y. 1991) (upholding classification of any particular source-identifying word or phrase that could by itself or in aggregate lead to disclosure of intelligence source) (decided under Executive Order 12,356); cf. Sims, 471 U.S. at 178 (recognizing that "the very nature of the intelligence apparatus of any country is to try to find out the concerns of others") (Exemption 3).

[219] Abbotts v. NRC, 766 F.2d 604, 608 (D.C. Cir. 1985) (quoting Afshar v. Dep't of State, 702 F.2d 1125, 1130 (D.C. Cir. 1983)) (decided under Executive Order 12,356).

[220] ACLU v. U.S. Dep't of Justice, 321 F. Supp. 2d 24, 37 (D.D.C. 2004) (quoting Sims, 471 U.S. at 178).

[221] Id. (quoting Ctr. for Nat'l Sec., 331 F.3d at 928).

[222] See Berman, 378 F. Supp. 2d at 1217 (holding, in context of Exemption 3, that agency's decision to employ a mosaic analysis is entitled to deference); see also Larson v. Dep't of State, No. 02-1937, 2005 WL 3276303, at *12 (D.D.C. Aug. 10, 2005) (allowing that "the CIA has the right to assume that foreign intelligence agencies are zealous ferrets" (citing Gardels, 689 F.2d at 1106)).

[223] See, e.g., Doherty v. U.S. Dep't of Justice, 775 F.2d 49, 53 (2d Cir.
(continued...)

release information that is "reasonably segregable"[224] applies in cases involving classified information as well as those involving nonclassified information.[225] In recent years, the D.C. Circuit has reemphasized the FOIA's segregation requirement in a series of decisions,[226] two of which involved

_____

[223](...continued)
1985); Paisley v. CIA, 712 F.2d 686, 700 (D.C. Cir. 1983); ACLU v. DOD, 406 F. Supp. 2d 330, 333 (D.D.C. 2006) (holding that a court "'cannot simply assume, over the well-documented and specific affidavits of the CIA to the contrary, that revelation of seemingly innocent information . . . is required under the FOIA'" (quoting Phillippi v. CIA, 655 F.2d 1325, 1330 (D.C. Cir. 1981))); Edmonds, 272 F. Supp. 2d at 57 (holding that agency may properly determine that release of any portion of document would result in harm to national security and on that basis classify entire document); Armstrong v. Executive Office of the President, 897 F. Supp. 10, 17 (D.D.C. 1995) (finding that Vaughn Index and supporting affidavits demonstrate that limited number of country captions and source citations contained in intelligence summaries are so "inextricably intertwined" with text of summaries as to be exempt from disclosure); Bevis v. Dep't of the Army, No. 87-1893, slip op. at 2 (D.D.C. Sept. 16, 1988) (ruling that redaction is not required when it would reduce balance of text to "unintelligible gibberish"); Am. Friends Serv. Comm. v. DOD, No. 83-4916, 1988 WL 82852, at *4 (E.D. Pa. Aug. 4, 1988) (holding that very fact that records sought would have to be extensively "reformulated, re-worked and shuffled" prior to any disclosure in and of itself established that nonexempt material was "inextricably intertwined" with exempt material), aff'd, 869 F.2d 587 (3d Cir. 1989) (unpublished table decision).

[224] 5 U.S.C. § 552(b) (2000 & Supp. IV 2004) (sentence immediately following exemptions).

[225] See, e.g., Oglesby v. U.S. Dep't of the Army, 920 F.2d 57, 66 n.12 (D.C. Cir. 1990) (dictum) (citing failure of Army affidavit to specify whether any reasonably segregable portions of 483-page document were withheld pursuant to Exemption 1); Ray v. Turner, 587 F.2d 1187, 1197 (D.C. Cir. 1978) (remanding for greater specificity in affidavit because agency may not rely on "exemption by document" approach even in Exemption 1 context); see also Harper v. DOD, No. 93-35876, 1995 WL 392032, at *2 (9th Cir. July 3, 1995) (reversing part of district court order that permitted agency to withhold entire report under Exemption 1, because district court failed to make "necessary findings" on segregability).

[226] See Trans-Pac. Policing Agreement v. U.S. Customs Serv., 177 F.3d 1022, 1028 (D.C. Cir. 1999); Kimberlin v. Dep't of Justice, 139 F.3d 944, 950 (D.C. Cir. 1998); Army Times Publ'g Co. v. Dep't of the Air Force, 998 F.2d 1067, 1068, 1071-72 (D.C. Cir. 1993); PHE, Inc. v. Dep't of Justice, 983 F.2d 248, 252-53 (D.C. Cir. 1993); Schiller v. NLRB, 965 F.2d 1205, 1210 (D.C. Cir. 1992).

records withheld pursuant to Exemption 1.[227] In the first of these two decisions, the D.C. Circuit, although upholding the district court's substantive
determination that the records contained information qualifying for Exemption 1 protection, nonetheless remanded the case to the district court because it had failed to "make specific findings of segregability for each of the
withheld documents."[228] In the second decision, the D.C. Circuit observed
that although the agency might have been "aware of its duties under FOIA
to disclose all nonsegregable information," it did not provide the court with
an "adequate explanation" on which to base such a finding.[229] Accordingly,
the D.C. Circuit also remanded the case to the district court for a more detailed description of the information withheld.[230] (For a further discussion
of this point, see Litigation Considerations, "Reasonably Segregable" Requirements, below.)

Additionally, agencies should also be aware of the FOIA's "(c)(3) exclusion."[231] This special records exclusion applies to certain especially sensitive records maintained by the Federal Bureau of Investigation, which
concern foreign intelligence, counterintelligence or international terrorism
matters: Where the existence of such records is itself a classified fact, the
FBI may, so long as the existence of the records remains classified, treat
the records as not subject to the requirements of the FOIA.[232] (See the discussion of this provision under Exclusions, below.)

## "Operational Files" Statutes

It is commonplace for intelligence agencies of the federal government
to maintain entire systems of records that contain almost exclusively rec-

---

[227] See Oglesby v. U.S. Dep't of the Army, 79 F.3d 1172, 1180-81 (D.C. Cir.
1996); Krikorian v. Dep't of State, 984 F.2d 461, 466-67 (D.C. Cir. 1993); see
also Canning v. U.S. Dep't of Justice, 848 F. Supp. 1037, 1049 n.2 (D.D.C.
1994) (applying Krikorian standard to specifically find that agency "carefully and methodically . . . respect[ed] FOIA's segregation] principle"); Bay
Area Lawyers Alliance for Nuclear Arms Control v. Dep't of State, No. C89-
1843, slip op. at 7-8, 11-12 (N.D. Cal. June 4, 1993) (applying same standard).

[228] Krikorian, 984 F.2d at 467; see also Greenberg v. U.S. Dep't of Treasury, 10 F. Supp. 2d 3, 14-15 (D.D.C. 1998) (ordering that CIA "more specifically" explain in subsequent Vaughn Index why portions of records withheld in full are not reasonably segregable); FOIA Update, Vol. XIV, No. 3, at
11-12 ("OIP Guidance: The 'Reasonable Segregation' Obligation").

[229] Oglesby, 79 F.3d at 1181.

[230] Id.

[231] 5 U.S.C. § 552(c)(3).

[232] Id.; see also Attorney General's Memorandum on the 1986 Amendments to the Freedom of Information Act 24-25 (Dec. 1987).

ords classified under Executive Order 12,958, as amended. Due to the sensitivity of these records systems, and owing to the fact that the information contained within them would be expected to be exempt from disclosure pursuant to Exemption 1, Congress has granted certain intelligence agencies special protections from disclosure through the enactment of specific "operational files" statutes implemented through Exemption 3 of the FOIA.[233] These "operational files" statutes remove records systems from the search and review requirements of the FOIA under well-defined circumstances when the system predominantly holds classified operational records.[234]

The rationale behind these special statutory provisions is that it would be a waste of time and money for the agency to conduct a search for and review of information that will almost invariably be exempt from disclosure under Exemption 1.[235] In eliminating the search and review requirement for records most unlikely to yield any releaseable information to a FOIA requester, Congress also sought to provide for the faster processing of unclassified material requested from intelligence agencies.[236] As these "operational files" statutes are predicated upon the classification status of the information, there is a close relationship between the protections offered "operational files" by Exemption 1 and Exemption 3. The distinction is that with "operational files" records systems, the five intelligence agencies that have been granted such FOIA protection through one of these special Exemption 3 statutes may determine as a preliminary, administrative matter that essentially the entire system would be exempt from disclosure under Exemption 1.[237]

While the Central Intelligence Agency was the first intelligence

---

[233] See, e.g., FOIA Update, Vol. V, No. 4, at 1-2 (explaining that an underlying principle of the Central Intelligence Agency Information Act of 1984, 50 U.S.C.A. § 431 (2003 & West Supp. 2006), is to free "the CIA of the burden of processing FOIA requests for" records that "would be almost entirely withholdable anyway, upon application of the FOIA's national security exemption, Exemption 1, together with the CIA's other statutory nondisclosure provisions under Exemption 3").

[234] Id.

[235] Id.; see also ACLU v. DOD, 351 F. Supp. 2d 265, 273 (S.D.N.Y. 2005) (commenting that Congress sought to eliminate the "unproductive process of searching and reviewing CIA operational records systems which contain little, if any, information releasable under the FOIA [and] absorbs a substantial amount of the time of experienced CIA operational personnel and scarce tax dollars" (citing H.R. Rep. No. 98-726, pt. 1, at 5 (1984))).

[236] Id. at 274.

[237] See FOIA Post, "Agencies Rely on Wide Range of Exemption 3 Statutes" (posted 12/16/03).

agency to receive "operational files" FOIA status in 1984,[238] four additional intelligence agencies have been granted such status relatively recently: the National Geospatial-Intelligence Agency;[239] the National Reconnaissance Office;[240] the National Security Agency;[241] and the Defense Intelligence Agency.[242] Each of their special statutes clearly outlines certain limited exceptions to its removal of file systems from the FOIA's search and review requirement,[243] and each requires the head of the agency to identify which "operational files" are considered to fall within the coverage of the statute in the first place.[244]

To date courts have had occasion to consider the application of these special national security-related Exemption 3 statutes in but a handful of cases,[245] and in so doing have suggested that there are varying degrees of deference that will be granted to agencies employing such special FOIA

---

[238] See 50 U.S.C.A. § 431 (removing from search and review provisions of FOIA certain files from the Directorate of Operations, Directorate for Science and Technology, and Office of Personnel Security); see also FOIA Update, Vol. V, No. 4, at 1-2.

[239] See 50 U.S.C.A. § 432 (West Supp. 2006) (removing agency's operational files from search and review provisions of FOIA).

[240] See 50 U.S.C.A. § 432a (removing agency's operational files from search and review provisions of FOIA).

[241] See 50 U.S.C.A. § 432b (removing from the search and review provisions of the FOIA certain files from the Signals Intelligence Directorate and the Research Associate Directorate "that document the means by which foreign intelligence or counterintelligence is collected through technical systems").

[242] See 50 U.S.C.A. § 432c (removing from search and review provisions of FOIA certain files from Directorate of Human Intelligence).

[243] See 50 U.S.C.A. § 431(b), (c), (d) (Central Intelligence Agency "operational files" definitions and limitations); id. § 432(a)(2)-(6) (National Geospatial-Intelligence Agency "operational files" definitions and limitations); id. § 432a(2)-(6) (National Reconnaissance Office "operational files" definitions and limitations); id. § 432b(b)(2), (c) (National Security Agency "operational files" definitions and limitations); id. § 432c(b)(2), (c) (Defense Intelligence Agency "operational files" definitions and limitations).

[244] See 50 U.S.C.A. § 431(a); id. § 432(a)(1); id. § 432a(a)(1); id. § 432b(a); id. § 432c(a).

[245] See Aftergood v. Nat'l Reconnaissance Office, No. 05-1307, 2006 WL 2048461, at *1 (D.D.C. July 24, 2006); ACLU v. DOD, 351 F. Supp. 2d 265, 271-72 (S.D.N.Y. 2005); Davy v. CIA, 357 F. Supp. 2d 76, 82 (D.D.C. 2004).

protection.[246]  In the most recent case to address the use of an "operational files" statute, the agency was denied any sort of special deference by the court, based upon its failure to properly identify what it considers to be operational files, as is required by each of these statues.[247]  In that case involving the National Reconnaissance Office, the court ultimately determined that while the agency's "operational files" statute validly protected certain material from the search and review provisions of the FOIA, the budget data at issue in this litigation triggered an exception to its "operational files" statutory provision.[248]  In a second recent decision, also involving a distinct statutory exception to "operational files" coverage, the same court held that such an exception to another agency's "operational files" statute was not triggered and that the special protection was properly applied.[249]

Although this is still a developing area of FOIA law, recent reviews by the courts suggest that intelligence agencies seeking to apply their special "operational files" protections granted by Congress should be aware that they will be held to the procedural requirements of and the particular exceptions within their "operational files" statutes. (For a further discussion of "operational files," see Exemption 3, "Operational Files" Provisions, below.)

## Homeland Security-Related Information

Due to the horrific events of September 11, 2001, and their aftermath throughout the world, no discussion of national security would be complete without emphasizing the efforts of the federal government to protect sensitive national security information, particularly regarding matters of critical infrastructure, weapons of mass destruction, and the general threat of terrorism.  In response to the attacks of September 11, 2001, the federal

---

[246] See Aftergood, 2006 WL 2048461, at *6 (rejecting usual grant of deference to agencies in national security cases, and advising that "courts should exercise a certain level of caution in reviewing an agency's written statements regarding the content of files for which the defendant claims § 432a's operational files exemption"); ACLU v. DOD, 351 F. Supp. 2d 265, 269 (S.D.N.Y. 2005) (determining that agency is not entitled to any special deference in its decision to handle "operational files" in relation to FOIA).

[247] See Aftergood, 2006 WL 2048461, at *6 (denying deference because "defendant has not yet publicly promulgated any official interpretation of § 432a's operational files exemption").

[248] See id. at 9 (finding that agency could not circumvent exceptions to "operational files" exemption contained within statute).

[249] See Davy v. CIA, 357 F. Supp. 2d 76, 83 (D.D.C. 2004) (holding that records had not been subject of investigation as outlined in agency's "operational files" statute and therefore were properly removed from FOIA's search and review requirement).

government has undergone its largest and most wide-ranging reorganization in more than fifty years.[250] This reorganization -- and the creation of the Department of Homeland Security, under the Homeland Security Act of 2002,[251] in addition to the Homeland Security Council within the White House[252] -- centralized the federal government's domestic national security efforts in order to protect Americans from the ever-increasing threat of terrorism. These changes have greatly impacted many aspects of the operation of the federal government, including the administration of the FOIA.[253] Today -- more than five years after the September 11, 2001 attacks -- the changes in how the federal government operates to protect national security continue.[254] Much greater emphasis is now placed on the protection of information that could expose the nation's critical infrastructure, military, government, and citizenry to an increased risk of attack.[255] As a result of these changes, federal departments and agencies should carefully consider the sensitivity of any information the disclosure of which could reasonably be expected to cause national security harm.[256]

On March 19, 2002, the White House Chief of Staff issued a directive

---

[250] See FOIA Post, "Homeland Security Law Contains New Exemption 3 Statute" (posted 1/27/03); FOIA Post, "Guidance on Homeland Security Information Issued" (posted 3/21/02); see also FOIA Post, "Annual Report Guidance for DHS-Related Agencies" (posted 8/8/03).

[251] See Homeland Security Act of 2002, 6 U.S.C. § 483 (2000 & Supp. IV 2004); see also Homeland Security Act Amendments of 2003, Pub. L. 108-7, 117 Stat. 526.

[252] See Exec. Order No. 13,228, § 5, 66 Fed. Reg. 51812 (Oct. 8, 2001) (creating Homeland Security Council).

[253] See FOIA Post, "Critical Infrastructure Regulations Issued by DHS" (posted 2/27/04); FOIA Post, "FOIA Officers Conference Held on Homeland Security" (posted 7/3/03); FOIA Post, "Homeland Security Law Contains New Exemption 3 Statute" (posted 1/27/03).

[254] See, e.g., USA PATRIOT Improvement and Reauthorization Act of 2005, Pub. L. No. 109-177, 120 Stat. 192 (2006) (amending USA PATRIOT Act and authorizing creation of National Security Division within Department of Justice).

[255] See Information Security Oversight Office Ann. Rep. 6 (2003) (cautioning that "if we are not attentive, the demands of war can distract us from doing what is necessary today to ensure the continued efficacy of the security classification system"); FOIA Post, "Guidance on Homeland Security Information Issued" (posted 3/21/02).

[256] See Attorney General's Memorandum for Heads of All Federal Departments and Agencies Regarding the Freedom of Information Act (Oct. 12, 2001), reprinted in FOIA Post (posted 10/15/01) (reminding agencies of importance of "safeguarding our national security" in FOIA decisionmaking).

to the heads of all federal departments and agencies addressing the need to safeguard and wherever appropriate protect such information.[257] This directive is implemented by an accompanying memorandum.[258] The implementing guidance contains two points that are especially relevant to amended Executive Order 12,958, though it was issued prior to the most recent amendment.

The first of these points concerns sensitive homeland security-related information that is currently classified; the classified status of such information should be maintained in accordance with applicable provisions of the amended Executive Order 12,958.[259] This includes extending the duration of classification as well as exempting such information from automatic declassification as appropriate.[260] The second point concerns previously unclassified or declassified information,[261] which may be classified or re-classified, as appropriate, pursuant to the amended executive order.[262] In this regard, if the information has been the subject of a previous access demand, such as a FOIA request, any such classification or re-classification is subject to the special requirements of section 1.7(d) of amended Executive Order 12,958.[263]

As a final note, agencies should be aware that although various government agencies today might use newly created terms to refer to catego-

---

[257] See White House Memorandum for Heads of Executive Departments and Agencies Concerning Safeguarding Information Regarding Weapons of Mass Destruction and Other Sensitive Documents Related to Homeland Security [hereinafter White House Homeland Security Memorandum] (Mar. 19, 2002), reprinted in FOIA Post (posted 3/21/02).

[258] See Memorandum from Acting Director of Information Security Oversight Office and Co-Directors of Office of Information and Privacy to Departments and Agencies [hereinafter ISOO/OIP Homeland Security Memorandum], reprinted in FOIA Post (posted 3/21/02) (citing Attorney General Ashcroft's FOIA Memorandum).

[259] See ISOO/OIP Homeland Security Memorandum (referring to sections 1.5, 1.6, and 3.4(b)(2) of original version of Executive Order 12,958 (authorizing information concerning weapons of mass destruction to be exempted from automatic declassification)).

[260] See id. (referring to sections 1.6(d)(2) and 3.4(b)(2) of original version of Executive Order 12,958).

[261] See id.

[262] See id. (explaining that initial classification or reclassification should be undertaken in accordance with Executive Order 12,958).

[263] See id.; Exec. Order No. 12,958, §§ 1.8(d); see also 42 U.S.C. § 2162 (2000) (governing classification of information concerning atomic weapons and other special nuclear material).

ries of homeland security-related information -- such as "Sensitive Homeland Security Information" (commonly referred to as "SHSI"),[264] "Sensitive But Unclassified Information" (sometimes referred to as "SBU information"),[265] or "Critical Infrastructure Information" (commonly referred to as "CII")[266] -- these categorical labels do not indicate classification pursuant to Executive Order 12,958.[267] Terms such as "SHSI" and "SBU" describe broad types of potentially sensitive information that might not even fall within any of the FOIA's exemptions.[268] It is significant to note that none of these new homeland security-related terms is included in Executive Order 12,958, as amended, and that the use of these labels alone does not provide for any protection from disclosure under any exemption, let alone Exemption 1.[269] A separate statute implements protections for "CII," and

---

[264] *FOIA Post*, "Critical Infrastructure Information Regulations Issued by DHS" (posted 2/27/04) (describing Department of Homeland Security report to Congress of February 20, 2004, which addresses development of policy and governmentwide procedures for handling "sensitive homeland security information"); see also *FOIA Post*, "FOIA Officers Conference Held on Homeland Security" (posted 7/3/03) (discussing FOIA officers conference conducted by Department of Justice on subject of homeland security-related FOIA issues).

[265] White House Homeland Security Memorandum, reprinted in *FOIA Post* (posted 3/21/02); see also ISOO/OIP Homeland Security Memorandum, reprinted in *FOIA Post* (posted 3/21/02).

[266] 6 U.S.C. § 131(3) (Supp. IV 2004) (defining "critical infrastructure information"); see also *FOIA Post*, "Critical Infrastructure Regulations Issued by DHS" (posted 2/27/04) (explaining implementation of section 214 of Homeland Security Act, which prohibits disclosure of certain "critical infrastructure information" and triggers protection of Exemption 3).

[267] Exec. Order No. 12,958, as amended, § 1.2(b) (providing that "no other terms shall be used to identify United States classified information").

[268] *FOIA Post*, "FOIA Officers Conference Held on Homeland Security" (posted 7/3/03) (emphasizing also that "primary emphasis [should be] on the safeguarding of information, where appropriate due to its particular sensitivity rather than on the basis of any catch-all label"); see also *FOIA Post*, "Executive Order 13,392 Implementation Guidance" (posted 04/27/06) (Part I.21.) (suggesting "[i]n-house training on 'safeguarding label'/FOIA exemption distinctions" as potential improvement area for agencies to address in their plans developed pursuant to Executive Order 13,392, 70 Fed. Reg. 75,373 (Dec. 14, 2005)).

[269] See *FOIA Post*, "FOIA Officers Conference Held on Homeland Security" (posted 7/3/03) (discussing "safeguarding" of information with identifying terms unrelated to classification); see also Presidential Memorandum for the Heads of Executive Departments and Agencies Concerning Guidelines and Requirements in Support of the Information Sharing Environment

(continued...)

these protections are incorporated into the FOIA through Exemption 3.[270] Indeed, it is worth reiterating in this regard that the protections afforded classified information under Exemption 1 can be applied only to information that has been properly classified under Executive Order 12,958, as amended. (For a further discussion of "safeguarding labels," see Exemption 2, Homeland Security-Related Information, below.)

## EXEMPTION 2

Exemption 2 of the FOIA exempts from mandatory disclosure records that are "related solely to the internal personnel rules and practices of an agency."[1] It is unique among the FOIA exemptions in that the courts have interpreted this one statutory phrase to encompass two very different categories of information:

(a)    internal matters of a relatively trivial nature -- often referred to as "low 2" information; and

(b)    more substantial internal matters, the disclosure of which would risk circumvention of a legal requirement -- often referred to as "high 2" information.[2]

In light of the threats posed by worldwide and domestic terrorism, this second category has come to play an essential role in providing necessary protection of information related to both national security most gener-

---

[269](...continued)
(Dec. 16, 2005), available at http://www.whitehouse.gov/news/releases/ 2005/12/20051216-10.html (setting out general guidelines for standardization of procedures related to "acquisition, access, retention, production, use, management, and sharing of Sensitive But Unclassified (SBU) information"), implemented by Information Sharing Environment Implementation Plan 94 (Nov. 16, 2006), available at http://www.ise.gov/docs/ ISE-impplan-200611.pdf (speaking of future plans to address existing difficulties with "the growing and non-standardized inventory of SBU designations and markings").

[270] 6 U.S.C. § 133 (2000 & Supp. IV 2004); see also FOIA Post, "Homeland Security Law Contains New Exemption 3 Statute" (posted 1/27/03) (summarizing provisions and operation of new Exemption 3 statute).

[1] 5 U.S.C. § 552(b)(2) (2000 & Supp. IV 2004).

[2] See FOIA Update, Vol. X, No. 3, at 3-4 ("OIP Guidance: Protecting Vulnerability Assessments Through Application of Exemption Two"); see, e.g., Schiller v. NLRB, 964 F.2d 1205, 1207 (D.C. Cir. 1992) (describing "low 2" and "high 2" aspects of exemption).

ally and homeland security in particular.[3] It is important that all agencies consider Exemption 2 carefully in properly evaluating -- and, where appropriate, withholding -- sensitive information, including critical infrastructure information,[4] that is of current law enforcement significance.[5] A comprehensive examination of that vital means of information protection follows the discussions below of Exemption 2's historical development and of the case law addressing the "low 2" aspect of Exemption 2. (See also the further discussion under Exemption 2, Homeland Security-Related Information, below.)

---

[3] See *FOIA Post*, "New Attorney General FOIA Memorandum Issued" (posted 10/15/01) (highlighting government's "need to protect critical systems, facilities, stockpiles, and other assets from security breaches"); see also White House Memorandum for Heads of Executive Departments and Agencies Concerning Safeguarding Information Regarding Weapons of Mass Destruction and Other Sensitive Documents Related to Homeland Security (Mar. 19, 2002) [hereinafter White House Homeland Security Memorandum], reprinted in *FOIA Post* (posted 3/21/02) (directing agencies, in accordance with accompanying memorandum from Information Security Oversight Office and Office of Information and Privacy, to review their documents in order to ensure that they are properly applying FOIA exemptions, specifically including Exemption 2, to information that is unclassified but nevertheless sensitive).

[4] See, e.g., USA PATRIOT Act of 2001, 42 U.S.C. § 5195c(e) (Supp. III 2003) (defining "critical infrastructure" as "systems and assets, whether physical or virtual, so vital to the United States that the incapacity or destruction of such systems and assets would have a debilitating impact on security, national economic security, national public health or safety, or any combination of those matters"); see also *FOIA Post*, "FOIA Officers Conference Held on Homeland Security" (posted 7/3/03) (discussing protection of "critical infrastructure information" within broader context of "protection of homeland security-related information").

[5] See Attorney General's Memorandum for Heads of All Federal Departments and Agencies Regarding the Freedom of Information Act (Oct. 12, 2001) [hereinafter Attorney General Ashcroft's FOIA Memorandum], reprinted in *FOIA Post* (posted 10/15/01) (emphasizing the importance of "enhancing the effectiveness of our law enforcement agencies" -- which agencies should "carefully consider . . . when making disclosure determinations under the FOIA"); see also White House Homeland Security Memorandum, reprinted in *FOIA Post* (posted 3/21/02) (calling upon agencies to identify and then safeguard "information that could be misused to harm the security of our nation and the safety of our people"); see also, e.g., Living Rivers, Inc. v. U.S. Bureau of Reclamation, 272 F. Supp. 2d 1313, 1322 (D. Utah 2003) (recognizing, in light of terrorism concerns, law enforcement significance of agency maps detailing results of multiple dam failures in post-9/11 context); cf. *FOIA Post*, "Critical Infrastructure Information Regulations Issued by DHS" (posted 2/27/04) (emphasizing critical distinction between "protecting" and "safeguarding" information).

Initial Considerations

Exemption 2's unique protection of two distinct categories of information can be traced back to the legislative history of the FOIA's enactment. For more than fifteen years after the passage of the Act four decades ago, much confusion existed concerning the intended coverage of Exemption 2 due to the differing approaches taken in the Senate and House Reports when the FOIA was enacted and the fact that these differences were not reconciled in a joint statement or report by both Houses of Congress. The Senate Report stated:

> Exemption No. 2 relates only to the internal personnel rules and practices of an agency. Examples of these may be rules as to personnel's use of parking facilities or regulation of lunch hours, statements of policy as to sick leave, and the like.[6]

The House Report provided a more expansive interpretation of Exemption 2's coverage, stating that it was intended to include:

> [o]perating rules, guidelines, and manuals of procedure for Government investigators or examiners . . . but [that] this exemption would not cover all "matters of internal management" such as employee relations and working conditions and routine administrative procedures which are withheld under the present law.[7]

The Supreme Court confronted the conflict in Exemption 2's coverage of routine internal matters in a case in which a requester sought to obtain case summaries of Air Force Academy ethics hearings, and it found the Senate Report to be more authoritative. In Department of the Air Force v. Rose,[8] the Supreme Court construed Exemption 2's somewhat ambiguous language as protecting internal agency matters so routine or trivial that they could not be "subject to . . . a genuine and significant public interest."[9] The Court declared that Exemption 2 was intended to relieve agencies of the burden of assembling and providing access to any "matter in which the public could not reasonably be expected to have an interest."[10] At the same time, presaging the eventual development of the "high 2" aspect of

---

[6] S. Rep. No. 89-813, at 8 (1965).

[7] H. Rep. No. 89-1497, at 10 (1966), reprinted in 1966 U.S.C.C.A.N. 2418, 2427; see also id. at 5 ("[P]remature disclosure of agency plans that are undergoing development . . . , particularly plans relating to expenditures, could have adverse effects upon both public and private interest[s].").

[8] 425 U.S. 352 (1976).

[9] Id. at 369.

[10] Id. at 369-70.

Exemption 2, discussed below, the Court also suggested in Rose that the approach taken in the House Report could permit an agency to withhold matters of some public interest "where disclosure may risk circumvention of agency regulation."[11]

The Supreme Court's ruling in Rose helped to define the contours of Exemption 2, but it did not dispel all the confusion about its scope. Early judicial opinions subsequent to this ruling, particularly in the Court of Appeals for the District of Columbia Circuit, demonstrated judicial ambivalence about whether the exemption covered only internal personnel rules and personnel practices of an agency or, on the other hand, an agency's internal personnel rules and more general internal practices.[12]

The confusion and uncertainty finally were laid to rest, at least in the D.C. Circuit, in Founding Church of Scientology v. Smith,[13] which set out specific steps for determining the applicability of Exemption 2. In this important 1983 decision, the D.C. Circuit articulated the following approach:

> First, the material withheld should fall within the terms of the statutory language as a personnel rule or internal practice of the agency. Then, if the material relates to trivial administrative matters of no genuine public interest, exemption would be automatic under the statute. If withholding frustrates legitimate public interest, however, the material should be released unless the government can show that disclosure would risk circumvention of lawful agency regulation.[14]

---

[11] Id. at 369.

[12] Compare Jordan v. U.S. Dep't of Justice, 591 F.2d 753, 764 (D.C. Cir. 1978) (en banc) (exemption covers "only internal personnel matters"), and Allen v. CIA, 636 F.2d 1287, 1290 (D.C. Cir. 1980) (exemption covers "nothing more than trivial administrative personnel rules"), with Lesar v. U.S. Dep't of Justice, 636 F.2d 472, 485 (D.C. Cir. 1980) (exemption covers routine matters of merely internal interest), and Cox v. U.S. Dep't of Justice, 601 F.2d 1, 4 (D.C. Cir. 1979) (per curiam) (same). See generally DeLorme Publ'g Co. v. NOAA, 917 F. Supp. 867, 875-76 & n.10 (D. Me. 1996) (describing debate among various circuit courts on meaning of Exemption 2's language), appeal dismissed per stipulation, No. 96-1601 (1st Cir. July 8, 1996).

[13] 721 F.2d 828 (D.C. Cir. 1983) (per curiam).

[14] Id. at 830-31 n.4 (citations omitted); see also Massey v. FBI, 3 F.3d 620, 622 (2d Cir. 1993) (holding that Exemption 2 applies to "non-employee" information, such as informant symbol numbers and file numbers); Schiller, 964 F.2d at 1208 (finding Exemption 2 appropriate to withhold Equal Access to Justice Act litigation strategies); Dirksen v. HHS, 803 F.2d 1456, 1458-59 (9th Cir. 1986) (approving use of Exemption 2 to withhold Medicare
(continued...)

In this decision, the D.C. Circuit thus made it clear that Exemption 2 allows the withholding of a great variety of internal rules, procedures, and guidelines -- effectively overruling its earlier decision in Allen v. CIA,[15] where it initially had indicated that Exemption 2 protection was intended for agency "personnel" records only. Consequently, agencies became free to consider withholding a wide range of information as appropriate under Exemption 2.[16]

Some differences among the courts of appeals for circuits other than the D.C. Circuit remain, however, with respect to the degree to which Exemption 2 information must be personnel-related as a threshold matter. Two 1997 appellate decisions, which are discussed in detail below -- see "High 2": Risk of Circumvention -- illustrate the narrow distinctions made in these jurisdictions, specifically the Courts of Appeals for the Ninth and Tenth Circuits, concerning this notion of "personnel-relatedness."[17] These decisions and their progeny, however, demonstrate the willingness[18] of the courts and Congress to accord appropriate protection to highly sensitive information under Exemption 2,[19] or otherwise.[20]

---

[14](...continued)
claims-processing guidelines); Canning v. U.S. Dep't of the Treasury, No. 94-2704, slip op. at 15 (D.D.C. May 7, 1998) (concluding that the Secret Service's reliance on Exemption 2 for nondisclosure of an internal listing of offices to contact after "an incident of interest" was proper).

[15] 636 F.2d at 1290 n.21 (taking unduly narrow position in rejecting agency argument that Exemption 2 should apply to any routine internal matters in which public lacks interest).

[16] See FOIA Update, Vol. V, No. 1, at 10 ("FOIA Counselor: The Unique Protection of Exemption 2") (advising that Founding Church "expressly" held that the Allen "personnel" restriction no longer applies); see also, e.g., Crooker v. ATF, 670 F.2d 1051, 1073 (D.C. Cir. 1981) (en banc) (concluding that "personnel" should not be read as narrowly as was suggested in Jordan); Judicial Watch, Inc. v. U.S. Dep't of Transp., No. 02-566, 2005 WL 1606915, at *9 (D.D.C. July 7, 2005) ("Exemption 2 is not limited to internal personnel rules and practices; rather, it is construed more generally to encompass documents that are used for predominantly internal purposes.").

[17] See Maricopa Audubon Soc'y v. U.S. Forest Serv., 108 F.3d 1082 (9th Cir. 1997); Audubon Soc'y v. U.S. Forest Serv., 104 F.3d 1201 (10th Cir. 1997).

[18] See Schwaner v. Dep't of the Air Force, 898 F.2d 793, 796 (D.C. Cir. 1990) ("Judicial willingness to sanction a weak relation to 'rules and practices' may be greatest when the asserted government interest is relatively weighty.").

[19] See, e.g., L.A. Times Commc'ns, LLC v. Dep't of the Army, 442 F. Supp. 2d 880, 901-02 (C.D. Cal. 2006) (finding that a database of Serious Incident
(continued...)

**EXEMPTION 2**

"Low 2":  Trivial Matters

Exemption 2 of the FOIA permits the withholding of internal matters that are of a relatively trivial nature.[21]  As its legislative and judicial history make clear, in this "low 2" aspect Exemption 2 is the only exemption in the FOIA having a conceptual underpinning totally unrelated to any harm caused by disclosure per se.[22]  Rather, this aspect of the exemption is based upon the rationale that the very task of processing and releasing

---

[19](...continued)
Reports submitted by private security contractors in Iraq to the Army Corps of Engineers was "maintained for a law enforcement purpose," and protecting the names of contractors within the database); Gordon v. FBI, 388 F. Supp. 2d 1028, 1035-36 (N.D. Cal. 2005) (protecting details of FBI's aviation "watch list" program -- including records discussing "selection criteria" for lists and handling and dissemination of lists, and "addressing perceived problems in security measures"); Coastal Delivery Corp. v. U.S. Customs Serv., 272 F. Supp. 2d 958, 965 (C.D. Cal.) (finding law enforcement purpose, as necessary under Ninth Circuit precedent to uphold application of Exemption 2, for protection of container-inspection statistics at Los Angeles/Long Beach seaport), reconsideration denied, 272 F. Supp. 2d at 966-68 (C.D. Cal. 2003), appeal dismissed voluntarily, No. 03-55833 (9th Cir. Aug. 26, 2003).

[20] See Living Rivers, Inc. v. U.S. Bureau of Reclamation, 272 F. Supp. 2d 1313, 1317-18, 1321-22 (D. Utah 2003) (affirming withholding of flood maps under Exemption 7(F), rather than Exemption 2, while acknowledging that court was bound by 1997 Tenth Circuit precedent severely limiting application of Exemption 2 to records regarding personnel rules and personnel practices); Sw. Ctr. for Biological Diversity v. USDA, 170 F. Supp. 2d 931, 943-47 (D. Ariz. 2000) (upholding protection for rare bird site-location information based on post-Maricopa Exemption 3 statute), aff'd, 314 F.3d 1060 (9th Cir. 2002); see also Abraham & Rose, P.L.C. v. United States, 138 F.3d 1075, 1082 (6th Cir. 1998) (holding that the evidence presented was "insufficient to create the significant, meaningful relationship with IRS internal personnel rules and practices required by" Exemption 2, while at the same time explicitly recognizing that "the sensitive nature of certain information such as FBI informant codes gives the government in such cases a significant interest in nondisclosure," and ultimately applying another FOIA exemption instead); cf. Jones v. FBI, 41 F.3d 238, 244-45 (6th Cir. 1994) (concluding that FBI properly redacted, under Exemption 2, symbol numbers used internally to identify confidential sources).

[21] See, e.g., Dep't of the Air Force v. Rose, 425 U.S. 352, 369-70 (1976); Lesar v. U.S. Dep't of Justice, 636 F.2d 472, 485 (D.C. Cir. 1980).

[22] See Rose, 425 U.S. at 369-70; see also, e.g., Edmonds v. FBI, 272 F. Supp. 2d 35, 51 (D.D.C. 2003) (observing that showings of "foreseeable adverse consequence[s]" are not necessary to withhold information that is trivial and of no public interest).

-262-

some requested records would place an administrative burden on the agency, a mere bother that would not be justified by any genuine public benefit.[23]

Accordingly, as a matter of longstanding practice, agencies have recognized that disclosing "low 2" information -- which by its very nature is nothing more than "trivial" -- is in many instances less burdensome than bothering to invoke the exemption to withhold it.[24] In practice, therefore, agencies may continue to disclose such information in the exercise of their administrative discretion.[25]

For information in a requested record to be properly withheld under the "low 2" aspect of Exemption 2, it must meet two criteria: First, the information must be "predominantly internal," and second, the information

---

[23] See FOIA Update, Vol. V, No. 1, at 10-11 ("FOIA Counselor: The Unique Protection of Exemption 2"); see also, e.g., Dirksen v. HHS, 803 F.2d 1456, 1460 (9th Cir. 1986) (observing that "the thrust of Exemption 2 [i.e., "low 2"] is . . . to relieve agencies of the burden of disclosing information in which the public does not have a legitimate interest"); Martin v. Lauer, 686 F.2d 24, 34 (D.C. Cir. 1982) (Exemption 2 "serves to relieve the agency from the administrative burden of processing FOIA requests when internal matters are not likely to be the subject of public interest."); Long v. U.S. Dep't of Justice, 450 F. Supp. 2d 42, 57 n.16 (D.D.C. 2006) (finding that the "limited public interest" in the withheld information was "outweighed by the government's interest in avoiding the significant burden involved in collecting and evaluating this information for release"), amended by 457 F. Supp. 2d 30 (D.D.C. 2006) (clarifying prior order), amended further on reconsideration, Nos. 00-0211 & 02-2467, 2007 WL 293508 (D.D.C. Feb. 2, 2007) (modifying amended order on other grounds), stay granted (D.D.C. Feb. 13, 2007); Carbe v. ATF, No. 03-1658, 2004 WL 2051359, at *6 (D.D.C. Aug. 12, 2004) ("'Low 2' information refers to internal procedures and practices of an agency where disclosure would constitute an administrative burden unjustified by any genuine and significant public benefit."); Fisher v. U.S. Dep't of Justice, 772 F. Supp. 7, 10 n.8 (D.D.C. 1991) (citing Martin, 686 F.2d at 34), aff'd, 968 F.2d 92 (D.C. Cir. 1992) (unpublished table decision).

[24] See Fonda v. CIA, 434 F. Supp. 498, 503 (D.D.C. 1977) (finding that where administrative burden is minimal and it would be easier to release information at issue, policy underlying Exemption 2 does not permit withholding); see also FOIA Update, Vol. V, No. 1, at 11 ("FOIA Counselor: The Unique Protection of Exemption 2") (advising agencies to invoke "low 2" aspect of Exemption 2 only where doing so truly avoids burden).

[25] See id.; accord Attorney General's Memorandum for Heads of All Federal Departments and Agencies Regarding the Freedom of Information Act (Oct. 12, 2001) [hereinafter Attorney General Ashcroft's FOIA Memorandum], reprinted in FOIA Post (posted 10/15/01) (recognizing continued agency practice of making discretionary disclosure determinations under the FOIA, upon careful consideration of all interests involved).

must be of a trivial nature and not of any "genuine public interest."[26] Thus, "low 2" shares in common with "high 2" the requirement that the information withheld be "predominantly internal."[27] However, for "low 2" in particular, agencies should pay attention to whether the information at issue "shed[s] significant light" on an agency personnel rule or practice.[28] As one court recently observed: "Information is 'predominantly internal' if it does not 'purport to regulate activities among members of the public or set standards to be followed by agency personnel in deciding whether to proceed against or take action affecting members of the public.'"[29] Accordingly, courts have held that routine internal personnel matters, such as performance standards and leave practices, for example, are covered under "low 2."[30]

Over time, courts have continued to include a wide variety of trivial administrative information within the "low 2" aspect of Exemption 2's coverage. This includes not only relatively minor pieces of information[31] -- e.g.,

---

[26] See Schiller v. NLRB, 964 F.2d 1205, 1207 (D.C. Cir. 1992) ("Predominantly internal documents that deal with trivial administrative matters fall under the 'low 2' exemption."); see also, e.g., ACLU v. FBI, 429 F. Supp. 2d 179, 189 (D.D.C. 2006) (explaining that "'low 2' [is designed] for materials related to trivial administrative matters of no genuine public interest").

[27] See, e.g., Schiller, 964 F.2d at 1207; Long, 450 F. Supp. 2d at 57 n.16; Edmonds, 272 F. Supp. 2d at 50.

[28] FOIA Update, Vol. XI, No. 2, at 2 (quoting Schwaner v. Dep't of the Air Force, 898 F.2d 793, 795 (D.C. Cir. 1990), and noting its stringent interpretation of Exemption 2); see also Canning v. U.S. Dep't of the Treasury, No. 94-2704, slip op. at 15 (D.D.C. May 7, 1998) (finding narrative information related to Secret Service contact list to be "clearly 'practices of an agency'" and therefore properly protected).

[29] Edmonds, 272 F. Supp. 2d at 50 (quoting Cox v. U.S. Dep't of Justice, 601 F.2d 1, 5 (D.C. Cir. 1979)).

[30] See, e.g., Small v. IRS, 820 F. Supp. 163, 168 (D.N.J. 1992) (employee service identification numbers); Pruner v. Dep't of the Army, 755 F. Supp. 362, 365 (D. Kan. 1991) (internal guidance regarding Army regulation governing discharge of conscientious objectors); FBI Agents Ass'n v. FBI, 3 Gov't Disclosure Serv. (P-H) ¶ 83,058, at 83,566-67 (D.D.C. Jan. 13, 1983) (information relating to performance ratings, recognition and awards, leave practices, transfers, travel expenses, and allowances); NTEU v. U.S. Dep't of the Treasury, 487 F. Supp. 1321, 1324 (D.D.C. 1980) (bargaining history and IRS interpretation of labor contract provisions).

[31] See, e.g., Hale v. U.S. Dep't of Justice, 973 F.2d 894, 902 (10th Cir. 1992) (permitting the withholding of "administrative markings and notations on documents; room numbers, telephone numbers, and FBI employees' identification numbers; a checklist form used to assist special agents
(continued...)

file or tracking numbers,[32] document routing information,[33] internal tele-

---

[31](...continued)
in consensual monitoring; personnel directories containing the names and addresses of FBI employees; and the dissemination page of Hale's 'rap sheet'"), cert. granted, vacated & remanded on other grounds, 509 U.S. 918 (1993); Scherer v. Kelley, 584 F.2d 170, 175-76 (7th Cir. 1978) (approving agency's withholding of "file numbers, initials, signature and mail routing stamps, references to interagency transfers, and data processing references"); Peter S. Herrick's Customs & Int'l Trade Newsletter v. U.S. Customs & Border Prot., No. 04-00377, 2006 WL 1826185, at *4 (D.D.C. June 30, 2006) (permitting withholding of twelve categories of "quintessentially internal" information, including file management procedures, paperwork completion instructions, and basic computer instructions); DiPietro v. Executive Office for U.S. Attorneys, 368 F. Supp. 2d 80, 82 (D.D.C. 2005) (holding that the agency properly withheld "an internal checklist of clerical actions, code numbers on a form for attorney time devoted to a task, a record of transmittals and receipts of records, a form used for inputting attorney work product data into a computer system, and identification and file numbers"); Changzhou Laosan Group v. U.S. Customs & Border Prot. Bureau, No. 04-1919, 2005 WL 913268, at *3 (D.D.C. Apr. 20, 2005) (upholding non-disclosure of "computer function codes, internal file numbers, computer system and report identity, internal operation information, and internal agency procedures").

[32] See, e.g., Middleton v. U.S. Dep't of Labor, No. 06-72, 2006 WL 2666300, at *6 (E.D. Va. Sept. 15, 2006) ("department control identification number"); Long, 450 F. Supp. 2d at 54-59 (concluding after an extensive analysis that "low 2" permits the withholding of "file numbers assigned by the agencies that have referred matters to [United States Attorneys' Offices]," and finding in the process that "compiling information to track an agency's performance of its core functions . . . is a quintessential agency practice"); Odle v. Dep't of Justice, No. 05-2711, 2006 WL 1344813, at *13 (N.D. Cal. May 17, 2006) (Office of Professional Responsibility case file numbers); Newry Ltd. v. U.S. Customs & Border Prot., No. 04-02110, 2005 WL 3273975, at *3 (D.D.C. July 29, 2005) (administrative markings related to "internal agency file control systems"); Delta Ltd. v. U.S. Customs & Border Prot. Bureau, 384 F. Supp. 2d 138, 147 (D.D.C.) ("internal file numbers" and "internal agency procedures and filing numbers"), partial reconsideration granted on other grounds, 393 F. Supp. 2d 15 (D.D.C. 2005); Envtl. Prot. Servs. v. EPA, 364 F. Supp. 2d 575, 583-84 (N.D. W. Va. 2005) ("Criminal Investigation Division tracking numbers"). But cf. Badalamenti v. U.S. Dep't of State, 899 F. Supp. 542, 547 (D. Kan. 1995) (determining that the agency's "bare assertion fails to demonstrate that the file and case numbers relate to an agency rule or practice or are otherwise encompassed within exemption 2"); cf. Fitzgibbon v. U.S. Secret Serv., 747 F. Supp. 51, 57 (D.D.C. 1990) (finding in the context of "high 2" analysis that "agencies have no generalized interest in keeping secret the method by which they store records").

phone and facsimile numbers,[34] and other similar administrative codes and markings[35] -- but also more extensive and substantive portions of adminis-

---

[33] See, e.g., Morley v. CIA, 453 F. Supp. 2d at 148-49 & n.2 (D.D.C. 2006) (concluding that "low 2" covers "materials that include 'citation to or discussion of CIA personnel rules and practices (including administrative routing information)'" (quoting agency declaration)); Wheeler v. U.S. Dep't of Justice, 403 F. Supp. 2d 1, 13 (D.D.C. 2005) (finding exempt from disclosure "information concerning the distribution of copies of documents" to an unnamed agency, because the interest in release was personal to the plaintiff and there was no evidence of bad faith in the processing of the plaintiff's FOIA request); Larson v. Dep't of State, No. 02-1937, 2005 WL 3276303, at *14 (D.D.C. Aug. 10, 2005) (finding that "low 2" covers "message routing data"); Coleman v. FBI, 13 F. Supp. 2d 75, 78 (D.D.C. 1998) (listing "mail routing stamps" among types of information properly withheld under "low 2"); Wilson v. Dep't of Justice, No. 87-2415, 1991 WL 111457, at *3 (D.D.C. June 13, 1991) (applying "low 2" to State Department transmittal slips from low-level officials).

[34] See, e.g., Ray v. FBI, 441 F. Supp. 2d 27, 33 (D.D.C. 2006) (internal FBI telephone number); Odle, 2006 WL 1344813, at *13 ("non-public [Office of Professional Responsibility] fax numbers and telephone numbers"); Morales Cozier v. FBI, No. 99-0312, slip op. at 13 (N.D. Ga. Sept. 25, 2000) ("facsimile numbers of FBI employees"); Germosen v. Cox, No. 98 Civ. 1294, 1999 WL 1021559, at *12 (S.D.N.Y. Nov. 9, 1999) (FBI telephone and facsimile numbers).

[35] See, e.g., Poulsen v. U.S. Customs & Border Prot., No. 06-1743, 2006 WL 2788239, at *6-9 (N.D. Cal. Sept. 26, 2006) (finding that certain information pertaining to agency computer network crash, such as "'incident i.d.' numbers" and administrative codes assigned to agency computers, was properly withheld); Baez v. FBI, 443 F. Supp. 2d 717, 727 (E.D. Pa. 2006) (concluding that the agency properly withheld administrative markings from an account statement, because they "could not be of any interest to the public"); Maydak v. U.S. Dep't of Justice, 362 F. Supp. 2d 316, 324 (D.D.C. 2005) (permitting withholding of "accounting numbers from purchase orders . . . because such information, similar to code numbers, is used for internal purposes and has no significant public interest"); Hamilton v. Weise, No. 95-1161, 1997 U.S. Dist. LEXIS 18900, at *17 (M.D. Fla. Oct. 1, 1997) (approving redaction of purely administrative Customs Service codes concerning individual pilot). But see Gerstein v. U.S. Dep't of Justice, No. C-03-4893, slip op. at 17-18 (N.D. Cal. Sept. 30, 2005) (ordering the disclosure of page numbers on records pertaining to delayed-notice searches, on the basis that "the public has an interest in learning about the aggregate length of notification delays" and "the redacted page numbers prevent [the requester] from linking documents together in a meaningful way"); Manna v. U.S. Dep't of Justice, 832 F. Supp. 866, 880 (D.N.J. 1993) (finding that "DEA failed to describe or explain what these 'internal markings' are . . . [and if they] relate to internal rules or practice and whether

(continued...)

trative records and, most significantly, entire documents.[36]

One particular type of administrative document -- federal personnel lists -- has caused the courts to struggle with the problem of determining when the threshold Exemption 2 requirement of being "related to" internal agency rules and practices is satisfied. Agencies had considered the use of Exemption 2 for such lists because the personal privacy protection of Exemption 6 -- successfully invoked to protect the names and home addresses of most federal employees[37] -- is generally unavailable to protect the names and duty addresses of federal employees inasmuch as there ordinarily is no privacy interest in such information. (See the discussion of this point under Exemption 6, below.)

In 1990, the Court of Appeals for the District of Columbia Circuit dispositively addressed the possible protection of federal personnel lists un-

---

[35](...continued)
these markings constitute trivial administrative matters of no public interest").

[36] See, e.g., Schiller v. NLRB, 964 F.2d at 1208 (internal time deadlines and procedures, recordkeeping directions, instructions on contacting agency officials for assistance and guidelines on agency decisionmaking); Nix v. United States, 572 F.2d 998, 1005 (4th Cir. 1978) (cover letters of merely internal significance); Melville v. U.S. Dep't of Justice, No. 05-0645, 2006 WL 2927575, at *6 (D.D.C. Oct. 12, 2006) (opening and closing forms from criminal prosecution); Geronimo v. Executive Office for U.S. Attorneys, No. 05-1057, 2006 WL 1992625, at *3 (D.D.C. July 14, 2006) (opening/closing form used for reporting to supervisory prosecutors); Gavin v. SEC, No. 04-4522, 2005 WL 2739293, at *5 (D. Minn. Oct. 24, 2005) (opening and closing reports from SEC investigation); Edmonds, 272 F. Supp. 2d at 50-51 (FBI internal rules and regulations for granting waivers from ordinary language-testing requirements); Amro v. U.S. Customs Serv., 128 F. Supp. 2d 776, 783 (E.D. Pa. 2001) ("record keeping directions, instructions on contacting agency officials for assistance and guidelines on agency decision making").

[37] See, e.g., FLRA v. U.S. Dep't of the Treasury, 884 F.2d 1446, 1452-53 (D.C. Cir. 1989) (relying on Exemption 6 to maintain protection of federal employees' home addresses); FOIA Update, Vol. III, No. 4, at 3 ("OIP Guidance: Privacy Protection Considerations") (delineating privacy protection considerations for federal employees); FOIA Update, Vol. VII, No. 3, at 3-4 ("FOIA Counselor: Protecting Federal Personnel Lists") (recognizing exceptions to disclosure of identities and work locations of certain law enforcement and military personnel); accord Attorney General's Memorandum for Heads of All Federal Departments and Agencies Regarding the Freedom of Information Act (Oct. 12, 2001) [hereinafter Attorney General Ashcroft's FOIA Memorandum], reprinted in FOIA Post (posted 10/15/01) (placing particular emphasis on personal privacy interests).

der Exemption 2 in Schwaner v. Department of the Air Force.[38] In a two-to-one decision, it held that a list of the names and duty addresses of military personnel stationed at Bolling Air Force Base does not meet the threshold requirement of being "related solely to the internal rules and practices of an agency."[39] The panel majority ruled that "the list does not bear an adequate relation to any rule or practice of the Air Force as those terms are used in exemption 2."[40] In so doing, it gave a new, stricter interpretation to the term "related to" under Exemption 2, for "low 2" purposes,[41] holding that if the information in question is not itself actually a "rule or practice," then it must "shed significant light" on a "rule or practice" in order to qualify.[42] The D.C. Circuit concluded that "lists do not necessarily (or perhaps even normally) shed significant light on a rule or practice; insignificant light is not enough."[43] Thus, under Schwaner, this aspect of Exemption 2 is not available to shield agencies from the burdens of processing requests for federal personnel lists.[44]

---

[38] 898 F.2d 793 (D.C. Cir. 1990).

[39] Id. at 794; see also Maydak, 362 F. Supp. 2d at 323 (holding Exemption 2 inapplicable to list of names and titles of prison staff; applying reasoning similar to that of Schwaner).

[40] Schwaner, 898 F.3d at 794.

[41] Id. at 796-97 (distinguishing agency practice of collecting information -- found to be insufficiently "related" to qualify for "low 2" protection -- from other agency practices, e.g., legitimate redaction of sensitive notations related to FBI informant symbol numbers (citing Lesar, 636 F.2d at 485-86)).

[42] Id. at 797; see also Audubon Soc'y v. U.S. Forest Serv., 104 F.3d 1201, 1204 (10th Cir. 1997) (concluding that maps of habitats of owls deemed "threatened" under Endangered Species Act are not sufficiently related to internal personnel rules and practices).

[43] Schwaner, 898 F.2d at 797; see DeLorme Publ'g Co. v. NOAA, 917 F. Supp. 867, 876 (D. Me. 1996) ("Nothing in Exemption 2 supports the proposition that government 'information may be withheld simply because it manifests an agency practice of collecting the information.'" (quoting Schwaner, 898 F.2d at 797)), appeal dismissed per stipulation, No. 96-1601 (1st Cir. July 8, 1996); see also Abraham & Rose, P.L.C. v. United States, 138 F.3d 1075, 1081, 1083 (6th Cir. 1998) (ruling that "information [contained in an IRS electronic database] . . . is not sufficiently related to a personnel rule or practice to satisfy . . . [the] Exemption 2 analysis," but can be protected under Exemptions 6 and 7(C)).

[44] See FOIA Update, Vol. XI, No. 2, at 2 (modifying prior guidance in light of controlling nature of ruling by D.C. Circuit, as circuit of "universal venue" under FOIA). But see Hale, 973 F.2d at 902 (ruling, in a post-Schwaner decision, that "personnel directories containing the names and [office] addresses of [most] FBI employees" are properly withheld as "trivial matters

(continued...)

In exceptional circumstances, however, information specific to individual federal employees, such as phone numbers and e-mail addresses, may be protectible under the "high 2" aspect of Exemption 2 on the basis that the consequences of disclosure would be harmful not only to the individuals but also to the effective operation of government offices.[45] (See also Exemption 2, "High 2": Risk of Circumvention, below.) Additionally, it is worth noting here that it is Department of Defense policy, based on specific statutory authority, and in coordination with the Office of Personnel Management, to accord extraordinary protection to the names and other identifying information of certain military service personnel under Exemption 6 of the FOIA.[46]

---

[44](...continued)
of no genuine public interest").

[45] See, e.g., Truesdale v. U.S. Dep't of Justice, No. 03-1332, 2005 WL 3294004, at *5 (D.D.C. Dec. 5, 2005) (protecting FBI Special Agents' telephone and facsimile numbers, because disclosure "would disrupt official business and could subject the FBI's employees to harassing telephone calls"); Queen v. Gonzales, No. 96-1387, 2005 WL 3204160, at *4 (D.D.C. Nov. 15, 2005) (finding that internal facsimile numbers of FBI Special Agents and support personnel involved in plaintiff's narcotics investigation were properly withheld); Pinnavaia v. FBI, No. 03-112, slip op. at 8 (D.D.C. Feb. 25, 2004) (holding that FBI Special Agents' beeper numbers and cell phone numbers were properly withheld, because their "disclosure . . . would disrupt official business" and "would serve no public benefit"); Edmonds, 272 F. Supp. at 51 (concluding that the FBI properly withheld secure facsimile numbers, because "this equipment would be worthless to the FBI in supporting its investigations" if the fax numbers were to be released); cf. Poulsen, 2006 WL 2788239, at *7-8 (concluding -- without citing to any case law on point -- that agency properly withheld names of employees involved in repairing computer network); The News-Press v. DHS, No. 05-CV-102, 2005 WL 2921952, at *10-11 (M.D. Fla. Nov. 4, 2005) (finding in unusual decision that names and signatures of low-level FEMA employees were properly redacted from disaster-assistance documents, falling "well within ['low 2' aspect of] Exemption 2").

[46] See 10 U.S.C. § 130b (2000 & Supp. IV 2004) (providing for nondisclosure of personally identifying information for personnel in overseas, sensitive, or routinely deployable units); Department of Defense Freedom of Information Act Program Regulations, 32 C.F.R. § 286.12(f)(2)(ii) (2006) (restating express authority to withhold names and duty addresses for such personnel); Memorandum from Department of Defense Directorate for Freedom of Information and Security Review 1 (Oct. 26, 1999) (applying same delineation for electronic mail addresses, on privacy-protection grounds); cf. Department of Defense Directorate for Administration and Management Memorandum Regarding Personally Identifying Information Under the Freedom of Information Act (Nov. 9, 2001), available at www.defenselink. mil/pubs/foi/withhold.pdf (urging careful consideration, given heightened
(continued...)

# EXEMPTION 2

The second part of the "low 2" formulation is whether there "is a genuine and significant public interest" in disclosure of the records requested.[47] When there is such an interest -- for example, with the honor code proceedings that were at issue in Department of the Air Force v. Rose -- the information is not covered by the "low 2" aspect of Exemption 2.[48] An illustration of how this "public interest" delineation has been drawn can be found in a decision in which large portions of a FOIA training manual used by the SEC were ruled properly withholdable as trivial and of no public interest,[49] while another portion, because of a discerned "public interest" in it, was

---

[46](...continued)
security concerns, before DOD disclosure of any lists of names and other personally identifying information of DOD personnel).

[47] Rose, 425 U.S. at 369.

[48] See id. at 367-70; see also, e.g., Vaughn v. Rosen, 523 F.2d 1136, 1140-43 (D.C. Cir. 1975) (refusing to allow agency to withhold evaluations of how effectively agency policies were being implemented); Gerstein, No. C-03-04893, slip op. at 17-18 (N.D. Cal. Sept. 30, 2005) (ordering disclosure of page numbers on records concerning delayed-notice searches, because the public has an interest in such searches and "the redacted page numbers prevent [the requester] from linking documents together in a meaningful way"); Carlson v. USPS, No. C-02-05471, 2005 WL 756573, at *5 (N.D. Cal. Mar. 31, 2005) (rejecting agency's application of "low 2" to records pertaining to mailbox locations, in part because agency had released records in response to prior similar requests and in part because of media coverage praising requester's efforts to obtain requested information); Church of Scientology v. IRS, 816 F. Supp. 1138, 1149 (W.D. Tex. 1993) (stating that "public is entitled to know how IRS is allocating" taxpayers' money as it pertains to IRS advance of travel funds to its employees), appeal dismissed per stipulation, No. 93-8431 (5th Cir. Oct. 21, 1993); Globe Newspaper Co. v. FBI, No. 91-13257, 1992 WL 396327, at *2-3 (D. Mass. Dec. 29, 1992) (finding that agency improperly invoked "low 2" for amount paid to FBI informant involved in "ongoing criminal activities"); News Group Boston, Inc. v. Nat'l R.R. Passenger Corp., 799 F. Supp. 1264, 1266-68 (D. Mass. 1992) (concluding that agency must disclose disciplinary actions taken against Amtrak employees), appeal dismissed, No. 92-2250 (1st Cir. Dec. 4, 1992); North v. Walsh, No. 87-2700, slip op. at 3 (D.D.C. June 25, 1991) (finding "low 2" inapplicable to travel vouchers of senior officials of Office of Independent Counsel); FBI Agents Ass'n, 3 Gov't Disclosure Serv. at 83,566-67 (concluding that standards of conduct, grievance procedures, and EEO procedures were improperly withheld under "low 2"); Ferris v. IRS, 2 Gov't Disclosure Serv. (P-H) ¶ 82,084, at 82,363 (D.D.C. Dec. 23, 1981) (holding that agency improperly withheld SES performance objectives).

[49] Am. Lawyer Media, Inc. v. SEC, No. 01-1967, 2002 U.S. Dist. LEXIS 16940, at *8 (D.D.C. Sept. 6, 2002) ("This information is the paradigmatic 'trivial administrative matter [that] is of no genuine public interest.'").

not.[50] This decision is reflective of the D.C. Circuit's admonition in Founding Church of Scientology v. Smith[51] that "a reasonably low threshold should be maintained for determining when withheld administrative material relates to significant public interests."[52]

The nature of this "public interest" in "low 2" cases was affected by the Supreme Court's decision in United States Department of Justice v. Reporters Committee for Freedom of the Press.[53] In Reporters Committee, the Supreme Court held that the "public interest" depended on the nature of the document sought and its relationship to "the basic purpose [of the FOIA] 'to open agency action to the light of public scrutiny."[54] The Court concluded that the FOIA's "core purposes" would not be furthered by disclosure of a record about a private individual, even if it "would provide details to include in a news story, [because] this is not the kind of public interest for which Congress enacted the FOIA."[55] It also emphasized that a particular FOIA requester's intended use of the requested information "has no bearing on the merits of his or her FOIA request" and that FOIA requesters therefore should be treated alike.[56] (See the further discussion of this decision under Exemption 6, The Reporters Committee Decision, below.)

Although the Supreme Court's decision in Reporters Committee was based on an analysis of Exemption 7(C), its interpretation of what constitutes "public interest" under the FOIA logically may be applicable under Exemption 2 as well.[57] After Reporters Committee, courts increasingly have focused upon the lack of any "legitimate public interest" when applying this aspect of Exemption 2 to information found to be related to an

---

[50] Id. at *16 (finding that certain definitions "contain[ing] general legal instruction to SEC staff on how to analyze FOIA requests . . . must be disclosed").

[51] 721 F.2d 828 (D.C. Cir. 1983).

[52] Id. at 830-31 n.4.

[53] 489 U.S. 749 (1989).

[54] Id. at 772 (quoting Rose, 425 U.S. at 372).

[55] Id. at 774.

[56] Id. at 771; see also FOIA Update, Vol. X, No. 2, at 5 ("OIP Guidance: Privacy Protection Under the Supreme Court's Reporters Committee Decision").

[57] See Schwaner, 898 F.2d at 800-01 (Revercomb, J., dissenting on issue not reached by majority) (relying on Reporters Committee's "core purposes" analysis and finding no "genuine" public interest in disclosure of names and duty addresses of military personnel).

agency's internal practices.[58] Indeed, a number of courts had already been taking such an approach in analyzing "low 2" cases before Reporters Committee.[59] Nevertheless, there remains the fact that this aspect of Exemption 2 simply does not cover any information in which there is "a genuine and significant public interest."[60]

---

[58] See Hale, 973 F.2d at 902 (finding no public interest in administrative markings and notations, personnel directories containing names and addresses of FBI employees, room and telephone numbers, employee identification numbers, consensual monitoring checklist form, and rap sheet-dissemination page); Morley, 453 F. Supp. 2d at 149 ("Simply stated, there is no legitimate public interest that would justify disclosure of CIA personnel rules and practices, including administrative routing information."); Middleton, 2006 WL 2666300, at *6 (concluding that "it is apparent" that "the redacted ID numbers [do not] constitute a matter of genuine public interest"); Gavin, 2005 WL 2739293, at *5 (finding that opening and closing reports of investigation were properly withheld because there is "no public interest" in them); Morales Cozier, No. 99-0312, slip op. at 13 (N.D. Ga. Sept. 25, 2000) (ruling that "facsimile numbers of FBI employees . . . constitute trivial matter that could not reasonably be expected to be of interest to the public"); Germosen, 1999 WL 1021559, at *12 (S.D.N.Y. Nov. 9, 1999) (finding no legitimate or genuine public interest in source symbol numbers and agent identification numbers, as well as in computer access codes, telephone and facsimile numbers, and numbers used to denote different categories of counterfeit currency), appeal dismissed, No. 00-6041 (2d Cir. Sept. 12, 2000); Voinche, 46 F. Supp. 2d at 30 (applying Exemption 2 to telephone number of FBI's Public Corruption Unit as "trivial administrative matter of no genuine public interest"); News Group Boston, 799 F. Supp. at 1268 (holding that there is no public interest in payroll and job title codes); Buffalo Evening News, Inc. v. U.S. Border Patrol, 791 F. Supp. 386, 390-93 (W.D.N.Y. 1992) (declaring that there is no public interest in "soundex" encoding of alien's family name, in whether or not alien is listed in Border Patrol Lookout Book, in codes used to identify deportability, in narratives explaining circumstances of apprehension, or in internal routing information).

[59] See, e.g., Martin, 686 F.2d at 34 (Exemption 2 "is in part designed to screen out illegitimate public inquiries into the functioning of an agency"); Lesar, 636 F.2d at 485-86 (public has "no legitimate interest" in FBI's mechanism for internal control of informant identities); Struth v. FBI, 673 F. Supp. 949, 959 (E.D. Wis. 1987) (plaintiff offered no evidence of public interest in source symbol or source file numbers). But see Tax Analysts v. U.S. Dep't of Justice, 845 F.2d 1060, 1064 n.8 (D.C. Cir. 1988) (Exemption 2 found inapplicable, without discussion, due to "public's obvious interest" in agency copies of court opinions), aff'd on other grounds, 492 U.S. 136 (1989).

[60] Rose, 425 U.S. at 369; see also FOIA Update, Vol. V, No. 1, at 11 ("FOIA Counselor: The Unique Protection of Exemption 2") (emphasizing "low threshold" for required disclosure of such information).

As a final matter under this aspect of Exemption 2, it also is worth noting that in some cases courts have conflated the "low 2" and "high 2" aspects of the exemption or have applied the incorrect one.[61] This is perhaps due in part to a lack of clarity in some agency declarations regarding which aspect of Exemption 2 the agency is invoking.[62] It therefore is important that agency declarations clearly specify whether "low 2" or "high 2" is being invoked for any particular piece of information and that they explain exactly how the exemption applies, any case law suggesting to the contrary notwithstanding.[63] (See also the further discussion of this point under Litigation Considerations, "Vaughn Index," below.)

"High 2": Risk of Circumvention

The second category of information covered by Exemption 2 -- inter-

---

[61] See, e.g., Baez, 443 F. Supp. 2d at 727 (holding that the agency properly withheld "allegedly sensitive" administrative markings, because they "could not be of any interest to the public"); Neuhausser v. U.S. Dep't of Justice, No. 6: 03-531, 2006 WL 1581010, at *10 (E.D. Ky. June 6, 2006) (discussing agency's "high 2" argument, but permitting redactions under "low 2" approach); Maydak v. U.S. Dep't of Justice, 254 F. Supp. 2d 23, 36 (D.D.C. 2003) (protecting Bureau of Prisons' internal codes for electronic systems on the ground that inmates "could access information regarding other inmates," and reiterating that courts have "consistently found no significant public interest in the disclosure of identifying codes"); Palacio v. U.S. Dep't of Justice, No. 00-1564, 2002 U.S. Dist. LEXIS 2198, at *15 (D.D.C. Feb. 11, 2002) (holding that FBI informant codes were properly withheld because "[t]he means by which the FBI refers to informants . . . is a matter of internal significance in which the public has no substantial interest" and "disclosure of the informant codes may . . . harm the FBI's legitimate investigative activities"), summary affirmance granted, No. 02-5247, 2003 U.S. App. LEXIS 1804 (D.C. Cir. Jan. 31, 2003); Voinche v. FBI, 46 F. Supp. 2d 26, 30 (D.D.C. 1999) (concluding that the "disclosure of [a telephone extension] could result in the circumvention of FBI law enforcement procedures and there is no significant public interest in [its] disclosure"); Coleman, 13 F. Supp. 2d at 79 (protecting FBI source symbol numbers and file numbers both as "low 2" "information [that] facilitates administrative operation and recordkeeping," and as "high 2" information, because disclosure could allow "criminals to redirect their activities [to] avoid legal intervention").

[62] See, e.g., Herrick's Newsletter, 2005 WL 3274073, at *2 (criticizing agency's "generic descriptions" and directing it to file new Vaughn Index that specifies whether information withheld under Exemption 2 is "low 2" or "high 2" information).

[63] See, e.g., Changzhou, 2005 WL 913268, at *3 ("[T]he Court is unaware of any authority requiring the government to designated [sic] whether a withholding falls within a 'low' or 'high' category.").

nal matters of a far more substantial nature[64] the disclosure of which would risk the circumvention of a statute or agency regulation -- has generated considerable controversy over the years. In Department of the Air Force v. Rose,[65] the Supreme Court specifically left open the question of whether such records fall within Exemption 2 coverage. Most of the courts wrestling with this question in the years after Rose did so in the context of law enforcement manuals containing sensitive staff instructions. For example, the Court of Appeals for the Eighth Circuit held that Exemption 2 does not apply to such matters, but that subsection (a)(2)(C) of the FOIA,[66] which arguably excludes law enforcement manuals from the automatic disclosure provisions of the FOIA, bars disclosure of manuals whose release to the public would significantly impede the law enforcement process.[67] Although tacitly approving the Eighth Circuit's argument, the Courts of Appeals for the Fifth and Sixth Circuits developed an alternative rationale for withholding law enforcement manuals: Disclosure would allow persons "simultaneously to violate the law and to avoid detection"[68] by impeding law enforcement efforts.[69]

However, the majority of the courts in other circuits that examined this issue in the first five years after Rose at least implicitly placed greater weight on the House Report in this respect[70] and accordingly held that Exemption 2 is applicable to internal administrative and personnel matters, including law enforcement manuals, to the extent that disclosure would risk circumvention of an agency regulation or statute or impede the

---

[64] See, e.g., Attorney General's Memorandum for Heads of All Federal Departments and Agencies Regarding the Freedom of Information Act (Oct. 12, 2001) [hereinafter Attorney General Ashcroft's FOIA Memorandum], reprinted in *FOIA Post* (posted 10/15/01) (citing safeguarding national security and enhancing effectiveness of law enforcement agencies as "fundamental values"); see also White House Memorandum for Heads of Executive Departments and Agencies Concerning Safeguarding Information Regarding Weapons of Mass Destruction and Other Sensitive Documents Related to Homeland Security (Mar. 19, 2002) [hereinafter White House Homeland Security Memorandum], reprinted in *FOIA Post* (posted 3/21/02) (directing agencies to identify sensitive homeland security-related information for appropriate safeguarding).

[65] 425 U.S. 352, 364, 369 (1976).

[66] 5 U.S.C. § 552(a)(2)(C) (2000 & Supp. IV 2004).

[67] See Cox v. Levi, 592 F.2d 460, 462-63 (8th Cir. 1979); Cox v. U.S. Dep't of Justice, 576 F.2d 1302, 1306-09 (8th Cir. 1978).

[68] Hawkes v. IRS, 467 F.2d 787, 795 (6th Cir. 1972).

[69] See, e.g., id.; Sladek v. Bensinger, 605 F.2d 899, 902 (5th Cir. 1979).

[70] H. Rep. No. 89-1497, at 10 (1966), reprinted in 1966 U.S.C.C.A.N. 2418, 2427.

effectiveness of an agency's law enforcement activities.[71]

The Court of Appeals for the District of Columbia Circuit firmly joined and solidified this majority approach when the full court addressed the issue in Crooker v. ATF, a case involving a law enforcement agents' training manual.[72] Although not explicitly overruling its earlier en banc decision in Jordan v. United States Department of Justice, which held that guidelines for the exercise of prosecutorial discretion were not properly withholdable,[73] the en banc decision in Crooker specifically rejected the rationale of Jordan that Exemption 2 could not protect law enforcement manuals or other documents whose disclosure would risk circumvention of the law.[74] The Crooker decision thus stands at the head of a long line of cases interpreting Exemption 2 to encompass protection for sensitive internal agency information.[75]

In Crooker, the D.C. Circuit fashioned a two-part test for determining which sensitive materials are exempt from mandatory disclosure under the "high 2" aspect of Exemption 2. This test requires both:

---

[71] See, e.g., Hardy v. ATF, 631 F.2d 653, 656 (9th Cir. 1980); Caplan v. ATF, 587 F.2d 544, 547 (2d Cir. 1978); Wilder v. Comm'r, 607 F. Supp. 1013, 1015 (M.D. Ala. 1985); Ferri v. Bell, No. 78-841, slip op. at 7-9 (M.D. Pa. Dec. 15, 1983); Fiumara v. Higgins, 572 F. Supp. 1093, 1102 (D.N.H. 1983); Watkins v. Comm'r, No. C81-0091J, slip op. at 1 (D. Utah Mar. 29, 1982); see also Crooker v. ATF, 670 F.2d 1051, 1070 n.50 (D.C. Cir. 1981) (en banc) (stating that the Courts of Appeals for the Fourth and Seventh Circuits had not yet addressed the issue of "whether Exemption 2 applies to documents whose disclosure would risk circumvention of the law").

[72] 670 F.2d at 1074.

[73] 591 F.2d 753, 771 (D.C. Cir. 1978) (en banc).

[74] See 670 F.2d at 1075 (repudiating rationale of Jordan "because it does not appear to comport with the full congressional intent underlying the FOIA").

[75] See, e.g., Massey v. FBI, 3 F.3d 620, 622 (2d Cir. 1993) (finding that disclosure of informant symbol numbers and source-identifying information "could do substantial damage to the FBI's law enforcement activities"); Schiller v. NLRB, 964 F.2d 1205, 1207-08 (D.C. Cir. 1992) (protecting records pertaining to agency's litigation strategy because disclosure "'would render those documents operationally useless'" (quoting NTEU v. U.S. Customs Serv., 802 F.2d 525, 530-31 (D.C. Cir. 1986)); Dirksen v. HHS, 803 F.2d 1456, 1458-59 (9th Cir. 1986) (affirming nondisclosure of claims-processing guidelines that could be used by healthcare providers to avoid audits); Hardy, 631 F.2d at 657 (holding that "law enforcement materials, disclosure of which may risk circumvention of agency regulation, are exempt from disclosure" under Exemption 2).

**EXEMPTION 2**

(1) that a requested document be "predominantly internal,"[76] and

(2) that its disclosure "significantly risks circumvention of agency regulations or statutes."[77]

Whether there is any public interest in disclosure is legally irrelevant under this "anti-circumvention" aspect of Exemption 2.[78] Rather, the concern under "high 2" is that a FOIA disclosure should not "'benefit those attempting to violate the law and avoid detection.'"[79] Thus, this aspect of Exemption 2 fundamentally rests upon a determination of reasonably expect-

---

[76] Crooker, 670 F.2d at 1074 (adopting mere "predominant internality" standard proposed by Judge Leventhal in concurrence in Vaughn v. Rosen, 523 F.2d 1136, 1151 (D.C. Cir. 1975)); see also Judicial Watch, Inc. v. U.S. Dep't of Transp., No. 02-566, 2005 WL 1606915, at *9 (D.D.C. July 7, 2005) ("Exemption 2 is not limited to internal personnel rules and practices; rather, it is construed more generally to encompass documents that are used for predominantly internal purposes.").

[77] Crooker, 670 F.2d at 1073-74; see also Peter S. Herrick's Customs & Int'l Trade Newsletter v. U.S. Customs & Border Prot., No. 04-0377, 2006 WL 1826185, at *5 (D.D.C. June 30, 2006) (rejecting the plaintiff's argument that an agency must show that circumvention "be almost certain," finding that instead "the test is satisfied so long as the information could assist individuals seeking to avoid or hinder lawful agency regulation"); Dorsett v. U.S. Dep't of the Treasury, 307 F. Supp. 2d 28, 36-37 (D.D.C. 2004) (upholding the applicability of "high 2" protection for Secret Service "internal protective investigative information," and reiterating that "'Congress evidenced a secondary purpose when it enacted FOIA of preserving the effective operation of governmental agencies'" (quoting Crooker, 670 F.2d at 1074)).

[78] See Gordon v. FBI, 388 F. Supp. 2d 1028, 1036 (N.D. Cal. 2005) (finding irrelevant the substantial public interest in records pertaining to aviation "watch lists," because "disclosing the information would assist terrorists in circumventing the purpose of the watch lists"); Judicial Watch, Inc. v. U.S. Dep't of Commerce, 337 F. Supp. 2d 146, 165 (D.D.C. 2004) ("In light of Exemption 2's anti-circumvention purpose, public interest in the disclosure is legally irrelevant."); Voinche v. FBI, 940 F. Supp. 323, 328 (D.D.C. 1996) (relying on Crooker test, where "public interest in disclosure is irrelevant," to find FBI information related to security of Supreme Court building and Supreme Court Justices properly withheld under Exemption 2), aff'd per curiam on other grounds, No. 96-5304, 1997 WL 411685 (D.C. Cir. June 19, 1997); Inst. for Policy Studies v. Dep't of the Air Force, 676 F. Supp. 3, 5 (D.D.C. 1987) (assuming "significant public interest," but nevertheless holding that classification procedures were properly withheld because of risk of circumvention in identifying vulnerabilities). But cf. Kaganove v. EPA, 856 F.2d 884, 889 (7th Cir. 1988) (suggesting that document might not meet Crooker test if its purpose were not "legitimate").

[79] Crooker, 670 F.2d at 1054 (quoting agency declaration).

ed harm.[80]

Essential to any determination of Exemption 2 applicability, of course, is consideration of the basic character of the records involved. Apart from the Tenth Circuit's decision in Audubon Society v. United States Forest Service,[81] discussed below, there is a common thread running through the cases that have considered the issue: Where the stakes are high -- e.g., the records at hand contain sensitive law enforcement or homeland security information -- judicial endorsement of "high 2" protection is commensurately highly likely.[82]

Indeed, in Crooker, the foundation case for "high 2" protection, the D.C. Circuit based its decision to uphold an agency's decision to protect a sensitive law enforcement training manual on "the overall design of FOIA, the explicit comments made in the House [legislative history], the caution-

---

[80] See, e.g., Judicial Watch, Inc. v. U.S. Dep't of Commerce, 83 F. Supp. 2d 105, 110 (D.D.C. 1999) (applying "high 2" based upon determination that disclosure of government credit card numbers "would present an opportunity for misuse and fraud"); see also H. Rep. No. 89-1497, at 5 (1966), reprinted in 1966 U.S.C.C.A.N. 2418, 2422 (emphasizing potential damage to public and private interests as basis for withholding agency plans); accord Attorney General Ashcroft's FOIA Memorandum], reprinted in FOIA Post (posted 10/15/01) (establishing governmentwide FOIA policy).

[81] 104 F.3d 1201 (10th Cir. 1997); cf. Maricopa Audubon Soc'y v. U.S. Forest Serv., 108 F.3d 1082, 1086-87 (9th Cir. 1997) (Ninth Circuit decision following counterpart Tenth Circuit decision on virtually identical facts, but only in that those facts did not involve anything that could be deemed "law enforcement material").

[82] See Schwaner v. Dep't of the Air Force, 898 F.2d 793, 796 (D.C. Cir. 1990) (acknowledging presciently that "[j]udicial willingness to sanction a weak relation to 'rules and practices' may be greatest when the asserted government interest is relatively weighty"); see also Lesar v. U.S. Dep't of Justice, 636 F.2d 472, 486 (D.C. Cir. 1980) (upholding Exemption 2 protection for FBI symbol numbers that are used to identify confidential informants, without evident regard for any relation to internal personnel rules or practices); cf. Maricopa, 108 F.3d at 1086-87 (distinguishing goshawk nesting site information, found to be unprotected by Exemption 2, from law enforcement records, such as claims-processing guidelines and training manuals, the disclosure of which was found to risk circumvention of law (citing Dirksen, 803 F.2d at 1458, and Hardy, 631 F.2d at 656)). See generally FOIA Post, "New Attorney General FOIA Memorandum Issued" (posted 10/15/01) (advising of "high 2" protection that is available for highly sensitive "critical infrastructure information" generated by federal agencies); cf. Ctr. for Nat'l Sec. Studies v. U.S. Dep't of Justice, 331 F.3d 918, 926 (D.C. Cir. 2003) (recognizing that agencies that specialize in law enforcement are entitled to deference when claiming law enforcement purpose under one of Exemption 7's subparts).

ary words of the Supreme Court in Rose, and even common sense."[83] Citing its seminal reliance on Exemption 2 to protect the informant codes that were at issue in Lesar,[84] the full D.C. Circuit in Crooker pointedly declared, once and for all, that "the scope of Exemption 2 [is not restricted] to minor employment matters."[85]

To meet the first part of the "high 2" Crooker standard, agencies must demonstrate that the information withheld is "predominantly internal."[86] While this is the same as for under "low 2," relatively speaking, because of the nature of the information protected by "high 2," courts might well be more willing to find that agencies have met the first part of the Crooker test" when considering the use of "high 2."[87] The D.C. Circuit established specific guidance on what constitutes an "internal" document in Cox v. United States Department of Justice, which held to be protectible information that

> does not purport to regulate activities among members of the public . . . [and] does [not] set standards to be followed by agency personnel in deciding whether to proceed against or to take action affecting members of the public. Differently stated, the unreleased information is not "secret law," the primary tar-

---

[83] 670 F.2d at 1074.

[84] 636 F.2d at 485-86.

[85] Crooker, 670 F.2d at 1069.

[86] See, e.g., Judicial Watch, Inc. v. U.S. Dep't of Transp., 2005 WL 1606915, at *11 (rejecting agency's application of Exemption 2 to letter from private company to FAA official, because agency did not explain how letter was "predominantly internal").

[87] See Schwaner, 898 F.2d at 796 ("Judicial willingness to sanction a weak relation to 'rules and practices' may be greatest when the asserted government interest is relatively weighty."); see also, e.g., Kaganove, 856 F.2d at 889 (finding that agency, like any employer, "reasonably would expect" applicant rating plan to be internal); NTEU v. U.S. Customs Serv., 802 F.2d 525, 531 (D.C. Cir. 1986) (holding that "appointments of individual members of the lower federal bureaucracy is primarily a question of 'internal' significance for the agencies involved"); Shanmugadhasan v. U.S. Dep't of Justice, No. 84-0079, slip op. at 31-34 (C.D. Cal. Feb. 18, 1986) (finding that DEA periodical distributed to more than 1700 state, federal, and foreign agencies was "predominantly internal," by reasoning that it did not "modify or regulate public behavior" and that DEA took "stringent steps" to ensure that it was distributed only to law enforcement agencies); Inst. for Policy Studies, 676 F. Supp. at 5 ("[I]t is difficult to conceive of a document that is more 'predominantly internal' than a guide by which agency personnel classify documents.").

get of [the FOIA's] broad disclosure provisions.[88]

Accordingly, federal law enforcement documents that were widely disseminated have been held to be sufficiently internal for purposes of Exemption 2 protection.[89] In one case that delineates the outer bounds of this concept, a law enforcement document distributed to 1700 state, federal, and foreign law enforcement agencies was held to meet the test of "predominant internality" when its dissemination was necessary for maximum law enforcement effectiveness and access by the general public was prohibited.[90]

Indeed, reflecting the high degree of deference that is implicitly accorded law enforcement activities under this substantive aspect of Exemption 2,[91] courts have treated a wide variety of information pertaining to

---

[88] 601 F.2d 1, 5 (D.C. Cir. 1979) (per curiam); see also Herrick's Newsletter, 2006 WL 1826185, at *7 ("The information properly withheld as 'high 2' does not purport to regulate interactions involving members of the public, and in no way constitutes the 'secret law' at which FOIA takes aim."); Sousa v. U.S. Dep't of Justice, No. 95-375, 1996 U.S. Dist. LEXIS 18627, at *11 (D.D.C. Dec. 9, 1996) (finding that "the exemption only applies to information 'used for a predominantly internal purpose'" (quoting Schiller, 964 F.2d at 1207)); cf. Gordon, 388 F. Supp. 2d at 1036-37 (requiring disclosure of "the legal basis for detaining someone whose name appears on a watch list").

[89] See, e.g., L.A. Times Commc'ns, LLC v. Dep't of the Army, 442 F. Supp. 2d 880, 901 (C.D. Cal. 2006) (rejecting plaintiff's arguments that the withheld information could not be "'predominantly internal'" because it had been "'widely disseminated'"; finding instead that the distribution to private contractors "does not negate th[e] fact" that the withheld information was "compiled for predominantly internal purposes," in part because of access restrictions placed on the private contractors).

[90] See Shanmugadhasan, No. 84-0079, slip op. at 31-34 (C.D. Cal. Feb. 18, 1986) (protecting sensitive portions of DEA periodical that contained drug-enforcement techniques and exchanges of law enforcement information); FOIA Post, "Critical Infrastructure Information Regulations Issued by DHS" (posted 2/27/04) (noting governmentwide applicability of safeguarding requirements for federal information required to be established pursuant to section 893 of Homeland Security Act of 2002, 6 U.S.C. § 483 (Supp. IV 2004)); cf. Presidential Memorandum for the Heads of Executive Departments and Agencies Concerning Guidelines and Requirements in Support of the Information Sharing Environment (Dec. 16, 2005), available at http://www.whitehouse.gov/news/releases/2005/12/20051216-10.html (discussing importance of, and establishing guidelines for, sharing "terrorism information" with state, local, tribal, and private entities).

[91] See Schwaner, 898 F.2d at 796 (acknowledging pragmatically and of
(continued...)

EXEMPTION 2

such activities as "internal," including:

(1) general guidelines for conducting investigations;[92]

(2) guidelines for conducting post-investigation litigation;[93]

---

[91](...continued)
necessity that "[j]udicial willingness to sanction a weak relation to 'rules and practices' may be greatest when the asserted government interest is relatively weighty"); Wiesenfelder v. Riley, 959 F. Supp. 532, 535 (D.D.C. 1997) (pointing out deference properly accorded law enforcement activities); cf. Ctr. for Nat'l Sec. Studies, 331 F.3d at 927-28 (recognizing need for deference to be afforded government's top counterterrorism officials who can best make "predictive judgment of harm that will result from disclosure of information" concerning ongoing national security investigation into 9/11 terrorist attacks) (Exemption 7(A)).

[92] See, e.g., PHE, Inc. v. U.S. Dep't of Justice, 983 F.2d 248, 251 (D.C. Cir. 1993) ("FBI guidelines as to what sources of information are available to its agents"); Sinsheimer v. DHS, 437 F. Supp. 2d 50, 56 (D.D.C. 2006) ("'agency procedures for the conduct of sexual harassment investigations'" (quoting agency declaration)); Sussman v. U.S. Marshals Serv., No. 03-0610, 2005 WL 3213912, at *5 (D.D.C. Oct. 13, 2005) ("guidelines for threat investigations and threat assessments") (appeal pending); Suzhou Yuanda Enter. v. U.S. Customs & Border Prot., 404 F. Supp. 2d 9, 12 (D.D.C. 2005) (internal instructions on handling seized property); Delta Ltd. v. U.S. Customs & Border Prot. Bureau, 384 F. Supp. 2d 138, 147-48 (D.D.C.) (same), partial reconsideration granted on other grounds, 393 F. Supp. 2d 15 (D.D.C. 2005); Becker v. IRS, No. 91-C-1203, 1992 WL 67849, at *6 n.1 (N.D. Ill. Mar. 27, 1992) (operational rules, guidelines, and procedures for law enforcement investigations and examinations), motion to amend denied (N.D. Ill. Apr. 12, 1993), aff'd in part & rev'd in part on other grounds, 34 F.3d 398 (7th Cir. 1994); Goldsborough v. IRS, No. 81-1939, 1984 WL 612, at *7 (D. Md. May 10, 1984) (manual with guidelines for criminal investigation).

[93] See, e.g., Schiller, 964 F.2d at 1207-08 (upholding the district court's finding that litigation strategy pertaining to the Equal Access to Justice Act passes Exemption 2's "threshold test" of being "predominantly internal"; rejecting the requester's contention that it does not simply because it "involves the [agency's] relations with outsiders"); Silber v. U.S. Dep't of Justice, No. 91-876, transcript at 19-20 (D.D.C. Aug. 13, 1992) (bench order) (deciding that agency's fraud litigation monograph was "predominantly internal," and observing that this phrase "has been read very broadly and expansively"); see also Shumaker, Loop & Kendrick, L.L.P. v. Commodity Futures Trading Comm'n, No. 97-7139, slip op. at 9 (N.D. Ohio May 27, 1997) (relying on Schiller to determine that agency settlement guidelines are similar to exempt litigation strategies, and implicitly finding that they are "predominantly internal"). But see Dayton Newspapers, Inc. v. Dep't of the Air Force, 107 F. Supp. 2d 912, 920 (S.D. Ohio 1999) (rejecting agencies' invoca-
(continued...)

(3) guidelines for identifying law violators;[94]

(4) a study of agency practices and problems pertaining to under-cover agents;[95]

(5) information related to prison security;[96] and

---

[93](...continued)
tion of Exemption 2 for individual malpractice case settlement amounts, which court treated as not covered by "'internal personnel rules and practices'" and, therefore, as "presum[ptively] . . . subject to disclosure" absent the applicability of any other exemption).

[94] See, e.g., Dirksen, 803 F.2d at 1458-59 (affirming nondisclosure of claims-processing guidelines that could be used by health care providers to avoid audits); Schwarz v. U.S. Dep't of Treasury, 131 F. Supp. 2d 142, 150 (D.D.C. 2000) ("personal characteristics used by the Secret Service in evaluating the dangerousness of a subject" found "clearly exempt from disclosure" under both Exemptions 2 and 7(E)), summary affirmance granted, No. 00-5453, 2001 WL 674636 (D.C. Cir. May 10, 2001); Voinche, 940 F. Supp. at 328-29 (protecting as internal manual describing techniques used by professional gamblers to evade prosecution); Church of Scientology Int'l v. IRS, 845 F. Supp. 714, 723 (C.D. Cal. 1993) (protecting "information about internal law enforcement techniques, practices, and procedures used by the IRS to coordinate the flow of information regarding Scientology"); Buffalo Evening News, Inc. v. U.S. Border Patrol, 791 F. Supp. 386, 393 (W.D.N.Y. 1992) (finding methods of apprehension and statement of ultimate disposition of case to be internal); Williston Basin Interstate Pipeline Co. v. FERC, No. 88-592, 1989 WL 44655, at *1-2 (D.D.C. Apr. 17, 1989) (holding portions of audit report to be "functional equivalent" of investigative techniques manual, and thus protectible under Exemptions 2 and 7(E), because disclosure would reveal techniques used by agency personnel to ascertain whether plaintiff was in compliance with federal law); Windels, Marx, Davies & Ives v. Dep't of Commerce, 576 F. Supp. 405, 409-10 (D.D.C. 1983) (protecting computer program under Exemptions 2 and 7(E) because it merely instructs computer how to detect possible law violations, rather than modifying or regulating public behavior).

[95] See Cox v. FBI, No. 83-3552, slip op. at 1 (D.D.C. May 31, 1984) (holding that a report concerning undercover agents "is exclusively an internal FBI document which does not affect the public and contains no 'secret law'"), appeal dismissed, No. 84-5364 (D.C. Cir. Feb. 28, 1985).

[96] See Miller v. Dep't of Justice, No. 87-0533, 1989 WL 10598, at *1-2 (D.D.C. Jan. 31, 1989) (finding "predominantly internal" sections of Bureau of Prisons manual that summarize procedures for security of prison control centers, including escape-prevention plans, control of keys and locks within prison, instructions regarding transportation of federal prisoners, and arms and defensive equipment inventories maintained in facility); see also
(continued...)

(6) vulnerability assessments.[97]

On the other hand, some courts have been reluctant to extend Exemption 2 protections in a non-law enforcement context without first finding that the records at issue are clearly "predominantly internal." In 1992, the District Court for the District of Columbia held that a computer-calculating technique used by the Department of Transportation to determine the safety rating for motor carriers was not purely internal because it was used to ascertain "whether and to what extent certain violations will have any legal effect or carry any legal penalty."[98] That same court held that documents relating to the procurement of telecommunications services by the federal government could not qualify as "primarily" internal because of the project's "massive" scale and significance.[99] Another district court, the United States District Court for the District of Oregon, held that a daily diary used to verify contract compliance did not contain internal instructions to government officials and therefore could not be withheld under Exemp-

---

[96](...continued)
Linn v. U.S. Dep't of Justice, No. 92-1406, 1995 WL 417810, at *19 (D.D.C. June 6, 1995) (protecting numerical symbols used for identifying prisoners, because disclosure could assist others in breaching prisoners' security); Kuffel v. U.S. Bureau of Prisons, 882 F. Supp. 1116, 1123 (D.D.C. 1995) (same).

[97] See, e.g., Inst. for Policy Studies, 676 F. Supp. at 5; see also FOIA Update, Vol. X, No. 3, at 3-4 ("OIP Guidance: Protecting Vulnerability Assessments Through Application of Exemption Two"); cf. Dorsett, 307 F. Supp. 2d at 36-37 (concluding that a Secret Service document used to "analyze and profile factual information concerning individuals" met the "predominantly internal" standard); Schwarz, 131 F. Supp. 2d at 150 (finding "the threat potential to individuals protected by the Secret Service" to be exempt from disclosure under both Exemptions 2 and 7(E)); Voinche, 940 F. Supp. at 328-29 (protecting as "predominantly internal" information relating to security of Supreme Court building and Supreme Court Justices); Ctr. for Nat'l Sec. Studies v. INS, No. 87-2068, 1990 WL 236133, at *5 (D.D.C. Dec. 19, 1990) (upholding on basis of Exemption 7(E) agency decision to protect final contingency plan in event of attack on United States).

[98] Don Ray Drive-A-Way Co. of Cal. v. Skinner, 785 F. Supp. 198, 200 (D.D.C. 1992). But see Wilder v. Comm'r, 601 F. Supp. 241, 242-43 (M.D. Ala. 1984) (determining that agreement between state and federal agencies concerning merely when to exchange information relevant to potential violations of tax laws is sufficiently internal procedure because it does not interpret substantive law).

[99] MCI Telecomms. Corp. v. GSA, No. 89-0746, 1992 WL 71394, at *5 (D.D.C. Mar. 25, 1992).

tion 2.[100]

In two decisions narrowly construing Exemption 2, the Courts of Appeals for the Ninth and Tenth Circuits refused to protect maps showing nest site locations of two different species of birds because the documents lacked sufficient "predominant internality" under a rigid interpretation of Exemption 2's language.[101] Declaring that the statutory phrase "internal personnel" modified both "rules" and "practices" of an agency, the Tenth Circuit turned down arguments from the Forest Service that the maps related to agency practices in that they helped Forest Service personnel perform their management duties.[102] Refusing to consider the potential harm from disclosure of such maps,[103] the Tenth Circuit declared that it would "stretch[] the language of the exemption too far to conclude that owl maps 'relate' to personnel practices of the Forest Service."[104] In reaching this decision, however, the Tenth Circuit relied on the D.C. Circuit case of Jordan v. United States Department of Justice,[105] even though the D.C. Circuit, sitting en banc, had explicitly repudiated the rationale of Jordan in this respect.[106]

Agreeing in a related case that such wildlife maps may not be protected from disclosure despite the potential risk of harm from their disclo-

---

[100] Tidewater Contractors, Inc. v. USDA, No. 95-541, 1995 WL 604112, at *3-4 (D. Or. Oct. 4, 1995), appeal dismissed voluntarily, No. 95-36238 (9th Cir. Mar. 5, 1996).

[101] See Maricopa Audubon Soc'y, 108 F.3d 1082; Audubon Soc'y, 104 F.3d 1201.

[102] Audubon Soc'y, 104 F.3d at 1204; see also Living Rivers, Inc. v. U.S. Bureau of Reclamation, 272 F. Supp. 2d 1313, 1317-18 (D. Utah 2003) (finding that "inundation maps," e.g., for Hoover Dam, do not meet extremely narrow "high 2" test used by Tenth Circuit requiring relation to "personnel practices").

[103] But see also Pease v. U.S. Dep't of Interior, No. 99CV113, slip op. at 2-4 (D. Vt. Sept. 17, 1999) (finding, on basis of National Park Omnibus Management Act of 1998, 16 U.S.C. § 5937 (2000), that agency properly withheld information pertaining to location of wildlife in Yellowstone National Park ecosystem) (Exemption 3).

[104] Audubon Soc'y, 104 F.3d at 1204; see also Thompson v. U.S. Dep't of Justice, No. 96-1118, slip op. at 30 (D. Kan. July 15, 1998) (following Audubon Society to deny protection to file numbers found not to qualify under rigid application of "personnel practices" requirement).

[105] See Audubon Soc'y, 104 F.3d at 1204 (citing Jordan, 591 F.2d at 764).

[106] See Crooker, 670 F.2d at 1075 (repudiating "the rationale of Jordan because it does not appear to comport with the full congressional intent underlying FOIA") (subsequent en banc action).

sure, the Ninth Circuit did not unqualifiedly accept the rationale of its circuit neighbor: Although declaring that the maps bore "no meaningful relationship to the 'internal personnel rules and practices' of the Forest Service,"[107] it instead stressed that the maps "do[] not tell the Forest Service how to catch lawbreakers [or] tell lawbreakers how to avoid the Forest Service's enforcement efforts," and it thereby specifically distinguished (and thus left undisturbed) its previous significant Exemption 2 decisions involving law enforcement records.[108] The Ninth Circuit's decision therefore has left much room for "high 2" protection of any information holding law enforcement significance.[109]

Once the "internality" of the information involved is established, courts readily move to the second "high 2" requirement and focus on what constitutes circumvention of legal requirements. As is discussed in more detail below, such legal requirements need not be criminally oriented and instead can be of a civil or regulatory nature.[110] Further, the potential law-

---

[107] Maricopa, 108 F.3d at 1086.

[108] Id. at 1087 (distinguishing Hardy, 631 F.2d at 656-57, and Dirksen, 803 F.2d at 1458-59).

[109] See Maricopa, 108 F.3d at 1087 (emphasizing that nest-site information "does not constitute 'law enforcement material'" entitled to protection under Exemption 2); see also, e.g., Lahr v. NTSB, 453 F. Supp. 2d 1153, 1171 (C.D. Cal. 2006) (reiterating Ninth Circuit's distinction between "law enforcement materials" and "administrative materials" in applying "high 2"); L.A. Times, 442 F. Supp. 2d at 901 (citing Hardy and Dirksen in finding that Army reconstruction efforts in Iraq had law enforcement purpose); Gordon, 388 F. Supp. 2d at 1035-36 (relying on Hardy in holding that FBI aviation "watch list" records were properly withheld under "high 2"); Coastal Delivery Corp. v. U.S. Customs Serv., 272 F. Supp. 2d 958, 965 (C.D. Cal.) (recognizing both protective room left by Ninth Circuit -- in that its Hardy rule remains "still in force today" -- and agency's consequently qualifying law enforcement purpose for container-inspection data at Los Angeles/Long Beach seaport), reconsideration denied, 272 F. Supp. 2d at 966-68 (C.D. Cal. 2003), appeal dismissed voluntarily, No. 03-55833 (9th Cir. Aug. 26, 2003).

[110] See, e.g., Schiller, 964 F.2d at 1208 ("[W]e have not limited the 'high 2' exemption to situations where penal or enforcement statutes could be circumvented."); cf. Jefferson v. Dep't of Justice, 284 F.3d 172, 178 (D.C. Cir. 2002) (reiterating that Exemption 7 "'covers investigatory files related to enforcement of all kinds of laws,' including those involving 'adjudicative proceedings'" (quoting Rural Hous. Alliance v. USDA, 498 F.2d 73, 81 n.46 (D.C. Cir. 1974)); Rugiero v. U.S. Dep't of Justice, 257 F.3d 534, 550 (6th Cir. 2001) (explaining that the "Court has adopted a per se rule" that Exemption 7 applies not only to records from criminal enforcement actions, but to "records compiled for civil enforcement purposes as well"); Gordon, 388 F. Supp. 2d at 1036 ("Exemption 7(E) is not limited to documents created in connection

(continued...)

breakers from whom the information is being protected need not be outside of the government -- meaning that information can be withheld to protect even against circumvention of legal requirements by agency employees.[111]

There are a number of different categories of information for which the risk of circumvention is readily apparent. Critically important are records that reveal the nature and extent of a particular investigation; these have been repeatedly held protectible on this "anti-circumvention" basis.[112] One common form of such information is sensitive administrative codes that contain information about agency investigations.[113]

---

[110](...continued)
with a criminal investigation.").

[111] See, e.g., Sinsheimer, 437 F. Supp. 2d at 56 (approving the withholding of "'agency procedures for the conduct of sexual harassment investigations'" because they could allow the subjects of such investigations (i.e., employees) to "'potentially foil investigative tactics'" (quoting agency declaration)); Judicial Watch, Inc. v. U.S. Dep't of Commerce, 337 F. Supp. 2d at 166 (holding that "guidelines for internal audits of Commerce expenses and travel vouchers" were properly withheld, because release "could enable Commerce employees to evade the law").

[112] See, e.g., Williams v. U.S. Dep't of Justice, No. 02-2452, slip op. at 6 (D.D.C. Feb. 4, 2004) (protecting FBI confidential source numbers because disclosure could reveal "the identity, scope, and location of FBI source coverage within a particular area"), reconsideration denied (D.D.C. Mar. 10, 2004), aff'd per curiam, 171 F. App'x 857 (D.C. Cir. 2005); Rosenberg v. Freeh, No. 97-0476, slip op. at 4-6 (D.D.C. May 12, 1998) (disclosure of FBI source numbers, banking codes, and code name would risk circumvention of law); Barkett v. U.S. Dep't of Justice, No. 86-2029, 1989 WL 930993, at *1 (D.D.C. July 18, 1989) ("The non-disclosure of information which reveals the nature and extent of a particular criminal investigation has been upheld under this exemption."); cf. KTVK-TV v. DEA, No. 89-379, 1989 U.S. Dist. LEXIS 10348, at *3 (D. Ariz. Aug. 29, 1989) (finding that disclosure of tape of speech by local police chief, given at seminar sponsored by DEA, which contained remarks on police department programs used or contemplated to discourage illegal drug use would "tend to discourage illegal use of drugs" rather than "enable drug users to avoid detection").

[113] See, e.g., Chavez-Arellano v. U.S. Dep't of Justice, No. 05-2503, 2006 WL 2346450, at *5-6 (D.D.C. Aug. 11, 2006) (protecting internal DEA codes because disclosure "would help identify the priority given to particular investigations" and "could allow suspects to avert detection and apprehension"); Neuhausser v. U.S. Dep't of Justice, No. 6: 03-531, 2006 WL 1581010, at *10 (E.D. Ky. June 6, 2006) (approving redaction of sensitive law enforcement codes); Wilson v. DEA, 414 F. Supp. 2d 5, 12 (D.D.C. 2006) (approving withholding of DEA Geographical Drug Enforcement Program (G-DEP)
(continued...)

# EXEMPTION 2

Another set of information that courts have recognized the importance of protecting is computer access codes, instructions, and programs used by agencies that might assist in gaining wrongful access to agencies' electronically stored information.[114] Nondisclosure of other sensitive information that might permit unauthorized access to agency computer or communications systems also has been upheld.[115]

---

[113](...continued)
codes); Butler v. U.S. Dep't of Justice, 368 F. Supp. 2d 776, 786 (E.D. Mich. 2005) (finding that disclosure of DEA "violator identifiers" could allow suspects to "decode this information and change their pattern of drug trafficking"), summary affirmance granted, No. 05-1922 (6th Cir. Jan. 25, 2006); Santos v. DEA, No. 02-0734, 2005 WL 555410, at *1 (D.D.C. Mar. 7, 2005) (concluding that disclosure of sensitive DEA codes "would compromise narcotics investigations by allowing drug users to alter their drug usage and exposing information regarding individuals cooperating with the agency"); Augarten v. DEA, No. 93-2192, 1995 WL 350797, at *1 (D.D.C. May 22, 1995) (acknowledging that release of "drug codes, information identification codes, and violator identification codes" would reveal nature and extent of specific investigations); Manna v. U.S. Dep't of Justice, 832 F. Supp. 866, 872, 880 (D.N.J. 1993) (finding that release of G-DEP and NADDIS numbers "would impede" investigative and enforcement efforts).

[114] See, e.g., Dirksen, 803 F.2d at 1457, 1459 (protecting instructions for computer coding); Masters v. ATF, No. 04-2274, slip op. at 8-9 (D.D.C. Sept. 25, 2006) (protecting computer data indicating "the terminal from which a query was made and the route by which the record was retrieved"); Doyharzabal v. Gal, No. 00-2995, 2001 WL 35810671, at *6, *10 (D.S.C. Apr. 25, 2001) (magistrate's recommendation) (protecting "an internal computer access code utilized by only [agency] employees in the course of their law enforcement duties"), adopted (D.S.C. Sept. 13, 2001), summary affirmance granted sub nom. Doyharzabal v. Fed. Bureau of Prisons, 31 F. App'x 144 (4th Cir. 2002); Boyd v. U.S. Marshal Serv., No. 99-2712, 2002 U.S. Dist. LEXIS 27734, at *6-7 (D.D.C. Mar. 15, 2002) (protecting unspecified computer codes), summary judgment granted, 2002 U.S. Dist. LEXIS 27735 (D.D.C. Oct. 7, 2002); Ferranti v. ATF, 177 F. Supp. 2d 41, 45 (D.D.C. 2001) (protecting "internal BATF computer codes" as "clearly fall[ing] within Exemption 2"); Kuffel, 882 F. Supp. at 1123 (protecting computer and teletype routing symbols, access codes, and computer option commands); Beckette v. USPS, No. 90-1246, 1993 WL 730711, at *4 (E.D. Va. Mar. 11, 1993) (protecting control file, which "is a set of instructions that controls the means by which data is entered and stored in the computer"), aff'd, 25 F.3d 1038 (4th Cir. 1994) (unpublished table decision); see also Windels, 576 F. Supp. at 412-14 (protecting computer program under Exemptions 2 and 7(E)); Kiraly v. FBI, 3 Gov't Disclosure Serv. (P-H) ¶ 82,465, at 83,135 (N.D. Ohio Feb. 17, 1982) (protecting computer codes under Exemptions 2 and 7(E)), aff'd, 728 F.2d 273 (6th Cir. 1984).

[115] See, e.g., Knight v. NASA, No. 2:04-cv-2054, 2006 WL 3780901, at *6
(continued...)

[115](...continued)
(E.D. Cal. Dec. 21, 2006) (observing that "high 2" protects "information facilitating a computer hacker's access to vulnerable agency databases, like file pathnames, keystroke instructions, directory address and other internal information," and approving agency's withholding of information that would reveal a server's "directory structure"); Poulsen v. U.S. Customs & Border Prot., No. 06-1743, 2006 WL 2788239, at *6-9 (N.D. Cal. Sept. 26, 2006) (holding that the agency properly withheld certain specific technical details of repairing a computer network, such as the "identifying codes for machines and workstations," the "names or other specific identifying information for databases or the patch installed," and the "work tickets" generated in response to employees' requests for assistance); Odle v. Dep't of Justice, No. 05-2711, 2006 WL 1344813, at *13 (N.D. Cal. May 17, 2006) (upholding agency's use of Exemption 2 to protect "'location codes, allegations codes, and computer pathnames that are used to access [agency's] computerized databases'" (quoting agency declaration)); Sussman, 2005 WL 3213912, at *5 (finding that agency properly withheld computer pathnames, which give location of files on computer network); Elec. Privacy Info. Ctr. v. DHS, 384 F. Supp. 2d 100, 109 (D.D.C. 2005) (protecting "information [that] would allow access to an otherwise secure database"); Truesdale v. U.S. Dep't of Justice, No. 03-1332, 2005 WL 3273093, at *7 (D.D.C. July 22, 2005) (finding that "internal administrative codes used in criminal law enforcement databases" were properly withheld because release "would allow individuals to circumvent the computer system"); Judicial Watch, Inc. v. U.S. Dep't of Commerce, 337 F. Supp. 2d at 166 (protecting file numbers and administrative markings because release could render computer system "vulnerable to hacking," and also protecting information pertaining to an internal DOD communication method); Robert v. U.S. Dep't of Justice, No. 99-3649, 2001 WL 34077473, at *5 (E.D.N.Y. Mar. 22, 2001) (recognizing necessity of redacting FBI file numbers to "protect against unauthorized access to [agency] computer system"), aff'd, 26 F. App'x 87 (2d Cir. 2002); Jefferson v. U.S. Dep't of Justice, No. 00-1489, slip op. at 3 (D.D.C. Nov. 30, 2000) (ruling that disclosure of case file numbers and computer pathnames "might be used to compromise the security" of agency's electronic databases and computer systems), aff'd in part & remanded in part on other grounds, 284 F.3d 172 (D.C. Cir. 2002); Bartolotta v. FBI, No. 99-1145, slip op. at 7 (D.D.C. July 13, 2000) (finding teletype access codes to be properly withheld because release "would enable individuals to interfere with [agency's] communications with other law enforcement agencies"); Linn, 1995 WL 417810, at *18-19, *21-22, *24-25 (protecting "access codes and routing symbols" withheld by Marshals Service because disclosure "could allow unauthorized access to and compromise of data in law enforcement communications systems," but refusing to protect similar information withheld by INTERPOL and Customs Service because asserted risks of compromising integrity of agencies' recordkeeping system were found to be "plainly insufficient"); Hall v. U.S. Dep't of Justice, No. 87-0474, 1989 WL 24542, at *2 (D.D.C. Mar. 8, 1989) (protecting various items that

(continued...)

**EXEMPTION 2**

Exemption 2's "anti-circumvention" protection also is readily applicable to vulnerability assessments, which are perhaps the quintessential type of record warranting protection on that basis; such records generally assess an agency's vulnerability (or that of another institution) to some form of outside interference or harm by identifying those programs or systems deemed the most sensitive and describing specific security measures that can be used to counteract such vulnerabilities.[116] A prime example of vulnerability assessments warranting protection under "high 2" are the computer security plans that all federal agencies are required by law to prepare.[117] In a decision involving such a document, for example, Schreibman v. United States Department of Commerce,[118] Exemption 2 was invoked to prevent unauthorized access to information which could result in "alternation [sic], loss, damage or destruction of data contained in the computer system."[119] It should be remembered, however, that even such a sensitive document must be reviewed to determine whether any "reasonably segregable" portion can be disclosed without harm.[120] (See the further

---

[115](...continued)
"could facilitate unauthorized access to [agency] communications systems"); Inst. for Policy Studies, 676 F. Supp. at 5 (according Exemption 2 protection to a record revealing the most sensitive portions of an agency system which "could be used to seek out the [system's] vulnerabilities"); see also FOIA Update, Vol. X, No. 3, at 3-4 ("OIP Guidance: Protecting Vulnerability Assessments Through Application of Exemption Two") (discussing case law according "protection to items of sensitive computer-related information").

[116] See FOIA Update, Vol. X, No. 3, at 3-4 ("OIP Guidance: Protecting Vulnerability Assessments Through Application of Exemption Two") (observing that "Exemption 2 should be fully available to protect vulnerability assessments, wherever it reasonably is determined that disclosure risks circumvention of the law or of some lawful requirement," and collecting cases); see also FOIA Post, "New Attorney General FOIA Memorandum Issued" (posted 10/15/01) (urging necessary protection of information regarding "critical systems, facilities, stockpiles, and other assets [which themselves hold potential for] use as weapons of mass destruction").

[117] See FOIA Update, Vol. X, No. 3, at 4 ("OIP Guidance: Protecting Vulnerability Assessments Through Application of Exemption Two") (citing Computer Security Act of 1987, Pub. L. No. 100-235, 101 Stat. 1724 (1988)).

[118] 785 F. Supp. 164 (D.D.C. 1991).

[119] Id. at 166.

[120] See id.; see also, e.g., PHE, 983 F.2d at 252 (remanding for "high 2" segregation; "district court clearly errs when it approves the government's withholding of information under the FOIA without making an express finding on segregability" (citing Schiller, 964 F.2d at 1210)); Wightman v. ATF, 755 F.2d 979, 982-83 (1st Cir. 1985) (remanding for determination on
(continued...)

discussions of this point under Procedural Requirements, "Reasonably Seg-regable" Obligation, above, and Litigation Considerations, "Reasonably Segregable" Requirements, below.)

Release of various categories of information other than those that already have been described above also has been found likely to result in harmful circumvention:

(1) information that would reveal the identities of informants;[121]

(2) information that would jeopardize undercover agents or op-

---

[120](...continued)
segregability); FOIA Update, Vol. XIV, No. 3, at 11-12 ("OIP Guidance: The 'Reasonable Segregation' Obligation"); Schrecker v. U.S. Dep't of Justice, 74 F. Supp. 2d 26, 32 (D.D.C. 1999) (finding that FBI properly "shield[ed] from disclosure [confidential informant] source codes [and] identifying data . . . no portion of [which] is reasonably segregable"), aff'd in part, rev'd & remanded in part, all on other grounds, 254 F.3d 162 (D.C. Cir. 2001); Archer v. HHS, 710 F. Supp. 909, 911-12 (S.D.N.Y. 1989) (upon in camera review, ordering disclosure of Medicare reimbursement-review criteria, but with specific audit trigger number segregated for protection).

[121] See, e.g., Davin v. U.S. Dep't of Justice, 60 F.3d 1043, 1065 (3d Cir. 1995) (upholding protection for informant codes); Jones v. FBI, 41 F.3d 238, 244-45 (6th Cir. 1994) (same); Massey, 3 F.3d at 622 (finding that disclosure of informant symbol numbers and source-identifying information "could do substantial damage to the FBI's law enforcement activities"); Lesar, 636 F.2d at 485 (finding that "informant codes plainly fall within the ambit of Exemption 2"); Williams, No. 02-2452, slip op. at 6 (D.D.C. Feb. 4, 2004) ("The release of the source symbol number could result in the disclosure of the informant's identity or the identity, scope, and location of FBI source coverage within a particular area."); Summers v. U.S. Dep't of Justice, No. 98-1837, slip op. at 13 (D.D.C. Mar. 10, 2003) (determining that informant designations and file numbers are properly covered by Exemption 2); Mack v. Dep't of the Navy, 259 F. Supp. 2d 99, 107 n.3 (D.D.C. 2003) (finding cooperating witness identification numbers to be "strictly internal and . . . sensitive because they conceal the identity of informants who were promised confidentiality in exchange for their cooperation"); Raulerson v. Ashcroft, 271 F. Supp. 2d 17, 24 (D.D.C. 2002) (finding FBI source symbol numbers to be properly withheld as category of information that is "amenable to non-specific explanation"); Shores v. FBI, 185 F. Supp. 2d 77, 83 (D.D.C. 2002) (recognizing that disclosing "informant symbol and file numbers," and thereby "compromising the identities of government informants," readily "could deter individuals from cooperating with the government"); Sinito v. U.S. Dep't of Justice, No. 87-0814, slip op. at 12 (D.D.C. July 12, 2000) (concluding that protection of source numbers continues even after death of informants); cf. Globe Newspaper Co. v. FBI, No. 91-13257, 1992 WL 396327, at *3 (D. Mass. Dec. 29, 1992) (ordering release of amount paid to FBI informant personally involved in continuing criminal activity).

# EXEMPTION 2

erations;[122]

(3) sensitive administrative codes and notations in law enforcement files;[123]

---

[122] See Peltier v. FBI, No. 02-4328, slip op. at 16-17 (D. Minn. Oct. 24, 2006) (magistrate's recommendation) (concluding that the FBI properly withheld "'the specific dollar amount of funds paid to an informant for his/her undercover operational expenses,'" and distinguishing Globe Newspaper, 1992 WL 396327 (quoting agency declaration)), adopted (D. Minn. Feb. 9, 2007); Russell v. FBI, No. 03-0611, slip op. at 8 (D.D.C. Jan. 9, 2004) (holding that release of "funds used for undercover operations . . . 'would impede the effectiveness of the FBI's internal law enforcement procedures'" (quoting agency declaration)), summary affirmance granted sub nom. Russell v. Dep't of Justice, No. 04-5036, 2004 WL 1701044 (D.C. Cir. July 29, 2004); Barkett, 1989 WL 930993, at *1 (finding that disclosure of "sensitive, detailed codes of current [DEA] activities could place the lives of undercover DEA agents in extreme peril"); Cox v. FBI, No. 83-3552, slip op. at 2 (D.D.C. May 31, 1984) (protecting report concerning FBI's undercover agent program because of potential for discovering identities of agents). But see also Homick v. U.S. Dep't of Justice, No. 98-00557, slip op. at 15 (N.D. Cal. Sept. 16, 2004) (ordering disclosure of twenty-two-year-old records concerning undercover vehicle because FBI failed to show that same type of vehicle was still being used), appeal dismissed voluntarily, No. 04-17568 (9th Cir. July 5, 2005).

[123] See, e.g., Founding Church of Scientology v. Smith, 721 F.2d 828, 830-31 (D.C. Cir. 1983) (protecting sensitive instructions regarding administrative handling of document); Boyd, 2002 U.S. Dist. LEXIS 27734, at *6-7 (protecting ATF "voucher numbers" and "law enforcement technique codes"); Coleman v. FBI, 13 F. Supp. 2d 75, 79 (D.D.C. 1998) (finding that the disclosure of file numbers "could potentially reveal a sequence of information including the dates, times, and identities of . . . informant transactions thereby exposing the depth of FBI's informant coverage"); Cappabianca v. Comm'r, U.S. Customs Serv., 847 F. Supp. 1558, 1563 (M.D. Fla. 1994) (protecting Customs Service file numbers "containing information such as the type and location of the case" because "if the code were cracked, [it] could reasonably lead to circumvention of the law"); Curcio v. FBI, No. 89-941, 1990 WL 179605, at *2 (D.D.C. Nov. 2, 1990) (protecting expense accounting in FBI criminal investigation). But see, e.g., Thompson, No. 96-1118, slip op. at 29-30 (D. Kan. July 15, 1998) (requiring release of Office of Professional Responsibility file numbers, even though recognizing their "sensitive and confidential" nature); Fitzgibbon v. U.S. Secret Serv., 747 F. Supp. 51, 57 (D.D.C. 1990) (rejecting the agency's argument regarding the integrity of its recordkeeping system, and finding that "agencies have no generalized interest in keeping secret the method by which they store records"); Wilkinson v. FBI, 633 F. Supp. 336, 342 & n.13 (C.D. Cal. 1986) (holding codes that identify law enforcement techniques not readily protectible under Exemption 2).

(4) security techniques used in prisons;[124]

(5) agency audit guidelines;[125]

(6) agency testing or employee rating materials;[126]

---

[124] See, e.g., Cox v. U.S. Dep't of Justice, 601 F.2d at 4-5 (upholding non-disclosure of weapon, handcuff, and transportation security procedures); Jimenez v. FBI, 938 F. Supp. 21, 27 (D.D.C. 1996) (approving nondisclosure of criteria for classification of prison gang member); Hall, 1989 WL 24542, at *2 (reasoning that disclosure of teletype routing symbols, access codes, and data entry codes maintained by Marshals Service "could facilitate unauthorized access to information in law enforcement communications systems, and [thereby] jeopardize [prisoners' security]"); Miller, 1989 WL 10598, at *1 (disclosure of sections of Bureau of Prisons (BOP) Custodial Manual that describe procedures for security of prison control centers would "necessarily facilitate efforts by inmates to frustrate [BOP's] security precautions"); cf. Thornburgh v. Abbott, 490 U.S. 401, 417 (1989) (rejecting requester's constitutional challenge to BOP regulation excluding publications that, although not necessarily likely to lead to violence, are determined by warden "to create an intolerable risk of disorder . . . at a particular prison at a particular time") (non-FOIA case). But see Linn v. U.S. Dep't of Justice, No. 92-1406, 1995 WL 631847, at *4-5 (D.D.C. Aug. 22, 1995) (rejecting as "conclusory" BOP's argument that release of case summary and internal memoranda would cause harm to safety of prisoners).

[125] See, e.g., Dirksen, 803 F.2d at 1458-59 (upholding protection of internal audit guidelines in order to prevent risk of circumvention of agency Medicare reimbursement regulations); Judicial Watch, Inc. v. U.S. Dep't of Commerce, 337 F. Supp. 2d at 166 (holding that agency properly withheld "guidelines for internal audits of Commerce expenses and travel vouchers"); Wiesenfelder, 959 F. Supp. at 535, 539 (protecting benchmarks signifying when enforcement action taken, errors identifying agency's tolerance for mistakes, and dollar amounts of potential fines); Archer, 710 F. Supp. at 911-12 (ordering Medicare reimbursement-review criteria disclosed, but protecting specific number that triggers audit); Windels, 576 F. Supp. at 412-13 (withholding computer program containing anti-dumping detection criteria). But see Don Ray Drive-A-Way, 785 F. Supp. at 200 (ordering disclosure based upon finding that knowledge of agency's regulatory priorities would allow regulated carriers to concentrate efforts on correcting most serious safety breaches).

[126] See, e.g., Patton v. FBI, 626 F. Supp. 445, 447 (M.D. Pa. 1985) (finding that testing materials were properly withheld because release would impair effectiveness of system and give future applicants unfair advantage), aff'd, 782 F.2d 1030 (3d Cir. 1986) (unpublished table decision); Oatley v. United States, 3 Gov't Disclosure Serv. (P-H) ¶ 83,274, at 84,065 (D.D.C. Aug. 16, 1983) (concluding that civil service testing materials satisfy two-part Crooker test); see also Kaganove, 856 F.2d at 890 (holding that disclo-
(continued...)

(7) codes that would identify intelligence targets;[127]

(8) agency credit card numbers;[128]

(9) an agency's unclassified manual detailing the categories of information that are classified, as well as their corresponding classification levels;[129]

(10) information concerning border security;[130]

---

[126](...continued)
sure of applicant rating plan would render it ineffectual and allow future applicants to "embellish" job qualifications); NTEU, 802 F.2d at 528-29 (determining that disclosure of hiring plan would give unfair advantage to some future applicants); Samble v. U.S. Dep't of Commerce, No. 92-225, slip op. at 12-13 (S.D. Ga. Sept. 22, 1994) (finding that release of evaluative criteria would compromise validity of rating process). But see Commodity News Serv. v. Farm Credit Admin., No. 88-3146, 1989 U.S. Dist. LEXIS 8848, at *13-16 (D.D.C. July 31, 1989) (holding the steps to be taken in selecting a receiver for liquidation of a failed federal land bank, including the sources an agency might contact when investigating candidates, to be not protectible under "high 2" because the agency did not demonstrate how the disclosure would allow any applicant to "gain an unfair advantage in the . . . process").

[127] See Tawalbeh v. U.S. Dep't of the Air Force, No. 96-6241, slip op. at 13 (C.D. Cal. Aug. 8, 1997) (finding that disclosure of Air Force internal intelligence collection codes "would allow unauthorized persons to decode classified . . . messages"); cf. Schrecker, 74 F. Supp. 2d at 32 (finding that the disclosure of identity of "governmental unit that submitted a particular document" could "risk circumvention of the ability of the [Defense Intelligence Agency] to collect or relay intelligence information").

[128] See Judicial Watch, Inc. v. U.S. Dep't of Commerce, 337 F. Supp. 2d at 166 (approving redaction of "government credit card numbers to prevent public access and misuse"); Boyd, 2002 U.S. Dist. LEXIS 27734, at *6-7 (finding that credit card account numbers were properly withheld under Exemption 2); Judicial Watch, Inc. v. U.S. Dep't of Commerce, 83 F. Supp. 2d at 110 (upholding protection of government credit card numbers based upon "realistic possibility of . . . misuse and fraud").

[129] See Inst. for Policy Studies, 676 F. Supp. at 5 (upholding the use of Exemption 2 to protect an Air Force security classification guide from which "a reader can gauge which components [of a classified emergency communication system] are the most sensitive and consequently the most important").

[130] See Herrick's Newsletter, 2006 WL 1826185, at *5 (approving withholding of portions of manual pertaining to seized property, in part because
(continued...)

(11) details of laboratory testing procedures;[131]

(12) law enforcement team and operation names;[132] and

(13) guidelines for protecting government officials.[133]

Even within sensitive law enforcement contexts, however, courts have rejected justifications for withholding when they fail to sufficiently articulate, with adequate evidentiary support, the potential harm from disclosure.[134] Similarly, in an exceptionally unusual decision, one court refused to

---

[130](...continued)
they could assist those wanting to smuggle contraband into country); Coastal Delivery Corp., 272 F. Supp. 2d at 965 (recognizing Exemption 2 protection for the number of inspections performed on shipping containers at a particular port by Customs Service, based on law enforcement purpose).

[131] See VoteHemp, Inc. v. DEA, No. 02-985, slip op. at 18-19 (D.D.C. Oct. 15, 2004) (concluding that DEA properly withheld "internal procedures for certifying a future [laboratory] testing procedure," because disclosure "could 'significantly risk future circumvention of federal drug control regulations'" (quoting agency declaration)).

[132] See Delta, 384 F. Supp. 2d at 148 (affording "high 2" protection to "law enforcement team or operation names and nomenclature"); Changzhou Laosan Group v. U.S. Customs & Border Prot. Bureau, No. 04-1919, 2005 WL 913268, at *3 (D.D.C. Apr. 20, 2005) (protecting "law enforcement investigation case name" and "investigation team name").

[133] See Judicial Watch, Inc. v. U.S. Dep't of Commerce, 337 F. Supp. 2d at 166 (finding that "guidelines for protecting the Secretary of Commerce on trade missions" were properly withheld, as disclosure "would compromise the Secretary's safety, making the Secretary subject to unlawful attacks"); Voinche, 940 F. Supp. at 329, 331 (approving nondisclosure of information relating to security of Supreme Court building and Justices).

[134] See, e.g., Gerstein v. U.S. Dep't of Justice, No. C-03-04893, slip op. at 18-21 (N.D. Cal. Sept. 30, 2005) (ordering disclosure of a compilation detailing each United States Attorney's Office's use of certain delayed-notice warrants, because the technique "is a matter of common knowledge" and disclosure would not reduce the technique's effectiveness); Larson v. Dep't of State, No. 02-1937, 2005 WL 3276303, at *14 (D.D.C. Aug. 10, 2005) (rejecting as "conclusory" agency's argument that release of documents concerning congressman's discussions with foreign officials "would reveal certain internal rules and practices" of agency; conjecturing that such an approach "would sweep into Exemption 2 nearly every record" maintained by agency); Carlson v. USPS, No. C-02-05471, 2005 WL 756573, at *6-7 (N.D. Cal. Mar. 31, 2005) (rejecting the agency's use of "high 2" to protect records
(continued...)

apply the "high 2" aspect of Exemption 2 to procedures that were designed to protect against any state agency's "circumventi[on]" of federal audit criteria for welfare reimbursement -- purely as a matter of special regard for the legal status of states.[135]

Under some circumstances, Exemption 2 may be applied to prevent potential circumvention through a "mosaic" approach -- information which would not by itself reveal sensitive law enforcement information can nonetheless be protected to prevent damage that could be caused by the assembly of different pieces of similar information by a requester.[136] This cir-

---

[134](...continued)
pertaining to mailbox locations, because the "plaintiff debunks defendant's efforts to show that releasing the information could be used to facilitate lawlessness" and because some of the agency's arguments were found to be "far-fetched," "speculative[,] and unsupported by evidence in the record"); Maydak v. U.S. Dep't of Justice, 362 F. Supp. 2d 316, 322 (D.D.C. 2005) (finding raw data from psychological test of prisoner not protectible under Exemptions 2 or 7(F) because agency's reasoning was "too speculative and not based upon competent evidence"); Homick, No. 98-00557, slip op. at 14-15 (N.D. Cal. Sept. 16, 2004) (ordering disclosure of information related to a twenty-year-old polygraph test because "the FBI has provided no statement that the type of machine, test, and number of charts used twenty years ago are the same or similar to those utilized today," and for similar reasons also ordering disclosure of information in twenty-two-year-old records related to an undercover vehicle).

[135] See Massachusetts v. HHS, 727 F. Supp. 35, 42 (D. Mass. 1989) ("The Act simply cannot be interpreted in such a way as to presumptively brand a sovereign state as likely to circumvent federal law. The second prong of Exemption 2 does not apply when it is [the state] itself that seeks the information.").

[136] See, e.g., Brunetti v. FBI, 357 F. Supp. 2d 97, 104 (D.D.C. 2004) (reasoning that FBI source symbol numbers and informant file numbers were properly withheld because "it would be possible . . . to discern patterns of information associated with particular sources," thereby allowing "[a]n individual with knowledge of the people and facts [to] be able to deduce the identities of these sources"); Dorsett, 307 F. Supp. 2d at 36 (concluding that certain Secret Service information, the disclosure of which in isolation would be "relatively harmless," could "in the aggregate" benefit those attempting to violate the law); Accuracy in Media v. FBI, No. 97-2107, slip op. at 5 (D.D.C. Mar. 31, 1999) (finding persuasive the FBI's argument that, with release of informant symbol numbers, "over time an informant may be identified by revealing . . . connections with dates, times, places, events"); Jan-Xin Zang v. FBI, 756 F. Supp. 705, 712 (W.D.N.Y. 1991) (ruling that source symbol and administrative identifiers were properly withheld on basis that "accumulation of information" known to be from same source could lead to detection); cf. Ctr. for Nat'l Sec. Studies, 331 F.3d at 928-29

(continued...)

cumstance first arose in the Exemption 2 context in a case involving a request for "Discriminant Function Scores" used by the IRS to select tax returns for examination.[137] Although the IRS conceded that release of any one individual's tax score would not disclose how returns are selected for audit, it took the position that the routine release of such scores would enable the sophisticated requester to discern, in the aggregate, its audit criteria, thus facilitating circumvention of the tax laws; the court accepted this rationale as an appropriate basis for affording protection under Exemption 2.[138] In a related case, one court upheld the denial of access to an IRS memorandum containing tolerance criteria used by the agency in its investigations, finding that disclosure would "undermine the enforcement of . . . internal revenue laws."[139] Increasingly, the "mosaic" approach has been used to protect information related to national security and homeland security, whether under Exemption 2,[140] or otherwise.[141] (See Exemption 1, Additional Considerations, above, for further discussion of the "mosaic"

---

[136](...continued)
(finding danger, in context of national security, based partly on "mosaic" concept); Davin, 60 F.3d at 1064-65 (remanding for agency to specify content of documents for which it raises "mosaic" argument).

[137] Ray v. U.S. Customs Serv., No. 83-1476, 1985 U.S. Dist. LEXIS 23091, at *10-11 (D.D.C. Jan. 28, 1985).

[138] See id.; see also Novotny v. IRS, No. 94-549, 1994 WL 722686, at *3 (D. Colo. Sept. 8, 1994); Wilder, 607 F. Supp. at 1015.

[139] O'Connor v. U.S. IRS, 698 F. Supp. 204, 206-07 (D. Nev. 1988). But cf. Archer, 710 F. Supp. at 911-12 (requiring careful segregation so that only truly sensitive portion of audit criteria is withheld).

[140] See, e.g., L.A. Times, 442 F. Supp. 2d at 898-99, 902 (using "mosaic" analysis in context of Exemptions 2 and 7(F) to find names of private security contractors protectible, because insurgents could use names in conjunction with other data "to organize attacks on vulnerable" companies and "to disrupt U.S. reconstruction efforts"); Coastal Delivery Corp., 272 F. Supp. 2d at 964-65 (concluding that the Customs Service had established that the release of seaport cargo-inspection data, combined with other known data, could -- through a "mosaic" analysis -- lead to the identification of highly sensitive security information and "risk circumvention of agency regulations as well as the law"); Inst. for Policy Studies, 676 F. Supp. at 5 (reasoning that classification guidelines could reveal which parts of sensitive communications system are most sensitive, which would enable foreign intelligence services to gather related unclassified records and seek out system's vulnerabilities).

[141] See, e.g., Ctr. for Nat'l Sec. Studies, 331 F.3d at 928-29 (finding danger, in context of national security and law enforcement, based partly on "mosaic" concept) (Exemption 7(A)); Halperin v. CIA, 629 F.2d 144, 150 (D.C. Cir. 1980) (applying "mosaic" analysis in context of Exemptions 1 and 3).

concept.)

Although originally, as in Crooker, the "anti-circumvention" protection afforded by Exemption 2 was applied almost exclusively to sensitive portions of criminal law enforcement manuals, it since has been extended to civil enforcement and regulatory matters, including some matters that are not law enforcement activities in the traditional sense.[142] In a pivotal case on this point, the National Treasury Employees Union sought documents known as "crediting plans," records used to evaluate the credentials of federal job applicants; the Customs Service successfully argued that disclosure of the plans would make it difficult to evaluate the applicants because they could easily exaggerate or even fabricate their qualifications, such falsifications would go undetected because the government lacked the resources necessary to verify each application, and unscrupulous future applicants could thereby gain an unfair competitive advantage.[143] The D.C. Circuit approved the withholding of such criteria under a refined application of Crooker, which focused directly on its second requirement, and held that the potential for circumvention of the selection program, as well as the general statutory and regulatory mandates to enforce applicable civil service laws, was sufficient to bring the information at issue within the protection of Exemption 2.[144] The agency demonstrated "circumvention" by showing that disclosure would either render the documents obsolete for their intended purpose, make the plan's criteria "operationally useless" or compromise the utility of the selection program.[145]

---

[142] See, e.g., Dirksen, 803 F.2d at 1459 (finding guidelines for processing Medicare claims properly withheld when disclosure could allow applicants to alter claims to fit them into certain categories and guidelines would thus "lose the utility they were intended to provide"); L.A. Times, 442 F. Supp. 2d at 901 (relying on Dirksen and Hardy in finding that the law enforcement purpose of the Army Corps of Engineers' Reconstruction Operations Center in Iraq was "to synthesize battlefield intelligence and make it available to military and [private security contractor] personnel in order to protect the lives of those individuals"); Wiesenfelder, 959 F. Supp. at 537-38 (finding trigger figures, error rate tolerances, and amounts of potential fines properly withheld because release would "substantially undermine" agency's regulatory efforts); Archer, 710 F. Supp. at 911 (protecting number of particular health procedures performed, which HHS contractor used to determine whether healthcare providers' claims for reimbursement under Medicare should be subjected to greater scrutiny; disclosure would allow providers "to avoid review and ensure automatic payment by submitting claims below the number . . . scrutinized").

[143] See NTEU, 802 F.2d at 528-29.

[144] See id. at 529-31.

[145] Id. at 530-31; cf. U.S. Dep't of Justice v. FLRA, 988 F.2d 1267, 1269 (D.C. Cir. 1993) (holding "crediting plans" to be also not subject to disclo-
(continued...)

This approach was expressly followed by the Court of Appeals for the Seventh Circuit in Kaganove to withhold from an unsuccessful job applicant the agency's merit promotion rating plan on the basis that disclosure of the plan "would frustrate the document's objective [and] render it ineffectual" for the very reasons noted in the NTEU case.[146] Similarly, the District Court for the District of Columbia permitted the Department of Education to withhold information consisting of trigger figures, error rates, and potential fines that provide "internal guidance to staff about how, when, and why they should concentrate their regulatory oversight."[147] The court agreed with the agency that "[g]iving institutions the wherewithal to engage in a cost/benefit analysis in order to choose their level of compliance would substantially undermine [its] regulatory efforts and thwart its program oversight."[148]

It is noteworthy that the Seventh Circuit in Kaganove,[149] the Ninth Circuit in Dirksen,[150] and the D.C. Circuit in NTEU[151] all reached their results even in the absence of any particular agency regulation or statute to be circumvented.[152] Thus, the second part of the Crooker test should properly be satisfied by a showing that disclosure would risk circumvention of general legal requirements.[153] In this regard, it is worth noting that the

---

[145](...continued)
sure under Federal Service Labor-Management Relations Act, 5 U.S.C. § 7114(b)(4)(B) (2000)).

[146] Kaganove, 856 F.2d at 889; see also Samble, No. CV192-225, slip op. at 12 (S.D. Ga. Sept. 22, 1994) (citing Kaganove, 856 F.2d at 889, to protect criteria used to evaluate job applicants).

[147] Wiesenfelder, 959 F. Supp. at 537.

[148] Id. at 537-38.

[149] 856 F.2d at 889.

[150] 803 F.2d at 1458-59.

[151] 802 F.2d at 529-31.

[152] See FOIA Update, Vol. X, No. 3, at 4 ("OIP Guidance: Protecting Vulnerability Assessments Through Application of Exemption Two") (advising that "the D.C. Circuit has expressly declined to impose any requirement that a particular statute or regulation be involved" (citing NTEU, 802 F.2d at 530-31)).

[153] See NTEU, 802 F.2d at 530-31 ("Where disclosure of a particular [record] would render [it] operationally useless, the Crooker analysis is satisfied whether or not the agency identifies a specific statute or regulation threatened by disclosure."); see also, e.g., Edmonds v. FBI, 272 F. Supp. 2d 35, 51 (D.D.C. 2003) (secure facsimile numbers found to be properly with-
(continued...)

EXEMPTION 2

District Court for the District of Columbia has expressly ruled, in the context of Exemption 2, that the "passage of time" does not necessarily "reduce[] the protections of a properly asserted exemption."[154]

Lastly, under the Freedom of Information Reform Act of 1986,[155] many of the materials previously protectible only on a "high 2" basis may be protectible also under Exemption 7(E).[156] Numerous post-amendment cases

---

[153](...continued) held because "this equipment would be worthless to the FBI in supporting its investigations" if the fax numbers were to be released); Knight v. DOD, No. 87-480, slip op. at 4 (D.D.C. Feb. 11, 1988) (memorandum detailing specific inventory audit guidelines held protectible because disclosure "would reveal [agency] rationale and strategy" for audit and would "create a significant risk that this information would be used by interested parties to frustrate ongoing or future . . . audits"); Boyce v. Dep't of the Navy, No. 86-2211, slip op. at 4 (C.D. Cal. Feb. 17, 1987) (routine hearing transcript properly withheld under Exemption 2 where disclosure would circumvent terms of contractual agreement entered into under labor-relations statutory scheme).

[154] Willis v. FBI, No. 96-1455, slip op. at 7 (D.D.C. Aug. 6, 1997) (magistrate's recommendation) (finding that DEA numbers -- G-DEP, NADDIS, and informant identifier codes -- are protectible even after case is long closed), adopted (D.D.C. Feb. 14, 1998), remanded on other grounds, 194 F.3d 175 (D.C. Cir. 1999) (unpublished table decision); see also Buckner v. IRS, 25 F. Supp. 2d 893, 899 (N.D. Ind. 1998) ("Because DIF scores are investigative techniques . . . still used by the IRS in evaluating tax returns . . . the age of the scores is of no consequence" in determining their releasability.) (Exemption 7(E)). But see Homick, No. 98-00557, slip op. at 14-15 (N.D. Cal. Sept. 16, 2004) (taking age of records into account in ordering disclosure because agency failed to show that same techniques currently were in use).

[155] Pub. L. No. 99-570, § 1802, 100 Stat. 3207, 3207-48, 3207-49 (codified as amended at 5 U.S.C. § 552(b)(2)).

[156] See, e.g., Kaganove, 856 F.2d at 888-89 (recognizing the congruence between the protection of information under Exemptions 2 and 7(E) based on the "risk [of] circumvention of the law"); Coastal Delivery Corp., 272 F. Supp. 2d at 965 (observing that the same reasons apply under both Exemptions 2 and 7(E) to protect from disclosure "information [that] has a law enforcement purpose . . . [where disclosure] would risk circumvention of agency regulations as well as the law"); see also Attorney General's Memorandum on the 1986 Amendments to the Freedom of Information Act 16-17 & n.32 (Dec. 1987) (observing that amendment of Exemption 7(E) in 1986 in some respects widened protections then available under Exemption 2); cf. NARA v. Favish, 541 U.S. 157, 169 (evincing Supreme Court's reliance on "Attorney General's consistent interpretation of" FOIA in successive such

(continued...)

have held such information to be exempt from disclosure under both Exemption 2 and Exemption 7(E).[157] Although Exemption 2 must still be used if any information fails to meet Exemption 7's "law enforcement" threshold, Exemption 2's history and judicial interpretations should be helpful in applying Exemption 7(E). (See the discussion of Exemption 7(E), below.)

## Homeland Security-Related Information

Since the horrific events of September 11, 2001, and given the potential for further terrorist activity in their aftermath, all federal agencies are concerned with the need to protect unclassified but sensitive information, including information pertaining to critical systems, facilities, stockpiles, and other assets (often referred to as "critical infrastructure") from security breaches and harm -- and in some instances from their potential use as weapons of mass destruction in and of themselves. Such protection efforts, of course, necessarily must include focus on any agency information that reasonably could be expected to enable someone to succeed in causing the feared harm, not all of which can appropriately be accorded national security classification protection as a practical matter.[158]

In addressing these heightened homeland security concerns, agency personnel responsible for reviewing documents responsive to FOIA requests prior to their disclosure should be sure to avail themselves of the full measure of Exemption 2's protection for national security- and home-

---

[156](...continued)
Attorney General memoranda), reh'g denied, 541 U.S. 1057 (2004).

[157] See, e.g., PHE, 983 F.2d at 251 (upholding FBI judgment, relying on both Exemptions 2 and 7(E), that release of "who would be interviewed, what could be asked, and what records or other documents would be reviewed" in FBI investigatory guidelines would risk circumvention of law); Gordon, 388 F. Supp. 2d at 1035-36 (holding that records concerning aviation "watch lists" were properly withheld under both Exemptions 2 and 7(E)); Schwarz, 131 F. Supp. 2d at 150 (finding Secret Service code names and White House gate numbers "clearly exempt from disclosure" under both Exemptions 2 and 7(E)); Peralta v. U.S. Attorney's Office, 69 F. Supp. 2d 21, 32, 35 (D.D.C. 1999) (applying both Exemptions 2 and 7(E) to radio channels used by FBI during physical surveillance); Voinche, 940 F. Supp. at 329, 331 (approving nondisclosure of information relating to security of Supreme Court building and Justices on basis of both Exemptions 2 and 7(E)).

[158] Cf. FOIA Post, "Executive Order on National Security Classification Amended" (posted 4/11/03) (noting coverage of "information that 'reveal[s] current vulnerabilities of systems, installations, infrastructures, or projects relating to national security,' in new Section 3.3(b)(8)" of Executive Order 12,958, as amended).

land security-related information.[159] That responsibility is of utmost importance when considering the need to protect particularly sensitive critical
infrastructure information from security breaches and harmful consequences.[160] In response to continued threats of terrorism, guidance issued by
the White House Chief of Staff in March 2002 highlighted the crucial nature
of that responsibility:

> The need to protect . . . sensitive information [related to
> America's homeland security] from inappropriate disclosure
> should be carefully considered, on a case-by-case basis,
> together with the benefits that result from the open and
> efficient exchange of scientific, technical, and like infor-
> mation.[161]

The types of information that may warrant Exemption 2 protection for
homeland security-related reasons include, for example, agency vulnerability assessments[162] and evaluations of items of critical infrastructure that

---

[159] See *FOIA Post*, "New Attorney General FOIA Memorandum Issued"
(posted 10/15/01) (emphasizing Exemption 2's applicability to homeland
security-related information, including "[a]ny agency assessment of, or
statement regarding, the vulnerability of" critical infrastructure); see also
*FOIA Post*, "FOIA Officers Conference Held on Homeland Security" (posted
7/3/03) (drawing attention to the "protection of homeland security-related
information [as] a subject of growing importance within all levels of government," and analyzing homeland security-related cases).

[160] See *FOIA Post*, "New Attorney General FOIA Memorandum Issued"
(posted 10/15/01).

[161] White House Memorandum for Heads of Executive Departments and
Agencies Concerning Safeguarding Information Regarding Weapons of
Mass Destruction and Other Sensitive Documents Related to Homeland Security (Mar. 19, 2002) [hereinafter White House Homeland Security Memo-
randum], reprinted in *FOIA Post* (posted 3/21/02) (directing agencies to
give "full and careful consideration to all applicable FOIA exemptions,"
through an attached memorandum from the National Archives and Records
Administration's Information and Security Oversight Office and the Department of Justice's Office of Information and Privacy that specifies Exemption
2 as a basis for protection of sensitive critical infrastructure information);
see also Attorney General Ashcroft's FOIA Memorandum, reprinted in
*FOIA Post* (posted 10/15/02) (emphasizing the importance of "safeguarding
our national security [and] enhancing the effectiveness of our law enforcement agencies"); cf. *FOIA Post*, "Critical Infrastructure Information Regulations Issued by DHS" (posted 2/27/04) (highlighting growing importance in
post-9/11 environment of safeguarding "sensitive homeland security information").

[162] See FOIA Update, Vol. X, No. 3, at 3-4 ("OIP Guidance: Protecting
(continued...)

are internal to the federal government.[163] Since September 11, 2001, nearly all courts that have considered nonclassified but nonetheless highly sensitive information have justifiably determined -- either under Exemption 2 or, upon a finding of a sufficient law enforcement connection,[164] under Exemptions 7(E) or 7(F)[165] -- that such information must be protected from disclo-

---

[162](...continued)
Vulnerability Assessments Through Application of Exemption Two"); see also, e.g., Inst. for Policy Studies v. Dep't of the Air Force, 676 F. Supp. 3, 5 (D.D.C. 1987) (upholding "use of Exemption 2 to withhold internal agency information on grounds of national security"); cf. Dorsett v. U.S. Dep't of the Treasury, 307 F. Supp. 2d 28, 36 (D.D.C. 2004) (concluding that a Secret Service document used to "analyze and profile factual information concerning individuals" could be "used to gain insight into the methods and criteria . . . [used] to identify and investigate persons of interest, and could alter such individuals' behavior to avoid detection"); Voinche v. FBI, 940 F. Supp. 323, 329, 332 (D.D.C. 1996) (approving nondisclosure of information relating to security of Supreme Court building and Supreme Court Justices on basis of both Exemptions 2 and 7(E)); Ctr. for Nat'l Sec. Studies v. INS, No. 87-2068, 1990 WL 236133, at *5-6 (D.D.C. Dec. 19, 1990) (approving an agency decision based on Exemption 7(E) to protect certain planning information developed for use in the event of an attack on the United States, because its "release . . . could assist terrorists in 'planning their attacks and escapes' and imperil the safety of Customs officers").

[163] See Homeland Security Presidential Directive (HSPD-7) 39 Weekly Comp. Pres. Doc. 1816 (Dec. 22, 2003) (defining "critical infrastructure" and "key resources," and also directing all Federal departments and agencies to "appropriately protect information . . . that would facilitate terrorist targeting of . . . [those] resources"), available at www.gpoaccess.gov/wcomp/v39no51.html; cf. FOIA Post, "Critical Infrastructure Information Regulations Issued by DHS" (posted 2/27/04) (detailing protection for certain information that is submitted to agencies by private-sector and other nonfederal entities, in contrast to information that is entirely internal to federal government).

[164] See Ctr. for Nat'l Sec. Studies v. U.S. Dep't of Justice, 331 F.3d 918, 926, 927-28 (D.C. Cir. 2003) (counseling "deference in national security matters," and finding law enforcement purpose established where agency demonstrated both "rational nexus" between agency investigation and its law enforcement duties as well as connection between person or incident and possible security risk or law violation).

[165] See, e.g., L.A. Times Commc'ns, LLC v. Dep't of the Army, 442 F. Supp. 2d 880, 900, 902 (C.D. Cal. 2006) (protecting names of private security contractors in Iraq under Exemptions 2 and 7(F)); Peter S. Herrick's Customs & Int'l Trade Newsletter v. U.S. Customs & Border Prot., No. 04-00377, 2006 WL 1826185, at *5 (D.D.C. June 30, 2006) (protecting, under Exemptions 2, 7(E), and 7(F), portions of law enforcement manual pertaining to

(continued...)

sure in order to avoid the harms described both in the Homeland Security Presidential Directive concerning "Critical Infrastructure Identification, Prioritization, and Protection"[166] and by Congress in the exemptions to the Freedom of Information Act.[167]

Such information found to be protected under Exemption 2 since the attacks of September 11, 2001 includes:

(1)  cargo container-inspection data from particular seaport;[168]

(2)  records pertaining to aviation "watch lists";[169]

(3)  the storage locations of explosives-detection equipment used in aviation security;[170]

---

[165](...continued)
handling of seized property); Living Rivers, Inc. v. U.S. Bureau of Reclamation, 272 F. Supp. 2d 1313, 1321-22 (D. Utah 2003) (concluding that maps of flooding likely to result from damage to Hoover Dam or Glen Canyon Dam were properly withheld under Exemption 7(F), instead of under Exemption 2 or Exemption 7(E), due largely to atypically narrow interpretation of law within particular judicial circuit).

[166] Homeland Security Presidential Directive (HSPD-7), 39 Weekly Comp. Pres. Doc. 1816 (Dec. 22, 2003).

[167] See Attorney General's Memorandum for Heads of All Federal Departments and Agencies Regarding the Freedom of Information Act (Oct. 12, 2001) [hereinafter Attorney General Ashcroft's FOIA Memorandum], reprinted in FOIA Post (posted 10/15/01) (encouraging agencies to carefully consider protecting sensitive information when making disclosure determinations).

[168] See Coastal Delivery Corp. v. U.S. Customs Serv., 272 F. Supp. 2d 958, 964-65 (C.D. Cal.) (quoting Crooker v. ATF, 670 F.2d 1051, 1074 (D.C. Cir. 1981) (en banc), as having "acknowledged the rule in the Ninth Circuit -- still in force today -- 'that law enforcement materials, disclosure of which may risk circumvention of agency regulation, are exempt from disclosure'"), reconsideration denied, 272 F. Supp. 2d at 966-68 (C.D. Cal. 2003), appeal dismissed voluntarily, No. 03-55833 (9th Cir. Aug. 26, 2003); cf. Living Rivers, 272 F. Supp. 2d at 1321-22 (recognizing importance of guarding against terrorist "target selection") (Exemption 7(F) case).

[169] See Gordon v. FBI, 388 F. Supp. 2d 1028, 1035-36 (N.D. Cal. 2005) (protecting details of FBI's aviation "watch list" program, including records detailing "selection criteria" for lists, describing handling and dissemination of lists, and providing guidance on "addressing perceived problems in security measures").

[170] See Judicial Watch, Inc. v. U.S. Dep't of Transp., No. 02-566, 2005 WL
(continued...)

(4) the names of private security contractors in a war zone;[171]

(5) guidelines for protecting high-ranking officials on overseas trips;[172] and

(6) records pertaining to the security of national borders.[173]

(See also the discussions of related exemptions under Exemption 7, Exemption 7(E), and Exemption 7(F), below.) However, in a limited number of recent contrary decision worth noting, courts have rejected agencies' "high 2" defenses pertaining to homeland security-related information because they concluded that the agencies did not sufficiently articulate the potential disclosure harm.[174] These exceptional cases stand as a reminder

---

[170](...continued) 1606915, at *9 (D.D.C. July 7, 2005) (agreeing with the agency that "release of this information would enable an individual or group to cause harm to the explosive detection systems prior to their installation").

[171] See L.A. Times, 442 F. Supp. 2d at 900, 902 (approving agency's withholding of such names under Exemptions 2 and 7(F) on basis that insurgents could target more vulnerable contractors, thereby putting lives in danger and "disrupt[ing] U.S. reconstruction efforts").

[172] See Judicial Watch, Inc. v. U.S. Dep't of Commerce, 337 F. Supp. 2d 146, 166 (D.D.C. 2004) (finding that "guidelines for protecting the Secretary of Commerce on trade missions" were properly withheld, as disclosure "would compromise the Secretary's safety, making the Secretary subject to unlawful attacks").

[173] See Elec. Info. Privacy Ctr. v. DHS, No. 04-1625, 2006 U.S. Dist. LEXIS 94615, at *16-19 (D.D.C. Dec. 22, 2006) (magistrate's recommendation) (approving agency's withholding of "'current and proposed operational practices'" that "'concern procedures for the detection . . . of illegal border crossing activities'" (quoting agency declaration)), adopted (D.D.C. Jan. 23, 2007); Herrick's Newsletter, 2006 WL 1826185, at *5 (acknowledging that withheld portions of property-seizure law enforcement manual are "intertwined with overarching concerns of national security" because "individuals seeking to evade capture by customs officials, to smuggle illegal contraband into the country, [or] to reclaim or otherwise obtain seized contraband . . . would be privy to the most effective ways in which to do so" if the manual were disclosed).

[174] See Poulsen v. U.S. Customs & Border Prot., No. 06-1743, 2006 WL 2788239, at *6-9 (N.D. Cal. Sept. 26, 2006) (holding that agency improperly withheld certain general information about computer network "crash," but also holding that it properly withheld specific technical information about repairing network); Carlson v. USPS, No. C-02-05471, 2005 WL 756573, at *6-7 (N.D. Cal. Mar. 31, 2005) (concluding that disclosure of data pertaining (continued...)

to agency personnel that the potential harms from disclosure must be clearly and sufficiently identified and articulated in order to properly withhold information under "high 2."[175]

Lastly, something connected to homeland security-related information is the fact that agencies use a variety of safeguarding labels for "sensitive information," which should not be confused with FOIA exemptions.[176] Whatever the safeguarding label that an agency might (or might not) use for the information maintained by it that has special sensitivity -- e.g., "for official use only" (FOUO), "sensitive but unclassified" (SBU), or "sensitive homeland security information" (SHSI)[177] -- whenever "predominantly" internal agency records may reveal information the disclosure of which could reasonably be expected to cause any of the harms described above, responsible federal officials should carefully consider the propriety of protect-

---

[174](...continued) to mailbox locations would not risk use of postal system to distribute biological or chemical agents because agency failed to demonstrate that such data actually could be used to determine mail collection routes); see also Gordon, 388 F. Supp. 2d at 1036-37 (requiring disclosure of "the legal basis for detaining someone whose name appears on a watch list").

[175] See, e.g., Poulsen, 2006 WL 2788239, at *7 ("Although defendant repeatedly asserts that this [descriptive] information [regarding the scope of the incident] would render the [agency] computer system vulnerable, defendant has not articulated how this general information would do so.").

[176] See, e.g., Presidential Memorandum for the Heads of Executive Departments and Agencies Concerning Guidelines and Requirements in Support of the Information Sharing Environment (Dec. 16, 2005), available at http://www.whitehouse.gov/news/releases/2005/12/20051216-10.html (setting out guidelines for standardization of procedures related to "acquisition, access, retention, production, use, management, and sharing of Sensitive But Unclassified (SBU) information"); see also Intelligence Reform and Terrorism Prevention Act of 2004, 6 U.S.C. § 485 (Supp. IV 2004) (establishing an "information sharing environment for the sharing of terrorism information in a manner consistent with national security and with applicable legal standards relating to privacy and civil liberties").

[177] See, e.g., Homeland Security Act of 2002, 6 U.S.C. § 482 (Supp. IV 2004) (directing implementation of procedures for safeguarding "sensitive homeland security information" in order to facilitate its sharing with appropriate state and local personnel); see also FOIA Post, "Critical Infrastructure Information Regulations Issued by DHS" (posted 2/27/04) (describing Department of Homeland Security report to Congress (dated Feb. 20, 2004) as addressing development of policy and procedures for handling "sensitive homeland security information").

ing such information under Exemption 2.[178] (See the additional discussion of such matters under Exemption 1, "Homeland Security-Related information," above.) Of course, such labels do <u>not</u> by themselves accord any necessary protection from disclosure under Exemption 2 (or any other FOIA exemption) -- meaning that agency personnel should ensure that both aspects of the "high 2" standard have been satisfied before withholding any information so labeled.[179]

## EXEMPTION 3

Exemption 3 of the FOIA incorporates the various nondisclosure provisions that are contained in other federal statutes. As enacted in 1966, Exemption 3 was broadly phrased so as to simply cover information "specifically exempted from disclosure by statute."[1] Nearly a decade later, in FAA v. Robertson, the Supreme Court interpreted this language as evincing a congressional intent to allow statutes which permitted the withholding of confidential information, and which were enacted prior to the FOIA, to remain unaffected by the disclosure mandate of the FOIA; it accordingly held that a broad withholding provision in the Federal Aviation Act which delegated almost unlimited discretion to agency officials to withhold specific documents in the "interest of the public" was incorporated within Exemption 3.[2] Fearing that this interpretation could allow agencies to evade the FOIA's disclosure intent, Congress in effect overruled the Supreme Court's decision by amending Exemption 3 in 1976.[3]

---

[178] See Attorney General Ashcroft's FOIA Memorandum (Oct. 12, 2001), reprinted in *FOIA Post* (posted 10/15/01) (urging all federal agencies to "consult with the Department of Justice's Office of Information and Privacy when significant FOIA issues arise"); cf. White House Security Memorandum, reprinted in *FOIA Post* (posted 3/21/02) (calling upon agencies to identify and then safeguard "information that could be misused to harm the security of our nation and the safety of our people").

[179] See *FOIA Post*, "Critical Infrastructure Information Regulations Issued by DHS" (posted 2/27/04) (emphasizing critical distinction between "protecting" and "safeguarding" information); see also *FOIA Post*, "Executive Order 13,392 Implementation Guidance" (posted 04/27/06) (Part I.21.) (suggesting "[i]n-house training on 'safeguarding label'/FOIA exemption distinctions" as potential improvement area for agencies to address in their plans developed pursuant to Exec. Order No. 13,392, 70 Fed. Reg. 75,373 (Dec. 14, 2005)).

[1] Pub. L. No. 89-487, 80 Stat. 250, 251 (1966) (subsequently amended).

[2] 422 U.S. 255, 266 (1975).

[3] See Pub. L. No. 94-409, 90 Stat. 1241, 1247 (1976) (single FOIA amendment enacted together with the Government in the Sunshine Act in 1976,

(continued...)

## EXEMPTION 3

As amended, Exemption 3 allows the withholding of information prohibited from disclosure by another statute only if one of two disjunctive requirements are met: the statute either "(A) requires that the matters be withheld from the public in such a manner as to leave no discretion on the issue, or (B) establishes particular criteria for withholding or refers to particular types of matters to be withheld."[4] A statute thus falls within the exemption's coverage if it satisfies any one of its disjunctive requirements,[5] though courts do not always specify under which subpart of Exemption 3 a statute qualifies. Additionally, as is detailed below, in the past several years the Exemption 3 landscape has been broadened significantly with FOIA-specific nondisclosure statutes, Appropriations Acts intended to have FOIA nondisclosure results, and an increasing number of statutes enacted to protect certain intelligence agencies' "operational files."

The Electronic Freedom of Information Act Amendments of 1996[6] require agencies to list the Exemption 3 statutes upon which they rely in their annual FOIA reports each year.[7] The Office of Information and Privacy reviews those reports for consistency in this respect as well as in others.[8]

### Initial Considerations

The Court of Appeals for the District of Columbia Circuit has held that records may be withheld under the authority of another statute pursu-

---

[3](...continued)
5 U.S.C. § 552b (2000 & Supp. III 2003)); see also FOIA Update, Vol. XV, No. 2, at 6 (connecting disclosure policies of Government in the Sunshine Act and FOIA).

[4] 5 U.S.C. § 552(b)(3) (2000 & Supp. IV 2004) (emphasis added).

[5] See Long v. IRS, 742 F.2d 1173, 1178 (9th Cir. 1984); Irons & Sears v. Dann, 606 F.2d 1215, 1220 (D.C. Cir. 1979); Am. Jewish Cong. v. Kreps, 574 F.2d 624, 628 (D.C. Cir. 1978).

[6] Pub. L. No. 104-231, 110 Stat. 3048.

[7] See 5 U.S.C. § 552(e)(1)(A)(ii) (2000 & Supp. IV 2004) (requiring annual FOIA reports as of Fiscal Year 1998); FOIA Update, Vol. XVIII, No. 3, at 5 (annual FOIA report guidelines issued by Department of Justice); see also FOIA Post, "FOIA Counselor Q&A: Annual FOIA Reports" (posted 12/19/03); FOIA Post, "Agencies Rely on Wide Range of Exemption 3 Statutes" (posted 12/16/03); FOIA Post, "Supplemental Guidance on Annual FOIA Reports" (posted 8/13/01).

[8] See FOIA Post, "GAO E-FOIA Implementation Report Issued" (posted 3/23/01) (describing OIP process of "reviewing all agency annual reports . . . and then contacting individual agencies to discuss and resolve any identified question or discrepancy"); see, e.g., FOIA Post, "Summary of Annual FOIA Reports for Fiscal Year 2003" (posted 7/29/04) (describing agency reliance upon Exemption 3 statutes during Fiscal Year 2003).

ant to Exemption 3 "if -- and only if -- that statute meets the requirements of Exemption 3, including the threshold requirement that it specifically exempt matters from disclosure."[9] The D.C. Circuit emphasized that:

> a statute that is claimed to qualify as an Exemption 3 withholding statute must, on its face, exempt matters from disclosure. We must find a congressional purpose to exempt matters from disclosure in the actual words of the statute (or at least in the legislative history of FOIA) -- not in the legislative history of the claimed withholding statute, nor in an agency's interpretation of the statute.[10]

That is not to say that the breadth and reach of the disclosure prohibition must be found on the face of the statute, but that the statute must at

---

[9] Reporters Comm. for Freedom of the Press v. U.S. Dep't of Justice, 816 F.2d 730, 734 (D.C. Cir.), modified on other grounds, 831 F.2d 1124 (D.C. Cir. 1987), rev'd on other grounds, 489 U.S. 749 (1989); see also Nat'l Ass'n of Home Builders v. Norton, 309 F.3d 26, 37 (D.C. Cir. 2002) (holding that statute failed to qualify as withholding statute under Exemption 3 because it did not refer to "nondisclosure of information"); Essential Info., Inc. v. USIA, 134 F.3d 1165, 1168 (D.C. Cir. 1998) (ruling that statute that prohibits "dissemination" and "distribution" of certain information within U.S. is qualifying "nondisclosure" statute).

[10] Reporters Comm., 816 F.2d at 735 (citation omitted); see also Anderson v. HHS, 907 F.2d 936, 951 n.19 (10th Cir. 1990) (holding that agency interpretation of statute not entitled to deference in determining whether statute qualifies under Exemption 3). But see Doe v. Veneman, 380 F.3d 807, 818 (5th Cir. 2004) (relying on legislative history of Federal Insecticide, Fungicide, and Rodenticide Act, 7 U.S.C. § 136i-1 (2000), as basis for determining that statute qualifies as Exemption 3 statute); Wis. Project on Nuclear Arms Control v. U.S. Dep't of Commerce, 317 F.3d 275, 284 (D.C. Cir. 2003) (finding that Congress made plain its intent to prevent the disclosure of export-application information by implementing a "comprehensive legislative scheme" and by granting the President the power to prevent a lapse of the statute's provisions, thereby satisfying Exemption 3's requirements); Times Publ'g Co. v. U.S. Dep't of Commerce, 236 F.3d 1286, 1291-92 (11th Cir. 2001) (considering the legislative history of a nondisclosure statute and related statute, together with a related executive order, to conclude that Congress intended to create a "comprehensive legislative scheme" prohibiting disclosure); Meyerhoff v. EPA, 958 F.2d 1498, 1501-02 (9th Cir. 1992) (looking to legislative history of withholding statute to determine that statutory amendment did not create new prohibition on disclosure, but rather clarified existing nondisclosure provision); cf. Essential Info., 134 F.3d at 1165-67 (surveying legislative history of Smith-Mundt Act, 22 U.S.C. § 1461-1a (2000), to bolster Exemption 3 ruling).

least "explicitly deal with public disclosure."[11] (Previously, the D.C. Circuit had found legislative history probative on the issue of whether an enactment was intended to serve as a withholding statute within the meaning of Exemption 3.[12]) More recently, the D.C. Circuit held that the Endangered Species Act[13] fails to "qualify as a withholding statute under Exemption 3" because "nothing in [the statute's] language refers to nondisclosure of information."[14] In any event, though, the legislative history of a newly enacted Exemption 3 statute may be considered in determining whether the statute is applicable to matters that are already pending.[15] And quite significantly, Exemption 3 statutes enacted during the pendency of a FOIA request or during FOIA litigation have been held to apply retroactively to the requested records.[16]

---

[11] Reporters Comm., 816 F.2d at 736; see, e.g., Cal-Almond, Inc. v. USDA, 960 F.2d 105, 108 (9th Cir. 1992) (finding disclosure prohibition sought to be effectuated through appropriations limitation to be inadequate under Exemption 3); see also Nat'l Ass'n of Home Builders, 309 F.3d at 37 ("Looking first to the 'plain language of the statute,' there is nothing in the Endangered Species Act that refers to withholding information." (quoting Ass'n of Retired R.R. Workers, Inc. v. U.S. R.R. Ret. Bd., 830 F.2d 331, 334 (D.C. Cir. 1987))).

[12] See Pub. Citizen Health Research Group v. FDA, 704 F.2d 1280, 1284 (D.C. Cir. 1983).

[13] 16 U.S.C. § 1533(a)(1) (2000 & Supp. IV 2004).

[14] Nat'l Ass'n of Home Builders, 309 F.3d at 37-38 (observing that the statute's plain language does not refer "to withholding information," and holding that the agency's reliance on "'legislative history will not avail if the language of the statute itself does not explicitly deal with public disclosure'" (quoting Reporter's Comm., 816 F.3d at 736)).

[15] See City of Chicago v. ATF, 384 F.3d 429 (7th Cir. 2004), vacated & remanded, 423 F.3d 777 (7th Cir. 2005) (considering congressional intent behind appropriations legislation that prohibited expenditure of appropriated funds for processing requests for firearms database information); Long v. IRS, 742 F.2d 1173, 1183-84 (9th Cir. 1984).

[16] See City of Chicago, 423 F.3d at 783 (holding that newly enacted appropriations legislation applies retroactively to requested records); Wis. Project, 317 F.3d at 284-85 (finding that agency properly relied upon statute to withhold information retroactively after Congress re-enacted statute during litigation); Sw. Ctr. for Biological Diversity v. USDA, 314 F.3d 1060, 1062 (9th Cir. 2002) (determining that agency can rely on newly enacted National Parks Omnibus Management Act, 16 U.S.C. § 5937 (2000), to withhold information, even though it was enacted after FOIA litigation had commenced); Times Publ'g, 236 F.3d at 1292 (finding that agency properly relied upon Export Administration Act, 50 app. U.S.C.A. § 2411(c)(1) (1991 & West Supp. 2006), to withhold information when Congress re-enacted

(continued...)

Exemption 3 generally is triggered only by federal statutes.[17] Federal rules of procedure, which are promulgated by the Supreme Court, ordinarily do not qualify under Exemption 3.[18] However, when a rule of procedure is subsequently modified and thereby specifically enacted into law by Congress, it may qualify under the exemption.[19] While the issue of whether a treaty can qualify as a statute under Exemption 3 has not yet been ruled on in any FOIA case, there is a sound policy basis for concluding that a treaty can so qualify.[20]

---

[16](...continued) statute during course of litigation, even though statute had lapsed at time of request); Chamberlain v. Kurtz, 589 F.2d 827, 835 (5th Cir. 1979) (applying amended version of Internal Revenue Code to pending case where court determined that no injustice would result); Am. Jewish Cong., 574 F.2d at 627 (applying amended version of Exemption 3 to pending case); Lee Pharm. v. Kreps, 577 F.2d 610, 614 (9th Cir. 1978) (same); FOIA Post, "Supreme Court Rules in Exemption 5 Case" (posted 4/4/01) (discussing Department of the Interior's legislative success with enactment of provision of National Parks Omnibus Management Act, 16 U.S.C. § 5937, as Exemption 3 statute that readily addressed problem of two appellate courts' refusal to protect nest-site locations of endangered species under Exemption 2).

[17] See Wash. Post Co. v. HHS, 2 Gov't Disclosure Serv. (P-H) ¶ 81,047, at 81,127 n.2 (D.D.C. Dec. 4, 1980) ("[A]n Executive Order . . . is clearly inadequate to support reliance on Exemption 3."), rev'd on other grounds, 690 F.2d 252 (D.C. Cir. 1982); cf. Wis. Project, 317 F.3d at 284-85 (determining that agency properly withheld records in reliance upon legislative scheme in which executive order operated to maintain effectiveness of intermittently lapsed Exemption 3 statute); Times Publ'g, 236 F.3d at 1291-92 (same).

[18] See Founding Church of Scientology v. Bell, 603 F.2d 945, 952 (D.C. Cir. 1979) (holding that Rule 26(c) of Federal Rules of Civil Procedure, governing issuance of protective orders, is not statute under Exemption 3).

[19] See, e.g., Fund for Constitutional Gov't v. Nat'l Archives & Records Serv., 656 F.2d 856, 867 (D.C. Cir. 1981) (concluding that Rule 6(e) of Federal Rules of Criminal Procedure, regulating disclosure of matters occurring before grand jury, satisfies Exemption 3's "statute" requirement because it was specially amended by Congress in 1977); Berry v. Dep't of Justice, 612 F. Supp. 45, 49 (D. Ariz. 1985) (determining that Rule 32 of Federal Rules of Criminal Procedure, governing disclosure of presentence reports, is "statute" for Exemption 3 purposes because it was affirmatively enacted into law by Congress in 1975); cf. Lykins v. U.S. Dep't of Justice, 725 F.2d 1455, 1462 n.7 (1984) (holding that standing "order" of court has no nondisclosure effect under FOIA).

[20] Cf. Whitney v. Robertson, 124 U.S. 190, 194 (1888) ("By the Constitution a treaty is placed on the same footing, and made of like obligation,
(continued...)

## EXEMPTION 3

Once it is established that a statute is a nondisclosure statute and that it meets at least one of the disjunctive requirements of Exemption 3, an agency next must establish that the records in question fall within the withholding provision of the nondisclosure statute.[21] This, in turn, often will require an interpretation of the nondisclosure statute.[22] Courts have been somewhat divided over whether to construe the withholding criteria of the nondisclosure statute narrowly, consistent with the strong disclosure policies specifically embodied in the FOIA,[23] or broadly, pursuant to deferential standards of general administrative law.[24] The Court of Appeals for the Second Circuit observed that "the Supreme Court has never applied a rule of [either] narrow or deferential construction to withholding statutes."[25] Consequently, it adopted a pragmatic, and essentially neutral, stance regarding interpretation of Exemption 3 statutes, "looking to the plain language of the statute and its legislative history, in order to deter-

---

[20](...continued)
with an act of legislation."); Pub. Citizen v. Office of the U.S. Trade Representative, 804 F. Supp. 385, 388 (D.D.C. 1992) (stating that trade agreement not ratified by Senate does not have status of "statutory law" and thus does not qualify under Exemption 3), appeal dismissed per stipulation, No. 93-5008 (D.C. Cir. Jan. 26, 1993).

[21] See CIA v. Sims, 471 U.S. 159, 167 (1985); A. Michael's Piano, Inc. v. FTC, 18 F.3d 138, 143 (2d Cir. 1994); Aronson v. IRS, 973 F.2d 962, 964 (1st Cir. 1992); Cal-Almond, 960 F.2d at 108; Fund for Constitutional Gov't, 656 F.2d at 868; Pub. Citizen Health Research Group, 704 F.2d at 1284; Goland v. CIA, 607 F.2d 339, 350 (D.C. Cir. 1978).

[22] See A. Michael's Piano, 18 F.3d at 143-45 (interpreting section 21(f) of FTC Act, 15 U.S.C. § 57b-2(f) (2000)); see also Aronson, 973 F.2d at 965-66 (giving deference to agency interpretation of withholding statute); Anderson v. HHS, 907 F.2d 936, 950-51 (10th Cir. 1990) (interpreting section 360j(c) of Medical Devices Act, 21 U.S.C.A. § 360j(c) (1999 & West Supp. 2006), and section 301(j) of Food, Drug, and Cosmetic Act, 21 U.S.C.A. § 331(j) (1999 & West Supp. 2006)); Grasso v. IRS, 785 F.2d 70, 74-75 (5th Cir. 1984) (interpreting section 6103 of Internal Revenue Code, 26 U.S.C.A. § 6103 (2002 & West Supp. 2006)).

[23] See Anderson, 907 F.2d at 951; Grasso, 785 F.2d at 75; Currie, 704 F.2d 523, 526-27 (11th Cir. 1983); DeLorme Publ'g Co. v. NOAA, 917 F. Supp. 867, 870-71 (D. Me. 1996).

[24] See Church of Scientology Int'l v. U.S. Dep't of Justice, 30 F.3d 224, 235 (1st Cir. 1994); Aronson, 973 F.2d at 967; White v. IRS, 707 F.2d 897, 900-01 (6th Cir. 1983) (holding that agency determination that documents in dispute fell within withholding provision of Internal Revenue Code was "neither arbitrary nor capricious"). But see DeLorme Publ'g, 917 F. Supp. at 871 (rejecting a deferential review when the statute at issue "ha[d] broad application and ha[d] been implemented by more than a dozen agencies").

[25] A. Michael's Piano, 18 F.3d at 144.

mine legislative purpose."[26]

Under Exemption 3, judicial review under the FOIA of agency action is limited to determinations that the withholding statute qualifies as an Exemption 3 statute and that the records fall within the statute's scope.[27] With respect to subpart (B) statutes -- which permit agencies some discretion to withhold or disclose records -- the agency's exercise of its discretion under the withholding statute is governed not by the FOIA, but by the withholding statute itself;[28] judicial review of that should not be within the FOIA's jurisdiction.[29]

Agencies and courts ordinarily specify the nondisclosure statute upon which Exemption 3 withholding is based. At least one court, however, found a need to conceal the nondisclosure statute that formed the basis for its ruling that the agency properly invoked Exemption 3, stating that "national security would be compromised and threats to the safety of individuals would arise" if it engaged in a specific discussion of the legal basis for Exemption 3's use in that exceptional case.[30]

---

[26] Id.

[27] See Aronson, 973 F.2d at 967; Ass'n of Retired R.R. Workers v. U.S. R.R. Ret. Bd., 830 F.2d 331, 335 (D.C. Cir. 1987). But see Long, 742 F.2d at 1181; DeLorme Publ'g, 917 F. Supp. at 871.

[28] See Aronson, 973 F.2d at 966; Ass'n of Retired R.R. Workers, 830 F.2d at 336.

[29] Cf. Roley v. Assistant Attorney Gen., No. 89-2774, slip op. at 8 (D.D.C. Mar. 9, 1990) (determining that court's grant of permission to disclose grand jury records pursuant to Rule 6(e)(3)(C)(i) of Federal Rules of Criminal Procedure does not govern disposition of same records in FOIA suit); Garside v. Webster, 733 F. Supp. 1142, 1147 (S.D. Ohio 1989) (same). But cf. DeLorme Publ'g, 917 F. Supp. at 871 (proceeding de novo when statute at issue was administered by numerous federal agencies); Palmer v. Derwinski, No. 91-197, slip op. at 3-4 (E.D. Ky. June 10, 1992) (holding that disclosure order issued by court pursuant to 38 U.S.C. § 7332(b) (2000) requires VA to disclose records under FOIA).

[30] Simpson v. Dep't of State, No. 79-0674, 2 Gov't Disclosure Serv. (P-H) ¶ 81,280, at 81,798 (D.D.C. Apr. 30, 1981) (concluding on remand that Exemption 3 authorized withholding of State Department's entire "Biographic Register" of federal employees involved in foreign policy activities, even though court of appeals had already ruled in Simpson v. Vance, 648 F.2d 10, 17 (D.C. Cir. 1980), that Exemption 6 did not cover all such information); see also Haddam v. FBI, No. 01-434, slip op. at 28 (D.D.C. Sept. 8, 2004) (protecting twenty-three pages of documents described in agency's in camera affidavit pursuant to Exemption 3, but declining to name nondisclosure statute that agency relied upon because "no further information as to this exemption should be disclosed on the public record").

# EXEMPTION 3

## Exemption 3 Statutes

A wide range of federal laws qualify as Exemption 3 statutes. In the past, courts usually placed emphasis on specifying whether a statute qualifies as an Exemption 3 statute under subpart (A) (which encompasses statutes that require information to be withheld and leave the agency no discretion on the issue) or subpart (B) (which encompasses statutes that either provide criteria for withholding information or refer to particular matters to be withheld, either explicitly or implicitly). (For a further discussion of specific statutes held to qualify as either "subpart (A)" or "subpart (B)" statutes, see below.) Although this practice is by no means obsolete, courts do not always specify exactly which subpart of Exemption 3 a statute qualifies under, instead simply determining whether a statute qualifies, or does not qualify, as an Exemption 3 statute generally.[31]

For example, in 2005 one district court held that the confidentiality provision in the Federal Election Campaign Act[32] qualifies as an Exemption 3 statute, but did not state whether it qualified under subpart (A) or (B) of Exemption 3.[33] Another district court held that sections 114(s)[34] and 40119(b)[35] of Title 49 of the United States Code, qualify as Exemption 3 statutes because they provide the authority for the Secretary of Transportation and the Undersecretary of the Transportation Security Administration to protect sensitive security information from disclosure, though the court did not specify under which subpart the statutes qualified.[36] Recently, a court held that section 3610(d) of the Fair Housing Act,[37] a provision that protects information concerning ongoing discrimination investigations, qualifies as a "disclosure-prohibiting statute," but likewise did not specify

---

[31] See, e.g., Nat'l Inst. of Military Justice v. DOD, 404 F. Supp. 2d 325, 335-37 (D.D.C. 2005) (holding that 10 U.S.C. § 130c (2000 & Supp. IV 2004) is an Exemption 3 statute without specifying under which subpart it qualifies); ACLU v. DOD, 389 F. Supp. 2d 547, 554 (S.D.N.Y. 2005) (same).

[32] 2 U.S.C. § 437g(a)(12)(A) (2000 & Supp. IV 2004).

[33] Citizens for Responsibility & Ethics in Wash. v. FEC, No. 04-1672, slip op. at 5 (D.D.C. May 16, 2005).

[34] 49 U.S.C.A. § 114(s) (West Supp. 2006).

[35] 49 U.S.C. § 40119(b) (2000 & Supp. III 2003).

[36] Gordon v. FBI, 390 F. Supp. 2d 897, 900 (N.D. Cal. 2004) (holding that "there is no dispute that these statutes fall within [the scope of] Exemption 3"); see also Tooley v. Bush, No. 06-306, 2006 WL 3783142, at *19 (D.D.C. Dec. 21, 2006) (holding that 49 U.S.C. § 114(s) qualifies as an Exemption 3 statute); Elec. Privacy Info. Ctr. v. DHS, 384 F. Supp. 2d 100, 110 n.10 (D.D.C. 2005) (finding that both 49 U.S.C. § 114(s) and 49 U.S.C. § 40119(b) qualify as Exemption 3 statutes generally).

[37] 42 U.S.C. § 3610(d) (2000).

either subpart of Exemption 3.[38]

Many statutes h**ave** been held to qualify as Exemption 3 statutes under the exemption's first subpart. A primary example is Rule 6(e) of the Federal Rules of Criminal Procedure,[39] which regulates disclosure of matters occurring before a grand jury and which satisfies the basic "statute" requirement of Exemption 3 because it was specially amended by Congress in 1977.[40] It is well established that "Rule 6(e) embodies a broad sweeping policy of preserving the secrecy of grand jury material regardless of the substance in which the material is contained."[41] Yet defining the parameters of Rule 6(e) protection is not always a simple task and has been the subject of much litigation. In Fund for Constitutional Government v. National Archives & Records Service, the Court of Appeals for the District of Columbia Circuit stated that the scope of the secrecy that must be afforded grand jury material "is necessarily broad" and, consequently, that "it encompasses not only the direct revelation of grand jury transcripts but also the disclosure of information which would reveal 'the identities of witnesses or jurors, the substance of the testimony, the strategy or direction of the investigation, the deliberations or questions of the jurors, and the like.'"[42]

---

[38] West v. Jackson, 448 F. Supp. 2d 207, 212-13 (D.D.C. 2006).

[39] Fed. R. Crim. P. 6(e).

[40] See Fund for Constitutional Gov't v. Nat'l Archives & Records Serv., 656 F.2d 856, 867 (D.C. Cir. 1981); see also Tel. Publ'g Co. v. U.S. Dep't of Justice, No. 95-521-M, slip op. at 16-18, 26-27 (D.N.H. Aug. 31, 1998) (citing Exemption 3 together with Rule 6(e) as a partial basis for protecting information related to a grand jury, including correspondence between the U.S. Attorney's Office and nongovernment attorneys pertaining to the grand jury, even where the correspondence was not shown to the grand jury and evidence notebooks were created by local police at the direction of an Assistant United States Attorney, because disclosure would "probably . . . reveal too much about evidence presented to the grand jury"); Greenberg v. U.S. Dep't of Treasury, 10 F. Supp. 2d 3, 27-28 (D.D.C. 1998) (permitting agency to withhold transcripts of conversations that were taped during course of FBI investigation and were subsequently subpoenaed by grand jury); McQueen v. United States, 179 F.R.D. 522, 528-30 (S.D. Tex. May 6, 1998) (holding that all matters occurring before grand jury are protected even if records predate grand jury investigation), aff'd, 176 F.3d 478 (5th Cir. 1999) (unpublished table decision).

[41] Iglesias v. CIA, 525 F. Supp. 547, 556 (D.D.C. 1981).

[42] 656 F.2d at 869 (quoting SEC v. Dresser Indus., Inc., 628 F.2d 1368, 1382 (D.C. Cir. 1980)); see also United States v. Kearse, 30 F. App'x 85 (4th Cir. 2002) (per curiam) (holding that Rule 6(e) prohibits FOIA disclosure of grand jury transcripts); Rugiero v. U.S. Dep't of Justice, 257 F.3d 534, 549 (continued...)

[42](...continued)
(6th Cir. 2001) (protecting grand jury transcripts, exhibits, and identities of witnesses), cert. denied, 534 U.S. 1134 (2002); Church of Scientology Int'l v. U.S. Dep't of Justice, 30 F.3d 224, 235 (1st Cir. 1994) ("[D]ocuments identified as grand jury exhibits, and whose contents are testimonial in nature or otherwise directly associated with the grand jury process, such as affidavits and deposition transcripts, ordinarily may be withheld simply on the basis of their status as exhibits."); McDonnell v. United States, 4 F.3d 1227, 1246 (3d Cir. 1993) (protecting "[i]nformation and records presented to a federal grand jury . . . names of individuals subpoenaed . . . [and] federal grand jury transcripts of testimony"); Silets v. U.S. Dep't of Justice, 945 F.2d 227, 230 (7th Cir. 1991) (concluding that "identity of witness before a grand jury and discussion of that witness' testimony" is exempt from disclosure, as it "falls squarely within" Rule 6(e)'s prohibition); Boyd v. ATF, No. 05-1096, 2006 U.S. Dist. LEXIS 71857, at *19 (D.D.C. Sept. 29, 2006) (protecting grand jury transcripts); Meserve v. U.S. Dep't of Justice, No. 04-1844, 2006 U.S. Dist. LEXIS 56732, at *9 n.5 (D.D.C. Aug. 14, 2006) (protecting grand jury "correspondence, witness subpoenas, transcripts, and evidence"); Peay v. Dep't of Justice, No. 04-1859, 2006 WL 1805616, at *2 (D.D.C. June 29, 2006) (holding that agency properly protected grand jury investigation request and referral, prosecutor's recommendation based on grand jury's investigation, and unsigned grand jury indictment; agency failed to show whether segregability requirements were met); Boyd v. Criminal Div., U.S. Dep't of Justice, No. 04-1100, 2005 WL 555412, at *6 (D.D.C. Mar. 9, 2005) (protecting identities of grand jury witnesses) (appeal pending); Brunetti v. FBI, 357 F. Supp. 2d 97, 105 (D.D.C. 2004) (protecting "grand jury subpoenas, names and identifying information of the individuals named in the subpoenas, records subpoenaed by the grand jury, and the dates of grand jury meetings"); Raulerson v. Ashcroft, 271 F. Supp. 2d 17, 24 (D.D.C. 2002) (finding that the "names of individuals subpoenaed to testify before the grand jury and the names of their employers clearly are matters 'occurring before the grand jury'" (quoting Fund for Constitutional Gov't, 656 F.2d at 869)); Germosen v. Cox, No. 98 Civ. 1294, 1999 WL 1021559, at *13 (S.D.N.Y. Nov. 9, 1999) (holding that identities of grand jury witnesses are protected by Rule 6(e)), appeal dismissed for failure to prosecute, No. 00-6041 (2d Cir. Sept. 12, 2000); Peralta v. U.S. Attorney's Office, 69 F. Supp. 2d 21, 33 (D.D.C. 1999) (determining that Rule 6(e) prohibited the release of identities of grand jury witnesses and descriptions of information obtained by federal grand jury subpoenas); Anderson v. U.S. Dep't of Justice, No. 95-1880, 1999 U.S. Dist. LEXIS 5048, at *8 (D.D.C. Apr. 12, 1999) (finding local police department line-up record properly withheld as it contained Assistant United States Attorney's handwritten notes regarding witness reactions to viewing individuals in line-up and, if released, would reveal "identities of witnesses or jurors"); Willis v. FBI, No. 96-1455, slip op. at 6 (D.D.C. Feb. 14, 1998) (declaring that a grand jury transcript was properly withheld even though "at one time [the requester's] counsel may have had a right of access to portions of the transcript for [witness impeachment purposes]"),

(continued...)

However, in its scrutiny of the scope of Rule 6(e) in <u>Senate of Puerto Rico v. United States Department of Justice</u>,[43] the D.C. Circuit firmly held that neither the fact that information was obtained pursuant to a grand jury subpoena, nor the fact that the information was submitted to the grand jury, is sufficient, in and of itself, to warrant the conclusion that disclosure is necessarily prohibited by Rule 6(e).[44] Rather, an agency must es-

---

[42](...continued)
<u>aff'd in part & remanded on other grounds</u>, 194 F.3d 175 (D.C. Cir. 1999) (unpublished table decision); <u>Twist v. Reno</u>, No. 95-258, 1997 U.S. Dist. LEXIS 8981, at *5 n.1 (D.D.C. May 12, 1997) (holding that agency properly withheld information that would reveal strategy or direction of grand jury investigation even though requester was previously on investigation team and had seen some of withheld information), <u>summary affirmance granted</u>, No. 97-5192, 1997 WL 811736 (D.C. Cir. Dec. 9, 1997); <u>Jimenez v. FBI</u>, 938 F. Supp. 21, 28 (D.D.C. 1996) (protecting notes written by Assistant United States Attorney in preparation for grand jury proceeding, records of third parties provided in course of proceeding, and notes concerning witnesses who testified); <u>Canning v. U.S. Dep't of Justice</u>, No. 92-0463, slip op. at 6 (D.D.C. June 26, 1995) (protecting "material that, while not directly mentioning the grand jury," nevertheless mentions witness names and describes witness testimony); <u>Helmsley v. U.S. Dep't of Justice</u>, No. 90-2413, slip op. at 4-6 (D.D.C. Sept. 25, 1992) (finding that Rule 6(e) protected records identifying witnesses who testified or were consulted, documents and evidence not presented but obtained through grand jury subpoenas, immunity applications and orders, exhibit lists, reports and memoranda discussing evidence, correspondence regarding compliance with subpoenas, documents, notes, and research relating to litigation regarding compliance with subpoenas, and letters among lawyers discussing grand jury proceedings).

[43] 823 F.2d 574 (D.C. Cir. 1987).

[44] <u>Id.</u> at 584; <u>see</u> <u>Wash. Post Co. v. U.S. Dep't of Justice</u>, 863 F.2d 96, 100 (D.C. Cir. 1988) (finding that record that was created before grand jury was impanelled did not independently reveal anything about grand jury and thus was not covered by Rule 6(e) -- even though record was subpoenaed by grand jury, was available to jurors, and was used by prosecutors to question grand jury witnesses); <u>see also</u> <u>John Doe Corp. v. John Doe Agency</u>, 850 F.2d 105, 109 (2d Cir. 1988) ("A document that is otherwise available to the public does not become confidential simply because it is before a grand jury."), <u>rev'd on other grounds</u>, 493 U.S. 146 (1989); <u>Germosen</u>, 1999 WL 1021559, at *13 (stating that Rule 6(e) imposes "no requirement that materials actually be presented to the grand jury in order to fall within the rule's scope"); <u>Tel. Publ'g</u>, No. 95-521-M, slip op. at 11 (D.N.H. Aug. 31, 1998) ("Exemption 3 . . . does not protect all information that is found in grand jury files since mere exposure to a grand jury does not, by itself, immunize information from disclosure."); <u>Isley v. Executive Office for U.S. At-</u>
(continued...)

tablish a nexus between the release of that information and "revelation of a protected aspect of the grand jury's investigation."[45] This requirement is particularly applicable to "extrinsic" documents that were created entirely independent of the grand jury process; for such a document, the D.C. Circuit emphasized in Washington Post Co. v. United States Department of Justice, the required nexus must be apparent from the information itself,

---

[44](...continued)
torneys, No. 96-0123, slip op. at 2-4 (D.D.C. Mar. 27, 1997) (ordering agency to provide further justification for withholding "transcripts, subpoenas, information provided in response to a grand jury subpoena, and information identifying who testified before a grand jury"), appeal dismissed, 203 F.3d 52 (D.C. Cir. 1997) (unpublished table decision); Butler v. U.S. Dep't of Justice, No. 86-2255, 1994 WL 55621, at *8 (D.D.C. Feb. 3, 1994) (holding descriptions of documents subpoenaed by grand jury not protected under Rule 6(e)), appeal dismissed, No. 94-5078 (D.C. Cir. Sept. 8, 1994); Astley v. Lawson, No. 89-2806, 1991 WL 7162, at *6 (D.D.C. Jan. 11, 1991) (ordering release of records even though requester might have been able to deduce purpose for which they were subpoenaed, because records on their face did not reveal grand jury's "inner workings").

[45] Senate of P.R., 823 F.2d at 584; see also Lopez v. Dep't of Justice, 393 F.3d 1345, 1349-51 (D.C. Cir. 2005) (holding that agency "failed to meet its burden of demonstrating some 'nexus between disclosure [of date of prosecutor's preliminary witness interview] and revelation of a protected aspect of the grand jury's investigation'" (quoting Senate of P.R., 823 F.2d at 584)); Tel. Publ'g, No. 95-521-M, slip op. at 11 (D.N.H. Aug. 31, 1998) (stating that agencies must show nexus between disclosure of withheld information and impermissible revelation of grand jury matters to invoke protection of Exemption 3); Burke v. DEA, No. 96-1739, slip op. at 7 (D.D.C. Mar. 30, 1998) (determining that agency established nexus by showing that release of name of subpoenaed individual and information relating to subpoenaed insurance claims would reveal information about inner workings of grand jury); Greenberg, 10 F. Supp. 2d at 27-28 (finding that a nexus was established because releasing transcripts of taped conversations would show "the direction or path the Grand Jury was taking"); Karu v. U.S. Dep't of Justice, No. 86-771, slip op. at 4-5 (D.D.C. Dec. 1, 1987) (finding that a nexus was established because "[w]ere this information to be released the very substance of the grand jury proceedings would be discernible"). But see Homick v. U.S. Dep't of Justice, No. 98-00557, slip op. at 16-17 (N.D. Cal. Sept. 16, 2004) (protecting "names and identifying information of grand jury witnesses," but ordering disclosure of information that the agency described only as "the type of records subpoenaed by the grand jury," because the agency failed to meet its burden of showing how such information "is exempt from disclosure"); Isley, No. 96-0123, slip op. at 4 (D.D.C. Mar. 27, 1997) (concluding that agency "has not sufficiently linked the exemption to the contents of the withheld documents"); LaRouche v. U.S. Dep't of Justice, No. 90-2753, 1993 WL 388601, at *5 (D.D.C. June 25, 1993) (holding that letter prepared by government attorney discussing upcoming grand jury proceedings did not reveal grand jury's "inner workings").

and "the government cannot immunize [it] by publicizing the link."[46] As a rule, an agency must be able to adequately document and support its determination that disclosure of the record in question would reveal a secret aspect of the grand jury proceeding.[47]

---

[46] 863 F.2d at 100.

[47] See, e.g., Lopez, 393 F.3d at 1349-51 (holding that although agency properly withheld grand jury subpoenas and the dates of grand jury subpoenas and post-testimony witness debriefings pursuant to Rule 6(e), it failed to demonstrate how disclosure of the date of prosecutor's preliminary witness interview would reveal a secret aspect of the grand jury proceeding); Maydak v. U.S. Dep't of Justice, 254 F. Supp. 2d 23, 42 (D.D.C. 2003) (stating that court could not determine whether agency properly invoked Exemption 3 when neither Vaughn Index nor agency's declaration described specific records withheld); Hronek v. DEA, 16 F. Supp. 2d 1260, 1276 (D. Or. 1998) (requiring agency to resubmit Vaughn Index and explain how disclosure of subpoenas would "compromise the integrity of the grand jury process"), aff'd, 7 F. App'x 591 (9th Cir. 2001); LaRouche v. U.S. Dep't of Treasury, No. 91-1655, slip op. at 19-20 (D.D.C. May 22, 1998) (rejecting agency's withholding of entire category of documents and requiring agency to submit Vaughn Index sufficient to show that disclosure would reveal protected aspect of grand jury proceeding), summary judgment granted in part (D.D.C. Mar. 31, 2000) (holding that agency affidavit ultimately demonstrated nexus between disclosure and revelation of secret aspects of grand jury for most records withheld under 6(e), but ordering release where agency failed to demonstrate nexus); Kronberg v. U.S. Dep't of Justice, 875 F. Supp. 861, 867-68 (D.D.C. 1995) (ordering grand jury material released where prior disclosure was made to defense counsel and where government had not met burden of demonstrating that disclosure would reveal inner workings of grand jury); Linn, 1995 WL 417810, at *7 ("[N]owhere in its affidavit does the DEA specifically link this exemption to the contents of the documents being withheld," but rather "merely states that it applied this exemption to withhold information that names witnesses and recounts testimony given to a federal grand jury."); Canning v. U.S. Dep't of Justice, 919 F. Supp. 451, 454-55 (D.D.C. 1994) (requiring government to produce affidavits "showing a basis for knowledge that the information came from grand jury" and explain how material is protected under Rule 6(e)); cf. Lion Raisins Inc. v. USDA, 354 F.3d 1072, 1082 n.10 (9th Cir. 2004) (lambasting counsel for not viewing the sealed documents at issue, because the court found "it perplexing that the government would choose to assign counsel to defend its position on appeal (both in its brief and at oral argument) who is totally unfamiliar with (and, presumably, denied access to) the facts upon which the government bases its claim to the law enforcement exemption") (Exemption 7(A) case incorrectly constrained administratively by grand jury secrecy); Ashton v. VA, No. 99-6018, 1999 U.S. App. LEXIS 22957, at *3 (2d Cir. Sept. 3, 1999) (finding agency affidavit sufficient because it showed that withheld records revealed "confidential materials from grand jury proceedings" and that records were within scope of Rule

(continued...)

And to do so, of course, agency FOIA personnel necessarily "must" be afforded unrestricted access to grand jury-protected information.[48]

A subsequent decision by the Court of Appeals for the First Circuit, Church of Scientology International v. United States Department of Justice, further clouds the precise contours of Rule 6(e).[49] Initially following Senate of Puerto Rico, the First Circuit rejected a position that the secrecy concerns protected by Rule 6(e) are automatically implicated for any materials "simply located in grand jury files."[50] Nevertheless, apparently operating under the premise that all grand jury exhibits constitute materials actually presented to the grand jurors, it further specified that, even with regard to "extrinsic documents," it would be "reasonable for an agency to withhold any document containing a grand jury exhibit sticker or that is otherwise explicitly identified on its face as a grand jury exhibit, as release of such documents reasonably could be viewed as revealing the focus of the grand

---

[47](...continued)
6(e) and Exemption 3); Local 32B-32J, Serv. Employees Int'l Union, AFL-CIO v. GSA, No. 97 Civ. 8509, 1998 WL 726000, at *7 (S.D.N.Y. Oct. 15, 1998) (concluding that agency's "sealed declaration makes clear the existence of a grand jury investigation and sufficiently describes the relation of the requested materials to such investigation" and that agency properly withheld grand jury exhibits and identities of grand jury witnesses); Sousa v. U.S. Dep't of Justice, No. 95-375, 1997 U.S. Dist. LEXIS 9010, at *10-11 (D.D.C. June 19, 1997) (holding that supplemental Vaughn Index adequately demonstrated that disclosure of grand jury witness subpoenas, Assistant United States Attorney's handwritten notes discussing content of witness testimony, evidence used, and strategies would reveal protected aspects of grand jury investigation).

[48] Canning v. U.S. Dep't of Justice, No. 92-0463, 1995 WL 1073434, at *2 (D.D.C. Feb. 26, 1995) (finding that FOIA officers are "among those with approved access to grand jury material" and that agency's FOIA officer therefore properly reviewed withheld documents in case at hand (citing United States Dep't of Justice, Fed. Grand Jury Practice 173 (Jan. 1993))); see also United States Dep't of Justice, Fed. Grand Jury Practice 57 (Aug. 2000) (recognizing that grand jury information properly may be disclosed to "administrative personnel who need to determine the applicability of Rule 6(e)'s disclosure prohibition for purposes of responding to requests for records under [the FOIA]"); FOIA Update, Vol. XIX, No. 3, at 2 (advising agencies of same in order to put any question on point entirely to rest); cf. Lion Raisins, 354 F.3d at 1082 & nn.10 & 12 (remanding case when agency was not prepared to present its Exemption 7(A) defense because counsel evidently was "denied access to . . . the facts," and even admitted to not knowing "what reasons justify the invocation of the law enforcement exemption," due to overly strict grand jury secrecy).

[49] 30 F.3d at 235-36.

[50] Id. at 236.

jury investigation."[51] Thus, the First Circuit has seemingly placed itself in at least some degree of conflict with the D.C. Circuit's Senate of Puerto Rico interpretation of the grand jury rule.[52]

The Court of Appeals for the Ninth Circuit has held that a provision of the Ethics in Government Act of 1978,[53] protecting the financial disclosure reports of special government employees, meets the requirements of subpart (A).[54] Another provision of the Ethics in Government Act, providing for the disclosure of financial disclosure reports of certain government employees,[55] was found to qualify as an Exemption 3 statute, allowing disclosure only if a requester met that statute's particular disclosure requirements.[56] While not actually distinguishing between the two subparts of Exemption 3, the Supreme Court in Baldrige v. Shapiro,[57] held that the Census Act[58] is an Exemption 3 statute because it requires that certain data be withheld in such a manner as to leave the Census Bureau with no discre-

---

[51] Id. at 235 n.15 (dictum); cf. Rugiero, 257 F.3d at 549 (holding that "documents identified as grand jury exhibits or containing testimony or other material directly associated with grand jury proceedings fall within [Exemption 3]" and "[d]ocuments created for reasons independent of a grand jury investigation do not," without acknowledging that many grand jury exhibits are created for "reasons independent" of a grand jury); Foster v. U.S. Dep't of Justice, 933 F. Supp. 687, 691 (E.D. Mich. 1996) (protecting "final prosecution report" when "[e]ach page containe[d] a 'grand jury' secrecy label").

[52] See Senate of P.R., 823 F.2d at 584; see also Crooker v. IRS, No. 94-0755, 1995 WL 430605, at *9 n.2 (D.D.C. Apr. 27, 1995) (observing that withholding documents on basis of grand jury exhibit labels "appears to be the type of per se withholding of grand jury material expressly rejected by the D.C. Circuit").

[53] 5 U.S.C. app. § 107 (2000).

[54] Meyerhoff v. EPA, 958 F.2d 1498, 1502 (9th Cir. 1992) (construing 1978 version of statute); see also Glascoe v. U.S. Dep't of Justice, No. 04-0486, 2005 WL 1139269, at *1 (D.D.C. May 15, 2005) (protecting Assistant United States Attorney's "confidential conflict of interest certification" based on nondisclosure requirement of section 107(a) of Ethics in Government Act).

[55] 5 U.S.C. app. § 205 (repealed as of Jan. 1, 1991).

[56] Church of Scientology of Tex. v. IRS, 816 F. Supp. 1138, 1152 (W.D. Tex. 1993), appeal dismissed per stipulation, No. 93-8431 (5th Cir. Oct. 21, 1993).

[57] 455 U.S. 345 (1982).

[58] 13 U.S.C. §§ 8(b), 9(a) (2000).

EXEMPTION 3

tion whatsoever.[59]

Sections 706(b) and 709(e) of Title VII of the Civil Rights Act of 1964[60] have also been held to meet the subpart (A) requirement because they allow the EEOC no discretion to publicly disclose matters pending before the Commission.[61] Similarly, the statute governing records pertaining to Currency Transaction Reports[62] has been found to meet the requirements of subpart (A).[63] The International Investment Survey Act of 1976[64] has been held to be a subpart (A) statute,[65] and certain portions of the overall public disclosure provisions of the Consumer Product Safety Act[66] likewise have been found to satisfy subpart (A)'s nondisclosure requirements.[67]

Additionally, the Hart-Scott-Rodino Antitrust Improvement Amendments to the Clayton Antitrust Act[68] prohibit public disclosure of premerger-notification materials submitted to the Department of Justice or the Federal Trade Commission.[69] Similarly, a provision of the Antitrust Civil

---

[59] 455 U.S. at 355.

[60] 42 U.S.C. §§ 2000e-5(b), 2000e-8(e) (2000).

[61] See Frito-Lay v. EEOC, 964 F. Supp. 236, 239-43 (W.D. Ky. 1997); Crump v. EEOC, No. 3:97-0275, slip op. at 5-6 (M.D. Tenn. May 30, 1997) (magistrate's recommendation), adopted (M.D. Tenn. June 18, 1997); Am. Centennial Ins. Co. v. EEOC, 722 F. Supp. 180, 183 (D.N.J. 1989); cf. EEOC v. City of Milwaukee, 54 F. Supp. 885, 893 (E.D. Wis. 1999) (noting that "any member of the public making a FOIA request" for materials at issue in this non-FOIA dispute "will be denied access, because Exemption 3 incorporates confidentiality provisions of sections 706(b) and 709(e) of Title VII).

[62] 31 U.S.C. § 5319 (2000 & Supp. III 2003).

[63] See Sciba v. Bd. of Governors of the Fed. Reserve Sys., No. 04-1011, 2005 WL 3201206, at *6 (D.D.C. Nov. 4, 2005); Linn, 1995 WL 631847, at *30; Small v. IRS, 820 F. Supp. 163, 166 (D.N.J. 1992); Vennes v. IRS, No. 5-88-36, slip op. at 6 (D. Minn. Oct. 14, 1988), aff'd, 890 F.2d 419 (8th Cir. 1989) (unpublished table decision).

[64] 22 U.S.C. § 3104(c) (2000).

[65] See Young Conservative Found. v. U.S. Dep't of Commerce, No. 85-3982, 1987 WL 9244, at *3-4 (D.D.C. Mar. 25, 1987).

[66] 15 U.S.C. § 2055(a)(2) (2000).

[67] See Mulloy v. Consumer Prod. Safety Comm'n, No. C-2-85-645, 1985 U.S. Dist. LEXIS 17194, at *2-5 (S.D. Ohio Aug. 2, 1985).

[68] 15 U.S.C. § 18a(h) (2000).

[69] See Lieberman v. FTC, 771 F.2d 32, 39, n.14 (2d Cir. 1985) (dictum)
(continued...)

Process Act,[70] which exempts from the FOIA transcripts of oral testimony taken in the course of investigations under that Act, has been held to qualify as a subpart (A) statute.[71] Likewise, a provision of the now-expired Independent Counsel Reauthorization Act,[72] was considered to qualify under Exemption 3, as the Department of Justice and the Independent Counsel had no discretion to disclose to the public materials supplied under it to the court.[73]

Also, a section of the Transportation Safety Act of 1974,[74] which states that the NTSB shall withhold from public disclosure cockpit voice recordings associated with accident investigations, was found to fall within subsection (A) of Exemption 3.[75] Similarly, information contained in the Social Security Administration's "Numident system," which was obtained from death certificates provided by state agencies, has been held exempt on the basis of subpart (A) on the grounds that the language of the statute[76] "leaves no room for agency discretion."[77]

In a decision construing the application of the identical Exemption 3

---

[69](...continued)
(explaining that premerger information "could not be disclosed under FOIA; Congress made that intention crystal clear") (non-FOIA case); Mattox v. FTC, 752 F.2d 116, 122 (5th Cir. 1985) (observing that premerger information is exempt from disclosure under the FOIA -- government agencies are not to be "clearing house[s] for the facts" concerning mergers) (non-FOIA case).

[70] 15 U.S.C. § 1314(g) (2000) (covering "[a]ny documentary material, answers to written interrogatories, or transcripts of oral testimony provided pursuant to any demand issued under this chapter").

[71] See Motion Picture Ass'n of Am. v. U.S. Dep't of Justice, No. 80 Civ. 6612, slip op. at 1 (S.D.N.Y. Oct. 6, 1981) (protecting transcripts of oral testimony under Exemption 3).

[72] 28 U.S.C. § 592(e) (2000) (expired as of June 30, 1999).

[73] Cf. Pub. Citizen v. Dep't of Justice, No. 82-2909 (D.D.C. May 18, 1983) (construing 1978 version of statute).

[74] 49 U.S.C. § 1114(c) (2000).

[75] McGilvra v. NTSB, 840 F. Supp. 100, 102 (D. Colo. 1993).

[76] 42 U.S.C.A. § 405(r) (2003 & West Supp. 2006).

[77] Int'l Diatomite Producers Ass'n v. U.S. Soc. Sec. Admin., No. 92-1634, 1993 WL 137286, at *3 (N.D. Cal. Apr. 28, 1993), appeal dismissed per stipulation, No. 93-16204 (9th Cir. Oct. 27, 1993).

EXEMPTION 3

language of the Government in the Sunshine Act[78] to the Defense Nuclear Facilities Safety Board Act[79] the D.C. Circuit has held that the latter statute allows no discretion with regard to the release of the Board's proposed recommendations, thus meeting the requirement of subpart (A).[80] By contrast, the D.C. Circuit found that the statute governing release by the FBI of criminal record information ("rap sheets")[81] fails to fulfill subpart (A)'s requirement of absolute withholding because the statute implies that the FBI has discretion to withhold records and, in fact, the FBI had exercised such discretion by its inconsistent manner of releasing "rap sheets" to the public.[82]

Traditionally, though, most Exemption 3 cases have involved subpart (B). For example, a provision of the Consumer Product Safety Act[83] has been held to set forth sufficiently definite withholding criteria for it to fall within the scope of subpart (B),[84] and the provision which prohibits the Commission from disclosing any information that is submitted to it pursuant to section 15(b) of the Act[85] has been held to meet the requirements of subpart (B) by referring to particular types of matters to be withheld.[86] Recently, a district court held that 10 U.S.C. § 130c,[87] a statute that protects from disclosure certain "sensitive information of foreign governments," qualifies as an Exemption 3 statute because it establishes particular criteria for withholding, thereby meeting the requirements of subpart (B).[88]

---

[78] 5 U.S.C. § 552b(c)(3) (2000 & Supp. III 2003).

[79] 42 U.S.C. § 2286 (2000).

[80] Natural Res. Def. Council v. Def. Nuclear Facilities Safety Bd., 969 F.2d 1248, 1249 (D.C. Cir. 1992).

[81] 28 U.S.C.A. § 534 (1993 & West Supp. 2006).

[82] See Reporters Comm. for Freedom of the Press v. U.S. Dep't of Justice, 816 F.2d 730, 736 n.9 (D.C. Cir.), modified on other grounds, 831 F.2d 1124 (D.C. Cir. 1987), rev'd on other grounds, 489 U.S. 749 (1989); see also Dayton Newspapers, Inc. v. FBI, No. C-3-85-815, slip op. at 6 (S.D. Ohio Feb. 9, 1993).

[83] 15 U.S.C. § 2055(b)(1).

[84] See Consumer Prod. Safety Comm'n v. GTE Sylvania, Inc., 447 U.S. 102, 122 (1980).

[85] 15 U.S.C. § 2055(b)(5).

[86] See Reliance Elec. Co. v. Consumer Prod. Safety Comm'n, No. 87-1478, slip op. at 16-17 (D.D.C. Sept. 19, 1989).

[87] (2000 & Supp. IV 2004).

[88] See Associated Press v. DOD, No. 05-5468, 2006 WL 2707395, at *9-10 (S.D.N.Y. Sept. 20, 2006).

Section 777 of the Tariff Act,[89] governing the withholding of "proprietary information," has been held to refer to particular types of information to be withheld and thus to be a subpart (B) statute.[90] Section 12(d) of the Railroad Unemployment Insurance Act[91] refers to particular types of matters to be withheld -- information which would reveal employees' identities -- and thus has been held to satisfy subpart (B).[92] Section 410(c)(2) of the Postal Reorganization Act,[93] governing the withholding of "information of a commercial nature . . . which under good business practice would not be publicly disclosed," has been held to refer to "particular types of matters to be withheld" and thus a subpart (B) statute.[94] Likewise, section

---

[89] 19 U.S.C. § 1677f (2000 & Supp. IV 2004).

[90] See Mudge Rose Guthrie Alexander & Ferdon v. U.S. Int'l Trade Comm'n, 846 F.2d 1527, 1530 (D.C. Cir. 1988).

[91] 45 U.S.C. § 362(d) (2000).

[92] See Ass'n of Retired R.R. Workers v. U.S. R.R. Ret. Bd., 830 F.2d 331, 334 (D.C. Cir. 1987); Nat'l Ass'n of Retired & Veteran Ry. Employees v. R.R. Ret. Bd., No. 87-117, slip op. at 5 (N.D. Ohio Feb. 20, 1991).

[93] 39 U.S.C.A. § 410(c)(2) (1980 & West Supp. 2006).

[94] Wickwire Gavin, P.C. v. USPS, 356 F.3d 588, 589, 597 (4th Cir. 2004) (holding that agency properly withheld "quantity and pricing" information related to contract for which requester was unsuccessful bidder); Reid v. USPS, No. 05-294, 2006 U.S. Dist. LEXIS 45538, at *17-26 (S.D. Ill. July 5, 2006) (finding that agency properly protected customer's postage statements and agency's daily financial statements); Carlson v. USPS, No. 03-4113, 2005 WL 756583, at *1, *4 (N.D. Cal. Mar. 31, 2005) (holding that USPS properly withheld aggregation of information in Post Office Locator database under 39 U.S.C.A. § 410(c)(2), because disclosure of such information "may be of potential benefit to [agency's] competitors" and disclosure would not be "good business practice") (appeal pending); Airline Pilots Ass'n, Int'l v. USPS, 2004 U.S. Dist. LEXIS 26067, at *4, *22 (D.D.C. June 24, 2004) (holding that USPS properly withheld pricing and rate information, methods of operation, performance requirements, and terms and conditions from transportation agreement with FedEx); Robinett v. USPS, No. 02-1094, 2002 WL 1728582, at *5 (E.D. La. July 24, 2002) (finding that the agency properly withheld job-applicant information under 39 U.S.C.A. § 410(c)(2) because it falls within the agency's regulatory definition of "information of a commercial nature"); Weres Corp. v. USPS, No. 94-1984, slip op. at 3-6 (D.D.C. Sept. 23, 1996) (finding that agency properly withheld "unit and total prices" submitted by unsuccessful offerors for government contracts); cf. Piper & Marbury, L.L.P. v. USPS, No. 99-2383, 2001 WL 214217, at *3-5 (D.D.C. Mar. 6, 2001) (magistrate's recommendation) (finding that even if requested contract contained some "commercial information" protectible under 39 U.S.C.A. § 410(c)(2), agency could not withhold entire contract under Exemption 3), adopted (D.D.C. Mar. 30, 2001), recon-
(continued...)

EXEMPTION 3

3509(d) of the Federal Victims' Protection and Rights Act,[95] governing the disclosure of information that would identify children who were victims of certain crimes or witnesses to crimes against others, has been held to qualify as an Exemption 3 statute because it "establishes particular criteria for withholding."[96]

Similarly, it has been held that section 12(c)(1) of the Export Administration Act, governing the disclosure of information from export licenses and applications,[97] authorizes the withholding of a sufficiently narrow class of information to satisfy the requirements of subpart (B) and thus qualifies as an Exemption 3 statute.[98] Likewise, the Collection and Publication of

---

[94](...continued)
sideration denied (D.D.C. Feb. 28, 2002); Nat'l W. Life Ins. Co. v. United States, 512 F. Supp. 454, 459, 462 (N.D. Tex. 1980) (concluding that list of names and duty stations of postal employees did not qualify as "commercial information" within scope of 39 U.S.C.A. § 410(c)(2)).

[95] 18 U.S.C. § 3509(d) (2000).

[96] Tampico v. Executive Office for U.S. Attorneys, No. 04-2285, slip op. at 8 (D.D.C. Apr. 29, 2005).

[97] 50 app. U.S.C.A. § 2411(c)(1) (1991 & West Supp. 2006) (statute which most recently expired on August 20, 2001, as required by the Export Administration Modification and Clarification Act of 2000, Pub. L. No. 106-508, 114 Stat. 2360 (2000), but has been re-extended several times in past, in substantially identical form).

[98] See Wis. Project on Nuclear Arms Control v. U.S. Dep't of Commerce, 317 F.3d 275, 284 (2003) (ruling that agency properly withheld export license application information under "comprehensive legislative scheme" through which expired Exemption 3 statute, Export Administration Act, 50 app. U.S.C.A. § 2411(c)(1), continued in operation by virtue of non-Exemption 3 statute that authorized the President to issue executive orders maintaining effectiveness of Act during repeated periods of lapse); Times Publ'g Co. v. U.S. Dep't of Commerce, 236 F.3d 1286, 1289-92 (11th Cir. 2001) (same); Armstrong v. Executive Office of the President, No. 89-142, slip op. at 30-35 (D.D.C. July 28, 1995) (same); Afr. Fund v. Mosbacher, No. 92 Civ. 289, 1993 WL 183736, at *6 (S.D.N.Y. May 26, 1993) (holding that Export Administration Act protection was properly applied to agency denial made after Act expired and before subsequent re-extension); see also Lessner v. U.S. Dep't of Commerce, 827 F.2d 1333, 1336-37 (9th Cir. 1987) (construing statute as effective in 1987); cf. Council for a Livable World v. U.S. Dep't of State, No. 96-1807, slip op. at 11 (D.D.C. Jan. 21, 1998) (finding that section 12(c)(1) of Export Administration Act, as specifically incorporated by reference into Arms Export Control Act, 22 U.S.C.A. § 2778(e) (2004 & West Supp. 2006), is Exemption 3 statute that protects information concerning export license applications -- without acknowledging that Export Adminis-
(continued...)

Foreign Commerce Act,[99] which explicitly provides for nondisclosure of shippers' export declarations, qualifies as an Exemption 3 statute under subpart (B).[100]

The Supreme Court has held that section 102(d)(3) of the National Security Act of 1947,[101] which required the Director of the CIA to protect "sources and methods," clearly refers to particular types of matters to be withheld and thus comes within the ambit of subpart (B),[102] and in some

---

[98](...continued)
tration Act had lapsed), amended (D.D.C. Nov. 23, 1998).

[99] 13 U.S.C. § 301(g) (2000 & Supp. IV 2004).

[100] See Afr. Fund, 1993 WL 183736, at *5; Young Conservative Found., 1987 WL 9244, at *2-3.

[101] Pub. L. No. 108-458, 118 Stat. 3643 (2004) (to be codified at 50 U.S.C. § 403-1(i)) (repealing Pub. L. No. 107-56, § 901, 115 Stat. 272 (2001), relating to responsibilities of Director of the CIA, and amending 50 U.S.C. § 403-1, thereby reassigning authority for protecting intelligence sources and methods to Director of National Intelligence).

[102] See CIA v. Sims, 471 U.S. 159, 167 (1985); see also Assassination Archives & Research Ctr. v. CIA, 334 F.3d 55, 60-61 (D.C. Cir. 2003) (affirming that release of CIA's five-volume compendium of biographical information on "Cuban Personalities" in its entirety would reveal intelligence sources and methods despite plaintiff's allegation that CIA previously released some of same information); Students Against Genocide v. Dep't of State, 257 F.3d 828, 835-36 (D.C. Cir. 2001) (finding that CIA properly withheld photographs purportedly taken by U.S. spy planes and satellites, including photographs that were shown to members of United Nations Security Council by U.S. Ambassador to U.N.); Maynard v. CIA, 986 F.2d 547, 554 (1st Cir. 1993) (stating that under § 403(d)(3) it is responsibility of Director of CIA to determine whether sources or methods should be disclosed); Krikorian v. Dep't of State, 984 F.2d 461, 465 (D.C. Cir. 1993) (same); Fitzgibbon v. CIA, 911 F.2d 755, 761 (D.C. Cir. 1990) (same); Morley v. CIA, 453 F. Supp. 2d 137, 149-51 (D.D.C. 2006) (protecting "intelligence sources and methods," cryptonyms, pseudonyms, and dissemination-control markings); Larson v. Dep't of State, No. 02-1937, 2005 WL 3276303, at *9-11 (D.D.C. Aug. 10, 2005) (protecting classification markings, dissemination control markings, organizational information, and information that could identify intelligence source); Aftergood v. CIA, 355 F. Supp. 2d 557, 562-64 (D.D.C. 2005) (finding that Exemption 3 statute protected CIA's historical budget information from 1947 to 1970, but noting that such protection did not extend to "1963 budget information" that CIA officially acknowledged in declassified "Cost Reduction Program Report"), amended, No. 01-2524, slip op. at 1 (D.D.C. Apr. 4, 2005) (ordering CIA to disclose officially acknowledged 1963 budget figure to plaintiff); Berman v. CIA, 378
(continued...)

instances provides a basis for an agency refusing to even confirm or deny the existence of records.[103]  (See the discussion of the use and origin of

---

[102](...continued)
F. Supp. 2d 1209, 1218 (E.D. Cal. 2005) (holding that CIA properly withheld two "President's Daily Briefs" prepared by CIA during President Johnson's term of office); Judicial Watch, Inc. v. Dep't of Commerce, 337 F. Supp. 2d 146, 167-68 (D.D.C. 2004) (protecting CIA intelligence sources and methods); Aftergood v. CIA, No. 02-1146 (D.D.C. Feb. 8, 2004) (finding that CIA properly withheld aggregate fiscal-year intelligence budget information); Hogan v. Huff, No. 00-Civ-6753, 2002 WL 1359722, at *9 (S.D.N.Y. June 21, 2002) (ruling that the CIA properly withheld information from investigative reports on the death of the requester's father because "disclosure of the information could subsequently put both informants and their families in a dangerous position"); Halpern v. FBI, No. 94-CV-365, slip op. at 16-17 (W.D.N.Y. Aug. 31, 2001) (magistrate's recommendation) (protecting locations of foreign CIA stations), adopted (W.D.N.Y. Oct. 12, 2001); Schrecker v. U.S. Dep't of Justice, 74 F. Supp. 2d 26, 32-33 (D.D.C. 1999) (ruling that CIA properly refused to disclose identity of deceased intelligence sources, allegedly of historical significance, and noting that privacy concerns are not relevant), aff'd in relevant part, rev'd & remanded on other grounds, 254 F.3d 162 (D.C. Cir. 2001); Aftergood v. CIA, No. 98-2107, 1999 U.S. Dist. LEXIS 18135, at *12-15 (D.D.C. Nov. 12, 1999) (permitting CIA to withhold total budget request for all intelligence and intelligence-related activities where Director of Central Intelligence determined that disclosure would "tend to reveal" sources and methods); Blazy v. Tenet, 979 F. Supp. 10, 23-24 (D.D.C. 1997) (protecting intelligence sources and methods located in requester's personnel file), summary affirmance granted, No. 97-5330 (D.C. Cir. May 12, 1998); Andrade v. CIA, No. 95-1215, 1997 WL 527347, at *3-5 (D.D.C. Aug. 18, 1997) (holding intelligence methods used in assessing employee fitness protectible), appeal voluntarily dismissed, No. 97-5251 (D.C. Cir. Dec. 18, 1997).

[103] See, e.g., Frugone v. CIA, 169 F.3d 772, 774-75 (D.C. Cir. 1999) (finding that CIA properly refused to confirm or deny existence of records concerning plaintiff's alleged employment relationship with CIA despite allegation that another government agency seemed to confirm plaintiff's status as former CIA employee); Minier v. CIA, 88 F.3d 796, 801 (9th Cir. 1996) (finding that agency properly refused to confirm or deny existence of records concerning deceased person's alleged employment relationship with CIA); Hunt v. CIA, 981 F.2d 1116, 1118 (9th Cir. 1992) (upholding agency's "Glomar" response to request on foreign national because acknowledgment of existence of any responsive record would reveal sources and methods); Knight v. CIA, 872 F.2d 660, 663 (5th Cir. 1989) (same); Riquelme v. CIA, 453 F. Supp. 2d 103, 105-06, 110-12 (D.D.C. 2006) (upholding CIA's "Glomar" response to request for records concerning its agents' alleged activities, involvement, and contacts in Paraguay during certain time period); ACLU, 389 F. Supp. 2d at 565 (upholding the CIA's "Glomar" response to requests for a Department of Justice memorandum specifying interrogation methods
(continued...)

the "Glomar" response under Exemption 1, In Camera Submissions, above.)

Of current significance in this regard is the fact that in December 2004, Congress enacted section 102A(i) of the National Security Act of 1947, as part of the Intelligence Reform and Terrorism Prevention Act,[104] and thereby transferred authority for protecting intelligence sources and methods from the Director of Central Intelligence to the Director of National Intelligence.[105] Courts subsequently have held that this new statute provides continued protection of the CIA's intelligence sources and meth-

---

[103](...continued)
that the CIA may use against top Al-Qaeda members and a "directive signed by President Bush granting the CIA the authority to set up detention facilities outside the United States and/or outlining interrogation methods that may be used against detainees"); Wolf v. CIA, 357 F. Supp. 2d 112, 117 (D.D.C. 2004) (concluding that the CIA properly refused to confirm or deny the existence of records on Jorge Elicier Gaitan, a Columbian presidential candidate assassinated in 1948, because such acknowledgment "could constitute a threat to national security or to the information-gathering process"), aff'd in pertinent part & remanded on other grounds, 473 F.3d 370 (D.C. Cir. 2007); Pipko v. CIA, 312 F. Supp. 2d 669, 678-79 (D.N.J. 2004) (holding that CIA properly refused to confirm or deny existence of records responsive to first-party request); Wheeler v. CIA, 271 F. Supp. 2d 132, 140-41 (D.D.C. 2003) (same); Kelly v. CIA, No. 00-2498, slip op. at 20 (D.D.C. Aug. 8, 2002) (finding that CIA properly refused to confirm or deny existence of any record reflecting any covert CIA relationship with UCLA); Arabian Shield Dev. Co. v. CIA, No. 3-98-CV-0624, 1999 WL 118796, at *4 (N.D. Tex. Feb. 26, 1999) (deferring to the CIA Director's determination that to confirm or deny the existence of any agency record pertaining to contract negotiations between a U.S. oil company and a foreign government would compromise intelligence sources and methods, while noting that the "Director [of Central Intelligence]'s determination in this regard is almost unassailable" and that "[a]bsent evidence of bad faith, the [CIA]'s determination 'is beyond the purview of the courts'") (quoting Knight v. CIA, 872 F.2d at 664); Earth Pledge Found. v. CIA, 988 F. Supp. 623, 627 (S.D.N.Y. 1996) (finding agency's "Glomar" response proper because acknowledgment of records would present "danger of revealing sources"), aff'd per curiam, 128 F.3d 788 (2d Cir. 1997); see also Tooley, 2006 WL 3783142, at *20-21 (upholding TSA's reliance on Exemption 3 and 49 U.S.C. § 114(s) in its "Glomar" response to first-party request for "TSA watch-list records"). But cf. ACLU, 389 F. Supp. 2d at 566 (declining to uphold CIA's "Glomar" denial of request for Justice Department memorandum interpreting Convention Against Torture, because acknowledgment of its existence does not implicate intelligence sources or methods), reconsideration denied, 396 F. Supp. 2d 459 (S.D.N.Y. 2005).

[104] Pub. L. No. 108-458, § 1011, 118 Stat. 3638 (2004).

[105] Id.

ods.[106]

Also, section 6 of the Central Intelligence Agency Act of 1949[107] -- protecting from disclosure "the organization, functions, names, official titles, salaries or numbers of personnel" employed by the CIA -- meets the requirements of subpart (B).[108] Likewise, the identities of Defense Intelligence Agency employees have been held to be protected from disclosure pursuant to 10 U.S.C. § 424.[109] Similarly, section 6 of Public Law No. 86-36,[110] pertaining to the organization, functions, activities, and personnel of the National Security Agency, has been held to qualify as a subpart (B) statute,[111] as has 18 U.S.C. § 798(a),[112] which criminalizes the disclosure of

---

[106] See e.g., Lahr v. NTSB, 453 F. Supp. 2d 1153, 1172 (C.D. Cal. 2006) (protecting CIA's intelligence sources and methods under 50 U.S.C.A. § 403-1(i) (West Supp. 2006)); Nat'l Sec. Archive Fund, Inc. v. CIA, 402 F. Supp. 2d 211, 222 (D.D.C. 2005) (protecting CIA's intelligence sources and methods documented in 2004 National Intelligence Estimate on Iraq).

[107] 50 U.S.C.A. § 403g (West Supp. 2006) (as amended by Pub. L. No. 108-458, §§ 1071(b)(1)(A), 1072(b), replacing "Director of Central Intelligence" with "Director of National Intelligence").

[108] See, e.g., Lahr, 453 F. Supp. 2d at 1172 (protecting names of CIA employees); Morley, 453 F. Supp. 2d at 150-51 (protecting CIA employee names and personal identifiers); Judicial Watch, Inc., 337 F. Supp. 2d at 167-68 (same); Minier, 88 F.3d at 801; Roman v. Dailey, No. 97-1164, 1998 U.S. Dist. LEXIS 6708, at *10-11 (D.D.C. May 11, 1998), appeal dismissed, No. 99-5083, 1999 WL 506683 (D.C. Cir. Jun. 3, 1999); Blazy, 979 F. Supp. at 23-24; Earth Pledge Found., 988 F. Supp. at 627-28; Campbell, 1996 WL 554511, at *6; Kronisch v. United States, No. 83-2458, 1995 WL 303625, at *4-6 (S.D.N.Y. May 18, 1995), aff'd on other grounds, 150 F.3d 112 (2d Cir. 1998); Hunsberger v. CIA, No. 92-2186, slip op. at 3 (D.D.C. Apr. 5, 1995); Rothschild v. CIA, No. 91-1314, 1992 WL 71393, at *2 (D.D.C. Mar. 25, 1992); Lawyers Comm. for Human Rights v. INS, 721 F. Supp. 552, 567 (S.D.N.Y. 1989); Pfeiffer v. CIA, 721 F. Supp. 337, 341-42 (D.D.C. 1989).

[109] (2000 & Supp. IV 2004); see, e.g., Larson v. Dep't of State, No. 02-1937, 2005 WL 3276303, at *15 (D.D.C. Aug. 10, 2005); Wickwire Gavin, P.C. v. Def. Intelligence Agency, 330 F. Supp. 2d 592, 601-02 (E.D. Va. 2004) (holding that agency properly withheld names of Defense Intelligence Agency employees).

[110] 50 U.S.C. § 402 note (2000).

[111] See Founding Church of Scientology v. NSA, 610 F.2d 824, 828 (D.C. Cir. 1979); Hayden v. NSA, 452 F. Supp. 247, 252 (D.D.C. 1978), aff'd, 608 F.2d 1381 (D.C. Cir. 1979); People for the Am. Way Found. v. NSA, 462 F. Supp. 2d 21, 28 (D.D.C. 2006) (treating statute as providing "absolute" protection); Lahr, 453 F. Supp. 2d at 1191-93 (holding, upon in camera inspection, that NSA properly protected a computer simulation program that "re-

(continued...)

any classified information "concerning the nature, preparation, or use of any code, cipher or cryptographic system of the United States."[113] And a provision of the Atomic Energy Act, prohibiting the disclosure of "restricted data" to the public,[114] refers to particular types of matters -- specifically, information pertaining to atomic weapons and special nuclear material[115] -- and thus has been held to qualify as a subpart (B) statute as well.[116]

Section 7332 of the Veterans Health Administration Patient Rights

---

[111](...continued)
lated to [its] core functions and activities"); Fla. Immigrant Advocacy Ctr. v. NSA, 380 F. Supp. 2d 1332, 1340 (S.D. Fla. 2005) (finding, upon in camera inspection, that NSA properly withheld one-page signal intelligence report because disclosure would reveal certain functions of NSA); see also 10 U.S.C. § 130b (2000 & Supp. IV 2004) (authorizing withholding of personally identifying information regarding any member of armed forces or employee of Department of Defense or of Coast Guard who is assigned to unit that is overseas, "sensitive," or "routinely deployable"); cf. O'Keefe v. DOD, 463 F. Supp. 2d 317, 325 (E.D.N.Y. 2006) (holding as improper DOD's blanket withholding of employees' names under 10 U.S.C. § 130b in the absence of any showing that those employees were "stationed with a 'routinely deployable unit' or any other unit within the ambit of [that statute]").

[112] (2000 & Supp. IV 2004).

[113] Winter v. NSA, 569 F. Supp. 545, 548 (S.D. Cal. 1983); see also Gilmore v. NSA, No. C 92-3646, 1993 U.S. Dist. LEXIS 7694, at *26-27 (N.D. Cal. May 3, 1993) (finding information on cryptography currently used by NSA to be "integrally related" to intelligence gathering and thus protectible).

[114] 42 U.S.C. § 2162 (2000 & Supp. III 2003).

[115] 42 U.S.C.A. § 2014(y) (2003 & West Supp. 2006) (defining "restricted data"); cf. FOIA Post, "Guidance on Homeland Security Information Issued" (posted 3/21/02) (reprinting Memorandum from Assistant to the President and Chief of Staff to the Heads of Executive Departments and Agencies (Mar. 19, 2002) (directing agencies to safeguard government information "that could reasonably be expected to assist in the development or use of weapons of mass destruction, including information about the current locations of stockpiles of nuclear materials that could be exploited for use in such weapons")).

[116] See Meeropol v. Smith, No. 75-1121, slip op. at 53-55 (D.D.C. Feb. 29, 1984), aff'd in relevant part & remanded in part sub nom. Meeropol v. Meese, 790 F.2d 942 (D.C. Cir. 1986). But see Gen. Elec. Co. v. NRC, 750 F.2d 1394, 1401 (7th Cir. 1984) (concluding that a provision of the Atomic Energy Act, 42 U.S.C.A. § 2133(b)(3) (2003 & West Supp. 2006), stating that technical information furnished by license applicants was to be used "only for the purposes of the common defense and security and to protect the health and safety of the public" lacked sufficient specificity to qualify as Exemption 3 statute).

# EXEMPTION 3

Statute[117] generally prohibits disclosure of even the abstract fact that medical records on named individuals are maintained pursuant to that section, but it provides specific criteria under which particular medical information may be released, and thus has been found to satisfy the requirements of subpart (B).[118] Records created by the Department of Veterans Affairs as part of a medical quality-assurance program[119] have similarly been held to qualify for Exemption 3 protection.[120] Likewise, one court has suggested that section 5038 of the Juvenile Delinquency Records Statute,[121] which generally prohibits disclosure of the existence of records compiled pursuant to that section, but which does provide specific criteria for releasing the information, qualifies as a subpart (B) statute.[122] Similarly, Section 207 of the National Park Omnibus Management Act of 1998,[123] which sets forth criteria for the Secretary of the Interior to apply when exercising discretion about release of "[i]nformation concerning the nature and specific location of [certain] National Park System resource[s]," including resources which are "endangered, threatened, rare, or commercially valuable," has been found to be within the scope of subpart (B).[124]

---

[117] 38 U.S.C. § 7332 (2000).

[118] See Palmer v. Derwinski, No. 91-197, slip op. at 3-4 (E.D. Ky. June 10, 1992).

[119] See 38 U.S.C. § 5705(a) (2000).

[120] See Schulte & Sun-Sentinel Co. v. VA, No. 86-6251, slip op. at 3-4 (S.D. Fla. Feb. 2, 1996) (allowing agency to withhold mortality statistics); see also Goodrich v. Dep't of the Air Force, 404 F. Supp. 2d 48, 50, 51 (D.D.C. 2005) (holding that 10 U.S.C. § 1102 (2000 & Supp. IV 2004), DOD's medical quality-assurance statute, qualifies as Exemption 3 statute protecting "minutes of Credentials Functions meetings and [Medical Practice Review Boards]"); Dayton Newspapers, Inc. v. Dep't of the Air Force, 107 F. Supp. 2d 912, 917 (S.D. Ohio 1999) (finding that 10 U.S.C. § 1102, qualifies as Exemption 3 statute protecting "all 'medical quality assurance records,' regardless of whether the contents of such records originated within or outside of a medical quality assurance program").

[121] 18 U.S.C. § 5038 (2000).

[122] See McDonnell v. United States, 4 F.3d 1227, 1251 (3d Cir. 1993) (holding that state juvenile delinquency records fall outside scope of statute).

[123] 16 U.S.C. § 5937 (2000).

[124] See Sw. Ctr. for Biological Diversity v. USDA, 314 F.3d 1060, 1061 (9th Cir. 2002) (approving withholding of information concerning specific nesting locations of northern goshawks); Hornbostel v. U.S. Dep't of the Interior, 305 F. Supp. 2d 21, 30 (D.D.C. 2003) (concluding that agency properly withheld information regarding "rare or commercially valuable" resources because resources were located within "public land" boundaries); Pease v.

(continued...)

The Court of Appeals for the District of Columbia Circuit has held that a portion of the Patent Act[125] satisfies subpart (B) because it identifies the types of matters -- patent applications and information concerning them -- intended to be withheld.[126] As well, the portion of the Civil Service Reform Act concerning the confidentiality of certain labor relations training and guidance materials,[127] has been held to qualify as a subpart (B) withholding statute.[128] In addition, the United States Information and Educational Exchange Act of 1948 (the "Smith-Mundt Act")[129] qualifies as a subpart (B) statute insofar as it prohibits the disclosure of certain overseas programming materials within the United States.[130] While the Smith-Mundt Act originally applied only to records prepared by the now-defunct United States Information Agency, the Foreign Affairs Reform and Restructuring Act of 1998 applied the relevant provisions of that statute to those

---

[124](...continued)
U.S. Dep't of Interior, No. 1:99CV113, slip op. at 2, 4 (D. Vt. Sept. 17, 1999) (finding that the agency properly withheld "certain information pertaining to the location, tracking and/or radio frequencies of grizzly bears" in the Yellowstone National Park ecosystem); cf. Maricopa Audubon Soc'y v. U.S. Forest Serv., 108 F.3d 1082, 1089 (9th Cir. 1997) (refusing to protect wildlife maps showing endangered species locations pursuant to Exemption 2); Audubon Soc'y v. U.S. Forest Serv., 104 F.3d 1201, 1204 (10th Cir. 1997) (same); FOIA Post, "Agencies Rely on Wide Range of Exemption 3 Statutes" (posted 12/16/03) (discussing National Park Omnibus Management Act of 1998, and citing Southwest Center for Biological Diversity); FOIA Post, "Supreme Court Rules in Exemption 5 Case" (posted 4/4/01) (noting possible need for additional nondisclosure legislation to protect confidential communications between Department of the Interior and Indian tribes); FOIA Update, Vol. XVI, No. 3, at 2 (describing difficulty of protecting endangered species locations under Exemption 2 prior to legislative enactment qualifying under Exemption 3).

[125] 35 U.S.C. § 122 (2000 & Supp. III 2003).

[126] Irons & Sears v. Dann, 606 F.2d 1215, 1220 (D.C. Cir. 1979); accord Leeds v. Quigg, 720 F. Supp. 193, 194 (D.D.C. 1989), summary affirmance granted, No. 89-5062, 1989 WL 386474 (D.C. Cir. Oct. 24, 1989).

[127] 5 U.S.C. § 7114(b)(4) (2000).

[128] See Dubin v. Dep't of the Treasury, 555 F. Supp. 408, 412 (N.D. Ga. 1981), aff'd, 697 F.2d 1093 (11th Cir. 1983) (unpublished table decision); NTEU v. OPM, No. 76-695, slip op. at 4 (D.D.C. July 9, 1979).

[129] 22 U.S.C. § 1461-1a (2000).

[130] See Essential Info., Inc. v. USIA, 134 F.3d 1165, 1168 (D.C. Cir. 1998) (holding that Smith-Mundt Act qualifies as nondisclosure statute even though "it does not prohibit all disclosure of records but only disclosure to persons in this country").

programs within the Department of State that absorbed USIA's functions.[131]

The Commodity Exchange Act,[132] which prohibits the disclosure of business transactions, market positions, trade secrets, or customer names of persons under investigation under the Act, has been held to refer to particular types of matters and thus to satisfy subpart (B).[133] The D.C. Circuit has held that a provision of the Federal Aviation Act,[134] relating to security data the disclosure of which would be detrimental to the safety of travelers, similarly shields that particular data from disclosure under the FOIA.[135] It also has been held that the DOD's "technical data" statute,[136] which protects technical information with "military or space application" for which an export license is required, satisfies subpart (B) because it refers to sufficiently particular types of matters.[137]

Further, the Federal Transfer Technology Act,[138] which allows federal agencies the discretion to protect for five years any commercial and confidential information that results from a Cooperative Research And Development Agreement (CRADA) with a nonfederal party, has been held to qual-

---

[131] See Foreign Affairs Reform and Restructuring Act of 1998, Pub. L. No. 105-277, 112 Stat. 2681 (codified as amended at 22 U.S.C. §§ 6501-6617) (abolishing USIA, 22 U.S.C. § 6531 (2000), transferring USIA functions to Department of State, 22 U.S.C. § 6532 (2000), and applying Smith-Mundt Act to USIA functions that were transferred to Department of State (22 U.S.C. § 6552(b)) (2000)).

[132] 7 U.S.C. § 12 (2000).

[133] See Hunt v. Commodity Futures Trading Comm'n, 484 F. Supp. 47, 49 (D.D.C. 1979).

[134] 49 U.S.C. § 40119 (2000 & Supp. III 2003), amended by Pub. L. No. 107-71, 115 Stat. 597, 603 (2001) (transferring statutory powers from Administrator of FAA to Under Secretary of Transportation for Security, and expanding criteria for nondisclosure).

[135] Pub. Citizen, Inc. v. FAA, 988 F.2d 186, 194 (D.C. Cir. 1993).

[136] 10 U.S.C. § 130 (2000).

[137] See Chenkin v. Dep't of the Army, No. 93-494, 1994 U.S. Dist. LEXIS 20907, at *8 (E.D. Pa. Jan. 14, 1994), aff'd, 61 F.3d 894 (3d Cir. 1995) (unpublished table decision); Colonial Trading Corp. v. Dep't of the Navy, 735 F. Supp. 429, 431 (D.D.C. 1990); see also Am. Friends Serv. Comm. v. DOD, No. 83-4916, 1986 WL 10659, at *4 (E.D. Pa. Sept. 25, 1986) (applying statute where only dispute was over coverage in relation to particular data at issue), rev'd on other grounds, 831 F.2d 441 (3d Cir. 1987).

[138] 15 U.S.C. § 3710a(c)(7) (2000 & Supp. IV 2004).

ify as an Exemption 3 statute.[139] Under a concurrent provision in that Act, the agency also is prohibited from disclosing any commercial and confidential information obtained from the CRADA's private-sector partner.[140] (See also the discussion of commercial information under Exemption 4, Commercial or Financial Information, below.)

By comparison, some statutes have been found to satisfy both Exemption 3 subparts. For example, while the Court of Appeals for the Third Circuit has held that section 222(f) of the Immigration and Nationality Act[141] sufficiently limits the category of information it covers -- records pertaining to the issuance or refusal of visas and permits to enter the United States -- to qualify as an Exemption 3 statute under subpart (B),[142] the Court of Appeals for the District of Columbia Circuit has held that the section satisfies subpart (A) as well as subpart (B).[143]

Similarly, Exemption 3 protection for information obtained by law enforcement agencies pursuant to the statute governing court-ordered wiretaps, Title III of the Omnibus Crime Control and Safe Streets Act of 1968,[144] has been recognized by district courts on a variety of bases.[145] However, in

---

[139] See Pub. Citizen Health Research Group v. NIH, 209 F. Supp. 2d 37, 43, 51 (D.D.C. 2002) (deciding that NIH properly withheld royalty rate information under 15 U.S.C. § 3710a(c)(7)(A), and noting that scope of Act's protection is "coterminous" with that of Exemption 4); DeLorme Publ'g Co. v. NOAA, 917 F. Supp. 867, 871 (D. Me. 1996) (finding that 15 U.S.C. § 3710a(c)(7)(A) qualifies as Exemption 3 statute), appeal dismissed per stipulation, No. 96-1601 (1st Cir. July 8, 1996).

[140] 15 U.S.C. § 3710a(c)(7)(B).

[141] 8 U.S.C. § 1202(f) (2000 & Supp. IV 2004).

[142] DeLaurentiis v. Haig, 686 F.2d 192, 194 (3d Cir. 1982); accord Smith v. Dep't of Justice, No. 81-CV-813, 1983 U.S. Dist. LEXIS 10878, at *13-14 (N.D.N.Y. Dec. 13, 1983).

[143] Medina-Hincapie v. Dep't of State, 700 F.2d 737, 741-42 (D.C. Cir. 1983); accord Perry-Torres v. U.S. Dep't of State, 404 F. Supp. 2d 140, 143-44 (D.D.C. 2005) (protecting "information regarding the denial of plaintiff's visa application"); Marulanda v. U.S. Dep't of State, No. 93-1327, slip op. at 4-6 (D.D.C. Jan. 31, 1996) (protecting documents relating to denial of plaintiff's visa even when agency previously released certain of those records that were determined not to breach confidentiality provision).

[144] See 18 U.S.C.A. §§ 2510-2520 (2000 & West Supp. 2006).

[145] See Mendoza v. DEA, 465 F. Supp. 2d 5, 11 (D.D.C. 2006) (protecting information obtained from authorized wiretap); Jennings v. FBI, No. 03-1651, slip op. at 11 (D.D.C. May 6, 2004) (protecting transcripts of wiretapped communications); Barreiro v. Executive Office for U.S. Attorneys,

(continued...)

**EXEMPTION 3**

Lam Lek Chong v. DEA,[146] the D.C. Circuit, finding that it "clearly identifies intercepted communications as the subject of its disclosure limitations," held that "Title III falls squarely within the scope of subsection (B)'s second prong, as a statute referring to 'particular matters to be withheld.'"[147]

---

[145](...continued)
No. 03-0720, slip op. at 5 (D.D.C. Dec. 31, 2003) (relying upon "wiretap statute" to protect information obtained through authorized wiretap, but not distinguishing between subparts (A) and (B) of Exemption 3), aff'd, No. 04-5071, 2004 WL 2451753, at *1 (D.C. Cir. Nov. 1, 2004); Sinito v. U.S. Dep't of Justice, No. 87-0814, slip op. at 12-14 (D.D.C. July 11, 2000) (implying that 18 U.S.C. § 2518(8)(b), which requires that Title III applications and orders be kept under court seal, is a subpart (A) statute in observing that "[t]he FBI has no discretion . . . to disclose Title III information that is under court seal"), aff'd, 22 F. App'x 1 (D.C. Cir. 2001); Gonzalez v. U.S. Dep't of Justice, No. 88-913, 1988 WL 120841, at *2 (D.D.C. Oct. 25, 1988) (holding that statute codified at 18 U.S.C. § 2511(2)(a)(ii), which regulates disclosure of existence of wiretap intercepts, meets requirements of subpart (A)); Docal v. Bennsinger, 543 F. Supp. 38, 43-44 (M.D. Pa. 1981) (relying upon entire statutory scheme of 18 U.S.C. §§ 2510-2520 but not distinguishing between Exemption 3 subparts); Carroll v. U.S. Dep't of Justice, No. 76-2038, slip op. at 2-3 (D.D.C. May 26, 1978) (holding that 18 U.S.C. § 2518(8), which regulates disclosure of contents of wiretap intercepts, meets requirements of subpart (A)).

[146] 929 F.2d 729 (D.C. Cir. 1991).

[147] Id. at 733 (quoting 5 U.S.C. § 552(b)(3) (2000 & Supp. IV 2004)); see also Willis v. FBI, No. 98-5071, 1999 WL 236891, at *1 (D.C. Cir. Mar. 19, 1999) (finding that FBI properly withheld two electronic surveillance tapes under Title III and Exemption 3); Payne v. U.S. Dep't of Justice, No. 96-30840, slip op. at 5-6 (5th Cir. July 11, 1997) (holding that tape recordings obtained pursuant to Title III "fall squarely" within scope of Exemption 3); Manna v. U.S. Dep't of Justice, No. 92-1840, slip op. at 3-4 (D.N.J. Aug. 25, 1993) (determining that analysis of audiotapes and identities of individuals conversing on tapes obtained pursuant to Title III is protected under Exemption 3), aff'd on other grounds, 51 F.3d 1158 (3d Cir. 1995); Barreiro, No. 03-0720, slip op. at 5 (D.D.C. Dec. 31, 2003) (protecting transcript of wiretapped communication); Manchester v. DEA, 823 F. Supp. 1259, 1267 (E.D. Pa. 1993) (ruling that wiretap applications and derivative information fall within broad purview of Title III), aff'd, 40 F.3d 1240 (3d Cir. 1994) (unpublished table decision); cf. Smith v. U.S. Dep't of Justice, 251 F.3d 1047, 1049 (D.C. Cir. 2001) (finding that audiotapes of telephone calls made by inmate on monitored prison telephone were not "interceptions" within scope of Title III and thus were improperly withheld); Cottone v. Reno, 193 F.3d 550, 554-56 (D.C. Cir. 1999) (noting that wiretapped recordings obtained pursuant to Title III ordinarily are exempt from disclosure under Exemption 3, but holding that Exemption 3 protection was waived when FOIA requester precisely identified specific tapes that had been played in open court by

(continued...)

Applications and orders for "pen registers" properly may be withheld pursuant to a sealing order issued by a court in accordance with 18 U.S.C. § 3123(d)[148] but once the sealing order is lifted, the statute no longer prohibits release under the FOIA.[149] In one case, information acquired through the use of a "pen register" was held to be protected from disclosure by Title III,[150] and was found to fall under Exemption 3.[151]

The withholding of tax return information has been approved under three different theories. The United States Supreme Court and most appellate courts that have considered the matter have held either explicitly or implicitly that section 6103 of the Internal Revenue Code[152] satisfies subpart (B) of Exemption 3.[153] The Courts of Appeals for the D.C., Fifth, Sixth, and Tenth Circuits have further reasoned that section 6103 is a subpart (A) statute to the extent that a person generally is not entitled to access to tax

---

[147](...continued)
prosecution as evidence during criminal trial).

[148] (2000 & Supp. IV 2004); see Jennings, No. 03-1651, slip op. at 11-12 (D.D.C. May 6, 2004) (protecting sealed pen register and conversation log sheets); Riley v. FBI, No. 00-2378, 2002 U.S. Dist. LEXIS 2632, at *5-6 (D.D.C. Feb. 11, 2002) (protecting sealed pen register applications and orders); Manna v. U.S. Dep't of Justice, 815 F. Supp. 798, 812 (D.N.J. 1993) (same), aff'd on other grounds, 51 F.3d 1158 (3d Cir. 1995).

[149] See 18 U.S.C. § 3123(d); see also Morgan v. U.S. Dep't of Justice, 923 F.2d 195, 197 (D.C. Cir. 1991) ("[T]he proper test for determining whether an agency improperly withholds records under seal is whether the seal, like an injunction, prohibits the agency from disclosing the records.").

[150] 18 U.S.C. §§ 2510-2520.

[151] McFarland v. DEA, No. 94-620, slip op. at 4 (D. Colo. Jan. 3, 1995) (protecting under Exemption 3 material "acquired through the use of a pen register").

[152] 26 U.S.C.A. § 6103 (2002 & West Supp. 2006).

[153] See, e.g., Church of Scientology v. IRS, 484 U.S. 9, 15 (1987); Aronson v. IRS, 973 F.2d 962, 964-65 (1st Cir. 1992) (finding that IRS lawfully exercised discretion to withhold street addresses pursuant to 26 U.S.C. § 6103(m)(1)); Long v. IRS, 891 F.2d 222, 224 (9th Cir. 1989) (holding that deletion of taxpayers' identification does not alter confidentiality of section 6103 information); DeSalvo v. IRS, 861 F.2d 1217, 1221 (10th Cir. 1988); Grasso v. IRS, 785 F.2d 70, 77 (3d Cir. 1986); Long v. IRS, 742 F.2d 1173, 1179 (9th Cir. 1984); Ryan v. ATF, 715 F.2d 644, 645 (D.C. Cir. 1983); Currie v. IRS, 704 F.2d 523, 527-28 (11th Cir. 1983); Willamette Indus. v. United States, 689 F.2d 865, 867 (9th Cir. 1982); Barney v. IRS, 618 F.2d 1268, 1274 n.15 (8th Cir. 1980) (dictum); Chamberlain v. Kurtz, 589 F.2d 827, 843 (5th Cir. 1979).

returns or return information of <u>other</u> taxpayers.[154] In 2003, however, the

---

[154] See <u>Stebbins v. Sullivan</u>, No. 90-5361, 1992 WL 174542, at *1 (D.C. Cir. July 22, 1992); <u>DeSalvo</u>, 861 F.2d at 1221 n.4; <u>Linsteadt v. IRS</u>, 729 F.2d 998, 1000 (5th Cir. 1984); <u>Fruehauf Corp. v. IRS</u>, 566 F.2d 574, 578 n.6 (6th Cir. 1977); see also <u>Tax Analysts v. IRS</u>, 410 F.3d 715, 717-22 (D.C. Cir. 2005) (finding that a "closing agreement" reached between an organization and the IRS did "not constitute a document submitted in support of the [organization's successful] application [for tax-exempt status]"; therefore, "closing agreement" is protected "return information" and is not subject to disclosure under section 6104); <u>Landmark Legal Found. v. IRS</u>, 267 F.3d 1132, 1135-37 (D.C. Cir. 2001) (determining that "return information" includes identities of tax-exempt organizations as well as information pertaining to third-party requests for audits or investigations of tax-exempt organizations); <u>Stanbury Law Firm v. IRS</u>, 221 F.3d 1059, 1062 (8th Cir. 2000) (ruling that names of contributors to public charity constitute tax return information and may not be disclosed); <u>Lehrfeld v. Richardson</u>, 132 F.3d 1463, 1467 (D.C. Cir. 1998) (protecting third-party "return information" submitted in support of application for tax-exempt status); <u>Tax Analysts v. IRS</u>, 117 F.3d 607, 611-16 (D.C. Cir. 1997) (holding that while Field Service Advice Memoranda contain some protectible "return information," any "legal analyses" contained therein do not constitute "return information" properly withholdable under Exemption 3); <u>Kamman v. IRS</u>, 56 F.3d 46, 49 (9th Cir. 1995) (holding appraisal of jewelry seized from third-party taxpayer and auctioned to satisfy tax liability was not "return information"); <u>Morley</u>, 453 F. Supp. 2d at 150-51 (protecting deceased person's W-4 tax withholding information); <u>Judicial Watch, Inc. v. Dep't of Justice</u>, 306 F. Supp. 2d 58 (D.D.C. 2004) (ruling that records related to bankruptcy of Enron Corporation constitute "return information"); <u>Hodge v. IRS</u>, No. 03-0269, 2003 U.S. Dist. LEXIS 17083, at *1-3 (D.D.C. Aug. 28, 2003) (ruling that agency withholding of third-party tax return information was proper despite claim that third party used plaintiff's social security number on third party's tax return); <u>Mays v. IRS</u>, No. 02-1191, 2003 WL 21518343, at *2 (D. Minn. May 21, 2003) (prohibiting disclosure of former bank's tax return information absent evidence of bank's corporate dissolution); <u>Andrews v. IRS</u>, No. 02-0973, 2003 U.S. Dist. LEXIS 10226, at *4-6 (D.D.C. Apr. 29, 2003) (approving agency's withholding of corporation's tax return information on basis that corporation had merged rather than dissolved); <u>Davis, Cowell & Bowe, LLP v. Soc. Sec. Admin.</u>, No. 01-4021, 2002 WL 1034058, at *5-7, *9 (N.D. Cal. May 16, 2002) (characterizing information on W-2 and W-3 wage forms, which were sent to and used by Social Security Administration for non-tax-related purposes before being sent to IRS, as confidential tax return information), <u>vacated as moot</u>, 281 F. Supp. 2d 1154 (N.D. Cal. 2003) (finding that Social Security Administration's declaration that it did not possess records that plaintiff requested rendered action moot); <u>McGinley v. U.S. Dep't of Treasury</u>, No. 01-09493, 2002 WL 1058115, at *3-4 (C.D. Cal. Apr. 15, 2002) (refusing to allow IRS employee access to record regarding contract between IRS and third party concerning corporate taxpayer's alleged audit, because

(continued...)

[154](...continued)
such record constituted tax return information); Chourre v. IRS, 203 F.
Supp. 2d 1196, 1200-02 (W.D. Wash. 2002) (finding that IRS properly redacted records containing information about plaintiff and third-party taxpayers); Leveto v. IRS, No. 98-285E, 2001 U.S. Dist. LEXIS 5791, at *21-22 (W.D.
Pa. Apr. 10, 2001) (ruling that IRS properly withheld information identifying
third-party taxpayers); Helmon v. IRS, No. 3-00-CV-0809-M, 2000 U.S. Dist.
LEXIS 17628, at *9-11 (N.D. Tex. Nov. 6, 2000) (magistrate's recommendation) (protecting third-party "return information" despite requester's claim
that she was administrator of estate of third party and thus was legally entitled to requested information, because proof of her relationship to deceased did not satisfy standard established by IRS regulations), adopted
(N.D. Tex. Nov. 30, 2000); Wewee v. IRS, No. 99-475, slip op. at 14-15 (D.
Ariz. Oct. 13, 2000) (magistrate's recommendation) (concluding that agency
properly withheld third-party tax return information, including individual
and business taxpayer names, income amounts, and deductions), adopted
(D. Ariz. Feb. 13, 2001); Allnutt v. U.S. Dep't of Justice, No. Y98-1722, 2000
U.S. Dist. LEXIS 4060, at *37-38 (D. Md. Mar. 6, 2000) (magistrate's recommendation) (recognizing that section 6103 prohibits disclosure of third-party taxpayer information even though IRS collected such information as part
of investigation of requester), adopted in pertinent part, 99 F. Supp. 2d 673,
675 (D. Md. 2000), renewed motion for summary judgment granted, 2000
WL 852455 (D. Md. Oct. 23, 2000), aff'd sub nom. Allnut v. Handler, 8 F.
App'x 225 (4th Cir. 2001) (per curiam); Murphy v. IRS, 79 F. Supp. 2d 1180,
1183-84 (D. Haw. 1999) (upholding agency decision to withhold third-party
return information despite requester's argument that he had "material interest" in information), appeal dismissed, No. 99-17325 (9th Cir. Apr. 17,
2000); Tax Analysts v. IRS, 53 F. Supp. 2d 449, 451-53 (D.D.C. 1999) (declaring that "closing agreements" releasing tax-exempt organizations from tax
liability constitute "tax return information" within scope of section 6103(a),
and that because they are distinct from "applications" or tax-exempt status,
which are open to public inspection under section 6104, they may not be
disclosed); Barmes v. IRS, 60 F. Supp. 2d 896, 900-01 (S.D. Ind. 1998) (protecting "transcripts containing a variety of tax data concerning third party
taxpayers"); Buckner v. IRS, 25 F. Supp. 2d 893, 899-900 (N.D. Ind. 1998)
(ruling that information properly was withheld where disclosure would reveal identity of third-party taxpayer); Crooker, 1995 WL 430605, at *3 (requiring IRS to confirm that redactions were not taken for aliases plaintiff
used in his tax-refund scheme); Gray, Plant, Mooty, Mooty & Bennett v.
IRS, No. 4-90-210, 1990 U.S. Dist. LEXIS 18799, at *8 (D. Minn. Dec. 18,
1990) (ordering public report released because it does not qualify as "return
information" as it does not include data in form which can be associated
with particular taxpayer), appeal dismissed, No. 91-1630 (8th Cir. May 14,
1991). But see also Ginsberg v. IRS, No. 96-2265, 1997 WL 882913, at *4
(M.D. Fla. Dec. 23, 1997) (magistrate's recommendation) (holding that the
bulk of a legal memorandum responding to a "Request for Technical Assistance" was not protectible "return information" because the document form-
(continued...)

D.C. Circuit held that "the IRS must disclose determinations denying or revoking tax exemptions, but do so in redacted form, thus protecting the privacy of the organizations involved."[155]

It should be noted that pursuant to sections 6103(c) and 6103(e)(7), individuals are not entitled to obtain tax return information even regarding themselves if it is determined that release would impair enforcement by the IRS.[156] Likewise, information that would provide insights into how

---

[154](...continued)
ed "the operative body of law found applicable to [the] taxpayers in this [case]"), adopted (M.D. Fla. Jan. 27, 1998).

[155] Tax Analysts v. IRS, 350 F.3d 100, 104 (D.C. Cir. 2003).

[156] See McQueen v. United States, 264 F. Supp. 2d 502, 516 (S.D. Tex. 2003) (reasoning that the release of plaintiff's records that "discussed specifics regarding the nature of the IRS case against . . . third parties" would "effectively thwart" federal tax administration); Carp v. IRS, No. 00-5992, 2002 WL 373448, at *4 (D.N.J. Jan. 28, 2002) (finding that documents submitted by IRS in support of search warrant application in a discontinued tax-fraud investigation were return information that could not be released to subject of investigation without impairing tax administration); Warren v. United States, No. 1:99CV1317, 2000 WL 1868950, at *6 (N.D. Ohio Oct. 31, 2000) (concluding that release of return information to taxpayer would inhibit investigation of taxpayer and impair tax administration); Youngblood v. Comm'r, No. 2:99-CV-9253, 2000 WL 852449, at *9-10 (C.D. Cal. Mar. 6, 2000) (declaring that criminal tax investigation report was properly withheld where IRS demonstrated that disclosure would seriously impair federal tax administration); Anderson v. United States Dep't of Treasury, No. 98-1112, 1999 WL 282784, at *2-3 (W.D. Tenn. Mar. 24, 1999) (finding that disclosure to taxpayer of IRS-prepared "checkspread" charting all checks written by taxpayer over two-year period would seriously impair tax administration, notwithstanding IRS agent's disclosure of "checkspread" to taxpayer during interview); Brooks v. IRS, No. 96-6284, 1997 WL 718473, at *9 (E.D. Cal. Aug. 28, 1997) (upholding protection of revenue agent's notes because release "would permit Plaintiff to ascertain the extent of [IRS's] knowledge and predict the direction of [its] examination"); Gibbs Int'l, Inc. v. IRS, No. 7:96-996-13, slip op. at 1 (D.S.C. Oct. 8, 1996) (stating that "disclosure of the documents would chill future cooperation with foreign government treaty partners"), aff'd, 129 F.3d 116 (4th Cir. 1997) (unpublished table decision); Holbrook v. IRS, 914 F. Supp. 314, 316-17 (S.D. Iowa 1996) (holding IRS agent's handwritten notes protectible because disclosure would interfere with enforcement proceedings and hence seriously impair tax administration); Pully v. IRS, 939 F. Supp. 429, 434-36 (E.D. Va. 1996) (holding documents relating to civil and criminal investigation of plaintiff protectible under Exemptions 3 and 7(A)); Fritz v. IRS, 862 F. Supp. 234, 236 (W.D. Wis. 1994) (finding that disclosure of name and address of purchaser of seized automobile would impair tax administration as "people

(continued...)

the IRS selects returns for audits has regularly been found to impair IRS's enforcement of tax laws.[157]  Of course, it also must be remembered that

[156](...continued)
would be less likely to purchase seized property" if their identities were revealed); Rollins v. U.S. Dep't of Justice, No. Civ.A. H-90-3170, 1992 WL 12014526, at *5-6 (S.D. Tex. June 30, 1992) (stating that IRS memoranda revealing scope and direction of investigation was properly withheld), aff'd, No. 92-2575 (5th Cir. Oct. 27, 1993); Starkey v. IRS, No. 91-20040, 1991 WL 330895, at *2-3 (N.D. Cal. Dec. 6, 1991) (same), appeal dismissed, No. 92-16162 (9th Cir. Nov. 23, 1992); Church of Scientology v. IRS, No. 89-5894, 1991 U.S. Dist. LEXIS 3008, at *3 (C.D. Cal. Mar. 4, 1991) (concluding that release of document referring to information obtainable under various treaties would chill future cooperation of foreign governments and tax-treaty partners); Casa Investors, Ltd. v. Gibbs, No. 88-2485, 1990 WL 180703, at *4 (D.D.C. Oct. 11, 1990) (holding that recommendation for settlement of tax controversies prepared by low-level IRS employees requires protection).  But see LeMaine v. IRS, No. 89-2914, 1991 WL 322616, at *5 (D. Mass. Dec. 10, 1991) (deciding that release of information commonly revealed to public in tax enforcement proceedings would not "seriously impair Federal tax administration" overall).

[157] See Gillin v. IRS, 980 F.2d 819, 822 (1st Cir. 1992) (per curiam) (holding that differential function scores, used to identify returns most in need of examination or audit, are exempt from disclosure); Long v. IRS, 891 F.2d at 224 (finding that computer tapes used to develop discriminant function formulas protected); Sutton v. IRS, No. 05-C-7177, 2007 WL 30547, at *3-4 (N.D. Ill. Jan. 4, 2007) (holding discriminant function scores properly exempt from disclosure); Coolman v. IRS, No. 98-6149, 1999 WL 675319, at *5 (W.D. Mo. July 12, 1999) (holding that section 6103(b)(2) permits IRS to withhold discriminant function scores), aff'd, No. 99-3963, 1999 WL 1419039 (8th Cir. Dec. 6, 1999); Buckner, 25 F. Supp. 2d at 898-99 (concluding that discriminant function scores were properly withheld under section 6103(b)(2), even where scores were seventeen years old, because IRS continued to use scores in determining whether to audit certain tax files); Wishart v. Comm'r, No. 97-20614, 1998 WL 667638, at *6 (N.D. Cal. Aug. 6, 1998) (holding discriminant function scores protectible), aff'd, 199 F.3d 1334 (9th Cir. 1999) (unpublished table decision); Cujas v. IRS, No. 1:97CV00741, 1998 WL 419999, at *5 (M.D.N.C. Apr. 15, 1998) (recognizing that requester was likely to disseminate information about his discriminant function score, "thus making it easier for taxpayers to avoid an audit of their return[s]"), aff'd, 162 F.3d 1154 (4th Cir. 1998) (unpublished table decision); Inman v. Comm'r, 871 F. Supp. 1275, 1278 (E.D. Cal. 1994) (holding discriminant function scores properly exempt); Lamb v. IRS, 871 F. Supp. 301, 304 (E.D. Mich. 1994) (same); In re Church of Scientology Flag Serv. Org./IRS FOIA Litig., No. 91-423, slip op. at 3-4 (M.D. Fla. May 19, 1993) (determining that "tolerance criteria" and discriminant function scores were properly withheld) (multidistrict litigation case); Small, 820 F. Supp. at 165-66 (holding discriminant function scores protected under both Exemption 3

(continued...)

section 6103 applies only to tax return information obtained by the Department of the Treasury, not to any such information maintained by other agencies that was obtained by means other than through the provisions of the Internal Revenue Code.[158]

Just over six years ago, Congress enacted section 6105 of the Internal Revenue Code,[159] which now governs the withholding of tax convention information such as bilateral agreements providing for, inter alia, the exchange of foreign "tax relevant information" with the United States and "mutual assistance in tax matters"; it, too, has been held to be an Exemption 3 statute.[160]

At least one court of appeals and several district courts have explicitly embraced a third theory based upon the reasoning of Zale Corp. v. IRS.[161] These courts have held that it is not necessary to view section 6103 as an Exemption 3 statute in order to withhold tax return information because the provisions of this tax code section are intended to operate as the sole standard governing the disclosure or nondisclosure of such information,

---

[157](...continued) and Exemption 7(E)); Ferguson v. IRS, No. C-89-4048, 1990 U.S. Dist. LEXIS 15293, at *4 (N.D. Cal. Oct. 31, 1990) (finding that standards and data used in selection and examination of returns are exempt from disclosure where they would impair IRS enforcement); see also 26 U.S.C.A. § 6103(b)(2)(D) (providing that no law "shall be construed to require the disclosure of standards used . . . for the selection of returns for examination . . . if the Secretary [of the Treasury] determines that such disclosure will seriously impair . . . enforcement under the internal revenue laws").

[158] See FOIA Update, Vol. IX, No. 2, at 5 (citing Stokwitz v. United States, 831 F.2d 893, 896-97 (9th Cir. 1987), for proposition that disclosure of tax returns that Navy obtained independently of IRS did not violate section 6103, and advising accordingly); see also 26 U.S.C.A. § 6103(b)(1)-(3) (defining "return," "return information," and "taxpayer return information" as information required by, or provided for, Secretary of the Treasury under title 26 of United States Code).

[159] Pub. L. No. 106-554, § 303, 114 Stat 2763 (2000) (codified as amended at 26 U.S.C. § 6105 (2000 & Supp. III 2003)).

[160] See Tax Analysts v. IRS, 217 F. Supp. 2d 23, 27-29 (D.D.C. 2002) (finding that IRS properly withheld international tax convention records considered confidential under such conventions but that otherwise would not be deemed confidential under laws of United States); Tax Analysts v. IRS, 152 F. Supp. 2d 1, 12 (D.D.C. 2001) (protecting record created by IRS to respond to foreign tax treaty partner's request for legal advice, because it consisted of tax convention information that treaty requires be kept confidential).

[161] 481 F. Supp. 486, 490 (D.D.C. 1979).

thereby "displacing" the FOIA.[162]

Viewing section 6103 as a "displacement" statute permitted some courts to avoid the de novo review required by the FOIA and to apply instead less stringent standards of review pursuant to the Administrative Procedure Act,[163] and could relieve agencies from certain procedural requirements of the FOIA, such as the time limitations for responding to requests and the duty to segregate and release nonexempt information.[164] Even under this approach, though, the government likely would be required to provide detailed <u>Vaughn</u> Indexes of the information being withheld, rather than general affidavits; the Sixth Circuit required this despite the fact that the court below had relied solely on the "displacement" theory for its decision.[165]

However, other courts have specifically refused to adopt this "displacement" analysis on the ground that to do so, once it is already evident that section 6103 is an Exemption 3 statute, "would be an exercise in judicial futility [requiring district courts] to engage in both FOIA and <u>Zale</u> analyses when confronted" with such cases.[166] Most significantly, the D.C. Circuit has squarely rejected the "displacement" argument on the basis that the procedures in section 6103 for members of the public to obtain access to IRS documents do not duplicate, and thus do not "displace," those of the

---

[162] See, e.g., <u>Cheek v. IRS</u>, 703 F.2d 271, 271 (7th Cir. 1983) (noting that section 6103 also "displaces" Privacy Act of 1974, 5 U.S.C. § 552a (2000 & Supp. IV 2004)); <u>King v. IRS</u>, 688 F.2d 488, 495 (7th Cir. 1982); <u>Kuzma v. IRS</u>, No. 81-600E, slip op. at 7-8 (W.D.N.Y. Dec. 31, 1984); see also <u>White v. IRS</u>, 707 F.2d 897, 900 (6th Cir. 1983) (indicating approval of <u>Zale</u>).

[163] 5 U.S.C. §§ 701-706 (2000).

[164] See <u>Grasso</u>, 785 F.2d at 73-74; <u>White</u>, 707 F.2d at 900; <u>Goldsborough v. IRS</u>, No. Y-81-1939, 1984 WL 612, at *5-6 (D. Md. May 10, 1984); <u>Green v. IRS</u>, 556 F. Supp. 79, 84 (N.D. Ind. 1982), aff'd, 734 F.2d 18 (7th Cir. 1984) (unpublished table decision); <u>Meyer v. Dep't of the Treasury</u>, 82-2 U.S. Tax Cas. (CCH) ¶ 9678, at 85,448 (W.D. Mich. Oct. 2, 1982); see also <u>Anderson v. U.S. Dep't of Treasury</u>, 1999 WL 282784, at *3 (acknowledging that if section 6103 pre-empted FOIA, then Administrative Procedure Act standard of review, rather than more stringent FOIA standard of review, would apply, but concluding that case did not require choice because agency action satisfied more stringent FOIA standard).

[165] <u>Osborn v. IRS</u>, 754 F.2d 195, 197-98 (6th Cir. 1985).

[166] <u>Currie</u>, 704 F.2d at 528; accord <u>Grasso</u>, 785 F.2d at 74; <u>Long</u>, 742 F.2d at 1181-82 (also rejecting section 701 of Economic Recovery Tax Act, 26 U.S.C.A. § 6103(b)(2), as "displacement" statute); <u>Linsteadt</u>, 729 F.2d at 1001-02; see also <u>Britt v. IRS</u>, 547 F. Supp. 808, 813 (D.D.C. 1982); <u>Tigar & Buffone v. CIA</u>, 2 Gov't Disclosure Serv. (P-H) ¶ 81,172, at 81,461 (D.D.C. Feb. 23, 1981).

## EXEMPTION 3

FOIA.[167]

The D.C. Circuit's rejection of the "displacement" theory in relation to section 6103 is consistent with previous D.C. Circuit decisions involving similar "displacement" arguments. For example, it had previously rejected a "displacement" argument involving the Department of State's Emergency Fund statutes[168] when it held that inasmuch as Exemption 3 is not satisfied by these statutes, information cannot be withheld pursuant to them, even though they were enacted after the FOIA.[169]

Yet the D.C. Circuit has held that the procedures of the Presidential Recordings and Materials Preservation Act[170] exclusively govern the disclosure of transcripts of the tape recordings of President Nixon's White House conversations, based upon that Act's comprehensive, carefully tailored procedure for releasing Presidential materials to the public.[171] Thus, the "displacement" theory may still be advanced for statutes which provide procedures for the release of information to the public that, in essence, duplicate the procedures provided by the FOIA,[172] or for statutes that com-

---

[167] Church of Scientology of Cal. v. IRS, 792 F.2d 146, 148-50 (D.C. Cir. 1986); see also Maxwell v. Snow, 409 F.3d 354, 358 (D.C. Cir. 2005) (holding that "FOIA still applies to [26 U.S.C.A.] § 6103 claims").

[168] 22 U.S.C. § 2671 (2000 & Supp. III 2003); 31 U.S.C. § 3526 (2000).

[169] See Wash. Post Co. v. U.S. Dep't of State, 685 F.2d 698, 703-04 & n.9 (D.C. Cir. 1982), cert. granted, 464 U.S. 812, vacated & remanded, 464 U.S. 979 (1983); see also FOIA Update, Vol. IV, No. 4, at 11 (noting that Supreme Court granted government's petition for certiorari, that Washington Post Company then withdrew its FOIA request (which had procedural effect of nullifying D.C. Circuit's decision), and that Supreme Court thus has never substantively reviewed issue); cf. U.S. Dep't of Justice v. Tax Analysts, 492 U.S. 136, 153-54 (1989) (holding that FOIA, not 28 U.S.C.A. § 1914 (1994 & West Supp. 2006), governs disclosure of court records in possession of government agencies); Paisley v. CIA, 712 F.2d 686, 697 (D.C. Cir. 1983) (stating that FOIA, not Speech or Debate Clause, is definitive word on disclosure of information within government's possession); Church of Scientology of Cal. v. USPS, 633 F.2d 1327, 1333 (9th Cir. 1980) (finding that postal statute does not displace more detailed and later-enacted FOIA absent specific indication of congressional intent to that effect).

[170] 44 U.S.C. § 2111 (2000).

[171] Ricchio v. Kline, 773 F.2d 1389, 1395 (D.C. Cir. 1985); cf. Katz v. NARA, 68 F.3d 1438, 1440-42 (D.C. Cir. 1995) (holding certain President John F. Kennedy autopsy material to be personal presidential papers not subject to FOIA).

[172] See Church of Scientology, 792 F.2d at 149 (dictum).

prehensively override the FOIA's access scheme.[173] In this connection, it should be noted that the FOIA's specific fee provision referring to other statutes that set fees for particular types of records[174] has the effect of causing those statutes to "displace" the FOIA's basic fee provisions.[175] (For a further discussion of this point, see Fees and Fee Waivers, below.)

---

[173] See Ricchio, 773 F.2d at 1395; cf. Essential Info., 134 F.3d at 1169-70 (Henderson, J., concurring) (suggesting displacement theory as alternate ground for affirming agency withholding); Long, 742 F.2d at 1178 (holding that FOIA does not apply to IRS private letter rulings, on basis that 26 U.S.C. § 6110 (2000) provides exclusive means of access); SDC Dev. Corp. v. Mathews, 542 F.2d 1116, 1120 (9th Cir. 1976) (reaching "displacement-type" result for records governed by the National Library of Medicine Act, a statute that later was repealed in 1993)); Jones v. OSHA, No. 94-3225, 1995 WL 435320 at *3-4 (W.D. Mo. June 6, 1995) (requiring release of employee complaints where Occupational Safety and Health Act, 29 U.S.C. § 657(f)(1) (2000), provided for disclosure; Gersh & Danielson v. EPA, 871 F. Supp. 407, 410 (D. Colo. 1994) (holding FOIA exemptions inapplicable where in conflict with disclosure provisions of Clean Water Act, 33 U.S.C. § 1251(e) (2000)); FOIA Update, Vol. XI, No. 3, at 7-8 n.32. But cf. Minier, 88 F.3d at 802-03 (finding that although the President John F. Kennedy Assassination Records Collection Act, 44 U.S.C. § 2107 note (2000 & Supp. III 2003), "requires agencies to release broader amounts of information relating to the Kennedy assassination" and "by its own terms, is an entirely separate scheme from the FOIA[,]" there is no indication "that Congress intended the JFK Act to override the CIA's ability to claim proper FOIA exemptions" (citing Assassination Archives & Research Ctr. v. Dep't of Justice, 43 F.3d 1542, 1544 (D.C. Cir. 1995))); accord Winterstein v. U.S. Dep't of Justice, 89 F. Supp. 2d 79, 82-83 (D.D.C. 2000) (ruling that existence of Nazi War Crimes Disclosure Act, 5 U.S.C. § 552 note (2000 & Supp. IV 2004), is not relevant to FOIA request for record pertaining to alleged Nazi war criminal except to extent that Congress's exclusion of particular class of records from Nazi War Crimes Disclosure Act was probative on subsidiary question of whether Congress considered withholding of record to be in public interest).

[174] 5 U.S.C. § 552(a)(4)(A)(vi).

[175] See Uniform Freedom of Information Act Fee Schedule and Guidelines, 52 Fed. Reg. 10,012 (1987) (implementing 5 U.S.C. § 552(a)(4)(A)(vi)); see also, e.g., Wade v. U.S. Dep't of Commerce, No. 96-0717, slip op. at 5-6 (D.D.C. Mar. 26, 1998) (recognizing that statute authorizing National Technical Information Service (NTIS) to establish its own fee schedule, 15 U.S.C. § 1153 (2000), supersedes standard FOIA fee provisions); FOIA Post, "NTIS: An Available Means of Record Disclosure" (posted 8/30/02; supplemented 9/23/02) (discussing operations of NTIS in relation to special FOIA fee provision).

# EXEMPTION 3

## FOIA-Specific Nondisclosure Statutes

Most Exemption 3 statutes contain a broad prohibition on disclosure that operates to prohibit disclosure of specified information by a federal agency generally and universally, which in turn is accommodated through Exemption 3 as a bar to public disclosure under the FOIA.[176] Increasingly, however, in the past several years, Congress has been enacting legislation specifically focused on prohibiting disclosure under the FOIA only.[177] The most common form of such a law directs that certain particular information, often information that is provided to or received by an agency pursuant to that statute, "shall be exempt from disclosure" under the FOIA in particular.[178] For instance, a provision of the Antitrust Civil Process Act[179] states

---

[176] See, e.g., 50 U.S.C.A. § 403-1(i) (West Supp. 2006) (requiring Director of National Intelligence to protect "intelligence sources and methods" from unauthorized disclosure); 18 U.S.C.A. §§ 2510-2520 (2000 & West Supp. 2006) (prohibiting disclosure of information obtained from court-ordered "Title III" wiretaps); Fed. R. Crim. P. 6(e) (establishing general rule of secrecy for matters occurring before a grand jury); 10 U.S.C. § 618(f) (2000) (prohibiting the disclosure of military promotion board proceedings "to any person not a member of the board").

[177] See, e.g., 42 U.S.C.A. § 299b-22 (West Supp. 2006) (prohibiting FOIA disclosure of patient safety work product) (enacted 2005); 6 U.S.C. § 133(a)(1)(A) (Supp. IV 2004) (prohibiting FOIA disclosure of critical infrastructure information voluntarily submitted to federal government for homeland security purposes) (enacted Nov. 25, 2002); 42 U.S.C. § 7412 (2000) (prohibiting FOIA disclosure of information submitted to EPA detailing "worst-case release scenarios" that might result from accidental or intentional releases of chemicals or fuels) (enacted Aug. 5, 1999); 16 U.S.C. § 5937 (2000) (prohibiting FOIA disclosure of information pertaining to National Park System resources such as endangered species) (enacted Nov. 13, 1998); 38 U.S.C. § 7451 (2000 & Supp. III 2003) (prohibiting FOIA disclosure of certain information collected by Department of Veterans Affairs in surveys of rates of compensation) (enacted Aug. 15, 1990); 31 U.S.C. § 5319 (2000 & Supp. III 2003) (preventing FOIA disclosure of Currency Transaction Reports) (enacted Sept. 13, 1982); 15 U.S.C. § 1314(g) (2000) (proscribing FOIA disclosure of certain records gathered in course of investigations under Antitrust Civil Process Act (enacted Sept. 30, 1976)).

[178] See, e.g., 42 U.S.C. § 300i-2 (2000 & Supp. IV 2004) (providing that certain public water system vulnerability assessments "shall be exempt from disclosure" under FOIA); 39 U.S.C. § 3016 (2000) (providing that any material provided pursuant to administrative subpoena issued by Postmaster General "shall be exempt from disclosure" under FOIA); 31 U.S.C. § 3733(k) (2000) (providing that information provided under "any civil investigation demand issued" pursuant to 31 U.S.C. § 3733(a) "shall be exempt from disclosure" under FOIA); 31 U.S.C. § 3729 (2000) (providing that certain information furnished pursuant to False Claims Act "shall be ex-
(continued...)

that "[a]ny documentary material, answers to written interrogatories, or transcripts of oral testimony provided pursuant to any demand issued under this [Act] shall be exempt from disclosure under section 552 of title 5."[180] Such language also can be found in section 214 of the Homeland Security Act of 2002,[181] which protects "critical infrastructure information" that is voluntarily submitted to the federal government for homeland security purposes, by specifically providing that it "shall be exempt from disclosure" under the FOIA.[182] Another such direct statutory approach used by Congress is where the law directs that "no information shall be disclosed" or that "information shall not be disclosed" under the FOIA.[183] Additionally, although it is not as direct an approach as prohibiting disclosure under the FOIA specifically, Congress created the same type of FOIA-specific statute

---

[178](...continued)
empt from disclosure" under FOIA); 15 U.S.C. § 4019(a) (2000) (providing that any information submitted in connection with export trade certificates of review "shall be exempt from disclosure" under FOIA); 15 U.S.C. § 57b-2 (2000) (providing that information received by FTC for investigative purposes "shall be exempt from disclosure" under FOIA); see also (*FOIA Post*, "Agencies Rely on Wide Range of Exemption 3 Statutes" (posted 12/16/03) (discussing "disclosure prohibitions that are not general in nature but rather are specifically directed toward disclosure under the FOIA in particular").

[179] 15 U.S.C. § 1314(g).

[180] 15 U.S.C. § 1314(g) (emphasis added).

[181] Pub. L. No. 107-296, 116 Stat. 2135 (codified at 6 U.S.C. § 133(a)(1)(A)); see *FOIA Post*, "Agencies Rely on Wide Range of Exemption 3 Statutes" (posted 12/16/03) (citing new Homeland Security Act Exemption 3 statute among statutes specifically directed at nondisclosure under FOIA); see also *FOIA Post*, "Critical Infrastructure Information Regulations Issued by DHS" (posted 2/27/04) (discussing breadth of implementation of new Exemption 3 statute).

[182] See 6 U.S.C. § 133(a)(1)(A); see also *FOIA Post*, "Homeland Security Law Contains New Exemption 3 Statute" (posted 1/27/03) (analyzing new Homeland Security Act Exemption 3 statute).

[183] See, e.g., 42 U.S.C.A. § 247d-6b(d) (2003 & West Supp. 2006) (providing directly that "[n]o Federal agency shall disclose under [the FOIA] any information identifying the location at which materials in the [strategic national] stockpile under subsection (a) are stored"); see also 41 U.S.C. § 254b(d)(2)(C) (2000) (providing that "[a] statement that any information received relating to commercial items that is exempt from disclosure under [the FOIA] shall not be disclosed by the Federal Government") (emphasis added).

when it enacted the Maritime Transportation Security Act of 2002,[184] which provides for the nondisclosure of security plans and port vulnerability assessments by mandating that such information "is not required to be disclosed to the public."[185] To the extent that such statutes have been challenged, courts have found that they qualify as Exemption 3 statutes,[186] though as yet no court has specifically discussed this more narrow legislative approach to nondisclosure.[187]

## Nondisclosure Results Under Appropriations Acts

Congress also has enacted legislation evidently aimed at achieving an Exemption 3 effect in an indirect fashion -- i.e., by limiting the funds that an agency may expend in responding to a FOIA request[188] The first such statute enacted was section 630 of the Agricultural, Rural Development, and Related Agencies Development Act, 1989, which states that "none of the funds provided in this Act may be expended to release information acquired from any handler under" the Act.[189] When section 630 was tested in Cal-Almond, Inc. v. United States Department of Agriculture, the Ninth Circuit did not decide whether this statute had the effect of triggering Exemption 3, but it reacted by observing that "if Congress intended to prohibit the release of the list under FOIA -- as opposed to the expenditure of funds in releasing the list -- it could easily have said so."[190]

---

[184] Pub. L. No. 107-295, § 113, 116 Stat. 2093 (codified at 46 U.S.C.A. § 70103).

[185] 46 U.S.C.A. § 70103(d) (2003 & West Supp. 2006).

[186] See, e.g., Sw. Ctr. for Biological Diversity, 170 F. Supp. 2d at 944-45 (holding that 16 U.S.C. § 5937 is Exemption 3 statute), aff'd, 314 F.3d 1060, 1062 (9th Cir. 2002); Linn v. U.S. Dep't of Justice, No. 92-1406, 1995 WL 631847, at *30 (D.D.C. Aug. 22, 1995) (holding that 31 U.S.C. § 5319 qualifies as Exemption 3 statute); Motion Picture Ass'n of Am. v. U.S. Dep't of Justice, No. 80 Civ. 6612, slip op. at 1 (S.D.N.Y. Oct. 6, 1981) (ruling that 15 U.S.C. § 1314(g) is Exemption 3 statute).

[187] See Gina Marie Stevens & Todd B. Tatelman, Protection of Security Related Information, Congressional Research Service, Sept. 27, 2006, at 8-9 (citing statutes "specifically directed toward the [FOIA]").

[188] See FOIA Post, "Supreme Court Vacates and Remands in ATF Database Case" (posted 3/25/03) (discussing Supreme Court's reaction to recently enacted statute that specifically prohibits ATF from using appropriated funds to comply with any FOIA request seeking certain firearms database records).

[189] Pub. L. No. 100-460, § 630, 102 Stat. 2229 (1988) (making appropriations for programs for Fiscal Year 1989).

[190] 960 F.2d at 108 (dictum) (opining on whether section 630 is "explicit" (continued...)

More recently, during the course of litigation in City of Chicago v. United States Department of Treasury,[191] Congress enacted three appropriations bills[192] that specifically prohibited the Bureau of Alcohol, Tobacco, Firearms, and Explosives from using appropriated funds to comply with any FOIA request seeking records relating to the contested firearms sales databases that are maintained by ATF.[193] The first of these laws was enacted shortly before the scheduled oral argument before the Supreme Court, whereupon the Court vacated the Seventh Circuit disclosure order that was on appeal and remanded the case for the lower court to consider the effect of this newly enacted provision.[194] By the time the case reached the circuit court for consideration on remand, Congress enacted the Consolidated Appropriations Act of 2004[195] that likewise prohibited ATF's use of appropriated funds to disclose the same type of firearms database information, and as a result, both appropriations laws were taken into consideration on remand.[196]

On remand, the appeals court determined that although both appropriations bills prohibited ATF from expending federal funds on retrieval of the information, there was no "irreconcilable conflict" between prohibiting such expenditure and granting plaintiff access to the databases.[197] While ATF's petition for a rehearing en banc was pending, Congress passed the

---

[190](...continued)
enough to qualify as Exemption 3 statute).

[191] 384 F.3d 429 (7th Cir. 2004), vacated & remanded, 423 F.3d 777 (7th Cir. 2005).

[192] Consolidated Appropriations Resolution of 2003, Pub. L. No. 108-7, § 644, 117 Stat. 11; Consolidated Appropriations Act of 2004, Pub. L. No. 108-199, 118 Stat 3; Consolidated Appropriations Act of 2005, Pub. L. No. 108-447, 118 Stat. 2809, 2859-2860 (2004).

[193] See id.

[194] See Dep't of Justice v. City of Chicago, 537 U.S. 1229, 1229 (2003); see also FOIA Post, "Supreme Court Vacates and Remands in ATF Database Case" (posted 3/25/03) (discussing extraordinary litigation development).

[195] Pub. L. No. 108-199, 118 Stat. 3 (likewise prohibiting use of appropriated funds to disclose same type of ATF firearms database information that was at issue in City of Chicago).

[196] City of Chicago, 384 F.3d at 431-32 (noting that "both parties to the litigation have rebriefed their arguments" due to the enactment of 2003 and 2004 appropriations legislation).

[197] Id. at 435-36 (ordering ATF to provide plaintiff access to the databases through novel use of court-appointed special master paid for by plaintiff).

EXEMPTION 3

Consolidated Appropriations Act of 2005,[198] which likewise prohibited the use of appropriated funds to disclose the same type of firearms database information, but added an appropriations rider providing that such data "shall be immune from judicial process."[199] On rehearing, the appeals court held that this new language "exempts from disclosure [firearms] data previously available to the public" and as such the new law qualified as an Exemption 3 statute.[200]

"Operational Files" Provisions

A closely related but somewhat different form of statutory protection can be found in special FOIA provisions that Congress has enacted to cover the "operational files" of individual intelligence agencies. For example, section 933(a) of the National Defense Authorization Act for Fiscal Year 2006[201] provides that "[t]he Director of the Defense Intelligence Agency, in coordination with the Director of National Intelligence, may exempt operational files of the Defense Intelligence Agency from the provisions of [the FOIA] which require publication, disclosure, search, or review in connection therewith."[202]

This special statutory protection is modeled after, and quite similar to, the CIA Information Act of 1984,[203] through which the Central Intelligence Agency was the first intelligence agency to obtain such exceptional FOIA treatment for its "operational files."[204] Three other such intelligence

---

[198] Pub. L. No. 108-447, 118 Stat. 2809, 2859-2860 (2004).

[199] Id.

[200] City of Chicago, 423 F.3d at 781-82; see also Antonelli v. ATF, No. 04-1180, 2006 WL 374312, at *2 (D.D.C. Dec. 18, 2006) (protecting "firearms trace reports" in their entireties under Consolidated Appropriations Act of 2005); Watkins v. ATF, No. 04-800, 2005 WL 2334277, at *1 (D.D.C. Sept. 1, 2005) (holding that Consolidated Appropriations Act of 2005 qualifies as Exemption 3 statute based on underlying legislative history). But cf. City of N.Y. v. Beretta U.S.A. Corp., 429 F. Supp. 2d 517, 528-29 (E.D.N.Y 2006) (distinguishing the City of Chicago litigation from this litigation, and holding that the firearms database appropriations legislation for 2005 (and 2006) does not prevent the disclosure of the firearms database information that already has been "obtained by explicit order of the court" during discovery) (non-FOIA case).

[201] Pub. L. No. 109-163, § 933(a), 119 Stat. 34 (2006) (codified at 50 U.S.C.A. § 432c (West Supp. 2006).

[202] 50 U.S.C.A. § 432c.

[203] 50 U.S.C.A. § 431 (2003 & West Supp. 2006).

[204] See FOIA Update, Vol. V, No. 4, at 1-2 (noting that an underlying prin-
(continued...)

agencies -- the National Security Agency, the National Reconnaissance Office, and the National Geospatial-Intelligence Agency -- have received similar FOIA protection under counterpart statutory provisions.[205] (For a further discussion of "operational files," see Exemption 1, "Operational Files" Statutes, above.)

Additional Considerations

Certain statutes fail to meet the requisites of either Exemption 3 prong. For instance, the Court of Appeals for the District of Columbia Circuit, in holding that provisions governing the FBI's sharing of "rap sheets"[206] do not qualify as an Exemption 3 statute because they do not expressly prohibit the disclosure of "rap sheets," explained that even if the provisions met the exemption's threshold requirement, they would not qualify as an Exemption 3 statute as they fail to satisfy either of its subparts.[207] Likewise, the Copyright Act of 1976[208] has been held to satisfy neither Exemption 3 subpart because, rather than prohibiting disclosure, it specifically permits public inspection of copyrighted documents.[209]

---

[204](...continued) ciple of the Central Intelligence Agency Information Act of 1984 is to free "the CIA of the burden of processing FOIA requests for" records that "would be almost entirely withholdable anyway, upon application of the FOIA's national security exemption, Exemption 1, together with the CIA's other statutory nondisclosure provisions under Exemption 3"); see also FOIA Post, "FOIA Amended by Intelligence Authorization Act" (posted 12/23/02) (commenting on similar rationale underlying the 2002 FOIA amendment, which made an exception to the FOIA's "any person" rule in certain circumstances for requests received by "elements of the intelligence community").

[205] See 50 U.S.C.A. § 432b (West Supp. 2006) (authorizing special "operational files" treatment for National Security Agency); 50 U.S.C.A. § 432a (West Supp. 2006) (same for National Reconnaissance Office); 50 U.S.C.A. § 432 (West Supp. 2006) (same for National Geospatial-Intelligence Agency); see also FOIA Post, "Agencies Rely on Wide Range of Exemption 3 Statutes" (posted 12/16/03).

[206] 28 U.S.C.A. § 534 (1993 & West Supp. 2006).

[207] Reporters Comm. for Freedom of the Press v. U.S. Dep't of Justice, 816 F.2d 730, 736 n.9 (D.C. Cir.), modified on other grounds, 831 F.2d 1124 (D.C. Cir. 1987), rev'd on other grounds, 489 U.S. 749 (1989).

[208] 17 U.S.C. § 705(b) (2000).

[209] See St. Paul's Benevolent Educ. & Missionary Inst. v. United States, 506 F. Supp. 822, 830 (N.D. Ga. 1980); see also FOIA Update, Vol. IV, No. 4, at 3-5 ("OIP Guidance: Copyrighted Materials and the FOIA") (emphasizing that Copyright Act should not be treated as Exemption 3 statute and that copyrighted records should be processed according to standards of Ex-

(continued...)

It has also been held that section 360j(h) of the Medical Device Amendments of 1976[210] is not an Exemption 3 statute because it does not specifically prohibit the disclosure of records,[211] nor is section 410(c)(6) of the Postal Reorganization Act,[212] because the broad discretion afforded the Postal Service to release or withhold records is not sufficiently specific.[213] Similarly, section 1106 of the Social Security Act[214] is not an Exemption 3 statute because it gives the Secretary of Health and Human Services wide discretion to enact regulations specifically permitting disclosure.[215] The Federal Insecticide, Fungicide, and Rodenticide Act[216] also does not satisfy either prong of Exemption 3 because the withholding of certain information is entirely discretionary under that Act.[217] Additionally, a district court has held that the "early warning disclosure provision" in the Transportation Recall Enhancement, Accountability, and Documentation Act[218] does not qualify as an Exemption 3 statute because it does not establish particular criteria for withholding information or refer to particular matters to be

---

[209](...continued)
emption 4 instead); accord Gilmore v. U.S. Dep't of Energy, 4 F. Supp. 2d 912, 922-23 (N.D. Cal. 1998) (alternate holding) (protecting copyrighted computer software pursuant to Exemption 4); FOIA Update, Vol. XVIII, No. 1, at 5-6 (cautioning agencies to "guard against the possibility that [Internet] dissemination of [reading room records] might be regarded as copyright infringement" in exceptional cases).

[210] 21 U.S.C.A. § 360j(h) (1999 & West Supp. 2006).

[211] See Pub. Citizen Health Research Group v. FDA, 704 F.2d 1280, 1286 (D.C. Cir. 1983).

[212] 39 U.S.C.A § 410(c)(6) (1980 & West Supp. 2006).

[213] See Church of Scientology v. USPS, 633 F.2d 1327, 1333 (9th Cir. 1980) (finding section 410(c)(6), which "permits the Postal Service total discretion" regarding the disclosure of its investigatory files, not to be an Exemption 3 statute because it provides "insufficient specificity" to allow its removal from the "impermissible range of agency discretion to make decisions rightfully belonging to the legislature").

[214] 42 U.S.C. § 1306 (2000).

[215] See Robbins v. HHS, No. 95-cv-3258, slip op. at 3-4 (N.D. Ga. Aug. 13, 1996), aff'd per curiam, 120 F.3d 275 (11th Cir. 1997) (unpublished table decision).

[216] 7 U.S.C. § 136h(d) (2000).

[217] See Nw. Coal. for Alternatives to Pesticides v. Browner, 941 F. Supp. 197, 201 (D.D.C. 1996). But see Doe v. Veneman, 380 F.3d 807, 818-19 (5th Cir. 2004) (holding that Federal Insecticide, Fungicide, and Rodenticide Act is Exemption 3 statute) (reverse FOIA suit).

[218] 49 U.S.C. § 30166(m) (2000).

withheld.[219]

A particularly difficult Exemption 3 issue was put to rest by the Supreme Court in 1988. In analyzing the applicability of Exemption 3 to the Parole Commission and Reorganization Act[220] and Rule 32 of the Federal Rules of Criminal Procedure, each of which governs the disclosure of presentence reports, the Supreme Court held that they are Exemption 3 statutes only in part.[221] The Court found that they do not permit the withholding of an entire presentence report, but rather only those portions of a presentence report pertaining to a probation officer's sentencing recommendations, certain diagnostic opinions, information obtained upon a promise of confidentiality, and information which, if disclosed, might result in harm to any person, and that "the remaining parts of the reports are not covered by this exemption, and thus must be disclosed unless there is some other exemption which applies to them."[222]

Another Exemption 3 issue concerns the Trade Secrets Act[223] which prohibits the unauthorized disclosure of certain commercial and financial information. Although the Supreme Court has declined to decide whether the Trade Secrets Act is an Exemption 3 statute,[224] most courts confronted with the issue have held that it is not.[225]

In 1987, the D.C. Circuit issued a decision that "definitively" resolved the issue by holding that the Trade Secrets Act does not satisfy either of Exemption 3's requirements and thus does not qualify as a separate with-

---

[219] Pub. Citizen, Inc. v. Mineta, 444 F. Supp. 2d 12, 17-18 (D.D.C. 2006) (appeal pending).

[220] 18 U.S.C. § 4208 (2000) (repealed as to offenses committed after November 1, 1987).

[221] U.S. Dep't of Justice v. Julian, 486 U.S. 1, 9 (1988).

[222] Id. at 11; see also FOIA Update, Vol. IX, No. 2, at 1-2.

[223] 18 U.S.C. § 1905 (2000 & Supp. IV 2004).

[224] Chrysler Corp. v. Brown, 441 U.S. 281, 319 n.49 (1979).

[225] See, e.g., Anderson v. HHS, 907 F.2d 936, 949 (10th Cir. 1990) ("[T]he broad and ill-defined wording of § 1905 fails to meet either of the requirements of Exemption 3."); Acumenics Research & Tech. v. U.S. Dep't of Justice, 843 F.2d 800, 805 n.6, 806 (4th Cir. 1988) (finding "no basis" for business submitter's argument that Exemption 3 and section 1905 prevent disclosure of information that is outside scope of Exemption 4) (reverse FOIA suit); Gen. Elec. Co. v. NRC, 750 F.2d 1394, 1401-02 (7th Cir. 1984) (same); accord FOIA Update, Vol. VI, No. 3, at 3 ("OIP Guidance: Discretionary Disclosure and Exemption 4"); see also 9 to 5 Org. for Women Office Workers v. Bd. of Governors of the Fed. Reserve Sys., 721 F.2d 1, 12 (1st Cir. 1983) (specifically declining to address issue).

holding statute.[226] First, its prohibition against disclosure is not absolute, as it prohibits only those disclosures that are "not authorized by law."[227] Because duly promulgated agency regulations can provide the necessary authorization for release, the agency "possesses discretion to control the applicability" of the Act.[228] The existence of this discretion precludes the Trade Secrets Act from satisfying subpart (A) of Exemption 3.[229] Moreover, the court held that the Trade Secrets Act fails to satisfy the first prong of subpart (B) because it "in no way channels the discretion of agency decisionmakers."[230] Indeed, the court concluded, this utter lack of statutory guidance renders the Trade Secrets Act susceptible to invocation at the "whim of an administrator."[231] Finally, it was held that the Act also fails to satisfy the second prong of subpart (B) because of the "encyclopedic character" of the material within its scope and the absence of any limitation on the agencies covered or the sources of data included.[232] Given all these elements, the court held that the Trade Secrets Act simply does not qualify as an Exemption 3 statute.[233] This followed the Department of Justice's stated policy position on the issue.[234]

The D.C. Circuit's decision on this issue is entirely consistent with the legislative history of the 1976 amendment to Exemption 3, which states that the Trade Secrets Act was not intended to qualify as a nondisclosure statute under the exemption and that any analysis of trade secrets and commercial or financial information should focus instead on the applicability of Exemption 4.[235] However, some confidential business information now may be protected by the National Defense Authorization Act for Fiscal

---

[226] See CNA Fin. Corp. v. Donovan, 830 F.2d 1132, 1137-43 (D.C. Cir. 1987).

[227] Id. at 1138.

[228] Id. at 1139.

[229] Id. at 1138.

[230] Id. at 1139.

[231] Id.

[232] Id. at 1140-41.

[233] Id. at 1141.

[234] See FOIA Update, Vol. VII, No. 3, at 6 (advising that Trade Secrets Act should not be regarded as Exemption 3 statute).

[235] See H.R. Rep. No. 94-880, at 23 (1976), reprinted in 1976 U.S.C.C.A.N. 2191, 2205; see also Anderson, 907 F.2d at 949-50; Acumenics, 843 F.2d at 805 n.6; CNA, 830 F.2d at 1142 n.70; Gen. Elec., 750 F.2d at 1401-02; Gen. Dynamics Corp. v. Marshall, 607 F.2d 234, 236-37 (8th Cir. 1979).

Year 1997.[236] This statute, enacted in 1996, amended both Titles 10 and 41 of the United States Code, and provides blanket protection for the proposals of unsuccessful offerors submitted in response to a solicitation for a competitive proposal.[237] Under it, a successful offeror's proposal is also protected if it is not "set forth or incorporated by reference" in the final contract;[238] the key determinant of exempt status is whether the proposal was actually set forth in or incorporated into the contract.[239] In 2003, the District Court for the District of Columbia firmly held it to be a subpart (B) statute in Hornbostel v. Department of the Interior.[240]

One court has incorrectly treated a provision of the Procurement Integrity Act[241] as an Exemption 3 statute.[242] That provision -- encompassing pre-award contractor bids, proposal information, and source selection information -- prohibits disclosures only "other than as provided by law," and it also provides that it "does not . . . limit the applicability of any . . . reme-

---

[236] Pub. L. No. 104-201, § 821, 110 Stat. 2422 (containing parallel measures applicable to armed services and most civilian agencies) (amending 10 U.S.C. § 2305 (2000) and 41 U.S.C. § 253b (2000)).

[237] See 10 U.S.C. § 2305(g) (encompassing all agencies listed in 10 U.S.C. § 2303 (2000), most notably NASA and Coast Guard); 41 U.S.C. § 253b(m) (encompassing civilian executive agencies); cf. Pohlman, Inc. v. SBA, No. 03-01241, slip op. at 26-27 (E.D. Mo. Sept. 30, 2005) (holding that 41 U.S.C. § 253b(m) "applies only to government procurement contracts, not to sales contracts" at issue in case); Ctr. for Pub. Integrity v. Dep't of Energy, 191 F. Supp. 2d 187, 190-94 (D.D.C. 2002) (rejecting applicability of 41 U.S.C. § 253b(m) to records relating to bids for sale of government property, on grounds that it applies only to government procurement contracts, not to contracts for sale of government property).

[238] Id.; see FOIA Update, Vol. XVIII, No. 1, at 2 (describing provisions of 10 U.S.C. § 2305(g) and 41 U.S.C. § 253b(m)).

[239] See id. (advising that the "underlying legislative history" of these statutory provisions "makes clear that it was Congress'[s] intent to alleviate the administrative burden imposed on agencies faced with the task of processing FOIA requests for contractor proposals").

[240] No. 02-2523, 2003 WL 23303294, at *5 (D.D.C. Aug. 7, 2003) (finding proposals to be properly withheld from disclosure because the statute "specifically prohibits the disclosure of 'a proposal in the possession or control of an agency'").

[241] 41 U.S.C. § 423 (2000 & Supp. III 2003).

[242] Legal & Safety Employer Research, Inc. v. U.S. Dep't of the Army, No. Civ. S001748, 2001 WL 34098652, at *3-4 (E.D. Cal. May 4, 2001) (dictum) (viewing statute as withholding statute under Exemption 3, but rejecting Exemption 3 applicability only because records at issue did not fall within scope of nondisclosure provision in Procurement Integrity Act).

dies established under any other law or regulation."[243] Although this one court failed to take notice of these applicable exceptions, another has found that they clearly evince congressional intent that the prohibition on disclosure is limited to those disclosures not contemplated by law, such as "leaks."[244]

Lastly, a controversial issue at one time was whether the Privacy Act of 1974[245] could serve as an Exemption 3 statute.[246] The Privacy Act authorizes an individual to obtain access to those federal records maintained under the individual's name or personal identifier, subject to certain broad, system-wide exemptions.[247] If the Privacy Act had been regarded as an Exemption 3 statute, records exempt from disclosure to first-party requesters under the Privacy Act also would have been exempt under the FOIA; if not, requesters would have been able to obtain information on themselves under the FOIA notwithstanding that such information was exempt under the Privacy Act. In the early 1980s, the Department of Justice took the position that the Privacy Act was an Exemption 3 statute within the first-party requester context.[248] When a conflict subsequently arose among the circuits that considered the proper relationship between these two access statutes, the Supreme Court agreed to resolve the issue.[249] However, these cases became moot when Congress, upon enacting the Central Intelligence Agency Information Act in 1984, explicitly provided that the Privacy

---

[243] 41 U.S.C. § 423(h).

[244] Pikes Peak Family Hous., LLC v. United States, 40 Fed. Cl. 673, 680-81 (Cl. Ct. 1998) (construing the phrase "other than as provided by law" in the Procurement Integrity Act as necessarily allowing disclosures in civil discovery and noting that the statute does not apply to legal disclosures but rather "is obviously directed at a situation in which a present or former government procurement officer secretly leaks information concerning a pending solicitation to an offeror participating therein") (non-FOIA case); cf. CNA Fin. Corp. v. Donovan, 830 F.2d 1132, 1152, n.139 (D.C. Cir. 1987) (noting that comparable language in Trade Secrets Act, 18 U.S.C. § 1905, interrelates with FOIA so as to render any statutory prohibition inapplicable because, under it, "FOIA would provide legal authorization for" disclosure).

[245] 5 U.S.C. § 552a (2000 & Supp. IV 2004).

[246] See FOIA Update, Vol. V, No. 2, at 8-9 (discussing legal position that subsequently was abandoned).

[247] See, e.g., 5 U.S.C. § 552a(j)(2).

[248] See FOIA Update, Vol. IV, No. 2, at 3.

[249] Provenzano v. U.S. Dep't of Justice, 717 F.2d 799 (3d Cir. 1983), cert. granted, 466 U.S. 926 (1984); Shapiro v. DEA, 721 F.2d 215 (7th Cir. 1983), cert. granted, 466 U.S. 926 (1984).

Act is not an Exemption 3 statute.[250] Thus, the Supreme Court dismissed the appeals in these cases and this issue has been placed to rest.[251]

## EXEMPTION 4

Exemption 4 of the FOIA protects "trade secrets and commercial or financial information obtained from a person [that is] privileged or confidential."[1] This exemption is intended to protect the interests of both the government and submitters of information.[2] Its very existence encourages submitters to voluntarily furnish useful commercial or financial information to the government and provides the government with an assurance that required submissions will be reliable.[3] The exemption also affords protection to those submitters who are required to furnish commercial or financial information to the government by safeguarding them from the competitive disadvantages that could result from disclosure.[4] The exemption covers two broad categories of information in federal agency records: (1) trade secrets; and (2) information that is (a) commercial or financial, and (b) obtained from a person, and (c) privileged or confidential.

### Trade Secrets

For purposes of Exemption 4, the Court of Appeals for the District of

---

[250] Pub. L. No. 98-477, § 2(c), 98 Stat. 2209, 2212 (1984) (amending what is now subsection (t) of Privacy Act).

[251] U.S. Dep't of Justice v. Provenzano, 469 U.S. 14 (1984); FOIA Update, Vol. V, No. 4, at 4. But see Hill v. Blevins, No. 92-0859, slip op. at 7 (M.D. Pa. Apr. 12, 1993) (holding that subsection (f)(3) of Privacy Act, which authorizes agency to establish procedures for disclosure of medical and psychological records, is "exempting" statute under FOIA), aff'd, 19 F.3d 643 (3d Cir. 1994) (unpublished table decision).

[1] 5 U.S.C. § 552(b)(4) (2000 & Supp. IV 2004).

[2] See, e.g., National Parks & Conservation Ass'n v. Morton, 498 F.2d 765, 767-70 (D.C. Cir. 1974) (concluding that the legislative history of the FOIA "firmly supports an inference that [Exemption 4] is intended for the benefit of persons who supply information as well as the agencies which collect it").

[3] See Critical Mass Energy Project v. NRC, 975 F.2d 871, 878 (D.C. Cir. 1992) (en banc).

[4] See National Parks, 498 F.2d at 768; see also Attorney General's Memorandum for Heads of All Federal Departments and Agencies Regarding the Freedom of Information Act (Oct. 12, 2001), reprinted in FOIA Post (posted 10/15/01) (recognizing fundamental societal value of "protecting sensitive business information").

Columbia Circuit in Public Citizen Health Research Group v. FDA,[5] has adopted a "common law" definition of the term "trade secret" that is narrower than the broad definition used in the Restatement of Torts.[6] The D.C. Circuit's decision in Public Citizen represented a distinct departure from what until then had been almost universally accepted by the courts -- that a "trade secret" encompasses virtually any information that provides a competitive advantage. In Public Citizen, a "trade secret" was more narrowly defined as "a secret, commercially valuable plan, formula, process, or device that is used for the making, preparing, compounding, or processing of trade commodities and that can be said to be the end product of either innovation or substantial effort."[7] This definition also incorporates a requirement that there be a "direct relationship" between the trade secret and the productive process.[8]

The Court of Appeals for the Tenth Circuit has expressly adopted the D.C. Circuit's narrower definition of the term "trade secret," finding it "more consistent with the policies behind the FOIA than the broad Restatement definition."[9] In so doing, the Tenth Circuit noted that adoption of the broader Restatement definition "would render superfluous" the remaining category of Exemption 4 information "because there would be no category of information falling within the latter" category that would be "outside" the reach of the trade secret category.[10] Like the D.C. Circuit, the Tenth Circuit was "reluctant to construe the FOIA in such a manner."[11] More recently, the Tenth Circuit declined to "address whether [it] should supplement" this narrower trade secret definition "to require a governmental showing that

---

[5] 704 F.2d 1280, 1288 (D.C. Cir. 1983).

[6] Restatement (First) of Torts § 757 cmt. b (1939) (stating that "[a] trade secret may consist of any formula, pattern, device or compilation of information which is used in one's business, and which gives him an opportunity to obtain an advantage over competitors who do not know or use it"), quoted in Pub. Citizen, 704 F.2d at 1284 n.7.

[7] 704 F.2d at 1288; see also Appleton v. FDA, 451 F. Supp. 2d 129, 142 & n.8 (D.D.C. 2006) (rejecting plaintiff's argument that trade secret, as defined in Public Citizen, requires "sole showing of 'innovation or substantial effort,'" and emphasizing that trade secret applies to information that constitutes the "'end product of either innovation or substantial effort'" (quoting Pub. Citizen, 704 F.2d at 1288)).

[8] Pub. Citizen, 704 F.2d at 1288; accord Ctr. for Auto Safety v. Nat'l Highway Traffic Safety Admin., 244 F.3d 144, 150-51 (D.C. Cir. 2001) (reiterating the Public Citizen definition and emphasizing that it "narrowly cabins trade secrets to information relating to the 'productive process' itself").

[9] Anderson v. HHS, 907 F.2d 936, 944 (10th Cir. 1990).

[10] Id.

[11] Id.

the documents in question are actually owned by the submitting entity or by any other party," finding that in the case before it, involving plans and specifications for an antique aircraft, the agency had shown a "corporate 'chain of ownership'" for the requested documents, leading from "the original owner and submitter" to the company currently claiming "trade secret" protection for them.[12]

Trade secret protection has been recognized for product manufacturing and design information,[13] but has been denied for general information concerning a product's physical or performance characteristics or a product

---

[12] Herrick v. Garvey, 298 F.3d 1184, 1191 (10th Cir. 2002) (declaring that the agency "need not show" that "ownership of these particular documents was specifically mentioned and transferred" with each corporate succession, because "such a requirement would be overly burdensome," and finding that the agency "need only show that there was a corporate successor that received the assets of the prior corporation").

[13] See, e.g., Appleton, 451 F. Supp. 2d at 142 & n.7 ("drug product manufacturing information, including manufacturing processes or drug chemical composition and processes"); Herrick v. Garvey, 200 F. Supp. 2d 1321, 1326 (D. Wyo. 2000) ("'technical blueprints depicting the design, materials, components, dimensions and geometry of'" 1935 aircraft (quoting agency declaration)), aff'd, 298 F.3d 1184, 1190 n.3 (10th Cir. 2002) (noting requester's concession at oral argument that blueprints remained commercially valuable); Heeney v. FDA, No. 97-5461, 1999 U.S. Dist. LEXIS 23365, at *25 & n.13 (C.D. Cal. Mar. 18, 1999) ("compliance testing" and "specification of the materials used in constructing" electrode catheter), aff'd, 7 F. App'x 770 (9th Cir. 2001); Sokolow v. FDA, No. 1:97-CV-252, slip op. at 7 (E.D. Tex. Feb. 19, 1998) (description of how drug is manufactured, including "analytical methods employed to assure quality and consistency" and "results of stability testing"), aff'd, 162 F.3d 1160 (5th Cir. 1998) (unpublished table decision); Citizens Comm'n on Human Rights v. FDA, No. 92-5313, 1993 WL 1610471, at *7 (C.D. Cal. May 10, 1993) ("information about how a pioneer drug product is formulated, chemically composed, manufactured, and quality controlled"), aff'd in part & remanded in part on other grounds, 45 F.3d 1325 (9th Cir. 1995); Pac. Sky Supply, Inc. v. Dep't of the Air Force, No. 86-2044, 1987 WL 25456, at *1 (D.D.C. Nov. 20, 1987) (design drawings of airplane fuel pumps developed by private company and used by Air Force), modifying No. 86-2044, 1987 WL 18214 (D.D.C. Sept. 29, 1987), on motion to amend judgment, No. 86-2044, 1987 WL 28485 (D.D.C. Dec. 16, 1987); see also Yamamoto v. IRS, No. 83-2160, slip op. at 2 (D.D.C. Nov. 16, 1983) (report on computation of standard mileage rate prepared by private company and used by IRS); cf. Myers v. Williams, 819 F. Supp. 919 (D. Or. 1993) (granting preliminary injunction to prevent FOIA requester from disclosing trade secret acquired through mistaken, but nonetheless official, FOIA release) (non-FOIA case). But see Wash. Research Project, Inc. v. HEW, 504 F.2d 238, 244-45 (D.C. Cir. 1974) (denying trade secret protection for "noncommercial scientist's research design"); Physicians Comm. for Responsible Med. v. NIH, 326 F. Supp. 2d 19, 23 (D.D.C. 2004) (same).

formula when release would not reveal the actual formula itself.[14] Moreover, one appellate court has concluded that "where the submitter or owner of documents held by the government grants the government permission
to loan or release those documents to the public, those documents are no
longer 'secret' for purposes of [trade secret protection under] Exemption 4"
and so must be released.[15]

## Commercial or Financial Information

If information does not qualify as a trade secret, it nonetheless may
be protected pursuant to Exemption 4 if it falls within its second, much
larger category. To be protected as such, the information must be commercial or financial, obtained from a person, and privileged or confidential.[16]
The overwhelming majority of Exemption 4 cases focus on this standard.

Courts have little difficulty in regarding information as "commercial or
financial" if it relates to business or trade.[17] The Court of Appeals for the

---

[14] See Ctr. for Auto Safety, 244 F.3d at 151 (airbag characteristics relating "only to the end product -- what features an airbag has and how it performs -- rather than to the production process"); Nw. Coal. for Alternatives
to Pesticides v. Browner, 941 F. Supp. 197, 201-02 (D.D.C. 1996) ("common
names and Chemical Abstract System . . . numbers of the inert ingredients"
contained in pesticide formulas).

[15] Herrick, 298 F.3d at 1194 & n.10 (distinguishing the facts of the case
before it, and upholding trade secret protection nonetheless, based upon
the subsequent revocation of that permission and the requester's failure to
challenge both whether such revocation could legally operate to "restore
the secret nature of the documents" and, if so, whether such revocation
could properly be made after the documents had been requested under the
FOIA).

[16] See, e.g., Gulf & W. Indus. v. United States, 615 F.2d 527, 529 (D.C. Cir.
1979); Consumers Union v. VA, 301 F. Supp. 796, 802 (S.D.N.Y. 1969), appeal dismissed as moot, 436 F.2d 1363 (2d Cir. 1971).

[17] See, e.g., Dow Jones Co. v. FERC, 219 F.R.D. 167, 176 (C.D. Cal. 2002)
(information relating "'to business decisions and practices regarding the
sale of power, and the operation and maintenance'" of generators (quoting
agency declaration)); Merit Energy Co. v. U.S. Dep't of the Interior, 180 F.
Supp. 2d 1184, 1188 (D. Colo. 2001) ("[i]nformation regarding oil and gas
leases, prices, quantities and reserves"), appeal dismissed, No. 01-1347
(10th Cir. Sept. 4, 2001); In Def. of Animals v. HHS, No. 99-3024, 2001 U.S.
Dist. LEXIS 24975, at *2, *29 (D.D.C. Sept. 28, 2001) (letter detailing "financial situation" of private primate research facility); Lepelletier v. FDIC, 977
F. Supp. 456, 459 (D.D.C. 1997) ("identities of businesses having unclaimed
deposits"), aff'd in part, rev'd in part & remanded on other grounds, 164
F.3d 37 (D.C. Cir. 1999); Cohen v. Kessler, No. 95-6140, slip op. at 9 (D.N.J.
(continued...)

District of Columbia Circuit has firmly held that these terms should be given their "ordinary meanings" and has specifically rejected the argument that the term "commercial" be confined to records that "reveal basic commercial operations," holding instead that records are commercial so long as the submitter has a "commercial interest" in them.[18] Such a commercial interest has been found, for example, for information pertaining to water rights held by Indian tribes in light of the tribes' interest in "maximizing" their position vis-a-vis this valuable resource.[19]

---

[17](...continued) Nov. 25, 1996) ("rat study's raw data" submitted to support application for approval of new animal drug); Bangor Hydro-Elec. Co. v. U.S. Dep't of the Interior, No. 94-0173-B, slip op. at 7 (D. Me. Apr. 17, 1995) ("information relating to proposed [land] usage charges"); Allnet Commc'n Servs. v. FCC, 800 F. Supp. 984, 987 (D.D.C. 1992) (software "output data and reports and extensive descriptive and instructional material"), aff'd, No. 92-5351 (D.C. Cir. May 27, 1994); RMS Indus. v. DOD, No. C-92-1545, slip op. at 3, 6 (N.D. Cal. Nov. 24, 1992) ("interim pricing, type and quality of machines owned" and names and background of key employees and suppliers "); ISC Group v. DOD, No. 88-0631, 1989 WL 168858, at *2-3 (D.D.C. May 22, 1989) (investigative report concerning allegations of overcharging on government contract); M/A-COM Info. Sys. v. HHS, 656 F. Supp. 691, 692 (D.D.C. 1986) (settlement negotiation documents reflecting "accounting and other internal procedures"); see also FOIA Update, Vol. VI, No. 1, at 3-4 ("OIP Guidance: Protecting Intrinsic Commercial Value"); FOIA Update, Vol. IV, No. 4, at 3-5 ("OIP Guidance: Copyrighted Materials and the FOIA").

[18] Pub. Citizen Health Research Group v. FDA, 704 F.2d 1280, 1290 (D.C. Cir. 1983) (citing Wash. Post Co. v. HHS, 690 F.2d 252, 266 (D.C. Cir. 1982), and Bd. of Trade v. Commodity Futures Trading Comm'n, 627 F.2d 392, 403 (D.C. Cir. 1980)); accord Baker & Hostetler LLP v. U.S. Dep't of Commerce, 473 F.3d 312, 319-20 (D.C. Cir. 2006) (citing Pub. Citizen Health Research Group, 704 F.2d at 1290, and finding that letters describing "favorable market conditions for domestic [lumber] companies" constituted "commercial information," because those companies "have a 'commercial interest' in such letters"); Judicial Watch, Inc. v. U.S. Dep't of Energy, 310 F. Supp. 2d 271, 308 (D.D.C. 2004) (holding that reports that "constitute work done for clients" are "'commercial' in nature"), aff'd in part & rev'd in part on other grounds, 412 F.3d 125 (D.C. Cir. 2005); Judicial Watch, Inc. v. Exp.-Imp. Bank, 108 F. Supp. 2d 19, 28 (D.D.C. 2000) (finding export-insurance applications containing detailed information on goods and customers to be "commercial or financial"); Brockway v. Dep't of the Air Force, 370 F. Supp. 738, 740 (N.D. Iowa 1974) (concluding that reports generated by commercial enterprise "must generally be considered commercial information"), rev'd on other grounds, 518 F.2d 1184 (8th Cir. 1975).

[19] Flathead Joint Bd. of Control v. U.S. Dep't of the Interior, 309 F. Supp. 2d 1217, 1221 (D. Mont. 2004) (declaring that "water rights themselves are an object of commerce . . . that is bought and sold," and holding that "infor-
(continued...)

# EXEMPTION 4

Nearly three decades ago, in a case involving a request for employee authorization cards submitted by a labor union, the Court of Appeals for the Second Circuit articulated a straightforward definition of the term "commercial," declaring that "surely [it] means [anything] pertaining or relating to or dealing with commerce."[20] In doing so, it categorically rejected the requester's argument that the information was "not commercial or financial because the [labor union did] not have profit as its primary aim."[21] The Second Circuit declared that such an "interpretation [would give] much too narrow a construction to the phrase in question."[22] Instead, the Second Circuit focused on the union's relationship with "commerce" and found that "[l]abor unions, and their representation of employees, quite obviously pertain to or are related to commerce and deal with the commercial life of the country."[23] Accordingly, the employee authorization cards were readily deemed to be "commercial."[24] Likewise, the D.C. Circuit has squarely held that a submitter's "nonprofit status is not determinative of the character of the information it reports," holding instead that "information may qualify as 'commercial' even if the provider's . . . interest in gathering, processing, and reporting the information is noncommercial."[25]

---

[19](...continued)
mation about the quantity available," or "information that creates the Tribes' negotiating position, supports their claims," or maximizes their position, "is all commercial information in function"), appeal dismissed, No. 04-35230 (9th Cir. Feb. 11, 2005); see also Starkey v. U.S. Dep't of Interior, 238 F. Supp. 2d 1188, 1195 (S.D. Cal. 2002) (concluding that "well and water related information" on an Indian reservation is "commercial or financial in nature" because "'water is a precious, limited resource'" and disclosure "'would adversely affect the Band's ability to negotiate its water rights or to litigate that issue'" (quoting agency declaration)).

[20] Am. Airlines, Inc. v. Nat'l Mediation Bd., 588 F.2d 863, 870 (2d Cir. 1978).

[21] Id.

[22] Id.

[23] Id.

[24] Id.; see also FlightSafety Servs. v. U.S. Dep't of Labor, No. 3:00CV 1285P, 2002 WL 368522, at *5 (N.D. Tex. Mar. 5, 2002) (protecting "information relating to the employment and wages of workers"), aff'd per curiam, 326 F.3d 607, 611 (5th Cir. 2003); Hustead v. Norwood, 529 F. Supp. 323, 326 (S.D. Fla. 1981) (same).

[25] Critical Mass Energy Project v. NRC, 830 F.2d 278, 281 (D.C. Cir. 1987) (finding that safety reports submitted by the nonprofit Institute for Nuclear Power Operations were "commercial," because the Institute's "'constituent utility companies [were] assuredly commercial enterprises engaged in the production and sale of electrical power for profit'" and "the commercial for-
(continued...)

Despite the widely accepted breadth of the term "commercial or financial," it is not without meaning and nevertheless remains a necessary element of Exemption 4 protection. For example, the D.C. Circuit recently rejected an agency's rather strained argument that data pertaining to the location of endangered pygmy owls qualified as "commercial or financial" information "simply because it was submitted pursuant to a government-to-government cooperative agreement" whereby a state agency provided "access to its database in return for money" from the federal government.[26] The D.C. Circuit reasoned that "[s]uch a quid-pro-quo exchange between governmental entities does not constitute a commercial transaction in the ordinary sense."[27] Moreover, the D.C. Circuit found, the requested "owl-sighting data itself [was] commercial neither by its nature (having been created by the government rather than in connection with a commercial enterprise) nor in its function (as there [was] no evidence that the parties who supplied the owl-sighting information [had] a commercial interest at stake in its disclosure)."[28] Consequently, the D.C. Circuit was "unpersuaded" that Exemption 4 applied.[29]

Similarly, a district court rejected an agency's attempt to convert "factual information regarding the nature and frequency of in-flight medical emergencies"[30] into "commercial information" for purposes of Exemption 4, finding instead that the "medical emergencies detailed in the [requested] documents [did] not naturally flow from commercial flight operations, but rather [were] chance events which happened to occur while the airplanes were in flight."[31] In delimiting the scope of the term "commercial," the court opined that "[t]he mere fact that an event occurs in connection with a commercial operation does not automatically transform documents regarding

---

[25](...continued)
tunes of [those] member utilities . . . could be materially affected by" disclosure (quoting district court)), vacated en banc on other grounds, 975 F.2d 871, 880 (D.C. Cir. 1992) (reiterating that it "agree[d] with the district court's conclusion that the information [contained in the nonprofit Institute's safety reports] is commercial in nature"); see also Sharyland Water Supply Corp. v. Block, 755 F.2d 397, 398 (5th Cir. 1985) (summarily declaring that audit reports submitted by nonprofit water supply company are "clearly commercial or financial").

[26] Nat'l Ass'n of Home Builders v. Norton, 309 F.3d 26, 38 (D.C. Cir. 2002).

[27] Id. at 38-39.

[28] Id. at 39.

[29] Id. at 38.

[30] Chi. Tribune Co. v. FAA, No. 97 C 2363, 1998 WL 242611, at *3 (N.D. Ill. May 7, 1998).

[31] Id. at *2.

that event into commercial information."[32]

Conversely, in an atypical ruling, the District Court for the Southern District of New York held that documents submitted by the General Electric Company (GE) to EPA supporting GE's alternative Hudson River dredging plan -- which would have been less costly to GE than the plan scheduled to be imposed on it by EPA -- were somehow not "commercial" under Exemption 4.[33] Despite the fact that GE "had a financial stake" in the matter and provided the documents in an effort "to convince the EPA to adopt its less expensive remedy," the court nonetheless held that EPA had "failed to establish that the information [had] any intrinsic commercial value."[34]

Interestingly, an agency's failure to establish the "commercial" character of requested information precluded Exemption 4 protection in the only appellate court decision to address the protection of information submitted by a scientist in connection with a grant application.[35] In that case, the D.C. Circuit found that research designs submitted as part of a grant application were not "commercial," despite claims that "[t]heir misappropriation," which "would be facilitated by premature disclosure, [would] deprive[ the researcher] of the career advancement and attendant material

---

[32] Id.; see also Maydak v. U.S. Dep't of Justice, 254 F. Supp. 2d 23, 48-49 (D.D.C. 2003) (rejecting an agency's argument that a company's report should be deemed "commercial" merely because it was "labeled" as "'proprietary and confidential,'" and denying Exemption 4 protection based upon the agency's failure to provide "any description of the report's content"), renewed motion for summary judgment granted in part & denied in part on other grounds, 362 F. Supp. 2d 316 (D.D.C. 2005); In Def. 2001 U.S. Dist. LEXIS 24975, at *29 (observing that "identities of [private] Foundation employees . . . standing alone, may not be commercial"); Animal Legal Def. Fund, Inc. v. Dep't of the Air Force, 44 F. Supp. 2d 295, 303 (D.D.C. 1999) (denying summary judgment when the agency's declaration merely "state[d]" that the company's "proposals contain 'commercial and financial information'" but failed to provide a "description of the documents to permit the [requester] or [the] Court to test the accuracy of that claim").

[33] N.Y. Pub. Interest Research Group v. EPA, 249 F. Supp. 2d 327, 332-34 (S.D.N.Y. 2003) (describing the documents as containing GE's "analyses of the costs, benefits, and environmental impact associated with the EPA's proposed remedy and GE's alternative remedy").

[34] Id. at 334 (finding also that EPA had not shown "that disclosure would jeopardize GE's commercial interests or reveal information about GE's ongoing operations, or that GE generated the information for a purpose other than advocating a policy to a governmental agency"); see also id. at 330 (noting that GE had neither submitted an affidavit nor "taken a position with regard to the documents").

[35] See Wash. Research Project, Inc. v. HEW, 504 F.2d 238, 244 (D.C. Cir. 1974).

rewards in which the academic and scientific market deals."[36] Finding that "the reach" of Exemption 4 "is not necessarily coextensive with the existence of competition in any form," the D.C. Circuit declared that "a noncommercial scientist's research design is not literally a trade secret or item of commercial information, for it defies common sense to pretend that the scientist is engaged in trade or commerce."[37] Although recognizing that a scientist may have "a preference for or an interest in nondisclosure of his research design," the D.C. Circuit held that if that interest is "founded on professional recognition and reward, it is surely more the interest of an employee than of an enterprise" and so is beyond the reach of Exemption 4.[38] Significantly, the D.C. Circuit noted that a given grantee "could conceivably be shown to have a commercial or trade interest in his research design," but it emphasized that "the burden of showing" such an interest "was on the agency."[39] Because the agency "did not introduce a single fact relating to the commercial character of any specific research project," the D.C. Circuit concluded that in that case, the agency had failed to "carr[y] its burden on this point."[40]

Lastly, protection for financial information is not limited to economic data generated solely by corporations or other business entities, but rather has been held to apply to personal financial information as well.[41] Examples of items usually regarded as commercial or financial information include: business sales statistics; research data; technical designs; customer and supplier lists; profit and loss data; overhead and operating

---

[36] Id. (observing that "the government has been at some pains to argue that biomedical researchers are really a mean-spirited lot who pursue self-interest as ruthlessly as the Barbary pirates did in their own chosen field").

[37] Id.

[38] Id. at 245.

[39] Id. at 244 n.6.

[40] Id.; see also Physicians Comm. for Responsible Med., 326 F. Supp. 2d 19, 24-25 (D.D.C. 2004) (citing Wash. Research Project, 504 F.2d at 244, and concluding "as a matter of law" that a noncommercial scientist's research designs did "not amount to commercial information," after finding that the scientist "never manufactured or marketed any drug . . . that was produced as a result of his research" and that "none of [his] research results have been marketed or used and subsequently subjected to additional study").

[41] See Wash. Post, 690 F.2d at 266; Defenders of Wildlife v. U.S. Dep't of the Interior, 314 F. Supp. 2d 1, 15 (D.D.C. 2004) (finding that draft severance agreements which contained "financial information surrounding [the Deputy Secretary's] separation from his former company . . . are within the common understanding of the term 'financial information'"); see also FOIA Update, Vol. IV, No. 4, at 14. But see Wash. Post, 690 F.2d at 266 (holding that mere "list of non-federal employment" is not "financial" within meaning of Exemption 4).

costs; and information on financial condition.[42]

## Obtained from a "Person"

The second of Exemption 4's specific criteria, that the information be "obtained from a person," is quite easily met in almost all circumstances. The term "person" refers to individuals as well as to a wide range of entities,[43] including corporations, banks, state governments, agencies of foreign governments, and Native American tribes or nations, who provide information to the government.[44] The reach of Exemption 4 is "sufficiently broad to encompass financial and commercial information concerning a third party" and protection is therefore available regardless of whether the information pertains directly to the commercial interests of the party that provided it -- as is typically the case -- or pertains to the commercial interests of another.[45] The courts have held, however, that information generat-

---

[42] See, e.g., Landfair v. U.S. Dep't of the Army, 645 F. Supp. 325, 327 (D.D.C. 1986).

[43] See, e.g., Nadler v. FDIC, 92 F.3d 93, 95 (2d Cir. 1996) (term "person" includes "'an individual, partnership, corporation, association, or public or private organization other than an agency'" (quoting definition found in Administrative Procedure Act, 5 U.S.C. § 551(2) (2000))); Dow Jones Co. v. FERC, 219 F.R.D. 167, 176 (C.D. Cal. 2002) (same).

[44] See, e.g., FlightSafety Servs. v. Dep't of Labor, 326 F.3d 607, 611 (5th Cir. 2003) (per curiam) (business establishments); Stone v. Exp.-Imp. Bank, 552 F.2d 132, 137 (5th Cir. 1977) (foreign government agency); Flathead Joint Bd. of Control v. U.S. Dep't of the Interior, 309 F. Supp. 2d 1217, 1221 (D. Mont. 2004) (Indian tribes (citing Indian Law Res. Ctr. v. Dep't of the Interior, 477 F. Supp. 144, 146 (D.D.C. 1979) (holding that an Indian tribe, "as a corporation that is not part of the Federal Government, is plainly a person within the meaning of the Act"))), appeal dismissed, No. 04-35230 (9th Cir. Feb. 11, 2005); Lepelletier v. FDIC, 977 F. Supp. 456, 459 (D.D.C. 1997) (banks), aff'd in part, rev'd in part & remanded on other grounds, 164 F.3d 37 (D.C. Cir. 1999); Hustead v. Norwood, 529 F. Supp. 323, 326 (S.D. Fla. 1981) (state government). See generally Merit Energy Co. v. U.S. Dep't of the Interior, 180 F. Supp. 2d 1184, 1189 (D. Colo. 2001) (rejecting Apache Tribe's claim of confidentiality for information "accumulated by the Tribe [pursuant to a cooperative agreement] that would otherwise be submitted by [oil and gas] lessees directly to the agency," and concluding that although the lessees could invoke Exemption 4, the Tribe could not), appeal dismissed, No. 01-1347 (10th Cir. Sept. 4, 2001).

[45] Bd. of Trade v. Commodity Futures Trading Comm'n, 627 F.2d 392, 405 (D.C. Cir. 1980) (holding that the "plain language" of Exemption 4 "does not in any way suggest that" the requested information "must relate to the affairs of the provider"); accord Critical Mass Energy Project v. NRC, 830 F.2d 278, 281 (D.C. Cir. 1987) (citing Board of Trade and protecting safety re-
(continued...)

ed by the federal government itself is not "obtained from a person" and is therefore excluded from Exemption 4's coverage.[46] Such information might possibly be protectible under Exemption 5, though, which incorporates a qualified privilege for sensitive commercial or financial information generated by the government.[47] (For a further discussion of the "commercial privilege," see Exemption 5, Other Privileges, below.)

Documents prepared by the government can still come within Exemption 4, however, if they simply contain summaries or reformulations of information supplied by a source outside the government,[48] or contain in-

---

[45](...continued)
ports submitted by power-plant consortium based on commercial interests of member utility companies), vacated en banc on other grounds, 975 F.2d 871 (D.C. Cir. 1992); see, e.g., Miami Herald Publ'g Co. v. SBA, 670 F.2d 610, 614 & n.7 (5th Cir. 1982) (analyzing Exemption 4 argument raised on behalf of borrowers even though no Exemption 4 argument was raised for lenders, who actually had "directly" supplied requested loan agreements to agency); see also Department of Justice FOIA Regulations, 28 C.F.R. § 16.8(a)(2) (2006) (defining a "submitter" as "any person or entity from whom the Department obtains business information, directly or indirectly").

[46] See Bd. of Trade, 627 F.2d at 404 (concluding that scope of Exemption 4 is "restrict[ed]" to information that has "not been generated within the Government"); Pohlman, Inc. v. SBA, No. 4:03-01241, slip op. at 20 (E.D. Mo. Sept. 30, 2005) (finding that information prepared by consultants hired by the agency and information generated by the agency in the course of its involvement with its borrowers was not "'obtained from a person'") (appeal pending); Allnet Comm'n Servs. v. FCC, 800 F. Supp. 984, 988 (D.D.C. 1992) (declaring that "person" under Exemption 4 "refers to a wide range of entities including corporations, associations and public or private organizations other than agencies"), aff'd, No. 92-5351 (D.C. Cir. May 27, 1994); see also, e.g., Maydak v. U.S. Dep't of Justice, 254 F. Supp. 2d 23, 49 (D.D.C. 2003), renewed motion for summary judgment granted in part & denied in part on other grounds, 362 F. Supp. 2d 316 (D.D.C. 2005); Judicial Watch, Inc. v. Exp.-Imp. Bank, 108 F. Supp. 2d 19, 28 (D.D.C. 2000); Buffalo Evening News, Inc. v. SBA, 666 F. Supp. 467, 469 (W.D.N.Y. 1987); Consumers Union v. VA, 301 F. Supp. 796, 803 (S.D.N.Y. 1969), appeal dismissed as moot, 436 F.2d 1363 (2d Cir. 1971).

[47] See Fed. Open Mkt. Comm. v. Merrill, 443 U.S. 340, 360 (1979); Morrison-Knudsen Co. v. Dep't of the Army of the U.S., 595 F. Supp. 352, 354-56 (D.D.C. 1984), aff'd, 762 F.2d 138 (D.C. Cir. 1985).

[48] See, e.g., OSHA Data/C.I.H., Inc. v. U.S. Dep't of Labor, 220 F.3d 153, 162 n.23 (3d Cir. 2000) (ratio calculated by agency, but based upon "individual components" supplied by private-sector employers); Gulf & W. Indus. v. United States, 615 F.2d 527, 529-30 (D.C. Cir. 1979) (contractor information contained in agency audit report); Dow Jones, 219 F.R.D. at

(continued...)

formation obtained through a plant inspection.[49] Moreover, the mere fact that the government supervises or directs the preparation of information submitted by sources outside the government does not preclude that information from being "obtained from a person."[50] Similarly, the District Court for the District of Columbia has held that the fact that particular information is "arrived at through negotiation" with the government does not preclude it from being regarded as "obtained from a person."[51]

---

[48](...continued)
170, 176 (power-plant information obtained by agency staff through interviews with "employees or representatives" of companies); Matthews v. USPS, No. 92-1208-CV-W-8, slip op. at 6 (W.D. Mo. Apr. 15, 1994) (technical drawings prepared by agency personnel, but based upon information supplied by computer company); BDM Corp. v. SBA, 2 Gov't Disclosure Serv. (P-H) ¶ 81,044, at 81,121 (D.D.C. Dec. 4, 1980) (contractor information contained in agency documents). But see Phila. Newspapers, Inc. v. HHS, 69 F. Supp. 2d 63, 67 (D.D.C. 1999) (characterizing an agency audit as "not simply a summary or reformulation of information supplied by a source outside the government" and finding that an analysis "prepared by the government" is not "'obtained from a person'" and so "may not be withheld under Exemption 4"), appeal dismissed per stipulation, No. 99-5335 (D.C. Cir. Mar. 17, 2000).

[49] Lion Raisins Inc. v. USDA, 354 F.3d 1072, 1076 (9th Cir. 2004) (quality assessment of raisins, "including weight, color, size, sugar content, and moisture" reflected in "Line Check Sheets" prepared by USDA inspectors during plant visits); Mulloy v. Consumer Prod. Safety Comm'n, No. 85-645, 1985 U.S. Dist. LEXIS 17194, at *2 (S.D. Ohio Aug. 2, 1985) (manufacturing and sales data compiled in establishment inspection report prepared by Commission investigator after on-site visit to plant), aff'd, No. 85-3720 (6th Cir. July 22, 1986).

[50] See High Country Citizens Alliance v. Clarke, No. 04-CV-00749, 2005 WL 2453955, at *5 (D. Colo. Sept. 29, 2005); Merit Energy Co. v. U.S. Dep't of the Interior, 180 F. Supp. 2d 1184, 1188 (D. Colo. 2001), appeal dismissed, No. 01-1347 (10th Cir. Sept. 4, 2001); Silverberg v. HHS, No. 89-2743, 1991 WL 633740, at *2 (D.D.C. June 14, 1991), appeal dismissed per stipulation, No. 91-5255 (D.C. Cir. Sept. 2, 1993); Daniels Mfg. Corp. v. DOD, No. 85-291, slip op. at 4 (M.D. Fla. June 3, 1986). But see Consumers Union, 301 F. Supp. at 803 (deciding that when "[t]he only things . . . obtained from outside the government were the hearing aids themselves," and the requested product testing on those hearing aids actually was performed by government personnel using their expertise and government equipment, the resulting data was not "obtained from a person" for purposes of Exemption 4).

[51] Pub. Citizen Health Research Group v. NIH, 209 F. Supp. 2d 37, 44 (D.D.C. 2002) (concluding that although a licensee's final royalty rate was the result of negotiation with the agency, that did "not alter the fact that the licensee is the ultimate source of [the] information," inasmuch as the

(continued...)

"Confidential" Information

The third requirement of Exemption 4 is met if the submitted information is "privileged or confidential." By far, most Exemption 4 litigation has focused on whether requested information is "confidential" for purposes of Exemption 4. In earlier years, courts based the application of Exemption 4 upon whether there was a promise of confidentiality by the government to the submitting party,[52] or whether the information was of the type not customarily released to the public by the submitter.[53]

These earlier tests were then superseded by National Parks & Conservation Ass'n v. Morton,[54] which significantly altered the test for confidentiality under Exemption 4 and became the leading case on the issue.[55] In National Parks, the Court of Appeals for the District of Columbia Circuit held that the test for confidentiality was an objective one.[56] Thus, whether information would customarily be disclosed to the public by the person from whom it was obtained was not considered dispositive.[57] Likewise, an agency's promise that information would not be released was not considered dispositive.[58] Instead, the D.C. Circuit declared in National Parks that the term "confidential" should be read to protect governmental and private interests in accordance with the following two-part test:

> To summarize, commercial or financial matter is "confidential" for purposes of the exemption if disclosure of the information is likely to have either of the following effects: (1) to impair the Government's ability to obtain necessary information in the future; or (2) to cause substantial harm to the competitive posi-

---

[51](...continued)
licensee "must provide the information in the first instance").

[52] See, e.g., GSA v. Benson, 415 F.2d 878, 881 (9th Cir. 1969).

[53] See, e.g., Sterling Drug, Inc. v. FTC, 450 F.2d 698, 709 (D.C. Cir. 1971); M.A. Schapiro & Co. v. SEC, 339 F. Supp. 467, 471 (D.D.C. 1972).

[54] 498 F.2d 765 (D.C. Cir. 1974).

[55] See, e.g., Burroughs v. Schlesinger, 403 F. Supp. 633, 637 (E.D. Va. 1975) (recognizing National Parks as "the leading case on defining the scope of" Exemption 4).

[56] Id. at 766.

[57] Id. at 767.

[58] See Wash. Post Co. v. HHS, 690 F.2d 252, 268 (D.C. Cir. 1982) (citing Nat'l Parks, 498 F.2d at 766).

tion of the person from whom the information was obtained.[59]

These two principal Exemption 4 tests, which apply disjunctively, have often been referred to in subsequent cases as the "impairment prong" and the "competitive harm prong." In National Parks, the D.C. Circuit expressly reserved the question of whether any other governmental interests -- such as compliance or program effectiveness -- might also be embodied in a "third prong" of the exemption.[60] (For a further discussion of this point, see Exemption 4, Third Prong of National Parks, below.)

Seventeen years later, in a surprising development, D.C. Circuit Court Judge Randolph, joined by Circuit Court Judge Williams, suggested in a concurring opinion in Critical Mass Energy Project v. NRC, that if it were a question of first impression, they would "apply the common meaning of [the word] 'confidential' and [would] reject" the National Parks test altogether.[61] Judges Randolph and Williams contended that there was no "legitimate basis" for the D.C. Circuit's addition of "some two-pronged 'objective' test" for determining if material was "confidential" in light of the unambiguous language of the exemption.[62] Nevertheless, they recognized that they were "not at liberty" to apply their "common sense" definition because the D.C. Circuit had "endorsed the National Parks definition many times," thus compelling them to follow it as well.[63] Thereafter, the government petitioned for, and was granted, an en banc rehearing in Critical Mass[64] so that the full D.C. Circuit could have an opportunity to consider whether the definition of confidentiality set forth in National Parks -- and followed by the panel majority in Critical Mass -- was indeed faithful to the language and legislative intent of Exemption 4.[65]

Fifteen years ago, the D.C. Circuit issued its en banc decision in Critical Mass. After examining the "arguments in favor of overturning National Parks, [the court] conclude[d] that none justifies the abandonment of so well established a precedent."[66] This ruling was founded on the principle of stare decisis -- which counsels against the overruling of an estab-

---

[59] 498 F.2d at 770.

[60] Id. at 770 n.17.

[61] 931 F.2d 939, 948 (D.C. Cir.) (Randolph & Williams, JJ., concurring), vacated & reh'g en banc granted, 942 F.2d 799 (D.C. Cir. 1991), grant of summary judgment to agency aff'd en banc, 975 F.2d 871 (D.C. Cir. 1992).

[62] Id.

[63] Id.

[64] 942 F.2d 799 (D.C. Cir. 1991).

[65] See FOIA Update, Vol. XIII, No. 4, at 1.

[66] 975 F.2d 871, 877 (D.C. Cir. 1992).

lished precedent.[67] The D.C. Circuit determined that "[i]n obedience to" stare decisis, it would not "set aside circuit precedent of almost twenty years' standing."[68] In so holding, it noted the "widespread acceptance of National Parks by [the] other circuits," the lack of any subsequent action by Congress that would remove the "'conceptual underpinnings'" of the decision, and the fact that the test had not proven to be "so flawed that [the court] would be justified in setting it aside."[69]

Although the National Parks test for confidentiality under Exemption 4 was thus reaffirmed, the full D.C. Circuit went on to "correct some misunderstandings as to its scope and application."[70] Specifically, the court "confined" the reach of National Parks and established an entirely new standard to be used for determining whether information "voluntarily" submitted to an agency is "confidential."[71] The United States Supreme Court declined to review the D.C. Circuit's en banc decision,[72] and it thus stands as the leading Exemption 4 case on this issue.[73] Indeed, almost ten years after rendering its decision, the D.C. Circuit remarked that it had had numerous occasions to address the applicable standards to be used under Exemption 4, but by far "[t]he judgment of the court sitting en banc in Critical Mass [was its] most significant statement on the subject."[74]

### The Critical Mass Decision

Through its en banc decision in Critical Mass Energy Project v. NRC, a seven-to-four majority of the Court of Appeals for the District of Columbia Circuit established two distinct standards to be used in determining whether commercial or financial information submitted to an agency is "confidential" under Exemption 4.[75] Specifically, the tests for confidentiality set forth in National Parks & Conservation Ass'n v. Morton,[76] were confined "to the category of cases to which [they were] first applied; namely, those

---

[67] See id. at 875.

[68] Id.

[69] Id. at 876-77 (quoting Patterson v. McLean Credit Union, 491 U.S. 164, 173 (1989)).

[70] Id. at 875.

[71] Id. at 871, 879.

[72] 507 U.S. 984 (1993).

[73] See FOIA Update, Vol. XIV, No. 2, at 1.

[74] Ctr. for Auto Safety v. Nat'l Highway Traffic Safety Admin., 244 F.3d 144, 147 (D.C. Cir. 2001).

[75] 975 F.2d 871, 879 (D.C. Cir. 1992).

[76] 498 F.2d 765, 770 (D.C. Cir. 1974).

in which a FOIA request is made for financial or commercial information a person was obliged to furnish the Government."[77] The D.C. Circuit announced an entirely new test for the protection of information that is "voluntarily" submitted: Such information is now categorically protected provided it is not "customarily" disclosed to the public by the submitter.[78]

In reaching this result, the D.C. Circuit first examined the bases for its decision in National Parks and then identified various interests of both the government and submitters of information that are protected by Exemption 4.[79] By so doing, it found that different interests are implicated depending upon whether the requested information was submitted voluntarily or under compulsion.[80] As to the government's interests, the D.C. Circuit found that when submission of the information is "compelled" by the government, the interest protected by nondisclosure is that of ensuring the continued reliability of the information.[81] On the other hand, it concluded, when information is submitted on a "voluntary" basis, the governmental interest protected by nondisclosure is that of ensuring the continued and full availability of the information.[82]

The D.C. Circuit found that this same dichotomy between compelled and voluntary submissions applies to the submitter's interests as well: When submission of information is compelled, the harm to the submitter's interest is the "commercial disadvantage" that is recognized under the Na-

---

[77] Critical Mass, 975 F.2d at 880.

[78] Id. at 879; accord Ctr. for Auto Safety v. Nat'l Highway Traffic Safety Admin., 244 F.3d 144, 147-48 (D.C. Cir. 2001) (emphasizing that there are two distinct standards to be used in determining confidentiality under Exemption 4, depending on whether information is provided on a "mandatory" or a "voluntary" basis); Bartholdi Cable Co. v. FCC, 114 F.3d 274, 281 (D.C. Cir. 1997) (reiterating that "[t]he test for whether information is 'confidential' depends in part on whether the information was voluntarily or involuntarily disclosed to the government") (non-FOIA case brought under Administrative Procedure Act, 5 U.S.C. §§ 701-706 (2000)); cf. Homeland Security Act of 2002, 6 U.S.C. § 133 (Supp. IV 2004) (establishing protection under Exemption 3, 5 U.S.C. § 552(b)(3) (2000 & Supp. IV 2004), for any properly marked "critical infrastructure information" that is voluntarily provided to the Department of Homeland Security); FOIA Post, "Critical Infrastructure Information Regulations Issued by DHS" (posted 2/27/04); FOIA Post, "Homeland Security Law Contains New Exemption 3 Statute" (posted 1/27/03).

[79] Critical Mass, 975 F.2d at 877-79.

[80] Id.

[81] Id. at 878.

[82] Id.

tional Parks "competitive injury" prong.[83] When information is volunteered, on the other hand, the exemption recognizes a different interest of the submitter, that of protecting information that "for whatever reason, 'would customarily not be released to the public by the person from whom it was obtained.'"[84]

Having delineated these various interests that are protected by Exemption 4, the D.C. Circuit then noted that the Supreme Court had "encouraged the development of categorical rules" in FOIA cases "whenever a particular set of facts will lead to a generally predictable application."[85] The court found that the circumstances of the Critical Mass case -- which involved voluntarily submitted reports -- lent themselves to such "categorical" treatment.[86]

Accordingly, the D.C. Circuit held that it was reaffirming the National Parks test for "determining the confidentiality of information submitted under compulsion," but was announcing a categorical rule for the protection of information provided on a voluntary basis.[87] It declared that such voluntarily provided information is "'confidential' for the purpose of Exemption 4 if it is of a kind that would customarily not be released to the public by the person from whom it was obtained."[88] It also emphasized that this categorical test for voluntarily submitted information is "objective" and that the agency invoking it "must meet the burden of proving the provider's custom."[89]

Applying this test to the information at issue in the Critical Mass case, the D.C. Circuit agreed with the district court's conclusion that the reports were commercial in nature, that they were provided to the agency on a voluntary basis, and that the submitter did not customarily release

---

[83] Id.

[84] Id. (quoting Sterling Drug, Inc. v. FTC, 450 F.2d 698, 709 (D.C. Cir. 1971)).

[85] Id. at 879 (citing U.S. Dep't of Justice v. Reporters Comm. for Freedom of the Press, 489 U.S. 749 (1989)).

[86] Id.

[87] Id.

[88] Id. But see Lee v. FDIC, 923 F. Supp. 451, 454 (S.D.N.Y. 1996) (characterizing the Critical Mass test for withholding voluntary submissions as including an additional requirement that "disclosure would likely impair the government's ability to obtain necessary information in the future").

[89] Critical Mass, 975 F.2d at 879.

them to the public.[90] Thus, the reports were found to be confidential and exempt from disclosure under this new test for Exemption 4.[91]

The D.C. Circuit concluded its opinion by addressing the objection raised by the requester in the case that the new test announced by the court "may lead government agencies and industry to conspire to keep information from the public by agreeing to the voluntary submission of information that the agency has the power to compel."[92] The court dismissed this objection on the grounds that there is "no provision in FOIA that obliges agencies to exercise their regulatory authority in a manner that will maximize the amount of information that will be made available to the public through that Act," and that it did not "see any reason to interfere" with an agency's "exercise of its own discretion in determining how it can best secure the information it needs."[93]

### Applying Critical Mass

The pivotal issue that has arisen as a result of the decision in Critical Mass Energy Project v. NRC[94] is the distinction that the court drew between information "required" to be submitted to an agency and information provided "voluntarily." Although the Court of Appeals for the District of Columbia Circuit never expressly articulated a definition of these two terms in its opinion in Critical Mass, the Department of Justice has issued policy guidance on this subject based upon an extensive analysis of the underlying rationale of the D.C. Circuit's decision, as well as several other

---

[90] Id. at 880 (citing first district court decision and first panel decision in Critical Mass, which recognized that submitter made reports available on confidential basis to individuals and organizations involved in nuclear power production process pursuant to explicit nondisclosure policy).

[91] Id.

[92] Id.

[93] Id.; see Animal Legal Def. Fund v. Sec'y of Agric., 813 F. Supp. 882, 892 (D.D.C. 1993) (finding, based upon this holding in Critical Mass, that there was "nothing" it could do, "however much it might be inclined to do so," to upset agency regulations that permitted regulated entities to keep documents "on-site," outside possession of agency, and thus unreachable under FOIA) (non-FOIA case brought under Administrative Procedure Act), vacated for lack of standing sub nom. Animal Legal Def. Fund, Inc. v. Espy, 29 F.3d 720 (D.C. Cir. 1994); cf. Inner City Press/Cmty. on the Move v. Bd. of Governors of the Fed. Reserve Sys., 463 F.3d 239, 245 n.6, 247 (2d Cir. 2006) (agreeing with this holding of Critical Mass, but declining to adopt its "amendment" to National Parks test for voluntarily submitted information).

[94] 975 F.2d 871 (D.C. Cir. 1992) (en banc).

indications of the court's intent.[95]

The Department of Justice has concluded that a submitter's voluntary participation in an activity -- such as seeking a government contract or applying for a grant or a loan -- does not govern whether any submissions made in connection with that activity are likewise "voluntary."[96] Rather than examining the nature of a submitter's participation in an activity, agencies are advised to focus on whether submission of the information at issue was required for those who chose to participate.[97] The Department of Justice's policy guidance also points out that information can be "required" to be submitted by a broad range of legal authorities, including informal mandates that call for submission as a condition of doing business with the government.[98] Furthermore, the existence of agency authority to require submission of information does not automatically mean such a submission is "required"; the agency authority must actually be exercised in order for a particular submission to be deemed "required."[99] By consistently

---

[95] See FOIA Update, Vol. XIV, No. 2, at 3-5 ("OIP Guidance: The Critical Mass Distinction Under Exemption 4"); see also id. at 6-7 ("Exemption 4 Under Critical Mass: Step-By-Step Decisionmaking"); accord McDonnell Douglas Corp. v. NASA, 895 F. Supp. 316, 317-18 (D.D.C. 1995) (noting that "[a]lthough no bright line rule exists for determining voluntariness, examination of the Critical Mass opinion sheds light on the type of information the D.C. Circuit Court contemplated as being voluntary") (reverse FOIA suit), aff'd on other grounds, No. 95-5290 (D.C. Cir. Sept. 17, 1996).

[96] See FOIA Update, Vol. XIV, No. 2, at 5.

[97] See id.; see also id. at 1 (pointing to significance of this guidance to procurement process and its development in coordination with Office of Federal Procurement Policy); accord Judicial Watch, Inc. v. Exp.-Imp. Bank, 108 F. Supp. 2d 19, 28 (D.D.C. 2000) (declaring that "when the government requires a private party to submit information as a condition of doing business with the government" the submission is deemed "required").

[98] See id. at 5; accord Lepelletier v. FDIC, 977 F. Supp. 456, 460 n.3 (D.D.C. 1997) ("Information is considered 'required' if any legal authority compels its submission, including informal mandates that call for the submission of the information as a condition of doing business with the government."), aff'd in part, rev'd in part & remanded on other grounds, 164 F.3d 37 (D.C. Cir. 1999); see also Sun-Sentinel Co. v. DHS, 431 F. Supp. 2d 1258, 1275 (S.D. Fla. 2006) (submission required by agency's contracts); Lykes Bros. S.S. Co. v. Peña, No. 92-2780, slip op. at 8-11 (D.D.C. Sept. 2, 1993) (submission "compelled" both by agency statute and by agency letter sent to submitters) (reverse FOIA suit).

[99] See FOIA Update, Vol. XIV, No. 2, at 5; accord Inner City Press/Cmty. on the Move v. Bd. of Governors of the Fed. Reserve Sys., 463 F.3d 239, 246-48 & nn. 7-8 (2d Cir. 2006); In Def. of Animals v. HHS, No. 99-3024, 2001 U.S. (continued...)

applying these principles to each item of information requested, agencies can best ensure that they are analytically distinguishing "voluntary" submissions from those that are "required," consistent with the D.C. Circuit's direction that the test is "objective."[100]

The D.C. Circuit rendered its first decision containing an extensive analysis of Critical Mass six years ago, in a case that did "not involve a typical voluntary information submission," but instead involved what the court characterized as a "mistaken submission."[101] The case, Center for Auto Safety v. National Highway Traffic Safety Administration, concerned an agency "Information Request" that was issued to airbag manufacturers and importers, and which "appeared mandatory on its face."[102] Not only did the request state that the agency "require[d]" submission of the specified information, it also included language indicating that "[f]ailure to respond promptly and fully . . . could subject [the recipient] to civil penalties."[103] Despite all of this, the D.C. Circuit upheld the district court's determination that this agency request had been issued in violation of the Paperwork Reduction Act,[104] because the agency had failed to "obtain prior approval from OMB."[105] As a result, the court held, the request could "be ignored without penalty," could not be enforced by the agency, and consequently could not "be considered mandatory."[106]

In making this determination, the D.C. Circuit held that "actual legal

---

[99] (...continued)
Dist. LEXIS 24975, at *33-35 (D.D.C. Sept. 28, 2001); Parker v. Bureau of Land Mgmt., 141 F. Supp. 2d 71, 78 n.6 (D.D.C. 2001); Gov't Accountability Project v. NRC, No. 86-1976, 1993 WL 13033518, at *5 (D.D.C. July 2, 1993) (dicta).

[100] See Critical Mass, 975 F.2d at 879; see also Ctr. for Auto Safety v. Nat'l Highway Traffic Safety Admin., 244 F.3d 144, 149 (D.C. Cir. 2001) (describing the "distinction between voluntary and mandatory submissions that was delineated in Critical Mass" as one "rooted in the importance of establishing clear tests in interpreting FOIA"); accord FOIA Update, Vol. XIV, No. 2, at 6-7 (setting forth detailed, step-by-step guidance for agency personnel to use in applying Critical Mass distinction).

[101] Ctr. for Auto Safety, 244 F.3d at 148.

[102] Id.

[103] Id.

[104] 44 U.S.C. § 3502(3)(A)(i) (2000 & Supp. III 2003) (requiring that OMB approve all agency forms seeking to collect information from ten or more persons or entities).

[105] Ctr. for Auto Safety, 244 F.3d at 148.

[106] Id. at 148-49.

authority, rather than the parties' beliefs or intentions, governs judicial assessments of the character of submissions."[107] The court "reject[ed] the argument" that it "should look to subjective factors," such as the submitting parties' beliefs, or "whether the agency, at the time it issued the request for information, considered the request to be mandatory."[108] Such a focus on the "parties' intentions," it declared, "would cause the court to engage in spurious inquiries into the mind" and would be at odds with the decision in Critical Mass, which emphasized that "the voluntary versus mandatory distinction [is] an objective test."[109]

In Center for Auto Safety, the D.C. Circuit also rejected the "argument that if a recipient does not assert that a submission is voluntary before submitting" requested information, it has somehow "waived" its ability to assert that the submission was voluntary.[110] This approach, too, was found to be at odds with Critical Mass, which recognized "an important policy interest in minimizing resistance" to agency requests for information.[111] Any agency insistence that submitters "identify and air legal objections" before responding to an agency's request for information would, the court found, "tend to frustrate" submitter cooperation.[112] The D.C. Circuit concluded that in this case, "the agency essentially 'flashed its badge' to gain entrance to a private sphere when it had no legal authority to do so," and that "[g]iven this unusual situation" it could not "treat the submissions as 'mandatory.'"[113]

When presented with a case involving essentially the opposite factual situation, the District Court for the District of Columbia applied this "objective test" and held that a submission made by a grant recipient was "required" -- even though it was submitted in response to an agency letter that, on its face, "merely requested, but did not require," that the information be provided.[114] The district court rejected the agency's argument that it "'did not send th[e] letter under any statutory or regulatory authority,'" that it did not consider it a "'demand [or] a threat,'" and that it viewed its

---

[107] Id. at 149.

[108] Id.

[109] Id.

[110] Id.

[111] Id.

[112] Id.

[113] Id. at 150.

[114] In Def., 2001 U.S. Dist. LEXIS 24975, at *32.

letter as "'merely a request for information.'"[115]  Rather, the court declared, it would "not attempt to discern the authors' intent in sending the letter" -- as the agency urged it to do -- "because [that] would require the [c]ourt to employ the exact [subjective] approach rejected by the Court of Appeals" in Center for Auto Safety.[116]  Examining the submission under an "objective test," the court concluded that because the agency had by regulation a "right of access" to any relevant documents maintained by grant recipients, it did in fact have "the legal authority to compel" the requested grant recipient's response.[117]  Moreover, the court found, the letter sent to the grant recipient sufficed as the agency's "exercise" of that authority.[118]  Accordingly, the court refused to look at the agency's subjective intent in sending the letter, and it held that because "the agency here did in fact send a letter requesting information that it had the legal authority to compel," the submission "was required."[119]

In a recent decision that relied extensively on the approach adopted by the D.C. Circuit in Center for Auto Safety, the District Court for the District of Columbia rejected the requester's argument that draft severance agreements provided by a Deputy Secretary nominee "were not voluntarily provided" to the agency, and instead it found particularly "persuasive" the agency's argument that although it had authority to require a nominee "to submit a description of [his] severance agreements," it had no "actual legal authority to compel him to submit" copies of them.[120]  The agency explained that if it had found the nominee's description of a given severance agreement to be lacking, "'the most [it] could have required him to do was to provide a more detailed description of the agreement's terms.'"[121]  In light of these facts, and utilizing "the objective test set forth in Center for Auto Safety," the court concluded that submission of the requested draft severance agreements themselves "must be considered voluntary."[122]

There are numerous other district court decisions that have applied

---

[115] Id. at *32 (quoting declarations from authors of letter).

[116] Id. at *34 (citing Ctr. for Auto Safety, 244 F.3d at 149); see also Parker, 141 F. Supp. 2d at 78 n.7 (likewise citing Center for Auto Safety and refusing to examine "subjective factors," such as submitter's belief at time of submission, when making determination on voluntariness).

[117] In Def., 2001 U.S. Dist. LEXIS 24975, at *35.

[118] Id. at *34.

[119] Id. at *35.

[120] Defenders of Wildlife v. U.S. Dep't of the Interior, 314 F. Supp. 2d 1, 16-17 (D.D.C. 2004) (appeal pending).

[121] Id. (quoting agency's brief).

[122] Id. at 17.

the Critical Mass distinction between "voluntary" and "required" submissions. In one of the first such cases, involving an application for approval to transfer a contract, the District Court for the District of Columbia found that the submission had been required both by the agency's statute -- which did not on its face apply to the submission at issue, but was found to apply based upon the agency's longstanding practice of interpreting the statute more broadly -- and by the agency's letter to the submitters which required them to "submit the documents as a condition necessary to receiving approval of their application."[123] Using the same approach as the Department of Justice's Critical Mass guidance, the court specifically held that "[u]nder Critical Mass, submissions that are required to realize the benefits of a voluntary program are to be considered mandatory."[124] Similarly, when the FDA conditioned its approval of a new drug on the manufacturer's submission of a post-marketing study, the protocol for that study (i.e., its design, hypotheses, and objectives) was deemed a required submission (even in the absence of agency regulations requiring manufacturers to conduct such post-marketing studies) because submission for that particular manufacturer had, in fact, been "necessary in order to obtain FDA approval" for the drug and that rendered it "required."[125]

In another case that also used the same approach as the Department of Justice's Critical Mass guidance, the District Court for the District of New Jersey found that when a submitter provided documents to agency officials during a meeting concerning its tax status, it did so voluntarily, because "if the submission of the documents were obligatory, there would be a controlling statute, regulation or written order."[126] In the absence of any such "mandate," the court concluded that the submission was volun-

---

[123] Lykes, No. 92-2780, slip op. at 9 (D.D.C. Sept. 2, 1993).

[124] Id. at 9 n.4; accord FOIA Update, Vol. XIV, No. 2, at 3-5; see also Judicial Watch, Inc. v. U.S. Dep't of Commerce, 337 F. Supp. 2d 146, 169 (D.D.C. 2004) (acknowledging that information "required of parties hoping to participate in" agency's trade missions was "compelled"); Lee v. FDIC, 923 F. Supp. 451, 454 (S.D.N.Y. 1996) (rejecting agency's attempt to characterize submission as "voluntary" when documents were "required to be submitted" in order to obtain government approval to merge two banks).

[125] Pub. Citizen Health Research Group v. FDA, 964 F. Supp. 413, 414 n.1 (D.D.C. 1997); see also, e.g., Pub. Citizen Health Research Group v. FDA, 997 F. Supp. 56, 62 n.3 (D.D.C. 1998) (concluding that information submitted in connection with New Drug Application was "required"), aff'd in pertinent part, 185 F.3d 898, 901, 903 (D.C. Cir. 1999); Sokolow v. FDA, No. 1:97-CV-252, slip op. at 6 (E.D. Tex. Feb. 19, 1998) (same), aff'd, 162 F.3d 1160 (5th Cir. 1998) (unpublished table decision).

[126] AGS Computers, Inc. v. U.S. Dep't of Treasury, No. 92-2714, slip op. at 10 (D.N.J. Sept. 16, 1993).

tary.[127]

In that case, the court rejected an argument advanced by the requester that despite the absence of a mandate requiring the submission, the court should "rule as a matter of law" that the documents were "required" to be submitted because submission was for the "benefit" of the submitter.[128] Finding that such an approach "results in putting the cart before the horse," the court noted that in Critical Mass, the D.C. Circuit decided first whether a submission was voluntary and only then did it apply the "less stringent standard for nondisclosure under the FOIA as an incentive for voluntary submitters to provide accurate and reliable information."[129] The requester's proposed test was "flawed," the court found, because it relied "too heavily on hindsight" and the court could "envision cases where someone at the time of submitting the documents is clearly doing so on a voluntary basis, but when a benefit analysis . . . is performed thereafter, the incorrect result is reached that the submission was compulsory."[130]

Three years ago, the District Court for the District of Columbia readily found documents provided by three different companies all to have been "voluntarily submitted," based primarily upon the representations made to the agency by the companies.[131] The court noted that the first submitter had "informed" the agency that its documents were provided "'as a voluntary public service with the view that these independent studies might be useful.'"[132] Similarly, the second submitter had "indicated" that its document was provided voluntarily "in order to resolve disputes with the government."[133] By contrast, the third submitter admitted that it was not "'certain[]'" how the agency "'came into possession of the report,'" but was able to state that the report had not been "'requested'" or paid for by any federal agency and that it did know that it had sent "courtesy" copies of it "'to various government officials.'"[134] Despite the requester's argument that as to this third submission the agency was unable to "state specifically how" the report was "obtained by the government," the court "agree[d]" with the agency's "conclusion" -- which was based upon the submitter's representa-

---

[127] Id. at 9-10.

[128] Id. at 10.

[129] Id.

[130] Id. at 10-11.

[131] Judicial Watch, Inc. v. U.S. Dep't of Energy, 310 F. Supp. 2d 271, 308-09 (D.D.C. 2004), aff'd in part & rev'd in part on other grounds, 412 F.3d 125 (D.C. Cir. 2005).

[132] Id. at 308 (quoting agency declaration).

[133] Id.

[134] Id. at 309 (quoting agency declaration).

tions -- that the documents were indeed "voluntarily provided."[135]

Another submission was deemed to be "voluntary" in a case involving a submitter which promptly "cooperated with agency officials" and provided agency inspectors "all the information" they requested "prior to the issuance of any subpoenas or warrants," which in turn ensured that the investigation "was neither delayed nor impeded in any manner."[136] In yet another case, a submission was found to be "voluntary" where the requester sought copies of the comments that a submitter had provided to the agency in response to the notice that it had been given concerning a FOIA request that had been made for its information.[137] In finding that such comments had been "voluntarily submitted" to the agency, the court focused on the agency's submitter-notice regulations and found that they "clearly did not require . . . [the submitter] to provide any comments whatsoever."[138] The court noted that under those regulations, the failure to submit objections to the disclosure of requested information did "not constitute a waiver" and that the agency was still obligated to review the information to determine whether release was appropriate.[139]

Other agencies do, in fact, expressly require submitters of information to provide comments if they have any objection to disclosure of their information in response to a FOIA request.[140] Such an approach is consistent with the submitter-notification process mandated by Executive Order 12,600,[141] and it ensures that when an agency is analyzing sensitive business information for Exemption 4 applicability it has the benefit of the submitter's expertise and viewpoint.[142] (These "required" submitter comments are themselves, of course, still entitled to all available Exemption 4 protection under the several tests for confidentiality set out in National Parks &

---

[135] Id.

[136] Shell Oil Co. v. U.S. Dep't of Labor, No. H-96-3113, slip op. at 13 (S.D. Tex. Mar. 30, 1998) (reverse FOIA suit), aff'd on other grounds, No. 98-20538 (5th Cir. Oct. 14, 1999).

[137] McDonnell Douglas Corp. v. NASA, No. 93-1540, 1993 WL 796612, at *1 (D.D.C. Nov. 17, 1993) (reverse FOIA suit).

[138] Id.

[139] Id. at *2 n.1.

[140] See, e.g., Department of Justice FOIA Regulations, 28 C.F.R. § 16.8(f) (2006); NLRB FOIA Regulations, 29 C.F.R. § 102.117(c)(2)(iv)(D) (2006).

[141] 3 C.F.R. 235 (1988), reprinted in 5 U.S.C. § 552 note (2000), and in FOIA Update, Vol. VIII, No. 2, at 2-3.

[142] Accord FOIA Update, Vol. III, No. 3, at 3 (emphasizing importance of establishing procedures for notifying submitters).

Conservation Ass'n v. Morton.[143] For a complete discussion of these tests, see Exemption 4, Impairment Prong of National Parks; Exemption 4, Competitive Harm Prong of National Parks; and Exemption 4, Third Prong of National Parks, below.)

There have been other decisions in which the wording of an agency's regulation was the key factor in determining whether a submission was "voluntary." The District Court for the District of Columbia has held that an agency properly determined that certain information relating to proposed pipeline projects was submitted "voluntarily," because the agency's regulations detailed specific items that were "required" to be included in the pipeline right-of-way applications, but then also specified items that an applicant "may submit" to "assist" in the processing of the application.[144] Because the information at issue did not fall within the list of items "required" for an application, the court concluded that it was "submitted voluntarily."[145]

In another case that turned on the wording of an agency's regulation, the same court found that the agency had demonstrated that the submission of information by kidney dialysis centers was voluntary and that the regulation relied on by the requester -- in support of its contention that the submission was required -- did not actually "require" the centers "to provide any particular information" and instead merely stated, "without further elaboration," that information "must be provided in the manner specified" by the agency's Secretary.[146] In that regard, the court found persuasive the agency's declaration that stated "unequivocally that the information was produced voluntarily and not subject to a statutory requirement."[147] By contrast, summary judgment was denied in another case when the agency's declaration entirely failed to indicate how the agency had received the requested documents.[148]

In a ruling that arguably takes the characterization of "voluntary" to

---

[143] 498 F.2d 765, 770 (D.C. Cir. 1974).

[144] Parker, 141 F. Supp. 2d at 77-78.

[145] Id. at 78 (rejecting as well requesters' argument that submitted information was "required" to be provided under NEPA regulations, when requesters failed to cite, and court could not find, any such mandatory provision in those regulations).

[146] Minntech Corp. v. HHS, No. 92-2720, slip op. at 8 (D.D.C. Nov. 17, 1993).

[147] Id.

[148] See Animal Legal Def. Fund, Inc. v. Dep't of the Air Force, 44 F. Supp. 2d 295, 303 (D.D.C. 1999) (observing that "nowhere in his declaration does [the agency declarant] aver that [the submitter's] submissions came to the [agency] 'voluntarily'").

its outermost reaches, the District Court for the Eastern District of Missouri held that a submission was voluntary even though the agency not only had the authority to issue a subpoena for the documents, but had in fact exercised that authority by actually issuing such a subpoena.[149] The court flatly rejected the agency's argument that the issuance of the subpoena rendered the submission "required," finding that that "conclusion ignore[d] the fact that subpoenaed parties may challenge [the subpoena], both administratively and through objections to enforcement proceedings."[150] Although no challenge to the subpoena was actually brought, the court found it "highly likely" that such a challenge would have been successful given the fact that the court had previously ruled that the same documents were privileged and hence did not have to be disclosed to private parties who were in litigation with the submitter.[151] "This," the court declared, "shows that the production in fact was voluntary, not required."[152]

Significantly, the District Court for the District of Columbia has issued a total of eight decisions that all hold -- consistent with the Department of Justice's policy guidance on this issue -- that prices submitted in response to a solicitation for a government contract are "required" submissions.[153]

---

[149] McDonnell Douglas Corp. v. EEOC, 922 F. Supp. 235, 242 (E.D. Mo. 1996) (reverse FOIA suit), appeal dismissed, No. 96-2662 (8th Cir. Aug. 29, 1996).

[150] Id.

[151] Id.

[152] Id.

[153] Canadian Commercial Corp. v. Dep't of the Air Force, 442 F. Supp. 2d 15, 29 (D.D.C. 2006) (reverse FOIA suit) (appeal pending); McDonnell Douglas Corp. v. U.S. Dep't of the Air Force, 215 F. Supp. 2d 200, 205 & n.3 (D.D.C. 2002) (reverse FOIA suit), aff'd in pertinent part & rev'd in part on other grounds, 375 F.3d 1182 (D.C. Cir. 2004), reh'g en banc denied, No. 02-5432 (D.C. Cir. Dec. 16, 2004); McDonnell Douglas Corp. v. NASA, 981 F. Supp. 12, 15 (D.D.C. 1997) (reverse FOIA suit), reconsideration denied, No. 96-2611, slip op. at 7-8 (D.D.C. May 1, 1998), rev'd on other grounds, 180 F.3d 303 (D.C. Cir. 1999), reh'g en banc denied, No. 98-5251 (D.C. Cir. Oct. 6, 1999), dismissed as moot on motion for entry of judgment, 102 F. Supp. 2d 21 (D.D.C.) (underlying FOIA request withdrawn after D.C. Circuit issued decision), reconsideration denied, 109 F. Supp. 2d 27 (D.D.C. 2000); Martin Marietta Corp. v. Dalton, 974 F. Supp. 37, 39 (D.D.C. 1997) (reverse FOIA suit); McDonnell Douglas, 895 F. Supp. at 317-18; McDonnell Douglas Corp. v. NASA, 895 F. Supp. 319, 325-26 (D.D.C. 1995) (reverse FOIA suit), vacated as moot, No. 95-5288 (D.C. Cir. Apr. 1, 1996); CC Distribs. v. Kinzinger, No. 94-1330, 1995 WL 405445, at *4 (D.D.C. June 28, 1995) (reverse FOIA suit); Chem. Waste Mgmt., Inc. v. O'Leary, No. 94-2230, 1995 WL 115894, at *4 (D.D.C. Feb. 28, 1995) (reverse FOIA suit); cf. MTB Group, Inc. (continued...)

In the first of these decisions, the court held that the submitter "had no choice but to submit the unit price information once it chose to submit its proposal," as the terms of the Request for Proposals (RFP) "compelled [it] to submit its unit prices."[154] Relying on that decision, the court reiterated in the second case that a contract "bidder only provides confidential information because the agency requires it [and that] once a firm has elected to bid, it must submit the mandatory information if it hopes to win the contract."[155]

In the third decision (which was subsequently vacated when the FOIA request was withdrawn while the case was on appeal),[156] the court again relied on the terms of the agency's RFP, which, it noted, "used language of compulsion in reference to pricing information."[157] There, the court also rejected as "temptingly simple" the submitter's argument that because it "did not have to enter into a contract, no information within the contract [should] be considered mandatory."[158] This "rather simplistic approach" was flatly rejected by the court as it "would result in classifying all government contractors as per se volunteers whose pricing information could easily be withheld from the public domain."[159]

In the fourth decision, after analyzing the Critical Mass decision, the

---

[153](...continued)
v. United States, 65 Fed. Cl. 516, 526-29 & n.22 (Fed. Cl. 2005) (concluding that the disclosure of "financial information in the bidding system is not voluntary" (citing as "persuasive authority" McDonnell Douglas, 215 F. Supp. 2d at 205, and Chem. Waste, 1995 WL 115894, at *4)) (non-FOIA case); Judicial Watch v. Dep't of the Army, 466 F. Supp. 2d 112, 125 (D.D.C. 2006) (noting that "price elements necessary to win a government contract" would be considered required, but finding that the information in question in the case before it was submitted voluntarily, because it was provided "not in an effort to bid for or obtain a contract but to negotiate the administration of [a] contract" already awarded); Judicial Watch, Inc. v. U.S. Dep't of Commerce, 337 F. Supp. 2d 146, 171-72 (D.D.C. 2004) (stating that "bidding information submitted at an agency's behest is required, but finding that the information at issue in the case before it was voluntarily provided, because it was submitted to foreign governments for consideration and was "not required by any United States legal authority").

[154] Chem. Waste, 1995 WL 115894, at *4.

[155] CC Distribs., 1995 WL 405445, at *4.

[156] See McDonnell Douglas Corp. v. NASA, No. 95-5288 (D.C. Cir. Apr. 1, 1996) (reverse FOIA suit).

[157] McDonnell Douglas, 895 F. Supp. at 325.

[158] Id.

[159] Id.

court expressly concluded "as a matter of law" that "the price elements necessary to win a government contract are not voluntary."[160] Once again faced with an argument by the submitter that its submission of a proposal and its entry into a government contract were "obviously voluntary acts," the court found that such contentions were simply "inapposite."[161] Declaring that "no one disputes that the process of offer and acceptance giving rise to contractual obligations is voluntary," the court held that the "focal point" must be "the information itself" and that there was no question that the agency "required that the contract itemize the prices for specific services."[162] The court then went on to somewhat sarcastically note that the submitter was "not doing the government a favor by providing the most basic information in a contract -- price" -- and it then observed that if "contractors want to win lucrative government contracts they must provide [agencies] with specific pricing elements for their goods and services."[163]

In the fifth decision, the court held that although the D.C. Circuit "has yet to address the issue, district court precedent in this Circuit uniformly and firmly points to the conclusion that the financial/commercial information found in the [submitter's] contracts was 'required' in the National Parks sense of the term by [the] Federal Acquisition Regulation[] . . . and therefore [was] subject to the National Parks test."[164] In so holding, the district court again noted that "[w]hether to compete for [the agency's] business at all was, of course, [the submitter's] option, but having elected to do so it was required to submit the information [the agency] insisted on having if it hoped to win the contract."[165]

The court relied on this case law in the sixth decision and held that "the relevant inquiry is whether the specific price elements and other information provided by [the submitter] were required to be submitted before [the agency] would award the contract."[166] Because the contract solicitation "included several statements indicating that bidders must submit certain information," the court determined that the agency "did not exceed the bounds of reasonableness in concluding that [the submitter] was 'required' to submit" the requested pricing information.[167]

---

[160] McDonnell Douglas, 895 F. Supp. at 318.

[161] Id.

[162] Id.

[163] Id.

[164] Martin Marietta, 974 F. Supp. at 39.

[165] Id.

[166] McDonnell Douglas, 981 F. Supp. at 15.

[167] Id.

In the seventh of these decisions, the court readily upheld the agency's determination that the submission of the requested contract pricing information was "not provided voluntarily."[168] After finding that the submitter
"was required to provide its cost and pricing information in order to complete the Air Force's Request for Proposal and be considered for the contract," the court reasoned that such a "factual situation is distinctly different" from that presented in the Critical Mass case, where information had
been volunteered "despite the fact that the disclosing entity was under no
obligation to provide the government with information."[169] By contrast, the
court firmly held, "[b]ecause contractors are required to submit cost and
pricing information if they wish to bid on a government contract, cases in
this district have found price and cost requirements to be compulsory, not
voluntary, submissions."[170]

Lastly, in the most recent of these decisions, the court relied on this
prior case law, which, it noted, "most often deemed" contract pricing information to be "a required element of government solicitations, and hence involuntarily submitted."[171] The court further relied on the terms of the agency's contract solicitation, which it found "support[ed] the conclusion that
[the] pricing information was required" and thus did "not warrant departure
from this line of precedent."[172]

Two other recent decisions by the District Court for the District of
Columbia -- while not directly ruling on the issue -- further support the
court's holdings in the above cases. In one case, in the course of distinguishing rebate and incentive information from unit prices, the court declared that "it is beyond dispute that unit pricing data is required to be
submitted in order to compete for a government contract."[173] In the other
case, the court, while holding that computer matrices containing millions
of pricing elements were not unit prices, nonetheless conducted an alternative analysis as if they were -- and it did so by utilizing the National
Parks competitive harm test, after earlier describing the matrices' submission to the agency as having been "required" in order to obtain the con-

---

[168] McDonnell Douglas, 215 F. Supp. 2d at 205.

[169] Id. at 205.

[170] Id. at 205 & n.3; see also FOIA Post, "New McDonnell Douglas Opinion Aids Unit Price Decisionmaking" (posted 10/4/02).

[171] Canadian Commercial, 442 F. Supp. 2d at 29 (citing Martin Marietta
Corp., 974 F. Supp. at 39, and McDonnell Douglas, 895 F. Supp. at 325-26).

[172] Id. at 29-30.

[173] Mallinckrodt v. West, 140 F. Supp. 2d 1, 5 (D.D.C. 2000) (reverse FOIA
suit), appeal dismissed voluntarily, No. 00-5330 (D.C. Cir. Dec. 12, 2000).

tract.[174]

The District Courts for the Eastern District of Missouri,[175] the Southern District of Alabama,[176] and the District of Colorado[177] likewise have ruled that contract submissions were not provided voluntarily and that, as a consequence, the greater protection afforded by Critical Mass for voluntary submissions was not applicable. In so holding, the Colorado court also specifically rejected the argument advanced by the submitter that because it had "voluntarily entered into the contract with the Government" the contract submission should be considered "voluntary."[178] In contrast, two cases decided in the Eastern District of Virginia immediately after Critical Mass reached the opposite conclusion and held that contract submissions were voluntarily provided.[179] (As noted below, however, one of those cases later was expressly repudiated by a subsequent court in that same district for failing to provide any justification whatsoever for its conclusion.[180])

Two years after the decision in Critical Mass, a case involving government contract prices reached the D.C. Circuit -- after having been decided by the lower court prior to the Critical Mass decision.[181] The D.C. Circuit, however, elected not to opine on the meaning of Critical Mass, or its

---

[174] MCI Worldcom, Inc. v. GSA, 163 F. Supp. 2d 28, 30, 35 (D.D.C. 2001) (reverse FOIA suit).

[175] See TRIFID Corp. v. Nat'l Imagery & Mapping Agency, 10 F. Supp. 2d 1087, 1098 (E.D. Mo. 1998) (relying on case law from the District Court for the District of Columbia) (reverse FOIA suit).

[176] Clearbrook, L.L.C. v. Ovall, No. 06-0629, 2006 U.S. Dist. LEXIS 81244, at *10 n.2 (S.D. Ala. Nov. 3, 2006) (denying plaintiff's motion for preliminary injunction) (citing Canadian Commercial, 442 F. Supp. 2d at 29), dismissed with prejudice per stipulation (S.D. Ala. Nov. 22, 2006) (reverse FOIA suit).

[177] See Source One Mgmt., Inc. v. U.S. Dep't of the Interior, No. 92-Z-2101, transcript at 6 (D. Colo. Nov. 10, 1993) (bench order) (reverse FOIA suit).

[178] Id. at 5.

[179] Envtl. Tech., Inc. v. EPA, 822 F. Supp. 1226, 1229 (E.D. Va. 1993) (summarily declaring that unit price information provided in connection with government contract was voluntarily submitted) (reverse FOIA suit); Cohen, Dunn & Sinclair, P.C. v. GSA, No. 92-0057-A, transcript at 28 (E.D. Va. Sept. 10, 1992) (bench order) (same).

[180] Comdisco, Inc. v. GSA, 864 F. Supp. 510, 517 n.8 (E.D. Va. 1994) (denigrating Envtl. Tech., 822 F. Supp. at 1229) (reverse FOIA suit); accord FOIA Update, Vol. XIV, No. 2, at 5 (same).

[181] McDonnell Douglas Corp. v. NASA, No. 92-5342, slip op. at 2 (D.C. Cir. Feb. 14, 1994) (reverse FOIA suit).

applicability to government contract submissions, and instead remanded the case to the district court with instructions for that court to "reexamine the applicability of exemption 4 to the contract prices at issue under our holding in Critical Mass."[182] (On remand, the district court found Critical Mass to be inapplicable to a government contract submission.[183]) Similarly, another case was remanded back to the agency -- which had made its Exemption 4 determination prior to the issuance of Critical Mass -- so that any voluntarily submitted information could be identified and then analyzed under the Critical Mass standards.[184]

   In McDonnell Douglas Corp. v. NASA, the D.C. Circuit once again declined to analyze this issue.[185] Although the submitter argued that "its submission of bidding information [was] part and parcel of the voluntary act of submitting a bid," the D.C. Circuit found that it was not necessary to decide that issue because "assuming arguendo" that the submission was "required," the court "believe[d that] the disputed line item price information [was] confidential commercial or financial information under the National Parks test" in any event.[186]

   There now have been two decisions by the District Court for the District of Columbia that have differentiated between discrete items contained in a government contract. In the first case, the court found that General and Administrative (G & A) rate ceilings were voluntarily provided to the government even though submission of actual G & A rates was "undisputed[ly] . . . a mandatory component" of an offeror's submission.[187] In so holding, the court rejected the agency's argument that because "submission of a cost proposal, including actual G & A rates was mandatory in order to compete for the contract," the G & A rate ceilings -- which had been requested by the contracting officer during negotiations -- "were also a

---

[182] Id.

[183] McDonnell Douglas, 895 F. Supp. at 318.

[184] Alexander & Alexander Servs. v. SEC, No. 92-1112, 1993 WL 439799, at *12 (D.D.C. Oct. 19, 1993) (reverse FOIA suit), appeal dismissed, No. 93-5398 (D.C. Cir. Jan. 4, 1996).

[185] McDonnell Douglas Corp. v. NASA, 180 F.3d 303 (D.C. Cir. 1999) (reverse FOIA suit), reh'g en banc denied, No. 98-5251 (D.C. Cir. Oct. 6, 1999), dismissed as moot on motion for entry of judgment, 102 F. Supp. 2d 21 (D.D.C.) (underlying FOIA request withdrawn after issuance of D.C. Circuit decision), reconsideration denied, 109 F. Supp. 2d 27 (D.D.C. 2000).

[186] Id. at 305-06 (referencing extensive Department of Justice guidance -- set forth at FOIA Update, Vol. XIV, No. 2, at 3-7 -- which thoroughly analyzes distinction between "voluntary" and "required" submissions).

[187] Cortez III Serv. Corp. v. NASA, 921 F. Supp. 8, 12 (D.D.C. 1996) (reverse FOIA suit), appeal dismissed voluntarily, No. 96-5163 (D.C. Cir. July 3, 1996).

mandatory part of the cost proposal."[188] Because the contract solicitation was "silent as to G & A rate ceilings," and in the absence of any firm evidence that the submitter "was required to provide G & A rate ceilings in order to continue to compete for the contract," the court concluded that their submission had been voluntary.[189]

Relying on this decision, the court in the second such case similarly rejected the agency's argument that "'all of the information submitted in an effort to win a government contract should be viewed as having been required by the contract solicitation.'"[190] Instead, the court distinguished those items that the contract solicitation stated "should" be included in a proposal from those that the solicitation stated "must" be included.[191] The court found that the rebate and incentive information at issue "may have made the bid more appealing or valuable to the government," but because it was not included within the list of items that the solicitation stated "must" be provided, it "was not required to be submitted within the meaning of Critical Mass."[192]

In contrast to the above cases, the District Court for the District of Columbia has found that where a contract resulted from "intense arms-length negotiations," as opposed to a solicitation by the government for a competitive bid, the contract terms (which included pricing and rate information) were voluntarily provided.[193] Because the government did not have the legal authority to compel the submission of the requested contract terms, and there was "no indication" of "any demand" by the government that specific terms had to be submitted for consideration, the court held that the information must "be judged according to Critical Mass."[194]

Other cases decided subsequent to Critical Mass have applied the voluntary/required distinction, but they have done so with only limited rationale or analysis for their conclusions on this pivotal issue. Instead, the information at issue was summarily found either to have been voluntarily

---

[188] Id.

[189] Id. at 12-13.

[190] Mallinckrodt, 140 F. Supp. 2d at 6 (quoting agency's brief).

[191] Id.

[192] Id. (rejecting the agency's argument that because the "solicitation required the submission of pricing information, it necessarily follows that rebates and incentives were [also] required to be submitted").

[193] Airline Pilots Ass'n, Int'l v. USPS, No. 03-2384, 2004 U.S. Dist. LEXIS 26067, at *4, *12-17 (D.D.C. June 24, 2004).

[194] Id. at *13-17 (citing Ctr. for Auto Safety, 244 F.3d at 149).

provided[195] or, conversely, to have been a required submission.[196] The D.C. Circuit had occasion to review one of these cases on appeal, but its unpublished opinion did not provide any further guidance on the Critical Mass distinction and instead merely affirmed the lower court's decision on that point.[197]

---

[195] See, e.g., Hull v. U.S. Dep't of Labor, No. 04-CV-01264, slip op. at 8 (D. Colo. Dec. 2, 2005) (noting that requester did "not dispute that this information was provided voluntarily"); Judicial Watch, Inc. v. U.S. Dep't of Justice, 306 F. Supp. 2d 58, 68 (D.D.C. 2004) (observing that the requester had failed to "offer a reason to support its belief that the documents in question were not submitted voluntarily," and deferring to the agency affidavits that said otherwise, as they were "the only evidence" before the court) (appeal pending); Pentagon Techs. Int'l v. United States, No. 98CIV.4831, 2000 WL 347165, at *3 (S.D.N.Y. Mar. 31, 2000) (alternative holding) (opining that the "information may be viewed as having been produced voluntarily in order to supplement the Government's understanding of the IBM proposal"); Clarkson v. Greenspan, No. 97-2035, slip op. at 9 (D.D.C. June 30, 1998) (holding that the information "was voluntarily provided in confidence, and, according to [the agency] its release could jeopardize the continued availability of such information"), summary affirmance granted, No. 98-5349, 1999 WL 229017 (D.C. Cir. Mar. 2, 1999); Allnet Commc'n Servs. v. FCC, 800 F. Supp. 984, 990 (D.D.C. 1992) (declaring that "[t]o the extent that the information sought was submitted voluntarily, the material was properly withheld"), aff'd, No. 92-5351, slip op. at 3 (D.C. Cir. May 27, 1994).

[196] See Nat'l Air Traffic Controllers Ass'n v. FAA, No. 06-53, 2007 WL 495798, at *2 (D.D.C. Feb. 12, 2007) (deciding that it "must use the more stringent standard for documents required to be submitted," because the parties failed to proffer evidence addressing whether the information at issue was voluntarily submitted or required by the agency); Trans-Pac. Policing Agreement v. U.S. Customs Serv., No. 97-2188, 1998 WL 34016806, at *2 (D.D.C. May 14, 1998) (concluding that information provided on import declaration form "is supplied under compulsion"), rev'd & remanded for segregability determination, 177 F.3d 1022 (D.C. Cir. 1999); Garren v. U.S. Dep't of the Interior, No. CV-97-273, slip op. at 12 n.10 (D. Or. Nov. 17, 1997) (magistrate's recommendation) (finding that information concerning purchase of river-rafting concession contract was required to be submitted), adopted (D. Or. Jan. 8, 1998); Afr. Fund v. Mosbacher, No. 92-289, 1993 WL 183736, at *7 & *8 n.3 (S.D.N.Y. May 26, 1993) (holding that information provided in export license applications was required to be submitted); Citizens Comm'n on Human Rights v. FDA, No. 92-5313, 1993 WL 1610471, at *8 (C.D. Cal. May 10, 1993) (finding that information concerning New Drug Application was required to be submitted), aff'd in part & remanded in part on other grounds, 45 F.3d 1325 (9th Cir. 1995).

[197] Allnet Commc'n Servs. v. FCC, No. 92-5351, slip op. at 3 (D.C. Cir. May 27, 1994) (finding no error in lower court's first concluding that requested information was exempt under standard for required submissions

(continued...)

In a case involving rather unusual factual circumstances, the District Court for the District of Columbia discussed the applicability of the Critical Mass distinction to documents that had been provided to the agency not by their originator, but as a result of the unauthorized action of a confidential source.[198] Although these documents were not actually at issue in the case, the court nevertheless elected to analyze their status under Critical Mass.[199] The court first noted that the decision in Critical Mass provided it with "little guidance" as those documents "had been produced voluntarily by the originator, without any intervening espionage."[200] The court nevertheless opined that in its case "the secret, unauthorized delivery" of the documents at issue made the submission "'involuntary' in the purest sense," but that application of the "more stringent standard for involuntary transfer would contravene the spirit" of Critical Mass.[201] Thus, the court declared that in such circumstances the proper test for determining the confidentiality of the documents should be the "more permissive standard" of Critical Mass, i.e., protection would be afforded if the information was of a kind that is not customarily released to the public by the submitter.[202]

The District Courts for the District of Maine, the Eastern District of Virginia, and most recently for the Southern District of New York and the Central District of California all have issued decisions that expressly declined to consider the possible applicability of Critical Mass to the information at issue because the Critical Mass distinction has not yet been adopted by their respective courts of appeals.[203] In so holding, the District Court

---

[197](...continued) and then also concluding that it would be exempt under standard for voluntary submissions).

[198] Gov't Accountability, 1993 WL 13033518, at *1.

[199] Id. at *4.

[200] Id. at *5.

[201] Id.

[202] Id.

[203] See Inner City Press/Cmty. on the Move v. Bd. of Governors of the Fed. Reserve Sys., 380 F. Supp. 2d 211, 216 n.2 (S.D.N.Y. 2005) (stating that the "Second Circuit has explicitly held off on determining whether it would accept the Critical Mass 'amendment' of the National Parks test"), reconsideration denied, No. 04 Civ. 8337, 2005 WL 2560396 (S.D.N.Y. Oct. 11, 2005), aff'd in part & remanded in part on other grounds, 463 F.3d 239, 246-47 n.8 (2d Cir. 2006); N.Y. Pub. Interest Research Group v. EPA, 249 F. Supp. 2d 327, 335 (S.D.N.Y. 2003) (noting that "[t]he Second Circuit has not commented on the Critical Mass modification of the National Parks test, and no circuit court has expressly adopted" it); Lahr v. NTSB, 453 F. Supp. 2d 1153, 1175 (C.D. Cal. 2006) (observing that "the Ninth Circuit has not ad-
(continued...)

for the Eastern District of Virginia noted that although a previous decision arising out of that same district had, in fact, "adopted the Critical Mass test," in its view that earlier opinion "provided little justification for its conclusion"; therefore, the court "decline[d] to follow" it.[204] In a 2003 decision addressing this issue, the District Court for the Southern District of New York similarly acknowledged that other courts in that district "have cited Critical Mass with approval," but nonetheless expressed the view that those other decisions gave "little justification for their conclusion."[205]

Years earlier, using a strictly pragmatic approach, the District Court for the Southern District of New York declared that it "need not decide whether Critical Mass is governing law in the Second Circuit" because the records at issue -- which were acquired by the FDIC by operation of law when it became receiver of a failed financial institution -- were "not produced voluntarily [and so] the Critical Mass standard simply [did] not apply."[206] On appeal, the Court of Appeals for the Second Circuit agreed with the lower court on this point, stating that because the records at issue were not provided voluntarily, the Critical Mass test simply was "irrelevant to the issue presented" by the appeal.[207] Similarly, the Court of Appeals for the Ninth Circuit has observed that the Critical Mass distinction between voluntary and required submissions "becomes relevant only when information is submitted to the government voluntarily."[208] Finding that the records at issue in the case before it were required to be submitted by the terms of the agency's contract solicitation, the Ninth Circuit declared that

---

[203](...continued) dressed the Critical Mass modification" of the National Parks test); Dow Jones Co. v. FERC, 219 F.R.D. 167, 178 (C.D. Cal. 2002) (remarking that "the test set forth in Critical Mass has not been adopted by any other circuit" and "is not consistent with Ninth Circuit jurisprudence"); Bangor Hydro-Elec. Co. v. U.S. Dep't of the Interior, No. 94-0173-B, slip op. at 9 n.3 (D. Me. Apr. 18, 1995) (observing that the "First Circuit . . . has not distinguished between information provided on a voluntary basis and that which must be disclosed" to the government); Comdisco, 864 F. Supp. at 517 (opining that "it is doubtful that the Fourth Circuit would be persuaded to embrace the Critical Mass standard with respect to voluntary submissions").

[204] Comdisco, 864 F. Supp. at 517 n.8 (referring to Envtl. Tech., 822 F. Supp. at 1226).

[205] N.Y. Pub. Interest Group, 249 F. Supp. 2d at 335 (referring to Pentagen, 2000 WL 347165, at *2, and Afr. Fund, 1993 WL 183736, at *7 n.3).

[206] Nadler v. FDIC, 899 F. Supp. 158, 161 (S.D.N.Y. 1995), aff'd, 92 F.3d 93 (2d Cir. 1996).

[207] Nadler v. FDIC, 92 F.3d 93, 96 n.1 (2d Cir. 1996).

[208] Frazee v. U.S. Forest Serv., 97 F.3d 367, 372 (9th Cir. 1996) (reverse FOIA suit).

in light of that fact, it "need not address" the Critical Mass distinction.[209]
More recently, the Court of Appeals for the Fourth Circuit declined to "decide which test governs within" that circuit, in a case where it found the
requested information to be properly withheld under Exemption 3 of the
FOIA,[210] which obviated any "need to reach the issue of Exemption 4's applicability."[211]

By contrast, using language that denoted its approval of the Critical
Mass distinction, the Court of Appeals for the Tenth Circuit began its analysis in a case by citing to Critical Mass and then declaring that the "first
step in an Exemption Four analysis is determining whether the information
submitted to the government agency was given voluntarily or involuntarily."[212] As with the earlier decisions in the Second and Ninth Circuits, however, the Tenth Circuit had no opportunity to actually address the application of the standard, because the parties agreed that the submission in
question was in fact "an involuntary one."[213]

In its most recent Exemption 4 decision, the District Court for the
Southern District of New York acknowledged that a portion of the records
in question were "provided voluntarily,"[214] but it nevertheless found that the
issue of the applicability of the Critical Mass analysis "need not be
reached."[215] In so deciding, the court again relied upon the fact that the
Second Circuit had "explicitly held off on determining whether it would accept" Critical Mass.[216] Moreover, it noted that the parties recognized that
the National Parks test applied.[217] Interestingly, the court opined in dicta
that in any event, "the Critical Mass amendment is merely a commonsensi-
cal extrapolation of the first prong of the National Parks test: If a person,
for any reason of substance, would not ordinarily wish a particular type of
information to be disclosed to the public and truly has a choice whether or
not to submit the information to the government, that person will likely

---

[209] Id.

[210] 5 U.S.C. § 552(b)(3) (2000 & Supp. IV 2004).

[211] Wickwire Gavin, P.C. v. USPS, 356 F.3d 588, 597 (4th Cir. 2004).

[212] Utah v. U.S. Dep't of the Interior, 256 F.3d 967, 969 (10th Cir. 2001).

[213] Id.

[214] Inner City Press, 380 F. Supp. 2d at 217-18 (ruling that a "telephonic
request" from an agency was "too amorphous" to be construed as a demand
for the submission of certain information, but that it sufficed "to qualify at
least a portion of the information provided as mandatory").

[215] Id. at 216 n.2.

[216] Id. (citing Nadler, 92 F.3d at 96 n.1).

[217] Id.

choose not to submit such information if the government may disclose it to the public."[218] On appeal, the Court of Appeals for the Second Circuit agreed with the district court that the information at issue on appeal was provided voluntarily.[219] However, it, too, eschewed the opportunity to consider the Critical Mass test on its merits, and instead it pragmatically bypassed Critical Mass on the grounds that the parties did "not argue for its adoption" and the district court "did not apply it in its decision."[220]

Under Critical Mass, once information is determined to be voluntarily provided, it is afforded protection as "confidential" information "if it is of a kind that would customarily not be released to the public by the person from whom it was obtained."[221] The D.C. Circuit observed in Critical Mass that this test was "objective" and that the agency invoking it "must meet the burden of proving the provider's custom."[222] The subsequent cases that have applied this "customary treatment" standard to information found to have been voluntarily submitted typically contain only perfunctory discussions of the showing necessary to satisfy it.[223]

---

[218] Id.

[219] Inner City Press, 463 F.3d at 248 (remarking that the agency's response to the submitter's telephone inquiry appeared to have been "merely informative," and, as the district court found, "'too amorphous'" to be considered a demand" for the disputed information (quoting Inner City Press, 380 F. Supp. 2d at 218)).

[220] Id. at 245 n.6.

[221] 975 F.2d at 879; accord Changzhou Laosan Group v. U.S. Customs & Border Prot. Bureau, 374 F. Supp. 2d 129, 132 (D.D.C. 2005) (reiterating the Critical Mass test and finding that the "current operating status of the submitting party has no effect on whether the information is of the type that would be publicly released").

[222] Id.; see Animal Legal Def. Fund, 44 F. Supp. 2d at 303 (noting that "unless [the agency declarant] would have personal knowledge about [the company's] customary practices, the [agency] will need an affidavit from an officer of [the company] to satisfy this final element of Critical Mass").

[223] See Delta Ltd. v. U.S. Customs & Border Prot. Bureau, 393 F. Supp. 2d 15, 18 (D.D.C. 2005) (finding that certain information was "of the type that would not be normally provided to the public at large," citing submitter's declaration); Judicial Watch, 310 F. Supp. 2d at 308 (remarking that the submitter "has indicated that [the requested documents] are not customarily disclosed to the public"), aff'd in part & rev'd in part on other grounds, 412 F.3d 125 (D.C. Cir. 2005); Cortez, 921 F. Supp. at 13 (noting that the submitter's "unrefuted sworn affidavits attest to the fact that G & A rate ceilings are the type of information that is not regularly disclosed to the public"); Thomas, No. 91-3278, slip op. at 6 (D.D.C. Oct. 7, 1994) (observing that the "uncontradicted affidavits reveal that the information is of a kind
(continued...)

Nevertheless, there are several decisions that contain a more detailed analysis of the standard. Most recently, the evidence that was provided to demonstrate the submitter's customary treatment consisted of a declaration from the submitter that averred that the company considered the documents to be "'proprietary financial information that it [had] never made available to the public,'" and that it had provided them to the agency "only after" receiving assurances that they "would remain confidential."[224] Similarly, the standard was found satisfied by the attestations made by submitters that described the limited distribution within the company on a "need to know" basis and attached as exhibits the confidentiality agreements that were entered into with outside contractors.[225] In another case, the evidence identified by the court to establish customary treatment consisted of a consulting contract, a protective order, and markings on the documents -- which the court deemed "most persuasive."[226] Similarly, the submitter's practice of "carefully guard[ing]" disclosure of the documents "even within the corporate structure," the markings on the documents, and the fact that the company "strenuously, and successfully, opposed their production in discovery in multiple civil cases" was found to establish customary treatment.[227]

---

[223](...continued) that the provider would not normally release to the public"); Minntech, No. 92-2720, slip op. at 8 n.3 (D.D.C. Nov. 17, 1993) (declaring that "[t]he Court accepts HHS's declarations that the type of information provided is not the type that dialysis centers would release to the public"); Gov't Accountability, 1993 WL 13033518, at *5 (opining that it "is not to be doubted" that the documents are "unavailable to the public"); Envtl. Tech., 822 F. Supp. at 1229 (finding that it is "readily apparent that the information is of a kind that [the submitter] would not customarily share with its competitors or with the general public"); Harrison v. Lujan, No. 90-1512, slip op. at 1 (D.D.C. Dec. 8, 1992) (deciding that the agency's "uncontradicted evidence . . . establishes that the documents at issue contain information that the provider would not customarily make available to the public"); Cohen, Dunn, No. 92-0057-A, transcript at 27 (E.D. Va. Sept. 10, 1992) (concluding that pricing information "is of a kind that would customarily not be released to the public by the entity from which it is obtained"); Allnet, 800 F. Supp. at 990 (holding that "it has been amply demonstrated that [the submitters] would not customarily release the information to the public").

[224] Defenders, 314 F. Supp. 2d at 17 (quoting submitter's declaration).

[225] Parker, 141 F. Supp. 2d at 79; see also Airline Pilots Ass'n, 2004 U.S. Dist. LEXIS 26067, at *17 (finding the standard met where the submitter's declaration described how the records at issue were subject to "very limited disclosure within the organization").

[226] AGS, No. 92-2714, slip op. at 11 (D.N.J. Sept. 16, 1993).

[227] McDonnell Douglas, 922 F. Supp. at 242.

In yet another case, the court found the standard satisfied by attestations made in agency affidavits, coupled with a detailed description of the documents that "reveal[ed] that they contain material that would not ordinarily be divulged to the general public."[228] Lastly, a court provided useful elaboration on this issue by specifically noting and then rejecting as "vague hearsay" the requester's contention that there had been "prior, unrestricted disclosure" of the information at issue.[229] In so doing, the court expressly found the requester's evidence to be "nonspecific" and lacking precision "regarding dates and times" of the alleged disclosures; conversely, it noted that the submitter had "provided specific, affirmative evidence that no unrestricted disclosure" had occurred.[230] Accordingly, the court concluded that it had been "amply demonstrated" that the information satisfied the "customary treatment" standard of Critical Mass.[231]

In the course of remanding another case for further proceedings based on the district court's "flawed" application of the "customary treatment" standard,[232] the D.C. Circuit nonetheless addressed several contentions concerning the standard. First, the court flatly rejected "the argument that the mere selling [of] a product on the open market can constitute evidence of customary disclosure."[233] Second, it rejected the argument "that a difference in level of detail is inadequate to establish a difference in type of information," finding instead that "substantial differences in level of

---

[228] Judicial Watch, 306 F. Supp. 2d at 68.

[229] Allnet, 800 F. Supp. at 989.

[230] Id.

[231] Id. at 990. But cf. Atlantis Submarines Haw., Inc. v. U.S. Coast Guard, No. 93-00986, slip op. at 9 (D. Haw. Jan. 28, 1994) (upholding an agency's decision to release a voluntarily submitted safety report that was provided to the agency in an effort to "influence" its "regulatory decisions"; although not expressly ruling on the "customary treatment" standard, finding that "after seeking to have its safety-related material incorporated into the [agency's] decision-making process," the submitter could not then "have the report exempted from public disclosure") (denying motion for preliminary injunction in reverse FOIA suit), dismissed per stipulation (D. Haw. Apr. 11, 1994).

[232] Ctr. for Auto Safety, 244 F.3d at 151-52 (finding that the district court had incorrectly equated the concept requiring release of information when "identical information" is already public, as a matter of exemption waiver, with the "customary treatment" standard, which allows Exemption 4 protection of voluntarily provided information if it "is of a kind" that would customarily not be released to the public").

[233] Id. ("The fact that airbags can be bought on the open market and inspected certainly does not establish that information describing the physical characteristics of every vehicle produced over many years is customarily disclosed.").

detail can produce a difference in type of information."[234] Finally, the D.C. Circuit directed the district court to review the submitters' declarations "and any other relevant responses" that they might supply, thereby endorsing the use of, and reliance upon, submitter declarations to establish customary treatment.[235]

In creating this "customary treatment" standard, the D.C. Circuit in Critical Mass articulated the test as dependent upon the treatment afforded the information by the individual submitter and not the treatment afforded the information by an industry as a whole.[236] This approach has been followed by all the cases applying the "customary treatment" standard thus far, although one court also found it "relevant" that the requester -- who was a member of the same industry as the submitters -- had, "up until the eve of trial," taken the position that the type of information at issue ought not to be released.[237] Further, as applied by the D.C. Circuit in Critical Mass, the "customary treatment" standard allows for some disclosures of the information to have been made, provided that such disclosures were not made to the general public.[238]

---

[234] Id. at 152.

[235] Id. at 153.

[236] 975 F.2d at 872, 878-80; accord Ctr. for Auto Safety, 244 F.3d at 148 (emphasizing that "in assessing customary disclosure, the court will consider how the particular party customarily treats the information, not how the industry as a whole treats the information"); Judicial Watch, 466 F. Supp. 2d at 126 (same); Parker, 141 F. Supp. 2d at 79 & n.8 (explaining that due to individualized nature of "customary treatment" standard, declaration concerning usual treatment by "petroleum industry" was "not probative"); see also FOIA Update, Vol. XIV, No. 2, at 7 (advising agencies applying "customary treatment" standard to examine treatment afforded information by individual submitter).

[237] Cohen, Dunn, No. 92-0057-A, transcript at 27 (E.D. Va. Sept. 10, 1992).

[238] See 975 F.2d at 880 (specifically citing to lower court decision that noted records had been provided to numerous interested parties under nondisclosure agreements, but had not been provided to public-at-large); accord Judicial Watch, 310 F. Supp. 2d at 309 (recognizing that although the requested document "was commissioned as a multiclient study," and the resulting report was "sold for $2,500," because its receipt was conditioned on the signing of "a confidentiality agreement," the report was deemed "not customarily disclosed to the public"); Ctr. for Auto Safety v. Nat'l Highway Traffic Safety Admin., 93 F. Supp. 2d 1, 17-18 (D.D.C. 2000) (emphasizing that "[l]imited disclosures, such as to suppliers or employees, do not preclude protection under Exemption 4, as long as those disclosures are not made to the general public"), remanded, 244 F.3d 144 (D.C. Cir. 2001); see also FOIA Update, Vol. XIV, No. 2, at 7 (advising agencies that

(continued...)

As a matter of sound administrative practice, the Department of Justice has advised agencies to employ procedures analogous to those set forth in Executive Order 12,600[239] when making determinations under the "customary treatment" standard.[240] (For further discussions of this executive order and its requirements, see Exemption 4, Competitive Harm Prong of National Parks, and "Reverse" FOIA, Executive Order 12,600, below.) Accordingly, whenever an agency is uncertain of a submitter's customary treatment of requested information, the submitter should be notified and given an opportunity to provide the agency with a description of its treatment of the information, including any disclosures that are customarily made and the conditions under which such disclosures occur.[241]

## Impairment Prong of National Parks

For information that is "required" to be submitted to an agency, the Court of Appeals for the District of Columbia Circuit has held that the tests for confidentiality originally established in National Parks & Conservation Ass'n v. Morton[242] continue to apply.[243] The first of these tests, the impairment prong, traditionally has been found to be satisfied when an agency demonstrates that the information at issue was provided voluntarily and that submitting entities would not provide such information in the future if

---

[238](...continued)
"customary treatment" standard allows submitter to have made some disclosures of information, provided such disclosures are not "public" ones).

[239] 3 C.F.R. 235.

[240] See FOIA Update, Vol. XIV, No. 2, at 7.

[241] See id.; accord Hull v. U.S. Dep't of Labor, No. 1:04-CV-01264, slip op. at 9-11 (D. Colo. Dec. 2, 2005) (concluding that agency had "failed to meet its burden" where agency's affiant lacked requisite "personal knowledge" about how submitter customarily handled certain documents; conversely, finding that agency had "met its burden" for other information at issue where submitter provided statements "specifically addressing" its customary treatment of such information); N.Y. Pub. Interest Group, 249 F. Supp. 2d at 337 (alternative holding) (finding that in the absence of "personal knowledge" the government had "not met its burden" under Critical Mass and that "without a statement" from the submitter "about its customary practice with regard to these documents, any finding of exemption would be based on agency speculation"); cf. Judicial Watch, Inc. v. U.S. Dep't of Commerce, 337 F. Supp. 2d 146, 171 (D.D.C. 2004) ("While affidavits from the information providers themselves or evidence of confidentiality agreements would carry more weight on the custom issue, it is sufficient for an agency to proceed solely on its sworn affidavits.").

[242] 498 F.2d 765, 770 (D.C. Cir. 1974).

[243] See Critical Mass Energy Project v. NRC, 975 F.2d 871, 880 (D.C. Cir. 1992) (en banc).

it were subject to public disclosure.[244] Conversely, protection under the

---

[244] See, e.g., FlightSafety Servs. v. Dep't of Labor, 326 F.3d 607, 612 (5th Cir. 2003) (per curiam) (protecting raw data reflecting salaries and wages, because disclosure "presents a serious risk that sensitive business information could be attributed to a particular submitting business [and such] attribution would indisputably impair [the agency's] future ability to obtain similar information from businesses [that] provide it under an explicit understanding that such information will be treated confidentially"); O'Harvey v. Comp. Programs Workers, No. 98-35106, 1999 WL 626633, at *1 (9th Cir. Aug. 16, 1999) (protecting information contained in a physician directory service database because disclosure "would impair the government's ability to purchase commercial data in the future" and to "obtain necessary medical information from physicians who would be unlikely to risk the dissemination of distorted data to the general public"); Bowen v. FDA, 925 F.2d 1225, 1228 (9th Cir. 1991) (protecting manufacturing formulas, processes, and quality-control and internal-security measures submitted voluntarily to FDA to assist with cyanide-tampering investigations because agencies relied heavily on such information and would be less likely to obtain it if businesses feared that it would be made public); Inner City Press/ Cmty. on the Move v. Bd. of Governors of the Fed. Reserve Sys., 380 F. Supp. 2d 211, 218 (protecting bank's client lists, loan terms, and similar data included with its merger application, because disclosure "would impair the [agency's] ability to collect such information"), aff'd in pertinent part & remanded on other grounds, 463 F.3d 239 (2d Cir. 2006); Kennedy v. DHS, No. 03-CV-6076, 2004 WL 2285058, at *7 (W.D.N.Y. Oct. 8, 2004) (protecting names and coding of inks provided voluntarily by ink manufacturers, because disclosure "would hinder future government efforts to obtain such information"); Forest Conservation Council v. U.S. Dep't of Labor, No. Civ. 011259, 2003 WL 21687927, at *3 (D.N.M. May 6, 2003) (protecting wage and employment data provided voluntarily by the State of New Mexico in accordance with a cooperative agreement that ensured confidentiality, because the agency's "ability to gather" such information "in the future is at risk"); Parker v. Bureau of Land Mgmt., 141 F. Supp. 2d 71, 81 (D.D.C. 2001) (alternative holding) (protecting detailed market studies relating to proposed pipeline projects because "if agencies seeking assistance from private parties in fulfilling their obligations under NEPA [could not] maintain the confidentiality of proprietary materials that have been submitted to [them], the government's ability to obtain such information would be impaired"); Heeney v. FDA, No. 97-5461, 1999 U.S. Dist. LEXIS 23365, at *31-32 (C.D. Cal. Mar. 18, 1999) (protecting name of withdrawn medical device because, if disclosed, "manufacturers would be loathe to provide" such data in future applications and agency's "ability to carry out its regulatory objectives would be thwarted"), aff'd, 7 F. App'x 770 (9th Cir. 2001); Gilmore v. U.S. Dep't of Energy, 4 F. Supp. 2d 912, 923 (N.D. Cal. 1998) (protecting videoconferencing software provided to an agency as part of a joint venture, as there "can be no doubt that corporations will be less likely to enter into joint ventures with the government to develop technology if that tech-

(continued...)

**EXEMPTION 4**

impairment prong traditionally has been denied when the court determines that disclosure will not, in fact, diminish the flow of information to the agency[245] -- for example, when it determines that the benefits associated with submission of particular information make it unlikely that the agency's ability to obtain future such submissions would be impaired.[246]

---

[244](...continued)
nology can be distributed freely").

[245] See, e.g., PETA v. USDA, No. 03-195, 2005 WL 1241141, at *5-6 (D.D.C. May 24, 2005) (finding no impairment because submission was required by federal regulations); Dow Jones Co. v. FERC, 219 F.R.D. 167, 178-79 (C.D. Cal. 2002) (no impairment based on asserted agreement of confidentiality because such agreements, "standing alone, are insufficient" and claim is undercut in any event because agency itself had previously "threatened [submitters] with disclosure" of very information at issue); Inter Ocean Free Zone, Inc. v. U.S. Customs Serv., 982 F. Supp. 867, 871 n.3 (S.D. Fla. 1997) (no impairment because "there can be no reasonable concern that those who are required by statute to submit [requested data] will risk violating the law"); Ctr. to Prevent Handgun Violence v. U.S. Dep't of the Treasury, 981 F. Supp. 20, 23 (D.D.C. 1997) (same), appeal dismissed, No. 97-5357 (D.C. Cir. Feb. 2, 1998); Pentagon Fed. Credit Union v. Nat'l Credit Union Admin., No. 95-1475-A, slip op. at 4 (E.D. Va. June 7, 1996) (no impairment based on "merely speculative fear" that "disclosure might discourage future responses from credit unions"); Nadler v. FDIC, 899 F. Supp. 158, 161 (S.D.N.Y. 1995) (dicta) (no impairment possible when agency "gained access to [submitter's] information by operation of law when it became receiver"), aff'd on other grounds, 92 F.3d 93 (2d Cir. 1996); Key Bank of Me., Inc. v. SBA, No. 91-362-P, 1992 U.S. Dist. LEXIS 22180, at *11 (D. Me. Dec. 31, 1992) (no impairment based on the speculative assertion that the public disclosure of Dun & Bradstreet reports will adversely affect a company's profits and thus make it "unlikely" that credit agencies will do business with the government; this "intimation regarding impairment of profits in no way speaks to the ability of affected credit agencies to continue to exist and supply needed data"); Wiley Rein & Fielding v. U.S. Dep't of Commerce, 782 F. Supp. 675, 677 (D.D.C. 1992) (no impairment given fact that requested documents contained no "sensitive information" and there was "no reason to believe" that such information would not be provided in future), appeal dismissed as moot, No. 92-5122 (D.C. Cir. Mar. 8, 1993).

[246] See, e.g., Lahr v. NTSB, 453 F. Supp. 2d 1153, 1175 (C.D. Cal. 2006) (no impairment from the release of information pertaining to "'flight characteristics and performance of a Boeing 747'" where the submitter did "not argue" that impairment would be likely, but instead simply "speculate[d] that [in the event of disclosure] it would reconsider its polices of providing information such as this to the government" (quoting submitter's declaration)); N.Y. Pub. Interest Research Group v. EPA, 249 F. Supp. 327, 336-37 (S.D.N.Y. 2003) (no impairment from release of submitter's alternative river-dredging analysis, because submitter "had significant external incen-
(continued...)

-398-

[246](...continued)
tives to provide" it, given that submitter was seeking "to convince" agency
to "abandon, or at least downscale," its own, more costly plan); McDonnell
Douglas Corp. v. U.S. Dep't of the Air Force, 215 F. Supp. 2d 200, 205 & n.3
(D.D.C. 2002) (no impairment from release of contract prices when even
submitter itself "at no point represent[ed] that should" the agency disclose
them, "it would no longer apply for government contracts") (reverse FOIA
suit), aff'd in part & rev'd in part on other grounds, 375 F.3d 1182 (D.C. Cir.
2004), reh'g en banc denied, No. 02-5342 (D.C. Cir. Dec. 16, 2004); Ctr. for
Pub. Integrity v. Dep't of Energy, 191 F. Supp. 2d 187, 196 (D.D.C. 2002) (no
impairment from release of the amounts of unsuccessful bids to buy government land, because "the benefits accruing to bidders from contracting
with the federal government make it unlikely that an agency's future contracting ability will suffer"); McDonnell Douglas Corp. v. NASA, 981 F.
Supp. 12, 15 (D.D.C. 1997) (no impairment from release of contract price
information, because "[g]overnment contracting involves millions of dollars
and it is unlikely that release of this information will cause [agency] difficulty in obtaining future bids") (reverse FOIA suit), rev'd on other grounds,
180 F.3d 303 (D.C. Cir. 1999), reh'g en banc denied, No. 98-5251 (D.C. Cir.
Oct. 6, 1999), dismissed as moot on motion for entry of judgment, 102 F.
Supp. 2d 21 (D.D.C.) (underlying FOIA request withdrawn after D.C. Circuit
issued decision), reconsideration denied, 109 F. Supp. 2d 27 (D.D.C. 2000);
Martin Marietta Corp. v. Dalton, 974 F. Supp. 37, 40 (D.D.C. 1997) (dictum)
(no impairment from release of cost, pricing, and management information
incorporated into a government contract, because contractors "will continue bidding for [agency] contracts despite the risk of revealing business
secrets if the price is right") (reverse FOIA suit); Cohen v. Kessler, No. 95-
6140, slip op. at 12 (D.N.J. Nov. 25, 1996) (no impairment from release of
raw research data submitted in support of an application for approval of a
new animal drug, "in light of the enormous profits that drug manufacturers
reap through product development and improvement"); Bangor Hydro-Elec.
Co. v. U.S. Dep't of the Interior, No. 94-0173-B, slip op. at 9 (D. Me. Apr. 18,
1995) (no impairment from release of financial information, because "it is in
the [submitter's] best interest to continue to supply as much information as
possible" in order to secure better usage charges for its lands); Buffalo
Evening News, Inc. v. SBA, 666 F. Supp. 467, 471 (W.D.N.Y. 1987) (no impairment from release of loan status information, because it is unlikely that
borrowers would decline benefits associated with obtaining loans simply
because status of loan was released); Daniels Mfg. Corp. v. DOD, No. 85-
291, slip op. at 6 (M.D. Fla. June 3, 1986) (no impairment from release of
product testing data when submission "virtually mandatory" if supplier
wished to do business with government); Badhwar v. U.S. Dep't of the Air
Force, 622 F. Supp. 1364, 1377 (D.D.C. 1985) (no impairment from release of
mishap reports when submission is "effectively mandatory" in order to do
business with government), aff'd in part & rev'd in part on other grounds,
829 F.2d 182 (D.C. Cir. 1987); Racal-Milgo Gov't Sys. v. SBA, 559 F. Supp. 4,
6 (D.D.C. 1981) (no impairment from release of contract prices, because "[i]t
(continued...)

## EXEMPTION 4

Under the categorical test announced by the D.C. Circuit in Critical Mass Energy Project v. NRC, the voluntary character of an information submission is sufficient to render it exempt, provided the information would not be customarily released to the public by the submitter.[247] (For a further discussion of this point, see Exemption 4, Applying Critical Mass, above.) In this regard, the D.C. Circuit has made it clear that an agency's unexercised authority, or mere "power to compel" submission of information, does not preclude such information from being provided to the agency "voluntarily."[248] This holding was compatible with several decisions rendered prior to Critical Mass that had protected information under the impairment prong despite the existence of agency authority that could have been used to compel its submission.[249]

---

[246](...continued) is unlikely that companies will stop competing for Government contracts if the prices contracted for are disclosed"). But see Orion Research, Inc. v. EPA, 615 F.2d 551, 554 (1st Cir. 1980) (finding impairment for technical proposals submitted in connection with government contract, because release "would induce potential bidders to submit proposals that do not include novel ideas"); Pentagen Techs. Int'l v. United States, No. 98CIV.4831, 2000 WL 347165, at *2-3 (S.D.N.Y. Mar. 31, 2000) (alternative holding) (finding impairment for "highly proprietary technical solution proposed by IBM" that, if "viewed as being required by the Government in order to full[y] comprehend the IBM bid, . . . would impair the Government's ability to obtain necessary information from bidders in the future" if it were disclosed); RMS, No. C-92-1545, slip op. at 7 (N.D. Cal. Nov. 24, 1992) (finding impairment for equipment descriptions, employee, customer, and subcontractor names submitted in connection with government contract, because "bidders only submit such information if it will not be released to their competitors"); Cohen, Dunn & Sinclair, P.C. v. GSA, No. 92-0057-A, transcript at 29 (E.D. Va. Sept. 10, 1992) (bench order) (finding impairment for detailed unit price information despite lack of "actual proof of a specific bidder being cautious in its bid or holding back").

[247] 975 F.2d at 879.

[248] Id. at 880; accord Parker, 141 F. Supp. 2d at 78 n.6 (noting that "in certain circumstances an agency may decline to require [submission of] information that it has the authority to compel and instead pursue voluntary compliance"); see FOIA Update, Vol. XIV, No. 2, at 5 ("OIP Guidance: The Critical Mass Distinction Under Exemption 4"); see also id. at 6-7 ("Exemption 4 Under Critical Mass: Step-By-Step Decisionmaking").

[249] See, e.g., Pub. Citizen Health Research Group v. FDA, 704 F.2d 1280, 1291 n.29 (D.C. Cir. 1983) (concluding that whether submissions are mandatory is a factor to be considered in an impairment claim, but that factor is "not necessarily dispositive"); Wash. Post Co. v. HHS, 690 F.2d 252, 268-69 (D.C. Cir. 1982). But see Teich v. FDA, 751 F. Supp. 243, 251 (D.D.C. 1990) (declaring that when "compelled cooperation will obtain precisely the same

(continued...)

The Court of Appeals for the Second Circuit likewise has rejected a requester's contention that the "mere legal authority to compel the production of information . . . is sufficient for that submission of information to be deemed mandatory."[250] The adoption of such a standard, it found, would result in an "undesirable general presumption against impairment."[251] The court further reasoned that "[i]f the vast majority of submissions" were "deemed mandatory," which "would seem to be the effective result" of the requester's suggested standard, then there would be "an overwhelming presumption against impairment."[252] This, in the court's view, would "essentially undermine[] Exemption 4's goal of protecting the government's ability to obtain information."[253] The requester, by contrast, offered "little reason for adopting such a broad rule."[254] Additionally, the court found that the adoption of the requester's proposed standard would "interfere[] with the government's discretion as to how to obtain information."[255] Like the D.C. Circuit, the Second Circuit saw "no reason for interfering with" such discretion."[256] Accordingly, it held that an agency "must both possess and exercise the legal authority to obtain information for the resulting submission of information to be deemed 'mandatory' under the National Parks

---

[249](...continued) results as voluntary cooperation, an impairment claim cannot be countenanced") (decided prior to Critical Mass and thus now overtaken by controlling precedent), appeal dismissed voluntarily, No. 91-5023 (D.C. Cir. July 2, 1992); see also Dow Jones, 219 F.R.D. at 178-79 (rejecting an impairment claim, based in part on the fact that the agency "retain[ed] subpoena and investigatory power," so that "even if disclosure [of the requested record] were to cause individuals to decide not to voluntarily disclose information in the future . . . [the agency] would still be able to access the relevant information") (decided after Critical Mass, but by court that declined to apply it).

[250] Inner City Press/Cmty. on the Move v. Bd. of Governors of the Fed. Reserve Sys., 463 F.3d 239, 246 (2d Cir. 2006).

[251] Id. at 246-47 (reiterating that "if a submission is deemed mandatory, then there is a presumption against impairment" (citing Nat'l Parks, 498 F.2d at 770)).

[252] Id. at 247.

[253] Id.

[254] Id.

[255] Id. (explaining that under requester's proposed standard, the agency "would be forced" to assert its authority "to compel information," because if the submitters knew "'that their information was subject to public disclosure, [they] would likely submit the bare minimum required'" (quoting Inner City Press, 380 F. Supp. 2d at 217 n.5)).

[256] Id. (citing Critical Mass, 975 F.2d at 880).

EXEMPTION 4

test."[257]

As a result of the D.C. Circuit's ruling in Critical Mass the significance of the impairment prong is undoubtedly diminished.[258] Nevertheless, the D.C. Circuit recognized that even when agencies require submission of information "there are circumstances in which disclosure could affect the reliability of such data."[259] Thus, after Critical Mass, the impairment prong of National Parks now applies to those more limited situations in which information is required to be provided, but where disclosure of that information under the FOIA will result in a diminution of the "reliability" or "quality" of what is submitted.[260]

---

[257] Id. at 247-48.

[258] See FOIA Update, Vol. XIV, No. 2, at 7.

[259] Critical Mass, 975 F.2d at 878 (citing Wash. Post, 690 F.2d at 268-69); see Goldstein v. HHS, No. 92-2013, slip op. at 5 (S.D. Fla. May 21, 1993) (magistrate's recommendation) (rejecting an argument that the decision in Critical Mass "essentially did away" with the impairment prong, and noting that under that decision "it is appropriate to consider whether or not disclosure of the information would undermine the government's interest in insuring its reliability"), adopted (S.D. Fla. July 21, 1993).

[260] See Critical Mass, 975 F.2d at 878; accord Judicial Watch, Inc. v. Exp.- Imp. Bank, 108 F. Supp. 2d 19, 29 (D.D.C. 2000) (protecting export-insurance applications that contained detailed financial information and customer lists, because "disclosure of such information might encourage exporters to be less forthcoming in their submissions"); Afr. Fund v. Mosbacher, No. 92 CIV. 289, 1993 WL 183736, at *7 (S.D.N.Y. May 26, 1993) (protecting information submitted with export license applications as it "fosters the provision of full and accurate information"); see also Goldstein, No. 92-2013, slip op. at 5, 7 (S.D. Fla. May 21, 1993) (protecting information concerning laboratory's participation in drug-testing program as it furthers agency's ability to continue to receive reliable information). But see Niagara Mohawk Power Corp. v. U.S. Dep't of Energy, 169 F.3d 16, 18 (D.C. Cir. 1999) (rejecting, as "inherently weak," a claim of qualitative impairment when the agency "secured the information under compulsion" and the data itself "appear[] to take the form of hard, cold numbers on energy use and production, the fudging of which may strain all but the deliberately mendacious"); Ctr. to Prevent Handgun Violence, 981 F. Supp. at 23 (rejecting, as "speculative" and unreasonable, agency's claim that accuracy of information required to be reported on multiple sales reports "would be jeopardized by public disclosure"); Pub. Citizen Health Research Group v. FDA, 964 F. Supp. 413, 415 (D.D.C. 1997) (rejecting, as "unsupported, even by an assertion of agency experience on the point," an agency's claim "that data submitted to the agency as part of its drug approval process 'would not be submitted as freely'" if the requested document were disclosed (quoting agency declaration)); Silverberg v. HHS, No. 89-2743, 1991 WL 633740, at
(continued...)

If an agency determines that release will not cause impairment, that decision should be given extraordinary deference by the courts.[261] In this regard there have been a few decisions addressing the feasibility of a submitter raising the issue of impairment on behalf of an agency. In one, the district court ruled that a submitter has "standing" to raise the issue of impairment.[262] Subsequently, however, the Court of Appeals for the Fourth Circuit refused to allow a submitter to make an impairment argument on

---

[260](...continued)
*4 (D.D.C. June 14, 1991) (rejecting, as "entirely speculative," claim of qualitative impairment based on contention that laboratory inspectors -- who work in teams of three and whose own identities are protected -- would fear litigation and thus be less candid if names of laboratories they inspected were released), appeal dismissed per stipulation, No. 91-5255 (D.C. Cir. Sept. 2, 1993); Teich, 751 F. Supp. at 252 (rejecting, as "absurd," a submitter's contention that companies would be less likely to conduct and report safety tests to the FDA for fear of public disclosure, because the companies' own interests in engendering good will and in avoiding product liability suits is sufficient assurance that they will conduct "the most complete testing program" possible).

[261] See, e.g., Gen. Elec. Co. v. NRC, 750 F.2d 1394, 1402 (7th Cir. 1984) (observing that there is not "much room for judicial review of the quintessentially managerial judgment" that disclosure will not cause impairment) (reverse FOIA suit); McDonnell Douglas, 215 F. Supp. 2d at 206 (holding that "[t]he managerial decision about how to best protect the government's interests in gathering information simply does not lend itself easily to judicial review"); McDonnell Douglas, 981 F. Supp. at 15-16 (declaring that "court should defer to the administrative agency's determination that release will not cause impairment"); CC Distribs. v. Kinzinger, No. 94-1330, 1995 WL 405445, at *4 (D.D.C. June 28, 1995) (same) (reverse FOIA suit); Chem. Waste Mgmt., Inc. v. O'Leary, No. 94-2230, 1995 WL 115894, at *4 (D.D.C. Feb. 28, 1995) (same) (reverse FOIA suit); AT&T Info. Sys. v. GSA, 627 F. Supp. 1396, 1401 (D.D.C. 1986) (finding that agency "'is in the best position to determine the effect of disclosure on its ability to obtain necessary technical information'" (quoting Orion, 615 F.2d at 554)) (reverse FOIA suit), rev'd on procedural grounds & remanded, 810 F.2d 1233 (D.C. Cir. 1987); cf. Ctr. for Pub. Integrity, 191 F. Supp. 2d at 196 (explaining that the rationale for showing deference is premised on the fact that "if the agency is willing to release information, it can be safely assumed that the agency is acting to protect" its interests; thus rejecting agency argument that it should be accorded deference when it invokes impairment prong to withhold information). But see Canadian Commercial Corp. v. Dep't of the Air Force, 442 F. Supp. 2d 15, 30 (D.D.C. 2006) (opining that case law does not endorse "blind acceptance of the government's vague and unsupported contentions" that disclosure was unlikely to impair its future interests) (reverse FOIA suit) (appeal pending).

[262] United Techs. Corp. v. HHS, 574 F. Supp. 86, 89 (D. Del. 1983).

the agency's behalf.[263] That appellate court decision was, in turn, subsequently relied on by a lower court which found that because "it is the government's interests that are protected" by the impairment prong, "it follows that it is the government that is best situated to make the determination of whether disclosure would inhibit future submissions."[264] That court reasoned that "it would be nonsense to block disclosure" of information "under the purported rationale of protecting government interests" when the government itself "wants to disclose" it.[265]

In Washington Post Co. v. HHS, the D.C. Circuit held that an agency must demonstrate that a threatened impairment is "significant," because a "minor" impairment is insufficient to overcome the general disclosure mandate of the FOIA.[266] Moreover, in Washington Post the D.C. Circuit held that the factual inquiry concerning the degree of impairment "necessarily involves a rough balancing of the extent of impairment and the importance of the information against the public interest in disclosure."[267] Because the case was remanded for further proceedings, the court found it unnecessary to decide the details of such a balancing test at that time.[268]

Five years later, in the first panel decision in Critical Mass, the D.C. Circuit cited Washington Post to reiterate that a threatened impairment must be significant, but it made no mention whatsoever of a balancing test.[269] The notion of a balancing test was resurrected in a subsequent decision of the D.C. Circuit in the Washington Post case.[270] This time, the D.C. Circuit elaborated on the balancing test -- even suggesting that it

[263] Hercules, Inc. v. Marsh, 839 F.2d 1027, 1030 (4th Cir. 1988); accord McDonnell Douglas, 215 F. Supp. 2d at 206 (holding that "[w]hen an agency makes the decision to disclose information, a party opposing disclosure makes little headway in raising the issue of impairment of information gathering on the agency's behalf").

[264] Comdisco, Inc. v. GSA, 864 F. Supp. 510, 515 (E.D. Va. 1994) (reverse FOIA suit).

[265] Id. at 516; accord McDonnell Douglas, 215 F. Supp. 2d at 206 (disparaging submitter's attempt to raise impairment claim even though agency itself had "determined that its interests [would] not be harmed" by disclosure, as "effectively telling [the agency] that [the submitter] knows better than [the agency] what is in [the agency's] long term interest").

[266] 690 F.2d at 269.

[267] Id.

[268] Id.

[269] 830 F.2d 278, 286 (D.C. Cir. 1987), vacated en banc, 975 F.2d 871 (D.C. Cir. 1992).

[270] 865 F.2d 320, 326-27 (D.C. Cir. 1989).

might apply to all aspects of Exemption 4, not just the impairment prong --
and held that "information will be withheld only when the affirmative interests in disclosure on the one side are outweighed by the factors identified
in National Parks I (and its progeny) militating against disclosure on the
other side."[271] Because the case was remanded once again (and ultimately
was settled), the court did not actually rule on the outcome of such a balancing process.[272]

The district court decision in Critical Mass, on remand from the first
panel decision of the D.C. Circuit, was the first decision to explicitly apply
a balancing test under the impairment prong of Exemption 4.[273] (Other decisions have utilized or made reference to a balancing test in ruling under
the competitive harm prong. For a further discussion of this point, see Exemption 4, Competitive Harm Prong of National Parks, below.) In Critical
Mass, the district court held that a consumer organization requesting information bearing upon the safety of nuclear power plants had "no particularized need of its own" for access to the information and thus was "remit-
ted to the general public interest in disclosure for disclosure's sake to support its request."[274] Although the court conceded that the public has an interest "of significantly greater moment than idle curiosity" in information
concerning the safety of nuclear power plants, that same interest was
shared by the NRC and the submitter of the information and their interest
in preventing disclosure was deemed to be of "a much more immediate and
direct nature."[275] Curiously, when this decision in Critical Mass was subsequently reviewed by both a second panel of the D.C. Circuit and then by

---

[271] Id. at 327.

[272] Id. at 328.

[273] 731 F. Supp. 554, 555-56 (D.D.C. 1990), rev'd in part on other grounds
& remanded, 931 F.2d 939 (D.C. Cir.), vacated & reh'g en banc granted, 942
F.2d 799 (D.C. Cir. 1991), grant of summary judgment to agency aff'd en
banc, 975 F.2d 871 (D.C. Cir. 1992); see also Pentagon Fed. Credit Union v.
Nat'l Credit Union Admin., No. 95-1475-A, slip op. at 4 (E.D. Va. June 7,
1996) (rejecting agency's impairment claim as "merely speculative," and in
so doing both referencing requester's citation to Washington Post balancing test and noting requester's assertion of "public interest" in disclosure of
documents).

[274] 731 F. Supp. at 556.

[275] Id.; see Gilmore, 4 F. Supp. 2d at 922-23 (declaring, for FOIA exemptions generally, that the court "must balance the public interest in disclosure against the interest Congress intended the exemption to protect" and,
upon determining that the requested video conferencing software fell within protection of both prongs of Exemption 4, the court balanced in favor of
protection, finding "no countervailing public interest" in disclosure of the
software inasmuch as it "sheds no light whatsoever on [agency's] performance of its duties").

the entire D.C. Circuit sitting en banc, no mention was made of any balancing test under Exemption 4.[276]

This issue appears to have been finally resolved by the D.C. Circuit in its decision in Public Citizen Health Research Group v. FDA.[277] There, the D.C. Circuit squarely rejected "a consequentialist approach to the public interest in disclosure" as "inconsistent with the '[b]alanc[e of] private and public interests' th[at] Congress struck in Exemption 4."[278] The court went on to state that "[t]hat balance is accurately reflected in the test of confidentiality" established by National Parks and that a requester cannot "bolster the case for disclosure by claiming an additional public benefit" in release.[279] "In other words," the D.C. Circuit declared, "the public interest side of the balance is not a function of the identity of the requester, . . . or of any potential negative consequences disclosure may have for the public, . . . nor likewise of any collateral benefits of disclosure."[280]

### Competitive Harm Prong of National Parks

The great majority of Exemption 4 cases have involved the competitive harm prong of the test for confidentiality established in National Parks & Conservation Ass'n v. Morton.[281] Information is "confidential" under this prong if disclosure "is likely . . . to cause substantial harm to the competitive position of the person from whom the information was obtained."[282] The Court of Appeals for the District of Columbia Circuit has "empha-

---

[276] 931 F.2d 939, 945-47 (D.C. Cir.), vacated & reh'g en banc granted, 942 F.2d 799 (D.C. Cir. 1991), grant of summary judgment to agency aff'd en banc, 975 F.2d 871 (D.C. Cir. 1992).

[277] 185 F.3d 898, 904 (D.C. Cir. 1999) (ruling under competitive harm prong, but applying rationale applicable to all prongs of Exemption 4).

[278] Id.

[279] Id.

[280] Id. (holding that "Congress has already determined the relevant public interest" by requiring disclosure of information under the FOIA unless it falls within "a specific exemption"); accord Lahr, 453 F. Supp. 2d at 1176 (rejecting the plaintiff's argument that "for any record falling under Exemption 4, the Court must apply a balancing test between the public interest in disclosure and the private interests protected by the exemption," and holding instead that the "only test" that it may apply "is that found in National Parks" (citing Pub. Citizen, 185 F.2d at 904)); Utah v. U.S. Dep't of the Interior, No. 2:98 CV 380, slip op. at 7 (D. Utah Nov. 3, 1999) (holding that "there is no balancing in applying Exemption 4 beyond the balancing that is inherent in the exemption itself").

[281] 498 F.2d 765, 770 (D.C. Cir. 1974).

[282] Id.

size[d]" that the "'important point for competitive harm in the FOIA context
. . . is that it be limited to harm flowing from the affirmative use of proprietary information by competitors'" and that this "'should not be taken to
mean simply any injury to competitive position, as might flow from customer or employee disgruntlement.'"[283]

In order for an agency to make a determination under this prong it is
essential that the submitter of the requested information be given an opportunity to provide the agency with its views on the possible competitive
harm that would be caused by disclosure. While such an opportunity had
long been voluntarily afforded submitters by several agencies and had
been recommended by the Department of Justice,[284] since 1987 it has been
expressly required by executive order.

Executive Order 12,600[285] requires, with certain limited exceptions,[286]
that agencies provide notification to submitters of confidential commercial

---

[283] Pub. Citizen Health Research Group v. FDA, 704 F.2d 1280, 1291 n.30
(D.C. Cir. 1983) (quoting Mark Q. Connelly, Secrets and Smokescreens: A
Legal and Economic Analysis of Government Disclosures of Business Data,
1981 Wis. L. Rev. 207, 235-36); accord CNA Fin. Corp. v. Donovan, 830 F.2d
1132, 1152 & n.158 (D.C. Cir. 1987) (reiterating "policy behind Exemption 4
of protecting submitters from external injury" and rejecting submitter objections that did "not amount to 'harm flowing from the affirmative use of
proprietary information by competitors'" (quoting Pub. Citizen, 704 F.2d at
1291 n.30)) (reverse FOIA suit). But see McDonnell Douglas Corp. v. NASA,
180 F.3d 303, 306-07 (D.C. Cir. 1999) (accepting as legally valid -- without
any reference to D.C. Circuit precedent to the contrary -- submitter's claim
that disclosure of government contract prices would cause submitter harm
by permitting its "commercial customers to bargain down ('ratchet down')
its prices more effectively") (reverse FOIA suit), reh'g en banc denied, No.
98-5251, slip op. at 2 (D.C. Cir. Oct. 6, 1999) (Silberman, J., concurring)
(attempting to explain the panel's acceptance of the submitter's claim by
opining that "[o]ther than in a monopoly situation anything that undermines a supplier's relationship with its customers must necessarily aid its
competitors"), dismissed as moot on motion for entry of judgment, 102 F.
Supp. 2d 21 (D.D.C.) (underlying FOIA request withdrawn after D.C. Circuit
issued decision), reconsideration denied, 109 F. Supp. 2d 27 (D.D.C. 2000).

[284] See FOIA Update, Vol. III, No. 3, at 3 (guidance issued in 1982 detailing steps that agencies should follow to notify submitters when their information is requested under the FOIA).

[285] 3 C.F.R. 235 (1988), reprinted in 5 U.S.C. § 552 note (2000), and in
FOIA Update, Vol. VIII, No. 2, at 2-3.

[286] See Exec. Order No. 12,600, § 8 (listing six circumstances in which
notice is not necessary -- for example, when agency determines that requested information should be withheld, or conversely, when it already is
public or its release is required by law).

information whenever an agency "determines that it may be required to disclose" such information under the FOIA.[287] Once submitters are notified, they must be given a "reasonable period of time" within which to object to disclosure of any of the requested information.[288] The executive order requires that agencies give careful consideration to the submitters' objections and provide them with a written statement explaining why any such objections are not sustained.[289] (For a further discussion of these procedures, see "Reverse" FOIA, Executive Order 12,600, below.)

As one court aptly emphasized, consultation with a submitter is "appropriate as one step in the evaluation process, [but it] is not sufficient to satisfy [an agency's] FOIA obligations."[290] Consequently, an agency is "required to determine for itself whether the information in question should be disclosed."[291] Indeed, when a submitter itself provided the requester with a copy of the requested document -- containing redactions made by the submitter, not by the agency -- the District Court for the District of Columbia held that the submitter's action "[did] not relieve" the agency of the obligation to make "an independent determination" as to the applicability of Exemption 4.[292] Without such an "independent assessment" by the agency "regarding the scope of [the submitter's] redactions," the court found that it could not properly make an Exemption 4 determination.[293]

---

[287] Exec. Order No. 12,600, § 1; cf. Venetian Casino Resort v. EEOC, No. 00-2890, 2006 WL 2806568, at *2, *5 (D.D.C. Sept. 29, 2006) (finding that in absence of FOIA request for submitter's information, Executive Order 12,600 had no applicability to action challenging agency's policy by which "it releases documents identified by submitting party as containing trade secrets and/or confidential information") (non-FOIA case). See generally OSHA Data/CIH, Inc. v. U.S. Dep't of Labor, 220 F.3d 153, 168 (3d Cir. 2000) (concluding that estimated $1.7 million costs for notifying more than 80,000 submitters was properly charged to FOIA requester seeking documents for commercial use).

[288] Exec. Order No. 12,600, § 4.

[289] Id. § 5.

[290] Lee v. FDIC, 923 F. Supp. 451, 455 (S.D.N.Y. 1996).

[291] Id.; accord Exec. Order No. 12,600, § 5 (notification procedures specifically contemplate that agency makes ultimate determination concerning release); see also Nat'l Parks, 498 F.2d at 767 (concluding that in justifying nondisclosure, the submitter's treatment of information is not "the only relevant inquiry"; rather, the agency must also be satisfied that the harms underlying the exemption are likely to occur).

[292] Nw. Coal. for Alternatives to Pesticides v. EPA, 254 F. Supp. 2d 125, 131 (D.D.C. 2003).

[293] Id. at 132, 134 (remanding case to agency for appropriate explanation
(continued...)

If an agency decides to invoke Exemption 4 and that decision is subsequently challenged in court by a FOIA requester, the submitter's objections to disclosure -- usually provided in an affidavit filed in conjunction with the agency's court papers, but sometimes provided separately if the submitter intervenes as a party in the lawsuit[294] -- will, in turn, be evaluated and relied upon by the court in determining the propriety of the exemption claim.[295] Courts have repeatedly rejected competitive harm claims

---

[293](...continued)
of agency's position). But see Anderson v. HHS, 907 F.2d 936, 940 (10th Cir. 1990) (accepting, without comment, the existing posture of the case in which the submitter had "intervened and [had] defended the action on behalf of the FDA").

[294] See, e.g., Pub. Citizen Health Research Group v. FDA, 185 F.3d 898, 900 (D.C. Cir. 1999) (noting that submitter had intervened in case); Appleton v. FDA, 310 F. Supp. 2d 194, 196-97 (D.D.C. 2004) (permitting submitters to intervene "as of right").

[295] See, e.g., Madison Mech., Inc. v. NASA, No. 99-2854, 2003 WL 1477014, at *5 (D.D.C. Mar. 20, 2003) (magistrate's recommendation) (grappling with the fact that the submitter "[m]ysteriously . . . merely submitted a brief letter stating that the information was deemed to be confidential business information," which, when coupled with the "conclusory statements" provided by the agency, compelled a finding "that there is nothing in the record" to support judgment for either party, and so recommending "an evidentiary hearing"), adopted, No. 99-2854, slip op. at 1 (D.D.C. Mar. 31, 2003) (denying both parties' cross-motions for summary judgment without prejudice "to further proceedings before" magistrate), removed from active calendar (D.D.C. Nov. 25, 2003); Pub. Citizen Health Research Group v. NIH, 209 F. Supp. 2d 37, 50 (D.D.C. 2002) (alternative holding) (finding -- when the agency sent notices to nearly five hundred submitters and fewer than two hundred responded -- that the "evidence of those who did respond was overwhelmingly against disclosure, which tips the scales heavily toward a conclusion that release of the information would likely cause substantial competitive injury"); Pub. Citizen Health Research Group v. FDA, 997 F. Supp. 56, 64 n.4 (D.D.C. 1998) (noting with approval submitter's "recognition that some of the requested documents may be safely released" and considering it "evidence that their claims of exemption . . . are grounded in good faith -- that the company is not reflexively resisting every request for disclosure"), aff'd in part, rev'd in part & remanded, 185 F.3d 898 (D.C. Cir. 1999); Teich v. FDA, 751 F. Supp. 243, 254 (D.D.C. 1990) (striking original declaration of submitter "on basic fairness grounds," and then finding submitter "not . . . able to support its position"), appeal dismissed voluntarily, No. 91-5023 (D.C. Cir. July 2, 1992); see also Durnan v. U.S. Dep't of Commerce, 777 F. Supp. 965, 967 (D.D.C. 1991) (rejecting challenge to agency's reliance on submitter's declaration, finding it entirely "relevant" to competitive harm determination); cf. Silverberg v. HHS, No. 89-2743, 1990 WL 599452, at *1 (D.D.C. June 26, 1990) (when only some submitters made

(continued...)

-- and even have ordered disclosure -- when those claims were advanced by agencies on their own.[296] The Court of Appeals for the Ninth Circuit upheld a competitive harm determination that was justified solely by an agency declarant, but in doing so it emphasized that this particular agency declarant was "'very familiar'" with the industry at issue and that he had experience that "put him in 'almost daily contact' with" it, all of which was found to lend "considerable weight to his testimony."[297] "More importantly," the Ninth Circuit emphasized, in that case the agency declarant had supported his conclusions with "detailed and specific descriptions" of the withheld information, including "the ways in which each category of informa-

---

[295](...continued) objections to disclosure, court permitted requester to obtain copies of those objections through discovery in order to enable him to substantiate his claim that not all submitters were entitled to Exemption 4 protection) (discovery order).

[296] See, e.g., N.C. Network for Animals v. USDA, No. 90-1443, slip op. at 8-9 (4th Cir. Feb. 5, 1991) (finding "evidence presented by" agency "insufficient to support" its burden, remanding case, and noting absence of sworn affidavits or detailed justification for withholding from submitters); Newry Ltd. v. U.S. Customs & Border Prot. Bureau, No. 04-02110, 2005 WL 3273975, at *4 & n.8 (D.D.C. July 29, 2005) (rejecting competitive harm argument advanced solely by agency), reconsideration granted (D.D.C. Mar. 30, 2006) (upholding competitive harm argument following agency's submission of supplemental declarations, including one from submitter); Pentagon Fed. Credit Union v. Nat'l Credit Union Admin., No. 95-1475-A, slip op. at 4-5 (E.D. Va. June 7, 1996) (rejecting competitive harm argument, noting failure of agency even to give notice to submitters who, in turn, ultimately provided sworn declarations to requester explicitly stating that disclosure would not cause them harm); Wiley Rein & Fielding v. U.S. Dep't of Commerce, 782 F. Supp. 675, 676 (D.D.C. 1992) (rejecting competitive harm argument, ordering disclosure, and emphasizing that "no evidence" was provided to indicate that submitters objected to disclosure), appeal dismissed as moot, No. 92-5122 (D.C. Cir. Mar. 8, 1993); Brown v. Dep't of Labor, No. 89-1220, 1991 U.S. Dist. LEXIS 1780, at *7 (D.D.C. Feb. 15, 1991) (denying competitive harm claim, ordering disclosure, and noting failure of submitters to object to disclosure), appeal dismissed, No. 91-5108 (D.C. Cir. Dec. 3, 1991); Black Hills Alliance v. U.S. Forest Serv., 603 F. Supp. 117, 121 (D.S.D. 1984) (finding agency affidavits inadequate, ordering disclosure, and noting that "[i]t is significant that [the submitter] itself has not submitted an affidavit addressing" issue of competitive harm); cf. N.Y. Pub. Interest Research Group v. EPA, 249 F. Supp. 2d 327, 330 (S.D.N.Y. 2003) (rejecting an agency's assertion that disclosure would impair its ability to obtain similar information in the future, ordering disclosure, and noting that the submitter had not provided "any affidavits or taken a position" on the documents at issue).

[297] Lion Raisins Inc. v. USDA, 354 F.3d 1072, 1080 (9th Cir. 2004) (quoting agency declaration).

tion could be turned to [the requester's] competitive advantage."[298]

The courts have tended to resolve issues of competitive harm on a case-by-case basis rather than by establishing general guidelines. For example, in some contexts customer names have been withheld because disclosure would cause substantial competitive harm[299] and in other contexts customer names have been ordered released because disclosure would not cause substantial competitive harm.[300] Similarly, in one case the table of contents and introductions to certain documents were withheld because the court found that their disclosure would "provide valuable descriptions of proprietary information,"[301] but in another case the court upheld an agency's decision to release a table of contents and other summary information because they revealed "only an outline" of the submitter's "operations and capabilities" and were "devoid of the detail which would be of value" to competitors.[302] The individualized and sometimes conflicting determinations indicative of competitive harm holdings is well illustrated in one case in which the D.C. Circuit originally affirmed a district court's decision which found that customer names of "CAT" scanner manufacturers were protected,[303] but subsequently vacated that decision upon the death of one of its judges.[304] On reconsideration, the newly constituted panel found that disclosure of the customer list raised a factual question as to the showing of competitive harm that precluded the granting of summary judgment after all.[305]

Factual disputes concerning the likelihood that disclosure of requested information would cause competitive harm precluded a ruling on summary judgment motions in two cases decided a decade ago by the District

---

[298] Id.

[299] See, e.g., RMS Indus. v. DOD, No. C-92-1545, slip op. at 7 (N.D. Cal. Nov. 24, 1992); Goldstein v. ICC, No. 82-1511, 1984 WL 3228, at *6-7 (D.D.C. July 31, 1985) (reopening case and protecting customer names); BDM Corp. v. SBA, 2 Gov't Disclosure Serv. (P-H) ¶ 81,044, at 81,120 (D.D.C. Dec. 4, 1980).

[300] See, e.g., Ivanhoe Citrus Ass'n v. Handley, 612 F. Supp. 1560, 1566 (D.D.C. 1985); Braintree Elec. Light Dep't v. Dep't of Energy, 494 F. Supp. 287, 290 (D.D.C. 1980).

[301] Allnet Commc'n Servs. v. FCC, No. 92-5351, slip op. at 5 (D.C. Cir. May 27, 1994).

[302] Dynalectron Corp. v. Dep't of the Air Force, No. 83-3399, 1984 WL 3289, at *5 (D.D.C. Oct. 30, 1984) (reverse FOIA suit).

[303] Greenberg v. FDA, 775 F.2d 1169, 1172-73 (D.C. Cir. 1985).

[304] Greenberg v. FDA, 803 F.2d 1213, 1215 (D.C. Cir. 1986).

[305] Id. at 1219.

Court for the District of Columbia.[306] In the first case, after reviewing the "claims made by the experts" for both parties, the court concluded that because the claims were "contradictory," summary judgment was "an inappropriate vehicle" for resolution of the case, and the court instead scheduled a bench trial.[307] (The case ultimately was settled, however, and no trial took place.[308]) In the second case, the court found that the record did "not present a clear picture as to the competitive injury, if any, that would result from releasing" the requested document -- a protocol (an outline of objectives and hypotheses) for a post-marketing study of a pharmaceutical drug.[309] Rather than proceeding to a trial, the court in that case ordered that the document and a memorandum supporting its withholding be submitted to the court in camera.[310] Thereafter, at the court's suggestion,[311] the document was also reviewed by "two experts identified by the parties and appointed by the court."[312] The experts then concluded, and the court agreed, that no competitive harm would "flow from the release" of the document, and disclosure was ordered.[313]

---

[306] Pub. Citizen Health Research Group v. FDA, 964 F. Supp. 413, 416 (D.D.C. 1997), review by expert witness suggested, No. 96-1650 (D.D.C. Mar. 18, 1997), summary judgment denied & document ordered released (D.D.C. Nov. 3, 1997); Pub. Citizen Health Research Group v. FDA, 953 F. Supp. 400, 402-03 (D.D.C. 1996), dismissed per stipulation, No. 94-0169, slip op. at 1 (D.D.C. Feb. 3, 1997); see also Madison, 2003 WL 1477014, at *5 (recommending the denial of both parties' summary judgment motions and the convening of an "evidentiary hearing" upon a finding that "there is nothing in the record which would allow any reasonable finder of fact to conclude in either party's favor") (case ultimately removed from active calendar).

[307] Pub. Citizen, 953 F. Supp. at 403.

[308] Pub. Citizen Health Research Group v. FDA, No. 94-0169, slip op. at 1 (D.D.C. Feb. 3, 1997) (agency agreed to release requested information as part of settlement).

[309] Pub. Citizen, 964 F. Supp. at 416.

[310] Id.

[311] See Pub. Citizen Health Research Group v. FDA, No. 96-1650, slip op. at 2 (D.D.C. Mar. 18, 1997) (concluding that an in camera submission had "disabled" the normal "adversary process," and so directing the parties to recommend candidates for appointment as expert witnesses who, under a protective order, could review material "and offer an opinion" as to the likelihood of competitive harm).

[312] Pub. Citizen Health Research Group v. FDA, No. 96-1650, slip op. at 1 (D.D.C. Nov. 3, 1997).

[313] Id. at 1-2.

Actual competitive harm need not be demonstrated for purposes of the competitive harm prong; rather, evidence of "actual competition and a likelihood of substantial competitive injury" is all that need be shown.[314] Although the requirement that a submitter face "actual competition" usually is readily satisfied,[315] the D.C. Circuit remanded a decision for further proceedings concerning the existence of "actual competition" and, in doing so, suggested that "a competitive injury is too remote for purposes of Exemption 4 if it can occur only in the occasional renegotiation of long-term contracts."[316]

---

[314] CNA, 830 F.2d at 1152 ; accord Frazee v. U.S. Forest Serv., 97 F.3d 367, 371 (9th Cir. 1996) (reverse FOIA suit); GC Micro Corp. v. Def. Logistics Agency, 33 F.3d 1109, 1113 (9th Cir. 1994); Gulf & W. Indus. v. United States, 615 F.2d 527, 530 (D.C. Cir. 1979); see, e.g., Judicial Watch v. U.S. Dep't of Commerce, 337 F. Supp. 2d 146, 169 (D.D.C. 2004) (rejecting plaintiff's contention that agency was required to submit "concrete evidence of specific harm," and finding instead that substantial harm need be only "'likely'" (quoting Nat'l Parks, 498 F.2d at 770)); NBC v. SBA, 836 F. Supp. 121, 124 n.3 (S.D.N.Y. 1993) (noting that agency "should have provided more details" regarding possible competitive harm, but ruling nonetheless that generalized sworn declaration from submitter was sufficient); Journal of Commerce, Inc. v. U.S. Dep't of the Treasury, No. 86-1075, 1987 WL 4922, at *2 (D.D.C. June 1, 1987) (holding that submitter was not required to document or pinpoint actual harm, but need only show its likelihood) (partial grant of summary judgment), renewed motion for summary judgment granted, No. 86-1075, 1998 U.S. Dist. LEXIS 17610 (D.D.C. Mar. 30, 1988), aff'd, 878 F.2d 1446 (Fed. Cir. 1989) (unpublished table decision); HLI Lordship Indus. v. Comm. for Purchase from the Blind & Other Severely Handicapped, 663 F. Supp. 246, 251 (E.D. Va. 1987) (concluding that competitive harm was likely, based upon fact that requester, who was a competitor of the submitter, had requested confidential treatment for its own similar submission).

[315] See, e.g., Lion Raisins, 354 F.3d at 1076, 1080 (characterizing the raisin industry as "highly competitive," and noting that "[t]he parties agree that there is actual competition in the relevant market"); PETA v. USDA, No. 03-195, 2005 WL 1241141, at *5-6 (D.D.C. May 24, 2005) (rejecting requester's argument that submitter's declaration was "too generic to show actual competition," when declaration listed number of competitors and described nature of competition but did not identify competitors by name); Pub. Citizen, 209 F. Supp. 2d at 47 (recognizing that the "pharmaceutical industry is a highly competitive market where companies routinely attempt to discover a possible advantage over their competitors"); Utah v. U.S. Dep't of the Interior, No. 2:98 CV 380, slip op. at 4-5 (D. Utah Nov. 3, 1999) (rejecting requester's argument that submitter had "no viable competitors," and finding that agency had "met its burden of justification" on that issue).

[316] Niagara Mohawk Power Corp. v. U.S. Dep't of Energy, 169 F.3d 16, 18 (D.C. Cir. 1999); see also Hercules, Inc. v. Marsh, 659 F. Supp. 849, 854

(continued...)

In this regard, a submitter's "admittedly weakened financial position" has been held "not [to] amount to a complete inability to suffer competitive harm," inasmuch as a "struggling, perhaps even failing, business remains entitled to the protections that Exemption Four affords to any company."[317] Moreover, it should be noted that the District Court for the Southern District of New York has held that the potential for competitive injury generally is measured "without regard to the total size or composition of the business whose competitive interests are at stake," but rather "in respect to the relevant market."[318]

In applying the competitive harm prong, one court has gone so far as to order disclosure based upon a "balancing test." Although it never expressly referred to it as such or cited to any supporting authority, this court found that disclosure of certain safety and effectiveness data pertaining to a medical device was "unquestionably in the public interest" and that the benefit of releasing this type of information "far outstrips the negligible competitive harm" alleged by the submitter.[319] In contrast, another court

---

[316](...continued)
(W.D. Va. 1987) (given fact that contract always awarded to submitter, protection under competitive harm prong unavailable as submitter failed to meet "threshold requirement" of facing competition) (reverse FOIA suit), aff'd, 839 F.2d 1027 (4th Cir. 1988).

[317] Inter Ocean Free Zone, Inc. v. U.S. Customs Serv., 982 F. Supp. 867, 872 (S.D. Fla. 1997); accord Nadler v. FDIC, 899 F. Supp. 158, 164 (S.D.N.Y. 1995) (determining that company in receivership was entitled to Exemption 4 protection), aff'd, 92 F.3d 93 (2d Cir. 1996); see also Changzhou Laosan Group v. U.S. Customs & Border Prot. Bureau, 374 F. Supp. 2d 129, 132 & n.3 (D.D.C. 2005) (noting in dicta that "it is not apparent that the operating status" of a company no longer in business "would be dispositive" in adjudicating the competitive harm issue).

[318] Inner City Press/Cmty. on the Move v. Bd. of Governors of the Fed. Reserve Sys., 380 F. Supp. 2d 211, 219-20 (S.D.N.Y. 2005) (finding that the competitive injury to "a small subset" of the submitter's business would be "substantial," notwithstanding the submitter's total assets worth approximately 418 billion dollars), aff'd in part & remanded in part on other grounds, 463 F.3d 239 (2d Cir. 2006); cf. Lion Raisins, 354 F.3d at 1079 (requiring a showing of actual competition "in the relevant market").

[319] Teich, 751 F. Supp. at 253; see also Pub. Citizen, 964 F. Supp. at 415 (citing Teich and stating that "an additional factor that may be considered is whether there is a strong public interest in release of the information") (insufficient record precluded court from actually ruling on claim of competitive harm and in camera inspection ordered). But cf. Citizens Comm'n on Human Rights v. FDA, No. 92-5313, 1993 WL 1610471, at *9 (C.D. Cal. May 10, 1993) (finding competitive harm and thus protecting research data used to support safety and effectiveness of pharmaceutical drug), aff'd in
(continued...)

employed a balancing test under Exemption 4, but that court balanced in favor of protection -- under both the impairment and competitive harm prongs -- declaring that "there is no countervailing public interest in disclosure [of the requested video conferencing software] because [the software] sheds no light whatsoever on [the agency's] performance of its duties."[320]

The Court of Appeals for the Ninth Circuit has cited to National Parks and then declared that it "agree[d] with the D.C. Circuit" that in making an Exemption 4 determination it "must balance the strong public interest in favor of disclosure against the right of private businesses to protect sensitive information."[321] Although the Ninth Circuit thus used the term "balance," it did so in the context of holding that the agency had entirely failed to meet its burden of showing that disclosure of the very general information at issue was likely to cause "any potential for competitive harm, let alone substantial harm," and as a result, the court stated, rather colloquially, that the "FOIA's strong presumption in favor of disclosure trumps the contractors' right to privacy."[322]

As discussed earlier, the D.C. Circuit appears to have dispositively resolved this issue in Public Citizen Health Research Group v. FDA, where it flatly rejected a requester's proposal that the court "should gauge whether the competitive harm done to the sponsor of an [Investigational New Drug] by the public disclosure of confidential information 'is outweighed by the strong public interest in safeguarding the health of human trial partici-

---

[319](...continued)
part & remanded in part on other grounds, 45 F.3d 1325 (9th Cir. 1995).

[320] Gilmore v. U.S. Dep't of Energy, 4 F. Supp. 2d 912, 923 (N.D. Cal. 1998); cf. Trans-Pac. Policing Agreement v. U.S. Customs Serv., No. 97-2188, 1998 U.S. Dist. LEXIS 7800, at *14 (D.D.C. May 14, 1998) (concluding, without actually using the word "balancing," that the agency's "proper application of Exemption 4 in this case does not offend the purposes of the FOIA"), rev'd & remanded for segregability determination, 177 F.3d 1022 (D.C. Cir. 1999).

[321] GC Micro, 33 F.3d at 1115.

[322] Id.; Garren v. U.S. Dep't of the Interior, No. CV-97-273, slip op. at 13 n.11 (D. Or. Nov. 17, 1997) (magistrate's recommendation) (referring to GC Micro and questioning "nature" of public interest to be considered in Exemption 4 cases, but declining to resolve that issue inasmuch as requested information was outside Exemption 4's protection), adopted (D. Or. Jan. 8, 1998); cf. Martin Marietta Corp. v. Dalton, 974 F. Supp. 37, 41 (D.D.C. 1997) (in context of holding that submitter had failed to demonstrate that it would suffer competitive harm from release of information incorporated into government contract, court notes importance of opening government procurement process to public scrutiny) (reverse FOIA suit).

pants."[323] Declaring that a requester cannot "bolster the case for disclosure by claiming an additional public benefit" in release, the D.C. Circuit held that Congress has already struck the appropriate balance between public and private interests and that "[t]hat balance is accurately reflected in the test of confidentiality set forth in National Parks."[324] (For a further discussion of this point, see Exemption 4, Impairment Prong of National Parks, above.) Despite this firm ruling by the D.C. Circuit, the Court of Appeals for the Tenth Circuit, without making any reference to the D.C. Circuit decision or its reasoning, observed that a requester had made a "strong public policy argument in favor of a 'rough balancing of interests' test under Exemption Four."[325] The court went on to agree with the requester that "the public interest in disclosure of information regarding the handling, storage, and disposal of dangerous materials such as spent nuclear fuel is high."[326] However, because the competitive harm from disclosure was "overwhelming" in that case, the court concluded that it "need not reach the issue of whether a balancing test is appropriate under Exemption Four."[327]

In assessing whether a submitter would suffer competitive harm, courts have held that "elaborate antitrust proceedings" are not required.[328]

---

[323] 185 F.3d at 903 (quoting requester's brief).

[324] Id. at 904; accord Lahr v. NTSB, 453 F. Supp. 2d 1153, 1176 (C.D. Cal. 2006) (rejecting the plaintiff's argument that "for any record falling under Exemption 4, the Court must apply a balancing test between the public interest in disclosure and the private interests protected by the exemption," and holding instead that the "only test" that it may apply "is that found in National Parks" (citing Pub. Citizen, 185 F.2d at 904)); Utah, No. 2:98 CV 380, slip op. at 7 (D. Utah Nov. 3, 1999) (holding that "there is no balancing in applying Exemption 4 beyond the balancing that is inherent in the exemption itself"); see also Pub. Citizen, 209 F. Supp. 2d at 45-51 (relying on D.C. Circuit's decision in Public Citizen, court uses phrase "rough balancing," but actually conducts disclosure analysis focused solely on harms recognized under Exemption 4); cf. NARA v. Favish, 541 U.S. 157, 172 (observing that under the FOIA's exemption scheme "the general interest in disclosure" is balanced in only "certain areas defined in the exemptions") (emphasis added) (Exemption 7(C) case), reh'g denied, 541 U.S. 1057 (2004).

[325] Utah v. U.S. Dep't of the Interior, 256 F.3d 967, 971 (10th Cir. 2001) (quoting Wash. Post Co. v. HHS, 865 F.2d 320, 326-28 (D.C. Cir. 1989) (decided a full ten years prior to the clarifying D.C. Circuit decision in Public Citizen and thus effectively overruled by that controlling precedent)).

[326] Id.

[327] Id.

[328] Nat'l Parks & Conservation Ass'n v. Kleppe, 547 F.2d 673, 681 (D.C. Cir. 1976); accord GC Micro, 33 F.3d at 1115 ("law does not require [agency] (continued...)

On the other hand, mere conclusory allegations of harm are unacceptable.[329] For example, the Ninth Circuit reversed a competitive harm determination made by the lower court which had protected, on a standard government form, the "percentage and dollar amount of work subcontracted out" to small disadvantaged businesses.[330] In so deciding, the Ninth Circuit rejected the contention advanced by the submitting contractors that disclosure would allow their competitors to "undercut future bids," holding that their "rather conclusory statements" to that effect were insufficient as the data was "made up of too many fluctuating variables for competitors to

---

[328](...continued)
to engage in a sophisticated economic analysis of the substantial competitive harm . . . that might result from disclosure"); Pub. Citizen, 704 F.2d at 1291.

[329] See, e.g., Pub. Citizen, 704 F.2d at 1291 ("[C]onclusory and generalized allegations of substantial competitive harm . . . cannot support an agency's decision to withhold requested documents."); Nw. Coal. for Alternatives to Pesticides v. Browner, 941 F. Supp. 197, 202 (D.D.C. 1996) (same); Lykes Bros. S.S. Co. v. Peña, No. 92-2780, slip op. at 13 (D.D.C. Sept. 2, 1993) (declaring that submitters are "required to make assertions with some level of detail as to the likelihood and the specific nature of the competitive harm they predict") (reverse FOIA suit); see also Nat'l Air Traffic Controllers Ass'n v. FAA, No. 06-53, 2007 WL 495798, at *2 (D.D.C. Feb. 12, 2007) (declaring that an agency "'is not required to provide a detailed economic analysis of the competitive environment, [but] it must provide affidavits that contain more than mere conclusory statements of competitive harm'" (quoting Gilda Indus., Inc. v. U.S. Customs & Border Prot. Bureau, 457 F. Supp. 2d 6, 10 (D.D.C. 2006))); Delta Ltd. v. U.S. Customs & Border Prot. Bureau, 384 F. Supp. 2d 138, 149 (D.D.C. 2005) (same), reconsideration granted in part on other grounds, 393 F. Supp. 2d 15, 19 (D.D.C. 2005); In Def. of Animals v. HHS, No. 99-3024, 2001 U.S. Dist. LEXIS 24975, at *38 (D.D.C. Sept. 28, 2001) (rejecting agency's "conclusory and vague statements" which provided "little more than speculation about potential problems in securing future contracts"); Pub. Citizen Health Research Group v. FDA, No. 99-0177, 2000 U.S. Dist. LEXIS 4108, at *6-9 (D.D.C. Jan. 19, 2000) (rejecting submitter's "conclusory" and "speculative" arguments regarding competitive harm); Heeney v. FDA, No. 97-5461, 1999 U.S. Dist. LEXIS 23365, at *36 (C.D. Cal. Mar. 18, 1999) (rejecting competitive harm argument when submitter "provide[d] no reason" for seeking to withhold requested information), aff'd on other grounds, 7 F. App'x 770 (9th Cir. 2001); Lee, 923 F. Supp. at 455 (rejecting competitive harm when the submitter failed to provide "adequate documentation of the specific, credible, and likely reasons why disclosure of the document would actually cause substantial competitive injury").

[330] GC Micro, 33 F.3d at 1115.

gain any advantage from the disclosure."[331]

Similarly, the District Court for the District of Columbia upheld an agency's decision to disclose three broad categories of information incorporated into a government contract -- specifically, "cost and fee information, including material, labor and overhead costs, as well as target costs, target profits and fixed fees"; "component and configuration prices, including unit pricing and contract line item numbers"; and "technical and management information, including subcontracting plans, asset allocation charts, and statements of the work necessary to accomplish certain system conversions" -- based upon the submitter's failure to specifically demonstrate that it would suffer competitive harm from their release.[332] In upholding release of this information, the court affirmed the agency's determination that "neither the revelation of cost and pricing data nor proprietary management strategies were likely to result in such egregious injury to [the submitter] as to disable it as an effective competitor for [the agency's] business in the future."[333]

Some courts have utilized a "mosaic" approach to sustain a finding of competitive harm, thereby protecting information that would not in and of itself cause harm, but which would be harmful when combined with information already available to the requester.[334] In one case -- where it was

---

[331] Id. at 1114-15; see also Berlin Steel Constr. Co. v. VA, No. 95-752, slip op. at 1, 5-6 (D. Conn. Sept. 30, 1996) (rejecting a competitive harm claim for "payment and progress reports" because the variables used by the contractor to reach its "final bid for this one project . . . remain unknown" and because no evidence was presented "that over the past years market fluctuations have remained substantially stable").

[332] Martin Marietta, 974 F. Supp. at 38, 40.

[333] Id. at 41.

[334] See, e.g., Gilda Indus., Inc. v. U.S. Customs & Border Prot. Bureau, 457 F. Supp. 2d 6, 11 (D.D.C. 2006) (protecting names and addresses of importers because when they were associated with a particular shipping time frame and Harmonized Tariff Schedule and when cross-referenced with publicly available vessel manifest information, disclosure would provide requester with "valuable knowledge regarding its competitors' business operations"); Trans-Pac., 1998 U.S. Dist. LEXIS 7800, at *10-11 (protecting Harmonized Tariff Numbers, which otherwise were publicly released, when they were linked to specific shipments of goods, because a "knowledgeable person can use [such] numbers to uncover information concerning the nature, cost, profit margin, and origin of shipments"); Lederle Lab. v. HHS, No. 88-0249, slip op. at 22-23 (D.D.C. July 14, 1988) (protecting scientific tests and identities of agency reviewers because disclosure would permit requester to "indirectly obtain that which is directly exempted from disclosure"); Timken Co. v. U.S. Customs Serv., 491 F. Supp. 557, 559

(continued...)

found that a company's labor costs would be revealed by disclosure of its wage rate and manhour information -- the court took the opposite approach and disaggregated the requested information, ordering release of the wage rates without the manhour information, because release of one without the other would not cause the company competitive harm.[335] In denying a competitive harm claim, another court noted that because the requested information pertained to every laboratory in a certain program, disclosure would not create a competitive advantage for any one of them because "each laboratory would have access to the same type of information as every other laboratory in the program."[336]

Many courts have held that if the information sought to be protected is itself publicly available through other sources, disclosure under the FOIA will not cause competitive harm and Exemption 4 is not applicable.[337]

---

[334](...continued) (D.D.C. 1980) (protecting data reflecting sales between a parent company and its subsidiary, because even if disclosure of such data "would be insufficient, standing by itself, to allow computation of the cost of production, this cost would be ascertainable when coupled with other information").

[335] Painters Dist. Council Six v. GSA, No. 85-2971, slip op. at 8 (N.D. Ohio July 23, 1986); see also Lykes, No. 92-2780, slip op. at 15 (D.D.C. Sept. 2, 1993) (submitter failed to show any harm given fact that proposed disclosures would "redact all price terms, financial terms, rates and the like"); San Jose Mercury News v. Dep't of Justice, No. 88-20504, slip op. at 4-5 (N.D. Cal. Apr. 17, 1990) (no harm once company name and other identifying information deleted from requested forms).

[336] Silverberg v. HHS, No. 89-2743, 1991 WL 633740, at *4 (D.D.C. June 14, 1991), appeal dismissed per stipulation, No. 91-5255 (D.C. Cir. Sept. 2, 1993); see also PETA, 2005 WL 1241141, at *7 (finding that a bank is not at a "competitive disadvantage" when "all banks would suffer the same alleged harm" if the type of information at issue were disclosed); Carolina Biological Supply Co. v. USDA, No. 93CV00113, slip op. at 8 (M.D.N.C. Aug. 2, 1993) (competitive harm unlikely when all companies involved in same business will have equal access to information in question) (reverse FOIA suit).

[337] See, e.g., Inner City Press/Cmty. on the Move v. Bd. of Governors of the Fed. Reserve Sys., 463 F.3d 239, 244 (2d Cir. 2006) (concluding that Exemption 4 does not apply "if identical information is otherwise in the public domain" (citing Niagara Mohawk Power, 169 F.3d at 19); Anderson v. HHS, 907 F.2d 936, 952 (10th Cir. 1990) (declaring that "no meritorious claim of confidentiality" can be made for documents that are in public domain); CNA, 830 F.2d at 1154 (holding that "[t]o the extent that any data requested under FOIA are in the public domain, the submitter is unable to make any claim to confidentiality -- a sine qua non of Exemption 4"); Cont'l Stock (continued...)

EXEMPTION 4

(The public availability of information has also defeated an agency's impairment claim,[338] as well as a submitter's protection under Critical Mass Energy Project v. NRC,[339] for a document that had been voluntarily provided.[340]) In addressing a claim of public availability, the District Court for the District of Columbia has declared that it is "[t]he party asserting public availability [who] must initially produce evidence to support its assertion,

---

[337](...continued)
Transfer & Trust Co. v. SEC, 566 F.2d 373, 375 (2d Cir. 1977) (concluding that "[n]o cognizable harm, much less any substantial harm," would occur from the release of information "almost all" of which already was readily available to the public); Newry, 2005 WL 3273975, at *4 n.8 (denying Exemption 4 protection for information that was "readily available" through search of database on agency's Web site); Lepelletier v. FDIC, 977 F. Supp. 456, 460 (D.D.C. 1997) (finding that when state laws provide for publication of names of depositors of abandoned accounts, "it is clear that Exemption 4 is not applicable, because depositors who abandon their funds likewise relinquish their claims to confidentiality"), aff'd in part, rev'd in part & remanded on other grounds, 164 F.3d 37 (D.C. Cir. 1999); MCI Telecomms. Corp. v. GSA, No. 89-0746, 1992 WL 71394, at *6 (D.D.C. Mar. 25, 1992) (holding that "publicly available documents cannot be considered confidential under exemption 4"), defendants' subsequent motion for summary judgment granted on basis of collateral estoppel, No. 89-0746 (D.D.C. Feb. 27, 1995); see also R & W Flammann GmbH v. United States, 339 F.3d 1320, 1323 (Fed. Cir. 2003) (finding that sealed bid, which was "publicly opened and became immediately available to the public as required by" procurement regulations, has entered the "public domain and is therefore not confidential under Exemption 4") (non-FOIA case brought under Administrative Procedure Act, 5 U.S.C. §§ 701-706 (2000)). Compare Lee, 923 F. Supp. at 455 (competitive injury claim rejected for information already available to public, albeit in different format), with Heeney, 1999 U.S. Dist. LEXIS 23365, at *38 (competitive injury claim accepted when the "context of the information in agency records is different than that in the marketplace").

[338] See Farmworkers Legal Servs. v. U.S. Dep't of Labor, 639 F. Supp. 1368, 1371 (E.D.N.C. 1986).

[339] 975 F.2d 871, 880 (D.C. Cir. 1992) (en banc).

[340] See Parker v. Bureau of Land Mgmt., 141 F. Supp. 2d 71, 80-81 (D.D.C. 2001) (ordering disclosure of an e-mail message that was provided voluntarily, because the court "agree[d] that [the] information is now publicly available [elsewhere] and [that] therefore [it] is not protected from disclosure under Exemption 4"). But cf. Baker & Hostetler LLP v. U.S. Dep't of Commerce, 473 F.3d 312, 320-21 (D.C. Cir. 2006) (rejecting plaintiff's argument that Tariff Act's official record requirement, found at 19 U.S.C. § 1516a(b)(2)(A)(i), required public disclosure of information that submitter had voluntary provided).

but the burden of <u>persuasion</u> remains on the opponent of disclosure."[341]

In applying this principle, one court has held that simply because individuals subject to a drug test had "a right of access to the performance and testing information" of the laboratory conducting their tests, that did "not make the [requested] information [concerning all certified laboratories] publicly available."[342] Similarly, release of a summary of a safety and effectiveness study was found not to waive Exemption 4 protection for the underlying raw data because the disclosed information did not "match the withheld information."[343] Significantly, when an agency had previously re-

---

[341] <u>Nw. Coal.</u>, 941 F. Supp. at 202 (citing <u>Occidental Petroleum Corp. v. SEC</u>, 873 F.2d 325, 342 (D.C. Cir. 1989)); <u>accord</u> <u>Inner City Press</u>, 463 F.3d at 245 & n.5 ("While the government retains the burden of persuasion that information is not subject to disclosure under FOIA, 'a party who asserts that material is publicly available carries the burden of <u>production</u> on that issue.'" (quoting <u>Davis v. U.S. Dep't of Justice</u>, 968 F.2d 1276, 1279 (D.C. Cir. 1992))); <u>Gilda</u>, 457 F. Supp. 2d at 12 (rejecting public domain argument where the requester showed "at most, only that the same general type of information" was publicly available); <u>Boyes v. U.S. Dep't of Energy</u>, No. 03-1756, 2005 WL 607882, at *7 (D.D.C. Mar. 16, 2005) (declaring that "[i]t is not enough for a requester to argue that some unspecified amount of the same information 'may' be public in some other forum"); <u>Campaign for Responsible Transplantation v. FDA</u>, No. 00-2849, slip op. at 10 (D.D.C. Sept. 24, 2004) (declaring that "the party favoring disclosure . . . has the burden of demonstrating that the information sought is identical to the information made public" (citing <u>Ctr. for Auto Safety v. Nat'l Highway Traffic Safety Admin.</u>, 244 F.3d 144, 151 (D.C. Cir. 2001))); <u>Heeney</u>, 1999 U.S. Dist. LEXIS 23365, at *27 (observing that "[w]hile it may generally be known" that a certain company manufactures catheters, the requester failed to supply "evidence that the information redacted in fact concerns" that company).

[342] <u>Silverberg</u>, 1991 WL 633740, at *3; <u>see also</u> <u>OSHA Data</u>, 220 F.3d at 163 n.25 (finding that the posting of a summary of data at the workplace and the placing of selected examples on an agency's Web site were nothing more than "limited disclosure[s] to a limited audience" and were "surely insufficient to render the data publicly available"); <u>N.Y. Times Co. v. U.S. Dep't of Labor</u>, 340 F. Supp. 2d 394, 401-02 (S.D.N.Y. 2004) (citing <u>OSHA Data</u> and likewise concluding that the posting of data at the workplace was not "public" disclosure).

[343] <u>Cohen v. Kessler</u>, No. 95-6140, slip op. at 12 (D.N.J. Nov. 25, 1996); <u>see also</u> <u>Herrick v. Garvey</u>, 200 F. Supp. 2d 1321, 1329 (D. Wyo. 2000) (finding that when company had reversed its prior authorization to disclose documents claimed as "trade secrets" and specific documents had not in fact been released previously, there was "no waiver of Exemption 4 protection"), <u>aff'd on other grounds</u>, 298 F.3d 1184, 1193-95 & n.10 (10th Cir. 2002) (explaining that the "[w]aiver doctrine" is distinct from the argument actually advanced by the requester -- who challenged the applicability of "trade se-
(continued...)

leased data without the submitter's "knowledge or consent," the District Court for the District of Columbia rejected the agency's argument that that data was "now in the public domain and no longer entitled to confidential treatment."[344] In rebuffing that proposition, the court held that "[t]he prior release of information to a limited number of requesters does not necessarily make the information a matter of common public knowledge, nor does it lessen the likelihood that [the submitter] might suffer competitive harm if it is disclosed again."[345]

Confidentiality was also upheld in a case where the requester argued that some of the withheld material had been disclosed "collaterally."[346] First, the D.C. Circuit declared that "assuming that certain information is available publicly," it saw "little reason why the government must go through the expense and burden of producing the information now; there is no benefit to . . . [the requester] or to the public that can be gained by imposing such a duplicative function on the government."[347] As to the requester's argument that there was "value to be gained from the juxtaposition" of that "public information within" the submitter's materials, the D.C. Circuit found that the requester's own argument "concedes the confidentiality" of the material, because the requester clearly wanted "not only the collaterally disclosed information, but the proprietary manner with which" it had been utilized.[348]

---

[343](...continued)
cret" protection "in the first place" when the submitting company, by virtue of giving its permission to the agency to disclose the information, thereby clearly "no longer intends" it to be "secret" -- and then assuming, "without deciding, that it was possible for the grant of permission to be revoked and the secret nature of the documents" to be restored, which in fact is what occurred).

[344] Martin Marietta, 974 F. Supp. at 40; accord Parker, 141 F. Supp. 2d at 80.

[345] Martin Marietta, 974 F. Supp. at 40; accord Trans-Pac., 1998 U.S. Dist. LEXIS 7800, at *13 (when "past release" of data "was isolated and unauthorized by" agency, such release found "not [to] affect the application of Exemption 4"); see also Pub. Citizen, 953 F. Supp. at 401, 405 (when submitter's document "inadvertently released" to requester by agency and subsequently filed on public record, court noted absence of evidence that anyone had "taken advantage" of that public access and issued protective order sealing court record and precluding requester from publicly disseminating document pending court's determination of Exemption 4 applicability).

[346] Allnet, No. 92-5351, slip op. at 4 (D.C. Cir. May 27, 1994).

[347] Id.

[348] Id.; see Pub. Citizen, 997 F. Supp. at 66 (recognizing that although some requested information "may be available because of overseas market-
(continued...)

The feasibility of "reverse engineering" (i.e., the process of independently recreating the requested information -- for example, by obtaining a finished product and dismantling it to learn its constituent elements) has been considered in evaluating a showing of competitive harm because it "is germane to the question whether information is in the public domain (and thus whether a showing of competitive harm can be made)."[349]  (Although in one case the court declined to even consider the requester's contention that reverse engineering was possible for  information protected as a "trade secret" under Exemption 4,[350] in a subsequent "trade secret" decision the court did consider such a claim.[351])

In Worthington Compressors, Inc. v. Costle,[352] the D.C. Circuit held that the cost of reverse engineering is a pertinent inquiry and that the test should be "whether release of the requested information, given its commercial value to competitors and the cost of acquiring it through other means, will cause substantial competitive harm to the business that submitted it."[353]  In that case, the D.C. Circuit pointed out that agency disclosures of

---

[348](...continued)
ing," the "context provided by" agency release renders it "different," and competitive harm is not "diminish[ed]").

[349] Nw. Coal., 941 F. Supp. at 202.

[350] See Pac. Sky Supply, Inc. v. Dep't of the Air Force, No. 86-2044, 1987 WL 28485, at *1 (D.D.C. Dec. 16, 1987) (refusing to consider feasibility of reverse engineering for documents withheld as trade secrets, because once trade secret determination is made, documents "'are exempt from disclosure, and no further inquiry is necessary'" (quoting Pub. Citizen, 704 F.2d at 1286)).

[351] See Ctr. for Auto Safety v. Nat'l Highway Traffic Safety Admin., 93 F. Supp. 2d 1, 15 (D.D.C. 2000) (considering, but rejecting, requester's argument that physical characteristics of air bags "are easily discernible" by "using simple hand tools to dismantle" them and finding instead that "[d]ismantling air bags to learn this information is dangerous, time-consuming, and expensive" and that therefore trade secret protection was appropriate), remanded on other grounds, 244 F.3d 144, 151 (D.C. Cir. 2001) (rejecting district court's conclusion that requested information qualified as a "trade secret," but holding that "it may nonetheless qualify for protection" as a voluntary submission).

[352] 662 F.2d 45 (D.C. Cir.), supplemental opinion sub nom. Worthington Compressors, Inc. v. Gorsuch, 668 F.2d 1371 (D.C. Cir. 1981).

[353] Id. at 52; accord Greenberg, 803 F.2d at 1218; Nw. Coal., 941 F. Supp. at 202; Daniels Mfg. Corp. v. DOD, No. 85-291, slip op. at 7-8 (M.D. Fla. June 3, 1986); Air Line Pilots Ass'n, Int'l v. FAA, 552 F. Supp. 811, 814 (D.D.C. 1982); see also Zotos Int'l v. Young, 830 F.2d 350, 353 (D.C. Cir. 1987) (if commercially valuable information has remained secret for many years, it is
(continued...)

information that benefit competitors at the expense of submitters deserve "close attention" by the courts.[354] As the court of appeals observed:

> Because competition in business turns on the relative costs and opportunities faced by members of the same industry, there is a potential windfall for competitors to whom valuable information is released under FOIA. If those competitors are charged only minimal FOIA retrieval costs for the information, rather than the considerable costs of private reproduction, they may be getting quite a bargain. Such bargains could easily have competitive consequences not contemplated as part of FOIA's principal aim of promoting openness in government.[355]

---

[353](...continued)
incongruous to argue that it may be readily reverse-engineered) (non-FOIA case); Heeney, No. 97-5461, 1999 U.S. Dist. LEXIS 23365, at *42 (rejecting the requester's claim that reverse engineering was possible, based on his failure to demonstrate "that he has the technical expertise to offer opinions about reverse-engineering of the devices at issue," and finding that the documents requested revealed "more than could be learned through reverse-engineering" in any event).

[354] 662 F.2d at 51.

[355] Id.; see, e.g., Pub. Citizen, 185 F.3d at 905 (declaring that Exemption 4 "clearly" is designed to protect against disclosures that would permit competitors "to eliminate much of the time and effort that would otherwise be required to bring to market a [competitive] product" (citing Webb v. HHS, 696 F.2d 101, 103 (D.C. Cir. 1982) ("If a [drug] manufacturer's competitor could obtain all the data in the manufacturer's [New Drug Application (NDA)], it could utilize them in its own NDA without incurring the time, labor, risk, and expense involved in developing them independently."))); Campaign for Responsible Transplantation, No. 00-2849, slip op. at 10 (protecting information contained in Investigational New Drug Application, because "sponsors would have much less incentive to make the enormous investments required . . . if other companies could [get a] free ride on their research developments and investments"); Parker, 141 F. Supp. 2d at 81 (alternative holding) (protecting detailed market studies relating to proposed pipeline projects because "the compilation and analysis of the publicly available data were undertaken at significant cost"); Pub. Citizen, 2000 U.S. Dist. LEXIS 4108, at *10-12 (protecting a company's investigators' names and the titles of unpublished articles because disclosure would permit competitors to "'eliminate much of the time and effort that would otherwise be required to bring to market'" a competitive product and because the company had "provid[ed] evidence that it would be costly for competitors to figure out through their own efforts all of the names and unpublished article titles at issue"); Sokolow v. FDA, No. 1:97-CV-252, slip op. at 7 (E.D. Tex. Feb. 19, 1998) (protecting drug safety and effectiveness information because it "could be used by competitors to develop clinical studies or
(continued...)

An agency's assertion of competitive harm for portions of a pesticide formula -- which admittedly was capable of being reverse engineered -- was rejected when the agency failed to explain "how difficult and costly" it would be to do so because, as the party "seeking to avoid disclosure," the agency was found not to have sustained its burden of "production and persuasion on that point."[356] Likewise, when information was found to be "freely or cheaply available from various sources," a court rejected a competitive harm claim, declaring that such information "cannot be considered protected confidential information."[357]

---

[355](...continued)
other research toward a competing product"), aff'd, 162 F.3d 1160 (5th Cir. 1998) (unpublished table decision); Cohen, No. 95-6140, slip op. at 12 (D.N.J. Nov. 25, 1996) (protecting raw data contained in a research study inasmuch as disclosure "would allow competitors to develop or refine their [own] products and avoid [incurring] the [corresponding] research and development costs because of the opportunity to piggy-back upon [the submitter's] development efforts," which "would therefore have [an] unwarranted deleterious impact on [the submitter's] competitive position"); Wash. Psychiatric Soc'y v. OPM, No. 87-1913, 1988 U.S. Dist. LEXIS 17069, at *6 (D.D.C. Oct. 13, 1988); Pac. Sky Supply, Inc. v. Dep't of the Air Force, No. 86-2044, 1987 WL 18214, at *4-5 (D.D.C. Sept. 29, 1987), modified, No. 86-2044 (D.D.C. Nov. 20, 1987), motion to amend judgment denied, No. 86-2044 (D.D.C. Dec. 16, 1987); Air Line Pilots Ass'n, Int'l v. FAA, 552 F. Supp. 811, 814 (D.D.C. 1982); see also Allnet, 800 F. Supp. at 988-89 (noting submitter's twenty-two-million-dollar investment and rejecting requester's argument that receipt of seven million dollars in annual sales revenue is somehow "de minimis"); SMS Data Prods. Group, Inc. v. U.S. Dep't of the Air Force, No. 88-0481, 1989 WL 201031, at *3 (D.D.C. Mar. 31, 1989) (noting that release would allow competitors access to information that they would otherwise have to spend "considerable funds" to develop on their own).

[356] Nw. Coal., 941 F. Supp. at 202; see also Lahr, 453 F. Supp. 2d at 1181-82 (noting submitter's claim that a competitor would need to invest twenty million dollars to reproduce its flight simulator training data, but rejecting competitive harm argument because requester countered that data could be independently reproduced at a cost of less than $33,000, and finding that court "was required" to "draw inferences in [requester's] favor").

[357] Frazee, 97 F.3d at 371 (upholding an agency decision to release a contractor's operating plan for managing recreational areas in a national forest, because a "large portion of the [requested] information, such as details regarding collection and handling of fees, operating season dates, rules, and law enforcement, is available to anyone using or visiting the facilities" and other information, "such as employee uniforms, maintenance equipment, and signs, is in public view daily" -- thereby making it unlikely that disclosure of the operating plan would cause competitive harm); see also Atlantis Submarines Haw., Inc. v. U.S. Coast Guard, No. 93-00986, slip

(continued...)

## EXEMPTION 4

Neither the willingness of the requester to restrict circulation of the information[358] nor a claim by the requester that it is not a competitor of the submitter[359] should logically defeat a showing of competitive harm.[360] The question is whether "public disclosure" would cause harm; there is no "middle ground between disclosure and nondisclosure."[361] Additionally the passage of time, while usually eroding the likelihood of competitive harm,[362]

---

[357](...continued)
op. at 8 (D. Haw. Jan. 28, 1994) (finding that disclosure of admittedly "readily-observable" procedures in submarine operations manual would not afford competitors "any substantial 'windfall'" and so would not cause competitive harm) (denying motion for preliminary injunction in reverse FOIA suit), dismissed per stipulation (D. Haw. Apr. 11, 1994).

[358] See Seawell, Dalton, Hughes & Timms v. Exp.-Imp. Bank, No. 84-241, slip op. at 2 (E.D. Va. July 27, 1984); cf. Schiffer v. FBI, 78 F.3d 1405, 1411 (9th Cir. 1996) ("limited access" to exempt records, subject to protective order, "not authorized by FOIA") (Exemption 7(C) case).

[359] See, e.g., Burke Energy Corp. v. Dep't of Energy for the United States, 583 F. Supp. 507, 512 (D. Kan. 1984) (characterizing the requester's "argument that it is not a competitor" as "totally without merit").

[360] See Heeney, No. 97-5461, 1999 U.S. Dist. LEXIS 23365, at *19 n.10 (explaining that the "identity of the requester is irrelevant . . . because once information has been released -- even to a private, noncompeting individual such as [this particular requester] -- the information has reached the public domain and cannot be withheld from subsequent requesters"); cf. NARA v. Favish, 541 U.S. at 172 (re-emphasizing that "[a]s a general rule, if the information is subject to disclosure, it belongs to all").

[361] Seawell, No. 84-241, slip op. at 2 (E.D. Va. July 27, 1984).

[362] See, e.g., Lahr, 453 F. Supp. 2d at 1180 (positing that information pertaining to the design and performance of an aircraft "developed in the 1960s" had "little or no remaining commercial value"); N.Y. Times, 340 F. Supp. 2d at 402 (rejecting competitive harm argument for number of employee hours worked four years previously, based partly on fact that contemporaneous information regarding hours was available); Ctr. for Pub. Integrity v. Dep't of Energy, 191 F. Supp. 2d 187, 195 (D.D.C. 2002) (rejecting a competitive harm claim for the amounts offered by unsuccessful bidders seeking to buy government land, because competitors would be "naive to assume that" the bidders' "business strategies and valuation methodologies remain the same over time in the face of changing market conditions"); Garren, No. CV-97-273, slip op. at 19-20 (D. Or. Nov. 17, 1997) (rejecting a competitive harm claim for sales prices for concessions sold "seven or eight years" ago, and finding that "price may be different for future transactions involving other parties and other companies and, potentially, a different operating environment"); Lee, 923 F. Supp. at 455 (rejecting competitive harm argument because the "financial information in question is given for

(continued...)

does not necessarily defeat Exemption 4 protection provided that disclosure of the material would still be likely to cause substantial competitive harm.[363] Finally, the D.C. Circuit has emphasized that it is incumbent upon the courts -- and, logically, upon agencies in the first instance -- to consider whether it is possible to redact requested information "in order to avoid application of Exemption 4."[364] (See the further discussions of this point under

---

[362](...continued)
[a period two years previously] and any potential detriment which could be caused by its disclosure would seem likely to have mitigated with the passage of time"); Teich, 751 F. Supp. at 253 (rejecting competitive harm claim based partly upon fact that documents were as many as twenty years old); see also Afr. Fund v. Mosbacher, No. 92-289, 1993 WL 183736, at *8 (S.D.N.Y. May 26, 1993) (rejecting argument that exemption permanently precludes release because passage of time might render later disclosures "of little consequence").

[363] See Ctr. for Auto Safety, 93 F. Supp. 2d at 16 (declaring that "[i]nformation does not become stale merely because it is old"); see also, e.g., Burke, 583 F. Supp. at 514 (nine-year-old data protected); Timken Co. v. U.S. Customs Serv., 3 Gov't Disclosure Serv. (P-H) ¶ 83,234, at 83,976 (D.D.C. June 24, 1983) (ten-year-old data protected); FOIA Update, Vol. IV, No. 4, at 14; cf. Herrick, 200 F. Supp. 2d at 1328 (protecting as "trade secret" technical blueprints for 1935 aircraft despite documents' "age or antiquity").

[364] Trans-Pac. Policing Agreement v. U.S. Customs Serv., 177 F.3d 1022, 1029 (D.C. Cir. 1999) (holding that although "[t]here is certainly no doubt" that Exemption 4 was properly applied to a ten-digit customs code, a remand was necessary to determine whether "disclosure of redacted [codes] poses a likelihood of substantial harm"); see also, e.g., FlightSafety Servs. v. Dep't of Labor, 326 F.3d 607, 612-13 (5th Cir. 2003) (per curiam) (adjudicating the requester's contention that the agency "should be required to redact any uniquely identifying private company descriptives and disclose the remainder of" the requested statistics regarding salary and wage data, and finding, after an "independent review" of the documentation submitted in camera, that "any disclosable information, is so inextricably intertwined with the exempt, confidential information that producing it would require substantial agency resources and produce a document of little informational value"); Pub. Citizen, 185 F.3d at 907 (remanding to determine "whether the documents the agency has withheld contain information that can be segregated and disclosed"); Elec. Privacy Info. Ctr. v. DHS, 384 F. Supp. 2d 100, 111 & n.12 (D.D.C. 2005) (performing segregability analysis even though parties did not raise issue and requester conceded proprietary of agency's Exemption 4 withholdings (citing Schiller v. NLRB, 964 F.2d 1205, 1210 (D.C. Cir. 1991)); In Def. of Animals v. USDA, No. 02-0557, slip op. at 2, 30-34 (D.D.C. Sept. 28, 2004) (deferring a ruling on the applicability of Exemption 4, because defendants provided "insufficient evidence" to permit the court to "entertain a segregability analysis"); Piper & Marbury, L.L.P. v. USPS, No. 99-2383, 2001 WL 214217, at *4 (D.D.C. Mar. 6, 2001) (magis-
(continued...)

EXEMPTION 4

Procedural Requirements, "Reasonably Segregable" Obligation, above, and Litigation Considerations, "Reasonably Segregable" Requirements, below.)

Numerous types of competitive injury have been identified by the courts as properly cognizable under the competitive harm prong, including the harms generally caused by disclosure of:

(1) detailed financial information such as a company's assets, liabilities, and net worth;[365]

(2) a company's actual costs, break-even calculations, profits and profit rates;[366]

(3) data describing a company's workforce that would reveal labor

---

[364](...continued)
trate's recommendation) (recommending full disclosure of contract when agency broadly claimed that it was exempt in its entirety; finding instead that Exemption 4 protects "particular knowledge, facts, or data, rather than entire documents"), adopted, No. 99-2383, slip op. at 4 (D.D.C. Mar. 30, 2001) (holding that "[i]n this circuit, an entire document simply does not qualify as 'information' ex[em]pted from disclosure under" the FOIA; concluding that although "particular 'information' may be redacted upon an adequate showing," the agency had "not pursued such a course in this case"; and, consequently, ordering release of the contract in its entirety), reconsideration denied (D.D.C. Feb. 28, 2002); Judicial Watch, Inc. v. U.S. Dep't of Commerce, 83 F. Supp. 2d 105, 111 (D.D.C. 1999) (deferring ruling on applicability of Exemption 4, despite finding that the affidavits "appear to support the withholding" of the documents, because they failed to provide enough detail "to permit the Court to conclude that documents withheld in their entirety do not contain any reasonably segregable information").

[365] See, e.g., Nat'l Parks, 547 F.2d at 684; Inner City Press/Cmty. on the Move v. Bd. of Governors of the Fed. Reserve Sys., No. 98 CIV. 4608, 1998 WL 690371, at *5 (S.D.N.Y. Sept. 30, 1998) ("capital situation, [company's] assets, cash flow, investments, leverage ratios, 'cross-selling strategy,' pretax earnings by product line, dividend capacity, revenues, and rate changes for its insurance operations"), aff'd, 182 F.3d 900 (2d Cir. 1999) (unpublished table decision).

[366] See, e.g., Gulf & W., 615 F.2d at 530; see also Hecht v. U.S. Agency for Int'l Dev., No. 95-263, 1996 WL 33502232, at *8-10 (D. Del. Dec. 18, 1996) (fringe benefits, overhead, and General and Administrative (G & A) costs); Cortez III Serv. Corp. v. NASA, 921 F. Supp. 8, 12 (D.D.C. 1996) (G & A rate ceilings that are "nearly identical" to actual G & A rates) (alternative holding) (reverse FOIA suit), appeal dismissed voluntarily, No. 96-5163 (D.C. Cir. July 3, 1996).

costs, profit margins, and competitive vulnerability;[367]

(4) a company's selling prices, purchase activity and freight charges;[368]

(5) shipper and importer names, type and quantity of freight hauled, routing systems, cost of raw materials, and information constituting the "bread and butter" of a manufacturing company;[369]

(6) type and volume of sales;[370]

(7) "currently unannounced and future products, proprietary technical information, pricing strategy, and subcontractor information," and similar data;[371]

---

[367] See, e.g., Westinghouse Elec. Corp. v. Schlesinger, 392 F. Supp. 1246, 1249 (E.D. Va. 1974), aff'd, 542 F.2d 1190 (4th Cir. 1976); see also Pub. Citizen, 209 F. Supp. 2d at 47 (royalty rate information when release "could easily lead to a competitor being able to make a rough calculation of a firm's profit margin on a particular drug").

[368] See, e.g., Braintree, 494 F. Supp. at 289; see also Destileria Serralles, Inc. v. Dep't of the Treasury, No. 85-0837, slip op. at 9 (D.P.R. Sept. 22, 1988) (purchase records, including prices paid for advertising).

[369] Journal of Commerce, Inc. v. U.S. Dep't of the Treasury, No. 86-1075, 1988 U.S. Dist. LEXIS 17610, at *9-10 (D.D.C. Mar. 30, 1988), aff'd, 878 F.2d 1446 (Fed. Cir. 1989) (unpublished table decision); see, e.g., Suzhou Yuanda Enter., Co. v. U.S. Customs & Border Prot., 404 F. Supp. 2d 9, 13 (D.D.C. 2005) (appeal pending); Inter Ocean Free Zone, 982 F. Supp. at 869, 873.

[370] Lion Raisins, 354 F.3d at 1081.

[371] SMS, 1989 WL 201031, at *4; see, e.g., Judicial Watch, Inc. v. Exp.-Imp. Bank, 108 F. Supp. 2d 19, 29 (D.D.C. 2000) (export-insurance documents when "transaction is in a highly competitive state," or is part of "an ongoing transaction"); Matthews v. USPS, No. 92-1208-CV-W-8, slip op. at 6 (W.D. Mo. Apr. 15, 1994) (technical drawings relating to computer system sold to government, technology for which still was being sold to others); RMS, No. C-92-1545, slip op. at 6-7 (N.D. Cal. Nov. 24, 1992) ("descriptions of equipment and the names of contacts, customers, key employees, and subcontractors"); BDM Corp. v. SBA, 2 Gov't Disclosure Serv. (P-H) ¶ 81,189, at 81,495 (D.D.C. Mar. 20, 1981) (names of consultants and subcontractors, and performance, cost, and equipment information); see also Nat'l Cmty. Reinvestment Coal. v. Nat'l Credit Union Admin., 290 F. Supp. 2d 124, 135 (D.D.C. 2003) (dicta) (business and marketing plans "would" be exempt) (non-FOIA case brought under Administrative Procedure Act). But see Nat'l Air Traffic Controllers Ass'n v. FAA, No. 06-53, 2007 WL 495798, at *3 (D.D.C. Feb. 12, 2007) (rejecting agency's withholding of names of contrac-

(continued...)

(8) raw research data used to support a pharmaceutical drug's safety and effectiveness, information regarding an unapproved application to market the drug in a different manner, and sales and distribution data of a drug manufacturer;[372] and

(9) technical proposals which are submitted, or could be used, in conjunction with offers on government contracts.[373]

The Tenth Circuit has upheld protection under the competitive harm prong for a lease entered into by a fuel storage company and the Skull Valley Band of Goshute Indians that would allow the company to store "spent nuclear fuel" on land owned by the Band.[374] Although the requester colorfully argued that "given 'the dangerous nature of the material [that] is the subject of the [l]ease . . . [most] regions would be about as anxious to attract a chance to store spent nuclear fuel as they would be to encourage an outbreak of leprosy,'" the Tenth Circuit found that competitive harm had been established because disclosure of the lease would weaken the negotiating positions of both the company and the Band in future such deals with other partners.[375] Similarly, protection has been recognized for information related to water rights held by Indian tribes inasmuch as disclosure

---

[371](...continued) tor's employees, because agency "only provided conclusory statements . . . about competitive harm to [submitter] due to employee raiding"); News-Press v. DHS, No. 2:05CV102, 2005 WL 2921952, at *20 (M.D. Fla. Nov. 4, 2005) (rejecting Exemption 4 protection for names of the contractor's "key personnel," because the contracts at issue had expired and the submitter's affidavits made "no reference to any attempts by their respective employers to protect their interest in key personnel, such as confidentiality agreements, non-compete agreements, or the like").

[372] See Citizens Comm'n, 1993 WL 1610471, at *9-10; see also Heeney v. FDA, 7 F. App'x 770, 771 (9th Cir. 2001); Sokolow, No. 1:97-CV-252, slip op. at 7-8 (E.D. Tex. Feb. 19, 1998); Cohen, No. 95-6140, slip op. at 11-12 (D.N.J. Nov. 25 1996).

[373] See, e.g., Boyes, 2005 WL 607882, at *7; Pentagon Techs. Int'l v. United States, No. 98CIV.4831, 2000 WL 347165, at *3 (S.D.N.Y. Mar. 31, 2000) (alternative holding); Hecht, 1996 WL 33502232, at *10; Joint Bd. of Control v. Bureau of Indian Affairs, No. 87-217, slip op. at 8 (D. Mont. Sept. 9, 1988); Landfair v. U.S. Dep't of the Army, 645 F. Supp. 325, 329 (D.D.C. 1986); Prof'l Review Org. v. HHS, 607 F. Supp. 423, 426 (D.D.C. 1985) (detailing manner in which professional services contract was to be conducted).

[374] Utah, 256 F.3d at 971.

[375] Id. at 970-71; accord Judicial Watch, 108 F. Supp. 2d at 29 (accepting competitive harm claim for export-insurance documents based upon threat of injury to submitters' "future negotiating position" in obtaining "financing on favorable terms").

would hurt their "negotiating position" in "real estate transactions, water leasing, and other commercial dealings."[376]

The District Court for the Southern District of New York has recognized protection under the competitive harm prong for documents pertaining to a proposed real estate venture, despite the fact that the harm that would flow from disclosure would come from a citizens group, rather than from competing real estate developers.[377] The court made its finding in light of the fact that the "avowed goal" of that group was "to drive the joint venture out of business."[378] The court found that irrespective of the identity of the requester, "the economic injury they may inflict on the joint venture is nonetheless a competitive injury" that would "jeopardize both the venture's relative position vis-a-vis other New York City real estate developers and its solvency."[379] This holding was affirmed by the Court of Appeals for the Second Circuit, which reiterated that "[t]he fact that [the] harm would result from active hindrance by the [requester] rather than directly by potential competitors does not affect the fairness considerations that underlie Exemption Four."[380]

The Second Circuit was faced with another "unusual question" concerning the applicability of the competitive harm prong when it decided a case involving a FOIA requester who "already [had] knowledge of the confidential information contained in the withheld documents."[381] The case concerned a request for design drawings that had been submitted by two

---

[376] Flathead Joint Bd. of Control v. U.S. Dep't of the Interior, 309 F. Supp. 2d 1217, 1221-22 (D. Mont. 2004) (explaining that tribes, "in developing a negotiating position with the State of Montana over the amount of their water rights, ought to be able to investigate the amount of water available to them as a part of creating their strategy"), appeal dismissed, No. 04-35230 (9th Cir. Feb. 11, 2005); see also Starkey v. U.S. Dep't of Interior, 238 F. Supp. 2d 1188, 1195 (S.D. Cal. 2002) (recognizing a competitive harm claim for "well and water related information" on an Indian reservation because release "would adversely affect the [Tribe's] ability to negotiate its water rights").

[377] Nadler v. FDIC, 899 F. Supp. 158, 163 (S.D.N.Y. 1995), aff'd, 92 F.3d 93 (2d Cir. 1996).

[378] Id.

[379] Id.

[380] Nadler v. FDIC, 92 F.3d 93, 97 (2d Cir. 1996). But cf. CNA, 830 F.2d at 1154 (observing, in the context of rejecting a competitive harm argument based on "anticipated displeasure of [submitter's] employees" and fear of "adverse public reaction," that such objections "simply do not amount to 'harm flowing from the affirmative use of proprietary information by competitors'" (quoting Pub. Citizen, 704 F.2d at 1291 n.30)).

[381] United Techs. Corp. v. FAA, 102 F.3d 688, 689 (2d Cir. 1996).

companies seeking approval to manufacture aircraft parts.[382] Those companies sought approval pursuant to "identicality" regulations, which permit a manufacturer to obtain approval for its parts based upon a showing that those parts are "identical" to parts which have already been approved; in this case, the approved parts were manufactured by the requester.[383] The requester argued that because the requested documents were "identical in all respects to the drawings" that it itself had previously submitted, they could not "be 'confidential' as to [the requester] within the meaning of FOIA Exemption 4."[384]

In rejecting that contention, the Second Circuit first noted that "[i]t is a basic principle under FOIA that the individuating circumstances of a requester are not to be considered in deciding whether a particular document should be disclosed."[385] Accordingly, the fact that the requester "already ha[d] knowledge of the information contained in the withheld documents" was found to be "irrelevant."[386] The Second Circuit also rejected the requester's argument that the Supreme Court's decision in United States Department of Justice v. Julian,[387] supported its contention "that confidentiality under Exemption 4 should be examined on a requester-specific basis," holding that because the requester was "not the party for whom the protections of Exemption 4 were intended, it ha[d] no claim of special access."[388] Inasmuch as the requester "'freely concede[d]' that it [could not] prevail if it must proceed" as if it were "any other member of the general public," the Second Circuit upheld the agency's decision to withhold the information.[389]

---

[382] Id.

[383] Id.

[384] Id. at 690.

[385] Id.

[386] Id. at 691.

[387] 486 U.S. 1 (1988) (holding that presentence report privilege, which is designed to protect subjects of such reports, cannot be invoked against those same subjects when they seek access to their own reports).

[388] United Techs., 102 F.3d at 691-92 (noting that the test for determining competitive harm "does not appear to contemplate its application on a requester-specific basis"); cf. Changzhou Laosan Group v. U.S. Customs & Border Prot. Bureau, No. 04-1919, 2005 WL 913268, at *6 (D.D.C. Apr. 20, 2005) (stating that the court was "unwilling to sustain a claim of Exemption 4 where the competitive harm, if any, is to the plaintiff, as opposed to a third party"), reconsideration granted in part & denied in part on other grounds, 374 F. Supp. 2d 129 (D.D.C. 2005).

[389] Id.; cf. Favish, 541 U.S. at 172 (reiterating that in FOIA cases "disclo-

(continued...)

On the other hand, protection under the competitive harm prong has been denied when the prospect of injury is remote[390] -- for example, when a government contract is not awarded competitively[391] -- or when the re-

---

[389](...continued)
sure does not depend on the identity of the requester").

[390] See, e.g., City of Chicago v. U.S. Dep't of the Treasury, No. 01 C 3835, 2002 WL 370216, at *2 (N.D. Ill. Mar. 8, 2002) (holding that the disclosure of information regarding firearms dealers "who shipped firearms that were lost or stolen from an interstate carrier" would not cause competitive harm to the carriers because the requested information pertaining to the dealers was not "otherwise linked in any way" to the carriers), rev'd & remanded on other grounds, No. 02-2259 (7th Cir. Nov. 29, 2005); Hecht, 1996 WL 33502232, at *8 (ruling that disclosure of "biographical information" about a contractor's employees would not cause competitive harm because the "possibility of another company recruiting away one's employees is present in nearly every industry," and opining that to "conclude that a competitor could determine, merely by looking at employee resumes, a company's technical and operational approach to a project would require a leap of logic that this court is unwilling to make"); Carolina, No. 93CV00113, slip op. at 9 (M.D.N.C. Aug. 2, 1993) (finding that disclosure of the number of animals sold by companies supplying laboratory specimens "will be simply a small addition to information available in the marketplace" and thus will not cause competitive harm); Teich, 751 F. Supp. at 254 (concluding that disclosure of safety and effectiveness data pertaining to medical device at "this late date" in product approval process "could not possibly help" competitors of submitter); see also PETA, 2005 WL 1241141, at *7 (concluding that certain financial information was not protected, because no showing was made that submitter would suffer "substantial competitive injury" if information were disclosed); Brown, 1991 U.S. Dist. LEXIS 1780, at *7 (concluding that certain wage information is not protected because no showing was made that submitter would suffer "'substantial' injury" if information were disclosed).

[391] See Hercules, Inc. v. Marsh, 839 F.2d 1027, 1030 (4th Cir. 1988) (reverse FOIA suit); see also Garren, No. CV-97-273, slip op. at 22 (D. Or. Nov. 17, 1997) (ordering the disclosure of sales price information for river-rafting concessions in Grand Canyon National Park as there was "very little competition, and [a] built-in preference favors existing concessioners and allows them to match any competing bid, thereby negating the potential competitive harm from disclosure of the information"); U.S. News & World Report v. Dep't of the Treasury, No. 84-2303, 1986 U.S. Dist. LEXIS 27634, at *14 (D.D.C. Mar. 26, 1986) (ordering disclosure of aggregate contract price for armored limousines for the President because release would not be competitively harmful given unique nature of contract and agency's role in design of vehicles); cf. Cove Shipping, Inc. v. Military Sealift Command, No. 84-2709, slip op. at 8-10 (D.D.C. Feb. 27, 1986) (ordering the release of a contract's wage and benefit breakdown because it related to "one isolated
(continued...)

quested information is too general in nature.[392] In addition, the D.C. Circuit, as well as several other courts, have held that the harms flowing from "embarrassing disclosure[s],"[393] or disclosures which could cause "customer or employee disgruntlement,"[394] are not cognizable under the competitive harm prong of Exemption 4.[395] (Moreover, such harms would not be cog-

---

[391](...continued)
contract, in an industry where labor contracts vary from bid to bid") (civil discovery case in which Exemption 4 case law was applied).

[392] See, e.g., GC Micro, 33 F.3d at 1111 (general information on the percentage and dollar amount of work subcontracted out to small disadvantaged businesses that does not reveal "breakdown of how the contractor is subcontracting the work, nor . . . the subject matter of the prime contract or subcontracts, the number of subcontracts, the items or services subcontracted, or the subcontractors' locations or identities"); N.C. Network, No. 90-1443, slip op. at 9 (4th Cir. Feb. 5, 1991) (general information regarding sales and pricing that would not reveal submitters' costs, profits, sources, or age, size, condition, or breed of animals sold); SMS, 1989 WL 201031, at *4 (general information regarding publicly held corporation's management structure, financial and production capabilities, corporate history and employees, most of which would be found in corporation's annual report and SEC filings and would in any event be readily available to any stockholder interested in obtaining such information); Davis Corp. v. United States, No. 87-3365, 1988 U.S. Dist. LEXIS 17611, at *10-11 (D.D.C. Jan. 19, 1988) (information contained in letters from contractor to agency regarding performance of contract that did not reveal contractor's suppliers or costs) (reverse FOIA suit); EHE Nat'l Health Serv. v. HHS, No. 81-1087, slip op. at 5 (D.D.C. Feb. 24, 1984) ("mundane" information regarding submitter's operation) (reverse FOIA suit); Am. Scissors Corp. v. GSA, No. 83-1562, 1983 U.S. Dist. LEXIS 11712, at *11 (D.D.C. Nov. 15, 1983) (general description of manufacturing process with no details) (reverse FOIA suit).

[393] Gen. Elec. Co. v. NRC, 750 F.2d 1394, 1402 (7th Cir. 1984) (reverse FOIA suit). But see Bauer v. United States, No. 92-0376, slip op. at 4 (D.D.C. Sept. 30, 1993) (upholding the deletion of the name of a corporation mentioned in an investigatory report on the basis that release of the name "in connection with a criminal investigation could cause undue speculation and commercial harm to that corporation"), remanded, No. 94-5205 (D.C. Cir. Apr. 14, 1995).

[394] Pub. Citizen, 704 F.2d at 1291 n.30 (declaring that competitive harm should "'be limited to harm flowing from the affirmative use of proprietary information by competitors'" and "'should not be taken to mean'" harms such as "'customer or employee disgruntlement'" or "'embarrassing publicity attendant upon public revelations concerning, for example, illegal or unethical payments to government officials'" (quoting law review article)).

[395] See, e.g., CNA, 830 F.2d at 1154 (declaring that "unfavorable publici-
(continued...)

nizable under Exemption 6 either, for it is well established that businesses have no "corporate privacy."[396] For a further discussion of this point, see Exemption 6, Privacy Considerations, below.) Nevertheless, the D.C. Circuit skirted this issue and expressly did not decide whether an allegation of harm flowing only from the embarrassing publicity associated with disclosure of a submitter's illegal payments to government officials would be

---

[395](...continued)
ty" and "demoralized" employees insufficient for showing of competitive harm); Ctr. to Prevent Handgun Violence v. U.S. Dep't of the Treasury, 981 F. Supp. 20, 23 (D.D.C. 1997) (denying competitive harm claim for disclosure that would cause "unwarranted criticism and harassment" inasmuch as harm must "flow from competitors' use of the released information, not from any use made by the public at large or customers"), appeal dismissed, No. 97-5357 (D.C. Cir. Feb. 2, 1998); Daisy Mfg. Co. v. Consumer Prod. Safety Comm'n, No. 96-5152, 1997 WL 578960, at *4 (W.D. Ark. Feb. 5, 1997) (declaring that court "cannot condone" use of FOIA "as shield[] against potentially negative, or inaccurate, publicity") (reverse FOIA suit), aff'd, 133 F.3d 1081 (8th Cir. 1998); Pub. Citizen, 964 F. Supp. at 415 n.2 (opining that it is "questionable whether the competitive injury associated with 'alarmism' qualifies under Exemption 4," because competitive harm does not encompass "adverse public reaction"); Martech USA, Inc. v. Reich, No. C-93-4137, slip op. at 5 (N.D. Cal. Nov. 24, 1993) (maintaining that although "information could damage . . . [submitter's] reputation, this is not the type of competitive harm protected by" Exemption 4) (denying motion for temporary restraining order in reverse FOIA suit); Silverberg, 1991 WL 633740, at *4 (discounting possibility that competitors might "distort" requested information and thus cause submitter embarrassment as insufficient for showing of competitive harm); Badhwar v. U.S. Dep't of the Air Force, 622 F. Supp. 1364, 1377 (D.D.C. 1985) (concluding that "fear of litigation" insufficient for showing of competitive harm), aff'd in part & rev'd in part on other grounds, 829 F.2d 182 (D.C. Cir. 1987); cf. Playboy Enters. v. U.S. Customs Serv., 959 F. Supp. 11, 17 (D.D.C. 1997) (finding, in context of awarding attorney fees, that when an agency initially withheld documents to protect the "commercial interests of an alleged counterfeiter," that position was so unreasonable as to be "devoid of any merit"), appeal dismissed, No. 97-5128 (D.C. Cir. June 18, 1997).

[396] See, e.g., Nat'l Parks, 547 F.2d at 685 n.44; cf. Judicial Watch, Inc. v. FDA, 407 F. Supp. 2d 70, 75 (D.D.C. 2005) (alternative holding) (protecting the names and addresses of manufacturers of an abortion drug because the plaintiff failed to create any genuine issue as to whether "abortion-related violence would, or could, cause harm to the drug sponsor's competitive position"), aff'd in part & remanded in part on other grounds, 449 F.3d 141, 150 (D.C. Cir. 2006) (declining to address district court's ruling on Exemption 4 after finding that information in question was protected under Exemption 6).

sufficient to establish competitive harm.[397] The court did go on to declare, however, that the submitter's "right to an exemption, if any, depends upon the competitive significance of whatever information may be contained in the documents" and that the submitter's motive for seeking confidential treatment, even if it was to avoid embarrassing publicity, was "simply irrelevant."[398]

Despite a wealth of previous case law upholding agency decisions to disclose government contract prices submitted as part of negotiated procurements, the D.C. Circuit has issued two decisions in the last seven years that have abruptly overturned -- in full or in part -- such agency decisions based on deficiencies in the underlying administrative record.[399]

In the first of these decisions, McDonnell Douglas v. NASA, the District Court for the District of Columbia had upheld NASA's decision to release contract prices based on the agency's thorough rebuttal of McDonnell Douglas's claims that release would cause it competitive harm.[400] The lower court reiterated the numerous grounds for NASA's disclosure decision, including the fact that release of contract pricing information "furthers the goals of FOIA."[401] In addition, the court held that NASA had effectively disputed McDonnell Douglas's contentions regarding competitive harm when it determined that contractors "compete on a variety of factors other than price," that foreign competitors were "not likely to be substantially aided by release," and that "any difficulty" McDonnell Douglas "may face in future commercial contract negotiations [did] not qualify as a substantial competitive injury and should be viewed as the cost of doing business with the

---

[397] Occidental Petroleum Corp. v. SEC, 873 F.2d 325, 341 (D.C. Cir. 1989) (reverse FOIA suit).

[398] Id.

[399] See McDonnell Douglas Corp. v. U.S. Dep't of the Air Force, 375 F.3d 1182 (D.C. Cir. 2004) (reverse FOIA suit), reh'g en banc denied, No. 02-5342 (Dec. 16, 2004); McDonnell Douglas Corp. v. NASA, 180 F.3d 303 (D.C. Cir. 1999) (reverse FOIA suit), reh'g en banc denied, No. 98-5251 (D.C. Cir. Oct. 6, 1999), dismissed as moot on motion for entry of judgment, 102 F. Supp. 2d 21 (D.D.C.) (underlying FOIA request withdrawn after D.C. Circuit issued decision), reconsideration denied, 109 F. Supp. 2d 27 (D.D.C. 2000).

[400] McDonnell Douglas Corp. v. NASA, 981 F. Supp. 12, 16 (D.D.C. 1997) (reverse FOIA suit), reconsideration denied, No. 96-2611, slip op. at 7-8 (D.D.C. May 1, 1998), rev'd, 180 F.3d 303 (D.C. Cir. 1999), reh'g en banc denied, No. 98-5251 (D.C. Cir. Oct. 6, 1999), dismissed as moot on motion for entry of judgment, 102 F. Supp. 2d 21 (D.D.C.) (underlying FOIA request withdrawn after D.C. Circuit issued decision), reconsideration denied, 109 F. Supp. 2d 27 (D.D.C. 2000).

[401] Id.

Government."[402]

The D.C. Circuit reversed, however, characterizing NASA's responses to McDonnell Douglas as "silly," "mystifying," "convoluted," and "even astonishing."[403] Without reference to any of the prior appellate court rulings on the issue,[404] or even to its own prior decisions limiting the type of harm recognized under the competitive harm prong to harm flowing from affirmative use of the information by competitors,[405] the D.C. Circuit declared McDonnell Douglas's arguments -- that release "would permit its commercial customers to bargain down ('ratchet down') its prices more effectively" and "would help its domestic and international competitors to underbid it" -- to be "indisputable."[406]

In response to the government's petition for rehearing -- which was denied -- D.C. Circuit Court Judge Silberman, the author of the opinion, ameliorated the government's concerns regarding prior D.C. Circuit precedent by first expressly clarifying that the McDonnell Douglas v. NASA decision did _not_ hold that "line item pricing would invariably" be protected.[407] Rather, he explained, the court had held "only that the agency's explanation of its position [in that particular case] bordered on the ridicu-

---

[402] Id.

[403] 180 F.3d at 306-07.

[404] See Pac. Architects & Eng'rs v. U.S. Dep't of State, 906 F.2d 1345, 1347 (9th Cir. 1990) (upholding disclosure of contract unit prices) (reverse FOIA suit); Acumenics Research & Tech., Inc. v. U.S. Dep't of Justice, 843 F.2d 800, 808 (4th Cir. 1988) (same) (reverse FOIA suit).

[405] See CNA, 830 F.2d at 1154; Pub. Citizen, 704 F.2d at 1291 n.30.

[406] McDonnell Douglas, 180 F.3d at 306-07; see also McDonnell Douglas Corp. v. NASA, No. 91-3134, transcript at 10 (D.D.C. Jan. 24, 1992) (bench order) (permanently enjoining disclosure of unit prices in light of "direct, specific" showing of competitive harm made by submitter and lack of "contrary information or evidence" in administrative record supporting release) (reverse FOIA suit), remanded for further consideration in light of Critical Mass, No. 92-5342 (D.C. Cir. Feb. 14, 1994), on remand, 895 F. Supp. 316, 319 (D.D.C. 1995) (finding Critical Mass inapplicable, denying agency opportunity to remedy "inadequacies" in record, and holding that permanent injunction "remains in place"), aff'd for agency failure to timely raise argument, No. 95-5290 (D.C. Cir. Sept. 17, 1996); Sperry Univac Div. v. Baldrige, 3 Gov't Disclosure Serv. (P-H) ¶ 83,265, at 84,052 (E.D. Va. June 16, 1982) (protecting unit prices on finding that they revealed submitter's pricing and discount strategy), appeal dismissed, No. 82-1723 (4th Cir. Nov. 22, 1982).

[407] See McDonnell Douglas Corp. v. NASA, No. 98-5251, slip op. at 2 (D.C. Cir. Oct. 6, 1999) (Silberman, J., concurring in denial of rehearing en banc).

lous."[408] Second, Judge Silberman seemingly sought to reconcile prior D.C. Circuit cases with the McDonnell Douglas v. NASA decision by commenting that "[o]ther than in a monopoly situation[,] anything that undermines a supplier's relationship with its customers must necessarily aid its competitors."[409]

In the first case to date to distinguish the results of McDonnell Douglas v. NASA, the Department of the Air Force initially prevailed in a challenge made to its decision to release contract prices.[410] In McDonnell Douglas v. Air Force, the District Court for the District of Columbia began its analysis by emphasizing that an "agency is not required to prove that its predictions of the effect of disclosure are superior" to those of the submitter's, but rather that "[i]t is enough that the agency's position is as plausible as the [submitter's] position."[411] The court than analyzed each of the three categories of Contract Line Item Number (CLIN) prices at issue in the case -- option prices, vendor prices, and "over and above" prices -- and found that the Air Force had "presented reasoned accounts of the effect of disclosure based on its experiences with government contracting."[412] The court concluded that the Air Force's "accounts are at least as compelling as [the submitter's"] accounts" and so readily upheld the Air Force's decision to disclose all three categories of prices, based upon its determination that disclosure would not be likely to cause substantial competitive harm.[413]

Most significantly, in issuing this ruling the court specifically found that the D.C. Circuit's McDonnell Douglas v. NASA decision did not require a different result.[414] The submitter had pressed such a position in its challenge to the Air Force's decision to release option prices, arguing that the D.C. Circuit had "rejected" the "exact argument" made by the Air Force to support its decision to release.[415] The district court soundly rejected the submitter's contention and found that the arguments that were made by the Air Force regarding disclosure of option prices, based upon its administrative record, "differ[ed] markedly" from those put forth by NASA in that

---

[408] Id.

[409] Id.

[410] See McDonnell Douglas v. U.S. Dep't of the Air Force, 215 F. Supp. 2d 200, 207-08 (D.D.C. 2002) (reverse FOIA suit), aff'd in part & rev'd in part, 375 F.3d 1182 (D.C. Cir. 2004), reh'g en banc denied, No. 02-5342 (D.C. Cir. Dec. 16, 2004).

[411] Id. at 205.

[412] Id. at 209.

[413] Id. at 206-09.

[414] Id. at 208.

[415] Id. at 207.

earlier D.C. Circuit case.[416]

This decision was in turn appealed to the D.C. Circuit, which then issued its second opinion addressing contract prices, in McDonnell Douglas v. Air Force.[417] On appeal, a divided panel of the D.C. Circuit reversed the district court's decision in part by holding that two of the categories of line item prices -- option prices and vendor prices -- could not be disclosed.[418] Unlike what had happened in its earlier decision in McDonnell Douglas v. NASA, however, the panel upheld the Air Force's decision to disclose a third category of line item prices, specifically "over and above" prices, finding that the agency's administrative record on that issue adequately "refute[d]" the arguments made by the submitter.[419] With respect to the option prices at issue in the case, McDonnell Douglas had argued that its competitors could "reverse-engineer" them and discern "sensitive" pricing factors.[420] The Air Force had responded that the base year prices and the option year prices were made up of too many factors and unknown variables for a competitor to be able to derive any sensitive information from them.[421] The panel majority did not address this aspect of the case, however.[422] Instead, it focused on and rejected outright the Air Force's judgment that McDonnell Douglas was not likely to suffer competitive harm from disclosure of the option prices where price would be only one of many factors used to evaluate any possible future bid.[423] It held, rather, that disclosure of the option prices "would significantly increase the probability McDonnell Douglas's competitors would underbid it in the event the Air Force rebids the contract" because, it declared, "price is the only objec-

---

[416] Id.

[417] 375 F.3d at 1182.

[418] See id.; see also FOIA Post, "Treatment of Unit Prices After McDonnell Douglas v. Air Force" (posted 9/8/05); FOIA Post, "Full Court Review Sought in McDonnell Douglas Unit Price Case (posted 10/7/04).

[419] See McDonnell Douglas, 375 F.3d at 1191-92; see also id. at 1200-01 & n.10 (Garland, J., dissenting) (pointing out that the court "did not explain why" its determination pertaining to over and above prices "should be any different with respect to the option years").

[420] See McDonnell Douglas, 375 F.3d at 1190 n.3.

[421] See id. at 1200 (Garland, J., dissenting)

[422] See McDonnell Douglas, 375 F.3d at 1190 n.3; see also id. at 1195 n.3, 1200 (Garland, J., dissenting) (noting that in the case of "line-item" prices," disclosure likely to result in substantial harm "only if a competitor is able to 'reverse-engineer' from the winning bidder's price to the sensitive strategic information upon which it is based" (citing Pac. Architects, 906 F.2d at 1347-48, and Acumenics Research, 843 F.2d at 808)).

[423] See id. at 1189.

tive, or at least readily quantified, criterion among the six criteria for awarding government contracts."[424] Despite the Air Force's uncontested factual showing that in any rebidding price would be considered together with five other factors, and then weighted equally with them, the panel majority nevertheless concluded that "[w]hether price will be but one of several factors to be weighted equally in any future [bidding process] . . . is necessarily somewhat speculative."[425]

Furthermore, the majority held that the Air Force's argument in this regard had already been "considered and rejected" by the D.C. Circuit in McDonnell Douglas Corp. v. NASA.[426] After first positing an entirely new definition of the term "underbidding," the panel proceeded to rule that the district court wrongly held that the Air Force's argument in this case "differs markedly" from the argument that had been rejected in McDonnell Douglas v. NASA.[427] On this basis, it held that the option prices in the contract were protected by Exemption 4 and could not be disclosed by the Air Force.[428]

Regarding the CLINs that McDonnell Douglas contended were made up primarily of vendor costs, McDonnell Douglas argued that its competitors probably obtained "the same or nearly the same" quotes from the same vendors and that disclosure of these unit prices therefore would allow them to calculate its "Vendor Pricing Factor."[429] The Air Force determined that disclosure of these CLINS would not cause McDonnell Douglas substantial competitive harm because in its experience it is "not uncommon" for a vendor to quote different prices to its different customers.[430] Rather than examine the evidence (or lack of it) behind McDonnell Douglas's argument, though, the panel majority instead stated that the Air Force had "provided no actual evidence" to support this proposition, and it then declared that it is "probable as a matter of economic theory" that a subcontractor would quote its prime contractors similar prices.[431] Based upon that theory of the case, and of the marketplace as well, the panel held that the Air Force's decision to disclose CLINs comprised of vendor prices was arbi-

---

[424] Id.

[425] Id.

[426] Id.

[427] Id.

[428] See id.

[429] Id. at 1190.

[430] Id.

[431] Id. at 1191.

trary and capricious.[432]

Lastly, as to the CLINs consisting of "over and above" rates in the contract -- i.e., rates that McDonnell Douglas agreed to charge the Air Force for work not priced in the basic contract -- McDonnell Douglas had argued that their disclosure would allow a competitor to calculate its labor markup because the wages McDonnell Douglas was paying were common knowledge.[433]

The Air Force refuted that claim and had determined that McDonnell Douglas's wages were not publicly known and that in fact McDonnell Douglas had submitted significantly different "over and above" rates in a contract to service another type of aircraft at the very same facility.[434] For this one category of prices, the panel agreed with the agency, holding that the Air Force "reasonably concluded [that] McDonnell Douglas failed to carry its burden of showing release of the Over and Above CLINs was likely to cause it substantial competitive harm. Therefore, the decision of the Air Force to release the[se] CLINs was not arbitrary and capricious."[435]

In dissent, Judge Garland strongly disagreed with the panel majority's decisions regarding both the option prices and the vendor prices, and he pointedly countered each of the stated justifications for those decisions.[436] Regarding the vendor pricing CLINs, Judge Garland pointed out that "it is the opponent of disclosure -- not the requester -- who bears the burden of proving whether substantial competitive harm is likely to result,"[437] but that in this case the panel majority "st[ood] the burden of proof on its head" by requiring the Air Force to provide special evidence to support its stated judgment.[438] Judge Garland also faulted the majority for using mere economic theory -- "a theory of the court's own invention" -- to support its decision that the vendor pricing CLINs are protected by Exemp-

---

[432] See id.

[433] See id. at 1191-92.

[434] See id. at 1192.

[435] Id.

[436] Id. at 1194-1204.

[437] Id. at 1195-96 (citing Occidental Petroleum, 873 F.2d at 342 (holding that the opponent of disclosure bears the "ultimate burden of persuasion"), and National Parks, 547 F.2d at 679 n.20 (declaring that "[t]he party seeking to avoid disclosure bears the burden of proving that the circumstances justify nondisclosure")).

[438] Id. at 1196.

tion 4.[439] Further, among other criticisms, Judge Garland stated that "unless we reverse the burden of proof and deny the Air Force the deference it is owed, there is no basis for overturning its conclusion that disclosure of the prices it paid for McDonnell Douglas's services is unlikely to cause substantial harm to the contractor's competitive position."[440]

Judge Garland also found errors in the majority's decision regarding the option prices in the contract. He recognized that the Air Force's argument regarding the option prices was not, in fact, the same argument that the D.C. Circuit had rejected in McDonnell Douglas v. NASA, and he observed that the panel majority was able to characterize the arguments in the two cases as the same only by "embellish[ing]" the definition of "underbidding."[441] Judge Garland further faulted the majority for simply dismissing the Air Force's determination that because price was only one of many evaluation factors used in awarding contracts the disclosure of option prices was not likely to cause substantial harm to McDonnell Douglas's competitive position.[442] He pointed out that the Air Force made clear in both its Request for Proposal (RFP) and final decision letter that multiple factors would be used to evaluate proposals, and therefore the majority was "wrong" to state its own view that whether or not "'price will be one of several factors to be weighted equally in any future RFP . . . is necessarily speculative.'"[443] He further observed that the contract at issue in this case was "not to supply cafeteria food, but to service planes that 'will be flown by American military personnel on highly dangerous missions,'" and that it therefore should not be surprising that "considerations of safety, quality, and confidence in an incumbent contractor would at least be the equal of price."[444] Judge Garland concluded that "[i]n dismissing the government's non-price factors argument and failing to address its reverse-engineering contention, my colleagues come perilously close to treating a contractor's claim of 'underbidding' as a talisman that bars disclosure of any line-item price."[445]

Notwithstanding this concern raised by Judge Garland, the panel majority in both of these McDonnell Douglas decisions expressly stated that the court was not creating a per se rule that prices in awarded govern-

---

[439] Id. at 1197.

[440] Id. at 1198 (citing CNA, 830 F.2d at 1155 (deferring to agency when presented with "no more than two contradictory views of what likely would ensue upon release of [the] information")).

[441] Id. at 1201.

[442] See id. at 1202.

[443] Id. (quoting majority opinion).

[444] Id. (quoting agency's brief).

[445] Id.

ment contracts must invariably be withheld.[446] Indeed, as discussed above, in the McDonnell Douglas v. Air Force decision, the court upheld the release of certain contract prices.[447] Thus, the net effect of these decisions is that agencies are best advised to continue both their practice of notifying all submitters of contract price information in order to obtain any objections to disclosure and to then carefully conducting a thorough competitive harm analysis on a case-by-case basis, thereby ensuring that they always have a sufficient administrative record on which to base and support their decisions.[448]

Subsequently, in its first unit price case decided since McDonnell Douglas v. Air Force, the District Court for the District of Columbia ruled similarly, and upheld the agency's decision to disclose "over and above" prices, but enjoined the agency from disclosing option year prices.[449] In so deciding, the court was presented with several arguments that the D.C. Circuit had declined to consider in McDonnell Douglas v. Air Force due to the parties' failure to raise them during the administrative process.[450]

With respect to option prices, the plaintiffs argued that disclosure would result in substantial competitive harm because competitors could submit unsolicited, lower bids to the Air Force, which the Air Force could then accept.[451] The court rejected the plaintiffs' argument, agreeing instead with the Air Force that under the FAR it could not accept an unsoli-

---

[446] See McDonnell Douglas v. Air Force, 375 F.3d at 1193; McDonnell Douglas v. NASA, No. 98-5251, slip op. at 2 (D.C. Cir. Oct. 6, 1999).

[447] See McDonnell Douglas v. Air Force, 375 F.3d at 1192.

[448] See FOIA Post, "Treatment of Unit Prices After McDonnell Douglas v. Air Force" (posted 9/8/05) (advising agencies that in light of D.C. Circuit's McDonnell Douglas v. Air Force decision they should continue their practice of conducting submitter notice in response to requests that seek unit prices and, where disclosure is required, creating a detailed administrative record to support their decisions) (supplementing FOIA Post, "Treatment of Unit Prices Under Exemption 4" (posted 5/29/02)) (emphasizing importance of undertaking submitter notice each time unit prices are requested and of carefully documenting agency rationale) (superseding FOIA Update, Vol. XVIII, No. 4, at 1, and FOIA Update, Vol. V, No. 4, at 4); see also FOIA Post, "New McDonnell Douglas Opinion Aids Unit Price Decisionmaking" (posted 10/4/02). See generally FOIA Update, Vol. IV, No. 4, at 10 (setting forth similar approach to handling requests for unit prices).

[449] Canadian Commercial Corp v. Dep't of the Air Force, 442 F. Supp. 2d 15, 41 (D.D.C. 2006) (reverse FOIA suit) (appeal pending).

[450] See id. at 38.

[451] Id. at 34; see also McDonnell Douglas v. Air Force, 375 F.3d at 1187-88 (declining to consider this argument because it was not made at the administrative level).

cited bid.[452] The plaintiffs also contended that the mere submission of unsolicited, lower-priced proposals by its competitors could induce the Air Force to issue a new solicitation for the option-year work, and that thereafter its competitors could make offers that would undercut the plaintiff's prices.[453] The Air Force countered that it "regularly and routinely" exercised options, and that the plaintiffs had failed to present any evidence to the contrary.[454] The court held that the Air Force had "improperly shifted" the burden to the plaintiffs, and that it was the Air Force, not the plaintiffs, that had failed to produce any evidence to support its argument.[455]

The Air Force had further argued that, pursuant to the FAR, a competitor's price would have to offset the transaction costs associated with changing contractors in order to persuade the Air Force not to exercise an option.[456] The court rejected this argument, concluding that it was just a "repackaging" of the "price is just one of many factors" argument which was rejected by the D.C. Circuit.[457] More specifically, the court found that the FAR "merely suggests that such considerations 'should' be taken into account, not that such a finding is required in order to decline to exercise an option."[458]

Although the court rejected the Air Force's disclosure decision with respect to option year prices, the court nonetheless addressed, and rejected, the plaintiffs' alternative argument that disclosure of option prices would allow their competitors to ascertain their pricing strategy and, consequently, to undercut their offers in future procurements.[459] Notably, the court pointed out that the burden was on plaintiffs to show that reverse-engineering was "not merely possible, but likely."[460] In this regard, the court found that the Air Force had refuted plaintiffs' arguments using "spe-

---

[452] Id. at 34 (citing 48 C.F.R. §§ 2.101, 15.603(c)).

[453] See id. at 34.

[454] Id. at 34-35

[455] Id. at 35-36.

[456] Id. at 38-39 (citing 48 C.F.R. § 17.207(c)); see also McDonnell Douglas, 375 F.3d at 1188-89 (refusing to consider such argument because it played no role in the agency's administrative decision).

[457] Canadian Commercial, 442 F. Supp. 2d at 35, 39.

[458] See id. at 38 (observing further that Air Force had failed to present any evidence that it had followed practice of requiring such finding notwithstanding FAR's permissive language).

[459] See id. at 33 & n.8.

[460] Id. at n.8.

cific and illustrative" reasoning.[461] Moreover, the court observed, the Air Force had highlighted the difficulty of accurately calculating plaintiffs' future offers, because of the "subjective variables that factor into cost analysis."[462] Given these circumstances, the court concluded that the plaintiffs had failed to show that competitors were "likely" to predict plaintiffs' future prices.[463]

Continuing this line of reasoning, the court upheld the agency's disclosure decision with respect to the "over and above" prices.[464] The plaintiffs had argued that their disclosure would allow their competitors' employees to learn, through their union memberships, the plaintiffs' negotiated pay rates.[465] This combination of pay rates and fixed hourly labor rates for over and above work CLINs, they further argued, would enable their competitors to deduce plaintiffs' overhead rates.[466] The court found that while such a "multi-step" occurrence might be "possible," the plaintiffs had failed to offer any evidence that this was "likely" to occur.[467] Therefore, for this category of prices, the court upheld the Air Force's decision that substantial competitive harm was not likely to result from its disclosure.[468]

In explaining the rationale for its decision, the court pointed out that it had not relied upon McDonnell Douglas v. Air Force to create "a strict mandate or per se rule" pertaining to unit prices.[469] Rather, the court explained, its conclusions were driven by the D.C. Circuit's analysis in that case, as well as by "the shortfalls in logic and evidence" in the Air Force's administrative decision in the case before it.[470] Thus, this decision further underscores the need for agencies to carefully evaluate competitive harm claims on a case-by-case basis and to carefully document their reasons for disclosing unit prices.

There are many well-reasoned decisions upholding agency determinations to disclose unit prices in the absence of convincing evidence of competitive harm. In a recent case, the submitter failed to present any ev-

---

[461] Id.

[462] Id. (citing Acumenics Research, 843 F.2d at 808).

[463] Id.

[464] See id. at 38 n.10.

[465] Id.

[466] See id.

[467] Id.

[468] See id.

[469] Id. at 39.

[470] Id.

idence showing how its unit prices could be reverse engineered by its competitors in order to allow them to determine the submitter's pricing strategy.[471] Similarly, the court found that the submitter had failed to demonstrate that the pricing structure for the contracts at issue would be relevant for "any potential future government contracts."[472] In another case, the submitter provided only "conclusory and generalized assertions" of harm, that "mainly detailed measures it took to guard and protect its pricing information," that the court found were "simply not relevant to the <u>National Parks</u> analysis."[473] An additional argument -- that the submitter would suffer harm because the "contract contemplates option years and may be rebid," was not raised before the agency and so was considered to be "outside the scope of the administrative record."[474] Nonetheless, the court addressed it in the alternative, finding it "unpersuasive," as the precedent primarily relied on by the submitter concerned the possibility of "rebidding a contract for unperformed work," a situation deemed "factually and legally distinguishable from" the case at hand.[475]

A similar challenge to an agency's decision to disclose, among other things, a contractor's unit price information was soundly rejected in yet another decision by the District Court for the District of Columbia.[476] In upholding the agency's decision to release the information, the court rejected the submitter's contention that disclosure would enable its competitors "to predict its costs and profit margin, significantly enhancing their ability to underbid."[477] Declaring that "[t]he public, including competitors who lost the business to the winning bidder, is entitled to know just how and why a government agency decided to spend public funds as it did; to be assured that the competition was fair; and indeed, even to learn how to be more effective competitors in the future," the court upheld the agency's decision to release the information because the submitter had "simply failed to demonstrate" how it would be competitively harmed by the information's disclo-

---

[471] Clearbrook, L.L.C. v. Ovall, No. 06-0629, 2006 U.S. Dist. LEXIS 81244, at *12 (S.D. Ala. Nov. 3, 2006) (denying plaintiff's motion for preliminary injunction), <u>dismissed with prejudice per stipulation</u> (S.D. Ala. Nov. 22, 2006) (reverse FOIA suit).

[472] Id.

[473] TRIFID Corp. v. Nat'l Imagery & Mapping Agency, 10 F. Supp. 2d 1087, 1099 (E.D. Mo. 1998) (reverse FOIA suit).

[474] Id.

[475] Id. at 1100.

[476] Martin Marietta, 974 F. Supp. at 38 (specifically, "cost and fee information," and "component and configuration prices" -- including unit pricing and contract line item numbers -- and "technical and management information").

[477] Id. at 40.

sure.[478] Although noting that the submitter "might prefer that less be known about its operations, and that the reasons for its past successes remain a mystery to be solved by the competitors on their own," the court held that the submitter had not shown "that it will in fact be unable to duplicate those successes unless [the agency] acquiesces in keeping the competition in the dark."[479]

The outcome of that case was consistent with the outcome in four cases concerning contract price information that were decided previously -- all of which were brought by submitters challenging agency decisions to disclose such information -- and in which none of the submitters were able to convince the court that disclosure of the prices charged the government would cause them to suffer competitive harm.[480] One of the cases was remanded back to the agency for further factfinding on that issue,[481] but in the remaining three cases the competitive harm arguments were rejected outright by the court.[482] (One of these cases subsequently was vacated after the FOIA request was withdrawn while the case was on appeal.[483])

---

[478] Id. at 41.

[479] Id.

[480] McDonnell Douglas Corp. v. NASA, 895 F. Supp. 319, 326 (D.D.C. 1995) (reverse FOIA suit), vacated as moot, No. 95-5288 (D.C. Cir. Apr. 1, 1996); CC Distribs. v. Kinzinger, No. 94-1330, 1995 WL 405445, at *5-6 (D.D.C. June 28, 1995) (reverse FOIA suit); Chem. Waste Mgmt., Inc. v. O'Leary, No. 94-2230, 1995 WL 115894, at *4-5 (D.D.C. Feb. 28, 1995) (reverse FOIA suit); Comdisco, Inc. v. GSA, 864 F. Supp. 510, 516 (E.D. Va. 1994) (reverse FOIA suit).

[481] Chem. Waste, 1995 WL 115894, at *5 (requiring the agency to correct its administrative record by addressing the submitter's "actual complaints of [competitive] harm," i.e., that when the contract was rebid, the new contractor "will be asked to perform the exact same -- and, as yet, unrendered -- services that were expected to be performed under" the existing contract).

[482] McDonnell Douglas, 895 F. Supp. at 326 (submitter "failed to show with any particularity how a competitor could use the information at issue to cause competitive injury"); CC Distribs., 1995 WL 405445, at *5 (submitter failed "to explain how its competitors could reverse-engineer its pricing methods and deduce its concessions from suppliers," which it had conclusorily claimed would occur if its unit prices were disclosed); Comdisco, 864 F. Supp. at 516 (submitter failed to satisfy standard that it "present persuasive evidence that disclosure of the unit prices would reveal some confidential piece of information, such as a profit multiplier or risk assessment, that would place the submitter at a competitive disadvantage").

[483] See McDonnell Douglas Corp. v. NASA, No. 95-5288 (D.C. Cir. Apr. 1, 1996).

Additionally, there are three other cases which contain a thorough analysis of the possible effects of disclosure of unit prices -- including two appellate decisions -- and in all three of these cases the courts likewise denied Exemption 4 protection, finding that disclosure of the prices would not directly reveal confidential proprietary information, such as a company's overhead, profit rates, or multiplier, and that the possibility of competitive harm was thus too speculative.[484] For example, the Court of Appeals for the Ninth Circuit denied Exemption 4 protection for the unit prices provided by a successful offeror despite the offeror's contention that competitors would be able to determine its profit margin by simply subtracting from the unit price the other component parts which are either set by statute or standardized within the industry.[485] The Ninth Circuit upheld the agency's determination that competitors would not be able to make this type of calculation, because the component figures making up the unit price were not, in fact, standardized, but instead were subject to fluctuation.[486]

Subsequent to the issuance of McDonnell Douglas v. NASA, but before the district court's decision in McDonnell Douglas v. Air Force, the District Court for the District of Columbia rendered an opinion in MCI Worldcom, Inc. v. GSA, that contained an alternative holding addressing the issue of disclosure of unit prices.[487] At issue in MCI Worldcom were tables containing complex matrices specifying millions of "pricing elements" for telecommunications services provided by contractors to the government.[488] The agency had informed the submitters that pursuant to a new policy, "it would now publicly disclose all 'contract unit prices'" pursuant to the disclosure provisions of the Federal Acquisition Regulation (FAR).[489] In overturning that agency decision, the court first ruled that the

---

[484] Pac. Architects, 906 F.2d at 1347; Acumenics, 843 F.2d at 808; J.H. Lawrence Co. v. Smith, No. 81-2993, slip op. at 8-9 (D. Md. Nov. 10, 1982).

[485] Pac. Architects, 906 F.2d at 1347.

[486] Id. at 1347-48; see RMS, No. C-92-1545, slip op. at 7 (N.D. Cal. Nov. 24, 1992) (declaring that the court was "unconvinced based on the evidence that the release of contract bid prices, terms and conditions whether interim or final will harm the successful bidders"); see also GC Micro, 33 F.3d at 1114-15 (relying on Pacific Architects, and ordering disclosure of percentage and dollar amount of work subcontracted out by defense contractors).

[487] 163 F. Supp. 2d 28, 35-36 (D.D.C. 2001) (reverse FOIA suit).

[488] Id. at 29-30.

[489] Id. at 30-31 (citing 48 C.F.R. §§ 15.503(b)(1), 15.506(d)(2) (currently at volume 2005), which mandate disclosure of unit prices in post-award notices and debriefings for contracts solicited after Jan. 1, 1998); see also Comdisco, 864 F. Supp. at 516 (noting that unit prices are "the sort of pricing information routinely disclosed under the [FAR]" (citing Acumenics, 843
(continued...)

tables did not, in fact, contain "unit prices," but instead "more closely re-semble[d] 'cost breakdowns,' which," it noted, "are specifically prohibited from disclosure by the very FAR provision relied upon" by the agency.[490] Noting the absence of any "standard definition of 'unit price'" in the FAR or in the case law, the court found that because the "pricing elements and components" at issue were "not separately purchased, ordered or billed to the government," they did not constitute the "price" for a "'good or ser-vice.'"[491] Accordingly, the court concluded that the tables did not contain "'unit price' information" within the meaning of the FAR.[492]

Although the court could have finished its decision with that holding, it nonetheless went on to rule that "even assuming" that the tables did con-tain "'unit price' information," the FAR did not "permit their disclosure."[493] Focusing on language contained in both of the FAR provisions relied on by

---

[489](...continued)
F.2d at 807-08)); JL Assocs., 90-2 CPD 261, B-239790 at 4 n.2 (Oct. 1, 1990) (Comptroller General decision rejecting argument that disclosure of option prices would cause submitter competitive harm by revealing pricing stra-tegy and decisionmaking process and noting that FAR "expressly advises awardees that the unit prices of awards will generally be disclosed to un-successful offerors"); cf. McDonnell Douglas Corp. v. Widnall, No. 94-0091, slip op. at 13 (D.D.C. Apr. 11, 1994) (ruling on different FAR disclosure pro-vision, and holding that that provision served as legal authorization for agency to release exercised option prices and that such prices thus were "not protected from disclosure by the Trade Secrets Act," 18 U.S.C. § 1905 (2000 & Supp. IV 2004), and that the court need not reach the issue of the applicability of Exemption 4), and McDonnell Douglas Corp. v. Widnall, No. 92-2211, slip op. at 8 (D.D.C. Apr. 11, 1994) (same), cases consolidated on appeal & remanded for further development of the record, 57 F.3d 1162, 1167 (D.C. Cir. 1995) (holding that because the agency's FAR "authorization argument is intertwined analytically" with the Exemption 4 coverage issue, a remand to the agency was necessary so that the court could "have one considered and complete statement of the Air Force's position" on the sub-mitter's claim that its prices were protected by Exemption 4) (non-FOIA cases brought under Administrative Procedure Act). See generally Flam-mann, 339 F.3d at 1323 (holding, in a pre-award bid protest case concern-ing unit prices contained in sealed bids -- as distinct from prices contained in proposals -- which were subject to the public opening requirement con-tained in a different FAR provision, that such bid prices "entered the public domain upon bid opening, and therefore . . . did not fall within Exemption 4 of FOIA").

[490] MCI Worldcom, 163 F. Supp. 2d at 33.

[491] Id. at 32-33.

[492] Id. at 34.

[493] Id.

the agency -- that prohibited "release of information that is confidential, trade secret, or otherwise exempt under FOIA Exemption 4" -- the court determined that the "unmistakable meaning" of the FAR provisions was that unit price information could be disclosed "only insofar as it" is not otherwise exempt from disclosure.[494] Moving to an analysis of whether the tables were protected under Exemption 4, the court relied on the D.C. Circuit's decision in McDonnell Douglas v. NASA, finding that the submitters had "set forth detailed facts" establishing that they would suffer "precisely the injuries that led [the D.C.] Circuit to declare that line item pricing was confidential information and not disclosable."[495] Most significantly, in making this determination, the court was greatly influenced by the fact that the agency was unable to "point[] to anything in the administrative record that establishes that the information is not confidential," as it had "never made any findings" on that issue.[496]

In a recent decision, the same court relied in part upon MCI Worldcom in holding that the Trade Secrets Act prohibited the disclosure of option year prices.[497] The agency in that case had argued that the FAR required it to disclose unit price information and therefore authorized its disclosure under the Trade Secrets Act.[498] Like in MCI Worldcom, however, the court determined that another provision of the FAR specifically "unauthorize[d]" the disclosure of any information that is protected by Exemption 4.[499] The agency had argued that the case law ultimately relied upon by the court, including MCI Worldcom, failed to address the history of the

---

[494] Id. at 34-35 (citing Mallinckrodt v. West, 140 F. Supp. 2d 1, 5-6 (D.D.C. 2000) (concluding that the FAR provisions "do no more than require the disclosure of information unless its disclosure would reveal information that is exempt from release under the FOIA") (reverse FOIA suit), appeal dismissed voluntarily, No. 00-5330 (D.C. Cir. Dec. 12, 2000)); accord Envtl. Tech., Inc. v. EPA, 822 F. Supp. 1226, 1229 n.4 (E.D. Va. 1993) (interpreting even less specific, pre-1998 version of unit price FAR provision to prohibit release of unit prices if such information "constitutes 'confidential business information'") (reverse FOIA suit).

[495] MCI Worldcom, 163 F. Supp. 2d at 36; see also Mallinckrodt, 140 F. Supp. 2d at 6 n.4 (dictum) (opining that it "need not reach" the issue, because the requested rebate and incentive information was protected as a voluntary submission, but nonetheless noting that "it appears" that it would be protected under the competitive harm test (citing McDonnell Douglas v. NASA,180 F.3d at 306)).

[496] MCI Worldcom, 163 F. Supp. 2d at 36 & n.10.

[497] See id. at 40.

[498] See id. at 40 (relying on 48 C.F.R. §§ 15.503(b)(1)(iv), 15.506(d)(2), and 5.303(b)(2)).

[499] Id. (citing 48 C.F.R. § 15.506(e), Mallinckrodt, 140 F. Supp. 2d at 5-6, and MCI Worldcom, 63 F. Supp. 2d at 34 & n.7).

FOIA and the FAR and accordingly should not guide the court's analysis.[500] The court found that argument "unconvincing," opining that the legislative history of the FOIA was "at best, ambiguous and inconclusive."[501] It further declared that "'[t]he FAR may not be interpreted in a way that contravenes [the] statutory prohibition on disclosure' that is contained in the FAR and its authorizing statute."[502]

More than a quarter-century ago, in the absence of a showing of competitive harm, the District Court for the District of Columbia denied Exemption 4 protection for the prices charged the government for computer equipment, and in so doing stated that "[d]isclosure of prices charged the Government is a cost of doing business with the Government."[503] This "cost of doing business" principle was later expressly recognized by the District Court for the District of Columbia as a "general proposition" that agencies may reasonably follow.[504] Although it is not applicable "to every case that arises,"[505] the court nevertheless found that it is "incumbent upon" a submitter challenging a contract price disclosure decision to "demonstrate that [an agency's] decision to follow this general proposition" -- namely, that disclosure of contract prices is a cost of doing business with the government -- is somehow arbitrary or capricious.[506] This ruling comports with the court's decision in an earlier unit price case in which it had recognized the "strong public interest in release of component and aggregate prices in Government contract awards."[507]

---

[500] See id.

[501] Id.

[502] Id. (quoting MCI Worldcom, 163 F. Supp. 2d at 34).

[503] Racal-Milgo Gov't Sys. v. SBA, 559 F. Supp. 4, 6 (D.D.C. 1981); accord CC Distribs., 1995 WL 405445, at *6; JL Assocs., 90-2 CPD 261, B-239790 at 4 (Oct. 1, 1990) (Comptroller General decision noting that "disclosure of prices charged the government is ordinarily a cost of doing business with the government"); see also EHE, No. 81-1087, slip op. at 4 (D.D.C. Feb. 24, 1984) ("[O]ne who would do business with the government must expect that more of his offer is more likely to become known to others than in the case of a purely private agreement.").

[504] CC Distribs., 1995 WL 405445, at *6.

[505] Id. (referring to Chem. Waste, 1995 WL 115894, at *5, where the prices at issue were those of a subcontractor who was "not in privity of contract" with the agency and thus was not, in fact, "doing business" with the government").

[506] Id.

[507] AT&T Info. Sys. v. GSA, 627 F. Supp. 1396, 1403 (D.D.C. 1986) (reverse FOIA suit); rev'd on other grounds & remanded, 810 F.2d 1233, 1236 (D.C.
(continued...)

Similarly, in a case involving unexercised option prices rather than "ordinary" unit prices the court expressly stated that it "generally agrees that '[d]isclosure of prices charged the Government is a cost of doing business with the Government.'"[508] It then upheld the agency's decision to release the option prices because "competitively sensitive information such as cost, overhead, or profit identifiers would not be revealed."[509] This decision was subsequently vacated by the D.C. Circuit, however,[510] after the FOIA requester withdrew its request while the case was pending on appeal. In the absence of a FOIA requester seeking access to the information, the court held that the case had become moot.[511]

The D.C. Circuit in McDonnell Douglas v. NASA noted that NASA had advised the submitter "that publication of line item prices is the 'price of doing business' with the government," but the court characterized the statement as one that "either assumes the conclusion, or else assumes a legal duty or authority on the government to publicize these prices," which NASA did not assert it had.[512] Nonetheless, the "cost of doing business" principle was again cited with approval by the District Court for the District of Columbia in an opinion issued five years ago that ordered disclosure of "the names of all entities that placed bids" to buy land that the government was selling, as well as "the amounts of all bids."[513] In rejecting the agency's competitive harm claim -- which was similar to the argument often made by submitters seeking to withhold unit prices, namely, that competitors could "reconstruct each factor in the bidder's calculations" by "comparing the total bid amount with information already in the public domain" -- the court relied on several of the district court decisions within the D.C. Circuit that "have viewed such arguments with skepticism" and have "required disclosure of both aggregate and unit prices," and then it ordered

---

(...continued)
Cir. 1987).

[508] Gen. Dynamics Corp. v. U.S. Dep't of the Air Force, 822 F. Supp. 804, 807 (D.D.C. 1992) (quoting Racal-Milgo, 559 F. Supp. at 6) (reverse FOIA suit), vacated as moot, No. 92-5186 (D.C. Cir. Sept. 23, 1993).

[509] Id.; see RMS, No. C-92-1545, slip op. at 7 (N.D. Cal. Nov. 24, 1992) (rejecting competitive harm claim for "interim" prices).

[510] Gen. Dynamics Corp. v. Dep't of the Air Force, No. 92-5186, slip op. at 1 (D.C. Cir. Sept. 23, 1993) (reverse FOIA suit).

[511] Id.

[512] McDonnell Douglas v. NASA, 180 F.3d at 306.

[513] Ctr. for Pub. Integrity, 191 F. Supp. 2d at 196 (citing Racal-Milgo, 559 F. Supp. at 6).

disclosure itself.[514] One of the principal cases relied upon to make this determination was <u>Brownstein Zeidman & Schomer v. Department of the Air Force</u>, in which the court had ordered disclosure of unit prices, rejecting as "highly speculative" the argument that their release would allow competitors to calculate the submitter's profit margin and thus be able to underbid it in future procurements.[515]

Fifteen years ago, in yet another case involving unit prices, the court found that it was a "fact-intensive question" whether the submitter would suffer competitive harm from release of its "price information" and it therefore declined to rule on the applicability of Exemption 4 in the context of a summary judgment motion.[516] (That case was never resolved on the merits by the District of Columbia court as the issue was first litigated by a party acting on behalf of the plaintiff in the Eastern District of Virginia[517] and the principle of collateral estoppel was then found to prevent the plaintiff from relitigating the issue in the District of Columbia.[518])

In the immediate wake of the decision by the D.C. Circuit in <u>Critical Mass Energy Project v. NRC</u>,[519] two decisions somewhat reflexively afforded protection to unit prices premised on the theory that contract submissions are "voluntary" and that such pricing terms are not customarily disclosed to the public.[520] These decisions appear to implicitly define voluntary submissions according to the nature of the activity to which they are connected and thus are contrary to the policy guidance issued by the Department of Justice concerning the voluntary/required distinction.[521] Indeed, one of these decisions[522] was expressly disclaimed by another judge in that same judicial district for failing to identify any justification

---

[514] <u>Id.</u> at 194, 196.

[515] 781 F. Supp. 31, 33 (D.D.C. 1991).

[516] <u>MCI</u>, 1992 WL 71394, at *6.

[517] <u>Cohen, Dunn & Sinclair, P.C. v. GSA</u>, No. 92-0057-A (E.D. Va. Sept. 10, 1992) (bench order).

[518] <u>MCI Telecomms. Corp. v. GSA</u>, No. 89-0746, slip op. at 4-9 (D.D.C. Feb. 27, 1995).

[519] 975 F.2d 871 (D.C. Cir. 1992) (en banc).

[520] <u>Envtl. Tech.</u>, 822 F. Supp. at 1229; <u>Cohen, Dunn</u>, No. 92-0057-A, transcript at 28 (E.D. Va. Sept. 10, 1992).

[521] <u>See</u> FOIA Update, Vol. XIV, No. 2, at 3-5 ("OIP Guidance: The <u>Critical Mass</u> Distinction Under Exemption 4"); <u>id.</u> at 6-7 ("Exemption 4 Under <u>Critical Mass</u>: Step-By-Step Decisionmaking").

[522] <u>Envtl. Tech.</u>, 822 F. Supp. at 1229.

whatsoever for its conclusion.[523] (For a further discussion of Critical Mass and its "voluntariness" standard, see Exemption 4, Applying Critical Mass, above.) In addition to affording protection to contract pricing information under Critical Mass, the other decision, in a rather cursory order issued from the bench, went on to alternatively afford protection under the competitive harm prong.[524]

None of the above cases concerning unit prices involved a request for pricing information submitted by an unsuccessful offeror. In the first decision to touch on this point, the court considered a situation in which the requester did not actually seek unit prices, but instead had requested the bottom-line price (total cumulative price) that an unsuccessful offeror had proposed for a government contract, as well as the bottom-line prices it had proposed for four years' worth of contract options.[525] Accepting the submitter's contention that disclosure of these bottom-line prices would cause it to suffer competitive harm by enabling competitors to deduce its pricing strategy, the court found that unsuccessful offerors had a different expectation of confidentiality than successful offerors, that the public interest in disclosure of pricing information concerning unawarded contracts was slight, and most importantly, that the unsuccessful offeror -- who would be competing with the successful offeror on the contract options as well as on future related contracts -- had demonstrated factually how the contract and option prices could be used by its competitors to derive data harmful to its competitive position.[526] By contrast, such a detailed explanation of harm was found lacking in an analogous case involving the sale of land by the government, and as a consequence the court ordered disclosure of the names of the unsuccessful bidders seeking to buy the land as well as the amounts of their bids.[527]

Congress addressed this issue in the procurement context with a statute that prohibits most agencies from disclosing solicited contract proposals -- which would contain proposed price information -- if those proposals have not become incorporated into an ensuing government con-

---

[523] Comdisco, 864 F. Supp. at 517 n.8.

[524] Cohen, Dunn, No. 92-0057-A, transcript at 29; Findings of Fact at 7-8 (E.D. Va. Sept. 10, 1992) (accepting argument that disclosure of detailed unit price information would reveal pricing strategy and permit future bids to be predicted and undercut).

[525] Raytheon Co. v. Dep't of the Navy, No. 89-2481, 1989 WL 550581, at *1 (D.D.C. Dec. 22, 1989).

[526] Id. at *5-6; see also FOIA Update, Vol. XI, No. 2, at 2; FOIA Update, Vol. IV, No. 4, at 10-11.

[527] Ctr. for Pub. Integrity, 191 F. Supp. 2d at 195-96.

tract.[528] This Exemption 3 statute[529] has the practical effect of providing statutory protection for the prices proposed by unsuccessful offerors because, by definition, that information is not incorporated into the resulting government contract.[530]

## Third Prong of National Parks

In addition to the impairment prong and the competitive harm prong of the test for confidentiality established in National Parks & Conservation Ass'n v. Morton, the decision specifically left open the possibility of a third prong that would protect other governmental interests, such as compliance and program effectiveness.[531] Several subsequent decisions reaffirmed this possibility in dicta[532] and, as discussed below, with its en banc decision in Critical Mass Energy Project v. NRC, the Court of Appeals for the District of Columbia Circuit conclusively recognized the existence of a "third prong" under National Parks.[533]

The third prong received its first thorough appellate court analysis and acceptance by the Court of Appeals for the First Circuit.[534] In 9 to 5

---

[528] National Defense Authorization Act for Fiscal Year 1997, Pub. L. No. 104-201, § 821, 110 Stat. 2422 (containing parallel measures applicable to armed services and most civilian agencies) (codified at 10 U.S.C. § 2305(g) (2000), amended by Pub. L. No. 106-65, 113 Stat. 512 (1999) (extending coverage of statute to all agencies listed in 10 U.S.C. § 2303 (2000), notably NASA and Coast Guard), and at 41 U.S.C. § 253b(m) (2000)); see Ctr. for Pub. Integrity, 191 F. Supp. 2d at 194 (construing the statute's coverage to include "a private party with whom the government has a procurement contract for products or services," but not "a private party purchasing government land").

[529] 5 U.S.C. § 552(b)(3) (2000 & Supp. IV 2004); see Hornbostel v. U.S. Dep't of the Interior, 305 F. Supp. 2d 21, 29-30 (D.D.C. 2003).

[530] See FOIA Update, Vol. XVIII, No. 1, at 2 (discussing statute and fact that key determinant of exempt status under it is whether proposal was incorporated into or otherwise set forth in resulting contract).

[531] 498 F.2d 765, 770 n.17 (D.C. Cir. 1974).

[532] Wash. Post Co. v. HHS, 690 F.2d 252, 268 n.51 (D.C. Cir. 1982); Nat'l Parks & Conservation Ass'n v. Kleppe, 547 F.2d 673, 678 n.16 (D.C. Cir. 1976); Pub. Citizen Health Research Group v. FDA, 539 F. Supp. 1320, 1326 (D.D.C. 1982), rev'd & remanded on other grounds, 704 F.2d 1280 (D.C. Cir. 1983).

[533] 975 F.2d 871, 879 (D.C. Cir. 1992); see also FOIA Update, Vol. XIV, No. 2, at 7 ("Exemption 4 Under Critical Mass: Step-By-Step Decisionmaking").

[534] 9 to 5 Org. for Women Office Workers v. Bd. of Governors of the Fed.

(continued...)

<u>Organization for Women Office Workers v. Board of Governors of the Federal Reserve System</u>, the First Circuit expressly admonished against using the two primary prongs of <u>National Parks</u> as "the exclusive criteria for determining confidentiality" and held that the pertinent inquiry is whether public disclosure of the information will harm an "identifiable private or governmental interest which the Congress sought to protect by enacting Exemption 4 of the FOIA."[535]

---

[534](...continued)
Reserve Sys., 721 F.2d 1 (1st Cir. 1983); <u>accord</u> Afr. Fund v. Mosbacher, No. 92-289, 1993 WL 183736, at *7 (S.D.N.Y. May 26, 1993) (finding the third prong satisfied when the agency "submitted extensive declarations that explain why disclosure of documents . . . would interfere with the export control system" (citing <u>Durnan v. U.S. Dep't of Commerce</u>, 777 F. Supp. 965, 967 (D.D.C. 1991))).

[535] <u>9 to 5</u>, 721 F.2d at 10; <u>see, e.g.</u>, <u>Judicial Watch, Inc. v. U.S. Dep't of Commerce</u>, 337 F. Supp. 2d 146, 170 (D.D.C. 2004) (protecting finance agreement, based partly upon third prong, because otherwise agency "would face difficulty negotiating future agreements with borrowers fearful of disclosure"); <u>Nadler v. FDIC</u>, 899 F. Supp. 158, 161-63 (S.D.N.Y. 1995) (protecting a joint venture agreement acquired when the FDIC became the receiver of a failed bank under the third prong because disclosure could "hurt the venture's prospects for financial success," which in turn would "reduce returns to the FDIC," and thereby "interfere significantly with the FDIC's receivership program, which aims to maximize profits on the assets acquired from failed banks"), <u>aff'd on other grounds</u>, 92 F.3d 93, 96 (2d Cir. 1996) (declining to consider applicability of the third prong and noting that while it had previously "adopted the <u>National Parks</u> formulation of Exemption 4," that previous "adoption did not encompass the speculation regarding 'program effectiveness'" that was set forth in <u>National Parks</u>); <u>Allnet Commc'n Servs. v. FCC</u>, 800 F. Supp. 984, 990 (D.D.C. 1992) (protecting computer models under third prong because disclosure would make providers of proprietary input data reluctant to supply such data to submitter, and without that data computer models would become ineffective, which, in turn, would reduce effectiveness of agency's program), <u>aff'd on other grounds</u>, No. 92-5351 (D.C. Cir. May 27, 1994); <u>Clarke v. U.S. Dep't of the Treasury</u>, No. 84-1873, 1986 WL 1234, at *2-3 (E.D. Pa. Jan. 24, 1986) (protecting identities of Flower Bond owners under third prong because government had legitimate interest in fulfilling "pre-FOIA contractual commitments of confidentiality" given to investors in order to ensure that pool of future investors willing to purchase government securities was not reduced; if that occurred, the pool of money from which government borrows would correspondingly be reduced, thereby harming national interest); <u>Comstock Int'l, Inc. v. Exp.-Imp. Bank</u>, 464 F. Supp. 804, 808 (D.D.C. 1979) (protecting loan applicant information under third prong on showing that disclosure would impair Bank's ability to promote U.S. exports); <u>see also</u> FOIA Update, Vol. IV, No. 4, at 15; <u>cf.</u> M/A-COM Info. Sys. v. HHS, 656 F. Supp. 691, 692 (D.D.C. 1986) (protecting settlement negotiation documents
(continued...)

Thereafter, the Department of Justice issued policy guidance regarding Exemption 4 protection for "intrinsically valuable" records -- records that are significant not for their content, but as valuable commodities which can be sold in the marketplace.[536] Because protection for such documents is well rooted in the legislative history of Exemption 4, the third prong of the National Parks test should permit the owners of such records to retain their full proprietary interest in them when release through the FOIA would result in a substantial loss of their market value.[537] Of course, this protection would be available only if there were sufficient evidence to demonstrate factually that potential customers would actually utilize the FOIA as a substitute for directly purchasing the records from the submitter.[538]

---

[535](...continued) upon a finding that "it is in the public interest to encourage settlement negotiations in matters of this kind and it would impair the ability of HHS to carry out its governmental duties if disclosure . . . were required"). But see News Group Boston, Inc. v. Nat'l R.R. Passenger Corp., 799 F. Supp. 1264, 1269 (D. Mass. 1992) (recognizing existence of third prong, but declining to apply it based on lack of specific showing that agency effectiveness would be impaired), appeal dismissed, No. 92-2250 (1st Cir. Dec. 4, 1992).

[536] See FOIA Update, Vol. VI, No. 1, at 3-4 ("OIP Guidance: Protecting Intrinsic Commercial Value").

[537] See id.; see also FOIA Update, Vol. IV, No. 4, at 3-5 (setting forth similar basis for protecting copyrighted materials against substantial adverse market effect caused by FOIA disclosure).

[538] See Cody Zeigler, Inc. v. U.S. Dep't of Labor, No. C2-00-134, 2002 WL 31159309, at *2-3 (S.D. Ohio Sept. 3, 2002) (recognizing that "there would be little reason for anyone else to purchase" the "Dodge Reports" sold by the McGraw-Hill Company "if they could be obtained for free from a government agency through a FOIA request," but refusing to accord Exemption 4 protection to the particular reports at issue due to the failure of McGraw-Hill to demonstrate that these "older" reports "retain[ed] any special value or significance today"); Brittany Dyeing & Printing Corp. v. EPA, No. 91-2711, slip op. at 10-12 (D.D.C. Mar. 12, 1993) (rejecting argument that FOIA disclosure of Dun & Bradstreet report would cause "loss of potential customers" because no evidence was presented to support contention that potential customers would use FOIA in such a manner, particularly in light of time involved in receiving information through FOIA process; nor was it shown how many such reports would be available through FOIA and court would not assume that majority, or even substantial number, could be so obtained); Key Bank of Me., Inc. v. SBA, No. 91-362-P, 1992 U.S. Dist. LEXIS 22180, at *11-12 (D. Me. Dec. 31, 1992) (denying protection for Dun & Bradstreet reports because "the notion that those who are in need of credit information will use the government as a source in order to save costs belies common sense").

Such a showing was made in a case concerning a request for copy-righted video conferencing software that the requester wanted to distribute on the Internet.[539] The court readily held that in such a situation "[t]here can be no doubt" that disclosure would cause "substantial commercial harm,"[540] because if the "technology is freely available on the Internet, there is no reason for anyone to license [it] from [its owner], and the value of [the owner's] copyright effectively will have been reduced to zero."[541]

The third prong was at issue in a case that concerned an agency that had the authority -- but had not yet had the time and resources -- to promulgate a regulation that would require submission of certain data.[542] During this interim period the agency was relying on companies to voluntarily submit the desired information.[543] In that case the court rejected the agency's argument that under these circumstances disclosure would impair its efficiency and effectiveness, holding instead that because Congress had "announced a preference for mandatory over voluntary submissions," the agency was "hard-pressed to support its claim that voluntary submissions are somehow more efficient."[544]

Thirteen years after the National Parks decision first raised the possibility that Exemption 4 could protect interests other than those reflected in the impairment and competitive harm prongs, a panel of the Court of Appeals for the District of Columbia Circuit embraced the third prong in the

---

[539] Gilmore v. U.S. Dep't of Energy, 4 F. Supp. 2d 912, 922-23 (N.D. Cal. 1998).

[540] Id. at 922 (protecting software, but not expressly doing so under "third prong").

[541] Id. at 923 (discounting the requester's argument that the copyright owner had "received only relatively meager royalties" and declaring that "there is a presumption of irreparable harm when a copyright is infringed"); see also FOIA Update, Vol. XVIII, No. 1, at 5-6 (cautioning agencies to "guard against the possibility that [Internet] dissemination of [reading room records] might be regarded as copyright infringement" in exceptional cases) (reiterated in FOIA Post, "FOIA Counselor Q&A: "Frequently Requested Records" (posted 7/25/03)); cf. Cody Zeigler, 2002 WL 31159309, at *3-4 (accommodating, with requester's acquiescence, copyright owner's preference that requested copyrighted reports, although not protected by Exemption 4, be made available for inspection only, not copying).

[542] Teich v. FDA, 751 F. Supp. 243, 251 (D.D.C. 1990), appeal dismissed voluntarily, No. 91-5023 (D.C. Cir. July 2, 1992).

[543] Id. at 251.

[544] Id. at 252-53.

first appellate decision in Critical Mass.[545] There, the panel adopted what it termed the "persuasive" reasoning of the First Circuit and expressly held that an agency may invoke Exemption 4 on the basis of interests other than the two principally identified in National Parks.[546]

Upon remand from the D.C. Circuit, the district court in Critical Mass found the requested information to be properly withheld pursuant to the third prong.[547] The court reached this decision based on the fact that if the requested information were disclosed, future submissions would not be provided until they were demanded under some form of compulsion -- which would then have to be enforced, precipitating "acrimony and some form of litigation with attendant expense and delay."[548] On appeal for the second time, a panel of the D.C. Circuit reversed the lower court on this point, but that decision was itself vacated when the D.C. Circuit decided to hear the case en banc.[549]

In its en banc decision in Critical Mass, the D.C. Circuit conducted an extensive review of the interests sought to be protected by Exemption 4 and expressly held that "[i]t should be evident from this review that the two interests identified in the National Parks test are not exclusive."[550] In addition, the D.C. Circuit went on to state that although it was overruling the first panel decision in Critical Mass, it "note[d]" that that panel had adopted the First Circuit's conclusion in 9 to 5 that Exemption 4 protects a "governmental interest in administrative efficiency and effectiveness."[551] Moreover, the D.C. Circuit specifically recognized yet another Exemption 4 interest -- namely, "a private interest in preserving the confidentiality of

---

[545] 830 F.2d 278, 282, 286 (D.C. Cir. 1987), vacated en banc, 975 F.2d 871 (D.C. Cir. 1992).

[546] Id. at 286.

[547] 731 F. Supp. 554, 557 (D.D.C. 1990), rev'd in part & remanded, 931 F.2d 939 (D.C. Cir.), vacated & reh'g en banc granted, 942 F.2d 799 (D.C. Cir. 1991), grant of summary judgment to agency aff'd en banc, 975 F.2d 871 (D.C. Cir. 1992).

[548] Id.

[549] 931 F.2d 939, 944-45 (D.C. Cir.), vacated & reh'g en banc granted, 942 F.2d 799 (D.C. Cir. 1991), grant of summary judgment to agency aff'd en banc, 975 F.2d 871 (D.C. Cir. 1992).

[550] 975 F.2d at 879.

[551] Id.; see also Allnet, 800 F. Supp. at 990 (recognizing, after Critical Mass, availability of third-prong protection to prevent impairment of agency effectiveness).

information that is provided the Government on a voluntary basis."[552] It declined to offer an opinion as to whether any other governmental or private interests might also fall within Exemption 4's protection.[553]

The District Court for the District of Columbia relied on the en banc decision in Critical Mass to hold that "impairment of the effectiveness of a government program is a proper factor for consideration in conducting an analysis under" Exemption 4.[554] The court utilized that test in a case involving a request for royalty rate information contained in licensing agreements that NIH entered into with pharmaceutical companies in accordance with a statutory mandate "to use the patent system to promote inventions arising from federally supported research."[555] The court upheld NIH's determination that it "'would cease to be an attractive or viable licensor of patented technology'" were it to disclose the royalty rate information.[556] The court found that "[s]uch a result obviously would hinder the agency in fulfilling its statutory mandate," and accordingly it afforded protection under the third prong of Exemption 4.[557] That same court issued a similar ruling in a case involving export-insurance documents, finding that disclosure "would interfere with the [Export-Import] Bank's ability to promote U.S. exports, and result in loss of business for U.S. exporters," which in turn would interfere with the agency's "ability to carry out its statutory purpose" of promoting the exchange of goods between the United States and foreign countries.[558]

### Privileged Information

The term "privileged" in Exemption 4 has been utilized by some courts as an alternative for protecting nonconfidential commercial or financial information. Indeed, the Court of Appeals for the District of Columbia Circuit has indicated that this term should not be treated as being merely synonymous with "confidential," particularly in light of the legislative history's explicit reference to certain privileges, e.g., the attorney-client and

---

[552] 975 F.2d at 879.

[553] Id.

[554] Pub. Citizen Health Research Group v. NIH, 209 F. Supp. 2d 37, 52 (D.D.C. 2002) (alternative holding).

[555] Id. at *42-43.

[556] Id. at *45 (quoting agency declaration).

[557] Id.

[558] Judicial Watch, Inc. v. Exp.-Imp. Bank, 108 F. Supp. 2d 19, 30 (D.D.C. 2000).

doctor-patient privileges.[559] Nevertheless, during the FOIA's first two decades, only two district court decisions discussed "privilege" in the Exemption 4 context.

In one case, the court upheld the Department of the Interior's withholding of detailed statements by law firms of work that they had done for the Hopi Indians on the ground that they were "privileged" because of their work-product nature within the meaning of Exemption 4: "The vouchers reveal strategies developed by Hopi counsel in anticipation of preventing or preparing for legal action to safeguard tribal interests. Such communications are entitled to protection as attorney work product."[560] In the second case, a legal memorandum prepared for a utility company by its attorney qualified as legal advice protectible under Exemption 4 as subject to the attorney-client privilege.[561] In both of these cases the information was also withheld as "confidential."

It was not until another five years had passed that a court protected material relying solely on the "privilege" portion of Exemption 4 -- specifically, by recognizing protection for documents subject to the "confidential report" privilege.[562] In a brief opinion, one court recognized Exemption 4 protection for settlement negotiation documents, but did not expressly characterize them as "privileged."[563] Another court subsequently recog-

---

[559] Wash. Post Co. v. HHS, 690 F.2d 252, 267 n.50 (D.C. Cir. 1982).

[560] Indian Law Res. Ctr. v. Dep't of the Interior, 477 F. Supp. 144, 148 (D.D.C. 1979).

[561] Miller, Anderson, Nash, Yerke & Wiener v. U.S. Dep't of Energy, 499 F. Supp. 767, 771 (D. Or. 1980).

[562] Wash. Post Co. v. HHS, 603 F. Supp. 235, 237-39 (D.D.C. 1985), rev'd on procedural grounds & remanded, 795 F.2d 205 (D.C. Cir. 1986).

[563] M/A-COM Info. Sys. v. HHS, 656 F. Supp. 691, 692 (D.D.C. 1986); see also FOIA Update, Vol. VI, No. 4, at 3-4 ("OIP Guidance: Protecting Settlement Negotiations"); Goodyear Tire & Rubber Co. v. Chiles Power Supply, Inc., 332 F.3d 976, 983 (6th Cir. 2003) (recognizing, after extensive discussion of its rationale, settlement negotiation privilege) (non-FOIA case); cf. FOIA Post, "Supreme Court Rules in Exemption 5 Case" (posted 4/4/01) (advising that viability of settlement privilege under Exemption 4 remained "entirely unaffected" by Supreme Court's decision in Dep't of the Interior v. Klamath Water Users Protective Ass'n, 532 U.S. 1 (2001)). But see In re Subpoena Issued to Commodity Futures Trading Comm'n, 370 F. Supp. 2d 201, 208-10 (D.D.C. 2005) (refusing to recognize settlement negotiations privilege) (non-FOIA case), aff'd in part on other grounds, 439 F.3d 740, 754-55 (D.C. Cir. 2006) (finding it unnecessary to decide whether federal settlement negotiations privilege exists, because proponent of privilege failed to meet its burden to show that disputed documents were created

(continued...)

nized Exemption 4 protection for documents subject to the critical self-evaluative privilege.[564]

Sixteen years after the first decision protecting attorney-client information under Exemption 4, the District Court for the Eastern District of Missouri issued the second such decision.[565] The court held that a company's "adverse impact analyses, [prepared] at the request of its attorneys, for the purpose of obtaining legal advice about the legal ramifications of [large scale] reductions in force,"[566] were protected by the attorney-client privilege.[567] In so holding, the court found that disclosure of the documents to the agency "constituted only a limited waiver and did not destroy the privilege."[568]

On the other hand, the Court of Appeals for the Tenth Circuit has held that documents subject to a state protective order entered pursuant to the State of Utah's equivalent of Rule 26(c)(7) of the Federal Rules of Civil Procedure -- which permits courts to issue orders denying or otherwise limiting the manner in which discovery is conducted so that a trade secret or other confidential commercial information is not disclosed or is only disclosed in a certain way -- were not "privileged" for purposes of Exemption 4.[569] While observing that discovery privileges "may constitute an additional ground for nondisclosure" under Exemption 4, the Tenth Circuit noted that those other privileges were for information "not otherwise specifically

---

[563](...continued)
for purpose of settlement discussions).

[564] Wash. Post Co. v. U.S. Dep't of Justice, No. 84-3581, 1987 U.S. Dist. LEXIS 14936, at *21 (D.D.C. Sept. 25, 1987) (magistrate's recommendation), adopted, No. 84-3581 (D.D.C. Dec. 15, 1987), rev'd in part on other grounds & remanded, 863 F.2d 96, 99 (D.C. Cir. 1988). But cf. Kan. Gas & Elec. Co. v. NRC, No. 87-2748, slip op. at 4 (D.D.C. July 2, 1993) (holding that because self-critical analysis privilege had been rejected previously in state court proceeding brought to suppress disclosure of documents, "doctrine of collateral estoppel" precluded "relitigation" of that claim in federal court) (reverse FOIA suit).

[565] McDonnell Douglas Corp. v. EEOC, 922 F. Supp. 235, 237, 242-43 (E.D. Mo. 1996) (alternative holding) (reverse FOIA suit), appeal dismissed, No. 96-2662 (8th Cir. Aug. 29, 1996).

[566] Id. at 237.

[567] Id. at 242-43.

[568] Id. at 243.

[569] Anderson v. HHS, 907 F.2d 936, 945 (10th Cir. 1990).

embodied in the language of Exemption 4."[570] By contrast, it concluded, recognition of a privilege for materials protected by a protective order under Rule 26(c)(7) "would be redundant and would substantially duplicate Exemption 4's explicit coverage of 'trade secrets and commercial or financial information.'"[571] Additionally, the Court of Appeals for the Fifth Circuit has "decline[d] to hold that the [FOIA] creates a lender-borrower privilege," despite the express reference to such a privilege in Exemption 4's legislative history.[572] (For a further discussion of atypical privileges, see Exemption 5, Other Privileges, below.)

## Interrelation with the Trade Secrets Act

Finally, it should be noted that the Trade Secrets Act[573] -- an extraordinarily broadly worded criminal statute -- prohibits the disclosure of much more than simply "trade secret" information and instead prohibits the unauthorized disclosure of all data protected by Exemption 4.[574] (See the discussion of this statute under Exemption 3, Additional Considerations, above.) Indeed, nearly every court that has considered the issue has found the Trade Secrets Act and Exemption 4 to be "coextensive."[575] In 1987, the Court of Appeals for the District of Columbia Circuit issued a long-awaited decision which contains an extensive analysis of the argument advanced by several commentators that the scope of the Trade Secrets Act is narrow, extending no more broadly than the scope of its three predecessor statutes.[576] The D.C. Circuit rejected that argument and held that the scope of the Trade Secrets Act is "at least co-extensive with that of Exemption 4."[577] Thus, the court held that if information falls within the

---

[570] Id.

[571] Id.

[572] Sharyland Water Supply Corp. v. Block, 755 F.2d 397, 400 (5th Cir. 1985).

[573] 18 U.S.C. § 1905 (2000).

[574] See CNA Fin. Corp. v. Donovan, 830 F.2d 1132, 1140 (D.C. Cir. 1987) (noting that the Trade Secrets Act "appears to cover practically any commercial or financial data collected by any federal employee from any source" and that the "comprehensive catalogue of items" listed in the Act "accomplishes essentially the same thing as if it had simply referred to 'all officially collected commercial information' or 'all business and financial data received'") (reverse FOIA suit).

[575] See, e.g., Gen. Elec. Co. v. NRC, 750 F.2d 1394, 1402 (7th Cir. 1984) (reverse FOIA suit).

[576] CNA, 830 F.2d at 1144-52.

[577] Id. at 1151; accord McDonnell Douglas Corp. v. U.S. Dep't of the Air
(continued...)

scope of Exemption 4, it also falls within the scope of the Trade Secrets Act.[578]

   The Trade Secrets Act, however, does not preclude disclosure of information "otherwise protected" by that statute, if the disclosure is "'authorized by law."'[579]   (For a further discussion of this point, see "Reverse" FOIA, below.)   For that reason, the D.C. Circuit has concluded that it need not "attempt to define the outer limits" of the Trade Secrets Act -- i.e., whether information falling outside the scope of Exemption 4 was nonetheless still within the scope of the Trade Secrets Act -- because the FOIA itself would provide authorization for release of any information falling outside the scope of an exemption.[580]

---

[577](...continued)
Force, 375 F.3d 1182, 1185-86 (D.C. Cir. 2004) (quoting CNA) (reverse FOIA suit), reh'g en banc denied, No. 02-5342 (D.C. Cir. Dec. 16, 2004); Bartholdi Cable Co. v. FCC, 114 F.3d 274, 281 (D.C. Cir. 1997) (citing CNA and declaring: "[W]e have held that information falling within Exemption 4 of FOIA also comes within the Trade Secrets Act.") (non-FOIA case brought under Administrative Procedure Act, 5 U.S.C. §§ 701-706 (2000)); Canadian Commercial Corp. v. Dep't of the Air Force, 442 F. Supp. 2d 15, 39 (D.D.C. 2006) (reverse FOIA suit) (appeal pending).   But see McDonnell Douglas Corp. v. Widnall, 57 F.3d 1162, 1165 n.2 (D.C. Cir. 1995) (noting in dicta that the court "suppose[s] it is possible that this statement [from CNA] is no longer accurate in light of [the court's] recently more expansive interpretation of the scope of Exemption 4" in Critical Mass Energy Project v. NRC, 975 F.2d 871, 879 (D.C. Cir. 1992)) (non-FOIA case brought under Administrative Procedure Act).

[578] CNA, 830 F.2d at 1151-52; see also McDonnell Douglas, 375 F.3d at 1185-86 (finding that the Trade Secrets Act "effectively prohibits an agency from releasing information subject to [Exemption 4]"); Bartholdi, 114 F.3d at 281 (declaring that when information is shown to be protected by Exemption 4, agencies are generally "precluded from releasing" it due to provisions of Trade Secrets Act); Canadian Commercial, 442 F. Supp. 2d at 39 (declaring that "if information is covered by Exemption 4, it must be withheld because the [Trade Secrets Act] prohibits disclosure"); Parker v. Bureau of Land Mgmt., 141 F. Supp. 2d 71, 77 n.5 (D.D.C. 2001) (noting that "[a]lthough FOIA exemptions are normally permissive rather than mandatory, the D.C. Circuit has held that the disclosure of material which is exempted under [Exemption 4 of the FOIA] is prohibited under the Trade Secrets Act").

[579] Bartholdi, 114 F.3d at 281 (quoting Trade Secrets Act).

[580] CNA, 830 F.2d at 1152 n.139; see also Chrysler Corp. v. Brown, 441 U.S. 281, 318-19 & n.49 (1979) (noting in dicta that "there is a theoretical possibility that material might be outside Exemption 4 yet within the [Trade Secrets Act]," but acknowledging that "that possibility is at most of
(continued...)

The practical effect of the Trade Secrets Act is to limit an agency's ability to make a discretionary release of otherwise-exempt material, because to do so in violation of the Trade Secrets Act would not only be a criminal offense, it would also constitute "a serious abuse of agency discretion" redressable through a reverse FOIA suit.[581] Thus, in the absence of a statute or properly promulgated regulation giving the agency authority to release the information -- which would remove the disclosure prohibition of the Trade Secrets Act -- a determination by an agency that information falls within Exemption 4 is "tantamount" to a decision that it cannot be released.[582]

## EXEMPTION 5

Exemption 5 of the FOIA protects "inter-agency or intra-agency memorandums or letters which would not be available by law to a party other than an agency in litigation with the agency."[1] The courts have construed this somewhat opaque language, with its sometimes confusing threshold requirement,[2] to "exempt those documents, and only those documents that are normally privileged in the civil discovery context."[3]

---

[580](...continued)
limited practical significance"); Frazee v. U.S. Forest Serv., 97 F.3d 367, 373 (9th Cir. 1996) (holding that because requested document was "not protected from disclosure under Exemption 4," it also was "not exempt from disclosure under the Trade Secrets Act") (reverse FOIA suit).

[581] Nat'l Org. for Women v. Soc. Sec. Admin., 736 F.2d 727, 743 (D.C. Cir. 1984) (Robinson, J., concurring); accord McDonnell Douglas, 57 F.3d at 1164 (holding that the Trade Secrets Act "can be relied upon in challenging agency action that violates its terms as 'contrary to law' within the meaning of the Administrative Procedure Act"); Pac. Architects & Eng'rs v. U.S. Dep't of State, 906 F.2d 1345, 1347 (9th Cir. 1990) (reverse FOIA suit); Charles River Park "A," Inc. v. HUD, 519 F.2d 935, 942 (D.C. Cir. 1975) (reverse FOIA suit); see also FOIA Update, Vol. VI, No. 3, at 3 ("OIP Guidance: Discretionary Disclosure and Exemption 4") (advising that the Trade Secrets Act is "a potent barrier to the disclosure of any information that falls within the protection of Exemption 4").

[582] CNA, 830 F.2d at 1144.

[1] 5 U.S.C. § 552(b)(5) (2000 & Supp. IV 2004).

[2] See, e.g., U.S. Dep't of Justice v. Julian, 486 U.S. 1, 19 n.1 (Scalia, J., dissenting on a point not reached by the majority) (discussing the "most natural reading" of the threshold and the "problem[s]" inherent in reading it in that way).

[3] NLRB v. Sears, Roebuck & Co., 421 U.S. 132, 149 (1975); see FTC v. Grolier Inc., 462 U.S. 19, 26 (1983); Martin v. Office of Special Counsel, 819 (continued...)

# EXEMPTION 5

Although originally it was "not clear that Exemption 5 was intended to incorporate every privilege known to civil discovery,"[4] the Supreme Court subsequently made it clear that the coverage of Exemption 5 is quite broad, encompassing both statutory privileges and those commonly recognized by case law, and that it is not limited to those privileges explicitly mentioned in its legislative history.[5] Accordingly, the Court of Appeals for the District of Columbia Circuit has stated that the statutory language "unequivocally" incorporates "all civil discovery rules into FOIA [Exemption 5]."[6] However, this incorporation of discovery privileges requires that a privilege be applied in the FOIA context exactly as it exists in the discovery context.[7] Thus, the precise contours of a privilege, with regard to applicable parties or the types of information that are protectible, are also incorporated into the FOIA.[8]

Additionally, it is not the "hypothetical litigation" between particular parties (in which relevance or need are appropriate factors) that governs Exemption 5's applicability;[9] rather, it is the circumstances in civil litigation in which memoranda would "routinely be disclosed."[10] Therefore, whether

---

[3](...continued)
F.2d 1181, 1184 (D.C. Cir. 1987); see also Attorney General's Memorandum for Heads of All Federal Departments and Agencies Regarding the Freedom of Information Act (Oct. 12, 2001), reprinted in FOIA Post (posted 10/15/01) (highlighting importance of protecting privileged information).

[4] Fed. Open Mkt. Comm. v. Merrill, 443 U.S. 340, 354 (1979).

[5] See U.S. v. Weber Aircraft Corp., 465 U.S. 792, 800 (1984); see also FOIA Update, Vol. V, No. 4, at 6. But see also Burka v. HHS, 87 F.3d 508, 517 (D.C. Cir. 1996) ("[T]o justify nondisclosure under Exemption 5, an agency must show that the type of material it seeks to withhold is generally protected in civil discovery for reasons similar to those asserted by the agency in the FOIA context.").

[6] Martin, 819 F.2d at 1185; see also Badhwar v. U.S. Dep't of the Air Force, 829 F.2d 182, 184 (D.C. Cir. 1987) ("Exemption 5 requires the application of existing rules regarding discovery.").

[7] See Burka v. HHS, 87 F.3d 508, 517 (D.C. Cir. 1996); see also Julian, 486 U.S. at 13 (1988) (holding that presentence report privilege, designed to protect report subjects, cannot be invoked against them as first-party requesters).

[8] See id.

[9] Sears, 421 U.S. at 149 n.16.

[10] H.R. Rep. No. 89-1497, at 10 (1966), reprinted in 1966 U.S.C.C.A.N. 2418.

the privilege invoked is absolute or qualified is of no significance.[11] Accordingly, no requester is entitled to greater rights of access under Exemption 5 by virtue of whatever special interests might influence the outcome of actual civil discovery to which he is a party.[12] Indeed, such an approach, combined with a careful application of Exemption 5's threshold language, is the only means by which the Supreme Court's firm admonition against use of the FOIA to circumvent discovery privileges can be given full effect.[13] Nevertheless, the fact that information is not generally discoverable does not necessarily mean that it is not discoverable by a specific class of parties in civil litigation, so just as the FOIA's privacy exemptions are not used against a first-party requester,[14] a privilege that is designed to pro-

---

[11] See Grolier, 462 U.S. at 27; see also FOIA Update, Vol. V, No. 4, at 6.

[12] See Grolier, 462 U.S. at 28; Sears, 421 U.S. at 149; see also, e.g., Martin, 819 F.2d at 1184 ("[T]he needs of a particular plaintiff are not relevant to the exemption's applicability."); Swisher v. Dep't of the Air Force, 660 F.2d 369, 371 (8th Cir. 1981) (observing that applicability of Exemption 5 is in no way diminished by fact that privilege may be overcome by showing of "need" in civil discovery context); MacLean v. DOD, No. 04-CV-2425, slip op. at 8-9 (S.D. Cal. June 2, 2005) ("[S]ince there is no 'need' determination under FOIA, there is no room for this Court to balance the public's interest in disclosure against defendants' interest in protecting the deliberative process."); Bilbrey v. U.S. Dep't of the Air Force, No. 00-0539, slip op. at 11 (W.D. Mo. Jan. 30, 2001) ("Once a government agency makes a prima facie showing of privilege, the analysis under FOIA Exemption 5 ceases, and does not proceed to the balancing of interests."), aff'd, No. 01-1789, 2001 WL 1222471, at *1 (8th Cir. Oct. 16, 2001) (unpublished table decision). But see In re Diet Drugs Prods. Liability Litig., No. 1203, 2000 WL 1545028, at *4 (E.D. Pa. Oct. 12, 2000) (stating that a court must balance the "relative interests of the parties" in determining the applicability of the deliberative process privilege under Exemption 5).

[13] See Weber Aircraft, 465 U.S. at 801-02 ("We do not think that Congress could have intended that the weighty policies underlying discovery privileges could be so easily circumvented."); see also Martin, 819 F.2d at 1186 (Where a requester is "unable to obtain those documents using ordinary civil discovery methods, . . . FOIA should not be read to alter that result."); Changzhou Laosan Group v. U.S. Customs & Border Prot. Bureau, No. Civ.A.04-1919, 2005 WL 913268, at *7 (D.D.C. Apr. 20, 2005) ("[T]he purpose of FOIA is not to serve as a tool for obtaining discovery for an administrative forfeiture proceeding."), reconsideration granted in part & denied in part on other grounds, 374 F. Supp. 2d 129 (D.D.C. 2005); cf. Nat'l Ass'n of Criminal Def. Lawyers, No. 97-372, slip op. at 8-10 (D.D.C. July 22, 1998) (holding that although agency made limited disclosures of report pursuant to criminal discovery rules, it was protectible because it was not "normally available by law" to party in litigation with agency).

[14] See H.R. Rep. No. 93-1380, at 13 (1974); see also FOIA Update, Vol. X,

(continued...)

tect a certain class of persons cannot be invoked against those persons as FOIA requesters.[15]

The three primary, most frequently invoked privileges that have been held to be incorporated into Exemption 5 are the deliberative process privilege (referred to by some courts, somewhat imprecisely, as "executive privilege"[16]), the attorney work-product privilege, and the attorney-client privilege.[17] First, however, Exemption 5's threshold requirement must be considered.

### "Inter-Agency or Intra-Agency" Threshold Requirement

The threshold issue under Exemption 5 is whether a record is of the type intended to be covered by the phrase "inter-agency or intra-agency memorandums" -- a phrase which, at first glance, would seem to encompass only documents generated by an agency and not documents circulated beyond the executive branch.[18] Six years ago, the Supreme Court shed much light on this issue when it ruled on the contours of Exemption 5's "inter-agency or intra-agency" threshold requirement for the first time in De-

---

[14](...continued)
No. 2, at 4.

[15] See Julian, 486 U.S. at 13 (holding that presentence report privilege, designed to protect reports' subjects, cannot be invoked against them as first-party requesters); see also United States v. Kipta, No. 97-638-1, 2001 WL 477153, at *1 (N.D. Ill. May 3, 2001) (following Julian).

[16] See, e.g., Marriott Int'l Resorts, L.P. v. United States, 437 F.3d 1302, 1305 (Fed. Cir. 2006) (noting that deliberative process privilege is one of many privileges that generally fall under rubric of "executive privilege") (non-FOIA case).

[17] See Sears, 421 U.S. at 149.

[18] See U.S. Dep't of Justice v. Julian, 486 U.S. 1, 19 n.1 (1988) (Scalia, J., dissenting on a point not reached by the majority) (observing that "the most natural meaning of the phrase 'intra-agency memorandum' is a memorandum that is addressed both to and from employees of a single agency -- as opposed to an 'inter-agency memorandum,' which would be a memorandum between employees of two different agencies"); see also, e.g., Maydak v. U.S. Dep't of Justice, 362 F. Supp. 2d 316, 322 (D.D.C. 2005) (ruling that documents exchanged between federal prisoner and prison staff do not meet threshold standard); Homick v. U.S. Dep't of Justice, No. C 98-00557, slip op. at 18 (N.D. Cal. Sept. 16, 2004) (holding that document exchanged between agency employee and private attorney does not qualify under threshold standard); Canning v. U.S. Dep't of Justice, No. 01-2215, slip op. at 16 (D.D.C. Mar. 9, 2004) (ruling that document in agency file that reflected communication between private client and attorney does not meet threshold standard).

partment of the Interior v. Klamath Water Users Protective Ass'n.[19] In a unanimous decision, the Court ruled that the threshold of Exemption 5 did not encompass communications between the Department of the Interior and several Indian tribes which, in making their views known to the Department on certain matters of administrative decisionmaking, not only had "their own, albeit entirely legitimate, interests in mind,"[20] but also were "seeking a Government benefit at the expense of other applicants."[21] Thus, records submitted to the agency by the Tribes, as "outside consultants," did not qualify for attorney work-product and deliberative process privilege protection in the case.[22]

Significantly, the Supreme Court's holding in Klamath rested on distinctly narrower grounds than did the appellate court's ruling below.[23] Before the case reached the Supreme Court, the Court of Appeals for the Ninth Circuit had held that Exemption 5's threshold could not accommodate communications between an agency and any "outside consultant" who has a "direct interest" in the subject of its "consultation" with the agency.[24] But this simplistic "direct interest" test did not survive the Supreme Court's review.[25]

Rather, while acknowledging that "consultants whose communications have typically been held exempt have not been communicating with the Government in their own interest" or on behalf of anyone else "whose interests might be affected by the Government action addressed by the consultant,"[26] the Supreme Court went one step further than the Ninth Circuit in its analysis. "While this fact alone distinguishes tribal communica-

---

[19] 532 U.S. 1 (2001); see also FOIA Post, "Supreme Court Rules in Exemption 5 Case" (posted 4/4/01) (discussing meaning, contours, and implications of Klamath decision).

[20] Klamath, 532 U.S. at 12.

[21] Id. at 12 n.4.

[22] Id. at 16.

[23] See FOIA Post, "Supreme Court Rules in Exemption 5 Case" (posted 4/4/01) (analyzing differences between Supreme Court's and Ninth Circuit's decisions).

[24] Klamath Water Users Protective Ass'n v. Department of the Interior, 189 F.3d 1034, 1038 (9th Cir. 1999), aff'd, 532 U.S. 1 (2001).

[25] See FOIA Post, "Supreme Court Rules in Exemption 5 Case" (posted 4/4/01) (emphasizing that "the Supreme Court ultimately applied an Exemption 5 threshold test rooted in . . . competition . . . not the Ninth Circuit's more general test that disqualified an outside party due to the existence of a self-interest alone").

[26] Klamath, 532 U.S. at 12.

tions from the consultants' examples recognized by several Courts of Appeals," the Court reasoned, "the distinction here is even sharper, in that the Tribes are <u>self-advocates at the expense of others seeking benefits inadequate to satisfy everyone.</u>"[27]

Indeed, by limiting its holding to only those communications in which the "outside consultant" has an interest in the outcome of the decisionmaking process <u>and</u> in which other existing parties have competing interests in "benefits inadequate to satisfy everyone," the Court pointedly refrained from adopting a rule any broader than the facts of the case required.[28] Rather, it limited its holding to situations involving the advocacy of competing external interests by those who might otherwise qualify as consultants for purposes of satisfying Exemption 5's threshold.[29]

During the years leading up to <u>Klamath</u>, in recognition of the necessities and practicalities of agency functioning, many courts had construed the scope of Exemption 5 to include various types of communications originating outside of agencies.[30] This pragmatic approach to the "inter-agency or intra-agency" threshold requirement, which in light of <u>Klamath</u> may be characterized as an "outside consultant" test, in the past often was characterized as a "functional test" for assessing the availability of Exemption 5 protection.[31] In <u>Klamath</u>, the Supreme Court assumed for purposes of its decision, and thereby implicitly strengthened, the pragmatic "outside consultant" approach to Exemption 5's threshold language.[32]

---

[27] <u>Id.</u> (emphasis added).

[28] <u>See id.</u> at 12 n.4 (declining to overrule <u>Pub. Citizen, Inc. v. U.S. Dep't of Justice</u>, 111 F.3d 168, 170-72 (D.C. Cir. 1997), and <u>Ryan v. Dep't of Justice</u>, 617 F.2d 781, 790 (D.C. Cir. 1980), both of which "arguably extend beyond" the "typical examples" of cases of consultants whose communications have been considered "intra-agency").

[29] <u>See</u> FOIA Post, "Supreme Court Rules in Exemption 5 Case" (posted 4/4/01) (pointing out that <u>Public Citizen</u> and <u>Ryan</u>, "and their potential progeny, stand apart from what clearly was rejected under the Court's bottom-line threshold test").

[30] <u>See</u> Burt A. Braverman & Francis J. Chetwynd, <u>Information Law: Freedom of Information, Privacy, Open Meetings, and Other Access Laws</u> § 9-3.1 (1985 & Supp. 1990).

[31] <u>See, e.g.</u>, <u>Durns v. Bureau of Prisons</u>, 804 F.2d 701, 704 n.5 (D.C. Cir. 1986) (employing "a functional rather than a literal test in assessing whether memoranda are 'inter-agency or intra-agency'"), <u>cert. granted, judgment vacated on other grounds & remanded</u>, 486 U.S. 1029 (1988).

[32] <u>See</u> <u>Klamath</u>, 532 U.S. at 9-11 (discussing cases involving communications from "outside consultants"); <u>see also</u> FOIA Post, "Supreme Court Rules in Exemption 5 Case" (posted 4/4/01) (pointing out that such "outside con-
(continued...)

Regarding records generated outside an agency but created through agency initiative, whether purchased or provided voluntarily without compensation, the Court of Appeals for the District of Columbia Circuit observed in Ryan v. Department of Justice[33] that "Congress apparently did not intend 'inter-agency or intra-agency' to be rigidly exclusive terms, but rather to include [nearly any record] that is part of the deliberative process."[34] Included in this category are such things as recommendations from Members of Congress,[35] recommendations from judges and special prosecutors,[36] recommendations from an agency to a commission established to assist another agency's policymaking,[37] and documents provided by an agency's contractor employees.[38]

Likewise, the D.C. Circuit has held that Exemption 5 applies to docu-

---

[32](...continued)
sultant" decisions "still stand as sound precedents for the satisfaction of Exemption 5's threshold requirement").

[33] 617 F.2d 781 (D.C. Cir. 1980).

[34] Id. at 790; see also Hooper v. Bowen, No. 88-1030, slip op. at 18 (C.D. Cal. May 24, 1989) ("courts have regularly construed this threshold test expansively rather than hypertechnically"); FOIA Update, Vol. III, No. 3, at 10 ("FOIA Counselor: Protecting 'Outside' Advice"); cf. Nat'l Ass'n of Criminal Def. Lawyers v. U.S. Dep't of Justice, No. 97-372, slip op. at 7-8 (D.D.C. July 22, 1998) (protecting agency-generated draft report circulated to nongovernmental parties for review and comment).

[35] See Ryan, 617 F.2d at 790 (protecting recommendations on judicial nomination process made by senators to Attorney General).

[36] See Lardner v. U.S. Dep't of Justice, No. 03-0180, U.S. Dist. LEXIS 5465, at *51-52 (D.D.C. Mar. 31, 2005).

[37] See Tigue v. U.S. Dep't of Justice, 312 F.3d 70, 78-79 (2d Cir. 2002) (protecting recommendations from a United States Attorney's Office to the Webster Commission, which was established to serve "as a consultant to the IRS").

[38] See Sakamoto v. EPA, 443 F. Supp. 2d 1182, 1191 (N.D. Cal. 2006) (upholding agency's invocation of Exemption 5 to protect documents prepared by private contractor hired to perform audit for agency); Hanson v. U.S. Agency for Int'l Dev., 372 F.3d 286, 292 (4th Cir. 2004) (applying privilege analysis to documents prepared by attorney hired by private company in contractural relationship with agency); Hertzberg v. Veneman, 273 F. Supp. 2d 67, 76 n. 2 (D.D.C. 2003) (holding that "witness statements from Forest Service contractor employees may be considered 'inter-agency or intra-agency' for the purpose of Exemption 5," citing Klamath, 532 U.S. at 10-11).

ments originating with a court.[39] Under this commonsense approach, documents generated by consultants outside of an agency were typically found to qualify for Exemption 5 protection because agencies, in the exercise of their primary functions, commonly have "a special need for the opinions and recommendations of temporary consultants."[40] Indeed, it has long been recognized under the FOIA that such advice can "play[] an integral function in the government's decision[making]."[41] And though frequently these consultants are called upon because there is no one readily available in the agency with the particular expertise that the consultant has,[42] there

---

[39] Durns, 804 F.2d at 704 & n.5 (applying Exemption 5 to presentence report prepared by probation officer for sentencing judge, with copies provided to Parole Commission and Bureau of Prisons); cf. Badhwar v. U.S. Dep't of the Air Force, 829 F.2d 182, 184-85 (D.C. Cir. 1987) (upholding application of Exemption 5 -- without even discussing "inter-agency or intra-agency" threshold -- to material supplied by outside contractors).

[40] Soucie v. David, 448 F.2d 1067, 1078 n.44 (D.C. Cir. 1971); cf. CNA Fin. Corp. v. Donovan, 830 F.2d 1132, 1161 (D.C. Cir. 1987) (recognizing importance of outside consultants in deliberative process privilege context).

[41] Hoover v. U.S. Dep't of the Interior, 611 F.2d 1132, 1138 (5th Cir. 1980) (protecting appraiser's report solicited by agency); see also, e.g., Lead Indus. Ass'n v. OSHA, 610 F.2d 70, 83 (2d Cir. 1979) (protecting consultant's report concerning safe levels of workplace lead exposure); Wu v. Nat'l Endowment for the Humanities, 460 F.2d 1030, 1032 (5th Cir. 1972) (protecting recommendations of volunteer consultants); Pohlman, Inc. v. SBA, No. 4:03-01241, slip op. at 23 (E.D. Mo. Sept. 30, 2005) (protecting market valuation report prepared for agency by outside consultant); Citizens Progressive Alliance v. U.S. Bureau of Indian Affairs, 241 F. Supp. 2d 1342, 1355 (D.N.M. 2002) (protecting recommendations provided by private company hired by BIA); cf. Rashid v. HHS, No. 98-0898, slip op. at 6-7 (D.D.C. Mar. 2, 2000) (holding correspondence sent by Assistant United States Attorney to expert witness, requesting evaluation of evidence in case, protectible under attorney work-product privilege); Gen. Elec. Co. v. EPA, 18 F. Supp. 2d 138, 142 (D. Mass. 1998) ("[L]etters from a federal agency to a state agency that solicit or respond to the state agency's input in an effort to coordinate and tailor joint regulatory efforts may be no less a part of the federal agency's deliberative processes than the state agency's recommendations or advice when acted upon at the federal level."); Judicial Watch, Inc. v. Comm'n on U.S.-Pac. Trade & Inv. Policy, No. 97-0099, slip op. at 9 (D.D.C. Sept. 30, 1999) (protecting recommendations from individuals outside government regarding proposed executive branch appointees); Hooper, No. 88-1030, slip op. at 17-19 (C.D. Cal. May 24, 1989) (protecting records originating with private insurance companies which acted as "fiscal intermediaries" for Health Care Financing Administration).

[42] See Formaldehyde Inst. v. HHS, 889 F.2d 1118, 1122-23 (D.C. Cir. 1989) (noting instances in which court had allowed agency consultations with

(continued...)

is no requirement that outside consultants be engaged in providing expertise unavailable within the agency for Exemption 5 to apply.[43]

While agencies often are the recipients of expert advice, they also occasionally provide it. In <u>Dow Jones & Co. v. Department of Justice</u>, the D.C. Circuit held that documents conveying advice from an agency to Congress for purposes of congressional decisionmaking are not "inter-agency" records under Exemption 5 for the simple reason that Congress is not an "agency" under the FOIA -- though the court also held that agencies may protect communications outside of an agency if they are "part and parcel of the <u>agency</u>'s deliberative process."[44]

In applying the basic rationale of the <u>Dow Jones</u> decision, the District Court for the District of Columbia found in 2004 that documents created by an agency to assist the decisionmaking process of a presidentially created commission, the National Energy Policy Development Group (NEPDG), could not be protected by Exemption 5.[45] The lower court ruled that just as Congress did not qualify as an "agency" for FOIA purposes, neither did the NEPDG, a White House entity likewise not subject to the FOIA.[46] However, this decision was overturned on appeal by the Court of Appeals for the District of Columbia Circuit.[47] The D.C. Circuit recognized that the NEPDG did

---

[42](...continued)
outside experts to meet Exemption 5 threshold test).

[43] See <u>Nat'l Inst. of Military Justice v. DOD</u>, 404 F. Supp. 2d 325, 345 (D.D.C. 2005) (holding that there is "no requirement . . . that outside consultants possess expertise not possessed by those inside the agency").

[44] 917 F.2d 571, 574-75 (D.C. Cir. 1990); <u>see also</u> <u>Texas v. ICC</u>, 889 F.2d 59, 61 (5th Cir. 1989) (holding that a document sent from an agency to an outside party did not meet the threshold standard because it was "a mere request for information, not a consultation or a solicitation of expert advice"); <u>Paisley v. CIA</u>, 712 F.2d 686, 699 n.54 (D.C. Cir. 1983) (presaging <u>Dow Jones</u> by suggesting that agency responses to congressional requests for information may not constitute protectible "inter-agency" communications); <u>cf.</u> <u>Hennessey v. U.S. Agency for Int'l Dev.</u>, No. 97-1133, 1997 WL 537998, at *3 (4th Cir. Sept. 2, 1997) (finding no "intra-agency 'deliberative process,'" as agency intended all interested parties to be involved in decision).

[45] See <u>Judicial Watch, Inc. v. U.S. Dep't of Energy</u>, 310 F. Supp. 2d 271, 315 (D.D.C. 2004).

[46] See <u>id.</u>

[47] See <u>Judicial Watch, Inc. v. U.S. Dep't of Energy</u>, 412 F.3d 125, 130-31 (D.C. Cir. 2005).

not qualify as an agency as defined by the FOIA,[48] yet it noted that the NEPDG was created specifically to advise the President on a policy issue and, therefore, that it would be "inconceivable" for Congress to have intended for Exemption 5 to apply to decisionmaking processes where the decisionmaker was an agency official subject to presidential oversight but not to decisionmaking processes where the decisionmaker is the President himself.[49] Underscoring the reading that the D.C. Circuit has traditionally given to the Exemption 5 threshold, the court firmly emphasized that "a document need not be created by an agency or remain in the possession of the agency in order qualify as 'intra-agency.'"[50]

In reversing this lower court decision, the D.C. Circuit acted consistently with the Supreme Court's 1973 decision in EPA v. Mink,[51] in which the Supreme Court declared that it was "beyond question that [agency documents prepared for a presidentially created committee organized to advise him on matters involving underground nuclear testing] are 'inter-agency or intra-agency' memoranda or 'letters' that were used in the decisionmaking processes of the Executive Branch."[52]

The D.C. Circuit's analysis in this case is entirely consistent with its analysis a year earlier in Judicial Watch, Inc. v. Department of Justice, in which it ruled that certain Department of Justice communications to the President or the Office of the President regarding pardons were properly protected under the presidential communications privilege.[53] The necessary implication of the D.C. Circuit's ruling was that these records were protected under Exemption 5 despite the fact that neither the President nor the Office of the President is an "agency" subject to the FOIA.[54]

---

[48] See id. at 129.

[49] See id. at 130.

[50] Id. (concluding, both implicitly and pragmatically, that its Dow Jones result was one thing for Congress, as the maker of laws under the Constitution, but would be quite another if applied to a President).

[51] 410 U.S. 74 (1973).

[52] Id. at 85 (emphasis added); see also Ryan, 617 F.2d at 786-87 (rejecting argument that Attorney General is not "agency" when acting in advisory capacity to President); Berman v. CIA, 378 F. Supp. 2d 1209, 1219-20 (E.D. Cal. 2005) (rejecting argument that documents prepared for President are not "inter-agency" simply because President is not "agency").

[53] No. 03-5098, 2004 WL 980826, at *11 (D.C. Cir. May 7, 2004).

[54] See, e.g., McDonnell v. Clinton, No. 97-1535, 1997 WL 33321085, at *1 (D.D.C. July 3, 1997) (holding that the "Office of the President, including its personal staff . . . whose sole function is to advise and assist the President, does not fall within the definition of agency" (citing Kissinger v. Reporters

(continued...)

In Formaldehyde Institute v. HHS,[55] the D.C. Circuit found that Exemption 5's "inter-agency or intra-agency" threshold requirement was satisfied even where no "formal relationship" existed between HHS and an outside scientific journal engaged in the process of reviewing an article that was submitted by an HHS scientist for possible publication.[56] The D.C. Circuit stated that the deciding factor was the "role" that the evaluative comments from the journal's reviewers played in the process of agency deliberations -- that is, they were regularly relied upon by agency authors and supervisors in making the agency's decisions.[57] More recently, in Public Citizen, Inc. v. U.S. Department of Justice,[58] the D.C. Circuit likewise protected the consultative relationship between former Presidents and agencies under the Presidential Records Act,[59] going so far as to conclude that "[c]onsultations under the Presidential Records Act are precisely the type that Exemption 5 was designed to protect."[60] It should be noted, moreover, that the Supreme Court in Klamath explicitly left open the continued viability of the D.C. Circuit's precedents in both Public Citizen and Ryan, noting that these two decisions "arguably extend" beyond the "typical examples" of cases in which communications of outside consultants have been held to satisfy "inter-agency or intra-agency" threshold.[61] It still remains to be seen exactly how such pre-Klamath precedents will develop further under Kla-

---

[54](...continued)
Comm. for Freedom of the Press, 445 U.S. 136, 150-55 (1980))), aff'd, 132 F.3d 1481 (D.C. Cir. 1997) (unpublished table decision); cf. AFL-CIO v. FEC, 177 F. Supp. 2d 48, 64 (D.D.C. 2002) (suggesting that FOIA might be "unconstitutional as applied" in particular context, while not reaching issue due to "judicial preference for resolving matters on non-constitutional grounds"), aff'd on other grounds, 333 F.2d 168 (D.C. Cir. 2003); accord Mink, 410 U.S. at 85 (avoiding constitutional infirmity, albeit sub silentio, through nondisclosure result).

[55] 889 F.2d 1118 (D.C. Cir. 1989).

[56] Id. at 1123-24.

[57] Id. (citing CNA, 830 F.2d at 1161); see also Weinstein v. HHS, 977 F. Supp. 41, 44-45 (D.D.C. 1997) (protecting evaluations by outside scientific experts utilized in "NIH's competitive grant application process"). But see Texas, 889 F.2d at 62 (embracing old "functional test" but finding it not satisfied for documents submitted by private party not standing in any consultative or advisory role with agency).

[58] 111 F.3d 168 (1997).

[59] 44 U.S.C. §§ 2201-07 (2000).

[60] 111 F.3d at 171.

[61] 532 U.S. at 12 n.4; see also FOIA Post, "Supreme Court Rules in Exemption 5 Case" (posted 4/4/01).

math in future cases involving the contours of Exemption 5's threshold.[62]

In two cases decided subsequent to Klamath, federal district courts have limited the threshold test as laid out by the Supreme Court. In Merit Energy Co. v. United States Department of the Interior,[63] the District Court for the District of Colorado held that communications between a Native American tribe and the agency did not meet the "inter or intra-agency" test, because the tribe was advocating its own interests.[64] The court did not expressly address the second part of the Klamath test -- namely, whether the tribe was advocating its interests at the expense of other parties.[65]

Similarly, in Center for International Environmental Law v. Office of the United States Trade Representative,[66] the District Court for the District of Columbia refused to allow the United States Trade Representative to protect documents exchanged by his office with the Government of Chile in the course of bilateral trade negotiations between the United States and the Chilean government.[67] The court made its ruling on the basis that the "critical factor" in the case before it was the "degree of self-interest" pursued by the outside party, "as compared to its interest in providing neutral advice"[68] -- and did not address the second component of the two-part test

---

[62] See FOIA Post, "Supreme Court Rules in Exemption 5 Case" (posted 4/4/01) (observing in this regard that Public Citizen and Ryan, "and their potential progeny, stand apart from" what the Supreme Court rejected in Klamath); see also Bangor Hydro-Elec. Co. v. U.S. Dep't of the Interior, No. 94-0173-B, slip op. at 5 (D. Me. Apr. 18, 1995) (presaging Klamath in holding that intra-agency threshold was not satisfied in case where party sought governmental benefit at expense of others' interests, and where agency "did not 'call upon' the [Penobscot] Nation to 'assist in internal decision-making'"; instead, "the Nation 'approached the government with their own interest in mind'" (quoting County of Madison v. U.S. Dep't of Justice, 641 F.2d 1036, 1042 (1st Cir. 1981))).

[63] 180 F. Supp. 2d 1184 (D. Colo. 2001).

[64] See id. at 1191.

[65] See id.; see also Flathead Joint Bd. of Control v. U.S. Dep't of the Interior, 309 F. Supp. 2d 1217, 1223-24 (D. Mont. 2004) (limiting discussion of Klamath's threshold test to its first component and then ordering disclosure, apparently based on understanding of waiver as result of prior disclosure).

[66] 237 F. Supp. 2d 17 (D.D.C. 2002).

[67] See id. at 25-27.

[68] Id. at 27.

announced in Klamath.[69]

Another application of the Klamath test can be found in Physicians Committee for Responsible Medicine v. National Institutes of Health.[70] In this 2004 case, the District Court for the District of Columbia ruled that Exemption 5 could not be used to protect documents submitted by an NIH grant applicant, because the applicant failed to qualify as a consultant under the test laid out in Klamath.[71] But in so ruling, the court referred to both of the aforementioned elements of the Klamath threshold test: that the applicant had submitted the grant application documents with his own interests in mind and that he was competing for a governmental benefit at the expense of other applicants, in a true multilateral situation.[72] This reading of Klamath was echoed by the District Court for the District of Columbia in Lardner v. U.S. Dep't of Justice,[73] in which the court explained that "[f]airly read, the holding of Klamath is only that a communication from an 'interested party' seeking a Government benefit 'at the expense of other applicants' is not an intra-agency record."[74]

Lastly, while state or local governments that voluntarily provide documents to federal agencies outside the contours of a formal state-federal partnership will likely not be considered consultants,[75] it still remains un-

---

[69] See Klamath, 532 U.S. at 12 ("[T]he dispositive point is that the apparent object of the Tribe's communications is a decision by an agency of the Government to support a claim by the Tribe that is necessarily adverse to the interests of competitors."); see also FOIA Post, "Supreme Court Rules in Exemption 5 Case" (posted 4/4/01) (explaining both content and contours of Klamath test). But see Judicial Watch v. Dep't of the Army, 435 F. Supp. 2d 81, 92 n.6 (D.D.C. 2006) (criticizing, in dicta, Justice Department's explanation of Klamath's two-part test in favor of decision in Center for International Environmental Law).

[70] 326 F. Supp. 2d 19, 29-30 (D.D.C. 2004).

[71] See id. at 30.

[72] See id.

[73] No. 03-0180, 2005 U.S. Dist. LEXIS 5465 (D.D.C. Mar. 31, 2005).

[74] Lardner, 2005 U.S. Dist. LEXIS 5465, at *51; accord FOIA Post "Supreme Court Rules in Exemption 5 Case" (posted 4/4/01) (discussing both elements of Supreme Court's Exemption 5 threshold standard).

[75] See Citizens for Pa.'s Future v. U.S. Dep't of Interior, No. 03-4498 (3d Cir. July 30, 2004) (vacating lower court decision protecting documents exchanged between state and federal agencies); Grand Cent. P'ship, Inc. v. Cuomo, 166 F.3d 473, 484 (2d Cir. 1999) (holding that letter sent from city councilman to agency did not meet threshold test, but specifically leaving open question of whether communication from state agency to federal

(continued...)

clear to what extent state or local governments acting in concert with federal agencies on joint regulatory matters will be considered consultants to the federal government for Exemption 5 purposes. Some courts have indicated a willingness to accept the idea that state governments can be consultants to the federal government under the Exemption 5 threshold.[76]

Deliberative Process Privilege

The most commonly invoked privilege incorporated within Exemption 5 is the deliberative process privilege, the general purpose of which is to "prevent injury to the quality of agency decisions."[77] Specifically, three policy purposes consistently have been held to constitute the bases for this privilege: (1) to encourage open, frank discussions on matters of policy between subordinates and superiors; (2) to protect against premature disclosure of proposed policies before they are finally adopted; and (3) to protect against public confusion that might result from disclosure of reasons and rationales that were not in fact ultimately the grounds for an agency's action.[78]

---

[75](...continued)
agency pursuant to joint state-federal operation might be).

[76] See Nat'l Ass'n of Home Builders v. Norton, 309 F.3d 26, 39 (D.C. Cir. 2002) (holding that particular documents provided by state agency to Department of Interior had not contributed to Department's deliberative process and therefore could not be protected by Exemption 5, but not disagreeing that such documents provided by state agency to federal agency could meet Exemption 5's threshold); cf. United States v. Allsteel, Inc., No. 87-C-4638, 1988 WL 139361, at *2 (N.D. Ill. Dec. 21, 1988) (protecting documents exchanged between federal and state co-regulators) (non-FOIA case).

[77] NLRB v. Sears, Roebuck & Co., 421 U.S. 132, 151 (1975); see also Attorney General's Memorandum for Heads of All Federal Departments and Agencies Regarding the Freedom of Information Act (Oct. 12, 2001) [hereinafter Attorney General Ashcroft's FOIA Memorandum], reprinted in FOIA Post (posted 10/15/01) (emphasizing importance of deliberative process privilege in protecting decisionmakers' ability to receive "confidential advice and counsel").

[78] See, e.g., Russell v. Dep't of the Air Force, 682 F.2d 1045, 1048 (D.C. Cir. 1982); Coastal States Gas Corp. v. Dep't of Energy, 617 F.2d 854, 866 (D.C. Cir. 1980); Jordan v. U.S. Dep't of Justice, 591 F.2d 753, 772-73 (D.C. Cir. 1978) (en banc); Kidd v. U.S. Dep't of Justice, 362 F. Supp. 2d 291, 296 (D.D.C. 2005) (protecting documents on basis that disclosure would "inhibit drafters from freely exchanging ideas, language choice, and comments in drafting documents") (internal quotation marks omitted); Heggestad v. U.S. Dep't of Justice, 182 F. Supp. 2d 1, 12 (D.D.C. 2000) (protecting memoranda containing recommendations based on perjured testimony, finding that they "have no probative value to the public since they are based on misrep-
(continued...)

Logically flowing from the foregoing policy considerations is the privilege's protection of the "decision making processes of government agencies."[79] In concept, the privilege protects not merely documents, but also the integrity of the deliberative process itself where the exposure of that process would result in harm.[80]

Indeed, in a major en banc decision, the Court of Appeals for the District of Columbia Circuit emphasized that even the mere status of an agency decision within an agency decisionmaking process may be protectible if the release of that information would have the effect of prematurely disclosing "the recommended outcome of the consultative process . . . as well

---

[78](...continued)
resentations"); AFGE v. HHS, 63 F. Supp. 2d 104, 108 (D. Mass. 1999) (holding that release of predecisional documents "could cause harm by providing the public with erroneous information"), aff'd, No. 99-2208, 2000 U.S. App. LEXIS 10993, at *3 (1st Cir. May 18, 2000). But see ITT World Commc'ns, Inc. v. FCC, 699 F.2d 1219, 1237-38 (D.C. Cir. 1983) (dictum) (suggesting that otherwise exempt predecisional material "may" be ordered released so as to explain actual agency positions), rev'd on other grounds, 466 U.S. 463 (1984).

[79] Sears, 421 U.S. at 150; see also Missouri ex rel. Shorr v. U.S. Army Corps of Eng'rs, 147 F.3d 708, 710 (8th Cir. 1998) ("The purpose of the deliberative process privilege is to allow agencies freely to explore alternative avenues of action and to engage in internal debates without fear of public scrutiny.").

[80] See, e.g., Nat'l Wildlife Fed'n v. U.S. Forest Serv., 861 F.2d 1114, 1119 (9th Cir. 1988) ("[T]he ultimate objective of exemption 5 is to safeguard the deliberative process of agencies, not the paperwork generated in the course of that process."); Schell v. HHS, 843 F.2d 933, 940 (6th Cir. 1988) ("Because Exemption 5 is concerned with protecting the deliberative process itself, courts now focus less on the material sought and more on the effect of the material's release."); Dudman Communications Corp. v. Dep't of the Air Force, 815 F.2d 1565, 1568 (D.C. Cir. 1987) ("Congress enacted Exemption 5 to protect the executive's deliberative processes -- not to protect specific materials."); Greenberg v. U.S. Dep't of Treasury, 10 F. Supp. 2d 3, 16 n.19 (D.D.C. 1998) (concluding that Exemption 5 "is not limited to preventing embarrassment or 'chilling' of the individual authors of deliberative documents" but is designed to prevent chilling of agency deliberations); Chem. Mfrs. Ass'n v. Consumer Prod. Safety Comm'n, 600 F. Supp. 114, 117 (D.D.C. 1984) (finding that ongoing regulatory process would be subject to "delay and disrupt[ion]" if preliminary analyses were prematurely disclosed). But cf. Bangor Hydro-Elec. Co. v. U.S. Dep't of the Interior, No. 94-0173-B, slip op. at 6 (D. Me. Apr. 18, 1995) (holding deliberative process privilege inapplicable when by regulation entire decisionmaking process is open to all interested parties) (alternative holding).

as the source of any decision."[81] This is particularly important to agencies involved in a regulatory process that specifically mandates public involvement in the decision process once the agency's deliberations are complete.[82] Moreover, the predecisional character of a document is not altered by the fact that an agency has subsequently made a final decision[83] or even has decided to not make a final decision.[84] Nor is it altered by the passage of time in general.[85]

---

[81] Wolfe v. HHS, 839 F.2d 768, 775 (D.C. Cir. 1988) (en banc).

[82] See id. at 776; see also Missouri, 147 F.3d at 710-11 (protecting intra-agency memorandum commenting on draft environmental impact statement and finding that "[a]lthough [the National Environmental Policy Act] contemplates public participation . . . NEPA's statutory language specifically indicates that disclosure to the public is to be in accord with FOIA, which includes Exemption 5"); Nat'l Wildlife, 861 F.2d at 1120-21 (draft forest plans and preliminary draft environmental impact statements protected); Chem. Mfrs., 600 F. Supp. at 118 (preliminary scientific data generated in connection with study of chemical protected).

[83] See, e.g., Fed. Open Mkt. Comm. v. Merrill, 443 U.S. 340, 360 (1979); May v. Dep't of the Air Force, 777 F.2d 1012, 1014-15 (5th Cir. 1985); Cuccaro v. Sec'y of Labor, 770 F.2d 355, 357 (3d Cir. 1985); Judicial Watch of Fla., Inc. v. U.S. Dep't of Justice, 102 F. Supp. 2d 6, 16 (D.D.C. 2000) (rejecting specious assertion that deliberative process privilege "expires" after deliberations have ended and relevant decision has been made); Elec. Privacy Info. Ctr. v. DHS, 384 F. Supp. 2d 100, 112-13 (D.D.C. 2005) (same); see also FOIA Update, Vol. XVI, No. 3, at 5 (dispelling "common misconception" about Exemption 5 on this point).

[84] See Sears, 421 U.S. at 151 n.18 (extending protection to records that are part of decisionmaking process even where process does not produce actual decision by agency); Hornbeck Offshore Transp., LLC v. U.S. Coast Guard, No. 04-1724, 2006 WL 696053, at *21 (D.D.C. Mar. 20, 2006) (rejecting plaintiff's claim that documents relating to action ultimately not taken did not qualify as predecisional); Judicial Watch, Inc. v. Clinton, 880 F. Supp. 1, 13 (D.D.C. 1995) (holding that to release deliberative documents because no final decision was issued would be "exalting semantics over substance"), aff'd on other grounds, 76 F.3d 1232 (D.C. Cir. 1996); cf. Elec. Privacy Info. Ctr., 384 F. Supp. 2d at 112 (holding that documents concerning now-abandoned agency program were nonetheless predecisional).

[85] See, e.g., AGS Computers, Inc. v. U.S. Dep't of Treasury, No. 92-2714, slip op. at 13 (D.N.J. Sept. 16, 1993) (holding that predecisional character is not lost through passage of time); Founding Church of Scientology v. Levi, 1 Gov't Disclosure Serv. (P-H) ¶ 80,155, at 80,374 (D.D.C. Aug. 12, 1980) ("There is nothing in the language of the provision to suggest that passage of time without more derogates from the exempt status of the deliberative material.").

Traditionally, the courts have established two fundamental require-ments, both of which must be met, for the deliberative process privilege to be invoked.[86] First, the communication must be predecisional, i.e., "ante-cedent to the adoption of an agency policy."[87] Second, the communication must be deliberative, i.e., "a direct part of the deliberative process in that it makes recommendations or expresses opinions on legal or policy mat-ters."[88] The burden is upon the agency to show that the information in question satisfies both requirements.[89]

In determining whether a document is predecisional, an agency does not necessarily have to point specifically to an agency final decision, but merely establish "what deliberative process is involved, and the role played by the documents in issue in the course of that process."[90] On this point,

---

[86] See Mapother v. Dep't of Justice, 3 F.3d 1533, 1537 (D.C. Cir. 1993) ("The deliberative process privilege protects materials that are both pre-decisional and deliberative." (citing Petroleum Info. Corp. v. U.S. Dep't of the Interior, 976 F.2d 1429, 1434 (D.C. Cir. 1992))).

[87] Jordan, 591 F.2d at 774.

[88] Vaughn v. Rosen, 523 F.2d 1136, 1143-44 (D.C. Cir. 1975).

[89] See Coastal States, 617 F.2d at 866.

[90] Id. at 868; see also Providence Journal Co. v. U.S. Dep't of the Army, 981 F.2d 552, 559 (1st Cir. 1992) (protecting IG's recommendations even though decisionmakers were not obligated to follow them); Formaldehyde Inst. v. HHS, 889 F.2d 1118, 1123 (D.C. Cir. 1989) (protecting recommenda-tions on suitability of article for publication, though decision on "whether and where" to publish article had not yet been made); Greenberg, 10 F. Supp. 2d at 17 (stating that "an evaluation of the legal status" of a case would be protected, but an "instruction from a senior to a junior official as to what legal action should be taken -- a final decision . . . does not merit Exemption 5 protection"); Horsehead Indus. v. EPA, No. 94-1299, slip op. at 14 (D.D.C. Oct. 1, 1996) ("In determining whether material is predecisional in nature, courts must look to see what role the material played in the deci-sionmaking process . . . . A statement of an opinion by an agency official or preliminary findings reported by a public affairs official do not necessarily constitute a statement of EPA policy or final opinion that has the force of law."); Knowles v. Thornburgh, No. 90-1294, slip op. at 5-6 (D.D.C. Mar. 11, 1992) (holding information generated during process preceding President's ultimate decision on application for clemency was predecisional); cf. Sw. Ctr. for Biological Diversity v. USDA, 170 F. Supp. 2d 931, 940 (D. Ariz. 2000) (rejecting as "tenuous" defendant's position that releasing informa-tion would "result in humans disturbing nesting goshawks," which in turn would alter agency's deliberative process by affecting results of scientific study), aff'd on other grounds, 314 F.3d 1060 (9th Cir. 2002); Animal Legal Def. Fund, Inc. v. Dep't of the Air Force, 44 F. Supp. 2d 295, 299 (D.D.C.

(continued...)

the Supreme Court has been very clear:

> Our emphasis on the need to protect pre-<u>decisional</u> documents
> does not mean that the existence of the privilege turns on the
> ability of an agency to identify a specific decision in connection
> with which a memorandum is prepared. Agencies are, and
> properly should be, engaged in a continuing process of examin-
> ing their policies; this process will generate memoranda con-
> taining recommendations which do not ripen into agency deci-
> sions; and the lower courts should be wary of interfering with
> this process.[91]

---

[90](...continued)
1999) (rejecting privilege claim because agency "utterly failed to specify
the role played by each withheld document" in policy-formulation process).

[91] Sears, 421 U.S. at 151 n.18; see also Schell, 843 F.2d at 941 ("When
specific advice is provided, . . . it is no less predecisional because it is accepted or rejected in silence, or perhaps simply incorporated into the thinking of superiors for future use."); Maydak v. U.S. Dep't of Justice, 362 F.
Supp. 2d 316, 326 (D.D.C. 2005) (protecting information concerning federal
inmate that was used by Bureau of Prison officials as part of continuing
process of making decisions regarding inmate's status); Hamilton Sec.
Group, Inc. v. HUD, 106 F. Supp. 2d 23, 30 (D.D.C. 2000) (protecting a draft
audit report that was never reviewed by an agency decisionmaker; holding
that "only those materials that are reviewed and approved by the District
Inspector General represent the agency's final position"), aff'd, No. 00-5331,
2001 WL 238162, at *1 (D.C. Cir. Feb. 23, 2001) (per curiam); Greenberg, 10
F. Supp. 2d at 16 (rejecting argument that documents were not deliberative
because not actually relied upon, observing that "[i]f the author had known
that the notes discussing the proposed questions and issues would be
subject to FOIA disclosure if not actually used, the author likely would
have been more cautious in what he or she recommended"); Brooks v. IRS,
No. CV-F-96-6284, 1997 U.S. Dist LEXIS 21075, at *23-24 (E.D. Cal. Nov. 17,
1997) ("governmental privilege does not hinge on whether or not the District Counsel relied on or accorded any weight to the information at issue
in rendering its final decision"); Perdue Farms, Inc. v. NLRB, No. 2:96-CV-
27-BO(1), 1997 U.S. Dist. LEXIS 14579, at *17 (E.D.N.C. Aug. 5, 1997) ("Although some [deliberative] processes do not ripen into agency decisions,
this does not preclude application of the deliberative process privilege.");
Hunt v. U.S. Marine Corp., 935 F. Supp. 46, 51 (D.D.C. 1996) (agency need
not point specifically to final decision made); Chem. Mfrs., 600 F. Supp. at
118 ("[t]here should be considerable deference to the [agency's] judgment
as to what constitutes . . . 'part of the agency give-and-take -- of the deliberative process -- by which the decision itself is made'" (quoting Vaughn,
523 F.2d at 1144)); Pfeiffer v. CIA, 721 F. Supp. 337, 340 (D.D.C. 1989) (court
"must give considerable deference to the agency's explanation of its decisional process, due to agency's expertise"). But see Carter v. U.S. Dep't of
Commerce, 186 F. Supp. 2d 1147, 1153-54 (D. Or. 2001) (holding that adjust-
(continued...)

Thus, so long as a document is generated as part of such a continuing process of agency decisionmaking, Exemption 5 can be applicable.[92] In

---

[91](...continued)
ed census data not examined by decisionmaker "cannot be said to have contributed" to decisionmaking process; and rejecting argument that data were nevertheless predecisional because agency was actively considering using them in future), aff'd, 307 F.3d 1084 (9th Cir. 2002); cf. Maricopa Audubon Soc'y v. U.S. Forest Serv., 108 F.3d 1089, 1094 (9th Cir. 1997) (declaring Supreme Court pronouncement to be merely "cautionary dictum"); Am. Small Bus. League v. SBA, No. C 04-4250, slip op. at 5 (N.D. Cal. Apr. 29, 2005) (following Maricopa's ruling that a document is not predecisional if it is only "part of a continuing process of agency self-examination," despite the Supreme Court's direct pronouncement to the contrary in Sears).

[92] See, e.g., Casad v. HHS, 301 F.3d 1247, 1252 (10th Cir. 2002) (holding that deliberative process privilege protects redacted portions of "summary statements" created prior to NIH's research grant funding decisions); Sierra Club v. U.S. Dep't of Interior, 384 F. Supp. 2d 1, 16 (D.D.C. 2004) (rejecting as "simplistic" plaintiff's claim that deliberative process privilege did not apply to documents generated after presidential policy decision but which reflected deliberations on how best to advocate President's policy proposals in Congress); Gordon v. FBI, 388 F. Supp. 2d 1028, 1038 (N.D. Cal. 2005) (protecting documents concerning government's "no-fly" list even after implementation of these lists, because withheld documents discussed potential revisions to relevant regulations); Tarullo v. DOD, 170 F. Supp. 2d 271, 277 (D. Conn. 2001) (rejecting an argument that a document was not predecisional, instead finding that it was merely "a description of how the agency performed under its then-existing policy," and concluding that although the memorandum "contains some objective description of the facts providing a basis for . . . opinions, it consists primarily of specific subjective recommendations about future agency conduct and policy"); Judicial Watch, Inc. v. Reno, No. 00-0723, slip op. at 6-7 (D.D.C. Mar. 30, 2001) (protecting communications regarding "continuing and follow-up issues" resulting from decision to repatriate Cuban emigré Elian Gonzalez); Felsen v. HHS, No. 95-975, slip op. at 90 (D. Md. Sept. 30, 1998) ("agency need not identify any specific decision, but merely must establish 'what deliberative process is involved, and the role played by the documents in issue in the course of that process'" (quoting Coastal States, 617 F.2d at 868)); Dayton Newspapers, Inc. v. U.S. Dep't of the Navy, No. C-3-95-328, slip op. at 55-56 (S.D. Ohio Sept. 12, 1996) (protecting communications that were postdecisional with respect to a specific agency decision but predecisional "in relation to their impact on broader policy decisions"); Md. Coal. for Integrated Educ. v. U.S. Dep't of Educ., No. 89-2851, slip op. at 6 (D.D.C. July 20, 1992) (finding material prepared during compliance review that goes beyond critique of reviewed program to discuss broader agency policy to be part of deliberative process), appeal dismissed voluntarily, No. 92-5346 (D.C. Cir. Dec. 13, 1993); Wash. Post Co. v. DOD, No. 84-2949, 1987 U.S. Dist LEXIS 16108, at *29 (D.D.C. Feb. 25, 1987) (holding that document generated in

(continued...)

a particularly instructive decision, Access Reports v. Department of Justice,[93] the D.C. Circuit emphasized the importance of identifying the larger process to which a document sometimes contributes. Further, "predecisional" documents are not only those circulated within the agency, but can also be those from an agency lacking decisional authority which advises another agency possessing such authority.[94] They even can be "documents which the agency decisionmaker herself prepared as part of her delibera-

---

[92](...continued)
continuing process of examining agency policy falls within deliberative process); Ashley v. U.S. Dep't of Labor, 589 F. Supp. 901, 908-09 (D.D.C. 1983) (holding that documents containing agency self-evaluations need not be shown to be part of clear process leading up to "assured" final decision so long as agency can demonstrate that documents were part of some deliberative process). Compare Parke, Davis & Co. v. Califano, 623 F.2d 1, 6 (6th Cir. 1980) (holding that document must be "essential element" of deliberative process), with Schell, 843 F.2d at 939-41 (appearing to reject, at least implicitly, "essential element" test), and AFGE, 63 F. Supp. 2d at 108-09 (rejecting proposed "essential functions" test). But see Maricopa, 108 F.3d at 1094 (dictum) ("agency must identify a specific decision where document is pre-decisional"); Senate of P.R. v. U.S. Dep't of Justice, 823 F.2d 574, 585 (D.C. Cir. 1987) (suggesting agency must specify final "decisions to which the advice or recommendations . . . contributed"); Nat'l Res. Def. Council v. DOD, 388 F. Supp. 2d 1086, 1098 (C.D. Cal. 2005) (holding that agency must identify specific decisonmaking process); Cook v. Watt, 597 F. Supp. 545, 550-52 (D. Alaska 1983) (refusing to extend privilege to documents originating in deliberative process merely because process held in abeyance and no decision reached).

[93] 926 F.2d 1192, 1196 (D.C. Cir. 1991); see also Taylor v. Dep't of the Treasury, No. C90-1928, slip op. at 3-4 (N.D. Cal. Jan. 20, 1991) (stating that deliberative process privilege covers "communications leading to the actual enactment of a law, not merely communications preceding a decision to commence the process of amending a law").

[94] See Renegotiation Bd. v. Grumman Aircraft Eng'g Corp., 421 U.S. 168, 188 (1975); Bureau of Nat'l Affairs, Inc. v. United States Dep't of Justice, 742 F.2d 1484, 1497 (D.C. Cir. 1984); Defenders of Wildlife v. United States Dep't of the Interior, No. 03-1192, 2004 WL 842374, at *11-12 (D.D.C. Apr. 13, 2004) (protecting documents relating to ethics investigation that were prepared by Department of the Interior and given to Office of Government Ethics, which had final authority over investigation). Compare Blazar v. OMB, No. 92-2719, slip op. at 14 (D.D.C. Apr. 15, 1994) (finding recommendations made from OMB to the President to be predecisional), with Am. Soc'y of Pension Actuaries v. IRS, 746 F. Supp. 188, 192 (D.D.C. 1990) (ordering disclosure after finding that IRS's budget assumptions and calculations were "relied upon by government" in making final estimate for President's budget).

tion and decisionmaking process,"[95] or documents that do not end up being considered by the agency decisonmaker at all.[96] Lastly, it has been held that the privilege is not limited to deliberations connected solely to agency activities that are specifically authorized by Congress.[97]

In contrast, however, are postdecisional documents. They generally embody statements of policy and final opinions that have the force of law,[98] that implement an established policy of an agency,[99] or that explain actions that an agency has already taken.[100] Exemption 5 ordinarily does not apply to postdecisional documents, as "the public is vitally concerned with the reasons which did supply the basis for an agency policy actually adopt-

---

[95] Judicial Watch, 102 F. Supp. 2d at 14 (protecting notes taken by Attorney General which she did not share with others).

[96] See Moye, O'Brien, O'Rourke, Hogan & Pickert v. Nat'l R.R. Passenger Corp., 376 F.3d 1270, 1279 (11th Cir. 2004) (reversing magistrate's ruling that documents that had contributed to decisionmaking process were not privileged just because they had not been considered by final decisionmaker; declaring that such ruling reflected magistrate's "too narrow" view of Exemption 5); see also Schell, 843 F.2d at 941 ("A subordinate who wishes to provide information candidly should not fear that the public will be privy to his views merely because his superiors have not yet acted on his recommendations.").

[97] See Enviro Tech Int'l, Inc. v. EPA, 371 F.3d 370, 376 (7th Cir. 2004) (protecting documents that contained EPA recommendations on workplace exposure limits to n-Propyl Bromide, despite fact that EPA lacks statutory authority to regulate such exposure limits); cf. Weissman v. CIA, 565 F.2d 692, 695-96 (D.C. Cir. 1977) (holding that CIA cannot use Exemption 7 to protect documents generated in course of law enforcement activity for which it has no statutory authorization).

[98] See, e.g., Taxation With Representation Fund v. IRS, 646 F.2d 666, 677-78 (D.C. Cir. 1981).

[99] See, e.g., Brinton v. Dep't of State, 636 F.2d 600, 605 (D.C. Cir. 1980); Nissei Sangyo Am., Ltd. v. IRS, No. 95-1019, 1997 U.S. Dist. LEXIS 22473, at *23-24 (D.D.C. May 8, 1997) (magistrate's recommendation) (declining to apply deliberative process privilege to results of tax audit in which agency was merely "applying published tax laws to factual information regarding a taxpayer"), adopted (D.D.C. Jan. 28, 1998).

[100] See, e.g., Sears, 421 U.S. at 153-54; Judicial Watch, Inc. v. HHS, 27 F. Supp. 2d 240, 245 (D.D.C. 1998) ("deliberative process privilege does not protect documents that merely state or explain agency decisions"); cf. Horowitz v. Peace Corps, No. 00-0848, slip op. at 9-10 (D.D.C. Oct. 12, 2001) (ordering parties to submit additional evidence of whether final decision had been made at time disputed memorandum was written). But cf. Murphy v. TVA, 571 F. Supp. 502, 505 (D.D.C. 1983) (protecting two "interim" decisions, which agency retains option of changing).

ed."[101] However, if a document is postdecisional in form but predecisional in its content, it may be protectible. For example, e-mail messages generated after a relevant agency decision has been made, but which merely reiterate the agency's predecisional deliberations and the author's own recommendations, are protectible under Exemption 5.[102]

Many courts have confronted the question of whether certain documents at issue were tantamount to agency "secret law," i.e., "orders and interpretations which [the agency] actually applies to cases before it,"[103] and which are "routinely used by agency staff as guidance."[104] Such documents should be disclosed because they are not in fact predecisional, but rather "discuss established policies and decisions."[105] Only those portions of a postdecisional document that discuss predecisional recommendations not expressly adopted can be protected.[106]

---

[101] Sears, 421 U.S. at 152.

[102] See Elec. Privacy Info. Ctr. v. DHS, No. 04-1625, 2006 U.S. Dist. LEXIS 94615, at *22-24 (D.D.C. Dec. 22, 2006) (protecting e-mail message generated after agency decision made which "recanted" deliberations preceding decision); N. Dartmouth Properties, Inc. v. HUD, 984 F. Supp. 65, 69 (D. Mass. 1997) (noting that author may not have known that final decision had been reached at time he composed message because "[n]o one would waste time preparing an e-mail message in an attempt to persuade someone to reach a conclusion if he knew that the conclusion he was advocating had already been reached").

[103] Sterling Drug, Inc. v. FTC, 450 F.2d 698, 708 (D.C. Cir. 1971).

[104] Coastal States, 617 F.2d at 869; see also Schlefer v. United States, 702 F.2d 233, 243-44 (D.C. Cir. 1983).

[105] Coastal States, 617 F.2d at 868; see also Safeway, Inc. v. IRS, No. 05-3182, 2006 WL 3041079, at *9 (N.D. Cal. Oct. 24, 2006) (ordering the release of documents characterized as an "intraagency discussion of how to apply established policy and law to the particular facts of Plaintiff's audit"); Evans v. OPM, 276 F. Supp. 2d 34, 40 (D.D.C. 2003) (holding that deliberative process privilege does not protect memorandum issued by OPM's Office of General Counsel that is "clear statement" of OPM's position on adoption of governmentwide hiring policy); Hansen v. U.S. Dep't of the Air Force, 817 F. Supp. 123, 124-25 (D.D.C. 1992) (ordering disclosure of draft document used by agency as final product); see also Carlton v. Dep't of Interior, No. 97-2105, slip op. at 15 n.7 (D.D.C. Sept. 3, 1998) (observing that court "need not find that the agency is withholding secret law . . . to conclude that the government has nevertheless failed to justify its withholdings under FOIA Exemption 5").

[106] See Sears, 421 U.S. at 151 (holding postdecisional documents subject to deliberative process privilege "as long as prior communications and the ingredients of the decisionmaking process are not disclosed"); see also

(continued...)

Several criteria have been fashioned to clarify the "often blurred" distinction between predecisional and postdecisional documents.[107] First, an agency should determine whether the document is a "final opinion" within the meaning of one of the two "automatic" disclosure provisions of the FOIA, subsection (a)(2)(A).[108] In an extensive consideration of this point, the Court of Appeals for the Fifth Circuit held that, inasmuch as subsection (a)(2)(A) specifies "the adjudication of [a] case[]," Congress intended "final opinions" to be only those decisions resulting from proceedings (such as that in Sears) in which a party invoked (and obtained a decision concerning) a specific statutory right of "general and uniform" applicability[109] However, the D.C. Circuit has stated that Field Service Advice memoranda ("FSAs") issued by the Internal Revenue Service's Office of Chief Counsel are not predecisional documents, because they constitute "statements of

---

[106](...continued)
Mead Data Cent., Inc. v. U.S. Dep't of the Air Force, 566 F.2d 242, 257 (D.C. Cir. 1977) ("It would exalt form over substance to exempt documents in which staff recommend certain action or offer their opinions on given issues but require disclosure of documents which only 'report' what those recommendations and opinions are."); Blazar, No. 92-2719, slip op. at 15 (D.D.C. Apr. 15, 1994) (deciding that President's indication of which alternative he adopted does not waive privilege for unadopted recommendations); cf. Steinberg v. U.S. Dep't of Justice, No. 91-2740, 1993 WL 385820, at *3 (D.D.C. Sept. 13, 1993) (holding that protection of exemption is not lost where decision to conduct particular type of investigation was merely intermediate step in larger process).

[107] See Schlefer, 702 F.2d at 237. See generally ITT, 699 F.2d at 1235; Arthur Andersen & Co. v. IRS, 679 F.2d 254, 258-59 (D.C. Cir. 1982); Tax Analysts v. IRS, No. 94-923, 1996 U.S. Dist. LEXIS 3259, at *4-8 (D.D.C. Mar. 15, 1996), aff'd, 117 F.3d 607 (D.C. Cir. 1997).

[108] 5 U.S.C. § 552(a)(2)(A) (2000 & Supp. IV 2004); see Fed. Open Mkt. Comm., 443 U.S. at 360-61 n.23.

[109] Skelton v. U.S. Postal Serv., 678 F.2d 35, 41 (5th Cir. 1982); cf. Rockwell Int'l Corp. v. U.S. Dep't of Justice, 235 F.3d 598, 602-03 (D.C. Cir. 2001) (concluding that a report was not a final opinion because it contained "conclusions of a voluntarily undertaken internal agency investigation, not a conclusion about agency action (or inaction) in an adversarial dispute with another party"); Common Cause v. IRS, 646 F.2d 656, 659-60 (D.C. Cir. 1981) (rejecting a claim that a document was a final opinion, because the agency's action involved "the voluntary suggestion, evaluation, and rejection of a proposed policy by an agency, not the agency's final, unappealable decision not to pursue a judicial remedy in an adversarial dispute"). But see Afshar v. Dep't of State, 702 F.2d 1125, 1142-43 (D.C. Cir. 1983) (holding that even single recommendation of no precedential value or applicability to rights of individual members of public loses protection if specifically adopted as basis for final decision).

an agency's legal position."[110] The court reached this conclusion even though the opinions were found to be "nonbinding" on the ultimate decisionmakers.[111]

Second, one must consider the nature of the decisionmaking authority vested in the office or person issuing the document.[112] If the author lacks "legal decision authority," the document is far more likely to be predecisional.[113] A crucial caveat in this regard, however, is that courts often look "beneath formal lines of authority to the reality of the decisionmaking

---

[110] Tax Analysts v. IRS, 117 F.3d 607, 617 (D.C. Cir. 1997); Evans, 276 F. Supp. 2d at 39 (finding documents at issue "indistinguishable" from records at issue in Tax Analysts for purposes of Exemption 5); cf. Tax Analysts v. IRS, 97 F. Supp. 2d 13, 17 (D.D.C. 2000) (protecting IRS Legal Memoranda, and distinguishing them from FSAs, on the basis that "[w]hereas [Legal Memoranda] flow 'upward' from staffers to reviewers, [FSAs] flow 'outward' from the Office of Chief Counsel to personnel in the field"); Ginsberg v. IRS, No. 96-2265-CIV-T-26E, 1997 WL 882913, at *4 & nn.4, 5 (M.D. Fla. Dec. 23, 1997) (magistrate's recommendation) ("Although the opinions of District Counsel may not represent final opinions or policy statements of the IRS . . . [they were] relied upon and specifically referenced" by the IRS agent in the conduct of the examination.), adopted (M.D. Fla. Jan. 27, 1998), appeal dismissed, No. 98-2384 (11th Cir. June 5, 1998).

[111] Tax Analysts, 117 F.3d at 617.

[112] See Pfeiffer, 721 F. Supp. at 340 ("What matters is that the person who issues the document has authority to speak finally and officially for the agency.").

[113] Grumman, 421 U.S. at 184-85; see also A. Michael's Piano, Inc. v. FTC, 18 F.3d 138, 147 (2d Cir. 1994) (finding staff attorney's recommendation predecisional as she had no authority to close investigation); Tax Analysts v. IRS, 152 F. Supp. 2d 1, 24-25 (D.D.C. 2001) (protecting memoranda "written by a component office without decisionmaking authority to a different component office" that had such authority), aff'd in part, rev'd in part on other grounds & remanded, 294 F.3d 71 (D.C. Cir. 2002); Tax Analysts, 97 F. Supp. 2d at 17 ("Because the drafters lack ultimate [decisionmaking] authority, their views are necessarily predecisional."); Badhwar v. U.S. Dep't of the Air Force, 615 F. Supp. 698, 702-03 (D.D.C. 1985) (concluding that Air Force safety board does not make decisions, only recommendations), aff'd in part & remanded in part on other grounds, 829 F.2d 182 (D.C. Cir. 1987); Am. Postal Workers Union v. Office of Special Counsel, No. 85-3691, slip op. at 6 (D.D.C. June 24, 1986) (protecting prosecutorial recommendations to special counsel which were not binding or dispositive). But see Tax Analysts, 117 F.3d at 617 (finding chief counsel's "nonbinding" FSAs to field offices to be not predecisional because they "constitute agency law").

process."[114] Hence, even an assertion by the agency that an official lacks ultimate decisionmaking authority might be "superficial" and unavailing if agency "practices" commonly accord decisionmaking authority to that official.[115] Conversely, an agency official who appears to have final authority may in fact not have such authority or may not be wielding that authority in a particular situation.[116]

Careful analysis of the decisionmaking process is sometimes required to determine whether the records reflect an earlier preliminary decision or recommendations concerning follow-up issues,[117] or whether the document

---

[114] Schlefer, 702 F.2d at 238; see also Nat'l Wildlife, 861 F.2d at 1123; cf. Goldstein v. Office of Indep. Counsel, No. 87-2028, 1999 WL 570862, at *7 (D.D.C. July 29, 1999) (protecting recommendations on possible criminal investigations from head of Department of Justice's Criminal Division to Director of FBI).

[115] Schlefer, 702 F.2d at 238, 241; see, e.g., Badran v. U.S. Dep't of Justice, 652 F. Supp. 1437, 1439 (N.D. Ill. 1987) (concluding that INS decision on plaintiff's bond was final, even though it was reviewable by immigration judge, because "immigration judges are independent from the INS, and no review of plaintiff's bond occurred within the INS").

[116] See, e.g., Nat'l Wildlife, 861 F.2d at 1122-23 (finding that headquarters' comments on regional plans were opinions and recommendations); Heggestad, 182 F. Supp. 2d at 10 (finding that top official in Department of Justice's Tax Division actually had made decision to prosecute despite fact that authority to make such decisions had been delegated to chief of Tax Division's Criminal Section); Nat'l Ass'n of Criminal Def. Lawyers v. U.S. Dep't of Justice, No. 97-372, slip op. at 10-13 (D.D.C. July 22, 1998) (deciding that predecisional character of draft IG report is not affected by fact that FBI took adverse personnel action against investigated employees after reviewing it); Jowett, Inc. v. Dep't of the Navy, 729 F. Supp. 871, 874 (D.D.C. 1989) (protecting audit reports prepared by entity lacking final decisionmaking authority).

[117] See, e.g., City of Va. Beach v. U.S. Dep't of Commerce, 995 F.2d 1247, 1254 (4th Cir. 1993) (protecting documents discussing past decision insofar as it influences future decision); Access Reports, 926 F.2d at 1196 (finding that staff attorney memorandum on how proposed FOIA amendments would affect future cases not postdecisional working law but opinion on how to handle pending legislative process); Sierra Club, 384 F. Supp. 2d at 16 (protecting documents discussing how to promote presidential decision in Congress); Gordon, 388 F. Supp. 2d at 1038 (upholding decision to withhold documents that concerned possible revisions to "no-fly" list regulations); The Wilderness Soc'y v. U.S. Dep't of the Interior, 344 F. Supp. 2d 1, 13-14 (D.D.C. 2004) (rejecting plaintiff's argument that mere fact that documents in question were created after relevant settlement agreement was concluded mandated holding that they were postdecisional; agency may

(continued...)

sought reflects a final decision or merely advice to a higher authority.[118] Thus, agency recommendations to OMB concerning the development of proposed legislation to be submitted to Congress are predecisional,[119] but descriptions of "agency efforts to ensure enactment of policies already established" are postdecisional.[120]

Third, it is useful to examine the direction in which the document flows along the decisionmaking chain. Naturally, a document "from a subordinate to a superior official is more likely to be predecisional"[121] than is

---

[117](...continued)
properly withhold documents evaluating prior agency decision); Hamrick v. Dep't of the Navy, No. 90-283, 1992 WL 739887, at *2 (D.D.C. Aug. 28, 1992) ("[D]ocuments prepared after [agency's] decision to dual source the F404 engines are not 'formal agency policy,' but, recommendations for future decisions relating to F404 procurement based upon lessons learned from the dual sourcing decisionmaking process."), appeal dismissed voluntarily, No. 92-5376 (D.C. Cir. Aug. 4, 1995); Dow, Lohnes & Albertson v. Presidential Comm'n on Broad. to Cuba, 624 F. Supp. 572, 574-75 (D.D.C. 1984) (holding records predecisional because, although documents discussed implementation of previous decision, issues discussed were "not mere details to be worked out but rather matters requiring further study and generating debate which culminated in the making of new policy"); cf. Wilkinson v. Chao, 292 F. Supp. 2d 288, 295 (D.N.H. 2003) (holding that agency's "final" decision was its decision not to give plaintiff overtime pay, rather than auditor's "determination" on appropriateness of decision, and that therefore documents generated after former but before latter were postdecisional).

[118] See, e.g., AFGE v. U.S. Dep't of Commerce, 907 F.2d 203, 208 (D.C. Cir. 1990); Bureau of Nat'l Affairs, 742 F.2d at 1497.

[119] See Bureau of Nat'l Affairs, 742 F.2d at 1497.

[120] Dow, Lohnes & Albertson v. USIA, No. 82-2569, slip op. at 15-16 (D.D.C. June 5, 1984), vacated in part, No. 84-5852 (D.C. Cir. Apr. 17, 1985); see also Badhwar v. United States Dep't of Justice, 622 F. Supp. 1364, 1372 (D.D.C. 1985) ("There is nothing predecisional about a recitation of corrective action already taken.").

[121] Coastal States, 617 F.2d at 868; see also Nadler v. U.S. Dep't of Justice, 955 F.2d 1479, 1491 (11th Cir. 1992) ("[A] recommendation to a supervisor on how to proceed is predecisional by nature."); Judicial Watch, No. 00-0723, slip op. at 8 (D.D.C. Mar. 30, 2001) (protecting "communications from subordinates to superiors" in Elian Gonzalez case); Students Against Genocide v. Dep't of State, No. 96-667, 1999 WL 699074, at *12 (D.D.C. Aug. 24, 1998) (magistrate's recommendation) (holding field notes of official analyzing factual information and making recommendations on U.S. foreign policy exempt), adopted (D.D.C. Sept. 29, 1998), aff'd in part & remanded in part on other grounds, 257 F.3d 828, 841 (D.C. Cir. 2001); Hayes v. Dep't of
(continued...)

one that travels in the opposite direction: "[F]inal opinions . . . typically flow from a superior with policymaking authority to a subordinate who carries out the policy."[122] However, under certain circumstances, recommendations can flow from the superior to the subordinate.[123] Indeed, even a policymaker's own predecisional notes to herself may be protectible.[124] In sum, perhaps the most important factor to consider is the "'role, if any, that the document plays in the process of agency deliberations.'"[125]

Finally, even if a document is clearly protected from disclosure by the deliberative process privilege, it may lose this protection if a final decision-

---

[121](...continued)
Labor, No. 96-1149-P-M, 1998 U.S. Dist. LEXIS 14120, at *18 (S.D. Ala. June 18, 1998) (magistrate's recommendation) ("[A] recommendation from a lower-level employee to a higher-level manager qualifies as a predecisional, deliberative document for purposes of exemption 5."), adopted (S.D. Ala. Aug. 10, 1998); Burke v. DEA, No. 96-1739, slip op. at 8 (D.D.C. Mar. 31, 1998) (protecting correspondence from postal inspector to Assistant United States Attorney who he was assisting in prosecution), appeal dismissed, No. 98-5113 (D.C. Cir. Mar. 31, 2000); Ginsberg, 1997 WL 882913, at *4-5 (holding protectible IRS agent's "request for technical assistance" and supervisor's addendum revealing "areas of concern of the two authors" during conduct of examination).

[122] Brinton, 636 F.2d at 605; see also AFGE v. U.S. Dep't of Commerce, 632 F. Supp. 1272, 1276 (D.D.C. 1986); Ashley, 589 F. Supp. at 908; cf. Shumaker, Loop & Kendrick v. Commodity Futures Trading Comm'n, No. 97-7139, slip op. at 14 (N.D. Ohio Nov. 27, 1997) (protecting an advisory document where there was "no indication that the author of the document had authority to establish agency policy").

[123] See Nat'l Wildlife, 861 F.2d at 1123 (finding comments from headquarters to regional office, under circumstances presented, to be advisory rather than directory); N. Dartmouth Properties, 984 F. Supp. at 70 (dictum) ("Conversation is, after all, a two-way street. A superior would be willing to engage a subordinate in candid debate only if he knows that his opinions will also be protected by the 'deliberative process' privilege.").

[124] See Judicial Watch, 102 F. Supp. 2d at 16 (protecting Attorney General's handwritten predecisional notes from meeting on campaign finance task force investigation); cf. Conoco Inc. v. U.S. Dep't of Justice, 687 F.2d 724, 727 (3d Cir. 1982) (rejecting the contention that only records "'circulated within the agency'" may be withheld under Exemption 5).

[125] Formaldehyde, 889 F.2d at 1122 (quoting CNA Fin. Corp. v. Donovan, 830 F.2d 1132, 1161 (D.C. Cir. 1987)); see also Judicial Watch, Inc. v. Reno, 154 F. Supp. 2d 17, 18 (D.D.C. 2001) ("It is not enough to say that a memorandum 'expresses the author's views' on a matter [because the] role played by the document in the course of the deliberative process must also be established.").

maker "chooses expressly to adopt or incorporate [it] by reference."[126] However, a few courts have suggested a less stringent standard of "formal or informal adoption."[127] Also, although mere "approval" of a predecisional document does not necessarily constitute adoption of it,[128] an inference of

---

[126] Sears, 421 U.S. at 161; see, e.g., Afshar, 702 F.2d at 1140 (finding recommendation expressly adopted in postdecisional memorandum); Niemeier v. Watergate Special Prosecution Force, 565 F.2d 967, 973 (7th Cir. 1977) (ordering disclosure of an "underlying memorandum" that was "expressly relied on in a final agency dispositional document"); Shumaker, No. 97-7139, slip op. at 14 (N.D. Ohio June 6, 2005) (ordering disclosure of advisory document written by agency general counsel and "thereafter adopted as the official position of the agency"); Bhd. of Locomotive Eng'rs v. Surface Transp. Bd., No. 96-1153, 1997 WL 446261, at *4-5 (D.D.C. July 31, 1997) (finding that staff recommendation was adopted in both written decision and commission vote); Burkins v. United States, 865 F. Supp. 1480, 1501 (D. Colo. 1994) (holding that final report's statement that findings are same as those of underlying memorandum constituted adoption of that document); Atkin v. EEOC, No. 91-2508, slip op. at 23-24 (D.N.J. July 14, 1993) (holding recommendation to close file not protectible where it was contained in agency's actual decision to close file); cf. Tax Analysts, 117 F.3d at 617 (finding that documents "routinely used" and "relied upon by agency personnel," in a particular factual setting, were "statements of the agency's legal position" and accordingly not protectible).

[127] Coastal States, 617 F.2d at 866; see Pentagon Fed. Credit Union v. Nat'l Credit Union Admin., No. 95-1475, slip op. at 5-8 (E.D. Va. June 7, 1996) (finding that board of directors' action "embracing" recommendations in "substantially same language" made documents postdecisional); Pension Actuaries, 746 F. Supp. at 192 (ordering disclosure simply on the basis that the IRS's budget assumptions and calculations were "relied upon by the government" in making its final estimate for the President's budget); cf. Skelton, 678 F.2d at 39 n.5 (declining to express opinion on whether reference must be to specific portion of document for express incorporation of that portion to occur).

[128] See, e.g., Mokhiber v. U.S. Dep't of Treasury, No. 01-1974, slip op. at 13 (D.D.C. Sept. 26, 2003) (protecting portions of document explaining recommended settlement amounts; ruling that decisionmaker's initialing of document signified only adoption of actual settlement amounts, not adoption of document author's reasoning); Hawkins v. U.S. Dep't of Labor, No. 3:05CV269J32, 2005 WL 2063811, at *4 (M.D. Fla. Aug. 19, 2005) (protecting documents that were used as part of basis for final agency decision, because there was no evidence of "clear adoption or incorporation" by agency); Rockwell Int'l v. U.S. Dep't of Justice, No. 98-761, slip op. at 8-9, 15 (D.D.C. Mar. 24, 1999) (finding no adoption where public memorandum merely referred to underlying documents as evidence supporting its conclusions and observing that "the memorandum is itself a discussion and statement of reasons [that] stands alone, independent of its supporting

(continued...)

incorporation or adoption has twice been found to exist where a decision-maker accepted a staff recommendation without giving a statement of reasons.[129] Nevertheless, where it is unclear whether a recommendation provided the basis for a final decision, the recommendation should be protectible.[130] (Though express incorporation and adoption are both sufficient to cause a document to lose Exemption 5 protection, it is important to note the distinction between the two terms: The former describes a scenario in which a decisionmaker expressly cites a previously predecisional document as the rationale for an agency's decision; in the latter, a document

---

[128](...continued)
documents"), aff'd on other grounds, 235 F.3d 598 (D.C. Cir. 2001); N. Dartmouth Properties, 984 F. Supp. at 69-70 (holding that fact that agency ultimately reached conclusion advocated by author of withheld document did not constitute adoption of author's reasoning); AFGE v. Dep't of the Army, 441 F. Supp. 1308, 1311 (D.D.C. 1977) (holding that decisionmaker's letter setting forth reasons for decision, not underlying report, constituted final agency decision).

[129] See Am. Soc'y of Pension Actuaries, 746 F. Supp. at 191; Martin v. MSPB, 3 Gov't Disclosure Serv. (P-H) ¶ 82,416, at 83,044 (D.D.C. Sept. 14, 1982). But see Blazar, No. 92-2719, slip op. at 14-15 (D.D.C. Apr. 15, 1994) (holding that no incorporation occurred when final decisionmaker approved one of several choices but did not indicate intention to adopt remainder of document in question); Am. Postal Workers Union, No. 85-3691, slip op. at 7-9 (D.D.C. June 24, 1986) (declining to infer incorporation).

[130] See Grumman, 421 U.S. at 184-85; Afshar, 702 F.2d at 1143 n.22; see also Casad, 301 F.3d at 1252 (protecting documents that were "important consideration" for final decisionmaker but were not "dispositive"); Sec. Fin. Life Ins. Co. v. U.S. Dep't of the Treasury, No. 03-102-SBC, 2005 WL 839543, at *7 (D.D.C. Apr. 12, 2005) (protecting documents where there was no evidence of express adoption by agency); Trans Union LLC v. FTC, No. 00-2384, 2001 U.S. Dist. LEXIS 4559, at *15 (D.D.C. Apr. 9, 2001) (following Grumman and rejecting argument that burden is on agency to prove that documents were not adopted as basis for policy); Perdue Farms, 1997 U.S. Dist. LEXIS 14579, at *20-23 (holding that fact that document was created only two days before issuance of final decision was insufficient to give rise to inference of adoption); Greyson v. McKenna & Cuneo, 879 F. Supp. 1065, 1069 (D. Colo. 1995) (deciding that use of phrase "the evidence shows" not enough for inference of adoption); Afr. Fund v. Mosbacher, No. 92-289, 1993 WL 183736, at *7 (S.D.N.Y. May 26, 1993) (concluding that record did not suggest either "adoption" or "final opinion" of agency); Wiley Rein & Fielding v. U.S. Dep't of Commerce, No. 90-1754, slip op. at 6 (D.D.C. Nov. 27, 1990) ("Denying protection to a document simply because the document expresses the same conclusion reached by the ultimate agency decisionmaker would eviscerate Exemption 5."); Ahearn v. U.S. Army Materials & Mechs. Research Ctr., 580 F. Supp. 1405, 1407 (D. Mass. 1984) (holding that fact that general officer reached same conclusion as report of investigation did not constitute adoption of report's reasoning).

comes to be used by the agency as an embodiment of the agency's policy.)[131]

In a significant decision on adoption during this past year, the Second Circuit Court of Appeals ordered the release of a Department of Justice memorandum concerning enforcement of immigration law by state and local law enforcement agencies.[132] While the court ordered the release of the memorandum, it was clear that this was ordered only because it was beyond reasonable dispute that the Justice Department had relied on the memorandum as a statement of agency policy, making repeated public references to the document in justifying its position on the matter in question.[133] This evidence of adoption went beyond "mere speculation," which certainly would have been insufficient.[134] Furthermore, the appeals court was careful to point out that mere "casual reference[s]" to an otherwise privileged document would not be enough to demonstrate incorporation, nor would the privilege have been lost had the Justice Department merely adopted the memorandum's conclusions.[135] Rather, the court found, the Justice Department had "publicly and repeatedly depended on the Memorandum as the primary legal authority justifying and driving . . . [its policy decision] and the legal basis therefor."[136] The Second Circuit noted that this distinguished the case from Grumman Aircraft,[137] where the Supreme Court ruled that there was no adoption because the "evidence [had] utterly fail[ed] to support the conclusion that the reasoning in the reports [had

---

[131] Compare Niemeier, 565 F.2d at 973 (ordering release of document that was "expressly relied on" in final agency decision document and thus "incorporated"), with Coastal States, 617 F.2d at 860 (upholding disclosure order for document that was in fact "regularly and consistently followed" by agency and thus was "adopted").

[132] Nat'l Council of La Raza v. U.S. Dep't of Justice, 411 F.3d 350, 361 (2d Cir. 2005).

[133] See id. at 358 (noting statements by agency official relying on document in question as sole means of explaining agency position on matter in question).

[134] See id. at 359 (comparing substantial evidence of adoption of memorandum in present case, as compared to other cases where such evidence was lacking).

[135] See id. at 358 ("Mere reliance on a document's conclusions does not necessarily involve reliance on a document's analysis[.]").

[136] Id.; see also Bronx Defenders v. DHS, No. 04 CV 8576, 2005 WL 3462725, at *4-5 (S.D.N.Y. Dec. 19, 2005) (ordering release of memorandum because government had cited it in multiple public documents as basis for government policy).

[137] 421 U.S. 168, 184 (1975).

been] adopted."[138]

A second primary limitation on the scope of the deliberative process privilege is that of course it applies only to "deliberative" documents and it ordinarily is inapplicable to purely factual matters, or to factual portions of otherwise deliberative memoranda.[139] Not only would factual material "generally be available for discovery,"[140] but its release usually would not threaten consultative agency functions.[141] This seemingly straightforward

---

[138] Id. at 184; see Robert v. HHS, No. 05-4660, 2007 U.S. App. LEXIS 3646, at *6 (2d Cir. Feb. 15, 2007) (rejecting plaintiff's claim of adoption or incorporation where there was "no evidence in the record" of either); La Raza, 411 F.3d at 359. But see Sussman v. U.S. Dep't of Justice, No. 03-3618, 2006 WL 2850608, at *18 (E.D.N.Y. Sept. 30, 2006) (denying summary judgment where government had "not addressed" whether predecisional, deliberative documents were adopted); Judicial Watch v. USPS, 297 F. Supp. 2d 252, 261 (D.D.C. 2004) (ruling oddly that agency had affirmative obligation to explicitly deny that draft documents had been adopted as agency policy); Wilderness Soc'y, 344 F. Supp. 2d at 14 (citing Judicial Watch, 297 F. Supp. 2d at 261, for same proposition).

[139] See, e.g., EPA v. Mink, 410 U.S. 73, 91 (1973) (refusing to extend deliberative process privilege protection to "factual material otherwise available on discovery merely [on the basis that] it was placed in a memorandum with matters of law, policy, or opinion"); Coastal States, 617 F.2d at 867 (citing Mink, 410 U.S. at 93); Bilbrey v. U.S. Dep't of the Air Force, No. 00-0539, slip op. at 10-11 (W.D. Mo. Jan. 30, 2001) (holding privilege inapplicable to factual statements underlying predecisional recommendations), aff'd, No. 01-1789, 2001 WL 1222471, at *1 (8th Cir. Oct. 16, 2001) (unpublished table decision); Sw. Ctr. for Biological Diversity, 170 F. Supp. 2d at 941 (concluding that release of "raw research data" would not expose agency's deliberative process, on grounds that such data were not recommendations, not subject to alteration upon further agency review, and not "selective" in character).

[140] 410 U.S. at 87-88 (1973).

[141] See Montrose Chem. Corp. v. Train, 491 F.2d 63, 66 (D.C. Cir. 1974); see also Dean v. FDIC, 389 F. Supp. 2d 780, 794 (E.D. Ky. 2005) (distinguishing between portions of documents containing opinions of inspector general investigators and sections that merely discuss substance of investigations); Rashid v. HHS, No. 98-0898, slip op. at 11-12 (D.D.C. Mar. 2, 2000) (declining to extend the privilege to agency requests for outside experts' evaluations on the basis that although "[t]he requests were predecisional, . . . they were not deliberative in that they did not 'reflect the give-and-take of the consultative process'" (quoting Coastal States, 617 F.2d at 866)); D.C. Technical Assistance Org. v. HUD, No. 98-0280, slip op. at 4-5 (D.D.C. July 29, 1999) (ordering release of factual portion of an otherwise deliberative record because it "does not evaluate the actions taken, but

(continued...)

distinction between deliberative and factual materials can blur, however, where the facts themselves reflect the agency's deliberative process[142] -- which has prompted the D.C. Circuit to observe that "the use of the factual matter/deliberative matter distinction produced incorrect outcomes in a small number of cases."[143]

In fact, the full D.C. Circuit has firmly declared that factual information should be examined "in light of the policies and goals that underlie" the privilege and in "the context in which the materials are used."[144] Following this approach, for example, the District Court for the District of Columbia recently allowed the Air Force to withhold "vote sheets" that were used in the process of determining retirement benefits.[145] Even though these vote sheets were factual in nature, the court found that they were used by agency personnel in developing recommendations to an agency decisionmaker and thus were "precisely the type of pre-decisional documents intended to fall under Exemption 5."[146]

Recognizing the shortcomings of a rigid factual/deliberative distinction, courts generally allow agencies to withhold factual material in an otherwise "deliberative" document under two general types of circum-

---

[141](...continued)
only describes them"); Horsehead, No. 94-1299, slip op. at 16 (D.D.C. Oct. 1, 1996) ("EPA has not demonstrated how the disclosure of either the testing processes . . . or the data from that testing involves [sic] its deliberative process.").

[142] See, e.g., Nat'l Wildlife, 861 F.2d at 1118 (rejecting simplistic fact/opinion distinction, and instead focusing on whether documents in question play role in agency's deliberative process); Skelton, 678 F.2d at 38-39 (explaining that focus should be on whether release of documents would reveal agency's evaluative process).

[143] Dudman, 815 F.2d at 1568.

[144] Wolfe, 839 F.2d at 774; see also Nat'l Wildlife, 861 F.2d at 1119 ("ultimate objective" of Exemption 5 is to safeguard agency's deliberative process); Sakomoto v. EPA, 443 F. Supp. 2d 1182, 1192 (N.D. Cal. 2006) (holding that facts may be withheld when they are "directly tied to the deliberative process").

[145] See Brannum v. Dominguez, 377 F. Supp. 2d 75, 83 (D.D.C. 2005).

[146] Id.; see also Bloomberg, L.P. v. SEC, No. 02-1582, 2004 U.S. Dist LEXIS 15111, at *34 (D.D.C. July 28, 2004) (protecting notes taken by SEC officials at meeting with companies subject to SEC oversight; finding that, though factual in form, notes would, if released, "severely undermine" SEC's ability to gather information from its regulatees and in turn undermine SEC's ability to deliberate on best means to address policymaking concerns in such areas).

stances.[147] The first circumstance occurs when the author of a document selects specific facts out of a larger group of facts and this very act is deliberative in nature. In Montrose Chemical Corp. v. Train, for example, the summary of a large volume of public testimony compiled to facilitate the EPA Administrator's decision on a particular matter was held to be part of the agency's internal deliberative process.[148] The D.C. Circuit held that the very act of distilling the testimony, of separating the significant facts from the insignificant facts, constitutes an exercise of judgment by agency personnel.[149] Such "selective" facts are therefore entitled to the same protection as that afforded to purely deliberative materials, as their release would "permit indirect inquiry into the mental processes,"[150] and so "expose" pre-

---

[147] See FOIA Update, Vol. VII, No. 3, at 6.

[148] 491 F.2d at 71.

[149] Id. at 68; see, e.g., Poll v. U.S. Office of Special Counsel, No. 99-4021, 2000 WL 14422, at *3 (10th Cir. Oct. 14, 1999) (protecting factual "distillation" which revealed significance that examiner attributed to various aspects of case); The Edmonds Inst. v. U.S. Dep't of Interior, No. 04-1560, 2006 WL 3059889, at *6 (D.D.C. Oct. 30, 2006) (protecting factual material considered for, but not utilized, in final report); Envtl. Prot. Servs. v. EPA, 364 F. Supp. 2d 575, 585 (N.D. W. Va. 2005) (protecting notes of agency investigator who previously had been briefed on investigation and had geared his queries accordingly, thereby making his notes selectively recorded information); Hamilton Sec. Group, 106 F. Supp. 2d at 33 (protecting facts in a draft audit report on the grounds that "any factual information that could be [released] would reveal decisions made by the auditor" and thereby chill future agency deliberations); Heggestad, 182 F. Supp. 2d at 12 n.10 (protecting facts "selected by authors from a larger body of factual material," because disclosure would reveal authors' deliberative processes); Melius v. Nat'l Indian Gaming Comm'n, No. 98-2210, 1999 U.S. Dist. LEXIS 17537, at *12 (D.D.C. Nov. 3, 1999) (affirming agency denial of "fact summaries that show the investigators' deliberation in determining [plaintiff's] suitability" for federal appointment); Mace, 37 F. Supp. 2d at 1150 (protecting factual "distillation" in otherwise deliberative EEOC report), aff'd, 197 F.3d 329 (8th Cir. 1999); Means v. Segal, No. 97-1301, slip op. at 10-11 (D.D.C. Mar. 18, 1998) (magistrate's recommendation) (holding that factual material "could not be released as segregable from the remainder, as the facts discussed in the investigative report reflect the value placed on each in forming the recommendation"), adopted (D.D.C. Apr. 15, 1998), aff'd per curiam, No. 98-5170 (D.C. Cir. Oct. 6, 1998); Atkin, No. 91-2508, slip op. at 21 (D.N.J. July 14, 1993) (holding exempt staff selection of certain factual documents to be used for report preparation); Bentson Contracting Co. v. NLRB, No. 90-451, slip op. at 3 (D. Ariz. Dec. 28, 1990) (finding that agency properly withheld document characterizing issues most important to parties and discussing how facts were analyzed in decisional process).

[150] Williams v. U.S. Dep't of Justice, 556 F. Supp. 63, 65 (D.D.C. 1982).

decisional agency deliberations.[151] Thus, to protect the factual materials, an agency must identify a process which "could reasonably be construed as predecisional and deliberative."[152]

A D.C. Circuit opinion concerning a report consisting of factual materials prepared for an Attorney General decision on whether to allow former U.N. Secretary General Kurt Waldheim to enter the United States provides an illustration of this factual/deliberative distinction and of the breadth of deliberative process privilege coverage under prevailing case law.[153] The D.C. Circuit found that "the majority of [the report's] factual material was assembled through an exercise of judgment in extracting pertinent material from a vast number of documents for the benefit of an official called upon to take discretionary action," and that it therefore fell within the delibera-

---

[151] Mead Data, 566 F.2d at 256; see also Providence Journal, 981 F.2d at 562 (revealing IG's factual findings would divulge substance of related recommendations); Lead Indus., 610 F.2d at 85 (disclosing factual segments of summaries would reveal deliberative process by "demonstrating which facts in the massive rule-making record were considered significant to the decisionmaker"); Judicial Watch, Inc. v. U.S. Dep't of Justice, No. 01-639, 2006 WL 2038513, at *7 (D.D.C. July 19, 2006) (quoting favorably from the government's declaration explanation that the "very act of selecting those facts which are significant from those that are not, is itself a deliberative process"); Farmworkers Legal Servs. v. U.S. Dep't of Labor, 639 F. Supp. 1368, 1373 (E.D.N.C. 1986) (holding that list of farmworker camps was "selective fact" and thus protectible).

[152] City of Va. Beach, 995 F.2d at 1255; see also Nat'l Ass'n of Home Builders v. Norton, 309 F.3d 26, 39 (D.C. Cir. 2002) (holding that documents listing locations of endangered species were not deliberative, despite fact that they were prepared partly to assist agency in making determinations under Endangered Species Act, 16 U.S.C. § 1653 (2000)); ITT, 699 F.2d at 1239 (holding that notes must be more than "straightforward factual narrations" to be protected); Playboy Enters. v. Dep't of Justice, 677 F.2d 931, 936 (D.C. Cir. 1982) (concluding that factual materials must be generated in course of agency's decisionmaking process to be protectible); Bryce v. OPIC, No. A-96-CA-595, slip op. at 17 (W.D. Tex. Sept. 28, 1998) (finding set of photographs to be "factual in nature" and rejecting argument that photographs are deliberative in that they embody agency consultant's "determination of those aspects of [a mining site] that it determined were of sufficient significance to bring to OPIC's attention"), appeal dismissed voluntarily, No. 99-50893 (5th Cir. Oct. 14, 1999); Lacy v. U.S. Dep't of the Navy, 593 F. Supp. 71, 78 (D. Md. 1984) (holding that photographs attached to deliberative report "do not become part of the deliberative process merely because some photographs were selected and others were not").

[153] Mapother, 3 F.3d at 1538-40.

tive process privilege.[154] By contrast, it also held that a chronology of Waldheim's military career was not deliberative, as it was "neither more nor less than a comprehensive collection of the essential facts" and "reflect[ed] no point of view."[155]

The second such circumstance is when factual information is so inextricably connected to the deliberative material that its disclosure would expose or cause harm to the agency's deliberations. If revealing factual information is tantamount to revealing the agency's deliberations, then the facts may be withheld.[156] For example, the D.C. Circuit has held

---

[154] Id. at 1539 (distinguishing and confining Playboy as involving report designed only to inform Attorney General of facts he would make available to Member of Congress, rather than one involving any decision he would have to make); see also City of Va. Beach, 995 F.2d at 1255 (observing similarly that in Playboy "[the] agency identified no decision in relation to the withheld investigative report"); Edmonds Inst. v. U.S. Dep't of Interior, 460 F. Supp. 2d 63, 71 (D.D.C. 2006) (protecting factual information considered, but not utilized in agency's final report, because release of such information "would reveal the editorial judgment" of agency employees); Phillips v. Immigration & Customs Enforcement, 385 F. Supp. 2d 296, 303 (S.D.N.Y. 2005) (citing Mapother and protecting notes taken in an interview that "reflect[ed] a selective recording of information"); Envtl. Prot. Servs., 364 F. Supp. 2d at 585 (protecting selectively assembled facts, on basis that such information could not be "severed from its context" (quoting Grand Cent. P'ship, Inc. v. Cuomo, 166 F.3d 473, 483 (2d Cir. 1999))).

[155] Mapother, 3 F.3d at 1539-40; see also D.C. Technical Assistance Org., No. 98-0280, slip op. at 5 (D.D.C. July 29, 1999) ("The order in which the [factual portions] are listed is apparently random, so that disclosing them reveals nothing of the decision making process or of the subjective assessment that follows.").

[156] See, e.g., Horowitz v. Peace Corps, 428 F.3d 271, 277 (D.C. Cir. 2005) (protecting a requested document where the decisonmaker's "thought processes are woven into the document to such an extent" that any attempt at segregating out information would reveal agency deliberations); Wolfe, 839 F.2d at 774-76 (protecting mere "fact" of status of proposal in deliberative process); Pohlman, Inc. v. SBA, No. 4:03-01241, slip op. at 25-26 (E.D. Mo. Sept. 30, 2005) (holding that to extent that portions of document could be considered factual, such information was inextricably intertwined with deliberative material and therefore were not subject to disclosure); Hawkins, 2005 WL 2063811, at *3 (protecting factual portions of a deliberative document that could not be "segregated in a meaningful way" from deliberative sections); Delta Ltd. v. U.S. Customs & Border Prot. Bureau, 384 F. Supp. 2d 138, 151-52 (D.D.C. 2005) (finding that factual portions of records were inextricably intertwined with deliberative portions and therefore were not releaseable); Tarullo, 170 F. Supp. 2d at 278 ("Although the document does summarize relevant facts, that summary is so

(continued...)

that the deliberative process privilege covers construction cost estimates, which the court characterized as "elastic facts," finding that their disclosure would reveal the agency's deliberations.[157]

Similarly, when factual or statistical information is actually an expression of deliberative communications, it may be withheld on the basis that to reveal that information would reveal the agency's deliberations.[158] Ex-

---

[156](...continued)
intertwined with . . . recommendations and opinions . . . that production of a redacted version would be incomprehensible, and the very selection of facts could also reveal the nature of those recommendations and opinions."); Brownstein Zeidman & Schomer v. Dep't of the Air Force, 781 F. Supp. 31, 36 (D.D.C. 1991) (holding that the release of summaries of negotiations would inhibit the free flow of information, as "summaries are not simply the facts themselves"); Jowett, 729 F. Supp. at 877 (determining that disclosing manner of selecting and presenting even most factual segments of audit reports would reveal process by which agency's final decision is made); Wash. Post Co. v. DOD, No. 84-2403, slip op. at 5 (D.D.C. Apr. 15, 1988) (finding factual assertions in briefing documents "thoroughly intertwined" with opinions and impressions); Wash. Post, 1987 U.S. Dist. LEXIS 16108, at *33 (holding that summaries and lists of materials relied upon in drafting report are "inextricably intertwined with the policymaking process"). But see Vaughn, 523 F.2d at 1145 (stating that survey results cannot be protected where they merely "provide the raw data upon which decisions can be made[ and] are not themselves a part of the decisional process"); Army Times Publ'g Co. v. Dep't of the Air Force, No. 90-1383, slip op. at 6-7 (D.D.C. Feb. 28, 1995) (citing Vaughn).

[157] Quarles v. Dep't of the Navy, 893 F.2d 390, 392-93 (D.C. Cir. 1990); see also Pohlman, No. 4:03-01241, slip op. at 24-25 (E.D. Mo. Sept. 30, 2005) (protecting "hold values" through which SBA estimated worth of assets); cf. Russell, 682 F.2d at 1048-49 (protecting documents prepared by Air Force group charged with developing agency's official report on herbicide use during Vietnam War). But see Natural Res. Def. Council v. Nat'l Marine Fisheries Serv., 409 F. Supp. 2d 379, 384-85 (S.D.N.Y. 2006) (deciding that "preliminary findings as to objective facts" are not protectible).

[158] See, e.g., Kennecott Utah Copper Corp. v. EPA, No. 94-162, slip op. at 4 (D.D.C. Sept. 11, 1995) (holding material relating to preparation of Hazard Ranking Scores part of deliberative process); SMS Data Prods. Group, Inc. v. U.S. Dep't of the Air Force, No. 88-481, 1989 WL 201031, at *1-2 (D.D.C. Mar. 31, 1989) (holding technical scores and technical rankings of competing contract bidders predecisional and deliberative); Nat'l Wildlife Fed'n v. U.S. Forest Serv., No. 86-1255, slip op. at 9 (D.D.C. Sept. 26, 1987) (protecting variables reflected in computer program's mathematical equation); Am. Whitewater Affiliation v. FERC, No. 86-1917, 1986 U.S. Dist. LEXIS 17067, at *10 (D.D.C. Dec. 2, 1986) ("[T]he cost and energy comparisons involved in this case are deliberative."); Brinderson Constructors, Inc. v. U.S. Army
(continued...)

emption 5 thus covers scientific reports that constitute the interpretation of technical data, insofar as "the opinion of an expert reflects the deliberative process of decision or policy making."[159] It has even been extended to cover successive reformulations of computer programs that were used to analyze scientific data.[160]

Indeed, the government interest in withholding technical data is even heightened if such material is requested at a time when disclosure of a scientist's "nascent thoughts . . . would discourage the intellectual risk-taking so essential to technical progress."[161] The Court of Appeals for the Ninth Circuit strongly echoed this view in National Wildlife Federation v. United States Forest Service, explaining as follows:

> Opinions on facts and [the] consequences of those facts form the grist for the policymaker's mill. Each opinion as to which of the great constellation of facts are relevant and important and each assessment of the implications of those facts suggests a different course of action by the agency. Before arriving at a final decision, the policymaker may alter his or her opinion regarding which facts are relevant or the likely consequences of these facts, or both. Tentative policies may undergo massive revisions based on a reassessment of these variables, during

---

[158](...continued)
Corps of Eng'rs, No. 85-905, 1986 WL 293230, at *5 (D.D.C. June 11, 1986) (holding that computations made in order to evaluate a claim for compensation "are certainly part of the deliberative process"); Prof'l Review Org., Inc. v. HHS, 607 F. Supp. 423, 427 (D.D.C. 1985) (observing that scores used to rate procurement proposals may be "numerical expressions of opinion rather than 'facts'"). But see Warren v. Soc. Sec. Admin., No. 98-CV-0116E, 2000 WL 1209383, at *3 (W.D.N.Y. Aug. 22, 2000) (holding that the privilege does not protect the ordered ranking of job applicants, and reasoning that such a ranking "is not pre-decisional . . . as [it is] the result of the panel's decisions" rather than an intermediate step in a multi-layered decisionmaking process), aff'd on other grounds, 10 F. App'x 20 (2d Cir. 2001).

[159] Parke, Davis, 623 F.2d at 6; see also Quarles, 893 F.2d at 392-93 (protecting cost estimates as "elastic facts"); Horsehead, No. 94-1299, slip op. at 15-20 (D.D.C. Oct. 1, 1996) (finding that agency scientists' "open discussion of the effectiveness of . . . testing results and frank exchanges of view regarding the interpretation of those results reside near the core of an agency's deliberative process"). But see Ethyl Corp. v. EPA, 478 F.2d 47, 50 (4th Cir. 1973) (characterizing such material as "technological data of a purely factual nature").

[160] See Cleary, Gottlieb, Steen & Hamilton v. HHS, 884 F. Supp. 770, 782-83 (D.D.C. 1993).

[161] Chem. Mfrs., 600 F. Supp. at 118.

which the agency may decide that certain initial projections are not reasonable or that the likely consequences of a given course of action have been over- or underestimated. Subjecting a policymaker to public criticism on the basis of such tentative assessments is precisely what the deliberative process privilege is intended to prevent.[162]

Likewise, it is noteworthy that the D.C. Circuit has stated that the "results of . . . factual investigations" may be within the protective scope of Exemption 5.[163] However, the D.C. Circuit also has emphasized that agencies bear the burden of demonstrating that disclosure of such information "would actually inhibit candor in the decision-making process."[164]

There are several categories of documents that routinely are protected by the deliberative process privilege. Among them are "advisory opinions, recommendations, and deliberations comprising part of a process by which governmental decisions and policies are formulated."[165] They are

---

[162] 861 F.2d at 1115, 1120 (protecting, e.g., "working drafts" of forest plan and "working drafts of environmental impact statements").

[163] Paisley v. CIA, 712 F.2d 686, 698 n.53 (D.C. Cir. 1983) (dictum); see also Brannum, 377 F. Supp. 2d at 82-83 (protecting factual "vote sheets" used as basis for recommendation to agency policymaker). But see Rashid, No. 98-0898, slip op. at 13-14 (D.D.C. Mar. 2, 2000) (opining without authority that "[t]he results of research are factual and not deliberative information").

[164] Army Times Publ'g Co. v. Dep't of the Air Force, 998 F.2d 1067, 1070 (D.C. Cir. 1993) (holding that agencies must show how process would be harmed where some factual material was released and similar factual material was withheld); see also Am. Petroleum Inst. v. EPA, 846 F. Supp. 83, 90-91 (D.D.C. 1994) (ordering agency to show how factual information could reveal deliberative process).

[165] Sears, 421 U.S. at 150; Humbarger v. EEOC, No. C 03-05818, 2005 U.S. Dist LEXIS 1707, at *5 (N.D. Cal. Jan. 28, 2005) (protecting investigative memoranda because they were predecisional and related to process of policy formation); Judicial Watch, Inc. v. Dep't of Justice, 306 F. Supp. 2d 58, 70 (D.D.C. 2004) (protecting "handwritten notes" on an invitation to the Attorney General, because disclosure "'would reveal what the staff member who wrote the notes considered to be important . . . and how the decision to attend the event may have been reached'" (quoting agency declaration)); Dorsett v. Dep't of the Treasury, 307 F. Supp. 2d. 28, 37-38 (D.D.C. 2004) (protecting Secret Service document evaluating threats presented by plaintiff and others to Secret Service protectees); Warren, 2000 WL 1209383, at *2 (protecting applicant scoresheets on basis that "[t]he decisions of a hiring panel to emphasize certain types of skills or how many points to award to an applicant for a particular educational experience or previous employ-
(continued...)

protected because, by their very nature, their release would likely "stifle honest and frank communication within the agency."[166]

Of a similar nature are "briefing materials" -- reports or other documents that summarize issues and advise superiors, either generally or in preparation for an event such as congressional testimony.[167] Though courts have not spoken with complete unanimity on this category, the overwhelming weight of authority, including a number of recent cases, now

---

[165](...continued)
ment experience are deliberative decisions in that they set the policy for the hiring process"); see also Jernigan v. Dep't of the Air Force, 1998 WL 658662, at *2 (9th Cir. Sept. 17, 1998) (protecting "opinions and recommendations" of agency investigating officer); Nat'l Wildlife, 861 F.2d at 1121 ("Recommendations on how to best deal with a particular issue are themselves the essence of the deliberative process."); Canning v. Dep't of the Treasury, No. 94-2704, slip op. at 7 (D.D.C. Mar. 21, 2001) ("Allowing disclosure of the pre-decisional opinions of Secret Service Special Agents on whether particular organizations pose protective security risks could compromise the agency's ability to complete its protective mission by stifling honest and frank communication within the agency."); Judicial Watch, 102 F. Supp. 2d at 16 (protecting notes taken by Attorney General at campaign finance task force meeting, but not shared with any other person, because their release "could reveal how the [Attorney General] prioritized different facts and considerations in deliberating whether or not to appoint an independent counsel . . . [and] reveal her interpretation of public policies which she deemed relevant" to decision whether to appoint independent counsel); Fine v. U.S. Dep't of Energy, No. 88-1033, slip op. at 9 (D.N.M. June 22, 1991) (finding that notes written in margins of documents constitute deliberations of documents' recipient); Jowett, 729 F. Supp. at 875 (protecting documents that are "part of the give-and-take between government entities"); Strang v. Collyer, 710 F. Supp. 9, 12 (D.D.C. 1989) (approving withholding of meeting notes that reflect the exchange of opinions between agency personnel or divisions of agency), aff'd sub nom. Strang v. DeSio, 899 F.2d 1268 (D.C. Cir. 1990) (unpublished table decision).

[166] Coastal States, 617 F.2d at 866; see also Missouri, 147 F.3d at 711 ("Perhaps a fuller description [of the record] and why it is exempt might have avoided this litigation, but it was not improper for the [agency] to conclude that open and frank intra-agency discussion would be 'chilled' by public disclosure."); Schell, 843 F.2d at 942 ("It is the free flow of advice, rather than the value of any particular piece of information, that Exemption 5 seeks to protect."); Fortson v. Harvey, 407 F. Supp. 2d 13, 16-17 (D.D.C. 2005) (rejecting plaintiff's argument that subordinate's report did not qualify as deliberative simply because it would be either accepted or rejected, and not debated, by superior).

[167] See, e.g., Judicial Watch, Inc. v. U.S. Dep't of Commerce, 337 F. Supp. 2d 146, 174 (D.D.C. 2004) (protecting "talking points" and recommendations on how to answer questions).

holds that briefing materials prepared by agencies for one purpose or another are properly protected under the deliberative process privilege.[168]

A category of documents particularly likely to be found exempt under the deliberative process privilege is "drafts,"[169] although it has been observed that such a designation "does not end the inquiry."[170] It should be

---

[168] See Sec. Fin. Life Ins. Co., No. 03-102-SBC, 2005 WL 839543, at *11 (D.D.C. Apr. 12, 2005) ("The undisputed evidence establishes that these [talking points] are deliberative."); Judicial Watch, Inc. v. U.S. Dep't of Energy, 310 F. Supp. 2d 271, 317 (D.D.C. 2004) (protecting briefing materials prepared for Secretary of the Interior), aff'd in part, rev'd in part on other grounds & remanded, 412 F.3d 125, 133 (D.C. Cir. 2005); Judicial Watch, 306 F. Supp. 2d at 71-72 (protecting e-mail created to prepare FERC chairman for upcoming congressional testimony); Thompson v. Dep't of the Navy, No. 95-347, 1997 WL 527344, at *4 (D.D.C. Aug. 18, 1997) (protecting materials created to brief senior officials who were preparing to respond to media inquiries, on the basis that "disclosure of materials reflecting the process by which the Navy formulates its policy concerning statements to and interactions with the press" could stifle frank communication within the agency), aff'd, No. 97-5292, 1998 WL 202253, at *1 (D.C. Cir. Mar. 11, 1998) (per curiam); Access Reports, 926 F.2d at 1196-97 (dictum); Klunzinger v. IRS, No. 5:96-CV-209, 1998 U.S. Dist. LEXIS 3226, at *31 (W.D. Mich. Mar. 3, 1998) (holding paper prepared to brief commissioner for meeting protectible); Hunt, 935 F. Supp. at 52 (holding "point papers" compiled to assist officers in formulating decision protectible); Wash. Post, 1987 U.S. Dist. LEXIS 16108, at *33 (holding summaries and lists of material compiled for general's report preparation protectible); Williams, 556 F. Supp. at 65 (holding "briefing papers prepared for the Attorney General prior to an appearance before a congressional committee" protectible); see also FOIA Update, Vol. IX, No. 4, at 5. But see Nat'l Sec. Archive v. FBI, No. 88-1507, 1993 WL 128499, at *2-3 (D.D.C. Apr. 15, 1993) (finding briefing papers to be not protectible).

[169] See, e.g., City of Va. Beach, 995 F.2d at 1253; Town of Norfolk v. U.S. Corps of Eng'rs, 968 F.2d 1438, 1458 (1st Cir. 1992); Dudman, 815 F.2d at 1569; Russell, 682 F.2d at 1048; Lead Indus., 610 F.2d 70, 85-86 (2d Cir. 1979); Judicial Watch, 337 F. Supp. 2d at 173 (protecting draft agreement and draft of letter from Secretary of Commerce); Judicial Watch, No. 00-0723, slip op. at 9-10 (D.D.C. Mar. 30, 2001); Judicial Watch, Inc. v. Exp.-Imp. Bank, 108 F. Supp. 2d 19, 36 (D.D.C. 2000); Hamilton Sec. Group, 106 F. Supp. 2d at 32; Snoddy v. Hawke, No. 99-1636, slip op. at 1-2 (D. Colo. Dec. 20, 1999), aff'd, No. 00-1384, 2001 WL 672263 (10th Cir. June 15, 2001); LaRouche, No. 91-1655, slip op. at 30 (D.D.C. May 22, 1998) (protecting draft search warrant affidavits and stating that "it is axiomatic that draft documents reflect some give and take on the part of those involved in the drafts").

[170] Arthur Andersen, 679 F.2d at 257 (citing Coastal States, 617 F.2d at
(continued...)

remembered, in this regard, that the very process by which a "draft" evolves into a "final" document can itself constitute a deliberative process warranting protection.[171] As a result, Exemption 5 protection can be avail-

---

[170](...continued)
866); see Heartwood, Inc. v. U.S. Forest Serv., 431 F. Supp. 2d 28, 37 (D.D.C. 2006) (ruling that draft reports prepared by Federal Advisory Committee Act committee for defendant agency could not be protected, because evidence showed that agency viewed draft reports as merely factual, not as containing "recommendations or policy judgments"); Judicial Watch, Inc. v. USPS, 297 F. Supp. 2d 252, 261 (D.D.C. 2004) (citing Arthur Andersen for proposition that "drafts are not presumptively privileged"); see also Petroleum Info., 976 F.2d at 1436 n.8 (suggesting harm standard for "mundane," nonpolicy-oriented documents, which can include drafts); Lee v. FDIC, 923 F. Supp. 451, 458 (S.D.N.Y. 1996) (declaring that a document's draft status is not a sufficient reason "to automatically exempt" it from disclosure where it has not been shown that disclosure would "inhibit the free flow of information" between agency personnel); cf. Hansen, 817 F. Supp. at 124-25 (concluding that an unpublished internal document lost its draft status when consistently treated by the agency as a finished product over many years).

[171] See, e.g., Nat'l Wildlife, 861 F.2d at 1122 ("To the extent that [the requester] seeks through its FOIA request to uncover any discrepancies between the findings, projections, and recommendations between the draft[s] prepared by lower-level [agency] personnel and those actually adopted, . . . it is attempting to probe the editorial and policy judgments of the decisionmakers."); Marzen v. HHS, 825 F.2d 1148, 1155 (7th Cir. 1987) ("[E]xemption protects not only the opinions, comments and recommendations in the draft, but also the process itself."); Dudman, 815 F.2d at 1569 ("[T]he disclosure of editorial judgments -- for example, decisions to insert or delete material or to change a draft's focus or emphasis -- would stifle the creative thinking and candid exchange of ideas necessary to produce good historical work."); Russell, 682 F.2d at 1048 ("Failure to apply the protections of Exemption (b)(5) to the . . . editorial review process would effectively make such discussion impossible."); Pies v. IRS, 668 F.2d 1350, 1353-54 (D.C. Cir. 1981) (ruling that disclosure of draft proposed regulation and draft transmittal memorandum that were ultimately not adopted as agency policy would be contrary to congressional intent in crafting Exemption 5); AFGE v. HHS, 63 F. Supp. 2d 104, 109 (D. Mass. 1999) (holding draft indoor air quality survey protectible because release would "enable a careful reader to determine the substance of HHS's proposed and adopted changes" and thereby "discourage candid discussion within the agency"), aff'd, No. 99-2208, 2000 U.S. App. LEXIS 10993 (1st Cir. May 18, 2000); Nat'l Ass'n of Criminal Def. Lawyers, No. 97-372, slip op. at 13-14 (D.D.C. July 22,1998) (holding draft inspector general report protectible because release "would uncover the [Office of the Inspector General's] deliberations regarding what should and should not have been included in the final report"); Horsehead, No. 94-1299, slip op. at 19 (D.D.C. Oct. 1, 1996) ("Comparing the draft
(continued...)

able to a draft document regardless of whether it differs from its final version.[172]

Following the 1990 census, the factual/deliberative distinction led to sharply contrasting decisions by two circuit courts of appeal, where the issue was the Commerce Department's withholding of numeric material.[173] Both the Assembly of the State of California and the Florida House of Representatives sought "adjusted" census figures for their respective states that were developed in the event that the Secretary of Commerce decided to adjust the 1990 census, a choice he opted against.[174] The Court of Appeals for the Eleventh Circuit applied a rigid "fact or opinion" test in determining whether such numerical data are protectible.[175] It viewed the census data as "opinion" that was ultimately rejected by the decisionmaker and therefore held them to be withholdable pursuant to the deliberative process privilege.[176]

Addressing the same issue, the Ninth Circuit, on the other hand, upheld a lower court's use of a "functional" test under which it found that the

---

[171](...continued) with the final version ultimately adopted by the agency would provide the requester with a picture window view into the agency's deliberations, the precise danger that Exemption 5 was crafted to avoid."); Rothschild v. CIA, No. 91-1314, slip op. at 6-7 (D.D.C. Mar. 25, 1992) (extending protection to "marginalia consisting of comments, opinions, further relevant information and associated notes" on drafts); Exxon, 585 F. Supp. at 698 (rejecting argument that agency must show how draft differs from final document, because such a requirement would "expose what occurred in the deliberative process between the draft's creation and the final document's issuance"); see also FOIA Update, Vol. VII, No. 2, at 2; FOIA Update, Vol. IV, No. 1, at 6.

[172] See Mobil Oil Corp. v. EPA, 879 F.2d 698, 703 (9th Cir. 1989) (dicta); Lead Indus., 610 F.2d at 86; see also Exxon, 585 F. Supp. at 698; City of West Chicago v. NRC, 547 F. Supp. 740, 751 (N.D. Ill. 1982); FOIA Update, Vol. VII, No. 2, at 2. But see Texaco, Inc. v. U.S. Dep't of Energy, 2 Gov't Disclosure Serv. (P-H) ¶ 81,296, at 81,833 (D.D.C. Oct. 13, 1981) (ruling to the contrary).

[173] Assembly of Cal. v. U.S. Dep't of Commerce, 968 F.2d 916 (9th Cir. 1992); Fla. House of Representatives v. U.S. Dep't of Commerce, 961 F.2d 941 (11th Cir. 1992).

[174] Assembly of Cal., 968 F.2d at 917-18; Fla. House of Representatives, 961 F.2d at 943-44.

[175] Fla. House of Representatives, 961 F.2d at 950.

[176] Id.

data, on "the continuum of deliberation and fact . . . fell closer to fact."[177] It ordered the California data released on the basis that disclosure would not reveal any of the Department of Commerce's deliberative processes.[178] The Ninth Circuit also reached a similar conclusion ten years later in a case brought about statistical estimates compiled as part of the 2000 census.[179] As none of these cases went to the Supreme Court, this narrow conflict remains.

In a case involving purely factual data found not to fall within the deliberative process privilege, Petroleum Information Corp. v. United States Department of the Interior,[180] the D.C. Circuit concluded that such factual information should be shielded by the privilege, or not, according to whether it involves "some policy matter."[181] It focused on "whether the agency has plausibly demonstrated the involvement of a policy judgment in the decisional process relevant to the requested documents,"[182] while at the same time suggesting that more "mundane" documents should be protected when "disclosure genuinely could be thought likely to diminish the candor of agency deliberations in the future."[183] This approach has been used by a few other courts.[184] However, in National Wildlife, the Ninth Circuit

---

[177] Assembly of Cal., 968 F.2d at 922.

[178] Id. at 923; see also Carter, 186 F. Supp. 2d at 1157 (following Assembly of California and ordering disclosure of adjusted data from 2000 census).

[179] See Carter v. U.S. Dep't of Commerce, 307 F.3d 1084, 1091-92 (9th Cir. 2002).

[180] 976 F.2d 1429 (D.C. Cir. 1992).

[181] Id. at 1435.

[182] Id. at 1436.

[183] Id. at 1436 n.8; accord Army Times, 998 F.2d at 1071, 1072 (concluding that "potentially harmful" factual information could be withheld if it were determined that it "would actually inhibit candor in the decision-making process if made available to the public").

[184] See Sun-Sentinel Co. v. DHS, 431 F. Supp. 2d 1258, 1277-78 (S.D. Fla. 2006) (refusing to protect e-mail communications containing advice to agency director merely because these messages contained recommendations on press relations, not on matters relating to agency's "mission"); Hennessey, 1997 WL 537998, at *5 (determining that the "report does not bear on a policy-oriented judgment of the kind contemplated by Exemption 5" (citing Petroleum Info., 976 F.2d at 1437)); Ethyl Corp. v. EPA, 25 F.3d 1241, 1248 (4th Cir. 1994) (concluding that the "privilege does not protect a document [that] is merely peripheral to actual policy formulation"); Legal & Safety Employer Research, Inc. v. U.S. Dep't of the Army, No. CIV. S-00-

(continued...)

flatly rejected the suggestion that it impose such a requirement that documents contain "recommendations on law or policy to qualify as deliberative," and other courts have followed that approach as well[185]

Lastly, protecting the very integrity of the deliberative process can, in

---

[184](...continued)
1748, 2001 WL 34098652, at *6 (E.D. Cal. May 4, 2001) (concluding that contractor performance evaluations, which were required to be considered in future government contract award determinations, were not "the type of policy decision contemplated by Exemption 5"); Chi. Tribune Co. v. HHS, No. 95 C 3917, 1997 U.S. Dist. LEXIS 2308, at *50 (N.D. Ill. Feb. 26, 1997) (magistrate's recommendation) (holding that scientific judgments are not protectible when they do not address agency policymaking), adopted (N.D. Ill. Mar. 28, 1997); Horsehead, No. 94-1299, slip op. at 19 (D.D.C. Oct. 1, 1996) (holding documents containing descriptions of scientific test results not protectible because they are "simply barren of any suggestion of advice or recommendations regarding policy judgments, and the factual information is easily segregated"); Larue v. IRS, No. 3-93-423, 1994 WL 315750, at *2 (E.D. Tenn. Jan. 27, 1994) (holding that privilege covers documents "actually related to the process by which policy is formed"); Md. Coal. for Integrated Educ. v. U.S. Dep't of Educ., No. 92-2178, slip op. at 2 (D.D.C. June 30, 1993) (rejecting position that deliberative process privilege applies to "all agency decisions"); see also Mapother, 3 F.3d at 1537-39 (discussing and harmonizing existing D.C. Circuit case law).

[185] 861 F.2d at 1118; see also Maricopa Audubon Soc'y v. U.S. Forest Serv., 108 F.3d 1089, 1095 (9th Cir. 1997) (ignoring the issue of "policy" and protecting a letter in which an employee was "fighting to preserve his job and reputation" by offering his "candid and confidential responses . . . to the head of his agency in order to rebut the charges made against him"); Providence Journal Co., 981 F.2d at 560 (citing National Wildlife and ruling that the agency's decision to discipline personnel for alleged misconduct is no less a "deliberative task . . . than the formulation or promulgation of agency disciplinary policy"); Ctr. for Biological Diversity v. Norton, No. Civ. 01-409 TUC, 2002 WL 32136200, at *2 (D. Ariz. 2002) (holding that limiting privilege to "'policy' decisions is overly narrow" and inconsistent with Ninth Circuit law); AFGE, AFL-CIO, Local 1164 v. HHS, 63 F. Supp. 2d 104, 109 (D. Mass. 1999) (rejecting plaintiff's contentions that a document must be related to an "essential function" of the agency in order to be protected, a claim "comparable" to the "law and policy" test rejected in Nat'l Wildlife); Citizens Comm'n on Human Rights v. FDA, No. 92CV5313, 1993 WL 1610471, at *11 (C.D. Cal. May 10, 1993) (citing National Wildlife and holding that appropriate test is simply whether document in question contributes to agency's deliberative process), aff'd in pertinent part & remanded in part, 45 F.3d 1325 (9th Cir. 1995); cf. Brockway v. Dep't of the Air Force, 518 F.2d 1184, 1192 (8th Cir. 1975) (rejecting plaintiff's contentions that accident witness statements are not part of agency's deliberations and that they should be released just because they are not policy memoranda).

some contexts, be the basis for the protection of factual information.[186] Similarly under some circumstances disclosure of even the identity of the author of a deliberative document could chill the deliberative process, thus warranting protection of that identity under Exemption 5,[187] even in circumstances in which a final version of the document in question has been released to the public.[188] Indeed, one court has specifically noted that the danger of revealing the agency's deliberations by disclosing facts is particularly acute when the document withheld is "short."[189] Factual information within a deliberative document also may be withheld when it is impossible to reasonably segregate meaningful portions of that factual information from the deliberative information.[190]

---

[186] See, e.g., Wolfe, 839 F.2d at 776 (revealing status of proposal in deliberative process "could chill discussions at a time when agency opinions are fluid and tentative"); Dudman, 815 F.2d at 1568 (revealing editorial judgments would stifle creative thinking).

[187] See, e.g., Brinton v. Dep't of State, 636 F.2d 600, 604 (D.C. Cir. 1980) (protecting identities of attorneys who provided legal advice to Secretary of State); Claudio, No. H-98-1911, slip op. at 8 (S.D. Tex. May 24, 2000) (accepting agency determination that release of identities of reports' authors would compromise integrity of agency decisionmaking process); Cofield v. City of LaGrange, No. 95-179, 1996 WL 32727, at *6 (D.D.C. Jan. 24, 1996) (finding internal routing notations possibly leading to identification of employees involved in decisionmaking protectible); Miscavige v. IRS, No. 91-1638, 1993 WL 389808, at *3 (N.D. Ga. June 15, 1992) (protecting handwritten signatures of agency employees involved in ongoing examination of church's claim of exempt status), aff'd on other grounds, 2 F.3d 366 (11th Cir. 1993); see also FOIA Update, Vol. VI, No. 2, at 6 (discussing circumstances under which it is appropriate to withhold name of author of requested document); cf. Wolfe, 839 F.2d at 775-76 (discussing how particularized disclosure can chill agency discussions); Greenberg, 10 F. Supp. 2d at 16 n.19 (holding that mere redaction of authors' names would not remove chilling effect on decisionmaking process).

[188] See City of W. Chi., 547 F. Supp at 750 (holding list of contributors to preliminary draft protectible even though names were in final version); Tax Reform Research Group v. IRS, 419 F. Supp. 415, 423-24 (D.D.C. 1976) (protecting identities of persons giving advice on policy matters even though substance of policy discussions had been released).

[189] Nadler, 955 F.2d at 1491 (dicta) (considering document "one and one-half pages in length").

[190] See Local 3, Int'l Bhd. of Elec. Workers v. NLRB, 845 F.2d 1177, 1180 (2d Cir. 1988) (concluding that short document would be rendered "nonsensical" by segregation); see also Lead Indus., 610 F.2d at 86 ("Instead of merely combing the documents for 'purely factual' tidbits, the court should have considered the segments in the context of the whole document and

(continued...)

**EXEMPTION 5**

## Attorney Work-Product Privilege

The second traditional privilege incorporated into Exemption 5 is the attorney work-product privilege, which protects documents and other memoranda prepared by an attorney in contemplation of litigation.[191] As its purpose is to protect the adversarial trial process by insulating the attorney's preparation from scrutiny,[192] the work-product privilege ordinarily does not attach until at least "some articulable claim, likely to lead to litigation," has arisen.[193] The privilege is not limited to civil proceedings, but rather extends to administrative proceedings[194] and to criminal matters as

---

[190](...continued)
that document's relation to the administrative process."); Linn v. U.S. Dep't of Justice, No. 92-1406, 1995 WL 631847, at *30-31 (D.D.C. Aug. 22, 1995) (holding that agency met burden in showing that in some instances factual material could not be segregated); Badhwar, 622 F. Supp. at 1375 (finding it impossible to "reasonably" segregate nondeliberative material from autopsy report); Morton-Norwich Prods., Inc. v. Mathews, 415 F. Supp. 78, 82 (D.D.C. 1976). But see Army Times, 998 F.2d at 1070 (emphasizing agency obligation to specifically address possible segregability and disclosure of factual information); accord FOIA Update, Vol. XIV, No. 3, at 10-11 ("OIP Guidance: The 'Reasonable Segregation' Obligation").

[191] See Hickman v. Taylor, 329 U.S. 495, 509-10 (1947); Fed. R. Civ. P. 26(b)(3) (codifying privilege in Federal Rules of Civil Procedure).

[192] See Jordan v. U.S. Dep't of Justice, 591 F.2d 753, 775 (D.C. Cir. 1978) (en banc).

[193] Coastal States Gas Corp. v. Dep't of Energy, 617 F.2d 854, 865 (D.C. Cir. 1980).

[194] See, e.g., Envtl. Prot. Servs. v. EPA, 364 F. Supp. 2d 575, 586 (N.D. W. Va. 2005) (EPA administrative enforcement proceeding); McErlean v. United States Dep't of Justice, No. 97-7831, 1999 WL 791680, at *7 (S.D.N.Y. Sept. 30, 1999) (INS deportation proceeding), amended (S.D.N.Y. Oct. 29, 1999); Means v. Segal, No. 97-1301, slip op. at 11-12 (D.D.C. Mar. 18, 1998) (magistrate's recommendation) (unfair labor practice determination), adopted (D.D.C. Apr. 15, 1998), aff'd per curiam, No. 98-5170 (D.C. Cir. Oct. 6, 1998); Williams v. McCausland, No. 90-Civ-7563, 1994 WL 18510, at *10 (S.D.N.Y. Jan. 18, 1994) (MSPB proceeding); Exxon Corp. v. Dep't of Energy, 585 F. Supp. 690, 700 (D.D.C. 1983) (regulatory audits and investigations); see also Judicial Watch, Inc. v. Rossotti, 285 F. Supp. 2d 17, 30-31 (D.D.C. 2003) (applying privilege to memorandum written by IRS associate chief counsel that discussed private financial information concerning prospective IRS employee); cf. Martin v. Office of Special Counsel, 819 F.2d 1181, 1187 (D.C. Cir. 1987) (reaching same result under Exemption (d)(5) of Privacy Act of 1974, 5 U.S.C. § 552a(d)(5) (2000)). But see MacLean v. DOD, No. 04-CV-2425, slip op. at 12-13 (S.D. Cal. June 2, 2005) (holding that privi-

(continued...)

well.[195] Similarly, the privilege has also been held applicable to documents

---

[194](...continued)
lege does not apply to records prepared for intra-agency review, even where such review could lead to discipline of agency employee).

[195] See, e.g., Rockwell Int'l Corp. v. U.S. Dep't of Justice, 235 F.3d 598, 604-05 (D.C. Cir. 2001) (applying privilege in case involving prosecution of environmental crimes); Nadler v. U.S. Dep't of Justice, 955 F.2d 1479, 1491-92 (11th Cir. 1992) (applying privilege in bribery investigation); Antonelli v. Sullivan, 732 F.2d 560, 561 (7th Cir. 1983) (ruling privilege applicable in bank-fraud prosecution); Butler v. U.S. Dep't of Justice, 368 F. Supp. 2d 776, 785-86 (E.D. Mich. 2005) (applying privilege to prosecution memorandum and draft indictment prepared as part of narcotics investigation); Williams v. U.S. Dep't of Justice, No. 02-2452, slip op. at 7 (D.D.C. Feb. 4, 2004) (protecting summaries of telephone conversations between Assistant United States Attorney and FBI official discussing various facets of criminal investigation); Kendrick v. Executive Office for U.S. Attorneys, No. 00-1809, slip op. at 5 (D.D.C. June 14, 2001) (holding privilege applicable to attorney notes prepared for grand jury proceedings, criminal indictment, and trial); Givner v. Executive Office for U.S. Attorneys, No. 99-3454, slip op. at 10-11 (D.D.C. Mar. 1, 2001) (approving application of privilege to "attorney notes, trial preparation materials, trial research, directives between government attorneys, witness related [sic] notes and materials, draft pleadings and draft letters" generated in criminal case); Bartolotta v. FBI, No. 99-1145, slip op. at 8 (D.D.C. July 13, 2000) (approving invocation of the privilege to protect a memorandum "prepared by an attorney of the Criminal Division that discusses and analyzes double jeopardy and collateral estoppel issues as they relate to the viability of contemplated litigation" under the RICO Act); Spannaus v. U.S. Dep't of Justice, No. 92-0372, slip op. at 4 (D.D.C. Sept. 30, 1999) (holding privilege applicable to a document prepared by an Assistant United States Attorney that discussed grand jury procedures in a criminal case, and stating that "[i]t is difficult to imagine a more direct application of the work product privilege"); Slater v. Executive Office for U.S. Attorneys, No. 98-1663, 1999 U.S. Dist. LEXIS 8399, at *9 (D.D.C. May 24, 1999) (protecting portions of letter from Assistant United States Attorney to FBI revealing investigative strategy in criminal case); Telegraph Publ'g Co. v. U.S. Dep't of Justice, No. 95-521, slip op. at 19-20 (D.N.H. Aug. 31, 1998) (holding privilege applicable to materials prepared by Assistant United States Attorney in preparation for criminal prosecution); Rzeslawski v. U.S. Dep't of Justice, No. 97-1156, slip op. at 9 (D.D.C. July 23, 1998) (affirming use of privilege for Assistant United States Attorney's handwritten notes reflecting trial preparation in criminal case), appeal dismissed, No. 00-5029 (D.C. Cir. Apr. 11, 2000); see also FOIA Update, Vol. V, No. 2, at 7 (discussing use of privilege in context of criminal law enforcement investigations). But cf. Powell v. Dep't of Justice, 584 F. Supp. 1508, 1520 (N.D. Cal. 1984) (suggesting, but not deciding, that attorney work-product materials generated in criminal case should be subject to disclosure under criminal discovery provisions).

generated in preparation of an amicus brief.[196]

This privilege sweeps very broadly in several respects.[197] First, litigation need never have actually commenced, so long as specific claims have been identified which make litigation probable.[198] Significantly, the Court of Appeals for the District of Columbia Circuit has ruled that the privilege "extends to documents prepared in anticipation of foreseeable litigation, even if no specific claim is contemplated."[199] The privilege also has been held to attach to records of law enforcement investigations, when the investigation is "based upon a specific wrongdoing and represent[s] an attempt to garner evidence and build a case against the suspected wrongdoer."[200]

---

[196] See Strang v. Collyer, 710 F. Supp. 9, 12-13 (D.D.C. 1989), aff'd sub nom. Strang v. DeSio, 899 F.2d 1268 (D.C. Cir. 1990) (unpublished table decision).

[197] See generally FOIA Update, Vol. IV, No. 3, at 6.

[198] See Kent Corp. v. NLRB, 530 F.2d 612, 623 (5th Cir. 1976); see, e.g., Hertzberg v. Veneman, 273 F. Supp. 2d 67, 80 (D.D.C. 2003) (applying privilege in situation where potential claimants had discussed possibility of pursuing claims); Tax Analysts v. IRS, 152 F. Supp. 2d 1, 19 (D.D.C. 2001) (protecting document written to assess "whether a particular case should be designated for litigation"), aff'd in part, rev'd in part on other grounds & remanded, 294 F.3d 71 (D.C. Cir. 2002); Blazy v. Tenet, 979 F. Supp. 10, 24 (D.D.C. 1997) (observing that communication between agency employee review panel and agency attorney throughout process of deciding whether to retain plaintiff "at the very least demonstrates that the [panel] was concerned about potential litigation"), summary affirmance granted, No. 97-5330 (D.C. Cir. May 12, 1998); Chemcentral/Grand Rapids Corp. v. EPA, No. 91-C-4380, 1992 WL 281322, at *3-4 (N.D. Ill. Oct. 6, 1992) (holding that privilege applies to legal advice given for specific agency cleanup sites); Savada v. DOD, 755 F. Supp. 6, 7 (D.D.C. 1991) (finding threat of litigation by counsel for adverse party sufficient); cf. Means, No. 97-1301, slip op. at 11-12 (D.D.C. Mar. 18, 1998) (holding privilege applicable to records prepared for unfair labor practice complaint that agency later dropped).

[199] Schiller v. NLRB, 964 F.2d 1205, 1208 (D.C. Cir. 1992); see also Delaney, Migdail & Young, Chartered v. IRS, 826 F.2d 124, 127 (D.C. Cir. 1987) (holding that privilege extends to documents prepared when identity of prospective litigation opponent unknown); Hertzberg, 273 F. Supp. 2d at 79 (protecting documents generated in light of "'strong probability of tort claims'" (quoting agency declaration)); Kelly v. CIA, No. 00-2498, slip op. at 32-36 (D.D.C. Aug. 8, 2002) (applying privilege to protect documents related to CIA's obligation to notify unwitting participants in drug-testing program and to claims that such individuals might raise in court).

[200] SafeCard Servs. v. SEC, 926 F.2d 1197, 1202 (D.C. Cir. 1991); see, e.g.,
(continued...)

However, the mere fact that it is conceivable that litigation might occur at some unspecified time in the future will not necessarily be sufficient
to protect attorney-generated documents; it has been observed that "the
policies of the FOIA would be largely defeated" if agencies were to withhold any documents created by attorneys "simply because litigation <u>might</u>
someday occur."[201] But when litigation is reasonably regarded as inevita-
ble under the circumstances, a specific claim need not yet have arisen,[202]

---

[200](...continued)
<u>Winterstein v. U.S.·Dep't of Justice</u>, 89 F. Supp. 2d 79, 81 (D.D.C. 2000) (pro-
tecting prosecution memorandum "prepared for the purpose of pursuing a
specific claim -- namely, the contemplated prosecution of Arthur Rudolph");
<u>Germosen v. Cox</u>, No. 98 Civ. 1294, 1999 WL 1021559, at *14 (S.D.N.Y. Nov.
9, 1999) (protecting correspondence between United States Attorney's Office and Postal Inspection Service regarding criminal investigative and prosecutive strategy), <u>appeal dismissed for failure to prosecute</u>, No. 00-6041
(2d Cir. Sept. 12, 2000); <u>Pentagen Techs. Int'l v. United States</u>, No. 98-4831,
1999 WL 378345, at *3 (S.D.N.Y. June 9, 1999) (upholding application of
privilege to attorney notes regarding qui tam suit in which government ultimately declined to intervene); <u>LaRouche v. U.S. Dep't of the Treasury</u>, No.
91-1655, slip op. at 24-26 (D.D.C. May 22, 1998) (holding that privilege covers letter from Assistant United States Attorney to IRS official requesting
IRS's participation in ongoing grand jury investigation of plaintiff); <u>Rosen-
berg v. Freeh</u>, No. 97-0476, slip op. at 7-8 (D.D.C. May 13, 1998) (protecting
documents generated by United States Attorney's Office during course of
considering prosecutive action against subjects of undercover operation);
<u>Sousa v. U.S. Dep't of Justice</u>, No. 95-375, 1997 U.S. Dist. LEXIS 9010, at *20
(D.D.C. June 19, 1997) (holding that documents were described sufficiently
to show that murder investigation, leading to potential prosecution, was
underway); <u>Feshbach v. SEC</u>, 5 F. Supp. 2d 774, 783 (N.D. Cal. 1997) (protecting documents pertaining to preliminary examination "based upon a
suspicion of specific wrongdoing and represent[ing] an effort to obtain evidence and to build a case against the suspected wrongdoer").

[201] <u>Senate of P.R. v. U.S. Dep't of Justice</u>, 823 F.2d 574, 587 (D.C. Cir.
1987) (emphasis added) (citing <u>Coastal States</u>, 617 F.2d at 865).

[202] <u>See</u> <u>In re Sealed Case</u>, 146 F.3d 881, 885-86 (D.C. Cir. 1998) (protecting document that provided legal advice intended to protect client from future litigation over particular transaction, even though no claim had yet
arisen) (non-FOIA case); <u>Schiller</u>, 964 F.2d at 1208 (holding documents that
provide tips and instructions for handling future litigation protectible); <u>De-
laney</u>, 826 F.2d at 127 (holding memoranda that "advise the agency of the
types of legal challenges likely to be mounted against a proposed program,
potential defenses available to the agency and the likely outcome" protectible); <u>Hertzberg</u>, 273 F. Supp. 2d at 78 (protecting documents from investigation where agency has determined that claims were likely to arise); <u>Ray-
theon Aircraft Co. v. U.S. Army Corps of Eng'rs</u>, 183 F. Supp. 2d 1280, 1289
(D. Kan. 2001) (protecting documents containing guidance for agency at-
(continued...)

and agencies can obtain necessary protection through the attorney work-product privilege.[203]

Further, it has been held that a document that was prepared for two disparate purposes was compiled in anticipation of litigation if "litigation was a major factor" in the decision to create it.[204] However, documents pre-

---

[202](...continued)
torneys on litigation of environmental law cases); Bhd. of Locomotive Eng'rs v. Surface Transp. Bd., No. 96-1153, 1997 WL 446261, at *6 (D.D.C. July 31, 1997) (finding future litigation "probable" when agency is aware that its legal interpretation will be contested in court); Direct Response Consulting Serv. v. IRS, No. 94-1156, 1995 WL 623282, at *2 (D.D.C. Aug. 21, 1995) (holding that articulable claim arose when agency became aware that its position was not accepted by taxpayers); Lacefield v. United States, No. 92-N-1680, 1993 WL 268392, at *8 (D. Colo. Mar. 10, 1993) (holding that agency's knowledge that adversary plans to challenge agency position constitutes sufficient anticipation of articulable claim); Silber v. U.S. Dep't of Justice, No. 91-876, transcript at 23-24 (D.D.C. Aug. 13, 1992) (bench order) (deciding that privilege covers monograph written to assist attorneys in prosecuting cases); Anderson v. U.S. Parole Comm'n, 3 Gov't Disclosure Serv. (P-H) ¶ 83,055, at 83,557 (D.D.C. Jan. 6, 1983) (deciding that privilege covers case digest of legal theories and defenses frequently used in litigation).

[203] See, e.g., Delaney, 826 F.2d at 127 (protecting "agency's attorneys' assessments of [a] program's legal vulnerabilities" crafted before specific litigation arose); Heggestad v. U.S. Dep't of Justice, 182 F. Supp. 2d 1, 8 (D.D.C. 2000) (noting that the privilege applies "even without a case already docketed or where the agency is unable to identify the specific claim to which the document relates"); see also Attorney General's Memorandum for Heads of All Federal Departments and Agencies Regarding the Freedom of Information Act (Oct. 12, 2001) [hereinafter Attorney General Ashcroft's FOIA Memorandum], reprinted in FOIA Post (posted 10/15/01) (emphasizing important role of attorney work-product privilege in ensuring that "lawyers' deliberations and communications are kept private").

[204] Wilson v. Dep't of Energy, No. 84-3163, slip op. at 7 n.1 (D.D.C. Jan. 28, 1985); see also Maine v. U.S. Dep't of the Interior, 298 F.3d 60, 68 (1st Cir. 2002) (amended opinion) (concluding that court's earlier opinion, which had required that litigation be primary factor in creation of documents for which attorney work-product privilege was claimed, was in error); Wood v. FBI, No. 3:02cv2058, 2004 U.S. Dist LEXIS 5525, at *13 (D. Conn. Mar. 31, 2004) (noting that the work-product privilege applies if the ""document can fairly be said to have been prepared or obtained because of the prospect of litigation"" (quoting United States v. Adlman, 134 F.3d 1194, 1202 (2d Cir. 1998) (quoting in turn Charles A. Wright, Arthur Miller, and Richard L. Marcus, 8 Federal Practice and Procedure 343 (1994)))); Hertzberg, 273 F. Supp. 2d at 80 (D.D.C. 2003) (rejecting "primary purpose" test); Maine v.
(continued...)

pared in an agency's ordinary course of business, not under circumstances sufficiently related to litigation, may not be accorded protection.[205]

The attorney work-product privilege also has been held to cover documents "relat[ing] to possible settlements" of litigation.[206] Logically, it can also protect the recommendation to close a litigation or prelitigation matter,[207] and even the final agency decision to terminate litigation.[208] But doc-

---

[204](...continued)
Norton, 208 F. Supp. 2d 63, 67 (D. Me. 2002) (applying privilege in civil discovery context to documents created in ordinary course of agency business, so long as agency could show that they were prepared in light of possible litigation); Brotherhood, 1997 WL 446261, at *6 (holding that privilege applies where document was created "in part" for litigation). But see United States v. Gulf Oil Corp., 760 F.2d 292, 296-97 (Temp. Emer. Ct. App. 1985) (holding, in non-FOIA case, that anticipation of litigation must be "the primary motivating purpose behind the creation of the document"); Pub. Citizen Inc. v. Dep't of State, 100 F. Supp. 2d 10, 30 (D.D.C. 2000) (requiring that litigation be "primary motivating purpose" in document's creation).

[205] See Hennessey v. U.S. Agency for Int'l Dev., No. 97-1113, 1997 WL 537998, at *6 (4th Cir. Sept. 2, 1997) (deciding that a report commissioned to complete a project was not prepared "because of the prospect of litigation," despite the threat of suit); Hill Tower, Inc. v. Dep't of the Navy, 718 F. Supp. 562, 567 (N.D. Tex. 1988) (concluding that aircraft accident investigation information in JAG Manual report was not created in anticipation of litigation).

[206] United States v. Metro. St. Louis Sewer Dist., 952 F.2d 1040, 1044-45 (8th Cir. 1992) (holding that it is "beyond doubt that draft consent decrees prepared by a federal government agency involved in litigation" are covered by Exemption 5, but remanding to determine if the privilege was waived); see also Tax Analysts, 152 F. Supp. 2d at 19 (protecting recommendations concerning settlement of case); Cities Serv. Co. v. FTC, 627 F. Supp. 827, 832 (D.D.C. 1984) ("attorney's notes or working papers which relate to . . . possible settlement discussions . . . are protected under the attorney work-product privilege"), aff'd, 778 F.2d 889 (D.C. Cir. 1985) (unpublished table decision); Church of Scientology v. IRS, No. 90-11069, slip op. at 20 (D. Mass. Apr. 22, 1992) (magistrate's recommendation) (holding that fact that parties were contemplating settlement does not foreclose application of attorney work-product privilege); cf. Carey-Canada, Inc. v. Aetna Cas. & Sur. Co., 118 F.R.D. 250, 251-52 (D.D.C. 1987) (upholding use of privilege, in non-FOIA case, for documents related to possible settlement of claims).

[207] See, e.g., A. Michael's Piano, Inc. v. FTC, 18 F.3d 138, 146-47 (2d Cir. 1994) (concluding that exemption still was applicable even if staff attorney was considering or recommending closing investigation); Heggestad, 182 F. Supp. 2d at 10-11 (holding privilege applicable to prosecution-declina-
(continued...)

uments prepared subsequent to the closing of a case are presumed, absent some specific basis for concluding otherwise, not to have been prepared in anticipation of litigation.[209] Moreover, documents not originally prepared in anticipation of litigation cannot assume the protection of the work-product privilege merely through their later placement in a litigation-related document.[210]

Second, Rule 26(b)(3) of the Federal Rules of Civil Procedure allows the privilege to be used to protect documents prepared "by or for another party or by or for that other party's representative." Not only do documents prepared by agency attorneys who are responsible for the litigation of a case which is being defended or prosecuted by the Department of Justice qualify for the privilege,[211] but also documents prepared by an attorney "not employed as a litigator,"[212] or even documents prepared by someone not

---

[207](...continued)
tion memoranda); cf. Tax Analysts v. IRS, No. 94-923, slip op. at 6 (D.D.C. Sept. 3, 1999) (protecting record containing "mental impressions" of agency attorney as to whether agency should continue to contest certain matters in litigation, or cease litigating case altogether); Grecco v. Dep't of Justice, No. 97-0419, slip op. at 12 (D.D.C. Apr. 1, 1999) (holding exemption applicable to records concerning determination whether to appeal lower court decision).

[208] See FOIA Update, Vol. VI, No. 3, at 5 (analyzing bases for privilege).

[209] See Senate of P.R., 823 F.2d at 586; Rashid v. U.S. Dep't of Justice, No. 99-2461, slip op. at 10-11 (D.D.C. June 12, 2001) (holding privilege inapplicable to documents drafted after case was settled); Canning v. Dep't of the Treasury, No. 94-2704, slip op. at 12 (D.D.C. May 7, 1998) (holding prosecutor's letter setting forth reasons relied upon in declining to prosecute case and "written after the conclusion of the investigation and after the decision to forgo litigation was made," not covered by privilege); Grine v. Coombs, No. 95-342, 1997 U.S. Dist. LEXIS 19578, at *10 (W.D. Pa. Oct. 10, 1997) (finding privilege inapplicable where no further agency enforcement action was contemplated at time of document's creation). But see Senate of P.R. v. U.S. Dep't of Justice, No. 84-1829, 1992 WL 119127, at *8 (D.D.C. May 13, 1992) (finding reasonable anticipation of litigation still existed after case was formally closed, because agency was carefully reevaluating it in light of new evidence).

[210] See Dow Jones & Co. v. Dep't of Justice, 724 F. Supp. 985, 989 (D.D.C. 1989), aff'd on other grounds, 917 F.2d 571 (D.C. Cir. 1990); MacLean, No. 04-2425, slip op. at 13 n.13 (S.D. Cal. June 2, 2005).

[211] See, e.g., Cook v. Watt, 597 F. Supp. 545, 548 (D. Alaska 1983).

[212] Ill. State Bd. of Educ. v. Bell, No. 84-337, slip op. at 9-10 (D.D.C. May 31, 1985).

employed primarily as an attorney.[213] Courts have also accorded work product protection to materials prepared by nonattorneys who are supervised by attorneys.[214] The premise in such cases is that work-product protection

---

[213] See, e.g., Hanson v. U.S. Agency for Int'l Dev., 372 F.3d 286, 293 (4th Cir. 2004) (upholding privilege even though attorney in question testified that he had been hired as engineer, not as attorney; finding that it was clear that despite being hired as engineer, attorney had exercised legal judgment in undertaking his analysis).

[214] See, e.g., United States v. Nobles, 422 U.S. 225, 238-39 (1975) (concluding, in a non-FOIA case, that "the realities of litigation" require that the privilege extend to material prepared by an attorney's agents); Diversified Indus. v. Meredith, 572 F.2d 596, 603 (8th Cir. 1977) ("While the 'work product' may be, and often is, that of an attorney, the concept of 'work product' is not confined to information or materials gathered or assembled by a lawyer.") (non-FOIA case); Shacket v. United States, 339 F. Supp. 2d 1092, 1096 (S.D. Cal. 2004) (holding it "irrelevant" that report withheld pursuant to work-product privilege was prepared by IRS Special Agent, not attorney; observing that the privilege extends to an attorney "or other representative of a party"); Hertzberg, 273 F. Supp. 2d at 76 (rejecting claim that privilege is limited to materials prepared by attorney, and citing Federal Rule of Civil Procedure 26(b)(3) for proposition that privilege extends to documents created at direction of attorney); Davis v. FTC, No. 96-CIV-9324, 1997 WL 73671, at *2 (S.D.N.Y. Feb. 20, 1997) (protecting material prepared by economists for administrative hearing); Creel v. U.S. Dep't of State, No. 6:92CV 559, 1993 U.S. Dist. LEXIS 21187, at *27 (E.D. Tex. Sept. 29, 1993) (magistrate's recommendation) (protecting special agent's notes made while assisting attorney in investigation), adopted (E.D. Tex. Dec. 30, 1993), aff'd, 42 F.3d 641 (5th Cir. 1995) (unpublished table decision); Durham v. U.S. Dep't of Justice, 829 F. Supp. 428, 432-33 (D.D.C. 1993) (protecting material prepared by government personnel under prosecuting attorney's direction), appeal dismissed for failure to timely file, No. 93-5354 (D.C. Cir. Nov. 29, 1994); Taylor v. Office of Special Counsel, No. 91-N-734, slip op. at 17 (D. Colo. Mar. 22, 1993) (holding that privilege covers telephone interview conducted by examiner at request of attorney); Joint Bd. of Control v. Bureau of Indian Affairs, No. 87-217, slip op. at 9-10 (D. Mont. Sept. 9, 1988) (protecting water studies produced by contract companies); Nishnic v. U.S. Dep't of Justice, 671 F. Supp. 771, 772-73 (D.D.C. 1987) (holding historian's research and interviews privileged); Wilson, No. 84-3163, slip op. at 8 (D.D.C. Jan. 28, 1995) (holding consultant's report privileged); Exxon Corp. v. FTC, 466 F. Supp. 1088, 1099 (D.D.C. 1978) (protecting economist's report), aff'd, 663 F.2d 120 (D.C. Cir. 1980). But see Boyd v. U.S. Marshals Serv., No. 99-2712, 2002 U.S. Dist. LEXIS 27734, at *8-9 (rejecting attorney work-product applicability where documents were prepared by nonattorney who merely "may" have been acting at direction of attorney); cf. Richman v. U.S. Dep't of Justice, No. 90-C-19-C, slip op. at 3 (W.D. Wis. Mar. 2, 1994) (holding that information not prepared "by a lawyer in preparation for litigation" was not entitled to any protection under Exemption 5 whatsoever); Brittany Dyeing
(continued...)

is appropriate when the nonattorney acts as the agent of the attorney; when that is not the case, the work-product privilege as incorporated by the FOIA has not been extended to protect the material prepared by the nonattorney.[215]

Third, the work-product privilege has been held to remain applicable when the information has been shared with a party holding a common interest with the agency.[216] The privilege remains applicable also when the document has become the basis for a final agency decision.[217]

---

[214](...continued)
& Printing Corp. v. EPA, No. 91-2711, slip op. at 7-8 (D.D.C. Mar. 12, 1993) (holding that witness statements taken by investigator at behest of counsel cannot be protected because they would "not expose agency decision-making process").

[215] See Hall v. Dep't of Justice, No. 87-474, 1989 WL 24542, at *7-8 (D.D.C. Mar. 8, 1989) (magistrate's recommendation) (concluding that agency's affidavit failed to show that prosecutorial report of investigation was prepared by Marshals Service personnel under direction of attorney), adopted (D.D.C. July 31, 1989); Nishnic, 671 F. Supp. at 810-11 (holding that summaries of witness statements taken by USSR officials for United States Department of Justice are not protectible).

[216] See, e.g., Gulf Oil, 760 F.2d at 295-96 (protecting documents shared between two companies contemplating merger); Chilivis v. SEC, 673 F.2d 1205, 1211-12 (11th Cir. 1982); Nishnic, 671 F. Supp. at 775 (protecting documents shared with foreign nation); cf. Dep't of the Interior v. Klamath Water Users Protective Ass'n, 532 U.S. 1, 15-16 (2001) (declining to extend Exemption 5 threshold to protect communications between agency and Indian tribes, despite fiduciary obligation of agency acting as trustee to protect confidentiality of such communications); Rashid, No. 99-2461, slip op. at 10 (D.D.C. June 12, 2001) (holding privilege inapplicable because agency failed to demonstrate common interest with third parties to whom it disclosed documents).

[217] See Wood v. FBI, 312 F. Supp. 2d 328, 344 (D. Conn. 2004) (noting prior rulings that incorporation or adoption do not vitiate work-product protection), aff'd in part, rev'd in part on other grounds & remanded, 432 F.3d 78 (2d Cir. 2005); Uribe v. Executive Office for U.S. Attorneys, No. 87-1836, 1989 U.S. Dist. LEXIS 5691, at *6-7 (D.D.C. May 23, 1989) (protecting criminal prosecution declination memorandum); Iglesias v. CIA, 525 F. Supp. 547, 559 (D.D.C. 1981) ("[A]ny argument to the effect that the attorney's opinions in question may have become the basis for final agency action is irrelevant [to the applicability of] the work-product privilege."); FOIA Update, Vol. VI, No. 3, at 5; see also Fed. Open Mkt. Comm. v. Merrill, 434 U.S. 340, 360 n.23 (1979) (protecting final determination under commercial privilege); cf. NLRB v. Sears, Roebuck & Co., 421 U.S. 132, 160 (1975) (holding that memoranda reflecting an agency decision to prosecute do not consti-
(continued...)

In <u>NLRB v. Sears, Roebuck & Co.</u>,[218] the Supreme Court allowed the withholding of a final agency decision on the basis that it was shielded by the work-product privilege,[219] but it also stated that Exemption 5 can never apply to final decisions and it expressed reluctance to "construe Exemption 5 to apply to documents described in FOIA subsection (a)(2),"[220] the "reading room" provision of the Act.[221] This result inevitably led to no small amount of confusion,[222] which was cleared up by the Supreme Court in <u>Federal Open Market Committee v. Merrill</u>.[223] In <u>Merrill</u>, the Court explained its statements in <u>Sears</u>,[224] and plainly stated that even if a document is a final opinion, and therefore falls within subsection (a)(2)'s mandatory disclosure requirements, it still may be withheld if it falls within the work-product privilege.[225] (For a discussion of the automatic disclosure require-

---

[217](...continued) .
tute a "final disposition" of the "case" within the meaning of subsection (a)(2) of the FOIA). <u>But see</u> <u>Grolier</u>, 462 U.S. at 32 n.4 (Brennan, J., concurring) ("[I]t is difficult to imagine how a final decision could be 'prepared in anticipation of litigation or for trial.'").

[218] 421 U.S. 132 (1975).

[219] <u>Id.</u> at 160.

[220] <u>Id.</u> at 153-54.

[221] <u>See</u> FOIA Update, Vol. XIII, No. 3, at 3-4 ("OIP Guidance: The 'Automatic' Disclosure Provisions of FOIA: Subsections (a)(1) & (a)(2)"); <u>see also</u> FOIA Update, Vol. XVII, No. 4, at 1-2 (describing amendments to subsection (a)(2)).

[222] <u>See, e.g.</u>, <u>Bristol-Meyers Co. v. FTC</u>, 598 F.2d 18, 24 n.11, 29 (D.C. Cir. 1978) (citing <u>Sears</u> for earlier proposition that document will lose work product protection if it is expressly adopted as agency policy or is incorporated into agency's "final opinion").

[223] 443 U.S. 340 (1979).

[224] <u>Id.</u> at 360 n.23 (clarifying that <u>Sears</u> observations were made in relation to privilege for predecisional communications only).

[225] <u>Id.</u> ("It should be obvious that the kind of mutually exclusive relationship between final opinions and statements of policy, on one hand, and predecisional communications, on the other, does not necessarily exist between final statements of policy and other Exemption 5 privileges."); <u>see also</u> Tax Analysts, 152 F. Supp. 2d at 29 (citing <u>Merrill</u> for the proposition that "agency working law contained in a privileged attorney work product is exempt material in and of itself" and, therefore, "need not be segregated and disclosed"). <u>But see</u> <u>SafeCard</u>, 926 F.2d at 1203-05, 1206 (mistakenly applying <u>Bristol-Meyers</u>, a pre-<u>Merrill</u> decision, in requiring the release of work product that memorializes a final decision); <u>Richman v. U.S. Dep't of</u>
(continued...)

ments of subsection (a)(2), see FOIA Reading Rooms and Web Sites, FOIA Reading Rooms, above.)

Fourth, the Supreme Court's decisions in United States v. Weber Aircraft Corp.[226] and FTC v. Grolier Inc.,[227] viewed in light of the traditional contours of the attorney work-product doctrine, afford sweeping attorney work-product protection to factual materials. Because factual work product enjoys qualified immunity from civil discovery, such materials are discoverable "only upon a showing that the party seeking discovery has substantial need" of materials which cannot be obtained elsewhere without "undue hardship."[228] In Grolier, the Supreme Court held that the "test under Exemption 5 is whether the documents would be 'routinely' or 'normally' disclosed upon a showing of relevance."[229] Because the rules of civil discovery require a showing of "substantial need" and "undue hardship" in order for a party to obtain any factual work-product,[230] such materials are not "routinely" or "normally" discoverable. This "routinely or normally discoverable" test was unanimously reaffirmed by the Supreme Court in Weber Aircraft.[231]

---

[225](...continued)
Justice, No. 90-C-19-C, slip op. at 9 (W.D. Wis. Feb. 2, 1994) (mistakenly concluding that work-product privilege applies only when information is predecisional).

[226] 465 U.S. 792 (1984).

[227] 462 U.S. 19 (1983).

[228] Fed. R. Civ. P. 26(b)(3).

[229] 462 U.S. at 26; see also Sears, 421 U.S. at 149 & n.16.

[230] Fed. R. Civ. P. 26(b)(3); see, e.g., Maine v. Norton, 208 F. Supp. 2d at 66-67 (holding, in civil discovery context, that civil litigants seeking discovery can show "particularized need" for documents withheld under deliberative process privilege, and "substantial need and undue hardship" for documents withheld under attorney work-product privilege, in order to overcome opponent's assertion of privilege).

[231] 465 U.S. at 799; see also Wood, 2004 U.S. Dist LEXIS, at *14 (noting that because in civil discovery context work-product privilege can be overcome only upon showing of substantial need, such documents are never "routinely disclosed" and hence are always protected in FOIA context); cf. In re England, 375 F.3d 1169, 1178-79 (D.C. Cir. 2004) (rejecting, in non-FOIA case, plaintiff's claim that statutory exemption from discovery rule could be overcome by bare assertion that protected documents would reveal agency wrongdoing); MacLean, No. 04-2425, slip op. at 7-9 (S.D. Cal. June 2, 2005) (refusing to accept plaintiff's contention that deliberative process privilege "disappears altogether" whenever there is "any reason" to believe that government engaged in misconduct). But see Martin v. U.S.
(continued...)

Although several pre-Weber Aircraft circuit court decisions limited attorney work-product protection to "deliberative" material,[232] no distinction between factual and deliberative work product should be applied.[233] During the past two years two lower federal courts held that agencies had an obligation to segregate out and disclose factual portions of work-product material.[234] However, in ruling on an appeal of one of these cases, the D.C. Circuit has explicitly repudiated any such holding, in a strong opinion clearly stating that the attorney work-product privilege does not distinguish between factual and deliberative materials.[235] This opinion firmly follows earlier precedents of that court, as well as those of numerous other federal courts,[236] and now should put any such question to rest.[237] It al-

---

[231](...continued)
Dep't of Justice, No. 96-2886, slip op. at 6-7 (D.D.C. Mar. 28, 2005) (reasoning that factual work-product documents are protected merely because of fact that plaintiff had made no showing of special need for documents, rather than fundamentally because work-product documents are not routinely discoverable and therefore never disclosable under FOIA in light of Weber Aircraft, 465 U.S. at 799, and Grolier, 462 U.S. at 26).

[232] See Robbins Tire & Rubber Co. v. NLRB, 563 F.2d 724, 735 (5th Cir. 1977), rev'd on other grounds, 437 U.S. 214 (1978); Deering Milliken, Inc. v. Irving, 548 F.2d 1131, 1138 (4th Cir. 1977); Title Guar. Co. v. NLRB, 534 F.2d 484, 492-93 n.15 (2d Cir. 1976).

[233] Cf. Judicial Watch, Inc. v. Dep't of Justice, 337 F. Supp. 2d 183, 186-87 (D.D.C. 2004) (holding that documents in question were properly withheld pursuant to attorney work-product privilege, but concluding that agency must still segregate unspecified portions for disclosure), rev'd, 432 F.3d 366, 372 (D.C. Cir. 2005).

[234] See Mone v. Dep't of the Navy, 353 F. Supp. 2d 193, 196 (D. Mass. 2005) (ordering in camera review of work-product document to determine if it contained segregable material); Judicial Watch, 337 F. Supp. 2d at 186-87 (claiming that circuit law on factual work-product material was "unclear").

[235] Judicial Watch, Inc. v. U.S. Dep't of Justice, 432 F.3d 366, 371 (D.C. Cir. 2005) ("[F]actual material is itself privileged when it appears within documents that are attorney work product. If a document is fully protected as work product, then segregability is not required.").

[236] See Martin, 819 F.2d at 1187 ("The work-product privilege simply does not distinguish between factual and deliberative material."); see also Tax Analysts v. IRS, 117 F.3d 607, 620 (D.C. Cir. 1997) (holding that district court was in error to limit protection to "the mental impressions, conclusions, opinions, or legal theories of an attorney"); A. Michael's Piano, 18 F.3d at 147 ("The work product privilege draws no distinction between materials that are factual in nature and those that are deliberative."); Norwood v. FAA, 993 F.2d 570, 576 (6th Cir. 1993) (holding that work-product privilege protects documents regardless of status as factual or deliberative);
(continued...)

ways should be remembered, though, that the agency has the burden of showing that the privilege applies to all withheld information in the first place.[238]

---

[236](...continued)
Nadler, 955 F.2d at 1492 ("[U]nlike the deliberative process privilege, the work-product privilege encompasses factual materials."); Raytheon, 183 F. Supp. 2d at 1292 (rejecting plaintiff's contention that agency must segregate and release factual work-product material); Allnutt v. U.S. Dep't of Justice, No. Civ. Y-98-901, 2000 WL 852455, at *9 (D. Md. Oct. 23, 2000) (recognizing that the attorney work-product privilege encompasses both deliberative materials and "all factual materials prepared in anticipation of the litigation"), aff'd, No. 01-1038, 2001 WL 468134, at *1 (4th Cir. May 3, 2001); May v. IRS, 85 F. Supp. 2d 939, 950 (W.D. Mo. 1999) (protecting both "the factual basis for [a] potential prosecution and an analysis of the applicable law"); Rugiero v. U.S. Dep't of Justice, 35 F. Supp. 2d 977, 984 (E.D. Mich. 1998) ("[T]he law is clear that . . . both factual and deliberative work product are exempt from release under FOIA."), aff'd in part & remanded in part on other grounds, 257 F.3d 534, 552-53 (6th Cir. 2001), cert. denied, 534 U.S. 1134 (2002); Manchester v. DEA, 823 F. Supp. 1259, 1269 (E.D. Pa. 1993) (deciding that segregation not required where "factual information is incidental to, and bound with, privileged" information); Manna v. U.S. Dep't of Justice, 815 F. Supp. 798, 814 (D.N.J. 1993) (following Martin), aff'd on other grounds, 51 F.3d 1158 (3d Cir. 1995); United Techs. Corp. v. NLRB, 632 F. Supp. 776, 781 (D. Conn. 1985) ("[I]f a document is attorney work product the entire document is privileged."), aff'd on other grounds, 777 F.2d 90 (2d Cir. 1985); accord FOIA Update, Vol. V, No. 4, at 6. But see Nickerson v. United States, No. 95-C-7395, 1996 WL 563465, at *3 (N.D. Ill. Oct. 1, 1996) (ruling that facts must be segregated under privilege); Fine v. U.S. Dep't of Energy, 830 F. Supp. 570, 574-76 (D.N.M. 1993) (refusing to follow Martin and instead following Robbins Tire and Deering Milliken); cf. Tax Analysts v. IRS, No. 94-923, 1998 WL 419755, at *3 (D.D.C. May 1, 1998) (requiring agency to disclose "agency working law, legal analysis, and conclusions, so long as the 'mental impressions, conclusions, opinions, or legal theories of an attorney' are protected" (quoting Tax Analysts, 117 F.3d at 619 (D.C. Cir. 1997)), because to allow otherwise would "eviscerate" the court of appeals' ruling that agency must release its field service advice memoranda to requester), appeal dismissed voluntarily, No. 94-00923 (D.C. Cir. Aug. 11, 1998).

[237] See Judicial Watch, 432 F.3d at 372 ("[B]ecause the e-mails at issue in this case are attorney work product, the entire contents of these documents . . . are exempt from disclosure under FOIA.").

[238] See, e.g., Linn v. U.S. Dep't of Justice, No. 92-1406, 1995 WL 417810, at *19, *29-30 (D.D.C. June 6, 1995) (requiring that agency specifically explain why material protected by privilege); Kronberg v. U.S. Dep't of Justice, 875 F. Supp. 861, 869 (D.D.C. 1995) (requiring agency to show how privilege applies); cf. Dayton Newspapers, Inc. v. U.S. Dep't of the Navy,
(continued...)

A collateral issue is the applicability of the attorney work-product privilege to witness statements. Within the civil discovery context, the Supreme Court has recognized at least a qualified privilege from civil discovery for such documents -- such material was held discoverable only upon a showing of necessity and justification.[239] Applying the "routinely and normally discoverable" test of Grolier and Weber Aircraft, the D.C. Circuit has firmly held that witness statements are protectible under Exemption 5.[240] Although some courts by contrast have held that witness statements are merely unprivileged factual information that must be segregated for disclosure,[241] the weight of authority supports the conclusion that the contours of Exemption 5's privilege incorporation are coextensive with the protective scope of the attorney work-product privilege.[242] Indeed, witness statements were the very records at issue in Hickman v. Taylor,[243] the seminal case in which the Supreme Court first articulated the attorney work-product privilege doctrine.[244]

Any such differences over the traditional protection accorded witness statements do not in any event affect the viability of protecting aircraft accident witness statements; such statements are protected under a distinct common law privilege that was first enunciated in Machin v. Zuckert[245] and

---

[238](...continued)
No. C-3-95-328, slip op. at 60-61 (S.D. Ohio Sept. 12, 1996) (ordering defendant to make affirmative showing that information for which it claimed privilege had been safeguarded against unauthorized disclosure).

[239] See Hickman, 329 U.S. at 511.

[240] See Martin, 819 F.2d at 1187.

[241] See, e.g., Uribe, 1989 U.S. Dist. LEXIS 5691, at *7 (declaring that statements made by plaintiff during his interrogation did not "represent the attorney's conclusions, recommendations and opinions"); Wayland v. NLRB, 627 F. Supp. 1473, 1476 (M.D. Tenn. 1986) (reasoning that because the witness statements in question were not shown to be other than an objective reporting of facts, they "do not reflect the attorney's theory of the case and his litigation strategy" and therefore cannot be protected).

[242] See FOIA Update, Vol. VIII, No. 2, at 4-5 ("OIP Guidance: Broad Protection for Witness Statements") (surveying case law on protection of witness statements).

[243] 329 U.S. 495 (1947).

[244] See id. at 512-13 ("Under ordinary conditions, forcing an attorney to repeat or write out all that witnesses have told him and to deliver the account to his adversary gives rise to grave dangers of inaccuracy and untrustworthiness. No legitimate purpose is served by such production.").

[245] 316 F.2d 336, 338 (D.C. Cir. 1963).

then was applied under the FOIA in Weber Aircraft.[246] (See the discussion under Exemption 5, Other Privileges, below.)

As a final point, it should be noted that the Supreme Court's decision in Grolier resolved a split in the circuits by ruling that the termination of litigation does not vitiate the protection for material otherwise properly categorized as attorney work-product.[247] Thus, as a matter of law, there is no temporal limitation on work-product protection under the FOIA.[248] However, such protection may be vitiated if the withholding of attorney work-product material would also shield from disclosure the unprofessional practices of an attorney by whom or under whose direction the material was prepared.[249] Otherwise, there is no "public interest" exception to the appli-

---

[246] 465 U.S. at 799; see also Badhwar v. U.S. Dep't of the Air Force, 829 F.2d 182, 185 (D.C. Cir. 1987) ("[T]he disclosure of 'factual' information that may have been volunteered would defeat the policy on which the Machin privilege is based.").

[247] 462 U.S. at 28; cf. Clark-Cowlitz Joint Operating Agency v. FERC, 798 F.2d 499, 502-03 (D.C. Cir. 1986) (en banc) (reaching same result under Government in the Sunshine Act, 5 U.S.C. § 552b (2000 & Supp. III 2003)).

[248] See Gutman v. U.S. Dep't of Justice, 238 F. Supp. 2d 284, 294-95 (D.D.C. 2003) (holding that attorney work-product privilege applies to documents prepared to advise Attorney General that government had appealed judge's decision to release requester on bond, even though by time of FOIA litigation requester had been convicted and was serving prison sentence); see also FOIA Update, Vol. IV, No. 3, at 1-2 (discussing Supreme Court's rejection in Grolier of any temporal limitation on attorney work-product privilege).

[249] See Moody v. IRS, 654 F.2d 795, 801 (D.C. Cir. 1981) (remanding to the district court for an evaluation of the attorney's conduct and, "if it is found [to be] in violation of professional standards, a determination of whether his breach of professional standards vitiated the work product privilege" otherwise applicable to the withheld material); see also Rashid, No. 99-2461, slip op. at 7-8 (D.D.C. June 12, 2001) ("While there are cases in which a lawyer's conduct may render inapplicable the work-product privilege . . . this is clearly not one of them."); cf. Alexander v. FBI, 198 F.R.D. 306, 311 (D.D.C. 2000) (holding, in non-FOIA case, that plaintiff could not overcome attorney-client privilege because it had not shown that defendant had sought counsel for purpose of furthering crime or fraud). But cf. NARA v. Favish, 541 U.S. 157, 174 (holding that where a FOIA requester makes an allegation of government misconduct in an effort to overcome a privacy interest under Exemption 7(C), "bare suspicion" is not enough, because "the requester must produce evidence that would warrant a belief by a reasonable person that the alleged Government impropriety might [actually] have occurred"), reh'g denied, 541 U.S. 1057 (2004); MacLean, No. 04-CV-2245, slip op. at 7-9 (S.D. Cal. June 6, 2005) (rejecting claim that deliberative

(continued...)

cation of the work-product privilege[250] under Exemption 5.[251]

## Attorney-Client Privilege

The third traditional privilege incorporated into Exemption 5 concerns "confidential communications between an attorney and his client relating to a legal matter for which the client has sought professional advice."[252] Unlike the attorney work-product privilege, the attorney-client privilege is not limited to the context of litigation.[253] Moreover, although it fundamentally applies to facts divulged by a client to his attorney, this privilege also encompasses any opinion given by an attorney to his client based upon, and thus reflecting, those facts,[254] as well as communications

---

[249](...continued)
process privilege is rendered inoperable if there is "any reason" to believe that governmental misconduct took place).

[250] See Winterstein, 89 F. Supp. 2d at 82.

[251] See Attorney General Ashcroft's FOIA Memorandum, reprinted in FOIA Post (posted 10/15/01) (emphasizing importance and viability of privileges that are applicable under Exemption 5).

[252] Mead Data Cent., Inc. v. U.S. Dep't of the Air Force, 566 F.2d 242, 252 (D.C. Cir. 1977).

[253] See, e.g., Mead Data, 566 F.2d at 252-53 (distinguishing attorney-client privilege from attorney work-product privilege, which is limited to litigation context); Elec. Privacy Info. Ctr. v. DHS, 384 F. Supp. 2d 100, 114 (D.D.C. 2005) (citing Mead Data and Crooker v. ATF); Crooker v. IRS, No. 94-0755, 1995 WL 430605, at *7 (D.D.C. Apr. 27, 1995) ("Unlike [with] the work product privilege, an agency may claim the attorney-client privilege for information outside the context of litigation.").

[254] See, e.g., Jernigan v. Dep't of the Air Force, No. 97-35930, 1998 WL 658662, at *2 (9th Cir. Sept. 17, 1998) (holding that privilege covers agency attorney's legal review of internal "Social Action" investigation); Schlefer v. United States, 702 F.2d 233, 244 n.26 (D.C. Cir. 1983) (observing that privilege "permits nondisclosure of an attorney's opinion or advice in order to protect the secrecy of the underlying facts"); Elec. Privacy Info. Ctr., 384 F. Supp. 2d at 114 (noting that privilege protects attorney's advice based upon facts provided by client); MacLean v. DOD, No. 04-2425, slip op. at 10 (S.D. Cal. June 2, 2005) (noting that privilege applies both to confidential facts supplied by client as well as to attorney's advice based on those facts); W & T Offshore, Inc. v. U.S. Dep't of Commerce, No. 03-2285, 2004 WL 2115418, at *4 (E.D. La. Sept. 21, 2004) (applying privilege to documents reflecting confidential communications between agency employees and agency counsel); Kelly v. CIA, No. 00-2498, slip op. at 21-22 (D.D.C. Aug. 8, 2002) (applying privilege to advice provided by CIA's counsel to CIA deputy director concerning CIA's budget, which is not matter of public
(continued...)

between attorneys[255] that reflect client-supplied information.[256] While the privilege typically involves a single client (even where the "client" is an agency) and his, her, or its attorneys, it also applies in situations where

---

[254](...continued)
record); Barmes v. IRS, 60 F. Supp. 2d 896, 901 (S.D. Ind. 1998) (protecting material "prepared by an IRS attorney in response to a request by a revenue officer to file certain liens pursuant to collection efforts against the plaintiffs"); Wishart v. Comm'r, No. 97-20614, 1998 U.S. Dist. LEXIS, at *16 (N.D. Cal. Aug. 6, 1998) (stating that privilege protects documents "created by attorneys and by the individually-named [defendant] employees for purposes of obtaining legal representation from the government"), aff'd, 1999 WL 985142 (9th Cir. Oct. 18, 1999); Cujas v. IRS, No. 1:97CV00741, 1998 U.S. Dist. LEXIS 6466, at *19 (M.D.N.C. Apr. 15, 1998) (holding that privilege encompasses "notes of a revenue officer . . . reflecting the confidential legal advice that the agency's District Counsel orally gave the officer in response to a proposed course of action"), aff'd, No. 98-1641 (4th Cir. Aug. 25, 1998); Ludsin v. SBA, No. 96-2865, slip op. at 3 (D.D.C. Apr. 24, 1997) (holding that privilege covers intra-agency memoranda containing agency attorney's "legal conclusions and reasoning"); Linn v. U.S. Dep't of Justice, No. 92-1406, 1995 WL 631847, at *32-33 (D.D.C. Aug. 22, 1995) (protecting confidential legal advice given in course of grand jury investigation); NBC v. SBA, 836 F. Supp. 121, 124-25 (S.D.N.Y. 1993) (holding that privilege covers "professional advice given by attorney that discloses" information given by client); cf. Direct Response Consulting Serv. v. IRS, No. 94-1156, 1995 WL 623282, at *3 (D.D.C. Aug. 21, 1995) (finding privilege inapplicable to attorney's memoranda to file which were never communicated to client). But see Lee v. FDIC, 923 F. Supp. 451, 457-58 (S.D.N.Y. 1996) (declaring that documents containing only "standard legal analysis" are not covered by privilege); cf. Brinton v. Dep't of State, 636 F.2d 600, 603 (D.C. Cir. 1980) ("[I]t is clear that when an attorney conveys to his client facts acquired from other persons or sources, those facts are not privileged" unless they reflect client confidences.).

[255] See Gordon v. FBI, 388 F. Supp. 2d 1028, 1039 (N.D. Cal. 2005) (holding that privilege did not extend to e-mail exchange where there was no evidence that attorney was party to it).

[256] See, e.g., Elec. Privacy Info. Ctr., 384 F. Supp. 2d at 114; Judicial Watch, Inc. v. U.S. Dep't of Commerce, 337 F. Supp. 2d 146, 174 (D.D.C. 2004) (applying privilege to documents written by agency attorneys to their superiors describing advice given to clients within agency); McErlean v. U.S. Dep't of Justice, No. 97-7831, 1999 WL 791680, at *7 (S.D.N.Y. Sept. 30, 1999); Buckner v. IRS, No. 1:97-CV-414, 1998 U.S. Dist. LEXIS 12449, at *19 (N.D. Ind. July 24, 1998); Green v. IRS, 556 F. Supp. 79, 85 (N.D. Ind. 1982), aff'd, 734 F.2d 18 (7th Cir. 1984) (unpublished table decision). But see Nat'l Res. Def. Council v. DOD, 388 F. Supp. 2d 1086, 1099 (C.D. Cal. 2005) (noting that privilege requires that withheld documents reflect confidential communication between agency and its attorneys, not merely that they be exchanges between agency and its attorneys).

there are multiple clients who share a common interest.[257]

The Supreme Court, in the civil discovery context, has emphasized the public policy underlying the attorney-client privilege -- "that sound legal advice or advocacy serves public ends and that such advice or advocacy depends upon the lawyer's being fully informed by the client."[258] As is set out in detail in the discussion of the attorney work-product privilege above, the Supreme Court held in United States v. Weber Aircraft Corp.[259] and in FTC v. Grolier Inc.[260] that the scopes of the various privileges are coextensive in the FOIA and civil discovery contexts.[261] Thus, any FOIA decision that might purport to expand or contract the privilege's contours according to whether the privilege is presented in a civil discovery or a FOIA context[262] does not accurately reflect the state of the law on this issue.[263] Finally, just as in the discovery context, the privilege can be waived by the client, who "owns" it, but it cannot be waived unilaterally by the at-

---

[257] See, e.g., Hanson v. U.S. Agency for Int'l Dev., 372 F.3d 286, 292 (4th Cir. 2004) (holding that privilege applies to documents created by attorney hired by private agency in contractual relationship with agency and, by agreement, then shared between contractor and agency, who had common interest in ongoing contractual dispute); Cavallaro v. United States, 284 F.3d 236, 249-50 (1st Cir. 2002) (discussing "common interest" doctrine invoked when multiple clients consult attorney on matter of mutual interest) (non-FOIA case); Sheet Metal Workers Int'l Ass'n v. Sweeney, 29 F.3d 120, 124 (4th Cir. 1994) (noting that "joint defense rule" protects confidential exchanges between parties having common interest in litigation) (non-FOIA case); Coffin v. Bowater, No. 03-227, 2005 WL 1412116, at *4 (D. Me. June 14, 2005) (citing Cavallaro as basis for evaluating privilege claim for documents exchanged between multiple parties) (non-FOIA case).

[258] Upjohn Co. v. United States, 449 U.S. 383, 389 (1981); see also FOIA Update, Vol. VI, No. 2, at 3-4 ("OIP Guidance: The Attorney-Client Privilege"); cf. Swidler & Berlin v. United States, 524 U.S. 399, 407 (1998) (addressing the privilege in the context of a criminal investigation, and observing that "there is no case authority for the proposition that the privilege applies differently [with respect to applicability after client's death] in criminal and civil cases").

[259] 465 U.S. 792 (1984).

[260] 462 U.S. 19 (1983).

[261] 465 U.S. at 799-800; 462 U.S. at 26-28; cf. In re Lindsey, 148 F.3d 1100, 1114 (D.C. Cir. 1998) (stating that, in criminal context, "government attorney-client privilege" does not shield "information related to criminal misconduct") (non-FOIA case); In re Grand Jury Subpoena Duces Tecum, 112 F.3d 910, 921 (8th Cir. 1997) (same) (non-FOIA case).

[262] See, e.g., Mead Data, 566 F.2d at 255 & n.28.

[263] See FOIA Update, Vol. VI, No. 2, at 3-4.

torney.[264]

The parallelism of a civil discovery privilege and Exemption 5 protection is particularly significant with respect to the concept of a "confidential communication" within the attorney-client relationship. To this end, one court has held that confidentiality may be inferred when the communications suggest that "'the government is dealing with its attorneys as would any private party seeking advice to protect personal interests.'"[265] In Upjohn Co. v. United States, the Supreme Court held that the attorney-client privilege covers attorney-client communications when the specifics of the communication are confidential, even though the underlying subject matter is known to third parties.[266] This decision effectively overruled several earlier decisions from the Court of Appeals for the District of Columbia Circuit

---

[264] See Hanson, 372 F.3d at 293-94 (holding that agency attorney's unauthorized release of otherwise privileged document, though it breached document's confidentiality, did not prevent agency from invoking privilege).

[265] Coastal States Gas Corp. v. Dep't of Energy, 617 F.2d 854, 863 (D.C. Cir. 1980)). But see also Maine v. U.S. Dep't of the Interior, 298 F.3d 60, 71-72 (1st Cir. 2002) (amended opinion) (holding that district court did not err in finding privilege inapplicable where defendants failed to show confidentiality of factual communications); Mead Data, 566 F.2d at 252-53 (requiring government to make affirmative showing of confidentiality for privilege to apply); Canning v. U.S. Dep't of Justice, No. 01-2215, slip op. at 16 (D.D.C. Mar. 9, 2004) (holding that, even apart from threshold concerns, privilege could not apply to document exchanged between private attorney and client but now properly held in agency files, because confidentiality had been breached); Dow, Lohnes & Albertson v. Presidential Comm'n on Broad. to Cuba, 624 F. Supp. 572, 578 (D.D.C. 1984) (holding that confidentiality must be shown in order to properly invoke Exemption 5); cf. Brinton v. Dep't of State, 636 F.2d 600, 605 (D.C. Cir. 1980) (holding district court record insufficient to support claim of privilege because it contained "no finding that the communications are based on or related to confidences from the client"); Dayton Newspapers, Inc. v. U.S. Dep't of the Navy, No. C-3-95-328, slip op. at 59 (S.D. Ohio Sept. 12, 1996) (ordering agency to make affirmative showing that information for which it claimed privilege had been safeguarded against unauthorized disclosure).

[266] 449 U.S. at 395-96; see also United States v. Cunningham, 672 F.2d 1064, 1073 n.8 (2d Cir. 1982); In re Diet Drugs Prods. Liability Litig., No. 1203, 2000 WL 1545028, at *5 (E.D. Pa. Oct. 12, 2000) ("While the underlying facts discussed in these communications may not be privileged, the communications themselves are privileged."); Judicial Watch, Inc. v. Comm'n on U.S.-Pac. Trade & Inv. Policy, No. 97-0099, slip op. at 17 (D.D.C. Sept. 30, 1999) (citing Upjohn); In re Ampicillin Antitrust Litig., 81 F.R.D. 377, 388 (D.D.C. 1978) (holding that privilege applies even where information in question was not confidential, so long as client intended that information be conveyed confidentially).

which had followed a different rule on this point.[267]

The Supreme Court in Upjohn concluded that the privilege encompasses confidential communications made to the attorney not only by decisionmaking "control group" personnel, but also by lower-echelon employees.[268] This broad construction of the attorney-client privilege acknowledges the reality that such lower-echelon personnel often possess information relevant to an attorney's advice-rendering function.[269] However, in 1997 the D.C. Circuit held that otherwise confidential agency memoranda are not protected under the privilege if they are authoritative interpretations of agency law,[270] a holding that was recently reinforced by the Second Circuit Court of Appeals.[271]

### Other Privileges

The FOIA neither expands nor contracts existing privileges, nor does it create any new privileges.[272] However, the Supreme Court has indicated that Exemption 5 may incorporate virtually all civil discovery privileges; if a document is immune from civil discovery, it is similarly protected from

---

[267] See, e.g., Brinton, 636 F.2d at 604; Mead Data, 566 F.2d at 255. But see Tax Analysts v. IRS, 117 F.3d 607, 618-20 (D.C. Cir. 1997) (following rule contrary to Upjohn); Schlefer, 702 F.2d at 245 (same).

[268] 449 U.S. at 392-97.

[269] See id.; see also Sherlock v. United States, No. 93-0650, 1994 WL 10186, at *3 (E.D. La. Jan. 12, 1994) (holding privilege applicable to communications from collection officer to district counsel); Murphy v. TVA, 571 F. Supp. 502, 506 (D.D.C. 1983) (holding that circulation of information within agency to employees involved in matter for which advice sought does not breach confidentiality); LSB Indus. v. Comm'r, 556 F. Supp. 40, 43 (W.D. Okla. 1982) (protecting information provided by agency investigators and used by agency attorneys).

[270] See Tax Analysts, 117 F.3d at 619-20.

[271] See Nat'l Council of La Raza v. U.S. Dep't of Justice, 411 F.3d 350, 360-61 (2d Cir. 2005) (stating that attorney-client privilege's rationale of protecting confidential communications is inoperative for documents that reflect actual agency policy); see also Robert v. HHS, No. 01-CV-4778, 2005 WL 1861755, at *5 (E.D.N.Y. Aug. 1, 2005) (citing La Raza though at same time finding that withheld documents did not reflect agency policy).

[272] See Ass'n for Women in Sci. v. Califano, 566 F.2d 339, 342 (D.C. Cir. 1977); see also Badhwar v. U.S. Dep't of the Air Force, 829 F.2d 182, 184 (D.C. Cir. 1987) ("To decide [whether a recognized privilege should be abandoned] in a FOIA case would be inappropriate, as Exemption 5 requires the application of existing rules regarding discovery, not their reformulation.").

mandatory disclosure under the FOIA.[273] Because Rule 501 of the Federal Rules of Evidence allows courts to create privileges as necessary,[274] there exists the potential for "new privileges" to be applied under Exemption 5.[275] However, one major caveat should be noted in the application of any discovery privilege under the FOIA: A privilege should not be used against a requester who would routinely receive such information in civil discovery.[276]

A quarter century ago, in Federal Open Market Committee v. Mer-

---

[273] See United States v. Weber Aircraft Corp., 465 U.S. 792, 799-800 (1984); FTC v. Grolier Inc., 462 U.S. 19, 26-27 (1983). But see Ctr. for Individual Rights v. U.S. Dep't of Justice, No. 03-1706, slip op. at 5 (D.D.C. June 29, 2004) (holding that documents protected from disclosure in another action pursuant to joint defense privilege could still be subject to disclosure under FOIA), dismissed as moot, slip op. at 11-12 (D.D.C. Sept. 21, 2004).

[274] See Trammel v. United States, 445 U.S. 40, 47 (1980); see, e.g., Goodyear Tire & Rubber Co. v. Chiles Power Supply, Inc., 332 F.3d 976, 980 (6th Cir. 2003) (recognizing, in a non-FOIA case, the settlement-negotiation privilege, which "fosters a more efficient, more cost-effective, and significantly less burdened judicial system"); Dellwood Farms, Inc. v. Cargill, Inc., 128 F.3d 1122, 1124-25 (7th Cir. 1997) (recognizing judge-fashioned "law enforcement investigatory privilege") (non-FOIA case); Kientzy v. McDonnell Douglas Corp., 133 F.R.D. 570, 571-73 (E.D. Mo. 1991) (recognizing "ombudsman privilege" under Rule 501 of Federal Rules of Evidence) (non-FOIA case); Shabazz v. Scurr, 662 F. Supp. 90, 92 (S.D. Iowa 1987) (same) (non-FOIA case); see also In re Sealed Case, 121 F.3d 729, 751-52 (D.C. Cir. 1997) (recognizing "presidential communications privilege" that applies to "communications made by presidential advisers in the course of preparing advice for the President . . . even when these communications are not made directly to the President") (non-FOIA case). But cf. In re Sealed Case, 148 F.3d 1073, 1079 (D.C. Cir. 1998) (declining to recognize proposed "protective function privilege") (non-FOIA case).

[275] See, e.g., FOIA Update, Vol. VI, No. 4, at 3-4 (suggesting that new privilege for settlement-negotiation records should be recognized under the FOIA). But see also Burka v. HHS, 87 F.3d 508, 517 (D.C. Cir. 1996) (holding that for record to be found privileged, agency must show that it is protected in discovery for reasons similar to those used by agency in FOIA context).

[276] See, e.g., U.S. Dep't of Justice v. Julian, 486 U.S. 1, 9 (1988) (holding that presentence report privilege, designed to protect report's subjects, cannot be invoked against them as first-party requesters); cf. Badhwar, 829 F.2d at 184 ("Exemption 5 requires application of existing rules regarding discovery, not their reformulation.").

rill,[277] the Supreme Court found an additional privilege incorporated within Exemption 5 based upon Federal Rule of Civil Procedure 26(c)(7), which provides that "for good cause shown . . . a trade secret or other confidential research, development or commercial information" is protected from discovery. This qualified privilege is available "at least to the extent that this information is generated by the Government itself in the process leading up to the awarding of a contract" and expires upon the awarding of the contract or upon the withdrawal of the offer.[278] The theory underlying the privilege is that early release of such information would likely put the government at a competitive disadvantage by endangering consummation of a contract; consequently, "the sensitivity of the commercial secrets involved, and the harm that would be inflicted upon the Government by premature disclosure should . . . serve as relevant criteria."[279]

This harm rationale has led one court to hold that the commercial privilege may be invoked when a contractor who has submitted proposed changes to the contract requests sensitive cost estimates.[280] Based upon this underlying theory, there is nothing in Merrill to prevent it from being read more expansively to protect the government from competitive disadvantage outside of the contract setting, as the issue in Merrill was not presented strictly within such a setting.[281] However, the Court of Appeals for the District of Columbia Circuit has declined to extend this privilege to scientific research, holding that the agency failed to show that such material is "generally protected in civil discovery for reasons similar to those asserted in the FOIA context."[282]

While the breadth of this privilege is still not fully established, a realty appraisal generated by the government in the course of soliciting buyers

---

[277] 443 U.S. 340 (1979).

[278] Id. at 360.

[279] Id. at 363.

[280] Taylor Woodrow Int'l v. United States, No. 88-429, 1989 WL 1095561, at *3 (W.D. Wash. Apr. 5, 1989) (concluding that disclosure would permit requester to take "unfair commercial advantage" of agency).

[281] See 443 U.S. at 360.

[282] Burka, 87 F.3d at 517; see also Sw. Ctr. for Biological Diversity v. USDA, 170 F. Supp. 2d 931, 942-43 (D. Ariz. 2000) (rejecting proposed "research data privilege" on basis that such information is routinely discoverable in civil litigation), aff'd on other grounds, 314 F.3d 1060 (9th Cir. 2002). But see Hornbostel v. U.S. Dep't of the Interior, 305 F. Supp. 2d 21, 32-33 (D.D.C. 2003) (citing Burka and recognizing privilege for "confidential research information," but refusing to allow withholding of documents under it because agency had not satisfied its burden of demonstrating that privilege was being used in FOIA context for reasons similar to its use in civil discovery context).

for its property has been held to fall squarely within it,[283] as have documents containing communications between agency personnel, potential buyers, and real estate agents concerning a proposed sale of government-owned real estate,[284] an agency's background documents which it used to calculate its bid in a "contracting out" procedure,[285] and portions of inter-agency cost estimates prepared by the government for use in the evaluation of construction proposals submitted by private contractors.[286] Quite clearly, however, purely legal memoranda drafted to assist contract-award deliberations are not encompassed by this privilege.[287]

The Supreme Court in United States v. Weber Aircraft Corp.[288] held that Exemption 5 incorporates the special privilege protecting witness statements generated during Air Force aircraft accident investigations.[289] Broadening the holding of Merrill that a privilege "mentioned in the legis-

---

[283] See Gov't Land Bank v. GSA, 671 F.2d 663, 665-66 (1st Cir. 1982) ("FOIA should not be used to allow the government's customers to pick the taxpayers' pockets.").

[284] See Marriott Employees' Fed. Credit Union v. Nat'l Credit Union Admin., No. 96-478-A, slip op. at 3 (E.D. Va. Dec. 24, 1996).

[285] See Morrison-Knudsen Co. v. Dep't of the Army of the United States, 595 F. Supp. 352, 354-56 (D.D.C. 1984), aff'd, 762 F.2d 138 (D.C. Cir. 1985) (unpublished table decision); see also FOIA Post, "FOIA Counselor Q&A" (posted 1/24/06) (discussing Morrison-Knudsen and advising that agencies may invoke commercial privilege to protect "A-76 documents," which reflect government's position in commercial bargaining process).

[286] See Hack v. Dep't of Energy, 538 F. Supp. 1098, 1104 (D.D.C. 1982); see also FOIA Update, Vol. IV, No. 4, at 14-15. But see Am. Soc'y of Pension Actuaries v. Pension Benefit Guar. Corp., No. 82-2806, slip op. at 3-4 (D.D.C. July 22, 1983) (distinguishing Merrill). See generally Steven W. Feldman, The Government's Commercial Data Privilege Under Exemption Five of the Freedom of Information Act, 105 Mil. L. Rev. 125 (1984); Theodore T. Belazis, The Government's Commercial Information Privilege: Technical Information and the FOIA's Exemption 5, 33 Admin. L. Rev. 415 (1981).

[287] See Shermco Indus. v. Sec'y of the Air Force, 613 F.2d 1314, 1319-20 n.11 (5th Cir. 1980); see also News Group Boston, Inc. v. Nat'l R.R. Passenger Corp., 799 F. Supp. 1264, 1270 (D. Mass. 1992) (finding affidavits insufficient to show why Amtrak payroll information is covered by privilege), appeal dismissed voluntarily, No. 92-2250 (1st Cir. Dec. 4, 1992).

[288] 465 U.S. at 799.

[289] See id. at 798-99 (noting that privilege for accident investigation privilege was first recognized in Machin v. Zuckert, 316 F.2d 336, 338 (D.C. Cir. 1963), and holding that it applies in FOIA context as well).

lative history of Exemption 5 is incorporated by the exemption,"[290] the Court held in Weber Aircraft that this long-recognized civil discovery privilege, even though not specifically mentioned in that legislative history, nevertheless falls within Exemption 5.[291] The "plain statutory language"[292] and the clear congressional intent to sustain claims of privilege when confidentiality is necessary to ensure efficient governmental operations[293] support this result.[294] This privilege also has been applied to protect statements made in Inspector General investigations.[295]

Similarly, in Hoover v. Department of the Interior, the Court of Appeals for the Fifth Circuit recognized an Exemption 5 privilege based on Federal Rule of Civil Procedure 26(b)(4), which limits the discovery of reports prepared by expert witnesses.[296] The document at issue in Hoover was an appraiser's report prepared in the course of condemnation proceedings.[297] In support of its conclusions, the Fifth Circuit stressed that such a report would not have been routinely discoverable and that premature release would jeopardize the bargaining position of the government.[298]

Most recently, in Judicial Watch, Inc. v. Department of Justice, the D.C. Circuit applied the presidential communications privilege under Ex-

---

[290] Weber Aircraft, 465 U.S. at 800.

[291] Id. at 804; see also FOIA Update, Vol. V, No. 2, at 12-13.

[292] 465 U.S. at 802.

[293] See id.

[294] See also Badhwar, 829 F.2d at 185 (privilege applied to contractor report).

[295] See Ahearn v. U.S. Army Materials & Mechs. Research Ctr., 583 F. Supp. 1123, 1124 (D. Mass. 1984); see also Walsh v. Dep't of the Navy, No. 91-C-7410, 1992 WL 67845, at *4 (N.D. Ill. Mar. 23, 1992); AFGE v. Dep't of the Army, 441 F. Supp. 1308, 1313 (D.D.C. 1977). But see Nickerson v. United States, No. 95-C-7395, 1996 WL 563465, at *3 (N.D. Ill. Oct. 1, 1996) (holding privilege not applicable to statements made in course of medical malpractice investigation); Wash. Post Co. v. U.S. Dep't of the Air Force, 617 F. Supp. 602, 606-07 (D.D.C. 1985) (finding privilege inapplicable when report format provided anonymity to witnesses).

[296] 611 F.2d 1132, 1141 (5th Cir. 1980).

[297] Id. at 1135.

[298] Id. at 1142; cf. Chem. Mfrs. Ass'n v. Consumer Prod. Safety Comm'n, 600 F. Supp. 114, 118-19 (D.D.C. 1984) (observing that Rule 26(b)(4) provides parallel protection in civil discovery for opinions of expert witnesses who do not testify at trial).

emption 5 of the FOIA to protect Department of Justice records regarding the President's exercise of his constitutional power to grant pardons.[299] This privilege, which protects communications among the President and his advisors, is unique among those recognized under Exemption 5 of the FOIA in that it is "'inextricably rooted in the separation of powers under the Constitution.'"[300] Although similar to the deliberative process privilege, it is broader in its coverage because it "'applies to documents in their entirety, and covers final and post-decisional materials as well as pre-deliberative ones.'"[301]

In a further exploration of the contours of this privilege, the District Court for the Eastern District of California rejected a FOIA requester's dual arguments that (1) the privilege must be invoked by the President himself[302] and (2) that the privilege could be lost simply due to the passage of time.[303] As the court noted, the privilege is itself a qualified privilege, meaning that in the civil discovery context it can be overcome by a showing of need.[304] In the FOIA context, however, such a requirement would impermissibly run afoul of the Supreme Court's "routinely and normally discoverable" test as set forth in FTC v. Grolier Inc.[305] and United States v. Weber Aircraft Corp.,[306] so the court accordingly ruled that the agency's invocation of the privilege had been proper.[307] One significant issue not yet ultimately resolved, though, is whether the privilege protects all records created within an agency to assist the President in the exercise of his non-delegable constitutional duties or is limited to those records that are "solicited and received by the President or his immediate advisers in the Office

---

[299] No. 03-5093, 2004 WL 980826, at *14 (D.C. Cir. May 7, 2004).

[300] 2004 WL 980826, at *4 (quoting United States v. Nixon, 418 U.S. 683, 708 (1974)).

[301] Id. (quoting In re Sealed Case, 121 F.3d at 745).

[302] See Berman v. CIA, 378 F. Supp. 2d 1209, 1220-21 (E.D. Cal. 2005) (concluding that such a requirement "would expose the President to considerable burden"); cf. Marriott Int'l Resorts, L.P. v. United States, 437 F.3d 1302, 1306-07 (Fed. Cir. 2006) (holding upon thorough review of question that authority to invoke deliberative process privilege need not be limited to head of agency, but rather may be delegated to another official) (non-FOIA case).

[303] See Berman, 378 F. Supp. 2d at 1221 (protecting documents created during Administration of President Lyndon B. Johnson).

[304] See id.

[305] 462 U.S. 19, 26 (1983).

[306] 465 U.S. 792, 799 (1984).

[307] See Berman, 378 F. Supp. 2d at 1222.

of the President."[308]

Prior to the Supreme Court's decision in <u>Department of the Interior v. Klamath Water Users Protective Association</u>,[309] several courts had held that communications reflecting settlement negotiations between the government and an adverse party, which are of necessity exchanged between the parties, could not be protected as "intra-agency" memoranda under Exemption 5.[310] However, several of those courts also recognized the great difficulties inherent in such a harsh Exemption 5 construction, especially in light of the "logic and force of [the] policy plea"[311] that the government's indispensable settlement mechanism can be impeded by such a result.[312]

---

[308] <u>Compare</u> <u>Judicial Watch</u>, 2004 WL 980826, at *14 (holding that privilege is limited to communications sent directly to the President or his immediate advisors in Office of the President), <u>with</u> <u>id.</u> at *19-22 (Randolph, J., dissenting) (urging that coverage be extended to intra-agency records that assist in the President's decisionmaking even though not sent to the President or his immediate staff).

[309] 532 U.S. 1 (2001).

[310] <u>See</u> <u>County of Madison v. U.S. Dep't of Justice</u>, 641 F.2d 1036, 1042 (1st Cir. 1981) (concluding that although "[w]e confess to feeling a sense of indecent exposure in countenancing a third[-]party adversary obtaining confidential exchanges between the Indians' attorneys and the government . . . we cannot agree that this means that [the] Indians are 'within' the Department of Justice"); <u>M/A-COM Info. Sys. v. HHS</u>, 656 F. Supp. 691, 692 (D.D.C. 1986) (applying the privilege under Exemption 4 but not under Exemption 5, on the basis that Exemption 5 "does not cover papers exchanged between a government agency and an outside adverse party . . . [but] by its terms covers only 'inter' or 'intra' agency documents"); <u>NAACP Legal Def. & Educ. Fund, Inc. v. U.S. Dep't of Justice</u>, 612 F. Supp. 1143, 1145-46 (D.D.C. 1985) (deciding that adversaries in litigation with an agency cannot "be viewed as being part of a federal agency or acting in consultation with the agency"); <u>Norwood v. FAA</u>, 580 F. Supp. 994, 1002-03 (W.D. Tenn. 1984) (citing <u>County of Madison</u> for proposition that settlement records are "not exempt as inter-agency or intra-agency memos") (on motion for clarification and reconsideration); <u>Ctr. for Auto Safety v. Dep't of Justice</u>, 576 F. Supp. 739, 747-49 (D.D.C. 1983) (holding that records "prepared by and disclosed or transmitted to" defendants in an antitrust case "are no longer 'inter-agency or intra-agency' documents and are [thus] beyond the scope" of Exemption 5).

[311] <u>County of Madison</u>, 641 F.2d at 1040.

[312] <u>See</u> <u>id.</u>; <u>see also, e.g.</u>, <u>Ctr. for Auto Safety</u>, 576 F. Supp. at 746 n.18 (quoting <u>County of Madison</u>, 641 F.2d at 1040); <u>Murphy v. TVA</u>, 571 F. Supp. 502, 506 (D.D.C. 1983) (observing that public policy favoring compromise over confrontation would be "seriously undermined" if internal doc-

(continued...)

Accordingly, one court has held that notes of an agency employee that reflected positions taken and issues raised in treaty negotiations had been properly withheld pursuant to Exemption 5 because their release would harm the agency's negotiation process.[313] Other courts have found the attorney work-product and deliberative process privileges to be properly invoked for documents prepared by agency personnel that reflected the substance of meetings between adverse parties and agency personnel in preparation for eventual settlement of a case.[314] Significantly, one court explicitly applied the settlement privilege to affirm the withholding of set-

---

[312](...continued)
uments reflecting employees' thoughts during course of negotiations were released); President George Washington, Message to United States House of Representatives, Mar. 30, 1796 (expounding authoritatively as well as presciently on need for secrecy in negotiations because of "pernicious influence" on future negotiations that could be occasioned by any public disclosure of such negotiations' substance); cf. Mark H. Grunewald, Freedom of Information and Confidentiality Under the Administrative Dispute Resolution Act, 9 Admin. L.J. 985 (1996) (discussing the governmental preference for settlement over litigation, the use of the Administrative Dispute Resolution Act, 5 U.S.C. §§ 571-83 (2000), to promote this goal, and the need for a statute protecting documents exchanged as part of ADRA proceedings from FOIA requests -- which was included as part of the 1996 amendments to the ADRA, 5 U.S.C. § 574(j) (2000)).

[313] Fulbright & Jaworski v. Dep't of the Treasury, 545 F. Supp. 615, 620 (D.D.C. 1982).

[314] See Coastal States Gas Corp. v. Dep't of Energy, 617 F.2d 854, 866 (D.C. Cir. 1980) (deliberative process privilege); Finkel v. HUD, No. 90-3106, 1995 WL 151790, at *3-4 (E.D.N.Y. Mar. 28, 1995) (deliberative process privilege), aff'd, No. 95-6112, 1996 U.S. App. LEXIS 2895, at *1 (2d Cir. Feb. 21, 1996); Wilson v. Dep't of Justice, No. 87-2415, slip op. at 8-11 (D.D.C. June 14, 1992) (attorney work-product privilege); Cities Serv. Co. v. FTC, 627 F. Supp. 827, 832 (D.D.C. 1984) (attorney work-product privilege), aff'd, 778 F.2d 889 (D.C. Cir. 1985) (unpublished table decision); see also FOIA Update, Vol. III, No. 3, at 10; cf. United States v. Metro. St. Louis Sewer Dist., 952 F.2d 1040, 1045 (8th Cir. 1992) (holding draft consent decrees covered by both deliberative process and attorney work-product privileges; remanded for determination of whether privileges waived); Greenberg v. U.S. Dep't of Treasury, 10 F. Supp. 2d 3, 17 (D.D.C. 1998) (remanding to agency for determination of whether document contained "evaluations" of settlement negotiation process covered by deliberative process privilege or merely nonprotectible "factual" descriptions). But cf. Mead Data Cent., Inc. v. U.S. Dep't of the Air Force, 566 F.2d 242, 257-58 (D.C. Cir. 1977) (finding that certain documents prepared by agency concerning negotiations failed to reveal any inter-agency deliberations and therefore were not withholdable).

tlement documents under Exemption 4.[315] Furthermore, Justice Brennan, noting the need for protecting attorney work-product information, specifically cited as a particular disclosure danger the ability of adverse parties to "gain insight into the agency's general strategic and tactical approach to deciding when suits are brought . . . and on what terms they may be settled."[316]

Finally, and most significantly, in 2003, the United States Court of Appeals for the Sixth Circuit was presented in Goodyear Tire & Rubber Co. v. Chiles Power Supply, Inc., a non-FOIA case, with the specific question of whether to recognize a civil discovery privilege for documents exchanged between parties in the course of settlement negotiations.[317] In making this determination, this appellate court quite properly considered the Supreme Court's directive to federal courts to recognize new discovery privileges when "reason and experience" show that there is a sufficiently strong public interest to be served by doing so.[318] Following this guidance by taking cognizance of the numerous and significant problems raised by the potential availability of settlement negotiation documents and of the inherent need to protect the confidentiality of such exchanges, the Sixth Circuit explicitly recognized a discovery privilege for documents exchanged between parties engaged in settlement negotiations.[319]

It is noteworthy in this regard that while earlier cases had not gone quite so far as to squarely recognize a settlement-negotiation privilege identified as such, many had ruled that parties making discovery demands for settlement communications would be required to make heightened, or "particularized," showings of relevancy in order to obtain them in civil dis-

---

[315] See M/A-COM, 656 F. Supp. at 692 (applying privilege under Exemption 4 to protect commercial information submitted to government in course of settlement negotiations).

[316] FTC v. Grolier Inc., 462 U.S. 19, 31 (1983) (Brennan, J., concurring) (emphasis added).

[317] 332 F.3d 976 (6th Cir. 2003).

[318] See Jaffee v. Redmond, 518 U.S. 1, 8-9 (1996) (discussing conditions under which new privileges may be recognized).

[319] See 332 F.3d at 981 ("[A]ny communications made in furtherance of settlement are privileged.") (emphasis added). But see In re Subpoena Issued to Commodity Futures Trading Comm'n, 370 F. Supp. 2d 201, 207 & n.7, 212 (D.D.C. 2005) (declining to recognize settlement privilege, in spite of Goodyear Tire), aff'd on alternative ground sub nom. In re Subpoena Duces Tecum Issued to Commodity Futures Trading Comm'n WD Energy Servs. Inc., 439 F.3d 740, 754-55 (D.C. Cir. 2006) (holding pointedly that "the district court lacked a sufficient factual context within which" to reach such a conclusion, and leaving the Sixth Circuit's recognition of the settlement privilege "open in this circuit").

covery.[320] Because settlement communications subject to such a discovery standard would not be "routinely and normally discoverable" under the test enunciated by the Supreme Court in Grolier[321] and Weber Aircraft,[322] they would also be protectible under Exemption 5 were the agency able to satisfy the elements of the threshold requirement.[323]

---

[320] See, e.g., Butta-Brinkman v. FCA Int'l, 164 F.R.D. 475, 477 (N.D. Ill. 1995) ("Absent a showing [that plaintiff] will be unable to obtain the relevant information through other discovery requests or interrogatories, we believe these settlement documents ought to retain their confidentiality."); SEC v. Thrasher, No. 92-6987, 1995 WL 552719, at *1 (S.D.N.Y. Sept. 18, 1995) (refusing to order production of settlement communications because discovering party failed to make compelling showing of need); Matsushita Elec. Corp. v. Loral Corp., No. 92-5461, 1995 WL 527640, at *4 (S.D.N.Y. Sept. 7, 1995) ("[I]t is reasonable to require that the discovering party, as the price for obtaining such potentially disruptive disclosure [of settlement communications], make a fairly compelling showing that it needs the information."); Riddell Sports, Inc. v. Brooks, No. 92-7851, 1995 WL 20260, at *1 (S.D.N.Y. Jan. 19, 1995) (holding that in absence of particularized showing that they are likely to lead to admissible evidence, documents concerning settlement are "presumed irrelevant and need not be produced"); Morse/ Diesel, Inc. v. Trinity Indus., Inc., 142 F.R.D. 80, 84 (S.D.N.Y. 1992) (concluding that the "particularized showing" requirement "places the burden of establishing relevance squarely on the party seeking production" of settlement communications); Bottaro v. Hatton Assocs., 96 F.R.D. 158, 159-60 (E.D.N.Y. 1982) (requiring a defendant to make "some particularized showing of a likelihood that admissible evidence will be generated by the dissemination of the terms of a settlement agreement"); see also FOIA Update, Vol. VI, No. 4, at 3-4 ("OIP Guidance: Protecting Settlement Negotiations") (establishing settlement-document protection policy); M/A-COM, 656 F. Supp. at 692 (applying privilege under Exemption 4); cf. Olin Corp. v. Ins. Co. of N. Am., 603 F. Supp. 445, 449-50 (S.D.N.Y. 1985) (affirming special master's determination that communications are protected by "settlement privilege"). But see Tribune Co. v. Purcigliotti, No. 93-7222, 1996 WL 337277, at *2 (S.D.N.Y. June 19, 1996) (concluding that "particularized showing" requirement "is neither binding on this Court nor has [it] been universally adopted in this Circuit"). See generally Richard L. Crisona & Richard A. Schwartz, For Discovery of Settlement Materials, Be Prepared to Demonstrate Relevance, 221 N.Y.L.J. 12 (1999) (criticizing "particularized showing" requirement, but noting its use by some courts).

[321] 462 U.S. 19, 26 (1983).

[322] 465 U.S. 792, 799 (1984).

[323] See FOIA Update, Vol. VI, No. 4, at 3-4 (describing judicial recognition of Exemption 5 privilege for settlement-negotiation communications); see also Attorney General Ashcroft's FOIA Memorandum, reprinted in FOIA Post (posted 10/15/01) (emphasizing importance of Exemption 5 in

(continued...)

Because Exemption 5 incorporates virtually all civil discovery privileges, courts also have recognized the applicability of other privileges, whether traditional or new, in the FOIA context.[324] Among those other privileges that are now recognized for purposes of the FOIA are the confidential report privilege,[325] the presentence report privilege,[326] the critical self-evaluative privilege,[327] the expert materials privilege,[328] and the federal

---

[323](...continued)
ensuring that "lawyers' deliberations and communications are kept private").

[324] See Martin v. Office of Special Counsel, 819 F.2d 1181, 1185 (D.C. Cir. 1987) (stating that Exemption 5 "unequivocally" incorporates "all civil discovery rules into FOIA"). But see also Burka v. HHS, 87 F.3d 508, 521 (D.C. Cir. 1996) (refusing to recognize the "confidential research information" privilege under the FOIA because it is not yet "established or well-settled . . . in the realm of civil discovery"); cf. Melendez-Colon v. Dep't of the Navy, 56 F. Supp. 2d 142, 145 (D.P.R. 1999) (rejecting the argument that the FOIA "creates a separate discovery or evidentiary privilege" that would bar plaintiff from using a document at an evidentiary hearing in a particular litigation case).

[325] See Wash. Post Co. v. HHS, 603 F. Supp. 235, 238-39 (D.D.C. 1985) (applying "confidential report" privilege under Exemption 4), rev'd on other grounds, 795 F.2d 205 (D.C. Cir. 1986).

[326] See Julian, 486 U.S. at 9 (recognizing privilege, but finding it applicable to third-party requesters only); United States v. Kipta, No. 97-638-1, 2001 WL 477153, at *1 (N.D. Ill. May 3, 2001) (citing Julian for proposition that, at least in absence of compelling justification, no third party "is to be given access to another person's [presentence investigation] report").

[327] See Wash. Post Co. v. U.S. Dep't of Justice, No. 84-3581, slip op. at 18-21 (D.D.C. Sept. 25, 1987) (magistrate's recommendation) (applying privilege under Exemption 4), adopted (D.D.C. Dec. 15, 1987), rev'd & remanded on other grounds, 863 F.2d 96 (D.C. Cir. 1988). But see Sangre de Cristo Animal Protection, Inc. v. Dep't of Energy, No. 96-1059, slip op. at 7-9 (D.N.M. Mar. 10, 1998) (declining to apply privilege to records of animal research facility, in light of Tenth Circuit's "cautious approach to expanding common law privileges"); cf. Tucker v. United States, 143 F. Supp. 2d 619, 626 (S.D. W. Va. 2001) (declining, in a non-FOIA case, to apply the privilege for medical peer review information, on the basis that "where Congress had the opportunity to create a privilege pursuant to statute, yet failed to do so, courts should be especially hesitant in recognizing a federal privilege").

[328] See Nissei Sangyo Am., Ltd. v. IRS, No. 95-1019, 1998 U.S. Dist. LEXIS 2966, at *2-3 (D.D.C. Jan. 28, 1998) (holding that because the Federal Rules of Civil Procedure "established a separate exception to discovery for expert materials . . . Exemption 5 of the FOIA . . . incorporates" it).

EXEMPTION 6

mediation privilege.[329]

Lastly, while it is evident that courts will continue to apply such civil discovery privileges under Exemption 5 of the FOIA, the mere fact that a particular privilege has been recognized by state law will not necessarily mean that it will be recognized by a federal court.[330]

## EXEMPTION 6

Personal privacy interests are protected by two provisions of the FOIA, Exemptions 6 and 7(C). While the application of Exemption 7(C), discussed below, is limited to information compiled for law enforcement purposes, Exemption 6 permits the government to withhold all information about individuals in "personnel and medical files and similar files" when the disclosure of such information "would constitute a clearly unwarranted invasion of personal privacy."[1] These exemptions are a vitally important part of the FOIA's statutory scheme,[2] but of course they cannot be invoked to withhold from a requester information pertaining only to himself.[3]

---

[329] See Sheldone v. Pa. Turnpike Comm'n, 104 F. Supp. 2d 511, 515 (W.D. Pa. 2000) (recognizing, in non-FOIA case, privilege for communications arising from mediation process); Folb v. Motion Picture Indus. Pension & Health Plans, 16 F. Supp. 2d 1164, 1180-81 (C.D. Cal. 1998) (holding, in non-FOIA case, that federal mediation privilege protects all communications exchanged in course of formal mediation proceeding), aff'd, 216 F.3d 1082 (9th Cir. 2000) (unpublished table decision); cf. 28 U.S.C. § 652(d) (2000) (requiring district courts to provide by local rule for confidentiality of alternative dispute resolution proceedings); 5 U.S.C. § 574(j) (2000) ("A dispute resolution communication which is between a neutral and a party and which may not be disclosed under this section shall also be exempt from disclosure under section 552(b)(3).").

[330] See, e.g., Sneirson v. Chem. Bank, 108 F.R.D. 159, 162 (D. Del. 1985) (non-FOIA case); Cincotta v. City of New York, No. 83-7506, 1984 WL 1210, at *1-2 (S.D.N.Y. Nov. 14, 1984) (non-FOIA case); cf. Brady-Lunny v. Massey, 185 F. Supp. 2d 928, 931 (C.D. Ill. 2002) (declining to order release under state law of any records that would be protected under FOIA).

[1] 5 U.S.C. § 552(b)(6) (2000 & Supp. IV 2004).

[2] See Attorney General's Memorandum for Heads of All Federal Departments and Agencies Regarding the Freedom of Information Act (Oct. 12, 2001), reprinted in FOIA Post (posted 10/15/01) (placing particular emphasis on the importance of "preserving personal privacy" among the other interests that are protected by the FOIA's exemptions).

[3] See H.R. Rep. No. 93-1380, at 13 (1974); U.S. Dep't of Justice v. Reporters Comm. for Freedom of the Press, 489 U.S. 749, 771 (1989) (citing U.S.
(continued...)

## Initial Considerations

To warrant protection under Exemption 6, information must first meet its threshold requirement; in other words, it must fall within the category of "personnel and medical files and similar files."[4] Personnel and medical files are easily identified, but there has not always been universal agreement about the meaning of the term "similar files." Prior to 1982, judicial interpretations of that phrase varied considerably and included a troublesome line of cases in the Court of Appeals for the District of Columbia Circuit, commencing with Board of Trade v. Commodity Futures Trading Commission,[5] which narrowly construed the term to encompass only "intimate" personal details.

In 1982, the Supreme Court acted decisively to resolve this controversy once and for all. In United States Department of State v. Washington Post Co.,[6] it firmly held, based upon a review of the legislative history of the FOIA, that Congress intended the term to be interpreted broadly, rather than narrowly.[7] The Court stated that the protection of an individual's privacy "surely was not intended to turn upon the label of the file which contains the damaging information."[8] Rather, the Court made clear that all information that "applies to a particular individual" meets the threshold requirement for Exemption 6 protection.[9] This means, of course, that this

---

[3](...continued)
Dep't of Justice v. Julian, 486 U.S. 1, 13-14 (1988)); Dean v. FDIC, 389 F. Supp. 2d 780, 794 (E.D. Ky. 2005) ("[T]o the extent that the defendants have redacted the 'name, address, and other identifying information' of the plaintiff himself in these documents . . . reliance on Exemption 6 or 7(C) would be improper."); see also FOIA Update, Vol. X, No. 2, at 5 (advising that, as a matter of sound administrative practice, "[a]n agency will not invoke an exemption to protect a requester from himself").

[4] 5 U.S.C. § 552(b)(6).

[5] 627 F.2d 392, 400 (D.C. Cir. 1980).

[6] 456 U.S. 595 (1982).

[7] Id. at 599-603 (citing H.R. Rep. No. 89-1497, at 11 (1966); S. Rep. No. 89-813, at 9 (1965); S. Rep. No. 88-1219, at 14 (1964)).

[8] Id. at 601 (citing H.R. Rep. No. 89-1497, at 11 (1966)); Judicial Watch, Inc. v. FDA, 449 F.3d 141, 152 (D.C. Cir. 2006) ("The Supreme Court has read Exemption 6 broadly, concluding the propriety of an agency's decision to withhold information does not 'turn upon the label of the file which contains the damaging information.'" (quoting Wash. Post, 456 U.S. at 601)).

[9] Id. at 602; see, e.g., Wood v. FBI, 432 F.3d 78, 86-87 (2d Cir. 2005) (overturning mistaken district court ruling by recognizing that personal information about government investigators appearing in investigative records are
(continued...)

[9](...continued)
indeed "similar files"); Lakin Law Firm, P.C. v. FTC, 352 F.3d 1122, 1123 (7th
Cir. 2003) (finding that consumer complaints filed with the FTC "clearly
fall[] within the exemption"), reh'g denied, No. 03-1689 (7th Cir. 2004); Sherman v. U.S. Dep't of the Army, 244 F.3d 357, 361 (5th Cir. 2001) (recognizing
that the "Supreme Court has interpreted exemption 6 'files' broadly to include any 'information which applies to a particular individual'" (quoting
Wash. Post, 456 U.S. at 601)); Strout v. U.S. Parole Comm'n, 40 F.3d 136, 139
(6th Cir. 1994) (protecting names and addresses of persons opposing parole of individual, without explicit discussion of threshold requirement);
O'Keefe v. DOD, 463 F. Supp. 2d 317, 326 (D.D.C. 2006) (concluding that investigative records at issue met threshold requirement for Exemption 6
protection); Balderrama v. DHS, No. 04-1617, 2006 WL 889778, at *9 (D.D.C.
Mar. 30, 2006) ("The Supreme Court has made clear that all information that
'applies to a particular individual' meets the threshold requirement for protection under Exemption 6."); Hornbeck Offshore Transp., LLC v. U.S. Coast
Guard, No. 04-1724, 2006 WL 696053, at *22 (D.D.C. Mar. 20, 2006) ("Courts
have broadly interpreted the term 'similar files' to include most information
applying to a particular individual."); Forest Serv. Employees for Envtl.
Ethics v. U.S. Forest Serv., No. 05-6015, 2005 WL 3488453, at *2 (D. Or. Dec.
21, 2005) (explaining that the Supreme Court "has given a broad definition
to 'similar file'"); In Def. of Animals v. HHS, No. 99-3024, 2001 U.S. Dist.
LEXIS 24975, at *15 (D.D.C. Sept. 28, 2001) (recognizing that names of research foundation members are "similar files"); Hecht v. U.S. Agency for Int'l
Dev., No. 95-263, 1996 WL 33502232, at *12 (D. Del. Dec. 18, 1996) ("We do
not think that Congress meant to limit Exemption 6 to a narrow class of
files containing only a discrete kind of personal information."). But see
Leadership Conference on Civil Rights v. Gonzales, 404 F. Supp. 2d 246,
257 (D.D.C. 2005) (finding erroneously that the names and work telephone
numbers of Justice Department paralegals do not meet the threshold for
Exemption 6 on the basis that information is not "similar to a 'personnel' or
'medical' file"), motion to amend denied, 421 F. Supp. 2d 104, 107-10 (D.D.C.
2006) (denying defendants' motion to alter or amend judgment; reaffirming
erroneous conclusion that Exemption 6 is inapplicable on basis that names
and telephone numbers of Justice Department paralegals are not similar to
"personnel" or "medical" files), appeal dismissed voluntarily, No. 06-5055,
2006 WL 1214937 (D.C. Cir. Apr. 28, 2006); Gordon v. FBI, 390 F. Supp. 2d
897, 902 (N.D. Cal. 2004) (deciding mistakenly that names of agency employees are not personal information about those employees that meets Exemption 6 threshold), summary judgment granted, 388 F. Supp. 2d 1028,
1040-42 (N.D. Cal. 2005) (concluding that Exemption 6 does not apply to
the names of agency's "lower-level" employees, and likewise opining that
"[t]he [agency] still has not demonstrated that an employee's name alone
makes a document a personnel, medical or 'similar file'"); Darby v. U.S. Dep't
of the Air Force, No. 00-0661, slip op. at 10-11 (D. Nev. Mar. 1, 2002) (rejecting redaction of names in IG report on basis that such documents "are not
'personnel or medical files[,]' nor are they 'similar' to such files"), aff'd on
(continued...)

threshold is met if the information applies to any particular, identifiable individual -- which makes it readily satisfied in all but the most unusual cases of questionable identifiability.[10]

The D.C. Circuit, sitting en banc, subsequently reinforced the Supreme Court's broad interpretation of this term by holding that a tape recording of the last words of the Space Shuttle Challenger crew, which "reveal[ed] the sound and inflection of the crew's voices during the last seconds of their lives . . . contains personal information the release of which is subject to the balancing of the public gain against the private harm at which it is purchased."[11] Not only did the D.C. Circuit determine that "lexi

---

[9](...continued)
other grounds sub nom. Darby v. DOD, 74 F. App'x 813 (9th Cir. 2003); Providence Journal Co. v. U.S. Dep't of the Army, 781 F. Supp. 878, 883 (D.R.I. 1991) (finding investigative report of criminal charges not to be "similar file," on basis that it was "created in response to specific criminal allegations" rather than as "regularly compiled administrative record"), modified & aff'd on other grounds, 981 F.2d 552 (1st Cir. 1992); see also Judicial Watch, Inc. v. United States, 84 F. App'x 335, 340-41 (4th Cir. 2004) (opining that IRS employee names do not meet Exemption 6 threshold) (Luttig, J., dissenting).

[10] See, e.g., Arieff v. U.S. Dep't of the Navy, 712 F.2d 1462, 1467-68 (D.C. Cir. 1983) (finding no protection under Exemption 6 for list of drugs ordered for use by some members of large group); VoteHemp, Inc. v. DEA, No. 02-985, slip op. at 13-16 (D.D.C. Oct. 15, 2004) (concluding without explication that redacted names of DEA employees who authored or received documents are not "similar files," but that names and addresses of third parties contained in documents constitute "similar files"); Na Iwi O Na Kupuna v. Dalton, 894 F. Supp. 1397, 1413 (D. Haw. 1995) (same for records pertaining to large group of Native Hawaiian human remains) (reverse FOIA case); see also FOIA Update, Vol. III, No. 4, at 1 (explaining that the Washington Post decision "revitalized the commonsense, practical approach of giving privacy considerations their full weight in the delicate balancing process"). But see Greenpeace USA, Inc. v. EPA, 735 F. Supp. 13, 14 (D.D.C. 1990) (opining narrowly that information pertaining to an employee's compliance with agency regulations regarding outside employment "does not go to personal information . . . [e]ven in view of the broad interpretation [of Exemption 6] enunciated by the Supreme Court").

[11] N.Y. Times Co. v. NASA, 920 F.2d 1002, 1005 (D.C. Cir. 1990) (en banc); see Forest Guardians v. FEMA, 410 F.3d 1214, 1218 (10th Cir. 2005) (finding that electronic Geographic Information System files containing "specific geographic location" of structures are "similar files"); Judicial Watch, Inc. v. USPS, No. 03-655, slip op. at 6 (D.D.C. Feb. 23, 2004) (assuming that audio portions of videotape are "similar files"), appeal dismissed voluntarily, No. 04-5153 (D.C. Cir. Aug. 25, 2004); Hertzberg v. Veneman, 273 F. Supp. 2d 67, 85 n.11 (D.D.C. 2003) (finding that requested videotapes
(continued...)

cal" and "non-lexical" information are subject to identical treatment under the FOIA,[12] it also concluded that Exemption 6 is equally applicable to the "author" and the "subject" of a file.[13]

Once it has been established that information meets the threshold requirement of Exemption 6, the focus of the inquiry turns to whether disclosure of the records at issue "would constitute a clearly unwarranted invasion of personal privacy."[14] This requires a balancing of the public's right to disclosure against the individual's right to privacy.[15] First, it must be ascertained whether a protectible privacy interest exists that would be threatened by disclosure. If no privacy interest is found, further analysis is unnecessary and the information at issue must be disclosed.[16]

On the other hand, if a privacy interest is found to exist, the public interest in disclosure, if any, must be weighed against the privacy interest in nondisclosure.[17] If no public interest exists, the information should be protected; as the D.C. Circuit has observed, "something, even a modest privacy interest, outweighs nothing every time."[18] Similarly, if the privacy interest outweighs the public interest, the information should be withheld; if

---

[11](...continued) "contain identifiable audio and video images of individual residents," and concluding that they of course are "similar files").

[12] 920 F.2d at 1005.

[13] Id. at 1007-08.

[14] 5 U.S.C. § 552(b)(6).

[15] See Dep't of the Air Force v. Rose, 425 U.S. 352, 372 (1976); Fund for Constitutional Gov't v. Nat'l Archives & Records Serv., 656 F.2d 856, 862 (D.C. Cir. 1981).

[16] See Ripskis v. HUD, 746 F.2d 1, 3 (D.C. Cir. 1984); Trentadue v. President's Council on Integrity & Efficiency, No. 2:03-CV-339, slip op. at 4 (D. Utah Apr. 26, 2004) (stating that agency made no showing of privacy interest, so names of government employees should be released) (Exemptions 6 and 7(C)); Holland v. CIA, No. 91-1233, 1992 WL 233820, at *16 (D.D.C. Aug. 31, 1992) (stating that information must be disclosed when there is no significant privacy interest, even if public interest is also de minimis).

[17] See Ripskis, 746 F.2d at 3; NARA v. Favish, 541 U.S. 157, 171 ("The term 'unwarranted' requires us to balance the family's privacy interest against the public interest in disclosure.") (Exemption 7(C)), reh'g denied, 541 U.S. 1057 (2004).

[18] Nat'l Ass'n of Retired Fed. Employees v. Horner, 879 F.2d 873, 879 (D.C. Cir. 1989); see also Int'l Bhd. of Elec. Workers Local No. 5 v. HUD, 852 F.2d 87, 89 (3d Cir. 1988) (perceiving no public interest in disclosure of employees' social security numbers).

the opposite is found to be the case, the information should be released.[19]

The Reporters Committee Decision

In 1989, the Supreme Court issued a landmark FOIA decision in United States Department of Justice v. Reporters Committee for Freedom of the Press,[20] which for the past eighteen years has governed all privacy-protection decisionmaking under the Act. The Reporters Committee case involved FOIA requests from members of the news media for access to any criminal history records -- known as "rap sheets" -- maintained by the FBI regarding certain persons alleged to have been involved in organized crime and improper dealings with a corrupt Congressman.[21] In holding "rap sheets" entitled to protection under Exemption 7(C), the Supreme Court set forth five guiding principles that govern the process by which determinations are made under both Exemptions 6 and 7(C) alike.

First, the Supreme Court made clear in Reporters Committee that substantial privacy interests can exist in personal information even though the information has been made available to the general public at some place and point in time. Establishing a "practical obscurity" standard,[22] the Court observed that if such items of information actually "were 'freely available,' there would be no reason to invoke the FOIA to obtain access to" them.[23]

Second, the Court articulated the general rule that the identity of a FOIA requester cannot be taken into consideration in determining what should be released under the Act. With the single exception that of course an agency will not invoke an exemption when the particular interest to be protected is the requester's own interest, the Court declared, "the identity of the requesting party has no bearing on the merits of his or her FOIA request."[24]

---

[19] See FOIA Update, Vol. X, No. 2, at 7 ("FOIA Counselor: Exemption 6 and Exemption 7(C): Step-by-Step Decisionmaking") (outlining mechanics of balancing process).

[20] 489 U.S. 749 (1989); see also FOIA Update, Vol. X, No. 2, at 3-6 ("OIP Guidance: Privacy Protection Under the Supreme Court's Reporters Committee Decision").

[21] 489 U.S. at 757.

[22] Id. at 762, 780.

[23] Id. at 764.

[24] Id. at 771; see also NARA v. Favish, 541 U.S. 157, 170-72 (reiterating that "[a]s a general rule, withholding information under FOIA cannot be predicated on the identity of the requester," but adding that this of course does not mean that a requester seeking to establish an overriding "public

(continued...)

Third, the Court declared that in determining whether any public interest would be served by a requested disclosure, one should no longer consider "the purposes for which the request for information is made."[25] Rather than turn on a requester's "particular purpose," circumstances, or proposed use, the Court ruled, such determinations "must turn on the nature of the requested document and its relationship to" the public interest overall.[26] (See the further discussions of this point under Exemption 6, Factoring in the Public Interest, and Exemption 7(C), below.)

Fourth, the Court narrowed the scope of the public interest to be considered under the Act's privacy exemptions, declaring for the first time that it is limited to "the kind of public interest for which Congress enacted the FOIA."[27] This "core purpose of the FOIA," as the Court termed it,[28] is to "shed[] light on an agency's performance of its statutory duties."[29]

Fifth, the Court established the proposition, under Exemption 7(C),

---

[24](...continued)
interest" in the disclosure of requested information "need not offer a reason for requesting the information") (Exemption 7(C)), reh'g denied, 541 U.S. 1057 (2004); Bassiouni v. CIA, 392 F.3d 244, 245-46 (7th Cir. 2004) (observing that "any member of the public may invoke FOIA, and the agency must disregard the requester's identity") (Exemption 1), cert. denied, 545 U.S. 1129 (2005).

[25] 489 U.S. at 771.

[26] Id. at 772; see also Favish, 541 U.S. at 175 (discussing "the nexus required between the requested documents and the purported public interest served by disclosure"); Sun-Sentinel Co. v. DHS, 431 F. Supp. 2d 1258, 1269-70 (S.D. Fla. 2006) (requiring nexus between information disclosable under FOIA and serving public interest); see also FOIA Post, "Supreme Court Rules for 'Survivor Privacy' in Favish" (posted 4/9/04) (elaborating on "nexus requirement"); FOIA Post, "FOIA Counselor Q&A" (posted 1/24/06) (explaining distinction between generalized public interest in broad subject area of FOIA request as opposed to specific public interest in particular documents at issue in FOIA request) (citing cases).

[27] 489 U.S. at 774.

[28] Id. at 775.

[29] Id. at 773; see also O'Kane v. U.S. Customs Serv., 169 F.3d 1308, 1310 (11th Cir. 1999) (per curiam) (affirming that Electronic Freedom of Information Act Amendments of 1996, Pub. L. No. 104-231, 110 Stat. 3048, do not "overrule" Reporters Committee definition of "public interest"); cf. Favish, 541 U.S. at 172 (reiterating the Reporters Committee "public interest" standard, and characterizing it as "a structural necessity in a real democracy" that "should not be dismissed" -- despite persistent arguments by amici in the case that Reporters Committee had been "overruled" by the Electronic FOIA amendments since 1996).

that agencies may engage in "categorical balancing" in favor of nondisclosure.[30] Under this approach, which builds upon the above principles, it may be determined, "as a categorical matter," that a certain type of information always is protectible under an exemption, "without regard to individual circumstances."[31]

---

[30] 489 U.S. at 776-80 & n.22; see also Favish, 541 U.S. at 173 (stressing need for "stability" in privacy balancing, lest balancing be too "ad hoc").

[31] 489 U.S. at 780; see, e.g., Reed v. NLRB, 927 F.2d 1249, 1252 (D.C. Cir. 1991) ("Exemption 6 protects 'Excelsior' lists [names and addresses of employees eligible to vote in union representation elections] as a category."); SafeCard Servs. v. SEC, 926 F.2d 1197, 1205-06 (D.C. Cir. 1991) (holding "categorically that, unless access to the names and addresses of private individuals appearing in files within the ambit of Exemption 7(C) is necessary in order to confirm or refute compelling evidence that the agency is engaged in illegal activity, such information is exempt from disclosure"); Johnson v. Comm'r, 239 F. Supp. 2d 1125, 1137 (W.D. Wash. 2002) (allowing categorical withholding of any identifying information about third parties and witnesses, as well as any information that they provided to IRS) (Exemption 7(C)), aff'd on other grounds, 68 F. App'x 839 (9th Cir. 2003); Grove v. Dep't of Justice, 802 F. Supp. 506, 511 (D.D.C. 1992) (Categorical balancing is appropriate for "information concerning criminal investigations of private citizens.") (Exemption 7(C)). But see Armstrong v. Executive Office of the President, 97 F.3d 575, 581-82 (D.C. Cir. 1996) (finding that agency had not adequately established basis for categorical rule for withholding identities of low-level FBI agents); Nation Magazine v. U.S. Customs Serv., 71 F.3d 885, 893-96 (D.C. Cir. 1995) (rejecting categorical issuance of "Glomar" response in case involving request for information concerning presidential candidate H. Ross Perot's offer "to help a federal agency fulfill its statutory duties to interdict drugs") (Exemption 7(C)); Associated Press v. DOD, 395 F. Supp. 2d 15, 20 (S.D.N.Y. 2005) (declining to take categorical approach to withholding of Guantanamo Bay detainees' identifying information), reconsideration denied, 395 F. Supp. 2d 17 (S.D.N.Y. 2005), subsequent decision, 410 F. Supp. 2d 147 (S.D.N.Y. 2006); Elec. Privacy Info. Ctr. v. DHS, 384 F. Supp. 2d 100, 116 (D.D.C. 2005) ("The fact that federal employees have an identifiable privacy interest in avoiding disclosures of information that could lead to annoyance or harassment, does not authorize a 'blanket exemption' for the names of all government employees in all records."); Konigsberg v. FBI, No. 02-2428, slip op. at 6 (D.D.C. May 27, 2003) (rejecting categorical withholding for records based on insufficient "eviden[tiary]" support); see also FOIA Update, Vol. XVII, No. 2, at 3-4 ("OIP Guidance: The Bifurcation Requirement for Privacy 'Glomarization'") (discussing need to bifurcate requests that ask for more than law enforcement records on a third party -- i.e., employing "Glomar" response for law enforcement records and treating non-law enforcement records under Exemption 6 in ordinary fashion).

EXEMPTION 6

Privacy Considerations

The first step in the Exemption 6 balancing process requires an assessment of the privacy interests at issue.[32] The relevant inquiry is whether public access to the information at issue would violate a viable privacy interest of the subject of such information.[33] In its Reporters Committee decision, the Supreme Court stressed that "both the common law and the literal understandings of privacy encompass the individual's control of information concerning his or her person,"[34] just as in National Archives & Records Administration v. Favish the Court drew upon the common law to find the principle of "survivor privacy" encompassed within the Act's privacy exemptions.[35] Indeed, in Reporters Committee the Court found a "strong privacy interest" in the nondisclosure of records of a private citizen's criminal history, "even where the information may have been at one time public."[36] Of course, information need not be intimate or embarrassing to qualify for Exemption 6 protection.[37]

And for its part, the Court of Appeals for the District of Columbia Circuit has emphasized the practical analytical point that under the FOIA's privacy-protection exemptions, "[t]he threat to privacy . . . need not be pa-

---

[32] See FOIA Update, Vol. X, No. 2, at 7.

[33] See Schell v. HHS, 843 F.2d 933, 938 (6th Cir. 1988); Ripskis v. HUD, 746 F.2d 1, 3 (D.C. Cir. 1984).

[34] 489 U.S. 749, 763 (1989).

[35] 541 U.S. 157, 165-70 ("[T]he concept of personal privacy . . . is not some limited or 'cramped notion' of that idea.") (Exemption 7(C)), reh'g denied, 541 U.S. 1057 (2004); see also FOIA Post, "Supreme Court Rules for 'Survivor Privacy' in Favish" (posted 4/9/04) (highlighting breadth of privacy protection principles in Supreme Court's decision).

[36] 489 U.S. at 767; see also DOD v. FLRA, 510 U.S. 487, 500 (1994) (finding privacy interest in federal employees' home addresses even though they "often are publicly available through sources such as telephone directories and voter registration lists"); FOIA Update, Vol. X, No. 2, at 4.

[37] See Dep't of State v. Wash. Post Co., 456 U.S. 595, 600 (1982); Horowitz v. Peace Corps, 428 F.3d 271, 279 (D.C. Cir. 2005) ("Even seemingly innocuous information can be enough to trigger the protections of Exemption 6."), cert. denied, 126 S. Ct. 1627 (2006); Nat'l Ass'n of Retired Fed. Employees v. Horner, 879 F.2d 873, 875 (D.C. Cir. 1989); Knight v. NASA, No. 2:04-2054, 2006 WL 3780901, at *5 (E.D. Cal. Dec. 21, 2006) ("Information need not be intimate or embarrassing to qualify for exemption under subdivision (b)(6)."); Appleton v. FDA, 451 F. Supp. 2d 129, 145 (D.D.C. 2006) ("Individuals have a privacy interest in personal information even if it is not of an embarrassing or intimate nature.").

tent or obvious to be relevant."[38] Therefore, as a general rule, the threat to privacy need only be real rather than speculative.[39] In some cases, this principle formerly was interpreted to mean that the privacy interest must be threatened by the very disclosure of information and not by any possible "secondary effects" of such release.[40] The D.C. Circuit, however, subsequently clarified its holding in Arieff v. United States Department of the Navy,[41] which had been read as stating that "secondary effects" were not cognizable under Exemption 6. In National Association of Retired Federal Employees v. Horner [hereinafter NARFE], the D.C. Circuit explained that the point in Arieff was that Exemption 6 was inapplicable because there was only "mere speculation" of a privacy invasion, i.e., only a slight possibility that the information, if disclosed, would be linked to a specific individual.[42]

---

[38] Pub. Citizen Health Research Group v. U.S. Dep't of Labor, 591 F.2d 808, 809 (D.C. Cir. 1978) (per curiam) (ruling that district court improperly refused to look beyond face of document at issue (i.e., to proffered in camera explanation of harm), which led it to fail to recognize underlying sensitivity).

[39] See Dep't of the Air Force v. Rose, 425 U.S. 352, 380 n.19 (1976) ("The legislative history is clear that Exemption 6 was directed at threats to privacy interests more palpable than mere possibilities."); Carter v. U.S. Dep't of Commerce, 830 F.2d 388, 391 (D.C. Cir. 1987) (stating that "[w]ithholding information to prevent speculative harm" is contrary to the FOIA's pro-disclosure policy); Arieff v. U.S. Dep't of the Navy, 712 F.2d 1462, 1467-68 (D.C. Cir. 1983) (finding that Exemption 6 did not apply when there was only a "'mere possibility'" that the medical condition of a particular individual would be disclosed by releasing a list of pharmaceuticals supplied to a congressional doctor (quoting Rose, 425 U.S. at 380 n.19)); Cawthon v. U.S. Dep't of Justice, No. 05-0567, 2006 WL 581250, at *3 (D.D.C. Mar. 9, 2006) ("To justify its exemption 6 withholdings, the defendant must show that the threat to employees' privacy is real rather than speculative.").

[40] See, e.g., S. Utah Wilderness Alliance, Inc. v. Hodel, 680 F. Supp. 37, 39 (D.D.C. 1988), vacated as moot, No. 88-5142 (D.C. Cir. Nov. 15, 1988).

[41] 712 F.2d at 1468.

[42] 879 F.2d at 878; see also ACLU v. DOD, 389 F. Supp. 2d 547, 571-72 (S.D.N.Y.) (concluding that possibility that Abu Ghraib prison detainees might recognize themselves or be recognized by members of public, despite redaction of requested photographs and videos, was "no more than speculati[on]"), reconsideration denied, 396 F. Supp. 2d 459 (S.D.N.Y. 2005), relief from judgment denied, 406 F. Supp. 2d 330 (S.D.N.Y. 2006); Fortson v. Harvey, 407 F. Supp. 2d 13, 17 (D.D.C. 2005) (deciding that potential harm to witnesses of unfavorable personnel evaluations and workplace harassment was "pure speculation"); Dayton Newspapers, Inc. v. Dep't of the Air Force, 107 F. Supp. 2d 912, 919 (S.D. Ohio 1999) (declining to protect medi-
(continued...)

Most recently, the Supreme Court did not at all concern itself with any issue of "secondary effects" or "derivative privacy interest" in Favish.[43] Rather, a unanimous Court in Favish readily found that the surviving family members of former Deputy White House Counsel Vincent Foster had a protectible privacy interest in his death-scene photographs, based in part on the family's fears of "intense scrutiny by the media."[44] In doing so, the Court did not view a privacy interest based on "limit[ing] attempts to exploit pictures of the deceased family member's remains for public purposes" as in any way too attenuated to qualify as a protectible privacy interest in the first place.[45] This means that any consideration of potential privacy invasions must include both what the requester might do with the information at hand and also what any other requester, or ultimate recipient, might do with it as well.[46]

Indeed, it has explicitly been recognized by the D.C. Circuit that "[w]here there is a substantial probability that disclosure will cause an interference with personal privacy, it matters not that there may be two or three links in the causal chain."[47] Even prior to the D.C. Circuit's clarifica-

---

[42](...continued) cal malpractice settlement figures based upon "mere possibility that factual information might be pieced together to supply 'missing link' and lead to personal identification" of claimants); Chi. Tribune Co. v. HHS, No. 95 C 3917, 1997 WL 1137641, at *10-11 (N.D. Ill. Feb. 26, 1997) (magistrate's recommendation) (finding "speculative at best" agency's argument that release of breast cancer patient data forms that identify patients only by nine-digit encoded "Study Numbers" could result in identification of individual patients), adopted (N.D. Ill. Mar. 28, 1997).

[43] 541 U.S. at 166.

[44] Id. at 167.

[45] Id.

[46] Id. at 174 ("It must be remembered that once there is disclosure, the information belongs to the general public."); see also FOIA Post, "Supreme Court Rules for 'Survivor Privacy' in Favish" (posted 4/9/04) (emphasizing that agencies must of course consider full range of potential privacy invasions).

[47] NARFE, 879 F.2d at 878; see, e.g., Favish v. Office of Indep. Counsel, 217 F.3d 1168, 1173 (9th Cir. 2000) (declaring that "it is not 'the production' of the records that would cause the harms, . . . but their exploitation by the media," a "probable consequence[] of the release" that is encompassed by "the statutory reference to what may 'reasonably be expected'"), rev'd on other grounds sub nom. NARA v. Favish, 541 U.S. 157, 167-70 (specifically taking into account "the consequences" of FOIA disclosure, including "public exploitation" of the records by either the requester or others), reh'g denied, 541 U.S. 1057 (2004); Judicial Watch, Inc. v. Dep't of the Army, 402 F. (continued...)

tion in NARFE, much less the Supreme Court's subsequent illustration of this point in Favish, one court pragmatically observed that to distinguish between the initial disclosure and unwanted intrusions as a result of that disclosure would be "to honor form over substance."[48]

Recently, the Court of Appeals for the Tenth Circuit, in Forest Guardians v. FEMA, decided that release of "electronic mapping files" would in-

---

[47](...continued)
Supp. 2d. 241, 251 (D.D.C. 2005) (granting defendant's motion for summary judgment as to information withheld pursuant to Exemption 6; finding that it is "likely" that the documents would be published on the Internet and that media reporters would seek out employees, and stating "[t]his contact is the very type of privacy invasion that Exemption 6 is designed to prevent"); Elec. Privacy Info. Ctr. v. DHS, 384 F. Supp. 2d 100, 117 (D.D.C. 2005) (finding that "DHS and TSA employees are likely to experience annoyance or harassment following disclosure of their involvement with the [Computer Assisted Passenger Prescreening System] program"); In Def. of Animals v. HHS, No. 99-3024, 2001 U.S. Dist. LEXIS 24975, at *18-20 (D.D.C. Sept. 28, 2001) (accepting that "threats and harassment . . . may reasonably be expected to be made" to members of research foundation); Hougan & Denton v. U.S. Dep't of Justice, No. 90-1312, slip op. at 3 (D.D.C. July 3, 1991) (concluding that solicitation by employers would invade privacy of participants in union's training program). But see U.S. Dep't of State v. Ray, 502 U.S. 164, 179-82 (1991) (Scalia, J., concurring in part) (suggesting that "derivative" privacy harm should not be relied upon in evaluating privacy interests, a position subsequently rejected sub silentio by a unanimous Supreme Court in Favish); Ctr. for Public Integrity v. OPM, No. 04-1274, 2006 WL 3498089, at *5 (D.D.C. Dec. 4, 2006) (finding that plaintiff's derivative theory of public interest was fatally flawed); Associated Press v. DOD, 410 F. Supp. 2d 147, 151 (D.D.C. 2006) (suggesting that "derivative" harms might not be cognizable under Exemption 6, based on Justice Scalia's concurring opinion in Ray); Forest Guardians v. U.S. Dep't of the Interior, No. 02-1003, 2004 WL 3426434, at *16-17 (D.N.M. Feb. 28, 2004) (deciding that agency did not meet its burden of establishing that names of financial institutions and amounts of individual loans in lienholder agreements could be used to trace individual permittees); Dayton Newspapers, Inc. v. VA, 257 F. Supp. 2d 988, 1001-05 (S.D. Ohio 2003) (rejecting argument based upon agency's concern that names of judges and attorneys could be used to search through databases to identify claimants and thereby invade privacy of claimants), reconsideration granted on other claims, No. 00-235, 2005 WL 2405992 (S.D. Ohio Sept. 29, 2005).

[48] Hudson v. Dep't of the Army, No. 86-1114, 1987 WL 46755, at *3 (D.D.C. Jan. 29, 1987) (protecting personal identifying information on the basis that its disclosure under the FOIA could ultimately lead to physical harm), aff'd, 926 F.2d 1215 (D.C. Cir. 1991) (unpublished table decision); see also, e.g., Hemenway v. Hughes, 601 F. Supp. 1002, 1006-07 (D.D.C. 1985) (same).

vade the privacy interest of homeowners.[49] The files contained the specific locations of insured structures that "could easily lead to the discovery of an individual's name and home address," as well as "unwanted and unsolicited mail, if not more."[50] Notably, the Tenth Circuit, like the Supreme Court and the D.C. Circuit, did not concern itself that these invasions of privacy might not occur immediately upon release of the mapping files.[51]

In some instances, the disclosure of information might involve no invasion of privacy because, fundamentally, the information is of such a nature that no expectation of privacy exists.[52] For example, civilian federal employees generally have no expectation of privacy regarding their names, titles, grades, salaries, and duty stations as employees[53] or regarding the

---

[49] 410 F.3d 1214, 1220-21 (10th Cir. 2005).

[50] Id. (finding that additional information, such as individual's decision to buy flood insurance, could be revealed through disclosure of requested files and thus also invade privacy).

[51] See id.

[52] See, e.g., Alliance for the Wild Rockies v. Dep't of the Interior, 53 F. Supp. 2d 32, 37 (D.D.C. 1999) (finding that commenters to proposed rulemaking could have no expectation of privacy when agency made clear that their identities would not be concealed); see also Memorandum for the President's Management Council 1 (Mar. 1, 2004) (providing guidance for federal agencies in implementing "E-Government initiative" and attaching NARA template for "Addresses" section of regulatory preambles that includes new policy that "[a]ll comments received will be posted without change . . . including any personal information provided"), available at www.whitehouse.gov/omb/inforeg/memo_pmc_egov.pdf.

[53] See 5 C.F.R. § 293.311 (2007) (OPM regulation specifying that certain information contained in federal employee personnel files is available to public); see also FLRA v. U.S. Dep't of Commerce, 962 F.2d 1055, 1059-61 (D.C. Cir. 1992) (noting that performance awards "have traditionally been subject to disclosure"); Core v. USPS, 730 F.2d 946, 948 (4th Cir. 1984) (finding no substantial invasion of privacy in information identifying successful federal job applicants); Leadership Conference on Civil Rights, 404 F. Supp. 2d 246, 257 (D.D.C. 2005) (noting that Justice Department paralegals' names and work numbers "are already publicly available from [OPM]"), motion to amend denied, 421 F. Supp. 2d 104, 107-10 (D.D.C. 2006), appeal dismissed voluntarily, No. 06-5055, 2006 WL 1214937 (D.C. Cir. Apr. 28, 2006); The News-Press v. DHS, No. 05-102, 2005 WL 2921952, at *11 (M.D. Fla. Nov. 4, 2005) (opining that "there is nothing about employment at FEMA or concurrence/non-concurrence in a [disaster relief] request that would invoke 'personal' privacy") (appeal pending); Nat'l W. Life Ins. v. United States, 512 F. Supp. 454, 461 (N.D. Tex. 1980) (discerning no expectation of privacy in names and duty stations of Postal Service employees);

(continued...)

parts of their successful employment applications that show their qualifications for their positions.[54] Historically, the Department of Defense, as a matter of policy, in most circumstances disclosed the name, rank, gross salary, duty assignments, duty phone numbers, source of commission, promotion sequence number, awards and decorations, professional military education, duty status, and other nonsensitive details of individual military personnel, as well as comparable information concerning individual civilian employees.[55] And by regulation, the Department of the Army discloses substantially the same information concerning its military and civilian personnel.[56] However, in light of recent terrorist activities around the world, the Department of Defense now regularly withholds personally identifying information about all particular military and civilian employees with re-

---

[53](...continued)
see also FOIA Update, Vol. III, No. 4, at 3 (discussing extent to which privacy of federal employees can be protected); cf. Tomscha v. GSA, No. 03-6755, 2004 WL 1234043, at *4-5 (S.D.N.Y. June 3, 2004) (deciding without discussion that amount of performance award was properly redacted when agency showed that there could be "mathematical linkage" between award and performance evaluation), aff'd, 158 F. App'x 329, 329 (2d Cir. 2005) (agreeing with the district court's finding that "the release of the justifications for [low-ranking GSA employee's] awards would constitute more than a de minimis invasion of privacy"). But see Ctr. for Pub. Integrity, 2006 WL 3498089, at *6 (finding that OPM properly withheld the names and duty stations of DOD and certain non-DOD federal personnel in sensitive occupations under Exemption 6).

[54] See Barvick v. Cisneros, 941 F. Supp. 1015, 1020 n.4 (D. Kan. 1996) (noting that the agency had "released information pertaining to the successful candidates' educational and professional qualifications, including letters of commendation and awards, as well as their prior work history, including federal positions, grades, salaries, and duty stations").

[55] See Department of Defense Freedom of Information Act Program Regulation, DOD 5400.7-R, 37-39 (Sept. 1998); see also Memorandum from Department of Defense Directorate for Freedom of Information and Security Review 1 (Oct. 26, 1999) (applying same analysis as in DOD 5400.7-R to electronic mail addresses, and authorizing withholding only for "personnel assigned to units that are sensitive, routinely deployable or stationed in foreign territories"); cf. 10 U.S.C. § 130b (2000 & Supp. IV 2004) (Department of Defense-wide provision); Department of Defense Freedom of Information Act Program Regulations, 32 C.F.R. § 286.12(f)(2)(ii) (2006) ("Names and duty addresses (postal and/or e-mail) . . . for personnel assigned to units that are sensitive, routinely deployable, or stationed in foreign territories are withholdable under [Exemption 6].").

[56] See Army Reg. 340-21, ¶ 3-3a(1), b(1), 5 July 1985; see also Army Reg. 25-55, ¶ 3-200, No. 6(b), 1 Nov. 1997 (providing for withholding of names and duty addresses of military personnel assigned to units that are "sensitive, routinely deployable or stationed in foreign territories").

spect to whom disclosure would "raise security or privacy concerns."[57]

Additionally, if the information at issue is particularly well known or is widely available within the public domain, there generally is no expectation of privacy.[58] Nor does an individual have any expectation of privacy

---

[57] Department of Defense Director for Administration and Management Memorandum 1-2 (Nov. 9, 2001), available at www.defenselink.mil/pubs/foi/withhold.pdf (noting that certain personnel's names can be released due to "the nature of their positions and duties," including public affairs officers and flag officers); see also O'Keefe v. DOD, 463 F. Supp. 2d 317, 327 (D.D.C. 2006) (upholding DOD's withholding of personal information of investigators as well as subjects of investigation found in United States Central Command Report); Ctr. for Pub. Integrity, 2006 WL 3498089, at *6 (protecting all information pertaining to DOD employees); Deichman v. United States, No. 05-680, 2006 WL 3000448, at *7 (E.D. Va. Oct. 20, 2006) (upholding United States Joint Forces Command's withholding of employee names and discussions of personnel matters relating to other employees under Exemption 6); MacLean v. DOD, No. 04-2425, slip op. at 18 (S.D. Cal. June 2, 2005) (protecting "names, initials, and other personal information" about Defense Hotline Investigators and other DOD personnel) (Exemptions 6 and 7(C)).

[58] See, e.g., Avondale Indus. v. NLRB, 90 F.3d 955, 961 (5th Cir. 1996) (finding that names and addresses of voters in union election were already disclosed in voluminous public record and that there was no showing that public record was compiled in such a way as to effectively obscure that information); Detroit Free Press, Inc. v. Dep't of Justice, 73 F.3d 93, 96-97 (6th Cir. 1996) (finding in singular decision no privacy rights in mug shots of defendants in ongoing criminal proceedings when names are public and defendants have appeared in open court) (Exemption 7(C)); Billington v. U.S. Dep't of Justice, 245 F. Supp. 2d 79, 85-86 (D.D.C. 2003) (finding that information about two persons contained in a reporter's notes given to the State Department was not protected by Exemption 6, because these persons "knew that they were speaking to a reporter on the record and therefore could not expect to keep private the substance of the interview"); Blanton v. U.S. Dep't of Justice, No. 93-2398, 1994 U.S. Dist. LEXIS 21444, at *11-12 (W.D. Tenn. July 14, 1994) ("The fact of [requester's former counsel's] representation is a matter of public record . . . . Whether an individual possesses a valid license to practice law is also a matter of public record and cannot be protected by any privacy interest."); Nat'l W. Life Ins., 512 F. Supp. at 461 (noting that names and duty stations of most federal employees are routinely published and available through Government Printing Office); cf. Doe v. FBI, 218 F.R.D. 256, 259-60 (D. Colo. 2003) (refusing to allow plaintiff to proceed with a case under a pseudonym or under seal, on the basis that his particular reputational interest does not "outweigh the public's interest in an open court system"). But see Times Picayune Publ'g Corp. v. U.S. Dep't of Justice, 37 F. Supp. 2d 472, 477-82 (E.D. La. 1999) (protecting the mug shot of a prominent individual despite wide publicity prior to his

(continued...)

with respect to information that she herself has made public.[59] On the other hand, if the information in question was at some time or place available to the public, but now is "hard-to-obtain information," the individual to whom it pertains may have a privacy interest in maintaining its "practical obscurity."[60]

---

[58](...continued)
guilty plea, and observing that a "mug is more than just another photograph of a person") (Exemption 7(C)); cf. Lakin Law Firm, P.C. v. FTC, 352 F.3d 1122, 1124-25 (7th Cir. 2003) (explaining that posting complaint advisory on Web site that warned consumers that "information provided may be subject to release under the FOIA" does not waive the privacy interests of consumer complainants) (emphasis added), reh'g denied, No. 03-1689 (7th Cir. 2004).

[59] See Nation Magazine v. U.S. Customs Serv., 71 F.3d 885, 896 (D.C. Cir. 1995) (finding no privacy interest in documents concerning presidential candidate H. Ross Perot's offer to aid federal government in drug interdiction, a subject about which Perot had made several public statements); see also Kimberlin v. Dep't of Justice, 139 F.3d 944, 949 (D.C. Cir 1998) (noting that government lawyer investigated by Department of Justice's Office of Professional Responsibility diminished his privacy interest by acknowledging existence of investigation but that he still retains privacy interest in nondisclosure of any details of investigation) (Exemption 7(C)); Judicial Watch, Inc. v. USPS, No. 03-655, slip op. at 7-8 (D.D.C. Feb. 23, 2004) (deciding that individuals had "minimal" privacy interests in their names when they identified themselves into microphones at "a public community meeting" attended by "'readily identifiable members of the local, regional and national media'"); cf. Showler v. Harper's Magazine Found., No. 05-178, slip op. at 5-8, 12-14 (E.D. Okla. Dec. 22, 2005) (finding no invasion of privacy of the family or First Amendment protection for a reporter who took a photograph of an open casket of a reservist killed in Iraq, because the family opened the funeral to the public, the funeral was attended by over 1200 people, including the governor of Oklahoma and members of the press, and the "photograph was the same scene the funeral attendees observed") (non-FOIA case).

[60] Reporters Comm., 489 U.S. at 780; see also Wash. Post, 456 U.S. at 603 n.5; Edwards v. Dep't of Justice, No. 04-5044, 2004 WL 2905342, at *1 (D.C. Cir. Dec. 15, 2004) (per curiam) (summarily affirming district court's decision to bar release of any responsive documents pursuant to Exemption 7(C); stating that the appellant's argument that the release of the documents was required because the government officially acknowledged the information contained therein fails because he "has failed to point to 'specific information in the public domain that appears to duplicate that being withheld'" (quoting Davis v. U.S. Dep't of Justice, 968 F.2d 1276, 1279 (D.C. Cir. 1992))); Fiduccia v. U.S. Dep't of Justice, 185 F.3d 1035, 1046-47 (9th Cir. 1999) (protecting information about two individuals whose homes were searched ten years previously despite publicity at that time and fact
(continued...)

Similarly, the mere fact that some of the information may be known to some members of the public does not negate the individual's privacy interest in preventing further dissemination to the public at large.[61] For exam-

---

[60](...continued)
that some information might be public in various courthouses) (Exemption 7(C)); Abraham & Rose, P.L.C. v. United States, 138 F.3d 1075, 1083 (6th Cir. 1998) (noting that there may be privacy interest in personal information even if "available on publicly recorded filings"); Leadership Conference on Civil Rights, 404 F. Supp. 2d at 257-59 (holding under Exemption 6 that law enforcement records that were previously given to symposium members fall within "practical obscurity" rule); Dayton Newspapers, Inc., 257 F. Supp. 2d at 1010 (reasoning that although modern search engines might make even otherwise obscure personal information more widely available, that "does not mean that [individuals] have lost all traits of privacy" in that information); Linn v. U.S. Dep't of Justice, No. 92-1406, 1995 WL 417810, at *31 (D.D.C. June 6, 1995) (declaring that even if "some of the names at issue were at one time released to the general public, individuals are entitled to maintaining the 'practical obscurity' of personal information that is developed through the passage of time"). But see Lardner v. U.S. Dep't of Justice, No. 03-0180, 2005 WL 758267, at *17 (D.D.C. Mar. 31, 2005) (ignoring Reporters Committee's "practical obscurity" rule in stating that "[t]he conviction that the pardon applicant is seeking to annul was itself public," and concluding that the "additional embarrassment beyond the original conviction" in an unsuccessful pardon application did not warrant Exemption 6 protection).

[61] See Isley v. Executive Office for U.S. Attorneys, No. 98-5098, 1999 WL 1021934, at *4 (D.C. Cir. Oct. 21, 1999) (finding no evidence that previously disclosed documents "continue to be 'freely available' in any 'permanent public record'") (Exemption 7(C)); ACLU v. FBI, 429 F. Supp. 2d 179, 193 (D.D.C. 2006) ("To the extent that a person may have retained a privacy interest in publicly made comments, that interest is certainly dissipated by the FBI's failure to redact his name from the entirety of the document."); Horowitz, 428 F.3d at 280 ("Even though the student did reveal his allegation to two Peace Corps workers . . . he still has an interest in avoiding further dissemination of his identity."); Pendergrass v. U.S. Dep't of Justice, No. 04-112, 2005 WL 1378724, at *4 (D.D.C. June 7, 2005) (reasoning that individual does not lose all privacy interest in telephone conversation even if she knew of potential for monitoring of such calls); Edmonds v. FBI, 272 F. Supp. 2d 35, 53 (D.D.C. 2003) (finding that media identification of persons mentioned in a law enforcement file "does not lessen their privacy interests or 'defeat the exemption,' for prior disclosure of personal information does not eliminate an individual's privacy interest in avoiding subsequent disclosure by the government") (Exemptions 6 and 7(C)), appeal dismissed voluntarily, No. 03-5364, 2004 WL 2806508 (D.C. Cir. Dec. 7, 2004); Mueller v. U.S. Dep't of the Air Force, 63 F. Supp. 2d 738, 743 (E.D. Va. 1999) (stating that existence of publicity surrounding events does not eliminate privacy interest) (Exemptions 6 and 7(C)); Chin v. U.S. Dep't of the Air Force,
(continued...)

ple, the Supreme Court in Favish did not diminish its estimation of "the weighty privacy interests involved" just because Vincent Foster's death occurred on national parkland and thus was "in public."[62] And one court has found that the subject of a photograph introduced into the court record "retained at least some privacy interest in preventing the further dissemination of the photographic image" when "[t]he photocopy in the Court record was of such poor quality as to severely limit its dissemination."[63]

However, the District Court for the Southern District of New York recently decided that military detainees at Guantanamo Bay had no privacy interest in their identifying information because they provided the information at formal legal proceedings before a tribunal and there was no evidence that the detainees "were informed that the proceedings would remain confidential in any respect."[64] Indeed, even though the tribunal records were not made available to the general public and press attendees had to agree to confidentiality requirements, it concluded that the detainees had no privacy interest in stopping further dissemination of their identifying information.[65] On reconsideration, the court went even further by stating, in dicta, that third parties had "even less of an expectation" of privacy in the disclosure of their identifying information by detainees at the tribunals.[66]

Along these same lines, that same court recently ordered the release

---

[61](...continued)
No. 97-2176, slip op. at 5 (W.D. La. June 24, 1999) (concluding that although "some of the events are known to certain members of the public . . . this fact is insufficient to place this record for dissemination into the public domain"), aff'd per curiam, No. 99-31237 (5th Cir. June 15, 2000); cf. Schiffer v. FBI, 78 F.3d 1405, 1411 (9th Cir. 1996) (treating requester's personal knowledge as irrelevant in assessing privacy interests).

[62] 541 U.S. at 171; see also FOIA Post, "Supreme Court Rules for 'Survivor Privacy' in Favish" (posted 4/9/04) (advising that "the Favish decision illustrates that the occurrence of an event in a public place is no disqualifying factor for privacy protection under the FOIA").

[63] Baltimore Sun v. U.S. Customs Serv., No. 97-1991, slip op. at 5 (D. Md. Nov. 21, 1997) (Exemption 7(C)).

[64] Associated Press, 410 F. Supp. 2d at 150 (distinguishing privacy interests involved with Guantanamo Bay detainees from those involved in Ray, based upon express promises of confidentiality that had been granted to Haitian "boat people").

[65] Id. at 156 & n.2 (opining that testifying detainees had no privacy interest in their testimony before tribunals because they did not know of confidentiality requirements, nor did government require such confidentiality in order to protect any privacy interest of detainees).

[66] Id. at 154.

of such detainees' names and other identifying information contained within documents regarding alleged abuse at Guantanamo Bay.[67] Finding the privacy interests of the detainees to be "minimal," the court concluded that the public interest in disclosing government malfeasance was great and, therefore, far outweighed any such minimal privacy interest.[68] The only piece of information that the court permitted to be withheld was the identifying information of a detainee's wife.[69] The court concluded that the detainee's wife "had a reasonable expectation of privacy that was not wholly eliminated by her husband's reluctant offer of the letter to the [Administrative Review Board] and that the competing interest of the Associated Press in obtaining her identity is modest."[70]

Most recently, the District Court for the Southern District of New York held that height and weight information concerning Guantanamo Bay detainees was not exempt from disclosure under Exemption 6.[71] Finding at best only a "modest" privacy interest in the nondisclosure of the information, the court acknowledged that prior cases involving height and weight information frequently resulted in decisions concluding that the privacy interest in the nondisclosure of such information is "quite weak."[72] After analyzing the privacy interest at issue, the court concluded that DOD had failed to make "any particularized showing that disclosure of this information is likely to lead to retaliation, harassment, or embarrassment."[73] Moreover, the court went further by suggesting that "at least some detainees would welcome having this information disclosed" due to the fact that the "immediate impetus" for the FOIA request concerned an investigation by the Associated Press of hunger strikes by detainees.[74] As for the public interest in disclosure of the information, the court stated that "there is a clear public interest in obtaining this information so as to assess, not only DOD's conduct with respect to the hunger strikes at Guantanamo, but more generally DOD's care and (literally) feeding of the detainees."[75] Weighing

---

[67] Associated Press v. DOD, No. 05-5468, 2006 WL 2707395, at *12 (S.D.N.Y. Sept. 20, 2006) (Exemptions 6 and 7(C)).

[68] Id. at *3-12.

[69] Id. at *11-12.

[70] Id. at *11.

[71] Associated Press v. DOD, 462 F. Supp. 2d 573, 577-78 (S.D.N.Y. 2006).

[72] Id. at 577 (citing cases).

[73] Id.

[74] Id.

[75] Id. (clarifying that information pertaining to both the height and weight of the detainees is necessary because "weight information only
(continued...)

this public interest in disclosure against the privacy interest in nondisclosure, the court concluded that the height and weight information contributes significantly to public understanding of the operations or activities of the government and this public interest in disclosure "more than outweighs the modest privacy interest, if any, here proffered by DOD."[76]

As another example, FOIA requesters, except when they are making first-party requests, do not ordinarily expect that their names will be kept private; therefore, release of their names would not cause even the minimal invasion of privacy necessary to trigger the balancing test.[77] Personal information about FOIA requesters, however, such as home addresses and home telephone numbers, should not be disclosed.[78] However, the identities of first-party requesters under the Privacy Act of 1974[79] should be protected because, unlike under the FOIA, an expectation of privacy can fairly be inferred from the personal nature of the records involved in those requests.[80]

The majority of courts to have considered the issue have held that individuals who write to the government expressing personal opinions generally do so with some expectation of confidentiality unless they are advised to the contrary in advance; their identities, but not necessarily the

---

[75](...continued)
takes on significance when paired with the corresponding information on height").

[76] Id. at 578.

[77] See FOIA Update, Vol. VI, No. 1, at 6; see also Holland v. CIA, No. 91-1233, 1992 WL 233829, at *15-16 (D.D.C. Aug. 31, 1992) (holding that researcher who sought assistance of presidential advisor in obtaining CIA files he had requested is comparable to FOIA requester whose identity is not protected by Exemption 6); Martinez v. FBI, No. 82-1547, slip op. at 7 (D.D.C. Dec. 19, 1985) (denying protection for identities of news reporters seeking information concerning criminal investigation) (Exemption 7(C)). But see Silets v. U.S. Dep't of Justice, 945 F.2d 227, 230 (7th Cir. 1991) (en banc) (protecting name of high school student who requested information about wiretaps on Jimmy Hoffa); see also FOIA Update, Vol. VII, No. 1, at 1 ("Surrogate FOIA Requests Increasing") (discussing the increasing popularity of surrogate FOIA requests -- "those made by persons or entities seeking federal records on behalf of others" -- whereby a corporation might want to be anonymous when seeking information about a competitor or a corporation, or an organization seeks to verify or disprove its suspicions that it might currently be under federal scrutiny).

[78] See FOIA Update, Vol. VI, No. 1, at 6.

[79] 5 U.S.C. § 552a (2000 & Supp. IV 2004).

[80] See FOIA Update, Vol. VI, No. 1, at 6.

substance of their letters, ordinarily should be withheld.[81] For instance, the Court of Appeals for the Fourth Circuit protected under Exemption 7(C) the

---

[81] See, e.g., Lakin Law Firm, 352 F.3d at 1125 (finding that the "core purposes" of the FOIA would not be served by the release of the names and addresses of persons who complained to the FTC about "cramming"); Strout v. U.S. Parole Comm'n, 40 F.3d 136, 139 (6th Cir. 1994) (articulating public policy against disclosure of names and addresses of people who write Parole Commission opposing convict's parole); Kidd v. Dep't of Justice, 362 F. Supp. 2d 291, 297 (D.D.C. 2005) (protecting names and addresses of constituents in letters written to their congressman); Butler v. Soc. Sec. Admin., No. 03-0810, slip op. at 5 (W.D. La. June 25, 2004) (finding that persons making complaints against an administrative law judge "have a privacy interest" in their complaints), aff'd on other grounds, No. 04-30854, 2005 WL 2055928 (5th Cir. Aug. 26, 2005); Save Our Springs Alliance v. Babbitt, No. A-97-CA-259, slip op. at 7-8 (W.D. Tex. Nov. 19, 1997) (concluding that release of home addresses and telephone numbers of government correspondents would not shed light on whether agency improperly considered writers' comments); Voinche v. FBI, 940 F. Supp. 323, 329-30 (D.D.C. 1996) ("There is no reason to believe that the public will obtain a better understanding of the workings of various agencies by learning the identities of . . . private citizens who wrote to government officials[.]"), aff'd per curiam, No. 96-5304, 1997 WL 411685 (D.C. Cir. June 19, 1997) Holy Spirit Ass'n v. U.S. Dep't of State, 526 F. Supp. 1022, 1032-34 (S.D.N.Y. 1981) (finding that "strong public interest in encouraging citizens to communicate their concerns regarding their communities" is fostered by protecting identities of writers); see also Holy Spirit Ass'n v. FBI, 683 F.2d 562, 564 (D.C. Cir. 1982) (concurring with the nondisclosure of correspondence because communications from citizens to their government "will frequently contain information of an intensely personal sort") (MacKinnon, J., concurring) (Exemptions 6 and 7(C)); cf. Ortiz v. HHS, 874 F. Supp. 570, 573-75 (S.D.N.Y.) (protecting letter to HHS alleging social security fraud) (Exemptions 7(C) and 7(D)), aff'd on Exemption 7(D) grounds, 70 F.3d 729 (2d Cir. 1995). But see also Memorandum for the President's Management Council 1 (Mar. 1, 2004) (providing guidance for federal agencies in implementing "E-Government initiative," and attaching NARA template for "Addresses" section of new regulatory preambles that includes new policy that "[a]ll comments received will be posted without change . . . including any personal information provided"), available at http://www.whitehouse.gov/omb/inforeg/memo_pmc_egov.pdf; see also U.S. Government, Regulations.gov, The Privacy and Use Notice Regarding Comment Submission, available at http://www.regulations.gov/fdmspublic/component/main (last visited Mar. 19, 2007) (establishing a government portal facilitating the location, review, and submission of comments on federal regulations published in the Federal Register that are open for public comment; stating that "[t]he general policy for comments and other submissions from members of the public is to make these submissions available for public viewing on the Internet as they are received and without change, including any personal identifiers or contact information").

names and addresses of people who wrote to the IRS expressing concerns about an organization's tax-exempt status.[82] Likewise, the District Court for the District of Columbia reached the same conclusion as the Fourth Circuit for the names and addresses of people who wrote to the IRS to comment on the same organization's tax-exempt status, both pro and con.[83] More recently, the District Court for the District of Columbia found that the names of persons who complained to the TSA and FBI about the TSA "watch list" were properly protected, as long as those individuals had not otherwise made their complaints public.[84] Nevertheless, in some circumstances courts have refused to accord privacy protection to such government correspondents.[85]

Additionally, neither corporations nor business associations possess

---

[82] Judicial Watch, Inc. v. United States, 84 F. App'x 335, 337 (4th Cir. 2004) (Exemption 7(C)).

[83] Judicial Watch, Inc. v. Rossotti, 285 F. Supp. 2d 17, 28 (D.D.C. 2003) (Exemption 7(C)).

[84] Gordon v. FBI, 388 F. Supp. 2d 1028, 1041-42, 1045 (N.D. Cal. 2005) (Exemptions 6 and 7(C)).

[85] See Lardner, 2005 WL 758267, at *17, *19 (requiring release of identities of unsuccessful pardon applicants, as well as of individuals mentioned in pardon documents, because they wrote letters in support of pardon applications or were listed as character references on pardon applications); Landmark Legal Found. v. IRS, 87 F. Supp. 2d 21, 27-28 (D.D.C. 2000) (granting Exemption 3 protection under 26 U.S.C. § 6103, but declining to grant Exemption 6 protection to citizens who wrote to IRS to express opinions or provide information; noting that "IRS has suggested no reason why existing laws are insufficient to deter any criminal or tortious conduct targeted at persons who would be identified"), aff'd on Exemption 3 grounds, 267 F.3d 1132 (D.C. Cir. 2001); Judicial Watch v. U.S. Dep't of Justice, 102 F. Supp. 2d 6, 17-18 (D.D.C. 2000) (allowing deletion of home addresses and telephone numbers but ordering release of identities of individuals who wrote to Attorney General about campaign finance or Independent Counsel issues), reconsideration denied temporarily pending in camera review, No. 97-CV-2869 (D.D.C. Aug. 17, 2000); Alliance for the Wild Rockies v. Dep't of the Interior, 53 F. Supp. 2d 32, 36-37 (D.D.C. 1999) (concluding that the agency "made it abundantly clear in its notice that the individuals submitting comments to its rulemaking would not have their identities concealed" when the rulemaking notice "specified that '[t]he complete file for this proposed rule is available for inspection'"); Cardona v. INS, No. 93-3912, 1995 WL 68747, at *3 (N.D. Ill. Feb. 15, 1995) (finding only "de minimis invasion of privacy" in release of name and address of individual who wrote letter to INS complaining about private agency that offered assistance to immigrants).

protectible privacy interests.[86] The closely held corporation or similar business entity, however, is an exception to this principle: "While corporations have no privacy, personal financial information is protected, including information about small businesses when the individual and corporation are identical."[87] Such an individual's expectation of privacy is, however, diminished with regard to matters in which he or she is acting in a business capacity.[88] In Doe v. Veneman, on the other hand, the District Court for the

---

[86] See, e.g., Sims v. CIA, 642 F.2d 562, 572 n.47 (D.C. Cir. 1980); Nat'l Parks & Conservation Ass'n v. Kleppe, 547 F.2d 673, 685 n.44 (D.C. Cir. 1976); Maydak v. U.S. Dep't of Justice, 362 F. Supp. 2d 316, 324-25 (D.D.C. 2005) (stating that Exemption 6 applies "'only to individuals'" (quoting Sims, 642 F.2d at 572 n.47)); cf. Forest Guardians v. U.S. Dep't of the Interior, 2004 WL 3426434, at *17 (reasoning that the identities of banks must be released because "that information is in the public domain"); Ivanhoe Citrus Ass'n v. Handley, 612 F. Supp. 1560, 1567 (D.D.C. 1985); see also Iowa Citizens for Cmty. Improvement v. USDA, No. 4-02-CV-10114, 2002 WL 32078275, at *5 n.10 (S.D. Iowa Aug. 13, 2002) (noting in dicta that "[i]t is not clear to this Court that a trust, any more than a corporation, has a privacy interest worthy of protection under the FOIA").

[87] Providence Journal Co. v. FBI, 460 F. Supp. 778, 785 (D.R.I. 1978), rev'd on other grounds, 602 F.2d 1010 (1st Cir. 1979); see also Beard v. Espy, No. 94-16748, 1995 WL 792071, at *1 (9th Cir. Dec. 11, 1995); Nat'l Parks, 547 F.2d at 685-86; Multi Ag Media LLC v. USDA, No. 05-1908, 2006 WL 2320941, at *2-3 (D.D.C. Aug. 9, 2006) ("[I]nformation withheld by the USDA pertains overwhelmingly to family-owed farms . . . the release of which would reveal personal information about those farms' owners."); Okla. Publ'g Co. v. HUD, No. CIV-87-1935-P, 1988 U.S. Dist. LEXIS 18643, at *4-5 (W.D. Okla. June 17, 1988); Atkinson v. FDIC, No. 79-1113, 1980 WL 355660, at *3 (D.D.C. Feb. 13, 1980) (protecting "personal financial information" of third parties), appeal dismissed voluntarily, No. 80-1409, 1980 WL 355810 (D.C. Cir. June 12, 1980); FOIA Update, Vol. III, No. 4, at 5 (advising that corporations do not have privacy, but that personal financial information is protectible when individual and corporation are identical). But see Long v. U.S. Dep't of Justice, 450 F. Supp. 2d 42, 72 (D.D.C.) ("At most, [the Department of Justice] ha[s] shown that disclosure of one record would reveal that an individual is associated with a business that in turn is a party to a legal proceeding. That fact, standing alone, does not implicate the FOIA's personal privacy concerns."), amended by 457 F. Supp. 2d 30 (D.D.C. 2006), amended further on reconsideration, Nos. 00-0211 & 02-2467, 2007 WL 293508 (D.D.C. Feb. 2, 2007), stay granted (D.D.C. Feb. 13, 2007).

[88] See, e.g., Or. Natural Desert Ass'n v. U.S. Dep't of the Interior, 24 F. Supp. 2d 1088, 1089 (D. Or. 1998) (concluding that cattle owners who violated federal grazing laws have "diminished expectation of privacy" in their names when such information relates to commercial interests) (Exemption 7(C)); Wash. Post Co. v. USDA, 943 F. Supp. 31, 34-36 (D.D.C. Oct. 18, 1996) (finding that farmers who received subsidies under cotton price support
(continued...)

Western District of Texas ruled that the Department of Agriculture had erroneously labeled individuals (who were taking part in a USDA program) as "businesses" based on either the number of livestock they owned or the fact that they had a name for their ranch, and it found that personally identifying information about those individuals was exempt from disclosure.[89]

The Supreme Court held unanimously in Favish that the "FOIA recognizes surviving family members' right to personal privacy with respect to their close relative's death-scene images."[90] This case involved a request for several death-scene photographs of Deputy White House Counsel Vincent Foster.[91] The government protected the photographs under the FOIA,

---

[88](...continued)
program have only minimal privacy interests in home addresses from which they also operate businesses), appeal dismissed voluntarily, No. 96-5373 (D.C. Cir. May 19, 1997); Ackerson & Bishop Chartered v. USDA, No. 92-1068, slip op. at 1 (D.D.C. July 15, 1992) (concluding that commercial mushroom growers operating under individual names have no expectation of privacy); Lawyers Comm. for Human Rights v. INS, 721 F. Supp. 552, 569 (S.D.N.Y. 1989) (stating that "disclosure [of names of State Department's officers and staff members involved in highly publicized case] merely establishes State [Department] employees' professional relationships or associates these employees with agency business"). But see Campaign for Family Farms v. Glickman, 200 F.3d 1180, 1187-89 (8th Cir. 2000) (protecting identities of pork producers who signed petition calling for abolishment of mandatory contributions to fund for marketing and advertising pork, because release would reveal position on referendum and "would vitiate petitioners' privacy interest in secret ballot") (reverse FOIA suit); Forest Guardians v. U.S. Forest Serv., No. 99-0615, slip op. at 39-45 (D.N.M. Jan. 29, 2001) (finding "'substantial' privacy interest" in personal loan information contained on escrow waiver forms that record ranchers' use of federal grazing permits as loan collateral) (reverse FOIA suit), appeal dismissed voluntarily, No. 01-2296 (10th Cir. Nov. 21, 2001); Hill v. USDA, 77 F. Supp. 2d 6, 8 (D.D.C. 1999) (finding privacy interest in records of business transactions between borrowers and partly owned family corporation relating to loans made by Farmers Home Administration to individual borrowers), summary affirmance granted, No. 99-5365, 2000 WL 520724, at *1 (D.C. Cir. Mar. 7, 2000).

[89] 230 F. Supp. 2d 739, 748-51 (W.D. Tex. 2002), aff'd in pertinent part on other grounds, 380 F.3d 807, 818 n.39 (5th Cir. 2004).

[90] 541 U.S. at 170; see also FOIA Post, "Supreme Court Rules for 'Survivor Privacy' in Favish" (posted 4/9/04) (highlighting full implications of Supreme Court's decision).

[91] 541 U.S. at 161.

but the lower courts ordered them disclosed.[92] Favish argued, relying on particular language in Reporter's Committee, that only the individual who was the direct "subject" of the records could have a privacy interest in those records.[93] The Court flatly rejected this argument, stating that "[t]he right to personal privacy is not confined, as Favish argues, to the 'right to control information about oneself.' Favish misreads [our opinion] in Reporter's Committee and adopts too narrow an interpretation of the case's holding."[94]

The Court then decided that "survivor privacy" was a valid privacy interest protected by Exemption 7(C), based on three factors. First, Reporter's Committee did not restrict personal privacy as "some limited or 'cramped notion' of that idea,"[95] so personal privacy is broad enough to protect surviving family members' "own privacy rights against public intrusions."[96] Second, the Court reviewed the long tradition at common law of "acknowledging a family's control over the body and death images of the deceased."[97] Third, the Court reasoned that Congress used that background in creating Exemption 7(C), including the fact that the government-wide FOIA policy memoranda of two Attorneys General had specifically extended privacy protection to families.[98]

Thus, the Supreme Court endorsed the holdings of several lower courts in recognizing that surviving family members have a protectible privacy interest in sensitive, often graphic, personal details about the circum-

---

[92] Id. at 161-64; see FOIA Post, "Supreme Court Decides to Hear 'Survivor Privacy' Case" (posted 5/13/03; supplemented 10/10/03) (chronicling case's history).

[93] 541 U.S. at 165.

[94] Id.

[95] Id. at 165.

[96] Id. at 167.

[97] Id. at 168. But cf. Showler, No. 05-178, slip op. at 6 (E.D. Okla. Dec. 22, 2005) (finding that a photograph of a deceased individual was distinguishable from the death-scene photographs in Favish because, inter alia, the photograph "was taken at a public, newsworthy event" and "was the same scene the funeral attendees observed").

[98] Id. at 169 (citing Attorney General's Memorandum on the Public Information Section of the Administrative Procedure Act (FOIA) 36 (June 1967) and Attorney General's Memorandum on the 1974 Amendments to the Freedom of Information Act 9-10 (Feb. 1975)); see also FOIA Post, "Supreme Court Rules for 'Survivor Privacy' in Favish" (posted 4/9/04) (noting that Supreme Court "dr[ew] additional support from two successive Attorney General memoranda on FOIA that specifically extended privacy protection to 'family members'").

stances surrounding an individual's death.[99] Further, while the Favish case involved graphic photographs, the Court's decision also supported the holdings of other courts that even information that is not so graphically sensitive in and of itself may be withheld to protect the privacy interests of surviving family members if disclosure would cause "'a disruption of their

---

[99] See, e.g., Hale v. U.S. Dep't of Justice, 973 F.2d 894, 902 (10th Cir. 1992) (perceiving "no public interest in photographs of the deceased victim, let alone one that would outweigh the personal privacy interests of the victim's family") (Exemption 7(C)), cert. granted, vacated & remanded on other grounds, 509 U.S. 918 (1993); Bowen v. FDA, 925 F.2d 1225, 1228 (9th Cir. 1991) (affirming nondisclosure of autopsy reports of individuals killed by cyanide-contaminated products); Badhwar v. U.S. Dep't of the Air Force, 829 F.2d 182, 186 (D.C. Cir. 1987) (noting that some autopsy reports might "shock the sensibilities of surviving kin"); Marzen v. HHS, 825 F.2d 1148, 1154 (7th Cir. 1987) (holding deceased infant's medical records exempt because their release "would almost certainly cause . . . parents more anguish"); Isley v. Executive Office for U.S. Attorneys, No. 96-0123, slip op. at 3-4 (D.D.C. Feb. 25, 1998) (approving the withholding of "medical records, autopsy reports and inmate injury reports pertaining to a murder victim as a way of protecting surviving family members"), aff'd on other grounds, 203 F.3d 52 (D.C. Cir. 1999) (unpublished table decision); Katz v. NARA, 862 F. Supp. 476, 483-86 (D.D.C. 1994) (holding that Kennedy family's privacy interests would be invaded by disclosure of "graphic and explicit" JFK autopsy photographs), aff'd on other grounds, 68 F.3d 1438 (D.C. Cir. 1995); N.Y. Times Co. v. NASA, 782 F. Supp. 628, 631-32 (D.D.C. 1991) (withholding audiotape of voices of Space Shuttle Challenger astronauts recorded immediately before their deaths, to protect family members from pain of hearing final words of loved ones). But see Journal-Gazette Co. v. U.S. Dep't of the Army, No. F89-147, slip op. at 8-9 (N.D. Ind. Jan. 8, 1990) (holding that because autopsy report of Air National Guard pilot killed in training exercise contained "concise medical descriptions of the cause of death," not "graphic, morbid descriptions," survivors' minimal privacy interest was were outweighed by public interest); see also FOIA Post, "Supreme Court Rules for 'Survivor Privacy' in Favish" (posted 4/9/04) (cautioning that "agencies applying this important principle must be mindful that it logically requires reasonable certainty that a survivor actually exists to merit such protection"); cf. Outlaw v. U.S. Dep't of the Army, 815 F. Supp. 505, 506 (D.D.C. 1993) (ordering disclosure in absence of evidence of existence of any survivor whose privacy would be invaded by release of murder-scene photographs of man murdered twenty-five years earlier); Kyle v. United States, No. 80-1038E, 1987 WL 13874, at *1-2 (W.D.N.Y. July 16, 1987) (ordering disclosure of medical records of all servicemen involved in accident alike, including two who died and one who was still alive); Rabbitt v. Dep't of the Air Force, 401 F. Supp. 1206, 1210 (S.D.N.Y. 1974) (ordering disclosure of medical records of two Air Force personnel involved in accident alike, including one who died and one who was still alive).

peace of minds.'"[100]

Also of significance is the fact that the Supreme Court's decision in Favish made it quite clear that the Court was not recognizing the "survivor privacy" principle on the basis of any surviving privacy interest of Mr. Foster, i.e., his "own posthumous reputation or some other interest personal to him."[101] Instead, the principle was applied based upon the Foster family's "own right and interest" in personal privacy protection.[102] The Court characterized this interest as the privacy interest of the family members in being "secure [in] their own refuge from a sensation-seeking culture[,] for their own peace of mind and tranquility."[103] Thus, the Court's adoption of "survivor privacy" does not alter the longstanding FOIA rule that death extinguishes one's privacy rights.[104] Most specifically, the Court in Favish

---

[100] 541 U.S. at 170-71 (quoting N.Y. Times Co., 782 F. Supp. at 631-32); see also Cowles Publ'g Co. v. United States, No. 90-349, slip op. at 6-7 (E.D. Wash. Dec. 20, 1990) (withholding identities of individuals who became ill or died from radiation exposure, in order to protect living victims and family members of deceased persons from intrusive contacts and inquiries); FOIA Post, "Supreme Court Rules for 'Survivor Privacy' in Favish" (posted 4/9/04) (discussing protection of records of Dr. Martin Luther King, Jr. assassination investigation); FOIA Update, Vol. III, No. 4, at 5 (advising more than twenty-five years ago that while privacy rights cannot be inherited, sensitive personal information pertaining to or affecting deceased persons may threaten privacy interests of surviving family members).

[101] 541 U.S. at 166; see also FOIA Post, "Supreme Court Rules for 'Survivor Privacy' in Favish" (posted 4/9/04) (advising that "the Court's 'survivor privacy' analysis in Favish eschewed" any such decedent-based approach).

[102] 541 U.S. at 166.

[103] Id.

[104] See, e.g., Na Iwi O Na Kupuna v. Dalton, 894 F. Supp. 1397, 1413 (D. Haw. 1995) (reverse FOIA suit); Tigar & Buffone v. U.S. Dep't of Justice, No. 80-2382, slip op. at 9-10 (D.D.C. Sept. 30, 1983) (Exemption 7(C)); Diamond v. FBI, 532 F. Supp. 216, 227 (S.D.N.Y. 1981), aff'd on other grounds, 707 F.2d 75 (2d Cir. 1983); see also FOIA Post, "Supreme Court Rules for 'Survivor Privacy' in Favish" (posted 4/9/04); FOIA Post, "Supreme Court Decides to Hear 'Survivor Privacy' Case" (posted 5/13/03; supplemented 10/10/03); FOIA Update, Vol. III, No. 4, at 5 (advising that "[a]fter death, a person no longer possesses privacy rights . . . [and that] privacy rights cannot be inherited by one heirs, [though] the disclosure of particularly sensitive personal information pertaining to a deceased person may well threaten the privacy interests of surviving family members or other close associates"); cf. United States v. Schlette, 842 F.2d 1574, 1581 (9th Cir.) (ordering disclosure of presentence report of deceased person pursuant to Rule 32(c) of Federal Rules of Criminal Procedure), amended, 854 F.2d 359 (9th Cir.

(continued...)

did not place any reliance on a recent potential variant of the concept that "focuse[d] on the interests of the deceased person even apart from the interests of his or her survivors."[105] That decedent-based approach has never been embraced as a matter of policy by the Department of Justice, and the Supreme Court likewise did not embrace it in Favish.[106]

On another point involved in Favish, public figures do not surrender all rights to privacy by placing themselves in the public eye, though certainly their expectations of privacy in general may be diminished. In some instances, "[t]he degree of intrusion is indeed potentially augmented by the fact that the individual is a well known figure."[107] It has been held that disclosure of sensitive personal information contained in investigative records about a public figure is appropriate "only where exceptional interests militate in favor of disclosure."[108] Thus, although one's status as a public figure

---

[104](...continued)
1988). But see Kiraly v. FBI, 728 F.2d 273, 277-78 (6th Cir. 1984) (adopting the district court's rationale, "which held: '. . . that the right to recovery for invasion of privacy lapses upon the person's death does not mean that the government must disclose inherently private information as soon as the individual dies'") (Exemption 7(C)).

[105] FOIA Post, "Supreme Court Decides to Hear 'Survivor Privacy' Case" (posted 5/13/03; supplemented 10/10/03) (discussing line of D.C. Circuit cases that suggested protecting post-mortem "reputational" interests).

[106] See 541 U.S. at 166 (distinguishing "survivor privacy" basis from any "reputation[al]" basis for privacy protection); see also FOIA Post, "Supreme Court Rules for 'Survivor Privacy' in Favish" (posted 4/9/04) (advising that "the proper application of [the 'survivor privacy'] principle involves protection of the interests of a decedent's survivors themselves").

[107] Fund for Constitutional Gov't v. Nat'l Archives & Records Serv., 656 F.2d 856, 865 (D.C. Cir. 1981) (emphasis added) (Exemption 7(C)); see Times Picayune, 37 F. Supp. 2d at 478-79 (noting that prominence of person "may well exacerbate the privacy intrusions") (Exemption 7(C)); cf. Wichlacz v. Dep't of Interior, 938 F. Supp. 325, 333-34 (E.D. Va. 1996) (recognizing that intense media scrutiny of death of Deputy White House Counsel Vincent Foster enhances privacy interests of individuals connected even remotely with investigation), aff'd, 114 F.3d 1178 (4th Cir. 1997) (unpublished table decision).

[108] Fund, 656 F.2d at 866; see also Nation Magazine v. Dep't of State, No. 92-2303, 1995 WL 17660254, at *8-11 & n.15 (D.D.C. Aug. 18, 1995) (holding that public interest in information about presidential candidate H. Ross Perot's dealings with government or whether he ever was investigated by FBI is not kind of public interest recognized by FOIA); Wilson v. Dep't of Justice, No. 87-2415, 1991 WL 111457, at *6 (D.D.C. June 13, 1991) (stating that even well-known Iran-Contra figure Richard Secord had privacy inter-
(continued...)

might in some circumstances factor into the privacy balance, a public figure does not, by virtue of his status, forfeit all rights of privacy.[109]

Indeed, in Favish, former Deputy White House Counsel Vincent Foster's status as both a public figure in the "Whitewater" matter and a high-level government official did not, in the Supreme Court's opinion, "detract"

---

[108](...continued)
est in fact that he was investigated; such investigation would reveal "little about 'what government is up to'"); cf. In re Espy, 259 F.3d 725, 729-30 (D.C. Cir. 2001) (granting motion, pursuant to Independent Counsel Statute, 28 U.S.C. § 594(h) (2000), to release final report concerning former Secretary of Agriculture). But see Wilson v. Dep't of Justice, No. 87-2415, 1991 WL 120052, at *4 (D.D.C. June 18, 1991) (ordering further declarations to determine whether any of the individuals investigated "are 'public figures' like the plaintiff whose involvement in Government operations would be of interest to the public").

[109] See Fund, 656 F.2d at 865; Phillips v. Immigration & Customs Enforcement, 385 F. Supp. 2d 296, 305 (S.D.N.Y. 2005) (disregarding requester's unsupported claim that former foreign government officials have no "legitimate privacy interest[s]"); Wolk v. United States, No. 04-832, 2005 WL 465382, at *5 (E.D. Pa. Feb. 28, 2005) ("[O]fficials do not surrender all of their rights to personal privacy when they accept a public appointment.") (Exemptions 6 and 7(C)); Elec. Privacy Info. Ctr. v. U.S. Dep't of Justice, No. 02-0063, slip op. at 10 n.7 (D.D.C. Mar. 11, 2004) (concluding that "government officials do not lose all personal private rights when they accept a public appointment"); Billington v. Dep't of Justice, 11 F. Supp. 2d 45, 62 (D.D.C. 1998) (finding that although public officials in some circumstances have diminished privacy, residual privacy interests militate against disclosure of nonpublic details), aff'd in pertinent part, 233 F.3d 581 (D.C. Cir. 2000); see also FOIA Update, Vol. III, No. 4, at 5 (advising on extent to which public figures are entitled to privacy protections); cf. Strassman v. U.S. Dep't of Justice, 792 F.2d 1267, 1268 (4th Cir. 1986) (protecting privacy interest of governor alleged to have invoked Fifth Amendment before grand jury) (Exemption 7(C)); McNamera v. U.S. Dep't of Justice, 974 F. Supp. 946, 959 (W.D. Tex. 1997) (stating that "[s]imply because an individual was once a public official does not mean that he retains that status throughout his life," and holding that three years after a disgraced sheriff resigned he was "a private, not a public figure") (Exemption 7(C)); Steinberg v. U.S. Dep't of Justice, No. 93-2409, slip op. at 11 (D.D.C. July 14, 1997) ("[E]ven widespread knowledge about a person's business dealings cannot serve to diminish his or her privacy interests in matters that are truly personal.") (Exemption 7(C)). But cf. Judicial Watch, Inc. v. U.S. Dep't of Justice, No. 00-745, 2001 U.S. Dist. LEXIS 25731, at *13 (D.D.C. Feb. 12, 2001) (suggesting that pardoned prisoners lost any privacy interests since they "arguably be-c[a]me public figures through their well-publicized pleas for clemency and [given] the speeches some have made since their release") (Exemption 7(C)).

at all from the "weighty privacy interests involved."[110] Likewise, a candidate for a political office, either federal or nonfederal, does not forfeit all rights to privacy.[111] It also should be noted in this regard that, unlike under the Privacy Act, foreign nationals are entitled to the same basic privacy rights under the FOIA as are U.S. citizens.[112]

Individuals do not waive their privacy rights merely by signing a document that states that information may be released to third parties under the FOIA.[113] As one court has observed, such a statement is not a waiver

---

[110] 541 U.S. at 171; see also FOIA Post, "Supreme Court Rules for 'Survivor Privacy' in Favish" (posted 4/9/04) (advising that the "fact that [Mr. Foster's] status did not at all 'detract' from those [privacy] interests in the Court's estimation means that they stood entirely undiminished despite it" and that "[i]n the future, other potential beneficiaries of the FOIA's privacy exemptions should be no less entitled to such treatment and commensurate privacy protection").

[111] See Nation Magazine, 71 F.3d at 894 & n.9 ("Although candidacy for federal office may diminish an individual's right to privacy . . . it does not eliminate it[.]"); Hunt v. U.S. Marine Corps, 935 F. Supp. 46, 54 (D.D.C. 1996) (finding that senatorial candidate Oliver North has unquestionable privacy interest in his military service personnel records and medical records); Nation Magazine, 1995 WL 17660254, at *10 (upholding refusal to confirm or deny existence of investigative records pertaining to presidential candidate H. Ross Perot); cf. Iowa Citizens for Cmty. Improvement v. USDA, 256 F. Supp. 2d 946, 954 (S.D. Iowa 2002) (ruling that nominee for position of Undersecretary of Agriculture for Rural Development does not forfeit all privacy rights).

[112] See Shaw v. U.S. Dep't of State, 559 F. Supp. 1053, 1067 (D.D.C. 1983); see also Ray, 502 U.S. at 175-79 (applying traditional analysis of privacy interests under FOIA to Haitian nationals); Ctr. for Nat'l Sec. Studies v. U.S. Dep't of Justice, 215 F. Supp. 2d 94, 105-06 (D.D.C. 2002) (recognizing, without discussion, the privacy rights of post-9/11 detainees who were unlawfully in the United States) (Exemption 7(C)), aff'd on other grounds, 331 F.3d 918 (D.C. Cir. 2003); Schiller v. INS, 205 F. Supp. 2d 648, 662 (W.D. Tex. 2002) (finding that "[a]liens [and] their families . . . have a strong privacy interest in nondisclosure of their names, addresses, and other information which could lead to revelation of their identities") (Exemption 7(C)); Judicial Watch, Inc. v. Reno, No. 00-0723, 2001 WL 1902811, at *8 (D.D.C. Mar. 30, 2001) (protecting asylum application filed on behalf of Cuban emigré Elian Gonzalez); Hemenway, 601 F. Supp. at 1005-07 (according Exemption 6 protection to citizenship information regarding news correspondents accredited to attend State Department press briefings); FOIA Update, Vol. VI, No. 3, at 5.

[113] See Hill, 77 F. Supp. 2d at 8; see also Lakin Law Firm, 352 F.3d at 1124-25 (explaining that a warning on Federal Trade Commission Web site

(continued...)

of the right to confidentiality, it is merely a warning by the agency and corresponding acknowledgment by the signers "that the information they were providing could be subject to release."[114] Similarly, individuals who sign a petition, knowing that those who sign afterward will observe their signatures, do not waive their privacy interests.[115] While such persons "would have no reason to be concerned that a limited number of like-minded individuals may have seen their names," they may well be concerned "that the petition not become available to the general public, including those opposing [the petitioners' position]."[116]

It also is important to remember that while the government may voluntarily or involuntarily waive its right to an exemption when its own interests are at stake, it cannot waive an individual's privacy interests under the FOIA by unilaterally publicizing information about that person.[117] The privacy interest inherent in Exemption 6 "belongs to the individual, not the agency holding the information," and "the fact that otherwise private information at one time or in some way may have been placed in the public domain does not mean that a person irretrievably loses his or her privacy interest in the information."[118]

---

[113](...continued)
that "information provided may be subject to release under the FOIA" cannot be construed as a waiver by consumers) (emphasis added).

[114] Hill, 77 F. Supp. 2d at 8 (rejecting argument that borrowers of Farmers Home Administration loans waived their privacy interests by signing loan-application documents that warned that information supplied could be subject to release to third parties). But cf. Associated Press, 410 F. Supp. 2d at 149-51 (finding that 317 Guantanamo Bay detainees had no cognizable privacy interests in their identifying information despite the fact that only sixty-three of them stated that they wanted their identifying information released when responding to a court-ordered survey that purportedly "aid[ed] the Court in resolving" its Exemption 6 analysis).

[115] See Campaign for Family Farms, 200 F.3d at 1188.

[116] Id.

[117] See Sherman v. U.S. Dep't of the Army, 244 F.3d 357, 363-64 (5th Cir. 2001) (protecting social security numbers of soldiers even though Army publicly disclosed SSNs in some circumstances, because individuals rather than government hold privacy interest in that information); see also Reporters Comm., 489 U.S. at 763-65 (emphasizing that privacy interest belongs to individual, not agency holding information pertaining to individual).

[118] Sherman, 244 F.3d at 363-64; accord Attorney General's Memorandum for Heads of All Federal Departments and Agencies Regarding the Freedom of Information Act (Oct. 12, 2001), reprinted in FOIA Post (posted 10/15/01) (emphasizing importance of "preserving personal privacy" under FOIA); FOIA Post, "New Attorney General FOIA Memorandum Issued" (continued...)

In addition, individuals who testify at criminal trials do not forfeit their rights to privacy except on those very matters that become part of the public record.[119] Nor do individuals who plead guilty to criminal charges lose all rights to privacy with regard to the proceedings against them.[120] Similarly, individuals who provide law enforcement agencies with reports of illegal conduct have well-recognized privacy interests, particularly when such persons reasonably fear reprisals for their assistance.[121] Even absent

---

[118](...continued)
(posted 10/15/01) (noting that the Ashcroft FOIA Memorandum "places particular emphasis on the right to privacy among the other interests that are protected by the FOIA's exemptions").

[119] See Isley, 1999 WL 1021934, at *4; Kiraly, 728 F.2d at 279; Brown v. FBI, 658 F.2d 71, 75 (2d Cir. 1981); see also Meserve v. U.S. Dep't of Justice, No. 04-1844, 2006 WL 2366427, at *7 (D.D.C. Aug. 14, 2006) ("[A] witness who testifies at trial does not waive her personal privacy."); Butler v. U.S. Dep't of Justice, 368 F. Supp. 2d 776, 783-84 (E.D. Mich. 2005) (protecting information about "informant who gave grand jury testimony implicating Plaintiff in crimes") (Exemptions 6 and 7(C)); Coleman v. FBI, 13 F. Supp. 2d 75, 80 (D.D.C. 1998); cf. Irons v. FBI, 880 F.2d 1446, 1454 (1st Cir. 1989) (en banc) (holding that disclosure of any source information beyond that actually testified to by confidential source is not required) (Exemption 7(D)).

[120] See Times Picayune, 37 F. Supp. 2d at 477-78 (refusing to order release of a mug shot, which with its "unflattering facial expressions" and "stigmatizing effect [that] can last well beyond the actual criminal proceedings . . . preserves, in its unique and visually powerful way, the subject individual's brush with the law for posterity"); see also McNamera, 974 F. Supp. at 959 (holding that convict's privacy rights are diminished only with respect to information made public during criminal proceedings against him) (Exemption 7(C)).

[121] See McCutchen v. HHS, 30 F.3d 183, 189 (D.C. Cir. 1994) ("The complainants [alleging scientific misconduct] have a strong privacy interest in remaining anonymous because, as 'whistle-blowers,' they might face retaliation if their identities were revealed.") (Exemption 7(C)); Holy Spirit, 683 F.2d at 564-65 (concurring opinion) (recognizing that writers of letters to authorities describing "'bizarre' and possibly illegal activities . . . could reasonably have feared reprisals against themselves or their family members") (Exemptions 6 and 7(C)); Balderrama v. DHS, No. 04-1617, 2006 WL 889778, at *9 (D.D.C. Mar. 30, 2006) ("[T]he individuals whose identities have been protected -- witnesses, undercover officers, informants -- maintain a substantial privacy interest in not being identified with law enforcement proceedings.") (Exemptions 6 and 7(C)); Forest Serv. Employees for Envtl. Ethics v. U.S. Forest Serv., No. 05-6015, 2005 WL 3488453, at *3 (D. Or. Dec. 21, 2005) (protecting identities of low-level and mid-level Forest Service employees who cooperated with accident investigation, because "these employees could face harassment"); Billington v. U.S. Dep't of Justice, 301 F.

(continued...)

any evidence of fear of reprisals, however, witnesses who provide information to investigative bodies -- administrative and civil, as well as criminal -- ordinarily are accorded privacy protection.[122] (For a more detailed discus-

---

[121](...continued)
Supp. 2d 15, 19-21 (D.D.C. 2004) (protecting identity of reporter who furnished interview notes to State Department, partly based upon existence of "substantial" fear of reprisal by Lyndon LaRouche followers); McQueen v. United States, 264 F. Supp. 2d 502, 519-20 (S.D. Tex. 2003) (protecting names and identifying information of grand jury witnesses and other sources when suspect had made previous threats against witnesses) (Exemption 7(C)), aff'd per curiam, 100 F. App'x 964 (5th Cir. 2004); Givner v. Executive Office for U.S. Attorneys, No. 99-3454, slip op. at 12-13 (D.D.C. Mar. 1, 2001) (finding withholding of juror and witness information "particularly appropriate" when "codefendents are either still fugitives or seeking a new trial"); Summers v. U.S. Dep't of Justice, No. 87-3168, slip op. at 4-15 (D.D.C. Apr. 19, 2000) (protecting identities of individuals who provided information to FBI Director J. Edgar Hoover concerning well-known people "because persons who make allegations against public figures are often subject to public scrutiny"); Ortiz, 874 F. Supp. at 573-75 (noting that probable close relationship between plaintiff and author of letter about her to HHS was likely to lead to retaliation); Cappabianca v. Comm'r, U.S. Customs Serv., 847 F. Supp. 1558, 1564-65 (M.D. Fla. 1994) (finding that the "opportunity for harassment or embarrassment is very strong" in a case involving the investigation of "allegations of harassment and retaliation for cooperation in a prior investigation") (Exemptions 6 and 7(C)); Manna v. U.S. Dep't of Justice, 815 F. Supp. 798, 809 (D.N.J. 1993) (concluding that because La Cosa Nostra "is so violent and retaliatory, the names of interviewees, informants, witnesses, victims and law enforcement personnel must be safeguarded") (Exemption 7(C)), aff'd, 51 F.3d 1158 (3d Cir. 1995).

[122] See, e.g., Perlman v. U.S. Dep't of Justice, 312 F.3d 100, 106 (2d Cir. 2002) (concluding that "[t]he public's interest in learning the identities of witnesses and other third parties is minimal because the information tells little or nothing about either the administration of the INS program or the Inspector General's conduct of its investigation") (Exemptions 6 and 7(C)), vacated & remanded, 541 U.S. 970, on remand, 380 F.3d 110 (2d Cir. 2004) (per curiam); Ford v. West, No. 97-1342, 1998 WL 317561, at *1-2 (10th Cir. June 12, 1998) (finding thoughts, sentiments, and emotions of co-workers questioned in investigation of racial harassment claim to be within protections of Exemptions 6 and 7(C)); Citizens for Responsibility & Ethics in Wash. v. Nat'l Indian Gaming Comm'n, No. 05-0806, 2006 U.S. Dist. LEXIS 89614, at *29 (D.D.C. Dec. 12, 2006) ("The fact that an individual supplied information to assist [National Indian Gaming Commission] in its investigations is exempt from disclosure under FOIA, regardless of the nature of the information supplied.") (Exemptions 6 and 7(C)); Brown v. EPA, 384 F. Supp. 2d 271, 278-80 (D.D.C. 2005) (protecting government employee-witnesses and informants because "[t]here are important principles at stake in the general rule that employees may come forward to
(continued...)

sion of the privacy protection accorded such law enforcement sources, see Exemption 7(C), below.)

An agency ordinarily is not required to conduct research to determine whether an individual has died or whether his activities have sufficiently become the subject of public knowledge so as to bar the application of Exemption 6.[123] The D.C. Circuit upheld the use of the FBI's "100-year rule,"

---

[122](...continued)
law enforcement officials with allegations of government wrongdoing and not fear that their identities will be exposed through FOIA") (Exemption 7(C)); Wolk, 2005 WL 465382, at *5 n.7 (recognizing that "interviewees who participate in FBI background investigations have a substantial privacy interest") (Exemptions 6 and 7(C)); Hayes v. U.S. Dep't of Labor, No. 96-1149, slip op. at 9-10 (S.D. Ala. June 18, 1998) (magistrate's recommendation) (protecting information that "would have divulged personal information or disclosed the identity of a confidential source" in an OSHA investigation) (Exemption 7(C)), adopted (S.D. Ala. Aug. 10, 1998); Tenaska Wash. Partners v. U.S. Dep't of Energy, No. 8:96-128, slip op. at 6-8 (D. Neb. Feb. 19, 1997) (protecting information that would "readily identify" individuals who provided information during routine IG audit); McLeod v. Peña, No. 94-1924, slip op. at 4 (D.D.C. Feb. 9, 1996) (protecting in their entireties memoranda and witness statements concerning investigation of plaintiff's former commanding officer when unit consisted of eight officers and twenty enlisted personnel) (Exemption 7(C)), summary affirmance granted sub nom. McLeod v. U.S. Coast Guard, No. 96-5071, 1997 WL 150096 (D.C. Cir. Feb. 10, 1997). But see Cooper Cameron Corp. v. U.S. Dep't of Labor, 280 F.3d 539, 553-54 (5th Cir. 2002) (ordering disclosure of information that could link witnesses to their OSHA investigation statements, because agency presented no evidence of "possibility of employer retaliation") (Exemption 7(C)); Fortson, 407 F. Supp. at 17 (deciding that witness statements compiled during an investigation of an equal employment opportunity complaint filed by the plaintiff must be released due to the following: the government previously released the names of persons who gave statements during the investigation; the agency offered only "pure speculation" of potential for harm to be caused by disclosure of the statements; and "witness statements made during a discrimination investigation are not the type of information that exemption 6 is designed to protect"); Fine v. U.S. Dep't of Energy, 823 F. Supp. 888, 896 (D.N.M. 1993) (ordering disclosure based partly upon the fact that the plaintiff no longer was employed by the agency and was "not in a position on-the-job to harass or intimidate employees of DOE/OIG and/or its contractors").

[123] See FOIA Update, Vol. V, No. 1, at 5; see also Davis v. Dep't of Justice, No. 04-5406, 2006 WL 2411393, at *10 (D.C. Cir. Aug. 22, 2006) ("In determining whether an agency's search is reasonable, a court must consider the likelihood that it will yield the sought-after information, the existence of readily available alternatives, and the burden of employing those alternatives.") (Exemption 7(C)); see also, e.g., Johnson v. Executive Office for U.S.
(continued...)

whereby the FBI assumes that an individual is alive unless his or her birth-date is more than 100 years ago, in making its privacy protection determi-nations.[124] This general rule is further strengthened by the Supreme Court's observations in Reporters Committee that "without regard to indi-vidual circumstances" certain categories of records will always warrant privacy protection and that "the standard virtues of bright-line rules are thus present, and the difficulties attendant to ad hoc adjudication may be avoided."[125] Before the D.C. Circuit's decision in that case several courts, faced with very old documents, refused to accept the presumption that all

---

[123](...continued)

Attorneys, 310 F.3d 771, 775-76 (D.C. Cir. 2002) (finding that agency's ef-forts to determine if individuals were alive or dead met "basic steps" nec-essary to determine information that could affect privacy interests, and concluding that "[w]e will not attempt to establish a brightline set of steps for agency to take" in determining whether an individual is dead); Manna v. U.S. Dep't of Justice, No. 92-1840, slip op. at 8 (D.N.J. Aug. 27, 1993) (find-ing government's obligation fulfilled by search of computerized index sys-tem and index cards for evidence of death of witness relocated more than twenty years ago), aff'd, 51 F.3d 1158 (3d Cir. 1995); Williams v. U.S. Dep't of Justice, 556 F. Supp. 63, 66 (D.D.C. 1982) (finding agency's good-faith processing, rather than extensive research for public disclosures, sufficient in lengthy, multifaceted judicial proceedings); cf. McGehee v. Casey, 718 F.2d 1137, 1141 n.9 (D.C. Cir. 1983) (recognizing that CIA cannot reason-ably bear burden of conducting exhaustive search to prove that particular items of classified information have never been published) (non-FOIA case).

[124] Schrecker v. U.S. Dep't of Justice, 349 F.3d 657, 662-65 (D.C. Cir. 2003) (holding decisively at long last that the FBI's administrative process of using its "100-year rule," searching the Social Security Death Index if an in-dividual's birthdate is in records, and using its institutional knowledge is reasonable and entirely sufficient in determining whether individuals men-tioned in requested records are deceased); see Davis, 2006 WL 2411393, at *5-6 (acknowledging FBI's use of "100-year rule"; finding that use of the rule was destined to fail when applied to audiotapes, as opposed to docu-ments, and stating that "[t]he reasonableness of [the "100-year rule"] de-pends upon the probability that the responsive records will contain the in-dividual's birth date . . . . [I]t seems highly unlikely that the participants in an audiotaped conversation would have announced their ages or dates of birth") (Exemption 7(C)); see also Piper v. U.S. Dep't of Justice, 428 F. Supp. 2d 1, 3 (D.D.C. Apr. 12, 2006) (observing that D.C. Circuit in Schrecker, 349 F.3d at 665, concluded that use of "100-year rule" was reasonable).

[125] 489 U.S. at 780; see also Favish, 541 U.S. at 173 (discussing the need for "stability with respect to both the specific category of privacy interests . . . and . . . public interests," because "[o]therwise, courts will be left to bal-ance in an ad hoc manner"); accord Halloran v. VA, 874 F.2d 315, 322 (5th Cir. 1989); see also FOIA Update, Vol. X, No. 2, at 4 (advising on "categori-cal balancing" principle that was enunciated in Reporters Committee).

individuals mentioned in such documents were alive.[126]

Faced with "reverse" FOIA challenges, several courts have had to consider whether to order agencies not to release records pertaining to individuals that agencies had determined should be disclosed.[127] In a case that reached the Court of Appeals for the Eighth Circuit, the signers of a petition requesting a referendum to abolish a mandatory payment by pork producers sued to prevent the Department of Agriculture from releasing their names pursuant to a FOIA request.[128] The Eighth Circuit agreed that,

---

[126] See Davin v. U.S. Dep't of Justice, 60 F.3d 1043, 1059 (3d Cir. 1995) ("[A]fter a sufficient passage of time . . . it would be unreasonable . . . not to assume that many of the individuals named in the requested records have died."); Diamond, 707 F.2d at 77 (requiring agency to review 200,000 pages outside scope of request to search for evidence as to whether subjects' privacy had been waived through death or prior public disclosure) (Exemption 7(C)); Outlaw, 815 F. Supp. at 506 (declining to withhold photographs of a victim murdered twenty-five years ago to protect the privacy of relatives when "[d]efendant's concern for the privacy of the decedent's surviving relatives has not extended to an effort to locate them . . . [and] there is no showing by defendant that, as of now, there are any surviving relatives of the deceased, or if there are, that they would be offended by the disclosure"); Wilkinson v. FBI, No. 80-1048, slip op. at 12-13 (C.D. Cal. June 17, 1987) (holding Exemption 7(C) inapplicable to documents more than thirty years old because the government relied on a presumption that "all persons [who are] the subject of FOIA requests are . . . living"); see also Summers v. Dep't of Justice, 140 F.3d 1077, 1085 (D.C. Cir. 1998) (Williams, J., concurring) (suggesting that "taking death into account only if the fact has happened to swim into their line of vision" might not be adequate if the FBI has access to "data bases that could resolve the issue") (Exemptions 6 and 7(C)); cf. Rosenfeld v. U.S. Dep't of Justice, 57 F.3d 803, 813 (9th Cir. 1995) (ordering disclosure of information based upon belief that it was not likely that anyone could be identified twenty-five years later) (Exemption 7(C)). But see Assassination Archives & Research Ctr. v. CIA, 903 F. Supp. 131, 133 (D.D.C. 1995) (protecting the identities of third parties in thirty-to-forty-year-old records based upon its finding "that the passage of time may actually increase privacy interests") (Exemption 7(C)).

[127] See, e.g., Nat'l Org. for Women v. Soc. Sec. Admin., 736 F.2d 727, 728 (D.C. Cir. 1984) (per curiam) (affirming district court's decision to enjoin release of affirmative action plans submitted to SSA) (Exemptions 4 and 6); Sonderegger v. U.S. Dep't of the Interior, 424 F. Supp. 847, 853-56 (D. Idaho 1976) (ordering temporary injunction of release of claimant names and amount claimed for victims of Teton Dam disaster, while allowing release of amount paid and category of payment with all personal identifying information deleted) (Exemptions 4 and 6).

[128] Campaign for Family Farms, 200 F.3d at 1182-84.

under the standards of the Administrative Procedure Act,[129] the Department of Agriculture's initial disclosure determination was not in accordance with law and the names must be withheld.[130]

In another decision involving the Department of Agriculture, arising in a reverse FOIA context, the District Court for the Southern District of Texas found that an agency decision to release identifying information about farmers and ranchers was incorrect and that this information must be withheld.[131] However, it went much further by issuing a permanent injunction that prohibited the agency from releasing this sort of information in any form.[132] On appeal, the Court of Appeals for the Fifth Circuit concluded that the district court lacked the jurisdiction to issue such a broad injunction because the Department of Agriculture had already agreed to not release the information at issue;[133] moreover, that injunction was found to be overbroad because it prohibited disclosures outside the context of the FOIA request that was at issue in that case.[134]

---

[129] 5 U.S.C. §§ 701-706 (2000) ("A person suffering legal wrong because of agency action, or adversely affected or aggrieved by agency action . . . is entitled to judicial review thereof."); see Chrysler v. Brown, 441 U.S. 281, 318 (1979) (deciding that judicial review based on administrative record according to "arbitrary, capricious, or not in accordance with law" standard applies to "reverse" FOIA cases).

[130] Campaign for Family Farms, 200 F.3d at 1184-89; see also Doe v. Veneman, 230 F. Supp. 2d at 749-51 (enjoining USDA from releasing ranch names and home addresses of ranchers, but mistakenly including within injunction releases through future FOIA requests and through non-FOIA matters); AFL-CIO v. Fed. Election Comm'n, 177 F. Supp. 2d 48, 61-63 (D.D.C. 2001) (finding, despite questionable standing of requester organization, agency's refusal to invoke Exemption 7(C) to withhold identities of individuals in its investigative files to be "arbitrary, capricious and contrary to law"), aff'd on other grounds, 333 F.3d 168 (D.C. Cir. 2003); Forest Guardians v. U.S. Forest Serv., No. 99-0615, slip op. at 39-45 (D.N.M. Jan. 29, 2001) (setting aside agency's decision to disclose personal financial information on escrow waiver forms that are used by banks to record use of federal grazing permits as loan collateral) (reverse FOIA suit).

[131] Doe v. Veneman, 230 F. Supp. 2d at 749-51.

[132] Doe v. Veneman, No. 99-335, slip op. at 4-5 (W.D. Tex. Feb. 14, 2003).

[133] Doe v. Veneman, 380 F.3d 807, 813-16 (5th Cir. 2004) ("Even though APHIS decided not to release personal . . . information [about participants in a livestock protection program], the district court enjoined the release of personal information contained in the . . . [management information system] database. By doing so, the district court acted without an actual controversy and exceeded the legal basis for review under the APA.").

[134] Id. at 818-20 (finding district court's injunction to be overbroad on

(continued...)

By contrast, a Native Hawaiian group brought suit to enjoin the Department of the Navy from making public certain information concerning a large group of Native Hawaiian human remains that had been inventoried pursuant to the Native American Graves Protection and Repatriation Act.[135] The court in that case held that the agency properly had determined that the information did not qualify for Exemption 6 protection and that it could be released.[136]

These privacy "reverse" FOIA cases are similar in posture to the more common "reverse" FOIA cases that are based upon a business submitter's claim that information falls within Exemption 4, cases which ordinarily are triggered by the "submitter notice" requirements of Executive Order 12,600.[137] (See the further discussion of this point under "Reverse" FOIA, below.) Despite this similarity, though, there is no requirement that an agency notify record subjects of the intent to disclose personal information about them or that it "track down an individual about whom another has requested information merely to obtain the former's permission to comply with the request."[138] Of course, a party seeking to protect his or her own

---

[134](...continued) several grounds).

[135] Na Iwi O Na Kupuna, 894 F. Supp. at 1402-04.

[136] Id. at 1412-13 (concluding that Exemption 6 was not intended to protect information pertaining to human remains, nor to protect information pertaining to large groups in which individuals are not identifiable).

[137] 3 C.F.R. 235 (1988), reprinted in 5 U.S.C. § 552 note (2000), and in FOIA Update, Vol. VIII, No. 2, at 2-3; see also FOIA Post, "Supreme Court Rules for 'Survivor Privacy' in Favish" (posted 4/9/04) (comparing the operation of the "submitter notice" provision to cases involving personal privacy, where the individuals whose privacy "interests are being protected under the FOIA rarely are aware of th[e FOIA] process, let alone involved in it").

[138] Blakey v. Dep't of Justice, 549 F. Supp. 362, 365 (D.D.C. 1982) (Exemption 7(C)), aff'd in part & vacated in part, 720 F.2d 215 (D.C. Cir. 1983); see Halpern v. FBI, No. 94-CV-365A, 2002 WL 31012157, at *10 (W.D.N.Y. Sept. 1, 2001) (magistrate's recommendation) (finding that there exists "no authority requiring the Government to contact [individuals mentioned in documents] for Exemption 6 to apply"), adopted (W.D.N.Y. Oct. 17, 2001); see also FOIA Post, "Supreme Court Rules for 'Survivor Privacy' in Favish" (posted 4/9/04) (noting that no formal objection is necessary for agencies to invoke FOIA's privacy exemptions to protect individuals); cf. Hemenway, 601 F. Supp. at 1007 (placing burden on requester, not agency, to contact foreign correspondents for requested citizenship information after receiving list of correspondents with office telephone numbers and addresses, and noting that correspondents are "free to decline to respond"). But see Associated Press v. DOD, 395 F. Supp. 2d 15, 16-17 & n.1 (S.D.N.Y. 2005) (re-
(continued...)

privacy interest always can move to intervene in an ongoing lawsuit between an agency and a FOIA requester.[139]

## Factoring in the Public Interest

Once it has been determined that a personal privacy interest is threatened by a requested disclosure, the second step in the balancing process comes into play; this stage of the analysis requires an assessment of the public interest in disclosure.[140] The burden of establishing that disclosure would serve the public interest is on the requester.[141] In its Reporters Committee decision, the Supreme Court limited the concept of public interest under the FOIA to the "core purpose" for which Congress enacted

---

[138](...continued)
quiring agency to ask (through unprecedented survey mechanism) Guantanamo Bay detainees whether they wished their identifying information to be released to plaintiff, based on exceptional fact that "detainees are in custody and therefore readily available"); cf. War Babes v. Wilson, 770 F. Supp. 1, 4-5 (D.D.C. 1990) (allowing agency sixty days to meet burden of establishing privacy interest by obtaining affidavits from World War II servicemembers who object to release of their addresses to British citizens seeking to locate their natural fathers).

[139] See, e.g., Jefferson v. U.S. Dep't of Justice, Office of the Inspector General, No. 01-1418, slip op. at 4-5 (D.D.C. Nov. 14, 2003) (allowing Department of Justice attorney to intervene to protect her personal privacy interests, on basis that she was at odds with plaintiff over release of information about her and that there was a question of the Department's ability to adequately represent her interests given past and ongoing employment discrimination matters) (Exemption 7(C)); cf. Doe v. Glickman, 256 F.3d 371, 375-81 (5th Cir. 2001) (holding that requester could intervene in "reverse" FOIA suit brought by individuals, in order to seek to block release of personally identifying information that requester sought in related FOIA suit); Pub. Citizen Health Research Group v. U.S. Dep't of Labor, 591 F.2d 808, 809 (D.C. Cir. 1978) (same, in FOIA suit).

[140] See FOIA Update, Vol. X, No. 2, at 7 ("FOIA Counselor: Exemption 6 and Exemption 7(C): Step-by-Step Decisionmaking").

[141] See Carter v. U.S. Dep't of Commerce, 830 F.2d 388, 391 nn.8 & 13 (D.C. Cir. 1987); see also NARA v. Favish, 541 U.S. 157, 175 (instructing that the balance does not even come "into play" when a requester has produced no evidence to "warrant a belief by a reasonable person that the alleged Government impropriety might have occurred") (Exemption 7(C)), reh'g denied, 541 U.S. 1057 (2004); Prison Legal News v. Lappin, 436 F. Supp. 2d 17, 22 (D.D.C. 2006) ("The burden of satisfying the 'public interest standard' is on the requester.").

it: To "shed[] light on an agency's performance of its statutory duties."[142] Information that does not directly reveal the operations or activities of the federal government,[143] the Supreme Court repeatedly has stressed, "falls outside the ambit of the public interest that the FOIA was enacted to serve."[144] If an asserted public interest is found to qualify under this stand-

---

[142] 489 U.S. 749, 773 (1989); see also O'Kane v. U.S. Customs Serv., 169 F.3d 1308, 1310 (11th Cir. 1999) (per curiam) (affirming that Electronic Freedom of Information Act Amendments of 1996, Pub. L. No. 104-231, 110 Stat. 3048, do not overrule Reporters Committee definition of "public interest"). But cf. Voinche v. FBI, 940 F. Supp. 323, 330 n.4 (D.D.C. 1996) (dictum) (speculating, based upon mere newspaper report of legislative action, that Electronic FOIA amendments would "effectively overrule" Reporters Committee), aff'd on other grounds per curiam, No. 96-5304, 1997 U.S. App. LEXIS 19089 (D.C. Cir. June 19, 1997).

[143] See Landano v. U.S. Dep't of Justice, 956 F.2d 422, 430 (3d Cir.) (There is "no FOIA-recognized public interest in discovering wrongdoing by a state agency.") (Exemption 7(C)), cert. denied on Exemption 7(C) question, 506 U.S. 868 (1992), & rev'd & remanded on other grounds, 508 U.S. 165 (1993); Phillips v. Immigration & Customs Enforcement, 385 F. Supp. 2d 296, 305 (S.D.N.Y. 2005) (observing that, although privacy interests of government officials may be lessened by countervailing public interest, that idea "would appear to be inapplicable to former foreign government officials"); McMillian v. Fed. Bureau of Prisons, No. 03-1210, 2004 WL 4953170, at 7 n.11 (D.D.C. July 23, 2004) (ruling that the plaintiff's argument that an audiotape would show the misconduct of the District of Columbia Board of Parole was irrelevant because "the FOIA is designed to support the public interest in how agencies of the federal government conduct business"); Garcia v. U.S. Dep't of Justice, 181 F. Supp. 2d 356, 374 (S.D.N.Y. 2002) (recognizing that the "discovery of wrongdoing at a state as opposed to a federal agency . . . is not a goal of FOIA") (Exemption 7(C)); see also FOIA Update, Vol. XII, No. 2, at 6 (advising that "government" should mean federal government); cf. Lissner v. U.S. Customs Serv., 241 F.3d 1220, 1223 & n.2 (9th Cir. 2001) (finding a public interest in the agency's treatment of city police officers arrested for smuggling steroids, but declining to "address the issue of whether opening up state and local governments to scrutiny also raises a cognizable public interest under the FOIA") (Exemption 7(C)); Dollinger v. USPS, No. 95-CV-6174T, slip op. at 3-4 (W.D.N.Y. Aug. 24, 1995) (finding "that the term 'government' as used in § 552(a)(4)(A)(iii) [i.e., the fee waiver provision] of the statute refers to the federal government").

[144] 489 U.S. at 775; see Bibles v. Or. Natural Desert Ass'n, 519 U.S. 355, 355-56 (1997); DOD v. FLRA, 510 U.S. 487, 497 (1994); see also, e.g., Piper v. U.S. Dep't of Justice, 428 F. Supp. 2d 1, 3 (D.D.C. 2006) (reasoning that "the public interest in knowing how the Department of Justice . . . handles its investigations 'is served whether or not the names and identifying information of third parties are redacted'"); Iowa Citizens for Cmty. Improvement v. USDA, 256 F. Supp. 2d 946, 951 (S.D. Iowa 2002) (declaring that while a
(continued...)

ard, it then must be accorded some measure of value so that it can be weighed against the threat to privacy.[145] And, as the Supreme Court in Favish pointedly emphasized, "the public interest sought to be advanced [must be] a significant one."[146]

Even prior to Reporters Committee the law was clear that disclosure must benefit the public overall and not just the requester himself. For example, a number of courts determined that a request made for purely commercial purposes does not further a public interest.[147] The Court of Appeals for the Ninth Circuit alone had adopted an approach that specifically factored the requester's personal interest in disclosure into the balancing

---

[144](...continued) presidential nominee's "fitness for public office may be of great popular concern to the public," such concern "does not translate into a real public interest that is cognizable . . . [under] the FOIA"); Gallant v. NLRB, No. 92-873, slip op. at 8-10 (D.D.C. Nov. 6, 1992) (concluding that disclosure of names of individuals to whom NLRB Member sent letters in attempt to secure reappointment would not add to understanding of NLRB's performance of its duties), aff'd on other grounds, 26 F.3d 168 (D.C. Cir. 1994); Andrews v. U.S. Dep't of Justice, 769 F. Supp. 314, 316-17 (E.D. Mo. 1991) (finding that although release of an individual's address, telephone number, and place of employment might serve a general public interest in the satisfaction of monetary judgments, "it does not implicate a public interest cognizable under the FOIA"); see also FOIA Update, Vol. XVIII, No. 1, at 1; FOIA Update, Vol. X, No. 2, at 4, 6; cf. FOIA Post, "Supreme Court Vacates and Remands in ATF Database Case" (posted 3/25/03) (discussing the Supreme Court's decision to vacate the Seventh Circuit opinion that erroneously found that "[t]he effectiveness of ATF's performance [of its statutory duties] impacts the City's interests" (citing City of Chicago v. U.S. Dep't of Treasury, 286 F.3d 628, 637 (7th Cir. 2002))).

[145] See, e.g., Dep't of the Air Force v. Rose, 425 U.S. 352, 372 (1976); Ripskis v. HUD, 746 F.2d 1, 3 (D.C. Cir. 1981); Fund for Constitutional Gov't v. Nat'l Archives & Records Serv., 656 F.2d 856, 862 (D.C. Cir. 1981).

[146] 541 U.S. at 172; see also FOIA Post, "Supreme Court Rules for 'Survivor Privacy' in Favish" (posted 4/9/04) (noting that the Supreme Court "emphasized" the requirement of "significan[ce]").

[147] See, e.g., Multnomah County Med. Soc'y v. Scott, 825 F.2d 1410, 1413 (9th Cir. 1987) (commercial solicitation of Medicare recipients); Wine Hobby USA, Inc. v. IRS, 502 F.2d 133, 137 (3d Cir. 1974) (individuals licensed to produce wine at home requested by distributor of amateur wine-making equipment); see also Aronson v. HUD, 822 F.2d 182, 185-86 (1st Cir. 1987) (Plaintiff's "commercial motivations are irrelevant for determining the public interest served by disclosure; they do, however, suggest one of the ways in which private interests could be harmed by disclosure and a reason why individuals would wish to keep the information confidential.").

process.[148]

In Reporters Committee, the Supreme Court approved the majority view that the requester's personal interest is irrelevant. First, as the Court emphasized, the requester's identity can have "no bearing on the merits of his or her FOIA request."[149] In so declaring, the Court ruled unequivocally that agencies should treat all requesters alike in making FOIA disclosure decisions; the only exception to this, the Court specifically noted, is that of course an agency should not withhold from a requester any information that implicates only that requester's own interest.[150] Furthermore, the "public interest" balancing required under the privacy exemptions should not include consideration of the requester's "particular purpose" in making the request.[151] Instead, the Court has instructed, the proper approach to the balancing process is to focus on "the nature of the requested document" and to consider "its relationship to" the public interest generally.[152] This approach thus does not permit attention to the special circumstances of any particular FOIA requester.[153] Rather, it necessarily involves a more

---

[148] See, e.g., Multnomah County Med. Soc'y, 825 F.2d at 1413; Van Bourg, Allen, Weinberg & Roger v. NLRB, 728 F.2d 1270, 1273 (9th Cir. 1984), vacated, 756 F.2d 692 (9th Cir.), reinstated, 762 F.2d 831 (9th Cir. 1985). But see also FOIA Post, "Supreme Court Rules for 'Survivor Privacy' in Favish" (posted 4/9/04) (noting a similar Ninth Circuit misinterpretation of Exemption 7(C) that had "left it alone among all circuit courts of appeals" until the Supreme Court repudiated its approach in Favish).

[149] 489 U.S. at 771; see also DOD v. FLRA, 510 U.S. at 496-501; Lowry v. Soc. Sec. Admin., No. 00-1616, 2001 U.S. Dist. LEXIS 23474, at *34 (D. Or. Aug. 29, 2001) (stating that "the identity of the requester and the purpose for which the records are sought cannot be taken into consideration in determining what should be released"); FOIA Update, Vol. X, No. 2, at 5-6.

[150] 489 U.S. at 771; see FOIA Update, Vol. X, No. 2, at 5; see also, e.g., Frets v. Dep't of Transp., No. 88-404-W-9, 1989 WL 222608, at *5-6 (W.D. Mo. Dec. 14, 1989) (withholding names of third parties mentioned in plaintiffs' own statements).

[151] 489 U.S. at 772; see also Favish, 541 U.S. at 172 (reiterating the Reporters Committee principle that "citizens should not be required to explain why they seek the information" at issue, but further elucidating that in a case where the requester's purported public interest revolves around an allegation of government wrongdoing, "the usual rule that the citizen need not offer a reason for requesting the information must be inapplicable"); DOD v. FLRA, 510 U.S. at 496-501.

[152] 489 U.S. at 772.

[153] See id. at 771-72 & n.20; see also Schiffer v. FBI, 78 F.3d 1405, 1410-11 (9th Cir. 1996) (noting that individual interest in obtaining information about oneself does not constitute public interest); Schwarz v. U.S. Dep't of
(continued...)

general "public interest" assessment based upon the contents and context of the records sought and their connection to any "public interest" that would be served by disclosure. In making such assessments, agencies should look to the possible effects of disclosure to the public in general.[154]

Accordingly, a request made for the purpose of obtaining "impeach-ment evidence, such as that required to be produced pursuant to Brady v. Maryland" does not further the public interest;[155] nor does a request made

---

[153](...continued)
State, No. 97-1342, slip op. at 1-5 (D.D.C. Mar. 20, 1998) (protecting address of individual despite prolific FOIA plaintiff's claim that she sought imag-ined "missing" husband's address so that she might "testify on his behalf and win his release from prison"), aff'd per curiam, 172 F.3d 921 (D.C. Cir. 1998) (unpublished table decision).

[154] See FOIA Update, Vol. X, No. 2, at 5-6; see also Favish, 541 U.S. at 174 ("It must be remembered that once there is a disclosure, the information belongs to the general public.").

[155] Curry v. DEA, No. 97-1359, slip op. at 5 (D.D.C. Mar. 30, 1998) (citing Brady v. Maryland, 373 U.S. 83 (1963)); see Neely v. FBI, 208 F.3d 461, 464 (4th Cir. 2000) (stating that "courts have sensibly refused to recognize, for purposes of FOIA, a public interest in nothing more than the fairness of a criminal defendant's own trial"); Cano v. DEA, No. 04-935, 2006 WL 1441383, at *4 (D.D.C. May 24, 2006) ("When weighing the privacy interests against plaintiff's purely personal interests in challenging his conviction, the balance clearly favors non-disclosure."); Cole-El v. U.S. Dep't of Justice, No. 03-1013, slip op. at 10 (D.D.C. Aug. 26, 2004) ("[Plaintiff's] interest in at-tacking his conviction does not constitute a public interest sufficient to overcome [a third party's] privacy interests.") (Exemption 7(C)), aff'd, No. 04-5329, 2005 U.S. App. LEXIS 7358, at *2-3 (D.C. Cir. Apr. 27, 2005) ("As appellant has not demonstrated a public interest in disclosure, the counter-vailing interest in privacy defeated his request for documents under the Freedom of Information Act."); Lora v. U.S. Dep't of Justice, No. 00-3072, slip op. at 13 (D.D.C. Apr. 9, 2004) ("Plaintiff's interest in attacking his convic-tion does not constitute a public interest sufficient to overcome the privacy interests of [third parties]."); Diaz v. Fed. Bureau of Prisons, No. 01-40070, slip op. at 10 (D. Mass. Dec. 20, 2001) (magistrate's recommendation) (find-ing that the public interest is not served by "the mere claim that disclosure would raise questions about the fairness" of the requester's trial), adopted (D. Mass. Feb. 7, 2002), aff'd, 55 F. App'x 5 (1st Cir. 2003); Martin v. U.S. Dep't of Justice, No. 96-2866, slip op. at 10 (D.D.C. Dec. 15, 1999) (noting that "courts have consistently found Brady violations to be outside the scope of the FOIA"); Billington v. Dep't of Justice, 11 F. Supp. 2d 45, 63 (D.D.C. 1998) (noting that "requests for Brady material are 'outside the proper role of FOIA'" (quoting Johnson v. Dep't of Justice, 758 F. Supp. 2, 5 (D.D.C. 1991))), aff'd in pertinent part, 233 F.3d 581 (D.C. Cir. 2000); cf. Hale v. U.S. Dep't of Justice, 226 F.3d 1200, 1204 n.4 (10th Cir. 2000) (finding that
(continued...)

in order to obtain or supplement discovery in a private lawsuit serve the public interest.[156] In fact, one court has observed that if the requester truly had a great need for the records for purposes of litigation, he or she should seek them in that forum, where it would be possible to provide them under an appropriate protective order.[157] Likewise, in Davy v. CIA, the requester's "personal crusade to unearth . . . information" that was the subject of a book that he wrote was found not to relate "in any way to a cognizable public interest."[158]

One purpose that the FOIA was designed for is to "check against corruption and to hold the governors accountable to the governed."[159] Indeed, information that would inform the public of violations of the public trust has a strong public interest and is accorded great weight in the balancing

---

[155](...continued)
plaintiff's Brady claim is irrelevant to Exemption 7(D) analysis).

[156] See Carpenter v. U.S. Dep't of Justice, 470 F.3d 434, 442 (1st Cir. 2006) (criminal trial) (Exemption 7(C)); Horowitz v. Peace Corps, 428 F.3d 271, 278-79 (D.C. Cir. 2005) (civil litigation); Brown v. FBI, 658 F.2d 71, 75 (2d Cir. 1981) (private litigation); Cappabianca v. Comm'r, U.S. Customs Serv., 847 F. Supp. 1558, 1564 (M.D. Fla. 1994) (job-related causes of action); Harry v. Dep't of the Army, No. 92-1654, slip op. at 7-8 (D.D.C. Sept. 10, 1993) (to appeal negative officer efficiency report); NTEU v. U.S. Dep't of the Treasury, 3 Gov't Disclosure Serv. (P-H) ¶ 83,224, at 83,948 (D.D.C. June 17, 1983) (grievance proceeding); FOIA Update, Vol. III, No. 4, at 6 (advising that requests from requesters who have clear personal interest in disclosure should be subject to careful scrutiny).

[157] Gilbey v. Dep't of the Interior, No. 89-0801, 1990 WL 174889, at *2 (D.D.C. Oct. 22, 1990); see also Billington, 11 F. Supp. 2d at 64 (noting that proper forum for challenging alleged illegal warrantless search is in district court where case was prosecuted); Bongiorno v. Reno, No. 95-72143, 1996 WL 426451, at *4 (E.D. Mich. Mar. 19, 1996) (observing that the proper place for a noncustodial parent to seek information about his child is the "state court that has jurisdiction over the parties, not a FOIA request or the federal court system"); cf. Favish, 541 U.S. at 174 ("There is no mechanism under FOIA for a protective order allowing only the requester to see whether the information bears out his theory, or for proscribing its general dissemination.").

[158] 357 F. Supp. 2d 76, 88 (D.D.C. 2004).

[159] Multnomah County Med. Soc'y, 825 F.2d at 1415 (quoting NLRB v. Robbins Tire & Rubber Co., 437 U.S. 214, 242 (1978)); see also Arieff v. U.S. Dep't of the Navy, 712 F.2d 1462, 1468 (D.C. Cir. 1983); Wash. Post Co. v. HHS, 690 F.2d 252, 264 (D.C. Cir. 1982); Nat'l Ass'n of Atomic Veterans, Inc. v. Dir., Def. Nuclear Agency, 583 F. Supp. 1483, 1487 (D.D.C. 1984).

process.[160] As a general rule, demonstrated wrongdoing of a serious and intentional nature by a high-level government official is of sufficient public interest to outweigh almost any privacy interest of that official.[161]

By contrast, less serious misconduct by low-level agency employees generally is not considered of sufficient public interest to outweigh the pri-

---

[160] See Favish, 541 U.S. at 172-73 (stressing that there should be a "necessary nexus between the requested information and the asserted public interest that would be advanced by disclosure"); see also *FOIA Post*, "Supreme Court Rules for 'Survivor Privacy' in Favish" (posted 4/9/04) (discussing the importance of establishing an "actual connection" between the particular information at issue and the qualifying public interest articulated by the requester).

[161] See, e.g., Cochran v. United States, 770 F.2d 949, 956-57 (11th Cir. 1985) (nonjudicial punishment findings and discipline imposed on Army major general for misuse of government personnel and facilities) (Privacy Act "wrongful disclosure" suit); Stern v. FBI, 737 F.2d 84, 93-94 (D.C. Cir. 1984) (name of high-level FBI official censured for deliberate and knowing misrepresentation) (Exemption 7(C)); Columbia Packing Co. v. USDA, 563 F.2d 495, 499 (1st Cir. 1977) (information about federal employees found guilty of accepting bribes); Chang v. Dep't of the Navy, 314 F. Supp. 2d 35, 42-45 (D.D.C. 2004) (information about Naval Commander's nonjudicial punishment for involvement in accident at sea) (Privacy Act "wrongful disclosure" suit); Wood v. FBI, 312 F. Supp. 2d 328, 345-51 (D. Conn. 2004) (identifying information linking FBI Supervisory Special Agent's name with specific findings and disciplinary action taken against him), aff'd in part & rev'd in part, 432 F.3d 78 (2d Cir. 2005); Lurie v. Dep't of the Army, 970 F. Supp. 19, 39-40 (D.D.C. 1997) (information concerning "mid- to high-level" Army medical researcher whose apparent misrepresentation and misconduct contributed to appropriation of $20,000,000 for particular form of AIDS research), appeal dismissed voluntarily, No. 97-5248 (D.C. Cir. Oct. 22, 1997); Sullivan v. VA, 617 F. Supp. 258, 260-61 (D.D.C. 1985) (reprimand of senior official for misuse of government vehicle and failure to report accident) (Privacy Act "wrongful disclosure" suit/Exemption 7(C)); Cong. News Syndicate v. U.S. Dep't of Justice, 438 F. Supp. 538, 544 (D.D.C. 1977) (misconduct by White House staffers); cf. Perlman v. U.S. Dep't of Justice, 312 F.3d 100, 107-08 (2d Cir. 2002) (finding public interest, even though misconduct was not proven, because "a substantial amount of evidence shows [that former INS General Counsel] allowed former INS officials . . . to exercise improper influence" and "the degree of wrongdoing alleged is fairly serious") (Exemptions 6 and 7(C)), vacated & remanded, 541 U.S. 970, on remand, 380 F.3d 110, 111 (2d Cir. 2004) (per curiam); Ferri v. Bell, 645 F.2d 1213, 1218 (3d Cir. 1981) (finding attempt to expose alleged deal between prosecutor and witness to be in public interest) (Exemption 7(C)), vacated & reinstated in part on reh'g, 671 F.2d 769 (3d Cir. 1982).

vacy interest of the employee.[162] Nor is there likely to be strong public interest in disclosure of the names of censured employees when the case has not "occurred against the backdrop of a well-publicized scandal" that has resulted in "widespread knowledge" that certain employees were disci-

---

[162] See, e.g., Rose, 425 U.S. at 381 (protecting names of cadets found to have violated Academy honor code); Hoyos v. United States, No. 98-4178, slip op. at 3 (11th Cir. Feb. 1, 1999) (finding "little public interest in access to [identities of individuals fired from the VA], especially when the reasons for removal -- the information that truly bears upon the agency's conduct, which is the focus of FOIA's concern -- were readily made available"); Beck v. Dep't of Justice, 997 F.2d 1489, 1493 (D.C. Cir. 1993) ("The identity of one or two individual relatively low-level government wrongdoers, released in isolation, does not provide information about the agency's own conduct.") (Exemptions 6 and 7(C)); Stern, 737 F.2d at 94 (protecting names of mid-level employees censured for negligence); Chamberlain v. Kurtz, 589 F.2d 827, 842 (5th Cir. 1979) (protecting names of disciplined IRS agents); Kimmel v. DOD, No. 04-1551, 2006 WL 1126812, at *3 (D.D.C. Mar. 31, 2006) (protecting names of civilian personnel below level of office director and of military personnel below rank of colonel (or captain in Navy); finding that disclosure of names would not shed any light on subject matter of FOIA request seeking release of documents related to posthumous advancement of Rear Admiral Husband E. Kimmel to rank of admiral on retired list of Navy); Buckley v. Schaul, No. 03-03233, slip op. at 8-9 (W.D. Wash. Mar. 8, 2004) (protecting identity of regional counsel alleged to have violated Privacy Act) (Exemptions 6 and 7(C)), aff'd, 135 F. App'x 929 (9th Cir. 2005); Chang, 314 F. Supp. 2d at 44-45 (protecting names and results of punishment of lower-level officers involved in collision of Navy vessel with another ship); Jefferson v. U.S. Dep't of Justice, Office of the Inspector General, No. 01-1418, slip op. at 11 (D.D.C. Nov. 14, 2003) ("A [nonsupervisory] Attorney-Advisor is not a government employee whose rank is so high that the public interest in disclosure of information pertaining to her performance of official government functions outweighs her personal privacy interest in protecting information about the details of a law enforcement investigation of her alleged misconduct.") (Exemption 7(C)); Gonzalez v. FBI, No. 99-5789, slip op. at 13-15 (E.D. Cal. Aug. 11, 2000) (declining to order agency to confirm or deny existence of records concerning any misconduct investigations against named federal employees) (Exemptions 6 and 7(C)), aff'd, 14 F. App'x 916 (9th Cir. 2001); Butler v. U.S. Dep't of Justice, No. 86-2255, 1994 WL 55621, at *10 (D.D.C. Feb. 3, 1994) (protecting identity of FBI Special Agent who received "mild admonishment" for conduct that "was not particularly egregious"), appeal dismissed, No. 94-5078 (D.C. Cir. Sept. 8, 1994); Cotton v. Adams, 798 F. Supp. 22, 26-27 (D.D.C. 1992) (finding that release of IG reports on conduct of low-level Smithsonian Institution employees would not allow public to evaluate Smithsonian's performance of mission); Heller v. U.S. Marshals Serv., 655 F. Supp. 1088, 1091 (D.D.C. 1987) (protecting names of agency personnel found to have committed "only minor, if any, wrongdoing") (Exemption 7(C)).

plined.[163]

And any asserted "public interest" in resolving mere allegations of wrongdoing cannot outweigh an individual's privacy interest in avoiding unwarranted association with such allegations.[164] Indeed, in Favish, the Supreme Court firmly held that mere allegations of wrongdoing are "insufficient" to satisfy the "public interest" standard required under the FOIA.[165]

---

[163] Beck, 997 F.2d at 1493-94; see Chin v. U.S. Dep't of the Air Force, No. 97-2176, slip op. at 3 (W.D. La. June 24, 1999) (finding a significant privacy interest in records that "document[] personal and intimate incidents of misconduct [that have] not previously been a part of the public domain"), aff'd per curiam, No. 99-31237 (5th Cir. June 15, 2000).

[164] See, e.g., McCutchen v. HHS, 30 F.3d 183, 187-89 (D.C. Cir. 1994) (protecting identities of scientists found not to have engaged in alleged scientific misconduct) (Exemption 7(C)); Hunt v. FBI, 972 F.2d 286, 288-90 (9th Cir. 1992) (protecting investigation of named FBI agent cleared of charges of misconduct) (Exemption 7(C)); Dunkelberger v. Dep't of Justice, 906 F.2d 779, 781-82 (D.C. Cir. 1990) (same) (Exemption 7(C)); Carter, 830 F.2d at 391 (protecting identities of attorneys subject to disciplinary proceedings that were later dismissed); Buckley, No. 03-03233, slip op. at 10-11 (W.D. Wash. Mar. 8, 2004) ("If these files were released, the public disclosure of allegations of impropriety against [regional counsel] and whomever else, without any findings of actual misconduct, could scar employees' personal and professional reputations.") (Exemptions 6 and 7(C)); Edmonds v. FBI, 272 F. Supp. 2d 35, 52 (D.D.C. 2003) (protecting identities of FBI clerical employees and FBI Special Agents because there was no reason to believe that their identities would shed light on alleged misconduct in FBI's language division) (Exemptions 6 and 7(C)), appeal dismissed voluntarily, No. 03-5364, 2004 WL 2806508 (D.C. Cir. Dec. 7, 2004); McQueen v. United States, 264 F. Supp. 2d 502, 533-34 (S.D. Tex. 2003) (deciding that public interest would not be served by "disclosure of information regarding unsubstantiated allegations" made against three government employees) (Exemptions 6 and 7(C)), aff'd, 100 F. App'x 964 (5th Cir. 2004) (per curiam); Pontecorvo v. FBI, No. 00-1511, slip op. at 40 (D.D.C. Sept. 30, 2001) (declining to order disclosure of the identity of an FBI Special Agent under investigation by the FBI Office of Professional Responsibility when the investigation was instituted solely "because of Plaintiff's own written request, not the independent determination of the Bureau") (Exemption 7(C)). But see Dobronski v. FCC, 17 F.3d 275, 278-80 (9th Cir. 1994) (ordering release of employee's sick leave slips despite fact that requester's allegations of abuse of leave time were wholly based upon unsubstantiated tips); see also FOIA Post, "Supreme Court Rules for 'Survivor Privacy' in Favish" (posted 4/9/04) (advising that Dobronksi is now discredited, if not effectively overruled, by Favish decision's total repudiation of Ninth Circuit's disclosure rationales).

[165] 541 U.S. at 173; see also Summers v. U.S. Dep't of Justice, No. 98-1837,
(continued...)

The Court observed that if "bare allegations" could be sufficient to satisfy the public interest requirement, then the exemption would be "transformed . . . into nothing more than a rule of pleading."[166] Indeed, if mere allegations were all that were necessary to override a personal privacy interest, then that privacy interest would become worthless.[167]

Moreover, even when the existence of an investigation of misconduct has become publicly known, the accused individual ordinarily has an overriding privacy interest in not having the further details of the matter disclosed.[168] And even where misconduct actually is found, the agency is not

---

[165](...continued)
slip op. at 19 (D.D.C. Apr. 13, 2004) (citing Favish and finding no merit to plaintiff's allegation that the FBI did not thoroughly investigate a case, because "plaintiff has not provided any evidence that the FBI acted improperly") (Exemption 7(C)); FOIA Post, "Supreme Court Rules for 'Survivor Privacy' in Favish" (posted 4/9/04) (discussing insufficiency of "mere allegations").

[166] 541 U.S. at 174; see also FOIA Post, "Supreme Court Rules for 'Survivor Privacy' in Favish" (posted 4/9/04) (discussing how privacy exemptions "could be swallowed whole" unless requesters alleging government wrongdoing are held to higher standards, because "[u]nfortunately, the government's decades of experience with FOIA administration teaches that there is no shortage of potential FOIA requesters who might be willing to make such allegations (even in what they would swear to be good faith, subjectively speaking) if that were all that it would take to gain disclosure").

[167] See U.S. Dep't of Justice v. Ray, 502 U.S. 164, 179 (1991) ("If a totally unsupported suggestion that the interest in finding out whether Government agents have been telling the truth justified disclosure of private materials, Government agencies would have no defenses against requests for production of private information."); see also Favish, 541 U.S. at 173 (emphasizing importance of "practical[ity]" in privacy-protection decisionmaking).

[168] See Kimberlin v. Dep't of Justice, 139 F.3d 944, 949 (D.C. Cir. 1998) (concluding that Assistant United States Attorney "did not, merely by acknowledging the investigation and making a vague references to its conclusion, waive all his interest in keeping the contents of the OPR file confidential") (Exemption 7(C)); Forest Serv. Employees for Envtl. Ethics v. U.S. Forest Serv., No. 05-6015, 2005 WL 3488453, at *3-4 (D. Or. Dec. 21, 2005) (protecting identities of low-level and mid-level employees facing discipline, because release "could subject them to embarrassment, shame, stigma and harassment," despite publicity given to fatalities caused by forest fire); MacLean v. DOD, No. 04-2425, slip op. at 16-17 (S.D. Cal. June 2, 2005) (finding that "substantial privacy interests" of individual found not to have committed professional misconduct outweighed any public interest) (Exemptions 6 and 7(C)); Mueller v. U.S. Dep't of the Air Force, 63 F. Supp. 2d

(continued...)

necessarily required to disclose every piece of information pertaining to the investigation.[169]

Prior to Reporters Committee, some courts held that the public interest in disclosure may be embodied in other federal statutes.[170] In light of Reporters Committee and National Association of Retired Federal Employ-

---

[168](...continued)
738, 743 (E.D. Va. 1999) (declaring that even given pre-existing publicity, "individuals have a strong interest in not being associated with alleged wrongful activity, particularly where, as here, the subject of the investigation is ultimately exonerated") (Exemptions 6 and 7(C)); see also Bast v. FBI, 665 F.2d 1251, 1255 (D.C. Cir. 1981) (explaining that publicity over an alleged transcript-alteration incident actually could exacerbate the harm to a privacy interest because "[t]he authoritative nature of such findings threatens much greater damage to an individual's reputation than newspaper articles or editorial columns" and "renewed publicity brings with it a renewed invasion of privacy"); Chin, No. 97-2176, slip op. at 5 (W.D. La. June 24, 1999) (finding that the fact "that some of the events are known to certain members of the public . . . is insufficient to place this record for dissemination into the public domain").

[169] See, e.g., Office of Capital Collateral Counsel, Northern Region of Fla. v. Dep't of Justice, 331 F.3d 799, 803-04 (11th Cir. 2003) (protecting AUSA's "private thoughts and feelings concerning her misconduct . . . and its effect on her, her family, and her career"); see also Kimberlin, 139 F.3d at 949 (finding that an AUSA "still has a privacy interest . . . in avoiding disclosure of the details of the investigation," despite the AUSA's acknowledgment that he was disciplined after the investigation); Halloran v. VA, 874 F.2d 315, 320-22 (5th Cir. 1989) (noting that employees of government contractor investigated by government for fraud did not lose privacy interests in comments transcribed in government investigatory files) (Exemption 7(C)); cf. LaRouche v. U.S. Dep't of Justice, No. 90-2753, slip op. at 14 (D.D.C. Aug. 8, 2002) (observing that the FBI "need not make a wholesale disclosure about an individual just because he is a publicly acknowledged FBI source") (Exemption 7(C)).

[170] See, e.g., Int'l Bhd. of Elec. Workers Local No. 5 v. HUD, 852 F.2d 87, 90 (3d Cir. 1988) (wage rates payable by federal contractors regulated by Davis-Bacon Act, 40 U.S.C. §§ 3141-3144, 3146-3147 (Supp. III 2003); USDA v. FLRA, 836 F.2d 1139, 1143 (8th Cir.) (names and addresses of federal employees under federal labor relations statute), cert. granted & remanded, 488 U.S. 1025 (1988), vacated, 876 F.2d 50 (8th Cir. 1989); Common Cause v. Nat'l Archives & Records Serv., 628 F.2d 179, 183-85 (D.C. Cir. 1980) (political campaign activities under Federal Corrupt Practices Act, 2 U.S.C. §§ 241-248, 252-256 (1970) (repealed 1972)) (Exemption 7(C)); Wash. Post, 690 F.2d at 265 (public disclosure of financial statements required by Ethics in Government Act of 1978, as amended, 28 U.S.C. § 591-599 (2000); see also Marzen v. HHS, 825 F.2d 1148, 1154 (7th Cir. 1987) (finding nondisclosure proper upon consideration of state statute mandating same).

ees v. Horner [hereinafter NARFE],[171] the Courts of Appeals for the District of Columbia, First, Second, Sixth, Seventh, Tenth, and Eleventh Circuits flatly rejected this approach, refusing to order disclosure of the home addresses of government employees on the explicit basis that the public interest in disclosure evidenced in the Federal Service Labor-Management Relations Act[172] [hereinafter FSLMRA] cannot be factored into the balance under the FOIA.[173] On the other hand, the Third, Fifth, and Ninth Circuit Courts of Appeals reached the opposite conclusion and ordered disclosure of the home addresses of bargaining unit employees to unions that requested them under the FSLMRA.[174] These circuit courts all declared that the Supreme Court had not considered specifically whether the public policy favoring collective bargaining embodied in the FSLMRA could be considered in balancing under the FOIA; consequently, none of these courts found an inconsistency between its holding and the teachings of Reporters Committee.[175]

Because of this split in the circuits, the Supreme Court granted certiorari in the Fifth Circuit case and finally resolved this issue in 1994.[176] The Court decisively reiterated the principles laid down in Reporters Committee and said the fact that it was looking at Exemption 6 rather than Exemption 7(C) in this case was "of little import"; the two exemptions differ in the "magnitude of the public interest that is required," not in the "identifi-

---

[171] 879 F.2d 873 (D.C. Cir. 1989).

[172] 5 U.S.C. §§ 7101-7106, 7111-7123, 7131-7135 (2000 & Supp. IV 2004).

[173] D.C. Circuit: FLRA v. U.S. Dep't of the Treasury, 884 F.2d 1446, 1453 (D.C. Cir. 1989); First Circuit: FLRA v. U.S. Dep't of the Navy, 941 F.2d 49, 56-57 (1st Cir. 1991); Second Circuit: FLRA v. VA, 958 F.2d 503, 511-12 (2d Cir. 1992); Sixth Circuit: FLRA v. Dep't of the Navy, 963 F.2d 124, 125 (6th Cir. 1992); Seventh Circuit: FLRA v. U.S. Dep't of the Navy, 975 F.2d 348, 354-55 (7th Cir. 1992); Tenth Circuit: FLRA v. DOD, 984 F.2d 370, 375 (10th Cir. 1993); Eleventh Circuit: FLRA v. DOD, 977 F.2d 545, 548 (11th Cir. 1992). See also Reed v. NLRB, 927 F.2d 1249, 1251 (D.C. Cir. 1991) (concluding that disclosure of "Excelsior" list (names and addresses of employees eligible to vote in union representation elections) would not reveal anything about NLRB's operations).

[174] Third Circuit: FLRA v. U.S. Dep't of the Navy, 966 F.2d 747, 758-59 (3d Cir. 1992) (en banc) (alternative holding); Fifth Circuit: FLRA v. DOD, 975 F.2d 1105, 1113-15 (5th Cir.), rev'd, 510 U.S. 487 (1994); Ninth Circuit: FLRA v. U.S. Dep't of the Navy, 958 F.2d 1490, 1497 (9th Cir. 1992), reh'g granted & opinion withdrawn, No. 90-70511 (9th Cir. Apr. 18, 1994); see also FLRA v. Dep't of Commerce, 954 F.2d 994, 997 (4th Cir. 1992), appeal dismissed per stipulation, No. 90-1852 (4th Cir. Apr. 6, 1995).

[175] FLRA v. U.S. Dep't of the Navy, 966 F.2d at 757-59; FLRA v. U.S. Dep't of the Navy, 958 F.2d at 1496-97.

[176] DOD v. FLRA, 510 U.S. 487 (1994).

cation of the relevant public interest."[177] The Court concluded that "because all FOIA requestors have an equal, and equally qualified, right to information, the fact that [FOIA requesters] are seeking to vindicate the policies behind the Labor Statute is irrelevant to the FOIA analysis."[178] The only relevant public interest under the FOIA remains, as set forth in Reporters Committee, "'the citizens' right to be informed about what their government is up to.'"[179]

On a related question concerning another federal statute -- the Davis-Bacon Act,[180] which requires that contractors on federal projects pay to their laborers no less than the wages prevailing for comparable work in their geographical area -- the D.C. and Second Circuits were the first post-Reporters Committee courts of appeals to confront this issue, and the Third and Tenth Circuits subsequently addressed it as well. These four courts have firmly held that although there may be a minimal public interest in facilitating the monitoring of compliance with federal labor statutes, disclosure of personal information that reveals nothing "directly about the character of a government agency or official" bears only an "attenuated . . . relationship to governmental activity."[181] Accordingly, it has been held that such an "attenuated public interest in disclosure does not outweigh the construction workers' significant privacy interest in [their names and addresses]."[182]

Overturning the decisions of two lower courts,[183] the Ninth Circuit characteristically took a different approach, but properly reached the same result.[184] The Ninth Circuit found a public interest in monitoring the agen-

---

[177] Id. at 496-97 & n.6.

[178] Id. at 499.

[179] Id. at 497 (quoting Reporters Comm., 489 U.S. at 773).

[180] 40 U.S.C. §§ 3141-3144, 3146-3147.

[181] Hopkins v. HUD, 929 F.2d 81, 88 (2d Cir. 1991); see Sheet Metal Workers Int'l Ass'n, Local No. 19 v. VA, 135 F.3d 891, 903-05 (3d Cir. 1998); Sheet Metal Workers Int'l Ass'n, Local No. 9 v. U.S. Air Force, 63 F.3d 994, 997-98 (10th Cir. 1995); Painting & Drywall Work Pres. Fund, Inc. v. HUD, 936 F.2d 1300, 1303 (D.C. Cir. 1991).

[182] Painting & Drywall, 936 F.2d at 1303; see Sheet Metal Workers, 63 F.3d at 997-98; Hopkins, 929 F.2d at 88.

[183] Painting Indus. of Haw. Mkt. Recovery Fund v. U.S. Dep't of the Air Force, 751 F. Supp. 1410, 1417 (D. Haw.), reconsideration denied, 756 F. Supp. 452 (D. Haw. 1990); Seattle Bldg. & Constr. Trades Council v. HUD, No. C89-1346C, slip op. at 10-11 (W.D. Wash. Oct. 30, 1990).

[184] Painting Indus. of Haw. Mkt. Recovery Fund v. U.S. Dep't of the Air

(continued...)

cy's "diligence in enforcing Davis-Bacon," but found the weight to be given that interest weakened when the public benefit was derived neither directly from the release of the information itself nor from mere tabulation of data or further research but rather from personal contact with the individuals whose privacy is at issue.[185]

Public oversight of government operations is the essence of public interest under the FOIA, and in the past courts have found that one who claims such a purpose must support his claim by more than mere allegation; he must show that the information in question is "of sufficient importance to warrant such" oversight,[186] and he had to show how the public interest would be served by disclosure in the particular case.[187] Moreover, the Supreme Court in Favish found the Ninth Circuit's reliance on mere allegations of government wrongdoing to be simply "insufficient."[188] The Court pointedly recognized that "allegations of misconduct are 'easy to al-

---

[184](...continued)
Force, 26 F.3d 1479, 1484-86 (9th Cir. 1994).

[185] Id. at 1485; see also Sheet Metal Workers, 63 F.3d at 997-98.

[186] Miller v. Bell, 661 F.2d 623, 630 (7th Cir. 1981); see also Accuracy in Media, Inc. v. Nat'l Park Serv., 194 F.3d 120, 124 (D.C. Cir. 1999) (discounting inconsistencies in multiple agency reports from complex crime scene as "hardly so shocking as to suggest illegality or deliberate government falsification") (Exemption 7(C)); Schiffer, 78 F.3d at 1410 (rejecting public interest argument absent evidence suggesting wrongdoing by FBI); Computer Prof'ls for Soc. Responsibility v. U.S. Secret Serv., 72 F.3d 897, 904-05 (D.C. Cir. 1996) ("[T]he public interest is insubstantial unless the requester puts forward compelling evidence that the agency denying the FOIA request is engaged in illegal activity and shows that the information sought is necessary in order to confirm or refute that evidence.") (Exemption 7(C)); LaRouche v. U.S. Dep't of Justice, No. 90-2753, slip op. at 22-23 (D.D.C. Nov. 17, 2000) ("[W]hile the public interest in possible corruption is great, mere inferences of a violation carry little weight."); Wichlacz v. Dep't of Interior, 938 F. Supp. 325, 333 (E.D. Va. 1996) (observing that plaintiff "has set forth no evidence to buttress his bald allegations" of cover-up in investigation of death of Deputy White House Counsel Vincent Foster, a theory substantially undercut by then-ongoing Independent Counsel investigation), aff'd, 114 F.3d 1178 (4th Cir. 1997) (unpublished table decision); Allard v. HHS, No. 4:90-CV-156, slip op. at 10-11 (W.D. Mich. Feb. 14, 1992) (finding that "conclusory allegations" of plaintiff -- a prisoner with violent tendencies -- concerning ex-wife's misuse of children's social security benefits do not establish public interest), aff'd, 972 F.2d 346 (6th Cir. 1992) (unpublished table decision).

[187] See Halloran, 874 F.2d at 323; Rashid v. U.S. Dep't of Justice, No. 99-2461, slip op. at 16-17 (D.D.C. June 12, 2001).

[188] 541 U.S. at 173.

lege and hard to disprove'"[189] and that courts therefore must require a "meaningful evidentiary showing" by the FOIA requester.[190] Therefore, the Court adopted a higher standard for evaluation of "agency wrongdoing" claims and held that "the requester must establish more than a bare suspicion in order to obtain disclosure. Rather, the requester must produce evidence that would warrant a belief by a reasonable person that the alleged Government impropriety might have occurred."[191] And in such cases, this higher standard applies above and beyond the "qualifying public interest" standard of Reporters Committee.[192]

Accordingly, assertions of "public interest" should be scrutinized carefully to ensure that they legitimately warrant the overriding of important privacy interests.[193] Indeed, in the past two years, several courts have applied this heightened standard to allegations of government misconduct and overwhelmingly have found that plaintiffs have not provided the requisite evidence required by Favish.[194]

---

[189] Id. at 175 (quoting Crawford-El v. Britton, 523 U.S. 574, 585 (1998)); see also Ray, 502 U.S. at 178-79 (holding that there is presumption of legitimacy given to government conduct, and noting that privacy interests would be worthless if only bare allegations could overcome these interests).

[190] 541 U.S. at 175.

[191] Id. at 174.

[192] See FOIA Post, "Supreme Court Rules for 'Survivor Privacy' in Favish" (posted 4/9/04) (advising that Favish's "additional new standard for determining the existence and magnitude of a public interest in 'agency wrongdoing' cases does not replace the basic Reporters Committee standard for determining the existence of any 'public interest' generally"); see also FOIA Update, Vol. X, No. 2, at 6-7.

[193] See, e.g., Favish, 541 U.S. at 172 (stressing the requirement that "the public interest sought to be advanced [be] a significant one"); see also FOIA Update, Vol. III, No. 4, at 6; accord Attorney General's Memorandum for Heads of All Federal Departments and Agencies Regarding the Freedom of Information Act (Oct. 12, 2001), reprinted in FOIA Post (posted 10/15/01) (placing particular emphasis on the right to privacy among the other interests that are protected by the FOIA's exemptions).

[194] See Carpenter, 470 F.3d at 442 (concluding that "the requester must produce evidence that would warrant a belief by a reasonable person that the alleged Government impropriety might have occurred") (Exemption 7(C)); Wood v. FBI, 432 F.3d 78, 89 (2d Cir. 2005) (finding that plaintiff's "unsupported allegations" do not overcome "presumption of legitimacy . . . [of] government actions"); Horowitz, 428 F.3d at 278 & n.1 (finding that the plaintiff offered "no further details to support these extremely speculative allegations" and did not "overcome the presumption that the Peace Corps's

(continued...)

As stated by the Second Circuit in Hopkins v. HUD, "[t]he simple invocation of a legitimate public interest . . . cannot itself justify the release of personal information. Rather, a court must first ascertain whether that interest would be served by disclosure."[195] The Second Circuit in Hopkins found a legitimate public interest in monitoring HUD's enforcement of prevailing wage laws generally, but found that disclosure of the names and addresses of workers employed on HUD-assisted public housing projects would shed no light on the agency's performance of that duty in particular.[196] Even the Ninth Circuit in Minnis v. USDA recognized a valid public

---

[194](...continued)
[sic] official conduct was proper"); Oguaju v. United States, 378 F.3d 1115, 1117 (D.C. Cir.) (ruling that plaintiff "failed to make the requisite showing" required by Favish), reh'g denied & amended, 386 F.3d 273 (D.C. Cir. 2004) (per curiam), cert. denied, 544 U.S. 983 (2005); Sonds v. Huff, 391 F. Supp. 2d 152, 159 (D.D.C. 2005) (finding that requester did not produce any "evidence of unlawful conduct or impropriety by government officials") (Exemption 7(C)); Brown v. EPA, 384 F. Supp. 2d 271, 279-80 (D.D.C. 2005) ("[P]laintiff can provide no evidence of agency wrongdoing.") (Exemption 7(C)); Manchester v. FBI, No. 96-0137, 2005 WL 3275802, at *7 (D.D.C. Aug. 9, 2005) ("The court finds that [requester] failed to make a specific allegation that government impropriety occurred.") (Exemptions 6 and 7(C)). But see also Homick v. U.S. Dep't of Justice, No. 98-00557, slip op. at 20 (N.D. Cal. Sept. 15, 2004) (finding that plaintiff provided requisite evidence required by Favish to support public interest assertion that government failed to provide him with impeachment and exculpatory evidence during prosecutions).

[195] 929 F.2d at 88 (citing Halloran, 874 F.2d at 323 (observing that "merely stating that the interest exists in the abstract is not enough; rather, the court should have analyzed how that interest would be served by compelling disclosure")); see also Favish, 541 U.S. at 172-73 (reminding agencies and courts alike of "the nexus required between the requested documents and the purported public interest served by disclosure"); FOIA Post, "Supreme Court Rules for 'Survivor Privacy' in Favish" (posted 4/9/04) (emphasizing that "Favish serves as a reminder of that requirement").

[196] Id.; see also Abraham & Rose, P.L.C. v. United States, 138 F.3d 1075, 1083 (6th Cir. 1998) (finding that information about individual taxpayers does not serve any possible public interest in "how the IRS exercises its power over the collection of taxes"); Sutton v. IRS, No. 05-7177, 2007 WL 30547, at *6 (N.D. Ill. Jan. 4, 2007) (upholding the IRS's withholding of personal information of third-party taxpayers and IRS personnel because "none of their personal information will give Plaintiff a greater understanding of how the agency is performing its duties"); Forest Guardians v. U.S. Dep't of the Interior, No. 02-1003, 2004 WL 3426434, at *17 (D.N.M. Feb. 28, 2004) (finding public interest served by release of financial value of loans and names of financial institutions that issued loans, but "protecting any arguably private personal financial or other information concerning indi-

(continued...)

[196](...continued)

vidual [Bureau of Land Management] grazing permittees"); Idaho v. U.S. Forest Serv., No. 97-0230-S, slip op. at 6 (D. Idaho Dec. 9, 1997) (determining that while disclosure of names and cities of residence of Forest Service land permit holders will show whether permits are being granted properly, disclosure of home addresses will provide no "additional insight into agency activities"); Save Our Springs Alliance v. Babbitt, No. A-97-CA-259, slip op. at 7-8 (W.D. Tex. Nov. 19, 1997) (finding that "context of the letters" shows nature of correspondents who commented on issue before agency; release of home addresses and telephone numbers would add nothing to understanding of agency's process); Hecht v. U.S. Agency for Int'l Dev., No. 95-263, 1996 WL 33502232, at *12 (D. Del. Dec. 18, 1996) (determining that the public interest is served by release of redacted contractor's employee data sheets without the names, addresses and other identifying information of the employees); Stabasefski v. United States, 919 F. Supp. 1570, 1575 (M.D. Ga. 1996) (finding that public interest is served by release of redacted vouchers showing amounts of Hurricane Andrew subsistence payment to FAA employees; disclosure of names of employees would shed no additional light on agency activities); Gannett Satellite Info. Network, Inc. v. U.S. Dep't of Educ., No. 90-1392, 1990 WL 251480, at *6 (D.D.C. Dec. 21, 1990) ("If in fact a student has defaulted, [his] name, address, and social security number would reveal nothing about the Department's attempts to collect on those defaulted loans. Nor would [they] reveal anything about the potential misuse of public funds."). But see Leadership Conference on Civil Rights v. Gonzales, 404 F. Supp. 2d 246, 256-57 (D.D.C. 2005) (failing to explain how "strong public interest in . . . protecting minorities against voter intimidation" would be served by release of Justice Department paralegal names and phone numbers merely listed as contacts for federal prosecutors to send materials for Attorney General voting integrity initiative); Gordon v. FBI, 388 F. Supp. 2d 1028, 1041 (N.D. Cal. 2005) (deciding that public interest is served by disclosure of individual agency employee names because their names show "who are making important government policy") (Exemptions 6 and 7(C)); Lardner v. U.S. Dep't of Justice, No. 03-0180, 2005 WL 758267, at *17 (D.D.C. Mar. 31, 2005) (finding, without explanation, that the public interest in analyzing the "circumstances in which the executive chooses to grant or deny a pardon and the factors that bear on that decision" would be served by the release of the names of unsuccessful pardon applicants); Homick, No. 98-00557, slip op. at 20-21 (N.D. Cal. Sept. 15, 2004) (ruling that plaintiff failed to establish any connection between release of personal information of third parties and public interest asserted) (Exemption 7(C)); Judicial Watch v. U.S. Dep't of Justice, 102 F. Supp. 2d 6, 17-18 (D.D.C. 2000) (allowing deletion of home addresses and telephone numbers, but ordering release of identities of individuals who wrote to Attorney General about campaign finance or Independent Counsel issues), reconsideration denied temporarily pending in camera review, No. 97-CV-2869 (D.D.C. Aug. 17, 2000); Or. Natural Desert Ass'n v. U.S. Dep't of the Interior, 24 F. Supp. 2d 1088, 1093 (D. Or. 1998) (finding that

(continued...)

interest in questioning the fairness of an agency lottery system that award-ed permits to raft down the Rogue River, but found, upon careful analysis, that the release of the names and addresses of the applicants would in no way further that interest.[197]  Similarly, in Heights Community Congress v.

---

[196](...continued)
public interest in knowing how agency is enforcing land-management laws is served by release of names of cattle owners who violated federal grazing laws) (Exemption 7(C)); Maples v. USDA, No. F 97-5663, slip op. at 14 (E.D. Cal. Jan. 13, 1998) (finding that release of names and addresses of permit holders would show public how permit process works and elimi-nate "suspicions of favoritism in giving out permits" for use of federal lands).

[197] 737 F.2d 784, 787 (9th Cir. 1984); see Wood, 432 F.3d at 89 ("Given that the FBI has already revealed the substance of the investigation and subsequent adjudication, knowledge of the names of the investigators would add little, if anything, to the public's analysis of whether the FBI dealt with the accused agents in an appropriate manner."); Larson v. Dep't of State, No. 02-01937, 2005 WL 3276303, at *29 (D.D.C. Aug. 10, 2005) (stating that the plaintiff did "not . . . adequately explain how disclosure of the identities of these particular sources would shed much, if any, light on the operations of [the Department of State]"); Summers, No. 98-1837, slip op. at 13 (D.D.C. Apr. 13, 2004) (concluding that "plaintiff has not estab-lished that disclosing the redacted names [of the FBI employees] will pro-vide any substantial additional information about the adequacy of the FBI's conduct"); Kelly v. CIA, No. 00-2498, slip op. at 49-50 (D.D.C. Sept. 25, 2002) (finding that although the "public interest in [the CIA's former] MKULTRA [program] is certainly very high," plaintiff had not demonstrated how dis-closing the names of individual test subjects would shed light on the MKULTRA program or CIA activities), appeal on adequacy of search dis-missed on procedural grounds, No. 02-5384, 2003 WL 21804101 (D.C. Cir. July 31, 2003); Times Picayune Publ'g Corp. v. U.S. Dep't of Justice, 37 F. Supp. 2d 472, 480-81 (E.D. La. 1999) (concluding that release of mug shot would not inform members of public about "activities of their government") (Exemption 7(C)); Baltimore Sun Co. v. U.S. Customs Serv., No. 97-1991, slip op. at 7 (D. Md. Nov. 21, 1997) (finding that the photograph of an individual who pled guilty to trafficking in child pornography was not "sufficiently probative of the fairness of [his] sentence that its disclosure [would] in-form[] the public of 'what the government is up to'") (Exemption 7(C)); N.Y. Times Co. v. NASA, 782 F. Supp. 628, 632-33 (D.D.C. 1991) (finding that re-lease of the audiotape of the Challenger astronauts' voices just prior to the explosion would not serve the "undeniable interest in learning about NASA's conduct before, during and after the Challenger disaster"). But see Detroit Free Press, Inc. v. Dep't of Justice, 73 F.3d 93, 97-98 (6th Cir. 1996) (saying that the agency's disclosure of the mug shots of indicted individu-als during the course of an ongoing criminal proceeding could reveal an "error in detaining the wrong person for an offense" or the "circumstances surrounding an arrest and initial incarceration"); Rosenfeld v. Dep't of Jus-
(continued...)

VA,[198] the Sixth Circuit found that the release of names and home addresses would result only in the "involuntary personal involvement" of innocent purchasers rather than appreciably furthering a concededly valid public interest in determining whether anyone had engaged in "racial steering."

Several courts, moreover, have observed that the minimal amount of information of interest to the public revealed by a single incident or investigation does not shed enough light on an agency's conduct to overcome the subject's privacy interest in his records.[199] In this vein, it is also important

---

[197] (...continued)
tice, 57 F.3d 803, 811-12 (9th Cir. 1995) (concluding that disclosure of the identities of individuals investigated would reveal whether the "FBI abused its law enforcement mandate by overzealously investigating a political protest movement to which some members of the government may then have objected") (Exemption 7(C)); Baltimore Sun v. U.S. Marshals Serv., 131 F. Supp. 2d 725, 729-30 (D. Md. 2001) (declaring that "[a]ccess to the names and addresses [of purchasers of seized property] would enable the public to assess law enforcement agencies' exercise of the substantial power to seize property, as well as USMS's performance of its duties regarding disposal of forfeited property") (Exemption 7(C)), appeal dismissed voluntarily, No. 01-1537 (4th Cir. June 25, 2001).

[198] 732 F.2d 526, 530 (6th Cir. 1984); Painting Indus., 26 F.3d at 1484-85 (protecting names and addresses of employees on payroll records, and stating that the "additional public benefit the requesters might realize through [contacting the employees] is inextricably intertwined with the invasions of privacy that those contacts will work"); The News-Press v. DHS, No. 05-102, 2005 WL 2921952, at *18-19 (M.D. Fla. Nov. 4, 2005) (deciding to protect the names and addresses of thousands of disaster relief claimants because the prospective utilization of this information by the plaintiff to find and interview the claimants "tips the scale towards the privacy invasion side").

[199] See Tomscha v. GSA, 158 F. App'x 329, 331 (2d Cir. 2005) (finding that disclosure of the justification for awards given to "a single low-ranking employee of the GSA . . . would not 'contribute significantly to the public understanding of the operations or activities of the government'" (quoting DOD v. FLRA, 510 U.S. at 495)); Oguaju v. United States, 288 F.3d 448, 451 (D.C. Cir. 2002) (declaring that "even if the records Oguaju seeks would reveal wrongdoing in his case, exposing a single, garden-variety act of misconduct would not serve the FOIA's purpose of showing 'what the Government is up to'") (Exemption 7(C)), vacated & remanded, 541 U.S. 970, on remand, 378 F.3d 1115 (D.C. Cir.), reh'g denied & amended, 386 F.3d 273 (D.C. Cir. 2004) (per curiam), cert. denied, 544 U.S. 983 (2005); Neely v. FBI, 208 F.3d 461, 464 (4th Cir. 2000) (observing that "courts have refused to recognize, for purposes of FOIA, a public interest in nothing more than the fairness of a criminal defendant's own trial") (Exemption 7(C)); Hunt, 972

(continued...)

to note that there is a logical distinction between the public interest that can exist within an overall subject that relates to a FOIA request, on the one hand, and the interest that might or might not be served by disclosure of the particular records that are responsive to that FOIA request, on the other.[200] The term "umbrella issue" has been utilized by agencies and courts when referring to this important distinction between showing public interest in only the general subject area of the request, as opposed to the public interest in the specific subject area of the disclosable portions of the requested records.[201] As a matter of sound policy, agencies should be aware of and address any "umbrella issue" in order to accurately weigh the public interest within applicable areas of FOIA decisionmaking, particularly in the balancing processes of both Exemption 6 and Exemption 7(C).[202]

---

[199](...continued)
F.2d at 289 (observing that disclosure of single internal investigation file "will not shed any light on whether all such FBI investigations are comprehensive or whether sexual misconduct by agents is common"); Mueller, 63 F. Supp. 2d at 745 ("[T]he interest of the public in the personnel file of one Air Force prosecutor is attenuated because information concerning a single isolated investigation reveals relatively little about the conduct of the Air Force as an agency.") (Exemptions 6 and 7(C)); Chin, No. 97-2176, slip op. at 5 (W.D. La. June 24, 1999) (finding only "marginal benefit to the public interest" in release of the facts of a single case, particularly "where alternative means exist -- such as statistical samples or generalized accounts -- to satisfy the public interest"). But see Cooper Cameron Corp. v. U.S. Dep't of Labor, 280 F.3d 539, 548-49 (5th Cir. 2002) (perceiving a "public interest in monitoring agencies' enforcement of the law in specific instances") (Exemption 7(C)).

[200] See FOIA Post, "FOIA Counselor Q&A" (posted 1/24/06) (explaining distinction between generalized public interest in broad subject area of FOIA request as opposed to specific public interest in particular documents at issue in FOIA request) (citing cases).

[201] Id. (identifying significance of "umbrella issue" under FOIA) (citing Elec. Privacy Info. Ctr. v. DOD, 355 F. Supp. 2d 98, 102 (D.D.C. 2004) (stating that "[t]he fact that [the requester] has provided evidence that there is some media interest in data mining as an umbrella issue does not satisfy the requirement that [the requester] demonstrate interest in the specific subject of [its] FOIA request"), and ACLU of N. Cal. v. Dep't of Justice, No. 04-4447, 2005 WL 588354, at *13 (N.D. Cal. Mar. 11, 2005) (ruling that "it was not sufficient for the plaintiffs to show [public] interest in only the general subject area of the request")); see also Schrecker v. Dep't of Justice, 349 F.3d 657, 661 (D.C. Cir. 2003) (stating that an inquiry regarding the public interest "should focus not on the general public interest in the subject matter of the FOIA request, but rather on the incremental value of the specific information being withheld") (Exemption 7(C)).

[202] FOIA Post, "FOIA Counselor Q&A" (posted 1/24/06) (citing KTVY-TV
(continued...)

Such approaches fully comport with the Supreme Court's emphasis on the required "nexus between the requested information and the asserted public interest that would be advanced by disclosure" in Favish,[203] and they are entirely consistent with the Court's determination in Reporters Committee that the "rap sheet" of a defense contractor, if such existed, would reveal nothing directly about the behavior of the Congressman with whom the contractor allegedly had an improper relationship, nor would it reveal anything about the conduct of the DOD.[204] The information must

---

[202](...continued)
v. United States, 919 F.2d 1465, 1470 (10th Cir. 1990) (Exemption 7(C)), NTEU v. Griffin, 811 F.2d 644, 648 (D.C. Cir. 1987) (fee waiver), and Cotton v. Heyman, 63 F.3d 1115, 1120 (D.C. Cir. 1995) (applying comparable approach to award of attorney fees)); see Morley v. CIA, 453 F. Supp. 2d 137, 155 (D.D.C. 2006) ("While plaintiff, in his FOIA request, claims that there is a public interest in the materials he seeks generally, he fails to establish that there is a public interest in the personal information claimed to be exempt here.") (Exemption 7(C)) (appeal pending); Long v. U.S. Dep't of Justice, 450 F. Supp. 2d 42, 69 (D.D.C.) (requiring that plaintiffs credibly demonstrate with sufficient specificity that disclosure of requested records would shed light on agency conduct), amended by 457 F. Supp. 2d 30, 31-32 (D.D.C. 2006), amended further on reconsideration, Nos. 00-0211 & 02-2467, 2007 WL 293508, at *1-5 (D.D.C. Feb. 2, 2007), stay granted (D.D.C. Feb. 13, 2007); PETA v. USDA, No. 03-195, 2006 WL 508332, at *3-4 (D.D.C. Mar. 3, 2006) (attorney fees); see also Attorney General's Memorandum for Heads of All Federal Departments and Agencies Regarding the Freedom of Information Act (Oct. 12, 2001) (urging "careful" decisionmaking), reprinted in FOIA Post (posted 10/15/01).

[203] 541 U.S. at 172-73.

[204] 489 U.S. at 774; see also NARFE, 879 F.2d at 879 (finding that names and home addresses of federal annuitants reveal nothing directly about workings of government); Halloran, 874 F.2d at 323 ("[M]erely stating that the interest exists in the abstract is not enough; rather, the court should have analyzed how that interest would be served by compelling disclosure."); Kimberlin v. Dep't of the Treasury, 774 F.2d 204, 208 (7th Cir. 1985) ("The record fails to reflect any benefit which would accrue to the public from disclosure and [the requester's] self-serving assertions of government wrongdoing and coverup do not rise to the level of justifying disclosure.") (Exemption 7(C)); Johnson v. U.S. Dep't of Justice, 739 F.2d 1514, 1519 (10th Cir. 1984) (finding that because allegations of improper use of law enforcement authority were not at all supported in requested records, disclosure of FBI special agent names would not serve public interest) (Exemption 7(C)); Stern, 737 F.2d at 92 (finding that certain specified public interests "would not be satiated in any way" by disclosure) (Exemption 7(C)); Miller, 661 F.2d at 630 (noting that plaintiff's broad assertions of government cover-up were unfounded as investigation was of consequence to plaintiff only and therefore did not "warrant probe of FBI efficiency") (Ex-
(continued...)

clearly reveal official government activities; it is not enough that the information would permit speculative inferences about the conduct of an agency or a government official,[205] or that it might aid the requester in lobbying efforts that would result in passage of laws and thus benefit the public in that respect.[206]

---

[204](...continued)
emption 7(C)); Brown v. EPA, 384 F. Supp. 2d at 279 (rejecting the "suggestion that the disclosure of names in government investigative files can somehow provide insight into the workings of the government") (Exemption 7(C)); Elec. Privacy Info. Ctr. v. DHS, 384 F. Supp. 2d 100, 117-18 (D.D.C. 2005) ("Names alone will not shed any light on how the agencies worked with the airlines."); Nation Magazine v. Dep't of State, No. 92-2303, 1995 WL 17660254, at *10 & n.15 (D.D.C. Aug. 18, 1995) ("[T]he public interest in knowing more about [presidential candidate H. Ross] Perot's dealings with the government is also not the type of public interest protected by the FOIA."). But see Nation Magazine v. U.S. Customs Serv., 71 F.3d 885, 895 (D.C. Cir. 1995) (finding that agency's response to presidential candidate H. Ross Perot's offer to assist in drug interdiction would serve public interest in agency's plans regarding "'privatization of government functions'").

[205] See Reporters Comm., 489 U.S. at 774, 766 n.18; see also Robbins v. HHS, No. 1:95-cv-3258, slip op. at 8-9 (N.D. Ga. Aug. 12, 1996) (ruling that the possibility that release of names and addresses of rejected social security disability claimants could ultimately reveal the agency's wrongful denial is "too attenuated to outweigh the significant invasion of privacy"), aff'd per curiam, No. 96-9000 (11th Cir. July 8, 1997); Gannett Satellite, No. 90-1392, slip op. at 12 (D.D.C. Dec. 21, 1990) (finding that names, addresses, and social security numbers of student loan defaulters would reveal nothing directly about Department of Education's administration of student loan program); FOIA Post, "Supreme Court Rules for 'Survivor Privacy' in Favish" (posted 4/9/04) (pointing out that "Favish now stands as a further bulwark against" speculation-wielding FOIA requesters). But see Avondale Indus. v. NLRB, 90 F.3d 955, 961-62 (5th Cir. 1996) (declaring that disclosure of marked unredacted voting lists in union representation election would give plaintiff information it needs to determine whether NLRB conducted election tainted with fraud and corruption); Int'l Diatomite Producers Ass'n v. U.S. Soc. Sec. Admin., No. C-92-1634, 1993 WL 137286, at *5 (N.D. Cal. Apr. 28, 1993) (finding that release of vital status information concerning diatomite industry workers serves "public interest in evaluating whether public agencies (OSHA, [Mine Safety and Health Administration], and EPA) carry out their statutory duties to protect the public from the potential health hazards from crystalline silica exposure"), appeal dismissed, No. 93-16723 (9th Cir. Nov. 1, 1993).

[206] See NARFE, 879 F.2d at 875; see also FOIA Update, Vol. X, No. 2, at 6 (discussing the narrowed "public interest" concept under Reporters Committee).

A very significant development concerning this issue occurred in United States Department of State v. Ray,[207] when the Supreme Court recognized a legitimate public interest in whether the State Department was adequately monitoring Haiti's promise not to prosecute Haitians who were returned to their country after failed attempts to enter the United States, but the Court determined that this public interest had been "adequately served" by release of redacted summaries of the agency's interviews with the returnees and that "[t]he addition of the redacted identifying information would not shed any additional light on the Government's conduct of its obligation."[208] Although the plaintiff claimed that disclosure of the identities of the unsuccessful emigrants would allow him to reinterview them and elicit further information concerning their treatment, the Court found "nothing in the record to suggest that a second set of interviews with the already-interviewed returnees would produce any relevant information. . . . Mere speculation about hypothetical public benefits cannot outweigh a demonstrably significant invasion of privacy."[209]

The Supreme Court expressly declined in Ray to decide whether a public interest that stems not from the documents themselves but rather from a "derivative use" to which the documents could be put could ever be weighed in the balancing process against a privacy interest.[210] Subsequently, however, several lower courts faced the "derivative use" issue and ordered the release of names and home addresses of private individuals in certain contexts despite the fact that the public benefit to be derived from release of the information depended upon the requesters' use of the lists to question those individuals concerning the government's diligence in performing its duties. These courts have found a "derivative use" public interest in the following contexts:

---

[207] 502 U.S. 164 (1991).

[208] Id. at 178; see also Pub. Citizen, Inc. v. RTC, No. 92-0010, 1993 WL 1617868, at *3-4 (D.D.C. Mar. 19, 1993) (adjudging public interest in agency's compliance with Affordable Housing Disposition Program to be served by release of information with identities of bidders and purchasers redacted). But see Rosenfeld, 57 F.3d at 811-12 (concluding that disclosure of names of investigative subjects would serve public interest in knowing whether FBI "overzealously" investigated political protest group by allowing comparison of investigative subjects to group's leadership roster) (Exemption 7(C)).

[209] 502 U.S. at 178-79; see also Navigator Publ'g v. U.S. Dep't of Transp., 146 F. Supp. 2d 68, 71 (D. Me. 2001) (concluding that release of addresses of merchant mariners licensed by United States would serve only "hypothetical 'derivative use'" that is far outweighed by "demonstrably significant invasion of privacy"), appeal dismissed, No. 01-1939 (1st Cir. Sept. 19, 2001).

[210] 502 U.S. at 178-79.

(1) a list of individuals who sold land to the Fish and Wildlife Service, which could be used to contact the individuals to determine how the agency acquires property throughout the United States;[211]

(2) a list of Haitian nationals returned to Haiti, which could be used for follow-up interviews with the Haitians to learn "whether the INS is fulfilling its duties not to turn away Haitians who may have valid claims for political asylum";[212]

(3) a list of citizens who reported wolf sightings, which could be used to monitor the Fish and Wildlife Service's enforcement of the Endangered Species Act;[213]

(4) the names of agents involved in the management and supervision of the FBI's 1972 investigation of John Lennon, which could be used to help determine whether the investigation was politically motivated;[214]

(5) the name and address of an individual who wrote a letter complaining about an immigration assistance company, which could be used to determine whether the INS acted upon the complaint;[215]

(6) the names and addresses of individuals who received property seized under federal law, which could enable the public to assess the government's exercise of its power to seize and dispose of property;[216] and

(7) the addresses of claimants awarded disaster assistance by FEMA based upon claims of damages from various hurricanes in Florida in 2004, which could be used to uncover further information pertaining to allegations of fraud and wasteful spending in the distribution of disaster

---

[211] Thott v. U.S. Dep't of the Interior, No. 93-0177-B, slip op. at 5-6 (D. Me. Apr. 14, 1994).

[212] Ray v. U.S. Dep't of Justice, 852 F. Supp. 1558, 1564-65 (S.D. Fla. 1994) (distinguishing Ray, 502 U.S. 164, on the basis that "in the instant case . . . the public interest is not adequately served by release of the redacted logs [and] this Court cannot say that interviewing the returnees would not produce any information concerning our government's conduct during the interdiction process").

[213] Urbigkit v. U.S. Dep't of the Interior, No. 93-CV-0232-J, slip op. at 13 (D. Wyo. May 31, 1994).

[214] Weiner v. FBI, No. 83-1720, slip op. at 5-7 (C.D. Cal. Dec. 6, 1995) (Exemptions 6 and 7(C)).

[215] Cardona v. INS, No. 93-3912, 1995 WL 68747, at *3 (N.D. Ill. Feb. 15, 1995).

[216] Baltimore Sun, 131 F. Supp. 2d at 729-30.

assistance by FEMA.[217]

However, the District Court for the District of Columbia reached a different result, with more cogent reasoning, in Hertzberg v. Veneman.[218] In that case, the plaintiff argued that disclosure of the names and identifying information that were withheld on witness statements would serve the public interest because, he said, it would allow him to contact the witnesses.[219] The court disagreed with this argument and it stated that "disclosure is not compelled under the FOIA [just] because the link between the request and the potential illumination of agency action is too attenuated. Plaintiff cites no case recognizing a derivative theory of public interest, and this Court does not understand the FOIA to encompass such a concept."[220] And now the Supreme Court's recent emphasis in Favish on "the necessary nexus between" the information requested and the "public interest" to be served, at a minimum, calls this "derivative use" notion into even greater question.[221]

---

[217] Sun-Sentinel, 431 F. Supp. 2d at 1269-73.

[218] 273 F. Supp. 2d 67, 86-87 (D.D.C. 2003).

[219] Id. at 87.

[220] Id.

[221] 541 U.S. at 172-73; see also Painting Indus., 26 F.3d at 1484-85 (finding that the public interest in monitoring an agency's enforcement of the Davis-Bacon Act is not served by disclosure of names and addresses on payroll records because an additional step of contacting employees is required and the "additional public benefit the requester might realize through these contacts is inextricably intertwined with the invasions of privacy that those contacts will work," but also reasoning that if yielding a public interest required only some further research by the requester, then the fact that the use is a "derivative" one should not detract from the strength of that public benefit); The News-Press, 2005 WL 2921952, at *18 (considering the possibility of a "derivative" public interest but ultimately concluding that "it does not tip the balance in favor of disclosure" and that it actually "does the opposite"); Sammis v. Barnhardt, No. C01-3973, 2002 WL 1285050, at *2 (N.D. Cal. June 6, 2002) ("If this court allowed disclosure, plaintiff would have to obtain the information, use it to contact applicants directly, and cause them to take action . . . . This derivative type of benefit is too tenuous to merit invading individuals' privacy."); Horsehead Indus. v. EPA, No. 94-1299, slip op. at 6 (D.D.C. Mar. 13, 1997) (acknowledging that disclosure of the identities of homeowners who volunteered to participate in a Superfund study might "provide a glimpse into EPA's activities," but finding that "this interest pales in comparison to the potential harm to the privacy" of study participants, based in part upon "reports of trespassers taking environmental samples"); Upper Peninsula Envtl. Coal. v. Forest Serv., No. 2:94-cv-021, slip op. at 10 (W.D. Mich. Sept. 28, 1994) (finding the
(continued...)

Finally, if alternative, less intrusive means are available to obtain information that would serve the public interest, there is less need to require disclosure of information that would cause an invasion of someone's privacy. Accordingly, "[w]hile [this is] certainly not a per se defense to a FOIA request," it is entirely appropriate, when assessing the public interest side of the balancing equation, to consider "the extent to which there are alternative sources of information available that could serve the public interest in disclosure."[222]

---

[221](...continued)
"derivative" public interest in gathering information that might assist the Forest Service in managing a wilderness area to be only "negligible," because "[i]t is not the purpose of the FOIA to allow private citizens to do the work of government agencies").

[222] DOD v. FLRA, 964 F.2d 26, 29-30 (D.C. Cir. 1992); see Office of the Capital Collateral Counsel, 331 F.3d at 804 (finding that there is substantial public information available about the AUSA's misconduct and that therefore any "public interest in knowing how DOJ responded to [the AUSA's] misconduct can be satisfied by this other public information"); Painting Indus., 26 F.3d at 1485 (union may "pass out fliers" or "post signs or advertisements soliciting information from workers about possible violations of the Davis-Bacon Act"); FLRA v. U.S. Dep't of Commerce, 962 F.2d 1055, 1060 n.2 (D.C. Cir. 1992) (union may "distribute questionnaires or conduct confidential face-to-face interviews" to obtain rating information about employees); Painting & Drywall, 936 F.2d at 1303 (contact at workplace is alternative to disclosing home addresses of employees); Multnomah County Med. Soc'y, 825 F.2d at 1416 (medical society can have members send literature to their patients as alternative to disclosure of identities of all Medicare beneficiaries); Chin, No. 97-2176, slip op. at 4-5 (W.D. La. June 24, 1999) (release of "statistical data and/or general accounts of incidents" would be an alternative to releasing investigative records of named individual to show whether government policies were "administered in an arbitrary manner"); Cowles Publ'g Co. v. United States, No. 90-349, slip op. at 8-9 (E.D. Wash. Dec. 20, 1990) (advertisements soliciting injured persons and their physicians, or direct contact with physicians, in region are viable alternatives to agency's releasing identities of persons injured by radiation exposure); Hemenway v. Hughes, 601 F. Supp. 1002, 1007 (D.D.C. 1985) (personal contact with individuals whose names and work addresses were released to plaintiff is alternative to agency's releasing personal information he seeks); cf. Heat & Frost Insulators & Asbestos Workers, Local 16 v. U.S. Dep't of the Air Force, No. S92-2173, slip op. at 3-4 (E.D. Cal. Oct. 4, 1993) (no alternative to union's request for payroll records -- with names, addresses, and social security numbers redacted -- would allow union to monitor agency's collection of records in compliance with federal regulations); Cotton, 798 F. Supp. at 27 n.9 (suggesting that request for all inspector general reports, from which identifying information could be redacted, would better serve public interest in overseeing discharge of inspector general duties than does request for only two specific investigative

(continued...)

EXEMPTION 6

In Favish, the Supreme Court recognized that the government had thoroughly investigated the suicide of Vincent Foster and that "[i]t would be quite extraordinary to say we must ignore the fact that five different inquiries into the Foster matter reached the same conclusion."[223] Indeed, if there are alternative sources, the D.C. Circuit has firmly ruled, the public interest in disclosure should be "discounted" accordingly.[224] Likewise, the Court of Appeals for the Tenth Circuit properly assigned no public interest value to a request to FEMA for "electronic map files" showing the locations of federally insured structures, because the electronic files were "merely cumulative of the information" that FEMA already had released in "hard copies" of the maps and because the requester already had a "plethora of information" with which "to evaluate FEMA's activities."[225]

Similarly, although courts ordinarily discuss the "public interest" as weighing in favor of disclosure, several courts have implicitly recognized that there can be a public interest in the nondisclosure of personal privacy information -- particularly, the public interest in avoiding the impairment of ongoing and future law enforcement investigations.[226] Most explicitly, the

---

[222](...continued)
reports involving known individuals).

[223] 541 U.S. at 175.

[224] DOD v. FLRA, 964 F.2d at 29-30.

[225] Forest Guardians v. FEMA, 410 F.3d 1214, 1219 & n.3 (10th Cir. 2005).

[226] See, e.g., Perlman, 312 F.3d at 106 ("The strong public interest in encouraging witnesses to participate in future government investigations offsets the weak public interest in learning witness and third party identities.") (Exemptions 6 and 7(C)); Strout v. U.S. Parole Comm'n, 40 F.3d 136, 139 (6th Cir. 1994) ("[T]here would appear to be a public policy interest against such disclosure, as the fear of disclosure to a convicted criminal could have a chilling effect on persons, particularly victims, who would otherwise provide the Commission with information relevant to a parole decision."); Miller v. Bell, 661 F.2d 623, 631 (7th Cir. 1981) (observing that the district court failed to consider "the substantial public interest in maintaining the integrity of future FBI undercover investigations") (Exemption 7(C)); Fund, 656 F.2d at 865-66 (protecting identities of government officials investigated but not charged with any crime in "Watergate" investigation) (Exemption 7(C)); Diaz, No. 01-40070, slip op. at 10 (D. Mass. Dec. 20, 2001) (deciding that there would be "chilling" effect if conversations between inmates and their attorneys were disclosed to public anytime they spoke on monitored prison telephones); Church of Scientology v. Dep't of State, 493 F. Supp. 418, 421 (D.D.C. 1980) (finding that Church of Scientology offered no public interest and that it had "practice of harassing its 'suppressors'") (Exemptions 6 and 7(C)); Flower v. FBI, 448 F. Supp. 567, 571-72 (W.D. Tex. 1978) (noting that "it is doubtful" that individuals would
(continued...)

D.C. Circuit, in Fund for Constitutional Government v. National Archives & Records Service, has recognized that the "public interest properly factors into both sides of the balance."[227]

### The Balancing Process

Once both the privacy interest at stake and the public interest in disclosure have been ascertained, the two competing interests must be weighed against one another.[228] In other words, it must be determined which is the greater result of disclosure: the harm to personal privacy or the benefit to the public.[229] In balancing these interests, "the 'clearly unwarranted' language of Exemption 6 weights the scales in favor of disclosure,"[230] but if the public benefit is weaker than the threat to privacy, the

---

[226](...continued)
cooperate with law enforcement if their privacy were not protected) (Exemption 7(C)); see also Favish, 541 U.S. at 170 (implying that nondisclosure result necessarily serves society's strong interest in denying "gruesome requests" made by "convicted felons" for photos of their victims); Tomscha v. GSA, No. 03-6755, 2004 WL 1234043, at *5 (S.D.N.Y. June 3, 2004) (finding that the agency has an interest "in encouraging managers and supervisors to comment candidly on an employee without fear their statements will become public," but assigning this interest to the privacy side of the balance); Kelly v. CIA, No. 00-2498, slip op. at 15 (D.D.C. Aug. 8, 2002) (observing that agency should factor in public interest at time that classification decision is made, and further noting that requester's asserted public interest in disclosure of requested information will not undermine proper classification because it certainly is in public interest to withhold information that would damage national security) (Exemption 1), modified in other respects, No. 00-2498, slip op. at 1 (D.D.C. Sept. 25, 2002), appeal on adequacy of search dismissed on procedural grounds, No. 02-5384, 2003 WL 21804101 (D.C. Cir. July 31, 2003).

[227] 656 F.2d at 865; see also FOIA Update, Vol. III, No. 4, at 5 (advising that there is a "sound basis" for agencies to look at the public interest in nondisclosure in order to "determine the 'net' public interest involved").

[228] See Dep't of the Air Force v. Rose, 425 U.S. 352, 372 (1976); Cawthon v. U.S. Dep't of Justice, No. 05-0567, 2006 WL 581250, at *4 (D.D.C. Mar. 9, 2006) (finding that the plaintiff's bare allegations fail to establish a public interest, and stating that "[a]bsent any evidence of agency impropriety, the balancing inquiry does not come 'into play'" (quoting NARA v. Favish, 541 U.S. 157, 175, reh'g denied, 541 U.S. 1057 (2004))).

[229] See Ripskis v. HUD, 746 F.2d 1, 3 (D.C. Cir. 1984); see FOIA Update, Vol. X, No. 2, at 7 ("FOIA Counselor: Exemption 6 and Exemption 7(C): Step-by-Step Decisionmaking").

[230] Ripskis, 746 F.2d at 3.

latter will prevail and the information should be withheld.[231] The threat to privacy need not be immediate or direct;[232] it need only outweigh the public interest.[233]

Although "the presumption in favor of disclosure is as strong [under Exemption 6] as can be found anywhere in the Act,"[234] the courts have most vigorously protected the personal, intimate details of an individual's life -- consistently protecting personal information that, if disclosed, is likely to cause the individual who is involved personal distress or embarrassment. Courts regularly uphold the nondisclosure of information concerning such things as:

(1) marital status;

(2) legitimacy of children;

(3) welfare payments;

(4) family fights and reputation;[235]

---

[231] See FOIA Update, Vol. X, No. 2, at 6 (emphasizing possible applicability of Privacy Act's disclosure prohibitions, particularly in light of Reporters Committee); see also Judicial Watch v. FDA, 449 F.3d 141, 153 (D.C. Cir. 2006) (upholding FDA's withholding names of agency personnel, private individuals, and companies who worked on approval of mifepristone (RU-486 abortion drug), as well as addresses of intervenors and all business partners associated with manufacturing of mifepristone; concluding that "[i]n the absence of a legitimate public interest, the private interest in avoiding harassment or violence tilts the scales"). But cf. Lahr v. NTSB, 453 F. Supp. 2d 1153, 1183-84 (C.D. Cal. 2006) (ordering the disclosure of names and identification numbers of eyewitnesses to TWA Flight 800 crash; concluding that eyewitnesses' privacy interests are outweighed by significant public interest in getting to the bottom of alleged "massive cover-up" by the government of alleged missile strike on Flight 800) (Exemptions 6 and 7(C)) (appeal pending).

[232] See Favish, 541 U.S. at 167 (relying, in finding threat to privacy, on expectation of renewed media exploitation if photographs were to be released).

[233] See Pub. Citizen Health Research Group v. U.S. Dep't of Labor, 591 F.2d 808, 809 (D.C. Cir. 1978) (finding that "[s]ince this is a balancing test, any invasion of privacy can prevail, so long as the public interest balanced against it is sufficiently weaker," and noting that the threat to privacy does not have to be "obvious").

[234] Wash. Post Co. v. HHS, 690 F.2d 252, 261 (D.C. Cir. 1982).

[235] See, e.g., Rural Hous. Alliance v. USDA, 498 F.2d 73, 77 (D.C. Cir.
(continued...)

(5)  medical condition;[236]

(6)  date of birth;[237]

(7)  religious affiliation;[238]

(8)  citizenship data;[239]

(9)  genealogical history establishing membership in a Native Ameri-

---

[235](...continued)
1974); see also Hardison v. Sec'y of VA, 159 F. App'x 93, 94 (11th Cir. 2005) (dates of marriage and spouses' names).

[236] See, e.g., McDonnell v. United States, 4 F.3d 1227, 1254 (3d Cir. 1993) ("living individual has a strong privacy interest in withholding his medical records"); Rural Hous. Alliance, 498 F.2d at 77; Pub. Employees for Envtl. Responsibility v. U.S. Dep't of the Interior, No. 06-182, 2006 U.S. Dist. LEXIS 85787, at *15 n.4 (D.D.C. Nov. 28, 2006) (noting that Department of the Interior properly invoked Exemption 6 in withholding information detailing employee's physical ailments and medical advice regarding those ailments); Sousa v. U.S. Dep't of Justice, No. 95-375, 1997 U.S. Dist. LEXIS 9010, at *22 (D.D.C. June 18, 1997) (withholding co-defendant's medical records); Robbins v. HHS, No. 1:95-cv-3258, slip op. at 8-9 (N.D. Ga. Aug. 12, 1996) (upholding nondisclosure of names, addresses, and claim denial letters of rejected social security disability claimants), aff'd per curiam, No. 96-9000 (11th Cir. July 8, 1997); Hunt v. U.S. Marine Corps, 935 F. Supp. 46, 54 (D.D.C. 1996) (observing that although public may have interest in a political candidate's fitness for office, disclosure of Oliver North's medical records would not shed light on conduct of Marine Corps).

[237] See, e.g., Hardison, 159 F. App'x at 93; Judicial Watch, Inc. v. U.S. Dep't of Commerce, 83 F. Supp. 2d 105, 112 (D.D.C. 1999), appeal dismissed voluntarily, No. 99-5054 (D.C. Cir. Sept. 10, 1999).

[238] See, e.g., Church of Scientology v. U.S. Dep't of the Army, 611 F.2d 738, 747 (9th Cir. 1979). But cf. Tangerine Rd. Assocs. v. U.S. Fish & Wildlife Serv., No. 02-614, slip op. at 3 (D. Ariz. May 5, 2004) (requiring release of pygmy owl locations because although Indian tribe considered pygmy owls sacred, defendant did not offer evidence showing that specific locations of the owls are sacred).

[239] See U.S. Dep't of State v. Wash. Post Co., 456 U.S. 595, 602 (1982) (passport information); Hemenway v. Hughes, 601 F. Supp. 1002, 1006 (D.D.C. 1985) ("Nationals from some countries face persistent discrimination . . . [and] are potential targets for terrorist attacks."); cf. Judicial Watch, Inc. v. Reno, No. 00-0723, 2001 WL 1902811, at *8 (D.D.C. Mar. 30, 2001) (asylum application); Judicial Watch, Inc. v. U.S. Dep't of Commerce, 83 F. Supp. 2d at 112 (visa and passport data).

can Tribe;[240]

    (10) social security numbers;[241]

    (11) criminal history records (commonly referred to as "rap sheets");[242]

    (12) incarceration of United States citizens in foreign prisons;[243]

    (13) sexual inclinations or associations;[244] and

    (14) financial status.[245]

Even "favorable information," such as details of an employee's outstanding performance evaluation, can be protected on the basis that it "may well

---

[240] Quinault Indian Nation v. Gover, No. C97-5625, transcript at 52-57 (W.D. Wash. Oct. 19, 1998), aff'd sub nom. Quinault Indian Nation v. Deer, 232 F.3d 896 (9th Cir. 2000) (unpublished table decision).

[241] See, e.g., Sherman v. U.S. Dep't of the Army, 244 F.3d 357, 365-66 (5th Cir. 2001); Norwood v. FAA, 993 F.2d 570, 575 (6th Cir. 1993); Peay v. Dep't of Justice, No. 04-1859, 2006 WL 1805616, at *2 (D.D.C. June 29, 2006) ("The IRS properly applied exemption 6 to the social security numbers of IRS personnel."); Dayton Newspapers, Inc. v. U.S. Dep't of the Navy, No. C-3-95-328, slip op. at 31-38 (S.D. Ohio Sept. 12, 1996); Kuffel v. U.S. Bureau of Prisons, 882 F. Supp. 1116, 1122 (D.D.C. 1995) (Exemption 7(C)); Fid. Nat'l Title Ins. Co. v. HHS, No. 91-5484, slip op. at 6-7 (C.D. Cal. Feb. 13, 1992).

[242] See, e.g., U.S. Dep't of Justice v. Reporters Comm. for Freedom of the Press, 489 U.S. 749, 780 (1989); Judicial Watch, Inc. v. U.S. Dep't of Justice, 365 F.3d 1108, 1124-26 (D.C. Cir. 2004) (protecting pardon applications, which include information about crimes committed).

[243] See Harbolt v. Dep't of State, 616 F.2d 772, 774 (5th Cir. 1980).

[244] See, e.g., Horowitz v. Peace Corps, 428 F.3d 271, 279-80 (D.C. Cir. 2005) (recognizing that "strong privacy interests are implicated when dealing with an individual's sexual activity, especially when the individual has reported a sexual assault"); Siminoski v. FBI, No. 83-6499, slip op. at 28 (C.D. Cal. Jan. 16, 1990).

[245] See, e.g., Beard v. Espy, No. 94-16748, 1995 WL 792071, at *1 (9th Cir. Dec. 11, 1995); Hill v. USDA, 77 F. Supp. 2d 6, 8-9 (D.D.C. 1999), summary affirmance granted, No. 99-5365, 2000 WL 520724, at *1 (D.C. Cir. Mar. 7, 2000); Green v. United States, 8 F. Supp. 2d 983, 998 (W.D. Mich. 1998), appeal dismissed, No. 98-1568 (6th Cir. Aug. 11, 1998); Stabasefski v. United States, 919 F. Supp. 1570, 1575 (M.D. Ga. 1996); Biase v. Office of Thrift Supervision, No. 93-2521, slip op. at 8-10 (D.N.J. Dec. 10, 1993); Okla. Publ'g Co. v. HUD, No. 87-1935-P, 1988 U.S. Dist. LEXIS 18643, at *4-5 (W.D. Okla. June 17, 1988).

embarrass an individual or incite jealousy" among co-workers.[246] Moreover, release of such information "reveals by omission the identities of employees who did not receive high ratings, creating an invasion of their privacy."[247]

A subject that has generated extensive litigation and that warrants special discussion is requests for compilations of names and home addresses of individuals. Prior to the Reporters Committee decision, the courts' analyses in "mailing list" cases ordinarily turned on the requester's purpose, or the "use" to which the requested information was intended to be put.[248] The Supreme Court in Reporters Committee, however, firmly repudiated any analysis based on the identity, circumstances, or intended

---

[246] Ripskis, 746 F.2d at 3; see Hardison, 159 F. App'x at 93 (performance appraisals); Tomscha v. GSA, 158 F. App'x 329, 331 (2d Cir. 2005) ("[W]e agree with the district court's finding that the release of the justifications for [plaintiff's] awards would constitute more than a de minimis invasion of privacy, as they necessarily include private, albeit positive, information regarding his job performance."); FLRA v. U.S. Dep't of Commerce, 962 F.2d 1055, 1059-61 (D.C. Cir. 1992) (performance appraisals); Lewis v. EPA, No. 06-2660, 2006 U.S. Dist. LEXIS 80936, at *17 (E.D. Pa. Nov. 3, 2006) (employee or candidate rankings and evaluations); Vunder v. Potter, No. 05-142, 2006 WL 162985, at *2-3 (D. Utah Jan. 20, 2006) (narrative of accomplishments submitted to superiors for consideration in performance evaluation); Tomscha v. GSA, No. 03-6755, 2004 WL 1234043, at *4 (S.D.N.Y. June 3, 2004) ("Both favorable and unfavorable assessments trigger a privacy interest."); Peralta v. U.S. Attorney's Office, 69 F. Supp. 2d 21, 33 (D.D.C. 1999) (letters of commendation for work on investigation of plaintiff). But see also Hardy v. DOD, No. CV-99-523, 2001 WL 34354945, at *9 (D. Ariz. Aug. 27, 2001) (finding concern with jealousy on parts of co-workers diminished by fact that subject employee had since retired).

[247] FLRA v. U.S. Dep't of Commerce, 962 F.2d at 1059.

[248] See, e.g., Aronson v. HUD, 822 F.2d 182, 185-87 (1st Cir. 1987) (holding that public interest in "the disbursement of funds the government owes its citizens" outweighs the privacy interest of such citizens to be free from others' attempts "to secure a share of that sum" when the government's efforts at disbursal are inadequate); Van Bourg, Allen, Weinberg & Roger v. NLRB, 728 F.2d 1270, 1273 (9th Cir. 1984) (identifying strong public interest in determining whether election fairly conducted), vacated, 756 F.2d 692 (9th Cir.), reinstated, 762 F.2d 831 (9th Cir. 1985); Getman v. NLRB, 450 F.2d 670, 675-76 (D.C. Cir. 1971) (holding public interest in need for study of union elections sufficient to warrant release to professor); Nat'l Ass'n of Atomic Veterans, Inc. v. Dir., Def. Nuclear Agency, 583 F. Supp. 1483, 1487-88 (D.D.C. 1984) (ordering disclosure of names and addresses of veterans involved in atomic testing because of public interest in increasing their knowledge of benefits and possible future health testing).

purpose of the particular FOIA requester at hand.[249] Rather, it said, the analysis must turn on the nature of the document and its relationship to the basic purpose of the FOIA.[250] Following Reporters Committee, the Court of Appeals for the District of Columbia Circuit found that those cases relying on the stated "beneficial" purpose of the requester were grounded on the now-disapproved proposition that "Exemption 6 carries with it an implicit limitation that the information, once disclosed, [may] be used only by the requesting party and for the public interest purpose upon which the balancing was based."[251]

Because agencies may neither distinguish between requesters nor limit the use to which disclosed information is put,[252] an analysis of the

---

[249] 489 U.S. at 771-72; see also Bibles v. Or. Natural Desert Ass'n, 519 U.S. 355, 355-56 (1997) (summarily rejecting argument that there is public interest in knowing to whom government is sending information so that those persons can receive information from other sources).

[250] 489 U.S. at 772; see also FOIA Update, Vol. X, No. 2, at 5-6 (advising that old "use" test has been overruled and should no longer be followed).

[251] Nat'l Ass'n of Retired Fed. Employees v. Horner, 879 F.2d 873, 875 (D.C. Cir. 1989) [hereinafter NARFE]; see also Prof'l Programs Group v. Dep't of Commerce, 29 F.3d 1349, 1353-55 (9th Cir. 1994) (withholding names and addresses of persons registered to take patent bar examination); Gannett Satellite Info. Network, Inc. v. U.S. Dep't of Educ., No. 90-1392, 1990 WL 251480, at *6-7 (D.D.C. Dec. 21, 1990) (denying access to names, social security numbers, and addresses of individuals who have defaulted on government-backed student loans); Schoettle v. Kemp, 733 F. Supp. 1395, 1397-98 (D. Haw. 1990) (relying upon both Reporters Committee's observation that "public interest" is not equivalent to "interesting or socially beneficial in some broad sense" and HUD's improved methods of tracing people, to withhold identities of mortgagors eligible for distributions of money); cf. Schiffer v. FBI, 78 F.3d 1405, 1411 (9th Cir. 1996) (ruling that FOIA does not authorize limited access to only one individual based upon that individual's personal knowledge of information contained in records). But see ACLU v. DOD, 389 F. Supp. 2d 547, 573 (S.D.N.Y.) (relying, in part, on the requester's desire "to inform and educate the public, and to spark debate" as relevant to the public interest found in the disclosure of photographs and videos of Abu Ghraib prison detainees), reconsideration denied, 396 F. Supp. 2d 459 (S.D.N.Y. 2005), relief from judgment denied, 406 F. Supp. 2d 330 (S.D.N.Y. 2006) (appeal pending); Aronson v. HUD, No. 88-1524, slip op. at 1 (1st Cir. Apr. 6, 1989) (affirming award of attorney fees to plaintiff on basis that disclosure of list of mortgagors to whom HUD owes money sheds light on agency's performance of its duty to reimburse those mortgagors).

[252] See Favish, 541 U.S. at 174 ("It must be remembered that once there is disclosure, the information belongs to the general public. There is no

(continued...)

consequences of disclosure of a mailing list cannot turn on the identity or purpose of the requester.[253] Thus, it was found to be irrelevant by the Supreme Court in Bibles v. Oregon Natural Desert Ass'n that the requester's purpose was to use the Bureau of Land Management mailing list to send information reflecting another viewpoint to people who had received newsletters reflecting the government's viewpoint.[254] In NARFE, it was found to be irrelevant that the requester's purpose was to use the list of federal retirees to aid in its lobbying efforts on behalf of those retirees.[255] While stopping short of creating a nondisclosure category encompassing all mailing lists, the D.C. Circuit in NARFE did hold that mailing lists consisting of names and home addresses of federal annuitants are categorically withholdable under Exemption 6.[256] (See discussion of "derivative use" theory under Exemption 6, Factoring in the Public Interest, above.)

------

[252](...continued)
mechanism under FOIA for a protective order allowing only the requester to see . . . the information . . . or for proscribing its general dissemination."); Bassiouni v. CIA, 392 F.3d 244, 246 (7th Cir. 2004) (stating that "any information available to [the requester] is available to North Korea's secret police and Iran's counterintelligence service too") (Exemption 1); see also FOIA Post, "Supreme Court Rules for 'Survivor Privacy' in Favish" (posted 4/9/04) (advising that "[i]n Favish, of course, this meant that the expected 'public exploitation' of the requested records through 'attempts to exploit pictures of the deceased family member's remains for public purposes' by the media . . . were properly taken into consideration").

[253] See NARFE, 879 F.2d at 875; see also Favish, 541 U.S. at 172 (explaining that "[a]s a general rule, if the information is subject to disclosure, it belongs to all").

[254] 519 U.S. at 355-56; see also FOIA Update, Vol. XVIII, No. 1, at 1.

[255] 879 F.2d at 879; see also Robbins, No. 1:95-cv-3258, slip op. at 8-9 (N.D. Ga. Aug. 12, 1996) (rejecting plaintiff's claim of intent to use the names and addresses of rejected social security disability claimants to represent them and "thereby 'promote the effective uniform administration of the disability program'" and ultimately reveal the agency's wrongful denials as "too attenuated" to outweigh a significant invasion of privacy (quoting plaintiff's papers)); Ctr. for Auto Safety v. Nat'l Highway Traffic Safety Admin., 809 F. Supp. 148, 150 (D.D.C. 1993) (finding that requester's function as "significant consumer rights advocate" does not imply a right to "take over the functions of NHTSA").

[256] NARFE, 879 F.2d at 879; see also Retired Officers Ass'n v. Dep't of the Navy, 744 F. Supp. 1, 2-3 (D.D.C. May 14, 1990) (holding names and home addresses of retired military officers exempt); cf. Reed v. NLRB, 927 F.2d 1249, 1251-52 (D.C. Cir. 1991) (categorically protecting "Excelsior" list (names and addresses of employees eligible to vote in union representation elections)).

Although the Supreme Court twice has specifically considered the issue and, without dissent, held that compilations of names and home addresses of United States residents are protectible under Exemption 6,[257] several lower courts nonetheless subsequently have ordered the disclosure of such lists. Some of these courts have found little or no privacy interest in the names and addresses.[258] Other courts have ordered the release of such personal information on the rationale that the names and addresses themselves would reveal (or lead to other information that would reveal) how the agency conducted some aspect of its business.[259] One court, in a parti-

---

[257] Bibles, 519 U.S. at 355-56 (mailing list of recipients of Bureau of Land Management publication); DOD v. FLRA, 510 U.S. 487, 494-502 (1994) (names and home addresses of federal employees in union bargaining units); U.S. Dep't of State v. Ray, 502 U.S. 164, 173-79 (1991) (withholding from interview summaries names and addresses of Haitian refugees interviewed by State Department about treatment upon return to Haiti).

[258] See Nat'l Ass'n of Home Builders v. Norton, 309 F.3d 26, 36 (D.C. Cir. 2002) (finding the privacy interest "relatively weak," and determining that the public interest in learning about an agency's use of owl data is served by release of the lot numbers of parcels of land where the owls have been spotted, even while acknowledging that the identities of landowners could be determined by use of this information), reconsideration denied, No. 01-5283 (D.C. Cir. Feb. 3, 2003) (per curiam); Avondale Indus. v. NLRB, 90 F.3d 955, 961 (5th Cir. 1996) (finding that names and addresses of voters in union election already were disclosed in voluminous public record); Baltimore Sun v. U.S. Marshals Serv., 131 F. Supp. 2d 725, 729 (D. Md. 2001) (declaring that purchasers of property previously seized by the government "voluntarily choose to participate in . . . a wholly legal commercial transaction" and "have little to fear in the way of 'harassment, annoyance, or embarrassment'") (Exemption 7(C)), appeal dismissed voluntarily, No. 01-1537 (4th Cir. June 25, 2001); Alliance for the Wild Rockies v. Dep't of the Interior, 53 F. Supp. 2d 32, 36-37 (D.D.C. 1999) (concluding that commenters to proposed rulemaking could have little expectation of privacy when rulemaking notice stated that complete file would be publicly available); Wash. Post Co. v. USDA, 943 F. Supp. 31, 34-36 (D.D.C. Oct. 18, 1996) (finding minimal privacy interest in home addresses at which farmers receiving subsidies under cotton price support program operate their businesses), appeal dismissed voluntarily, No. 96-5373 (D.C. Cir. May 19, 1997); Ackerson & Bishop Chartered v. USDA, No. 92-1068, slip op. at 1 (D.D.C. July 15, 1992) (finding no privacy interest in names of commercial mushroom growers operating under own names). But cf. Dream Palace v. County of Maricopa, 384 F.3d 990, 1010-12 (9th Cir. 2004) (recognizing privacy interest of exotic dancers in their names, addresses, and telephone numbers appearing on work-permit applications, due to potential harassment that could arise from public disclosure of such information) (non-FOIA case).

[259] See Baltimore Sun, 131 F. Supp. 2d at 729-30 (names and addresses of purchasers of property seized by government found to allow public to as-

(continued...)

cularly unusual decision, ordered disclosure of the names and cities of residence of individuals granted permits to use Forest Service lands to "aid in determining whether improper influence is used to obtain permits or whether permits are being granted to those with a past history of environmental abuses," but affirmed the withholding of street addresses because there was "no showing that knowledge of the street addresses will provide additional insight into agency activities that would not be revealed with disclosure of names and cities of residence alone."[260]

Another recently decided case, Sun-Sentinel Co. v. United States Department of Homeland Security, contains a useful delineation between what should be withheld and what should be disclosed.[261] In Sun-Sentinel, the District Court for the Southern District of Florida ordered the disclosure of the addresses of claimants awarded disaster relief by FEMA, but found

---

[259](...continued)
sess agencies' exercise of their power to seize property and their duty to dispose of such property) (Exemption 7(C)); Or. Natural Desert Ass'n v. U.S. Dep't of the Interior, 24 F. Supp. 2d 1088, 1093 (D. Or. 1998) (names of cattle owners who violated federal grazing laws found to reveal "how government is enforcing and punishing violations of land management laws") (Exemption 7(C)); Maples v. USDA, No. 97-5663, slip op. at 14 (E.D. Cal. Jan. 13, 1998) (names and addresses of permit holders for use of federal lands "would provide the public with an understanding of how the permit process works"); Urbigkit v. U.S. Dep't of the Interior, No. 93-CV-0232-J, slip op. at 13 (D. Wyo. May 31, 1994) (list of citizens who reported wolf sightings found to show agency activities "with respect to the duties imposed upon it by the Endangered Species Act"); Ray v. U.S. Dep't of Justice, 852 F. Supp. 1558, 1564-65 (S.D. Fla. 1994) (names and addresses of interdicted Haitians might reveal "information concerning our government's conduct during the interdiction process"); Thott v. U.S. Dep't of the Interior, No. 93-0177-B, slip op. at 5-6 (D. Me. Apr. 14, 1994) (list of individuals who sold land to Fish and Wildlife Service found to inform the public "about the methods used by FWS in acquiring property throughout the United States").

[260] Idaho v. U.S. Forest Serv., No. 97-0230-S, slip op. at 6 (D. Idaho Dec. 9, 1997); see Judicial Watch v. U.S. Dep't of Justice, 102 F. Supp. 2d 6, 17-18 (D.D.C. 2000) (allowing withholding of home addresses and telephone numbers of individuals who wrote to Attorney General about campaign finance or Independent Counsel issues, but concluding that in the event any individuals were elected officials their identities might possibly reveal information to the public "which could suggest that their Justice Department had been steered by political pressure rather than by relevant facts and law"), reconsideration denied temporarily pending in camera review, No. 97-CV-2869 (D.D.C. Aug. 17, 2000).

[261] 431 F. Supp. 2d at 1267-75 (involving records pertaining to FEMA's recovery activities during 2004 hurricane season in Florida).

that the <u>names</u> of the recipients deserved privacy.[262] It also ordered the release of the names and identification numbers of FEMA inspectors.[263]

In <u>Sun-Sentinel</u>, noting that there is "a substantial privacy interest in a home address,"[264] the court found that "there is a substantial and legitimate public interest in FEMA's handling of disaster assistance in the wake of recent hurricanes."[265] Upon balancing the two interests, it permitted the release of the disaster claimants' addresses because the public interest outweighed the privacy interest as "[t]he release of these addresses will shed light on the activities and operations of FEMA; namely, the extent to which ineffective quality controls and processing of aid applications may have resulted in wasteful spending of taxpayer dollars by FEMA."[266] The court went on to state that "[m]erely knowing the number of claimants and the amount of relief awarded to claimants within a geographic area as large as a zip code does not provide sufficient data for an interested citizen to evaluate the manner in which FEMA carried out its statutory responsibilities."[267] Finding that "the privacy interest in names equals the privacy interest in home addresses,"[268] the court did not permit the release of the names of disaster claimants, concluding that "that the release of names would not serve the public interest of demonstrating the operations and activities of FEMA" because "the possibility of finding fraud through the release of names is speculative."[269] Explaining its reasoning, the court stated that "[w]hereas the addresses go to the heart of whether FEMA improperly disbursed funds to property that sustained no damage, the names of disaster claimants are not as probative."[270]

---

[262] <u>Id.</u> at 1267-73.

[263] <u>Id.</u> at 1273-75.

[264] <u>Id.</u> at 1269.

[265] <u>Id.</u> ("As a result of the 2004 hurricane season, FEMA disbursed billions of dollars to approximately 1.2 million applicants . . . . [S]everal investigations unearthed that FEMA's disbursement of assistance was rife with fraud and waste.").

[266] <u>Id.</u> at 1270, 1273 n.12 (stating that the court "believes that the release of the these addresses, despite the substantial privacy interest, is uniquely important under the facts of this case").

[267] <u>Id.</u> at 1270.

[268] <u>Id.</u>

[269] <u>Id.</u> at 1271-72.

[270] <u>Id.</u> at 1271 (reasoning that "[o]nce the addresses are released, the inquiry would concern whether the property sustained the damage claimed and the name of the disaster claimant would not shed additional

(continued...)

Then, the court in <u>Sun-Sentinel</u> addressed the release of the names and identification numbers of FEMA inspectors, concluding that the public interest outweighed privacy.[271] It found that "the record demonstrates that there is a strong public interest in the disclosure of the identities of the FEMA inspectors."[272] The court concluded that the release of the names and identification numbers of FEMA inspectors would be in the public interest because it would "allow the public to examine fully whether the process of selecting FEMA inspectors should be improved and whether these inspectors violated the public's trust in awarding disaster assistance."[273] On the privacy side of the balance, the court also specifically noted FEMA's failure to provide any case law showing that the release would constitute a "clearly unwarranted" invasion of privacy.[274] In fact, the court was "hard pressed to understand how revealing that an individual works for a government contractor would constitute an invasion of privacy."[275]

In another exceptional decision, the D.C. Circuit remanded a case to the district court to determine whether some of the names of individual depositors with unclaimed funds at banks for which the FDIC is now the receiver should be released to a professional money finder.[276] Introducing a new element into the balancing test for this particular type of information, the D.C. Circuit held that the standard test "is inapposite here, i.e., where the individuals whom the government seeks to protect have a clear interest in the release of the requested information."[277] As guidance to the lower court charged with applying this novel approach, the D.C. Circuit ordered, first, that "release of names associated with unclaimed deposits

---

[270](...continued)
light on this inquiry").

[271] Id. at 1274.

[272] Id. at 1273-74 (pointing to record evidence consisting of findings by Inspector General and Homeland Security and Government Affairs Committee showing that FEMA inspectors were poorly trained, lacked oversight, and filled out forms without examining purportedly damaged property; finding further that record evidence showed that significant number of inspectors had criminal records); cf. CEI Wash. Bureau, Inc. v. Dep't of Justice, No. 05-5446, slip op. at 2-5 (D.C. Cir. Nov. 21, 2006) (remanding and vacating lower court decision for "affidavits [or] evidentiary hearings sufficient to resolve the factual disputes" on existing privacy-protection record).

[273] Id. at 1274.

[274] Id.

[275] Id.

[276] Lepelletier v. FDIC, 164 F.3d 37, 48-49 (D.C. Cir. 1999).

[277] Id. at 48.

should not be matched with the amount owed to that individual" and, second, that "on remand, the District Court must determine the dollar amount below which an individual's privacy interest should be deemed to outweigh his or her interest in discovering his or her money, such that the names of depositors with lesser amounts may be redacted."[278] It is unclear, however, whether this highly unconventional privacy balancing analysis can be squared with the subsequent analysis of personal privacy protection that was adopted by the Supreme Court in Favish.[279]

Other courts, more in line with the teachings of the Supreme Court, have protected compilations of names and addresses. For example, when the request clearly is for the purpose of soliciting business or for other commercial purposes, most courts readily have found mailing lists to be protectible.[280] Even when there is no apparent commercial interest at stake, other courts have found the possible public interest too attenuated to overcome the clear privacy interest an individual has in his name and home ad-

---

[278] Id.; see also Pub. Citizen, Inc. v. Dep't of Educ., No. 01-2351, slip op. at 5-12 (D.D.C. June 17, 2002) (relying on Lepelletier and finding both "substantial benefits" to borrowers by disclosure and a public interest benefit in showing the extent of compliance with statutory duties). But see Reporters Comm., 489 U.S. at 772 n.20 (noting that Congress made no statement that the FOIA was designed for broader uses to serve the "social good"); Schoettle, 733 F. Supp. at 1397-98 (relying on Reporters Committee's observation that "public interest" is not equivalent to "interesting or socially beneficial in some broad sense," in protecting identities of mortgagors eligible for distributions of money); cf. Doe v. FBI, 218 F.R.D. 256, 259 (D. Colo. 2003) (rejecting plaintiff's argument that even if his own privacy interest is not compelling the court should consider other parties' privacy interests, and concluding that "the Court will not allow Plaintiff to piggyback on their privacy interests" in order to achieve an unconventional nondisclosure result) (non-FOIA case).

[279] See 541 U.S. at 174-75 (instructing that "counterweight" necessary to balance against privacy interest exists only when requester provides sufficient evidence); cf. FOIA Post, "Supreme Court Rules for 'Survivor Privacy' in Favish" (posted 4/9/04) (explaining that Favish discredits "or effectively overrules" several prior decisions that ordered disclosure based on allegations of wrongdoing).

[280] See, e.g., Prof'l Programs, 29 F.3d at 1353-55 (withholding names and addresses of persons registered to take patent bar examination from business offering patent bar exam preparation courses to lawyers); Robbins, No. 1:95-cv-3258, slip op. at 8-9 (N.D. Ga. Aug. 12, 1996) (withholding names and addresses of rejected social security disability claimants from attorney hoping to solicit business); Schoettle, 733 F. Supp. at 1397-98 (declining to order release of identities of mortgagors eligible for distributions of money).

dress.[281] Yet other courts have protected mailing lists, emphasizing the increased privacy interest inherent in a list that reveals sensitive information beyond the mere names and addresses of the individuals found on the list.[282] And when a requester seeks the address of a named individual for a

---

[281] See Reed, 927 F.2d at 1252 (protecting names and addresses of employees eligible to vote in union representation elections); Navigator Publ'g v. U.S. Dep't of Transp., 146 F. Supp. 2d 68, 71 (D. Me. 2001) (concluding that "significant" privacy interest in mariners' addresses outweighs "hypothetical" public interest in matching addresses against criminal records to permit evaluation of Coast Guard performance of its licensing duties), appeal dismissed, No. 01-1939 (1st Cir. Sept. 19, 2001); Judicial Watch v. Reno, 2001 WL 1902811, at *8 (discerning no public interest in disclosure of names and telephone numbers of nongovernment attendees at meeting with federal immigration officials); Fort Hall Landowners Alliance, Inc. v. Bureau of Indian Affairs, No. 99-00052, slip op. at 13 (D. Idaho Mar. 17, 2000) (protecting list of landowner names, addresses, and ownership interests on basis that there is no qualifying public interest in facilitating attorney representation of landowners in right-of-way negotiations); Dayton Newspapers, Inc. v. Dep't of the Air Force, 35 F. Supp. 2d 1033, 1035 (S.D. Ohio 1998) (redacting "claimants' names, social security numbers, home addresses, home/work telephone numbers and places of employment" from militarywide medical tort-claims database), reh'g denied in pertinent part, No. C-97-78, slip op. at 13-14 (S.D. Ohio Mar. 26, 1999); Horsehead Indus. v. EPA, No. 94-1299, slip op. at 6 (D.D.C. Mar. 13, 1997) (finding that the possible "glimpse into EPA's activities" that would accrue from disclosure of identities of homeowners who volunteered to participate in a Superfund study "pales in comparison to the potential harm to the privacy" of study participants); Stabasefski, 919 F. Supp. at 1575 (determining that disclosure of names of FAA employees who received Hurricane Andrew subsistence payments would shed no brighter light on agency activities than vouchers that were released showing amounts of payments); Upper Peninsula Envtl. Coal. v. Forest Serv., No. 2:94-cv-021, slip op. at 9-10 (W.D. Mich. Sept. 28, 1994) (concluding that information already provided about wilderness campers (i.e., dates, campsite, number in party, state of auto registration) sheds sufficient light on agency's performance of duties without disclosure of names and addresses of campers); Gannett Satellite, 1990 WL 251480, at *6-7 (concluding that names, social security numbers, and addresses of individuals who defaulted on government-backed student loans do not themselves directly reveal anything about student loan programs).

[282] See Ray, 502 U.S. at 176 (observing that disclosure of a list of Haitian refugees interviewed by the State Department about their treatment upon return to Haiti "would publicly identify the interviewees as people who cooperated with a State Department investigation"); Campaign for Family Farms v. Glickman, 200 F.3d 1180, 1187-88 (8th Cir. 2000) (protecting list of pork producers who signed petition that declared their position on referendum that was sought by petition) (reverse FOIA suit); NARFE, 879 F.2d at 876 (characterizing the list at issue as revealing that each individual on it
(continued...)

purely private purpose, courts have found the privacy interest to be at its zenith and the public interest to be at its nadir.[283]

Another area that merits particular discussion is the applicability of Exemption 6 to requests for information about civilian and military federal employees. Generally, civilian employees' names, present and past position titles, grades, salaries, and duty stations are releasable as no viable privacy interest exists in such data.[284] The Department of Justice recommends the release of additional items, particularly those relating to professional qualifications for federal employment.[285] By regulation, the Department of the Army discloses the name, rank, date of rank, gross salary, duty assignments, office telephone number, source of commission, promotion sequence number, awards and decorations, educational level, and duty status of most of its military personnel and the name, past and present position titles, grades, salaries, and duty stations of its civilian employ-

---

[282](...continued)
"is retired or disabled (or the survivor of such a person) and receives a monthly annuity check from the federal Government"); Minnis v. USDA, 737 F.2d 784, 787 (9th Cir. 1984) ("Disclosure would reveal not only the applicants' names and addresses, but also their personal interests in water sports and the out-of-doors.").

[283] See, e.g., Schwarz v. Dep't of State, No. 97-1342, slip op. at 5 (D.D.C. Mar. 20, 1998) (stating, despite plaintiff's claim that she needed the address of a third party to assist her, that the "merits of an agency's FOIA determinations do not rest on the identity of the requester or the purpose for which the information is intended to be used"), aff'd per curiam, 172 F.3d 921 (D.C. Cir. 1998) (unpublished table decision); Bongiorno v. Reno, No. 95-72143, 1996 WL 426451, at *14 (E.D. Mich. Mar. 19, 1996) (noting that the requester sought personal information concerning his adopted daughter "for his own purposes, as understandable as they may be, and not to shine a public light into the recesses of the federal bureaucracy"); Andrews v. U.S. Dep't of Justice, 769 F. Supp. 314, 316-17 (E.D. Mo. 1991) (declining to release individual's address, telephone number, and place of employment to requester seeking it for purpose of satisfying monetary judgment).

[284] See 5 C.F.R. § 293.311 (2007); see also FOIA Update, Vol. VII, No. 3, at 3.

[285] See FOIA Update, Vol. III, No. 4, at 3; see also Core v. USPS, 730 F.2d 946, 948 (4th Cir. 1984) (qualifications of successful federal applicants); Samble v. U.S. Dep't of Commerce, No. 1:92-225, slip op. at 11 (S.D. Ga. Sept. 22, 1994) (far-reaching decision requiring disclosure of successful job applicant's "undergraduate grades; private sector performance awards; foreign language abilities; and his answers to questions concerning prior firings, etc., convictions, delinquencies on federal debt, and pending charges against him"); Associated Gen. Contractors, Inc. v. EPA, 488 F. Supp. 861, 863 (D. Nev. 1980) (education, former employment, academic achievements, and employee qualifications).

ees.[286] Historically, the entire Department of Defense disclosed the same information and other nonsensitive data concerning most of its service-members and civilian employees.[287]

By statutory enactment as well as by regulation, certain military personnel throughout the Department of Defense are properly afforded greater privacy protection than other servicemembers and nonmilitary employees.[288] Even prior to enactment of such special statutory protection, courts had found that because of the threat of terrorism, military servicemembers stationed outside the United States have a greater expectation of privacy.[289] Courts have, however, ordered the release of names of military personnel stationed in the United States.[290] In light of terrorist activities with

---

[286] Army Reg. 340-21, ¶ 3-3a(1), b(1), 5 July 1985; see also Army Reg. 25-55, ¶ 3-200, No. 6(b), 1 Nov. 1997 (providing for withholding of names and duty addresses of military personnel assigned to units that are "sensitive, routinely deployable or stationed in foreign territories").

[287] See Department of Defense Freedom of Information Act Program Regulation, DOD 5400.7-R, 37-39 (Sept. 1998); Memorandum from Department of Defense Directorate for Freedom of Information and Security Review 1 (Oct. 26, 1999) (applying same analysis as DOD 5400.7-R to electronic mail addresses, and authorizing withholding only for "personnel assigned to units that are sensitive, routinely deployable or stationed in foreign territories").

[288] See 10 U.S.C. § 130b (2000 & Supp. IV 2004); Department of Defense Freedom of Information Act Program Regulations, 32 C.F.R. § 286.12(f)(2)(ii) (2006) ("Names and duty addresses (postal and/or e-mail) . . . for personnel assigned to units that are sensitive, routinely deployable, or stationed in foreign territories are withholdable under [Exemption 6].").

[289] See Jernigan v. Dep't of the Air Force, No. 97-35930, 1998 WL 658662, at *1 (9th Cir. Sept. 17, 1998) (agreeing with the Air Force that "'[i]dentifying [its] personnel overseas increases the threat of terrorism and the likelihood that they will be targeted for attack'"); Hudson v. Dep't of the Army, No. 86-1114, 1987 WL 46755, at *3-4 (D.D.C. Jan. 29, 1987) (finding threat of terrorism creates privacy interest in names, ranks, and addresses of Army personnel stationed in Europe, Middle East, and Africa), aff'd, 926 F.2d 1215 (D.C. Cir. 1991) (unpublished table decision); Falzone v. Dep't of the Navy, No. 85-3862, 1988 WL 128474, at *1-2 (D.D.C. Nov. 21, 1988) (finding same with respect to names and addresses of naval officers serving overseas or in classified, sensitive, or readily deployable positions).

[290] See Hopkins v. Dep't of the Navy, No. 84-1868, 1985 WL 17673, at *2 (D.D.C. Feb. 5, 1985) (ordering disclosure of "names, ranks and official duty stations of servicemen stationed at Quantico" to life insurance salesman); Jafari v. Dep't of the Navy, 3 Gov't Disclosure Serv. (P-H) ¶ 83,250, at 84,014 (E.D. Va. May 11, 1983) (finding no privacy interest in "duty status" or at-

(continued...)

in the United States and the resulting heightened security awareness nationwide, however, the Department of Defense now withholds personally identifying information concerning its military and civilian personnel stationed within the United States whenever release would "raise security or privacy concerns."[291]

This new practice now has been upheld by the District Court for the District of Columbia: In Judicial Watch, Inc. v. Department of the Army, that court protected the names and duty stations of DOD employees named in documents concerning no-bid contracts awarded following the 2003 invasion of Iraq.[292] Additionally, certain other federal employees such as law enforcement personnel and Internal Revenue Service employees possess, by virtue of the nature of their work, protectible privacy interests in their identities and work addresses.[293] (See the further discussions of these is-

---

[290](...continued)
tendance records of reserve military personnel) (Privacy Act "wrongful disclosure" suit), aff'd on other grounds, 728 F.2d 247 (4th Cir. 1984).

[291] See Department of Defense Director for Administration and Management Memorandum 1-2 (Nov. 9, 2001), available at www.defenselink.mil/pubs/foi/withhold.pdf.

[292] 402 F. Supp. 2d at 250-52 (finding that "[t]he privacy interest of civilian federal employees includes the right to control information related to themselves"); see also MacLean v. DOD, No. 04-2425, slip op. at 18 (S.D. Cal. June 2, 2005) (protecting "names, initials, and other personal information" about Defense Hotline Investigators and other DOD personnel) (Exemptions 6 and 7(C)).

[293] See Wood v. FBI, 432 F.3d 78, 87-89 (2d Cir. 2005) (protecting investigative personnel of FBI's Office of Professional Responsibility); Judicial Watch, Inc. v. United States, 84 F. App'x 335, 338-39 (4th Cir. 2004) (protecting names of lower-level clerical workers at IRS); New England Apple Council v. Donovan, 725 F.2d 139, 142-44 (1st Cir. 1984) (protecting identities of nonsupervisory Inspector General investigators who participated in grand jury investigation of requester) (Exemption 7(C)); Lesar v. U.S. Dep't of Justice, 636 F.2d 472, 487-88 (D.C. Cir. 1980) (protecting identities of FBI Special Agents) (Exemption 7(C)); Elec. Privacy Info. Ctr. v. DHS, No. 04-1625, 2006 U.S. Dist. LEXIS 94615, at *30 (D.D.C. Dec. 22, 2006) (protecting names of employees from United States Customs and Border Protection and DHS involved in anti-terrorism efforts); Voinche v. FBI, 412 F. Supp. 2d 60, 66-69 (D.D.C.) (protecting identities of FBI Special Agents, nonagent FBI personnel, and state and local law enforcement officials) (Exemptions 6 and 7(C)), summary judgment granted, 425 F. Supp. 2d 134 (D.D.C. 2006) (Exemption 7(C)); Gonzalez v. ATF, No. 04-2281, 2005 WL 3201009, at *7-8 (D.D.C. Nov. 9, 2005) (same) (Exemptions 6 and 7(C)); Van Mechelen v. U.S. Dep't of the Interior, No. 05-5393, 2005 WL 3007121, at *4-5 (W.D. Wash. Nov. 9, 2005) (protecting identifying information of lower-level Office of In-
(continued...)

sues under Exemption 2, "Low 2": Trivial Matters, above, and Exemption 7(C), below.)

Purely personal details pertaining to government employees are protectible under Exemption 6.[294] Indeed, courts generally have recognized

[293](...continued)
spector General and Bureau of Indian Affairs employees in report of investigation) (Exemptions 6 and 7(C)); Judicial Watch, Inc. v. FDA, 407 F. Supp. 2d 70, 76-77 (D.D.C. 2005) (finding that HHS employees named in records concerning abortion drug testing were properly protected pursuant to Exemption 6 in order to ensure employees' safety), aff'd in pertinent part, 449 F.3d 141, 152-54 (D.C. Cir. 2006); Davy v. CIA, 357 F. Supp. 2d 76, 87-88 (D.D.C. 2004) (protecting CIA employee names); Pons v. U.S. Customs Serv., No. 93-2094, 1998 U.S. Dist. LEXIS 6084, at *13-14 (D.D.C. Apr. 27, 1998) (protecting identities of lower- and mid-level agency employees who worked on asset forfeiture documents); Lampkin v. IRS, No. 1:96-138, 1997 WL 373717, at *2 (W.D.N.C. Feb. 24, 1997) (protecting identities of IRS employees who, by nature of employment, are subject to harassment and annoyance) (Exemption 7(C)); Lawyers Comm. for Human Rights v. INS, 721 F. Supp. 552, 565, 569 (S.D.N.Y. 1989) (permitting withholding of the identities of FBI agents and support staff, who "have a particularly strong interest in maintaining their privacy in the present action due to the divided public opinion and heightened interest in [this] case") (Exemptions 6 and 7(C)); see also FOIA Update, Vol. VII, No. 3, at 3-4. But see Lahr v. NSTB, No. 03-8023, 2006 WL 2854314, at *14-15 (C.D. Cal. Oct. 4, 2006) (ordering the release of the names of FBI Special Agents involved in the investigation of the crash of TWA Flight 800 on the basis that it is "unlikely that the FBI Special Agents will be subjected to harassment or annoyance" inasmuch as there is "no aggrieved 'target' or defendant" due to the investigation's conclusion that there was no criminal wrongdoing) (Exemptions 6 and 7(C)).

[294] See, e.g., DOD v. FLRA, 510 U.S. 487, 500 (1994) (employees' home addresses); Am. Fed'n of Gov't Employees v. United States, 712 F.2d 931, 932-33 (4th Cir. 1983) (same); Singleton v. Executive Office for United States Attorneys, No. 05-2413, slip op. at 4 (D.D.C. Nov. 1, 2006) ("Disclosure of the [Assistant United States Attorneys'] home addresses would constitute a clearly unwarranted invasion of personal privacy."); Brannum v. Dominguez, 377 F. Supp. 2d 75, 84 (D.D.C. 2005) (names and signatures of Air Force Personnel Board members); Kidd v. Dep't of Justice, 362 F. Supp. 2d 291, 296-97 (D.D.C. 2005) (home telephone number); Barvick v. Cisneros, 941 F. Supp. 1015, 1020-21 (D. Kan. 1996) (personal information such as home addresses and telephone numbers, social security numbers, dates of birth, insurance and retirement information, reasons for leaving prior employment, and performance appraisals); Stabasefski, 919 F. Supp. at 1575 (names of FAA employees who received Hurricane Andrew assistance payments); Plain Dealer Publ'g Co. v. U.S. Dep't of Labor, 471 F. Supp. 1023, 1028-30 (D.D.C. 1979) (medical, personnel, and related documents of em-
(continued...)

the sensitivity of information contained in personnel-related files and have accorded protection to the personal details of a federal employee's service.[295] In addition, the identities of persons who apply but are not selected for federal government employment may be protected.[296] Even sugges-

---

[294](...continued)
ployees filing claims under Federal Employees Compensation Act); Info. Acquisition Corp. v. Dep't of Justice, 444 F. Supp. 458, 463-64 (D.D.C. 1978) ("core" personal information such as marital status and college grades). But see Wash. Post v. HHS, 690 F.2d at 258-65 (holding personal financial information required for appointment as HHS scientific consultant not exempt when balanced against need for oversight of awarding of government grants); Trupei v. DEA, No. 04-1481, slip op. at 3-5 (D.D.C. Sept. 27, 2005) (ordering disclosure of signature where name of retired DEA agent was already released, because "speculative" possibility of misuse of signature did not establish cognizable privacy interest); Husek v. IRS, No. 90-CV-923, 1991 U.S. Dist. LEXIS 20971, at *1 (N.D.N.Y. Aug. 16, 1991) (holding citizenship, date of birth, educational background, and veteran's preference of federal employees not exempt), aff'd, 956 F.2d 1161 (2d Cir. 1992) (unpublished table decision).

[295] See, e.g., Ripskis, 746 F.2d at 3-4 (names and identifying data contained on evaluation forms of HUD employees who received outstanding performance ratings); Warren v. Soc. Sec. Admin., No. 98-CV-0116E, 2000 WL 1209383, at *4 (W.D.N.Y. Aug. 22, 2000) (award nomination forms for specific employees), aff'd, 10 F. App'x 20 (2d Cir. 2001); Rothman v. USDA, No. 94-8151, slip op. at 6 (C.D. Cal. June 17, 1996) (settlement agreement related to charge of employment discrimination that "could conceivably lead to embarrassment or friction with fellow employees or supervisors"); Resendez v. Runyon, No. 94-434F, slip op. at 6-7 (W.D. Tex. Aug. 11, 1995) (names of applicants for supervisory training who have not yet been accepted or rejected); McLeod v. U.S. Coast Guard, No. 94-1924, slip op. at 8-10 (D.D.C. July 25, 1995) (Coast Guard officer's evaluation report), summary affirmance granted, No. 96-5071, 1997 WL 150096 (D.C. Cir. Feb. 10, 1997); Putnam v. U.S. Dep't of Justice, 873 F. Supp. 705, 712-13 (D.D.C. 1995) (names of FBI employees mentioned in "circumstances outside of their official duties," such as attending training classes and as job applicants); Ferri v. U.S. Dep't of Justice, 573 F. Supp. 852, 862-63 (W.D. Pa. 1983) (FBI background investigation of Assistant United States Attorney); Dubin v. Dep't of the Treasury, 555 F. Supp. 408, 412 (N.D. Ga. 1981) (studies of supervisors' performance and recommendations for performance awards), aff'd, 697 F.2d 1093 (11th Cir. 1983) (unpublished table decision); see also FLRA v. U.S. Dep't of Commerce, 962 F.2d at 1060 (distinguishing personnel "ratings," which traditionally have not been disclosed, from "performance awards," which ordinarily are disclosed); cf. Prof'l Review Org., Inc. v. HHS, 607 F. Supp. 423, 427 (D.D.C. 1985) (résumé data of proposed staff of government contract bidder).

[296] See Core, 730 F.2d at 948-49 (protecting identities and qualifications
(continued...)

tions submitted to an Employee Suggestion Program may be withheld to protect employees with whom the suggestions are identifiable from the embarrassment that might occur from disclosure.[297]

Similarly, the courts customarily have extended protection to the identities of mid- and low-level federal employees accused of misconduct, as well as to the details and results of any internal investigations into such allegations of impropriety.[298] The D.C. Circuit has reaffirmed this position

---

[296](...continued)
of unsuccessful applicants for federal employment); Judicial Watch, Inc. v. U.S. Dep't of Commerce, 337 F. Supp. 2d 146, 177 (D.D.C. 2004) (holding that résumé of individual interested in project that never "got out of the embryonic stages" was properly withheld); Warren, 2000 WL 1209383, at *4 (protecting identities of unsuccessful job applicants); Judicial Watch, Inc. v. Exp.-Imp. Bank, 108 F. Supp. 2d 19, 38 (D.D.C. 2000) (protecting résumés of individuals whose applications for insurance were withdrawn or denied); Judicial Watch, Inc. v. Comm'n on U.S. Pac. Trade & Inv. Policy, No. 97-0099, 1999 WL 33944413, at *11-12 (D.D.C. Sept. 30, 1999) (protecting identities of individuals considered for but not appointed to Commission); Rothman, No. 94-8151, slip op. at 8-9 (C.D. Cal. June 17, 1996) ("Disclosure of information in the applications of persons who failed to get a job may 'embarrass or harm' them."); Barvick, 941 F. Supp. at 1021-22 (protecting all information about unsuccessful federal job applicants because any information about members of "select group" that applies for such jobs could identify them); Voinche v. FBI, 940 F. Supp. 323, 329-30 (D.D.C. 1996) (protecting identities of possible candidates for Supreme Court vacancies), aff'd per curiam, No. 96-5304, 1997 U.S. App. LEXIS 19089 (D.C. Cir. June 19, 1997); Putnam, 873 F. Supp. at 712-13 (protecting identities of FBI personnel who were job candidates); Holland v. CIA, No. 91-1233, 1992 WL 233820, at *13-15 (D.D.C. Aug. 31, 1992) (protecting identity of person not selected as CIA general counsel).

[297] See Matthews v. USPS, No. 92-1208-CV-W-8, slip op. at 5 (W.D. Mo. Apr. 15, 1994).

[298] See, e.g., Stern v. FBI, 737 F.2d 84, 94 (D.C. Cir. 1984) (protecting identities of mid-level employees censured for negligence, but requiring disclosure of identity of high-level employee found guilty of serious, intentional misconduct) (Exemption 7(C)); Chamberlain v. Kurtz, 589 F.2d 827, 841-42 (5th Cir. 1979) (names of disciplined IRS agents); Cawthon, 2006 WL 581250, at *2-4 (protecting information about two Federal Bureau of Prisons doctors, including records pertaining to malpractice and disciplinary matters); Forest Serv. Employees for Envtl. Ethics v. U.S. Forest Serv., No. 05-6015, 2005 WL 3488453, at *4 (D. Or. Dec. 21, 2005) ("USFS employees are publically employed . . . [and] the names of the employees . . . holds little or no expectation of privacy. The expectation, however, increases when attached to stigmatizing events."); Mueller v. U.S. Dep't of the Air Force, 63 F. Supp. 2d 738, 743-45 (E.D. Va. 1999) (unsubstantiated allegations of

(continued...)

in <u>Dunkelberger v. Department of Justice</u>.[299]  It made very clear in <u>Dunkel-berger</u> that, even post-<u>Reporters Committee</u>, the D.C. Circuit's decision in <u>Stern v. FBI</u> remains solid guidance for the balancing of the privacy inter-ests of federal employees found to have committed wrongdoing against the public interest in shedding light on agency activities.[300]

---

[298](...continued)
prosecutorial misconduct) (Exemptions 6 and 7(C)); <u>Chin v. U.S. Dep't of the Air Force</u>, No. 97-2176, slip op. at 3-5 (W.D. La. June 24, 1999) (investiga-tions of fraternization), <u>aff'd per curiam</u>, No. 99-31237 (5th Cir. June 15, 2000); <u>Lurie v. Dep't of the Army</u>, 970 F. Supp. 19, 40 (D.D.C. 1997) (identi-ties of HIV researchers who played minor role in possible scientific miscon-duct), <u>appeal dismissed voluntarily</u>, No. 97-5248 (D.C. Cir. Oct. 22, 1997); <u>McLeod v. Peña</u>, No. 94-1924, slip op. at 4-6 (D.D.C. Feb. 9, 1996) (investi-gation of Coast Guard officer for alleged use of government resources for personal religious activities) (Exemption 7(C)), <u>summary affirmance grant-ed sub nom.</u> <u>McLeod v. U.S. Coast Guard</u>, No. 96-5071, 1997 WL 150096 (D.C. Cir. Feb. 10, 1997); <u>Cotton v. Adams</u>, 798 F. Supp. 22, 25-28 (D.D.C. 1992) (report of Inspector General's investigation of low-level employees of Smithsonian Institution museum shops); <u>Schonberger v. Nat'l Transp. Safe-ty Bd.</u>, 508 F. Supp. 941, 944-45 (D.D.C.) (results of complaint by employee against supervisor), <u>aff'd</u>, 672 F.2d 896 (D.C. Cir. 1981) (unpublished table decision); <u>Iglesias v. CIA</u>, 525 F. Supp. 547, 561 (D.D.C. 1981) (agency attor-ney's response to Office of Professional Responsibility misconduct allega-tions); <u>see also</u> <u>McCutchen v. HHS</u>, 30 F.3d 183, 187-89 (D.C. Cir. 1994) (identities of both federally and privately employed scientists investigated for possible scientific misconduct protected) (Exemption 7(C)); <u>cf.</u> <u>Heller v. U.S. Marshals Serv.</u>, 655 F. Supp. 1088, 1091 (D.D.C. 1987) ("extremely strong interest" in protecting privacy of individual who cooperated with in-ternal investigation of possible criminal activity by fellow employees).  <u>But see</u> <u>Gannett River States Publ'g Corp. v. Bureau of the Nat'l Guard</u>, No. J91-0455, 1992 WL 175235, at *5-6 (S.D. Miss. Mar. 2, 1992) (given previous dis-closure of investigative report of helocasting accident, disclosure of actual discipline received would result in "insignificant burden" on soldiers' priva-cy interests).

[299] 906 F.2d 779, 782 (D.C. Cir. 1990) (upholding FBI's refusal to confirm or deny existence of letters of reprimand or suspension for alleged miscon-duct by undercover agent) (Exemption 7(C)); <u>Favish</u>, 541 U.S. at 175 (noting realistically that "[a]llegations of government misconduct are 'easy to al-lege and hard to disprove'" (quoting <u>Crawford-El v. Britton</u>, 523 U.S. 574, 585 (1998)).

[300] <u>Id.</u> at 781; <u>see also</u> <u>Ford v. West</u>, No. 97-1342, 1998 WL 317561, at *2-3 (10th Cir. June 12, 1998) (protecting information about discipline of co-worker and finding that redacted information would not inform public about agency's response to racial harassment claim); <u>Kimberlin v. Dep't of Justice</u>, 139 F.3d 944, 949 (D.C. Cir. 1998) (protecting information about in-vestigation of staff-level attorney for allegations of unauthorized disclosure
(continued...)

During the 1980s, a peculiar line of cases began to develop within the D.C. Circuit regarding the professional or business conduct of an individual. Specifically, the courts began to require the disclosure of information concerning an individual's business dealings with the federal government; indeed, even embarrassing information, if related to an individual's professional life, was subject to disclosure.[301] Similarly, the Court of Appeals for the Sixth Circuit suggested that the disclosure of a document prepared by a government employee during the course of his employment "will not constitute a clearly unwarranted invasion of personal privacy simply because it would invite a negative reaction or cause embarrassment in the sense that a position is thought by others to be wrong or inadequate."[302]

---

[300](...continued)
of information to media) (Exemption 7(C)); Beck v. Dep't of Justice, 997 F.2d 1489, 1494 (D.C. Cir. 1993) (upholding agency's refusal to either confirm or deny existence of records concerning alleged wrongdoing of named DEA agents) (Exemptions 6 and 7(C)); Hunt v. FBI, 972 F.2d 286, 288-90 (9th Cir. 1992) (protecting contents of investigative file of nonsupervisory FBI agent accused of unsubstantiated misconduct) (Exemption 7(C)); Early v. Office of Prof'l Responsibility, No. 95-0254, slip op. at 2-3 (D.D.C. Apr. 30, 1996) (upholding Office of Professional Responsibility's refusal to confirm or deny existence of complaints or investigations concerning performance of professional duties of one United States district court judge and two Assistant United States Attorneys) (Exemption 7(C)), summary affirmance granted, No. 96-5136, 1997 WL 195523 (D.C. Cir. Mar. 31, 1997).

[301] See, e.g., Wash. Post Co. v. U.S. Dep't of Justice, 863 F.2d 96, 100-01 (D.C. Cir. 1988) (information relating to business judgments and decisions made during development of pharmaceutical) (Exemption 7(C)); Sims v. CIA, 642 F.2d 562, 574 (D.C. Cir. 1980) (names of persons who conducted scientific and behavioral research under contracts with or funded by CIA); Bd. of Trade v. Commodity Futures Trading Comm'n, 627 F.2d 392, 399-400 (D.C. Cir. 1980) (identities of trade sources who supplied information to Commission); Cohen v. EPA, 575 F. Supp. 425, 430 (D.D.C. 1983) (names of suspected EPA "Superfund" violators) (Exemption 7(C)); Stern v. SBA, 516 F. Supp. 145, 149 (D.D.C. 1980) (names of agency personnel accused of discriminatory practices); see also Judicial Watch, Inc. v. Exp.-Imp. Bank, 108 F. Supp. 2d at 37-38 (résumés of executives of businesses approved for insurance by Export-Import Bank); Or. Natural Desert Ass'n, 24 F. Supp. 2d at 1093-94 (names of cattle owners who violated federal grazing laws; concluding that "the [professional or business] relationship of the individual and the government does weigh in favor of disclosure") (Exemption 7(C)).

[302] Schell v. HHS, 843 F.2d 933, 939 (6th Cir. 1988); see also Kurzon v. HHS, No. 00-395, 2001 WL 821531, at *7-11 (D.N.H. July 17, 2001) (ordering disclosure of names and business addresses of unsuccessful National Institute of Mental Health grant applicants, relying in part upon privacy analysis in Kurzon v. HHS, 649 F.2d 65, 69 (1st Cir. 1981), which court found "instructive" despite fact that First Circuit's "similar files" holding is no longer

(continued...)

In five later cases, however, the D.C. Circuit reached firm nondisclosure decisions, with no discussion of this consideration at all.[303] Then it clarified that any such lack of privacy an individual has in his business dealings applies only to purely "'business judgments and relationships.'"[304] Indeed, an individual has a very strong interest in allegations of wrongdoing or in the fact that he or she was a target of a law enforcement investigation, even when the alleged wrongdoing occurred in the course of the

---

[302](...continued)
good law post-Washington Post, 456 U.S. 595), appeal dismissed voluntarily, No. 01-2319 (1st Cir. Oct. 5, 2001); Physicians Comm. for Responsible Med. v. Glickman, 117 F. Supp. 2d 1, 5-6 (D.D.C. 2000) (finding that "asserted stigma of rejection is significantly diluted when shared among approximately 140" nonappointed applicants for membership in federal advisory committee); Lawyers Comm. for Human Rights, 721 F. Supp. at 569 (finding that "disclosure [of names of State Department's officers and staff members involved in highly publicized case] merely establishes State [Department] employees' professional relationships or associates these employees with agency business" because agency provided "no substantial evidence of . . . security or privacy interests"; however, protecting the names of FBI Special Agents and support staff from other documents because of "strong" privacy interests) (Exemptions 6 and 7(C)).

[303] Beck, 997 F.2d at 1492 (finding that when no evidence of wrongdoing exists, there is "no public interest to be balanced against the two [DEA] agents' obvious interest in the continued confidentiality of their personnel records"); Dunkelberger, 906 F.2d at 781-82 (recognizing that FBI Special Agent has privacy interest in protecting his employment records against public disclosure); Carter v. U.S. Dep't of Commerce, 830 F.2d 388, 391-92 (D.C. Cir. 1987) (withholding identities of private-sector attorneys subject to Patent and Trademark Office disciplinary investigations); Stern, 737 F.2d at 91 (recognizing that federal employees have privacy interest in information about their employment); Ripskis, 746 F.2d at 3-4 (identifying "substantial privacy interests" in performance appraisals of federal employees); see also Hill, 77 F. Supp. 2d at 7-8 (shielding business information related to Farmers Home Administration loans to individuals); Prof'l Review Org., 607 F. Supp. at 427 (finding protectible privacy interests in résumés of professional staff of successful government contract applicant sought by unsuccessful bidder); Hemenway, 601 F. Supp. at 1006 (protecting citizenship information on journalists accredited to attend press briefings).

[304] McCutchen, 30 F.3d at 187-88 (quoting Wash. Post, 863 F.2d at 100); see also Fortson v. Harvey, 407 F. Supp. 2d 13, 17-18 (D.D.C. 2005) (finding no privacy interest in witness statements made during discrimination investigation, and relying on Sims v. CIA, 642 F.2d at 574, for proposition that Exemption 6 does not protect business-related information). But see Campaign for Family Farms, 200 F.3d at 1187-89 (finding privacy interest in pork producers' signatures on petition that declared signers' intended voting positions on controversial pork-production issue).

individual's professional activities.[305] Moreover, under <u>Reporters Committee</u>, an individual doing business with the federal government certainly may have some protectible privacy interest, and such dealings with the government do not alone necessarily implicate a public interest that furthers the purpose of the FOIA.[306]

In applying Exemption 6, it must be remembered that all reasonably segregable, nonexempt portions of requested records must be released.[307]

---

[305] See, e.g., <u>McCutchen</u>, 30 F.3d at 187-88; <u>Fund for Constitutional Gov't v. Nat'l Archives & Records Serv.</u>, 656 F.2d 856, 865-66 (D.C. Cir. 1981) (protecting identities of government officials investigated but not prosecuted in "Watergate" investigation) (Exemption 7(C)); <u>cf.</u> <i>FOIA Post</i>, "Supreme Court Rules for 'Survivor Privacy' in <u>Favish</u>" (posted 4/9/04) (discussing "public figure" status and its realistic effect on privacy considerations).

[306] <u>See</u> 489 U.S. at 774 (ruling that information concerning a defense contractor, if such exists, would reveal nothing directly about the behavior of the congressman with whom he allegedly dealt or about the conduct of the Department of Defense in awarding contracts to his company); <u>accord</u> <u>Halloran v. VA</u>, 874 F.2d 315, 324 (5th Cir. 1989) (finding that public interest in learning about VA's relationship with its contractor is served by release of documents with redactions of identities of company employees suspected of fraud). <u>But cf.</u> <u>Or. Natural Desert Ass'n</u>, 24 F. Supp. 2d at 1093 (holding that privacy interests of cattle owners who violated federal grazing laws are outweighed by public interest in knowing how government enforces land-management laws) (Exemption 7(C)); <u>Commodity News Serv. v. Farm Credit Admin.</u>, No. 88-3146, 1989 WL 910244, at *2 (D.D.C. July 31, 1989) (declining to protect personal résumé of appointed receiver of failed bank under Exemption 6).

[307] <u>See</u> 5 U.S.C. § 552(b) (2000 & Supp. IV 2004) (sentence immediately following exemptions); <u>see, e.g.</u>, <u>Kimberlin</u>, 139 F.3d at 949-50 (declining to affirm withholding of the entire file pertaining to an Office of Professional Responsibility investigation of an Assistant United States Attorney without "more specification of the types of material in the file" and specific findings on segregability by the district court); <u>Patterson v. IRS</u>, 56 F.3d 832, 838-40 (7th Cir. 1995) (refusing to permit agency to withhold entire document under Exemption 6 if only "portions" are exempt); <u>Hronek v. DEA</u>, 16 F. Supp. 2d 1260, 1270, 1278 (D. Or. 1998) ("Blanket explanations . . . do not meet FOIA's [segregability] requirements and do not permit the court to make the necessary findings . . . . The government fails to indicate why the privacy interests at stake could not be protected simply by redacting particular identifying information."), <u>aff'd</u>, 7 F. App'x 591 (9th Cir. 2001); <u>see also</u> <u>Trans-Pac. Policing Agreement v. U.S. Customs Serv.</u>, 177 F.3d 1022, 1026-29 (D.C. Cir. 1999) (imposing upon district courts "an affirmative duty to consider the segregability issue sua sponte" even if not raised by the requester) (Exemption 4); <u>Krikorian v. Dep't of State</u>, 984 F.2d 461, 466-67 (D.C. Cir. 1993) ("'The "segregability" requirement applies to all documents

(continued...)

## EXEMPTION 6

(See the discussions of this issue under Procedural Requirements, "Reasonably Segregable" Obligation, above, and Litigation Considerations, "Reasonably Segregable" Requirements, below.) For example, in Department of the Air Force v. Rose, the Supreme Court ordered the release of case summaries of disciplinary proceedings, provided that personal identifying information was deleted.[308] Likewise, circuit courts of appeals have upheld the nondisclosure of the names and identifying information of employee-witnesses when disclosure would link each witness to a particular previously disclosed statement,[309] have ordered the disclosure of computerized lists of numbers and types of drugs routinely ordered by the congressional

---

[307](...continued)
and all exemptions in the FOIA.'" (quoting Ctr. for Auto Safety v. EPA, 731 F.2d 16, 21 (D.C. Cir. 1984))) (Exemptions 1, 3, and 5); Judicial Watch, Inc. v. U.S. Dep't of Commerce, 83 F. Supp. 2d at 109 ("[D]istrict courts are required to consider segregability issues even when the parties have not specifically raised such claims."); Lowry v. Soc. Sec. Admin., No. 00-1616, 2001 U.S. Dist. LEXIS 23474, at *34-36 (D. Or. Aug. 29, 2001) (requiring the agency to "provide copies of the hearing tapes up to the point of the first question to the claimant" because those portions of the tapes take place "before any personal information about a claimant is revealed"); FOIA Update, Vol. XIV, No. 3, at 11-12 ("OIP Guidance: The 'Reasonable Segregation' Obligation").

[308] 425 U.S. at 380-81; see also FOIA Update, Vol. VII, No. 1, at 6; cf. Ripskis, 746 F.2d at 4 (agency voluntarily released outstanding performance rating forms with identifying information deleted); Aldridge v. U.S. Comm'r of Internal Revenue, No. 7:00-CV-131, 2001 WL 196965, at *3 (N.D. Tex. Feb. 23, 2001) (determining that privacy interests of employees recommended for discipline could be protected by redacting their names); Hecht v. U.S. Agency for Int'l Dev., No. 95-263, 1996 WL 33502232, at *12 (D. Del. Dec. 18, 1996) (finding that privacy interests of government contractor's employees could be protected by withholding their names and addresses from biographical data sheets); cf. Church of Scientology v. IRS, 816 F. Supp. 1138, 1160 (W.D. Tex. 1993) (ordering agency to protect employees' privacy interests in their handwriting by typing handwritten records at requester's expense).

[309] See L&C Marine Transp., Ltd. v. United States, 740 F.2d 919, 923 (11th Cir. 1984) (Exemption 7(C)); cf. Ray, 502 U.S. at 175-76 (concluding that de minimis privacy invasion from release of personal information about unidentified person becomes significant when information is linked to particular individual). But see also Cooper Cameron Corp. v. U.S. Dep't of Labor, 280 F.3d 539, 553-54 (5th Cir. 2002) (ordering disclosure of information that could link witnesses to their OSHA investigation statements, because agency presented no evidence of "possibility of employer retaliation") (Exemption 7(C)).

pharmacy after deletion of any item identifiable to a specific individual,[310] and have ordered the disclosure of documents concerning disciplined IRS employees, provided that all names and other identifying information were deleted.[311]

Nevertheless, in some situations the deletion of personal identifying information may not be adequate to provide necessary privacy protection.[312] It is significant in this regard that in <u>Department of the Air Force v. Rose</u>, the Supreme Court specifically admonished that if it were determined on remand that the deletions of personal references were not sufficient to safeguard privacy, then the summaries of disciplinary hearings should not be released.[313]

---

[310] See <u>Arieff v. U.S. Dep't of the Navy</u>, 712 F.2d 1462, 1468-69 (D.C. Cir. 1983); <u>cf.</u> <u>Dayton Newspapers</u>, 35 F. Supp. 2d at 1035 (ordering release of militarywide medical tort-claims database with "claimants' names, social security numbers, home addresses, home/work telephone numbers and places of employment" redacted); <u>Chi. Tribune Co. v. HHS</u>, No. 95 C 3917, 1997 WL 1137641, at *18-19 (N.D. Ill. Feb. 26, 1997) (magistrate's recommendation) (ordering release of breast cancer patient data forms that identify patients only by nine-digit encoded "Study Numbers"), <u>adopted</u> (N.D. Ill. Mar. 28, 1997); <u>Minntech Corp. v. HHS</u>, No. 92-2720, slip op. at 5 (D.D.C. Nov. 17, 1993) (ordering release of FDA studies concerning mortality rates and use of kidney dialyzers with names, addresses, places of birth, and last four digits of social security numbers deleted); <u>Frets v. Dep't of Transp.</u>, No. 88-404-W-9, 1989 WL 222608, at *5 (W.D. Mo. Dec. 14, 1989) (ordering disclosure of urinalysis reports of air traffic controllers with identities deleted); <u>Citizens for Envtl. Quality v. USDA</u>, 602 F. Supp. 534, 538-39 (D.D.C. 1984) (ordering disclosure of health test results because identity of single agency employee tested could not, after deletion of his name, be ascertained from any information known outside appropriate part of agency (citing <u>Rose</u>, 425 U.S. at 380 n.19 (dicta))).

[311] See <u>Chamberlain</u>, 589 F.2d at 841-42; <u>cf.</u> <u>Senate of P.R. v. Dep't of Justice</u>, No. 84-1829, 1993 WL 364696, at *10-11 (D.D.C. Aug. 24, 1993) (ordering release of information concerning cooperating inmate after redaction of identifying details).

[312] See, e.g., <u>Harry v. Dep't of the Army</u>, No. 92-1654, slip op. at 9 (D.D.C. Sept. 13, 1993) (concluding that redaction of ROTC personnel records was not possible because "intimate character" of ROTC corps at university would make records recognizable to requester who was in charge of university's ROTC program); <u>see also</u> <u>Alirez v. NLRB</u>, 676 F.2d 423, 428 (10th Cir. 1982) (finding that deletion of names and other identifying data pertaining to small group of co-workers was simply inadequate to protect them from embarrassment or reprisals because requester could still possibly identify individuals) (Exemption 7(C)).

[313] 425 U.S. at 381; <u>see also, e.g.</u>, <u>ACLU v. DOD</u>, 389 F. Supp. 2d at 572

(continued...)

Despite the admonition of the Supreme Court in Rose, though, a few isolated courts later permitted redaction only of information that directly identified the individuals to whom it pertains. In ordering the disclosure of information pertaining to air traffic controllers who were reinstated in their jobs shortly after their 1982 strike, the Sixth Circuit, in Norwood v. FAA, held that only items that "by themselves" would identify the individual -- names, present and pre-removal locations, and social security numbers -- could be withheld.[314] It later modified its opinion to state that, although there might be instances in which an agency could justify the withholding of "information other than 'those items which "by themselves" would identify the individuals,'" the FAA in this case had "made no such particularized effort, relying generally on the claim that 'fragments of information' might be able to be pieced together into an identifiable set of circumstances."[315]

Similarly, the District Court for the Northern District of California ordered the disclosure of application packages for candidates for an Air Force graduate degree program with the redaction of only the applicants' names, addresses, and social security numbers.[316] Although the packets regularly contained detailed descriptions of the applicants' education, careers, projects, and achievements, the court concluded that it could not "discern how there is anything more than a 'mere possibility' that [the requester] or others will be able to discern to which particular applicant each redacted application corresponds."[317] And more recently, the District Court for the Southern District of Ohio found "much too speculative" the Air Force's argument that disclosure of medical malpractice settlement figures could permit researchers to "comb local news articles, possibly discovering

---

[313](...continued)
(declaring that for certain photographic and video images, "where the context compelled the conclusion that individual recognition could not be prevented without redaction so extensive as to render the images meaningless, I [am] order[ing] those images not to be produced").

[314] 993 F.2d 570, 575 (6th Cir. 1993), modified, No. 92-5820 (6th Cir. July 9, 1993), reh'g denied (6th Cir. Aug. 12, 1993); see also Dayton Newspapers, Inc. v. VA, 257 F. Supp. 2d 988, 1006 (S.D. Ohio 2003) (ordering release of birthdates of individuals in claims database on basis that birthdates alone cannot be used to identify individuals).

[315] Norwood v. FAA, No. 92-5820, slip op. at 1 (6th Cir. July 9, 1993).

[316] Manos v. U.S. Dep't of the Air Force, No. C-92-3986, slip op. at 2-5 (N.D. Cal. Mar. 24, 1993), reconsideration denied (N.D. Cal. Apr. 9, 1993).

[317] Id. at 3; cf. Heat & Frost Insulators & Asbestos Workers, Local 16 v. U.S. Dep't of the Air Force, No. S92-2173, slip op. at 2-4 (E.D. Cal. Oct. 4, 1993) (ordering release of certified payroll records -- with names, addresses, social security numbers, race, and gender deleted -- even though number of characteristics revealed and small number of workers would make it likely that knowledgeable person could identify workers).

the identity of claimants and interfering with their privacy rights."[318] That court concluded that "[t]he mere possibility that factual information might be pieced together to supply the 'missing link,' and lead to personal identification, does not exempt such information from disclosure" under Exemption 6.[319] The same court, in a different case brought by the same FOIA requester, even went so far as to rule that the government cannot rely on the sophistication of modern online search engines as a justification to withhold information under Exemption 6.[320]

The Supreme Court recognized the power of "computer[ization]" as itself a powerful privacy-protection factor in Reporters Committee.[321] Indeed the overwhelming majority of courts take a much broader view of the redaction process.[322] For example, to protect those persons who were the subjects of disciplinary actions that were later dismissed, the D.C. Circuit has upheld the nondisclosure of public information contained in such disciplinary files when the redaction of personal information would not be adequate to protect the privacy of the subjects because the requester could easily obtain and compare unredacted copies of the documents from public sources.[323] When the information in question concerns a small group of individuals who are known to each other and easily identifiable from the details contained in the information, redaction might not adequately protect

---

[318] Dayton Newspapers, Inc. v. Dep't of the Air Force, 107 F. Supp. 2d 912, 919 (S.D. Ohio 1999).

[319] Id.

[320] Dayton Newspapers, Inc., 257 F. Supp. 2d at 1001-05 & n.19 (rejecting government's argument that names could be used as search terms in online databases in order to learn identities of claimants).

[321] Reporters Comm., 489 U.S. at 765, 770-71 (recognizing threats to privacy from data stored in computerized databases).

[322] See, e.g., Judicial Watch, Inc. v. U.S. Dep't of Commerce, 337 F. Supp. 2d at 178 (recognizing realistically that "[i]nformation beyond a person's name can identify that person").

[323] Carter, 830 F.2d at 391; see also, e.g., Marzen v. HHS, 825 F.2d 1148, 1152 (7th Cir. 1987) (concluding that redaction of "identifying characteristics" would not protect the privacy of a deceased infant's family because others could ascertain the identity and "would learn the intimate details connected with the family's ordeal"); Campaign for Family Farms v. Veneman, No. 99-1165, 2001 WL 1631459, at *3 (D. Minn. July 19, 2001) (finding that disclosure of zip codes and dates of signatures could identify signers of petition); Ligorner v. Reno, 2 F. Supp. 2d 400, 405 (S.D.N.Y. 1998) (finding that redaction of a complaint letter to the Office of Professional Responsibility would be inadequate to protect the identities of the individual accused of misconduct and of the accuser, because "public could deduce the identities of the individuals whose names appear in the document from its context").

privacy interests.[324]

Likewise, when the information is "unique and specific" to the subjects of a record, "individual identities may become apparent from the specific details set forth in [the] documents," so that "deletion of personal identifying information . . . may not be adequate to provide the necessary privacy protection."[325] Indeed, a determination of what constitutes identifying

---

[324] See, e.g., Alirez, 676 F.2d at 428 (finding that mere deletion of names and other identifying data concerning small group of co-workers inadequate to protect them from embarrassment or reprisals because requester could still possibly identify individuals) (Exemption 7(C)); Karantsalis v. U.S. Dep't of Educ., No. 05-22088, slip op. at 4 n.4 (S.D. Fla. Dec. 19, 2005) (reasoning that because the requested document dealt "with a particular, small workplace, and since the contents of the report deal exclusively with confidential personnel matters, it is not possible, as in some cases, merely to excise personally identifying information"); Butler v. Soc. Sec. Admin., No. 03-0810, slip op. at 6 (W.D. La. June 25, 2004) (protecting complaints made against the requester, "because the employee or employees who complained could have been easily identified by the fact scenarios described in the documents"), aff'd on other grounds, 146 F. App'x 752 (5th Cir. 2005); Rothman, No. 94-8151, slip op. at 8-9 (C.D. Cal. June 17, 1996) (protecting information in employment applications that pertains to knowledge, skills, and abilities of unsuccessful applicants, because the "field of candidates for this particular position (canine officer) is specialized and is limited to about forty persons who work in same agency and may know each other personally"); McLeod, No. 94-1924, slip op. at 6 (D.D.C. Feb. 9, 1996) (concluding that redaction of investigative memoranda and witness statements would not protect privacy when "community of possible witnesses and investigators is very small" -- eight officers and twenty enlisted personnel) (Exemption 7(C)); Barvick, 941 F. Supp. at 1021-22 (protecting all information about unsuccessful federal job applicants because any information about members of "select group" that applies for such job could identify them); Harry, No. 92-1654, slip op. at 9 (D.D.C. Sept. 13, 1993) (concluding that removal of all identifying marks from university's ROTC personnel records was impossible because of "intimate character" of ROTC corps); Frets, 1989 WL 222608, at *4 (determining that disclosure of handwritten statements would identify those who came forward with information concerning drug use by air traffic controllers even if names were redacted); see also Forest Guardians v. U.S. Dep't of the Interior, 2004 WL 3426434, at *16 ("minimiz[ing] the risk" identified by agency that the release of nonidentifying information for each individual grazing allotment could still identify individual permittees due to the small number of permittees on each allotment, and saying the same about requiring the release of information at the field office level, based upon the fact that "no field office will have only one permittee").

[325] Rashid v. U.S. Dep't of Justice, No. 99-2461, slip op. at 15-16 (D.D.C. June 12, 2001); see Whitehouse v. U.S. Dep't of Labor, 997 F. Supp. 172, 175

(continued...)

information requires both an objective analysis and an analysis "from the vantage point of those familiar with the mentioned individuals."[326] Of course, when a FOIA request is of such character that by its very terms it is limited to privacy-sensitive information pertaining to an identified or identifiable individual, redaction is not possible.[327]

---

[325](...continued)
(D. Mass. 1998) (discerning "no practical way" to sanitize "personal and unique" medical evaluation reports to prevent identification by knowledgeable reader); Ortiz v. HHS, 874 F. Supp. 570, 573-75 (S.D.N.Y.) (finding that factors such as type style, grammar, syntax, language usage, writing style, and mention of facts "that would reasonably be known only by a few persons" could lead to identification of the author if an anonymous letter were released) (Exemptions 7(C) and 7(D)), aff'd on Exemption 7(D) grounds, 70 F.3d 729 (2d Cir. 1995); cf. Schulte v. VA, No. 86-6251, slip op. at 11 (S.D. Fla. Feb. 2, 1996) (finding that disclosure of mortality data for cardiac surgery programs compiled by VA as part of medical quality assurance program would be identified with head cardiac surgeon at any VA facility with only one attending head surgeon) (Exemption 3 (38 U.S.C. § 5705 (2000 & Supp. III 2003))).

[326] Cappabianca v. Comm'r, U.S. Customs Serv., 847 F. Supp. 1558, 1565 (M.D. Fla. 1994). But see also ACLU v. DOD, 389 F. Supp. 2d at 572 ("If, because someone sees the redacted pictures and remembers from earlier versions leaked to, or otherwise obtained by, the media that his image, or someone else's, may have been redacted from the picture, the intrusion into personal privacy is marginal and speculative, arising from the event itself and not the redacted image.").

[327] See, e.g., Hunt, 972 F.2d at 288 (holding that "public availability" of an accused FBI agent's name does not defeat privacy protection and "would make redactions of [the agent's name in] the file a pointless exercise"); MacLean, No. 04-2425, slip op. at 18 (S.D. Cal. June 2, 2005) (pointing out that deletion of identity of named subject of request from professional responsibility file "would be pointless") (Exemptions 6 and 7(C)); Buckley v. Schaul, No. 03-03233, slip op. at 9 (W.D. Wash. Mar. 8, 2004) (finding that even with redactions, the "disclosure of investigative files coupled with the public availability of Plaintiff's FOIA request naming [regional counsel]" would not adequately protect privacy interests) (Exemptions 6 and 7(C)); Claudio v. Soc. Sec. Admin., No. H-98-1911, 2000 WL 33379041, at *8 (S.D. Tex. May 24, 2000) (observing that redaction of documents concerning named subject "would prove meaningless"); Mueller, 63 F. Supp. 2d at 744 (noting that when requested documents relate to a specific individual, "deleting [her] name from the disclosed documents, when it is known that she was the subject of the investigation, would be pointless"); Chin, No. 97-2176, slip op. at 5 (W.D. La. June 24, 1999) (observing that deletion of identifying information "fails to protect the identity of [the individual] who is named in the FOIA request"); Cotton, 798 F. Supp. at 27 (determining that releasing any portion of the documents would "abrogate the privacy
(continued...)

# EXEMPTION 6

When a request is focused on records concerning an identifiable individual and the records are of a particularly sensitive nature, it may be necessary to go a step further than withholding in full without segregation: It may be necessary to follow special "Glomarization" procedures to protect the "targeted" individual's privacy. (See the discussion of the use and origin of the "Glomar" response under Exemption 1, In Camera Submissions, above.) If a request is formulated in such a way that even acknowledgment of the existence of responsive records would cause harm, then the subject's privacy can be protected only by refusing to confirm or deny that responsive records exist. This special procedure is a widely accepted method of protecting, for example, even the mere mention of a person in law enforcement records.[328] (For a more detailed explanation of such privacy "Glomarization," see the discussion under Exemption 7(C), below.)

This procedure is equally applicable to protect an individual's privacy interest in sensitive non-law enforcement records.[329] For example, many agencies maintain an employee assistance program for their employees, operating it on a confidential basis in which privacy is assured. An agency would release neither a list of the employees who participate in such a program nor any other information concerning the program without redacting the names of participants. Logically, then, in responding to a request for any employee assistance counseling records pertaining to a named employee, the agency could protect the privacy of that individual only by refusing to confirm or deny the existence of responsive records.[330]

Similarly, the "Glomarization" approach would be appropriate in responding to a request targeting such matters as a particular citizen's welfare records or the disciplinary records of an employee accused of relatively minor misconduct.[331] Generally, this approach is proper whenever mere

---

[327](...continued)
interests" when the request is for documents pertaining to two named individuals); Schonberger, 508 F. Supp. at 945 (stating that no segregation was possible when request was for one employee's file).

[328] See, e.g., Reporters Comm., 489 U.S. at 757, 780; Dunkelberger, 906 F.2d at 782; Antonelli v. FBI, 721 F.2d 615, 617-19 (7th Cir. 1983); see also FOIA Update, Vol. VII, No. 1, at 3.

[329] See FOIA Update, Vol. VII, No. 2, at 2 (discussing "Glomarization" in context of non-law enforcement records).

[330] See, e.g., U.S. Dep't of State v. Wash. Post Co., 456 U.S. 595, 596 (1982) (describing agency's denial of request for any documentation of any United States citizenship status of two Iranian nationals, which amounted to "Glomarization").

[331] See, e.g., Beck, 997 F.2d at 1493 (refusing to confirm or deny existence of disciplinary records pertaining to named DEA agents) (Exemptions
(continued...)

acknowledgment of the existence of records would be tantamount to disclosing an actual record the disclosure of which "would constitute a clearly unwarranted invasion of personal privacy."[332] It must be remembered, however, that this response is effective only so long as it is given consistently for a distinct category of requests.[333] If it were to become known that an agency gave a "Glomar" response only when records do exist and gave a "no records" response otherwise, then the purpose of this special approach would be defeated.[334]

---

[331](...continued)
6 and 7(C)); Dunkelberger, 906 F.2d at 782 (refusing to confirm or deny existence of letter of reprimand or suspension of FBI agent) (Exemption 7(C)); Jefferson v. U.S. Dep't of Justice, Office of Inspector General, No. 01-1418, slip op. at 11-13 (D.D.C. Nov. 14, 2003) (deciding that although OIG had released documents about officially confirmed investigation into employee, agency correctly refused to confirm or deny existence of any other OIG record about employee) (Exemption 7(C)); Claudio, 2000 WL 33379041, at *8-9 (affirming agency's refusal to confirm or deny existence of any record reflecting any investigation of administrative law judge); Early, No. 95-0254, slip op. at 2-3 (D.D.C. Apr. 30, 1996) (upholding Office of Professional Responsibility's refusal to confirm or deny existence of complaints or investigations concerning performance of professional duties of one United States district court judge and two Assistant United States Attorneys) (Exemption 7(C)); Cotton, 798 F. Supp. at 26 n.8 (suggesting that "the better course would have been for the Government to refuse to confirm or deny the existence of responsive materials"); Ray v. U.S. Dep't of Justice, 778 F. Supp. 1212, 1213-15 (S.D. Fla. 1991) (upholding agency's refusal to confirm or deny existence of investigative records concerning federal immigration officer) (Exemptions 6 and 7(C)). But see Jefferson v. Dep't of Justice, 284 F.3d 172, 174 (D.C. Cir. 2002) (declining to uphold OPR's use of the "Glomar response as to all of its files in the absence of an evidentiary showing" that it maintained no "non-law enforcement files regarding" the subject of the request); Kimberlin, 139 F.3d at 946-47 (regarding "Glomar" response as inapplicable once subject publicly acknowledges investigation).

[332] See FOIA Update, Vol. VII, No. 2, at 2; see also Ray v. U.S. Dep't of Justice, 558 F. Supp. 226, 228 (D.D.C. 1982) (dicta) (upholding agency's refusal to confirm or deny existence of records pertaining to plaintiff's former attorney), aff'd, 720 F.2d 216 (D.C. Cir. 1983) (unpublished table decision).

[333] See FOIA Update, Vol. VII, No. 1, at 3 (explaining that "only through the consistent application of this masked response to third-party requests . . . can the privacy of those who are in fact mentioned in [particularly sensitive agency] files be protected").

[334] See id.

## EXEMPTION 7

Exemption 7 of the FOIA, as amended both in 1974 and in 1986, protects from disclosure "records or information compiled for law enforcement purposes, but only to the extent that the production of such law enforcement records or information (A) could reasonably be expected to interfere with enforcement proceedings, (B) would deprive a person of a right to a fair trial or an impartial adjudication, (C) could reasonably be expected to constitute an unwarranted invasion of personal privacy, (D) could reasonably be expected to disclose the identity of a confidential source, including a State, local, or foreign agency or authority or any private institution which furnished information on a confidential basis, and, in the case of a record or information compiled by a criminal law enforcement authority in the course of a criminal investigation, or by an agency conducting a lawful national security intelligence investigation, information furnished by a confidential source, (E) would disclose techniques and procedures for law enforcement investigations or prosecutions, or would disclose guidelines for law enforcement investigations or prosecutions if such disclosure could reasonably be expected to risk circumvention of the law, or (F) could reasonably be expected to endanger the life or physical safety of any individual."[1]

The threshold requirement for Exemption 7 has been modified by Congress twice since the enactment of the FOIA. In its original form, this exemption simply permitted the withholding of "investigatory files compiled for law enforcement purposes except to the extent available by law to a party other than an agency."[2] As such, it was consistently construed to exempt all material contained in an investigatory file, regardless of the status of the underlying investigation or the nature of the documents requested.[3]

In 1974, Congress rejected the application of a "blanket" exemption for investigatory files and narrowed the scope of Exemption 7 by requiring that withholding be justified by one of six specified types of harm.[4] Under this revised Exemption 7 structure, an analysis of whether a record was protected by this exemption involved two steps: First, the record had to qualify as an "investigatory record compiled for law enforcement purposes"; second, its disclosure had to be found to threaten one of the enumerated

---

[1] 5 U.S.C. § 552(b)(7) (2000 & Supp. IV 2004).

[2] Pub. L. No. 90-23, 81 Stat. 54, 55 (1967) (subsequently amended).

[3] See, e.g., Weisberg v. U.S. Dep't of Justice, 489 F.2d 1195, 1198-1202 (D.C. Cir. 1973).

[4] Pub. L. No. 93-502, 88 Stat. 1561, 1563 (1974) (subsequently amended).

harms of Exemption 7's six subparts.[5]

Congress amended Exemption 7 again in 1986, retaining its basic structure as established by the 1974 FOIA amendments but significantly broadening the protection given to law enforcement records virtually throughout the exemption and its subparts.[6] The Freedom of Information Reform Act of 1986, often referred to as the 1986 FOIA amendments, modified the threshold requirement of Exemption 7 in several distinct respects; it deleted the word "investigatory" and added the words "or information," such that Exemption 7 protections are now potentially available to all "records or information compiled for law enforcement purposes."[7] And, except for Exemption 7(B) and part of Exemption 7(E), it altered the requirement that an agency demonstrate that disclosure "would" cause the harm each subsection seeks to prevent, to the lesser standard that disclosure "could reasonably be expected to" cause the specified harm.[8]

---

[5] See FBI v. Abramson, 456 U.S. 615, 622 (1982).

[6] Freedom of Information Reform Act of 1986, Pub. L. No. 99-570, § 1802, 100 Stat. 3207, 3207-48; see U.S. Dep't of Justice v. Reporters Comm. for Freedom of the Press, 489 U.S. 749, 756 n.9 (1989) (recognizing that the shift from "would constitute" standard to "could reasonably be expected to constitute" standard "represents a congressional effort to ease considerably a Federal law enforcement agency's burden in invoking [Exemption 7]"); Tax Analysts v. IRS, 294 F.3d 71, 79 (D.C. Cir. 2002) (explaining that 1986 FOIA amendments changed threshold for Exemption 7 to delete "any requirement" that information be investigatory and that exemption therefore can be applied more widely); Hopkinson v. Shillinger, 866 F.2d 1185, 1222 n.27 (10th Cir. 1989) ("The 1986 amendment[s] broadened the scope of exemption 7's threshold requirement . . . ."); North v. Walsh, 881 F.2d 1088, 1098 n.14 (D.C. Cir. 1989) (stating that Congress in 1986 "changed the threshold requirement for withholding information under exemption 7" so that "it now applies more broadly"); Wash. Post Co. v. U.S. Dep't of Justice, No. 84-3581, 1987 U.S. Dist. LEXIS 14936, at *26 (D.D.C. Sept. 25, 1987) (magistrate's recommendation) (noting that an "[a]gency's burden of proof in this threshold test has been lightened considerably"), adopted (D.D.C. Dec. 15, 1987), rev'd in part on other grounds & remanded, 863 F.2d 96 (D.C. Cir. 1988).

[7] § 1802, 100 Stat. at 3207-48; see also Tax Analysts, 294 F.3d at 79 (emphasizing that the "legislative history makes it clear that Congress intended the amended exemption to protect both investigatory and non-investigatory materials, including law enforcement manuals and the like" (citing S. Rep. No. 98-221, at 23 (1983))).

[8] Id.; see Attorney General's Memorandum on the 1986 Amendments to the Freedom of Information Act 9-13 (Dec. 1987) [hereinafter Attorney General's 1986 Amendments Memorandum]; cf. NARA v. Favish, 541 U.S. 157, 169 (evincing the Supreme Court's reliance on "the Attorney General's con-
(continued...)

Exemption 7's expansion to cover "information" compiled for law enforcement purposes extended protection to compilations of information as they are preserved in particular records and also to information within the record itself, so long as that information was compiled for law enforcement purposes.[9] It plainly was designed "to ensure that sensitive law enforcement information is protected under Exemption 7 regardless of the particular format or record in which [it] is maintained."[10] It was intended to avoid use of any mechanical process for determining the purpose for which a physical record was created and to instead establish a focus on the purpose for which information contained in a record has been generated.[11] In making their determinations of threshold Exemption 7 applicability, agencies should focus on the content and compilation purpose of each item of information involved, regardless of the overall character of the record in which it happens to be maintained.[12]

---

[8](...continued)
sistent interpretation of" the FOIA in successive such Attorney General memoranda), reh'g denied, 541 U.S. 1057 (2004).

[9] Attorney General's 1986 Amendments Memorandum at 5.

[10] S. Rep. No. 98-221, at 23 (1983).

[11] See id.

[12] See id.; Abramson, 456 U.S. at 630-32; accord Jefferson v. Dep't of Justice, 284 F.3d 172, 176-77 (D.C. Cir. 2002) (reiterating that "this circuit has long emphasized that the focus is on how and under what circumstances the requested files were compiled"); Melville v. U.S. Dep't of Justice, No. 05-0645, 2006 WL 2927575, at *7 (D.D.C. Oct. 12, 2006) (repeating that to assess "whether records are compiled for law enforcement purposes, the 'focus is on how and under what circumstances the requested files were compiled'" (quoting Jefferson, 284 F.3d at 176-77)); Masters v. ATF, No. 04-2274, slip op. at 12 (D.D.C. Sept. 25, 2006) (explaining that the "'focus is on how and under what circumstances the requested files were compiled, and whether the files sought relate to anything that can fairly be characterized as an enforcement proceeding'" (quoting Jefferson, 284 F.3d at 176-77)); Meserve v. U.S. Dep't of Justice, No. 04-1844, 2006 U.S. Dist. LEXIS 56732, at *13 (D.D.C. Aug. 14, 2006) (reiterating that "[i]n assessing whether records are compiled for law enforcement purposes, the 'focus is on how and under what circumstances the required files were compiled'" (quoting Jefferson, 284 F.3d at 176-77)); Deglace v. DEA, No. 05-2276, 2007 WL 521896, at *2 (D.D.C. Feb. 15, 2007) (explaining that records located in DEA's Investigative Reporting and Filing System, Planning and Inspection Division, and Operations Files satisfy threshold because such systems pertain to "misconduct," criminal activity, and "confidential source" information) (appeal pending); see, e.g., Sinsheimer v. DHS, 437 F. Supp. 2d 50, 55 (D.D.C. June 16, 2006) (stressing that "[i]t is the purpose of the record, not the role of the agency, that is determinative"); Living Rivers, Inc. v. U.S. Bureau of

(continued...)

This amendment of Exemption 7 shifted its focus from a "record" to an item of "information," building upon the approach to Exemption 7's threshold that was employed by the Supreme Court in FBI v. Abramson,[13] in which the Court pragmatically focused on the "kind of information" contained in the law enforcement records before it. The amendment essentially codified prior judicial determinations that an item of information originally compiled by an agency for a law enforcement purpose does not lose Exemption 7 protection merely because it is maintained in or recompiled into a non-law enforcement record.[14] This properly places "emphasis on the

---

[12](...continued)
Reclamation, 272 F. Supp. 1313, 1319 (D. Utah 2003) (finding that records created to protect dams from terrorism satisfy Exemptions 7's threshold, and reasoning that "the context in which an agency has currently compiled a document . . . determines whether it is 'compiled for law enforcement purposes'" (quoting John Doe Agency v. John Doe Corp., 493 U.S. 146, 153-54 (1989))); Hogan v. Huff, No. 00 Civ. 6753, 2002 WL 1359722, at *11 (S.D.N.Y. June 21, 2002) (declaring that "[d]ue to the nature of the origin" of the documents used to determine a target's "status as a potential unregistered agent for the Cuban government, the documents in question meet the requirement of being gathered for law enforcement purposes"); Ctr. to Prevent Handgun Violence v. U.S. Dep't of the Treasury, 981 F. Supp. 20, 22-23 (D.D.C. 1997) (finding that because reports of gun sales are "starting points for investigations of illegal gun trafficking," such reports are "clearly law enforcement records"); cf. Avondale Indus. v. NLRB, 90 F.3d 955, 962 (5th Cir. 1996) (finding no evidence in the requested record or in case law that union "voting lists were, in any way, compiled for a law enforcement purpose").

[13] 456 U.S. at 626.

[14] See id. at 631-32 ("We hold that information initially contained in a record made for law enforcement purposes continues to meet the threshold requirements of Exemption 7 where that recorded information is reproduced or summarized in a new document for a non-law-enforcement purpose."); Lesar v. U.S. Dep't of Justice, 636 F.2d 472, 487 (D.C. Cir. 1980) (holding that documents from review of previous FBI surveillance meet threshold); see also Assassination Archives & Research Ctr. v. CIA, 903 F. Supp. 131, 132-33 (D.D.C. 1995) (finding that information from criminal investigations recompiled into administrative file to assist FBI in responding to Senate committee hearings "certainly satisfies" threshold requirement), dismissed without prejudice, No. 94-0655 (D.D.C. May 31, 1996); Exner v. U.S. Dep't of Justice, 902 F. Supp. 240, 242 & n.3 (D.D.C. 1995) (protecting law enforcement document even if copy is maintained in non-law enforcement file), appeal dismissed, No. 95-5411, 1997 WL 68352 (D.C. Cir. Jan. 15, 1997). But cf. Rosenfeld v. U.S. Dep't of Justice, 57 F.3d 803, 811 (9th Cir. 1995) (affirming district court's refusal to apply Abramson principle to documents originally compiled for law enforcement purposes but "channelized" into non-law enforcement files when principle raised as defense for first

(continued...)

contents, and not the physical format of documents."[15]

The scope of Exemption 7 was further expanded by the 1986 FOIA amendments, which removed the requirement that records or information be "investigatory" in character in order to qualify for Exemption 7 protection.[16] Under the former formulations, agencies and courts considering Exemption 7 issues often found themselves struggling with the "investigatory" requirement, which held the potential for disqualifying sensitive law enforcement information from Exemption 7 protection.[17] Courts construing this statutory term generally interpreted it as requiring that the records in question result from specifically focused law enforcement inquiries as opposed to more routine monitoring or oversight of government programs.[18]

---

[14](...continued)
time in motion for reconsideration).

[15] Ctr. for Nat'l Sec. Studies v. CIA, 577 F. Supp. 584, 590 (D.D.C. 1983) (applying Abramson to hold that duplicate copy of congressional record maintained in agency files is not "agency record"); see, e.g., Ctr. for Nat'l Sec. Studies v. U.S. Dep't of Justice, 331 F.3d 918, 926 (D.C. Cir. 2003) (explaining that although the requested documents are of a type that "have traditionally been public . . . [a]s compiled, they constitute a comprehensive diagram of the law enforcement investigation" and thus are "[c]learly" compiled for law enforcement purposes); Ponder v. Reno, No. 98-3097, slip op. at 4-5 (D.D.C. Jan. 22, 2001) (concluding that "the agency's purpose in compiling the records, not their ultimate use of the documents, determines if they meet the Exemption 7 threshold"); Exner, 902 F. Supp. at 242 n.3 (explaining that documents compiled in the course of an FBI investigation into "underworld/criminal activities" involving federal antiracketeering statutes "clearly constitute records or information compiled for law enforcement purposes" even if "a copy of the documents might also be found in a non-law enforcement file"); ISC Group v. DOD, No. 88-631, 1989 WL 168858, at *5 (D.D.C. May 22, 1989) (failing to protect the investigatory report prepared by a private company expressly for the agency's criminal investigation pursuant to Exemption 7 "would elevate form over substance and frustrate the purpose of the exemption"); cf. In re Sealed Case, 856 F.2d 268, 271 (D.C. Cir. 1988) (explaining that law enforcement privilege protects testimony about contents of files which would themselves be protected, because public interest in safeguarding ongoing investigations is identical in both situations); Weinstein v. HHS, 977 F. Supp. 41, 45 (D.D.C. 1997) (applying Abramson to protect sensitive information under Exemption 5).

[16] See Attorney General's 1986 Amendments Memorandum at 6.

[17] See id.

[18] Compare, e.g., Sears, Roebuck & Co. v. GSA, 509 F.2d 527, 529-30 (D.C. Cir. 1974) (deciding that records submitted for mere monitoring of employment discrimination are not "investigatory"), with Ctr. for Nat'l Poli-
(continued...)

The distinction between "investigatory" and "noninvestigatory" law enforcement records, was not always so clear.[19] Moreover, the "investigatory" requirement per se was frequently blurred together with the "law enforcement purposes" aspect of the exemption, so that it sometimes became difficult to distinguish between the two.[20] Law enforcement manuals containing sensitive information about specific procedures and guidelines followed by an agency were held not to qualify as "investigatory records" because they had not originated in connection with any specific investigation, even though they clearly had been compiled for law enforcement purposes.[21]

The 1986 FOIA amendments were a response to such troublesome distinctions, and they broadened the potential sweep of the exemption's coverage considerably.[22] Under those FOIA amendments, the protections of Exemption 7's six subparts were made available to all records or information compiled for "law enforcement purposes."[23] Even records generated pursuant to routine agency activities that previously could not be regarded as "investigatory" now should qualify for Exemption 7 protection when those activities involve a law enforcement purpose; this certainly includes records generated for general law enforcement purposes that do not necessarily relate to specific investigations, although some relatively recent decisions still carelessly contain the pre-1986 FOIA amendment "investigatory" language.[24] Records such as law enforcement manuals, for ex-

---

[18](...continued)
cy Review on Race & Urban Issues v. Weinberger, 502 F.2d 370, 373 (D.C. Cir. 1974) (ruling that records of agency review of public schools suspected of discriminatory practices are "investigatory").

[19] Compare, e.g., Gregory v. FDIC, 470 F. Supp. 1329, 1334 (D.D.C. 1979) (finding that bank examination report "typifies routine oversight" and thus is not "investigatory"), rev'd on other grounds, 631 F.2d 896 (D.C. Cir. 1980), with Copus v. Rougeau, 504 F. Supp. 534, 538 (D.D.C. 1980) (holding that compliance review forecast report is "clearly" investigative record).

[20] See, e.g., Rural Hous. Alliance v. USDA, 498 F.2d 73, 81 & n.47 (D.C. Cir. 1974).

[21] See Sladek v. Bensinger, 605 F.2d 899, 903 (5th Cir. 1979) (holding Exemption 7 inapplicable to DEA manual that "was not compiled in the course of a specific investigation"); Cox v. U.S. Dep't of Justice, 576 F.2d 1302, 1310 (8th Cir. 1978) (same).

[22] See Attorney General's 1986 Amendments Memorandum at 7.

[23] Id.

[24] See Boyd v. DEA, No. 01-0524, slip op. at 7-8 (D.D.C. Mar. 8, 2002) (finding that agency could withhold highly sensitive research analysis in intelligence report pursuant to Exemption 7(E)); Tran v. U.S. Dep't of Jus-
(continued...)

ample which previously were found unqualified for Exemption 7 protection only because they were not "investigatory" in character,[25] now readily satisfy the exemption's threshold requirement.[26] Of course, all law enforce-

---

[24](...continued)
tice, No. 01-0238, 2001 WL 1692570, at *3 (D.D.C. Nov. 20, 2001) (concluding that INS form was properly withheld under Exemption 7(E) because it would reveal law enforcement techniques); see, e.g., Allnutt v. Dep't of Justice, 99 F. Supp. 2d 673, 680 (D. Md. 2000) (stating that the Tax Division records at issue "must generally arise during the course of an investigation" and "must involve the detection or punishment of violations of law" to satisfy the Exemption 7 threshold), renewed motion for summary judgment granted, No. Y-98-901, 2000 WL 852455, at *20-21 (D. Md. Oct. 23, 2000), aff'd sub nom. Allnutt v. Handler, 8 F. App'x 225 (4th Cir. 2001); Morales Cozier v. FBI, No. 1:99-0312, slip op. at 15 (N.D. Ga. Sept. 25, 2000) (finding that records "generated through an investigation" initiated by an invitation to an official of the Cuban government to speak in the United States were compiled for law enforcement purposes).

[25] See, e.g., Sladek, 605 F.2d at 903; Cox, 576 F.2d at 1310.

[26] See Attorney General's 1986 Amendments Memorandum at 7; see, e.g., Tax Analysts, 294 F.3d at 79 (explaining that "the legislative history makes it clear that Congress intended the amended exemption to protect both investigatory and non-investigatory materials, including law enforcement manuals and the like"); PHE, Inc. v. Dep't of Justice, 983 F.2d 248, 249, 251 (D.C. Cir. 1993) (holding portions of FBI's Manual of Investigative Operations and Guidelines properly withheld pursuant to Exemption 7(E)); Peter S. Herrick's Custom & Int'l Trade Newsletter v. U.S. Customs & Border Prot., No. 04-0377, 2006 U.S. Dist. LEXIS 44802, at *1, *20-21 (D.D.C. June 30, 2006) (explaining that "if the personnel oversight and investigation procedures [in the agency's forfeiture handbook] concern misconduct that violates the law, then the information may be deemed to meet the threshold requirement of Exemption 7"); Sussman v. U.S. Marshals Serv., No. 03-610, 2005 WL 3213912, at *9 (D.D.C. Oct. 13, 2005) (finding that "administrative and operational guidelines and procedures" that are used to investigate threats against federal court employees satisfy law enforcement requirement), summary judgment granted in pertinent part, No. 06-5085, 2006 U.S. App. LEXIS 26317 (D.C. Cir. Oct. 20, 2006); Mosby v. U.S. Marshals Serv., No. 04-2083, 2005 U.S. Dist. LEXIS, at *13-14 (D.D.C. Sept. 1, 2005) (explaining that "administrative and operational guidelines and procedures" meet the threshold, because "[t]his information facilitates monitoring investigations, the flow and maintenance of investigative records, and aids in detecting and apprehending fugitives"); Ctr. for Nat'l Sec. Studies v. INS, No. 87-2068, 1990 WL 236133, at *6 (D.D.C. Dec. 19, 1990) (reiterating that documents relating to INS's law enforcement procedures meet threshold requirement as "purpose in preparing these documents relat[es] to legitimate concerns that federal immigration laws have been or may be violated"). But see Maydak, 254 F. Supp. 2d 23, 38 (D.D.C. 2003) (finding
(continued...)

ment records found qualified for exemption protection under the pre-1986 language of Exemption 7 undoubtedly remain so.[27]

Thus, the sole issue remaining is the application of the phrase "law enforcement purposes" in the context of Exemption 7 as amended. Courts have held that Exemption 7's law enforcement purpose encompasses a wide variety of records and information, as can be seen in the following examples:

(1) records compiled in the "investigations of crimes";[28]

---

[26](...continued)
that Bureau of Prisons failed to satisfy law enforcement threshold for records in its Inmate Central Records System, which it described as concerning day-to-day activities and events occurring during inmates' confinement); Cowsen-El v. U.S. Dep't of Justice, 826 F. Supp. 532, 533 (D.D.C. 1992) (explaining that threshold is not met by Bureau of Prisons guidelines covering how prison officials should count and inspect prisoners).

[27] See Rural Hous., 498 F.2d at 80-82 (finding that threshold of Exemption 7 met if investigation focuses directly on specific illegal acts which could result in civil or criminal penalties); Southam News v. INS, 674 F. Supp. 881, 887 (D.D.C. 1987) (finding that, based upon pre-1986 language, INS Lookout Book used to assist in exclusion of inadmissible aliens satisfies threshold requirement); U.S. News & World Report v. Dep't of the Treasury, No. 84-2303, 1986 U.S. Dist. LEXIS 27634, at *5 (D.D.C. Mar. 26, 1986) (reasoning that records pertaining to acquisition of two armored limousines for President meet threshold test when activities involved investigation of how best to safeguard President); Nader v. ICC, No. 82-1037, slip op. at 10-11 (D.D.C. Nov. 23, 1983) (deciding that disbarment proceedings meet Exemption 7 threshold because they are "quasi-criminal" in nature).

[28] Baez v. FBI, 443 F. Supp. 2d 717, 724 (E.D. Pa. 2006) (declaring that "there is no question" that documents pertaining to "investigation of crimes," were compiled for law enforcement purposes); see, e.g., Associated Press v. DOD, No. 05-5468, 2006 WL 2707395, at *3 (S.D.N.Y. Sept. 20, 2006) (stating that "records of investigations to determine whether to charge U.S. military personnel with misconduct . . . were compiled for law enforcement purposes" (citing Aspin v. DOD, 491 F.2d 24, 26-28 (D.C. Cir. 1973) (explaining that records from an investigation "directed toward discovering and toward obtaining evidence of possible offenses under the Uniform Code of Military Justice" were compiled for law enforcement purposes)); Long v. U.S. Dep't of Justice, No. 00-0211, 2006 WL 2578755, at *17 n.20 (D.D.C. Sept. 8, 2006) (accepting agency's uncontested assertion that records are compiled for law enforcement purposes when government is in role of prosecutor or plaintiff); Maydak v. U.S. Dep't of Justice, No. 00-0562, 2006 U.S. LEXIS 58409, at *8-9 (D.D.C. Aug. 21, 2006) (observing that records concerning fraudulent access device applications and unauthorized
(continued...)

(2) investigatory files and file systems;[29]

(3) audits;[30] and, more generally,

(4) records responsive to a particular type of FOIA request (i.e., given

---

[28](...continued)
telecommunications access devices satisfy law enforcement threshold); Ray v. FBI, 441 F. Supp. 2d 27, 33-34 (D.D.C. 2006) (determining that documents generated by FBI efforts to prevent distribution of pornography, combat insurance fraud, and battle drug trafficking meet law enforcement threshold); Watkins Motor Lines, Inc. v. EEOC, No. 8:05-1065, 2006 WL 905518, at *3 (M.D. Fla. Apr. 7, 2006) (stating that because "the records were compiled while the EEOC was investigating an alleged violation of federal law, the records were compiled for law enforcement purposes"); Delta Ltd. v. U.S. Customs & Border Prot., 384 F. Supp. 2d 138, 142-43, 152 (D.D.C. July 26, 2005) (finding "no question" that records created during seizure of merchandise exported from China were compiled for law enforcement purpose); Maydak v. U.S. Dep't of Justice, 362 F. Supp. 2d 316, 323 (D.D.C. 2005) (finding "no dispute" that records involving alleged or actual assaults at federal penitentiary were compiled for law enforcement purposes).

[29] See Deglace, 2007 WL 521896, at *2 (finding that DEA records systems pertaining to personnel misconduct, criminal activity, and confidential sources satisfy threshold); Balderrama v. DHS, No. 04-1616, 2006 WL 889778, at *1, *7-9 (D.D.C. Mar. 30, 2006) (explaining that "Pre-Sentencing Investigation Reports," which are routinely prepared regarding all convicted felons during prosecution process, are part of law enforcement file and thus satisfy law enforcement requirement); Butler v. DEA, No. 05-1798, 2006 WL 398653, at *3 (D.D.C. Feb. 16, 2006) (noting that records maintained in DEA's Investigative Reporting and Filing System and in DEA's Operations File satisfy threshold because they contain information on individuals investigated by agency and identities and details regarding confidential sources); see also Melville, 2006 WL 2927575, at *7 (describing records of investigation and prosecution of narcotics-related activity as being maintained in Criminal Case File System and thus qualifying as "law enforcement records for purposes of Exemption 7"); Antonelli v. ATF, No. 04-1180, 2006 WL 141732, at *4 (D.D.C. Jan. 18, 2006) (stating that records "maintained in the Prisoner Processing and Population Management/Prison Tracking System and in the Warrant Information Network" were complied for ATF's law enforcement purposes of processing and transporting prisoners, executing arrest warrants, and investigating fugitive matters, and that they "therefore satisfy . . . [the] threshold requirement").

[30] Faiella v. IRS, No. 05-CV-238, 2006 WL 2040130, at *4 (D.N.H. July 20, 2006) (observing that "an IRS audit is a law enforcement activity"); cf. Van Mechelen v. U.S. Dep't of the Interior, No. C05-5393, 2005 WL 3007121, at *1, *4 (W.D. Wash. Nov. 9, 2005) (explaining that reports generated by investigation into building leases satisfy law enforcement threshold).

the "nature" of the request).[31]

However, even with such wide latitude, courts do not determine automatically that records involving "wrongdoing" necessarily satisfy the law enforcement threshold.[32] Therefore, agencies in litigation still should describe in some detail the law enforcement purpose behind the compilation of the requested records.[33] (For further discussion of this point, see Litiga-

---

[31] Valdez v. U.S. Dep't of Justice, No. 04-0950, 2007 U.S. Dist. LEXIS 10566, at *10 (D.D.C. Feb. 16, 2007) ("Given the nature of plaintiff's FOIA request and the descriptions of the systems of records where responsive records likely would be located, the Court concludes that any responsive records would be law enforcement records."); Boyd v. ATF, No. 05-1096, 2006 U.S. Dist. LEXIS 71857, at *1, *22 (D.D.C. Sept. 29, 2006) (stating that it is "evident from the nature of the . . . requests" for criminal investigative file and policies/procedures on confidential informants that the "relevant records were compiled for law enforcement purposes"); Wilson v. DEA, No. 04-1814, 2006 WL 212138, at *1, *5, *7 (D.D.C. Jan. 27, 2006) (stating that "[g]iven the nature of the request" for conspiracy records and drug laboratory reports, "DEA clearly meets the threshold requirement"); Dipietro v. Executive Office for U.S. Attorneys, 357 F. Supp. 2d 177, 184 (D.D.C. 2004) (declaring that "[g]iven the nature of [the] request" for criminal files including confidential informant records, the requested records satisfy the "law enforcement" threshold), summary judgment granted, 386 F. Supp. 2d 80 (D.D.C. 2005); cf. Hogan, 2002 WL 1359722, at *11 (explaining that the requested records satisfy Exemption 7's threshold "due to the nature of [their] origin").

[32] See, e.g., Cawthon v. U.S. Dep't of Justice, No. 05-0567, 2006 WL 581250, at *4 (D.D.C. Mar. 9, 2006) (explaining that malpractice records for two Bureau of Prison doctors "appear to come from personnel records" and therefore do not meet Exemption 7's law enforcement threshold); Leadership Conference on Civil Rights v. Gonzales, 404 F. Supp. 2d 246, 257 (D.D.C. 2005) (finding "no evidence that the paralegal names and work numbers" appearing in communications related to monitoring federal elections were "compiled for law enforcement purposes"), motion to amend denied, 421 F. Supp. 2d 104 (D.D.C. 2006); Maydak, 362 F. Supp. 2d at 321-23 (concluding that psychological test maintained in Bureau of Prisons files, documents pertaining to accidents and injuries sustained in recreation department at prison, and list of staff names and titles of prison employees were not compiled for law enforcement purposes); Phillips v. Immigration & Customs Enforcement, 385 F. Supp. 2d 296, 306 (S.D.N.Y. 2005) (finding law enforcement requirement not met for report involving immigration status of two former military officials from El Salvador accused of atrocities, because report "was prepared for Congress").

[33] See, e.g., Cawthon, 2006 WL 581250, at *4 (finding agency's declaration to be insufficient to satisfy threshold); Antonelli v. ATF, No. 04-1180, 2005 U.S. Dist. LEXIS 17089, at *26 (D.D.C. Aug. 16, 2005) (noting that the

(continued...)

tion Considerations, Vaughn Index, below.)

    For instance, the question of whether the Federal Bureau of Prison's practice of recording telephone calls made by prison inmates to individuals outside the prison facility satisfies the law enforcement threshold arose after the Court of Appeals for the District of Columbia Circuit ruled that such recordings did not qualify for Title III protection[34] and therefore could not be withheld pursuant to Exemption 3 of the FOIA.[35] (This statute -- Title III of the Omnibus Crime Control and Safe Street Act of 1968 -- governs wiretaps and makes it unlawful, except under certain conditions, to intercept wire, oral, or electronic communications; the statute places restrictions on the release of the intercepted information.[36]) The D.C. Circuit in Smith v. United States Department of Justice thus held that telephone recordings of the inmates were "not a product of an 'interception' consensual or otherwise."[37] However, courts in subsequent cases specifically addressing whether the recordings of these telephone calls satisfy Exemption 7's threshold, have found consistently that these recordings were compiled for law enforcement purposes, thus satisfying that requirement and permitting the application of Exemption 7(C) to such records.[38]

---

[33](...continued)
defendant agencies "have proffered no evidence from which the Court may find for them on the threshold requirement"); Flores v. U.S. Dep't of Justice, No. 03-2105, slip op. at 4 (D.D.C. Aug. 31, 2004) (finding that while the "description of the records suggests that a criminal investigation was conducted, [the] mere suggestion" is not sufficient to meet the threshold of "law enforcement"), summary judgment granted (D.D.C. Feb. 7, 2005), summary affirmance granted, No. 05-5074, 2005 U.S. App. LEXIS 24159 (D.C. Cir. Nov. 8, 2005), cert. denied, 126 S. Ct. 2316 (2006).

[34] See Smith v. U.S. Dep't of Justice, 251 F.3d 1047, 1049 (D.C. Cir. 2001) (finding that tapes of telephone calls made by inmates are not within of scope of Title III).

[35] 5 U.S.C. § 552(b)(3).

[36] Title III of the Omnibus Crime Control and Safe Street Act of 1968, 18 U.S.C. §§ 2510-2520 (2000 & Supp. IV 2004).

[37] 251 F.3d at 1049.

[38] See, e.g., Swope v. U.S. Dep't of Justice, 439 F. Supp. 2d 1, 6 (D.D.C. July 3, 2006) (stating that "such telephone recordings are the functional equivalent of law enforcement records"); Thomas v. U.S. Dep't of Justice, No. 1:04-112, 2006 WL 722141, at *2 (E.D. Tex. Mar. 15, 2006) (reiterating that telephone calls are monitored "to preserve the security of the institution and to protect the public" and that the recordings thus satisfy the law enforcement requirement); Butler v. Fed. Bureau of Prisons, No. 05-643, 2005 WL 3274573, at *3 (D.D.C. Sept. 27, 2005) (finding that "BOP is a law enforcement agency," and explaining that because inmate telephone calls
(continued...)

Thus, overall, the "law" to be enforced within the meaning of the term "law enforcement purposes" includes both civil[39] and criminal stat-

---

[38](...continued)
are monitored to preserve security and orderly management of the institution and to protect the public, "such telephone recordings are the functional equivalent of law enforcement records"); Pendergrass v. U.S. Dep't of Justice, No. 04-112, 2005 WL 1378724, at *4 (D.D.C. June 7, 2005) (explaining that prisons monitor and record telephone calls in order "to preserve the security and orderly management of the institution and to protect the public"; consequently, the recordings are "the functional equivalent of law enforcement"); Jones v. Fed. Bureau of Prisons, No. 03-1647, slip op. at 1 (D.D.C. Oct. 6, 2004) (declaring that "monitoring and taping of inmate telephone calls [do] serve a law enforcement purpose"); Monaco v. Dep't of Justice, No. 02-1843, slip op. at 6 (D.D.C. Sept. 24, 2003) (concluding that BOP tapes of telephone conversations "are law enforcement records for purposes of Exemption 7").

[39] See, e.g., Rugiero v. U.S. Dep't of Justice, 257 F.3d 534, 550 (6th Cir. 2001) (explaining that the "Court has adopted a per se rule" that applies not only to criminal enforcement actions, but to "records compiled for civil enforcement purposes as well"); Rural Hous., 498 F.2d at 81 & n.46 (holding that the "character of the statute violated would rarely make a material distinction, because the law enforcement purposes . . . include both civil and criminal purposes"); Morley v. CIA, No. 03-2545, 2006 WL 2806561, at *14 (D.D.C. Sept. 29, 2006) (mentioning that law enforcement "extends to civil investigations and proceedings"); Envtl. Prot. Servs. v. EPA, 364 F. Supp. 2d 575, 587 (N.D. W. Va. 2005) (reiterating that law enforcement standard includes "civil laws"); Martinez v. EEOC, No. 04-CA-0391, 2004 WL 2359895, at *2 (W.D. Tex. Oct. 19, 2004) (restating that requirement of "law enforcement purpose" is satisfied by both criminal and civil laws); Black & Decker Corp. v. United States, No. 02-2070, 2004 WL 500847, at *3 (D. Md. Feb. 19, 2004) (stating that "law enforcement" includes both civil and criminal matters); Judicial Watch, Inc. v. Rossotti, No. 01-2672, U.S. Dist. 2002 LEXIS 25213, at *19-20 (D. Md. Dec. 16, 2002) (ruling that letters written by citizens concerned about plaintiff's compliance with IRS laws were compiled for "civil law enforcement purposes"), aff'd sub nom. Judicial Watch, Inc. v. United States, 84 F. App'x 335 (4th Cir. 2004); Schiller v. INS, 205 F. Supp. 2d 648, 659 (W.D. Tex. 2002) (stating that "[l]aw enforcement for purposes of the FOIA is not limited strictly to criminal investigations but also includes within its scope civil investigations" (citing Rugiero, 257 F.3d at 550)); Baltimore Sun v. U.S. Marshals Serv., 131 F. Supp. 2d 725, 728 n.2 (D. Md. 2001) (reasoning that United States Marshals Service forfeiture records satisfy threshold because agency is responsible for "enforcement of civil and criminal seizure and forfeiture laws"); Youngblood v. Comm'r of Internal Revenue, No. 2:99-9253, 2000 WL 852449, at *10 (C.D. Cal. Mar. 7, 2000) (holding that IRS "investigations or proceedings in the civil or criminal context" satisfy the threshold).

utes,[40] as well as those statutes authorizing administrative (i.e., regulatory) proceedings.[41]

---

[40] See, e.g., Beard v. Espy, No. 94-16748, 1995 WL 792071, at *1 (9th Cir. Dec. 11,1995) (protecting complaint letter and notes compiled during criminal investigation involving USDA loans); Ortiz v. HHS, 70 F.3d 729, 730 (2d Cir. 1995) (holding that unsigned, unsolicited letter used to launch criminal investigation by Social Security Administration meets threshold for law enforcement purposes, although no charges filed against target); Judicial Watch v. U.S. Dep't of Justice, No. 99-1883, slip op. at 2-3, 11 (D.D.C. June 9, 2005) (finding that information from databases and computer systems created by Civil Rights Division task force members in response to abortion clinic violence satisfies law enforcement threshold, because evidence gathered relates to violations of federal criminal statutes); Oliver v. FBI, No. 02-0012, slip op. at 4 (D.D.C. Mar. 8, 2004) (finding that records compiled during investigation into, and criminal prosecution for, kidnaping and transporting minor across state lines satisfy law enforcement threshold), aff'd per curiam, No. 04-5445, 2005 U.S. App. LEXIS 13991 (D.C. Cir. July 8, 2005); Oguaju v. Executive Office for U.S. Attorneys, No. 00-1930, slip op. at 3 n.2 (D.D.C. Sept. 25, 2003) (finding that threshold requirement was satisfied when information was compiled as part of "criminal investigation, prosecution and conviction" of requester), summary affirmance granted, No. 04-5407, 2005 U.S. App. LEXIS 23891 (D.C. Cir. Nov. 3, 2005); Solar Sources v. United States, No. 96-0772, slip op. at 5 (S.D. Ind. Mar. 10, 1997) (holding that criminal antitrust investigation of explosives industry was "indisputably" compiled for law enforcement purposes), aff'd, 142 F.3d 1033 (7th Cir. 1998); Hoffman v. Brown, No. 1:96-53, slip op. at 4 (W.D.N.C. Nov. 26, 1996) (finding that information compiled by VA police canvassing plaintiff's neighbors regarding "alleged criminal activity of plaintiff at home" meets threshold), aff'd, 145 F.3d 1324 (4th Cir. 1998) (unpublished table decision); Mavadia v. Caplinger, No. 95-3542, 1996 WL 592742, at *2 (E.D. La. Oct. 11, 1996) (finding that both civil and criminal investigations of possible violations of immigration laws satisfy threshold); Cappabianca v. Comm'r. U.S. Customs Serv., 847 F. Supp. 1558, 1565 (M.D. Fla. 1994) (stating that records of internal investigation focusing specifically on alleged acts that could result in civil or criminal sanctions were compiled for law enforcement purposes); Stone v. Def. Investigative Serv., 816 F. Supp. 782, 787 (D.D.C. 1993) (protecting foreign counterintelligence investigation and investigation into possible violation of federal statute), appeal dismissed for failure to prosecute, No. 93-5178 (D.C. Cir. Mar. 11, 1994); Buffalo Evening News, Inc. v. U.S. Border Patrol, 791 F. Supp. 386, 394 (W.D.N.Y. 1992) (reasoning that USBP form meets threshold because it is generated in investigations of violations of federal immigration law).

[41] See, e.g., Jefferson, 284 F.3d at 178 (reiterating that Exemption 7 "'covers investigatory files related to enforcement of all kinds of laws,' including those involving 'adjudicative proceedings'" (quoting Rural Hous., 498 F.2d at 81 n.46)); Ctr. for Nat'l Policy Review, 502 F.2d at 373 (holding that administrative determination has "salient characteristics of 'law enforcement'

(continued...)

Most significantly, the courts recognize that "law enforcement" within the meaning of Exemption 7 extends beyond these traditional realms into the realms of national security and homeland security-related government activities as well.[42] For example, in Center for National Security Studies v.

---

[41](...continued)
contemplated" by Exemption 7 threshold requirement); Envtl. Prot. Servs., 364 F. Supp. 2d at 587 (stating that records compiled in EPA's administrative proceeding satisfy law enforcement threshold, because Exemption 7 applies to "enforcement of civil laws, such as regulations"); Schiller, 205 F. Supp. 2d at 559 (stating that "law enforcement" for purposes of FOIA includes regulatory proceedings (citing Rugiero, 257 F.3d at 550)); Hidalgo v. Bureau of Prisons, No. 00-1229, slip op. at 3 (D.D.C. June 6, 2001) (determining that records compiled during investigation of prisoner for violating institutional rules and regulations satisfy threshold), summary affirmance granted, No. 01-5257, 2002 WL 1997999 (D.C. Cir. Aug. 29, 2002); McErlean v. Dep't of Justice, No. 97-7831, 1999 WL 791680, at *8 (S.D.N.Y. Sept. 30, 1999) (stating that "it is well-settled that documents compiled by the INS in connection with the administrative proceedings authorized by the Immigration and Naturalization Act are documents compiled for 'law enforcement purposes'"); Gen. Elec. Co. v. EPA, 18 F. Supp. 2d 138, 143-44 (D. Mass. 1998) (reasoning that EPA decision to classify a site as contaminated "is not an enforcement action at all but rather ordinary informal rulemaking," which would ordinarily not meet Exemption 7 threshold, though in this case it did because "it is entirely reasonable for the agency to anticipate that enforcement proceedings are in the offing"); Johnson v. DEA, No. 97-2231, 1998 U.S. Dist. LEXIS 9802, at *9 (D.D.C. June 25, 1998) (reiterating that "law being enforced may be . . . regulatory"); Straughter v. HHS, No. 94-0567, slip op. at 4 (S.D. W. Va. Mar. 31, 1995) (magistrate's recommendation) (finding threshold met by records compiled by HHS's Office of Civil Rights in course of investigation of handicap discrimination as violation of Rehabilitation Act), adopted (S.D. W. Va. Apr. 17, 1995); Kay v. FCC, 867 F. Supp. 11, 16-18 (D.D.C. 1994) (explaining that FCC's statutory authority to revoke licenses or deny license applications is qualifying law enforcement purpose); Aircraft Gear Corp. v. NLRB, No. 92-C-6023, slip op. at 10 (N.D. Ill. Mar. 14, 1994) (stating that documents created in connection with NLRB unfair labor practices cases and union representation case meet threshold); Ehringhaus v. FTC, 525 F. Supp. 21, 22-23 (D.D.C. 1980) (deciding that documents prepared as part of FTC investigation into advertising practices of cigarette manufacturers meet threshold); cf. Gordon v. FBI, 388 F. Supp. 2d 1028, 1036 (N.D. Cal. 2005) (explaining that law enforcement is not limited to criminal law, but can encompass "internal guidelines" (citing Dirksen v. HHS, 803 F.2d 1456, 1459 (9th Cir. 1986)).

[42] See Ctr. for Nat'l Sec. Studies, 331 F.3d at 926 (finding law enforcement threshold met by records compiled in course of investigation into "breach of this nation's security"); Gordon, 388 F. Supp. 2d at 1036 (extending the law enforcement threshold to include memoranda and e-mail messages created by the FBI in its handling of various aviation "watch lists"

(continued...)

**EXEMPTION 7**

United States Department of Justice, the D.C. Circuit recently explained that the names of post-9/11 detainees, found on documents that traditionally have been public, are properly withheld because they were compiled for the law enforcement purpose of pursuing a "heinous violation of federal law as well as a breach of national security."[43] Indeed, in accepting arguments that terrorists could use information previously considered innocuous and safe for public release, courts have shown a new sensitivity to the needs of homeland security by recognizing the law enforcement nexus for certain documents that readily could be used by terrorists to assess the likelihood of detection, to analyze the degree of damage inflicted by striking one particular target instead of another, or even to intimidate witnesses and/or the families of witnesses.[44]

---

[42](...continued)
created to "protect the American flying public from terrorists"); Living Rivers, 272 F. Supp. 2d at 1321 (finding that terrorists could make use of downstream flooding projections from agency's dam "inundation maps," and obliquely referring to "a dam failure as [seeking] a 'weapon of mass destruction'"); Coastal Delivery Corp. v. U.S. Customs Serv., 272 F. Supp. 2d 958, 964-65 (C.D. Cal. 2003) (ruling that terrorists could use information to avoid detection and to direct "merchandise to vulnerable ports"), reconsideration denied, No. 02-3838, 2002 WL 21507775 (C.D. Cal. June 13, 2003), appeal dismissed voluntarily, No. 03-55833 (9th Cir. Aug. 26, 2003); see also Pratt v. Webster, 673 F.2d 408, 421 (D.C. Cir. 1982) (explaining that "to pass the FOIA Exemption 7 threshold," agencies must establish that their activities are based on a concern that "federal laws have been or may be violated or that national security may be breached" (emphasis added)); cf. Morley, 2006 WL 2806561, at *13 (stretching Exemption 7's law enforcement purpose to include documents "which are the product of a CIA investigatory process"); Lahr v. NTSB, No. 03-8023, 2006 WL 2789870, at *1, *4, *22 (C.D. Cal. Aug. 31, 2006) (extending the law enforcement purpose to cover CIA documents compiled to analyze the mid-air explosion of TWA Flight 800 that could possibly have been result of terrorist activity, because "it was the FBI that compiled" the records).

[43] 331 F.3d at 926, 929.

[44] See id. at 929 ("While the name of any individual detainee may appear innocuous or trivial, it could be of great use to al Qaeda in plotting future terrorist attacks or intimidating witnesses in the present investigation."); Living Rivers, 272 F. Supp. 2d at 1321 (reasoning that terrorists could use "inundation maps" to aid in carrying out attacks on dams both in choosing potential targets and in selecting particular, more vulnerable features of certain dams); Coastal Delivery, 272 F. Supp. 2d at 964, 966 (explaining that information that appears to be "innocuous on its own" could reasonably be used by "potential terrorists and smugglers" to circumvent law enforcement procedures); see also FOIA Post, "FOIA Officers Conference Held on Homeland Security" (posted 7/3/03) (discussing recent case law developments, and advising on the "increasing significance of both information
(continued...)

As another recent example, in <u>Los Angeles Times Communications v. Department of the Army</u>,[45] the District Court for the Central District of California ruled that incident reports from private security contractors in Iraq meet the law enforcement threshold because the purpose of compiling and maintaining such incident reports "falls within a cognizable law enforcement mandate in Iraq [of tracking] insurgent attacks on and other unlawful activities against Coalition forces [and contract employees] to improve intelligence information that will enhance security."[46] Furthermore, in an analysis similar to that of the courts in <u>Center for National Security Studies</u>[47] and <u>Coastal Delivery Corp.</u>,[48] this court significantly went on to uphold the withholding of even the names of the companies mentioned in the reports, pursuant to Exemption 7(F),[49] explaining that "[t]he test is not whether the [contractor] company names alone are sufficient to directly result in a threat to the safety of military and [contractor] personnel," but rather whether or not "'information [that] is not of obvious importance in itself . . . in a mosaic analysis, it could lead to identification of substantive information.'"[50]

In fact, the courts that have uniformly determined that documents related to national or homeland security satisfy Exemption 7's law enforce-

---

[44](...continued)
sharing and information safeguarding in connection with sensitive homeland security information"); <u>cf.</u> <i>FOIA Post</i>, "Guidance on Homeland Security Information Issued" (posted 3/21/02) (stressing need for safeguarding not only classified records but also "sensitive information related to America's homeland security that might not meet" classification standards).

[45] 442 F. Supp. 2d 880 (C.D. Cal. 2006).

[46] <u>Id.</u> at *13.

[47] 331 F.3d at 926 (explaining that while similar documents have traditionally been public, in the instant case, the names "constitute a comprehensive diagram of the law enforcement investigation").

[48] 272 F. Supp. 2d at 964-65 (explaining that "[w]hile it is true that knowing the rate of examination at different ports may not be the best way" for terrorists and smugglers to avoid detection, arguments that they "could not and would not use the information [to direct activities to vulnerable ports] is unpersuasive," and further explaining that while the information is not of obvious importance, if it were released and combined "'with other known data, in a 'mosaic' analysis, it could lead'" to substantive information (quoting <u>Davin v. U.S. Dep't of Justice</u>, 60 F.3d 1043, 1064-65 (3d Cir. 1995))).

[49] <u>L.A. Times</u>, 442 F. Supp. 2d at 898-99 (explaining that to qualify for Exemption 7(F) protection, information must satisfy the threshold and in addition the agency must establish that disclosure "would reasonably be expected to endanger the life or physical safety of any individual").

[50] <u>Id.</u> (quoting <u>Davin</u>, 60 F.3d at 1064-65.

ment requirement have discussed repeatedly that the agencies' mandates to protect society and to prevent violence are key to establishing the threshold's satisfaction[51] -- making "homeland security," as a practicable matter in the post-9/11 world, virtually synonymous with "law enforcement."[52]

---

[51] See Ctr. for Nat'l Sec. Studies, 331 F.3d at 926, 928 (explaining that "America faces an enemy" and that the terrorism investigation into this "heinous violation" is one of the Department of Justice's chief law enforcement duties); Gordon, 388 F.2d at 1045 ("[T]he information was compiled in connection with maintaining the watch lists to prevent another terrorist attack on civil aviation. There is nothing in the redacted information that suggests that the FBI's assertion of a law enforcement purpose is pretextual, that is, that the FBI is placing names on the watch lists because of a person's First Amendment activities rather than for a law enforcement purpose."); Living Rivers, 272 F. Supp. 2d at 1320 (concluding that "inundation maps" were compiled for law enforcement purposes because they are used for homeland security as part of the Department of the Interior's "Emergency Action Plans and to protect and alert potentially threatened people"); see also Pratt, 673 F.2d at 410, 422-23 (finding that documents gathered during the investigation of the Black Panther Party, "an allegedly subversive and violent domestic organization," met law enforcement threshold because investigation involved "prevention of violence" on American soil); Ayyad v. U.S. Dep't of Justice, No. 00-960, 2002 WL 654133, at *8-12 (S.D.N.Y. Apr. 17, 2002) (ruling that the information satisfies Exemption 7's threshold, because it "is clearly related to law enforcement proceedings and was compiled by the FBI to investigate" the 1993 World Trade Center bombing); Judicial Watch, Inc. v. Reno, No. 00-0723, slip op. at 21 (D.D.C. Mar. 30, 2001) (stating that "information related to an investigation of possible terrorist threats . . . is sufficient to meet" the threshold); Morales Cozier, No. 99-0312, slip op. at 14-15 (N.D. Ga. Sept. 25, 2000) (explaining that the law enforcement threshold is met by an investigation of activities that "could have presented an interference with United States foreign policy or national security"); cf. Jabara v. Webster, 691 F.2d 272, 279-80 (6th Cir. 1982) (clarifying, in a Privacy Act case, that an investigation encompassing the exercise of First Amendment rights is not barred if it is relevant to an authorized criminal, civil, administrative, or intelligence investigation).

[52] See, e.g., Ctr. for Nat'l Sec. Studies, 331 F.3d at 926 (concluding that investigations of persons detained in the wake of breach of national security by 9/11 terror attack meet law enforcement standard easily); Gordon, 388 F. Supp. 2d at 1036 (concluding that "law enforcement purpose" cannot be read "too narrowly" and that "watch lists" used to protect American flying public from terrorism were created for law enforcement purposes); Living Rivers, 272 F.2d at 1320 (finding that inundation maps meet law enforcement threshold); Coastal Delivery, 272 F. Supp. 2d at 964-65 (reasoning that law enforcement requirement is satisfied by cargo-inspection data at seaports where disclosure could permit terrorists to direct activities to "vulnerable ports"); see also FOIA Post, "FOIA Officers Conference Held on

(continued...)

Furthermore, in this area courts pointedly emphasize the propriety of judicial deference; indeed, in Center for National Security Studies, the D.C. Circuit observed that it was acting fully "in accord with several federal courts that have wisely respected the executive judgments in prosecuting the national response to terrorism" by deferring to the executive on "decisions of national security," especially in establishing the law enforcement purpose and in foreseeing the harm from disclosure.[53] (For further discussions of homeland security-related matters, see Exemption 1, Homeland Security-Related Information, above, and Exemption 2, Homeland Security-Related Information, above.)

In addition to all such matters of federal law enforcement, Exemption

---

[52](...continued)
Homeland Security" (posted 7/3/03) (explaining amendments to Executive Order 13292, memorandum pertaining to homeland security, and recent case law); FOIA Post, "Guidance on Homeland Security Information Issued" (posted 3/21/02) (discussing recent events concerning safeguarding information); cf. L.A. Times, 442 F. Supp. 2d at 898 (explaining that there is "a cognizable law enforcement mandate in Iraq" of improving intelligence information that will enhance security).

[53] 331 F.3d at 932; see also L.A. Times, 442 F. Supp. 2d at 899 (deferring to agency's predictive judgments and explaining that it is "'well-established' that the judiciary owes some measure of deference to the executive in cases implicating national security'" (quoting Ctr. for Nat'l Sec. Studies, 331 F.2d at 926-27)); Zadvydas v. Davis, 533 U.S. 678, 696 (2001) (noting that circumstances of "terrorism" can warrant heightened deference) (non-FOIA case); Dep't of the Navy v. Egan, 484 U.S. 518, 530 (1988) (stating that courts are reluctant to intrude into "national security affairs") (non-FOIA case); cf. N. Jersey Media Group v. Ashcroft, 308 F.3d 198, 200-03 (3d Cir. 2002) (holding that closure of "special interest" deportation hearings involving detainees with alleged connections to terrorism does not violate First Amendment when "open hearings might impair national security" by disclosing potentially sensitive information) (non-FOIA case); Gordon, 388 F. Supp. 2d at 1036, 1045 (admitting that "[i]t is not too difficult to believe" that the release of the requested information would be useful to terrorists, and stressing that "[t]here is nothing in the redacted information that suggests that the FBI's assertion of a law enforcement purpose is pretextual"). But see Lahr, 2006 WL 2789870, at *1, *5, *16 (declaring in a case involving allegations that "the government acted improperly in its investigation of Flight 800," which exploded in mid-air in 1996; stating that there is "a presumption of legitimacy accorded to a government official's conduct," but nevertheless finding that there is evidence "sufficient to permit Plaintiff to proceed based on his claims [that there was a] massive cover-up" by government officials of plaintiff's theorized "fact" that the explosion was caused by an errant missile launched by the United States military).

7 also applies to records compiled to enforce state law,[54] and even foreign law.[55] There is no requirement that the matter culminate in actual adminis-

---

[54] See Hopkinson, 866 F.2d at 1222 n.27 (holding that Exemption 7 applies "to FBI laboratory tests conducted at the request of local law enforcement authorities"); Leadership, 404 F. Supp. 2d at 257-58 (determining that "local police arrest reports [and] bail bond information" met threshold); Antonelli, 2005 U.S. Dist. LEXIS 17089, at *12 (declaring that records "compiled during the course of an investigation by a local police department, with ATFE assistance," satisfy threshold); Franklin v. DEA, No. 97-1225, slip op. at 7 (S.D. Fla. June 26, 1998) (stating that documents compiled for "federal or state" law enforcement purposes meet threshold); Code v. FBI, No. 95-1892, 1997 WL 150070, at *5 (D.D.C. Mar. 26, 1997) (finding that documents compiled in connection with FBI's efforts to assist local police in homicide investigations meet threshold); Butler, 888 F. Supp. at 180, 182 (finding that Air Force personnel background report -- requested by local law enforcement agency for its investigation into murder -- was compiled for law enforcement purposes); Kuffel v. Bureau of Prisons, 882 F. Supp. 1116, 1124 (D.D.C. 1995) (ruling that information from state law enforcement agency investigating various state crimes qualifies); Wojtczak v. U.S. Dep't of Justice, 548 F. Supp. 143, 146-48 (E.D. Pa. 1982) ("This Court must therefore interpret the statute as written and concludes that Exemption 7 applies to all law enforcement records, federal, state, or local, that lie within the possession of the federal government"); see also Shaw v. FBI, 749 F.2d 58, 64 (D.C. Cir. 1984) (explaining that authorized federal investigation into commission of state crime constitutes valid criminal law enforcement investigation, which qualifies confidential source-provided information for protection under second half of Exemption 7(D)); Palacio v. U.S. Dep't of Justice, No. 00-1564, 2002 U.S. Dist. LEXIS 2198, at *16 (D.D.C. Feb. 11, 2002) (explaining that records of investigation conducted by city task force were "created or compiled" for law enforcement purposes and thus satisfy threshold), summary affirmance granted, No. 02-5247, 2003 U.S. App. LEXIS 1804 (D.C. Cir. Jan. 31, 2003); Rojem v. U.S. Dep't of Justice, 775 F. Supp. 6, 10 (D.D.C. 1991) (determining that material provided to FBI by state law enforcement agency for assistance in that state agency's criminal investigation is "compiled for law enforcement purposes"), appeal dismissed for failure to timely file, No. 92-5088 (D.C. Cir. Nov. 4, 1992).

[55] See, e.g., Bevis v. Dep't of State, 801 F.2d 1386, 1388 (D.C. Cir. 1986) (finding no distinction between foreign and domestic enforcement purposes in language of statute); Zevallos-Gonzalez v. DEA, No. 97-1720, slip op. at 9 (D.D.C. Sept. 25, 2000) (concluding that documents generated during an investigation conducted under the "authority of Peruvian laws and under the authority granted to the DEA under the Controlled Substance Act to pursue the agency's law enforcement obligations under both United States statutes and international agreements . . . were compiled for law enforcement purposes"); Schwarz v. U.S. Dep't of Justice, No. 95-2162, slip op. at 6 (D.D.C. May 31, 1996) (stating that information compiled by INTERPOL at behest of foreign government meets requirement), summary affirmance
(continued...)

trative, civil, or criminal enforcement.[56] However, if the agency lacks the authority to pursue a particular law enforcement matter, Exemption 7 protection may not be afforded in certain instances,[57] but may nevertheless

---

[55](...continued)
granted, No. 96-5183 (D.C. Cir. Oct. 23, 1996); Donovan v. FBI, 579 F. Supp. 1111, 1119-20 (S.D.N.Y. 1983) (stating that an FBI investigation undertaken and laboratory tests performed in support of a foreign government's efforts to identify and prosecute perpetrators of crimes satisfy threshold, and reasoning that "refusing to apply Exemption 7 to foreign law enforcement might have the practical effect of interfering with cooperation and information sharing"), vacated on other grounds on motion for reconsideration, 579 F. Supp. 1124 (S.D.N.Y.), appeal dismissed as moot, 751 F.2d 368 (2d Cir. 1984); see also FOIA Update, Vol. V, No. 2, at 6-7 (reasoning that records compiled for "nonfederal" investigations satisfy threshold, because "Exemption 7's threshold requirement . . . makes no reference to federal investigations, nor can any such limitation logically be inferred").

[56] See, e.g., Ponder, No. 98-3097, slip op. at 5 (D.D.C. Jan. 22, 2001) (ruling that records were compiled for law enforcement purpose despite fact that subject was never prosecuted); Goldstein v. Office of Indep. Counsel, No. 87-2028, 1999 WL 570862, at *8-9 (D.D.C. July 29, 1999) (magistrate's recommendation) (determining that investigation of perennial presidential candidate Lyndon LaRouche for possible criminal violations was for legitimate law enforcement purpose even if that investigation "went nowhere"); cf. Wolk v. United States, No. 04-CV-832, 2005 WL 465382, at *4 (E.D. Pa. Feb. 28, 2005) (stating that "[w]e construe the term 'enforcement' to encompass the conducting of a security background check of a federal judicial nominee" even when the process reveals no improprieties, because "[i]t is impossible, ex ante, to determine whether an FBI investigation will reveal troubling information about a specific nominee").

[57] See, e.g., Rosenfeld, 57 F.3d at 808-09 (finding no law enforcement purpose when "documents all support a conclusion that . . . any asserted purpose for compiling these documents was pretextual"); Weissman v. CIA, 565 F.2d 692, 696 (D.C. Cir. 1977) (ruling that the CIA's "full background check within the United States of a citizen who never had any relationship with the CIA is not authorized and the law enforcement exemption is accordingly unavailable"); Taylor v. U.S. Dep't of Justice, 257 F. Supp. 2d 101, 108 (D.D.C. 2003) (stating that investigations must be "'within the agency's law enforcement authority'" (quoting Whittle v. Moschella, 756 F. Supp. 589, 593 (D.D.C. 1991))), reconsideration denied, 268 F. Supp. 2d 34 (D.D.C. 2003), appeal dismissed for failure to prosecute, No. 03-5111, 2003 WL 2205968 (D.C. Cir. Aug. 19, 2003); Enviro Tech Int'l v. EPA, No. 02 C 4650, 2003 U.S. Dist. LEXIS 25493, at *22 (N.D. Ill. Mar. 11, 2003) (describing Exemption 7 as having "hook" that can in some cases restrict its use to "only those documents relating to specifically authorized agency activities"), aff'd, 371 F.3d 370 (7th Cir. 2004) (distinguishing again important differences between "ultra vires" for Exemption 5 and for Exemption 7); (continued...)

still be afforded in other situations.[58]

Additionally, "[b]ackground security investigations by governmental units which have authority to conduct such functions"[59] have been held by most courts to meet the threshold tests under the succeeding formulations of Exemption 7.[60] And further, personnel investigations of government em-

---

[57](...continued)
Miscavige v. IRS, No. 91-3721, slip op. at 2, 5 (C.D. Cal. Dec. 9, 1992) (finding no law enforcement purpose for post-1986 documents because IRS investigation concluded in 1985); cf. Kuzma v. IRS, 775 F.2d 66, 69 (2d Cir. 1985) (declaring that unauthorized or illegal investigative tactics may not be shielded from public by use of FOIA exemptions).

[58] Pratt, 673 F.2d at 422-23 (explaining that "Exemption 7 refers to purposes rather than methods" and that "[w]hile many of the FBI's goals and methods in its COINTELPRO activities against the [Black Panther Party] give us serious pause," such as the goal to prevent "militant black nationalist groups and leaders from gaining respectability by discrediting them," these questionable methods do not defeat the exemption's coverage when law enforcement is the primary purpose because, "[f]rom the record before us, we cannot conclude that [the FBI's concern about violence] was implausible or irrational"); Hrones v. CIA, 685 F.2d 13, 19 (1st Cir. 1982) (legality of agency's actions in national security investigation falls outside scope of judicial review in FOIA action); Dean v. FDIC, 389 F. Supp. 2d 780, 790 (E.D. Ky. 2005) (finding that "a 13-month, overzealous investigation" into a possible conflict of interest that "negatively impacted" an employee's career, yet concluded that no wrongdoing had occurred, was authorized because the Office of Inspector General (OIG) "has the authority and responsibility to investigate even potential criminal violations relating to FDIC programs" and that the "overboard" response by the OIG "does not require the conclusion that the investigation was undertaken in bad faith"); Peltier v. FBI, No. 03-CV-905S, 2005 WL 735964, at *14 (W.D.N.Y. Mar. 31, 2005) (stating that "the rule in this Circuit is that the Government need only show that the records were compiled by a law enforcement agency in the course of a criminal investigation [because t]he legitimacy of the investigation is immaterial"); cf. Mettetal v. U.S. Dep't of Justice, No. 2:04-410, 2006 U.S. Dist. LEXIS 64157, at *11 (E.D. Tenn. Sept. 7, 2006) (explaining that the "Sixth Circuit has adopted a per se rule under which any document compiled by a law enforcement agency" is compiled for a law enforcement purpose) (emphasis added).

[59] S. Conf. Rep. No. 93-1200, at 12 (1974), reprinted in 1974 U.S.C.C.A.N. 6267, 6291.

[60] See, e.g., Mittleman v. OPM, 76 F.3d 1240, 1241-43 (D.C. Cir. 1996) (OPM background investigation); Rosenfeld, 57 F.3d at 809 ("FBI government appointment investigations"); Wolk, 2005 WL 465382, at *4 (concluding that "enforcement" encompasses conducting a "security background (continued...)

ployees also are compiled for law enforcement purposes if they focus on "specific and potentially unlawful activity by particular employees" of a civil or criminal nature.[61]

---

[60](...continued)
check" by reasoning that "'enforcement of the law fairly includes not merely the detection and punishment of violations of law but their prevention'" (quoting Miller v. United States, 630 F. Supp. 347, 349 (E.D.N.Y. 1986)); Pontecorvo v. FBI, No. 00-1511, slip op. at 37-38 (D.D.C. Sept. 30, 2001) (background investigation of potential employee); Melius v. Nat'l Indian Gaming Comm'n, No. 92-2210, 1999 U.S. Dist. LEXIS 17537, at *6, *15 (D.D.C. Nov. 3, 1999) ("suitability investigations" for gaming contracts); Assassination Archives, 903 F. Supp. at 132 (FBI "background investigations"); Bostic v. FBI, No. 1:94 CV 71, slip op. at 2, 11 (W.D. Mich. Dec. 16, 1994) (FBI pre-employment investigation); Doe v. U.S. Dep't of Justice, 790 F. Supp. 17, 20-21 (D.D.C. 1992) (background investigation of individual conditionally offered employment as attorney); Miller, 630 F. Supp. at 349 (USIA background-security investigation of federal job applicant); Koch v. Dep't of Justice, 376 F. Supp. 313, 315 (D.D.C. 1974) (background investigations fall within Exemption 7 because they involve determinations as to whether applicants engaged in criminal conduct that would disqualify them for federal employment); see also FOIA Update, Vol. VI, No. 4, at 6.

[61] Stern v. FBI, 737 F.2d 84, 89 (D.C. Cir. 1984); see Perlman v. U.S. Dep't of Justice, 312 F.3d 100, 103, 105 (2d Cir. 2002) (discussing allegations of preferential treatment and undue access and influence in INS Investor Visa Program by former INS general counsel, and finding that records compiled during investigation into allegations satisfy Exemption 7's threshold, because such acts could subject him to criminal or civil penalties), aff'd, 380 F.3d 110 (2d Cir. 2004); Kimberlin v. Dep't of Justice, 139 F.3d 944, 947-48 (D.C. Cir. 1998) (concluding that an investigation "conducted in response to and focused upon a specific, potentially illegal release of information by a particular, identified official" satisfies the threshold); Strang v. Arms Control & Disarmament Agency, 864 F.2d 859, 862 (D.C. Cir. 1989) (characterizing agency investigation into employee violation of national security laws as law enforcement); O'Keefe v. DOD, 463 F. Supp. 2d 317, 320, 324 (E.D.N.Y. 2006) (finding that report detailing investigation of complaint alleging misconduct by commanding officers on multiple occasions was compiled for law enforcement purposes); Lewis v. United States, No. 02-3249, slip op. at 1, 6 (C.D. Cal. June 2, 2003) (finding that investigation of alleged unauthorized collection action by IRS employees was for law enforcement purposes); Mueller v. Dep't of the Air Force, 63 F. Supp. 2d 738, 742 (E.D. Va. 1999) (holding that the investigation into prosecutorial misconduct was for law enforcement purposes because "'an agency investigation of its own employees is for law enforcement purposes . . . if it focuses directly on specifically alleged illegal acts, illegal acts of a particular identified official, acts which could, if proved, result in civil or criminal sanctions'" (quoting Stern, 737 F.2d at 89)); Hayes v. U.S. Dep't of Labor, No. 96-1149, 1998 U.S. Dist. LEXIS 14120, at *11-12 (S.D. Ala. June 10, 1998) (ex-
(continued...)

Indeed, in Jefferson v. Department of Justice, the D.C. Circuit Court, in clarifying the mixed-function nature of the Department of Justice's Office of Professional Responsibility (OPR), stated that "OPR conducts both law enforcement and non-law enforcement activities," and it elaborated at length on the difference between the two types of files that "government agencies compile: (1) files in connection with government oversight of the performance of duties by its employees, and (2) files in connection with investigations that focus directly on specific alleged illegal acts which could result in civil or criminal sanction."[62] The D.C. Circuit declined to find that all OPR records were compiled for law enforcement purposes, particularly because the "Department's regulations describe OPR as a mixed-function agency with responsibilities that embrace not only investigations of violations of law and breaches of professional standards that may result in civil liability . . . but breaches of internal Department guidelines that may lead to disciplinary proceedings . . . of such non-law violations."[63] Thus, courts

---

[61](...continued)
plaining that records of "internal agency investigations are considered to be compiled for 'law enforcement purposes' when the investigations focus on specifically alleged acts, which, if proved, could amount to violations of civil or criminal law"), adopted (S.D. Ala. Aug. 10, 1998); Lurie v. Dep't of the Army, 970 F. Supp. 19, 36 (D.D.C. 1997) (explaining that threshold met because investigation focused directly on specifically alleged illegal acts of identified officials (citing Rural Hous., 498 F.2d at 81)), appeal dismissed voluntarily, No. 97-5248 (D.C. Cir. Oct. 22, 1997); Linn v. U.S. Dep't of Justice, No. 92-1406, 1995 WL 631847, at *22 (D.D.C. Aug. 22, 1995) ("[D]ocuments compiled for purposes of internal discipline of employees are not compiled for law enforcement purposes . . . [b]ut such internal monitoring of employees may be 'for law enforcement purposes' if the focus of the investigation concerns acts that could result in civil or criminal sanctions." (quoting Stern, 737 F.2d at 89)), appeal dismissed voluntarily, No. 97-5122 (D.C. Cir. July 14, 1997); Housley v. U.S. Dep't of the Treasury, 697 F. Supp. 3, 5 (D.D.C. 1988) (reiterating that investigation concerning misconduct by special agent which, if proved, could have resulted in federal civil or criminal sanctions qualifies as law enforcement); cf. Favish, 541 U.S. at 175 (recognizing realistically that "[a]llegations of government misconduct are 'easy to allege and hard to disprove'" (quoting Crawford-El v. Britton, 523 U.S. 574, 585 (1998))); In re Dep't of Investigation of N.Y., 856 F.2d 481, 485 (2d Cir. 1988) (explaining that the law enforcement privilege applies in the discovery context when the investigation served the "dual purposes of evaluating conduct in office and enforcing the criminal law") (non-FOIA case).

[62] Jefferson, 284 F.3d at 176-77 (citing Rural Hous., 498 F.2d at 81).

[63] Id. at 179; see also Sakamoto v. EPA, 443 F. Supp. 2d 1182, 1194 (N.D. Cal. 2006) (discussing difference between supervision and law enforcement by explaining that "'[i]f the investigation is for a possible violation of law, then the inquiry is for law enforcement purposes, as distinct from cus-
(continued...)

continue to distinguish between mere supervision of federal employees for performance of their assigned duties, on one hand, and investigations of federal employees for law enforcement purposes, on the other -- finding repeatedly that "an agency's general monitoring of its own employees to ensure compliance with the agency's statutory mandate and regulations" does not satisfy Exemption 7's threshold requirement.[64]

---

[63](...continued)
tomary surveillance of the performance of duties by government employees'" (quoting Jefferson, 284 F.3d at 177)).

[64] Stern, 737 F.2d at 89 (dictum) (reminding that "it is necessary to distinguish between those investigations conducted 'for a law enforcement purpose' and those in which an agency, acting as the employer, simply supervises its own employees"); see also Jefferson, 284 F.3d at 177-78 (ruling that agencies must distinguish between records based on "allegations that could lead to civil or criminal sanctions" and records "maintained in the course of general oversight of government employees"); Patterson v. IRS, 56 F.3d 832, 837-38 (7th Cir. 1995) (holding that the "general citation to an entire body of statutes contained in the United States Code under the heading 'Equal Employment Opportunity statutes'" does not establish a law enforcement purpose, and declaring that the agency must "'distinguish between internal investigations conducted for law enforcement purposes and general agency monitoring'" (quoting Stern, 727 F.2d at 89)); Rural Hous., 498 F.2d at 81 (distinguishing between agency oversight of performance of employees and investigations focusing on specific illegal acts of employees); Wood v. FBI, 312 F. Supp. 2d 328, 345 (D. Conn. 2004) (reiterating that "'an investigation conducted by a federal agency for the purpose of determining whether to discipline employees for activity which does not constitute a violation of law is not for law enforcement purposes under Exemption 7'" (quoting Stern, 737 F.2d at 90)), aff'd in part & rev'd in part on other grounds, 432 F.3d 78 (2d Cir. 2005); Jefferson v. U.S. Dep't of Justice, No. 01-1418, slip op. at 16 (D.D.C. Mar. 31, 2003) (finding that Office of Inspector General records concerning particular federal employee were not oversight records of internal agency monitoring, because they were compiled during investigation into her failure to comply with court order), aff'd, 168 F. App'x 448 (D.C. Cir. 2005); Varville v. Rubin, No. 3:96CV00629, 1998 WL 681438, at *14 (D. Conn. Aug. 18, 1998) (explaining that the threshold was not met by a report discussing possible ethical violations and prohibited personnel practices because the inquiry "more closely resembles an employer supervising its employees than an investigation for law enforcement purposes"); Lurie, 970 F. Supp. at 36 ("The general internal monitoring by an agency of its own employees is not shielded from public scrutiny under Exemption 7, because 'protection of all such internal monitoring under Exemption 7 would devastate FOIA.'" (quoting Stern, 737 F.2d at 89)); Fine v. U.S. Dep't of Energy, 823 F. Supp. 888, 907-08 (D.N.M. 1993) (ruling that threshold met by agency with both administrative and law enforcement functions when documents were compiled during investigation of specific allegations and not as part of routine oversight); Cotton v. Adams, 798 F.

(continued...)

Thus, while the line between mere employee monitoring and an investigation of an employee that satisfies the threshold requirement of Exemption 7 is narrow, the following examples satisfying the threshold shed useful light on this distinction:

(1) an investigation of an employee's allegations of misconduct and gross incompetence;[65]

(2) an investigation triggered by a complaint letter alleging that particular government prosecutors had withheld certain information during

---

[64](...continued)
Supp. 22, 25 (D.D.C. 1992) (holding that agency's internal investigation of its own employees satisfies threshold only if it focuses directly on illegal acts that could result in criminal or civil sanctions; Greenpeace USA, Inc. v. EPA, 735 F. Supp. 13, 15 (D.D.C. 1990) (threshold was not met by internal investigation into whether employee complied with agency conflict-of-interest regulations). But cf. Nagel v. HEW, 725 F.2d 1438, 1441 (D.C. Cir. 1984) (holding that the "employer's determination whether a federal employee is performing his job adequately constitutes an authorized law enforcement activity" within the meaning of subsection (e)(7) of the Privacy Act of 1974, 5 U.S.C. § 552a (2000 & Supp. IV 2004)).

[65] Edmonds v. FBI, 272 F. Supp. 2d 35, 42, 54 (D.D.C. 2003); see also Jefferson v. Dep't of Justice, No. 04-5226, 2005 U.S. App. LEXIS 23360, at *2 (D.C. Cir. Oct. 26, 2005) (affirming district court's ruling that law enforcement threshold is met by investigation concerning Department of Justice attorney accused of official misconduct); Trentadue v. Integrity Comm., No. 2:03-339, 2006 WL 1184636, at *5 (D. Utah May 2, 2006) (finding threshold met by documents prepared in course of investigation of allegations against federal employee); Pagan v. Treasury Inspector Gen. for Tax Admin., No. 04-4179, slip op. at 6 (E.D.N.Y. Jan. 31, 2006) (finding that documents created as result of specific allegations of misuse of government equipment and of conducting personal business while on official duty qualify as law enforcement documents); MacLean v. DOD, No. 04-2425, slip op. at 14 (S.D. Cal. June 2, 2005) (finding that documents created in response to allegations of professional misconduct against prosecutor satisfy law enforcement threshold); Judicial Watch v. U.S. Dep't of Commerce, 337 F. Supp. 2d 146, 179 (D.D.C. 2004) (finding that investigations of certain agency personnel for possible violations of campaign finance laws and trade mission improprieties qualify as law enforcement); cf. Herrick's Newsletter, 2006 U.S. Dist. LEXIS 44802, at *1, *20-21 (explaining that "if the personnel oversight and investigation procedures concern misconduct that violates the law, then the information may be deemed to meet the threshold requirement of Exemption 7"); Dohse v. Potter, No. 8:04CV355, 2006 WL 398653, at *1, *7 (D. Neb. Feb. 15, 2006) (ruling that investigation by Postal Service of independent contractor for "interpersonal conflicts," including "alleged threats to postal personnel," satisfies law enforcement threshold).

litigation;[66]

(3) an investigation of a particular Assistant United States Attorney for disclosing confidential information about the alleged use of cocaine by a suspect;[67] and

(4) an investigation triggered by an allegation of racial harassment.[68]

On the other hand, examples of matters that do not satisfy the threshold are:

(1) an investigation into whether an employee who spoke at a meeting sponsored by a regulated company violated agency regulations when the case focused on "whether an agency employee has complied with agency regulations";[69]

(2) records concerning an employee who had been disciplined because the agency was participating "as an employer" and not as an "agency enforcing the revenue laws";[70] and

---

[66] Ligorner v. Reno, 2 F. Supp. 2d 400, 402-03 (S.D.N.Y. 1998).

[67] Kimberlin, 139 F.3d at 946-47.

[68] Ford v. West, No. 97-1342, 1998 WL 317561, at *1-2 (10th Cir. June 12, 1998); see also Martinez v. EEOC, No. 04-CA-0271, 2005 U.S. Dist. LEXIS 3864, at *2, *11 (W.D. Tex. Mar. 3, 2005) (finding that information compiled in relation to charges of "a racially hostile work environment" meets the law enforcement threshold); cf. Sakamoto, 443 F. Supp. 2d at 1194 (discussing files "compiled by the EPA as part of the internal investigatory or adjudicatory proceedings associated with the EEOC process for complaints of discrimination in accordance with Title VII of the Civil Rights Act," and concluding that the agency "has met its burden" to show that the records were compiled for law enforcement purposes); Sinsheimer, 437 F. Supp 2d at 52, 55 (declaring that investigations into allegations of sexual misconduct in the workplace meet the law enforcement threshold, even when the charges were dropped, because "the investigations were carried out to enforce federal civil rights laws"); Watkins, 2006 WL 905518, at *1-3 (reasoning that records compiled during an investigation into an allegation of employment discrimination -- based on a company's denial of employment to a person convicted of aggravated sexual abuse -- "were compiled for a law enforcement purpose," because the EEOC investigated "a charge that [the company] violated federal law by discriminating"); Martinez, 2004 WL 2359895, at *2 (stating that "investigation into charges of discrimination" met law enforcement threshold).

[69] Greenpeace, 735 F. Supp. at 14-15.

[70] Patterson, 56 F.3d at 837.

(3) an investigation conducted by an Office of Inspector General that the agency merely asserted "must" have been for law enforcement purposes even though the Inspector General "also investigates internal matters concerning agency inefficiency and mismanagement."[71]

The common thread running through all these cases is the one first established in Rural Housing and then reiterated in Stern: It is imperative that an agency articulate the purpose of its actions and, as necessary, "distinguish [between] two types of files relating to government employees."[72] Most especially, as noted above, entities such as an Office of Inspector General and the Department of Justice's Office of Professional Responsibility need to take particular care in describing the different types of personnel investigations that they conduct, because such entities routinely conduct both law enforcement and non-law enforcement investigations of agency employees.[73]

---

[71] Cotton, 798 F. Supp. at 25; see also Jefferson, 284 F.3d at 178-79 (stating that oversight of performance, including review of violations of agency rules, does not qualify as "law enforcement" within meaning of Exemption 7); Wood, 312 F. Supp. 2d at 346 (finding that employee conduct at issue involved only "violations of agency policy" and thus did not satisfy threshold).

[72] Rural Hous., 498 F.2d at 82 (stating that the "purpose of the 'investigatory files' is thus the critical factor," and reiterating that an agency must distinguish between its "surveillance of the performance of duties by government employees [and its] inquiry as to an identifiable possible violation of law"); Stern, 737 F.2d at 89 (emphasizing that an agency's "general internal monitoring of its own employees to insure compliance with the agency's statutory mandate and regulations is not protected from public scrutiny under Exemption 7 . . . [and that] an agency's investigation of its own employees is for 'law enforcement purposes' only if it focuses 'directly on specifically alleged illegal acts, illegal acts of particular identified officials, acts which could, if proved, result in civil or criminal sanctions'" (quoting Rural Hous., 498 F.2d at 81)).

[73] See, e.g., Jefferson, 284 F.3d at 176 (finding, based upon then-existing regulations, that Department of Justice's Office of Professional Responsibility conducts "both law enforcement and non-law enforcement activities"); Cotton, 798 F. Supp. at 25 (stating that while "the [Office of] Inspector General has the ability to conduct investigations," it also looks into "internal matters concerning agency inefficiency and mismanagement," so its documents "could merely" pertain to an alleged violation of the agency's own rules); Greenpeace, 735 F. Supp. at 15 (finding that documents at issue concerned mere compliance with agency regulations). But see Dean, 389 F. Supp. 2d at 785, 790 (finding that an inquiry into whether an agency employee, who "as a private citizen" violated any ethical standards by developing certain software concepts, satisfied the law enforcement threshold, and explaining that "the Court is of the opinion that the OIG has the authority and responsibility to investigate even potential criminal violations").

Similarly, determining whether a record concerning matters other than an agency's own activities and personnel was "compiled for law enforcement purposes" under Exemption 7, the courts have generally distinguished between agencies with both law enforcement and administrative functions and those whose principal function is criminal law enforcement.[74] An agency whose functions are "mixed" usually has to show that the records at issue involved the enforcement of a statute or regulation within its authority.[75] Courts have additionally required that the records be compiled

---

[74] See Attorney General's 1986 Amendments Memorandum at 7; see also Sciba v. Bd. of Governors of the Fed. Reserve Sys., No. 04-1011, 2005 WL 3201206, at *7 (D.D.C. Nov. 4, 2005) (finding that Board is law enforcement agency, because it has responsibility not only to monitor for compliance but also to detect and prosecute crimes and violations of federal statutes within its sphere, including Bank Secrecy Act); Moye, O'Brien, O'Rourke, Hogan & Pickert v. Nat'l R.R. Passenger Corp., No. 6:02-CV-126, 2003 WL 21146674, at *17 (M.D. Fla. May 13, 2003) (reiterating that an agency "with mixed law enforcement and non-law enforcement functions requires the Court to consider the purpose of the investigation and to determine whether the information was gathered as part of an inquiry about a potential violation of the law, rather than in the course of the agency's administrative function of overseeing compliance with its rules and regulations"), remanded on other grounds, 376 F.3d 1270 (11th Cir. 2004), cert. denied, 543 U.S. 1121 (2005); cf. Mayer, Brown, Rowe & Maw v. IRS, No. 04-2187, 2006 U.S. Dist. LEXIS 58410, at *23 (D.D.C. Aug. 21, 2006) (saying that IRS "combines administrative and law enforcement functions").

[75] See Lewis v. IRS, 823 F.2d 375, 379 (9th Cir. 1987) (holding the threshold met when the IRS "had a purpose falling within its sphere of enforcement authority in compiling particular documents"); Birch v. USPS, 803 F.2d 1206, 1210-11 (D.C. Cir. 1986) (explaining that threshold was met because enforcement of laws regarding use of mails falls within statutory authority of Postal Service); Church of Scientology v. U.S. Dep't of the Army, 611 F.2d 738, 748 (9th Cir. 1979) (remanding to Naval Investigative Service for it to show that investigation involved enforcement of statute or regulation within its authority); Irons v. Bell, 596 F.2d 468, 473 (1st Cir. 1979) (determining that mixed-function agency must demonstrate purpose falling within its sphere of enforcement authority); Sutton v. IRS, No. 05-7177, 2007 WL 30547, at *5 (N.D. Ill. Jan. 4, 2007) (stating that "whenever the IRS is enforcing the revenue laws, it is completely obvious that it is proceeding with an enforcement purpose" and adding that here, IRS investigated violations of Internal Revenue Code regarding alimony deduction); see also Cooper Cameron Corp. v. Dep't of Labor, 280 F.3d 539, 545 (5th Cir. 2002) (observing that "Congress obviously intended OSHA inspections to be part of an enforcement program," particularly when the agency is responding to a workplace accident); Coulter v. Reno, No. 98-35170, 1998 WL 658835, at *1 (9th Cir. Sept. 17, 1998) (holding threshold met by records of Navy criminal investigation into allegations of lewd and lascivious conduct by Navy personnel); Church of Scientology Int'l v. IRS, 995 F.2d 916, 919 (9th Cir. 1993) (continued...)

for "adjudicative or enforcement purposes."[76]

---

[75](...continued)
("This court has clearly held that the IRS has the 'requisite law enforcement mandate'" through its enforcement provisions of the federal tax code (quoting Lewis, 823 F.2d at 379)); Faiella, 2006 WL 2040130, at *1, *4 (noting that civil audit qualifies as law enforcement activity through IRS's enforcement provisions); Martinez, 2005 U.S. Dist. LEXIS 3864, at *8, *11 (explaining that the "EEOC bears burden of showing that it compiled records for a law enforcement purpose and establishing its entitlement to the exemption"); Carp v. IRS, No. 00-5992, 2002 WL 373448, at *4-5 (D.N.J. Jan. 28, 2002) (determining that IRS investigation targeting individual for possible violation of federal tax law satisfies threshold); Wayne's Mech. & Maint. Contractor, Inc. v. Dep't of Labor, No. 1:00-45, slip op. at 7 n.2 (N.D. Ga. May 7, 2001) (concluding that records compiled by OSHA during investigation of industrial accident were within agency's statutory law enforcement mandate); Phila. Newspapers, Inc. v. HHS, 69 F. Supp. 2d 63, 67 (D.D.C. 1999) (holding that investigative records created in response to specific allegations of Medicare fraud by physicians at a teaching hospital were compiled for law enforcement purposes).

[76] Rural Hous., 498 F.2d at 81; see Pac. Energy Inst. v. IRS, No. 94-36172, 1996 WL 14244, at *1 (9th Cir. Jan. 16, 1996) (accepting that investigations involving enforcement of Internal Revenue Code satisfy threshold); Becker v. IRS, 34 F.3d 398, 407 (7th Cir. 1994) (holding that IRS has "law enforcement purpose in investigating potential illegal tax protester activity"); Church of Scientology, 995 F.2d at 919 (finding that IRS Exempt Organizations Division "performs law enforcement function by enforcing provisions of the federal tax code"); Citizens for Responsibility & Ethics in Wash. v. Nat'l Indian Gaming Comm'n, No. 05-0806, 2006 U.S. Dist. LEXIS 89614, at *21-22 (D.D.C. Dec. 12, 2006) (holding that National Indian Gaming Commission's investigation into alleged misuse of tribal gaming revenues satisfied Exemption 7 threshold); Odle v. Dep't of Justice, No. 05-2771, 2006 WL 1344813, at *5-6 (N.D. Cal. May 17, 2006) (explaining that the Department of Justice's Office of Professional Responsibility is a mixed-function agency and thus has "the burden of demonstrating the records in question were compiled 'for adjudicative or enforcement purposes'"; finding that records compiled for an investigation into "misrepresentation to the court, violation of a court order, misrepresentation to defense counsel, subornation of perjury, and failure to correct false testimony" meet the threshold (quoting Church of Scientology, 611 F.2d at 748)); Suzhou Yuanda Enter. Co. v. U.S. Customs & Border Prot., 404 F. Supp. 2d 9, 14 (D.D.C. 2005) (finding law enforcement threshold met by investigation into suspected scheme to import merchandise, because agency is charged with enforcing federal laws regarding proper importation of merchandise); Millhouse v. IRS, No. 03-1418, 2005 U.S. Dist LEXIS 1290, at *6-7 (D.D.C. Jan. 3, 2005) (holding that records compiled during IRS investigation of "money laundering and narcotics trafficking activities" were compiled for law enforcement purposes); Means v. Segal, No. 97-1301, slip op. at 12 (D.D.C. Mar. 18, 1998) (magis-
(continued...)

However, in two relatively recent cases involving agencies with "mixed" functions, courts have applied the phrase "law enforcement purpose" quite broadly.[77] In Living Rivers, Inc. v. United States Bureau of Reclamation, the court explained that before it could determine if "dam inundation" maps created by the Department of the Interior's Bureau of Reclamation (BOR) were withheld properly pursuant to either Exemption 7(E) or Exemption 7(F), it first had to determine whether Exemption 7's threshold requirement was met.[78] Reiterating the differences between "per se" law enforcement agencies and those with both administrative and law enforcement functions, the court pragmatically acknowledged that "Congress has provided the BOR with express 'law enforcement authority' to 'maintain law and order and protect persons and property within Reclamation projects and on Reclamation lands.'"[79] After endorsing this express grant of law enforcement authority, the court next addressed the "compilation" aspect of the threshold requirement, finding that the "context in which an agency has currently compiled a document, rather than the purpose for which the document was originally created, determines whether it is 'compiled for law enforcement purposes.'"[80] Based upon this pragmatic, post-9/11 analysis, the court ruled that "the inundation maps are presently used and were compiled in direct relation to the BOR's statutory law enforcement mandate. The BOR therefore satisfies the first prong of Exemption 7."[81]

Similarly, in Coastal Delivery v. United States Customs Service, the court recognized readily that "Customs has a law enforcement mandate" regarding the "number of examinations it performed on merchandise arriv-

---

[76](...continued)
trate's recommendation) (holding that Federal Labor Relations Authority is charged with statutory responsibility to conduct investigations related to unfair labor practices and records related to this duty meet threshold), adopted (D.D.C. Apr. 15, 1998), aff'd on other grounds, No. 98-5170 (D.C. Cir. Oct. 6, 1998); cf. Reed v. NLRB, 927 F.2d 1249, 1252 (D.C. Cir. 1991) (noting "skepticism" of government's alternative argument regarding application of Exemption 7(C)'s threshold to lists of names and addresses of eligible voters in union representative election compiled for NLRB compliance purposes).

[77] Living Rivers, 272 F. Supp. 2d at 1318-20; Coastal Delivery, 272 F. Supp. 2d at 963.

[78] 272 F. Supp. 2d at 1318.

[79] Id. at 1318-19 (quoting "General Authority of Secretary of the Interior," 43 U.S.C.A. § 373b(a) (2000 & Supp. III 2003), pertaining to law enforcement authority granted to Bureau of Reclamation, specifically regarding public safety).

[80] Id. at 1319-20.

[81] Id. (quoting John Doe Agency, 493 U.S. at 153-54).

ing into the Los Angeles/Long Beach seaport."[82]  Accordingly, it found a sufficient Exemption 7 nexus, in support of both Exemption 2 and Exemption 7(E) protection, because the agency's cargo container inspection numbers "allow Customs to track the overall effectiveness of its examination technique, and evaluate both its commercial enforcement strategy and its border security responsibilities."[83]

In the case of criminal law enforcement agencies, the courts have accorded the government varying degrees of special deference when considering whether their particular records meet the threshold requirement of Exemption 7.[84]  Indeed, the First, Second, Sixth, Eighth, and Eleventh Circuit Courts of Appeals have adopted a per se rule that qualifies all "investigative" records of criminal law enforcement agencies for protection under Exemption 7.[85]  Other courts, while according significant deference to

---

[82] 272 F. Supp. 2d at 963; see also Favish, 541 U.S. at 164 (stating succinctly that "[i]t is common ground among the parties that the death-scene photographs in OIC's possession are 'records or information compiled for law enforcement purposes' as that phrase is used in Exemption 7C"); Suzhou, 404 F. Supp. 2d at 14 (declaring that "Customs is a law enforcement agency charged with enforcing federal law regarding the proper entry of merchandise into the United States" and that the agency "properly applied Exemption 7"); cf. Ctr. for Nat'l Sec. Studies, 331 F.3d at 926 (recognizing that the "terrorism investigation [into the events of September 11, 2001] is one of DOJ's chief 'law enforcement duties' at this time," and thereby pragmatically merging national security and homeland security concerns into "law enforcement purposes").

[83] 272 F. Supp at 963.

[84] Compare, e.g., Pratt, 673 F.2d at 418 (declaring that "a court can accept less exacting proof from [a law enforcement agency]"), with Kuehnert v. FBI, 620 F.2d 662, 667 (8th Cir. 1980) (holding that "Exemption 7 extends to all investigative files of a criminal law enforcement agency").

[85] See First Circuit:  Curran v. Dep't of Justice, 813 F.2d 473, 475 (1st Cir. 1987) (holding that investigatory records of law enforcement agencies are "inherently" compiled for law enforcement purposes); Irons, 596 F.2d at 474-76 (holding that "investigatory records of law enforcement agencies are inherently records compiled for 'law enforcement purposes' within the meaning of Exemption 7"); Second Circuit:  Halpern v. FBI, 181 F.3d 279, 296 (2d Cir. 1999) (applying rule that when records are compiled in course of law enforcement investigation, purpose of investigation is not subject of review by court); Ferguson v. FBI, 957 F.2d 1059, 1070 (2d Cir. 1992) (finding that there is "no room for [a] district court's inquiry into whether the FBI's asserted law enforcement purpose was legitimate"); Williams v. FBI, 730 F.2d 882, 884-85 (2d Cir. 1984) (ruling that records of a law enforcement agency are given "absolute protection" even if "records were compiled in the course of an unwise, meritless or even illegal investigation"); Peltier, 2005 WL

(continued...)

criminal law enforcement agencies, have held that an agency must demonstrate some specific nexus[86] between the records and a proper law en-

---

[85](...continued)
735964, at *14 (explaining that the "legitimacy of the investigation is immaterial [because] the rule in this Circuit is that the Government need only show that the records were compiled by a law enforcement agency in the course of a criminal investigation"); Sixth Circuit: Detroit Free Press, Inc. v. Dep't of Justice, 73 F.3d 93, 96 (6th Cir. 1996) (holding that "mug shots" are created for law enforcement purpose, and applying per se rule adopted previously in Jones v. FBI, 41 F.3d 238, 246 (6th Cir. 1994) (adopting a per se rule that the FBI is "archetypical" federal law enforcement agency and that "concern about overbroad withholding should therefore be addressed by proper scrutiny of the claimed exemptions themselves and not by use of a blunt instrument at the threshold")); Eighth Circuit: Miller v. USDA, 13 F.3d 260, 263 (8th Cir. 1993) (tardiness in working on case does not eliminate law enforcement purpose); Kuehnert, 620 F.2d at 666 (FBI need not show law enforcement purpose of particular investigation as precondition to invoking Exemption 7); Eleventh Circuit: Robinson v. Dep't of Justice, No. 00-11182, slip op. at 10 (11th Cir. Mar. 15, 2001) (holding that investigative records concerning search and seizure of drug-carrying vessel are "'inherently records compiled for law enforcement purposes'" (quoting Curran, 813 F.2d at 475)); Arenberg v. DEA, 849 F.2d 579, 581 (11th Cir. 1988) (suggesting that courts should be "hesitant" to reexamine law enforcement agency's decision to investigate if there is plausible basis for agency's decision); see also Binion v. U.S. Dep't of Justice, 695 F.2d 1189, 1193-94 (9th Cir. 1983) (holding that "a fortiori" approach is appropriate when FBI pardon investigation was "clearly legitimate").

[86] See, e.g., Davin v. U.S. Dep't of Justice, 60 F.3d 1043, 1056 (3d Cir. 1995) (applying "adaptation" of two-pronged rational nexus test and holding FBI's "simple recitation of statutes, orders and public laws" insufficient; agency must describe nexus between "each document" and particular investigation), on remand, No. 92-1122, slip op. at 11-13 (W.D. Pa. Apr. 9, 1998) (finding that government demonstrated connection between target and "potential violation of law or security risk" for each investigation), aff'd, 176 F.3d 471, 471 (3d Cir. 1999) (unpublished table decision); Van Mechelen, 2005 WL 3007121, at *4 (reiterating that the phrase "'law enforcement purpose'" applies to records "created in the course of an investigation 'related to the enforcement of federal laws . . . and that [the] nexus between [the] investigation and [the] agency's law enforcement duties [is] based on information sufficient to support at least a colorable claim of its rationality'" (quoting Pratt, 673 F.2d at 420-21)); Gordon, 388 F.2d at 1035 (finding that because "[t]he FBI 'has a clear law enforcement mandate, [it] need only establish a rational nexus between enforcement of federal law and the document for which [a law enforcement] exemption is claimed'" (quoting Rosenfeld, 57 F.3d at 808)); Wolk, 2005 WL 465382, at *3 (stating that "[t]he Third Circuit has adopted a rational nexus test" requiring the agency to "(1) detail the connection between the individual under investigation and a potential
(continued...)

forcement purpose.[87]

---

[86](...continued)
violation of law or security risk; and (2) show 'that this relationship is based upon information'" sufficient to support a colorable claim of rationality (quoting Davin, 60 F.3d at 1056)); Beneville v. U.S. Dep't of Justice, No. 98-6137, slip op. at 17 (D. Or. June 11, 2003) (declaring that the agency "has established that it is a law enforcement agency" and that it satisfied the threshold requirement by showing a "rational nexus between the enforcement of a federal law and the documents for which the exemption is claimed"); Kern v. FBI, No. 94-0208, slip op. at 9 (C.D. Cal. Sept. 14, 1998) (rejecting FBI's Vaughn Index as inadequate because it did not demonstrate nexus between duty to investigate espionage and documents sought); Franklin, No. 97-1225, slip op. at 7-8 (S.D. Fla. June 26, 1998) (reiterating the need for a "nexus between the records and the enforcement of federal or state law"); Grine v. Coombs, No. 95-342, 1997 U.S. Dist. LEXIS 19578, at *14-18 (W.D. Pa. Oct. 10, 1997) (holding that the "proper test is the 'rational nexus' test," and determining that investigatory reports triggered by complaints of dumping hazardous waste satisfy test), appeal dismissed for failure to prosecute, 98 F. App'x 178 (3d Cir. 2004); Crompton v. DEA, No. 95-8771, slip op. at 12-13 (C.D. Cal. Mar. 25, 1997) (stating that agencies with "clear law enforcement mandate such as the DEA need only establish a 'rational nexus' between enforcement of a federal law and the document for which a law enforcement exemption is claimed," and holding that there is a such nexus between DEA's "law enforcement duties to manage the national narcotics intelligence system" and information withheld). But see Poulsen v. Customs & Border Prot., No. 06-1743, 2006 WL 2788239, at *6 (N.D. Cal. Sept. 26, 2006) (explaining that while Customs "has a clear law enforcement mandate" and need only establish a "'rational nexus between enforcement of a federal law and the document for which an exemption is claimed,'" records that the agency generated in response to a computer virus "were not created as part of an investigation, or in connection with CBP's enforcement of a federal law" and thus did not satisfy the law enforcement threshold (quoting Church of Scientology, 611 F.2d at 748)).

[87] See, e.g., Marriott Employees' Fed. Credit Union v. Nat'l Credit Union Admin., No. 96-478-A, 1996 WL 33497625, at *4 (E.D. Va. Dec. 24, 1996) (finding that documents compiled by NCUA pursuant to administration of Federal Credit Union Act satisfy standard, because NCUA "is empowered" by Congress to enforce Act by conducting necessary "investigations and litigation"); Blanton v. U.S. Dep't of Justice, No. 93-2398, slip op. at 5-8 (W.D. Tenn. July 14, 1994) (finding that information concerning the validity of plaintiff's counsel's purported license to practice law does not meet the threshold because law licenses are matter of public record and that the government failed to prove that records were "compiled for a law enforcement purpose"); Rosenfeld v. U.S. Dep't of Justice, 761 F. Supp. 1440, 1445-48 (N.D. Cal. 1991) (explaining that FBI investigation of Free Speech Movement "was begun in good faith and with a plausible basis," but ceased to have "colorable claim [of rationality] as the evidence accumulated" and be-
(continued...)

The Supreme Court in 1990 resolved a conflict in lower court decisions[88] by decisively holding that information not initially obtained or generated for law enforcement purposes may still qualify under Exemption 7 if it is subsequently compiled for a valid law enforcement purpose at any time prior to "when the Government invokes the Exemption."[89] Rejecting

---

[87](...continued)
came "a case of routine monitoring . . . for intelligence purposes"; date at which FBI's initial law enforcement-related suspicions were "demonstrably unfounded" was "cut-off point for the scope of a law enforcement purpose" under Exemption 7), aff'd in pertinent part, rev'd in part & remanded, 57 F.3d 803 (9th Cir. 1995); Friedman v. FBI, 605 F. Supp. 306, 321 (N.D. Ga. 1984) (finding that the FBI was "'gathering information with the good faith belief that the subject may violate or has violated federal law' rather than 'merely monitoring the subject for purposes unrelated to enforcement of federal law'" (quoting Lamont v. Department of Justice, 475 F. Supp. 761, 770 (S.D.N.Y. 1979))).

[88] Compare Crowell & Moring v. DOD, 703 F. Supp. 1004, 1009-10 (D.D.C. 1989) (holding that solicitation and contract bids may be protected), and Gould Inc. v. GSA, 688 F. Supp. 688, 691 (D.D.C. 1988) (finding that routine audit reports may be protected), with John Doe Corp. v. John Doe Agency, 850 F.2d 105, 109 (2d Cir. 1988) (ruling that routine audit reports are not protectible), rev'd & remanded, 493 U.S. 146 (1989), and Hatcher v. USPS, 556 F. Supp. 331, 335 (D.D.C. 1982) (holding that routine contract negotiation and oversight material is not protectible).

[89] John Doe Agency, 493 U.S. at 153; see also KTVY-TV v. United States, 919 F.2d 1465, 1469 (10th Cir. 1990) (per curiam) (applying John Doe Agency to hold that information regarding personnel interview conducted before investigation commenced and later recompiled for law enforcement purposes satisfied Exemption 7 threshold); ACLU v. DOD, 389 F. Supp. 2d 547, 570 (S.D.N.Y.) (ruling that photographs taken for "personal use" were compiled for law enforcement purposes, because Army Criminal Investigation Command opened investigation immediately upon receipt of photographs and agents used them to conduct that investigation), reconsideration denied, 396 F. Supp. 2d 459 (S.D.N.Y. 2005); Kansi v. U.S. Dep't of Justice, 11 F. Supp. 2d 42, 44 (D.D.C. 1998) (explaining that once documents become assembled for law enforcement purposes, "all [such] documents qualify for protection under Exemption 7 regardless of their original source"); Hayes, 1998 U.S. Dist. LEXIS 14120, at *12 ("Records that are incorporated into investigatory files also qualify . . . even though those records may not have been created originally for law enforcement purposes."); Perdue Farms, Inc. v. NLRB, No. 2:96-27, 1997 U.S. Dist. LEXIS 14579, at *37 (E.D.N.C. Aug. 5, 1997) (magistrate's recommendation) (stating that the language of the statute "contains no requirement that the compilation be effected at a specific time" (citing John Doe Agency, 493 U.S. at 153)), adopted (E.D.N.C. Jan. 20, 1998); Butler v. Dep't of the Air Force, 888 F. Supp. 174, 179-80, 182 (D.D.C. 1995) (holding Air Force personnel background report -- requested by local (continued...)

the distinction between documents originally compiled or obtained for law enforcement purposes and those later assembled for such purposes, the Court held that the term "compiled" must be accorded its ordinary meaning -- which includes "materials collected and assembled from various sources or other documents" -- and it found that the plain meaning of the statute contains "no requirement that the compilation be effected at a specific time."[90]

The existing standard for review of criminal law enforcement records in the Court of Appeals for the District of Columbia Circuit is somewhat more stringent than the per se rule discussed above. The D.C. Circuit held in Pratt v. Webster that records generated as part of a counterintelligence program of questionable legality which was part of an otherwise clearly authorized law enforcement investigation met the threshold requirement for Exemption 7 and rejected the per se approach.[91] Instead, it adopted a two-part test for determining whether the threshold for Exemption 7 has been met: (1) whether the agency's investigatory activities that give rise to the documents sought are related to the enforcement of federal laws or to the maintenance of national security; and (2) whether the nexus between the investigation and one of the agency's law enforcement duties is based on information sufficient to support at least a colorable claim of rationality.[92]

---

[89](...continued)
law enforcement agency for its investigation into murder -- to be compiled for law enforcement purposes), aff'd per curiam, No. 96-5111 (D.C. Cir. May 6, 1997).

[90] John Doe Agency, 493 U.S. at 153.

[91] 673 F.2d at 416 n.17.

[92] Id. at 420-21; see, e.g., Campbell v. U.S. Dep't of Justice, 164 F.3d 20, 32 (D.C. Cir. 1998) (requiring nexus between agency activities and law enforcement duties, and finding that most FBI files of 1960s investigations of James Baldwin -- believed to be associated with subversive organizations -- meet threshold, but elaborating that law enforcement agency may not simply rely on file names to satisfy threshold); Summers v. U.S. Dep't of Justice, 140 F.3d 1077, 1083 (D.C. Cir. 1998) (to show nexus, FBI must link names redacted from former FBI Director J. Edgar Hoover's telephone logs to law enforcement activities); Quiñon v. FBI, 86 F.3d 1222, 1228-29 (D.C. Cir. 1996) (reiterating that agency's basis for connection between object of investigation and asserted law enforcement duty cannot be pretextual or wholly unbelievable and remanding because FBI's affidavits were insufficient to show that Pratt nexus test satisfied when only specific fact cited is filing of motion; "filing of a non-fraudulent pleading cannot, taken alone, form the basis for a legitimate obstruction of justice investigation"); Computer Prof'ls for Soc. Responsibility v. U.S. Secret Serv., 72 F.3d 897, 902, 904 (D.C. Cir. 1996) (investigation into allegations of telecommunications
(continued...)

Since the removal of the word "investigatory" from the threshold requirement of Exemption 7 in 1986, the D.C. Circuit has had few opportunities to reconsider the Pratt test, a portion of which expressly requires a nexus between requested records and an investigation.[93] In Keys v. United States Department of Justice, however, the D.C. Circuit modified the language of the Pratt test to reflect those amendments and to require that an agency demonstrate the existence of a nexus "between [its] activity" (rather than its investigation) "and its law enforcement duties."[94] Although not

---

[92](...continued)
fraud satisfies threshold, as do documents pertaining to police breakup of public meeting of computer hackers club); King v. U.S. Dep't of Justice, 830 F.2d 210, 229 (D.C. Cir. 1987) (supporting Pratt two-part test by stating that agency must identify particular individual/incident as object of its investigation and specify connection between individual/incident and possible security risk or violation of federal law and that agency must then demonstrate that relationship is based on information sufficient to support colorable claim of rationality); Founding Church of Scientology v. Smith, 721 F.2d 828, 829 n.1 (D.C. Cir. 1983) (holding that "Pratt is the law of this circuit insofar as it interprets the threshold requirement of exemption 7"); Wheeler v. U.S. Dep't of Justice, 403 F. Supp. 2d 1, 14 (D.D.C. 2005) (describing how the agency established a nexus when it "clearly identified the particular individual who was the object of its investigation" and stated that it was authorized to conduct investigation and that it "investigated him to see if he were acting on behalf of the Cuban government," thus providing "'information sufficient to support at least a colorable claim of its rationality'" (quoting Pratt, 673 F.2d at 420-21)); Judicial Watch, 337 F. Supp. 2d at 179 ("A 'law enforcement purpose' exists where there is a 'rational nexus' between the compiled document and a law enforcement duty of the agency and where there is 'a connection between an individual or incident and a possible security risk or violation of federal law.'" (quoting Ctr. for Nat'l Sec. Studies, 331 F.3d at 926)); Wichlacz v. U.S. Dep't of Interior, 938 F. Supp. 325, 330 (E.D. Va. 1996) (observing that "investigative activities giving rise to the compilation of the records must be related to the enforcement of federal law, and there must be a rational connection between the investigative activities and the agency's law enforcement duties"), aff'd, 114 F.3d 1178 (4th Cir. 1997) (unpublished table decision); Exner, 902 F. Supp. at 242-43 (finding that investigatory activities were based on legitimate concern that federal laws were being violated and that activities connected rationally to target); cf. CEI, 404 F. Supp. 2d at 178 (describing two-part nexus test and finding that "individuals' A-numbers and FBI numbers" maintained in agency database satisfy nexus requirement).

[93] See, e.g., King, 830 F.2d at 229 n.141 (dictum) (holding that the 1986 FOIA amendments did not "qualif[y] the authority of Pratt" test).

[94] 830 F.2d 337, 340 (D.C. Cir. 1987); see also Rochon v. Dep't of Justice, No. 88-5075, slip op. at 3 (D.C. Cir. Sept. 14, 1988) (holding that agency must demonstrate nexus between its compilation of records and its law

(continued...)

specifically relying on the amended statutory language, the D.C. Circuit in Keys held that records compiled solely because the subject had a known affiliation with organizations that were strongly suspected of harboring Communists met the Exemption 7 threshold.[95] As no appellate decision has yet employed the modified Pratt test adopted by Keys, the impact of this change in the threshold is not yet fully realized.

Even under the test enunciated in Pratt,[96] significant deference has

---

[94](...continued)
enforcement duties); Hall v. U.S. Dep't of Justice, 63 F. Supp. 2d 14, 16 (D.D.C. 1999) (holding that Davin "is not persuasive authority" because "Third Circuit standard is more permissive" than established D.C. Circuit standard (referring to Campbell, 164 F.3d at 32)), reconsideration denied, No. 96-2306, slip op. at 2 (D.D.C. May 29, 2003); Code, 1997 WL 150070, at *4-5 (reiterating requirement for nexus between activities and law enforcement duties); Wickline v. FBI, No. 92-1189, 1994 WL 549756, at *2 (D.D.C. Sept. 30, 1994) (finding that requirement for "nexus between the agency's activity and its law enforcement duties" was met when FBI compiled requested information through its investigation of series of murders involving organized crime); Abdullah v. FBI, No. 92-0356, slip op. at 3 (D.D.C. Aug. 10, 1992) (holding that "law enforcement agencies such as the FBI must show that the records at issue are related to the enforcement of federal laws and that the law enforcement activity was within the law enforcement duty of that agency"); Beck v. U.S. Dep't of Justice, No. 87-3356, slip op. at 26-27 (D.D.C. Nov. 7, 1989) ("[D]efendants must merely establish that the nexus between the agency's activity and its law enforcement duty" is based on a "colorable claim of rationality."). But see Simon v. Dep't of Justice, 980 F.2d 782, 783 (D.C. Cir. 1992) (stating that agency must demonstrate nexus between investigation and one of its law enforcement duties (citing Pratt, 673 F.2d at 420-21)); Reiter v. DEA, No. 96-0378, 1997 WL 470108, at *3 (D.D.C. Aug. 13, 1997) (describing how the nexus "requires an agency to establish a connection between the individual under investigation and a possible violation of a federal law"), summary affirmance granted, No. 97-5246 (D.C. Cir. Mar. 3, 1998); Keenan v. Dep't of Justice, No. 94-1909, slip op. at 12-15 (D.D.C. Mar. 2, 1997) (ruling that the agency had not established the required nexus, because it was "unclear as to whether an investigation was conducted at all"); Assassination Archives & Research Ctr. v. U.S. Dep't of Justice, No. 92-2193, 1993 WL 763547, at *6-7 (D.D.C. Apr. 29, 1993) (declaring that government must establish that investigation related to enforcement of federal law raises colorable claim "rationally related" to one or more of agency's law enforcement duties).

[95] 830 F.2d at 341-42.

[96] 673 F.2d at 421 (A court should be "hesitant to second-guess a law enforcement agency's decision to investigate if there is a plausible basis" for its decision.).

been accorded criminal law enforcement agencies.[97] Nevertheless, the D.C. Circuit has indicated in Pratt and elsewhere that if an investigation is shown to have been in fact conducted for an improper purpose, Exemption 7 may not be applicable to the records of that investigation.[98]

---

[97] See, e.g., Rosenfeld, 57 F.3d at 808 (ruling that Pratt's rational nexus test requires "a degree of deference to a law enforcement agency's decision to investigate"); King, 830 F.2d at 230-32 (finding that subject's close association with "individuals and organizations . . . of investigative interest to the FBI" and its consequent investigation of the subject during the McCarthy era for possible violation of national security laws meets the threshold in the absence of evidence supporting the existence of an improper purpose); Campbell v. Dep't of Justice, 193 F. Supp. 2d 29, 39-40 (D.D.C. 2001) (clarifying that law enforcement purpose must be evaluated as of the time that the records are compiled, even if history now questions the legal basis for investigation today); Simon v. U.S. Dep't of Justice, 752 F. Supp. 14, 18 (D.D.C. 1990) (Given the subject's prior pacifist activities, it was not "irrational or implausible for [the FBI] -- operating in the climate existing during the early 1950s -- [to conduct] what appears to have been a brief criminal investigation into the possibility that the plaintiff harbored Communist affiliations."), aff'd on other grounds, 980 F.2d 782 (D.C. Cir. 1992); see also Ctr. for Nat'l Sec. Studies, 331 F.3d at 927-28 (declaring that "[j]ust as we have deferred to the executive when it invokes FOIA Exemptions 1 and 3 in national security cases, we owe the same deference under Exemption 7(A) in appropriate cases"). But see also Jefferson, 284 F.3d at 178 (limiting deference when an agency relies on a "bare assertion to justify invocation of an exemption"); Summers, 140 F.3d at 1082, 1084 (suggesting that deference to agency may be overcome when records, such as J. Edgar Hoover's "official and confidential" (O&C) files, were "not readily available to field agents" and "contain[ed] scandalous material on public figures to be used for political blackmail"), on remand, No. 87-3168, slip op. at 3 & n.4 (D.D.C. Apr. 19, 2000) (finding, after in camera review of 4000 pages of the O&C files, that the FBI "ha[d] adequately established" that Exemption 7's "threshold requirement" was met).

[98] See Pratt, 673 F.2d at 420-21 (reiterating that Exemption 7 is not intended to "include investigatory activities wholly unrelated to law enforcement agencies' legislated functions of preventing risks to the national security and violations of the criminal laws and of apprehending those who do violate the laws"); see also Quiñon, 86 F.3d at 1228-29 (explaining that agency's connection between object of investigation and asserted law enforcement duty cannot be pretextual or wholly unbelievable and holding FBI affidavits insufficient to demonstrate legitimate basis for obstruction of justice charge; "cryptic allusion to 'certain events' is especially problematic" when events "may be nothing more sinister than . . . criticisms"); Shaw, 749 F.2d at 63 (stating that the "mere existence of a plausible criminal investigatory reason to investigate would not protect the files of an inquiry explicitly conducted . . . for purposes of harassment"); Lesar, 636 F.2d at 487 (questioning whether records that were generated after investigation

(continued...)

## EXEMPTION 7

With the broadening of Exemption 7 in the 1986 FOIA amendments, all federal agencies should consider which records of a noninvestigatory character may qualify for protection because they relate sufficiently to a law enforcement mission assigned to the agency.[99] Agencies may now be able to apply Exemption 7 protection, for example, to law enforcement manuals, program oversight reports, and other similar documents because of their relationship to the agency's law enforcement mission.[100] The full effects of these amendments will be realized only upon the case-by-case identification of particular items of noninvestigatory law enforcement information the disclosure of which could cause one of the harms specified in Exemption 7's six subparts.[101]

For example, emerging case law supports the use of Exemption 7 to

---

[98](...continued)
"wrongly strayed beyond its original law enforcement scope" would meet threshold test for Exemption 7); Enviro Tech, 2003 U.S. Dist. LEXIS 25493, at *21-22 (discussing the consequences of "ultra vires decisions," and explaining that Exemption 7 has a "hook that might restrict the exemption to only those documents relating to specifically authorized agency activities") (dicta); Warren v. United States, No. 1:99-1317, 2000 WL 1868950, at *6 (N.D. Ohio Oct. 31, 2000) (determining that despite fact that IRS investigator may have aggressively gathered information during civil audit, this had clear law enforcement purpose and was not beyond authority of agency). But see, e.g., Sinito v. U.S. Dep't of Justice, No. 87-0814, 2000 U.S. Dist. LEXIS 22504, at *27 (D.D.C. July 11, 2000) (declaring that plaintiff's "[u]nanswered questions and inflammatory accusations regarding alleged governmental agent corruption . . . do not persuade this Court" that records were not compiled for law enforcement purposes).

[99] See PHE, 983 F.2d at 249, 251, 253 (holding portions of FBI's Manual of Investigative Operations & Guidelines properly withheld pursuant to Exemption 7(E)); Herrick's Newsletter, 2006 U.S. Dist. LEXIS 44802, at *1, *20-21 (ruling that portions of the agency's "Fines, Penalties & Forfeitures Handbook" that concern "possible tampering with and theft of evidence" satisfy the threshold requirement).

[100] See Attorney General's 1986 Amendments Memorandum at 8-9; see also Guerrero v. DEA, No. 93-2006, slip op. at 14-15 (D. Ariz. Feb. 22, 1996) (approving nondisclosure of portions of DEA Agents Manual); Church of Scientology Int'l v. IRS, 845 F. Supp. 714, 723 (C.D. Cal. 1993) (concluding that parts of IRS Law Enforcement Manual were exempt from disclosure pursuant to Exemption 7(E)).

[101] Accord Attorney General's Memorandum for Heads of All Federal Departments and Agencies Regarding the Freedom of Information Act (Oct. 12, 2001), reprinted in FOIA Post (posted 10/15/01) (instructing agencies to protect national security and their law enforcement missions by undertaking "full and deliberate consideration of the institutional, commercial, and personal privacy interests that could be implicated by disclosure").

protect integrated intelligence and law enforcement information -- which might not previously have been categorized as collected for law enforcement purposes -- particularly in situations where agencies have gathered information for purposes of combating terrorism and protecting homeland security.[102] Such case law finds its antecedent in the "national security" framework found in Pratt[103] and logically applies Exemption 7 to protect intelligence data that relates to an agency's law enforcement mission.[104] Indeed, at least three post-9/11 FOIA decisions have recognized this newer "national security" framework and have applied it to protect sensitive, homeland security-related information -- explaining that terrorists could use the information to increase the risk of an attack or to increase the dam-

---

[102] See, e.g., Owens v. U.S. Dep't of Justice, No. 04-1701, 2006 WL 3490790, at *5 (D.D.C. Dec. 1, 2006) (noting that "threshold showing has been made" because records were "generated during an investigation into terrorist attacks" and defendant agencies are "statutorily authorized to investigate activities of this type"); Ayyad, WL 654133, at *3 (holding that records concerning the 1993 terrorist bombing of the World Trade Center satisfy the threshold when "the Government may need [information from the requester's file] to use to detect threats to the integrity of the nation's security"); Judicial Watch, Inc. v. FBI, No. 00-745, slip op. at 6-7 (D.D.C. Apr. 20, 2001) (finding that FBI has shown nexus between investigation related to domestic security/terrorism and its assigned law enforcement mission); Judicial Watch, No. 00-0723, slip op. at 21 (D.D.C. Mar. 30, 2001) (finding that records concerning "the investigation of terrorist threats" involved "a legitimate law enforcement duty" and satisfied the threshold). But see also Weissman, 565 F.2d at 695-96 (finding that the CIA's authority was limited by Congress to intelligence matters abroad, and holding that the agency was not authorized to conduct "investigations of private American nationals who had no contact with the CIA, [merely] on the grounds that eventually their activities might threaten the Agency").

[103] Pratt, 673 F.2d at 420 (applying a two-part test, and allowing that the threshold may be satisfied if the agency's investigatory activities "relate[] to the enforcement of federal laws or to the maintenance of national security").

[104] See, e.g., Morales Cozier, No. 99-0312, slip op. at 14-15 (N.D. Ga. Sept. 25, 2000) (stating that the threshold was satisfied under either the "per se" test or the Pratt test because "[p]laintiff's activities in contacting an official of a government with which the United States has no official relations and inviting him to the United States could have presented an interference with United States foreign policy or national security in an area where the FBI has an investigatory or enforcement interest"); cf. White House Memorandum for Heads of Executive Departments and Agencies Concerning Safeguarding Information Regarding Weapons of Mass Destruction and Other Sensitive Documents Related to Homeland Security (Mar. 19, 2002), reprinted in FOIA Post (posted 3/21/02) (emphasizing need to protect information "that could reasonably be expected to assist" terrorist activity).

age done by an attack.[105]

Nevertheless, agencies should be mindful that while the FOIA's policy goals strongly support protecting intelligence information as part of the preventative law enforcement mission under Exemption 7,[106] courts may require some showing of a rational nexus between such activities and an agency's law enforcement functions.[107] Accordingly, agencies should care-

---

[105] See Ctr. for Nat'l Sec. Studies, 331 F.3d at 928-29 (explaining that "disclosure of [post-9/11] detainees' names would enable al Qaeda or other terrorist groups to map the course of the investigation [and] could be of great use to al Qaeda in plotting future terrorists attacks or intimidating witnesses"); Living Rivers, 272 F. Supp. 2d at 1321 (stating that terrorists could use "inundation maps" to aid both in target selection and in carrying out terrorist attacks by analyzing downstream harm from projected extent of flooding); Coastal Delivery, 272 F. Supp. 2d at 964 (finding that terrorists could use information about rate of examinations at ports to avoid detection by selecting those ports with relatively low rates of examinations); see also Campbell, 164 F.3d at 31-33 (discussing whether 1960s investigations of subversive organizations believed to be threat to U.S. security meet threshold); Pratt, 673 F.2d at 421 (explaining that investigation into breach of national security qualifies as law enforcement); L.A. Times, 442 F. Supp. 2d at 898 (finding that collection of "intelligence information" was compiled for "cognizable law enforcement purposes" (citing Ctr. for Nat'l Sec. Studies, 331 F.3d at 926)); Simon, 752 F. Supp. at 18 (explaining that given the "climate existing during the early 1950's [the court] cannot conclude that it was irrational or implausible" to take into account "earlier passivist activities" and conduct a "criminal investigation into the possibility that [the subject] harbored Communist affiliations," and therefore finding that the records met the law enforcement threshold); FOIA Post, "FOIA Officers Conference Held on Homeland Security" (posted 7/3/03) (discussing use of FOIA's law enforcement exemptions where necessary to protect homeland security-related information); cf. Maydak v. United States, No. 02-5168, slip op. at 7 (D.C. Cir. Apr. 20, 2004) (reiterating that "[a]lthough the Privacy Act does not define 'law enforcement authority,' we have interpreted the phrase broadly," and given the Bureau of Prison's mandate to preserve prison security, "we have no doubt that examining photographs for conduct that may threaten that security is pertinent to and within the scope of an authorized law enforcement activity").

[106] See Attorney General Ashcroft's FOIA Memorandum, reprinted in FOIA Post (posted 10/15/01) (describing a FOIA policy goal of "safeguarding our national security [and] enhancing the effectiveness of our law enforcement agencies").

[107] See Pratt, 673 F.2d at 420. But see also Ctr. for Nat'l Sec. Studies, 331 F.3d at 921, 926 (seemingly going beyond Pratt for homeland security/terrorism purposes by finding that although names of detainees traditionally are made public, names that were gathered in "response to the terrorist

(continued...)

fully examine their law enforcement purposes in determining that a "sound legal basis" exists for applying Exemption 7 and gaining its broad protections under the six subparts discussed below.[108] And while agencies must establish this "connection" between their activities and their institutional mandates in general, they can be mindful that the courts have properly given deference to agency expertise in this area -- particularly in post-9/11 judicial decisions, which repeatedly advert to the tragic events of that day and to how "American life [has] changed drastically and dramatically."[109]

## EXEMPTION 7(A)

The first subpart of Exemption 7, Exemption 7(A), authorizes the withholding of "records or information compiled for law enforcement purposes, but only to the extent that production of such law enforcement records or information . . . could reasonably be expected to interfere with en-

---

[107](...continued)
attacks of September 11, 2001 . . . constitute a comprehensive diagram of the law enforcement investigation" and thus were compiled for law enforcement purposes and properly withheld).

[108] Attorney General Ashcroft's FOIA Memorandum, reprinted in *FOIA Post* (posted 10/15/01).

[109] N.J. Media Group, 308 F.3d at 202-03 (discussing First Amendment rights, and recognizing that the "case arises in the wake of September 11, 2001, a day on which American life changed drastically and dramatically . . . . Since the primary national policy must be self-preservation, it seems elementary that, to the extent open deportation hearings might impair national security," the special interest deportation hearings were properly closed); see Ctr. for Nat'l Sec. Studies, 331 F.3d at 926, 932 (referring to 9/11 terrorism as a "heinous violation," and stating that "the courts must defer to the executive on [such] decisions of national security"); L.A. Times, 442 F. Supp. 2d at 899 (explaining that the "Court defers" to the agency because its position is "reasonably detailed," and that it is "'well-established that the judiciary owes some measure of deference to the executive in cases implicating national security, a uniquely executive purview'" (quoting Ctr. for Nat'l Sec. Studies, 331 F.3d at 926-27)); Coastal Delivery, 272 F. Supp. 2d at 960-61, 964 (pointing to the existence of "new anti-terrorism programs" in approving protection of the type of information released prior to 9/11, and stating that "plaintiff's arguments that potential terrorists and smugglers could not and would not use the information" are simply "unpersuasive" in that context); see also, e.g., Edmonds, 272 F. Supp. at 55 (stating that the "deference that has historically been extended to the executive when it invokes FOIA Exemption 1" must be extended to Exemption 7 in the national security area); cf. Zadvydas, 533 U.S. at 696 (recognizing that terrorism can warrant "heightened deference").

forcement proceedings."[1] The Freedom of Information Reform Act of 1986, often referred to as the 1986 FOIA amendments, lessened the showing of harm required from a demonstration that release "would interfere with" to "could reasonably be expected to interfere with" enforcement proceedings.[2] The courts have recognized repeatedly that the change in the language for this exemption effectively broadens its protection.[3]

---

[1] 5 U.S.C. § 552(b)(7)(A) (2000 & Supp. IV 2004).

[2] Pub. L. No. 99-570, § 1802, 100 Stat. 3207, 3207-48; see Attorney General's Memorandum on the 1986 Amendments to the Freedom of Information Act 10 (Dec. 1987) [hereinafter Attorney General's 1986 Amendments Memorandum]; see also NARA v. Favish, 541 U.S. 157, 169 (evincing the Supreme Court's reliance on "the Attorney General's consistent interpretation of" the FOIA in successive such Attorney General memoranda), reh'g denied, 541 U.S. 1057 (2004).

[3] See Robinson v. Dep't of Justice, No. 00-11182, slip op. at 8 n.5 (11th Cir. Mar. 15, 2001) (noting that 1986 FOIA amendments changed the standard from "would" interfere to "could reasonably be expected to" interfere); Manna v. U.S. Dep't of Justice, 51 F.3d 1158, 1164 n.5 (3d Cir. 1995) (stating that Congress amended the statute to "relax significantly the standard for demonstrating interference"); Alyeska Pipeline Serv. v. EPA, 856 F.2d 309, 311 n.18 (D.C. Cir. 1988) (treating the lower court's improper reliance on the pre-amendment version of Exemption 7(A) as irrelevant as it simply "required EPA to meet a higher standard than FOIA now demands"); Wright v. OSHA, 822 F.2d 642, 647 (7th Cir. 1987) (explaining that amended language creates broad protection); Curran v. Dep't of Justice, 813 F.2d 473, 474 n.1 (1st Cir. 1987) ("[T]he drift of the changes is to ease -- rather than to increase -- the government's burden in respect to Exemption 7(A)."); In Def. of Animals v. HHS, No. 99-3024, 2001 U.S. Dist. LEXIS, at *9 (D.D.C. Sept. 28, 2001) (reiterating that "'could reasonably' . . . represents a relaxed standard; before 1986, the government had to show that disclosure 'would' interfere with law enforcement"); Gould Inc. v. GSA, 688 F. Supp. 689, 703 n.33 (D.D.C. 1988) (The "1986 amendments relaxed the standard of demonstrating interference with enforcement proceedings."); see also Spannaus v. U.S. Dep't of Justice, 813 F.2d 1285, 1288 (4th Cir. 1987) (explaining that an "agency's showing under the amended statute, which in part replaces 'would' with 'could reasonably be expected to,' is to be measured by a standard of reasonableness, which takes into account the 'lack of certainty in attempting to predict harm'" (quoting S. Rep. No. 98-221, at 24 (1983)); cf. John Doe Agency v. John Doe Corp., 493 U.S. 146, 157 (1989) (taking "practical approach" when confronted with interpretation of FOIA and applying "workable balance" between interests of public in greater access and needs of government to protect certain kinds of information); U.S. Dep't of Justice v. Reporters Comm. for Freedom of the Press, 489 U.S. 749, 777-78 n.22 (1989) (declaring that Congress intended the identical modification of the language of Exemption 7(C) to provide greater "flexibility in responding to FOIA requests for law enforcement records" and that it replaced "a focus on

(continued...)

Determining the applicability of this Exemption 7 subsection thus requires a two-step analysis focusing on (1) whether a law enforcement proceeding is pending or prospective, and (2) whether release of information about it could reasonably be expected to cause some articulable harm.[4] The courts have held that the mere pendency of enforcement pro-

---

[3](...continued)
the effect of a particular disclosure" with a "standard of reasonableness" that supports a "categorical" approach to records of similar character).

[4] See, e.g., NLRB v. Robbins Tire & Rubber Co., 437 U.S. 214, 224 (1978) (holding that the government must show how the records "would interfere with a pending enforcement proceeding"); Manna, 51 F.3d at 1164 ("To fit within Exemption 7(A), the government must show that (1) a law enforcement proceeding is pending or prospective and (2) release of the information could reasonably be expected to cause some articulable harm."); Campbell v. HHS, 682 F.2d 256, 259 (D.C. Cir. 1982) (stating that agency must demonstrate interference with pending enforcement proceeding); Long v. U.S. Dep't of Justice, No. 00-0211, 2006 WL 2578755, at *26 (D.D.C. Sept. 8, 2006) (reiterating that an "agency must demonstrate" that an enforcement proceeding is pending or prospective and that the "disclosure of the information could reasonably be expected to cause some articulable harm to the proceeding"); Beneville v. U.S. Dep't of Justice, No. 98-6137, slip op. at 22 (D. Or. June 11, 2003) (explaining that simply satisfying the law enforcement purpose "does not establish the remainder of the requirement . . . that disclosure of the documents could reasonably be expected to interfere with law enforcement proceedings" (citing Lewis v. IRS, 823 F.2d 375, 379 (9th Cir. 1987))); Judicial Watch v. FBI, No. 00-745, 2001 U.S. Dist. LEXIS 25732, at *14 (D.D.C. Apr. 20, 2001) ("Once the agency establishes that an enforcement proceeding is pending, the agency must show that release of the withheld documents is likely to cause some distinct harm."); Scheer v. U.S. Dep't of Justice, 35 F. Supp. 2d 9, 13 (D.D.C. 1999) (stating that agency "must first prove" existence of law enforcement proceeding and "must next prove" harm), appeal dismissed per stipulation, No. 99-5317 (D.C. Cir. Nov. 2, 2000); Franklin v. U.S. Dep't of Justice, No. 97-1225, slip op. at 7 (S.D. Fla. June 15, 1998) (magistrate's recommendation) (two-part test), adopted (S.D. Fla. June 26, 1998), aff'd, 189 F.3d 485 (11th Cir. 1999) (unpublished table decision); Hamilton v. Weise, No. 95-1161, 1997 U.S. Dist. LEXIS 18900, at *25 (M.D. Fla. Oct. 1, 1997) (same); Butler v. Dep't of the Air Force, 888 F. Supp. 174, 183 (D.D.C. 1995) (same), aff'd per curiam, No. 96-5111 (D.C. Cir. May 6, 1997); see also Attorney General's Memorandum for Heads of All Federal Departments and Agencies Regarding the Freedom of Information Act (Oct. 12, 2001), reprinted in FOIA Post (posted 10/15/01) (emphasizing the importance of "enhancing the effectiveness of our law enforcement agencies"); cf. Va. Dep't of State Police v. Wash. Post, No. 04-1375, 2004 WL 2198327, at *5, *9 (4th Cir. 2004) (agreeing with the "general principle that a compelling governmental interest exists in protecting the integrity of an ongoing law enforcement investigation," and explaining that "law enforcement agencies must be able
(continued...)

ceedings is an inadequate basis for the invocation of Exemption 7(A); the government must also establish that some distinct harm could reasonably be expected to result if the record or information requested were disclosed.[5] For example, the Court of Appeals for the District of Columbia

---

[4](...continued)
to investigate crime without the details of the investigation being released to the public in a manner that compromises the investigation") (non-FOIA case).

[5] See, e.g., Lion Raisins Inc. v. USDA, 354 F.3d 1072, 1085 (9th Cir. 2004) [hereinafter Lion I] (stating that the "USDA cannot argue that revealing the information would allow Lion premature access to the evidence" or harm its investigation, because "Lion already has copies of the documents it seeks"); Neill v. Dep't of Justice, No. 93-5292, 1994 WL 88219, at *1 (D.C. Cir. Mar. 9, 1994) (explaining that conclusory affidavit lacked specificity of description necessary to ensure meaningful review of agency's Exemption 7(A) claims); Miller v. USDA, 13 F.3d 260, 263 (8th Cir. 1993) (holding that government must make specific showing of why disclosure of documents could reasonably be expected to interfere with enforcement proceedings); Crooker v. ATF, 789 F.2d 64, 65-67 (D.C. Cir. 1986) (finding that agency failed to demonstrate that disclosure would interfere with enforcement proceedings); Grasso v. IRS, 785 F.2d 70, 77 (3d Cir. 1986) (stating that the "government must show, by more than conclusory statement, how the particular kinds of investigatory records requested would interfere with a pending enforcement proceeding"); Dow Jones Co. v. FERC, 219 F.R.D. 167, 173 (C.D. Cal. 2002) (illustrating that an agency cannot easily demonstrate harm to its proceedings when "the subjects of the investigation . . . have copies" of the record in question); Scheer, 35 F. Supp. 2d at 13-14 (finding that the agency's assertion that disclosure to the requester would harm its investigation "is belied" by the agency's full disclosure to the target of the investigation; therefore, the agency "has not met its burden of offering clear proof that disclosure . . . would have interfered with a law enforcement proceeding within the meaning of FOIA exemption 7(A)"); Jefferson v. Reno, No. 96-1284, 1997 U.S. Dist. LEXIS 3064, at *10 (D.D.C. Mar. 17, 1997) (ruling that neither agency's declaration nor its checklist "describes how the release of any or all responsive documents could reasonably be expected to interfere with these enforcement proceedings"); ACLU Found. v. U.S. Dep't of Justice, 833 F. Supp. 399, 407 (S.D.N.Y. 1993) (explaining that possibility of interference was not so evident when investigations referred to closed or "generalized class" of cases; accordingly, government must provide sufficient information for court to decide whether disclosure will actually threaten similar, ongoing enforcement proceedings); see also FOIA Post, "Supreme Court Vacates and Remands in ATF Database Case" (posted 3/25/03) (advising of Supreme Court decision to vacate -- i.e., render "null and void" -- Seventh Circuit's Exemption 7(A) decision in City of Chicago v. U.S. Dep't of the Treasury, 287 F.3d 628 (7th Cir.), amended upon denial of reh'g en banc, 297 F.3d 672 (7th Cir. 2002), vacated & remanded sub nom. U.S. Dep't of Justice v. City of Chicago, 537 U.S. 1229 (2003), in light of new
(continued...)

Circuit has held that the fact that a judge in a criminal trial specifically delayed disclosure of certain documents until the end of the trial is alone insufficient to establish interference with that ongoing proceeding.[6]

It is beyond question that Exemption 7(A) is temporal in nature and is not intended to "endlessly protect material simply because it [is] in an investigatory file."[7] Thus, as a general rule, Exemption 7(A) may be invoked so long as the law enforcement proceeding involved remains pending,[8] or

---

[5](...continued)
legislation), vacated & remanded, 432 F.3d 777 (7th Cir. 2005); cf. Lion Raisins Inc. v. USDA, No. 05-0062, 2005 WL 2704879, at *7-9 (E.D. Cal. Oct. 19, 2005) [hereinafter Lion II] (distinguishing Lion I because "[h]ere, the worksheets are not identical" to the ones in Lion's possession, and while agreeing that USDA's litigation strategy has been revealed in its prior actions and that "it is unlikely that Lion will now try to extricate itself from these accusations of fraudulent fabrication by fabricating more documents," nevertheless finding that the falsified document and ongoing proceedings establish that disclosure of "this kind of evidence" would interfere with ongoing law enforcement proceedings).

[6] North v. Walsh, 881 F.2d 1088, 1100 (D.C. Cir. 1989) (stating that the standard is "whether disclosure can reasonably be expected to interfere in a palpable, particular way" with enforcement proceedings); see also Goodman v. U.S. Dep't of Labor, No. CV-01-515-ST, 2001 U.S. Dist. LEXIS 22748, at *13 (D. Or. Dec. 12, 2001) (magistrate's recommendation) (explaining that "the scope of discovery . . . is not the issue," and that the withholding was proper under FOIA standards), adopted (D. Or. Jan. 14, 2002); Warren v. United States, No. 1:99-1317, 2000 U.S. Dist. LEXIS 17660, at *18 (N.D. Ohio Oct. 13, 2000) (explaining that although plaintiffs "will likely be entitled to release of all the documents at issue in this proceeding, through the criminal discovery process, that fact does not prohibit reliance on Exemption 7 in the context of this case").

[7] Robbins Tire, 437 U.S. at 230; see Solar Sources, Inc. v. United States, 142 F.3d 1033, 1037 (7th Cir. 1998) (stating that "Exemption 7(A) does not permit the Government to withhold all information merely because that information was compiled for law enforcement purposes"); Dickerson v. Dep't of Justice, 992 F.2d 1426, 1431 (6th Cir. 1993) (reiterating that when investigation is over and purpose of it has expired, information should be disclosed); Hamilton, 1997 U.S. Dist. LEXIS 18900, at *25-26 (declaring that Exemption 7(A) was enacted "mainly to overrule judicial decisions that prohibited disclosure of investigatory files in 'closed' cases"); cf. Kay v. FCC, 976 F. Supp. 23, 37-38 (D.D.C. 1997) (explaining that an agency "may continue to invoke Exemption 7(A) to withhold the requested documents until . . . [the law enforcement proceeding] comes to a conclusion"), aff'd, 172 F.3d 919 (D.C. Cir. 1998) (unpublished table decision).

[8] See, e.g., Seegull Mfg. Co. v. NLRB, 741 F.2d 882, 886-87 (6th Cir. 1984)
(continued...)

so long as an enforcement proceeding is fairly regarded as prospective[9] or

---

[8](...continued)
(finding that NLRB administrative practice of continuing to assert Exemption 7(A) for six-month "buffer period" after termination of proceedings "arbitrary and capricious"); Barney v. IRS, 618 F.2d 1268, 1273-74 (8th Cir. 1980) (explaining that once enforcement proceedings are "either concluded or abandoned, exemption 7(A) will no longer apply"); City of Chicago v. U.S. Dep't of the Treasury, No. 01-C-3835, 2002 WL 370216, at *4 (N.D. Ill. Mar. 8, 2002) (rejecting again, in a second case, the agency's argument that release of the information "would allow members of the general public to 'connect the dots'" in a case in which the agency "does not know whether an investigation is ongoing [but] nevertheless releases the information [routinely] after a fixed period of time"), rev'd & remanded on other grounds, No. 02-2259 (7th Cir. Nov. 29, 2005); W. Journalism Ctr. v. Office of the Indep. Counsel, 926 F. Supp. 189, 192 (D.D.C. 1996) ("By definition until his or her work is completed, an Independent Counsel's activities are ongoing . . . and once the task is completed . . . all the records . . . are required to be turned over to the Archivist and at that time would be subject to FOIA requests."), aff'd, No. 96-5178, 1997 WL 195516 (D.C. Cir. Mar. 11, 1997); Linn v. U.S. Dep't of Justice, No. 92-1406, 1995 WL 417810, at *25 (D.D.C. June 6, 1995) (ruling that Exemption 7(A) is not applicable when there is "no evidence before the Court that any investigation exists"), appeal dismissed voluntarily, No. 97-5122 (D.C. Cir. July 14, 1997); Kilroy v. NLRB, 633 F. Supp. 136, 142-43 (S.D. Ohio 1985) (holding that Exemption 7(A) "applies only when a law enforcement proceeding is pending"), aff'd, 823 F.2d 553 (6th Cir. 1987) (unpublished table decision); Antonsen v. U.S. Dep't of Justice, No. K-82-008, slip op. at 9-10 (D. Alaska Mar. 20, 1984) ("It is difficult to conceive how the disclosure of these materials could have interfered with any enforcement proceedings" after a criminal defendant had been tried and convicted.).

[9] See, e.g., Boyd v. Criminal Div., U.S. Dep't of Justice, No. 05-5142, 2007 WL 328064, at *3 (D.C. Cir. Feb. 6, 2007) (stating that government's identification of targets of investigation satisfies concrete prospective law enforcement proceeding requirement); Manna, 51 F.3d at 1165 (ruling that when "prospective criminal or civil (or both) proceedings are contemplated," information is protected from disclosure); In Def. of Animals, 2001 U.S. Dist. LEXIS 24975, at *8 ("Previous USDA investigations of animal deaths at the Foundation resulted in formal charges . . . and there is no evidence that the agency would treat its most recent investigation differently."); Judicial Watch, 2001 U.S. Dist. LEXIS 25732, at *16 (explaining that "[a]lthough no enforcement proceedings are currently pending, the FBI has represented that such proceedings may become necessary as the investigation progresses"); Gen. Elec. Co. v. EPA, 18 F. Supp. 2d 138, 144 (D. Mass. 1998) (explaining that "it is entirely reasonable for the [a]gency to anticipate that enforcement proceedings are in the offing"); Kay, 976 F. Supp. at 38 ("Moreover, if the proceeding is not pending, an agency may continue to invoke Exemption 7(A) so long as the proceeding is regarded as prospective.");

(continued...)

as preventative.[10]

Although Exemption 7(A) is temporal in nature, it nevertheless remains viable throughout the duration of long-term investigations.[11] For ex-

---

[9](...continued)
Foster v. U.S. Dep't of Justice, 933 F. Supp. 687, 692 (E.D. Mich. 1996) (holding that disclosure "could impede ongoing government investigation (and prospective prosecution)"); Cudzich v. INS, 886 F. Supp. 101, 106 (D.D.C. 1995) (stating that "where disclosure of information would cause impermissible harm to a concrete prospective law enforcement proceeding, such a situation is also within the protective scope of Exemption 7(A)"); Richman v. U.S. Dep't of Justice, No. 90-C-19, slip op. at 13 (W.D. Wis. Feb. 2, 1994) (finding that files pertaining to "pending and prospective" criminal enforcement proceedings are protected); Southam News v. INS, 674 F. Supp. 881, 887 (D.D.C. 1987) (recognizing that Service Lookout Book, containing "names of violators, alleged violators and suspected violators," is protected as proceedings clearly are at least prospective against each violator); Marzen v. HHS, 632 F. Supp. 785, 805 (N.D. Ill. 1985) (concluding that Exemption 7(A) prohibits disclosure of law enforcement records when their release "would interfere with enforcement proceedings, pending, contemplated, or in the future."), aff'd, 825 F.2d 1148 (7th Cir. 1987).

[10] See, e.g., Ctr. for Nat'l Sec. Studies v. U.S. Dep't of Justice, 331 F.3d 918, 928 (D.C. Cir. 2003) (determining that release of information at issue could allow terrorists to "more easily formulate or revise counter-efforts" and could be of "great use to al Qaeda in plotting future terrorist attacks"); Moorefield v. U.S. Secret Serv., 611 F.2d 1021, 1026 (5th Cir. 1980) (holding broadly that material pertaining to "Secret Service investigations carried out pursuant to the Service's protective function" -- to prevent harm to protectees -- is eligible for Exemption 7(A) protection); cf. Living Rivers, Inc. v. U.S. Bureau of Reclamation, 272 F. Supp. 2d 1313, 1322 (D. Utah 2003) (recognizing that the use of the dam inundation maps "could increase risk of an attack on the dams" by enabling terrorists to assess prospective damage) (Exemption 7(F) case).

[11] See Antonelli v. U.S. Parole Comm'n, No. 93-0109, slip op. at 3-4 (D.D.C. Feb. 23, 1996) (reiterating that courts repeatedly find "lengthy, delayed or even dormant investigations" covered by Exemption 7(A) and holding that release of eight-year-old investigative file "would interfere with possible proceedings"); Butler v. U.S. Dep't of Justice, No. 86-2255, 1994 WL 55621, at *24 (D.D.C. Feb. 3, 1994) (stating that agency "leads" were not stale simply because they were several years old given that indictee remained at large), appeal dismissed voluntarily, No. 94-5078 (D.C. Cir. Sept. 8, 1994); Afr. Fund v. Mosbacher, No. 92-289, 1993 WL 183736, at *4 (S.D.N.Y. May 26, 1993) (finding that documents that would interfere with lengthy or delayed investigation fall within protective ambit of Exemption 7(A)); see also Davoudlarian v. Dep't of Justice, No. 93-1787, 1994 WL 423845, at *2-3 (4th Cir. Aug. 15, 1994) (unpublished table decision) (continued...)

ample, in 1993 it was held applicable to the FBI's continuing investigation into the 1975 disappearance of Jimmy Hoffa.[12] And in 2005, the continued use of Exemption 7(A) was held proper in the FBI's long-term investigation of the 1971 airplane hijacking by "D.B. Cooper," who infamously parachuted out of that plane with a satchel of money.[13] Indeed, even when an investigation is dormant, Exemption 7(A) has been held to be applicable because of the possibility that the investigation could lead to a "prospective law enforcement proceeding."[14] The "prospective" proceeding, however, must be a concrete possibility, rather than a mere hypothetical one.[15]

---

[11](...continued)
(holding that records of open investigation of decade-old murder remained protectible).

[12] Dickerson, 992 F.2d at 1432 (affirming district court's conclusion that FBI's investigation into 1975 disappearance of Jimmy Hoffa remained ongoing and therefore was still "prospective" law enforcement proceeding). But see Detroit Free Press v. U.S. Dep't of Justice, 174 F. Supp. 2d 597, 600 (E.D. Mich. 2001) (ordering an in camera inspection of FBI's records of the Hoffa disappearance investigation in light of the "inordinate amount of time that [it] has remained an allegedly pending and active investigation").

[13] Cook v. U.S. Dep't of Justice, No. 04-2542, 2005 WL 2237615, at *2 (W.D. Wash. Sept. 13, 2005) (stressing that "the mere fact that this crime remains unsolved . . . do[es] not establish, or even raise a genuine issue of material fact, regarding the pendency of this investigation").

[14] See, e.g., Nat'l Pub. Radio v. Bell, 431 F. Supp. 509, 514-15 (D.D.C. 1977) (explaining that although the investigation into the death of nuclear-industry whistleblower Karen Silkwood is "dormant," it "will hopefully lead to a 'prospective law enforcement proceeding'" and that disclosure "presents the very real possibility of a criminal learning in alarming detail of the government's investigation of his crime before the government has had the opportunity to bring him to justice" (emphasis added)); see also FOIA Update, Vol. V, No. 2, at 6.

[15] See In Def. of Animals, 2001 U.S. Dist. LEXIS 24975, at *9 (stating that an "anticipated filing satisfies FOIA's requirement of a reasonably anticipated, concrete prospective law enforcement proceeding"); Judicial Watch, 2001 U.S. Dist. LEXIS 25732, at *16 (accepting agency's representation that "proceedings may become necessary as investigation progresses" as sufficient to establish concrete possibility); ACLU Found., 833 F. Supp. at 407 (finding that possibility of interference not so evident for investigative documents related to generalized categories of cases; agency must show that disclosure would actually threaten similar, ongoing enforcement proceedings); Badran v. U.S. Dep't of Justice, 652 F. Supp. 1437, 1440 (N.D. Ill. 1987) (relying on pre-amendment language, court held that mere possibility that person mentioned in file might some day violate law was insufficient to invoke Exemption 7(A)); Nat'l Pub. Radio, 431 F. Supp. at 514 (holding that
(continued...)

Further, even after an enforcement proceeding is closed, courts have ruled that the continued use of Exemption 7(A) may be proper in certain instances. One such instance involves "related" proceedings, i.e., those instances in which information from a closed law enforcement proceeding will be used again in other pending or prospective law enforcement proceedings -- for example, when charges are pending against additional defendants[16] or when additional charges are pending against the original de-

---

[15](...continued)
"dormant" investigation "is nonetheless an 'active' one," which justifies continued Exemption 7(A) applicability); see also 120 Cong. Rec. S9329 (daily ed. May 30, 1974) (statement of Sen. Hart).

[16] See Solar Sources, 142 F.3d at 1040 (explaining that although the government has "closed" its cases against certain defendants by obtaining plea agreements and convictions, withholding is proper because the information "compiled against them is part of the information" in ongoing cases against other targets); New England Med. Ctr. Hosp. v. NLRB, 548 F.2d 377, 385-86 (1st Cir. 1976) (finding Exemption 7(A) applicable when a "closed file is essentially contemporary with, and closely related to, the pending open case" against another defendant; applicability of exemption does not hinge on "open" or "closed" label agency places on a file); Givner v. Executive Office for U.S. Attorneys, No. 99-3454 slip op. at 3, 7 (D.D.C. Mar. 1, 2001) (explaining that although plaintiff is "serving his sentence," withholding is proper because "release of prosecutorial documents could potentially jeopardize" pending trial and habeas action of co-conspirators); Cucci v. DEA, 871 F. Supp. 508, 512 (D.D.C. 1994) (finding protection proper when information pertains to "multiple intermingled investigations and not just the terminated investigation" of subject); Engelking v. DEA, No. 91-0165, slip op. at 6 (D.D.C. Nov. 30, 1992) (reasoning that information in inmate's closed file was properly withheld because fugitive discussed in requester's file is still at large; explaining that records from closed file can relate to law enforcement efforts which are still active or in prospect), summary affirmance granted in pertinent part, vacated in part & remanded, No. 93-5091, 1993 U.S. Dist. LEXIS 33824 (D.C. Cir. Oct. 6, 1993); Warmack v. Huff, No. 88-H-1191-E, slip op. at 22-23 (N.D. Ala. May 16, 1990) (finding that Exemption 7(A) applicable to documents in multi-defendant case involving four untried fugitives), aff'd, 949 F.2d 1162 (11th Cir. 1991) (unpublished table decision); Freedberg v. Dep't of the Navy, 581 F. Supp. 3, 4 (D.D.C. 1982 ) (holding that Exemption 7(A) remained applicable when two murderers were convicted but two other remained at large). But see Linn, 1995 WL 417810, at *9 (explaining that the statement that "some unspecified investigation against a fugitive, or perhaps more than one fugitive, was ongoing . . . without any explanation of how release" of the information would interfere with "efforts to apprehend this (or these) fugitive (or fugitives) is patently insufficient to justify the withholding of information").

fendant.[17]

Another circumstance in which the continued use of Exemption 7(A) has been held proper involves post-conviction motions, i.e., those instances in which the requester has filed a motion for a new trial or has otherwise appealed the court's action.[18] The extent of protection in such a circumstance, however, varies; some courts have limited Exemption 7(A) protection to only the material not used at the first trial,[19] while other courts in

---

[17] See Pinnavaia v. FBI, No. 04-5115, 2004 WL 2348155, at *1 (D.C. Cir. Oct. 19, 2004) (explaining that although FBI San Diego Field Office's investigation was closed, its New York Field Office records were part of investigatory files for separate, ongoing investigation, so use of Exemption 7(A) therefore was proper); Franklin v. U.S. Dep't of Justice, No. 98-5339, slip op. at 3 (11th Cir. July 13, 1999) (holding that "disclosure could have reasonably been expected to interfere with [defendant's] federal appeal and state criminal trial"); Hoffman v. U.S. Dep't of Justice, No. 98-1733-A, slip op. at 3 (W.D. Okla. Sept. 21, 2001) (explaining that although the federal trial was completed, a decision to proceed with a state prosecution "convinces the Court" that the requested records should not be disclosed); Cudzich, 886 F. Supp. at 106-07 (holding that while INS investigation is complete, parts of file "containing information pertaining to pending investigations of other law enforcement agencies" are properly withheld); Kuffel v. U.S. Bureau of Prisons, 882 F. Supp. 1116, 1126 (D.D.C. 1995) (ruling that Exemption 7(A) remains applicable when inmate has criminal prosecutions pending in other cases); Dickie v. Dep't of the Treasury, No. 86-649, slip op. at 8 (D.D.C. Mar. 31, 1987) (holding that release of documents from closed federal prosecution could jeopardize state criminal proceedings).

[18] See, e.g., Kansi v. U.S. Dep't of Justice, 11 F. Supp. 2d 42, 44 (D.D.C. 1998) (explaining that the "potential for interference . . . that drives the 7(A) exemption . . . exists at least until plaintiff's conviction is final"; thus, plaintiff's pending motion for new trial is pending law enforcement proceeding for purposes of FOIA); see also Keen v. Executive Office for U.S. Attorneys, No. 96-1049, slip op. at 7 (D.D.C. July 14, 1999) (magistrate's recommendation) (reasoning that pending motion to redetermine sentence qualifies as "pending enforcement proceeding for purposes of FOIA Exemption 7(A)"), adopted (D.D.C. Mar. 28, 2000); Burke v. DEA, No. 96-1739, slip op. at 5 (D.D.C. Mar. 31, 1998) (finding that post-conviction appeal qualifies as law enforcement proceeding).

[19] See Pons v. U.S. Customs Serv., No. 93-2094, 1998 U.S. Dist. LEXIS 6084, at *14 (D.D.C. Apr. 23, 1998) (ruling that disclosure of information not used in plaintiff's prior trials could "interfere with another enforcement proceeding"); Hemsley v. U.S. Dep't of Justice, No. 90-2413, slip op. at 10 (D.D.C. Sept. 24, 1992) (holding that Exemption 7(A) protection applied when the "only pending criminal proceeding" was an appeal of the denial of a new trial motion; "[k]nowledge of potential witnesses and documentary evidence that were not used during the first trial" could "genuinely harm

(continued...)

some cases have extended Exemption 7(A) protection to all of the information compiled during all of the law enforcement proceedings.[20]

Similarly, Exemption 7(A) also may be invoked when an investigation has been terminated but an agency retains oversight or some other continuing enforcement-related responsibility.[21] For example, it has been found to have been invoked properly to protect impounded ballots where their disclosure could "interfere with the authority of the NLRB" to conduct and process future collective bargaining representation elections.[22] If, however, there is no such ongoing agency oversight or continuing enforcement-related responsibility, courts do not permit an agency to continue the use

---

[19](...continued)
government's case"); cf. Senate of P.R. v. U.S. Dep't of Justice, 823 F.2d 574, 578 (D.C. Cir. 1987) (relying on language of statute prior to 1986 FOIA amendments to remand case for additional explanation of why no segregable portions of documents could be released without interfering with related proceedings); Narducci v. FBI, No. 93-0327, slip op. at 3-4 (D.D.C. Sept. 22, 1995) (explaining that Exemption 7(A) remains applicable "in light of retrial, not yet scheduled, of several defendants," when agency had "adequately identified" how disclosure would interfere with retrial; however, agency must release all "public source documents").

[20] See Keen, No. 96-1049, slip op. at 6-8 (D.D.C. July 14, 1999) (finding use of Exemption 7(A) proper to withhold entire criminal file while motion to "redetermine" sentence is pending); Kansi, 11 F. Supp. 2d at 44 (holding that Exemption 7(A) protection "exists at least until plaintiff's conviction is final"); Burke, No. 96-1739, slip op. at 5 (D.D.C. Mar. 31, 1998) (ruling that protection of records "compiled for . . . prosecution of plaintiff in a previous criminal trial" is proper in light of plaintiff's post-conviction appeal because "disclosure of these records could harm the government's prosecution of the plaintiff's appeal"); Crooker v. ATF, No. 83-1646, slip op. at 1-2 (D.D.C. Apr. 30, 1984) (finding "no question that Exemption 7(A) is controlling" while motion to withdraw guilty plea is still pending).

[21] See, e.g., Alaska Pulp Corp. v. NLRB, No. 90-1510D, slip op. at 2 (W.D. Wash. Nov. 4, 1991) (stating that Exemption 7(A) remains applicable when corporation found liable for unfair labor practices, but parties remain embroiled in controversy as to compliance); Erb v. U.S. Dep't of Justice, 572 F. Supp. 954, 956 (W.D. Mich. 1983) (finding withholding proper when investigation "concluded 'for the time being'" and then subsequently reopened); ABC Home Health Servs. v. HHS, 548 F. Supp. 555, 556, 559 (N.D. Ga. 1982) (holding documents protected when "final settlement" was subject to re-evaluation for at least three years); Timken v. U.S. Customs Serv., 531 F. Supp. 194, 199-200 (D.D.C. 1981) (finding protection proper when final determination could be challenged or appealed); Zeller v. United States, 467 F. Supp. 487, 501 (S.D.N.Y. 1979) (finding that records compiled to determine whether party is complying with consent decree were protectible).

[22] Injex Indus. v. NLRB, 699 F. Supp. 1417, 1419-20 (N.D. Cal. 1986).

of Exemption 7(A) to protect information.[23]

The types of "law enforcement proceedings" to which Exemption 7(A) may be applicable have been interpreted broadly by the courts.[24] Such proceedings have been held to include not only criminal actions,[25] but civil actions[26] and regulatory proceedings[27] as well. They include "cases in which

---

[23] See, e.g., Phila. Newspapers, Inc. v. HHS, 69 F. Supp. 2d 63, 66-67 (D.D.C. 1999) (finding that release of audit statistics and details of settlement from closed investigation of one hospital would not interfere with possible future settlements with other institutions when none were being investigated); Ctr. for Auto Safety v. Dep't of Justice, 576 F. Supp. 739, 751-55 (D.D.C. 1983) (rejecting the agency's argument that "disclosures which make consent decree negotiations more difficult" qualify as "interference" with law enforcement proceedings because "release at this time of the documents at issue will occur after the termination of any proceeding to which the documents are relevant"), partial reconsideration granted, No. 82-0714, 1983 WL 1955 (D.D.C. July 7, 1983); see also Van Bourg, Allen, Weinberg & Roger v. NLRB, 751 F.2d 982, 985 (9th Cir. 1985) (stating that documents from unfair labor practice are not protected by Exemption 7(A) when no claim is pending or contemplated); Poss v. NLRB, 565 F.2d 654, 656-58 (10th Cir. 1977) (same); cf. Linn, 1995 WL 417810, at *9 (finding that an unspecified possible investigation against an unknown number of fugitives "is patently insufficient to justify the withholding of information"); Badran, 652 F. Supp. at 1440 (calling the agency's position "bewildering and indefensible" when it argued that Exemption 7(A) was proper because it "could use [the information] against a person who might some day violate immigration laws").

[24] See, e.g., Ctr. for Nat'l Sec. Studies, 331 F.3d at 926 (stating that law enforcement proceeding requirement is met by investigation into "breach of this nation's security"); Edmonds v. FBI, 272 F. Supp. 2d 35, 54-55 (D.D.C. 2003) (concluding that agency justified its withholding of records under Exemption 7(A) in case involving "national security issues").

[25] See, e.g., Manna, 51 F.3d at 1165 (finding that criminal law enforcement proceedings involving La Cosa Nostra and its "long, sordid and bloody history of racketeer domination and exploitation" meets threshold); Delviscovo v. FBI, 903 F. Supp. 1, 3 (D.D.C. 1995) (explaining that ongoing criminal investigation of organized crime activities including narcotics, gambling, stolen property, and loan sharking satisfies threshold), summary affirmance granted, No. 95-5388 (D.C. Cir. Jan. 24, 1997); Gould, 688 F. Supp. at 703 (ruling that post-award audit reports pertaining to ongoing criminal investigation into pricing discounts qualify); Nat'l Pub. Radio, 431 F. Supp. at 510, 513-15 (reasoning that documents relating to a nuclear-safety whistleblower's plutonium contamination, given the "possibility of obstruction of justice," fall "within the protective scope of Exemption 7(A)").

[26] See, e.g., Manna, 51 F.3d at 1165 (stating that disclosure would inter-
(continued...)

---

the agency has the initiative in bringing an enforcement action and those
. . . in which it must be prepared to respond to a third party's challenge."[28]
Enforcement proceedings in state courts[29] and foreign courts[30] also qualify

---

[26](...continued)
fere with contemplated civil proceedings); Judicial Watch v. Rossotti, 285
F. Supp. 2d 17, 29 (D.D.C. 2003) (concluding that the "documents in question relate to an ongoing civil investigation by IRS and are exempt under
Exemption 7(A)"); Bender v. Inspector Gen. NASA, No. 90-2059, slip op. at
1-2, 8 (N.D. Ohio May 24, 1990) (explaining that information relating to "official reprimand" was reasonably expected to interfere with government's
proceeding to recover damages "currently pending" before same court).

[27] See, e.g., Envtl. Prot. Servs. v. EPA, 364 F. Supp. 2d 575, 588 (N.D. W.
Va. 2005) (stating that the disclosure of records compiled as part of EPA's
investigation into violations of its Toxic Substance Control Act "would prematurely reveal the EPA's case . . . in the administrative proceeding that is
currently pending"); Graves v. EEOC, No. CV 02-6842, slip op. at 10 (C.D.
Cal. Apr. 4, 2003) (finding employment dispute and pending EEOC charge
sufficient to meet law enforcement standard), aff'd, 144 F. App'x 626 (9th
Cir. 2005); Johnson v. DEA, No. 97-2231, 1998 U.S. Dist. LEXIS 9802, at *9
(D.D.C. June 25, 1998) (reiterating that "law being enforced may be . . . regulatory"); Rosenglick v. IRS, No. 97-747-18A, 1998 U.S. Dist. LEXIS 3920, at
*6 (M.D. Fla. Mar. 10, 1998) (confirming that phrase "law enforcement pur-
poses" includes "civil, criminal, and administrative statutes and regulations
such as those promulgated and enforced by the IRS"); Farm Fresh, Inc. v.
NLRB, No. 91-603-N, slip op. at 1, 7-9 (E.D. Va. Nov. 15, 1991) (holding that
NLRB's unfair labor practice action constitutes law enforcement proceedings); Alaska Pulp, No. 90-1510D, slip op. at 2, 5 (W.D. Wash. Nov. 4, 1991)
(explaining that after finding of unfair labor practice, compliance investigation to determine back pay awards constitutes enforcement proceedings);
Concrete Constr. Co. v. U.S. Dep't of Labor, No. 2-89-649, slip op. at 2-6 (S.D.
Ohio Oct. 26, 1990) (ruling that Department of Labor's regulation and inspection of construction sites constitute enforcement proceedings); Injex,
699 F. Supp. at 1419 (finding that NLRB's responsibility to process collective bargaining representation elections constitutes law enforcement proceedings); Fedders Corp. v. FTC, 494 F. Supp. 325, 327-28 (S.D.N.Y.) (concluding that FTC investigation into allegations of unfair advertising and offering of equipment warranties constitutes law enforcement proceedings),
aff'd, 646 F.2d 560 (2d Cir. 1980) (unpublished table decision).

[28] Mapother v. Dep't of Justice, 3 F.3d 1533, 1540 (D.C. Cir. 1993).

[29] See, e.g., Shaw v. FBI, 749 F.2d 58, 64 (D.C. Cir. 1984) (holding that "an
authorized federal investigation into the commission of state crime [the
JFK assassination] qualifies"); Hoffman, No. 98-1733-A, slip op. at 3 (W.D.
Okla. Sept. 21, 2001) (stating that although federal proceedings were completed, a decision to proceed with state prosecution qualifies); Butler, 888
F. Supp. at 182-83 (explaining that release could jeopardize pending state
(continued...)

for Exemption 7(A) protection.

It is well established that in order to satisfy the "law enforcement proceedings" requirement of Exemption 7(A), an agency must be able to point to a specific pending or contemplated law enforcement proceeding that could be harmed by disclosure.[31] By comparison, while some courts have extended the attorney work-product privilege of Exemption 5 to instances of "foreseeable litigation, even if no specific claim is contemplated,"[32] courts have not likewise extended the protection of Exemption 7(A).[33]

---

[29](...continued)
criminal proceeding).

[30] See, e.g., Bevis v. Dep't of State, 801 F.2d 1386, 1388 (D.C. Cir. 1986) (stating that the "language of the statute makes no distinction between foreign and domestic enforcement purposes" (citing Shaw, 749 F.2d at 64)); Zevallos-Gonzalez v. DEA, No. 97-1720, slip op. at 11-13 (D.D.C. Sept. 25, 2000) (explaining that even though no indictment in United States was likely, disclosure of information sought would "interfere with efforts of Peruvian officials" to investigate and prosecute).

[31] See Mapother, 3 F.3d at 1542 ("We believe that a categorical approach is appropriate in determining the likelihood of enforcement proceedings in cases where an alien is excluded from entry into the United States because of his alleged participation in Nazi persecutions or genocide. Otherwise, we must exercise our faculties as mind-readers."); Nat'l Sec. Archive v. FBI, 759 F. Supp. 872, 883 (D.D.C. 1991) (reasoning that FBI's justification that disclosure would interfere with its overall counterintelligence program "must be rejected" as too general to be type of proceeding cognizable under Exemption 7(A), and permitting FBI to demonstrate whether there existed any specific pending or contemplated law enforcement proceedings).

[32] Schiller v. NLRB, 964 F.2d 1205, 1208 (D.C. Cir. 1992); see also, e.g., Delaney, Migdail & Young, Chartered v. IRS, 826 F.2d 124, 127 (D.C. Cir. 1987) (extending attorney work-product privilege to documents prepared at time when identity of prospective litigation opponent was not yet known).

[33] See Phila. Newspapers, 69 F. Supp. at 66-67 (rejecting agency's argument that disclosure of audit statistics would interfere with possible future action because "investigation is over"); Ctr. for Auto Safety, 576 F. Supp. at 751-55 (stating that modification of consent decree from closed proceeding not protected when not being used in ongoing proceeding; rejecting agency's argument that disclosure would make future negotiations more difficult); see also Van Bourg, Allen, Weinberg & Roger, 751 F.2d at 985 (finding that Exemption 7(A) does not apply to documents from closed proceeding when no other claim is pending or contemplated); Poss, 565 F.2d at 656-58 (same); Linn,1995 WL 417810, at *25 (ruling that Exemption 7(A) is not applicable when no investigation exists); Badran, 652 F. Supp. at 1440
(continued...)

As one court has observed, "[i]f an agency could withhold information whenever it could imagine circumstances where the information might have some bearing on some hypothetical enforcement proceeding, the FOIA would be meaningless."[34] Rather, it is the existence of a pending or prospective law enforcement proceeding against other investigative targets that permits the continued use of Exemption 7(A) when law enforcement proceedings against initial investigatory target are "closed."[35] Thus, information cannot properly be protected just because a law enforcement agency asserts, without a firm basis, that release would interfere with future actions.[36]

With respect to judicial deference to agency judgments under Exemption 7(A), the courts can be quite pragmatic. Indeed, in a significant decision involving post-September 11 detainees, the D.C. Circuit in Center for National Security Studies v. United States Department of Justice not

---

[33](...continued)
(rejecting agency's attempt to equate "might some day" with "pending").

[34] Badran, 652 F. Supp. at 1440.

[35] See, e.g., Solar Sources, 142 F.3d at 1040 (finding use of Exemption 7(A) proper in closed case when there is ongoing case against other targets); New England Med. Ctr. Hosp., 548 F.2d at 385-86 (stating that protection of closed file is proper when it relates to pending open case); Givner, No. 99-3454, slip op. at 3, 7 (D.D.C. Mar. 1, 2001) (explaining that although plaintiff is "serving his sentence," impeding trial of two co-conspirators and habeas action of convicted co-conspirator "clearly satisfy" requirement); Concrete Constr., No. 2-89-649, slip op. at 3-5 (S.D. Ohio Oct. 26, 1990) (approving use of Exemption 7(A) when release of program plans would permit prospective targets to gauge "potential of being investigated"); see also Engelking, No. 91-0165, slip op. at 6 (D.D.C. Nov. 30, 1992) (ruling that inmate's file was properly withheld when fugitive was involved); Warmack, No. 88-H-1191-E, slip op. at 22-23 (N.D. Ala. May 16, 1990) (holding Exemption 7(A) applicable to documents involving fugitives).

[36] See, e.g., Dow Jones, 219 F.R.D. at 174 (stating that the "defendant fails to cite, and the Court was unable to locate, any case in which a court upheld an agency's determination to withhold disclosure pursuant to Exemption 7(A) because disclosure would interfere with settlement discussions or impede the willingness of targets of the investigation to voluntarily disclose additional information"); Ctr. for Auto Safety, 576 F. Supp. at 751-55 (holding that records concerning a modification of a consent decree from a closed proceeding are not protectible when not "being used in an on-going investigation"; disclosure would not interfere with future settlements); see also Van Bourg, Allen, Weinberg & Roger, 751 F.2d at 985 (stating that documents from unfair labor practice are not protected by Exemption 7(A) when no claim is pending or contemplated); Poss, 565 F.2d at 656-58 (same).

long ago declared that "the courts must defer to the executive on decisions of national security" under Exemption 7(A) as well as elsewhere.[37] Explaining that "America faces an enemy just as real as its former Cold War foes,"[38] the D.C. Circuit stressed the concept of deference repeatedly in this case, citing both to its own prior decisions and to Supreme Court precedent.[39] Further, it said that it would "reject any attempt to artificially limit the long-recognized deference to the executive on national security issues," which means that this deference now clearly has been extended to the law enforcement realm.[40] Thus, there is a strong connection between law enforcement, national security, and homeland security when it comes to combating the threat of domestic terrorism,[41] particularly insofar as courts "have wisely respected the executive's judgment in prosecuting the national response to terrorism."[42]

Further, regarding an agency's specific evaluation of harm, the D.C. Circuit in Center for National Security Studies also recognized that "Exemption 7(A) explicitly requires a predictive judgment of the harm that will re-

---

[37] Ctr. for Nat'l Sec. Studies, 331 F.3d at 928, 932 (emphasizing that "we owe the same deference under Exemption 7(A) in appropriate cases, such as this one"); cf. L.A. Times Commc'ns v. Dep't of the Army, 442 F. Supp. 880, 899 (C.D. Cal. 2006) (stating that "[t]he Court defers" to Army officer's evaluation of how release of information could benefit insurgents in Iraq). But see Haddam v. FBI, No. 01-434, slip op. at 23-27 (D.D.C. Sept. 8, 2004) (stating that "[a]s with national security matters, this Court generally does not question the FBI's expert assessment that disclosure of the requested information could interfere with pending or prospective law enforcement proceedings," but nevertheless declaring that the agency "has not shown how naming certain statutory provisions upon which [d]efendant plans to rely after the 7(A) exemption lapses would jeopardize the ongoing investigation or national security more generally").

[38] Ctr. for Nat'l Sec. Studies, 331 F. 3d at 928.

[39] See id. at 926-28 (citing Zadvydas v. Davis, 533 U.S. 678, 696 (2001) (stating that terrorism warrants heightened deference) (non-FOIA case); Dep't of the Navy v. Egan, 484 U.S. 518, 530 (1988) (concluding that courts should be reluctant to intrude into national security affairs) (non-FOIA case); CIA v. Sims, 471 U.S. 159, 179 (1985) (explaining that the CIA is familiar with "the whole picture" so its decisions merit deference); King v. U.S. Dep't of Justice, 830 F.2d 210, 217 (D.C. Cir. 1987) (stating that "the court owes substantial weight to detailed agency explanations in the national security context").

[40] Ctr. for Nat'l Sec. Studies, 331 F.3d at 928-30.

[41] See FOIA Post, "FOIA Officers Conference Held on Homeland Security" (posted 7/3/03) (discussing "the safeguarding and protection of homeland security-related information").

[42] Ctr. for Nat'l Sec. Studies, 331 F.3d at 932.

sult from disclosure of information."[43] While its discussion of the concept of Exemption 7(A)'s "predictive judgment" in this particular case involved an agency's judgment in the national security arena, the D.C. Circuit never-theless carefully reviewed the government's submissions and found that they readily met Exemption 7(A)'s standards.[44] Thus, agencies should keep in mind the D.C. Circuit's deferential "predictive judgment" approach when determining the applicability of Exemption 7(A) among other FOIA exemp-tions, when describing the agency expertise brought to bear on such deter-minations, and when articulating the harm envisioned by the release of withheld information, whether or not the case involves particularly sensi-tive national security issues.[45]

More generally, with respect to the showing of harm to law enforce-ment proceedings required to invoke Exemption 7(A), the Supreme Court in NLRB v. Robbins Tire & Rubber Co. rejected the position that "interference" must always be established on a document-by-document basis, and held that a determination of the exemption's applicability may be made "generi-cally," based on the categorical types of records involved.[46] Indeed, the Su-preme Court in United States Department of Justice v. Reporters Commit-tee for Freedom of the Press emphatically affirmed the vitality of its Rob-bins Tire approach and further extended it to include situations arising un-der other FOIA exemptions in which records can be entitled to protection on a "categorical" basis.[47]

Along these lines, in a recent case involving a request for a particular agency form used for wiretapping, it was found that the defendant agency initially "denied the request pursuant to Exemption 7(A) . . . before deter-

---

[43] Id. at 928; see also L.A. Times, 442 F. Supp. at 899 (stating that "[t]he Court defers to [Army officer's] predictive judgments" about Exemption 7(A) harm in insurgency setting); Edmonds, 272 F. Supp. 2d at 55 (address-ing the issue of harm regarding "the likelihood of intimidation of individuals involved in the investigation").

[44] Ctr. for Nat'l Sec. Studies, 331 F.3d at 926 (quoting Campbell v. U.S. Dep't of Justice, 164 F.3d 20, 32 (D.C. Cir. 1998), and Pratt v. Webster, 673 F.2d 408, 419 (D.C. Cir. 1982)).

[45] See, e.g., FOIA Post, "FOIA Officers Conference Held on Homeland Security" (posted 7/3/03) (emphasizing importance of protecting sensitive homeland security-related information under FOIA's law enforcement ex-emptions); see also Ctr. for Nat'l Sec. Studies, 331 F.3d at 928 (discussing government's descriptions of harm flowing from release of particular types of information, and finding that "government's expectation [of harm] is rea-sonable").

[46] 437 U.S. at 236.

[47] Reporters Comm., 489 U.S. at 776-80 (Exemption 7(C)).

mining that the document in question [actually] did not exist in its files."[48] Accepting this approach, the court observed that it is "well-established that the government may justify its withholdings by reference to generic categories of documents, rather than document-by-document," and it further explained that the "government's explanation for initially withholding the document under Exemption 7(A) was proper [because] 'with respect to particular kinds of enforcement proceedings, disclosure of particular kinds of investigatory records while a case is pending would generally interfere with enforcement proceedings.'"[49] Indeed, almost all courts have accepted affidavits in Exemption 7(A) cases that specify the distinct, generic categories of documents at issue and the harm that would result from their release, rather than requiring extensive, detailed itemizations of each document.[50]

---

[48] Powers v. U.S. Dep't of Justice, No. 03-C-893, 2006 U.S. Dist. LEXIS 62756, at *1 (E.D. Wis. Sept. 1, 2006).

[49] Id. (quoting Solar Sources, 142 F.3d at 1038 (citing Robbins Tire, 437 U.S. at 236)); cf. Watkins Motor Lines, Inc. v. EEOC, No. 8:05-1065, 2006 WL 905518, at *5 (M.D. Fla. Apr. 7, 2006) (finding, in a case in which the EEOC continued to investigate even after the charging party withdrew the complaint, that the agency's use of Exemption 7(A) was proper because "'with respect to particular kinds of enforcement proceedings, disclosure of particular kinds of investigatory records while a case is pending would generally interfere with enforcement proceedings'" (quoting Robbins Tire, 437 U.S. at 236)).

[50] See, e.g., Moye, O'Brien, O'Rourke, Hogan & Pickert v. Nat'l R.R. Passenger Corp., No. 03-14823, slip op. at 6-7 (11th Cir. June 24, 2004) (declaring that "[a]ll Amtrak has to do is show a reasonable expectation of 'interference' from release of the category of documents involved here, as opposed to having to do a document by document or page by page analysis," and noting supporting decisions in the Sixth, Eighth, and Ninth Circuits); Lynch v. Dep't of the Treasury, No. 99-1697, 2000 WL 123236, at *2 (9th Cir. Jan. 28, 2000) (explaining that "government need not 'make a specific factual showing with respect to each withheld document'" (quoting Lewis, 823 F.2d at 380)); Solar Sources, 142 F.3d at 1038 (reiterating that government "may justify its withholdings by reference to generic categories of documents, rather than document-by-document"); In re Dep't of Justice, 999 F.2d 1302, 1308 (8th Cir. 1993) (en banc) (The "Supreme Court has consistently interpreted Exemption 7 of the FOIA (specifically so far subsections 7(A), 7(C), and 7(D))" to permit the government to proceed on a "categorical basis" and to not require a document-by-document Vaughn Index.), on remand sub nom. Crancer v. U.S. Dep't of Justice, No. 89-234, slip op. at 6 (E.D. Mo. Oct. 4, 1994) (magistrate's recommendation) (approving FBI's "generic" affidavit as sufficient and denying plaintiff's requests for methodology of document review and accounting of time spent reviewing documents), adopted (E.D. Mo. Nov. 7, 1994); Dickerson, 992 F.2d at 1431 (stating that it is "often feasible for courts to make 'generic determinations'
(continued...)

[50](...continued)
about interference"); Lewis, 823 F.2d at 380 (holding that IRS need only make general showing and is not required to make specific factual showing with respect to each withheld page); Wright, 822 F.2d at 646 (explaining that "a detailed listing is generally not required under Exemption 7(A)"); Spannaus, 813 F.2d at 1288 (stating that Supreme Court accepts generic determinations); Curran, 813 F.2d at 475 (holding that generic determinations permitted); Bevis, 801 F.2d at 1389 (finding that agency may take "generic approach, grouping documents into relevant categories"); Crooker, 789 F.2d at 67 ("Because generic determinations are permitted, the government need not justify its withholdings document-by-document; it may instead do so category-of-document by category-of-document."); Campbell, 682 F.2d at 265 (recognizing that "government may focus upon categories of records"); Newry Ltd. v. U.S. Customs & Border Prot. Bureau, No. 04-2110, 2005 WL 3273975, at *5 (D.D.C. July 29, 2005) (explaining that "[a]n agency need not detail the potential interference on a document-by-document basis," but may group documents into relevant categories that are "'sufficiently distinct to allow a court to grasp'" how release of the information in question would interfere with law enforcement proceedings (quoting Bevis, 801 F.2d at 1389)); Changzhou Laosan Group v. U.S. Customs & Border Prot. Bureau, No. 04-1919, 2005 WL 913268, at *8 (D.D.C. Apr. 20, 2005) (stating that agency may take generic approach and group documents into relevant categories that allow court to grasp how release would interfere with proceedings); Envtl. Prot., 364 F. Supp. 2d at 588 (stating that an "agency is not required to establish on a document-by-document basis the interference that would result from the disclosure of each document," but instead may take a generic approach "based on categorical types of records" (citing Robbins Tire, 437 U.S. at 232)); Edmonds, 272 F. Supp. 2d at 54 (explaining that the agency may group documents into categories, but that "[i]n order to utilize this categorical approach, [an agency] must 'conduct a document-by-document review' of all responsive documents to assign documents to the proper category and 'explain to the court how the release of each category would interfere with enforcement proceedings'" (quoting Bevis, 801 F.2d 1389-90)); Sandgrund v. SEC, 215 F. Supp. 2d 178, 180-81 (D.D.C. 2002) (acknowledging that generic or categorical approach is proper, but finding some descriptions to be "too broad or generic" to satisfy "government's Vaughn obligation" and to permit meaningful court review); ACLU Found., 833 F. Supp. at 407 (An agency "must supply sufficient facts about the alleged interference . . . . This does not, however, necessarily require an individualized showing for each document."); see also FOIA Update, Vol. V, No. 2, at 3-4 ("FOIA Counselor: The 'Generic' Aspect of Exemption 7(A)") (advising agencies on most efficient and practical uses of Exemption 7(A)); cf. Robinson, No. 00-11182, slip op. at 8-9 (11th Cir. Mar. 15, 2001) (reiterating that while courts can accept generic determinations of interference with enforcement proceedings, government must "make at least some minimal showing"; because the district court ruled sua sponte, it "lacked an adequate factual basis for its deci-
(continued...)

Nevertheless, in a recent decision discussing the procedures necessary to use such a categorical approach, a court stressed the importance of a document-by-document review.[51] In explaining the necessity of reviewing Exemption 7(A) records prior to placing them in categories, it described by comparison the different treatment accorded to Exemption 5's attorney work-product privilege and Exemption 7(A), observing that the "work-product doctrine is broadly construed and applies to facts, law, opinions, and analysis. Thus, where a document is withheld pursuant to the work-product doctrine, there is no reasonably segregable portion to release."[52] The court stated that it "decline[d] to leap that far" for Exemption 7(A) and declared that such a broad application "would eviscerate the segregation requirement under Exemption 7(A)."[53]

Likewise, in another recent case discussing the categorical approach under Exemption 7(A), another court first stated that the "FOIA permits agencies to craft rules exempting certain categories of records from disclosure under Exemption 7(A) instead of making a record-by-records showing," but then added that an "agency's ability to rely on categorical rules, however, has limits."[54] The court continued to describe the proper approach to categorizing records by explaining that agencies bear the burden of "identifying either specific documents or functional categories of information that are exempt from disclosure, and disclosing any reasonably segreable, non-exempt" portions, because to do otherwise "would eviscerate the principles of openness in government that the FOIA embodies."[55]

Thus, agencies sometimes are cautioned by courts to review all requested documents in order to know the character and content of all records being placed into particular generic categories, as was made clear by the District Court for the District of Minnesota in Gavin v. Securities & Ex-

---

[50](...continued)
sion"); Beneville, No. 98-6137, slip op. 22-23 (D. Or. June 11, 2003) (holding that "Exemption 7(A) does not authorize 'blanket exemptions' for 'all records relating to an ongoing investigation,'" and instructing agency to "submit additional briefing" describing why it did not segregate and release records such as newspapers and magazine articles in its initial response (quoting Campbell, 682 F.2d at 259)).

[51] Gavin v. SEC, No. 04-4522, 2006 U.S. LEXIS 75227, at *13 (D. Minn. Oct. 13, 2006).

[52] Id.

[53] Id.; cf. Judicial Watch v. Dep't of Justice, 432 F.3d 366, 371 (D.C. Cir. 2005) (declaring that "the Circuit's case law is clear" and reiterating that if "a document is fully protected as work product, then segregability is not required").

[54] Long, 2006 WL 2578755, at *27.

[55] Id. at *27, *29.

change Commission.[56] In Gavin, the court explained that while "[n]umerous courts, including the Eighth Circuit, hold that an agency may utilize the categorical approach to justify its burden with regard to FOIA Exemption 7(A)," a document-by-document review to categorize the documents is required.[57] In a subsequent decision in the same case, this court reiterated that an agency's ability to place documents into categories "does not obviate the requirement that an agency conduct a document-by-document review"; rather, it must conduct a document-by-document review in order to assign documents to proper categories.[58]

Then, in yet a third ruling in this case, the court chastised the Securities and Exchange Commission by stating that it "has continually and deliberately stalled in fulfilling its obligations to conduct a document-by-document review of material it seeks to withhold pursuant to Exemption 7(A). In doing so, the SEC has attempted to play by its own rules and disregard the law."[59] This insistence on at least some review of the documents in order to place them in the proper category is, indeed, in line with the general rule in the D.C. Circuit as well as in other jurisdictions.[60]

---

[56] Gavin v. SEC, No. 04-4522, 2005 WL 2739293, at *3-4 (D. Minn. Oct. 24, 2005), partial reconsideration denied, No. 04-4522, 2006 WL 208783 (D. Minn. Jan. 26, 2006), clarification & stay denied, No. 04-4522, 2006 WL 1738417 (D. Minn. June 20, 2006); summary judgment granted in part, 2006 U.S. Dist. LEXIS 75227 (Oct. 13, 2006).

[57] Id.

[58] Gavin v. SEC, No. 04-4522, 2006 WL 208783, at *2 (D. Minn. Jan. 26, 2006) (citing In re Dep't of Justice, 999 F.2d at 1305-09).

[59] Gavin v. SEC, No. 04-4522, 2006 WL 1738417, at *3 (D. Minn. June 20, 2006); see also Gavin, 2006 U.S. Dist. LEXIS 75227, at *11-13 (approving the agency's withholding of that portion of records for which the agency finally conducted a document-by-document review, but denying the agency's motion as to the remaining documents for which it had not conducted such a review).

[60] See, e.g., Bevis, 801 F.2d at 1389 (stating that although an agency need not justify its withholding on a document-by-document basis, "it must review each document to determine the category in which it properly belongs"); see also In re Dep't of Justice, 999 F.2d at 1309 (explaining that agency must conduct document-by-document review to assign documents to proper categories); Crooker, 789 F.2d at 67 (describing review of documents file-by-file as unnecessary, but stressing review of documents for category-by-category assignment as necessary); Barney, 618 F.2d at 1273 (reiterating that agency is not required to make specific factual showing with respect to each withheld document, but instead may focus on particular categories of documents); Inst. for Justice & Human Rights v. Executive Office of the U.S. Attorney, No. 96-1469, 1998 U.S. Dist. LEXIS 3709, (continued...)

**EXEMPTION 7(A)**

Specific guidance has been provided by the Courts of Appeals for the First, Fourth, and D.C. Circuits as to what constitutes an adequate "generic category" in an Exemption 7(A) affidavit.[61] The general principle uniting their decisions is that affidavits must provide at least a general, "functional" description of the types of documents at issue sufficient to indicate the type of interference threatening the law enforcement proceeding.[62] It

---

[60](...continued)
at *16-17 (N.D. Cal. Mar. 18, 1998) (stating that declarations need to establish that each document was reviewed); Kay, 976 F. Supp. at 35 (explaining that agency must conduct document-by-document review in order to assign each document to proper category); Jefferson, 1997 U.S. Dist. LEXIS 3064, at *10 n.1 (explaining need for document-by-document review of responsive records); Hillcrest Equities, Inc. v. U.S. Dep't of Justice, No. CA3-85-2351-R, slip op. at 7 (N.D. Tex. Jan. 26, 1987) (declaring that government must review each document to determine category to which it belongs).

[61] See Spannaus, 813 F.2d at 1287, 1289 (stating that "details regarding initial allegations giving rise to this investigation; notification of [FBI Headquarters] of the allegations and ensuing investigation; interviews with witnesses and subjects; investigative reports furnished to the prosecuting attorneys," and similar categories are all sufficient); Curran, 813 F.2d at 476 (same); Bevis, 801 F.2d at 1390 (explaining that "identities of possible witnesses and informants, reports on the location and viability of potential evidence, and polygraph reports" are sufficient; categories "identified only as 'teletypes,' 'airtels,' or 'letters'" are insufficient); see also Cucci, 871 F. Supp. at 511-12 (holding that "evidentiary matters category" -- described as "witness statements, information exchanged between the FBI and local law enforcement agencies, physical evidence, evidence obtained pursuant to search warrants and documents related to the case's documentary and physical evidence" is sufficient); cf. Solar Sources, 142 F.3d at 1036-39 (explaining that agency's six broad categories and eight subcategories "may have provided a sufficient factual basis" for judicial review, but cautioning that "we might give some weight to appellants' argument [that categories did not provide functional descriptions] had the district court not conducted a thorough in camera review").

[62] See, e.g., Lion I, 354 F.3d at 1084 (explaining that its holding does "not imply that the government must disclose facts that would undermine the very purpose of its withholding," but that particularly if the agency wants the court to rely on an in camera declaration, it must justify its exemption position "in as much detail as possible"); Curran, 813 F.2d at 475 ("Withal, a tightrope must be walked: categories must be distinct enough to allow meaningful judicial review, yet not so distinct as prematurely to let the cat out of the investigative bag."); Crooker, 789 F.2d at 67 ("The hallmark of an acceptable Robbins category is thus that it is functional; it allows the court to trace a rational link between the nature of the document and the alleged likely interference."); Owens v. U.S. Dep't of Justice, No. 04-1701, 2006 WL 3490790, at *6 (D.D.C. Dec. 1, 2006) (observing that "courts reviewing the

(continued...)

should be noted, however, that both the First and the Fourth Circuits have approved a "miscellaneous" category of "other sundry items of information."[63] Although the D.C. Circuit has not yet specifically addressed an af-

---

[62](...continued)
withholding of agency records under Exemption 7 cannot demand categories 'so distinct as prematurely to let the cat out of the investigative bag,'" but finding that the agency's categories in this case did not provide "so much as a bare sketch of the information" and that the agency therefore had not met its burden under Exemption 7(A) (quoting Curran, 813 F.2d at 475)); Gavin, 2005 WL 2739293, at *3 (stating that the "[p]roper utilization of the categorical approach requires" categories to be "functional," which is defined as allowing "'the court to trace a rational link between the nature of the document and the alleged likely interference'" (quoting Bevis, 801 F.2d at 1389)); Pinnavaia v. FBI, No. 03-112, slip op. at 11 (D.D.C. Feb. 25, 2004) (stating that the declaration provides an "adequate basis to find that disclosure of the withheld information would interfere with law enforcement proceedings"), summary affirmance granted, No. 04-5115, 2004 WL 2348155, at *1 (D.C. Cir. Oct. 19, 2004) (explaining that "FBI's affidavits have substantiated its claim" that release could reasonably be expected to interfere with enforcement proceedings (citing Ctr. for Nat'l Sec. Studies, 331 F.3d at 928)); Voinche v. FBI, 46 F. Supp. 2d 26, 31 (D.D.C. 1999) (explaining that generic approach is appropriate, but that agency must demonstrate how each category of documents, if disclosed, could reasonably be expected to interfere with law enforcement proceedings); Hoffman v. U.S. Dep't of Justice, No. 98-1733-A, slip op. at 15, 18 (W.D. Okla. Dec. 15, 1999) (explaining that while Supreme Court has approved categorical approach, responsive documents must be grouped into "categories that can be linked to cogent reasons for nondisclosure"); Kitchen v. DEA, No. 93-2035, slip op. at 12-13 (D.D.C. Oct. 11, 1995) (approving categorical descriptions when court can trace rational link between nature of document and likely interference); cf. Inst. for Justice & Human Rights, 1998 U.S. Dist. LEXIS 3709, at *14-15 (explaining that four categories -- confidential informant, agency reports, co-defendant extradition documents, and attorney work product -- are too general to be functional and ordering government to "recast" categories to show how documents in "new categories would interfere with the pending proceedings"); Putnam v. U.S. Dep't of Justice, 873 F. Supp. 705, 714 (D.D.C. 1995) (stating that agency "administrative inquiry file" is "patently inadequate" description); SafeCard Servs. v. SEC, No. 84-3073, slip op. at 6 n.3 (D.D.C. May 19, 1988) (holding that agency "file" is not sufficient generic category to justify withholding), aff'd in part, rev'd in part on other grounds & remanded, 926 F.2d 1197 (D.C. Cir. 1991); Pruitt Elec. Co. v. U.S. Dep't of Labor, 587 F. Supp. 893, 895-96 (N.D. Tex. 1984) (explaining that disclosure of reference material consulted by investigator that might aid an unspecified target in unspecified manner found not to cause interference).

[63] Spannaus, 813 F.2d at 1287, 1289; Curran, 813 F.2d at 476 (finding that wide range of records made some degree of generality "understandable --

(continued...)

fidavit containing such a category, a subsequent decision of the District Court for the District of Columbia held that documents categorized as "Other Agency Records," and described in agency affidavits as "material evidence that was the basis for the conviction," were described "sufficient[ly] to allow the court to determine that the files were properly withheld."[64]

The functional test set forth by the D.C. Circuit does not require a detailed showing that release of the records is likely to interfere with the law enforcement proceedings; it is sufficient for the agency to make a generalized showing that release of these particular kinds of documents would generally interfere with enforcement proceedings.[65] Indeed, publicly revealing too many details about an ongoing investigation could jeopardize the government's ability to protect such information.[66] Also, it should be

---

[63](...continued)
and probably essential").

[64] Keen, No. 96-1049, slip op. at 10 (D.D.C. July 14, 1999).

[65] See, e.g., Judicial Watch, 285 F. Supp. 2d at 29-30 (approving the IRS's use of Exemption 7(A) to withhold names of specific employees because "[c]ollecting taxes is an unpopular job, to put it mildly, and IRS 'lower level' employees are entitled to some identity protection"); Kay, 976 F. Supp. at 39 (stating that agency "need not establish that witness intimidation is certain to occur, only that it is a possibility"); Pully v. IRS, 939 F. Supp. 429, 436 (E.D. Va. 1996) ("All that is required is an objective showing that interference could reasonably occur as the result of the documents' disclosure."); Wichlacz v. U.S. Dep't of Interior, 938 F. Supp. 325, 331 (E.D. Va. 1996) (holding that a "particularized showing of interference is not required; rather, the government may justify nondisclosure in a generic fashion"), aff'd, 114 F.3d 1178 (4th Cir. 1997) (unpublished table decision); Gould, 688 F. Supp. at 703-04 n.34 (describing functional test as steering "middle ground" between detail required by Vaughn Index and blanket withholding); Alyeska Pipeline Serv. v. EPA, No. 86-2176, 1987 WL 17081, at *2-3 (D.D.C. Sept. 9, 1987) (explaining that the government need not "show that intimidation will certainly result," but that it must "show that the possibility of witness intimidation exists"), aff'd, 856 F.2d 309 (D.C. Cir. 1988).

[66] See Detroit Free Press, 174 F. Supp. 2d at 600-01 (concluding that information published in a newspaper -- including quotes from the FBI Special Agent-in-Charge of the Detroit Field Office -- "details some of the evidence developed and being developed, and the direction and scope" of the twenty-seven-year-long Hoffa disappearance investigation and thus "calls into question the veracity of the FBI's justification for withholding"; in camera review ordered); cf. Va. Dep't of State Police, 2004 WL 2198327, at *5 (recognizing that "law enforcement agencies must be able to investigate crime without the details of the investigation being released to the public in a manner that compromises the investigation"); Cook, 2005 WL 2237615,
(continued...)

remembered that making this showing is easier than in the past due to the current language of the statute.[67]

However, it is important to note that the D.C. Circuit in Bevis v. Department of State, held that even though an agency "need not justify its withholding on a document-by-document basis in court, [it] must itself review each document to determine the category in which it properly belongs."[68] Indeed, when an agency elects to use the "generic" approach, the court stated, the agency "has a three-fold task. First, it must define its categories functionally. Second, it must conduct a document-by-document review in order to assign the documents to the proper category. Finally, it must explain to the court how the release of each category would interfere with enforcement proceedings."[69] (For a further discussion, see Litigation

---

[66](...continued)
at *2 (stating that "[t]he Court is persuaded, however, that disclosure of the non-public information contained in the existing records could reasonably be expected to hinder the investigation" and not, as contended, facilitate help from the public in apprehending the 1971 airplane hijacker).

[67] See Manna, 51 F.3d at 1164 n.5 ("Congress amended this exemption to relax significantly the standard for demonstrating interference with enforcement proceedings."); Gould, 688 F. Supp. at 703 n.33 (explaining that the 1986 FOIA amendments "relaxed the standard of demonstrating interference with enforcement proceedings").

[68] 801 F.2d at 1389; see also Crooker, 789 F.2d at 67 (explaining that while government can justify its withholding category-by-category, government cannot justify its withholdings file-by-file); accord In re Dep't of Justice, 999 F.2d at 1309 (The "government may meet its burden by . . . conducting a document-by-document review to assign documents to proper categories."); Gavin, 2006 WL 208783, at *2 (emphasizing that the categorical approach "does not obviate the requirement that an agency conduct a document-by-document review" in order to assign documents to the proper category); Inst. for Justice, 1998 U.S. Dist. LEXIS 3709, at *16-17 (determining that declarations "do not establish that each document was reviewed"); Kay, 976 F. Supp. at 35 (explaining that an "agency must conduct a document-by-document review in order to assign each document to a proper category" (citing Bevis, 801 F.2d at 1389-90)); Jefferson, 1997 U.S. Dist. LEXIS 3064, at *10 n.1 (stating that "it would appear from a review of their declaration that Defendants may have never conducted a document-by-document review of responsive material," and denying the government's motion for summary judgment pending further submission); Hillcrest Equities, No. CA3-85-2351-R, slip op. at 7 (N.D. Tex. Jan. 26, 1987) (declaring that government must review each document to determine category in which it belongs).

[69] Bevis, 801 F.2d at 1389-90; see also Newry, 2005 WL 3273975, at *5 (referring to three-fold task); Beneville, No. 98-6137, slip op. at 17-18 (D. Or. (continued...)

Considerations, "Vaughn Index," below.)

The courts have long accepted that Congress intended that Exemption 7(A) apply "whenever the government's case in court would be harmed by the premature release of evidence or information,"[70] or when disclosure

---

[69](...continued)
June 11, 2003) (same); Judicial Watch, 2001 U.S. Dist. LEXIS 25732, at *13-16 (same); Voinche, 46 F. Supp. 2d at 31 (same); Kay, 976 F. Supp. at 35 (same); Jefferson, 1997 U.S. Dist. LEXIS 3064, at *12 (same); Maccaferri Gabions, Inc. v. U.S. Dep't of Justice, No. 95-2576, slip op. at 11-13 (D. Md. Mar. 26, 1996) (same), appeal dismissed voluntarily, No. 96-1513 (4th Cir. Sept. 19, 1996); Cudzich, 886 F. Supp. at 106 (same); Cucci, 871 F. Supp. at 511 (same).

[70] Robbins Tire, 437 U.S. at 232; see, e.g., Mapother, 3 F.3d at 1543 (holding that release of prosecutor's index of all documents he deems relevant would provide "critical insights into [government's] legal thinking and strategy"); Faiella v. IRS, No. 05-238, 2006 WL 2040130, at *3 (D.N.H. July 20, 2006) (stating that "disclosing information under active consideration" in a criminal investigation could undermine any future prosecution by "prematurely disclosing the government's potential theories, issues, and evidentiary requirements"); Suzhou Yuanda Enter. Co. v. U.S. Customs & Border Prot., 404 F. Supp. 2d 9, 14 (D.D.C. 2005) (agreeing that release of information "would interfere with an agency investigation [by] informing the public of the evidence sought and scrutinized by this type of investigation"); Envtl. Prot., 364 F. Supp. 2d at 588 (explaining that disclosure "would prematurely reveal the EPA's case"); Judicial Watch v. U.S. Dep't of Commerce, 337 F. Supp. 2d 146, 179 (D.D.C. 2004) (finding that agency has demonstrated that law enforcement proceedings are pending and that release of agent notes and information concerning export violations could "reasonably be expected to interfere" with proceedings); Rosenberg v. Freeh, No. 97-0476, slip op. at 1, 9 (D.D.C. May 13, 1998) (stating that release of code name would be "premature and damaging"); Rosenglick, 1998 U.S. Dist. LEXIS 3920, at *7-8 (explaining that "courts have liberally interpreted the term interference" and holding that "[s]uch an interpretation makes sense" because early access could "aid a wrongdoer in secreting or tampering with evidence [as well as reveal] the nature, scope, strategy and direction of the investigation"); Palmer Commc'ns v. U.S. Dep't of Justice, No. 96-M-777, slip op. at 4 (D. Colo. Oct. 30, 1996) (finding that release would harm "court's ability to control the use of discovery materials . . . [resulting in] an unacceptable interference with a law enforcement proceeding"); Durham v. USPS, No. 91-2234, 1992 WL 700246, at *1 (D.D.C. Nov. 25, 1992) (deciding that release of investigative memoranda, witness files, and electronic surveillance material would substantially interfere with pending homicide investigation by impeding government's ability to prosecute its strongest case), aff'd, No. 92-5511 (D.C. Cir. July 27, 1993); cf. Cecola v. FBI, No. 94 C 4866, 1995 WL 143548, at *2 (N.D. Ill. Mar. 30, 1995) (disallowing deposition of agency affiant when it might alert plaintiff to
(continued...)

would impede any necessary investigation prior to the enforcement proceeding.[71] In Robbins Tire, the Supreme Court found that the NLRB had

---

[70](...continued)
government's investigative strategy). But see LeMaine v. IRS, No. 89-2914, 1991 U.S. Dist. LEXIS 18651, at *13 (D. Mass. Dec. 10, 1991) (finding that agency failed to demonstrate that release would "seriously impair any ongoing effort to collect taxes or penalties . . . or to pursue criminal charges").

[71] See, e.g., Lynch, 2000 WL 123236, at *2 (stating that agency declarations "made clear" that release of records could harm "efforts at corroborating witness statements . . . alert potential suspects . . . [and] interfere with surveillance"); Solar Sources, 142 F.3d at 1039 (stating that disclosure could interfere by revealing "scope and nature" of investigation); Dickerson, 992 F.2d at 1429 (holding that public disclosure of information in Hoffa kidnapping file could reasonably be expected to interfere with enforcement proceedings); Citizens for Responsibility & Ethics in Wash. v. Nat'l Indian Gaming Comm'n, No. 05-00806, 2006 U.S. Dist. LEXIS 89614, at *21-24 (D.D.C. Dec. 12, 2006) (finding that release of records regarding alleged misuse of tribal gaming revenues during investigation could allow targets to ascertain direction of investigations, to identify potential charges to be brought, and to expose state and nature of current investigations, thereby undermining federal investigations); Gerstein v. U.S. Dep't of Justice, No. C-03-04893, slip op. at 11 (N.D. Cal. Sept. 30, 2005) (explaining that release of sealed warrants "could reasonably be expected to interfere" with ongoing investigation); Elec. Privacy Info. Ctr. v. DHS, 384 F. Supp. 2d 100, 119 (D.D.C. 2005) (holding that "release of this information could undermine the effectiveness" of the agency's investigation); Judicial Watch v. U.S. Dep't of Justice, 306 F. Supp. 2d 58, 75-76 (D.D.C. 2004) (observing that release of documents during course of investigation could damage agency's ability to obtain information); Kay, 976 F. Supp. at 38-39 (holding that the agency "specifically established that release" would permit the requester to gain insight into the FCC's evidence against him, to discern the narrow focus of the investigation, to assist in circumventing the investigation, and to create witness intimidation, and that disclosure would "reveal the scope, direction and nature" of the investigation); Pully, 939 F. Supp. at 436 (explaining that the requester's promise not to interfere with the investigation is of "no consequence" because government "need not take into account the individual's propensity or desire to interfere"; objective showing that disclosure could lead to interference found sufficient); W. Journalism, 926 F. Supp. at 192 (noting that disclosure could "contaminate the investigative process"); Butler, 888 F. Supp. at 182-83 (finding that disclosure would interfere with pending investigations by local police department of requester for stalking and murder); Kay v. FCC, 867 F. Supp. 11, 19 (D.D.C. 1994) (holding that documents, including letters to FCC from informants, would reveal scope of investigation and strength of case against plaintiff; disclosure of documents, "even redacted to exclude proper names," could lead to retaliatory action and intimidation of witnesses); Vosburgh v. IRS, No. 93-1493, 1994 WL 564699, at *2-3 (D. Or. July 5, 1994) (stating that dis-
(continued...)

established interference with its unfair labor practice enforcement proceeding by showing that release of its witness statements would create a great potential for witness intimidation and could deter their cooperation.[72]

---

[71](...continued)
closure of "DMV" record, memoranda of interview, police report, and portions of search warrants could interfere with IRS's investigation by revealing nature, scope, and direction of investigation, evidence obtained, government's strategies, and by providing requester with opportunity to create defenses and tamper with evidence); Int'l Collision Specialists, Inc. v. IRS, No. 93-2500, 1994 WL 395310, at *2, 4 (D.N.J. Mar. 2, 1994) (ruling that disclosure could reasonably be expected to interfere with enforcement proceedings by enabling requester "to determine nature, source, direction, and limits" of IRS investigation and to "fabricate defenses and tamper with evidence"); Church of Scientology Int'l v. IRS, 845 F. Supp. 714, 721 (C.D. Cal. 1993) (finding that disclosure likely to interfere with IRS's ability to investigate requester pursuant to Church Audit Procedures Act, 26 U.S.C. § 7611 (2000)); Church of Scientology v. IRS, 816 F. Supp. 1138, 1157 (W.D. Tex. 1993) (stating that disclosure could reasonably be expected to interfere with enforcement proceedings, subject IRS employees to harassment or reprisal, and reveal direction and scope of IRS investigation); Nat'l Pub. Radio, 431 F. Supp. at 514-15 (explaining that disclosure would impair agency's continued, long-term investigation into suspicious death of nuclear-safety whistleblower).

[72] 437 U.S. at 239; see also Ctr. for Nat'l Sec. Studies, 331 F.3d at 929 (reasoning that requested list of names "could be of great use" by terrorists in "intimidating witnesses"); Solar Sources, 142 F.3d at 1039 (stating that disclosure could result in "chilling and intimidation of witnesses"); Judicial Watch, Inc. v. U.S. Dep't of Justice, 102 F. Supp. 6, 19-20 (D.D.C. 2000) (reiterating that prematurely disclosing documents related to witnesses could result in witness tampering or intimidation and could discourage continued cooperation); Anderson v. U.S. Dep't of Treasury, No. 98-1112, 1999 U.S. Dist. LEXIS 20877, at *10 (W.D. Tenn. Mar. 24, 1999) (finding that disclosure allows "possibility of witness intimidation" and interference with proceedings); Accuracy in Media, Inc. v. Nat'l Park Serv., No. 97-2109, 1998 U.S. Dist. LEXIS 18373, at *26 (D.D.C. Nov. 13, 1998) (acknowledging that "disclosure of witnesses' statements and reports acquired by law enforcement personnel may impede the [Office of Independent Counsel's] investigation"), aff'd on other grounds, 194 F.3d 120 (D.C. Cir. 1999); Kansi, 11 F. Supp. 2d at 44 (holding that disclosure provides "potential for interference with witnesses and highly sensitive evidence"); Anderson v. USPS, 7 F. Supp. 2d 583, 586 (E.D. Pa. 1998) (explaining that release "would expose actual or prospective witnesses to undue influence or retaliation"), aff'd, 187 F.3d 625 (3d Cir. 1999) (unpublished table decision); Rosenglick, 1998 U.S. Dist. LEXIS 3920, at *7-8 (reasoning that disclosure "could aid a wrongdoer in secreting or tampering with evidence or witnesses"); Wichlacz, 938 F. Supp. at 331 (finding Independent Counsel "justified in concluding that there are substantial risks of witnesses intimidation or har-

(continued...)

Similarly, in a 2005 decision involving the FBI's still-ongoing investigation into a 1971 airplane hijacking, the court discussed the difficulties with gathering reliable information from witnesses by first noting that disclosure of nonpublic information "could reasonably be expected to hinder the investigation," rather than, as contended by the FOIA plaintiff, advance the public's help in solving the crime.[73] This court went on to describe in detail the kinds of harm that could that could result from the release of nonpublic information, and thus hinder the investigation, by enumerating that the requested FOIA disclosure could make it "far more difficult" for the FBI:

> (a) to verify and corroborate future witness statements and evidence, (b) to discern which tips, leads, and confession have merit and deserve further investigation and which are inconsistent with the known facts and can be safely ignored, and (c) to conduct effective interrogations of suspects.[74]

Other courts have ruled that interference has been established when, for example, the disclosure of information could prevent the government from obtaining data in the future.[75] Indeed, the D.C. Circuit in Alyeska

---

[72](...continued)
assment [and] reduced witness cooperation" in investigation which remains active and ongoing); Holbrook v. IRS, 914 F. Supp. 314, 316 (S.D. Iowa 1996) (releasing information might permit targets of pending investigation to "tamper with or intimidate potential witnesses"); cf. Franklin, No. 98-5339, slip op. at 2-3 (11th Cir. July 13, 1999) (ruling that "district court correctly determined" that disclosure of statements made by eight government witnesses who testified at criminal trial "could have reasonably been expected to interfere with . . . appeal and state criminal trial").

[73] Cook, 2005 WL 2237615, at *2.

[74] Id.

[75] See, e.g., Ctr. for Nat'l Sec. Studies, 331 F.3d at 930 (recognizing that witnesses "would be less likely to cooperate" and that a "potential witness or informant may be much less likely to come forward and cooperate with the investigation if he believes his name will be made public"); Watkins Motor Lines, 2006 WL 905518, at *8-9 (noting that the fact that a witness does not object to disclosure of notes from interviews "is not dispositive," as disclosure could reasonably be expected to cause harm, and adding that "the possibility of harm from disclosure of witness statements arises regardless of whether the witness is favorable to the person seeking disclosure" (citing Robbins Tire, 437 U.S. at 241-42)); Kay, 976 F. Supp. at 38-39 (finding potential for "witness intimidation and discourage[ment of] future witness cooperation" in ongoing investigation of alleged violation of FCC's rules); Wichlacz, 938 F. Supp. at 331 (reducing cooperation of potential witnesses when they learn of disclosure, thus interfering with ongoing investigation); Dow Jones & Co. v. U.S. Dep't of Justice, 880 F. Supp. 145, 150

(continued...)

**EXEMPTION 7(A)**

<u>Pipeline Service v. EPA</u>, ruled that disclosure of documents pertaining to a corporation under investigation that might identify which of that corporation's employees had provided those documents to a private party (who in turn had provided them to EPA) would "thereby subject them to potential reprisals and deter them from providing further information to [the] EPA."[76]

The exemption has been held to be properly invoked when release would hinder an agency's ability to control or shape investigations,[77] would

---

[75](...continued)
(S.D.N.Y. 1995) (Disclosing "statements by interviewees . . . might affect the testimony or statements of other witnesses and could severely hamper the Independent Counsel's ability to elicit untainted testimony."), <u>vacated on other grounds</u>, 907 F. Supp. 79 (S.D.N.Y. 1995); <u>Kay</u>, 867 F. Supp. at 19 (explaining that witness "intimidation would likely dissuade informants from cooperating with the investigation as it proceeds"); <u>Manna v. U.S. Dep't of Justice</u>, 815 F. Supp. 798, 808 (D.N.J. 1993) (disclosing FBI reports could result in chilling effect on potential witnesses), <u>aff'd</u>, 51 F.3d 1158, 1165 (finding "equally persuasive the district court's concern for persons who have assisted or will assist law enforcement personnel"); <u>Crowell & Moring v. DOD</u>, 703 F. Supp. 1004, 1011 (D.D.C. 1989) (holding that disclosure of identities of witnesses would impair grand jury's ability to obtain cooperation and would impede government's preparation of its case); <u>Gould</u>, 688 F. Supp. at 703 (disclosing information would have chilling effect on sources who are employees of requester); <u>Nishnic v. U.S. Dep't of Justice</u>, 671 F. Supp. 776, 794 (D.D.C. 1987) (disclosing identity of foreign source would end its ability to provide information in unrelated ongoing law enforcement activities); <u>Timken</u>, 531 F. Supp. at 199-200 (Disclosure of investigation records would interfere with the agency's ability "in the future to obtain this kind of information.").

[76] 856 F.2d at 311. <u>But cf. Clyde v. U.S. Dep't of Labor</u>, No. 85-139, slip op. at 6 (D. Ariz. July 3, 1986) (describing possible reluctance of contractors to enter into voluntary conciliations with government if substance of negotiations released does not constitute open law enforcement proceeding when specific conciliation process has ended); <u>Cohen v. EPA</u>, 575 F. Supp. 425, 428-29 (D.D.C. 1983) (holding Exemption 7(A) inapplicable to protect letters sent to entities suspected of unlawfully releasing hazardous substances when such disclosure not shown to deter parties from cooperating with voluntary cleanup programs).

[77] <u>See, e.g., Swan v. SEC</u>, 96 F.3d 498, 500 (D.C. Cir. 1996) (holding that the release "could reveal much about the focus and scope" of the investigation); <u>J.P. Stevens & Co. v. Perry</u>, 710 F.2d 136, 143 (4th Cir. 1983) (finding that premature disclosure would "hinder [agency's] ability to shape and control investigations"); <u>Cal-Trim, Inc. v. IRS</u>, No. 05-2408, slip op. at 6-8 (D. Ariz. Feb. 6, 2007) (finding that release of documents would reveal nature, direction, scope, and limits of tax investigation); <u>Watkins Motor Lines</u>, 2006 905518, at *6 (explaining that document release would give insight into

(continued...)

enable targets of investigations to elude detection[78] or to suppress or fabricate evidence,[79] or would prematurely reveal evidence or strategy in the

---

[77](...continued)
progress, scope, and direction of investigation); Judicial Watch, 306 F.
Supp. 2d at 75 (finding that release could reveal status of investigation and
agency's assessment of evidence (citing Swan, 96 F.3d at 500)); Youngblood v. Comm'r, No. 2:99-cv-9253, 2000 U.S. Dist. LEXIS 5083, at *36 (C.D.
Cal. Mar. 6, 2000) (holding that disclosure "could reveal the nature, scope,
direction and limits" of the investigation); Kay, 976 F. Supp. at 38-39 (discussing how release would reveal scope, direction, and nature of investigation).

[78] See, e.g., Moorefield, 611 F.2d at 1026 (explaining that disclosure of
the requested information would enable targets "to elude the scrutiny of
the [Secret] Service").

[79] See, e.g., Solar Sources, 142 F.3d at 1039 (stating that disclosure
"could result in destruction of evidence"); Mendoza v. DEA, No. 06-0591,
2006 WL 3734365, at *4 (D.D.C. Dec. 20, 2006) (reiterating that disclosure
could assist fugitives and other targets to avoid apprehension and to develop false alibis); Watkins Motor Lines, 2006 WL 905518, at *8 (finding
that "even if the Court disregards the allegation that Plaintiff may falsify or
dispose of records, Defendants have made a sufficient showing of harm
that could reasonably be expected to result from disclosure"); Lion II, 2005
WL 2704879, at *7-8 (agreeing that it is "unlikely that Lion will now try to
extricate itself from these accusation of fraudulent fabrication by fabricating more documents directly under the nose of USDA," yet ruling that the
documents nevertheless were properly withheld); Alyeska Pipeline, 856
F.2d at 312 (ruling that disclosure could allow for destruction or alteration
of evidence, fabrication of alibis, and identification of witnesses); Accuracy
in Media, Inc. v. U.S. Secret Serv., No. 97-2108, 1998 WL 185496, at *4
(D.D.C. Apr. 16, 1998) (explaining that release could permit witnesses to
modify, tailor, or fabricate testimony); Cujas v. IRS, No. 1:97-00741, U.S.
Dist. LEXIS 6466, at *14 (M.D.N.C. Apr. 15, 1998) (finding that release of
information would "alert" plaintiff to scope and direction of case and provide "opportunity to dispose" of assets), aff'd, 162 F.3d 1154 (4th Cir. 1998)
(unpublished table decision); Rosenglick, 1998 U.S. Dist. LEXIS 3920, at *7
(reiterating that disclosure "could aid wrongdoer in secreting or tampering
with evidence"); Maccaferri, No. 95-2576, slip op. at 14 (D. Md. Mar. 26,
1996) (determining that disclosure of information could provide plaintiff
with opportunity to alter or destroy evidence); Holbrook, 914 F. Supp. at
316 (releasing information could allow targets to construct defenses); Nishnic, 671 F. Supp. at 794 (releasing information might allow subjects to suppress or fabricate evidence); see also Manna v. U.S. Dep't of Justice, No. 92-
1840, slip op. at 11 n.3 (D.N.J. Aug. 25, 1993) (finding that possible sup-
pression of evidence manifest when copy of search warrant was left on
body of gangland-style murder victim), aff'd, 51 F.3d 1158, 1162, 1164-65
(3d Cir. 1995); cf. Lion I, 354 F.3d at 1085 (explaining that the agency's con-
(continued...)

government's case.[80]  Additionally, information that would reveal investigative trends, emphasis, and targeting schemes has been determined to be eligible for protection under Exemption 7(A) in those instances when disclosure would provide targets with the ability to perform a "cost/benefit

---

[79](...continued)
cerns that disclosure would provide the target with "an opportunity to forge or falsify" the documents at issue are "speculative and farfetched" in a situation in which "there is no possibility that Lion could tamper with or falsify the authentic USDA-retained originals . . . because Lion seeks only copies").

[80] See, e.g., Ctr. for Nat'l Sec. Studies, 331 F.3d at 928 (stating that the requested information "would enable al Qeada or other terrorist groups to map the course of the investigation," thus giving terrorist organizations "a composite picture"); Solar Sources, 142 F.3d at 1039 (determining that disclosure could result in "revelation of the scope and nature of the Government's investigation"); Mapother, 3 F.3d at 1543 (holding that release of prosecutor's index of all documents he deems relevant would afford a "virtual roadmap through the [government's] evidence . . . which would provide critical insights into its legal thinking and strategy"); Suzhou, 404 F. Supp. 2d at 14 (agreeing that disclosure could "inform the public of the evidence sought and scrutinized in this type of investigation"); Hambarian v. Comm'r, No. 99-9000, 2000 U.S. Dist. LEXIS 6217, at *7 (C.D. Cal. Feb. 16, 2000) (explaining that disclosure would reveal agency's theories and analysis of evidence); McErlean v. U.S. Dep't of Justice, No. 97-7831, 1999 WL 791680, at *8 (S.D.N.Y. Sept. 30, 1999) (finding that release of memoranda would reveal substance of information gathered and thus interfere with enforcement proceedings); Anderson, 1999 U.S. Dist. LEXIS 20877, at *10 (reasoning that the disclosure of the requested "checkspread" (the agency's compilation of checks written by the requester) "could very well jeopardize the proceedings by more fully revealing the scope and nature" of the government's case; Anderson, 7 F. Supp. 2d at 586 (stating that the release of the requested information "would disclose the focus" of the government's investigation); Maccaferri, No. 95-2576, slip op. at 14 (D. Md. Mar. 26, 1996) (reasoning that disclosure of the records requested would give "premature insight into the Government's strategy and strength of its position"); Cecola, 1995 WL 143548, at *3 (finding that release of information in ongoing criminal investigation might alert plaintiff to government's investigative strategy); Afr. Fund, 1993 WL 183736, at *4 (explaining that the disclosure sought "risks alerting targets to the existence and nature" of the investigation); Manna, 815 F. Supp. at 808 (holding that disclosure would obstruct justice by revealing agency's strategy and extent of its knowledge); Raytheon Co. v. Dep't of the Navy, 731 F. Supp. 1097, 1101 (D.D.C. 1989) (holding that the requested information "could be particularly valuable to [an investigative target] in the event of settlement negotiations"); Ehringhaus v. FTC, 525 F. Supp. 21, 22-23 (D.D.C. 1980) (stating that disclosure would reveal the focus, "important aspects of the planned strategy of [FTC] attorneys, [and] the strengths and weaknesses of the government's case").

analysis" of compliance with agency regulations.[81] Still other courts have indicated that any premature disclosure, by and of itself, can constitute interference with an enforcement proceeding.[82] In contrast, the D.C. Circuit has held that the mere fact that defendants in related ongoing criminal proceedings might obtain documents through the FOIA that were ruled unavailable "through discovery, or at least before [they] could obtain them through discovery," does not itself "constitute interference with a law enforcement proceeding."[83]

Furthermore, Exemption 7(A) ordinarily will not afford protection

---

[81] Concrete Constr., No. 2-89-649, slip op. at 3-5 (S.D. Ohio Oct. 26, 1990) (holding that disclosure of past fiscal year's Field Operation Program Plans, containing projections for inspections and areas of concentration, would be "obviously a detriment to the enforcement objectives of the Department of Labor" because disclosure "takes away the guessing" about the potential of being investigated); see also Farmworkers Legal Servs. v. U.S. Dep't of Labor, 639 F. Supp. 1368, 1374 (E.D.N.C. 1986) (approving the use of Exemptions 7(A) and 7(E) for information pertaining to the agency's "targeting scheme," the disclosure of which "would 'reveal the amount of investigative resources targeted and allocated'" for inspections (quoting agency declaration)).

[82] See Robbins Tire, 437 U.S. at 224-25, 234-37 (concluding that disclosure of "witness statements in pending unfair labor practice proceedings" would generally interfere with enforcement proceedings); Lewis, 823 F.2d at 380 (agreeing with the "reasoning of the Eight Circuit" that the "'government is not required to make a specific factual showing [of harm] with respect to each withheld document'" (quoting Barney, 618 F.2d at 1273)); Barney, 618 F.2d at 1273 (stating that disclosure "prior to the institution of civil or criminal tax enforcement proceedings, would necessarily interfere with such proceedings"); Safeway, Inc. v. IRS, No. C05-3182, 2006 WL 3041079, at *5 (N.D. Cal. Oct. 24, 2006) (explaining that "'under exemption 7(A) the government is not required to make a specific factual showing with respect to each withheld document,'" and thus agency's "general concern that revealing the scope of [its] case could frustrate its ability to pursue it" is sufficient (quoting Barney, 618 F.2d at 1273)); Steinberg v. IRS, 463 F. Supp. 1272, 1273 (S.D. Fla. 1979) (explaining that the "premature disclosure of [requested] records could seriously hamper the ongoing investigations and prejudice the government's prospective case").

[83] North, 881 F.2d at 1097; see also Goodman, 2001 U.S. Dist. LEXIS 22748, at *13 (explaining that scope of permissible discovery is of no consequence under Exemption 7(A)); Warren, 2000 U.S. LEXIS 17660, at *18 (stating that "discovery process" is not relevant to applicability of Exemption 7(A)); cf. Senate of P.R., 823 F.2d at 589 (finding that trial court's failure to describe harm from release of undescribed documents developed for closed law enforcement investigation, but assertedly relevant to open criminal law enforcement proceeding, did not permit upholding Exemption 7(A) applicability).

when the target of the investigation has possession of or submitted the information in question.[84] Nevertheless, it is increasingly clear that agencies can properly withhold information if they can demonstrate that its "selectivity of recording" information provided by the target would suggest the nature and scope of the investigation,[85] or if it can articulate with specificity how each category of documents, if disclosed, would cause interference.[86] Indeed, in a case in which two clients requested statements that

---

[84] See, e.g., Lion I, 354 F.3d at 1085 (stating-- in a situation in which the investigatory target already possessed copies of the documents sought -- that "[b]ecause Lion already has copies . . . USDA cannot argue that revealing the information would allow Lion premature access to the evidence upon which it intends to rely at trial"); Wright, 822 F.2d at 646 (observing that disclosure of information provided by plaintiff would not provide plaintiff "with any information that it does not already have"); Dow Jones, 219 F.R.D. at 174 (stating that there cannot be harm, because "each target company has a copy . . . and therefore is on notice as to the government's possible litigation strategy and potential witnesses"); Scheer, 35 F. Supp. 2d at 14 (declaring that agency assertions of harm and "concern proffered . . . cannot stand" when agency itself disclosed information to target); Ginsberg v. IRS, No. 96-2265-CIV-T-26E, 1997 WL 882913, at *3 (M.D. Fla. Dec. 23, 1997) (reiterating that "where the documents requested are those of the [requester] rather than the documents of a third party . . . 'it is unlikely that their disclosure could reveal . . . anything [the requester] does not know already'" (quoting Grasso, 785 F.2d at 77)); see also Oncology Servs. Corp. v. NRC, No. 93-0939, slip op. at 17 (W.D. Pa. Feb. 7, 1994) (finding that agency may not categorically withhold transcribed interviews, conducted in presence of requester's attorney, for these interviewed individuals who consented to release of their own transcripts); cf. Campbell, 682 F.2d at 262 (discussing the legislative history of Exemption 7(A), and distinguishing between records generated by the government and those "submitted to the government by such targets").

[85] See Willard v. IRS, 776 F.2d 100, 103 (4th Cir. 1985) (concluding that "selectivity in recording" those portions of interviews that agents considered relevant "would certainly provide clues . . . of the nature and scope of the investigation"); see also Gould, 688 F. Supp. at 704 n.37 (reiterating that "disclosure of which records were selected by investigators from the universe of available materials for copying or compiling would reveal the nature, scope and focus of the government's investigation").

[86] See Linsteadt v. IRS, 729 F.2d 998, 1004 & n.10, 1005 (5th Cir. 1984) (stating that release would frustrate the investigation by revealing reliance government placed upon particular evidence and by aiding targets in tampering with evidence); see also Grasso, 785 F.2d at 76-77 (tempering its order to release records where the "IRS had not shown" that disclosure could interfere with the investigation by adding that, in some circumstances, a "memorandum of the individual's own statement may be exempt from disclosure, as, for example, when it discloses the direction of [a] po-

(continued...)

their attorney made to the SEC and argued that the "information their attorney conveyed to the [agency] must be treated as coming from them," it was held that the "harm in releasing this information flows mainly from the fact that it reflects the [agency] staff's selective recording . . . and thereby reveals the scope and focus of the investigation."[87]

Because Exemption 7(A) is temporal in nature, it generally has been recognized that once Exemption 7(A) applicability ceases with a change in underlying circumstances an agency then may invoke other applicable exemptions; therefore, agencies ordinarily do not determine what other, underlying exemptions are appropriate until the underlying investigation reaches a point at which the documents no longer merit Exemption 7(A) protection.[88]

In fact, the Supreme Court, the D.C. Circuit, and other circuit courts of appeals have approved the generic approach and the functional test for Ex-

---

[86](...continued)
tential investigation"); cf. Alyeska Pipeline, 856 F.2d at 314 (explaining that mere assertions that requester knows scope of investigation are not sufficient to present genuine issue of material fact that would preclude summary judgment).

[87] Swan, 96 F.3d at 500-01.

[88] See Computer Prof'ls for Soc. Responsibility v. U.S. Secret Serv., 72 F.3d 897, 906-07 (D.C. Cir. 1996) (permitting agency on remand to apply exemptions other than Exemption 7(A) for records of investigation which was terminated during litigation); Dickerson, 992 F.2d at 1430 n.4 (explaining that "when exemption (7)(A) has become inapplicable," records may still be protected under other exemptions); Senate of P.R., 823 F.2d at 589 (finding that the "district court did not abuse its discretion in permitting the DOJ to press additional FOIA exemptions after its original, all-encompassing (7)(A) exemption claim became moot"); Chilivis v. SEC, 673 F.2d 1205, 1208 (11th Cir. 1982) (holding government not barred from invoking other exemptions after reliance on Exemption 7(A) rendered untenable by conclusion of underlying law enforcement proceeding); W. Journalism, 926 F. Supp. at 192 (explaining that once the Independent Counsel's task is completed, the documents are "turned over to the Archivist and at that time would be subject to FOIA [disclosure]"); Curcio v. FBI, No. 89-0941, slip op. at 4-6 (D.D.C. Mar. 24, 1995) (permitting the agency to invoke new exemptions when Exemption 7(A) is no longer applicable, because the agency has "made a clear showing of what the changed circumstances are and how they justify permitting the agency to raise new claims of exemption" and has "proffered a legitimate reason why it did not previously argue all applicable exemptions"); cf. Miller Auto Sales, Inc. v. Casellas, No. 97-0032, slip op. at 3 (W.D. Va. Jan. 6, 1998) (remanding to give the agency an "opportunity to make a new FOIA determination at the administrative level now that enforcement proceedings have ended").

emption 7(A),[89] and in multiple rulings have approved the continued use of Exemption 7(A) where necessary even after initial enforcement proceedings are closed.[90] Notwithstanding this widely accepted practice, however, the D.C. Circuit seven years ago ruled that the government must prove its case with respect to any other, underlying FOIA exemptions "at the same time" in the original court proceedings "in an Exemption 7(A) case in such a manner that the district court can rule on the issue,"[91] and it denied the defendant agency's motion to remand a case back to the district

---

[89] See, e.g., Robbins Tire, 437 U.S. at 223-24, 236 (explaining that applicability of Exemption 7(A) may be made generically, based on categories); Lynch, 2000 WL 123236, at *2 (stating that specific factual showing is not necessary); Solar Sources, 142 F.3d at 1038 (reiterating that government may use generic categories); In re Dep't of Justice, 999 F.2d at 1308 (approving use of categorical bases for nondisclosure); Spannaus, 813 F.2d at 1288 (stating that the "Supreme Court has rejected . . . particularized showings of interference, holding instead that the Government may justify nondisclosure in a generic fashion"); Bevis, 801 F.2d at 1389 (explaining that the agency may take generic approach); Crooker, 789 F.2d at 67 (describing an acceptable Robbins Tire category as "functional," allowing "the court to trace a rational link between the nature of the document and the alleged interference"); Campbell, 682 F.2d at 265 (stating that categories are permitted); see also Gould, 688 F. Supp. at 703-04 & n.34 (approving use of "functional test set forth in Bevis and Crooker"); cf. Reporters Comm., 489 U.S. 776-80 (holding that FOIA exemption determinations sometimes may be made "categorically" (citing Robbins Tire, 437 U.S. at 214)).

[90] See Franklin, No. 98-5339, slip op. at 2-3 (11th Cir. July 13, 1999) (approving continued use of Exemption 7(A) during federal appeal of conviction and pending state criminal trial); Solar Sources, 142 F.3d at 1035, 1037, 1040 (approving continued use of Exemption 7(A) although case closed against certain defendants); New England Med. Ctr. Hosp., 548 F.2d at 385-86 (approving continued use of Exemption 7(A) when "closed file records" related to pending case); Keen, No. 96-1049, slip op. at 6-8 (D.D.C. July 14, 1999) (stating that motion to redetermine sentence qualifies records for Exemption 7(A) protection); Kansi, 11 F. Supp. 2d at 45 (approving continued use of Exemption 7(A) while inmate's appeal of sentence is pending); Pons, 1998 U.S. Dist. LEXIS 6084, at *14 (approving continued use of Exemption 7(A) for certain information not used in requester's prior trials); Burke, No. 96-1739, slip op. at 5 (D.D.C. Mar. 31, 1998) (holding that records were properly withheld in light of plaintiff's post-conviction appeal); Cudzich, 886 F. Supp. at 106-07 (approving continued use of Exemption 7(A) because there were "pending investigations of other law enforcement agencies"); Kuffel, 882 F. Supp. at 1126 (ruling that Exemption 7(A) properly applies while other cases pending against defendant); Timken, 531 F. Supp. at 199-200 (finding that Exemption 7(A) remains applicable as long as determination still could be appealed).

[91] Maydak v. U.S. Dep't of Justice, 218 F.3d 760, 765 (D.C. Cir. 2000) [hereinafter Maydak I].

court once Exemption 7(A) became inapplicable.[92]

This decision by the D.C. Circuit was a departure from its prior rulings,[93] as well as the prior rulings of the District Court for the District of Columbia and other circuit courts,[94] and did not permit any accommodation based on the temporal nature of the exemption.[95] The D.C. Circuit in Maydak v. United States Department of Justice further ruled that the nature of the burden of proof under Exemption 7(A) does not relieve an agency from having to prove its case with respect to other, underlying exemptions in

---

[92] See id. at 769.

[93] See Computer Prof'ls, 72 F.3d at 906-07 (permitting application of exemptions other than Exemption 7(A) when underlying circumstances changed); Senate of P.R., 823 F.2d at 589 (approving district court's exercise of its discretion in remanding to agency for agency "to press additional FOIA exemptions" after Exemption 7(A)'s circumstances changed).

[94] See, e.g., Dickerson, 992 F.2d at 1430 n.4 (explaining that if Exemption 7(A) has become inapplicable, records may still be protected by other exemptions); Chilivis, 673 F.2d at 1208 (finding that government was not barred from invoking other exemptions after reliance on Exemption 7(A) was rendered untenable by changed circumstances); Curcio, No. 89-0941, slip op. at 4-6 (D.D.C. Mar. 24, 1995) (permitting agency to invoke new exemptions when Exemption 7(A) became no longer applicable); see also Bevis, 801 F.2d at 1390 (remanding to permit the agency to "reformulate its generic categories in accordance with the Crooker requirement"); Crooker, 789 F.2d at 66-67 (explaining that the agency's affidavit did not adequately establish applicability of Exemption 7(A), and remanding so that agency could "make a presentation"); Campbell, 682 F.2d at 265 (finding agency affidavits insufficient; remanding for the agency to demonstrate how release of information "would interfere with the investigation").

[95] See Maydak I, 218 F.3d at 766 (disagreeing with the government's view that once "Exemption 7(A) is inapplicable, then the government should be allowed to start back at the beginning" -- by declaring that Exemption 7(A) is not "so unique" and should not be "singled out for preferential treatment"); see also FOIA Post, "Supreme Court Declines to Review Waiver Case" (posted 8/7/01) (discussing temporal nature of Exemption 7(A)); cf. Delta Ltd. v. U.S. Customs & Border Prot., 384 F. Supp. 2d 138, 153 (D.D.C.) ("Plaintiff seems to argue that because it is the subject of the investigation, it is afforded a special right to the information withheld pursuant to Exemption 7(A). No such right exists."), partial reconsideration granted, 393 F. Supp. 2d 15 (D.D.C. 2005); Changzhou Laosan, 2005 WL 913268, at *8 (stating that "plaintiff appears to believe that it is entitled [to information b]ut there is no such exception to 7(A) for the benefit of targets").

the original district court proceedings.[96] Indeed, the Court rebuffed the agency's reliance on longstanding Exemption 7(A) practice and supporting case law by declaring that "nothing" in existing case law "should be construed as supporting the proposition that, when the government withdraws its reliance on Exemption 7(A) <u>after the district court has reached a final decision and an appeal has been filed</u>, the appropriate course of action is necessarily remand to the agency for reprocessing of the FOIA request in question."[97] In fact, in <u>Maydak I</u>, the court went so far as to declare that "merely stating that 'for example' an exemption might apply is inadequate to raise a FOIA exemption," even when underlying a uniquely temporal one such as Exemption 7(A).[98]

Prior to the <u>Maydak I</u> decision, when agencies found themselves in litigation in which "changed circumstances" (i.e., the end of underlying law enforcement proceedings) had placed into question the continuing viability of Exemption 7(A), they either voluntarily "reprocessed" the requested records using all other appropriate exemptions or were ordered to do so by the court.[99] Now, however, whenever invoking Exemption 7(A) in litigation, agencies may choose to seek and receive permission from the district court to invoke Exemption 7(A) alone (thereby reserving all other poten-

---

[96] See <u>Maydak I</u>, 218 F.3d at 765-66.

[97] <u>Id.</u> at 767 (emphasis added); cf. <u>Jefferson v. Dep't of Justice</u>, 284 F.3d 172, 179 (D.C. Cir. 2002) (following <u>Maydak I</u> and ruling that the agency may not raise Exemption 6 for the first time on remand after ruling that the only exemption raised by the agency did not cover all potential records within the scope of the request); <u>Smith v. U.S. Dep't of Justice</u>, 251 F.3d 1047, 1050 (D.C. Cir. 2001) (holding -- in a situation in which the government initially relied on Exemption 3 only, subsequently "changed its position," and then requested a remand to raise other exemptions -- that the government "'must assert all exemptions at the same time, in the original district court proceedings'" (quoting <u>Maydak I</u>, 218 F.3d at 764)).

[98] <u>Id.</u> (citing <u>Ryan v. Dep't of Justice</u>, 617 F.2d 781, 792 n.38a (D.C. Cir. 1980)).

[99] See, e.g., <u>Computer Prof'ls for Soc. Responsibility</u>, 72 F.3d at 906-07 (permitting use of exemptions other than Exemption 7(A) when investigation was terminated during course of FOIA litigation); <u>Dickerson</u>, 992 F.2d at 1430 n.4 (explaining that when Exemption 7(A) has become inapplicable, records may be processed using other FOIA exemptions); <u>Senate of P.R.</u>, 823 F.2d at 589 (finding that the district court properly permitted the Department of Justice to raise underlying FOIA exemptions once Exemption 7(A) ceased to apply); <u>Chilivis</u>, 673 F.2d at 1208 (holding government may invoke other exemptions after Exemption 7(A) was rendered untenable by conclusion of underlying law enforcement proceeding).

tially invokable exemptions)[100] or undertake the time-consuming process of invoking Exemption 7(A) together with all other, underlying, exemptions in their initial Vaughn declarations.[101] Indeed, in a recent case that attempted a third approach by describing "the exemptions being invoked solely on an in camera, ex parte basis," the District Court for the District of Columbia, relying on Maydak I, ruled that "[t]his Circuit requires a defendant agency to 'genuinely assert' the exemptions upon which it plans to rely after Exemption 7(A) no longer is available to withhold information," and added that it could "find[] no precedent to permit a defendant agency to name and rely on the exemptions being invoked solely on an in camera, ex parte basis."[102] With any of these approaches, however, it is important to note that an agency is not bound by the exemptions it relied on at the administrative stage, as courts have routinely held that the need to raise all applicable exemptions only arises once the request goes to litigation.[103]

---

[100] Accord Senate of P.R., 823 F.2d at 589 (evincing that the district court maintains such discretion by explicitly holding "that the district court did not abuse its discretion in permitting [the agency] to press additional FOIA exemptions after its original, all-encompassing (7)(A) exemption claim became moot").

[101] See, e.g., Ayyad v. U.S. Dep't of Justice, No. 00 Civ. 960, 2002 U.S. Dist. LEXIS 6925, at *4 n.2 (S.D.N.Y. Apr. 18, 2002) (noting that agency invoked exemptions in addition to Exemption 7(A) "because of Maydak").

[102] Haddam, No. 01-434, slip op. at 26-27 (D.D.C. Sept. 8, 2004).

[103] See, e.g., Ford v. West, No. 97-1342, 1998 WL 317561, at *1 (10th Cir. June 12, 1998) (adjudicating exemption not raised at administrative level and raised for first time in litigation); Young v. CIA, 972 F.2d 536, 538 (4th Cir. 1992) (stating that "an agency does not waive FOIA exemptions by not raising them during the administrative process"); Pohlman, Inc. v. SBA, No. 4:03-01231, slip op. at 26 (E.D. Mo. Sept. 30, 2005) (agreeing that an agency is "not precluded from relying on Exemption 3 simply because [it was not raised] at the administrative level"); Leforce & McCombs v. HHS, No. 04-176, slip op. at 13 (E.D. Okla. Feb. 3, 2005) (emphasizing that even if the agency had "failed to invoke the attorney-client privilege in the administrative proceeding, the Court would nevertheless be free to consider [it]"); Boyd v. U.S. Marshals Serv., No. 99-2712, 2002 U.S. Dist. LEXIS 27734, at *6 (D.D.C. Mar. 15, 2002) (stating that although the defendant did not raise exemptions other than Exemption 7(A) at the administrative level, it did not have to do so because the "government must assert all applicable exemptions [only] in the district court proceedings"), summary judgment granted on other grounds, 2004 U.S. Dist. LEXIS 27406 (D.D.C. Sept. 22, 2004); Living Rivers, 272 F.2d at 1318 (recognizing that although "at the administrative level" the agency "did not cite Exemption 7 . . . an agency may raise a particular exemption for the first time in the district court"); Dubin v. Department of the Treasury, 555 F. Supp. 408, 412 (N.D. Ga. 1981) (explaining that agency did not waive FOIA exemptions in litigation by not raising

(continued...)

Notwithstanding the above Maydak I "solutions" of receiving permission to raise other applicable exemptions later or "Vaughning" and briefing fully all possible exemptions at the onset of litigation,[104] it is highly significant that several post-Maydak I cases have permitted agencies to raise exemptions not invoked initially in litigation.[105] In two of these cases, the courts relied on Senate of Puerto Rico v. United States Department of Justice[106] and interpreted Maydak I liberally to permit "later" exemption claims.[107] In fact, in August v. FBI, the D.C. Circuit itself distinguished Maydak I, harmonized it with Senate of Puerto Rico, and declared that "we have repeatedly acknowledged that there are some 'extraordinary' circumstances in which courts of appeals may exercise their authority . . . to require 'such further proceedings to be had as may be just under the circumstances,' in order to allow the government to raise FOIA exemption claims it failed to raise the first time around."[108] Indeed, it carefully explained that "[g]iven the drafters' recognition that the harms of disclosure may in some cases outweigh its benefits, we have avoided adopting a 'rigid press it at the threshold, or lose it for all times' approach to . . . agenc[ies'] FOIA ex-

---

[103](...continued)
them during administrative process), aff'd, 697 F.2d 1093 (11th Cir. 1983) (unpublished table decision).

[104] See FOIA Post, "Supreme Court Declines to Review Waiver Case" (8/7/01) (advising of practical implications of, and response to, Maydak I upon its issuance).

[105] See generally Trentadue v. Integrity Comm., No. 04-4200 (10th Cir. Sept. 27, 2005); August, 328 F.3d 697; Gavin, 2005 WL 2739293; Piper v. U.S. Dep't of Justice, 374 F. Supp. 2d 73 (D.D.C. 2005), on remand, 428 F. Supp. 2d 1 (D.C. 2006); Sciba v. Bd. of Governors of the Fed. Reserve Sys., No. 04-1011, 2005 WL 758260 (D.D.C. Apr. 1, 2005), summary judgment granted, 2005 WL 3201206 (D.D.C. Nov. 4, 2005); Maydak v. U.S. Dep't of Justice, 362 F. Supp. 2d 316 (D.D.C. 2005) [hereinafter Maydak II]; Summers, No. 98-1837 (D.D.C. Apr. 13, 2004).

[106] August, 328 F.3d at 699, 701 (reiterating that courts have avoided adopting "rigid" approach and that courts have discretion to permit government to invoke other FOIA exemptions after underlying basis for Exemption 7(A) ceases to exist (citing Senate of P.R., 823 F.2d at 581)); Summers, No. 98-1837, slip op. at 7 (D.D.C. Apr. 13, 2004) (permitting the government "to assert new exemptions prior to the district court issuing final judgment" (citing generally Senate of P.R., 823 F.2d 574)).

[107] August, 328 F.3d at 700-02 (distinguishing Maydak I by stressing that government's behavior in August was more consistent with simple human error than with "tactical maneuvering" and that therefore "remand is particularly appropriate in this case"); Summers, No. 98-1837, slip op. at 7 (D.D.C. Apr. 13, 2004) (interpreting Maydak I as permitting government to invoke new exemptions at any time during "district court proceedings").

[108] 328 F.3d at 700 (quoting Maydak I, 218 F.3d at 767).

emption claims."[109]

This recognition of "the harms of disclosure" mentioned in August was at the forefront of the court's reasoning two years ago in Piper v. United States Department of Justice.[110] While the District Court for the District of Columbia in this case chastised the agency for its "sluggish neglect" and its "bungled . . . litigation," it nevertheless found that "in certain FOIA cases where the judgment will impinge on rights of third parties that are expressly protected by FOIA . . . district courts not only have the discretion, but sometimes the obligation to consider newly presented facts and to grant relief."[111] Thus, the court concluded that it would reconsider its prior ruling to determine if the "redactions, newly justified" were proper.[112]

Indeed, in Summers v. United States Department of Justice, that court, following August and relying on Senate of Puerto Rico, pragmatically re-cast Maydak I completely.[113] It stated that "Maydak, however, provides that the government is required to raise all claimed exemptions at the district court proceedings, but does not hold that all exemptions must be raised at the same time"[114] -- whereas Maydak I in fact had stated that "[w]e have plainly and repeatedly told the government that, as a general rule, it must assert all exemptions at the same time."[115] The result of this recasting of Maydak I allowed the agency in Summers to "substitute" exemptions in the not uncommon situation of the underlying factual circumstances changing during the course of litigation.[116] However, even where

---

[109] Id. at 699 (quoting Senate of P.R., 823 F.2d at 581, and by way of clarification, harmonizing Maydak I with it).

[110] 374 F. Supp. 2d 73, 78 (D.D.C. June 1, 2005).

[111] Id. at 78-79 & n.1 (citing August, 328 F.3d at 699-702); accord Senate of P.R., 823 F.2d at 581.

[112] Id. at 79.

[113] Summers, No. 98-1837, slip op. at 7 (D.D.C. Apr. 13, 2004).

[114] Id.

[115] Maydak I, 218 F.3d at 764 (citing Wash. Post v. HHS, 795 F.2d 205, 208 (D.C. Cir. 1986); Ryan, 617 F.2d at 789, 792; Holy Spirit Ass'n v. CIA, 636 F.2d 838, 846 (D.C. Cir. 1980)); see also Jefferson, 284 F.3d at 179 (finding that "Glomar response was inappropriate" and ordering release of all "non-law enforcement records" unless covered by FOIA exemptions invoked already, because "invocation on appeal of Exemption 6 comes too late").

[116] Summers, No. 98-1837, slip op. at 7-8 (D.D.C. Apr. 13, 2004) (discussing agency's "failure to claim the correct exemption" and the consequences of disclosure of information by stating that the "'law does not require that third parties pay for the Government's mistakes'" (quoting August, 328 F.3d
(continued...)

circumstances have changed, some courts have gone so far as to judge the applicability of Exemption 7(A) as of the time that the agency made its determination as to its applicability.[117]

In its trend of relaxing the rule announced in Maydak I and permitting agencies to "substitute" exemptions due to changed circumstances during litigation, the District Court for the District of Columbia continues to pragmatically treat the Maydak I decision[118] by de-emphasizing the "at the same time" portion of the phrase used in Maydak I to instruct federal agencies to "assert all exemptions at the same time, in the same original district court proceeding."[119] Indeed, this court recently found that exemptions raised for the first time in a renewed summary judgment motion were proper "in any event," because the new exemptions were being raised in the original district court proceedings.[120] Likewise, exemptions not raised in an Answer, but claimed in later district court filings have been held to be

---

[116](...continued)
at 701)).

[117] See Tellier v. Executive Office for U.S. Attorneys, No. 96-5323, 1997 WL 362497, at *1 (D.C. Cir. May 15, 1997) (per curiam) (finding a law enforcement proceeding pending at the time of the request; affirming the withholding of the documents because "'[t]o require an agency to adjust or modify its FOIA responses on post-response occurrences could create an endless cycle of . . . reprocessing'" (quoting Bonner v. U.S. Dep't of State, 928 F.2d 1148, 1152 (D.C. Cir. 1991))); Goodman, 2001 U.S. Dist. LEXIS 22748, at *9 ("The determination as to whether a release of records could reasonably be expected to interfere with enforcement proceedings is to be made as of the time the agency decided to withhold the documents." (citing Bonner, 928 F.2d at 1152)); Gomez v. U.S. Attorney, No. 93-2530, 1996 U.S. Dist. LEXIS 6439, at *2 (D.D.C. May 13, 1996) (reasoning that Exemption 7(A) is claimed properly as of the receipt of the request and that when circumstances change, a plaintiff is "free to file a new FOIA request"), appeal dismissed voluntarily, No. 96-5185 (D.C. Cir. May 12, 1997); Lynch, 2000 WL 123236, at *3 (stating that judicial review is to be made as of time agency decided to withhold documents); Keen, No. 96-1049, slip op. at 6-7 (D.D.C. July 14, 1999) (maintaining that court review is limited to time at which agency made its exemption determination); Local 32B-32J, Serv. Employees Int'l Union v. GSA, No. 97-8509, 1998 WL 726000, at *8 (S.D.N.Y. Oct. 15, 1998) (stating that judicial review of agency's decision must be made in light of status of enforcement proceedings at time at which agency responded).

[118] See generally Trentadue, No. 04-4200 (10th Cir. Sept. 27, 2005); Sciba, 2005 WL 758260; Maydak II, 362 F. Supp. 2d 316.

[119] Maydak I, 218 F.3d at 765.

[120] Maydak II, 362 F. Supp. 2d at 318-19.

properly before the court.[121]

Along these same lines, in two recent cases in which Exemption 7(A) became no longer applicable because the investigations had closed, the courts in both instances explained at length the special circumstances surrounding the situations that justified remands for further exemption consideration.[122] In Trentadue v. Integrity Committee, the Court of Appeals for the Tenth Circuit specifically stated that it would "retain jurisdiction" and ordered a "limited remand" after the law enforcement proceeding terminated because, though the agency raised other exemptions at the district court level, the "district court did not rule on these alternate bases for exemption."[123] In Gavin v. SEC, the court simply remanded the case back to the agency.[124]

The D.C. Circuit likewise did not apply Maydak I rigidly in two other relatively recent cases in which the agencies did not invoke all applicable exemptions at the district court level.[125] In LaCedra v. Executive Office for United States Attorneys, the agency, due to its misreading of a FOIA request, conducted a limited search and processed only a portion of the requested records.[126] But stating that "[n]othing in Maydak requires an agency to invoke any exemption applicable to a record that the agency in good faith believes has not been requested," the D.C. Circuit specifically permit-

---

[121] See Sciba, 2005 WL 758260, at *1 n.3 (permitting the agency to later invoke exemptions not raised in its Answer, and reiterating that an "exemption only need be raised at a point in the district court proceedings that gives the court an adequate opportunity to consider it," and further noting that "an agency only waives FOIA exemptions by failing to claim them in the original proceedings before the district court"); see also Lawrence v. United States, 355 F. Supp. 2d 1307, 1310-11 (M.D. Fla. 2004) (finding that the defendant agency filed its Answer before its FOIA review was complete, and explaining that "[u]nder these circumstances, Defendant's untimeliness in failing to assert the FOIA exemptions in its answer is excused"); accord Senate of P.R., 823 F.2d at 589 (reasoning that district court did not abuse its discretion by permitting agency to raise other FOIA exemptions after original invocation of Exemption (7)(A) became moot).

[122] Trentadue, No. 04-4200, slip op. at 4 (10th Cir. Sept. 27, 2005); Gavin, 2005 WL 2739293, at *2.

[123] Trentadue, No. 04-4200, slip op. at 4 (10th Cir. Sept. 27, 2005).

[124] Gavin, 2005 WL 2739293, at *2 & n.2.

[125] See generally United We Stand Am., 359 F.3d 595 (D.C. Cir. 2004); LaCedra v. Executive Office for U.S. Attorneys, 317 F.3d 345 (D.C. Cir. 2003).

[126] LaCedra, 317 F.3d at 348 (stating that agency's interpretation of request was "implausible" and "erroneous").

ted the agency to invoke all applicable exemptions on remand.[127]

In United We Stand America v. IRS, the request concerned a document that the IRS prepared at the direction of a congressional committee and which the agency maintained was not an "agency record" subject to the FOIA.[128] The agency simply stated to the district court that "'[s]hould the Court determine that the documents in question constitute agency records for purposes of the FOIA . . . the defendant reserves the right, pursuant to the statute, to assert any applicable exemption claim(s), prior to disclosure, and to litigate further any such exemption claims.'"[129] The D.C. Circuit concluded that "only those portions of the IRS response that would reveal the congressional request are not subject to FOIA," and it then specifically remanded "with instructions" for the agency "to release any segregable portions that are not otherwise protected by one of FOIA's nine exemptions."[130]

As a final Exemption 7(A)-related matter, agencies should be aware of the "(c)(1) exclusion,"[131] which was enacted by the FOIA Reform Act in 1986.[132] This special record exclusion applies to situations in which the very fact of a criminal investigation's existence is as yet unknown to the in-

---

[127] Id. (explicitly rejecting plaintiff's argument that Maydak I required "exemption waiver" result).

[128] 359 F.3d at 597 (presenting fact pattern very much akin to that of Ryan, 617 F.2d at 781).

[129] Id. at 598 (quoting government's brief).

[130] Compare United We Stand Am., 359 F.3d at 597, 605 (remanding case to release segregable portions of agency records commingled in file with congressional records not subject to FOIA), with Maydak I, 218 F.3d at 765 ("We have said explicitly in the past that merely stating that 'for example' an exemption might apply is inadequate to raise a FOIA exemption." (citing Ryan, 617 F.2d at 792 n.38a)); see also Senate of P.R., 823 F.2d at 580-81 (reiterating that "fairness to parties seeking disclosure ordinarily requires that they be accorded a full and concentrated opportunity to challenge and test comprehensively the agency's evidence regarding all claimed exemptions" and that the agency "'should be able to cite all possible relevant exemptions well before the appellate stage'" (quoting Jordan v. U.S. Dep't of Justice, 591 F.2d 753, 780 (D.C. Cir. 1978) (en banc))); FOIA Post, "Supreme Court Declines to Review Waiver Case" (posted 8/7/01) (discussing difficulty of raising all FOIA exemptions in original district court proceedings, and stressing that "raising" means invoking exemptions in such manner that court can rule on their applicability); accord August, 328 F.3d at 701 (permitting agency to raise additional exemptions, and harmonizing Maydak I with language in Senate of P.R. by emphasizing court's existing discretion).

[131] 5 U.S.C. § 552(c)(1).

[132] Pub. L. No. 99-570, § 1802, 100 Stat. at 3207-49.

vestigation's subject, and disclosure of the existence of the investigation (which would be revealed by any acknowledgment of the existence of responsive records) could reasonably be expected to interfere with enforcement proceedings.[133] In such circumstances, an agency may treat the records as not subject to the requirements of the FOIA. (See the discussion of the operation of subsection (c)(1) under Exclusions, below.)


## EXEMPTION 7(B)


Exemption 7(B) of the FOIA, which is aimed at preventing prejudicial pretrial publicity that could impair a court proceeding, protects "records or information compiled for law enforcement purposes [the disclosure of which] would deprive a person of a right to a fair trial or an impartial adjudication."[1] Despite the possible constitutional significance of its function, in practice this exemption is not often invoked -- for example, it was used just over 200 times by all federal departments and agencies during Fiscal Year 2006.[2] In the situation in which it would most logically be employed -- i.e., an ongoing law enforcement proceeding -- an agency's application of Exemption 7(A) to protect its institutional law enforcement interests invariably would serve to protect the interests of the defendants to the prosecution as well. Even in the non-law enforcement realm, the circumstances that call for singular reliance upon Exemption 7(B) occur only rarely.

Consequently, Exemption 7(B) has been featured prominently in only one FOIA case to date, Washington Post Co. v. United States Department of Justice.[3] At issue there was whether public disclosure of a pharmaceutical company's internal self-evaluative report, submitted to the Justice Department in connection with a grand jury investigation, would jeopardize the company's ability to receive a fair and impartial civil adjudication of several personal injury cases pending against it.[4] In remanding the case

---

[133] See Attorney General's 1986 Amendments Memorandum at 18-22.

[1] 5 U.S.C. § 552(b)(7)(B) (2000 & Supp. IV 2004).

[2] See Governmentwide Compilation of All Departments' and Agencies' Annual FOIA Reports, Fiscal Year 2006, available at http://www.usdoj. gov/oip/fy06.html.

[3] 863 F.2d 96, 101-02 (D.C. Cir. 1988); see also Alexander & Alexander Servs. v. SEC, No. 92-1112, 1993 WL 439799, at *10-11 (D.D.C. Oct. 19, 1993) (citing Washington Post to find that company "failed to meet its burden of showing how release of particular documents would deprive it of the right to a fair trial") ("reverse" FOIA suit), appeal dismissed, No. 93-5398 (D.C. Cir. Jan. 4, 1996).

[4] Wash. Post, 863 F.2d at 99; see also Palmer Commc'ns v. U.S. Dep't of Justice, No. 96-M-777, slip op. at 4 (D. Colo. Oct. 30, 1996) ("[T]he unavoid-
(continued...)

for further consideration, the Court of Appeals for the District of Columbia Circuit articulated a two-part standard to be employed in determining Exemption 7(B)'s applicability: "(1) that a trial or adjudication is pending or truly imminent; and (2) that it is more probable than not that disclosure of the material sought would seriously interfere with the fairness of those proceedings."[5] Although the D.C. Circuit in Washington Post offered a sin--gle example of proper Exemption 7(B) applicability -- i.e., when "disclosure through FOIA would furnish access to a document not available under the discovery rules and thus would confer an unfair advantage on one of the parties" -- it did not limit the scope of the exemption to privileged documents only.[6]

## EXEMPTION 7(C)

Exemption 7(C) provides protection for personal information in law enforcement records. This exemption is the law enforcement counterpart to Exemption 6, which is the FOIA's fundamental privacy exemption. (See the discussions of the primary privacy-protection principles that apply to both exemptions under Exemption 6, above.) Exemption 7(C) provides protection for law enforcement information the disclosure of which "could reasonably be expected to constitute an unwarranted invasion of personal privacy."[1] Despite their similarities in language, though, the relative sweep of the two exemptions can be significantly different.

Whereas Exemption 6 routinely requires an identification and balancing of the relevant privacy and public interests, Exemption 7(C) can be even more "categorized" in its application. Indeed, the Court of Appeals for

---

[4](...continued)
able conclusion is that granting the requested relief would harm this court's ability to control the use of discovery materials in the criminal case. That is an unacceptable interference with a law enforcement proceeding as defined by Exemption 7(A). Moreover, disclosure of the material sought under these circumstances would seriously interfere with the fairness of the procedures as defined by Exemption 7(B).").

[5] 863 F.2d at 102; cf. Dow Jones Co. v. FERC, 219 F.R.D. 167, 175 (C.D. Cal. 2002) (finding that there is "no evidence that any trial or adjudication" is pending and that the agency has not demonstrated that release "would generate pretrial publicity that could deprive the companies or any of their employees of their right to a fair trial," and accordingly ruling that the exemption did not apply).

[6] Wash. Post, 863 F.2d at 102.

[1] 5 U.S.C. § 552(b)(7)(C) (2000 & Supp. IV 2004).

the District of Columbia Circuit held in SafeCard Services v. SEC[2] that based upon the traditional recognition of the strong privacy interests inherent in law enforcement records,[3] and the logical ramifications of United States Department of Justice v. Reporters Committee for Freedom of the Press,[4] the "categorical withholding" of information that identifies third parties in law enforcement records will ordinarily be appropriate under Exemption 7(C).[5] (See the discussion of the Supreme Court's Reporters

---

[2] 926 F.2d 1197 (D.C. Cir. 1991).

[3] See Attorney General's Memorandum for Heads of All Federal Departments and Agencies Regarding the Freedom of Information Act (Oct. 12, 2001) [hereinafter Attorney General Ashcroft's FOIA Memorandum], reprinted in *FOIA Post* (posted 10/15/01) (evincing government commitment to enhancing effectiveness of law enforcement agencies).

[4] 489 U.S. 749 (1989); see also Attorney General Ashcroft's FOIA Memorandum, reprinted in *FOIA Post* (posted 10/15/01) (emphasizing the importance of protecting personal privacy among the other interests that are protected by the FOIA's exemptions); FOIA Update, Vol. X, No. 2, at 3-7 (discussing mechanics of privacy-protection decisionmaking process employed under Exemptions 6 and 7(C)).

[5] 926 F.2d at 1206; see, e.g., Blanton v. U.S. Dep't of Justice, 64 F. App'x 787, 789 (D.C. Cir. 2003) (protecting identities of third parties contained in FBI files categorically, including those assumed to be deceased); Fiduccia v. U.S. Dep't of Justice, 185 F.3d 1035, 1047-48 (9th Cir. 1999) (protecting records concerning FBI searches of house of two named individuals categorically); Nation Magazine v. U.S. Customs Serv., 71 F.3d 885, 896 (D.C. Cir. 1995) (restating that those portions of records in investigatory files which would reveal subjects, witnesses, and informants in law enforcement investigations are categorically exempt (citing SafeCard)); Long v. U.S. Dep't of Justice, 450 F. Supp. 2d 42, 68 (D.D.C.) (finding categorical principle established in Reporters Committee to be "particularly applicable" where information at issue is maintained by government in computerized compilations), amended by 457 F. Supp. 2d 30 (D.D.C. 2006), amended further on reconsideration, Nos. 00-0211 & 02-2467, 2007 WL 293508 (D.D.C. Feb. 2, 2007) (modifying amended order on other grounds), stay granted (D.D.C. Feb. 13, 2007); Mack v. Dep't of the Navy, 259 F. Supp. 2d 99, 106 (D.D.C. 2003) (protecting identities of law enforcement agents, victims, witnesses, subjects of investigative interest, and third parties contained in investigative records categorically); Carp v. IRS, No. 00-5992, 2002 WL 373448, at *4-5 (D.N.J. Jan. 28, 2002) (holding that all information that identifies third parties is categorically exempt); Pusa v. FBI, No. CV-00-12384, slip op. at 8 (C.D. Cal. May 4, 2001) (finding certain information pertaining to third parties to be categorically exempt), aff'd, 31 F. App'x 567 (9th Cir. 2002); Coolman v. IRS, No. 98-6149, 1999 WL 675319, at *5 (W.D. Mo. July 12, 1999) (finding categorical withholding of third-party information in law enforcement records to be proper), summary affirmance

(continued...)

**EXEMPTION 7(C)**

Committee decision under Exemption 6, The Reporters Committee Decision, above.)

Certain other distinctions between Exemption 6 and Exemption 7(C) are apparent: in contrast with Exemption 6, Exemption 7(C)'s language establishes a lesser burden of proof to justify withholding in two distinct re-

---

[5](...continued)
granted, 1999 WL 1419039 (8th Cir. 1999); Ctr. to Prevent Handgun Violence v. U.S. Dep't of the Treasury, 981 F. Supp. 20, 23 (D.D.C. 1997) (stating that "categorical exclusion from release of names in law enforcement reports applies only to subjects, witnesses, or informants in law enforcement investigations"); McNamera v. U.S. Dep't of Justice, 974 F. Supp. 946, 957-60 (W.D. Tex. 1997) (allowing categorical withholding of information concerning criminal investigation of private citizens); Tanks v. Huff, No. 95-568, 1996 U.S. Dist. LEXIS 7266, at *12-13 (D.D.C. May 28, 1996) (holding that absent compelling evidence of agency wrongdoing, criminal histories and other personal information about informants are categorically exempt), appeal dismissed voluntarily, No. 96-5180 (D.C. Cir. Aug. 13, 1996); Straughter v. HHS, No. 94-0567, slip op. at 5 (S.D. W. Va. Mar. 31, 1995) (magistrate's recommendation) (affording per se protection under Exemption 7(C) for witnesses and third parties when requester has identified no public interest), adopted (S.D. W. Va. Apr. 17, 1995); cf. AFL-CIO v. FEC, 177 F. Supp. 2d 48, 61 (D.D.C. 2001) (applying "this Circuit['s]" categorical rule that requires withholding under Exemption 7(C) of names of, and identifying information about, private individuals appearing in law enforcement files, even though action was brought under Administrative Procedure Act, 5 U.S.C. § 706(2)(A) (2000), and despite questionable standing of plaintiff organization to assert any such privacy interest), aff'd on other grounds, 333 F.3d 168 (D.C. Cir. 2003); Alexander & Alexander Servs. v. SEC, No. 92-1112, 1993 WL 439799, at *10 (D.D.C. Oct. 19, 1993) (requiring categorical withholding of personal information, even when records concern only professional activity of subjects, when no compelling evidence of illegal agency activity exists) ("reverse" FOIA case), appeal dismissed, No. 93-5398 (D.C. Cir. Jan. 4, 1996). But see Kimberlin v. U.S. Dep't of Justice, 139 F.3d 944, 948 (D.C. Cir. 1998) (eschewing the categorical rule of nondisclosure for Office of Professional Responsibility files, and suggesting the use of a case-by-case balancing test involving consideration of the "rank of public official involved and the seriousness of misconduct alleged"); Davin v. U.S. Dep't of Justice, 60 F.3d 1043, 1060 (3d Cir. 1995) (ruling that the "government must conduct a document by document fact-specific balancing"); Konigsberg v. FBI, No. 02-2428, slip op. at 5-7 (D.D.C. May 27, 2003) (refusing to apply categorical rule to records on informant who allegedly was protected from prosecution by FBI, based upon exceptional circumstances presented); Baltimore Sun v. U.S. Marshals Serv., 131 F. Supp. 2d 725, 730 n.5 (D. Md. 2001) (declining to accord categorical protection to third parties who purchased federally forfeited property), appeal dismissed voluntarily, No. 01-1537 (4th Cir. June 25, 2001).

spects.[6] First, it is well established that the omission of the word "clearly" from the language of Exemption 7(C) eases the burden of the agency and stems from the recognition that law enforcement records are inherently more invasive of privacy than "personnel and medical files and similar files."[7] Indeed, the "'strong interest' of individuals, whether they be suspects, witnesses, or investigators, 'in not being associated unwarrantedly with alleged criminal activity'" has been repeatedly recognized.[8]

---

[6] See NARA v. Favish, 541 U.S. 157, 165-66 (distinguishing between Exemption 6's and Exemption 7(C)'s language), reh'g denied, 541 U.S. 1057 (2004).

[7] See Cong. News Syndicate v. U.S. Dep't of Justice, 438 F. Supp. 538, 541 (D.D.C. 1977) ("[A]n individual whose name surfaces in connection with an investigation may, without more, become the subject of rumor and innuendo."); see also, e.g., Iglesias v. CIA, 525 F. Supp. 547, 562 (D.D.C. 1981).

[8] Fitzgibbon v. CIA, 911 F.2d 755, 767 (D.C. Cir. 1990) (quoting Stern v. FBI, 737 F.2d 84, 91-92 (D.C. Cir. 1984)); see also Neely v. FBI, 208 F.3d 461, 464-66 (4th Cir. 2000) (finding that FBI Special Agents and third-party suspects have "substantial interest[s] in nondisclosure of their identities and their connection[s] to particular investigations"); Quiñon v. FBI, 86 F.3d 1222, 1230 (D.C. Cir. 1996) (ruling that "'[p]ersons involved in FBI investigations -- even if they are not the subject of the investigation -- "have a substantial interest in seeing that their participation remains secret"'" (quoting Fitzgibbon, 911 F.2d at 767 (quoting, in turn, King v. U.S. Dep't of Justice, 830 F.2d 210, 233 (D.C. Cir. 1987)))); Schiffer v. FBI, 78 F.3d 1405, 1410 (9th Cir. 1996) (stating that persons named in FBI files have "strong interest in 'not being associated unwarrantedly with alleged criminal activity'" (quoting Fitzgibbon, 911 F.2d at 767)); Computer Prof'ls for Soc. Responsibility v. U.S. Secret Serv., 72 F.3d 897, 904 (D.C. Cir. 1996) (finding that release of names of individuals, including nonsuspects, who attended public meeting that attracted attention of law enforcement officials would impinge upon their privacy); Hunt v. FBI, 972 F.2d 286, 288 (9th Cir. 1992) (finding that association of FBI "agent's name with allegations of sexual and professional misconduct could cause the agent great personal and professional embarrassment"); Dunkelberger v. Dep't of Justice, 906 F.2d 779, 781 (D.C. Cir. 1990) (refusing to confirm or deny existence of letter of reprimand or suspension of named FBI Special Agent); Bast v. U.S. Dep't of Justice, 665 F.2d 1251, 1254-55 (D.C. Cir. 1981) (ruling that government officials do not surrender all rights to personal privacy by virtue of public appointment); Leveto v. IRS, No. 98-285E, 2001 U.S. Dist. LEXIS 5791, at *17-18 (W.D. Pa. Apr. 10, 2001) (recognizing privacy interests of suspects, witnesses, interviewees, and investigators); Morales Cozier v. FBI, No. 1:99 CV 0312, slip op. at 16-17 (N.D. Ga. Sept. 25, 2000) (protecting identities of FBI support personnel and individuals who provided information to FBI; citing 'well-recognized and substantial privacy interest' in nondisclosure (quoting Neely, 208 F.3d at 464)); Franklin v. U.S. Dep't of Justice, No. 97-1225, slip op. at 10 (S.D. Fla. June 15, 1998) (magistrate's recommendation) (stating law en-

(continued...)

## EXEMPTION 7(C)

Second, the Freedom of Information Reform Act of 1986 further broadened the protection afforded by Exemption 7(C) by lowering the risk-of-harm standard from "would" to "could reasonably be expected to."[9] This amendment to the Act eased the standard for evaluating a threatened privacy invasion through disclosure of law enforcement records.[10] One court, in interpreting the amended language, pointedly observed that it affords the agency "greater latitude in protecting privacy interests" in the law enforcement context.[11] Such information "is now evaluated by the agency under a more elastic standard; exemption 7(C) is now more comprehensive."[12]

---

[8](...continued) forcement officers, suspects, witnesses, innocent third parties, and individuals named in investigative files have substantial privacy interests in nondisclosure (citing Wichlacz v. U.S. Dep't of Interior, 938 F. Supp. 325, 330 (E.D. Va. 1996))), adopted (S.D. Fla. June 26, 1998), aff'd per curiam, 189 F.3d 485 (11th Cir. 1999); Buros v. HHS, No. 93-571, slip op. at 10 (W.D. Wis. Oct. 26, 1994) (refusing to confirm or deny existence of criminal investigatory records concerning county official, even though subject's alleged mishandling of funds already known to public; "confirming . . . federal criminal investigation brushes the subject with an independent and indelible taint of wrongdoing"). But see Davin v. U.S. Dep't of Justice, No. 92-1122, slip op. at 9 (W.D. Pa. Apr. 9, 1998) (concluding that individuals' privacy interests became diluted during more than twenty years that had passed since investigation was conducted), aff'd, 176 F.3d 471 (3d Cir. 1999) (unpublished table decision).

[9] Pub. L. No. 99-570, § 1802, 100 Stat. 3207, 3207-48; see Attorney General's Memorandum on the 1986 Amendments to the Freedom of Information Act 9-12 (Dec. 1987) [hereinafter Attorney General's 1986 Amendments Memorandum]; see also Favish, 541 U.S. at 169 (evincing the Supreme Court's reliance on "the Attorney General's consistent interpretation of" the FOIA in successive such Attorney General memoranda).

[10] See Reporters Comm., 489 U.S. at 756 n.9; Stone v. FBI, 727 F. Supp. 662, 665 (D.D.C. 1990) (stating that the 1986 FOIA amendments have "eased the burden of an agency claiming that exemption"), aff'd, No. 90-5065 (D.C. Cir. Sept. 14, 1990).

[11] Wash. Post Co. v. U.S. Dep't of Justice, No. 84-3581, 1987 U.S. Dist. LEXIS 14936, at *32 (D.D.C. Sept. 25, 1987) (magistrate's recommendation), adopted (D.D.C. Dec. 15, 1987), rev'd on other grounds & remanded, 863 F.2d 96 (D.C. Cir. 1988).

[12] Id.; see also Keys v. U.S. Dep't of Justice, 830 F.2d 337, 346 (D.C. Cir. 1987) (finding that the "government need not 'prove to a certainty that release will lead to an unwarranted invasion of personal privacy,'" at least not after the 1986 FOIA amendments (quoting Reporters Comm., 816 F.2d 730, 738 (D.C. Cir. 1987))); Nishnic v. Dep't of Justice, 671 F. Supp. 776, 788 (D.D.C. 1987) (holding phrase "could reasonably be expected to" to be more

(continued...)

Under the balancing test that traditionally has been applied to both Exemption 6 and Exemption 7(C), the agency must first identify and evaluate the privacy interest(s), if any, implicated in the requested records.[13] But in the case of records related to investigations by criminal law enforcement agencies, the case law has long recognized, either expressly or implicitly, that "'the mention of an individual's name in a law enforcement file will engender comment and speculation and carries a stigmatizing connotation.'"[14]

---

[12](...continued)
easily satisfied standard than phrase "likely to materialize").

[13] See e.g., Straughter, No. 94-0567, slip op. at 5 (S.D. W. Va. Mar. 31, 1995) (observing that agency must first identify and evaluate particular privacy interest implicated); Albuquerque Publ'g Co. v. U.S. Dep't of Justice, 726 F. Supp. 851, 855 (D.D.C. 1989) ("Our preliminary inquiry is whether a personal privacy interest is involved."); see also FOIA Update, Vol. X, No. 2, at 7 (advising that there first must be a viable privacy interest of an identifiable, living person in the requested information for any further consideration of privacy-exemption protection to be appropriate).

[14] Fitzgibbon, 911 F.2d at 767 (quoting Branch v. FBI, 658 F. Supp. 204, 209 (D.D.C. 1987)); see also Massey v. FBI, 3 F.3d 620, 624 (2d Cir. 1993) (same); Miller v. Bell, 661 F.2d 623, 631-32 (7th Cir. 1981) ("real potential for harassment"); Lesar v. U.S. Dep't of Justice, 636 F.2d 472, 488 (D.C. Cir. 1980) ("'It is difficult if not impossible, to anticipate all respects in which disclosure might damage reputation or lead to personal embarrassment and discomfort.'" (quoting Lesar v. U.S. Dep't of Justice, 455 F. Supp. 921, 925 (D.D.C. 1978))); Palacio v. U.S. Dep't of Justice, No. 00-1564, 2002 U.S. Dist. LEXIS 2198, at *9 (D.D.C. Feb. 11, 2002) (finding that release of individual's name in connection with criminal investigation may carry stigma and subject him to unnecessary public attention or harassment), summary affirmance granted, No. 02-5247, 2003 WL 242751 (D.C. Cir. Jan. 31, 2003); Morley v. U.S. CIA, 453 F. Supp. 2d 137, 155 (D.D.C. 2006) (recognizing that D.C. Circuit "has found a considerable stigma inherent in being associated with law enforcement proceedings"); Brady-Lunny v. Massey, 185 F. Supp. 2d 928, 932 (C.D. Ill. 2002) (deciding that release of names of federal inmates, some of whom had not been charged with or convicted of crimes, would "stigmatize these individuals and cause what could be irreparable damage to their reputations"); Perlman v. U.S. Dep't of Justice, No. 00 Civ. 5842, 2001 WL 910406, at *6 (S.D.N.Y. Aug. 13, 2001) (finding that release of names of individuals who provided information during investigation would subject them to "embarrassment, harassment or threats of reprisal"), aff'd in pertinent part, 312 F.3d 100, 106 (2d Cir. 2002) (recognizing that witnesses and third parties have "strong privacy interests" in not being identified as having been part of law enforcement investigation), vacated & remanded, 541 U.S. 970, on remand, 380 F.3d 110, 111-12 (2d Cir. 2004) (per curiam) (affirming previous holding); Times Picayune Publ'g Corp. v. U.S. Dep't of Justice, 37 F. Supp. 2d 472, 477 (E.D. La. 1999) (recognizing
(continued...)

Thus, Exemption 7(C) has been regularly applied to withhold references to persons who are not targets of investigations and who were merely mentioned in law enforcement files,[15] as well as to persons of "investiga-

---

[14](...continued)
that a "mug shot's stigmatizing effect can last well beyond the actual criminal proceeding"); Abraham & Rose, P.L.C. v. United States, 36 F. Supp. 2d 955, 957 (E.D. Mich. 1998) (noting that filing of tax lien against individual could cause "comment, speculation and stigma"); Thompson v. U.S. Dep't of Justice, No. 96-1118, slip op. at 24 (D. Kan. July 14, 1998) (finding that release of third-party names could invite harassment, embarrassment, or annoyance); Anderson v. USPS, 7 F. Supp. 2d 583, 586 (E.D. Pa. 1998) (disclosing identities of interviewees and witnesses may result in embarrassment and harassment), aff'd, 187 F.3d 625 (3d Cir. 1999) (unpublished table decision); Cujas v. IRS, No. 1:97-00741, 1998 U.S. Dist. LEXIS 6466, at *9 (M.D.N.C. Apr. 15, 1998) (finding that "third parties named in these law enforcement records have a very strong privacy interest in avoiding the stigma and embarrassment resulting from their identification as a person that is or was under investigation"), summary affirmance granted, No. 98-1641, 1998 WL 539686 (4th Cir. Aug. 25, 1998); Hamilton v. Weise, No. 95-1161, 1997 U.S. Dist. LEXIS 18900, at *20 (M.D. Fla. Oct. 1, 1997) (protecting third-party names to avoid harassment, embarrassment, and unwanted public attention); McNamera, 974 F. Supp. at 958 (rejecting argument that individual already investigated by one agency cannot be stigmatized by acknowledgment of investigation by another agency); Dayton Newspapers, Inc. v. U.S. Dep't of the Navy, No. C-3-95-328, slip op. at 51 (S.D. Ohio Sept. 13, 1996) (withholding records concerning acquitted criminal defendants because disclosure "can cause not only extreme embarrassment and humiliation, but also severe professional and economic hardship"); Southam News v. INS, 674 F. Supp. 881, 887 (D.D.C. 1987) (finding disclosure of identities of individuals excludable from U.S. "would result in derogatory inferences about and possible embarrassment to those individuals"); cf. Cerveny v. CIA, 445 F. Supp. 772, 776 (D. Colo. 1978) (finding mere mention of individual's name as subject of CIA file could be damaging to his or her reputation) (Exemption 6). But see Associated Press v. DOD, No. 05-5468, 2006 WL 2707395, at *4 (S.D.N.Y. Sept. 20, 2006) (concluding that prison detainees have severely diminished expectation of privacy and actually might want their identities publicized in response to FOIA request for any documents pertaining to abuse they are alleged to have suffered) (Exemptions 6 and 7(C)); Blanton v. U.S. Dep't of Justice, No. 93-2398, 1994 U.S. Dist. LEXIS 21444, at *8-12 (W.D. Tenn. July 14, 1993) (holding that there is no privacy interest in mere mention of defense attorney's name in criminal file or in validity of law license when attorney represented requester at criminal trial) (Exemptions 6 and 7(C)).

[15] See SafeCard, 926 F.2d at 1206 (protecting names of third parties); Fabiano v. McIntyre, 146 F. App'x 549, 550 (3d Cir. 2005) (per curiam) (affirming district court decision protecting names of victims in child pornography photographs); Rugiero v. U.S. Dep't of Justice, 257 F.3d 534, 552

(continued...)

[15](...continued)
(6th Cir. 2001) (protecting identifying information about third parties); Shaf-izadeh v. ATF, No. 99-5727, 2000 WL 1175586, at *2 (6th Cir. Aug. 10, 2000) (protecting names of, and identifying information about, private individuals); Neely, 208 F.3d at 464 (withholding names of third parties mentioned or interviewed in course of investigation); Halpern v. FBI, 181 F.3d 279, 297 (2d Cir. 1999) (same); Johnston v. U.S. Dep't of Justice, No. 97-2173, 1998 U.S. App. LEXIS 18557, at *2 (8th Cir. Aug. 10, 1998) (same); Gabel v. IRS, 134 F.3d 377, 377 (9th Cir. 1998) (protecting third-party names in Department of Motor Vehicles computer printout included in plaintiff's IRS file); Computer Prof'ls, 72 F.3d at 904 (finding that release of names of any individuals who attended public meeting that attracted attention of law enforcement officials would impinge upon their privacy); Sutton v. IRS, No. 05-7177, 2007 WL 30547, at *6 (N.D. Ill. Jan. 4, 2007) (finding that third-party taxpayers and IRS personnel have an interest in maintaining the privacy of their personal information); Romero-Cicle v. U.S. Dep't of Justice, No. 05-2303, 2006 WL 3361747, at *5 (D.D.C. Nov. 20, 2006) (protecting personal information that would identify prison visitors and third-party inmates); Bogan v. FBI, No. 04-C-532-C, 2005 WL 1367214, at *7 (W.D. Wis. June 7, 2005) (protecting names of third parties merely mentioned in investigative file); Envtl. Prot. Servs. v. EPA, 364 F. Supp. 2d 575, 588-89 (N.D. W. Va. 2005) (protecting private information about homeowners who were interviewed and whose homes were tested as part of EPA investigation); Chourre v. IRS, 203 F. Supp. 2d 1196, 1201 (W.D. Wash. 2002) (holding that redaction of third-party taxpayer information was proper); Amro v. U.S. Customs Serv., 128 F. Supp. 2d 776, 787 (E.D. Pa. 2001) (withholding names of "non-suspects arising during investigations"); Diaz v. Fed. Bureau of Prisons, No. 01-40070, slip op. at 6 (D. Mass. Dec. 20, 2001) (magistrate's recommendation) (withholding audiotape of monitored telephone conversation between plaintiff (a prison inmate) and his former trial attorney), adopted (D. Mass. Feb. 7, 2002), aff'd, 55 F. App'x 5 (1st Cir. 2003); Morales Cozier, No. 99-CV-0312, slip op. at 17 (N.D. Ga. Sept. 25, 2000) (protecting identities of third parties mentioned in law enforcement documents); Comer v. IRS, No. 97-CV-76329, slip op. at 2 (E.D. Mich. Aug. 17, 2000) (approving withholding of third party's driver's license information); Bartolotta v. FBI, No. 99-1145, slip op. at 6 (D.D.C. July 13, 2000) (withholding personal information regarding potential visitors to inmate-plaintiff); W. Ctr. for Journalism v. IRS, 116 F. Supp. 2d 1, 12 (D.D.C. 2000) (protecting address of complainant and "unrelated, incidental medical information about a third party"), aff'd, 22 F. App'x 14 (D.C. Cir. 2001); Murphy v. IRS, 79 F. Supp. 2d 1180, 1185 (D. Haw. 1999) (protecting identities of third parties); Crump v. EEOC, No. 97-0275, slip op. at 6 (M.D. Tenn. May 30, 1997) (magistrate's recommendation) (protecting personal information of third parties who filed charges with EEOC), adopted (M.D. Tenn. June 18, 1997); Feshbach v. SEC, 5 F. Supp. 2d 774, 785 (N.D. Cal. 1997) (withholding identities of third parties against whom SEC did not take action); Ajluni v. FBI, 947 F. Supp. 599, 604-05 (N.D.N.Y. 1996) (protecting identities of third parties merely

(continued...)

tory interest" to a criminal law enforcement agency.[16] Indeed, the Supreme

---

[15](...continued)
mentioned in FBI files); Perrone v. FBI, 908 F. Supp. 24, 26-27 (D.D.C. 1995) (holding that release of names of persons mentioned in law enforcement files could lead to "stigmatizing public attention and even harassment"); Fritz v. IRS, 862 F. Supp. 234, 236 (W.D. Wis. 1994) (protecting name and address of person who purchased requester's seized car). But see City of Chicago v. U.S. Dep't of the Treasury, 287 F.3d 628, 636 (7th Cir. 2002) (declining to find "any legitimate privacy concerns" in names and addresses of firearm purchasers), vacated & remanded, 537 U.S. 1229 (2003); Baltimore Sun, 131 F. Supp. 2d at 729 (rejecting protection of names and addresses of purchasers of forfeited property); see also FOIA Post, "Supreme Court Vacates and Remands in ATF Database Case" (posted 3/25/03) (discussing impact of vacatur in City of Chicago case).

[16] See, e.g., Neely, 208 F.3d at 464 (withholding names and identifying information of third-party suspects); Halpern, 181 F.3d at 297 (finding strong privacy interest in material that suggests person has at one time been subject to criminal investigation); O'Kane v. U.S. Customs Serv., 169 F.3d 1308, 1309 (11th Cir. 1999) (protecting home addresses of individuals whose possessions were seized by government); Spirko v. USPS, 147 F.3d 992, 998-99 (D.C. Cir. 1998) (protecting suspects' palm- and fingerprints, their interviews and discussions with law enforcement officers, and photographs of former suspects and their criminal histories); Computer Prof'ls, 72 F.3d at 904 (holding potential suspects would have their privacy impinged if names disclosed); Massey, 3 F.3d at 624 (finding third parties' privacy interests in nondisclosure "potentially greater" than those of law enforcement officers); McDonnell v. United States, 4 F.3d 1227, 1255 (3d Cir. 1993) (finding suspects have "obvious privacy interest in not having their identities revealed"); Maynard v. CIA, 986 F.2d 547, 566 (1st Cir. 1993) (reiterating "potential for harassment, reprisal or embarrassment" if names of individuals investigated by FBI disclosed); Davis v. U.S. Dep't of Justice, 968 F.2d 1276, 1281 (D.C. Cir. 1992) (deciding that "embarrassment and reputational harm" would result from disclosure of taped conversations of individuals with boss of New Orleans organized crime family); Silets v. U.S. Dep't of Justice, 945 F.2d 227, 230 (7th Cir. 1991) (en banc) (protecting associates of Jimmy Hoffa who were subjects of electronic surveillance); Fund for Constitutional Gov't v. Nat'l Archives & Records Serv., 656 F.2d 856, 861-66 (D.C. Cir. 1981) (withholding identities of persons investigated but not charged, unless "exceptional interests militate in favor of disclosure"); Del-Turco v. FAA, No. 04-281, slip op. at 6-7 (D. Ariz. July 11, 2005) (protecting information concerning airline employees who were investigated for safety violations but against whom charges never were brought); Garcia v. U.S. Dep't of Justice, 181 F. Supp. 2d 356, 371 (S.D.N.Y. 2002) (protecting names, identities, addresses, and information pertaining to third parties who were of investigatory interest); Amro, 128 F. Supp. 2d at 784 (finding that disclosure of names of third parties of investigatory interest to Customs Service would "undermine the privacy interests of these individuals"); Willis v. FBI,
(continued...)

Court in Reporters Committee placed strong emphasis on the propriety of broadly protecting the interests of private citizens whose names or identifying information is in a record that the government "happens to be storing."[17] More recently, in NARA v. Favish, the Supreme Court likewise recognized that law enforcement files often contain information on individuals by "mere happenstance," and it strongly reinforced the protection available under Exemption 7(C).[18] Hence, the small minority of older district court decisions that failed to appreciate the strong privacy interests inherent in the association of an individual with a law enforcement investigation should no longer be regarded as authoritative.[19]

The identities of federal, state, and local law enforcement personnel referenced in investigatory files are also routinely withheld, usually for reasons similar to those described quite aptly by the Court of Appeals for the Fourth Circuit:

---

[16](...continued)
No. 99-CV-73481, slip op. at 18 (E.D. Mich. July 11, 2000) (magistrate's recommendation) (protecting identifying information concerning subject of FBI investigation), adopted (E.D. Mich. Sept. 26, 2000); Phila. Newspapers, Inc. v. HHS, 69 F. Supp. 2d 63, 68 (D.D.C. 1999) (protecting names of doctors "investigated for -- but not charged with -- Medicare fraud"); Thompson, No. 96-1118, slip op. at 24 (D. Kan. July 14, 1998) (withholding names of complainant, information provided by third-party subject, and names of individuals interviewed); Tawalbeh v. U.S. Dep't of the Air Force, No. 96-6241, slip op. at 7 (C.D. Cal. Aug. 8, 1997) (protecting names of third parties who were potential targets of criminal investigation); Buros, No. 93-571, slip op. at 10 (W.D. Wis. Oct. 26, 1994) (finding that even though subject's alleged mishandling of funds already known to public, confirming federal criminal investigation "brushes the subject with an independent and indelible taint of wrongdoing").

[17] 489 U.S. at 380; see also id. at 774-75 (declaring with no small amount of emphasis that "it should come as no surprise that in none of our cases construing the FOIA have we found it appropriate to order a Government agency to honor a FOIA request for information about a particular private citizen").

[18] Favish, 541 U.S. at 166 (explicating in full that "law enforcement documents obtained by Government investigators often contain information about persons interviewed as witnesses or initial suspects but whose link to the official inquiry may be the result of mere happenstance"); see also FOIA Post, "Supreme Court Rules for 'Survivor Privacy' in Favish" (posted 4/9/04) (emphasizing breadth of privacy protection enunciated by Supreme Court in Favish).

[19] See, e.g., Silets v. FBI, 591 F. Supp. 490, 498 (N.D. Ill. 1984); Cunningham v. FBI, 540 F. Supp. 1, 2 (N.D. Ohio 1981), rev'd & remanded with order to vacate, No. 84-3367 (6th Cir. May 9, 1985); Lamont v. Dep't of Justice, 475 F. Supp. 761, 778 (S.D.N.Y. 1979).

# EXEMPTION 7(C)

One who serves his state or nation as a career public servant is not thereby stripped of every vestige of personal privacy, even with respect to the discharge of his official duties. Public identification of any of these individuals could conceivably subject them to harassment and annoyance in the conduct of their official duties and in their private lives.[20]

---

[20] Nix v. United States, 572 F.2d 998, 1006 (4th Cir. 1978); see FOIA Update, Vol. V, No. 2, at 5; see, e.g., Favish, 541 U.S. at 171 (finding privacy interests to be undiminished by deceased's status as high-level public official); Fabiano, 146 F. App'x at 549 (affirming withholding of names and telephone numbers of FBI Special Agent, FBI support employees, and non-FBI federal employee); Rugiero, 257 F.3d at 552 (upholding nondisclosure of identifying information about DEA agents and personnel); Robert v. Nat'l Archives, 1 F. App'x 85, 86 (2d Cir. 2001) (protecting government employee's name); Shafizadeh, 2000 WL 1175586, at *2 (withholding names of, and identifying information about, federal law enforcement personnel); Neely, 208 F.3d at 464 (withholding FBI Special Agents' names); Fiduccia, 185 F.3d at 1043-45 (withholding DEA and INS agents' names); Halpern, 181 F.3d at 296 (protecting identities of nonfederal law enforcement officers); Johnston, 1998 U.S. App. LEXIS 18557, at *2 (protecting names of DEA agents and personnel and local law enforcement personnel); Manna v. U.S. Dep't of Justice, 51 F.3d 1158, 1166 (3d Cir. 1995) (finding law enforcement officers have substantial privacy interest in nondisclosure of names, particularly when requester held high position in La Cosa Nostra); Jones v. FBI, 41 F.3d 238, 246 (6th Cir. 1994) (protecting names of FBI Special Agents and federal, state, and local law enforcement personnel); Becker v. IRS, 34 F.3d 398, 405 n.23 (7th Cir. 1994) (protecting initials, names, and phone numbers of IRS employees); Church of Scientology Int'l v. IRS, 995 F.2d 916, 920-21 (9th Cir. 1993) (deciding privacy interest exists in handwriting of IRS agents in official documents); Maynard, 986 F.2d at 566 (protecting names and initials of low-level FBI Special Agents and support personnel); Hale v. U.S. Dep't of Justice, 973 F.2d 894, 902 (10th Cir. 1992) (finding FBI employees have substantial privacy interest in concealing their identities), vacated & remanded on other grounds, 509 U.S. 918 (1993); Davis, 968 F.2d at 1281 (holding that "undercover agents" have protectible privacy interests); New England Apple Council v. Donovan, 725 F.2d 139, 142-44 (1st Cir. 1984) (inspector general investigator has "interest in retaining the capability to perform his tasks effectively by avoiding untoward annoyance or harassment"); Miller, 661 F.2d at 630 ("It is not necessary that harassment rise to the level of endangering physical safety before the protections of 7(C) can be invoked."); Lesar, 636 F.2d at 487-88 (annoyance or harassment); O'Keefe v. DOD, 463 F. Supp. 2d 317, 324 (E.D.N.Y. 2006) (protecting identities of DOD investigators); Mettetal v. U.S. Dep't of Justice, No. 2:04-CV-410, 2006 U.S. Dist. LEXIS 64157, at *10-12 (E.D. Tenn. Sept. 7, 2006) (protecting names of local law enforcement and non-FBI government personnel involved in plaintiff's criminal prosecution) (Exemptions 6 and 7(C)); Trentadue v. Integrity Comm., No. 2:03-CV-339, 2006 WL 1184636, at

(continued...)

It should be noted that prior to the <u>Reporters Committee</u> and <u>Safe-Card</u> decisions, courts ordinarily held that because Exemption 7(C) involves a balancing of the private and public interests on a case-by-case basis, there existed no "blanket exemption for the names of all [law en-

---

[20](...continued)
*5-6 (D. Utah May 2, 2006) (protecting identities of mid- and low-level law enforcement personnel); <u>Gavin v. SEC</u>, No. 04-4522, 2005 WL 2739293, at *5-6 (D. Minn. Oct. 24, 2005) (protecting names of SEC staff involved in investigation); <u>Summers v. U.S. Dep't of Justice</u>, No. 98-1837, slip op. at 15 (D.D.C. Mar. 10, 2003) (approving FBI's decision to distinguish between low-level (or first-line) supervisors and high-level supervisors who may be more knowledgeable about investigation); <u>Aldridge v. U.S. Comm'r of Internal Revenue</u>, No. 7:00-CV-131, 2001 WL 196965, at *2 (N.D. Tex. Feb. 23, 2001) (withholding IRS employees' social security numbers, home addresses, phone numbers, birthdates, and direct dial telephone number of acting chief of IRS's Examinations Division); <u>Times Picayune</u>, 37 F. Supp. 2d at 478 (noting that one's status "as a 'public figure' does not eviscerate" one's privacy interest under the FOIA); <u>Ortiz v. U.S. Dep't of Justice</u>, No. 97-140, slip op. at 5 (M.D. La. Aug. 25, 1998) (magistrate's recommendation) (protecting names and identifying information pertaining to local and foreign law enforcement officers), <u>adopted</u> (M.D. La. Oct. 1, 1998); <u>see also</u> <u>Sosa v. FBI</u>, No. 93-1126, slip op. at 8 (D.D.C. Apr. 9, 1998) (protecting murdered law enforcement officer's autopsy reports). <u>But see</u> <u>Lissner v. U.S. Customs Serv.</u>, 241 F.3d 1220, 1224 (9th Cir. 2001) (ordering release of physical description of state law enforcement officers involved in smuggling incident); <u>Lahr v. NTSB</u>, No. 03-8023, 2006 WL 2854314, at *14 (C.D. Cal. Oct. 4, 2006) (concluding that absent aggrieved "target" or defendant, and with ten years having elapsed since investigation, it is unlikely that FBI Special Agents would be subject to harassment or annoyance) (appeal pending); <u>Homick v. U.S. Dep't of Justice</u>, No. 98-00557, slip op. at 19-27 (N.D. Cal. Sept. 16, 2004) (ordering disclosure of identities of FBI Special Agents, government support personnel, and foreign, state, and local law enforcement officers), <u>reconsideration denied</u> (N.D. Cal. Oct. 27, 2004), <u>appeal dismissed voluntarily</u>, No. 04-17568 (9th Cir. July 5, 2005); <u>Trentadue v. President's Council on Integrity & Efficiency</u>, No. 03-339, slip op. at 4 (D. Utah Apr. 26, 2004) (refusing to find any privacy interest and therefore ordering release of names of mid-level government employees involved in investigation of Justice Department IG despite failure of requester to demonstrate any public interest); <u>Darby v. U.S. Dep't of the Air Force</u>, No. CV-S-00-0661, slip op. at 11-12 (D. Nev. Mar. 1, 2002) (ordering release of names of DOD IG investigators and other government employees involved in investigation), <u>aff'd sub nom.</u> Darby v. DOD, 74 F. App'x 813 (9th Cir. 2003); <u>Hardy v. FBI</u>, No. 95-883, slip op. at 21, 28 (D. Ariz. July 29, 1997) (ordering release of names of ATF supervisory agents involved in raid at Waco); <u>see also</u> FOIA Post, "Supreme Court Rules for 'Survivor Privacy' in <u>Favish</u>" (posted 4/9/04) (discussing privacy expectations of individual identified as "public figure").

forcement] personnel in all documents."[21] Nonetheless, absent a demonstration of significant misconduct on the part of law enforcement personnel or other government officials,[22] the overwhelming majority of courts have declared their identities exempt from disclosure pursuant to Exemption 7(C).[23] Those few decisions ordering disclosure of the names of govern-

---

[21] Lesar, 636 F.2d at 487.

[22] See, e.g., Perlman, 312 F.3d at 107-09 (ordering release of extensive details concerning IG investigation of former INS general counsel who was implicated in wrongdoing, and enunciating unique five-factor test to balance government employee's privacy interest against public interest in disclosure, including employee's rank, degree of wrongdoing and strength of evidence, availability of information, whether information sheds light on government activity, and whether information is related to job function or is personal in nature); Stern, 737 F.2d at 94 (ordering release of name of FBI Special Agent-in-Charge who directly participated in intentional wrongdoing, while protecting names of two mid-level agents whose negligence incidentally furthered cover-up); Chang v. Dep't of the Navy, 314 F. Supp. 2d 35, 42-45 (D.D.C. 2004) (approving disclosure of details of nonjudicial punishment and letter of reprimand of commander of ship punished for dereliction of duty) (Privacy Act "wrongful disclosure" decision interpreting Exemption 6); Wood v. FBI, 312 F. Supp. 2d 328, 350-51(D. Conn. 2004) (applying Perlman standard in disallowing Exemption 6 protection and ordering release of information identifying FBI Special Agent with supervisory authority who was investigated for wrongdoing, but withholding names of investigators under Exemption 7(C)); see also Jefferson v. U.S. Dep't of Justice, No. 01-1418, slip op. at 11 (D.D.C. Nov. 14, 2003) (protecting details of IG investigation of government attorney-advisor with no decisionmaking authority as employee whose rank was not so high that public interest in disclosure could outweigh personal privacy interest in learning of any investigated alleged misconduct).

[23] See, e.g., Manna, 51 F.3d at 1166 (finding unfounded complaints of government misconduct insufficient to outweigh law enforcement officers' substantial privacy interests); Hale, 973 F.2d at 901 (holding unsubstantiated allegations of government wrongdoing do not justify disclosing law enforcement personnel names); Davis, 968 F.2d at 1281 ("undercover agents"); In re Wade, 969 F.2d 241, 246 (7th Cir. 1992) (FBI Special Agent); Patterson v. FBI, 893 F.2d 595, 601 (3d Cir. 1990) (FBI personnel); Johnson v. U.S. Dep't of Justice, 739 F.2d 1514, 1519 (10th Cir. 1984) (deciding that FBI Special Agents' identities are properly protectible absent evidence of impropriety in undisclosed material); MacLean v. DOD, No. 04-2425, slip op. at 16-17 (S.D. Cal. June 6, 2005) (protecting prosecutor's professional responsibility file because disclosure would associate him with alleged wrongful activity of which he was ultimately cleared); Wolk v. United States, No. 04-832, 2005 WL 465382, at *5-7 (E.D. Pa. Feb. 28, 2005) (protecting personal background information about federal judicial nominee absent proven allegations of wrongdoing); Dorsett v. U.S. Dep't of the

(continued...)

ment investigators -- other than when demonstrated misconduct has been involved -- either predate <u>Reporters Committee</u>[24] (not to mention <u>Favish</u>) or else find an unusually significant public interest in disclosure.[25]

---

[23](...continued)
<u>Treasury</u>, 307 F. Supp. 2d 28, 38-39 (D.D.C. 2004) (withholding names of Secret Service Agents and personnel, FBI Special Agents, and other employees in face of allegations of misconduct); <u>Lopez v. U.S. Dep't of Justice</u>, No. 99-1722, slip op. at 10-12 (D.D.C. Jan. 21, 2003) (protecting names of government employees absent evidence of misconduct), <u>summary affirmance granted in pertinent part</u>, No. 03-5192, 2004 WL 626726 (D.C. Cir. Mar. 29, 2004); <u>Pontecorvo v. FBI</u>, No. 00-1511, slip op. at 41 (D.D.C. Sept. 30, 2001) (withholding identity of FBI Special Agent who conducted plaintiff's background investigation, absent sufficient evidence of misconduct); <u>Robert v. Dep't of Justice</u>, No. 99-CV-3649, slip op. at 16 (E.D.N.Y. Mar. 22, 2001) (withholding employees' names and personal information because disclosure could cause embarrassment in light of "plaintiff's far[-]reaching allegations of departmental wrongdoing"); <u>Ray v. U.S. Dep't of Justice</u>, 778 F. Supp. 1212, 1215 (S.D. Fla. 1991) (affirming government may neither confirm nor deny existence of records concerning results of INS investigation of alleged misconduct of employee); <u>see also</u> <u>Favish</u>, 541 U.S. at 173-75 (holding that requester who asserts a "government misconduct public interest" must produce evidence that would be deemed believable by a "reasonable person" for there to exist a "counterweight on the FOIA scale for the court to balance against the cognizable privacy interests in the requested records"); <u>Aldridge</u>, No. 7:00-CV-131, 2001 WL 196965, at *3 (ordering disclosure of recommendation concerning potential disciplinary action against IRS employees, with only their names redacted, based upon public's "interest in knowing how well a particular agency's employees behave on the job").

[24] <u>See, e.g.,</u> <u>Castañeda v. United States</u>, 757 F.2d 1010, 1012 (9th Cir. 1985) (treating USDA investigator's privacy interest as "not great," based upon novel reasoning that his "name would be discoverable in any civil case brought [against the agency]"), <u>amended upon denial of panel reh'g</u>, 773 F.2d 251 (9th Cir. 1985); <u>Iglesias</u>, 525 F. Supp. at 563 (disclosing names of government employees involved in conducting investigation); <u>Canadian Javelin, Ltd. v. SEC</u>, 501 F. Supp. 898, 904 (D.D.C. 1980) (releasing names of SEC investigators). <u>But see also</u> <u>FOIA Post</u>, "Supreme Court Rules for 'Survivor Privacy' in <u>Favish</u>" (posted 4/9/04) (discussing viability of <u>Castañeda</u> decision in light of Supreme Court's repudiation of Ninth Circuit's privacy jurisprudence).

[25] <u>See</u> <u>Lissner</u>, 241 F.3d at 1223 (ordering disclosure of physical description of state law enforcement officers, and citing only general public interest in ensuring reliability of government investigations); <u>Hardy</u>, No. 95-883, slip op. at 21 (D. Ariz. July 29, 1997) (releasing identities of supervisory ATF agents and other agents publicly associated with Waco incident, finding that public's interest in Waco raid "is greater than in the normal case

(continued...)

## EXEMPTION 7(C)

The history of one case in the District Court for the District of Columbia illustrates the impact of the Reporters Committee decision in this area of law. In Southam News,[26] the district court initially held that the identities of FBI clerical personnel who performed administrative tasks with respect to requested records could not be withheld under Exemption 7(C). Even then, this position was inconsistent with other, contemporaneous decisions.[27] Following the Supreme Court's decision in Reporters Committee, the government sought reconsideration of the Southam News decision. Agreeing that revelation of identities and activities of low-level agency personnel ordinarily will shed no light on government operations, as required by Reporters Committee, the district court reversed its earlier disclosure order and held the names to be properly protected.[28] Significantly, the court also recognized that "the only imaginable contribution that this information could make would be to enable the public to seek out individuals who had been tangentially involved in investigations and to question them for unauthorized access to information as to what the investigation entailed and what other FBI personnel were involved."[29] The same district

---

[25](...continued)
where release of agent names affords no insight into an agency's conduct or operations"); Butler, 1994 WL 55621, at *13 (releasing identities of supervisory FBI personnel upon finding of "significant" public interest in protecting requester's due process rights); cf. Weiner v. FBI, No. 83-1720, slip op. at 7 (C.D. Cal. Dec. 6, 1995) (finding public interest in release of names and addresses of agents involved in management and supervision of FBI investigation of music legend John Lennon) (applying FOIA analysis in civil discovery context). But see FOIA Post, "Supreme Court Rules for 'Survivor Privacy' in Favish" (posted 4/9/04) (pointing out that Lissner decision is now "discredit[ed] or effectively overrule[d]" by Supreme Court's repudiation of Ninth Circuit's privacy jurisprudence).

[26] 674 F. Supp. at 888.

[27] See, e.g., Doherty v. U.S. Dep't of Justice, 775 F.2d 49, 52 (2d Cir. 1985) (protecting identities of FBI Special Agents and nonagent personnel); Kirk v. U.S. Dep't of Justice, 704 F. Supp. 288, 292 (D.D.C. 1989) ("Just like FBI [S]pecial [A]gents, administrative and clerical personnel could be subject to harassment, questioning, and publicity, and the Court concludes that the FBI did not need to separate the groups of employees for purposes of explaining why disclosure of their identities was opposed.").

[28] Southam News v. INS, No. 85-2721, slip op. at 3 (D.D.C. Aug. 30, 1989).

[29] Id.; see also Judicial Watch v. United States, 84 F. App'x 335, 339 (4th Cir. 2004) (protecting names and home addresses of lower-level IRS employees absent compelling evidence of agency corruption, in order to avoid potential harassment) (Exemption 6); Halpern, 181 F.3d at 296 (concluding that disclosure of names of law enforcement personnel could subject them to "harassment in the conduct of their official duties"); Manna, 51 F.3d at
(continued...)

court has strongly reaffirmed that identities of both FBI clerical personnel and low-level FBI Special Agents are properly withheld as a routine matter under Exemption 7(C), even when they take part in a highly publicized investigation.[30]

---

[29](...continued)
1166 (holding law enforcement officers involved in La Cosa Nostra investigation have substantial privacy interest in nondisclosure of their names); Cal-Trim, Inc. v. IRS, No. 05-2408, slip op. at 8 (D. Ariz. Feb. 6, 2007) (protecting personal privacy of lower-level IRS employees); Joyce v. FBI, 152 F. Supp. 2d 32, 36 (D.D.C. 2001) (approving the redaction of names of, and identifying information about, law enforcement personnel, given the "potential for harassment and the infringement on the private lives of law-enforcement officials"); Morales Cozier, No. 99-CV-0312, slip op. at 17 (N.D. Ga. Sept. 25, 2000) (withholding identities of FBI Special Agents who investigated requester after her professional contact with Cuban citizen; citing potential for "harassment, surveillance, or [undue] investigation of these [Special A]gents by foreign governments"); Bartolotta, No. 99-1145, slip op. at 9 (D.D.C. July 13, 2000) (accepting that disclosing identities of two Criminal Division attorneys could result in harassment or reprisals, and could make it more difficult for them to perform duties that require low profile); Hambarian v. IRS, No. 99-9000, 2000 U.S. Dist. LEXIS 6317, at *10 (C.D. Cal. Feb. 15, 2000) (protecting names and identification numbers of IRS employees "who participated in the investigation of" the requester); Ortiz, No. 97-140, slip op. at 7 (M.D. La. Aug. 25, 1998) (magistrate's recommendation) (finding that disclosure of names of FBI personnel could subject them to "harassment and annoyance"), adopted (M.D. La. Oct. 1, 1998); Smith v. ATF, 977 F. Supp. 496, 499 (D.D.C. 1997) (finding disclosure of law enforcement officers' names "might seriously prejudice their effectiveness in conduct of investigations"); Harvey v. U.S. Dep't of Justice, No. 96-0509, 1997 WL 669640, at *3 (D.D.C. Oct. 23, 1997) (recognizing that release of names of DEA support personnel could target them for "'harassing inquiries for unauthorized access' to information"); Simon v. U.S. Dep't of Justice, 752 F. Supp. 14, 19 (D.D.C. 1990) (protecting identities of FBI Special Agents and other government personnel involved in processing FOIA request), aff'd, 980 F.2d 782 (D.C. Cir. 1992).

[30] See Stone, 727 F. Supp. at 663 n.1 (protecting identities of FBI Special Agents and clerical employees who participated in investigation of assassination of Robert F. Kennedy); Hoffman v. Brown, No. 97-1145, 1998 WL 279575 (4th Cir. May 19, 1998) (per curiam) (withholding portions of transcript of unauthorized audiotaped conversations of Veterans Administration Medical Center employees made during IG investigation); Wichlacz, 938 F. Supp. at 334 (E.D. Va. 1996) (protecting names of Park Police officers who investigated suicide of Deputy White House Counsel Vincent Foster, as well as psychiatrists who were listed on paper found in Foster's wallet, because disclosure would cause "onslaught of media attention" and could cause camera crews to "besiege" their workplaces and homes), aff'd per curiam, 114 F.3d 1178 (4th Cir. 1997) (unpublished table decision); Exner v.
(continued...)

On the other hand, the Court of Appeals for the Ninth Circuit has twice failed to follow the Reporters Committee decision.[31] In two decisions, Lissner v. United States Customs Service[32] and Favish v. Office of Independent Counsel,[33] the Ninth Circuit inexplicably ignored very well-recognized privacy interests and refused to adhere to the narrowed definition of public interest set forth in Reporters Committee.[34] In Lissner, the Ninth Circuit ordered disclosure of the "general physical description" of two state law enforcement officers who were involved in smuggling steroids.[35] In so doing, it neglected to consider the fact that the physical descriptions of these persons would shed no light on the activities of the United States Customs Service.[36]

Likewise, in Favish v. Office of Independent Counsel, when attempting to balance the interests involved in ten photographs of the scene of Deputy White House Counsel Vincent Foster's suicide, the Ninth Circuit sent the case to the district court for it to view the photographs in camera

---

[30](...continued)
U.S. Dep't of Justice, 902 F. Supp. 240, 243-45 (D.D.C. 1995) (protecting identities of deceased former FBI Special Agent and his two sons, one of whom FBI may have observed "in criminally suspect behavior" at requester's apartment, which requester claimed had been searched for political reasons involving her alleged relationship with President Kennedy), appeal dismissed, No. 95-5411, 1997 WL 68352 (D.C. Cir. Jan. 15, 1997); cf. Armstrong v. Executive Office of the President, 97 F.3d 575, 581-82 (D.C. Cir. 1996) (finding that agency had not adequately defended categorical rule for withholding identities of low-level FBI Special Agents) (Exemption 6).

[31] See, e.g., Bibles v. Or. Natural Desert Ass'n, 83 F.3d 1168, 1172 (9th Cir. 1996) (Fernandez, J., dissenting) ("Once again we are asked to bridle at and practically ignore the FOIA teachings of the United States Supreme Court."), summarily rev'd & remanded per curiam, 519 U.S. 355 (1997) (Exemption 6); see also FOIA Update, Vol. XVIII, No. 1, at 1 (discussing Supreme Court's extraordinary action in summarily reversing Ninth Circuit's decision in Bibles).

[32] 241 F.3d 1220 (9th Cir. 2001).

[33] 217 F.3d 1168 (9th Cir. 2000), summary judgment granted on remand, No. CV 97-1479, 2001 WL 770410 (C.D. Cal. Jan. 11, 2001), aff'd, 37 F. App'x 863 (9th Cir. 2002), rev'd sub nom. NARA v. Favish, 541 U.S. 157, reh'g denied, 541 U.S. 1057 (2004).

[34] See FOIA Update, Vol. X, No. 2, at 3 (analyzing Supreme Court's Reporters Committee decision).

[35] 241 F.3d at 1224.

[36] See Reporters Comm., 489 U.S. at 774 ("[T]he FOIA's central purpose is to ensure that the Government's activities be opened to the sharp eye of public scrutiny . . . .").

and inevitably order disclosure under highly flawed standards[37] -- doing so even though those very photographs had been held to be protected by Exemption 7(C) in a previous case.[38] Further, in analyzing the public interest in disclosure, the Ninth Circuit purported to follow Reporters Committee yet based its finding of public interest in disclosure of the photographs merely upon plaintiff's "doubts" regarding the adequacy of the government's investigation into the suicide[39] -- leading to an order from the district court to disclose five of the death-scene photographs.[40]

The Supreme Court rejected the Ninth Circuit's views of privacy protection, and its acceptance of such public interest arguments, when it unanimously reversed the Ninth Circuit in NARA v. Favish.[41] It ruled that while the Ninth Circuit had recognized the family's privacy interest and the nature of the asserted public interest, the Ninth Circuit had failed to properly balance the two when it required no credible evidence showing actual government wrongdoing.[42] Such a reading of the Reporters Committee public interest standard in this context, the Court said, "leaves Exemption 7(C) with little force or content."[43] So under the Supreme Court's ruling in Favish, and its decision to protect the photographs at issue, a FOIA re-

---

[37] See 217 F.3d at 1174.

[38] See Accuracy in Media, Inc. v. Nat'l Park Serv., 194 F.3d 120, 122-23 (D.C. Cir. 1999) (finding that the spouse, parents, and children of Deputy White House Counsel Vincent Foster have a discernible privacy interest in not having his death-scene photographs made public; holding that to show that an invasion of privacy is not unwarranted, the plaintiff must produce "'compelling evidence that the agency denying the FOIA request is engaged in illegal activity, and access to the [photograph] is necessary in order to confirm or refute that evidence'" (quoting SafeCard, 926 F.2d at 1205-06)); see also Accuracy in Media, Inc. v. Office of Indep. Counsel, 61 F. App'x 712, 712-13 (D.C. Cir. 2003) (per curiam) (ruling that requester had "once again failed to demonstrate" that agency engaged in illegal activity, and finding that same privacy interest in nondisclosure of photograph of hand and description of body existed as in Accuracy in Media, 194 F.3d at 122).

[39] 217 F.3d at 1174; see also id. at 1184 (Pregerson, J., dissenting) (observing that "Favish has made no showing that anyone connected with the OIC's investigations . . . engaged in wrongful conduct"; explaining that the requester bears the burden of advancing the public interest, and that this requester "has failed to do so").

[40] Favish, 2001 WL 770410, at *1 (ordering five of ten photographs at issue released to plaintiff).

[41] 541 U.S. 157.

[42] Id. at 173-74.

[43] Id. at 173.

quester's assertion of a public interest based on "government wrongdoing" now must meet a distinctly higher standard.[44] Indeed, the Supreme Court's repudiation of the Ninth Circuit's decision in Favish is sweeping enough to discredit (or effectively overrule) that circuit court's previous aberrational privacy jurisprudence.[45] (See also the further discussions of Favish's fundamental privacy-protection principles under Exemption 6, above.)

In Reporters Committee, the Supreme Court found that substantial privacy interests can exist in personal information such as is contained in "rap sheets," even though the information has been made available to the general public at some place and point in time. Applying a "practical obscurity" standard,[46] the Court observed that if such items of information actually "were 'freely available,' there would be no reason to invoke the FOIA to obtain access to [them]."[47] (See Exemption 7(D), below, for a discussion

---

[44] Id. at 174-75; see also FOIA Post, "Supreme Court Rules for 'Survivor Privacy' in Favish" (posted 4/9/04) (discussing higher standard, as well as continued need for showing of Reporters Committee-type public interest even when requester successfully alleges government wrongdoing). But cf. Detroit Free Press, Inc. v. Dep't of Justice, 73 F.3d 93, 97-98 (6th Cir. 1996) (suggesting in dicta that there might be significant public interest in disclosure of "mug shots" in limited circumstances without requester demonstrating with particularity any actual government misconduct); Beacon Journal Publ'g Co. v. Gonzalez, No. 05-1396, slip op. at 2 (N.D. Ohio Nov. 16, 2005) (ordering disclosure of "mug shots" under Sixth Circuit's decision in Detroit Free Press); Detroit Free Press, Inc. v. U.S. Dep't of Justice, No. 05-71601, slip op. at 1 (E.D. Mich. Oct. 7, 2005) (same); Times Picayune, 37 F. Supp. 2d at 477 (pre-Favish decision protecting "mug shot" beyond confines of Sixth Circuit).

[45] See, e.g., Lissner, 241 F.3d at 1224; Rosenfeld, 57 F.3d at 812; Dobronski v. FCC, 17 F.3d 275, 278 (9th Cir. 1994); see Dow Jones Co., Inc. v. FERC, 219 F.R.D. 167, 175-76 (C.D. Cal. 2003) (ordering disclosure of names of individuals who cooperated with investigation, expressly based upon Ninth Circuit's now-repudiated Favish ruling, merely because they were not accused of criminal activity); see also FOIA Post, "Supreme Court Rules for 'Survivor Privacy' in Favish" (posted 4/9/04) (analyzing Favish decision's sweeping impact on Ninth Circuit case law).

[46] 489 U.S. at 762-63, 780.

[47] Id. at 764; see Edwards v. Dep't of Justice, No. 04-5044, 2004 WL 2905342, at *1 (D.C. Cir. 2004) (per curiam) (summarily affirming district court decision withholding information where plaintiff failed to point to specific information in public domain that duplicated withheld information); Fiduccia, 185 F.3d at 1047 (protecting FBI records reflecting information that is also available in "various courthouses"); Abraham & Rose, P.L.C. v. United States, 138 F.3d 1075, 1083 (6th Cir. 1998) (stating that clear privacy interest exists with respect to names, addresses, and other identify-

(continued...)

of the status of open-court testimony under that exemption.)

All but one court of appeals to have addressed the issue have found protectible privacy interests in conjunction with or in lieu of protection under Exemption 7(D) -- in the identities of individuals who provide information to law enforcement agencies.[48] Consequently, the names of witnesses

---

[47](...continued)
ing information, even if already available in publicly recorded filings (citing DOD v. FLRA, 510 U.S. 487, 500 (1994) (Exemption 6))); Harrison v. Executive Office for U.S. Attorneys, 377 F. Supp. 2d 141, 147-48 (D.D.C. 2005) (protecting names and addresses of criminal defendants, case captions and numbers, attorney names and addresses, and case initiation, disposition, and sentencing dates even though information could be found by searches of public records); Leadership Conference on Civil Rights v. Gonzales, 404 F. Supp. 2d 246, 257-59 (D.D.C. 2005) (finding privacy interest in information concerning private individuals even though documents were previously distributed in unredacted form to symposium participants); Times Picayune, 37 F. Supp. 2d at 478-79 (holding that public dissemination of "mug shot" after trial would trigger renewed publicity and renewed invasion of privacy of subject); Billington v. U.S. Dep't of Justice, 11 F. Supp. 2d 45, 61 (D.D.C. 1998) (finding that "agency is not compelled to release information just because it may have been disclosed previously"), aff'd in pertinent part, 233 F.3d 581 (D.C. Cir. 2000); Greenberg v. U.S. Dep't of Treasury, No. 87-898, 1998 U.S. Dist. LEXIS 9803, at *55 (D.D.C. July 1, 1998) (finding third party's privacy interest not extinguished because public may be aware he was target of investigation); Baltimore Sun Co. v. U.S. Customs Serv., No. 97-1991, slip op. at 4 (D. Md. Nov. 12, 1997) (holding that inclusion of poor copy of defendant's photograph in publicly available court record did not eliminate privacy interest in photo altogether); Lewis v. USPS, No. 96-3467, slip op. at 2 (D. Md. Apr. 30, 1997) (holding that fact that complainant's name is already known, whether disclosed by investigating agency or otherwise, is irrelevant; declaring that "limited oral disclosure" does not constitute waiver of exemption). But see Lardner v. U.S. Dep't of Justice, No. 03-0180, 2005 U.S. Dist. LEXIS 5465, at *55-61 (D.D.C. Mar. 31, 2005) (ignoring element of "practical obscurity" in ordering release of names of unsuccessful pardon applicants and names of private individuals who supported clemency applications) (Exemption 6).

[48] See, e.g., Hoffman, 1998 WL 279575 (protecting "private citizen identifiers" in VA investigative report); Beard v. Espy, No. 94-16748, 1995 U.S. App. LEXIS 38269, at *2 (9th Cir. Dec. 11, 1995) (protecting complaint letter); Manna, 51 F.3d at 1166 (holding that interviewees and witnesses involved in criminal investigation have substantial privacy interest in nondisclosure of their names, particularly when requester held high position in La Cosa Nostra); McDonnell, 4 F.3d at 1256 (protecting identities of witnesses and third parties involved in criminal investigation of maritime disaster); Massey, 3 F.3d at 624 (declaring that disclosure of names of cooperating witnesses and third parties, including cooperating law enforcement offi-
(continued...)

and their home and business addresses have been held properly protectible under Exemption 7(C).[49] Additionally, Exemption 7(C) protection has

---

[48](...continued)
cials, could subject them to "embarrassment and harassment"); KTVY-TV v. United States, 919 F.2d 1465, 1469 (10th Cir. 1990) (per curiam) (withholding interviewees' names as "necessary to avoid harassment and embarrassment"); Cleary v. FBI, 811 F.2d 421, 424 (8th Cir. 1987) (deciding disclosure would subject "sources to unnecessary questioning concerning the investigation [and] to subpoenas issued by private litigants in civil suits incidentally related to the investigation"); Cuccaro v. Sec'y of Labor, 770 F.2d 355, 359 (3d Cir. 1985) ("privacy interest of . . . witnesses who participated in OSHA's investigation outweighs public interest in disclosure"); L&C Marine Transp., Ltd. v. United States, 740 F.2d 919, 923 (11th Cir. 1984) (reasoning that disclosure of identities of employee-witnesses in OSHA investigation could cause "problems at their jobs and with their livelihoods"); New England Apple, 725 F.2d at 144-45 ("Disclosure could have a significant, adverse effect on this individual's private or professional life."); Kiraly v. FBI, 728 F.2d 273, 279 (6th Cir. 1984) (finding that, in absence of public benefit in disclosure, informant's personal privacy interests do not lapse at death); Holy Spirit Ass'n v. FBI, 683 F.2d 562, 564-65 (D.C. Cir. 1982) (concurring opinion) (citing "risk of harassment" and fear of reprisals); Alirez v. NLRB, 676 F.2d 423, 427 (10th Cir. 1982) (holding that disclosure would result in "embarrassment or reprisals"); Lesar, 636 F.2d at 488 ("'Those cooperating with law enforcement should not now pay the price of full disclosure of personal details.'" (quoting Lesar, 455 F. Supp. at 925)); cf. Grand Cent. P'ship v. Cuomo, 166 F.3d 473, 486 (2d Cir. 1999) (finding that HUD failed to prove that disclosure of documents would identify individuals). But see Cooper Cameron Corp. v. U.S. Dep't of Labor, 280 F.3d 539, 554 (5th Cir. 2002) (rebuffing idea of retaliation against employees who gave statements to OSHA investigator, and ordering disclosure of source-identifying content of statements despite fact that identifiable employee-witnesses' names already had been released in separate civil proceeding).

[49] See Coulter v. Reno, No. 98-35170, 1998 WL 658835, at *1 (9th Cir. Sept. 17, 1998) (protecting names of witnesses and of requester's accusers); Spirko, 147 F.3d at 998 (protecting notes and phone messages concerning witnesses); Computer Prof'ls, 72 F.3d at 904 (protecting names of witnesses); Manna, 51 F.3d at 1166 (deciding witnesses in La Cosa Nostra case have "substantial" privacy interest in nondisclosure of their names); L&C Marine, 740 F.2d at 922 ("employee-witnesses . . . have a substantial privacy interest"); Antonelli v. Sullivan, 732 F.2d 560, 562 (7th Cir. 1984) ("[The requester] has mentioned no legitimate need for the witnesses' phone numbers and we can well imagine the invasions of privacy that would result should he obtain them."); Sinsheimer v. DHS, 437 F. Supp. 2d 50, 54-56 (D.D.C. 2006) (protecting names of witnesses and of plaintiff's coworkers because of public interest in encouraging cooperation and participation of agency employees in investigations of civil rights violations); Brown v. EPA, 384 F. Supp. 2d 271, 278 (D.D.C. 2005) (recognizing that fed-
(continued...)

been afforded to the identities of informants,[50] even when it was shown

---

[49](...continued)
eral employees who were witnesses in an internal investigation have a
"broad right to be protected from mischief -- within the workplace and
without -- that could follow from the public disclosure of their identit[ies]
as witnesses in a criminal investigation"); Dean v. FDIC, 389 F. Supp. 2d
780, 794-96 (E.D. Ky. 2005) (withholding identifying information of third
parties and witnesses in IG investigation); Johnson v. Comm'r of Internal
Revenue, 239 F. Supp. 2d 1125, 1137 (W.D. Wash. 2002) (protecting identifying information of third parties and witnesses contacted during IRS investigation); Hogan v. Huff, No. 00-6753, 2002 WL 1359722, at *9-10
(S.D.N.Y. June 21, 2002) (protecting identities of witnesses); Wayne's
Mech. & Maint. Contractor, Inc. v. U.S. Dep't of Labor, No. 1:00-CV-45, slip
op. at 9 (N.D. Ga. May 7, 2001) ("In the context of OSHA investigations,
employee-witnesses have a substantial privacy interest regarding statements given about a work-related accident in light of the potential for embarrassment and retaliation that disclosure of their identity could cause.");
Heggestad v. U.S. Dep't of Justice, 182 F. Supp. 2d 1, 13 (D.D.C. 2000)
(withholding identities of certain grand jury witnesses); Foster v. U.S. Dep't
of Justice, 933 F. Supp. 687, 692 (E.D. Mich. 1996) (protecting prospective
witnesses); Crooker v. Tax Div. of the U.S. Dep't of Justice, No. 94-30129,
1995 WL 783236, at *18 (D. Mass. Nov. 17, 1995) (magistrate's recommendation) (holding names of witnesses and individuals who cooperated with
government protected to prevent "undue embarrassment and harassment"),
adopted (D. Mass. Dec. 15, 1995), aff'd per curiam, 94 F.3d 640 (1st Cir.
1996) (unpublished table decision); Cappabianca v. Comm'r, U.S. Customs
Serv., 847 F. Supp. 1558, 1566 (M.D. Fla. 1994) (witnesses, investigators,
and other subjects of investigation have "substantial privacy interests");
Farese v. U.S. Dep't of Justice, 683 F. Supp. 273, 275 (D.D.C. 1987) (protecting names and number of family members of participants in Witness Security Program, as well as funds authorized to each, because disclosure
"would pose a possible danger to the persons named" or "might subject
those persons to harassment"); cf. Brown v. FBI, 658 F.2d 71, 75-76 (2d Cir.
1981) (protecting information concerning witness who testified against requester) (Exemption 6). But see Cooper Cameron, 280 F.3d at 545, 554
(holding names of three employee-witnesses exempt, yet inconsistently ordering release of source-identifying content of their statements); Lahr, 2006
WL 2854314, at *14 (stating "the public interest in uncovering alleged
agency malfeasance and wrongdoing in the investigation of the crash of
Flight 800 outweighs the privacy interest that conceivably exists in eyewitness names"); Lipman v. United States, No. 3:97-667, slip op. at 3 (M.D.
Pa. June 3, 1998) (releasing names of witnesses who testified at trial based
upon assumption defendant had already received information under
Jencks v. United States, 353 U.S. 657 (1957)), appeal dismissed voluntarily,
No. 98-7489 (3d Cir. Feb. 23, 1999).

[50] See Fiduccia, 185 F.3d at 1044 (withholding names of informants);
Quiñon, 86 F.3d at 1227, 1231 (protecting informants' identities in absence
(continued...)

[50](...continued)
of agency misconduct); Schiffer, 78 F.3d at 1410 (protecting names of persons who provided information to FBI); Computer Prof'ls, 72 F.3d at 904-05 (protecting names of informants, including name of company that reported crime to police, because disclosure might permit identification of corporate officer who reported crime); Manna, 51 F.3d at 1162 (safeguarding names of informants in La Cosa Nostra case); Jones, 41 F.3d at 246 (protecting informants' identities); McCutchen v. HHS, 30 F.3d 183, 189 (D.C. Cir. 1994) (protecting names of individuals alleging scientific misconduct); Koch v. USPS, No. 93-1487, 1993 U.S. App. LEXIS 26130, at *2 (8th Cir. Oct. 8, 1993) ("The informant's interest in maintaining confidentiality is considerable [because] the informant risked embarrassment, harassment, and emotional and physical retaliation."); Nadler v. U.S. Dep't of Justice, 955 F.2d 1479, 1490 (11th Cir. 1992) ("Disclosure of the identities of the FBI's sources will disclose a great deal about those sources but in this case will disclose virtually nothing about the conduct of the government."); Coleman v. U.S. Dep't of Justice, No. 02-79-A, slip op. at 11 (E.D. Va. Oct. 7, 2002) (protecting names and identifying information of people who aided in investigation of Ruby Ridge incident); LaRouche v. U.S. Dep't of Justice, No. 90-2753, 2001 U.S. Dist. LEXIS 25416, at *21 (D.D.C. July 5, 2001) (finding that informant's hanwritten drawings could reveal identity); Gonzalez v. FBI, No. CV F 99-5789, slip op. at 18 (E.D. Cal. Aug. 11, 2000) (finding that privacy interest is not invalidated merely because person is confirmed informant); Unger v. IRS, No. 99-698, 2000 U.S. Dist. LEXIS 5260, at *12 (N.D. Ohio Mar. 28, 2000) (protecting "identities of private citizens who provided information to law enforcement officials"); Petterson v. IRS, No. 98-6020, slip op. at 8 (W.D. Mo. Apr. 22, 1999) (protecting informant's personal data); Pfannenstiel v. FBI, No. 98-0386, slip op. at 7 (D.N.M. Feb. 18, 1999) (withholding identities of confidential informants); Schlabach v. IRS, No. 98-0075, 1998 U.S. Dist. LEXIS 19579, at *2 (E.D. Wash. Nov. 10, 1998) (withholding personal information obtained from private citizens during investigation); Local 32B-32J, Serv. Employees Int'l Union v. GSA, No. 97-8509, 1998 WL 726000, at *9 (S.D.N.Y. Oct. 15, 1998) (finding that disclosure of names of individuals who provided information during investigation may subject them to threats of reprisal); Billington, 11 F. Supp. 2d at 63 (finding that witnesses' privacy interests outweigh public interest, even when witnesses appeared in court or participated in media interview); Thompson, No. 96-1118, slip op. at 24 (D. Kan. July 14, 1998) (protecting names and identifying information about individuals who provided or could provide information concerning investigation); Rosenberg, No. 97-0476, slip op. at 10 (D.D.C. May 13, 1998) (protecting names of individuals who cooperated and actively participated in investigation, as well as of "individuals who provided assistance to the operation because of their occupation or use of their property"); Steinberg v. U.S. Dep't of Justice, 179 F.R.D. 357, 363 (D.D.C. 1998) (withholding informants' names, alias names, and portions of interview regarding terrorist activities); see also Wrenn v. Vanderbilt Univ. Hosp., No. 3:91-1005, slip op. at 14-15 (M.D. Tenn. June 10, 1993) (protect-
(continued...)

that "the information provided to law enforcement authorities was knowingly false."[51]

Although on occasion a pre-Reporters Committee decision found that an individual's testimony at trial precluded Exemption 7(C) protection,[52] under the Reporters Committee "practical obscurity" standard trial testimony should not diminish Exemption 7(C) protection.[53] Plainly, if a person

---

[50](...continued)
ing identity of person who alleged discrimination), aff'd, 16 F.3d 1224 (6th Cir. 1994) (unpublished table decision).

[51] Gabrielli v. U.S. Dep't of Justice, 594 F. Supp. 309, 313 (N.D.N.Y. 1984); see also Block v. FBI, No. 83-813, slip op. at 11 (D.D.C. Nov. 19, 1984) ("[The requester's] personal interest in knowing who wrote letters concerning him . . . is not sufficient to demonstrate a public interest.") (Exemption 6).

[52] Compare Myers, No. 85-1746, 1986 U.S. Dist. LEXIS 20058, at *4-7 (D.D.C. Sept. 22, 1986) ("no privacy interest exists" as to names of law enforcement personnel who testified at requester's trial), with Prows v. U.S. Dep't of Justice, No. 87-1657, 1989 WL 39288, at *3 (D.D.C. Apr. 13, 1989) ("[T]he protection of Exemption 7(C) is not waived by the act of testifying at trial."), summary affirmance granted, No. 89-5185 (D.C. Cir. Feb. 26, 1990).

[53] See Jones, 41 F.3d at 247 (holding fact that law enforcement employee chose to testify or was required to testify or otherwise come forward in other settings does not amount to waiver of personal privacy); Burge v. Eastburn, 934 F.2d 577, 579 (5th Cir. 1991) (affirming refusal, under Exemption 7(C), to confirm or deny existence of information in FBI files regarding individuals who testified at plaintiff's murder trial); Melville v. U.S. Dep't of Justice, No. 05-0645, 2006 WL 2927575, at *9 (D.D.C. Oct. 9, 2006) (emphasizing that privacy interest of law enforcement personnel or other third parties mentioned in responsive records is not diminished by fact they may have testified at trial); McDade v. Executive Office for U.S. Attorneys, No. 03-1946, slip op. at 11 (D.D.C. Sept. 29, 2004) ("A witness who testifies at a trial does not waive personal privacy."), summary affirmance granted, No. 04-5378, 2005 U.S. App. LEXIS 15259 (D.C. Cir. July 25, 2005), cert. denied, 126 S. Ct. 791 (2005); Boyd v. U.S. Marshals Serv., No. 99-2712, slip op. at 5 (D.D.C. Mar. 30, 2001) (finding that plaintiff's assertion that informant and others who testified at his criminal trial waived their right to privacy by testifying is "simply wrong"); Galpine, No. 99-1032, slip op. at 12 (E.D.N.Y. Apr. 28, 2000) (reiterating that Exemption 7(C) protects "identities of individuals who testified at [requester's] criminal trial"); Rivera v. FBI, No. 98-0649, slip op. at 5 (D.D.C. Aug. 31, 1999) ("Individuals who testify at trial do not waive their privacy interest[s] beyond the scope of the trial record."); Robinson v. DEA, No. 97-1578, slip op. at 9 (D.D.C. Apr. 2, 1998) (stating that "[t]he disclosure during a trial of otherwise exempt information does not make the information public for all purposes"); Baltimore Sun, No. 97-

(continued...)

who actually testifies retains a substantial privacy interest, the privacy of someone who is identified only as a potential witness likewise should be preserved.[54]

Moreover, courts have repeatedly recognized that the passage of time will not ordinarily diminish the applicability of Exemption 7(C).[55] This

---

[53](...continued)
1991, slip op. at 5 (D. Md. Nov. 21, 1997) (reasoning that request for original photograph of defendant because court's copy was unreproducible is evidence that "substance of photograph had not been fully disclosed to the public," so defendant retained privacy interest in preventing further dissemination); Dayton Newspapers, No. C-3-95-328, slip op. at 42 (S.D. Ohio Sept. 12, 1996) (finding that victims who testified at trial retain privacy interests in their identities); Tanks, 1996 U.S. Dist. LEXIS 7266, at *10 (holding that requester's knowledge of identities of informants who testified against him does not diminish their privacy interests); cf. Bey v. FBI, No. 01-0299, slip op. at 4 (D.D.C. Aug. 2, 2002) (releasing most of list of telephone numbers (captured on court-ordered "pen register") that were dialed from telephone in plaintiff's house, because numbers were made public in open-court testimony at plaintiff's criminal trial). But see Linn v. U.S. Dep't of Justice, No. 92-1406, 1997 U.S. Dist. LEXIS 9321, at *17 (D.D.C. May 29, 1997) (finding no justification for withholding identities of witnesses who testified against requester at trial) (Exemptions 7(C) and 7(F)), appeal dismissed voluntarily, No. 97-5122 (D.C. Cir. July 14, 1997).

[54] See Rosenglick v. IRS, No. 97-747-18A, 1998 U.S. Dist. LEXIS 3920, at *9 (M.D. Fla. Mar. 10, 1998); Watson v. U.S. Dep't of Justice, 799 F. Supp. 193, 196 (D.D.C. 1992).

[55] See, e.g., Halpern, 181 F.3d at 297 ("Confidentiality interests cannot be waived through . . . the passage of time."); McDonnell, 4 F.3d at 1256 (deciding that passage of forty-nine years does not negate individual's privacy interest); Maynard, 986 F.2d at 566 n.21 (finding effect of passage of time upon individual's privacy interests to be "simply irrelevant"); Fitzgibbon, 911 F.2d at 768 (concluding that passage of more than thirty years irrelevant when records reveal nothing about government activities); Keys, 830 F.2d at 348 (holding that passage of forty years did not "dilute the privacy interest as to tip the balance the other way"); King, 830 F.2d at 234 (rejecting argument that passage of time diminished privacy interests at stake in records more than thirty-five years old); Diamond v. FBI, 707 F.2d 75, 77 (2d Cir. 1983) ("the danger of disclosure may apply to old documents"); Ray v. FBI, 441 F. Supp. 2d 27, 35 (D.D.C. 2006) (rejecting argument that passage of time and retirement of FBI Special Agents diminish their privacy interests); Sinito v. U.S. Dep't of Justice, No. 87-0814, 2000 U.S. Dist. LEXIS 22504, at *35 (D.D.C. July 12, 2000) (concluding that the "passage of time ordinarily does not diminish the applicability of Exemption 7(C)"); Franklin, No. 97-1225, slip op. at 12 (S.D. Fla. June 15, 1998) (magistrate's recommendation) (rejecting argument that passage of time vitiates individual's pri-

(continued...)

may be especially true in instances in which the information was obtained through questionable law enforcement investigations.[56] In fact, the "practical obscurity" concept expressly recognizes that the passage of time may actually <u>increase</u> the privacy interest at stake when disclosure would revive information that was once public knowledge but has long since faded from memory.[57]

---

[55](...continued)
vacy interest in nondisclosure), <u>adopted</u> (S.D. Fla. June 26, 1998); <u>Stone</u>, 727 F. Supp. at 664 (explaining that FBI Special Agents who participated in an investigation over twenty years earlier, even one as well known as the RFK assassination, "have earned the right to be 'left alone' unless an important public interest outweighs that right"); <u>see also</u> <u>Exner</u>, 902 F. Supp. at 244 n.7 (holding that fact that incidents in question "occurred more than thirty years ago may, but does not necessarily, diminish the privacy interest"); <u>Branch</u>, 658 F. Supp. at 209 (The "privacy interests of the persons mentioned in the investigatory files do not necessarily diminish with the passage of time."); <u>cf.</u> <u>Schrecker v. U.S. Dep't of Justice</u>, 349 F.3d 657, 664-65 (D.C. Cir. 2003) (approving FBI's use of "100-year rule," which presumes that individual is dead if birthdate appeared in documents responsive to request and was more than 100 years old, to determine if subject of requested record is still alive and has privacy interest); <u>Oglesby v. U.S. Dep't of the Army</u>, 79 F.3d 1172, 1183 (D.C. Cir. 1996) (ruling that "mere passage of time is not a per se bar to reliance on [E]xemption 1"). <u>But see</u> <u>Davin</u>, 60 F.3d at 1058 (finding that for some individuals, privacy interest may become diluted by passage of over sixty years, though under certain circumstances potential for embarrassment and harassment may endure); <u>Outlaw v. U.S. Dep't of the Army</u>, 815 F. Supp. 505, 506 (D.D.C. Mar. 25, 1993) (ordering release of twenty-five-year-old photographs of murder victim with no known surviving next of kin); <u>Silets</u>, 591 F. Supp. at 498 ("[W]here documents are exceptionally old, it is likely that their age has diminished the privacy interests at stake.").

[56] <u>See, e.g.</u>, <u>Dunaway v. Webster</u>, 519 F. Supp. 1059, 1079 (N.D. Cal. 1981) ("[The target of a McCarthy era investigation] may . . . deserve greater protection, because the connection to such an investigation might prove particularly embarrassing or damaging."); <u>see also</u> <u>Campbell v. U.S. Dep't of Justice</u>, 193 F. Supp. 2d 29, 40-41 (D.C. Cir. 2001) (finding that "the persons who were involved in [investigation of 1960s writer and civil rights activist James Baldwin] deserve protection of their reputations as well as recognition that they were simply doing a job that the cultural and political climate at the time dictated").

[57] <u>See</u> <u>Reporters Comm.</u>, 489 U.S. at 767 ("[O]ur cases have also recognized the privacy interest inherent in the nondisclosure of certain information even when the information may at one time have been public."); <u>Rose v. Dep't of the Air Force</u>, 495 F.2d 261, 267 (2d Cir. 1974) ("[A] person's privacy may be as effectively infringed by reviving dormant memories as by imparting new information.") (Exemption 6), <u>aff'd</u>, 425 U.S. 352 (1976); <u>see</u>
(continued...)

**EXEMPTION 7(C)**

An individual's Exemption 7(C) privacy interest likewise is not extinguished merely because a requester might on his own be able to "piece together" the identities of third parties whose names have been deleted.[58] Nor do persons mentioned in law enforcement records lose all their rights

---

[57](...continued)
also Assassination Archives & Research Ctr. v. CIA, 903 F. Supp. 131, 133 (D.D.C. 1995) (finding that passage of thirty or forty years "may actually increase privacy interests, and that even a modest privacy interest will suffice" to protect identities). See generally Favish, 541 U.S. at 173-74 (according full privacy protection without any hesitation, notwithstanding passage of ten years since Vincent Foster's death).

[58] Weisberg v. U.S. Dep't of Justice, 745 F.2d 1476, 1491 (D.C. Cir. 1984); see also Carpenter v. U.S. Dep't of Justice, 470 F.3d 434, 440 (1st Cir. 2006) (finding that privacy interest of subject is not terminated even if his identity as an informant could arguably be determined from another source); Ford v. West, No. 97-1342, 1998 WL 317561, at *3 (10th Cir. June 12, 1998) (holding fact that requester obtained some information through other channels does not change privacy protection under FOIA and no waiver of third parties' privacy interests due to "inadequate redactions"); L&C Marine, 740 F.2d at 922 ("An individual does not lose his privacy interest under 7(C) because his identity . . . may be discovered through other means."); Judicial Watch, Inc. v. FBI, No. 00-745, 2001 U.S. Dist. LEXIS 25732, at *20 (D.D.C. Apr. 20, 2001) ("The fact that the requester might be able to figure out the individuals' identities through other means or that their identities have been disclosed elsewhere does not diminish their privacy interests . . . ."); Voinche v. FBI, No. 99-1931, slip op. at 13 n.4 (D.D.C. Nov. 17, 2000) ("The fact that Mr. Voinche [might have] learned of the identity of these individuals by reading a publication does not impair the privacy rights enjoyed by these three people."); Billington v. Dep't of Justice, 69 F. Supp. 2d 128, 137 (D.D.C. 1999) (deciding that disclosure of unredacted records due to administrative error did not "diminish the magnitude of the privacy interests of the individuals" involved), aff'd in pertinent part, 233 F.3d 581, 583 (D.C. Cir. 2000) (stating there was "nothing to add to the district court's sound reasoning" with respect to the withholdings under Exemption 7(C)); Cujas, 1998 U.S. Dist. LEXIS 6466, at *9 (reiterating that fact that information available elsewhere does not diminish third-party privacy interests in such law enforcement records); Smith, 977 F. Supp. at 500 (finding fact that plaintiff "can guess" names withheld does not waive privacy interest); Master v. FBI, 926 F. Supp. 193, 198-99 (D.D.C. 1996) (protecting subjects of investigative interest even though plaintiffs allegedly know their names), summary affirmance granted, 124 F.3d 1309 (D.C. Cir. 1997) (unpublished table decision). But see Cooper Cameron, 280 F.3d at 553 (refusing to protect the content of three employee-witness statements after release of the witnesses' names, even though disclosure would result in linking each employee to his or her statement).

to privacy merely because their names have been disclosed.[59]

---

[59] See, e.g., Fiduccia, 185 F.3d at 1047 (concluding that privacy interests are not lost by reason of earlier publicity); Halpern, 181 F.3d at 297 ("Confidentiality interests cannot be waived through prior public disclosure . . . ."); Kimberlin, 139 F.3d at 949 (finding that even after subject's public acknowledgment of charges and sanction against him, he retained privacy interest in nondisclosure of "'details of investigation, of his misconduct, and of his punishment,'" and in "preventing speculative press reports of his misconduct from receiving authoritative confirmation from official source" (citing Bast, 665 F.2d at 1255)); Schiffer, 78 F.3d at 1410-11 (deciding fact that much of information in requested documents was made public during related civil suit does not reduce privacy interest); Jones, 41 F.3d at 247 (holding fact that law enforcement employee chose to testify or was required to testify or otherwise come forward in other settings does not amount to personal privacy waiver); Hunt, 972 F.2d at 288 ("public availability" of accused FBI Special Agent's name does not defeat privacy protection and "would make redaction of [the agent's name in] the file a pointless exercise"); Fitzgibbon, 911 F.2d at 768 (concluding fact that CIA or FBI may have released information about individual elsewhere does not diminish the individual's "substantial privacy interests"); Bast, 665 F.2d at 1255 (finding that "previous publicity amounting to journalistic speculation cannot vitiate the FOIA privacy exemption"); Wiggins v. Nat'l Credit Union Admin., No. 05-2332, 2007 U.S. Dist. LEXIS 6367, at *21 (D.D.C. Jan. 30, 2007) (deciding fact that identities of third parties were disclosed in a related criminal trial does not diminish privacy interest); Swope v. U.S. Dep't of Justice, 439 F. Supp. 2d 1, 6 (D.D.C. 2006) (stating that individual's awareness that telephone conversation is being monitored does not negate privacy rights in further disclosure of personal information); Odle v. Dep't of Justice, No. 05-2711, 2006 WL 1344813, at *10 (N.D. Cal. May 17, 2006) (finding that public's knowledge of subject's involvement in trial does not eliminate any privacy interest in further disclosure); Shores v. FBI, 185 F. Supp. 2d 77, 83 (D.D.C. 2002) (deciding that privacy interests are not diminished by the fact that plaintiff "may deduce the identities of individuals through other means or that their identities have already been disclosed" (citing Fitzgibbon, 911 F.2d at 768, and Weisberg, 745 F.2d at 1491)); LaRouche, 2001 U.S. Dist. LEXIS 25416, at *30 (holding that "release of similar information in another case does not warrant disclosure of otherwise properly exempted material"); Ponder v. Reno, No. 98-3097, slip op. at 6 (D.D.C. Jan. 22, 2001) (deciding that the fact that the government "failed to fully redact all agents' names does not constitute a waiver of Exemption 7(C)"); McGhghy v. DEA, No. C 97-0185, slip op. at 11 (N.D. Iowa May 29, 1998) (holding that "mere fact that individuals named in withheld documents may have previously waived their confidentiality interests, either voluntarily or involuntarily, does not mandate disclosure of withheld documents"), aff'd per curiam, No. 98-2989, 1999 U.S. App. LEXIS 16709 (8th Cir. July 13, 1999); Thomas v. Office of U.S. Attorney, 928 F. Supp. 245, 250 & n.8 (E.D.N.Y. 1996) (holding that despite public disclosure of some information about attorney's connec-
(continued...)

Similarly, "[t]he fact that one document does disclose some names . . . does not mean that the privacy rights of these or others are waived; it has been held that [requesters] do not have the right to learn more about the activities and statements of persons merely because they are mentioned once in a public document about the investigation."[60]

Under the traditional Exemption 7(C) analysis, once a privacy interest has been identified and its magnitude has been assessed, it is balanced against the magnitude of any recognized public interest that would be served by disclosure.[61] And under Reporters Committee, the standard of

_____

[59](...continued)
tion with crime family, he still retains privacy interests in preventing further disclosure), appeal dismissed, No. 93-CV-3128 (2d Cir. Oct. 29, 1996); Crooker, 1995 WL 783236, at *18 (holding that despite fact that requester may have learned identities of third parties through criminal discovery, Exemption 7(C) protection remains); see also ACLU v. FBI, 429 F. Supp. 2d 179, 193 (D.D.C. 2006) ("To the extent that a person may have retained a privacy interest in publically made comments, that interest is certainly dissipated by the FBI's failure to redact his name from the entirety of the document."). But see Detroit Free Press, 73 F.3d at 98 (finding no unwarranted invasion of privacy in disclosure of "mug shots" of indicted individuals who had already appeared in court and had their names divulged); Steinberg v. U.S. Dep't of Justice, 179 F.R.D. 366, 371 (D.D.C. 1998) (holding content of sources' interviews must be disclosed once agency disclosed their identities); cf. Grove v. CIA, 752 F. Supp. 28, 32 (D.D.C. 1990) (ordering FBI to further explain Exemption 7(C) withholdings in light of highly publicized nature of investigation and fact that CIA and Secret Service released other records pertaining to same individuals).

[60] Kirk, 704 F. Supp. at 292; see also Favish, 541 U.S. at 171 (holding that "the fact that other pictures had been made public [does not] detract[] from the weighty privacy interests" in the remaining pictures); Kimberlin, 139 F.3d at 949 (reasoning that merely because subject of investigation acknowledged existence of investigation -- thus breaking bulwark level of "Glomarization" -- does not constitute waiver of subject's interest in keeping contents of Office of Professional Responsibility report confidential).

[61] See Schiffer, 78 F.3d at 1410 (explaining once agency shows that privacy interest exists, court must balance it against public's interest in disclosure); Computer Prof'ls, 72 F.3d at 904 (finding after privacy interest found, court must identify public interest to be served by disclosure); Massey, 3 F.3d at 624-25 (holding once agency establishes that privacy interest exists, that interest must be balanced against value of information in furthering FOIA's disclosure objectives); Church of Scientology, 995 F.2d at 921 (remanding case because district court failed to determine whether public interest in disclosure outweighed privacy concerns); Grine v. Coombs, No. 95-342, 1997 U.S. Dist. LEXIS 19578, at *19 (W.D. Pa. Oct. 10, 1997) (requiring balancing of privacy interest and extent to which it is in-
(continued...)

public interest to consider is one specifically limited to the FOIA's "core purpose" of "shed[ding] light on an agency's performance of its statutory duties."[62] Accordingly, for example, the courts have consistently refused to recognize any public interest, as defined by Reporters Committee, in disclosure of information to assist a convict in challenging his conviction.[63]

---

[61](...continued)
vaded against public benefit that would result from disclosure); Thomas, 928 F. Supp. at 250 (observing that since personal privacy interest in information is implicated, court must inquire whether any countervailing factors exist that would warrant invasion of that interest); Globe Newspaper Co. v. FBI, No. 91-13257, 1992 WL 396327, at *4 (D. Mass. Dec. 29, 1992) (finding public interest in disclosing amount of money government paid to officially confirmed informant guilty of criminal wrongdoing outweighs informant's de minimis privacy interest); Church of Scientology, 816 F. Supp. at 1160 (concluding while employees have privacy interest in their handwriting, that interest does not outweigh public interest in disclosure of information contained in documents not otherwise exempt); see also Favish, 541 U.S. at 174-75 (holding that "only when the FOIA requester has produced evidence to satisfy [a belief by a reasonable person] will there exist a counterweight on the FOIA scale for the court to balance against the cognizable privacy interests in the requested records"); Lawyers Comm. for Human Rights v. INS, 721 F. Supp. 552, 571 (S.D.N.Y. 1989) (balancing plaintiff's interest in disclosure of names of individuals listed in INS Lookout Book on basis of ideological exclusion provision against excluded individuals' privacy interests); FOIA Post, "Supreme Court Rules for 'Survivor Privacy' in Favish" (posted 4/9/04) (discussing balancing of privacy interests and public interest); FOIA Update, Vol. X, No. 2, at 7.

[62] 489 U.S. at 773; see also Dayton Newspapers, Inc. v. U.S. Dep't of the Navy, 109 F. Supp. 2d 768, 775 (S.D. Ohio 1999) (concluding that questionnaire responses by court-martial members were properly withheld because the "information contained therein sheds no light on the workings of the government").

[63] See, e.g., Oguaju v. United States, 288 F.3d 448, 450 (D.C. Cir. 2002) (finding that plaintiff's "personal stake in using the requested records to attack his convictions does not count in the calculation of the public interest"), vacated & remanded, 541 U.S. 970, on remand, 378 F.3d 1115 (D.C. Cir.) (reaffirming prior decision), reh'g denied, 386 F.3d 273 (D.C. Cir. 2004), cert. denied, 544 U.S. 983 (2005); Neely, 208 F.3d at 464 (ruling that requester's wish to establish his own innocence does not create FOIA-recognized public interest); Hale, 973 F.2d at 901 (finding no FOIA-recognized public interest in death-row inmate's allegation of unfair trial); Landano v. U.S. Dep't of Justice, 956 F.2d 422, 430 (3d Cir. 1991) (finding no public interest in disclosure of identities of individuals involved in murder investigation because such release would not shed light on how FBI fulfills its responsibilities), cert. denied on Exemption 7(C) grounds, 506 U.S. 868 (1992), rev'd & remanded on other grounds, 508 U.S. 165 (1993); Burge, 934
(continued...)

Indeed, a FOIA requester's private need for information in connection with litigation plays no part whatsoever in determining whether disclosure is warranted.[64] So in NARA v. Favish, the Supreme Court further reinforced

---

[63](...continued)
F.2d at 580 ("requester's need, however significant, does not warrant disclosure"); Trentadue, 2006 WL 1184636, at *6 (reiterating that the reason the FOIA request was made does not govern, but "rather it is whether disclosure would serve the core purpose of FOIA -- letting the citizens know what the[ir] government is up to"); Taylor v. U.S. Dep't of Justice, 257 F. Supp. 2d 101, 110 (D.D.C. 2003) (finding no public interest in disclosure of third-party information that requester asserted might assist him in challenging his conviction), reconsideration denied, 268 F. Supp. 2d 34 (D.D.C. 2003), appeal dismissed sub nom. Taylor v. FBI, No. 03-5111, 2003 WL 22005968 (D.C. Cir. Aug. 19, 2003); Boyd, No. 99-2712, slip op. at 5 (D.D.C. Mar. 30, 2001) (finding requests for Brady material to be outside proper role of FOIA); Galpine, No. 99-1032, slip op. at 13 (E.D.N.Y. Apr. 28, 2000) (restating that requests for exculpatory evidence are "'outside the proper role of FOIA'" (quoting Colon, 1998 WL 695631, at *5)); Fedrick v. U.S. Dep't of Justice, 984 F. Supp. 659, 664 (W.D.N.Y. 1997) (magistrate's recommendation) (finding that requester's personal interest in seeking information for use in collateral challenge to his conviction does not raise "FOIA-recognized interest"), adopted, No. 95-558 (W.D.N.Y. Oct. 28, 1997), aff'd sub nom. Fedrick v. Huff, 165 F.3d 13 (2d Cir. 1998) (unpublished table decision); Trupei, 1998 WL 8986, at *3 (concluding that request for Brady material is not within role of FOIA); Smith, 977 F. Supp. at 499 (holding that requester's personal interest in obtaining exculpatory statements does not give him greater rights under FOIA); Thomas, 928 F. Supp. at 251 (holding that prisoner's personal interest in information to challenge his conviction "does not raise a FOIA-recognized interest that should be weighed against the subject's privacy interests"); Durham v. USPS, No. 91-2234, 1992 WL 700246, at *2 (D.D.C. Nov. 25, 1992) (holding "Glomar" response appropriate even though plaintiff argued that information would prove his innocence), summary affirmance granted, No. 92-5511 (D.C. Cir. July 27, 1993); Johnson, 758 F. Supp. at 5 ("Resort to Brady v. Maryland as grounds for waiving confidentiality [under Exemptions 7(C) and 7(D)] is . . . outside the proper role of the FOIA. Exceptions cannot be made because of the subject matter or [death-row status] of the requester."). But see Lipman, No. 3:97-667, slip op. at 4 (M.D. Pa. June 3, 1998) (making exceptional finding of public interest in plaintiff's quest to discover whether government withheld Brady material).

[64] See Massey, 3 F.3d at 625 ("[The] mere possibility that information may aid an individual in the pursuit of litigation does not give rise to a public interest."); Joslin v. U.S. Dep't of Labor, No. 88-1999, slip op. at 8 (10th Cir. Oct. 20, 1989) (finding no public interest in release of documents sought for use in private tort litigation); Sakamoto v. EPA, 443 F. Supp. 2d 1182, 1197 (N.D. Cal. 2006) (finding no public interest in disclosure of documents sought for use in plaintiff's employment discrimination case); Me-
(continued...)

the FOIA principle that a requester's <u>identity</u> generally is irrelevant in the processing of a FOIA request,[65] but it at the same time made clear that a requester's <u>reason</u> for making a FOIA request, insofar as an evidentiary showing on an asserted "public interest" is required, can of course affect Exemption 7(C) decisionmaking.[66]

It is also important to note that there is a logical distinction between the public interest that can exist in an overall subject that relates to a

---

[64](...continued)
serve v. U.S. Dep't of Justice, No. 04-1844, 2006 U.S. Dist. LEXIS 56732, at *23-24 (D.D.C. Aug. 14, 2006) (holding that request seeking information in order to pursue motion for new trial and motion to vacate or set aside sentence does not involve qualifying public interest); <u>Garcia</u>, 181 F. Supp. 2d at 372 (holding that a request seeking information in furtherance of private litigation falls outside "the ambit of FOIA's goal of public disclosure of agency action"); <u>Exner</u>, 902 F. Supp. at 244 & n.8 (explaining requester's interest in pursuing legal remedies against person who entered her apartment does not pertain to workings of government); <u>Bruscino</u>, No. 94-1955, 1995 WL 444406, at *9 (D.D.C. May 12, 1995) (concluding no public interest in release of information concerning other inmates sought for use in private litigation); <u>Andrews v. U.S. Dep't of Justice</u>, 769 F. Supp. 314, 317 (E.D. Mo. 1991) (deciding no public interest in satisfaction of private judgments). <u>But see</u> <u>Butler</u>, No. 86-2255, 1994 WL 55621, at *5-6 (D.D.C. Feb. 3, 1994) (ordering identities of supervisory FBI personnel disclosed because of "significant" public interest in protecting requester's due process rights in his attempt to vacate sentence).

[65] <u>See</u> <u>Favish</u>, 541 U.S. at 170 ("As a general rule, withholding information under FOIA cannot be predicated on the identity of the requester."); <u>see also</u> FOIA Post, "Supreme Court Rules for 'Survivor Privacy' in <u>Favish</u>" (posted 4/9/04) (pointing out that "<u>Favish</u> thus stands as a reminder to all agencies that their consideration of potential privacy invasions must include both what the requester might do with the information at hand and also what any other requester (or ultimate recipient) might do with it as well").

[66] <u>See</u> <u>Favish</u>, 541 U.S. at 172 (stating that when the privacy concerns of Exemption 7(C) apply, an agency can require the requester "to establish a sufficient reason for the disclosure" by having the requester demonstrate both "that the public interest sought to be advanced [by disclosure] is a significant one" and that disclosure of the "information [requested] is likely to advance that interest"); <u>see also</u> FOIA Post, "Supreme Court Rules for 'Survivor Privacy' in <u>Favish</u> (posted 4/9/04) (discussing public interest standard adopted in <u>Favish</u>, as well as required "nexus" between requested information and public interest asserted); <u>cf.</u> CEI Wash. Bureau, Inc. v. Dep't of Justice, No, 05-5446, slip op. at 4-5 (D.C. Cir. Nov. 21, 2006) (remanding for possible "evidentiary hearing[]" needed to resolve "factual disputes" regarding "extent of" both privacy interests and public interests involved).

FOIA request and the public interest that might or might not be served by disclosure of the actual records that are at hand in that particular FOIA request.[67] The term "umbrella issue" is used by agencies and courts alike to make this important distinction when considering public interest issues under the FOIA.[68] This approach of carefully distinguishing the general from the specific has ready application in determining whether particular record portions at hand are of such nature that their disclosure actually would serve an identified general public interest and therefore warrant the overriding of a personal privacy interest in the Exemption 7(C) balancing process.[69]

Furthermore, unsubstantiated allegations of official misconduct are simply insufficient to establish a public interest in disclosure: The Supreme Court in NARA v. Favish made it very clear that "bare suspicion" is completely inadequate and that a requester must produce evidence that would be credible in the eyes of a reasonable person.[70] Now, one who

---

[67] See FOIA Post, "FOIA Counselor Q&A" (posted 1/24/06) (explaining distinction between generalized public interest in broad subject area of FOIA request as opposed to specific public interest in particular documents at issue in that FOIA request) (citing cases).

[68] Id. (discussing meaning of "umbrella issue" under FOIA (citing Elec. Privacy Info. Ctr. v. DOD, 365 F. Supp. 2d 98, 102 (D.D.C. 2004) (stating that "[t]he fact that [the requester] has provided evidence that there is some media interest in data mining as an umbrella issue does not satisfy the requirement that [it] demonstrate interest in the specific subject of [its] FOIA request"), and ACLU of N. Cal. v. Dep't of Justice, No. 04-4447, 2005 WL 588354, at *13 (N.D. Cal. Mar. 11, 2005) (ruling that "it was not sufficient for the plaintiffs to show [public] interest in only the general subject area of the request"))).

[69] See, e.g., KTVY-TV v. United States, 919 F.2d 1465, 1470 (10th Cir. 1990) (rejecting an assertion that "the public interest at stake is the right of the public to know" about a controversial event, because on careful analysis the particular record segments at issue "do not provide information about" that subject).

[70] 541 U.S. at 172; see, e.g., Boyd v. Criminal Div. of the U.S. Dep't of Justice, Nos. 05-5142 & 04-5369, 2007 WL 328064, at *4 (D.C. Cir. Feb. 6, 2007) (stating that an alleged single instance of a Brady violation would not suffice to show a pattern of government wrongdoing); Oguaju, 288 F.3d at 451 (holding that "bald accusations" of prosecutorial misconduct are insufficient to establish public interest); Spirko, 147 F.3d at 999 (finding no public interest in names and information pertaining to suspects and law enforcement officers absent any evidence of alleged misconduct by agency); Enzinna v. U.S. Dep't of Justice, No. 97-5078, 1997 WL 404327, at *1 (D.C. Cir. June 30, 1997) (finding that without evidence that Assistant United States Attorney made misrepresentation at trial, public interest in dis-

(continued...)

[70](...continued)
closure is insubstantial); Quiñon, 86 F.3d at 1231 (holding that in absence
of evidence FBI engaged in wrongdoing, public interest is "insubstantial");
Schiffer, 78 F.3d at 1410 (finding "little to no" public interest in disclosure
when requester made unsubstantiated claim that FBI's decision to investigate him had been affected by "undue influence"); McCutchen, 30 F.3d at
189 (finding "negligible" public interest in disclosure of identities of agency
scientists who did not engage in scientific misconduct); Beck v. Dep't of
Justice, 997 F.2d 1489, 1492-94 (D.C. Cir. 1993) (holding that agency properly "Glomarized" request for records concerning alleged wrongdoing by
two named employees; no public interest absent any evidence of wrongdoing or widespread publicity of investigation); KTVY-TV, 919 F.2d at 1470
(allegations of "possible neglect"); Nat'l Ass'n of Criminal Def. Lawyers v.
U.S. Dep't of Justice, No. 04-0697, 2006 U.S. Dist. LEXIS 63853, at *14-16
(D.D.C. Sept. 7, 2006) (stating that knowing what, if anything, went wrong
in an individual case would not shed any light on the government's operations as a whole); Geronimo v. Executive Office for U.S. Attorneys, No. 05-
1057, 2006 WL 1992625, at *6 (D.D.C. July 14, 2006) (stating that the plaintiff did not "contend that the withheld information is necessary to confirm
or refute unlawful activity by EOUSA and therefore has failed to trigger the
balancing requirement"); Odle, 2006 WL 1344813, at *9 (finding no public
interest because the records at issue "would shed little light on the ability
of the DOJ and its employees to competently perform their duties"); Butler
v. DEA, No. 05-1798, 2005 U.S. Dist. LEXIS 40942, at *13-14 (D.D.C. Feb. 16,
2006) (finding that plaintiff's bald assertions of misconduct were not sufficient to establish public interest), aff'd, No. 06-5084, 2006 U.S. App. LEXIS
20472 (D.C. Cir. Aug. 7, 2006); Brown, 384 F. Supp. 2d at 279-81 (applying
Favish and holding that the plaintiff failed to produce "evidence that would
warrant a belief by a reasonable person that the alleged [g]overnment impropriety might have occurred"); Peltier v. FBI, No. 03-905, 2005 WL 735964,
at *15 (W.D.N.Y. Mar. 31, 2005) (applying Favish and finding "no evidence
of any illegality on the part of the FBI," despite opinions from two courts of
appeals recognizing government misconduct during the investigation and
prosecution of plaintiff's underlying criminal case); Shores, 185 F. Supp. 2d
at 83 (finding no public interest in unsubstantiated assertion that certain
FBI Special Agents committed unlawful acts); Ligorner, 2 F. Supp. 2d at
405 (when considering privacy interests of person accused of misconduct,
public interest is "de minimis"); Greenberg v. U.S. Dep't of Treasury, 10 F.
Supp. 2d 3, 25 (D.D.C. 1998) (rejecting plaintiffs' "post-hoc rationalization of
public interest" in FBI investigation because they had not even suggested
FBI wrongdoing during investigation); Exner, 902 F. Supp. at 244-45 & n.9
(finding allegation of FBI cover-up of "extremely sensitive political operation" provides "minimal at best" public interest); Triestman v. U.S. Dep't of
Justice, 878 F. Supp. 667, 673 (S.D.N.Y. 1995) (finding no substantial public
interest in disclosure when request seeks information concerning possible
investigations of wrongdoing by named DEA agents); Buros, No. 93-571,
slip op. at 10 (W.D. Wis. Oct. 26, 1994) (holding even though subject's po-

(continued...)

asserts government misconduct as the public interest is held to a higher standard: Such a FOIA requester must make a "meaningful evidentiary showing" in order to provide even a public interest "counterweight" to the privacy interest and require a balancing of the two.[71] Additionally, the requester must establish some "nexus" between the requested documents and the asserted "significant" public interest in disclosure.[72]

It also has been held that no public interest exists in federal records that pertains to alleged misconduct by state officials;[73] such an attenuated

---

[70](...continued)
tential mishandling of funds already known to public, "confirming . . . federal criminal investigation brushes the subject with an independent and indelible taint of wrongdoing"); Williams v. McCausland, No. 90-7563, 1994 WL 18510, at *12 (S.D.N.Y. Jan. 18, 1994) (protecting identities of government employees accused of improper conduct) (Exemptions 6 and 7(C)). But see Providence Journal Co. v. U.S. Dep't of the Army, 981 F.2d 552, 567-69 (1st Cir. 1992) (making finding of public interest in disclosure of unsubstantiated allegations against two senior officials); ACLU v. DOD, 389 F. Supp. 2d 547, 573 (S.D.N.Y. 2005) (finding "substantial public interest" in release of photos of government misconduct at prison in Iraq) (Exemptions 6 and 7(C)), reconsideration denied, 396 F. Supp. 2d 459 (S.D.N.Y. 2005) (appeal pending); McLaughlin v. Sessions, No. 9244, 1993 U.S. Dist. LEXIS 13817, at *18 (D.D.C. Sept. 22, 1993) (reasoning that because request seeks information to determine whether FBI investigation was improperly terminated, requester's interest in scope and course of investigation constitutes recognized public interest which must be balanced against privacy interests of named individuals).

[71] Favish, 541 U.S. at 173-75 (stating that Court cannot ignore fact that five different investigations into Foster matter reached same conclusion, and noting that Favish failed to produce any evidence of government impropriety that would be believable by reasonable person); see also FOIA Post, "Supreme Court Rules for 'Survivor Privacy' in Favish" (posted 4/9/04) (discussing specific public interest standard as enunciated in Favish).

[72] 541 U.S. at 175; see also FOIA Post, "Supreme Court Rules for 'Survivor Privacy' in Favish" (posted 4/9/04) (discussing necessary nexus between requested information and asserted public interest).

[73] See Landano, 956 F.2d at 430 (discerning "no FOIA-recognized public interest in discovering wrongdoing by a state agency"); Garcia, 181 F. Supp. 2d at 374 ("The discovery of wrongdoing at a state as opposed to a federal agency . . . is not the goal of FOIA."); LaRouche, 2001 U.S. Dist. LEXIS 25416, at *20 ("The possible disclosures of state government misconduct is not information that falls within a public interest FOIA [was] intended to protect."); Thomas, 928 F. Supp. at 251 (recognizing that FOIA cannot serve as basis for requests about conduct of state agency). But see also Lissner, 241 F.3d at 1223 (rationalizing that public interest exists in
(continued...)

interest "falls outside the ambit of the public interest the FOIA was enacted to serve."[74] Moreover, it should be remembered that any special expertise claimed by the requester is irrelevant in assessing any public interest in disclosure.[75]

It also is important to remember that a requester must do more than identify a public interest that qualifies for consideration under Reporters Committee: The requester must demonstrate that the public interest in disclosure is sufficiently compelling to, on balance, outweigh legitimate privacy interests.[76] Of course, "[w]here the requester fails to assert a public

---

[73](...continued)
Custom Service's handling of smuggling incident despite fact that information pertained to actions of state law enforcement officers).

[74] Reporters Comm., 489 U.S. at 775; see also FOIA Update, Vol. XII, No. 2, at 6 (explaining that "government activities" in Reporter's Committee standard means activities of federal government).

[75] See Ford, 1998 WL 317561, at *3 (holding that plaintiff's prior EEO successes against agency do not establish public interest in disclosure of third-party names in this investigation); Massey, 3 F.3d at 625 (finding that the identity of the requesting party and the use that that party plans to make of the requested information have "no bearing on the assessment of the public interest served by disclosure"); Stone, 727 F. Supp. at 668 n.4 (stating that court looks to public interest served by release of information, "not to the highly specialized interests of those individuals who understandably have a greater personal stake in gaining access to that information"). But cf. Manna, 51 F.3d at 1166 (deciding that although court does not usually consider requester's identity, fact that requester held high position in La Cosa Nostra is certainly material to protection of individual privacy).

[76] See Senate of P.R., 823 F.2d at 588 (holding that general interest of legislature in "getting to the bottom" of a controversial investigation is not sufficient to overcome "substantial privacy interests"); Morales Cozier, No. 1:99-CV-0312, slip op. at 18 (N.D. Ga. Sept. 25, 2000) (concluding that public interest in knowing what government is up to in relation to investigation of individuals having contact with Cubans is not furthered by disclosing government employees' names and identifying information); Schrecker v. U.S. Dep't of Justice, 74 F. Supp. 2d 26, 34 (D.D.C. 1999) (finding requester's "own personal curiosity" about names of third parties and agents insufficient to outweigh privacy interests), rev'd on other grounds, 254 F.3d 162, 166 (D.C. Cir. 2001); Times Picayune, 37 F. Supp. 2d at 482 (describing public interest in public figure's "mug shot" as "purely speculative" and therefore readily outweighed by privacy interest); Ajluni, 947 F. Supp. 605 ("In the absence of any strong countervailing public interest in disclosure, the privacy interests of the individuals who are the subjects of the redacted material must prevail."); Fitzgibbon v. U.S. Secret Serv., 747 F. Supp. 51, 59

(continued...)

interest purpose for disclosure, even a less-than-substantial invasion of another's privacy is unwarranted."[77] In the wake of Reporters Committee, the public interest standard ordinarily will not be satisfied when FOIA requesters seek law enforcement information pertaining to living persons.[78]

---

[76](...continued)
(D.D.C. 1990) (holding public interest in alleged plot in United States by agents of now deposed dictatorship insufficient to overcome "strong privacy interests"); Stone, 727 F. Supp. at 667-68 n.4 ("[N]ew information considered significant by zealous students of the RFK assassination investigation would be nothing more than minutia of little or no value in terms of the public interest."); see also Associated Press, 2006 WL 2707395, at *5 (finding minimal privacy interest in identifying detainees at Guantanamo Bay compared to public interest in evaluating allegations of abuse and DOD's response to it); ACLU, 389 F. Supp. 2d at 571-73 (finding possibility of invasion of privacy in redacted photographs to be "no more than speculative" and to be outweighed by "substantial public interest"); Ctr. to Prevent Handgun Violence, 981 F. Supp. at 23-24 (finding "minuscule privacy interest" in identifying sellers in multiple-sales gun reports in comparison to public interest in scrutinizing ATF's performance of its duty to enforce gun control laws and to curtail illegal interstate gun trafficking); Steinberg, 1998 WL 384084, at *3 (finding significant public interest in criminal investigation of alleged counterterrorist activities, which outweighs privacy interests of informants known to plaintiff). But see Cooper Cameron, 280 F.3d at 547, 554 (viewing a "general public interest in monitoring" a specific OSHA investigation as sufficient to overcome employee-witnesses' privacy interests against employer retaliation); Lardner, 2005 U.S. Dist. LEXIS 5465, at *62-64 (finding that release of identities of unsuccessful pardon applicants would shed light on government's exercise of pardon power in "important ways" without establishing required nexus).

[77] King v. U.S. Dep't of Justice, 586 F. Supp. 286, 294 (D.D.C. 1983), aff'd, 830 F.2d 210 (D.C. Cir. 1987); see also Beck, 997 F.2d at 1494 (observing that because request implicates no public interest at all, court "'need not linger over the balance; something . . . outweighs nothing every time'" (quoting Nat'l Ass'n of Retired Fed. Employees v. Horner, 879 F.2d 873, 879 (D.C. Cir. 1989)) (Exemptions 6 and 7(C)); Fitzgibbon, 911 F.2d at 768 (same); Shoemaker v. U.S. Dep't of Justice, No. 03-1258, slip op. at 7 (C.D. Ill. May 19, 2004) (concluding that documents were properly withheld where the plaintiff could not identify a public interest, "let alone any substantial public interest to outweigh the privacy concerns claimed by [the government]"), aff'd, 121 F. App'x 127 (7th Cir. 2004); FOIA Update, Vol. X, No. 2, at 7.

[78] See, e.g., Abraham & Rose, 138 F.3d at 1083 (stating that public may have interest in learning how IRS exercises its power over collection of taxes but that this does not mean that identity or other personal information concerning taxpayers will shed light on agency's performance) (Exemption 6); Spirko, 147 F.3d at 999 (recognizing strong privacy interests of
(continued...)

[78](...continued)
suspects and law enforcement officers when requested documents neither
confirm nor refute plaintiff's allegations of government misconduct); Quiñon, 86 F.3d at 1231 (finding insufficient public interest in disclosing individuals mentioned in FBI files when no evidence of wrongdoing; even if individuals had engaged in wrongdoing, such misconduct would have to
shed light on agency's action); Schiffer, 78 F.3d at 1410 (recognizing "little
to no" public interest in disclosure of persons in FBI file, including some
who provided information to FBI, when no evidence of FBI wrongdoing);
Schwarz v. INTERPOL, No. 94-4111, 1995 U.S. App. LEXIS 3987, at *7 (10th
Cir. Feb. 28, 1995) (ruling that disclosure of any possible information about
whereabouts of requester's "alleged husband" is not in public interest);
Maynard, 986 F.2d at 566 (disclosing information concerning low-level FBI
employees and third parties not in public interest); Fitzgibbon, 911 F.2d at
768 ("[T]here is no reasonably conceivable way in which the release of one
individual's name . . . would allow citizens to know 'what their government
is up to.'" (quoting Reporters Comm., 489 U.S. at 773)); Pemco Aeroplex, Inc.
v. U.S. Dep't of Labor, No. 01-AR-1421, slip op. at 5 (N.D. Ala. Dec. 11, 2001)
(finding no public interest in disclosing identities of employees who completed race-discrimination questionnaire); Greenberg, 10 F. Supp. 2d at 29
(holding that privacy interests of individuals mentioned in FBI surveillance
tapes and transcripts obtained in arms-for-hostages investigation clearly
outweigh any public interest in disclosure); McNamera, 974 F. Supp. at
958-61 (finding, where no evidence of agency wrongdoing, no public interest in disclosure of information concerning criminal investigations of private citizens); Stone, 727 F. Supp. at 666-67 (stating that disclosing identities of low-level FBI Special Agents who participated in RFK assassination investigation is not in public interest); see also KTVY-TV, 919 F.2d at
1470 (stating that disclosing identities of witnesses and third parties
would not further plaintiff's unsupported theory that post office shootings
could have been prevented by postal authorities); Halloran v. VA, 874 F.2d
315, 323 (5th Cir. 1989) ("[M]erely stating that the interest exists in the abstract is not enough; rather, the court should have analyzed how that interest would be served by compelling disclosure."); FOIA Update, Vol. X, No.
2, at 6; cf. Nation Magazine, 71 F.3d at 895 (finding that "in some, perhaps
many" instances when third party seeks information on named individual
in law enforcement files, public interest will be "negligible"; but when individual had publicly offered to help agency, disclosure of records concerning that fact might be in public interest by reflecting "agency activity" in
how it responded to offer of assistance); Associated Press, 2006 WL
2707395, at *5 (finding existing public interest to be "great" and ordering
release of detainees' names and other identifying information contained
within documents regarding abuse at Guantanamo Bay detention facility);
ACLU, 389 F. Supp. 2d at 568-74 (finding substantiated public interest in
production of redacted photographs concerning abuse of detainees at Abu
Ghraib prison). But cf. Favish, 541 U.S. at 166-70 (recognizing "survivor privacy" principle, and holding that family of deceased individual has own

(continued...)

## EXEMPTION 7(C)

In order to protect the privacy interest of any individual who might be living, agencies may use many different kinds of tests or research methods to determine whether that person is still living or has died. For instance, the D.C. Circuit approved the Federal Bureau of Investigation's methods for doing this in Schrecker v. U.S. Dep't of Justice.[79] The FBI uses several steps to determine whether an individual mentioned in a record is alive or dead, including looking up the individual's name in Who Was Who, employing its "100-year rule" (which presumes that an individual is dead if his or her birthdate appears in the responsive documents and he or she would be over 100 years old), and using previous FOIA requests (institutional knowledge), a search of the Social Security Death Index (when the Social Security number appears in the responsive documents), and other "internal" sources.[80]

The Schrecker decision, however, now should be viewed together with the D.C. Circuit's subsequent decision in Davis v. Department of Justice.[81] In Davis, the D.C. Circuit was presented with an unusual fact pattern in which the request was for audiotapes, not documents.[82] It accordingly determined that the steps outlined in Schrecker were insufficient

---

[78](...continued) right and interest in personal privacy protection with respect to decedent's death-scene photographs due to their exceptional sensitivity); Accuracy in Media, 194 F.3d at 123 (protecting autopsy and death-scene photographs arising out of the investigation of Deputy White House Counsel Vincent Foster's suicide, and rejecting plaintiff's categorical argument that the "FOIA's protection of personal privacy ends upon the death of the individual depicted"); FOIA Post, "Supreme Court Rules for 'Survivor Privacy' in Favish" (posted 4/9/04) (discussing "survivor privacy" principle and its exceptional contours).

[79] 349 F.3d at 663 (approving FBI's usual method of determining whether individual is living or dead); see also Johnson v. Executive Office for U.S. Attorneys, 310 F.3d 771, 775 (D.C. Cir. 2002) (approving of the agency's inquiries concerning the subject of a request, and refusing to establish a "brightline set of steps for an agency" to determine whether he or she is living or dead). But see also Davis v. Dep't of Justice, 460 F.3d 92, 103 (D.C. Cir. 2006) (clarifying that court's holding in Schrecker did not purport to affirm any set of search methodologies as per se sufficient).

[80] Schrecker, 349 F.3d at 663-66; see also Peltier v. FBI, No. 02-4328, slip op. at 21 (D. Minn. Oct. 24, 2006) (magistrate's recommendation) (finding that FBI properly determined whether individuals were living or deceased by following steps set out in Schrecker), adopted (D. Minn. Feb. 9, 2007); Peltier, 2005 WL 735964, at *14 (same); Piper v. U.S. Dep't of Justice, 428 F. Supp. 2d 1, 3-4 (D.D.C. 2006) (same).

[81] 460 F.3d 92.

[82] Id. at 95.

when analyzing the tapes, as there is "virtually no chance that a speaker will announce" any personal identifiers during an oral conversation.[83] The court concluded that "[i]n determining whether an agency's search is reasonable," courts must consider several factors, specifically "the likelihood that it will yield the sought-after information, the existence of readily available alternatives, and the burden of employing those alternatives."[84] The court remanded the case in Davis "to permit the agency an opportunity to evaluate the alternatives and either to conduct a further search or to explain satisfactorily why it should not be required to do so."[85]

In Reporters Committee, the Supreme Court also emphasized the propriety and practicability of "categorical balancing" under Exemption 7(C) as a means of achieving "workable rules" for processing FOIA requests.[86] In so doing, it recognized that entire categories of cases can properly receive uniform disposition "without regard to individual circumstances; the standard virtues of bright-line rules are thus present, and the difficulties attendant to ad hoc adjudication may be avoided."[87] This approach, in conjunction with other elements of Reporters Committee and traditional Exemption 7(C) principles, subsequently led the D.C. Circuit to largely eliminate the need for case-by-case balancing in favor of "categorical" withholding of individuals' identities in law enforcement records.[88]

In SafeCard, the plaintiff sought information pertaining to an SEC investigation of manipulation of SafeCard stock, including "names and addresses of third parties mentioned in witness interviews, of customers listed in stock transaction records obtained from investment companies, and of persons in correspondence with the SEC."[89] Recognizing the fundamentally inherent privacy interest of individuals mentioned in any way in law enforcement files,[90] the D.C. Circuit found that the plaintiff's asserted public interest -- providing the public "with insight into the SEC's conduct with

---

[83] Id. at 104.

[84] See id. at 105.

[85] Id.

[86] 489 U.S. at 776-80.

[87] Id. at 780. But see also Cooper Cameron, 280 F.3d at 553 (acknowledging that statements to OSHA by employee-witnesses are "a characteristic genus suitable for categorical treatment," yet declining to use categorical approach).

[88] SafeCard, 926 F.2d at 1206.

[89] Id. at 1205.

[90] Id. (recognizing privacy interests of suspects, witnesses, and investigators).

respect to SafeCard" -- was "not just less substantial [but] insubstantial."[91] Based upon the Supreme Court's endorsement of categorical rules in Reporters Committee, it then further determined that the identities of individuals who appear in law enforcement files would virtually never be "very probative of an agency's behavior or performance."[92] It observed that such information would serve a "significant" public interest only if "there is compelling evidence that the agency . . . is engaged in illegal activity."[93] Con-

---

[91] Id.

[92] Id.

[93] Id. at 1206; see also Oguaju, 288 F.3d at 451 (finding that "exposing a single, garden-variety act of misconduct would not serve the FOIA's purpose of showing 'what the Government is up to'" (quoting Reporters Comm., 489 U.S. at 780)); Quiñon, 86 F.3d at 1231 (finding insufficient public interest in revealing individuals mentioned in FBI files absent evidence of wrongdoing; even if individuals had engaged in wrongdoing, such misconduct would have to shed light on agency's action); McCutchen, 30 F.3d at 188 ("Mere desire to review how an agency is doing its job, coupled with allegations that it is not, does not create a public interest sufficient to override the privacy interests protected by Exemption 7(C)."); Davis, 968 F.2d at 1282 ("[W]hen . . . governmental misconduct is alleged as the justification for disclosure, the public interest is 'insubstantial' unless the requester puts forward 'compelling evidence that the agency denying the FOIA request is engaged in illegal activity' and shows that the information sought 'is necessary in order to confirm or refute that evidence.'" (quoting Safe-Card, 926 F.2d at 1205-06)); Goldstein v. Office of Indep. Counsel, No. 87-2028, 1999 WL 570862, at *9 (D.D.C. July 29, 1999) (magistrate's recommendation) (finding "significant public interest" in documents relating to FBI's terrorism investigations but concluding that withholding of third-party names is proper absent compelling evidence of illegal activity by FBI); Chasse v. U.S. Dep't of Justice, No. 98-207, slip op. at 11 (D. Vt. Jan. 12, 1999) (magistrate's recommendation) (deciding that Exemption 7(C) does not apply to information regarding job-related activities of high-level INS officials alleged to have deceived members of congressional task force), adopted (D. Vt. Feb. 9, 1999), aff'd, No. 99-6059 (2d Cir. Apr. 6, 2000) (Privacy Act wrongful disclosure case); McGhghy, No. C 97-0185, slip op. at 10 (N.D. Iowa May 29, 1998) (holding that there is "no compelling public interest rationale" for disclosing the names of law enforcement officers, private individuals, investigative details, or suspects' names from DEA files); cf. Nation Magazine, 71 F.3d at 895-96 (noting that when individual had publicly offered to help agency, disclosure of records concerning that fact might be in public interest by reflecting "agency activity" in how it responded to offer of assistance); Dunkelberger, 906 F.2d at 782 (finding some cognizable public interest in "FBI Special Agent's alleged participation in a scheme to entrap a public official and in the manner in which the agent was disciplined"); Or. Natural Desert Ass'n v. U.S. Dep't of the Interior, 24 F. Supp. 2d 1088, 1093-94 (D. Or. 1998) (finding that public interest in

(continued...)

sequently, the D.C. Circuit held that "unless access to the names and addresses of private individuals appearing in files within the ambit of Exemption 7(C) is necessary in order to confirm or refute compelling evidence that the agency is engaged in illegal activity, such information is [categorically] exempt from disclosure."[94] This all now should be viewed, though, together with the standard applied by the Supreme Court in NARA v. Favish regarding any specific evaluation of an asserted "agency wrongdoing public interest."[95] In any event, of course, agencies should be sure to redact their law enforcement records so that only identifying information is withheld

---

[93](...continued)
knowing how government enforces and punishes violations of land-management laws outweighs privacy interests of cattle trespassers who admitted violations) (Exemptions 6 and 7(C)). But see Detroit Free Press, 73 F.3d at 98 (finding, despite no evidence of government wrongdoing, public interest in disclosure of "mug shots" of indicted individuals who had already appeared in court and had their names divulged) (dicta); Rosenfeld, 57 F.3d at 811-12 (making finding of public interest in disclosure of names of subjects of investigatory interest because disclosure would serve public interest by shedding light on FBI actions and showing whether and to what extent FBI "abused its law enforcement mandate by overzealously investigating a political protest movement"); Providence Journal, 981 F.2d at 567-69 (making finding of public interest in disclosure of unsubstantiated allegations); Homick, No. 98-00557, slip op. at 19-20, 22-23 (N.D. Cal. Sept. 16, 2004) (making finding of public interest in disclosure of names of FBI and DEA Special Agents, and of state, local, and foreign law enforcement officers, on basis that disclosure would show whether government officials acted negligently or perhaps otherwise improperly in performance of their duties); Bennett v. DEA, 55 F. Supp. 2d 36, 41 (D.D.C. 1999) (ordering release of informant's rap sheet after finding "very compelling" evidence of "extensive government misconduct" in handling "career" informant); Davin, No. 92-1122, slip op. at 9 (W.D. Pa. Apr. 9, 1998) (ordering disclosure of names and addresses of individuals in records of FBI investigation of Workers Alliance of America conducted between 1938 and 1964).

[94] SafeCard, 926 F.2d at 1206; see also Neely, 208 F.3d at 464 (adopting SafeCard approach). But see Baltimore Sun, 131 F. Supp. 2d at 730 n.5 (determining that "plaintiff need not provide compelling evidence of government wrongdoing in light of the inapplicability of the categorical rule of SafeCard" to this case; deciding that "[a] more general public interest in what a government agency is up to is sufficient here").

[95] See FOIA Post, "Supreme Court Rules for 'Survivor Privacy' in Favish" (posted 4/9/04) (advising that the Supreme Court "has explained that in seeking to apply some 'clear' or 'compelling' evidence test in such a case an agency now specifically should consider whether the requester has 'produced any evidence that would warrant a belief by a reasonable person that the alleged [g]overnment impropriety might have occurred'" (quoting Favish, 541 U.S. at 174)).

under Exemption 7(C).[96] (See the further discussion of privacy redaction under Exemption 6, The Balancing Process, above.)

Protecting the privacy interests of individuals who are the targets of FOIA requests and are named in investigatory records requires special procedures. Most agencies with criminal law enforcement responsibilities follow the approach of the FBI, which is generally to respond to FOIA requests for records concerning other individuals by refusing to confirm or deny whether such records exist. Such a response is necessary because, as previously discussed, members of the public may draw adverse inferences from the mere fact that an individual is mentioned in the files of a criminal law enforcement agency.[97]

Therefore, the abstract fact that records exist (or not) can be protec-

---

[96] See, e.g., Church of Scientology Int'l v. U.S. Dep't of Justice, 30 F.3d 224, 230-31 (1st Cir. 1994) (deciding that Vaughn Index must explain why documents entirely withheld under Exemption 7(C) could not have been released with identifying information redacted); Maydak v. U.S. Dep't of Justice, 362 F. Supp. 2d 316, 325 (D.D.C. 2005) (ordering release of prisoner housing unit information, but withholding inmate names and register numbers because agency did not proffer evidence that released information could be used to identify inmates); Canning v. U.S. Dep't of Justice, No. 01-2215, slip op. at 19 (D.D.C. Mar. 9, 2004) (finding application of Exemption 7(C) to entire documents rather than to personally identifying information within documents to be overly broad); Prows v. U.S. Dep't of Justice, No. 90-2561, 1996 WL 228463, at *3 (D.D.C. Apr. 25, 1996) (concluding that rather than withholding documents in full, agency simply can delete identifying information about third-party individuals to eliminate stigma of being associated with law enforcement investigation); Lawyers Comm., 721 F. Supp. at 571 (finding a middle ground in balancing of interest in disclosure of names in INS Lookout Book on basis of "ideological exclusion" provision against individuals' privacy interest by ordering release of only the occupation and country of excluded individuals); see also Aldridge, No. 7:00-CV-131, 2001 WL 196965, at *2-3 (deciding that privacy of IRS employees could be adequately protected by redacting their names from recommendation concerning potential disciplinary action against them).

[97] See Ray, 778 F. Supp. at 1215; FOIA Update, Vol. X, No. 3, at 5; FOIA Update, Vol. VII, No. 1, at 3-4 ("OIP Guidance: Privacy 'Glomarization'"); FOIA Update, Vol. III, No. 4, at 2; see also Antonelli v. FBI, 721 F.2d 615, 617 (7th Cir. 1983) ("even acknowledging that certain records are kept would jeopardize the privacy interests that the FOIA exemptions are intended to protect"); Burke v. U.S. Dep't of Justice, No. 96-1739, 1999 WL 1032814, at *5 (D.D.C. Sept. 30, 1999) (permitting agency to "simply 'Glomarize'" as to portion of request that seeks investigatory records); McNamera, 974 F. Supp. at 957-60 (allowing FBI and INTERPOL to refuse to confirm or deny whether they have criminal investigatory files on private individuals who have "great privacy interest" in not being associated with stigma of criminal investigation).

ted in this context. Except when the third-party subject is deceased or provides a written waiver of his privacy rights, law enforcement agencies ordinarily "Glomarize" such third-party requests -- refusing either to confirm or deny the existence of responsive requests -- in order to protect the personal privacy interests of those who are in fact the subject of or mentioned in investigatory files.[98] Indeed, courts have endorsed this "Glomar" response by an agency in a variety of law enforcement situations: For instance, this response is found appropriate when responding to requests for documents regarding alleged government informants,[99] trial witnesses,[100]

---

[98] See, e.g., Antonelli, 721 F.2d at 617 (deciding that "Glomar" response is appropriate for third-party requests when requester has identified no public interest in disclosure); McDade, No. 03-1946, slip op. at 11-12 (D.D.C. Sept. 29, 2004) (holding that agency's "Glomar" response was appropriate for third-party request concerning ten named individuals); Boyd v. DEA, No. 01-0524, slip op. at 3-4 (D.D.C. Mar. 8, 2002) ("The FBI's Glomar response was appropriate because the subject of the FOIA request was a private individual in law enforcement records and plaintiff's claim of his misconduct would not shed light on the agency's conduct."); Daley v. U.S. Dep't of Justice, No. 00-1750, slip op. at 2-3 (D.D.C. Mar. 9, 2001) (holding "Glomar" response proper when request seeks information related to third party who has not waived privacy rights); McNamera, 974 F. Supp. at 954 (deciding that "Glomar" response concerning possible criminal investigatory files on private individuals is appropriate where records would be categorically exempt); see also FOIA Update, Vol. X, No. 3, at 5; FOIA Update, Vol. VII, No. 1, at 3-4. But cf. Jefferson v. Dep't of Justice, 284 F.3d 172, 178-79 (D.C. Cir. 2002) (declining to affirm district court's approval of "Glomar" response to request for Office of Professional Responsibility records pertaining to Assistant United States Attorney, because of possibility that some non-law enforcement records were within scope of request); see also Hidalgo v. FBI, No. 04-0562, slip op. at 4-5 (D.D.C. Sept. 29, 2005) (finding "Glomar" response to be not appropriate when informant is not stigmatized by public confirmation of his FBI file and plaintiff has provided evidence to support allegations of government misconduct).

[99] See, e.g., Butler, 2006 U.S. Dist. LEXIS 40942 (finding that agency properly refused to confirm or deny the existence of records pertaining to alleged DEA informants); Flores v. U.S. Dep't of Justice, No. 03-2105, slip op. at 4-5 (D.D.C. Feb. 7, 2005) (finding that agency properly gave "Glomar" response to third-party request for information on private individuals and alleged informants), summary affirmance granted, No. 05-5074, 2005 U.S. App. LEXIS 24159 (D.C. Cir. Nov. 8, 2005), cert. denied, 126 S. Ct. 2316 (2006); Tanks, 1996 U.S. Dist. LEXIS 7266, at *12-13 (permitting FBI to refuse to confirm or deny existence of any law enforcement records, unrelated to requester's case, concerning informants who testified against requester).

[100] See, e.g., Oguaju, 288 F.3d at 451 (approving the government's use of "Glomar" response for a third-party request for any information on an indi-

(continued...)

subjects of investigations,[101] or individuals who may merely be mentioned in a law enforcement record.[102]

In employing privacy "Glomarization," however, agencies must be

---

[100](...continued)
vidual who testified at the requester's trial when the requester provided no public interest rationale); Enzinna, 1997 WL 404327, at *2 (finding government's "Glomar" response appropriate because acknowledging existence of responsive documents would associate witnesses with criminal investigation); Juste v. U.S. Dep't of Justice, No. 03-723 (D.D.C. Jan. 30, 2004) (finding that agency properly refused to confirm or deny existence of records on third parties who testified at plaintiff's trial); see also Meserve, 2006 U.S. Dist. LEXIS 56732, at *19-22 (concluding that while agency confirmed existence of records relating to third party's participation at public trial, it also properly provided "Glomar" response for any additional documents concerning third party).

[101] See, e.g., Reporters Comm., 489 U.S. at 775 (upholding FBI's refusal to confirm or deny that it maintained "rap sheets" on named individual); Greenberg, 10 F. Supp. 2d at 24 (holding "Glomar" response appropriate when existence of records would link named individuals with taking of American hostages in Iran and disclosure would not shed light on agency's performance); Schwarz, 1995 U.S. App. LEXIS 3987, at *7 (holding "Glomar" response proper for third-party request for file of requester's "alleged husband" when no public interest shown); Massey, 3 F.3d at 624 ("individuals have substantial privacy interests in information that either confirms or suggests that they have been subject to criminal investigations or proceedings"); Schwarz v. U.S. Dep't of Treasury, 131 F. Supp. 2d 142, 150 (D.D.C. 2000) (finding that "Glomar" response is proper in connection with request for third party's law enforcement records); Claudio v. Soc. Sec. Admin., No. H-98-1911, slip op. at 16 (S.D. Tex. May 24, 2000) (holding "Glomar" response proper when request sought any investigatory records about administrative law judge); Early v. Office of Prof'l Responsibility, No. 95-0254, slip op. at 3 (D.D.C. Apr. 30, 1996) (concluding that "Glomar" response concerning possible complaints against or investigations of judge and three named federal employees was proper absent any public interest in disclosure), summary affirmance granted, No. 96-5136, 1997 WL 195523 (D.C. Cir. Mar. 31, 1997); Latshaw v. FBI, No. 93-571, slip op. at 1 (W.D. Pa. Feb. 21, 1994) (deciding that FBI may refuse to confirm or deny existence of any law enforcement records on third party), aff'd, 40 F.3d 1240 (3d Cir. 1994) (unpublished table decision).

[102] See, e.g., Jefferson v. Dep't of Justice, 168 F. App'x 448 (D.C. Cir. 2005) (affirming district court judgment that agency, after processing responsive documents, could refuse to confirm or deny existence of any additional mention of third party in its investigative database); Nation Magazine, 71 F.3d at 894 (stating that privacy interest in keeping secret the fact that individual was subject to law enforcement investigation extends to third parties who might be mentioned in investigatory files).

careful to use it only to the extent that is warranted by the terms of the particular FOIA request at hand.[103] For a request that involves more than just a law enforcement file, the agency must take a "bifurcated" approach to it, distinguishing between the exceptionally sensitive law enforcement part of the request and any part that is not so sensitive as to require "Glomarization."[104] In so doing, agencies apply the following general rules:

---

[103] See, e.g., Nation Magazine, 71 F.3d at 894-96 (holding categorical "Glomar" response concerning law enforcement files on individual inappropriate when individual had publicly offered to help agency; records discussing reported offers of assistance to the agency by former presidential candidate H. Ross Perot "may implicate a less substantial privacy interest than any records associating Perot with criminal activity," so conventional processing is required for such records); see also FOIA Update, Vol. XVII, No. 2, at 3-4 ("OIP Guidance: The Bifurcation Requirement for Privacy 'Glomarization'").

[104] See, e.g., Jefferson, 284 F.3d at 178-79 (refusing to allow categorical Exemption 7(C) "Glomar" response to request for Office of Professional Responsibility records concerning Assistant United States Attorney because agency did not bifurcate for separate treatment of its non-law enforcement records); Nation Magazine, 71 F.3d at 894-96 (deciding that "Glomar" response is appropriate only as to existence of records associating former presidential candidate H. Ross Perot with criminal activity), on remand, 937 F. Supp. 39, 45 (D.D.C. 1996) (finding that "Glomar" response as to whether Perot was subject, witness, or informant in law enforcement investigation appropriate after agency searched law enforcement files for records concerning Perot's efforts to assist agency), further proceedings, No. 94-00808, slip op. at 9-11 (D.D.C. Feb. 14, 1997) (ordering agency to file in camera declaration with court explaining whether it ever assigned informant code to named individual and results of any search performed using that code; agency not required to state on record whether individual was ever assigned code number), further proceedings, No. 94-00808, slip op. at 9-10 (D.D.C. May 21, 1997) (accepting agency's in camera declaration that search of its records using code number assigned to named individual uncovered no responsive documents); Manchester v. FBI, No. 96-0137, 2005 WL 3275802, at *6 (D.D.C. Aug. 9, 2005) (finding that agency properly bifurcated request between information related to acknowledged investigation and third-party information outside scope of investigation); Meserve, 2006 U.S. Dist. LEXIS 56732, at *19-22 (concluding that while agency confirmed existence of certain records relating to third party's participation at public trial, it properly provided "Glomar" response for any additional documents concerning third party); Burke, 1999 WL 1032814, at *5 (finding no need to bifurcate request that "specifically and exclusively" sought investigative records on third parties); Tanks, 1996 U.S. Dist. LEXIS 7266, at *4 (upholding privacy "Glomarization" after agency bifurcated between aspects of request); Nation Magazine v. Dep't of State, No. 92-2303, slip op. at 23-24 (D.D.C. Aug. 18, 1995) (requiring FBI to search for any "noninvestigative" files on Perot); Grove, 802 F. Supp. at 510-11 (finding agency conducted

(continued...)

(1) FOIA requests that merely seek law enforcement records pertaining to a named individual, without any elaboration, can be given a standard "Glomarization" response; (2) any request that is specifically and exclusively directed to an agency's non-law enforcement files (e.g., one aimed at personnel files only) should receive purely conventional treatment, without "Glomarization"; and (3) FOIA requests that do more than simply seek law enforcement records on a named individual (e.g., ones that encompass personnel or possible administrative files as well) must be bifurcated for conventional as well as "Glomarization" treatment.[105] The "Glomar" response also is appropriate when one government agency has officially acknowledged the existence of an investigation but the agency that received the third-party request has never officially acknowledged undertaking an investigation into that matter.[106]

Prior to Reporters Committee, before an agency could give a "Glomarization" response, it was required to check the requested records, if any existed, for any official acknowledgment of the investigation (e.g., as a result of a prosecution) or for any overriding public interest in disclosure that would render "Glomarization" inapplicable. However, in Reporters Committee, the Supreme Court eliminated the need to consider whether there has been a prior acknowledgment when it expressly "recognized the priva-

---

[104](...continued)
search for administrative records sought but "Glomarized" part of request concerning investigatory records); accord Reporters Comm., 489 U.S. at 757 (involving "Glomarization" bifurcation along "public interest" lines); Gardels v. CIA, 689 F.2d 1100, 1102-03 (D.C. Cir. 1982) (approving "Glomarization" bifurcation that acknowledged overt contacts with educational institution but refused to confirm or deny covert contacts) (Exemptions 1 and 3); cf. Jefferson, 284 F.3d at 179 (requiring Office of Professional Responsibility to determine nature of records contained in file pertaining to Assistant United States Attorney before giving categorical "Glomar" response).

[105] Accord FOIA Update, Vol. XVII, No. 2, at 3-4; see, e.g., Nation Magazine, 937 F. Supp. at 45 (finding that "Glomar" response as to whether presidential candidate H. Ross Perot was subject, witness, or informant in law enforcement investigation appropriate after agency searched law enforcement files for less sensitive law enforcement records); Tanks, 1996 U.S. Dist. LEXIS 7266, at *4 (finding that agency properly bifurcated between aspects of request); Grove, 802 F. Supp. at 510-14 (allowing Navy to bifurcate between "administrative documents" and those held by its investigative component, Naval Investigative Service).

[106] See McNamera, 974 F. Supp. at 958 (finding that "Glomar" response is proper so long as agency employing it has not publicly identified individual as subject of investigation); cf. Frugone v. CIA, 169 F.3d 772, 774-75 (D.C. Cir. 1999) (finding that CIA properly "Glomarized" existence of records concerning plaintiff's alleged employment relationship with CIA despite allegation that another government agency seemingly confirmed plaintiff's status as former CIA employee) (Exemptions 1 and 3).

cy interest inherent in the nondisclosure of certain information even when the information may have been at one time public."[107] Further, as the very fact of an arrest and conviction of a person, as reflected in his FBI "rap sheet," creates a cognizable privacy interest, any underlying investigative file, containing a far more detailed account of the subject's activities, gives rise to an even greater privacy interest.[108]

At the litigation stage, the agency must demonstrate to the court, either through a Vaughn affidavit or an in camera submission, that its refusal to confirm or deny the existence of responsive records is appropriate.[109] Although this "refusal to confirm or deny" approach is now widely accepted in the case law,[110] several cases have illustrated the procedural difficulties

---

[107] 489 U.S. at 767.

[108] See FOIA Update, Vol. X, No. 3, at 5 (stating that under Reporters Committee, Exemption 7(C) "Glomarization" can be undertaken without review of any responsive records, in response to third-party requests for routine law enforcement records pertaining to living private citizens who have not given consent to disclosure); see also FOIA Update, Vol. XII, No. 2, at 6 (warning agencies not to notify requesters of identities of other agencies to which record referrals are made, in any exceptional case in which doing so would reveal sensitive abstract fact about existence of records).

[109] See Valdez v. Dep't of Justice, No. 05-5184, 2006 U.S. App. LEXIS 1042, at *1-2 (D.C. Cir. Jan. 12, 2006) (per curiam) (denying government's motion for summary affirmance because agency failed to adequately demonstrate need for "Glomar" response); Ely v. FBI, 781 F.2d 1487, 1492 n.4 (11th Cir. 1986) ("the government must first offer evidence, either publicly or in camera to show that there is a legitimate claim"); McNamera, 974 F. Supp. at 957-58 (finding agencies' affidavits sufficient to support "Glomar" response); Nation Magazine, No. 94-00808, slip op. at 9-11 (D.D.C. Feb. 14, 1997) (ordering agency to file in camera declaration with court explaining whether it ever assigned informant code to named individual and results of any search performed using that code); Grove, 752 F. Supp. at 30 (requiring agency to conduct search to properly justify use of "Glomar" response in litigation).

[110] See, e.g., Reporters Comm., 489 U.S. at 757 (request for any "rap sheet" on individual defense contractor); Oguaju, 288 F.3d at 451 (request for information on individual who testified at requester's trial); Schwarz, 1995 U.S. App. LEXIS 3987, at *7 (request for file on "alleged husband"); Beck, 997 F.2d at 1493-94 (request for records concerning alleged wrongdoing by two named DEA agents); Dunkelberger, 906 F.2d at 780, 782 (request for information that could verify alleged misconduct by undercover FBI Special Agent); Freeman v. U.S. Dep't of Justice, No. 86-1073, slip op. at 2 (4th Cir. Dec. 29, 1986) (request for alleged FBI informant file of Teamsters president); Strassman v. U.S. Dep't of Justice, 792 F.2d 1267, 1268 (4th Cir. 1986) (request for records allegedly indicating whether governor of

(continued...)

involved in defending a "Glomar" response when the requester's "speculation" as to the contents of the records (if any exist) raises a qualifying public interest.[111]

The significantly lessened certainty of harm now required under Exemption 7(C) and the approval of "categorical" withholding of privacy-related law enforcement information in most instances should permit agencies to afford full protection to the personal privacy interests of those mentioned in law enforcement files[112] whenever those interests are threatened

---

[110](...continued)
West Virginia threatened to invoke Fifth Amendment); Antonelli, 721 F.2d at 616-19 (request seeking files on eight third parties); Voinche, No. 99-1931, slip op. at 12-13 (D.D.C. Nov. 17, 2000) (request for information on three individuals allegedly involved in Oklahoma City bombing); Greenberg, 10 F. Supp. 2d at 10 (request for information relating to involvement of named individuals in "October Surprise" allegations); Early, No. 95-0254, slip op. at 3 (D.D.C. Apr. 30, 1996) (request for complaints against or investigations of judge and three named federal employees); Triestman, 878 F. Supp. at 669 (request by prisoner seeking records of investigations of misconduct by named DEA agents); Ray, 778 F. Supp. at 1215 (request for any records reflecting results of INS investigation of alleged employee misconduct); Knight Publ'g Co. v. U.S. Dep't of Justice, No. 84-510, slip op. at 1-2 (W.D.N.C. Mar. 28, 1985) (request by newspaper seeking any DEA investigatory file on governor, lieutenant governor, or attorney general of North Carolina); Ray v. U.S. Dep't of Justice, 558 F. Supp. 226, 228-29 (D.D.C. 1982) (request by convicted killer of Dr. Martin Luther King, Jr., seeking any file on requester's former attorney or Congressman Louis Stokes), aff'd, 720 F.2d 216 (D.C. Cir. 1983) (unpublished table decision); Blakey v. Department of Justice, 549 F. Supp. 362, 365-66 (D.D.C. 1982) (request by professor seeking any records relating to minor figure in investigation of assassination of President Kennedy who was indexed under topics other than Kennedy assassination), aff'd in part & vacated in part, 720 F.2d 215 (D.C. Cir. 1983) (unpublished table decision).

[111] See Shaw v. FBI, 604 F. Supp. 342, 344-45 (D.D.C. 1985) (seeking any investigatory files on individuals whom requester believed participated in assassination of President Kennedy); Flynn v. U.S. Dep't of Justice, No. 83-2282, slip op. at 1-3 (D.D.C. Feb. 18, 1984) (alleging that documents reflect judicial bias), summary judgment for agency granted (D.D.C. Apr. 6, 1984); see also Knight Publ'g, No. 84-510, slip op. at 2 (W.D.N.C. Mar. 28, 1985) (unsealing of in camera affidavit on motion to compel).

[112] Favish, 541 U.S. at 166 (noting that "law enforcement documents obtained by Government investigators often contain information about persons interviewed as witnesses or initial suspects but whose link to the official inquiry may be the result of mere happenstance").

by a contemplated FOIA disclosure.[113]

## EXEMPTION 7(D)

Exemption 7(D) provides protection for "records or information compiled for law enforcement purposes [which] could reasonably be expected to disclose the identity of a confidential source, including a State, local, or foreign agency or authority or any private institution which furnished information on a confidential basis, and, in the case of a record or information compiled by a criminal law enforcement authority in the course of a criminal investigation or by an agency conducting a lawful national security intelligence investigation, information furnished by a confidential source."[1]

It has long been recognized that Exemption 7(D) affords the most comprehensive protection of all of the FOIA's law enforcement exemptions.[2] Indeed, both Congress and the courts have clearly manifested their appreciation that a "robust" Exemption 7(D)[3] is important to ensure that "confidential sources are not lost through retaliation against the sources for past disclosure or because of the sources' fear of future disclosure."[4]

---

[113] See Attorney General's 1986 Amendments Memorandum at 9-12; see also Favish, 541 U.S. at 169 (evincing the Supreme Court's reliance on "the Attorney General's consistent interpretation of" the FOIA in successive such Attorney General memoranda); accord Attorney General Ashcroft's FOIA Memorandum, reprinted in FOIA Post (posted 10/15/01) (stressing importance of protecting law enforcement interests).

[1] 5 U.S.C. § 552(b)(7)(D) (2000 & Supp. IV 2004).

[2] Billington v. U.S. Dep't of Justice, 301 F. Supp. 2d 15, 21 (D.D.C. 2004) (stating that "Exemption 7(D) has long been recognized as affording the most comprehensive protection of all FOIA's law enforcement exemptions" (citing Voinche v. FBI, 940 F. Supp. 323, 331 (D.D.C. 1996)); accord Irons v. FBI, 880 F.2d 1446, 1451 (1st Cir. 1989).

[3] See Brant Constr. Co. v. EPA, 778 F.2d 1258, 1262 (7th Cir. 1985) (recognizing that Exemption 7(D) is intended to ensure that law enforcement agencies are not unduly hampered in their investigations).

[4] Id.; see, e.g., Ortiz v. HHS, 70 F.3d 729, 732 (2d Cir. 1995) (stating that "Exemption 7(D) is meant to . . . protect confidential sources from retaliation that may result from the disclosure of their participation in law enforcement activities"); McDonnell v. United States, 4 F.3d 1227, 1258 (3d Cir. 1993) (finding that the "goal of Exemption 7(D) [is] to protect the ability of law enforcement agencies to obtain the cooperation of persons having relevant information and who expect a degree of confidentiality in return for their cooperation"); Providence Journal Co. v. U.S. Dep't of the Army, 981 F.2d 552, 563 (1st Cir. 1992) (explaining that Exemption 7(D) is intended to

(continued...)

## EXEMPTION 7(D)

Sources' identities are protected wherever they have provided information either under an express promise of confidentiality[5] or "under circumstances from which such an assurance could be reasonably inferred."[6] As the Supreme Court in 1993 made clear in United States Department of Justice v. Landano,[7] not all sources furnishing information in the course of

---

[4](...continued)
avert "drying-up" of sources); Nadler v. U.S. Dep't of Justice, 955 F.2d 1479, 1486 (11th Cir. 1992) (observing that the "fear of exposure would chill the public's willingness to cooperate with the FBI . . . [and] would deter future cooperation" (citing Irons, 880 F.2d at 1450-51)); Shaw v. FBI, 749 F.2d 58, 61 (D.C. Cir. 1984) (holding that the purpose of Exemption 7(D) is "to prevent the FOIA from causing the 'drying up' of sources of information in criminal investigations"); Citizens for Responsibility & Ethics in Wash. v. Nat'l Indian Gaming Comm'n, No. 05-00806, 2006 U.S. Dist. LEXIS 89614, at *30 (D.D.C. Dec. 12, 2006) (reiterating that "'if current informants are exposed, future potential informants might be deterred'" (quoting agency declaration)); Wilson v. DEA, 414 F. Supp. 2d 5, 7 (D.D.C. 2006) (concluding that release of names of DEA sources could jeopardize DEA criminal investigative operations and deter cooperation of future potential DEA sources); Garcia v. U.S. Dep't of Justice, 181 F. Supp. 2d 356, 375 (S.D.N.Y. 2002) (holding that "Exemption 7(D) [en]sures that confidential sources are protected from retaliation in order to prevent the loss of valuable sources of information"); Givner v. Executive Office for U.S. Attorneys, No. 99-3454, slip op. at 15 (D.D.C. Mar. 1, 2001) (recognizing that "[c]ourts have granted a broad interpretation of Exemption 7(D) in order to protect sources").

[5] See Rosenfeld v. U.S. Dep't of Justice, 57 F.3d 803, 814 (9th Cir. 1995) ("[A]n express promise of confidentiality is 'virtually unassailable' [and is] easy to prove: 'The FBI need only establish the informant was told his name would be held in confidence.'" (quoting Wiener v. FBI, 943 F.2d 972, 986 (9th Cir. 1991))); Jones v. FBI, 41 F.3d 238, 248 (6th Cir. 1994) (stating that "sources who spoke with express assurances of confidentiality are always 'confidential' for FOIA purposes"); McDonnell, 4 F.3d at 1258 (holding that "identity of and information provided by [persons given express assurances of confidentiality] are exempt from disclosure under the express language of Exemption 7(D)").

[6] S. Conf. Rep. No. 93-1200, at 13 (1974), reprinted in 1974 U.S.C.C.A.N. 6285, 6291; see Dohse v. Potter, No. 04-355, 2006 WL 379901, at *7 (D. Neb. Feb. 15, 2006) (concluding that because public safety concerns are significant in context of disgruntled postal employees or contractors, source's "assurance of confidentiality could be inferred"); Farrugia v. Executive Office for U.S. Attorneys, No. 04-0298, 2006 WL 335771, at *8 (D.D.C. Feb. 14, 2006) (reasoning that "based on the nature of crime for which plaintiff was convicted and circumstances surrounding his arrest . . . it [was] reasonable to infer existence of an implicit grant of confidentiality").

[7] 508 U.S. 165 (1993).

criminal investigations are entitled to a "presumption" of confidentiality.[8] Instead, the Supreme Court ruled that source confidentiality must be determined on a case-by-case basis,[9] particularly noting that such a presumption should not be applied automatically to cooperating law enforcement agencies.[10]

The term "source" is meant to include a wide variety of individuals and institutions. The legislative history of the 1974 amendments to the FOIA indicates that the term "confidential source" was chosen by design to encompass a broader group than would have been included had the word "informer" been used.[11] This was reinforced in the Freedom of Information Reform Act of 1986,[12] which added to the statute specific categories of individuals and institutions to be included in the term "source."[13]

By its own terms, however, this statutory enumeration is not exhaustive. Indeed, courts have interpreted the term "source" to include a broad range of individuals and institutions that are not necessarily specified on the face of the statute -- such as crime victims;[14] citizens providing unsolicited allegations of misconduct;[15] citizens responding to inquiries from law enforcement agencies;[16] private employees responding to OSHA investigators about the circumstances of an industrial accident;[17] and employees

---

[8] Id. at 175.

[9] Id. at 179-80.

[10] Id. at 176; see also FOIA Update, Vol. XIV, No. 3, at 10.

[11] See S. Conf. Rep. No. 93-1200, at 13.

[12] Freedom of Information Reform Act of 1986, Pub. L. No. 99-570, § 1802, 100 Stat. 3207, 3207-48.

[13] Id.

[14] See, e.g., Coleman v. FBI, No. 89-2773, slip op. at 21 (D.D.C. Dec. 10, 1991), summary affirmance granted, No. 92-5040, 1992 WL 373976 (D.C. Cir. Dec. 4, 1992); Gula v. Meese, 699 F. Supp. 956, 960 (D.D.C. 1988).

[15] See, e.g., Brant Constr., 778 F.2d at 1263; Pope v. United States, 599 F.2d 1383, 1386-87 (5th Cir. 1979); Almy v. Dep't of Justice, No. 90-0362, 1995 WL 476255, at *12-13 (N.D. Ind. Apr. 13, 1995), aff'd, 114 F.3d 1191 (7th Cir. 1997) (unpublished table decision).

[16] See, e.g., Providence Journal, 981 F.2d at 565; Miller v. Bell, 661 F.2d 623, 627-28 (7th Cir. 1981); Kowalczyk v. O'Brien, No. 94-1333, slip op. at 2 (D.D.C. Jan. 30, 1996); Augarten v. DEA, No. 93-2192, 1995 WL 350797, at *2 (D.D.C. May 22, 1995); Almy, 1995 WL 476255, at *21, 23.

[17] See, e.g., L&C Marine Transp., Ltd. v. United States, 740 F.2d 919, 924-25 (11th Cir. 1984); Wayne's Mech. & Maint. Contractor, Inc. v. U.S. Dep't of

(continued...)

providing information about their employers.[18] Courts have likewise interpreted it to include prisoners;[19] mental healthcare facilities;[20] medical personnel;[21] commercial or financial institutions[22] and employees;[23] social organizations' officials and employees;[24] state and local law enforcement agencies[25] and employees;[26] and foreign law enforcement agencies.[27] By

---

[17](...continued)
Labor, No. 1:00-45, slip op. at 18-19 (N.D. Ga. May 7, 2001). But cf. Cooper Cameron Corp. v. U.S. Dep't of Labor, 280 F.3d 539, 552 (5th Cir. 2002) (stating that "[f]or us to hold . . . that OSHA's investigative records, as a category, are implicitly confidential would be unwarranted and would plow new ground").

[18] See, e.g., United Techs. Corp. v. NLRB, 777 F.2d 90, 94 (2d Cir. 1985); Gov't Accountability Project v. NRC, No. 86-3201, slip op. at 9-10 (D.D.C. June 30, 1993).

[19] See, e.g., Williams v. FBI, No. 99-0899, slip op. at 1-2 (D.D.C. July 31, 2000); Johnson v. Fed. Bureau of Prisons, No. 90-H-645, 1990 U.S. Dist. LEXIS 18358, at *9 (N.D. Ala. Nov. 1, 1990).

[20] See, e.g., Sanders v. U.S. Dep't of Justice, No. 91-2263, 1992 WL 97785, at *4-5 (D. Kan. Apr. 21, 1992).

[21] See, e.g., Putnam v. U.S. Dep't of Justice, 873 F. Supp. 705, 716 (D.D.C. 1995).

[22] See, e.g., Halpern v. FBI, 181 F.3d 279, 300 (2d Cir. 1999); Davin v. U.S. Dep't of Justice, No. 98-3343, slip op. at 9 (3d Cir. Jan. 27, 1999); Williams v. FBI, 69 F.3d 1155, 1158 (D.C. Cir. 1995); Jones, 41 F.3d at 248; Biase v. Office of Thrift Supervision, No. 93-2521, slip op. at 11 (D.N.J. Dec. 10, 1993); McCoy v. Moschella, No. 89-2155, 1991 WL 212208, at *1 (D.D.C. Sept. 30, 1991); Founding Church of Scientology v. Levi, 579 F. Supp. 1060, 1063 (D.D.C. 1982), aff'd, 721 F.2d 828 (D.C. Cir. 1983); Biberman v. FBI, 528 F. Supp. 1140, 1143 (S.D.N.Y. 1982); Dunaway v. Webster, 519 F. Supp. 1059, 1082 (N.D. Cal. 1981).

[23] See, e.g., Hunsberger v. U.S. Dep't of Justice, No. 92-2587, slip op. at 6-7 (D.D.C. July 22, 1997) (upholding confidential source protection for employee of financial institution).

[24] See Halpern, 181 F.3d at 300.

[25] See, e.g., Halpern, 181 F.3d at 299; Williams, 69 F.3d at 1160 (local law enforcement agency); Jones, 41 F.3d at 248 (law enforcement agencies); Bell v. FBI, No. 93-1485, 1993 U.S. App. LEXIS 27235, at *5 (6th Cir. Oct. 18, 1993) (local law enforcement agencies and their officers); Ferguson v. FBI, 957 F.2d 1059, 1068 (2d Cir. 1992) (local police department); Hopkinson v. Shillinger, 866 F.2d 1185, 1222 & n.27 (10th Cir. 1989) (state law enforcement agencies); Parton v. U.S. Dep't of Justice, 727 F.2d 774, 775-77 (8th

(continued...)

contrast, neither federal law enforcement agencies nor federal employees acting in their official capacities should receive any "confidential source" protection.[28]

The same underlying considerations that mandate that a broad spectrum of individuals and institutions be encompassed by the term "source" also require that the adjective "confidential" be given a similarly broad construction: It signifies that the "source furnished information with the understanding that the . . . [agency] would not divulge the communication except to the extent the . . . [agency] thought necessary for law enforcement purposes."[29]

---

[25](...continued)
Cir. 1984) (state prison officials interviewed in connection with civil rights investigation); Lesar v. U.S. Dep't of Justice, 636 F.2d 472, 489-91 (D.C. Cir. 1980) (local police departments); Meserve v. U.S. Dep't of Justice, No. 04-1844, 2006 U.S. Dist. LEXIS 56732, at *29-30 (D.D.C. Aug. 14, 2006) (state and local law enforcement agencies); Manchester v. FBI, No. 96-0137, 2005 WL 3275802, at *8 (D.D.C. Aug. 9, 2005) (state and local law enforcement agencies); Peralta v. U.S. Dep't of Justice, 69 F. Supp. 2d 21, 35 (D.D.C. 1999) (state and local authorities).

[26] See Garcia, 181 F. Supp. 2d at 377 (protecting identity of "state governmental employee" who provided "professional opinions as well as observations" regarding "plaintiff and his criminal activities").

[27] See, e.g., Billington v. U.S. Dep't of Justice, 233 F.3d 581, 585 n.5 (D.C. Cir. 2000) (foreign agencies); Halpern, 181 F.3d at 299; Shaw, 749 F.2d at 62 (foreign law enforcement agencies); Weisberg v. U.S. Dep't of Justice, 745 F.2d 1476, 1491-92 (D.C. Cir. 1984) (same); Founding Church of Scientology v. Regan, 670 F.2d 1158, 1161-62 (D.C. Cir. 1981) (foreign INTERPOL national bureaus); Brunskill v. U.S. Dep't of Justice, No. 99-3316, slip op. at 7 (D.D.C. Mar. 19, 2001) (foreign law enforcement agencies), summary affirmance granted, No. 01-5135, 2001 WL 1488634 (D.C. Cir. 2001); Schwarz v. U.S. Dep't of Justice, No. 95-2162, slip op. at 7-8 (D.D.C. May 31, 1996) (foreign INTERPOL national bureaus), summary affirmance granted, No. 96-5183 (D.C. Cir. Oct. 23, 1996); Badalamenti v. Dep't of State, 899 F. Supp. 542, 549 (D. Kan. 1995) (foreign law enforcement officials); Linn v. U.S. Dep't of Justice, No. 92-1406, 1995 WL 417810, at *11, *22, *32 (D.D.C. June 6, 1995) (foreign law enforcement agencies, including foreign INTERPOL national bureaus).

[28] See Retail Credit Co. v. FTC, No. 75-0895, 1976 WL 1206, at *4 n.3 (D.D.C. 1976); see also FOIA Update, Vol. V, No. 2, at 7. But see Kuzma v. IRS, 775 F.2d 66, 70 (2d Cir. 1985) (finding that Exemption 7(D) can protect identities of some federal government employees who served as confidential sources).

[29] Landano, 508 U.S. at 174; Envtl. Prot. Servs. v. EPA, 364 F. Supp. 2d (continued...)

## EXEMPTION 7(D)

Most significantly, "the question is not whether the requested <u>docu-ment</u> is of the type that the agency usually treats as confidential, but whether the particular <u>source</u> spoke with an understanding that the communication would remain confidential."[30] And because the applicability of this exemption hinges on the circumstances under which the information is provided, and not on the harm resulting from disclosure (in contrast to Exemptions 6 and 7(C)), no balancing test is applied under the case law of Exemption 7(D).[31]

---

[29](...continued)
575, 588 (N.D. W. Va. 2005) (reiterating that source is deemed confidential if source furnished information with understanding that government agency would not divulge information except to extent necessary for law enforcement purposes).

[30] <u>Id.</u> at 172; <u>see</u> <u>Billington</u>, 233 F.3d at 585 (holding that the "confidentiality analysis proceeds from the perspective of an informant, not [that of] the law enforcement agency"); <u>Ortiz</u>, 70 F.3d at 733 (finding that although agency did not solicit letter from letter writer, it was writer's expectation that letter would be kept secret); <u>McDonnell</u>, 4 F.3d at 1258 (holding that a "content based test [is] not appropriate in evaluating a document for Exemption 7(D) status[;] rather the proper focus of the inquiry is on the <u>source</u> of the information"); <u>Providence Journal</u>, 981 F.2d at 563 (explaining that "confidentiality depends not on [document's] contents but on the terms and circumstances under which" agency acquired information); <u>Ferguson</u>, 957 F.2d at 1069 (observing that "Exemption 7(D) is concerned not with the content of the information, but only with the circumstances in which the information was obtained"); <u>Weisberg</u>, 745 F.2d at 1492 (stating that availability of Exemption 7(D) depends not upon factual contents of document sought, but upon whether source was confidential); <u>Shaw</u>, 749 F.2d at 61 (same); <u>Lesar</u>, 636 F.2d at 492 (noting that applicability of Exemption 7(D) does not depend on factual content of document); <u>Envtl. Prot. Servs.</u>, 364 F. Supp. 2d at 590-91 (declaring that "witnesses would not have been forthright with EPA had they not thought their comments were being held in strict confidence"); <u>Santos v. DEA</u>, No. 02-0734, 2005 WL 555410, at *4 (D.D.C. Mar. 7, 2005) (concluding that sources who provided information to DEA would not have done so without assurances of confidentiality); <u>Gordon v. Thornberg</u>, 790 F. Supp. 374, 377 (D.R.I. 1992) (defining "confidential" as "provided in confidence or trust; neither the information nor the source need be 'secret'").

[31] <u>See, e.g.</u>, <u>Jones</u>, 41 F.3d at 247 (clarifying that Exemption 7(D) "does not involve a balancing of public and private interests; if the source was confidential, the exemption may be claimed regardless of the public interest in disclosure"); <u>McDonnell</u>, 4 F.3d at 1257 (stating that Exemption "7(D) does not entail a balancing of public and private interests"); <u>Nadler</u>, 955 F.2d at 1487 n.8 (holding that "[o]nce a source has been found to be confidential, Exemption 7(D) does not require the Government to justify its decision to withhold information against the competing claim that the public

(continued...)

Courts have uniformly recognized that express promises of confidentiality deserve protection under Exemption 7(D),[32] but they usually require

---

[31](...continued)
interest weighs in favor of disclosure"); Parker v. Dep't of Justice, 934 F.2d 375, 380 (D.C. Cir. 1991) (stating that "judiciary is not to balance interests under Exemption 7(D)"); Schmerler v. FBI, 900 F.2d 333, 336 (D.C. Cir. 1990) (declaring that "statute admits no such balancing"); Irons v. FBI, 811 F.2d 681, 685 (1st Cir. 1987) (stating that "the judiciary is not permitted to undertake a balancing of conflicting interests, but is required to uphold a claimed 7(D) exemption so long as the statutory criteria are met"); Katz v. FBI, No. 87-3712, slip op. at 9 (5th Cir. Mar. 30, 1988) (noting that "unlike [with] the privacy exemption, no balancing of interests is allowed once material qualifies for the confidential source exemption"); Brant Constr., 778 F.2d at 1262-63 (observing that "[n]o judicial 'balancing' of the competing interests is permitted" under Exemption 7(D)); Cuccaro v. Sec'y of Labor, 770 F.2d 355, 360 (3d Cir. 1985) (noting that "Exemption 7(D) provides that [information furnished by] confidential sources may be withheld and the court is not required to engage in the balancing test of Exemption 7(C)"); Sands v. Murphy, 633 F.2d 968, 971 (1st Cir. 1980) (stating that "a judicial balancing test is not appropriate in applying Exemption 7(D)"); Carbe v. ATF, No. 03-1658, 2004 U.S. Dist. LEXIS 17339, at *16 (D.D.C. Aug. 12, 2004) (Exemption 7(D) "does not involve a balancing of public and private interests; if the source was confidential, the exemption could be claimed regardless of public interest in disclosure." (citing Jones, 41 F.3d at 247)).

[32] See, e.g., Williams, 69 F.3d at 1159 (finding information provided under express assurances of confidentiality to be exempt from disclosure); Jones, 41 F.3d at 248 ("[o]n the basis of [court's] in camera review," express confidentiality justified); KTVY-TV v. United States, 919 F.2d 1465, 1470 (10th Cir. 1990) (upholding express assurances of confidentiality given interviewees who provided information regarding postal employee who shot and killed fellow workers); Birch v. USPS, 803 F.2d 1206, 1212 (D.C. Cir. 1986) (withholding found proper when "informant requested and received express assurances of confidentiality prior to assisting the investigation"); Citizens for Responsibility & Ethics in Wash., 2006 U.S. Dist. LEXIS 89614, at *30 (finding agency's application of Exemption 7(D) proper when "'the person ha[d] been given an express guarantee'" (quoting agency declaration); Judicial Watch v. U.S. Dep't of Justice, No. 99-1883, slip op. at 14-15 (D.D.C. June 9, 2005) (concluding that the agency properly invoked Exemption 7(D) to protect information that a witness provided "under an express pledge of confidentiality"); Flowserve U.S., Inc. v. Dep't of Labor, No. 04-0868, 2004 WL 2451829, at *3 (N.D. Tex. Nov. 2, 2004) (finding that agency's verbal assurance, buttressed by private nature of interviews, did create express assurance of confidentiality that warranted Exemption 7(D) protection); Pfannenstiel v. Dir. of the FBI, No. 98-0386, slip op. at 7 (D.N.M. Feb. 18, 1999) (finding withholding proper when FBI "entered express verbal agreements . . . by promising [sources] that their identities would be kept confidential"); Colon v. Executive Office for U.S. Attorneys, No. 98-0180,

(continued...)

affidavits specifically demonstrating the firm existence of such an express promise.[33] Express promises can be supported by notations made on the

---

[32](...continued)
1998 WL 695631, at *5 (D.D.C. Sept. 29, 1998) (ruling that information provided by informant referred to as "CI" may be withheld pursuant to express promise of confidentiality); Franklin v. U.S. Dep't of Justice, No. 97-1225, slip op. at 13-15 (S.D. Fla. June 15, 1998) (magistrate's recommendation) (withholding of "identities and information provided by coded and non-coded sources based upon express promises of confidentiality" was proper), adopted (S.D. Fla. June 26, 1998), aff'd, 189 F.3d 485 (11th Cir. 1999) (unpublished table decision); Fedrick v. U.S. Dep't of Justice, 984 F. Supp. 659, 665 (W.D.N.Y. 1997) (magistrate's recommendation) (withholding upheld when express promises of confidentiality were given to informants "in accordance with DEA policy and procedure"), adopted, No. 95-558 (W.D.N.Y. Oct. 28, 1997), aff'd sub nom. Fedrick v. Huff, 165 F.3d 13 (2d Cir. 1998) (unpublished table decision); Mittleman v. OPM, No. 92-0158, slip op. at 2 & n.2 (D.D.C. Jan. 18, 1995) (withholding proper when sources given express promise of confidentiality during OPM's background investigation), aff'd on other grounds per curiam, 76 F.3d 1240 (D.C. Cir. 1996); Cappabianca v. Comm'r, U.S. Customs Serv., 847 F. Supp. 1558, 1566 (M.D. Fla. 1994) (explaining that "application of Landano to a case where a witness [to an internal investigation] gave full cooperation only after receiving an express assurance of confidentiality . . . clearly leads to the conclusion that the witness is a confidential source"); Simon v. U.S. Dep't of Justice, 752 F. Supp. 14, 21 (D.D.C. 1991) (withholding proper when "source explicitly requested that his identity be kept confidential"), aff'd, 980 F.2d 782 (D.C. Cir. 1992).

[33] See, e.g., Boyd v. Criminal Div., of U.S. Dep't. of Justice, No. 05-5142, 2007 WL 328064, at *6 (D.C. Cir. 2007) (finding that ATF's affidavit properly demonstrated that confidential source received an express promise); Citizens for Responsibility & Ethics in Wash., 2006 U.S. Dist. LEXIS 89614, at *30-31 (finding sufficient agency's declaration that indicates "'confidential source . . . has been given an express guarantee that personal and contact information will not be disclosed to the public'" (quoting agency declaration); Chavez-Arellano v. U.S. Dep't of Justice, No. 05-2503, 2006 U.S. Dist. LEXIS 56104, at *27 (D.D.C. Aug. 11, 2006) (holding that affidavit and exhibits provided sufficient evidence that source was given express promise of confidentiality); Sussman v. U.S. Marshals Serv., No. 03-0610, 2005 WL 3213912, at *8 (D.D.C. Oct. 13, 2005) (finding that USMS's declaration adequately showed that confidential sources were given express promises of confidentiality), summary affirmance granted, No. 06-5085 (D.C. Cir. Oct. 20, 2006); Judicial Watch, No. 99-1883, slip op. at 15 (D.D.C. June 9, 2005) (concluding that FBI's declaration demonstrated that disclosure of document would identify source who received express promise of confidentiality); Sukup v. Executive Office for U.S. Attorneys, No. 02-0355, slip op. at 10 (D.D.C. Jan. 13, 2005) (concluding that agency properly applied Exemption 7(D) to "information that was provided with an express assurance of confidentiality'" (quoting agency declaration)); DiPietro v. Executive Office
(continued...)

face of documents indicating that the information in them is to be kept confidential pursuant to an express promise;[34] by statements from the agents

---

[33](...continued)
for U.S. Attorneys, 357 F. Supp. 2d 177, 185 (D.D.C. 2004) (reiterating that when an agency relies on an express assurance of confidentiality to invoke Exemption 7(D), it must offer "probative evidence that the source did in fact receive an express grant of confidentiality"); Summers v. U.S. Dep't of Justice, No. 98-1837, slip op. at 17 (D.D.C. Mar. 10, 2003) (determining that FBI properly "withheld information about and information furnished by individuals who were given express assurances of confidentiality"); Guccione v. Nat'l Indian Gaming Comm'n, No. 98-CV-164, 1999 U.S. Dist. LEXIS 15475, at *8 (S.D. Cal. Aug. 4, 1999) (declaring that express confidentiality can be found to exist when the agency's declaration "provides sufficient context and explanation of the [withheld] documents' contents"). But see Hudson v. Dep't of Justice, No. 04-4079, 2005 WL 1656909, at *6 (N.D. Cal. July 11, 2005) (rejecting FBI's "bare assertions" of express confidentiality absent sufficiently detailed declaration demonstrating that such promise of confidentiality was provided); cf. Hronek v. DEA, 16 F. Supp. 2d 1260, 1275 (D. Or. 1998) (ordering submission of a supplemental declaration because the agency failed to sufficiently "discuss the [express] grant of confidentiality"), aff'd, No. 99-36055, 2001 WL 291035 (9th Cir. Mar. 12, 2001).

[34] See, e.g., Neely v. FBI, 208 F.3d 461, 466 (4th Cir. 2000) (remanding with instructions that if the "district court finds that the [withheld] documents . . . do in fact, as the FBI claims, bear evidence 'on their face' of 'express promises of confidentiality,' . . . then the FBI would most likely be entitled to withhold such documents" (quoting government's brief)); King v. U.S. Dep't of Justice, 830 F.2d 210, 235 (D.C. Cir. 1987) (finding express confidentiality when the agency showed that the "documents [were] marked 'confidential informant' at the time of their compilation"); Peltier v. FBI, No. 02-4328, slip op. at 23 (D. Minn. Oct. 24, 2006) (finding that FBI established that records themselves "constitute contemporaneous evidence reflecting express grants of confidentiality"), adopted (D. Minn. Feb. 9, 2007); Peltier v. FBI, No. 03-905S, 2005 WL 735964, at *18 (W.D.N.Y. Mar. 31, 2005) (finding that evidence of express confidentiality was present when documents, contained designations "PROTECT," "protect identity," and "protect by request"); Martinez v. EEOC, No. 04-0271, 2005 U.S. Dist. LEXIS 3864, at *11 n.27 (W.D. Tex. Mar. 3, 2005) (recognizing that courts have held that words such as "confidential[ity] requested by witness" on face of document are sufficient to justify nondisclosure); Homick v. Dep't of Justice, No. 98-0557, slip op. at 30 (N.D. Cal. Sept. 16, 2004) (determining that "protect" or "protect identity by request," followed by name of interviewee, was indicative of express grant of confidentiality); Barber v. Office of Info. & Privacy, No. 02-1748, slip op. at 7 (D.D.C. Sept. 4, 2003) (determining that documents "stamped 'Confidential Property of F.D.L.E. Released to U.S. Attorney No. Dist. . . . Its Contents Are Not To Be Distributed Outside of Your Agency'" certainly evidence express promises of confidentiality), summary affirmance granted, No. 03-5266, 2004 WL 344040 (D.C. Cir. May 7, 2004);

(continued...)

or sources involved in which they attest to their personal knowledge of an express promise;[35] by specific agency practices or procedures regarding the routine treatment of confidential sources,[36] including those for "symbol-

---

[34](...continued)
Rosenberg v. Freeh, No. 97-0476, slip op. at 13 (D.D.C. May 13, 1998) (ruling that agency demonstrated express confidentiality when "protect identity" was written next to informant's name).

[35] See, e.g., Neuhausser v. U.S. Dep't of Justice, No. 03-531, 2006 WL 1581010, at *7 (E.D. Ky. June 6, 2006) (finding that DEA's declaration delineated between those informants who received express assurances of confidentiality and those who received implied assurances of confidentiality); Wheeler v. U.S. Dep't of Justice, 403 F. Supp. 2d 1, 16 (D.D.C. 2005) (finding that FBI's declaration sufficiently demonstrated that agent had personal knowledge of express promise given to confidential source); Millhouse v. IRS, No. 03-1418, 2005 U.S. Dist. LEXIS 1290, at *7-8 (D.D.C. Jan. 3, 2005) (concluding that the IRS's declaration was sufficient to meet the government's burden that "information obtained from th[e] informant in connection with [the IRS's] investigation was provided under the express understanding that the informant's identity would be held confidential"); Billington, 301 F. Supp. 2d at 22 (finding that an in camera affidavit of the source "confirms that the source . . . was assured [with] an express grant of confidentiality").

[36] See, e.g., Neuhausser, 2006 WL 1581010, at *7 (finding that DEA has longstanding confidential source policy which provides that coded sources receive express assurances of confidentiality); Millhouse, 2005 U.S. Dist. LEXIS 1290, at *5 (finding that IRS's Special Agent followed IRS procedures for providing confidential sources with express grants of confidentiality); Pinnavaia v. FBI, No. 03-112, slip op. at 12 (D.D.C. Feb. 25, 2004) (withholding confidential source number identifiers because FBI policy assigns such numbers only pursuant to express grant of confidentiality); Rugiero v. U.S. Dep't of Justice, 234 F. Supp. 2d 697, 702 (E.D. Mich. 2002) (relying on detailed affidavits by DEA indicating that sources given express confidentiality were assigned codes and recorded as such), appeal dismissed voluntarily, No. 03-2455 (6th Cir. Feb. 8, 2005); Campbell v. U.S. Dep't of Justice, No. 89-3016, slip op. at 23 (D.D.C. Sept. 28, 2001) (finding express promise of confidentiality to be established in part by "Bureau Bulletins issued by the FBI headquarters" and the FBI's "Manuals of Rules and Regulations that deal with confidential sources [and which] were in effect at the time the information . . . was gathered"); Wayne's Mech. & Maint. Contractor, No. 1:00-45, slip op. at 18-19 (N.D. Ga. May 7, 2001) (stating that "employee-witnesses are covered by Exemption 7(D) because OSHA representatives did ensure . . . that their statements would be confidential, according to standard OSHA practice"). But see Homick, No. 98-0557, slip op. at 28 (N.D. Cal. Sept. 16, 2004) (finding that FBI's 1993 policy guidelines for source symbol numbers were not applicable to requested information).

numbered" sources;[37] or by some combination of the above.[38]

---

[37] See, e.g., Mays v. DEA, 234 F.3d 1324, 1329 (D.C. Cir. 2000) (holding that an agency affidavit that "plainly refers to 'notations on the face of [the] withheld document[s]' -- specifically, the DEA confidential informant code -- indicat[es] that [the] source received an express assurance of confidentiality" (quoting Campbell v. U.S. Dep't of Justice, 164 F.3d 20, 34 (D.C. Cir. 1998))); Manna v. U.S. Dep't of Justice, 51 F.3d 1158, 1167 (3d Cir. 1995) (finding that express confidentiality exists as to sources "assigned numbers" who provided information regarding organized crime); McDonnell, 4 F.3d at 1258 (reasoning that a "source was considered so sensitive that he or she was assigned a symbol source number and was never referred to by name in the file [leading to the] conclusion that [the information is] exempt from disclosure under the express language of Exemption 7(D)"); Mendoza v. DEA, No. 06-0591, 2006 WL 3734365, at *6 (D.D.C. Dec. 20, 2006) (explaining DEA's practice that coded sources are expressly assured confidentiality); Chavez-Arellano, 2006 U.S. Dist. LEXIS 56104, at *26 (describing how notes on face of document demonstrated that coded sources were expressly assured confidentiality); Ray v. FBI, 441 F. Supp. 2d 27, 36 (D.D.C. 2006) (explaining FBI practice that confidential sources who receive permanent source symbol numbers are provided express assurances of confidentiality); Neuhausser, 2006 WL 1581010, at *7 (holding that DEA's declaration indicated "coded informants" received express assurances of confidentiality and were assigned identification codes to be used in place of names); Antonelli v. ATF, No. 04-1180, 2006 WL 367893, at *6 (D.D.C. Feb. 16, 2006) (affirming invocation of Exemption 7(D) for coded sources); Wheeler, 403 F. Supp. 2d at 16 (agreeing that FBI's declaration showed that informant with source symbol number received express grant of confidentiality); Jones v. DEA, No. 04-1690, 2005 WL 1902880, at *3 (D.D.C. July 13, 2005) (finding that defendant properly justified withholding document given necessary DEA policy of debriefing coded confidential source); Piper v. U.S. Dep't of Justice, No. 98-1161, 2005 WL 1384337, at *6 (D.D.C. June 13, 2005) (determining that agency practice regarding assigned source symbol numbers showed express assurance of confidentiality); Butler v. U.S. Dep't of Justice, 368 F. Supp. 2d 776, 785 (E.D. Mich. 2005) (recognizing that "coded informants" are assured by DEA that their identities and information they provide will remain confidential); Halpern v. FBI, No. 94-365A(F), slip op. at 24-26 (W.D.N.Y. Aug. 31, 2001) (magistrate's recommendation) (finding sufficient the FBI's consistent policy of assigning source symbol numbers to informants who "report to the FBI on a regular basis and with the understanding that their identities would be held in the strictest confidence," and indicating that protection extends also to instances in which "the same informants are referred to not by their assigned codes and symbols, but by their names and other identifying information"), adopted (W.D.N.Y. Oct. 12, 2001); Galpine v. FBI, No. 99-1032, slip op. at 16 (E.D.N.Y. Apr. 28, 2000) (finding confidentiality to be established through the agency's "expression of a consistent policy" of assigning "source symbol numbers . . . to those informants who report information to the FBI on a

(continued...)

Further, courts have held that the identities of persons providing statements in response to routinely given "unsolicited assurances of confidentiality" are protectible under Exemption 7(D) as well.[39] However,

---

[37](...continued)
regular basis pursuant to an express assurance of confidentiality"); Green v. DEA, No. 98-0728, slip op. at 10 (D.D.C. Sept. 30, 1999) (finding to be sufficient agency's attestation that written policy in effect at time that sources supplied information required that individuals who became informants be issued "cooperating individual" codes and be given express assurances of confidentiality), aff'd in pertinent part & remanded in part, No. 99-5356, 2000 WL 271988 (D.C. Cir. Feb. 17, 2000). But see Davin v. U.S. Dep't of Justice, 60 F.3d 1043, 1062 (3d Cir. 1995) (stating that "government . . . must produce evidence of its alleged policy and practice of giving all symbol numbered informants or code name sources express assurances of confidentiality, evidence that the policy was in force throughout the [time] spanned by the documents . . . and evidence that the policy was applied to each of the separate investigations and in each case in which a document or portion has been withheld"), aff'd on appeal after remand, 176 F.3d 471 (3d Cir. 1999) (unpublished table decision); Rosenfeld, 57 F.3d at 81 (determining that FBI affidavits did not demonstrate that symbol-numbered sources were given express promises of confidentiality); McCoy v. United States, No. 04-101, 2006 WL 463106, at *6 (N.D. W. Va. Feb. 24, 2006) (rejecting adequacy of affidavit that indicated that coded sources "generally" receive express assurances of confidentiality because agency failed to show that individuals in question were given express assurances of confidentiality); cf. Billington v. U.S. Dep't of Justice, 245 F. Supp. 2d 79, 89 (D.D.C. 2003) (finding that "the mere fact that reports provided by a source have been assigned to a numbered file does not establish that he or she has been provided with assurances that the reports will remain confidential"), on reconsideration, 301 F. Supp. 2d 15 (D.D.C. 2004) (upholding agency application of Exemption 7(D) following in camera inspection).

[38] See, e.g., Davin, No. 98-3343, slip op. at 8 (3d Cir. Jan. 27, 1999) (finding express confidentiality to be established when a "source is referred to as a 'confidential informant,' coupled with the FBI Manuals' policy that confidential informants should be given express assurances of confidentiality"); Neuhausser, 2006 WL 1581010, at *7 (concluding that DEA's policy sufficiently established that coded sources received express assurances of confidentiality).

[39] See, e.g., Brant Constr., 778 F.2d at 1264 (concluding that transmission of information did not carry with it implicit request for confidentiality, but that it is unlikely that sources would have made allegations had they thought that agency would not keep them in strictest confidence); L&C Marine, 740 F.2d at 925 n.8 (finding that "the identity of a person . . . may be protected if the person provided information under an . . . assurance of confidentiality"); Pope, 599 F.2d at 1386-87 (concluding that sources of information would hardly have made charges unless they were confident

(continued...)

vague declarations, unsupported statements asserting the existence of an express promise from third parties who are, without direct knowledge, or generalized recitations of harm are generally insufficient to support Exemption 7(D) protection for any source.[40]

---

[39](...continued)
that their identities would remain concealed); Borton, Inc. v. OSHA, 566 F. Supp. 1420, 1422 (E.D. La. 1983) (magistrate's recommendation published as "appendix"); see also Church of Scientology Int'l v. U.S. Dep't of Justice, 30 F.3d 224, 239 (1st Cir. 1994) (ruling that "investigator's policy of affording confidentiality in interviews is an adequate basis upon which the government may consider the information provided . . . confidential"); Providence Journal, 981 F.2d at 555, 565 (finding express promises of confidentiality for twenty-four individuals based upon inspector general regulation); Badalamenti, 899 F. Supp. at 549 (withholding proper when agency attests that expectation of confidentiality for information about criminal activity documented by governing body of INTERPOL by resolutions); Kuffel v. U.S. Bureau of Prisons, 882 F. Supp. 1116, 1125 (D.D.C. 1995) (discussing how "ongoing understanding" between local law enforcement agencies and FBI that information shared about criminal investigation conducted by local agency would remain confidential alone could support conclusion that explicit grant of confidentiality existed). But cf. Cooper Cameron, 280 F.3d at 550 (refusing to "presume regularity in [OSHA] inspector's actions" despite agency's "established policy explicitly to assure employee-witnesses of confidentiality").

[40] See, e.g., Cooper Cameron, 280 F.3d at 550 (holding that express promise of confidentiality is not established by "internally inconsistent, self-contradictory" declaration that "vaguely states that according to standard procedure, OSHA assured the [sources] that their statements would remain confidential"); Billington, 233 F.3d at 584-85 (requiring the FBI "at the very least" to "indicate where [express] assurances of confidentiality are memorialized"); Halpern, 181 F.3d at 299 (finding to be insufficient the agency's "bare assertions that express assurances were given to the sources in question, and that the information received was treated in a confidential manner during and subsequent to its receipt"); Campbell, 164 F.3d at 34-35 (remanding the case to the district court because the agency's affidavit "simply asserts that various sources received express assurances of confidentiality without providing any basis for the declarant's knowledge of this alleged fact"); McCoy, 2006 WL 463106, at *6 (holding that DEA declaration failed to demonstrate that information was provided with express assurance of confidentiality); Homick, No. 98-0557, slip op. at 31 (N.D. Cal. Sept. 16, 2004) (finding that agency's vague justification for withholding documents was facially insufficient); Goldstein v. Office of Indep. Counsel, No. 87-2028, 1999 WL 570862, at *13 (D.D.C. July 29, 1999) (magistrate's recommendation) (warning agency "that the generic, 'cookie-cutter,' one size fits all declaration . . . which speaks generally of policies and procedures but does not specifically indicate when, where, and by whom each confidential source was in fact expressly promised confiden-

(continued...)

## EXEMPTION 7(D)

In contrast to the situation involving express confidentiality, a particularly difficult issue under Exemption 7(D) involves the circumstances under which an expectation of confidentiality should be inferred. Over the years, a number of courts of appeals employed a "presumption" of confidentiality in criminal cases, particularly those involving the FBI.[41] Historically, these courts applied a "categorical" approach to this aspect of Exemption 7(D), of the type generally approved by the Supreme Court in United States Department of Justice v. Reporters Committee for Freedom of the Press,[42] thereby eliminating the burdensome task for criminal law enforcement agencies of proving implied confidentiality on a case-by-case basis. In its landmark Exemption 7(D) decision in Landano, however, the Supreme Court effectively reversed all of these cases on this point of evidentiary presumption.[43]

At issue in Landano was "whether the Government is entitled to a presumption that all sources supplying information to the Federal Bureau of Investigation . . . in the course of a criminal investigation are confidential sources."[44] In Landano, the Supreme Court first made it clear that its decision affects only implied assurances of confidentiality[45] and that a source

---

[40](...continued)
tiality, will not do"); Voinche, 46 F. Supp. 2d at 34 (rejecting an agency's "general arguments for protecting confidential informants as well as [its] unsupported assertion . . . that the FBI made an express promise of confidentiality to the informant").

[41] D.C. Circuit: Parker, 934 F.2d at 378; Dow Jones & Co. v. Dep't of Justice, 917 F.2d 571, 576 (D.C. Cir. 1990); Schmerler, 900 F.2d at 337; Second Circuit: Donovan v. FBI, 806 F.2d 55, 61 (2d Cir. 1986); Diamond v. FBI, 707 F.2d 75, 78 (2d Cir. 1983); Sixth Circuit: Ingle v. Dep't of Justice, 698 F.2d 259, 269 (6th Cir. 1983); Seventh Circuit: Kimberlin v. Dep't of the Treasury, 774 F.2d 204, 208 (7th Cir. 1985); Miller, 661 F.2d at 627; Eighth Circuit: Parton, 727 F.2d at 776; Tenth Circuit: KTVY-TV, 919 F.2d at 1470; Hopkinson, 866 F.2d at 1222-23; Eleventh Circuit: Nadler, 955 F.2d at 1486 & n.7. But see Third Circuit: Lame v. U.S. Dep't of Justice, 654 F.2d 917, 928 (3d Cir. 1981) (requiring "detailed explanations relating to each alleged confidential source" so that court can determine whether Exemption 7(D) withholding appropriate as to "each source"); Ninth Circuit: Wiener, 943 F.2d at 986 (observing that "a claim that confidentiality was impliedly granted . . . requires the court to engage in a highly contextual, fact-based inquiry").

[42] 489 U.S. 749 (1989).

[43] See 508 U.S. at 179-80.

[44] Id. at 167.

[45] See id. at 172 (acknowledging that "precise question before us . . . is how the Government can meet its burden of showing that a source provided information on an implied assurance of confidentiality"); see Rosenfeld,
(continued...)

need not have an expectation of "total secrecy" in order to be deemed a confidential source.[46] However, the Court found that it was not Congress's intent to provide for a "universal" presumption or broad categorical withholding under Exemption 7(D);[47] rather, it declared, a "more particularized approach" is required.[48] Under this refined approach, agencies seeking to

---

[45](...continued)
57 F.3d at 814 (stating that "Landano did not affect the application of Exemption 7(D) to sources and information covered by an express assurance of confidentiality").

[46] Landano, 508 U.S. at 174 (observing that "an exemption so limited that it covered only sources who reasonably could expect total anonymity would be, as a practical matter, no exemption at all"); see Cappabianca, 847 F. Supp. at 1566 (stating that "[t]he Landano Court noted that 'confidential' does not necessarily mean completely secret, but that a statement may still be made in confidence when the speaker knows it will be shared with limited others"); Butler v. U.S. Dep't of Justice, No. 86-2255, 1994 WL 55621, at *6 (D.D.C. Feb. 3, 1994) (holding that "source need not be promised total secrecy . . . for material to be covered by [Exemption 7(D)]"), appeal dismissed voluntarily, No. 94-5078 (D.C. Cir. Sept. 8, 1994).

[47] Landano, 508 U.S. at 174-78; see Rosenfeld, 57 F.3d at 814 (reiterating that the "presumption of confidentiality [no longer] attaches from the mere fact of an FBI investigation . . . [Instead,] the confidentiality determination turns on the circumstances under which the subject provided the requested information."); Jones, 41 F.3d at 247 (observing that the "[Supreme] Court unanimously held that the government is not entitled to a presumption that all sources supplying information to the FBI in the course of a criminal investigation are confidential within the meaning of Exemption 7(D)"); cf. Rugiero v. U.S. Dep't of Justice, 257 F.3d 534, 552 (6th Cir. 2001) (rebuking DEA for "appl[ying] an incorrect standard" where "the affidavit indicates that the DEA has adopted a blanket rule that any informant who has not received an express assurance of confidentiality will be treated as having received an implied assurance of confidentiality").

[48] Landano, 508 U.S. at 179-80; see Quiñon v. FBI, 86 F.3d 1222, 1231 (D.C. Cir. 1996) (restating that the "[Supreme] Court rejected . . . a broad presumption of confidentiality in favor of a 'particularized approach' that looks to 'factors such as the nature of the crime that was investigated and the source's relation to it' in order to determine whether a promise of confidentiality may be inferred" (quoting Landano, 508 U.S. at 179-80)); Steinberg v. U.S. Dep't of Justice, 23 F.3d 548, 549 (D.C. Cir. 1994) (stating that Landano requires government to make "more particularized showing" of confidentiality"); Spirko v. USPS, No. 96-0458, slip op. at 7 (D.D.C. Feb. 25, 1997) (stating that the "government must make a 'particularized' showing as to each source of information"), aff'd on other grounds, 147 F.3d 992 (D.C. Cir. 1998); cf. Computer Prof'ls for Soc. Responsibility v. U.S. Secret Serv., 72 F.3d 897, 906 (D.C. Cir. 1996) (holding that "the manner in which an agency
(continued...)

invoke Exemption 7(D) must prove expectations of confidentiality based upon the "circumstances" of each case.[49]

Such specific showings of confidentiality, the Supreme Court indicated, can be made on a "generic" basis,[50] when "certain circumstances characteristically support an inference of confidentiality."[51] Throughout Lan-

---

[48](...continued)
'routinely' handles information is not sufficient to establish an implied assurance of confidentiality").

[49] Landano, 508 U.S. at 180; see Cooper Cameron, 280 F.3d at 552 (declaring that "implied confidentiality can arise . . . through the specific circumstances of a particular investigation"); Billington, 233 F.3d at 585 (finding that the "circumstances under which the FBI receives information might support a finding of an implied assurance of confidentiality"); Hale v. U.S. Dep't of Justice, 226 F.3d 1200, 1204 (10th Cir. 2000) (holding that "[a] source's reluctance to speak directly with the FBI is a clear sign that the source wanted to remain confidential"); Hale v. U.S. Dep't of Justice, 99 F.3d 1025, 1030 (10th Cir. 1996) (explaining that inferences of confidentiality "should be evaluated on a case-by-case basis"); see also FOIA Update, Vol. XIV, No. 3, at 10; Maydak v. U.S. Dep't of Justice, 362 F. Supp. 2d 316, 323 (D.D.C. 2005) (noting that source who witnessed assault provided information under circumstances from which confidentiality reasonably could be inferred); Homick v. Dep't of Justice, No. 98-0557, slip op. at 9 (N.D. Cal. Oct. 27, 2004) (finding that eyewitnesses to narcotics transactions and other criminal conduct were entitled to confidentiality), appeal dismissed voluntarily, No. 04-17568 (9th Cir. July 5, 2005). But see Ortiz v. U.S. Dep't of Justice, No. 97-140-A-3, slip op. at 9 (M.D. La. Aug. 25, 1998) (magistrate's recommendation) (relying on pre-Landano cases for proposition that assurance of confidentiality, either express or implied, can be assumed when individual gives information to criminal law enforcement official unless circumstances indicate otherwise), adopted (M.D. La. Oct. 1, 1998), aff'd, 194 F.3d 1309 (5th Cir. 1999) (unpublished table decision).

[50] Landano, 508 U.S. at 179.

[51] Id. at 177; see Mays, 234 F.3d at 1331 (observing that there is "no doubt that a source of information about a conspiracy to distribute cocaine typically faces a sufficient threat of retaliation that the information he provides should be treated as implicitly confidential"); Halpern, 181 F.3d at 299-300 (holding that "fear of retaliation" in meat-packing industry during union movement in 1930s and 1940s satisfied Landano standard); Prescott v. Dep't of Justice, No. 00-0187, slip op. at 4 (D.D.C. Aug. 10, 2001) (finding implied confidentiality where agency attested that sources "had a specific personal or business relationship with plaintiff . . . [who] was investigated for possession and distribution of major quantities of narcotics as well as possession of extremely violent weapons including machine guns and grenades"); Billington v. Dep't of Justice, 11 F. Supp. 2d 45, 67 (D.D.C. 1998)
(continued...)

dano, the Court stressed two "factors" to be applied in deciding whether implicit confidentiality exists: "the nature of the crime . . . and the source's relation to it."[52] It also pointed to five lower court rulings in which courts highlighted the potential for harm to the witnesses involved, as examples of decisions in which courts have correctly applied these two factors.[53]

The courts that have addressed this during the past fourteen years under the Landano rule have recognized the nature of the crime and the source's relation to it as the primary factors in determining whether im-

---

[51](...continued)
(concluding that investigation of violent organization involved "exactly the type of serious offenses which would warrant" an inference of implied confidentiality), aff'd in part, vacated in part & remanded on other grounds, 233 F.3d 581 (D.C. Cir. 2000); Coleman v. FBI, 13 F. Supp. 2d 75, 81-82 (D.D.C. 1998) ("Where there is an ongoing relationship between an informant and the Bureau and their communication occurs via secret rendezvous, it is reasonable to infer confidentiality."); Greenberg v. U.S. Dep't of Treasury, 10 F. Supp. 2d 3, 19 (D.D.C. 1998) (ruling that implied assurance can be inferred when source advised agency he received threat to life); Steinberg v. U.S. Dep't of Justice, 179 F.R.D. 357, 365 (D.D.C. Apr. 28, 1998) (finding "generic circumstances" met when source would speak to FBI only through intermediary); Butler v. Dep't of the Treasury, No. 95-1931, 1997 U.S. Dist. LEXIS 802, at *10 (D.D.C. Jan. 14, 1997) (emphasizing that the monitoring of conversations in a prison setting between cooperating sources and plaintiff "is precisely the situation contemplated by the 'generic' circumstances of confidentiality" in Landano); see also McNamera v. U.S. Dep't of Justice, 974 F. Supp. 946, 963 (W.D. Tex. 1997) (ruling that major narcotics conspiracy case involved circumstances that characteristically support inference of confidentiality).

[52] Landano, 508 U.S. at 179.

[53] Id. at 179-80 (citing Keys v. U.S. Dep't of Justice, 830 F.2d 337, 345-46 (D.C. Cir. 1987) (believing that individuals providing information regarding possible Communist sympathies, criminal activity, and murder by foreign operatives would have worried about retaliation); Donovan, 806 F.2d at 60-61 (ruling that individuals providing information about four American churchwomen murdered in El Salvador will likely face fear of disclosure); Parton, 727 F.2d at 776-77 (reasoning that prison officials providing information regarding alleged attack on inmate faced "high probability of reprisal"); Nix v. United States, 572 F.2d 998, 1003-04 (4th Cir. 1978) (finding implicit confidentiality when guards and prison inmates providing information about guards who allegedly beat another inmate face risk of reprisal); Miller, 661 F.2d at 628 (determining that individuals providing information about self-proclaimed litigious subject seeking to enlist them in "antigovernment crusades" faced "strong potential for harassment").

plied confidentiality exists.[54] They have uniformly recognized that a key consideration is of course the potential for retaliation against the source, whether based on actual threats of retaliation by defendants or requesters,[55] prior retaliatory acts by perpetrators or against sources,[56] the possi-

---

[54] See Cooper Cameron, 280 F.3d at 551-52; Hale, 226 F.3d at 1203; Grand Cent. P'ship v. Cuomo, 166 F.3d 473, 486-87 (2d Cir. 1999); Hale, 99 F.3d at 1030; Quiñon, 86 F.3d at 1231; Ortiz, 70 F.3d at 733; Williams, 69 F.3d at 1159; Davin, 60 F.3d at 1063; Rosenfeld, 57 F.3d at 814; Jones, 41 F.3d at 247-48; Koch v. USPS, No. 93-1487, 1993 U.S. App. LEXIS 26130, at *3-4 (8th Cir. Oct. 8, 1993); McDonnell, 4 F.3d at 1260; Massey v. FBI, 3 F.3d 620, 623 (2d Cir. 1993); Peralta, 69 F. Supp. 2d at 34; cf. Mays, 234 F.3d at 1330 (concluding that the Supreme Court in Landano did not find that "the source need have any particular relationship to the crime in order for the information [that] he supplies to be deemed confidential," and further concluding that "whatever his 'relation to the crime,' an informant is at risk to the extent that the criminal enterprise he exposes is of a type inclined toward violent retaliation"); Oliver v. FBI, No. 02-0012, slip op. at 8 (D.D.C. Mar. 8, 2004) (rejecting the FBI's contention that implied confidentiality existed, because the sources "placed themselves in harm's way should the assailant become aware of their cooperation with the FBI"), summary judgment granted (D.D.C. Nov. 15, 2004) (holding, after in camera review, that FBI properly invoked Exemption 7(D) to withhold entire records).

[55] See, e.g., Masters v. ATF, No. 04-2274, slip op. at 17 (D.D.C. Sept. 25, 2006) (explaining that "violations of Federal firearms law . . . and individuals who provide information concerning these crimes face a very real possibility of violent reprisal"); Dohse, 2006 WL 379901, at *7 (concluding that "in light of the nature of the alleged threats . . . the informant could reasonably be assumed to suffer reprisal if his identity were disclosed"); Wilson, 414 F. Supp. 2d at 7 (finding it "reasonable to infer that individuals [who] provided information about [trade of illicit substances] would fear for their safety if their identities or the information they provided was revealed" (citing Quiñon, 86 F.3d at 1222)); Peltier, 2005 WL 735964, at *19 (concluding that "sources are precisely the type of individuals who reasonably would fear retaliation in the event of disclosure . . . given the highly charged emotions, ongoing exposure, and public attention in th[is] case"); Carbe, 2004 U.S. Dist. LEXIS 17339, at *14 (acknowledging that confidential source faced possible retaliation if documents were released); Jennings v. FBI, No. 03-1651, slip op. at 18 (D.D.C. May 6, 2004) (agreeing that "in the type of prosecution involved here -- armed bank robbery -- it is reasonable to infer that source would fear reprisal"); Blanton v. U.S. Dep't of Justice, 182 F. Supp. 2d 81, 87 (D.D.C. 2002) (recognizing that "[e]ven though plaintiff is incarcerated, his threats against persons responsible for his arrest and . . . his conviction make it possible that these individuals could be targets of physical harm should their identities be revealed"), aff'd, 64 F. App'x 787 (D.C. Cir. 2003); Linn v. U.S. Dep't of Justice, No. 92-1406, 1995 WL 631847, at *34 (D.D.C. Aug. 22, 1995) (finding withholding proper when "persons associated with the investigation and prosecution were subject to threats (continued...)

bility of reprisals by third parties,[57] the specific dangers faced by prison informants,[58] or the violent or intimidating nature of the crime itself.[59]

---

[55](...continued)
of harm when their cooperation was divulged"); Putnam, 873 F. Supp. at 716 (fearing retribution, FBI properly withheld "names and information provided by relatives and close associates of the victim and the plaintiff" when former FBI Special Agent pled guilty to first degree manslaughter of an informant); see also Germosen v. Cox, No. 98 CIV 1294, 1999 WL 1021559, at *17 (S.D.N.Y. Nov. 9, 1999) (observing that requester sought names of confidential informants "for the specific purpose of inflicting the precise harm that Exemption 7(D) seeks to prevent -- harassment of the confidential source"), appeal dismissed for failure to prosecute, No. 00-6041 (2d Cir. Sept. 12, 2000). But see Hidalgo v. FBI, No. 04-0562, slip op. at 5 (D.D.C. Sept. 29, 2005) (finding that government initially failed to make necessary showing that disclosure of source's identity would subject him or her to "harassment and actual danger"), summary judgment granted (D.D.C. Sept. 22, 2006).

[56] See, e.g., Garcia, 181 F. Supp. 2d at 377 (holding that "sources expected their identities to be kept private in order to avoid retaliation by" a plaintiff who had been "convicted of two violent felonies, including conspiring to kill an individual who had testified against him at his robbery trial"); Jimenez v. FBI, 938 F. Supp. 21, 30 (D.D.C. 1996) (finding withholding of name and identifying information of source to be proper when plaintiff had previously harassed and threatened government informants).

[57] See, e.g., Hale, 226 F.3d at 1204-05 (stating that "people who provided detailed information surrounding [a kidnaping and murder], information that would only be known to a few people, would logically be fearful of retribution," in part because "[a]t the time the FBI conducted the[] interviews it was unclear if [plaintiff] had acted alone . . . or whether he may have worked with accomplices who might have violent propensities"); Coleman, 13 F. Supp. 2d at 82 (recognizing potential for "third party retaliation" even when imprisoned murderer, rapist, and kidnapper has "slim likelihood" of freedom); Landano v. U.S. Dep't of Justice, 873 F. Supp. 884, 888 (D.N.J. 1994) (stating on remand from the Supreme Court that "the violent nature of the crime, the potential involvement of the motorcycle gang, and the broad publication of the murder persuade the court that an implied assurance of confidentiality is warranted"); Gonzalez v. ATF, No. 04-2281, 2005 WL 3201009, at *9 (D.D.C. Nov. 9, 2005) (finding FBI's use of Exemption 7(D) proper to withhold sources' names and information because it was reasonable that sources would fear reprisal).

[58] See, e.g., Maydak, 362 F. Supp. 2d at 324 (concluding that "an individual providing confidential information about inmate-on-inmate sexual assault [would] only [speak with] an express or an implied grant of confidentiality"); Hazel v. Dep't of Justice, No. 95-01992, slip op. at 11 (D.D.C. July 2, 1998) (identifying risk of reprisal in "close-quarter context of prison" for

(continued...)

Moreover, they have recognized that the "danger of retaliation encompasses more than the source's physical safety."[60]

---

[58](...continued)
sources who provided information about "cold-blooded murder" of inmate); Butler, 1997 U.S. Dist. LEXIS 802, at *10 (recognizing danger of cooperating with prison or law enforcement officials).

[59] See, e.g., Mays, 234 F.3d at 1331 (emphasizing "[t]hat a conspiracy to distribute cocaine is typically a violent enterprise, in which a reputation for retaliating against informants is a valuable asset, [and] is enough to establish the inference of implied confidentiality for those who give information about such a conspiracy"); Hale, 99 F.3d at 1031 (recognizing that nature of crime supports inference of confidentiality when "discrete aspects" of it "make it particularly likely" for source to fear reprisal); Williams, 69 F.3d at 1159 (finding withholding justified based on "risk of retaliation, harassment and bodily harm"); Koch, 1993 U.S. App. LEXIS 26130, at *3-4 (finding withholding proper as to whistleblower who reported another employee's threat to bring grenade in to work because of "nature of alleged threat" and possibility of retaliation); Meserve, 2006 U.S. Dist. LEXIS 56732, at *30 (concluding that agency properly applied Exemption 7(D) to protect eyewitness statements regarding armed robbery due to threats of harm made); Gansterer v. U.S. Dep't of Justice, No. 95-1614, slip op. at 21 (C.D. Cal. July 6, 1998) (magistrate's recommendation) (recognizing that criminals engaged in drug trafficking are often "heavily armed, making violent retaliation a very real fear for those who provide information to the government"), adopted (C.D. Cal. Aug. 24, 1998); McQueen v. United States, 179 F.R.D. 522, 531 (S.D. Tex. May 6, 1998) (considering requester's ability to harm informants in upholding Exemption 7(D) protection); Campbell v. U.S. Dep't of Justice, No. 89-3016, 1996 WL 554511, at *9 (D.D.C. Sept. 19, 1996) (approving consideration of sources' fears of retribution), subsequent decision, No. 89-3016, slip op. at 6 (D.D.C. Aug. 6, 1997), rev'd & remanded on other grounds, 164 F.3d 20, 34-35 (D.C. Cir. 1998); Wickline v. FBI, 923 F. Supp. 1, 3 (D.D.C. 1996) (finding withholding proper based on violent nature of crime when requester had been convicted of multiple dismemberment murders); Perrone v. FBI, 908 F. Supp. 24, 27 (D.D.C. 1995) (withholding proper when those interviewed face fear of retribution or harm based on fact of their cooperation with FBI). But see Sukup, No. 02-0355, slip op. at 10 (D.D.C. Jan. 13, 2005) (rejecting agency's vague assertions that nature of crimes investigated were such that implied confidentially was automatic).

[60] Ortiz, 70 F.3d at 733 (citing Irons, 880 F.2d at 1451); see Grand Cent. P'ship, 166 F.3d at 487 (recognizing that retaliation "may constitute work place harassment, demotions, job transfers or loss of employment"); LaRouche v. U.S. Dep't of Justice, No. 90-2753, slip op. at 11 (D.D.C. Nov. 17, 2000) (observing that "[f]ear of financial retribution is valid in considering whether information was given confidentially"); Schrecker v. U.S. Dep't of Justice, 74 F. Supp. 2d 26, 35 (D.D.C. 1999) (finding implied confidentiality in case involving passport fraud and contempt of Congress when disclo-
(continued...)

Indeed, in post-Landano cases, courts have found implied confidentiality in circumstances involving organized crime,[61] murder,[62] drug trafficking,[63] extortion,[64] illegal possession of firearms,[65] domestic terrorism,[66] na-

---

[60](...continued)
sure of source's identity "would likely subject him to potential reprisal from others"), aff'd in part, rev'd in part & remanded on other grounds, 254 F.3d 162 (D.C. Cir. 2001); see also United Techs., 777 F.2d at 94 (concluding that "[a]n employee-informant's fear of employer retaliation can give rise to a justified expectation of confidentiality"). But cf. LaRouche, No. 90-2753, slip op. at 23 (D.D.C. July 5, 2001) (finding that the agency "failed to meet its burden of proof" for implied confidentiality where the "information furnished by the[] informants did not pertain to dangerous crimes associated with violence" -- i.e., it pertained to "white collar offenses" -- and where the government "made no showing that indicates release of the[] documents would subject the sources to retaliation").

[61] See, e.g., Homick, No. 98-0557, slip op. at 29 (N.D. Cal. Sept. 16, 2004) (agreeing with agency's position that confidentiality was "reasonably inferred" because of "violent nature of plaintiff and his associates, and his connections with members of organized crime"); Brunetti v. FBI, 357 F. Supp. 2d 97, 107 (D.D.C. 2004) (inferring confidentiality based on plaintiff's forty-year conviction for Racketeering Influenced and Corrupt Organizations crimes); Pray v. FBI, No. 95-0380, 1998 WL 440843, at *4-5 (S.D.N.Y. Aug. 3, 1998) (racketeering investigation); Wickline, 923 F. Supp. at 3 (organized crime case); Delviscovo v. FBI, 903 F. Supp. 1, 3 (D.D.C. 1995) (major racketeering investigation), summary affirmance granted, No. 95-5388 (D.C. Cir. Jan. 24, 1997); Cudzich v. INS, 886 F. Supp. 101, 107 (D.D.C. 1995) (suspected alien smuggling ring); Landano, 873 F. Supp. at 888 (possible motorcycle gang-related violence); Anderson v. DEA, No. 92-0225, slip op. at 11 (W.D. Pa. May 18, 1994) (magistrate's recommendation) (gang-related shootings), adopted (W.D. Pa. June 27, 1994), appeal dismissed, No. 94-3387 (3d Cir. Sept. 12, 1994); Manna v. U.S. Dep't of Justice, 832 F. Supp. 866, 876 (D.N.J. 1993) (organized crime activity), aff'd, 51 F.3d 1158 (3d Cir. 1995);

[62] See, e.g., Hale, 226 F.3d at 1204-05; Engelking v. DEA, 119 F.3d 980 (D.C. Cir. 1997); Peltier, No. 02-4328, slip op. at 24 (D. Minn. Oct. 24, 2006); Peltier, 2005 WL 735964, at *18-19; Shores v. FBI, No. 98-2728, 2002 WL 230756, at *4 (D.D.C. Feb. 4, 2002); Burke v. U.S. Dep't of Justice, No. 96-1739, 1999 WL 1032814, at *8 (D.D.C. Sept. 30, 1999); Green, No. 98-0728, slip op. at 10-11 (D.D.C. Sept. 30, 1999); Russell v. Barr, No. 92-2546, slip op. at 11 (D.D.C. Aug. 28, 1998); Coleman, 13 F. Supp. 2d at 82; Isley, No. 96-0123, slip op. at 8 (D.D.C. Mar. 27, 1997); Wickline, 923 F. Supp. at 3; Eagle Horse v. FBI, No. 92-2357, slip op. at 1, 5 (D.D.C. July 28, 1995); LeGrand v. FBI, No. 94-0300, slip op. at 12 (S.D.N.Y. July 10, 1995); Linn, 1995 WL 417810, at *11; Putnam, 873 F. Supp. at 716; Landano, 873 F. Supp. at 888.

[63] See, e.g., Ibarra-Cortez v. DEA, 36 F. App'x 598, 598 (9th Cir. 2002);
(continued...)

tional security,[67] loan sharking and gambling,[68] armed bank robbery,[69] bribery,[70] interstate transportation of stolen property,[71] tax evasion,[72] kidnap-

---

[63](...continued)
Mays, 234 F.3d 1324; Bell, 1993 U.S. App. LEXIS 27235, at *5; Mendoza, 2006 WL 3734365, at *6; McCoy, 2006 WL 463106, at *11; Queen v. Gonzales, No. 96-1387, 2005 WL 3204160, at *5 (D.D.C. Nov. 15, 2005); Gonzalez, 2005 WL 3201009, at *9; Jones, 2005 WL 1902880, at *4; Butler, 368 F. Supp. 2d at 786; Juste v. U.S. Dep't of Justice, No. 03-723, slip op. at 12 (D.D.C. Jan. 30, 2004); Barreiro v. Executive Office for U.S. Attorneys, No. 03-0720, 2004 WL 2451753, at *9 (D.D.C. Dec. 31, 2003); Rubis v. DEA, No. 01-1132, slip op. at 6 (D.D.C. Sept. 30, 2002); Rugiero, 234 F. Supp. 2d at 702; Gansterer, No. 95-1614, slip op. at 16, 21 (C.D. Cal. July 6, 1998); McNamera, 974 F. Supp. at 963; Jimenez, 938 F. Supp. at 29; Perrone, 908 F. Supp. at 27; Delviscovo, 903 F. Supp. at 3; Badalamenti, 899 F. Supp. at 549; Linn, 1995 WL 417810, at *11.

[64] See, e.g., Rugiero, 234 F. Supp. 2d at 702; Perrone, 908 F. Supp. at 27; Delviscovo, 903 F. Supp. at 3.

[65] See Mendoza, 2006 WL 3734365, at *6; Rugiero, 234 F. Supp. 2d at 702; Perrone, 908 F. Supp. at 27.

[66] See, e.g., Judicial Watch, Inc. v. Reno, No. 00-0723, 2001 WL 1902811, at *9 (D.D.C. Mar. 30, 2001) (finding implied confidentiality to be established for "confidential informant who reported a possible terrorist threat against the INS Miami District Office"); Blanton v. U.S. Dep't of Justice, 63 F. Supp. 2d 35, 49 (D.D.C. 1999) (finding implied confidentiality for sources who assisted in an investigation of a bombing of an African-American church "during a time of great unrest in the South"), on motion for partial reconsideration, 182 F. Supp. 2d 81, 88 (D.D.C. 2002), aff'd, 64 F. App'x 787 (D.C. Cir. 2003); Ajluni v. FBI, 947 F. Supp. 599, 602, 606 (N.D.N.Y. 1996); Steinberg v. U.S. Dep't of Justice, No. 93-2409, slip op. at 24 (D.D.C. Oct. 31, 1995).

[67] See Campbell, 1996 WL 554511, at *9 (finding an implied confidential relationship "given the customary trust" that exists for relaying information between nonfederal and foreign law enforcement agencies and the FBI); Pinnavaia, No. 03-112, slip op. at 14 (D.D.C. Feb. 25, 2004).

[68] See Delviscovo, 903 F. Supp. at 3.

[69] See Jennings, No. 03-1651, slip op. at 18 (D.D.C. May 6, 2004) (finding that sources who provided information regarding details of bank robbery are entitled to "implied confidentiality" to protect their identities); Anderson v. U.S. Dep't of Justice, No. 95-1880, 1999 U.S. Dist. LEXIS 5048, at *9 n.8 (D.D.C. Apr. 12, 1999) (finding Exemption 7(D) properly applied when witnesses to armed bank robbery provided information during police line-up).

[70] See Melius v. Nat'l Indian Gaming Comm'n, No. 98-2210, 1999 U.S.
(continued...)

ping,[73] financial crimes,[74] corruption by law enforcement officials of state and local governments,[75] and passport fraud and contempt of Congress.[76] Courts also have found that a possibility of retaliation exists for paid infor-

---

[70](...continued)
Dist. LEXIS 17537, at *17-18 (D.D.C. Nov. 3, 1999) (holding that criminal investigation involving allegations of bribery suggests an implied promise of confidentiality).

[71] See Delviscovo, 903 F. Supp. at 3.

[72] See McQueen v. United States, 264 F. Supp. 2d 502, 523 (S.D. Tex. 2003) (holding that a diesel tax fraud operation inspired "very real" fear in agency's confidential sources, and then reasoning that "[t]his particular kind of tax fraud -- involving big dollars, complex operations, vast numbers of transactions, and many people -- is not qualitatively unlike other crimes on the 'categorical list,' such as organized crime, loan sharking and gambling, and bribery").

[73] See Hale, 226 F.3d at 1204-05; Canning v. U.S. Dep't of Justice, No. 01-2215, slip op. at 13 (D.D.C. Mar. 9, 2004) (concluding that agency had "adequate justification for nondisclosure" due to nature of kidnapping information contained in responsive documents); Piper v. U.S. Dep't of Justice, 294 F. Supp. 2d 16, 29 (D.D.C. 2003); cf. Oliver, No. 02-0012, slip op. at 8 (D.D.C. Mar. 8, 2004) (concluding that agency failed to demonstrate confidential source's relation to the kidnapping crime to warrant "implied confidentiality"), summary judgment granted (D.D.C. Nov. 15, 2004) (holding, after in camera review, that FBI properly invoked Exemption 7(D) to withhold entire records).

[74] See LaRouche, No. 90-2753, slip op. at 11-12 (D.D.C. Nov. 17, 2000). But see also Billington, 233 F.3d at 586 n.7 (stating in dicta that "[w]e have doubts that [the LaRouche political organization's] members' participation in financial crimes [after the organization publicly disavowed violence], without more, would support an inference that sources received an implied assurance of confidentiality"); Canning, No. 01-2215, slip op. at 11 (D.D.C. Mar. 9, 2004) (reasoning that "the prior convictions of members of the LaRouche organization for financial crimes does not rise to the level of creating . . . an implied assurance of confidentiality"); Davis v. U.S. Dep't of Justice, No. 00-2457, slip op. at 20 (D.D.C. Mar. 21, 2003) (requiring agency to provide more detail regarding circumstances of interviews with sources for nonviolent financial crimes).

[75] See Garcia, 181 F. Supp. 2d at 377 (finding implied confidentiality in a case involving "investigation . . . into serious allegations of corruption within the state police").

[76] See Schrecker, 74 F. Supp. 2d at 35 (upbraiding requester for "cavalier suggestion" that "passport fraud and contempt of Congress are not serious enough crimes to warrant . . . implied confidentiality").

mants,[77] for anonymous sources,[78] and for symbol-numbered sources.[79]

Moreover, implied confidentiality has been found where former members of targeted organizations disclosed self-incriminating information,[80] where sources provided information as a result of plea-bargains,[81] where sources provided information in response to a subpoena,[82] where sources were interviewed during an unfair labor practice investigation,[83] and where an employee provided information about an employer.[84] Additionally, the Court of Appeals for the Second Circuit found implied confidentiality for sources who furnished information in connection with a civil law enforcement investigation of a company that was alleged to have harassed homeless persons.[85]

---

[77] See, e.g., Jones, 41 F.3d at 248; Anderson, No. 92-0225, slip op. at 11 (W.D. Pa. May 18, 1994); Lesar, No. 92-2219, slip op. at 11 (D.D.C. Oct. 18, 1993).

[78] See, e.g., Ortiz, 70 F.3d at 733; Hamilton v. Weise, No. 95-1161, 1997 U.S. Dist. LEXIS 18900, at *28 (M.D. Fla. Oct. 1, 1997).

[79] See, e.g., Jones, 41 F.3d at 248; Tamayo v. U.S. Dep't of Justice, 932 F. Supp. 342, 345 (D.D.C. 1996), summary affirmance granted, No. 96-5234, 1997 U.S. App. LEXIS 16367 (D.C. Cir. May 22, 1997); Putnam, 873 F. Supp. at 716.

[80] See Campbell, 1996 WL 554511, at *9.

[81] See Homick, No. 98-0557, slip op. at 8 (N.D. Cal. Oct. 27, 2004) (finding that "informant and attorney [names] are properly withheld under Exemption 7(D) due to an inference of confidentiality from the proffer discussion"); Engelking v. DEA, No. 91-0165, 1997 U.S. Dist. LEXIS 1881, at *6 (D.D.C. Feb. 21, 1997) (finding implied confidentiality and observing that plea bargains frequently are only way to obtain information about other suspected criminals).

[82] See LaRouche v. U.S. Dep't of Justice, No. 90-2753, slip op. at 15 (D.D.C. Aug. 8, 2002) (stating that "the need for a subpoena indicates the desire for confidentiality").

[83] See Means v. Segal, No. 97-1301, slip op. at 14-15 (D.D.C. Mar. 18, 1998) (magistrate's recommendation) (finding withholding consistent with written policy of FLRA), adopted (D.D.C. Apr. 14, 1998), aff'd per curiam on other grounds, No. 98-5170 (D.C. Cir. Oct. 6, 1998).

[84] See, e.g., Government Accountability Project, No. 86-3201, slip op. at 9-10 (D.D.C. June 30, 1993).

[85] Grand Cent. P'ship, 166 F.3d at 487-88 (stating that "[t]hough the HUD investigation was civil in nature, the allegations of misconduct contained in the sources' documents are 'serious and damaging' and led to the impo-

(continued...)

Some courts, however, have found the agency attestations before them as to the circumstances surrounding a claim of implied confidentiality to be insufficient, holding that a more "specific" showing as to the nature of the crime and the source's relation to it is required under <u>Landano</u>.[86] For

---

[85](...continued)
sition of civil sanctions" and reasoning that "[i]f the identities of the sources . . . were disclosed, they would face an objectively real and substantial risk of retaliation, reprisal or harassment").

[86] <u>See, e.g.</u>, <u>Billington</u>, 233 F.3d at 585-86 (instructing the FBI on remand to "supply evidence that informants predicated their assistance on an implied assurance of confidentiality" where the organization about which information was provided had "publicly disavowed violence"); <u>Neely</u>, 208 F.3d at 467 (remanding with observation that "district court would be well within its discretion to require the FBI . . . to fully shoulder its responsibility -- which to date it has not done -- to provide specific justifications" for claim of implied confidentiality); <u>Hale</u>, 99 F.3d at 1033 (finding that government's claim of implied confidentiality lacked particularized justification); <u>DiPietro</u>, 357 F. Supp. 2d at 186 (rejecting agency's unsupported assertion of expressed and implied assurances of confidentiality); <u>Raulerson v. Ashcroft</u>, 271 F. Supp. 2d 17, 27 (D.D.C. 2002) (ruling that "the dispositive issue must be . . . more than simply whether the crime is violent," and that an agency cannot generalize circumstances from one source to all but rather must demonstrate fear of retaliation for each source); <u>Morales Cozier v. FBI</u>, No. 1:99-0312, slip op. at 19 (N.D. Ga. Sept. 25, 2000) (holding that the FBI's "mere[] state[ment] that the sources were associates or acquaintances of plaintiff with knowledge of her activities" is insufficient to justify an inference of confidentiality); <u>Hall v. U.S. Dep't of Justice</u>, 26 F. Supp. 2d 78, 81 (D.D.C. 1998) (finding that "FBI's generalized assertion of crimes relating to Communist Party activities is not enough to support . . . 'reasonable assumption'" that sources expected confidentiality); <u>Kern v. FBI</u>, No. 94-0208, slip op. at 11-12 (C.D. Cal. Sept. 14, 1998) (stating that agency's justification for the application of Exemption 7(D) is "vague and fails to sufficiently describe the circumstances from which an inference of implied confidentiality could be made"); <u>see also</u> <u>Computer Prof'ls</u>, 72 F.3d at 906 (holding that agency offered no evidence that fear of retaliation was "sufficiently widespread" to justify inference of confidentiality for sources of information and information they provided); <u>Ajluni v. FBI</u>, No. 94-CV-325, slip op. at 13 (N.D.N.Y. July 13, 1996) (finding agency's statements "unacceptably conclusory" when circumstances surrounding its receipt of information were not described), <u>summary judgment granted</u>, 947 F. Supp. 599, 606 (N.D.N.Y. 1996) (holding, after in camera review, that information was provided under implied assurance of confidentiality). <u>But see</u> <u>Blanton v. Dep't of Justice</u>, 64 F. App'x 787, 790 (D.C. Cir. 2003) (relying on FBI affidavits regarding the nature of the crime to find that "<u>Landano</u> does not require that both the nature of the crime and the relationship of the source must be investigated in all implied confidentiality situations; instead it only emphasized that the government could not rely on a blanket presumption that all infor-
(continued...)

example, the Court of Appeals for the First Circuit has held that "[i]t is not enough . . . for the government simply to state blandly that the source's relationship to the crime permits an inference of confidentiality. Rather, the government has an obligation to spell out that relationship . . . [without] compromising the very interests it is seeking to protect."[87]

Therefore, law enforcement agencies seeking to invoke Exemption 7(D) for "implied confidentiality" sources must specifically address both factors in order to meet Landano's higher evidentiary standard on a case-by-case basis.[88] The Supreme Court specifically stated that when "institutional" sources -- such as local law enforcement agencies and private commercial enterprises -- are involved, greater disclosure should occur, because these sources typically provide a "wide variety of information" under circumstances that do not necessarily warrant confidentiality.[89] Accordingly, federal agencies now have the burden of determining and proving through the use of detailed affidavits in litigation that cooperating law enforcement agencies have provided information under either an express[90] or an implied

---

[86](...continued)
mation . . . was covered by an implied confidentiality agreement").

[87] Church of Scientology Int'l, 30 F.3d at 224.

[88] 508 U.S. at 180; see also FOIA Update, Vol. XIV, No. 3, at 10 (discussing Landano evidentiary requirements).

[89] 508 U.S. at 176; see, e.g., Hale, 99 F.3d at 1033 (finding that agency did not adequately justify withholding information provided by commercial and financial institutions); Linn, 1995 WL 417810, at *32 (noting that agency disclosed "much of the information it previously withheld . . . in light of Landano," but ordering disclosure of institutional source document, "particularly in light of the fact that this document obviously originated from the Louisiana state authorities, and the application of Exemption 7(D) depends on the source of the information rather than its contents"); see also FOIA Update, Vol. XIV, No. 3, at 10 (discussing applicability of Landano standards to "institutional" sources).

[90] See, e.g., Peltier, 2005 WL 735964, at *16 (finding that "the FBI had an agreement with foreign law enforcement agencies that expressly forbids dissemination of information provided to the FBI"); Maydak v. U.S. Dep't of Justice, 254 F. Supp. 2d 23, 44 (D.D.C. 2003) (finding that subsequent statements by local law enforcement agency source requesting confidentiality were insufficient to establish express confidentiality as of time that information was provided); LaRouche, No. 90-2753, slip op. at 21 (D.D.C. July 5, 2001) (finding express confidentiality where agency affidavit "sufficiently details the relationships the FBI has with the foreign governments in question, . . . specifically refers to written agreements the agency has with these governments, . . . explains the differing types of agreements the agency has with governments[,] and details the levels of restriction gov-

(continued...)

promise of confidentiality.[91]

Before Landano, there existed conflict in the case law as to the availability of Exemption 7(D) protection for sources who were advised that they might be called to testify if a trial eventually were to take place.[92] However, in Landano, the Supreme Court resolved this conflict by holding that "[a] source should be deemed confidential if the source furnished information with the understanding that the [agency] would not divulge the communication except to the extent . . . thought necessary for law enforcement purposes."[93] (It should be noted that the effect of a source's actual

---

[90](...continued)
ernments place on the release of information given to the FBI"); Linn, 1995 WL 417810, at *32 (ruling that agency's conclusory attestation that "'policy of confidentiality . . . between [local and federal] law enforcement justifies nondisclosure' . . . [is] insufficient to justify withholding").

[91] See, e.g., Davin, No. 98-3343, slip op. at 9 (3d Cir. Jan. 27, 1999) (upholding a finding of implied assurances of confidentiality for state or local bureaus or agencies and a financial institution "accustomed to maintaining confidential files, and as to which a policy of routinely granting confidentiality was cited"); Savage v. FBI, No. C2-90-797, slip op. at 15 (S.D. Ohio Mar. 8, 1996) (finding implied confidentiality when the agency attested that local law enforcement authorities suggested that they might "revisit the extent of their cooperation with the FBI if confidentiality is not maintained") aff'd, 124 F.3d 199 (6th Cir. 1997) (unpublished table decision); Beard v. Dep't of Justice, 917 F. Supp. 61, 63 (D.D.C. 1996) (finding implied confidentiality when the agency attested that "[t]he FBI requested permission from the [local law enforcement agency] to release the information [and t]he request was denied"); Putnam, 873 F. Supp. at 717 (finding implied confidentiality when the agency attested that "documents provided by [state police] are not accessible to the public absent authorization from the state law enforcement agency"); Cucci v. DEA, 871 F. Supp. 508, 513 (D.D.C. 1994) (finding implied confidentiality when the agency attested that a document was stamped "not to be distributed outside your agency" and a state police representative stated that state police "provide . . . law enforcement records to other agencies based upon an express understanding of confidentiality"); see also FOIA Update, Vol. XIV, No. 3, at 10 (advising agencies that they should pay particular attention under Landano to "institutional sources").

[92] Compare Van Bourg, Allen, Weinberg & Roger v. NLRB, 751 F.2d 982, 986 (9th Cir. 1985) (no confidentiality recognized), and Poss v. NLRB, 565 F.2d 654, 658 (10th Cir. 1977) (same), with Irons, 811 F.2d at 687 (confidentiality recognized), Schmerler, 900 F.2d at 339 (same), and United Techs., 777 F.2d at 95 (same).

[93] 508 U.S. at 174 (clarifying that "'confidential,' as used in Exemption 7(D), refers to a degree of confidentiality less than total secrecy"); see also
(continued...)

<u>testimony</u> upon continued Exemption 7(D) protection presents a distinctly different issue,[94] which is addressed below together with other issues regarding waiver of this exemption.)

The first clause of Exemption 7(D), with respect to any civil or criminal law enforcement records, focuses upon the identity of a confidential source, rather than the information furnished by the source. The 1974 legislative history of Exemption 7(D), though, plainly evidences Congress's intention to absolutely and comprehensively protect the identity of anyone who provided information to a government agency in confidence.[95] Thus, this exemption's first clause protects "both the identity of the informer and information which might reasonably be found to lead to disclosure of such identity."[96] Consequently, the courts have readily recognized that the first clause of Exemption 7(D) safeguards not only such obviously identifying information as an informant's name and address,[97] but also all information that would "tend to reveal" the source's identity,[98] including telephone

---

[93](...continued)
<u>Leveto v. IRS</u>, No. 98-285, 2001 U.S. Dist. LEXIS 5791, at *20 (W.D. Pa. Apr. 10, 2001) (finding confidentiality established for sources who were "assured that their identities would not be disclosed except to the extent necessary to obtain a search warrant, or at a future grand jury proceeding or criminal trial"); <u>Jefferson v. O'Brien</u>, No. 96-1365, slip op. at 2 (D.D.C. July 3, 2000) (rejecting as inconsequential "[p]laintiff's evidence that law enforcement officers recognized the potential need to have confidential informants available to testify at trial when they were interviewed").

[94] <u>See</u> <u>Parker</u>, 934 F.2d at 381 (distinguishing cases in which a source actually testifies from cases "consider[ing] whether a source, knowing he is likely to testify at the time he furnishes information to [an] agency, is, or remains after testimony, a 'confidential source'").

[95] <u>See</u> S. Conf. Rep. No. 93-1200, at 13.

[96] 120 Cong. Rec. 17033 (1974) (statement of Sen. Hart).

[97] <u>See, e.g.</u>, <u>Cuccaro</u>, 770 F.2d at 359-60; <u>Piper</u>, 2005 WL 1384337, at *6 (protecting name and address); <u>Crooker v. IRS</u>, No. 94-0755, 1995 WL 430605, at *6 (D.D.C. Apr. 27, 1995) (protecting names and addresses); <u>Ferreira v. DEA</u>, 874 F. Supp. 15, 16 (D.D.C. 1995) (protecting names); <u>Cleveland & Vicinity Dist. Council v. U.S. Dep't of Labor</u>, No. 1:87-2384, slip op. at 12-14 (N.D. Ohio Apr. 22, 1992) (magistrate's recommendation) (protecting names and addresses), <u>adopted</u> (N.D. Ohio May 11, 1992).

[98] <u>See</u> <u>Pollard v. FBI</u>, 705 F.2d 1151, 1155 (9th Cir. 1983) (holding that entire document properly was withheld where disclosure "would tend to reveal [source's] identity"); <u>Ajluni</u>, 947 F. Supp. at 606 (finding information properly withheld where disclosure could result in narrowing sources "to a limited group of individuals"); <u>Mavadia v. Caplinger</u>, No. 95-3542, 1996 WL 592742, at *3 (E.D. La. Oct. 11, 1996) (ordering protection for information

(continued...)

numbers,[99] the time and place of events or meetings,[100] and information provided by the source that could allow the source's identity to be deduced.[101]

---

[98](...continued)
that would identify informants); Kitchen v. FBI, No. 93-2382, slip op. at 13 (D.D.C. Mar. 18, 1996) (ruling that "Exemption 7(D) protects more than the names of confidential sources; it protects information . . . that might identify such sources"); see, e.g., Lodi v. IRS, No. 96-2095, slip op. at 4-5 (E.D. Cal. Apr. 14, 1998) (finding entire pages of material properly withheld because release would disclose identity of confidential source); Spirko, No. 96-0458, slip op. at 2 (D.D.C. Apr. 11, 1997) (ruling that agency properly withheld location where certain event took place and specific information imparted by informant because release would allow a "knowledgeable person to deduce informant's identity"), aff'd on other grounds, 147 F.3d 992 (D.C. Cir. 1998); Doe v. U.S. Dep't of Justice, 790 F. Supp. 17, 21 (D.D.C. 1992) (stating that where source is well known to investigated applicant, agency must protect "even the most oblique indications of identity"); Palacio v. U.S. Dep't of Justice, No. 00-1564, 2002 U.S. Dist. LEXIS 2198, at *25 n.15 (D.D.C. Feb. 8, 2002) (permitting withholding of cooperating witness' "aliases, date of birth, address, identification numbers, . . . physical description, and [information which sets] forth his or her involvement in other investigations"), summary affirmance granted, No. 02-5247, 2003 U.S. App. LEXIS 1804 (D.C. Cir. Jan. 31, 2003).

[99] See Crooker, 1995 WL 430605, at *6 (determining that the agency properly "deleted . . . telephone numbers, recent activities, and other information tending to reveal the identity of confidential informants").

[100] See, e.g., Halpern, No. 94-365A(F), slip op. at 25-26 (W.D.N.Y. Aug. 31, 2001) (protecting times and places that information was obtained); Accuracy in Media v. FBI, No. 97-2107, slip op. at 5 (D.D.C. Mar. 31, 1999) (reasoning that "an informant may be identified by . . . dates, times, places, events, or names connected with certain cases").

[101] See, e.g., Ibarra-Cortez, 36 F. App'x at 598 (withholding documents where the requester "might be able to deduce the identity of the informants because they deal with specific events and circumstances"); Hale, 226 F.3d at 1204 n.2 (finding that "public dissemination of the documents [supplied by sources] would reveal the[ir] identit[ies]" because the "case took place in a small town where most everyone knew everyone else"); Billington v. Dep't of Justice, 69 F. Supp. 2d 128, 138 (D.D.C. 1999) (finding that the "FBI is well within its rights to withhold [the city of origin of various teletypes] where revealing the city would reveal the identity of the source," and protecting the identities of foreign agencies that requested law enforcement information where disclosure would "reveal that they have also agreed to provide such information in return" and therefore would "betray these foreign entities' status as confidential sources"), aff'd in pertinent part, vacated in part & remanded on other grounds, 233 F.3d 581 (D.C. Cir. 2000); see

(continued...)

**EXEMPTION 7(D)**

Accordingly, protection for source-identifying information, such as source symbol numbers,[102] extends well beyond information that is merely a substitute for the source's name; for example, as necessary to prevent indirect identification of a source, even the name of a third party who is not a confidential source -- but who acted as an intermediary for the source in his dealings with the agency -- can be withheld.[103] And when circumstances warrant, a law enforcement agency may employ a "Glomar" response -- refusing to confirm or deny the very existence of records about a particular individual or possible source entity -- if a more specific response to a narrowly targeted request would reflect the fact of whether he, she, or it acted as a confidential source.[104]

---

[101](...continued)
also Judicial Watch, Inc. v. FBI, No. 00-745, slip op. at 14 (D.D.C. Apr. 20, 2001) (recognizing the "substantial likelihood in many cases that the identity of a source can be determined from an analysis of the information furnished by the source himself, especially where the analysis is made by a person familiar with the facts and circumstances on which the investigation is predicated"); cf. Alirez v. NLRB, 676 F.2d 423, 427 (10th Cir. 1982) (protecting identifying information that could "potentially subject[] Board informants . . . to . . . reprisals" due to close familiarity within the workplace setting) (Exemption 7(C)); Harry v. Dep't of the Army, No. 92-1654, slip op. at 9 (D.D.C. Sept. 10, 1993) (finding segregation of ROTC personnel records impossible given small size of campus ROTC program) (Exemption 6).

[102] See Brunetti, 357 F. Supp. 2d at 107 (holding "that the FBI's internal numbering system for confidential informants is appropriately withheld . . . especially when release might lead to discovery of confidential informant's identity"); Halpern, No. 94-365A(F), slip op. at 25-26 (W.D.N.Y. Aug. 31, 2001) (accepting FBI's assertion that release of source symbol designations would permit "individuals who were the target of the investigations . . . to determine dates, times and places that information pertaining to them was obtained, resulting in knowledge as to the informant's identity"); Accuracy in Media, No. 97-2107, slip op. at 5 (D.D.C. Mar. 31, 1999) (reasoning that if informant symbol numbers "were routinely released, over time an informant may be identified by revealing the informant's connections with dates, times, places, events, or names connected with certain cases"); Putnam, 873 F. Supp. at 716 (finding "coded identification numbers, file numbers and information that could be used to identify sources" properly withheld); see also Lesar, 636 F.2d at 485-86 (reasoning that Exemption 2 was properly applied in tandem with Exemption 7(D) to provide necessary source protection in face of requester's avowed purpose of correlating information in manner that would risk source).

[103] See Birch, 803 F.2d at 1212; United Techs., 777 F.2d at 95.

[104] See, e.g., Benavides v. DEA, 769 F. Supp. 380, 381-82 (D.D.C. 1990), rev'd & remanded on procedural grounds, 968 F.2d 1243 (D.C. Cir.), modified, 976 F.2d 751 (D.C. Cir. 1992).

Even greater source-identification protection is provided by the "(c)(2) exclusion,"[105] which permits a criminal law enforcement agency to entirely exclude records from the FOIA under specified circumstances when necessary to avoid divulging the existence of a source relationship. (See the discussion of this provision under Exclusions, below.) Additionally, information provided by a source may be withheld under this first clause of Exemption 7(D) wherever disclosure of that information would permit the "linking" of a source to specific source-provided material.[106]

The second clause of Exemption 7(D) first broadly protects all information furnished to criminal law enforcement authorities by confidential sources[107] in the course of criminal investigations.[108] Thus, the statutory requirement of an "investigation," while not a component of Exemption 7's threshold language, is "a predicate of exemption under the second clause of paragraph (D)."[109] For the purposes of this clause, criminal law enforcement authorities include federal agencies' inspectors general.[110]

---

[105] 5 U.S.C. § 552(c)(2).

[106] See L&C Marine, 740 F.2d at 923-25; see, e.g., Stone v. Def. Investigative Serv., 816 F. Supp. 782, 788 (D.D.C. 1993) (protecting "information so singular that to release it would likely identify the individual"); Barrett v. OSHA, No. C2-90-147, slip op. at 13 (S.D. Ohio Oct. 18, 1990) (protecting statements obtained from witnesses regarding single incident involving only three or four persons).

[107] See Ferguson, 957 F.2d at 1069 (finding that "[o]nce it is shown that information was provided by a confidential source [during a criminal or lawful national security intelligence investigation], the information itself is protected from disclosure, despite the fact that there is no danger that the identity of the source could be divulged"); Reiter v. DEA, No. 96-0378, 1997 WL 470108, at *6-7 (D.D.C. Aug. 13, 1997) (holding all source-supplied information protectible under Exemption 7(D)'s second clause when source is confidential), summary affirmance granted, No. 97-5246, 1998 WL 202247 (D.C. Cir. Mar. 3, 1998).

[108] See Shaw, 749 F.2d at 63-65 (articulating standard for determining if law enforcement undertaking satisfies "criminal investigation" threshold); see also Pray v. Dep't of Justice, No. 95-5383, 1996 WL 734142, at *1 (D.C. Cir. Nov. 20, 1996) (per curiam) (upholding agency's use of Exemption 7(D) for source information); Kuffel, 882 F. Supp. at 1126 ("qualifying criminal investigation" exists when "FBI gather[s] information on criminals who violated specific state crimes for the purpose of using the information as possible leads in investigations of robberies and burglaries that could be in violation of federal law").

[109] Keys, 830 F.2d at 343.

[110] See Ortiz, 70 F.3d at 732 (ruling that Exemption 7(D) properly applied when "HHS's Office of Inspector General . . . use[d anonymous] letter to

(continued...)

## EXEMPTION 7(D)

In an important elaboration on the definition of a "criminal investigation," courts have recognized that information originally compiled by local law enforcement authorities in conjunction with a nonfederal criminal investigation fully retains its criminal investigatory character when subsequently obtained by federal authorities,[111] even if received solely for use in a federal civil enforcement proceeding.[112] In addition, protection for source-provided information has been extended to information supplied to federal officials by state or local enforcement authorities seeking assistance in pursuing a nonfederal investigation.[113]

The second clause of Exemption 7(D) additionally protects "records or information compiled for law enforcement purposes . . . by an agency conducting a lawful national security intelligence investigation" that "could reasonably be expected to disclose the identity of a confidential source and . . . information furnished by a confidential source."[114] This broad national security clause applies to any agency and covers all law enforcement in-

---

[110](...continued)
launch a criminal investigation"); Providence Journal, 981 F.2d at 563 n.13 (deeming inspectors general same as criminal law enforcement authorities); Brant Constr., 778 F.2d at 1265 (recognizing "substantial similarities between the activities of the FBI and the OIGs").

[111] See Harvey v. U.S. Dep't of Justice, 747 F. Supp. 29, 38 (D.D.C. 1990).

[112] See Martinez v. EEOC, No. 04-0391, 2004 WL 2359895, at *2 (W.D. Tex. Oct. 19, 2004) (rejecting plaintiff's argument that Exemption 7(D) should not apply to EEOC civil investigations); Cleveland, No. 1:87-2384, slip op. at 12 n.3 (N.D. Ohio Apr. 22, 1992) (holding that Exemption 7(D) "clearly applies to information obtained from confidential sources in all investigations, both civil and criminal"); Dayo v. INS, No. C-2-83-1422, slip op. at 5-6 (S.D. Ohio Dec. 31, 1985).

[113] See, e.g., Hopkinson, 866 F.2d at 1222 (protecting state law enforcement agency's request for FBI laboratory evaluation of evidence submitted by state agency and results of FBI's analysis); Gordon, 790 F. Supp. at 377-78 (emphasizing that "when a state law enforcement agency sends material to an FBI lab for testing, confidentiality is 'inherently implicit'" and that "all information from another agency must be protected to provide the confidence necessary to law enforcement cooperation"); Rojem v. U.S. Dep't of Justice, 775 F. Supp. 6, 12 (D.D.C. 1991) (finding that disclosure of criminal files provided to FBI by state authorities "would unduly discourage" states from enlisting FBI's assistance), appeal dismissed for failure to timely file, No. 92-5088 (D.C. Cir. Nov. 4, 1992); Payne v. U.S. Dep't of Justice, 722 F. Supp. 229, 231 (E.D. Pa. 1989) (stating that "requirement is met . . . [when] the documents sought are FBI laboratory and fingerprint examinations of evidence collected by local law enforcement agencies"), aff'd, 904 F.2d 695 (3d Cir. 1990) (unpublished table decision).

[114] 5 U.S.C. § 552(b)(7)(D).

formation either identifying or that was provided by the confidential source.[115] Protection for sources under this clause of Exemption 7(D) has readily been found in cases regarding domestic terrorism,[116] foreign intelligence services,[117] agents of foreign governments,[118] and national security investigations.[119] No court has ever found a lawful national security intelligence investigation not to involve a law enforcement purpose.[120]

Although courts considering an agency's use of this clause of Exemption 7(D) may require an agency to establish that a particular investigation is related to national security or intelligence activities, "substantial deference" is given to an agency regarding national security concerns.[121] Such

---

[115] See Attorney General's 1986 Amendments Memorandum at 14; see also NARA v. Favish, 541 U.S. 157, 169 (evincing the Supreme Court's reliance on "the Attorney General's consistent interpretation of" the FOIA in successive Attorney General memoranda), reh'g denied, 541 U.S. 1057 (2004).

[116] See, e.g., Judicial Watch, 2001 WL 1902811, at *9; Blanton, 63 F. Supp. 2d at 49; Ajluni, 947 F. Supp. at 602; Steinberg, No. 93-2409, slip op. at 24 (D.D.C. Oct. 31, 1995).

[117] See Meeropol v. Smith, No. 75-1121, slip op. at 76-78 (D.D.C. Feb. 29, 1984) (protecting information obtained during intelligence investigations), aff'd in pertinent part & remanded in part on other grounds sub nom. Meeropol v. Meese, 790 F.2d 942 (D.C. Cir. 1986); Campbell, 1996 WL 554511, at *9 (finding implied confidentiality for foreign law enforcement agencies); Shaw, 749 F.2d at 62 (same); Pinnavaia, No. 03-112, slip op. at 14 (D.D.C. Feb. 25, 2004) (finding that "the agreement between New Scotland Yard and the FBI expressly forbids the disclosure of information provided to the FBI").

[118] See Hogan v. Huff, No. 00 Civ. 6753, 2002 WL 1359722, at *11 (S.D.N.Y. June 21, 2002) (finding that law enforcement purpose exists where documents were gathered to determine if subject was unregistered agent for Cuban Government).

[119] See Hudson, 2005 WL 1656909, at *5 (finding that the FBI "has an agreement with this confidential . . . source under which security and/or criminal law enforcement information is exchanged"); Pinnavaia, No. 03-112, slip op. at 12 (D.D.C. Feb. 25, 2004).

[120] Cf. Weissman v. CIA, 565 F.2d 692, 695 (D.C. Cir. 1977) (concluding that because "[t]he Agency simply has no [legal] authority in the guise of law enforcement," records compiled for "background checks" are not protected by Exemption 7).

[121] Hogan, 2002 WL 1359722, at *11 ("Courts have a 'well-settled' obligation to grant 'substantial deference' to agency affidavits that implicate national security." (quoting Doherty v. U.S. Dep't of Justice, 775 F.2d 49, 52

(continued...)

agency deference is similar to that given under Exemptions 1 and 3.[122] (For a further discussion of this point, see Exemption 1, Deference to Agency Expertise, above.)

Under the case law, the confidential source information that falls within the broad coverage of this second clause of Exemption 7(D) need not necessarily be source-identifying.[123] Thus, under the second clause of Exemption 7(D), courts have permitted the withholding of confidential information even after the source's identity has been officially divulged or acknowledged,[124] or when the requester knows the source's identity.[125] Simi-

---

[121](...continued)
(2d Cir. 1985) (Exemption 7(C))); cf. Ctr. for Nat'l Sec. Studies v. U.S. Dep't of Justice, 331 F.3d 918, 926-27 (D.C. Cir. 2003) (granting deference to agency for national-security related Exemption 7(A) concerns specifically, and discussing such deference for FOIA exemptions in general (citing Zadvydas v. Davis, 533 U.S. 678, 696 (2001) (non-FOIA, terrorism-related case); CIA v. Sims, 471 U.S. 159, 180 (1985) (Exemption 3); McGehee v. Casey, 718 F.2d 1137, 1148 (D.C. Cir. 1983) (Exemption 1))).

[122] See Ctr. for Nat'l Sec. Studies, 331 F.3d at 927-28 (stating more broadly that "[we cannot] conceive of any reason to limit deference to the executive in its area of expertise to certain FOIA exemptions so long as the government's declarations raise legitimate concerns that disclosure would impair national security").

[123] See, e.g., Parker, 934 F.2d at 375; Shaw, 749 F.2d at 61-62; Radowich v. U.S. Attorney, Dist. of Md., 658 F.2d 957, 964 (4th Cir. 1981); Duffin v. Carlson, 636 F.2d 709, 712 (D.C. Cir. 1980); Simon, 752 F. Supp. at 22; see also FOIA Update, Vol. XIV, No. 3, at 10 (pointing out breadth of Exemption 7(D) coverage). See generally Attorney General's Memorandum for Heads for All Federal Departments and Agencies Regarding the Freedom of Information Act (Oct. 12, 2001) [hereinafter Attorney General Ashcroft's FOIA Memorandum], reprinted in FOIA Post (posted 10/15/01) (underscoring the federal government's commitment to "enhancing the effectiveness of our law enforcement agencies").

[124] See, e.g., Neely, 208 F.3d at 466 (holding that district court erred to extent it denied withholding based on belief that Exemption 7(D) cannot be claimed to protect identities of confidential sources whose identities previously have been disclosed); Ferguson, 957 F.2d at 1068 (holding that the subsequent disclosure of a source's identity or of some of the information provided by the source does not require "full disclosure of information provided by such a source"); Cleary v. FBI, 811 F.2d 421, 423 (8th Cir. 1987) (rejecting plaintiff's argument that "the confidential source exemption is unavailable because the identities of the confidential sources have been disclosed to him by the FBI"); Shafmaster Fishing Co. v. United States, 814 F. Supp. 182, 185 (D.N.H. 1993) (ruling that source's identity or information provided need not be "secret" to justify withholding); Church of Scientology
(continued...)

larly, information provided by an anonymous source is eligible for protection.[126] Moreover, even when source-provided information has been revealed and the identities of some of the confidential sources have been independently divulged, Exemption 7(D) can protect against the matching of witnesses' names with the specific information that they supplied.[127]

---

[124](...continued)
v. IRS, 816 F. Supp. 1138, 1161 (W.D. Tex. 1993) (declaring it "irrelevant that the identity of the confidential source is known").

[125] See, e.g., Jones, 41 F.3d at 249 (explaining that Exemption 7(D) "focuses on the source's intent, not the world's knowledge"); Radowich, 658 F.2d at 960 (declaring that Exemption 7(D) applies even when "identities of confidential sources . . . [are] known"); see also L&C Marine, 740 F.2d at 923, 925 (noting that fact that employee witnesses "could be matched to their statements" does not diminish Exemption 7(D) protection); Keeney v. FBI, 630 F.2d 114, 119 n.2 (2d Cir. 1980) (ruling that Exemption 7(D) applies to "local law enforcement agencies [that] have now been identified"); Butler v. U.S. Dep't of Justice, Crim. Div., No. 02-0412, slip op. at 8 (D.D.C. Mar. 29, 2004) (finding Exemption 7(D) properly invoked to withhold information regardless of fact that confidential sources are known); Ortiz, No. 97-140-A-3, slip op. at 10 (M.D. La. Aug. 25, 1998) (stating that "[i]t is irrelevant that the identity of the confidential source is known"); Crooker, 1995 WL 430605, at *6 (stating that "an agency may withhold confidential information even if the requester or the public know[s] the source's identity"); Wickline v. FBI, No. 92-1189, 1994 WL 549756, at *4 n.8 (D.D.C. Sept. 30, 1994) (reiterating that "confidentiality is not waived or revoked when a [requester] already knows the protected names"); Shafmaster Fishing, 814 F. Supp. at 185 (stating that source's identity need not be secret to justify withholding information under Exemption 7(D)).

[126] See Ortiz, 70 F.3d at 735 (reasoning that extending confidentiality to anonymous hotline communications "reflects a common sense judgment" given the importance of encouraging public cooperation in combatting fraud); Providence Journal, 981 F.2d at 565-67 (extending confidentiality to unsolicited anonymous letters regarding investigation of officers in Rhode Island Army National Guard); Hamilton, 1997 U.S. Dist. LEXIS 18900, at *28 (finding it "reasonable to assume" that anonymous caller expected confidentiality); Mitchell v. Ralston, No. 81-4478, slip op. at 2 (S.D. Ill. Oct. 14, 1982) (ruling that anonymity of source does not negate confidentiality).

[127] See Spannaus v. U.S. Dep't of Justice, No. 92-0372, slip op. at 16 (D.D.C. June 20, 1995) (determining that any "plaintiff asserting a claim of prior disclosure must designate specific information in the public domain that duplicates what is being withheld"), summary affirmance granted in part, vacated in other part & remanded, No. 95-5267, 1996 WL 523814 (D.C. Cir. Aug. 16, 1996); Kirk v. U.S. Dep't of Justice, 704 F. Supp. 288, 293 (D.D.C. 1989); see also L&C Marine, 740 F.2d at 925 (ruling that the names of employee-witnesses in OSHA accident investigation were properly withheld...)

(continued...)

**EXEMPTION 7(D)**

Because the phrase "confidential information furnished only by the confidential source" sometimes caused confusion in the past, the 1986 FOIA amendments unequivocally clarified the congressional intent by deleting the word "confidential" as a modifier of "information" and omitting the word "only" from this formulation.[128] Even prior to that legislative change, courts regularly employed this portion of Exemption 7(D) to protect all information provided by a confidential source, both because such withholdings were anticipated by the language and legislative history of the statute,[129] and in recognition of the fact that disclosure of any of this material would jeopardize the system of confidentiality that ensures a free flow of information from sources to investigatory agencies.[130] Now, however, courts need look no further than the Act's literal language to see that all source-provided information is covered in criminal and national security in-

---

[127](...continued)
held "even if use of civil discovery procedures might provide plaintiffs-appellees with information sufficient to match the workers with their statements").

[128] See Freedom of Information Reform Act of 1986, Pub. L. No. 99-570, § 1802, 100 Stat. 3207, 3207-48; see also FOIA Update, Vol. VII, No. 4, at 3-6 (setting out statute in its amended form, interlineated to show exact changes made).

[129] See Irons, 880 F.2d at 1450-51.

[130] See id. at 1449; see also, e.g., Ortiz, 70 F.3d at 732 (reiterating that "Exemption 7(D) is meant to . . . 'encourage cooperation with law enforcement agencies by enabling the agencies to keep their informants' identities confidential'" (quoting United Techs., 777 F.2d at 94)); Duffin, 636 F.2d at 712-13 (reiterating Congress's belief that disclosure of confidential information would discourage cooperation from sources); Kennedy v. DEA, No. 92-2731, 1994 U.S. Dist. LEXIS 2275, at *14-15 (D.D.C. Feb. 28, 1994) (stating that release of information would "jeopardize [agency's] ability to conduct future law enforcement operations premised upon promises of confidentiality"); Biase, No. 93-2521, slip op. at 11 n.14 (D.N.J. Dec. 10, 1993) (stating that the "goal of Exemption 7(D) [is] to protect the ability of law enforcement agencies to obtain the cooperation of persons having relevant information"); Church of Scientology, 816 F. Supp. at 1161 (explaining that Exemption 7(D) was enacted "to ensure that the FOIA did not impair federal law enforcement agencies' ability to gather information"); Dayton Newspapers, Inc. v. FBI, No. C-3-85-815, slip op. at 13 (S.D. Ohio Feb. 9, 1993) (noting that the "purpose of Exemption 7(D) is to ensure that the FOIA did not impair the ability of federal law enforcement agencies to gather information, thus to ensure that information continued to flow to those agencies"); Shafmaster Fishing, 814 F. Supp. at 185 (stating that the object of Exemption 7(D) is "'not simply to protect the source, but also to protect the flow of information to the law enforcement agency'" (quoting Irons, 880 F.2d at 1449)).

vestigations.[131]

Once courts determine the existence of confidentiality under Exemption 7(D), they are reluctant to find a subsequent waiver of the exemption's protections.[132] This restraint stems both from the potentially adverse repercussions that may result from additional disclosures and from a recognition that any "judicial effort[] to create a 'waiver' exception" to exemption 7(D)'s language runs afoul of the statute's intent to provide "workable rules."[133] It therefore has been recognized that a waiver of Exemption 7(D)'s protections should be only found upon "'absolutely solid evidence showing that the source of an FBI interview in a law enforcement investigation has manifested complete disregard for confidentiality.'"[134]

Thus, even authorized or official disclosure of some information provided by a confidential source does not open the door to disclosure of any of the other information the source has provided.[135] In this vein, it is well

---

[131] See, e.g., Irons, 880 F.2d at 1448.

[132] See, e.g., Reiter, 1997 WL 470108, at *6 ("[O]nce an informant's confidentiality has been established, almost nothing can eviscerate Exemption 7(D) protection.").

[133] Parker, 934 F.2d at 380; see also Neely, 208 F.3d at 466 (observing that "the statute by its terms does not provide for . . . waiver"); Irons, 880 F.2d at 1455-56 (citing Reporters Comm., 489 U.S. at 779).

[134] Parker, 934 F.2d at 378 (quoting Dow Jones & Co. v. Dep't of Justice, 908 F.2d 1006, 1011 (D.C. Cir.), superseded, 917 F.2d 571 (D.C. Cir. 1990)); see, e.g., Billington, 69 F. Supp. 2d at 139 (concluding that plaintiff's allegation that source was "unafraid," even if true, does not constitute "absolutely solid evidence" that source "manifested complete disregard for confidentiality"); Billington, 11 F. Supp. 2d at 69 (finding that alleged source did not exhibit "complete disregard for confidentiality" by giving newspaper interview); Freeman v. U.S. Dep't of Justice, No. 92-0557, 1993 WL 260694, at *3-4 (D.D.C. June 28, 1993) (ruling that the "fact that federal, state, and local authorities were publicly cooperating in the . . . investigation, or that certain individuals publicly acknowledged that they were 'working closely' with the investigation . . . does not 'manifest complete disregard for confidentiality'"), vacated in other part on denial of reconsideration, No. 92-0557, 1994 WL 35871 (D.D.C. Jan. 26, 1994). But see Ray, 441 F. Supp. 2d at 37 (stating that court is not inclined to protect plaintiff's confidentiality, because plaintiff clearly stated that "he ha[d] waived any reliance he may have had" and that " FBI has no such duty to afford plaintiff" continued confidentiality against his will).

[135] See Brant Constr., 778 F.2d at 1265 n.8 (ruling that "subsequent disclosure of the information, either partially or completely, does not affect its exempt status under 7(D)"); Shaw, 749 F.2d at 62 (holding that "[d]isclosure
(continued...)

established that source-identifying and source-provided information remains protected even when some of it has been the subject of testimony in open court.[136] Moreover, in order to demonstrate a waiver by disclosure

---

[135](...continued)
of one piece of information received from a particular party -- and even the disclosure of that party as its source -- does not prevent that party from being a 'confidential source' for other purposes"); Johnson v. Dep't of Justice, 758 F. Supp. 2, 5 (D.D.C. 1991) (stating that the fact that someone made public statement concerning incident "does not constitute a waiver of the Bureau's confidential file [because a] . . . press account may be erroneous or false or, more likely, incomplete").

[136] See, e.g., Neely, 208 F.3d at 466 (recognizing that a source can "remain a 'confidential source' . . . even if the source's communication with [the agency] is subsequently disclosed at trial"); Jones, 41 F.3d at 249 (holding that Exemption 7(D) "provides for nondisclosure of all sources who provided information with an understanding of confidentiality, not for protection of only those sources whose identity remains a secret at the time of future FOIA litigation [because they do not testify]"); Davis v. U.S. Dep't of Justice, 968 F.2d 1276, 1281 (D.C. Cir. 1992) (concluding that an informant's testimony in open court did not "'waive the [government's] right to invoke Exemption 7(D)'" (quoting Parker, 934 F.2d at 379-80)); Ferguson, 957 F.2d at 1068 (affirming that local law enforcement officer does not lose status as confidential source by testifying in court); Parker, 934 F.2d at 379-81 (stating that "government agency is not required to disclose the identity of a confidential source or information conveyed to the agency in confidence in a criminal investigation notwithstanding the possibility that the informant may have testified at a public trial"); Irons, 880 F.2d at 1454 (recognizing that "[t]here is no reason grounded in fairness for requiring a source who disclosed information during testimony to reveal, against his will (or to have the FBI reveal for him), information that he did not disclose in public"); Kimberlin, 774 F.2d at 209 (determining that "disclosure [prior to or at trial] of information given in confidence does not render non-confidential any of the information originally provided"); Canning, No. 01-2215, slip op. at 12 (D.D.C. Mar. 9, 2004) (rejecting plaintiff's argument that confidentiality was waived by informant's subsequent act of testifying in court); Doolittle v. U.S. Dep't of Justice, 142 F. Supp. 2d 281, 285-86 (N.D.N.Y. 2001) (protecting identities of confidential sources that "prosecutors [had] disclosed . . . in open court during [plaintiff's] sentencing hearing"); Daniel v. U.S. Dep't of Justice, No. 99-2423, slip op. at 4 (D.D.C. Mar. 30, 2001) (holding that Exemption 7(D) remains applicable even though source information was "produced at or before trial pursuant to . . . criminal discovery rules"); Jefferson, No. 96-1365, slip op. at 2 (D.D.C. July 3, 2000); Coleman, 13 F. Supp. 2d at 82; Guerrero v. DEA, No. 93-2006, slip op. at 10 (D. Ariz. Feb. 21, 1996); Johnson, 1990 U.S. Dist. LEXIS 18358, at *8-9; see also LaRouche, No. 90-2753, slip op. at 12 (D.D.C. Nov. 17, 2000) (noting that an agency is not obliged to identify sources "[e]ven if another agency ha[s]" done so); cf. Sanderson v. IRS, No. 98-2369, 1999 WL 35290, at *3 (E.D. La. Jan. 25, 1999) (continued...)

through authorized channels, the requester must demonstrate <u>both</u> that "'the exact information given to the [law enforcement authority] has already become public, and the fact that the informant gave the same information to the [law enforcement authority] is also public.'"[137] Consequently, one court has found that the government is not required even to "confirm or deny that persons who testify at trial are also confidential informants."[138]

The lengths to which it is proper to go when necessary to guard against informant identification through informant-provided information are illustrated by one decision holding that letters shown to a suspect for the purpose of prompting a confession were properly denied to the suspect under the FOIA -- even though the suspect was the very author of the letters (which, in turn, had been provided to authorities by a third party).[139] Similarly, the release of informant-related material to a party aligned with an agency in an administrative proceeding in no way diminishes the government's ability to invoke Exemption 7(D) in response to a subsequent request by a nonallied party.[140] Logically, this principle should be extended to encompass parties aligned with the government in actual litigation as well.

Nor is the protection of Exemption 7(D) forfeited by "court-ordered

---

[136](...continued) (concluding that source's deposition testimony in civil action did not act as "wholesale waiver" of information provided to agency). <u>But see</u> <u>Homick</u>, No. 98-0557, slip op. at 4 (N.D. Cal. Oct. 27, 2004) (concluding that FBI's source waived confidentiality by later testifying).

[137] <u>Parker</u>, 934 F.2d at 378; <u>Dow Jones</u>, 917 F.2d at 577; <u>see also</u> <u>Davis</u>, 968 F.2d at 1280 (holding that government is entitled to withhold tapes obtained through informant's assistance "unless it is specifically shown that those tapes, or portions of them, were played during the informant's testimony"); <u>Sanderson</u>, 1999 WL 35290, at *3-4 (ordering disclosure of "exact information to which [source] testified in her deposition"); <u>cf.</u> <u>Hale v. U.S. Dep't of Justice</u>, No. 89-1175, slip op. at 6 (W.D. Okla. Jan. 17, 1995) (stating that "individuals who testified in court could not be expected to have their identities or the topic of their testimony withheld"), <u>rev'd in part on other grounds</u>, 99 F.3d 1025 (10th Cir. 1996).

[138] <u>Schmerler</u>, 900 F.2d at 339 (reasoning that testimony by source does not automatically waive confidentiality because source may be able "'to camouflage his true role notwithstanding his court appearance'" (quoting <u>Irons</u>, 811 F.2d at 687)); <u>see also</u> <u>Parker</u>, 934 F.2d at 381.

[139] See <u>Gula</u>, 699 F. Supp. at 960.

[140] See <u>United Techs.</u>, 777 F.2d at 95-96; <u>see also</u> <u>FOIA Update</u>, Vol. IV, No. 2, at 6.

and court-supervised" disclosure to an opponent in civil discovery.[141] Although it previously had been held that when the government fails to object in any way to such discovery and then consciously and deliberately puts confidential source information into the public record a waiver of the exemption will be found to have occurred,[142] subsequent Exemption 7(D) decisions have undermined such a conclusion.[143] As noted above, however, "if the exact information given to the [law enforcement agency] has already become public, and the fact that the informant gave the same information to the [agency] is also public, there would be no grounds to withhold."[144]

Obviously, if no waiver of Exemption 7(D) results from authorized release of relevant information, "[t]he per se limitation on disclosure under 7(D) does not disappear if the identity of the confidential source becomes known through other means."[145] It should be observed that in the unusual situation in which an agency elects to publicly disclose source-identifying or source-provided information as necessary in furtherance of an important agency function, it "has no duty to seek the witness's permission to waive his confidential status under the Act."[146] Conversely, because Exemption 7(D) "mainly seeks to protect law enforcement agencies in their efforts to

---

[141] Donohue v. U.S. Dep't of Justice, No. 84-3451, 1987 U.S. Dist. LEXIS 15185, at *14 (D.D.C. Dec. 23, 1987).

[142] See Nishnic v. U.S. Dep't of Justice, 671 F. Supp. 776, 812 (D.D.C. 1987).

[143] See Glick v. Dep't of Justice, No. 89-3279, 1991 WL 118263, at *4 (D.D.C. June 20, 1991) (finding that disclosure "pursuant to discovery in another case . . . does not waive the confidentiality of the information or those who provided it"); see also Parker, 934 F.2d at 380 (observing that judicial efforts to create "waiver" exception run "contrary to statute's intent to provide workable rules" (citing Irons, 811 F.2d at 1455-56)); Sinito v. U.S. Dep't of Justice, No. 87-0814, slip op. at 24 (D.D.C. July 12, 2000) (holding that "[n]o further release of information . . . is warranted" even though "the names of certain informants were made a matter of public record through release of civil discovery material"), summary affirmance granted in pertinent part, No. 00-5321 (D.C. Cir. Apr. 11, 2001).

[144] Dow Jones, 917 F.2d at 577.

[145] L&C Marine, 740 F.2d at 925 (citing Radowich, 658 F.2d at 960); see, e.g., Lesar, 636 F.2d at 491 (finding that no waiver of confidentiality occurs when confidential information finds its way into public domain); Keeney, 630 F.2d at 119 n.2 (declaring that Exemption 7(D) continues to protect confidential sources even after their identification).

[146] Borton, 566 F. Supp. at 1422; see, e.g., Doe, 790 F. Supp. at 21-22 (declaring that "the FBI is not required to try to persuade people to change their minds" and that any such requirement "would undermine the Bureau's effectiveness").

find future sources,"[147] acts of "'waiver' by 'sources' will not automatically prove sufficient to release the [source-provided] information."[148] (See the discussion of this point under Discretionary Disclosure and Waiver, below.)

Under the case law, Exemption 7(D)'s protection for sources and the information they have provided also is in no way diminished by the fact that an investigation has been closed.[149] Indeed, because of the vital role that Exemption 7(D) plays in promoting effective law enforcement, courts have consistently recognized that its protections cannot be lost through

---

[147] Irons, 880 F.2d at 1453; see, e.g., Koch v. USPS, No. 92-0233, slip op. at 12 (W.D. Mo. Dec. 17, 1992) (stating that individuals would be less likely to come forward with information in future investigations if informants' identities were disclosed), aff'd, 7 F.3d 1042 (8th Cir. 1993) (unpublished table decision).

[148] Irons, 880 F.2d at 1452; see, e.g., Canning, No. 01-2215, slip op. at 12 (D.D.C. Mar. 9, 2004) (stating that "an informant's later actions do not waive an agency's right to withhold information"); Guerrero, No. 93-2006, slip op. at 10 (D. Ariz. Feb. 21, 1996) (holding that "full disclosure of information provided by confidential informant . . . not required simply because" informant made "public statements"); Spurlock v. FBI, No. 91-5602, slip op. at 2 (C.D. Cal. Nov. 29, 1993) (concluding that the "fact that [source] had any sense of braggadocio in his telling the world he had talked to the FBI cannot vitiate the protections of the exemption and the nature of his statements to the FBI as confidential"), rev'd on other grounds, 69 F.3d 1010 (9th Cir. 1995). But see Providence Journal, 981 F.2d at 567 n.16 (holding that express waiver of confidentiality by source vitiates Exemption 7(D) protection); Blanton, 63 F. Supp. 2d at 49 (ruling that sources "have waived any assurance of confidentiality, express or implied, by writing books about their experiences as confidential FBI informants").

[149] See Ortiz, 70 F.3d at 733 ("the status of the investigation is . . . immaterial to the application of the exemption"); KTVY-TV, 919 F.2d at 1470-71; Akron Standard Div. of Eagle-Picher Indus. v. Donovan, 780 F.2d 568, 573 (6th Cir. 1986); Ortiz, No. 97-140-A-3, slip op. at 10 (E.D. La. Aug. 25, 1998) ("information and/or identity of the individual remains confidential subject to Exemption 7(D) after the investigation is concluded"); Foster v. U.S. Dep't of Justice, 933 F. Supp. 687, 693 (E.D. Mich. 1996) (Exemption 7(D) "may be claimed even when an investigation generating records containing information concerning a confidential source has been closed"); Almy, 1995 WL 476255, at *13 (protection "not diminished" when investigation closed); Church of Scientology, 816 F. Supp. at 1161 (source identity and information provided "remains confidential . . . after the investigation is concluded"); Soto v. DEA, No. 90-1816, slip op. at 7 (D.D.C. Apr. 13, 1992) ("[i]t is of no consequence that these sources provided information relating to a criminal investigation which has since been completed"); Gale v. FBI, 141 F.R.D. 94, 98 (N.D. Ill. 1992) (statements protected even "while no investigation is pending" under Exemption 7(D)).

the mere passage of time.[150]   Additionally, unlike with Exemption 7(C),[151] the safeguards of Exemption 7(D) remain wholly undiminished by the death of the source.[152]

---

[150] See, e.g., Halpern, 181 F.3d at 300 (declaring that "it makes no difference in our analysis whether now, in hindsight, the objective need for confidentiality has diminished; what counts is whether then, at the time the source communicated with the FBI, the source understood that confidentiality would attach"); Schmerler, 900 F.2d at 336 (indicating that Exemption 7(D) "contains no sunset provision"); Keys, 830 F.2d at 346 (stating that "'Congress has not established a time limitation for exemption (7)(D) and it would be both impractical and inappropriate for the Court to do so.'" (quoting Keys v. Dep't of Justice, No. 85-2588, slip op. at 9 (D.D.C. May 12, 1986))); King, 830 F.2d at 212-13, 236 (protecting interviews conducted in 1941 and 1952); Irons, 811 F.2d at 689 (applying Exemption 7(D) protection to information regarding 1948-1956 Smith Act trials); Brant Constr., 778 F.2d at 1265 n.8 (emphasizing that "policy of [Exemption] 7(D) [is] to protect future sources of information" and that passage of time "does not alter status" of source-provided information); Diamond, 707 F.2d at 76-77 (protecting McCarthy-era documents); Piper, 294 F. Supp. 2d at 29 (protecting sources in thirty-year-old investigation); Fitzgibbon v. U.S. Secret Serv., 747 F. Supp. 51, 60 (D.D.C. 1990) (protecting information regarding alleged 1961 plot against President Kennedy by Trujillo regime in Dominican Republic); Abrams v. FBI, 511 F. Supp. 758, 762-63 (N.D. Ill. 1981) (protecting twenty-seven-year-old documents).

[151] See, e.g., Schrecker, 14 F. Supp. 2d at 118 (noting that "the FBI does not withhold third party information concerning Exemption 7(C) if it can determine that the third party's age would exceed 100 years").

[152] See, e.g., Blanton, 64 F. App'x at 790 (rejecting plaintiff's "claim that the death of a confidential source eliminates the applicability of Exemption 7(D)"); McDonnell, 4 F.3d at 1258 (holding that issue of whether source is "deceased does not extend to the information withheld pursuant to Exemption 7(D)"); Schmerler, 900 F.2d at 336 ("that the sources may have died is of no moment to the analysis"); Kiraly v. FBI, 728 F.2d 273, 279 (6th Cir. 1984) (finding information provided by deceased source who also testified at trial properly withheld); Cohen v. Smith, No. 81-5365, slip op. at 4 (9th Cir. Mar. 25, 1983); Sinito, No. 87-0814, slip op. at 24 (D.D.C. July 12, 2000) (holding that "[i]t is settled that the protection for sources and information they provide is not diminished because of death"); Schrecker v. U.S. Dep't of Justice, 14 F. Supp. 2d 111, 118 (D.D.C. 1998) (finding identity of informant withholdable "regardless of whether he/she is alive"); see also FOIA Update, Vol. IV, No. 3, at 5; cf. Swidler & Berlin v. United States, 524 U.S. 399, 407 (1998) (recognizing that "posthumous disclosure of [attorney-client] communications may be as feared as disclosure during the client's lifetime") (non-FOIA case); Allen v. DOD, 658 F. Supp. 15, 20 (D.D.C. 1986) (protecting identities of deceased intelligence sources under Exemption 1). But see Homick, No. 98-0557, slip op. at 4 (N.D. Cal. Oct. 27, 2004) (concluding

(continued...)

In sum, Exemption 7(D) traditionally has been afforded a broad construction by the courts in recognition of the compelling law enforcement need to "protect sources and prevent critical information from 'drying up.'"[153] To this end, all federal agencies maintaining law enforcement information should be sure to carefully apply Exemption 7(D)[154] wherever necessary to provide adequate confidential source protection.[155]

## EXEMPTION 7(E)

Exemption 7(E) affords protection to all law enforcement information that "would disclose techniques and procedures for law enforcement investigations or prosecutions, or would disclose guidelines for law enforcement investigations or prosecutions if such disclosure could reasonably be expected to risk circumvention of the law."[1] As discussed below, an ever-growing body of case law demonstrates that this exemption applies to a very broad range of law enforcement information, including national security- and homeland security-related information,[2] insofar as it meets the

---

[152](...continued)
that Exemption 7(D) is inapplicable to deceased source).

[153] Givner, No. 99-3454, slip op. at 15 (D.D.C. Mar. 1, 2001) (citing Shaw, 749 F.2d at 61); see also Attorney General's 1986 Amendments Memorandum at 13.

[154] Accord Attorney General Ashcroft's FOIA Memorandum, reprinted in FOIA Post (posted 10/15/01) (encouraging agencies to carefully consider the protection of the "fundamental values that are held by our society" -- including that of "enhancing the effectiveness of our law enforcement agencies" -- "when making disclosure determinations under the FOIA").

[155] See Sluby v. U.S. Dep't of Justice, No. 86-1503, 1987 WL 10509, at *2-3 (D.D.C. Apr. 30, 1987) ("'robust' reading of [E]xemption 7(D) is supported by . . . Congressional events"); Randle v. Comm'r, 866 F. Supp. 1080, 1085 (N.D. Ill. 1994) (although most exemptions construed narrowly, confidential source exemption applied "'robustly'"); accord Irons, 811 F.2d at 687-89 (post-1986-amendment decision extending Exemption 7(D) protection to sources who received only conditional assurances of confidentiality).

[1] 5 U.S.C. § 552(b)(7)(E) (2000 & Supp. IV 2004).

[2] See, e.g., Morley v. CIA, No. 03-2545, 2006 WL 2806561, at *14 (D.D.C. Sept. 29, 2006) (recognizing that Exemption 7's threshold requirement that records be compiled for "'law enforcement purpose' includes national security-related government activities"); Coastal Delivery Corp. v. U.S. Customs Serv., 272 F. Supp. 2d 958, 963-65 (C.D. Cal. 2003) (affording Exemption 7(E) protection to seaport inspection data because release could lead to identification of "vulnerable ports"), reconsideration denied, id. at 966-68 (C.D. Cal. 2003), appeal dismissed voluntarily, No. 03-55833 (9th Cir. Aug.
(continued...)

# EXEMPTION 7(E)

law enforcement threshold requirement for all of Exemption 7.[3]

Exemption 7(E) is comprised of two distinct protective clauses. The first clause permits the withholding of "records or information compiled for law enforcement purposes . . . [that] would disclose techniques and procedures for law enforcement investigations or prosecutions."[4] This clause is phrased in such a way so as to not require a showing of any particular determination of harm -- or risk of circumvention of law -- that would be caused by disclosure of the records or information within its coverage.[5] Rather, it is designed to provide "categorical" protection to the information

---

[2](...continued)
26, 2003); Ctr. for Nat'l Sec. Studies v. INS, No. 87-2068, 1990 WL 236133, at *5 (D.D.C. Dec. 19, 1990) (upholding agency decision to protect final contingency plan in event of attack on United States, as one of several documents that agency withheld that "relate directly to . . . agency's law enforcement duties"); see also FOIA Post, "FOIA Officers Conference Held on Homeland Security" (posted 7/3/03) (summarizing authority for protecting homeland security-related information up to that date).

[3] See, e.g., Living Rivers, Inc. v. U.S. Bureau of Reclamation, 272 F. Supp. 2d 1313, 1320 (D. Utah 2003) (determining that agency's use of flood maps to develop emergency action plans for homeland security purposes readily met "compiled for law enforcement purpose" requirement); see also Ctr. for Nat'l Sec. Studies v. U.S. Dep't of Justice, 331 F.3d 918, 928-29 (D.C. Cir. 2003) (recognizing need for deference to be afforded government's top counterterrorism officials who can best make "predictive judgment of harm that will result from disclosure of information" concerning ongoing national security investigation into 9/11 terrorist attacks) (Exemption 7(A)).

[4] 5 U.S.C. § 552(b)(7)(E).

[5] See, e.g., Peter S. Herrick's Customs & Int'l Trade Newsletter v. U.S. Customs & Border Prot., No. 04-00377, 2006 WL 1826185, at *7 (D.D.C. June 30, 2006) (acknowledging that first clause of Exemption 7(E) "requir[es] no demonstration of harm or balancing of interests"); Burke v. U.S. Dep't of Justice, No. 96-1739, 1999 WL 1032814, at *8 (D.D.C. Sept. 30, 1999) (holding that Exemption 7(E) "does not require the FBI to show that disclosure of [FBI Form FD-515] ratings [of effectiveness of investigative techniques] would cause any particular harm"); Coleman v. FBI, No. 89-2773, slip op. at 25 (D.D.C. Dec. 10, 1991), summary affirmance granted, No. 92-5040, 1992 WL 373976 (D.C. Cir. Dec. 4, 1992) (per curiam) ("The first clause of this exemption . . . does not require a determination that harm . . . would be caused by disclosure of the records or information within its coverage."). But see Davin v. U.S. Dep't of Justice, 60 F.3d 1043, 1064 (3d Cir. 1995) (requiring, in an atypical decision, that an agency submit "evidence that specific documents it has withheld contain secret information about techniques for recruiting informants [the disclosure of which] would risk circumvention of the law").

so described.[6]

Notwithstanding the broad scope of Exemption 7(E)'s protection, in order for the first clause of the exemption to apply the technique or procedure at issue ordinarily must not be well known to the public.[7] Accordingly, techniques such as "[i]nterception of wire, oral, and electronic communi-

---

[6] See Attorney General's Memorandum on the 1986 Amendments to the Freedom of Information Act 16 n.27 (Dec. 1987) [hereinafter Attorney General's 1986 Amendments Memorandum]; see, e.g., Judicial Watch, Inc. v. U.S. Dep't of Commerce, 337 F. Supp. 2d 146, 181 (D.D.C. 2004) (reiterating that first clause of Exemption 7(E) provides "'categorical protection'" for law enforcement techniques and procedures (quoting Judicial Watch, Inc. v. FBI, No. 00-745, 2001 U.S. Dist. LEXIS 25732, at *26-27 (D.D.C. Apr. 20, 2001)); Rivera v. FBI, No. 98-0649, slip op. at 9-10 (D.D.C. Aug. 31, 1999) (upholding categorical protection for bank security measures); Smith v. ATF, 977 F. Supp. 496, 501 (D.D.C. 1997) ("Exemption 7(E) provides categorical protection to information related to law enforcement techniques."); Fisher v. U.S. Dep't of Justice, 772 F. Supp. 7, 12 n.9 (D.D.C. 1991) (explicitly recognizing categorical protection for law enforcement techniques and procedures), aff'd, 968 F.2d 92 (D.C. Cir. 1992) (unpublished table decision); see also FOIA Update, Vol. XV, No. 2, at 3 (distinguishing between Exemption 7(E)'s two clauses).

[7] See Attorney General's 1986 Amendments Memorandum at 16 n.27 (citing S. Rep. No. 98-221, at 25 (1983) (citing, in turn, H.R. Rep. No. 93-1380, at 12 (1974)); see also Rugiero v. U.S. Dep't of Justice, 257 F.3d 534, 551 (6th Cir. 2001) (stating that the first clause of Exemption 7(E) "protects [only] techniques and procedures not already well-known to the public"); Becker v. IRS, 34 F.3d 398, 405 (7th Cir. 1994) (concluding that the "investigative techniques used by the IRS with respect to tax protesters . . . unquestionably fall under [Exemption 7(E)]," and implicitly upholding the district court's finding that the techniques at hand were not publicly known); Judicial Watch, Inc. v. U.S. Dep't of Commerce, 337 F. Supp. 2d at 179, 181 (recognizing exemption's protection for techniques "not well-known to the public"); Campbell v. U.S. Dep't of Justice, No. 89-3016, slip op. at 6-7 (D.D.C. Aug. 6, 1997) (declaring that Exemption 7(E) applies to "obscure or secret techniques," and refusing to apply it to "basic" techniques), rev'd & remanded on other grounds, 164 F.3d 20 (D.C. Cir. 1998); Albuquerque Publ'g Co. v. U.S. Dep't of Justice, 726 F. Supp. 851, 858 (D.D.C. 1989) (stating that agencies "should avoid burdening the Court . . . [with] techniques that are commonly described or depicted in movies, popular novels, stories or magazines, or on television").

cations,[8] "mail covers" and the "use of post office boxes,"[9] "'security flashes' or the tagging of fingerprints,'"[10] pretext telephone calls,[11] and "planting transponders on aircraft suspected of smuggling'"[12] have been denied protection under Exemption 7(E) when courts have found them to be generally known to the public.

However, even commonly known procedures have been protected from disclosure when "'the circumstances of their usefulness . . . may not be widely known,'"[13] or their use "in concert with other elements of an investi-

---

[8] Pub. Employees for Envtl. Responsibility v. EPA, 978 F. Supp. 955, 963 (D. Colo. 1997), appeal dismissed voluntarily, No. 97-1384 (10th Cir. Nov. 25, 1997).

[9] Dunaway v. Webster, 519 F. Supp. 1059, 1083 (N.D. Cal. 1981); see also Billington v. U.S. Dep't of Justice, 69 F. Supp. 2d 128, 140 (D.D.C. 1999) (observing as general matter that "wiretaps or use of post office boxes" are "commonly known" for purposes of Exemption 7(E)), aff'd in pertinent part, vacated in part & remanded on other grounds, 233 F.3d 581 (D.C. Cir. 2000).

[10] Ferguson v. Kelley, 448 F. Supp. 919, 926 (N.D. Ill. 1978) (supplemental opinion), reconsideration denied in pertinent part, 455 F. Supp. 324, 326 (N.D. Ill. 1978) (reiterating that methods used that are generally well known to public do not warrant Exemption 7(E) protection).

[11] Rosenfeld v. U.S. Dep't of Justice, 57 F.3d 803, 815 (9th Cir. 1995); see also Campbell, No. 89-3016, slip op. at 7-8 (D.D.C. Aug. 6, 1997) (ordering disclosure of information pertaining to "various pretexts" because information is known to public, requested records do not describe details of techniques, and disclosure would not undermine techniques' effectiveness); Struth v. FBI, 673 F. Supp. 949, 970 (E.D. Wis. 1987) (dismissing pretext as merely "garden variety ruse or misrepresentation"). But see Nolan v. U.S. Dep't of Justice, No. 89-2035, 1991 WL 36547, at *8 (D. Colo. Mar. 18, 1991) (concluding that disclosure of information surrounding pretext phone call could harm ongoing investigations because similar calls might be used again), aff'd on other grounds, 973 F.2d 843 (10th Cir. 1992).

[12] Hamilton v. Weise, No. 95-1161, 1997 U.S. Dist. LEXIS 18900, at *30 (M.D. Fla. Oct. 1, 1997).

[13] Wickline v. FBI, No. 92-1189, 1994 WL 549756, at *5 (D.D.C. Sept. 30, 1994) (quoting Parker v. U.S. Dep't of Justice, No. 88-0760, slip op. at 8 (D.D.C. Feb. 28, 1990), aff'd in pertinent part, No. 90-5070 (D.C. Cir. June 28, 1990)); see, e.g., Brunetti v. FBI, 357 F. Supp. 2d 97, 108 (D.D.C. 2004) (agreeing with FBI's assessment that release of notations regarding "efficacy [of techniques used] would allow criminals to adapt their activities and methods in order to avoid future detection"); Delviscovo v. FBI, 903 F. Supp. 1, 3 (D.D.C. 1995) (declaring withholding of FBI accomplishment report (containing information on use and effectiveness of investigative tech-

(continued...)

gation and in their totality directed toward a specific investigative goal constitute a 'technique' which merits protection."[14] Moreover, courts have endorsed the withholding of the details of a wide variety of commonly known procedures -- for example, polygraph examinations,[15] undercover

---

[13](...continued)
niques) to be "well established" and "proper"), summary affirmance grant-ed, No. 95-5388 (D.C. Cir. Jan. 24, 1997); Buffalo Evening News, Inc. v. U.S. Border Patrol, 791 F. Supp. 386, 392 n.5, 393 n.6 (W.D.N.Y. 1992) (finding that Exemption 7(E) protects fact of whether alien's name is listed in INS Lookout Book and method of apprehension of alien); see also Biase v. Office of Thrift Supervision, No. 93-2521, slip op. at 12 (D.N.J. Dec. 16, 1993) (up-holding protection of "investigative techniques and procedures that are either not commonly known to the public, or if publicly known, their disclo-sure could lessen their effectiveness"). But see Goldstein v. Office of Indep. Counsel, No. 87-2028, 1999 WL 570862, at *14 (D.D.C. July 29, 1999) (find-ing that portions of two documents were improperly withheld, because they did not contain "a secret or an exceptional investigative technique," nor would their disclosure risk circumvention of law, and treating the age of the documents (ten and sixteen years old) as a significant factor).

[14] PHE, Inc. v. U.S. Dep't of Justice, No. 90-1461, slip op. at 7 (D.D.C. Jan. 31, 1991), aff'd in pertinent part, rev'd in part & remanded, 983 F.2d 248 (D.C. Cir. 1993); see, e.g., Judicial Watch, Inc. v. U.S. Dep't of Commerce, 337 F. Supp. 2d at 181-82 (approving withholding of "firearm specifications" and "radio frequencies" used by agents protecting Secretary of Commerce); Judicial Watch, Inc. v. FBI, No. 00-745, 2001 U.S. Dist. LEXIS 25732, at *29-30 (D.D.C. Apr. 20, 2001) (protecting the "identities of two types of records concerning prison inmates which are often checked by FBI special agents," because even identifying the records would enable inmates "to alter their activities[,] thus hindering the effectiveness of this technique"); Hassan v. FBI, No. 91-2189, 1992 U.S. Dist. LEXIS 22655, at *13 (D.D.C. July 13, 1992) (protecting common techniques used with uncommon technique to achieve unique investigative goal), summary affirmance granted, No. 92-5318 (D.C. Cir. Mar. 17, 1993); Beck v. U.S. Dep't of Treasury, No. 88-493, slip op. at 26-27 (D.D.C. Nov. 8, 1989) (approving nondisclosure of certain documents, in-cluding map, because disclosure would reveal surveillance technique used by Customs Service, as well as why certain individuals were contacted with regard to investigations), aff'd, 946 F.2d 1563 (D.C. Cir. 1992) (unpub-lished table decision).

[15] See, e.g., Hale v. U.S. Dep't of Justice, 973 F.2d 894, 902-03 (10th Cir. 1992) (concluding that disclosure of "polygraph matters" could lessen effec-tiveness), cert. granted, vacated & remanded on other grounds, 509 U.S. 918 (1993); Piper v. U.S. Dep't of Justice, 294 F. Supp. 2d 16, 30 (D.D.C. 2003) (declaring that polygraph materials were properly withheld because their release would reveal sensitive "logistical considerations"), reconsider-ation denied on other grounds, 312 F. Supp. 2d 17 (D.D.C. 2004); Edmonds v. FBI, 272 F. Supp. 2d 35, 56 (D.D.C. 2003) (deciding that the FBI's declara-
(continued...)

operations,[16] surveillance techniques,[17] and bank security measures[18] -- on

---

[15](...continued)
tion "convincingly describes how the release of [polygraph] information might create a risk of circumvention of the law"); Shores v. FBI, 185 F. Supp. 2d 77, 85 (D.D.C. 2002) (determining that FBI properly withheld polygraph information to preserve effectiveness of polygraph examinations); Blanton v. U.S. Dep't of Justice, 63 F. Supp. 2d 35, 49-50 (D.D.C. 1999) (finding that disclosing certain polygraph information -- e.g., "sequence of questions" -- would allow individuals to employ countermeasures), aff'd, 64 F. App'x 787 (D.C. Cir. 2003); Coleman, 13 F. Supp. 2d at 83 (holding that disclosure of behavioral science analysis and details of polygraph examination would frustrate enforcement of law); Perrone v. FBI, 908 F. Supp. 24, 28 (D.D.C. 1995) (finding that release of precise polygraph questions and their sequence would allow circumvention of examination). But see Homick v. U.S. Dep't of Justice, No. 98-00557, slip op. at 14-15, 32 (N.D. Cal. Sept. 16, 2004) (ordering the disclosure of the details of a twenty-year-old polygraph test, including "the type of test given, the number of charts, and the serial number of the polygraph machine," because "the FBI has provided no statement that the type of machine, test, and number of charts used twenty years ago are the same or similar to those utilized today"), appeal dismissed voluntarily, No. 04-17568 (9th Cir. July 5, 2005).

[16] See, e.g., LaRouche v. U.S. Dep't of Justice, No. 90-2753, slip op. at 21 (D.D.C. Nov. 17, 2000) (rejecting plaintiff's argument that information regarding techniques for undercover work must be released, because even "widely known techniques" are entitled to protection when their disclosure would negatively affect future investigations); Sinito v. U.S. Dep't of Justice, No. 87-0814, 2000 U.S. Dist. LEXIS 22504, at *45-48 (D.D.C. July 12, 2000) (holding that the disclosure of information about an "electronic recording device" (a body microphone) "would impair the FBI's ability to conduct future investigations"), summary affirmance granted, 22 F. App'x 1 (D.C. Cir. 2001); Rosenberg v. Freeh, No. 97-0476, slip op. at 17 (D.D.C. May 13, 1998) (protecting "information on the use of false identities for undercover special agents," because disclosure "could significantly reduce [the] future effectiveness of this investigative technique"), aff'd, No. 99-5209, 1999 WL 1215961 (D.C. Cir. Nov. 12, 1999) (per curiam); Foster v. U.S. Dep't of Justice, 933 F. Supp. 687, 693 (E.D. Mich. 1996) (holding that release of techniques and guidelines used in undercover operations would diminish their effectiveness); Wagner v. FBI, No. 90-1314, 1991 U.S. Dist. LEXIS 7506, at *7 (D.D.C. June 4, 1991) (holding that exemption protects detailed surveillance and undercover investigative methods and techniques), summary affirmance granted, No. 91-5220 (D.C. Cir. Aug. 3, 1992). But see also Homick, No. 98-00557, slip op. at 33 (N.D. Cal. Sept. 16, 2004) (ordering the release of records generally related to the "establishment of a nationwide undercover program utilized by the FBI," because the FBI's "justification [for withholding] is wholly conclusory").

[17] See, e.g., Masters v. ATF, No. 04-2274, slip op. at 18-19 (D.D.C. Sept.
(continued...)

the basis that disclosure could reduce or even nullify the effectiveness of such procedures.[19] As one court recently observed pragmatically, this is

---

[17](...continued)
25, 2006) (protecting details of electronic surveillance techniques not widely known to public -- including their circumstances, timing, and location -- and finding that plaintiff "merely speculates" that public is aware of such details); Shores, 185 F. Supp. 2d at 85 (protecting details of surveillance operations at federal prison, including information about telephone system); Burke v. DEA, No. 96-1739, slip op. at 9 (D.D.C. Mar. 31, 1998) (upholding Postal Service's refusal to disclose detailed description of surveillance techniques); Steinberg v. U.S. Dep't of Justice, No. 93-2409, slip op. at 15-16 (D.D.C. July 14, 1997) (approving nondisclosure of precise details of telephone and travel surveillance despite fact that criminals know that such techniques are used generally); Butler v. Dep't of the Treasury, No. 95-1931, 1997 WL 138720, at *4 (D.D.C. Jan. 14, 1997) (reasoning that disclosing methods of monitoring and type of equipment used could enable future targets to avoid surveillance).

[18] See, e.g., Maguire v. Mawn, No. 02 Civ. 2164, 2004 WL 1124673, at *3 (S.D.N.Y. May 19, 2004) (protecting the details of a bank's use of "bait money," although it is a publicly known technique, because "disclosure . . . could reasonably make the [b]ank more susceptible to robberies in the future"); Williams v. U.S. Dep't of Justice, No. 02-2452, slip op. at 11-12 (D.D.C. Feb. 4, 2004) (protecting "serial numbers on bait money" because disclosing this aspect of this "technique would undercut its usefulness"), reconsideration denied (D.D.C. Mar. 10, 2004), aff'd per curiam, 171 F. App'x 857 (D.C. Cir. 2005); Rivera, No. 98-0649, slip op. at 9-10 (D.D.C. Aug. 31, 1999) (upholding categorical protection for bank security measures); Dayton Newspapers, Inc. v. FBI, No. C-3-85-815, 1993 WL 1367435, at *6 (S.D. Ohio Feb. 9, 1993) (concluding that FBI properly withheld details of bank security devices and equipment used in bank robbery investigation); Malloy v. U.S. Dep't of Justice, 457 F. Supp. 543, 545 (D.D.C. 1978) (protecting details concerning "bait money" and "bank security devices").

[19] See, e.g., Hale, 973 F.2d at 902-03 (concluding that disclosure of use of security devices and their modus operandi could lessen their effectiveness); Bowen v. FDA, 925 F.2d 1225, 1229 (9th Cir. 1991) (deciding that release of specifics of cyanide-tracing techniques would present serious threat to future product-tampering investigations); Cal-Trim, Inc. v. IRS, No. 05-2408, slip op. at 6-8 (D. Ariz. Feb. 6, 2007) (protecting certain records from ongoing IRS investigation because release could allow the individuals under investigation "to craft explanations or defenses based on the [IRS] agent's analysis or enable them the opportunity to disguise or conceal the transactions that are under investigation"); Whitfield v. U.S. Dep't of the Treasury, No. 04-0679, 2006 WL 2434923, at *5-6 (D.D.C. Aug. 22, 2006) (concluding that details of arrest procedures were properly withheld because disclosure could assist suspects in avoiding arrest) (appeal pending); Judicial Watch, Inc. v. Dep't of Commerce, 337 F. Supp. 2d at 181-82
(continued...)

especially true "when the method employed is meant to operate clandes-tinely, unlike [other techniques] that serve their crime-prevention purpose by operating in the open."[20]

Indeed, because of the nature of the underlying information, defend-ing nondisclosures under the first clause of Exemption 7(E) often must be approached with special care; accordingly, courts have permitted agencies

---

[19](...continued)
(protecting details of techniques used to "identify parties and transactions that should be monitored for violations of [agency] regulations," as disclo-sure would indicate "'what kinds of action [agency] categorizes as signifi-cant and what kinds of action may be considered less significant'" (quoting agency declaration)); Maydak v. U.S. Dep't of Justice, 362 F. Supp. 2d 316, 320 (D.D.C. 2005) (holding that the Bureau of Prisons properly withheld techniques that were "used to detect that plaintiff was sending requests to security agencies while claiming he was a staff member," because disclo-sure "'would assist an inmate in correlating the use of a particular investi-gative technique with its corresponding effectiveness'" (quoting agency declaration)); Piper, 294 F. Supp. 2d at 31 (observing that the public's "[g]eneral, non-specific knowledge that the FBI possesses capabilities to electronically monitor the movement of automobiles . . . is not the same as identifying the actual device, its function, and its capabilities"); Peralta v. U.S. Attorney's Office, 69 F. Supp. 2d 21, 35 (D.D.C. 1999) (upholding redac-tion of FBI Forms FD-515, which rank effectiveness of techniques, as well as information that would identify radio channels used during surveillance and transmitter numbers used to monitor conversations, in order "to pre-vent potential harm to future law enforcement activities"); Pons v. U.S. Cus-toms Serv., No. 93-2094, 1998 U.S. Dist. LEXIS 6084, at *20 (D.D.C. Apr. 23, 1998) (protecting "cooperative arrangements between Customs and other law enforcement agencies" to keep them effective); Code v. FBI, No. 95-1892, 1997 WL 150070, at *8 (D.D.C. Mar. 26, 1997) (recognizing that disclo-sure of criminal personality profiles could assist criminals in evading detec-tion); Pray v. Dep't of Justice, 902 F. Supp. 1, 4 (D.D.C. 1995) (concluding that release of information about particular investigative techniques and their effectiveness in FBI accomplishment report could enable criminals to employ countermeasures to neutralize their effectiveness), summary affirm-ance granted in pertinent part, 1996 WL 734142 (D.C. Cir. Nov. 20, 1996); Fisher v. U.S. Dep't of Justice, 772 F. Supp. 7, 12 (D.D.C. 1991) (finding that disclosure could alert subjects of investigation about FBI techniques); see also FOIA Update, Vol. V, No. 2, at 5 (discussing scope of Exemption 7(E) protection as encompassing "obscure or secret techniques" (quoting Jaffe v. CIA, 573 F. Supp. 377, 387 (D.D.C. 1983))). But cf. Gerstein v. U.S. Dep't of Justice, No. 03-04893, 2005 U.S. Dist. LEXIS 41276, at *38-43 (N.D. Cal. Sept. 30, 2005) (ordering the release of a compilation detailing each United States Attorney's Office's use of certain delayed-notice warrants, because the technique "is a matter of common knowledge" and disclosure would not reduce the technique's effectiveness).

[20] Maguire, 2004 WL 1124673, at *3.

to describe secret law enforcement techniques in only general terms, where necessary, while withholding the full details.[21] Of course, this does not obviate an agency's duty to provide the most complete public declaration possible, as demonstrated by several court decisions finding agencies' declarations to be inadequate.[22] In many circumstances, though, it is not

---

[21] See, e.g., Bowen, 925 F.2d at 1229 (ruling that release of specifics of cyanide-tracing techniques would present serious threat to future product-tampering investigations); Cohen v. Smith, No. 81-5365, slip op. at 8 (9th Cir. Mar. 25, 1983) (protecting details of telephone interviews); Carbe v. ATF, No. 03-1658, 2004 WL 2051359, at *11 (D.D.C. Aug. 12, 2004) (finding that "electronic surveillance request forms and asset forfeiture reimbursement forms . . . [are] [c]ertainly . . . protected from release by Exemption 7(E)," as disclosure "might reveal the nature of electronic equipment and the sequence of its uses"); Peyton v. Reno, No. 98-1457, 2000 WL 141282, at *1 (D.D.C. Jan. 6, 2000) (protecting Discriminant Function Scores used to select tax returns for evaluation); Klunzinger v. IRS, 27 F. Supp. 2d 1015, 1027-28 (W.D. Mich. 1998) (upholding protection of documents which, if disclosed, would "reveal confidential information regarding when the IRS would undertake compliance activity"); Laroque v. U.S. Dep't of Justice, No. 86-2677, 1988 WL 75942, at *3 (D.D.C. July 12, 1988) (protecting "Reason and Source codes" in State Department "lookout notices," which are not generally known to public); U.S. News & World Report v. Dep't of the Treasury, No. 84-2303, 1986 U.S. Dist. LEXIS 27634, at *8 (D.D.C. Mar. 26, 1986) (protecting Secret Service's contract specifications for President's armored limousine); Hayward v. U.S. Dep't of Justice, 2 Gov't Disclosure Serv. (P-H) ¶ 81,231, at 81,646 (D.D.C. July 14, 1981) (protecting methods and techniques used by Marshals Service to relocate protected witnesses); Ott v. Levi, 419 F. Supp. 750, 752 (E.D. Mo. 1976) (protecting laboratory techniques used in arson investigation).

[22] See, e.g., Boyd v. ATF, No. 05-1096, 2006 WL 2844912, at *9 (D.D.C. Sept. 29, 2006) (criticizing the agency's "inadequate" Vaughn Index, as it "tend[s] to recite the language of the FOIA exemption and refer to the Vaughn indices, without explaining why the release of the information would compromise law enforcement"); Long v. U.S. Dep't of Justice, 450 F. Supp. 2d 42, 79 (D.D.C.) (rejecting the agency's Exemption 7(E) argument, which essentially restated the statutory standard, because it "failed to identify any law enforcement technique or procedure that would be disclosed upon release of the information"), amended by 457 F. Supp. 2d 30 (D.D.C. 2006), amended further on reconsideration, Nos. 00-0211 & 02-2467, 2007 WL 293508 (D.D.C. Feb. 2, 2007), stay granted (D.D.C. Feb. 13, 2007); Homick, No. 98-00557, slip op. at 14-15, 32 (N.D. Cal. Sept. 16, 2004) (ordering disclosure of records concerning twenty-year-old polygraph test because FBI failed to show that similar techniques were still in use at time of withholding); Prescott v. Dep't of Justice, No. 00-187, slip op. at 5, 11-12 (D.D.C. Aug. 10, 2001) (upholding the redaction of FBI Form FD-515 because the FBI specified the potential harm from release, while rejecting another agency's invocation of Exemption 7(E) to withhold other "'informa-

(continued...)

possible to describe secret law enforcement techniques even in general terms without disclosing the very information sought to be withheld.[23] A court's in camera review of the documents at issue may be required to demonstrate the propriety of nondisclosure in such cases.[24]

---

[22](...continued)
tion regarding investigative techniques and procedures'" (quoting agency's declaration), because the other agency "merely reiterated the statutory language"); Smith, 977 F. Supp. at 501 (explaining that although an agency might not be able to discuss the details of certain techniques, "that does not excuse the agency from providing the Court with information sufficient for it to decide whether the material is properly withheld under Exemption 7(E)," and rejecting the agency's declaration as "conclusory"); Feshbach v. SEC, 5 F. Supp. 2d 774, 786-87 & n.11 (N.D. Cal. 1997) (finding the SEC's reasons for withholding checklists and internal database to be conclusory and insufficient); Linn v. U.S. Dep't of Justice, No. 92-1406, 1995 WL 417810, at *26 (D.D.C. June 6, 1995) (rejecting invocation of Exemption 7(E) because no justification was provided to show how release of commonly known technique could interfere with future law enforcement efforts).

[23] See Boyd, 2006 WL 2844912, at *9; Morley, 2006 WL 2806561, at *14; Smith, 977 F. Supp. at 501; see also, e.g., Gonzalez v. ATF, No. 04-2281, 2005 WL 3201009, at *9-10 (D.D.C. Nov. 9, 2005) (permitting the withholding of information pertaining to an unspecified law enforcement technique, and accepting the agency's attestations that disclosure "could limit its future effectiveness" and "would allow criminals to develop countermeasures against the technique"); McQueen v. United States, 264 F. Supp. 2d 502, 521 (S.D. Tex. 2003) (finding that requested documents show "details [that], by themselves, would reveal law enforcement techniques" and thus were properly withheld), summary affirmance granted on other grounds, 100 F. App'x 964 (5th Cir. 2004); Butler, 1997 WL 138720, at *4 (observing that "[i]t is sometimes impossible to describe secret law enforcement techniques without disclosing the information sought to be withheld"); Coleman, 13 F. Supp. 2d at 83 (permitting the FBI to withhold the "manner and circumstances" of identified techniques, because "[f]urther explanation of these techniques . . . would effectively expose the core of information sought to be protected"); Soto v. DEA, No. 90-1816, slip op. at 7 (D.D.C. Apr. 13, 1992) (concluding that detailed description of technique pertaining to detection of drug traffickers would effectively disclose it); cf. Schwaner v. Dep't of the Air Force, 898 F.2d 793, 796 (D.C. Cir. 1990) (observing that under the "high 2" aspect of Exemption 2, "courts have also exempted materials that are so closely related to rules and practices that disclosure could lead to disclosure of the rule or practice itself").

[24] See, e.g., Jones v. FBI, 41 F.3d 238, 249 (6th Cir. 1994) (concluding, upon in camera review, that investigative techniques were properly withheld); Mayer, Brown, Rowe & Maw LLP v. IRS, No. 04-2187, 2006 WL 2425523, at *8 (D.D.C. Aug. 21, 2006) (directing the defendant agency to submit "a representative sample of the [withheld] records for in camera re-

(continued...)

Prior to the enactment of the Freedom of Information Reform Act of 1986,[25] Exemption 7(E) protected law enforcement techniques and procedures only when they could be regarded as "investigatory" or "investigative" in character,[26] but this limitation was removed by those FOIA amendments.[27] Exemption 7(E), as amended in 1986, simply covers "techniques

---

[24](...continued)
view" because the agency's declaration did not have sufficient detail to permit a ruling on the applicability of Exemption 7(E)), further opinion, No. 04-2187, slip op. at 2-3 (D.D.C. Oct. 24, 2006) (concluding after in camera review that Exemption 7(E) was properly applied); ACLU v. FBI, No. 05-1004, 2006 WL 2303103, at *1 (D.D.C. Aug. 9, 2006) (granting summary judgment to the defendant agency after "conduct[ing] an in camera, ex parte review of the disputed documents"); Palacio v. U.S. Dep't of Justice, No. 00-1564, 2002 U.S. Dist. LEXIS 2198, at *29 (D.D.C. Feb. 11, 2002) (ordering the FBI to provide greater detail concerning information withheld under Exemption 7(E), or to submit for in camera review either the documents at issue or a detailed declaration "[i]f the necessary detail would disclose the very information it seeks to withhold"), summary affirmance granted on other grounds, No. 02-5247, 2003 WL 242751 (D.C. Cir. Jan. 31, 2003); Allnutt v. U.S. Dep't of Justice, No. 98-901, 2000 WL 852455, at *1-2 (D. Md. Oct. 23, 2000) (finding, upon in camera review, that computer command codes used to access federal databases were properly withheld), aff'd sub nom. Allnutt v. Handler, 8 F. App'x 225 (4th Cir. 2001); Smith, 977 F. Supp. at 501 (concluding that agency must either provide greater detail about records withheld or submit records for in camera review); Pub. Employees for Envtl. Responsibility, 978 F. Supp. at 961-62 (concluding, upon in camera review, that certain documents must be released while others may be withheld); Campbell v. U.S. Dep't of Justice, No. 89-3016, 1996 WL 554511, at *10 (D.D.C. Sept. 19, 1996) (directing in camera submission of technique information at issue), rev'd & remanded on other grounds, 164 F.3d 20 (D.C. Cir. 1998); Linn v. U.S. Dep't of Justice, No. 92-1406, 1997 WL 577586, at *4 (D.D.C. May 29, 1997) (determining that in camera inspection was necessary because DEA had not provided specific, nonconclusory explanation to justify withholding of what it identified as law enforcement technique); Rojem v. U.S. Dep't of Justice, 775 F. Supp. 6, 12 (D.D.C. 1991) (ordering in camera inspection), subsequent decision, No. 90-3021, 1991 WL 241931, at *1 (D.D.C. Oct. 31, 1991) (upholding Exemption 7(E) upon in camera inspection), appeal dismissed for failure to timely file, No. 92-5088 (D.C. Cir. Nov. 4, 1992); Nat'l Sec. Archive v. FBI, 759 F. Supp. 872, 885 (D.D.C. 1991) (ordering the agency to submit a supplemental affidavit describing the information withheld, but finding that "[d]ue to the sensitive nature of this subject, that affidavit may be submitted in camera if necessary").

[25] Pub. L. No. 99-570, § 1802, 100 Stat. 3207, 3207-48, 3207-49.

[26] Pub. L. No. 93-502, 88 Stat. 1561, 1563 (1974).

[27] See, e.g., Tax Analysts v. IRS, 294 F.3d 71, 79 (D.C. Cir. 2002) (discuss-
(continued...)

and procedures for law enforcement investigations or prosecutions."[28] As such, it authorizes the withholding of information consisting of, or reflecting, a law enforcement "technique" or a law enforcement "procedure," wherever it is used "for law enforcement investigations or prosecutions" generally.[29] Law enforcement manuals, including those that pertain to the "prosecutions" stage of the law enforcement process, accordingly meet the re-

---

[27](...continued)
ing effects of 1986 FOIA amendments on Exemption 7(E)); Gordon v. FBI, 388 F. Supp. 2d 1028, 1036 (N.D. Cal. 2005) (rejecting the plaintiff's "narrow[]" reading of the "law enforcement purpose" requirement of Exemption 7(E), and noting that it "is not limited to documents created in connection with a criminal investigation").

[28] 5 U.S.C. § 552(b)(7)(E).

[29] Id.; see Attorney General's 1986 Amendments Memorandum at 15; see also Nowak v. IRS, 210 F.3d 384 (9th Cir. 2000) (unpublished table decision) (affirming the district court's conclusion "that the redacted information, if disclosed, 'would significantly hamper the defendant's tax collection and law enforcement functions, and facilitate taxpayer circumvention of federal Internal Revenue laws'" (quoting agency declaration)); Mosby v. U.S. Marshals Serv., No. 04-2083, 2005 WL 3273974, at *5 (D.D.C. Sept. 1, 2005) (finding that "administrative and operational guidelines and procedures" were properly withheld, as the contents "would provide assistance to persons threatening individuals and property protected by the USMS and allow fugitives to avoid apprehension"); Tran v. U.S. Dep't of Justice, No. 01-0238, 2001 WL 1692570, at *3 (D.D.C. Nov. 20, 2001) (concluding that INS form -- used when agencies share information from immigration records -- was properly withheld because it would reveal law enforcement techniques); Unger v. Dist. Disclosure Office IRS, No. 99-698, 2000 WL 1009493, at *4 (N.D. Ohio Mar. 28, 2000) (finding that IRS properly withheld references to "specific dollar tolerance" used as "threshold in determining whether to prosecute"); Guerrero v. DEA, No. 93-2006, slip op. at 14-15 (D. Ariz. Feb. 22, 1996) (holding that Exemption 7(E) properly protects portions of DEA Agents Manual concerning undercover operations, confidential informant codes, surveillance devices, and enforcement and security procedures); Hammes v. U.S. Customs Serv., No. 94 Civ. 4868, 1994 WL 693717, at *1 (S.D.N.Y. Dec. 9, 1994) (protecting Customs Service criteria used to determine which passengers to stop and examine); Windels, Marx, Davies & Ives v. Dep't of Commerce, 576 F. Supp. 405, 414 (D.D.C. 1983) (finding "consistent with other cases . . . that Exemption 7(E) shields computer codes" and programs because their disclosure "would reveal investigative procedures"). But see Herrick's Newsletter, 2006 WL 1826185, at *8 (holding that a portion of an agency manual pertaining to the destruction of seizure of property is not related to a law enforcement investigation and instead "relate[s] only to the conservation of the agency's physical and monetary resources"); Cowsen-El v. U.S. Dep't of Justice, 826 F. Supp. 532, 533-34 (D.D.C. 1992) (finding Bureau of Prisons program statement to be internal policy document wholly unrelated to investigations or prosecutions).

quirements for withholding under Exemption 7(E) to the extent that they consist of, or reflect, law enforcement techniques and procedures that are confidential and must remain so in order to preserve their effectiveness.[30]

The second clause of Exemption 7(E) protects "guidelines for law enforcement investigations or prosecutions if [their] disclosure could reasonably be expected to risk circumvention of the law."[31] As such, it has a distinct harm standard built into it -- not unlike the "anti-circumvention," "high 2" aspect of Exemption 2 -- and it indeed has considerable overlap with this aspect of Exemption 2 in general.[32] (See the discussion under Exemption 2, "High 2": Risk of Circumvention, above.) This distinct protection is intended to ensure proper protection for the type of law enforcement guideline in-

---

[30] See Attorney General's 1986 Amendments Memorandum at 16; accord Attorney General's Memorandum for Heads of All Federal Departments and Agencies Regarding the Freedom of Information Act (Oct. 12, 2001) [hereinafter Attorney General Ashcroft's FOIA Memorandum], reprinted in FOIA Post (posted 10/15/01) (emphasizing the fundamental societal value of "enhancing the effectiveness of our law enforcement agencies"); see, e.g., Herrick's Newsletter, 2006 WL 1826185, at *7 (protecting many portions of a manual pertaining to seized property, including details of "the transport, seizure, storage, testing, physical security, evaluation, maintenance, and cataloguing of, as well as access to, seized property"); Guerrero, No. 93-2006, slip op. at 14-15 (D. Ariz. Feb. 22, 1996) (approving nondisclosure of portions of DEA Agents Manual); Church of Scientology Int'l v. IRS, 845 F. Supp. 714, 723 (C.D. Cal. 1993) (concluding that parts of IRS Law Enforcement Manual concerning "procedures for handling applications for tax exemption and examinations of Scientology entities" and memorandum regarding application of such procedures were properly withheld); Williston Basin Interstate Pipeline Co. v. FERC, No. 88-0592, 1989 WL 44655, at *2 (D.D.C. Apr. 17, 1989) (finding portions of a regulatory audit describing the significance of each page in an audit report, investigatory technique utilized, and the auditor's conclusions to constitute "the functional equivalent of a manual of investigative techniques").

[31] 5 U.S.C. § 552(b)(7)(E).

[32] See, e.g., Coastal Delivery Corp., 272 F. Supp. 2d at 965 (concluding that agency properly applied Exemption 2 for same reasons that it applied Exemption 7(E)); Schwarz v. U.S. Dep't of Treasury, 131 F. Supp. 2d 142, 150 (D.D.C. 2000) (finding Secret Service information evaluating personal characteristics and threat potential of individuals to be "clearly exempt from disclosure" under both Exemptions 2 and 7(E)), summary affirmance granted, No. 00-5453, 2001 WL 674636 (D.C. Cir. May 10, 2001); see also Berg v. Commodity Futures Trading Comm'n, No. 93 C 6741, slip op. at 11 n.2 (N.D. Ill. June 23, 1994) (magistrate's recommendation) ("[I]t would appear that exemption (b)(7)(E) is essentially a codification of the 'high 2' exemption[.]"), accepted & dismissed per stipulation (N.D. Ill. July 26, 1994); see also FOIA Update, Vol. XV, No. 2, at 3 (discussing the "firm 'harm' requirement already built into" Exemptions 2 and 7(E), among others).

formation found ineligible to be withheld in the en banc decision of the Court of Appeals for the District of Columbia Circuit in Jordan v. Department of Justice,[33] a case involving guidelines for prosecutions. It reflects a dual concern with the need to remove any lingering effect of that decision, while at the same time ensuring that agencies do not unnecessarily maintain "secret law" establishing standards that are used to regulate societal behavior.[34]

This clause of Exemption 7(E) therefore is available to protect any "law enforcement guideline" information of the type involved in Jordan, whether it pertains to the prosecution or basic investigative stage of a law enforcement matter, whenever it is determined[35] that its disclosure "could reasonably be expected to risk circumvention of the law."[36] In taking this

---

[33] 591 F.2d 753, 771 (D.C. Cir. 1978) (en banc).

[34] See S. Rep. No. 98-221, at 25 (1983); Attorney General's 1986 Amendments Memorandum at 16-17; see also Gordon, 388 F. Supp. 2d at 1036-37 (requiring disclosure of "the legal basis for detaining someone whose name appears on a watch list"); Don Ray Drive-A-Way Co. of Cal. v. Skinner, 785 F. Supp. 198, 200 (D.D.C. 1992) (finding that disclosure of safety ratings system is necessary to permit regulated entities to know what agency considers to be most serious safety breaches).

[35] See Buckner v. IRS, 25 F. Supp. 2d 893, 899 (N.D. Ind. 1998) (finding that "the age of the [DIF] scores is of no consequence" in upholding protection of Discriminant Function Scores used to evaluate tax returns). But see also Homick, No. 98-00557, slip op. at 14-15, 32 (N.D. Cal. Sept. 16, 2004) (taking age of records into account in ordering disclosure because agency failed to show that same technique was currently in use).

[36] See, e.g., PHE, Inc. v. Dep't of Justice, 983 F.2d 248, 251 (D.C. Cir. 1993) (holding that "release of FBI guidelines as to what sources of information are available to its agents might encourage violators to tamper with those sources of information and thus inhibit investigative efforts"); Sussman v. U.S. Marshall Serv., No. 03-610, 2005 WL 3213912, at *9 (D.D.C. Oct. 13, 2005) (protecting "procedures utilized in investigation [of] threats against federal court employees," because release "could create a risk of circumvention of the law") (appeal pending); Carp v. IRS, No. 00-5992, 2002 WL 373448, at *6 (D.N.J. Jan. 28, 2002) (concluding, after in camera review, that disclosure "would risk circumvention of the law by exposing specific, non-routine investigative techniques used by the IRS to uncover tax fraud"); Tax Analysts v. IRS, 152 F. Supp. 2d 1, 17 (D.D.C. 2001) (determining that disclosure of agency summary of tax-avoidance scheme, "including identification of vulnerabilities" in IRS operations, could risk circumvention of law), rev'd & remanded on other grounds, 294 F.3d 71 (D.C. Cir. 2002); Wishart v. Comm'r, No. 97-20614, 1998 WL 667638, at *6 (N.D. Cal. Aug. 6, 1998) (protecting Discriminant Function Scores to avoid possibility that "taxpayers could manipulate" return information to avoid IRS audits), aff'd,

(continued...)

approach, Congress notably employed the more relaxed harm standard used in most of Exemption 7, also making clear that it was "guided by the 'circumvention of the law' standard"[37] that had been established by the D.C. Circuit in Crooker v. ATF.[38]

Accordingly, in applying this second clause of Exemption 7(E) to law enforcement manuals, agencies should focus on the portions of those guidelines that correlate to particular harm to law enforcement efforts[39]

---

[36](...continued)
199 F.3d 1334 (9th Cir. 1999) (unpublished table decision); Voinche v. FBI, 940 F. Supp. 323, 331 (D.D.C. 1996) (upholding nondisclosure of Criminal Intelligence Digest used to assist and guide FBI personnel), aff'd per curiam, No. 96-5304, 1997 WL 411685 (D.C. Cir. June 19, 1997); Jimenez v. FBI, 938 F. Supp. 21, 30 & n.6 (D.D.C. 1996) (approving invocation of Exemption 7(E) to protect gang-validation criteria used by Bureau of Prisons to determine whether individual is gang member); Pully v. IRS, 939 F. Supp. 429, 437 (E.D. Va. 1996) (finding that the release of Discriminant Function Scores would enable taxpayers to "develop techniques to avoid 'flagging' [by] the IRS computers"); Silber v. U.S. Dep't of Justice, No. 91-876, transcript at 25 (D.D.C. Aug. 13, 1992) (bench order) (ruling that disclosure of a Department of Justice monograph on fraud litigation "would present the specter of circumvention of the law"); Ctr. for Nat'l Sec. Studies, 1990 WL 236133, at *5-6 (recognizing that release of INS plans to be deployed in event of attack on U.S. could assist terrorists in circumventing border control). But see also Church of Scientology v. IRS, 816 F. Supp. 1138, 1162 (W.D. Tex. 1993) (holding that the IRS did not establish how release of records "regarding harassment of Service employees" written during an investigation "could reasonably be expected to circumvent the law"), appeal dismissed per stipulation, No. 93-8431 (5th Cir. Oct. 21, 1993).

[37] S. Rep. No. 98-221, at 25 (1983); see Attorney General's 1986 Amendments Memorandum at 17; see also NARA v. Favish, 541 U.S. 157, 169 (evincing the Supreme Court's reliance on "the Attorney General's consistent interpretation of" the FOIA in successive such Attorney General memoranda), reh'g denied, 541 U.S. 1057 (2004).

[38] 670 F.2d 1051 (D.C. Cir. 1981) (en banc).

[39] See, e.g., PHE, 983 F.2d at 252 (finding that the Department of Justice's National Obscenity Enforcement Unit failed to submit an affidavit containing "precise descriptions of the nature of the redacted material and providing reasons why releasing each withheld section would create a risk of circumvention of the law"); Antonelli v. ATF, No. 04-1180, 2005 U.S. Dist. LEXIS 17089, at *30 (D.D.C. Aug. 16, 2005) (rejecting the agency's general averments of harm, because a "mere recitation of the statutory language does not satisfy its burden of proof"), summary judgment granted in pertinent part, No. 04-1180, 2006 WL 3147675, at *1 (D.D.C. Nov. 1, 2006) (protecting "'collection techniques used [by the Bureau of Prisons] to conduct
(continued...)

and at the same time should make every effort to meet their obligations to disclose all reasonably segregable, nonexempt information.[40] (See the further discussions of this point under Procedural Requirements, "Reasonably Segregable" Obligation, above, and Litigation Considerations, "Reasonably Segregable" Requirements, below.)

Overall, it also is worth focusing on the potential role of both clauses of Exemption 7(E) in protecting homeland security-related information. In the current post-September 11, 2001 environment, law enforcement information that might be covered by this exemption should be viewed in light of its potential for causing harm -- or risking danger -- to individuals or to the public collectively.[41] It is vitally important in all instances to conduct a careful review of any information of homeland security sensitivity in order to evaluate any likelihood of disclosure harm, either in the form of potential danger to a person or persons or as a consequence of circumvention of law

---

[39](...continued)
an investigation'" because disclosure could risk circumvention of the law (quoting agency declaration)); Leveto v. IRS, No. 98-285, 2001 U.S. Dist. LEXIS 5791, at *21 (W.D. Pa. Apr. 10, 2001) (protecting dollar amount budgeted for agency to investigate particular individual, because release could allow others to learn agency's monetary limits and undermine such investigations in future); Linn, 1995 WL 417810, at *32 (affirming nondisclosure of one page from Drug Agent's Guide to Forfeiture of Assets on basis that agency explained harm).

[40] See PHE, 983 F.2d at 252 (remarking that the agency's "vague and conclusory" affidavit might have "established a legitimate basis for withholding" had it "clearly indicated why disclosable material could not be segregated from exempted material"); see, e.g., Wightman v. ATF, 755 F.2d 979, 982-83 (1st Cir. 1985) (remanding for determination of segregability) (Exemption 2); Voinche v. FBI, 412 F. Supp. 2d 60, 69 (criticizing the agency's "conclusory statements," and ordering it to "either release the information withheld . . . or provide a satisfactory Vaughn index, including a proper segregability analysis"), summary judgment granted, 425 F. Supp. 2d 134, 135 & n.2 (D.D.C. 2006) (noting that agency ultimately released information at issue in its entirety); cf. Schreibman v. U.S. Dep't of Commerce, 785 F. Supp. 164, 166 (D.D.C. 1991) (requiring agency to segregate and release portions of documents that merely identify computer systems rather than contain security plans, which remain protected as vulnerability assessments) (Exemption 2); see also FOIA Update, Vol. XIV, No. 3, at 11-12 ("OIP Guidance: The 'Reasonable Segregation' Obligation").

[41] See Attorney General Ashcroft's FOIA Memorandum, reprinted in FOIA Post (posted 10/15/01) (emphasizing that agencies should "carefully consider the protection of," inter alia, law enforcement interests when reviewing law enforcement records).

or regulation.[42]

Indeed, courts increasingly are recognizing the appropriate application of Exemption 7(E) to such sensitive information, including:

(1) guidelines for response to terrorist attacks;[43]

(2) records pertaining to aviation "watch lists";[44]

(3) inspection statistics of an international seaport;[45]

(4) analyses of security procedures;[46] and

(5) records pertaining to domestic terrorism investigations.[47]

---

[42] See FOIA Post, "FOIA Officers Conference Held on Homeland Security" (posted 7/3/03) (summarizing authority for protecting homeland security-related information up to that date); accord Attorney General Ashcroft's FOIA Memorandum, reprinted in FOIA Post (posted 10/15/01) ("I encourage your agency to carefully consider the protection of all [applicable] values and interests when making disclosure determinations under the FOIA.").

[43] See Ctr. for Nat'l Sec. Studies, 1990 WL 236133, at *5-6 (according Exemption 7(E) protection to final contingency plan in event of attack on United States, to guidelines for response to terrorist attacks, and to contingency plans for immigration emergencies).

[44] See Gordon, 388 F. Supp. 2d at 1035-36 (protecting details of FBI's aviation "watch list" program -- including records detailing "selection criteria" for lists and handling and dissemination of lists, and "addressing perceived problems in security measures").

[45] See Coastal Delivery Corp., 272 F. Supp. 2d at 963-65 (protecting number of examinations at particular seaport because information could be used in conjunction with other publicly available information to discern rates of inspection at that port, thereby allowing for identification of "vulnerable ports" and target selection).

[46] See, e.g., Voinche, 940 F. Supp. at 329, 332 (approving the nondisclosure of information "relating to the security of the Supreme Court building and the security procedures for Supreme Court Justices" on the basis of both Exemptions 2 and 7(E)); cf. U.S. News & World Report, 1986 U.S. Dist. LEXIS 27634, at *8 (upholding protection of Secret Service's contract specifications for President's armored limousine); Hayward, 2 Gov't Disclosure Serv. (P-H), at 81,646 (protecting methods and techniques used by Marshals Service to relocate protected witnesses).

[47] See ACLU v. FBI, 429 F. Supp. 2d 179, 194 (D.D.C. 2006) (holding that the agency properly withheld certain records the release of which "could allow individuals 'to develop countermeasures' that could defeat the effec-

(continued...)

Furthermore, these types of records may well be protected from disclosure under more than one FOIA exemption,[48] and it also is possible that such sensitive law enforcement records, even if technically not covered by Exemption 7(E), may be covered by other FOIA exemptions.[49] (See the discussions of this point under Exemption 2, Homeland Security-Related Information, above, and Exemption 7(F), below.)

In sum, law enforcement agencies -- including the wide range of agencies that discharge national security- and homeland security-related responsibilities[50] -- may avail themselves of the distinct protections provided in Exemption 7(E)'s two clauses.[51] Their law enforcement records, to

---

[47](...continued) tiveness of the agency's domestic terrorism investigations" (quoting agency declaration)).

[48] See, e.g., Gordon, 388 F. Supp. 2d at 1035-36 (applying Exemptions 2 and 7(E) to same information); Coastal Delivery Corp., 272 F. Supp. 2d at 963-65 (concluding that records were properly withheld under both Exemptions 2 and 7(E)); Voinche, 940 F. Supp. at 329, 332 (approving the nondisclosure of information "relating to the security of the Supreme Court building and the security procedures for Supreme Court Justices" on the basis of both Exemptions 2 and 7(E)).

[49] See, e.g., Herrick's Newsletter, 2006 WL 1826185, at *8 (holding that portion of agency manual pertaining to destruction of seized property is not related to any law enforcement investigation or prosecution and cannot be withheld under Exemption 7(E), but can be withheld under Exemption 2); Living Rivers, 272 F. Supp. 2d at 1321-22 (concluding that maps of flooding likely to result from failure of Hoover Dam or Glen Canyon Dam were properly withheld under Exemption 7(F), instead of under Exemption 2 or Exemption 7(E), due largely to atypically narrow interpretation of law within particular judicial circuit).

[50] See, e.g., Morley, 2006 WL 2806561, at *14 (discussing application of Exemption 7(E) to CIA procedures, and observing that "'law enforcement purpose' includes national security-related government activities"); Living Rivers, 272 F. Supp. 2d at 1320-22 (treating Department of the Interior's Bureau of Reclamation as readily falling into FOIA's "law enforcement" category, even though protection was afforded under Exemption 7(F) rather than under Exemption 7(E)); cf. FOIA Post, "New Attorney General FOIA Memorandum Issued" (posted 10/15/01) (discussing the "need to protect critical systems, facilities, stockpiles, and other assets from security breaches and harm -- and in some instances from their potential use as weapons of mass destruction in and of themselves," as well as "any agency information that could enable someone to succeed in causing the feared harm").

[51] See Boyd v. DEA, No. 01-0524, slip op. at 7-8 (D.D.C. Mar. 8, 2002) (upholding protection under both clauses of Exemption 7(E) for highly sensi-
(continued...)

the extent that they can be regarded as reflecting techniques or procedures, are entitled to categorical protection under Exemption 7(E)'s first
clause.[52] In addition, law enforcement guidelines that satisfy the broad
"could reasonably be expected to risk circumvention of law" standard can
be protected under Exemption 7(E)'s second clause.[53] (See the discussion
of Exemption 2's overlapping "anti-circumvention" protection under Exemption 2, "High 2": Risk of Circumvention, above.)

## EXEMPTION 7(F)

Exemption 7(F) permits the withholding of law enforcement-related
information necessary to protect the physical safety of a wide range of individuals. This exemption provides broad protection to "any individual"
when disclosure of information about him "could reasonably be expected to
endanger [his] life or physical safety."[1]

Prior to the 1986 FOIA amendments,[2] Exemption 7(F) by its former
terms protected records that "would . . . endanger the life or physical safety
of law enforcement personnel,"[3] and it had been invoked to protect both
federal and local law enforcement officers.[4] Cases decided after the 1986

---

[51](...continued)
tive research analysis in intelligence report properly withheld by FinCEN,
Financial Crimes Enforcement Network of United States Department of the
Treasury); see also Hammes, 1994 WL 693717, at *1 (protecting Customs
Service criteria used to determine which passengers to stop and examine).

[52] See Attorney General's 1986 Amendments Memorandum at 15-16 &
n.27 (explaining that 1986 FOIA amendments eliminated requirement that
law enforcement information be "investigatory" in order to be withheld under any subpart of Exemption 7); see also Smith, 977 F. Supp. at 501 ("Exemption 7(E) provides categorical protection to information related to law
enforcement techniques.").

[53] See Attorney General's 1986 Amendments Memorandum at 17 & n.31.

[1] 5 U.S.C. § 552(b)(7)(F) (2000 & Supp. IV 2004).

[2] Pub. L. No. 99-570, § 1802, 100 Stat. 3207, 3207-48 to 3207-49 (1986).

[3] Pub. L. No. 93-502, 88 Stat. 1561, 1563 (1974) (subsequently amended).

[4] See, e.g., Maroscia v. Levi, 569 F.2d 1000, 1002 (7th Cir. 1977) (FBI Special Agents and also "other law enforcement personnel"); Barham v. Secret
Serv., No. 82-2130, slip op. at 5 (W.D. Tenn. Sept. 13, 1982) (Secret Service
agents); Docal v. Bennsinger, 543 F. Supp. 38, 48 (M.D. Pa. 1981) (DEA special agents, supervisory special agents, and local law enforcement officers); Nunez v. DEA, 497 F. Supp. 209, 212 (S.D.N.Y. 1980) (DEA special
agents); Ray v. Turner, 468 F. Supp. 730, 735 (D.D.C. 1979) (U.S. Customs
(continued...)

**EXEMPTION 7(F)**

FOIA amendments continue this strong protection for law enforcement agents.[5]

---

[4](...continued)
Service agent).

[5] See, e.g., Rugiero v. U.S. Dep't of Justice, 257 F.3d 534, 552 (6th Cir. 2001) (protecting names of DEA agents), cert. denied, 534 U.S. 1134 (2002); Johnston v. U.S. Dep't of Justice, No. 97-2173, 1998 U.S. App. LEXIS 18557, at *2 (8th Cir. Aug. 10, 1998) (protecting names of DEA agents); Housley v. DEA, No. 92-16946, 1994 U.S. App. LEXIS 11232, at *4 (9th Cir. May 4, 1994) (finding Exemption 7(F) properly used to protect "physical safety"); Peter S. Herrick's Customs & Int'l Trade Newsletter v. U.S. Customs & Border Prot., No. 04-0377, 2006 WL 1826185, at *9 (D.D.C. June 30, 2006) (finding that disclosure of U.S. Customs officials' identities and information regarding seized contraband could endanger life or physical safety of both Customs officials and innocent bystanders); McCoy v. United States, No. 04-101, 2006 WL 463106, at *11 (N.D. W. Va. Feb. 24, 2006) (magistrate's recommendation) (finding that DEA properly withheld names of DEA Special Agents, Deputy U.S. Marshals, and state and local law enforcement officers); Blanton v. U.S. Dep't of Justice, 182 F. Supp. 2d 81, 87 (D.D.C. 2002) (acknowledging that disclosure of identities of FBI Special Agents could endanger their safety), aff'd, 64 F. App'x 787 (D.C. Cir. 2003); Rubis v. DEA, No. 01-1132, slip op. at 4, 7 (D.D.C. Sept. 30, 2002) (protecting identities of DEA agents who routinely deal with violators, because disclosure would place them in danger); Garcia v. U.S. Dep't of Justice, 181 F. Supp. 2d 356, 378 (S.D.N.Y. 2002) (protecting names of FBI Special Agents and other government agents); Amro v. U.S. Customs Serv., 128 F. Supp. 2d 776, 788 (E.D. Pa. 2001) (protecting names of DEA supervisory agents and other law enforcement officers); Hronek v. DEA, 16 F. Supp. 2d 1260, 1275 (D. Or. 1998) (protecting names and identities of DEA agents, supervisory agents, and other law enforcement officers), aff'd, 7 F. App'x 591 (9th Cir. 2001); Hazel v. Dep't of Justice, No. 95-01992, slip op. at 13 (D.D.C. July 2, 1998) (protecting correctional officers' names); Johnson v. DEA, No. 97-2231, 1998 U.S. Dist. LEXIS 9802, at *14 (D.D.C. June 25, 1998) (protecting DEA agents' names because disclosure could have detrimental effect on operations), aff'd in pertinent part, 1999 U.S. App. LEXIS 7332 (D.C. Cir. Mar. 2, 1999); Franklin v. U.S. Dep't of Justice, No. 97-1225, slip op. at 15 (S.D. Fla. June 15, 1998) (magistrate's recommendation) ("It is in the public interest not to disclose the identity of [DEA] Special Agents so that they may continue to effectively pursue undercover and investigative assignments."), adopted (S.D. Fla. June 26, 1998), aff'd per curiam, 189 F.3d 485 (11th Cir. 1999); McGhghy v. DEA, No. C 97-0185, slip op. at 12 (N.D. Iowa May 29, 1998) (finding that DEA "established a clear nexus between disclosure and harm to agents and officers"), aff'd per curiam, No. 98-2989 (8th Cir. July 19, 1999); Fedrick v. U.S. Dep't of Justice, 984 F. Supp. 659, 665 (W.D.N.Y. 1997) (magistrate's recommendation) (protecting names of DEA agents, supervisory agents, and other law enforcement personnel), adopted, No. 95-558 (W.D.N.Y. Oct. 28, 1997), aff'd sub nom. Fedrick v. Huff, 165 F.3d 13 (2d Cir. (continued...)

Under the amended language of Exemption 7(F), courts have applied the broader coverage now offered by the exemption, holding that it can afford protection of the "names and identifying information of . . . federal employees, and third persons who may be unknown" to the requester in connection with particular law enforcement matters.[6] Withholding such infor-

---

[5](...continued)
1998) (unpublished table decision); Jimenez v. FBI, 938 F. Supp. 21, 30-31 (D.D.C. 1996) (holding that disclosure of names of DEA special agents, supervisors, and local law enforcement officer could result in "physical attacks, threats, or harassment"; disclosure of DEA's investigative personnel would endanger lives of its agents and have "detrimental effect" on its operations); Badalamenti v. U.S. Dep't of State, 899 F. Supp. 542, 550 (D. Kan. 1995) (protecting names of law enforcement personnel); Almy v. Dep't of Justice, No. 90-362, slip op. at 26 (N.D. Ind. Apr. 13, 1995) (protecting names of DEA agents, supervisory agents, and other law enforcement personnel), aff'd, 114 F.3d 1191 (7th Cir. 1997) (unpublished table decision); Manchester v. DEA, 823 F. Supp. 1259, 1273 (E.D. Pa. 1993) (protecting names and identities of DEA special agents, supervisory special agents, and other law enforcement officers). But see Pub. Employees for Envtl. Responsibility v. EPA, 978 F. Supp. 955, 964 (D. Colo. 1997) (finding no risk to agency investigators in disclosing EPA Inspector General guidelines).

[6] Luther v. IRS, No. 5-86-130, slip op. at 6 (D. Minn. Aug. 13, 1987); see also Johnston, 1998 U.S. App. LEXIS 18557, at *2 (protecting names of DEA personnel, local law enforcement personnel, and third parties); Herrick's Newsletter, 2006 WL 1826185, at *9 (holding that the release of information concerning seized contraband and Customs' officials could reasonably be expected to endanger the physical safety of those officials and "innocent third parties located in the vicinity of Customs' officials, activities, or seized contraband"); McQueen v. United States, 264 F. Supp. 2d 502, 521 (S.D. Tex. 2003) (protecting identities of informants and undercover agents participating in plaintiff's criminal investigation), aff'd, 100 F. App'x 964 (5th Cir. 2004); Brady-Lunny v. Massey, 185 F. Supp. 2d 928, 932 (C.D. Ill. 2002) (finding that release of list of detainees' names would endanger life and physical safety given security risks that always are present in inmate populations); Garcia, 181 F. Supp. 2d at 378 (protecting "names and/or identifying information concerning private citizens and third parties who provided information" to FBI); Hidalgo v. Bureau of Prisons, No. 00-1229, slip op. at 4 (D.D.C. June 6, 2001) (withholding information about inmate-plaintiff's "separatees"), summary affirmance granted, No. 01-5257 (D.C. Cir. Aug. 29, 2002); Bartolotta v. FBI, No. 99-1145, slip op. at 5-6 (D.D.C. July 13, 2000) (protecting identities of inmate-plaintiff's "separatees"); Willis v. FBI, No. 99-CV-73481, slip op. at 20-21 (E.D. Mich. July 11, 2000) (magistrate's recommendation) (protecting names and identifying information of federal employees and third parties), adopted (E.D. Mich. Sept. 29, 2000); Russell v. Barr, No. 92-2546, slip op. at 11-12 (D.D.C. Aug. 28, 1998) (protecting identities of individuals who cooperated in investigation and prosecution involving spousal murder when agency demonstrated requester's reputation for

(continued...)

mation can be necessary in order to protect such persons from possible harm by a requester who has threatened them in the past.[7] Indeed, many

---

[6](...continued)
violent behavior); Isley v. Executive Office for U.S. Attorneys, No. 96-0123, slip op. at 8-9 (D.D.C. Mar. 27, 1997) (upholding agency's nondisclosure of identifying information about individuals who provided information during murder investigation when there was reasonable likelihood that disclosure would threaten their lives), appeal dismissed, No. 97-5105 (D.C. Cir. Sept. 8, 1997); Anderson v. U.S. Marshals Serv., 943 F. Supp. 37, 40 (D.D.C. 1996) (protecting identity of individual who required separation from incarcerated requester when disclosure could endanger his safety); Sanders v. U.S. Dep't of Justice, No. 91-2263, 1992 WL 97785, at *4 (D. Kan. Apr. 21, 1992) (finding that disclosing identities of medical personnel who prepared requester's mental health records would endanger their safety, in view of requester's mental difficulties); Pfeffer v. Dir., Bureau of Prisons, No. 89-899, slip op. at 4 (D.D.C. Apr. 18, 1990) (holding that information about smuggling weapons into prisons could reasonably be expected to endanger physical safety of "some individual" and therefore is properly withheld). But see Long v. U.S. Dep't of Justice, 450 F. Supp. 2d 42, 80 (D.D.C.) (finding government's assertion that disclosure of "program category" information "will increase the chances that third parties will be harmed in some way" to be conclusory), amended by 457 F. Supp. 2d 30 (D.D.C. 2006), amended further on reconsideration, Nos. 00-0211 & 02-2467, 2007 WL 293508 (D.D.C. Feb. 2, 2007), stay granted (D.D.C. Feb. 13, 2007); Maydak v. U.S. Dep't of Justice, 362 F. Supp. 2d 316, 320 (D.D.C. 2005) (ordering release of psychological testing data and list of prison staff to inmate requester because such information ordinarily is released to public); Trupei v. Huff, No. 96-2850, 1998 WL 8986, at *4 (D.D.C. Jan. 7, 1998) (finding government's concern for safety of individuals whose identities are unknown to requester to be "conclusory," warranting only Exemption 7(C) protection); Linn v. U.S. Dep't of Justice, No. 92-1406, 1995 WL 631847, at *9 (D.D.C. Aug. 22, 1995) (finding that the agency "has not established even a minimal nexus" between the withheld information and harm to persons discussed in the file).

[7] See, e.g., Brunetti v. FBI, 357 F. Supp. 2d 97, 109 (D.D.C. 2004) (approving the withholding of the identities of individuals who cooperated with the FBI, given the "violent nature of the La Cosa Nostra organization"); Ortloff v. U.S. Dep't of Justice, No. 98-2819, slip op. at 10 (D.D.C. Mar. 22, 2002) (finding the withholding of the "name of one witness who was identified as being potentially subject to future harm" proper, given plaintiff's conviction for violent acts); Shores v. FBI, 185 F. Supp. 2d 77, 85 (D.D.C. 2002) (approving the nondisclosure of names of, and identifying information about, three cooperating witnesses when information obtained from one of those witnesses led to plaintiff's murder conviction and "prompted [p]laintiff to attempt to have a member of that witness' [sic] family murdered"); Blanton, 182 F. Supp. 2d at 87 (protecting identities of FBI Special Agents and non-law enforcement personnel assisting in investigation, because "[e]ven though [requester] is incarcerated, his threats against persons responsible
(continued...)

courts have held that the very expansive language of "any individual" encompasses the protection of the identities of informants.[8]

Significantly, Exemption 7(F) protection has been held to remain applicable even after a law enforcement officer subsequently retired.[9] Moreover, it has been held that Exemption 7(F) can be employed to protect even

---

[7](...continued)
for his arrest and now his conviction make it possible that these individuals could be targets of physical harm"); Burke v. U.S. Dep't of Justice, No. 96-1739, 1999 WL 1032814, at *9 (D.D.C. Sept. 30, 1999) (finding that disclosing identities of "agents, other agencies' personnel and sources could expose [them] to violent retaliation," given requester's violent history); Anderson v. U.S. Dep't of Justice, No. 95-1888, 1999 U.S. Dist. LEXIS 4731, at *10-11 (D.D.C. Mar. 31, 1999) (finding that releasing witnesses' names could subject them to harassment and threats, given requester's history of carrying firearms); Crooker v. IRS, No. 94-0755, 1995 WL 430605, at *5 (D.D.C. Apr. 27, 1995) (protecting confidential informants when requester has history of harassing, intimidating, and abusing witnesses); Manna v. U.S. Dep't of Justice, 815 F. Supp. 798, 810 (D.N.J. 1993) (finding that releasing FBI reports would endanger life or physical safety of associates of requester in organized crime case), aff'd on other grounds, 51 F.3d 1158 (3d Cir. 1995); Author Servs. v. IRS, No. 90-2187, slip op. at 7 (C.D. Cal. Nov. 14, 1991) (withholding identities of third parties and handwriting and identities of IRS employees in view of previous conflict and hostility between parties). But see Homick v. U.S. Dep't of Justice, No. 98-557, slip op. at 33-34 (N.D. Cal. Sept. 16, 2004) (ordering disclosure of information that would identify FBI informants despite evidence of requester's violent nature), reconsideration denied (N.D. Cal. Oct. 27, 2004), appeal dismissed, No. 04-17568 (9th Cir. July 5, 2005).

[8] Housley v. FBI, No. 87-3231, 1988 WL 30751, at *3 (D.D.C. Mar. 24, 1988) (protecting identities of informants); see also Butler v. U.S. Dep't of Justice, 368 F. Supp. 2d 776, 786 (E.D. Mich. 2005) (protecting information that could endanger lives of individuals who provided information to DEA); Bartolotta, No. 99-1145, slip op. at 5-6 (D.D.C. July 13, 2000) (protecting name of, and identifying information about, confidential inmate-source); Pray v. FBI, No. 95-0380, 1998 WL 440843, at *3 (S.D.N.Y. Aug. 3, 1998) (protecting names of sources); Jimenez, 938 F. Supp. at 30-31 (protecting names and identifying information furnished by confidential sources); Bruscino v. Fed. Bureau of Prisons, No. 94-1955, 1995 WL 444406, at *11 (D.D.C. May 12, 1995) (protecting investigatory information obtained from sources whose lives would be endangered by disclosure, especially in view of "rough justice" to be rendered upon informants should identities be disclosed), summary affirmance granted in pertinent part, vacated & remanded in part, No. 95-5213, 1996 WL 393101 (D.C. Cir. June 24, 1996).

[9] See Moody v. DEA, 592 F. Supp. 556, 559 (D.D.C. 1984).

the identities of individuals who testified at the requester's criminal trial.[10] And one court approved a rather novel, but certainly appropriate, application of this exemption to a description in an FBI laboratory report of a homemade machine gun because its disclosure would create the real possibility that law enforcement officers would have to face "individuals armed with homemade devices constructed from the expertise of other law enforcement people."[11]

When Exemption 7(F) was broadened by the 1986 FOIA amendments, that action created a broader potential for the exemption that obviously had yet to be fully realized.[12] Notably, it expanded the set of individ-

---

[10] See Linn v. U.S. Dep't of Justice, No. 92-1406, 1997 U.S. Dist. LEXIS 9321, at *17 (D.D.C. May 29, 1997) (protecting witnesses who testified) (Exemptions 7(C) and 7(F)), appeal dismissed voluntarily, No. 97-5122 (D.C. Cir. July 14, 1997); Beck v. U.S. Dep't of Justice, No. 88-3433, 1991 U.S. Dist. LEXIS 1179, at *10-11 (D.D.C. July 24, 1991) (finding that exemption was not necessarily waived when information revealed at public trial); Prows v. U.S. Dep't of Justice, No. 87-1657, 1989 WL 39288, at *2 (D.D.C. Apr. 13, 1989) (finding, as under Exemption 7(C), DEA agents' identities protectible even though they testified at trial), aff'd, No. 89-5185 (D.C. Cir. Feb. 26, 1990). But see Myers v. U.S. Dep't of Justice, No. 85-1746, 1986 U.S. Dist. LEXIS 20058, at *6 (D.D.C. Sept. 22, 1986) (declining to protect law enforcement personnel who testified) (Exemptions 7(C) and 7(F)).

[11] LaRouche v. Webster, No. 75-6010, 1984 WL 1061, at *8 (S.D.N.Y. Oct. 23, 1984); accord FOIA Post, "New Attorney General FOIA Memorandum Issued" (posted 10/15/01) (discussing use of Exemption 2 to protect critical systems, facilities, stockpiles, and other assets from security breaches and harm given their potential for use as weapons of mass destruction in and of themselves); see also Pfeffer, No. 89-899, slip op. at 4 (D.D.C. Apr. 14, 1990) (approving withholding of information on smuggling of weapons into prison); cf. FOIA Post, "Guidance on Homeland Security Information Issued" (posted 3/21/02) (instructing agencies to take appropriate action to safeguard information related to America's homeland security by giving careful consideration to all applicable FOIA exemptions, such as Exemption 2); Lawyers Comm. for Human Rights v. INS, 721 F. Supp. 552, 571 (S.D.N.Y. 1989) (declining to identify individuals listed in INS Lookout Book on basis of "ideological exclusion" provision other than by occupation and country, because "some individuals could be placed in grave danger in their own countries if it were learned that the American government suspects them of being affiliated with terrorist organizations") (Exemption 7(C)).

[12] See Attorney General's Memorandum on the 1986 Amendments to the Freedom of Information Act 18 (Dec. 1987) [hereinafter Attorney General's 1986 Amendments Memorandum] (discussing the amendments, and stating that agencies should consider the modifications of Exemption 7(F) as a signal to rely on it "whenever there is any reasonable likelihood of a FOIA disclosure endangering any person"); see also NARA v. Favish, 541 U.S.

(continued...)

uals entitled to Exemption 7(F) protection from "law enforcement person-nel" only, to begin with, to the all-encompassing formulation of "any per-son," without limitation.[13] By removing that earlier limitation on which in-dividuals merit protection, Congress authorized agencies to exercise their sound judgment in protecting "any person" whose life or safety is at risk in sensitive law enforcement records.[14] As was pointedly observed in the At-torney General's implementation memorandum on the 1986 FOIA amend-ments at the time: "Exemption 7(F) is now available to provide necessary protection for the full range of persons whose personal physical safety can be at stake in sensitive law enforcement files."[15]

Now, in the current post-September 11, 2001 homeland security envi-ronment, Exemption 7(F) provides vital new avenues of protection for sen-sitive information that could prove deadly if obtained by those seeking to do harm to the public on a large scale.[16] Indeed, Exemption 7(F) has now been found readily available to protect against disclosure of "inundation maps" that showed projected patterns in which downstream areas would be catastrophically flooded in the event of breaches in nearby dams.[17] The

---

[12](...continued)
157, 169 (evincing the Supreme Court's reliance on "the Attorney General's consistent interpretation of" the FOIA in successive such Attorney General memoranda), reh'g denied, 541 U.S. 1057 (2004).

[13] See Freedom of Information Reform Act of 1986, §§ 1801-04 of Pub. L. No. 99-570, 100 Stat. 3207-48 (1986); Attorney General's 1986 Amendments Memorandum 18.

[14] See, e.g., Garcia, 181 F. Supp. 2d at 378 ("In evaluating the validity of an agency's invocation of Exemption 7(F), the court should 'within limits, defer to the agency's assessment of danger.'" (quoting Linn, 1995 WL 631847, at *9)); see also Ctr. for Nat'l Security Studies v. U.S. Dep't of Jus-tice, 331 F.3d 918, 926-27 (D.C. Cir. 2003) (recognizing in analogous context under Exemption 7(A), that agency's judgment in this respect is entitled to great deference from courts).

[15] Attorney General's 1986 Amendments Memorandum 18; see also Fav-ish, 541 U.S. at 169 (citing, with approval, "the Attorney General's consist-ent interpretation of" the FOIA in such Attorney General FOIA memoran-da).

[16] Cf. FOIA Post, "New Attorney General FOIA Memorandum Issued" (posted 10/15/01) (discussing the "need to protect critical systems, facili-ties, stockpiles, and other assets from security breaches and harm -- and in some instances from their potential use as weapons of mass destruction in and of themselves," as well as "any agency information that could enable someone to succeed in causing the feared harm").

[17] Living Rivers, Inc. v. U.S. Bureau of Reclamation, 272 F. Supp. 2d 1313, 1321-22 (D. Utah 2003) (finding that disclosure of inundation maps could
(continued...)

court reasoned that releasing such information in the face of current homeland security concerns "could increase the risk of an attack" on one dam
over another, and on such dam targets overall, because terrorists would be
able to use these maps to estimate the amount of damage and carnage
caused by flooding.[18]

Courts have continued to address this and to find that Exemption
7(F)'s protective ambit broadly encompasses any unspecified individual
whose safety could reasonably be endangered by a disclosure.[19] This rationale was recently used to protect information regarding seized contraband, and information concerning U.S. Customs' employees involved in the

---

[17](...continued)
reasonably be expected to place at risk lives of individuals in downstream
areas that would be flooded by breach of dams by increasing risk of terrorist attacks on dams); see also Ctr. for Nat'l Sec. Studies v. U.S. Dep't of
Justice, 215 F. Supp. 2d 94, 106, 108-09 (D.D.C. 2002) (holding that while
Exemption 7(F) does not protect names of individuals detained after terrorist attack, or identities of their attorneys, it does protect dates and locations of their detention, arrest, and release), rev'd in other part, aff'd in part
on other grounds & remanded, 331 F.3d 918 (D.C. Cir. 2003) (Exemption
7(A)).

[18] Living Rivers, 272 F. Supp. 2d at 1321-22 (concluding that the requested FOIA disclosure could "aid in carrying out a terrorist attack").

[19] See, e.g., L.A. Times Commc'ns, LLC v. Dep't of the Army, 442 F. Supp.
2d 880, 898-900 (C.D. Cal. 2006) (applying Exemption 7(F) where disclosure
of private security contractor company names could endanger the life or
physical safety of many individuals); Herrick's Newsletter, 2006 WL
1826185, at *9 (finding that Exemption 7(F) encompasses the protection of
innocent third parties located in the vicinity of Customs' officials, activities,
or seized contraband); Brady-Lunny, 185 F. Supp. 2d at 932 (upholding use
of Exemption 7(F) in order to protect against risk of violence on a broad
range of unspecified individuals if information on prisoners was released);
Ctr. for Nat'l Sec. Studies, 215 F. Supp. 2d at 108 (finding that disclosure of
location of detention facilities holding suspects in September 11 attacks
"would make detention facilities vulnerable to retaliatory attacks, and
'place at risk not only . . . detainees, but the facilities themselves and their
employees'"), aff'd in part & rev'd in part on other grounds, 331 F. 3d 918
(D.C. Cir. 2003); see also LaRouche, 1984 WL 1061, at *8 (applying even the
unamended form of Exemption 7(F) to an FBI laboratory report on home-
made machine guns, because unknown current or future law enforcement
officers could have to face "individuals armed with [such] home-made devices" if disclosure were compelled). But see ACLU v. DOD, 389 F. Supp.
2d 547, 578 (S.D.N.Y. 2005) (declining to apply Exemption 7(F) to withhold
photographs depicting the treatment of detainees, in part because of the
"education and debate [the] publicity [of the photographs] will foster").

seizure, storage, and evaluation of the contraband.[20] Applying Exemption 7(F), the court reasoned that the release of this information could place at risk innocent third parties located in the vicinity of U.S. Customs' officials, activities, or the seized contraband.[21] Similarly, Exemption 7(F) was used to protect the company names of private security contractors (PSC) operating in concert with U.S. military forces in Iraq.[22] In that case, the court accepted the government's specific "assessment that disclosure of the PSC company names might very well be expected to endanger the life or safety of miliary personnel, PSC employees, and civilians of Iraq."[23]

Although Exemption 7(F)'s coverage is in large part duplicative of that afforded by Exemption 7(C), it is potentially broader in that no balancing is required for withholding under Exemption 7(F),[24] so agencies should give careful consideration to the added measure of protection that it affords in all law enforcement contexts.[25] Indeed, it is difficult to imagine any circumstance in which the public's interest in disclosure could outweigh the personal safety of any individual.[26]

---

[20] Herrick's Newsletter, 2006 WL 1826185, at *8-9.

[21] Id. at 9 (citing Garcia, 181 F. Supp. 2d at 378).

[22] L.A. Times, 442 F. Supp. 2d at 898-900.

[23] Id. at 900.

[24] See Raulerson v. Ashcroft, 271 F. Supp. 2d 17, 29 (D.D.C. 2002) ("Unlike Exemption 7(C), which involves a balancing of societal and individual privacy interests, 7(F) is an absolute ban against certain information and, arguably, an even broader protection than 7(C)."); Shores, 185 F. Supp. 2d at 85 (stating that Exemption 7(F), while covering material that also may be subject to Exemption 7(C), "does not require any balancing test"); LaRouche, 1984 WL 1061, at *8 (stating Exemption 7(F) was properly asserted after the danger to law enforcement personnel was identified); see also FOIA Update, Vol. V, No. 2, at 5. But see ACLU, 389 F. Supp. 2d at 578 (dicta) (rejecting the principle that once threat to life or safety is discerned, no balancing is required in Exemption 7(F) analysis).

[25] Accord Attorney General's Memorandum for Heads of All Federal Departments and Agencies Regarding the Freedom of Information Act (Oct. 12, 2001) [hereinafter Attorney General Ashcroft's FOIA Memorandum], reprinted in FOIA Post (posted 10/15/01) ("I encourage your agency to carefully consider the protection of all [applicable] values and interests when making disclosure determinations under the FOIA."); see also FOIA Post, "FOIA Officers Conference Held on Homeland Security" (posted 7/3/03) (identifying homeland security context as within realm of law enforcement for purposes of FOIA protection, and discussing Exemption 7(F) as basis for protecting sensitive homeland security-related information).

[26] See Colon v. Executive Office for U.S. Attorneys, No. 98-0180, 1998 WL (continued...)

In sum, Exemption 7(F) has proven to be of great utility to law enforcement agencies, given the lessened "could reasonably be expected" harm standard now in effect.[27] It will apply whenever an agency determines that there is a reasonable likelihood that disclosure risks physical harm to anyone.[28]

## EXEMPTION 8

Exemption 8 of the FOIA protects matters that are "contained in or related to examination, operating, or condition reports prepared by, on behalf of, or for the use of an agency responsible for the regulation or supervision of financial institutions."[1]

---

[26](...continued)
695631, at *6 (D.D.C. Sept. 29, 1998) (reiterating that it is not in public interest to disclose identities of law enforcement officers); Franklin, No. 97-1225, slip op. at 15 (S.D. Fla. June 15, 1998) (magistrate's recommendation) (finding that "it is in the public interest" to protect names of DEA agents), adopted (S.D. Fla. June 26, 1998).

[27] See, e.g., Spirko v. USPS, 147 F.3d 992, 994 (D.C. Cir. 1998) (protecting handwritten notes about suspects); Brady-Lunny, 185 F. Supp. 2d at 932 (recognizing risk to physical safety present in inmate populations, "given inmates' gang ties, interest in escape, and motive for violence against informants and rivals"; finding that disclosure of detainees' names could threaten security); L.A. Times, 442 F. Supp. 2d at 900 (finding that disclosure of private security contractor (PSC) company names could reasonably be expected to endanger lives of military personnel, PSC employees, and civilians in Iraq); Blanton, 182 F. Supp. 2d at 86 (withholding the identities of "non-law enforcement persons who assist the government in its criminal investigation (such as persons in the Witness Protection Program)"); Garcia, 181 F. Supp. 2d at 373 (protecting the personal information of any of the agents or other witnesses whose identities are contained in a file); Crompton, No. 95-8771, slip op. at 16 (C.D. Cal. Mar. 26, 1997) (finding withholding of agents' names, signatures, and identifying information proper).

[28] See Attorney General's 1986 Amendments Memorandum 18 & n.34 (Dec. 1987) (suggesting that Exemption 7(F) as amended be applied whenever there is any likelihood of harm); see also, e.g., Dickie v. Dep't of the Treasury, No. 86-649, slip op. at 13 (D.D.C. Mar. 31, 1987) (upholding application of Exemption 7(F) as amended based upon agency judgment of "very strong likelihood" of harm); see also FOIA Update, Vol. XV, No. 2, at 3; Attorney General Ashcroft's FOIA Memorandum, reprinted in FOIA Post (posted 10/15/01) (emphasizing federal government's commitment to enhancing effectiveness of law enforcement agencies).

[1] 5 U.S.C. § 552(b)(8) (2000 & Supp. IV 2004).

This exemption received little judicial attention during the first dozen years of the FOIA's operation. The only significant decision during that period was M.A. Schapiro & Co. v. SEC, in which the District Court for the District of Columbia held that national securities exchanges and broker-dealers are not "financial institutions" within the meaning of the exemption.[2] Fourteen years later, after passage of the Government in the Sunshine Act[3] -- the legislative history of which broadly defines the term "financial institutions" -- that same court disavowed its early narrow interpretation of the term and held that stock exchanges qualify as "financial institutions" under Exemption 8.[4] As a result, subsequent attempts by FOIA requesters to have courts rely on the ruling in M.A. Schapiro have been unsuccessful.[5]

Instead, courts interpreting Exemption 8 have largely declined to restrict the "particularly broad, all-inclusive" scope of the exemption.[6] The Court of Appeals for the District of Columbia Circuit has led the way by declaring that "if Congress has intentionally and unambiguously crafted a particularly broad, all-inclusive definition, it is not [the courts'] function, even in the FOIA context, to subvert that effort."[7] As another court has

---

[2] 339 F. Supp. 467, 470 (D.D.C. 1972).

[3] 5 U.S.C. § 552b (2000 & Supp. III 2003).

[4] Mermelstein v. SEC, 629 F. Supp. 672, 673-75 (D.D.C. 1986).

[5] See Feshbach v. SEC, 5 F. Supp. 2d 774, 781 (N.D. Cal. 1997) (rejecting argument that court should follow M.A. Schapiro definition of term "financial institutions" because "the same district court [had] noted [in Mermelstein] that [M.A. Schapiro] was no longer good law"); Berliner, Zisser, Walter & Gallegos v. SEC, 962 F. Supp. 1348, 1351 n.5 (D. Colo. 1997) (likewise rejecting cramped reading of term "financial institutions" because court in Mermelstein had noted that "subsequent passage of the Sunshine Act" rendered decision in M.A. Schapiro "no longer good law").

[6] Consumers Union of the U.S., Inc. v. Office of the Comptroller of the Currency, No. 86-1841, slip op. at 2 (D.D.C. Mar. 11, 1988); McCullough v. FDIC, No. 79-1132, 1980 U.S. Dist. LEXIS 17685, at *2-3 (D.D.C. July 28, 1980) (observing that "Congress has left no room for a narrower interpretation of Exemption 8"). But see Forest Guardians v. U.S. Forest Serv., No. 99-615, slip op. at 51 (D.N.M. Jan. 29, 2001) (declaring that Exemption 8 does not "shield everything banking institutions accumulate . . . that might be reviewed in the process of a bank examination," and opining that "[s]uch a vague and sweeping definition of what Exemption 8 encompasses can only be regarded as antithetic to . . . FOIA's disclosure requirements"), appeal dismissed voluntarily, No. 01-2296 (10th Cir. Nov. 21, 2001).

[7] Consumers Union of the U.S., Inc. v. Heimann, 589 F.2d 531, 533 (D.C. Cir. 1978); see also Sharp v. FDIC, 2 Gov't Disclosure Serv. (P-H) ¶ 81,107, at 81,270 (D.D.C. Jan. 28, 1981); McCullough, 1980 U.S. Dist. LEXIS 17685, at

(continued...)

stated: "Exemption 8 was intended by Congress -- and has been interpreted by courts -- to be very broadly construed."[8]

Indeed, the D.C. Circuit has gone so far as to state that in Exemption 8 Congress has provided "absolute protection regardless of the circumstances underlying the regulatory agency's receipt or preparation of examination, operating or condition reports."[9] Similarly, in a major Exemption 8 decision, the D.C. Circuit broadly construed the term "financial institutions" and held that it is not limited to "depository" institutions.[10] In turn, the District Court for the District of Colorado relied upon that D.C. Circuit decision when ruling that an "investment advisor company" is a "financial institution" under Exemption 8, observing that "investment advisors, as a matter of common practice, are fiduciaries of their clients who direct, and in reality make, important investment decisions."[11] The District Court for the Northern District of California, "following the logic" of these earlier cases, broadly held "that the term 'financial institutions' encompasses brokers and dealers of securities or commodities as well as self-regulatory organiza-

---

[7](...continued)
*2-3.

[8] Pentagon Fed. Credit Union v. Nat'l Credit Union Admin., No. 95-1475, slip op. at 8-9 (E.D. Va. June 7, 1996); accord Attorney General's Memorandum for Heads of All Federal Departments and Agencies Regarding the Freedom of Information Act (Oct. 12, 2001), reprinted in FOIA Post (posted 10/15/01) (emphasizing importance of protecting institutional and commercial information); FOIA Post, "New Attorney General Memorandum Issued" (posted 10/15/01) (discussing the need for agencies to fully, deliberately, and carefully consider the institutional, commercial, and personal privacy interests that can be implicated by any disclosure of government information).

[9] Gregory v. FDIC, 631 F.2d 896, 898 (D.C. Cir. 1980); see also Clarkson v. Greenspan, No. 97-2035, slip op. at 14-15 (D.D.C. June 30, 1998) (extending Exemption 8 protection to records of examinations conducted by Federal Reserve Banks for Board of Governors of Federal Reserve System), summary affirmance granted, No. 98-5349, 1999 WL 229017 (D.C. Cir. Mar. 2, 1999).

[10] Pub. Citizen v. Farm Credit Admin., 938 F.2d 290, 293-94 (D.C. Cir. 1991) (per curiam) (holding that National Consumer Cooperative Bank (NCCB) is "financial institution" for purposes of Exemption 8 and that exemption protects audit reports prepared by Farm Credit Administration (FCA) for submission to Congress regarding NCCB, even though FCA does not regulate or supervise NCCB).

[11] Berliner, 962 F. Supp. at 1352 (relying on the "legislative history of the [Government in the] Sunshine Act" in the absence of any "unambiguous definition of financial institutions provided in FOIA's text or legislative history").

tions, such as the [National Association of Securities Dealers]."[12]

Courts have consistently discerned two purposes underlying Exemption 8[13]-- a primary purpose of "ensur[ing] the security of financial institutions," which could be undermined by frank evaluations of such institutions, and a secondary purpose of safeguarding "the relationship between the banks and their supervising agencies."[14] Accordingly, different types of documents have been held to fall within the broad confines of Exemption 8.

First and foremost, the authority of federal agencies to withhold bank examination reports prepared by federal bank examiners has not been questioned.[15] Further, matters that are "related to" such reports -- that is,

---

[12] Feshbach, 5 F. Supp. 2d at 781.

[13] See Nat'l Cmty. Reinvestment Coal. v. Nat'l Credit Union Admin., 290 F. Supp. 2d 124, 135-36 (D.D.C. 2003) (affirming that two purposes of Exemption 8 are "to safeguard public confidence . . . which could be undermined by candid evaluations of financial institutions" and "to ensure that [banks] continue to cooperate . . . without fear that their confidential information will be disclosed"); Berliner, 962 F. Supp. at 1353 (delineating Exemption 8's "dual purposes" as "protecting the integrity of financial institutions and facilitating cooperation between [agencies] and the entities regulated by [them]"); Atkinson v. FDIC, No. 79-1113, 1980 WL 355660, at *1 (D.D.C. Feb. 13, 1980) (recognizing Exemption 8's purposes of protecting security of financial institutions and "promot[ing] cooperation and communication between bank employees and examiners").

[14] Consumers Union, 589 F.2d at 534 (identifying primary reason for adoption of Exemption 8 as protecting disclosure of examination, operation, and condition reports -- which, if disclosed, might undermine public confidence in financial institutions -- and secondary reason as safeguarding relationship between supervisory agencies and banks, because banks would be less likely to cooperate with federal examiners if examinations were freely available to competitors and to public); Feinberg v. Hibernia Corp., No. 90-4245, 1993 WL 8620, at *4 (E.D. La. Jan. 6, 1993) (identifying Exemption 8's dual purposes, including primary purpose of protecting operation and condition reports containing frank evaluations of investigated banks and secondary purpose of protecting relationship between financial institutions and supervisory government agencies) (non-FOIA case); Fagot v. FDIC, 584 F. Supp. 1168, 1173 (D.P.R. 1984) (recognizing primary purpose of Exemption 8 in protecting information containing frank evaluations which might undermine public confidence and secondary purpose in protecting relationship between financial institutions and supervisory agencies), aff'd in pertinent part & rev'd in part, 760 F.2d 252 (1st Cir. 1985) (unpublished table decision).

[15] See Sharp, 2 Gov't Disclosure Serv. (P-H) at 81,270; Atkinson, 1980 WL 355660, at *1; see also Clarkson, No. 97-2035, slip op. at 14-15 (D.D.C. June
(continued...)

documents that "represent the foundation of the examination process, the findings of such an examination, or its follow-up" -- have also been held exempt from disclosure.[16] Likewise, Exemption 8 has been employed to withhold portions of documents -- such as internal memoranda and policy statements -- that contain specific information about named financial institutions.[17]

Bank examination reports and related documents prepared by state regulatory agencies have been found protectible under Exemption 8 on more than one ground. The purposes of the exemption are plainly served by withholding such material because of the "interconnected" purposes

---

[15](...continued)
30, 1998) (holding that Board of Governors of Federal Reserve System may withhold records of examinations prepared by Federal Reserve Banks); cf. Feinberg v. Hibernia Corp., No. 90-4245, 1992 WL 54738, at *6-7 (E.D. La. Mar. 9, 1992) (noting, in the context of a civil discovery dispute in a lawsuit unrelated to the FOIA, that "[t]here is no question that the bank examination reports themselves fall within the purview" of what would be protected by Exemption 8) (non-FOIA case).

[16] Atkinson, 1980 WL 355660, at *1; see, e.g., Parsons v. Freedom of Info. Act Officer, Office of Consumer Affairs SEC, No. 96-4128, 1997 WL 461320, at *1 (6th Cir. Aug. 12, 1997) (summarily holding that "all communication[s] between" SEC and National Association of Securities Dealers (NASD), including "any SEC audits" of NASD, "were exempt from disclosure"); Abrams v. Office of the Comptroller of the Currency, No. 05-2433, 2006 WL 1450525, at *4 (N.D. Tex. May 25, 2006) (ruling that OCC Order of Investigation was withholdable even if it lacked "direct connection" with examination report, so long as it was "related to" such examination report); Biase v. Office of Thrift Supervision, No. 93-2521, slip op. at 12 (D.N.J. Dec. 16, 1993); Teichgraeber v. Bd. of Governors, Fed. Reserve Sys., No. 87-2505, 1989 WL 32183, at *1 (D. Kan. Mar. 20, 1989); Consumers Union, No. 86-1841, slip op. at 2-3 (D.D.C. Mar. 11, 1988); Folger v. Conover, No. 82-4, slip op. at 5-8 (E.D. Ky. Oct. 25, 1983); Sharp, 2 Gov't Disclosure Serv. (P-H) at 81,270-71; cf. In re Knoxville News-Sentinel Co., 723 F.2d 470, 476 (6th Cir. 1983) (citing Exemption 8 as support for conclusion that agency's questioning of bank employees is to be shielded from civil discovery) (non-FOIA case). But see Forest Guardians, No. 99-615, slip op. at 51-52 (D.N.M. Jan. 29, 2001) (declining to extend Exemption 8 protection to escrow waivers, and ruling they are not "reports of or related to a bank examination").

[17] Wachtel v. Office of Thrift Supervision, No. 3-90-833, slip op. at 19-20, 23, 26-28, 30, 33 (M.D. Tenn. Nov. 20, 1990) (protecting portions of documents containing information about two named financial institutions -- specifically, names of institutions, names of officers and agents, any references to their geographic locations, and specific information about their financial conditions).

and operations of federal and state banking authorities.[18] In one case, a state agency report, transferred to a federal agency strictly for its confidential use and thus still within the control of the state agency, was held as a threshold matter not even to be an "agency record" under the FOIA subject to disclosure.[19] In general, "all records, regardless of the source,"[20] concerning "a bank's financial condition and operations [that are] in the possession of a federal agency 'responsible for the regulation or supervision of financial institutions,' are exempt."[21]

Indeed, even records pertaining to banks that are no longer in operation can be withheld under Exemption 8 in order to serve the policy of promoting "frank cooperation" between bank and agency officials.[22] The ex-

---

[18] Atkinson, 1980 WL 355660, at *1.

[19] McCullough, 1980 U.S. Dist. LEXIS 17685, at *7-8.

[20] Id. (quoting Admin. Procedure Act: Hearing on S. 1663 Before the Subcomm. on Admin. Practice & Procedure of the Senate Comm. on the Judiciary, 88th Cong. 2d Sess. 179 (1964)); see also Consumers Union, No. 86-1841, slip op. at 2-3 (D.D.C. Mar. 11, 1988) (finding examination report protectible even if its contents originate with consumers rather than financial institutions or regulators).

[21] McCullough, 1980 U.S. Dist. LEXIS 17685, at *7-8 (quoting Admin. Procedure Act: Hearing on S. 1663 Before the Subcomm. on Admin. Practice & Procedure of the Senate Comm. on the Judiciary, 88th Cong. 2d Sess. 179 (1964)); see also Snoddy v. Hawke, No. 99-1636, slip op. at 2 (D. Colo. Dec. 20, 1999) (holding that electronic mail, notes, and correspondence pertaining to matters discussed by employees of Citibank and Office of Comptroller of Currency were properly withheld as "matters prepared by or for the [regulating] agency . . . [and pertaining to] examination, operating or condition reports"), aff'd on other grounds, 13 F. App'x 768 (10th Cir. 2001); Clarkson, No. 97-2035, slip op. at 15 (D.D.C. June 30, 1998) (finding that records of examinations conducted by Federal Reserve Banks for the Board of Governors of the Federal Reserve System were properly withheld because the "examinations were done by or for the agency responsible for regulating Reserve Banks"). But see Forest Guardians, No. 99-615, slip op. at 51 (D.N.M. Jan. 29, 2001) (rejecting the agency's argument that because the Farm Credit Administration is a financial institution responsible for regulating Farm Credit Banks, and escrow waivers submitted by lenders contained information contained in or related to bank examination or condition reports, those escrow waivers fall within Exemption 8: "Were the argument to be taken as meritorious, it would shield everything banking institutions accumulate if any possibility existed the information might be reviewed in the process of examination.").

[22] Gregory, 631 F.2d at 899; accord Berliner, 962 F. Supp. at 1353 (upholding applicability of Exemption 8 to documents relating to company

(continued...)

emption protects even bank examination reports and related memoranda relating to insolvency proceedings.[23] Documents relating to cease-and-desist orders that issue after a bank examination as the result of a closed administrative hearing are also properly exempt.[24] Also, reports examining bank compliance with consumer laws and regulations have been held to "fall squarely within the exemption."[25]

Moreover, in keeping with this expansive construction of Exemption 8, courts have generally not required agencies to segregate and disclose portions of documents unrelated to the financial state of the institution. As one court has observed, "an entire examination report, not just that related to the 'condition of the bank' may properly be withheld."[26] Although some courts have declined to extend the protection of Exemption 8 to "purely factual material,"[27] the District Court for the District of Columbia has consist-

---

[22](...continued) that had "been defunct for at least four years" and declining to adopt argument that passage of time abated "need for confidentiality"). But cf. In re Sunrise Sec. Litig., 109 B.R. 658, 664-67 (E.D. Pa. 1990) (holding that Federal Home Loan Bank of Atlanta could not rely upon regulation implementing Exemption 8 as independent evidentiary "bank examination privilege," and finding that even under more general "official information privilege" there exists no absolute protection for internal working papers and other documents generated in government's examination of failed bank) (non-FOIA case).

[23] See, e.g., Tripati v. U.S. Dep't of Justice, No. 87-3301, 1990 U.S. Dist. LEXIS 6249, at *2-3 (D.D.C. May 18, 1990).

[24] See, e.g., Atkinson, 1980 WL 355660, at *2.

[25] Id.; see also Snoddy, No. 99-1636, slip op. at 2 (D. Colo. Dec. 20, 1999) (holding that e-mail, notes, and other correspondence pertaining to whether Citibank violated regulation fell within purview of Exemption 8); Consumers Union, No. 86-1841, slip op. at 2-3 (D.D.C. Mar. 11, 1988) (finding that reports fall within Exemption 8 "because they analyze and summarize information concerning consumer complaints"); cf. Consumers Union, 589 F.2d at 534-35 (concluding that Truth in Lending Act, 15 U.S.C. § 1601 (2000), does not narrow Exemption 8's broad language).

[26] Atkinson, 1980 WL 355660, at *2. But see Fagot v. FDIC, No. 84-1523, slip op. at 5-6 (1st Cir. Mar. 27, 1985) (finding that portion of document which does not relate to bank report or examination cannot be withheld); see also FOIA Update, Vol. XIV, No. 3, at 11-12 ("OIP Guidance: The 'Reasonable Segregation' Obligation").

[27] Pentagon Fed., No. 95-1476, slip op. at 9 (E.D. Va. June 7, 1996) (declining to extend Exemption 8 protection to "purely factual material"); see Lee v. FDIC, 923 F. Supp. 451, 459 (S.D.N.Y. 1996) (likewise denying protection for information found to be "primarily factual"), dismissed, No. 1:95 CV
(continued...)

ently protected factual material, most recently in its decision in <u>Bloomberg</u> <u>v. SEC</u>,[28] where it pointedly noted the absence of any controlling case law to support a "distinction between factual versus analytical or deliberative material under [Exemption 8]."[29] Relying on an earlier decision of the same court, <u>Bloomberg</u> made clear that any consideration of the bank examination privilege has no place in an Exemption 8 case.[30] Indeed, in light of the broad construction traditionally given to Exemption 8,[31] its underlying purposes,[32] and the distinct possibility that the bank examination privilege is most aptly considered under Exemption 5,[33] at least for records that qualify

---

[27](...continued)
7963 (S.D.N.Y. Sept. 15, 1997); <u>cf.</u> <u>Schreiber v. Soc'y for Sav. Bancorp, Inc.</u>, 11 F.3d 217, 220 (D.C. Cir. 1993) (declaring, in context of civil discovery, that "bank examination privilege protects only agency opinions and recommendations from disclosure; purely factual information falls outside the privilege") (non-FOIA case); <u>In re Subpoena</u>, 967 F.2d 630, 634 (D.C. Cir. 1992) ("The bank examination privilege, like the deliberative process privilege, shields from discovery only agency opinions or recommendations; it does not protect purely factual material.") (non-FOIA case).

[28] 357 F. Supp. 2d 156 (D.D.C. 2004).

[29] <u>Id.</u> at 170.

[30] <u>See</u> <u>id.</u> (citing <u>Nat'l Cmty. Reinvestment Coal.</u>, 290 F. Supp. 2d at 136 n.5).

[31] <u>See, e.g.</u>, <u>Consumers Union</u>, 589 F.2d at 533 (emphasizing that courts should not "subvert" Congress's "intentionally and unambiguously crafted . . . broad, all-inclusive definition" in Exemption 8 context).

[32] <u>See</u> <u>Bloomberg</u>, 357 F. Supp. 2d at 170 (reasoning that withholding both factual and other material under Exemption 8 better serves its twin purposes of safeguarding public stature of financial institutions and encouraging cooperation between regulatory agencies and their regulated institutions); <u>cf.</u> <u>Marriott Employees' Fed. Credit Union v. Nat'l Credit Union Admin.</u>, No. 96-478-A, 1996 WL 33497625, at *5 (E.D. Va. Dec. 24, 1996) (protecting factual information, despite the court's belief that Exemption 8 generally does not shield factual information, because "disclosure of [the particular information at issue] would undermine the spirit of cooperation between banks and regulating agencies that Exemption 8 attempts to foster").

[33] <u>See, e.g.</u>, <u>United States v. Weber Aircraft Corp.</u>, 465 U.S. 792, 800 (1984) (recognizing that Exemption 5 applies to both statutory and common law privileges and that it is not limited to those listed in Exemption 5's legislative history); <u>Burka v. HHS</u>, 87 F.3d 508, 516 (D.C. Cir. 1996) (construing Exemption 5 to cover those privileges mentioned in FOIA's legislative history and "other generally recognized civil discovery protections"); <u>In re</u> <u>Subpoena Served Upon the Comptroller of the Currency</u>, 967 F.2d 630, 633

(continued...)

as inter-agency or intra-agency records under Exemption 5's threshold requirement,[34] Bloomberg reflects a strongly protective approach for the treatment of factual material under Exemption 8.

Lastly, it should be noted that a provision of the Federal Deposit Insurance Corporation Improvement Act of 1991 explicitly limits Exemption 8's applicability with respect to specific reports prepared pursuant to it.[35] That statute requires all federal banking agency inspectors general to conduct a review and to make a written report when a deposit insurance fund incurs a material loss with respect to an insured depository institution.[36] The statute further provides that, with the exception of information that would reveal the identity of any customer of the institution, the federal banking agency "shall disclose the report upon request under [the FOIA] without excising . . . any information about the insured depository institution under [Exemption 8]."[37]

## EXEMPTION 9

Exemption 9 of the FOIA covers "geological and geophysical information and data, including maps, concerning wells."[1] This exemption has rarely been invoked or interpreted,[2] so its contours remain to be fully defined. As few courts have examined Exemption 9 in any depth, it is still not clear exactly what types of geological or geophysical information are protected from disclosure under the exemption, or whether it was intended to apply to all types of "wells."

More than twenty years ago, one court held in Black Hills Alliance v. United States Forest Service that Exemption 9 applies only to "well information of a technical or scientific nature," and not to general mineral exploration data -- such as the location, depth, or number of exploration drill

---

[33](...continued)
(D.C. Cir. 1992) (observing that courts have "long recognized" bank examination privilege).

[34] 5 U.S.C. § 552(b)(5).

[35] 12 U.S.C.A. § 1831o(k) (2001 & West Supp. 2006).

[36] Id. § 1831o(k)(1).

[37] Id. § 1831o(k)(4).

[1] 5 U.S.C. § 552(b)(9) (2000 & Supp. IV 2004).

[2] See, e.g., Nat'l Broad. Co. v. SBA, 836 F. Supp. 121, 124 n.2 (S.D.N.Y. 1993) (noting merely that document withheld under Exemption 4 "also contains geographic or geological information which is exempted from disclosure pursuant to FOIA Exemption 9").

holes.[3] It is significant that this court pointed to the legislative history of the FOIA -- specifically, to evidence that Congress intended through Exemption 9 to protect the oil and gas exploration and extraction industry from unfair competitive harm by "speculators" -- in support of its decision to order the release of generalized well data where a competitive harm argument could not readily be supported.[4]

Two recent decisions, however, give greater depth to Exemption 9. In Starkey v. United States Department of Interior[5] the District Court for the Southern District of California held that information related to the presence of groundwater -- including "ground water inventories, [water] well yield in gallons per minute, and the thickness of the decomposed granite aquifer" -- was exempt from disclosure under both Exemption 4[6] and Exemption 9.[7] Though the court discussed the two exemptions separately, with Exemption 9 receiving very little analysis, it emphasized that "water is a precious, limited resource" and that release of well data would place one party at a

---

[3] 603 F. Supp. 117, 122 (D.S.D. 1984) (requiring government to disclose number, locations, and depths of proposed uranium exploration drill holes in national forest under federally approved program, and noting that this geological exploration information "falls short of the technical and scientific information envisioned by Congress").

[4] Id. (stating that disclosure of "exploratory findings of oil companies would give speculators an unfair advantage over the companies which spent millions of dollars in exploration" (citing H.R. Rep. No. 89-1497, at 9 (1966), reprinted in 1966 U.S.C.C.A.N. 2418, 2428)); see also Admin. Procedure Act: Hearing on S. 1160, S. 1336, S. 1758 and S. 1879 Before the Subcomm. on Admin. Practice and Procedure of the Senate Comm. on the Judiciary, 89th Cong. 536-38 (1965) (statement of W. Oil & Gas Ass'n) (lobbying for protection of information furnished to government by oil and gas industries, resulting in later adoption of Exemption 9, despite proposed Exemption 4's protection of confidential commercial information, due to concerns that Exemption 4 might be narrowly construed); cf. Petroleum Exploration v. Comm'r, 193 F.2d 59, 62 (4th Cir. 1951) (recognizing commercial value of information related to mineral exploration and extraction) (non-FOIA case); Prohosky v. Prudential Ins. Co. of Am., 584 F. Supp. 1337, 1340 (N.D. Ind. 1984) (acknowledging longstanding legal doctrine that subterranean water, oil, and natural gas are considered to be "ferae naturae" until actually pierced with well) (non-FOIA case).

[5] 238 F. Supp. 2d 1188 (S.D. Cal. 2002).

[6] 5 U.S.C. § 552(b)(4) (protecting "trade secrets and commercial or financial information [that is] obtained from a person [and that is] privileged or confidential").

[7] 238 F. Supp. 2d at 1196 (affirming action of agency in withholding commercially sensitive portions of "preliminary draft supplemental environmental assessment" related to groundwater tables and wells).

disadvantage in negotiations over its use.[8]

In National [sic] Resources Defense Council v. DOD,[9] the District Court for the District of Columbia made it clear that the FOIA does not distinguish between well information pertaining to privately and publicly owned water wells.[10] Rejecting the plaintiff's claim that a statement in Exemption 9's legislative history seemed to favor such a distinction,[11] it relied on the well-known legal principle that "'reference to legislative history is inappropriate when the text of the statute is unambiguous.'"[12] By emphasizing the text of the FOIA over its legislative history, it clearly diverged from the Black Hills Alliance court's analysis and broadened Exemption 9's potential scope. Two other decisions have mentioned Exemption 9, both did so in the context of the regulation of natural gas producers; however, neither case discussed its scope or application in significant detail.[13]

Thus, the relatively few cases decided under Exemption 9 to date suggest that its boundaries are not defined clearly by the type of information protectible, and only broadly by the type of well.[14] In fact, what is

---

[8] Id. at 1195.

[9] 388 F. Supp. 2d 1086 (C.D. Cal. 2005).

[10] Id. at 1107-08.

[11] Id. at 1108 (noting plaintiff's reliance on H.R. Rep. No. 89-1497, at 11 (1966), which states that Exemption 9 was created because geological maps based on explorations by private oil companies were not "covered" by existing "trade secrets" laws).

[12] Id. (quoting United States v. Sioux, 362 F.3d 1241, 1246-47 (9th Cir. 2004)).

[13] See Superior Oil Co. v. FERC, 563 F.2d 191, 203-04 & n.20 (5th Cir. 1977) (accepting without discussion that agency may choose to withhold information concerning regulated natural gas exploration and production by private companies under Exemption 9, but ruling that agency also may make discretionary disclosure of certain information despite risk of competitive harm) (non-FOIA case); Pennzoil Co. v. Federal Power Comm'n, 534 F.2d 627, 629-30 & n.2 (5th Cir. 1976) (ruling without significant discussion that Exemption 9 may allow, but does not require, agency to withhold information concerning natural gas "reserve data" reported by regulated private companies) (non-FOIA case); see also Ecee, Inc. v. FERC, 645 F.2d 339, 348-49 (5th Cir. 1981) (holding requirement that producers of natural gas submit confidential geological data to be valid) (non-FOIA case).

[14] See Superior Oil Co., 563 F.2d at 197 (natural gas exploration expenditure data); Pennzoil Co., 534 F.2d at 629 (natural gas reserve estimate data); Nat'l Res. Def. Council, 388 F. Supp. 2d at 1107-08 (public and private water well location map data); Starkey, 238 F. Supp. at 1195 (water

(continued...)

clear from the Exemption 9 decisions thus far is that courts have applied it to all types of wells and to various information about these wells.[15] It also is reasonable to assume that both agencies and courts may apply Exemption 9 to protect well data in other compelling circumstances, such as when Exemption 9 protection is necessary to guard against an attack upon pooled natural resources intended to cause harm to the public.[16]

## EXCLUSIONS

In amending the Freedom of Information Act in 1986, Congress created a novel mechanism for protecting certain especially sensitive law enforcement matters, under subsection (c) of the Act.[1] These three special protection provisions, referred to as record "exclusions," expressly authorize federal law enforcement agencies, for especially sensitive records under certain specified circumstances, to "treat the records as not subject to the requirements of [the FOIA]."[2] Today, more than twenty years after the creation of these special record exclusions, it must be remembered that the procedures that are required to properly employ them still are by no means straightforward and must be implemented with the utmost care.[3] Any agency considering employing an exclusion or having a question as to their

---

[14](...continued)
table levels and well-yield data); Black Hills Alliance, 603 F. Supp. at 122 (uranium exploration test drilling data).

[15] Id.

[16] See Living Rivers, Inc. v. U.S. Bureau of Reclamation, 272 F. Supp. 2d 1313, 1321-22 (D. Utah 2003) (finding that disclosure of "inundation maps" could reasonably be expected to place at risk lives of individuals in downstream areas, which would be flooded by breach of dams, through increasing risk of terrorist attack on dams) (Exemption 7(F)); cf. White House Memorandum for Heads of Executive Departments and Agencies Concerning Safeguarding Information Regarding Weapons of Mass Destruction and Other Sensitive Documents Related to Homeland Security (Mar. 19, 2002), reprinted in FOIA Post (posted 3/21/02) (emphasizing "obligation to safeguard" homeland security-related records).

[1] See Attorney General's Memorandum on the 1986 Amendments to the Freedom of Information Act 18-30 (Dec. 1987) [hereinafter Attorney General's 1986 Amendments Memorandum]; cf. NARA v. Favish, 541 U.S. 157, 169 (evincing the Supreme Court's reliance on "the Attorney General's consistent interpretation of" the FOIA in successive such Attorney General memoranda), reh'g denied, 541 U.S. 1057 (2004).

[2] 5 U.S.C. § 552(c)(1), (c)(2), (c)(3) (2000 & Supp. IV 2004); see Tanks v. Huff, No. 95-568, 1996 WL 293531, at *5 (D.D.C. May 28, 1996), appeal dismissed, No. 96-5180 (D.C. Cir. Aug. 13, 1996).

[3] See Attorney General's 1986 Amendments Memorandum at 27 n.48.

implementation should first consult with the Office of Information and Privacy, at (202) 514-3642.[4]

At the outset, it is important to recognize the somewhat subtle, but very significant, distinction between the result of employing a record exclusion and the concept that is colloquially known as "Glomarization."[5] That latter term refers to the situation in which an agency expressly refuses to confirm or deny the existence of records responsive to a request.[6] (A more detailed discussion of "Glomarization" can be found under Exemption 1, In Camera Submissions, above, and also under Exemption 7(C), above.) The application of one of the three record exclusions, on the other hand, results in a response to the FOIA requester stating that no records responsive to his FOIA request exist.[7] While "Glomarization" remains adequate to provide necessary protection in certain situations, these special record exclusions are invaluable in addressing the exceptionally sensitive situations in which even "Glomarization" is inadequate to the task.

## The (c)(1) Exclusion

The first of these novel provisions, known as the "(c)(1) exclusion," provides as follows:

Whenever a request is made which involves access to records described in subsection (b)(7)(A) and (A) the investigation or proceeding involves a possible violation of criminal law; and (B) there is reason to believe that (i) the subject of the investigation or proceeding is not aware of its pendency, and (ii) disclosure of the existence of the records could reasonably be expected to interfere with enforcement proceedings, the agency may, during

---

[4] See id.; accord Attorney General's Memorandum for Heads of All Federal Departments and Agencies Regarding the Freedom of Information Act (Oct. 12, 2001) [hereinafter Attorney General Ashcroft's FOIA Memorandum], reprinted in FOIA Post (posted 10/15/01) (advising agencies to consult with Office of Information and Privacy on all "significant FOIA issues").

[5] See id. at 26 & n.47; see also Benavides v. DEA, 968 F.2d 1243, 1246-48 (D.C. Cir.) (initially confusing exclusion mechanism with "Glomarization"), modified, 976 F.2d 751, 753 (D.C. Cir. 1992); Valencia-Lucena v. DEA, No. 99-0633, slip op. at 8 (D.D.C. Feb. 8, 2000) (recognizing that Benavides "was subsequently clarified"), summary affirmance granted sub nom. Lucena v. DEA, No. 00-5117, 2000 WL 1582743 (D.C. Cir. Sept. 7, 2000).

[6] See, e.g., Gardels v. CIA, 689 F.2d 1100, 1103 (D.C. Cir. 1982); Phillippi v. CIA, 546 F.2d 1009, 1013 (D.C. Cir. 1976).

[7] See Attorney General's 1986 Amendments Memorandum at 18 (cited in Tanks, 1996 WL 293531, at *5); see also Steinberg v. U.S. Dep't of Justice, No. 93-2409, 1997 WL 349997, at *1 (D.D.C. June 18, 1997) ("[T]he government need not even acknowledge the existence of excluded information.").

only such time as that circumstance continues, treat the records as not subject to the requirements of this section.[8]

In most cases, the protection of Exemption 7(A) is sufficient to guard against any impairment of law enforcement investigations or proceedings through the FOIA. To avail itself of Exemption 7(A), however, an agency must routinely specify that it is doing so -- first administratively and then, if sued, in court -- even when it is invoking the exemption to withhold all responsive records in their entireties. Thus, in specific situations in which the very fact of an investigation's existence is yet unknown to the investigation's subject, invoking Exemption 7(A) in response to a FOIA request for pertinent records permits an investigation's subject to be "tipped off" to its existence. By the same token, any person (or entity) engaged in criminal activities could use a carefully worded FOIA request to try to determine whether he, she, or it is under federal investigation. An agency response that does not invoke Exemption 7(A) to withhold law enforcement files tells such a requester that his activities have thus far escaped detection.

The (c)(1) exclusion authorizes federal law enforcement agencies, under specified circumstances, to shield the very existence of records of ongoing investigations or proceedings by excluding them entirely from the FOIA's reach.[9] To qualify for such exclusion from the FOIA, the records in question must be those which would otherwise be withheld in their entireties under Exemption 7(A). Further, they must relate to an "investigation or proceeding [that] involves a possible violation of criminal law."[10] Hence, any records pertaining to a purely civil law enforcement matter cannot be excluded from the FOIA under this provision, although they may qualify for ordinary Exemption 7(A) withholding. However, the statutory requirement that there be only a "possible violation of criminal law," by its very terms, admits a wide range of investigatory files maintained by more than just criminal law enforcement agencies.[11]

Next, the statute imposes two closely related requirements which go to the very heart of the particular harm addressed through this record exclusion. An agency determining whether it can employ (c)(1) protection must consider whether it has "reason to believe" that the investigation's

---

[8] 5 U.S.C. § 552(c)(1) (2000 & Supp. IV 2004).

[9] See Attorney General's Memorandum on the 1986 Amendments to the Freedom of Information Act 18-22 (Dec. 1987) [hereinafter Attorney General's 1986 Amendments Memorandum].

[10] 5 U.S.C. § 552(c)(1)(A).

[11] See Attorney General's 1986 Amendments Memorandum at 20 & n.37 (files of agencies that are not primarily engaged in criminal law enforcement activities may be eligible for protection if they contain information about potential criminal violations that are pursued with the possibility of referral to Department of Justice for further prosecution).

## EXCLUSIONS

subject is not aware of its pendency and that, most fundamentally, the agency's disclosure of the very existence of the records in question "could reasonably be expected to interfere with enforcement proceedings."[12]

Obviously, where all investigatory subjects are already aware of an investigation's pendency, the "tip off" harm sought to be prevented through this record exclusion is not of concern. Accordingly, the language of this exclusion expressly obliges agencies contemplating its use to consider the level of awareness already possessed by the investigative subjects involved. It is appropriate that agencies do so, as the statutory language provides, according to a good-faith, "reason to believe" standard -- which very much comports with the "could reasonably be expected to" standard utilized both elsewhere in this exclusion and in the amended language of Exemption 7(A).[13]

This "reason to believe" standard for considering a subject's present awareness should afford agencies all necessary latitude in making such determinations. As the exclusion is phrased, this requirement is satisfied so long as an agency determines that it affirmatively has a "reason to believe" that such awareness does not in fact exist. While it is always possible that an agency might possess somewhat conflicting or even contradictory indications on such a point, unless an agency can resolve that a subject is aware of an investigation, it should not risk impairing that investigation through a telling FOIA disclosure.[14] Moreover, agencies are not obligated to accept any bald assertions by investigative subjects that they "know" of ongoing investigations against them; such assertions might well constitute no more than sheer speculation. Because such a ploy, if accepted, could defeat the exclusion's clear statutory purpose, agencies should rely upon their own objective indicia of subject awareness and consequent harm.[15]

In the great majority of cases, invoking Exemption 7(A) will protect the interests of law enforcement agencies in responding to FOIA requests for active law enforcement files. The (c)(1) exclusion should be employed only in the exceptional case in which an agency reaches the judgment that, given its belief of the subject's unawareness of the investigation, the mere invocation of Exemption 7(A) could reasonably be expected to cause harm -- a judgment that should be reached distinctly and thoughtfully.[16]

Finally, the clear language of this exclusion specifically restricts its

---

[12] 5 U.S.C. § 552(c)(1)(B).

[13] See Attorney General's 1986 Amendments Memorandum at 21.

[14] See id.

[15] See id. at n.38.

[16] See id. at 21.

applicability to "during only such time" as the above required circumstances continue to exist. This limitation comports with the extraordinary nature of the protection afforded by the exclusion, as well as with the basic temporal nature of Exemption 7(A) underlying it. It means, of course, that an agency that has employed the exclusion in a particular case is obligated to cease doing so once the circumstances warranting it cease to exist.

Once a law enforcement matter reaches a stage at which all subjects are aware of its pendency, or at which the agency otherwise determines that the public disclosure of that pendency no longer could lead to harm, the exclusion should be regarded as no longer applicable. If the FOIA request that triggered the agency's use of the exclusion remains pending administratively at such time, the excluded records should be identified as responsive to that request and then processed in an ordinary fashion.[17] In the exceptional event that this occurs during the pendency of litigation, the court should exercise its discretion to permit the agency to employ all applicable exemptions for the protection of sensitive portions of the underlying records.[18] (See also the discussions of this basic point under Exemption 7(A), above, and Litigation Considerations, Waiver of Exemptions in Litigation, below.) However, an agency is under no legal obligation to spontaneously reopen a closed FOIA request, or a litigation case, even though records were excluded during its entire pendency: By operation of law, the records simply were not subject to the FOIA during the pendency of the request.[19]

Where all of these requirements are met, and an agency reaches the judgment that it is necessary and appropriate that the (c)(1) exclusion be

---

[17] See id. at 22.

[18] See August v. FBI, 328 F.3d 697, 699 (D.C. Cir. 2003) (explaining that "[g]iven the drafters' recognition that the harms of disclosure may in some cases outweigh its benefits, we have avoided adopting a 'rigid press it at the threshold, or lose it for all times' approach to . . . agenc[ies'] FOIA exemption claims'" (quoting Senate of P.R. v. U.S. Dep't of Justice, 823 F.2d 574, 581 (D.C. Cir. 1987))); LeCedra v. Executive Office for U.S. Attorneys, 317 F.3d 345, 348 (D.C. Cir. 2003) (holding that agency acting in good faith should be permitted to raise underlying exemptions); Senate of P.R., 823 F.2d at 589 (finding that "district court did not abuse its discretion in permitting the [agency] to press additional FOIA exemptions after its original, all-encompassing (7)(A) exemption claim became moot"). But see FOIA Post, "Supreme Court Is Asked to Review Law Enforcement Case" (posted 5/30/01) (discussing Maydak v. U.S. Dep't of Justice, 218 F.3d 760, 765-68 (D.C. Cir. 2000), in which the Court of Appeals for the District of Columbia Circuit held that an agency had waived other FOIA exemptions by failing to raise them prior to the expiration of Exemption 7(A) applicability); see also FOIA Post, "Supreme Court Declines to Review Waiver Case" (posted 8/7/01) (cautioning agencies further in light of Maydak case).

[19] See Attorney General's 1986 Amendments Memorandum at 22 n.39.

employed in connection with a request, the records in question will be treated, as far as the FOIA requester is concerned, as if they did not exist.[20] Where it is the case that the excluded records are just part of the totality of records responsive to a FOIA request, the request will be handled as a seemingly routine one, with the other responsive records processed as if they were the only responsive records in existence. Where the only records responsive to a request fall within the exclusion, the requester will lawfully be told that no records responsive to his FOIA request exist.[21]

In order to maintain the integrity of an exclusion, each agency that employs it must ensure that its FOIA responses are consistent throughout. Therefore, all agencies that could possibly employ at least one of the three record exclusions should ensure that their FOIA communications are consistently phrased so that a requester cannot ever discern the existence of any excluded records, or of any matter underlying them, through the agency's response to his FOIA request.

### The (c)(2) Exclusion

The second exclusion applies to a narrower situation, involving the threatened identification of confidential informants in criminal proceedings.[22] The "(c)(2) exclusion" provides as follows:

> Whenever informant records maintained by a criminal law enforcement agency under an informant's name or personal identifier are requested by a third party according to the informant's name or personal identifier, the agency may treat the records as not subject to the requirements of [the FOIA] unless the informant's status as an informant has been officially confirmed.[23]

This exclusion contemplates the situation in which a sophisticated requester could try to identify an informant by forcing a law enforcement agency into a position in which it otherwise would have no lawful choice but to tellingly invoke Exemption 7(D) in response to a request which en-

---

[20] See id. at 22.

[21] See id.

[22] See Attorney General's Memorandum on the 1986 Amendments to the Freedom of Information Act 22-24 (Dec. 1987) [hereinafter Attorney General's 1986 Amendments Memorandum]; see also Tanks v. Huff, No. 95-568, 1996 WL 293531, at *5 (D.D.C. May 28, 1996), appeal dismissed, No. 96-5180 (D.C. Cir. Aug. 13, 1996).

[23] 5 U.S.C. § 552(c)(2) (2000 & Supp. IV 2004).

compasses informant records maintained on a named person.[24] In the ordinary situation, Exemption 7(D), as amended, should adequately allow a law enforcement agency to withhold all items of information necessary to prevent the identification of any of its confidential sources.[25]

But as with Exemption 7(A), invoking Exemption 7(D) in response to a FOIA request tells the requester that somewhere within the records encompassed by his particular request there is reference to at least one confidential source. Again, under ordinary circumstances the disclosure of this fact poses no direct threat. But under certain extraordinary circumstances, this disclosure could result in devastating harms to the source and to the system of confidentiality existing between sources and criminal law enforcement agencies.

The scenario in which the exclusion is most likely to be employed is one in which the ringleaders of a criminal enterprise suspect that they have been infiltrated by a source and therefore force all participants in the criminal venture either to directly request that any law enforcement files on them be disclosed to the organization or to execute privacy waivers authorizing disclosure of their files in response to a request from the organization. Absent the (c)(2) exclusion, a law enforcement agency could effectively be forced to disclose information to the subject organization (i.e., through the very invocation of Exemption 7(D)) indicating that the named individual is a confidential source.[26]

The (c)(2) exclusion is principally intended to address this unusual, but dangerous situation by permitting an agency to escape the necessity of giving a response that would be tantamount to identifying a named party as a law enforcement source.[27] Any criminal law enforcement agency is authorized to treat such requested records, within the extraordinary context of such a FOIA request, as beyond the FOIA's reach. As with the (c)(1)

---

[24] See Attorney General's 1986 Amendments Memorandum at 23.

[25] See, e.g., Keys v. U.S. Dep't of Justice, 830 F.2d 337, 345-46 (D.C. Cir. 1987); see also U.S. Dep't of Justice v. Landano, 508 U.S. 165, 179-81 (1993) (Although "the Government is not entitled to a presumption that a source is confidential within the meaning of Exemption 7(D) whenever the source provides information to the FBI in the course of a criminal investigation," it should "often" be able to identify circumstances supporting an inference of confidentiality.); FOIA Update, Vol. XIV, No. 3, at 10.

[26] See Attorney General's 1986 Amendments Memorandum at 23; Tanks, No. 95-568, 1996 WL 293531, at *5-6.

[27] See Attorney General's 1986 Amendments Memorandum at 23-24; Tanks, 1996 WL 293531, at *6 (stating that "[t]he (c)(2) exclusion is principally intended to permit an agency to avoid giving a response that would identify a named party as a source" (citing Attorney General's 1986 Amendments Memorandum at 23)).

exclusion, the agency would have "no obligation to acknowledge the existence of such records in response to such request."[28]

By its terms, the exclusion simply becomes inapplicable if and when the individual's status as a source has been officially confirmed.[29] But by merely confirming a source's status as such, a law enforcement agency does not thereby obligate itself to confirm the existence of any specific records regarding that source.[30] Thus, the (c)(2) exclusion cannot be read to automatically require disclosure of source-related information once a source has been officially acknowledged,[31] so long as such information may properly be protected under a FOIA exemption.[32]

---

[28] S. Rep. No. 98-221, at 25 (1983).

[29] See 5 U.S.C. § 552(c)(2); Gonzalez v. FBI, No. 99-5789, slip op. at 18 (E.D. Cal. Aug. 11, 2000) (recognizing that subsection (c)(2) "requires an agency to treat the records as subject to the requirements of [the FOIA] if the informant's status as an informant has been officially confirmed"), aff'd, 14 F. App'x 916 (9th Cir. 2001); Valencia-Lucena v. DEA, No. 99-0633, slip op. at 8 (D.D.C. Feb. 8, 2000) (concluding that "[subs]ection (c)(2) is irrelevant to the resolution of this action" because the subject's status as an informant was "officially confirmed at [the requester's] criminal trial"); Tanks, 1996 WL 293531, at *5 (holding that "given the fact that the status of [the subjects] as government informants in Plaintiff's case is confirmed, the (c)(2) exclusion simply has no bearing on the instant case").

[30] See Gonzalez, No. 99-5789, slip op. at 18 (E.D. Cal. Aug. 11, 2000) (finding that "nowhere within [subsection (c)(2)] does it state that the privacy exemptions found at subsections (b)(6) and (b)(7) are invalidated because a person is a confirmed informant"); Valencia-Lucena, No. 99-0633, slip op. at 8 (D.D.C. Feb. 8, 2000) (rejecting plaintiff's argument that "when FOIA [subs]ection (c)(2) does not apply, the agency must confirm the existence of responsive records"); Tanks, 1996 WL 293531, at *5-6 (same).

[31] See Benavides v. DEA, 968 F.2d 1243, 1248 (D.C. Cir.) ("There is no evidence that Congress intended subsection (c)(2) to repeal or supersede the other enumerated FOIA exemptions or to require disclosure whenever the informant's status has been officially confirmed."), modified on other grounds, 976 F.2d 751, 753 (D.C. Cir. 1992); cf. Valencia-Lucena, No. 99-0633, slip op. at 8-9 (D.D.C. Feb. 8, 2000) (holding that once subsection (c)(2) was rendered inapplicable by official confirmation of source's status as such, FBI appropriately relied on Exemptions 6 and 7(C) as basis for new refusal to confirm or deny existence of any responsive records).

[32] See Benavides, 968 F.2d at 1248 ("The legislative history suggests, in fact, that Congress intended to permit the DEA to withhold documents under 7(C) and 7(D), even if the agency must, under subsection (c)(2), acknowledge their existence."); Tanks, 1996 WL 293531, at *6 ("Accepting the status of [two named individuals] as government informants, the FBI ex-

(continued...)

A criminal law enforcement agency forced to employ this exclusion should do so in the same fashion as it would employ the (c)(1) exclusion discussed above.[33] It is imperative that all information that ordinarily would be disclosed to a first-party requester, other than information which would reflect that an individual is a confidential source, be disclosed. If, for example, the Federal Bureau of Investigation were to respond to a request for records pertaining to an individual having a known record of federal prosecutions by replying that "there exist no records responsive to your FOIA request," the interested criminal organization would surely recognize that its request had been afforded extraordinary treatment and would draw its conclusions accordingly. Therefore, the (c)(2) exclusion must be employed in a manner entirely consistent with its clear source-protection objective.

## The (c)(3) Exclusion

The third of these special record exclusions pertains only to certain law enforcement records that are maintained by the FBI.[34] The "(c)(3) exclusion" provides as follows:

> Whenever a request is made which involves access to records maintained by the Federal Bureau of Investigation pertaining to foreign intelligence or counterintelligence, or international terrorism, and the existence of the records is classified information as provided in [Exemption 1], the Bureau may, as long as the existence of the records remains classified information, treat the records as not subject to the requirements of [the FOIA].[35]

This exclusion recognizes the exceptional sensitivity of the FBI's activities in the areas of foreign intelligence, counterintelligence, and the battle against international terrorism, as well as the fact that the classified files of these activities can be particularly vulnerable to targeted FOIA requests. Sometimes, within the context of a particular FOIA request, the very fact that the FBI does or does not hold any records on a specified person or subject can itself be a sensitive fact, properly classified in accordance with the applicable executive order on the protection of national se-

---

[32](...continued)
plained why disclosure of any information in its files unrelated to the Plaintiff and his prosecution would constitute an unwarranted invasion of personal privacy pursuant to Exemption 7(C), 5 U.S.C. § 552(b)(7)(C).").

[33] See Attorney General's 1986 Amendments Memorandum at 24.

[34] See Attorney General's Memorandum on the 1986 Amendments to the Freedom of Information Act 24-27 (Dec. 1987) [hereinafter Attorney General's 1986 Amendments Memorandum].

[35] 5 U.S.C. § 552(c)(3) (2000 & Supp. IV 2004).

curity information[36] and protectible under FOIA Exemption 1.[37] Once again, however, the mere invocation of Exemption 1 to withhold such information can provide information to the requester which would have an extremely adverse effect on the government's interests. In some possible contexts, the furnishing of an actual "no records" response, even in response to a seemingly innocuous "first-party" request, could compromise sensitive activities.[38]

Congress took cognizance of this through the (c)(3) exclusion, in which it authorizes the FBI to protect itself against such harm in connection with any of its records pertaining to these three, especially sensitive, areas. To do so, the FBI must of course reach the judgment, in the context of a particular request, that the very existence or nonexistence of responsive records is itself a classified fact and that it need employ this record exclusion to prevent its disclosure.[39] By the terms of this provision, the excluded records may be treated as such so long as their existence, within the context of the request, "remains classified information."[40]

Additionally, it should be noted that while the statute refers to records maintained by the FBI, exceptional circumstances could possibly arise in which it would be appropriate for another component of the Department of Justice or another federal agency to invoke this exclusion on a derivative basis as well.[41] Such a situation could occur where information in records of another component or agency is derived from FBI records which fully qualify for (c)(3) exclusion protection. In such extraordinary circumstances,

---

[36] See Exec. Order No. 12,958, as amended, § 3.6(a), 68 Fed. Reg. 15,315 (Mar. 28, 2003), reprinted in 50 U.S.C. § 435 note (2000 & Supp. III 2003) and summarized in FOIA Post (posted 4/11/03).

[37] See 5 U.S.C. § 552(b)(1); see also Attorney General's 1986 Amendments Memorandum at 25.

[38] See id. (suggesting that especially with the passage of time, such sensitive records or information might be "maintained elsewhere" (e.g., by the ODNI's National Counterterrorism Center) in which case this exclusion should nonetheless apply, in order to "avoid an anomalous result").

[39] See id.; see also id. at n.44 (addressing overlap with subsection (c)(1)).

[40] 5 U.S.C. § 552(c)(3); see FOIA Update, Vol. XVI, No. 2, at 1-2, 11 (noting that executive order places emphasis on limited classification and automatic declassification); see also FOIA Post, "Executive Order on National Security Classification Amended" (posted 4/11/03) (noting substantive changes to Executive Order 12,958).

[41] See Attorney General's 1986 Amendments Memorandum at 25 n.45 (explaining anticipatorily that although this exclusion was created primarily for use by the FBI, "it is conceivable that records derived from such FBI records might be maintained elsewhere, potentially in contexts in which the harm sought to be prevented by this exclusion is no less threatened").

the agency processing the derivative information should consult with the FBI regarding the possible joint invocation of the exclusion in order to avoid a potentially damaging inconsistent response.[42]

## Procedural Considerations

Several procedural considerations regarding the implementation and operation of these special record exclusions should be noted. First, it should be self-evident that the decision to employ an exclusion in response to a particular request must not be reflected on anything made available to the requester. This, of course, requires careful attention to the handling of a request at its earliest stages in order to ensure that an agency does not mistakenly speak of the existence (or even of the possible existence) of responsive records in its early administrative correspondence with the requester. And when an agency reaches the judgment that it is necessary to employ an exclusion, it should do so as a specific official determination that is reviewed carefully by appropriate supervisory agency officials.[43] The particular records covered by an exclusion action should be concretely and carefully identified and segregated from any responsive records that are to be processed according to ordinary procedures.[44]

It must be remembered that providing a "no records" response as part of an exclusion strategy does not insulate the agency from either administrative or judicial review of the agency's action. The recipient of a "no records" response might challenge it because he believes that the agency has failed to conduct a sufficiently detailed search to uncover the requested records.[45] Alternately, any requester, mindful of the exclusion mechanism and seeking information of a nature which could possibly trigger an exclusion action, could seek judicial review in an effort to pursue his suspicions and to have a court determine whether an exclusion, if in fact used, was employed appropriately.

Moreover, because the very objective of the exclusions is to preclude the requester from learning that there exist such responsive records, all administrative appeals and court cases involving a "no records" response

---

[42] See id.; cf. *FOIA Post*, "FOIA Amended by Intelligence Authorization Act" (posted 12/23/02) (discussing the enactment of a provision in the Intelligence Authorization Act of 2003, 5 U.S.C. § 552(a)(3)(E) (2000 & Supp. IV 2004), that precludes the making of certain "foreign" FOIA requests to any "element[] of the intelligence community").

[43] See Attorney General's Memorandum on the 1986 Amendments to the Freedom of Information Act 27 (Dec. 1987) [hereinafter Attorney General's 1986 Amendments Memorandum].

[44] See id.

[45] See id. at 29; see also Oglesby v. U.S. Dep't of the Army, 920 F.2d 57, 67 (D.C. Cir. 1990).

must receive extremely careful attention. If one procedure is employed in adjudicating appeals or litigating cases in which there actually are no responsive records, and any different course is followed where an exclusion is in fact being used, sophisticated requesters could quickly learn to distinguish between the two and defeat the exclusion's very purpose.[46]

Consequently, agencies should prepare in advance a uniform procedure to handle administrative appeals and court challenges that seek review of the possibility that an exclusion was employed in a given case. In responding to administrative appeals from "no record" responses,[47] agencies should accept any clear request for administrative appellate review of the possible use of an exclusion and specifically address it in evaluating and responding to the appeal.[48]

In the exceptional case in which an exclusion was in fact invoked, the appellate review authority should examine the correctness of that action and come to a judgment as to the exclusion's continued applicability as of that time.[49] In the event that an exclusion is found to have been improperly employed or to be no longer applicable, the appeal should be remanded for prompt conventional processing of all formerly excluded records, with the requester advised accordingly.[50] When it is determined either that an exclusion was properly employed or that, as in the overwhelming bulk of cases, no exclusion was used, the result of the administrative appeal should be, by all appearances, the same: The requester should be specifically advised that this aspect of his appeal was reviewed and found to be without merit.[51]

Such administrative appeal responses, of course, necessarily must be stated in such a way that does not indicate whether an exclusion was in fact invoked.[52] Moreover, in order to preserve the exclusion mechanism's effectiveness, requesters who inquire in any way whether an exclusion has been used should routinely be advised that it is the agency's standard poli-

---

[46] See Attorney General's 1986 Amendments Memorandum at 29.

[47] See FOIA Update, Vol. XII, No. 2, at 5 ("OIP Guidance: Procedural Rules Under the D.C. Circuit's Oglesby Decision") (requiring agency to advise any requester who receives "no record" response of its procedures for filing administrative appeal) (superseding FOIA Update, Vol. V, No. 3, at 2).

[48] See Attorney General's 1986 Amendments Memorandum at 29 (superseded in part by FOIA Update, Vol. XII, No. 2, at 5).

[49] See id. at 28.

[50] See id.

[51] See id. at 28-29.

[52] See id. at 29.

cy to refuse to confirm or deny that an exclusion was employed in any particular case.[53]

Exclusion issues in court actions must be handled with similarly careful and thoughtful preparation.[54] First, it need be recognized that any judicial review of a suspected exclusion determination must of course be conducted ex parte, based upon an in camera court filing submitted directly to the judge.[55] Second, it is essential to the integrity of the exclusion mechanism that requesters not be able to determine whether an exclusion was employed at all in a given case based upon how any case is handled in court. Thus, it is critical that the in camera defenses of exclusion issues raised in FOIA cases occur not merely in those cases in which an exclusion actually was employed and is in fact being defended.[56]

Accordingly, it is the government's standard litigation policy in the defense of FOIA lawsuits that, whenever a FOIA plaintiff raises a distinct claim regarding the suspected use of an exclusion, the government will routinely submit an in camera declaration addressing that claim, one way or the other.[57] When an exclusion was in fact employed, the correctness of that action will be justified to the court. When an exclusion was not in fact employed, the in camera declaration will state simply that it is being submitted to the court so as to mask whether or not an exclusion is being em-

---

[53] See id. at 29 & n.52; Steinberg v. U.S. Dep't of Justice, No. 93-2409, 1997 WL 349997, at *1 (D.D.C. June 18, 1997) (refusing to "confirm[] or deny[] the existence of any exclusion . . . and conclud[ing] that if an exclusion was invoked, it was and remains amply justified"); cf. NARA v. Favish, 541 U.S. 157, 170 (reminding of the "general rule" that withholding information under the FOIA "cannot be predicated on the identity of the requester"), reh'g denied, 541 U.S. 1057 (2004).

[54] Accord Attorney General's Memorandum for Heads of All Federal Departments and Agencies Regarding the Freedom of Information Act (Oct. 12, 2001), reprinted in FOIA Post (posted 10/15/01) (reminding agencies to "carefully consider" the handling of all FOIA requests, including matters in litigation).

[55] See Attorney General's 1986 Amendments Memorandum at 29; see also Steinberg, 1997 WL 349997, at *1 (approving use of agency in camera declaration where plaintiff "alleged that certain requested information may have been excluded pursuant to [sub]section 552(c)").

[56] See Attorney General's 1986 Amendments Memorandum at 29.

[57] See id. at 30; see also, e.g., Steinberg, 1997 WL 349997, at *1 ("[T]he government is permitted to file an in camera declaration, which explains either that no exclusion was invoked or that the exclusion was invoked appropriately."); Steinberg v. U.S. Dep't of Justice, No. 91-2740, 1993 WL 524528, at *2 (D.D.C. Dec. 2, 1993) (agency "volunteered an in camera submission related to the allegation of covert reliance on § 552(c)").

ployed, thus preserving the integrity of the exclusion process overall.[58] In either case, the government will of course urge the court to issue a public decision which does not indicate whether it is or is not an actual exclusion case. Such a public decision, like an administrative appeal determination of an exclusion-related request for review, should specify only that a full review of the claim was had and that, if an exclusion was in fact employed, it was, and remains, amply justified.[59]

## DISCRETIONARY DISCLOSURE AND WAIVER

The Freedom of Information Act is an information disclosure statute which, through its exemption structure, strikes a balance between information disclosure and nondisclosure,[1] with an emphasis on the "fullest responsible disclosure."[2] Inasmuch as the FOIA's exemptions are discretion-

---

[58] See Attorney General's 1986 Amendments Memorandum at 30.

[59] See id.; see also, e.g., Steinberg, 1997 WL 349997, at *1 (where plaintiff alleged possible use of exclusion, "without confirming or denying the existence of any exclusion, the Court finds and concludes [after review of agency's in camera declaration] that if an exclusion was invoked, it was and remains amply justified"); Beauman v. FBI, No. CV-92-7603, slip op. at 2 (C.D. Cal. Apr. 12, 1993) ("'In response to the plaintiff's claim of the (c)(1) exclusion being utilized in this action, . . . [w]ithout confirming or denying that any such exclusion was actually invoked by the defendant, the Court finds and concludes [after review of an in camera declaration] that if an exclusion was in fact employed, it was, and remains, amply justified.'") (adopting agency's proposed conclusion of law).

[1] See John Doe Agency v. John Doe Corp., 493 U.S. 146, 153 (1989) ("Congress sought 'to reach a workable balance between the right of the public to know and the need of the Government to keep information in confidence'" (citing H.R. Rep. No. 1497, at 6 (1966))); see also NARA v. Favish, 541 U.S. 157, 172 (observing that while under the FOIA government information "belongs to citizens to do with as they choose," this is balanced against statutory "limitations that compete with the general interest in disclosure, and that, in appropriate cases, can overcome it"), reh'g denied, 541 U.S. 1057 (2004).

[2] S. Rep. No. 89-813, at 3 (1965) (stating the FOIA's statutory objective as that of achieving "the fullest responsible disclosure"); see also Attorney General's Memorandum on the 1986 Amendments to the Freedom of Information Act 30 (Dec. 1987) [hereinafter Attorney General's 1986 Amendments Memorandum] (same) (quoting Chrysler Corp. v. Brown, 441 U.S. 281, 293 (1979)); FOIA Update, Vol. IX, No. 3, at 14 (same); cf. 5 U.S.C. § 552b note (2000 & Supp. III 2003) (policy statement enacted as part of the Government in the Sunshine Act specifying that it is "the policy of the United States that the public is entitled to the fullest practicable information

(continued...)

ary, not mandatory,[3] agencies may make "discretionary disclosures" of exempt information, as a matter of their administrative discretion, where they are not otherwise prohibited from doing so.[4]

In October 2001, a statement of governmentwide FOIA policy was issued by Attorney General John Ashcroft.[5] The Ashcroft FOIA Memorandum recognizes the continued agency practice of considering whether to make "discretionary disclosures" of information that is exempt under the Act, while at the same time emphasizing that agencies should do so only

---

[2](...continued)
regarding the decisionmaking processes of the Federal Government") (emphasis added).

[3] See Chrysler, 441 U.S. at 293 (reasoning that the application of agency FOIA policies may require "some balancing and accommodation," and noting that "Congress did not design the FOIA exemptions to be mandatory bars to disclosure"); Bartholdi Cable Co. v. FCC, 114 F.3d 274, 282 (D.C. Cir. 1997) (stating that the "FOIA's exemptions simply permit, but do not require, an agency to withhold exempted information").

[4] See CNA Fin. Corp. v. Donovan, 830 F.2d 1132, 1334 n.1 (D.C. Cir. 1987) (explaining that an agency's FOIA disclosure decision can "be grounded either in its view that none of the FOIA exemptions applies, and thus that disclosure is mandatory, or in its belief that release is justified in the exercise of its discretion, even though the data fall within one or more of the statutory exemptions."); see also, e.g., Chenkin v. Dep't of the Army, No. 94-7109, slip op. at 1 (3d Cir. June 7, 1995) (deciding that discretionary disclosure of documents during appellate litigation process renders case moot as to those documents); see also FOIA Update, Vol. VI, No. 3, at 3 ("[A]gencies generally have discretion under the Freedom of Information Act to decide whether to invoke applicable FOIA exemptions."); FOIA Update, Vol. XIII, No. 2, at 5-6 (discussing exercise of agency discretion in processing of requests for information maintained in electronic form); cf. FOIA Post, "The Use of Contractors in FOIA Administration" (posted 09/30/04) (advising of general rule that agencies may "contract out" tasks involved in FOIA administration by "allowing contractors to do any work that does not require discretionary decisionmaking").

[5] See Attorney General's Memorandum for Heads of All Federal Departments and Agencies Regarding the Freedom of Information Act (Oct. 12, 2001) [hereinafter Attorney General Ashcroft's FOIA Memorandum], reprinted in FOIA Post (posted 10/15/01) (emphasizing the public interest in protecting fundamental societal values, "[a]mong [which] are safeguarding our national security, enhancing the effectiveness of our law enforcement agencies, protecting sensitive business information and, not least, preserving personal privacy").

upon "full and deliberate consideration" of all interests involved.[6] It reminds agencies "to carefully consider the protection of all [applicable] values and interests when making disclosure determinations under the FOIA."[7]

When agencies make discretionary disclosures of exempt information upon such "full and deliberate" consideration of all of the interests involved in accordance with Attorney General Ashcroft's FOIA Memorandum,[8] they should not be held to have "waived" their ability to invoke applicable FOIA exemptions for similar or related information in the future. In other situations, however, various types of agency conduct and circumstances can reasonably be held to result in exemption waiver.

Discretionary Disclosure

As a general rule, an agency's ability to make a discretionary disclosure of exempt information, as recognized in Attorney General Ashcroft's

---

[6] Attorney General Ashcroft's FOIA Memorandum, reprinted in *FOIA Post* (posted 10/15/01); see also *FOIA Post*, "New Attorney General FOIA Memorandum Issued" (posted 10/15/01) (adding that much FOIA-exempt information is subject to statutory disclosure prohibitions as well as to prudential nondisclosure considerations).

[7] Attorney General Ashcroft's FOIA Memorandum, reprinted in *FOIA Post* (posted 10/15/01); see also, e.g., White House Memorandum for Heads of Executive Departments and Agencies Concerning Safeguarding Information Regarding Weapons of Mass Destruction and Other Sensitive Documents Related to Homeland Security (Mar. 19, 2002), reprinted in *FOIA Post* (posted 3/21/02) (focusing on need to protect sensitive homeland security-related information); *FOIA Post*, "FOIA Officers Conference Held on Homeland Security" (posted 7/3/03) (noting that though Attorney General Ashcroft's FOIA Memorandum "was developed well before the events of September 11, 2001, its issuance highlighted the importance of carefully considering the applicability of FOIA exemptions to information viewed as sensitive through a post-9/11 lens"); *FOIA Post*, "New Attorney General FOIA Memorandum Issued" (posted 10/15/01) (highlighting government's "need to protect critical systems, facilities, stockpiles, and other assets from security breaches and harm -- and in some instances from their potential use as weapons of mass destruction in and of themselves"); accord Presidential Memorandum for Heads of Departments and Agencies Regarding the Freedom of Information Act, 29 Weekly Comp. Pres. Doc. 1999 (Oct. 4, 1993), reprinted in FOIA Update, Vol. XIV, No. 3, at 3.

[8] Attorney General Ashcroft's FOIA Memorandum, reprinted in *FOIA Post* (posted 10/15/01); see also *FOIA Post*, "New Attorney General FOIA Memorandum Issued" (posted 10/15/01) (pointing out significance of "discretionary disclosure" element of Attorney General Ashcroft's FOIA Memorandum).

FOIA Memorandum,[9] will vary according to the nature of the FOIA exemption and the underlying interests involved. First, while the FOIA does not itself prohibit the disclosure of any information,[10] an agency's ability to make a discretionary disclosure of information covered by a FOIA exemption can hinge on whether there exists any legal barrier to disclosure of that information. Some of the FOIA's exemptions -- such as Exemption 2,[11] and Exemption 5,[12] for example -- protect a type of information that is not subject to any such disclosure prohibition. Other FOIA exemptions -- most notably Exemption 3[13] -- directly correspond to, and serve to accommodate, distinct prohibitions on information disclosure that operate independently of the FOIA or are given nondisclosure effect under it. Agencies are constrained from making a discretionary FOIA disclosure of the types of information covered by the following FOIA exemptions:

Exemption 1 of the FOIA protects from disclosure national security information concerning the national defense or foreign policy, provided that it has been properly classified in accordance with both the substantive and procedural requirements of an existing executive order.[14] As a rule, an agency official holding classification authority determines whether information requires classification and then that determination is implemented under the FOIA through the invocation of Exemption 1.[15] Thus, if information is in fact properly classified, and therefore is exempt from disclosure under Exemption 1, it is not appropriate for discretionary FOIA disclosure. (See the discussion of Exemption 1, above.)

Exemption 3 of the FOIA explicitly accommodates the nondisclosure provisions that are contained in a variety of other federal statutes.[16] Some

---

[9] Attorney General's Memorandum for Heads of All Federal Departments and Agencies Regarding the Freedom of Information Act (Oct. 12, 2001) [hereinafter Attorney General Ashcroft's FOIA Memorandum], reprinted in FOIA Post (posted 10/15/01); see also Exec. Order No. 13,392, 70 Fed. Reg. 75,373 (Dec. 14, 2005) (addressing procedural aspects of governmentwide FOIA administration).

[10] See 5 U.S.C. § 552(d) (2000 & Supp. IV 2004).

[11] Id. § 552(b)(2).

[12] Id. § 552(b)(5).

[13] Id. § 552(b)(3).

[14] Id. § 552(b)(1) (implementing Executive Order 12,958, as amended, 68 Fed. Reg. 15,315 (Mar. 28, 2003), reprinted in 50 U.S.C. § 435 (2000 & Supp. III 2003) and summarized in FOIA Post (posted 4/11/03)).

[15] See generally FOIA Update, Vol. VI, No. 1, at 1-2.

[16] See 5 U.S.C. § 552(b)(3); see also FOIA Post, "Agencies Rely on Wide
(continued...)

of these statutory nondisclosure provisions, such as those pertaining to grand jury information[17] and census data,[18] categorically prevent disclosure harm and establish absolute prohibitions on agency disclosure; others leave agencies with some discretion as to whether to disclose certain information, but such administrative discretion generally is exercised independently of the FOIA.[19] (See the discussion of Exemption 3, above.) Therefore, agencies ordinarily do not make discretionary disclosure under the FOIA of information that falls within the scope of Exemption 3.[20]

Exemption 4 of the FOIA protects "trade secrets and commercial or financial information obtained from a person [that is] privileged or confidential."[21] For the most part, Exemption 4 protects information implicating private commercial interests that would not ordinarily be the subject of discretionary FOIA disclosure. (See the discussions of Exemption 4, above, and "Reverse" FOIA, below.) Even more significantly, a specific criminal statute, the Trade Secrets Act,[22] prohibits the unauthorized disclosure of most (if not all) of the information falling within Exemption 4; its practical effect is to constrain an agency's ability to make a discretionary disclosure of Exemption 4 information,[23] absent an agency regulation (based upon a

---

[16](...continued)
Range of Exemption 3 Statutes" (posted 12/16/03).

[17] See Fed. R. Crim. P. 6(e) (enacted as statute in 1977).

[18] See 13 U.S.C. § 8(b), 9(a) (2000).

[19] See, e.g., Aronson v. IRS, 973 F.2d 962, 966 (1st Cir. 1992).

[20] See, e.g., Ass'n of Retired R.R. Workers v. Railroad Retirement Bd., 830 F.2d 331, 335 (D.C. Cir. 1987) (deciding that FOIA jurisdiction does not extend to exercise of agency disclosure discretion within Exemption 3 statute); see also FOIA Update, Vol. XV, No. 4, at 7 (describing firm limitation imposed on disclosure of "tax return information" under 26 U.S.C.A. § 6103 (2002 & West. Supp. 2006)). But see Palmer v. Derwinski, No. 91-197, slip op. at 3-4 (E.D. Ky. June 10, 1992) (exceptional FOIA case in which court ordered Veterans Administration to disclose existence of certain medical records pursuant to discretionary terms of 38 U.S.C. § 7332(b) (2000)); see also, e.g., Craig v. United States, 131 F.3d 99, 101-07 (2d Cir. 1997) (articulating factors according to which courts make discretionary disclosure determinations for grand jury information) (non-FOIA case).

[21] 5 U.S.C. § 552(b)(4) (2000 & Supp. IV 2004).

[22] 18 U.S.C. § 1905 (2000 & Supp. IV 2004).

[23] See CNA Fin. Corp. v. Donovan, 830 F.2d 1132, 1144 (D.C. Cir. 1987); see also FOIA Update, Vol. VI, No. 3, at 3 ("OIP Guidance: Discretionary Disclosure and Exemption 4").

federal statute) that expressly authorizes disclosure.[24] (See the discussion of this point under "Reverse" FOIA, below.)

Exemptions 6 and 7(C) of the FOIA protect personal privacy interests, in non-law enforcement records[25] and law enforcement records,[26] respectively. As with private commercial information covered by Exemption 4, the personal information protected by Exemptions 6 and 7(C) is not the type of information ordinarily considered appropriate for discretionary FOIA disclosure; with these exemptions, a balancing of public interest considerations is built into the determination of whether the information is exempt in the first place.[27] (See the discussions of this point under Exemption 6, above, and Exemption 7(C), above.)

Moreover, the personal information covered by Exemptions 6 and 7(C) in many cases falls within the protective coverage of the Privacy Act of 1974,[28] which mandates that any such information concerning U.S. citizens and permanent-resident aliens that is maintained in a "system of records"[29] not be disclosed unless that disclosure is permitted under one of the specific exceptions to the Privacy Act's general disclosure prohibition.[30] Inasmuch as the FOIA-disclosure exception in the Privacy Act permits only those disclosures that are "required" under the FOIA,[31] the making of discretionary FOIA disclosures of personal information is fundamentally incompatible with the Privacy Act and, in many instances, is prohibited by

---

[24] See Chrysler v. Brown, 441 U.S. 281, 295-96 (1979); see, e.g., St. Mary's Hosp., Inc. v. Harris, 604 F.2d 407, 409-10 (5th Cir. 1979).

[25] 5 U.S.C. § 552(b)(6).

[26] Id. § 552(b)(7)(C).

[27] See NARA v. Favish, 541 U.S. 157, 171 (holding that agency must balance privacy interests of persons affected by disclosure against public interest in disclosure), reh'g denied, 541 U.S. 1057 (2004).

[28] 5 U.S.C. § 552a (2000 & Supp. IV 2004).

[29] Id. § 552a(a)(5).

[30] Id. § 552a(b)(1)-(12).

[31] Id. § 552a(b)(2). But see also Bartel v. FAA, 725 F.2d 1403 (D.C. Cir. 1984) (holding that the exception applies "[o]nly when the agency is faced with a FOIA request," which in practice means that the Privacy Act disclosure prohibition "could turn on the wholly fortuitous circumstance of whether a FOIA request for records has been lodged"), reh'g en banc denied, No. 82-2473 (D.C. Cir. Mar. 23, 1984); FOIA Update, Vol. V, No. 3, at 2 (discussing interplay between FOIA and Privacy Act under Bartel).

it.[32]

With the exception of information that is subject to the disclosure prohibitions accommodated by the above FOIA exemptions, agencies may make discretionary disclosures of any information that is exempt under the FOIA. A prime example is the type of administrative information that can fall within the "low 2" aspect of Exemption 2, which is uniquely designed to shield agencies from sheer administrative burden rather than from any substantive disclosure harm. (See the discussion of Exemption 2, above.) In many instances, especially when the information in question is a portion of a document page not otherwise exempt in its entirety, it is more efficient simply to release the information than to withhold it.[33]

Perhaps the most common examples of information that an agency might disclose as a matter of administrative discretion can be found under Exemption 5, which incorporates discovery privileges that almost always protect only the institutional interests of the agency possessing the information. (See the discussion of Exemption 5, above.) Information that otherwise could be withheld under the deliberative process privilege to protect an agency deliberative process might be disclosed with the passage of time, for example.[34] Some litigation-related records that otherwise might routinely be withheld under Exemption 5's attorney work-product privilege can be discretionarily disclosed if the agency determines that it is appropriate to do so, as this privilege broadly covers practically all information prepared in connection with litigation without any temporal limitation whatsoever. (See the discussion of Exemption 5, Attorney Work-Product Privilege, above.) This is theoretically possible even for information covered by the attorney-client privilege of Exemption 5 as well, but all agencies should be careful to heed the fundamental importance of "these

---

[32] See DOD v. FLRA, 964 F.2d 26, 30-31 n.6 (D.C. Cir. 1992) (discussing Privacy Act's limitations on discretionary FOIA disclosure); see also FOIA Update, Vol. V, No. 3, at 2; cf. Crumpton v. United States, 843 F. Supp. 751, 756 (D.D.C. 1994) (holding that disclosure under FOIA of personal information that is not subject to Privacy Act creates no liability under Federal Tort Claims Act (FTCA), due to applicability of FTCA's discretionary function exception), aff'd on other grounds sub nom. Crumpton v. Stone, 59 F.3d 1400 (D.C. Cir. 1995).

[33] See FOIA Update, Vol. V, No. 1, at 11-12 ("FOIA Counselor: The Unique Protection of Exemption 2") (advising agencies not to invoke exemption needlessly); accord Exec. Order No. 13,392, Sec. 1(c) (requiring agencies to "process requests under the FOIA in an efficient and appropriate manner").

[34] See FOIA Update, Vol. 1, No. 1, at 4 (identifying "age" of document of document as something logically taken into account in FOIA decisionmaking).

privileges and the sound policies underlying them."[35]

The potential held by other FOIA exemptions for discretionary disclosure necessarily varies from exemption to exemption -- but in all cases agencies should remember that any such action should be taken, as stated in Attorney General Ashcroft's FOIA Memorandum, "only after full and deliberate consideration of the institutional, commercial, and personal privacy interests that could be implicated by disclosure of the information."[36]

For purposes of any discretionary disclosure that an agency considers, it also may be remembered that the FOIA requires agencies to focus on individual portions of records in connection with the applicability of all exemptions of the Act and to disclose all individual, "reasonably segregable" record portions that are not covered by an exemption.[37] (See the discussions of this issue under Procedural Requirements, "Reasonably Segregable" Obligation, above, and Litigation Considerations, "Reasonably Segregable" Requirements, below.) The satisfaction of this important statutory requirement sometimes involves an onerous delineation process, one that can lend itself to the making of discretionary disclosures, particularly at the

---

[35] Attorney General Ashcroft's FOIA Memorandum, reprinted in *FOIA Post* (posted 10/15/01).

[36] Id.; see also Exec. Order No. 13,392, Sec. 4(a) (procedural directive speaking of Attorney General's authority regarding "release of public information").

[37] 5 U.S.C. § 552(b) (sentence immediately following exemptions); see also, e.g., Trans-Pac. Policing Agreement v. U.S. Customs Serv., 177 F.3d 1022, 1028 (D.C. Cir. 1999) (holding that district courts have affirmative duty to consider issue of segregability sua sponte even if issue has not been specifically raised by plaintiff); Kimberlin v. Dep't of Justice, 139 F.3d 944, 946, 949-51 (D.C. Cir. 1998) (holding that district court erred in approving agency's withholding of entire documents without making specific finding on segregability); PHE, Inc. v. Dep't of Justice, 983 F.2d 248, 252 (D.C. Cir. 1993) (holding that both agency and court must determine whether any nonexempt information can be segregated from exempt information and released); Hronek v. DEA, 16 F. Supp. 2d 1260, 1270 (D. Or. 1998) (making extensive finding on segregability and stating that "[b]lanket explanations . . . do not meet FOIA's requirements and do not permit the court to make the necessary findings"); Steinberg v. U.S. Dep't of Justice, 179 F.R.D. 357, 364 (D.D.C. 1998) (requiring agency to submit documents for in camera review of segregability where "substantial segments of material -- several consecutive paragraphs or pages" -- were withheld "based on assurances that the entirety of each redaction would identify a third-party [sic] with a privacy interest"); Brooks v. IRS, No. CV-F-96-6284, 1997 WL 842415 at *2 (E.D. Cal. Nov. 19, 1997) ("The court may not simply approve the withholding of an entire document without entering a finding on segregability.").

margins of FOIA exemption applicability.[38]

When an agency considers making a discretionary disclosure of exempt information under the FOIA, it may do so without undue concern that in exercising its administrative discretion with respect to particular information it is impairing its ability to invoke applicable FOIA exemptions for any arguably similar information in the future. Indeed, in the leading judicial pronouncement on this point, Mobil Oil Corp. v. EPA,[39] a FOIA requester argued that by making a discretionary disclosure of certain records that could have been withheld under Exemption 5 the agency had waived its right to invoke that exemption for a group of "related" records that the requester sought.[40] In soundly rejecting such a waiver argument, however, the Court of Appeals for the Ninth Circuit surveyed the law of waiver under the FOIA and found "no case . . . in which the release of certain documents waived the exemption as to other documents. On the contrary, [courts] generally have found that the release of certain documents waives FOIA exemptions only for those documents released."[41]

Such a general rule of nonwaiver through discretionary disclosure is supported by sound policy considerations, as the Ninth Circuit in Mobil Oil discussed at some length:

---

[38] See, e.g., Army Times Publ'g Co. v. U.S. Dep't of the Air Force, 998 F.2d 1067, 1071 (D.C. Cir. 1993) (emphasizing significance of segregation requirement in connection with deliberative process privilege under Exemption 5); Wightman v. ATF, 755 F.2d 979, 983 (1st Cir. 1985) (finding that "detailed process of segregation" was not unreasonable for request involving thirty-six pages).

[39] 879 F.2d 698 (9th Cir. 1989).

[40] Id. at 700.

[41] Id. at 701; see Salisbury v. United States, 690 F.2d 966, 971 (D.C. Cir. 1982) ("[D]isclosure of a similar type of information in a different case does not mean that the agency must make its disclosure in every case."); Stein v. U.S. Dep't of Justice, 662 F.2d 1245, 1259 (7th Cir. 1981) (holding that exercise of discretion should waive no right to withhold records of "similar nature"); Schiller v. NLRB, No. 87-1176, slip op. at 7 (D.D.C. July 10, 1990) ("Discretionary release of a document pertains to that document alone, regardless of whether similar documents exist."), rev'd on other grounds, 964 F.2d 1205 (D.C. Cir. 1992); see also, e.g., U.S. Student Ass'n v. CIA, 620 F. Supp. 565, 571 (D.D.C. 1985) (rejecting waiver through prior disclosure, except as to "duplicate" information); Dow, Lohnes & Albertson v. Presidential Comm'n on Broad. to Cuba, 624 F. Supp. 572, 578 (D.D.C. 1984) (same); cf. Silber v. U.S. Dep't of Justice, No. 91-876, transcript at 18 (D.D.C. Aug. 13, 1992) (bench order) (reasoning that no waiver would be found even if it were to be established that other comparable documents had been disclosed).

Implying such a waiver could tend to inhibit agencies from making any disclosures other than those explicitly required by law because voluntary release of documents exempt from disclosure requirements would expose other documents [of a related nature] to risk of disclosure. An agency would have an incentive to refuse to release all exempt documents if it wished to retain an exemption for any documents . . . . [R]eadily finding waiver of confidentiality for exempt documents would tend to thwart the [FOIA's] underlying statutory purpose, which is to implement a policy of broad disclosure of government records.[42]

In fact, this rule was presaged by the Court of Appeals for the District of Columbia Circuit many years ago, when it observed:

Surely this is an important consideration. The FOIA should not be construed so as to put the federal bureaucracy in a defensive or hostile position with respect to the Act's spirit of open government and liberal disclosure of information.[43]

As another court phrased it: "A contrary rule would create an incentive against voluntary disclosure of information."[44]

---

[42] 879 F.2d at 701; see also Army Times, 998 F.2d at 1068 (articulating general principle of no waiver of exemption simply because agency released "information similar to that requested" in past); Halkin v. Helms, 598 F.2d 1, 9 (D.C. Cir. 1978) ("The government is not estopped from concluding in one case that disclosure is permissible while in another case it is not.").

[43] Nationwide Bldg. Maintenance, Inc. v. Sampson, 559 F.2d 704, 712 n.34 (D.C. Cir. 1977).

[44] Mehl v. EPA, 797 F. Supp. 43, 47 (D.D.C. 1992); see also Military Audit Project v. Casey, 656 F.2d 724, 754 (D.C. Cir. 1981) (reasoning that an agency should not be penalized for declassifying and releasing documents during litigation; otherwise, there would be "a disincentive for an agency to reappraise its position and, when appropriate, release documents previously withheld"); Greenberg v. U.S. Dep't of Treasury, 10 F. Supp. 2d 3, 23-24 (D.D.C. 1998) ("Penalizing agencies by holding that they waive their exhaustion defense if they make a discretionary document release after the time for an administrative appeal had expired would not advance the underlying purpose of the FOIA -- the broadest possible responsible disclosure of government documents."); Shewchun v. INS, No. 95-1920, slip op. at 8 (D.D.C. Dec. 10, 1995) (to find agency bad faith after agency conducted new search and released more information "would create a disincentive for agencies to conduct reviews of their initial searches"), summary affirmance granted, No. 97-5044, 1997 WL 404711 (D.C. Cir. June 5, 1997); Berg v. U.S. Dep't of Energy, No. 94-0488, slip op. at 8 (D.D.C. Nov. 7, 1994) (stating that release of information after initial search does not prove inadequacy of search and that to hold otherwise would end "laudable agency practice of

(continued...)

# DISCRETIONARY DISCLOSURE AND WAIVER

By the same token, moreover, in cases in which discretionary disclosures are made by agencies, courts have found that they do not constitute a basis for awarding attorneys fees under the Act -- especially insofar as they involve no "court-ordered" relief.[45] Agencies may make discretionary

---

[44](...continued)
updating and reconsidering the release of information after the completion of the initial FOIA search"); Gilmore v. NSA, No. 92-3646, 1993 U.S. Dist. LEXIS 22027, at *29 (N.D. Cal. May 3, 1993) (following Military Audit and declining to penalize agency), aff'd on other grounds, 76 F.3d 386 (9th Cir. 1995) (unpublished table decision); Stone v. FBI, 727 F. Supp. 662, 666 (D.D.C. 1990) (reasoning that agencies should be free to make "voluntary" disclosures without concern that they "could come back to haunt" them in other cases); cf. Pub. Citizen v. Dep't of State, 11 F.3d 198, 203 (D.C. Cir. 1993) (holding that agency should not be required to disclose "related materials" where "to do so would give the Government a strong disincentive ever to provide its citizenry with briefings of any kind on sensitive topics"). But see Billington v. U.S. Dep't of Justice, 11 F. Supp. 2d 45, 59 (D.D.C. 1998) (citing Bonner v. Dep't of State, 928 F.2d 1148, 1151 (D.C. Cir. 1991), for the proposition that "[w]hile a full release of documents previously withheld does not demonstrate bad faith, doubt may be cast on the agency's original exemption claim when the information in question is found releasable within two years" and that a district court in such a case must accordingly "examine closely the initial exemption claims"), summary judgment granted in pertinent part, 69 F. Supp. 2d 128, 135 (D.D.C. 1999), aff'd in part, vacated in part & remanded on other grounds, 233 F.3d 581 (D.C. Cir. 2000).

[45] Davis v. Dep't of Justice, 460 F.3d 92, 105-06 (D.C. Cir. 2006) (applying Oil, Chem. & Atomic Workers, and rejecting requester's claim for attorneys fees as there had been no finding on merits for requester); Oil, Chem. & Atomic Workers Int'l Union, AFL-CIO v. Dep't of Energy, 288 F.3d 452, 454-55 (D.C. Cir. 2002) (applying Supreme Court precedent, Buckhannon Bd. & Care Home, Inc. v. W. Va. Dep't of Health & Human Res., 532 U.S. 598, 603 (2001), to hold that "for plaintiffs in FOIA actions to become eligible for an award of attorney's fees, they must have 'been awarded some relief by [a] court'"); see, e.g., Lovell v. Alderete, 630 F.2d 428, 432 & n.4 (5th Cir. 1980) (alternative holding) ("[The] Government's compliance with [plaintiff's] request was not caused mainly by the institution of the suit, but rather was also affected by a change in the United States Attorney General's [May 5, 1977] guidelines concerning disclosure of exempted materials."); Lissner v. U.S. Customs Serv., No. 98-7438, slip op. at 7 (C.D. Cal. Aug. 19, 1999) (refusing to award attorney fees because such an award would punish the agency "for its disclosure of information it believed was exempt [and would] . . . lead to the undesirable result that agencies would simply entrench themselves in their original positions, for fear that releasing subsequent documents would subject them to attorney fees liability"), rev'd on other grounds, 241 F.3d 1220 (9th Cir. 2001); cf. Bubar v. FBI, 3 Gov't Disclosure Serv. (P-H) ¶ 83,218, at 89,930-31 (D.D.C. June 13, 1983) (declining
(continued...)

dis-closures of exempt information, at any stage of the FOIA administrative or litigative process, without concern for such consequences.[46] In fact, one court had occasion to express this principle in broad terms:

> Were the courts to construe disclosure of a document as an agency's concession of wrongful withholding, . . . agencies would be forced to either never disclose a document once withheld or risk being assessed fees. This result would frustrate the policy of encouraging disclosure that prompted enactment of the FOIA and its amendments. . . . Penalizing an agency for disclosure at any stage of the proceedings is simply not in the spirit of the FOIA.[47]

Agencies should be mindful, though, that these principles apply to true discretionary disclosures made under the FOIA -- which should be made available, if at all, to anyone -- as distinguished from any "selective" disclosure made more narrowly outside the realm of the FOIA.[48] Such non-FOIA disclosures can lead to more difficult waiver questions.

### Waiver

Sometimes when a FOIA exemption is being invoked, a further inquiry must be undertaken to determine whether the applicability of the exemption has been waived through some prior disclosure, or perhaps even as the result of an express authorization from the party or parties affected by the disclosure. Resolution of this inquiry requires a careful analysis of the specific nature of, and circumstances surrounding, the prior disclosure

---

[45](...continued)
to award attorney fees when disclosure was caused by administrative reprocessing of request "pursuant to newly-adopted procedures").

[46] See Nationwide, 559 F.2d at 712 n.34 ("Certainly where the government can show that information disclosed . . . was nonetheless exempt from the FOIA a plaintiff should not be awarded attorney fees."); cf. Pub. Law Educ. Inst. v. U.S. Dep't of Justice, 744 F.2d 181, 183-84 (D.C. Cir. 1984) (denying attorney fees award when agency disclosed requested records discretionarily in related proceeding).

[47] Am. Commercial Barge Lines v. NLRB, 758 F.2d 1109, 1112 (6th Cir. 1985).

[48] See, e.g., North Dakota ex rel. Olson v. Andrus, 581 F.2d 177, 182 (8th Cir. 1978) (finding waiver when agency made "selective" disclosure to one interested party only); Comm. to Bridge the Gap v. Dep't of Energy, No. 90-3568, transcript at 5 (C.D. Cal. Oct. 11, 1991) (bench order) (finding waiver when agency gave preferential treatment to interested party; such action is "offensive" to FOIA and "fosters precisely the distrust of government the FOIA was intended to obviate"), aff'd on other grounds, 10 F.3d 808 (9th Cir. 1993) (unpublished table decision).

and may even vary according to the particular exemption involved.[49]

There are some well-established rules for determining whether an agency has waived its right to use FOIA exemptions with regard to requested information.[50] As a general rule, the government may not rely on an otherwise valid exemption to justify withholding information that officially has entered the public domain.[51] The Court of Appeals for the District of Columbia Circuit has adopted this rule because ordinarily an "exemption can serve no purpose once information . . . becomes public."[52] To have been "officially" released, however, information generally must have been disclosed under circumstances in which an authoritative government official allowed the information to be made public.[53] Further, courts have

---

[49] See FOIA Update, Vol. IV, No. 2, at 6 (advising of fundamental approach to waiver questions by agencies and courts); see also Mobil Oil Corp. v. EPA, 879 F.2d 698, 700 (9th Cir. 1989) ("The inquiry into whether a specific disclosure constitutes a waiver is fact specific."); Carson v. U.S. Dep't of Justice, 631 F.2d 1008, 1016 n.30 (D.C. Cir. 1980) ("[T]he extent to which prior agency disclosure may constitute a waiver of the FOIA exemptions must depend both on the circumstances of prior disclosure and on the particular exemptions claimed.").

[50] See Fitzgibbon v. CIA, 911 F.2d 755, 765 (D.C. Cir. 1990) (explaining criteria for official agency acknowledgment of publicly disclosed information (citing Afshar v. Dep't of State, 702 F.2d 1125, 1133 (D.C. Cir. 1983))); James Madison Project v. NARA, No. 98-2737, slip op. at 7 n.5 (D.D.C. Mar. 5, 2002) (collecting cases that describe elements of waiver), summary affirmance granted in pertinent part & remanded in part, No. 02-5089, 2002 WL 31296220 (D.C. Cir. Oct. 11, 2002).

[51] Students Against Genocide v. Dep't of State, 257 F.3d 828, 836 (D.C. Cir. 2001) (emphasizing that "[f]or the public domain doctrine to apply, the specific information sought must have already been 'disclosed and preserved in a permanent public record'" (citing Cottone v. Reno, 193 F.3d 550, 554-55 (D.C. Cir. 1999))); Callahan v. Executive Office for U.S. Attorneys, No. 98-1826, slip op. at 3 (D.D.C. Apr. 18, 2002) (ordering release of court-filed documents on basis that they already were in public domain).

[52] Cottone, 193 F.3d at 555 (noting also that a court "must be confident that the information sought is truly public and that the requester receives no more than what is publicly available"). But cf. Fitzgibbon, 911 F.2d at 766 (suggesting that the "'fact that [national security] information resides in the public domain does not eliminate the possibility that further disclosures can cause harm to intelligence sources, methods and operations'"); see also Edmonds v. FBI, 272 F. Supp. 2d 35, 48 (D.D.C. 2003) (same).

[53] See, e.g., Wolf v. CIA, 473 F. 3d 370, 379-380 (D.C. Cir. 2007) (holding that former CIA director's testimony before congressional subcommittee, which included reading from dispatch mentioning individual who was

(continued...)

consistently held that it is the FOIA plaintiff who bears the burden of demonstrating that the withheld information has been officially disclosed.[54]

With regard to prior disclosure, courts have consistently held that the prior public disclosure must "match" the exempt information in question; otherwise, the difference between the two might itself be a sufficient basis for reaching the conclusion that no waiver has occurred.[55] For example, if

---

[53](...continued)
subject of request, waived CIA's ability to refuse to confirm or deny existence of responsive records pertaining to that individual); Myles-Pirzada v. Dep't of the Army, No. 91-1080, slip op. at 6 (D.D.C. Nov. 23, 1992) (finding that privilege was waived when agency official read report to requester); see also Frugone v. CIA, 169 F.3d 772, 774 (D.C. Cir. 1999) (ruling that disclosure made by employee from agency other than one from which information was sought is not official and thus does not constitute waiver).

[54] See, e.g., Pub. Citizen v. Dep't of State, 276 F.3d 634, 645 (D.C. Cir. 2002) (reaffirming that burden is on requester to establish that specific record in public domain duplicates that being withheld (citing Afshar, 702 F.2d at 1132)); Deglace v. DEA, No. 05-2276, 2007 WL 521896, at *2 (D.D.C. Feb. 15, 2007) (finding no waiver when plaintiff produced circumstantial evidence that records have entered the public domain, but not the records themselves) (appeal pending); Bronx Defenders v. DHS, No. 04 CV 8576, 2005 WL3462725, at *3 (S.D.N.Y. Dec. 19, 2005) (finding that release of excerpts from document does not replicate whole document and create waiver); Shores v. FBI, 185 F. Supp. 2d 77, 86-87 (D.D.C. 2002) (finding no waiver when plaintiff failed to demonstrate that specific information had entered public domain). But see Natural Res. Def. Council v. DOD, 442 F. Supp. 2d 857, 865-66 (C.D. Cal. Mar. 21, 2006) (rejecting government's argument that records were "leaked" to lobbying firm in light of facts that agency failed "to take affirmative steps to inhibit . . . further dissemination" and agency staff discussed content of records with firm's representatives).

[55] See, e.g., Wolf, 473 F. 3d at 379-380 (distinguishing official acknowledgment of the record's existence from official acknowledgment of the record's content and emphasizing that content needed to have been entered into public domain in order to be considered waived); Heeney v. FDA, 7 F. App'x 770, 772 (9th Cir. 2001) (concluding that "[b]ecause . . . FDA's previous disclosures involved unrelated files . . . the information [at issue] was properly withheld"); Nowak v. IRS, No. 98-56656, 2000 WL 60067, at *2 (9th Cir. Jan. 21, 2000) (determining that in order for FOIA plaintiff to establish waiver of FOIA exemption, he must be able to establish that information in his possession originated from same documents as those released in prior disclosure); Davis v. U.S. Dep't of Justice, 968 F.2d 1276, 1280 (D.C. Cir. 1992) (finding no waiver as plaintiff failed to demonstrate that "exact portions" of records sought are in public domain); Fitzgibbon, 911 F.2d at 766 (finding no waiver when withheld information "pertain[s] to a time period later than the date of the publicly documented information"); Afshar, 702

(continued...)

the information that already is available to the public is less specific than that at issue, the agency still may properly invoke an exemption to protect the more detailed information.[56] Likewise, the fact that an agency has re-

---

[55](...continued)
F.2d at 1132 (finding that "withheld information is in some material respect different" from that which requester claimed had been released previously); Hertzberg v. Veneman, 273 F. Supp. 2d 67, 81-82 (D.D.C. 2003) (holding that "selective" disclosure of some withheld material does not waive use of exemptions to protect similar, but undisclosed, information); Enviro Tech Int'l, Inc. v. EPA, No. 02-C-4650, slip op. at 15 (N.D. Ill. Mar. 11, 2003) (holding that agency "summarization" disclosure of withheld information could waive use of exemptions only for limited information contained within summary, not for all related records), aff'd, 371 F.3d 370 (7th Cir. 2004); Starkey v. U.S. Dep't of the Interior, 238 F. Supp. 2d 1188, 1193 (S.D. Cal. 2002) (finding waiver of exemptions for two documents filed with, and publicly available through, local county government); Assassination Archives & Research Ctr. v. CIA, 177 F. Supp. 2d 1, 10 (D.D.C. 2001) (holding that plaintiff had not demonstrated that information at issue matched documents previously disclosed or released by CIA under JFK Act), aff'd, 334 F.3d 55 (D.C. Cir. 2003); Nat'l Sec. Archive Fund, Inc. v. CIA, No. 99-1160, slip op. at 14 (D.D.C. July 31, 2000 ) (reiterating that CIA's prior release of several declassified biographies of world leaders did not compel it to disclose whether it maintained other information on those world leaders); Pease v. U.S. Dep't of Interior, No. 1:99CV113, slip op. at 7 (D. Vt. Sept. 11, 1999) (disclosing similar records prior to enactment of Exemption 3 statute does not result in waiver of current records covered by that statute); Kay v. FCC, 867 F. Supp. 11, 20-21 (D.D.C. 1994) (inadvertent disclosure of some informants' names does not waive Exemption 7(A) protection for information about other informants); cf. Herrick v. Garvey, 200 F. Supp. 2d 1321, 1329 (D. Wyo. Dec. 12, 2000) (finding no waiver where corporation reversed its earlier decision to disclose materials and disputed items had not been released by FAA previously), aff'd, 298 F.3d 1184 (10th Cir. 2002). But see Comm. to Bridge the Gap v. Dep't of Energy, No. 90-3568, transcript at 2-5 (C.D. Cal. Oct. 11, 1991) (bench order) (distinguishing Mobil Oil and finding deliberative process privilege waived for draft order by prior voluntary disclosure of earlier draft order to interested party; agency ordered to release earlier draft order and all subsequent revisions), aff'd on other grounds, 10 F.3d 808 (9th Cir. 1993) (unpublished table decision).

[56] See Edmonds v. FBI, 272 F. Supp. 2d 35, 49 (D.D.C. 2003) (holding that because the withheld information is far more detailed than that in the public domain, "its release could provide a composite picture, or at least additional information, that would be harmful to national security"); Kelly v. CIA, No. 00-2498, slip op. at 12 (D.D.C. Aug. 8, 2002) (holding that agency had not waived use of exemptions, because prior public disclosure was less specific and detailed than information withheld); Heeney v. FDA, No. 97-5461, slip op. at 19 (C.D. Cal. Mar. 16, 1999) (holding that mere fact that withheld documents may contain information previously released is insuffi-
(continued...)

leased to the public general information concerning a subject does not preclude the agency from invoking an exemption to protect the more specific information concerning that same subject.[57] Indeed, courts have consistently "refused to find that the discretionary disclosure of a document effectuates a waiver of other related documents."[58]

Furthermore, general or limited public discussion of a subject by agency officials usually does not lead to waiver with respect to specific information or records.[59] Courts ordinarily do not penalize agency officials for

---

[56](...continued)
cient because context in which documents were previously released may differ from context in which documents are currently being withheld), aff'd, 7 F. App'x 770 (9th Cir. 2001); Baltimore Sun Co. v. U.S. Customs Serv., No. 97-1191 (D. Md. Nov. 21, 1997) (ruling that public disclosure of "a poor quality photograph" did not waive the agency's ability to protect a clear copy where there was greater sensitivity in the latter); see also Cottone, 193 F.3d at 555-56 (finding waiver where plaintiff had identified specific tapes in public domain).

[57] See Assassination Archives & Research Ctr. v. CIA, 334 F.3d 55, 61 (D.C. Cir. 2003) (holding that previous generalized disclosures did not result in waiver, because they "did not precisely track the records sought to be released"); Coastal Delivery Corp. v. U.S. Customs Serv., 272 F. Supp. 2d 958, 966 (C.D. Cal. 2003) (rejecting the requester's waiver argument because the withheld information was "merely the same category of information, not the exact information" as that previously disclosed); Ctr. for Int'l Envtl. Law v. Office of the U.S. Trade Representative, 237 F. Supp. 2d 17, 23 (D.D.C. 2002) (holding that public availability of "similar but not identical information" does not lead to waiver for all information on same subject).

[58] Enviro Tech, No. 02-C-4650, slip op. at 15 (N.D. Ill. Mar. 11, 2003), aff'd, 371 F.3d 370 (7th Cir. 2004); see also Wood v. FBI, 312 F. Supp. 2d 328, 344 (D. Conn. 2004) (ruling that agency official could not possibly have waived exemptions applicable to memorandum that he had not even seen), aff'd in pertinent part, 432 F.3d 78 (2d Cir. 2005); see also Riquelme v. CIA, 453 F. Supp. 2d 103, 115 (D.D.C. 2006) (holding that declassification of records pertaining to Chilean and Argentinian involvement in regional intelligence initiative does not result in waiver as to possible Paraguayan involvement in same intelligence initiative).

[59] See, e.g., Students Against Genocide, 257 F.3d at 836 (holding that government did not waive its right to "invoke . . . FOIA exemptions by displaying the withheld photographs to the delegates of . . . foreign governments . . . [because they] were not released to the general public"); Kimberlin v. Dep't of Justice, 139 F.3d 944, 949 (D.C. Cir. 1998) (holding that public acknowledgment of investigation and "vague reference to its conclusion" does not waive use of Exemption 7(C) to protect "details of the investigation"); Goodman v. U.S. Dep't of Labor, No. 01-515, 2001 WL 34039487, at *4

(continued...)

DISCRETIONARY DISCLOSURE AND WAIVER

sharing information concerning government activities with the public in general terms.[60]

Under some circumstances, though, an agency certainly can waive the applicability of a FOIA exemption through the public discussion of information by agency official.[61] In this context, one district court held that

---

[59](...continued)
(D. Or. Dec. 21, 2001) (finding no waiver, because agency official was merely describing disputed documents, rather than releasing them); Billington v. Dep't of Justice, 11 F. Supp. 2d 45, 55 (D.D.C. 1999) (finding no waiver where requester failed to show that "exact activities" claimed to be in public domain "have been disclosed in these documents"), aff'd on other grounds, 233 F.3d 581 (D.C. Cir. 2000); Rothschild v. Dep't of Energy, 6 F. Supp. 2d 38, 40-41 (D.D.C. 1998) (finding no waiver where requester failed to specify how public discussion of particular economic theory revealed agency deliberative process with respect to long-term, wide-ranging study); Marriott Employees' Fed. Credit Union v. Nat'l Credit Union Admin., No. 96-478-A, 1996 WL 33497625, at *2 (E.D. Va. Dec. 24, 1996) (finding no waiver because "[a]lthough the existence and general subject of the investigations is known to the public, there is no evidence in the record indicating that specific information concerning these investigations has been shared with unauthorized parties"); Blazar v. OMB, No. 92-2719, slip op. at 11-12 (D.D.C. Apr. 15, 1994) (following Public Citizen and finding no waiver of Exemptions 1 and 3 when published autobiography refers to information sought but provides no more than general outline of it). But see Wash. Post Co. v. U.S. Dep't of the Air Force, 617 F. Supp. 602, 605 (D.D.C. 1985) (disclosure of document's conclusions waived privilege for body of document).

[60] See, e.g., Pub. Citizen v. Dep't of State, 11 F.3d 198, 201 (D.C. Cir. 1993) (finding that an "agency official does not waive FOIA exemption 1 by publicly discussing the general subject matter of documents which are otherwise properly exempt from disclosure"); Dow Jones & Co. v. U.S. Dep't of Justice, 880 F. Supp. 145, 151 (S.D.N.Y. 1995) (holding that agency's "limited, general and cursory discussions" of investigative subject matter during press conference did not waive Exemption 7(A)), vacated on other grounds, 907 F. Supp. 79 (S.D.N.Y. 1995); see also Military Audit Project v. Casey, 656 F.2d 724, 754 (D.C. Cir. 1981) (resisting any rule that would be "a disincentive for an agency to reappraise its position and, when appropriate, release documents previously withheld"); Greenberg, 10 F. Supp. 2d at 23-24 (resisting likewise any rule that "would not advance the underlying purpose of the FOIA -- the broadest possible responsible disclosure of government documents.").

[61] See, e.g., Wolf, 473 F. 3d at 379-380 (finding waiver of "Glomar" response where agency head had discussed subject of request in congressional testimony); Myles-Pirzada, No. 91-1080, slip op. at 6 (D.D.C. Nov. 23, 1992) (finding waiver when agency official read report to requester over

(continued...)

information that was the subject of an "off-the-record" disclosure to the press by an agency official cannot be protected under Exemption 1.[62] Such waiver can occur even in a telephone conversation,[63] though the District Court for the District of Columbia has limited the waiver to the information actually made public.[64] In one case, for example, it was held that an agency official's oral disclosure of only the conclusion reached in a predecisional document "does not, without more, waive the [deliberative process] privilege."[65] In another, an agency disclosure to a small group of nongovernmental personnel, with no copies permitted, was held not to inhibit agency decisionmaking, so the deliberative process privilege was not waived.[66] Even in the context of civil litigation, a court has held that the discussion of classified information with a plaintiff's uncleared counsel did not amount to a waiver.[67]

---

[61](...continued)
telephone); Comm. to Bridge the Gap, No. 90-3568, transcript at 3-5 (C.D. Cal. Sept. 9, 1991) (bench order) (ruling that agency waived deliberative process privilege by voluntarily providing draft order to interested party).

[62] Lawyers Comm. for Human Rights v. INS, 721 F. Supp. 552, 569 (S.D.N.Y. 1989), motion for reargument denied, No. 87-Civ-1115, slip op. at 1-3 (S.D.N.Y. May 23, 1990); see also Grand Cent. P'ship v. Cuomo, 166 F.3d 473, 484 (2d Cir. 1999) (refusing to extend Exemption 5 protection to "[a] letter [which] appear[ed] to report matters that were aired at a public hearing"); Shell Oil Co. v. IRS, 772 F. Supp. 202, 211 (D. Del. 1991) (finding waiver when agency employee read aloud entire draft document at public meeting).

[63] See, e.g., Catchpole v. Dep't of Transp., No. 97-8058, slip op. at 5-7 (11th Cir. Feb. 25, 1998) (remanding to determine if official read memorandum to requester over telephone, thereby waiving privilege).

[64] See Myles-Pirzada, No. 91-1080, slip op. at 6 (D.D.C. Nov. 23, 1992).

[65] Morrison v. U.S. Dep't of Justice, No. 87-3394, 1988 WL 47662, at *1 (D.D.C. Apr. 29, 1988).

[66] Dow, Lohnes & Albertson v. Presidential Comm'n on Broad. to Cuba, 624 F. Supp. 572, 577-78 (D.D.C. 1984); see also Am. Lawyer Media, Inc. v. SEC, No. 01-1967, 2002 U.S. Dist. LEXIS 16940, at *4 (D.D.C. Sept. 6, 2002) (holding that agency did not waive right to withhold portions of training manual by permitting requester to review manual during public training conference); Brinderson Constructors, Inc. v. Army Corps of Eng'rs, No. 85-0905, 1986 WL 293230, at *5 (D.D.C. June 11, 1986) (requester's participation in agency enterprise did not entitle requester to all related documents).

[67] Edmonds v. U.S. Dep't of Justice, 405 F. Supp. 2d 23, 31 (D.D.C. Dec. 19, 2005) (distinguishing partial disclosure to plaintiff's counsel during meeting, on one hand, from making entire compendium of information used
(continued...)

## DISCRETIONARY DISCLOSURE AND WAIVER

Further, it is important to note that "[t]he fact that [a FOIA requester] can guess which names have been deleted from the released documents does not act as a waiver to disclosure."[68] This holds true even when a requester has personal knowledge of the facts, such as by observing or participating in the events detailed in government records.[69] Indeed, even if a requester could piece together information from different sources and potentially develop a complete picture of withheld facts, that does not compel the waiver of applicable exemptions.[70] In sum, a FOIA plaintiff's personal knowledge of information contained within a government record does not alone mean that an agency has made (or should make) any official disclosure to the public.[71]

---

[67](...continued)
by FBI publicly available, on another hand).

[68] Valencia-Lucena v. DEA, No. 99-0633, slip op. at 7 (D.D.C. Feb. 8, 2000) (citing Weisberg v. U.S. Dep't of Justice, 745 F.2d 1476, 1491 (D.C. Cir. 1984)); see also LaRouche v. U.S. Dep't of Justice, No. 90-2753, slip op. at 15-16 (D.D.C. July 5, 2001) (holding that mere fact that plaintiff purported that he was able to identify witness names from other sources did not diminish privacy interests held); LaRouche v. U.S. Dep't of Justice, No. 90-2753, slip op. at 11-12 (D.D.C. Nov. 17, 2000) (finding that Exemption 7(D) protection for confidential sources who provided information was not waived just because plaintiff might well identify sources from documents disclosed by different agency).

[69] See, e.g., Rubis v. DEA, No. 01-1132, slip op. at 7 (D.D.C. Sept. 30, 2002) (reaffirming that exemption is not waived by fact that plaintiff might well already know identities of individuals); Tanks v. Huff, No. 95-568, 1996 U.S. Dist. LEXIS 7266, at *10 (D.D.C. May 28, 1996) (holding that requester's knowledge of identities of informants who testified against him does not affect ability of agency to invoke exemption).

[70] See, e.g., Whalen v. U.S. Marine Corps, 407 F. Supp. 2d 54, 60 (D.D.C. 2005) (holding that government did not waive Exemptions 1 and 3 merely because plaintiff might well surmise what redacted information was by using knowledge obtained from nonfiction books written by private authors); see also Gilda Indus., Inc. v. U.S. Customs & Border Prot. Bureau, 457 F. Supp. 2d 6, 12 (D.D.C. 2006) (finding no waiver even though requester could compare two publicly available lists and deduce correlation bearing upon withheld information; information therefore was properly protected under Exemption 4).

[71] See U.S. Dep't of Justice v. Reporters Comm. for Freedom of the Press, 489 U.S. 749, 770 (1989) (holding that "the identity of the requesting party has no bearing on the merits of his or her FOIA request"); see also FOIA Update, Vol. X, No. 2, at 3-6 ("OIP Guidance: Privacy Protection Under the Supreme Court's Reporters Committee Decision") (advising that "a requester's particular knowledge of the information in question or its underlying

(continued...)

It also should be noted that courts are generally sympathetic to the necessities of effective agency functioning when confronted with an issue of waiver.[72] For example, courts have recognized that agencies ordinarily

---

[71](...continued)
circumstances (perhaps due to his relationship with the interested party, for example) should not be taken into account"); accord NARA v. Favish, 541 U.S. 157 (reiterating that "disclosure does not depend on the identity of the requester," and reminding that information subject to disclosure "belongs to all"), reh'g denied, 541 U.S. 1057 (2004); see also FOIA Post, "Supreme Court Rules for 'Survivor Privacy' in Favish" (posted 4/9/04) (observing that well-known maxim under FOIA that "release to one is release to all" was firmly reinforced by Supreme Court in its Favish decision).

[72] See, e.g., Isley v. Executive Office for U.S. Attorneys, No. 98-5098, 1999 WL 1021934, at *4 (D.C. Cir. Oct. 21, 1999) (finding that witnesses' testimony at trial does not waive the "government's right to withhold specific information about matters as to which [the witnesses have] testified" at trial); Schiffer v. FBI, 78 F.3d 1405, 1410-11 (9th Cir. 1996) (finding no waiver of FBI's right to invoke Exemption 7(C) for information made public during related civil action); Massey v. FBI, 3 F.3d 620, 624 (2d Cir. 1993) (ruling that individuals did not waive "strong privacy interests in government documents containing information about them even where the information may have been public at one time"); Cooper v. Dep't of the Navy, 558 F.2d 274, 278 (5th Cir. 1977) (finding that prior disclosure of aircraft accident investigation report to aircraft manufacturer did not constitute waiver); Summers v. U.S. Dep't of Justice, No. 98-1837, slip op. at 15-16 (D.D.C. Apr. 13, 2004) (determining that agency did not waive applicability of Exemption 7(C) by disclosure of third-party names from separate documents); Hornbostel v. U.S. Dep't of the Interior, 305 F. Supp. 2d 21, 28-29 (D.D.C. 2003) (holding that defendant's failure to respond to request within statutory time limit certainly does not waive exemptions and "has little substantive effect"); Dayton Newspapers, Inc. v. VA, 257 F. Supp. 2d 988, 1010 (S.D. Ohio Jan. 23, 2003) (noting that modern information technology has altered understanding of personal privacy, and observing generally that requesters "cannot claim that private records are no longer private simply because they are accessible through other means"); Nat'l Sec. Archive, No. 99-1160, slip op. at 13 (D.D.C. July 31, 2001) (concluding that disclosure of CIA-produced biographies by other agencies did not "preempt the CIA's ability to withhold [them]"); Doolittle v. U.S. Dep't of Justice, 142 F. Supp. 2d 281, 286 (N.D.N.Y. 2001) (declaring that "the [g]overnment's promise of confidentiality to an informant is intended to apply notwithstanding the type of limited disclosure present here [a sentencing hearing]," and finding that "such disclosure should not constitute a waiver of the [g]overnment's promise to keep the informant's identity confidential"); McGilvra v. Nat'l Transp. Safety Bd., 840 F. Supp. 100, 102 (D. Colo. 1993) (citing Cooper and finding that release of cockpit voice recorder tapes to parties to accident investigation is not "public" disclosure under FOIA); Medera Cmty. Hosp. v. United States, No. 86-542, slip op. at 6-9 (E.D. Cal. June 28, 1988) (finding no waiver

(continued...)

should be granted special latitude in matters of national security[73] and criminal law enforcement,[74] because of the inherent sensitivity of such activities and information. And in the national security context, this latitude can lead to an especially pragmatic view of what amounts to a waiver by the government,[75] with one appellate court even deciding that the passage of time should properly be considered when determining whether public disclosure of national security information has resulted in waiver.[76]

In the law enforcement context, it has been firmly held that the mere fact that a confidential source testifies at a trial does not waive Exemption 7(D) protection for any source-provided information not actually revealed in public.[77]

---

[72](...continued)
where memoranda interpreting agency's regulations were sent to state auditor involved in enforcement proceeding); Erb v. U.S. Dep't of Justice, 572 F. Supp. 954, 956 (W.D. Mich. 1983) (upholding nondisclosure under Exemption 7(A) despite "limited disclosure" of FBI criminal investigative report to defense attorney and state prosecutor).

[73] See Ctr. for Nat'l Sec. Studies v. U.S. Dep't of Justice, 331 F.3d 918, 928 (D.C. Cir. 2003) (emphasizing need for deference to agencies in all national security-related matters); Students Against Genocide, 257 F.3d at 835 (reiterating that sharing of classified information with foreign government does not result in waiver); Van Atta v. Def. Intelligence Agency, No. 87-1508, 1988 WL 73856, at *2 (D.D.C. July 6, 1988) (same).

[74] See Neely v. FBI, 208 F.3d 461, 466 (4th Cir. 2000) (holding that "public availability [does not] effect a waiver of the government's right" to invoke Exemption 7(D)); Irons v. FBI, 880 F.2d 1446, 1456-57 (1st Cir. 1989) (en banc) (finding good public policy reasons why public testimony by confidential source should not waive FBI's right to withhold information pursuant to Exemption 7(D)); Garcia v. U.S. Dep't of Justice, 181 F. Supp. 2d 356, 377 (S.D.N.Y. 2002) (finding that inadvertent disclosure of names of confidential sources does not waive government's right to invoke Exemption 7(D)).

[75] See Edmonds, 405 F. Supp. 2d at 29 (finding that even agency's disclosure to plaintiff's counsel at meeting did not amount to affirmative step toward declassification action with regard to information withheld under Exemption 1); Nat'l Sec. Archive v. CIA, No. 99-1160, slip op. at 12-13 (D.D.C. July 31, 2000) (ruling that Exemption 1 can be waived only through official action of CIA, not by disclosure by other agencies or presence of related information in public domain).

[76] Bassiouni v. CIA, 392 F.3d 244, 247 (7th Cir. 2004) (rejecting plaintiff's argument that agency acknowledgment of existence of records fourteen years earlier waived FOIA protection), cert. denied, 545 U.S. 1129 (2005).

[77] See Isley, 1999 WL 1021934, at *4 (finding that the fact that a witness
(continued...)

As a sound general rule, agencies making an official disclosure of information outside the executive branch should be able to do so without risking waiver of that information under circumstances in which the agency can demonstrate a legitimate purpose for the disclosure, and is able to establish that the disclosure was made with a restriction on further dissemination.[78] Generally speaking, if an agency is able to establish these two fundamental anti-waiver elements, its later claim of exemption will

---

[77](...continued)
testifies "only bars the government from withholding the [witnesses'] testimony itself"); Housley v. DEA, No. 92-16946, 1994 WL 168278, at *2 (9th Cir. May 4, 1994) (fact that some information may have been disclosed at criminal trial does not result in waiver as to other information); see also Jones v. FBI, 41 F.3d 238, 249 (6th Cir. 1994) (Exemption 7(D) "focuses on the source's intent, not the world's knowledge . . . . [H]old[ing] otherwise would discourage sources from cooperating with the FBI because of fear of revelation via FOIA."); Davoudlarian v. Dep't of Justice, No. 93-1787, 1994 WL 423845, at *3 (4th Cir. Aug. 15, 1994) (per curiam) (requester must demonstrate that specific witness statements were disclosed at civil trial in order to show waiver); Parker v. Dep't of Justice, 934 F.2d 375, 379 (D.C. Cir. 1991) (finding that "government agency is not required to disclose the identity of a confidential source or information conveyed to the agency in confidence in a criminal investigation notwithstanding the possibility that the informant may have testified at a public trial"); Larouche v. U.S. Dep't of Justice, No. 90-2753, slip op. at 6 (D.D.C. Aug. 8, 2002) (noting that "[a]lthough the government may not withhold information that is in the public domain, it need not make a wholesale disclosure about an individual just because he is a publicly acknowledged FBI source"); Daniel v. U.S. Dep't of Justice, No. 99-2423, slip op. at 3-4 (D.D.C. Mar. 30, 2001) (finding Exemption 7(D)'s protection not waived regarding previously undisclosed information furnished by witnesses who testified at trial under grant of immunity); Coleman v. FBI, 13 F. Supp. 2d 75, 80 (D.D.C. 1998) (finding that "an individual who testifies at trial does not waive this privacy interest beyond the scope of the trial[;] . . . [to] hold otherwise would discourage essential witness testimony"); cf. Reiter v. DEA, No. 96-0378, 1997 WL 470108, at *6 (D.D.C. Aug. 13, 1997) ("An agency may . . . continue to invoke Exemption 7(D) in the event that the requester learns of the source's identity and the information supplied by him through the source's open court testimony."), aff'd, No. 97-5246, 1998 WL 202247 (D.C. Cir. Apr. 27, 1998).

[78] See FOIA Update, Vol. IV, No. 2, at 6 ("The Effect of Prior Disclosure: Waiver of Exemptions"); see, e.g., Judicial Watch v. USPS, 297 F. Supp. 2d 252, 268 (D.D.C. 2004) (observing that a "disclosure to a third party that promotes the client's trial strategy and is consistent with maintaining secrecy against trial opponents does not waive the privilege"); McSheffrey v. Executive Office for U.S. Attorneys, No. 02-5239, 2003 WL 179840, at *1 (D.C. Cir. Jan. 24, 2003) (affirming that individuals who provided personal information to prison officials during visit with inmate did not waive personal privacy protection).

likely prevail.[79]

By contrast, however, courts <u>do</u> look harshly upon such prior disclosures, particularly seemingly "selective disclosures," that result in unfairness.[80] Indeed, in one case addressing the potential unfairness of selective disclosures, a commercial life insurance company sought access to records maintained by the United States Navy reflecting the name, rank, and duty locations of servicemen stationed at Quantico Marine Corps Base.[81] The district court, while not technically applying the doctrine of waiver, rejected the agency's privacy arguments on the grounds that virtually the same information -- officers' reassignment stations -- had been routinely published in the <u>Navy Times</u> and that the Dep't of Defense had previously disclosed the names and addresses of 1.4 million service members to a politi-

---

[79] See <u>Heggestad v. U.S. Dep't of Justice</u>, 182 F. Supp. 2d 1, 12-13 (D.D.C. 2000) (finding no waiver of deliberative process or attorney work-product privileges where information was disclosed to congressman); <u>see, e.g.</u>, <u>Rashid v. HHS</u>, No. 98-0898, slip op. at 7 (D.D.C. Mar. 2, 2000) (disclosure of memorandum to expert witnesses in anticipation of their testimony at trial); <u>McGilvra</u>, 840 F. Supp. at 102 (release of cockpit voice recorder tapes to parties in accident investigation); <u>Badhwar v. U.S. Dep't of the Air Force</u>, 629 F. Supp. 478, 481 (D.D.C. 1986) (disclosure to outside person held necessary to assemble report in first place), <u>aff'd in part & remanded in part on other grounds</u>, 829 F.2d 182 (D.C. Cir. 1987); <u>see also</u> <u>FOIA Update</u>, Vol. V, No. 1, at 4 (discussing congressional access to government records under the FOIA); <u>cf.</u> <u>FOIA Update</u>, Vol. IV, No. 2, at 6 (cautioning that "where such a disclosure is made not in furtherance of a legitimate governmental purpose, especially where it is not authorized under agency regulations, courts have been particularly unsympathetic to agencies").

[80] See, e.g., <u>Natural Res. Def. Council v. DOD</u>, 442 F. Supp. 2d 857, 865-66 (C.D. Cal. Mar. 21, 2006) (rejecting agency's leak argument where evidence of selective disclosure and preferential treatment was substantial); <u>North Dakota ex rel. Olson v. Andrus</u>, 581 F.2d 177, 182 (8th Cir. 1978) (finding "selective disclosure" of record to one party in litigation to be "offensive" to FOIA and sufficient to prevent agency's subsequent invocation of Exemption 5 against other party to litigation); <u>Nw. Envtl. Def. Ctr. v. U.S. Forest Serv.</u>, No. 91-125, slip op. at 12 (D. Or. Aug. 23, 1991) (magistrate's recommendation) (determining that agency waived deliberative process privilege as to portion of agency report that was discussed with "interested" third party), <u>adopted</u> (D. Or. Feb. 12, 1992); <u>Comm. to Bridge the Gap</u>, No. 90-3568, transcript at 3-5 (C.D. Cal. Sept. 9, 1991) (bench order) (finding waiver of deliberative process privilege for draft order by prior voluntary disclosure of earlier draft order to interested party; selective disclosure is "offensive" to FOIA).

[81] <u>Hopkins v. Dep't of the Navy</u>, No. 84-1868, 1985 WL 17673, at *1 (D.D.C. Feb. 5, 1985).

cal campaign committee.[82]

While "selective" disclosure does not always result in waiver, courts do often consider the overall fairness of the prior disclosure in question. For example, the Court of Appeals for the Fifth Circuit has held that while "selective disclosure" is of concern "with respect to those exemptions that protect the government's interest in non-disclosure of information . . . [that] concern [is] not implicated when a government agency relies on exemption 6 . . . to prevent disclosure of personal information."[83] Courts also expect an agency to adhere to its own policies and regulations concerning the disclosure of information contained within its records systems. Accordingly, an agency's failure to heed its own regulations regarding circulation of internal agency documents has been found sufficient to warrant a finding of waiver.[84] Similarly, an agency's regulation requiring disclosure of the information,[85] an agency's carelessness in permitting access to certain information,[86] and an agency's mistaken disclosure of the contents of a document[87] all have resulted in waiver.[88]

---

[82] Id. at *3; see also In re Subpoena Duces Tecum, 738 F.2d 1367, 1371-74 (D.C. Cir. 1984) (voluntary disclosure by private party of information to one agency waived attorney work-product and attorney-client privileges when same information was sought by second agency) (non-FOIA case).

[83] Sherman v. U.S. Dep't of the Army, 244 F.3d 357, 363-64 (5th Cir. 2001) ("only the individual whose informational privacy interests are protected by exemption 6 can effect a waiver of those privacy interests"); accord Attorney General's Memorandum for Heads of All Federal Departments and Agencies Regarding the Freedom of Information Act (Oct. 12, 2001), reprinted in FOIA Post (posted 10/15/01) (emphasizing importance of protecting personal privacy).

[84] Shermco Indus. v. Sec'y of the Air Force, 613 F.2d 1314, 1320 (5th Cir. 1980).

[85] See Johnson v. HHS, No. 88-243-5, slip op. at 10-11 (E.D.N.C. Feb. 7, 1989), aff'd, 905 F.2d 1530 (4th Cir. 1990) (unpublished table decision).

[86] See, e.g., Cooper v. Dep't of the Navy, 594 F.2d 484, 488 (5th Cir. 1978) (finding it "intolerable that such confidential documents should be furnished to one side of a lawsuit and not to the other," but noting that even "an unauthorized filching of the document would not in the normal course operate as a waiver of the [agency's] right to withhold it"); Haddam v. INS, No. 99-3371, slip op. at 5 (D.D.C. Feb. 15, 2001) (holding that INS's mistaken disclosure of document protected by attorney-client privilege to plaintiff's attorney waived that privilege for that document).

[87] See, e.g., Dresser Indus. Valve Operations, Inc. v. EEOC, 2 Gov't Disclosure Serv. (P-H) ¶ 82,197, at 82,575 (W.D. La. Jan. 19, 1982).

[88] See also Gannett River States Publ'g Corp. v. Bureau of the Nat'l

(continued...)

DISCRETIONARY DISCLOSURE AND WAIVER

On the other hand, and as a matter of practicality, courts have followed a general rule that waiver is not necessarily found when an agency makes an entirely mistaken disclosure of information.[89] Similarly, they also

---

[88](...continued)
Guard, No. J91-0455-L, 1992 WL 175235, at *6 (S.D. Miss. Mar. 2, 1992) (finding privacy interests in withholding identities of soldiers disciplined for causing accident to be de minimis because agency previously released much identifying information); Powell v. United States, 584 F. Supp. 1508, 1520-21 (N.D. Cal. 1984) (suggesting that attorney work-product privilege may be waived when agency made earlier release of such information which "reflect[ed] positively" on agency, and later may have withheld work-product information on same matter which did not reflect so "positively" on agency).

[89] See Ford v. West, No. 97-1342, 1998 WL 317561, at *3 (10th Cir. June 12, 1998) (rejecting claim that defendant's inadvertent release of names constituted waiver: "[D]efendant's inadequate redactions do not operate to waive the personal privacy interests of the individuals discussed in the investigative file."); Garcia, 181 F. Supp.2d at 377 (ruling that inconsistent redactions of names of confidential sources does not waive government's ability to invoke Exemption 7(D)); Am. Lawyer Media, 2002 U.S. Dist. LEXIS 16940, at *4 (holding that agency did not waive right to withhold portions of training manual by permitting plaintiff's employee to review manual during public training conference, because plaintiff had not shown that manual is in public domain); Fort Hall Landowners Alliance, Inc. v. Bureau of Indian Affairs, No. 99-00052, slip op. at 13-14 (D. Idaho Mar. 17, 2000) (noting that "an agency's inadvertent or mistaken disclosure does not necessarily constitute a waiver," and declining to find waiver when agency recognized its error and took corrective action); LaRouche v. U.S. Dep't of Justice, No. 90-2753, slip op. at 24 (D.D.C. July 5, 2001) (holding that inadvertent disclosure of information to another FOIA requester does not warrant disclosure of properly exempt information); Ponder v. Reno, No. 98-3097, slip op. at 6 (D.D.C. Jan. 22, 2001) (reaffirming principle that inadvertent disclosure does not constitute a waiver of Exemption 7(C)); Sinito v. U.S. Dep't of Justice, No. 87-0814, slip op. at 29-30 (D.D.C. July 12, 2000) (finding that documents inadvertently disclosed and briefly released to public did not "erase every vestige" of the privacy interests at stake), summary affirmance granted, 22 F. App'x 1 (D.C. Cir. 2001); Billington, 11 F. Supp. 2d at 66 (finding no waiver of Exemption 7(D) protection in case involving more than 40,000 documents where agency mistakenly released one withheld document to previous requester, and observing: "One document in such an enormous document request is merely a needle in a haystack. That one FBI agent may have redacted a document differently than another, or that the same FBI agent did not redact a document in precisely the same manner in different years, did not constitute bad faith."); Pub. Citizen Health Research Group v. FDA, 953 F. Supp. 400, 404-06 (D.D.C. 1996) (finding no waiver where material accidently released and information not disseminated by requester); Nation Magazine v. Dep't of State, 805 F. Supp. 68, 73 (D.D.C. (continued...)

have held that an agency does not waive its use of FOIA exemptions when an agency official mistakenly promises to make a disclosure.[90]

When an agency has been compelled to share information with Congress without making an official disclosure of information to the public, courts have consistently ruled that this exchange of information does not result in waiver, especially for information relating to national security.[91]

---

[89](...continued)
1992) (dicta) ("[N]o rule of administrative law requires an agency to extend erroneous treatment of one party to other parties, 'thereby turning an isolated error into a uniform misapplication of the law.'" (quoting Sacred Heart Med. Ctr. v. Sullivan, 958 F.2d 537, 548 n.24 (3d Cir. 1992))); Astley v. Lawson, No. 89-2806, 1991 WL 7162, at *8 (D.D.C. Jan. 11, 1991) (holding that inadvertent placement of documents into public record did not waive exemption when it was remedied immediately upon agency's awareness of mistake); cf. Kay, 867 F. Supp. at 23-24 (inadvertent disclosure of documents caused entirely by clerical error has no effect on remaining material at issue); Fleet Nat'l Bank v. Tonneson & Co., 150 F.R.D. 10, 16 (D. Mass. 1993) (holding that inadvertent production of one volume of three-volume report did not constitute waiver of attorney work-product privilege as to that volume, nor as to remaining two volumes of report) (non-FOIA case); Myers v. Williams, 819 F. Supp. 919, 921 (D. Or. 1993) (granting preliminary injunction prohibiting FOIA requester from disclosing original and all copies of erroneously disclosed document containing trade secrets) (non-FOIA case).

[90] See Hertzberg, 273 F. Supp. 2d at 82 (concluding that agency official's assurances that information would be released did not waive Exemption 5); Anderson v. U.S. Dep't of the Treasury, No. 98-1112, 1999 WL 282784, at *4 (W.D. Tenn. Mar. 24, 1999) (finding that the mere promise of an IRS agent to disclose a document to a FOIA requester did not constitute waiver, because "[n]othing in [the] FOIA . . . make[s] such a statement binding and irrevocable").

[91] See Rockwell v. U.S. Dep't of Justice, 235 F.3d 598, 604-05 (D.C. Cir. 2001) (finding no waiver when agency secured promise of confidentiality from congressional subcommittee); Pub. Citizen, 11 F.3d at 201 (finding no waiver when agency official publicly discussed only general subject matter of documents in congressional testimony); Fitzgibbon, 911 F.2d at 765 (holding that prior disclosure in a congressional report does not waive "information pertaining to a time period later than the date of the publicly documented information"); Edmonds v. FBI, 272 F. Supp. 2d at 49 (affirming that disclosure of classified material to congressional committee "does not deprive the [agency] of the right to classify the information under Exemption 1" (citing Fitzgibbon, 911 F.2d at 766)); see also Afshar, 702 F.2d at 1131-32 (finding no waiver when withheld information is in some respect materially different); cf. Heeney, No. 97-5461, slip op. at 19 (C.D. Cal. Mar. 16, 1999) (finding no waiver where documents at issue contained informa-

(continued...)

## DISCRETIONARY DISCLOSURE AND WAIVER

Furthermore, disclosure in a congressional report does not waive Exemption 1 applicability if the agency itself has never publicly acknowledged the information.[92] Most significantly, in deference to the common agency practice of disclosing specifically requested information to a congressional committee,[93] or to the General Accounting Office (an arm of Congress),[94] such disclosures generally do not result in waiver.

---

[91](...continued)
tion that previously was released in different context).

[92] See Earth Pledge Found. v. CIA, 988 F. Supp. 623, 627 (S.D.N.Y. 1996), aff'd, 128 F.3d 788 (2d Cir. 1997); see also Salisbury v. United States, 690 F.2d 966, 971 (D.C. Cir. 1982) (holding that information in Senate report "cannot be equated with disclosure by the agency itself"); Military Audit Project, 656 F.2d at 744 (finding that publication of Senate report does not constitute official release of agency information); Students Against Genocide, 50 F. Supp. 2d at 25 (affirming principle that only agency that is original source of information in question can waive applicability of FOIA exemption).

[93] See, e.g., Rockwell, 235 F.3d at 604 (finding no waiver for documents provided to congressional oversight subcommittee, in accordance with FOIA's specific congressional-disclosure provision, found at 5 U.S.C. § 552(d)); Fla. House of Representatives v. U.S. Dep't of Commerce, 961 F.2d 941, 946 (11th Cir. 1992) (holding no waiver of exemption due to court-ordered disclosure, involuntary disclosure to Congress, or disclosure of related information); Aspin v. DOD, 491 F.2d 24, 26 (D.C. Cir. 1973) (accepting that military criminal investigation records related to "My Lai Massacre," during Vietnam War, were exempt from disclosure, despite release to Armed Services Committees of both Houses of Congress); Edmonds, 272 F. Supp. 2d at 49 (affirming that disclosure of classified material to congressional committee "does not deprive the [agency] of the right to classify the information under Exemption 1" (citing Fitzgibbon 911 F.2d at 766)); Wash. Post Co. v. DOD, No. 84-2949, 1987 U.S. Dist. LEXIS 16108, at *25 n.9 (D.D.C. Feb. 25, 1987) ("unprincipled disclosure" by Members of Congress who had signed statements of confidentiality "cannot be the basis to compel disclosure" by the agency); see also Eagle-Picher Indus. v. United States, 11 Ct. Cl. 452, 460-61 (1987) (holding that work-product privilege is not waived in nonspecific congressional testimony "if potentially thousands of documents need be reviewed to determine if the gist or a significant part of documents were revealed") (non-FOIA case); FOIA Update, Vol. V, No. 1, at 3-4 ("OIP Guidance: Congressional Access Under FOIA") (analyzing Murphy v. Dep't of the Army, 613 F.2d 1151 (D.C. Cir. 1979), and advising that "[e]ven where a FOIA request is made by a Member clearly acting in a completely official capacity, such a request does not properly trigger the special access rule of subsection ([d]) unless it is made by a committee or subcommittee chairman, or otherwise under the authority of a committee or subcommittee").

[94] See, e.g., Shermco, 613 F.2d at 1320-21.

In addition, when an agency has been compelled to disclose a document under limited and controlled conditions, such as under a protective order in an administrative proceeding, its authority to withhold the document thereafter is not diminished.[95] This applies as well to disclosures made in the criminal discovery context.[96]

---

[95] See, e.g., Lead Indus. Ass'n v. OSHA, 610 F.2d 70, 79 n.13 (2d Cir. 1979) (permitting OSHA to withhold records that it previously shared with consultant for decisionmaking purposes); see also Allnet Commc'n Servs. v. FCC, 800 F. Supp. 984, 989 (D.D.C. 1992) (finding no waiver where information was disclosed under "strict confidentiality"), aff'd, No. 92-5351 (D.C. Cir. May 27, 1994); Abrams v. Office of the Comptroller of the Currency, No. 3:05-CV-2433, 2006 WL 1450525 at *5 (N.D. Tex. May 25, 2006) (concluding that agency did not waive Exemption 8 protection when it released information to limited number of people for limited purpose of demonstrating authority to issue subpoenas); see also Silverberg v. HHS, No. 89-2743, 1991 WL 633740, at *3 (D.D.C. June 14, 1991) (ruling that fact that individual who is subject of drug test by particular laboratory has right of access to its performance and testing information does not render such information publicly available), appeal dismissed per stipulation, No. 91-5255 (D.C. Cir. Sept. 2, 1993).

[96] See, e.g., Hronek, 7 F. App'x 591, 592 (9th Cir. 2001) (rejecting contention that DEA waived claimed exemptions where documents at issue "relate[d] to documents released to [plaintiff during] the course of his criminal conviction."); Cottone, 193 F.3d at 556 (limiting finding of waiver to specific wiretapped recordings played in open court and refusing to extend finding of waiver to wiretapped recordings provided to plaintiff's counsel as Brady material); Ferguson v. FBI, 957 F.2d 1059, 1068 (2d Cir. 1992) (holding that fact that local police department released records pursuant to New York Freedom of Information Law and one of its officers testified at length in court did not to waive police department's status as confidential source under Exemption 7(D)); Parker, 934 F.2d at 379 (affirming nondisclosure under Exemption 7(D) even though confidential informant may have testified at requester's trial); Nat'l Ass'n of Criminal Def. Lawyers v. U.S. Dep't of Justice, No. 97-372, slip op. at 8-10 (D.D.C. July 22, 1998) (ruling that limited disclosure of draft report to defendants pursuant to criminal discovery rules does not waive Exemption 5 protection); Willis v. FBI, No. 96-1455, slip op. at 2-6 (D.D.C. Feb. 14, 1998) ("The mere fact that at one time the Plaintiff's counsel may have had a right of access to portions of the transcript for a limited purpose hardly suffices to show that all of the requested transcripts now are a part of the public domain."), aff'd in part & remanded in part on other grounds, 194 F.3d 175 (D.C. Cir. 1999) (unpublished table decision); Fisher v. U.S. Dep't of Justice, 772 F. Supp. 7, 12 (D.D.C. 1991) (even if some of withheld information has appeared in print, nondisclosure is proper because disclosure from official source would confirm unofficial information and thereby cause harm to third parties); Beck v. U.S. Dep't of Justice, No. 88-3433, slip op. at 2 (D.D.C. July 24, 1991) ("Exemption 7(C) is not necessarily waived where an individual has testified at trial."), summa-
(continued...)

# DISCRETIONARY DISCLOSURE AND WAIVER

Of course, circulation of a document within an agency does not waive an exemption.[97] Nor does disclosure among federal agencies,[98] or to advisory committees (even those including members of the public).[99] Similarly, properly controlled disclosure to state or local law enforcement officials,[100]

---

[96](...continued)
ry affirmance granted in pertinent part & denied in part, No. 91-5292 (D.C. Cir. Nov. 19, 1992); Erb, 572 F. Supp. at 956 (nondisclosure to third party upheld under Exemption 7(A) even though document provided to defendant through criminal discovery); cf. Johnston v. U.S. Dep't of Justice, No. 97-2173, 1998 WL 518529, at *1-2 (8th Cir. Aug. 10, 1998) ("'[T]he fact that an agent decided or was required to testify . . . does not give plaintiff a right under FOIA to documents revealing the fact and nature of [agent's] employment.'" (quoting Jones, 41 F.3d at 246-47)). But see Kronberg v. U.S. Dep't of Justice, 875 F. Supp. 861, 867 (D.D.C. 1995) (waiver of exemption found when agency had previously released same documents during requester's criminal trial).

[97] See, e.g., Direct Response Consulting Serv. v. IRS, No. 94-1156, 1995 WL 623282, at *5 (D.D.C. Aug. 21, 1995) (attorney-client privilege not waived when documents sent to other divisions within agency); Chemcentral/Grand Rapids Corp. v. EPA, No. 91-C-4380, 1992 WL 281322, at *7 (N.D. Ill. Oct. 6, 1992) (no waiver of attorney-client privilege when documents in question were circulated to only those employees who needed to review legal advice contained in them); Lasker-Goldman Corp. v. GSA, 2 Gov't Disclosure Serv. (P-H) ¶ 81,125, at 81,322 (D.D.C. Feb. 27, 1981) (no waiver when document was circulated to management officials within agency).

[98] See, e.g., Chilivis v. SEC, 673 F.2d 1205, 1211-12 (11th Cir. 1982) (agency does not automatically waive exemption by releasing documents to other agencies); Silber v. U.S. Dep't of Justice, No. 91-876, transcript at 10-18 (D.D.C. Aug. 13, 1992) (bench order) (distribution of manual to other agencies does not constitute waiver). But cf. Lacefield v. United States, No. 92-N-1680, 1993 WL 268392, at *6 (D. Colo. Mar. 10, 1993) (attorney-client privilege waived with respect to letter from City of Denver attorney to Colorado Department of Safety because letter was circulated to IRS).

[99] See, e.g., Aviation Consumer Action Project v. Washburn, 535 F.2d 101, 107-08 (D.C. Cir. 1976).

[100] See, e.g., Gen. Elec. Co. v. EPA, 18 F. Supp. 2d 138, 143 (D. Mass. 1998) (finding that because EPA is obligated to consult with state agencies in formulating federal policy, disclosures made pursuant to that obligation do not constitute waiver of applicability of FOIA exemption); Kansi v. U.S. Dep't of Justice, 11 F. Supp. 2d 42, 44-45 (D.D.C. 1998) (stating that even if plaintiff had adduced evidence that information was actually disclosed to local prosecutor, such disclosure would not have waived Exemption 7(A) protection); Erb, 572 F. Supp. at 956 (holding that disclosure of FBI report to local prosecutor did not cause waiver of Exemption 7(A)).

or to state attorneys general,[101] does not waive FOIA exemption protection.[102]

The one circumstance in which an agency's failure to treat information in a responsible, appropriate fashion should not result in waiver is when the failure is not fairly attributable to the agency -- i.e., when an agency employee has made an unauthorized disclosure, a "leak" of information.[103] Recognizing that a finding of waiver in such circumstances would only lead to "exacerbation of the harm created by the leaks,"[104] the courts have invariably refused to penalize agencies by ruling that a waiver has occurred due to such conduct.[105]

---

[101] See Interco, Inc. v. FTC, 490 F. Supp. 39, 44 (D.D.C. 1979).

[102] See FOIA Update, Vol. IV, No. 2, at 6.

[103] See, e.g., Favish, 541 U.S. at 158 (accepting that unofficial leak and subsequent publication of death-scene photograph of body of presidential aide did not prevent agency from invoking Exemption 7(C) to protect privacy of surviving family members); see also FOIA Post, "Supreme Court Rules for 'Survivor Privacy' in Favish" (posted 4/9/04) (observing that waiver issue regarding "leaked" photograph was quickly "dispatched" by Court "in no uncertain terms"); see also Hanson v. U.S. Agency for Int'l Dev., 372 F.3d 286, 294 (4th Cir. 2004) (finding no waiver when attorney consulting for federal agency unilaterally released documents that he authored during course of attorney-client relationship between him and agency).

[104] Murphy, 490 F. Supp. at 1142.

[105] See, e.g., Simmons v. U.S. Dep't of Justice, 796 F.2d 709, 712 (4th Cir. 1986) (unauthorized disclosure does not constitute waiver); Medina-Hincapie v. Dep't of State, 700 F.2d 737, 742 n.20 (D.C. Cir. 1983) (official's ultra vires release does not constitute waiver); Edmonds, 272 F. Supp. 2d at 49 (holding that because information in public domain was leaked, agency may continue to withhold identical information because "'release would amount to official confirmation or acknowledgment of [its] accuracy'" (quoting Wash. Post v. DOD, 766 F. Supp. 1, 9 (D.D.C. 1991))); Trans-Pac. Policing Agreement v. U.S. Customs Serv., No. 97-2188, 1998 WL 34016806, at *4 (D.D.C. May 14, 1998) (finding no waiver from "isolated and unauthorized" disclosures that were not "in accordance with [agency] regulations or directions"), rev'd & remanded on other grounds, 177 F.3d 1022 (D.C. Cir. 1999); Harper v. Dep't of Justice, No. 92-462, slip op. at 19 (D. Or. Aug. 9, 1993) ("alleged, unauthorized, unofficial, partial disclosure" in private publication does not waive Exemption 1), aff'd in part, rev'd in part & remanded on other grounds sub nom. Harper v. DOD, 60 F.3d 833 (9th Cir. 1995) (unpublished table decision); LaRouche v. U.S. Dep't of Justice, No. 90-2753, 1993 WL 388601, at *7 (D.D.C. June 25, 1993) (fact that some aspects of grand jury proceeding were leaked to press has "no bearing" on FOIA litigation); RTC v. Dean, 813 F. Supp. 1426, 1429-30 (D. Ariz. 1993) (no waiver

(continued...)

## DISCRETIONARY DISCLOSURE AND WAIVER

On the other hand, "official" disclosures -- i.e., direct acknowledgments by authoritative government officials -- may well waive an otherwise applicable FOIA exemption.[106]

---

[105](...continued)
of attorney-client privilege when agency took precautions to secure confidentiality of document, but inexplicable leak nonetheless occurred) (non-FOIA case); Laborers' Int'l Union v. U.S. Dep't of Justice, 578 F. Supp. 52, 58 n.3 (D.D.C. 1983) (finding that unauthorized disclosure of document "resembling" one at issue does not waive invocation of exemptions), aff'd, 772 F.2d 919, 921 n.1 (D.C. Cir. 1984) (noting that disclosure would "enable the [plaintiff] to verify whether the report in its possession is an authentic copy"); Safeway Stores, Inc. v. FTC, 428 F. Supp. 346, 347-48 (D.D.C. 1977) (finding no waiver where congressional committee leaked report to press); cf. Hunt v. CIA, 981 F.2d 1116, 1120 (9th Cir. 1992) (agency not required to confirm or deny accuracy of information released by other government agencies regarding its interest in certain individuals); Rush v. Dep't of State, 748 F. Supp. 1548, 1556 (S.D. Fla. 1990) (finding that author of agency documents, who had since left government service, did not have authority to waive Exemption 5 protection). But cf. In re Engram, No. 91-1722, 1992 WL 120211, at *5 (4th Cir. June 2, 1992) (per curiam) (permitting discovery as to circumstances of suspected leak).

[106] See Wolf, 473 F. 3d at 379-380 (holding that agency waived ability to refuse to confirm or deny existence of responsive records pertaining to individual because agency head had discussed that individual during congressional testimony); Moye, O'Brien, O'Rourke, Hogan & Pickert v. Nat'l R.R. Passenger Corp., No. 6:02-CV-126, slip op. at 21 (M.D. Fla. Aug. 18, 2003) (ruling that agency waived deliberative process privilege when it shared results of draft audit report with subject of audit), rev'd on other grounds, 376 F.3d 1270 (11th Cir. 2004), cert. denied, 543 U.S. 1121 (2005); Starkey, 238 F. Supp. 2d at 1193 (finding that public availability of documents filed with local government waived exemptions); Melendez-Colon v. U.S. Dep't of the Navy, 56 F. Supp. 2d 142, 145 (D.P.R. 1999) (finding in civil discovery dispute that because Navy previously disclosed document in question pursuant to FOIA, that prior disclosure waived Navy's privilege claim); Kimberlin v. Dep't of Justice, 921 F. Supp. 833, 835-36 (D.D.C. 1996) (holding exemption waived when material was released pursuant to "valid, albeit misunderstood, authorization"), aff'd in pertinent part & remanded in other part, 139 F.3d 944 (D.C. Cir. 1998); Quinn v. HHS, 838 F. Supp. 70, 75 (W.D.N.Y. 1993) (attorney work-product privilege waived where "substantially identical" information was previously released to requester); Schlesinger v. CIA, 591 F. Supp. 60, 66 (D.D.C. 1984); see also Krikorian v. Dep't of State, 984 F.2d 461, 467-68 (D.C. Cir. 1993) (court on remand must determine whether redacted portions of document has been "officially acknowledged"); cf. Abbotts v. NRC, 766 F.2d 604, 607 (D.C. Cir. 1985) (holding agency's official "level of threat nuclear facility should guard against" is not waived by prior public estimates of appropriate level by congressional and other agency reports); Isley, 1999 WL 1021934, at *4 (finding no waiver

(continued...)

Similarly, an individual's express disclosure authorization with respect to his own interests implicated in requested records can also result in a waiver.[107] By the same token, it has been held that "only the individual whose informational privacy interests are protected . . . can effect a waiver of th[e] privacy interest[] when they are threatened by a[] FOIA request . . . because the privacy interest at stake belongs to the individual, [and] not the agency holding the information."[108] Accordingly, even if an agency has

---

[106](...continued)
where plaintiff failed to demonstrate that documents at issue were a part of permanent public record); Afshar, 702 F.2d at 1133 (books by former agency officials do not constitute "an official and documented disclosure"); Armstrong v. Executive Office of the President, No. 89-142, slip op. at 16-17 (D.D.C. Aug. 29, 1995) (holding that book by former agency official containing information "substantially different" from documents sought is not official disclosure); Holland v. CIA, No. 92-1233, 1992 WL 233820, at *7 (D.D.C. Aug. 31, 1992) (applying Afshar and finding that requester has not demonstrated that specific information in public domain has been "officially acknowledged").

[107] See, e.g., Providence Journal Co. v. U.S. Dep't of the Army, 981 F.2d 552, 567 (1st Cir. 1992) (source statements not entitled to Exemption 7(D) protection when individuals expressly waived confidentiality); Blanton v. U.S. Dep't of Justice, 63 F. Supp. 2d 35, 47 (D.D.C. 1999) (finding that FBI confidential sources waive their privacy interests where they extensively publicize their status as confidential sources); Key Bank of Me., Inc. v. SBA, No. 91-362, 1992 U.S. Dist. LEXIS 22180, at *25-26 (D. Me. Dec. 31, 1992) (given that subject of documents has specifically waived any privacy interest she might have in requested information, agency has not demonstrated that release of information would harm any privacy interest) (Exemption 6); cf. Wiley v. VA, 176 F. Supp. 2d 747, 753 (E.D. Mich. 2001) (observing that "[p]laintiff might well have forfeited his Privacy Act protection through his own selective disclosure and reference to his VA records"). But cf. McSheffrey, 2003 WL 179840, at *1 (determining that prison visitors do not waive privacy interest in information provided to prison officials for security purposes); Campaign for Family Farms v. Glickman, 200 F.3d 1180, 1188 (8th Cir. 1999) (finding that although parties who signed petition in question did so with knowledge that subsequent signatories would be able to view their names, they did not waive their privacy interests under FOIA) ("reverse" FOIA suit); Kimberlin, 139 F.2d at 949 (holding that fact that employee publicly acknowledged that he had been investigated and disciplined by Office of Professional Responsibility did not "waive all his interest in keeping the contents of the OPR file confidential"); Church of Scientology Int'l v. IRS, 995 F.2d 916, 921 (9th Cir. 1993) (IRS agents' purported waivers of privacy interests held insufficient to compel disclosure).

[108] Sherman, 244 F.3d at 363-64; see also Wiley, 176 F. Supp. 2d at 753 (finding that "[t]he case law on this subject, though extremely limited, indicates that an individual can waive the privacy interest that the [Privacy

(continued...)

previously disclosed such information, that disclosure may not waive the individual's privacy interest in that information.[109]

As mentioned above, the government is not required to demonstrate in a FOIA case that it has positively determined that not a single disclosure of any withheld information has occurred.[110] Indeed, the burden is on the plaintiff to show that the information sought is public.[111] As the D.C.

---

[108](...continued)
Act] is meant to safeguard by . . . disclosing otherwise confidential information"); Wayne's Mech. & Maint. Contractor, Inc. v. U.S. Dep't of Labor, No. 1:00-CV-45, slip op. at 18 (N.D. Ga. May 7, 2001) (reiterating that "[o]nly the witness, not the Department of Labor or OSHA, has the power to waive Exemption 7(D)'s protection of confidentiality"); Judicial Watch v. Reno, No. 00-0723, 2001 WL 1902811, at *7 (D.D.C. Mar. 30, 2001) (holding that the privacy interest belongs to individual whose interest is at stake and agency cannot surrender that interest). But see Iowa Citizens for Cmty. Improvement v. USDA, 256 F. Supp. 2d 946, 955 (S.D. Iowa Aug. 13, 2002) (noting that "common sense dictates that prior disclosure -- either by the government, the news media or private individuals -- does lessen an individual's expectation of privacy").

[109] Sherman, 244 F.3d at 364; see, e.g., Wayne's Mech. & Maint. Contractor, No. 1:00-CV-45, slip op. at 18 (N.D. Ga. May 7, 2001) (noting that "[o]nly the witness, not the Dep't of Labor or OSHA, has the power to waive Exemption 7(D)'s protection of confidentiality"); Judicial Watch, No. 00-0723, 2001 WL 1902811, at *7 (D.D.C. Mar. 30, 2001) (noting that "the privacy interest belongs to [subject], and defendants cannot surrender it"); cf. Kimberlin, 139 F.2d at 949 (holding that an employee's acknowledgment that he had been investigated by the Office of Professional Responsibility (OPR) did not "waive all his interest in keeping the contents of the OPR file confidential"); LaRouche, No. 90-2753, slip op. at 14 (D.D.C. Aug. 8, 2002) (observing that the FBI "need not make a wholesale disclosure about an individual just because he is a publicly acknowledged FBI source") (Exemption 7(C)).

[110] See Williams v. U.S. Dep't of Justice, 556 F. Supp. 63, 66 (D.D.C. 1982) (court refused, in a FOIA action brought by a former senator convicted in the Abscam investigation, to impose upon the agency a duty to search for the possibility that privacy interests "may have been partially breached in the course of many-faceted proceedings occurring in different courts over a period of prior years," for to do so "would defeat the exemption in its entirety or at least lead to extended delay and uncertainty"); cf. McGehee v. Casey, 718 F.2d 1137, 1141 n.9 (D.C. Cir. 1983) (in a non-FOIA case involving CIA's prepublication review, observing that an agency "cannot reasonably bear the burden of conducting an exhaustive search to prove that a given piece of information is not published anywhere" else).

[111] See, e.g., Lopez, 2004 WL 626726, at *1 at (ruling that plaintiff failed
(continued...)

[111](...continued)
to demonstrate that specific information is in public domain); James Madison Project, 2002 WL 31296220, at *1 (holding that a FOIA plaintiff "bears the burden of showing that the specific information at issue has been officially disclosed"); Pub. Citizen, 276 F.3d at 645 (finding that plaintiff has burden of demonstrating that specific information is in public domain); Cottone, 193 F.3d at 555 (holding that requester has burden of demonstrating "precisely which tapes . . . were played" in open court and that because trial transcript clearly indicated precise date and time of particular conversations in question, plaintiff had discharged his burden of production by pointing to those specific tapes); Isley, 1999 WL 1021934, at *4 (holding that party may gain access to information on waiver basis only if it can point to specific information identical to information which is currently being withheld); Nowak, 2000 WL 60067, at *2 (holding that "[i]n order to establish a waiver, the [plaintiff must be able to demonstrate that the previous disclosure was] authorized and voluntary"); Davoudlarian, 1994 WL 423845, at *3 (requester has burden of demonstrating that specific information was disclosed at trial); Pub. Citizen, 11 F.3d at 201 (applying Afshar and holding "plaintiffs cannot simply show that similar information has been released, but must establish that a specific fact already has been placed in the public domain"); Wood, 312 F. Supp. 2d at 344 (ruling that plaintiff has not demonstrated waiver of attorney work-product privilege); Edmonds, 272 F. Supp. 2d at 48-49 (noting that plaintiff has failed to show that this specific information has been released to public); Assassination Archives, 334 F.3d at 60 (holding that plaintiff must show that previous disclosure duplicates specificity of withheld material); Enviro Tech, No. 02-C-4650, slip op. at 15 (N.D. Ill. Mar. 11, 2003) (holding that plaintiff has not demonstrated that information at issue is exactly same as what is in public domain); Ctr. for Int'l Envtl. Law v. Office of the U.S. Trade Representative, 237 F. Supp. 2d 17, 20 (D.D.C. 2002) (holding that plaintiff failed to show that information was in public domain merely by pointing to other publicly available documents that deal with same general subject); Shores, 185 F. Supp. 2d at 86 (citing Cottone, 193 F.3d at 554, and finding that party seeking disclosure bears initial burden of production to identify specific information in public domain that is duplicative of information being withheld); Scott v. CIA, 916 F. Supp. 42, 50-51 (D.D.C. 1996) (requiring requester to compile list of any public source material believed to mirror withheld information); Freeman v. U.S. Dep't of Justice, No. 02-0557, 1993 WL 260694, at *3-4 (D.D.C. June 28, 1993) (finding that requester failed to demonstrate that agencies have shown "complete disregard for confidentiality" and had not shown that information available to public duplicated that being withheld); Pfeiffer v. CIA, 721 F. Supp. 337, 342 (D.D.C. 1989) (declaring that a plaintiff must do more than simply identify "information that happens to find its way into a published account" to meet this burden). But see also Dean, 813 F. Supp. at 1429 ("[A] party seeking to invoke the attorney-client privilege has the burden of affirmatively demonstrating non-waiver.") (non-FOIA case); Wash. Post, 766 F. Supp. at 12-13 (suggesting that agency has

(continued...)

Circuit has pointedly observed: "It is far more efficient, and obviously fairer, to place the burden of production on the party who claims that the information is publicly available."[112] In another case, the D.C. Circuit reasoned that the burden of production should fall upon the requester "because the task of proving the negative -- that the information has <u>not</u> been revealed -- might require the government to undertake an exhaustive, potentially limitless search"[113] If a plaintiff meets the burden of production, it is then "up to the government, if it so chooses, to rebut the plaintiff's proof [and demonstrate] that the specific . . . [records] identified" are not publicly available."[114] When a record may be publicly available in theory, but is so hard to obtain that no objective disclosure or waiver arguably has occurred, the burden is on the requester to prove that the records are in fact obtainable.[115]

(The related issue of whether an agency waives its ability to invoke an exemption in litigation by not raising it at an early stage of the proceedings is discussed under Litigation Considerations, Waiver of Exemptions in Litigation, below.)

## LITIGATION CONSIDERATIONS

It has been said that "[t]he FOIA is intended to work without court intervention."[1] While this may be true most of the time, it nevertheless is the case that when a FOIA lawsuit is filed, litigants frequently find that

---

[111](...continued)
ultimate burden of proof when comparing publicly is identical and, if not, determining whether release of slightly different information would harm national security).

[112] <u>Occidental Petroleum Corp. v. SEC</u>, 873 F.2d 325, 342 (D.C. Cir. 1989) (reverse FOIA suit).

[113] <u>Davis</u>, 968 F.2d at 1279-82.

[114] <u>Cottone</u>, 193 F.3d at 556.

[115] See <u>U.S. Dep't of Justice v. Reporters Comm. for Freedom of the Press</u>, 489 U.S. 749, 764 (1989) (applying test of availability to contents of "rap sheets" scattered among different courthouses and police stations, and viewing requested "rap sheet" as unavailable to general public in spite of requester's claims to contrary); see also <u>Inner City Press/Cmty. on the Move v. Bd. of Governors of the Fed. Reserve Sys.</u>, 463 F.3d 239, 251 (2d Cir. 2006) (applying availability test and distinguishing from record involved in <u>Reporters Committee</u> any record that could be obtained via single visit to single federal agency Web site).

[1] <u>Landmark Legal Found. v. EPA</u>, 272 F. Supp. 2d 70, 85 (D.D.C. 2003).

"Freedom of Information Act cases are peculiarly difficult."[2] To help simplify these peculiar difficulties and to provide a general overview of FOIA litigation considerations, this discussion will follow a rough chronology of a typical FOIA lawsuit -- from the threshold question of whether jurisdictional prerequisites have been met, to the assessment of costs on appeal.

In considering litigation under the FOIA, it is important to bear in mind that in accordance with the Attorney General's FOIA Memorandum of October 12, 2001, it is the Department of Justice's policy to defend an agency's decisions made under the FOIA "unless they lack a sound legal basis or present an unwarranted risk of adverse impact on the ability of other agencies to protect other important records."[3] It should be remembered that this is not unlike the comparable litigation-defense standards employed in earlier years of the FOIA's administration.[4]

## Jurisdiction, Venue, and Other Preliminary Matters

The United States district courts are vested with exclusive jurisdiction over FOIA cases by section (a)(4)(B) of the Act, which provides in pertinent part:

> On complaint, the district court of the United States in the district in which the complainant resides, or has his principal place of business, or in which the agency records are situated, or in the District of Columbia, has jurisdiction to enjoin the agency from withholding agency records and to order the production of any agency records improperly withheld from the complainant.[5]

---

[2] Miscavige v. IRS, 2 F.3d 366, 367 (11th Cir. 1993); see also Summers v. Dep't of Justice, 140 F.3d 1077, 1080 (D.C. Cir. 1998) (noting "peculiar nature of the FOIA"); Nat'l Res. Def. Council v. DOD, 388 F. Supp. 2d 1086, 1095 (C.D. Cal. 2005) ("The peculiar nature of a FOIA dispute poses unique problems."); cf. Exec. Order No. 13,392, Sec. 1(d), 70 Fed. Reg. 75,373 (Dec. 14, 2005) (seeking to strengthen individual agency compliance with FOIA in order to "help avoid disputes and related litigation").

[3] Attorney General's Memorandum for Heads of All Federal Departments and Agencies Regarding the Freedom of Information Act (Oct. 12, 2001) [hereinafter Attorney General Ashcroft's FOIA Memorandum], reprinted in FOIA Post (posted 10/15/01).

[4] See FOIA Post, "New Attorney General FOIA Memorandum Issued" (posted 10/15/01) (discussing new Attorney General FOIA Memorandum in context of previous such memoranda); cf. FOIA Update, Vol. XIV, No. 3, at 1 ("President and Attorney General Issue New FOIA Policy Memoranda").

[5] 5 U.S.C. § 552(a)(4)(B) (2000 & Supp. IV 2004); see also Clark v. United States, 116 F. App'x 278, 279 (Fed. Cir. 2004) (explaining that FOIA suits

(continued...)

## LITIGATION CONSIDERATIONS

This provision has been held to govern judicial review under all three of the FOIA's access provisions.[6] Because of its specific reference to the "complainant," however, the Court of Appeals for the District of Columbia Circuit has held that this language limits relief under the FOIA to disclosure of records to a particular requester.[7] Consequently, it does not appear to authorize a court to order the publication of information, even informa-

---

[5](...continued)
are not within subject matter jurisdiction of Court of Federal Claims); Arriaga v. West, No. 00-1171, 2000 WL 870867, at *2 (Vet. App. June 21, 2000) (commenting that Court of Appeals for Veterans Claims has no jurisdiction over FOIA claims); Bernard v. United States, 59 Fed. Cl. 497, 503 (2004) (declaring that Court of Federal Claims has no jurisdiction over FOIA matters), aff'd, 98 F. App'x 860 (Fed. Cir. 2004), reh'g denied, No. 04-5039 (Fed. Cir. May 5, 2004); In re Lucabaugh, 262 B.R. 900, 905 (E.D. Pa. 2000) (finding FOIA claims insufficient to confer jurisdiction on bankruptcy court). But cf. U.S. Ass'n of Imps. of Textiles & Apparel v. United States, 366 F. Supp. 2d 1280, 1283 n.2 (Ct. Int'l Trade 2005) (concluding that Court of International Trade has jurisdiction under 28 U.S.C. § 1581(i) to consider claims implicating FOIA's affirmative publication provisions, 5 U.S.C. § 552(a)(1)-(2)).

[6] See Kennecott Utah Copper Corp. v. U.S. Dep't of the Interior, 88 F.3d 1191, 1202 (D.C. Cir. 1996) ("The 'judicial review provisions apply to requests for information under subsections (a)(1) and (a)(2) of section 552 as well as under subsection (a)(3).'" (quoting Am. Mail Line v. Gulick, 411 F.2d 696, 701 (D.C. Cir. 1969))).

[7] See Kennecott, 88 F.3d at 1203 (holding that remedial provision of FOIA limits relief to ordering disclosure of documents); Dietz v. O'Neill, No. 00-3440, 2001 U.S. Dist. LEXIS 3222, at *2 (D. Md. Feb. 15, 2001) (holding that remedial provision of FOIA limits relief to ordering disclosure of documents), aff'd per curiam, 15 F. App'x 42 (4th Cir. 2001); Green v. NARA, 992 F. Supp. 811, 817 (E.D. Va. 1998) (concluding that unless agency records have been improperly withheld, "'a district court lacks jurisdiction to devise remedies to force an agency to comply with FOIA's disclosure requirements'" (quoting U.S. Dep't of Justice v. Tax Analysts, 492 U.S. 136, 142 (1989))). But cf. Pub. Citizen v. Dep't of State, 276 F.3d 634, 645 (D.C. Cir. 2002) (declaring that agency's "cut-off" policy for conducting FOIA record searches is unreasonable "both generally and as applied to [plaintiff's] request"); Pa. Dep't of Pub. Welfare v. United States, No. 99-175, 1999 WL 1051963, at *2 (W.D. Pa. Oct. 12, 1999) (suggesting that "[Administrative Procedure Act] review is available to enforce provisions of the FOIA for which the FOIA provides no express remedy"); Pub. Citizen v. Lew, No. 97-2891, slip op. at 4 (D.D.C. July 14, 1998) (refusing to dismiss claim alleging noncompliance with FOIA requirement to publish descriptions of "major information systems" compiled under Paperwork Reduction Act, 44 U.S.C.A. §§ 3501-3520 (1991 & West Supp. 2006), because even in the absence of an express judicial review provision in the FOIA, the Administrative Procedure Act, 5 U.S.C. §§ 701-706 (2000), provides a "strong presumption that Congress intend[ed] judicial review of administrative action").

tion required to be published under subsection (a)(1) of the FOIA.[8] Nor does it appear to empower a court to order an agency to make records available for public inspection and copying in an agency reading room under subsection (a)(2).[9] Similarly, the FOIA does not provide a jurisdictional vehicle for a court to consider Bivens-type constitutional tort claims against FOIA officers.[10] Instead, its statutory language, as the Supreme Court ruled in Kissinger v. Reporters Committee for Freedom of the Press, makes federal jurisdiction dependent upon a showing that an agency has

---

[8] See Kennecott, 88 F.3d at 1203 ("We think it significant, however, that § 552(a)(4)(B) is aimed at relieving the injury suffered by the individual complainant, not by the general public. It allows district courts to order 'the production of any agency records improperly withheld from the complainant,' not agency records withheld from the public." (quoting 5 U.S.C. § 552(a)(4)(B) (emphasis added by court))); cf. Perales v. DEA, 21 F. App'x 473, 474-75 (7th Cir. 2001) (dismissing an action brought to obtain an "implementing regulation," because such a request "described only material that would be available in the public domain," not material "properly covered" by the FOIA). But see Pa. Dep't of Pub. Welfare v. United States, No. 99-175, 2001 U.S. Dist. LEXIS 3492, at *28 (W.D. Pa. Feb. 7, 2001) (deciding that the Administrative Procedure Act confers jurisdiction on a court to order publication of an index under subsection (a)(2) of the FOIA even though the FOIA itself does not), appeal dismissed voluntarily, No. 01-1868 (3d Cir. Apr. 24, 2002); cf. Ass'n of Imps., 366 F. Supp. 2d at 1283 n.2 (opining that 28 U.S.C. § 1581(i) confers Court of International Trade with jurisdiction to hear claims seeking publication under subsection (a)(1) of FOIA).

[9] See Kennecott, 88 F.3d at 1203 ("Section 552(a)(4)(B) authorizes district courts to order "production" of agency documents, not 'publication.'"); see also Tax Analysts v. IRS, 117 F.3d 607, 610 (D.C. Cir. 1997) (treating as "conceded for the purposes of this case only" that sole remedy under section 552(a)(4)(B) is order directing agency to produce records to complaining party). But see Tax Analysts v. IRS, No. 94-923, 1998 WL 419755, at *4-6 (D.D.C. May 1, 1998) (ordering disclosure of exceptionally large volume of records upon remand and also ordering uniquely fashioned remedy that, in accordance with 5 U.S.C. § 552(a)(2)(D), such FOIA-processed records be placed in reading room on weekly basis as they are processed), appeal dismissed voluntarily, No. 98-5252 (D.C. Cir. Aug. 11, 1998); cf. Ass'n of Imps., 366 F. Supp. 2d at 1283 n.2 (opining that 28 U.S.C. § 1581(i) confers Court of International Trade with jurisdiction to hear claims implicating subsection (a)(2) of FOIA).

[10] Johnson v. Executive Office for U.S. Attorneys, 310 F.3d 771, 777 (D.C. Cir. 2002) (explaining that the "FOIA precludes the creation of a Bivens remedy"); Thomas v. FAA, No. 05-2391, 2007 WL 219988, at *3 (D.D.C. Jan. 25, 2007) (noting that a plaintiff "cannot obtain a Bivens remedy for an alleged violation of FOIA"). But cf. O'Shea v. NLRB, No. 2:05-2808, 2006 WL 1977152, at *5 (D.S.C. July 11, 2006) (recognizing that agency employees who arbitrarily and capriciously withhold information may be subject to disciplinary action).

(1) "improperly"; (2) "withheld"; (3) "agency records." Judicial authority to devise remedies and enjoin agencies can only be invoked, under the jurisdictional grant conferred by § 552, if the agency has contravened all three components of this obligation.[11]

As a consequence, a plaintiff who does not allege any improper withholding of agency records fails to state a claim over which a court has subject matter jurisdiction within the meaning of Rule 12(b)(1) of the Federal Rules of Civil Procedure[12] or, alternatively, fails to state a claim upon which relief could be granted under Rule 12(b)(6).[13] Regardless of the exact legal

---

[11] 445 U.S. 136, 150 (1980).

[12] See, e.g., Segal v. Whitmyre, No. 04-80795, 2005 WL 1406171, at *3 (S.D. Fla. Apr. 6, 2005) (finding lack of jurisdiction over FOIA claim because plaintiff failed to allege improper withholding of agency records); Ellis v. IRS, No. 02-1976, 2003 U.S. Dist. LEXIS 24829, at *11 (D. Colo. Dec. 29, 2003) (dismissing claim for lack of subject matter jurisdiction because all documents were released prior to lawsuit); Armstead v. Gray, No. 3-03-1350, 2003 WL 21730737, at *1-2 (N.D. Tex. July 23, 2003) (finding no basis for jurisdiction under FOIA when plaintiff alleged only that agency employees "improperly accessed" plaintiff's records); Tota v. United States, No. 99-0445E, 2000 WL 1160477, at *2 (W.D.N.Y. July 31, 2000) (dismissing claim for lack of subject matter jurisdiction because the "[p]laintiff has not provided any evidence that the FBI improperly withheld any agency records"); Shafmaster Fishing Co. v. United States, 814 F. Supp. 182, 184 (D.N.H. 1993) ("The court thus lacks subject matter jurisdiction if the information was properly withheld under FOIA exemptions."); see also Goldgar v. Office of Admin., 26 F.3d 32, 34 (5th Cir. 1994) (per curiam) (pointing out that where agency had no records responsive to plaintiff's request, court had no jurisdiction under FOIA); Rae v. Hawk, No. 98-1099, slip op. at 3 (D.D.C. Mar. 7, 2001) (finding no subject matter jurisdiction over claims against agencies that received no FOIA request from plaintiff); Unigard Ins. Co. v. Dep't of the Treasury, 997 F. Supp. 1339, 1341 (S.D. Cal. 1997) ("The court presumes a lack of jurisdiction until the party asserting [it] proves otherwise."); cf. Kennecott, 88 F.3d at 1202 (dismissing, for lack of jurisdiction, claim seeking court-ordered publication of information, when court concluded that no such remedy exists under FOIA).

[13] Williams v. Reno, No. 95-5155, 1996 WL 460093, at *2 (D.C. Cir. Aug. 7, 1996) (disagreeing that the district court lacked jurisdiction over a FOIA claim, because the plaintiff alleged improper withholding and, in any event, "the district court has subject matter jurisdiction over FOIA claims" (citing Sweetland v. Walters, 60 F.3d 852, 855 (D.C. Cir. 1996))); Torres v. CIA, 39 F. Supp. 2d 960, 962 n.3 (N.D. Ill. 1999) (suggesting that an agency's "summary judgment motion" predicated on a lack of subject matter jurisdiction was "an imprecise use of the notion of 'jurisdiction' [and that if the] CIA's position were sound, no court could ever decide a FOIA case in favor of a governmental defendant on the merits, for it would lose jurisdic-

(continued...)

basis used, however, if an agency has not improperly withheld records, a FOIA suit should be dismissed.[14]

For the jurisdictional requirements for a FOIA case to be met, "an agency first must either have created or obtained a record as a prerequisite to its becoming an 'agency record' within the meaning of the FOIA."[15] Of course, if an agency does not have, nor ever had, possession and control of the requested record, then there can be no improper withholding.[16] Rec-

---

[13](...continued)
tion as soon as it found that no documents responsive to a plaintiff's FOIA request had been improperly withheld"); Mace v. EEOC, 37 F. Supp. 2d 1144, 1146 (E.D. Mo. 1999) (deciding that dismissal for lack of jurisdiction was "inappropriate," but that dismissal for failure to state a claim was applicable because court lacked further jurisdiction to grant relief), aff'd, 197 F.3d 329 (8th Cir. 1999); Prado v. Ilchert, No. 95-1497, 1997 WL 383239, at *3 (N.D. Cal. June 10, 1997) (dismissing for failure to state claim upon which relief can be granted under FOIA when agency to which request was made lacked responsive records); see also Hart v. FBI, No. 95-2110, 1996 WL 403016, at *3 n.11 (7th Cir. July 16, 1996) (although plaintiff's "los[s] on the merits does not retroactively revoke a district court's jurisdiction," district court's grant of summary judgment to government deprived it of further jurisdiction to act).

[14] See, e.g., Kissinger, 445 U.S. at 139 ("When an agency has demonstrated that it has not "withheld" requested records in violation of the standards established by Congress, the federal courts have no authority to order the production of such records under the FOIA."); Bloom v. Soc. Sec. Admin., 72 F. App'x 733, 735 (10th Cir. July 3, 2003) (finding that once documents were released, "there existed no 'case or controversy' sufficient to confer subject matter jurisdiction on the federal court").

[15] Forsham v. Harris, 445 U.S. 169, 182 (1980), overruled in part by Omnibus Consolidated and Emergency Supplemental Appropriations Act, 1999, Pub. L. No. 105-277, 112 Stat. 2681 (1998) (making certain research data generated by private federal grantees subject to FOIA requests); Judicial Watch, Inc. v. U.S. Dep't of Energy, 412 F.3d 125, 132 (D.C. Cir. 2005) (holding that records created or obtained by agency employees while detailed to the National Energy Policy Development Group, a unit of the Executive Office of the President, "are not 'agency records' within the meaning of the FOIA"); see also Apel v. CIA, No. 3:06-CV-136, 2006 WL 1446874, at *1-2 (N.D. Fla. May 23, 2006) (holding that messages sent "through" CIA's Web site are not agency records for purposes of FOIA, because they were not created by CIA).

[16] See U.S. Dep't of Justice v. Tax Analysts, 492 U.S. 136, 145 (1989); Kissinger, 445 U.S. at 155 n.9 ("[T]here is no FOIA obligation to retain records prior to [receipt of a FOIA] request."); Lechliter v. Rumsfeld, No. 05-4381, 2006 WL 1506717, at *2 (3d Cir. June 1, 2006) (finding no improper with-
(continued...)

ords that are created by or come into the possession of an agency after a

---

<sup>16</sup>(...continued)
holding where agency destroyed documents for reason that "'is not itself suspect'" (citing SafeCard Servs. v. SEC, 926 F.2d 1197, 1201 (D.C. Cir. 1991))); Wilbur v. CIA, 355 F.3d 675, 678 (D.C. Cir. 2004) (per curiam) ("[T]he fact that responsive documents once existed does not mean that they remain in the [agency's] custody today or that the [agency] had a duty under FOIA to retain the records."); Jones v. FBI, 41 F.3d 238, 249 (6th Cir. 1994) (finding no remedy for records destroyed prior to FOIA request); Sliney v. Fed. Bureau of Prisons, No. 04-1812, 2005 WL 839540, at *5 (D.D.C. Apr. 11, 2005) ("The fact that the agency once possessed documents that have been destroyed does not preclude the entry of summary judgment for the agency."); Piper v. U.S. Dep't of Justice, 294 F. Supp. 2d 16, 22 (D.D.C. 2003) ("FOIA does not impose a document retention requirement on government agencies."), reconsideration denied, 312 F. Supp. 2d 17 (D.D.C. 2004); Graves v. EEOC, Nos. 02-6842, 02-6306, slip op. at 10-11 (C.D. Cal. Apr. 4, 2003) (providing no relief to plaintiff where agency properly destroyed records prior to receiving his FOIA request); Blanton v. U.S. Dep't of Justice, 182 F. Supp. 2d 81, 85 (D.D.C. 2002) (rejecting plaintiff's contention that agency should have contacted former employees about location of responsive records, and awarding agency summary judgment), aff'd, 64 F. App'x 787 (D.C. Cir. 2003) (per curiam), reh'g en banc denied, Nos. 02-5115, 02-5296 (D.C. Cir. July 22, 2003); Folstad v. Bd. of Governors of the Fed. Reserve Sys., No. 1:99-124, 1999 U.S. Dist. LEXIS 17852, at *5 (W.D. Mich. Nov. 16, 1999) (declaring that the FOIA "does not independently impose a retention obligation on the agency and that "[e]ven if the agency failed to keep documents that it should have kept, that failure would create neither responsibility under FOIA to reconstruct those documents nor liability for the lapse"), aff'd, 234 F.3d 1268 (6th Cir. 2000) (unpublished table decision); Bartlett v. U.S. Dep't of Justice, 867 F. Supp. 314, 316 (E.D. Pa. 1994) (dismissing case for lack of jurisdiction after finding that "[plaintiff's] request seeks presently nonexistent material"); cf. Morris v. Comm'r, No. F-97-5031, 1997 WL 842413, at *4 (E.D. Cal. Nov. 25, 1997) (finding that a request for determination of tax status "was not a request for a document in existence" and thus was not "a valid FOIA request"). But see also Cal-Almond, Inc. v. USDA, No. 89-574, slip op. at 2-3 (E.D. Cal. Mar. 12, 1993) (ruling that when agency returned requested records to submitter four days after denying requester's administrative appeal, in violation of its own records-retention requirements, and court determined that such records were required to be disclosed, agency must seek return of records from submitter for disclosure to requester), appeal dismissed per stipulation, No. 93-16727 (9th Cir. Oct. 26, 1994); OMB Circular A-110, "Uniform Administrative Requirements for Grants and Agreements with Institutions of Higher Education, Hospitals, and Other Non-Profit Organizations," 64 Fed. Reg. 54,926 (Oct. 8, 1999) (requiring agencies to respond to FOIA requests for certain grantee research data by first obtaining that data from grantee, in implementation of Omnibus Consolidated and Emergency Supplemental Appropriations Act, 1999).

FOIA request is received but before the search for responsive records is conducted, however, may be considered "agency records" for purposes of such FOIA request depending upon the agency's "scope-of-search cut-off" policy.[17] An agency's failure to consider these records when responding to the FOIA request may be considered an improper withholding.[18] (For further discussions of "cut-off" dates and determining the scope of a FOIA request, see Procedural Requirements, Proper FOIA Requests, above.)

Further, the term "record" includes "any information that would be an agency record subject to the [FOIA] when maintained by an agency in any format, including an electronic format."[19] This definition thus broadly encompasses within the concept of "agency record" information maintained by agencies in electronic form.[20] Of course, the FOIA provides no jurisdiction over records other than those held by a federal agency.[21] (For further

---

[17] See FOIA Post, "Use of 'Cut-Off' Dates for FOIA Searches" (posted 5/6/04) (explaining importance of agency "cut-off" dates, and advising that "date-of-search cut-off" should be used absent compelling circumstances); see also 28 C.F.R. § 16.4(a) (2006) (Department of Justice FOIA regulation specifying that its standard "cut-off" practice "include[s] only records in its possession as of the date [that it] begins its search for them") (emphasis added).

[18] See Pub. Citizen, 276 F.3d at 643-44 (refusing to approve agency's "date-of-request cut-off" policy, and pointing out that it effectively results in withholding of potentially large number of relevant agency records); McGehee v. CIA, 697 F.2d 1095, 1110 (D.C. Cir. 1983) (cautioning agencies against adopting policies the net effect of which "is significantly to impair the requester's ability to obtain the records or significantly to increase the amount of time he must wait to obtain them"), vacated on other grounds on panel reh'g & reh'g en banc denied, 711 F.2d 1076 (D.C. Cir. 1983).

[19] 5 U.S.C. § 552(f)(2).

[20] See FOIA Update, Vol. XVII, No. 4, at 2 (discussing applicability of FOIA to electronic records).

[21] See, e.g., Megibow v. Clerk of U.S. Tax Court, 432 F.3d 387, 388 (2d Cir. 2005) (ruling that United States Tax Court is not subject to FOIA); Blankenship v. Claus, 149 F. App'x 897, 898 (11th Cir. 2005) (affirming dismissal of FOIA claim brought against state authority); Wright v. Curry, 122 F. App'x 724, 725 (5th Cir. 2004) (emphasizing that FOIA "applies to federal agencies, not state agencies"); United States v. Alcorn, 6 F. App'x 315, 316-17 (6th Cir. 2001) (affirming the dismissal of a FOIA claim against a district court "because the federal courts are specifically excluded from FOIA's definition of 'agency'"); McDonnell v. Clinton, No. 97-5179, 1997 WL 812536, at *1 (D.C. Cir. Dec. 29, 1997) (dismissing FOIA claim brought solely against the President); Ortez v. Wash. County, 88 F.3d 804, 811 (9th Cir. 1996) (dismissing FOIA claims against county and county officials); Simon v. Miami (continued...)

**LITIGATION CONSIDERATIONS**

discussions of the terms "agency" and "agency records," see Procedural Requirements, Entities Subject to the FOIA, above, and Procedural Requirements, "Agency Records," above.)

Whether an agency has "improperly" withheld records usually turns on whether one or more exemptions applies to the documents at issue.[22] If

---

[21](...continued)
County Incarceration Facility, No. 3:05-CV-191, 2006 WL 1663689, at *1 (S.D. Ohio May 5, 2006) (magistrate's recommendation) (explaining that because telecommunications company is not federal agency, it is not subject to FOIA), adopted, 2006 WL 1663689 (S.D. Ohio May 12, 2006); Cruz v. Superior Court Judges, No. 3:04-CV-1103, 2006 WL 547930, at *1 (D. Conn. Mar. 1, 2006) (holding that municipal police department is not subject to FOIA, which "applies [only] to federal agencies"); Davis v. Johnson, No. 05-2060, 2005 U.S. Dist. LEXIS 12475, at *1 (N.D. Cal. June 20, 2005) (disallowing FOIA claim against deputy public defender who represented plaintiff in state criminal trial); Benjamin v. Fuller, No. 3:05-cv-941, 2005 WL 1136864, at *1 (M.D. Pa. May 13, 2005) (dismissing a FOIA suit against a district court because the FOIA's definition of "'agency' does not include the courts of the United States"); Carter v. U.S. 6th Circuit Court of Appeal, No. 3:05-cv-134, 2005 WL 1138828, at *1 (E.D. Tenn. May 12, 2005) (dismissing claim against appellate court and explaining that FOIA applies only to executive branch agencies); Yoonessi v. N.Y. State Bd. for Prof'l Med. Conduct, No. 03-cv-871, 2005 WL 645223, at *26 (W.D.N.Y. Mar. 21, 2005) ("[T]he plain language of the FOIA precludes its application to state and local agencies or to individuals."); Slovinec v. Ill. Dep't of Human Servs., No. 02-4124, 2005 WL 442555, at *7 (N.D. Ill. Feb. 22, 2005) (explaining that the "FOIA has no application to the States"); Troyer v. McCallum, No. 03-0143, 2002 WL 32365922, at *1 (W.D. Wis. Mar. 14, 2002) (holding that FOIA "creates no obligations for state agencies"); Allnut v. U.S. Dep't of Justice, 99 F. Supp. 2d 673, 678 (D. Md. 2000) (ruling that trustees of bankruptcy estates are "private" and thus are not subject to FOIA), aff'd sub. nom. Allnutt v. Handler, 8 F. App'x 225 (4th Cir. 2001); Anderson v. Fed. Pub. Defender, No. 95-1485, slip op. at 1 (D.D.C. Mar. 28, 1996) (The "Federal Public Defender is not an agency subject to the requirements of the Freedom of Information Act."); cf. Moye, O'Brien, O'Rourke, Hogan & Pickert v. National R.R. Passenger Corp., No. 6:02-CV-126, 2003 WL 21146674, at *6 (M.D. Fla. May 13, 2003) ("Although Amtrak is not a federal agency, it must comply with FOIA pursuant to statute."), rev'd & remanded on other grounds, 116 F. App'x 251 (11th Cir. 2004), cert. denied, 543 U.S. 1121 (2005). See generally Price v. County of San Diego, 165 F.R.D. 614, 620 (S.D. Cal. 1996) (emphasizing that the FOIA applies only "to authorities of the Government of the United States").

[22] See Tax Analysts, 492 U.S. at 151 (generalizing that "agency records which do not fall within one of the exemptions are improperly withheld"); Abraham & Rose, P.L.C. v. United States, 138 F.2d 1075, 1078 (6th Cir. 1998) (indicating that agency denying FOIA request bears burden of establishing (continued...)

the agency can establish that no responsive records exist, then there is of course no "improper" withholding, and judgment for the agency should be granted.[23] The same is true if all responsive records have been released in full to the requester,[24] though a court still may grant equitable relief if it

<hr>

[22](...continued)
lishing that requested information falls within exemption and remanding case for consideration of appropriate exemptions).

[23] See, e.g., Perales v. DEA, 21 F. App'x 473, 474 (7th Cir. Oct. 17, 2001) (affirming dismissal because information requested does not exist); Coal. on Political Assassinations v. DOD, 12 F. App'x 13, 14 (D.C. Cir. 2001) (finding search to be adequate even though no records were located; "[t]hat responsive documents may have once existed does not establish that they remain in the DOD's custody today"); Sorrells v. United States, No. 97-5586, 1998 WL 58080, at *1 (6th Cir. Feb. 6, 1998) (finding no improper withholding when agency does not have document with "full, legible signature"); Jones v. FBI, 41 F.3d 238, 249 (6th Cir. 1994) (finding no remedy for records destroyed prior to FOIA request); Cal-Almond, Inc. v. USDA, 960 F.2d 105, 108-09 (9th Cir. 1992) (adjudging that absent improper conduct by government, FOIA does not require recreation of destroyed records); see also FOIA Update, Vol. XII, No. 2, at 5 (advising agencies to afford administrative appeal rights to FOIA requesters in "no record" situations (citing Oglesby v. U.S. Dep't of the Army, 920 F.2d 57, 67 (D.C. Cir. 1990))); cf. Urban v. United States, 72 F.3d 94, 95 (8th Cir. 1995) (holding that district court erred by dismissing Complaint prior to service on ground that no records existed; case remanded for submission of evidence as to existence of responsive records). But cf. Satterlee v. IRS, No. 05-3181, 2006 WL 561485, at *1-2 (W.D. Mo. Mar. 6, 2006) (refusing to grant motion to dismiss, and concluding that court has jurisdiction -- despite agency's failure to locate responsive records -- but inviting government to "reframe" its motion as seeking summary judgment).

[24] See, e.g., Gabel v. Comm'r, No. 94-16245, 1995 WL 267203, at *2 (9th Cir. May 5, 1995) (finding no improper withholding because "it was uncontested" that agency provided complete response to request); Burr v. Huff, No. 04-C-53, 2004 WL 253345, at *2 (W.D. Wis. Feb. 6, 2004) ("If no documents exist, nothing can be withheld, and jurisdiction cannot be established."), aff'd, No. 04-1466, 2004 U.S. App. LEXIS 22476, at *2-3 (7th Cir. Oct. 14, 2004), cert. denied, 544 U.S. 1004 (2005); Ferranti v. Gilfillan, No. 04-cv-339, 2005 WL 1366446, at *2 (D. Conn. May 31, 2005) (dismissing suit for lack of jurisdiction after agency fully released all requested records); Reg'l Mgmt. Corp. v. Legal Servs. Corp., 10 F. Supp. 2d 565, 573-74 (D.S.C. 1998) (concluding that "no case or controversy exists" because agency produced all requested documents); D'Angelica v. IRS, No. S-94-1998, 1996 U.S. Dist. LEXIS 6681, at *3 (E.D. Cal. Apr. 25, 1996) (granting agency summary judgment when all requested records either did not exist or were fully disclosed); cf. Martinez v. Fed. Bureau of Prisons, 444 F.3d 620, 624 (D.C. Cir. 2006) (holding that agency fulfilled its FOIA obligations by affording
(continued...)

finds in an exceptional case that the agency maintains an unlawful FOIA "policy or practice" threatening to impair the requester's ability to obtain records in the future, upon application of a strict "capable of repetition but evading review" standard.[25] This narrow situation, however, is far different from the issuance of declaration, following disclosure of all requested records, that an agency's initial withholding violated the FOIA.[26] The D.C. Circuit has held that such a declaratory judgment would constitute an advisory opinion that courts lack the jurisdiction to issue.[27]

---

[24](...continued)
prisoner-plaintiff "meaningful opportunity to review" his presentence reports and to take notes on them); Howell v. U.S. Dep't of Justice, No. 04-0479, 2006 WL 890674, at *2 (D.D.C. Apr. 4, 2006) (finding no improper withholding where, pursuant to Federal Bureau of Prisons policy, inmate was afforded opportunity to review his presentence investigation report (citing Martinez)).

[25] See Payne Enters. v. United States, 837 F.2d 486, 490-92 (D.C. Cir. 1988) (finding repeated, unacceptably long agency delays in providing nonexempt information sufficient to create jurisdiction where such delays are likely to recur absent immediate judicial intervention); Pub. Citizen v. Office of the U.S. Trade Representative, 804 F. Supp. 385, 387 (D.D.C. 1992) (deciding that a court has jurisdiction to consider an "agency's policy to withhold temporarily, on a regular basis, certain types of documents"); cf. Gavin v. SEC, No. 04-4552, 2005 WL 2739293, at *6 (D. Minn. Oct. 24, 2005) (rejecting request to enjoin SEC from using "Glomar" response, because "future harm is merely speculative in nature, and injunctive relief is [therefore] inappropriate"); Ctr. for Individual Rights v. U.S. Dep't of Justice, No. 03-1706, slip op at 11-12 (D.D.C. Sept. 21, 2004) (finding a lack of jurisdiction to grant equitable relief -- after the agency made full disclosure during the course of litigation -- because the plaintiff failed to establish an unlawful FOIA policy or otherwise "articulate what documents it might seek in the future or in what way future requests would mirror the circumstances of its original request").

[26] Payne Enters., 837 F.2d at 491 (distinguishing between the issuance of "[a] declaration that an agency's initial refusal to disclose requested information was unlawful, after the agency made that information available, [which] would constitute an advisory opinion in contravention of Article III of the Constitution," and a grant of equitable relief, following full disclosure, where an agency maintains an otherwise-unreviewable "policy or practice that will impair . . . lawful access to information in the future").

[27] Id.; see also Pagosans for Pub. Lands v. U.S. Forest Serv., No. 06-cv-00556, 2007 WL 162745, at *3 (D. Colo. Jan. 18, 2007) ("There is no jurisdiction under FOIA for a declaratory judgment."). But see Or. Natural Desert Ass'n v. Gutierrez, 409 F. Supp. 2d 1237, 1248 (D. Or. 2006) (issuing, after the agency's disclosure of all requested records, a declaratory judgment that its failure "to make a timely determination resulted in an improper

(continued...)

Once a court determines that information has been properly withheld pursuant to a FOIA exemption, the court has no inherent, equitable power to order disclosure absent some other statute mandating disclosure.[28] The converse of this rule, however -- that a court has inherent, equitable power to refuse to order disclosure of nonexempt information -- has not been established with the same degree of certainty.[29]

Similarly, an agency has not improperly withheld records when it is prohibited from disclosing them by a pre-existing court order.[30] While the

---

[27](...continued)
withholding under the Act"); Beacon Journal Publ'g Co. v. Gonzalez, No. 05-CV-1396, 2005 U.S. Dist. LEXIS 28109, at *3-4 (N.D. Ohio Nov. 16, 2005) (pronouncing, following an agency's disclosure of the requested photographs, that its initial withholding was "contrary to the FOIA").

[28] See Spurlock v. FBI, 69 F.3d 1010, 1016-18 (9th Cir. 1995) (concluding that when court finds records exempt under FOIA, it has no "inherent" authority to order disclosure of agency information just because it might conflict with depositions or other public statements of informant).

[29] See Maricopa Audubon Soc'y v. U.S. Forest Serv., 108 F.3d 1082, 1087 (9th Cir. 1997) ("We conclude that a district court lacks inherent power, equitable or otherwise, to exempt materials that FOIA itself does not exempt."); Weber Aircraft Corp. v. United States, 688 F.2d 638, 645 (9th Cir. 1982) ("The careful balancing of interests which Congress attempted to achieve in the FOIA would be upset if courts could exercise their general equity powers to authorize nondisclosure of material not covered by a specific exemption."), rev'd on other grounds, 465 U.S. 792 (1984); see also Abraham & Rose, 138 F.3d at 1077 ("Basing a denial of a FOIA request on a factor unrelated to any of the[] nine exemptions clearly contravenes [the FOIA]."); cf. Halperin v. U.S. Dep't of State, 565 F.2d 699, 706 (D.C. Cir. 1977) ("The power of a court to refuse to order the release of information that does not qualify for one of the nine statutory exemptions exists, if at all, only in "exceptional circumstances." (citing Soucie v. David, 448 F.2d 1067, 1077 (D.C. Cir. 1971))). But see Renegotiation Bd. v. Bannercraft Clothing Co., 415 U.S. 1, 20 (1973) (suggesting, in dicta, that the FOIA does not "limit the inherent powers of an equity court"); Campos v. INS, 32 F. Supp. 2d 1337, 1345-46 (S.D. Fla. 1998) (same).

[30] See, e.g., GTE Sylvania, Inc. v. Consumers Union, 445 U.S. 375, 387 (1980) ("To construe the lawful obedience of an injunction issued by a federal district court with jurisdiction to enter such a decree as 'improperly' withholding documents under the Freedom of Information Act would do violence to the common understanding of the term 'improperly' and would extend the Act well beyond the intent of Congress."); Freeman v. U.S. Dep't of Justice, 723 F. Supp. 1115, 1120 (D. Md. 1988) (refusing to order the release of records covered by pre-existing nondisclosure order of sister district court); see also FOIA Update, Vol. IV, No. 3, at 5 (counseling that re-

(continued...)

validity of such a pre-existing court order does not depend upon whether it is based upon FOIA exemptions,[31] it is the agency's burden to demonstrate that the order was intended to operate as an injunction against the agency, rather than as a mere court seal.[32]

---

[30](...continued)
quests for records subject to court order forbidding disclosure ordinarily should be denied). But see also FOIA Update, Vol. XIII, No. 3, at 5 (advising that "protective orders" issued by agency administrative law judges do not qualify as court orders); cf. Riley v. FBI, No. 00-2378, 2002 U.S. Dist. LEXIS 2632, at *7 (D.D.C. Feb. 12, 2002) (finding that "pen register" materials were sealed and therefore were properly withheld on basis of Exemption 3).

[31] See Wagar v. U.S. Dep't of Justice, 846 F.2d 1040, 1047 (6th Cir. 1988) (holding that validity of nondisclosure orders does not depend on their being based on FOIA exemptions).

[32] See, e.g., Morgan v. U.S. Dep't of Justice, 923 F.2d 195, 197 (D.C. Cir. 1991) ("[T]he proper test for determining whether an agency improperly withholds records under seal is whether the seal, like an injunction, prohibits the agency from disclosing the records."); Odle v. Dep't of Justice, No. 05-2771, 2006 WL 1344813, at *14 (N.D. Cal. May 17, 2006) (concluding that agency may not withhold information pursuant to sealing order unless that court order prohibits disclosure in response to FOIA requests); Gerstein v. U.S. Dep't of Justice, No. 03-04893, slip op. at 10-11 (N.D. Cal. Sept. 30, 2005) (determining that sealing orders pertaining to search and seizure warrants prohibited FOIA disclosure, because they were intended to prevent investigative targets "from learning about the warrant[s]"); Armstrong v. Executive Office of the President, 830 F. Supp. 19, 23 (D.D.C. 1993) ("[I]t is also clear that the Protective Order was not intended to act as a limitation on the Government's ability to determine the final disposition of these classified materials."); Senate of P.R. v. U.S. Dep't of Justice, No. 84-1829, 1993 U.S. Dist. LEXIS, at *18-19 (D.D.C. Aug. 24, 1993) (finding that agency declaration failed to satisfy Morgan test, and requiring more detailed explanation of intended effect of sealing order); McDonnell Douglas Corp. v. NASA, No. 91-3134, slip op. at 1-2 (D.D.C. July 12, 1993) ("While this court's sealing Order temporarily precluded release, that order was not intended to operate as the functional equivalent of an injunction prohibiting release. It was only approved by the court for the purposes of expediting this litigation and protecting information . . . until this lawsuit was resolved."); see also Lykins v. U.S. Dep't of Justice, 725 F.2d 1455, 1460-61 & n.7 (D.C. Cir. 1984) (determining that a federal district court policy -- one "now enshrined in an order [that was] not issued as part of a concrete case or controversy before [that] court" -- does not constitute the type of "court order" contemplated in GTE Sylvania); cf. Pansy v. Borough of Stroudsburg, 23 F.3d 772, 791 (3d Cir. 1994) ("[W]here it is likely that information is accessible under a relevant freedom of information law, a strong presumption exists against granting or maintaining an order of confidentiality whose scope would pre-
(continued...)

Further, because the Supreme Court has clearly instructed that, as a general rule, "the identity of the requesting party" does not have any bearing on the proper disclosure of information under the FOIA,[33] it is well settled that it is not appropriate for a court to order disclosure of information to a FOIA requester with a special restriction, either explicit or implicit, that the requester not further disseminate the information received.[34] As the Supreme Court recently put it: "There is no mechanism under FOIA for a protective order allowing only the requester to see whether the information bears out his theory, or for proscribing its general dissemination."[35]

The venue provision of the FOIA, quoted above, provides requesters with a broad choice of forums in which to bring suit.[36] When a requester sues in a jurisdiction other than the District of Columbia, however, he is obliged to allege the nexus giving rise to proper venue in that jurisdiction.[37]

---

[32](...continued)
vent disclosure of that information pursuant to the relevant freedom of information law.").

[33] U.S. Dep't of Justice v. Reporters Comm. for Freedom of the Press, 489 U.S. 749, 771-72 (1989); see also FOIA Update, Vol. X, No. 2, at 3-4 (discussing Reporters Committee decision).

[34] See, e.g., Chin v. U.S. Dep't of the Air Force, No. 99-3127, 2000 WL 960515, at *2 (5th Cir. June 15, 2000) (refusing to allow disclosure of exempt information under protective order); Schiffer v. FBI, 78 F.3d 1405, 1411 (9th Cir. 1996) (overruling district court's order limiting access to persons other than plaintiff "is not authorized by FOIA"); Spurlock, 69 F.3d at 1016 (finding that district court erred when, after determining that requested material was exempt, it nevertheless ordered disclosure of any "falsified statements" made to FBI about requester); cf. Maricopa, 108 F.3d at 1088-89 (rejecting, as irrelevant, plaintiff's offer to agree not to further disclose requested information: "FOIA does not permit selective disclosure of information only to certain parties . . . . [O]nce the information is disclosed to [this requester], it must also be made available to all members of the public who request it.").

[35] NARA v. Favish, 541 U.S. 157, 174, reh'g denied, 541 U.S. 1057 (2004); see also FOIA Post, "Supreme Court Rules for 'Survivor Privacy' in Favish" (posted 4/9/04) (observing that the Court firmly reinforced the general FOIA rule that "release to one is release to all").

[36] See 5 U.S.C. § 552(a)(4)(B) (providing for venue in any of four locations).

[37] See Gaylor v. U.S. Dep't of Justice, No. 05-CV-414, 2006 WL 1644681, at *1 (D.N.H. June 14, 2006) (finding venue lacking in New Hampshire, where plaintiff, who claimed to be resident of Texas, was incarcerated and was general partner in company that was no longer in good standing in New Hampshire); Cosio v. INS, No. 97-5380, slip op. at 3 (C.D. Cal. Dec. 29, 1997)
(continued...)

## LITIGATION CONSIDERATIONS

Largely due to the statutory designation of the District of Columbia as an appropriate forum for any FOIA action,[38] the District Court for the District of Columbia and Court of Appeals for the District of Columbia Circuit have, over the years, decided a great many of the leading cases under the FOIA.[39]

The District Court for the District of Columbia has been held to be the sole appropriate forum for cases in which the requester resides and works outside the United States and the records requested are located in the District of Columbia.[40] As a related matter, aliens are treated the same as U.S. citizens for FOIA venue purposes.[41] And on another technical venue matter, even though the District Court for the District of Columbia is the "uni-

---

[37](...continued)
(finding venue improper for plaintiffs who do not reside or have their principal places of business in judicial district and who do not allege that their records were maintained there); Schwarz v. IRS, 998 F. Supp. 201, 203 (N.D.N.Y. 1998) (finding venue improper where agency maintains regional office unless substantial part of activity complained of also occurred there), appeal dismissed for lack of merit, No. 98-6065 (2d Cir. July 30, 1998); Handlery Hotels, Inc. v. U.S. Consumer Prod. Safety Comm'n, No. 97-1100, slip op. at 3 (S.D. Cal. Dec. 5, 1997) (finding venue improper where based on location of plaintiff's counsel); Keen v. FBI, No. 97-2657, 1997 U.S. Dist. LEXIS 16220, at *2 (N.D. Cal. Oct. 17, 1997) (finding venue improper where pro se plaintiff housed temporarily); see also Morrell v. U.S. Dep't of Justice, No. 96-4356, 1996 WL 732499, at *1 (N.D. Cal. Dec. 16, 1996) (transferring pro se action improperly filed in Northern District of California to Eastern District of California, where plaintiff resided); cf. McHale v. FBI, No. 99-1628, slip op. at 8-9 (D.D.C. Nov. 7, 2000) (dismissing case under "first-filed" rule in favor of similar litigation pending in another jurisdiction).

[38] See, e.g., FOIA Update, Vol. XI, No. 2, at 2 (citing "universal venue" provision of FOIA, 5 U.S.C. § 552(a)(4)(B)).

[39] See, e.g., Gaylor, 2006 WL 1644681, at *1 (transferring suit to District Court for District of Columbia, because of its "special expertise in FOIA matters"); Matlack, Inc. v. EPA, 868 F. Supp. 627, 630 (D. Del. 1994) ("The United States Court of Appeals for the District of Columbia Circuit has long been on the leading edge of interpreting the parameters of what a federal agency must disclose and may withhold consistent with the terms of FOIA."); see also FOIA Update, Vol. VI, No. 3, at 1-2 (describing FOIA litigation process within D.C. Circuit).

[40] See Akutowicz v. United States, 859 F.2d 1122, 1126 (2d Cir. 1988).

[41] See, e.g., Arevalo-Franco v. INS, 889 F.2d 589, 590-91 (5th Cir. 1989) (ruling that resident alien may bring FOIA suit in district where he in fact resides).

versal" venue for FOIA lawsuits,[42] it is not settled whether the Tennessee Valley Authority is amenable to FOIA suit either in Washington, D.C. or else only in the Northern District of Alabama (the venue set by statute for that wholly owned government corporation).[43]

The judicial doctrine of forum non conveniens, as codified in 28 U.S.C. § 1404(a),[44] can permit the transfer of a FOIA case to a different judicial district.[45] The courts have invoked this doctrine to transfer FOIA cases under a variety of circumstances.[46] Similarly, when the requested records are the

---

[42] See, e.g., FOIA Update, Vol. VI, No. 3, at 2 (noting that under the FOIA's "universal venue provision," 5 U.S.C. § 552(a)(4)(B), any FOIA lawsuit can be filed in the District Court for the District of Columbia).

[43] Compare Jones v. NRC, 654 F. Supp. 130, 132 (D.D.C. 1987) (declaring that "Congress has made clear [in 16 U.S.C. § 831g(a) (2000 & Supp. IV 2004)] that the venue statute that permits [service of] process against federal agencies [i.e., 28 U.S.C. § 1391(e) (2000 & Supp. III 2003)] does not apply to TVA"), with Murphy v. TVA, 559 F. Supp. 58, 59 (D.D.C. 1983) (finding a "strong presumption that Congress intended FOIA actions against the TVA to be maintainable in the District of Columbia").

[44] (2000).

[45] See generally Ross v. Reno, No. 95-CV-1088, 1996 WL 612457, at *3-4 (E.D.N.Y. Aug. 13, 1996) (discussing factors in favor of and in opposition to transfer of case to neighboring jurisdiction).

[46] See, e.g., Carpenter v. U.S. Dep't of Justice, No. 3:05-CV-172, 2005 WL 1290678, at *2 (D. Conn. Apr. 28, 2005) (transferring FOIA suit to district in which plaintiff's criminal case was pending, because request sought records from that proceeding); Cecola v. FBI, No. 94 C 4866, 1995 WL 645620, at *3 (N.D. Ill. Nov. 1, 1995) (transferring remainder of case to district where remaining records and government's declarant are located, where plaintiff operates business, and where activities described in requested records presumably took place); Southmountain Coal Co. v. Mine Safety & Health Admin., No. 94-0110, slip op. at 2-3 (D.D.C. Mar. 10, 1994) (justifying transfer of suit to district where corporate requester resides and has principal place of business and where criminal case on which request is based is pending, on grounds that "a single court [handling] both FOIA and criminal discovery would obviate the possibility of contradictory rulings, and would prevent the use of FOIA as a mere substitute for criminal discovery"); Bauer v. United States, No. 91-374A, slip op. at 3 (W.D.N.Y. Feb. 3, 1992) (finding venue improper where pro se suit filed; action transferred to jurisdiction where records located); Housley v. U.S. Dep't of Justice, No. 89-436, slip op. at 3-4 (D.D.C. Nov. 13, 1989) (transferring case to district where criminal proceeding against plaintiff was held and where evidence obtained by government's electronic surveillance allegedly was improperly withheld); cf. Envtl. Crimes Project v. EPA, 928 F. Supp. 1, 1-2 (D.D.C. 1995) (finding

(continued...)

subject of pending FOIA litigation in another judicial district, the related doctrine of "federal comity" can permit a court to defer to the jurisdiction of the other court, in order to avoid unnecessarily burdening the federal judiciary and delivering conflicting FOIA judgments.[47]

In a decision involving a somewhat related issue, the Court of Appeals for the Eighth Circuit upheld the removal of a state FOIA case to a federal court because the records at issue actually belonged to the United States Attorney's Office, which had intervened to protect its interests.[48]

---

[46](...continued)
that "[t]he interest of justice clearly favors transfer of this case," but absent "precise" information as to location of records sought, declining to order transfer in view of "substantial weight due to plaintiff's choice of forum"). But see In re Scott, 709 F.2d 717, 721-22 (D.C. Cir. 1983) (issuing writ of mandamus and remanding case when district court sua sponte transferred case, without determination of whether venue was proper in other forum, merely in effort to reduce burden of "very large number of in forma pauperis cases"); Haswell v. Nat'l R.R. Passenger Corp., No. 05-723, 2006 WL 839067, at *3-4 (D. Ariz. Mar. 28, 2006) (denying government's request to transfer venue to District of Columbia, because plaintiff was resident of Arizona, even though agency and all responsive records were located in Washington, D.C.; reasoning that "case [likely] will be decided on summary judgment" based upon affidavits).

[47] See, e.g., City of Chicago v. U.S. Dep't of the Treasury, No. 01 C 3835, 2001 WL 1173331, at *3 (N.D. Ill. Oct. 4, 2001) (finding "comity" inapposite when a related case seeking much of the same information at issue is before a court of appeals); see also McHale v. FBI, No. 99-1628, slip op. at 8-9 (D.D.C. Nov. 7, 2000) (applying "first-filed" rule to dismiss case when similar litigation was already pending in another jurisdiction); Hunsberger v. U.S. Dep't of Justice, No. 93-1945, slip op. at 1 (D.D.C. Mar. 16, 1994) (concluding that lack of responsiveness of court in which similar action was previously filed is "inadequate" ground to maintain independent action in second court); Beck v. U.S. Dep't of Justice, No. 88-3433, 1991 U.S. Dist. LEXIS 1179, at *15-16 (D.D.C. Jan. 31, 1991), summary affirmance granted in pertinent part & denied in part, No. 91-5292 (D.C. Cir. Nov. 19, 1992), aff'd on remaining issues, 997 F.2d 1489 (D.C. Cir. 1993); see also Envtl. Crimes Project, 928 F. Supp. at 2 (denying government's transfer motion, but ordering stay of proceedings pending resolution of numerous discovery disputes in related cases in other jurisdiction); FOIA Update, Vol. VI, No. 3, at 6 ("[G]iving a [FOIA] litigant more than one opportunity in court is a 'luxury that cannot be afforded.'" (quoting Charles Alan Wright, Law of Federal Courts 678 (4th ed. 1983))).

[48] See United States v. Todd, 245 F.3d 691, 693 (8th Cir. 2001) (finding a "colorable defense" based on the FOIA, which justified removal); see also, e.g., Brady-Lunny v. Massey, 185 F. Supp. 2d 928, 930, 932 (C.D. Ill. 2002) (indicating that United States removed state FOIA case pursuant to "feder-
(continued...)

The Eighth Circuit explained that not only does the federal removal statute, 28 U.S.C. § 1442(a)(1),[49] establish an independent basis for federal court jurisdiction, but the FOIA itself raises a "colorable defense" to the state action.[50] (For a further discussion of such removal actions under the federal pre-emption doctrine, see Discretionary Disclosure and Waiver, above.)

On occasion, FOIA plaintiffs have attempted to expedite judicial consideration of their suits by seeking a preliminary injunction to "enjoin" the agency from continuing to withhold the requested records.[51] When such extraordinary relief is sought, the court does not adjudicate the parties' substantive claims, but rather weighs: (1) whether the plaintiff is likely to prevail upon the merits; (2) whether the plaintiff will be irreparably harmed absent relief; (3) whether the defendant will be substantially harmed by the issuance of injunctive relief; and (4) whether the public interest will be

---

[48](...continued)
al question doctrine," and ultimately finding that information at issue was exempt under FOIA and therefore should not be disclosed).

[49] (2000).

[50] 245 F.3d at 693.

[51] See U.S. Dep't of Commerce v. Assembly of Cal., 501 U.S. 1272 (1991) (staying preliminary injunction); Aronson v. HUD, 869 F.2d 646, 648 (1st Cir. 1989) (denying preliminary injunction); Carlson v. USPS, No. 02-5471, 2005 WL 756573, at *8 (N.D. Cal. Mar. 31, 2005) (denying request for injunction sought to compel "timely" response to FOIA request); Robbins v. U.S. Bureau of Land Mgmt., 219 F.R.D. 685, 687 (D. Wyo. 2004) (denying as premature a motion to compel production of documents that were the subject of multiple FOIA requests); Beta Steel Corp. v. NLRB, No. 2:97 CV 358, 1997 WL 836525, at *2 (N.D. Ind. Oct. 22, 1997) (denying preliminary injunction); see also Cullinane v. Arnold, No. 97-779, 1998 U.S. Dist. LEXIS 5575, at *4 (C.D. Cal. Mar. 24, 1998) (denying writ of mandamus because FOIA provides adequate remedy); see also Al-Fayed v. CIA, No. 00-2092, slip op. at 18 (D.D.C. Dec. 11, 2000) (reminding plaintiffs, who twice before had petitioned for a temporary restraining order, that a preliminary injunction amounts to "extraordinary" relief, which must be granted "sparingly"), aff'd on other grounds, 254 F.3d 300 (D.C. Cir. 2001); cf. Dorsett v. U.S. Dep't of Justice, 307 F. Supp. 2d 28, 42 (D.D.C., 2004) (describing plaintiff's motion for injunction to prevent agency from "not taking any action honoring or denying" FOIA request, but dismissing it because court has no jurisdiction to make "advisory findings" regarding agency conduct towards FOIA requesters); Wiedenhoeft v. United States, 189 F. Supp. 2d 295, 296-97 (D. Md. 2002) (refusing to issue temporary restraining order to force "immediate compliance" with plaintiff's FOIA requests by moving them "to the head of the queue forthwith").

benefitted by such relief.[52]

In a FOIA case, the granting of such an injunction would necessarily force the government to disclose the very information that is the subject of the litigation, without affording it any opportunity to fully and fairly litigate its position on the merits; such an injunction would moot the government's claims before they could ever be adjudicated and would effectively destroy any possibility of appellate review.[53] Consequently, the government would presumptively sustain irreparable harm in any instance in which a preliminary injunction were issued in a FOIA case.[54]

Moreover, because a court can exercise FOIA jurisdiction only after it has first found an improper withholding, a substantial question exists as to whether the FOIA even empowers a court to issue a preliminary injunction

---

[52] See Elec. Privacy Info. Ctr. v. Dep't of Justice, 416 F. Supp. 2d 30, 36 (D.D.C. 2006); Long v. DHS, 436 F. Supp. 2d 38, 43 (D.D.C. 2006); Al-Fayed v. CIA, No. 00-2092, 2000 WL 34342564, at *2 (D.D.C. Sept. 20, 2000); Aguilera v. FBI, 941 F. Supp. 144, 147 (D.D.C. 1996); Ray v. Reno, No. 94-1384, slip op. at 3 (D.D.C. Oct. 24, 1995), appeal dismissed for lack of prosecution, No. 96-5005 (D.C. Cir. Dec. 26, 1996); Hunt v. U.S. Marine Corps, No. 94-2317, slip op. at 2 (D.D.C. Oct. 28, 1994); Nation Magazine v. U.S. Dep't of State, 805 F. Supp. 68, 72 (D.D.C. 1992); see also Mayo v. U.S. Gov't Printing Office, 839 F. Supp. 697, 700 (N.D. Cal. 1992) (finding fact that FOIA expressly authorizes injunctive relief does not divest district court of obligation to "exercise its sound discretion," relying on traditional legal standards, in granting such relief (citing Weinberger v. Romero Barcelo, 456 U.S. 305, 312 (1982))), aff'd, 9 F.3d 1450 (9th Cir. 1993).

[53] See Aronson, 869 F.2d at 648 ("To issue the preliminary injunction discloses the names, permanently injuring the interest HUD seeks to protect[.]"); see also Long, 436 F. Supp. 2d at 44 (refusing to issue a preliminary injunction to compel the production of records, because "[t]he government has not yet had a chance to review its files, prepare and file a dispositive motion, and provide the Court the information necessary to make a decision on any material that might be subject to an exemption"); Hunt, No. 94-2317, slip op. at 5 (D.D.C. Oct. 28, 1994) (denying temporary restraining order, in part on basis of strong "public interest in an 'orderly, fair and efficient administration of the FOIA'" (quoting Nation Magazine, 805 F. Supp. at 74)); cf. Maine v. U.S. Dep't of the Interior, No. 00-122, 2001 WL 98373, at *3 (D. Me. Feb. 5, 2001) (granting stay because "the loss of the right to appeal alone convinces this Court that this factor weighs strongly in favor of Defendants"), aff'd & vacated in part on the merits, 285 F.3d 126 (1st Cir.), amended & superseded, 298 F.3d 60 (1st Cir. 2002).

[54] See generally FOIA Update, Vol. XII, No. 3, at 1-2 (discussing comparable situation of "unstayed" disclosure orders).

to begin with.[55] These considerations lead to the conclusion that the extraordinary mechanism of preliminary injunctive relief should not be available in FOIA cases, although expedited processing may be appropriate.[56] Indeed, the FOIA itself contemplates expedited processing of requests in cases of "compelling need" and in other cases that are determined by agency regulation to warrant such processing.[57]

However, even the timing of an agency's response to an expedited processing request itself has been subject to a preliminary injunction.[58] Such was the case in a ruling by the District Court for the District of Columbia in Electronic Privacy Information Center (EPIC) v. Department of Justice, which involved a request for records concerning the government's terrorist surveillance program.[59] In EPIC, the court ruled that courts have the jurisdictional authority to impose "concrete deadlines" on any agency that "delay[s]" the processing of an expedited FOIA request beyond what arguably is "as soon as practicable,"[60] i.e., the statutory standard applicable to

---

[55] See Kissinger, 455 U.S. at 150 (absent improper withholding, FOIA confers no "[j]udicial authority to devise remedies and enjoin agencies"); NLRB v. Sears, 421 U.S. 132, 147-48 (1975) (once it is determined that withheld information falls within one of FOIA's exemptions, FOIA "'does not apply' to such documents" (quoting Act)). But see Wash. Post v. DHS, 459 F. Supp. 2d 61, 76 (D.D.C. 2006) (granting plaintiff's motion for preliminary injunction on basis of "expedited action" rationale), stay granted, No. 06-5337 (D.C. Cir. Nov. 1, 2006).

[56] See Leadership Conference on Civil Rights v. Gonzales, 404 F. Supp. 2d 246, 260 (D.D.C. 2005) (ordering Department of Justice to expedite processing and to produce requested documents within ten months); Perdue Farms, Inc. v. NLRB, 927 F. Supp. 897, 906 (E.D.N.C. 1996) (granting injunction mandating processing of month-old FOIA request pertaining to challenged union election "immediately and with all deliberate speed").

[57] 5 U.S.C. § 552(a)(6)(E)(i)(I)-(II); see, e.g., 22 C.F.R. § 171.12(c)(4) (2006) (Department of State regulation under which expedited processing may be granted if "[s]ubstantial humanitarian concerns would be harmed by the [agency's] failure to process [the requested records] immediately"); cf. Aguilera, 941 F. Supp. at 152-53 (granting the plaintiff's motion for a preliminary injunction to compel expedited processing on the basis that the plaintiff "made a strong showing of exceptional and urgent need in this case to fall within the exception . . . [and] to warrant an expedition of his FOIA request").

[58] See Elec. Privacy Info. Ctr., 416 F. Supp. 2d at 42 (granting preliminary injunction to accelerate agency's processing of expedited request).

[59] See id. at 33.

[60] Id. at 38.

expedition.[61] It then issued an injunction to accelerate the processing of EPIC's FOIA request (which the Department of Justice already had agreed to handle on an expedited basis) by requiring production of records within twenty days of its order.[62]

In reaching this decision, the court focused on the "twenty-day deadline applicable to standard FOIA requests" and opined that if an agency fails to meet this deadline, it "presumptively also fails to" meet the expedition standard.[63] Because the Department of Justice had surpassed the "standard" twenty-day deadline -- and had as yet presented no "credible evidence" justifying its "delay" -- the court found that EPIC's "right to expedition" would be lost if a preliminary injunction were not issued.[64] Despite this ruling, it is worth reiterating that the FOIA provides no specific time frame within which an expedited request must be processed, but rather, as mentioned above, requires only that the processing be accomplished "as soon as practicable."[65] (See the further discussions of expedited processing under Procedural Requirements, Time Limits, above, and Litigation Considerations, "Open America" Stays of Proceedings, below.)

In any event, a FOIA plaintiff -- even one who is proceeding pro se

---

[61] See 5 U.S.C. § 552(a)(6)(E)(iii).

[62] See Elec. Privacy Info. Ctr., 416 F. Supp. 2d at 40; see also Gerstein v. CIA, No. 06-4643, 2006 WL 3462659, at *4-5 (N.D. Cal. Nov. 29, 2006) (granting plaintiff's motion for preliminary injunction and ordering agencies to process plaintiff's FOIA requests within thirty days); Wash. Post, 459 F. Supp. 2d at 68 n.4, 76 (granting the plaintiff's motion for a preliminary injunction "to complete the processing of the plaintiff's . . . FOIA requests and produce or identify all responsive records within 10 days," and to provide a Vaughn Index, despite the agency's prior expedited review of plaintiff's FOIA request). But cf. Long, 436 F. Supp. 2d at 44 (denying, given the "broad scope of plaintiff's requests," a motion for a preliminary injunction to compel processing within twenty days, and explaining that "[t]he government has not yet had a chance to review its files, prepare and file a dispositive motion, and provide the Court the information necessary to make a decision on any material that might be subject to an exemption").

[63] Elec. Privacy Info. Ctr., 416 F. Supp. 2d at 39.

[64] Id. at 40-41.

[65] 5 U.S.C. § 552(a)(6)(E)(iii); see also S. Rep. 104-272, 1996 WL 262861, at *17 (May 15, 1996) ("The goal [of expedited processing] is not to get the request processed within a specific time period, but to give the request priority in processing more quickly than would otherwise occur." (emphasis added)); ACLU v. DOD, 339 F. Supp. 2d 501, 503 (S.D.N.Y. 2004) ("While it would appear that expedited processing would necessarily require compliance in fewer than 20 days, Congress provided that the executive was to 'process as soon as practicable' any expedited request.").

-- must file suit before expiration of the applicable statute of limitations, just like any other plaintiff.[66] In Spannaus v. Department of Justice, the D.C. Circuit applied the general federal statute of limitations, which is found at 28 U.S.C. § 2401(a),[67] to FOIA actions.[68] Section 2401(a) states, in pertinent part, that "every action commenced against the United States shall be barred unless the complaint is filed within six years after the right of action first accrues." In Spannaus it was held that the FOIA cause of action accrued -- and, therefore, that the statute of limitations began to run -- once the plaintiff had "constructively" exhausted his administrative remedies (see the discussion of Exhaustion of Administrative Remedies, below) and not when all administrative appeals had been finally adjudicated.[69] In accordance with the Spannaus decision, the National Archives and Records Administration issued General Records Schedule 14,[70] which sets the

---

[66] See, e.g., Wilbur v. CIA, 273 F. Supp. 2d 119, 123 (D.D.C. 2003) ("Although [plaintiff] is now without a lawyer, he is still required to follow the basic rules of court procedure."), aff'd on other grounds, 355 F.3d 675 (D.C. Cir. 2004) (per curiam), reh'g denied, No. 03-5142 (D.C. Cir. Apr. 7, 2004).

[67] (2000).

[68] 824 F.2d 52, 55-56 (D.C. Cir. 1987); see also, e.g., Harris v. Freedom of Info. Unit, DEA, No. 3:06-0176, 2006 WL 3342598, at *6 (N.D. Tex. Nov. 17, 2006) (holding that plaintiff's suit is barred by six-year statute of limitations and further concluding that plaintiff is not entitled to equitable tolling); Aftergood v. CIA, 225 F. Supp. 2d 27, 29 (D.D.C. 2002) (noting that section 2401(a) is a "jurisdictional condition attached to the government's waiver of sovereign immunity," and dismissing Complaint filed five months too late because the statute of limitations "must be strictly construed"); Lighter v. IRS, No. 00-00289, 2001 U.S. Dist. LEXIS 3483, at *4 (D. Haw. Feb. 27, 2001) (dismissing Complaint filed eight years after plaintiff exhausted his administrative remedies, two years too late); McClain v. U.S. Dep't of Justice, No. 97-C-0385, 1999 WL 759505, at *4 (N.D. Ill. Sept. 1, 1999) (dismissing Complaint after calculating that cause of action was filed three years after statute of limitations expired), aff'd, 17 F. App'x 471 (7th Cir. 2001); Madden v. Runyon, 899 F. Supp. 217, 226 (E.D. Pa. 1995) (finding that even assuming plaintiff exhausted his administrative remedies, statute of limitations would have expired four years prior to commencement of suit); see also Peck v. CIA, 787 F. Supp. 63, 66 (S.D.N.Y. 1992) (refusing to waive the statute of limitations because to do so would be "a waiver of sovereign immunity," which "cannot be relaxed based on equitable considerations," but noting that "there is nothing in the statute that prevents plaintiff from refiling an identical request . . . and thereby restarting the process").

[69] 824 F.2d at 57-59; see Peck, 787 F. Supp. at 65-66 (once constructive exhaustion period has run, statute of limitations is not tolled while request for information is pending before agency).

[70] Nat'l Archives & Records Admin., General Records Schedule, Schedule
(continued...)

record-retention period at six years for all correspondence and supporting documentation relating to denied FOIA requests.[71]

Lastly, where a pro se FOIA plaintiff seeks appointment of counsel, a district court has wide discretion to decide whether to grant that request under 28 U.S.C. § 1915(e)(1).[72] A court should consider several factors in making this decision: (1) the nature and complexity of the action; (2) the potential merit of the claims; (3) the inability of a pro se party to obtain counsel by other means; and (4) the degree to which the interests of justice will be served by appointment of counsel.[73] If a court denies counsel, it should provide reasons for its decision.[74] (For a discussion of the availability of attorney fees in the event that counsel is appointed, see Attorney Fees, below.) Finally, it should be noted that the FOIA does not provide a plaintiff, pro se or otherwise, with a right to a jury trial.[75]

### Pleadings

An agency has thirty days from the date of service of process to an-

---

[70](...continued)
14 (1998).

[71] Id.; see also Attorney General's Memorandum on the 1986 Amendments to the Freedom of Information Act 28 n.51 (Dec. 1987) (advising that agencies should be sure to maintain any "excluded" records for purposes of possible further review (citing FOIA Update, Vol. V, No. 4, at 4 (advising same regarding "personal" records))); FOIA Update, Vol. XVIII, No. 1, at 5-6 (advising that particular provision of Electronic FOIA amendments, 5 U.S.C. § 552(a)(3)(B), does not require agencies to alter their records-disposition or records-maintenance practices).

[72] (2000); see, e.g., Schwarz v. U.S. Dep't of the Treasury, No. 00-5453, 2001 WL 674636, at *1 (D.C. Cir. May 10, 2001) (declaring that "appellants are not entitled to appointment of counsel when they have not demonstrated sufficient likelihood of success on the merits").

[73] See, e.g., Willis v. FBI, 274 F.3d 531, 532-33 (D.C. Cir. 2001) (citing local court rules as most appropriate basis upon which to decide a question of appointment of counsel in a FOIA case; Jackson v. County of McLean, 953 F.2d 1070, 1072 (7th Cir. 1992) (providing "nonexclusive" list of factors to be considered on questions of appointment of counsel) (non-FOIA case); Long v. Shillinger, 927 F.2d 525, 527 (10th Cir. 1991) (same) (non-FOIA case).

[74] See Willis v. FBI, No. 98-5071, 1999 WL 236891, at *1 (D.C. Cir. Mar. 19, 1999) (requiring remand when no reasons were provided for refusal to appoint counsel).

[75] See, e.g., Buckles v. Indian Health Serv./Belcourt Serv. Unit, 268 F. Supp. 2d 1101, 1102 (D.N.D. 2003).

swer a FOIA Complaint,[76] not the usual sixty days that are otherwise permitted by Federal Rule of Civil Procedure 12(a). While courts are not required to automatically accord expedited treatment to FOIA lawsuits, they may do so "if good cause therefor is shown."[77]

FOIA lawsuits are adjudicated according to standards and procedures that are atypical within the field of administrative law. First, the usual "substantial evidence" standard of review of agency action is replaced in the FOIA by a de novo review standard.[78] Second, the burden of proof is on the defendant agency, which must justify its decision to withhold any information.[79] When Exemption 1 is invoked, however, most courts have applied a highly deferential standard of review for classified documents in order to avoid compromising national security.[80] (See the

---

[76] See 5 U.S.C. § 552(a)(4)(C) (2000 & Supp. IV 2004).

[77] Federal Courts Improvement Act, 28 U.S.C. § 1657 (2000) (repealing 5 U.S.C. § 552(a)(4)(D) (1982), which provided that FOIA proceedings generally "take precedence over all cases on the docket and shall be . . . expedited in every way"); see also Freedom Commc'ns, Inc. v. FDIC, 157 F.R.D. 485, 487 (C.D. Cal. 1994) ("The Court offers its assurance to all concerned that it will continue to handle all matters in this action in an expeditious manner. However, we do not see the value in issuing an order that does no more than reiterate policies already announced by statute and the Court itself."); FOIA Update, Vol. VI, No. 2, at 6 (explaining statutory revision regarding expedition of FOIA actions).

[78] See 5 U.S.C. § 552(a)(4)(B); see also Halpern v. FBI, 181 F.3d 279, 288 (2d Cir. 1999) (observing that de novo standard of review comports with congressional intent); Summers v. Dep't of Justice, 140 F.3d 1077, 1080 (D.C. Cir. 1998) (explaining that review is "de novo").

[79] See 5 U.S.C. § 552(a)(4)(B); Solar Sources, Inc. v. United States, 142 F.3d 1033, 1037 (7th Cir. 1998) ("The government bears the burden of justifying its decision to withhold the requested information pursuant to a FOIA exemption."); Church of Scientology Int'l v. U.S. Dep't of Justice, 30 F.3d 224, 228 (1st Cir. 1994) (same); cf. Trenerry v. U.S. Dep't of the Treasury, No. 92-5053, 1993 WL 26813, at *5 (10th Cir. Feb. 5, 1993) (recognizing that although district court used phrase "arbitrary and capricious" in discussing scope of review, its decision should be upheld if "reviewing the entire order clearly reveals that the court performed a de novo review and correctly placed the burden on IRS").

[80] See, e.g., Students Against Genocide v. Dep't of State, 257 F.3d 828, 833 (D.C. Cir. 2001) (reiterating that agency affidavits in Exemption 1 cases are entitled to "substantial weight" (citing Goland v. CIA, 607 F.2d 339, 352 (D.C. Cir. 1978))); Snyder v. CIA, 230 F. Supp. 2d 17, 22 (D.D.C. 2002) (describing "substantial weight" to be given to agency declarations and affidavits concerning classification, provided declarations "'contain reasonable

(continued...)

**LITIGATION CONSIDERATIONS**

discussion under Exemption 1, Standard of Review, above.) Fee waiver issues also are reviewed under the de novo standard of review, but the scope of review is specifically limited by statute to the record before the agency.[81] (For a further discussion of fee waiver review standards, see Fees and Fee Waivers, above.)

Additionally, agency decisions to refuse to expedite the processing of FOIA requests in instances where requesters claim the statutorily based "compelling need"[82] are reviewed under the de novo standard of review,[83] but any such decisions that are based on individual agency regulations providing other grounds for expedition will be "entitled to judicial deference."[84] A major exception to the de novo standard of review is "reverse" FOIA lawsuits, in which courts apply the more deferential "arbitrary and capricious" standard under the Administrative Procedure Act.[85] (See the discussion of this point under "Reverse" FOIA, Standard of Review, below.)

Only federal agencies are proper party defendants in FOIA litigation.[86] Consequently, neither the agency head nor other agency officials

---

[80](...continued)
specificity [of] detail'" (quoting Halperin v. CIA, 629 F.2d 144, 148 (D.C. Cir. 1980))); Halpern v. FBI, No. 94-365, 2002 WL 31012157, at *7 (W.D.N.Y. Aug. 31, 2001) (magistrate's recommendation) ("'[S]ubstantial deference' must be given to Vaughn affidavits in the context of national security." (quoting Diamond v. FBI, 707 F.2d 75, 79 (2d Cir. 1983))), adopted (W.D.N.Y. Oct. 16, 2001); see also Ctr. for Nat'l Sec. Studies v. U.S. Dep't of Justice, 331 F.3d 918, 928 (D.C. Cir. 2003) (observing that "the judiciary is in an extremely poor position to second-guess the executive's judgment in this area") (Exemption 7 case).

[81] 5 U.S.C. § 552(a)(4)(A)(vii); see, e.g., Judicial Watch, Inc. v. U.S. Dep't of Justice, 122 F. Supp. 2d 13, 16 (D.D.C. 2000).

[82] 5 U.S.C. § 552(a)(6)(E)(i)(I).

[83] See Al-Fayed v. CIA, 254 F.3d 300, 306-08 (D.C. Cir. 2001) (holding, in a case of first impression, that "a district court must review de novo an agency's denial of a request for expedition under FOIA"); ACLU v. U.S. Dep't of Justice, 321 F. Supp. 2d 24, 29 (D.D.C. 2004) (same).

[84] Al-Fayed, 254 F.3d at 307 n.7.

[85] 5 U.S.C. §§ 701-706 (2000).

[86] See 5 U.S.C. § 552(a)(4)(B) (granting district courts "jurisdiction to enjoin the agency from withholding agency records improperly withheld from complainant"); 5 U.S.C. § 552(f)(1) (defining the term "agency"); see also Megibow v. Clerk of U.S. Tax Court, 432 F.3d 387, 387 (2d Cir. 2005) (concluding, on issue of first impression, that United States Tax Court is not subject to FOIA); United States v. Casas, 376 F.3d 20, 22 (1st Cir. 2004)
(continued...)

are proper parties to a FOIA suit,[87] nor is "the United States" as such.[88] (For

---

[86](...continued)
(stating that judicial branch is not subject to FOIA); United States v. Choate, 102 F. App'x 634, 635 (10th Cir. 2004) (same); Dunnington v. DOD, No. 06-0925, 2007 WL 60902, at *1 (D.D.C. Jan. 8, 2007) ("Neither branch of Congress is an executive agency subject to FOIA."); Pena v. U.S. Dep't of Prob., No. 06 CV 2481, 2006 WL 2806383, at *1 (E.D.N.Y. Sept. 28, 2006) (dismissing for lack of subject matter jurisdiction because "[t]he Probation Department, an administrative unit of the judiciary, is not subject to the disclosure obligations of FOIA"); Boyd v. Criminal Div., U.S. Dep't of Justice, No. 04-1100, 2005 WL 555412, at *4 (D.D.C. Mar. 9, 2005) (same), aff'd, 475 F.3d 381 (D.C. Cir. 2007); Ali v. Przbyl, No. 04-CV-0459E, 2004 WL 1682774, at *2 (W.D.N.Y. July 26, 2004) ("FOIA does not apply to state or local agencies or state or local individuals."); Woodruff v. Office of the Pub. Defender, No. 03-791, slip op. at 3-4 (N.D. Cal. June 3, 2004) (dismissing defendants Office of Federal Public Defender and Clerk of U.S. District Court because federal courts and organizations under control of courts are not subject to FOIA); Mount of Olives Paralegals v. Bush, No. 04 C 620, 2004 WL 1102315, at *2 (N.D. Ill. May 6, 2004) (noting that state agencies are not subject to federal FOIA).

[87] See, e.g., Thompson v. Walbran, 990 F.2d 403, 405 (8th Cir. 1993) (per curiam) (dismissing suit brought against prosecutor, because plaintiff "sued the wrong party"); Petrus v. Bowen, 833 F.2d 581, 582 (5th Cir. 1987) ("Neither the Freedom of Information Act nor the Privacy Act creates a cause of action for a suit against an individual employee of a federal agency."); Harrison v. Lappin, No. 04-0061, 2005 WL 752186, at *3 (D.D.C. Mar. 31, 2005) (same); Buckles v. Indian Health Serv./Belcourt Serv. Unit, 268 F. Supp. 2d 1101, 1102 (D.N.D. 2003) (same); Eison v. Kallstrom, 75 F. Supp. 2d 113, 115-16 (S.D.N.Y. 1999) (recognizing that FOIA creates no cause of action against individual defendants, but allowing pro se plaintiff to amend Complaint to substitute agency as defendant); Barvick v. Cisneros, 941 F. Supp. 1015, 1017 n.2 (D. Kan. 1996) (ruling that the only proper party defendant in a FOIA action is the agency, not an individual federal official); see also Payne v. Minihan, No. 97-0266SC, slip op. at 14-15 (D.N.M. Apr. 30, 1998) (agreeing with majority view that agency personnel are not proper parties to FOIA suit, but nevertheless declining to dismiss action, because agency did "not challenge" suit on basis of improper party and was "on notice" of suit), aff'd sub nom. Payne v. NSA, 232 F.3d 902 (10th Cir. 2000) (unpublished table decision); cf. Thomas v. FAA, No. 05-2391, 2007 WL 219988, at *3 (D.D.C. Jan. 25, 2007) (noting that proper defendant in FOIA case is federal agency and, "[t]herefore, Plaintiff cannot obtain a Bivens remedy for an alleged violation of FOIA by the [individual] defendants").

[88] See Sanders v. United States, No. 96-5372, 1997 WL 529073, at *1 (D.C. Cir. July 3, 1997) (dismissing Complaint because "United States" is not agency subject to FOIA); United States v. Trenk, No. 06-1004, 2006 WL 3359725, at *8 (D.N.J. Nov. 20, 2006) ("The United States is not a proper

(continued...)

a further discussion of which entities are subject to the FOIA, see Procedural Requirements, Entities Subject to the FOIA, above). This rule derives from the plain language of the Act, which vests the district courts with jurisdiction to enjoin "the agency" from withholding records.[89] Similarly, there is a sound general rule that only the person who has actually submitted a FOIA request at the administrative level can be the proper party plaintiff in any subsequent court action based on that request.[90]

---

[88](...continued)
party in a FOIA action."); Huertas v. United States, No. 04-3361, 2005 WL 1719143, at *7 (D.N.J. July 21, 2005) (granting defendants' motion for summary judgment because United States and individual defendants were only defendants named); Lawrence v. United States, No. 8:03-CV-660, 2004 U.S. Dist. LEXIS 15445, at *6-7 (M.D. Fla. July 8, 2004) (ruling that "all parts of [plaintiff's FOIA case] as brought against the United States of America are hereby dismissed for lack of jurisdiction").

[89] 5 U.S.C. § 552(a)(4)(B) (emphasis added); see, e..g,, Pri-Har v. Dep't of Justice, No. 04-1448, 2005 WL 3273550, at *1 n.1 (D.D.C. Sept. 27, 2005) (noting that "[a]lthough the plaintiff lists both the Executive Office for the United States Attorneys and the Department of Justice as defendants in this action, the only proper defendant is the Department of Justice"); Brooks v. Bureau of Prisons, No. 04-0055, 2005 WL 623229, at *2 (D.D.C. Mar. 17, 2005) ("The proper defendant in a FOIA or Privacy Act case is the agency, in this case, the Department of Justice of which BOP is a component."); Judicial Watch, Inc. v. FBI, 190 F. Supp. 2d 29, 30 n.1 (D.D.C. 2002) (stating that the proper defendant is the Department of Justice "rather than the FBI, which is a component of DOJ and therefore not an 'agency' within the statutory definition"); Peralta v. U.S. Attorney's Office, No. 94-760, slip op. at 1-3 (D.D.C. May 17, 1999) (permitting Department of Justice to be substituted as proper defendant, as Department of Justice is "agency" under FOIA, and accordingly vacating order that had joined Executive Office for United States Attorneys and FBI as necessary parties). But see Peralta v. U.S. Attorney's Office, 136 F.3d 169, 173 (D.C. Cir. 1998) (dictum) (suggesting, despite both statutory language and agency structure, that "the FBI is subject to the FOIA in its own name"); Prison Legal News v. Lappin, 436 F. Supp. 2d 17, 22 (D.D.C. 2006) (finding that the Bureau of Prisons "exercises 'substantial independent authority'" and that, accordingly, the Bureau of Prisons, "despite its status as a component agency of the DOJ, is a proper defendant in this FOIA action"); Lair v. Dep't of the Treasury, No. 03-827, 2005 WL 645228, at *3 (D.D.C. Mar. 21, 2005) (relying on D.C. Circuit's dictum in Peralta and on district court's vacated memorandum opinion in Peralta to hold that Secret Service, Bureau of Alcohol, Tobacco, and Firearms, and Executive Office for United States Attorneys were proper defendants), reconsideration denied, 2005 WL 1330722 (D.D.C. June 3, 2005).

[90] See Trenk, 2006 WL 3359725, at *9 (concluding that plaintiff lacks standing to bring FOIA action because "[h]is name does not appear on the document requests, and he is not the client for which the requests were

(continued...)

It is clear that an agency in possession of records originating with another agency cannot refuse to process those records merely by advising the requester to seek them directly from the other agency.[91] In litigation,

---

[90](...continued)
made"); The Haskell Co. v. U.S. Dep't of Justice, No. 05-1110, 2006 WL 627156, at *2 (D.D.C. Mar. 13, 2006) (dismissing case because plaintiff had no standing to sue agency on FOIA request submitted solely by its law firm); Three Forks Ranch Corp. v. Bureau of Land Mgmt., 358 F. Supp. 2d 1, 2 (D.D.C. 2005) (holding that "a FOIA request made by an attorney must clearly indicate that it is being made 'on behalf of' the corporation to give that corporation standing to bring a FOIA challenge"); Mahtesian v. OPM, 388 F. Supp. 2d 1047, 1050 (N.D. Cal. 2005) (finding that attorney's reference to anonymous client in FOIA request does not confer standing on that client); Maxxam, Inc. v. FDIC, No. 98-0989, 1999 WL 33912624, at *2 (D.D.C. Jan. 29, 1999) (finding that only plaintiff's attorney was real party in interest when FOIA request was made in attorney's, not plaintiff's, name); Payne, No. 97-0266SC, slip op. at 12-14 (D.N.M. Apr. 30, 1998) (dismissing plaintiff who sued as "concerned citizen" because "[i]t is the filing of his requests and their actual or constructive denials which distinguishes the harm suffered by [the actual requester] from the harm incurred by [the concerned citizen]"); Wade v. Dep't of Commerce, No. 96-0717, slip op. at 4 (D.D.C. Mar. 26, 1998) (finding failure to exhaust administrative remedies because plaintiff was not "'the person making'" the FOIA request (quoting 5 U.S.C. § 552(a)(6)(A)(i))); Unigard Ins. Co. v. Dep't of the Treasury, 997 F. Supp. 1339, 1342 (S.D. Cal. 1997) ("A person whose name does not appear on the request for disclosure lacks standing to sue under FOIA, even if his interest was asserted in the request." (citing United States v. McDonnell, 4 F.3d 1227, 1237 (3d Cir. 1993))); cf. Burka v. HHS, 142 F.3d 1286, 1290-91 (D.C. Cir. 1998) (refusing to award attorney fees to plaintiff who claimed he was suing for unnamed party, because of "dangers inherent in recognizing an 'undisclosed' client as the real plaintiff"); Doe v. FBI, 218 F.R.D. 256, 260 (D. Colo. 2003) (refusing to allow FOIA plaintiff to proceed pseudonymously). But see Archibald v. Roche, No. 01-1492, slip op. at 2 (D.D.C. Mar. 29, 2002) (allowing a plaintiff whose name did not appear on the initial FOIA request to amend his complaint in order to name a proper plaintiff, "in the interest of justice"); Olsen v. U.S. Dep't of Transp. Fed. Transit Admin., No. 02-00673, 2002 WL 31738794, at *2 n.2 (N.D. Cal. Dec. 2, 2002) (refusing to find lack of standing when plaintiff was not identified by his attorney in initial request, because agency's administrative appeal response itself acknowledged plaintiff's identity).

[91] See, e.g., In re Wade, 969 F.2d 241, 247-48 (7th Cir. 1992) (explaining that agency cannot avoid request or withhold documents merely by referring requester to another agency where documents originated); see also FOIA Update, Vol. XV, No. 3, at 6 (advising agencies of record-referral responsibilities); cf. Hardy v. DOD, No. 99-523, 2001 WL 34354945, at *11 (D. Ariz. Aug. 27, 2001) (ruling that an agency was not required to forward a FOIA request for personnel records about one of its retired employees to

(continued...)

the defendant agency ordinarily will include in its own court submissions affidavits from the originating agency to address any contested withholdings in these records.[92] (For a further discussion of agency referral practices, see Procedural Requirements, Referrals and Consultations, above.)

Lastly, although Rule 15(a) of the Federal Rules of Civil Procedure counsels that leave to amend complaints "shall be freely given when justice so requires,"[93] the decision to grant such leave is entrusted to the sound discretion of the district court.[94] Courts have recognized limitations on a plaintiff's ability to amend a FOIA Complaint, even when the plaintiff is proceeding pro se.[95] In particular, courts have rejected attempts to amend Complaints due to the plaintiff's undue delay,[96] when the Complaint

---

[91](...continued)
OPM, where the records were now maintained). But cf. Snyder v. CIA, 230 F. Supp. 2d 17, 25 (D.D.C. 2002) (noting with approval agency's practice of closing pending requests that require coordination with other agencies even before coordination has been completed).

[92] See, e.g., Williams v. FBI, No. 92-5176, slip op. at 2 (D.C. Cir. May 7, 1993); Oglesby v. U.S. Dep't of the Army, 920 F.2d 57, 69 & n.15 (D.C. Cir. 1990); Fitzgibbon v. CIA, 911 F.2d 755, 757 (D.C. Cir. 1990); Greenberg v. U.S. Dep't of Treasury, 10 F. Supp. 2d 3, 11, 18 (D.D.C. 1998) (requiring agency or component that referred documents to justify nondisclosure); Jan-Xin Zang v. FBI, 756 F. Supp. 705, 706-07 & n.1 (W.D.N.Y. 1991); see also FOIA Update, Vol. XII, No. 3, at 3-4 ("OIP Guidance: Referral and Consultation Procedures"); FOIA Update, Vol. XIV, No. 3, at 6-8 (Department of Justice memorandum setting forth White House consultation process); cf. Peralta, 136 F.3d at 175 (remanding for consideration of whether referral procedures could result in "improper withholding" of referred documents).

[93] See Foman v. Davis, 371 U.S. 178, 182 (1962) (non-FOIA case); Katzman v. Sessions, 156 F.R.D. 35, 38 (E.D.N.Y. 1994) (holding that to defeat a motion to supplement pleadings, "the nonmovant must demonstrate either bad faith on the part of the moving party, the futility of the claims asserted within the application, or undue prejudice to the nonmovant") (non-FOIA case).

[94] See, e.g., Miss. Ass'n of Coops. v. Farmers Home Admin., 139 F.R.D. 542, 543 (D.D.C. 1991).

[95] See, e.g., Brown v. U.S. Patent & Trademark Office, No. 06-14716, 2007 WL 446601, at *1 (11th Cir. Feb. 13, 2007) (noting that "[a]lthough pro se pleadings are to be liberally construed, . . . ordinary rules of procedure and summary judgment still apply"). But see Eison, 75 F. Supp. 2d at 116 n.2 (recognizing that plaintiffs proceeding pro se are given "considerable latitude to correct superficial pleading errors").

[96] See Friedman v. FBI, 605 F. Supp. 306, 314-15 (N.D. Ga. 1984) (denying amendment when sought six years into litigation without sufficient cause);
(continued...)

as amended still would fail to state a justiciable claim,[97] when the plaintiff sought to dramatically alter the scope and nature of the FOIA litigation,[98] or when the plaintiff sought to add an unreasonable number of claims.[99]

## Exhaustion of Administrative Remedies

Under the FOIA, administrative remedies must be exhausted prior to judicial review. When a FOIA plaintiff attempts to obtain judicial review without first properly undertaking full and timely administrative exhaus-

---

[96](...continued)
see also Becker v. IRS, 1992 WL 67849, at *3 (N.D. Ill. Mar. 27, 1992) ("Any attempt by the [plaintiffs] to expand the nature of the search at this late date must be rejected.").

[97] See, e.g., Beech v. Comm'r, 190 F. Supp. 2d 1183, 1187 (D. Ariz. 2001) (dismissing Complaint with prejudice because it "could not be made viable by amendment"); Rzeslawski v. U.S. Dep't of Justice, No. 97-1156, slip op. at 7 (D.D.C. Mar. 16, 1999) (disallowing amendment to add defendants because administrative remedies were not exhausted); Lanter v. Dep't of Justice, No. 93-34, slip op. at 1-2 (W.D. Okla. Aug. 30, 1993) (noting that plaintiffs' amended complaint does "not show exhaustion of their administrative remedies, or other exception to the exhaustion requirements"), aff'd on other grounds, 19 F.3d 33 (10th Cir. 1994) (unpublished table decision).

[98] See, e.g., Caton v. Norton, No. 04-CV-439, 2005 WL 1009544, at *4 (D.N.H. May 2, 2005) (denying motion to amend Complaint where plaintiff sought to add claims barred by doctrines of sovereign immunity and exhaustion of administrative remedies); Szymanski v. DEA, No. 93-1314, 1993 WL 433592, at *2 (D.D.C. Oct. 6, 1993) ("This Court will not permit a F.O.I.A. complaint, properly filed, to become the narrow edge of a wedge which forces open the court house door to unrelated claims against unrelated parties."); Miss. Ass'n, 139 F.R.D. at 544 ("Where, however, the complaint, as amended, would radically alter the scope and nature of the case and bears no more than a tangential relationship to the original action, leave to amend should be denied."); see also Trenerry v. IRS, No. 90-C-444, 1993 WL 565354, at *3 (N.D. Okla. Oct. 28, 1993) ("Plaintiff's motion to amend the pleadings is untimely, seeks to add a new unrelated cause of action and appears on its face to be frivolous."). But see also Eison, 75 F. Supp. 2d at 114, 117 (allowing plaintiff to amend original Complaint in order to allege improper withholding of records, where original Complaint had asked for injunction against "pattern and practice" of delayed agency responses, which court deemed "now moot").

[99] Allnutt v. U.S. Trustee, No. 97-02414, slip op. at 8 (D.D.C. July 31, 1999) (allowing an amendment seeking to add six FOIA claims, but noting that further attempts to amend would be disallowed in order to prevent plaintiff from advancing "a never-ending case by perpetually amending his complaint to add the latest FOIA request"), appeal dismissed for lack of juris., No. 99-5410 (D.C. Cir. Feb. 2, 2000).

tion, the lawsuit is subject to ready dismissal because "exhaustion of administrative remedies is a mandatory prerequisite to a lawsuit under FOIA."[100] Exhaustion allows top-level officials of an agency to correct possible mistakes made at lower levels and thereby obviate unnecessary judicial review.[101]

Many courts have held that dismissal is appropriate under Rule 12(b)(1) of the Federal Rules of Civil Procedure, treating exhaustion under the FOIA as essentially the same as a jurisdictional requirement.[102] Inas-

---

[100] Wilbur v. CIA, 355 F.3d 675, 676 (D.C. Cir. 2004) (per curiam) (citing Oglesby v. U.S. Dep't of the Army, 920 F.2d 57, 61-64, 65 n.9 (D.C. Cir. 1990)); see, e.g., Almy v. U.S. Dep't of Justice, No. 96-1207, 1997 WL 267884, at *3 (9th Cir. May 7, 1997) ("[T]he FOIA requires exhaustion of administrative remedies before the filing of a lawsuit."); Taylor v. Appleton, 30 F.3d 1365, 1367 (11th Cir. 1994) ("The FOIA clearly requires a party to exhaust all administrative remedies before seeking redress in the federal courts."); McDonnell v. United States, 4 F.3d 1227, 1240, 1241 (3d Cir. 1993) (same); Voinche v. U.S. Dep't of the Air Force, 983 F.2d 667, 669 (5th Cir. 1993) ("We conclude that the FOIA should be read to require that a party must present proof of exhaustion of administrative remedies prior to seeking judicial review."); see also Scherer v. U.S. Dep't of Educ., 78 F. App'x 687, 690 (10th Cir. 2003) (affirming dismissal based on failure to exhaust because while plaintiff's "labors may have been exhausting . . . he failed to pursue any of his requests as far as he could").

[101] Oglesby, 920 F.2d at 61; see also Taylor, 30 F.3d at 1369 ("Allowing a FOIA requester to proceed immediately to court to challenge an agency's initial response would cut off the agency's power to correct or rethink initial misjudgments or errors."); Martin v. Court Servs. & Offender Supervision Agency, No. 05-853, 2005 WL 3211536, at *3 (D.D.C. Nov. 17, 2005) (recognizing that administrative exhaustion "[g]ives the parties and the courts the benefit of the agency's experience and expertise"); Hogan v. Huff, No. 00-Civ.-6753, 2002 WL 1359722, at *4 (S.D.N.Y. June 21, 2002) (explaining that administrative appeal procedures "provide agencies an opportunity to correct internal mistakes").

[102] See, e.g., McDonnell, 4 F.3d at 1240 & n.9 (affirming dismissal for lack of subject matter jurisdiction because plaintiff failed to exhaust administrative remedies); Trenerry v. IRS, No. 95-5150, 1996 WL 88459, at *1 (10th Cir. Mar. 1, 1996) (confirming that district court lacked subject matter jurisdiction "where plaintiff has failed to exhaust her administrative remedies"); Hymen v. MSPB, 799 F.2d 1421, 1423 (9th Cir. 1986) (same); Hardy v. Daniels, No. 05-955, 2006 WL 176531, at *1 (D. Or. Jan. 23, 2006) ("Where a plaintiff has failed to exhaust . . . the district court will dismiss the case for lack of jurisdiction."); Robert VIII v. Dep't of Justice, No. 05-CV-2543, 2005 WL 3371480, at *7 (E.D.N.Y. Dec. 12, 2005) ("[A] court lacks subject matter jurisdiction over a requester's claim where the requester has failed to exhaust the administrative remedies provided under the FOIA statute."); Sny-
(continued...)

much as exhaustion is required by the Administrative Procedure Act,[103] of which the FOIA is a part, this approach is well founded. Indeed, even those courts that term exhaustion as "prudential" in nature because the FOIA itself does not expressly require it nevertheless enforce the administrative exhaustion principle under the FOIA, albeit that they often view Rule 12(b)(6) as the appropriate vehicle for dismissal.[104] Regardless of the

---

[102](...continued)
der v. DOD, No. 03-4992, slip op. at 5 (N.D. Cal. Feb. 2, 2005) ("[E]xhaustion goes to court's subject matter jurisdiction[.]"); Thomas v. IRS, No. 03-CV-2080, 2004 WL 3185320, at *1 (M.D. Pa. Nov. 16, 2004) (concluding that court lacks jurisdiction because plaintiff failed to exhaust his administrative remedies), aff'd, 153 F. App'x 89 (3d Cir. 2005); McMillan v. Togus Reg'l Office, VA, No. 03-CV-1074, 2003 WL 23185665, at *1 (E.D.N.Y. Nov. 18, 2003) (dismissing unexhausted FOIA claim because "[s]ubject matter jurisdiction is lacking"), aff'd, 120 F. App'x 849 (2d Cir. 2005); Scherer v. United States, 241 F. Supp. 2d 1270, 1277 (D. Kan. 2003) (granting government's motion to dismiss under Rule 12(b)(1) because plaintiff failed to exhaust administrative remedies), aff'd, 78 F. App'x 687 (10th Cir. 2003); Redding v. Christian, 161 F. Supp. 2d 671, 674 (W.D.N.C. 2001) ("[W]hen this action was filed, this court lacked jurisdiction over the subject matter of this case as a matter of law because plaintiff had not sought any administrative remedies, much less exhausted them."); Maples v. USDA, No. 97-5663, slip op. at 6 (E.D. Cal. Jan. 15, 1998) ("When a complaint contains an unexhausted request in its prayer for relief, the court must dismiss this portion for lack of subject matter jurisdiction."); Rabin v. U.S. Dep't of State, 980 F. Supp. 116, 119 (E.D.N.Y. 1997) (suggesting that defense of failure to exhaust is most properly raised in FRCP Rule 12(b)(1) dismissal motion); Thomas v. Office of the U.S. Attorney, 171 F.R.D. 53, 55 (E.D.N.Y. 1997) ("Failure to properly exhaust . . . precludes a federal court of subject matter jurisdiction over a requester's claims."); Jones v. Shalala, 887 F. Supp. 210, 214 (S.D. Iowa 1995) (declaring that failure to exhaust administrative remedies deprives court of jurisdiction to compel disclosure of records).

[103] See 5 U.S.C. § 704 (2000) (authorizing judicial review only of "[a]gency action made reviewable by statute and every final agency action for which there is no other adequate remedy in a court") (emphasis added); see also Darby v. Cisneros, 509 U.S. 137, 153 (1993) (explaining that exhaustion of administrative remedies is "effectively codified" in Administrative Procedure Act) (non-FOIA case).

[104] See, e.g., Hildalgo v. FBI, 344 F.3d 1256, 1258-59 (D.C. Cir. 2003) (opining that the exhaustion requirement is not jurisdictional because "the FOIA does not unequivocally make it so," but then explaining that exhaustion is required if "'the purposes of exhaustion' and the 'particular administrative scheme' support such a bar" (quoting Oglesby, 920 F.2d at 61)); Taylor, 30 F.3d at 1367 n.3 (stating that an unexhausted FOIA claim "should have been dismissed pursuant to Rule 12(b)(6) for failure to state a claim upon which relief can be granted"); Scherer v. Balkema, 840 F.2d 437, 443

(continued...)

stated basis for dismissal, though, when a requester attempts to seek judicial review before the agency has had an opportunity to exercise its discretion and expertise on the matter and to make a factual record to support its decision, the Complaint should be dismissed for failure to exhaust administrative remedies.[105]

A plaintiff cannot evade proper FOIA administrative procedures by

---

[104](...continued)
(7th Cir. 1988) (ruling that plaintiff failed to state a claim when he failed to allege exhaustion of administrative remedies); Bestor v. CIA, No. 04-2049, 2005 WL 3273723, at *3 (D.D.C. Sept. 1, 2005) (dismissing Complaint under Rule 12(b)(6) where plaintiff failed to "allege or demonstrate" that he exhausted his administrative remedies); Flowers v. IRS, 307 F. Supp. 2d 60, 66 (D.D.C. 2004) (stating that "the exhaustion requirement is a prudential consideration, not a jurisdictional prerequisite"); Gambini v. U.S. Customs Serv., No. 5:01-CV-300, 2001 U.S. Dist. LEXIS 21336, at *4-5 (N.D. Tex. Dec. 21, 2001) (dismissing Complaint under Rule 12(b)(6) because plaintiff had not exhausted administrative remedies); see also Jones v. U.S. Dep't of Justice, No. 04-1729, 2005 U.S. Dist. LEXIS 20097, at *2 (D.D.C. Sept. 12, 2005) (characterizing exhaustion as "jurisprudential doctrine" rather than jurisdictional requirement); Boyd v. Criminal Div., U.S. Dep't of Justice, No. 04-1100, 2005 WL 555412, at *4 (D.D.C. Mar. 9, 2005) (dismissing Complaint because plaintiff failed to exhaust his administrative remedies, but saying that "exhaustion requirement . . . is not jurisdictional"), aff'd, 475 F.3d 381 (D.C. Cir. 2007); Kennedy v. DHS, No. 03-6076, 2004 WL 2285058, at *4-5 (W.D.N.Y. Oct. 8, 2004) (noting that "[t]he precise nature of the exhaustion requirement is not well-settled," but concluding that it is "not jurisdictional"); cf. Sweetland v. Walters, 60 F.3d 852, 855 (D.C. Cir. 1995) (per curiam) (declaring it inappropriate for district court to find lack of jurisdiction, because federal defendant is not an agency for FOIA purposes; dismissal for failure "to state a claim upon which relief could be granted" found proper). But see, e.g., Oglesby, 920 F.2d at 61-62 ("Courts have consistently confirmed that the FOIA requires exhaustion . . . before an individual may seek relief in the courts.").

[105] See, e.g., Judicial Watch, Inc. v. FBI, 190 F. Supp. 2d 29, 33 (D.D.C. 2002) (citing Oglesby, 920 F.2d at 61-62); Makuch v. FBI, No. 99-1094, 2000 WL 915640, at *2 (D.D.C. Jan. 5, 2000) ("Under FOIA, a party must exhaust available administrative remedies before seeking judicial review." (citing Dettmann v. U.S. Dep't of Justice, 802 F.2d 1472, 1476-77 (D.C. Cir. 1986))); Schoenman v. FBI, No. 04-2202, 2006 WL 1582253, at *9 (D.D.C. June 5, 2006) ("[E]xhaustion of administrative remedies is required before a party can seek judicial review . . . ."); Trueblood v. U.S. Dep't of Treasury, 943 F. Supp. 64, 68 (D.D.C. 1996). But cf. Jones, No. 03-1647, slip op. at 3 (D.D.C. May 18, 2004) (allowing plaintiff to maintain unexhausted claim that was "substantially similar" to exhausted claim, because reaching its merits would not undermine purposes of administrative review), summary affirmance granted, No. 04-5498 (D.C. Cir. Jan. 20, 2006).

attempting to file his FOIA request as part of a judicial proceeding[106] or in the course of administratively appealing a previously filed FOIA request,[107] though he certainly may narrow the scope of an existing request at any time.[108] Along similar lines, a FOIA claim may well be dismissed on exhaustion grounds if the defendant agency is unable to locate the request in its files -- unless, of course, the plaintiff produces sufficient evidence that a

---

[106] See Gillin v. IRS, 980 F.2d 819, 822-23 (1st Cir. 1992) (per curiam) (ruling that when "flawed" request was predicated upon a misunderstanding with agency but, within one week after submission, information provided by agency should have prompted requester to revise his request, requester cannot salvage request by clarification in litigation); Hillman v. Comm'r, No. 1:97-cv-760, 1998 U.S. Dist. LEXIS 12431, at *15 (W.D. Mich. July 10, 1998) (rejecting plaintiff's attempt to have discovery demand treated as access request because "a governmental agency is not required to respond to interrogatories disguised as a FOIA request"); Smith v. Reno, No. C-93-1316, 1996 U.S. Dist. LEXIS 5594, at *8 n.3 (N.D. Cal. Apr. 23, 1996) ("A request for documents in a complaint does not constitute a proper discovery request, much less a proper FOIA request."), aff'd sub nom. Smith v. City of Berkeley, 133 F.3d 929 (9th Cir. 1998) (unpublished table decision); Juda v. U.S. Dep't of Justice, No. 94-1521, slip op. at 4, 6 (D.D.C. Mar. 28, 1996) (plaintiff cannot interpose new request through vehicle of "motion for leave to pursue discovery"); Pray v. Dep't of Justice, 902 F. Supp. 1, 2-3 (D.D.C. 1995) (disallowing request to FBI field office "made only in response to the government's motion for summary judgment"), aff'd in part & remanded in part on other grounds, No. 95-5383, 1996 WL 734142, at *1 (D.C. Cir. Nov. 20, 1996); Pollack v. U.S. Dep't of Justice, No. 89-2569, 1993 WL 293692, at *4 (D. Md. July 23, 1993) (court lacks subject matter jurisdiction when request not submitted until after litigation filed), aff'd on other grounds, 49 F.3d 115 (4th Cir. 1995); see also Kowalczyk v. Dep't of Justice, 73 F.3d 386, 388 (D.C. Cir. 1996) ("Requiring an additional search each time the agency receives a letter that clarifies a prior request could extend indefinitely the delay in processing new requests."); cf. Payne, No. 97-0266SC, slip op. at 12 (D.N.M. Apr. 30, 1998) ("The FOIA creates a cause of action only for persons who have followed its procedures.").

[107] See Thomas, 171 F.R.D. at 55; see also Moore v. Aspin, 916 F. Supp. 32, 36 (D.D.C. 1996) ("Sending an appeal to a different agency does not initiate a proper FOIA request for that agency to conduct a search.").

[108] See Forest Guardians v. U.S. Dep't of the Interior, No. 02-1003, 2004 WL 3426434, at *11 (D.N.M. Feb. 28, 2004) (rejecting an agency's argument that the plaintiff's attempt to narrow the scope of its request -- during the course of litigation -- was tantamount to a failure to exhaust; "there is no evidence in record that the [agency] would reach a different conclusion if given the opportunity to decide a more narrow FOIA request"), rev'd & remanded on other grounds, 416 F.3d 1173 (10th Cir. 2005); cf. 5 U.S.C. § 552(a)(6)(B)(ii) (2000 & Supp. IV 2004) (providing that agency must allow requester opportunity to modify his request if it needs to extend its twenty-day time limit for processing by more than ten additional days).

request actually was made.[109] (For a further discussion of the proper submission of requests, see Procedural Requirements, Proper FOIA Requests, above.)

The FOIA permits requesters to treat an agency's failure to comply with its specific time limits as full, or "constructive," exhaustion of administrative remedies.[110] Thus, when an agency does not respond to a perfected request within the twenty-day (excepting Saturdays, Sundays, and legal

---

[109] See, e.g., Arnold v. U.S. Secret Serv., No. 05-0450, 2006 WL 2844238, at *2 (D.D.C. Sept. 29, 2006) (holding that a "certified mail return receipt is not competent evidence of plaintiff's compliance with the FOIA's exhaustion requirement"); Schoenman v. FBI, No. 04-2202, 2006 WL 1126813, at *13 (D.D.C. Mar. 31, 2006) (dismissing FOIA claims where agencies contended that they never received requests, and noting that plaintiff provided no proof that draft requests on his counsel's computer were ever mailed and received; "[w]ithout a copy of a stamped envelope . . . or a returned receipt . . . [p]laintiff cannot meet the statutory requirements under FOIA"); Schoenman, 2006 WL 1582253, at *12 (dismissing claims where agency stated that appeals were never received, and finding that plaintiff failed to present clear evidence that draft appeal letters on his counsel's computer "were ever mailed to and received" by agency); Antonelli v. ATF, No. 04-1180, 2005 WL 3276222, at *5 (D.D.C. Aug. 16, 2005) (finding that plaintiff failed to sufficiently demonstrate that FOIA requests were submitted to agency, which could not locate them in its files, even though plaintiff produced copies of requests and asserted that he mailed them); see also Roum v. Bush, 461 F. Supp. 2d 40, 47 n.3 (D.D.C. 2006) (implying that plaintiff produced sufficient evidence that request actually was made when plaintiff provided receipt from U.S. Postal Service indicating that request was delivered to FBI); Linn v. U.S. Dep't of Justice, No. 92-1406, 1995 WL 631847, at *15-16 (D.D.C. Aug. 22, 1995) (ruling that when plaintiff introduces copy of appeal letter and attests that it was sent, case should not be dismissed for failure to exhaust administrative remedies). But see also Reyes v. U.S. Customs Serv., No. 05-173, 2005 WL 3274563, at *2 (D.D.C. July 28, 2005) (concluding, without elaboration, that plaintiff presented genuine issue of material fact as to whether his request was received by defendant agency, which had no record of it); Hammie v. Soc. Sec. Admin., 765 F. Supp. 1224, 1226 (E.D. Pa. 1991) (stating that in considering government's dismissal motion, court is required to accept plaintiff's averments that he submitted requests).

[110] See 5 U.S.C. § 552(a)(6)(C); see also FOIA Update, Vol. XVII, No. 4, at 2 (describing Electronic FOIA amendments' modification of Act's basic time limit from ten to twenty working days); Nurse v. Sec'y of the Air Force, 231 F. Supp. 2d 323, 328 (D.D.C. 2002) ("The FOIA is considered a unique statute because it recognizes a constructive exhaustion doctrine for purposes of judicial review upon the expiration of certain relevant FOIA deadlines.").

public holidays) statutory time limit set forth in the Act,[111] the requester is deemed to have exhausted his administrative remedies and can seek immediate judicial review, even though the requester has not filed an administrative appeal.[112] If a requester files suit before the twenty-day period has expired, the suit must be dismissed even if the agency still has failed to respond to the request after the twenty day period has expired because "the Court will only consider those facts and circumstances that existed at the time of the filing of the complaint, and not subsequent events."[113] In-

---

[111] 5 U.S.C. § 552(a)(6)(A)(i).

[112] See, e.g., Pollack, 49 F.3d at 118-19 ("Under FOIA's statutory scheme, when an agency fails to comply in a timely fashion with a proper FOIA request, it may not insist on the exhaustion of administrative remedies unless the agency responds to the request before suit is filed."); Campbell v. Unknown Power Superintendent of the Flathead Irrigation & Power Project, No. 91-35104, 1992 WL 84315, at *1 (9th Cir. Apr. 22, 1992) (noting that exhaustion is deemed to have occurred if agency fails to respond to request within statutory time limit); Accuracy in Media, Inc. v. NTSB, No. 03-0024, 2006 WL 826070, at *6 (D.D.C. Mar. 29, 2006) (finding constructive exhaustion because plaintiff filed its FOIA Complaint seven months after NTSB received its request and before NTSB complied with it); Hall v. CIA, No. 04-0614, 2005 WL 850379, at *2 & n.6 (D.D.C. Apr. 13, 2005) (finding constructive exhaustion where plaintiff filed suit prior to CIA's belated response to his request, and rejecting agency's "novel" argument that it was somehow excused from FOIA's statutory time limit while awaiting final outcome of plaintiff's previous FOIA suit); see also FOIA Update, Vol. IV, No. 1, at 6 (discussing exhaustion); cf. Or. Natural Desert Ass'n, 409 F. Supp. 2d at 1247 (finding constructive exhaustion with respect to "cut-off" date challenge, even though plaintiff did not raise such claim in its administrative appeal, because document production from agency and referral agencies continued after plaintiff filed suit and plaintiff could not have foreseen effect of "cut-off" policy at time appeal was filed); Anderson v. USPS, 7 F. Supp. 2d 583, 586 (E.D. Pa. 1998) (finding that "vague positive response" from agency received after statutory time limit allows plaintiff to claim "constructive" exhaustion), aff'd, 187 F.3d 625 (3d Cir. 1999) (unpublished table decision).

[113] Judicial Watch, Inc. v. FBI, No. 01-1216, slip op. at 8 (D.D.C. July 26, 2002) (citing Judicial Watch, Inc. v. U.S. Dep't of Justice, No. 97-2089, slip op. at 11 (D.D.C. July 14, 1998) (citing, in turn, Newman-Green, Inc. v. Alfonzo-Larrain, 490 U.S. 826, 830 (1989) ("The existence of federal jurisdiction ordinarily depends on the facts as they exist when the complaint is filed."))); cf. Dorn v. Comm'r, No. 2:03CV539, 2005 WL 1126653, at *3-4 (M.D. Fla. May 12, 2005) (dismissing lawsuit where Complaint was filed prematurely, even though agency ultimately responded after twenty-day period), reconsideration denied, 2005 WL 2248857 (M.D. Fla. June 1, 2005). But cf. Judicial Watch, Inc. v. U.S. Dep't of Energy, 191 F. Supp. 2d 138, 139 (D.D.C. 2002) (erroneously permitting premature Complaint to be cured by filing of

(continued...)

disputably, though, an agency's failure to comply with the statutory deadline neither requires nor empowers a court to ignore the agency's right to invoke applicable statutory exemptions and summarily order disclosure of any or all information sought.[114]

The special right to immediate judicial review that arises from the lack of a timely response lapses if an agency responds to a request at any time before the requester's FOIA suit is filed; in that situation, the requester <u>must</u> administratively appeal a denial and wait at least twenty working days for the agency to adjudicate that appeal -- as is required by 5 U.S.C. § 552(a)(6)(A)(ii) -- before commencing litigation.[115] This latter point was well established by the Court of Appeals for the District of Columbia Circuit in <u>Oglesby v. U.S. Dep't of the Army</u>, which held that "an administrative appeal is mandatory if the agency cures its failure to respond within the statutory period by responding to the FOIA request before suit is filed."[116] Thus, under <u>Oglesby</u>, if a FOIA requester waits beyond the twenty-day period for the agency's initial response and then, in fact, receives that response before suing the agency, the requester must exhaust his ad-

---

[113](...continued)
"supplemental" Complaint).

[114] See <u>Judicial Watch, Inc. v. USPS</u>, 297 F. Supp. 2d 252, 270 (D.D.C. 2004) (refusing to grant plaintiff's request for immediate disclosure of documents as remedy for insufficient declaration); <u>Barvick v. Cisneros</u>, 941 F. Supp. 1015, 1019-20 (D. Kan. 1996) ("This court is persuaded that an agency's failure to respond within ten days does not automatically entitle a FOIA requester to summary judgment."); <u>M.K. v. U.S. Dep't of Justice</u>, No. 96 CIV. 1307, 1996 WL 509724, at *3 (S.D.N.Y. Sept. 9, 1996) ("[T]he government's failure to respond to M.K.'s request within the statutory . . . time limit does not give M.K. the right to obtain the requested documents; it merely amounts to an exhaustion of administrative remedies and allows M.K. to bring this lawsuit."). But cf. <u>Hornes v. Executive Office for U.S. Attorneys</u>, No. 04-2190, 2006 WL 2792680, at *3 (D.D.C. Sept. 27, 2006) (finding constructive exhaustion where plaintiff lodged his in forma pauperis application with court prior to agency's belated response -- even though, due to "administrative delay," Complaint was not filed by clerk until afterward).

[115] See, e.g., <u>Oglesby</u>, 920 F.2d at 63 (ruling that if requester receives agency response before filing suit -- even one that is untimely -- requester must submit an administrative appeal before filing suit); <u>Smith v. FBI</u>, 448 F. Supp. 2d 216, 220 (D.D.C. 2006) (same); <u>Judicial Watch, Inc. v. Rossotti</u>, 285 F. Supp. 2d 17, 26 (D.D.C. 2003) (same); see also <u>FOIA Update</u>, Vol. XII, No. 2, at 3-5 ("OIP Guidance: Procedural Rules Under the D.C. Circuit's <u>Oglesby</u> Decision").

[116] 920 F.2d at 63.

ministrative appeal rights before litigating the matter.[117] If an agency makes an adverse determination after the requester has filed suit, however, the requester need not first administratively appeal that determination before pressing forward with the court action.[118]

Regardless of whether the agency's response is timely, the requester's exhaustion obligation may be excused if the agency's response fails to supply notice of the right to file an administrative appeal, as required by 5 U.S.C. § 552(a)(6)(A)(i),[119] or ultimately to supply notice of the right to

---

[117] Id. at 63-64; see, e.g., Almy v. U.S. Dep't of Justice, No. 96-1207, 1997 WL 267884, at *2-3 (7th Cir. May 7, 1997) (requester's failure to appeal agencies' "no records" responses constitutes a "failure to exhaust his administrative remedies"); Taylor, 30 F.3d at 1369 ("We therefore join the District of Columbia Circuit and the Third Circuit on this issue."); McDonnell, 4 F.3d at 1240 (applying Oglesby); Yang v. IRS, No. 06-1547, 2006 WL 2927548, at *2 (D. Minn. Oct. 12, 2006) (same); Hardy v. Lappin, No. 03-1949, 2005 WL 670753, at *1 (D.D.C. Mar. 21, 2005) (same); Allen v. IRS, No. 03-1698, 2004 WL 1638155, at *1 (D. Ariz. June 15, 2004) (same), aff'd on other grounds, 137 F. App'x 22 (9th Cir. 2005); Judicial Watch, Inc. v. FBI, 190 F. Supp. 2d 29, 33 (D.D.C. 2002) (same); Samuel v. U.S. Dep't of Justice, No. 93-0348, slip op. at 3-4 (D. Idaho Feb. 3, 1995) (same); Sloman v. U.S. Dep't of Justice, 832 F. Supp. 63, 66-67 (S.D.N.Y. 1993) (same); see also FOIA Update, Vol. XII, No. 2, at 3-5 ("OIP Guidance: Procedural Rules Under the D.C. Circuit's Oglesby Decision"). But cf. Or. Natural Desert Ass'n, 409 F. Supp. 2d at 1247 (finding some "difficulty in applying Oglesby" when agency responds in piecemeal fashion).

[118] See Pollack, 49 F.3d at 119 ("[I]t was error for the district court to conclude that it was somehow deprived of jurisdiction because [the requester] failed to file administrative appeals . . . during the litigation."); Crooker v. Tax Div. of the U.S. Dep't of Justice, No. 94-30129, 1995 WL 783236, at *8 (D. Mass. Nov. 17, 1995) (magistrate's recommendation) ("Plaintiff's complaint, in seeking the 'disclos[ure of] agency records being improperly withheld' remained alive to test the adequacy of the disclosures, once made."), adopted (D. Mass. Dec. 15, 1995), aff'd on other grounds per curiam, No. 96-1094 (1st Cir. Aug. 20, 1996). But see Voinche v. FBI, 999 F.2d 962, 963-64 (5th Cir. 1993) (holding that in action based on agency's failure to comply with FOIA's time limits for responses, disclosures made only after litigation commenced rendered action moot).

[119] See Ruotolo v. Dep't of Justice, 53 F.3d 4, 9 (2d Cir. 1995); Oglesby, 920 F.2d at 65; Leinbach v. U.S. Dep't of Justice, No. 05-744, 2006 WL 1663506, at *6 (D.D.C. June 14, 2006) (excusing the plaintiff's failure to file an administrative appeal, because the agency's response letter failed to provide him with "[correct] information regarding the administrative process to be followed"); Nurse, 231 F. Supp. 2d at 327-28 (finding constructive exhaustion because agency failed to inform requester of his right to appeal adverse decision); Lamb v. IRS, 871 F. Supp. 301, 303 (E.D. Mich. 1994) (de-

(continued...)

seek court review at the conclusion of the administrative appeal process.[120] However, so long as such notice is given, there is no particular formula or set of "magic words" that the agency must employ in giving it.[121] (For a further discussion of administrative notification requirements, see Procedural Requirements, Responding to FOIA Requests, above.) Furthermore, Oglesby counsels that a requester must file an administrative appeal within the time limit specified in an agency's FOIA regulations or else face dismissal for failure to exhaust administrative remedies.[122]

---

[119](...continued)
claring that failure to inform requester of his right to appeal constitutes failure to comply with statutory time limits, thus permitting lawsuit); see also FOIA Update, Vol. VI, No. 4, at 6 (advising of consequences of agency failure to provide requester with statement of administrative appeal rights). But cf. Envtl. Prot. Info. Ctr. & Forest Issues Group v. U.S. Forest Serv., No. 03-cv-449, slip op. at 8 (N.D. Cal. Oct. 14, 2003) (holding that "[t]he requirements under 5 U.S.C. § 552(a)(6)(A)(i) pertain [only] to the agency's decision whether or not to release the requested files," not to its decision to provide records in a format different from that requested), rev'd & remanded on other grounds, 432 F.3d 945 (9th Cir. 2005).

[120] See Nurse, 231 F. Supp. 2d at 328-29 (chiding three agency offices for all failing to notify plaintiff of his right to judicial review of denial of administrative appeal).

[121] See Kay v. FCC, 884 F. Supp. 1, 2-3 (D.D.C. 1995) (letter which "gave the Plaintiff notice of his right to secure further agency review of the adverse determination, of the manner in which he could exercise that right, of the time limits for filing such request, and of the regulatory provisions containing general procedures pertaining to review applications 'held to' more than adequately fulfill[] the purposes behind the notice provision"); see also Jones, No. 94-2294, slip op. at 5 (D. Md. Jan. 18, 1995) (requester not relieved of appeal obligation simply because agency response included statement that requester would be notified if missing records were later located; response letter also advised that it constituted "final action" of agency component and notified plaintiff of right to administratively appeal).

[122] See Oglesby, 920 F.2d at 65 n.9 (citing regulations of agencies involved); Hamilton Sec. Group, Inc. v. HUD, 106 F. Supp. 2d 23 (D.D.C. 2000) (finding that requester failed to exhaust administrative remedies when it submitted administrative appeal one day after agency's regulatory time period had expired), summary affirmance granted, No. 00-5331, 2001 WL 238162 (D.C. Cir. Feb. 23, 2001) (per curiam); Voinche v. CIA, No. 96-1708, slip op. at 3 (W.D. La. Nov. 25, 1996) (plaintiff's filing of administrative appeal eleven months after agency's response justifies dismissal notwithstanding delay of almost four years by agency in responding to request), appeal dismissed as frivolous, 119 F.3d 3 (5th Cir. 1997) (unpublished table decision); Jones v. U.S. Dep't of Justice, No. 94-2294, slip op. at 6 (D. Md.
(continued...)

An agency response that merely acknowledges receipt of a request does not constitute a "determination" under the FOIA in that it neither denies records nor grants the right to appeal the agency's determination.[123] Significantly, though, the twenty-day time period does not run until the request is received by the appropriate office in the agency,[124] as set forth in

---

[122](...continued)

Jan. 18, 1995) (awarding summary judgment to government when time limit prescribed by agency regulations for administrative appeal had expired); Lanter v. Dep't of Justice, No. 93-0034, slip op. at 2 (W.D. Okla. July 30, 1993) (court compelled to dismiss FOIA claim when plaintiff's administrative appeal from agency's response not filed in timely manner), aff'd, 19 F.3d 33 (10th Cir. 1994) (unpublished table decision); see also FOIA Update, Vol. XII, No. 2, at 4-5 (analyzing procedural requirements in light of Oglesby decision). But cf. Kennedy v. U.S. Dep't of Justice, No. 93-0209, slip op. at 2-3 (D.D.C. July 12, 1993) (when requester's affidavit attests to mailing of timely administrative appeal but agency affidavit denies receipt, court may permit requester additional time to submit another appeal and agency additional time to respond; "nothing in the FOIA statute or regulations requires the Plaintiff to do more than mail his administrative appeal in a timely fashion").

[123] See Martinez v. FBI, 3 Gov't Disclosure Serv. (P-H) ¶ 83,005, at 83,435 (D.D.C. Dec. 1, 1982); FOIA Update, Vol. XIII, No. 3, at 5 (advising that acknowledgment letters simply do not constitute responses for purposes of statutory deadlines); cf. Dickstein v. IRS, 635 F. Supp. 1004, 1006 (D. Alaska 1986) (letter referring requester to alternative "procedures which involved less red tape and bureaucratic hassle" not deemed to be denial). But cf. N.Y. Times Co. v. U.S. Dep't of Labor, 340 F. Supp. 2d 394, 399 (S.D.N.Y. 2004) (concluding that letter from agency that merely informed requester that submitter notice to 13,000 businesses would be required before final disclosure decision could be made was implicit denial of his administrative appeal).

[124] See Schoenman, 2006 WL 1126813, at *12 (recognizing that twenty-day period does not begin to run until agency receives request); Hutchins v. Dep't of Justice, No. 00-2349, 2005 WL 1334941, at *2 (D.D.C. June 6, 2005) ("Without any showing that the agency received the request, the agency has no obligation to respond to it."); see also FOIA Post, "Anthrax Mail Emergency Delays FOIA Correspondence" (posted 11/30/01) (noting that "[t]he processing of a FOIA request, with all applicable statutory deadlines, is triggered by an agency's 'receipt of . . . such request'" (quoting 5 U.S.C. § 552(a)(6)(A)(i))). But see Lion Raisins Inc. v. USDA, 354 F.3d 1072, 1077 n.5 (9th Cir. 2004) (holding without evident basis that constructive exhaustion occurred despite fact that plaintiff's administrative appeal was not received because agency mailroom became contaminated with anthrax spores).

the agency's regulations.[125] In fact, when an agency has regulations requiring that requests be made to specific offices for specific records,[126] a request will not be deemed received -- and no search for responsive records need be performed -- if the requester does not follow those regulations.[127]

---

[125] See Brumley v. U.S. Dep't of Labor, 767 F.2d 444, 445 (8th Cir. 1985) (noting that request needed to be forwarded to proper office, so one or two day slippage in response time therefore was justified); Judicial Watch, Inc. v. U.S. Dep't of Justice, No. 97-2089, slip op. at 9-11 (D.D.C. July 14, 1998) (dismissing Complaint filed "prior to the existence of any statutory obligation" because FOIA offices had not even received request that was improperly addressed prior to suit being filed); Kessler v. United States, 899 F. Supp. 644, 645 (D.D.C. 1995) (because plaintiff submitted request to IRS Headquarters, not district office where he resided, "it is as if he had made no request at all on which the IRS could render a determination"); United States v. Agunbiade, No. 90-610, 1995 WL 351058, at *6 (E.D.N.Y. May 10, 1995) ("In failing to direct his requests, in accordance with agency-specific rules, to the appropriate parties and agencies from which he sought information, [the requester] ignored the most fundamental dictates of FOIA."), aff'd sub nom. United States v. Osinowo, Nos. 95-1334, 95-1519, 1996 WL 20514 (2d Cir. Jan. 19, 1996). But cf. Nat'l Ass'n of Criminal Def. Lawyers v. U.S. Dep't of Justice, No. 97-372, slip op. at 13 (D.D.C. June 26, 1998) (while acknowledging that complaint was amended to add request for which "the administrative process had [not] run its course," nevertheless awarding interim attorney fees based upon notion that lawsuit, not pre-existing administrative process, resulted in release of records in question), interlocutory appeal dismissed for lack of juris., 182 F.3d 981 (D.C. Cir. 1999).

[126] See, e.g., Department of Justice FOIA Regulations, 28 C.F.R. § 16.3 (2006).

[127] See Church of Scientology v. IRS, 792 F.2d 146, 150 (D.C. Cir. 1986); Flowers, 307 F. Supp. 2d at 68-69 (ruling that failure to file FOIA request that comports with agency's rules constitutes failure to exhaust administrative remedies); Leytman v. N.Y. Stock Exch., No. 95 CV 902, 1995 WL 761843, at *2 (E.D.N.Y. Dec. 6, 1995); see also Antonelli, 2005 WL 3276222, at *6 (dismissing FOIA claims because plaintiff submitted requests to confinement facility officials rather than to Federal Bureau of Prison's FOIA office as required by regulation); Matsey v. U.S. Dep't of Justice, No. 03-00889, 2005 WL 1017687, at *7 (D.D.C. May 2, 2005) (finding that plaintiff failed to exhaust because he did not send properly marked letter to particular official specified in agency regulations); Thomas, 2004 WL 3185320, at *1 (finding that plaintiff did not exhaust administrative remedies, because he did not send FOIA request to proper agency location in accordance with regulations); West v. Jackson, 448 F. Supp. 2d 207, 212 n.1 (D.D.C. 2006) (same); Nash v. U.S. Dep't of Justice, 992 F. Supp. 447, 449 (D.D.C. 1998) (rejecting plaintiff's argument that location of one agency component's records in second component's files necessitates separate search of first component's files, in absence of proper FOIA request to first component), sum-
(continued...)

(For a further discussion of time limits, see Procedural Requirements, Time Limits, above.) Additionally, even when a requester has "constructively" exhausted his administrative remedies by the agency's failure to respond determinatively to the request within the statutory time limits, the requester is not entitled to a Vaughn Index during the administrative process.[128]

Whether the agency has met or exceeded its twenty-day time limit for the processing of initial responses to a request, its twenty-day time limit for the processing of administrative appeals, or its ten-day extension of either time limit,[129] requesters have been deemed not to have constructively exhausted administrative remedies when they have failed to comply with necessary requirements of the FOIA's administrative process. This has been the case, for example, when requesters have failed to:

(1)  provide required proof of identity[130] in first-party requests[131] or

---

[127](...continued)
mary affirmance granted, No. 98-5096 (D.C. Cir. July 20, 1998); Rogers v. U.S. Nat'l Reconnaissance Office, No. 94-B-2934, slip op. at 5 (N.D. Ala. Sept. 13, 1995) (holding dismissal of Air Force appropriate when request is made to Department of Defense: "It is the plaintiff's burden to make his FOIA request to the agency component which he believes possesses responsive material. Plaintiff has provided no basis to shift that burden to the agency."). But cf. Lehrfeld v. Richardson, 132 F.3d 1463, 1466 (D.C. Cir. 1998) (assuming that proper FOIA request was made, rather than deciding "whether reference to a Vaughn index in a request for information suffices to put the agency on notice that the request is being made pursuant to the FOIA").

[128] See, e.g., Schaake v. IRS, No. 91-958, 1992 U.S. Dist. LEXIS 9418, at *11 (S.D. Ill. June 3, 1992); SafeCard Servs. v. SEC, No. 84-3073, slip op. at 3-5 (D.D.C. Apr. 21, 1986); see also FOIA Update, Vol. VII, No. 3, at 6 (counseling that Vaughn Index is not required at administrative level); Judicial Watch, Inc. v. Clinton, 880 F. Supp. 1, 11 (D.D.C. 1995) ("Agencies need not provide a Vaughn Index until ordered by a court after the plaintiff has exhausted the administrative process."), aff'd on other grounds, 76 F.3d 1232 (D.C. Cir. 1996).

[129] See 5 U.S.C. § 552(a)(6)(A)-(B).

[130] See Summers v. U.S. Dep't of Justice, 999 F.2d 570, 572-73 (D.C. Cir. 1993) (holding that authorization for release of records need not be notarized, but can be attested to under penalty of perjury pursuant to 28 U.S.C. § 1746 (2000)); Lee v. U.S. Dep't of Justice, 235 F.R.D. 274, 286 (W.D. Pa. 2006) (dismissing FOIA claims because plaintiff failed to verify his identity in accordance with agency regulations by omitting his full name and place of birth from his request); Davis v. U.S. Attorney, Dist. of Md., No. 92-3233, slip op. at 2-3 (D. Md. July 5, 1994) (dismissing suit without prejudice when plaintiff failed to provide identification by notarized consent, attesta-
(continued...)

## LITIGATION CONSIDERATIONS

disclosure authorization by third parties;[132]

(2) "reasonably describe" the records sought;[133]

---

[130](...continued)
tion under 28 U.S.C. § 1746, or alternative form of identification in conformity with agency regulations).

[131] See, e.g., Lilienthal v. Parks, 574 F. Supp. 14, 17-18 (E.D. Ark. 1983).

[132] See Pusa v. FBI, No. 99-04603, slip op. at 5 (C.D. Cal. Aug. 5, 1999) (dismissing case because plaintiff did not comply with agency regulations concerning third-party requests); Harvey v. U.S. Dep't of Justice, No. CV 92-176, slip op. at 17-18 (D. Mont. Jan. 9, 1996) (declining to grant motion for production of third-party records because plaintiff failed to submit authorization at the administrative level), aff'd on other grounds, 116 F.3d 484 (9th Cir. June 3, 1997) (unpublished table decision); Freedom Magazine v. IRS, No. 91-4536, 1992 U.S. Dist. LEXIS, at *10-13 (C.D. Cal. Nov. 13, 1992) (finding that court lacked jurisdiction when, prior to filing suit, plaintiff failed to provide waivers for third-party records as required by IRS regulations). But see Martin v. U.S. Dep't of Justice, No. 96-2866, slip op. at 7-8 (D.D.C. Dec. 15, 1999) (ruling that agency was not justified in refusing to process third-party request in absence of privacy waiver because agency's regulation on privacy waivers was permissive, not mandatory, but nevertheless dismissing complaint because all records would be subject to Exemption 7(C) protection in any event); Tanoue v. IRS, 904 F. Supp. 1161, 1165 (D. Haw. 1995) (finding exhaustion despite plaintiff's failure to provide third-party waiver for IRS "return information" because agency ignored request in mistaken belief that no action was necessary inasmuch as information was unreleasable without consent in any case); LaRouche v. U.S. Dep't of Justice, No. 90-2753, 1993 WL 388601, at *7 (D.D.C. June 25, 1993) (although third-party waivers were not submitted during administrative process, "they present solely legal issues which can properly be resolved by [the] Court").

[133] See, e.g., Gillin, 980 F.2d at 822-23 (deciding that a request for records "used as a basis to conclude there was a deficiency in [requester's] tax return" did not "reasonably describe" the records of the agency's field examination of requester's tax return, since the agency concluded after completion of its field examination that there was no deficiency); Marks v. U.S. Dep't of Justice, 578 F.2d 261, 263 (9th Cir. 1978); Dale v. IRS, 238 F. Supp. 2d 99, 104-05 (D.D.C. 2002) (finding that an agency is "under no obligation to release records that have not been reasonably described" and that a request that failed to conform to agency requirements "amounted to an all-encompassing fishing expedition . . . at taxpayer expense"); see also Voinche v. U.S. Dep't of the Air Force, 983 F.2d 667, 669 n.5 (5th Cir. 1993) (concluding that administrative remedies on fee waiver request were not exhausted when requester failed to amend request to achieve specificity required by agency regulations).

(3) comply with fee requirements;[134]

---

[134] See, e.g., Pietrangelo v. U.S. Dep't of the Army, 155 F. App'x 526 (2d Cir. 2005) (affirming dismissal for failure to exhaust, despite agency's untimely response, because plaintiff neither paid nor requested waiver of assessed fees); Pollack, 49 F.3d at 119-20 (rejecting plaintiff's novel argument that untimeliness of agency response required it to provide documents free of charge); Kumar v. U.S. Dep't of Justice, No. 06-714, 2007 WL 537723, at *3 (D.D.C. Feb. 16, 2007) (concluding that "plaintiff failed to exhaust his administrative remedies because he did not pay the required fees associated with the search for records responsive to his FOIA request"); Ivey v. Snow, No. 05-CV-1095, 2006 WL 2051339, at *4 (D.D.C. July 20, 2006) (finding that plaintiff failed to exhaust administrative remedies, because he neither paid fees associated with requests nor sought fee waiver); Hicks v. Hardy, No. 04-769, 2006 WL 949918, at *2 (D.D.C. Apr. 12, 2006) (holding that "plaintiff cannot maintain his claim without paying the assessed fee," and explaining that this holds true "[r]egardless of whether . . . plaintiff 'filed' suit before or after receiving a request for payment"); Thorn v. United States, No. 04-1185, 2005 WL 3276285, at *1-2 (D.D.C. Aug. 11, 2005) (finding that plaintiff's administrative remedies were not exhausted, because he failed to pay assessed fees, and noting that "[c]ommencement of a civil action pursuant to FOIA does not relieve a requester of his obligation to pay any required fees"); Farrugia v. Executive Office for U.S. Attorneys, 366 F. Supp. 2d 56, 57 (D.D.C. 2005) (dismissing Complaint for failure to exhaust, because plaintiff failed to pay search fees that agency requested after it processed his request and properly informed him that records were available upon payment); Jeanes v. U.S. Dep't of Justice, 357 F. Supp. 2d 119, 123 (D.D.C. 2004) ("[E]xhaustion of administrative remedies does not occur until the required fees are paid or an appeal is taken from the denial of a request for a fee waiver."); Dale, 238 F. Supp. 2d at 107 (dismissing Complaint for failure to claim or establish entitlement to fee waiver or, alternatively, to commit to payment of fees); Ctr. to Prevent Handgun Violence, 981 F. Supp. at 23 (rejecting requester's "equitable tolling" argument; requester's agreement to accept sampling of documents for free does not excuse noncompliance with exhaustion requirement in subsequent fee waiver suit covering all records); Trueblood v. U.S. Dep't of the Treasury, 943 F. Supp. 64, 68 (D.D.C. 1996) ("Regardless of whether the plaintiff 'filed' suit before or after receiving a request for payment, the plaintiff has an obligation to pay for the reasonable copying and search fees assessed by the defendant."); Kuchta v. Harris, No. 92-1121, 1993 WL 87750, at *3-4 (D. Md. Mar. 25, 1993) (failure to either pay fees or request fee waiver halts administrative process and precludes exhaustion); Centracchio v. FBI, No. 92-0357, slip op. at 5 (D.D.C. Mar. 16, 1993) ("Plaintiff's failure to pay the deposit or request a waiver is fatal to his claim and requires dismissal . . . ."); Atkin v. EEOC, No. 91-2508, slip op. at 21-22 (D.N.J. Dec. 4, 1992) ("[E]xhaustion does not occur where the requester has failed to pay the assessed fees, even though the agency failed to timely process a request."), appeal dismissed for failure to prosecute, No. 93-5548 (3d Cir. Dec.

(continued...)

(4) pay authorized fees incurred in a prior request before making new requests;[135]

(5) present for review at the administrative appeal level any objection to earlier processing practices;[136]

(6) administratively request a waiver of fees;[137] or

(7) challenge a fee waiver denial at the administrative appeal

---

[134](...continued)
6, 1993); see also Kong On Imp. & Exp. Co. v. U.S. Customs & Border Prot. Bureau, No. 04-2001, 2005 WL 1458279, at *2 (D.D.C. June 20, 2005) (dismissing Complaint for failure to exhaust administrative remedies because plaintiff did not pay processing fees until after he filed suit) (appeal pending); Atkin v. EEOC, No. 92-5522, slip op. at 5 n.3 (D.N.J. Jan. 24, 1994) (subject matter jurisdiction determined as of date that Complaint was filed; fact that plaintiff paid fees after suit was instituted does not confer jurisdiction); cf. Wiggins v. Nat'l Credit Union Admin., No. 05-2332, 2007 WL 259941, at *5 (D.D.C. Jan. 30, 2007) (finding that, despite plaintiff's failure to exhaust, "no purpose would be served by having this matter delayed until plaintiff pays the required fee" because agency "has already considered and processed plaintiff's request"); Sliney v. Fed. Bureau of Prisons, No. 04-1812, 2005 WL 839540, at *4 (D.D.C. Apr. 11, 2005) (recognizing that the plaintiff's failure to pay requested fees "constitutes a failure to exhaust," but excusing that failure to pay that duplication fee because the agency "produced no evidence" that it ever informed him of the fee amount). But see Hemmings v. Freeh, No. 95-738, 2005 WL 975626, at *3 (D.D.C. Apr. 25, 2005) (denying defendant's motion to dismiss, because plaintiff "cured" his failure to exhaust by paying assessed fees, even though he did so only after government filed its dismissal motion).

[135] See, e.g., Trenerry v. IRS, No. 95-5150, 1996 WL 88459, at *1 (10th Cir. Mar. 1, 1996); Crooker, 577 F. Supp. at 1219-20; Mahler v. Dep't of Justice, 2 Gov't Disclosure Serv. (P-H) ¶ 82,032, at 82,262 (D.D.C. Sept. 29, 1981).

[136] See, e.g., Halpern v. FBI, 181 F.3d 279, 289 (2d Cir. 1999) (approving FBI practice of seeking clarification of requester's possible interest in "cross-references," and dismissing portion of suit challenging failure to process those records when plaintiff did not dispute agency action until after suit was filed); Dettmann, 802 F.2d at 1477 (same); Lair v. Dep't of Treasury, No. 03-827, 2005 WL 645228, at *3 (D.D.C. Mar. 21, 2005) (determining that plaintiff exhausted his administrative remedies as to certain aspects of agency's action on his request, but not as to others), reconsideration denied, 2005 WL 1330722 (D.D.C. June 3, 2005).

[137] See, e.g., Ivey, 2006 WL 2051339, at *4; Antonelli, 2005 WL 3276222, at *8; Trenerry, 1996 WL 88459, at *2; Voinche, 983 F.2d at 669.

stage.[138]

Although it is not yet a settled point of law, the only possible exception to the FOIA's firm exhaustion requirement concerns requests for expedited access to records -- for which the agency has a ten-calendar-day response deadline.[139] Despite statutory language referring to administrative appeals of such requests,[140] the few courts that have considered the issue thus far have ruled that exhaustion of administrative remedies is not required prior to seeking court review of an agency's denial of requested expedited access.[141] In any event, however, the denial of expedited access

---

[138] See, e.g., Fulton v. Executive Office for U.S. Attorneys, No. 05-1300, 2006 WL 1663526, at *3-4 (D.D.C. June 15, 2006) (dismissing Complaint because plaintiff did not pay fees or appeal denial of his fee waiver request); Boyd, 2005 WL 555412, at *4 ("Failure to pay the requested fees or to appeal the denial from a refusal to waive fees constitutes a failure to exhaust administrative remedies."); Oguaju v. Executive Office for U.S. Attorneys, No. 00-1930, slip op. at 1 n.1 (D.D.C. Sept. 25, 2003) (refusing to consider plaintiff's "motion to waive fees," because he failed to administratively appeal fee waiver denial), summary affirmance granted, No. 04-5407, 2005 U.S. App. LEXIS 23891 (D.C. Cir. Nov. 3, 2005); Mells v. IRS, No. 99-2030, 2001 U.S. Dist. LEXIS 1262, at *5 (D.D.C. Jan. 23, 2001) (deciding that plaintiff must pay fee or seek waiver from agency before challenging government's response concerning fees), subsequent opinion denying fee waiver, 2002 U.S. Dist. LEXIS 24275 (D.D.C. Nov. 21, 2002); Schwarz v. U.S. Dep't of Treasury, 131 F. Supp. 2d 142, 148 (D.D.C. 2000) ("Exhaustion of administrative remedies . . . includes payment of required fees or an appeal within the agency from a decision refusing to waive fees."), summary affirmance granted, No. 00-5453 (D.C. Cir. May 10, 2001); Tinsley v. Comm'r, No. 3:96-1769-P, 1998 WL 59481, at *4 (N.D. Tex. Feb. 9, 1998) (finding no exhaustion because plaintiff failed to appeal fee waiver denial).

[139] 5 U.S.C. § 552(a)(6)(E)(ii)(I).

[140] See 5 U.S.C. § 552(a)(6)(E)(ii)(II) (referring to "expeditious consideration of administrative appeals of such determinations of whether to provide expedited processing").

[141] See ACLU v. U.S. Dep't of Justice, 321 F. Supp. 2d 24, 28-29 (D.D.C. 2004) (concluding that FOIA does not require administrative appeal of agency's denial of expedition request); Elec. Privacy Info. Ctr. v. U.S. Dep't of Justice, No. 03-2078, slip op. at 5 (D.D.C. Dec. 19, 2003) (finding that administrative appeal of refusal to grant expedited processing of request is required by "neither the statute nor applicable case law"); Judicial Watch, Inc. v. FBI, No. 01-1216, slip op. at 6 (D.D.C. July 26, 2002) (noting that the statutory language "provides for direct judicial review of an agency's failure to timely respond to a request for expedited processing"); Al-Fayed v. CIA, No. 00-2092, 2000 U.S. District LEXIS 21476, at *8 (D.D.C. Sept. 20, 2000) (concluding that "[n]othing in the statute or its legislative history" indicates

(continued...)

to records, or the failure to act on such a request within ten days, certainly should not entitle a requester to seek immediate judicial review of the agency's failure to respond to the underlying request for records as well; if a requester files suit seeking access to records prior to the twenty-day time period within which an agency must respond to that underlying request, that suit is subject to ready dismissal for failure to exhaust administrative remedies.[142]

## "Open America" Stays of Proceedings

When a requester who has constructively exhausted administrative remedies due to an agency's failure to comply with the FOIA's time deadlines files a suit in court, the court may retain jurisdiction over the case -- ordinarily through issuance of a stay of proceedings -- while allowing the agency additional time to complete its processing of the request. The FOIA itself explicitly permits such a stay if it can be shown that "exceptional circumstances exist and that the agency is exercising due diligence in responding to the request."[143] This provision of the FOIA provides an important "safety valve" for agencies that have been, and continue to be, overwhelmed by increasing numbers of FOIA requests.[144]

---

[141](...continued)
that an administrative appeal of a denial of expedited processing is required before an applicant may seek judicial review), aff'd on other grounds, 254 F.3d 300 (D.C. Cir. 2001).

[142] See Dorn, 2005 WL 1126653, at *3-4 (dismissing lawsuit where Complaint was filed prematurely, even though agency ultimately responded after twenty-day period); Judicial Watch, Inc., No. 01-1216, slip op. at 8 (D.D.C. July 26, 2002) (dismissing plaintiff's Complaint seeking release of requested records, because it was filed prematurely; although the agency failed to timely respond to the Complaint, for dismissal purposes "the Court will only consider those facts and circumstances that existed at the time of the filing of the complaint, and not subsequent events"). But cf. Elec. Privacy Info. Ctr. v. Dep't of Justice, 416 F. Supp. 2d 30, 38-39 (D.D.C. 2006) (explaining that courts have "authority to impose concrete deadlines" on any agency that delays processing of expedited request beyond what is "as soon as practicable," and reasoning that delay is presumed when agency fails to respond to such request within twenty days).

[143] 5 U.S.C. § 552(a)(6)(C)(i)-(iii) (2000 & Supp. IV 2004).

[144] See Manna v. U.S. Dep't of Justice, No. 93-81, 1994 WL 808070, at *10 (D.N.J. Apr. 13, 1994) (noting "huge number of FOIA requests that have overwhelmed [agency's] human and related resources"); Cohen v. FBI, 831 F. Supp. 850, 854 (S.D. Fla. 1993) (explaining that court "cannot focus on theoretical goals alone, and completely ignore the reality that these agencies cannot possibly respond to the overwhelming number of requests received within the time constraints imposed by FOIA"); see also Natural
(continued...)

The leading case construing this FOIA provision is <u>Open America v. Watergate Special Prosecution Force</u>.[145] In <u>Open America</u>, the Court of Appeals for the District of Columbia Circuit held that "exceptional circumstances" may exist when an agency can show that it "is deluged with a volume of requests for information vastly in excess of that anticipated by Congress [and] when the existing resources are inadequate to deal with the volume of such requests within the time limits of subsection (6)(A)."[146]

The Electronic Freedom of Information Act Amendments of 1996 explicitly redefined the term "exceptional circumstances" to exclude any "delay that results from a predictable agency workload of requests . . . unless the agency demonstrates reasonable progress in reducing its backlog of pending requests."[147] This definition of "exceptional circumstances" makes it difficult for agencies seeking a stay of proceedings to argue only the existence of a FOIA backlog as the basis for a stay.[148] At the same time, in

---

[144](...continued)
<u>Res. Def. Council v. Dep't of Energy</u>, 191 F. Supp. 2d 41, 42 (D.D.C. 2002) (while noting that "it is commonly accepted that no federal agency can meet the impossibly rigorous timetable set forth in the [FOIA]," nevertheless granting motion for expedited release of records); FOIA Post, "Summary of Annual FOIA Reports for Fiscal Year 2003" (posted 7/29/04) (reporting that over three million requests were received governmentwide in Fiscal Year 2003); FOIA Post, "Supplemental Guidance on Annual FOIA Reports" (posted 8/13/01) (addressing backlog-related statistical compilations in annual FOIA reports); cf. FOIA Post, "Executive Order 13,392 Implementation Guidance" (posted 4/27/06) (observing that Executive Order 13,392 obliges agencies to "identify ways to eliminate or reduce" backlogs, which "have long been a concern under the FOIA").

[145] 547 F.2d 605 (D.C. Cir. 1976).

[146] <u>Id.</u> at 616.

[147] Electronic Freedom of Information Act Amendments of 1996, Pub. L. No. 104-231, § 7(c), 110 Stat. 3048 (codified as amended at 5 U.S.C. § 552(a)(6)(C)(ii)); <u>see also</u> FOIA Update, Vol. XVIII, No. 3, at 3-7 (advising agencies regarding reporting of backlog-related information in annual FOIA reports, as of Fiscal Year 1998).

[148] <u>See</u> H.R. Rep. No. 104-795, at 18-19 (1996); <u>see also</u> <u>Leadership Conference on Civil Rights v. Gonzales</u>, 404 F. Supp. 2d 246, 259 n.4 (D.D.C. 2005) ("An agency must show more than a great number of requests to establish[] exceptional circumstances under the FOIA."); <u>Donham v. U.S. Dep't of Energy</u>, 192 F. Supp. 2d 877, 882 (S.D. Ill. 2002) (refusing to accept agency's argument that its backlog qualifies as "exceptional circumstances" because "then the 'exceptional circumstances' provision would render meaningless the twenty-day response requirement"); <u>Al-Fayed v. CIA</u>, No. 00-2092, slip op. at 5 (D.D.C. Jan. 16, 2001) ("Rather than overturn <u>Open</u>

(continued...)

enacting the Electronic FOIA amendments, Congress specifically contemplated that other factors may be relevant to a court's determination as to whether "exceptional circumstances" exist: An agency's efforts to reduce its pending request backlog; the size and complexity of other requests being processed by the agency; the amount of classified material involved; and the number of requests for records by courts or administrative tribunals that are also pending.[149] Furthermore, the amendments include a companion provision that specifies that a requester's "refusal . . . to reasonably modify the scope of a request or arrange for an alternative time frame for processing . . . shall be considered as a factor in determining whether exceptional circumstances exist."[150]

In Open America, the D.C. Circuit ruled that the "due diligence" requirement in the FOIA may be satisfied by an agency's good faith processing of all requests on a "first-in/first-out" basis and that a requester's right to have his request processed out of turn requires a particularized showing of "exceptional need or urgency."[151] In so ruling, the D.C. Circuit rejected the notion that the mere filing of a lawsuit was a basis for such expedited treatment.[152] The Electronic FOIA amendments modified this first in/first

---

[148](...continued)
America, the 1996 amendments merely explain that predictable agency workload and a backlog alone, will not justify a stay."), aff'd on other grounds, 254 F.3d 300 (D.C. Cir. 2001); Eltayib v. U.S. Coast Guard, No. 99-1033, slip op. at 3 (D.D.C. Nov. 11, 1999) (explaining intent of Electronic FOIA amendments' modification of FOIA's "exceptional circumstances" provision), aff'd on other grounds, 53 F. App'x 127 (D.C. Cir. 2002) (per curiam); see also FOIA Update, Vol. XVII, No. 4, at 10 (describing provisions of Electronic FOIA amendments).

[149] See H.R. Rep. No. 104-795, at 24-25, 1996 U.S.C.C.A.N. 3448, 3468 (1996) (specifying factors that may be considered in determining whether "exceptional circumstances" exist).

[150] 5 U.S.C. § 552(a)(6)(C)(iii); see also Sierra Club v. U.S. Dep't of Justice, 384 F. Supp. 2d 1, 31 (D.D.C. 2004) (finding that plaintiff's refusal to reasonably modify "extremely broad" request or to arrange alternate time frame for disclosure constituted "unusual circumstances" and relieved agency of statutory timeliness requirements); Peltier v. FBI, No. 02-4328, slip op. at 8 (D. Minn. Aug. 15, 2003) (granting a stay and explaining that the plaintiff's refusal "to modify the scope of his request supports a finding of exceptional circumstances"); Al-Fayed, No. 00-2092, slip op. at 6, 12 (D.D.C. Jan. 16, 2001) (granting an Open America stay and denigrating plaintiffs' ostensible efforts to limit scope of their requests as "more symbolic than substantive"), aff'd on other grounds, 254 F.3d 300 (D.C. Cir. 2001).

[151] See Open Am., 547 F.2d at 616.

[152] Id. at 615; see also Fiduccia v. U.S. Dep't of Justice, 185 F.3d 1035,
(continued...)

out rule by explicitly allowing agencies to establish "multitrack" processing for requests, based on the amount of time and/or work involved in a particular request.[153] The amendments nevertheless preserved the principle that, within such multiple tracks, an agency's "due diligence" in handling its FOIA requests is shown by its consideration of those requests on a first-in, first-out basis.[154]

When the requirements of the statute and Open America -- as modified by the 1996 amendments -- are met, courts have readily granted agency motions to stay judicial proceedings to allow for additional time to complete the administrative processing of a request.[155] By contrast, such mo-

---

[152](...continued)
1040-41 (9th Cir. 1999) (refusing to approve automatic preference for FOIA requesters who file suit, because it "would generate many pointless and burdensome lawsuits"); Cohen, 831 F. Supp. at 854 ("[L]ittle progress would result from allowing FOIA requesters to move to the head of the line by filing a lawsuit. This would do nothing to eliminate the FOIA backlog; it would merely add to the judiciary's backlog."); cf. Hunsberger v. U.S. Dep't of Justice, No. 94-0168, 1994 U.S. Dist. LEXIS, at *1-2 (D.D.C. May 3, 1994), summary affirmance granted, No. 94-5234 (D.C. Cir. Apr. 10, 1995) (forbidding requester from circumventing Open America stay by filing new complaint based on same request). But see Exner v. FBI, 542 F.2d 1121, 1123 (9th Cir. 1976) (adopting the approach of a concurring opinion in Open America, and holding that the filing of a suit can move a requester "up the line").

[153] Electronic Freedom of Information Act Amendments of 1996, Pub. L. No. 104-231, § 7(a), 110 Stat. 3048 (codified at 5 U.S.C. § 552(a)(6)(D)(i)).

[154] Id. § 7(a)(D)(ii) (codified at 5 U.S.C. § 552(a)(6)(D)(ii)).

[155] See, e.g., Ctr. for Pub. Integrity v. U.S. Dep't of State, No. 05-2313, 2006 WL 1073066, at *5 (D.D.C. Apr. 24, 2006) (finding exceptional circumstances where an agency experienced an unpredictable "increase in the number of FOIA requests for the two most recent fiscal years and also the unforseen increase in . . . [its FOIA staff's] other information access duties"); Elec. Privacy Info. Ctr. v. U.S. Dep't of Justice, No. 02-0063, 2005 U.S. Dist. LEXIS 18876, at *12-17 (D.D.C. Aug. 31, 2005) (approving stay where FBI faced "unanticipated amount of lengthy FOIA requests," showed "reasonable progress" in reducing its backlog, and demonstrated due diligence by adopting three-tiered processing system, as well as certain electronic processing techniques); Bower v. FDA, No. 03-224, 2004 WL 2030277, at *3 (D. Me. Aug. 30, 2004) (granting stay where FDA faced "enormous litigation demands" and demonstrated reasonable progress with its FOIA backlog); Appleton v. FDA, 254 F. Supp. 2d 6, 10-11 (D.D.C. 2003) (approving an Open America stay generally, but requiring parties to confer about precise scope of plaintiff's request and to propose appropriate length of stay); Cooper v. FBI, No. 99-2305, slip op. at 2, 4 (D.D.C. June 28, 2000) (granting

(continued...)

tions have predictably proven unsuccessful when agencies have failed to set forth sufficient facts to demonstrate the propriety of such a stay.[156]

---

[155](...continued)
defendant's stay motion for "at least" four months); Judicial Watch, Inc. v. U.S. Dep't of State, No. 99-1130, slip op. at 2 (D.D.C. Feb. 17, 2000) (approving ten-month stay because "unanticipated workload, the inadequate resources of the agency, and the complexity of many of the requests" constitute exceptional circumstances), appeal dismissed as interlocutory, No. 00-5095 (D.C. Cir. June 2, 2000); Emerson v. CIA, No. 99-0274, 1999 U.S. Dist. LEXIS 19511, at *3-4 (D.D.C. Dec. 16, 1999) (granting two-year stay because of "extraordinary circumstances" and multiple agency efforts to alleviate FOIA backlog); Summers v. CIA, No. 98-1682, slip op. at 4 (D.D.C. July 26, 1999) (finding that FBI's FOIA procedures are "fair and expeditious" and that exceptional circumstances exists, warranting six-month stay of proceedings); Judicial Watch, Inc. v. U.S. Dep't of Justice, No. 97-2869, slip op. at 6-8 (D.D.C. Aug. 25, 1998) (finding that agency exercised due diligence when both parties agreed that exceptional circumstances existed and requester failed to show exceptional need for records); Narducci v. FBI, No. 98-0130, slip op. at 1 (D.D.C. July 17, 1998) (ordering thirty-four-month stay because of "deluge[]" of requests coupled with "reasonable progress" in reducing backlog). See generally FOIA Update, Vol. XIX, No. 4, at 7 (describing FBI effort to reduce backlog through use of negotiation team); FOIA Update, Vol. XIX, No. 3, at 5-6 (describing Department of Justice efforts at backlog reduction).

[156] See, e.g., Leadership Conference on Civil Rights, 404 F. Supp. at 259 (rejecting agency's stay request predicated on "large backlog of pending FOIA requests, including 16 requests which take much longer to process than other[s]," reallocation of resources to respond to court orders, and "personnel issues"); The Wilderness Soc'y v. U.S. Dep't of the Interior, No. 04-0650, 2005 WL 3276256, at *10 (D.D.C. Sept. 12, 2005) (denying stay because agency failed to present any evidence to support claim that it faced unanticipated volume of FOIA requests); Eltayib, No. 99-1033, slip op. at 4 (D.D.C. Nov. 11, 1999) (denying stay and taking agency to task for failing to take any measures to comport with statutory requirements for showing reasonable progress); Los Alamos Study Group v. Dep't of Energy, No. 99-201, slip op. at 4-5 (D.N.M. Oct. 26, 1999) (declining to approve stay of proceedings predicated on agency's need to review sensitive materials, because such review "is part of the predictable agency workload of requests"); cf. Hall v. CIA, No. 04-0814, 2005 WL 850379, at *5 (D.D.C. Apr. 13, 2005) (refusing to accept the CIA's argument that a stay was warranted while the agency awaited "final guidance from the Court" on the plaintiff's previous lawsuit); Homick v. U.S. Dep't of Justice, No. 98-00557, slip op. at 2 (N.D. Cal. Oct. 27, 2004) (denying FBI's motion for stay because it "repeatedly failed to meet various [court imposed] deadlines . . . over more than two years"). But cf. Nat'l Sec. Archive v. U.S. Dep't of the Air Force, No. 05-571, 2006 WL 1030152, at *5 (D.D.C. Apr. 19, 2006) (finding that agency failed to process plaintiff's requests with due diligence, but declining to

(continued...)

Even in those instances in which some additional processing time is appropriate, courts have undertaken increasing scrutiny of agency claims that long delays are warranted.[157]

Of course, any stay necessarily includes the time required to consult with other agencies whose information is included in the responsive records, particularly when such review by the originating agency is mandatory.[158] In addition, an "Open America" stay should, when necessary, in-

---

[156](...continued)
order immediate disclosure of unprocessed documents because they first had to be reviewed for declassification; "[r]elease of classified documents cannot be ordered without such review no matter how dilatory an agency might be").

[157] See Fiduccia, 185 F.3d at 1041 (overturning stay of proceedings allowed by district court, because delay was only "ordinary and expected"); Hendricks v. U.S. Dep't of Justice, No. 05-05-H, slip op. at 13 (D. Mont. Aug. 18, 2005) (concluding that FBI did not demonstrate exceptional circumstances sufficient to warrant stay for full length of time requested); Bower, 2004 WL 2030277, at *3 (approving seven-month stay, rather than leaving FDA "to its own, unmonitored devices" for full two-and-one-half-year period that it had requested); Ruiz v. U.S. Dep't of Justice, No. 00-0105, slip op. at 3 (D.D.C. Sept. 27, 2001) (acknowledging that the agency made "a satisfactory showing that a stay . . . is warranted," but reducing the stay's length from the thirty-three months requested to only seven months); Beneville v. U.S. Dep't of Justice, No. 98-6137, slip op. at 8 (D. Or. Dec. 17, 1998) (declining to approve full stay of proceedings requested by FBI regarding Unabomber files); Grecco v. Dep't of Justice, No. 97-0419, slip op. at 2 (D.D.C. Aug. 24, 1998) (granting two-year stay rather than four-year stay that was requested by FBI); see also Peralta v. FBI, No. 94-760, slip op. at 2 (D.D.C. June 6, 1997) (reducing Open America stay by four months because of enactment of Electronic FOIA amendments, and requiring that agency justify additional time needed for processing on basis of new statutory standard), vacated & remanded on other grounds, 136 F.3d 169 (D.C. Cir. 1998); cf. Donham, 192 F. Supp. 2d at 884 (refusing to set processing deadline, but also refusing to grant open-ended stay of proceedings); Gilmore v. U.S. Dep't of Energy, 4 F. Supp. 2d 912, 925 (N.D. Cal. 1998) ("Where a pattern and practice of late responses is alleged . . . a normal, predictable workload cannot constitute 'exceptional circumstances.'"), dismissed per stipulation, No. 95-0285 (N.D. Cal. Apr. 3, 2000).

[158] See, e.g., Gilmore v. U.S. Dep't of State, No. C 95-1098, slip op. at 25-26, 29 (N.D. Cal. Feb. 9, 1996) (An "agency receiving requests for information classified by another agency 'shall refer copies . . . to the originating agency for processing.'" (quoting Exec. Order No. 12,958 § 3.7(b), 3 C.F.R. 333 (1996), reprinted in 50 U.S.C. § 435 note (2000), and reprinted in abridged form in FOIA Update, Vol. XVI, No. 2, at 5-10); cf. Nat'l Sec. Archive, 2006 WL 1030152, at *4-5 (concluding that agency failed to exercise
(continued...)

clude the time required for preparation of a <u>Vaughn</u> Index.[159] While the <u>Open America</u> decision itself does not address the additional time needed by an agency to justify nondisclosure of any withheld records once they are processed, courts have, as a practical matter, tended to merge the record-processing and affidavit-preparation stages of a case when issuing stays of proceedings under <u>Open America</u>.[160] And when there is a large volume of responsive documents that have not been processed, a court may grant a stay of proceedings that provides for interim or "timed" releases and/or interim status reports on agency processing efforts.[161]

An "<u>Open America</u>" stay always may be denied when the requester can show an "exceptional need or urgency" for having his request processed out of turn.[162] Traditionally, such a showing was found if the requester's life or personal safety, or substantial due process rights, would be jeopard-

---

[158](...continued)
due diligence in responding to plaintiff's requests, but nevertheless recognizing that it must complete declassification review process, which entails "referral to multiple agencies").

[159] See <u>FOIA Update</u>, Vol. IX, No. 4, at 5 (discussing relevant cases).

[160] See, e.g., <u>Lisee</u>, 741 F. Supp. at 989-90 ("<u>Open America</u>" stay granted for both processing records and preparing <u>Vaughn</u> Index); <u>Ettlinger v. FBI</u>, 596 F. Supp. 867, 878-79 (D. Mass. 1984) (same); <u>Shaw v. Dep't of State</u>, 1 Gov't Disclosure Serv. (P-H) ¶ 80,250, at 80,630 (D.D.C. July 31, 1980) (same).

[161] See, e.g., <u>Al-Fayed v. CIA</u>, No. 00-2092, slip op. at 12 (D.D.C. Jan. 16, 2001) (granting stays for four agencies, but requiring status reports every sixty days), <u>aff'd on other grounds</u>, 254 F.3d 300 (D.C. Cir. 2001); <u>Raulerson v. Reno</u>, No. 95-2053, slip op. at 1 (D.D.C. Sept. 11, 1998) (approving thirty-month stay to process over 19,000 pages, but ordering four interim status reports); <u>Samuel Gruber Educ. Project v. U.S. Dep't of Justice</u>, No. 90-1912, slip op at 6 (D.D.C. Feb. 8, 1991) (granting nearly two-year stay, but requiring six-month progress reports); <u>Hinton v. FBI</u>, 527 F. Supp. 223, 223-25 (E.D. Pa. 1981) (staying proceedings, but ordering interim releases at ninety-day intervals); <u>cf. Bower</u>, 2004 WL 2030277, at *3 (requiring FDA to produce status report at end of seven-month stay, which included estimated time by which document production would be completed).

[162] See <u>Open Am.</u>, 547 F.2d at 616; <u>see also Edmonds v. FBI</u>, No. 02-1294, 2002 WL 32539613, at *4 (D.D.C. Dec. 3, 2002) (denying motion for an <u>Open America</u> stay even though it was justified by exceptional circumstances, and ordering expedited processing); <u>Aguilera v. FBI</u>, 941 F. Supp. 144, 149-52 (D.D.C. 1996) (finding initially that FBI satisfied "exceptional circumstances-due diligence test" warranting eighty-seven-month delay, but subsequently granting expedited access due to exigent circumstances), <u>appeal dismissed</u>, No. 98-5035 (D.C. Cir. Mar. 18, 1998).

ized by the failure to process a request immediately.[163] The Department of Justice, as a matter of administrative policy, also expedited FOIA requests when there was "widespread and exceptional media interest" in information which "involve possible questions about the government's integrity which affect public confidence."[164]

The Electronic FOIA amendments generally codified these requirements.[165] Under them, agencies must have regulations providing for the granting of expedited treatment in cases of "compelling need" or "in other cases determined by the agency."[166] "Compelling need" is defined by law to encompass a situation in which withholding of the requested records "could reasonably be expected to pose an imminent threat to the life or

---

[163] See, e.g., Neely v. FBI, No. 97-0786, slip op. at 9 (W.D. Va. July 27, 1998) (granting expedited processing of FOIA request where plaintiff has pending motion for new criminal trial based on alleged false trial testimony and needs documents for proof), vacated & remanded on other grounds, 208 F.3d 461 (4th Cir. 2000); Ferguson v. FBI, 722 F. Supp. 1137, 1141-44 (S.D.N.Y. 1989) (need for documents, not otherwise available, in post-conviction challenge and upcoming criminal trial); Cleaver v. Kelley, 427 F. Supp. 80, 81 (D.D.C. 1976) (plaintiff facing multiple criminal charges carrying possible death penalty in state court); see also FOIA Update, Vol. IV, No. 3, at 3 ("OIP Guidance: When to Expedite FOIA Requests"); cf. Kitchen v. FBI, No. 94-5159, 1995 WL 311615, at *1 (D.C. Cir. Apr. 27, 1995) (per curiam) (requester has not shown sufficiently serious harm to warrant interlocutory appeal when deportation hearing not yet scheduled (citing Ray, 770 F. Supp. at 1550-51)); Billington v. U.S. Dep't of Justice, No. 92-462, slip op. at 3-5 (D.D.C. July 27, 1992) (expedited treatment denied despite pendency of prosecutions, when requester had not shown any likelihood that files contain "materially exculpatory information"). Compare Freeman v. U.S. Dep't of Justice, No. 92-557, slip op. at 6 (D.D.C. Oct. 2, 1992) (expedited processing granted when scope of request limited, Jencks Act material unavailable in state prosecution, and information useful to plaintiff's criminal defense might have been contained in requested documents), with Freeman v. U.S. Dep't of Justice, No. 92-557, 1993 WL 260694, at *5 (D.D.C. June 28, 1993) (denying further expedited treatment when processing "would require a hand search of approximately 50,000 pages, taking approximately 120 days"). But see Gilmore v. FBI, No. 93-2117, slip op. at 1, 3 (N.D. Cal. July 26, 1994) (expediting request despite showing of due diligence and exceptional circumstances, based upon perfunctory finding that "[p]laintiff has sufficiently shown that the information he seeks will become less valuable if the FBI processes his request on a first-in, first-out basis").

[164] Department of Justice FOIA Regulations, 28 C.F.R. § 16.5(d)(iv) (1996).

[165] See FOIA Update, Vol. XVII, No. 4, at 10 (describing Electronic FOIA amendment provisions).

[166] 5 U.S.C. § 552(a)(6)(E)(i); see also FOIA Update, Vol. XVII, No. 4, at 10.

physical safety of an individual."[167]  Additionally, the Electronic FOIA amendments specify that expedited processing will be granted when there exists, "with respect to a request made by a person primarily engaged in disseminating information, urgency to inform the public concerning actual or alleged Federal Government activity."[168]

The D.C. Circuit, in discussing the second part of this statutory standard, has observed that "'[g]iven the finite resources generally available for filling FOIA requests, unduly generous use of the expedited processing procedure would unfairly disadvantage other requesters who do not qualify for its treatment.'"[169]  It then held that a request for records pertaining to the deaths of Princess Diana and Dodi Al-Fayed did not satisfy the "urgency to inform" standard because the events at issue were over two years old, and "[a]lthough these topics may continue to be newsworthy, none of the events at issue is the subject of a currently unfolding story."[170] Lower courts have similarly limited the reach of this expedited access standard.[171]

---

[167] 5 U.S.C. § 552(a)(6)(E)(v)(I).

[168] Id. § 552(a)(6)(E)(v)(II); see also 28 C.F.R. § 16.5(d) (specifying procedures for expedited processing, including when there is "[a]n urgency to inform the public about an actual or alleged federal government activity, if made by a person primarily engaged in disseminating information"); Tripp v. DOD, 193 F. Supp. 2d 229, 241 (D.D.C. 2002) (finding that plaintiff does not meet the criteria for expedited processing, because while she "has been the object of media attention," she is not primarily engaged in disseminating information to the media); cf. Appleton, 254 F. Supp. 2d at 10 n.5 (ruling that the plaintiff's advanced age is not a basis contemplated by the FOIA for expedited access).

[169] Al-Fayed v. CIA, 254 F.3d 300, 310 (D.C. Cir. 2001) (quoting H.R. Rep. No. 104-795, at 26).

[170] Id. at 311 (observing further that "[e]ven if the information sought is properly characterized as 'current,' it cannot fairly be said to concern a matter of 'exigency to the American public,'" and noting that "[t]here is no evidence in the record that there is substantial interest, either on the part of the American public or the media, in this particular aspect of plaintiff's allegations") (footnote omitted).

[171] See Tripp, 193 F. Supp. 2d at 242 (ruling that inasmuch as events giving rise to FOIA request were three years old, there was no "great news media interest" and thus no "urgent need" for requested information); see also IEEE Spectrum v. Dep't of Justice, No. 05-0865, slip op. at 2 (D.D.C. Feb. 16, 2006) (denying expedited processing where the plaintiff, a magazine, made only self-serving statements that the subject of the request was "a currently unfolding story" and "newsworthy"); Elec. Privacy Info. Ctr. v. DOD, 355 F. Supp. 2d 98, 102 (D.D.C. 2004) (denying expedited processing

(continued...)

Absent truly exceptional circumstances, though, courts have generally declined to order expedited processing when records are "needed" for post-judgment attacks on criminal convictions,[172] or for use in other civil litigation.[173] Employing an extremely unusual tactic, one plaintiff sought in

---

[171](...continued)
where plaintiff failed to show interest in particular data-mining software that was subject of its request, and instead relied on general public interest in "umbrella" subject of data mining); Elec. Privacy Info. Ctr. v. U.S. Dep't of Justice, No. 03-2078, slip op. at 10 (D.D.C. Dec. 19, 2003) (deciding that there was no urgency to inform the public that warranted expedited access, because "[t]he appearance of thirty-one newspaper articles does not make a story a matter of 'current exigency'"); see also FOIA Post, "FOIA Counselor Q&A" (posted 1/24/06) (discussing the meaning of the term "umbrella issue," and advising of its use "when considering public interest issues under the FOIA").

[172] See, e.g., Ruiz v. U.S. Dep't of Justice, No. 00-0105, slip op. at 3 (D.D.C. Sept. 27, 2001) ("To the extent that records are intended for use in an attack on plaintiff's criminal conviction, this situation does not constitute an exceptional need."); Edmond v. U.S. Attorney, 959 F. Supp. 1, 4 (D.D.C. 1997) (explaining that a "mere challenge to a conviction" is not sufficient to warrant expedited processing); Schweihs v. FBI, 933 F. Supp. 719, 723 (N.D. Ill. 1996) (denying expedited processing of records related to plaintiff's conviction, despite plaintiff's claims of ill health); Russell v. Barr, No. 92-2546, slip op. at 2 (D.D.C. Mar. 5, 1993) (holding "[p]laintiff's claim that the requested information may 'minister [his] defense in the civil proceeding and motion for a new trial' in his criminal proceeding" to be inadequate to justify expedition). But see Aguilera, 941 F. Supp. at 152-53 (ordering expedited processing for a request not scheduled for completion for nearly ninety months, because "[p]laintiff has demonstrated that he faces grave punishment, his reason to believe the documents may assist in his defense has been corroborated by objective proof, his request is limited in scope, and the criminal discovery process is unavailable").

[173] See, e.g., Price v. CIA, No. 90-1507, 1990 WL 141480, at *1 (4th Cir. Oct. 2, 1990) (affirming denial of expedited access to documents claimed to be needed for lawsuit soon to be barred by statute of limitations); Rogers v. U.S. Nat'l Reconnaissance Office, No. 94-B-2934, slip op. at 17 (N.D. Ala. Sept. 13, 1995) ("Courts have consistently rejected claims of urgency based on private litigation concerns."); Cohen, 831 F. Supp. at 854 (refusing to order expedited access for records needed in civil lawsuit); cf. Armstrong v. Bush, 807 F. Supp. 816, 819 (D.D.C. 1992) (according priority to additional FOIA requests added to those already subject of litigation, when responsive records might otherwise be destroyed). But see Edmonds, No. 02-1294, slip op. at 7 (D.D.C. Dec. 3, 2002) (granting expedition even though a pending lawsuit is what motivated plaintiff's requests, based upon the questionable reasoning that "[n]othing in the DOJ's regulation disqualified a plaintiff from obtaining expedited processing where the documents may

(continued...)

lieu of seeking expedited processing of his FOIA request to have a federal court stay his state habeas corpus proceedings pending a response to his FOIA request.[174] Rejecting such a novel stay application, the court found that it was constrained by the constitutional doctrine of Younger v. Harris[175] from interfering in the state court proceedings.[176] (See also further discussion under Procedural Requirements, Expedited Processing, above.)

## Adequacy of Search

In many FOIA suits, the defendant agency will face challenges not only to its reliance on particular exemptions, but also to the nature and extent of its search for responsive documents. Sometimes, that is all that a plaintiff will dispute.[177] (For discussions of administrative considerations in conducting searches, see Procedural Requirements, Searching for Records, above.) To prevail in a FOIA action, the agency must show that it made "'a good-faith effort to conduct a search for the requested records, using methods which can be reasonably expected to produce the information requested.'"[178] The fundamental question is not "'whether there might

---

[173](...continued)
assist her in another lawsuit, nor is there any basis to conclude that a whistleblower who has brought suit against a government agency as a result of her firing cannot also satisfy the DOJ's regulation for expedited processing").

[174] See Sosa v. FBI, No. 93-1126, slip op. at 1 (D.D.C. Nov. 4, 1993); see also Arriaga v. West, No. 00-1171, 2000 WL 870867, at *2 (Vet. App. June 21, 2000) (dismissing for lack of jurisdiction plaintiff's mandamus petition that was filed in his attempt to require Secretary of Veterans Affairs to release records requested under FOIA and to stay proceedings before administrative board until his petition was decided).

[175] 401 U.S. 37 (1971).

[176] See Sosa, No. 93-1126, slip op. at 1 (D.D.C. Nov. 4, 1993).

[177] See, e.g., Iturralde v. Comptroller of Currency, 315 F.3d 311, 313 (D.C. Cir. 2003) (explaining that adequacy of agency's search is at issue); Perry v. Block, 684 F.2d 121, 126 (D.C. Cir. 1982) (noting that plaintiff contested only adequacy of search).

[178] Nation Magazine v. U.S. Customs Serv., 71 F.3d 885, 890 (D.C. Cir. 1995) (quoting Oglesby v. U.S. Dep't of the Army, 920 F.2d 57, 68 (D.C. Cir. 1990)); see Tavakoli-Nouri v. CIA, No. 00-3620, 2001 U.S. App. LEXIS 24676, at *7 (3d Cir. Oct. 18, 2001) (same); Maynard v. CIA, 986 F.2d 547, 559 (1st Cir. 1993) (noting that "crucial" search issue is whether agency's search was "'reasonably calculated to discover the requested documents'" (quoting SafeCard Servs. v. SEC, 926 F.2d 1197, 1201 (D.C. Cir. 1991))); Maydak v. U.S. Dep't of Justice, 254 F. Supp. 2d 23, 38 (D.D.C. Mar. 21, 2003) ("In determining the adequacy of a FOIA search, the Court is guided by principles
(continued...)

exist any other documents possibly responsive to the request, but rather whether the search for those documents was adequate.'"[179] In other words, simply put, "the focus of the adequacy inquiry is not on the results."[180]

---

[178](...continued)
of reasonableness.").

[179] Steinberg v. U.S. Dep't of Justice, 23 F.3d 548, 551 (D.C. Cir. 1994) (quoting Weisberg v. U.S. Dep't of Justice, 745 F.2d 1476, 1485 (D.C. Cir. 1984)); see Citizens Comm'n on Human Rights v. FDA, 45 F.3d 1325, 1328 (9th Cir. 1995) (same); Nation Magazine, 71 F.3d at 892 n.7 (explaining that "there is no requirement that an agency [locate] all responsive documents"); Ethyl Corp. v. EPA, 25 F.3d 1241, 1246 (4th Cir. 1994) ("In judging the adequacy of an agency search for documents the relevant question is not whether every single potentially responsive document has been unearthed."); In re Wade, 969 F.2d 241, 249 n.11 (7th Cir. 1992) (declaring that issue is not whether other documents might exist, but whether search was adequate); Van Mechelen v. U.S. Dep't of the Interior, No. 05-5393, 2005 WL 3007121, at *2 (W.D. Wash. Nov. 9, 2005) (same); Atkin v. IRS, No. 04-CV-0080, 2005 WL 1155127, at *5 (N.D. Ohio Mar. 30, 2005) (same); Sephton v. FBI, 365 F. Supp. 2d 91, 101 (D. Mass. 2005) (explaining that FOIA does not require review of "every single file that might conceivably contain responsive information"), aff'd, 442 F.3d 27 (1st Cir. 2006); Snyder v. CIA, 230 F. Supp. 2d 17, 21 (D.D.C. 2002) (stipulating that FOIA does not require a search of "every conceivable area where responsive records might be found"); cf. Raulerson v. Reno, No. 96-120, slip op. at 5 (D.D.C. Feb. 26, 1999) (suggesting that agency's failure to locate complaints filed by plaintiff, the existence of which agency did not dispute, "casts substantial doubt" on adequacy of agency's search), summary affirmance granted, No. 99-5300 (D.C. Cir. Nov. 23, 1999).

[180] Hornbostel v. U.S. Dep't of the Interior, 305 F. Supp. 2d 21, 28 (D.D.C. 2003), aff'd, No. 03-5257, 2004 WL 1900562 (D.C. Cir. Aug. 25, 2004); see Grand Cent. P'ship v. Cuomo, 166 F.3d 473, 489 (2d Cir. 1999) ("'[T]he factual question . . . is whether the search was reasonably calculated to discover the requested documents, not whether it actually uncovered every document extant.'" (quoting SafeCard Servs., 926 F.2d at 1201)); In re Wade, 969 F.2d at 249 n.11 (declaring that issue is not whether other documents may exist, but whether search was adequate); Meeropol v. Meese, 790 F.2d 942, 952-53 (D.C. Cir. 1986) ("[A] search is not unreasonable simply because it fails to produce all relevant material; no search of this [large] size . . . will be free from error."); Elliot v. U.S. Attorney Gen., No. 06-1128, 2006 WL 3191234, at *3 (D.D.C. Nov. 2, 2006) (concluding that agency "conducted a search that was reasonable," even though no records were located); Judicial Watch v. Rossotti, 285 F. Supp. 2d 17, 26 (D.D.C. 2003) ("Perfection is not the standard by which the reasonableness of a FOIA search is measured."); Garcia v. U.S. Dep't of Justice, 181 F. Supp. 2d 356, 368 (S.D.N.Y. 2002) ("The agency is not expected to take extraordinary measures to find the requested records."); Citizens Against UFO Secrecy, Inc. v. DOD, No.

(continued...)

## LITIGATION CONSIDERATIONS

The adequacy of any FOIA search, of course, is necessarily "dependent upon the circumstances of the case."[181] Searches through agency or component indices, for example, which contain records in which a requester is the subject of the record, have been held to be adequate in almost all instances.[182] With respect to the processing of "cross references" or "see

---

[180](...continued)
99-00108, slip op. at 8 (D. Ariz. Mar. 30, 2000) (declaring that "[a] fruitless search result is immaterial if [d]efendant can establish that it conducted a search reasonably calculated to uncover all relevant documents"), aff'd, 21 F. App'x 774 (9th Cir. 2001); Boggs v. United States, 987 F. Supp. 11, 20 (D.D.C. 1997) (noting that the role of the court is to determine the reasonableness of the search, "not whether the fruits of the search met plaintiff's aspirations"); Freeman v. U.S. Dep't of Justice, No. 90-2754, slip op. at 3 (D.D.C. Oct. 16, 1991) ("The FOIA does not require that the government go fishing in the ocean for fresh water fish."). But see Raulerson, No. 96-120, slip op. at 5 (D.D.C. Feb. 26, 1999) (suggesting that the agency's failure to locate complaints filed by plaintiff, the existence of which the agency did not dispute, "casts substantial doubt" on the adequacy of the agency's search).

[181] Davis v. Dep't of Justice, 460 F.3d 92, 103 (D.C. Cir. 2006) ("The 'adequacy of an agency's search is measured by a standard of reasonableness, and is dependent upon the circumstances of the case.'" (quoting Schrecker v. Dep't of Justice, 349 F.3d 657, 663 (D.C. Cir. 2003))); Truitt v. Dep't of State, 897 F.2d 540, 542 (D.C. Cir. 1990); see Rugiero v. U.S. Dep't of Justice, 257 F.3d 534, 547 (6th Cir. 2001) ("The FOIA requires a reasonable search tailored to the nature of the request."); Campbell v. U.S. Dep't of Justice, 164 F.3d 20, 28 (D.C. Cir. 1998) (same); Maynard, 986 F.2d at 559 (explaining that adequacy of search "depends upon the facts of each case"); Gavin v. SEC, No. 04-4522, 2005 WL 2739293, at *7 (D. Minn. Oct. 24, 2005) (finding the agency's search sufficient "in light of the facts of this case"); Landmark Legal Found. v. EPA, 272 F. Supp. 2d 59, 62 (D.D.C. 2003) (citing Weisberg, 745 F.2d at 1485); LaRouche v. U.S. Dep't of Justice, No. 90-2753, 2001 U.S. Dist. LEXIS 25416, at *5 (D.D.C. July 5, 2001) ("An examination of the . . . search must take into account the totality of the circumstances.").

[182] See, e.g., Church of Scientology Int'l v. U.S. Dep't of Justice, 30 F.3d 224, 230 (1st Cir. 1994) (finding to be sufficient agency's search of United States Attorney's Office computerized record system); Maynard, 986 F.2d at 562 (concluding that Treasury Department properly limited its search to its automated Treasury Enforcement Communications System (TECS)); Truesdale v. U.S. Dep't of Justice, No. 03-1332, 2005 WL 3273093, at *6 (D.D.C. July 22, 2005) (upholding DEA's search of its Narcotics and Dangerous Drugs Information System, which "identifies individuals by name, social security number, and/or date of birth" and provides "means for obtaining DEA investigative files"); Ledesma v. U.S. Marshals Serv., No. 04-1413, 2005 WL 405452, at *3 (D.D.C. Feb. 18, 2005) (finding that the United States Marshals Service properly searched for records concerning the plaintiff's deten-
(continued...)

references" -- records in which the subject of the request is just mentioned -- only those parts of the file that pertain directly to the subject of the request ordinarily are considered within the scope of the request.[183] Further,

---

[182](...continued)
tion by using "the Prisoner Processing and Population Management/Prisoner Tracking . . . and Warrant Information Network systems"), summary affirmance granted, No. 05-5150, 2006 U.S. App. LEXIS 11218 (D.C. Cir. Apr. 19. 2006); Barreiro v. Executive Office for U.S. Attorneys, No. 03-0720, slip op. at 5 (D.D.C. Dec. 31, 2003) (upholding search for records concerning plaintiff's criminal case using computerized case-tracking system that permits retrieval of all prosecution records), aff'd, No. 04-5071, 2004 WL 2451753 (D.C. Cir. Nov. 1, 2004); Raulerson v. Ashcroft, 271 F. Supp. 2d 17, 22 (D.D.C. 2002) ("[I]f the FBI believes that a search of its [Central Records System] is sufficient, it need not go further."), dismissed for lack of prosecution, No. 03-5054 (D.C. Cir. Apr. 4, 2003); Blanton v. U.S. Dep't of Justice, 63 F. Supp. 2d 35, 41 (D.D.C. 1999) (finding no requirement to search informant files for references to individual when such references would be "flagged" by agency's "cross-reference" search for records about that individual), motion for partial reconsideration granted on other grounds, No. 93-1789 (D.D.C. June 2, 2000), aff'd, 64 F. App'x 787 (D.C. Cir. 2003) (per curiam); Murphy v. IRS, 79 F. Supp. 2d 1180, 1185 (D. Haw. 1999) (noting that because technical advice memoranda all would be logged into Technical Management Information System, search of that database was adequate); see also Campbell, 164 F.3d at 28 ("[T]he FBI need not conduct ELSUR (electronic surveillance) and tickler (temporary file) searches when the FOIA requester does not expressly ask it to do so. [It] has discretion to conduct a standard search in response to a general request . . . ."); Piper v. U.S. Dep't of Justice, 294 F. Supp. 2d 16, 24 (D.D.C. 2003) (refusing to fault an FBI Central Index search despite the fact that it did not turn up twenty-eight missing records; the possibility that "some documents may have slipped through the bureaucratic cracks of the vast administrative structure that is the FBI" does not make the FBI's search unreasonable), reconsideration denied, 312 F. Supp. 2d 17 (D.D.C. 2004). But see Summers v. U.S. Dep't of Justice, No. 89-3300, slip op. at 6 (D.D.C. June 13, 1995) (holding the agency's search inadequate despite the retrieval of over 30,000 responsive pages pertaining to former FBI Director J. Edgar Hoover's telephone logs and appointment calendars, because the agency's declaration did "not explain the search terms used, the type of search performed[,] and [did] not aver 'that all files likely to contain responsive materials . . . were searched'"); Steinberg v. U.S. Dep't of the Treasury, No. 93-2348, slip op. at 8 (D.D.C. Sept. 18, 1995) (declaring that search solely of TECS was inadequate when "it is reasonable to conclude that additional systems exist," that TECS does not include these record systems, and that it would not be unduly burdensome to search other systems).

[183] See Romero-Cicle v. U.S. Dep't of Justice, No. 05-2303, slip op. at 6 (D.D.C. Nov. 20, 2006) (declaring that "[s]ince plaintiff failed to raise the scope of the search issue in his administrative appeal, he is precluded from

(continued...)

agencies that maintain field offices in various locations ordinarily are not obligated to search offices other than those to which the request has been directed.[184]

---

[183](...continued)
challenging [the agency's] decision to limit its search for responsive records" now in litigation); Posner v. Dep't of Justice, 2 Gov't Disclosure Serv. (P-H) ¶ 82,229, at 82,650 (D.D.C. Mar. 9, 1982); see also FOIA Update, Vol. XVI, No. 3, at 3 (providing policy guidance on "scoping" of requests, and suggesting that an important consideration is that of fashioning ways "to devote [an agency's] limited resources to serving . . . FOIA requesters as efficiently and economically as reasonably possible"); accord Attorney General Ashcroft's FOIA Memorandum, reprinted in FOIA Post (posted 10/15/01) (emphasizing the importance of maintaining "a government that is fully functional and efficient").

[184] See, e.g., Kowalczyk v. Dep't of Justice, 73 F.3d 386, 389 (D.C. Cir. 1996) (stating that when "the requester clearly states that he wants all agency records . . . regardless of their location, but fails to direct the agency's attention to any particular office other than the one receiving the request, then the agency need pursue only a lead . . . that is both clear and certain"); Church of Scientology v. IRS, 792 F.2d 146, 150 (D.C. Cir. 1986) (finding that when agency regulations require requests be made to specific offices for specific records, there is no need to search additional offices when those regulations are not followed); Marks v. U.S. Dep't of Justice, 578 F.2d 261, 263 (9th Cir. 1978) (finding no duty to search FBI field offices when requester directed request only to FBI Headquarters and did not specify which field offices he wanted searched); Tooley v. Bush, No. 06-306, 2006 WL 3783142, at *13 (D.D.C. Dec. 21, 2006) ("Where a requester submits his request only to the FBI headquarters and not to individual field offices, the FBI is under no obligation to search all of its field offices."); Dayton Newspapers, Inc. v. VA, 257 F. Supp. 2d 988, 999-1001 (S.D. Ohio 2003) (granting summary judgment to agency because requested records were maintained by agency's regional offices, not central office where request was erroneously submitted); Maydak, 254 F. Supp. 2d at 44-45 (refusing to find search inadequate because agency has "no statutory obligation to proceed with a search of all of its field offices"); Prescott v. Dep't of Justice, No. 00-0187, slip op. at 7 (D.D.C. Aug. 10, 2001) (finding search of FBI Headquarters reasonable, based on Department of Justice regulations requiring requesters to direct their requests to individual FBI field offices in the first instance); Domingues v. FBI, No. 98-74612, slip op. at 7 (E.D. Mich. June 23, 1999) (magistrate's recommendation) (alternative holding) (suggesting that request to agency headquarters that does not ask for field office search does not "reasonably describe" field office records, so headquarters search is all that is required), adopted (E.D. Mich. July 29, 1999), aff'd, No. 99-1976, 2000 WL 1140594, at *1 (6th Cir. Aug. 7, 2000); AFGE v. U.S. Dep't of Commerce, 632 F. Supp. 1272, 1278 (D.D.C. 1986) (holding that agency's refusal to perform canvass of 356 bureau offices for multitude of files was justified), aff'd, 907 F.2d 203 (D.C. Cir. 1990). But see Krikorian v.
(continued...)

It is incumbent upon an agency, of course, not to interpret the scope of a FOIA request too narrowly.[185] For example, a request that asks for all

---

[184](...continued)

U.S. Dep't of State, 984 F.2d 461, 468-69 (D.C. Cir. 1993) (remanding so district court could explain why it was unnecessary for agency to search eleven regional security offices identified in article that formed basis for plaintiff's request); Kennedy v. U.S. Dep't of Justice, No. 03-6077, 2004 WL 2284691, at *4 (W.D.N.Y. Oct. 8, 2004) (holding that FBI was obliged to search its Buffalo Field Office, because it was "specifically mentioned" in request sent to FBI Headquarters -- even though plaintiff was informed that he could request records from Buffalo Field Office directly); Conteh v. FBI, No. 01-1330, slip op. at 5 (D.D.C. Apr. 1, 2002) (ordering defendant to explain why it failed to advise plaintiff that responsive records were located in two field offices so that plaintiff could submit his requests there); see also 28 C.F.R. §§ 16.3(a), 16.41(a) (2006) (specifying that FOIA and Privacy Act requests for records held by the FBI field offices must be submitted to the field office directly); cf. Friends of Blackwater v. U.S. Dep't of the Interior, 391 F. Supp. 2d 115, 122 (D.D.C. 2005) (determining that Interior Department regulations required Fish and Wildlife Service to forward request to Office of Secretary of Interior because that office likely maintained responsive records); Nat'l Res. Def. Council v. DOD, 388 F. Supp. 2d 1086, 1102 (C.D. Cal. 2005) (finding that DOD should have directed request for records concerning perchlorate (a chemical substance) to Air Force because DOD had appointed Air Force as lead component for perchlorate issues but had not informed public of that decision); The Wilderness Soc'y v. U.S. Dep't of the Interior, 344 F. Supp. 2d 1, 19, 20 (D.D.C. 2004) (finding, based on agency's own regulations, that it had "affirmative duty" to forward request to components that it reasonably knew might have responsive records, even though plaintiff -- an experienced FOIA requester -- directed its inquiry solely to four specific offices); FOIA Post, "FOIA Counselor Q&A" (posted 1/24/06) (discussing issue of whether agencies are obligated to forward incorrectly directed FOIA requests to other agencies and further explaining holding in Blackwater).

[185] See, e.g., Judicial Watch, Inc. v. DOD, No. 05-00390, 2006 WL 1793297, at *3 (D.D.C. June 28, 2006) (recognizing that "agencies have a duty to construe FOIA requests liberally," but finding "no compelling reason to construe Judicial Watch's request as covering all files related to strategic communication"); Wilderness Soc'y v. U.S. Bureau of Land Mgmt., No. 01-CV-2210, 2003 WL 255971, at *5 (D.D.C. Jan. 15, 2003) (refusing to grant summary judgment due to agency's narrow interpretation of request); Hemenway v. Hughes, 601 F. Supp. 1002, 1005 (D.D.C. 1985) (while recognizing ambiguity of request, rejecting agency conclusion that it had no record of "citizenship data" of foreign news correspondents when it maintained such information on "application forms" that were required to be filed by such correspondents); cf. FOIA Update, Vol. XVI, No. 3, at 3 (advising agencies to "interpret FOIA requests 'liberally' when determining which records are responsive to them" (quoting Nation Magazine, 71 F.3d

(continued...)

records pertaining to a specific subject and then, in addition, enumerates certain items within that subject should be interpreted broadly, according to a ruling by the Court of Appeals for the District of Columbia Circuit.[186] Chiding the agency for its "implausible reading," the D.C. Circuit explained that "[t]he drafter of a FOIA request might reasonably seek all of a certain set of documents while nonetheless evincing a heightened interest in a specific subset thereof,"[187] but it emphasized that the reverse would not be true: "We think it improbable, however, that a person who wanted only the subset would draft a request that first asks for the full set."[188] (For a further discussion of determining the scope of a FOIA request, see Procedural Requirements, Proper FOIA Requests, above.)

On another search-related point, the D.C. Circuit has expressly held that an agency "is not obligated to look beyond the four corners of the request for leads to the location of responsive documents."[189] Similarly, "[b]ecause the scope of a search is limited by a plaintiff's FOIA request, there is no general requirement that an agency search secondary references or variant spellings."[190] Nor is an agency required to undertake a new search

---

[185](...continued)
at 890)).

[186] See LaCedra v. Executive Office for U.S. Attorneys, 317 F.3d 345, 348 (D.C. Cir. 2003); see also Fla. Immigration Advocacy Ctr. v. NSA, 380 F. Supp. 2d 1332, 1345 (S.D. Fla. 2005) (upholding an agency's search for records concerning the migration of "third country nationals," because the "[p]laintiff requested such a broad search," even though his request also listed countries of particular interest).

[187] LaCedra, 317 F.3d at 348.

[188] Id.

[189] Kowalczyk, 73 F.3d at 389 (holding that agency is not required to speculate about potential leads); see Williams v. Ashcroft, 30 F. App'x 5, 6 (D.C. Cir. 2002) (deciding that agency need not look for records not sought in initial FOIA request); Sheridan v. Dep't of the Navy, 9 F. App'x 55, 56 (2d Cir. 2001) (citing Kowalczyk); Gilchrist v. Dep't of Justice, No. 05-1540, 2006 WL 3091534, at *3 (D.D.C. Oct. 30, 2006) ("It was not unreasonable for EOUSA and USAO-MD staff to limit the searches to the specific document plaintiff identified in his FOIA request."); see also W. Ctr. for Journalism v. IRS, 116 F. Supp. 2d 1, 9 (D.D.C. 2000) (concluding that diligent search was shown when, even though not required to do so, agency searched for records beyond scope of request); cf. Nurse v. Sec'y of the Air Force, 231 F. Supp. 2d 323, 330 (D.D.C. 2002) (declaring that agency was not required to have "clairvoyant capabilities" in order to determine nature of request).

[190] Maynard, 986 F.2d at 560; Russell v. Barr, No. 92-2546, 1998 U.S. Dist. LEXIS 14515, at *6-7 (D.D.C. Aug. 28, 1998) (ruling that agency was not required to search for records under requester's wife's maiden name when re-

(continued...)

based on a subsequent "clarification" of a request, especially after the requester has examined the released documents.[191] Indeed, the D.C. Circuit has explicitly observed that "[r]equiring an additional search each time the agency receives a letter that clarifies a prior request could extend indefinitely the delay in processing new requests,"[192] and that "if the requester discovers leads in the documents he receives from the agency, he may pursue those leads through a second FOIA request."[193]

---

[190](...continued)
quester provided only her married name); cf. Lowe v. FBI, No. 96-512, slip op. at 2-3 (E.D. Okla. July 31, 1998) (finding no improper withholding of records when plaintiff failed to provide agency with additional information requested in order to conduct a more thorough search); Spannaus, No. 92-372, slip op. at 6-7 (D.D.C. June 20, 1995) (holding that agency was not required to search files of individual known to be connected with bankruptcy proceedings when request sought records on proceedings, not on individual). But see Canning v. U.S. Dep't of Justice, 919 F. Supp. 451, 461 (D.D.C. 1994) (when records on subject of request filed under two different names and agency is aware of the dual filing, agency obligated to search under both names, especially after requester brought second name to agency's attention).

[191] See Kowalczyk, 73 F.3d at 388 ("A reasonable effort to satisfy [a] request does not entail an obligation to search anew based upon a subsequent clarification."); see also McQueen v. United States, 179 F.R.D. 522, 525 n.5 (S.D. Tex. 1998) ("FOIA contains no provision which obligates an agency to update FOIA disclosures." (citing U.S. Dep't of Justice v. Tax Analysts, 492 U.S. 136, 139-40 (1989))).

[192] Kowalczyk, 73 F.3d at 388; cf. Bonner v. U.S. Dep't of State, 928 F.2d 1148, 1152 (D.C. Cir. 1991) ("To require an agency to adjust or modify its FOIA responses based on post-response occurrences could create an endless cycle of judicially mandated reprocessing."); FOIA Post, "Use of 'Cut-Off' Dates for FOIA Searches" (posted 5/6/04) (advising agencies that it is "entirely reasonable" to search for records that are in their possession only as of the date upon which they commence a search, because otherwise they would be subject to a "potentially endless" cycle of searching).

[193] Id. at 389; see Nash v. U.S. Dep't of Justice, 992 F. Supp. 447, 449 (D.D.C.) ("The fact that some EOUSA information was located in BOP files when the BOP conducted its search for records maintained by the BOP does not require the EOUSA to conduct a separate search of its own files, absent receipt of a FOIA request submitted to the EOUSA."), summary affirmance granted, No. 98-5096, 1998 WL 545424 (D.C. Cir. July 20, 1998). But see Kefalos v. IRS, No. 2-97-117, 1998 WL 419983, at *9-10 (S.D. Ohio Apr. 3, 1998) (refusing to grant summary judgment because affidavit inadequate in face of allegation by plaintiff that documents released reference existence of other documents), subsequent opinion granting summary judgment to agency, No. 2-97-117, 1998 U.S. Dist. LEXIS 10432 (S.D. Ohio

(continued...)

## LITIGATION CONSIDERATIONS

The proper scope of an agency's search is limited not only by what the requester asks for but also by the date the agency uses as a temporal limit for its search. Referred to as "cut-off" dates, these temporal limits are used to determine which agency records are encompassed within the scope of a request.[194] Courts have held that an agency's use of an inappropriate "cut-off" date can unduly restrict a FOIA request's temporal scope, thereby rendering the agency's subsequent search for responsive records unreasonable.[195] Searches conducted using a "cut-off" based on the date that the search begins (i.e., a "date-of-search cut-off") have been viewed by the courts much more favorably than a search that uses a less inclusive "cut-off," such as one based on the date of the request or of the request's receipt (i.e., a "date-of-request cut-off").[196]

---

[193](...continued)
May 19, 1998).

[194] See FOIA Post, "Use of 'Cut-Off' Dates for FOIA Searches" (posted 5/6/04) (explaining importance of proper use of "cut-off" dates).

[195] See, e.g., Pub. Citizen v. Dep't of State, 276 F.3d 634, 643-44 (D.C. Cir. 2002) (finding an agency's search to be inadequate because the agency unjustifiably failed to use a later "cut-off" date that "might have resulted in the retrieval of more [responsive] documents"); McGehee v. CIA, 697 F.2d 1095, 1101 (D.C. Cir. 1983) (observing that "a temporal limit pertaining to FOIA searches . . . is only valid when the limitation is consistent with the agency's duty to take reasonable steps to ferret out requested documents"), vacated on other grounds on panel reh'g & reh'g en banc denied, 711 F.2d 1076 (D.C. Cir. 1983).

[196] See, e.g., Van Strum v. EPA, No. 91-35404, 1992 WL 197660, at *2 (9th Cir. Aug. 17, 1992) (agreeing that a date-of-search "cut-off" date is "the most reasonable date for setting the temporal cut-off in this case"); McGehee, 697 F.2d at 1104 (favoring a "date-of-search cut-off" because it "results in a much fuller search and disclosure" than does a "date-of-request cut-off"); see also Or. Natural Desert Ass'n v. Gutierrez, 409 F. Supp. 2d 1284, 1288 (D. Or. 2006) (suggesting that a date-of-search "cut-off" date might be more reasonable than a date-of-request "cut-off" date); Defenders of Wildlife v. U.S. Dep't of the Interior, 314 F. Supp. 2d 1, 12 n.10 (D.D.C. 2004) (recognizing that because the agency's FOIA regulations established a "date-of-search cut-off," records created after the agency's "FOIA search began . . . are not covered by [the FOIA] request"); cf. Ctr. for Biological Diversity v. U.S. Marine Corps, No. 00-2387, slip op. at 14 (D.D.C. Aug. 21, 2003) (ordering agency to disclose particular documents prepared after date of request, but noting that such action in this particular case would not require "any additional searches" because such documents "have already been identified"). But cf. Hall v. CIA, No. 98-1319, slip op. at 10 (D.D.C. Aug. 10, 2000) (explaining that "under CIA policy a search is [required] to be conducted [only] up to the date on which the agency sent out a letter acknowledging receipt of the FOIA request").

A date-of-search approach also has been preferred to a more expansive, but simply unworkable, "cut-off" based on the date that documents actually are released.[197] Indeed, one court realistically described a "date-of-release cut-off" as "inherently flawed," because it creates "an ever moving target for the production of documents under FOIA."[198] (For a further discussion of the proper scope of a FOIA request, see Procedural Requirements, Proper FOIA Requests, above.)

In extraordinarily onerous cases, an agency may not be compelled to undertake even an initially requested search that is of such range or magnitude as to make it "unreasonably burdensome."[199] Indeed, "it is the requester's responsibility to frame requests with sufficient particularity to ensure that searches are not unreasonably burdensome . . . [because the] FOIA was not intended to reduce government agencies to full-time investigators on behalf of requesters."[200]

---

[197] See Edmonds Inst. v. U.S. Dep't of the Interior, 383 F. Supp. 2d 105, 111 (D.D.C. 2005) (rejecting date-of-release "cut-off" date in favor of one based on date of search).

[198] Id.; cf. Bonner, 928 F.2d at 1152 ("To require an agency to adjust or modify its FOIA responses based on post-response occurrences could create an endless cycle of judicially mandated reprocessing.").

[199] Nation Magazine, 71 F.3d at 891-92 (rejecting demand that agency search "through 23 years of unindexed files for records pertaining" to subject, while remanding for focus on narrower search for dated memorandum in files indexed chronologically); see also AFGE v. U.S. Dep't of Commerce, 907 F.2d 203, 209 (D.C. Cir. 1990) (holding that a request that would require an agency "to locate, review, redact, and arrange for inspection a vast quantity of material" is "so broad as to impose an unreasonable burden upon the agency" (citing Goland v. CIA, 607 F.2d 339, 353 (D.C. Cir. 1978))); Brophy v. DOD, No. 05-360, 2006 WL 571901, at *6 (D.D.C. Mar. 8, 2006) (finding it "unduly burdensome" to impose broader search on agency, because request was "vague and indistinct"); Schrecker v. U.S. Dep't of Justice, 217 F. Supp. 2d 29, 35 (D.D.C. 2002) (rejecting as unreasonable requested search that would have required "hand-search through 574,726 linear feet" of unindexed records), aff'd, 349 F.3d 657 (D.C. Cir. 2003); cf. Lowry v. Soc. Sec. Admin., No. 00-1616, 2001 U.S. Dist. LEXIS 23474, at *29 (D. Or. Aug. 29, 2001) (recognizing that agencies need not conduct "unreasonably burdensome" searches, but concluding that agency's search is not "unreasonable" where it can be performed by "two employees working one 40-hour week" using "existing agency technology").

[200] Judicial Watch, Inc. v. Exp.-Imp. Bank, 108 F. Supp. 2d 19, 27 (D.D.C. 2000) (quoting Assassination Archives & Research Ctr. v. CIA, 720 F. Supp. 217, 219 (D.D.C. 1989)); see also 5 U.S.C. § 552(a)(3)(A) (requiring that a request "reasonably describe[]" the records sought); Campbell, 164 F.3d at 29 (explaining that a requester must establish a "sufficient predicate" to justify

(continued...)

On the other hand, while "[t]here is no requirement that an agency search every record system,"[201] an agency "'cannot limit its search to only one record system if there are others that are likely to turn up the information requested.'"[202] Stated another way, "if an agency has reason to know that certain places might well contain responsive documents, it is obligated under FOIA to search [those places] barring an undue burden."[203] Of

---

[200](...continued)
searching for a particular type of record).

[201] Oglesby, 920 F.2d at 68 (citing cases); see Chamberlain, 957 F. Supp. at 294; Moore v. Aspin, 916 F. Supp. 32, 35 (D.D.C. 1996); see also Sheridan, 9 F. App'x 55, 58 (2d Cir. 2001) (suggesting that agency is under no obligation to search for records in place not initially specified by requester); Wheeler v. U.S. Dep't of Justice, No. 02-604, slip op. at 8 (D.D.C. Nov. 21, 2006) (stating that search was, by plaintiff's "own definition, reasonable").

[202] Campbell, 164 F.3d at 28 (quoting Oglesby, 920 F.2d at 68); see Negley v. FBI, 169 F. App'x 591, 595 (D.C. Cir. 2006) (reversing grant of summary judgment, because FBI did not specifically demonstrate that it searched for particular file designated by plaintiff); Wolf v. CIA, 357 F. Supp. 2d 112, 119 (D.D.C. 2004) (finding, based on references in documents independently obtained by plaintiff, that FBI should have searched particular file that likely contained responsive records), aff'd in part, rev'd in part & remanded all on other grounds, 473 F.3d 370 (D.C. Cir. 2007); Comer v. IRS, No. 97-76329, 1999 WL 1922219, at *1 (E.D. Mich. Sept. 30, 1999) (questioning agency's search because it failed to justify why it would not be feasible to search specific places that plaintiff requested be searched), subsequent opinion, 2000 WL 1566279 (E.D. Mich. Aug. 17, 2000), motion for reconsideration denied, 2000 WL 172771 (E.D. Mich. Oct. 5, 2000); cf. Davis, 460 F.3d at 105 ("[T]he methodology employed by the agency was extremely unlikely to produce the needed information, and it appears -- although we do not know for certain -- that there are readily available alternatives that would not impose an undue burden on the government."); Conteh, No. 01-1330, slip op. at 4-5 (D.D.C. Apr. 1, 2002) (chastising agency for not advising plaintiff of existence of records in field offices, reference to which was found when initial search was conducted; "[i]nstead, the parties and this Court unnecessarily are forced to expend time and resources to litigate the matter").

[203] Valencia-Lucena v. U.S. Coast Guard, 180 F.3d 321, 327 (D.C. Cir. 1999); see Jefferson v. U.S. Dep't of Justice, 168 F. App'x 448, 450 (D.C. Cir. 2005) (concluding that search was inadequate because it did not include particular database that agency acknowledged "might have files" responsive to request); Juda v. U.S. Customs Serv., No. 99-5333, 2000 WL 1093326, at *1-2 (D.C. Cir. June 19, 2000) (per curiam) (reversing grant of summary judgment where agency "fail[ed] to pursue clear leads to other existing records"); Hornbeck Offshore Transp., LLC v. U.S. Coast Guard, No. 04-1724, 2006 WL 696053, at *9-11 (D.D.C. Mar. 20, 2006) (finding that the

(continued...)

course, those places should be within the agency[204] or in a federal records center at which the agency has stored its records."[205]

When documents that are located as a result of an initial search suggest other fruitful areas to search, an agency might be required to explore those areas, because "the court evaluates the reasonableness of an agen-

---

[203](...continued)
agency's search, which was limited to one office, "was reasonable, especially in light of its policies and the relevant time constraints, and the affidavits produced by the [a]gency detailing the searches employed and methodologies used"); Pub. Citizen v. Dep't of Educ., 292 F. Supp. 2d 1, 7-8 (D.D.C. 2003) (refusing to approve computerized search for records when those records did not contain requested information, but ordering instead manual review of 25,000 paper files).

[204] See Williams v. U.S. Attorney's Office, No. 03-CV-674, 2006 WL 717474, at *5 (N.D. Okla. Mar. 16, 2006) (noting that FOIA requires agency to search its own records and not those of third party, such as county jail records); Duggan v. U.S. Dep't of Justice, No. 03-10260, slip op. at 2 (D. Mass. Jan. 28, 2004) ("FOIA does not entitle the plaintiff to direct the Criminal Division [of the Department of Justice] to search the records of other agencies and agency components[.]"), aff'd, 109 F. App'x 439 (1st Cir. 2004) (per curiam); Garcia v. U.S. Dep't of Justice, 181 F. Supp. 2d 356, 368 (S.D.N.Y. 2002) ("The agency is not expected to take extraordinary measures to find the requested records."); Blanton v. U.S. Dep't of Justice, 182 F. Supp. 2d 81, 85 (D.D.C. 2001) ("FOIA does not impose an obligation on defendant to contact former employees to determine whether they know of the whereabouts of records that might be response to a FOIA request."), aff'd, 64 F. App'x 787 (D.C. Cir. 2003) (per curiam); Brunskill v. U.S. Dep't of Justice, No. 99-3316, slip op. at 4-5 (D.D.C. Mar. 19, 2001) (concluding that FBI has no obligation to search for records at Customs Service, because "there is no basis to compel defendant to conduct its search outside its own systems of records"). Contra Jackson v. U.S. Attorney's Office, 362 F. Supp. 2d 39, 42 (D.D.C. 2005) (suggesting that agency should have contacted former Assistant United States Attorney regarding whereabouts of directive that she authored); Comer v. IRS, No. 97-76329, 2001 U.S. Dist. LEXIS 16996, at *10 (E.D. Mich. Sept. 25, 2001) (deciding that "it is not unreasonable to attempt to question a former employee about the possible existence of documents related to one request," even while recognizing that the former employee might not remember the document or that the agency might be unable to locate him; cf. People for the Am. Way Found. v. U.S. Dep't of Justice, 451 F. Supp. 2d 6, 16 (D.D.C. 2006) (concluding that court-administered database (PACER) could and should be used as search tool) (appeal pending).

[205] See, e.g., Valencia-Lucena, 180 F.3d at 327 ("Pursuant to the regulations of the National Archives and Records Administration . . . agency records stored at a federal record center are deemed 'to be maintained by the agency which deposited the record.'" (quoting 36 C.F.R. § 1229.162 (1998))).

cy's search based on what the agency knew at [the search's] conclusion rather than what the agency speculated at its inception."[206] Of course, when a requester has set limitations on the scope of his request, either at the administrative stage[207] or in the course of litigation,[208] he cannot subsequently challenge the adequacy of the search on the ground that the agency limited its search accordingly. Moreover, the D.C. Circuit has held that when the subject of a request is involved in several separate matters, but information is sought regarding only one of them, an agency is not obligated to extend its search to other files or to other documents that are referenced in records retrieved in response to the initial search, so long as that search was reasonable and complete in and of itself.[209]

To prove the adequacy of its search, as in sustaining its use of ex-

---

[206] Campbell, 164 F.3d at 28; see Truitt, 897 F.2d at 545-46 (admonishing agency to "admit and correct error when error is revealed" and conduct additional searches if requester suggests other areas in which to look). But cf. Hall v. U.S. Dep't of Justice, 63 F. Supp. 2d 14, 18 (D.D.C. 1999) (inviting plaintiff to make another FOIA request for records the existence of which were only "suggested" by documents already released).

[207] See Lechliter v. DOD, 371 F. Supp. 2d 589, 595 (D. Del. 2005) ("A requestor may not challenge the adequacy of a search after an agency limits the scope of a search in response to direction from the requestor."); Votehemp, Inc. v. DEA, No. 02-985, slip op. at 8-9 (D.D.C. Oct. 15, 2004) (concluding that narrowed search was adequate as agency and plaintiff had agreed to search of only three offices); Nation Magazine v. Dep't of State, No. 92-2303, 1995 WL 17660254, at *7 (D.D.C. Aug. 18, 1995) (holding search, which was limited to single DEA field office based on information supplied in request, to be "particularly appropriate here due to the fact that DEA must manually search its noninvestigative records").

[208] See Nation Magazine, 1995 WL 17660254, at *7-8 (holding that plaintiff was bound to scope of request as narrowed in litigation).

[209] Steinberg, 23 F.3d at 552 (concluding that "[otherwise] an agency . . . might be forced to examine virtually every document in its files, following an interminable trail of cross-referenced documents like a chain letter winding its way through the mail"); see also Davy v. CIA, 357 F. Supp. 2d 76, 84 (D.D.C. 2004) (finding that adequacy of agency's search was not undermined by fact that records referenced in released documents were not provided to plaintiff; the "FOIA cannot be used to troll for documents, which, if they even exist, appear barely tangential to the subject of" a request); Canning v. U.S. Dep't of Justice, 848 F. Supp. 1037, 1050 (D.D.C. 1994) (adequacy of search not undermined by fact that requester has received additional documents mentioning subject through separate request, when such documents are "tagged" to name of subject's associate). See generally Campbell, 164 F.3d at 28 ("[T]he proper inquiry is whether the requesting party has established a sufficient predicate to justify searching for a particular type of record.").

emptions, an agency relies upon its declarations, which should be "relatively detailed, nonconclusory, and submitted in good faith."[210] Such declarations should show "that the search method was reasonably calculated to uncover all relevant documents."[211] This ordinarily is accomplished by a

---

[210] Pollack v. Bureau of Prisons, 879 F.2d 406, 409 (8th Cir. 1989); see Miller v. U.S. Dep't of State, 779 F.2d 1378, 1383 (8th Cir. 1986) ("An agency may prove the reasonableness of its search through affidavits of responsible agency officials so long as the affidavits are relatively detailed, nonconclusory, and submitted in good faith."); Weisberg v. U.S. Dep't of Justice, 705 F.2d 1344, 1351 (D.D.C. 1983) (same); Perry, 684 F.2d at 127 ("[A]ffidavits that explain in reasonable detail the scope and method of the search conducted by the agency will suffice to demonstrate compliance with the obligations imposed by the FOIA."); Goland, 607 F.2d at 352 (finding agency's description of withheld material to be "specifically described and justified"); Triestman v. U.S. Dep't of Justice, 878 F. Supp. 667, 672 (S.D.N.Y. 1995) ("[A]ffidavits attesting to the thoroughness of an agency search of its records and its results are presumptively valid."); see also FOIA Update, Vol. IV, No. 1, at 6 (discussing what constitutes "adequate search"); cf. FOIA Post, "Use of 'Cut-Off' Dates for FOIA Searches" (posted 5/6/04) (explaining importance of proper use of "cut-off" dates in determining appropriate temporal limits of search).

[211] Oglesby, 920 F.2d at 68 (declaring that although agency was not required to search "every" record system, "[a]t the very least, [it] was required to explain in its affidavit that no other record system was likely to produce responsive documents"); see Church of Scientology, 792 F.2d at 151 (ruling that agency affidavit should describe general structure of agency's file system, which makes further search difficult); Ferranti v. ATF, 177 F. Supp. 2d 41, 47 (D.D.C. 2001) ("Affidavits that include search methods, locations of specific files searched, descriptions of searches of all files likely to contain responsive documents, and names of agency personnel conducting the search are considered presumptively sufficient."), summary affirmance granted, No. 01-5451, 2002 WL 31189766, at *1 (D.C. Cir. Oct. 2, 2002); see also Papa v. United States, 281 F.3d 1004, 1013 (9th Cir. 2002) (reversing grant of summary judgment because "nothing in the record certif[ies] that all the records . . . have been produced"); Steinberg, 23 F.3d at 552 (finding description of search inadequate when it failed "to describe in any detail what records were searched, by whom, and through what process"); Oglesby, 920 F.2d at 68; Peay v. U.S. Dep't of Justice, No. 04-1859, 2006 WL 83497, at *2 (D.D.C. Jan. 12, 2006) (denying summary judgment because agency did not describe Federal Records Center search or explain why particular archival box that it located and focused on there "would likely contain all responsive documents"); Judicial Watch v. FDA, 407 F. Supp. 2d 70, 74 (D.D.C. 2005) (finding that agency declarations sufficiently described search by detailing "scope and method used" to search for records and by providing "details about the specific offices" searched), aff'd in pertinent part, rev'd in other part & remanded on other grounds, 449 F.3d 141 (D.C. Cir. 2006); Antonelli v. ATF, No. 04-1180, 2005 WL 3276222, at *11 (D.D.C.
(continued...)

LITIGATION CONSIDERATIONS

declaration that identifies the types of files that an agency maintains, states the search terms that were employed to search through the files selected for the search, and contains an averment that all files reasonably expected to contain the requested records were, in fact, searched.[212] In re-

---

[211](...continued)
Aug. 16, 2005) (rejecting an agency's declaration that merely stated which offices were "contacted in an attempt to locate any responsive documents" but that did not "describe the searches undertaken or the file systems searched"); Tarullo v. DOD, 170 F. Supp. 2d 271, 274 (D. Conn. 2001) (deciding that absence in agency's declaration of description of scope and nature of search "makes it impossible" to find that search was reasonable); Judicial Watch, Inc. v. U.S. Dep't of Commerce, 34 F. Supp. 2d 28, 46 (D.D.C. 1998) (denying unprecedented partial summary judgment motion filed by agency against itself and requiring "restrictive and rigorous" search because of "egregious" agency conduct); Law Firm of Tidwell Swaim & Assocs. v. Herrmann, No. 3:97-2097, 1998 WL 740765, at *4 (N.D. Tex. Oct. 16, 1998) (denying summary judgment because of dispute as to proper scope of agency search). But see Maynard, 986 F.2d at 560 (refusing to find that district court abused its discretion when it denied as untimely plaintiff's motion for reconsideration based on allegation that agency "improperly limited its search").

[212] See, e.g., Iturralde, 315 F.3d at 313-14 (explaining requirements for adequate search); Valencia-Lucena, 180 F.3d at 326 (same); Schmidt v. DOD, No. 3:04-1159, 2007 WL 196667, at *2 (D. Conn. Jan. 23, 2007) (finding that agency conducted adequate search based on the agency's affidavits which detailed "the timeliness of the search, the manner in which the search was conducted, the specific places that were searched, and the retrieval of the relevant documents"); McCoy v. United States, No. 1:04-CV-101, 2006 WL 463106, at *13 (N.D. W. Va. Feb. 24, 2006) (denying the Executive Office for United States Attorneys' motion for summary judgment as to the adequacy of its search, because the declaration "failed to set forth the methods and records systems used by the EOUSA to conduct [its] search"); Gilchrist v. Dep't of Justice, No. 05-1540, 2006 WL 463257, at *3 (D.D.C. Feb. 24, 2006) (denying an agency's motion for summary judgment because its declaration "neither describes the records searched nor the method by which agency staff conducted the search"); Citizens for Responsibility & Ethics in Wash. v. U.S. Dep't of Justice, 405 F. Supp. 2d 2, 3 (D.D.C. 2005) (concluding that agency conducted adequate search, because its declarations "set forth the terms and nature of . . . [the] search and, perhaps even more significantly, they state[d] that the locations most likely to contain responsive documents were extensively searched"); Kidd v. U.S. Dep't of Justice, 362 F. Supp. 2d 291, 295 (D.D.C. Mar. 30, 2005) (finding an agency's search adequate because its declaration sufficiently described "records and databases searched . . . general processes employed in the searches . . . dates the searches were performed . . . the offices which conducted searches . . . and the records located"); Landmark Legal Found., 272 F. Supp. 2d at 66 (finding a search affidavit to be suffi-

(continued...)

cent years, courts have been increasingly stringent in enforcing this requirement.[213]

It is not necessary that the agency employee who actually performed the search supply an affidavit describing the search; rather, the affidavit of an official responsible for supervising or coordinating the search efforts should be sufficient in any FOIA litigation case to fulfill the "personal knowledge" requirement of Rule 56(e) of the Federal Rules of Civil Procedure.[214] (For a further discussion of this "personal knowledge" requirement,

---

[212](...continued)
cient because it "identifi[ed] the affiants and their roles in the agency, discuss[ed] how the FOIA request was disseminated with their office and the scope of the search, which particular files were searched, and the chronology of the search"); Garcia v. U.S. Dep't of Justice, 181 F. Supp. 2d 356, 368 (S.D.N.Y. 2002) ("To fulfill the adequate search requirement of the [FOIA], the government should identify the searched files and recite facts which enable the district court to satisfy itself that all appropriate files have been searched.").

[213] See, e.g., Toolasprashad v. Bureau of Prisons, No. 06-1187, 2006 U.S. Dist. LEXIS 82397, at *3-4 (D.D.C. Nov. 13, 2006) (denying agency's motion for summary judgment because declaration neither described search that yielded records nor specified "search terms" used); Jefferson v. Bureau of Prisons, No. 05-848, 2006 WL 3208666, at *7 (D.D.C. Nov. 7, 2006) (concluding that the agencies' declarations were inadequate because they did not "describe the systems of records each agency maintains, detailed the method of retrieving records, or averred that the agency identified and searched all files reasonably likely to contain responsive records"); Friends of Blackwater, 391 F. Supp. 2d at 122 (concluding that agency's failure to locate documents known to exist, when combined with affidavit that did not specify terms used in conducting search, rendered search inadequate); Maydak v. U.S. Dep't of Justice, 362 F. Supp. 2d 316, 326 (D.D.C. Mar. 30, 2005) (finding an agency's declaration to be inadequate where it contained "no information about the search terms and the specific files searched" and failed to specifically aver that "all files likely to contain responsive records were searched"); Boyd v. U.S. Marshals Serv., No. 99-2712, 2002 U.S. Dist. LEXIS 27734, at *2-3 (D.D.C. Mar. 15, 2002) (rejecting declarations that did not identify search terms used, locations searched, and reasons for searching only particular locations).

[214] See, e.g., Carney v. U.S. Dep't of Justice, 19 F.3d 807, 814 (2d Cir. 1994) ("An affidavit from an agency employee responsible for supervising a FOIA search is all that is needed to satisfy Rule 56(e); there is no need for the agency to supply affidavits from each individual who participated in the actual search."); Maynard, 986 F.2d at 560 (same); SafeCard, 926 F.2d at 1202 (ruling that employee "in charge of coordinating the [agency's] search and recovery efforts [is] most appropriate person to provide a comprehensive affidavit"); see also Patterson v. IRS, 56 F.3d 832, 841 (7th Cir. 1995)

(continued...)

**LITIGATION CONSIDERATIONS**

see Litigation Considerations, Summary Judgment, below.)

While the initial burden certainly rests with an agency to demonstrate the adequacy of its search,[215] once that obligation is satisfied, the

---

[214](...continued)
(holding appropriate declarant's reliance on standard search form completed by his predecessor); Lewis v. EPA, No. 06-2660, 2006 WL 3227787, at *3 (E.D. Pa. Nov. 3, 2006) (holding that the agency employee's declaration was admissible because the employee's "statements [were] based either on 'personal examination' of the responsive documents or on information provided to him by employees under his supervision"); Brophy, 2006 WL 571901, at *5 ("Although the government's declarants here did not physically perform the searches for responsive records, they satisfy the requirement of personal knowledge and qualify as competent witnesses concerning the FOIA searches."); Judicial Watch, Inc. v. U.S. Dep't of Commerce, 337 F. Supp. 2d 146, 160-61 (D.D.C. 2004) (ruling that declarations from employee who coordinated agency's searches satisfied personal knowledge requirement); Kay v. FCC, 976 F. Supp. 23, 33 n.29 (D.D.C. 1997) ("Generally, declarations accounting for searches of documents that contain hearsay are acceptable."), aff'd, 172 F.3d 919 (D.C. Cir. 1998) (unpublished table decision); Mehl v. EPA, 797 F. Supp. 43, 46 (D.D.C. 1992) (ruling that agency employee with "firsthand knowledge" of relevant files was appropriate person to supervise search undertaken by contractor); Spannaus v. U.S. Dep't of Justice, No. 85-1015, slip op. at 7 (D. Mass. July 13, 1992) (finding affidavit of agency employee sufficient when third party claimed to have knowledge of additional documents and employee contacted that individual); cf. Bingham v. U.S. Dep't of Justice, No. 05-0475, 2006 WL 3833950, at *3-4 (D.D.C. Dec. 29, 2006) (concluding that the declarant had sufficient knowledge of the subject matter and, "therefore, need not have been employed by the responding agency at the time of the facts underlying the requested records"); Homer J. Olsen, Inc. v. U.S. Dep't of Transp. Fed. Transit Admin., No. 02-00673, 2002 WL 31738794, at *5 n.4 (N.D. Cal. Dec. 2, 2002) (sustaining objection to declaration from employee who had no personal knowledge about what records were produced by regional office in response to a request). But see Katzman v. CIA, 903 F. Supp. 434, 438-39 (E.D.N.Y. 1995) (finding declaration from agency's FOIA coordinator inadequate when agency initially misidentified requester's attorney as subject of request, and requiring declarations from supervisors in each of agency's three major divisions attesting that search was conducted for correct subject).

[215] See Patterson, 56 F.3d at 840; Maynard, 986 F.2d at 560; Miller, 779 F.2d at 1378; Weisberg, 705 F.2d at 1351; see also Santos v. DEA, 357 F. Supp. 2d 33, 37 (D.D.C. 2004) ("Conclusory statements that the agency has reviewed the relevant files are insufficient to support summary judgment."); Williams v. U.S. Attorney's Office, No. 96-1367, slip op. at 5 (D.D.C. Sept. 21, 1999) (explaining that to prove adequacy of search, agency's affidavit should describe "where and how it looked for responsive records" and
(continued...)

agency's position can be rebutted "only by showing that the agency's search was not made in good faith,"[216] because agency declarations are "entitled to a presumption of good faith."[217] Consequently, a requester's

---

[215](...continued) "what it was looking for"); Bennett v. DEA, 55 F. Supp. 2d 36, 40 (D.D.C. 1999) (pointing out that affidavit must provide details of scope of search; "simply stating that 'any and all records' were searched is insufficient").

[216] Maynard, 986 F.2d at 560 (citing Miller, 779 F.2d at 1383); see, e.g., Carney, 19 F.3d at 812; Weisberg, 705 F.2d at 1351-52; Wilson v. DEA, 414 F. Supp. 2d 5, 12 (D.D.C. 2006) (finding that the plaintiff failed to rebut the agency's "initial showing of a good faith search"); Graves v. EEOC, No. 02-6842, slip op. at 11 (C.D. Cal. Mar. 26, 2004) (declaring that once agency demonstrates adequacy of its search, burden shifts to plaintiff "to supply direct evidence of bad faith" to defeat summary judgment), aff'd, 144 F. App'x 626 (9th Cir. 2005), cert. denied, 126 S. Ct. 1800 (2006); Windel v. United States, No. 3:02-CV-306, 2004 WL 3363406, at *3 (D. Alaska Sept. 30, 2004) (concluding that plaintiff's "mere recitation" that several individuals should have been contacted as part of agency's search did not constitute evidence of bad faith); Tota v. United States, No. 99-0445E, 2000 WL 1160477, at *2 (W.D.N.Y. 2000) (explaining that to avoid summary judgment in favor of agency, plaintiff must show "bad faith," by "presenting specific facts showing that documents exist" that were not produced); cf. Accuracy in Media, Inc., No. 03-00024, 2006 WL 826070, at *9-10 (D.D.C. Mar. 29, 2006) (reasoning that "a requester cannot challenge the adequacy of a search based on the underlying actions that are the subject of the request, [and that] it may challenge the adequacy of a search by arguing that the search itself, rather than the underlying agency actions, was conducted in bad faith"); Brophy, 2006 WL 571901, at *8 (finding that an agency's search was conducted in good faith, even though the agency "was deplorably tardy in releasing the documents that were found"); Judicial Watch, Inc., 337 F. Supp. 2d at 161 (finding that plaintiff's attempt to discredit search with its own declaration was "insufficient to overcome the personal knowledge-based" declarations submitted by agency, which fully described its search; concluding further that any failings associated with the agency's first search did not undermine its second search, which was "sufficient under the law"); Harvey v. U.S. Dep't of Justice, No. 92-176, slip op. at 10 (D. Mont. Jan. 9, 1996) ("The purported bad faith of government agents in separate criminal proceedings is irrelevant to [the] question of the adequate, good faith search for documents responsive to a FOIA request."), aff'd on other grounds, 116 F.3d 484 (9th Cir. 1997) (unpublished table decision).

[217] Chilingirian v. U.S. Attorney Executive Office, 71 F. App'x 571, 572 (6th Cir. 2003) (citing U.S. Dep't of State v. Ray, 502 U.S. 164, 179 (1991)); see, e.g., Coyne v. United States, 164 F. App'x 141, 142 (2d Cir. 2006) (per curiam) (citing Grand Cent. P'ship, 166 F.3d at 489); Peltier v. FBI, No. 03-CV-9055, 2005 WL 735964, at *4 (W.D.N.Y. Mar. 31, 2005) (citing Carney, 19 F.3d at 812); Butler v. Soc. Sec. Admin., No. 03-0810, slip op. at 5 (W.D. La. (continued...)

"'[m]ere speculation that as yet uncovered documents may exist does not undermine the finding that the agency conducted a reasonable search for them.'"[218] Even when a requested document indisputably exists or once

---

[217](...continued)
June 25, 2004), aff'd on other grounds, No. 04-30854, 2005 WL 2055928 (5th Cir. Aug. 26, 2005); Wood v. FBI, 312 F. Supp. 2d 328, 340 (D. Conn. 2004) (citing Carney, 19 F.3d at 812), aff'd in part, rev'd in part on other grounds & remanded, 432 F.3d 78 (2d Cir. 2005); Piper, 294 F. Supp. 2d at 24 (citing Ground Saucer Watch, Inc. v. CIA, 692 F.2d 770, 771 (D.C. Cir. 1981)).

[218] Steinberg, 23 F.3d at 552 (quoting SafeCard, 926 F.2d at 1201); see Kucernak v. FBI, No. 96-17143, 1997 WL 697377, at *1 (9th Cir. Nov. 4, 1997) ("Mere allegations that the government is shielding or destroying documents does [sic] not undermine the adequacy . . . of the search."); Oglesby, 920 F.2d at 67 n.13 ("[H]ypothetical assertions are insufficient to raise a material question of fact with respect to the adequacy of the agency's search."); Nat'l Inst. of Military Justice v. DOD, 404 F. Supp. 2d 325, 350 (D.D.C. 2005) (upholding the agency's search, and explaining that the plaintiff's "conclusory assertion" failed to overcome "the detailed declarations submitted by the [agency]"); Citizens for Responsibility & Ethics in Wash., 405 F. Supp. 2d at 5 (rejecting plaintiff's assertion that additional documents must exist "given the magnitude of the [alleged] scandal" that was the subject of its request); Lair v. U.S. Dep't of the Treasury, No. 03-827, 2005 WL 645228, at *4 (D.D.C. Mar. 21, 2005) (explaining that the plaintiff's "insistence that the ATF controls specific additional documents . . . does not alter the court's determination of adequacy"), reconsideration denied, 2005 WL 1330722, at *2 (D.D.C. June 3, 2005); Martinale v. CIA, No. 03-1632, 2005 WL 327119, at *3 (D.D.C. Feb. 9, 2005) ("Plaintiff's strong belief that defendants possess responsive documents beyond those disclosed is nothing more than speculation, and therefore is insufficient to raise a genuine issue of material fact with respect to the adequacy of the searches[.]"); Jones-Edwards v. Appeal Bd. of the NSA/Cent. Sec. Serv., 352 F. Supp. 2d 420, 422 (S.D.N.Y. 2005) (alternative holding) ("Plaintiff's belief . . . that the NSA did not make a reasonable search -- because if it had it would have found something -- is not enough to withstand . . . [the agency's] motion for summary judgment."), aff'd, No. 05-0962, 2006 WL 2620313, at *2 (2d Cir. Sept. 12, 2006); Flowers v. IRS, 307 F. Supp. 2d 60, 67 (D.D.C. 2004) (stating that "'purely speculative claims about the existence and discoverability of other documents'" are not enough to rebut presumption of good faith (quoting SafeCard, 926 F.2d at 1200)); Bay Area Lawyers Alliance for Nuclear Arms Control v. Dep't of State, 818 F. Supp. 1291, 1295 (N.D. Cal. 1992) ("Plaintiff's incredulity at the fact that no responsive documents were uncovered . . . does not constitute evidence of unreasonableness or bad faith."); see also Students Against Genocide v. Dep't of State, 257 F.3d 828, 839 (D.C. Cir. 2001) ("[T]hat the Department gave SAGE more information than it requested does not undermine the conclusion that its search was reasonable and adequate."); Boyd, 2005 WL 555412, at *4 (D.D.C. Mar. 9, 2005) (rejecting claims that searches were inadequate as

(continued...)

existed, summary judgment will not be defeated by an unsuccessful search for the document, so long as the search was diligent.[219] Indeed, "[n]othing

---

[218](...continued)
plaintiff did not identify any particular missing records or suggest that there were other files that should have been searched); cf. NARA v. Favish, 541 U.S. 157, 174 (noting realistically that "[a]llegations of government misconduct are easy to 'allege and hard to disprove'" (quoting Crawford-El v. Britton, 523 U.S. 574, 585 (1998) (non-FOIA case))), reh'g denied, 541 U.S. 1057 (2004). But see Meyer v. Fed. Bureau of Prisons, 940 F. Supp. 9, 14 (D.D.C. 1996) (reference to responsive pages in agency memorandum, coupled with equivocal statement in declaration that it "appears" responsive pages do not exist, requires further clarification by agency); Katzman v. Freeh, 926 F. Supp. 316, 320 (E.D.N.Y. 1996) (because additional documents were referenced in released documents, summary judgment was withheld "until defendant releases these documents or demonstrates that they either are exempt from disclosure or cannot be located").

[219] See Twist v. Gonzales, 171 F. App'x 855, 855 (D.C. Cir. 2005) (ruling that failure to locate specific documents does not render search inadequate or demonstrate that search was conducted in bad faith); Nation Magazine, 71 F.3d at 892 n.7 ("Of course, failure to turn up [a specified] document does not alone render the search inadequate."); Citizens Comm'n, 45 F.3d at 1328 (adequacy of search not undermined by inability to locate 137 out of 1000 volumes of responsive material, absent evidence of bad faith, and when affidavit contained detailed, nonconclusory account of search); Maynard, 986 F.2d at 564 ("'The fact that a document once existed does not mean that it now exists; nor does the fact that an agency created a document necessarily imply that the agency has retained it.'" (quoting Miller, 779 F.2d at 1385)); Elliott v. NARA, No. 06-1246, 2006 WL 3783409, at *3 (D.D.C. Dec. 21, 2006) ("An agency's search is not presumed unreasonable because it fails to find all the requested information."); Burnes v. CIA, No. 05-242, 2005 WL 3275895, at *2 (D.D.C. Sept. 14, 2005) ("An agency's failure to find a particular document does not undermine the determination that the search was adequate."); Judicial Watch v. U.S. Dep't of Transp., No. 02-566, 2005 WL 1606915, at *7 (D.D.C. July 7, 2005) (upholding search even though some responsive records, which once existed, were destroyed prior to plaintiff's request); People for the Ethical Treatment of Animals v. USDA, No. 03-195, 2005 WL 1241141, at *4 (D.D.C. May 24, 2005) (rejecting plaintiff's argument that search was inadequate simply because disclosed documents refer to others that were not produced or listed in Vaughn Index); Barfield v. U.S. Dep't of Justice, No. 04-0636, 2005 WL 551808, at *6 (D.D.C. Mar. 8, 2005) (finding an agency's search to be adequate, despite its failure to locate particular documents, because it was "directed to the locations where such records might reasonably be expected to be located, if they exist or ever existed"); Allen v. U.S. Secret Serv., 335 F. Supp. 2d 95, 99 (D.D.C. 2004) ("[T]he fact that plaintiff [independently] discovered one document that possibly should have been located by the Service does not render the search process unreasonable."); DiPietro v. Executive Office for U.S. Attor-

(continued...)

in the law requires the agency to document the fate of documents it cannot find."[220] And when an agency does subsequently locate additional docu-

---

[219](...continued)
neys, 357 F. Supp. 2d 177, 182 (D.D.C. 2004) ("An agency's unsuccessful search for records that once may have existed does not render the search inadequate."); Piper, 294 F. Supp. 2d at 23-24 (stating that because the "inquiry regarding the adequacy of a search is the search itself and not the results thereof," the fact that documents were missing is insufficient to rebut otherwise-adequate affidavits demonstrating the reasonableness of the search); Grace v. Dep't of Navy, No. 99-4306, 2001 WL 940908, at *4 (N.D. Cal. Aug. 13, 2001) (finding "more than reasonably adequate" an agency search for misplaced personnel records); Tolotti v. IRS, No. 97-003, 2000 WL 1274235, at *1 (D. Nev. July 14, 2000) ("Obviously the agency cannot produce destroyed documents."); Coal. on Political Assassinations v. DOD, No. 99-0594, slip op. at 7 (D.D.C. Mar. 29, 2000) (reasoning that even if the agency once possessed responsive records, the agency's unsuccessful search was nevertheless thorough and well-explained and thus the agency "fulfilled its obligation under the FOIA"), aff'd, 12 F. App'x 13 (D.C. Cir. 2001); Kay, 976 F. Supp. at 33 (explaining that search not inadequate simply because plaintiff received in discovery documents not produced in response to FOIA request; discovery "may differ from FOIA disclosure procedures"); Antonelli v. U.S. Parole Comm'n, No. 93-0109, slip op. at 2 (D.D.C. Feb. 23, 1996) ("While it is undisputed that [plaintiff] provided the U.S. Marshals Service with a copy of the document he now seeks, the fact that the USMS cannot find it is not evidence of an insufficient search."); Shewchun v. INS, No. 95-1920, slip op. at 7 (D.D.C. Dec. 10, 1996) ("Nor does plaintiff's identification of undisclosed documents that he has obtained through other sources render the search unreasonable."), summary affirmance granted, No. 97-5044 (D.C. Cir. June 5, 1997). But see Boyd, 2002 U.S. Dist. LEXIS 27734, at *4 (stating that the agency's declaration should have explained why a particular report, which was known to exist, was not located, and requiring the agency to "explain its failure to locate this report in a future motion"); Trentadue v. FBI, No. 04-772, slip op. at 5-6 (D. Utah May 5, 2004) (finding search insufficient in light of specific evidence proffered by plaintiff that certain documents do exist and were not found through FBI's automated search); Tran v. U.S. Dep't of Justice, No. 01-0238, 2001 U.S. Dist. LEXIS 21552, at *12-13 (D.D.C. Nov. 20, 2001) (finding that "it is not enough for [an agency] to simply state that [the] documents are destroyed or missing" without providing more explanation), motion for summary judgment granted, 2002 WL 535815 (D.D.C. Mar. 12, 2002); Kronberg, 875 F. Supp. at 870-71 (requiring government to provide additional explanation for absence of documentation required by statute and agency regulations to be created, when plaintiff presented evidence that other files, reasonably expected to contain responsive records, were not identified as having been searched).

[220] Roberts v. U.S. Dep't of Justice, No. 92-1707, 1995 WL 356320, at *2 (D.D.C. Jan. 28, 1993); see Miller, 779 F.2d at 1385 ("Thus, the Department
(continued...)

ments, or documents initially believed to have been lost or destroyed, courts generally have accepted this as evidence of the agency's good-faith efforts.[221]

---

[220](...continued)
is not required by the Act to account for documents which the requester has in some way identified if it has made a diligent search for those documents in places in which they might be expected to be found."); Ferranti v. U.S. Dep't of Justice, No. 03-2385, 2005 WL 3040823, at *2 (D.D.C. Jan. 28, 2005) (rejecting plaintiff's "contention that EOUSA should account for previously possessed records"); see also Physicians Comm. for Responsible Med. v. Glickman, 117 F. Supp. 2d 1, 4 (D.D.C. 2000) (while acknowledging that individuals might have had personal "emails and telephone conversations," nevertheless declaring that "[t]here is no evidence . . . that the agency ever had [these] records," despite plaintiff's insistence to the contrary). But see Valencia-Lucena, 180 F.3d at 328 (suggesting that unless it would be "fruitless" to do so, agency is required to seek out employee responsible for record "when all other sources fail to provide leads to the missing record" and when "there is a close nexus . . . between the person and the particular record").

[221] See Maynard, 986 F.2d at 565 ("Rather than bad faith, we think that the forthright disclosure by the INS that it had located the misplaced file suggests good faith on the part of the agency."); Meeropol, 790 F.2d at 953 (rejecting the argument that later-produced records call the adequacy of a search into question, because "[i]t would be unreasonable to expect even the most exhaustive search to uncover every responsive file"); Goland, 607 F.2d at 370 (refusing to undermine validity of agency's prior search because one week following decision by court of appeals agency had discovered numerous, potentially responsive, additional documents several months earlier); Peay v. Dep't of Justice, No. 04-1859, 2006 WL 1805616, at *1 (D.D.C. June 29, 2006) (noting that newly discovered responsive records were not evidence of agency bad faith, but rather was "oversight and, at worst, ineptness on the part of the previous reviewer"); Nat'l Inst. of Military Justice, 404 F. Supp. 2d at 333-34 (stating that "[a]lthough the agency was not initially diligent, that alone does not demonstrate bad faith, especially in light of the subsequent efforts to search for responsive records"); Corbeil v. U.S. Dep't of Justice, No. 04-2265, 2005 WL 3275910, at *3 (D.D.C. Sept. 26, 2005) ("[A]n agency's prompt report of the discovery of additional responsive materials may be viewed as evidence of its good faith efforts to comply with its obligations under FOIA."); Lechliter, 371 F. Supp. 2d at 593 (finding that agency acted in good faith by locating additional documents after error associated with its initial search was corrected); Landmark Legal Found., 272 F. Supp. 2d at 63 (emphasizing that the "continuing discovery and release of documents does not provide that the original search was inadequate, but rather shows good faith on the part of the agency that it continues to search for responsive documents"); Campaign for Responsible Transplantation v. FDA, 219 F. Supp. 2d 106, 111 (D.D.C. 2002) (suggesting that the discovery of fifty-five additional documents amounted to a "pro-

(continued...)

## Mootness and Other Grounds for Dismissal

As is generally the case in any other civil litigation, a FOIA lawsuit may be barred from consideration on its merits due to mootness or the doctrines of issue or claim preclusion, or because some other factor warrants dismissal.

In a FOIA lawsuit, the courts can grant a requester relief only when an agency has improperly withheld agency records.[222] Therefore, if, during litigation, it is determined that all documents found responsive to the underlying FOIA request have been released in full to the requester, the suit should be dismissed as moot because there is no justiciable case or controversy.[223] Similarly, if a FOIA plaintiff's Complaint alleges only an unreason-

---

[221](...continued)
verbial 'drop in the bucket'" in light of the voluminous number of documents located as a result of the agency's search); Torres v. CIA, 39 F. Supp. 2d 960, 963 (N.D. Ill. 1999) (rejecting challenge to the adequacy of search when "a couple of pieces of paper -- having no better than marginal relevance" -- were uncovered during additional searches); Klunzinger v. IRS, 27 F. Supp. 2d 1015, 1024 (W.D. Mich. 1998) (concluding that continued release of responsive documents attests to agency's good faith in providing complete response); Gilmore v. NSA, No. 92-3646, 1993 U.S. Dist. LEXIS 7694, at *27 (N.D. Cal. Apr. 30, 1993) (acceptance of plaintiff's "'perverse theory that a forthcoming agency is less to be trusted in its allegations than an unyielding agency'" would "'work mischief in the future by creating a disincentive for the agency to reappraise its position'" (quoting Military Audit Project v. Casey, 656 F.2d 724, 754 (D.C. Cir. 1981))), aff'd, 76 F.3d 386 (9th Cir. 1995) (unpublished table decision); cf. Envtl. Prot. Servs. v. EPA, 364 F. Supp. 2d 575, 583 (D.D.C. 2005) (concluding that EPA conducted reasonable searches despite discovery of documents not initially found; stating that while EPA's initial searches were flawed, EPA had remedied such preliminary deficiencies).

[222] See 5 U.S.C. § 552(a)(4)(B) (2000 & Supp. IV 2004); see also Kissinger v. Reporters Comm. for Freedom of the Press, 445 U.S. 136, 150 (1980); Summers v. Dep't of Justice, 140 F.3d 1077, 1080 (D.C. Cir. 1998) ("When an agency declines to produce a requested document, the agency bears the burden . . . of proving the applicability of claimed statutory exemptions.").

[223] See, e.g., Hall v. CIA, 437 F.3d 94, 99 (D.C. Cir. 2006) (finding that the agency's release of documents without seeking payment mooted plaintiff's "arguments that the district court's denial of a fee waiver was substantively incorrect"); Brown v. U.S. Dep't of Justice, 169 F. App'x 537, 540 (11th Cir. 2006) (per curiam) (holding that FOIA claim became moot when documents were released); Parenti v. IRS, 70 F. App'x 470, 471 (9th Cir. 2003) (holding that FOIA claim is moot if search was adequate and all responsive documents were produced); Lepelletier v. FDIC, 23 F. App'x 4, 6 (D.C. Cir. 2001) (refusing to consider case further because plaintiff "received all -- indeed
(continued...)

able delay in responding to a FOIA request and the agency subsequently responds by processing the requested records, the FOIA lawsuit should be dismissed as moot.[224]

---

[223](...continued)
more than -- the relief he initially sought . . . [c]onsequently, his appeal is moot . . . ."); Anderson v. HHS, 3 F.3d 1383, 1384 (10th Cir. 1993) (citing Carter v. VA, 780 F.2d 1479, 1481 (9th Cir. 1986), and DeBold v. Stimson, 735 F.2d 1037, 1040 (7th Cir. 1984)); Walsh v. VA, No. 03-C-0225, slip op. at 2 (E.D. Wis. Feb. 10, 2004) (pointing out that "'[i]n FOIA cases, mootness occurs when requested documents have already been produced'" (quoting Matter of Wade, 969 F.2d 241, 248 (7th Cir. 1992))); cf. Haji v. ATF, No. 03 Civ. 8479, 2004 WL 1783625, at *2-3 (S.D.N.Y. Aug. 10, 2004) (holding that plaintiff's request is moot because requested files, if ever in existence, were destroyed at World Trade Center during attacks of September 11, 2001); Long v. ATF, 964 F. Supp. 494, 497-98 (D.D.C. 1997) (holding that agency's grant of fee waiver renders moot issue of requester's status for purposes of assessing fees on that request). But see also Marin Inst. for the Prevention of Drug & Other Alcohol Problems v. HHS, No. 98-17345, 2000 WL 964620, at *1 (9th Cir. July 11, 2000) (finding no mootness when release of document at issue was "surreptitious[]" and not necessarily document plaintiff requested); Hudson v. FBI, No. 04-4079, 2005 WL 2347117, at *1-2 (N.D. Cal. Sept. 26, 2005) (refusing to dismiss plaintiff's Complaint as moot because, although disputed documents were released and FOIA claims were resolved, related Privacy Act access claims had yet to be adjudicated); Nw. Univ. v. USDA, 403 F. Supp. 2d 83, 86 (D.D.C. 2005) (finding no mootness despite belated release of documents because plaintiff challenged adequacy of defendant's document production); Boyd v. U.S. Marshals Serv., No. 99-2712, 2000 U.S. Dist. LEXIS 14025, at *2 (D.D.C. Sept. 25, 2000) (refusing to dismiss case despite fact that all responsive, nonexempt records were released, because agency "[has] yet to explain [its] redactions or withholdings"); Looney v. Walters-Tucker, 98 F. Supp. 2d 1, 3 (D.D.C. 2000) (refusing to dismiss a case as moot where all records located as responsive were produced, because "[i]n a FOIA case, courts always have jurisdiction to determine the adequacy of search"), aff'd per curiam sub nom. Looney v. FDIC, 2 F. App'x 8 (D.C. Cir. 2001); cf. Anderson v. HHS, 907 F.2d 936, 941 (10th Cir. 1990) (declaring that although plaintiff had already obtained all responsive documents in private civil litigation, albeit subject to protective order, plaintiff's FOIA litigation to obtain documents free from any such restriction remained viable).

[224] See, e.g., Voinche v. FBI, 999 F.2d 962, 963 (5th Cir. 1993) (dismissing case as moot because only issue in case was "tardiness" of agency response, which was made moot by agency disclosure determination); Atkins v. Dep't of Justice, No. 90-5095, 1991 WL 185084, at *1 (D.C. Cir. Sept. 18, 1991) ("The question whether DEA complied with the [FOIA's] time limitation in responding to [plaintiff's] request is moot because DEA has now responded to this request."); Tijerina v. Walters, 821 F.2d 789, 799 (D.C. Cir. 1987) ("'[H]owever fitful or delayed the release of information, . . . if we are

(continued...)

# LITIGATION CONSIDERATIONS

In <u>Payne Enterprises v. United States</u>,[225] however, the Court of Appeals for the District of Columbia Circuit held that when records are routinely withheld at the initial processing level, but consistently released after an administrative appeal, and when this situation results in continuing injury to the requester, a lawsuit challenging that practice is ripe for adjudication and is not subject to dismissal on the basis of mootness.[226] The defendant agency's "voluntary cessation" of that practice in <u>Payne</u> did not moot the case when the plaintiff challenged the agency's <u>policy</u> as an

---

[224](...continued)
convinced appellees have, however belatedly, released all nonexempt material, we have no further judicial function to perform under the FOIA.'" (quoting <u>Perry v. Block</u>, 684 F.2d 121, 125 (D.C. Cir. 1982))); <u>Amaya-Flores v. DHS</u>, No. 06-CA-225, 2006 WL 3098777, at *3 (W.D. Tex. Oct. 30, 2006) (finding that <u>Voinche</u> is controlling precedent because "a review of Plaintiff's Complaint shows that her allegations relate only to a delay in obtaining a FOIA response and not [to] the improper withholding of documents"); <u>Walsh</u>, No. 03-C-0225, slip op. at 3-4 (E.D. Wis. Feb. 10, 2004) (finding a claim for declaratory relief to be "without merit" because although the agency failed to respond within the FOIA's time limits, it released all records, thus ending any "actual controversy between the parties") (internal quotations omitted); <u>Potts v. U.S. Dep't of the Treasury</u>, No. 3:02-1599, 2003 WL 22872408, at *2 (N.D. Tex. Oct. 8, 2003) (magistrate's recommendation) ("To the extent that Plaintiffs' complaint is based on the tardiness of Defendant's response to their FOIA requests, their claim has been rendered moot because the [agency] produced the documents."), <u>adopted</u>, 2003 WL 22952825 (N.D. Tex. Nov. 5, 2003); <u>Gambini v. U.S. Customs Serv.</u>, No. 5:01-CV-300, 2001 U.S. Dist. LEXIS 21336, at *4 (N.D. Tex. Dec. 21, 2001) (same); <u>Fisher v. FBI</u>, 94 F. Supp. 2d 213, 216 (D. Conn. 2000) (finding the lawsuit moot and explaining that "[t]he fact that the records came after some delay is not necessarily tantamount to an improper denial of the records; rather, it is an unfortunate consequence of the kind of repetitious requests made by plaintiff").

[225] 837 F.2d 486 (D.C. Cir. 1988).

[226] <u>Id.</u> at 488-93; <u>see also</u> <u>Gilmore v. U.S. Dep't of Energy</u>, 4 F. Supp. 2d 912, 924 (N.D. Cal. 1998) (finding "independent cause of action" for agency's failure to respond within statutory time limits, despite correctness of agency's disclosure determination), <u>dismissed per stipulation</u>, No. 95-0285 (N.D. Cal. Apr. 3, 2000). <u>But see</u> <u>Walsh v. VA</u>, 400 F.3d 535, 537 (7th Cir. 2005) (holding that theoretical possibility of plaintiff having to wait again for records in future FOIA request is insufficient to keep plaintiff's claim alive); <u>OSHA Data/CIH, Inc. v. U.S. Dep't of Labor</u>, 105 F. Supp. 2d 359, 368 (D.N.J. 1999) (refusing to permit claim to go forward when no proof existed that agency would routinely refuse to release data for period of time), <u>aff'd</u>, 220 F.3d 153 (3d Cir. 2000); <u>Reg'l Mgmt. Corp. v. Legal Servs. Corp.</u>, 10 F. Supp. 2d 565, 573 (D.S.C. 1998) (refusing to permit further consideration of moot claim as there was no evidence of continuing injury to requester from "isolated event"), <u>aff'd</u>, 186 F.3d 457 (4th Cir. 1999).

unlawful wrong that otherwise would continue unremedied.[227] Although Payne has been used as the springboard for suits by plaintiffs contending that individual agencies have engaged in a "pattern and practice" of ignoring their obligations under the FOIA, in most of these cases plaintiffs have not found a sympathetic reception to their complaints.[228]

---

[227] Payne Enters., 837 F.2d at 491; see also, e.g., Hercules, Inc. v. Marsh, 839 F.2d 1027, 1028 (4th Cir. 1988) (holding that threat of disclosure of agency telephone directory not mooted by release because new request for subsequent directory pending; agency action thus "capable of repetition yet evading review") (reverse FOIA suit); Better Gov't Ass'n v. Dep't of State, 780 F.2d 86, 90-91 (D.C. Cir. 1986) (holding that challenge to fee waiver standards as applied was moot, but challenge to facial validity of standards was ripe and not moot); Or. Natural Desert Ass'n v. Gutierrez, 409 F. Supp. 2d 1237, 1244-45 (D. Or. 2006) (refusing to find mootness, despite release of documents, due to plaintiff's concern regarding future ability to obtain documents in light of agency's "cut-off" and referral regulations); Pub. Citizen v. Office of the U.S. Trade Representative, 804 F. Supp. 385, 387 (D.D.C. 1992) (stating that despite the disclosure of the specific records requested, a court retains jurisdiction when a plaintiff challenges an "agency's policy to withhold temporarily, on a regular basis, certain types of documents"). But see Atkins v. Dep't of Justice, 1991 WL 185084, at *1 (D.C. Cir. Sept. 18, 1991) ("The question whether DEA complied with the [FOIA's] time limitation in responding to [plaintiff's] request is moot because DEA has now responded to this request."); cf. McDonnell Douglas Corp. v. NASA, 109 F. Supp. 2d 27, 29 (D.D.C. 2000) (holding that the "voluntary cessation" doctrine does not apply in the "reverse" FOIA context; when "the FOIA request underlying the litigation" is withdrawn, the case is moot).

[228] See, e.g., Reg'l Mgmt. Corp. v. Legal Servs. Corp., 186 F.3d 457, 464-65 (4th Cir. 1999) (refusing to consider challenge to alleged policy of non-disclosure of documents relating to ongoing investigations because claim was not "ripe"); Gilmore v. NSA, No. 94-16165, 1995 WL 792079, at *1 (9th Cir. Dec. 11, 1995) (refusing to grant injunction for alleged "systemic agency abuse" in responding to FOIA requests where system of handling requests was "reasonable" and records were "diverse and complex," requiring "painstaking review"); Pub. Employees for Envtl. Responsibility v. U.S. Dep't of the Interior, No. 06-182, 2006 WL 3422484, at *9-10 (D.D.C. Nov. 28, 2006) (denying injunctive relief as there is neither evidence of a policy or practice violating FOIA, nor a cognizable danger that alleged FOIA violation will recur); Ctr. for Individual Rights v. U.S. Dep't of Justice, No. 03-1706, slip op. at 10-12 (D.D.C. Sept. 21, 2004) (denying declaratory and injunctive relief that had been sought to prevent agency's delayed responses to plaintiff's future FOIA requests); Swan View Coal. v. USDA, 39 F. Supp. 2d 42, 47 (D.D.C. 1999) (refusing to grant declaratory relief where agency's failure to timely respond was "an aberration"); cf. Eison v. Kallstrom, 75 F. Supp. 2d 113, 114, 117 (S.D.N.Y. 1999) (allowing plaintiff to amend original complaint in order to allege improper withholding of records, where original com-

(continued...)

## LITIGATION CONSIDERATIONS

Dismissal of a FOIA lawsuit also can be appropriate when the plaintiff fails to prosecute the suit,[229] or records are publicly available under a separate statutory scheme upon payment of fees,[230] or if the claims presented are not ripe.[231] Additionally, a FOIA plaintiff's status as a fugitive

---

[228](...continued)
plaint had asked for injunction against "pattern and practice" of delayed agency responses, which court deemed "now moot"). But see Gutierrez, 409 F. Supp. 2d at 1245 (finding the case not moot because the plaintiff was "concerned about [his] ability to obtain documents in light of the ["cut-off" and referral] regulations"); Gilmore v. U.S. Dep't of Energy, 33 F. Supp. 2d 1184, 1189 (N.D. Cal. 1998) (allowing discovery on "pattern and practice" claim of agency delay in processing FOIA requests), dismissed per stipulation, No. 95-0285 (N.D. Cal. Apr. 3, 2000).

[229] See, e.g., Antonelli v. Executive Office for U.S. Attorneys, No. 92-2416, 1994 WL 245567, at *1 (7th Cir. June 6, 1994) (affirming district court's dismissal of Complaint when, seven months after plaintiff's Complaint was found defective for lack of specificity, plaintiff had failed to amend); Fuller v. FCI Fort Dix, No. 03-1676, 2006 WL 1550000, at *1 (D.D.C. June 1, 2006) (holding that summary judgment was conceded where the plaintiff "failed to file a response by the extended deadline"); Colon v. Huff, No. 00-0201, slip op. at 2-3 (M.D. Pa. June 2, 2000) (dismissing suit for plaintiff's failure to prosecute and failure to keep court apprised of his current address); Nuzzo v. FBI, No. 95-1708, 1996 WL 741587, at *2 (D.D.C. Oct. 8, 1996) (after appropriate warning, dismissing action against several defendants because of plaintiff's failure to respond to motions for summary judgment).

[230] See Kleinerman v. Patent & Trademark Office, No. 82-295, 1983 WL 658, at *1 (D. Mass. Apr. 25, 1983) (dismissing FOIA action because Patent and Trademark Act gave plaintiff independent right of access provided he paid for records); cf. Perales v. DEA, 21 F. App'x 473, 474 (7th Cir. 2001) (dismissing a suit brought to obtain access to an "implementing regulation," because "§ 552(a)(3) of the FOIA does not cover material already made available through publication in the Federal Register").

[231] See, e.g., Odle v. Dep't of Justice, No. 05-2711, 2005 WL 2333833, at *2 (N.D. Cal. Sept. 22, 2005) (holding that, as the defendants no longer assert a "Glomar" defense, the plaintiff's claim regarding defendants' use of that defense became moot, and that the plaintiff's contention that the defendants were unlawfully withholding documents was not ripe for adjudication as the defendants were in the midst of reviewing and processing the requested documents); Doe v. Veneman, 230 F. Supp. 2d 739, 746 (W.D. Tex. 2002) (dismissing claims regarding "other pending FOIA requests" as "too broad for the Court to effectively review because such requests are numerous, request a variety of information, and are still pending with administrative agencies"); Rodrequez v. USPS, No. 90-1886, 1991 WL 212202, at *2 (D.D.C. Oct. 2, 1991) (finding case not yet ripe, absent submission of further information enabling identification of plaintiff's records from among those
(continued...)

may warrant dismissal under the "fugitive disentitlement doctrine."[232] (For a further discussion of fugitives and their FOIA requests, see Procedural Requirements, FOIA Requesters, above). However, dismissal is not necessarily appropriate when a plaintiff dies, as a FOIA claim may be continued by a properly substituted party.[233]

Another reason for dismissing a FOIA lawsuit involves the doctrine of res judicata, sometimes also referred to as "claim preclusion."[234] Res judicata precludes relitigation of an action when it is brought by a plaintiff against the same agency for the same documents, the withholding of which previously has been adjudicated.[235] Res judicata does not prevent

---

[231](...continued)
of thirty-six persons with same name); Nat'l Sec. Archive v. U.S. Dep't of Commerce, No. 87-1581, 1987 WL 27208, at *1 (D.D.C. Nov. 25, 1987) (dismissing a fee waiver case because "of the incomplete nature of the administrative record and the lack of a final administrative decision").

[232] See Maydak v. U.S. Dep't of Educ., 150 F. App'x 136, 138 (3d Cir. 2005) (affirming the district court's dismissal of plaintiff's FOIA suit under the "fugitive disentitlement doctrine" because "there was enough of a connection between Maydak's fugitive status and his FOIA case to justify application of the doctrine" (citing Ortega-Rodriguez v. United States, 507 U.S. 234, 246-49 (1993) (concluding that "absent some connection between a defendant's fugitive status and his appeal, as provided when a defendant is at large during 'the ongoing appellate process,' the justifications advanced for dismissal of fugitives' pending appeals generally will not apply) (citation omitted))); see also Doyle v. U.S. Dep't of Justice, 668 F.2d 1365, 1365 (D.C. Cir. 1981) (upholding the district court's dismissal of the plaintiff's FOIA Complaint, and noting that so long as the plaintiff remains a federal fugitive "it is the general rule that he may not demand that a federal court service his complaint").

[233] See Sinito v. U.S. Dep't of Justice, 176 F.3d 512, 515-16 (D.C. Cir. 1999) (finding that FOIA cause of action survives death of original requester, but restricting substitution of parties to successor or representative of deceased, pursuant to Rule 25 of Federal Rules of Civil Procedure); D'Aleo v. Dep't of the Navy, No. 89-2347, 1991 U.S. Dist. LEXIS, at *2-4 (D.D.C. Mar. 27, 1991) (appointing as plaintiff deceased plaintiff's sister, who was executrix of his estate). But cf. Hayles v. U.S. Dep't of Justice, No. H-79-1599, slip op. at 3 (S.D. Tex. Nov. 2, 1982) (dismissing case upon death of plaintiff when no timely motion for substitution was filed).

[234] See generally FOIA Update, Vol. VI. No. 3, at 6 (discussing "preclusion doctrines" under the FOIA).

[235] See Schwarz v. Nat'l Inst. of Corr., No. 98-1230, 1998 WL 694510, at *1 (10th Cir. Oct. 15, 1998) (affirming dismissal of case because plaintiff's argument that defendant was not party to earlier action was found to be
(continued...)

consideration of a FOIA lawsuit, though, when the plaintiff in the earlier, non-FOIA case involving the same records could not raise a FOIA claim.[236]

---

[235](...continued)
without factual basis); Wrenn v. Shalala, No. 94-5198, 1995 WL 225234, at *1 (D.C. Cir. Mar. 8, 1995) (affirming dismissal of requests that were subject of plaintiff's previous litigation, but reversing dismissal on "claims that were not and could not have been litigated in that prior action"); Hanner v. Stone, No. 92-2565, 1993 WL 302206, at *1 (6th Cir. Aug. 6, 1993) (holding that under doctrine of res judicata, "a final judgment on the merits of an action precludes the parties or their privies from relitigating issues that were or could have been raised in a prior action") (emphasis added); NTEU v. IRS, 765 F.2d 1174, 1177 (D.C. Cir. 1985) (refusing to consider successive FOIA suits for documents that were "identical except for the year involved"); Lane v. Dep't of Justice, No. 1:02-CV-06555, 2006 WL 1455459, at *6 (E.D.N.Y. May 22, 2006) (holding that res judicata barred the plaintiff's claims against the FBI because the claims had already been adjudicated and because the plaintiff "failed to take the necessary action to contest that decision"); Taylor v. Blakey, No. 03-0173, 2005 U.S. Dist. LEXIS 40594, at *12-14 (D.D.C. May 12, 2005) (dismissing suit based on res judicata because plaintiff's interests were legally identical to those of plaintiff's virtual representative who litigated and lost identical FOIA request in Tenth Circuit); Tobie v. Wolf, No. 01-3899, 2002 WL 1034061, at *1 (N.D. Cal. May 8, 2002) (finding privity between "officers of the same government," and therefore dismissing the suit, because the plaintiff previously litigated the same issues against a component of the agency named as a co-defendant in a later suit); Katz v. U.S. Dep't of Justice, 596 F. Supp. 196, 196 (E.D. Mo. 1984) (declaring that, of course, "[a] plaintiff cannot continuously relitigate the same cause of action against the same defendant"); Church of Scientology v. IRS, 569 F. Supp. 1165, 1169 (D.D.C. 1983) ("Where the issues, documents, and plaintiffs are identical in both the prior and present FOIA litigation, the issue of exemption cannot be relitigated.") (internal quotations omitted), vacated & remanded on other grounds, 792 F.2d 146 (D.C. Cir. 1986); see also Greyshock v. U.S. Coast Guard, No. 94-563, slip op. at 2-3 (D. Haw. Jan. 25, 1996) ("All of the claims brought in the instant actions were undeniably claims which either were or could have been brought in this first action in the District Court for the District of Columbia. For that reason alone, plaintiff is precluded from any further pursuit of these claims in this or any other court."), aff'd in part & rev'd in part on other grounds, 107 F.3d 16 (9th Cir. 1997) (unpublished table decision); cf. Peltier v. FBI, No. 02-4328, slip op. at 4-5 (D. Minn. Oct. 24, 2006) (magistrate's recommendation) (dictum) (finding that plaintiff's New York FOIA action appears to preclude the instant case pursuant to the principles of claim and issue preclusion, and further finding that although "the New York FOIA action is presently on appeal[, this] does not undermine the preclusive effect of the [New York] district court's final judgment"), adopted (D. Minn. Feb. 9, 2007).

[236] See North v. Walsh, 881 F.2d 1088, 1093-95 (D.C. Cir. 1989) (deciding
(continued...)

In addition, res judicata is not applicable where there has been a change in the factual circumstances or legal principles applicable to the lawsuit.[237]

When parallel FOIA suits are brought by the same party for the same records, dismissal may be appropriate by operation of the "first-filed" rule.[238] This rule holds that "[w]hen lawsuits involving the same controversy are filed in more than one jurisdiction, the general rule is that the court that first acquired jurisdiction has priority."[239] The "first-filed" rule differs from res judicata because in the latter a case involving the same parties already has been decided, whereas in the former the cases are still pend-

---

[236](...continued)
that claim for records under FOIA was not barred by prior discovery prohibition for same records in criminal case in which FOIA claim could not have been interposed).

[237] See, e.g., Negley v. FBI, 169 F. App'x 591, 594 (D.C. Cir. 2006) (holding that res judicata was inapplicable because both lawsuits -- one to obtain records from Sacramento office and other to obtain records from San Francisco office -- did not involve same "nucleus of facts"; declaring further that the "FOIA does not limit a party to a single request, and because the records maintained by an FBI office may change over time, a renewal of a previous request inevitably raises new factual questions"); Croskey v. U.S. Office of Special Counsel, No. 96-5114, 1997 WL 702364, at *3 (D.C. Cir. Oct. 17, 1997) (finding res judicata inapplicable because document was not in existence when earlier litigation was brought); Hanner v. Stone, No. 92-1579, 1992 WL 361382, at *1 (6th Cir. Dec. 8, 1992) (determining that present claim was not precluded under doctrine of res judicata when appellate court had previously adjudicated claim that was similar, but involved different issue); ACLU v. U.S. Dep't of Justice, 321 F. Supp. 2d 24, 34 (D.D.C. 2004) (finding res judicata inapplicable where changed circumstances -- namely, Attorney General's decision to declassify records in question -- altered legal issues surrounding plaintiff's FOIA request); Wolfe v. Froehlke, 358 F. Supp. 1318, 1319 (D.D.C. 1973) (stating that lawsuit was not barred where national security status had changed), aff'd, 510 F.2d 654 (D.C. Cir. 1974); cf. Primorac v. CIA, 277 F. Supp. 2d 117, 120 (D.D.C. 2003) (dismissing case on basis of res judicata despite plaintiff's argument that automatic declassification section of Executive Order 12,958 was unavailable to him in previous lawsuit for same records and fact that it was still unavailable because it was not yet effective); Bernson v. ICC, 635 F. Supp. 369, 371 (D. Mass. 1986) (refusing to accept argument that changed circumstances rendered inapplicable previous decision affirming invocation of FOIA exemption, and dismissing claim based on res judicata).

[238] See McHale v. FBI, No. 99-1628, slip op. at 8-9 (D.D.C. Nov. 7, 2000) (dismissing "essentially duplicative action").

[239] Biochem Parma, Inc. v. Emory Univ., 148 F. Supp. 2d 11, 13 (D.D.C. 2001) (citing Columbia Plaza Corp. v. Sec. Nat'l Bank, 525 F.2d 620, 627 (D.C. Cir. 1975)) (non-FOIA cases).

ing, but both rules proceed from the same goal -- to minimize redundant litigation and thereby conserve judicial resources.[240]

Collateral estoppel, or "issue preclusion," also may foreclose further consideration of a FOIA suit.[241] Collateral estoppel precludes relitigation of an issue previously litigated by one party to the action.[242] For example, if an agency's search for records already has been found to be adequate, a plaintiff should not be able to question that same search in a subsequent action.[243] While collateral estoppel may be somewhat more problematic in the FOIA context where there is not necessarily an express or implied legal relationship between the plaintiff in the first action and the plaintiff in the successive suit,[244] the risk of conflicting decisions on the same set of rec-

---

[240] See McHale, No. 99-1628, slip op. at 3 (D.D.C. Nov. 7, 2000) (describing purpose of "first-filed" rule as "conserv[ation of] judicial resources"); see also Flynn v. Place, 63 F. Supp. 2d 18, 25 (D.D.C. 1999) (explaining that purpose of res judicata doctrine is to "protect[] adversaries from expensive and vexatious multiple lawsuits, [and] conserve[] judicial resources") (non-FOIA case).

[241] See generally FOIA Update, Vol. VI, No. 3, at 6.

[242] See Yamaha Corp. of Am. v. United States, 961 F.2d 245, 254 (D.C. Cir. 1992) (non-FOIA case); Church of Scientology v. U.S. Dep't of the Army, 611 F.2d 738, 750-51 (9th Cir. 1980) (declaring that complete identity of plaintiff and document at issue precludes relitigation); see also FOIA Update, Vol. VI, No. 3, at 6; cf. Cotton v. Heyman, 63 F.3d 1115, 1118 nn.1-2 (D.C. Cir. 1995) (holding that doctrine of direct estoppel, which precludes relitigating issue finally decided in "separate proceeding" within same suit, prevented Smithsonian Institution from challenging district court determination that it is subject to FOIA on appeal from award of attorney fees; however, "Smithsonian is free to relitigate the issue against another party in a separate proceeding"). But see North, 881 F.2d at 1093-95 (finding issue preclusion inapplicable when exemption issues raised in FOIA action differ from relevancy issues raised in prior action for discovery access to same records); Hall v. CIA, No. 04-00814, 2005 WL 850379, at *3 (D.D.C. Apr. 13, 2005) (holding doctrine of collateral estoppel inapplicable where plaintiff previously challenged adequacy of search and exemption's validity but in instant case, by contrast, sought immediate production of documents and reduction or waiver of fees).

[243] See, e.g., Allnutt v. U.S. Dep't of Justice, 99 F. Supp. 2d 673, 677 (D. Md. 2000) (refusing, "[i]n accord with basic res judicata principles," to reconsider adequacy of search issue that was decided by another court), aff'd per curiam sub nom. Allnut v. Handler, 8 F. App'x 225 (4th Cir. 2001).

[244] See Favish v. Office of Indep. Counsel, 217 F.3d 1168, 1171 (9th Cir. 2000) (refusing to find that an attorney who represented the plaintiff in a previous case was precluded from relitigating the releasability of death-
(continued...)

ords suggests that relaxed notions of privity -- which courts have allowed in other contexts[245] -- are particularly appropriate in FOIA cases.[246] As with the doctrine of res judicata, collateral estoppel is not applicable to a subsequent lawsuit if there is an intervening material change in the law or factual predicate.[247]

---

[244](...continued)
scene photographs of former Deputy White House Counsel Vincent Foster, because the identity of interests was viewed by the second appellate court as only "an abstract interest in enforcement of FOIA") (internal quotations omitted), rev'd on other grounds sub nom. NARA v. Favish, 541 U.S. 157, reh'g denied, 541 U.S. 1057 (2004); see also FOIA Post, "Supreme Court to Hear FOIA and Privacy Act Cases Back-to-Back" (posted 9/30/03; supplemented 10/10/03) (describing unusual circumstances of Favish case); cf. Doe v. Glickman, 256 F.3d 371, 380 (5th Cir. 2001) (permitting third-party intervention in "reverse" FOIA suit in order to avoid collateral estoppel effect of decision potentially adverse to third-party interests); Robertson v. DOD, 402 F. Supp. 1342, 1347 (D.D.C. 1973) (concluding that private citizen's interest in subsequent FOIA action was not protected by government in prior "reverse" FOIA suit over same documents, because interests were not "congruent").

[245] See, e.g., Montana v. United States, 440 U.S. 147, 155-56 (1979) (finding that that government was estopped from rearguing a question that was "definitely and actually litigated and adjudged" in a state court decision, even though the government was not a party to that state court action, because the government had a "sufficient laboring oar" in the state court proceeding "to actuate principles of estoppel") (internal quotations omitted) (non-FOIA case).

[246] Compare Accuracy in Media, Inc. v. Nat'l Park Serv., 194 F.3d 120, 123 (D.C. Cir. 1999) (affirming district court denial of access to photographs of former Deputy White House Counsel Vincent Foster death scene, on basis of invasion of privacy), with Favish, 217 F.3d at 1174 (remanding case to district court to view same photographs in camera in order to balance asserted "public interest" against surviving family's privacy interests).

[247] See, e.g., Croskey, 1997 WL 702364, at *5 (concluding that access to investigator's notes and impressions of witnesses adjudicated in prior proceeding was "sufficiently different" from witness statements themselves to bar application of collateral estoppel); Minnis v. USDA, 737 F.2d 784, 786 n.1 (9th Cir. 1984) (declaring that "an intervening Supreme Court decision clarifying an issue that had been uncertain in the lower courts defeats collateral estoppel"); McQueen v. United States, 264 F. Supp. 2d 502, 513-14 (S.D. Tex. 2003) (refusing to find that collateral estoppel prevented plaintiff from litigating "requests for information that may not be essentially identical," despite agency's argument that the contested documents were "the same kinds . . . but for different years").

## LITIGATION CONSIDERATIONS

### "Vaughn Index"

A distinguishing feature of FOIA litigation is that the defendant agency bears the burden of sustaining its action of withholding records.[248] The most commonly used device for meeting this burden of proof is the "Vaughn Index," fashioned by the Court of Appeals for the District of Columbia Circuit in a case entitled Vaughn v. Rosen.[249]

The Vaughn decision requires agencies to prepare an itemized index, correlating each withheld document (or portion) with a specific FOIA exemption and the relevant part of the agency's nondisclosure justification.[250] Such an index allows the trial court "to make a rational decision [about] whether the withheld material must be produced without actually viewing the documents themselves . . . [and] to produce a record that will render [its] decision capable of meaningful review on appeal."[251] It also helps to

---

[248] See 5 U.S.C. § 552(a)(4)(B) (2000 & Supp. IV 2004); see also Natural Res. Def. Council v. NRC, 216 F.3d 1180, 1190 (D.C. Cir. 2000) (explaining that the "FOIA itself places the burden on the agency to sustain the lawfulness of specific withholdings in litigation") (Government in the Sunshine Act case); Brady-Lunny v. Massey, 185 F. Supp. 2d 928, 931 (C.D. Ill. 2002) ("Since the Government is the party refusing to produce the documents, it bears the burden of showing that the documents are not subject to disclosure.").

[249] 484 F.2d 820 (D.C. Cir. 1973); see, e.g., Canning v. U.S. Dep't of Justice, 848 F. Supp. 1037, 1042 (D.D.C. 1994) ("Agencies are typically permitted to meet [their] heavy burden by 'filing affidavits describing the material withheld and the manner in which it falls within the exemption claimed.'" (quoting King v. U.S. Dep't of Justice, 830 F.2d 210, 217 (D.C. Cir. 1987))).

[250] See Vaughn, 484 F.2d at 827; accord King, 830 F.2d at 217.

[251] King, 830 F.2d at 219; see, e.g., Maine v. U.S. Dep't of the Interior, 298 F.3d 60, 65 (1st Cir. 2002); Rugiero v. U.S. Dep't of Justice, 257 F.3d 534, 544 (6th Cir. 2001) (explaining that Vaughn Index enables court to make "independent assessment" of agency's exemption claims), Campaign for Responsible Transplantation v. FDA, 219 F. Supp. 2d 106, 116 (D.D.C. 2002) ("Without a proper Vaughn index, a requester cannot argue effectively for disclosure and this court cannot rule effectively."); Cucci v. DEA, 871 F. Supp. 508, 514 (D.D.C. 1994) ("An adequate Vaughn index facilitates the trial court's duty of ruling on the applicability of certain invoked FOIA exemptions, gives the requester as much information as possible that he may use to present his case to the trial court and thus enables the adversary system to operate."); cf. Antonelli v. Sullivan, 732 F.2d 560, 562 (7th Cir. 1984) (holding that no Vaughn Index is required when small number of documents is at issue and affidavit contains sufficient detail); Moye, O'Brien, O'Rourke, Hogan & Pickert v. Nat'l R.R. Passenger Corp., No. 02-126, 2003 WL 21146674, at *6 (M.D. Fla. May 13, 2003) ("'Vaughn indexes are most

(continued...)

"create balance between the parties."[252]

Thus, if a court finds that an index is not sufficiently detailed, it should require one that is more detailed.[253] Alternatively, if a <u>Vaughn</u> In-

---

[251](...continued)
useful in cases involving thousands of pages of documents.'" (quoting <u>Miscavige v. IRS</u>, 2 F.3d 366, 368 (11th Cir. 1993))), <u>rev'd & remanded on other grounds</u>, 116 F. App'x 251 (11th Cir. 2004), <u>cert. denied</u>, 543 U.S. 1121 (2005).

[252] <u>Long v. U.S. Dep't of Justice</u>, 10 F. Supp. 205, 209 (N.D.N.Y. 1998); <u>see, e.g.</u>, <u>Judicial Watch, Inc. v. FDA</u>, 449 F.3d 141, 146 (D.C. Cir. 2006) (noting that the agency would have "a nearly impregnable defensive position" but for its burden to justify nondisclosure); <u>Odle v. Dep't of Justice</u>, No. 05-2711, 2006 WL 1344813, at *5 (N.D. Cal. May 17, 2006) (observing that <u>Vaughn</u> Index "afford[s] the person making a FOIA request a meaningful opportunity to contest the soundness of withholding"); <u>Peter S. Herrick's Customs & Int'l Trade Newsletter v. U.S. Customs & Border Prot.</u>, No. 04-0377, 2005 WL 3274073, at *2 (D.D.C. Sept. 22, 2005) ("The purpose of the <u>Vaughn</u> index is to provide fertile ground upon which to germinate the seeds of adversarial challenge."); <u>Edmonds v. FBI</u>, 272 F. Supp. 2d 35, 44 (D.D.C. 2003) (explaining that affidavits must "'strive to correct the asymmetrical distribution of knowledge that characterizes FOIA litigation'" (quoting <u>King</u>, 830 F.2d at 218)); <u>see also</u> <u>Kern v. FBI</u>, No. 94-0208, slip op. at 5 (C.D. Cal. Sept. 14, 1998) (opining that one purpose of <u>Vaughn</u> Index is "to afford the requester an opportunity to intelligently advocate release of the withheld documents"); <u>cf.</u> <u>Fiduccia v. U.S. Dep't of Justice</u>, 185 F.3d 1035, 1042 (9th Cir. 1999) (pointing out that <u>Vaughn</u> Index is not required where it is unnecessary to be particularly concerned about adversarial balance).

[253] <u>See</u> <u>Davin v. U.S. Dep't of Justice</u>, 60 F.3d 1043, 1065 (3d Cir. 1995) (remanding case for further proceedings and suggesting that another, more detailed <u>Vaughn</u> Index be required); <u>Church of Scientology Int'l v. U.S. Dep't of Justice</u>, 30 F.3d 224, 230-40 (1st Cir. 1994) (same); <u>Wiener v. FBI</u>, 943 F.2d 972, 979 (9th Cir. 1991) (remanding case for a more thorough <u>Vaughn</u> Index); <u>Herrick's Newsletter</u>, 2005 WL 3274073, at *2 (directing agency to "re-file the <u>Vaughn</u> index with specific identifications of 'low 2' and 'high 2' status for the information that is withheld under Exemption 2"); <u>Antonelli v. ATF</u>, No. 04-1180, 2005 WL 3276222, at *9 n.8 (D.D.C. Aug. 16, 2005) (directing the agency "to file a less confusing, detailed declaration and corresponding <u>Vaughn</u> index"); <u>Elec. Privacy Info. Ctr. v. DHS</u>, 384 F. Supp. 2d 100, 120 (D.D.C. 2005) (permitting agencies to submit revised <u>Vaughn</u> Index to correct inadequacies in original); <u>Nat'l Res. Def. Council v. DOD</u>, 388 F. Supp. 2d 1086, 1089 (C.D. Cal. 2005) (ordering submission of new <u>Vaughn</u> Index because original was too conclusory to support exemption claims); <u>Santos v. DEA</u>, 357 F. Supp. 2d 33, 37-38 (D.D.C. 2004) (requiring supplemental declaration because initial one failed to provide "sufficient detail" to establish connection between exemptions invoked and doc-
(continued...)

dex is inadequate to support withholding, it certainly may be supplemented through the court's in camera review of the withheld material.[254] (See

---

[253](...continued)
uments withheld); Madison Mech., Inc. v. NASA, No. 99-2854, 2003 WL
1477014, at *4 (D.D.C. Mar. 20, 2003) (magistrate's recommendation) (recommending that another Vaughn Index be required because of deficiencies
in first one), adopted (D.D.C. Mar. 31, 2003); Wilderness Soc'y v. Bureau of
Land Mgmt., No. 01-2210, 2003 WL 255971, at *7 (D.D.C. Jan. 15, 2003),
modified (D.D.C. Feb. 4, 2003) (requiring supplemental Vaughn Index to
correct conclusory and generalized exemption claims); Coleman v. FBI, 972
F. Supp. 5, 9 (D.D.C. 1997) (rejecting narratives on "deleted page sheets"
that apply to multiple documents and requiring agency to redo index to "inform the court as to the contents of individual documents and the applicability of the various Exemptions"); see also Bryce v. Overseas Private Inv.
Corp., No. 96-595, slip op. at 10 (W.D. Tex. Sept. 28, 1998) ("An agency may
submit a revised index at any time prior to the summary judgment hearing." (citing Coastal States Gas Corp. v. Dep't of Energy, 644 F.2d 969, 971,
981 (3d Cir. 1981))); cf. Windel v. United States, No. A02-306, 2004 WL
3363406, at *4 (D. Alaska Sept. 30, 2004) (rejecting the government's attempt to justify withholdings with a letter that "describes in general terms,
the exemptions claimed," and ordering submission "of a proper Vaughn index" that contains "sufficient detail regarding the bases for exemption").

[254] See, e.g., Lion Raisins Inc. v. USDA, 354 F.3d 1072, 1082 (9th Cir.
2004) (acknowledging that "[u]nder certain limited circumstances, we have
endorsed the use of in camera review of government affidavits as the basis
for FOIA decisions"); Fiduccia, 185 F.3d at 1042-43 (suggesting likewise
that notwithstanding Wiener, 943 F.2d at 979, in camera inspection could
by itself be sufficient); Maynard v. CIA, 986 F.2d 547, 557 (1st Cir. 1993)
("Where, as here, the agency, for good reason, does not furnish publicly the
kind of detail required for a satisfactory Vaughn index, a district court may
review the documents in camera."); Simon v. U.S. Dep't of Justice, 980 F.2d
782, 784 (D.C. Cir. 1992) (holding that despite inadequacy of Vaughn Index,
in camera review, "although admittedly imperfect . . . is the best way to
[en]sure both that the agency is entitled to the exemption it claims and
that the confidential source is protected"); see also High Country Citizens
Alliance v. Clarke, No. 04-CV-00749, 2005 WL 2453955, at *8 (D. Colo. Sept.
29, 2005) (finding in camera review necessary due to insufficient descriptions of withheld documents in Vaughn Index); Carbe v. ATF, No. 03-1658,
2004 WL 2051359, at *8 n.5 (D.D.C. Aug. 12, 2004) (denying plaintiff's request for in camera inspection, because Vaughn Index adequately described withheld information); Twist v. Ashcroft, 329 F. Supp. 2d 50, 54
(D.D.C. 2004) ("[I]n camera review of the withheld documents (or of the portions withheld) is proper if the agency affidavits are insufficiently detailed
to permit review of exemption claims[.]"), aff'd per curiam on other grounds,
171 F. App'x 855 (D.C. Cir. Nov. 16, 2004); Nat'l Wildlife Fed'n v. U.S. Forest
Serv., 861 F.2d 1114, 1116 (9th Cir. 1988) ("[W]here a trial court properly reviewed contested documents in camera, an adequate factual basis for the
(continued...)

the further discussion of this point under Litigation Considerations, In Camera Inspection, below.)

There is no set formula for a Vaughn Index; instead, it is the function, not the form that is important.[255] Indeed, the D.C. Circuit has eloquently

---

[254](...continued)
decision exists."); Hornbostel v. U.S. Dep't of the Interior, 305 F. Supp. 2d 21, 30 (D.D.C. 2003) (commenting that while Vaughn Index description of documents was "slightly ambiguous," correctness of exemption claims was demonstrated through in camera examination), aff'd, No. 03-5257, 2004 WL 1900562 (D.C. Cir. Aug. 25, 2004); cf. Judicial Watch, Inc. v. Dep't of the Army, 402 F. Supp. 2d 241, 249 & n.6 (D.D.C. 2005) (ordering in camera inspection to review accuracy of agency's descriptions of withheld information after inadvertent disclosure revealed existence of discrepancies and inaccuracies in Vaughn Index), summary judgment granted in part, 435 F. Supp. 2d 81 (D.D.C. 2006); Fla. Immigrant Advocacy Ctr. v. NSA, 380 F. Supp. 2d 1332, 1338 (S.D. Fla. 2005) (conducting in camera inspection "to satisfy an 'uneasiness' or 'doubt' that the exemption claim may be over-broad given the nature of the Plaintiff's arguments"). But see also Wiener, 943 F.2d at 979 (suggesting that "[i]n camera review of the withheld documents by the [district] court is not an acceptable substitute for an adequate Vaughn index"); cf. Peltier v. FBI, No. 03-CV-905, 2005 WL 735964, at *11 (W.D.N.Y. Mar. 31, 2005) (acknowledging that "in camera review is particularly frowned upon in the context of Exemption 1 withholdings . . . [h]owever, Defendant's insufficient Vaughn index leaves this Court with no choice but to conduct further review"), renewed mot. for summary judgment granted, 2006 WL 462096, at *2 (W.D.N.Y. Feb. 24, 2006), aff'd, No. 06-1405, 2007 WL 627534 (2d Cir. Feb. 23, 2007).

[255] Jones v. FBI, 41 F.3d 238, 242 (6th Cir. 1994); see Fiduccia, 185 F.3d at 1044 ("Any form . . . may be adequate or inadequate, depending on the circumstances."); Church of Scientology, 30 F.3d at 231 (agreeing that there is no set formula for a Vaughn Index); Gallant v. NLRB, 26 F.3d 168, 172-73 (D.C. Cir. 1994) (holding that justification for withholding provided by agency may take any form as long as agency offers "reasonable basis to evaluate [it]s claim of privilege"); Vaughn v. United States, 936 F.2d 862, 867 (6th Cir. 1991) ("A court's primary focus must be on the substance, rather than the form, of the information supplied by the government to justify withholding requested information."); Hornbeck v. U.S. Coast Guard, No. 04-1724, 2006 WL 696053, at *6 (D.D.C. Mar. 20, 2006) ("[T]he precise form of the agency's submission -- whether it be an index, a detailed declaration, or a narrative -- is immaterial."); Voinche v. FBI, 412 F. Supp. 2d 60, 65 (D.D.C.) ("[I]t is the function of a Vaughn index rather than its form that is important, and a Vaughn index is satisfactory as long as it allows a court to conduct a meaningful de novo review of the agency's claim of exemption."), summary judgment granted, 425 F. Supp. 2d 134 (D.D.C. 2006) (appeal pending); Tax Analysts v. IRS, 414 F. Supp. 2d 1, 4-5 (D.D.C. 2006) (recognizing that substance of government's justification for withholding

(continued...)

observed that "a <u>Vaughn</u> index is not a work of literature; agencies are not graded on the richness or evocativeness of their vocabularies."[256] Likewise, the sufficiency of a <u>Vaughn</u> Index is not determined by reference to the length of its document descriptions.[257] What "'is required is that the requester and the trial judge be able to derive from the index a clear explanation of why each document or portion of a document withheld is putatively exempt from disclosure.'"[258] As one court has explained:

> A true <u>Vaughn</u> index identifies discrete portions of documents and identifies the exemption pertaining to each portion of the document. In most cases, such an index provides the date, source, recipient, subject matter and nature of each document in sufficient detail to permit the requesting party to argue effectively against the claimed exemptions and for the court to assess the applicability of the claimed exemptions.[259]

---

[255](...continued)
takes precedence over form in which it is presented) (appeal pending); <u>cf.</u> <u>People for the Ethical Treatment of Animals v. USDA</u>, No. 03-195, 2005 WL 1241141, at *4 (D.D.C. May 24, 2005) (stating that the agency "may submit other materials to supplement its <u>Vaughn</u> index, such as affidavits, that give the court enough information to determine whether the claimed exemptions are properly applied" (citing <u>Judicial Watch, Inc. v. USPS</u>, 297 F. Supp. 2d 252, 257 (D.D.C. 2004))).

[256] <u>Landmark Legal Found. v. IRS</u>, 267 F.3d 1132, 1138 (D.C. Cir. 2001); <u>see</u> <u>Coldiron v. U.S. Dep't of Justice</u>, 310 F. Supp. 2d 44, 52 (D.D.C. 2004) ("Rarely does the court expect to find in briefs, much less <u>Vaughn</u> indices, anything resembling poetry.").

[257] <u>See</u> <u>Judicial Watch, Inc.</u>, 449 F.3d at 146 ("[W]e focus on the functions of the <u>Vaughn</u> index, not the length of the document descriptions, as the touchstone of our analysis.").

[258] <u>Manna v. U.S. Dep't of Justice</u>, 832 F. Supp. 866, 873 (D.N.J. 1993) (quoting <u>Hinton v. Dep't of Justice</u>, 844 F.2d 126, 129 (3d Cir. 1988)), <u>aff'd</u>, 51 F.3d 1158 (3d Cir. 1995); <u>see</u> <u>Jones</u>, 41 F.3d at 242 (holding an agency's <u>Vaughn</u> Index adequate when it "'enables the court to make a reasoned independent assessment of the claim[s] of exemption'" (quoting <u>Vaughn</u>, 936 F.2d at 866-67)). <u>But see</u> <u>People for the Am. Way Found. v. NSA</u>, No. 06-206, slip op. at 11 n.5 (D.D.C. Nov. 20, 2006) (reminding that "a <u>Vaughn</u> index is not required . . . where it 'could cause the very harm that [the exemption] was intended to prevent'" (quoting <u>Linder v. NSA</u>, 94 F.3d 693, 697 (D.C. Cir. 1996) (non-FOIA case)).

[259] <u>St. Andrews Park, Inc. v. U.S. Dep't of Army Corps of Eng'rs</u>, 299 F. Supp. 2d 1264, 1271 (S.D. Fla. 2003); <u>see also</u> <u>Cole v. U.S. Dep't of Justice</u>, No. 05-674, 2006 WL 2792681, at *5 (D.D.C. Sept. 27, 2006) (noting that index specified: "(1) the type of document, (2) the exact location of the

(continued...)

When a <u>Vaughn</u> Index meets these criteria, it is "'accorded a presumption of good faith.'"[260] Of course, "[t]he degree of specificity of itemization, justification, and correlation required in a particular case will . . . depend on the nature of the document at issue and the particular exemption assert-

---

[259](...continued)
withheld information in the document, (3) the applicable FOIA exemptions for all withheld information, and (4) a brief description of the withheld information"); <u>Edmonds Inst. v. U.S. Dep't of the Interior</u>, 383 F. Supp. 2d 105, 109 (D.D.C. 2005) (explaining that <u>Vaughn</u> Index "should contain a short description of the content of each individual document sufficient to allow" its exemption use to be tested); <u>Dorsett v. U.S. Dep't of the Treasury</u>, 307 F. Supp. 2d 28, 34 (D.D.C. 2004) (describing adequate <u>Vaughn</u> Index).

[260] <u>Carney v. U.S. Dep't of Justice</u>, 19 F.3d 807, 812 (2d Cir. 1994) (quoting <u>SafeCard Servs. v. SEC</u>, 926 F.2d 1197, 1200 (D.C. Cir. 1991)); <u>see, e.g.</u>, <u>Jones</u>, 41 F.3d at 242 (reiterating that agency affidavits entitled to presumption of good faith); <u>Cohen v. FBI</u>, No. 93-1701, slip op. at 4 (D.D.C. Oct. 11, 1994) ("[M]inor contradictions in defendants' affidavits do not evince intentional misrepresentation on their part."); <u>see also</u> <u>Church of Scientology</u>, 30 F.3d at 233 (explaining that a good-faith presumption is applicable only "when the agency has provided a reasonably detailed explanation for its withholdings . . . court may not without good reason second-guess an agency's explanation, but it also cannot discharge its de novo review obligation unless that explanation is sufficiently specific"); <u>Coastal Delivery Corp. v. U.S. Customs Serv.</u>, 272 F. Supp. 2d 958, 962 (C.D. Cal. 2003) (explaining that a plaintiff's disagreement with the conclusions reached in a <u>Vaughn</u> Index is not a sufficient basis for challenging it, and observing that "such a challenge is . . . appropriate [only] when the defendant does not provide sufficient explanation of its position to allow for disagreement"), <u>appeal dismissed voluntarily</u>, No. 03-55833 (9th Cir. 2003); <u>Butler v. DEA</u>, No. 05-1798, 2006 WL 398653, at *2 (D.D.C. Feb. 16, 2006) (noting presumption of good faith accorded to agency affidavits); <u>Dean v. FDIC</u>, 389 F. Supp. 2d 780, 791 (D. Ky. 2005) (concluding that the agency's <u>Vaughn</u> Index was entitled to a presumption of good faith because it contained sufficient detail "to permit the court to make a fully informed decision" about the propriety of the agency's nondisclosure); <u>Caton v. Norton</u>, No. 04-CV-439, 2005 WL 3116613, at *11 (D.N.H. Nov. 21, 2005) (concluding that mistakes in processing FOIA request, which agency "convincingly explained," were not sufficient to overcome "presumption of good faith" given to its declaration); <u>cf.</u> <u>NARA v. Favish</u>, 541 U.S. 157, 174-75 (requiring "meaningful evidentiary showing" to overcome "presumption of legitimacy accorded to the Government's official conduct," because "[a]llegations of government misconduct are easy to 'allege and hard to disprove'" (quoting <u>Crawford-El v. Britton</u>, 523 U.S. 574, 585 (1998) (non-FOIA case))), <u>reh'g denied</u>, 541 U.S. 1057 (2004); <u>FOIA Post</u>, "Supreme Court Rules for 'Survivor Privacy' in <u>Favish</u>" (posted 4/9/04) (discussing how unsubstantiated allegations of official misconduct are insufficient to establish "public interest" in disclosure of third-party records, as enunciated in <u>Favish</u>).

ed."[261]

A document specifically denominated as a "Vaughn Index" per se is not even essential, so long as the nature of the withheld information is adequately attested to by the agency.[262] What is essential, however, is that

---

[261] Info. Acquisition Corp. v. Dep't of Justice, 444 F. Supp. 458, 462 (D.D.C. 1978); see, e.g., Landmark Legal Found., 267 F.3d at 1138 (chiding plaintiff for his criticism of repetitive nature of Vaughn Index, given that "thousands of documents belonged in the same category"); Citizens Comm'n on Human Rights v. FDA, 45 F.3d 1325, 1328 (9th Cir. 1995) (finding adequate, for responsive records consisting of 1000 volumes of 300 to 400 pages each, agency's volume-by-volume summary when Vaughn Indexes "specifically describe the documents' contents and give specific reasons for withholding them"); Davis v. U.S. Dep't of Justice, 968 F.2d 1276, 1282 n.4 (D.C. Cir. 1992) (opining that precise matching of exemptions with specific withheld items "may well be unnecessary" when all government's generic claims have merit); Vaughn, 936 F.2d at 868 (approving category-of-document approach when over 1000 pages were withheld under Exemptions 3, 5, 7(A), 7(C), 7(D), and 7(E)); Odle, 2006 WL 1344813, at *9 (recognizing that "the detail required in a Vaughn index depends on the specific exemption claimed"); Tax Analysts, 414 F. Supp. 2d at 4 (concluding that agency need not justify withholdings on a document-by-document basis because it invoked only one exemption); Coldiron, 310 F. Supp. 2d at 52 (explaining that repetition in Vaughn Index is to be expected, especially when "each redacted passage concerns the same, classified subject"); NTEU v. U.S. Customs Serv., 602 F. Supp. 469, 473 (D.D.C. 1984) (reasoning that the fact that only one exemption is involved "nullif[ies] the need to formulate the type of itemization and correlation system required by the Court of Appeals in Vaughn"); aff'd, 802 F.2d 525 (D.C. Cir. 1986); Agee v. CIA, 517 F. Supp. 1335, 1337-38 (D.D.C. 1981) (accepting index listing fifteen categories when more specific index would compromise national security); cf. Lardner v. U.S. Dep't of Justice, No. 03-0180, 2005 WL 758267, at *20 (D.D.C. Mar. 31, 2005) (finding that agency need not amend Vaughn Index to include names of clemency applicants who were subjects of withheld advisory letters, because that would shed no light on whether categorical withholding under Exemption 5 was proper).

[262] See, e.g., Judicial Watch, Inc., 449 F.3d at 146 (stating that an agency may "submit other measures in combination with or in lieu of the index itself," such as supporting affidavits, or seek in camera review of the documents); Wishart v. Comm'r, No. 98-17248, 1999 WL 985142, at *1 (9th Cir. Oct. 27, 1999) (suggesting that Vaughn Index is unnecessary if declarations are detailed enough); Miscavige v. IRS, 2 F.3d 366, 368 (11th Cir. 1993) (deciding that separate document expressly designated as "Vaughn Index" is unnecessary when agency "declarations are highly detailed, focus on the individual documents, and provide a factual base for withholding each document at issue"); Voinche, 412 F. Supp. 2d at 65 (explaining that an agency "does not have to provide an index per se, but can satisfy its

(continued...)

the Vaughn Index expressly indicate for each document that any reasonably segregable information has been disclosed.[263] In this connection, the Court of Appeals for the District of Columbia Circuit has repeatedly held that it is reversible error for a district court not to make a finding of segregability.[264]

Indeed, the D.C. Circuit has even ruled that if the segregability issue

---

[262](...continued)
burden by other means, such as submitting the documents in question for an in camera review or by providing a detailed affidavit or declaration"); Queen v. Gonzales, No. 96-1387, 2005 WL 3204160, at *2 (D.D.C. Nov. 15, 2005) (explaining that "[a]gency affidavits can satisfy Vaughn's requirements" if they are detailed sufficiently to permit de novo review) (appeal pending); Doyharzabal v. Gal, No. 7:00-2995-24, 2004 WL 2444124, at *3 (D.S.C. Sept. 13, 2004) (finding agency's affidavit to be "equivalent" to Vaughn Index); Judicial Watch, 297 F. Supp. 2d at 257 (noting that agency may submit materials in "'any form'" as long as reviewing court has reasonable basis to evaluate exemption claim (quoting Gallant, 26 F.3d at 173)); Goulding v. IRS, No. 97 C 5728, 1998 WL 325202, at *7 (N.D. Ill. June 8, 1998) ("A Vaughn index is not necessary in every case, so long as the function it serves is sufficiently performed by the agency's affidavits or declarations."); Ferri v. U.S. Dep't of Justice, 573 F. Supp. 852, 856-57 (W.D. Pa. 1983) (holding that 6000 pages of unindexed grand jury testimony were sufficiently described); cf. Minier v. CIA, 88 F.3d 796, 804 (9th Cir. 1996) ("[W]hen a FOIA requester has sufficient information to present a full legal argument, there is no need for a Vaughn index.").

[263] See, e.g., Isley v. Executive Office for U.S. Attorneys, No. 98-5098, 1999 WL 1021934, at *7 (D.C. Cir. Oct. 21, 1999) ("The segregability requirement applies to all documents and all exemptions in the FOIA."); Krikorian v. Dep't of State, 984 F.2d 461, 467 (D.C. Cir. 1993) (remanding for segregability determination for "each of the withheld documents"); Edmonds Inst., 383 F. Supp. 2d at 108 ("The Vaughn index should contain a description of the segregability analysis . . . ."); Nat'l Res. Def. Council, 388 F. Supp. 2d at 1105 (denying summary judgment because agency "completely fail[ed] to analyze segregability"); The Wilderness Soc'y v. U.S. Dep't of the Interior, 344 F. Supp. 2d 1, 19 (D.D.C. 2004) (rejecting a "blanket declaration that all facts are so intertwined [as] to prevent disclosure under the FOIA" (citing Animal Legal Def. Fund, Inc. v. Dep't of the Air Force, 44 F. Supp. 2d 295, 301-02 (D.D.C. 1999))).

[264] See Kimberlin v. Dep't of Justice, 139 F.3d 944, 950 (D.C. Cir. 1998) (stating that it is reversible error for district court to fail to make segregability finding, and remanding for such a finding); Schiller v. NLRB, 964 F.2d 1205, 1210 (D.C. Cir. 1992) (same); see also Animal Legal Def. Fund, 44 F. Supp. 2d at 299 (chastising agency for failing to discharge "its duty under § 552(b)"); FOIA Update, Vol. XIV, No. 3, at 11-12 ("OIP Guidance: The 'Reasonable Segregation' Obligation") (urging agencies to heed this requirement, based upon emerging case law).

has not first been raised by the parties, the district court has "an affirmative duty" to consider the matter "sua sponte."[265] (For further discussions of this issue, see Procedural Requirements, "Reasonably Segregable" Obligation, above, and Litigation Considerations, "Reasonably Segregable" Requirements, below.) Questions regarding segregability also may be resolved through in camera inspection of documents by the district court, when necessary.[266] (For a further discussion of in camera inspection, see Litigation Considerations, In Camera Inspection, below.)

When voluminous records are at issue, courts have approved the use of Vaughn Indexes based upon representative samplings of the withheld documents.[267] This special procedure "allows the court and the parties to

---

[265] Trans-Pac. Policing Agreement v. U.S. Customs Serv., 177 F.3d 1022, 1028 (D.C. Cir. 1999); see also Hornbeck, 2006 WL 696053, at *7 ("[D]istrict courts are required to consider segregability issues even when the parties have not specifically raised such claims."); Perry-Torres v. U.S. Dep't of State, 404 F. Supp. 2d 140, 144 (D.D.C. 2005) (noting court's sua sponte duty to consider segregability); Elec. Privacy Info. Ctr., 384 F. Supp. 2d at 111 n.4 (same).

[266] See Solar Sources, Inc. v. United States, 142 F.3d 1033, 1039 (7th Cir. 1998) (finding that in camera review, coupled with sworn agency declaration, "provided the district court with a sufficient factual basis to determine that the documents were properly withheld"); Becker v. IRS, 34 F.3d 398, 406 (7th Cir. 1994) (finding remand unnecessary as judge "did not simply rely on IRS affidavits describing the documents, but conducted an in camera review" (citing Hopkins v. HUD, 929 F.2d 81, 85 (2d Cir. 1991) (holding that absence of district court's findings on segregability warrants "remand with instructions to the district court to examine the inspector reports in camera"))).

[267] See, e.g., Neely v. FBI, 208 F.3d 461, 467 (4th Cir. 2000) (suggesting that, on remand, district court "resort to the well-established practice . . . of randomly sampling the documents in question"); Solar Sources, 142 F.3d at 1038-39 (approving use of sample of 6000 pages out of five million); Jones, 41 F.3d at 242 (approving sample comprising two percent of total number of documents at issue); Meeropol v. Meese, 790 F.2d 942, 956-57 (D.C. Cir. 1986) (allowing sampling of every 100th document when approximately 20,000 documents were at issue); Weisberg v. U.S. Dep't of Justice, 745 F.2d 1476, 1490 (D.C. Cir. 1984) (approving index of sampling of withheld documents, with over 60,000 pages at issue, even though no example of certain exemptions was provided); Hornbeck, 2006 WL 696053, at *6 ("When dealing with voluminous records, a court will sanction an index or agency declaration that describes only a representative sample of the total number of documents."); Nat'l Res. Def. Council, 388 F. Supp. 2d at 1089 (ordering parties to agree upon "representative sample" from more than 6500 documents that will provide basis for Vaughn Index); Jefferson v. O'Brien, No. 96-1365, slip op. at 5 (D.D.C. Feb. 22, 2000) (approving sample index of

(continued...)

reduce a voluminous FOIA exemption case to a manageable number of items" for the Vaughn Index and, "[i]f the sample is well-chosen, a court can, with some confidence, 'extrapolate its conclusions from the represent-ative sample to the larger group of withheld materials.'"[268] Once a repre-sentative sampling of the withheld documents is agreed to, however, the agency's subsequent release of some of those documents may destroy the representativeness of the sample and thereby raise questions about the propriety of withholding other responsive documents that were not includ-ed in the sample.[269] In recognition of this danger, the D.C. Circuit has held

---

[267](...continued)
approximately four percent of responsive records); see also Wash. Post v. DOD, 766 F. Supp. 1, 15-16 (D.D.C. 1991) (deciding that with more than 14,000 pages of responsive material involved, agency should produce de-tailed Vaughn Index for sample of files, such sample to be determined by parties or court); cf. Piper v. U.S. Dep't of Justice, 294 F. Supp. 2d 16, 20 (D.D.C. 2003) (noting that the parties agreed to sample of 357 pages out of 80,000 to be discussed in Vaughn Index); Kronisch v. United States, No. 83 CIV. 2458, 1995 WL 303625, at *1, *13 n.1 (S.D.N.Y. May 18, 1995) (holding sampling of fifty documents selected by plaintiff, out of universe of approxi-mately 30,000 pages, to be appropriate basis for resolution of discovery dis-pute). But see Martinson v. Violent Drug Traffickers Project, No. 95-2161, 1996 WL 571791, at *8 (D.D.C. Aug. 7, 1996) ("This Court does not believe that 173 pages of located documents is even close to being 'voluminous.'"); SafeCard Servs. v. SEC, No. 84-3073, 1988 WL 58910, at *3-5 (D.D.C. May 19, 1988) (concluding that burden of indexing relatively small number of re-quested documents (approximately 200) was insufficient to justify sam-pling).

[268] Bonner v. U.S. Dep't of State, 928 F.2d 1148, 1151 (D.C. Cir. 1991) (quoting Fensterwald v. CIA, 443 F. Supp. 667, 669 (D.D.C. 1977)); see FlightSafety Servs. Corp. v. Dep't of Labor, 326 F.3d 607, 612-13 (5th Cir. 2003) (per curiam) (approving use of representative sample that was of-fered to district court for in camera inspection, because sample was "ade-quate" to demonstrate that no reasonably segregable information could be extracted from withheld records); Campaign for Responsible Transplanta-tion v. FDA, 180 F. Supp. 2d 29, 34 (D.D.C. 2001) (approving representative sampling of one of many applications for investigational new drugs, all of which are "essentially uniform," but allowing plaintiff to select one to be sampled); cf. Halpern v. FBI, No. 94-365, 2002 WL 31012157, at *14 (W.D.N.Y. Aug. 31, 2001) (magistrate's recommendation) (opining in dicta that sampling would be inappropriate for the 116 pages at issue), adopted (W.D.N.Y. Oct. 16, 2001).

[269] See Bonner, 928 F.2d at 1153-54 (explaining that the sample should "uncover[] no excisions or withholdings improper when made," but also noting that "[t]he fact that some documents in a sample set become releas-able with the passage of time does not, by itself, indicate any agency lapse"); Meeropol, 790 F.2d at 960 (finding error rate of twenty-five percent
(continued...)

that an agency "must justify its initial withholdings and is not relieved of that burden by a later turnover of sample documents," and that "the district court must determine whether the released documents were properly redacted [when] initially reviewed."[270]

Many agencies use "coded" Vaughn Indexes -- which break certain FOIA exemptions into several categories, explain the particular nondisclosure rationales for each category, and then mark the exemption and category on the particular documents at issue.[271] Courts have generally accepted the use of such "coded" indexes when "[e]ach deletion was correlated specifically and unambiguously to the corresponding exemption . . . [which] was adequately explained by functional categories . . . [so as to] place[] each document into its historical and investigative perspective."[272]

---

[269](...continued)
"unacceptably high"); Schrecker v. U.S. Dep't of Justice, 14 F. Supp. 2d 111, 117 (D.D.C. 1998) (ordering reprocessing of all documents because of problems with representative sampling).

[270] Bonner, 928 F.2d at 1154; see also Davin, 60 F.3d at 1053 (plaintiff's agreement to sampling does not relieve government of obligation to disclose reasonably segregable, nonexempt material in all responsive documents, including those not part of sample).

[271] See, e.g., Jones, 41 F.3d at 242-43 (noting that coded indices "have become accepted practice"); Maynard, 986 F.2d at 559 & n.13 (noting use by FBI and explaining format); Queen, 2005 WL 3204160, at *2 (same); accord 5 U.S.C. § 552(b) (second and third sentences following exemptions; requiring document markings as part of initial administrative processing).

[272] Keys v. U.S. Dep't of Justice, 830 F.2d 337, 349-50 (D.C. Cir. 1987); see, e.g., Judicial Watch, Inc., 449 F.3d at 147 (explaining that a Vaughn Index may utilize "codes and categories," so long as they are "sufficiently particularized to carry the agency's burden of proof"); Blanton v. Dep't of Justice, 64 F. App'x 787, 789 (D.C. Cir. 2003) (stating that "coding . . . adequately describes the documents and justifies the exemptions"); Maynard, 986 F.2d at 559 n.13 (explaining that "use of coded indices has been explicitly approved by several circuit courts"); Garcia v. U.S. Dep't of Justice, 181 F. Supp. 2d 356, 370 (S.D.N.Y. 2002) (accepting adequacy of agency's coded Vaughn Index); Baez v. FBI, 443 F. Supp. 2d 717, 723 (E.D. Pa. 2006) (upholding use of coded Vaughn Index where agency "redacted only identifying information and administrative markings"); Heeney v. FDA, No. 97-5461, 1999 U.S. Dist. LEXIS 23365, at *23 (C.D. Cal. Mar. 16, 1999) (finding agency's coded declaration to be sufficient), aff'd, 7 F. App'x 770 (9th Cir. 2001); Canning, 848 F. Supp. at 1043 ("[T]here is nothing inherently improper about the use of a coding system."); Steinberg v. U.S. Dep't of Justice, 801 F. Supp. 800, 803 (D.D.C. 1992), aff'd in pertinent part & remanded in part, 23 F.3d 548 (D.C. Cir. 1994) (refusing to find coded Vaughn Index inadequate); cf. Fiduccia, 185 F.3d at 1043-44 (observing that "[t]he form of
(continued...)

Innovative formats for "coded" affidavits have been found acceptable, so long as they enhance the ultimate goal of overall "descriptive accuracy" of the affidavit.[273]

The D.C. Circuit has gone so far as to hold that the district court judge's review of only the expurgated documents -- an integral part of the "coded" affidavit -- was sufficient in a situation in which the applicable exemption was obvious from the face of the documents.[274] However, this approach has been found inadequate when the coded categories are too "far ranging" and more detailed subcategories could be provided.[275] Indeed, when numerous pages of records are withheld in full, a "coded" affidavit

---

[272](...continued)
disclosure is not critical" and that "redacted documents [can be] an entirely satisfactory (perhaps superior) alternative to a Vaughn index or affidavit performing this function"); Davin, 60 F.3d at 1051 ("While the use of the categorical method does not per se render a Vaughn index inadequate, an agency using justification codes must also include specific factual information concerning the documents withheld and correlate the claimed exemptions to the withheld documents."), on remand, No. 92-1122, slip op. at 6 (W.D. Pa. Apr. 9, 1998) (approving revised coded Vaughn Index), aff'd, 176 F.3d 471 (3d Cir. 1999) (unpublished table decision). But see Wiener, 943 F.2d at 978-79 (rejecting coded affidavits on belief that such categorical descriptions fail to give requester sufficient opportunity to contest withholdings); Samuel Gruber Educ. Project v. U.S. Dep't of Justice, 24 F. Supp. 2d 1, 8 (D.D.C. 1998) (magistrate's recommendation) (suggesting that coded Vaughn Indexes have been "near[ly] universal[ly] condemnation"), adopted with modifications, No. 90-1912 (D.D.C. Mar. 17, 1998).

[273] See Nat'l Sec. Archive v. Office of the Indep. Counsel, No. 89-2308, 1992 WL 1352663, at *3-4 (D.D.C. Aug. 28, 1992) (finding "alphabetical classification" properly employed to facilitate coordination of agency justifications where information was withheld by multiple agencies under various exemptions); see also King, 830 F.2d at 225; Canning, 848 F. Supp. at 1043.

[274] Delaney, Migdail & Young, Chartered v. IRS, 826 F.2d 124, 128 (D.C. Cir. 1987); see Whittle v. Moschella, 756 F. Supp. 589, 595 (D.D.C. 1991) ("For two large redactions, the contents are not readily apparent, but since the information there redacted was provided by confidential sources, it is entirely protected from disclosure."); see also King, 830 F.2d at 221 ("Utilization of reproductions of the material released to supply contextual information about material withheld is clearly permissible, but caution should be exercised in resorting to this method of description."); cf. Fiduccia, 185 F.3d at 1043 (recognizing that a Vaughn Index is "a superfluity" when the plaintiff and the court can ascertain the nature of information withheld by reviewing the redacted documents).

[275] See King, 830 F.2d at 221-22. But see Canning, 848 F. Supp. at 1044-45 (approving coded Vaughn Index for classified information and differentiating it from that filed in King).

that does not specifically correlate multiple exemption claims to particular portions of the pages withheld has been found to be impermissibly conclusory.[276]

Agencies employing "coded" indexes ordinarily attach copies of the records released in part -- i.e., the "expurgated" documents -- as part of their public Vaughn submission.[277] But agencies seeking to justify withholding records from first-party FOIA requesters should be mindful of the fact that the public filing of expurgated documents about the individual requester (or even detailed descriptions of them in briefs) may constitute a "disclosure" under subsection (b) of the Privacy Act of 1974.[278] Unless proceeding under seal, or with the prior written consent of the requester, an agency should strive to make such a disclosure only in accordance with one of the exceptions set forth in the Privacy Act -- such as its "routine use" exception or its "court order" exception.[279]

Although an agency ordinarily must justify its withholdings on a

---

[276] See Coleman v. FBI, No. 89-2773, 1991 WL 333709, at *4 (D.D.C. Apr. 3, 1991) (allowing "coded" affidavit for expurgated pages, but rejecting it as to pages withheld in full), summary affirmance granted, No. 92-5040, 1992 WL 373976 (D.C. Cir. Dec. 4, 1992); see also Williams v. FBI, No. 90-2299, 1991 WL 163757, at *3-4 (D.D.C. Aug. 6, 1991) (finding "coded" affidavit insufficiently descriptive as to documents withheld in their entireties).

[277] See, e.g., Maynard, 986 F.2d at 559 n.13 (explaining coded Vaughn procedure); Queen, 2005 WL 3204160, at *3 (noting that the agency attached redacted pages to its coded declaration and "labeled each redaction with an exemption code").

[278] 5 U.S.C. § 552a(b) (2000 & Supp. IV 2004); see, e.g., Krohn v. U.S. Dep't of Justice, No. 78-1536, slip op. at 2-7 (D.D.C. Mar. 19, 1984), vacated in part on other grounds (D.D.C. Nov. 29, 1984); Citizens Bureau of Investigation v. FBI, No. C78-80, slip op. at 3 (N.D. Ohio Dec. 12, 1979); see also Laningham v. U.S. Navy, No. 83-3238, slip op. at 2-3 (D.D.C. Sept. 25, 1984), summary judgment granted (D.D.C. Jan. 7, 1985), aff'd per curiam, 813 F.2d 1236 (D.C. Cir. 1987).

[279] 5 U.S.C. § 552a(b)(3), (11); see also, e.g., 66 Fed. Reg. 36593, 36593 (July 12, 2001) (listing routine uses applicable to records in Justice Department's Civil Division Case File System); 63 Fed. Reg. 8666, 8667-68 (Feb. 20, 1998) (listing routine uses applicable to records in United States Attorneys' Offices' Civil Case Files); cf. Blazy v. Tenet, 979 F. Supp. 10, 27 (D.D.C. 1997) (agreeing to an uncontested order to seal Privacy Act-protected documents released pursuant to a routine use, while chiding the plaintiff that "[h]aving obtained three volumes of released documents through this litigation, [he] somewhat ironically complains that the government improperly filed these documents with the Court in violation of his privacy rights"), summary affirmance granted, No. 97-5330, 1998 WL 315583 (D.C. Cir. May 12, 1998).

page-by-page or document-by-document basis, under certain circumstances courts have approved withholdings of entire, but discrete, categories of records which encompass similar information.[280] Most commonly, courts have permitted the withholding of records under Exemption 7(A) on a category-by-category or "generic" basis.[281] While the outermost contours

---

[280] See Judicial Watch, Inc., 449 F.3d at 148 (concluding that the agency's "decision to tie each document to one or more claimed exemptions in its index and then summarize the commonalities of the documents in a supporting affidavit is a legitimate way of serving those functions"); NLRB v. Robbins Tire & Rubber Co., 437 U.S. 214, 223-24 (1978) (stating that language of Exemption 7(A) "appears to contemplate that certain generic determinations may be made"); Crooker v. ATF, 789 F.2d 64, 66-67 (D.C. Cir. 1986) (distinguishing between unacceptable "blanket" exemptions and permissible generic determinations); Pully v. IRS, 939 F. Supp. 429, 433-38 (E.D. Va. 1996) (accepting categorization of 5624 documents into twenty-six separate categories protected under several exemptions); see also U.S. Dep't of Justice v. Landano, 508 U.S. 165, 179 (1993) ("There may well be other generic circumstances in which an implied assurance of confidentiality fairly can be inferred."); U.S. Dep't of Justice v. Reporters Comm. for Freedom of the Press, 489 U.S. 749, 776 (1989) (instructing that "categorical decisions may be appropriate and individual circumstances disregarded when a case fits into a genus in which the balance characteristically tips in one direction"); cf. Coleman v. FBI, 972 F. Supp. 5, 8 (D.D.C. 1997) ("For an agency to break from the norm of a document-by-document index, the agency must at least argue that a 'categorical' index is warranted.").

[281] See, e.g., Robbins Tire, 437 U.S. at 218-23 (endorsing government's position "that a particularized, case-by-case showing is neither required nor practical, and that witness statements in pending unfair labor practice proceedings are exempt as a matter of law from disclosure [under Exemption 7(A)] while the hearing is pending"); Solar Sources, 142 F.3d at 1040 (reiterating that detailed Vaughn Index is not generally required in Exemption 7(A) cases); In re Dep't of Justice, 999 F.2d 1302, 1309 (8th Cir. 1993) (en banc); Dickerson v. Dep't of Justice, 992 F.2d 1426, 1428, 1433-34 (6th Cir. 1993) (approving FBI justification of Exemption 7(A) for documents pertaining to disappearance of Jimmy Hoffa on "category-of-document" basis by supplying "a general description of the contents of the investigatory files, categorizing the records by source or function"); Lewis v. IRS, 823 F.2d 375, 389 (9th Cir. 1987) ("The IRS need only make a general showing that disclosure of its investigatory records would interfere with its enforcement proceedings."); Bevis v. Dep't of State, 801 F.2d 1386, 1389 (D.C. Cir. 1986); W. Journalism Ctr. v. Office of the Indep. Counsel, No. 96-5178, 1997 WL 195516, at *1 (D.C. Cir. Mar. 11, 1997) ("[A]ppellee was not required to describe the records retrieved in response to appellants' request, or the harm their disclosure might cause, on a document-by-document basis, as appellee's description of the information contained in the three categories it devised is sufficient to permit the court to determine whether the information retrieved is exempt from disclosure."); see also Citizens Comm'n, 45

(continued...)

of what constitutes acceptable "generic" Exemption 7(A) <u>Vaughn</u> declarations are sometimes unclear,[282] it appears well established that if the agency has (1) defined its Exemption 7(A) categories functionally, (2) conducted a document-by-document review in order to assign documents to the proper category, and (3) explained how the release of each category of information would interfere with the enforcement proceedings, the description will be found sufficient.[283] (See the discussion of <u>Vaughn</u> Indexes under Exemption 7(A), above.) Moreover, when "a claimed FOIA exemption consists of a generic [exemption], dependent upon the category of records rather than the subject matter which each individual record contains [so

---

[281](...continued)
F.3d at 1328 (for responsive records consisting of 1000 volumes of 300 to 400 pages each, volume-by-volume summary held adequate when <u>Vaughn</u> Indexes sufficiently describe the documents' contents and give specific reasons for withholding them"); <u>Gavin v. SEC</u>, No. 04-4522, 2005 WL 2739293, at *3 (D. Minn. Oct. 24, 2005) (recognizing propriety of categorical approach to justify use of Exemption 7(A)); <u>FOIA Update</u>, Vol. V, No. 2, at 3-4 (describing appropriate affidavits for cases involving Exemption 7(A)). But see <u>Detroit Free Press v. U.S. Dep't of Justice</u>, 174 F. Supp. 2d 597, 601 (E.D. Mich. 2001) (ordering in camera review because <u>Vaughn</u> Index statements concerning potential harm from release of any information about disappearance of former Teamsters president Jimmy Hoffa were undermined by publication of specifics concerning Hoffa investigation); cf. <u>Inst. for Justice & Human Rights v. Executive Office of the U.S. Attorney</u>, No. C 96-1469, 1998 WL 164965, at *6-7 (N.D. Cal. Mar. 18, 1998) (refusing to permit agency to justify Exemption 7(A) withholdings by category when it had already submitted <u>Vaughn</u> Indexes justifying withholdings on document-by-document basis).

[282] <u>Compare</u> <u>Curran v. Dep't of Justice</u>, 813 F.2d 473, 476 (1st Cir. 1987) (approving category entitled "other sundry items of information" because "[a]bsent a 'miscellaneous' category of this sort, the FBI would, especially in the case of one-of-a-kind records, have to resort to just the sort of precise description which would itself compromise the exemption"), <u>and</u> <u>May v. IRS</u>, No. 90-1123-CV-W-2, 1991 WL 328041, at *2-3 (W.D. Mo. Dec. 9, 1991) (approving categories of "intra-agency memoranda" and "work sheets"), <u>with</u> <u>Bevis</u>, 801 F.2d at 1390 ("categories identified only as 'teletypes,' or 'airtels,' or 'letters'" held inadequate).

[283] <u>See</u> <u>In re Dep't of Justice</u>, 999 F.2d at 1309 (citing <u>Bevis</u>, 801 F.2d at 1389-90); <u>Manna v. U.S. Dep't of Justice</u>, 815 F. Supp. 798, 806 (D.N.J. 1993); see also <u>Dickerson</u>, 992 F.2d at 1433 (enumerating categories of information withheld); <u>Judicial Watch, Inc. v. FBI</u>, No. 00-745, 2001 WL 35612541, at *5 (D.D.C. Apr. 20, 2001) (same); <u>Curran</u>, 813 F.2d at 476 (same); <u>May</u>, 1991 WL 328041, at *3-4 (same); <u>Docal v. Bennsinger</u>, 543 F. Supp. 38, 44 n.12 (M.D. Pa. 1981) (enumerating categories of "interference"); cf. <u>Curran</u>, 813 F.2d at 476 (stating that FBI affidavit met <u>Bevis</u> test and therefore finding it unnecessary to determine whether <u>Bevis</u> test is too demanding).

that] resort to a Vaughn index is futile,"[284] such generic descriptions can also satisfy an agency's Vaughn obligation with regard to other exemptions as well.[285]

In a broad range of contexts, most courts have refused to require agencies to file public Vaughn Indexes that are so detailed as to reveal sensitive information the withholding of which is the very issue in the litigation.[286] Therefore, in camera affidavits are frequently utilized in Exemp-

---

[284] Church of Scientology v. IRS, 792 F.2d 146, 152 (D.C. Cir. 1986).

[285] See Reporters Comm., 489 U.S. at 779-80 (authorizing "categorical" protection of information under Exemption 7(C)); Gallant, 26 F.3d at 173 (approving categorical withholding of names under Exemption 6); Church of Scientology, 792 F.2d at 152 (finding generic exemption under IRS Exemption 3 statute, 26 U.S.C. § 6103 (2000), appropriate if "affidavit sufficiently detailed to establish that the document or group of documents in question actually falls into the exempted category"); Antonelli v. FBI, 721 F.2d 615, 617-19 (7th Cir. 1983) (holding that no index required in third-party request for records when agency categorically neither confirmed nor denied existence of records on particular individuals absent showing of public interest in disclosure); Brown v. FBI, 658 F.2d 71, 74 (2d Cir. 1981) (protecting personal information under Exemption 6); Pully, 939 F. Supp. at 433-38 (accepting categorical descriptions for documents protected under Exemptions 3 (in conjunction with 26 U.S.C. § 6103(a)), 5 (attorney-client privilege), 7(A), 7(C), and 7(E) -- 5624 documents arranged into twenty-six categories); May, 1991 WL 328041, at *3-4 (protecting withholdings under both Exemption 7(A) and Exemption 3 (in conjunction with 26 U.S.C. § 6103)); NTEU, 602 F. Supp. at 472-73 (finding no index required for forty-four crediting plans withheld under Exemption 2); see also FOIA Update, Vol. X, No. 2, at 6 (discussing categorical Exemption 7(C) balancing under Reporters Committee). But see Judicial Watch, Inc., 402 F. Supp. 2d at 251 ("The fact that federal employees have an identifiable privacy interest in avoiding disclosures of information that could lead to annoyance or harassment . . . does not authorize a 'blanket exemption' for the names of all government employees."); McNamara v. U.S. Dep't of Justice, 949 F. Supp. 478, 483 (W.D. Tex. 1996) (rejecting apparent categorical indices for criminal files on third parties that were withheld under Exemptions 6 and 7(C) because "there is no way for the court to tell whether some, a portion of some, or all the documents being withheld fall within any of the exemptions claimed"); cf. Church of Scientology, 30 F.3d at 234 ("[A] categorical approach to nondisclosure is permissible only when the government can establish that, in every case, a particular type of information may be withheld regardless of the specific surrounding circumstances.").

[286] See, e.g., Landano, 508 U.S. at 180 ("To the extent that the Government's proof may compromise legitimate interests, of course, the Government still can attempt to meet its burden with in camera affidavits."); Bassiouni v. CIA, 392 F.3d 244, 246 (7th Cir. 2004) ("The risk to intelligence
(continued...)

tion 1 cases when a public description of responsive documents would compromise national security.[287] (For a further discussion of this point, see

---

[286](...continued)
sources and methods comes from the details that would appear in a Vaughn index . . . ."), cert. denied, 545 U.S. 1129 (2005); Lion Raisins, 354 F.3d at 1084 (vouching that an agency need not "disclose facts that would undermine the very purpose of its withholding"); Maricopa Audubon Soc'y v. U.S. Forest Serv., 108 F.3d 1089, 1093 (9th Cir. 1997) ("Indeed we doubt that the agency could have introduced further proof without revealing the actual contents of the withheld materials."); Oglesby v. U.S. Dep't of the Army, 79 F.3d 1172, 1176 (D.C. Cir. 1996) ("The description and explanation the agency offers should reveal as much detail as possible as to the nature of the document without actually disclosing information that deserves protection."); Maynard, 986 F.2d at 557 (emphasizing that although public declaration "lacked specifics, a more detailed affidavit could have revealed the very intelligence sources or methods that the CIA wished to keep secret"); Lewis, 823 F.2d at 380 ("[A] Vaughn index of the documents here would defeat the purpose of Exemption 7(A). It would aid [the requester] in discovering the exact nature of the documents supporting the government's case against him earlier than he otherwise would or should."); Curran, 813 F.2d at 476 (agency should not be forced "to resort to just the sort of precise description which would itself compromise the exemption"); Church of Scientology v. U.S. Dep't of the Army, 611 F.2d 738, 742 (9th Cir. 1980) (recognizing that "the government need not specify its objections in such detail as to compromise the secrecy of the information"); Baez, 443 F. Supp. 2d at 723 ("[I]t is hard to see how the government could have provided . . . more information about the redactions without disclosing the redacted information itself."); Odle, 2006 WL 1344813, at *9 (explaining that the Vaughn Index must "disclose 'as much as possible without thwarting the claimed exemption's purposes'" (quoting Wiener, 943 F.2d at 977)); Herrick's Newsletter, 2005 WL 3274073, at *4 ("The Court will not require an agency to describe the withheld material with such specificity as to result in the constructive equivalent of actual disclosure."); Berman v. CIA, 378 F. Supp. 2d 1209, 1215-16 (E.D. Cal. 2005) (recognizing that because the CIA's declaration "is part of the public record," it must of necessity support the withholding of intelligence sources and methods through the use of "terms that are general").

[287] See, e.g., Doyle v. FBI, 722 F.2d 554, 556 (9th Cir. 1983) (approving use of in camera affidavits in certain cases involving national security exemption); Edmonds, 272 F. Supp. 2d at 46 (approving the use of an in camera affidavit because "extensive public justification would threaten to reveal the very information for which a FOIA exemption is claimed"); Pub. Educ. Ctr., Inc. v. DOD, 905 F. Supp. 19, 22 (D.D.C. 1995) (same); Keys v. U.S. Dep't of Justice, No. 85-2588, slip op. at 3 (D.D.C. May 12, 1986) (noting "the inherent problems that necessarily arise whenever a FOIA affiant is confronted with the need to be circumspect" due to national security concerns), aff'd on other grounds, 830 F.2d at 337; Peltier v. FBI, No. 03-CV-905,

(continued...)

Litigation Considerations, In Camera Inspection, below.) This same important principle also has been applied to other FOIA exemptions -- for example, in Exemption 5 cases,[288] in Exemption 7(A) cases,[289] in Exemption 7(C) cases,[290] and in Exemption 7(D) cases.[291] However, in all cases in which explanations for withholding are presented in camera, the agency is obliged to ensure that it first has set forth on the public record an explanation that

---

[287](...continued)
2006 WL 462096, at *1 (W.D.N.Y. Feb. 24, 2006) (allowing submission of in camera Vaughn Index to justify withholding pursuant to Exemption 1), aff'd, No. 06-1405, 2007 WL 627534 (2d Cir. Feb. 23, 2007); see also CIA v. Sims, 471 U.S. 159, 179 (1985) (recognizing that "the mere explanation of why information must be withheld can convey [harmful] information").

[288] See, e.g., Ethyl Corp. v. EPA, 25 F.3d 1241, 1250 (4th Cir. 1994) ("If the district court is satisfied that the EPA cannot describe documents in more detail without breaching a properly asserted confidentiality, then the court is still left with the mechanism provided by the statute -- to conduct an in camera review of the documents."); Wolfe v. HHS, 839 F.2d 768, 771 n.3 (D.C. Cir. 1988) (en banc) ("Where the index itself would reveal significant aspects of the deliberative process, this court has not hesitated to limit consideration of the Vaughn index to in camera inspection.").

[289] See, e.g., Alyeska Pipeline Serv. v. EPA, No. 86-2176, 1987 WL 17071, at *3 (D.D.C. Sept. 9, 1987) ("[R]equiring a Vaughn index in this matter will result in exactly the kind of harm to defendant's law enforcement proceedings which it is trying to avoid under exemption 7(A)."), aff'd on other grounds, 856 F.2d 309 (D.C. Cir. 1988); Dickerson v. Dep't of Justice, No. 90-60045, 1991 WL 337422, at *3 (E.D. Mich. July 31, 1991), aff'd, 992 F.2d 1426 (6th Cir. 1993).

[290] See Canning v. Dep't of Justice, No. 01-2215, slip op. at 6 (D.D.C. May 27, 2005) (permitting agency to file portion of declaration in camera in order to avoid compromising Exemption 7(C) position).

[291] See, e.g., Carpenter v. U.S. Dep't of Justice, 470 F.3d 434, 442 (1st Cir. 2006) (explaining that, in the instant Exemption 7(C) case, "[e]ven if [plaintiff] had asserted a valid public interest, the appropriate method for a detailed evaluation of the competing interests would have been through an in camera review because a standard Vaughn index might result in disclosure of the very information that the government attempted to protect"); Landano, 508 U.S. at 180 (ruling that government can meet its burden with in camera affidavits in order to avoid identification of sources in Exemption 7(D) withholdings); Church of Scientology, 30 F.3d at 240 n.23 (same); Keys, 830 F.2d at 349 (announcing that there is no requirement to produce Vaughn Index in "degree of detail that would reveal precisely the information that the agency claims it is entitled to withhold"); Doe v. U.S. Dep't of Justice, 790 F. Supp. 17, 21 (D.D.C. 1992) ("[A] meaningful description beyond that provided by the Vaughn code utilized in this case would probably lead to disclosure of the identity of sources.").

is as complete as possible without compromising the sensitive information.[292]

With regard to the timing of the creation of a Vaughn Index, it is well settled that a requester is not entitled to receive one during the administrative process.[293] Furthermore, courts generally do not require the submission of a Vaughn Index prior to the time at which a dispositive motion is filed; this standard practice is based upon the need to maintain an orderly and efficient adjudicative process in FOIA cases, and upon the practical reality that some form of affidavit, declaration, or index virtually always accompanies the defendant agency's motion for summary judgment.[294] Efforts to compel the preparation of Vaughn Indexes prior to the filing of an agency's dispositive motion are typically denied as premature.[295]

---

[292] See Lion Raisins, 354 F.3d at 1084 (overturning district court decision that relied on in camera review of sealed declaration, and remanding for creation of Vaughn Index); Armstrong v. Executive Office of the President, 97 F.3d 575, 580-81 (D.C. Cir. 1996) (citing Lykins v. U.S. Dep't of Justice, 725 F.2d 1455, 1465 (D.C. Cir. 1984)); Philippi v. CIA, 546 F.2d 1009, 1013 (D.C. Cir. 1976); cf. Al Najjar v. Ashcroft, No. 00-1472, slip op. at 7 (D.D.C. July 22, 2003) (rejecting agencies' overly broad in camera submissions, and requiring agencies to augment public record before any ruling is made on dispositive motions).

[293] See, e.g., Schwarz v. U.S. Dep't of Treasury, 131 F. Supp. 2d 142, 147 (D.D.C. 2000) ("[T]here is no requirement that an agency provide a . . . 'Vaughn' index on an initial request for documents."); Edmond v. U.S. Attorney, 959 F. Supp. 1, 5 (D.D.C. 1997) (rejecting, as premature, request for Vaughn Index when agency had not processed plaintiff's request); see also FOIA Update, Vol. VII, No. 3, at 6; cf. Judicial Watch, Inc. v. Clinton, 880 F. Supp. 1, 11 (D.D.C. 1995); Schaake v. IRS, No. 91-958, slip op. at 7-8 (S.D. Ill. June 3, 1992).

[294] See, e.g., Tannehill v. Dep't of the Air Force, No. 87-1335, slip op. at 1 (D.D.C. Aug. 20, 1987) (noting that standard practice is to await filing of agency's dispositive motion before deciding whether additional indexes will be necessary); British Airports Auth. v. CAB, 2 Gov't Disclosure Serv. (P-H) ¶ 81,234, at 81,654 (D.D.C. June 25, 1981) (explaining that "standard practice which has developed is for the Court to commit the parties to a schedule for briefing summary judgment motions," with "defendant typically fil[ing] first and simultaneously with or in advance of filing submit[ting] supporting affidavits and indices").

[295] See, e.g., Miscavige, 2 F.3d at 369 ("The plaintiff's early attempt in litigation of this kind to obtain a Vaughn Index . . . is inappropriate until the government has first had a chance to provide the court with the information necessary to make a decision on the applicable exemptions."); Gerstein v. CIA, No. 06-4643, 2006 WL 3462659, at *5 (N.D. Cal. Nov. 29, 2006) (denying plaintiff's request for Vaughn Index because agencies had not yet

(continued...)

## "Reasonably Segregable" Requirements

The FOIA requires that "[a]ny reasonably segregable portion of a record shall be provided to any person requesting such a record after deletion of the portions which are exempt."[296] Added as part of the 1974 FOIA amendments,[297] this important provision was designed to narrow the focus of the application of exemptions from documents to specific segments of information within them.[298] Of course, the segments of information, if dis-

---

[295](...continued)
begun responding to plaintiff's FOIA requests); Bassiouni v. CIA, 248 F. Supp. 2d 795, 797 (N.D. Ill. 2003) (finding plaintiff's request for a Vaughn Index premature because the case was "only in the initial stages"); Pyne v. Comm'r, No. 98-00253, 1999 WL 112532, at *3 (D. Haw. Jan. 6, 1999) (denying motion to compel submission of Vaughn Index as "premature" when agency had not yet refused to release records or provided supporting affidavit for nondisclosure); Stimac v. U.S. Dep't of Justice, 620 F. Supp. 212, 213 (D.D.C. 1985) (denying as premature motion to compel Vaughn Index on ground that "filing of a dispositive motion, along with detailed affidavits, may obviate the need for indexing the withheld documents"); see also Payne v. U.S. Dep't of Justice, No. 95-2968, 1995 WL 601112, at *1 (E.D. La. Oct. 11, 1995) (refusing to order Vaughn Index at "nascent" stage of litigation, i.e., when defendants had not even answered plaintiff's Complaint); Cohen v. FBI, 831 F. Supp. 850, 855 (S.D. Fla. 1993) (confirming that Vaughn Index is not required when "Open America" stay is granted "because no documents have been withheld on the grounds that they are exempt from disclosure"). But see Keeper of Mountains Found. v. U.S. Dep't of Justice, No. 06-cv-00098, 2006 WL 1666262, at *3 (S.D. W. Va. June 14, 2006) (granting the plaintiff's request for a Vaughn Index prior to the agency's dispositive motion, because production "at this stage of the litigation, rather than later at the summary judgment stage, is the more efficient and fair approach"); Providence Journal Co. v. U.S. Dep't of the Army, 769 F. Supp. 67, 69 (D.R.I. 1991) (finding contention that Vaughn Index must await dispositive motion to be "insufficient and sterile" when agency "has not even indicated when it plans to file such a motion"); cf. Schulz v. Hughes, 250 F. Supp. 2d 470, 475 (E.D. Pa. 2003) (ruling that upon payment of fees, agency should prepare Vaughn Index for any documents it refuses to release); ACLU v. DOD, 339 F. Supp. 2d 501, 504-05 (S.D.N.Y. 2004) (ordering production of a Vaughn Index prior to the filing of the defendants' dispositive motion, due to the "glacial pace at which defendant agencies have been responding to the plaintiffs' requests," which evinces "an indifference to the commands of FOIA and fails to afford accountability of government").

[296] 5 U.S.C. § 552(b) (2000 & Supp. IV 2004) (sentence immediately following exemptions).

[297] Pub. L. No. 93-502, 88 Stat. 1561.

[298] See Billington v. U.S. Dep't of Justice, 233 F.3d 581, 586 (D.C. Cir.
(continued...)

closed, must have some meaning.[299] Furthermore, it must be technically feasible within the particular form of the requested record to segregate the exempt information from the nonexempt information.[300]

---

[298](...continued)
2000) (emphasizing that the FOIA's segregability requirement limits exemption claims to "discrete units of information; to withhold an entire document, all units of information in that document must [be exempt]"); Schiller v. NLRB, 964 F.2d 1205, 1209 (D.C. Cir. 1992) ("'The focus in the FOIA is information not documents and an agency cannot justify withholding an entire document simply by showing that it contains some exempt material.'" (quoting Mead Data Cent., Inc. v. U.S. Dep't of the Air Force, 566 F.2d 242, 260 (D.C. Cir. 1977))); see also Attorney General's Memorandum on the 1974 Amendments to the Freedom of Information Act 14 (Feb. 1975); FOIA Update, Vol. XIV, No. 3, at 11-12 ("OIP Guidance: The 'Reasonable Segregation' Obligation"). But cf. Piper & Marbury, L.L.P. v. USPS, No. 99-2383, 2001 WL 214217, at *4 (D.D.C. Mar. 6, 2001) (magistrate's recommendation) (erroneously extrapolating from the segregability mandate the notion that "there is no authority for the proposition that entire documents are exempt from FOIA"), adopted (D.D.C. Mar. 30, 2001).

[299] See Thomas v. U.S. Dep't of Justice, No. 1:04-CV-112, 2006 WL 722141, at *4 (E.D. Tex. Mar. 15, 2006) (noting that redacting telephone recordings for segregable information "would have left nothing meaningful to release"); Nat'l Sec. Archive Fund, Inc. v. CIA, 402 F. Supp. 2d 211, 220-21 (D.D.C. 2005) (concluding that no reasonably segregable information exists, because "the non-exempt information would produce only incomplete, fragmented, unintelligible sentences composed of isolated, meaningless words"); Givner v. Executive Office for U.S. Attorneys, No. 99-3454, slip op. at 17-18 (D.D.C. Mar. 1, 2001) (deciding that agencies may withhold nonexempt information if it amounts to "'essentially meaningless words and phrases'" (quoting Neufield v. IRS, 646 F.2d 661, 663 (D.C. Cir. 1981))); Warren v. Soc. Sec. Admin., No. 98-0116E, 2000 WL 1209383, at *5 (W.D.N.Y. Aug. 22, 2000) (reasoning that documents are not reasonably segregable when the only nonexempt information amounts to "little more than templates"), aff'd in pertinent part, 10 F. App'x 20 (2d Cir. 2001); Pub. Citizen v. Dep't of State, 100 F. Supp. 2d 10, 25 (D.D.C. 2000) ("'The district court judge 'is not called upon to take on the role of censor going through a line-by-line analysis for each document and removing particular words.'" (quoting Ray v. Turner, 587 F.2d 1187, 1197 (D.C. Cir. 1978))), aff'd in part, rev'd in part & remanded on other grounds, 276 F.3d 674 (D.C. Cir. 2002); cf. Solar Sources, Inc. v. United States, 142 F.3d 1033, 1039 (7th Cir. 1998) ("[C]ourts should not order segregation when such a process would be significantly unwieldy.").

[300] See, e.g., Swope v. U.S. Dep't of Justice, 439 F. Supp. 2d 1, 7 (D.D.C. 2006) (concluding that "the exempt and nonexempt portions of the telephone conversations could not be reasonably segregated," based on the Bureau of Prisons' explanation that it lacked the technical capability to do

(continued...)

As a general rule, "[t]he 'segregability requirement applies to all documents and all exemptions in the FOIA.'"[301] To meet this requirement, agency declarations must address the issue "with reasonable specificity."[302] Indeed, conclusory language in agency declarations that does not provide a specific basis for segregability findings by district courts may be found inadequate.[303] Nevertheless, a court might be able to make its own segre-

---

[300](...continued)
so); Butler v. Fed. Bureau of Prisons, No. 05-643, 2005 WL 3274573, at *5 (D.D.C. Sept. 27, 2005) (holding that because the agency relied on a rudimentary tape recorder to segregate information "the exempt and nonexempt portions of telephone conversation could not be reasonably segregated"); see also McMillian v. Fed. Bureau of Prisons, No. 03-1210, 2004 WL 4953170, at *8 (D.D.C. July 23, 2004) (upholding defendant's position that exempt and nonexempt portions of telephone conversation were inextricably intertwined because even if tape was made of only plaintiff's side of conversation, comments would be out of context and misleading); cf. 5 U.S.C. § 552(a)(4)(B) (codifying standard of "technical feasibility" in several parts of Act, including subsection (b), as practical matter; speaking also of "substantial weight" to be given agency "feasibility" determinations).

[301] Hornbostel v. U.S. Dep't of the Interior, 305 F. Supp. 2d 21, 34 (D.D.C. 2003) (quoting Ctr. for Auto Safety v. EPA, 731 F.2d 16, 21 (D.C. Cir. 1984)); see McSheffrey v. Executive Office for U.S. Attorneys, 13 F. App'x 3, 4 (D.C. Cir. 2001) (remanding with explicit instructions that the district court "determine whether any portion of these documents can be segregated for release"); Mays v. DEA, 234 F.3d 1324, 1328 (D.C. Cir. 2000) (remanding to determine whether "any intelligible portion of the contested pages can be segregated for release"). But see Judicial Watch, Inc. v. U.S. Dep't of Justice, 432 F.3d 366, 371 (D.C. Cir. 2005) (holding that "[i]f a document is fully protected as [attorney] work product, then segregability is not required").

[302] Elec. Privacy Info Ctr. v. TSA, No. 03-1846, 2006 WL 626925, at *8 (D.D.C. Mar. 12, 2006) (explaining that a "line-by-line" review is not required as the court considers "a variety of factors to determine if Defendants' segregability justifications [are] sufficiently detailed and reasonable, rather than requiring a specific checklist of form language"); Animal Legal Def. Fund v. Dep't of the Air Force, 44 F. Supp. 2d 295, 301 (D.D.C. 1999) (citing Armstrong v. Executive Office of the President, 97 F.3d 575, 578 (D.C. Cir. 1996)); see Judicial Watch v. HHS, 27 F. Supp. 2d 240, 246 (D.D.C. 1998) ("If a court is to make specific findings of segregability without conducting in camera review in every FOIA case, the government simply must provide more specific information in its Vaughn affidavits.").

[303] See Pa. Dep't of Pub. Welfare v. HHS, No. 05-1285, 2006 WL 3792628, at *17 (W.D. Pa. Dec. 21, 2006) (concluding that agency's declaration is too broad and fails to provide factual recitation as to segregability); Voinche v. FBI, 412 F. Supp. 2d 60, 69 (D.D.C. 2006) (denying summary judgment as to Exemption 7(E) because the agency provided "nothing but conclusory

(continued...)

gability determination, even in the absence of an adequate analysis in an agency's declaration.[304]

---

[303](...continued)
statements as to the impossibility of segregating any portions of the re-leased material without even citing specifically which withheld documents it was referring to") (appeal pending); Nat'l Res. Def. Council v. DOD, 388 F. Supp. 2d 1086, 1106 (C.D. Cal. 2005) (finding that the segregability analysis is not met based on a "boilerplate statement . . . , which conclusorily as-serts [that] all reasonably segregable information has been released"); Gavin v. SEC, No. 04-4522, 2005 WL 2739293, at *4 (D. Minn. Oct. 24, 2005) (ordering agency to provide detailed affidavits as record is insufficient to enable determination as to whether agency has sustained its burden of reasonable segregability), reconsideration denied, 2006 WL 208783 (D.D.C. Jan. 26, 2006); Edmonds Inst. v. U.S. Dep't of the Interior, 383 F. Supp. 2d 105, 110 (D.D.C. 2005) (directing defendant to produce more detailed Vaughn Index because its "generalized paragraph on segregability" does not suffice); The Wilderness Soc'y v. U.S. Dep't of the Interior, 344 F. Supp. 2d 1, 19 (D.D.C. 2004) (holding that "a blanket declaration that all facts are so intertwined to prevent disclosure . . . does not constitute a sufficient ex-planation of non-segregability"); Wiener v. FBI, No. 83-1720, slip op. at 13 (C.D. Cal. Sept. 27, 2004) (finding that agency's conclusory justifications fail to meet agency's burden of proof regarding segregability); Dorsett v. U.S. Dep't of the Treasury, 307 F. Supp. 2d 28, 41 (D.D.C. 2004) (denying sum-mary judgment in part "[b]ecause of [agency's] inadequate and conclusory segregability explanation," and ordering renewed motion with affidavit solely addressing segregability); Animal Legal Def. Fund, 44 F. Supp. 2d at 301 (holding that conclusory statement regarding segregability is "patently insufficient"); see also Patterson v. IRS, 56 F.3d 832, 839 (7th Cir. 1995) ("[B]ecause the [agency declaration] lumps all of the withheld information together in justifying nondisclosure, the district court could not have inde-pendently evaluated whether exempt information alone was being with-held or deleted in each instance.").

[304] See, e.g., Becker v. IRS, 34 F.3d 398, 406 (7th Cir. 1994) (finding re-mand unnecessary because judge "did not simply rely on IRS affidavits de-scribing the documents, but conducted an in camera review"); Gutman v. U.S. Dep't of Justice, 238 F. Supp. 2d 284, 296 (D.D.C. 2003) (approving dec-laration that justified segregability determination based on inclusion of facts from withheld documents); Ferranti v. ATF, 177 F. Supp. 2d 41, 47 (D.D.C. 2001) (while recognizing a "substantial defect" in a declaration that fails to refer explicitly to segregability, nevertheless determining independ-ently that the segregability requirement met by the "narrow scope of the categorical withholdings[,] . . . the good faith declaration that only such properly withheld information was redacted, and a careful review of the ac-tual documents that plaintiff submitted"), summary affirmance granted, No. 01-5451, 2002 WL 31189766, at *1 (D.C. Cir. Oct. 2, 2002); see also Rugiero v. U.S. Dep't of Justice, 234 F. Supp. 2d 697, 710 (E.D. Mich. 2002) (ordering in camera review because "plaintiff has raised enough doubt" about segre-
(continued...)

Traditionally, the district court's segregability obligation arose upon a plaintiff's specific complaint or argument about the defendant agency's compliance with that statutory requirement.[305] In Trans-Pacific Policing Agreement v. United States Customs Service,[306] however, the Court of Appeals for the District of Columbia Circuit treated this obligation as a sua sponte requirement for the district court -- i.e., one to be met automatically even if the plaintiff had not raised the issue -- and it reversed a district court judgment on that basis alone.[307]

This means that even in the absence of a specific challenge by a FOIA plaintiff, an agency's Vaughn declaration readily can be found insufficient if it attempts to "justify withholding an entire document simply by showing that it contains some exempt material."[308] As a result, summary judgment may be denied to an agency if its declarations do not adequately demonstrate that all reasonably segregable, nonexempt information has been disclosed.[309] (For a further discussion of summary judgment require-

---

[304](...continued)
gability issue); see also Campaign for Family Farms v. Veneman, No. 99-1165, 2001 WL 1631459, at *3 (D. Minn. July 19, 2001) (deciding sua sponte that zip codes and dates of signature entries on petition are not "reasonably segregable," because of "distinct possibility" that release of that information would thwart protected privacy interest).

[305] See, e.g., Summers v. Dep't of Justice, 140 F.3d 1077, 1081 (D.C. Cir. 1998); Judicial Watch v. HHS, 27 F. Supp. 2d 240, 246-47 & n.2 (D.D.C. 1998).

[306] 177 F.3d 1022 (D.C. Cir. 1999).

[307] Id. at 1027 (indicating that district court had duty to consider reasonable segregability even though requester never sought segregability finding); see Isley v. Executive Office for U.S. Attorneys, No. 98-5098, 1999 WL 1021934, at *7 (D.C. Cir. Oct. 21, 1999) (explaining that district court erred in failing to make segregability finding even though plaintiff failed to raise issue at trial); Brunetti v. FBI, 357 F. Supp. 2d 97, 111 (D.D.C. 2004) (noting that the district court "has a duty to consider the segregability of the withheld information sua sponte"); Schrecker v. U.S. Dep't of Justice, 74 F. Supp. 2d 26, 29 (D.D.C. 1999) ("[D]istrict courts are required to consider segregability issues even when the parties have not specifically raised such claims."), aff'd in pertinent part & rev'd in part, 254 F.3d 162 (D.C. Cir. 2001). But cf. Nicolaus v. FBI, 24 F. App'x 807, 809 (9th Cir. 2001) (refusing to consider plaintiff's segregability argument because he failed to raise it in his opening appellate brief).

[308] Mead Data, 566 F.2d at 260; see Kimberlin v. Dep't of Justice, 139 F.3d 944, 950 (D.C. Cir. 1998).

[309] See, e.g., Nat'l Res. Def. Council, 388 F. Supp. 2d at 1105-06 (denying defendants' motion for summary judgment, in part, because Vaughn Index
(continued...)

ments, see Litigation Considerations, Summary Judgment, below.) Moreover, a district court decision may be remanded entirely on procedural grounds -- even if it correctly rules for the agency in all substantive exemption respects -- if it fails to make segregability findings.[310]

Ultimately, the agency's duty to deal with "reasonably segregable," nonexempt portions of records arises first at the administrative level and, indeed, an agency's careful action at this level may forestall problems later on. (For a discussion of document segregation at the administrative level, see Procedural Requirements, "Reasonably Segregable" Obligation, above.) This is so because, as previously noted, "regardless of whether a particular FOIA request proceeds to litigation, the obligation nonetheless is the same -- it 'applies to all documents and all exemptions in the FOIA.'"[311]

<u>In Camera Inspection</u>

The FOIA specifically authorizes in camera examination of docu-

---

[309](...continued)
failed to provide segregability analysis); <u>Wilderness Soc'y</u>, 344 F. Supp. 2d at 19 (same); <u>Animal Legal Def. Fund</u>, 44 F. Supp. 2d at 301 (denying government's motion for summary judgment, in part, because declaration was insufficient on segregability issue). <u>But see</u> <u>ACLU v. DOD</u>, 389 F. Supp. 2d 547, 567-68 (S.D.N.Y. 2005) (granting government's motion for summary judgment with regard to segregability based on in camera review of <u>Vaughn</u> Index and classified declarations).

[310] <u>See, e.g.</u>, <u>James Madison Project v. NARA</u>, No. 02-5089, 2002 WL 31296220, at *1 (D.C. Cir. Oct. 11, 2002) (per curiam) (remanding, despite ruling in favor of the government on exemptions, for a "more precise finding" on segregability); <u>McSheffrey v. Executive Office for U.S. Attorneys</u>, 13 F. App'x 3, 4 (D.C. Cir. 2001) (remanding with explicit instructions that the district court "determine whether any portion of these documents can be segregated for release"); <u>Isley</u>, 1999 WL 1021934, at *7 (remanding case for segregability finding); <u>Kimberlin</u>, 139 F.3d at 950 ("[W]e must remand this case to the district court to determine whether any of the withheld documents contains material that can be segregated and disclosed . . . ."); <u>Wiener v. FBI</u>, 943 F.2d 972, 988 (9th Cir. 1991) (holding that "district court erred by failing to make specific findings on the issue of segregability" and remanding for "specific finding that no information contained in each document or substantial portion of a document withheld is segregable"); <u>cf.</u> <u>Johnson v. Executive Office for U.S. Attorneys</u>, 310 F.3d 771, 777 (D.C. Cir. 2002) (approving of district court's sua sponte segregability determination). <u>But see</u> <u>Carpenter v. U.S. Dep't of Justice</u>, 470 F.3d 434, 443 (1st Cir. 2006) (concluding that, although district court failed to find expressly that there were no reasonably segregable portions, the district court's in camera inspection afforded it an opportunity to make this determination).

[311] <u>FOIA Update</u>, Vol. XIV, No. 3, at 12 (quoting <u>Ctr. for Auto Safety</u>, 731 F.2d at 21).

ments,[312] but whether to employ this tool of judicial review is a matter firmly committed to the "'broad discretion of the trial court judge.'"[313] Courts typically exercise their discretionary authority to order in camera inspection in exceptional rather than routine cases,[314] primarily because in cam-

---

[312] See 5 U.S.C. § 552(a)(4)(B); see also S. Conf. Rep. No. 93-1200, at 9 (1974), reprinted in 1974 U.S.C.C.A.N. 6267, 6287.

[313] Horowitz v. Peace Corps, 428 F.3d 271, 282 (D.C. Cir. 2005) (quoting Spirko v. USPS, 147 F.3d 992, 996 (D.C. Cir. 1998) (quoting, in turn, Lam Lek Chong v. DEA, 929 F.2d 729, 735 (D.C. Cir. 1991) (quoting, in turn, Carter v. U.S. Dep't of Commerce, 830 F.2d 388, 392 (D.C. Cir. 1987)))); accord Quiñon v. FBI, 86 F.3d 1222, 1227 (D.C. Cir. 1996); see, e.g., NLRB v. Robbins Tire & Rubber Co., 437 U.S. 214, 224 (1978) ("The in camera review provision is discretionary by its terms[.]"); Halpern v. FBI, 181 F.3d 279, 295 (2d Cir. 1999) (noting that in camera "review would have been appropriate," but leaving this to "the trial court's discretion on remand"), on remand, No. 94-CV-365A, 2002 WL 31012157, at *14 (W.D.N.Y. Aug. 31, 2002) (magistrate's recommendation) (denying plaintiff's motion for in camera inspection), adopted (W.D.N.Y. Oct. 17, 2002); Jernigan v. Dep't of the Air Force, No. 97-35930, 1998 WL 658662, at *1 n.3 (9th Cir. Sept. 14, 1998) ("Section 552(a)(4)(B) empowers, but does not require, a district court to examine the contents of agency records in camera . . . ."); Parsons v. Freedom of Info. Act Officer, No. 96-4128, 1997 WL 461320, at *1 (6th Cir. Aug. 12, 1997) (explaining that district court has discretion to conduct in camera inspection, but that it is neither "favored nor necessary" so long as adequate factual basis for decision exists); Armstrong v. Executive Office of the President, 97 F.3d 575, 579 (D.C. Cir. 1996) (finding that district court did not abuse its discretion when it undertook in camera review of one document, but not of another (similarly characterized) document); Miscavige v. IRS, 2 F.3d 366, 368 (11th Cir. 1993) (holding that in camera review "is discretionary and not required, absent an abuse of discretion"); Ingle v. Dep't of Justice, 698 F.2d 259, 267 (6th Cir. 1983) (listing four factors courts should consider before exercising discretion to review records in camera); Pons v. U.S. Customs Serv., No. 93-2094, 1998 U.S. Dist. LEXIS 6084, at *4 (D.D.C. Apr. 23, 1998) ("The ultimate criterion is whether the district judge believes that in camera inspection is necessary to make a responsible de novo determination on the agency's compliance with the FOIA statute.").

[314] See, e.g., Robbins Tire, 437 U.S. at 224 (explaining that in camera review provision "is designed to be invoked when the issue before the District Court could not be otherwise resolved"); PHE, Inc. v. U.S. Dep't of Justice, 983 F.2d 248, 252-53 (D.C. Cir. 1993) (observing that in camera review is generally disfavored, but permissible on remand arising from inadequate affidavit); Elec. Privacy Info. Ctr. v. DHS, 384 F. Supp. 2d 100, 119 (D.D.C. 2005) ("[C]ourts disfavor in camera inspection and it is more appropriate in only the exceptional case."); Iowa Citizens for Cmty. Improvement v. USDA, 256 F. Supp. 2d 946, 957 (S.D. Iowa 2002) (declaring that court should not be "super-administrator" that conducts in camera review in every FOIA

(continued...)

era review "circumvents the adversarial process,"[315] but also because of the burdens involved.[316]

In camera review is unnecessary and inappropriate when agencies meet their burden of proof by means of sufficiently detailed affidavits.[317] In

---

[314](...continued)
case); Animal Legal Def. Fund, Inc. v. Dep't of the Air Force, 44 F. Supp. 2d 295, 304 (D.D.C. 1999) ("'[I]n camera review should not be resorted to as a matter of course . . . .'" (quoting Quiñon, 86 F.3d at 1228)); Guccione v. Nat'l Indian Gaming Comm'n, No. 98-CV-164, 1999 U.S. Dist. LEXIS 15475, at *3 (S.D. Cal. Aug. 5, 1999) ("[I]n camera review is a last resort, to be used only when the propriety of the withholding cannot otherwise be determined.").

[315] Jones v. FBI, 41 F.3d 238, 243 (6th Cir. 1994) (citing Vaughn v. United States, 936 F.2d 862, 866 (6th Cir. 1991)); see McNamera v. U.S. Dep't of Justice, 974 F. Supp. 946, 956 (W.D. Tex. 1997) (suggesting that Vaughn Index is preferable to in camera inspection because "it keeps in tact [sic] our system of adversarial dispute resolution").

[316] See, e.g., Ray v. Turner, 587 F.2d 1187, 1195 (D.C. Cir. 1978) ("In camera inspection requires effort and resources and therefore a court should not resort to it routinely on the theory that 'it can't hurt.'"); Robert v. HHS, No. 01-CV-4778, 2005 WL 1861755, at *6 (E.D.N.Y. Aug. 1, 2005) (declaring that courts should not "spend scarce judicial resources for in camera review where defendant's affidavits are sufficiently descriptive and make clear that the privileges asserted apply").

[317] See, e.g., Nowak v. United States, No. 98-56656, 2000 WL 60067, at *2 (9th Cir. Jan. 21, 2000) (finding in camera review unnecessary where affidavits were sufficiently detailed); Young v. CIA, 972 F.2d 536, 538 (4th Cir. 1992) (rejecting in camera inspection when affidavits and Vaughn Indexes were sufficiently specific); Silets v. U.S. Dep't of Justice, 945 F.2d 227, 229-32 (7th Cir. 1991) (en banc) (same); Vaughn v. United States, 936 F.2d 862, 869 (6th Cir. 1991) (finding in camera review "neither favored nor necessary where other evidence provides adequate detail and justification"); Local 3, Int'l Bhd. of Elec. Workers v. NLRB, 845 F.2d 1177, 1180 (2d Cir. 1988) (rejecting in camera review because "detailed affidavit was sufficient"); Safeway, Inc. v. IRS, No. 05-3182, 2006 WL 3041079, at *10 (N.D. Cal. Oct. 24, 2006) (denying the plaintiff's request for in camera review because the agency "has sustained its burden of proof with respect to the documents as to which the Court has granted summary judgment"); Elec. Privacy, 384 F. Supp. 2d at 120 (finding in camera review unnecessary based on defendants' descriptions and justifications); Ocean Conservancy v. Evans, 260 F. Supp. 2d 1162, 1189-90 (M.D. Fla. 2003) (holding that the "[c]ourt's primary role in reviewing a government's claimed exemption under FOIA is not to conduct in camera review," and finding affidavits sufficient to justify exemption claims); Taylor v. U.S. Dep't of Justice, 257 F. Supp. 2d 101, 114 (D.D.C. 2003) (finding in camera review to be unnecessary because of ade-
(continued...)

camera review is one of several options that may be ordered, however, when agency affidavits are insufficiently detailed to permit meaningful review of exemption claims.[318]

In camera review also may be ordered in other circumstances.[319] If

---

[317](...continued)
quacy of defendant's affidavit and Vaughn Index); Falwell v. Executive Office of the President, 158 F. Supp. 2d 734, 738 (W.D. Va. 2001) (finding "no justification" for in camera review because the agency's affidavit provides "more than sufficient information to make a reasoned decision" as to the agency's compliance with the FOIA); Ligorner v. Reno, 2 F. Supp. 2d 400, 405 (S.D.N.Y. 1998) ("In camera review is only necessary when the evidence presented by the government is insufficient on its face to establish that non-disclosure is required, or when there is some evidence of agency bad faith.").

[318] See, e.g., Halpern, 181 F.3d at 295 (observing that "[in camera] review would have been appropriate" because agency affidavit was conclusory, but noting that "such action is one best left to the trial court's discretion"; Spirko, 147 F.3d at 997 ("If the agency fails to provide a sufficiently detailed explanation to enable the district court to make a de novo determination of the agency's claims of exemption, the district court then has several options, including inspecting the documents in camera."); Quiñon, 86 F.3d at 1229 ("[W]here an agency's affidavits merely state in conclusory terms that documents are exempt from disclosure, an in camera review is necessary."); In re Dep't of Justice, 999 F.2d 1302, 1310 (8th Cir. 1993) (en banc) ("If the [Vaughn Index] categories remain too general, the district court may also examine the disputed documents in camera to make a first hand determination."); Judicial Watch, Inc. v. Dep't of the Army, 435 F. Supp. 2d 81, 92 (D.D.C. 2006) (stating that the court "undertook an onerous in camera review" because the agency failed to provide a detailed Vaughn Index, and further declaring that the "FOIA mandates broad disclosure, and the right to withholding information constitute a narrow exception, not an exploitable rule"); Dohse v. Potter, No. 8:04CV355, 2005 WL 2180090, at *1 (D. Neb. Sept. 8, 2005) (granting plaintiff's motion for in camera review because of defendant's insufficiently detailed declaration). But cf. J.P. Stevens & Co. v. Perry, 710 F.2d 136, 142 (4th Cir. 1983) (holding that district court erred in conducting in camera inspection because Exemption 7(A) Vaughn affidavit was sufficient to show "interference" on category-by-category basis); Associated Builders & Contractors v. NLRB, No. 98-612, slip op. at 4 (S.D. Ohio Feb. 21, 2001) (deciding that in camera inspection is not required even if the agency's Vaughn Index is inadequate, so long as the court "is able to make an independent, reasoned judgment about the contents of the documents at issue and the applicability of the exemptions asserted").

[319] Cole v. U.S. Dep't of Justice, No. 05-674, 2006 WL 2792681, at *5 (D.D.C. Sept. 27, 2006) (stating that in camera review is appropriate when "the affidavit is 'insufficiently detailed to permit meaningful review of ex-
(continued...)

the number of records involved is relatively small, in camera review may be utilized to save both the court and the parties time and resources.[320]  In this regard, in camera review of a small sample of a larger set of documents

---

[319](...continued)
emption claims' . . . where there is evidence of bad faith on the part of the agency, or where the judge wishes to resolve an uneasiness about the government's 'inherent tendency to resist disclosure'") (citations omitted); Hull v. U.S. Dep't of Labor, No. 04-cv-01264, slip op. at 16 (D. Colo. Dec. 2, 2005) (explaining that the following factors are considered in deciding whether to grant in camera review: "whether the affidavits submitted by the agency [were] too vague to allow review of the agency's claims, whether the number and size of the documents at issue would place an 'onerous burden' on the Court, and any evidence of agency bad faith in withholding the documents"); Dean v. FDIC, 389 F. Supp. 2d 780, 789 (E.D. Ky. 2005) (stating that the following factors should be considered when determining whether in camera review is appropriate: "'(1) judicial economy; (2) actual agency bad faith, either in the FOIA action or in the underlying activities that generated the records requested; (3) strong public interest; and (4) whether the parties request in camera review'" (quoting Rugiero v. U.S. Dep't of Justice, 257 F.3d 534, 543 (6th Cir. 2001))).

[320] See Quiñon, 86 F.3d at 1228 (suggesting that number of documents is "another . . . factor to be considered" when determining whether in camera review is appropriate); Maynard v. CIA, 986 F.2d 547, 558 (1st Cir. 1993) ("In camera review is particularly appropriate when the documents withheld are brief and limited in number."); Currie v. IRS, 704 F.2d 523, 530 (11th Cir. 1983) ("Thorough in camera inspection of the withheld documents where the information is extensive and the claimed exemptions are many . . . is not the preferred method of determining the appropriateness of the government agency's characterization of the withheld information."); Tax Analysts v. IRS, No. 94-923, 1999 U.S. Dist. LEXIS 19514, at *14 (D.D.C. Nov. 3, 1999) (noting, as factor justifying in camera review, minimal burden on court where only one sentence is to be reviewed); Local 32B-32J, Serv. Employees Int'l Union, AFL-CIO v. GSA, No. 97 Civ. 8509, 1998 WL 726000, at *11 (S.D.N.Y. Oct. 15, 1998) (observing that in camera review is "ordered most often in cases in which only a small number of documents are to be examined"); Steinberg v. U.S. Dep't of Justice, 179 F.R.D. 357, 364 (D.D.C. Apr. 28, 1998) (ordering in camera inspection of seven documents "[i]n the interests of efficiency"); see also Klunzinger v. IRS, 27 F. Supp. 2d 1015, 1028 (W.D. Mich. 1998) ("The withheld documents in this case are far too numerous to be considered the proper subject of an in camera inspection."); Animal Legal Def. Fund, 44 F. Supp. 2d at 304 (rejecting in camera review, but requiring agency to "submit a more detailed affidavit" in order to conserve judicial resources); Smith v. ATF, 977 F. Supp. 496, 503 (D.D.C. 1997) (finding that "judicial economy is best served" by allowing correction of deficient affidavits rather than by in camera review of two documents).

may be warranted.[321] Additionally, when a discrepancy is found to exist between representations in an agency's affidavit and other information that the agency has publicly disclosed about the withheld records, in camera inspection may be an appropriate method to resolve that discrepancy.[322]

Similarly, in camera inspection may be ordered in cases in which the plaintiff alleges that the government has waived its right to claim an exemption.[323] Further, in camera inspection may be used to verify that an agency has released all reasonably segregable information,[324] or to ascertain whether a district court properly ruled on the merits of a case.[325] (For a further discussion of appellate matters, see Litigation Considerations, Considerations on Appeal, below.)

------

[321] See, e.g., Carter, 830 F.2d at 393 n.16 (suggesting that for voluminous documents, "selective inspection of . . . documents [is] often an appropriate compromise"); N.Y. Pub. Interest Research Group v. EPA, 249 F. Supp. 2d 327, 331 (S.D.N.Y. 2003) (discussing fact that in camera review was conducted of representative sample of documents); Wilson v. CIA, No. 89-3356, 1991 WL 226682, at *3 (D.D.C. Oct. 15, 1991) (ordering fifty-document sample of approximately 1000 pages withheld in whole or in part, selected equally by parties, for in camera examination); Wilson v. Dep't of Justice, No. 87-2415, 1991 WL 120052, at *4 (D.D.C. June 18, 1991) (requiring sample of eight of approximately eighty withheld documents, to be selected equally by each side, for detailed in camera description); Agee v. CIA, 517 F. Supp. 1335, 1336 (D.D.C. 1981) (utilizing "random" in camera review); cf. Young, 972 F.2d at 549 (rejecting a per se rule that would require in camera review "whenever the examination could be completed quickly"). But cf. Lame v. U.S. Dep't of Justice, 654 F.2d 917, 927 (3d Cir. 1981) (holding in camera sampling of law enforcement documents insufficient).

[322] See Mehl v. EPA, 797 F. Supp. 43, 46 (D.D.C. 1992) (conducting in camera inspection because affidavits contradicted published report).

[323] See Pub. Citizen v. U.S. Dep't of State, 787 F. Supp. 12, 13 (D.D.C. 1992) (finding exemptions properly invoked after reviewing records in camera), aff'd, 11 F.3d 198 (D.C. Cir. 1993).

[324] Jefferson v. U.S. Dep't of Justice, No. 01-1418, slip op. at 31 n.13 (D.D.C. Mar. 31, 2003) (deciding to hold in abeyance a segregability determination for documents claimed to be exempt on the basis of Exemption 5 of the FOIA until in camera inspection is completed); Citizens Progressive Alliance v. U.S. Bureau of Indian Affairs, 241 F. Supp. 2d 1342, 1359 (D.N.M. 2002) (noting that "all segregable portions of the documents have been released," a finding verified by in camera inspection).

[325] See, e.g., FlightSafety Servs. Corp. v. Dep't of Labor, 326 F.3d 607, 612 (5th Cir. 2003) (per curiam) (affirming district court's judgment after reviewing documents in camera); Tax Analysts v. IRS, 294 F.3d 71, 73 (D.C. Cir. 2002) (same).

# LITIGATION CONSIDERATIONS

In camera review is most likely to be ordered when there is actual evidence of bad faith on the part of the agency;[326] indeed, in this circumstance, in camera review may be "particularly appropriate."[327] Moreover, even with the submission of adequately detailed affidavits -- and in the absence of any bad faith in the agency's FOIA processing -- in camera inspection may be undertaken based upon "evidence of bad faith or illegality with regard to the underlying activities which generated the documents at issue."[328] The Court of Appeals for the Sixth Circuit, in particular, has rea-

---

[326] Rugiero v. U.S. Dep't of Justice, 257 F.3d 534, 547 (6th Cir. 2001) (finding that the requester failed to demonstrate "strong evidence of bad faith that calls into question the district court's decision not to conduct an in camera review").

[327] Quiñon, 86 F.3d at 1228; see, e.g., Jones, 41 F.3d at 242-43 (reviewing, at request of both parties, documents compiled as part of FBI's widely criticized COINTELPRO operations during 1960s and 1970s because of "evidence of bad faith or illegality with regard to the underlying activities which generated the documents at issue"); cf. Ford v. West, No. 97-1342, 1998 WL 317561, at *3 (10th Cir. June 12, 1998) ("'[M]ere allegations of bad faith' should not 'undermine the sufficiency of agency submissions.'" (quoting Minier v. CIA, 88 F.3d 796, 803 (9th Cir. 1996))); Silets, 945 F.2d at 231 (finding mere assertion, as opposed to actual evidence, of bad faith on part of agency insufficient to warrant court's in camera review); Askew v. United States, No. 05-CV-200, 2006 WL 3307469, at *7 (E.D. Ky. Nov. 13, 2006) (holding that "the plaintiff has not overcome the presumption of good faith attending the Vaughn Index and, thus, . . . a wholesale in camera inspection of the documents is not necessary"); Neuhausser v. U.S. Dep't of Justice, No. 6:03-531, 2006 WL 1581010, at *4 (E.D. Ky. June 6, 2006) (finding in camera review to be unnecessary because defendant provided detailed Vaughn Index and plaintiff failed to present substantial evidence of bad faith); McCoy v. United States, No. 04-CV-101, 2006 WL 463106, at *16 (N.D. W. Va. Feb. 24, 2006) (magistrate's recommendation) (finding in camera review to be unwarranted "[b]ecause the defendant has sufficiently demonstrated that the claimed exemptions apply, and because there is no showing of bad faith"), adopted (N.D. W. Va. Aug. 23, 2006); Kennedy v. U.S. Dep't of Justice, No. 03-CV-6077, 2004 WL 2284691, at *5 (W.D.N.Y. Oct. 8, 2004) (finding in camera review to be unnecessary because plaintiff presented no substantial evidence of bad faith). But see Hull, No. 1:04-cv-01264, slip op. at 19-20 (D. Colo. Dec. 2, 2005) (stating that although the plaintiff's evidence of bad faith "is not sufficient to disturb [the court's] findings regarding the documents withheld under Exemption 4," the plaintiff's evidence, coupled with the defendant's conclusory and vague affidavits, strengthens the court's conclusion on the necessity for in camera review of the documents withheld under Exemption 5).

[328] Jones, 41 F.3d at 242-43; see Detroit Free Press v. U.S. Dep't of Justice, 174 F. Supp. 2d 597, 601 (E.D. Mich. 2001) (ordering in camera submissions because of questions about "the veracity of" the agency's justification
(continued...)

soned that in camera review is appropriate in such a case in order to reassure the plaintiff and the public that justice has been served.[329]

In camera review often is employed in cases involving national security, where detailed public affidavits may be impracticable.[330] (For a further discussion of in camera review of classified materials, see Exemption
1, In Camera Submissions, above.) Even in national security cases, however, it has been observed that "a district court exercises a wise discretion
when it limits the number of documents it reviews in camera."[331] Sometimes in these cases, in addition to in camera inspection, an agency will
employ in camera declarations to explain the basis for its withholdings.[332]

---

[328](...continued)
for withholding documents, which "rais[e] questions of bad faith"); see also
Summers v. Dep't of Justice, 140 F.3d 1077, 1085 (D.C. Cir. 1998) (Silberman, J., concurring) (urging in camera review of the "Official and Confidential" files of former FBI Director J. Edgar Hoover "to fully understand the
enormous public interest in these materials"). But see, e.g., Accuracy in
Media, Inc. v. Nat'l Park Serv., 194 F.3d 120, 125 (D.C. Cir. 1999) (holding
that alleged "evidentiary discrepancies" identified in published materials
concerning highly publicized suicide of Deputy White House Counsel Vincent Foster was not evidence of bad faith warranting in camera review of
death-scene and autopsy photographs).

[329] See Jones, 41 F.3d at 242-43.

[330] See, e.g., Pub. Citizen v. Dep't of State, 11 F.3d 198, 200-01 (D.C. Cir.
1993) (tacitly approving use of in camera inspection to determine whether
Exemption 1 protection waived); Weberman v. NSA, 668 F.2d 676, 678 (2d
Cir. 1982) (finding in camera inspection of classified affidavit appropriate
when "[d]isclosure of the details . . . might result in serious consequences
to the nation's security"); Edmonds v. FBI, 272 F. Supp. 2d 35, 46-47 (D.D.C.
2003) (agreeing, after reviewing "the extensive confidential material submitted [for in camera review, that] this is one of those 'occasion[s] when
extensive public justification would threaten to reveal the very information
for which a FOIA exemption is claimed'" (quoting Lykins v. United States,
725 F.2d 1455, 1463 (D.C. Cir. 1984))).

[331] Armstrong, 97 F.3d at 580 ("First, [limited in camera review] makes it
less likely that sensitive information will be disclosed. Second, if there is
an unauthorized disclosure, having reduced the number of people with access to the information makes it easier to pinpoint the source of the leak.").

[332] See, e.g., Maynard, 986 F.2d at 557 (noting that in camera declarations filed); Hunt v. CIA, 981 F.2d 1116, 1118 (9th Cir. 1992) (same); ACLU
v. DOD, 389 F. Supp. 2d 547, 567-68 (S.D.N.Y. 2005) (concluding that there
is no segregable information based on in camera review of two classified
declarations and Vaughn Index); Peltier v. FBI, No. 03-CV-905, 2005 WL
735964, at *11 (W.D.N.Y. Mar. 31, 2005) (finding need for supplemental
(continued...)

## LITIGATION CONSIDERATIONS

Although in camera declarations should be used sparingly,[333] government agencies defending cases since the events of September 11, 2001, have found it increasingly necessary to rely on in camera declarations due to the sensitive matters at issue.[334]

To be sure, it has been held that a district court may properly review in camera declarations only if it publicly explains its rationale for so doing and ensures that the agency has provided as complete a public explanation as possible without jeopardizing the sensitive, exempt information.[335]

---

[332](...continued)
Vaughn Index, in camera declaration, or traditional in camera review) (appeal pending); Haddam v. FBI, No. 01-434, slip op. at 12 (D.D.C. Sept. 8, 2004) (noting that "[f]requently the issue of in camera, ex parte affidavits arises in FOIA cases involving Exemption 1"); Edmonds, 272 F. Supp. 2d at 43 (noting agency use of in camera supplement to public declaration); Springmann v. U.S. Dep't of State, No. 93-1238, slip op. at 2-3 (D.D.C. Feb. 24, 2000) (granting renewed motion for summary judgment after reviewing in camera affidavit); see also Dow Jones Co. v. FERC, 219 F.R.D. 167, 171 (C.D. Cal. 2003) (explaining that agency submitted disputed record in camera); cf. Canning v. Dep't of Justice, No. 01-2215, slip op. at 6 (D.D.C. May 27, 2005) (granting the agency's motion for leave to file a declaration in camera because the "declaration is very personal in nature, and releasing any additional information would seriously compromise the secrecy claimed in this case").

[333] See Armstrong, 97 F.3d at 580-81 ("[T]he use of in camera affidavits has generally been disfavored."); Pub. Citizen v. Dep't of State, 100 F. Supp. 2d 10, 27 (D.D.C. 2000) (explaining that "[w]hile . . . in camera declarations are disfavored as a first line of defense," the agency had already submitted "three public declarations" amounting to a "threshold showing on the public record"), aff'd in pertinent part & rev'd in part on other grounds, 276 F.3d 674 (D.C. Cir. 2002).

[334] See, e.g., Edmonds, 272 F. Supp. 2d at 43 (noting use of ex parte supplementary affidavit and extensive in camera Vaughn Index in case involving problems after September 11, 2001 in FBI's translation unit); ACLU, 389 F. Supp. 2d at 567-68 (approving use of in camera classified declarations and Vaughn Index in case involving records related to CIA requesting DOD to detain Iraqi suspect without identifying him); Al Najjar v. Ashcroft, No. 00-1472, slip op. at 2 (D.D.C. July 22, 2003) (noting that three Department of Justice components submitted "substantial portions of their moving papers and Vaughn index in camera and ex parte" in case involving secret, classified evidence pertaining to detainee).

[335] See Lion Raisins Inc. v. USDA, 354 F.3d 1072, 1083 (9th Cir. 2004) (holding that "resort to in camera review is appropriate only after [agency] has submitted as much detail in the form of public affidavits and testimony as possible"); Armstrong, 97 F.3d at 580 (holding that district court "must
(continued...)

Additionally, in limited circumstances, in camera, ex parte oral testimony may be permitted, but when it is taken, it should be transcribed and maintained under seal.[336] Regardless of whether the court inspects documents or receives testimony in camera, however, counsel for the plaintiff ordinarily is not entitled to participate in these in camera proceedings.[337]

---

[335](...continued)
both make its reasons for [relying on an in camera declaration] clear and make as much as possible of the in camera submission available to the opposing party" (citing Lykins, 725 F.2d at 1465)); Phillippi v. CIA, 546 F.2d 1009, 1013 (D.C. Cir. 1976) (requiring "as complete a public record as is possible" before examining classified affidavits in camera); see also Haddam, No. 01-434, slip op. at 15 (D.D.C. Sept. 8, 2004) (declaring that, after a full in camera review of the record, the court believed that the instant case "involves a set of circumstances necessitating the use of in camera, ex parte submission of affidavits, Vaughn indices and other material normally provided in the public record," and accordingly allowing the agency to rely on these submissions to justify invoking Exemption 1); Al Najjar, No. 00-1472, slip op. at 7 (D.D.C. July 22, 2003) (requiring agencies to "create a more complete public record of their responses to plaintiffs' FOIA requests"); cf. Pub. Citizen Health Research Group v. U.S. Dep't of Labor, 591 F.2d 808, 809 (D.C. Cir. 1978) (ruling that the district court should not have refused to examine an affidavit proffered in camera in an Exemption 6 case, because the affidavit was "the only matter available . . . that would have enabled [the court] to properly decide de novo the propriety of" the agency's exemption claim).

[336] See Pollard v. FBI, 705 F.2d 1151, 1154 (9th Cir. 1983) (acknowledging that ex parte testimony was not recorded, and advising that "wiser course" for future cases would be to record it); Physicians for Soc. Responsibility v. U.S. Dep't of Justice, No. 85-0169, slip op. at 3 (D.D.C. Aug. 23, 1985) (noting that the transcript of in camera review was ordered "sealed and secured"); cf. Martin v. U.S. Dep't of Justice, No. 85-3091, slip op. at 3 (3d Cir. July 2, 1986) (ordering nonexempt portion of in camera transcript disclosed).

[337] See Solar Sources, Inc. v. United States, 142 F.3d 1033, 1040 (7th Cir. 1998) ("[T]he general rule is that counsel are not entitled to participate in in camera FOIA proceedings."); Arieff, 712 F.2d at 1470-71 & n.2 (prohibiting participation by plaintiff's counsel even when information withheld was personal privacy information); Pollard, 705 F.2d at 1154 (finding no reversible error when court not only reviewed affidavit and documents in camera, but also received authenticating testimony ex parte); Salisbury v. United States, 690 F.2d 966, 973 n.3 (D.C. Cir. 1982); Weberman, 668 F.2d at 678; cf. Ellsberg v. Mitchell, 709 F.2d 51, 61 (D.C. Cir. 1983) (holding that plaintiff's counsel is not permitted to participate in in camera review of documents arguably covered by state secrets privilege) (non-FOIA case). But cf. Lederle Labs. v. HHS, No. 88-249, 1988 WL 47649, at *1-2 (D.D.C. May 2, 1988) (issuing a restrictive protective order in an Exemption 4 case that ap-
(continued...)

# LITIGATION CONSIDERATIONS

If a court undertakes in camera inspection, it necessarily establishes an adequate factual basis for determining the applicability of the claimed exemptions.[338] This should be true regardless of the adequacy of an agency's affidavit.[339]

## Summary Judgment

Summary judgment is the procedural vehicle by which nearly all FOIA cases are resolved,[340] because "in FOIA cases there is rarely any fac-

---

[337](...continued)
peared to permit counsel for the requester to review contested business information).

[338] See Nat'l Wildlife Fed'n v. U.S. Forest Serv., 861 F.2d 1114, 1116 (9th Cir. 1988) ("[W]here a trial court properly reviewed contested documents in camera, an adequate factual basis for the decision exists."); City of Va. Beach v. U.S. Dep't of Commerce, 995 F.2d 1247, 1252 n.12 (4th Cir. 1993) ("By conducting in camera review, the district court established an adequate basis for its decision."); see also Lissner v. U.S. Customs Serv., 241 F.3d 1220, 1223 (9th Cir. 2001) (reversing district court decision on Exemption 7(C) applicability because appellate court's own in camera review revealed "nothing in the unredacted documents that is particularly personal").

[339] See, e.g., Church of Scientology, Inc. v. U.S. Dep't of the Army, 611 F.2d 738, 743 (9th Cir. 1979) (holding that despite "conclusory" affidavits, after in camera inspection trial court had "adequate factual basis" for its decision); see also Lion Raisins, 354 F.3d at 1082 ("Under certain limited circumstances, we have endorsed the use of in camera review of government affidavits as the basis for FOIA decisions."); Fiduccia v. U.S. Dep't of Justice, 185 F.3d 1035, 1042-43 (9th Cir. 1999) (suggesting, notwithstanding Wiener v. FBI, 943 F.2d 972, 979 (9th Cir. 1991), that in camera inspection could by itself be sufficient); Spirko, 147 F.3d at 997 (ruling that in camera inspection is one alternative for district court when agency fails sufficiently to detail its exemption claims). But see Wiener, 943 F.2d at 979 ("In camera review of the withheld documents by the court is not an acceptable substitute for an adequate Vaughn index."); St. Andrews Park, Inc. v. U.S. Dep't of the Army Corps of Eng'rs, 299 F. Supp. 2d 1264, 1271 & 1272 n.5 (S.D. Fla. 2003) (declaring in camera review to be "not dispositive" when agency's affidavit found to be inadequate, even while suggesting that exemption claims "appear . . . to be justified").

[340] See, e.g., Wickwire Gavin, P.C. v. USPS, 356 F.3d 588, 591 (4th Cir. 2004) (declaring that FOIA cases are generally resolved on summary judgment); Cooper Cameron Corp. v. U.S. Dep't of Labor, 280 F.3d 539, 543 (5th Cir. 2002) ("Summary judgment resolves most FOIA cases."); Harrison v. Executive Office for U.S. Attorneys, 377 F. Supp. 2d 141, 145 (D.D.C. 2005) ("FOIA cases are typically and appropriately decided on motions for sum-
(continued...)

tual dispute . . . only a legal dispute over how the law is to be applied to the documents at issue."[341] Motions for summary judgment are governed by Rule 56 of the Federal Rules of Civil Procedure, which provides, in part, that the "judgment sought shall be rendered forthwith if the pleadings, depositions, answers to interrogatories, and admissions on file, together with the affidavits, if any, show that there is no genuine issue as to any material fact."[342] So long as there are no material facts at issue and no facts susceptible to divergent inferences bearing upon an issue critical to disposition of the case," summary judgment is appropriate.[343] Of course, an agency's failure to respond to a FOIA request in a timely manner does not, by itself, jus-

---

[340](...continued)
mary judgment."); Raytheon Aircraft Co. v. U.S. Army Corps of Eng'rs, 183 F. Supp. 2d 1280, 1283 (D. Kan. 2001) ("FOIA cases . . . are especially amenable to summary judgment because the law, rather than the facts, is the only matter in dispute."); Sanderson v. IRS, No. 98-2369, 1999 WL 35290, at *2 (E.D. La. Jan. 25, 1999) (observing that summary judgment is the usual means for disposing of FOIA cases); Pub. Employees for Envtl. Responsibility v. EPA, 978 F. Supp. 955, 959 (D. Colo. 1997) ("FOIA claims are typically resolved on summary judgment[.]"), appeal dismissed voluntarily, No. 97-1384 (10th Cir. Nov. 25, 1997); Cappabianca v. Comm'r, U.S. Customs Serv., 847 F. Supp. 1558, 1562 (M.D. Fla. 1994) ("[O]nce documents in issue are properly identified, FOIA cases should be handled on motions for summary judgment." (citing Miscavige v. IRS, 2 F.3d 366, 369 (11th Cir. 1993))).

[341] Gray v. Sw. Airlines, Inc., 33 F. App'x 865, 869 n.1 (9th Cir. 2002) (Reinhardt, J., dissenting) (citing Schiffer v. FBI, 78 F.3d 1405, 1409 (9th Cir. 1996)) (non-FOIA case).

[342] Fed. R. Civ. P. 56(c); see, e.g., McClain v. U.S. Dep't of Justice, 17 F. App'x 471, 474 (7th Cir. 2001) ("[T]he purpose of summary judgment is to isolate and dispose of factually unsupported claims[.]").

[343] Alyeska Pipeline Serv. v. EPA, 856 F.2d 309, 314 (D.C. Cir. 1988); see, e.g., Plazas-Martinez v. DEA, 891 F. Supp. 1, 3 (D.D.C. 1995) ("Plaintiff's submission does create a dispute on an issue of fact; it is not a material issue, however."); Kuffel v. U.S. Bureau of Prisons, 882 F. Supp. 1116, 1122 (D.D.C. 1995) (holding that plaintiff's disagreement with application of exemptions does not constitute a dispute as to material facts precluding summary judgment "because he does not put forth any facts to prove that they were wrongfully applied"); Patterson v. IRS, No. 90-1941, 1992 WL 477021, at *1 (S.D. Ind. Nov. 3, 1992) ("[T]he disputed fact must be outcome determinative."), aff'd in part, rev'd & remanded in part on other grounds, 56 F.3d 841 (7th Cir. 1995); cf. Horowitz v. Peace Corps, No. 00-0848, slip op. at 9-10 (D.D.C. Oct. 12, 2001) (denying both parties' motions for summary judgment because of conflicting evidence on the timing of a decision -- a "significant material fact" with respect to the applicability of Exemption 5), aff'd in pertinent part & rev'd in other part, 428 F.3d 271 (D.C. Cir. 2005).

tify an award of summary judgment to the requester.[344]

The Court of Appeals for the District of Columbia Circuit has held that "a motion for summary judgment adequately underpinned is not defeated simply by bare opinion or an unaided claim that a factual controversy persists."[345] For example, summary judgment will not be defeated by unsupported claims that an agency is withholding information that already is in the public domain.[346] Nor will summary judgment necessarily be precluded by discrepancies in the agency's page counts, particularly when the

---

[344] See Tri-Valley CAREs v. U.S. Dep't of Energy, No. 03-3926, 2004 WL 2043034, at *18 (N.D. Cal. Sept. 10, 2004) ("[A] lack of timeliness does not preclude summary judgment for an agency in a FOIA case."), aff'd in pertinent part & remanded, No. 04-17232, 2006 WL 2971651 (9th Cir. Oct. 16, 2006); Hornbostel v. U.S. Dep't of the Interior, 305 F. Supp. 2d 21, 28 (D.D.C. 2003) (same); St. Andrews Park, Inc. v. U.S. Dep't of the Army Corps. of Eng'rs, 299 F. Supp. 2d 1264, 1269 (S.D. Fla. 2003) ("Defendant's exceeding the prescribed 20-day time limit to adjudicate the FOIA denial appeal does not entitle Plaintiffs to [summary] judgment."); Iacoe v. IRS, No. 98-C-0466, 1999 WL 675322, at *4 (E.D. Wis. July 23, 1999) ("The effect of the agency's failure to meet the time limit is merely to permit the requester to bring an action in district court . . . ."); Barvick v. Cisneros, 941 F. Supp. 1015, 1019-20 (D. Kan. 1996) ("This court is persuaded that an agency's failure to respond within [the statutory time limits] does not automatically entitle a FOIA requester to summary judgment.").

[345] Alyeska Pipeline, 856 F.2d at 314; see Mace v. EEOC, 197 F.3d 329, 330 (8th Cir. 1999) ("[S]peculative claims about [the] existence of other documents cannot rebut [the] presumption of good faith afforded [to] agency affidavits." (citing SafeCard Servs. v. SEC, 926 F.2d 1197, 1200 (D.C. Cir. 1991))); Germosen v. Cox, No. 98 Civ. 1294, 1999 WL 1021559, at *18-19 (S.D.N.Y. Nov. 9, 1999) (ruling that plaintiff cannot defeat summary judgment by speculating that further evidence will develop to support his allegations), appeal dismissed for failure to prosecute, No. 00-6041 (2d Cir. Sept. 12, 2000); Iacoe, 1999 WL 675322, at *4 ("Plaintiff's speculations about a cover-up are insufficient to overcome the presumption of good faith to which the agency's declaration is entitled."); Judicial Watch, Inc. v. HHS, 27 F. Supp. 2d 240, 243-44 (D.D.C. 1998) (explaining that plaintiff's "bare suspicion" will not call into question adequacy of agency's search); Gale v. FBI, 141 F.R.D. 94, 96 (N.D. Ill. 1992) (holding that plaintiff's "own self-serving statements [alone] are insufficient to create a genuine issue of material fact barring summary judgment"); see also Marks v. United States, 578 F.2d 261, 263 (9th Cir. 1978) ("Conclusory allegations unsupported by factual data will not create a triable issue of fact.").

[346] See Steinberg v. U.S. Dep't of Justice, 179 F.R.D. 357, 360 (D.D.C. 1998) (finding that summary judgment is not defeated "with pure conjecture about the possible content of withheld information, raising 'some metaphysical doubt as to the material facts'" (quoting Matsushita Elec. Indus. v. Zenith Radio Corp., 475 U.S. 574, 586 (1986))).

agency has processed a voluminous number of pages, so long as the agency has supplied a "well-detailed and clear" explanation for the differences.[347] Moreover, a plaintiff -- even one appearing pro se -- will be found to have conceded the government's factual assertions if he fails to contest them, once it is clear that he understands his responsibility to do so.[348]

In a FOIA case, the agency has the burden of justifying nondisclosure,[349] and it must sustain its burden by submitting detailed affidavits[350]

---

[347] Master v. FBI, 926 F. Supp. 193, 197-98 (D.D.C. 1996), summary affirmance granted, 124 F.3d 1309 (D.C. Cir. 1997) (unpublished table decision); see also Piper v. U.S. Dep't of Justice, 294 F. Supp. 2d 16, 23-24 (D.D.C. 2003) (finding "no material issue to rebut the Government's good faith presumption in the processing of [plaintiff's] FOIA request" merely because of "gaps in the serialization of the files").

[348] See McNamara v. Nat'l Credit Union Ass'n, 264 F. Supp. 2d 1, 4 (D.D.C. 2002) (treating as conceded defendant's statement of material facts because plaintiff filed motion to dismiss without prejudice rather than opposition to summary judgment motion); Knight v. FDA, No. 95-4097, 1997 WL 109971, at *1 (D. Kan. Feb. 11, 1997) (accepting as "reasonable and fair" agency's processing of plaintiff's request and granting agency summary judgment "[i]n the absence of any argument from the plaintiff"); Nuzzo v. FBI, No. 95-1708, 1996 WL 741587, at *2 (D.D.C. Oct. 8, 1996) (granting defendant agency's unopposed summary judgment motion); Butler v. Dep't of the Air Force, 888 F. Supp. 174, 179 (D.D.C. 1995) (ruling that because plaintiff failed to controvert agency's factual assertions, they must be accepted as true), aff'd per curiam, No. 96-5111 (D.C. Cir. May 6, 1997); see also Hart v. FBI, No. 94 C 6010, 1995 WL 170001, at *2 (N.D. Ill. Apr. 7, 1995) (holding that "plaintiff has not asserted any facts which convince this Court that the FBI has any records which relate to him or has failed to conduct an adequate search"), aff'd, 91 F.3d 146 (7th Cir. July 16, 1996) (unpublished table decision); cf. Ruotolo v. IRS, 28 F.3d 6, 8-9 (2d Cir. 1994) (finding that although plaintiffs were generally aware of summary judgment rules, district court should have specifically notified them of consequences of not complying with litigation deadlines before dismissing case).

[349] See 5 U.S.C. § 552(a)(4)(B) (2000 & Supp. IV 2004); see, e.g., U.S. Dep't of Justice v. Reporters Comm. for Freedom of the Press, 489 U.S. 749, 755 (1989); Wishart v. Comm'r, No. 98-17248, 1999 WL 985142, at *1 (9th Cir. June 25, 1999); Coastal States Gas Corp. v. Dep't of Energy, 617 F.2d 854, 868 (D.C. Cir. 1980); Judicial Watch, Inc. v. Dep't of the Army, 402 F. Supp. 2d 241, 245 (D.D.C. 2005) (stating that "the defendant agency has the burden of justifying nondisclosure"); Dean v. FDIC, 389 F. Supp. 2d 780, 789 (E.D. Ky. 2005) ("The government bears the burden of proving that its withholdings under FOIA were lawful.").

[350] See, e.g., O'Harvey v. Office of Workers' Compensation Programs, No. 96-33015, 1997 WL 31589, at *1 (9th Cir. Jan. 21, 1997) (holding that when

(continued...)

that identify the documents at issue and explain why they fall under the claimed exemptions.[351] (A federal statute specifically permits unsworn declarations (i.e., without notarizations) to be utilized in all cases in which affidavits otherwise would be required.[352]) The widespread use of Vaughn Indexes, of course, means that affidavits, in the form of Vaughn Indexes, will nearly always be submitted in FOIA lawsuits, notwithstanding Rule 56's language making affidavits optional in general. (For a further discussion of Vaughn Indexes, see Litigation Considerations, Vaughn Index, above.)

As one court has put it, "[s]ummary judgment is available to the defendant in a FOIA case when the agency proves that it has fully discharged its obligations under the FOIA, after the underlying facts and the inferences to be drawn from them are construed in the light most favorable to the FOIA requester."[353] Summary judgment may be granted solely on the basis of agency affidavits if they are clear, specific, and reasonably detailed, if they describe the withheld information in a factual and nonconclusory manner, and if there is no contradictory evidence on the record or evidence of agency bad faith.[354] If all of these requisites are met, such affida-

---

[350](...continued)
the district court relied on the agency's denial letter "[w]ithout an affidavit or oral testimony, [it] lacked a factual basis to make its decision"); Judicial Watch, 402 F. Supp. 2d at 245 (noting that an agency may meet its burden "by providing the requester with a Vaughn index, adequately describing each withheld document and explaining the exemption's relevance").

[351] See Summers v. Dep't of Justice, 140 F.3d 1077, 1080 (D.C. Cir. 1998); King v. U.S. Dep't of Justice, 830 F.2d 210, 217 (D.C. Cir. 1987); Vaughn v. Rosen, 484 F.2d 820, 826-28 (D.C. Cir. 1973); cf. McClain, 17 F. App'x at 474 (holding that there is no entitlement to Vaughn Index unless plaintiff shows that he made specific request for records and agency withheld them pursuant to FOIA exemptions); Harrison, 377 F. Supp. 2d at 145-46 (reasoning that a court may grant summary judgment based on the agency's affidavits or declarations if they describe "'the documents and the justifications for nondisclosure with reasonably specific detail, demonstrate that the information withheld logically falls within the claimed exemption, and are not controverted by either contrary evidence in the record nor by evidence of agency bad faith'" (quoting Military Audit Project v. Casey, 656 F. 2d 724, 738 (D.C. Cir. 1981))).

[352] 28 U.S.C. § 1746 (2000); see Summers v. U.S. Dep't of Justice, 999 F.2d 570, 572-73 (D.C. Cir. 1993).

[353] Miller v. U.S. Dep't of State, 779 F.2d 1378, 1382 (8th Cir. 1985).

[354] See, e.g., L.A. Times Commc'ns v. Dep't of the Army, 442 F. Supp. 2d 880, 899-900 (C.D. Cal. 2006) (granting summary judgment based on the agency's detailed and nonconclusory declarations, and noting that the

(continued...)

vits are usually accorded substantial weight by the courts.[355]

---

[354](...continued)
agency's position "is not controverted by contrary evidence in the record or any evidence of agency bad faith"); Lane v. Dep't of Justice, No. 1:02-CV-06555, 2006 WL 1455459, at *11 (E.D.N.Y. May 22, 2006) (granting summary judgment "because the defendants provide a detailed and non-conclusory affidavit that indicates there is no genuine factual dispute"); Assassination Archives & Research Ctr. v. CIA, 177 F. Supp. 2d 1, 8 (D.D.C. 2001) (pointing out that a "mere assertion of bad faith is not sufficient to overcome a motion for summary judgment" (citing Hayden v. NSA, 608 F.2d 1381, 1387 (D.C. Cir. 1979))), aff'd, 334 F.3d 55 (D.C. Cir. 2003); Barvick, 941 F. Supp. at 1018 (declaring that summary judgment is available "when the agency offers adequate affidavits establishing that it has complied with its FOIA obligations"); Hemenway v. Hughes, 601 F. Supp. 1002, 1004 (D.D.C. 1985) (recognizing that in FOIA cases, summary judgment does not hinge on existence of genuine issue of material fact, but rather on whether agency affidavits are reasonably specific, demonstrate logical use of exemptions, and are not controverted by evidence in record or by bad faith) (applying standard developed in national security context to Exemption 6); cf. Niagara Mohawk Power Corp. v. U.S. Dep't of Energy, 169 F.3d 16, 18 (D.C. Cir. 1999) (finding agency affidavits conclusory and denying summary judgment despite plaintiff's failure to controvert agency assertions by remaining silent); Kamman v. IRS, 56 F.3d 46, 49 (9th Cir. 1995) (finding that agency failed to satisfy burden of proof and awarding summary judgment to plaintiff when agency affidavits "are nothing more than 'conclusory and generalized allegations'"); Voinche v. FBI, 46 F. Supp. 2d 26, 30 (D.D.C. 1999) (denying summary judgment when agency provided conclusory affidavit to support invocation of Exemption 7(A)); Demma v. U.S. Dep't of Justice, No. 93 C 7296, 1995 WL 360731, at *3 (N.D. Ill. June 15, 1995) (denying summary judgment when affidavits addressed only one subject of plaintiff's multiple-subject request), appeal dismissed voluntarily, No. 96-1231 (7th Cir. June 12, 1996).

[355] See, e.g., In re Wade, 969 F.2d 241, 246 (7th Cir. 1992) ("Without evidence of bad faith, the veracity of the government's submissions regarding reasons for withholding the documents should not be questioned."); Gardels v. CIA, 689 F.2d 1100, 1104 (D.C. Cir. 1982); Taylor v. Dep't of the Army, 684 F.2d 99, 106-07 (D.C. Cir. 1982); Judicial Watch, Inc. v. Clinton, 880 F. Supp. 1, 10 (D.D.C. 1995), aff'd on other grounds, 76 F.3d 1232 (D.C. Cir. 1996); see also Sephton v. FBI, 365 F. Supp. 2d 91, 97 (D. Mass. 2005) (declaring that the plaintiff's evidence "is insufficient to rebut the presumption of good faith" given to the agency's affidavits), aff'd, 442 F.3d 27 (1st Cir. 2006); Piper, 294 F. Supp. 2d at 20 ("Upon a finding that the affidavits are sufficient, the court need not conduct further inquiry into their veracity."); Coastal Delivery Corp. v. U.S. Customs Serv., 272 F. Supp. 2d 958, 962 (C.D. Cal. 2003) ("Disagreeing with the [agency's] conclusion [concerning applicability of an exemption] is not a reason to challenge the Vaughn Index."), appeal dismissed voluntarily, No. 03-55833 (9th Cir. Aug. 26, 2003).

## LITIGATION CONSIDERATIONS

In certain circumstances, opinions or conclusions may be asserted in agency affidavits, especially in cases in which disclosure would compromise national security.[356] On the other hand, "[c]ourts have consistently held that a requester's opinion disputing the risk created by disclosure is not sufficient to preclude summary judgment for the agency when the agency possessing the relevant expertise has provided sufficiently detailed affidavits."[357]

Rule 56(e) of the Federal Rules of Civil Procedure provides that the affidavit must be based upon the personal knowledge of the affiant, must demonstrate the affiant's competency to testify as to matters stated, and must set forth only facts that would be admissible in evidence.[358] "Gratuitous recitations of the affiant's own interpretation of the law," however, are

---

[356] See Ctr. for Nat'l Sec. Studies v. U.S. Dep't of Justice, 331 F.3d 918, 927 (D.C. Cir. 2003) (crediting the government's predictive judgments concerning harm to national security that could result from release of requested information); Gardels, 689 F.2d at 1106 (recognizing that there is "necessarily a region for forecasts in which informed judgment as to potential harm should be respected"); Halperin v. CIA, 629 F.2d 144, 149 (D.C. Cir. 1980) (declaring that "courts must take into account . . . that any affidavit of threatened harm to national security will always be speculative"); Hoch v. CIA, 593 F. Supp. 675, 683-84 (D.D.C. 1984), aff'd, 807 F.2d 1227 (D.C. Cir. 1990) (unpublished table decision); see also Moore v. FBI, No. 83-1541, slip op. at 2 (D.D.C. Aug. 30, 1984) (finding that "particular incident" was sufficiently identified given national security nature of documents), aff'd, 762 F.2d 138 (D.C. Cir. 1985) (unpublished table decision).

[357] Struth v. FBI, 673 F. Supp. 949, 954 (E.D. Wis. 1987); see, e.g., Goldberg v. U.S. Dep't of State, 818 F.2d 71, 78-79 (D.C. Cir. 1987) (Exemption 1); Spannaus v. U.S. Dep't of Justice, 813 F.2d 1285, 1289 (4th Cir. 1987) (Exemption 7(A)); Curran v. Dep't of Justice, 813 F.2d 473, 477 (1st Cir. 1987) (Exemption 7(A)); Gardels, 689 F.2d at 1106 n.5 (Exemptions 1 and 3); People for the Am. Way Found. v. NSA/Cent. Sec. Serv., 462 F. Supp. 2d 21, 33-34 (D.D.C. 2006) (Exemption 1); Edmonds v. U.S. Dep't of Justice, 405 F. Supp. 2d 23, 27-30 (D.D.C. 2005) (Exemption 1); Whalen v. U.S. Marine Corps, 407 F. Supp. 2d 54, 56-59 (D.D.C. 2005) (Exemptions 1 and 3); Wheeler v. U.S. Dep't of Justice, 403 F. Supp. 2d 1, 6-7, 10-12 (D.D.C. 2005) (Exemption 1); Windels, Marx, Davies & Ives v. Dep't of Commerce, 576 F. Supp. 405, 410-11 (D.D.C. 1983) (Exemptions 2 and 7(E)); see also Sephton, 365 F. Supp. 2d at 101 (stating that the plaintiff's speculation "is not adequate to rebut the presumption of good faith generated by the agency's affidavits in the context of litigation pursuant to FOIA"); Lindsey v. NSC, No. 84-3897, slip op. at 3 (D.D.C. July 12, 1985) (holding that a FOIA plaintiff cannot defeat summary judgment by saying that he will raise genuine issue "at a time of his own choosing").

[358] Fed. R. Civ. P. 56(e).

inappropriate.[359]

The affidavit or declaration of an agency official who is knowledge-able about the way in which information is processed and is familiar with the documents at issue satisfies the personal knowledge requirement.[360]

---

[359] Doolittle v. U.S. Dep't of Justice, 142 F. Supp. 2d 281, 285 n.5 (N.D.N.Y. 2001) ("The practice of submitting legal arguments through the declaration . . . is improper, and such arguments will not be considered."); Peters v. IRS, No. 00-2143, slip op. at 5 (D.N.J. Feb. 23, 2001) ("Argument of the facts and the law shall not be contained in the affidavits."); Alamo Aircraft Sup-ply, Inc. v. Weinberger, No. 85-1291, 1986 U.S. Dist. LEXIS 29010, at *3 (D.D.C. Feb. 21, 1986) (reproving agency declaration for "several gratuitous recitations of the affiant's own interpretation of the law").

[360] See, e.g., Spannaus, 813 F.2d at 1289 (holding that declarant's attes-tation "to his personal knowledge of the procedures used in handling [the] request and his familiarity with the documents in question" is sufficient); Schrecker v. U.S. Dep't of Justice, 217 F. Supp. 2d 29, 35 (D.D.C. 2002) (re-jecting argument that affidavit was hearsay because affiant was "respon-sible for the FBI's compliance with FOIA litigation and is therefore not merely speculating about the FBI activities"), aff'd, 349 F.3d 657 (D.C. Cir. 2003); Gerstein v. U.S. Dep't of Justice, No. 03-04893, 2005 U.S. Dist. LEXIS 41276, at *13-14 (N.D. Cal. Sept. 30, 2005) (denying the plaintiff's motion to strike the agency's declaration, inasmuch as the declarant permissibly in-cluded "facts relayed from individuals who had first-hand knowledge," and because the declarant had "first-hand knowledge of what happens when a court seals a warrant"); Hoffman v. U.S. Dep't of Justice, No. 98-1733, slip op. at 7 (W.D. Okla. Apr. 16, 1999) (finding personal knowledge require-ment was met because declarant was "aware of what was done by virtue of information provided to him in his official capacity"); Cucci v. DEA, 871 F. Supp. 508, 513 (D.D.C. 1994) (finding that declarant "had the requisite per-sonal knowledge based on her examination of the records and her discus-sion with a representative of the [state police]" to attest that information was provided with express understanding of confidentiality); Laborers' Int'l Union v. U.S. Dep't of Justice, 578 F. Supp. 52, 55-56 (D.D.C. 1983) (finding affiant competent when observations were based on review of investiga-tive report and upon general familiarity with nature of investigations simi-lar to that documented in requested report), aff'd, 772 F.2d 919 (D.C. Cir. 1984); see also Madison Mech., Inc. v. NASA, No. 99-2854, 2003 WL 1477014, at *6 (D.D.C. Mar. 20, 2003) (magistrate's recommendation) (re-quiring agency to submit revised affidavits stating "fully and precisely" declarant's basis for personal knowledge), adopted (D.D.C. Mar. 31, 2003); Avondale Indus. v. NLRB, No. 96-1227, 1998 WL 34064938, at *3 (E.D. La. Mar. 23, 1998) (holding that there is no requirement that author of records prepare Vaughn Index); Coleman v. FBI, No. 89-2773, slip op. at 8-9 (D.D.C. Dec. 10, 1991) ("The law does not require the affiant preparing a Vaughn Index to be personally familiar with more than the procedures used in proc-essing the particular request."), summary affirmance granted, No. 92-5040

(continued...)

Similarly, in instances in which an agency's search is questioned, an affidavit of an agency employee responsible for coordinating the search efforts satisfies the personal knowledge requirement.[361] Likewise, in justifying the withholding of classified information under Exemption 1, the affiant is required only to possess document-classification authority for the records in question, not personal knowledge of the particular substantive area that is the subject of the request.[362] However, affiants must establish that they

---

[360](...continued)
(D.C. Cir. Dec. 4, 1992); cf. Kamman, 56 F.3d at 49 (rejecting affidavit that revealed that signer "did not even review the actual documents at issue" and attested only "that the documents are in a file that is marked with the name of a taxpayer other than [plaintiff]"); Canning v. Dep't of Justice, No. 92-0463, slip op. at 4-5 (D.D.C. June 26, 1995) (finding personal knowledge requirement was met where affidavit established affiant's authority to review withheld grand jury records, and affiant personally reviewed such records); FOIA Update, Vol. XIX, No. 3, at 2 (advising that agency FOIA officers are authorized to review grand jury materials for purposes of FOIA administration, notwithstanding strict secrecy requirements of Rule 6(e) of Federal Rules of Criminal Procedure (citing Canning)).

[361] See, e.g., Carney v. U.S. Dep't of Justice, 19 F.3d 807, 814 (2d Cir. 1994), aff'g in pertinent part, rev'g & remanding in part, No. 92-CV-6204, slip op. at 12 (W.D.N.Y. Apr. 27, 1993) ("There is no basis in either the statute or the relevant caselaw to require that an agency effectively establish by a series of sworn affidavits a 'chain of custody' over its search process. The format of the proof submitted by defendant -- declarations of supervisory employees, signed under penalty of perjury -- is sufficient for purposes of both the statute and Fed. R. Civ. P. 56."); Maynard v. CIA, 986 F.2d 547, 560 (1st Cir. 1993) ("[A]n agency need not submit an affidavit from the employee who actually conducted the search. Instead, an agency may rely on an affidavit of an agency employee responsible for supervising the search."); SafeCard, 926 F.2d at 1202 (finding that employee "in charge of coordinating the [agency's] search and recovery efforts [is the] most appropriate person to provide a comprehensive affidavit"); Perry-Torres v. U.S. Dep't of State, 404 F. Supp. 2d 140, 142 (D.D.C. 2005) (stating that "affidavits may be submitted by an official who coordinated the search, and need not be from each individual who participated in the search"); Inner City Press/Cmty. on the Move v. Bd. of Governors of the Fed. Reserve Sys., No. 98 Civ. 4608, 1998 WL 690371, at *4 (S.D.N.Y. Sept. 30, 1998) ("[I]t is even routine to accept affidavits from agency officials who have supervised but not personally conducted a FOIA search."), aff'd, 182 F.3d 900 (2d Cir. 1999) (unpublished table decision).

[362] See Holland v. CIA, No. 92-1233, 1992 WL 233820, at *8-9 (D.D.C. Aug. 31, 1992); McTigue v. U.S. Dep't of Justice, No. 84-3583, slip op. at 8-9 (D.D.C. Dec. 3, 1985), aff'd, 808 F.2d 137 (D.C. Cir. 1987).

are personally familiar with all of the withheld records,[363] and they should not be selected solely on the basis that they occupy particular positions in the agency.[364]

## Discovery

Discovery is the exception, not the rule, in FOIA cases.[365] If it occurs -- and determinations of whether and under what conditions discovery is permitted are always vested in the sound discretion of the district court[366]

---

[363] See Kamman, 56 F.3d at 49 (rejecting affidavit that revealed that signer "did not even review the actual documents at issue," and that attested only "that the documents are in a file that is marked with the name of a taxpayer other than [plaintiff]"); Sellar v. FBI, No. 84-1611, slip op. at 3 (D.D.C. July 22, 1988).

[364] See Timken Co. v. U.S. Customs Serv., 3 Gov't Disclosure Serv. (P-H) ¶ 83,234, at 83,975 n.9 (D.D.C. June 24, 1983) (rejecting attestations of affiant who merely sampled documents that staff had reviewed for him); cf. Marriott Int'l Resorts, L.P. v. United States, 437 F.3d 1302, 1308 (Fed. Cir. 2006) (holding that "the head of an Agency can, when [the step is] carefully undertaken, delegate authority to invoke the deliberative process privilege on the Agency's behalf") (non-FOIA case).

[365] See, e.g., Heily v. U.S. Dep't of Commerce, 69 F. App'x 171, 174 (4th Cir. 2003) (per curiam) ("It is well-established that discovery may be greatly restricted in FOIA cases."); Van Mechelen v. U.S. Dep't of the Interior, No. 05-5393, 2005 WL 3007121, at *5 (W.D. Wash. Nov. 9, 2005) (observing that "discovery is not ordinarily part of a FOIA case"); Wheeler v. CIA, 271 F. Supp. 2d 132, 139 (D.D.C. 2003) ("Discovery is generally unavailable in FOIA actions."); Hardy v. DOD, No. 99-523, 2001 WL 3435945, at *4 (D. Ariz. Aug. 27, 2001) ("[D]iscovery is not favored in FOIA cases."); Judicial Watch, Inc. v. Exp.-Imp. Bank, 108 F. Supp. 2d 19, 25 (D.D.C. 2000) ("[D]iscovery in a FOIA action is generally inappropriate."); Pub. Citizen Health Research Group v. FDA, 997 F. Supp. 56, 72 (D.D.C. 1998) ("Discovery is to be sparingly granted in FOIA actions."), aff'd in part, rev'd in part & remanded, 185 F.3d 898 (D.C. Cir. 1999); Katzman v. Freeh, 926 F. Supp. 316, 319 (E.D.N.Y. 1996) ("[D]iscovery in a FOIA action is extremely limited . . . .").

[366] See Wood v. FBI, 432 F.3d 78, 84-85 (2d Cir. 2005) (recognizing that "[a] district court has broad discretion to manage pre-trial discovery" (citing Grand Cent. P'ship v. Cuomo, 166 F.3d 473, 488 (2d Cir. 1999))); Becker v. IRS, 34 F.3d 398, 406 (7th Cir. 1994); Maynard v. CIA, 986 F.2d 547, 567 (1st Cir. 1993); Gillin v. IRS, 980 F.2d 819, 823 (1st Cir. 1992) (per curiam); Nolan v. U.S. Dep't of Justice, 973 F.2d 843, 849 (10th Cir. 1992); N.C. Network for Animals, Inc. v. USDA, No. 90-1443, 1991 WL 10757, at *4 (4th Cir. Feb. 5, 1991) ("The district court should exercise its discretion to limit discovery in this as in all FOIA cases, and may enter summary judgment on the basis of agency affidavits when they are sufficient to resolve issues . . . ."); Petrus v. (continued...)

-- discovery ordinarily is limited to the scope of an agency's search, its indexing and classification procedures, and similar factual matters.[367] The

---

[366](...continued)
Brown, 833 F.2d 581, 583 (5th Cir. 1987) ("A trial court has broad discretion
and inherent power to stay discovery until preliminary questions that may
dispose of the case are determined."); Meeropol v. Meese, 790 F.2d 942,
960-61 (D.C. Cir. 1986) (same, with respect to broad district court discretion); see also Anderson v. HHS, 80 F.3d 1500, 1507 (10th Cir. 1996) (holding that district court did not abuse its discretion in denying plaintiff discovery on attorney fees issue).

[367] See Heily, 69 F. App'x at 174 (explaining that when discovery is permitted, generally it is "limited to the scope of agency's search and its indexing and classification procedures"); see, e.g., Tax Analysts v. IRS, 214 F.3d
179, 185 (D.C. Cir. 2000) (remanding for discovery on "narrow and fact-specific question" concerning disclosability of specific type of document); Ruotolo v. Dep't of Justice, 53 F.3d 4, 11 (2d Cir. 1995) (holding that discovery
on scope of burden that search would entail should have been granted);
Weisberg v. U.S. Dep't of Justice, 627 F.2d 365, 371 (D.C. Cir. 1980) (finding
discovery appropriate to inquire into adequacy of document search); Ban-
goura v. U.S. Dep't of the Army, No. 05-0311, 2006 WL 3734164, at *6
(D.D.C. Dec. 8, 2006) (allowing limited discovery regarding adequacy of
agency's search); MacLean v. DOD, No. 04CV2425, 2005 WL 628021, at *1
(S.D. Cal. Mar. 16, 2005) (granting limited discovery on the basis that the
discovery that the plaintiff seeks "is necessary to support an argument that
the claimed exemptions are inapplicable, and . . . the information sought is
within the exclusive province of the Government"); Judicial Watch, Inc. v.
U.S. Dep't of Commerce, 127 F. Supp. 2d 228, 230 (D.D.C. 2000) (permitting
depositions to be taken about parameters of FOIA search); Long v. U.S.
Dep't of Justice, 10 F. Supp. 2d 205, 210 (N.D.N.Y. 1998) (finding discovery
appropriate to test adequacy of search); Pub. Citizen, 997 F. Supp. at 72
(holding that discovery is limited to "investigating the scope of the agency
search for responsive documents, the agency's indexing procedures, and
the like"); see also Wash. Post Co. v. U.S. Dep't of Justice, No. 84-3581, slip
op. at 1-2 (D.D.C. Aug. 2, 1990) (permitting discovery, in Exemption 7(B)
case, on issue of whether it is more probable than not that disclosure
would seriously interfere with fairness of pending or "truly imminent" trial
or adjudication); Silverberg v. HHS, No. 89-2743, 1990 WL 599452, at *1-2
(D.D.C. June 26, 1990) (permitting discovery, in Exemption 4 case, of responses by private drug-testing laboratories to agency's inquiry concerning whether their "performance test results" are customarily released to
public); ABC, Inc. v. USIA, 599 F. Supp. 765, 768-70 (D.D.C. 1984) (ordering
agency head to submit to deposition on issue of whether transcripts of
tape-recorded telephone calls constitute "personal records" or "agency records"); cf. United States v. Owens, 54 F.3d 271, 277 (6th Cir. 1995) (allowing
discovery on issue of ownership of joint state/federal task force records in
action by United States to enjoin state court disclosure order under state
public records law). But see Pa. Dep't of Pub. Welfare v. United States, No.
(continued...)

major exception to this limited scope of discovery is when the plaintiff raises a sufficient question as to the agency's good faith in processing documents or any other respect.[368] In any case, however, before being permit-

---

[367](...continued)
99-175, 1999 WL 1051963, at *3 (W.D. Pa. Oct. 12, 1999) (allowing limited discovery "regarding the authenticity and completeness of the material produced by HHS, as well as the methodology used to compile it," because plaintiff "'does not know the contents of the information sought and is, therefore, helpless to contradict the government's description of the information or assist the trial judge'" (quoting Davin v. U.S. Dep't of Justice, 60 F.3d 1043, 1049 (3d Cir. 1995))), appeal dismissed voluntarily, No. 01-1886 (3d Cir. Apr. 24, 2002).

[368] See, e.g., Carney v. U.S. Dep't of Justice, 19 F.3d 807, 812 (2d Cir. 1994) ("In order to justify discovery once the agency has satisfied its burden, the plaintiff must make a showing of bad faith on the part of the agency sufficient to impugn the agency's affidavits or declarations, or provide some tangible evidence that an exemption claimed by the agency should not apply or summary judgment is otherwise inappropriate.") (citations omitted); Citizens for Responsibility & Ethics in Wash. v. U.S. Dep't of Justice, No. 05-2078, 2006 WL 1518964, at *3-6 (D.D.C. June 1, 2006) (granting the plaintiff's motion for discovery in the form of time-limited depositions because the plaintiff raised a sufficient question of bad faith on the part of government to "warrant limited discovery for the purpose of exploring the reasons behind [purported] delays in processing [plaintiff's] FOIA requests"); Caton v. Norton, No. 04-CV-439, 2005 WL 1009544, at *5 (D.N.H. May 2, 2005) (holding that plaintiff's showing of bad faith entitled him to limited discovery regarding allegedly altered document); Gilmore v. U.S. Dep't of Energy, 33 F. Supp. 2d 1184, 1190 (N.D. Cal. 1998) (permitting discovery when plaintiff claimed existence of pattern and practice of unreasonable delay in responding to FOIA requests, but limiting discovery to agency's "policies and practices for responding to FOIA requests, and the resources allocated to ensure its compliance the FOIA time limitations"); Judicial Watch, Inc. v. U.S. Dep't of Commerce, 34 F. Supp. 2d 28, 46 (D.D.C. 1998) (allowing discovery "under the rigorous supervision of a Magistrate Judge" concerning alleged illegal destruction and removal of records subsequent to plaintiff's FOIA request), partial summary judgment granted, 83 F. Supp. 2d 105 (D.D.C. 1999); Hawthorn Mgmt. Servs. v. HUD, No. 3:96CV2435, 1997 WL 821767, at *3 (D. Conn. Dec. 18, 1997) (permitting discovery because affiant's failure to disclose all pertinent information concerning bidding process in initial declaration amounted to "bad faith"); cf. Accuracy in Media, Inc. v. Nat'l Park Serv., 194 F.3d 120, 124 (D.C. Cir. 1999) (upholding denial of discovery based on "speculative criticism" of agency's search); Grand Cent. P'ship, 166 F.3d at 489 (finding discovery unwarranted based on plaintiff's "speculation that there must be more documents" and that agency acted in "bad faith" by not producing them); Jones v. FBI, 41 F.3d 238, 249 (6th Cir. 1994) (finding discovery unwarranted when court convinced that agency "has acted in good faith and has prop-
(continued...)

## LITIGATION CONSIDERATIONS

ted discovery, a FOIA plaintiff must adequately explain to the court exactly how the specific discovery requested will uncover information that would create a genuine issue of material fact.[369]

Even if a FOIA plaintiff surmounts this considerable barrier to discovery, there are certain areas that nevertheless are not within the permissible bounds of discovery in any event. A FOIA plaintiff should not be permitted to extend his discovery efforts into the agency's thought processes for claiming particular exemptions.[370] Moreover, discovery should not

---

[368](...continued)
erly withheld responsive material"; declaring fact that agency destroyed documents prior to receipt of FOIA request was not evidence of lack of "good faith"); Voinche v. FBI, 412 F. Supp. 2d 60, 72 (D.D.C. 2006) (denying discovery because the plaintiff neither provided evidence of bad faith nor established a "relationship between the testimony he seeks and the present FOIA action") (appeal pending).

[369] See O'Neill v. U.S. Dep't of Justice, No. 06-0671, 2006 WL 3538991, at *2 (E.D. Wis. Dec. 7, 2006) (denying plaintiff's motion to compel discovery as information sought is irrelevant to instant FOIA case); Morley v. CIA, No. 03-2545, 2006 WL 280645, at *2 (D.D.C. Feb. 6, 2006) (stating that the plaintiff's Rule 56(f) declaration merely addresses "his and the public's interest in the disclosure of documents relating to the assassination of President John F. Kennedy, rather than [his] inability to file his opposition to Defendant's motion for summary judgment," and finding that the plaintiff's argument therefore is not a basis for allowing discovery); Judicial Watch, Inc. v. U.S. Dep't of Justice, No. 99-1883, slip op. at 16 (D.D.C. June 9, 2005) (denying discovery under Fed. R. Civ. P. 56(f) because plaintiff did not adequately demonstrate any need for discovery); Ctr. for Nat'l Sec. Studies v. Dep't of Justice, No. 01-2500, 2002 U.S. Dist. LEXIS 2983, at *5 (D.D.C. Feb. 21, 2002) ("In order to obtain discovery under Fed. R. Civ. P. 56(f), a plaintiff must demonstrate that 'it cannot for reasons stated present by affidavit facts essential to justify [its] opposition.'" (quoting Carpenter v. Fed. Nat'l Mortgage Ass'n, 174 F.3d 231, 237 (D.C. Cir. 1999))), rev'd on other grounds, 331 F.3d 918 (D.C. Cir. 2003); Code v. FBI, No. 95-1892, 1997 WL 150070, at *8 (D.D.C. Mar. 26, 1997) (citing Strang v. U.S. Arms Control & Disarm. Agency, 864 F.2d 859, 861 (D.C. Cir. 1989)); SMS Data Prod. Group v. U.S. Dep't of the Air Force, No. 88-0481, 1989 WL 201031, at *5 (D.D.C. May 11, 1989) ("In the absence of substantial questions concerning the substantive content of defendant's affidavits, further discovery is inappropriate."); accord Fed. R. Civ. P. 56(f) (describing procedure for summary judgment when affidavits are unavailable).

[370] See Ajluni v. FBI, 947 F. Supp. 599, 608 (N.D.N.Y. 1996) (explaining that discovery not permitted into the "thought processes of [the] agency in deciding to claim a particular FOIA exemption"); Murphy v. FBI, 490 F. Supp. 1134, 1136 (D.D.C. 1980) (stating that "discovery is limited to factual disputes . . . [and that] the thought processes of the agency in deciding to
(continued...)

be permitted when a plaintiff seeks by it to obtain the contents of withheld documents -- the matter that lies at the very heart of a FOIA case.[371]

Discovery also should not be permitted when the plaintiff is plainly using the FOIA lawsuit as a means of questioning investigatory action taken by the agency or the underlying reasons for undertaking such investigations.[372] Courts will refuse to "allow [a] plaintiff to use this limited discov-

---

[370](...continued)
claim a particular FOIA exemption . . . are protected from disclosure").

[371] See, e.g., Tax Analysts v. IRS, 410 F.3d 715, 722 (D.C. Cir. 2005) (reasoning that "[Appellant's] demand for further inquiry into the substance of the documents would, if granted, turn FOIA on its head, awarding Appellant in discovery the very remedy for which it seeks to prevail in the suit"); Local 3, Int'l Bhd. of Elec. Workers v. NLRB, 845 F.2d 1177, 1179 (2d Cir. 1988) (finding plaintiff not entitled to discovery that would be tantamount to disclosure of contents of exempt documents); Pollard v. FBI, 705 F.2d 1151, 1154 (9th Cir. 1983) (affirming denial of discovery when directed to substance of withheld documents at issue); Fla. Immigrant Advocacy Ctr. v. NSA, 380 F. Supp. 2d 1332, 1343 (S.D. Fla. 2005) (observing that discovery is impermissible when the plaintiff is seeking to obtain "information [that] would not be available to it under the FOIA and may be classified or otherwise protected by disclosure by statute"); Schiller v. INS, 205 F. Supp. 2d 648, 654 (W.D. Tex. 2002) (refusing to permit discovery that sought "information . . . for which [plaintiffs] filed the FOIA request"); Pub. Citizen, 997 F. Supp. at 73 (same); Katzman, 926 F. Supp. at 319 (same); Moore v. FBI, No. 83-1541, slip op. at 6 (D.D.C. Mar. 9, 1984) (denying discovery requests that "would have to go to the substance of the classified materials" at issue, and noting that "[t]his is precisely the case when the court can and should exercise its discretion to deny that discovery"), aff'd, 762 F.2d 138 (D.C. Cir. 1985) (unpublished table decision); Laborers' Int'l Union v. U.S. Dep't of Justice, 578 F. Supp. 52, 56 (D.D.C. 1983) (sustaining government's objections to interrogatories when answers would "serve to confirm or deny the authenticity of the document held by plaintiff"), aff'd, 772 F.2d 919 (D.C. Cir. 1984).

[372] See RNR Enters. v. SEC, 122 F.3d 93, 98 (2d Cir. 1997) (finding no abuse of discretion in district court denial of discovery propounded for "investigative purposes"); Flowers v. IRS, 307 F. Supp. 2d 60, 72 (D.D.C. 2004) (scolding plaintiff, who "may be unhappy with the search results," for seeking discovery in her FOIA case in order to conduct investigation of the agency's rationale for tax audit); Cecola v. FBI, No. 94 C 4866, 1995 WL 143548, at *3 (N.D. Ill. Mar. 31, 1995) (disallowing deposition concerning factual basis for assertion of Exemption 7(A), because "there is concern that the subject of the investigation not be alerted to the government's investigative strategy"); Williams v. FBI, No. 90-2299, 1991 WL 163757, at *3 (D.D.C. Aug. 6, 1991) ("An agency's rationale for undertaking an investigation of the Plaintiff is not the proper subject of FOIA discovery requests.");

(continued...)

ery opportunity as a fishing expedition [for] investigating matters related to separate lawsuits."[373]

Discovery should be denied altogether if the court is satisfied from the agency's affidavits that "no factual dispute remains,"[374] and when the

---

[372](...continued)
see also Freedman v. Dep't of Justice, No. 78-4257, slip op. at 3-4 (D. Kan. Jan. 3, 1990) (denying discovery concerning electronic surveillance investigative practices).

[373] Changzhou Laosan Group v. U.S. Customs & Border Prot. Bureau, No. 04-1919, 2005 WL 913268, at *7 (D.D.C. Apr. 20, 2005) (denying the plaintiff's request for discovery because "the purpose of FOIA is not to serve as a tool for obtaining discovery for an administrative forfeiture proceeding"); Tannehill v. Dep't of the Air Force, No. 87-1335, 1987 WL 25657, at *2 (D.D.C. Nov. 12, 1987) (limiting discovery to determination of FOIA issues, not to underlying personnel decision); see Al-Fayed v. CIA, No. 00-2092, slip op. at 17 (D.D.C. Dec. 11, 2000) (terming plaintiff's discovery request "a fishing expedition" and refusing to grant it), aff'd on other grounds, 254 F.3d 300 (D.C. Cir. 2001); Immanuel v. Sec'y of Treasury, No. 94-884, 1995 WL 464141, at *1 (D. Md. Apr. 4, 1995) (rejecting discovery that would constitute "a fishing expedition into all the possible funds held by the Department of [the] Treasury which may fall within the terms of [plaintiff's] broad FOIA request. Such an expedition is certainly not going to come at the government's expense when it is evident that [plaintiff] seeks this information only for his own commercial use."), aff'd on other grounds, No. 95-1953, 1996 WL 157732 (4th Cir. Apr. 5, 1996); cf. Carpenter v. U.S. Dep't of Justice, No. 3:05CV172, 2005 WL 1290678, at *2 (D. Conn. Apr. 28, 2005) (noting that the plaintiff is seeking discovery for a criminal case pending in another district, and finding therefore that the plaintiff's argument -- to keep cases in two separate districts in order to minimize any inappropriate impact -- is unpersuasive because if the "plaintiff can find a way of using any such documents to his advantage, he will inject them into the criminal case"); United States v. Chrein, 368 F. Supp. 2d 278, 284 (S.D.N.Y. 2005) (explaining that "a FOIA request cannot be used as simply a way to get around discovery rules, and limitations, of a civil action"); Ctr. for Individual Rights v. U.S. Dep't of Justice, No. 03-1706, slip op. at 5-6 (D.D.C. June 29, 2004) ("'FOIA rights are unaffected by the requester's involvement in other litigation; an individual may therefore obtain under FOIA information that may be useful in non-FOIA litigation, even when the documents sought could not be obtained through discovery.'" (quoting North v. Walsh, 881 F.2d 1088, 1099 (D.C. Cir. 1989))).

[374] Schrecker v. U.S. Dep't of Justice, 217 F. Supp. 2d 29, 35 (D.D.C. 2002), aff'd, 349 F.3d 657 (D.C. Cir. 2003); see Goland v. CIA, 607 F.2d 339, 352 (D.C. Cir. 1978), vacated in other part & reh'g denied, 607 F.2d 367 (D.C. Cir. 1979); Van Mechelen, 2005 WL 3007121, at *5 (finding discovery to be unwarranted because government satisfied its burden of proof); see also
(continued...)

affidavits are "relatively detailed" and submitted in good faith.[375] Consequently, discovery should routinely be denied when the plaintiff's "efforts
are made with [nothing] more than a 'bare hope of falling upon something
that might impugn the affidavits'" submitted by the defendant agency.[376]

---

[374](...continued)
Becker, 34 F.3d at 406 (finding that district court did not err by granting
summary judgment to government without addressing plaintiff's motion for
discovery; explaining that the judge "must have been satisfied that discovery was unnecessary when she concluded that the IRS's search was reasonable and ruled in favor of the IRS on summary judgment").

[375] See Wood, 432 F.3d at 85 (affirming denial of discovery, and holding
that the "district court did not abuse its discretion in finding [plaintiff's
conjectural] assertion insufficient to overcome the government's good faith
showing"); SafeCard, 926 F.2d at 1200-02 (affirming decision to deny discovery as to adequacy of search, on ground that agency's affidavits were
sufficiently detailed); Military Audit Project v. Casey, 656 F.2d 724, 751
(D.C. Cir. 1981) (affirming trial court's refusal to permit discovery when
plaintiffs had failed to raise "substantial questions concerning the substantive content of the [defendants'] affidavits"); Citizens for Responsibility &
Ethics in Wash. v. Nat'l Indian Gaming Comm'n, No. 05-00806, 2006 WL
3628954, at *11 (D.D.C. Dec. 12, 2006) (finding no extraordinary basis to
grant discovery because alleged deficiencies in agency's affidavits are not
legally significant and there is no evidence of bad faith); Reid v. USPS, No.
05-cv-294, 2006 WL 1876682, at *5 (S.D. Ill. July 5, 2006) (denying discovery
because "[d]efendant's submissions are adequate on their face"); Fla. Immigrant Advocacy Ctr., 380 F. Supp. 2d at 1343 (denying discovery because
agency's affidavit was "sufficiently detailed, nonconclusory and submitted
in good faith"); Allen v. U.S. Secret Serv., 335 F. Supp. 2d 95, 100 (D.D.C.
2004) (denying discovery because the "[p]laintiff has not established that
the affidavits are incomplete or made in bad faith"); Broaddrick v. Executive
Office of the President, 139 F. Supp. 2d 55, 64 (D.D.C. 2001) (denying discovery because agency affidavits were sufficiently detailed) (Privacy Act
case); Pease v. U.S. Dep't of Interior, No. 1:99CV113, slip op. at 6 (D. Vt.
Sept. 11, 1999) ("'[D]iscovery relating to the agency's search and the exemptions it claims for withholding records generally is unnecessary if the agency's submissions are adequate on their face.'" (quoting Carney, 19 F.3d at
812)); Hunt v. U.S. Marine Corps, 935 F. Supp. 46, 50 (D.D.C. 1996) (denying
discovery because "defendants have met their burden of showing that they
made a good faith effort to conduct a search for the requested records, using methods reasonably expected to produce the desired information"); cf.
Animal Legal Def. Fund, Inc. v. Dep't of the Air Force, 44 F. Supp. 2d 295,
304 (D.D.C. 1999) (finding agency affidavit insufficient but ordering more
detailed affidavit and Vaughn Index rather than permitting discovery);
Long, 10 F. Supp. 2d at 210 (allowing discovery because agency affidavit
was found to be insufficient).

[376] Pub. Citizen, 997 F. Supp. at 73 (quoting Founding Church of Scientol-
(continued...)

In any event, "'curtailment of discovery' is particularly appropriate where the court makes an in camera inspection."[377] Permissible discovery should take place, if at all, only after the government moves for summary judgment and submits its supporting affidavits and memorandum of law, which contain its evidentiary proof in the case.[378]

---

[376] (...continued)
ogy v. NSA, 610 F.2d 824, 836-37 n.101 (D.C. Cir. 1979)); see Military Audit Project, 656 F.2d at 751-52; Kay v. FCC, 976 F. Supp. 23, 34 n.35 (D.D.C. 1997) (concluding that because plaintiff failed to submit "concrete evidence of bad faith," discovery was actually sought only to discredit agency declaration), affd, 172 F.3d 919 (D.C. Cir. 1998) (unpublished table decision); see also Physicians Comm. for Responsible Med. v. Glickman, 117 F. Supp. 2d 1, 4 (D.D.C. 2000) ("Discovery to pursue a suspicion or a hunch is unwarranted.") (Federal Advisory Committee Act case).

[377] Ajluni v. FBI, 947 F. Supp. 599, 608 (N.D.N.Y. 1996) (quoting Katzman, 926 F. Supp. at 320); see Mehl v. EPA, 797 F. Supp. 43, 46 (D.D.C. 1992) (employing in camera review, rather than discovery, to resolve inconsistency between representations in Vaughn Index and agency's prior public statements); Laborers' Int'l, 772 F.2d at 921.

[378] See, e.g., Miscavige v. IRS, 2 F.3d 366, 369 (11th Cir. 1993) ("The plaintiff's early attempt in litigation of this kind . . . to take discovery depositions is inappropriate until the government has first had a chance to provide the court with the information necessary to make a decision on the applicable exemptions."); see Farese v. U.S. Dep't of Justice, No. 86-5528, slip op. at 6 (D.C. Cir. Aug. 12, 1987) (affirming denial of discovery filed prior to affidavits, because the discovery "sought to short-circuit the agencies' review of the voluminous amount of documentation requested"); Simmons v. U.S. Dep't of Justice, 796 F.2d 709, 711-12 (4th Cir. 1986) (approving district court's decision denying discovery because agency affidavit filed with summary judgment motion made need for discovery "moot"); Military Audit Project, 656 F.2d at 750 (finding no abuse of discretion where agency affidavits were not "inadequate . . . let alone conclusory"); Piron v. Dep't of Justice, No. C00-1287, slip. op. at 2-3 (W.D. Wash. Jan. 10, 2001) (quoting Department of Justice's Freedom of Information Act Guide & Privacy Act Overview 597-98 (May 2000) to the effect that "[p]ermissible discovery . . . should take place, if at all, only after the government moves for summary judgment," in denying discovery on the ground that the government had not yet submitted its summary judgment motion), subsequent opinion (W.D. Wash. May 9, 2001); Founding Church of Scientology v. U.S. Marshals Serv., 516 F. Supp. 151, 156 (D.D.C. 1980) (barring discovery until defendant has opportunity to submit second Vaughn affidavit). But see Long, 10 F. Supp. 2d at 210 (allowing discovery prior to government's motion for summary judgment only to test adequacy of search); Ctr. for Nat'l Sec. Studies v. INS, No. 87-2068, slip op. at 2 (D.D.C. July 27, 1988) (permitting discovery on issue of agency's "due diligence" in processing responsive records even prior to filing of government's affidavit because of discerned "discrepan-
(continued...)

Lastly, it is worth noting that the courts have held that, in appropriate cases, the government can conduct discovery against a FOIA plaintiff,[379] though case law is split on the question of whether in a FOIA case a party can take discovery against a private citizen.[380]

## Waiver of Exemptions in Litigation

Because the FOIA directs district courts to review agency actions de novo,[381] an agency is not barred from invoking a particular exemption in litigation merely because that exemption was not cited in responding to the

---

[378](...continued)
cies" in agency's representations as to when processing would be completed), summary judgment granted, 1990 WL 236133 (D.D.C. Dec. 19, 1990).

[379] See, e.g., In re Engram, No. 91-1722, 1992 WL 120211, at *3 (4th Cir. June 2, 1992) (per curiam) (permitting discovery regarding how plaintiff obtained defendant's document as relevant to issue of waiver under Exemption 5); Weisberg v. U.S. Dep't of Justice, 749 F.2d 864, 868 (D.C. Cir. 1984) (ruling that agency "should be able to use the discovery rules in FOIA suits like any other litigant"); McSheffrey v. Executive Office for U.S. Attorneys, No. 98-0650, slip op. at 3 (D.D.C. Sept. 8, 1999) (recognizing that by conducting discovery against plaintiff, government could have confirmed receipt of agency's response to FOIA request), aff'd on other grounds, 13 F. App'x 3 (D.C. Cir. 2001). But cf. Kurz-Kasch, Inc. v. DOD, 113 F.R.D. 147, 148 (S.D. Ohio 1986) (indicating mistakenly that "only . . . agencies of the government" can be subject to discovery in FOIA cases).

[380] Compare In re Shackelford, No. 93-25, slip op. at 1 (D.D.C. Feb. 19. 1993) ("[P]laintiff's effort to depose two former FBI Special Agents, now retired, concerning the purpose and conduct of the investigation of John Lennon over twenty years ago, is beyond the scope of allowable discovery in a [FOIA] action."), with Judicial Watch, Inc. v. U.S. Dep't of Commerce, No. 95-133, 2000 WL 33243469, at *1-2 (D.D.C. Dec. 5, 2000) (allowing discovery to be taken regarding White House e-mails sent to and from the Department of Commerce and the Democratic National Committee "that would reasonably lead to evidence that the DOC was not complying with [plaintiff's] first FOIA request"), and Judicial Watch, 34 F. Supp. 2d at 33-35 (noting in passing that depositions had been taken of several former agency employees); see also Kurz-Kasch, 113 F.R.D. at 148 (refusing, in a case of first impression, to allow a FOIA plaintiff to depose a private citizen, on the mistaken ground that under the FOIA "discovery rules . . . apply . . . only against agencies of the government"); cf. Forest Guardians v. U.S. Forest Serv., No. 99-615, slip op. at 4 (D.N.M. Mar. 29, 2000) (disallowing discovery by information submitters against FOIA requesters, who had received submitted records from defendant agency in redacted form, when discovery was sought for purpose of determining whether requesters made further disclosures) (reverse FOIA case).

[381] 5 U.S.C. § 552(a)(4)(B) (2000 & Supp. IV 2004).

request at the administrative level.[382] Failure to raise an exemption in a timely fashion in litigation at the district court level, however, may result in its waiver.[383]

Although an agency should not be required to plead its exemptions in its Answer to a Complaint,[384] it has been held that "'agencies [may] not

---

[382] See, e.g., Young v. CIA, 972 F.2d 536, 538-39 (4th Cir. 1992) ("an agency does not waive FOIA exemptions by not raising them during the administrative process" (citing Dubin v. Dep't of Treasury, 555 F. Supp. 408, 412 (N.D. Ga. 1981)), aff'd, 697 F.2d 1093 (11th Cir. 1983)); Living Rivers, Inc. v. U.S. Bureau of Reclamation, 272 F. Supp. 2d 1313, 1318 (D. Utah 2003) (citing Young); Sinito v. U.S. Dep't of Justice, No. 87-0814, 2000 U.S. Dist. LEXIS 22504, at *25 (D.D.C. July 12, 2000) ("[A]n agency is not barred from invoking a particular exemption in litigation merely because that exemption was not cited in responding to the request at the administrative level."); Frito-Lay v. EEOC, 964 F. Supp. 236, 239 (W.D. Ky. 1997) ("[A]n agency's failure to raise an exemption at any level of the administrative process does not constitute a waiver of that defense."); Farmworkers Legal Servs. v. U.S. Dep't of Labor, 639 F. Supp. 1368, 1370-71 (E.D.N.C. 1986) ("The relevant cases universally hold that exemption defenses are not too late if initially raised in the district court."); see also Pohlman, Inc. v. SBA, No. 4:03CV01241, slip op. at 26 (E.D. Mo. Sept. 30, 2005) (concluding that agency was not barred from invoking Exemption 3 in litigation merely because Exemption 3 was not raised at administrative level); Leforce & McCombs, P.C. v. HHS, No. 04-176, slip op. at 13 (E.D. Okla. Feb. 3, 2005) (explaining that privilege claim under Exemption 5 is not waived by agency's failure to invoke it at administrative stage); Conoco Inc. v. U.S. Dep't of Justice, 521 F. Supp. 1301, 1306 (D. Del. 1981) (holding that agency is not barred from asserting work-product claim under Exemption 5 merely because it had not acceded to plaintiff's demand for Vaughn Index at administrative level), aff'd in part, rev'd in part & remanded, 687 F.2d 724 (3d Cir. 1982). But cf. AT&T Info. Sys. v. GSA, 810 F.2d 1233, 1236 (D.C. Cir. 1987) (holding that in "reverse" FOIA context -- when standard of review is "arbitrary [and] capricious" standard based upon "whole" administrative record -- agency may not at litigation stage initially offer its reasons for refusal to withhold material); Gilday v. U.S. Dep't of Justice, No. 85-292, slip op. at 5 (D.D.C. July 22, 1985) (ruling that agency rationale asserted initially in litigation in defense of denial of fee waiver cannot correct shortcomings of administrative record).

[383] See, e.g., Ryan v. Dep't of Justice, 617 F.2d 781, 792 & n.38a (D.C. Cir. 1980) (refusing to allow an agency to invoke an exemption not previously "raised," proclaiming instead that "an agency must identify the specific statutory exemptions relied upon, and do so at least by the time of the district court proceedings").

[384] See, e.g., Sciba v. Bd. of Governors of the Fed. Reserve Sys., No. 04-1011, 2005 WL 758260, at *1 n.3 (D.D.C. Apr. 1, 2005) (recognizing that
(continued...)

make new exemption claims to a district court after the judge has ruled in the other party's favor,' nor may they 'wait until appeal to raise additional claims of exemption or additional rationales for the same claim."[385] Thus, an agency's failure to preserve its exemption positions can lead to serious

---

[384](...continued)
agency is not required to raise any exemption in its Answer); Lawrence v. United States, 355 F. Supp. 2d 1307, 1311 (M.D. Fla. 2004) (finding that IRS did not waive its right to invoke exemptions when it did not include them in its Answer to plaintiff's Amended Complaint); Frito-Lay, 964 F. Supp. at 239 & n.4 (distinguishing between affirmative defenses, which are waived if not raised, and FOIA exemption claims, which are not waived, and declaring that "[p]laintiff has had ample notice of and opportunity to rebut Defendant's defenses"); Johnson v. Fed. Bureau of Prisons, No. 90-H-645-E, slip op. at 4-5 (N.D. Ala. Nov. 1, 1990); Farmworkers Legal Servs., 639 F. Supp. at 1371; Berry v. Dep't of Justice, 612 F. Supp. 45, 47 (D. Ariz. 1985); see also AFGE v. U.S. Dep't of Commerce, 907 F.2d 203, 206-07 (D.C. Cir. 1990). But see Ray v. U.S. Dep't of Justice, 908 F.2d 1549, 1557 (11th Cir. 1990) (suggesting that all exemptions must be raised by defendant agency "'in a responsive pleading'" (quoting Chilivis v. SEC, 673 F.2d 1205, 1208 (11th Cir. 1982))), rev'd on other grounds sub nom. U.S. Dep't of State v. Ray, 502 U.S. 164 (1991); Maccaferri Gabions, Inc. v. U.S. Dep't of Justice, No. 95-2576, slip op. at 4-6 (D. Md. Mar. 26, 1996) (holding that government's withholding pursuant to FOIA exemption constitutes affirmative defense which must be set forth in its Answer, but finding that government's reference to exemption in its Answer and requester's knowledge of basis for withholding cured any pleading defect), appeal dismissed voluntarily, No. 96-1513 (4th Cir. Sept. 19, 1996); cf. Kansi v. U.S. Dep't of Justice, 11 F. Supp. 2d 42, 43 (D.D.C. 1998) (finding that requester lost entitlement to litigate fee waiver claim by not raising issue in Complaint).

[385] Senate of P.R. v. U.S. Dep't of Justice, 823 F.2d 574, 580 (D.C. Cir. 1987) (quoting Holy Spirit Ass'n v. CIA, 636 F.2d 838, 846 (D.C. Cir. 1980)); Tax Analysts v. IRS, 152 F. Supp. 2d 1, 25-26 (D.D.C. 2001) (citing Grumman Aircraft Eng'g Corp. v. Renegotiation Bd., 482 F.2d 710, 721-22 (D.C. Cir. 1973)), aff'd in pertinent part, rev'd in part, 294 F.3d 71 (D.C. Cir.), reh'g en banc denied (D.C. Cir. Aug. 5, 2002). But see Williams v. FBI, No. 91-1054, 1997 WL 198109, at *2 (D.D.C. Apr. 16, 1997) (distinguishing the rule in a case where exemption was raised first in a motion for reconsideration, because the "policy militating against piecemeal litigation is less weighty where the district court proceedings are not yet completed"), appeal dismissed, No. 98-5249 (D.C. Cir. Oct. 7, 1998); Judicial Watch of Fla., Inc. v. U.S. Dep't of Justice, 102 F. Supp. 2d 6, 12 & n.4 (D.D.C. 2000) (explaining that agency may not raise exemption for first time in brief replying to plaintiff's response to motion for summary judgment, but may raise it in future motion for summary judgment, thereby affording plaintiff opportunity to respond); cf. Steinberg v. U.S. Dep't of Justice, No. 93-2409, slip op. at 10 (D.D.C. July 14, 1997) (offering agency option of either further justifying withholding documents in full under Exemption 7(C) or invoking another exemption, such as Exemption 7(D)).

waiver consequences as FOIA litigation progresses -- not only during the initial district court proceedings,[386] but also at the appellate level,[387] and even following a remand.[388]

---

[386] See, e.g., Rosenfeld v. U.S. Dep't of Justice, 57 F.3d 803, 811 (9th Cir. 1995) (holding new exemption claims waived when raised for first time after district court ruled against government on its motion for summary judgment); Ray, 908 F.2d at 1551 (same); Scheer v. U.S. Dep't of Justice, No. 98-1613, slip op. at 4-5 (D.D.C. July 24, 1999) (denying a motion for reconsideration to present new exemption claims, partly because defendant did not show "why, through the exercise of due diligence, it could not have presented this evidence before judgment was rendered"), remanded per stipulation, No. 99-5317 (D.C. Cir. Nov. 2, 2000); Miller v. Sessions, No. 77-C-3331, 1988 WL 45519, at *1-2 (N.D. Ill. May 2, 1988) (holding "misunderstanding" on part of government counsel of court's order to submit additional affidavits insufficient to overcome waiver, and denying motion for reconsideration); Powell v. U.S. Dep't of Justice, No. C-82-326, slip op. at 4 (N.D. Cal. June 14, 1985) (holding that government may not raise Exemption 7(D) for documents declassified during pendency of case when only Exemption 1 was raised at outset); cf. Judicial Watch, Inc. v. U.S. Dep't of Energy, No. 01-0981, slip op. at 3-4 (D.D.C. May 26, 2004) (purporting to refuse to allow the government to "raise[] the presidential communication privilege" after summary judgment was granted to plaintiff, based upon the wholly mistaken belief that the government was seeking to do so when in fact it merely was citing to a recent such case as an example of the flawed analysis undertaken by the court on the matter of threshold Exemption 5 applicability) (on motion for reconsideration). But cf. Piper v. U.S. Dep't of Justice, 374 F. Supp. 2d 73, 78 (D.D.C. 2005) (opining that while FOIA exemptions not raised at the initial district court proceedings ordinarily may be waived, if disclosure "will impinge on rights of third parties that are expressly protected by FOIA . . . district courts not only have the discretion, but sometimes the obligation to consider newly presented facts and to grant" post-judgment relief); accord Senate of P.R., 823 F.2d at 581 (holding firmly and portentiously that "the district judge did not abuse his discretion when he evaluated the situation at hand as one inappropriate for application of a rigid 'press it at the threshold, or lose it for all times' approach to the agency's FOIA exemption claims").

[387] See, e.g., Jordan v. U.S. Dep't of Justice, 591 F.2d 753, 779-80 (D.C. Cir. 1978) (en banc) (refusing to consider government's Exemption 7 claim first raised in "supplemental memorandum" filed one month prior to appellate oral argument).

[388] See, e.g., Fendler v. Parole Comm'n, 774 F.2d 975, 978 (9th Cir. 1985) (barring government from raising Exemption 5 on remand to protect presentence report because it was raised for first time on appeal); Ryan, 617 F.2d at 792 & n.38a (holding government barred from invoking Exemption 6 on remand because it was "raised" for first time on appeal, and defining "raised" to mean, in effect, "fully Vaughned"); cf. Benavides v. U.S. Bureau of

(continued...)

This lesson was underscored by the Court of Appeals for the District of Columbia Circuit's decision in Maydak v. United States Department of Justice.[389] In Maydak, the D.C. Circuit refused to allow the defendant agency to invoke underlying FOIA exemptions when its initial Exemption 7(A) basis for nondisclosure became no longer applicable due to the completion of the underlying law enforcement proceedings.[390] While recognizing that it previously had allowed agencies to raise new exemptions when there was "a substantial change in the factual context of the case,"[391] the D.C. Circuit ruled that the termination of underlying enforcement proceedings and the resultant expiration of the applicability of Exemption 7(A) did not meet this standard.[392]

Indeed, in Maydak the D.C. Circuit refused to recognize that the temporal nature of Exemption 7(A) necessitates a practical approach to processing investigatory law enforcement records.[393] Rather, it denied the

---

[388](...continued)
Prisons, 995 F.2d 269, 273 (D.C. Cir. 1993) ("[T]he government is not entitled to raise defenses to requests for information seriatim until it finds a theory that the court will accept, but must bring all its defenses at once before the district court.") (Privacy Act access case). Compare Wash. Post Co. v. HHS, 795 F.2d 205, 208-09 (D.C. Cir. 1986) (finding that "privilege" prong of Exemption 4 may not be raised for first time on remand -- even though "confidential" prong was previously raised -- absent sufficient extenuating circumstances), and Wash. Post Co. v. HHS, 865 F.2d 320, 327 (D.C. Cir. 1989) (prohibiting agency from raising new aspect of previously raised prong of Exemption 4), with Lame v. U.S. Dep't of Justice, 767 F.2d 66, 71 n.7 (3d Cir. 1985) (permitting new exemptions to be raised on remand, as compared to raising new exemptions on appeal). But see also Morgan v. U.S. Dep't of Justice, 923 F.2d 195, 199 n.5 (D.C. Cir. 1991) (remanding for the district court to determine whether a sealing order actually prohibits disclosure under the FOIA, but noting that the government can invoke other exemptions "if the court determines that the seal does not prohibit disclosure").

[389] 218 F.3d 760 (D.C. Cir. 2000).

[390] Id. at 767.

[391] Id. (citing, e.g., Senate of P.R., 823 F.2d at 580-81).

[392] Id. at 767-68 (proclaiming that the only change in the "factual context" of the case was the "simple resolution of other litigation, hardly an unforeseeable difference").

[393] See FOIA Post, "Supreme Court Is Asked to Review Law Enforcement Case" (posted 5/30/01) (describing the D.C. Circuit's approach to Exemption 7(A) in the Maydak case); see also Senate of P.R., 823 F.2d at 581 (describing circumstances in which, "[f]rom a practical standpoint," further proceedings might well be required in order to allow the agency to invoke

(continued...)

agency the ability to invoke any FOIA exemption that had not been "raised" at the district court level.[394] "Raising" an exemption means more than merely identifying, noting, or generally describing it, according to the D.C. Circuit: It means invoking it "as a defense in a manner in which the district court could rule on the issue."[395]

The Maydak ruling, though, may have been a direct result of the D.C. Circuit's perception of "tactical maneuvering" by the government at the FOIA requester's expense.[396] Indeed, when another D.C. Circuit panel subsequently was presented with a similar situation, in August v. FBI, it took pains to point out that it did not intend to "adopt[] a rigid 'press it at the threshold or lose it for all times' approach to . . . agenc[ies'] FOIA exemption claims."[397] Significantly, that panel emphasized the fact that the full court in Jordan v. United States Department of Justice[398] had adopted a "flexible approach to handling belated invocations of FOIA exemptions," which it said actually was "affirmed" in Maydak.[399] The D.C. Circuit in August acknowledged three circumstances that might permit the government belatedly to invoke FOIA exemptions: a substantial change in the factual context of a case; an interim development in an applicable legal doctrine; or pure mistake.[400]

Moreover, in two rulings issued shortly after August, another panel of

---

[393](...continued)
other exemptions once Exemption 7(A) no longer is applicable).

[394] 218 F.3d at 765.

[395] Id. (citing Ryan, 617 F.2d at 792 n.38a). But see United We Stand Am., Inc. v. IRS, 359 F.3d 595, 598, 603 (D.C. Cir. 2004) (leaving to the district court on remand the question of "[w]hether one of the nine exemptions applies" to the disputed record despite the fact that the agency only "reserve[d] the right . . . to assert any applicable exemption claim(s)").

[396] August v. FBI, 328 F.3d 697, 701 (D.C. Cir. 2003) (characterizing agency's conduct in Maydak).

[397] Id. at 699 (quoting Senate of P.R., 823 F.2d at 581).

[398] 591 F.2d 753 (D.C. Cir. 1978) (en banc).

[399] August, 328 F.3d at 700 (harmonizing Maydak and Jordan); see also Summers v. U.S. Dep't of Justice, No. 98-1837, slip op. at 7 (D.D.C. Apr. 13, 2004) (interpreting Maydak to require the government to raise all claimed exemptions at some time during the district court proceedings -- but not requiring "that all exemptions . . . be raised at the same time").

[400] August, 328 F.3d at 700 (citing Jordan); see, e.g., Judicial Watch v. Dep't of the Army, 466 F. Supp. 2d 112, 124 (D.D.C. 2006) (granting reconsideration to correct agency's error and afford intervenor an opportunity to raise exemptions).

the D.C. Circuit suggested that an agency's belated raising of FOIA exemptions might be appropriate under an additional circumstance -- namely, when the legal basis for an agency's initial decision on a FOIA request is rejected in litigation. In United We Stand America, Inc. v. IRS,[401] the primary issue was whether a requested record should be considered a congressional document or an "agency record."[402] At the district court level, the agency actually "reserved the right" to invoke exemptions if the court disagreed with the agency's determination that the record was a congressional document and thus not subject to the FOIA.[403] On appeal, the D.C. Circuit determined that the document was at least partially an "agency record," and it remanded the case to the district court to decide the applicability of any exemption claims that the agency previously had "reserved."[404] Similarly, in LaCedra v. Executive Office for United States Attorneys,[405] the D.C. Circuit found as a matter of law that the agency's interpretation of a FOIA request was "implausible," but nonetheless explicitly permitted the agency on remand to raise exemption claims for the additional records that would be considered responsive, on the basis that "[n]othing in Maydak requires an agency to invoke any exemption applicable to a record the agency in good faith believes has not been requested."[406]

The consequence of this line of cases is that, especially within the D.C. Circuit, agencies should be sure to carefully coordinate with their principal litigation counsel in any FOIA lawsuit in which underlying FOIA exemptions or overlapping FOIA defenses are involved.[407] As a matter of general practice, a prudent course of action would be to obtain the court's permission to raise the threshold defense first in order to specifically reserve the right to invoke the remaining exemptions at a later date, if necessary.[408] Of course, if for some reason the district court does not permit

---

[401] 359 F.3d 295 (D.C. Cir. 2004).

[402] Id. at 597.

[403] Id. at 598.

[404] Id. at 603.

[405] 317 F.3d 345 (D.C. Cir. 2003).

[406] Id. at 348.

[407] See FOIA Post, "Supreme Court Declines to Review Waiver Case" (posted 8/7/01) (advising agencies to give especially careful attention to litigation-waiver issues in wake of Maydak).

[408] See United We Stand Am., 359 F.3d at 598 (permitting agency to raise on remand exemptions reserved in its district court papers, in which it stated: "Should the Court determine that the documents in question constitute agency records for purposes of the FOIA . . . the defendant reserves the right, pursuant to the statute, to assert any applicable exemption

(continued...)

this pragmatic approach, then the agency, in order to guard against any possible finding of waiver, could raise all applicable exemption claims in its initial district court summary judgment submissions.[409] (See the further discussion of this issue under Exemption 7(A), above.) Although the failure to submit an entirely adequate Vaughn affidavit will not necessarily result in a waiver of exemptions and justify the granting of summary judg-

---

[408](...continued)
claim(s), prior to disclosure, and to litigate further any such exemption claims"); accord Senate of P.R., 823 F.2d at 581 (holding that "the district judge did not abuse his discretion when he evaluated the situation at hand as one inappropriate for application of a rigid 'press it at the threshold, or lose it for all times' approach to the agency's FOIA exemption claims").

[409] See Jefferson v. Dep't of Justice, 284 F.3d 172, 179 (D.C. Cir. 2002) (foreclosing government's ability to invoke Exemption 6 in allowing remand only to determine whether records meet law enforcement threshold for invocation of Exemption 7(C); "the government's invocation on appeal of Exemption 6 comes too late"); Smith v. U.S. Dep't of Justice, 251 F.3d 1047, 1051-52 (D.C. Cir. 2001) (rejecting agency's Exemption 3 claim and refusing to remand to the district court to allow the agency "there for the first time raise certain other exemptions from the FOIA" (citing Maydak)); Ayyad v. U.S. Dep't of Justice, No. 00-960, 2002 WL 654133, at *4 n.6 (S.D.N.Y. Apr. 18, 2002) (finding no need to decide the applicability of "numerous additional claims of exemption" that were thoroughly raised by the agency (out of its concern with waiver), because the "documents are so clearly covered by exemption 7(A)"); see also Trentadue v. Integrity Comm., No. 04-4200, slip op. at 4-5 (10th Cir. Sept. 27, 2005) (remanding case due to termination of law enforcement investigation upon which Exemption 7(A) claim was based, and directing district court to consider applicability of other exemptions that were raised in district court proceedings but never were ruled upon); Sciba, 2005 WL 758260, at *1 n.3 (explaining that to avoid waiver, an exemption must be "raised at a point in the district court proceedings that gives the court an adequate opportunity to consider it"); cf. Boyd v. U.S. Marshals Serv., No. 99-2712, 2002 U.S. Dist. LEXIS 27734, at *6 (D.D.C. Mar. 15, 2002) (finding that while the defendant agencies relied exclusively on Exemption 7(A) at the administrative level, they avoided waiver of other exemptions by invoking them "after being served with the complaint"); Pub. Citizen v. Dep't of Educ., 292 F. Supp. 2d 1, 4-5 (D.D.C. 2003) (rejecting agency's argument that fees should be paid for broad-based search because it was raised for first time in court, which the court claimed would "frustrate . . . the efficient and prompt administration of the FOIA"). But see also Cotner v. U.S. Parole Comm'n, 747 F.2d 1016, 1018-19 (5th Cir. 1984) (recognizing that new exemptions may be raised on remand due to a "fundamental" change in the government's position that was "not calculated to gain any tactical advantage in this particular case"); Chilivis v. SEC, 673 F.2d 1205, 1208 (11th Cir. 1982) (deciding that government is not barred from invoking other exemptions after reliance on Exemption 7(A) was rendered untenable by conclusion of underlying law enforcement proceeding).

ment against an agency,[410] the most prudent practice for agency defendants is to ensure that their initial Vaughn affidavits contain sufficiently detailed justifications of every exemption that they plan to invoke on the basis of all known facts.[411]

## Sanctions

The FOIA does not authorize any award of monetary damages to a requester,[412] either for an agency's unjustified refusal to release requested

---

[410] See Coastal States Gas Corp. v. Dep't of Energy, 644 F.2d 969, 982 (3d Cir. 1981) (finding it abuse of discretion to refuse to consider revised index and instead award "partial judgment" to plaintiff, even though corrected index was submitted one day before oral argument on plaintiff's "partial judgment" motion); cf. Wilkinson v. FBI, No. 80-1048, slip op. at 3 (C.D. Cal. June 17, 1987) (providing government thirty days to further justify exemptions but, after reviewing subsequent declarations, finding same faults with new declarations as with original ones and ordering in camera review). But see Carroll v. IRS, No. 82-3524, slip op. at 28 (D.D.C. Jan. 31, 1986) (holding affidavits insufficient and affording agencies no further opportunities to reassert their claims because "[a]fter years of litigation, the suit must be resolved").

[411] See Maine v. U.S. Dep't of the Interior, 285 F.3d 126, 137 (1st Cir.) (refusing to afford the defendant an opportunity on remand to remedy an affidavit insufficiency discerned by the appellate court), aff'd in pertinent part & rev'd & vacated in other part on reh'g, 298 F.3d 60 (1st Cir. 2002); Coastal States, 644 F.2d at 981 (suggesting that agencies might be restricted to one Vaughn affidavit); see also ABC, Inc. v. USIA, 599 F. Supp. 765, 768 (D.D.C. 1984) (denying government's request to first litigate "agency record" issue and to raise other exemptions only if threshold defense fails); cf. Homick v. U.S. Dep't of Justice, No. 98-00557, slip op. at 3-4 (N.D. Cal. Oct. 27, 2004) (refusing to allow the submission of an additional Vaughn Index for a group of documents not processed prior to the hearing date, and noting that the "[p]laintiff requested this information in 1992 and filed a FOIA complaint in 1998").

[412] See Eltayib v. U.S. Coast Guard, 53 F. App'x 127, 127 (D.C. Cir. 2002) (declaring that the FOIA "does not authorize the collection of damages"); O'Toole v. IRS, 52 F. App'x 961, 962 (9th Cir. 2002) (same); O'Meara v. IRS, No. 97-3383, 1998 WL 123984, at *1 (7th Cir. Mar. 12, 1998) ("FOIA . . . does not authorize sanctions as a remedy for failure to disclose documents. Instead, courts are limited to ordering the production of agency records, and assessing reasonable attorney fees and litigation costs against the United States."); Ross v. United States, No. 06-0963, 2006 WL 3250831, at *10 (D.D.C. Nov. 10, 2006) ("It is well-settled that monetary damages are not available under FOIA."); Serrano v. U.S. Dep't of Justice INS, No. 01-0521, 2001 WL 1190993, at *2 n.1 (E.D. La. Oct. 5, 2001) ("FOIA does not authorize an action for money damages against the agency or its personnel."); Butler

(continued...)

records[413] or for alleged improper disclosure of information.[414] The Act does, however, provide that in certain narrowly prescribed circumstances agency employees who arbitrarily or capriciously withhold information may be subject to disciplinary action. Specifically, subsection (a)(4)(F) of the FOIA, as amended, provides:

> Whenever the court orders the production of any agency records improperly withheld from the complainant and assesses against the United States reasonable attorney fees and other litigation costs, and the court additionally issues a written finding that the circumstances surrounding the withholding raise questions whether agency personnel acted arbitrarily or capriciously with respect to the withholding, the [United States Office of] Special Counsel shall promptly initiate a proceeding to determine whether disciplinary action is warranted against the officer or employee who was primarily responsible for the with-

---

[412](...continued)
v. Nelson, No. 96-48, 1997 WL 580331, at *3 (D. Mont. May 16, 1997) ("Section 552 of Title 5 includes a comprehensive and defined list of remedies available; the conspicuous absence of a provision allowing an action for money damages convinces the court that Plaintiff may not seek damages under the FOIA."); Stabasefski v. United States, 919 F. Supp. 1570, 1573 (M.D. Ga. 1996) ("[T]he remedial measures available under the Freedom of Information Act are limited to injunctive relief, costs, and attorney's fees." (citing 5 U.S.C. § 552(a)(4)(B), (E))); see also Whitfield v. U.S. Dep't of the Treasury, No. 04-0679, 2006 WL 2434923, at *7 (D.D.C. Aug. 22, 2006) (commenting that "[p]laintiff's request for damages would fail" because FOIA provides injunctive relief only).

[413] See Schwartz v. U.S. Patent & Trademark Office, No. 95-5349, 1996 U.S. App. LEXIS 4609, at *2-3 (D.C. Cir. Feb. 22, 1996); Thompson v. Walbran, 990 F.2d 403, 405 (8th Cir. 1993); Wren v. Harris, 675 F.2d 1144, 1147 (10th Cir. 1982); Gilbert v. Soc. Sec. Admin., No. 93-C-1055, slip op. at 10 (E.D. Wis. Dec. 28, 1994); Bologna v. Dep't of the Treasury, No. 93-1495, 1994 WL 381975, at *4 (D.N.J. Mar. 29, 1994); Duffy v. United States, No. 87-C-10826, slip op. at 31-32 (N.D. Ill. May 29, 1991); Daniels v. St. Louis Veterans Admin. Reg'l Office, 561 F. Supp. 250, 251 (E.D. Mo. 1983); Diamond v. FBI, 532 F. Supp. 216, 233 (S.D.N.Y. 1981), aff'd on other grounds, 707 F.2d 75 (2d Cir. 1983).

[414] See Crumpton v. Stone, 59 F.3d 1400, 1406 (D.C. Cir. 1995) (holding that agency decision to disclose information under FOIA constitutes "a discretionary function exempt from suit under the [Federal Tort Claims Act]"); Sterling v. United States, 798 F. Supp. 47, 48 & n.2 (D.D.C. 1992) (ruling that neither FOIA nor Administrative Procedure Act, 5 U.S.C. §§ 701-706 (2000), authorizes award of monetary damages for alleged improper disclosure), summary affirmance granted, No. 93-5264 (D.C. Cir. Mar. 11, 1994).

holding.[415]

Thus, there are three distinct jurisdictional prerequisites to the initiation of a Special Counsel investigation under the FOIA: (1) the court must order the production of agency records found to be improperly withheld; (2) it must award attorney fees and litigation costs; and (3) it must issue a specific "written finding" of suspected arbitrary or capricious conduct. The imposition of sanctions, when all three prerequisites have been met, has occurred infrequently.[416] Nevertheless, agency FOIA personnel should not

---

[415] 5 U.S.C. § 552(a)(4)(F) (2000 & Supp. IV 2004); see 5 U.S.C. § 1211 (2000) (establishing "Office of Special Counsel" independent of Merit Systems Protection Board); see also 1978 FOIA Amendment, Pub. L. No. 95-454, 92 Stat. 1111 (changing "Civil Service Commission" to "Special Counsel").

[416] See, e.g., O'Shea v. NLRB, No. 2:05-2808, 2006 WL 1977152, at *6 (D.S.C. July 11, 2006) (holding that referral to Office of Special Counsel was unwarranted because defendant agency was not improperly withholding documents); Hull v. U.S. Dep't of Labor, No. 04-1264, 2006 U.S. Dist. LEXIS 35054, at *21 (D. Colo. May 30, 2006) (concluding that, despite "bureaucratic mistakes," defendant did not lie or disobey or ignore court orders, and that defendant's conduct therefore did not warrant referral to Office of Special Counsel); Defenders of Wildlife v. USDA, 311 F. Supp. 2d 44, 61 (D.D.C. 2004) (declining to find that agency acted arbitrarily and capriciously, because court did not find that agency withheld nonexempt records); Al-Fayed v. CIA, No. 00-2092, slip op. at 3 (D.D.C. Apr. 25, 2002) (rejecting plaintiff's contention that agency document releases were unreasonably dilatory and thus refusing to impose sanctions when agency "released all responsive documents within the Court ordered time"); Chourre v. IRS, 203 F. Supp. 2d 1196, 1202 (W.D. Wash. 2002) (denying request for sanctions because there was "nothing in the record to suggest that [defendant] acted arbitrarily or capriciously"); Kempker-Cloyd v. U.S. Dep't of Justice, No. 5:97-253, 1999 U.S. Dist. LEXIS 4813, at *23 (W.D. Mich. Mar. 12, 1999) (finding that even though agency's action was "incomplete and untimely" and "not in good faith," there was no evidence of arbitrary or capricious behavior), motion for fees & costs granted, slip op. at 14 (W.D. Mich. Apr. 2, 1999) (magistrate's recommendations), adopted (W.D. Mich. Aug. 17, 1999); Judicial Watch, Inc. v. U.S. Dep't of Commerce, 34 F. Supp. 2d 28, 43 n.9 (D.D.C.) (finding "merit in the view that the district court should be more willing to refer disciplinary matters to the Office of Special Counsel when agencies act arbitrarily and capriciously," but declining to consider appropriateness of referral until conclusion of litigation), further discovery ordered, 34 F. Supp. 2d 47 (D.D.C. 1998), partial summary judgment granted, 83 F. Supp. 2d 105 (D.D.C. 1999); Gabel v. IRS, No. 97-1653, 1998 WL 817758, at *5-6 (N.D. Cal. June 25, 1998) (declining to issue "sanctions" finding when all requested records had been produced and thus no records improperly were withheld); cf. Norwood v. FAA, No. 83-2315, slip op. at 20 (W.D. Tenn. Dec. 11, 1991) (finding that when a court denies fees on the

(continued...)

overlook the importance and viability of this sanction provision.[417]

In addition, a provision of the Whistleblower Protection Act of 1989[418] authorizes the Office of Special Counsel to investigate certain allegations concerning arbitrary or capricious withholding of information requested under the FOIA. Unlike subsection (a)(4)(F) of the FOIA, this provision does not even require a judicial finding; indeed, no lawsuit need even be filed to invoke this other sanction mechanism.[419]

Further, as in all civil cases, courts may exercise their discretion to impose sanctions on FOIA litigants[420] as well as on government counsel[421]

---

[416](...continued)
ground that the plaintiff is proceeding pro se, "the issuance of written findings pursuant to 5 U.S.C. § 552(a)(4)(F) would be inappropriate since both prerequisites have not been met"), aff'd in part & rev'd in part on other grounds, 993 F.2d 570 (6th Cir. 1993); Miller v. Webster, No. 77-C-3331, slip op. at 4 (N.D. Ill. Oct. 27, 1983) (refusing to refer "alleged violation" to Merit Systems Protection Board because violation was "de minimis"), summary judgment granted (N.D. Ill. Feb. 29, 1984).

[417] See Judicial Watch, Inc. v. U.S. Dep't of Commerce, 337 F. Supp. 2d 146, 182-83 (D.D.C. 2004) (inviting the plaintiff to file an application for attorney fees and "to move for the Court to make any findings needed to cause referral of the DOC's activities to the Office of Special Counsel, pursuant to 5 U.S.C. § 552(a)(4)(F)," because of the agency's poor handling of the plaintiff's initial requests); Ray v. U.S. Dep't of Justice, 716 F. Supp. 1449, 1451-52 (S.D. Fla. 1989) (holding "court order" requirement satisfied even though no record was found to be improperly withheld); FOIA Update, Vol. IV, No. 3, at 5 (discussing FOIA provision mandating MSPB Special Counsel investigation in all qualifying cases of suspected "arbitrary and capricious" withholding).

[418] 5 U.S.C. § 1216(a)(3) (2000).

[419] See generally H.R. Rep. No. 95-1717, at 137 (1978), reprinted in 1978 U.S.C.C.A.N. 2723, 2870 ("[T]his provision is not intended to require that an administrative or court decision be rendered concerning withholding of information before the Special Counsel may investigate allegations of such a prohibited practice.").

[420] See, e.g., Johnson v. Comm'r, 68 F. App'x 839, 840 (9th Cir. 2003) (granting agency's motion for sanctions because appeal was "frivolous"); Taylor v. Blakey, No. 03-0173, 2006 WL 279103, at *7-8 (D.D.C. Feb. 6, 2006) (noting that res judicata bars the plaintiff's case, and warning the plaintiff's counsel that "his zeal fostered carelessness, which took him to the edge of acceptability, and to the brink of an unpleasant rendezvous with Rule 11"); Nash v. U.S. Dep't of Justice, 992 F. Supp. 447, 450 (D.D.C. 1998) (alternative holding) (dismissing suit as sanction for "continuing violation" of Rule
(continued...)

who have violated court rules or shown disrespect for the judicial process. One court has even referred an Assistant United States Attorney who handled a FOIA requester's criminal case to the Department of Justice's Office of Professional Responsibility following a finding that he prematurely "destroyed records responsive to [the] FOIA request while [the FOIA] litigation was pending."[422] In general, claims of "bad faith" actions by a govern-

---

[420](...continued)
11 of Federal Rules of Civil Procedure by plaintiff's counsel), summary affirmance granted, No. 98-5096 (D.C. Cir. July 20, 1998).

[421] See, e.g., Pac. Fisheries, Inc. v. IRS, No. 04-2436, 2006 WL 1635706, at *5 (W.D. Wash. June 1, 2006) (ordering agency to show cause why pursuant to 28 U.S.C. § 1927 attorney fees in form of sanctions should not be assessed, as it appeared that agency "unreasonably and vexatiously multiplied proceedings"); Landmark Legal Found. v. EPA, 272 F. Supp. 2d 70, 87 (D.D.C. 2003) (awarding attorney fees and costs as sanction for agency's violation of court order intended to preserve FOIA-requested records); Allen v. FBI, No. 00-342, slip op. at 9-10 (D.D.C. Aug. 26, 2002) (finding "inexcusable" the fact that the defendant agency "took no steps to preserve" records requested under the FOIA, and requiring it not only to pay plaintiff's litigation costs, but also to provide responsive records free of charge); cf. Nat'l Sec. Archive Fund, Inc. v. U.S. Dep't of the Air Force, No. 05-571, 2006 WL 1030152, at *5-6 (D.D.C. Apr. 19, 2006) (admonishing the Air Force for its mismanaged FOIA operations, and ordering the parties to meet at a status conference during which the Air Force was to present "an officer of sufficient rank over the 11th Communications Squadron to have the ability to order that things be done and to achieve results") (emphasis added); Elec. Privacy Info. Ctr. v. Dep't of Justice, No. 05-845, 2005 U.S. Dist. LEXIS 40318, at *3-4 (D.D.C. Nov. 16, 2005) (characterizing agency's efforts as "unnecessarily slow and inefficient," and ordering agency to "complete processing of 1500 pages every 15 calendar days"). But see Hull, 2006 U.S. Dist. LEXIS 35054, at *21-22 (declining to impose attorney fees in form of sanctions under 28 U.S.C. § 1927, because plaintiff asserted claim specifically against agency and "[r]elief under § 1927 is available only against attorneys"); Long v. U.S. Dep't of Justice, 207 F.R.D. 4, 7 (D.D.C. 2002) (declining to impose Rule 11 sanction for repeated errors in the defendant agency's summary judgment motions, but warning the agency that "further delays created by erroneous factual representations . . . may require the Court to revisit" the sanctions issue); Jefferson v. Reno, No. 96-1284, slip op. at 1 (D.D.C. Mar. 16, 2001) (rescinding a monetary sanction that had been imposed on the government "for the purpose of deterring future violations and highlighting the importance of [agency] complying with . . . [the] FOIA," because such a fine is, in fact, barred by sovereign immunity).

[422] Jefferson v. Reno, 123 F. Supp. 2d 1, 5 (D.D.C. 2000); cf. Miller v. Holzman, No. 95-01231, 2007 WL 172327, at *5-7 (D.D.C. Jan. 17, 2007) (magistrate's recommendation) (finding that agency's destruction of records -- collected in response to FOIA request and deemed non-responsive or exempt (continued...)

ment agency ordinarily are considered in administrative proceedings or in judicial decisions on whether to grant attorney fees.[423]

In determining whether to impose sanctions on plaintiffs, district courts ordinarily review the number and content of court filings and their effect on the courts as indicia of frivolousness or harassment.[424] For exam-

---

[422](...continued)
from disclosure -- was "potentially sanctionable").

[423] See, e.g., Schanen v. U.S. Dep't of Justice, 798 F.2d 348, 350 (9th Cir. 1986) (upholding exemption claims, but ordering government to pay plaintiff's attorney fees and costs due to government counsel's failure to competently defend claims); Landmark Legal Found., 272 F. Supp. 2d at 87 (ordering agency to pay plaintiff's attorney fees and costs because of its "contumacious" violation of order to preserve records); Jefferson, 123 F. Supp. 2d at 5 (assessing attorney fees and costs associated with reconstruction of records, following violation of court order that had required that records be reconstructed and sent to both plaintiff and his attorney); Ellis v. United States, 941 F. Supp. 1068, 1081 (D. Utah 1996); Okla. Publ'g Co. v. HUD, No. 87-1935-P, slip op. at 7 (W.D. Okla. June 17, 1988) (attorney fees assessed against government when counsel failed to comply with scheduling and disclosure orders); see also Allen v. Fed. Bureau of Prisons, No. 00-342, slip op. at 9-10 (D.D.C. Aug. 26, 2002) (imposing sanctions on agency in form of "reimbursement of Plaintiff of his filing fee and all postage and copying costs," and prohibiting agency from charging fee for processing of few remaining records after it "inexcusabl[y]" destroyed majority of requested records); Hill v. Dep't of the Air Force, No. 85-1485, slip op. at 7 (D.N.M. Sept. 4, 1987) (ordering documents processed at no further cost to plaintiff because of unreasonable delay in processing FOIA request), aff'd on other grounds, 844 F.2d 1407 (10th Cir. 1988). But see also Carlson v. USPS, No. 02-5471, 2005 WL 756573, at *9-10 (N.D. Cal. Mar. 31, 2005) (denying plaintiff's motion for sanctions because agency's "conduct did not rise to level of bad faith").

[424] See, e.g., Schwarz v. NSA, 526 U.S. 122, 122 (1999) (barring plaintiff from further filings, citing thirty-five frivolous petitions for certiorari); Schwarz v. USDA, 22 F. App'x 9, 10 (D.C. Cir. 2001) (affirming district court prohibition against plaintiff's filing of any further civil actions without first obtaining leave of court, because of her long and unwavering history of frivolous claims and litigation abuses); Schwarz v. CIA, No. 99-4016, 1999 WL 330237, at *1 (10th Cir. May 25, 1999) (admonishing plaintiff for "frivolousness" in light of "recurring pattern of similarly unsuccessful FOIA actions" and warning that "future frivolous filings . . . will result in sanctions"); see also, e.g., Hoyos v. VA, No. 98-4178, slip op. at 4 (11th Cir. Feb. 1, 1999) (affirming district court's order barring plaintiff from future filings without court's permission, and noting that plaintiff "has frivolously sued just about everyone even remotely associated with the VA . . . and has burdened the district court with over 130 motions and notices, many of them duplica-
(continued...)

ple, as a sanction under Rule 11 of the Federal Rules of Civil Procedure, a frequent FOIA requester who filed nearly fifty FOIA lawsuits over the course of eight years and who routinely failed to oppose motions to dismiss was ordered to show cause in any subsequent lawsuit why the principle of res judicata did not bar the intended suit.[425] As a general rule, however, "mere litigiousness alone does not support the issuance of an injunction" against filing further lawsuits.[426]

---

[424](...continued)
tive"); Goldgar v. Office of Admin., 26 F.3d 32, 35-36 & n.3 (5th Cir. 1994) (warning plaintiff that subsequent filing or appeal of FOIA lawsuits without jurisdictional basis may result in assessment of costs, attorney's fees and proper sanctions or that plaintiff may be required to "obtain judicial preapproval of all future filings"); Robert VIII v. Dep't of Justice, No. 05-CV-2543, 2005 WL 3371480, at *12-15 (E.D.N.Y. Dec. 12, 2005) (enjoining plaintiff from filing future actions without leave of court, as the plaintiff's "litigation history in the EDNY is vexatious," based on the twenty-four FOIA cases filed in the EDNY, which "have required a substantial use of judicial resources at considerable expense to Defendants"); Schwarz v. U.S. Dep't of the Treasury, 131 F. Supp. 2d 142, 148 (D.D.C. 2000) (threatening plaintiff with dismissal of claims as "malicious" if she makes any future attempts to litigate claims that already have been resolved against her), summary affirmance granted, No. 00-5453 (D.C. Cir. May 10, 2001); Peck v. Merletti, 64 F. Supp. 2d 599, 603 (E.D. Va. 1999) (noting plaintiff's "continued pursuit of nonexistent information . . . and the drain on valuable judicial and law enforcement resources," requiring that plaintiff's future filings comply with "Federal Rule of Civil Procedure 8 in regards to 'a short and plain statement of the claim'" (quoting Fed. R. Civ. P. 8(a)(2))); Wrenn v. Gallegos, No. 92-3358, slip op. at 1-2 (D.D.C. May 26, 1994) (barring plaintiff's future filings absent prior leave of court, because plaintiff "has been adjudicated a vexatious litigant in several other forums and remains so in this court").

[425] See Crooker v. U.S. Marshals Serv., 641 F. Supp. 1141, 1143 (D.D.C. 1986); see also Crooker v. ATF, No. 96-01790, slip op. at 1-2 (D.D.C. Nov. 22, 1996) (dismissing Complaint for failure to comply with requirements of Crooker v. United States Marshals Service).

[426] In re Powell, 851 F.2d at 434; cf. Zemansky v. EPA, 767 F.2d 569, 573-74 (9th Cir. 1995) (holding that district court exceeded its authority by requiring frequent requester, whose requests included "questions, commentary, narrative" and other extraneous material, to make future requests in "'separate document which is clearly defined as an FOIA request' and not 'intertwined with non-FOIA matters'"). But see Robert VIII, 2005 WL 3371480, at *15 (enjoining FOIA plaintiff from filing future actions without leave of court, in order "to disallow future complaints that do not comport with the Federal Rules or that lack merit or are duplicative"); Schwarz v. USDA, No. 01-1464, slip op. at 2-3 (D.D.C. Aug. 3, 2001) (enjoining plaintiff from filing civil actions unless plaintiff obtains leave of court), aff'd, 22 F. App'x 9, 10 (D.C. Cir. 2001); Hunsberger v. U.S. Dep't of Energy, No. 96-

(continued...)

# LITIGATION CONSIDERATIONS

In a related vein, the Prison Litigation Reform Act of 1995[427] provides that an action in forma pauperis cannot be filed by a prisoner who, on three or more prior occasions while incarcerated, "brought an action or appeal in a court of the United States that was dismissed on the grounds that it is frivolous, malicious, or fails to state a claim upon which relief may be granted."[428] Although this statute applies only to suits that have been brought in federal court, it applies both to federal prisoners and to state prisoners alike.[429]

## Considerations on Appeal

As noted previously, an exceptionally large percentage of FOIA cases are decided by means of summary judgment.[430] While a decision on a motion for summary judgment usually is immediately appealable, not all orders granting judgment to a party on a FOIA issue are immediately appealable.[431] The grant of an Open America stay of proceedings, for example, is

---

[426](...continued)
0455, slip op. at 2 (D.D.C. Mar. 14, 1996) (enjoining plaintiff from filing any further civil actions without first obtaining leave of court because "[p]laintiff's numerous actions have demanded countless hours from this Court").

[427] 28 U.S.C. § 1915A (2000).

[428] Id. § 1915A(b)(1); see, e.g., Wiggins v. Huff, No. C 98-1072, 1998 WL 226300, at *1 (N.D. Cal. Apr. 28, 1998) (denying request -- from prisoner who had three or more prior dismissals -- to proceed in forma pauperis, and dismissing FOIA action without prejudice to refiling it with payment of filing fee).

[429] See Wiggins, 1998 WL 226300, at *11 (dismissing state prisoner's FOIA suit against federal agency); Willis v. FBI, No. 2:96-cv-276, slip op. at 1-2 (W.D. Mich. Oct. 21, 1996) (ordering warden of state prison to "place a hold on plaintiff's prisoner account" to provide for payment of filing fee).

[430] See, e.g., Pub. Employees for Envtl. Responsibility v. EPA, 978 F. Supp. 955, 959 (D. Colo. 1997) (explaining that "FOIA claims are typically resolved on summary judgment" (citing KTVY-TV v. United States, 919 F.2d 1465, 1468 (10th Cir. 1990))); Cappabianca v. U.S. Customs Serv., 847 F. Supp. 1558, 1562 (M.D. Fla. 1994) ("[O]nce documents in issue are properly identified, FOIA cases should be handled on motions for summary judgment." (citing Miscavige v. IRS, 2 F.3d 366, 369 (11th Cir. 1993))).

[431] See, e.g., Loomis v. U.S. Dep't of Energy, No. 99-6084, 1999 WL 1012451, at *1 (2d Cir. Oct. 14, 1999) (holding that partial grant of summary judgment is not final order); Church of Scientology Int'l v. IRS, 995 F.2d 916, 921 (9th Cir. 1993) (ruling that document is "not exempt," without accompanying disclosure order, held nonappealable); Ferguson v. FBI, 957 F.2d 1059, 1063-64 (2d Cir. 1992) (noting that while "partial disclosure orders in FOIA cases are appealable," fact that district court may have erred in de-
(continued...)

not an appealable final decision.[432] Similarly, it has been held that an "interim" award of attorney fees is not appealable until the conclusion of the district court proceedings in the case.[433]

Once a case properly is on appeal, though, the government ordinarily must obtain a stay of any trial court disclosure order if disclosure is re-

---

[431](...continued)
ciding question of law does not vest jurisdiction in appellate court when no disclosure order has yet been entered and, consequently, no irreparable harm would result); Ctr. for Nat'l Sec. Studies v. CIA, 711 F.2d 409, 413-14 (D.C. Cir. 1983) (finding no appellate jurisdiction to review court order granting summary judgment to defendant on only one of twelve counts in Complaint, because order did not affect "predominantly all" of merits of case and plaintiffs did not establish that denial of relief under 28 U.S.C. § 1292(a)(1) (2000) would cause them irreparable injury); Hinton v. FBI, 844 F.2d 126, 129-33 (3d Cir. 1988) (declining to review district court order that a Vaughn Index be filed); In re Motion to Compel filed by Steele, 799 F.2d 461, 464-65 (9th Cir. 1986); cf. Judicial Watch, Inc. v. Dep't of Energy, 412 F.3d 125, 128 (D.C. Cir. 2005) (denying motion to dismiss appeal because, although district court's order was not final as it did not resolve all issues, it was injunctive in nature and therefore appealable under 28 U.S.C. § 1292(a)(1)); John Doe Corp. v. John Doe Agency, 850 F.2d 105, 107-08 (2d Cir. 1988) (finding district court order denying motion for disclosure of documents, preparation of Vaughn Index, and answers to interrogatories appealable, and thereupon reversing on merits), rev'd on other grounds, 493 U.S. 146 (1989); Irons v. FBI, 811 F.2d 681, 683 (1st Cir. 1987) (allowing government to appeal motion for partial summary judgment for plaintiff, stating that appellate jurisdiction vests at time order requiring government to disclose records is issued).

[432] See Summers v. U.S. Dep't of Justice, 925 F.2d 450, 453 (D.C. Cir. 1991); Al-Fayed v. CIA, No. 00-2092, slip op. at 4 (D.D.C. Jan. 16, 2001) (refusing to treat plaintiff's motion for a stay as "akin" to a motion for summary judgment, because "in stark contrast to a motion for summary judgment, a motion for a stay does not evaluate the merits of a case"), aff'd on other grounds, 254 F.3d 300 (D.C. Cir. 2001).

[433] See Nat'l Ass'n of Criminal Def. Lawyers v. U.S. Dep't of Justice, 182 F.3d 981, 984-85 (D.C. Cir. 1999) (finding that award of "interim" attorney fees is appealable neither as final judgment nor as collateral order); Judicial Watch, Inc. v. U.S. Dep't of Justice, No. 01-5019, 2001 WL 800022, at *1 (D.C. Cir. June 13, 2001) (per curiam) (dismissing the appeal because the "district court's order holding that appellee is a representative of the news media for purposes of 5 U.S.C. § 552(a)(4)(A)(ii)(II) is not final in the traditional sense and does not meet the requirements of the collateral order doctrine").

quired by a date certain or, even worse, "forthwith."[434] The government's motion for such a stay should be granted as a matter of course as denial would destroy the status quo and would cause irreparable harm to the government appellant by mooting the issue on appeal.[435] In comparison,

---

[434] But see Cooper Cameron Corp. v. U.S. Dep't of Labor, No. 00-21077, slip op. at 1 (5th Cir. Jan. 21, 2002) (refusing to stay a judgment because, according to the Fifth Circuit, "'forthwith' does not affect the time period for filing a petition for rehearing or rehearing en banc, during the running of which the mandate cannot issue").

[435] See, e.g., Rosenfeld v. U.S. Dep't of Justice, 501 U.S. 1227, 1227 (1991) (granting full stay pending appeal); John Doe Agency v. John Doe Corp., 488 U.S. 1306, 1307 (Marshall, Circuit Justice 1989) (granting stay based upon "balance of the equities"); see also Wash Post v. DHS, No. 06-5337 (D.C. Cir. Nov. 1, 2006) ("[Agency] has satisfied the stringent standards required for a stay pending appeal."); Nat'l Council of La Raza v. Dep't of Justice, No. 04-5474, slip op. at 2 (2d Cir. Dec. 20, 2004) (granting stay for duration of appeal, but subject to expedited briefing schedule); Providence Journal Co. v. FBI, 595 F.2d 889, 890 (1st Cir. 1979); Ctr. for Nat'l Sec. Studies v. U.S. Dep't of Justice, 217 F. Supp. 2d 58, 58 (D.D.C. 2002) (explaining that "stays are routinely granted in FOIA cases," and granting stay because disclosure of detainee names would "effectively moot any appeal"), aff'd in part, rev'd in part & remanded, 331 F.3d 918 (D.C. Cir. 2003); Maine v. U.S. Dep't of the Interior, No. 00-122, 2001 WL 98373, at *3 (D. Me. Feb. 5, 2001) (relying on Providence Journal to grant stay pending appeal, and finding "most persuasive in this regard" irreparable harm to agency's right to appeal court's disclosure order); Antonelli v. FBI, 553 F. Supp. 19, 25 (N.D. Ill. 1982). But see Manos v. U.S. Dep't of the Air Force, No. 93-15672, slip op. at 2 (9th Cir. Apr. 28, 1993) (denying stay of district court disclosure order when government "failed to demonstrate . . . any possibility of success on the merits of its appeal," despite appellate court's recognition that such denial would render appeal moot); Sears, Roebuck & Co. v. GSA, 509 F.2d 527, 530 (D.C. Cir. 1974) (dissolving the district court's stay because the plaintiff "failed to demonstrate the probable success on the merits of its appeal required for continuance of the stay") ("reverse" FOIA suit); see also Long v. IRS, No. 74-724, 2006 WL 2222274, at *3 (W.D. Wash. Aug. 2, 2006) (denying motion for stay because motion was confusing, was ill-timed, and determinative factors for issuing stay did not tip in favor of agency); ACLU v. DOD, 357 F. Supp. 2d 708, 709 (S.D.N.Y. 2005) (denying motion for stay as defendant failed to demonstrate likelihood to suffer prejudice or to succeed on merits); Armstrong v. Executive Office of the President, 877 F. Supp. 750, 752-53 (D.D.C. 1995) (denying stay of its determination (later reversed on appeal) that National Security Council is an "agency" under FOIA); cf. Piper v. U.S. Dep't of Justice, 374 F. Supp. 2d 73, 81 (D.D.C. 2005) (noting that during pendency of plaintiff's appeal district court has no jurisdiction to entertain agency's Rule 60(b) motion even though motion seeks to protect third parties' interests); Bright v. Attorney Gen. John Ashcroft, 259 F. Supp. 2d 502, 502 (E.D. La. 2003) (disclosing contested material gratuitous-
(continued...)

granting such a stay causes relatively minimal harm to the appellee.[436]

The circuit courts of appeals do not have uniform legal standards governing the scope of appellate review of FOIA decisions. The Courts of Appeals for the District of Columbia,[437] Second,[438] Sixth,[439] and Eighth Cir-

---

[435](...continued)
ly and thus obviating government's appeal). See generally FOIA Update, Vol. XII, No. 3, at 1-2 (describing emergency Supreme Court action staying court-ordered disclosures in two FOIA cases).

[436] See Moye, O'Brien, O'Rourke, Hogan & Pickert v. Nat'l RR Passenger Corp., No. 02-126, slip op. at 2 (M.D. Fla. Sept. 4, 2003) (deciding to grant the defendant agency a stay "to test the merits of its arguments on appeal," and discerning "no evidence of a specific harm" to plaintiff from a delay in the disclosure of records); cf. Ctr. for Int'l Envtl. Law v. Office of the U.S. Trade Representative, 240 F. Supp. 2d 21, 23 (D.D.C. 2003) (recognizing harm to plaintiff if stay is granted, but granting it conditioned on agency seeking expedited review because of "serious legal question" at issue and irreparable harm to agency).

[437] See Assassination Archives & Research Ctr. v. CIA, 334 F.3d 55, 57 (D.C. Cir. 2003) ("We review the district court's grant of summary judgment de novo."); Landmark Legal Found. v. IRS, 267 F.3d 1132, 1134 (D.C. Cir. 2001) (referring to standard of review as "de novo"); Summers v. Dep't of Justice, 140 F.3d 1077, 1079 (D.C. Cir. 1998) ("[I]t is well-understood law that '[w]e review orders granting summary judgment de novo.'" (quoting Gallant v. NLRB, 26 F.3d 168, 171 (D.C. Cir. 1994))); Kimberlin v. Dep't of Justice, 139 F.3d 944, 947 (D.C. Cir. 1998) ("We review de novo the district court's grant of summary judgment, applying the same standards that governed the district court's decision."); see also Petroleum Info. Corp. v. U.S. Dep't of the Interior, 976 F.2d 1429, 1433 & n.3 (D.C. Cir. 1992) ("This circuit applies in FOIA cases the same standard of appellate review applicable generally to summary judgments." (explicitly contrasting Ninth Circuit's "clearly erroneous" standard, and more favorably citing Wash. Post Co. v. HHS, 865 F.2d 320, 325-26 & n.8 (D.C. Cir. 1989))).

[438] See Nat'l Council of La Raza v. Dep't of Justice, 411 F.3d 350, 355 (2d Cir. 2005) (reviewing "de novo a district court's grant of summary judgment in a FOIA case"); Tigue v. U.S. Dep't of Justice, 312 F.3d 70, 75 (2d Cir. 2002) (same); Perlman v. U.S. Dep't of Justice, 312 F.3d 100, 104 (2d Cir. 2002) ("We review an agency's decision to withhold records under FOIA de novo . . . ."); Halpern v. FBI, 181 F.3d 279, 287 (2d Cir. 1999) (applying de novo standard in FOIA cases "to determine whether there are genuine issues of material fact requiring trial").

[439] See Rugiero v. U.S. Dep't of Justice, 257 F.3d 534, 543 (6th Cir. 2001) ("[T]his court reviews the propriety of a district court's grant of summary judgment in a FOIA proceeding de novo."), cert. denied, 534 U.S. 1134

(continued...)

cuits,[440] have applied a purely de novo standard of review. Such a standard is entirely consistent with the nearly universal practice of adjudicating FOIA cases on the basis of summary judgment motions -- which generally are utilized only in the absence of any material factual disputes when the moving party is entitled to a judgment as a matter of law.[441]

By contrast, the Courts of Appeals for the Third,[442] Fifth,[443] and Seventh Circuits,[444] while recognizing that issues of law generally are re-

---

[439](...continued)
(2002); Sorrells v. United States, No. 97-5586, 1998 WL 58080, at *1 (6th Cir. Feb. 6, 1998) (deciding appeal "[u]pon de novo review"); Abraham & Rose, P.L.C. v. United States, 138 F.3d 1075, 1077 (6th Cir. 1998) (holding that grant of summary judgment is reviewed de novo on appeal). But see Vonderheide v. IRS, No. 98-4277, 1999 WL 1000875, at *1 (6th Cir. Oct. 28, 1999) ("Where an appeal concerns a factual attack on subject matter jurisdiction, this court reviews the factual findings of the district court for clear error and the legal conclusions de novo.").

[440] See Missouri v. U.S. Dep't of the Interior, 297 F.3d 745, 749 n.2 (8th Cir. 2002) (aligning the court with the Sixth, Tenth, and D.C. Circuits in "establish[ing] the de novo standard of review generally applicable in summary judgment cases"); see also Bilbrey v. U.S. Dep't of the Air Force, 20 F. App'x 597, 598 (8th Cir. 2001) (referring to "careful de novo review of the record"). But see also Johnston v. U.S. Dep't of Justice, No. 97-2173, 1998 WL 518529, at *1 (8th Cir. Aug. 10, 1998) ("We review the district court's factual findings for clear error and its legal conclusions de novo.").

[441] See Fed. R. Civ. P. 56(c).

[442] See, e.g., Sheet Metal Workers Int'l Ass'n v. VA, 135 F.3d 891, 896 & n.3 (3d Cir. 1998) (describing "two-tiered test" while recognizing that review standard is not uniform among circuits); McDonnell v. United States, 4 F.3d 1227, 1241-42 (3d Cir. 1993) (pointing to "unique configuration" of summary judgment in FOIA cases as basis for rejecting "familiar standard of appellate review" for summary judgment cases).

[443] See FlightSafety Servs. Corp. v. Dep't of Labor, 326 F.3d 607, 610-11 & n.2 (5th Cir. 2003) (per curiam) (applying de novo standard of review to district court's legal conclusions while recognizing potential applicability of different standard for factual determinations); Avondale Indus., Inc. v. NLRB, 90 F.3d 955, 958 (5th Cir. 1996) (finding de novo review appropriate when parties' dispute focuses "'not upon the unique facts of [the] case, but upon categorical rules,'" a question of law to which district court is not entitled to deference (quoting Halloran v. VA, 874 F.2d 315, 320 (5th Cir. 1989))).

[444] See Enviro Tech Int'l, Inc. v. EPA, 371 F.3d 370, 373-74 (7th Cir. 2004) (stating that "clearly erroneous" standard remains norm for FOIA cases in Seventh Circuit); Solar Sources, Inc. v. United States, 142 F.3d 1033, 1038

(continued...)

viewed de novo, hold that review of FOIA cases, because of their "unique nature,"[445] should be undertaken under a two-pronged deferential standard: Whether the district court had an adequate factual basis for its decision and, if so, whether that decision is clearly erroneous. Similarly, the Fourth,[446] Ninth,[447] Tenth,[448] and Eleventh Circuits[449] distinguish between

---

[444](...continued)
(7th Cir. 1998) ("[W]e continue to believe that the clearly erroneous standard remains appropriate in light of the unique circumstances presented by FOIA exemption cases."); Becker v. IRS, 34 F.3d 398, 402 (7th Cir. 1994) (explaining that whether withheld material fits within established standards of exemption reviewed is under two-pronged, deferential test).

[445] Minier v. CIA, 88 F.3d 796, 800 (9th Cir. 1996); see also Solar Sources, 142 F.3d at 1038 (referring to "the unique circumstances presented by FOIA exemption cases").

[446] See United States v. Mitchell, No. 03-6938, 2002 WL 22999456, at *1 (4th Cir. Dec. 23, 2004) (articulating the standard of review in this case as "limited to determining whether the district court had an adequate factual basis for its decision and whether upon this basis the decision was clearly erroneous"); Ethyl Corp. v. EPA, 25 F.3d 1241, 1246 (4th Cir. 1994) ("Although any factual conclusions that place a document within a stated exemption of FOIA are reviewed under a clearly erroneous standard, 'the question of whether a document fits within one of FOIA's prescribed exemptions is one of law, upon which the district court is entitled to no deference.'" (quoting City of Va. Beach v. Dep't of Commerce, 995 F.2d 1247, 1252 n.12 (4th Cir. 1993))); cf. Hanson v. Agency for Int'l Dev., 372 F.3d 286, 290 (4th Cir. 2004) (stating that grant of summary judgment in FOIA action is issue of law, which is reviewed de novo); Heily v. U.S. Dep't of Commerce, 69 F. App'x 171, 173 (4th Cir. July 3, 2003) (per curiam) (same).

[447] See Envtl. Prot. Info. Ctr. v. U.S. Forest Serv., 432 F.3d 945, 947 (9th Cir. 2005) (stating that district court is given deference on factual findings, which are reviewed only for clear error, but that application of particular FOIA exemption is reviewed de novo); Shors v. Treasury Inspector Gen. for Tax Admin., 68 F. App'x 99, 100 (9th Cir. June 9, 2003) (describing "two-part standard of review"); Carter v. U.S. Dep't of Commerce, 307 F.3d 1084, 1088 (9th Cir. 2002) (advising that "standard of review is not simply de novo," and that factual findings are reviewed for clear error, while legal conclusions are reviewed de novo); Klamath Water Users Protective Ass'n v. U.S. Dep't of the Interior, 189 F.3d 1034, 1036 (9th Cir. 1999) (explaining that standard is whether district judge had an adequate factual basis for decision; if so, district court's conclusions are reviewed de novo), aff'd on other grounds, 532 U.S. 1 (2001); Schiffer v. FBI, 78 F.3d 1405, 1409 (9th Cir. 1996) ("[W]hile we review the underlying facts supporting the district court's decision for clear error, we review de novo its conclusion [regarding the applicability of specific exemptions]."). But see Frazee v. U.S. Forest Serv., 97 F.3d 367, 370 (9th Cir. 1996) (describing "special standard" of re-
(continued...)

the district court's factual basis for its decision, which is reviewed under a clearly erroneous standard, and the district court's application of FOIA exemptions to approve withholding of documents -- which, in these circuits, most often is reviewed de novo.[450] The end result has caused some confu-

---

[447](...continued)
view of factual issues, i.e., whether adequate factual basis supports district court's ruling, appellate court overturns only if ruling "is clearly erroneous").

[448] See Casad v. HHS, 301 F.3d 1247, 1251 (10th Cir. 2002) (explaining that review is first "whether the district court had an adequate factual basis" for its decision, and then "de novo [of] the district court's legal conclusions that the requested materials are covered by the relevant FOIA exemptions"); Utah v. U.S. Dep't of the Interior, 256 F.3d 967, 969 (10th Cir. 2001) (same); Sheet Metal Workers Int'l Ass'n v. U.S. Air Force, 63 F.3d 994, 997 (10th Cir. 1995) ("[O]ur court reviews de novo any legal determinations made by the district court once we have assured ourselves that the district court 'had an adequate factual basis upon which to base its decision.'" (quoting Anderson v. HHS, 907 F.2d 936, 942 (10th Cir. 1990))).

[449] See Office of the Capital Collateral Counsel v. Dep't of Justice, 331 F.3d 799, 802 (11th Cir. 2003) (applying the de novo standard of review because "issues in this appeal are limited to the legal application of [a] FOIA exemption"); Catchpole v. Dep't of Transp., No. 97-8058, slip op. at 2 (11th Cir. Feb. 25, 1998) (applying de novo standard of review to FOIA case (citing Hale v. Tallapoosa County, 50 F.3d 1579, 1581 (11th Cir. 1995), and McGuire Oil Co. v. Mapco, Inc., 958 F.2d 1552, 1557 (11th Cir. 1992)) (non-FOIA cases)). But see Brown v. U.S. Dep't of Justice, 169 F. App'x 537, 539 (11th Cir. 2006) (stating that a "district court's determinations under the FOIA are reviewed for clear error"); O'Kane v. U.S. Customs Serv., 169 F.3d 1308, 1309 (11th Cir. 1999) (while acknowledging that grants of summary judgment are reviewed de novo, states that "district court determinations under FOIA" are reviewed for "clear error"); see also Robinson v. Dep't of Justice, No. 00-11182, slip op. at 9 (11th Cir. Mar. 15, 2001) (without deciding the applicability of an exemption, vacating the district court opinion because the court "lacked an adequate factual basis for its decision").

[450] See, e.g., Office of the Capital Collateral Counsel, 331 F.3d at 802 (explaining that factual findings "would ordinarily be reviewed for clear error" but that the legal application of a FOIA exemption is reviewed de novo); Sheet Metal Workers Int'l Ass'n v. VA, 135 F.3d 891, 896 (3d Cir. 1998) ("The two tiered standard review of the district court's determination that a particular document is or is not properly subject to exemption does not, of course, preclude plenary review of issues of law."); Ethyl Corp., 25 F.3d at 1246 ("[T]he question of whether a document fits within one of FOIA's prescribed exemptions is one of law, upon which the district court is entitled to no deference.").

sion in the standard for appellate review for FOIA cases,[451] because it is difficult to distinguish between the review standard for "any factual conclusions that place a document within a stated exemption of FOIA" (which is "clearly erroneous" in these circuits[452]) and the review standard for "whether a document fits within one of FOIA's prescribed exemptions"[453] (which is de novo).

This confusion is further illustrated by FOIA decisions of the First Circuit. In an early ruling, that circuit court eschewed any deference to the district court's decision in FOIA matters.[454] Then, in two decisions issued less than five months apart, it appeared to articulate opposite standards.[455] It applied a de novo standard of review in considering the district court's determination of whether the government supplied an adequate Vaughn Index.[456] This issue, however, logically falls within the category of whether the district court had an adequate factual basis for its determination, a question which is subject to de novo review even in those circuits employing the more deferential, two-pronged test.[457] In a recent opinion, though,

---

[451] Schiffer, 78 F.3d at 1408 ("Determining the appropriate standard of review to apply to summary judgment in FOIA cases . . . has caused some confusion because of the peculiar circumstances presented by such cases.").

[452] Id. (quoting Ethyl Corp., 25 F.3d at 1246).

[453] Id.

[454] See New England Apple Council v. Donovan, 725 F.2d 139, 141 n.2 (1st Cir. 1984) ("Appellees incorrectly state that this court may reverse the district court only if its conclusions are 'clearly erroneous.' In summary judgment there can be no review of factual issues, because Rule 56(c) bars the district court from resolving any disputed factual issues at the summary judgment stage.").

[455] Compare Aronson v. HUD, 822 F.2d 182, 188 (1st Cir. 1987) ("In reviewing a district court's grant of summary judgment, we apply the same standard as the district court."), with Irons, 811 F.2d at 684 ("where the conclusions of the trial court depend on its . . . choice of which competing inferences to draw from undisputed basic facts, appellate courts should defer to such fact-intensive findings, absent clear error"; however, questions of pure legal interpretation reviewed de novo).

[456] See Church of Scientology Int'l v. U.S. Dep't of Justice, 30 F.3d 224, 231 (1st Cir. 1994).

[457] See, e.g., Davin v. U.S. Dep't of Justice, 60 F.3d 1043, 1048-49 (3d Cir. 1995) (explaining that review of adequacy of factual basis for district court's decision "is de novo and requires us to examine the affidavits below"); Wiener v. FBI, 943 F.2d 972, 978 (9th Cir. 1991) ("Whether the government's public affidavits constituted an adequate Vaughn index is a ques-

(continued...)

the First Circuit alluded to its use of a "clearly erroneous" standard of review.[458]

In sum, the case law on this point simply cannot be reconciled among the various circuits, and conflicting decisions are not uncommon even within the same circuit.[459]

On another issue involving appeal considerations, the Court of Appeals for the District of Columbia Circuit, in a case of first impression, ruled that the standard of review of a district court decision on that portion of the FOIA's expedited access provision -- which authorizes expedited access "in cases in which the person requesting the records demonstrates a compelling need"[460] -- is de novo.[461] "Precisely because FOIA's terms apply nationwide," the D.C. Circuit decided not to accord deference to any particular agency's interpretation of this provision of the FOIA.[462] At the same time, however, the D.C. Circuit held that if an agency were to issue a rule consistent with the statutory language that permits expedition "in other cases determined by the agency,"[463] that rule would be entitled to judicial deference.[464] In any event, once an agency has acted upon the underlying request for which expedited access was requested, the FOIA itself removes

---

[457](...continued)
tion of law reviewed de novo.").

[458] See Maine v. U.S. Dep't of the Interior, 285 F.3d 126, 134 (1st Cir) (stating that "we cannot say that the district court erred in this case" and also that "[w]e perceive no error by the court"), aff'd on reh'g, 298 F.3d 60 (1st Cir. 2002).

[459] See Enviro Tech Int'l, Inc., 371 F.3d at 374 (recognizing split amongst circuits as to appropriate standard of review in FOIA cases, and further noting inconsistencies within Seventh Circuit).

[460] 5 U.S.C. § 552(a)(6)(E)(i) (2000 & Supp. IV 2004).

[461] Al-Fayed v. CIA, 254 F.3d 300, 305 (D.C. Cir. 2001) (deciding that "the logical conclusion is that de novo review is the proper standard for a district court to apply to a denial of expedition"); see Tripp v. DOD, 193 F. Supp. 2d 229, 241 (D.D.C. 2002) (citing Al-Fayed).

[462] Id. at 307.

[463] Id. at 307 n.7 (citing portion of subsection 5 U.S.C. § 552(a)(6)(E)(i) that allows for expedition "in other cases determined by the agency").

[464] See Al-Fayed, 254 F.3d at 307 n.7 ("A regulation promulgated in response to such an express delegation of authority to an individual agency is entitled to judicial deference . . . as is each agency's reasonable interpretation of its own regulations.").

court oversight of the agency's decision on the issue of expedition.[465]

In contrast, it is well settled that a trial court decision refusing to allow discovery will be reversed only if the court abused its discretion.[466] Similarly, a "reverse" FOIA case -- which is brought under the Administrative Procedure Act[467] -- is reviewed only with reference to whether the agency acted in a manner that was "arbitrary, capricious, an abuse of discretion, or otherwise not in accordance with law," based upon the "whole [administrative] record."[468] (For a further discussion of this point, see "Reverse" FOIA, Standard of Review, below.)

It is noteworthy that in a routine FOIA case where the merits and law of the case are so clear as to justify summary disposition, summary affirmance or reversal may be appropriate.[469] An otherwise routine case, how-

---

[465] See 5 U.S.C. § 552(a)(6)(E)(iii); see also Judicial Watch, Inc. v. U.S. Naval Observatory, 160 F. Supp. 2d 111, 112 (D.D.C. 2001) ("[B]ecause defendant has . . . provided a complete response to the request for records, this Court no longer has subject matter jurisdiction over the claim that defendant failed to expedite processing of plaintiff's request.").

[466] See Anderson v. HHS, 80 F.3d 1500, 1507 (10th Cir. 1996) (holding that district court decision to deny further discovery on attorney fees issue "was not an abuse of discretion"); Church of Scientology v. IRS, 991 F.2d 560, 562 (9th Cir. 1993), vacated in part on other grounds & remanded, No. 91-15730 (9th Cir. July 14, 1994); Meeropol v. Meese, 790 F.2d 942, 960 (D.C. Cir. 1986); Northrop Corp. v. McDonnell Douglas Corp., 751 F.2d 395, 399 (D.C. Cir. 1988).

[467] 5 U.S.C. §§ 701-706 (2000).

[468] AT&T Info. Sys. v. GSA, 810 F.2d 1233, 1236 (D.C. Cir. 1987) (citing Chrysler Corp. v. Brown, 441 U.S. 281, 318 (1979)); see Reliance Elec. Co. v. Consumer Prod. Safety Comm'n, 924 F.2d 274, 277 (D.C. Cir. 1991) (explaining that agency decisions to release information under FOIA are "informal adjudications" reviewed under arbitrary and capricious standard of Administrative Procedure Act); Daisy Mfg. Co. v. Consumer Prod. Safety Comm'n, 133 F.3d 1081, 1083 (8th Cir. 1998) (same); see also Doe v. Veneman, 230 F. Supp. 2d 739, 747 (W.D. Tex. 2002) (recognizing that "reverse" FOIA suits are "cognizable under the Administrative Procedures [sic] Act") aff'd in pertinent part & rev'd in part on other grounds, 380 F.3d 807, 813-14 (5th Cir. 2004); cf. Campaign for Family Farms v. Glickman, 200 F.3d 1180, 1187 n.6 (8th Cir. 2000) (explaining that review ordinarily is based upon administrative record, but noting that de novo review could be appropriate if it is shown that agency's "factfinding procedures in ["reverse"] FOIA cases are inadequate").

[469] See, e.g., Barreiro v. Executive Office for U.S. Attorneys, No. 04-5071, 2004 WL 2451753, at *1 (D.C. Cir. Nov. 1, 2004) (granting summary affirm-

(continued...)

ever, could be remanded if the district court fails to make a segregability finding -- even if the district court's decision is in all other respects entirely correct.[470] (For a further discussion of this point, see Litigation Considerations, "Reasonably Segregable" Requirements, above.) Other procedures are available for discharging the appellate court's functions in unusual procedural circumstances.[471]

It also is noteworthy that courts ordinarily will not consider issues raised for the first time on appeal by FOIA litigants.[472] For this reason,

---

[469](...continued)
ance); Pinnavaia v. FBI, No. 04-5115, 2004 WL 2348155, at *1 (D.C. Cir. Oct. 19, 2004) (same); Hayden v. Dep't of Justice, No. 03-5078, 2003 WL 22305071, at *1 (D.C. Cir. Oct. 6, 2003) (same); Daniel v. Dep't of Justice, No. 01-5119, 2001 WL 1029156, at *1 (D.C. Cir. Aug. 28, 2001) (citing Taxpayers Watchdog, Inc. v. Stanley, 819 F.2d 294, 297 (D.C. Cir. 1987) (per curiam), and Walker v. Washington, 627 F.2d 541, 545 (D.C. Cir. 1980) (per curiam)).

[470] See, e.g., James Madison Project v. NARA, No. 02-5089, 2002 WL 31296220, at *1 (D.C. Cir. Oct. 11, 2002) (denying summary affirmance in part and remanding for "a more precise finding by the district court as to segregability"); Trans-Pac. Policing Agreement v. U.S. Customs Serv., 177 F.3d 1022, 1028 (D.C. Cir. 1999) ("[T]he District Court had an affirmative duty to consider the segregability issue sua sponte."); Kimberlin, 139 F.3d at 949-50 (remanding because district court failed to make segregability finding).

[471] See, e.g., Constangy, Brooks & Smith v. NLRB, 851 F.2d 839, 842 (6th Cir. 1988) (determining that it is inappropriate to vacate district court order, after fully complied with, when attorney fees issue pending; proper procedure is to dismiss appeal); Larson v. Executive Office for U.S. Attorneys, No. 85-6226, slip op. at 4 (D.C. Cir. Apr. 6, 1988) (concluding that when only issue on appeal is mooted, initial lower court order should be vacated without prejudice and case remanded).

[472] See, e.g., Judicial Watch, Inc. v. United States, 84 F. App'x 335, 338 (4th Cir. 2004) (refusing to entertain new arguments from appellant on adequacy of agency's search, despite appellant's characterization of them as "further articulation" of points made below); Blanton v. Dep't of Justice, 64 F. App'x 787, 789 (D.C. Cir. 2003) (per curiam) (rebuffing appellant's efforts to challenge adequacy of agency's Vaughn Index, because issue was not raised in district court); Iturralde v. Comptroller, 315 F.3d 311, 314 (D.C. Cir. 2003) (rejecting appellant's efforts to challenge sufficiency of agency's affidavits, because he did not raise issue in district court); James Madison Project, 2002 WL 31296220, at *1 (deciding that appellant waived challenges to agency's invocation of FOIA exemptions by failing to address arguments supporting withholding that were made in agency's summary affirmance motion); Greyshock v. U.S. Coast Guard, No. 96-15266, 1997 WL

(continued...)

agencies should ensure that they raise or preserve all exemption claims at the district court level.[473] Failure to do so might result in waiver of these claims.[474] (See Litigation Considerations, Waiver of Exemptions in Litigation, above.)

Lastly, Rule 39(a) of the Federal Rules of Appellate Procedure is applied to award costs to the government when it is successful in a FOIA appeal; the D.C. Circuit has held that this rule's presumption favoring such awards of costs is fully applicable in FOIA cases.[475]

---

[472](...continued)
51514, at *3 (9th Cir. Feb. 5, 1997) (declining to consider a challenge to a separate FOIA request that was not "mentioned in the complaint or any other pleading before the district court"); McCutchen v. HHS, 30 F.3d 183, 186-87 (D.C. Cir. 1994) (refusing to consider correctness of agency's interpretation of FOIA request when issue was raised for first time on appeal); see also Students Against Genocide v. Dep't of State, 257 F.3d 828, 835 (D.C. Cir. 2001) (refusing to consider argument made for first time in appellate reply brief); OSHA/Data/CIH, Inc. v. U.S. Dep't of Labor, 220 F.3d 153, 169 n.35 (3d Cir. 2000) (refusing to permit supplementation of record on appeal). But see also Trans-Pac., 177 F.3d at 1027 (allowing segregability issue to be raised for first time on appeal, because "appellants' failure to raise segregability certainly was not a knowing waiver of that argument"); Carter v. U.S. Dep't of Commerce, 830 F.2d 388, 390 n.8 (D.C. Cir. 1987) (considering sua sponte new theories of public interest in Exemption 6 balancing that were not raised by plaintiff at district court); Farese v. U.S. Dep't of Justice, No. 86-5528, slip op. at 9-10 (D.C. Cir. Aug. 12, 1987) (finding plaintiff not estopped from challenging use of specific exemptions at appellate stage when he argued at trial court level merely that agency had failed to meet its burden of establishing that documents were exempt).

[473] See FOIA Post, "Supreme Court Declines to Review Waiver Case" (posted 8/7/01) (advising agencies to pay special attention to "the issue of waiver of FOIA exemptions during the course of litigation"); see also Ryan v. Dep't of Justice, 617 F.2d 781, 792 n.38a (D.C. Cir. 1980) (explaining that "raising" an exemption means "identifying it at the district court level" and then demonstrating the applicability of any pertinent exemption).

[474] Tax Analysts v. IRS, 152 F. Supp. 2d 1, 25-26 (D.D.C. 2001) (refusing to allow an agency to invoke an exemption that it had previously abandoned, based upon rule forbidding new exemption claims after "the judge has ruled in the other party's favor" (citing Grumman Aircraft Eng'g Corp. v. Renegotiation Bd., 482 F.2d 710, 721-22 (D.C. Cir. 1973)), aff'd in part & rev'd in part, 294 F.3d 71 (D.C. Cir. 2002); see also, e.g., FOIA Post, "Supreme Court Is Asked to Review Law Enforcement Case" (posted 5/30/01) (discussing circumstances of D.C. Circuit's Maydak decision, and describing its approach to Exemption 7(A)).

[475] See Baez v. U.S. Dep't of Justice, 684 F.2d 999, 1005-07 (D.C. Cir. 1982)
(continued...)

ATTORNEY FEES

The FOIA is one of more than a hundred different federal statutes that contain a "fee-shifting" provision permitting the trial court to award reasonable attorney fees and litigation costs to a plaintiff who has "substantially prevailed."[1] The FOIA's attorney fees provision, added as subsection (a)(4)(E) of the Act as part of the 1974 FOIA amendments, requires courts to engage in a two-step substantive inquiry: (1) Is the plaintiff eligible for an award of fees and/or costs? (2) If so, is the plaintiff entitled to the award?[2] Even if a plaintiff meets both of these tests, the award of fees and costs is entirely within the discretion of the court.[3]

Attorney Fees and Litigation Costs: Eligibility Generally

The FOIA's attorney fees provision limits an award to fees and costs incurred in litigating a case brought pursuant to the FOIA;[4] accordingly,

---

[475](...continued)
(en banc); see also Scherer v. United States, 78 F. App'x 687, 690 (10th Cir. 2003) (upholding district court's award of costs to agency); Johnson v. Comm'r, 68 F. App'x 839, 840 (9th Cir. 2003) (awarding costs to agency because requester's appeal was frivolous).

[1] 5 U.S.C. § 552(a)(4)(E) (2000 & Supp. IV 2004).

[2] 5 U.S.C. § 552(a)(4)(E); see, e.g., Tax Analysts v. U.S. Dep't of Justice, 965 F.2d 1092, 1093 (D.C. Cir. 1992); Church of Scientology v. USPS, 700 F.2d 486, 489 (9th Cir. 1983); see also Wheeler v. IRS, 37 F. Supp. 2d 407, 411 n.1 (W.D. Pa. 1998) ("The test for whether the court should award a FOIA plaintiff litigation costs is the same as the test for whether attorney fees should be awarded.").

[3] See, e.g., Lissner v. U.S. Customs Serv., 56 F. App'x 330, 331 (9th Cir. 2002) (stating that review of attorney fee award is for abuse of discretion); Anderson v. HHS, 80 F.3d 1500, 1504 (10th Cir. 1996) ("Assessment of attorney's fees in an FOIA case is discretionary with the district court."); Detroit Free Press, Inc. v. Dep't of Justice, 73 F.3d 93, 98 (6th Cir. 1996) ("We review the court's determination [to grant fees] for an abuse of discretion."); Young v. Dir., No. 92-2561, 1993 WL 305970, at *2 (4th Cir. 1993) (noting that court has discretion to deny fees even if eligibility threshold is met); Maynard v. CIA, 986 F.2d 547, 567 (1st Cir. 1993) (holding that a decision on whether to award attorney fees "will be reversed only for an abuse of . . . discretion"); Tax Analysts, 965 F.2d at 1094 ("sifting of those [fee] criteria over the facts of a case is a matter of district court discretion"); Bangor Hydro-Elec. Co. v. U.S. Dep't of the Interior, 903 F. Supp. 160, 170 (D. Me. 1995) ("Awards of litigation costs and attorney fees under FOIA are left to the sound discretion of the trial court.").

[4] See Nichols v. Pierce, 740 F.2d 1249, 1252-54 (D.C. Cir. 1984) (refusing
(continued...)

fees and other costs may not be awarded for services rendered at the administrative level.[5] Furthermore, the Court of Appeals for the District of Columbia Circuit recently held that FOIA litigation costs related to disputes with third parties, "who are not within the government's authority or control, with respect to litigation issues that were neither raised nor pursued by the government, cannot form the basis of a fee award under 5 U.S.C. § 552(a)(4)(E)."[6]

A threshold eligibility matter concerns precisely who can qualify for

---

[4](...continued)
to award fees for plaintiff's success under Administrative Procedure Act, 5 U.S.C. §§ 701-706 (2000), in forcing agency to issue regulations, despite plaintiff's claim of victory under FOIA subsection (a)(1)), because Complaint failed to assert claim under or rely specifically on FOIA); Sinito v. U.S. Dep't of Justice, No. 87-0814, slip op. at 3 n.2 (D.D.C. Mar. 23, 2001) (declining to consider fee-entitlement argument based on Equal Access to Justice Act, 5 U.S.C. § 504 (2000), because plaintiff relied on only FOIA in his motion), summary affirmance granted, No. 01-5168 (D.C. Cir. Oct. 15, 2001).

[5] See AutoAlliance Int'l, Inc. v. U.S. Customs Serv., No. 02-72369, slip op. at 3 (E.D. Mich. Mar. 23, 2004) (denying attorney fees for time spent on "administrative appeals that should have been completed prior to filing suit"); Inst. for Wildlife Prot. v. U.S. Fish & Wildlife Serv., No. 02-6178, slip op. at 6 (D. Or. Dec. 3, 2003) (deducting hours spent on FOIA administrative process for fee-calculation purposes); Nw. Coal. for Alternatives to Pesticides v. Browner, 965 F. Supp. 59, 65 (D.D.C. 1997) ("FOIA does not authorize fees for work performed at the administrative stage."); Associated Gen. Contractors v. EPA, 488 F. Supp. 861, 864 (D. Nev. 1980) (concluding that attorney fees are unavailable for work performed at administrative level); cf. Kennedy v. Andrus, 459 F. Supp. 240, 244 (D.D.C. 1978) (rejecting attorney fees claim for services rendered at administrative level under Privacy Act, 5 U.S.C. § 552a (2000)), aff'd, 612 F.2d 586 (D.C. Cir. 1980) (unpublished table decision). But see Or. Natural Desert Ass'n v. Gutierrez, No. 05-210, 2006 WL 2318610, at *4 (D. Or. Aug. 24, 2006) (awarding fees for work performed at the administrative level, on the rationale that "exhaustion of remedies is required and provides a sufficient record for the civil action") (appeal pending); McCoy v. Fed. Bureau of Prisons, No. 03-383, 2005 WL 1972600, at *4 (E.D. Ky. Aug. 16, 2005) (permitting fees for work on plaintiff's administrative appeal, on the rationale that it "was necessary to exhaust administrative remedies"), reconsideration denied, No. 03-383 (E.D. Ky. Oct. 6, 2005); cf. Tule River Conservancy v. U.S. Forest Serv., No. 97-5720, slip op. at 16-17 (E.D. Cal. Sept. 12, 2000) (allowing attorney fees for pre-litigation research on "how to exhaust [plaintiff's] administration remedies prior to filing suit" and on "how to file FOIA complaint").

[6] Judicial Watch, Inc. v. U.S. Dep't of Commerce, 470 F.3d 363, 373 (D.C. Cir. 2006).

an award of attorney fees. The Supreme Court's decision in Kay v. Ehrler[7] clearly establishes that subsection (a)(4)(E) does not authorize the award of fees to a pro se nonattorney plaintiff, because "the word 'attorney,' when used in the context of a fee-shifting statute, does not encompass a layperson proceeding on his own behalf."[8] In order to be eligible for attorney fees, therefore, a FOIA plaintiff must have a representational relationship with an attorney.[9]

Furthermore, Kay stands for the proposition that no award of attorney fees should be made to a pro se plaintiff who also is an attorney.[10] Because the fee-shifting provision of the FOIA was intended "'to encourage potential claimants to seek legal advice before commencing litigation,'"[11] and because a pro se attorney, by definition, does not seek out the "'detached and

---

[7] 499 U.S. 432 (1991).

[8] Benavides v. Bureau of Prisons, 993 F.2d 257, 259 (D.C. Cir. 1993) (explaining Kay decision); see Bensman v. U.S. Fish & Wildlife Serv., 49 F. App'x 646, 647 (7th Cir. 2002) ("Even when a pro se litigant performs the same tasks as an attorney, he is not entitled to reimbursement for his time."); Deichman v. United States, No. 2:05cv680, 2006 WL 3000448, at *7 (E.D. Va. Oct. 20, 2006) (holding that pro see litigant cannot recover attorney fees under FOIA); Lair v. Dep't of the Treasury, No. 03-827, 2005 WL 645228, at *6 (D.D.C. Mar. 21, 2005) (explaining that "pro-se non-attorney . . . may not collect attorney fees" (citing Benavides)), reconsideration denied, 2005 WL 1330722 (D.D.C. June 3, 2005).

[9] See Kooritzky v. Herman, 178 F.3d 1315, 1323 (D.C. Cir. 1999) (holding that for all similarly worded fee-shifting statutes, "the term 'attorney' contemplates an agency relationship between a litigant and an independent lawyer"); see also Blazy v. Tenet, 194 F.3d 90, 94 (D.C. Cir. 1999) (concluding that attorney need not file formal appearance in order for litigant to claim fees for consultations, so long as attorney-client relationship existed) (Privacy Act case); cf. Anderson v. U.S. Dep't of the Treasury, 648 F.2d 1, 3 (D.C. Cir. 1979) (indicating that when an organization litigates through in-house counsel, any payable attorney fees should not "exceed[] the expenses incurred by [that party] in terms of [in-house counsel] salaries and other out-of-pocket expenses").

[10] 499 U.S. at 438 ("The statutory policy of furthering the successful prosecution of meritorious claims is better served by a rule that creates an incentive to retain counsel in every case.") (emphasis added). But see Baker & Hostetler LLP v. U.S. Dep't of Commerce, 473 F.3d 312, 324 (D.C. Cir. 2006) (holding that law firm representing itself is eligible for attorney's fees).

[11] Id. at 434 n.4 (quoting Falcone v. IRS, 714 F.2d 646, 647 (6th Cir. 1983)).

objective perspective necessary"' to litigate his FOIA case,[12] the over-whelming majority of courts have agreed with Kay and have held that a pro se attorney is not eligible for a fee award that otherwise would have had to be paid to counsel.[13] This is particularly so because "[a]n award of attor-ney's fees was intended to relieve plaintiffs of the burden of legal costs, not reward successful claimants or penalize the government."[14]

A pro se attorney who claims that his or her status is merely "techni-cal" because he or she represents an undisclosed client is looked upon with disfavor. In rejecting such a claim, the D.C. Circuit has declared that "stat-us as both attorney and litigant may be a 'technicality,' but it is a legally meaningful one and not to be ignored."[15] Finding that the pro se attorney "controlled the legal strategy and presentation" of the case, the D.C. Circuit similarly denied fees for the services of that pro se attorney's lawyer-col-leagues who worked under his direction, "because there was no attorney-client relationship between them."[16] Of course, if an attorney actually re-tains outside counsel to represent him or her, those fees may be compen-

---

[12] Id.

[13] See, e.g., Burka v. HHS, 142 F.3d 1286, 1289 (D.C. Cir. 1998) ("It is . . . impossible to conclude otherwise than that pro se litigants who are attor-neys are not entitled to attorney's fees under FOIA."); Ray v. U.S. Dep't of Justice, 87 F.3d 1250, 1252 (11th Cir. 1996) (deciding that principles an-nounced in Kay apply with "equal force" in FOIA case); Albino v. USPS, No. 01-563, 2002 WL 32345674, at *8 (W.D. Wis. May 20, 2002) (agreeing that pro se plaintiffs who are attorneys are barred from receiving attorney fees under the rationale of Kay); Manos v. Dep't of the Air Force, 829 F. Supp. 1191, 1193 (N.D. Cal. 1993) (stating that "fairness and sound policy" compel same treatment of attorney and nonattorney pro se FOIA plaintiffs); Wha-len v. IRS, No. 92C 4841, 1993 WL 532506, at *11 (N.D. Ill. Dec. 20, 1993) (finding "no satisfactory distinction between pro se FOIA litigants who are lawyers and those who are not for the propose of awarding fees"). But see Texas v. ICC, 935 F.2d 728, 731 (5th Cir. 1991) (pointing out that "lawyers who represent themselves in FOIA actions may recover under the fee-shifting provision"); cf. Chin v. U.S. Dep't of the Air Force, No. 99-31237, slip op. at 3 (5th Cir. June 15, 2000) (assuming, but not deciding, that Cazalas v. U.S. Dep't of Justice, 709 F.2d 1051 (5th Cir. 1983), which awarded fee to a pro se attorney, has been "rendered moribund"); Barrett v. U.S. Dep't of Justice, No. 3:95-264, slip op. at 5 (S.D. Miss. Mar. 17, 1997) (declining to decide whether Fifth Circuit would overrule Cazalas in light of Kay deci-sion, because alternative ground existed for deciding fee issue at hand), aff'd, No. 97-60223 (5th Cir. Nov. 20, 1997).

[14] Burka, 142 F.3d at 1289-90; see Dixie Fuel Co. v. Callahan, 136 F. Supp. 2d 659, 661 (E.D. Ky. 2001).

[15] Burka, 142 F.3d at 1291.

[16] Id.

sable.[17]

However, it is worth noting that in a recent case, the D.C. Circuit, relying on dictum in Kay, held that a law firm representing itself is eligible for attorney's fees.[18] In its analysis, the D.C. Circuit explained that the Supreme Court was clear that "the exception for individual plaintiffs who represent themselves does not apply to organizations."[19] As the Supreme Court made no distinction between law firms and other types of organizations represented by in-house counsel, the D.C. Circuit concluded that a law firm representing itself is eligible for an award of attorney fees.[20]

Unlike attorney fees, the costs of litigating a FOIA suit can reasonably be incurred by, and awarded to, even a pro se litigant who is not an attorney.[21] Although a particular federal statute, 28 U.S.C. § 1920,[22] lists certain items that may be taxed as costs,[23] in some instances FOIA costs have been awarded independently of this statute.[24] "Costs" in a FOIA case

---

[17] See, e.g., Ray v. U.S. Dep't of Justice, 856 F. Supp. 1576, 1582 (S.D. Fla. 1994), aff'd, 87 F.3d 1250 (11th Cir. 1996); Whalen, 1993 WL 532506, at *11.

[18] Baker & Hostetler LLP v. U.S. Dep't of Commerce, 473 F.3d 312, 324 (D.C. Cir. 2006) (panel rehearing pending).

[19] Id. at 325.

[20] Id. at 326.

[21] See Carter v. VA, 780 F.2d 1479, 1481-82 (9th Cir. 1986); DeBold v. Stimson, 735 F.2d 1037, 1043 (7th Cir. 1984); Clarkson v. IRS, 678 F.2d 1368, 1371 (11th Cir. 1983); Crooker v. U.S. Dep't of Justice, 632 F.2d 916, 921-22 (1st Cir. 1980); Dorn v. Comm'r, No. 03-CV5-39, 2005 WL 1126653, at *4 (M.D. Fla. May 12, 2005) (recognizing that pro se litigant "could be entitled to costs," but denying such award because "plaintiff did not substantially prevail"); Albino, 2002 WL 32345674, at *1 (awarding costs because pro se plaintiff substantially prevailed); Malone v. Freeh, No. 97-3043, slip op. at 3 (D.D.C. July 12, 1999) (awarding pro se plaintiff $200 for costs); Wheeler, 37 F. Supp. 2d at 411.

[22] (2000).

[23] 28 U.S.C. § 1920 ("A judge or clerk . . . may tax as costs the following: (1) Fees of the clerk and marshal; (2) Fees of the court reporter . . . ; (3) Fees and disbursements for printing and witnesses; (4) Fees for exemplification and copies of papers necessarily obtained for use in the case; (5) Docket fees under section 1923 of this title; (6) Compensation of court appointed experts[.]").

[24] See Blazy, 194 F.3d at 95 (stating that "§ 1920 does not serve as a limit on recovery of litigation costs under either FOIA or the Privacy Act"); Kuzma v. IRS, 821 F.2d 930, 933 (2d Cir. 1987) (concluding that "the policies un-
(continued...)

have been interpreted to include photocopying, postage, typing, transcription, parking, and transportation expenses, in addition to routine filing costs and marshals' fees paid at the trial level,[25] as well as the fees paid to a special master appointed by the court to review documents on its behalf.[26] However, a plaintiff cannot seek to have work done by an attorney compensated under the guise of "costs."[27]

Any FOIA plaintiff, including a corporation or even a State, that does engage the services of an attorney for litigation is eligible to seek an award of attorney fees and costs.[28] By the same token, if it prevails, even a defendant agency may recover its costs pursuant to Rule 54(d) of the Federal

---

[24](...continued)
derlying § 1920 are antithetical to the remedial purpose" of the FOIA); Comer v. IRS, No. 97-76329, 2002 WL 31835437, at *2 (E.D. Mich. Oct. 30, 2002) (refusing to limit costs under FOIA to those contained in 28 U.S.C. § 1920); Tax Analysts v. IRS, No. 94-923, 1998 WL 283207, at *3 (D.D.C. Mar. 17, 1998) (same).

[25] See Kuzma, 821 F.2d at 931-34 (finding that costs may include photocopying, postage, covers, exhibits, typing, transportation, and parking fees, but not "cost of law books readily available in libraries"); Williams v. Dep't of the Army, No. 92-20088, 1993 WL 372245, at *6 (N.D. Cal. Sept. 13, 1993) (agreeing that such costs are recoverable if "they are reasonable"). But see Carpa v. FBI, No. 00-2025, slip op. at 2 (D.D.C. Oct. 15, 2001) (denying pro se plaintiff reimbursement for costs of postage and office supplies because such costs "not typically recoverable" under local court rule); Trenerry v. IRS, No. 90-C-444, 1994 WL 25877, at *1 (N.D. Okla. Jan. 26, 1994) (refusing to allow costs for transportation, supplies, or "any other costs not properly taxed pursuant to 28 U.S.C. § 1920").

[26] See Wash. Post v. DOD, 789 F. Supp. 423, 424 (D.D.C. 1992) (apportioning special master's fees equally between plaintiff and government).

[27] See Anderson, 80 F.3d at 1508 (suggesting that work done by attorneys is not "properly a cost item"); see also Comer, 2002 WL 31835437, at *2 (rejecting pro se plaintiff's costs-reimbursement request for "paralegal fees").

[28] See, e.g., Texas, 935 F.2d at 733 ("[T]he goal of encouraging litigation of meritorious FOIA claims is doubtlessly furthered by reimbursing the legal fees of all complainants who substantially prevail and who meet the traditional criteria -- even those complainants, such as corporations or states, who could finance their own lawsuit."); Assembly of Cal. v. U.S. Dep't of Commerce, No. Civ-S-91-990, 1993 WL 188328, at *6 (E.D. Cal. May 28, 1993) ("Although the Assembly may have more resources than some private citizens, this does not mean the Assembly is any less restricted with respect to allocating its resources.").

Rules of Civil Procedure, although such recoveries are uncommon.[29]

### Attorney Fees and Litigation Costs:  The Buckhannon  Standard

Assuming that a plaintiff qualifies for eligibility as described above, the next step is to determine whether the plaintiff is actually eligible for a fee award under the circumstances of the case.  This, in turn, requires a determination that the plaintiff has "substantially prevailed" within the meaning of subsection (a)(4)(E) of the FOIA -- as limited by the Supreme Court's decision in Buckhannon Board & Care Home, Inc. v. West Virginia Department of Health & Human Resources.[30]

This eligibility determination once consumed a considerable amount of judicial attention, as courts applied the "catalyst theory" for awarding attorney fees, which held that a plaintiff could be awarded attorney fees if his lawsuit served as a "catalyst" in achieving a voluntary change in the defendant's conduct.[31]  This produced a wide variety of decisions describing what circumstances were sufficient to find eligibility for attorney fees.[32]  The catalyst theory was specifically rejected, however, when the Supreme Court, in Buckhannon, held that a plaintiff must obtain a judicially sanctioned "alteration in the legal relationship of the parties" before fees will be awarded.[33]

Although the FOIA was not the particular statute at issue in Buckhannon, the Supreme Court there repeated its oft-expressed view that the numerous federal fee-shifting statutes, including the FOIA, should be interpreted consistently.[34]  Two years after the Buckhannon decision, the Court of Appeals for the D.C. Circuit expressly applied Buckhannon's holding to the FOIA.  In Oil, Chemical & Atomic Workers International Union

---

[29] See, e.g., Chin, No. 99-31237, Order at 1 (5th Cir. June 15, 2000) (ordering plaintiff to pay defendant's costs on appeal); Donohue v. U.S. Dep't of Justice, No. 84-3451, slip op. at 1-2 (D.D.C. Mar. 7, 1988) (granting government's bill of costs for reimbursement of reporter, witness, and deposition expenses); Medoff v. CIA, No. 78-733, Order at 1 (D.N.J. Mar. 13, 1979) (awarding government, as prevailing party, its litigation costs in full amount of $93, effectively against ACLU, in accordance with statutory authorization contained in 28 U.S.C. § 1920); see also Baez v. U.S. Dep't of Justice, 684 F.2d 999, 1005-06 (D.C. Cir. 1982) (en banc) (assessing against unsuccessful plaintiff all costs of appeal).

[30] 532 U.S. 598 (2001) (non-FOIA case).

[31] See Buckhannon, 532 U.S. at 600 (explaining "catalyst theory").

[32] See id. at 602 n.3 (collecting cases).

[33] Id. at 605.

[34] Id. at 603 n.4 (citing Hensley v. Eckerhart, 461 U.S. 424, 433 n.7 (1983)).

(OCAW) v. Department of Energy,[35] the D.C. Circuit declared that the "substantially prevails" language of the FOIA is the "functional equivalent of the "prevailing party" language that is found in other fee-shifting statutes.[36] Extrapolating from this conclusion and thus applying Buckhannon, the D.C. Circuit ruled that "in order for plaintiffs in FOIA actions to become eligible for an award of attorney's fees, they must have 'been awarded some relief by [a] court' either in a judgment on the merits or in a court-ordered consent decree."[37] In other words, unless a FOIA plaintiff obtains court-ordered relief on the merits of his complaint that results in a material alteration of the legal relationship between the parties,[38] there can be no eligibility for attorney fees[39] or costs.[40]

Indeed, in OCAW, the D.C. Circuit ultimately held that the plaintiff had not prevailed "[u]nder the rule of Buckhannon."[41] While the D.C. Circuit in OCAW found that a court-endorsed stipulation "arguably changed the legal status of the parties" insofar as it required the agency "to complete its record review in 60 days," that order did not in its eyes constitute "judicial relief on the merits of the [plaintiff's] complaint."[42] In its view, that order simply was an interim "procedural ruling," because both prior to and after its issuance the agency was not obliged "to turn over any documents."[43]

---

[35] 288 F.3d 452 (D.C. Cir. 2002).

[36] Id. at 455-56.

[37] Id. (quoting Buckhannon, 532 U.S. at 603); see also Campaign for Responsible Transplantation v. FDA, 448 F. Supp. 2d 146, 150 (D.D.C. 2006) (holding that plaintiff did not "substantially prevail," because FDA released documents voluntarily, not by any type of order).

[38] See id. at 458-59 (discussing Buckhannon's requirements).

[39] See id. at 457 ("Because Buckhannon controls, the existing law of our circuit must give way."); see also Davis v. Dep't of Justice, 460 F.3d 92, 106 (D.C. Cir. 2006) (denying fee eligibility where FBI released requested audiotapes voluntarily, rather than "pursuant to any judgment or order").

[40] See, e.g., McSheffrey v. Executive Office for U.S. Attorneys, No. 02-5401, 2003 WL 21538054, at *1 (D.C. Cir. July 2, 2003) (per curiam) (finding no distinction between the requirements for recovering attorney fees and litigation costs, and ruling that to obtain either there must be a "judgment on the merits or . . . a court-ordered consent decree" (citing OCAW, 288 F.3d at 456-57)).

[41] OCAW, 288 F.3d at 459.

[42] Id. at 458.

[43] Id.; see also Davis, 2006 WL 2411393, at *11 (holding that an appellate court order remanding the case for a segregability determination "is insuf-

(continued...)

## ATTORNEY FEES

In two significant decisions following <u>OCAW</u>, though, the D.C. Circuit found that fee eligibility had been established under the <u>Buckhannon</u> standard. Two years ago, in <u>Edmonds v. FBI</u>,[44] it found that <u>Buckhannon</u>'s requirements can be satisfied even where there is no "judgment by the court regarding the legality of the government's withholding of documents."[45] It concluded there that a district court order that compelled expedited processing and directed production of nonexempt records by a specific date altered the legal relationship of the parties and provided the plaintiff with relief on the merits.[46] Specifically, according to the D.C. Circuit in that case, the order did so by moving the plaintiff's request "to the head of the line" -- thereby providing "full relief" on a statutorily-provided expedited-processing claim -- and by mandating disclosure under "the court-designated deadline."[47] This, in turn, rendered the plaintiff eligible for an award of attorney fees.[48]

A year later, in <u>Davy v. CIA</u>,[49] the D.C. Circuit held that a district court order (memorializing a joint stipulation) that simply required production of nonexempt records by particular dates also satisfied <u>Buckhannon</u>.[50] It reached this conclusion even though the order, unlike the one at issue in <u>Edmonds</u>, did not concern expedited processing,[51] which is an independent cause of action under the FOIA.[52] The D.C. Circuit in <u>Davy</u> reasoned that the legal relationship of the parties had been altered because the order required the CIA to take an action that it otherwise had no duty to take

---

[43](...continued)
ficient to satisfy the <u>OCAW</u> test").

[44] 417 F.3d 1319 (D.C. Cir. 2005).

[45] <u>Id.</u> at 1323; <u>see also</u> <u>Cooke v. Ronald Reagan Presidential Library</u>, No. 05-6518, slip op. at 7-8 (C.D. Cal. Sept. 1, 2006) (awarding fees based upon "lenient" application of <u>Buckhannon</u> in Ninth Circuit (citing <u>Carbonell v. INS</u>, 429 F.3d 894, 898 (9th Cir. 2005) (non-FOIA case)).

[46] <u>See id.</u> at 1322-23.

[47] <u>Id.</u> at 1323-24.

[48] <u>Id.</u> at 1324.

[49] 456 F.3d 162 (D.C. Cir. 2006), <u>reh'g en banc denied</u>, No. 05-5151 (D.C. Cir. Sept. 18, 2006).

[50] <u>See id.</u> at 165.

[51] <u>See id.</u> at 164-65

[52] <u>See</u> 5 U.S.C. § 552(a)(6)(E)(i); <u>see also</u> <u>Edmonds</u>, 417 F.3d at 1324 (explaining that "right of expedition [is] judicially enforceable").

-- "producing documents by specific dates."[53]  Further, it said, the order amounted to "relief on the merits," as opposed to a mere procedural ruling, because it provided the plaintiff with the "precise relief [that] his complaint sought" -- prompt disclosure of the requested records.[54]  Notably, the D.C. Circuit attempted to distinguish its prior opinion in OCAW, which had denied fee eligibility by explaining that the OCAW order merely required the agency to conduct a search.[55]  As the dissent in OCAW had pointed out, however, the order in that case not only required the agency to complete its record review, it also directed the agency to disclose nonexempt portions of any documents within sixty-days.[56]

Following the D.C. Circuit's overall lead, an increasing number of courts have similarly recognized Buckhannon's applicability in the FOIA context.[57]  A few courts, however, have continued to adhere to the catalyst

---

[53] Davy, 456 F.3d at 165; see also Piper v. U.S. Dep't of Justice, 339 F. Supp. 2d 13, 19 (D.D.C. 2004) (concluding that an order reducing the FBI's Open America stay from four years to two years "changed the parties' legal status" by requiring processing of documents two years earlier than planned).  But see Nw. Coal. For Alternatives to Pesticides v. EPA, No. 99-437, 2007 U.S. Dist. LEXIS 8763, at *6-8 (D.D.C. Feb. 7, 2007) (finding that under Davy plaintiff has not "substantially prevailed" because, although Court's 2003 order remanding case to agency had changed legal relationship of parties, plaintiff was not awarded relief on merits of his claim when Court later found that agency had properly withheld contested documents); Campaign, 448 F. Supp. 2d at 151 (finding that order requiring FDA to produce more detailed Vaughn Index was "a procedural, rather than [a] substantive order," and that it did not change any legal relationship or provide the plaintiff with relief on merits).

[54] Davy, 456 F.3d at 165; see also Jarno v. DHS, 365 F. Supp. 2d 733, 737 (E.D. Va. 2005) (finding fee eligibility under Buckhannon, because the court-approved settlement agreement provided for release of nonexempt records by certain dates, and declaring that the plaintiff received "the relief he sought in his claim" -- documents responsive to his request).

[55] See Davy, 456 F.3d at 165 (distinguishing order in OCAW as one that "was procedural -- conduct a search[,] as opposed to substantive -- produce documents").

[56] See OCAW, 288 F.3d at 465 (Rogers, J., dissenting) (summarizing district court order).

[57] See, e.g., Union of Needletrades v. INS, 336 F.3d 200, 206 (2d Cir. 2003) (declaring that although plaintiff "accomplished the objective it sought to achieve" by bringing a FOIA suit, "its failure to secure either a judgment on the merits or a court-ordered consent decree renders it ineligible for an award of attorney's fees"); Poulsen v. U.S. Customs & Border Prot., No. 06-1743, 2007 WL 160945, at *1 (N.D. Cal. Jan. 17, 2007) (following Buckhan-
(continued...)

theory of fee eligibility.[58]

---

[57](...continued)

non standard to determine whether plaintiff is eligible for attorney fees); Peter S. Herrick's Customs & Int's Trade Newsletter v. United States Customs & Border Prot., No. 04-0377, 2006 WL 3060012, at *3 (D.D.C. Oct. 26, 2006) (applying Buckhannon standard to determine plaintiff's eligibility for fee award); Or. Natural Desert Ass'n, 2006 WL 2318610, at *1 (explaining that Buckhannon applies to fee eligibility determination in FOIA cases); Roberts v. Principi, No. 02:02-166, 2006 WL 169726, at *11 (E.D. Tenn. June 16, 2006) (finding, under Buckhannon standard, that plaintiff did not substantially prevail, because VA voluntarily disclosed requested records); Pac. Fisheries, Inc. v. IRS, No. 04-2436, 2006 WL 1635706, at *5 (W.D. Wash. June 1, 2006) (denying fees, even though the "lawsuit was necessary to compel the Service to provide an appropriate response to the FOIA request"); McCoy, 2005 WL 1972600, at *1 (finding plaintiff eligible for fee award under Buckhannon standard); Kahn v. Comm'r, No. 03-CV-6169, 2005 WL 1123733, at *2 (S.D.N.Y. May 11, 2005) (applying Buckhannon and finding that plaintiff was not prevailing party, because he obtained records sought in his Amended Complaint "without Court intervention"); Martinez v. EEOC, No. 04-CA-0271, 2005 U.S. Dist. LEXIS 3864, at *19 (W.D. Tex. Mar. 3, 2005) (rejecting plaintiff's assertion that he substantially prevailed based on mere fact that his suit prompted agency to release records); W&T Offshore, Inc. v. U.S. Dep't of Commerce, No. 03-2285, 2004 WL 2984343, at *2-3 (E.D. La. Dec. 23, 2004) (applying Buckhannon to reject plaintiff's claim for fees predicated on catalyst theory); Landers v. Dep't of the Air Force, 257 F. Supp. 2d 1011, 1012 (S.D. Ohio 2003) (finding no entitlement to attorney fees, despite the fact that lawsuit caused release of documents, because plaintiff "obtained no relief from this Court").

[58] See, e.g., Windel v. United States, No. 3:02-CV-306, 2006 WL 1036786, at *3 (D. Alaska Apr. 19, 2006) (explaining that fee eligibility is based on whether filing a lawsuit was "necessary" to obtain information and whether it had "a substantial causative effect on the delivery of information"); Pohlman, Inc. v. SBA, No. 4:03-CV-1241, slip op. at 27 (E.D. Mo. Sept. 30, 2005) (suggesting that plaintiff substantially prevailed because, in addition to court-ordered disclosure of some records, his lawsuit appeared to prompt agency's earlier voluntary release of other information); AutoAlliance Int'l, Inc. v. U.S. Customs Serv., 300 F. Supp. 2d 509, 513-14 (E.D. Mich. 2004) (declaring that Buckhannon standard applies to fee awards under FOIA, but finding eligibility based only on court-ordered agency review of records after which agency made voluntary disclosures), aff'd on other grounds, 155 F. App'x 226 (6th Cir. 2005); Read v. FAA, 252 F. Supp. 2d 1108, 1110-11 (W.D. Wash. 2003) (same); cf. Beacon Journal Publ'g Co. v. Gonzalez, No. 05-CV-1396, 2005 U.S. Dist. LEXIS 28109, at *3-8 (N.D. Ohio Nov. 16, 2005) (finding fee eligibility based on grant of summary judgment in favor of plaintiff, which followed agency's voluntary production of requested "mug shot" photographs); Albino, 2002 WL 32345674, at *8 (applying catalyst theory to find that plaintiff substantially prevailed because agency re-

(continued...)

Attorney Fees and Litigation Costs:  Entitlement

Even if a plaintiff satisfies the threshold eligibility standards, a court still must exercise its equitable discretion in separately determining whether that plaintiff is entitled to an attorney fee award.[59]  This discretion ordinarily is guided by four traditional criteria that derive from the FOIA's legislative history.[60]  These factors are:  (1) the public benefit derived from the case; (2) the commercial benefit to the complainant; (3) the nature of the complainant's interest in the records sought; and (4) whether the government's withholding had a reasonable basis in law.[61]  These four entitlement factors, of course, have nothing to do with determining an appropriate fee amount; therefore, they cannot be considered in that entirely sepa-

---

[58](...continued)
sponded to FOIA request after suit was filed, but denying fees because plaintiff was proceeding pro se).

[59] See Young v. Dir., No. 92-2561,1993 WL 305970, at *2 (4th Cir. Aug. 10, 1993) ("Even if a plaintiff substantially prevails, however, a district court may nevertheless, in its discretion, deny the fees."); Texas v. ICC, 935 F.2d 728, 733 (5th Cir. 1991) ("The district court did not specify which of the criteria [plaintiff] failed to satisfy.  But so long as the record supports the court's exercise of discretion, the decision will stand.").

[60] See S. Rep. No. 93-854, at 19 (1974); cf. Cotton v. Heyman, 63 F.3d 1115, 1123 (D.C. Cir. 1995) (declining to review remaining factors after finding no public benefit from release and recognizing reasonableness of agency's position).  But cf. Judicial Watch, Inc. v. Dep't of Commerce, 384 F. Supp. 2d 163, 169 (D.D.C. 2005) (suggesting that "in addition to the four factors," the agency's conduct -- which was found to have "likely" involved the destruction and removal of documents, and which was deemed to have demonstrated a "lack of respect for the FOIA process -- would tip the balance in favor of a fee award").

[61] See Detroit Free Press, Inc. v. Dep't of Justice, 73 F.3d 93, 98 (6th Cir. 1996); Cotton, 63 F.3d at 1117; Tax Analysts v. U.S. Dep't of Justice, 965 F.2d 1092, 1093 (D.C. Cir. 1992); Church of Scientology v. USPS, 700 F.2d 486, 492 (9th Cir. 1983); Fenster v. Brown, 617 F.2d 740, 742-45 (D.C. Cir. 1979); Cuneo v. Rumsfeld, 553 F.2d 1360, 1364-66 (D.C. Cir. 1977).  But see also Burka v. HHS, 142 F.3d 1286, 1293 (D.C. Cir. 1998) (Randolph, J., concurring) ("Although we have applied these criteria in the past, they deserve another look."); see also Herrick's Newsletter, 2006 WL 3060012, at *11 (holding that an award of attorney fees is inappropriate "[g]iven the modest amount of court-ordered relief, the minimal public benefit conferred by the released information, plaintiff's overriding commercial and professional interest in the materials, and Customs' reasonable and largely correct legal position").

rate analysis.[62]

While any FOIA disclosure hypothetically benefits the public by generally increasing public knowledge about the government, this "broadly defined benefit" is not what Congress had in mind when it provided for awards of attorney fees.[63] Rather, the "public benefit" factor ""speaks for an award [of attorney fees] when the complainant's victory is likely to add to the fund of information that citizens may use in making vital political choices.""[64] Such a determination, which necessarily entails an evaluation of the nature of the specific information disclosed,[65] has led to findings of "public benefit" in a variety of contexts.[66] Highly pertinent considerations in this "public benefit" inquiry are "the degree of dissemination and [the] likely public impact that might be expected from a particular disclosure."[67] When

---

[62] See Long v. IRS, 932 F.2d 1309, 1315-16 (9th Cir. 1991).

[63] Cotton, 63 F.3d at 1120 (citing Fenster, 617 F.2d at 744); see Klamath Water Users Protective Ass'n v. U.S. Dep't of the Interior, 18 F. App'x 473, 475 (9th Cir. 2001) (declining to award attorney fees for the release of documents "having marginal public interest and little relevance to the making of political choices by citizens").

[64] Cotton, 63 F.3d at 1120 (quoting Fenster, 617 F.2d at 744 (quoting, in turn, Blue v. Bureau of Prisons, 570 F.2d 529, 534 (5th Cir. 1978))).

[65] See Cotton, 63 F.3d at 1120.

[66] See, e.g., Hull v. U.S. Dep't of Labor, No. 04-CV-1264, 2006 U.S. Dist. LEXIS 35054, at *6 (D. Colo. May 30, 2006) (finding public benefit from disclosure of records concerning Department of Labor's investigation of corporate pension plan, because "millions of Americans" have interest in agency's effort to ensure "that private pension plans remain solvent and viable"); PETA v. USDA, No. 03-195, 2006 WL 508332, at *3 (D.D.C. Mar. 3, 2006) (recognizing public benefit in disclosure of records that permit public to "assess" whether USDA complied with regulations when it made loan guarantee to large distributor of puppies); McCoy v. Fed. Bureau of Prisons, No. 03-383, 2005 WL 1972600, at *1 (E.D. Ky. Aug. 16, 2005) (concluding that the release of records concerning the death of an inmate in the Bureau of Prisons' custody served the public's interest "in ensuring that the BOP fulfills its statutory duty to safeguard the well-being of individuals in its custody"), reconsideration denied (E.D. Ky. Oct. 6, 2005); Jarno v. DHS, 365 F. Supp. 2d 733, 738 (E.D. Va. 2005) (finding public interest to have been served by release of records regarding DHS's handling of plaintiff's high-profile asylum case); Piper v. U.S. Dep't of Justice, 339 F. Supp. 2d 13, 21 (D.D.C. 2004) (finding public benefit through disclosure of information concerning allegations of evidence tampering by FBI personnel).

[67] Blue, 570 F.2d at 533; Church of Scientology, 769 F. Supp. at 331 (recognizing a public interest in "the apparently improper designation of a religion as a 'tax shelter' project"); see Polynesian Cultural Ctr. v. NLRB, 600

(continued...)

the information released is already in the public domain, of course, this factor does not weigh in favor of a fee award.[68]

On the other hand "[m]inimal, incidental and speculative public benefit will not suffice" to satisfy the requirements of subsection (a)(4)(E).[69] It is

---

[67](...continued)
F.2d 1327, 1330 (9th Cir. 1979) (per curiam) (denying fees when "disclosure was unlikely to result in widespread dissemination, or substantial public benefit"); Hull, 2006 U.S. Dist. LEXIS 35054, at *5 (finding planned dissemination -- free of charge -- through posting on association's Web site to be "key factor" in public benefit analysis); Long v. IRS, No. 74-724, 2006 WL 1041818, at *5 (W.D. Wash. Apr. 3, 2006) (finding public benefit based on plaintiff's assertion that statistical data requested from IRS was "critical" to her organization's "efforts to monitor and [publicly] disseminate information on IRS activities") (appeal pending); Jarno, 365 F. Supp. 2d at 738-40 ("The wide dissemination to the press and public . . . establish[ed] that the public benefitted from the government's FOIA response."); OCAW v. U.S. Dep't of Energy, 141 F. Supp. 2d 1, 5 & n.7 (D.D.C. 2001) (concluding that public benefit factor was met by wide dissemination of information released as result of lawsuit), rev'd on other grounds, 288 F.3d 452 (D.C. Cir. 2002). Compare Piper, 339 F. Supp. 2d at 22 (accepting "plaintiff's unequivocal representations . . . that he is going to write a book," and viewing it as "unlikely that plaintiff would continually engage in this litigious battle had he just planned to store . . . 80,000 documents in a room somewhere and browse through them at his leisure"), with Frydman v. Dep't of Justice, 852 F. Supp. 1497, 1503 (D. Kan. 1994) (deciding that requester's suggestion that he might write book was "too speculative to warrant much weight"), aff'd, 57 F.3d 1080 (10th Cir. 1995) (unpublished table decision).

[68] See, e.g., Tax Analysts, 965 F.2d at 1094 (affirming district court's finding that more prompt reporting by Tax Analysts of additional twenty-five percent of publicly available district court tax decisions was "less than overwhelming" contribution to public interest); Laughlin v. Comm'r, 117 F. Supp. 2d 997, 1002 (S.D. Cal. 2000) (declining to award fees for disclosure of document that is "readily accessible commercially"); Petroleum Info. Corp. v. U.S. Dep't of the Interior, No. 89-3173, slip op. at 5-6 (D.D.C. Nov. 16, 1993) (holding that public benefit is only "slight" where litigation resulted in disclosure of information in electronic form that was previously publicly available in printed form). But cf. PETA, 2006 WL 508332, at *4 (finding the existence of a "limited" public benefit, despite the agency's release of "the bulk of the requested information" before the lawsuit was commenced).

[69] Aviation Data Serv. v. FAA, 687 F.2d 1319, 1323 (10th Cir. 1982); see Ellis v. United States, 941 F. Supp. 1068, 1078 (D. Utah 1996) ("[T]he successful FOIA plaintiff always achieves some degree of public benefit by bringing the government into compliance with FOIA and by the benefit assumed to flow from public disclosure of government information."); Bangor
(continued...)

similarly unavailing to show simply that the prosecution of the suit has compelled an agency to improve the efficiency of its FOIA processing.[70]

Moreover, it has been held by the D.C. Circuit that the notion of "public benefit" should not be grounded solely on "the potential release of present and future information" resulting from the legal precedent set by the case in which fees are sought.[71] As the D.C. Circuit perceptively noted in

---

[69](...continued)
Hydro-Elec. Co. v. U.S. Dep't of the Interior, 903 F. Supp. 169, 171 (D. Me. 1995) ("[B]y definition a successful FOIA plaintiff always confers some degree of benefit on the public by bringing the government into compliance with FOIA . . . ."); Texas, 935 F.2d at 733-34 (suggesting that there is "little public benefit" in disclosure of documents that fail to reflect agency wrongdoing: "Texas went fishing for bass and landed an old shoe. Under the circumstances, we decline to require the federal government to pay the cost of tackle."). But see Cottone v. FBI, No. 94-1598, slip op. at 3 (D.D.C. Mar. 16, 2001) (citing Williams v. FBI, 17 F. Supp. 2d 6, 9 (D.D.C. 1997), to justify awarding fees in order to encourage service on Civil Pro Bono Counsel panel), appeal dismissed voluntarily, No. 01-5159 (D.C. Cir. July 26, 2001); Landano v. U.S. Dep't of Justice, 873 F. Supp. 884, 892 (D.N.J. 1994) ("Here, the public clearly benefits from this disclosure since it has an interest in the fair and just administration of the criminal justice system as [applied to the plaintiff].").

[70] See Read v. FAA, 252 F. Supp. 2d 1108, 1110-11 (W.D. Wash. 2003) (refusing to find that mere act of bringing lawsuit without resultant release of records conferred public benefit warranting attorney fees); Solone v. IRS, 830 F. Supp. 1141, 1143 (N.D. Ill. 1993) ("While the public would benefit from the court's imprimatur to the IRS to comply voluntarily with the provisions of the FOIA, this is not the type of benefit that FOIA attorneys' fees were intended to generate."); Muffoletto v. Sessions, 760 F. Supp. 268, 277 (E.D.N.Y. 1991) (maintaining that public benefit in compelling FBI to act more expeditiously is insufficient).

[71] Cotton, 63 F.3d at 1120; see Chesapeake Bay Found. v. USDA, 108 F.3d 375, 377 (D.C. Cir. 1997) ("Nor is the establishment of a legal right to information a public benefit for the purpose of awarding attorneys' fees." (citing Cotton, 63 F.3d at 1120)); see also Bangor Hydro-Elec., 903 F. Supp. at 170 (rejecting argument that public benefitted by precedent that would "allow other utilities to easily acquire similar documents for the benefit of those utilities ratepayers"). But see Church of Scientology, 700 F.2d at 493 (declaring that an appellate ruling that a specific statutory provision does not qualify under Exemption 3 "in our view, benefits the public"); Aronson v. HUD, 866 F.2d 1, 3 (1st Cir. 1989) (suggesting that public interest is served by disclosure to "private tracer" of information concerning mortgagors who were owed "distributive share" refunds); Cottone, No. 94-1598, slip op. at 2 (D.D.C. Mar. 16, 2001) (accepting plaintiff's argument of public benefit deriving from the "precedential effect of [his] victory," while at the
(continued...)

one case: "Such an inherently speculative observation is . . . inconsistent with the structure of FOIA itself."[72]

The second factor -- the commercial benefit to the plaintiff -- requires an examination of whether the plaintiff had an adequate private commercial incentive to litigate its FOIA demand even in the absence of an award of attorney fees. If so, then fees should be denied,[73] except in the case of news media interests, which generally "should not be considered commercial interests."[74]

---

[71](...continued)
same time recognizing "binding circuit precedent" to the contrary).

[72] Cotton, 63 F.3d at 1120.

[73] See, e.g., Klamath, 18 F. App'x at 475 (finding that plaintiff association sought documents to advance and protect interests of its members, and recognizing that fact that members might be "nonprofit" does not make their interests less commercial for FOIA purposes); Fenster, 617 F.2d at 742-44 (affirming denial of fees to law firm that obtained disclosure of government auditor's manual used in reviewing contracts of the type entered into by firm's clients); Chamberlain v. Kurtz, 589 F.2d 827, 842-43 (5th Cir. 1979) (concluding that plaintiff who faced $1.8 million deficiency claim for back taxes and penalties "needed no additional incentive" to bring FOIA suit against IRS for documents relevant to his defense); Horsehead Indus. v. EPA, 999 F. Supp. 59, 69 (D.D.C. 1998) (finding that requester would have brought suit regardless of availability of fees); Viacom Int'l v. EPA, No. 95-2243, 1996 WL 515505, at *2 (E.D. Pa. Aug. 29, 1996) (dismissing as "divorced from reality" corporation's contention that its "'knowing the extent of its potential liability will not promote any commercial interests'"); Frye v. EPA, No. 90-3041, 1992 WL 237370, at *4 (D.D.C. Aug. 31, 1992) (denying fees where "plaintiff does not effectively dispute that the prime beneficiaries of the information requested will be commercial entities with commercial interests that either are, or might become, his clients"); Hill Tower, Inc. v. Dep't of the Navy, 718 F. Supp. 568, 572 (N.D. Tex. 1989) (ruling that a plaintiff who had filed tort claims against the government arising from aircraft crash "had a strong commercial interest in seeking [related] information [as] it was [its] antenna that was damaged by the crash"). But see Aronson, 866 F.2d at 3 (finding that the "potential for commercial personal gain did not negate the public interest served" by private tracer's lawsuit since "failure of HUD to comply reasonably with its reimbursement duty would probably only be disclosed by someone with a specific interest in ferreting out unpaid recipients"); Windel v. United States, No. 3:02-CV-306, 2006 WL 1036786, at *3 (D. Alaska Apr. 19, 2006) (awarding portion of requested fees, even though plaintiff's FOIA request "clearly implicated her own pecuniary interests" in obtaining documents concerning her gender discrimination claim).

[74] S. Rep. No. 93-854, at 19 (1974), quoted in Fenster, 617 F.2d at 742 n.4;
(continued...)

The third factor -- the nature of the plaintiff's interest in the records -- often is evaluated in tandem with the second factor[75] and militates against awarding fees in cases where the plaintiff had an adequate personal incentive to seek judicial relief.[76] To disqualify a fee applicant under the second and third factors, "a motive need not be strictly commercial; any private interest will do."[77] In this regard, the use of the FOIA as a substitute for dis-

---

[74](...continued)
accord FOIA Update, Vol. VIII, No. 1, at 10 ("New Fee Waiver Policy Guidance").

[75] See, e.g., Church of Scientology, 700 F.2d at 494 (noting that it is "logical to read the two criteria together where a private plaintiff has pursued a private interest").

[76] See, e.g., Polynesian Cultural Ctr., 600 F.2d at 1330 (ruling that attorney fees award should not "'merely subsidize a matter of private concern' at taxpayer expense" (quoting Blue, 570 F.2d at 533-34)); Nw. Univ. v. USDA, 403 F. Supp. 2d 83, 88 & n.7 (D.D.C. 2005) (denying fee award where plaintiff sought records concerning investigations into its activities for apparent purpose of challenging agency's findings); Tran v. U.S. Dep't of Justice, No. 01-0238, 2001 U.S. Dist. LEXIS 21552, at *15 (D.D.C. Nov. 20, 2001) (refusing to award fees, because suit was brought "entirely for [plaintiff's] own benefit, [his] having requested only documents and records pertaining to himself"); Viacom, 1996 WL 515505, at *2 ("[W]e harbor strong doubts that Viacom entered into this proceeding to foster the public interest in disclosure. Its motivation, as evinced by its conduct of this litigation, was to assert its own interests as a potentially responsible party to the clean up operation."); Abernethy v. IRS, 909 F. Supp. 1562, 1569 (N.D. Ga. 1995) (suggesting that when plaintiff sought records of investigation of which he was target to challenge his removal from management position, his "strong personal motivation for filing this lawsuit outweigh[ed] any public interest which may result from disclosure"); Frydman, 852 F. Supp. at 1504 ("Although plaintiff's interest in the information in this case is not pecuniary, it is strictly personal."). But see Crooker v. U.S. Parole Comm'n, 776 F.2d 366, 368 (1st Cir. 1985) (finding the third factor to favor plaintiff where the "interest was neither commercial nor frivolous, [but] to ensure that the Parole Commission relied on accurate information in making decisions affecting his liberty"); Piper, 339 F. Supp. 2d at 21-22 (concluding that because plaintiff's "distinct personal interest" in writing book about his mother's kidnapping was not separable from public interest in this "scholarly endeavor," second factor will not weigh against fee award); Williams, 17 F. Supp. 2d at 9 (awarding fees "[e]ven if [the requester's] own interest in the records is personal," in order to "serve the larger public purpose of encouraging" representation by pro bono counsel).

[77] Tax Analysts, 965 F.2d at 1095 ("'[P]laintiff was not motivated simply by altruistic instincts, but rather by its desire for efficient, easy access to [tax] decisions.'" (quoting Tax Analysts v. U.S. Dep't of Justice, 759 F. Supp.
(continued...)

covery has routinely been found to constitute the pursuit of a private, non-compensable interest.[78] And if a FOIA plaintiff's motives, in a rare case, should change over the course of the litigation, in that case a court should bifurcate the fee award on the basis of such shifting interests.[79]

The fourth factor -- the reasonableness of the agency's withholding -- counsels against a fee award when the agency had a reasonable basis in law for concluding that the information in issue was exempt. If an agency's position is correct as a matter of law, this factor should be disposi-

---

[77](...continued)
28, 31 (D.D.C. 1991))); see Bangor Hydro-Elec., 903 F. Supp. at 171 (rejecting public utility's argument that it incurred no commercial benefit because under "'traditional regulatory principles'" utility would be obliged to pass any commercial gain on to its ratepayers); Mosser Constr. Co. v. U.S. Dep't of Labor, No. 93CV7525, slip op. at 4 (N.D. Ohio Mar. 29, 1994) (explaining that factor weighs against not-for-profit organization whose actions are motivated by commercially related concerns on behalf of its members). But see Assembly of Cal v. U.S. Dep't of Commerce, No. Civ-S-91-990, 1993 WL 188328, at *5 (E.D. Cal. May 28, 1993) (refusing to preclude fees where state legislature sought information to challenge federal census count, even though benefits could accrue to state, because "plaintiffs did not stand to personally benefit but acted as public servants").

[78] See, e.g., Ellis, 941 F. Supp. at 1079 (compiling cases); Muffoletto, 760 F. Supp. at 275 (rejecting plaintiff's entitlement to fees on grounds that "[t]he plaintiff's sole motivation in seeking the requested information was for discovery purposes, namely, to assist him in the defense of a private civil action"); Republic of New Afrika v. FBI, 645 F. Supp. 117, 121 (D.D.C. 1986) (stating that purely personal motives of plaintiff -- to exonerate its members of criminal charges and to circumvent civil discovery -- dictated against award of fees), aff'd sub nom. Provisional Gov't of the Republic of New Afrika v. ABC, 821 F.2d 821 (D.C. Cir. 1987) (unpublished table decision); Simon v. United States, 587 F. Supp. 1029, 1033 (D.D.C. 1984) (articulating that use of FOIA as substitute for civil discovery "is not proper and this court will not encourage it by awarding fees"). But see McCoy, 2005 WL 1972600, at *2 (finding fee entitlement, even though plaintiff's FOIA request "served her personal interest in obtaining . . . evidence" for use in related tort litigation); cf. Jarno, 365 F. Supp. 2d at 740 (concluding that plaintiff's interest in the requested documents "support[ed] an award of attorney's fees," despite his motivation to seek disclosure in order to "facilitate the fair adjudication of his political asylum claim").

[79] See, e.g., Anderson v. HHS, 80 F.3d 1500, 1504-05 (10th Cir. 1996) (affirming district court's denial of fees for first phase of litigation -- when plaintiff's primary motive was to obtain records for state court action, while approving them for second phase -- when plaintiff's primary interest in records was public dissemination).

tive.[80] The converse, however, also may be true -- namely, that "[r]ecalcitrant and obdurate behavior 'can make the last factor dispositive without consideration of any of the other factors.'"[81]

Of course, if an agency had even so much as a "colorable basis in law" for withholding information, then this factor should be weighed with other relevant considerations to determine entitlement.[82] In general, an agency's

---

[80] See Chesapeake Bay Found. v. USDA, 11 F.3d 211, 216 (D.C. Cir. 1993) ("If the Government was right in claiming that the [records] were exempt from disclosure under FOIA, then no fees are recoverable."); Cotton, 63 F.3d at 1117 ("[T]here can be no doubt that a party is not entitled to fees if the government's legal basis for withholding requested records is correct."); Polynesian Cultural Ctr., 600 F.2d at 1330 (denying fees, despite court-ordered disclosure, because "[t]he Board's claim of exemption was not only reasonable, but correct," based upon subsequent Supreme Court decision); Horsehead Indus., 999 F. Supp. at 64 (ruling that "fees will not be awarded" when agency's withholding "is correct as a matter of law"); see also Wheeler v. IRS, 37 F. Supp. 2d 407, 413 (W.D. Pa. 1998) (finding that reasons for government's refusal to disclose records "may even be dispositive"). But see Cottone, No. 94-1598, slip op. at 3-4 (D.D.C. Mar. 16, 2001) (awarding fees even though agency's position was reasonable; relying on fact that agency's defense was "determined, dilatory, and expensive to confront"); Williams, 17 F. Supp. 2d at 8 (stating that "'courts must be careful not to give any particular factor dispositive weight'" (quoting Nationwide Bldg. Maint., Inc. v. Sampson, 559 F.2d 704, 714 (D.C. Cir. 1977))); cf. Nw. Coal. for Alternatives to Pesticides v. EPA, 421 F. Supp. 2d 123, 128-29 (D.D.C. 2006) (finding plaintiff entitled to a fee award, even though the court never ruled that the agency's withholdings were improper, on the basis that a previous remand order obligated the EPA to articulate its reasons for withholding and "[a]t that juncture . . . the EPA had not demonstrated a reasonable basis for withholding").

[81] Read, 252 F. Supp. 2d at 1112 (quoting Horsehead Indus., 999 F. Supp. at 68); see also Allen v. INS, No. 80-2246 (D.D.C. July 20, 1981) (awarding attorney fees based upon single factor of "reasonableness").

[82] Tax Analysts, 965 F.2d at 1097 (quoting Cuneo, 553 F.2d at 1365-66)); Educ./Instruccion, Inc. v. HUD, 649 F.2d 4, 8 (1st Cir. 1981) (government's withholding must "have 'a colorable basis in law' and not appear designed 'merely to avoid embarrassment or to frustrate the requester'" (quoting S. Rep. No. 93-854, at 19)); LaSalle Extension Univ. v. FTC, 627 F.2d 481, 484-86 (D.C. Cir. 1980); Fenster, 617 F.2d at 744; Hull v. U.S. Dep't of Labor, No. 04-CV-1264, 2006 U.S. Dist. LEXIS 35054, at *11 (D. Colo. May 30, 2006) (finding agency's withholding determination, based on "colorable legal argument," to be reasonable, but concluding that other factors weighed in favor of fee award); Ellis, 941 F. Supp. at 1080 (government need show only "reasonable or colorable basis for the withholding" and that it has not engaged in recalcitrant or obdurate behavior); Solone, 830 F. Supp. at 1143

(continued...)

legal basis for withholding is "reasonable" if pertinent authority exists to support the claimed exemption.[83] Even in the absence of supporting authority, withholding may also be "reasonable" where no precedent directly contradicts the agency's position.[84]

In an illustrative example, the D.C. Circuit upheld a district court's finding of reasonableness in a case in which there was "no clear precedent on the issue,"[85] even though the district court's decision in favor of the agency's withholding was reversed unanimously by the court of appeals, which decision, in turn, was affirmed by a near-unanimous decision of the Supreme Court.[86] Similarly, the mere fact that an agency foregoes an appeal on the merits of a case and complies with a district court disclosure order does not foreclose it from asserting the reasonableness of its original position in opposing a subsequent fee claim.[87] When the delay in releasing records, rather than the agency's substantive claim of exemption, is challenged, that delay does not favor a fee award so long as the agency has not

---

[82](...continued)
(government acted reasonably when agency had "at least a colorable basis in law for its decision to withhold" and there are no allegations of harassment of requester or avoidance of embarrassment by the agency).

[83] See Adams v. United States, 673 F. Supp. 1249, 1259-60 (S.D.N.Y. 1987); see also Am. Commercial Barge Lines v. NLRB, 758 F.2d 1109, 1112-14 (6th Cir. 1985); Republic of New Afrika, 645 F. Supp. at 122. But see United Ass'n of Journeymen & Apprentices, Local 598 v. Dep't of the Army, 841 F.2d 1459, 1462-64 (9th Cir. 1988) (withholding held unreasonable where agency relied on one case that was "clearly distinguishable" and where "strong contrary authority [was] cited by the [plaintiff]"); Nw. Coal. for Alternatives to Pesticides v. Browner, 965 F. Supp. 59, 64 (D.D.C. 1997) (finding that an EPA decision "to rely solely on manufacturers' claims of confidentiality, rather than conduct more extensive questioning of the manufacturers' claims or make its own inquiry . . . was essentially a decision not to commit resources to questioning claims of confidentiality but instead to confront issues as they arise in litigation -- and to pay attorneys' fees if EPA loses").

[84] See Frydman, 852 F. Supp. at 1504 ("Although the government did not offer case authority to support its position regarding the [records], we believe the government's position had a colorable basis. There is little, if any, case authority which directly holds contrary to the government's position.").

[85] Tax Analysts, 965 F.2d at 1096-97.

[86] Tax Analysts v. Dep't of Justice, 492 U.S. 136 (1989).

[87] See Cotton, 63 F.3d at 1119.

engaged in "obdurate behavior or bad faith."[88] But an agency's decision to withhold entire documents when it could have redacted them relatively easily has been found "unreasonable" for purposes of the entitlement analysis.[89] (For further discussions of an agency's obligation to segregate and

---

[88] Ellis, 941 F. Supp. at 1080 (noting that agency was "in frequent contact with plaintiffs' counsel" and that "[d]ue to the scope of plaintiffs' request, some delay was inherent"); see Hull, 2006 U.S. Dist. LEXIS 35054, at *12 (viewing agency delays as "more suggestive of ineptitude than bad faith"); Read, 252 F. Supp. 2d at 1112 ("[D]elay due to bureaucratic ineptitude alone is not sufficient to weigh in favor of an award of attorney's fees."); Horsehead Indus. 999 F. Supp. at 66 (finding that narrow reading of request is not "bad faith"); Republic of New Afrika v. FBI, 645 F. Supp. at 122; Smith v. United States, No. 95-1950, 1996 WL 696452, at *7 (E.D. La. Dec. 4, 1996) (finding that "[t]he government did not act with due diligence, and has offered no reason to find that the delay was 'unavoidable[,]'" but holding in favor of the government on this factor as "[t]he evidence in this case is that the Coast Guard's noncompliance was due to administrative ineptitude rather than any unwillingness to comply with [plaintiff's] FOIA request"), aff'd, No. 97-30184 (5th Cir. Sept. 12, 1997); Frye, No. 90-3041, 1992 WL 237370, at *3 (explaining that although agency failed to adequately explain plaintiff's more-than-two-year wait for final response (such delay previously having been found "unreasonable" by court), agency's voluntary disclosure of documents two days before Vaughn Index deadline did not warrant finding of "obdurate" behavior absent affirmative evidence of bad faith). But see Jarno, 365 F. Supp. 2d at 740 (determining that the fourth factor favored a fee award, because the agency "failed to comply with the requirements of [the] FOIA by not responding to Plaintiff's request for information within the statutory time frame"); Miller v. U.S. Dep't of State, 779 F.2d 1378, 1390 (8th Cir. 1985) ("While these reasons [for delay] are plausible, and we do not find them to be evidence of bad faith . . . they are practical explanations, not reasonable legal bases."); Claudio v. Soc. Sec. Admin., No. H-98-1911, 2000 WL 33379041, at *11 (S.D. Tex. May 24, 2000) (despite finding all four factors unmet, nevertheless awarding fees because of "the Government's action in not delivering the majority of the documents until after suit was filed and in failing to provide a Vaughn Index until after ordered to do so by the Court"); United Merchants & Mfrs. v. Meese, No. 87-3367, slip op. at 3 (D.D.C. Aug. 10, 1988) (declaring it unnecessary for plaintiff to show "that defendant was obdurate in order to prevail" where there was "no reasonable basis for defendant to have failed to process plaintiff's [FOIA request] for nearly a year").

[89] See Poulsen, 2007 WL 160945, at *2 (holding that agency's position was not substantially justified because, in many instances, agency's redactions were "inconsistent and seemingly without reasoned basis"); Long, 2006 WL 1041818, at *4-5 (concluding that IRS lacked reasonable basis to fully withhold audit statistics on grounds that disclosure could somehow identify individual taxpayer returns; if necessary, "IRS could [have] redact-[ed]" this information); McCoy, 2005 WL 1972600, at *2 (finding that the Bu-
(continued...)

release nonexempt information, see Procedural Requirements, "Reasonably Segregable" Obligation, above, and Litigation Considerations, "Reasonably Segregable" Requirements, above.)

Typically, FOIA plaintiffs seek attorney fees only at the conclusion of a case. Even when the underlying action has been decided, a petition for attorney fees "survive[s] independently under the court's equitable jurisdiction."[90] The fact that an attorney fees petition is pending, moreover, does not preclude appellate review of the district court's decision on the merits.[91]

Some FOIA plaintiffs, however, have sought "interim" attorney fees before the conclusion of a case -- although such relief has been termed "inefficient"[92] and "piecemeal."[93] It is almost always clearer at the end of a FOIA case whether a plaintiff has "substantially prevailed," but sometimes a plaintiff can point to a threshold determination concerning eligibility to receive records that sufficiently supports eligibility to an interim award.[94] Of course, a plaintiff still must prove entitlement to an interim award.[95] If

---

[89](...continued)
reau of Prisons had no reasonable basis to withhold requested documents in their entireties in order to protect the privacy of third parties; "[w]hile the duty to withhold certain identifying information . . . is supported by case law, withholding the information in its entireties was not necessary").

[90] Carter v. VA, 780 F.2d 1479, 1481 (9th Cir. 1986); see Anderson v. HHS, 3 F.3d 1383, 1385 (10th Cir. 1993) ("[T]he fee issue is ancillary to the merits of the controversy.").

[91] See McDonnell v. United States, 4 F.3d 1227, 1236 (3d Cir. 1993) ("Even if a motion for attorney's fees is still pending in the district court, that motion does not constitute a bar to our exercise of jurisdiction under § 1291." (citing Budinich v. Becton Dickinson & Co., 486 U.S. 196, 198-202 (1988))).

[92] Biberman v. FBI, 496 F. Supp. 263, 265 (S.D.N.Y. 1980) (noting "inefficiency" of interim fee award); see Allen v. FBI, 716 F. Supp. 667, 669-72 (D.D.C. 1989) (recognizing that although court may order payment of interim fees, it should be done only "in limited circumstances").

[93] Hydron Labs., Inc. v. EPA, 560 F. Supp. 718, 722 (D.R.I. 1983) (refusing to deal "piecemeal" with questions concerning entitlement to attorney fees).

[94] See Wash. Post v. DOD, 789 F. Supp. 423, 424-26 (D.D.C. 1992) (awarding interim fees for special master whose work established plaintiff's right to receive certain records); Allen v. DOD, 713 F. Supp. 7, 12-13 (D.D.C. 1989) (awarding interim fees, but only "for work leading toward the threshold release of non-exempt documents").

[95] See Nat'l Ass'n of Criminal Def. Lawyers v. U.S. Dep't of Justice, No.
(continued...)

interim fees are approved, payment of the fees need not await final judgment in the action.[96] If an agency wishes to appeal an interim award, however, it must wait for a final court decision on the underlying merits of the case.[97]

### Attorney Fees and Litigation Costs:  Calculations

If a court decides to make a fee award -- either interim or otherwise -- its next task is to determine an appropriate fee amount, based upon attorney time shown to have been reasonably expended.  Fee claims should be supported by well-documented, contemporaneous billing records;[98] while

---

[95](...continued)
97-372, slip op. at 2 (D.D.C. June 26, 1998) (awarding interim fees based on court's conclusion that, inter alia, even brief litigation had "imposed concrete hardship on Plaintiff's counsel"), interlocutory appeal dismissed for lack of juris., 182 F.3d 981 (D.C. Cir. 1999); Allen v. FBI, 716 F. Supp. at 671 (suggesting that interim fee awards should be made only in unusual case of protracted litigation and financial hardship); Powell v. U.S. Dep't of Justice, 569 F. Supp. 1192, 1200 (N.D. Cal. 1983) (listing four factors to be considered in court's discretion for award of interim fees).

[96] See Rosenfeld v. United States, 859 F.2d 717, 727 (9th Cir. 1988); Wash. Post, 789 F. Supp. at 425.

[97] See Nat'l Ass'n of Criminal Def. Lawyers v. U.S. Dep't of Justice, 182 F.3d 981, 986 (D.C. Cir. 1999) (concluding that prior to conclusion of case in district court, appellate court has no jurisdiction to review attorney fees award); see also Petties v. District of Columbia, 227 F.3d 469, 472 (D.C. Cir. 2000) (emphasizing that interim review of attorney fees decision is unavailable until final judgment is reached) (non-FOIA case).

[98] See Blazy v. Tenet, 194 F.3d 90, 92 (D.C. Cir. 1999) (rejecting otherwise-valid claim for attorney fees "for want of substantiation"); Nat'l Ass'n of Concerned Veterans v. Sec'y of Def., 675 F.2d 1319, 1327 (D.C. Cir. 1982) (per curiam) ("Attorneys who anticipate making a fee application must maintain contemporaneous, complete and standardized time records which accurately reflect the work done by each attorney."); Pohlman, Inc. v. SBA, No. 4:03-CV-1241, slip op. at 27-28 (E.D. Mo. Sept. 30, 2005) (chiding plaintiff for failing to support fee request with documentation of time expended on lawsuit); Ajluni v. FBI, No. 94-CV-325, 1997 WL 196047, at *2 (N.D.N.Y. Apr. 14, 1997) ("Moreover, '[t]he rule in this Circuit prohibits the submission of reconstructed records, where no contemporaneous records have been kept.'" (quoting Lenihan v. City of N.Y., 640 F. Supp. 822, 824 (S.D.N.Y. 1986))); cf. Poulsen, 2007 WL 160945, at *3 (finding that agency's "challenge to the reasonableness of plaintiff's fee request is conclusory and that [agency] did not meet its 'burden of providing specific evidence to challenge the accuracy and reasonableness of the hours charged'" (quoting McGrath v. County of Nevada, 67 F.3d 248, 255 (9th Cir. 1995))).

some courts will consider reconstructed records,[99] the amount ultimately awarded may be reduced accordingly.[100]

The starting point in setting a fee award is to multiply the number of hours reasonably expended by a reasonable hourly rate -- a calculation that yields the "lodestar."[101] Not all hours expended in litigating a case will be deemed to have been "reasonably" expended. For example, courts have directed attorneys to subtract hours spent litigating claims upon which the party seeking the fee ultimately did not prevail.[102] In such cases, a distinction has been made between a loss on a legal theory where "the issue was

---

[99] See, e.g., Judicial Watch, Inc. v. Dep't of Commerce, 384 F. Supp. 2d 163, 173-74 (D.D.C. 2005) (awarding fees based on records reconstructed by former colleague of attorney who handled FOIA suit).

[100] See Anderson v. HHS, 80 F.3d 1500, 1506 (10th Cir. 1996) ("Reconstructed records generally do not accurately reflect the actual time spent; and we have directed district courts to scrutinize such records and adjust the hours if appropriate."). But see Judicial Watch, 384 F. Supp. 2d at 174 (declining to reduce a fee award where billing records were reconstructed from transcripts and videotapes, which "though not contemporaneous time records in the traditional sense, nonetheless . . . indicate[d] precisely the length and nature of the work done" and were deemed to be "perhaps even more reliable . . . than a mere time record").

[101] See Hensley v. Eckerhart, 461 U.S. 424, 433 (1982) (civil rights case); Copeland v. Marshall, 641 F.2d 880, 891 (D.C. Cir. 1980) (en banc) (Title VII case); Lindy Bros. Builders, Inc. v. Am. Radiator & Standard Sanitary Corp., 487 F.2d 161, 168 (3d Cir. 1973) (describing the product of a reasonable hourly rate and the hours actually worked as "the lodestar of the court's fee determination") (non-FOIA case).

[102] See, e.g., Hensley, 461 U.S. at 434-40; Anderson, 80 F.3d at 1506; Copeland, 641 F.2d at 891-92; Nw. Coal. for Alternatives to Pesticides v. EPA, 421 F. Supp. 2d 123, 129-30 (D.D.C. 2006) (holding that the "plaintiff should not be compensated for its unnecessary and unsuccessful 'Motion for Entry of Judgment'"); Ajluni, 947 F. Supp. at 611 (limiting fees to those incurred up to point at which "the last of the additional documents were released"); McDonnell v. United States, 870 F. Supp. 576, 589 (D.N.J. 1994). But see Lissner v. U.S. Customs Serv., 56 F. App'x 330, 331 (9th Cir. 2003) (permitting award for preparation of initial attorney fees motion, even though it was unsuccessful, because it was "necessary step to . . . ultimate victory"); see also FOIA Post, "Supreme Court Rules for 'Survivor Privacy' in Favish" (posted 4/5/04) (describing Supreme Court's truly ultimate repudiation of bases for Ninth Circuit's ruling); cf. Judicial Watch, 384 F. Supp. 2d at 171 (awarding attorney fees for the discovery phase of litigation, even though it "was not productive in the sense of getting tangible results," because it gave "effect to" the court's prior order granting the plaintiff an opportunity "to reconstruct or discover documents" that the agency "destroyed or removed" during its initial search).

all part and parcel of one [ultimately successful] matter,"[103] and a rejected claim that is "truly fractionable" from the successful claim.[104] In some cases when the plaintiff's numerous claims are so intertwined that the court can discern "no principled basis for eliminating specific hours from the fee award," courts have employed a "general reduction method," allowing only a percentage of fees commensurate with the estimated degree to which that plaintiff had prevailed.[105]

---

[103] Copeland, 641 F.2d at 892 n.18; see Nat'l Ass'n of Concerned Veterans, 675 F.2d at 1327 n.13; Nat'l Ass'n of Atomic Veterans v. Dir., Def. Nuclear Agency, No. 81-2662, slip op. at 7 (D.D.C. July 15, 1987) (deciding that because plaintiff "clearly prevailed" on its only claim for relief, it is "entitled to recover fees for time expended on the few motions upon which it did not prevail").

[104] See, e.g., Weisberg v. Webster, No. 78-322, slip op. at 3 (D.D.C. June 13, 1985); Newport Aeronautical Sales v. Dep't of the Navy, No. 84-0120, slip op. at 10-11 (D.D.C. Apr. 17, 1985); see also Weisberg v. U.S. Dep't of Justice, 745 F.2d 1476, 1499 (D.C. Cir. 1984) (declining to award fees for issues on which plaintiff did "not ultimately prevail" and for "non-productive time"); Piper v. U.S. Dep't of Justice, 339 F. Supp. 2d 13, 24 (D.D.C. 2004) (refusing to grant fees for time spent on claims that ultimately were unsuccessful); Steenland v. CIA, 555 F. Supp. 907, 911 (W.D.N.Y. 1983) (declaring that award for work performed after release of records, where all claims of exemptions subsequently upheld, "would assess a penalty against defendants which is clearly unwarranted"); Agee v. CIA, No. 79-2788, slip op. at 1 (D.D.C. Nov. 3, 1982) ("[P]laintiff is not entitled to fees covering work where he did not substantially prevail."); Dubin v. Dep't of Treasury, 555 F. Supp. 408, 413 (N.D. Ga. 1981) (holding that fees awarded "should not include fees for plaintiffs' counsel for their efforts after the release of documents by the Government . . . since they failed to prevail on their claims at trial"), aff'd, 697 F.2d 1093 (11th Cir. 1983) (unpublished table decision); cf. Anderson, 80 F.3d at 1504 (affirming district court's denial of fees for portion of lawsuit during which plaintiff's primary motivation was her personal interest, while allowing fees for remainder of suit when public interest was paramount motivation). But see Badhwar v. U.S. Dep't of the Air Force, No. 84-154, slip op. at 3 (D.D.C. Dec. 11, 1986) ("[D]efendants' attempts to decrease [fees] on the grounds that the plaintiffs did not prevail as to all issues raised . . . are not persuasive. [The FOIA] requires only that the plaintiff should have 'substantially prevailed.'").

[105] See, e.g., Hull v. U.S. Dep't of Labor, No. 04-CV-1264, 2006 U.S. Dist. LEXIS 35054, at *20 (D. Colo. May 30, 2006) (reducing number of hours for which plaintiff may recover fees by sixty percent, because she was only "about forty percent successful"); Kempker-Cloyd v. U.S. Dep't of Justice, No. 5:97-253, slip op. at 14 (W.D. Mich. Apr. 2, 1999) (magistrate's recommendation) (dividing claimed amount of attorney fees in half, because "[s]egregating litigation efforts spent on intertwined issues . . . is impracticable, if not impossible"), adopted (W.D. Mich. Aug. 17, 1999); McDonnell,

(continued...)

Additionally, prevailing plaintiffs' counsel are obligated to exercise sound billing judgment. This means that "[c]ounsel for the prevailing party should make a good-faith effort to exclude from a fee request hours that are excessive, redundant, or otherwise unnecessary."[106] Furthermore, the D.C. Circuit has admonished that "[s]ome expense items, though perhaps not unreasonable between a first class law firm and a solvent client, are not supported by indicia of reasonableness sufficient to allow us justly to tax the same against the United States."[107] Although "contests over fees should not be permitted to evolve into exhaustive trial-type proceedings,"[108] when attorney fees are awarded, the hours expended by counsel for the plaintiff pursuing the fee award also are ordinarily compensable.[109]

---

[105](...continued)
870 F. Supp. at 589 (reducing plaintiff's requested award by sixty percent because "the amount of relief denied was greater than that awarded").

[106] Hensley, 461 U.S. at 434, quoted in Assembly of Cal. v. U.S. Dep't of Commerce, No. Civ-S-91-990, 1993 WL 188328, at *11 (E.D. Cal. May 28, 1993); see AutoAlliance Int'l, Inc. v. U.S. Customs Serv., 155 F. App'x 226, 228 (6th Cir. 2005) (upholding district court's twenty-five percent reduction of fees for "general excessiveness in billing" in this "relatively unexceptional FOIA case"); Am. Small Bus. League v. SBA, No. 04-4250, 2005 WL 2206486, at *1 (N.D. Cal. Sept. 12, 2005) (reducing fees for "unnecessary" time that was spent "thinking about, researching and drafting" fee petition); McCoy v. Fed. Bureau of Prisons, No. 03-383, 2005 WL 1972600, at *3-4 (E.D. Ky. Aug. 16, 2005) (reducing fees by approximately thirty percent because some of the hours submitted were "duplicative, unnecessary to the outcome of the case, and excessive for an experienced attorney"), reconsideration denied (E.D. Ky. Oct. 6, 2005); Smith v. Ashcroft, No. 02-CV-0043, 2005 WL 1309149, at *4 (W.D. Mich. May 25, 2005) (reducing fees by twenty-five percent because the amount sought included compensation for "work not reasonably necessary to prosecute the case," such as "attorney time spent responding to media inquiries"); City of Detroit, No. 93-CV-72310, slip op. at 3-4 (E.D. Mich. Mar. 24, 1995) (reducing requested fees by sixty percent because city employed eight attorneys when two would have sufficed, utilized two principal litigators when one would have sufficed, and generated nearly half of all fees sought in connection with its fees petition).

[107] In re North (Schultz Fee Application), 8 F.3d 847, 852 (D.C. Cir. 1993) (non-FOIA case).

[108] Nat'l Ass'n of Concerned Veterans, 675 F.2d at 1324.

[109] See Lissner, 56 F. App'x at 331; Copeland, 641 F.2d at 896; see also AutoAlliance Int'l, 155 F. App'x at 228 (affirming district court's limitation of "fees on fees" to three percent of hours in main case, absent unusual circumstances); Or. Natural Desert Ass'n v. Gutierrez, No. 05-210, 2006 WL 2318610, at *6 (D. Or. Aug. 24, 2006) (reducing "fees on fees" by fifteen percent "to match the reduction for [plaintiff's] partial success") (appeal pend-
(continued...)

To determine a reasonable hourly rate -- which has been defined "as that prevailing in the community for similar work"[110] -- courts will accept affidavits from local attorneys to support hourly rate claims, but they should be couched in terms of specific market rates for particular types of litigation and they must be well supported.[111] The pertinent legal market, for purposes of calculating legal fees, is the jurisdiction in which the district court sits.[112] Within the D.C. Circuit, the standard rate most often employed is an updated version of the "Laffey Matrix," based on the eponymous court case of that name.[113]

The lodestar calculation is strongly presumed to yield the reasonable fee. Indeed, the Supreme Court has clarified that such enhancements are not available under statutes authorizing an award of attorney fees to a

---

[109](...continued)
ing); McCoy, 2005 WL 1972600, at *3 (allowing fees for time spent "reviewing entitlement to fees and drafting the related motion"); Am. Small Bus. League, 2005 WL 2206486, at *1 (allowing portion of fees for "time spent on the fee motion"); Nat'l Veterans Legal Servs. Program v. VA, No. 96-1740, 1999 WL 33740260, at *5 (D.D.C. Apr. 13, 1999) (approving award of "fees-on-fees"); Assembly of Cal. v. Dep't of Commerce, No. S91-990, 1993 WL 188328, at *16 (E.D. Cal. May 28, 1993); Katz v. Webster, No. 82-1092, slip op. at 4-5 (S.D.N.Y. Feb. 1, 1990).

[110] Nat'l Ass'n of Concerned Veterans, 675 F.2d at 1323.

[111] See id.; McCoy, 2005 WL 1972600, at *3 (requiring plaintiff to verify reasonableness of requested hourly rate by submitting "one or more affidavits from area attorneys who are experienced in and familiar with reasonable hourly rates in similar cases"); Inst. for Wildlife Prot. v. U.S. Fish & Wildlife Serv., No. 02-6178, slip op. at 5 (D. Or. Dec. 3, 2003) (reducing plaintiff's claimed hourly rate due to counsel's lack of FOIA experience and noncomplexity of case); Confederated Tribes v. Babbitt, No. 96-197, slip op at 3 (D. Or. Sept. 30, 1997) (rejecting plaintiff's proposed use of the area market rate for calculation of fees because plaintiff's attorneys in fact contracted to work for their client at a substantially lower rate).

[112] See, e.g., AutoAlliance Int'l, 155 F. App'x at 127 (affirming district court's use of market rate for judicial district within which it sits); Nw. Coal. for Alternatives to Pesticides v. Browner, 965 F. Supp. 59, 65 (D.D.C. 1997) (explaining that fees are properly calculated based on the legal market for the jurisdiction "in which the district court sits").

[113] Laffey v. Nw. Airlines, 746 F.2d 4, 24-25 (D.C. Cir. 1984), overruled in part on other grounds by Save Our Cumberland Mountains, Inc. v. Hodel, 857 F.2d 1516, 1524 (D.C. Cir. 1988 (en banc); see, e.g., Covington v. District of Columbia, 57 F.3d 1101, 1109 (D.C. Cir. 1995) (noting circuit court approval of use of "Laffey Matrix") (non-FOIA case).

"prevailing or substantially prevailing party," such as the FOIA.[114] More-over, FOIA fee awards may not be increased to provide plaintiffs' attorneys "interest" to compensate for delays in their receipt of payments for legal services rendered.[115] Also, if a case has been in litigation for a prolonged period of time, "[a]ttorneys' fees awarded against the United States must be based on the prevailing market rates at the time the services were per-formed, rather than rates current at the time of the award."[116]

Lastly, in ruling on a petition for attorney fees and costs, a court should provide a concise but clear explanation of its reasons for any award encompassing eligibility, entitlement, and the rationale for its calcula-tions.[117] Upon appeal, such rulings are reviewed for abuse of discretion.[118]

## "REVERSE" FOIA

The Court of Appeals for the District of Columbia Circuit has defined a "reverse" FOIA action as one in which the "submitter of information -- usually a corporation or other business entity" that has supplied an agency with "data on its policies, operations or products -- seeks to prevent the agency that collected the information from revealing it to a third party in

---

[114] City of Burlington v. Dague, 505 U.S. 557, 562 (1992) (prohibiting con-tingency enhancement in environmental fee-shifting statutes and noting that case law "construing what is a 'reasonable' fee applies uniformly to all [federal fee-shifting statutes]"); see Ray v. U.S. Dep't of Justice, 856 F. Supp. 1576, 1583 (S.D. Fla. 1994) (noting that "Dague calls into question the appli-cability of an enhancement for contingency cases," but declining to decide whether the decision also forbids a fee enhancement for "exceptional" cases by holding that this FOIA case result was not exceptional), aff'd, 87 F.3d 1250 (11th Cir. 1996); Judicial Watch, 384 F. Supp. 2d at 174 (denying a request for an enhancement, because the plaintiff failed to explain "why the lodestar does not offer sufficient compensation"); Assembly of Cal., 1993 WL 188328, at *14 (refusing to grant approval for any upward adjust-ment in the lodestar calculation).

[115] See Library of Cong. v. Shaw, 478 U.S. 310, 314 (1986) ("In the ab-sence of express congressional consent to the award of interest separate from a general waiver of immunity to suit, the United States is immune from an interest award."); Weisberg v. U.S. Dep't of Justice, 848 F.2d 1265, 1272 (D.C. Cir. 1988).

[116] Nw. Coal., 965 F. Supp. at 66 ("Contrary to plaintiffs' assertions, it is not proper to adjust historic rates to take inflation into account." (citing Library of Cong., 478 U.S. at 322)).

[117] Hensley, 461 U.S. at 437; Union of Concerned Scientists v. NRC, 824 F.2d 1219, 1228 (D.C. Cir. 1987).

[118] See Weisberg, 848 F.2d at 1272 (citing Copeland, 641 F.2d at 901).

response to the latter's FOIA request."[1] Such "reverse" FOIA challenges generally arise from situations involving pending FOIA requests, but on occasion they are brought by parties challenging other types of prospective agency disclosures as well.[2]

An agency's decision to release submitted information in response to a FOIA request ordinarily will "be grounded either in its view that none of the FOIA exemptions applies, and thus that disclosure is mandatory, or in its belief that release is justified in the exercise of its discretion, even though the information falls within one or more of the statutory exemptions."[3] Typically, the submitter contends that the requested information falls within Exemption 4 of the FOIA,[4] but submitters have also challenged, with mixed results, the contemplated disclosure of information that they

---

[1] CNA Fin. Corp. v. Donovan, 830 F.2d 1132, 1133 n.1 (D.C. Cir. 1987); accord Mallinckrodt Inc. v. West, 140 F. Supp. 2d 1, 4 (D.D.C. 2000) (declaring that "[i]n a 'reverse FOIA' case, the court has jurisdiction when a party disputes an agency's decision to release information under FOIA"), appeal dismissed voluntarily, No. 00-5330 (D.C. Cir. Dec. 12, 2000); Cortez III Serv. Corp. v. NASA, 921 F. Supp. 8, 11 (D.D.C. 1996) (holding that in reverse FOIA actions "courts have jurisdiction to hear complaints brought by parties claiming that an agency decision to release information adversely affects them"), appeal dismissed voluntarily, No. 96-5163 (D.C. Cir. July 3, 1996).

[2] See, e.g., AFL-CIO v. FEC, 333 F.3d 168, 172 (D.C. Cir. 2003) (submitter organization challenged, albeit with questionable standing, agency decision to place investigatory file, which included information on individuals, in agency's public reading room); Bartholdi Cable Co. v. FCC, 114 F.3d 274, 279 (D.C. Cir. 1997) (submitter challenged agency order requiring it to publicly disclose information, which was issued in context of federal licensing requirements); McDonnell Douglas Corp. v. Widnall, No. 94-0091, slip op. at 13 (D.D.C. Apr. 11, 1994) (submitter challenged agency release decision that was based upon disclosure obligation imposed by Federal Acquisition Regulation (FAR)), and McDonnell Douglas Corp. v. Widnall, No. 92-2211, slip op. at 8 (D.D.C. Apr. 11, 1994) (same), cases consolidated on appeal & remanded for further development of the record, 57 F.3d 1162, 1167 (D.C. Cir. 1995); cf. Tripp v. DOD, 193 F. Supp. 2d 229, 233 (D.D.C. 2002) (plaintiff challenged disclosure of federal job-related information pertaining to herself, but did so after disclosure already had been made to media).

[3] CNA, 830 F.2d at 1134 n.1; see Alexander & Alexander Servs. v. SEC, No. 92-1112, 1993 WL 439799, at *9, *11-12 (D.D.C. Oct. 19, 1993) (agency determined that Exemptions 4, 7(B), and 7(C) did not apply to certain requested information and "chose not to invoke" Exemption 5 for certain other requested information), appeal dismissed, No. 93-5398 (D.C. Cir. Jan. 4, 1996).

[4] 5 U.S.C. § 552(b)(4) (2000 & Supp. IV 2004).

contended was exempt under other FOIA exemptions as well.[5] (For a further discussion of other such "reverse" FOIA cases, see Exemption 6, Priva-

---

[5] See, e.g., Doe v. Veneman, 380 F.3d 807, 816-18 & n.39 (5th Cir. 2004) (agreeing with plaintiffs that the requested information was protected under Exemption 3, but finding it unnecessary to decide the applicability of Exemption 6 or the Privacy Act, 5 U.S.C. § 552a (2000 & Supp. IV 2004), because "the result would be the same"); Campaign for Family Farms v. Glickman, 200 F.3d 1180, 1182 (8th Cir. 2000) (agreeing with submitter that Exemption 6 should have been invoked, and ordering permanent injunction requiring agency to withhold requested information); Bartholdi, 114 F.3d at 282 (denying the submitter's request for an injunction based on a claim that agency's balancing of interests under Exemption 6 was "arbitrary or capricious," and holding that "even were [the submitter] correct that its submissions fall within Exemption 6, the [agency] is not required to withhold the information from public disclosure," because the "FOIA's exemptions simply permit, but do not require, an agency to withhold exempted information"); Tripp, 193 F. Supp. 2d at 238-39 (dismissing plaintiff's claim that the agency's prior disclosure of information about her somehow "violated" Exemptions 5, 6, 7(A), and 7(C); concluding that with the exception of information covered by Exemption 7(C) -- which was found inapplicable to the information at issue -- a plaintiff could "not rely on a claim that a FOIA exemption requires the withholding" of information, inasmuch as the FOIA merely permits withholding but does not "require" it); AFL-CIO v. FEC, 177 F. Supp. 2d 48, 61-63 (D.D.C. 2001) (agreeing with plaintiffs that the identities of third parties mentioned in an agency's investigative files should have been afforded protection under Exemption 7(C); rejecting the agency's argument that "the public interest in disclosure outweighs the privacy interest" of the named individuals," because the D.C. Circuit "has established a categorical rule" for the protection of such information; and finding the agency's "refusal to apply Exemption 7(C) to bar release" to be "arbitrary, capricious and contrary to law" (citing SafeCard Servs. v. SEC, 926 F.2d 1197 (D.C. Cir. 1991))), aff'd on other grounds, 333 F.3d 168 (D.C. Cir. 2003); Na Iwi O Na Kupuna v. Dalton, 894 F. Supp. 1397, 1411-13 (D. Haw. 1995) (denying plaintiff's request to enjoin release of information that plaintiff contended was exempt pursuant to Exemptions 3 and 6); Church Universal & Triumphant, Inc. v. United States, No. 95-0163, slip op. at 2, 3 & n.3 (D.D.C. Feb. 8, 1995) (rejecting the submitter's argument "that the documents in question are 'return information' that is protected from disclosure under" Exemption 3, but sua sponte asking the agency "to consider whether any of the materials proposed for disclosure are protected by" Exemption 6); Alexander, 1993 WL 439799, at *10-12 (agreeing with the submitter that Exemption 7(C) should have been invoked, and ordering the agency to withhold additional information; finding that the submitter failed to "timely provide additional substantiation" to justify its claim that Exemption 7(B) applied; and finding that the deliberative process privilege of Exemption 5 "belongs to the governmental agency to invoke or not," and noting the "absence of any record support" suggesting that the agency, "as a general matter, arbitrarily declined to invoke that privilege").

**"REVERSE" FOIA**

cy Considerations, above.)

Five years ago the District Court for the District of Columbia issued opinions in two reverse FOIA cases involving claims that disclosure would be in violation of the Privacy Act of 1974.[6] In one, the court held that the plaintiffs had "properly asserted a cause of action" because the information at issue was protected by Exemption 7(C) of the FOIA and therefore could not be disclosed under the Privacy Act -- inasmuch as that statute generally prohibits public disclosure of Privacy Act-covered information that falls within a FOIA exemption.[7] In the second case -- which was brought <u>after</u> the disclosure had been made -- the court held that the plaintiff could not rely on an alleged violation of the Privacy Act to bring an independent "reverse" FOIA claim against the agency.[8] (See the further discussion of this issue under Exemption 6, Privacy Considerations, above.)

In a "reverse" FOIA suit, the party seeking to prevent the disclosure of information the government intends to release assumes the burden of justifying the nondisclosure of the information.[9] A submitter's challenge to an

---

[6] 5 U.S.C. § 552a.

[7] Recticel Foam Corp. v. U.S. Dep't of Justice, No. 98-2523, slip op. at 9-10 (D.D.C. Jan. 31, 2002) (enjoining disclosure of FBI's criminal investigative files pertaining to plaintiffs), appeal dismissed, No. 02-5118 (D.C. Cir. Apr. 25, 2002); see also Doe v. Veneman, 230 F. Supp. 2d 739, 751-53 (W.D. Tex. 2002) (recognizing claim that disclosure of the identities of ranchers utilizing livestock-protection collars would be a "violation of" the Privacy Act, after concluding that the "FOIA does not require release of the information"), aff'd in part & rev'd in part on other grounds, 380 F.3d 807, 816-18 & n.39 (5th Cir. 2004) (declining to consider applicability of either Exemption 6 or Privacy Act after concluding that Exemption 3 protects requested information).

[8] Tripp, 193 F. Supp. 2d at 238-40 (rejecting plaintiff's argument that her "reverse" FOIA claim was properly predicated on her "'reverse FOIA' request" that she previously sent to the President and the Attorney General requesting "DOD's compliance with its obligations" under the FOIA and the Privacy Act).

[9] See Martin Marietta Corp. v. Dalton, 974 F. Supp. 37, 40 n.4 (D.D.C. 1997); accord Frazee v. U.S. Forest Serv., 97 F.3d 367, 371 (9th Cir. 1996) (declaring that the "party seeking to withhold information under Exemption 4 has the burden of proving that the information is protected from disclosure"); Occidental Petroleum Corp. v. SEC, 873 F.2d 325, 342 (D.C. Cir. 1989) (explaining that the "statutory policy favoring disclosure requires that the opponent of disclosure" bear the burden of persuasion); TRIFID Corp. v. Nat'l Imagery & Mapping Agency, 10 F. Supp. 2d 1087, 1097 (E.D. Mo. 1998) (same); see also McDonnell Douglas Corp. v. U.S. Dep't of the Air Force, 375 F.3d 1182, 1195 (D.C. Cir. 2004) (Garland, J., dissenting), reh'g
(continued...)

agency's disclosure decision is reviewed in light of the "basic policy" of the FOIA to "'open agency action to the light of public scrutiny'" and in accordance with the "narrow construction" afforded to the FOIA's exemptions.[10] If the underlying FOIA request is subsequently withdrawn, the basis for the court's jurisdiction will dissipate and the case will be dismissed as moot.[11] By the same token, a court lacks jurisdiction if an agency has not made a final determination to release requested information.[12]

---

[9](...continued)
en banc denied, No. 02-5342 (D.C. Cir. Dec. 16, 2004); cf. Kan. Gas & Elec. Co. v. NRC, No. 87-2748, slip op. at 4 (D.D.C. July 2, 1993) (holding that submitter's "unsuccessful earlier attempt" to suppress disclosure in state court "effectively restrains it" from raising same arguments again in reverse FOIA action).

[10] Martin Marietta, 974 F. Supp. at 40 (quoting U.S. Dep't of the Air Force v. Rose, 425 U.S. 352, 372 (1976)); see, e.g., TRIFID, 10 F. Supp. 2d at 1097 (reviewing the submitter's claims in light of the FOIA principle that "[i]nformation in the government's possession is presumptively disclosable unless it is clearly exempt"); Daisy Mfg. Co. v. Consumer Prod. Safety Comm'n, No. 96-5152, 1997 WL 578960, at *1 (W.D. Ark. Feb. 5, 1997) (examining the submitter's claims in light of "the policy of the United States government to release records to the public except in the narrowest of exceptions," and observing that "[o]penness is a cherished aspect of our system of government"), aff'd, 133 F.3d 1081 (8th Cir. 1998).

[11] See McDonnell Douglas Corp. v. NASA, No. 95-5288, slip op. at 1 (D.C. Cir. Apr. 1, 1996) (ordering a reverse FOIA case "dismissed as moot in light of the withdrawal of the [FOIA] request at issue"); Gen. Dynamics Corp. v. Dep't of the Air Force, No. 92-5186, slip op. at 1 (D.C. Cir. Sept. 23, 1993) (same); Gulf Oil Corp. v. Brock, 778 F.2d 834, 838 (D.C. Cir. 1985) (same); McDonnell Douglas Corp. v. NASA, 102 F. Supp. 2d 21, 24 (D.D.C.) (dismissing case after underlying FOIA request was withdrawn, which in turn occurred after case already had been decided by D.C. Circuit and was before district court on motion for entry of judgment), reconsideration denied, 109 F. Supp. 2d 27 (D.D.C. 2000); cf. Sterling v. United States, 798 F. Supp. 47, 48 (D.D.C. 1992) (declaring that once a record has been released, "there are no plausible factual grounds for a 'reverse FOIA' claim"), aff'd, No. 93-5264 (D.C. Cir. Mar. 11, 1994).

[12] See, e.g., Doe, 380 F.3d at 814-15 (reversing injunction after finding that district court had "exceeded its jurisdiction" by enjoining release of information that agency had in fact decided "not to release"); United States v. N.Y. City Bd. of Educ., No. 96-0374, 2005 WL 1949477, at *1 (E.D.N.Y. Aug. 15, 2005) (holding that the court "did not have jurisdiction to enjoin disclosure of" requested documents until "a final determination to disclose the documents" had been made by the agency, and consequently denying a motion for injunctive relief) (non-FOIA case); cf. Dresser Indus., Inc. v. United States, 596 F.2d 1231, 1234, 1238 (5th Cir. 1979) (finding that agencies'
(continued...)

## "REVERSE" FOIA

    The landmark case in the reverse FOIA area is <u>Chrysler Corp. v. Brown</u>, in which the Supreme Court held that jurisdiction for a reverse FOIA action cannot be based on the FOIA itself because "Congress did not design the FOIA exemptions to be mandatory bars to disclosure" and, as a result, the FOIA "does not afford" a submitter "any right to enjoin agency disclosure."[13] Moreover, the Supreme Court held that jurisdiction cannot be based on the Trade Secrets Act[14] (a broadly worded criminal statute prohibiting the unauthorized disclosure of "practically any commercial or financial data collected by any federal employee from any source"[15]), because it is a criminal statute that does not afford a "private right of action."[16] Instead, the Court found that review of an agency's "decision to dis-

---

[12](...continued)
asserted failure to "assure" plaintiff that requested information was exempt from disclosure was not "reviewable by statute" or "final" -- which court described as "exhaustion of administrative remedies requirement" of Administrative Procedure Act, 5 U.S.C. §§ 701-706 (2000), and not "jurisdictional requirement" -- and dismissing count of Complaint seeking declaratory judgment that agencies abused their discretion).

[13] 441 U.S. 281, 293-94 (1979); <u>accord</u> <u>Campaign for Family Farms</u>, 200 F.3d at 1185 (concluding that an "agency has discretion to disclose information within a FOIA exemption, unless something independent of FOIA prohibits disclosure"); <u>Bartholdi</u>, 114 F.3d at 281 (declaring that the "mere fact that information falls within a FOIA exemption does not of itself bar an agency from disclosing the information"); <u>RSR Corp. v. Browner</u>, 924 F. Supp. 504, 509 (S.D.N.Y. 1996) (holding that the "FOIA itself does not provide a cause of action to a party seeking to enjoin an agency's disclosure of information, even if the information requested falls within one of FOIA's exemptions"), <u>aff'd</u>, No. 96-6186, 1997 WL 134413 (2d Cir. Mar. 26, 1997), <u>affirmance vacated without explanation</u>, No. 96-6186 (2d Cir. Apr. 17, 1997); <u>Kan. Gas</u>, No. 87-2748, slip op. at 3 (D.D.C. July 2, 1993) (finding that any "party seeking to prevent disclosure . . . must rely on other sources of law, independent of FOIA, to justify enjoining disclosure"). <u>But see</u> <u>AFL-CIO</u>, 177 F. Supp. 2d at 61-63 (concluding, without evident legal basis because of questionable standing, that due to "categorical" nature of Exemption 7(C), a reverse FOIA plaintiff can state claim that agency's decision not to invoke that exemption is unlawful or arbitrary and capricious); <u>accord</u> <u>Tripp</u>, 193 F. Supp. 2d at 239 (observing with mistaken imprecision that the district court's decision in <u>AFL-CIO</u> "goes only so far as to say that FOIA prohibits the release of the limited category of 7(C) information").

[14] 18 U.S.C. § 1905 (2000 & Supp. IV 2004).

[15] <u>CNA</u>, 830 F.2d at 1140.

[16] <u>Chrysler</u>, 441 U.S. at 316-17; <u>accord</u> <u>McDonnell Douglas v. Air Force</u>, 375 F.3d at 1186 n.1 (citing <u>Chrysler</u>).

close" requested records[17] can be brought under the Administrative Procedure Act (APA).[18] Accordingly, reverse FOIA plaintiffs ordinarily argue that an agency's contemplated release would violate the Trade Secrets Act and thus would "not be in accordance with law" or would be "arbitrary and capricious" within the meaning of the APA.[19]

In Chrysler, the Supreme Court specifically did not address the "relative ambits" of Exemption 4 and the Trade Secrets Act, nor did it determine whether the Trade Secrets Act qualified as an Exemption 3[20] statute.[21] Almost a decade later, the D.C. Circuit, after repeatedly skirting these difficult issues, "definitively" resolved them.[22] With regard to the Trade Secrets Act and Exemption 3, the D.C. Circuit held that the Trade Secrets Act does not qualify as an Exemption 3 statute under either of that exemption's subparts, particularly as it acts only as a prohibition against "unauthorized"

---

[17] Chrysler, 441 U.S. at 318.

[18] 5 U.S.C. §§ 701-706; see, e.g., CC Distribs. v. Kinzinger, No. 94-1330, 1995 WL 405445, at *2 (D.D.C. June 28, 1995) (holding that "neither [the] FOIA nor the Trade Secrets Act provides a cause of action to a party who challenges an agency decision to release information . . . [but] a party may challenge the agency's decision" under the APA); Comdisco, Inc. v. GSA, 864 F. Supp. 510, 513 (E.D. Va. 1994) (finding that the "sole recourse" of a "party seeking to prevent an agency's disclosure of records under FOIA" is review under the APA); Atlantis Submarines Haw., Inc. v. U.S. Coast Guard, No. 93-00986, slip op. at 5 (D. Haw. Jan. 28, 1994) (concluding that in a reverse FOIA suit, "an agency's decision to disclose documents over the objection of the submitter is reviewable only under" the APA) (denying motion for preliminary injunction), dismissed per stipulation (D. Haw. Apr. 11, 1994); Envtl. Tech., Inc. v. EPA, 822 F. Supp. 1226, 1228 (E.D. Va. 1993) (same).

[19] See, e.g., McDonnell Douglas v. Air Force, 375 F.3d at 1186 n.1 (noting that a submitter "may seek review of an agency action that violates the Trade Secrets Act on the ground that it is 'contrary to law'" under the APA); McDonnell Douglas Corp. v. Widnall, 57 F.3d 1162, 1164 (D.C. Cir. 1995) (same); Acumenics Research & Tech. v. Dep't of Justice, 843 F.2d 800, 804 (4th Cir. 1988) (same); Gen. Elec. Co. v. NRC, 750 F.2d 1394, 1398 (7th Cir. 1984) (same); Mallinckrodt, 140 F. Supp. 2d at 4 (declaring that "[a]lthough FOIA exemptions are normally permissive rather than mandatory," the Trade Secrets Act "independently prohibits the disclosure of confidential information"); Cortez, 921 F. Supp. at 11; Gen. Dynamics Corp. v. U.S. Dep't of the Air Force, 822 F. Supp. 804, 806 (D.D.C. 1992), vacated as moot, No. 92-5186 (D.C. Cir. Sept. 23, 1993); Raytheon Co. v. Dep't of the Navy, No. 89-2481, 1989 WL 550581, at *1 (D.D.C. Dec. 22, 1989).

[20] 5 U.S.C. § 552(b)(3).

[21] 441 U.S. at 319 n.49.

[22] CNA, 830 F.2d at 1134.

disclosures.[23] Indeed, because "agencies conceivably could control the frequency and scope of its application through regulations adopted on the strength of statutory withholding authorizations which do not themselves survive the rigors of Exemption 3," the D.C. Circuit found it inappropriate to classify the Trade Secrets Act as an Exemption 3 statute.[24] (For a further discussion of this point, see Exemption 3, Additional Considerations, above.)

In addition, the D.C. Circuit ruled that the scope of the Trade Secrets Act is not narrowly limited to that of its three predecessor statutes and that, instead, its scope is "at least co-extensive with that of Exemption 4."[25] Thus, information falling within the ambit of Exemption 4 would also fall within the scope of the Trade Secrets Act.[26] Accordingly, in the absence of

---

[23] Id. at 1141.

[24] Id. at 1139-40.

[25] Id. at 1151; accord McDonnell Douglas v. Air Force, 375 F.3d at 1185-86 (quoting CNA); Bartholdi, 114 F.3d at 281 (citing CNA and declaring: "[W]e have held that information falling within Exemption 4 of FOIA also comes within the Trade Secrets Act."); Canadian Commercial Corp. v. Dep't of the Air Force, 442 F. Supp. 2d 15, 39 (D.D.C. 2006) (appeal pending); Alexander, 1993 WL 439799, at *9; Gen. Dynamics, 822 F. Supp. at 806. But see Chrysler, 441 U.S. 281, 318-19 & n.49 (stating in dicta that "there is a theoretical possibility that material might be outside Exemption 4 yet within the [Trade Secrets Act]," but noting that "that possibility is at most of limited practical significance"); McDonnell Douglas v. Air Force, 375 F.3d at 1204 & n.17 (Garland, J., dissenting) (suggesting that an "agency's agreement to expend a specified amount of public funds . . . may represent a case in which [Exemption 4] and the Trade Secrets Act should not be regarded as coextensive"); McDonnell Douglas, 57 F.3d at 1165 n.2 (noting in dicta that "we suppose it is possible that this statement [from CNA] is no longer accurate in light of [the court's] recently more expansive interpretation of the scope of Exemption 4" in Critical Mass Energy Project v. NRC, 975 F.2d 871, 879 (D.C. Cir. 1992) (en banc)).

[26] See, e.g., McDonnell Douglas v. Air Force, 375 F.3d at 1185-86 (finding that the Trade Secrets Act "effectively prohibits an agency from releasing information [that is] subject to [Exemption 4]"); Bartholdi, 114 F.3d at 281 (concluding that when information is shown to be protected by Exemption 4, the government is generally "precluded from releasing" it by the Trade Secrets Act); Canadian Commercial, 442 F. Supp. 2d at 39 (declaring that "if information is covered by Exemption 4, it must be withheld because the [Trade Secrets Act] prohibits disclosure"); Mallinckrodt, 140 F. Supp. 2d at 4 (declaring that "the Trade Secrets Act affirmatively prohibits the disclosure of information covered by Exemption 4"); McDonnell Douglas Corp. v. NASA, 895 F. Supp. 319, 322 n.4 (D.D.C. 1995) (finding that because the two provisions are "co-extensive," it is "unnecessary to perform a redundant
(continued...)

a statute or properly promulgated regulation giving an agency authority to release the information -- which would remove the Trade Secrets Act's disclosure prohibition[27] -- a determination that requested material falls within Exemption 4 is tantamount to a determination that the material cannot be released, because the Trade Secrets Act "prohibits" disclosure.[28] To the extent that information falls outside the scope of Exemption 4, the D.C. Cir-

---

[26](...continued)
analysis"), vacated as moot, No. 95-5288 (D.C. Cir. Apr. 1, 1996); Chem. Waste Mgmt., Inc. v. O'Leary, No. 94-2230, 1995 WL 115894, at *6 n.1 (noting that the "analysis under either regime is identical"); Raytheon, 1989 WL 550581, at *1.

[27] See, e.g., St. Mary's Hosp., Inc. v. Harris, 604 F.2d 407, 410 (5th Cir. 1979) (finding that a disclosure made pursuant to a Social Security Administration regulation "was authorized by law within the meaning of the Trade Secrets Act"); RSR, 924 F. Supp. at 512 (finding that Clean Water Act, 33 U.S.C. § 1318(b) (2000), and "regulations promulgated under it permit disclosure" of submitter's "effluent data" and that agency's contemplated disclosure of such data is authorized by law); Jackson v. First Fed. Sav., 709 F. Supp. 887, 890-94 (E.D. Ark. 1989) (concluding that a Federal Home Loan Bank Board regulation was "sufficient [under the Trade Secrets Act] to authorize" the release of certain bank-examination documents); see also Qwest Commc'ns Int'l v. FCC, 229 F.3d 1172, 1173 (D.C. Cir. 2000) (finding that a provision of the Communications Act of 1934, 47 U.S.C. § 220(f) (2002), "provides sufficient authorization for disclosure of trade secrets," but nevertheless remanding for further proceedings because the agency "failed to explain how its [disclosure order was] consistent with its policy regarding the treatment of confidential [audit] information"); cf. McDonnell Douglas Corp. v. NASA, 180 F.3d 303, 306 (D.C. Cir. 1999) (repeatedly noting absence of agency reliance on "any independent legal authority to release" requested information as basis for concluding that it was subject to Trade Secrets Act's disclosure prohibition); Canadian Commercial, 442 F. Supp. 2d at 40-41 (rejecting agency's reliance on FAR provisions as authority to disclose unit price information). See generally Bartholdi, 114 F.3d at 281-82 (rejecting challenge to validity of disclosure regulation for failure to first exhaust issue before agency); S. Hills Health Sys. v. Bowen, 864 F.2d 1084, 1093 (3d Cir. 1988) (rejecting challenge to validity of disclosure regulation as unripe).

[28] CNA, 830 F.2d at 1151-52; see, e.g., Pac. Architects & Eng'rs v. U.S. Dep't of State, 906 F.2d 1345, 1347 (9th Cir. 1990) (holding that when release of requested information is barred by Trade Secrets Act, agency "does not have discretion to release it"); Envtl. Tech., 822 F. Supp. at 1228 (concluding that Trade Secrets Act "bars disclosure of information that falls within Exemption 4"); Gen. Dynamics, 822 F. Supp. at 806 (declaring that the Trade Secrets Act "is an independent prohibition on the disclosure of information within its scope"); see also FOIA Update, Vol. VI, No. 3, at 3 (discussing Trade Secrets Act bar to discretionary disclosure under Exemption 4).

cuit found that there was no need to determine whether it nonetheless still fits within the outer boundaries of the Trade Secrets Act.[29] Such a ruling was unnecessary, the court found, because the FOIA itself would provide the necessary authorization to release any information not falling within one of its exemptions.[30]

## Standard of Review

In Chrysler Corp. v. Brown, the Supreme Court held that the Administrative Procedure Act's predominant scope and standard of judicial review -- review on the administrative record according to an arbitrary and capricious standard -- should "ordinarily" apply to reverse FOIA actions.[31] Indeed, the Court of Appeals for the District of Columbia Circuit has strongly emphasized that judicial review in reverse FOIA cases should be based on the administrative record, with de novo review reserved for only those cases in which an agency's administrative procedures were "severely defective."[32]

---

[29] CNA, 830 F.2d at 1152 n.139.

[30] Id.; see Frazee, 97 F.3d at 373 (emphasizing that the submitters gave "no reason as to why the Trade Secrets Act should, in their case, provide protection from disclosure broader than the protection provided by Exemption 4 of FOIA," and finding that because the requested document was "not protected from disclosure under Exemption 4," it also was "not exempt from disclosure under the Trade Secrets Act"); Alexander, 1993 WL 439799, at *9 (declaring that "if the documents are not deemed confidential pursuant to Exemption 4, they will not be protected under the Trade Secrets Act").

[31] 441 U.S. 281, 318 (1979); accord Campaign for Family Farms v. Glickman, 200 F.3d 1180, 1184 (8th Cir. 2000); Reliance Elec. Co. v. Consumer Prod. Safety Comm'n, 924 F.2d 274, 277 (D.C. Cir. 1991); Gen. Dynamics Corp. v. U.S. Dep't of the Air Force, 822 F. Supp. 804, 806 (D.D.C. 1992), vacated as moot, No. 92-5186 (D.C. Cir. Sept. 23, 1993); Davis Corp. v. United States, No. 87-3365, 1988 U.S. Dist. LEXIS 17611, at *5-6 (D.D.C. Jan. 19, 1988); see also McDonnell Douglas Corp. v. NASA, No. 91-3134, transcript at 6 (D.D.C. Jan. 24, 1992) (bench order) (recognizing that court has "very limited scope of review"), remanded, No. 92-5342 (D.C. Cir. Feb. 14, 1994).

[32] Nat'l Org. for Women v. Social Sec. Admin., 736 F.2d 727, 745 (D.C. Cir. 1984) (per curiam) (McGowan & Mikva, JJ., concurring in result); accord Campaign for Family Farms v. Glickman, 200 F.3d at 1186 n.6; Acumenics Research & Tech. v. U.S. Dep't of Justice, 843 F.2d 800, 804-05 (4th Cir. 1988); RSR Corp. v. Browner, 924 F. Supp. 504, 509 (S.D.N.Y. 1996), aff'd, No. 96-6186, 1997 WL 134413 (2d Cir. Mar. 26, 1997), affirmance vacated without explanation, No. 96-6186 (2d Cir. Apr. 17, 1997); Comdisco, Inc. v. GSA, 864 F. Supp. 510, 513 (E.D. Va. 1994); Burnside-Ott Aviation Training Ctr. v. United States, 617 F. Supp. 279, 282-84 (S.D. Fla. 1985); cf. Alcolac, Inc. v.

(continued...)

The D.C. Circuit subsequently reaffirmed its position on the appropriate scope of judicial review in reverse FOIA cases, holding that the district court "behaved entirely correctly" when it rejected the argument advanced by the submitter -- that it was entitled to de novo review because the agency's factfinding procedures were inadequate -- and instead confined its review to an examination of the administrative record.[33] The Court of Appeals for the Ninth Circuit, similarly rejecting a submitter's challenge to an agency's factfinding procedures, also has held that judicial review in a reverse FOIA suit is properly based on the administrative record.[34]

---

[32](...continued)
Wagoner, 610 F. Supp. 745, 749 (W.D. Mo. 1985) (upholding agency's decision to deny claim of confidentiality as "rational"). But see McDonnell Douglas v. Air Force, 375 F.3d at 1197, 1201-02 (Garland, J., dissenting) (criticizing the panel majority for substituting its own facts and rationales for those contained in the case's administrative record, including its reliance upon an economic theory "of the court's own invention"); Carolina Biological Supply Co. v. USDA, No. 93CV00113, slip op. at 4 & n.2 (M.D.N.C. Aug. 2, 1993) (applying de novo review after observing that standard of review issue presented close "judgment call"); Artesian Indus. v. HHS, 646 F. Supp. 1004, 1005-06 (D.D.C. 1986) (flatly rejecting position advanced by both parties that it should base its decision on agency record according to arbitrary and capricious standard).

[33] CNA Fin. Corp. v. Donovan, 830 F.2d 1132, 1162 (D.C. Cir. 1987); see, e.g., TRIFID Corp. v. Nat'l Imagery & Mapping Agency, 10 F. Supp. 2d 1087, 1092-96 (E.D. Mo. 1998) (finding the agency's factfinding procedures to be adequate when the submitter "received notice of the FOIA request and was given the opportunity to object," and holding that challenges to the brevity of the agency's disclosure decision, the lack of an administrative appeal right, as well as "procedural irregularities" concerning the time period allotted for providing objections, as well as a dispute over the appropriate decisionmaker, did not justify de novo review); RSR, 924 F. Supp. at 509 (finding the agency's factfinding procedures to be adequate when the submitter was "promptly notified" of the FOIA request and "given an opportunity to object to disclosure" and "to substantiate [those] objections" before the agency decision was made); Comdisco, 864 F. Supp. at 514 (finding the agency's factfinding procedures to be adequate when the submitter was "accorded a full and fair opportunity to state and support its position on disclosure"); see also CC Distribs. v. Kinzinger, No. 94-1330, 1995 WL 405445, at *3 (D.D.C. June 28, 1995) (confining its review to the record when the submitter did "not actually challenge the agency's factfinding procedures," but instead challenged how the agency "applied" those procedures); Chem. Waste Mgmt., Inc. v. O'Leary, No. 94-2230, 1995 WL 115894, at *6 n.4 (D.D.C. Feb. 28, 1995) (confining its review to the record even when the agency's factfinding itself was found to be "inadequate," because the agency's "factfinding procedures" were not challenged).

[34] See Pac. Architects & Eng'rs v. U.S. Dep't of State, 906 F.2d 1345, 1348
(continued...)

Review on the administrative record is a "deferential standard of review [that] only requires that a court examine whether the agency's decision was 'based on a consideration of the relevant factors and whether there has been a clear error of judgment.'"[35] Under this standard "[a] reviewing court does not substitute its judgment for the judgment of the agency" and instead "simply determines whether the agency action constitutes a clear error of judgment."[36] Significantly, "[a]n agency is not required to prove that its predictions of the effect of disclosure are superior"; rather, it "is enough that the agency's position is as plausible as the contesting party's position."[37] Indeed, as one court has recently held, "[t]he harm from disclosure is a matter of speculation, and when a reviewing court finds that an agency has supplied an equally reasonable and thorough prognosis, it is for the agency to choose between the contesting party's prognosis and its own."[38]

Because judicial review is based on the agency's administrative record, it is vitally important that agencies take care to develop a comprehensive one.[39] Indeed, the Court of Appeals for the Seventh Circuit once chas-

---

[34](...continued)
(9th Cir. 1990).

[35] McDonnell Douglas Corp. v. NASA, 981 F. Supp. 12, 14 (D.D.C. 1997) (quoting Citizens to Preserve Overton Park v. Volpe, 401 U.S. 402, 416 (1971)), rev'd on other grounds, 180 F.3d 303 (D.C. Cir. 1999); accord Campaign for Family Farms, 200 F.3d at 1187 (likewise quoting Citizens to Preserve Overton Park); Clearbrook, L.L.C. v. Ovall, No. 06-0629, 2006 U.S. Dist. LEXIS 81244, at *7 (S.D. Ala. Nov. 3, 2006) (same); McDonnell Douglas Corp. v. U.S. Dep't of the Air Force, 215 F. Supp. 2d 200, 204 (D.D.C. 2002) (same), aff'd in part & rev'd in part, 375 F.3d 1182 (D.C. Cir. 2004), reh'g en banc denied, No. 02-5342 (D.C. Cir. Dec. 16, 2004); Mallinckrodt Inc. v. West, 140 F. Supp. 2d 1, 4 (D.D.C. 2000) (same), appeal dismissed voluntarily, No. 00-5330 (D.C. Cir. Dec. 12, 2000).

[36] McDonnell Douglas, 215 F. Supp. 2d at 204; accord Bartholdi Cable Co. v. FCC, 114 F.3d 274, 279 (D.C. Cir. 1997); GS New Mkts. Fund, L.L.C. v. U.S. Dep't of the Treasury, 407 F. Supp. 2d 21, 24 (D.D.C. 2005).

[37] McDonnell Douglas, 215 F. Supp. 2d at 205; accord CNA, 830 F.2d at 1155 (deferring to agency when presented with "no more than two contradictory views of what likely would ensue upon release of [the] information").

[38] McDonnell Douglas, 215 F. Supp. 2d at 205; accord CNA, 830 F.2d at 1155) (upholding agency's release decision, and finding that agency's "explanations of anticipated effects were certainly no less plausible than those advanced by" submitter).

[39] See Reliance, 924 F.2d at 277 (insisting that the court "cannot properly perform" its review "unless the agency has explained the reasons for its de-
(continued...)

tised an agency for failing to develop an adequate record in a reverse FOIA action.[40] Similarly, the D.C. Circuit has remanded several reverse FOIA cases back to the agency for development of a more complete administrative record. In one, the D.C. Circuit ordered a remand so that it would have the benefit of "one considered and complete statement" of the agency's position on disclosure.[41] In another, the D.C. Circuit reversed the decision of the district court, which had permitted an inadequate record to be supplemented in court by an agency affidavit, holding that because the agency had failed at the administrative level to give a reason for its refusal to withhold certain price information, it was precluded from offering a "post-hoc

---

[39](...continued)
cision"); MCI Worldcom, Inc. v. GSA, 163 F. Supp. 2d 28, 30, 36 & n.10 (D.D.C. 2001) (ruling against the agency when it "never made any findings" regarding the confidentiality of the requested pricing information and could "not point[] to anything in the administrative record that establishes that the information is not confidential"); see also McDonnell Douglas, 981 F. Supp. at 14 (ordering record supplemented to include "additional comments" provided by submitter as well as agency's "lengthy response" because submitter's comments, though untimely, were considered by agency); McDonnell Douglas Corp. v. NASA, 895 F. Supp. 319, 323-24 (D.D.C. 1995) (ordering the record supplemented after finding that certain documents "specifically referenced" in the submitter's letter to the agency "were improperly omitted from the administrative record" and holding that even though those referenced documents had not been examined by the agency, the letter itself was, and agency "cannot pick and choose what information in the document will be considered"), vacated as moot, No. 95-5288 (D.C. Cir. Apr. 1, 1996); FOIA Post, "Treatment of Unit Prices After McDonnell Douglas v. Air Force" (posted 9/8/05) (emphasizing importance of agencies conducting submitter notice each time unit prices are requested, thoroughly analyzing specific arguments presented by submitter, and clearly setting forth agency rationale in administrative record (supplementing FOIA Post, "Treatment of Unit Prices Under Exemption 4" (posted 5/29/02)); FOIA Update, Vol. VIII, No. 2, at 1; FOIA Update, Vol. IV, No. 4, at 10; FOIA Update, Vol. III, No. 3, at 3. Compare McDonnell Douglas, No. 91-3134, transcript at 6 (D.D.C. Jan. 24, 1992) (finding agency's action to be arbitrary and capricious based on insufficient agency record), with Gen. Dynamics, 822 F. Supp. at 806 (deeming agency's action to be not arbitrary and capricious based upon existence of agency's "lengthy and thorough" administrative record).

[40] Gen. Elec. Co. v. NRC, 750 F.2d 1394, 1403-04 (7th Cir. 1984) (rejecting agency's competitive harm decision consisting of "one short sentence," and remanding case for elaboration of basis for agency's decision).

[41] McDonnell Douglas Corp. v. Widnall, 57 F.3d 1162, 1167 (D.C. Cir. 1995) (inexplicably deeming case to have come to court in "unusual posture" with "confusing administrative record" stemming from "intersection" of FOIA actions and contract award announcements).

rationalization" for the first time in court.[42]

Likewise, the court ordered a remand after holding that an "agency's administrative decision must stand or fall upon the reasoning advanced by the agency therein" and that an "agency cannot gain the benefit of hindsight in defending its decision" by advancing a new argument once the matter gets to litigation.[43] Thus, the D.C. Circuit has emphasized that judicial review in reverse FOIA cases must be conducted on the basis of the "administrative record compiled by the agency in advance of litigation."[44] Of course, agency affidavits that do "no more than summarize the administrative record" have been found to be permissible.[45]

In another case remanded to the agency for further proceedings due to an inadequate record, the D.C. Circuit rejected the argument proffered by the agency that a reverse FOIA plaintiff bears the burden of proving the

---

[42] AT&T Info. Sys. v. GSA, 810 F.2d 1233, 1236 (D.C. Cir. 1987).

[43] Data-Prompt, Inc. v. Cisneros, No. 94-5133, slip op. at 3 (D.C. Cir. Apr. 5, 1995); cf. McDonnell Douglas v. Air Force, 375 F.3d at 1188 & n.2 (declaring that it did not rely upon the agency's "post hoc rationale" for upholding its decision, and explaining that the court would remand a matter to an agency "where the agency's initial explanation of its decision was inadequate," but that it would "not typically remand to permit the agency an opportunity to adopt an entirely new explanation first suggested on appeal").

[44] AT&T, 810 F.2d at 1236; see also TRIFID, 10 F. Supp. 2d at 1097 (refusing to consider affidavits proffered by the submitter as they "were not submitted to [the agency] during the administrative process"); CC Distribs., 1995 WL 405445, at *3 (same); Chem. Waste, 1995 WL 115894, at *6 n.4 (same); Alexander & Alexander Servs. v. SEC, No. 92-1112, 1993 WL 439799, at *13 n.9 (D.D.C. Oct. 19, 1993) (same), appeal dismissed, No. 93-5398 (D.C. Cir. Jan. 4, 1996); Gen. Dynamics, 822 F. Supp. at 805 n.1 (same); accord Clearbrook, 2006 U.S. Dist. LEXIS 81244, at *10 (same). But cf. Canadian Commercial, 442 F. Supp. 2d at 27-29 (accepting the agency's second decision letter, which was issued after litigation commenced, because the plaintiff "acquiesced in the reconsideration of the earlier decision").

[45] Hercules, Inc. v. Marsh, 839 F.2d 1027, 1030 (4th Cir. 1988); accord McDonnell Douglas Corp. v. EEOC, 922 F. Supp. 235, 238 n.2 (E.D. Mo. 1996) (permitting the submission of an agency affidavit that "helps explain the administrative record"), appeal dismissed, No. 96-2662 (8th Cir. Aug. 29, 1996); Lykes Bros. S.S. Co. v. Peña, No. 92-2780, slip op. at 16 (D.D.C. Sept. 2, 1993) (permitting the submission of an agency affidavit that "merely elaborates" upon the basis for the agency decision and "provides a background for understanding the redactions"); see also, e.g., Int'l Computaprint v. U.S. Dep't of Commerce, No. 87-1848, slip op. at 12 n.36 (D.D.C. Aug. 16, 1988) ("The record in this case has been supplemented with explanatory affidavits that do not alter the focus on the administrative record.").

"non-public availability" of information, finding that it is "far more efficient, and obviously fairer" for that burden to be placed on the party who claims that the information is public.[46] The D.C. Circuit also upheld the district court's requirement that the agency prepare a document-by-document explanation for its denial of confidential treatment.[47] Specifically, the D.C. Circuit found that the agency's burden of justifying its decision "cannot be shirked or shifted to others simply because the decision was taken in a reverse-FOIA rather than a direct FOIA context."[48] Moreover, it observed, in cases in which the public availability of information is the basis for an agency's decision to disclose, the justification of that position is "inevitably document-specific."[49] Similarly, the District Court for the District of Columbia ordered a remand in a case in which the agency "never did acknowledge," let alone "respond to," the submitter's competitive harm argument.[50]

Rather than order a remand, however, that same district court, in an earlier case, simply ruled against the agency -- even going so far as to permanently enjoin it from releasing the requested information -- on the basis of a record that it found insufficient under the standards of the APA.[51] Specifically, the court noted that the agency "did not rebut any of the evidence produced" by the submitter, "did not seek or place in the record any contrary evidence, and simply ha[d] determined" that the evidence offered by the submitter was "insufficient or not credible."[52] This, the court found, "is classic arbitrary and capricious action by a government agency."[53] When

---

[46] Occidental Petroleum Corp. v. SEC, 873 F.2d 325, 342 (D.C. Cir. 1989).

[47] Id. at 343-44.

[48] Id. at 344.

[49] Id.

[50] Chem. Waste, 1995 WL 115894, at *5.

[51] McDonnell Douglas, No. 91-3134, transcript at 5-6, 10 (D.D.C. Jan. 24, 1992).

[52] Id. at 6.

[53] Id.; see, e.g., McDonnell Douglas, 922 F. Supp. at 241-42 (declaring an agency to be "arbitrary and capricious" because its "finding that the documents [at issue] were required [to be submitted was] not supported by substantial evidence in the agency record," and elaborating that it was "not at all clear" that the agency "even made a factual finding on [that] issue" and "to the extent" that it "did consider the facts of [the] case, it viewed only the facts favorable to its predetermined position"); Cortez III Serv. Corp. v. NASA, 921 F. Supp. 8, 13 (D.D.C. 1996) (declaring an agency decision to be "not in accordance with law" when "[n]either the administrative decision nor the sworn affidavits submitted by the [agency] support the conclusion that [the submitter] was required to provide" the requested information),

(continued...)

the agency subsequently sought an opportunity to "remedy" those "inadequacies in the record" by seeking a remand, the court declined to permit one, reasoning that the agency was "not entitled to a second bite of the apple just because it made a poor decision [for,] if that were the case, administrative law would be a never ending loop from which aggrieved parties would never receive justice."[54]

This same court -- when later presented with an administrative record that "differ[ed] substantially" from that earlier case and which "rebutted [the submitter's] arguments with detailed analysis" and indicated that the agency had "consulted" experienced individuals who were "intimately familiar with [the submitter's] arguments and evidence" -- readily upheld the agency's disclosure decision.[55] When the submitter sought reconsideration of the court's ruling, contending that the court improperly sustained the agency's decision on the basis of "'secret testimony from anonymous witnesses,'" the court dismissed those contentions as "inapposite and inaccurate," reasoning that "none of the issues before the court concerned the relative prestige of the experts on each party's side."[56] Rather, the court held, the "more appropriate concern [was] whether [the agency's] factual decisions [were] supported by substantial evidence" in the administrative record.[57] This decision was, nevertheless, abruptly overturned on appeal for what the court of appeals tersely characterized as the agency's "illogical application of the competitive harm test," with no mention made of the extensive evidence in the agency's administrative record.[58]

Another agency's disclosure determination was readily upheld when it was based on an administrative record that the court found plainly demonstrated that the agency "specifically considered" and "understood" the

---

[53](...continued)
appeal dismissed voluntarily, No. 96-5163 (D.C. Cir. July 3, 1996). See generally Envtl. Tech., Inc. v. EPA, 822 F. Supp. 1226, 1230 (E.D. Va. 1993) (granting submitter's motion for permanent injunction perfunctorily, without even addressing adequacy of agency record).

[54] McDonnell Douglas Corp. v. NASA, 895 F. Supp. 316, 319 (D.D.C. 1995) (permanent injunction ordered to "remain[] in place"), aff'd for agency failure to timely raise argument, No. 95-5290 (D.C. Cir. Sept. 17, 1996).

[55] McDonnell Douglas, 981 F. Supp. at 16.

[56] McDonnell Douglas Corp. v. NASA, No. 96-2611, slip op. at 3 (D.D.C. May 1, 1998) (quoting submitter's brief), rev'd on other grounds, 180 F.3d 303 (D.C. Cir. 1999).

[57] Id. at 4.

[58] McDonnell Douglas Corp. v. NASA, 180 F.3d 303, 307 (D.C. Cir. 1999) (dismissing agency's disclosure determination brusquely); see also FOIA Update, Vol. XX, No. 1, at 2.

arguments of the submitter and "provided reasons for rejecting them."[59] In so ruling, the court took note of the "lengthy and thorough" administrative process, during which the agency "repeatedly solicited and welcomed" the submitter's views on whether a FOIA exemption applied.[60] This record demonstrated that the agency's action was not arbitrary or capricious.[61]

Similarly, when an agency provided a submitter with "numerous opportunities to substantiate its confidentiality claim," afforded it "vastly more than the amount of time authorized" by its regulations, and "explain[ed] its reasons for [initially] denying the confidentiality request," the court found that the agency had "acted appropriately by issuing its final decision denying much of the confidentiality request on the basis that it had not received further substantiation."[62] In so holding, the court specifically rejected the submitter's contention that "it should have received even

---

[59] Gen. Dynamics, 822 F. Supp. at 807.

[60] Id. at 806.

[61] Id. at 807; see, e.g., GS New Mkts. Fund, 407 F. Supp. 2d at 25 (concluding that the agency "carefully considered the nature of the FOIA requests and the basis for the [submitter's] objections before rationally concluding that it should release portions of" the requested records); McDonnell Douglas, 215 F. Supp. 2d at 202-03 (noting that agency "requested comments from" submitter three times, that submitter actually "provided comments eleven times," and that after considering those comments agency "presented reasoned accounts" of its position and so, its "decision to disclose was not arbitrary or capricious"); Atlantis Submarines Haw., Inc. v. U.S. Coast Guard, No. 93-00986, slip op. at 10-11 (D. Haw. Jan. 28, 1994) (finding that the agency "appears to have fully examined the evidence and carefully followed its own procedures," that its decision to disclose "was conscientiously undertaken," and that it thus was not "arbitrary or capricious") (denying motion for preliminary injunction), dismissed per stipulation (D. Haw. Apr. 11, 1994); Source One Mgmt., Inc. v. U.S. Dep't of the Interior, No. 92-Z-2101, transcript at 4 (D. Colo. Nov. 10, 1993) (bench order) (declaring that the "Government has certainly been open in listening to" the submitter's arguments "and has made a decision which . . . is rational and is not an abuse of discretion and is not arbitrary and capricious"); Lykes Bros., No. 92-2780, slip op. at 15 (D.D.C. Sept. 2, 1993) (noting that the agency "provided considerable opportunity" for the submitters to "contest the proposed disclosures, and provided sufficient reasons on the record for rejecting" the submitters' arguments).

[62] Alexander, 1993 WL 439799, at *5-6; see CC Distribs., 1995 WL 405445, at *6 n.2 (ruling that the agency's procedures were adequate when the agency gave the submitter "adequate notice" of the existence of the FOIA request, afforded it "numerous opportunities to explain its position," repeatedly advised it to state its objections "with particularity," and "at least, provided [the submitter] with occasion to make the best case it could").

more assistance" from the agency and held that the agency was "under no obligation to segregate the documents into categories or otherwise organize the documents for review."[63] The court also specifically noted that the agency's acceptance of some of the submitter's claims for confidentiality in this matter "buttresses" the conclusion that its decision was "rational."[64]

## Executive Order 12,600

Administrative practice in potential reverse FOIA situations is generally governed by an executive order issued nearly two decades ago. Executive Order 12,600 requires federal agencies to establish certain predisclosure notification procedures which will assist agencies in developing adequate administrative records.[65] The executive order recognizes that submitters of proprietary information have certain procedural rights and it therefore requires, with certain limited exceptions,[66] that notice be given to submitters of confidential commercial information when they mark it as such,[67] or more significantly, whenever the agency "determines that it may

---

[63] Alexander, 1993 WL 439799, at *5 & 13 n.5.

[64] Id. at *13 n.6; accord Daisy Mfg. Co. v. Consumer Prod. Safety Comm'n, No. 96-5152, 1997 WL 578960, at *3 (W.D. Ark. Feb. 5, 1997) (finding it significant that the record revealed that the agency had been "careful in its selection of records for release, and in fact [had] denied the release of some records"), aff'd, 133 F.3d 1081 (8th Cir. 1998); Source One, No. 92-Z-2101, transcript at 4 (D. Colo. Nov. 10, 1993) (noting with approval that "there were certain things that [the agency had] excised").

[65] 3 C.F.R. 235 (1988) (applicable to all executive branch departments and agencies), reprinted in 5 U.S.C. § 552 note (2000), and in FOIA Update, Vol. VIII, No. 2, at 2-3; see, e.g., Department of Justice FOIA Regulations, 28 C.F.R. § 16.8(a)(2) (2006) (defining "submitter" as "any person or entity from whom the Department obtains business information, directly or indirectly").

[66] Exec. Order No. 12,600, § 8 (listing six circumstances in which notice is not necessary -- for example, when an agency determines that the requested information should be withheld, or conversely, when it already is public or its release is required by law); cf. FOIA Post, "Supreme Court Rules for 'Survivor Privacy' in Favish" (posted 4/9/04) (observing that in contrast to the notice that is routinely afforded to submitters of business information, "as a matter of longstanding practice born of practicality, individuals whose personal privacy interests are being protected under the FOIA rarely are aware of that process, let alone involved in it").

[67] Exec. Order No. 12,600, § 3 (establishing procedures for submitter marking of information); cf. Homeland Security Act of 2002, 6 U.S.C. § 133 (2000 & Supp. IV 2004) (establishing protection under Exemption 3, 5 U.S.C. § 552(b)(3) (2000 & Supp. IV 2004), for "critical infrastructure infor-

(continued...)

be required to disclose" the requested data.[68]

---

[67](...continued)
mation" that is properly marked as such and is voluntarily provided to Department of Homeland Security); *FOIA Post*, "Critical Infrastructure Information Regulations Issued by DHS" (posted 2/27/04) (advising of potential governmentwide implementation); *FOIA Post*, "Homeland Security Law Contains New Exemption 3 Statute" (posted 1/27/03) (comparing requirements of statute to those of Executive Order 12,600).

[68] Exec. Order No. 12,600, § 1; see Judicial Watch v. Dep't of the Army, 466 F. Supp. 2d 112, 122-24 & n. 7 (D.D.C. 2006) (permitting intervenor to raise Exemption 4 after the court had ordered the release of documents, because the agency had neglected to follow its submitter notice regulation); Delta Ltd. v. U.S. Customs & Border Prot. Bureau, 393 F. Supp. 2d 15, 18 (D.D.C. 2005) (stating that agency was "putting third parties at risk" by failing to follow its regulations that require it to contact submitters); MCI Worldcom, Inc. v. GSA, 163 F. Supp. 2d 28, 37 (D.D.C. 2001) (finding that an agency acted arbitrarily and capriciously when it "failed to follow" its submitter-notice regulations and did not afford the submitter "the opportunity to submit any comments as to how disclosure of the [requested information] would cause [it] substantial competitive harm"); see also *FOIA Post*, "Treatment of Unit Prices After McDonnell Douglas v. Air Force" (posted 9/8/05) (supplementing *FOIA Post*, "New McDonnell Douglas Opinion Aids Unit Price Decisionmaking" (posted 10/4/02)); *FOIA Post*, "Treatment of Unit Prices Under Exemption 4" (posted 5/29/02) (setting forth new guidance on handling requests for unit prices, directing agencies once again to conduct full submitter notice each time unit prices are requested, and advising agencies to carefully evaluate any claims of competitive harm on a case-by-case basis) (superseding *FOIA Update*, Vol. XVIII, No. 4, at 1, and *FOIA Update*, Vol. V, No. 4, at 4); *FOIA Update*, Vol. VIII, No. 2, at 1; *FOIA Update*, Vol. IV, No. 4, at 10; *FOIA Update*, Vol. III, No. 3, at 3; cf. Forest Guardians v. U.S. Forest Serv., No. 99-615, slip op. at 57 (D.N.M. Jan. 29, 2001) (finding that although the agency "failed to undertake procedures required by its own regulations, to engage in sufficient fact finding[,] or to utilize a rational and consistent decision-making process," the court could not "agree" that these facts rendered the agency's conduct "contrary to law" or arbitrary and capricious, because there were "insufficient concrete and uncontested facts" to make a determination on the applicability of any FOIA exemption) (case ultimately settled by the parties and agency agreed to provide notice to affected submitters). But cf. McDonnell Douglas Corp. v. NASA, 895 F. Supp. 319, 323 (D.D.C. 1995) (finding that an agency "simply does not have the authority to require [the submitter] to justify again and again why information, the disclosure of which has been enjoined by a federal court, should continue to be enjoined," and holding that the agency must instead take steps to "have the existing injunction modified or dissolved"), vacated as moot, No. 95-5288 (D.C. Cir. Apr. 1, 1996). See generally OSHA Data/CIH, Inc. v. U.S. Dep't of Labor, 220 F.3d 153, 168 (3d Cir. 2000) (concluding that estimated $1.7 million cost of notifying more
(continued...)

When submitters are given notice under this procedure, they must be given a "reasonable period of time" within which to object to disclosure of any of the requested material.[69] As one court has emphasized, however, this consultation is "appropriate as one step in the evaluation process, [but] is not sufficient to satisfy [an agency's] FOIA obligations."[70] Consequently, an agency is "required to determine for itself whether the information in question should be disclosed."[71]

If the submitter's objection is not, in fact, sustained by the agency, the submitter must be notified in writing and given a brief explanation of the agency's decision.[72] Such a notification must be provided a "reasonable number of days prior to a specified disclosure date," which gives the submitter an opportunity to seek judicial relief.[73] Executive Order 12,600 mirrors the policy guidance issued by the Office of Information and Privacy in 1982,[74] and for most federal agencies it reflects what already had been existing practice.[75]

This executive order predates the decision of the Court of Appeals for

---

[68](...continued)
than 80,000 submitters was properly charged to requester seeking documents for commercial use).

[69] Exec. Order No. 12,600, § 4; see McDonnell Douglas, 895 F. Supp. at 328 (holding that submitter is "not denied due process of law just because [agency] regulations do not allow cumulative opportunities to submit justifications and to refute agency decisions").

[70] Lee v. FDIC, 923 F. Supp. 451, 455 (S.D.N.Y. 1996).

[71] Id.; accord Exec. Order No. 12,600, § 5 (specifically contemplating that after affording notice to submitter agency makes ultimate determination concerning release); see also Nat'l Parks & Conservation Ass'n v. Morton, 498 F.2d 765, 767 (D.C. Cir. 1974) (concluding that in justifying nondisclosure, the submitter's treatment of the information is not "the only relevant inquiry," and finding that agency must be satisfied that harms underlying exemption are likely to occur).

[72] Exec. Order No. 12,600, § 5; see TRIFID Corp. v. Nat'l Imagery & Mapping Agency, 10 F. Supp. 2d 1087, 1093 (E.D. Mo. 1998) ("An agency's explanation of its decision may be 'curt,'" provided that it "indicate[s] the determinative reason for the action taken.").

[73] Exec. Order No. 12,600, § 5.

[74] See FOIA Update, Vol. III, No. 3, at 3 ("OIP Guidance: Submitters' Rights").

[75] See FOIA Update, Vol. IV, No. 4, at 1 (describing agency submitter notice practice); see also FOIA Update, Vol. VIII, No. 2, at 1 (same).

the District of Columbia Circuit in Critical Mass Energy Project v. NRC,[76] and thus does not contain any procedures for notifying submitters of voluntarily provided information in order to determine if that information is "of a kind that would customarily not be released to the public by the person from whom it was obtained."[77] (For a further discussion of this "customary treatment" standard, see Exemption 4, Applying Critical Mass, above.) As a matter of sound administrative practice, however, agencies should employ procedures analogous to those set forth in Executive Order 12,600 when making determinations under this "customary treatment" standard.[78]

Accordingly, if an agency is uncertain of the submitter's customary treatment of information, the submitter should be notified and given an opportunity to provide the agency with a description of its treatment -- including any disclosures that are customarily made and the conditions under which such disclosures occur.[79] The agency should then make an objective determination as to whether or not the "customary treatment" standard is satisfied.[80] Of course, in the event a submitter challenges an agency's threshold determination under Critical Mass concerning whether the submission is "required" or "voluntary," the agency should be careful to include in the administrative record a full justification for its position on that issue as well.[81]

---

[76] 975 F.2d 871 (D.C. Cir. 1992) (en banc).

[77] Id. at 879.

[78] See FOIA Update, Vol. Vol. XIV, No. 2, at 6-7 ("Exemption 4 Under Critical Mass: Step-By-Step Decisionmaking"); see also id. at 3-5 ("OIP Guidance: The Critical Mass Distinction Under Exemption 4").

[79] See id. at 7; accord Ctr. for Auto Safety v. Nat'l Highway Traffic Safety Admin., 244 F.3d 144, 153 (D.C. Cir. 2001) (directing the district court, on remand, to review the submitters' declarations "and any other relevant responses" that they might provide to establish their customary treatment of the requested information); Hull v. U.S. Dep't of Labor, No. 1:04-CV-01264, slip op. at 9-11 (D. Colo. Dec. 2, 2005) (finding that agency had "met its burden" to show that information was not "customarily released" by submitter where agency provided statements from submitters "specifically addressing" its customary treatment of such information; conversely, finding that agency had "failed to meet its burden" on customary treatment issue where submitter failed to address it and agency's affiant lacked requisite "personal knowledge" about submitter's practices); cf. Judicial Watch, Inc. v. U.S. Dep't of Commerce, 337 F. Supp. 2d 146, 171 (D.D.C. 2004) ("While affidavits from the information providers themselves or evidence of confidentiality agreements would carry more weight on the custom issue, it is sufficient for an agency to proceed solely on its sworn affidavits.").

[80] See FOIA Update, Vol. XIV, No. 2, at 7.

[81] See McDonnell Douglas Corp. v. EEOC, 922 F. Supp. 235, 241-42 (E.D.
(continued...)

## "REVERSE" FOIA

The procedures set forth in Executive Order 12,600 do not provide a submitter with a formal evidentiary hearing.[82] This is entirely consistent with what has now become well-established law -- i.e., that an agency's procedures for resolving a submitter's claim of confidentiality are not inadequate simply because they do not afford the submitter a right to an evidentiary hearing.[83] Agencies should be aware, though, that confusion and litigation can result from using undocumented conversations as a short-cut method of avoiding scrupulous adherence to these submitter-notice procedures.[84]

Similarly, procedures in the executive order do not provide for an administrative appeal of an adverse decision on a submitter's claim for confidentiality. The lack of such an appeal right has not been considered by the D.C. Circuit, but it has been addressed by the District Court for the District of Columbia, which has flatly rejected a submitter's contention that an agency's decision to disclose information "<u>must</u>" be subject to an administrative appeal.[85]

---

[81](...continued)
Mo. 1996) (concluding that the agency's finding that the submission was required was "not supported by substantial evidence," and consequently finding the agency decision to be "arbitrary, capricious, [an] abuse of discretion and contrary to the law"), appeal dismissed, No. 96-2662 (8th Cir. Aug. 29, 1996); Cortez III Serv. Corp. v. NASA, 921 F. Supp. 8, 13 (D.D.C. 1996) (explaining that agency's failure to provide "support" for its conclusion that submission was required rendered its decision "not in accordance with law"), appeal dismissed voluntarily, No. 96-5163 (D.C. Cir. July 3, 1996).

[82] See FOIA Update, Vol. VIII, No. 2, at 1 (describing basic procedural protections afforded to submitters under Executive Order 12,600, none of which includes evidentiary hearing).

[83] See CNA Fin. Corp. v. Donovan, 830 F.2d 1132, 1159 (D.C. Cir. 1987); Nat'l Org. for Women v. Social Sec. Admin., 736 F.2d 727, 746 (D.C. Cir. 1984) (per curiam) (McGowan & Mikva, JJ., concurring in result); McDonnell Douglas Corp. v. NASA, No. 96-2611, slip op. at 4 (D.D.C. May 1, 1998), rev'd on other grounds, 180 F.3d 303 (D.C. Cir. 1999).

[84] See Fed. Elec. Corp. v. Carlucci, 687 F. Supp. 1, 5 (D.D.C. 1988) (involving disappointed bidder who brought action seeking to have solicitation declared void after agency had released its cost data, in absence of submitter objections to release, which submitter claimed was due to "apparent misunderstanding as to what was actually going to be released"), grant of summary judgment to agency aff'd, 866 F.2d 1530 (D.C. Cir. 1989).

[85] Lykes Bros. S.S. Co. v. Peña, No. 92-2780, slip op. at 6 (D.D.C. Sept. 2, 1993); see also TRIFID, 10 F. Supp. 2d at 1093-94 (noting the lack of an appeal provision in the executive order, and concluding that the "absence of
(continued...)

The Court of Appeals for the Fourth Circuit had an opportunity to confront this issue in Acumenics Research & Technology v. Department of Justice.[86] There, in analyzing Department of Justice regulations which do not provide for an administrative appeal, the Fourth Circuit found that the procedures provided for in the regulations -- namely, notice of the request, an opportunity to submit objections to disclosure, careful consideration of those objections by the agency, and issuance of a written statement describing the reasons why any objections were not sustained -- in combination with a "face-to-face meeting that, in essence, amounted to an opportunity to appeal [the agency's] tentative decision in favor of disclosure," were adequate.[87] The Fourth Circuit, however, expressly declined to render an opinion as to whether the procedures implemented by the regulations alone would have been adequate.[88]

Likewise, the Court of Appeals for the Ninth Circuit has upheld the adequacy of an agency's factfinding procedures that did not provide for an administrative appeal per se.[89] In that case, the agency's procedures provided for notice and an opportunity to object to disclosure, for consideration of the objection by the agency, for a written explanation as to why the objection was not sustained, and then for another opportunity for the submitter to provide information in support of its objection.[90] After independently reviewing the record, the Ninth Circuit found that such procedures were adequate, and it accordingly held that the agency's decision to disclose the information did not require review in a trial de novo.[91]

## BASIC FOIA REFERENCES

The following is a list of primary reference materials pertaining to the Freedom of Information Act, 5 U.S.C. § 552 (2000 & Supp. IV 2004).

A growing number of reference materials pertaining to the FOIA are available to the public electronically through FOIA-related sites on the World Wide Web. The Department of Justice maintains a comprehensive

---

[85](...continued)
an appeal mechanism and a formal mechanism to provide additional information [did] not render [the agency's] procedures defective").

[86] 843 F.2d 800, 805 (4th Cir. 1988).

[87] Id.

[88] Id. at 805 n.4.

[89] See Pac. Architects & Eng'rs v. U.S. Dep't of State, 906 F.2d 1345, 1348 (9th Cir. 1990).

[90] Id.

[91] Id.

## BASIC FOIA REFERENCES

FOIA Web site (www.usdoj.gov/oip) -- which contains links to many of the basic reference materials listed below, including all Justice Department FOIA-related reference materials. *See, e.g.*, Mount of Olives' Paralegals v. Bush, No. 04-CV-044, 2004 U.S. Dist. LEXIS 8504, at *6 (S.D. Ill. Jan. 23, 2004) ("The Court suggests that [plaintiff] consult the FOIA reference guide on the DOJ website at www.usdoj.gov for guidance. . . . [T]he DOJ website should be helpful in this regard as well.").

The Department of Justice's FOIA Web site also contains links to the FOIA Web sites of other federal agencies; it lists the names, addresses, and telephone numbers of the FOIA contacts at all federal agencies; and it serves as a single electronic access point for linkage to the annual FOIA reports and the FOIA Improvement Plans (filed in accordance with Executive Order 13,392) of all federal agencies. *See FOIA Post*, "Executive Order 13,392 Implementation Guidance" (posted 4/27/06). In order to best facilitate public access to FOIA-related materials, individual electronic addresses are included below and the Office of Information and Privacy adds additional electronic addresses to this list as they become available. *See FOIA Update*, Vol. XVIII, No. 3, at 2.

Another basic reference tool is the cumulative index to *FOIA Update*, covering issues of that periodical through 1997. *See FOIA Update*, Vol. XVIII, No. 4, at i-ix. All issues of *FOIA Update*, from 1979-2000, also are available electronically on the Department of Justice's FOIA Web site. Its successor publication, *FOIA Post*, is made available through the Department's FOIA Web site as well. *See, e.g.*, *FOIA Post*, "Electronic Compilation of E-FOIA Implementation Guidance" (posted 2/28/03). Further reference materials also can be found in the extensive list of related law review articles that is contained in the Department of Justice's *Freedom of Information Case List* (2002 ed.), which also is available on the Department's FOIA Web site.

### Congressional References

House of Representatives Committee on Government Operations, *Clarifying and Protecting the Right of the Public to Information.* H.R. Rep. No. 1497, 89th Cong., 2d Sess. (1966), 14 pages. Out of print. Available at most law libraries.

House of Representatives Committee on Government Operations, *Freedom of Information Act (Compilation and Analysis of Department Regulations Implementing 5 U.S.C. § 552).* Committee Print, 90th Cong., 2d Sess. (1968), 303 pages with appendices. Out of print. Available at most law libraries.

House of Representatives Committee on Government Operations and Senate Committee on the Judiciary, *Freedom of Information Act and Amendments of 1974 (P.L. 93-502).* Joint Committee Print, 94th Cong., 1st Sess. (1975), 571 pages. Known as the "Joint Source Book." Out of print. Available at most law libraries.

House of Representatives Committee on Government Operations, *Freedom of Information Act Requests for Business Data and Reverse FOIA Lawsuits.* H.R. Rep. No. 1382, 95th Cong., 2d Sess. (1978), 67 pages. Out of print. Available at most law libraries.

House of Representatives Committee on Government Operations, Subcommittee on Government Information, Justice, and Agriculture, *The Freedom of Information Reform Act: Hearings on S. 774.* 98th Cong., 2d Sess. (1984), 1155 pages. Available at Federal Depository Libraries.

House of Representatives Committee on Government Operations, Subcommittee on Government Information, Justice, and Agriculture, *Federal Information Dissemination Policies and Practices.* 101st Cong., 1st Sess. (1989), 904 pages. Available at most law libraries.

House of Representatives Committee on the Judiciary, Subcommittee on Civil and Constitutional Rights, *FBI Oversight and Authorization Request for Fiscal Year 1991.* Committee Print, 101st Cong., 2d Sess. (1990), 566 pages. Available at most law libraries.

House of Representatives Committee on Government Reform and Oversight, *Electronic Freedom of Information Amendments of 1996.* H.R. Rep. No. 795, 104th Cong., 2d Sess. (1996), 40 pages. Available at most law libraries. Also available on the World Wide Web (thomas.loc.gov/cgi-bin/cpquery/z?cp104:hr795.104:).

House of Representatives Committee on Government Reform and Oversight, *Federal Information Policy Oversight.* 104th Cong., 2d Sess. (1996), 485 pages. Available at most law libraries.

House of Representatives Committee on Government Reform, *A Citizen's Guide on Using the Freedom of Information Act and the Privacy Act of 1974 to Request Government Records.* H.R. Rep. No. 226, 109th Cong., 1st Sess. (2005), 33 pages and appendices. Available on the World Wide Web (www.fas.org/sgp/foia/citizen.html).

House of Representatives Committee on Government Reform, Subcommittee on Government Management, Finance, and Accountability, *Information Policy in the 21st Century: A Review of the Freedom of Information Act.* 109th Cong., 1st Sess. (2005), 57 pages and appendices. Available on the World Wide Web (http://frwebgate.access.gpo.gov/cgi-bin/getdoc.cgi?dbname=109_house_hearings&docid=22705.wais.pdf).

Implementing FOIA [Freedom of Information Act] - Assessing Agency Efforts to meet FOIA Requirements: Hearing Before the Subcommittee on Information Policy, Census, and National Archives of the Committee on Oversight and Government Reform, 110th Cong. (2007) (statement of Melanie Ann Pustay, Acting Director, Office of Information and Privacy), (http://www.usdoj.gov/oip /foia30.pdf).

Senate Committee on the Judiciary, *Clarifying and Protecting the Right of the Public to Information, and Other Purposes*. S. Rep. No. 813, 89th Cong., 1st Sess. (1965), 10 pages. Out of print. Available at most law libraries.

Senate Committee on the Judiciary, *Freedom of Information Act Source Book: Legislative Materials, Cases, Articles*. S. Doc. No. 82, 93d Cong., 2d Sess. (1974), 432 pages on the Act prior to the 1974 Amendments. Out of print. Available at most law libraries.

Senate Committee on the Judiciary, Subcommittee on Criminal Laws and Procedures, *The Erosion of Law Enforcement Intelligence and Its Impact on the Public Security*. Committee Print, 95th Cong., 2d Sess. (1978), 179 pages. Out of print. Available at most law libraries.

Senate Committee on the Judiciary, *Freedom of Information: A Compilation of State Laws*. Committee Print, 95th Cong., 2d Sess. (1978), 475 pages. Out of print. Available at most law libraries.

Senate Committee on the Judiciary, *Agency Implementation of the 1974 Amendments to the Freedom of Information Act*. Committee Print, 95th Cong., 2d Sess. (1980), 188 pages. Out of print. Available at most law libraries.

Senate Committee on the Judiciary, Subcommittee on the Constitution, *Freedom of Information Act*, Vols. 1-2. Committee Print, 97th Cong., 1st Sess. (1981), 1147 pages and appendix. Available at most law libraries.

Senate Committee on the Judiciary, Subcommittee on the Constitution, *Freedom of Information Reform Act Report, Together with Supplemental Views, to Accompany S. 1730*. Committee Print 97-690, 97th Cong., 2d Sess. (1982), 17 pages. Available at most law libraries.

Senate Committee on the Judiciary, Subcommittee on the Constitution, *Freedom of Information Reform Act Report (on S. 774)*. Committee Print 98-221, 98th Cong., 1st Sess. (1983), 48 pages. Available at most law libraries.

Senate Committee on the Judiciary, Subcommittee on Technology and the Law, *The Freedom of Information Act*. Committee Print, 100th Cong., 2d Sess. (1988), 244 pages. Out of print. Available at most law libraries.

Senate Committee on the Judiciary, *Electronic Freedom of Information Improvement Act of 1994*. S. Rep. No. 1365, 103d Cong., 2d Sess. (1994), 28 pages. Available at most law libraries.

Senate Committee on the Judiciary, *Electronic Freedom of Information Improvement Act of 1995*. S. Rep. No. 272, 104th Cong., 2d Sess. (1996), 39 pages. Available at most law libraries. Also available on the

World Wide Web (www.fas.org/irp/congress/1996_rpt/s104272.htm).

Senate Committee on the Judiciary, Subcommittee on Terrorism, Technology and Homeland Security, *Hearing: Openness in Government and Freedom of Information: Examining the OPEN Government Act of 2005.* 109th Cong., 1st Sess. (2005). Available on the World Wide Web (judiciary. senate.gov/hearing.cfm?id=1417).

United States Government Accounting Office, *Report to Congressional Requesters: Information Management: Progress in Implementing the 1996 Electronic Freedom of Information Act Amendments.* GAO-01-378, March 16, 2001, 50 pages. Available on the World Wide Web (www.gao.gov/new. items/d01378.pdf).

United States Government Accounting Office, *Report to Congressional Requesters: Information Management: Update on Implementation of the 1996 Freedom of Information Act Amendments.* GAO-02-493, August 30, 2002, 99 pages. Available on the World Wide Web (www.gao.gov/new. items/d02493.pdf).

United States Government Accounting Office, *Report to the Ranking Minority Member, Committee on the Judiciary, U.S. Senate: Freedom of Information Act: Agency Views on Changes Resulting From New Administration Policy.* GAO-03-981, September 3, 2003, 39 pages. Available on the World Wide Web (www.gao.gov/new.items/d03981.pdf).

United States Government Accounting Office, *Testimony before the Subcommittee on Government Management, Finance and Accountability, Committee on Government Reform, House of Representatives: Information Management: Implementation of the Freedom of Information Act.* GAO-05-648T, May 11, 2005, 27 pages. Available on the World Wide Web (www. gao.gov/new.items/d05648t.pdf).

United States Government Accounting Office, *Testimony Before the Subcommittee on Government Management, Finance, and Accountability, Committee on Government Reform, House of Representatives, Freedom of Information Act: Preliminary Analysis of Processing Trends Shows Importance of Improvement Plans.* GAO-06-1022T, July 26, 2006, 64 pages. Available on the World Wide Web (www.gao.gov/new.items/d061022t. pdf).

## Executive Branch Materials

*Attorney General's Memorandum on the Public Information Section of the Administrative Procedure Act (FOIA)*, June 1967, 40 pages. Out of print. Reprinted in Gov't Disclosure Serv. (Prentice-Hall), Vol. 1, ¶ 300,601. Available on the Department of Justice's FOIA Web site at www.usdoj. gov/oip/67agmemo.htm.

*Attorney General's Memorandum on the 1974 Amendments to the*

## BASIC FOIA REFERENCES

*Freedom of Information Act*, February 1975, 26 pages and appendices. Available on the Department of Justice's FOIA Web site at www.usdoj. gov/oip/74agmemo.htm.

*Attorney General's Memorandum on the 1986 Amendments to the Freedom of Information Act*, December 1987, 30 pages and appendices. Available on the Department of Justice's FOIA Web site at www.usdoj. gov/oip/86agmemo.htm.

Attorney General's Memorandum for Heads of All Departments and Agencies Regarding the Freedom of Information Act, October 12, 2001. Available on the Department of Justice's FOIA Web site at www.usdoj. gov/oip/011012.htm. Also reprinted in *FOIA Post* (posted 10/15/01).

Attorney General's Report to the President Pursuant to Executive Order 13,392, entitled "Improving Agency Disclosure of Information," October 16, 2006. Available on the Department of Justice's FOIA Web site at www. usdoj.gov/oip/ag_report_to_president_13392.pdf.

Compendium of all federal agencies' FOIA Improvement Plans, submitted in accordance with Executive Order 13,392. *See FOIA Post*, "Agency FOIA Improvement Plans Posted" (posted 6/20/06). Available on the Department of Justice's FOIA Web site at www.usdoj.gov/04foia/agency_ improvement.html.

Compiled Freedom of Information Act Decisions, a feature of *FOIA Post*. Compilations of summaries of FOIA decisions received by the Office of Information and Privacy prior to the inception of *FOIA Post* in 2001. Prepared in retrospective compilations covering six-month periods, extending back twelve years prior to 2000. *See FOIA Post*, "Compilations of FOIA Decisions Now Cover Past Fifteen Years" (posted 12/31/03). Available on the Department of Justice's FOIA Web site at www.usdoj.gov/oip/foiapost/ mainpage.htm.

Department of Justice's Basic FOIA Training Manual, a comprehensive compilation of current FOIA training materials. *See FOIA Post*, "Basic FOIA Training Manual Now Available On-Line" (posted 11/26/04). Available on the Department of Justice's FOIA Web site at www.usdoj.gov/oip/ trainingmaterials.htm.

Department of Justice's FOIA Improvement Plan Pursuant to Executive Order 13,392. Available on the Department of Justice's FOIA Web site at www.usdoj.gov/04foia/ourplan.htm.

Department of Justice's Freedom of Information Act and Privacy Act Regulations, 28 C.F.R. Part 16 (2006), published by the Office of the Federal Register, but primarily available on the Department of Justice's FOIA Web site at www.usdoj.gov/oip/04_1_1.html.

Department of Justice Freedom of Information Act Reference Guide

(2006). Available in paper form from the Office of Information and Privacy, but primarily available on the Department of Justice's FOIA Web site at www.usdoj.gov/oip/04_3.html.

Executive Order 13,392, "Improving Agency Disclosure of Information," December 14, 2005. Available on the White House Web site at www.whitehouse.gov/news/releases/2005/12/print/20051214-4.html.

*FOIA Update*, a newsletter of information and guidance for federal agencies that was published by the Office of Information and Privacy, Department of Justice, from 1979-2000. Available (with exclusive search engine) on the Department of Justice's FOIA Web site at www.usdoj.gov/oip/foi-upd.htm.

*FOIA Post*, a Web-based successor to *FOIA Update* that is published by the Office of Information and Privacy, Department of Justice, as of 2001. *FOIA Post* contains articles of information and policy guidance pertaining to the Freedom of Information Act that are electronically published on an as-needed basis throughout the year. Available on the Department of Justice's FOIA Web site at www.usdoj.gov/oip/foiapost/mainpage.htm.

*Freedom of Information Case List*, a compilation of judicial decisions that was published by the Office of Information and Privacy, Department of Justice, up to and including 2002, containing decisions, both published and unpublished, under the Freedom of Information Act, the Privacy Act of 1974, the Federal Advisory Committee Act, and the Government in the Sunshine Act, as well as a list of "reverse" FOIA decisions. The final edition, published in May 2002, is available on the Department of Justice's FOIA Web site at www.usdoj.gov/oip/cl-tofc.html.

New Freedom of Information Act Decisions, a feature of *FOIA Post* beginning in of 2001. A quarterly compilation of summaries of all FOIA decisions received by the Office of Information and Privacy. Available on the Department of Justice's FOIA Web site at www.usdoj.gov/oip/foiapost/mainpage.htm.

Presidential Memorandum for Heads of Departments and Agencies Regarding the Freedom of Information Act, October 4, 1993. Published at 29 Weekly Compilation of Presidential Documents 1999 (Oct. 4, 1993). Reprinted in *FOIA Update*, Vol. XIV, No. 3, at 3. Also still available on the Department of Justice's FOIA Web site at www/usdoj.gov/oip/93clntmem.htm.

White House Memorandum for Heads of Executive Departments and Agencies Concerning Safeguarding Information Related to Homeland Security, with an accompanying memorandum from the Acting Director of the Information Security Oversight Office and the Co-Directors of the Department of Justice's Office of Information and Privacy, March 19, 2002. Available on the Department of Justice's FOIA Web site at www.usdoj.gov/oip/foiapost/2002foiapost10.htm. Also reprinted in *FOIA Post* (posted 3/21/02).

**BASIC FOIA REFERENCES**

*Your Right to Federal Records* (2006), a joint publication of the General Services Administration and the Department of Justice. Available from the Consumer Information Center, Department 320L, Pueblo, CO 81009. (Publication number: 320N; price: $1.00.) Available on the Department of Justice's FOIA Web site at www.usdoj.gov/oip/04_7.html.

<u>Nongovernment Publications</u>

*Access Reports*, a biweekly newsletter published (together with *Access Reports Reference File*) by Access Reports, Inc., Lynchburg, VA 24503. World Wide Web address www.accessreports.com.

*Federal Information Disclosure* (3d ed. 2000), James T. O'Reilly, West Group, Rochester, NY 14694. Biannual supplements. World Wide Web address www.west.thomson.com.

*Getting and Protecting Competitive Business Information: A Business Guide to Using the Freedom of Information Act* (1997), Burt A. Braverman, Frances J. Chetwynd, and Harry A. Hammitt, Management Concepts, Inc., Vienna, VA 22182. Out of print.

*Government Disclosure Service ("GDS")*, Prentice-Hall, Englewood Cliffs, NJ 07632. A monthly summary of FOIA-related matters that included full-text publication of FOIA and Privacy Act decisions from 1980 through October 1983, most of which are not published elsewhere. (Discontinued as of October 1983.)

*Guidebook to the Freedom of Information and Privacy Acts* (2d ed. 1986), Justin D. Franklin and Robert F. Bouchard, West Group, Rochester, NY 14694. Supplement published in 2006. World Wide Web address www.west.thomson.com.

*How to Use the Federal FOI Act* (9th ed. 2004), Reporters Committee for Freedom of the Press, Arlington, VA 22209. Complete set also available on CD-ROM. World Wide Web address www.rcfp.org.

*Information Law: Freedom of Information, Privacy, Open Meetings, and Other Access Laws* (1985), Burt A. Braverman and Frances J. Chetwynd, Practising Law Institute, New York City, NY 10019. Two volumes. Supplement published in 1990. World Wide Web address www.crblaw.com.

*Litigation Under the Federal Open Government Laws* (2d ed. 2004), Harry A. Hammitt, David L. Sobel, and Tiffany A. Stedman, Electronic Privacy Information Center and the James Madison Project, Washington, D.C. 20009. World Wide Web address www.epic.org.

Open Government Guide (2006), Reporters Committee for Freedom of the Press, Arlington, VA 22209. Available as a complete set or on a state-by-state basis. Complete set also available on CD-ROM. World Wide Web address www.rcfp.org.

*Privacy Times*, a newsletter that reports Privacy Act/Freedom of Information Act news, published biweekly by Privacy Times, Inc., P.O. Box 302, Cabin John, MD 20818. World Wide Web address www.privacytimes. com.

*Step-By-Step Guide to Using the Freedom of Information Act* (2000), American Civil Liberties Union Foundation, Washington, D.C. 20002. World Wide Web address www.aclu.org. Out of print.

THE FREEDOM OF INFORMATION ACT

5 U.S.C. § 552

As Amended

§ 552. Public information; agency rules, opinions, orders, records, and proceedings

(a)  Each agency shall make available to the public information as follows:

(1)  Each agency shall separately state and currently publish in the Federal Register for the guidance of the public --

(A)  descriptions of its central and field organization and the established places at which, the employees (and in the case of a uniformed service, the members) from whom, and the methods whereby, the public may obtain information, make submittals or requests, or obtain decisions;

(B)  statements of the general course and method by which its functions are channeled and determined, including the nature and requirements of all formal and informal procedures available;

(C)  rules of procedure, descriptions of forms available or the places at which forms may be obtained, and instructions as to the scope and contents of all papers, reports, or examinations;

(D)  substantive rules of general applicability adopted as authorized by law, and statements of general policy or interpretations of general applicability formulated and adopted by the agency; and

(E)  each amendment, revision, or repeal of the foregoing.

Except to the extent that a person has actual and timely notice of the terms thereof, a person may not in any manner be required to resort to, or be adversely affected by, a matter required to be published in the Federal Register and not so published. For the purpose of this paragraph, matter reasonably available to the class of persons affected thereby is deemed published in the Federal Register when incorporated by reference therein with the approval of the Director of the Federal Register.

(2)  Each agency, in accordance with published rules, shall make available for public inspection and copying --

(A)  final opinions, including concurring and dissenting opinions, as well as orders, made in the adjudication of cases;

(B) those statements of policy and interpretations which have been adopted by the agency and are not published in the Federal Register;

(C) administrative staff manuals and instructions to staff that affect a member of the public;

(D) copies of all records, regardless of form or format, which have been released to any person under paragraph (3) and which, because of the nature of their subject matter, the agency determines have become or are likely to become the subject of subsequent requests for substantially the same records; and

(E) a general index of the records referred to under subparagraph (D);

unless the materials are promptly published and copies offered for sale. For records created on or after November 1, 1996, within one year after such date, each agency shall make such records available, including by computer telecommunications or, if computer telecommunications means have not been established by the agency, by other electronic means. To the extent required to prevent a clearly unwarranted invasion of personal privacy, an agency may delete identifying details when it makes available or publishes an opinion, statement of policy, interpretation, staff manual, instruction, or copies of records referred to in subparagraph (D). However, in each case the justification for the deletion shall be explained fully in writing, and the extent of such deletion shall be indicated on the portion of the record which is made available or published, unless including that indication would harm an interest protected by the exemption in subsection (b) under which the deletion is made. If technically feasible, the extent of the deletion shall be indicated at the place in the record where the deletion was made. Each agency shall also maintain and make available for public inspection and copying current indexes providing identifying information for the public as to any matter issued, adopted, or promulgated after July 4, 1967, and required by this paragraph to be made available or published. Each agency shall promptly publish, quarterly or more frequently, and distribute (by sale or otherwise) copies of each index or supplements thereto unless it determines by order published in the Federal Register that the publication would be unnecessary and impracticable, in which case the agency shall nonetheless provide copies of such index on request at a cost not to exceed the direct cost of duplication. Each agency shall make the index referred to in subparagraph (E) available by computer telecommunications by December 31, 1999. A final order, opinion, statement of policy, interpretation, or staff manual or instruction that affects a member of the public may be relied on, used, or cited as precedent by an agency against a party other than an agency only if --

(i) it has been indexed and either made available or published as provided by this paragraph; or

(ii)  the party has actual and timely notice of the terms thereof.

(3)(A)  Except with respect to the records made available under paragraphs (1) and (2) of this subsection, and except as provided in subparagraph (E), each agency, upon any request for records which (i) reasonably describes such records and (ii) is made in accordance with published rules stating the time, place, fees (if any), and procedures to be followed, shall make the records promptly available to any person.

(B)  In making any record available to a person under this paragraph, an agency shall provide the record in any form or format requested by the person if the record is readily reproducible by the agency in that form or format.  Each agency shall make reasonable efforts to maintain its records in forms or formats that are reproducible for purposes of this section.

(C)  In responding under this paragraph to a request for records, an agency shall make reasonable efforts to search for the records in electronic form or format, except when such efforts would significantly interfere with the operation of the agency's automated information system.

(D)  For purposes of this paragraph, the term "search" means to review, manually or by automated means, agency records for the purpose of locating those records which are responsive to a request.

(E)  An agency, or part of an agency, that is an element of the intelligence community (as that term is defined in section 3(4) of the National Security Act of 1947 (50 U.S.C. 401a(4))) shall not make any record available under this paragraph to --

(i)  any government entity, other than a State, territory, commonwealth, or district of the United States, or any subdivision thereof; or

(ii)  a representative of a government entity described in clause (i).

(4)(A)(i)  In order to carry out the provisions of this section, each agency shall promulgate regulations, pursuant to notice and receipt of public comment, specifying the schedule of fees applicable to the processing of requests under this section and establishing procedures and guidelines for determining when such fees should be waived or reduced.  Such schedule shall conform to the guidelines which shall be promulgated, pursuant to notice and receipt of public comment, by the Director of the Office of Management and Budget and which shall provide for a uniform schedule of fees for all agencies.

(ii) Such agency regulations shall provide that --

(I) fees shall be limited to reasonable standard charges for document search, duplication, and review, when records are requested for commercial use;

(II) fees shall be limited to reasonable standard charges for document duplication when records are not sought for commercial use and the request is made by an educational or noncommercial scientific institution, whose purpose is scholarly or scientific research; or a representative of the news media; and

(III) for any request not described in (I) or (II), fees shall be limited to reasonable standard charges for document search and duplication.

(iii) Documents shall be furnished without any charge or at a charge reduced below the fees established under clause (ii) if disclosure of the information is in the public interest because it is likely to contribute significantly to public understanding of the operations or activities of the government and is not primarily in the commercial interest of the requester.

(iv) Fee schedules shall provide for the recovery of only the direct costs of search, duplication, or review. Review costs shall include only the direct costs incurred during the initial examination of a document for the purposes of determining whether the documents must be disclosed under this section and for the purposes of withholding any portions exempt from disclosure under this section. Review costs may not include any costs incurred in resolving issues of law or policy that may be raised in the course of processing a request under this section. No fee may be charged by any agency under this section --

(I) if the costs of routine collection and processing of the fee are likely to equal or exceed the amount of the fee; or

(II) for any request described in clause (ii)(II) or (III) of this subparagraph for the first two hours of search time or for the first one hundred pages of duplication.

(v) No agency may require advance payment of any fee unless the requester has previously failed to pay fees in a timely fashion, or the agency has determined that the fee will exceed $250.

(vi) Nothing in this subparagraph shall supersede fees chargeable under a statute specifically providing for setting the level of fees for particular types of records.

(vii) In any action by a requester regarding the waiver of fees under this section, the court shall determine the matter de novo: Provided, That the court's review of the matter shall be limited to the record before the agency.

(B) On complaint, the district court of the United States in the district in which the complainant resides, or has his principal place of business, or in which the agency records are situated, or in the District of Columbia, has jurisdiction to enjoin the agency from withholding agency records and to order the production of any agency records improperly withheld from the complainant. In such a case the court shall determine the matter de novo, and may examine the contents of such agency records in camera to determine whether such records or any part thereof shall be withheld under any of the exemptions set forth in subsection (b) of this section, and the burden is on the agency to sustain its action. In addition to any other matters to which a court accords substantial weight, a court shall accord substantial weight to an affidavit of an agency concerning the agency's determination as to technical feasibility under paragraph (2)(C) and subsection (b) and reproducibility under paragraph (3)(B).

(C) Notwithstanding any other provision of law, the defendant shall serve an answer or otherwise plead to any complaint made under this subsection within thirty days after service upon the defendant of the pleading in which such complaint is made, unless the court otherwise directs for good cause is shown.

[(D) Repealed by Pub. L. 98-620, Title IV, § 402(2), Nov. 8, 1984, 98 Stat. 3357.]

(E) The court may assess against the United States reasonable attorney fees and other litigation costs reasonably incurred in any case under this section in which the complainant has substantially prevailed.

(F) Whenever the court orders the production of any agency records improperly withheld from the complainant and assesses against the United States reasonable attorney fees and other litigation costs, and the court additionally issues a written finding that the circumstances surrounding the withholding raise questions whether agency personnel acted arbitrarily or capriciously with respect to the withholding, the Special Counsel shall promptly initiate a proceeding to determine whether disciplinary action is warranted against the officer or employee who was primarily responsible for the withholding. The Special Counsel, after investigation and consideration of the evidence submitted, shall submit his findings and recommendations to the administrative authority of the agency concerned and shall send copies of the findings and recommendations to the officer or employee or his representative. The administrative authority shall take the corrective action that the Special Counsel recommends.

(G) In the event of noncompliance with the order of the court, the district court may punish for contempt the responsible employee, and in the case of a uniformed service, the responsible member.

(5) Each agency having more than one member shall maintain and make available for public inspection a record of the final votes of each member in every agency proceeding.

(6)(A) Each agency, upon any request for records made under paragraph (1), (2), or (3) of this subsection, shall --

(i) determine within 20 days (excepting Saturdays, Sundays, and legal public holidays) after the receipt of any such request whether to comply with such request and shall immediately notify the person making such request of such determination and the reasons therefor, and of the right of such person to appeal to the head of the agency any adverse determination; and

(ii) make a determination with respect to any appeal within twenty days (excepting Saturdays, Sundays, and legal public holidays) after the receipt of such appeal. If on appeal the denial of the request for records is in whole or in part upheld, the agency shall notify the person making such request of the provisions for judicial review of that determination under paragraph (4) of this subsection.

(B)(i) In unusual circumstances as specified in this subparagraph, the time limits prescribed in either clause (i) or clause (ii) of subparagraph (A) may be extended by written notice to the person making such request setting forth the unusual circumstances for such extension and the date on which a determination is expected to be dispatched. No such notice shall specify a date that would result in an extension for more than ten working days, except as provided in clause (ii) of this subparagraph.

(ii) With respect to a request for which a written notice under clause (i) extends the time limits prescribed under clause (i) of subparagraph (A), the agency shall notify the person making the request if the request cannot be processed within the time limit specified in that clause and shall provide the person an opportunity to limit the scope of the request so that it may be processed within that time limit or an opportunity to arrange with the agency an alternative time frame for processing the request or a modified request. Refusal by the person to reasonably modify the request or arrange such an alternative time frame shall be considered as a factor in determining whether exceptional circumstances exist for purposes of subparagraph (C).

(iii) As used in this subparagraph, "unusual circumstances" means, but only to the extent reasonably necessary to the proper processing of the particular requests --

(I) the need to search for and collect the requested records from field facilities or other establishments that are separate from the office processing the request;

(II) the need to search for, collect, and appropriately examine a voluminous amount of separate and distinct records which are demanded in a single request; or

(III) the need for consultation, which shall be conducted with all practicable speed, with another agency having a substantial interest in the determination of the request or among two or more components of the agency having substantial subject matter interest therein.

(iv) Each agency may promulgate regulations, pursuant to notice and receipt of public comment, providing for the aggregation of certain requests by the same requestor, or by a group of requestors acting in concert, if the agency reasonably believes that such requests actually constitute a single request, which would otherwise satisfy the unusual circumstances specified in this subparagraph, and the requests involve clearly related matters. Multiple requests involving unrelated matters shall not be aggregated.

(C)(i) Any person making a request to any agency for records under paragraph (1), (2), or (3) of this subsection shall be deemed to have exhausted his administrative remedies with respect to such request if the agency fails to comply with the applicable time limit provisions of this paragraph. If the Government can show exceptional circumstances exist and that the agency is exercising due diligence in responding to the request, the court may retain jurisdiction and allow the agency additional time to complete its review of the records. Upon any determination by an agency to comply with a request for records, the records shall be made promptly available to such person making such request. Any notification of denial of any request for records under this subsection shall set forth the names and titles or positions of each person responsible for the denial of such request.

(ii) For purposes of this subparagraph, the term "exceptional circumstances" does not include a delay that results from a predictable agency workload of requests under this section, unless the agency demonstrates reasonable progress in reducing its backlog of pending requests.

(iii) Refusal by a person to reasonably modify the scope of a request or arrange an alternative time frame for processing the request (or a modified request) under clause (ii) after being given an opportunity to do so by the agency to whom the person made the request shall be considered as a factor in determining whether exceptional circumstances exist for purposes of this subparagraph.

(D)(i) Each agency may promulgate regulations, pursuant to notice and receipt of public comment, providing for multitrack processing of requests or records based on the amount of work or time (or both) involved in processing requests.

(ii) Regulations under this subparagraph may provide a person making a request that does not qualify for the fastest multitrack processing an opportunity to limit the scope of the request in order to qualify for faster processing.

(iii) This subparagraph shall not be considered to affect the requirement under subparagraph (C) to exercise due diligence.

(E)(i) Each agency shall promulgate regulations, pursuant to notice and receipt of public comment, providing for expedited processing of requests for records --

(I) in cases in which the person requesting the records demonstrates a compelling need; and

(II) in other cases determined by the agency.

(ii) Notwithstanding clause (i), regulations under this subparagraph must ensure --

(I) that a determination of whether to provide expedited processing shall be made, and notice of the determination shall be provided to the person making the request, within 10 days after the date of the request; and

(II) expeditious consideration of administrative appeals of such determinations of whether to provide expedited processing.

(iii) An agency shall process as soon as practicable any request for records to which the agency has granted expedited processing under this subparagraph. Agency action to deny or affirm denial of a request for expedited processing pursuant to this subparagraph, and failure by an agency to respond in a timely manner to such a request shall be subject to judicial review under paragraph (4), except that the judicial review shall be based on the record before the agency at the time of the determination.

(iv) A district court of the United States shall not have jurisdiction to review an agency denial of expedited processing of a request for records after the agency has provided a complete response to the request.

(v) For purposes of this subparagraph, the term "compelling need" means --

(I) that a failure to obtain requested records on an expedited basis under this paragraph could reasonably be expected to pose an imminent threat to the life or physical safety of an individual; or

(II) with respect to a request made by a person primarily engaged in disseminating information, urgency to inform the public concerning actual or alleged Federal Government activity.

(vi) A demonstration of a compelling need by a person making a request for expedited processing shall be made by a statement certified by such person to be true and correct to the best of such person's knowledge and belief.

(F) In denying a request for records, in whole or in part, an agency shall make a reasonable effort to estimate the volume of any requested matter the provision of which is denied, and shall provide any such estimate to the person making the request, unless providing such estimate would harm an interest protected by the exemption in subsection (b) pursuant to which the denial is made.

(b) This section does not apply to matters that are --

(1)(A) specifically authorized under criteria established by an Executive order to be kept secret in the interest of national defense or foreign policy and (B) are in fact properly classified pursuant to such Executive order;

(2) related solely to the internal personnel rules and practices of an agency;

(3) specifically exempted from disclosure by statute (other than section 552b of this title), provided that such statute (A) requires

that the matters be withheld from the public in such a manner as to leave no discretion on the issue, or (B) establishes particular criteria for withholding or refers to particular types of matters to be withheld;

(4) trade secrets and commercial or financial information obtained from a person and privileged or confidential;

(5) inter-agency or intra-agency memorandums or letters which would not be available by law to a party other than an agency in litigation with the agency;

(6) personnel and medical files and similar files the disclosure of which would constitute a clearly unwarranted invasion of personal privacy;

(7) records or information compiled for law enforcement purposes, but only to the extent that the production of such law enforcement records or information (A) could reasonably be expected to interfere with enforcement proceedings, (B) would deprive a person of a right to a fair trial or an impartial adjudication, (C) could reasonably be expected to constitute an unwarranted invasion of personal privacy, (D) could reasonably be expected to disclose the identity of a confidential source, including a State, local, or foreign agency or authority or any private institution which furnished information on a confidential basis, and, in the case of a record or information compiled by criminal law enforcement authority in the course of a criminal investigation or by an agency conducting a lawful national security intelligence investigation, information furnished by a confidential source, (E) would disclose techniques and procedures for law enforcement investigations or prosecutions, or would disclose guidelines for law enforcement investigations or prosecutions if such disclosure could reasonably be expected to risk circumvention of the law, or (F) could reasonably be expected to endanger the life or physical safety of any individual;

(8) contained in or related to examination, operating, or condition reports prepared by, on behalf of, or for the use of an agency responsible for the regulation or supervision of financial institutions; or

(9) geological and geophysical information and data, including maps, concerning wells.

Any reasonably segregable portion of a record shall be provided to any person requesting such record after deletion of the portions which are exempt under this subsection. The amount of information deleted shall be indicated on the released portion of the record, unless including that indication would harm an interest protected by the exemption in this subsection under which the deletion is made. If technically feasible, the amount of the information deleted shall be indicated at the place in the record where such deletion is made.

(c)(1) Whenever a request is made which involves access to records described in subsection (b)(7)(A) and --

> (A) the investigation or proceeding involves a possible violation of criminal law; and

> (B) there is reason to believe that (i) the subject of the investigation or proceeding is not aware of its pendency, and (ii) disclosure of the existence of the records could reasonably be expected to interfere with enforcement proceedings, the agency may, during only such time as that circumstance continues, treat the records as not subject to the requirements of this section.

> (2) Whenever informant records maintained by a criminal law enforcement agency under an informant's name or personal identifier are requested by a third party according to the informant's name or personal identifier, the agency may treat the records as not subject to the requirements of this section unless the informant's status as an informant has been officially confirmed.

> (3) Whenever a request is made which involves access to records maintained by the Federal Bureau of Investigation pertaining to foreign intelligence or counterintelligence, or international terrorism, and the existence of the records is classified information as provided in subsection (b)(1), the Bureau may, as long as the existence of the records remains classified information, treat the records as not subject to the requirements of this section.

(d) This section does not authorize withholding of information or limit the availability of records to the public, except as specifically stated in this section. This section is not authority to withhold information from Congress.

(e)(1) On or before February 1 of each year, each agency shall submit to the Attorney General of the United States a report which shall cover the preceding fiscal year and which shall include --

> (A) the number of determinations made by the agency not to comply with requests for records made to such agency under subsection (a) and the reasons for each such determination;

> (B)(i) the number of appeals made by persons under subsection (a)(6), the result of such appeals, and the reason for the action upon each appeal that results in a denial of information; and

> > (ii) a complete list of all statutes that the agency relies upon to authorize the agency to withhold information under subsection (b)(3), a description of whether a court has upheld the de-

cision of the agency to withhold information under each such statute, and a concise description of the scope of any information withheld;

(C) the number of requests for records pending before the agency as of September 30 of the preceding year, and the median number of days that such requests had been pending before the agency as of that date;

(D) the number of requests for records received by the agency and the number of requests which the agency processed;

(E) the median number of days taken by the agency to process different types of requests;

(F) the total amount of fees collected by the agency for processing requests; and

(G) the number of full-time staff of the agency devoted to processing requests for records under this section, and the total amount expended by the agency for processing such requests.

(2) Each agency shall make each such report available to the public including by computer telecommunications, or if computer telecommunications means have not been established by the agency, by other electronic means.

(3) The Attorney General of the United States shall make each report which has been made available by electronic means available at a single electronic access point. The Attorney General of the United States shall notify the Chairman and ranking minority member of the Committee on Government [Reform] of the House of Representatives and the Chairman and ranking minority member of the Committees on Governmental Affairs and the Judiciary of the Senate, no later than April 1 of the year in which each such report is issued, that such reports are available by electronic means.

(4) The Attorney General of the United States, in consultation with the Director of the Office of Management and Budget, shall develop reporting and performance guidelines in connection with reports required by this subsection by October 1, 1997, and may establish additional requirements for such reports as the Attorney General determines may be useful.

(5) The Attorney General of the United States shall submit an annual report on or before April 1 of each calendar year which shall include for the prior calendar year a listing of the number of cases arising under this section, the exemption involved in each case, the disposition of such case, and the cost, fees, and penalties assessed under subparagraphs (E), (F), and (G) of subsection (a)(4). Such

report shall also include a description of the efforts undertaken by the Department of Justice to encourage agency compliance with this section.

(f)  For purposes of this section, the term --

(1)  "agency" as defined in section 551(1) of this title includes any executive department, military department, Government corporation, Government controlled corporation, or other establishment in the executive branch of the Government (including the Executive Office of the President), or any independent regulatory agency; and

(2)  "record" and any other term used in this section in reference to information includes any information that would be an agency record subject to the requirements of this section when maintained by an agency in any format, including an electronic format.

(g)  The head of each agency shall prepare and make publicly available upon request, reference material or a guide for requesting records or information from the agency, subject to the exemptions in subsection (b), including --

(1)  an index of all major information systems of the agency;

(2)  a description of major information and record locator systems maintained by the agency; and

(3)  a handbook for obtaining various types and categories of public information from the agency pursuant to chapter 35 of title 44, and under this section.

G:O: US GOVERNMENT PRINTING OFFICE : 2007—337-437

Santa Clara County
**LIBRARY**

Renewals:
(800) 471-0991
www.santaclaracountylib.org